Linux Undercover

Linux Secrets as Revealed by the Linux Documentation Project

Edited by
Eric S. Raymond

Red Hat Software, Inc.
Research Triangle Park, North Carolina

Revision 1.0, February 1998

Red Hat Software, Inc.
4201 Research Commons, Suite 100
79 T. W. Alexander Drive
P. O. Box 13588
Research Triangle Park, NC 27709
(919) 547-0012
redhat@redhat.com
http://www.redhat.com

Preface

This first edition of "Linux Undercover" is the first LDP compendium to be brought to you with the new "just-in-time" production method. Previous editions often included stale HOWTOs that had been superseded by new versions during the production of the book. We have attacked this problem by dramatically shortening the production time – essentially, this book was printed straight from the on-line master documents.

To accomplish this, Red Hat and I redesigned the production process, and then I added features to SGML-Tools to support the new process. Instead of hand-editing the TeX generated from their SGML and LaTeX masters each time, we now make changes to the masters themselves and pass them back to the authors. The book index is no longer re-compiled by hand each time, but instead generated from index markup in the authors' document masters.

None of this would have been possible without a new level of cooperation from the HOWTO authors. We gratefully acknowledge the enthusiasm, dedication, and perseverence they have brought to the service of the Linux community.

The scripts I used to compile and produce this book will be available in the contrib directory of the SGML-tools distribution, which you can find at any major Linux archive site. If you choose to produce your own Linux book with them, feel free – but please bear in mind that it is customary to return a due portion of the profits to the LDP authors or charities of their choice.

This book omits some HOWTOs in order to fit within the fixed maximum pagecount supported by our printers. The omitted ones mostly fall into several broad categories, which we list here to give some indication of what else may be available on the LDP Website:

- *Internationalization.* HOWTOs on customizing Linux for Chinese, Cyrillic, Danish, Finnish, French, German, Hebrew, Italian, Polish, Slovenian, Spanish and Thai have been omitted.

- *Non-Intel hardware.* We don't cover the Alpha, Amiga, Atari, or Power Mac in this book.

- *Non-TCP/IP Networking* LDP includes some resources on non-IP protocols such as SMB and IPX which we don't carry in this book.

- *Old News* HOWTOs on Linux facilities that used to be optional add-ons but are now part of all standard distributions – ELF, shadow passwords, PCI support, etc.

- *Commercial add-ons.* We have omitted HOWTOs describing how to use Linux with expensive commercial software or hardware out of reach of normal home and small-business PC users.

For the full set of HOWTOs, see the master archive site at the Linux Documentation Project: http://sunsite.unc.edu/LDP.

This book reflects the state of that archive on 24 Feb 1998.

— Eric S. Raymond <esr@snark.thyrsus.com>

Table Of Contents

Tux – Linux's penguin mascot

Linux Installation and Getting Started

Version 3.0, 30 November 1997.

This book is an installation and new-user guide for the Linux system, meant for UNIX novices and gurus alike. Contained herein is information on how to obtain Linux, installation of the software, a beginning tutorial for new UNIX users, and an introduction to system administration. It is meant to be general enough to be applicable to any distribution of the Linux software.

Contents

Preface

"You are in a maze of twisty little passages, all alike."

Before you looms one of the most complex and utterly intimidating systems ever written. Linux, the free UNIX clone for the personal computer, produced by a mishmash team of UNIX gurus, hackers, and the occasional loon. The system itself reflects this complex heritage, and although the development of Linux may appear to be a disorganized volunteer effort, the system is powerful, fast, and free. It is a true 32-bit operating system solution.

My own experiences with Linux began several years ago, when I sat down to figure out how to install the only "distribution" available at the time—a couple of diskettes made available by H.J. Lu. I downloaded a slew of files and read pages upon pages of loosely-organized installation notes. Somehow, I managed to install this basic system and get everything working together. This was long before you could buy the Linux software on CD-ROM from worldwide distributors; before, in fact, Linux even knew how to access a CD-ROM drive. This was before XFree86, before Emacs, before commercial software support, and before Linux became a true rival to MS-DOS, Microsoft Windows, and OS/2 in the personal computer market.

You hold in your very hands the map and guidebook to the world of Linux. It is my hope that this book will help you to get rolling with what I consider to be the fastest, most powerful operating system for the personal computer. Setting up your own Linux system can be a great deal of fun—so grab a cup of coffee, sit back, and read on.

Grab a cup for me, too, while you're at it. I've been up hacking Linux for days.

Audience

This book is for any personal computer user who wants to install and use Linux on their system. We assume that you have basic knowledge about personal computers and operating systems such as MS-DOS. No previous knowledge about Linux or UNIX is assumed.

Despite this, we strongly suggest that UNIX novices invest in one of the many good UNIX books out there. Several of them are listed in Appendix A.

Organization

This book contains the following chapters.

Chapter 1, *Introduction to Linux*, gives a general introduction to what Linux is, what it can do for you, and what is required to run it on your system. It also provides helpful hints for getting help and reducing overall stress.

Chapter 2, *Obtaining and Installing Linux*, explains how to obtain the Linux software, as well as how to install it—from repartitioning your drive, creating filesystems, and loading the software on the system. It contains instructions meant to be general for any distribution of Linux, and relies on the documentation provided for your particular release to fill in any gaps.

Chapter 3, *Linux Tutorial*, is a complete introduction to using the Linux system for UNIX novices. If you have previous UNIX experience, most of this material should be familiar.

Chapter 4, *System Administration*, introduces many of the important concepts of system administration under Linux. This will also be of interest to UNIX system administrators who want to know about the Linux-specific issues of running a system.

Chapter 5, *Advanced Features*, introduces the reader to a number of advanced features supported by Linux, such as the X Window System and TCP/IP networking. A complete guide to configuring XFree86-3.1 is included.

Appendix A, *Sources of Linux Information*, is a listing of other sources of information about Linux, including newsgroups, mailing lists, online documents, and books.

Appendix B, *Linux Vendor List*, provides a short list of software vendors offering Linux software and services.

Appendix C, *FTP Tutorial and Site List*, is a tutorial for downloading files from the Internet with FTP. This appendix also includes a listing of FTP archive sites which carry Linux software.

Appendix D, *Linux BBS List*, is a listing of bulletin board systems worldwide which carry Linux software. Because most Linux users are do not have access to the Internet, it is important that information on BBS systems becomes available.

Appendix E, *The GNU General Public License*, contains a copy of the GNU GPL, the license agreement under which Linux is distributed. It is very important that Linux users understand the GPL; many disagreements over the terms of the GPL have been raised in recent months.

Acknowledgments

This book has been long in the making, and many people are responsible for the outcome. In particular, I would like to thank Larry Greenfield and Karl Fogel for their work on the first version of Chapter 3, and to Lars Wirzenius for his work on Chapter 4. Thanks to Michael K. Johnson for his assistance with the LDP and the LATEX conventions used in this manual, and to Ed Chi, who sent me a printed copy of the book for edition.

Thanks to Melinda A. McBride at SSC, Inc., who did an excellent job completing the index for Chapters 3, 4, and 5. I would also like to thank Andy Oram, Lar Kaufman, and Bill Hahn at O'Reilly and Associates for their assistance with the Linux Documentation Project.

Thanks to Linux Systems Labs, Morse Telecommunications, Yggdrasil Computing, and others for their support of the Linux Documentation Project through sales of this book and other works.

Much thanks to the many activists, including (in no particular order) Linus Torvalds, Donald Becker, Alan Cox, Remy Card, Ted T'so, H.J. Lu, Ross Biro, Drew Eckhardt, Ed Carp, Eric Youngdale, Fred van Kempen, Steven Tweedie, and a score of others, for devoting so much time and energy to this project, and without whom there wouldn't be anything to write a book about.

Special thanks to the myriad of readers who have sent their helpful comments and corrections. There are far too many to list here. Who needs a spell checker, when you have an audience?

Matt Welsh
13 January 1994

Credits and Legalese

The Linux Documentation Project is a loose team of writers, proofreaders, and editors who are working on a set of definitive Linux manuals. The overall coordinator of the project is Matt Welsh, aided by Lars Wirzenius and Michael K. Johnson.

This manual is but one in a set of several being distributed by the Linux Documentation Project, including a Linux User's Guide, System Administrator's Guide, Network Administrator's Guide, and Kernel Hacker's Guide. These manuals are all available in LaTeX source format and Postscript output for anonymous FTP from sunsite.unc.edu, in the directory /pub/Linux/docs/LDP.

We encourage anyone with a penchant for writing or editing to join us in improving Linux documentation. If you have Internet e-mail access, you can join the linux-doc mailing list sending mail to

    majordomo@vger.rutgers.edu

with the line

    subscribe linux-doc

as the first line of the message body.

Feel free to get in touch with the author and coordinator of this manual if you have questions, postcards, money, or ideas. Matt Welsh can be reached via Internet e-mail at mdw@sunsite.unc.edu, or in real life at

    Computer Science Department
    Cornell University
    4130 Upson Hall
    Ithaca, NY 14853
    USA

For complete contact information, please visit the World Wide Web page at the URL:

    http://www.cs.cornell.edu/home/mdw/mdw.html

UNIX is a trademark of X/Open.

Linux is not a trademark, and has no connection to UNIX™ or X/Open.

The X Window System is a trademark of the Massachusetts Institute of Technology.

MS-DOS and Microsoft Windows are trademarks of Microsoft, Inc.

Documentation Conventions

These conventions should be obvious, but we'll include them here for the pedantic.

Bold   Used to mark **new concepts**, **WARNINGS**, and **keywords** in a language.

italics   Used for *emphasis* in text, and occasionally for quotes or introductions at the beginning of a section. Also used to indicate commands for the user to type when showing screen interaction (see below).

⟨slanted⟩   Used to mark **meta-variables** in the text, especially in representations of the command line. For example,

        ls -l ⟨foo⟩

where ⟨foo⟩ would "stand for" a filename, such as /bin/cp.

`Typewriter`   Used to represent screen interaction, as in

```
$ ls -l /bin/cp
-rwxr-xr-x  1 root     wheel     12104 Sep 25 15:53 /bin/cp
```

Also used for code examples, whether it is C code, a shell script, or something else, and to display general files, such as configuration files. When necessary for clarity's sake, these examples or figures will be enclosed in thin boxes.

`Key`   Represents a key to press. You will often see it in this form:

        Press `return` to continue.

◇   A diamond in the margin, like a black diamond on a ski hill, marks "danger" or "caution." Read paragraphs marked this way carefully.

Chapter 1

Introduction to Linux

Linux is quite possibly the most important achievement of free software since the original *Space War*, or, more recently, Emacs. It has developed into the operating system for businesses, education, and personal productivity. Linux is no longer just for UNIX wizards who sit for hours in front of the glowing console (although we assure you that quite a number of users fall into this category). This book will help you get the most out of it.

Linux (pronounced with a short *i*, as in *LIH-nucks*) is a clone of the UNIX operating system that runs on Intel 80386 and 80486 computers. It supports a wide range of software, from TEX to X Windows to the GNU C/C++ compiler to TCP/IP. It's a versatile, bona fide implementation of UNIX, freely distributed by the terms of the GNU General Public License (see Appendix E).

Linux can turn any 386 or 486 PC into a workstation. It will give you the full power of UNIX at your fingertips. Businesses are installing Linux on entire networks of machines, using the operating system to manage financial and hospital records, a distributed user computing environment, telecommunications, and more. Universities worldwide are using Linux for teaching courses on operating systems programming and design. And, of course, computing enthusiasts everywhere are using Linux at home, for programming, productivity, and all-around hacking.

What makes Linux so different is that it is a *free* implementation of UNIX. It was and still is developed by a group of volunteers, primarily on the Internet, exchanging code, reporting bugs, and fixing problems in an open-ended environment. Anyone is welcome to join in the Linux development effort: all it takes is interest in hacking a free UNIX clone and some kind of programming know-how. The book that you hold in your hands is your tour guide.

1.1 About This Book

This book is an installation and entry-level guide to the Linux system. The purpose is to get new users up and running with the system by consolodating as much important material as possible into one book. Instead of covering many of the volatile technical details, those things which tend to change with rapid development, we give you enough background to find out more on your own.

Linux is not difficult to install and use. However, as with any implementation of UNIX, there is often some black magic involved to get everything working correctly. We hope that this book will get you on the Linux tourbus and show you how groovy this operating system can be.

In this book, we cover the following topics.

9

- What is Linux? The design and philosophy of this unique operating system, and what it can do for you.

- All of the details of what is needed to run Linux, including suggestions on what kind of hardware configuration is recommended for a complete system.

- How to obtain and install Linux. There are many distributions of the Linux software. We present a general discussion of Linux software distributions, how to obtain them, and generic instructions for installing the software (which should be applicable to any distribution).

  This edition also contains specific instructions for the Slackware distribution of Linux.

- A brief introductory UNIX tutorial, for those users who have never had experience with UNIX before. This tutorial should, hopefully, provide enough material for complete novices to have enough basic know-how to find their way around the system.

- An introduction to systems administration with Linux. This covers the most important tasks that new Linux administrators will need to be familiar with, such as creating users, managing filesystems, and so forth.

- Information on configuring more advanced aspects of Linux, such as the X Window System, networking with TCP/IP and SLIP, and the setup of electronic mail and news systems.

This book is for the personal computer user wishing to get started with Linux. We don't assume previous UNIX experience, but do expect novices to refer to other materials along the way. For those unfamiliar with UNIX, a list of useful sources of information is given in Appendix A. In general, this book is meant to be read along with another book on basic UNIX concepts.

1.2   A Brief History of Linux

UNIX is one of the most popular operating systems worldwide because of its large support base and distribution. It was originally developed as a multitasking system for minicomputers and mainframes in the mid-1970's, but has since grown to become one of the most widely used operating systems anywhere, despite its sometimes confusing interface and lack of central standardization.

The real reason for UNIX's popularity? Many hackers feel that UNIX is the Right Thing—the One True Operating System. Hence, the development of Linux by an expanding group of UNIX hackers who want to get their hands dirty with their own system.

Versions of UNIX exist for many systems—ranging from personal computers to supercomputers such as the Cray Y-MP. Most versions of UNIX for personal computers are quite expensive and cumbersome. At the time of this writing, a one-machine version of AT&T's System V for the 386 runs at about US$1500.

Linux is a freely distributable version of UNIX developed primarily by Linus Torvalds [1] at the University of Helsinki in Finland. Linux was developed with the help of many UNIX programmers and wizards across the Internet, allowing anyone with enough know-how and gumption the ability to develop and change the system. The Linux kernel uses no code from AT&T or any other proprietary source, and much of the software available for Linux is developed by the GNU project at the Free Software Foundation in Cambridge, Massachusetts. However, programmers all over the world have contributed to the growing pool of Linux software.

Linux was originally developed as a hobby project by Linus Torvalds. It was inspired by Minix, a small UNIX system developed by Andy Tanenbaum, and the first discussions about Linux were on the USENET newsgroup comp.os.minix. These discussions were concerned mostly with the development of a small, academic UNIX system for Minix users who wanted more.

The very early development of Linux was mostly dealing with the task-switching features of the 80386 protected-mode interface, all written in assembly code. Linus writes,

---

[1] torvalds@kruuna.helsinki.fi.

"After that it was plain sailing: hairy coding still, but I had some devices, and debugging was easier. I started using C at this stage, and it certainly speeds up developement. This is also when I start to get serious about my megalomaniac ideas to make 'a better Minix than Minix'. I was hoping I'd be able to recompile `gcc` under Linux some day...

"Two months for basic setup, but then only slightly longer until I had a disk-driver (seriously buggy, but it happened to work on my machine) and a small filesystem. That was about when I made 0.01 available [around late August of 1991]: it wasn't pretty, it had no floppy driver, and it couldn't do much anything. I don't think anybody ever compiled that version. But by then I was hooked, and didn't want to stop until I could chuck out Minix."

No announcement was ever made for Linux version 0.01. The 0.01 sources weren't even executable: they contained only the bare rudiments of the kernel source, and assumed that you had access to a Minix machine to compile and play with them.

On 5 October 1991, Linus announced the first "official" version of Linux, version 0.02. At this point, Linus was able to run `bash` (the GNU Bourne Again Shell) and `gcc` (the GNU C compiler), but not very much else was working. Again, this was intended as a hacker's system. The primary focus was kernel development—none of the issues of user support, documentation, distribution, and so on had even been addressed. Today, the Linux community still seems to treat these ergonomic issues as secondary to the "real programming"—kernel development.

Linus wrote in `comp.os.minix`,

"Do you pine for the nice days of Minix-1.1, when men were men and wrote their own device drivers? Are you without a nice project and just dying to cut your teeth on a OS you can try to modify for your needs? Are you finding it frustrating when everything works on Minix? No more all-nighters to get a nifty program working? Then this post might be just for you.

"As I mentioned a month ago, I'm working on a free version of a Minix-lookalike for AT-386 computers. It has finally reached the stage where it's even usable (though may not be depending on what you want), and I am willing to put out the sources for wider distribution. It is just version 0.02... but I've successfully run `bash`, `gcc`, `gnu-make`, `gnu-sed`, `compress`, etc. under it."

After version 0.03, Linus bumped the version number up to 0.10, as more people started to work on the system. After several further revisions, Linus increased the version number to 0.95, to reflect his expectation that the system was ready for an "official" release very soon. (Generally, software is not assigned the version number 1.0 until it is theoretically complete or bug-free.) This was in March of 1992. Almost a year and a half later, in late December of 1993, the Linux kernel was still at version 0.99.pl14—asymptotically approaching 1.0. As of the time of this writing, the current kernel version is 1.1 patchlevel 52, and 1.2 is right around the corner.

Today, Linux is a complete UNIX clone, capable of running X Windows, TCP/IP, Emacs, UUCP, mail and news software, you name it. Almost all of the major free software packages have been ported to Linux, and commercial software is becoming available. Much more hardware is supported than in original versions of the kernel. Many people have executed benchmarks on 80486 Linux systems and found them comparable with mid-range workstations from Sun Microsystems and Digital Equipment Corporation. Who would have ever guessed that this "little" UNIX clone would have grown up to take on the entire world of personal computing?

1.3 System Features

Linux supports most of the features found in other implementations of UNIX, plus quite a few that aren't found elsewhere. This section is a nickel tour of the Linux kernel features.

Linux is a complete multitasking, multiuser operating system (just like all other versions of UNIX). This means that many users can be logged into the same machine at once, running multiple programs simultaneously.

The Linux system is mostly compatible with a number of UNIX standards (inasmuch as UNIX has standards) on the source level, including IEEE POSIX.1, System V, and BSD features. It was developed with source portability in mind: therefore, you are most likely to find commonly-used features in the Linux system which are shared across multiple implementations. A great deal of free UNIX software available on the Internet and elsewhere compiles on Linux out of the box. In addition, all source code for the Linux system, including the kernel, device drivers, libraries, user programs, and development tools, is freely distributable.

Other specific internal features of Linux include POSIX job control (used by shells such as `csh` and `bash`), pseudoterminals (`pty` devices), and support for national or customized keyboards using dynamically-loadable keyboard drivers. Linux also supports **virtual consoles**, which allow you to switch between multiple login sessions from the system console in text mode. Users of the "`screen`" program will find the Linux virtual console implementation familiar.

The kernel is able to emulate 387-FPU instructions itself, so that systems without a math coprocessor can run programs that require floating-point math instructions.

Linux supports various filesystem types for storing data. Various filesystems, such as the *ext2fs* filesystem, have been developed specifically for Linux. Other filesystem types, such as the Minix-1 and Xenix filesystems, are also supported. The MS-DOS filesystem has been implemented as well, allowing you to access MS-DOS files on hard drive or floppy directly. The ISO 9660 CD-ROM filesystem type, which reads all standard formats of CD-ROMs, is also supported. We'll talk more about filesystems in Chapters 2 and 4.

Linux provides a complete implementation of TCP/IP networking. This includes device drivers for many popular Ethernet cards, SLIP (Serial Line Internet Protocol, allowing you to access a TCP/IP network via a serial connection), PLIP (Parallel Line Internet Protocol), PPP (Point-to-Point Protocol), NFS (Network File System), and so on. The complete range of TCP/IP clients and services is supported, such as FTP, `telnet`, NNTP, and SMTP. We'll talk more about networking in Chapter 5.

The Linux kernel is developed to use the special protected-mode features of the Intel 80386 and 80486 processors. In particular, Linux makes use of the protected-mode descriptor-based memory management paradigm and many of the other advanced features of these processors. Anyone familiar with 80386 protected-mode programming knows that this chip was designed for a multitasking system such as UNIX (or, actually, Multics). Linux exploits this functionality.

The Linux kernel supports demand-paged loaded executables. That is, only those segments of a program which are actually used are read into memory from disk. Also, copy-on-write pages are shared among executables, meaning that if several instances of a program are running at once, they will share pages in physical memory, reducing overall memory usage.

In order to increase the amount of available memory, Linux also implements disk paging: that is, up to 256 megabytes of "swap space"[2] can be allocated on disk. When the system requires more physical memory, it will swap out inactive pages to disk, thus allowing you to run larger applications and support more users at once. However, swap is no substitute for physical RAM—it is much slower due to drive access latency times.

The kernel also implements a unified memory pool for user programs and disk cache. In this way, all free memory is used for caching, and the cache is reduced when running large programs.

Executables use dynamically linked shared libraries, meaning that executables share common library code in a single library file found on disk, not unlike the SunOS shared library mechanism. This allows executable files to occupy much less space on disk, especially those that use many library functions. There are also statically-linked libraries for those who wish to use object debugging or maintain "complete" executables

---

[2]Swap space is inappropriately named: entire processes are not swapped, but rather individual pages. Of course, in many cases entire processes will be swapped out, but this is not neccessarily always the case.

without the need for shared libraries to be in place. Linux shared libraries are dynamically linked at run-time, allowing the programmer to replace modules of the libraries with their own routines.

To facilitate debugging, the Linux kernel does core dumps for post-mortem analysis. Using a core dump and an executable linked with debugging support, it is possible to determine what caused a program to crash.

1.4 Software Features

In this section, we'll introduce you to many of the software applications available for Linux, and talk about a number of common computing tasks. After all, the most important part of the system is the wide range of software available for it. The fact that most of this software is freely distributable is even more impressive.

1.4.1 Basic commands and utilities

Virtually every utility that you would expect to find on standard implementations of UNIX has been ported to Linux. This includes basic commands such as `ls`, `awk`, `tr`, `sed`, `bc`, `more`, and so on. You name it, Linux has it. Therefore, you can expect your familiar working environment on other UNIX systems to be duplicated on Linux. All of the standard commands and utilities are there. (Novice Linux users should see Chapter 3 for an introduction to these basic UNIX commands.)

Many text editors are available, including `vi`, `ex`, `pico`, `jove`, as well as GNU Emacs and variants such as Lucid Emacs (which incorporates extensions for use under X Windows) and `joe`. Whatever text editor you're accustomed to using has more than likely been ported to Linux.

The choice of a text editor is an interesting one. Many UNIX users still use "simple" editors such as `vi` (in fact, the author wrote this book using `vi` under Linux). However, `vi` has many limitations, due to its age, and more modern (and complex) editors such as Emacs are gaining popularity. Emacs supports a complete LISP-based macro language and interpreter, a powerful command syntax, and other fun-filled extensions. Emacs macro packages exist to allow you to read electronic mail and news, edit the contents of directories, and even engage in an artificially intelligent psychotherapy session (indispensible for stressed-out Linux hackers).

One interesting note is that most of the basic Linux utilities are GNU software. These GNU utilities support advanced features not found in the standard versions from BSD or AT&T. For example, GNU's version of the `vi` editor, `elvis`, includes a structured macro language which differs from the original AT&T implementation. However, the GNU utilities strive to remain compatible with their BSD and System V counterparts. Many people consider the GNU versions of these programs superior to the originals.

The most important utility to many users is the **shell**. The shell is a program which reads and executes commands from the user. In addition, many shells provide features such as **job control** (allowing the user to manage several running processes at once—not as Orwellian as it sounds), input and output redirection, and a command language for writing **shell scripts**. A shell script is a file containing a program in the shell command language, analogous to a "batch file" under MS-DOS.

There are many types of shells available for Linux. The most important difference between shells is the command language. For example, the **C Shell** (`csh`) uses a command language somewhat like the C programming language. The classic **Bourne Shell** uses a different command language. One's choice of a shell is often based on the command language that it provides. The shell that you use defines, to some extent, your working environment under Linux.

No matter what shell you're accustomed to, some version of it has probably been ported to Linux. The most popular shell is the GNU Bourne Again Shell (`bash`), a Bourne shell variant which includes many advanced features, such as job control, command history, command and filename completion, an Emacs-like interface for editing the command line, and powerful extensions to the standard Bourne shell language.

Another popular shell is `tcsh`, a version of the C Shell with advanced functionality similar to that found in `bash`. Other shells include `zsh`, a small Bourne-like shell; the Korn shell (`ksh`); BSD's `ash`; and `rc`, the Plan 9 shell.

What's so important about these basic utilities? Linux gives you the unique opportunity to tailor a custom system to your needs. For example, if you're the only person who uses your system, and you prefer to exclusively use the `vi` editor, and `bash` as your shell, there's no reason to install other editors or shells. The "do it yourself" attitude is prevalent among Linux hackers and users.

1.4.2   Text processing and word processing

Almost every computer user has a need for some kind of document preparation system. (How many computer enthusiasts do you know who still use pen and paper? Not many, we'll wager.) In the PC world, *word processing* is the norm: it involves editing and manipulating text (often in a "What-You-See-Is-What-You-Get" environment) and producing printed copies of the text, complete with figures, tables, and other garnishes.

In the UNIX world, *text processing* is much more common, which is quite different than the classical concept of word processing. With a text processing system, text is entered by the author using a "typesetting language", which describes how the text should be formatted. Instead of entering the text within a special word processing environment, the source may be modified with any text editor such as `vi` or Emacs. Once the source text (in the typesetting language) is complete, the user formats the text with a separate program, which converts the source to a format suitable for printing. This is somewhat analogous to programming in a language such as C, and "compiling" the document into a printable form.

There are many text processing systems available for Linux. One is `groff`, the GNU version of the classic `nroff` text formatter originally developed by Bell Labs and still used on many UNIX systems worldwide. Another modern text processing system is TeX, developed by Donald Knuth of computer science fame. Dialects of TeX, such as LaTeX, are also available.

Text processors such as TeX and `groff` differ mostly in the syntax of their formatting languages. The choice of one formatting system over another is also based upon what utilities are available to satisfy your needs, as well as personal taste.

For example, some people consider the `groff` formatting language to be a bit obscure, so they use TeX, which is more readable by humans. However, `groff` is capable of producing plain ASCII output, viewable on a terminal, while TeX is intended primarily for output to a printing device. However, various programs exist to produce plain ASCII from TeX-formatted documents, or to convert TeX to `groff`, for example.

Another text processing system is `texinfo`, an extension to TeX used for software documentation by the Free Software Foundation. `texinfo` is capable of producing a printed document, or an online-browsable hypertext "Info" document from a single source file. Info files are the main format of documentation used by GNU software such as Emacs.

Text processors are used widely in the computing community for producing papers, theses, magazine articles, and books (in fact, this book was produced using LaTeX). The ability to process the source language as a plain text file opens the door to many extensions to the text processor itself. Because source documents are not stored in an obscure format, readable only by a particular word processor, programmers are able to write parsers and translators for the formatting language, extending the system.

What does such a formatting language look like? In general, the formatting language source consists mostly of the text itself, along with "control codes" to produce a particular effect, such as changing fonts, setting margins, creating lists, and so on.

As an example, take the following text:

Mr. Torvalds:

We are very upset with your current plans to implement *post-hypnotic suggestion* in the **Linux** terminal driver code. We feel this way for three reasons:

1. Planting subliminal messages in the terminal driver is not only immoral, it is a waste of time;
2. It has been proven that "post-hypnotic suggestions" are ineffective when used upon unsuspecting UNIX hackers;
3. We have already implemented high-voltage electric shocks, as a security measure, in the code for `login`.

We hope you will reconsider.

This text would appear in the LaTeX formatting language as the following:

```
\begin{quote}
Mr. Torvalds:

We are very upset with your current plans to implement {\em post-hypnotic
suggestion\/} in the {\bf Linux} terminal driver code. We feel this
way for three reasons:
\begin{enumerate}
\item Planting subliminal messages in the kernel driver is not only
      immoral, it is a waste of time;
\item It has been proven that ``post-hypnotic suggestions'' are ineffective
      when used upon unsuspecting UNIX hackers;
\item We have already implemented high-voltage electric shocks, as a
      security measure, in the code for {\tt login}.
\end{enumerate}
We hope you will reconsider.
\end{quote}
```

The author enters the above "source" text using any text editor, and generates the formatted output by processing the source with LaTeX. At first glance, the typesetting language may appear to be obscure, but it's actually quite easy to learn. Using a text processing system enforces typographical standards when writing. For example, all enumerated lists within a document will look the same, unless the author modifies the definition of the enumerated list "environment". The primary goal is to allow the author to concentrate on writing the actual text, instead of worrying about typesetting conventions.

WYSIWYG word processors are attractive for many reasons; they provide a powerful (and sometimes complex) visual interface for editing the document. However, this interface is inherently limited to those aspects of text layout which are accessible to the user. For example, many word processors provide a special "format language" for producing complicated expressions such as mathematical formulae. This is identical text processing, albeit on a much smaller scale.

The subtle benefit of text processing is that the system allows you to specify exactly what you mean. Also, text processing systems allow you to edit the source text with any text editor, and the source is easily converted to other formats. The tradeoff for this flexibility and power is the lack of a WYSIWYG interface.

Many users of word processors are used to seeing the formatted text as they edit it. On the other hand, when writing with a text processor, one generally does not worry about how the text will appear when formatted. The writer learns to expect how the text should look from the formatting commands used in the source.

There are programs which allow you to view the formatted document on a graphics display before printing. For example, the `xdvi` program displays a "device independent" file generated by the TeX system under the X Windows environment. Other software applications, such as xfig, provide a WYSIWYG graphics interface for drawing figures and diagrams, which are subsequently converted to the text processing language for inclusion in your document.

Admittedly, text processors such as nroff were around long before word processing was available. However, many people still prefer to use text processing, because it is more versatile and independent of a graphics environment. In either case, the idoc word processor is also available for Linux, and before long we expect to see commercial word processors becoming available as well. If you absolutely don't want to give up word processing for text processing, you can always run MS-DOS, or some other operating system, in addition to Linux.

There are many other text-processing-related utilities available. The powerful METAFONT system, used for designing fonts for TEX, is included with the Linux port of TEX. Other programs include ispell, an interactive spell checker and corrector; makeindex, used for generating indicies in LATEX documents; as well as many groff and TEX-based macro packages for formatting many types of documents and mathematical texts. Conversion programs to translate between TEX or groff source to a myriad of other formats are available.

1.4.3   Programming languages and utilities

Linux provides a complete UNIX programming environment, including all of the standard libraries, programming tools, compilers, and debuggers that you would expect to find on other UNIX systems. Within the UNIX software development world, applications and systems programming is usually done in C or C++. The standard C and C++ compiler for Linux is GNU's gcc, which is an advanced, modern compiler supporting many options. It is also capable of compiling C++ (including AT&T 3.0 features) as well as Objective-C, another object-oriented dialect of C.

Besides C and C++, many other compiled and interpreted programming languages have been ported to Linux, such as Smalltalk, FORTRAN, Pascal, LISP, Scheme, and Ada (if you're masochistic enough to program in Ada—we're not going to stop you). In addition, various assemblers for writing protected-mode 80386 code are available, as are UNIX hacking favorites such as Perl (the script language to end all script languages) and Tcl/Tk (a shell-like command processing system including support for developing simple X Windows applications).

The advanced gdb debugger has been ported, which allows you to step through a program to find bugs, or examine the cause for a crash using a core dump. gprof, a profiling utility, will give you performance statistics for your program, letting you know where your program is spending most of its time executing. The Emacs text editor provides an interactive editing and compilation environment for various programming languages. Other tools include GNU make and imake, used to manage compilation of large applications; and RCS, a system for source locking and revision control.

Linux implements dynamically-linked shared libraries, which allow binaries to be much smaller as the subroutine code is linked at run-time. These DLL libraries also allow the applications programmer to override function definitions with their own code. For example, if a programmer wished to write her own version of the malloc() library routine, the linker would use the programmer's new routine instead of the one found in the libraries.

Linux is ideal for developing UNIX applications. It provides a modern programming environment with all of the bells and whistles. Various standards such as POSIX.1 are supported, allowing software written for Linux to be easily ported to other systems. Professional UNIX programmers and system administrators can use Linux to develop software at home, and then transfer the software to UNIX systems at work. This not only can save a great deal of time and money, but will also let you work in the comfort of your own home.[3] Computer Science students can use Linux to learn UNIX programming and to explore other aspects of the system, such as kernel architecture.

---

[3]The author uses his Linux system to develop and test X Windows applications at home, which can be directly compiled on workstations elsewhere.

With Linux, not only do you have access to the complete set of libraries and programming utilities, but you also have the complete kernel and library source code at your fingertips.

1.4.4   The X Window System

The X Window System is the standard graphics interface for UNIX machines. It is a powerful environment supporting many applications. Using X Windows, the user can have multiple terminal windows on the screen at once, each one containing a different login session. A pointing device such as a mouse is often used with the X interface, although it isn't required.

Many X-specific applications have been written, such as games, graphics utilities, programming and documentation tools, and so on. With Linux and X, your system is a bona fide workstation. Coupled with TCP/IP networking, you can even display X applications running on other machines on your Linux display, as is possible with other systems running X.

The X Window System was originally developed at MIT, and is freely distributable. However, may commercial vendors have distributed proprietary enhancements to the original X Windows software. The version of X Windows available for Linux is known as XFree86, a port of X11R5 made freely distributable for 80386-based UNIX systems such as Linux. XFree86 supports a wide range of video hardware, including VGA, Super VGA, and a number of accelerated video adaptors. This is a complete distribution of the X Windows software, containing the X server itself, many applications and utilities, programming libraries, and documentation.

Standard X applications include xterm (a terminal emulator used for most text-based applications within an X window); xdm (the X Session Manager, which handles logins); xclock (a simple clock display); xman (an X-based man page reader), and more. The many X applications available for Linux are too numerous to mention here, but the base XFree86 distribution includes the "standard" applications found in the original MIT release. Many others are available separately, and theoretically any application written for X Windows should compile cleanly under Linux.

The look and feel of the X Windows interface is controlled to a large extent by the **window manager**. This friendly program is in charge of the placement of windows, the user interface for resizing, iconifying, and moving windows, the appearance of window frames, and so on. The standard XFree86 distribution includes twm, the classic MIT window manager, although more advanced window managers such as the Open Look Virtual Window Manager (olvwm) are available as well. One window manager that is popular among Linux users is fvwm. This is a small window manager, requiring less than half of the memory used by twm. It provides a 3-D appearance for windows, as well a virtual desktop—if the user moves the mouse to the edge of the screen, the entire desktop is shifted as if the display were much larger than it actually is. fvwm is greatly customizable, and allows all functions to be accessed from the keyboard as well as the mouse. Many Linux distributions use fvwm as the standard window manager.

The XFree86 distribution contains programming libraries and include files for those wily programmers who wish to develop X applications. Various widget sets, such as Athena, Open Look, and Xaw3D are supported. All of the standard fonts, bitmaps, man pages, and documentation are included. PEX (a programming interface for 3-D graphics) is also supported.

Many X applications programmers use the proprietary Motif widget set for development. Several vendors sell single and multiple-user licenses for a binary version of Motif for Linux. Because Motif itself is relatively expensive, not many Linux users own it. However, binaries statically linked with Motif routines may be freely distributed. Therefore, if you write a program using Motif and wish to distribute it freely, you may provide a binary so that users without Motif can use the program.

The only major caveats with X Windows are the hardware and memory requirements. A 386 with 4 megabytes of RAM is capable of running X, but 8 megabytes or more of physical RAM are needed to use it comfortably. A faster processor is nice to have as well, but having enough physical RAM is much more important. In addition, to achieve really slick video performance, an accelerated video card (such as a local bus S3-chipset card) is strongly recommended. Performance ratings in excess of 140,000 xstones have been acheived with Linux and XFree86. With sufficient hardware, you'll find that running X and Linux is as fast, or faster, than running X on other UNIX workstations.

In Chapter 5 we'll discuss how to install and use X on your system.

1.4.5   Networking

Interested in communicating with the world? Yes? No? Maybe? Linux supports the two primary networking protocols for UNIX systems: **TCP/IP** and **UUCP**. TCP/IP (Transmission Control Protocol/Internet Protocol, for acronym aficionados) is the set of networking paradigms that allow systems all over the world to communicate on a single network known as the Internet. With Linux, TCP/IP, and a connection to the network, you can communicate with users and machines across the Internet via electronic mail, USENET news, file transfers with FTP, and more. There are many Linux systems currently on the Internet.

Most TCP/IP networks use Ethernet as the physical network transport. Linux supports many popular Ethernet cards and interfaces for personal computers, including the D-Link pocket Ethernet adaptor for laptops.

However, because not everyone has an Ethernet drop at home, Linux also supports **SLIP** (Serial Line Internet Protocol), which allows you to connect to the Internet via modem. In order to use SLIP, you'll need to have access to a SLIP server, a machine connected to the network which allows dial-in access. Many businesses and universities provide such SLIP servers. In fact, if your Linux system has an Ethernet connection as well as a modem, you can configure it as a SLIP server for other hosts.

NFS (Network File System) allows your system to seamlessly share files with other machines on the network. FTP (File Transfer Protocol) allows you to transfer files between other machines. Other applications include `sendmail`, a system for sending and receiving electronic mail using the SMTP protocol; NNTP-based electronic news systems such as C-News and INN; `telnet`, `rlogin`, and `rsh`, which allow you to login and execute commands on other machines on the network; and `finger`, which allows you to get information on other Internet users. There are literally tons of TCP/IP-based applications and protocols out there.

The full range of mail and news readers are available for Linux, such as `elm`, `pine`, `rn`, `nn`, and `tin`. Whatever your preference, you can configure your Linux system to send and receive electronic mail and news from all over the world.

If you have experience with TCP/IP applications on other UNIX systems, Linux will be very familiar to you. The system provides a standard socket programming interface, so virtually any program which uses TCP/IP can be ported to Linux. The Linux X server also supports TCP/IP, allowing you to display applications running on other systems on your Linux display.

In Chapter 5 we'll discuss configuration and setup of TCP/IP, including SLIP, for Linux.

UUCP (UNIX-to-UNIX Copy) is an older mechanism used to transfer files, electronic mail, and electronic news between UNIX machines. Classically, UUCP machines connected to each other over the phone lines via modem, but UUCP is able to transport over a TCP/IP network as well. If you do not have access to a TCP/IP network or a SLIP server, you can configure your system to send and receive files and electronic mail using UUCP. See Chapter 5 for more information.

1.4.6   Telecommunications and BBS software

If you have a modem, you will be able to communicate with other machines using one of the telecommunications packages available for Linux. Many people use telecommunications software to access bulletin board systems (BBSs), as well as commercial online services such as Prodigy, CompuServe, and America On-Line. Other people use their modems to connect to a UNIX system at work or school. You can even use your modem and Linux system to send and receive facsimiles. Telecommunications software under Linux is very similar to that found under MS-DOS or other operating systems. Anyone who has ever used a telecommunications package will find the Linux equivalent familiar.

One of the most popular communications packages for Linux is Seyon, an X application providing a customizable, ergonomic interface, with built-in support for various file transfer protocols such as Kermit, ZModem, and so on. Other telecommunications programs include C-Kermit, pcomm, and minicom. These are similar to communications programs found on other operating systems, and are quite easy to use.

If you do not have access to a SLIP server (see the previous section), you can use term to multiplex your serial line. term will allow you to open multiple login sessions over the modem connection to a remote machine. term will also allow you to redirect X client connections to your local X server, through the serial line, allowing you to display remote X applications on your Linux system. Another software package, KA9Q, implements a similar SLIP-like interface.

Running a bulletin board system (BBS) is a favorite hobby (and means of income) for many people. Linux supports a wide range of BBS software, most of which is more powerful than what is available for other operating systems. With a phone line, a modem, and Linux, you can turn your system into a BBS, providing dial-in access to your system to users worldwide. BBS software for Linux includes XBBS and the UniBoard BBS packages.

Most BBS software locks the user into a menu-based system where only certain functions and applications are available. An alternative to BBS access is full UNIX access, which would allow users to dial into your system and login as a regular user. While this would require a fair amount of maintenance on the part of the system administrator, it can be done, and providing public UNIX access from your Linux system is not difficult to do. Along with a TCP/IP network, you can provide electronic mail and news access to users on your system.

If you do not have access to a TCP/IP network or UUCP feed, Linux will also allow you to communicate with a number of BBS networks, such as FidoNet, with which you can exchange electronic news and mail via the phone line. More information on telecommunications and BBS software under Linux can be found in Chapter 5.

1.4.7 Interfacing with MS-DOS

Various utilities exist to interface with the world of MS-DOS. The most well-known application is the Linux MS-DOS Emulator, which allows you to run many MS-DOS applications directly from Linux. Although Linux and MS-DOS are completely different operating systems, the 80386 protected-mode environment allows certain tasks to behave as if they were running in 8086-emulation mode, as MS-DOS applications do.

The MS-DOS emulator is still under development, yet many popular applications run under it. Understandably, however, MS-DOS applications which use bizarre or esoteric features of the system may never be supported, because it is only an emulator. For example, you wouldn't expect to be able to run any programs which use 80386 protected-mode features, such as Microsoft Windows (in 386 enhanced mode, that is).

Applications which run successfully under the Linux MS-DOS Emulator include 4DOS (a command interpreter), Foxpro 2.0, Harvard Graphics, MathCad, Stacker 3.1, Turbo Assembler, Turbo C/C++, Turbo Pascal, Microsoft Windows 3.0 (in *real* mode), and WordPerfect 5.1. Standard MS-DOS commands and utilities (such as PKZIP, and so on) work with the emulator as well.

The MS-DOS Emulator is meant mostly as an ad hoc solution for those people who need MS-DOS only for a few applications, but use Linux for everything else. It's not meant to be a complete implementation of MS-DOS. Of course, if the Emulator doesn't satisfy your needs, you can always run MS-DOS as well as Linux on the same system. Using the LILO boot loader, you can specify at boot time which operating system to start. Linux can coexist with other operating systems, such as OS/2, as well.

Linux provides a seamless interface for transferring files between Linux and MS-DOS. You can mount an MS-DOS partition or floppy under Linux, and directly access MS-DOS files as you would any other.

Currently under development is a project known as **WINE**—a Microsoft Windows emulator for the X Window System under Linux. Once WINE is complete, users will be able to run MS-Windows applications directly from Linux. This is similar to the proprietary WABI Windows emulator from Sun Microsystems. At the time of this writing, WINE is still in the early stages of development, but the outlook is good.

In Chapter 5 we'll talk about the MS-DOS tools available for Linux.

1.4.8   Other applications

A host of miscellany is available for Linux, as one would expect from such a hodgepodge operating system. Linux's primary focus is currently for personal UNIX computing, but this is rapidly changing. Business and scientific software is expanding, and commercial software vendors are beginning to contribute to the growing pool of applications.

Several relational databases are available for Linux, including Postgres, Ingres, and Mbase. These are full-featured, professional client/server database applications similar to those found on other UNIX platforms. /rdb, a commercial database system, is available as well.

Scientific computing applications include FELT (a finite element analysis tool); gnuplot (a plotting and data analysis application); Octave (a symbolic mathematics package, similar to MATLAB); xspread (a spreadsheet calculator); xfractint, an X-based port of the popular Fractint fractal generator; xlispstat (a statistics package), and more. Other applications include Spice (a circuit design and analysis tool) and Khoros (an image/digital signal processing and visualization system).

Of course, there are many more such applications which have been, and can be, ported to run on Linux. Whatever your field, porting UNIX-based applications to Linux should be quite straightforward. Linux provides a complete UNIX programming interface, sufficient to serve as the base for any scientific application.

As with any operating system, Linux has its share of games. These include classic text-based dungeon games such as Nethack and Moria; MUDs (multi-user dungeons, which allow many users to interact in a text-based adventure) such as DikuMUD and TinyMUD; as well as a slew of X games such as xtetris, netrek, and Xboard (the X11 version of gnuchess). The popular shoot-em-up arcade-style *Doom* has also been ported to Linux.

For audiophiles, Linux has support for various sound cards and related software, such as CDplayer (a program which can control a CD-ROM drive as a conventional CD player, surprisingly enough), MIDI sequencers and editors (allowing you to compose music for playback through a synthesizer or other MIDI-controlled instrument), and sound editors for digitized sounds.

Can't find the application you're looking for? The Linux Software Map, described in Appendix A, contains a list of many software packages which have been written and ported to Linux. While this list is far from complete, it contains a great deal of software. Another way to find Linux applications is to look at the INDEX files found on Linux FTP sites, if you have Internet access. Just by poking around you'll find a great deal of software just waiting to be played with.

If you absolutely can't find what you need, you can always attempt to port the application from another platform to Linux. Most freely distributable UNIX-based software will compile on Linux with few problems. Or, if all else fails, you can write the application yourself. If it's a commercial application you're looking for, there may be a free "clone" available. Or, you can encourage the software company to consider releasing a Linux binary version. Several individuals have contacted software companies, asking them to port their applications to Linux, and have met with various degrees of success.

1.5 About Linux's Copyright

Linux is covered by what is known as the GNU *General Public License*, or *GPL*. The GPL was developed for the GNU project by the Free Software Foundataion. It makes a number of provisions for the distribution and modification of "free software". "Free" in this sense refers to freedom, not just cost. The GPL has always been subject to misinterpretation, and we hope that this summary will help you to understand the extent and goals of the GPL and its effect on Linux. A complete copy of the GPL is included in Appendix E.

Originally, Linus Torvalds released Linux under a license more restrictive than the GPL, which allowed the software to be freely distributed and modified, but prevented any money changing hands for its distribution and use. On the other hand, the GPL allows people to sell and make profit from free software, but does not allow them to restrict the right for others to distribute the software in any way.

First, it should be explained that "free software" covered by the GPL is *not* in the public domain. Public domain software is software which is not copyrighted, and is literally owned by the public. Software covered by the GPL, on the other hand, is copyrighted to the author or authors. This means that the software is protected by standard international copyright laws, and that the author of the software is legally defined. Just because the software may be freely distributed does not mean that it is in the public domain.

GPL-licensed software is also not "shareware". Generally, "shareware" software is owned and copyrighted by the author, but the author requires users to send in money for its use after distribution. On the other hand, software covered by the GPL may be distributed and used free of charge.

The GPL also allows people to take and modify free software, and distribute their own versions of the software. However, any derived works from GPL software must also be covered by the GPL. In other words, a company could not take Linux, modify it, and sell it under a restrictive license. If any software is derived from Linux, that software must be covered by the GPL as well.

The GPL allows free software to be distributed and used free of charge. However, it also allows a person or organization to distribute GPL software for a fee, and even to make a profit from its sale and distribution. However, in selling GPL software, the distributor cannot take those rights away from the purchaser; that is, if you purchase GPL software from some source, you may distribute the software for free, or sell it yourself as well.

This might sound like a contradiction at first. Why sell software for profit when the GPL allows anyone to obtain it for free? As an example, let's say that some company decided to bundle a large amount of free software on a CD-ROM and distribute it. That company would need to charge for the overhead of producing and distributing the CD-ROM, and the company may even decide to make profit from the sales of software. This is allowed by the GPL.

Organizations which sell free software must follow certain restrictions set forth in the GPL. First, they cannot restrict the rights of users who purchase the software. This means that if you buy a CD-ROM of GPL software, you can copy and distribute that CD-ROM free of charge, or resell it yourself. Secondly, distributors must make it obvious to users that the software is indeed covered by the GPL. Thirdly, distributors must provide, free of charge, the complete source code for the software being distributed. This will allow anyone who purchases GPL software to make modifications of that software.

Allowing a company to distribute and sell free software is a very good thing. Not everyone has access to the Internet to download software, such as Linux, for free. The GPL allows companies to sell and distribute software to those people who do not have free (cost-wise) access to the software. For example, many organizations sell Linux on diskette, tape, or CD-ROM via mail order, and make profit from these sales. The developers of Linux may never see any of this profit; that is the understanding that is reached between the developer and the distributor when software is licensed by the GPL. In other words, Linus knew that companies may wish to sell Linux, and that he may not see a penny of the profits from those sales.

In the free software world, the important issue is not money. The goal of free software is always to develop and distribute fantastic software and to allow anyone to obtain and use it. In the next section, we'll discuss how this applies to the development of Linux.

1.6   The Design and Philosophy of Linux

When new users encounter Linux, they often have a few misconceptions and false expectations of the system. Linux is a unique operating system, and it is important to understand its philosophy and design in order to use it effectively. Time enough for a soapbox. Even if you are an aged UNIX guru, what follows is probably of interest to you.

In commercial UNIX development houses, the entire system is developed with a rigorous policy of quality assurance, source and revision control systems, documentation, and bug reporting and resolution. Developers are not allowed to add features or to change key sections of code on a whim: they must validate the change as a response to a bug report and consequently "check in" all changes to the source control system, so that the changes can be backed out if necessary. Each developer is assigned one or more parts of the system code, and only that developer may alter those sections of the code while it is "checked out".

Internally, the quality assurance department runs rigorous regression test suites on each new pass of the operating system, and reports any bugs. It is the responsibility of the developers to fix these bugs as reported. A complicated system of statistical analysis is employed to ensure that a certain percentage of bugs are fixed before the next release, and that the operating system as a whole passes certain release criteria.

In all, the process used by commercial UNIX developers to maintain and support their code is very complicated, and quite reasonably so. The company must have quantitative proof that the next revision of the operating system is ready to be shipped; hence, the gathering and analysis of statistics about the operating system's performance. It is a big job to develop a commercial UNIX system, often large enough to employ hundreds (if not thousands) of programmers, testers, documentors, and administrative personel. Of course, no two commercial UNIX vendors are alike, but you get the general picture.

With Linux, you can throw out the entire concept of organized development, source control systems, structured bug reporting, or statistical analysis. Linux is, and more than likely always will be, a hacker's operating system.[4]

Linux is primarily developed as a group effort by volunteers on the Internet from all over the world. Across the Internet and beyond, anyone with enough know-how has the opportunity to aid in developing and debugging the kernel, porting new software, writing documentation, or helping new users. There is no single organization responsible for developing the system. For the most part, the Linux community communicates via various mailing lists and USENET newsgroups. A number of conventions have sprung up around the development effort: for example, anyone wishing to have their code included in the "official" kernel should mail it to Linus Torvalds, which he will test and include in the kernel (as long as it doesn't break things or go against the overall design of the system, he will more than likely include it).

The system itself is designed with a very open-ended, feature-minded approach. While recently the number of new features and critical changes to the system have diminished, the general rule is that a new version of the kernel will be released about every few months (sometimes even more frequently than this). Of course, this is a very rough figure: it depends on a several factors including the number of bugs to be fixed, the amount of feedback from users testing pre-release versions of the code, and the amount of sleep that Linus has had this week.

Let it suffice to say that not every single bug has been fixed, and not every problem ironed out between releases. As long as the system appears to be free of critical or oft-manifesting bugs, it is considered "stable" and new revisions will be released. The thrust behind Linux development is not an effort to release perfect, bug-free code: it is to develop a free implementation of UNIX. Linux is *for* the developers, more than anyone else.

Anyone who has a new feature or software application to add to the system generally makes it available in

---

[4]What I mean by "hacker" is a feverishly dedicated programmer, a person who enjoys exploiting computers and generally doing interesting things with them. This is in contrast to the common denotation of "hacker" as a computer wrongdoer or outlaw.

an "alpha" stage—that is, a stage for testing by those brave or unwary users who want to bash out problems with the initial code. Because the Linux community is largely based on the Internet, alpha software is usually uploaded to one or more of the various Linux FTP sites (see Appendix C) and a message posted to one of the Linux USENET newsgroups about how to get and test the code. Users who download and test alpha software can then mail results, bug fixes, or questions to the author.

After the initial problems in the alpha code have been fixed, the code enters a "beta" stage, in which it is usually considered stable but not complete (that is, it works, but not all of the features may be present). Otherwise, it may go directly to a "final" stage in which the software is considered complete and usable. For kernel code, once it is complete the developer may ask Linus to include it in the standard kernel, or as an optional add-on feature to the kernel.

Keep in mind that these are only conventions—not rules. Some people feel so confident with their software that they don't need to release an alpha or test version. It is always up to the developer to make these decisions.

You might be amazed that such a nonstructured system of volunteers, programming and debugging a complete UNIX system, could get anything done at all. As it turns out, it is one of the most efficient and motivated development efforts ever employed. The entire Linux kernel was written *from scratch*, without employing any code from proprietary sources. A great deal of work was put forth by volunteers to port all of the free software under the sun to the Linux system. Libraries were written and ported, filesystems developed, and hardware drivers written for many popular devices.

The Linux software is generally released as a *distribution*, which is a set of pre-packaged software making up an entire system. It would be quite difficult for most users to build a complete system from the ground up, starting with the kernel, adding utilities, and installing all of the necessary software by hand. Instead, there are a number of software distributions including everything that you need to install and run a complete system. Again, there is no standard distribution—there are many, each with their own advantages and disadvantages. We'll talk more about the various available Linux distributions in Section 2.1.

Despite the completeness of the Linux software, you will still need a bit of UNIX know-how to install and run a complete system. No distribution of Linux is completely bug-free, so you may be required to fix small problems by hand after installation. Running a UNIX system is not an easy task, not even for commercial versions of UNIX. If you're serious about Linux, bear in mind that it will take a considerable amount of effort and attention on your part to keep the system running and take care of things: this is true of *any* UNIX system, and Linux is no exception. Because of the diversity of the Linux community and the many needs which the software is attempting to meet, not eveything can be taken care of for you all of the time.

1.6.1 Hints for UNIX novices

Installing and using your own Linux system does not require a great deal of background in UNIX. In fact, many UNIX novices successfully install Linux on their systems. This is a worthwhile learning experience, but keep in mind that it can be very frustrating to some. If you're lucky, you will be able to install and start using your Linux system without any UNIX background. However, once you are ready to delve into the more complex tasks of running Linux—installing new software, recompiling the kernel, and so forth—having background knowledge in UNIX is going to be a necessity.

Fortunately, by running your own Linux system you will be able to learn the essentials of UNIX necessary for these tasks. This book contains a good deal of information to help you get started—Chapter 3 is a tutorial covering UNIX basics, and Chapter 4 contains information on Linux system administration. You may wish to read these chapters before you attempt to install Linux at all—the information contained therein will prove to be invaluable should you run into problems.

Nobody can expect to go from being a UNIX novice to a UNIX system administrator overnight. No implementation of UNIX is expected to run trouble- and maintenance-free. You must be aptly prepared for the journey which lies ahead. Otherwise, if you're new to UNIX, you may very well become overly frustrated with the system.

1.6.2   Hints for UNIX gurus

Even those people with years of UNIX programming and systems administration experience may need assistance before they are able to pick up and install Linux. There are still aspects of the system that UNIX wizards will need to be familiar with before diving in. For one thing, Linux is not a commercial UNIX system. It does not attempt to uphold the same standards as other UNIX systems you have may have come across. To be more specific, while stability is an important factor in the development of Linux, it is not the *only* factor.

More important, perhaps, is functionality. In many cases, new code will make it into the standard kernel even though it is still buggy and not functionally complete. The assumption is that it is more important to release code which users can test and use than delay a release until it is "complete". As an example, WINE (the Microsoft Windows Emulator for Linux) had an "official" alpha release before it was completely tested. In this way, the Linux community at large had a chance to work with the code, test it, and help develop it, while those who found the alpha code "good enough" for their needs could use it. Commercial UNIX vendors rarely, if ever, release software in this manner.

If you have been a UNIX systems administrator for more than a decade, and have used every commercial UNIX system under the Sun (no pun intended), Linux may take some getting used to. The system is very modern and dynamic. A new kernel release is made approximately every few months. New software is constantly being released. One day your system may be completely up-to-date with the current trend, and the next day the same system is considered to be in the Stone Age.

With all of this dynamic activity, how can you be expected to keep up with the ever-changing Linux world? For the most part, it is best to upgrade incrementally; that is, upgrade only those parts of the system that *need* upgrading, and then only when you think an upgrade is necessary. For example, if you never use Emacs, there is little reason to continuously install every new release of Emacs on your system. Furthermore, even if you are an avid Emacs user, there is usually no reason to upgrade it unless you find that some feature is missing that is in the next release. There is little or no reason to always be on top of the newest version of software.

We hope that Linux will meet or exceed your expectations of a homebrew UNIX system. At the very core of Linux is the spirit of free software, of constant development and growth. The Linux community favors expansion over stability, and that is a difficult concept to swallow for many people, especially those so steeped in the world of commercial UNIX. You cannot expect Linux to be perfect; nothing ever is in the free software world. However, we believe that Linux really is as complete and useful as any other implementation of UNIX.

1.7   Differences Between Linux and Other Operating Systems

It is important to understand the differences between Linux and other operating systems, such as MS-DOS, OS/2, and other implementations of UNIX for the personal computer. First of all, it should be made clear that Linux will coexist happily with other operating systems on the same machine: that is, you can run MS-DOS and OS/2 along with Linux on the same system without problems. There are even ways to interact between the various operating systems, as we'll see.

1.7.1   Why use Linux?

Why use Linux instead of a well-known, well-tested, and well-documented commercial operating system? We could give you a thousand reasons. One of the most important, however, is that Linux is an excellent choice for personal UNIX computing. If you're a UNIX software developer, why use MS-DOS at home? Linux will allow you to develop and test UNIX software on your PC, including database and X Windows applications. If you're a student, chances are that your university computing systems run UNIX. With Linux, you can run your own UNIX system and tailor it to your own needs. Installing and running Linux is also an excellent way to learn UNIX if you don't have access to other UNIX machines.

But let's not lose sight. Linux isn't just for personal UNIX users. It is robust and complete enough to handle large tasks, as well as distributed computing needs. Many businesses—especially small ones—are moving to Linux in lieu of other UNIX-based workstation environments. Universities are finding Linux to be perfect for teaching courses in operating systems design. Larger commercial software vendors are starting to realize the opportunities that a free operating system can provide.

The following sections should point out the most important differences between Linux and other operating systems. We hope that you'll find that Linux can meet your computing needs, or (at least) enhance your current computing environment. Keep in mind that they best way to get a taste for Linux is just to try it out—you needn't even install a complete system to get a feel for it. In Chapter 2, we'll show you how.

1.7.2   Linux vs. MS-DOS

It's not uncommon to run both Linux and MS-DOS on the same system. Many Linux users rely on MS-DOS for applications such as word processing. While Linux provides its own analogues for these applications (for example, TEX), there are various reasons why a particular user would want to run MS-DOS as well as Linux. If your entire dissertation is written using WordPerfect for MS-DOS, you may not be able to easily convert it to TEX or some other format. There are many commercial applications for MS-DOS which aren't available for Linux, and there's no reason why you can't use both.

As you might know, MS-DOS does not fully utilize the functionality of the 80386 and 80486 processors. On the other hand, Linux runs completely in the processor's protected mode, and exploits all of the features of the processor. You can directly access all of your available memory (and beyond, using virtual RAM). Linux provides a complete UNIX interface not available under MS-DOS—developing and porting UNIX applications under Linux is easily done, while under MS-DOS you are limited to a small subset of the UNIX programming functionality. Because Linux is a true UNIX system, you do not have these limitations.

We could debate the pros and cons of MS-DOS and Linux for pages on end. However, let it suffice to say that Linux and MS-DOS are completely different entities. MS-DOS is inexpensive (compared to other commercial operating systems), and has a strong foothold in the PC computing world. No other operating system for the PC has reached the level of popularity of MS-DOS—largely because the cost of these other operating systems is unapproachable to most personal computer users. Very few PC users can imagine spending $1000 or more on the operating system alone. Linux, however, is free, and you finally have the chance to decide.

We will allow you to make your own judgments of Linux and MS-DOS based on your expectations and needs. Linux is not for everybody. If you have always wanted to run a complete UNIX system at home, without the high cost of other UNIX implementations for the PC, Linux may be what you're looking for.

There are tools available to allow you to interact between Linux and MS-DOS. For example, it is easy to access MS-DOS files from Linux. There is also an MS-DOS emulator available, which allows you to run many popular MS-DOS applications. A Microsoft Windows emulator is currently under development.

1.7.3   Linux vs. The Other Guys

A number of other advanced operating systems are on the rise in the PC world. Specifically, IBM's OS/2 and Microsoft's Windows NT are becoming very popular as more users move away from MS-DOS.

Both OS/2 and Windows NT are full multitasking operating systems, much like Linux. Technically, OS/2, Windows NT, and Linux are quite similar: they support roughly the same features in terms of user interface, networking, security, and so forth. However, the real difference between Linux and The Other Guys is the fact that Linux is a version of UNIX, and hence benefits from the contributions of the UNIX community at large.

What makes UNIX so important? Not only is it the most popular operating system for multiuser machines, it is also the foundation for the majority of the free software world. If you have access to the Internet, nearly all of the free software available there is written specifically for UNIX systems. (The Internet itself is largely UNIX-based.)

There are many implementations of UNIX, from many vendors, and no single organization is responsible for distribution. There is a large push in the UNIX community for standardization in the form of open systems, but no single corporation controls this design. Hence, any vendor (or, as it turns out, any hacker) may implement these standards in an implementation of UNIX.

OS/2 and Windows NT, on the other hand, are proprietary systems. The interface and design are controlled by a single corporation, and only that corporation may implement that design. (Don't expect to see a free version of OS/2 anytime in the near future.) In one sense, this kind of organization is beneficial: it sets a strict standard for the programming and user interface unlike that found even in the open systems community. OS/2 is OS/2 wherever you go—the same holds for Windows NT.

However, the UNIX interface is constantly developing and changing. Several organizations are attempting to standardize the programming model, but the task is very difficult. Linux, in particular, is mostly compliant with the POSIX.1 standard for the UNIX programming interface. As time goes on, it is expected that the system will adhere to other such standards, but standardization is not the primary issue in the Linux development community.

1.7.4   Other implementations of UNIX

There are several other implementations of UNIX for the 80386 and 80486. The 80386 architecture lends itself to the UNIX design, and a number of vendors have taken advantage of this.

Feature-wise, other implementations of UNIX for the PC are quite similar to Linux. You will see that almost all commercial versions of UNIX support roughly the same software, programming environment, and networking features. However, there are some strong differences between Linux and commercial versions of UNIX.

First of all, Linux supports a different range of hardware from commercial implementations. In general, Linux supports the most well-known hardware devices, but support is still limited to that hardware which developers actually have access to. However, commercial UNIX vendors generally have a wider support base, and tend to support more hardware, although Linux is not far behind. We'll cover the hardware requirements for Linux in Section 1.8.

Secondly, commercial implementations of UNIX usually come bundled with a complete set of documentation as well as user support from the vendor. In contrast, most of the documentation for Linux is limited to documents available on the Internet—and books such as this one. In Section 1.9 we'll list sources of Linux documentation and other information.

As far as stability and robustness are concerned, many users have reported that Linux is at least as stable as commercial UNIX systems. Linux is still under development, and certain features (such TCP/IP networking) are less stable but improve as time goes by.

The most important factor to consider for many users is price. The Linux software is free, if you have access to the Internet (or another computer network) and can download it. If you do not have access to such a network, you may need to purchase it via mail order on diskette, tape, or CD-ROM (see Appendix B).

Of course, you may copy Linux from a friend who may already have the software, or share the cost of purchasing it with someone else. If you are planning to install Linux on a large number of machines, you need only purchase a single copy of the software—Linux is not distributed on a "single machine" license.

The value of commercial UNIX implementations should not be demeaned: along with the price of the software itself, one usually pays for documentation, support, and assurance of quality. These are very important factors for large institutions, but personal computer users may not require these benefits. In any case, many businesses and universities are finding that running Linux on a lab of inexpensive personal computers is preferrable to running a commercial version of UNIX in a lab of workstations. Linux can provide the functionality of a workstation on PC hardware at a fraction of the cost.

As a "real-world" example of Linux's use within the computing community, Linux systems have travelled the high seas of the North Pacific, managing telecommunications and data analysis for an oceanographic research vessel. Linux systems are being used at research stations in Antarctica. As a more mundane example, perhaps, several hospitals are using Linux to maintain patient records. It is proving to be as reliable and useful as other implementations of UNIX.

There are other free or inexpensive implementations of UNIX for the 386 and 486. One of the most well-known is 386BSD, an implementation and port of BSD UNIX for the 386. 386BSD is comparable to Linux in many ways, but which one is "better" depends on your own personal needs and expectations. The only strong distinction that we can make is that Linux is developed openly (where any volunteer can aid in the development process), while 386BSD is developed within a closed team of programmers who maintain the system. Because of this, serious philosophical and design differences exist between the two projects. The goals of the two projects are entirely different: the goal of Linux is to develop a complete UNIX system from scratch (and have a lot of fun in the process), and the goal of 386BSD is in part to modify the existing BSD code for use on the 386.

NetBSD is another port of the BSD NET/2 distribution to a number of machines, including the 386. NetBSD has a slightly more open development structure, and is comparable to 386BSD in many respects.

Another project of note is HURD, an effort by the Free Software Foundation to develop and distribute a free version of UNIX for many platforms. Contact the Free Software Foundation (the address is given in Appendix E) for more information about this project. At the time of this writing, HURD is still in early stages of development.

Other inexpensive versions of UNIX exist as well, such as Coherent (available for about $99) and Minix (an academic but useful UNIX clone upon which early development of Linux was based). Some of these implementations are of mostly academic interest, while others are full-fledged systems for real productivity. Needless to say, however, many personal UNIX users are moving to Linux.

1.8 Hardware Requirements

Now you must be convinced of how wonderful Linux is, and all of the great things that it can do for you. However, before you rush out and install the software, you need to be aware of the hardware requirements and limitations that Linux has.

Keep in mind that Linux was developed by its users. This means, for the most part, that the hardware which is supported by Linux is only the hardware which the users and developers actually have access to. As it turns out, most of the popular hardware and peripherals for 80386/80486 systems are supported (in fact, Linux supports more hardware than some commercial implementations of UNIX). However, some of the more obscure and esoteric devices aren't supported yet. As time goes on, a wider range of hardware is supported, so if your favorite devices aren't listed here, chances are that support for them is forthcoming.

Another drawback for hardware support under Linux is that many companies have decided to keep the hardware interface proprietary. The upshot of this is that volunteer Linux developers simply can't write drivers for those devices (if they could, those drivers would be owned by the company that owned the interface, which would violate the GPL). The companies that maintain proprietary interfaces write their own drivers for operating systems such as MS-DOS and Microsoft Windows; the end user (that's you) never needs to know about the interface. Unfortunately, this does not allow Linux developers to write drivers for those devices.

There is very little that can be done about the situation. In some cases, programmers have attempted to write hackish drivers based on assumptions about the interface. In other cases, developers will work with the company in question and attempt to obtain information about the device interface, with varying degrees of success.

In the following sections, we'll attempt to summarize the hardware requirements for Linux. The Linux *Hardware HOWTO* (see Section 1.9) contains a more complete listing of hardware supported by Linux.

Disclaimer: a good deal of hardware support for Linux is currently in the development stage. Some distributions may or may not support these experimental features. This section primarily lists hardware which has been supported for some time and is known to be stable. When in doubt, consult the documentation for the distribution of Linux you are using (see Section 2.1 for more information on Linux distributions).

1.8.1   Motherboard and CPU requirements

Linux currently supports systems with an Intel 80386, 80486, or Pentium CPU. This includes all variations on this CPU type, such as the 386SX, 486SX, 486DX, and 486DX2. Non-Intel "clones", such as AMD and Cyrix processors, work with Linux as well.

If you have a 80386 or 80486SX, you may also wish to use a math coprocessor, although one isn't required (the Linux kernel can do FPU emulation if you do not have a math coprocessor). All standard FPU couplings are supported, such as IIT, Cyrix FasMath, and Intel coprocessors.

The system motherboard must use ISA or EISA bus architecture. These terms define how the system interfaces with peripherals and other components on the main bus. Most systems sold today are either ISA or EISA bus. IBM's MicroChannel (MCA) bus, found on machines such as the IBM PS/2, is not currently supported.

Systems which use a local bus architecture (for faster video and disk access) are supported as well. It is suggested that you have a standard local bus architecture such as the VESA Local Bus ("VLB").

1.8.2   Memory requirements

Linux requires very little memory to run compared to other advanced operating systems. You should have at the very least 2 megabytes of RAM; however, it is strongly suggested that you have 4 megabytes. The more memory you have, the faster the system will run.

Linux can support the full 32-bit address range of the 386/486; in other words, it will utilize all of your RAM automatically.

Linux will run happily with only 4 megabytes of RAM, including all of the bells and whistles such as X Windows, Emacs, and so on. However, having more memory is almost as important as having a faster processor. 8 megabytes is more than enough for personal use; 16 megabytes or more may be needed if you are expecting a heavy user load on the system.

Most Linux users allocate a portion of their hard drive as swap space, which is used as virtual RAM. Even if you have a great deal of physical RAM in your machine, you may wish to use swap space. While swap space is no replacement for actual physical RAM, it can allow your system to run larger applications by swapping out inactive portions of code to disk. The amount of swap space that you should allocate depends on several factors; we'll come back to this question in Section 2.2.3.

1.8.3 Hard drive controller requirements

You do not need to have a hard drive to run Linux; you can run a minimal system completely from floppy. However, this is slow and very limited, and many users have access to hard drive storage anyway. You must have an AT-standard (16-bit) controller. There is support in the kernel for XT-standard (8 bit) controllers; however, most controllers used today are AT-standard. Linux should support all MFM, RLL, and IDE controllers. Most, but not all, ESDI controllers are supported—only those which do ST506 hardware emulation.

The general rule for non-SCSI hard drive and floppy controllers is that if you can access the drive from MS-DOS or another operating system, you should be able to access it from Linux.

Linux also supports a number of popular SCSI drive controllers, although support for SCSI is more limited because of the wide range of controller interface standards. Supported SCSI controllers include the Adaptec AHA1542B, AHA1542C, AHA1742A (BIOS version 1.34), AHA1522, AHA1740, AHA1740 (SCSI-2 controller, BIOS 1.34 in Enhanced mode); Future Domain 1680, TMC-850, TMC-950; Seagate ST-02; UltraStor SCSI; Western Digital WD7000FASST. Clones which are based on these cards should work as well.

1.8.4 Hard drive space requirements

Of course, to install Linux, you'll need to have some amount of free space on your hard drive. Linux will support multiple hard drives in the same machine; you can allocate space for Linux across multiple drives if necessary.

The *amount* of hard drive space that you will require depends greatly on your needs and the amount of software that you're installing. Linux is relatively small as UNIX implementations go; you could run a complete system in 10 to 20 megabytes of space on your drive. However, if you want to have room for expansion, and for larger packages such as X Windows, you will need more space. If you plan to allow multiple users to use the machine, you will need to allocate storage for their files.

Also, unless you have a large amount of physical RAM (16 megabytes or more), you will more than likely want to allocate swap space, to be used as virtual RAM. We will discuss all of the details of installing and using swap space in Section 2.2.3.

Each distribution of Linux usually comes with some literature that should help you to gauge the precise amount of required storage depending on the amount of software you plan to install. You can run a minimal system with less than 20 megabytes; a complete system with all of the bells and whistles in 80 megabytes or less; and a very large system with room for many users and space for future expansion in the range of 100-150 megabytes. Again, these figures are meant only as a ballpark approximation; you will have to look at your own needs and goals in order to determine your specific storage requirements.

1.8.5 Monitor and video adapator requirements

Linux supports all standard Hercules, CGA, EGA, VGA, IBM monochrome, and Super VGA video cards and monitors for the default text-based interface. In general, if the video card and monitor coupling works under another operating system such as MS-DOS, it should work fine with Linux. Original IBM CGA cards suffer from "snow" under Linux, which is not pleasant to use.

Graphical environments such as the X Window System have video hardware requirements of their own. Instead of listing these requirements here, we relegate the discussion to Section 5.1.1. In short, to run the

X Window System on your Linux machine, you will need one of the video cards listed in that section.

1.8.6 Miscellaneous hardware

The above sections described the hardware which is required to run a Linux system. However, most users have a number of "optional" devices such as tape and CD-ROM storage, sound boards, and so on, and are interested in whether or not this hardware is supported by Linux. Read on.

1.8.6.1 Mice and other pointing devices

For the most part, you will only be using a mouse under a graphical environment such as the X Window System. However, several Linux applications not associated with a graphics environment do make use of the mouse.

Linux supports all standard serial mice, including Logitech, MM series, Mouseman, Microsoft (2-button) and Mouse Systems (3-button). Linux also supports Microsoft, Logitech, and ATIXL busmice. The PS/2 mouse interface is supported as well.

All other pointing devices, such as trackballs, which emulate the above mice, should work as well.

1.8.6.2 CD-ROM storage

Almost all CD-ROM drives use the SCSI interface. As long as you have a SCSI adaptor supported by Linux, then your CD-ROM drive should work. A number of CD-ROM drives have been verified to work under Linux, including the NEC CDR-74, Sony CDU-541, and Texel DM-3024. The Sony internal CDU-31a and the Mistsumi CD-ROM drives are supported by Linux as well.

Linux supports the standard ISO-9660 filesystem for CD-ROMs.

1.8.6.3 Tape drives

There are several types of tape drives available on the market. Most of them use the SCSI interface, all of which should be supported by Linux. Among the verified SCSI tape drives are the Sankyo CP150SE; Tandberg 3600; Wangtek 5525ES, 5150ES, and 5099EN with the PC36 adaptor. Other QIC-02 drives should be supported as well.

Drivers are currently under development for various other tape devices, such as Colorado drives which hang off of the floppy controller.

1.8.6.4 Printers

Linux supports the complete range of parallel printers. If you are able to access your printer via the parallel port from MS-DOS or another operating system, you should be able to access it from Linux as well. The Linux printing software consists of the UNIX standard lp and lpr software. This software also allows you to print remotely via the network, if you have one available.

1.8.6.5 Modems

As with printer support, Linux supports the full range of serial modems, both internal and external. There is a great deal of telecommunications software available for Linux, including Kermit, pcomm, minicom, and

Seyon. If your modem is accessible from another operating system on the same machine, you should be able to access it from Linux with no difficulty.

1.8.7   Ethernet cards

Many popular Ethernet cards and LAN adaptors are supported by Linux. These include:

- 3com 3c503, 3c503/16
- Novell NE1000, NE2000
- Western Digital WD8003, WD8013
- Hewlett Packard HP27245, HP27247, HP27250
- D-Link DE-600

The following clones are reported to work:

- LANNET LEC-45
- Alta Combo
- Artisoft LANtastic AE-2
- Asante Etherpak 2001/2003,
- D-Link Ethernet II
- LTC E-NET/16 P/N 8300-200-002
- Network Solutions HE-203,
- SVEC 4 Dimension Ethernet
- 4-Dimension FD0490 EtherBoard 16

Clones which are compatible with any of the above cards should work as well.

1.9   Sources of Linux Information

As you have probably guessed, there are many sources of information about Linux available apart from this book. In particular, there are a number of books, not specific to Linux but rather about UNIX in general, that will be of importance, especially to those readers without previous UNIX experience. If you are new to the UNIX world, we seriously suggest that you take the time to peruse one of these books before you attempt to brave the jungles of Linux. Specifically, the book *Learning the UNIX Operating System*, by Grace Todino and John Strang, is a good place to start.

Many of the following sources of information are available online in some electronic form. That is, you must have access to an online network, such as the Internet, USENET, or Fidonet, in order to access the information contained therein. If you do not have online access to any of this material, you might be able to find someone kind enough to give you hardcopies of the documents in question. Read on.

1.9.1   Online documents

If you have access to the Internet, there are many Linux documents available via anonymous FTP from archive sites all over the world. If you do not have direct Internet access, these documents may still be available to you: many Linux distributions on CD-ROM contain all of the documents mentioned here. Also, they are distributed on many other networks, such as Fidonet and CompuServe. If you are able to send mail to Internet sites, you may be able to retrieve these files using one of the `ftpmail` servers which will electronically mail you the documents or files from FTP archive sites. See Appendix C for more information on using `ftpmail`.

There is a great number of FTP archive sites which carry Linux software and related documents. A list of well-known Linux archive sites is given in Appendix C. In order to reduce network traffic, you should always use the FTP site which is geographically (network-wise) closest to you.

Appendix A contains a listing of some of the Linux documents which are available via anonymous FTP. The filenames will differ depending on the archive site in question; most sites keep Linux-related documents in the `docs` subdirectory of their Linux archive space. For example, on the FTP site `sunsite.unc.edu`, Linux files are stored in the directory `/pub/Linux`, with Linux-related documentation being found in `/pub/Linux/docs`.

Examples of available online documents are the *Linux FAQ*, a collection of frequently asked questions about Linux; the Linux *HOWTO* documents, each describing a specific aspect of the system—including the *Installation HOWTO*, the *Printing HOWTO*, and the *Ethernet HOWTO*; and, the Linux META-FAQ, a list of other sources of Linux information on the Internet.

Most of these documents are also regularly posted to one or more Linux-related USENET newsgroups; see Section 1.9.4 below.

1.9.2   Linux on the World Wide Web

The Linux Documentation Home Page is available for World Wide Web users at the URL

    http://sunsite.unc.edu/mdw/linux.html

This page contains many HOWTOs and other documents in HTML format, as well as pointers to other sites of interest to Linux users.

1.9.3   Books and other published works

At this time, there are few published works specifically about Linux. Most noteworthy are the books from the Linux Documentation Project, a project carried out over the Internet to write and distribute a bona fide set of "manuals" for Linux. These manuals are analogues to the documentation sets available with commercial versions of UNIX: they cover everything from installing Linux, to using and running the system, programming, networking, kernel development, and more.

The Linux Documentation Project manuals are available via anonymous FTP from the Internet, as well as via mail order from several sources. Appendix A lists the manuals which are available and covers means of obtaining them in detail.

There are not many books specifically about Linux currently available. However, there are a large number of books about UNIX in general which are certainly applicable to Linux—as far as using and programming the system is concerned, Linux does not differ greatly from other implementations of UNIX. In short, almost everything you want to know about using and programming Linux can be found in sources meant for a general UNIX audience. In fact, this book is meant to be complemented by the large library of UNIX books currently available; here, we present the most important Linux-specific details and hope that you will look to other sources for more in-depth information.

Armed with a number of good books about using UNIX, as well as the book you hold in your hands, you should be able to tackle just about anything. Appendix A includes a list of highly-recommended UNIX books, both for UNIX newcomers and UNIX wizards alike.

There is also a monthly magazine about Linux, called the *Linux Journal*. It is distributed worldwide, and is an excellent way to keep in touch with the many goings-on in the Linux community—especially if you do not have access to USENET news (see below). See Appendix A for information on subscribing to the *Linux Journal*.

1.9.4   USENET newsgroups

USENET is a worldwide electronic news and discussion forum with a heavy contingent of so-called "newsgroups"—discussion areas devoted to a particular topic. Much of the development of Linux has been done over the waves of the Internet and USENET, and not suprisingly there are a number of USENET newsgroups available for discussions about Linux.

The original Linux newsgroup was `alt.os.linux`, and was created to move some of the discussions about Linux out of `comp.os.minix` and the various mailing lists. Soon, the traffic on `alt.os.linux` grew to be large enough that a newsgroup in the `comp` hierarchy was warranted; a vote was taken in February of 1992, and `comp.os.linux` was created.

`comp.os.linux` quickly became one of the most popular (and loudest) USENET groups; more popular than any other `comp.os` group. In December of 1992, a vote was taken to split the newsgroup in order to reduce traffic; only `comp.os.linux.announce` passed this vote. In July of 1993, the group was finally split into the new hierarchy. Almost 2000 people voted in the `comp.os.linux` reorganization, making it one of the largest USENET Call For Votes ever.

If you do not have direct USENET access, but are able to send and receive electronic mail from the Internet, there are mail-to-news gateways available for each of the newsgroups below.

`comp.os.linux.announce`

> `comp.os.linux.announce` is a moderated newsgroup for announcements and important postings about the Linux system (such as bug reports, important patches to software, and so on). If you read any Linux newsgroups at all, read this one. Often, the important postings in this group are not crossposted to other groups. This group also contains many periodic postings about Linux, including many of the online documents described in the last section and listed in Appendix A.

> Postings to this newsgroup must be approved by the moderators, Matt Welsh and Lars Wirzenius. If you wish to submit and article to this group, in most cases you can simply post the article as you normally would (using `Pnews` or whatever posting software that you have available); the news software will automatically forward the article to the moderators for approval. However, if your news system is not set up correctly, you may need to mail the article directly; the submission address is `linux-announce@tc.cornell.edu`.

> The rest of the Linux newsgroups listed below are unmoderated.

`comp.os.linux.help`

> This is the most popular Linux newsgroup. It is for questions and answers about using, setting up, or otherwise running a Linux system. If you are having problems with Linux, you may post to this newsgroup, and hopefully receive a reply from someone who might be able to help. However, it is strongly suggested that you read all of the available Linux documentation before posting questions to this newsgroup.

`comp.os.linux.admin`

> This newsgroup is for questions and discussion about running a Linux system, most commonly in an active, multi-user environment. Any discussion about administrative issues of Linux (such as packaging software, making backups, handling users, and so on) is welcome here.

`comp.os.linux.development`

> This is a newsgroup for discussions about development of the Linux system. All issues related to kernel and system software development should be discussed here. For example,

if you are writing a kernel driver and need help with certain aspects of the programming, this would be the place to ask. This newsgroup is also for discussions about the direction and goals behind the Linux development effort, as described (somewhat) in Section 1.6.

It should be noted that this newsgroup is not (technically) for discussions about development of software *for* Linux, but rather for discussions of development *of* Linux. That is, issues dealing with applications programming under Linux should be discussed in another Linux newsgroup; `comp.os.linux.development` is about developing the Linux system itself, including the kernel, system libraries, and so on.

`comp.os.linux.misc`

This newsgroup is for all discussion which doesn't quite fit into the other available Linux groups. In particular, advocacy wars (the incessant "Linux versus Windows NT" thread, for example), should be waged here, as opposed to in the technical Linux groups. Any non-technical or metadiscourse about the Linux system should remain in `comp.os.linux.misc`.

It should be noted that the newsgroup `comp.os.linux`, which was originally the only Linux group, has been superseded by the new hierarchy of groups. If you have access to `comp.os.linux`, but not to the newer Linux groups listed above, encourage your news administrator to create the new groups on your system.

1.9.5   Internet mailing lists

If you have access to Internet electronic mail, you can participate in a number of mailing lists even if you do not have USENET access. Note that if you are not directly on the Internet, you can join one of these mailing lists as long as you are able to exchange electronic mail with the Internet (for example, UUCP, FidoNET, CompuServe, and other networks all have access to Internet mail).

The "Linux Activists" mailing list is primarily for Linux developers and people interested in aiding the development process. This is a "multi-channel" mailing list, in which you join one or more "channels" based on your particular interests. Some of the available channels include: NORMAL, for general Linux-related issues; KERNEL, for kernel development; GCC, for discussions relating to the gcc compiler and library development; NET, for discussions about the TCP/IP networking code; DOC, for issues relating to writing and distributing Linux documentation; and more.

For more information about the Linux Activists mailing list, send mail to

    linux-activists@niksula.hut.fi

You will receive a list of currently available channels, including information on how to subscribe and unsubscribe to particular channels on the list.

Quite a few special-purpose mailing lists about and for Linux exist as well. The best way to find out about these is to watch the Linux USENET newsgroups for announcements, as well as to read the list of publicly-available mailing lists, periodically posted to the USENET group news.answers.

1.10   Getting Help

You will undoubtedly require some degree of assistance during your adventures in the Linux world. Even the most wizardly of UNIX wizards occasionally is stumped by some quirk or feature of Linux, and it's important to know how and where to find help when you need it.

The primary means of getting help in the Linux world are via Internet mailing lists and USENET newsgroups, as discussed in Section 1.9. If you don't have online access to these sources, you might be able to find comparable Linux discussion forums on other online services, such as on local BBS's, CompuServe, and so on.

A number of businesses are providing commercial support for Linux. This will allow you to pay a "subscription fee" which will allow you to call the consultants for help with your Linux problems. Appendix B contains a list of Linux vendors, some of which provide commercial support. However, if you have access to USENET and Internet mail, you may find the free support found there to be just as useful.

Keeping the following suggestions in mind will greatly improve your experiences with Linux and will guarantee you more success in finding help to your problems.

Consult all available documentation...first! The first thing you should do when encountering a problem is consult the various sources of information listed in Section 1.9 and Appendix A. These documents were laboriously written for people like you—people who need help with the Linux system. Even books written for UNIX in general are applicable to Linux, and you should take advantage of them. More than likely, you will find the answer to your problems somewhere in this documentation, as impossible as it may seem.

If you have access to USENET news or any of the Linux-related mailing lists, be sure to actually *read* the information there before posting for help with your problem. Many times, solutions to common problems are not easy to find in documentation, and instead are well-covered in the newsgroups and mailing lists devoted to Linux. If you only post to these groups, and don't actually read them, you are asking for trouble.

Learn to appreciate self-maintenance. In most cases, it is preferable to do as much independent research and investigation into the problem as possible before seeking outside help. After all, you asked for it, by running Linux in the first place! Remember that Linux is all about hacking and fixing problems yourself. It is not a commercial operating system, nor does it try to look like one. Hacking won't kill you. In fact, it will teach you a great deal about the system to investigate and solve problems yourself—maybe even enough to one day call yourself a Linux guru. Learn to appreciate the value of hacking the system, and how to fix problems yourself. You can't expect to run a complete, homebrew Linux system without some degree of handiwork.

Remain calm. It is vital to refrain from getting frustrated with the system, at all costs. Nothing is earned by taking an axe—or worse, a powerful electromagnet—to your Linux system in a fit of anger. The authors have found that a large punching bag or similar inanimate object is a wonderful way to relieve the occasional stress attack. As Linux matures and distributions become more reliable, we hope that this problem will go away. However, even commercial UNIX implementations can be tricky at times. When all else fails, sit back, take a few deep breaths, and go after the problem again when you feel relaxed. Your mind and conscience will be clearer.

Refrain from posting spuriously. Many people make the mistake of posting or mailing messages pleading for help prematurely. When encountering a problem, do not—we repeat, do *not*—rush immediately to your nearest terminal and post a message to one of the Linux USENET newsgroups. Often, you will catch your own mistake five minutes later and find yourself in the curious situation of defending your own sanity in a public forum. Before posting anything any of the Linux mailing lists or newsgroups, first attempt to resolve the problem yourself and be absolutely certain what the problem is. Does your system not respond when switched on? Perhaps the machine is unplugged.

If you do post for help, make it worthwhile. If all else fails, you may wish to post a message for help in any of the number of electronic forums dedicated to Linux, such as USENET newsgroups and mailing lists. When posting, remember that the people reading your post are not there to help you. The network is not your personal consulting service. Therefore, it is important to remain as polite, terse, and informative as possible.

How can one accomplish this? First, you should include as much (relevant) information about your system and your problem as possible. Posting the simple request, "I cannot seem to get e-mail to work" will probably get you nowhere unless you include information on your system, what software you are using, what you have attempted to do so far and what the results were. When including technical information, it is usually a good idea to include general information on the version(s) of your software (Linux kernel version, for example), as well as a brief summary of your hardware configuration. However, don't overdo it—including information on the brand and type of monitor that you have probably is irrelevant if you're trying to configure networking software.

Secondly, remember that you need to make some attempt—however feeble—at solving your problem before you go to the Net. If you have never attempted to set up electronic mail, for instance, and first decide to ask folks on the Net how to go about doing it, you are making a big mistake. There are a number of documents available (see the Section 1.9) on how to get started with many common tasks under Linux. The idea is to get as far along as possible on your own and *then* ask for help if and when you get stuck.

Also remember that the people reading your message, however helpful, may occasionally get frustrated by seeing the same problem over and over again. Be sure to actually read the Linux newsgroups and mailing lists before posting your problems. Many times, the solution to your problem has been discussed repeatedly, and all that's required to find it is to browse the current messages.

Lastly, when posting to electronic newsgroups and mailing lists, try to be as polite as possible. It is much more effective and worthwhile to be polite, direct, and informative—more people will be willing to help you if you master a humble tone. To be sure, the flame war is an art form across many forms of electronic communication, but don't allow that to preoccupy your and other people's time. Save the network undue wear and tear by keeping bandwidth as low as possible, and by paying as much attention to other sources of information which are available to you. The network is an excellent way to get help with your Linux problems—but it is important to know how to use the network *effectively*.

Chapter 2

Obtaining and Installing Linux

In this chapter, we'll describe how to obtain the Linux software, in the form of one of the various pre-packaged distributions, and how to install the distribution that you choose.

As we have mentioned, there is no single "official" distribution of the Linux software; there are, in fact, many distributions, each of which serves a particular purpose and set of goals. These distributions are available via anonymous FTP from the Internet, on BBS systems worldwide, and via mail on diskette, tape, and CD-ROM.

Here, we present a general overview of the installation process. Each distribution has its own specific installation instructions, but armed with the concepts presented here you should be able to feel your way through any installation. Appendix A lists sources of information for installation instructions and other help, if you're at a total loss.

This book contains additional sections detailing the Slackware distribution of Linux.

2.1   Distributions of Linux

Because Linux is free software, no single organization or entity is responsible for releasing and distributing the software. Therefore, anyone is free to put together and distribute the Linux software, as long as the restrictions in the GPL are observed. The upshot of this is that there are many distributions of Linux, available via anonymous FTP or via mail order.

You are now faced with the task of deciding upon a particular distribution of Linux which suits your needs. Not all distributions are alike. Many of them come with just about all of the software you'd need to run a complete system—and then some. Other Linux distributions are "small" distributions intended for users without copious amounts of diskspace. Many distributions contain only the core Linux software, and you are expected to install larger software packages, such as the X Window System, yourself. (In Chapter 4 we'll show you how.)

The Linux *Distribution HOWTO* (see Appendix A) contains a list of Linux distributions available via the Internet as well as mail order. Appendix B also lists contact addresses for a number of Linux mail-order vendors. If you purchased this book in printed the form, the publisher should also be able to provide you with a Linux distribution or tell you who can.

How can you decide among all of these distributions? If you have access to USENET news, or another computer conferencing system, you might want to ask there for personal opinions from people who have installed Linux. Even better, if you know someone who has installed Linux, ask them for help and advice. There are many factors to consider when choosing a distribution, however, everyone's needs and opinions are different. In actuality, most of the popular Linux distributions contain roughly the same set of software, so the distribution that you select is more or less arbitrary.

This book contains information on installing the popular Slackware and Slackware Pro distributions of Linux.

2.1.1   Getting Linux from the Internet

If you have access to the Internet, the easiest way to obtain Linux is via anonymous FTP.[1] Appendix C lists a number of FTP archive sites which carry Linux software. One of these is `sunsite.unc.edu`, and the various Linux distributions can be found in the directory

          /pub/Linux/distributions

there.

Many distributions are released via anonymous FTP as a set of disk images. That is, the distribution consists of a set of files, and each file contains the binary image of a floppy. In order to copy the contents of the image file onto the floppy, you can use the `RAWRITE.EXE` program under MS-DOS. This program copies, block-for-block, the contents of a file to a floppy, without regard for disk format.[2]

`RAWRITE.EXE` is available on the various Linux FTP sites, including `sunsite.unc.edu` in the directory

          /pub/Linux/system/Install/rawrite

Therefore, in many cases, you simply download the set of diskette images, and use `RAWRITE.EXE` with each image in turn to create a set of diskettes. You boot from the so-called "boot diskette" and you're ready to roll. The software is usually installed directly from the floppies, although some distributions allow you to install from an MS-DOS partition on your hard drive. Some distributions allow you to install over a TCP/IP network. The documentation for each distribution should describe these installation methods if they are available.

Other Linux distributions are installed from a set of MS-DOS format floppies. For example, the Slackware distribution of Linux requires only the boot and root diskettes to be created using `RAWRITE.EXE`. The rest of the diskettes are copied to MS-DOS format diskettes using the MS-DOS `COPY` command. The system installs the software directly from the MS-DOS floppies. This saves you the trouble of having to use `RAWRITE.EXE` for many image files, although it requires you to have access to an MS-DOS system to create the diskettes.

Each distribution of Linux available via anonymous FTP should include a `README` file describing how to download and prepare the diskettes for installation. Be sure to read all of the available documentation for the release that you are using.

When downloading the Linux software, be sure to use *binary* mode for all file transfers (with most FTP clients, the command "`binary`" enables this mode).

See Section 2.1.4, below, for information on obtaining the Slackware distribution from the Internet.

---

[1]If you do not have direct Internet access, you can obtain Linux via the `ftpmail` service, provided that you have the ability to exchange e-mail with the Internet. See Appendix C for details.

[2]If you have access to a UNIX workstation with a floppy drive, you can also use the `dd` command to copy the file image directly to the floppy. A command such as "`dd of=/dev/rfd0 if=foo bs=18k`" will "raw write" the contents of the file `foo` to the floppy device on a Sun workstation. Consult your local UNIX gurus for more information on your system's floppy devices and the use of `dd`.

2.1.2 Getting Linux from other online sources

If you have access to another computer network such as CompuServe or Prodigy, there may be a means to download the Linux software from these sources. In addition, many bulletin board (BBS) systems carry Linux software. A list of Linux BBS sites is given in Appendix D. Not all Linux distributions are available from these computer networks, however—many of them, especially the various CD-ROM distributions, are only available via mail order.

2.1.3 Getting Linux via mail order

If you don't have Internet or BBS access, many Linux distributions are available via mail order on diskette, tape, or CD-ROM. Appendix B lists a number of these distributors. Many of them accept credit cards as well as international orders, so if you're not in the United States or Canada you still should be able to obtain Linux in this way.

Linux is free software, although distributors are allowed by the GPL to charge a fee for it. Therefore, ordering Linux via mail order might cost you between US$30 and US$150, depending on the distribution. However, if you know someone who has already purchased or downloaded a release of Linux, you are free to borrow or copy their software for your own use. Linux distributors are not allowed to restrict the license or redistribution of the software in any way. If you are thinking about installing an entire lab of machines with Linux, for example, you only need to purchase a single copy of one of the distributions, which can be used to install all of the machines.

2.1.4 Getting Slackware

Slackware is a popular distribution of Linux maintained by Patrick Volkerding.[3] It is easy to install and fairly complete, and may be obtained both from the Internet as well as on CD-ROM from a number of vendors (see Appendix B).

The Slackware distribution consists of a number of "disk sets", each one containing a particular type of software (for example, the d disk set contains development tools such as the gcc compiler, and the x disk set contains the X Window System software). You can elect to install whatever disk sets you like, and can install new ones later.

The version of Slackware described here is 2.0.0, of 25 June 1994. Installation of later versions of Slackware should be very similar to the information given here.

2.1.4.1 Slackware disk sets

Unfortunately, Slackware does not maintain a complete list of diskspace requirements for each disk set. You need at least 7 megabytes to install just the "A" series of disks; a very rough estimate of the required diskspace would be 2 or 2.5 megabytes per disk.

The following disk sets are available:

A   The base system. Enough to get up and running and have elvis and comm programs available. Based around the 1.0.9 Linux kernel, and the new filesystem standard (FSSTND).

These disks are known to fit on 1.2M disks, although the rest of Slackware won't. If you have only a 1.2M floppy, you can still install the base system, download other disks you want and install them from your hard drive.

---

[3]Patrick Volkerding can be reached on the Internet at volkerdi@mhd1.moorhead.msus.edu.

AP	Various applications and add ons, such as the manual pages, **groff**, **ispell** (GNU and international versions), **term**, **joe**, **jove**, **ghostscript**, **sc**, **bc**, and the quota patches.
D	Program development. GCC/G++/Objective C 2.5.8, **make** (GNU and BSD), **byacc** and GNU **bison**, **flex**, the 4.5.26 C libraries, **gdb**, kernel source for 1.0.9, **SVGAlib**, **ncurses**, **clisp**, **f2c**, **p2c**, **m4**, **perl**, **rcs**.
E	GNU Emacs 19.25.
F	A collection of FAQs and other documentation.
I	Info pages for GNU software. Documentation for various programs readable by **info** or Emacs.
N	Networking. TCP/IP, UUCP, **mailx**, **dip**, **deliver**, **elm**, **pine**, **smail**, **cnews**, **nn**, **tin**, **trn**.
OOP	Object Oriented Programming. GNU Smalltalk 1.1.1, and the Smalltalk Interface to X (STIX).
Q	Alpha kernel source and images (currently contains Linux 1.1.18).
TCL	Tcl, Tk, TclX, blt, itcl.
Y	Games. The BSD games collection, and Tetris for terminals.
X	The base XFree86 2.1.1 system, with **libXpm**, **fvwm** 1.20, and **xlock** added.
XAP	X applications: X11 **ghostscript**, **libgr13**, **seyon**, **workman**, **xfilemanager**, **xv** 3.01, GNU **chess** and **xboard**, **xfm** 1.2, **ghostview**, and various X games.
XD	X11 program development. X11 libraries, server linkkit, PEX support.
XV	Xview 3.2 release 5. XView libraries, and the Open Look virtual and non-virtual window managers.
IV	Interviews libraries, include files, and the **doc** and **idraw** apps.
OI	ParcPlace's Object Builder 2.0 and Object Interface Library 4.0, generously made available for Linux developers according to the terms in the "copying" notice found in these directories. Note that these only work with **libc-4.4.4**, but a new version may be released once **gcc** 2.5.9 is available.
T	The TeX and LaTeX text formatting systems.

You must get the "A" disk set; the rest are optional. We suggest installing the **A**, **AP**, and **D** sets, as well as the **X** set if you plan to run the X Window System.

2.1.4.2   Getting Slackware from the Internet

The Slackware release of Linux may be found on any number of FTP sites worldwide. Appendix C lists several of the Linux FTP sites; we suggest that you try to find the software on the FTP site nearest you, to reduce net traffic. However, two of the major Linux FTP archives are **sunsite.unc.edu** and **tsx-11.mit.edu**.

The Slackware release may be found at least on the following sites:

- **sunsite.unc.edu:/pub/Linux/distributions/slackware**
- **tsx-11.mit.edu:/pub/linux/packages/slackware**
- **ftp.cdrom.com:/pub/linux/slackware**

`ftp.cdrom.com` is Slackware's home site.

2.1.4.2.1 Downloading the files

You should download the following files using FTP. Be sure to use binary mode when transferring. Appendix C contains a complete tutorial on using FTP.

- The various `README` files, as well as `SLACKWARE_FAQ`. Be sure to read these files before attempting to install the software, to get any updates or changes to this document.
- A bootdisk image. This is a file that you will write to a floppy to create the Slackware boot disk. If you have a 1.44 megabyte boot floppy (3.5"), look in the directory `bootdsks.144`. If you have a 1.2 megabyte boot floppy (5.25"), look in the directory `bootdsks.12`.

  You need one of the following bootdisk files.

  - `bare.gz`. This is a boot floppy that has only IDE hard drive drivers. (No SCSI, CD-ROM, or networking support.) Use this if you only have an IDE hard drive controller and aren't going to be installing over the network or from CD-ROM.
  - `cdu31a.gz`. Contains IDE, SCSI, and the Sony CDU31A/33A driver.
  - `mitsumi.gz`. Contains IDE, SCSI, and the Mitsumi CD-ROM driver.
  - `modern.gz`. An experimental boot disk with a newer kernel, and all drivers except those for network cards and the Sony 535 CD-ROM.
  - `net.gz`. Contains IDE and network drivers.
  - `sbpcd.gz`. Contains IDE, SCSI, and SoundBlaster Pro/Panasonic CD-ROM drivers.
  - `scsi.gz`. Contains IDE, SCSI, and SCSI CD-ROM drivers.
  - `scsinet.gz`. Contains IDE, SCSI, SCSI CD-ROM, and network drivers.
  - `sony535.gz`. Contains IDE, SCSI, and Sony 535/531 CD-ROM drivers.
  - `xt.gz`. Contains IDE and XT hard drive drivers.

  You need only *one* of the above bootdisk images, depending on the hardware that you have in your system.

  The issue here is that some hardware drivers conflict with each other in strange ways, and instead of attempting to debug hardware problems on your system it's easier to use a boot floppy image with only certain drivers enabled. Most users should try `scsi.gz` or `bare.gz`.

- A rootdisk image. This is a file that you will write to a floppy to create the Slackware installation disk. As with the bootdisk image, look in `rootdsks.144` or `rootdsks.12` depending on the type of boot floppy drive that you have.

  You need one of the following files:

  - `color144.gz`. The menu-based color installation disk for 1.44 megabyte drives. Most users should use this rootdisk.
  - `umsds144.gz`. A version of the `color144` disk for installing with the UMSDOS filesystem, which allows you to install Linux onto a directory of an MS-DOS filesystem. This installation method is not discussed in detail here, but it will prevent you from having to repartition your drive. More on this later.
  - `tty144.gz`. The terminal-based installation disk for 1.44 megabyte drives. If `color144.gz` doesn't work for you, try `tty144.gz` instead.
  - `colrlite.gz`. The menu-based color installation disk for 1.2 megabyte drives.
  - `umsds12.gz`. A version of the `colrlite` disk for installing with the UMSDOS filesystem. See the description of `umsds144.gz`, above.
  - `tty12.gz`. The terminal-based installation disk for 1.2 megabyte drives. Use this rootdisk if you have a 1.2 megabyte boot floppy and `colrlite.gz` doesn't work for you.

Again, you need only *one* of the above rootdisk images, depending on the type of boot floppy drive that you have.

- `GZIP.EXE`. This is an MS-DOS executable of the `gzip` compression program used to compress the boot and rootdisk files (the `.gz` extension on the filenames indicates this). This can be found in the `install` directory.

- `RAWRITE.EXE`. This is an MS-DOS program that will write the contents of a file (such as the boot and rootdisk images) directly to a floppy, without regard to format. You will use `RAWRITE.EXE` to create the boot and root floppies. This can be found in the `install` directory as well.

  You only need `RAWRITE.EXE` and `GZIP.EXE` if you plan to create the boot and root floppies from an MS-DOS system. If you have access to a UNIX workstation with a floppy drive instead, you can create the floppies from there, using the `dd` command. See the man page for `dd` and ask your local UNIX administrators for assistance.

- The files in the directories `slakware/a1`, `slakware/a2`, and `slakware/a3`. These files make up the "A" disk set of the Slackware distribution. They are required. Later, you will copy these files to MS-DOS floppies for installation (or, you can install from your hard drive). Therefore, when you download these files, keep them in separate directories; don't mix the `a1` files with the `a2` files, and so on.

  Be sure that you get the files without periods in the filenames as well. That is, within FTP, use the command "`mget *`" instead of "`mget *.*`".

- The files in the directories `ap1`, `ap2`, etc., depending on what disk sets you are installing. For example, if you are installing the "X" disk series, get the files in the directories `x1` through `x5`. As with the "A" disk set, above, be sure to keep the files in separate directories when you download them.

2.1.4.3   Getting Slackware on CD-ROM

Slackware is also available on CD-ROM. Most Slackware CD-ROMs simply contain a copy of the files as they appear on the FTP archive sites, as described above. Therefore, if you have a Slackware CD-ROM, you have all of the files that you need.

You will have to create a boot and root floppy from the files on the CD-ROM. See Section 2.1.4.2.1, above, for a discussion on the available boot and root disk images.

First, decide which boot and root disk images you will use. They should all be on the CD-ROM. Below, we will describe how to create these floppies.

2.1.4.4   Installation methods

Slackware provides several different means of installing the software. The most popular is installing from an MS-DOS partition on your hard drive; another is to install from a set of MS-DOS floppies created from the disk sets that you downloaded.

If you have Slackware on a CD-ROM, you can install the files directly from there. The Slackware Pro distribution, from Morse Telecommunications, allows you to install Slackware so that many files are accessed directly on the CD-ROM. This can save a great deal of space on your hard drive, with the tradeoff that running certain applications will be slower.

2.1.4.4.1   Creating the boot and root floppies   You must create floppies from the bootdisk and rootdisk images that you downloaded (or have on CD-ROM), no matter what type of installation you will be doing.

On an MS-DOS system, you must uncompress the bootdisk and rootdisk images using `GZIP.EXE`. For example, if you're using the `bare.gz` bootdisk image, issue the MS-DOS command:

```
C:\> GZIP -D BARE.GZ
```

which will uncompress `bare.gz` and leave you with the file `bare`. If you are installing from CD-ROM, you can copy the bootdisk image (such as `bare.gz`) to you hard drive, and run `GZIP.EXE` from the CD-ROM to uncompress it.

You must similarly uncompress the rootdisk image. For example, if you are using the rootdisk `color144.gz`, issue the command:

```
C:\> GZIP -D COLOR144.GZ
```

which will uncompress the file and leave you with `color144`.

Next, you must have two *high-density* MS-DOS formatted floppies. (They must be of the same type; that is, if your boot floppy drive is a 3.5" drive, both floppies must be high-density 3.5" disks.) You will use `RAWRITE.EXE` to write the boot and rootdisk images to the floppies.

Issue the command:

```
C:\> RAWRITE
```

Answer the prompts for the name of the file to write (such as `bare`, or `color144`) and the floppy to write it to (such as `A:`). `RAWRITE` will copy the file, block-by-block, directly to the floppy. Also use `RAWRITE` for the root disk image. When you're done, you'll have two floppies: one containing the boot disk, the other containing the root disk. Note that these two floppies will no longer be readable by MS-DOS (they are "Linux format" floppies, in some sense).

Be sure that you're using brand-new, error-free floppies. The floppies must have no bad blocks on them.

Note that you do not need to be running MS-DOS in order to install Slackware. However, running MS-DOS makes it easier to create the boot and root floppies, and it makes it easier to install the software (as you can install directly from an MS-DOS partition on your system). If you are not running MS-DOS on your system, you can use someone else's MS-DOS system just to create the floppies, and install from there.

It is not necessary to use `GZIP.EXE` and `RAWRITE.EXE` under MS-DOS to create the boot and root floppies, either. You can use the `gzip` and `dd` commands on a UNIX system to do the same job. (For this, you will need a UNIX workstation with a floppy drive, of course.) For example, on a Sun workstation with the floppy drive on device `/dev/rfd0`, you can use the commands:

```
$ gunzip bare.gz
$ dd if=bare of=/dev/rfd0 obs=18k
```

You must provide the appropriate block size argument (the `obs` argument) on some workstations (e.g., Suns) or this will fail. If you have problems the man page for `dd` will be instructive.

2.1.4.4.2 Preparing for installation from hard drive

If you're planning on installing the Slackware software directly from the hard drive (which is often faster and more reliable than a floppy installation), you will need an MS-DOS partition on the system that you're installing Slackware to.

Note: If you plan to install Slackware from an MS-DOS partition, that partition must NOT be compressed with DoubleSpace, Stacker, or any other MS-DOS drive compression utility. Linux currently cannot read DoubleSpace/Stacker MS-DOS partitions directly. (You can access them via the MS-DOS Emulator, but that is not an option when installing the Linux software.)

To prepare for hard drive installation, simply create a directory on the hard drive to store the Slackware files. For example,

```
C:\> MKDIR SLACKWAR
```

will create the directory `C:\SLACKWAR` to hold the Slackware files. Under this directory, you should create subdirectories `A1`, `A2`, and so on, for each disk set that you downloaded, using the `MKDIR` command. All of the files from the `A1` disk should go into the directory `SLACKWAR\A1`, and so forth.

2.1.4.4.3   Preparing for floppy installation   If you wish to install Slackware from floppies instead of the hard drive, you'll need to have one blank, MS-DOS formatted floppy for each Slackware disk that you downloaded. These disks must be high-density format.

The A disk set (disks A1 through A3) may be either 3.5" or 5.25" floppies. However, the rest of the disk sets must be 3.5" disks. Therefore, if you only have a 5.25" floppy drive, you'll need to borrow a 3.5" drive from someone in order to install disk sets other than A. (Or, you can install from the hard drive, as explained in the previous section.)

To make the disks, simply copy the files from each Slackware directory onto an MS-DOS formatted floppy, using the MS-DOS COPY command. As so:

```
C:\> COPY A1\*.* A:
```

will copy the contents of the A1 disk to the floppy in drive A:. You should repeat this for each disk that you downloaded.

You do *not* need to modify or uncompress the files on the disks in any way; you merely need to copy them to MS-DOS floppies. The Slackware installation procedure takes care of uncompressing the files for you.

2.1.4.4.4   Preparing for CD-ROM installation   If you have Slackware on a CD-ROM, you are ready to install the software once you have created the boot and root floppies. The software will be installed directly from CD.

2.2   Preparing to Install Linux

After you have obtained a distribution of Linux, you're ready to prepare your system for installation. This takes a certain degree of planning, especially if you're already running other operating systems. In the following sections we'll describe how to plan for the Linux installation.

2.2.1   Installation overview

While each release of Linux is different, in general the method used to install the software is as follows:

1. **Repartition your hard drive(s).** If you have other operating systems already installed, you will need to *repartition* the drives in order to allocate space for Linux. This is discussed in Section 2.2.4, below.

2. **Boot the Linux installation media.** Each distribution of Linux has some kind of installation media—usually a "boot floppy"—which is used to install the software. Booting this media will either present you with some kind of installation program, which will step you through the Linux installation, or allow you to install the software by hand.

3. **Create Linux partitions.** After repartitioning to allocate space for Linux, you create Linux partitions on that empty space. This is accomplished with the Linux fdisk program, covered in Section 2.3.3.

4. **Create filesystems and swap space.** At this point, you will create one or more *filesystems*, used to store files, on the newly-created partitions. In addition, if you plan to use swap space, you will create the swap space on one of your Linux partitions. This is covered in Sections 2.3.4 and 2.3.5.

5. **Install the software on the new filesystems.** Finally, you will install the Linux software on your newly-created filesystems. After this, it's smooth sailing—if all goes well. This is covered in Section 2.3.6. Later, in Section 2.5, we describe what to do if anything goes wrong.

Many distributions of Linux provide an installation program which will step you through the installation process, and automate one or more of the above steps for you. Keep in mind throughout this chapter that any number of the above steps may be automated for you, depending on the distribution.

The Slackware distribution of Linux, covered in this book, only requires you to repartition your drive, using `fdisk`, and use the `setup` program to accomplish the other steps.

Important hint: While preparing to install Linux, the best advice that we can give is to *take notes* during the entire procedure. Write down everything that you do, everything that you type, and everything that you see that might be out of the ordinary. The idea here is simple: if (or when!) you run into trouble, you want to be able to retrace your steps and find out what went wrong. Installing Linux isn't difficult, but there are many details to remember. You want to have a record of all of these details so that you can experiment with other methods if something goes wrong. Also, keeping a notebook of your Linux installation experience is useful when you want to ask other people for help, for example, when posting a message to one of the Linux-related USENET groups. Your notebook is also something that you'll want to show to your grandchildren someday.[4]

2.2.2 Repartitioning concepts

In general, hard drives are divided into *partitions*, where a single partition is devoted to a single operating system. For example, on one hard drive, you may have several separate partitions—one devoted to, say, MS-DOS, another to OS/2, and another to Linux.

If you already have other software installed on your system, you may need to resize those partitions in order to free up space for Linux. You will then create one or more Linux partitions on the resulting free space for storing the Linux software and swap space. We call this process *repartitioning*.

Many MS-DOS systems utilize a single partition inhabiting the entire drive. To MS-DOS, this partition is known as `C:`. If you have more than one partition, MS-DOS names them `D:`, `E:`, and so on. In a way, each partition acts like a separate hard drive.

On the first sector of the disk is a **master boot record** along with a **partition table**. The boot record (as the name implies) is used to boot the system. The partition table contains information about the locations and sizes of your partitions.

There are three kinds of partitions: **primary**, **extended**, and **logical**. Of these, primary partitions are used most often. However, because of a limit in the size of the partition table, you can only have four primary partitions on any given drive.

The way around this four-partition limit is to use an extended partition. An extended partition doesn't hold any data by itself; instead, it acts as a "container" for logical partitions. Therefore, you could create one extended partition, covering the entire drive, and within it create many logical partitions. However, you may have only one extended partition per drive.

2.2.3 Linux partition requirements

Before we explain how to repartition your drives, you need to have an idea of how much space you will be allocating for Linux. We will be discussing how to create these partitions later, in Section 2.3.3.

On UNIX systems, files are stored on a **filesystem**, which is essentially a section of the hard drive (or other medium, such as CD-ROM or diskette) formatted to hold files. Each filesystem is associated with a specific part of the directory tree; for example, on many systems, there is a filesystem for all of the files

---

[4]The author shamefully admits that he kept a notebook of all of his tribulations with Linux for the first few months of working with the system. It is now gathering dust on his bookshelf.

in the directory /usr, another for /tmp, and so on. The **root filesystem** is the primary filesystem, which corresponds to the topmost directory, /.

Under Linux, each filesystem lives on a separate partition on the hard drive. For instance, if you have a filesystem for / and another for /usr, you will need two partitions to hold the two filesystems.

Before you install Linux, you will need to prepare filesystems for storing the Linux software. You must have at least one filesystem (the root filesystem), and therefore one partition, allocated to Linux. Many Linux users opt to store all of their files on the root filesystem, which is in most cases easier to manage than several filesystems and partitions.

However, you may create multiple filesystems for Linux if you wish—for example, you may want to use separate filesystems for /usr and /home. Those readers with UNIX system administration experience will know how to use multiple filesystems creatively. In Chapter 4 we discuss the use of multiple partitions and filesystems.

Why use more than one filesystem? The most commonly stated reason is safety; if, for some reason, one of your filesystems is damaged, the others will (usually) be unharmed. On the other hand, if you store all of your files on the root filesystem, and for some reason the filesystem is damaged, then you may lose all of your files in one fell swoop. This is, however, rather uncommon; if you backup the system regularly you should be quite safe.[5]

Another reason to use multiple filesystems is to divvy up storage between multiple hard drives. If you have, say, 40 megabytes free on one hard drive, and 50 megabytes free on another, you might want to create a 40-megabyte root filesystem on the first drive and a 50-megabyte /usr filesystem on the other. Currently it is not possible for a single filesystem to span multiple drives; if your free hard drive storage is fragmented between drives you will need to use multiple filesystems to utilize it all.

In summary, Linux requires at least one partition, for the root filesystem. If you wish to create multiple filesystems, you will need a separate partition for each additional filesystem. Some distributions of Linux automatically create partitions and filesystems for you, so you may not need to worry about these issues at all.

Another issue to consider when planning your partitions is swap space. If you wish to use swap space with Linux, you have two options. The first is to use a *swap file* which exists on one of your Linux filesystems. You will create the swap file for use as virtual RAM after you install the software. The second option is to create a *swap partition*, an individual partition to be used only as swap space. Most people use a swap partition instead of a swap file.

A single swap file or partition may be up to 16 megabytes in size. If you wish to use more than 16 megabytes of swap, you can create multiple swap partitions or files—up to eight in all. For example, if you need 32 megabytes of swap, you can create two 16-megabyte swap partitions.

Setting up a swap partition is covered in Section 2.3.4, and setting up a swap file in Chapter 4.

Therefore, in general, you will create at least two partitions for Linux: one for use as the root filesystem, and the other for use as swap space. There are, of course, many variations on the above, but this is the minimal setup. You are not required to use swap space with Linux, but if you have less than 16 megabytes of physical RAM it is strongly suggested that you do.

Of course, you need to be aware of how much *space* these partitions will require. The size of your Linux filesystems (containing the software itself) depends greatly on how much software you're installing and what distribution of Linux you are using. Hopefully, the documentation that came with your distribution will give you an approximation of the space requirements. A small Linux system can use 20 megabytes or less; a larger system anywhere from 80 to 100 megabytes, or more. Keep in mind that in addition to the space required by the software itself, you need to allocate extra space for user directories, room for future expansion, and so forth.

The size of your swap partition (should you elect to use one) depends on how much virtual RAM you

---

[5]The author uses a single 200-megabyte filesystem for all of his Linux files, and hasn't had any problems (so far).

require. A rule of thumb is to use a swap partition that is twice the space of your physical RAM; for example, if you have 4 megabytes of physical RAM, an 8-megabyte swap partition should suffice. Of course, this is mere speculation—the actual amount of swap space that you require depends on the software which you will be running. If you have a great deal of physical RAM (say, sixteen megabytes or more), you may not wish to use swap space at all.

Important note: Because of BIOS limitations, it is usually not possible to boot from partitions using cylinders numbered over 1023. Therefore, when setting aside space for Linux, keep in mind that you may not want to use a partition in the >1023-cylinder range for your Linux root filesystem. Linux can still *use* partitions with cylinders numbered over 1023, however, you may not be able to *boot* Linux from such a partition. This advice may seem premature, but it is important to know while planning your drive layout.

If you absolutely must use a partition with cylinders numbered over 1023 for your Linux root filesystem, you can always boot Linux from floppy. This is not so bad, actually—it only takes a few seconds longer to boot than from the hard drive. At any rate, it's always an option.

2.2.4 Repartitioning your drives

In this section, we'll describe how to resize your current partitions (if any) to make space for Linux. If you are installing Linux on a "clean" hard drive, you can skip this section and proceed to Section 2.3, below.

The usual way to resize an existing partition is to delete it (thus destroying all of the data on that partition) and recreate it. Before repartitioning your drives, *backup your system*. After resizing the partitions, you can reinstall your original software from the backup. However, there are several programs available for MS-DOS which are able to resize partitions nondestructively. One of these is known as "FIPS", and can be found on many Linux FTP sites.

Also, keep in mind that because you'll be shrinking your original partitions, you may not have space to reinstall everything. In this case, you need to delete enough unwanted software to allow the rest to fit on the smaller partitions.

The program used to repartition is known as `fdisk`. Each operating system has its own analogue of this program; for example, under MS-DOS, it is invoked with the `FDISK` command. You should consult your documentation for whatever operating systems you are currently running for information on repartitioning. Here, we'll discuss how to resize partitions for MS-DOS using `FDISK`, but this information should be easily extrapolated to other operating systems.

Please consult the documentation for your current operating systems before repartitioning your drive. This section is meant to be a general overview of the process; there are many subtleties that we do not cover here. You can lose all of the software on your system if you do not repartition the drive correctly.

A warning: Do not modify or create partitions for any other operating systems (including Linux) using `FDISK` under MS-DOS. You should only modify partitions for a particular operating system with the version of `fdisk` included with that operating system; for example, you will create Linux partitions using a version of `fdisk` for Linux. Later, in Section 2.3.3, we describe how to create Linux partitions, but for now we are concerned with resizing your current ones.

Let's say that you have a single hard drive on your system, currently devoted entirely to MS-DOS. Hence, your drive consists of a single MS-DOS partition, commonly known as "C:". Because this repartitioning method will destroy the data on that partition, you need to create a bootable MS-DOS "system disk" which contains everything necessary to run `FDISK` and restore the software from backup after the repartitioning is complete.

In many cases, you can use the MS-DOS installation disks for this purpose. However, if you need to create your own system disk, format a floppy with the command

```
FORMAT /s A:
```

Copy onto this floppy all of the necessary MS-DOS utilities (usually most of the software in the directory \DOS on your drive), as well as the programs FORMAT.COM and FDISK.EXE. You should now be able to boot this floppy, and run the command

        FDISK C:

to start up FDISK.

Use of FDISK should be self-explanatory, but consult the MS-DOS documentation for details. When you start FDISK, use the menu option to display the partition table, and *write down* the information displayed there. It is important to keep a record of your original setup in case you want to back out of the Linux installation.

To delete an existing partition, choose the FDISK menu option "Delete an MS-DOS Partition or Logical DOS Drive". Specify the type of partition that you wish to delete (primary, extended, or logical) and the number of the partition. Verify all of the warnings. Poof!

To create a new (smaller) partition for MS-DOS, just choose the FDISK option "Create an MS-DOS Partition or Logical DOS Drive". Specify the type of partition (primary, extended, or logical), and the size of the partition to create (specified in megabytes). FDISK should create the partition and you're ready to roll.

After you're done using FDISK, you should exit the program and reformat any new partitions. For example, if you resized the first DOS partition on your drive (C:) you should run the command

        FORMAT /s C:

You may now reinstall your original software from backup.

2.3   Installing the Linux software

After you have resized your existing partitions to make space for Linux, you are ready to install the software. Here is a brief overview of the procedure:

- Boot the Linux installation media;
- Run fdisk under Linux to create Linux partitions;
- Run mke2fs and mkswap to create Linux filesystems and swap space;
- Install the Linux software;
- Finally, either install the LILO boot loader on your hard drive, or create a boot floppy in order to boot your new Linux system.

As we have said, one (or more) of these steps may be automated for you by the installation procedure, depending on the distribution of Linux which you are using. Please consult the documentation for your distribution for specific instructions.

2.3.1   Booting Linux

The first step is to boot the Linux installation media. In most cases, this is a "boot floppy" which contains a small Linux system. Upon booting the floppy, you will be presented with an installation menu of some kind which will lead you through the steps of installing the software. On other distributions, you will be presented with a login prompt when booting this floppy. Here, you usually login as root or install to begin the installation process.

The documentation which came with your particular distribution will explain what is necessary to boot Linux from the installation media.

If you are installing the Slackware distribution of Linux, all that is required is to boot the boot floppy which you created in the previous section.

Most distributions of Linux use a boot floppy which allows you to enter hardware parameters at a boot prompt, to force hardware detection of various devices. For example, if your SCSI controller is not detected when booting the floppy, you will need to reboot and specify the hardware parameters (such as I/O address and IRQ) at the boot prompt.

Likewise, IBM PS/1, ThinkPad, and ValuePoint machines do not store drive geometry in the CMOS, and you must specify it at boot time.

The boot prompt is often displayed automatically when booting the boot floppy. This is the case for the Slackware distribution. Other distributions require you to hold down $\boxed{\texttt{shift}}$ or $\boxed{\texttt{ctrl}}$ while booting the floppy. If successful, you should see the prompt

> `boot:`

and possibly other messages.

To try booting without any special parameters, just press **enter** at the boot prompt.

Watch the messages as the system boots. If you have a SCSI controller, you should see a listing of the SCSI hosts detected. If you see the message

> `SCSI: 0 hosts`

then your SCSI controller was not detected, and you will have to use the following procedure.

Also, the system will display information on the drive partitions and devices detected. If any of this information is incorrect or missing, you will have to force hardware detection.

On the other hand, if all goes well and you hardware seems to be detected, you can skip to the following section, Section 2.3.2.

To force hardware detection, you must enter the appropriate parameters at the boot prompt, using the following syntax:

> `ramdisk` ⟨*parameters...*⟩

There are a number of such parameters available; here are some of the most common.

hd=⟨*cylinders*⟩,⟨*heads*⟩,⟨*sectors*⟩
> Specify the harddrive geometry. Required for systems such as the IBM PS/1, ValuePoint, and ThinkPad. For example, if your drive has 683 cylinders, 16 heads, and 32 sectors per track, enter
>
> > `ramdisk hd=683,16,32`

tmc8xx=⟨*memaddr*⟩,⟨*irq*⟩
> Specify address and IRQ for BIOS-less Future Domain TMC-8xx SCSI controller. For example,
>
> > `ramdisk tmc8xx=0xca000,5`
>
> Note that the 0x prefix must be used for all values given in hexadecimal. This is true for all of the following options.

st0x=⟨*memaddr*⟩,⟨*irq*⟩
> Specify address and IRQ for BIOS-less Seagate ST02 controller.

t128=⟨*memaddr*⟩,⟨*irq*⟩
> Specify address and IRQ for BIOS-less Trantor T128B controller.

ncr5380=⟨*port*⟩,⟨*irq*⟩,⟨*dma*⟩ Specify port, IRQ, and DMA channel for generic NCR5380
controller.

aha152x=⟨*port*⟩,⟨*irq*⟩,⟨*scsi_id*⟩,1
> Specify port, IRQ, and SCSI ID for BIOS-less AIC-6260 controllers. This includes Adaptec
> 1510, 152x, and Soundblaster-SCSI controllers.

For each of these, you must enter `ramdisk` followed by the parameter that you wish to use.

If you have questions about these boot-time options, please read the Linux *SCSI HOWTO*, which should
be available on any Linux FTP archive site (or from wherever you obtained this book), as well as the Linux
CD-ROM HOWTO. These documents describe hardware compatibility in much more detail.

2.3.2   Drives and partitions under Linux

Many distributions require you to create Linux partitions by hand using the `fdisk` program. Others may
automatically create partitions for you. Either way, you should know the following information about Linux
partitions and device names.

Drives and partitions under Linux are given different names than their counterparts under other operating
systems. Under MS-DOS, floppy drives are referred to as A: and B:, while hard drive partitions are named
C:, D:, and so on. Under Linux, the naming convention is quite different.

Device drivers, found in the directory `/dev`, are used to communicate with devices on your system
(such as hard drives, mice, and so on). For example, if you have a mouse on your system, you access it
through the driver `/dev/mouse`. Floppy drives, hard drives, and individual partitions are all given individual
device drivers of their own. Don't worry about the device driver interface for now; it is important only to
understand how the various devices are named in order to use them.

Table 2.1 lists the names of these various device drivers.

A few notes about this table. Note that `/dev/fd0` corresponds to the first floppy drive (A: under MS-
DOS) and `/dev/fd1` corresponds to the second floppy (B:).

Also, SCSI hard drives are named differently than other drives. IDE, MFM, and RLL drives are accessed
through the devices `/dev/hda`, `/dev/hdb`, and so on. The individual partitions on the drive `/dev/hda` are
`/dev/hda1`, `/dev/hda2`, and so on. However, SCSI drives are named `/dev/sda`, `/dev/sdb`, etc., with partition
names such as `/dev/sda1` and `/dev/sda2`.

Here's an example. Let's say that you have a single IDE hard drive, with 3 primary partitions. The first
two are set aside for MS-DOS, and the third is an extended partition which contains two logical partitions,
both for use by Linux. The devices referring to these partitions would be:

First MS-DOS partition (C:)	/dev/hda1
Second MS-DOS partition (D:)	/dev/hda2
Extended partition	/dev/hda3
First Linux logical partition	/dev/hda5
Second Linux logical partition	/dev/hda6

Note that `/dev/hda4` is skipped; it corresponds to the fourth primary partition, which we don't
have in this example. Logical partitions are named consecutively starting with `/dev/hda5`.

Device	Name
First floppy (A:)	/dev/fd0
Second floppy (B:)	/dev/fd1
First hard drive (entire drive)	/dev/hda
First hard drive, primary partition 1	/dev/hda1
First hard drive, primary partition 2	/dev/hda2
First hard drive, primary partition 3	/dev/hda3
First hard drive, primary partition 4	/dev/hda4
First hard drive, logical partition 1	/dev/hda5
First hard drive, logical partition 2	/dev/hda6
⋮	
Second hard drive (entire drive)	/dev/hdb
Second hard drive, primary partition 1	/dev/hdb1
⋮	
First SCSI hard drive (entire drive)	/dev/sda
First SCSI hard drive, primary partition 1	/dev/sda1
⋮	
Second SCSI hard drive (entire drive)	/dev/sdb
Second SCSI hard drive, primary partition 1	/dev/sdb1
⋮	

Table 2.1: Linux partition names

2.3.3   Creating Linux partitions

Now you are ready to create Linux partitions with the fdisk command. As described in Section 2.2.3, in general you will need to create at least one partition for the Linux software itself, and another partition for swap space.

After booting the installation media, run fdisk by typing

    fdisk ⟨drive⟩

where ⟨drive⟩ is the Linux device name of the drive you plan to add partitions to (see Table 2.1). For instance, if you want to run fdisk on the first SCSI disk in your system, use the command fdisk /dev/sda. /dev/hda (the first IDE drive) is the default if you don't specify one.

If you are creating Linux partitions on more than one drive, run fdisk once for each drive.

    # fdisk /dev/hda

    Command (m for help):

Here fdisk is waiting for a command; you can type m to get a list of options.

```
Command (m for help):  m
Command action
a toggle a bootable flag
d delete a partition
l list known partition types
m print this menu
n add a new partition
p print the partition table
q quit without saving changes
t change a partition's system id
u change display/entry units
v verify the partition table
w write table to disk and exit
x extra functionality (experts only)

Command (m for help):
```

The n command is used to create a new partition. Most of the other options you won't need to worry about. To quit fdisk without saving any changes, use the q command. To quit fdisk and write the changes to the partition table to disk, use the w command.

The first thing you should do is display your current partition table and write the information down, for later reference. Use the p command.

```
Command (m for help):  p
Disk /dev/hda:  16 heads, 38 sectors, 683 cylinders
Units = cylinders of 608 * 512 bytes

    Device Boot  Begin   Start    End  Blocks   Id  System
/dev/hda1    *       1       1    203   61693    6  DOS 16-bit >=32M

Command (m for help):
```

In this example, we have a single MS-DOS partition on /dev/hda1, which is 61693 blocks (about 60 megs).[6] This partition starts at cylinder number 1, and ends on cylinder 203. We have a total of 683 cylinders in this disk; so there are 480 cylinders left to create Linux partitions on.

To create a new partition, use the n command. In this example, we'll create two primary partitions (/dev/hda2 and /dev/hda3) for Linux.

```
Command (m for help):  n
Command action
e extended
p primary partition (1-4)
p
```

---

[6] A block, under Linux, is 1024 bytes.

Here, `fdisk` is asking the type of the partition to create: extended or primary. In our example, we're creating only primary partitions, so we choose p.

```
Partition number (1-4):
```

`fdisk` will then ask for the number of the partition to create; since partition 1 is already used, our first Linux partition will be number 2.

```
Partition number (1-4):  2
First cylinder (204-683):
```

Now enter the starting cylinder number of the partition. Since cylinders 204 through 683 are unused, we'll use the first available one (numbered 204). There's no reason to leave empty space between partitions.

```
First cylinder (204-683):  204
Last cylinder or +size or +sizeM or +sizeK (204-683):
```

`fdisk` is asking for the size of the partition to create. We can either specify an ending cylinder number, or a size in bytes, kilobytes, or megabytes. Since we want our partition to be 80 megs in size, we specify +80M. When specifying a partition size in this way, `fdisk` will round the actual partition size to the nearest number of cylinders.

```
Last cylinder or +size or +sizeM or +sizeK (204-683):  +80M
Warning: Linux cannot currently use 33090 sectors of this partition
```

If you see a warning message such as this, it can be ignored. `fdisk` prints the warning because it's an older program, and dates before the time that Linux partitions were allowed to be larger than 64 megabytes.

Now we're ready to create our second Linux partition. For sake of demonstration, we'll create it with a size of 10 megabytes.

```
Command (m for help):  n
Command action
e extended
p primary partition (1-4)
p
Partition number (1-4):  3
First cylinder (474-683):  474
Last cylinder or +size or +sizeM or +sizeK (474-683):  +10M
```

At last, we'll display the partition table. Again, write down all of this information—especially the block sizes of your new partitions. You'll need to know the sizes of the partitions when creating filesystems, later. Also, verify that none of your partitions overlap.

```
Command (m for help):  p

Disk /dev/hda:  16 heads, 38 sectors, 683 cylinders
Units = cylinders of 608 * 512 bytes

     Device Boot   Begin   Start   End   Blocks   Id  System
   /dev/hda1    *      1       1    203   61693    6  DOS 16-bit >=32M
   /dev/hda2          204     204    473   82080   81  Linux/MINIX
   /dev/hda3          474     474    507   10336   81  Linux/MINIX
```

As you can see, /dev/hda2 is now a partition of size 82080 blocks (which corresponds to about 80 megabytes), and /dev/hda3 is 10336 blocks (about 10 megs).

Note that many distributions (such as Slackware) require you to use the t command in fdisk to change the type of the swap partition to "Linux swap", which is usually numbered 82. You can use the L command to print a list of known partition type codes, and then use t to set the type of the swap partition to that which corresponds to "Linux swap".

In this way, the installation software will be able to automatically find your swap partitions based on type. If the installation software doesn't seem to recognize your swap partition, you might want to re-run fdisk and use the t command on the partition in question.

In the example above, the remaining cylinders on the disk (numbered 508 to 683) are unused. You may wish to leave unused space on the disk, in case you wish to create additional partitions later.

Finally, we use the w command to write the changes to disk and exit fdisk.

```
Command (m for help):  w

#
```

Keep in mind that none of the changes you make while running fdisk will take effect until you give the w command, so you can toy with different configurations and save them when you're done. Also, if you want to quit fdisk at any time without saving the changes, use the q command. Remember that you shouldn't modify partitions for operating systems other than Linux with the Linux fdisk program.

Remember that you may not be able to boot Linux from a partition using cylinders numbered over 1023. Therefore, you should try to create your Linux root partition within the sub-1024 cylinder range. Again, if this is impossible, you can simply boot Linux from floppy.

Some Linux distributions require you to reboot the system after running fdisk. This is to allow the changes to the partition table to take effect before installing the software. Newer versions of fdisk automatically update the partition information in the kernel, so rebooting isn't necessary. To be on the safe side, after running fdisk you should reboot the installation media, as before, before proceeding.

2.3.4   Creating the swap space

If you are planning to use a swap partition for virtual RAM, you're ready to prepare it for use.[7] In Chapter 4 we will discuss the preparation of a swap file in case you don't want to use an individual partition.

Many distributions require you to create and activate swap space before installing the software. If you have a small amount of physical RAM, the installation procedure may not be successful unless you have some amount of swap space enabled.

The Slackware distribution requires you to create swap space, before installation, if you have 4 megabytes of RAM or less. If this is not the case, the Slackware installation procedure can be used to prepare swap space automatically. If in doubt, go ahead and follow the procedure described here; it can't hurt.

The command used to prepare a swap partition is `mkswap`, and it takes the form

    mkswap -c ⟨partition⟩ ⟨size⟩

where ⟨partition⟩ is the name of the swap partition, and ⟨size⟩ is the size of the partition, in blocks.[8] For example, if your swap partition is /dev/hda3 and is 10336 blocks in size, use the command

    # mkswap −c /dev/hda3 10336

The `-c` option tells `mkswap` to check for bad blocks on the partition when creating the swap space.

If you are using multiple swap partitions, you will need to execute the appropriate `mkswap` command for each partition.

After formatting the swap space, you need to enable it for use by the system. Usually, the system automatically enables swap space at boot time. However, because you have not yet installed the Linux software, you need to enable it by hand.

The command to enable swap space is `swapon`, and it takes the form

    swapon ⟨partition⟩

In the example above, to enable the swap space on /dev/hda3, we use the command

    # swapon /dev/hda3

---

[7]Again, some distributions of Linux will prepare the swap space automatically for you, or via an installation menu option.

[8]This is the size as reported by `fdisk`, using the `p` menu option. A block under Linux is 1024 bytes.

2.3.5   Creating the filesystems

Before you can use your Linux partitions to store files, you must create **filesystems** on them. Creating a filesystem is analogous to formatting a partition under MS-DOS or other operating systems. We discussed filesystems briefly in Section 2.2.3.

There are several types of filesystems available for Linux. Each filesystem type has its own format and set of characteristics (such as filename length, maximum file size, and so on). Linux also supports several "third-party" filesystem types such as the MS-DOS filesystem.

The most commonly used filesystem type is the **Second Extended Filesystem**, or *ext2fs*. The *ext2fs* is one of the most efficient and flexible filesystems; it allows filenames up to 256 characters and filesystem sizes of up to 4 terabytes. In Chapter 4, we'll discuss the various filesystem types available for Linux. Initially, however, we suggest that you use the *ext2fs* filesystem.

If you are installing the Slackware distribution, filesystems are created automatically for you by the installation procedure described in the next section. If you wish to create your filesystems by hand, however, follow the procedure described here.

To create an *ext2fs* filesystem, use the command

        mke2fs -c ⟨partition⟩ ⟨size⟩

where ⟨*partition*⟩ is the name of the partition, and ⟨*size*⟩ is the size of the partition in blocks. For example, to create a 82080-block filesystem on **/dev/hda2**, use the command

        # *mke2fs -c /dev/hda2 82080*

If you're using multiple filesystems for Linux, you'll need to use the appropriate **mke2fs** command for each filesystem.

If you have encountered any problems at this point, see Section 2.5 at the end of this chapter.

2.3.6   Installing the software

Finally, you are ready to install the software on your system. Every distribution has a different mechanism for doing this. Many distributions have a self-contained program which will step you through the installation. On other distributions, you will have to **mount** your filesystems in a certain subdirectory (such as **/mnt**) and copy the software to them by hand. On CD-ROM distributions, you may be given the option to install a portion of the software on your hard drives, and leave most of the software on the CD-ROM.

Some distributions offer several different ways to install the software. For example, you may be able to install the software directly from an MS-DOS partition on your hard drive, instead of from floppies. Or, you may be able to install over a TCP/IP network via FTP or NFS. See your distribution's documentation for details.

For example, the Slackware distribution only requires you to create partitions with `fdisk`, optionally create swap space with `mkswap` and `swapon` (if you have 4 megs or less of RAM), and then run the `setup` program. `setup` leads you through a very self-explanatory menu system to install the software. Use of `setup` is described in detail below.

The exact method used to install the Linux software differs greatly with each distribution. We're hoping that installing the Linux software should be self-explanatory, as it is with most distributions.

2.3.6.1 Installing Slackware with `setup`

If you are installing Slackware, after creating partitions (and possibly swap space), use the command

    `# setup`

This will present you will a menu-based procedure to walk you through the remaining steps of installation.

The procedure described here corresponds to that found on the `color144` and `colrlite` root disks; the other root disks may have slightly different procedures.

The `setup` menu consists of the following items. Use the arrow keys to move over the items, and press `enter` or `spacebar` to select an item.

Help	View the `setup` help file.
Keymap	This option allows you to specify the keyboard mapping for your system if you do not have a US keyboard. A list of keymaps will be presented; select the appropriate item from the list.
Quick	This allows you to select between "quick" and "verbose" installation modes. "Verbose" is the default, and is recommended for most installations (unless you've installed Slackware a dozen times, in which case you already know this).
Make tags	This allows Slackware installation experts to create customized "tag files" for preselecting packages. This is only necessary for customizing the installation procedure in some way; you shouldn't have to concern yourself with this.
Addswap	This will be the first item that most users will select to install Slackware. A list of available swap partitions will be displayed (those partitions with type "Linux swap" as set in `fdisk`). You will be able to specify which partitions you wish to use for swap space. You will then be asked if you wish to run `mkswap` on these partitions.
	If you have already executed `mkswap` and `swapon` (as described in Section 2.3.4) on your swap partitions, then you should *not* allow `setup` to execute `mkswap` on these partitions.

Even if you have already executed `mkswap` and `swapon`, it is necessary to use the `Addswap` menu item: This ensures that your swap partitions will be available once you have the system installed.

◇ Be warned! Creating swap space on a partition will destroy data on that partition. Be sure that you're not wiping out data that you want to keep.

If you select this menu item, you will be automatically prompted if you wish to proceed with the following items. In general, you should do this.

Target   This item allows you to specify the partitions upon which Linux is to be installed. A list of available partitions (those with type "Linux native", as specified by `fdisk`) will be displayed, and you will be asked to enter the name of your Linux root partition, such as `/dev/hda2`. You will then be prompted for the type of filesystem that you wish to create; we suggest using the `ext2fs` filesystem type as described in Section 2.3.5. This will create a filesystem on the named partition—somewhat analogous to "formatting" the partition under MS-DOS.

You will also be prompted for any other partitions that you might wish to use for Linux. For example, if you created a separate partition for `/usr` (see Section 2.2.3), you will be able to specify the name of the partition and the location where it should be mounted (as in `/usr` or `/usr/bin`).

◇ Be warned! Creating a filesystem on a partition will destroy all data on that partition. Be sure that you're not wiping out data that you want to keep.

Even if you already created your filesystems using `mke2fs` (see Section 2.3.5), you must use the `Target` menu item to specify the partitions where Linux will be installed.

Source   This menu item allows you to specify where you will be installing Slackware from, such as floppy, hard drive, or CD-ROM.

If you are installing from hard drive, you will be asked what partition the Slackware files are found on, as well as the type of partition. For example, if you have the Slackware files on an MS-DOS partition, enter the name of the partition (such as `/dev/hda1`) and select `MS-DOS FAT` as the type. You will then be asked what directory the files may be found under on this partition. For example, if you have the Slackware files stored under the directory `C:\SLACK` on your MS-DOS partition, enter

        `/slack`

as the location. Note that you should use forward slashes, not backslashes, in the pathname.

If you are installing from CD-ROM, you will be asked the type of CD-ROM device that you are using, as well as what directory on the CD-ROM the files may be found in. Many CD-ROMs have the files contained within the directory `/slakware`, but this depends on the release.

If you are installing Slackware Professional,[9] two directories are used on the CD-ROM. slakware is used for the standard system which will install the files directly to your hard drive. slackpro is used for the CD-ROM-based system where many files are accessed directly from the CD-ROM. This can save diskspace, but accessing many files is also noticeably slower. Several other Slackware vendors provide the ability to run the software from the CD-ROM as well. However, if you have the diskspace to spare, we recommend not running Slackware from the CD-ROM itself. Performance is generally slower.

If you are attempting a hard drive or CD-ROM install, Slackware may report that there is a mount error at this point. This is usually an indication that there was a problem accessing the hard drive or CD-ROM. See Section 2.5.3 for more information if you see such an error message.

Disk sets This menu option allows you to select the disk sets that you wish to install. You must install at least the A disk set. Simply use the arrow keys and spacebar to select which disk sets you wish to install.

Note that selecting a particular disk set does not mean that all packages on the disk set will be installed; you will be prompted before installing packages on the disk set marked as "optional" or "recommended."

Install At long last, this menu item will install the software on your system. You will be prompted for the prompting method; most users should select "normal." For each disk set that you selected, the "required" packages will be installed, and you will be prompted when installing the "optional" and "recommended" packages. If you are installing from floppy you will be asked to insert each floppy in succession.

As each package is installed a short description will be printed. Unless you have background in UNIX or Linux, many of these descriptions will not mean much to you. Take note of which packages are being installed, so you know what's there, but don't worry about trying to jot down everything that's printed on the display.

The most common error encountered here is that a file cannot be found on a floppy, or an I/O error when attempting to read the floppy. The former is an indication that the files on your floppy might be corrupted or incomplete; the latter that the floppy itself is bad. Any floppies which give these errors should be replaced, and you should re-install the disk set containing those floppies. See Section 2.5.3 for suggestions.

You may also have read errors when attempting to access a CD-ROM; be sure that the CD-ROM is clean, has no fingerprints, etc.

---

[9]Slackware Professional is a version of Slackware available from Morse Telecommunications.

Configure   This menu item performs some post-installation configuration of your system. This
                is covered in the following section.

2.3.7   Creating the boot floppy or installing LILO

Every distribution provides some means of booting your new Linux system after you have installed
the software. In many cases, the installation procedure will create a "boot floppy" which contains
a Linux kernel configured to use your newly-created root filesystem. In order to boot Linux, you
would boot from this floppy, and control would be transferred to your hard drive after booting. On
other distributions, this "boot floppy" is the installation floppy itself.

Many distributions give you the option of installing **LILO** on your hard drive. LILO is a program
that is installed on your drive's master boot record. It is able to boot a number of operating systems,
including MS-DOS and Linux, and allows you to select at startup time which to boot.

For the Slackware distribution, the Configure item in the setup menu will allow you to create a
boot floppy as well as install LILO. These options should be fairly self-explanatory. The Configure
menu item also allows you to specify your modem, mouse, and timezone information.

In order for LILO to be installed successfully, it needs to know a good deal of information about
your drive configuration—for example, which partitions contain which operating systems, how to
boot each operating system, and so on. Many distributions, when installing LILO, attempt to
"guess" at the appropriate parameters for your configuration. Although it's not often, the automated
LILO installation provided by some distributions can fail, and leave your master boot record in
shambles (although it's very doubtful that any damage to the actual data on your hard drive will
take place). In particular, if you use OS/2's Boot Manager, you should *not* install LILO using the
automated procedure—there are special instructions for using LILO with the Boot Manager, which
will be covered later.

In many cases, it is best to use a boot floppy, until you have a chance to configure LILO yourself,
by hand. If you're feeling exceptionally trustworthy, though, you can go ahead with the automated
LILO installation if it is provided with your distribution.

In Chapter 4, we'll cover in detail how to configure and install LILO for your particular setup.

If everything goes well, then congratulations! You have just installed Linux on your system. Go
have a Diet Coke or something—you deserve it.

In case you did run into any trouble, the next section will describe the most common sticking
points for Linux installations, and how to get around them.

2.3.8   Additional installation procedures

Some distributions of Linux provide a number of additional installation procedures, allowing you
to configure various software packages such as TCP/IP networking, the X Window System, and so

on. If you are provided with these configuration options during installation, you may wish to read ahead in this book for more information on how to configure this software. Otherwise, you should put off these installation procedures until you have a complete understanding of how to configure the software.

It's up to you; if all else fails, just go with the flow and see what happens. It's very doubtful that anything that you do incorrectly now cannot be undone in the future. (Knock on wood.)

2.4 Postinstallation procedures

After you have completed installing the Linux software, there should be very little left to do before you can begin to use the system. In most cases, you should be able to reboot the system, login as **root**, and begin exploring the system. (Each distribution has a slightly different method for doing this.)

At this point it's a good idea to explain how to reboot and shutdown the system as you're using it. You should never reboot or shutdown your Linux system by pressing the reset switch or with the old "Vulcan Nerve Pinch"—that is, by pressing $\boxed{\texttt{ctrl-alt-del}}$ in unison.[10] You shouldn't simply switch off the power, either. As with most UNIX systems, Linux caches disk writes in memory. Therefore, if you suddenly reboot the system without shutting down "cleanly", you can corrupt the data on your drives, causing untold damage.

The easiest way to shut down the system is with the **shutdown** command. As an example, to shutdown and reboot the system immediately, use the following command as **root**:

```
# shutdown -r now
```

This will cleanly reboot your system. The man page for **shutdown** describes the other command-line arguments that are available.[11]

Note, however, that many Linux distributions do not provide the **shutdown** command on the installation media. This means that the first time you reboot your system after installation, you may need to use the $\boxed{\texttt{ctrl-alt-del}}$ combination after all. Thereafter, you should always use the **shutdown** command.

After you have a chance to explore and use the system, there are several configuration chores that you should undertake. The first is to create a user account for yourself (and, optionally, for any other users that might have access to the system). Creating user accounts is described in Section 4.4. Usually, all that you have to do is login as **root**, and run the **adduser** (sometimes **useradd**) program. This will lead you through several prompts to create a new user account.

---

[10]On most Linux systems, however, $\boxed{\texttt{ctrl-alt-del}}$ will cause the system to shutdown gracefully, as if you had used the **shutdown** command.

[11]Use the command **man shutdown** to see the manual page for **shutdown**.

If you created more than one filesystem for Linux, or if you're using a swap partition, you may need to edit the file /etc/fstab in order for those filesystems to be available automatically after rebooting. (For example, if you're using a separate filesystem for /usr, and none of the files that should be in /usr appear to be present, you may simply need to mount that filesystem.) Section 4.8 describes this procedure. Note that the Slackware distribution of Linux automatically configures your filesystems and swap space at installation time, so this usually isn't necessary.

2.5   Running Into Trouble

Almost everyone runs into some kind of snag or hangup when attempting to install Linux the first time. Most of the time, the problem is caused by a simple misunderstanding. Sometimes, however, it can be something more serious, such as an oversight by one of the developers, or a bug.

This section will describe some of the most common installation problems, and how to solve them. If your installation appears to be successful, but you received unexpected error messages during the installation, these are described here as well.

2.5.1   Problems with booting the installation media

When attempting to boot the installation media for the first time, you may encounter a number of problems. These are listed below. Note that the following problems are *not* related to booting your newly-installed Linux system. See Section 2.5.4 for information on these kinds of pitfalls.

- **Floppy or media error when attempting to boot.**

  The most popular cause for this kind of problem is a corrupt boot floppy. Either the floppy is physically damaged, in which case you should re-create the disk with a *brand new* floppy, or the data on the floppy is bad, in which case you should verify that you downloaded and transferred the data to the floppy correctly. In many cases, simply re-creating the boot floppy will solve your problems. Retrace your steps and try again.

  If you received your boot floppy from a mail order vendor or some other distributor, instead of downloading and creating it yourself, contact the distributor and ask for a new boot floppy— but only after verifying that this is indeed the problem.

- **System "hangs" during boot or after booting.**

  After the installation media boots, you will see a number of messages from the kernel itself, indicating which devices were detected and configured. After this, you will usually be presented with a login prompt, allowing you to proceed with installation (some distributions instead drop you right into an installation program of some kind). The system may appear to "hang" during several of these steps. During all of these steps, be patient; loading software from floppy is very slow. In many cases, the system has not hung at all, but is merely taking a long time.

Verify that there is no drive or system activity for at least several minutes before assuming that the system is hung.

1. After booting from the LILO prompt, the system must load the kernel image from floppy. This may take several seconds; you will know that things are going well if the floppy drive light is still on.

2. While the kernel boots, SCSI devices must be probed for. If you do not have any SCSI devices installed, the system will "hang" for up to 15 seconds while the SCSI probe continues; this usually occurs after the line

    ```
    lp_init: lp1 exists (0), using polling driver
    ```

    appears on your screen.

3. After the kernel is finished booting, control is transferred to the system bootup files on the floppy. Finally, you will be presented with a login prompt, or be dropped into an installation program. If you are presented with a login prompt such as

    ```
    Linux login:
    ```

    you should then login (usually as root or install—this varies with each distribution). After entering the username, the system may pause for 20 seconds or more while the installation program or shell is being loaded from floppy. Again, the floppy drive light should be on. Don't assume that the system is hung.

Any of the above items may be the source of your problem. However, it is possible that the system actually may "hang" while booting, which can be due to several causes. First of all, you may not have enough available RAM to boot the installation media. (See the following item for information on disabling the ramdisk to free up memory.)

The cause of many system hangs is hardware incompatibility. Section 1.8 in the last chapter presented an overview of supported hardware under Linux. Even if your hardware is supported, you may run into problems with incompatible hardware configurations which are causing the system to hang. See Section 2.5.2, below, for a discussion of hardware incompatibilities.

- **System reports out of memory errors while attempting to boot or install the software.**

This item deals with the amount of RAM that you have available. On systems with 4 megabytes of RAM or less, you may run into trouble booting the installation media or installing the software itself. This is because many distributions use a "ramdisk", which is a filesystem loaded directly into RAM, for operations while using the installation media. The entire image of the installation boot floppy, for example, may be loaded into a ramdisk, which may require more than a megabyte of RAM.

The solution to this problem is to disable the ramdisk option when booting the install media. Each release has a different procedure for doing this; on the SLS release, for example, you type "floppy" at the LILO prompt when booting the a1 disk. See your distribution's documentation for details.

You may not see an "out of memory" error when attempting to boot or install the software; instead, the system may unexpectedly hang, or fail to boot. If your system hangs, and none of the explanations in the previous section seem to be the cause, try disabling the ramdisk.

Keep in mind that Linux itself requires at least 2 megabytes of RAM to run at all; some distributions of Linux require 4 megabytes or more.

- **The system reports an error such as "permission denied" or "file not found" while booting.**

  This is an indication that your installation bootup media is corrupt. If you attempt to boot from the installation media (and you're sure that you're doing everything correctly), you should not see any errors such as this. Contact the distributor of your Linux software and find out about the problem, and perhaps obtain another copy of the boot media if necessary. If you downloaded the bootup disk yourself, try re-creating the bootup disk, and see if this solves your problem.

- **The system reports the error "VFS: Unable to mount root" when booting.**

  This error message means that the root filesystem (found on the boot media itself), could not be found. This means that either your boot media is corrupt in some way, or that you are not booting the system correctly.

  For example, many CD-ROM distributions require that you have the CD-ROM in the drive when booting. Also be sure that the CD-ROM drive is on, and check for any activity. It's also possible that the system is not locating your CD-ROM drive at boot time; see Section 2.5.2 for more information.

  If you're sure that you are booting the system correctly, then your bootup media may indeed be corrupt. This is a very uncommon problem, so try other solutions before attempting to use another boot floppy or tape.

2.5.2 Hardware problems

The most common form of problem when attempting to install or use Linux is an incompatibility with hardware. Even if all of your hardware is supported by Linux, a misconfiguration or hardware conflict can sometimes cause strange results—your devices may not be detected at boot time, or the system may hang.

It is important to isolate these hardware problems if you suspect that they may be the source of your trouble. In the following sections we will describe some common hardware problems and how to resolve them.

2.5.2.1 Isolating hardware problems

If you experience a problem that you believe to be hardware-related, the first thing that you should do is attempt to isolate the problem. This means eliminating all possible variables and (usually) taking the system apart, piece-by-piece, until the offending piece of hardware is isolated.

This is not as frightening as it may sound. Basically, you should remove all nonessential hardware from your system, and then determine which device is actually causing the trouble—possibly by reinserting each device, one at a time. This means that you should remove all hardware other than the floppy and video controllers, and of course the keyboard. Even innocent-looking devices such as mouse controllers can wreak unknown havoc on your peace of mind unless you consider them nonessential.

For example, let's say that the system hangs during the Ethernet board detection sequence at boot time. You might hypothesize that there is a conflict or problem with the Ethernet board in your machine. The quick and easy way to find out is to pull the Ethernet board, and try booting again. If everything goes well, then you know that either (a) the Ethernet board is not supported by Linux (see Section 1.8 for a list of compatible boards), or (b) there is an address or IRQ conflict with the board.

"Address or IRQ conflict?" What on earth does that mean? All devices in your machine use an *IRQ*, or *interrupt request line*, to tell the system that they need something done on their behalf. You can think of the IRQ as a cord that the device tugs when it needs the system to take care of some pending request. If more than one device is tugging on the same cord, the kernel won't be able to detemine which device it needs to service. Instant mayhem.

Therefore, be sure that all of your installed devices are using unique IRQ lines. In general the IRQ for a device can be set by jumpers on the card; see the documentation for the particular device for details. Some devices do not require the use of an IRQ at all, but it is suggested that you configure them to use one if possible (the Seagate ST01 and ST02 SCSI controllers being good examples).

In some cases, the kernel provided on your installation media is configured to use a certain IRQ for certain devices. For example, on some distributions of Linux, the kernel is preconfigured to use IRQ 5 for the TMC-950 SCSI controller, the Mitsumi CD-ROM controller, and the bus mouse driver. If you want to use two or more of these devices, you'll need to first install Linux with only one of these devices enabled, then recompile the kernel in order to change the default IRQ for one of them. (See Chapter 4 for information on recompiling the kernel.)

Another area where hardware conflicts can arise is with DMA (direct memory access) channels, I/O addresses, and shared memory addresses. All of these terms describe mechanisms through which the system interfaces with hardware devices. Some Ethernet boards, for example, use a shared memory address as well as an IRQ to interface with the system. If any of these are in conflict with other devices, then the system may behave unexpectedly. You should be able to change the DMA channel, I/O or shared memory addresses for your various devices with jumper settings. (Unfortunately, some devices don't allow you to change these settings.)

The documentation for your various hardware devices should specify the IRQ, DMA channel, I/O address, or shared memory address that the devices use, and how to configure them. Again, the simple way to get around these problems is just to temporarily disable the conflicting devices until you have time to determine the cause of the problem.

Table 2.2 is a list of IRQ and DMA channels used by various "standard" devices found on most systems. Almost all systems will have some of these devices, so you should avoid setting the IRQ or DMA of other devices in conflict with these values.

Device	I/O address	IRQ	DMA
ttyS0 (COM1)	3f8	4	n/a
ttyS1 (COM2)	2f8	3	n/a
ttyS2 (COM3)	3e8	4	n/a
ttyS3 (COM4)	2e8	3	n/a
lp0 (LPT1)	378 - 37f	7	n/a
lp1 (LPT2)	278 - 27f	5	n/a
fd0, fd1 (floppies 1 and 2)	3f0 - 3f7	6	2
fd2, fd3 (floppies 3 and 4)	370 - 377	10	3

Table 2.2: Common device settings

2.5.2.2   Problems recognizing hard drive or controller

When Linux boots, you should see a series of messages on your screen such as:

```
Console:  colour EGA+ 80x25, 8 virtual consoles
Serial driver version 3.96 with no serial options enabled
tty00 at 0x03f8 (irq = 4) is a 16450
tty03 at 0x02e8 (irq = 3) is a 16550A
lp_init:  lp1 exists (0), using polling driver
...
```

Here, the kernel is detecting the various hardware devices present on your system. At some point, you should see the line

```
Partition check:
```

followed by a list of recognized partitions, for example:

```
Partition check:
hda:  hda1 hda2
hdb:  hdb1 hdb2 hdb3
```

If, for some reason, your drives or partitions are not recognized, then you will not be able to access them in any way.

There are several things that can cause this to happen:

- **Hard drive or controller not supported.** If you are using a hard drive controller (IDE, SCSI, or otherwise) that is not supported by Linux, the kernel will not recognize your partitions at boot time.

- **Drive or controller improperly configured.** Even if your controller is supported by Linux, it may not be configured correctly. (This is particularly a problem for SCSI controllers; most non-SCSI controllers should work fine without any additional configuration).

  Refer to the documentation for your hard drive and/or controller for information on solving these kinds of problems. In particular, many hard drives will need to have a jumper set if they are to be used as a "slave" drive (for example, as the second hard drive). The acid test for this kind of condition is to boot up MS-DOS, or some other operating system, known to work with your drive and controller. If you can access the drive and controller from another operating system, then it is not a problem with your hardware configuration.

  See Section 2.5.2.1, above, for information on resolving possible device conflicts, and Section 2.5.2.3, below, for information on configuring SCSI devices.

- **Controller properly configured, but not detected.** Some BIOS-less SCSI controllers require the user to specify information about the controller at boot time. Section 2.5.2.3, below, describes how to force hardware detection for these controllers.

- **Hard drive geometry not recognized.** Some systems, such as the IBM PS/ValuePoint, do not store hard drive geometry information in the CMOS memory, where Linux expects to find it. Also, certain SCSI controllers need to be told where to find drive geometry in order for Linux to recognize the layout of your drive.

  Most distributions provide a bootup option to specify the drive geometry. In general, when booting the installation media, you can specify the drive geometry at the LILO boot prompt with a command such as:

  boot: *linux hd=⟨cylinders⟩,⟨heads⟩,⟨sectors⟩*

  where ⟨cylinders⟩, ⟨heads⟩, and ⟨sectors⟩ correspond to the number of cylinders, heads, and sectors per track for your hard drive.

  After installing the Linux software, you will be able to install LILO, allowing you to boot from the hard drive. At that time, you can specify the drive geometry to the LILO installation procedure, making it unnecessary to enter the drive geometry each time you boot. See Chapter 4 for more about LILO.

2.5.2.3   Problems with SCSI controllers and devices

Presented here are some of the most common problems with SCSI controllers and devices such as CD-ROMs, hard drives, and tape drives. If you are having problems getting Linux to recognize your drive or controller, read on.

The Linux SCSI HOWTO (see Appendix A) contains much useful information on SCSI devices in addition to that listed here. SCSI can be particularly tricky to configure at times.

- **A SCSI device is detected at all possible ID's.** This is caused by strapping the device to the same address as the controller. You need to change the jumper settings so that the drive uses a different address from the controller itself.

- **Linux reports sense errors, even if the devices are known to be error-free.** This can be caused by bad cables, or by bad termination. If your SCSI bus is not terminated at both ends, you may have errors accessing SCSI devices. When in doubt, always check your cables.

- **SCSI devices report timeout errors.** This is usually caused by a conflict with IRQ, DMA, or device addresses. Also check that interrupts are enabled correctly on your controller.

- **SCSI controllers using BIOS are not detected.** Detection of controllers using BIOS will fail if the BIOS is disabled, or if your controller's "signature" is not recognized by the kernel. See the Linux SCSI HOWTO for more information about this.

- **Controllers using memory mapped I/O do not work.** This is caused when the memory-mapped I/O ports are incorrectly cached. Either mark the board's address space as uncacheable in the XCMOS settings, or disable cache altogether.

- **When partitioning, you get a warning that "cylinders > 1024", or you are unable to boot from a partition using cylinders numbered above 1023.** BIOS limits the number of cylinders to 1024, and any partition using cylinders numbered above this won't be accessible from the BIOS. As far as Linux is concerned, this affects only booting; once the system has booted you should be able to access the partition. Your options are to either boot Linux from a boot floppy, or boot from a partition using cylinders numbered below 1024. See Section 2.3.7 for information on creating a boot diskette or installing LILO.

- **CD-ROM drive or other removeable media devices are not recognized at boot time.** Try booting with a CD-ROM (or disk) in the drive. This is necessary for some devices.

If your SCSI controller is not recognized, you may need to force hardware detection at boot time. This is particularly important for BIOS-less SCSI controllers. Most distributions allow you to specify the controller IRQ and shared memory address when booting the installation media. For example, if you are using a TMC-8xx controller, you may be able to enter

```
boot:   linux tmx8xx=⟨interrupt⟩,⟨memory-address⟩
```

at the LILO boot prompt, where ⟨interrupt⟩ is the IRQ of controller, and ⟨memory-address⟩ is the shared memory address. Whether or not you will be able to do this depends on the distribution of Linux you are using; consult your documentation for details.

2.5.3 Problems installing the software

Actually installing the Linux software should be quite trouble-free, if you're lucky. The only problems that you might experience would be related to corrupt installation media or lack of space on your Linux filesystems. Here is a list of these common problems.

- **System reports "Read error", "file not found", or other errors while attempting to install the software.** This is indicative of a problem with your installation media. If you are installing from floppy, keep in mind that floppies are quite succeptible to media errors of this type. Be sure to use brand-new, newly-formatted floppies. If you have an MS-DOS partition on your drive, many Linux distributions allow you to install the software from the hard drive. This may be faster and more reliable than using floppies.

  If you are using a CD-ROM, be sure to check the disc for scratches, dust, or other problems which might cause media errors.

  The cause of the problem may be that the media is in the incorrect format. For example, if using floppies, many Linux distributions require that the floppies be formatted in high-density MS-DOS format. (The boot floppy is the exception; it is not in MS-DOS format in most cases.) If all else fails, either obtain a new set of floppies, or recreate the floppies (using new diskettes) if you downloaded the software yourself.

- **System reports errors such as "tar: read error" or "gzip: not in gzip format".** This problem is usually caused by corrupt files on the installation media itself. In other words, your floppy may be error-free, but the data on the floppy is in some way corrupted. For example, if you downloaded the Linux software using text mode, rather than binary mode, then your files will be corrupt, and unreadable by the installation software.

- **System reports errors such as "device full" while installing.** This is a clear-cut sign that you have run out of space when installing the software. Not all Linux distributions will be able to cleanly pick up the mess; you shouldn't be able to abort the installation and expect the system to work.

  The solution is usually to re-create your filesystems (with the `mke2fs` command) which will delete the partially-installed software. You can then attempt to re-install the software, this time selecting a smaller amount of software to install. In other cases, you may need to start completely from scratch, and rethink your partition and filesystem sizes.

- **System reports errors such as "read_intr: 0x10" while accessing the hard drive.** This is usually an indication of bad blocks on your drive. However, if you receive these errors while using `mkswap` or `mke2fs`, the system may be having trouble accessing your drive. This can either be a hardware problem (see Section 2.5.2), or it might be a case of poorly specified geometry. If you used the

      hd=⟨cylinders⟩,⟨heads⟩,⟨sectors⟩

option at boot time to force detection of your drive geometry, and incorrectly specified the geometry, you could be prone to this problem. This can also happen if your drive geometry is incorrectly specified in the system CMOS.

- **System reports errors such as "file not found" or "permission denied".** This problem can occur if not all of the necessary files are present on the installation media (see the next paragraph) or if there is a permissions problem with the installation software. For example, some distributions of Linux have been known to have bugs in the installation software itself. These are usually fixed very rapidly, and are quite infrequent. If you suspect that the distribution software contains bugs, and you're sure that you have not done anything wrong, contact the maintainer of the distribution to report the bug.

If you have other strange errors when installing Linux (especially if you downloaded the software yourself), be sure that you actually obtained all of the necessary files when downloading. For example, some people use the FTP command

    mget *.*

when downloading the Linux software via FTP. This will download only those files that contain a ".", in their filenames; if there are any files without the ".", you will miss them. The correct command to use in this case is

    mget *

The best advice is to retrace your steps when something goes wrong. You may think that you have done everything correctly, when in fact you forgot a small but important step somewhere along the way. In many cases, just attempting to re-download or re-install the Linux software can solve the problem. Don't beat your head against the wall any longer than you have to!

Also, if Linux unexpectedly hangs during installation, there may be a hardware problem of some kind. See Section 2.5.2 for hints.

2.5.4   Problems after installing Linux

You've spent an entire afternoon installing Linux. In order to make space for it, you wiped your MS-DOS and OS/2 partitions, and tearfully deleted your copies of SimCity and Wing Commander. You reboot the system, and nothing happens. Or, even worse, *something* happens, but it's not what should happen. What do you do?

In Section 2.5.1, we covered some of the most common problems that can occur when booting the Linux installation media—many of those problems may apply here. In addition, you may be victim to one of the following maladies.

2.5.4.1 Problems booting Linux from floppy

If you are using a floppy to boot Linux, you may need to specify the location of your Linux root partition at boot time. This is especially true if you are using the original installation floppy itself, and not a custom boot floppy created during installation.

While booting the floppy, hold down boxed shift or boxed ctrl. This should present you with a boot menu; press boxed tab to see a list of available options. For example, many distributions allow you to type

  boot: *linux hd=⟨partition⟩*

at the boot menu, where ⟨*partition*⟩ is the name of the Linux root partition, such as /dev/hda2. Consult the documentation for your distribution for details.

2.5.4.2 Problems booting Linux from the hard drive

If you opted to install LILO, instead of creating a boot floppy, then you should be able to boot Linux from the hard drive. However, the automated LILO installation procedure used by many distributions is not always perfect. It may make incorrect assumptions about your partition layout, in which case you will need to re-install LILO to get everything right. Installing LILO is covered in Chapter 4.

- **System reports** "Drive not bootable---Please insert system disk." You will get this error message if the hard drive's master boot record is corrupt in some way. In most cases, it's harmless, and everything else on your drive is still intact. There are several ways around this:

  1. While partitioning your drive using fdisk, you may have deleted the partition that was marked as "active". MS-DOS and other operating systems attempt to boot the "active" partition at boot time (Linux pays no attention to whether the partition is "active" or not). You may be able to boot MS-DOS from floppy and run FDISK to set the active flag on your MS-DOS parition, and all will be well.

     Another command to try (with MS-DOS 5.0 and higher) is

     FDISK /MBR

     This command will attempt to rebuild the hard drive master boot record for booting MS-DOS, overwriting LILO. If you no longer have MS-DOS on your hard drive, you'll need to boot Linux from floppy and attempt to install LILO later.

  2. If you created an MS-DOS partition using Linux's version of fdisk, or vice versa, you may get this error. You should create MS-DOS partitions only using MS-DOS's version FDISK. (The same applies to operating systems other than MS-DOS.) The best solution here is either to start from scratch and repartition the drive correctly, or to merely delete and re-create the offending partitions using the correct version of fdisk.

3. The LILO installation procedure may have failed. In this case, you should either boot from your Linux boot floppy (if you have one), or from the original installation media. Either of these should provide options for specifying the Linux root partition to use when booting. Hold down `shift` or `ctrl` at boot time, and press `tab` from the boot menu for a list of options.

- **When booting the system from the hard drive, MS-DOS (or another operating system) starts instead of Linux.** First of all, be sure that you actually installed LILO when installing the Linux software. If not, then the system will still boot MS-DOS (or whatever other operating system you may have) when you attempt to boot from the hard drive. In order to boot Linux from the hard drive, you will need to install LILO (see Chapter 4).

On the other hand, if you *did* install LILO, and another operating system boots instead of Linux, then you have LILO configured to boot that other operating system by default. While the system is booting, hold down `shift` or `ctrl`, and press `tab` at the boot prompt. This should present you with a list of possible operating systems to boot; select the appropriate option (usually just "`linux`") to boot Linux.

If you wish to select Linux as the default operating system to boot, you will need to re-install LILO. See Chapter 4.

It also may be possible that you attempted to install LILO, but the installation procedure failed in some way. See the previous item.

2.5.4.3   Problems logging in

After booting Linux, you should be presented with a login prompt, like so:

```
linux login:
```

At this point, either the distribution's documentation or the system itself will tell you what to do. For many distributions, you simply login as **root**, with no password. Other possible usernames to try are **guest** or **test**.

Most newly-installed Linux systems should not require a password for the initial login. However, if you are asked to enter a password, there may be a problem. First, try using a password equivalent to the username; that is, if you are logging in as **root**, use "**root**" as the password.

If you simply can't login, there may be a problem. First, consult your distribution's documentation; the username and password to use may be buried in there somewhere. The username and password may have been given to you during the installation procedure, or they may be printed on the login banner.

One cause of this may be a problem with installing the Linux login and initialization files. If this is the case, you may need to reinstall (at least parts of) the Linux software, or boot your installation media and attempt to fix the problem by hand—see Chapter 4 for hints.

2.5.4.4 Problems using the system

If login is successful, you should be presented with a shell prompt (such as "#" or "$") and can happily roam around your system. However, there are some initial problems with using the system that sometimes creep up.

The most common initial configuration problem is incorrect file or directory permissions. This can cause the error message

```
Shell-init:  permission denied
```

to be printed after logging in (in fact, any time you see the message "permission denied" you can be fairly certain that it is a problem with file permissions).

In many cases, it's a simple matter of using the chmod command to fix the permissions of the appropriate files or directories. For example, some distributions of Linux once used the (incorrect) file mode 0644 for the root directory (/). The fix was to issue the command

```
# chmod 755 /
```

as root. However, in order to issue this command, you needed to boot from the installation media and mount your Linux root filesystem by hand—a hairy task for most newcomers.

As you use the system, you may run into places where file and directory permissions are incorrect, or software does not work as configured. Welcome to the world of Linux! While most distributions are quite trouble-free, very few of them are perfect. We don't want to cover all of those problems here. Instead, throughout the book we help you to solve many of these configuration problems by teaching you how to find them and fix them yourself. In Chapter 1 we discussed this philosophy in some detail. In Chapter 4, we give hints for fixing many of these common configuration problems.

Chapter 3

Linux Tutorial

3.1 Introduction

New users of UNIX and Linux may be a bit intimidated by the size and apparent complexity of the system before them. There are many good books on using UNIX out there, for all levels of expertise from novice to expert. However, none of these books covers, specifically, an introduction to using Linux. While 95% of using Linux is exactly like using other UNIX systems, the most straightforward way to get going on your new system is with a tutorial tailored for Linux. Herein is such a tutorial.

This chapter does not go into a large amount of detail or cover many advanced topics. Instead, it is intended to get the new Linux user running, on both feet, so that he or she may then read a more general book about UNIX and understand the basic differences between other UNIX systems and Linux.

Very little is assumed here, except perhaps some familiarity with personal computer systems, and MS-DOS. However, even if you're not an MS-DOS user, you should be able to understand everything here. At first glance, UNIX looks a lot like MS-DOS (after all, parts of MS-DOS were modeled on the CP/M operating system, which in turn was modeled on UNIX). However, only the very superficial features of UNIX resemble MS-DOS in any way. Even if you're completely new to the PC world, this tutorial should be of help.

And, before we begin: *Don't be afraid to experiment.* The system won't bite you. You can't destroy anything by working on the system. UNIX has some amount of security built in, to prevent "normal" users (the role which you will now assume) from damaging files which are essential to the system. Even so, the absolute worst thing that can happen is that you'll delete all of your files—and you'll have to go back and re-install the system. So, at this point, you have nothing to lose.

3.2 Basic UNIX Concepts

UNIX is a multitasking, multiuser operating system. This means that there can be many people using one computer at the same time, running many different applications. (This differs from MS-DOS, where only one person can use the system at any one time.) Under UNIX, for users to identify themselves to the system, they must **log in**, which entails two steps: Entering your **login name** (the name which the system identifies you as), and entering your **password**, which is your personal secret key to logging into your account. Because only you know your password, no one else can login to the system under your username.

On traditional UNIX systems, the system administrator will assign you a username and an initial password when you are given an account on the system. However, because you are the system administrator, you must set up your own account before you can login—see Section 3.2.1, below. For the following discussions, we'll use the imaginary username "`larry`".

In addition, each UNIX system has a **hostname** assigned to it. It is this hostname that gives your machine a name, gives it character and charm. The hostname is used to identify individual machines on a network, but even if your machine isn't networked, it should have a hostname. In Section 4.10.2 we'll cover setting your system's hostname. For our examples, below, the system's hostname is "`mousehouse`".

3.2.1 Creating an account

Before you can use the system, you must set up a user account for yourself. This is because it's usually not a good idea to use the `root` account for normal use. The `root` account should be reserved for running privileged commands and for maintaining the system, as discussed in Section 4.1.

In order to create an account for yourself, you need to login as `root` and use the `useradd` or `adduser` command. See Section 4.4 for information on this procedure.

3.2.2 Logging in

At login time, you'll see a prompt resembling the following on your screen:

```
mousehouse login:
```

Here, enter your username, and press the Return key. Our hero, `larry`, would type the following:

```
mousehouse login: larry
Password:
```

Now, enter your password. It won't be echoed to the screen when you login, so type carefully. If you mistype your password, you'll see the message

```
Login incorrect
```

and you'll have to try again.

Once you have correctly entered the username and password, you are officially logged into the system, and are free to roam.

3.2.3   Virtual consoles

The system's **console** is the monitor and keyboard connected directly to the system. (Because UNIX is a multiuser operating system, you may have other terminals connected to serial ports on your system, but these would not be the console.) Linux, like some other versions of UNIX, provides access to **virtual consoles** (or VC's), which allow you to have more than one login session from your console at a time.

To demonstrate this, login to your system (as demonstrated above). Now, press ⌐alt-F2⌐. You should see the `login:` prompt again. You're looking at the second virtual console—you logged into the first. To switch back to the first VC, press ⌐alt-F1⌐. *Voila!* You're back to your first login session.

A newly-installed Linux system probably allows you to access the first four VC's, using ⌐alt-F1⌐ through ⌐alt-F4⌐. However, it is possible to enable up to 12 VC's—one for each function key on your keyboard. As you can see, use of VC's can be very powerful—you can be working on several different VC's at once.

While the use of VC's is somewhat limiting (after all, you can only be looking at one VC at a time), it should give you a feel for UNIX's multiuser capabilities. While you're working on VC #1, you can switch over to VC #2 and start working on something else.

3.2.4   Shells and commands

For most of your explorations in the world of UNIX, you'll be talking to the system through the use of a **shell**. A shell is just a program which takes user input (e.g., commands which you type) and translates them into instructions. This can be compared to the `COMMAND.COM` program under MS-DOS, which does essentially the same thing. The shell is just one interface to UNIX. There are many possible interfaces—such as the X Window System, which lets you run commands by using the mouse and keyboard in conjunction.

As soon as you login, the system starts the shell, and you can type commands to it. Here's a quick example. Here, Larry logs in, and is left sitting at the shell **prompt**.

```
mousehouse login:  larry
Password:  larry's password
Welcome to Mousehouse!
```

```
/home/larry#
```

"`/home/larry#`" is the shell's prompt, indicating that it's ready to take commands. (More on what the prompt itself means later.) Let's try telling the system to do something interesting:

```
/home/larry# make love
make: *** No way to make target 'love'.  Stop.
/home/larry#
```

Well, as it turns out `make` was the name of an actual program on the system, and the shell executed this program when given the command. (Unfortunately, the system was being unfriendly.)

This brings us to one burning question: What are commands? What happens when you type "`make love`"? The first word on the command line, "`make`", is the name of the command to be executed. Everything else on the command line is taken as arguments to this command. Examples:

```
/home/larry# cp foo bar
```

Here, the name of the command is "`cp`", and the arguments are "`foo`" and "`bar`".

When you type a command, the shell does several things. First of all, it looks at the command name, and checks to see if it is a command which is internal to the shell. (That is, a command which the shell knows how to execute itself. There are a number of these commands, and we'll go into them later.) The shell also checks to see if the command is an alias, or substitute name, for another command. If neither of these conditions apply, the shell looks for a program, on the disk, with the command's name. If it finds such a program, the shell runs it, giving the program the arguments specified on the command line.

In our example, the shell looks for the program called `make`, and runs it with the argument `love`. `Make` is a program often used to compile large programs, and it takes as arguments the name of a "target" to compile. In the case of "`make love`", we instructed `make` to compile the target `love`. Because `make` can't find a target by this name, it fails with a humorous error message, and we are returned to the shell prompt.

What happens if we type a command to a shell, and the shell can't find a program with the command name to run? Well, we can try it:

```
/home/larry# eat dirt
eat: command not found
/home/larry#
```

Quite simply, if the shell can't find a program with the name given on the command line (here, "`eat`"), it prints an error message which should be self-explanatory. You'll often see this error message if you mistype a command (for example, if you had typed "`mkae love`" instead of "`make love`").

3.2.5 Logging out

Before we delve much further, we should tell you how to log out of the system. At the shell prompt, use the command

```
/home/larry# exit
```

to logout. There are other ways of logging out as well, but this is the most foolproof one.

3.2.6 Changing your password

You should also be aware of how to change your password. The command `passwd` will prompt you for your old password, and your new password. It will ask you to reenter the new password for validation. Be careful not to forget your password—if you do, you will have to ask the system administrator to reset it for you. (If you're the system administrator, see Section 4.4.)

3.2.7 Files and directories

Under most operating systems (UNIX included), there is the concept of a **file**, which is just a bundle of information which is given a name (called a **filename**). Examples of files would be your history term paper, an e-mail message, or an actual program which can be executed. Essentially, anything which is saved on disk is saved in an individual file.

Files are identified by their filenames. For example, the file containing your history paper might be saved with the filename `history-paper`. These names usually identify the file and its contents in some form which is meaningful to you. There is no standard format for filenames as there is under MS-DOS and other operating systems; in general, filenames may contain any character (except /—see the discussion of pathnames, below), and are limited to 256 characters in length.

With the concept of files comes the concept of directories. A **directory** is just a collection of files. It can be thought of as a "folder" which contains many different files. Directories themselves are given names, with which you can identify them. Furthermore, directories are maintained in a tree-like structure; that is, directories may contain other directories.

A file may be referred to by its **pathname**, which is made up of the filename, preceded by the name of the directory which contains the file. For example, let's say that Larry has a directory called `papers`, which contains three files: `history-final`, `english-lit`, and `masters-thesis`. (Each of these three files contains information for three of Larry's ongoing projects.) To refer to the file `english-lit`, Larry can specify the file's pathname:

```
papers/english-lit
```

As you can see, the directory and file names are separated by a single slash (/). For this reason, filenames themselves cannot contain the / character. MS-DOS users will find this convention familiar, although in the MS-DOS world, the backslash (\) is used instead.

As mentioned, directories can be nested within each other as well. For example, let's say that Larry has another directory, within **papers**, called **notes**. This directory contains the files **math-notes** and **cheat-sheet**. The pathname of the file **cheat-sheet** would be

    papers/notes/cheat-sheet

Therefore, the pathname really is a "path" which you take to locate a certain file. The directory above a given subdirectory is known as the **parent directory**. Here, the directory **papers** is the parent of the **notes** directory.

3.2.8 The directory tree

Most UNIX systems have a standard layout for files, so that system resources and programs can be easily located. This layout forms a directory tree, which starts at the "/" directory, also known as "the root directory". Directly underneath / are some important subdirectories: **/bin**, **/etc**, **/dev**, and **/usr**, among others. These directories in turn contain other directories which contain system configuration files, programs, and so on.

In particular, each user has a **home directory**, which is the directory set aside for that user to store his or her files. In the examples above, all of Larry's files (such as **cheat-sheet** and **history-final**) were contained in Larry's home directory. Usually, user home directories are contained under **/home**, and are named for the user who owns that directory. Therefore, Larry's home directory is **/home/larry**.

In Figure 3.2.8 a sample directory tree is represented. It should give you some idea of how the directory tree on your system is organized.

3.2.9 The current working directory

At any given time, commands that you type to the shell are given in terms of your **current working directory**. You can think of your working directory as the directory in which you are currently "located". When you first login, your working directory is set to your home directory—**/home/larry** in our case. Whenever you reference a file, you may refer to it in relationship to your current working directory, instead of specifying the full pathname of the file.

Here's an example. Larry has the directory **papers**, and **papers** contains the file **history-final**. If Larry wants to look at this file, he can use the command

    /home/larry# *more /home/larry/papers/history-final*

The **more** command simply displays a file, one screen at a time. However, because Larry's current working directory is **/home/larry**, he can instead refer to the file *relative* to his current location. The command would be

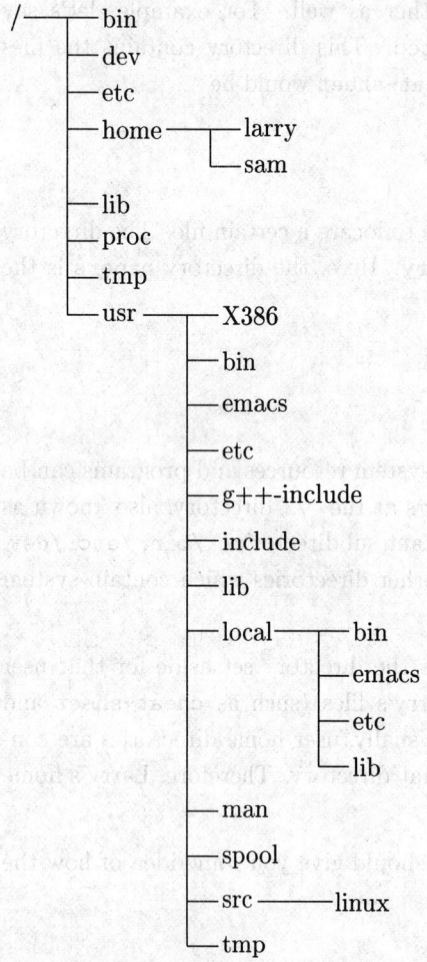

Figure 3.1: A typical (abridged) Unix directory tree.

`/home/larry#` *more papers/history-final*

Therefore, if you begin a filename (such as `papers/final`) with a character other than "/", the system assumes that you're referring to the file in terms relative to your current working directory. This is known as a **relative pathname**.

On the other hand, if you begin a filename with a "/", the system interprets this as a full pathname—that is, a pathname including the entire path to the file, starting from the root directory, /. This is known as an **absolute pathname**.

3.2.10 Referring to home directories

Under both `tcsh` and `bash`,[1] your home directory can be referred to using the tilde character ("~").
For example, the command

> `/home/larry#` *more ~/papers/history-final*

is equivalent to

> `/home/larry#` *more /home/larry/papers/history-final*

The "~" character is simply replaced with the name of your home directory by the shell.

In addition, you can specify other user's home directories with the tilde as well. The pathname
"`~karl/letters`" translates to "`/home/karl/letters`" by the shell (if `/home/karl` is karl's home
directory). The use of the tilde is simply a shortcut; there is no directory named "~"—it's just
syntactic sugar provided by the shell.

3.3   First Steps into UNIX

Before we begin, it is important to note that all file and command names on a UNIX system are
case-sensitive (unlike operating systems such as MS-DOS). For example, the command `make` is very
different than `Make` or `MAKE`. The same hold for file and directory names.

3.3.1   Moving around

Now that we can login, and know how to refer to files using pathnames, how can we change our
current working directory, to make life easier?

The command for moving around in the directory structure is `cd`, short for "change directory".
You'll notice that many often-used Unix commands are two or three letters. The usage of the `cd`
command is:

> `cd` ⟨*directory*⟩

where ⟨*directory*⟩ is the name of the directory which you wish to change to.

As we said, when you login, you begin in your home directory. If Larry wanted to move down
into the `papers` subdirectory, he'd use the command

> `/home/larry#` *cd papers*
> `/home/larry/papers#`

---

[1]`tcsh` and `bash` are two *shells* running under Linux. The shell is the program which reads user commands and
executes them; most Linux systems enable either `tcsh` or `bash` for new user accounts.

As you can see, Larry's prompt changes to reflect his current working directory (so he knows where he is). Now that he's in the **papers** directory, he can look at his history final with the command

```
/home/larry/papers# more history-final
```

Now, Larry is stuck in the **papers** subdirectory. To move back up to the parent directory, use the command

```
/home/larry/papers# cd ..
/home/larry#
```

(Note the space between the "cd" and the "..".) Every directory has an entry named ".." which refers to the parent directory. Similarly, every directory has an entry named "." which refers to itself. Therefore, the command

```
/home/larry/papers# cd .
```

gets us nowhere.

You can also use absolute pathnames in the **cd** command. To **cd** into Karl's home directory, we can use the command

```
/home/larry/papers# cd /home/karl
/home/karl#
```

Also, using **cd** with no argument will return you to your own home directory.

```
/home/karl# cd
/home/larry#
```

3.3.2 Looking at the contents of directories

Now that you know how to move around directories you probably think, "So what?" The basic skill of moving around directories is fairly useless, so let's introduce a new command, **ls**. **ls** prints a listing of files and directories, by default from your current directory. For example:

```
/home/larry# ls
Mail
letters
papers
/home/larry#
```

Here we can see that Larry has three entries in his current directory: `Mail`, `letters`, and `papers`. This doesn't tell us much—are these directories or files? We can use the `-F` option on the `ls` command to tell us more.

```
/home/larry# ls -F
Mail/
letters/
papers/
/home/larry#
```

From the / appended to each filename, we know that these three entries are in fact subdirectories.

Using `ls -F` may also append "*" to the end of a filename. This indicates that the file is an **executable**, or a program which can be run. If nothing is appended to the filename using `ls -F`, the file is a "plain old file", that is, it's neither a directory, or an executable.

In general, each UNIX command may take a number of options in addition to other arguments. These options usually begin with a "-", as demonstrated above with `ls -F`. The `-F` option tells `ls` to give more information about the type of the files involved—in this case, printing a / after each directory name.

If you give `ls` a directory name, it will print the contents of that directory.

```
/home/larry# ls -F papers
english-lit
history-final
masters-thesis
notes/
/home/larry#
```

Or, for a more interesting listing, let's see what's in the system's /etc directory.

```
/home/larry# ls /etc
```

Images	ftpusers	lpc	rc.new	shells
adm	getty	magic	rc0.d	startcons
bcheckrc	gettydefs	motd	rc1.d	swapoff
brc	group	mount	rc2.d	swapon
brc~	inet	mtab	rc3.d	syslog.conf
csh.cshrc	init	mtools	rc4.d	syslog.pid
csh.login	init.d	pac	rc5.d	syslogd.reload
default	initrunlvl	passwd	rmt	termcap
disktab	inittab	printcap	rpc	umount
fdprm	inittab.old	profile	rpcinfo	update
fstab	issue	psdatabase	securetty	utmp
ftpaccess	lilo	rc	services	wtmp

```
/home/larry#
```

(For those MS-DOS users out there, notice how the filenames can be longer than 8 characters, and can contain periods in any position. It is even possible to have more than one period in a filename.)

Let's cd up to the top of the directory tree, using "cd ..", and then down to another directory: /usr/bin.

```
/home/larry# cd ..
/home# cd ..
/# cd usr
/usr# cd bin
/usr/bin#
```

You can also move into directories in multiple steps, as in cd /usr/bin.

Try moving around various directories, using ls and cd. In some cases, you may run into a foreboding "Permission denied" error message. This is simply the concept of UNIX security kicking in: in order to ls or to cd into a directory, you must have permission to do so. We'll talk more about this in   Section 3.9.

3.3.3   Creating new directories

It's time to learn how to create directories. This involves the use of the mkdir command. Try the following:

```
/home/larry# mkdir foo
/home/larry# ls -F
Mail/
foo/
letters/
papers/
/home/larry# cd foo
/home/larry/foo# ls
/home/larry/foo#
```

Congrats! You've just made a new directory and moved into it. Since there aren't any files in this new directory, let's learn how to copy files from one place to another.

3.3.4   Copying files

Copying files is done with the command cp:

```
/home/larry/foo# cp /etc/termcap .
/home/larry/foo# cp /etc/shells .
/home/larry/foo# ls -F
shells      termcap
/home/larry/foo# cp shells bells
/home/larry/foo# ls -F
bells       shells       termcap
/home/larry/foo#
```

The `cp` command copies the files listed on the command line to the file or directory given as the last argument. Notice how we use the directory "." to refer to the current directory.

3.3.5 Moving files

A new command named `mv` moves files, instead of copying them. The syntax is very straightforward.

```
/home/larry/foo# mv termcap sells
/home/larry/foo# ls -F
bells       sells       shells
/home/larry/foo#
```

Notice how `termcap` no longer exists, but in its place is the file `sells`. This can be used to rename files, as we have just done, but also to move a file to a completely new directory.

Note: `mv` and `cp` will overwrite the destination file (if it already exists) without asking you. Be careful when you move a file into another directory: there may already be a file with the same name in that directory, which you'll overwrite!

3.3.6 Deleting files and directories

You now have an ugly rhyme developing with the use of the `ls` command. To delete a file, use the `rm` command. ("rm" stands for "remove").

```
/home/larry/foo# rm bells sells
/home/larry/foo# ls -F
shells
/home/larry/foo#
```

We're left with nothing but shells, but we won't complain. Note that `rm` by default won't prompt you before deleting a file—so be careful.

A related command to `rm` is `rmdir`. This command deletes a directory, but only if the directory is empty. If the directory contains any files or subdirectories, `rmdir` will complain.

3.3.7   Looking at files

The commands `more` and `cat` are used for viewing the contents of files. `more` displays a file, one screenful at a time, while `cat` displays the whole file at once.

To look at the file `shells`, we can use the command

> `/home/larry/foo#` *more shells*

In case you're interested what `shells` contains, it's a list of valid shell programs on your system. On most systems, this includes /bin/sh, /bin/bash, and /bin/csh. We'll talk about these different types of shells later.

While using `more`, press $\boxed{\text{Space}}$ to display the next page of text, and $\boxed{\text{b}}$ to display the previous page. There are other commands available in `more` as well, these are just the basics. Pressing $\boxed{\text{q}}$ will quit `more`.

Quit `more` and try `cat /etc/termcap`. The text will probably fly by much too quickly for you to read it. The name "cat" actually stands for "concatenate", which is the real use of the program. The `cat` command can be used to concatenate the contents of several files and save the result to another file. This will be discussed later.

3.3.8   Getting online help

Almost every UNIX system, Linux included, provides a facility known as "manual pages", or "man pages" for short. These man pages contain online documentation for all of the various system commands, resources, configuration files, and so on.

The command used to access man pages is `man`. For example, if you're interested in finding out about the other options of the `ls` command, you can type

> `/home/larry#` *man ls*

and the man page for `ls` will be displayed.

Unfortunately, most of the man pages out there are written for those who already have some idea of what the command or resource does. For this reason, man pages usually only contain the hardcore technical details of the command, without a lot of tutorial. However, man pages can be an invaluable resource for jogging your memory if you forget the syntax of a command. Man pages will also tell you a lot about the commands which we won't tell you in this book.

I suggest that you try `man` for the commands we've already gone over, and whenever I introduce a new command. You'll notice some of these commands won't have man pages. This could be for several reasons. For one, the man pages haven't been written yet (the Linux Documentation Project is responsible for man pages under Linux as well. We are gradually accumulating most of the man pages available for the system). Secondly, the the command might be an internal shell command, or an alias (as discussed in Section 3.2.4), in which case it would not have a man page of its own. One example is cd, which is a shell internal command. The shell actually processes the cd—there is no separate program which contains this command.

3.4 Summary of Basic Commands

This section introduces some of the most useful basic commands on a UNIX system, including those covered in the last section.

Note that options usually begin with a "-", and in most cases multiple one-letter options may be combined using a single "-". For example, instead of using the command ls -l -F, it is adequate to use ls -1F.

Instead of listing all of the options available for each of these commands, we'll only talk about those which are useful or important at this time. In fact, most of these commands have a large number of options (most of which you'll never use). You can use man to see the manual pages for each command, which list all of the available options.

Also note that many of these commands take a list of files or directories as arguments, denoted by "⟨file1⟩ ... ⟨fileN⟩". For example, the cp command takes as arguments a list of files to copy, followed by the destination file or directory. When copying more than one file, the destination must be a directory.

cd   Change the current working directory.
Syntax: cd ⟨directory⟩
⟨directory⟩ is the directory to change to. ("." refers to the current directory, ".." the parent directory.)
Example: cd ../foo sets the current directory to ../foo.

ls   Displays information about the named files and directories.
Syntax: ls ⟨file1⟩ ⟨file2⟩ ... ⟨fileN⟩
Where ⟨file1⟩ through ⟨fileN⟩ are the filenames or directories to list. Options: There are more options than you want to think about. The most commonly used are -F (used to display some information about the type of the file), and -l (gives a "long" listing including file size, owner, permissions, and so on. This will be covered in detail later.)
Example: ls -lF /home/larry will display the contents of the directory /home/larry.

cp   Copies file(s) to another file or directory.
Syntax: cp ⟨file1⟩ ⟨file2⟩ ... ⟨fileN⟩ ⟨destination⟩
Where ⟨file1⟩ through ⟨fileN⟩ are the files to copy, and ⟨destination⟩ is the destination file or directory.
Example: cp ../frog joe copies the file ../frog to the file or directory joe.

mv   Moves file(s) to another file or directory. This command does the equivalent of a
            copy followed by the deletion of the original. This can be used to rename files, as
            in the MS-DOS command RENAME.
            Syntax: mv ⟨*file1*⟩ ⟨*file2*⟩ ...⟨*fileN*⟩ ⟨*destination*⟩
            Where ⟨*file1*⟩ through ⟨*fileN*⟩ are the files to move, and ⟨*destination*⟩ is the desti-
            nation file or directory.
            Example: mv ../frog joe moves the file ../frog to the file or directory joe.

rm   Deletes files. Note that when files are deleted under UNIX, they are unrecoverable
            (unlike MS-DOS, where you can usually "undelete" the file).
            Syntax: rm ⟨*file1*⟩ ⟨*file2*⟩ ...⟨*fileN*⟩
            Where ⟨*file1*⟩ through ⟨*fileN*⟩ are the filenames to delete.
            Options: -i will prompt for confirmation before deleting the file.
            Example: rm -i /home/larry/joe /home/larry/frog deletes the files joe and
            frog in /home/larry.

mkdir   Creates new directories.
            Syntax: mkdir ⟨*dir1*⟩ ⟨*dir2*⟩ ...⟨*dirN*⟩
            Where ⟨*dir1*⟩ through ⟨*dirN*⟩ are the directories to create.
            Example: mkdir /home/larry/test creates the directory test under
            /home/larry.

rmdir   This command deletes empty directories. When using rmdir, your current working
            directory must not be within the directory to be deleted.
            Syntax: rmdir ⟨*dir1*⟩ ⟨*dir2*⟩ ...⟨*dirN*⟩
            Where ⟨*dir1*⟩ through ⟨*dirN*⟩ are the directories to delete.
            Example: rmdir /home/larry/papers deletes the directory /home/larry/papers,
            if it is empty.

man   Displays the manual page for the given command or resource (that is, any system
            utility which isn't a command, such as a library function.) Syntax: man ⟨*command*⟩
            Where ⟨*command*⟩ is the name of the command or resource to get help on.
            Example: man ls gives help on the ls command.

more   Displays the contents of the named files, one screenful at a time.
            Syntax: more ⟨*file1*⟩ ⟨*file2*⟩ ...⟨*fileN*⟩
            Where ⟨*file1*⟩ through ⟨*fileN*⟩ are the files to display.
            Example: more papers/history-final displays the file papers/history-final.

cat   Officially used to concatenate files, cat is also used to display the entire contents
            of a file at once.
            Syntax: cat ⟨*file1*⟩ ⟨*file2*⟩ ...⟨*fileN*⟩
            Where ⟨*file1*⟩ through ⟨*fileN*⟩ are the files to display.
            Example: cat letters/from-mdw displays the file letters/from-mdw.

echo   Simply echoes the given arguments.

          Syntax: echo ⟨arg1⟩ ⟨arg2⟩ ...⟨argN⟩

          Where ⟨arg1⟩ through ⟨argN⟩ are the arguments to echo.

          Example: echo "Hello world" displays the string "Hello world".

grep   Display all of the lines in the named file(s) matching the given pattern.

          Syntax: grep ⟨pattern⟩ ⟨file1⟩ ⟨file2⟩ ...⟨fileN⟩

          Where ⟨pattern⟩ is a regular expression pattern, and ⟨file1⟩ through ⟨fileN⟩ are the
          files to search.

          Example: grep loomer /etc/hosts will display all lines in the file /etc/hosts
          which contain the pattern "loomer".

3.5   Exploring the File System

The **file system** is the collection of files and the hierarchy of directories on your system. I promised
before to escort you around the filesystem and the time has come.

You have the skills and the knowledge to make sense out of what I'm saying, and you have a
roadmap. (Refer to Figure 3.2.8 on page 80).

First, change to the root directory (cd /), and do an ls -F. You'll probably see these directories[2]:
bin, dev, etc, home, install, lib, mnt, proc, root, tmp, user, usr, and var.

Let's take a look at each of these directories.

/bin   /bin is short for "binaries", or executables. This is where many essential system
          programs reside. Use the command "ls -F /bin" to list the files here. If you look
          down the list you may see a few commands that you recognize, such as cp, ls,
          and mv. These are the actual programs for these commands. When you use the cp
          command, you're running the program /bin/cp.

          Using ls -F, you'll see that most (if not all) of the files in /bin have an asterisk
          ("*") appended to their filenames. This indicates that the files are executables, as
          described in Section 3.3.2.

/dev   Next on our stop is /dev. Take a look, again with ls -F.

          The "files" in /dev are known as **device drivers**—they are used to access system
          devices and resources, such as disk drives, modems, memory, and so on. For exam-
          ple, just as you can read data from a file, you can read input from the mouse by
          accessing /dev/mouse.

          The filenames beginning with fd are floppy disk devices. fd0 is the first floppy disk

---

[2]You may see others, and you might not see all of them. Don't worry. Every release of Linux differs in some
respects.

drive, fd1 the second. Now, the astute among you will notice that there are more floppy disk devices then just the two I've listed above: they represent specific types of floppy disks. For example, fd1H1440 will access high-density, 3.5" diskettes in drive 1.

Here is a list of some of the most commonly used device files. Note that even though you may not have some of the devices listed below, the chances are that you'll have entries in /dev for them anyway.

- /dev/console refers to the system's console—that is, the monitor connected directly to your system.

- The various /dev/ttyS and /dev/cua devices are used for accessing serial ports. For example, /dev/ttyS0 refers to "COM1" under MS-DOS. The /dev/cua devices are "callout" devices, which are used in conjunction with a modem.

- The device names beginning with hd access hard drives. /dev/hda refers to the *whole* first hard disk, while hda1 refers to the first *partition* on /dev/hda.

- The device names beginning with sd are SCSI drives. If you have a SCSI hard drive, instead of accessing it through /dev/hda, you would access /dev/sda. SCSI tapes are accessed via st devices, and SCSI CD-ROM via sr devices.

- The device names beginning with lp access parallel ports. /dev/lp0 refers to "LPT1" in the MS-DOS world.

- /dev/null is used as a "black hole"—any data sent to this device is gone forever. Why is this useful? Well, if you wanted to suppress the output of a command appearing on your screen, you could send that output to /dev/null. We'll talk more about this later.

- The device names beginning with /dev/tty refer to the "virtual consoles" on your system (accessed via by pressing alt-F1 , alt-F2 , and so on). /dev/tty1 refers to the first VC, /dev/tty2 refers to the second, and so on.

- The device names beginning with /dev/pty are "pseudo-terminals". They are used to provide a "terminal" to remote login sessions. For example, if your machine is on a network, incoming telnet logins would use one of the /dev/pty devices.

/etc   /etc contains a number of miscellaneous system configuration files. These include /etc/passwd (the user database), /etc/rc (the system initialization script), and so on.

/sbin   sbin is used for storing essential system binaries, to be used by the system administrator.

/home	/home contains user's home directories. For example, /home/larry is the home directory for the user "larry". On a newly-installed system, there may not be any users in this directory.
/lib	/lib contains **shared library images**. These files contain code which many programs share in common. Instead of each program containing its own copy of these shared routines, they are all stored in one common place, in /lib. This makes executable files smaller, and saves space on your system.
/proc	/proc is a "virtual filesystem", the files in which are stored in memory, not on the drive. They refer to the various **processes** running on the system, and allow you to get information about what programs and processes are running at any given time. We'll go into more detail in Section 3.11.1.
/tmp	Many programs have a need to generate some information and store it in a temporary file. The canonical location for these files is in /tmp.
/usr	/usr is a very important directory. It contains a number of subdirectories which in turn contain some of the most important and useful programs and configuration files used on the system.
	The various directories described above are essential for the system to operate, but most of the things found in /usr are optional for the system. However, it is those optional things which make the system useful and interesting. Without /usr, you'd more or less have a boring system, only with programs like cp and ls. /usr contains most of the larger software packages and the configuration files which accompany them.
/usr/X386	/usr/X386 contains The X Window System, if you installed it. The X Window System is a large, powerful graphical environment which provides a large number of graphical utilities and programs, displayed in "windows" on your screen. If you're at all familiar with the Microsoft Windows or Macintosh environments, X Windows will look very familiar. The /usr/X386 directory contains all of the X Windows executables, configuration files, and support files. This will be covered in more detail in Section 5.1.
/usr/bin	/usr/bin is the real warehouse for software on any UNIX system. It contains most of the executables for programs not found in other places, such as /bin.
/usr/etc	Just as /etc contained miscellaneous system programs and configuration files, /usr/etc contains even more of these utilities and files. In general, the files found in /usr/etc are not essential to the system, unlike those found in /etc, which are.
/usr/include	/usr/include contains **include files** for the C compiler. These files (most of which end in .h, for "header") declare data structure names, subroutines, and constants used when writing programs in C. Those files found in /usr/include/sys

are generally used when programming on the UNIX system level. If you are familiar with the C programming language, here you'll find header files such as `stdio.h`, which declares functions such as `printf()`.

`/usr/g++-include`

`/usr/g++-include` contains include files for the C++ compiler (much like `/usr/include`).

`/usr/lib`

`/usr/lib` contains the "stub" and "static" library equivalents to the files found in `/lib`. When compiling a program, the program is "linked" with the libraries found in `/usr/lib`, which then directs the program to look in `/lib` when it needs the actual code in the library. In addition, various other programs store configuration files in `/usr/lib`.

`/usr/local`

`/usr/local` is a lot like `/usr`—it contains various programs and files not essential to the system, but which make the system fun and exciting. In general, those programs found in `/usr/local` are specialized for your system specifically—that is, `/usr/local` differs greatly between UNIX systems.

Here, you'll find large software packages such as TEX (a document formatting system) and Emacs (a large and powerful editor), if you installed them.

`/usr/man`

This directory contains the actual man pages. There are two subdirectories for every man page "section" (use the command `man man` for details). For example, `/usr/man/man1` contains the source (that is, the unformatted original) for man pages in section 1, and `/usr/man/cat1` contains the formatted man pages for section 1.

`/usr/src`

`/usr/src` contains the source code (the uncompiled program) for various programs on your system. The most important thing here is `/usr/src/linux`, which contains the source code for the Linux kernel.

`/var`

`/var` holds directories that often change in size or tend to grow. Many of those directories used to reside in `/usr`, but since we are trying to keep it relatively unchangeable, the directories that change often have been moved to `/var`. Some of those directories are:

`/var/adm`

`/var/adm` contains various files of interest to the system administrator, specifically system logs, which record any errors or problems with the system. Other files record logins to the system, as well as failed login attempts. This will be covered in Chapter 4.

`/var/spool`

`/var/spool` contains files which are to be "spooled" to another program. For example, if your machine is connected to a network, incoming mail will be stored in `/var/spool/mail`, until you read it or delete it. Outgoing or incoming news articles may be found in `/var/spool/news`, and so on.

3.6   Types of shells

As I have mentioned too many times before, UNIX is a multitasking, multiuser operating system. Multitasking is *very* useful, and once you get used to it, you'll use it all of the time. Before long, you'll be able to run programs in the "background", switch between multiple tasks, and "pipeline" programs together to achieve complicated results with a single command.

Many of the features we'll be covering in this section are features provided by the shell itself. Be careful not to confuse UNIX (the actual operating system) with the shell—the shell is just an interface to the underlying system. The shell provides a great deal of functionality on top of UNIX itself.

The shell is not only an interpreter for your interactive commands, which you type at the prompt. It is also a powerful programming language, which allows you to write **shell scripts**, to "batch" several shell commands together in a file. MS-DOS users will recognize the similarity to "batch files". Use of shell scripts is a very powerful tool, which will allow you to automate and expand your usage of UNIX. See Section 3.13.1 for more information.

There are several types of shells in the UNIX world. The two major types are the "Bourne shell" and the "C shell". The Bourne shell uses a command syntax like the original shell on early UNIX systems, such as System III. The name of the Bourne shell on most UNIX systems is /bin/sh (where sh stands for "shell"). The C shell (not to be confused with sea shell) uses a different syntax, somewhat like the programming language C, and on most UNIX systems is named /bin/csh.

Under Linux, there are several variations of these shells available. The two most commonly used are the Bourne Again Shell, or "Bash" (/bin/bash), and Tcsh (/bin/tcsh). Bash is a form of the Bourne shell with many of the advanced features found in the C shell. Because Bash supports a superset of the Bourne shell syntax, any shell scripts written in the standard Bourne shell should work with Bash. For those who prefer to use the C shell syntax, Linux supports Tcsh, which is an expanded version of the original C shell.

The type of shell that you decide to use is mostly a religious issue. Some folks prefer the Bourne shell syntax with the advanced features of Bash, and some prefer the more structured C shell syntax. As far as normal commands, such as cp and ls, are concerned, the type of shell you're using doesn't matter—the syntax is the same. Only when you start to write shell scripts or use some of the advanced features of the shell do the differences between shell types begin to matter.

As we're discussing some of the features of the shell, below, we'll note those differences between Bourne and C shells. However, for the purposes of this manual, most of those differences are minimal. (If you're really curious at this point, read the man pages for bash and tcsh).

3.7   Wildcards

A key feature of most Unix shells is the ability to reference more than one filename using special characters. These so-called **wildcards** allow you to refer to, say, all filenames which contain the character "n".

The wildcard "*" refers to any character or string of characters in a filename. For example, when you use the character "*" in a filename, the shell replaces it with all possible substitutions from filenames in the directory which you're referencing.

Here's a quick example. Let's suppose that Larry has the files frog, joe, and stuff in his current directory.

```
/home/larry# ls
frog      joe      stuff
/home/larry#
```

To access all files with the letter "o" in the filename, we can use the command

```
/home/larry# ls *o*
frog      joe
/home/larry#
```

As you can see, the use of the "*" wildcard was replaced with all substitutions which matched the wildcard from filenames in the current directory.

The use of "*" by itself simply matches all filenames, because all characters match the wildcard.

```
/home/larry# ls *
frog      joe      stuff
/home/larry#
```

Here are a few more examples.

```
/home/larry# ls f*
frog
/home/larry# ls *ff
stuff
/home/larry# ls *f*
frog      stuff
/home/larry# ls s*f
stuff
/home/larry#
```

The process of changing a "*" into filenames is called **wildcard expansion** and is done by the shell. This is important: the individual commands, such as ls, *never* see the "*" in their list of parameters. The shell expands the wildcard to include all of the filenames which match. So, the command

```
/home/larry# ls *o*
```

is expanded by the shell to actually be

```
/home/larry# ls frog joe
```

One important note about the "*" wildcard. Using this wildcard will *not* match filenames which begin with a single period ("."). These files are treated as "hidden" files—while they are not really hidden, they don't show up on normal ls listings, and aren't touched by the use of the "*" wildcard.

Here's an example. We already mentioned that each directory has two special entries in it: "." refers to the current directory, and ".." refers to the parent directory. However, when you use ls, these two entries don't show up.

```
/home/larry# ls
frog     joe      stuff
/home/larry#
```

If you use the -a switch with ls, however, you can display filenames which begin with ".". Observe:

```
/home/larry# ls -a
.     ..     .bash_profile     .bashrc     frog     joe     stuff
/home/larry#
```

Now we can see the two special entries, "." and "..", as well as two other "hidden" files—.bash_profile and .bashrc. These two files are startup files used by bash when larry logs in. More on them in Section 3.13.3.

Note that when we use the "*" wildcard, none of the filenames beginning with "." are displayed.

```
/home/larry# ls *
frog     joe      stuff
/home/larry#
```

This is a safety feature: if the "*" wildcard matched filenames beginning with ".", it would also match the directory names "." and "..". This can be dangerous when using certain commands.

Another wildcard is "?". The "?" wildcard will only expand a single character. Thus, "ls ?" will display all one character filenames, and "ls termca?" would display "termcap" but *not* "termcap.backup". Here's another example:

```
/home/larry# ls j?e
joe
/home/larry# ls f??g
frog
```

```
/home/larry# ls ????f
stuff
/home/larry#
```

As you can see, wildcards allow you to specify many files at one time. In the simple command summary, in Section 3.4, we said that the `cp` and `mv` commands actually can copy or move multiple files at one time. For example,

```
/home/larry# cp /etc/s* /home/larry
```

will copy all filenames in `/etc` beginning with "s" to the directory `/home/larry`. Therefore, the format of the `cp` command is really

cp ⟨file1⟩ ⟨file2⟩ ⟨file3⟩ ...⟨fileN⟩ ⟨destination⟩

where ⟨file1⟩ through ⟨fileN⟩ is a list of filenames to copy, and ⟨destination⟩ is the destination file or directory to copy them to. `mv` has an identical syntax.

Note that if you are copying or moving more than one file, the ⟨destination⟩ must be a directory. You can only copy or move a *single* file to another file.

3.8   UNIX Plumbing

3.8.1   Standard input and output

Many UNIX commands get input from what is known as **standard input** and send their output to **standard output** (often abbreviated as "stdin" and "stdout"). Your shell sets things up so that standard input is your keyboard, and standard output is the screen.

Here's an example using the command `cat`. Normally, `cat` reads data from all of the filenames given on the command line and sends this data directly to stdout. Therefore, using the command

```
/home/larry/papers# cat history-final masters-thesis
```

will display the contents of the file `history-final` followed by `masters-thesis`.

However, if no filenames are given to `cat` as parameters, it instead reads data from stdin, and sends it back to stdout. Here's an example.

```
/home/larry/papers# cat
Hello there.
Hello there.
Bye.
Bye.
```

> ctrl-D
>
> /home/larry/papers#

As you can see, each line that the user types (displayed in italics) is immediately echoed back by the `cat` command. When reading from standard input, commands know that the input is "finished" when they receive an EOT (end-of-text) signal. In general, this is generated by pressing ctrl-D .

Here's another example. The command `sort` reads in lines of text (again, from stdin, unless files are given on the command line), and sends the sorted output to stdout. Try the following.

> /home/larry/papers# *sort*
> *bananas*
> *carrots*
> *apples*
> ctrl-D
> apples
> bananas
> carrots
> /home/larry/papers#

Now we can alphabetize our shopping list... isn't UNIX useful?

3.8.2 Redirecting input and output

Now, let's say that we wanted to send the output of `sort` to a file, to save our shopping list elsewhere. The shell allows us to **redirect** standard output to a filename, using the ">" symbol. Here's how it works.

> /home/larry/papers# *sort > shopping-list*
> *bananas*
> *carrots*
> *apples*
> ctrl-D
> /home/larry/papers#

As you can see, the result of the `sort` command isn't displayed, instead it's saved to the file `shopping-list`. Let's look at this file.

> /home/larry/papers# *cat shopping-list*
> apples
> bananas
> carrots
> /home/larry/papers#

Now we can sort our shopping list, and save it, too! But let's suppose that we were storing our unsorted, original shopping list in the file items. One way of sorting the information and saving it to a file would be to give sort the name of the file to read, in lieu of standard input, and redirect standard output as we did above. As so:

```
/home/larry/papers# sort items > shopping-list
/home/larry/papers# cat shopping-list
apples
bananas
carrots
/home/larry/papers#
```

However, there's another way of doing this. Not only can we redirect standard output, but we can redirect standard *input* as well, using the "<" symbol.

```
/home/larry/papers# sort < items
apples
bananas
carrots
/home/larry/papers#
```

Technically, sort < items is equivalent to sort items, but the former allows us to demonstrate the point: sort < items behaves as if the data in the file items was typed to standard input. The shell handles the redirection. sort wasn't given the name of the file (items) to read; as far as sort is concerned, it was still reading from standard input as if you had typed the data from your keyboard.

This introduces the concept of a **filter**. A filter is a program which reads data from standard input, processes it in some way, and sends the processed data to standard output. Using redirection, standard input and/or standard output can be referenced from files. sort is a simple filter: it sorts the incoming data and sends the result to standard output. cat is even simpler: it doesn't do anything with the incoming data, it simply outputs whatever was given to it.

3.8.3   Using pipes

We've already demonstrated how to use sort as a filter. However, these examples assumed that you had data in a file somewhere, or were willing to type the data to standard input yourself. What if the data you wanted to sort came from the output of another command, such as ls? For example, using the -r option with sort sorts the data in reverse-alphabetical order. If you wanted to list the files in your current directory in reverse order, one way to do it would be:

```
/home/larry/papers# ls
english-list
history-final
```

```
masters-thesis
notes
/home/larry/papers# ls > file-list
/home/larry/papers# sort -r file-list
notes
masters-thesis
history-final
english-list
/home/larry/papers#
```

Here, we saved the output of ls in a file, and then ran sort -r on that file. But this is unwieldy and causes us to use a temporary file to save the data from ls.

The solution is to use **pipelining**. Pipelining is another feature of the shell which allows you to connect a string of commands in a "pipe", where the stdout of the first command is sent directly to the stdin of the second command, and so on. Here, we wish to send the stdout of ls to the stdin of sort. The "|" symbol is used to create a pipe:

```
/home/larry/papers# ls | sort -r
notes
masters-thesis
history-final
english-list
/home/larry/papers#
```

This command is much shorter, and obviously easier to type.

Another useful example—using the command

```
/home/larry/papers# ls /usr/bin
```

is going to display a long list a files, most of which will fly past the screen too quickly for you to read them. Instead, let's use more to display the list of files in /usr/bin.

```
/home/larry/papers# ls /usr/bin | more
```

Now you can page down the list of files at your own leisure.

But the fun doesn't stop here! We can pipe more than two commands together. The command head is a filter which displays the first lines from an input stream (here, input from a pipe). If we wanted to display the last filename in alphabetical order in the current directory, we can use:

```
/home/larry/papers# ls | sort -r | head -1
notes
/home/larry/papers#
```

where `head -1` simply displays the first line of input that it receives (in this case, the stream of reverse-sorted data from `ls`).

3.8.4 Non-destructive redirection

Using ">" to redirect output to a file is destructive: in other words, the command

> `/home/larry/papers#` *ls > file-list*

overwrites the contents of the file `file-list`. If, instead, you redirect with the symbol ">>", the output will be appended to the named file, instead of overwriting it.

> `/home/larry/papers#` *ls >> file-list*

will append the output of the `ls` command to `file-list`.

Just keep in mind that redirection and using pipes are features provided by the shell—the shell provides this handy syntax using ">" and ">>" and "|". It has nothing to do with the commands themselves, but the shell.

3.9 File Permissions

3.9.1 Concepts of file permissions

Because there are multiple users on a UNIX system, in order to protect individual user's files from tampering by other users, UNIX provides a mechanism known as **file permissions**. This mechanism allows files and directories to be "owned" by a particular user. As an example, because Larry created the files in his home directory, Larry owns those files, and has access to them.

UNIX also allows files to be shared between users and groups of users. If Larry so desired, he could cut off access to his files, such that no other user could access them. However, on most systems the default is to allow other users to read your files, but not modify or delete them in any way.

As explained above, every file is owned by a particular user. However, files are also owned by a particular **group**, which is a system-defined group of users. Every user is placed into at least one group when that user is created. However, the system administrator may also grant the user access to more than one group.

Groups are usually defined by the type of users which access the machine. For example, on a university UNIX system, users may be placed into the groups `student`, `staff`, `faculty` or `guest`. There are also a few system-defined groups (such as `bin` and `admin`) which are used by the system itself to control access to resources—very rarely do actual users belong to these system groups.

Permissions fall into three main divisions: read, write, and execute. These permissions may be granted to three classes of users: the owner of the file, the group to which the file belongs, and to all users, regardless of group.

Read permission allows a user to read the contents of the file, or in the case of directories, to list the contents of the directory (using `ls`). Write permission allows the user to write to and modify the file. For directories, write permission allows the user to create new files or delete files within that directory. Finally, execute permission allows the user to run the file as a program or shell script (if the file happens to be a program or shell script, that is). For directories, having execute permission allows the user to `cd` into the directory in question.

3.9.2   Interpreting file permissions

Let's look at an example to demonstrate file permissions. Using the `ls` command with the `-l` option will display a "long" listing of the file, including file permissions.

```
/home/larry/foo# ls -l stuff


-rw-r--r--   1 larry     users          505 Mar 13 19:05 stuff

/home/larry/foo#
```

The first field printed in the listing represents the file permissions. The third field is the owner of the file (`larry`), and the fourth field is the group to which the file belongs (`users`). Obviously, the last field is the name of the file (`stuff`), and we'll cover the other fields later.

This file is owned by `larry`, and belongs to the group `users`. Let's look at the file permissions. The string `-rw-r--r--` lists, in order, the permissions granted to the file's owner, the file's group, and everybody else.

The first character of the permissions string ("`-`") represents the type of file. A "`-`" just means that this is a regular file (as opposed to a directory or device driver). The next three letters ("`rw-`") represent the permissions granted to the file's owner, `larry`. The "`r`" stands for "read" and the "`w`" stands for "write". Thus, `larry` has read and write permission to the file `stuff`.

As we mentioned, besides read and write permission, there is also "execute" permission— represented by an "`x`". However, there is a "`-`" here in place of the "`x`", so Larry doesn't have execute permission on this file. This is fine, the file `stuff` isn't a program of any kind. Of course, because Larry owns the file, he may grant himself execute permission for the file if he so desires. This will be covered shortly.

The next three characters, `r--`, represent the group's permissions on the file. The group which owns this file is `users`. Because only an "`r`" appears here, any user which belongs to the group `users` may read this file.

The last three characters, also `r--`, represent the permissions granted to every other user on the system (other than the owner of the file and those in the group `users`). Again, because only an "r" is present, other users may read the file, but not write to it or execute it.

Here are some other examples of group permissions.

`-rwxr-xr-x`   The owner of the file may read, write, and execute the file. Users in the file's group, and all other users, may read and execute the file.

`-rw-------`   The owner of the file may read and write the file. No other user can access the file.

`-rwxrwxrwx`   All users may read, write, and execute the file.

3.9.3   Dependencies

It is important to note that the permissions granted to a file also depend on the permissions of the directory in which the file is located. For example, even if a file is set to `-rwxrwxrwx`, other users cannot access the file unless they have read and execute access to the directory in which the file is located. For example, if Larry wanted to restrict access to all of his files, he could simply set the permissions on his home directory `/home/larry` to `-rwx------`. In this way, no other user has access to his directory, and all files and directories within it. Larry doesn't need to worry about the individual permissions on each of his files.

In other words, to access a file at all, you must have execute access to all directories along the file's pathname, and read (or execute) access to the file itself.

Usually, users on a UNIX system are very open with their files. The usual set of permissions given to files is `-rw-r--r--`, which will allow other users to read the file, but not change it in any way. The usual set of permissions given to directories is `-rwxr-xr-x`, which will allow other users to look through your directories, but not create or delete files within them.

However, many users wish to keep other users out of their files. Setting the permissions of a file to `-rw-------` will not allow any other user to access the file. Likewise, setting the permissions of a directory to `-rwx------` will keep other users out of the directory in question.

3.9.4   Changing permissions

The command `chmod` is used to set the permissions on a file. Only the owner of a file may change the permissions on that file. The syntax of `chmod` is:

    chmod {a,u,g,o}{+,-}{r,w,x} ⟨filenames⟩

Briefly, you supply one or more of **a**ll, **u**ser, **g**roup, or **o**ther. Then you specify whether you are adding rights (**+**) or taking them away (**-**). Finally, you specify one or more of **r**ead, **w**rite, and **e**xecute. Some examples of legal commands are:

`chmod a+r stuff`

> Gives all users read access to the file.

`chmod +r stuff`

> Same as above—if none of a, u, g, or o is specified, a is assumed.

`chmod og-x stuff`

> Remove execute permission from users other than the owner.

`chmod u+rwx stuff`

> Allow the owner of the file to read, write, and execute the file.

`chmod o-rwx stuff`

> Remove read, write, and execute permission from users other than the owner and users in the file's group.

3.10 Managing file links

Links allow you to give a single file multiple names. Files are actually identified to the system by their **inode number**, which is just the unique filesystem identifier for the file[3]. A directory is actually a listing of inode numbers with their corresponding filenames. Each filename in a directory is a **link** to a particular inode.

3.10.1 Hard links

The `ln` command is used to create multiple links for one file. For example, let's say that you have the file `foo` in a directory. Using `ls -i`, we can look at the inode number for this file.

```
# ls -i foo
22192 foo
#
```

Here, the file `foo` has an inode number of 22192 in the filesystem. We can create another link to `foo`, named `bar`:

```
# ln foo bar
```

With `ls -i`, we see that the two files have the same inode.

```
# ls -i foo bar
22192 bar    22192 foo
#
```

---

[3]The command `ls -i` will display file inode numbers.

Now, accessing either `foo` or `bar` will access the same file. If you make changes to `foo`, those changes will be made to `bar` as well. For all purposes, `foo` and `bar` are the same file.

These links are known as *hard links* because they directly create a link to an inode. Note that you can only hard-link files on the same filesystem; symbolic links (see below) don't have this restriction.

When you delete a file with `rm`, you are actually only deleting one link to a file. If you use the command

   # *rm foo*

then only the link named `foo` is deleted; `bar` will still exist. A file is only actually deleted on the system when it has no links to it. Usually, files have only one link, so using the `rm` command deletes the file. However, if a file has multiple links to it, using `rm` will only delete a single link; in order to delete the file, you must delete all links to the file.

The command `ls -l` will display the number of links to a file (among other information).

```
# ls -l foo bar
-rw-r--r--    2 root      root         12 Aug  5 16:51 bar
-rw-r--r--    2 root      root         12 Aug  5 16:50 foo
#
```

The second column in the listing, "2", specifies the number of links to the file.

As it turns out, a directory is actually just a file containing information about link-to-inode translations. Also, every directory has at least two hard links in it: "." (a link pointing to itself), and ".." (a link pointing to the parent directory). The root directory (/) ".." link just points back to /.

3.10.2   Symbolic links

Symbolic links are another type of link, which are somewhat different than hard links. A symbolic link allows you to give a file another name, but it doesn't link the file by inode.

The command `ln -s` will create a symbolic link to a file. For example, if we use the command

   # *ln -s foo bar*

we will create the symbolic link `bar` pointing to the file `foo`. If we use `ls -i`, we will see that the two files have different inodes, indeed.

```
# ls -i foo bar
22195 bar   22192 foo
#
```

However, using `ls -l`, we see that the file `bar` is a symlink pointing to `foo`.

```
# ls -l foo bar
lrwxrwxrwx    1 root      root            3 Aug  5 16:51 bar -> foo
-rw-r--r--    1 root      root           12 Aug  5 16:50 foo
#
```

The permission bits on a symbolic link are not used (they always appear as `rwxrwxrwx`). Instead, the permissions on the symbolic link are determined by the permissions on the target of the symbolic link (in our example, the file `foo`).

Functionally, hard links and symbolic links are similar, but there are some differences. For one thing, you can create a symbolic link to a file which doesn't exist; the same is not true for hard links. Symbolic links are processed by the kernel differently than hard links are, which is just a technical difference but sometimes an important one. Symbolic links are helpful because they identify what file they point to; with hard links, there is no easy way to determine which files are linked to the same inode.

Links are used in many places on the Linux system. Symbolic links are especially important to the shared library images in `/lib`. See Section 4.7.2 for more information.

3.11 Job Control

3.11.1 Jobs and processes

Job control is a feature provided by many shells (Bash and Tcsh included) which allows you to control multiple running commands, or **jobs**, at once. Before we can delve much further, we need to talk about **processes**.

Every time you run a program, you start what is known as a *process*—which is just a fancy name for a running program. The command `ps` displays a list of currently running processes. Here's an example:

```
/home/larry# ps

  PID TT STAT  TIME COMMAND
   24  3 S     0:03 (bash)
  161  3 R     0:00 ps

/home/larry#
```

The `PID` listed in the first column is the **process ID**, a unique number given to every running process. The last column, `COMMAND`, is the name of the running command. Here, we're only looking at the processes which Larry is currently running[4]. These are `bash` (Larry's shell), and the `ps` command itself. As you can see, `bash` is running concurrently with the `ps` command. `bash` executed `ps` when Larry typed the command. After `ps` is finished running (after the table of processes is displayed), control is returned to the `bash` process, which displays the prompt, ready for another command.

A running process is known as a *job* to the shell. The terms *process* and *job* are interchangeable. However, a process is usually referred to as a "job" when used in conjunction with **job control**—a feature of the shell which allows you to switch between several independent jobs.

In most cases users are only running a single job at a time—that being whatever command they last typed to the shell. However, using job control, you can run several jobs at once, switching between them as needed. How might this be useful? Let's say that you're editing a text file and need to suddenly interrupt your editing and do something else. With job control, you can temporarily suspend the editor, and back at the shell prompt start to work on something else. When you're done, you can start the editor back up, and be back where you started, as if you never left the editor. This is just one example. There are many practical uses for job control.

3.11.2 Foreground and background

Jobs can either be in the **foreground** or in the **background**. There can only be one job in the foreground at any one time. The foreground job is the job which you interact with—it receives input from the keyboard and sends output to your screen. (Unless, of course, you have redirected input or output, as described in Section 3.8). On the other hand, jobs in the background do not receive input from the terminal—in general, they run along quietly without need for interaction.

Some jobs take a long time to finish, and don't do anything interesting while they are running. Compiling programs is one such job, as is compressing a large file. There's no reason why you should sit around being bored while these jobs complete their tasks; you can just run them in the background. While the jobs are running in the background, you are free to run other programs.

Jobs may also be **suspended**. A suspended job is a job that is not currently running, but is temporarily stopped. After you suspend a job, you can tell the job to continue, in the foreground or the background as needed. Resuming a suspended job will not change the state of the job in any way—the job will continue to run where it left off.

Note that suspending a job is not equal to *interrupting* a job. When you interrupt a running process (by hitting your interrupt key, which is usually $\boxed{\texttt{ctrl-C}}$)[5], it kills the process, for good. Once the job is killed, there's no hope of resuming it; you'll have to re-run the command. Also note that some programs trap the interrupt, so that hitting $\boxed{\texttt{ctrl-C}}$ won't immediately kill the job. This is to allow the program to perform any necessary cleanup operations before exiting. In fact, some programs simply don't allow you to kill them with an interrupt at all.

---

[4]There are many other processes running on the system as well—"`ps -aux`" lists them all.

[5]The interrupt key can be set using the `stty` command. The default on most systems is $\boxed{\texttt{ctrl-C}}$, but we can't guarantee the same for your system.

3.11.3   Backgrounding and killing jobs

Let's begin with a simple example. The command **yes** is a seemingly useless command which sends an endless stream of y's to standard output. (This is actually useful. If you piped the output of **yes** to another command which asked a series of yes and no questions, the stream of y's would confirm all of the questions.)

Try it out.

```
/home/larry# yes
y
y
y
y
y
```

The y's will continue *ad infinitum*. You can kill the process by hitting your interrupt key, which is usually ctrl-C . So that we don't have to put up with the annoying stream of y's, let's redirect the standard output of **yes** to **/dev/null**. As you may remember, **/dev/null** acts as a "black hole" for data. Any data sent to it will disappear. This is a very effective method of quieting an otherwise verbose program.

```
/home/larry# yes > /dev/null
```

Ah, much better. Nothing is printed, but the shell prompt doesn't come back. This is because **yes** is still running, and is sending those inane y's to **/dev/null**. Again, to kill the job, hit the interrupt key.

Let's suppose that we wanted the **yes** command to continue to run, but wanted to get our shell prompt back to work on other things. We can put **yes** into the background, which will allow it to run, but without need for interaction.

One way to put a process in the background is to append an "**&**" character to the end of the command.

```
/home/larry# yes > /dev/null &
[1] 164
/home/larry#
```

As you can see, we have our shell prompt back. But what is this "[1] 164"? And is the **yes** command really running?

The "[1]" represents the **job number** for the **yes** process. The shell assigns a job number to every running job. Because **yes** is the one and only job that we're currently running, it is assigned job number 1. The "164" is the process ID, or PID, number given by the system to the job. Either number may be used to refer to the job, as we'll see later.

You now have the `yes` process running in the background, continuously sending a stream of y's to /dev/null. To check on the status of this process, use the shell internal command `jobs`.

```
/home/larry# jobs
[1]+  Running                 yes >/dev/null   &
/home/larry#
```

Sure enough, there it is. You could also use the `ps` command as demonstrated above to check on the status of the job.

To terminate the job, use the command `kill`. This command takes either a job number or a process ID number as an argument. This was job number 1, so using the command

```
/home/larry# kill %1
```

will kill the job. When identifying the job with the job number, you must prefix the number with a percent ("%") character.

Now that we've killed the job, we can use `jobs` again to check on it:

```
/home/larry# jobs

[1]+  Terminated              yes >/dev/null

/home/larry#
```

The job is in fact dead, and if we use the `jobs` command again nothing should be printed.

You can also kill the job using the process ID (PID) number, which is printed along with the job ID when you start the job. In our example, the process ID is 164, so the command

```
/home/larry# kill 164
```

is equivalent to

```
/home/larry# kill %1
```

You don't need to use the "%" when referring to a job by its process ID.

3.11.4 Stopping and restarting jobs

There is another way to put a job into the background. You can start the job normally (in the foreground), **stop** the job, and then restart it in the background.

First, start the `yes` process in the foreground, as you normally would:

```
/home/larry# yes > /dev/null
```

Again, because `yes` is running in the foreground, you shouldn't get your shell prompt back.

Now, instead of interrupting the job with `ctrl-C`, we'll *suspend* the job. Suspending a job doesn't kill it: it only temporarily stops the job until you restart it. To do this, you hit the suspend key, which is usually `ctrl-Z`.

```
/home/larry# yes > /dev/null
ctrl-Z
[1]+  Stopped                 yes >/dev/null
/home/larry#
```

While the job is suspended, it's simply not running. No CPU time is used for the job. However, you can restart the job, which will cause the job to run again as if nothing ever happened. It will continue to run where it left off.

To restart the job in the foreground, use the command `fg` (for "foreground").

```
/home/larry# fg
yes >/dev/null
```

The shell prints the name of the command again so you're aware of which job you just put into the foreground. Stop the job again, with `ctrl-Z`. This time, use the command `bg` to put the job into the background. This will cause the command to run just as if you started the command with "&" as in the last section.

```
/home/larry# bg
[1]+ yes >/dev/null &
/home/larry#
```

And we have our prompt back. `jobs` should report that `yes` is indeed running, and we can kill the job with `kill` as we did before.

How can we stop the job again? Using `ctrl-Z` won't work, because the job is in the background. The answer is to put the job in the foreground, with `fg`, and then stop it. As it turns out you can use `fg` on either stopped jobs or jobs in the background.

There is a big difference between a job in the background and a job which is stopped. A stopped job is not running—it's not using any CPU time, and it's not doing any work (the job still occupies system memory, although it may be swapped out to disk). A job in the background is running, and using memory, as well as completing some task while you do other work. However, a job in the background may try to display text on to your terminal, which can be annoying if you're trying to work on something else. For example, if you used the command

```
/home/larry# yes &
```

without redirecting stdout to /dev/null, a stream of y's would be printed to your screen, without any way of interrupting it (you can't use ctrl-C to interrupt jobs in the background). In order to stop the endless y's, you'd have to use the fg command, to bring the job to the foreground, and then use ctrl-C to kill it.

Another note. The fg and bg commands normally foreground or background the job which was last stopped (indicated by a "+" next to the job number when you use the command jobs). If you are running multiple jobs at once, you can foreground or background a specific job by giving the job ID as an argument to fg or bg, as in

    /home/larry# *fg %2*

(to foreground job number 2), or

    /home/larry# *bg %3*

(to background job number 3). You can't use process ID numbers with fg or bg.

Furthermore, using the job number alone, as in

    /home/larry# *%2*

is equivalent to

    /home/larry# *fg %2*

Just remember that using job control is a feature of the shell. The commands fg, bg and jobs are internal to the shell. If for some reason you use a shell which does not support job control, don't expect to find these commands available.

In addition, there are some aspects of job control which differ between Bash and Tcsh. In fact, some shells don't provide job control at all—however, most shells available for Linux support job control.

3.12   Using the vi Editor

A **text editor** is simply a program used to edit files which contain text, such as a letter, C program, or a system configuration file. While there are many such editors available for Linux, the only editor which you are guaranteed to find on any UNIX system is vi— the "visual editor". vi is not the easiest editor to use, nor is it very self-explanatory. However, because it is so common in the UNIX world, and at times you may be required to use it, it deserves some documentation here.

Your choice of an editor is mostly a question of personal taste and style. Many users prefer the baroque, self-explanatory and powerful **Emacs**—an editor with more features than any other single program in the UNIX world. For example, Emacs has its own built-in dialect of the LISP programming language, and has many extensions (one of which is an "Eliza"-like AI program). However, because Emacs and all of its support files are relatively large, you may not have access to it on many systems. vi, on the other hand, is small and powerful, but more difficult to use. However, once you know your way around vi, it's actually very easy. It's just the learning curve which is sometimes difficult to cross.

This section is a coherent introduction to vi—we won't discuss all of its features, just the ones you need to know to get you started. You can refer to the man page for vi if you're interested in learning about more of this editor's features. Or, you can read the book *Learning the* vi *Editor* from O'Reilly and Associates. See Appendix A for information.

3.12.1 Concepts

While using vi, at any one time you are in one of three modes of operation. These modes are known as *command mode*, *insert mode*, and *last line mode*.

When you start up vi, you are in *command mode*. This mode allows you to use certain commands to edit files or to change to other modes. For example, typing "x" while in command mode deletes the character underneath the cursor. The arrow keys move the cursor around the file which you're editing. Generally, the commands used in command mode are one or two characters long.

You actually insert or edit text within *insert mode*. When using vi, you'll probably spend most of your time within this mode. You start insert mode by using a command such as "i" (for "insert") from command mode. While in insert mode, you are inserting text into the document from your current cursor location. To end insert mode and return to command mode, press ⌑esc⌑.

Last line mode is a special mode used to give certain extended commands to vi. While typing these commands, they appear on the last line of the screen (hence the name). For example, when you type ":" from command mode, you jump into last line mode, and can use commands such as "wq" (to write the file and quit vi), or "q!" (to quit vi without saving changes). Last line mode is generally used for vi commands which are longer than one character. In last line mode, you enter a single-line command and press ⌑enter⌑ to execute it.

3.12.2 Starting vi

The best way to understand these concepts is to actually fire up vi and edit a file. In the example "screens" below, we're only going to show a few lines of text, as if the screen was only six lines high (instead of twenty-four).

The syntax for vi is

    vi ⟨filename⟩

where ⟨filename⟩ is the name of the file that you wish to edit.

Start up `vi` by typing

    `/home/larry#` *vi test*

which will edit the file `test`. You should see something like

```
~
~
~
~
~
~
~
"test" [New file]
```

The column of "~" characters indicates that you are the end of the file.

3.12.3   Inserting text

You are now in command mode; in order to insert text into the file, press i (which will place you into insert mode), and begin typing.

```
Now is the time for all good men to come to the aid of the party._
~
~
~
~
```

While inserting text, you may type as many lines as you wish (pressing return after each, of course), and may correct mistakes using the backspace key.

To end insert mode, and return to command mode, press esc .

While in command mode, you can use the arrow keys to move around the file. Here, because we only have one line of text, trying to use the up- or down-arrow keys will probably cause `vi` to beep at you.

There are several ways to insert text, other than using the i command. For example, the a command inserts text beginning *after* the current cursor position, instead of on the current cursor position. For example, use the left arrow key to move the cursor between the words "good" and "men".

```
Now is the time for all good_men to come to the aid of the party.
~
~
~
~
~
```

Press `a`, to start insert mode, type "wo", and then hit `esc` to return to command mode.

```
Now is the time for all good women to come to the aid of the party.
~
~
~
~
~
```

To begin inserting text at the line below the current one, use the o command. For example, press `o` and type another line or two:

```
Now is the time for all good women to come to the aid of the party.
Afterwards, we'll go out for pizza and beer.
~
~
~
~
```

Just remember that at any time you're either in command mode (where commands such as i, a, or o are valid), or in insert mode (where you're inserting text, followed by `esc` to return to command mode), or last line mode (where you're entering extended commands, as discussed below).

3.12.4 Deleting text

From command mode, the x command deletes the character under the cursor. If you press `x` five times, you'll end up with:

```
Now is the time for all good women to come to the aid of the party.
Afterwards, we'll go out for pizza and_
~
~
~
~
```

Now press `a`, insert some text, followed by `esc`:

```
Now is the time for all good women to come to the aid of the party.
Afterwards, we'll go out for pizza and Diet Coke.
~
~
~
~
```

You can delete entire lines using the command `dd` (that is, press [d] twice in a row). If your cursor is on the second line, and you type `dd`,

```
Now is the time for all good women to come to the aid of the party.
~
~
~
~
~
```

To delete the word which the cursor is on, use the `dw` command. Place the cursor on the word "good", and type `dw`.

```
Now is the time for all women to come to the aid of the party.
~
~
~
~
~
```

3.12.5 Changing text

You can replace sections of text using the `R` command. Place the cursor on the first letter in "party", press [R], and type the word "hungry".

```
Now is the time for all women to come to the aid of the hungry.
~
~
~
~
~
```

Using `R` to edit text is much like the `i` and `a` commands, but `R` overwrites text, instead of inserting it.

The `r` command replaces the single character under the cursor. For example, move the cursor to the beginning of the word "Now", and type `r` followed by `C`, you'll have:

```
Cow is the time for all women to come to the aid of the hungry.
~
~
~
~
~
```

The "~" command changes the case of the letter under the cursor from upper- to lower-case, and vise versa, For example, if you place the cursor on the "o" in "Cow", above, and repeatedly press ~ , you'll end up with:

```
COW IS THE TIME FOR ALL WOMEN TO COME TO THE AID OF THE HUNGRY.
~
~
~
~
~
```

3.12.6 Moving commands

You already know how to use the arrow keys to move around the document. In addition, you can use the h, j, k, and l commands to move the cursor left, down, up, and right, respectively. This comes in handy when (for some reason) your arrow keys aren't working correctly.

The w command moves the cursor to the beginning of the next word; the b moves it to the beginning of the previous word.

The 0 (that's a zero) command moves the cursor to the beginning of the current line, and the $ command moves it to the end of the line.

When editing large files, you'll want to move forwards or backwards through the file a screenful at a time. Pressing ctrl-F moves the cursor one screenful forward, and ctrl-B moves it a screenful back.

In order to move the cursor to the end of the file, type G. You can also move to an arbitrary line; for example, typing the command 10G would move the cursor to line 10 in the file. To move to the beginning of the file, use 1G.

You can couple moving commands with other commands, such as deletion. For example, the command d$ will delete everything from the cursor to the end of the line; dG will delete everything from the cursor to the end of the file, and so on.

3.12.7 Saving files and quitting vi

To quit vi without making changes to the file, use the command :q!. When you type the ":", the cursor will move to the last line on the screen; you'll be in last line mode.

```
COW IS THE TIME FOR ALL WOMEN TO COME TO THE AID OF THE HUNGRY.
~
~
~
~
~
:_
```

In last line mode, certain extended commands are available. One of them is q!, which quits vi without saving. The command :wq saves the file and then exits vi. The command ZZ (from command mode, without the ":") is equivalent to :wq. Remember that you must press ⌈enter⌉ after a command entered in last line mode.

To save the file without quitting vi, just use :w.

3.12.8   Editing another file

To edit another file, use the :e command. For example, to stop editing test, and edit the file foo instead, use the command

```
COW IS THE TIME FOR ALL WOMEN TO COME TO THE AID OF THE HUNGRY.
~
~
~
~
~
:e foo_
```

If you use :e without saving the file first, you'll get the error message

```
No write since last change (":edit!" overrides)
```

which simply means that vi doesn't want to edit another file until you save the first one. At this point, you can use :w to save the original file, and then use :e, or you can use the command

```
COW IS THE TIME FOR ALL WOMEN TO COME TO THE AID OF THE HUNGRY.
~
~
~
~
~
:e!  foo_
```

The "!" tells vi that you really mean it—edit the new file without saving changes to the first.

3.12.9 Including other files

If you use the :r command, you can include the contents of another file in the current file. For example, the command

```
:r foo.txt
```

would insert the contents of the file foo.txt in the text at the current cursor location.

3.12.10 Running shell commands

You can also run shell commands from within vi. The :r! command works like :r, but instead of reading a file, it inserts the output of the given command into the buffer at the current cursor location. For example, if you use the command

```
:r! ls -F
```

you'll end up with

```
COW IS THE TIME FOR ALL WOMEN TO COME TO THE AID OF THE HUNGRY.
letters/
misc/
papers/
~
~
```

You can also "shell out" of vi, in other words, run a command from within vi, and return to the editor when you're done. For example, if you use the command

```
:! ls -F
```

the ls -F command will be executed, and the results displayed on the screen, but not inserted into the file which you're editing. If you use the command

```
:shell
```

vi will start an instance of the shell, allowing you to temporarily put vi "on hold" while you execute other commands. Just logout of the shell (using the exit command) to return to vi.

3.12.11 Getting help

vi doesn't provide much in the way of interactive help (most UNIX programs don't), but you can always read the man page for vi. vi is a visual front-end to the ex editor; it is ex which handles many of the last-line mode commands in vi. So, in addition to reading the man page for vi, see ex as well.

3.13   Customizing your Environment

The shell provides many mechanisms to customize your work environment. As we've mentioned before, the shell is more than a command interpreter—it is also a powerful programming language. While writing shell scripts is an extensive subject, we'd like to introduce you to some of the ways that you can simplify your work on a UNIX system by using these advanced features of the shell.

As we have mentioned before, different shells use different syntaxes when executing shell scripts. For example, Tcsh uses a C-like syntax, while Bourne shells use another type of syntax. In this section, we won't be running into many of the differences between the two, but we will assume that shell scripts are executed using the Bourne shell syntax.

3.13.1   Shell scripts

Let's say that you use a series of commands often, and would like to shorten the amount of required typing by grouping all of them together into a single "command". For example, the commands

```
/home/larry#  cat chapter1 chapter2 chapter3 > book
/home/larry#  wc -l book
/home/larry#  lp book
```

would concatenate the files chapter1, chapter2, and chapter3 and place the result in the file book. Then, a count of the number of lines in book would be displayed, and finally book would be printed with the lp command.

Instead of typing all of these commands, you could group them into a **shell script**. We described shell scripts briefly in Section 3.13.1. The shell script used to run all of these commands would look like

```
#!/bin/sh
# A shell script to create and print the book

cat chapter1 chapter2 chapter3 > book
wc -l book
lp book
```

If this script was saved in the file makebook, you could simply use the command

```
/home/larry#  makebook
```

to run all of the commands in the script. Shell scripts are just plain text files; you can create them with an editor such as emacs or vi [6].

---

[6] vi is covered in Section 3.12.

Let's look at this shell script. The first line, "#!/bin/sh", identifies the file as a shell script, and tells the shell how to execute the script. It instructs the shell to pass the script to /bin/sh for execution, where /bin/sh is the shell program itself. Why is this important? On most UNIX systems, /bin/sh is a Bourne-type shell, such as Bash. By forcing the shell script to run using /bin/sh, we are ensuring that the script will run under a Bourne-syntax shell (instead of, say, a C shell). This will cause your script to run using the Bourne syntax even if you use Tcsh (or another C shell) as your login shell.

The second line is a *comment*. Comments begin with the character "#" and continue to the end of the line. Comments are ignored by the shell—they are commonly used to identify the shell script to the programmer.

The rest of the lines in the script are just commands, as you would type them to the shell directly. In effect, the shell reads each line of the script and runs that line as if you had typed it at the shell prompt.

Permissions are important for shell scripts. If you create a shell script, you must make sure that you have execute permission on the script in order to run it[7]. The command

/home/larry# *chmod u+x makebook*

can be used to give yourself execute permission on the shell script makebook.

3.13.2 Shell variables and the environment

The shell allows you to define **variables**, as most programming languages do. A variable is just a piece of data which is given the name.

◇   Note that Tcsh, as well as other C-type shells, use a different mechanism for setting variables than is described here. This discussion assumes the use of a Bourne shell, such as Bash (which you're probably using). See the Tcsh man page for details.

When you assign a value to a variable (using the "=" operator), you can access the variable by prepending a "$" to the variable name, as demonstrated below.

/home/larry# *foo="hello there"*

The variable foo is given the value "hello there". You can now refer to this value by the variable name, prefixed with a "$" character. The command

```
/home/larry# echo $foo
hello there
/home/larry#
```

[7]When you create text files, the default permissions usually don't include execute permission.

produces the same results as

```
/home/larry# echo "hello there"
hello there
/home/larry#
```

These variables are internal to the shell. This means that only the shell can access these variables. This can be useful in shell scripts; if you need to keep track of a filename, for example, you can store it in a variable, as above. Using the command set will display a list of all defined shell variables.

However, the shell allows you to **export** variables to the **environment**. The environment is the set of variables which all commands that you execute have access to. Once you define a variable inside the shell, exporting it makes that variable part of the environment as well. The export command is used to export a variable to the environment.

◇   Again, here we differ between Bash and Tcsh. If you're using Tcsh, another syntax is used for setting environment variables (the setenv command is used). See the Tcsh man page for more information.

The environment is very important to the UNIX system. It allows you to configure certain commands just by setting variables which the commands know about.

Here's a quick example. The environment variable PAGER is used by the man command. It specifies the command to use to display man pages one screenful at a time. If you set PAGER to be the name of a command, it will use that command to display the man pages, instead of more (which is the default).

Set PAGER to "cat". This will cause output from man to be displayed to the screen all at once, without breaking it up into pages.

```
/home/larry# PAGER="cat"
```

Now, export PAGER to the environment.

```
/home/larry# export PAGER
```

Try the command man ls. The man page should fly past your screen without pausing for you.

Now, if we set PAGER to "more", the more command will be used to display the man page.

```
/home/larry# PAGER="more"
```

Note that we don't have to use the export command after we change the value of PAGER. We only need to export a variable once; any changes made to it thereafter will automatically be propagated to the environment.

The man pages for a particular command will tell you if the command uses any environment variables; for example, the man man page explains that PAGER is used to specify the pager command. Some commands share environment variables; for example, many commands use the EDITOR environment variable to specify the default editor to use when one is needed.

The environment is also used to keep track of important information about your login session. An example is the HOME environment variable, which contains the name of your home directory.

```
/home/larry/papers# echo $HOME
/home/larry
```

Another interesting environment variable is PS1, which defines the main shell prompt. For example,

```
/home/larry# PS1="Your command, please: "
Your command, please:
```

To set the prompt back to our usual (which contains the current working directory followed by a "#" symbol),

```
Your command, please:  PS1="\w# "
/home/larry#
```

The bash man page describes the syntax used for setting the prompt.

3.13.2.1 The PATH environment variable

When you use the ls command, how does the shell find the ls executable itself? In fact, ls is found in /bin/ls on most systems. The shell uses the environment variable PATH to locate executable files for commands which you type.

For example, your PATH variable may be set to:

```
/bin:/usr/bin:/usr/local/bin:.
```

This is a list of directories for the shell to search, each directory separated by a ":". When you use the command ls, the shell first looks for /bin/ls, then /usr/bin/ls, and so on.

Note that the PATH has nothing to do with finding regular files. For example, if you use the command

```
/home/larry# cp foo bar
```

The shell does not use PATH to locate the files foo and bar—those filenames are assumed to be complete. The shell only uses PATH to locate the cp executable.

This saves you a lot of time; it means that you don't have to remember where all of the command executables are stored. On many systems, executables are scattered about in many places, such as /usr/bin, /bin, or /usr/local/bin. Instead of giving the command's full pathname (such as /usr/bin/cp), you can simply set PATH to the list of directories that you want the shell to automatically search.

Notice that PATH contains ".", which is the current working directory. This allows you to create a shell script or program and run it as a command from your current directory, without having to specify it directly (as in ./makebook). If a directory isn't on your PATH, then the shell will not search it for commands to run—this includes the current directory.

3.13.3 Shell initialization scripts

In addition to shell scripts that you create, there are a number of scripts that the shell itself uses for certain purposes. The most important of these are your **initialization scripts**, scripts automatically executed by the shell when you login.

The initialization scripts themselves are simply shell scripts, as described above. However, they are very useful in setting up your environment by executing commands automatically when you login. For example, if you always use the mail command to check your mail when you login, you place the command in your initialization script so it will be executed automatically.

Both Bash and Tcsh distinguish between a **login shell** and other invocations of the shell. A login shell is a shell invoked at login time; usually, it's the only shell which you'll use. However, if you "shell out" of another program, such as vi, you start another instance of the shell, which isn't your login shell. In addition, whenever you run a shell script, you automatically start another instance of the shell to execute the script.

The initialization files used by Bash are: /etc/profile (set up by the system administrator, executed by all Bash users at login time), $HOME/.bash_profile (executed by a login Bash session), and $HOME/.bashrc (executed by all non-login instances of Bash). If .bash_profile is not present, .profile is used instead.

Tcsh uses the following initialization scripts: /etc/csh.login (executed by all Tcsh users at login time), $HOME/.tcshrc (executed a login time and by all new instances of Tcsh), and $HOME/.login (executed at login time, following .tcshrc). If .tcshrc is not present, .cshrc is used instead.

To fully understand the function of these files, you'll need to learn more about the shell itself. Shell programming is a complicated subject, far beyond the scope of this book. See the man pages for bash and/or tcsh to learn more about customizing your shell environment.

3.14 So You Want to Strike Out on Your Own?

Hopefully we have provided enough information to give you a basic idea of how to use the system. Keep in mind that most of the interesting and important aspects of Linux aren't covered here—these are the very basics. With this foundation, before long you'll be up and running complicated applications and fulfilling the potential of your system. If things don't seem exciting at first, don't despair—there is much to be learned.

One indispensable tool for learning about the system is to read the man pages. While many of the man pages may appear confusing at first, if you dig beneath the surface there is a wealth of information contained therein.

We also suggest reading a complete book on using a UNIX system. There is much more to UNIX than meets the eye—unfortunately, most of it is beyond the scope of this book. Some good UNIX books to look at are listed in Appendix A.

Chapter 4

System Administration

This chapter is an overview to Linux system administration, including a number of advanced features which aren't necessarily for system administrators only. Just as every dog has its day, every system has its administrator, and running the system is a very important and sometimes time-consuming job, even if you're the only user on your system.

We have tried to cover here the most important things about system administration you need to know when you use Linux, in sufficient detail to get you comfortably started. In order to keep it short and sweet, we have only covered the very basics, and have skipped many an important detail. You should read the *Linux System Administrator's Guide* if you are serious about running Linux. It will help you understand better how things work, and how they hang together. At least skim through it so that you know what it contains and know what kind of help you can expect from it.

4.1 About Root, Hats, and the Feeling of Power

As you know, UNIX differentiates between different users, so that what they do to each other and to the system can be regulated (one wouldn't want anybody to be able to read one's love letters, for instance). Each user is given an **account**, which includes a username, home directory, and so on. In addition to accounts given to real people, there are special system-defined accounts which have special privileges. The most important of these is the **root account**, for the username root.

4.1.1 The root account

Ordinary users are generally restricted so that they can't do harm to anybody else on the system, just to themselves. File permissions on the system are arranged such that normal users aren't allowed to delete or modify files in directories shared by all users (such as /bin and /usr/bin. Most users also protect their own files with the appropriate file permissions so that other users can't access or modify those files.

There are no such restrictions on `root`. The user `root` can read, modify, or delete any file on the system, change permissions and ownerships on any file, and run special programs, such as those which partition the drive or create filesystems. The basic idea is that the person or persons who run and take care of the system logs in as `root` whenever it is necessary to perform tasks that cannot be executed as a normal user. Because `root` can do anything, it is easy to make mistakes that have catastrophic consequences when logged in using this account.

For example, as a normal user, if you inadvertently attempt to delete all of the files in `/etc`, the system will not permit you to do so. However, when logged in as `root`, the system won't complain at all. It is very easy to trash your system when using `root`. The best way to prevent accidents is to:

- Sit on your hands before you press $\boxed{\text{return}}$ on a command which may cause damage. For example, if you're about to clean out a directory, before hitting $\boxed{\text{return}}$, re-read the entire command and make sure that it is correct.

- Don't get accustomed to using `root`. The more comfortable you are in the role of the `root` user, the more likely you are to confuse your privileges with those of a normal user. For example, you might *think* that you're logged in as `larry`, when you're really logged in as `root`.

- Use a different prompt for the `root` account. You should change `root`'s `.bashrc` or `.login` file to set the shell prompt to something other than your regular user prompt. For example, many people use the character "$" in prompts for regular users, and reserve the character "#" for the `root` user prompt.

- Only login as `root` when absolutely necessary. And, as soon as you're finished with your work as `root`, log out. The less you use the `root` account, the less likely you'll be to do damage on your system.

Of course, there is a breed of UNIX hackers out there who use `root` for virtually everything. But every one of them has, at some point, made a silly mistake as `root` and trashed the system. The general rule is, until you're familiar with the lack of restrictions on `root`, and are comfortable using the system without such restrictions, login as `root` sparingly.

Of course, everyone makes mistakes. Linus Torvalds himself once accidentally deleted the entire kernel directory tree on his system. Hours of work were lost forever. Fortunately, however, because of his knowledge of the filesystem code, he was able to reboot the system and reconstruct the directory tree by hand on disk.

Put another way, if you picture using the `root` account as wearing a special magic hat that gives you lots of power, so that you can, by waving your hand, destroy entire cities, it is a good idea to be a bit careful about what you do with your hands. Since it is easy to move your hand in a destructive way by accident, it is not a good idea to wear the magic hat when it is not needed, despite the wonderful feeling.

4.1.2 Abusing the system

Along with the feeling of power comes the tendency to do harm. This is one of the grey areas of UNIX system administration, but everyone goes through it at some point in time. Most users of UNIX systems never have the ability to wield this power—on university and business UNIX systems, only the highly-paid and highly-qualified system administrators ever login as root. In fact, at many such institutions, the root password is a highly guarded secret: it is treated as the Holy Grail of the institution. A large amount of hubbub is made about logging in as root; it is portrayed as a wise and fearsome power, given only to an exclusive cabal.

This kind of attitude towards the root account is, quite simply, the kind of thing which breeds malice and contempt. Because root is so fluffed-up, when some users have their first opportunity to login as root (either on a Linux system or elsewhere), the tendency is to use root's privileges in a harmful manner. I have known so-called "system administrators" who read other user's mail, delete user's files without warning, and generally behave like children when given such a powerful "toy".

Because root has such privilege on the system, it takes a certain amount of maturity and self-control to use the account as it was intended—to run the system. There is an unspoken code of honor which exists between the system administrator and the users on the system. How would you feel if your system administrator was reading your e-mail or looking over your files? There is still no strong legal precedent for electronic privacy on time-sharing computer systems. On UNIX systems, the root user has the ability to forego all security and privacy mechanisms on the system. It is important that the system administrator develop a trusting relationship with the users on the system. I can't stress that enough.

4.1.3 Dealing with users

UNIX security is rather lax by design. Security on the system was an afterthought—the system was originally developed in an environment where users intruding upon other users was simply unheard of. Because of this, even with security measures, there is still the ability for normal users to do harm.

System administrators can take two stances when dealing with abusive users: they can be either paranoid or trusting. The paranoid system administrator usually causes more harm than he or she prevents. One of my favorite sayings is, "Never attribute to malice anything which can be attributed to stupidity." Put another way, most users don't have the ability or knowledge to do real harm on the system. 90% of the time, when a user is causing trouble on the system (by, for instance, filling up the user partition with large files, or running multiple instances of a large program), the user is simply unaware that what he or she is doing is a problem. I have come down on users who were causing a great deal of trouble, but they were simply acting out of ignorance—not malice.

When you deal with users who are causing potential trouble, don't be accusative. The old rule of "innocent until proven guilty" still holds. It is best to simply talk to the user, and question about the trouble, instead of causing a confrontation. The last thing you want to do is be on the user's bad side. This will raise a lot of suspicion about you—the system administrator—running the system correctly. If a user believes that you distrust or dislike them, they might accuse you of deleting files or breaching privacy on the system. This is certainly not the kind of position that you want to be in.

If you do find that a user has been attempting to "crack" the system, or was intentionally doing harm to the system, don't return the malicious behavior with malice of your own. Instead, simply provide a warning—but be flexible. In many cases, you may catch a user "in the act" of doing harm to the system—give them a warning. Tell them not to let it happen again. However, if you *do* catch them causing harm again, be absolutely sure that it is intentional. I can't even begin to describe the number of cases where it appeared as though a user was causing trouble, when in fact it was either an accident or a fault of my own.

4.1.4   Setting the rules

The best way to run a system is not with an iron fist. That may be how you run the military, but UNIX was not designed for such discipline. It makes sense to lay down a simple and flexible set of guidelines for users—but remember, the fewer rules you have, the less chance there is of breaking them. Even if your rules for using the system are perfectly reasonable and clear, users will always at times break these rules without intending to. This is especially true in the case of new UNIX users, who are just learning the ropes of the system. It's not patently obvious, for example, that you shouldn't download a gigabyte of files and mail them to everyone on the system. Users need help understanding the rules, and why they are there.

If you do specify usage guidelines for your system, make sure that the reason behind a particular guideline is made clear. If you don't, then users will find all sorts of creative ways to get around the rule, and not know that they are in fact breaking it.

4.1.5   What it all means

We can't tell you how to run your system to the last detail. Most of the philosophy depends on how you're using the system. If you have many users, things are much different than if you only have a few users, or if you're the only user on the system. However, it's always a good idea—in any situation—to understand what being the system administrator really means.

Being the system administrator doesn't make you a UNIX wizard. There are many system admins out there who know very little about UNIX. Likewise, there are many "normal" users out there who know more about UNIX than any system administrator could. Also, being the system administrator does not allow you to use malice against your users. Just because the system gives you the privilege to mess with user files does not mean that you have any right to do so.

Lastly, being the system administrator is really not a big deal. It doesn't matter if your system is a little 386 or a Cray supercomputer. Running the system is the same, regardless. Knowing the root password isn't going to earn you money or fame. It will allow you to maintain the system, and keep it running. That's it.

4.2   Booting the System

There are several ways to boot the system, either from floppy or from the hard drive.

4.2.1   Using a boot floppy

Many people boot Linux using a "boot floppy" which contains a copy of the Linux kernel. This kernel has the Linux root partition coded into it, so it will know where to look on the hard drive for the root filesystem. (The rdev command can be used to set the root partition in the kernel image; see below.) This is the type of floppy created by Slackware during installation, for example.

To create your own boot floppy, first locate the kernel image on your hard disk. It should be in the file /Image or /etc/Image. Some installations use the file /vmlinux for the kernel.

You may instead have a compressed kernel. A compressed kernel uncompresses itself into memory at boot time, and takes up much less space on the hard drive. If you have a compressed kernel, it may be found in the file /zImage or /etc/zImage.

Once you know where the kernel is, set the root device in the kernel image to the name of your Linux root partition with the rdev command. The format of the command is

    rdev ⟨kernel-name⟩ ⟨root-device⟩

where ⟨kernel-name⟩ is the name of the kernel image, and ⟨root-device⟩ is the name of the Linux root partition. For example, to set the root device in the kernel /etc/Image to /dev/hda2, use the command

    # rdev /etc/Image /dev/hda2

rdev can set other options in the kernel as well, such as the default SVGA mode to use at boot time. Just use "rdev -h" to get a help message.

After setting the root device, you can simply copy the kernel image to the floppy. Whenever copying data to a floppy, it's a good idea to MS-DOS format the floppy first. This lays down the sector and track information on the floppy, so it can be detected as either high or low density.

For example, to copy the kernel in the file /etc/Image to the floppy in /etc/fd0, use the command

    # cp /etc/Image /dev/fd0

This floppy should now boot Linux.

4.2.2 Using LILO

Another method of booting is to use LILO, a program which resides in the boot sector of your hard disk. This program is executed when the system is booted from the hard disk, and can automatically boot up Linux from a kernel image stored on the hard drive itself.

LILO can also be used as a first-stage boot loader for several operating systems, allowing you to select at boot time which operating system (such as Linux or MS-DOS) to boot. When you boot using LILO, the default operating system is booted unless you press $\boxed{\texttt{ctrl}}$, $\boxed{\texttt{alt}}$, or $\boxed{\texttt{shift}}$ during the bootup sequence. If you press any of these keys, you will be provided with a boot prompt, at which you type the name of the operating system to boot (such as "linux" or "msdos"). If you press $\boxed{\texttt{tab}}$ at the boot prompt, a listing of available operating systems will be provided.

The easy way to install LILO is to edit the configuration file, /etc/lilo.conf, and then run the command

  # */sbin/lilo*

The LILO configuration file contains a "stanza" for each operating system that you want to boot. The best way to demonstrate this is with an example LILO config file. The below setup is for a system which has a Linux root partition on /dev/hda1, and an MS-DOS partition on /dev/hda2.

```
# Tell LILO to modify the boot record on /dev/hda (the first
# non-SCSI hard drive). If you boot from a drive other than /dev/hda,
# change the following line.
boot = /dev/hda

# Name of the boot loader. No reason to modify this unless you're doing
# some serious hacking on LILO.
install = /boot/boot.b

# Have LILO perform some optimization.
compact

# Stanza for Linux root partition on /dev/hda1.
image = /etc/Image    # Location of kernel
   label = linux      # Name of OS (for the LILO boot menu)
   root = /dev/hda1   # Location of root partition
   vga = ask          # Tell kernel to ask for SVGA modes at boot time

# Stanza for MSDOS partition on /dev/hda2.
other = /dev/hda2     # Location of partition
   table = /dev/hda   # Location of partition table for /dev/hda2
   label = msdos      # Name of OS (for boot menu)
```

The first operating system stanza in the config file will be the default OS for LILO to boot. You can select another OS to boot at the LILO boot prompt, as discussed above.

Remember that every time you update the kernel image on disk, you should rerun /sbin/lilo in order for the changes to be reflected on the boot sector of your drive.

Also note that if you use the "root =" line, above, there's no reason to use rdev to set the root partition in the kernel image. LILO sets it for you at boot time.

The Linux FAQ (see Appendix A) provides more information on LILO, including how to use LILO to boot with OS/2's Boot Manager.

4.3   Shutting Down

Shutting down a Linux system is a bit tricky. Remember that you should never just turn off the power or hit the reset switch while the system is running. The kernel keeps track of disk I/O in memory buffers. If you reboot the system without giving the kernel the chance to write its buffers to disk, you can corrupt your filesystems.

Other precautions are taken at shutdown time as well. All processes are sent a signal, which allows them to die gracefully (writing and closing all files, and so on). Filesystems are unmounted for safety. If you wish, the system can also alert users that the system is going down and give them a change to log off.

The easiest way to shutdown is with the shutdown command. The format of the command is

    shutdown ⟨time⟩ ⟨warning-message⟩

The ⟨time⟩ argument is the time to shutdown the system (in the format hh:mm:ss), and ⟨warning-message⟩ is a message displayed on all user's terminals before shutdown. Alternately, you can specify the ⟨time⟩ as "now", to shutdown immediately. The -r option may be given to shutdown to reboot the system after shutting down.

For example, to shutdown the system at 8:00pm, use the command

    # *shutdown -r 20:00*

The command halt may be used to force an immediate shutdown, without any warning messages or grace period. halt is useful if you're the only one using the system, and want to shut down the system and turn it off.

◇   Don't turn off the power or reboot the system until you see the message:

    The system is halted

It is very important that you shutdown the system "cleanly" using the shutdown or halt commands. On some systems, pressing ctrl-alt-del will be trapped and cause a shutdown; on other systems, however, using the "Vulcan nerve pinch" will reboot the system immediately and may cause disaster.

4.4   Managing Users

Whether or not you have many users on your system, it's important to understand the aspects of user management under Linux. Even if you're the only user, you should presumably have a separate account for yourself (an account other than root to do most of your work).

Each person using the system should have his or her own account. It is seldom a good idea to have several people share the same account. Not only is security an issue, but accounts are used to uniquely identify users to the system. You need to be able to keep track of who is doing what.

4.4.1   User management concepts

The system keeps track of a number of pieces of information about each user. They are summarized below.

username   The username is the unique identifier given to every user on the system. Examples of usernames are larry, karl, and mdw. Letters and digits may be used, as well as the characters "_" (underscore) and "." (period). Usernames are usually limited to 8 characters in length.

user ID   The user ID, or UID, is a unique number given to every user on the system. The system usually keeps track of information by UID, not username.

group ID   The group ID, or GID, is the ID of the user's default group. In Section 3.9 we discussed group permissions; each user belongs to one or more groups defined by the system administrator. More about this below.

password   The system also stores the user's encrypted password. The passwd command is used to set and change user passwords.

full name   The user's "real name" or "full name" is stored along with the username. For example, the user schmoj may have the name "Joe Schmo" in real life.

home directory
                   The home directory is the directory in which the user is initially placed at login time. Every user should have his or her own home directory, usually found under /home.

login shell   The user's login shell is the shell which is started for the user at login time. Examples are /bin/bash and /bin/tcsh.

The file /etc/passwd contains this information about users. Each line in the file contains information about a single user; the format of each line is

```
username:encrypted password:UID:GID:full name:home directory:login shell
```

An example might be:

```
kiwi:Xv8Q981g71oKK:102:100:Laura Poole:/home/kiwi:/bin/bash
```

As we can see, the first field, "kiwi", is the username.

The next field, "Xv8Q981g71oKK", is the encrypted password. Passwords are not stored on the system in any human-readable format. The password is encrypted using itself as the secret key. In other words, you need to know the password to decrypt it. This form of encryption is fairly secure.

Some systems use "shadow password" in which password information is relegated to the file /etc/shadow. Because /etc/passwd is world-readable, /etc/shadow provides some degree of extra security because it is not. Shadow password provides some other features such as password expiration and so on; we will not go into these features here.

The third field, "102", is the UID. This must be unique for each user. The fourth field, "100", is the GID. This user belongs to the group numbered 100. Group information, like user information, is stored in the file /etc/group. See Section 4.4.5 for more information.

The fifth field is the user's full name, "Laura Poole". The last two fields are the user's home directory (/home/kiwi) and login shell (/bin/bash), respectively. It is not required that the user's home directory be given the same name as the username. It does help identify the directory, however.

4.4.2   Adding users

When adding a user, there are several steps to be taken. First, the user must be given an entry in /etc/passwd, with a unique username and UID. The GID, fullname, and other information must be specified. The user's home directory must be created, and the permissions on the directory set so that the user owns the directory. Shell initialization files must be provided in the new home directory and other system-wide configuration must be done (for example, setting up a spool for incoming e-mail for the new user).

While it is not difficult to add users by hand (I do), when you are running a system with many users it is easy to forget something. The easiest way to add users is to use an interactive program which asks you for the required information and updates all of the system files automatically. The name of this program is useradd or adduser, depending on what software was installed. The man pages for these commands should be fairly self-explanatory.

4.4.3   Deleting users

Similarly, deleting users can be accomplished with the commands `userdel` or `deluser` depending on what software was installed on the system.

If you'd like to temporarily "disable" a user from logging into the system (without deleting the user's account), you can simply prepend an asterisk ("`*`") to the password field in `/etc/passwd`. For example, changing `kiwi`'s `/etc/passwd` entry to

```
kiwi:*Xv8Q981g71oKK:102:100:Laura Poole:/home/kiwi:/bin/bash
```

will restrict `kiwi` from logging in.

4.4.4   Setting user attributes

After you have created a user, you may need to change attributes for that user, such as home directory or password. The easiest way to do this is to change the values directly in `/etc/passwd`. To set a user's password, use the `passwd` command. For example,

```
# passwd larry
```

will change `larry`'s password. Only `root` may change other user's password in this manner. Users can change their own passwords with `passwd` as well.

On some systems, the commands `chfn` and `chsh` will be available to allow users to set their own fullname and login shell attributes. If not, they will have to ask the system administrator to change these attributes for them.

4.4.5   Groups

As we have mentioned, each user belongs to one or more groups. The only real importance of group relationships pertains to file permissions, as you'll recall from Section 3.9, each file has a "group ownership" and a set of group permissions which defines how users in that group may access the file.

There are several system-defined groups such as `bin`, `mail`, and `sys`. Users should not belong to any of these groups; they are used for system file permissions. Instead, users should belong to an individual group such as `users`. If you want to be cute, you can maintain several groups of users such as `student`, `staff`, and `faculty`.

The file `/etc/group` contains information about groups. The format of each line is

```
group name:password:GID:other members
```

Some example groups might be:

```
root:*:0:
users:*:100:mdw,larry
guest:*:200:
other:*:250:kiwi
```

The first group, `root`, is a special system group reserved for the `root` account. The next group, `users`, is for regular users. It has a GID of 100. The users `mdw` and `larry` are given access to this group. Remember that in `/etc/passwd` each user was given a default GID. However, users may belong to more than one group, by adding their usernames to other group lines in `/etc/group`. The `groups` command lists what groups you are given access to.

The third group, `guest`, is for guest users, and `other` is for "other" users. The user `kiwi` is given access to this group as well.

As you can see, the "password" field of `/etc/group` is rarely used. It is sometimes used to set a password on group access. This is seldom necessary. To protect users from changing into priveleged groups (with the `newgroup` command), set the password field to "*".

The commands `addgroup` or `groupadd` may be used to add groups to your system. Usually, it's easier just to add entries in `/etc/group` yourself, as no other configuration needs to be done to add a group. To delete a group, simply delete its entry in `/etc/group`.

4.5 Archiving and Compressing Files

Before we can talk about backups, we need to introduce the tools used to archive files and software on UNIX systems.

4.5.1 Using tar

The `tar` command is most often used to archive files.

The format of the `tar` command is

    tar ⟨options⟩ ⟨file1⟩ ⟨file2⟩ ...⟨fileN⟩

where ⟨options⟩ is the list of commands and options for `tar`, and ⟨file1⟩ through ⟨fileN⟩ is the list of files to add or extract from the archive.

For example, the command

    # *tar cvf backup.tar /etc*

would pack all of the files in /etc into the tar archive `backup.tar`. The first argument to `tar`— "cvf"—is the `tar` "command". "c" tells `tar` to create a new archive file. The "v" option forces `tar` into verbose mode—printing each filename as it is archived. The "f" option tells `tar` that the next argument—`backup.tar`—is the name of the archive to create. The rest of the arguments to `tar` are the file and directory names to add to the archive.

The command

> # *tar xvf backup.tar*

will extract the tar file `backup.tar` in the current directory. This can sometimes be dangerous—when extracting files from a tar file, old files are overwritten.

Furthermore, before extracting tar files it is important to know where the files should be unpacked. For example, let's say you archived the following files: `/etc/hosts`, `/etc/group`, and `/etc/passwd`. If you use the command

> # *tar cvf backup.tar /etc/hosts /etc/group /etc/passwd*

the directory name `/etc/` is added to the beginning of each filename. In order to extract the files to the correct location, you would need to use the following commands:

> # *cd /*
> # *tar xvf backup.tar*

because files are extracted with the pathname saved in the archive file.

If, however, you archived the files with the command

> # *cd /etc*
> # *tar cvf hosts group passwd*

the directory name is not saved in the archive file. Therefore, you would need to "`cd /etc`" before extracting the files. As you can see, how the tar file is created makes a large difference in where you extract it. The command

> # *tar tvf backup.tar*

may be used to display an "index" of the tar file before unpacking it. In this way you can see what directory the filenames in the archive are stored relative to, and can extract the archive from the correct location.

4.5.2 gzip and compress

Unlike archiving programs for MS-DOS, `tar` does not automatically compress files as it archives them. Therefore, if you are archiving two 1-megabyte files, the resulting tar file will be two megabytes in size. The `gzip` command may be used to compress a file (the file to compress need not be a tar file). The command

```
# gzip -9 backup.tar
```

will compress `backup.tar` and leave you with `backup.tar.gz`, the compressed version of the file. The `-9` switch tells `gzip` to use the highest compression factor.

The `gunzip` command may be used to uncompress a gzipped file. Equivalently, you may use "`gzip -d`".

`gzip` is a relatively new tool in the UNIX community. For many years, the `compress` command was used instead. However, because of several factors[1], `compress` is being phased out.

`compressed` files end in the extension `.Z`. For example, `backup.tar.Z` is the compressed version of `backup.tar`, while `backup.tar.gz` is the gzipped version[2]. The `uncompress` command is used to expand a `compressed` file; `gunzip` knows how to handle `compressed` files as well.

4.5.3 Putting them together

Therefore, to archive a group of files and compress the result, you can use the commands:

```
# tar cvf backup.tar /etc
# gzip -9 backup.tar
```

The result will be `backup.tar.gz`. To unpack this file, use the reverse set of commands:

```
# gunzip backup.tar.gz
# tar xvf backup.tar
```

Of course always make sure that you are in the correct directory before unpacking a tar file.

You can use some UNIX cleverness to do all of this on one command line, as in the following:

```
# tar cvf - /etc | gzip -9c > backup.tar.gz
```

Here, we are sending the tar file to "`-`", which stands for `tar`'s standard output. This is piped to `gzip`, which compresses the incoming tar file, and the result is saved in `backup.tar.gz`. The `-c` option to `gzip` tells `gzip` to send its output to stdout, which is redirected to `backup.tar.gz`.

A single command used to unpack this archive would be:

```
# gunzip -c backup.tar.gz | tar xvf -
```

---

[1]These factors include a software patent dispute against the `compress` algorithm and the fact that `gzip` is much more efficient than `compress`.

[2]To add further confusion, for some time the extension `.z` (lowercase "z") was used for gzipped files. The official `gzip` extension is now `.gz`.

Again, `gunzip` uncompresses the contents of `backup.tar.gz` and sends the resulting tar file to stdout. This is piped to `tar`, which reads "`-`", this time referring to `tar`'s standard input.

Happily, the `tar` command also includes the `z` option to automatically compress/uncompress files on the fly, using the `gzip` compression algorithm.

For example, the command

> # *tar cvfz backup.tar.gz /etc*

is equivalent to

> # *tar cvf backup.tar /etc*
> # *gzip backup.tar*

Just as the command

> # *tar xvfz backup.tar.Z*

may be used instead of

> # *uncompress backup.tar.Z*
> # *tar xvf backup.tar*

Refer to the man pages for `tar` and `gzip` for more information.

4.6 Using Floppies and Making Backups

Floppies are usually used as backup media. If you don't have a tape drive connected to your system, floppy disks can be used (although they are slower and somewhat less reliable).

You may also use floppies to hold individual filesystems—in this way, you can **mount** the floppy to access the data on it.

4.6.1 Using floppies for backups

The easiest way to make a backup using floppies is with `tar`. The command

> # *tar cvfzM /dev/fd0 /*

will make a complete backup of your system using the floppy drive `/dev/fd0`. The "M" option to `tar` allows the backup to be a multivolume backup; that is, when one floppy is full, `tar` will prompt for the next. The command

tar xvfzM /dev/fd0

can be used to restore the complete backup. This method can also be used if you have a tape drive
(/dev/rmt0) connected to your system.

Several other programs exist for making multiple-volume backups; the backflops program found
on tsx-11.mit.edu may come in handy.

Making a complete backup of the system can be time- and resource-consuming. Most system
administrators use a incremental backup policy, in which every month a complete backup is taken,
and every week only those files which have been modified in the last week are backed up. In this case,
if you trash your system in the middle of the month, you can simply restore the last full monthly
backup, and then restore the last weekly backups as needed.

The find command can be useful in locating files which have changed since a certain date.
Several scripts for managing incremental backups can be found on sunsite.unc.edu.

4.6.2   Using floppies as filesystems

You can create a filesystem on a floppy just as you would on a hard drive partition. For example,

mke2fs /dev/fd0 1440

creates a filesystem on the floppy in /dev/fd0. The size of the filesystem must correspond to the
size of the floppy. High-density 3.5" disks are 1.44 megabytes, or 1440 blocks, in size. High-density
5.25" disks are 1200 blocks.

In order to access the floppy, you must **mount** the filesystem contained on it. The command

mount -t ext2 /dev/fd0 /mnt

will mount the floppy in /dev/fd0 on the directory /mnt. Now, all of the files on the floppy will
appear under /mnt on your drive. The "-t ext2" specifies an ext2fs filesystem type. If you created
another type of filesystem on the floppy, you'll need to specify its type to the mount command.

The "mount point" (the directory where you're mounting the filesystem) needs to exist when
you use the mount command. If it doesn't exist, simply create it with mkdir.

See Section 4.8 for more information on filesystems, mounting, and mount points.

◇   Note that any I/O to the floppy is buffered just as hard disk I/O is. If you change data on the
floppy, you may not see the drive light come on until the kernel flushes its I/O buffers. It's important
that you not remove a floppy before you unmount it; this can be done with the command

umount /dev/fd0

Do not simply switch floppies as you would on an MS-DOS system; whenever you change floppies,
umount the first one and mount the next.

4.7 Upgrading and Installing New Software

Another duty of the system administrator is upgrading and installing new software.

The Linux community is very dynamic. New kernel releases come out every few weeks, and other software is updated almost as often. Because of this, new Linux users often feel the need to upgrade their systems constantly to keep up the the rapidly changing pace. Not only is this unnecessary, it's a waste of time: to keep up with all of the changes in the Linux world, you would be spending all of your time upgrading and none of your time using the system.

So, when should you upgrade? Some people feel that you should upgrade when a new distribution release is made—for example, when Slackware comes out with a new version. Many Linux users completely reinstall their system with the newest Slackware release every time. This, also, is a waste of time. In general, changes to Slackware releases are small. Downloading and reinstalling 30 disks when only 10% of the software has been actually modified is, of course, pointless.

The best way to upgrade your system is to do it by hand: only upgrade those software packages which you know that you should upgrade. This scares a lot of people: they want to know what to upgrade, and how, and what will break if they don't upgrade. In order to be successful with Linux, it's important to overcome your fears of "doing it yourself"— which is what Linux is all about. In fact, once you have your system working and all software correctly configured, reinstalling with the newest release will no doubt wipe all of your configuration and things will be broken again, just as they were when you first installed your system. Setting yourself back in this manner is unnecessary—all that is needed is some know-how about upgrading your system, and how to do it right.

You'll find that when you upgrade one component of your system, other things should not break. For example, most of the software on my system is left over from an ancient 0.96 MCC Interim installation. Yet, I run the newest version of the kernel and libraries with this software with no problem. For the most part, senselessly upgrading to "keep up with the trend" is not important at all. This isn't MS-DOS or Microsoft Windows. There is no important reason to run the newest version of all of the software. If you find that you would like or need features in a new version, then upgrade. If not, then don't. In other words, only upgrade what you have to, and when you have to. Don't just upgrade for the sake of upgrading. That will waste a lot of time and effort trying to keep up.

The most important software to upgrade on your system is the kernel, the libraries, and the gcc compiler. These are the three essential parts of your system, and in some cases they all depend on each other for everything to work successfully. Most of the other software on your system does not need to be upgraded periodically.

4.7.1 Upgrading the kernel

Upgrading the kernel is simply a matter of getting the sources and compiling them yourself. You must compile the kernel yourself in order to enable or disable certain features, as well as to ensure that the kernel will be optimized to run on your machine. The process is quite painless.

The kernel sources may be retrieved from any of the Linux FTP sites (see Section C for a list). On sunsite.unc.edu, for instance, the kernel sources are found in /pub/Linux/kernel. Kernel versions are numbered using a version number and a patchlevel. For example, kernel version 0.99 patchlevel 11 is usually written as 0.99.pl11, or just 0.99.11.

The kernel sources are released as a gzipped tar file[3]. For example, the file containing the 0.99.pl11 kernel sources is linux-0.99.11.tar.gz.

Unpack this tar file from the directory /usr/src; it creates the directory /usr/src/linux which contains the kernel sources. You should delete or rename your existing /usr/src/linux before unpacking the new version.

Once the sources are unpacked, you need to make sure that two symbolic links in /usr/include are correct. To create these links, use the commands

    # ln -sf /usr/src/linux/include/linux /usr/include/linux
    # ln -sf /usr/src/linux/include/asm /usr/include/asm

Once you have created these links once, there is no reason to create them again when you install the next version of the kernel sources. (See Section 3.10 for more about symbolic links.)

Note that in order to compile the kernel, you must have the gcc and g++ C and C++ compilers installed on your system. You may need to have the most recent versions of these compilers: see Section 4.7.3, below, for more information.

To compile the kernel, first cd to /usr/src/linux. Run the command make config. This command will prompt you for a number of configuration options, such as what filesystem types you wish to include in the new kernel.

Next, edit /usr/src/linux/Makefile. Be sure that the definition for ROOT_DEV is correct—it defines the device used as the root filesystem at boot time. The usual definition is

    ROOT_DEV = CURRENT

Unless you are changing your root filesystem device, there is no reason to change this.

Next, run the command make dep to fix all of the source dependencies. This is a very important step.

Finally, you're ready to compile the kernel. The command make Image will compile the kernel and leave the new kernel image in the file /usr/src/linux/Image. Alternately, the command make zImage will compile a compressed kernel image, which uncompresses itself at boot time and uses less drive space.

---

[3]Often, a patch file is also released for the current kernel version which allows you to patch your current kernel sources from the last patchlevel to the current one (using the program patch). In most cases, however, it's usually easier to install the entire new version of the kernel sources.

Once you have the kernel compiled, you need to either copy it to a boot floppy (with a command such as "cp Image /dev/fd0") or install it using LILO to boot from your hard drive. See Section 4.2.2 for more information.

4.7.2 Upgrading the libraries

As mentioned before, most of the software on the system is compiled to use shared libraries, which contain common subroutines shared among different programs.

If you see the message

```
Incompatible library version
```

when attempting to run a program, then you need to upgrade to the version of the libraries which the program requires. Libraries are back-compatible; that is, a program compiled to use an older version of the libraries should work with the new version of the libraries installed. However, the reverse is not true.

The newest version of the libraries can be found on the Linux FTP sites. On sunsite.unc.edu, they are located in /pub/Linux/GCC. The "release" files there should explain what files you need to download and how to install them. Briefly, you should get the files image-*version*.tar.gz and inc-*version*.tar.gz where *version* is the version of the libraries to install, such as 4.4.1. These are gzipped tar files; the image file contains the library images to install in /lib and /usr/lib. The inc file contains include files to install in /usr/include

The release-*version*.tar.gz should explain the installation procedure in detail (the exact instructions vary for each release). In general you need to install the library .a and .sa files in /usr/lib. These are the libraries used at compilation time.

In addition, the shared library image files, libc.so.*version* are installed in /lib. These are the shared library images loaded at runtime by programs using the libraries. Each library has a symbolic link using the major version number of the library in /lib.

For example, the libc library version 4.4.1 has a major version number of 4. The file containing the library is libc.so.4.4.1. A symbolic link of the name libc.so.4 is also in /lib pointing to this file. You need to change this symbolic link when upgrading the libraries. For example, when upgrading from libc.so.4.4 to libc.so.4.4.1, you need to change the symbolic link to point to the new version.

◇ It is very important that you change the symbolic link in one step, as given below. If you somehow delete the symbolic link libc.so.4, then programs which depend on the link (including basic utilities like ls and cat) will stop working. Use the following command to update the symbolic link libc.so.4 to point to the file libc.so.4.4.1:

```
# ln -sf /lib/libc.so.4.4.1 /lib/libc.so.4
```

You also need to change the symbolic link `libm.so.`*version* in the same manner. If you are upgrading to a different version of the libraries substitute to appropriate filenames above. The library release notice should explain the details. (See Section 3.10 for more information about symbolic links.)

4.7.3 Upgrading gcc

The gcc C and C++ compiler is used to compile software on your system, most importantly the kernel. The newest version of gcc is found on the Linux FTP sites. On `sunsite.unc.edu`, it is found in the directory `/pub/Linux/GCC` (along with the libraries). There should be a `release` file for the gcc distribution detailing what files you need to download and how to install them.

4.7.4 Upgrading other software

Upgrading other software is usually just a matter of downloading the appropriate files and installing them. Most software for Linux is distributed at gzipped tar files, including either sources or binaries or both. If binaries are not included in the release, you may need to compile them yourself; usually, this means typing `make` in the directory where the sources are held.

Reading the USENET newsgroup `comp.os.linux.announce` for announcements of new software releases is the easiest way to find out about new software. Whenever you are looking for software on an FTP site, downloading the `ls-lR` index file from the FTP site and using `grep` to find the files in question is the easiest way to locate software. If you have `archie` available to you, it can be of assistance as well[4]. See Appendix A for more details.

One handy source of Linux software is the Slackware distribution disk images. Each disk contains a number of `.tgz` files which are simply gzipped tar files. Instead of downloading the disks, you can download the desired `.tgz` files from the Slackware directories on the FTP site and install them directly. If you run the Slackware distribution, the `setup` command can be used to automatically load and install a complete series of disks.

Again, it's usually not a good idea to upgrade by reinstalling with the newest version of Slackware, or another distribution. If you reinstall in this way, you will no doubt wreck your current installation, including user directories and all of your customized configuration. The best way to upgrade software is piecewise; that is, if there is a program that you use often that has a new version, upgrade it. Otherwise, don't bother. Rule of thumb: If it ain't broke, don't fix it. If your current software works, there's no reason to upgrade.

---

[4]If you don't have `archie`, you can telnet to an `archie` server such as `archie.rutgers.edu`, login as "archie" and use the command "`help`"

4.8 Managing Filesystems

Another task of the system administrator is taking care of filesystems. Most of this job entails periodically checking the filesystems for damage or corrupted files; many systems automatically check the filesystems at boot time.

4.8.1 Mounting filesystems

First, a few concepts about filesystems. Before a filesystem is accessible to the system, it must be **mounted** on some directory. For example, if you have a filesystem on a floppy, you must mount it under some directory, say /mnt, in order to access the files on it (see Section 4.6.2). After mounting the filesystem, all of the files in the filesystem appear in that directory. After unmounting the filesystem, the directory (in this case, /mnt) will be empty.

The same is true of filesystems on the hard drive. The system automatically mounts filesystems on your hard drive for you at bootup time. The so-called "root filesystem" is mounted on the directory /. If you have a separate filesystem for /usr, for example, it is mounted on /usr. If you only have a root filesystem, all files (including those in /usr) exist on that filesystem.

The command mount is used to mount a filesystem. The command

```
    mount -av
```

is executed from the file /etc/rc (which is the system initialization file executed at boot time; see Section 4.10.1). The mount -av command obtains information on filesystems and mount points from the file /etc/fstab. An example fstab file appears below.

```
    # device        directory       type       options
    /dev/hda2       /               ext2       defaults
    /dev/hda3       /usr            ext2       defaults
    /dev/hda4       none            swap       sw
    /proc           /proc           proc       none
```

The first field is the device—the name of the partition to mount. The second field is the mount point. The third field is the filesystem type—such as ext2 (for ext2fs) or minix (for Minix filesystems). Table 4.1 lists the various filesystem types available for Linux.[5] Not all of these filesystem types may be available on your system; your kernel must have support for them compiled in. See Section 4.7 for information on building the kernel.

The last field of the fstab file contains mount options—usually, this is set to "defaults".

As you can see, swap partitions are included in /etc/fstab as well. They have a mount directory of none, and type swap. The swapon -a command, executed from /etc/rc as well, is used to enable swapping on all swap devices listed in /etc/fstab.

---

[5]This table is current as of kernel version 1.1.37.

Filesystem	Type name	Comment
Second Extended Filesystem	ext2	Most common Linux filesystem.
Extended Filesystem	ext	Superseded by ext2.
Minix Filesystem	minix	Original Minix filesystem; rarely used.
Xia Filesystem	xia	Like ext2, but rarely used.
UMSDOS Filesystem	umsdos	Used to install Linux on an MS-DOS partition.
MS-DOS Filesystem	msdos	Used to access MS-DOS files.
/proc Filesystem	proc	Provides process information for ps, etc.
ISO 9660 Filesystem	iso9660	Format used by most CD-ROMs.
Xenix Filesystem	xenix	Used to access files from Xenix.
System V Filesystem	sysv	Used to access files from System V variants for the x86.
Coherent Filesystem	coherent	Used to access files from Coherent.
HPFS Filesystem	hpfs	Read-only access for HPFS partitions (DoubleSpace).

Table 4.1: Linux Filesystem Types

The fstab file contains one special entry—for the /proc filesystem. As mentioned in Section 3.11.1, the /proc filesystem is used to store information about system processes, available memory, and so on. If /proc is not mounted, commands such as ps will not work.

◇   The mount command may only be used by root. This is to ensure security on the system; you wouldn't want regular users mounting and unmounting filesystems on a whim. There are several software packages available which allow regular users to mount and unmount filesystems (floppies in particular) without compromising system security.

The mount -av command actually mounts all filesystems other than the root filesystem (in the table above, /dev/hda2). The root filesystem is automatically mounted at boot time by the kernel.

Instead of using mount -av, you can mount a filesystem by hand. The command

> # *mount -t ext2 /dev/hda3 /usr*

is equivalent to mounting the filesystem with the entry /dev/hda3 in the fstab example file above.

In general, you should never have to mount or unmount filesystems by hand. The mount -av command in /etc/rc takes care of mounting the filesystems at boot time. Filesystems are automatically unmounted by the shutdown or halt commands before bringing the system down.

4.8.2   Checking filesystems

It is usually a good idea to check your filesystems for damage or corrupt files every now and then. Some systems automatically check their filesystems at boot time (with the appropriate commands in /etc/rc).

The command used to check a filesystem depends on the type of the filesystem in question. For ext2fs filesystems (the most commonly used type), this command is e2fsck. For example, the command

> # *e2fsck -av /dev/hda2*

will check the ext2fs filesystem on **/dev/hda2** and automatically correct any errors.

It is usually a good idea to unmount a filesystem before checking it. For example, the command

> # *umount /dev/hda2*

will unmount the filesystem on **/dev/hda2**, after which you can check it. The one exception is that you cannot unmount the root filesystem. In order to check the root filesystem when it's unmounted, you should use a maintenance boot/root diskette (see Section 4.11.1). You also cannot unmount a filesystem if any of the files in it are "busy"—that is, being used by a running process. For example, you cannot unmount a filesystem if any user's current working directory is on that filesystem. You will receive a "**Device busy**" error if you attempt to unmount a filesystem which is in use.

Other filesystem types use different forms of the e2fsck command, such as **efsck** and **xfsck**. On some systems, you can simply use the command **fsck**, which will determine the filesystem type and execute the appropriate command.

It is important that you reboot your system immediately after checking a mounted filesystem if any corrections were made to that filesystem. (However, in general, you shouldn't check filesystems while they are mounted.) For example, if e2fsck reports that it corrected any errors with the filesystem, you should immediately **shutdown -r** in order to reboot the system. This is to allow the system to re-sync its information about the filesystem when e2fsck modifies it.

The **/proc** filesystem never needs to be checked in this manner. **/proc** is a memory filesystem, managed directly by the kernel.

4.9   Using a swap file

Instead of reserving an individual partition for swap space, you can use a file. However, to do so you'll need install the Linux software and get everything going *before* you create the swap file.

If you have a Linux system installed, you can use the following commands to create a swap file. Below, we're going to create a swap file of size 8208 blocks (about 8 megs).

> # *dd if=/dev/zero of=/swap bs=1024 count=8208*

This command creates the swap file itself. Replace the "**count=**" with the size of the swap file in blocks.

```
# mkswap /swap 8208
```

This command will initialize the swapfile; again, replace the name and size of the swapfile with the appropriate values.

```
# /etc/sync
# swapon /swap
```

Now we are swapping on the file **/swap** which we have created, after syncing, which ensures that the file has been written to disk.

The one major drawback to using a swapfile in this manner is that all access to the swap file is done through the filesystem. This means that the blocks which make up the swap file may not be contiguous. Therefore, performance may not be as great as using a swap partition, for which blocks are always contiguous and I/O requests are done directly to the device.

Another drawback in using a swapfile is the chance to corrupt your filesystem data—when using large swap files, there is the chance that you can corrupt your filesystem if something goes wrong. Keeping your filesystems and swap partitions separate will prevent this from happening.

Using a swap file can be very useful if you have a temporary need for more swap space. For example, if you're compiling a large program and would like to speed things up somewhat, you can temporarily create a swap file and use it in addition to your regular swap space.

To get rid of a swap file, first use **swapoff**, as in

```
# swapoff /swap
```

And you can safely delete the file.

```
# rm /swap
```

Remember that each swap file (or partition) may be as large as 16 megabytes, but you may use up to 8 swap files or partitions on your system.

4.10   Miscellaneous Tasks

Believe it or not, there are a number of housekeeping tasks for the system administrator which don't fall into any major category.

4.10.1   System startup files

When the system boots, a number of scripts are executed automatically by the system before any user logs in. Here is a description of what happens.

At bootup time, the kernel spawns the process /etc/init. init is a program which reads its configuration file, /etc/inittab, and spawns other processes based on the contents of this file. One of the important processes started from inittab is the /etc/getty process started on each virtual console. The getty process grabs the VC for use, and starts a login process on the VC. This allows you to login on each VC; if /etc/inittab does not contain a getty process for a certain VC, you will not be able to login on that VC.

Another process executed from /etc/inittab is /etc/rc, the main system initialization file. This file is a simple shell script which executes any initialization commands needed at boot time, such as mounting the filesystems (see Section 4.8) and initializing swap space.

Your system may execute other initialization scripts as well, such as /etc/rc.local. /etc/rc.local usually contains initialization commands specific to your own system, such as setting the hostname (see the next section). rc.local may be started from /etc/rc or from /etc/inittab directly.

4.10.2 Setting the hostname

In a networked environment, the hostname is used to uniquely identify a particular machine, while in a standalone environment the hostname just gives the system personality and charm. It's like naming a pet: you can always address to your dog as "The dog," but it's much more interesting to assign the dog a name such as Spot or Woofie.

Setting the system's hostname is a simple matter of using the hostname command. If you are on a network, your hostname should be the full hostname of your machine, such as goober.norelco.com. If you are not on a network of any kind, you can choose an arbitrary host and domainname, such as loomer.vpizza.com, shoop.nowhere.edu, or floof.org.

When setting the hostname, the hostname must appear in the file /etc/hosts, which assigns an IP address to each host. Even if your machine is not on a network, you should include your own hostname in /etc/hosts.

For example, if you are not on a TCP/IP network, and your hostname is floof.org, simply include the following line in /etc/hosts:

```
127.0.0.1       floof.org localhost
```

This assigns your hostname, floof.org, to the loopback address 127.0.0.1 (used if you're not on a network). The localhost alias is also assigned to this address.

If you are on a TCP/IP network, however, your real IP address and hostname should appear in /etc/hosts. For example, if your hostname is goober.norelco.com, and your IP address is 128.253.154.32, add the following line to /etc/hosts:

```
128.253.154.32       goober.norelco.com
```

If your hostname does not appear in /etc/hosts, you will not be able to set it.

To set your hostname, simply use the hostname command. For example, the command

> # *hostname -S goober.norelco.com*

sets the hostname to goober.norelco.com. In most cases, the hostname command is executed from one of the system startup files, such as /etc/rc or /etc/rc.local. Edit these two files and change the hostname command found there to set your own hostname; upon rebooting the system the hostname will be set to the new value.

4.11 What To Do In An Emergency

On some occasions, the system administrator will be faced with the problem of recovering from a complete disaster, such as forgetting the root password or trashing filesystems. The best advice is, *don't panic*. Everyone makes stupid mistakes—that's the best way to learn about system administration: the hard way.

Linux is not an unstable version of UNIX. In fact, I have had fewer problems with system hangs than with commercial versions of UNIX on many platforms. Linux also benefits from a strong complement of wizards who can help you get out of a bind.

The first step in investigating any problem is to attempt to fix it yourself. Poke around, see how things work. Too much of the time, a system administrator will post a desperate plea for help before looking into the problem at all. Most of the time, you'll find that fixing problems yourself is actually very easy. It is the path to guruhood.

There are very few cases where reinstalling the system from scratch is necessary. Many new users accidentally delete some essential system file, and immediately reach for the installation disks. This is not a good idea. Before taking such drastic measures, investigate the problem and ask others to help fix things up. In almost all cases, you can recover your system from a maintenance diskette.

4.11.1 Recovering using a maintenance diskette

One indispensable tool for the system administrator is the so called "boot/root disk"—a floppy which can be booted for a complete Linux system, independent of your hard drive. Boot/root disks are actually very simple—you create a root filesystem on the floppy, place all of the necessary utilities on it, and install LILO and a bootable kernel on the floppy. Another technique is to use one floppy for the kernel and another for the root filesystem. In any case, the result is the same: you are running a Linux system completely from floppy.

The canonical example of a boot/root disk is the Slackware boot disks[6]. These diskettes contain

---

[6]See Section 2.1.1 for information on downloading these from the Internet. For this procedure, you don't need to download the entire Slackware release—only the boot and root diskettes.

a bootable kernel and a root filesystem, all on floppy. They are intended to be used to install the Slackware distribution, but come in very handy when doing system maintenance.

The H.J Lu boot/root disk, available from `/pub/Linux/GCC/rootdisk` on `sunsite.unc.edu`, is another example of such a maintenance disk. Or, if you're ambitious, you can create your own. In most cases, however, using a pre-made boot/root disk is much easier and will probably be more complete.

Using a boot/root disk is very simple. Just boot the disk on your system, and login as `root` (usually no password). In order to access the files on your hard drive, you will need to mount your filesystems by hand. For example, the command

> # *mount -t ext2 /dev/hda2 /mnt*

will mount an ext2fs filesystem on `/dev/hda2` under `/mnt`. Remember that `/` is now on the boot/root disk itself; you need to mount your hard drive filesystems under some directory in order to access the files. Therefore, `/etc/passwd` on your hard drive is now `/mnt/etc/passwd` if you mount your root filesystem on `/mnt`.

4.11.2   Fixing the root password

If you forget your root password, no problem. Just boot the boot/root disk, mount your root filesystem on `/mnt`, and blank out the password field for `root` in `/mnt/etc/passwd`, as so:

> `root::0:0:root:/:/bin/sh`

Now `root` has no password; when you reboot from the hard drive you should be able to login as `root` and reset the password using `passwd`.

Aren't you glad you learned how to use `vi`? On your boot/root disk, other editors such as Emacs probably aren't available, but `vi` should be.

4.11.3   Fixing trashed filesystems

If you somehow trash your filesystems, you can run `e2fsck` (if you use the ext2fs filesystem type, that is) to correct any damaged data on the filesystems from floppy. Other filesystem types use different forms of the `fsck` command; see Section 4.8 for details.

When checking your filesystems from floppy, it's best for the filesystems to not be mounted.

One common cause of filesystem damage is superblock corruption. The *superblock* is the "header" of the filesystem that contains information on the filesystem status, size, free blocks, and so forth. If you corrupt your superblock (for example, by accidentally writing data directly to the filesystem's partition), the system may not recognize the filesystem at all. Any attempt to mount the filesystem could fail, and `e2fsck` won't be able to fix the problem.

Happily, the *ext2fs* filesystem type saves copies of the superblock at "block group" boundaries on the drive—usually, every 8K blocks. In order to tell e2fsck to use a copy of the superblock, you can use a command such as

> # *e2fsck -b 8193 ⟨partition⟩*

where ⟨*partition*⟩ is the partition on which the filesystem resides. The -b 8193 option tells e2fsck to use the copy of the superblock stored at block 8193 in the filesystem.

4.11.4   Recovering lost files

If you accidentally deleted important files on your system, there's no way to "undelete" them. However, you can copy the relevant files from the floppy to your hard drive. For example, if you deleted /bin/login on your system (which allows you to login), simply boot the boot/root floppy, mount the root filesystem on /mnt, and use the command

> # *cp -a /bin/login /mnt/bin/login*

The -a option tells cp to preserve the permissions on the file(s) being copied.

Of course, if the files you deleted weren't essential system files which have counterparts on the boot/root floppy, you're out of luck. If you made backups, you can always restore from them.

4.11.5   Fixing trashed libraries

If you accidentally trashed your libraries or symbolic links in /lib, more than likely commands which depended on those libraries will no longer run (see Section 4.7.2). The easiest solution is to boot your boot/root floppy, mount your root filesystem, and fix the libraries in /mnt/lib.

Chapter 5

Advanced Features

This chapter will introduce you to some of the more interesting features of Linux. This assumes that you have at least basic UNIX experience, and understand the information contained in the previous chapters.

The most important aspect of Linux that distinguishes it from other implementations of UNIX is its open design and philosophy. Linux was not developed by a small team of programmers driven by a marketing committee with a single goal in mind. It was developed by a heterogenous mob of hackers, putting what they wanted into a homebrew UNIX system.

Consequently, the diversity of design in the Linux world is large. Some people dislike this lack of uniformity and conformity—on the other hand, others call it one of the strongest qualities of Linux.

5.1 The X Window System

The X Window System is a large and powerful (and somewhat complex) graphics environment for UNIX systems. The original X Window System code was developed at MIT; commercial vendors have since made X the industry standard for UNIX platforms. Virtually every UNIX workstation in the world runs some variant of the X Window system.

A free port of the MIT X Window System version 11, release 6 (X11R6) for 80386/80486/Pentium UNIX systems has been developed by a team of programmers originally headed by David Wexelblat[1]. The release, known as XFree86[2], is available for System V/386, 386BSD, and other x86 UNIX implementations, including Linux. It includes all of the required binaries, support files, libraries, and tools.

Configuring and using the X Window System is far beyond the scope of this book. You are encouraged to read *The X Window System: A User's Guide*—see Appendix A for information on this

---

[1]David may be reached on the Internet at `dwex@XFree86.org`.

[2]XFree86 is a trademark of The XFree86 Project, Inc.

book. In this section, we'll give a step-by-step description of how to install and configure XFree86 for Linux, but you will have to fill in some of the details yourself by reading the documentation released with XFree86 itself. (This documentation is discussed below.) The Linux *XFree86 HOWTO* is another good source of information.

5.1.1 Hardware requirements

As of XFree86 version 3.1, released in September 1994, the following video chipsets are supported. The documentation included with your video adaptor should specify the chipset used. If you are in the market for a new video card, or are buying a new machine that comes with a video card, have the vendor find out exactly what the make, model, and chipset of the video card is. This may require the vendor to call technical support on your behalf; in general vendors will be happy to do this. Many PC hardware vendors will state that the video card is a "standard SVGA card" which "should work" on your system. Explain that your software (mention Linux and XFree86!) does not support all video chipsets and that you must have detailed information.

You can also determine your videocard chipset by running the `SuperProbe` program included with the XFree86 distribution. This is covered in more detail below.

The following standard SVGA chipsets are supported:

- Tseng ET3000, ET4000AX, ET4000/W32

- Western Digital/Paradise PVGA1

- Western Digital WD90C00, WD90C10, WD90C11, WD90C24, WD90C30, WD90C31, WD90C33

- Genoa GVGA

- Trident TVGA8800CS, TVGA8900B, TVGA8900C, TVGA8900CL, TVGA9000, TVGA9000i, TVGA9100B, TVGA9200CX, TVGA9320, TVGA9400CX, TVGA9420

- ATI 18800, 18800-1, 28800-2, 28800-4, 28800-5, 28800-6, 68800-3, 68800-6, 68800AX, 68800LX, 88800

- NCR 77C22, 77C22E, 77C22E+

- Cirrus Logic CLGD5420, CLGD5422, CLGD5424, CLGD5426, CLGD5428, CLGD5429, CLGD5430, CLGD5434, CLGD6205, CLGD6215, CLGD6225, CLGD6235, CLGD6420

- Compaq AVGA

- OAK OTI067, OTI077

- Avance Logic AL2101

- MX MX68000, MX680010

- Video 7/Headland Technologies HT216-32

The following SVGA chipsets with accelerated features are also supported:

- 8514/A (and true clones)

- ATI Mach8, Mach32

- Cirrus CLGD5420, CLGD5422, CLGD5424, CLGD5426, CLGD5428, CLGD5429, CLGD5430, CLGD5434, CLGD6205, CLGD6215, CLGD6225, CLGD6235

- S3 86C911, 86C924, 86C801, 86C805, 86C805i, 86C928, 86C864, 86C964

- Western Digital WD90C31, WD90C33

- Weitek P9000

- IIT AGX-014, AGX-015, AGX-016

- Tseng ET4000/W32, ET4000/W32i, ET4000/W32p

Video cards using these chipsets are supported on all bus types, including VLB and PCI.

All of the above are supported in both 256 color and monochrome modes, with the exception of the Avance Logic, MX and Video 7 chipsets, which are only supported in 256 color mode. If your video card has enough DRAM installed, many of the above chipsets are supported in 16 and 32 bits-per-pixel mode (specifically, some Mach32, P9000, S3 and Cirrus boards). The usual configuration is 8 bits per pixel (that is, 256 colors).

The monochrome server also supports generic VGA cards, the Hercules monochrome card, the Hyundai HGC1280, Sigma LaserView, and Apollo monochrome cards. On the Compaq AVGA, only 64k of video memory is supported for the monochrome server, and the GVGA has not been tested with more than 64k.

This list will undoubtedly expand as time passes. The release notes for the current version of XFree86 should contain the complete list of supported video chipsets.

One problem faced by the XFree86 developers is that some video card manufacturers use non-standard mechanisms for determining clock frequencies used to drive the card. Some of these manufacturers either don't release specifications describing how to program the card, or they require developers to sign a non-disclosure statement to obtain the information. This would obviously restrict the free distribution of the XFree86 software, something that the XFree86 development team is not willing to do. For a long time, this has been a problem with certain video cards manufactured by Diamond, but as of release 3.1 of XFree86, Diamond has started to work with the development team to release free drivers for these cards.

The suggested setup for XFree86 under Linux is a 486 machine with at least 8 megabytes of RAM, and a video card with a chipset listed above. For optimal performance, we suggest using an accelerated card, such as an S3-chipset card. You should check the documentation for XFree86 and verify that your particular card is supported before taking the plunge and purchasing expensive hardware. Benchmark ratings comparisons for various video cards under XFree86 are posted routinely to the USENET newsgroups `comp.windows.x.i386unix` and `comp.os.linux.misc`.

As a side note, my personal Linux system is a 486DX2-66, 20 megabytes of RAM, and is equipped with a VLB S3-864 chipset card with 2 megabytes of DRAM. I have run X benchmarks on this machine as well as on Sun Sparc IPX workstations. The Linux system is roughly 7 times faster than the Sparc IPX (for the curious, XFree86-3.1 under Linux, with this video card, runs at around 171,000 xstones; the Sparc IPX at around 24,000). In general, XFree86 on a Linux system with an accelerated SVGA card will give you much greater performance than that found on commercial UNIX workstations (which usually employ simple framebuffers for graphics).

Your machine will need at least 4 megabytes of physical RAM, and 16 megabytes of virtual RAM (for example, 8 megs physical and 8 megs swap). Remember that the more physical RAM that you have, the less that the system will swap to and from disk when memory is low. Because swapping is inherently slow (disks are very slow compared to memory), having 8 megabytes of RAM or more is necessary to run XFree86 comfortably. A system with 4 megabytes of physical RAM could run *much* (up to 10 times) more slowly than one with 8 megs or more.

5.1.2   Installing XFree86

The Linux binary distribution of XFree86 can be found on a number of FTP sites. On `sunsite.unc.edu`, it is found in the directory `/pub/Linux/X11`. (As of the time of this writing, the current version is 3.1; newer versions are released periodically).

It's quite likely that you obtained XFree86 as part of a Linux distribution, in which case downloading the software separately is not necessary.

If you are downloading XFree86 directly, This table lists the files in the XFree86-3.1 distribution.

One of the following servers is required:

File	Description
`XF86-3.1-8514.tar.gz`	Server for 8514-based boards.
`XF86-3.1-AGX.tar.gz`	Server for AGX-based boards.
`XF86-3.1-Mach32.tar.gz`	Server for Mach32-based boards.
`XF86-3.1-Mach8.tar.gz`	Server for Mach8-based boards.
`XF86-3.1-Mono.tar.gz`	Server for monochrome video modes.
`XF86-3.1-P9000.tar.gz`	Server for P9000-based boards.
`XF86-3.1-S3.tar.gz`	Server for S3-based boards.
`XF86-3.1-SVGA.tar.gz`	Server for Super VGA-based boards.
`XF86-3.1-VGA16.tar.gz`	Server for VGA/EGA-based boards.
`XF86-3.1-W32.tar.gz`	Server for ET4000/W32-based boards.

All of the following files are required:

File	Description
XF86-3.1-bin.tar.gz	The rest of the X11R6 binaries.
XF86-3.1-cfg.tar.gz	Config files for xdm, xinit and fs.
XF86-3.1-doc.tar.gz	Documentation and manpages.
XF86-3.1-inc.tar.gz	Include files.
XF86-3.1-lib.tar.gz	Shared X libraries and support files.
XF86-3.1-fnt.tar.gz	Basic fonts.

The following files are optional:

File	Description
XF86-3.1-ctrb.tar.gz	Selected contrib programs.
XF86-3.1-extra.tar.gz	Extra XFree86 servers and binaries.
XF86-3.1-lkit.tar.gz	Server linkkit for customization.
XF86-3.1-fnt75.tar.gz	75-dpi screen fonts.
XF86-3.1-fnt100.tar.gz	100-dpi screen fonts.
XF86-3.1-fntbig.tar.gz	Large Kanji and other fonts.
XF86-3.1-fntscl.tar.gz	Scaled fonts (Speedo, Type1).
XF86-3.1-man.tar.gz	Manual pages.
XF86-3.1-pex.tar.gz	PEX binaries, includes and libraries.
XF86-3.1-slib.tar.gz	Static X libraries and support files.
XF86-3.1-usrbin.tar.gz	Daemons which reside in /usr/bin.
XF86-3.1-xdmshdw.tar.gz	Shadow password version of xdm.

The XFree86 directory should contain README files and installation notes for the current version.

All that is required to install XFree86 is to obtain the above files, create the directory /usr/X11R6 (as root), and unpack the files from /usr/X11R6 with a command such as:

```
# gzip –dc XF86-3.1-bin.tar.gz | tar xfB –
```

Remember that these tar files are packed relative to /usr/X11R6, so it's important to unpack the files there.

After unpacking the files, you first need to link the file /usr/X11R6/bin/X to the server that you're using. For example, if you wish to use the SVGA color server, /usr/bin/X11/X should be linked to /usr/X11R6/bin/XF86_SVGA. If you wish to use the monochrome server instead, relink this file to XF86_MONO with the command

```
# ln –sf /usr/X11R6/bin/XF86_MONO  /usr/X11R6/bin/X
```

The same holds true if you are using one of the other servers.

If you aren't sure which server to use, or don't know your video card chipset, you can run the SuperProbe program found in /usr/X11R6/bin (included in the XF86-3.1-bin listed above). This

156   Chapter 5.   Advanced Features

program will attempt to determine your video chipset type and other information; write down its output for later reference.

You need to make sure that `/usr/X11R6/bin` is on your path. This can be done by editing your system default `/etc/profile` or `/etc/csh.login` (based on the shell that you, or other users on your system, use). Or you can simply add the directory to your personal path by modifying `/etc/.bashrc` or `/etc/.cshrc`, based on your shell.

You also need to make sure that `/usr/X11R6/lib` can be located by `ld.so`, the runtime linker. To do this, add the line

```
/usr/X11R6/lib
```

to the file `/etc/ld.so.conf`, and run `/sbin/ldconfig`, as `root`.

5.1.3   Configuring XFree86

Setting up XFree86 is not difficult in most cases. However, if you happen to be using hardware for which drivers ar under development, or wish to obtain the best performance or resolution from an accelerated graphics card, configuring XFree86 can be somewhat time-consuming.

In this section we will describe how to create and edit the `XF86Config` file, which configures the XFree86 server. In many cases it is best to start out with a "basic" XFree86 configuration, one which uses a low resolution, such as 640x480, which should be supported on all video cards and monitor types. Once you have XFree86 working at a lower, standard resolution, you can tweak the configuration to exploit the capabilities of your video hardware. The idea is that you want to know that XFree86 works at all on your system, and that something isn't wrong with your installation, before attempting the sometimes difficult task of setting up XFree86 for real use.

In addition to the information listed here, you should read the following documentation:

- The XFree86 documentation in `/usr/X11R6/lib/X11/doc` (contained within the `XFree86-3.1-doc` package). You should especially see the file `README.Config`, which is an XFree86 configuration tutorial.

- Several video chipsets have separate `README` files in the above directory (such as `README.Cirrus` and `README.S3`). Read one of these if applicable.

- The man page for `XFree86`.

- The man page for `XF86Config`.

- The man page for the particular server that you are using (such as `XF86_SVGA` or `XF86_S3`).

The main XFree86 configuration file is `/usr/X11R6/lib/X11/XF86Config`. This file contains information on your mouse, video card parameters, and so on. The file `XF86Config.eg` is provided with the XFree86 distribution as an example. Copy this file to `XF86Config` and edit it as a starting point.

The `XF86Config` man page explains the format of this file in detail. Read this man page now, if you have not done so already.

We are going to present a sample `XF86Config` file, piece by piece. This file may not look exactly like the sample file included in the XFree86 distribution, but the structure is the same.

◇   Note that the `XF86Config` file format may change with each version of XFree86; this information is only valid for XFree86 version 3.1.

◇   Also, you should not simply copy the configuration file listed here to your own system and attempt to use it. Attempting to use a configuration file which doesn't correspond to your hardware could drive the monitor at a frequency which is too high for it; there have been reports of monitors (especially fixed-frequency monitors) being damaged or destroyed by using an incorrectly configured `XF86Config` file. The bottom line is this: Make absolutely sure that your `XF86Config` file corresponds to your hardware before you attempt to use it.

Each section of the `XF86Config` file is surrounded by the pair of lines `Section "⟨section-name⟩"`...`EndSection`. The first part of the `XF86Config` file is `Files`, which looks like this:

```
Section "Files"
    RgbPath      "/usr/X11R6/lib/X11/rgb"
    FontPath     "/usr/X11R6/lib/X11/fonts/misc/"
    FontPath     "/usr/X11R6/lib/X11/fonts/75dpi/"
EndSection
```

The `RgbPath` line sets the path to the X11R6 RGB color database, and each `FontPath` line sets the path to a directory containing X11 fonts. In general you shouldn't have to modify these lines; just be sure that there is a `FontPath` entry for each font type that you have installed (that is, for each directory in `/usr/X11R6/lib/X11/fonts`).

The next section is `ServerFlags`, which specifies several global flags for the server. In general this section is empty.

```
Section "ServerFlags"
# Uncomment this to cause a core dump at the spot where a signal is
# received.  This may leave the console in an unusable state, but may
# provide a better stack trace in the core dump to aid in debugging
#    NoTrapSignals

# Uncomment this to disable the <Crtl><Alt><BS> server abort sequence
#    DontZap
EndSection
```

Here, we have all lines within the section commented out.

The next section is `Keyboard`. This should be fairly intuitive.

```
Section "Keyboard"
    Protocol    "Standard"
    AutoRepeat  500 5
    ServerNumLock
EndSection
```

Other options are available as well—see the `XF86Config` file if you wish to modify the keyboard configuration. The above should work for most systems.

The next section is `Pointer` which specifies parameters for the mouse device.

```
Section "Pointer"

    Protocol    "MouseSystems"
    Device      "/dev/mouse"

# Baudrate and SampleRate are only for some Logitech mice
#     BaudRate   9600
#     SampleRate 150

# Emulate3Buttons is an option for 2-button Microsoft mice
#     Emulate3Buttons

# ChordMiddle is an option for some 3-button Logitech mice
#     ChordMiddle

EndSection
```

The only options that you should concern yourself with now are `Protocol` and `Device`. `Protocol` specifies the mouse *protocol* that your mouse uses (not the make or brand of mouse). Valid types for `Protocol` (under Linux—there are other options available for other operating systems) are:

- BusMouse

- Logitech

- Microsoft

- MMSeries

- Mouseman

- MouseSystems

- PS/2

- `MMHitTab`

`BusMouse` should be used for the Logitech busmouse. Note that older Logitech mice should use `Logitech`, but newer Logitech mice use either `Microsoft` or `Mouseman` protocols. This is a case in which the protocol doesn't necessarily have anything to do with the make of the mouse.

`Device` specifies the device file where the mouse can be accessed. On most Linux systems, this is `/dev/mouse`. `/dev/mouse` is usually a link to the appropriate serial port (such as `/dev/cua0`) for serial mice, or to the appropriate busmouse device for busmice. At any rate, be sure that the device file listed in `Device` exists.

The next section is `Monitor`, which specifies the characteristics of your monitor. As with other sections in the `XF86Config` file, there may be more than one `Monitor` section. This is useful if you have multiple monitors connected to a system, or use the same `XF86Config` file under multiple hardware configurations. In general, though, you will need a single `Monitor` section.

```
Section "Monitor"

    Identifier  "CTX 5468 NI"

    # These values are for a CTX 5468NI only! Don't attempt to use
    # them with your monitor (unless you have this model)

    Bandwidth    60
    HorizSync    30-38,47-50
    VertRefresh  50-90

    # Modes: Name       dotclock  horiz             vert

    ModeLine "640x480"  25        640 664 760 800   480 491 493 525
    ModeLine "800x600"  36        800 824 896 1024  600 601 603 625
    ModeLine "1024x768" 65        1024 1088 1200 1328  768 783 789 818

EndSection
```

The `Identifier` line is used to give an arbitrary name to the `Monitor` entry. This can be any string; you will use it to refer to the `Monitor` entry later in the `XF86Config` file.

they are listed below.

`HorizSync` specifies the valid horizontal sync frequencies for your monitor, in kHz. If you have a multisync monitor, this can be a range of values (or several comma-separated ranges), as seen above. If you have a fixed-frequency monitor, this will be a list of discrete values, such as:

```
HorizSync    31.5, 35.2, 37.9, 35.5, 48.95
```

Your monitor manual should list these values in the technical specifications section. If you do not have this information available, you should either contact the manufacturer or vendor of your monitor to obtain it. There are other sources of information, as well;

VertRefresh specifies the valid vertical refresh rates (or vertical synchronization frequencies) for your monitor, in Hz. Like HorizSync this can be a range or a list of discrete values; your monitor manual should list them.

HorizSync and VertRefresh are used only to double-check that the monitor resolutions that you specify are in valid ranges. This is to reduce the chance that you will damage your monitor by attempting to drive it at a frequency for which it was not designed.

The ModeLine directive is used to specify a single resolution mode for your monitor. The format of ModeLine is

> ModeLine ⟨name⟩ ⟨clock⟩ ⟨horiz-values⟩ ⟨vert-values⟩

⟨name⟩ is an arbitrary string, which you will use to refer to the resolution mode later in the file. ⟨dot-clock⟩ is the driving clock frequency, or "dot clock" associated with the resolution mode. A dot clock is usually specified in MHz, and is the rate at which the video card must send pixels to the monitor at this resolution. ⟨horiz-values⟩ and ⟨vert-values⟩ are four numbers each which specify when the electron gun of the monitor should fire, and when the horizontal and vertical sync pulses fire during a sweep.

How can you determine the ModeLine values for your monitor? The file VideoModes.doc, included with the XFree86 distribution, describes in detail how to determine these values for each resolution mode that your monitor supports. First of all, ⟨clock⟩ must correspond to one of the dot clock values that your video card can produce. Later in the XF86Config file you will specify these clocks; you can only use video modes which have a ⟨clock⟩ value supported by your video card.

There are two files included in the XFree86 distribution which may include ModeLine data for your monitor. These files are modeDB.txt and Monitors, both of which are found in /usr/X11R6/lib/X11/doc.

You should start with ModeLine values for the VESA standard monitor timings, which most monitors support. modeDB.txt includes timing values for VESA standard resolutions. In that file, you will see entries such as

```
# 640x480@60Hz Non-Interlaced mode
# Horizontal Sync = 31.5kHz
# Timing: H=(0.95us, 3.81us, 1.59us), V=(0.35ms, 0.064ms, 1.02ms)
#
# name      clock   horizontal timing      vertical timing      flags
  "640x480" 25.175  640  664  760  800     480  491  493  525
```

This is a VESA standard timing for a 640x480 video mode. It uses a dot clock of 25.175, which your video card must support to use this mode (more on this later). To include this entry in the XF86Config file, you'd use the line

```
ModeLine "640x480"  25.175   640 664 760 800   480 491 493 525
```

Note that the ⟨name⟩ argument to ModeLine (in this case "640x480") is an arbitrary string—the convention is to name the mode after the resolution, but ⟨name⟩ can technically be anything descriptive which describes the mode to you.

For each ModeLine used the server will check that the specifications for the mode fall within the range of values specified with Bandwidth, HorizSync and VertRefresh. If they do not, the server will complain when you attempt to start up X (more on this later). For one thing, the dot clock used by the mode should not be greater than the value used for Bandwidth. (However, in many cases it is safe to use modes with a slightly higher bandwidth than your monitor can support.)

If the VESA standard timings do not work for you (you'll know after trying to use them later) then the files modeDB.txt and Monitors include specific mode values for many monitor types. You can create ModeLine entries from the values found in those two files as well. Be sure to only use values for the specific model of monitor that you have. Note that many 14 and 15-inch monitors cannot support higher resolution modes, and often resolutions of 1024x768 at low dot clocks. This means that if you can't find high resolution modes for your monitor in these files, then your monitor probably does not support those resolution modes.

If you are completely at a loss, and can't find working ModeLine values for your monitor, you can follow the instructions in the VideoModes.doc file included in the XFree86 distribution to generate ModeLine values from the specifications listed in your monitor's manual. While your mileage will certainly vary when attempting to generate ModeLine values by hand, this is a good place to look if you can't find the values that you need. VideoModes.doc also describes the format of the ModeLine directive and other aspects of the XFree86 server in gory detail.

Lastly, if you do obtain ModeLine values which are almost, but not quite, right, then it may be possible to simply modify the values slightly to obtain the desired result. For example, if while running XFree86 the image on the monitor is shifted slightly, or seems to "roll", you can follow the instructions in the VideoModes.doc file to try to fix these values. Also, be sure to check the knobs and controls on the monitor itself! In many cases it is necessary to change the horizontal or vertical size of the display after starting up XFree86 in order for the image to be centered and be of the appropriate size. Having these controls on the front of the monitor can certainly make life easier.

◇   You shouldn't use monitor timing values or ModeLine values for monitors other than the model that you own. If you attempt to drive the monitor at a frequency for which it was not designed, you can damage or even destroy it.

The next section of the XF86Config file is Device, which specifies parameters for your video card. Here is an example.

```
Section "Device"
        Identifier "#9 GXE 64"

        # Nothing yet; we fill in these values later.
```

```
EndSection
```

This section defines properties for a particular video card. `Identifier` is an arbitrary string describing the card; you will use this string to refer to the card later.

Initially, you don't need to include anything in the `Device` section, except for `Identifier`. This is because we will be using the X server itself to probe for the properties of the video card, and entering them into the `Device` section later. The XFree86 server is capable of probing for the video chipset, clocks, RAMDAC, and amount of video RAM on the board.

Before we do this, however, we need to finish writing the `XF86Config` file. The next section is `Screen`, which specifies the monitor/video card combination to use for a particular server.

```
Section "Screen"
    Driver      "Accel"
    Device      "#9 GXE 64"
    Monitor     "CTX 5468 NI"
    Subsection "Display"
        Depth       16
        Modes       "1024x768" "800x600" "640x480"
        ViewPort    0 0
        Virtual     1024 768
    EndSubsection
EndSection
```

The `Driver` line specifies the X server that you will be using. The value values for `Driver` are:

- Accel: For the XF86_S3, XF86_Mach32, XF86_Mach8, XF86_8514, XF86_P9000, XF86_AGX, and XF86_W32 servers;

- SVGA: For the XF86_SVGA server;

- VGA16: For the XF86_VGA16 server;

- VGA2: For the XF86_Mono server;

- Mono: For the non-VGA monochrome drivers in the XF86_Mono and XF86_VGA16 servers.

You should be sure that /usr/X11R6/bin/X is a symbolic link to the server that you are using.

The `Device` line specifies the `Identifier` of the `Device` section corresponding to the video card to use for this server. Above, we created a `Device` section with the line

```
Identifier "#9 GXE 64"
```

Therefore, we use "#9 GXE 64" on the `Device` line here.

Similarly, the `Monitor` line specifies the name of the `Monitor` section to be used with this server. Here, "CTX 5468 NI" is the `Identifier` used in the `Monitor` section described above.

`Subsection "Display"` defines several properties of the XFree86 server corresponding to your monitor/video card combination. The `XF86Config` file describes all of these options in detail; most of them are icing on the cake and not necessary to get the system working.

The options that you should know about are:

- `Depth`. Defines the number of color planes—the number of bits per pixel. Usually, `Depth` is set to 8. For the `VGA16` server, you would use a depth of 4, and for the monochrome server a depth of 1. If you are using an accelerated video card with enough memory to support more bits per pixel, you can set `Depth` to 16, 24, or 32. If you have problems with depths higher than 8, set it back to 8 and attempt to debug the problem later.

- `Modes`. This is the list of video mode names which have been defined using the `ModeLine` directive in the `Monitor` section. In the above section, we used `ModeLines` named "1024x768", "800x600", and "640x48"0. Therefore, we use a `Modes` line of

      Modes   "1024x768" "800x600" "640x480"

  The first mode listed on this line will be the default when XFree86 starts up. After XFree86 is running, you can switch between the modes listed here using the keys `ctrl` `alt` `numeric +` and `ctrl` `alt` `numeric -` .

  It might be best, when initially configuring XFree86, to use lower resolution video modes, such as 640x480, which tend to work on most systems. Once you have the basic configuration working you can modify `XF86Config` to support higher resolutions.

- `Virtual`. Sets the virtual desktop size. XFree86 has the ability to use any additional memory on your video card to extend the size of your desktop. When you move the mouse pointer to the edge of the display, the desktop will scroll, bringing the additional space into view. Therefore, even if you are running at a lower video resolution such as 800x600, you can set `Virtual` to the total resolution which your video card can support (a 1-megabyte video card can support 1024x768 at a depth of 8 bits per pixel; a 2-megabyte card 1280x1024 at depth 8, or 1024x768 at depth 16). Of course, the entire area will not be visible at once, but it can still be used.

  The `Virtual` feature is a nice way to utilize the memory of your video card, but it is rather limited. If you want to use a true virtual desktop, we suggest using `fvwm`, or a similar window manager, instead. `fvwm` allows you to have rather large virtual desktops (implemented by hiding windows, and so forth, instead of actually storing the entire desktop in video memory at once). See the man pages for `fvwm` for more details about this; most Linux systems use `fvwm` by default.

- `ViewPort`. If you are using the `Virtual` option described above, `ViewPort` sets the coordinates of the upper-left-hand corner of the virtual desktop when XFree86 starts up. `Virtual 0 0` is often used; if this is unspecified then the desktop is centered on the virtual desktop display (which may be undesirable to you).

Many other options for this section exist; see the XF86Config man page for a complete description. In practice these other options are not necessary to get XFree86 initially working.

5.1.4   Filling in video card information

Your XF86Config file is now ready to go, with the exception of complete information on the video card. What we're going to do is use the X server to probe for the rest of this information, and fill it into XF86Config.

Instead of probing for this information with the X server, the XF86Config values for many cards are listed in the files modeDB.txt, AccelCards, and Devices. These files are all found in /usr/X11R6/lib/X11/doc. In addition, there are various README files for certain chipsets. You should look in these files for information on your video card, and use that information (the clock values, chipset type, and any options) in the XF86Config file. If any information is missing, you can probe for it as described here.

In these examples we will demonstrate configuration for a #9 GXE 64 video card, which uses the XF86_S3 chipset. This card happens to be the one which the author uses, but the discussion here applies to any video card.

The first thing to do is to determine the video chipset used on the card. Running SuperProbe (found in /usr/X11R6/bin) will tell you this information, but you need to know the chipset name as it is known to the X server.

To do this, run the command

```
X -showconfig
```

This will give the chipset names known to your X server. (The man pages for each X server list these as well.) For example, with the accelerated XF86_S3 server, we obtain:

```
XFree86 Version 3.1 / X Window System
(protocol Version 11, revision 0, vendor release 6000)
Operating System: Linux
Configured drivers:
  S3: accelerated server for S3 graphics adaptors (Patchlevel 0)
      mmio_928, s3_generic
```

The valid chipset names for this server are mmio_928 and s3_generic. The XF86_S3 man page describes these chipsets and which videocards use them. In the case of the #9 GXE 64 video card, mmio_928 is appropriate.

If you don't know which chipset to use, the X server can probe it for you. To do this, run the command

```
X -probeonly > /tmp/x.out 2>&1
```

if you use bash as your shell. If you use csh, try:

```
X -probeonly &> /tmp/x.out
```

You should run this command while the system is unloaded, that is, while no other activity is occurring on the system. This command will also probe for your video card dot clocks (as seen below), and system load can throw off this calculation.

The output from the above (in /tmp/x.out should contain lines such as the following:

```
XFree86 Version 3.1 / X Window System
(protocol Version 11, revision 0, vendor release 6000)
Operating System: Linux
Configured drivers:
  S3: accelerated server for S3 graphics adaptors (Patchlevel 0)
      mmio_928, s3_generic
```
Several lines deleted...
```
(--) S3: card type: 386/486 localbus
(--) S3: chipset:   864 rev. 0
(--) S3: chipset driver: mmio_928
```

Here, we see that the two valid chipsets for this server (in this case, XF86_S3) are mmio_928 and s3_generic. The server probed for and found a video card using the mmio_928 chipset.

In the Device section of the XF86Config file, add a Chipset line, containing the name of the chipset as determined above. For example,

```
Section "Device"
        # We already had Identifier here...
        Identifier "#9 GXE 64"
        # Add this line:
        Chipset "mmio_928"
EndSection
```

Now we need to determine the driving clock frequencies used by the video card. A driving clock frequency, or dot clock, is simply a rate at which the video card can send pixels to the monitor. As we have seen, each monitor resolution has a dot clock associated with it. Now we need to determine which dot clocks are made available by the video card.

First you should look into the files (modeDB.txt, and so forth) mentioned above and see if your card's clocks are listed there. The dot clocks will usually be a list of 8 or 16 values, all of which are in MHz. For example, when looking at modeDB.txt we see an entry for the Cardinal ET4000 video board, which looks like this:

```
# chip    ram    virtual   clocks                       default-mode  flags
ET4000   1024   1024 768    25  28  38  36  40  45  32  0  "1024x768"
```

As we can see, the dot clocks for this card are 25, 28, 38, 36, 40, 45, 32, and 0 MHz.

In the `Devices` section of the `XF86Config` file, you should add a `Clocks` line containing the list of dot clocks for your card. For example, for the clocks above, we would add the line

```
          Clocks 25 28 38 36 40 45 32 0
```

to the `Devices` section of the file, after `Chipset`. Note that the order of the clocks is important! Don't resort the list of clocks or remove duplicates.

If you cannot find the dot clocks associated with your card, the X server can probe for these as well. Using the `X -probeonly` command described above, the output should contain lines which look like the following:

```
  (--) S3: clocks:  25.18  28.32  38.02  36.15  40.33  45.32  32.00  00.00
```

We could then add a `Clocks` line containing all of these values, as printed. You can use more than one `Clocks` line in `XF86Config` should all of the values (sometimes there are more than 8 clock values printed) not fit onto one line. Again, be sure to keep the list of clocks in order as they are printed.

Be sure that there is no `Clocks` line (or that it is commented out) in the `Devices` section of the file when using `X -probeonly` to probe for the clocks. If there is a `Clocks` line present, the server will *not* probe for the clocks—it will use the values given in `XF86Config`.

Note that some accelerated video boards use a programmable clock chip. (See the `XF86_Accel` man page for details; this generally applies to S3, AGX, and XGA-2 boards.) This chip essentially allows the X server to tell the card which dot clocks to use. If this is the case, then you may not find a list of dot clocks for the card in any of the above files. Or, the list of dot clocks printed when using `X -probeonly` will only contain one or two discrete clock values, with the rest being duplicates or zero.

For boards which use a programmable clock chip, you would use a `ClockChip` line, instead of a `Clocks` line, in your `XF86Config` file. `ClockChip` gives the name of the clock chip as used by the video card; the man pages for each server describe what these are. For example, in the file `README.S3`, we see that several S3-864 video cards use an "ICD2061A" clock chip, and that we should use the line

```
          ClockChip "icd2061a"
```

instead of `Clocks` in the `XF86Config` file. As with `Clocks`, this line should go in the `Devices` section, after `Chipset`.

Similarly, some accelerated cards require you to specify the RAMDAC chip type in the XF86Config file, using a Ramdac line. The XF86_Accel man page describes this option. Usually, the X server will correctly probe for the RAMDAC.

Some video card types require you to specify several options in the Devices section of XF86Config. These options will be described in the man page for your server, as well as in the various files (such as README.cirrus or README.S3. These options are enabled using the Option line. For example, the #9 GXE 64 card requires two options:

```
        Option "number_nine"
        Option "dac_8_bit"
```

Usually, the X server will work without these options, but they are necessary to obtain the best performance. There are too many such options to list here, and they each depend on the particular video card being used. If you must use one of these options, fear not—the X server man pages and various files in /usr/X11R6/lib/X11/doc will tell you what they are.

So, when you're finished, you should end up with a Devices section which looks something like this:

```
    Section "Device"
        # Device section for the #9 GXE 64 only !
        Identifier "#9 GXE 64"
        Chipset "mmio_928"
        ClockChip "icd2061a"
        Option "number_nine"
        Option "dac_8_bit"
    EndSection
```

Most video cards will require a Clocks line, instead of ClockChip, as described above. The above Device entry is only valid for a particular video card, the #9 GXE 64. It is given here only as an example.

There are other options that you can include in the Devices entry. Check the X server man pages for the gritty details, but the above should suffice for most systems.

5.1.5 Running XFree86

With your XF86Config file configured, you're ready to fire up the X server and give it a spin. First, be sure that /usr/X11R6/bin is on your path.

The command to start up XFree86 is

```
startx
```

This is a front-end to `xinit` (in case you're used to using `xinit` on other UNIX systems).

This command will start the X server and run the commands found in the file `.xinitrc` in your home directory. `.xinitrc` is just a shell script containing X clients to run. If this file does not exist, the system default `/usr/X11R6/lib/X11/xinit/xinitrc` will be used.

A standard `.xinitrc` file looks like this:

```
#!/bin/sh

xterm -fn 7x13bold -geometry 80x32+10+50 &
xterm -fn 9x15bold -geometry 80x34+30-10 &
oclock -geometry 70x70-7+7 &
xsetroot -solid midnightblue &

exec twm
```

This script will start up two `xterm` clients, an `oclock`, and set the root window (background) color to `midnightblue`. It will then start up `twm`, the window manager. Note that `twm` is executed with the shell's `exec` statement; this causes the `xinit` process to be replaced with `twm`. Once the `twm` process exits, the X server will shut down. You can cause `twm` to exit by using the root menus: depress mouse button 1 on the desktop background—this will display a pop up menu which will allow you to `Exit Twm`.

Be sure that the last command in `.xinitrc` is started with `exec`, and that it is not placed into the background (no ampersand on the end of the line). Otherwise the X server will shut down as soon as it has started the clients in the `.xinitrc` file.

Alternately, you can exit X by pressing `ctrl`-`alt`-`backspace` in combination. This will kill the X server directly, exiting the window system.

The above is a very, very simple desktop configuration. Many wonderful programs and configurations are available with a bit of work on your `.xinitrc` file. For example, the `fvwm` window manager will provide a virtual desktop, and you can customize colors, fonts, window sizes and positions, and so forth to your heart's content. Although the X Window System might appear to be simplistic at first, it is extremely powerful once you customize it for yourself.

If you are new to the X Window System environment, we strongly suggest picking up a book such as *The X Window System: A User's Guide*. Using and configuring X is far too in-depth to cover here. See the man pages for `xterm`, `oclock`, and `twm` for clues on getting started.

5.1.6   Running into trouble

Often, something will not be quite right when you initially fire up the X server. This is almost always caused by a problem in your `XF86Config` file. Usually, the monitor timing values are off, or the video card dot clocks set incorrectly. If your display seems to roll, or the edges are fuzzy, this is a clear indication that the monitor timing values or dot clocks are wrong. Also be sure that you are correctly specifying your video card chipset, as well as other options for the `Device` section of `XF86Config`. Be absolutely certain that you are using the right X server and that `/usr/X11R6/bin/X` is a symbolic link to this server.

If all else fails, try to start X "bare"; that is, use a command such as:

```
X > /tmp/x.out 2>&1
```

You can then kill the X server (using the $\boxed{\texttt{ctrl}}$ $\boxed{\texttt{alt}}$ $\boxed{\texttt{backspace}}$ key combination) and examine the contents of `/tmp/x.out`. The X server will report any warnings or errors—for example, if your video card doesn't have a dot clock corresponding to a mode supported by your monitor.

The file `VideoModes.doc` included in the XFree86 distribution contains many hints for tweaking the values in your `XF86Config` file.

Remember that you can use $\boxed{\texttt{ctrl}}$ $\boxed{\texttt{alt}}$ $\boxed{\texttt{numeric +}}$ and $\boxed{\texttt{ctrl}}$ $\boxed{\texttt{alt}}$ $\boxed{\texttt{numeric -}}$ to switch between the video modes listed on the `Modes` line of the `Screen` section of `XF86Config`. If the highest resolution mode doesn't look right, try switching to lower resolutions. This will let you know, at least, that those parts of your X configuration are working correctly.

Also, check the vertical and horizontal size/hold knobs on your monitor. In many cases it is necessary to adjust these when starting up X. For example, if the display seems to be shifted slightly to one side, you can usually correct this using the monitor controls.

The USENET newsgroup `comp.windows.x.i386unix` is devoted to discussions about XFree86. It might be a good idea to watch that newsgroup for postings relating to your video configuration— you might run across someone with the same problems as your own.

5.2   Accessing MS-DOS Files

If, for some twisted and bizarre reason, you should have need to access files from MS-DOS, it's quite easily done under Linux.

If all you need is to copy a file to or from an MS-DOS floppy disk, the simplest way may be to use the `Mtools` software. The `Mtools` commands `mcd`, `mdir`, and `mcopy` all behave as their MS-DOS counterparts; they even allow you to specify MS-DOS-style drive and file names to work on. If you installed `Mtools`, there should be man pages available for these commands.

If you need to do more complex operations, like interactively editing files on an MS-DOS volume from Linux, you can mount an MS-DOS partition or floppy under Linux. This will allow you to access the files directly through the Linux filesystem. For example, if you have an MS-DOS floppy in `/dev/fd0`, the command

```
# mount -t msdos /dev/fd0 /mnt
```

will mount it under /mnt. See Section 4.6.2 for more information on mounting floppies.

You can also mount an MS-DOS partition of your hard drive for access under Linux. If you have an MS-DOS partition on /dev/hda1, the command

    # *mount -t msdos /dev/hda1 /mnt*

will mount it. Be sure to umount the partition when you're done using it. You can have your MS-DOS partitions automatically mounted at boot time if you include entries for them in /etc/fstab; see Section 4.8 for details. For example, the following line in /etc/fstab will mount an MS-DOS partition on /dev/hda1 on the directory /dos.

    /dev/hda1   /dos   msdos   defaults

Accessing MS-DOS files is one thing; running MS-DOS programs from Linux is another. There is an MS-DOS Emulator under development for Linux; it is widely available, and included with most distributions. It can be retrieved from a number of locations, including the various Linux FTP sites (see Appendix C for details). The MS-DOS Emulator is reportedly powerful enough to run a number of applications, including Wordperfect, from Linux. However, Linux and MS-DOS are vastly different operating systems. The power of any MS-DOS emulator under UNIX is somewhat limited.

In addition, work is underway on a Microsoft Windows emulator (called WINE) to run under X Windows. Watch the newsgroups and FTP sites for more information.

5.3   Networking with TCP/IP

Linux supports a full implementation of the TCP/IP (Transport Control Protocol/Internet Protocol) networking protocols. TCP/IP has become the most successful mechanism for networking computers worldwide. With Linux and an Ethernet card, you can network your machine to a local area network, or (with the proper network connections), to the Internet—the worldwide TCP/IP network.

Hooking up a small LAN of UNIX machines is easy. It simply requires an Ethernet controller in each machine and the appropriate Ethernet cables and other hardware. Or, if your business or university provides access to the Internet, you can easily add your Linux machine to this network.

The current implementation of TCP/IP and related protocols for Linux is called "NET-3". This has no relationship to the so-called NET-3 release of BSD UNIX; instead, "NET-3" in this context means the third implementation of TCP/IP for Linux.

Linux NET-3 also supports SLIP—Serial Line Internet Protocol. SLIP allows you to have dialup Internet access using a modem. If your business or university provides SLIP access, you can dial in to the SLIP server and put your machine on the Internet over the phone line. Alternately, if your Linux machine also has Ethernet access to the Internet, you can set up your Linux box as a SLIP server.

For complete information on setting up TCP/IP under Linux, we encourage you to read the Linux NET-3 HOWTO, available via anonymous FTP from `sunsite.unc.edu`. The NET-3 HOWTO is a complete guide to configuring TCP/IP, including Ethernet and SLIP connections, under Linux. The Linux Ethernet HOWTO is a related document that describes configuration of various Ethernet card drivers for Linux. The *Linux Network Administrator's Guide*, from the Linux Documentation Project, is also available. See Appendix A for more information on these documents.

Also of interest is the book *TCP/IP Network Administration*, by Craig Hunt. It contains complete information on using and configuring TCP/IP on UNIX systems.

5.3.1 Hardware Requirements

You can use Linux TCP/IP without any networking hardware at all—configuring "loopback" mode allows you to talk to yourself. This is necessary for some applications and games which use the "loopback" network device.

However, if you want to use Linux with an Ethernet TCP/IP network, you need a compatible Ethernet card. The following types are known to work: 3com 3c503, 3c503/16; Novell NE1000, NE2000; Western Digital WD8003, WD8013; Hewlett Packard HP27245, HP27247, HP27250.

The following clones are reported to work: WD-80x3 clones: LANNET LEC-45; NE2000 clones: Alta Combo, Artisoft LANtastic AE-2, Asante Etherpak 2001/2003, D-Link Ethernet II, LTC E-NET/16 P/N 8300-200-002, Network Solutions HE-203, SVEC 4 Dimension Ethernet, 4-Dimension FD0490 EtherBoard 16, and D-Link DE-600, SMC Elite 16.

See the Linux Ethernet HOWTO at

```
http://sunsite.unc.edu/LDP/HOWTO/Ethernet-HOWTO.html for a more
```

complete discussion of Linux Ethernet hardware compatibility.

Linux also supports SLIP and PPP, which allows you to use a modem to access the Internet over the phone line. In this case, you'll need a modem compatible with your SLIP/PPP server—most servers require a 14.4kbps or 28.8kbps V.32bis modem.

5.3.2 Configuring TCP/IP on your system

In this section we're going to discuss how to configure an Ethernet TCP/IP connection on your system. Note that this method should work for many systems, but certainly not all. This discussion should be enough to get you on the right path to configuring the network parameters of your machine, but there are numerous caveats and fine details not mentioned here. We direct you to the *Linux Network Administrators' Guide* and the NET-3-HOWTO for more information.[3]

---

[3]Some of this information is adapted from the NET-3-HOWTO

First of all, we assume that you have a Linux system that has the TCP/IP software installed. This includes basic clients such as `telnet` and `ftp`, system administration commands such as `ifconfig` and `route` (usually found in `/etc`), and networking configuration files (such as `/etc/hosts`). The other Linux-related networking documents described above explain how to go about installing the Linux networking software if you do not have it already.

We also assume that your kernel has been configured and compiled with TCP/IP support enabled. See Section 4.7 for information on compiling your kernel. To enable networking, you must answer "yes" to the appropriate questions during the `make config` step, and rebuild the kernel.

Once this has been done, you must modify a number of configuration files used by NET-3. For the most part this is a simple procedure. Unfortunately, however, there is wide disagreement between Linux distributions as to where the various TCP/IP configuration files and support programs should go. Much of the time, they can be found in `/etc`, but in other cases may be found in `/usr/etc`, `/usr/etc/inet`, or other bizarre locations. In the worst case you'll have to use the `find` command to locate the files on your system. Also note that not all distributions keep the NET-3 configuration files and software in the same location—they may be spread across several directories.

The following information applies primarily to Ethernet connections. If you're planning to use SLIP, read this section to understand the concepts, and follow the SLIP-specific instructions in the following section.

5.3.2.1 Your network configuration

Before you can configure TCP/IP, you need to determine the following information about your network setup. In most cases, your local network administrator can provide you with this information.

- IP address. This is the unique machine address in dotted-decimal format. An example is 128.253.153.54. Your network admins will provide you with this number.

  If you're only configuring loopback mode (i.e. no SLIP, no ethernet card, just TCP/IP connections to your own machine) then your IP address is 127.0.0.1.

- Your network mask ("netmask"). This is a dotted quad, similar to the IP address, which determines which portion of the IP address specifies the subnetwork number, and which portion specifies the host on that subnet. (If you're shaky on these TCP/IP networking terms, we suggest reading some introductory material on network administration.) The network mask is a pattern of bits, which when overlayed onto an address on your network, will tell you which subnet that address lives on. This is very important for routing, and if you find, for example, that you can happily talk to people outside your network, but not to some people within your network, there is a good chance that you have an incorrect mask specified.

  Your network administrators will have chosen the netmask when the network was designed, and therefore they should be able to supply you with the correct mask to use. Most networks are class C subnetworks which use 255.255.255.0 as their netmask. Other Class B networks use 255.255.0.0. The NET-3 code will automatically select a mask that assumes no subnetting as a default if you do not specify one.

This applies as well to the loopback port. Since the loopback port's address is always 127.0.0.1, the netmask for this port is always 255.0.0.0. You can either specify this explicitly or rely on the default mask.

- Your network address. This is your IP address masked bitwise-ANDed the netmask. For example, if your netmask is 255.255.255.0, and your IP address is 128.253.154.32, your network address is 128.253.154.0. With a netmask of 255.255.0.0, this would be 128.253.0.0.

If you're only using loopback, you don't have a network address.

- Your broadcast address. The broadcast address is used to broadcast packets to every machine on your subnet. Therefore, if the host number of machines on your subnet is given by the last byte of the IP address (netmask 255.255.255.0), your broadcast address will be your network address ORed with 0.0.0.255.

For example, if your IP address is 128.253.154.32, and your netmask is 255.255.255.0, your broadcast address is 128.253.154.255.

Note that for historical reasons, some networks are setup to use the network address as the broadcast address, if you have any doubt, check with your network administrators. (In many cases, it will suffice to duplicate the network configuration of other machines on your subnet, substituting your own IP address, of course.)

If you're only using loopback, you don't have a broadcast address.

- Your gateway address. This is the address of the machine which is your "gateway" to the outside world (i.e. machines not on your subnet). In many cases the gateway machine has an IP address identical to yours but with a ".1" as its host address; e.g., if your IP address is 128.253.154.32, your gateway might be 128.253.154.1. Your network admins will provide you with the IP address of your gateway.

In fact, you may have multiple gateways. A *gateway* is simply a machine that lives on two different networks (has IP addresses on different subnets), and routes packets between them. Many networks have a single gateway to "the outside world" (the network directly adjacent to your own), but in some cases you will have multiple gateways—one for each adjacent network.

If you're only using loopback, you don't have a gateway address. The same is true if your network is isolated from all others.

- Your nameserver address. Most machines on the net have a name server which translates hostnames into IP addresses for them. Your network admins will tell you the address of your name server. You can also run a server on your own machine by running named, in which case the nameserver address is 127.0.0.1. Unless you absolutely *must* run your own name server, we suggest using the one provided to you on the network (if any). Configuration of named is another issue altogether; our priority at this point is to get you talking to the network. You can deal with name resolution issues later.

If you're only using loopback, you don't have a nameserver address.

SLIP users: You may or may not require any of the above information, except for a nameserver address. When using SLIP, your IP address is usually determined in one of two ways: Either (a) you have a "static" IP address, which is the same every time you connect to the network, or (b) you have a "dynamic" IP address, which is allocated from a pool available addresses when you connect to the server. In the following section on SLIP configuration this is covered in more detail.

NET-3 supports full routing, multiple routes, subnetworking (at this stage on byte boundaries only), the whole nine yards. The above describes most basic TCP/IP configurations. Yours may be quite different: when in doubt, consult your local network gurus and check out the man pages for `route` and `ifconfig`. Configuring TCP/IP networks is very much beyond the scope of this book; the above should be enough to get most people started.

5.3.2.2   The networking `rc` files

`rc` files are systemwide configuration scripts executed at boot time by `init`, which start up all of the basic system daemons (such as `sendmail`, `cron`, etc.) and configure things such as the network parameters, system hostname, and so on. `rc` files are usually found in the directory `/etc/rc.d` but on other systems may be in `/etc`.

Here, we're going to describe the `rc` files used to configure TCP/IP. There are two of them: `rc.inet1` and `rc.inet2`. `rc.inet1` is used to configure the basic network parameters (such as IP addresses and routing information) and `rc.inet2` fires up the TCP/IP daemons (`telnetd`, `ftpd`, and so forth).

Many systems combine these two files into one, usually called `rc.inet` or `rc.net`. The names given to your `rc` files doesn't matter, as long as they perform the correct functions and are executed at boot time by `init`. To ensure this, you may need to edit `/etc/inittab` and uncomment lines to execute the appropriate `rc` file(s). In the worst case you will have to create the `rc.inet1` and `rc.inet2` files from scratch and add entries for them to `/etc/inittab`.

As we said, `rc.inet1` configures the basic network interface. This includes your IP and network address, and the routing table information for your network. The routing tables are used to route outgoing (and incoming) network datagrams to other machines. On most simple configurations, you have three routes: One for sending packets to your own machine, another for sending packets to other machines on your network, and another for sending packets to machines outside of your network (through the gateway machine). Two programs are used to configure these parameters: `ifconfig` and `route`. Both of these are usually found in `/etc`.

`ifconfig` is used for configuring the network device interface with the parameters that it requires to function, such as the IP address, network mask, broadcast address and the like. `route` is used to create and modify entries in the routing table.

For most configurations, an `rc.inet1` file that looks like the following should work. You will, of course, have to edit this for your own system. Do *not* use the sample IP and network addresses listed here for your own system; they correspond to an actual machine on the Internet.

```sh
#!/bin/sh
# This is /etc/rc.d/rc.inet1 -- Configure the TCP/IP interfaces

# First, configure the loopback device

HOSTNAME=`hostname`

/etc/ifconfig lo 127.0.0.1        # uses default netmask 255.0.0.0
/etc/route add 127.0.0.1          # a route to point to the loopback device

# Next, configure the ethernet device. If you're only using loopback or
# SLIP, comment out the rest of these lines.

# Edit for your setup.
IPADDR="128.253.154.32"           # REPLACE with YOUR IP address
NETMASK="255.255.255.0"           # REPLACE with YOUR netmask
NETWORK="128.253.154.0"           # REPLACE with YOUR network address
BROADCAST="128.253.154.255"       # REPLACE with YOUR broadcast address, if you
                                  # have one. If not, leave blank and edit below.
GATEWAY="128.253.154.1"           # REPLACE with YOUR gateway address!

/etc/ifconfig eth0 ${IPADDR} netmask ${NETMASK} broadcast ${BROADCAST}

# If you don't have a broadcast address, change the above line to just:
# /etc/ifconfig eth0 ${IPADDR} netmask ${NETMASK}

/etc/route add ${NETWORK}

# The following is only necessary if you have a gateway; that is, your
# network is connected to the outside world.
/etc/route add default gw ${GATEWAY} metric 1

# End of Ethernet Configuration
```

Again, you may have to tweak this file somewhat to get it to work. The above should be sufficient for the majority of simple network configurations, but certainly not all.

rc.inet2 starts up various servers used by the TCP/IP suite. The most important of these is inetd. inetd sits in the background and listens to various network ports. When a machine tries to make a connection to a certain port (for example, the incoming telnet port), inetd forks off a copy of the appropriate daemon for that port (in the case of the telnet port, inetd starts in.telnetd). This is simpler than running many separate, standalone daemons (e.g., individual copies of telnetd, ftpd, and so forth)—inetd starts up the daemons only when they are needed.

syslogd is the system logging daemon—it accumulates log messages from various applications
and stores them into log files based on the configuration information in /etc/syslogd.conf. routed
is a server used to maintain dynamic routing information. When your system attempts to send
packets to another network, it may require additional routing table entries in order to do so. routed
takes care of manipulating the routing table without the need for user intervention.

Our example rc.inet2, below, only starts up the bare minimum of servers. There are many
other servers as well—many of which have to do with NFS configuration. When attempting to
setup TCP/IP on your system, it's usually best to start with a minimal configuration and add more
complex pieces (such as NFS) when you have things working.

Note that in the below file, we assume that all of the network daemons are held in /etc. As
usual, edit this for your own configuration.

```
#! /bin/sh
# Sample /etc/rc.d/rc.inet2

# Start syslogd
if [ -f /etc/syslogd ]
then
      /etc/syslogd
fi

# Start inetd
if [ -f /etc/inetd ]
then
      /etc/inetd
fi

# Start routed
if [ -f /etc/routed ]
then
      /etc/routed -q
fi

# Done!
```

Among the various additional servers that you may want to start in rc.inet2 is named. named
is a name server—it is responsible for translating (local) IP addresses to names, and vice versa. If
you don't have a nameserver elsewhere on the network, or want to provide local machine names to
other machines in your domain, it may be necessary to run named. (For most configurations it is
not necessary, however.) named configuration is somewhat complex and requires planning; we refer
interested readers to a good book on TCP/IP network administration.

5.3.2.3 /etc/hosts

/etc/hosts contains a list of IP addresses and the hostnames that they correspond to. In general, /etc/hosts only contains entries for your local machine, and perhaps other "important" machines (such as your nameserver or gateway). Your local name server will provide address-to-name mappings for other machines on the network, transparently.

For example, if your machine is loomer.vpizza.com with the IP address 128.253.154.32, your /etc/hosts would look like:

```
127.0.0.1              localhost
128.253.154.32         loomer.vpizza.com loomer
```

If you're only using loopback, the only line in /etc/hosts should be for 127.0.0.1, with both localhost and your hostname after it.

5.3.2.4 /etc/networks

The /etc/networks file lists the names and addresses of your own, and other, networks. It is used by the route command, and allows you to specify a network by name, should you so desire.

Every network you wish to add a route to using the route command (generally called from rc.inet1—see above) *must* have an entry in /etc/networks.

As an example,

```
default 0.0.0.0 # default route     - mandatory
loopnet 127.0.0.0 # loopback network - mandatory
mynet 128.253.154.0 # Modify for your own network address
```

5.3.2.5 /etc/host.conf

This file is used to specify how your system will resolve hostnames. It should contain the two lines:

```
order hosts,bind
multi on
```

These lines tell the resolve libraries to first check the /etc/hosts file for any names to lookup, and then ask the nameserver (if one is present). The multi entry allows you to have multiple IP addresses for a given machine name in /etc/hosts.

5.3.2.6 /etc/resolv.conf

This file configures the name resolver, specifying the address of your name server (if any) and your domain name. Your domain name is your fully-qualified hostname (if you're a registered machine

on the Internet, for example), with the hostname chopped off. That is, if your full hostname is
`loomer.vpizza.com`, your domain name is just `vpizza.com`.

For example, if your machine is `goober.norelco.com`, and has a nameserver at the address
128.253.154.5, your `/etc/resolv.conf` would look like:

```
domain       norelco.com
nameserver   127.253.154.5
```

You can specify more than one nameserver—each must have a `nameserver` line of its own in
`resolv.conf`.

5.3.2.7   Setting your hostname

You should set your system hostname with the `hostname` command. This is usually called from
`/etc/rc` or `/etc/rc.local`; simply search your system `rc` files to determine where it is invoked.
For example, if your (full) hostname is `loomer.vpizza.com`, edit the appropriate `rc` file to execute
the command:

```
/bin/hostname loomer.vpizza.com
```

Note that the `hostname` executable may not be found in `/bin` on your system.

5.3.2.8   Trying it out

Once you have all of these files set up, you should be able to reboot your new kernel and attempt
to use the network. There are many places where things can go wrong, so it's a good idea to test
individual aspects of the network configuration (e.g., it's probably not a good idea to test your
network configuration by firing up Mosaic over a network-based X connection).

You can use the `netstat` command to display your routing tables; this is usually the source of
the most trouble. The `netstat` man page describes the exact syntax of this command in detail. In
order to test network connectivity, we suggest using a client such as `telnet` to connect to machines
both on your local subnetwork and external networks. This will help to narrow down the source
of the problem. (For example, if you're unable to connect to local machines, but can connect to
machines on other networks, more than likely there is a problem with your netmask and routing
table configuration). You can also invoke the `route` command directly (as `root`) to play with the
entries in your routing table.

You should also test network connectivity by specifying IP addresses directly, instead of hostnames. For example, if you have problems with the command

```
$ telnet shoop.vpizza.com
```

the cause may be incorrect nameserver configuration. Try using the actual IP address of the machine in question; if that works, then you know that your basic network setup is (more than likely) correct, and the problem lies in your specification of the name server address.

Debugging network configurations can be a difficult task, and we can't begin to cover it here. If you are unable to get help from a local guru we strongly suggest reading the *Linux Network Administrators' Guide* from the LDP.

5.3.3 SLIP Configuration

SLIP (Serial Line Internet Protocol) allows you to use TCP/IP over a serial line, be that a phone line, with a dialup modem, or a leased asynchronous line of some sort. Of course, to use SLIP you'll need access to a dial-in SLIP server in your area. Many universities and businesses provide SLIP access for a modest fee.

There are two major SLIP-related programs available—dip and slattach. Both of these programs are used to initiate a SLIP connection over a serial device. It is *necessary* to use one of these programs in order to enable SLIP—it will not suffice to dial up the SLIP server (with a communications program such as kermit) and issue ifconfig and route commands. This is because dip and slattach issue a special *ioctl()* system call to seize control of the serial device to be used as a SLIP interface.

dip can be used to dial up a SLIP server, do some handshaking to login to the server (exchanging your username and password, for example) and then initate the SLIP connection over the open serial line. slattach, on the other hand, does very little other than grab the serial device for use by SLIP. It is useful if you have a permanent line to your SLIP server and no modem dialup or handshaking is necessary to initiate the connection. Most dialup SLIP users should use dip, on the other hand.

dip can also be used to configure your Linux system as a SLIP server, where other machines can dial into your own and connect to the network through a secondary Ethernet connection on your machine. See the documentation and man pages for dip for more information on this procedure.

SLIP is quite unlike Ethernet, in that there are only two machines on the "network"—the SLIP host (that's you) and the SLIP server. For this reason, SLIP is often referred to as a "point-to-point" connection. A generalization of this idea, known as PPP (Point to Point Protocol) has also been implemented for Linux.

When you initiate a connection to a SLIP server, the SLIP server will give you an IP address based on (usually) one of two methods. Some SLIP servers allocate "static" IP addresses—in which case your IP address will be the same every time you connect to the server. However, many SLIP servers allocate IP addresses dynamically—in which case you receive a different IP address each time you connect. In general, the SLIP server will print the values of your IP and gateway addresses when you connect. dip is capable of reading these values from the output of the SLIP server login session and using them to configure the SLIP device.

Essentially, configuring a SLIP connection is just like configuring for loopback or ethernet. The main differences are discussed below. Read the previous section on configuring the basic TCP/IP files, and apply the changes described below.

5.3.3.1   Static IP address SLIP connections using dip

If you are using a static-allocation SLIP server, you may want to include entries for your IP address and hostname in /etc/hosts. Also, configure these files listed in the above section: rc.inet2, host.conf, and resolv.conf.

Also, configure rc.inet1, as described above. However, you only want to execute ifconfig and route commands for the loopback device. If you use dip to connect to the SLIP server, it will execute the appropriate ifconfig and route commands for the SLIP device for you. (If you're using slattach, on the other hand, you *will* need to include ifconfig/route commands in rc.inet1 for the SLIP device—see below.)

dip *should* configure your routing tables appropriately for the SLIP connection when you connect. In some cases, however, dip's behavior may not be correct for your configuration, and you'll have to run ifconfig or route commands by hand after connecting to the server with dip (this is most easily done from within a shell script that runs dip and immediately executes the appropriate configuration commands). Your gateway is, in most cases, the address of the SLIP server. You may know this address before hand, or the gateway address will be printed by the SLIP server when you connect. Your dip chat script (described below) can obtain this information from the SLIP server.

ifconfig may require use of the pointopoint argument, if dip doesn't configure the interface correctly. For example, if your SLIP server address is 128.253.154.2, and your IP address is 128.253.154.32, you may need to run the command

```
ifconfig sl0 128.253.154.32 pointopoint 128.253.154.2
```

as root, after connecting with dip. The man pages for ifconfig will come in handy.

Note that SLIP device names used with the ifconfig and route commands are sl0, sl1 and so on (as opposed to eth0, eth1, etc. for Ethernet devices).

In Section 5.3.4, below, we explain how to configure dip to connect to the SLIP server.

5.3.3.2   Static IP address SLIP connections using slattach

If you have a leased line or cable running directly to your SLIP server, then there is no need to use dip to initiate a connection. slattach can be used to configure the SLIP device instead.

In this case, your /etc/rc.inet1 file should look something like the following:

```
#!/bin/sh
IPADDR="128.253.154.32"          # Replace with your IP address
REMADDR="128.253.154.2" # Replace with your SLIP server address
```

```
# Modify the following for the appropriate serial device for the SLIP
# connection:
slattach -p cslip -s 19200 /dev/ttyS0
/etc/ifconfig sl0 $IPADDR pointopoint $REMADDR up
/etc/route add default gw $REMADDR
```

slattach allocates the first unallocated SLIP device (sl0, sl1, etc.) to the serial line specified.

Note that the first parameter to slattach is the SLIP protocol to use. At present the only valid values are slip and cslip. slip is regular SLIP, as you would expect, and cslip is SLIP with datagram header compression. In most cases you should use cslip; however, if you seem to be having problems with this, try slip.

If you have more than one SLIP interface then you will have routing considerations to make. You will have to decide what routes to add, and those decisions can only be made on the basis of the actual layout of your network connections. A book on TCP/IP network configuration, as well as the man pages to route, will be of use.

5.3.3.3 Dynamic IP address SLIP connections using dip

If your SLIP server allocates an IP address dynamically, then you certainly don't know your address in advance—therefore, you can't include an entry for it in /etc/hosts. (You should, however, include an entry for your host with the loopback address, 127.0.0.1.)

Many SLIP servers print your IP address (as well as the server's address) when you connect. For example, one type of SLIP server prints a string such as,

```
Your IP address is 128.253.154.44.
Server address is 128.253.154.2.
```

dip can capture these numbers from the output of the server and use them to configure the SLIP device.

See Section 5.3.3.1, above, for information on configuring your various TCP/IP files for use with SLIP. Below, we explain how to configure dip to connect to the SLIP server.

5.3.4 Using dip

dip can simplify the process of connecting to a SLIP server, logging in, and configuring the SLIP device. Unless you have a leased line running to your SLIP server, dip is the way to go.

To use dip, you'll need to write a "chat script" which contains a list of commands used to communicate with the SLIP server at login time. These commands can automatically send your username/password to the server, as well as get information on your IP address from the server.

Here is an example `dip` chat script, for use with a dynamic IP address server. For static servers, you will need to set the variables `$local` and `$remote` to the values of your local IP address and server IP address, respectively, at the top of the script. See the `dip` man page for details.

```
main:
  # Set Maximum Transfer Unit. This is the maximum size of packets
  # transmitted on the SLIP device. Many SLIP servers use either 1500 or
  # 1006; check with your network admins when in doubt.
  get $mtu 1500

  # Make the SLIP route the default route on your system.
  default

  # Set the desired serial port and speed.
  port cua03
  speed 38400

  # Reset the modem and terminal line. If this causes trouble for you,
  # comment it out.
  reset

  # Prepare for dialing. Replace the following with your
  # modem initialization string.
  send ATT&C1&D2\\N3&Q5%M3%C1N1W1L1S48=7\r
  wait OK 2
  if $errlvl != 0 goto error
  # Dial the SLIP server
  dial 2546000
  if $errlvl != 0 goto error
  wait CONNECT 60
  if $errlvl != 0 goto error

  # We are connected.  Login to the system.
login:
  sleep 3
  send \r\n\r\n
  # Wait for the login prompt
  wait login: 10
  if $errlvl != 0 goto error

  # Send your username
  send USERNAME\n

  # Wait for password prompt
  wait ord: 5
  if $errlvl != 0 goto error
```

```
     # Send password.
     send PASSWORD\n

     # Wait for SLIP server ready prompt
     wait annex: 30
     if $errlvl != 0 goto error

     # Send commands to SLIP server to initate connection.
     send slip\n
     wait Annex 30

     # Get the remote IP address from the SLIP server. The 'get...remote'
     # command reads text in the form xxx.xxx.xxx.xxx, and assigns it
     # to the variable given as the second argument (here, $remote).
     get $remote remote
     if $errlvl != 0 goto error
     wait Your 30

     # Get local IP address from SLIP server, assign to variable $local.
     get $local remote
     if $errlvl != 0 goto error

     # Fire up the SLIP connection
done:
     print CONNECTED to $remote at $rmtip
     print GATEWAY address $rmtip
     print LOCAL address $local
     mode SLIP
     goto exit
error:
     print SLIP to $remote failed.

   exit:
```

dip automatically executes ifconfig and route commands based on the values of the variables
$local and $remote. Here, those variables are assigned using the get...remote command, which
obtains text from the SLIP server and assigns it to the named variable.

If the ifconfig and route commands that dip runs for you don't work, you can either run the
correct commands in a shell script after executing dip, or modify the source for dip itself. Running
dip with the -v option will print debugging information while the connection is being set up, which
should help you to determine where things might be going awry.

Now, in order to run dip and open the SLIP connection, you can use a command such as:

```
/etc/dip/dip -v /etc/dip/mychat 2>&1
```

Where the various dip files, and the chat script (mychat.dip), are stored in /etc/dip.

The above discussion should be enough to get you well on your way to talking to the network, either via Ethernet or SLIP. Again, we strongly suggest looking into a book on TCP/IP network configuration, especially if your network has any special routing considerations, other than those mentioned here.

5.4   Networking with UUCP

UUCP (UNIX-to-UNIX Copy) is an older mechanism used to transfer information between UNIX systems. Using UUCP, UNIX systems dial each other up (using a modem) and transfer mail messages, news articles, files, and so on. If you don't have TCP/IP or SLIP access, you can use UUCP to communicate with the world. Most of the mail and news software (see Sections 5.5 and 5.6) can be configured to use UUCP to transfer information to other machines. In fact, if there is an Internet site nearby, you can arrange to have Internet mail sent to your Linux machine via UUCP from that site.

The *Linux Network Administrator's Guide* contains complete information on configuring and using UUCP under Linux. Also, the Linux UUCP HOWTO, available via anonymous FTP from sunsite.unc.edu, should be of help. Another source of information on UUCP is the book *Managing UUCP and USENET*, by Tim O'Reilly and Grace Todino. See Appendix A for more information.

5.5   Electronic Mail

Like most UNIX systems, Linux provides a number of software packages for using electronic mail. E-mail on your system can either be local (that is, you only mail other users on your system), or networked (that is, you mail, using either TCP/IP or UUCP, users on other machines on a network). E-mail software usually consists of two parts: a *mailer* and a *transport*. The mailer is the user-level software which is used to actually compose and read e-mail messages. Popular mailers include elm, tt pine, and mutt. The transport is the low-level software which actually takes care of delivering the mail, either locally or remotely. The user never sees the transport software; they only interact with the mailer. However, as the system administrator, it is important to understand the concepts behind the transport software and how to configure it.

The most popular transport software for Linux is Smail. This software is easy to configure, and is able to send both local and remote TCP/IP and UUCP e-mail. The more powerful sendmail transport is used on most UNIX systems, however, because of its complicated setup mechanism, many Linux systems don't use it.

The Linux Mail HOWTO gives more information on the available mail software for Linux and how to configure it on your system. If you plan to send mail remotely, you'll need to understand either TCP/IP or UUCP, depending on how your machine is networked (see Sections 5.3 and 5.4).

The UUCP and TCP/IP documents listed in Appendix A should be of help there.

Most of the Linux mail software can be retrieved via anonymous FTP from `sunsite.unc.edu` in the directory `/pub/Linux/system/mail`.

5.6   News and USENET

Linux also provides a number of facilities for managing electronic news. You may choose to set up a local news server on your system, which will allow users to post "articles" to various "newsgroups" on the system... a lively form of discussion. However, if you have access to a TCP/IP or UUCP network, then you will be able to participate in USENET—a worldwide network news service.

There are two parts to the news software—the *server* and the *client*. The news server is the software which controls the newsgroups and handles delivering articles to other machines (if you are on a network). The news client, or *newsreader*, is the software which connects to the server to allow users to read and post news.

There are several forms of news servers available for Linux. They all follow the same basic protocols and design. The two primary versions are "C News" and "INN". There are many types of newsreaders, as well, such as `slrn` and `tin`. The choice of newsreader is more or less a matter of taste; all newsreaders should work equally well with different versions of the server software. That is, the newsreader is independent of the server software, and vice versa.

If you only want to run news locally (that is, not as part of USENET), then you will need to run a server on your system, as well as install a newsreader for the users. The news server will store the articles in a directory such as `/usr/spool/news`, and the newsreader will be compiled to look in this directory for news articles.

If instead you wish to run news over the network, there are several options open to you. TCP/IP network-based news uses a protocol known as NNTP (Network News Transmission Protocol). NNTP allows a newsreader to read news over the network, on a remote machine. NNTP also allows news servers to send articles to each other over the network—this is the software upon which USENET is based. Most businesses and universities have one or more NNTP servers set up to handle all of the USENET news for that site. Every other machine at the site runs an NNTP-based newsreader to read and post news over the network via the NNTP server. This means that only the NNTP server actually stores the news articles on disk.

Here are some possible scenarios for news configuration.

- You run news locally. That is, you have no network connection, or no desire to run news over the network. In this case, you need to run C News or INN on your machine, and install a newsreader to read the news locally.

- You have access to a TCP/IP network and an NNTP server. If your organization has an NNTP news server set up, you can read and post news from your Linux machine by simply installing an NNTP-based newsreader. (Most newsreaders available can be configured to run locally or use NNTP). In this case, you do not need to install a news server or store news articles on your system. The newsreader will take care of reading and posting news over the network. Of course, you will need to have TCP/IP configured and have access to the network (see Section 5.3).

- You have access to a TCP/IP network but have no NNTP server. In this case, you can run an NNTP news server on your Linux system. You can install either a local or an NNTP-based newsreader, and the server will store news articles on your system. In addition, you can configure the server to communicate with other NNTP news servers to transfer news articles.

- You want to transfer news using UUCP. If you have UUCP access (see Section 5.4), you can participate in USENET as well. You will need to install a (local) news server and a news reader. In addition, you will need to configure your UUCP software to periodically transfer news articles to another nearby UUCP machine (known as your "news feed"). UUCP does not use NNTP to transfer news; simply, UUCP provides its own mechanism for transferring news articles.

Most of the "standard" news software (available via anonymous FTP from `ftp.uu.net` in the directory `/news`) will compile out-of-the box on Linux.

The LDP's *Linux Network Administrator's Guide* contains complete information on configuring news software for Linux. The book *Managing UUCP and Usenet*, by Tim O'Reilly and Grace Todino, is an excellent guide to setting up news software. Also of interest is the USENET document "How to become a USENET site," available from `ftp.uu.net`, in the directory `/usenet/news.announce.newusers`.

Appendix A

Sources of Linux Information

This appendix contains information on various sources of Linux information, such as online documents, books, and more. Many of these documents are available either in printed form, or electronically from the Internet or BBS systems. Many Linux distributions also include much of this documentation in the distribution itself, so after you have installed Linux these files may be present on your system.

A.1 Online Documents

These documents should be available on any of the Linux FTP archive sites (see Appendix C for a list). If you do not have direct access to FTP, you may be able to locate these documents on other online services (such as CompuServe, local BBS's, and so on). If you have access to Internet mail, you can use the `ftpmail` service to receive these docucments. See Appendix C for more information.

In particular, the following documents may be found on `sunsite.unc.edu` in the directory `/pub/Linux/docs`. Many sites mirror this directory; however, if you're unable to locate a mirror site near you, this is a good one to fall back on.

You can also access Linux files and documentation using `gopher`. Just point your `gopher` client to port 70 on `sunsite.unc.edu`, and follow the menus to the Linux archive. This is a good way to browse Linux documentation interactively.

The Linux Frequently Asked Questions List

> The Linux Frequently Asked Questions list, or "FAQ", is a list of common questions (and answers!) about Linux. This document is meant to provide a general source of information about Linux, common problems and solutions, and a list of other sources of information. Every new Linux user should read this document. It is available in a number of formats, including plain ASCII, PostScript, and Lout typesetter format. The Linux FAQ is maintained by Ian Jackson, `ijackson@nyx.cs.du.edu`.

The Linux META-FAQ

> The META-FAQ is a collection of "metaquestions" about Linux; that is, sources of information about the Linux system, and other general topics. It is a good starting place for the Internet user wishing to find more information about the system. It is maintained by Michael K. Johnson, `johnsonm@sunsite.unc.edu`.

The Linux INFO-SHEET

> The Linux INFO-SHEET is a technical introduction to the Linux system. It gives an overview of the system's features and available software, and also provides a list of other sources of Linux information. The format and content is similar in nature to the META-FAQ; incidentally, it is also maintained by Michael K. Johnson.

The Linux Software Map

> The Linux Software Map is a list of many applications available for Linux, where to get them, who maintains them, and so forth. It is far from complete—to compile a complete list of Linux software would be nearly impossible. However, it does include many of the most popular Linux software packages. If you can't find a particular application to suit your needs, the LSM is a good place to start. It is maintained by Lars Wirzenius, `lars.wirzenius@helsinki.fi`.

The Linux HOWTO Index

> The Linux HOWTOs are a collection of "how to" documents, each describing in detail a certain aspect of the Linux system. They are maintained by Matt Welsh, `mdw@sunsite.unc.edu`. The HOWTO Index lists the HOWTO documents which are available (several of which are listed below).

The Linux Installation HOWTO

> The Linux Installation HOWTO describes how to obtain and install a distribution of Linux, similar to the information presented in Chapter 2.

The Linux Distribution HOWTO

> This document is a list of Linux distributions available via mail order and anonymous FTP. It also includes information on other Linux-related goodies and services. Appendix B contains a list of Linux vendors, many of which are listed in the *Distribution HOWTO*.

The Linux XFree86 HOWTO

> This document describes how to install and configure the X Window System software for Linux. See the section "5.1" for more about the X Window System.

The Linux Mail, News, and UUCP HOWTOs

> These three HOWTO documents describe configuration and setup of electronic mail, news, and UUCP communications on a Linux system. Because these three subjects are often intertwined, you may wish to read all three of these HOWTOs together.

The Linux Hardware HOWTO

> This HOWTO contains an extensive list of hardware supported by Linux. While this list is far from complete, it should give you a general picture of which hardware devices should be supported by the system.

The Linux SCSI HOWTO

> The Linux SCSI HOWTO is a complete guide to configuration and usage of SCSI devices under Linux, such as hard drives, tape drives and CD-ROM.

The Linux NET-2-HOWTO

> The Linux NET-2-HOWTO describes installation, setup, and configuration of the "NET-2" TCP/IP software under Linux, including SLIP. If you want to use TCP/IP on your Linux system, this document is a must read.

The Linux Ethernet HOWTO

> Closely related to the NET-2-HOWTO, the Ethernet HOWTO describes the various Ethernet devices supported by Linux, and explains how to configure each of them for use by the Linux TCP/IP software.

The Linux Printing HOWTO

> This document describes how to configure printing software under Linux, such as lpr. Configuration of printers and printing software under UNIX can be very confusing at times; this document sheds some light on the subject.

Other online documents

> If you browse the docs subdirectory of any Linux FTP site, you'll see many other documents which are not listed here: A slew of FAQ's, interesting tidbits, and other important information. This miscellany is difficult to categorize here; if you don't see what you're looking for on the list above, just take a look at one of the Linux archive sites listed in Appendix C.

A.2 Linux Documentation Project Manuals

The Linux Documentation Project is working on developing a set of manuals and other documentation for Linux, including man pages. These manuals are in various stages of development, and any help revising and updating them is greatly appreciated. If you have questions about the LDP, please contact Matt Welsh (mdw@sunsite.unc.edu).

These books are available via anonymous FTP from a number of Linux archive sites, including sunsite.unc.edu in the directory /pub/Linux/docs/LDP. A number of commercial distributors are selling printed copies of these books; in the future, you may be able to find the LDP manuals on the shelves of your local bookstore.

Linux Installation and Getting Started, by Matt Welsh

> A new user's guide for Linux, covering everything the new user needs to know to get started. You happen to hold this book in your hands.

The Linux System Administrators' Guide, by Lars Wirzenius

> This is a complete guide to running and configuring a Linux system. There are many issues relating to systems administration which are specific to Linux, such as needs for supporting a user community, filesystem maintenance, backups, and more. This guide covers them all.

The Linux Network Administrators' Guide, by Olaf Kirch

> An extensive and complete guide to networking under Linux, including TCP/IP, UUCP, SLIP, and more. This book is a very good read; it contains a wealth of information on many subjects, clarifying the many confusing aspects of network configuration.

The Linux Kernel Hackers' Guide, by Michael Johnson

> The gritty details of kernel hacking and development under Linux. Linux is unique in that the complete kernel source is available. This book opens the doors to developers who wish to add or modify features within the kernel. This guide also contains comprehensive coverage of kernel concepts and conventions used by Linux.

A.3   Books and Other Published Works

Linux Journal is a monthly magazine for and about the Linux community, written and produced by a number of Linux developers and enthusiasts. It is distributed worldwide, and is an excellent way to keep in touch with the dynamics of the Linux world, especially if you don't have access to USENET news.

At the time of this writing, subscriptions to *Linux Journal* are US$19/year in the United States, US$24 in Canada, and US$29 elsewhere. To subscribe, or for more information, write to Linux Journal, PO Box 85867, Seattle, WA, 98145-1867, USA, or call +1 206 527-3385. Their FAX number is +1 206 527-2806, and e-mail address is `linux@ssc.com`. You can also find a *Linux Journal* FAQ and sample articles via anonymous FTP on `sunsite.unc.edu` in `/pub/Linux/docs/linux-journal`.

As we have said, not many books have been published dealing with Linux specifically. However, if you are new to the world of UNIX, or want more information than is presented here, we suggest that you take a look at the following books which are available.

A.3.1   Using UNIX

Title: *Learning the UNIX Operating System*

Author:	Grace Todino & John Strang
Publisher:	O'Reilly and Associates, 1987
ISBN:	0-937175-16-1, $9.00

A good introductory book on learning the UNIX operating system. Most of the information should be applicable to Linux as well. I suggest reading this book if you're new to UNIX and really want to get started with using your new system.

Title:	*Learning the* vi *Editor*
Author:	Linda Lamb
Publisher:	O'Reilly and Associates, 1990
ISBN:	0-937175-67-6, $21.95

This is a book about the vi editor, a powerful text editor found on every UNIX system in the world. It's often important to know and be able to use vi, because you won't always have access to a "real" editor such as Emacs.

A.3.2 Systems Administration

Title:	*Essential System Administration*
Author:	Æleen Frisch
Publisher:	O'Reilly and Associates, 1991
ISBN:	0-937175-80-3, $29.95

From the O'Reilly and Associates Catalog, "Like any other multi-user system, UNIX requires some care and feeding. *Essential System Administration* tells you how. This book strips away the myth and confusion surrounding this important topic and provides a compact, manageable introduction to the tasks faced by anyone responsible for a UNIX system." I couldn't have said it better myself.

Title:	*TCP/IP Network Administration*
Author:	Craig Hunt
Publisher:	O'Reilly and Associates, 1990
ISBN:	0-937175-82-X, $24.95

A complete guide to setting up and running a TCP/IP network. While this book is not Linux-specific, roughly 90% of it is applicable to Linux. Coupled with the Linux NET-2-

HOWTO and *Linux Network Administrator's Guide*, this is a great book discussing the concepts and technical details of managing TCP/IP.

Title: *Managing UUCP and Usenet*
Author: Tim O'Reilly and Grace Todino
Publisher: O'Reilly and Associates, 1991
ISBN: 0-937175-93-5, $24.95

This book covers how to install and configure UUCP networking software, including configuration for USENET news. If you're at all interested in using UUCP or accessing USENET news on your system, this book is a must-read.

A.3.3 The X Window System

Title: *The X Window System: A User's Guide*
Author: Niall Mansfield
Publisher: Addison-Wesley
ISBN: 0-201-51341-2, ??

A complete tutorial and reference guide to using the X Window System. If you installed X windows on your Linux system, and want to know how to get the most out of it, you should read this book. Unlike some windowing systems, a lot of the power provided by X is not obvious at first sight.

A.3.4 Programming

Title: *The C Programming Language*
Author: Brian Kernighan and Dennis Ritchie
Publisher: Prentice-Hall, 1988
ISBN: 0-13-110362-8, $25.00

This book is a must-have for anyone wishing to do C programming on a UNIX system. (Or any system, for that matter.) While this book is not obstensibly UNIX-specific, it is quite applicable to programming C under UNIX.

Title: *The Unix Programming Environment*
Author: Brian Kernighan and Bob Pike

Publisher: Prentice-Hall, 1984
ISBN: 0-13-937681-X, ??

An overview to programming under the UNIX system. Covers all of the tools of the trade; a good read to get acquainted with the somewhat amorphous UNIX programming world.

Title: *Advanced Programming in the UNIX Environment*
Author: W. Richard Stevens
Publisher: Addison-Wesley
ISBN: 0-201-56317-7, $50.00

This mighty tome contains everything that you need to know to program UNIX at the system level—file I/O, process control, interprocess communication, signals, terminal I/O, the works. This book focuses on various UNI standards, including POSIX.1, which Linux mostly adheres to.

A.3.5   Kernel Hacking

Title: *The Design of the UNIX Operating System*
Author: Maurice J. Bach
Publisher: Prentice-Hall, 1986
ISBN: 0-13-201799-7, ??

This book covers the algorithms and internals of the UNIX kernel. It is not specific to any particular kernel, although it does lean towards System V-isms. This is the best place to start if you want to understand the inner tickings of the Linux system.

Title: *The Magic Garden Explained*
Author: Berny Goodheart and James Cox
Publisher: Prentice-Hall, 1994
ISBN: 0-13-098138-9, ??

This book describes the System V R4 kernel in detail. Unlike Bach's book, which concentrates heavily on the algorithms which make the kernel tick, this book presents the SVR4 implementation on a more technical level. Although Linux and SVR4 are distant cousins, this book can give you much insight into the workings of an actual UNIX kernel implementation. This is also a very modern book on the UNIX kernel—published in 1994.

Appendix B

Linux Vendor List

This appendix lists contact information for a number of vendors which sell Linux on diskette, tape, and CD-ROM. Many of them provide Linux documentation, support, and other services as well. This is by no means a complete listing; if you purchased this book in printed form, it's very possible that the vendor or publishing company also provides Linux software and services.

The author makes no guarantee as to the accuracy of any of the information listed in this Appendix. This information is included here only as a service to readers, not as an advertisement for any particular organization.

Fintronic Linux Systems
1360 Willow Rd., Suite 205
Menlo Park, CA 94025 USA
Tel: +1 415 325-4474
Fax: +1 415 325-4908
linux@fintronic.com

InfoMagic, Inc.
PO Box 30370
Flagstaff, AZ 86003-0370 USA
Tel: +1 800 800-6613, +1 602 526-9565
Fax: +1 602 526-9573
Orders@InfoMagic.com

Lasermoon Ltd
2a Beaconsfield Road, Fareham,
Hants, England. PO16 0QB.
Tel: +44 (0) 329 826444.
Fax: +44 (0) 329 825936.
info@lasermoon.co.uk

Linux Journal
P.O. Box 85867
Seattle, WA 98145-1867 USA
Tel: +1 206 527-3385
Fax: +1 206 527-2806
linux@ssc.com

Linux Systems Labs
18300 Tara Drive
Clinton Twp, MI 48036 USA
Tel: +1 313 954-2829, +1 800 432-0556
Fax: +1 313 954-2806
info@lsl.com

Morse Telecommunication, Inc.
26 East Park Avenue, Suite 240
Long Beach, NY 11561 USA
Tel: +1 800 60-MORSE
Fax: +1 516 889-8665
Linux@morse.net

Nascent Technology
Linux from Nascent CDROM
P.O. Box 60669
Sunnyvale CA 94088-0669 USA
Tel: +1 408 737-9500
Fax: +1 408 241-9390
nascent@netcom.com

Red Hat Software
P.O. Box 4325
Chapel Hill, NC 27515 USA
Tel: +1 919 309-9560
redhat@redhat.com

SW Technology
251 West Renner Suite 229
Richardson, TX 75080 USA
Tel: +1 214 907-0871
swt@netcom.com

Takelap Systems Ltd.
The Reddings, Court Robin Lane,

Llangwm, Usk, Gwent, United Kingdom NP5 1ET.
Tel: +44 (0)291 650357
Fax: +44 (0)291 650500
info@ddrive.demon.co.uk

Trans-Ameritech Enterprises, Inc.
2342A Walsh Ave
Santa Clara, CA 95051 USA
Tel: +1 408 727-3883
roman@trans-ameritech.com

Unifix Software GmbH
Postfach 4918
D-38039 Braunschweig
Germany
Tel: +49 (0)531 515161
Fax: +49 (0)531 515162

Yggdrasil Computing, Incorporated
4880 Stevens Creek Blvd., Suite 205
San Jose, CA 95129-1034 USA
Tel: +1 800 261-6630, +1 408 261-6630
Fax: +1 408 261-6631
info@yggdrasil.com

Appendix C

FTP Tutorial and Site List

FTP ("File Transfer Protocol") is the set of programs that are used for transferring files between systems on the Internet. Most UNIX, VMS, and MS-DOS systems on the Internet have a program called `ftp` which you use to transfer these files, and if you have Internet access, the best way to download the Linux software is by using `ftp`. This appendix covers basic `ftp` usage—of course, there are many more functions and uses of `ftp` than are given here.

At the end of this appendix there is a listing of FTP sites where Linux software can be found. Also, if you don't have direct Internet access but are able to exchange electronic mail with the Internet, information on using the `ftpmail` service is included below.

If you're using an MS-DOS, UNIX, or VMS system to download files from the Internet, then `ftp` is a command-driven program. However, there are other implementations of `ftp` out there, such as the Macintosh version (called `Fetch`) with a nice menu-driven interface, which is quite self-explanatory. Even if you're not using the command-driven version of `ftp`, the information given here should help.

`ftp` can be used to both upload (send) or download (receive) files from other Internet sites. In most situations, you're going to be downloading software. On the Internet there are a large number of publicly-available **FTP archive sites**, machines which allow anyone to `ftp` to them and download free software. One such archive site is `sunsite.unc.edu`, which has a lot of Sun Microsystems software, and acts as one of the main Linux sites. In addition, FTP archive sites **mirror** software to each other—that is, software uploaded to one site will be automatically copied over to a number of other sites. So don't be surprised if you see the exact same files on many different archive sites.

C.1 Starting `ftp`

Note that in the example "screens" printed below I'm only showing the most important information, and what you see may differ. Also, commands in *italics* represent commands that you type;

everything else is screen output.

To start `ftp` and connect to a site, simply use the command

```
ftp ⟨hostname⟩
```

where ⟨*hostname*⟩ is the name of the site you are connecting to. For example, to connect to the mythical site `shoop.vpizza.com` we can use the command

```
ftp shoop.vpizza.com
```

C.2 Logging In

When `ftp` starts up we should see something like

```
Connected to shoop.vpizza.com.
220 Shoop.vpizza.com FTPD ready at 15 Dec 1992 08:20:42 EDT
Name (shoop.vpizza.com:mdw):
```

Here, `ftp` is asking us to give the username that we want to login as on `shoop.vpizza.com`. The default here is `mdw`, which is my username on the system I'm using FTP from. Since I don't have an account on `shoop.vpizza.com` I can't login as myself. Instead, to access publicly-available software on an FTP site you login as `anonymous`, and give your Internet e-mail address (if you have one) as the password. So, we would type

```
Name (shoop.vpizza.com:mdw): anonymous
331-Guest login ok, send e-mail address as password.
Password: mdw@sunsite.unc.edu
230- Welcome to shoop.vpizza.com.
230- Virtual Pizza Delivery[tm]:  Download pizza in 30 cycles or less
230- or you get it FREE!
ftp>
```

Of course, you should give your e-mail address, instead of mine, and it won't echo to the screen as you're typing it (since it's technically a "password"). `ftp` should allow us to login and we'll be ready to download software.

C.3 Poking Around

Okay, we're in. `ftp>` is our prompt, and the `ftp` program is waiting for commands. There are a few basic commands you need to know about. First, the commands ls ⟨file⟩

and

dir ⟨file⟩

both give file listings (where ⟨file⟩ is an optional argument specifying a particular filename to list). The difference is that ls usually gives a short listing and dir gives a longer listing (that is, with more information on the sizes of the files, dates of modification, and so on).

The command

cd ⟨directory⟩

will move to the given directory (just like the cd command on UNIX or MS-DOS systems). You can use the command

cdup

to change to the parent directory[1].

The command

help ⟨command⟩

will give help on the given ftp ⟨command⟩ (such as ls or cd). If no command is specified, ftp will list all of the available commands.

If we type dir at this point we'll see an initial directory listing of where we are.

```
ftp> dir
200 PORT command successful.
150 Opening ASCII mode data connection for /bin/ls.
total 1337

dr-xr-xr-x  2 root     wheel        512 Aug 13 13:55 bin
drwxr-xr-x  2 root     wheel        512 Aug 13 13:58 dev
drwxr-xr-x  2 root     wheel        512 Jan 25 17:35 etc
drwxr-xr-x 19 root     wheel       1024 Jan 27 21:39 pub
drwxrwx-wx  4 root     ftp-admi    1024 Feb  6 22:10 uploads
drwxr-xr-x  3 root     wheel        512 Mar 11  1992 usr

226 Transfer complete.
921 bytes received in 0.24 seconds (3.7 Kbytes/s)
ftp>
```

---
[1]The directory above the current one.

Each of these entries is a directory, not an individual file which we can download (specified by the d in the first column of the listing). On most FTP archive sites, the publicly available software is under the directory /pub, so let's go there.

```
ftp> cd pub
ftp> dir
200 PORT command successful.
150 ASCII data connection for /bin/ls (128.84.181.1,4525) (0 bytes).
total 846

-rw-r--r--   1 root     staff      1433 Jul 12  1988 README
-r--r--r--   1 3807     staff     15586 May 13  1991 US-DOMAIN.TXT.2
-rw-r--r--   1 539      staff     52664 Feb 20  1991 altenergy.avail
-r--r--r--   1 65534    65534     56456 Dec 17  1990 ataxx.tar.Z
-rw-r--r--   1 root     other   2013041 Jul  3  1991 gesyps.tar.Z
-rw-r--r--   1 432      staff     41831 Jan 30  1989 gnexe.arc
-rw-rw-rw-   1 615      staff     50315 Apr 16  1992 linpack.tar.Z
-r--r--r--   1 root     wheel     12168 Dec 25  1990 localtime.o
-rw-r--r--   1 root     staff      7035 Aug 27  1986 manualslist.tblms
drwxr-xr-x   2 2195     staff       512 Mar 10 00:48 mdw
-rw-r--r--   1 root     staff      5593 Jul 19  1988 t.out.h

226 ASCII Transfer complete.
2443 bytes received in 0.35 seconds (6.8 Kbytes/s)
ftp>
```

Here we can see a number of (interesting?) files, one of which is called README, which we should download (most FTP sites have a README file in the /pub directory).

C.4   Downloading files

Before downloading files, there are a few things that you need to take care of.

- **Turn on hash mark printing.** *Hash marks* are printed to the screen as files are being transferred; they let you know how far along the transfer is, and that your connection hasn't hung up (so you don't sit for 20 minutes, thinking that you're still downloading a file). In general, a hash mark appears as a pound sign (#), and one is printed for every 1024 or 8192 bytes transferred, depending on your system.

  To turn on hash mark printing, give the command hash.

  ```
  ftp> hash
  Hash mark printing on (8192 bytes/hash mark).
  ftp>
  ```

- **Determine the type of file which you are downloading.** As far as FTP is concerned, files come in two flavors: *binary* and *text*. Most of the files which you'll be downloading are binary files: that is, programs, compressed files, archive files, and so on. However, many files (such as READMEs and so on) are text files.

  Why does the file type matter? Only because on some systems (such as MS-DOS systems), certain characters in a text file, such as carriage returns, need to be converted so that the file will be readable. While transferring in binary mode, no conversion is done—the file is simply transferred byte after byte.

  The commands bin and ascii set the transfer mode to binary and text, respectively. *When in doubt, always use binary mode to transfer files.* If you try to transfer a binary file in text mode, you'll corrupt the file and it will be unusable. (This is one of the most common mistakes made when using FTP.) However, you can use text mode for plain text files (whose filenames often end in .txt).

  For our example, we're downloading the file README, which is most likely a text file, so we use the command

  ```
  ftp> ascii
  200 Type set to A.
  ftp>
  ```

- **Set your local directory.** Your *local directory* is the directory on your system where you want the downloaded files to end up. Whereas the cd command changes the remote directory (on the remote machine which you're FTPing to), the lcd command changes the local directory.

  For example, to set the local directory to **/home/db/mdw/tmp**, use the command

  ```
  ftp> lcd /home/db/mdw/tmp
  Local directory now /home/db/mdw/tmp
  ftp>
  ```

Now you're ready to actually download the file. The command

```
get ⟨remote-name⟩ ⟨local-name⟩
```

is used for this, where ⟨remote-name⟩ is the name of the file on the remote machine, and ⟨local-name⟩ is the name that you wish to give the file on your local machine. The ⟨local-name⟩ argument is optional; by default, the local filename is the same as the remote one. However, if for example you're downloading the file README, and you already have a README in your local directory, you'll want to give a different ⟨local-filename⟩ so that the first one isn't overwritten.

For our example, to download the file README, we simply use

```
ftp> get README
200 PORT command successful.
```

```
150 ASCII data connection for README (128.84.181.1,4527) (1433 bytes).
#
226 ASCII Transfer complete.
local:  README remote:  README
1493 bytes received in 0.03 seconds (49 Kbytes/s)
ftp>
```

C.5   Quitting FTP

To end your FTP session, simply use the command

    quit

The command

    close

can be used to close the connection with the current remote FTP site; the open command can then
be used to start a session with another site (without quitting the FTP program altogether).

    ftp> *close*
    221 Goodbye.
    ftp> *quit*

C.6   Using ftpmail

ftpmail is a service which allows you to obtain files from FTP archive sites via Internet electronic
mail. If you don't have direct Internet access, but are able to send mail to the Internet (from a
service such as CompuServe, for example), ftpmail is a good way to get files from FTP archive
sites. Unfortunately, ftpmail can be slow, especially when sending large jobs. Before attempting
to download large amounts of software using ftpmail, be sure that your mail spool will be able to
handle the incoming traffic. Many systems keep quotas on incoming electronic mail, and may delete
your account if your mail exceeds this quota. Just use common sense.

    sunsite.unc.edu, one of the major Linux FTP archive sites, is home to an ftpmail server. To
use this service, send electronic mail to

    ftpmail@sunsite.unc.edu

with a message body containing only the word:

    help

This will send you back a list of `ftpmail` commands and a brief tutorial on using the system.

For example, to get a listing of Linux files found on `sunsite.unc.edu`, send mail to the above address containing the text

```
open sunsite.unc.edu
cd /pub/Linux
dir
quit
```

You may use the `ftpmail` service to connect to any FTP archive site; you are not limited to `sunsite.unc.edu`. The next section lists a number of Linux FTP archives.

C.7   Linux FTP Site List

Table C.1 is a listing of the most well-known FTP archive sites which carry the Linux software. Keep in mind that many other sites mirror these, and more than likely you'll run into Linux on a number of sites not on this list.

Site name	IP Address	Directory
tsx-11.mit.edu	18.172.1.2	/pub/linux
sunsite.unc.edu	152.2.22.81	/pub/Linux
nic.funet.fi	128.214.6.100	/pub/OS/Linux
ftp.mcc.ac.uk	130.88.200.7	/pub/linux
fgb1.fgb.mw.tu-muenchen.de	129.187.200.1	/pub/linux
ftp.informatik.tu-muenchen.de	131.159.0.110	/pub/Linux
ftp.dfv.rwth-aachen.de	137.226.4.105	/pub/linux
ftp.informatik.rwth-aachen.de	137.226.112.172	/pub/Linux
ftp.ibp.fr	132.227.60.2	/pub/linux
kirk.bu.oz.au	131.244.1.1	/pub/OS/Linux
ftp.uu.net	137.39.1.9	/systems/unix/linux
wuarchive.wustl.edu	128.252.135.4	/systems/linux
ftp.win.tue.nl	131.155.70.100	/pub/linux
ftp.ibr.cs.tu-bs.de	134.169.34.15	/pub/os/linux
ftp.denet.dk	129.142.6.74	/pub/OS/linux

Table C.1: Linux FTP Sites

`tsx-11.mit.edu`, `sunsite.unc.edu`, and `nic.funet.fi` are the "home sites" for the Linux software, where most of the new software is uploaded. Most of the other sites on the list mirror some combination of these three. To reduce network traffic, choose a site that is geographically closest to you.

Appendix D

Linux BBS List

Printed here is a list of bulletin board systems (BBS) which carry Linux software. Zane Healy (`healyzh@holonet.net`) maintains this list. If you know of or run a BBS which provides Linux software which isn't on this list, you should get in touch with him.

The Linux community is no longer an Internet-only society. In fact, it is now estimated that the majority of Linux users don't have Internet access. Therefore, it is especially important that BBSs continue to provide and support Linux to users worldwide.

D.1 United States

Citrus Grove Public Access, 916-381-5822. ZyXEL 16.8/14.4 Sacramento, CA. Internet: `citrus.sac.ca.us`

Higher Powered BBS, 408-737-7040. ? CA. RIME ->HIGHER

hip-hop, 408-773-0768. 19.2k Sunnyvale, CA. USENET access

hip-hop, 408-773-0768. 38.4k Sunnyvale, CA.

Unix Online, 707-765-4631. 9600 Petaluma, CA. USENET access

The Outer Rim, 805-252-6342. Santa Clarita, CA.

Programmer's Exchange, 818-444-3507. El Monte, CA. Fidonet

Programmer's Exchange, 818-579-9711. El Monte, CA.

Micro Oasis, 510-895-5985. 14.4k San Leandro, CA.

Test Engineering, 916-928-0504. Sacramento, CA.

Slut Club, 813-975-2603. USR/DS 16.8k HST/14.4K Tampa, FL. Fidonet 1:377/42

Lost City Atlantis, 904-727-9334. 14.4k Jacksonville, FL. FidoNet

Aquired Knowledge, 305-720-3669. 14.4k v.32bis Ft. Lauderdale, FL. Internet, UUCP

The Computer Mechanic, 813-544-9345. 14.4k v.32bis St. Petersburg, FL. Fidonet, Sailnet, MXBBSnet

AVSync, 404-320-6202. Atlanta, GA.

Information Overload, 404-471-1549. 19.2k ZyXEL Atlanta, GA. Fidonet 1:133/308

Atlanta Radio Club, 404-850-0546. 9600 Atlanta, GA.

Rebel BBS, 208-887-3937. 9600 Boise, ID.

Rocky Mountain HUB, 208-232-3405. 38.4k Pocatello, ID. Fionet, SLNet, CinemaNet

EchoMania, 618-233-1659. 14.4k HST Belleville, IL. Fidonet 1:2250/1, f'req LINUX

UNIX USER, 708-879-8633. 14.4k Batavia, IL. USENET, Internet mail

PBS BBS, 309-663-7675. 2400 Bloomington, IL.

Third World, 217-356-9512. 9600 v.32 IL.

Digital Underground, 812-941-9427. 14.4k v.32bis IN. USENET

The OA Southern Star, 504-885-5928. New Orleans, LA. Fidonet 1:396/1

Channel One, 617-354-8873. Boston, MA. RIME ->CHANNEL

VWIS Linux Support BBS, 508-793-1570. 9600 Worcester, MA.

WayStar BBS, 508-481-7147. 14.4k V.32bis USR/HST Marlborough, MA. Fidonet 1:333/14

WayStar BBS, 508-481-7293. 14.4k V.32bis USR/HST Marlborough, MA. Fidonet 1:333/15

WayStar BBS, 508-480-8371. 9600 V.32bis or 14.4k USR/HST Marlborough, MA. Fidonet 1:333/16

Programmer's Center, 301-596-1180. 9600 Columbia, MD. RIME

Brodmann's Place, 301-843-5732. 14.4k Waldorf, MD. RIME ->BRODMANN, Fidonet

Main Frame, 301-654-2554. 9600 Gaithersburg, MD. RIME ->MAINFRAME

1 Zero Cybernet BBS, 301-589-4064. MD.

WaterDeep BBS, 410-614-2190. 9600 v.32 Baltimore, MD.

Harbor Heights BBS, 207-663-0391. 14.4k Boothbay Harbor, ME.

Part-Time BBS, 612-544-5552. 14.4k v.32bis Plymouth, MN.

The Sole Survivor, 314-846-2702. 14.4k v.32bis St. Louis, MO. WWIVnet, WWIVlink, etc

MAC's Place, 919-891-1111. 16.8k, DS modem Dunn, NC. RIME ->MAC

Digital Designs, 919-423-4216. 14.4k, 2400 Hope Mills, NC.

Flite Line, 402-421-2434. Lincoln, NE. RIME ->FLITE, DS modem

Legend, 402-438-2433. Lincoln, NE. DS modem

MegaByte Mansion, 402-551-8681. 14.4 V,32bis Omaha, NE.

Mycroft QNX, 201-858-3429. 14.4k NJ.

Steve Leon's, 201-886-8041. 14.4k Cliffside Park, NJ.

Dwight-Englewood BBS, 201-569-3543. 9600 v.42 Englewood, NJ. USENET

The Mothership Cnection, 908-940-1012. 38.4k Franklin Park, NJ.

The Laboratory, 212-927-4980. 16.8k HST, 14.4k v.32bis NY. FidoNet 1:278/707

Valhalla, 516-321-6819.   14.4k HST v.32 Babylon, NY. Fidonet (1:107/255), UseNet (die.linet.org)

Intermittent Connection, 503-344-9838. 14.4k HST v.32bis Eugene, OR. 1:152/35

Horizon Systems, 216-899-1086. USR v.32 Westlake, OH.

Horizon Systems, 216-899-1293. 2400 Westlake, OH.

Centre Programmers Unit, 814-353-0566. 14.4k V.32bis/HST Bellefonte, PA.

Allentown Technical, 215-432-5699. 9600 v.32/v.42bis Allentown, PA. WWIVNet 2578

Tactical-Operations, 814-861-7637. 14.4k V32bis/V42bis State College, PA. Fidonet 1:129/226,

`tac_ops.UUCP`
North Shore BBS, 713-251-9757. Houston, TX.
The Annex, 512-575-1188. 9600 HST TX. Fidonet 1:3802/217
The Annex, 512-575-0667. 2400 TX. Fidonet 1:3802/216
Walt Fairs, 713-947-9866. Houston, TX. FidoNet 1:106/18
CyberVille, 817-249-6261. 9600 TX. FidoNet 1:130/78
splat-ooh, 512-578-2720. 14.4k Victoria, TX.
splat-ooh, 512-578-5436. 14.4k Victoria, TX.
alaree, 512-575-5554. 14.4k Victoria, TX.
Ronin BBS, 214-938-2840. 14.4 HST/DS Waxahachie (Dallas), TX. RIME, Intelec, Smartnet, etc.
VTBBS, 703-231-7498. Blacksburg, VA.
MBT, 703-953-0640. Blacksburg, VA.
NOVA, 703-323-3321. 9600 Annandale, VA. Fidonet 1:109/305
Rem-Jem, 703-503-9410. 9600 Fairfax, VA.
Enlightend, 703-370-9528. 14.4k Alexandria, VA. Fidonet 1:109/615
My UnKnown BBS, 703-690-0669. 14.4k V.32bis VA. Fidonet 1:109/370
Georgia Peach BBS, 804-727-0399. 14.4k Newport News, VA.
Top Hat BBS, 206-244-9661. 14.4k WA. Fidonet 1:343/40
victrola.sea.wa.us, 206-838-7456. 19.2k Federal Way, WA. USENET

D.2 Outside of the United States

Galaktische Archive, 0043-2228303804. 16.8 ZYX Wien, Austria. Fidonet 2:310/77 (19:00-7:00)
Linux-Support-Oz, +61-2-418-8750. v.32bis 14.4k Sydney, NSW, Austrailia. Internet/Usenet, E-Mail/News
500cc Formula 1 BBS, +61-2-550-4317. V.32bis Sydney, NSW, Australia.
Magic BBS, 403-569-2882. 14.4k HST/Telebit/MNP Calgary, AB, Canada. Internet/Usenet
Logical Solutions, 299-9900 through 9911. 2400 AB, Canada.
Logical Solutions, 299-9912, 299-9913. 14.4k Canada.
Logical Solutions, 299-9914 through 9917. 16.8k v.32bis Canada.
V.A.L.I.S., 403-478-1281. 14.4k v.32bis Edmonton, AB, Canada. USENET
The Windsor Download, (519)-973-9330. v32bis 14.4 ON, Canada.
r-node, 416-249-5366. 2400 Toronto, ON, Canada. USENET
Synapse, 819-246-2344. 819-561-5268 Gatineau, QC, Canada. RIME->SYNAPSE
Radio Free Nyongwa, 514-524-0829. v.32bis ZyXEL Montreal, QC, Canada. USENET, Fidonet
DataComm1, +49.531.132-16. 14.4 HST Braunschweig, NDS, Germany. Fido 2:240/550, LinuxNet
DataComm2, +49.531.132-17. 14.4 HST Braunschweig, NDS, Germany. Fido 2:240/551, LinuxNet
Linux Server /Braukmann, +49.441.592-963. 16.8 ZYX Oldenburg, NDS, Germany. Fido

2:241/2012, LinuxNet

MM's Spielebox, +49.5323.3515. 14.4 ZYX Clausthal-Zfd., NDS, Germany. Fido 2:241/3420

MM's Spielebox, +49.5323.3516. 16.8 ZYX Clausthal-Zfd., NDS, Germany. Fido 2:241/3421

MM's Spielebox, +49.5323.3540. 9600 Clausthal-Zfd., NDS, Germany. Fido 2:241/3422

Bit-Company / J. Bartz, +49.5323.2539. 16.8 ZYX MO Clausthal-Zfd., NDS, Germany. Fido 2:241/3430

Fractal Zone BBS /Maass, +49.721.863-066. 16.8 ZYX Karlsruhe, BW, Germany. Fido 2:241/7462

Hipposoft /M. Junius, +49.241.875-090. 14.4 HST Aachen, NRW, Germany. Fido 2:242/6, 4:30-7,8-23:30

UB-HOFF /A. Hoffmann, +49.203.584-155. 19.2 ZYX+ Duisburg, Germany. Fido 2:242/37

FORMEL-Box, +49.4191.2846. 16.8 ZYX Kaltenkirchen, SHL, Germany. Fido 2:242/329, LinuxNet (6:00-20:00)

BOX/2, +49.89.601-96-77. 16.8 ZYX Muenchen, BAY, Germany. Fido 2:246/147, info magic: LINUX (22-24,0:30-2,5-8)

Die Box Passau 2+1, +49.851.555-96. 14.4 V32b Passau, BAY, Germany. Fido 2:246/200 (8:00-3:30)

Die Box Passau Line 1, +49.851.753-789. 16.8 ZYX Passau, BAY, Germany. Fido 2:246/2000 (8:00-3:30)

Die Box Passau Line 3, +49.851.732-73. 14.4 HST Passau, BAY, Germany. Fido 2:246/202 (5:00-3:30)

Die Box Passau ISDN, +49.851.950-464. 38.4/64k V.110/X.75 Passau, BAY, Germany. Fido 2:246/201 (8:00-24:00,1:00-3:30)

Public Domain Kiste, +49.30.686-62-50. 16.8 ZYX BLN, Germany. Fido 2:2403/17

CS-Port / C. Schmidt, +49.30.491-34-18. 19.2 Z19 Berlin, BLN, Germany. Fido 2:2403/13

BigBrother / R. Gmelch, +49.30.335-63-28. 16.8 Z16 Berlin, BLN, Germany. Fido 2:2403/36.4 (16-23:00)

CRYSTAL BBS, +49.7152.240-86. 14.4 HST Leonberg, BW, Germany. Fido 2:2407/3, LinuxNet

Echoblaster BBS #1, +49.7142.213-92. HST/V32b Bietigheim, BW, Germany. Fido 2:2407/4, LinuxNet (7-19,23-01h

Echoblaster BBS #2, +49.7142.212-35. V32b Bietigheim, BW, Germany. Fido 2:2407/40, LinuxNet (20h-6h)

LinuxServer / P. Berger, +49.711.756-275. 16.8 HST Stuttgart, BW, Germany. Fido 2:2407/34, LinuxNet (8:3-17:5,19-2)

Rising Sun BBS, +49.7147.3845. 16.8 ZYX Sachsenheim, BW, Germany. Fido 2:2407/41, LinuxNet (5:30-2:30)

bakunin.north.de,   +49.421.870-532.   14.4   D   2800 Bremen,   HB,   Germany. kraehe@bakunin.north.de

oytix.north.de, +49.421.396-57-62. ZYX HB, Germany. mike@oytix.north.de, login as gast

Fiffis Inn BBS, +49-89-5701353. 14.4-19.2 Munich, Germany. FidoNet 2:246/69,Internet,USENET,LinuxNet

The Field of Inverse Chaos, +358 0 506 1836. 14.4k v32bis/HST Helsinki, Finland. USENET;

ichaos.nullnet.fi

Modula BBS, +33-1 4043 0124. HST 14.4 v.32bis Paris, France.

Modula BBS, +33-1 4530 1248. HST 14.4 V.32bis Paris, France.

STDIN BBS, +33-72375139. v.32bis Lyon, Laurent Cas, France. FidoNet 2:323/8

Le Lien, +33-72089879. HST 14.4/V32bis Lyon, Pascal Valette, France. FidoNet 2:323/5

Basil, +33-1-44670844. v.32bis Paris, Laurent Chemla, France.

Cafard Naum, +33-51701632. v.32bis Nantes, Yann Dupont, France.

DUBBS, +353-1-6789000. 19.2 ZyXEL Dublin, Ireland. Fidonet 2:263/167

Galway Online, +353-91-27454. 14.4k v32b Galway, Ireland. RIME, @iol.ie

Nemesis' Dungeon, +353-1-324755 or 326900. 14.4k v32bis Dublin, Ireland. Fidonet 2:263/150

nonsolosoftware, +39 51 6140772. v.32bis, v.42bis Italy. Fidonet 2:332/407

nonsolosoftware, +39 51 432904. ZyXEL 19.2k Italy. Fidonet 2:332/417

Advanced Systems, +64-9-379-3365. ZyXEL 16.8k Auckland, New Zealand. Singet, INTLnet, Fidonet.

Thunderball Cave, 472567018. Norway. RIME ->CAVE

DownTown BBS Lelystad, +31-3200-48852. 14.4k Lelystad, Netherlands. Fido 2:512/155, UUCP

MUGNET Intl-Cistron BBS, +31-1720-42580. 38.4k Alphen a/d Rijn, Netherlands. UUCP

The Controversy, (65)560-6040. 14.4k V.32bis/HST Singapore. Fidonet 6:600/201

Pats System, +27-12-333-2049. 14.4k v.32bis/HST Pretoria, South Africa. Fidonet 5:71-1/36

Gunship BBS, +46-31-693306. 14.4k HST DS Gothenburg Sweden.

Baboon BBS, +41-62-511726. 19.2k Switzerland. Fido 2:301/580 and /581

The Purple Tentacle, +44-734-590990. HST/V32bis Reading, UK. Fidonet 2:252/305

A6 BBS, +44-582-460273. 14.4k Herts, UK. Fidonet 2:440/111

On the Beach, +444-273-600996. 14.4k/16.8k Brighton, UK. Fidonet 2:441/122

Appendix E

The GNU General Public License

Printed below is the GNU General Public License (the *GPL* or *copyleft*), under which Linux is licensed. It is reproduced here to clear up some of the confusion about Linux's copyright status—Linux is *not* shareware, and it is *not* in the public domain. The bulk of the Linux kernel is copyright ©1993 by Linus Torvalds, and other software and parts of the kernel are copyrighted by their authors. Thus, Linux *is* copyrighted, however, you may redistribute it under the terms of the GPL printed below.

GNU GENERAL PUBLIC LICENSE
Version 2, June 1991

Copyright ©1989, 1991 Free Software Foundation, Inc. 675 Mass Ave, Cambridge, MA 02139, USA Everyone is permitted to copy and distribute verbatim copies of this license document, but changing it is not allowed.

E.1 Preamble

The licenses for most software are designed to take away your freedom to share and change it. By contrast, the GNU General Public License is intended to guarantee your freedom to share and change free software–to make sure the software is free for all its users. This General Public License applies to most of the Free Software Foundation's software and to any other program whose authors commit to using it. (Some other Free Software Foundation software is covered by the GNU Library General Public License instead.) You can apply it to your programs, too.

When we speak of free software, we are referring to freedom, not price. Our General Public Licenses are designed to make sure that you have the freedom to distribute copies of free software (and charge for this service if you wish), that you receive source code or can get it if you want it, that you can change the software or use pieces of it in new free programs; and that you know you can do these things.

To protect your rights, we need to make restrictions that forbid anyone to deny you these rights or to ask you to surrender the rights. These restrictions translate to certain responsibilities for you if you distribute copies of the software, or if you modify it.

For example, if you distribute copies of such a program, whether gratis or for a fee, you must give the recipients all the rights that you have. You must make sure that they, too, receive or can get the source code. And you must show them these terms so they know their rights.

We protect your rights with two steps: (1) copyright the software, and (2) offer you this license which gives you legal permission to copy, distribute and/or modify the software.

Also, for each author's protection and ours, we want to make certain that everyone understands that there is no warranty for this free software. If the software is modified by someone else and passed on, we want its recipients to know that what they have is not the original, so that any problems introduced by others will not reflect on the original authors' reputations.

Finally, any free program is threatened constantly by software patents. We wish to avoid the danger that redistributors of a free program will individually obtain patent licenses, in effect making the program proprietary. To prevent this, we have made it clear that any patent must be licensed for everyone's free use or not licensed at all.

The precise terms and conditions for copying, distribution and modification follow.

E.2 Terms and Conditions for Copying, Distribution, and Modification

0. This License applies to any program or other work which contains a notice placed by the copyright holder saying it may be distributed under the terms of this General Public License. The "Program", below, refers to any such program or work, and a "work based on the Program" means either the Program or any derivative work under copyright law: that is to say, a work containing the Program or a portion of it, either verbatim or with modifications and/or translated into another language. (Hereinafter, translation is included without limitation in the term "modification".) Each licensee is addressed as "you".

   Activities other than copying, distribution and modification are not covered by this License; they are outside its scope. The act of running the Program is not restricted, and the output from the Program is covered only if its contents constitute a work based on the Program (independent of having been made by running the Program). Whether that is true depends on what the Program does.

1. You may copy and distribute verbatim copies of the Program's source code as you receive it, in any medium, provided that you conspicuously and appropriately publish on each copy an appropriate copyright notice and disclaimer of warranty; keep intact all the notices that refer to this License and to the absence of any warranty; and give any other recipients of the Program a copy of this License along with the Program.

You may charge a fee for the physical act of transferring a copy, and you may at your option offer warranty protection in exchange for a fee.

2. You may modify your copy or copies of the Program or any portion of it, thus forming a work based on the Program, and copy and distribute such modifications or work under the terms of Section 1 above, provided that you also meet all of these conditions:

   a. You must cause the modified files to carry prominent notices stating that you changed the files and the date of any change.

   b. You must cause any work that you distribute or publish, that in whole or in part contains or is derived from the Program or any part thereof, to be licensed as a whole at no charge to all third parties under the terms of this License.

   c. If the modified program normally reads commands interactively when run, you must cause it, when started running for such interactive use in the most ordinary way, to print or display an announcement including an appropriate copyright notice and a notice that there is no warranty (or else, saying that you provide a warranty) and that users may redistribute the program under these conditions, and telling the user how to view a copy of this License. (Exception: if the Program itself is interactive but does not normally print such an announcement, your work based on the Program is not required to print an announcement.)

These requirements apply to the modified work as a whole. If identifiable sections of that work are not derived from the Program, and can be reasonably considered independent and separate works in themselves, then this License, and its terms, do not apply to those sections when you distribute them as separate works. But when you distribute the same sections as part of a whole which is a work based on the Program, the distribution of the whole must be on the terms of this License, whose permissions for other licensees extend to the entire whole, and thus to each and every part regardless of who wrote it.

Thus, it is not the intent of this section to claim rights or contest your rights to work written entirely by you; rather, the intent is to exercise the right to control the distribution of derivative or collective works based on the Program.

In addition, mere aggregation of another work not based on the Program with the Program (or with a work based on the Program) on a volume of a storage or distribution medium does not bring the other work under the scope of this License.

3. You may copy and distribute the Program (or a work based on it, under Section 2) in object code or executable form under the terms of Sections 1 and 2 above provided that you also do one of the following:

   a. Accompany it with the complete corresponding machine-readable source code, which must be distributed under the terms of Sections 1 and 2 above on a medium customarily used for software interchange; or,

b. Accompany it with a written offer, valid for at least three years, to give any third party, for a charge no more than your cost of physically performing source distribution, a complete machine-readable copy of the corresponding source code, to be distributed under the terms of Sections 1 and 2 above on a medium customarily used for software interchange; or,

c. Accompany it with the information you received as to the offer to distribute corresponding source code. (This alternative is allowed only for noncommercial distribution and only if you received the program in object code or executable form with such an offer, in accord with Subsection b above.)

The source code for a work means the preferred form of the work for making modifications to it. For an executable work, complete source code means all the source code for all modules it contains, plus any associated interface definition files, plus the scripts used to control compilation and installation of the executable. However, as a special exception, the source code distributed need not include anything that is normally distributed (in either source or binary form) with the major components (compiler, kernel, and so on) of the operating system on which the executable runs, unless that component itself accompanies the executable.

If distribution of executable or object code is made by offering access to copy from a designated place, then offering equivalent access to copy the source code from the same place counts as distribution of the source code, even though third parties are not compelled to copy the source along with the object code.

4. You may not copy, modify, sublicense, or distribute the Program except as expressly provided under this License. Any attempt otherwise to copy, modify, sublicense or distribute the Program is void, and will automatically terminate your rights under this License. However, parties who have received copies, or rights, from you under this License will not have their licenses terminated so long as such parties remain in full compliance.

5. You are not required to accept this License, since you have not signed it. However, nothing else grants you permission to modify or distribute the Program or its derivative works. These actions are prohibited by law if you do not accept this License. Therefore, by modifying or distributing the Program (or any work based on the Program), you indicate your acceptance of this License to do so, and all its terms and conditions for copying, distributing or modifying the Program or works based on it.

6. Each time you redistribute the Program (or any work based on the Program), the recipient automatically receives a license from the original licensor to copy, distribute or modify the Program subject to these terms and conditions. You may not impose any further restrictions on the recipients' exercise of the rights granted herein. You are not responsible for enforcing compliance by third parties to this License.

7. If, as a consequence of a court judgment or allegation of patent infringement or for any other reason (not limited to patent issues), conditions are imposed on you (whether by court order, agreement or otherwise) that contradict the conditions of this License, they do not excuse you

from the conditions of this License. If you cannot distribute so as to satisfy simultaneously your obligations under this License and any other pertinent obligations, then as a consequence you may not distribute the Program at all. For example, if a patent license would not permit royalty-free redistribution of the Program by all those who receive copies directly or indirectly through you, then the only way you could satisfy both it and this License would be to refrain entirely from distribution of the Program.

If any portion of this section is held invalid or unenforceable under any particular circumstance, the balance of the section is intended to apply and the section as a whole is intended to apply in other circumstances.

It is not the purpose of this section to induce you to infringe any patents or other property right claims or to contest validity of any such claims; this section has the sole purpose of protecting the integrity of the free software distribution system, which is implemented by public license practices. Many people have made generous contributions to the wide range of software distributed through that system in reliance on consistent application of that system; it is up to the author/donor to decide if he or she is willing to distribute software through any other system and a licensee cannot impose that choice.

This section is intended to make thoroughly clear what is believed to be a consequence of the rest of this License.

8. If the distribution and/or use of the Program is restricted in certain countries either by patents or by copyrighted interfaces, the original copyright holder who places the Program under this License may add an explicit geographical distribution limitation excluding those countries, so that distribution is permitted only in or among countries not thus excluded. In such case, this License incorporates the limitation as if written in the body of this License.

9. The Free Software Foundation may publish revised and/or new versions of the General Public License from time to time. Such new versions will be similar in spirit to the present version, but may differ in detail to address new problems or concerns.

Each version is given a distinguishing version number. If the Program specifies a version number of this License which applies to it and "any later version", you have the option of following the terms and conditions either of that version or of any later version published by the Free Software Foundation. If the Program does not specify a version number of this License, you may choose any version ever published by the Free Software Foundation.

10. If you wish to incorporate parts of the Program into other free programs whose distribution conditions are different, write to the author to ask for permission. For software which is copyrighted by the Free Software Foundation, write to the Free Software Foundation; we sometimes make exceptions for this. Our decision will be guided by the two goals of preserving the free status of all derivatives of our free software and of promoting the sharing and reuse of software generally.

NO WARRANTY

11. BECAUSE THE PROGRAM IS LICENSED FREE OF CHARGE, THERE IS NO WAR-
RANTY FOR THE PROGRAM, TO THE EXTENT PERMITTED BY APPLICABLE
LAW. EXCEPT WHEN OTHERWISE STATED IN WRITING THE COPYRIGHT HOLD-
ERS AND/OR OTHER PARTIES PROVIDE THE PROGRAM "AS IS" WITHOUT WAR-
RANTY OF ANY KIND, EITHER EXPRESSED OR IMPLIED, INCLUDING, BUT NOT
LIMITED TO, THE IMPLIED WARRANTIES OF MERCHANTABILITY AND FITNESS
FOR A PARTICULAR PURPOSE. THE ENTIRE RISK AS TO THE QUALITY AND PER-
FORMANCE OF THE PROGRAM IS WITH YOU. SHOULD THE PROGRAM PROVE
DEFECTIVE, YOU ASSUME THE COST OF ALL NECESSARY SERVICING, REPAIR
OR CORRECTION.

12. IN NO EVENT UNLESS REQUIRED BY APPLICABLE LAW OR AGREED TO IN WRIT-
ING WILL ANY COPYRIGHT HOLDER, OR ANY OTHER PARTY WHO MAY MODIFY
AND/OR REDISTRIBUTE THE PROGRAM AS PERMITTED ABOVE, BE LIABLE TO
YOU FOR DAMAGES, INCLUDING ANY GENERAL, SPECIAL, INCIDENTAL OR CON-
SEQUENTIAL DAMAGES ARISING OUT OF THE USE OR INABILITY TO USE THE
PROGRAM (INCLUDING BUT NOT LIMITED TO LOSS OF DATA OR DATA BEING
RENDERED INACCURATE OR LOSSES SUSTAINED BY YOU OR THIRD PARTIES
OR A FAILURE OF THE PROGRAM TO OPERATE WITH ANY OTHER PROGRAMS),
EVEN IF SUCH HOLDER OR OTHER PARTY HAS BEEN ADVISED OF THE POSSI-
BILITY OF SUCH DAMAGES.

END OF TERMS AND CONDITIONS

E.3 Appendix: How to Apply These Terms to Your New Programs

If you develop a new program, and you want it to be of the greatest possible use to the public, the best way to achieve this is to make it free software which everyone can redistribute and change under these terms.

To do so, attach the following notices to the program. It is safest to attach them to the start of each source file to most effectively convey the exclusion of warranty; and each file should have at least the "copyright" line and a pointer to where the full notice is found.

⟨one line to give the program's name and a brief idea of what it does.⟩ Copyright ©19yy ⟨name of author⟩

This program is free software; you can redistribute it and/or modify it under the terms of the GNU General Public License as published by the Free Software Foundation; either version 2 of the License, or (at your option) any later version.

This program is distributed in the hope that it will be useful, but WITHOUT ANY WARRANTY; without even the implied warranty of MERCHANTABILITY or FIT-

NESS FOR A PARTICULAR PURPOSE. See the GNU General Public License for more details.

You should have received a copy of the GNU General Public License along with this program; if not, write to the Free Software Foundation, Inc., 675 Mass Ave, Cambridge, MA 02139, USA.

Also add information on how to contact you by electronic and paper mail.

If the program is interactive, make it output a short notice like this when it starts in an interactive mode:

```
Gnomovision version 69, Copyright (C) 19yy name of author Gnomovision comes with
ABSOLUTELY NO WARRANTY; for details type 'show w'.  This is free software, and
you are welcome to redistribute it under certain conditions; type 'show c' for
details.
```

The hypothetical commands 'show w' and 'show c' should show the appropriate parts of the General Public License. Of course, the commands you use may be called something other than 'show w' and 'show c'; they could even be mouse-clicks or menu items–whatever suits your program.

You should also get your employer (if you work as a programmer) or your school, if any, to sign a "copyright disclaimer" for the program, if necessary. Here is a sample; alter the names:

Yoyodyne, Inc., hereby disclaims all copyright interest in the program 'Gnomovision' (which makes passes at compilers) written by James Hacker.

⟨*signature of Ty Coon*⟩, 1 April 1989
Ty Coon, President of Vice

This General Public License does not permit incorporating your program into proprietary programs. If your program is a subroutine library, you may consider it more useful to permit linking proprietary applications with the library. If this is what you want to do, use the GNU Library General Public License instead of this License.

Linux System Administrators' Guide

Lars Wirzenius

This is version 0.6 of the Linux System Administrators' Guide.
Published November 15, 1997.

The LaTeX source code and other machine readable formats can be found on the Internet via anonymous ftp on `sunsite.unc.edu`, in the directory `/pub/Linux/docs/LDP`. Also available are at least Postscript and TeX .DVI formats. The official home page for the book is `http://www.iki.fi/liw/linux/sag/`. The current version can always be found at that location.

This page is dedicated to a future dedication.

In the mean time...I'd like someone who knows him let Terry Pratchett know that his way of using footnotes is rather inspiring.

This page is dedicated to a future dedication.

Chapter 1

Introduction

> *In the beginning, the file was without form, and void; and*
> *emptiness was upon the face of the bits. And the Fingers of*
> *the Author moved upon the face of the keyboard. And the Author*
> *said, Let there be words, and there were words.*

This manual, the Linux System Administrators' Guide, describes the system administration aspects of using Linux. It is intended for people who know next to nothing about system administration (as in "what is it?"), but who have already mastered at least the basics of normal usage. This manual also doesn't tell you how to install Linux; that is described in the Installation and Getting Started document. See below for more information about Linux manuals.

System administration is all the things that one has to do to keep a computer system in a useable shape. It includes things like backing up files (and restoring them if necessary), installing new programs, creating accounts for users (and deleting them when no longer needed), making certain that the filesystem is not corrupted, and so on. If a computer were, say, a house, system administration would be called maintenance, and would include cleaning, fixing broken windows, and other such things. System administration is not called maintenance, because that would be too simple.[1]

The structure of this manual is such that many of the chapters should be usable independently, so that if you need information about, say, backups, you can read just that chapter.[2] This hopefully makes the book easier to use as a reference manual, and

---

[1] There are some people who *do* call it that, but that's just because they have never read this manual, poor things.

[2] If you happen to be reading a version that has a chapter on backups, that is.

makes it possible to read just a small part when needed, instead of having to read everything. However, this manual is first and foremost a tutorial, and a reference manual only as a lucky coincidence.

This manual is not intended to be used completely by itself. Plenty of the rest of the Linux documentation is also important for system administrators. After all, a system administrator is just a user with special privileges and duties. A very important resource are the manual pages, which should always be consulted when a command is not familiar.

While this manual is targeted at Linux, a general principle has been that it should be useful with other UNIX based operating systems as well. Unfortunately, since there is so much variance between different versions of UNIX in general, and in system administration in particular, there is little hope to cover all variants. Even covering all possibilities for Linux is difficult, due to the nature of its development.

There is no one official Linux distribution, so different people have different setups, and many people have a setup they have built up themselves. This book is not targeted at any one distribution, even though I use the Debian GNU/Linux system almost exclusively. When possible, I have tried to point out differences, and explain several alternatives.

I have tried to describe how things work, rather than just listing "five easy steps" for each task. This means that there is much information here that is not necessary for everyone, but those parts are marked as such and can be skipped if you use a pre-configured system. Reading everything will, naturally, increase your understanding of the system and should make using and administering it more pleasant.

Like all other Linux related development, the work was done on a volunteer basis: I did it because I thought it might be fun and because I felt it should be done. However, like all volunteer work, there is a limit to how much effort I have been able to spend, and also on how much knowledge and experience I have. This means that the manual is not necessarily as good as it would be if a wizard had been paid handsomely to write it and had spent a few years to perfect it. I think, of course, that it is pretty nice, but be warned.

One particular point where I have cut corners is that I have not covered very thoroughly many things that are already well documented in other freely available manuals. This applies especially to program specific documentation, such as all the details of using mkfs). I only describe the purpose of the program, and as much of its usage as is necessary for the purposes of this manual. For further information, I refer the gentle reader to these other manuals. Usually, all of the referred to documentation is part of the full Linux documentation set.

While I have tried to make this manual as good as possible, I would really like to hear from you if you have any ideas on how to make it better. Bad language, factual errors, ideas for new areas to cover, rewritten sections, information about how various UNIX versions do things, I am interested in all of it. My contact information is available via the World Wide Web at `http://www.iki.fi/liw/mail-to-lasu.html`. You need to read this web page to bypass my junkmail filters.

Many people have helped me with this book, directly or indirectly. I would like to especially thank Matt Welsh for inspiration and LDP leadership, Andy Oram for getting me to work again with much-valued feedback, Olaf Kirch for showing me that it can be done, and Adam Richter at Yggdrasil and others for showing me that other people can find it interesting as well.

Stephen Tweedie, H. Peter Anvin, Rémy Card, Theodore Ts'o, and Stephen Tweedie have let me borrow their work[3] (and thus make the book look thicker and much more impressive). I am most grateful for this, and very apologetic for the earlier versions that sometimes lacked proper attribution.

In addition, I would like to thank Mark Komarinski for sending his material in 1993 and the many system administration columns in Linux Journal. They are quite informative and inspirational.

Many useful comments have been sent by a large number of people. My miniature black hole of an archive doesn't let me find all their names, but some of them are, in alphabetical order: Paul Caprioli, Ales Cepek, Marie-France Declerfayt, Dave Dobson, Olaf Flebbe, Helmut Geyer, Larry Greenfield and his father, Stephen Harris, Jyrki Havia, Jim Haynes, York Lam, Timothy Andrew Lister, Jim Lynch, Michael J. Micek, Jacob Navia, Dan Poirier, Daniel Quinlan, Jouni K Seppänen, Philippe Steindl, G.B. Stotte. My apologies to anyone I have forgotten.

Typographical conventions

Bold   Used to mark **new concepts**, **WARNINGS**, and **keywords** in a language.

italics   Used for *emphasis* in text, and occasionally for quotes or introductions

---

[3] A comparison between the xia and ext2 filesystems, the device list and a description of the ext2 filesystem. These aren't part of the book any more.

at the beginning of a section.

slanted   Used to mark **meta-variables** in the text, especially in representations
                   of the command line. For example,

```
ls -l foo
```

where *foo* would "stand for" a filename, such as `/bin/cp`.

Typewriter   Used to represent screen interaction, as in

```
$ ls -l /bin/cp
-rwxr-xr-x  1 root     wheel     12104 Sep 25 15:53 /bin/cp
```

Also used for code examples, whether it is C code, a shell script, or
something else, and to display general files, such as configuration files.
When necessary for clarity's sake, these examples or figures will be
enclosed in thin boxes.

Key   Represents a key to press. You will often see it in this form:

Press return to continue.

The Linux Documentation Project

The Linux Documentation Project, or LDP, is a loose team of writers, proofreaders,
and editors who are working together to provide complete documentation for the
Linux operating system. The overall coordinator of the project is Greg Hankins.

This manual is one in a set of several being distributed by the LDP, including a
Linux Users' Guide, System Administrators' Guide, Network Administrators' Guide,
and Kernel Hackers' Guide. These manuals are all available in LaTeX source format,
.dvi format, and postscript output by anonymous FTP from `sunsite.unc.edu`, in
the directory `/pub/Linux/docs/LDP`.

We encourage anyone with a penchant for writing or editing to join us in improving
Linux documentation. If you have Internet e-mail access, you can contact Greg
Hankins at `gregh@sunsite.unc.edu`.

The LDP Rhyme[4]

A wondrous thing,
and beautiful,
'tis to write,
a book.

I'd like to sing,
of the sweat,
the blood and tear,
which it also took.

It started back in,
nineteen-ninety-two,
when users whined,
"we can nothing do!"

They wanted to know,
what their problem was,
and how to fix it
(by yesterday).

We put the answers in,
a Linux f-a-q,
hoped to get away,
from any more writin'.

"That's too long,
it's hard to search,
and we don't read it,
any-which-way!"

Then a few of us,
joined together
(virtually, you know),
to start the LDP.

We started to write,
or plan, at least,
several books,
one for every need.

The start was fun,
a lot of talk,
an outline,
then a slew.

Then silence came,
the work began,
some wrote less,
others more.

A blank screen,
oh its horrible,
it sits there,
laughs in the face.

We still await,
the final day,
when everything,
will be done.

Until then,
all we have,
is a draft,
for you to comment on.

---

[4]The author wishes to remain anonymous. It was posted to the LDP mailing list by Matt Welsh.

Chapter 2

Overview of a Linux System

> *God looked over everything he had made,*
> *and saw that it was very good.*
> *Genesis 1:31*

This chapter gives an overview of a Linux system. First, the major services provided by the operating system are described. Then, the programs that implement these services are described with a considerable lack of detail. The purpose of this chapter is to give an understanding of the system as a whole, so that each part is described in detail elsewhere.

2.1   Various parts of an operating system

A UNIX operating system consists of a **kernel** and some **system programs**. There are also some **application programs** for doing work. The kernel is the heart of the operating system[1]. It keeps track of files on the disk, starts programs and runs them concurrently, assigns memory and other resources to various processes, receives packets from and sends packets to the network, and so on. The kernel does very little by itself, but it provides tools with which all services can be built. It also prevents anyone from accessing the hardware directly, forcing everyone to use the tools it provides. This way the kernel provides some protection for users from each other. The tools provided by the kernel are used via **system calls**; see manual page section 2 for more information on these.

---

[1]In fact, it is often mistakenly considered to be the operating system itself, but it is not. An operating system provides many more services than a plain kernel.

The system programs use the tools provided by the kernel to implement the various services required from an operating system. System programs, and all other programs, run 'on top of the kernel', in what is called the **user mode**. The difference between system and application programs is one of intent: applications are intended for getting useful things done (or for playing, if it happens to be a game), whereas system programs are needed to get the system working. A word processor is an application; `telnet` is a system program. The difference is often somewhat blurry, however, and is important only to compulsive categorizers.

An operating system can also contain compilers and their corresponding libraries (GCC and the C library in particular under Linux), although not all programming languages need be part of the operating system. Documentation, and sometimes even games, can also be part of it. Traditionally, the operating system has been defined by the contents of the installation tape or disks; with Linux it is not as clear since it is spread all over the FTP sites of the world.

2.2   Important parts of the kernel

The Linux kernel consists of several important parts: process management, memory management, hardware device drivers, filesystem drivers, network management, and various other bits and pieces. Figure 2.1 shows some of them.

Probably the most important parts of the kernel (nothing else works without them) are memory management and process management. Memory management takes care of assigning memory areas and swap space areas to processes, parts of the kernel, and for the buffer cache. Process management creates processes, and implements multitasking by switching the active process on the processor.

At the lowest level, the kernel contains a hardware device driver for each kind of hardware it supports. Since the world is full of different kinds of hardware, the number of hardware device drivers is large. There are often many otherwise similar pieces of hardware that differ in how they are controlled by software. The similarities make it possible to have general classes of drivers that support similar operations; each member of the class has the same interface to the rest of the kernel but differs in what it needs to do to implement them. For example, all disk drivers look alike to the rest of the kernel, i.e., they all have operations like 'initialize the drive', 'read sector N', and 'write sector N'.

Some software services provided by the kernel itself have similar properties, and can therefore be abstracted into classes. For example, the various network protocols

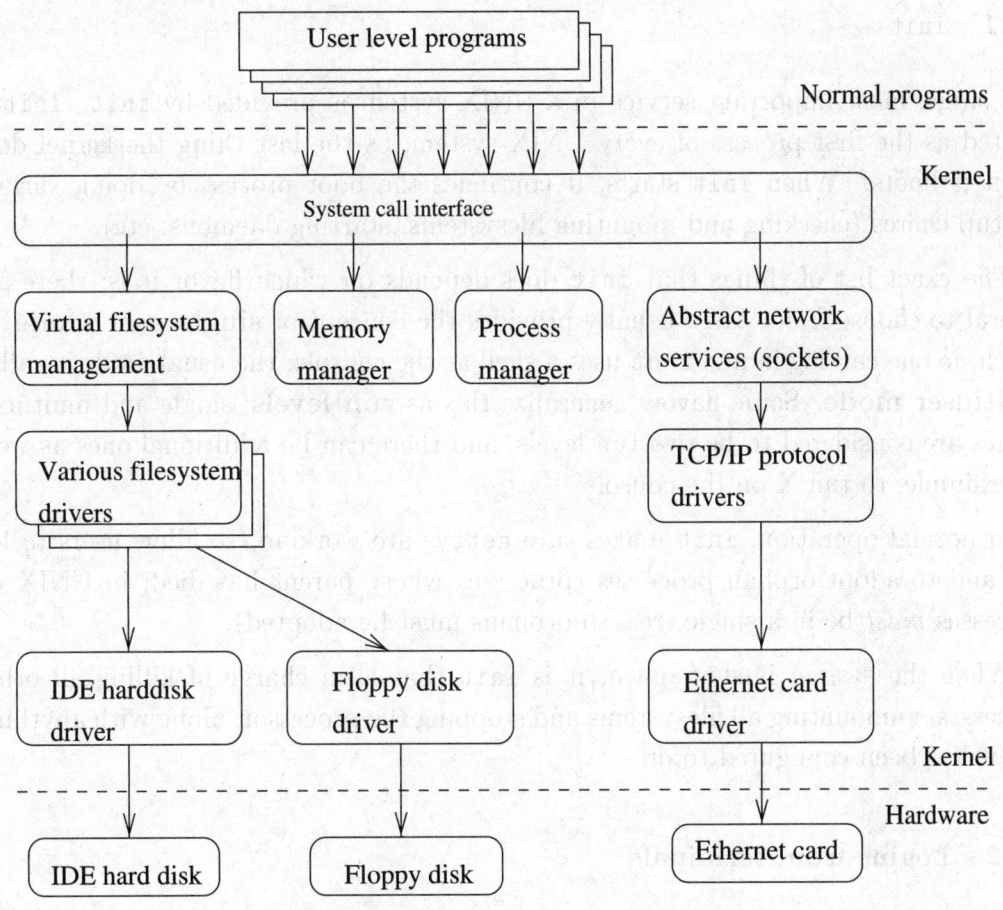

Figure 2.1: Some of the more important parts of the Linux kernel.

have been abstracted into one programming interface, the BSD socket library. Another example is the **virtual filesystem** (VFS) layer that abstracts the filesystem operations away from their implementation. Each filesystem type provides an implementation of each filesystem operation. When some entity tries to use a filesystem, the request goes via the VFS, which routes the request to the proper filesystem driver.

2.3 Major services in a UNIX system

This section describes some of the more important UNIX services, but without much detail. They are described more thoroughly in later chapters.

2.3.1   `init`

The single most important service in a UNIX system is provided by `init`. `init` is started as the first process of every UNIX system, as the last thing the kernel does when it boots. When `init` starts, it continues the boot process by doing various startup chores (checking and mounting filesystems, starting daemons, etc).

The exact list of things that `init` does depends on which flavor it is; there are several to choose from. `init` usually provides the concept of **single user mode**, in which no one can log in and `root` uses a shell at the console; the usual mode is called **multiuser mode**. Some flavors generalize this as **run levels**; single and multiuser modes are considered to be two run levels, and there can be additional ones as well, for example, to run X on the console.

In normal operation, `init` makes sure `gettys` are working (to allow users to log in), and to adopt orphan processes (processes whose parent has died; in UNIX *all* processes *must* be in a single tree, so orphans must be adopted).

When the system is shut down, it is `init` that is in charge of killing all other processes, unmounting all filesystems and stopping the processor, along with anything else it has been configured to do.

2.3.2   Logins from terminals

Logins from terminals (via serial lines) and the console (when not running X) are provided by the `getty` program. `init` starts a separate instance of `getty` for each terminal for which logins are to be allowed. `getty` reads the username and runs the `login` program, which reads the password. If the username and password are correct, `login` runs the shell. When the shell terminates, i.e., the user logs out, or when `login` terminated because the username and password didn't match, `init` notices this and starts a new instance of `getty`. The kernel has no notion of logins, this is all handled by the system programs.

2.3.3   Syslog

The kernel and many system programs produce error, warning, and other messages. It is often important that these messages can be viewed later, even much later, so they should be written to a file. The program doing this is `syslog`. It can be configured to sort the messages to different files according to writer or degree of importance. For example, kernel messages are often directed to a separate file from the others, since kernel messages are often more important and need to be read regularly to spot problems.

2.3.4 Periodic command execution: `cron` and `at`

Both users and system administrators often need to run commands periodically. For example, the system administrator might want to run a command to clean the directories with temporary files (`/tmp` and `/var/tmp`) from old files, to keep the disks from filling up, since not all programs clean up after themselves correctly.

The `cron` service is set up to do this. Each user has a `crontab`, where he lists the commands he wants to execute and the times they should be executed. The `cron` daemon takes care of starting the commands when specified.

The `at` service is similar to `cron`, but it is once only: the command is executed at the given time, but it is not repeated.

2.3.5 Graphical user interface

UNIX and Linux don't incorporate the user interface into the kernel; instead, they let it be implemented by user level programs. This applies for both text mode and graphical environments.

This arrangement makes the system more flexible, but has the disadvantage that it is simple to implement a different user interface for each program, making the system harder to learn.

The graphical environment primarily used with Linux is called the X Window System (X for short). X also does not implement a user interface; it only implements a window system, i.e., tools with which a graphical user interface can be implemented. The three most popular user interface styles implemented over X are Athena, Motif, and Open Look.

2.3.6 Networking

Networking is the act of connecting two or more computers so that they can communicate with each other. The actual methods of connecting and communicating are slightly complicated, but the end result is very useful.

UNIX operating systems have many networking features. Most basic services—filesystems, printing, backups, etc—can be done over the network. This can make system administration easier, since it allows centralized administration, while still reaping in the benefits of microcomputing and distributed computing, such as lower costs and better fault tolerance.

However, this book merely glances at networking; see the Linux Network Administrators' Guide for more information, including a basic description of how networks operate.

2.3.7   Network logins

Network logins work a little differently than normal logins. There is a separate physical serial line for each terminal via which it is possible to log in. For each person logging in via the network, there is a separate virtual network connection, and there can be any number of these[2]. It is therefore not possible to run a separate `getty` for each possible virtual connection. There are also several different ways to log in via a network, `telnet` and `rlogin` being the major ones in TCP/IP networks.

Network logins have, instead of a herd of `getty`s, a single daemon per way of logging in (`telnet` and `rlogin` have separate daemons) that listens for all incoming login attempts. When it notices one, it starts a new instance of itself to handle that single attempt; the original instance continues to listen for other attempts. The new instance works similarly to `getty`.

2.3.8   Network file systems

One of the more useful things that can be done with networking services is sharing files via a **network file system**. The one usually used is called the Network File System, or NFS, developed by Sun.

With a network file system any file operations done by a program on one machine are sent over the network to another computer. This fools the program to think that all the files on the other computer are actually on the computer the program is running on. This makes information sharing extremely simple, since it requires no modifications to programs.

---

[2]Well, at least there can be many. Network bandwidth still being a scarce resource, there is still some practical upper limit to the number of concurrent logins via one network connection.

2.3.9 Mail

Electronic mail is usually the most important method for communicating via computer. An electronic letter is stored in a file using a special format, and special mail programs are used to send and read the letters.

Each user has an **incoming mailbox** (a file in the special format), where all new mail is stored. When someone sends mail, the mail program locates the receiver's mailbox and appends the letter to the mailbox file. If the receiver's mailbox is in another machine, the letter is sent to the other machine, which delivers it to the mailbox as it best sees fit.

The mail system consists of many programs. The delivery of mail to local or remote mailboxes is done by one program (the **mail transfer agent** or **MTA**, e.g., `sendmail` or `smail`), while the programs users use are many and varied (**mail user agent** or **MUA**, e.g., `pine` or `elm`). The mailboxes are usually stored in `/var/spool/mail`.

2.3.10 Printing

Only one person can use a printer at one time, but it is uneconomical not to share printers between users. The printer is therefore managed by software that implements a **print queue**: all print jobs are put into a queue and whenever the printer is done with one job, the next one is sent to it automatically. This relieves the users from organizing the print queue and fighting over control of the printer.[3]

The print queue software also **spools** the printouts on disk, i.e., the text is kept in a file while the job is in the queue. This allows an application program to spit out the print jobs quickly to the print queue software; the application does not have to wait until the job is actually printed to continue. This is really convenient, since it allows one to print out one version, and not have to wait for it to be printed before one can make a completely revised new version.

2.4   The filesystem layout

The filesystem is divided into many parts; usually along the lines of a root filesystem with `/bin`, `/lib`, `/etc`, `/dev`, and a few others; a `/usr` filesystem with programs and unchanging data; a `/var` filesystem with changing data (such as log files); and a `/home`

---

[3]Instead, they form a new queue *at* the printer, waiting for their printouts, since no one ever seems to be able to get the queue software to know exactly when anyone's printout is really finished. This is a great boost to intra-office social relations.

filesystem for everyone's personal files. Depending on the hardware configuration and the decisions of the system administrator, the division can be different; it can even be all in one filesystem.

Chapter 3 describes the filesystem layout in some detail; the Linux Filesystem Standard covers it in somewhat more detail.

Chapter 3

Overview of the Directory Tree

> *Two days later, there was Pooh,*
> *sitting on his branch, dangling his*
> *legs, and there, beside him, were four*
> *pots of honey...*
> *(A.A. Milne)*

This chapter describes the important parts of a standard Linux directory tree, based on the FSSTND filesystem standard. It outlines the normal way of breaking the directory tree into separate filesystems with different purposes and gives the motivation behind this particular split. Some alternative ways of splitting are also described.

3.1 Background

This chapter is loosely based on the Linux filesystem standard, FSSTND, version 1.2 (see the bibliography, [?]), which attempts to set a standard for how the directory tree in a Linux system is organized. Such a standard has the advantage that it will be easier to write or port software for Linux, and to administer Linux machines, since everything will be in their usual places. There is no authority behind the standard that forces anyone to comply with it, but it has got the support of most, if not all, Linux distributions. It is not a good idea to break with the FSSTND without very compelling reasons. The FSSTND attempts to follow Unix tradition and current trends, making Linux systems familiar to those with experience with other Unix systems, and vice versa.

This chapter is not as detailed as the FSSTND. A system administrator should also read the FSSTND for a complete understanding.

This chapter does not explain all files in detail. The intention is not to describe every file, but to give an overview of the system from a filesystem point of view. Further information on each file is available elsewhere in this manual or the manual pages.

The full directory tree is intended to be breakable into smaller parts, each on its own disk or partition, to accomodate to disk size limits and to ease backup and other system administration. The major parts are the root, /usr, /var, and /home filesystems (see figure 3.1). Each part has a different purpose. The directory tree has been designed so that it works well in a network of Linux machines which may share some parts of the filesystems over a read-only device (e.g., a CD-ROM), or over the network with NFS.

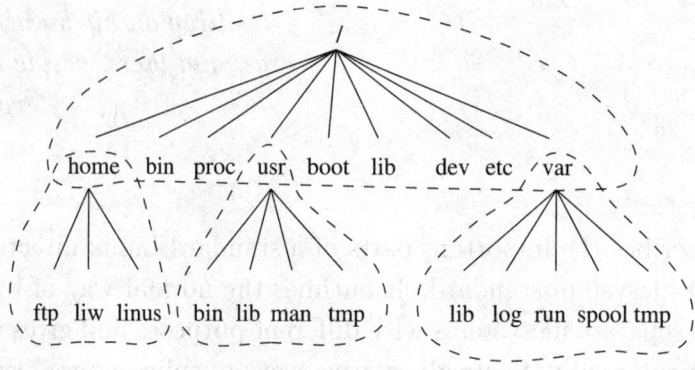

Figure 3.1: Parts of a Unix directory tree. Dashed lines indicate partition limits.

The roles of the different parts of the directory tree are described below.

- The root filesystem is specific for each machine (it is generally stored on a local disk, although it could be a ramdisk or network drive as well) and contains the files that are necessary for booting the system up, and to bring it up to such a state that the other filesystems may be mounted. The contents of the root filesystem will therefore be sufficient for the single user state. It will also contain tools for fixing a broken system, and for recovering lost files from backups.

- The /usr filesystem contains all commands, libraries, manual pages, and other unchanging files needed during normal operation. No files in /usr should be specific for any given machine, nor should they be modified during normal use. This allows the files to be shared over the network, which can be cost-effective since it saves disk space (there can easily be hundreds of megabytes in /usr), and can make administration easier (only the master /usr needs to be changed when updating an application, not each machine separately). Even if the filesystem is on a local disk, it could be mounted read-only, to lessen the chance of filesystem corruption during a crash.

- The /var filesystem contains files that change, such as spool directories (for mail, news, printers, etc), log files, formatted manual pages, and temporary files. Traditionally everything in /var has been somewhere below /usr, but that made it impossible to mount /usr read-only.

- The /home filesystem contains the users' home directories, i.e., all the real data on the system. Separating home directories to their own directory tree or filesystem makes backups easier; the other parts often do not have to be backed up, or at least not as often (they seldom change). A big /home might have to be broken on several filesystems, which requires adding an extra naming level below /home, e.g., /home/students and /home/staff.

Although the different parts have been called filesystems above, there is no requirement that they actually be on separate filesystems. They could easily be kept in a single one if the system is a small single-user system and the user wants to keep things simple. The directory tree might also be divided into filesystems differently, depending on how large the disks are, and how space is allocated for various purposes. The important part, though, is that all the standard *names* work; even if, say, /var and /usr are actually on the same partition, the names /usr/lib/libc.a and /var/adm/messages must work, for example by moving files below /var into /usr/var, and making /var a symlink to /usr/var.

The Unix filesystem structure groups files according to purpose, i.e., all commands are in one place, all data files in another, documentation in a third, and so on. An alternative would be to group files files according to the program they belong to, i.e., all Emacs files would be in one directory, all TeX in another, and so on. The problem with the latter approach is that it makes it difficult to share files (the program directory often contains both static and shareable and changing and non-shareable files), and sometimes to even find the files (e.g., manual pages in a huge number of places, and making the manual page programs find all of them is a maintenance nightmare).

3.2   The root filesystem

The root filesystem should generally be small, since it contains very critical files and a small, infrequently modified filesystem has a better chance of not getting corrupted. A corrupted root filesystem will generally mean that the system becomes unbootable except with special measures (e.g., from a floppy), so you don't want to risk it.

The root directory generally doesn't contain any files, except perhaps the standard boot image for the system, usually called /vmlinuz. All other files are in subdirectories in the root filesystems:

/bin   Commands needed during bootup that might be used by normal users (probably after bootup).

/sbin   Like /bin, but the commands are not intended for normal users, although they may use them if necessary and allowed.

/etc   Configuration files specific to the machine.

/root   The home directory for user root.

/lib   Shared libraries needed by the programs on the root filesystem.

/lib/modules Loadable kernel modules, especially those that are needed to boot the system when recovering from disasters (e.g., network and filesystem drivers).

/dev   Device files.

/tmp   Temporary files. Programs running after bootup should use /var/tmp, not /tmp, since the former is probably on a disk with more space.

/boot   Files used by the bootstrap loader, e.g., LILO. Kernel images are often kept here instead of in the root directory. If there are many kernel images, the directory can easily grow rather big, and it might be better to keep it in a separate filesystem. Another reason would be to make sure the kernel images are within the first 1024 cylinders of an IDE disk.

/mnt   Mount point for temporary mounts by the system administrator. Programs aren't supposed to mount on /mnt automatically. /mnt might be divided into subdirectories (e.g., /mnt/dosa might be the floppy drive

using an MS-DOS filesystem, and **/mnt/exta** might be the same with
an ext2 filesystem).

/proc, /usr, /var, /home Mount points for the other filesystems.

3.2.1 The /etc directory

The **/etc** directory contains a lot of files. Some of them are described below. For
others, you should determine which program they belong to and read the manual
page for that program. Many networking configuration files are in **/etc** as well, and
are described in the Networking Administrators' Guide.

/etc/rc or **/etc/rc.d** or **/etc/rc?.d** Scripts or directories of scripts to run at startup or when changing the run level. See the chapter on **init** for further
information.

/etc/passwd The user database, with fields giving the username, real name, home
directory, encrypted password, and other information about each user.
The format is documented in the *passwd* manual page.

/etc/fdprm Floppy disk parameter table. Describes what different floppy disk formats look like. Used by **setfdprm**. See the *setfdprm* manual page for
more information.

/etc/fstab Lists the filesystems mounted automatically at startup by the **mount**
-a command (in **/etc/rc** or equivalent startup file). Under Linux, also
contains information about swap areas used automatically by **swapon**
-a. See section 4.8.5 and the *mount* manual page for more information.

/etc/group Similar to **/etc/passwd**, but describes groups instead of users. See the
group manual page for more information.

/etc/inittab Configuration file for **init**.

/etc/issue Output by **getty** before the login prompt. Usually contains a short
description or welcoming message to the system. The contents are up
to the system administrator.

/etc/magic The configuration file for **file**. Contains the descriptions of various
file formats based on which **file** guesses the type of the file. See the
magic and *file* manual pages for more information.

/etc/motd   The **message of the day**, automatically output after a successful login. Contents are up to the system administrator. Often used for getting information to every user, such as warnings about planned downtimes.

/etc/mtab   List of currently mounted filesystems. Initially set up by the scripts, and updated automatically by the `mount` command. Used when a list of mounted filesystems is needed, e.g., by the `df` command.

/etc/shadow   Shadow password file on systems with shadow password software installed. The shadow password feature moved the encrypted password from /etc/passwd into /etc/shadow; the latter is not readable by anyone except `root`. This makes it harder to crack passwords.

/etc/login.defs   Configuration file for the `login` command.

/etc/printcap   Like /etc/termcap, but intended for printers. Different syntax.

/etc/profile, /etc/csh.login, /etc/csh.cshrc   Files executed at login or startup time by the Bourne or C shells. These allow the system administrator to set global defaults for all users. See the manual pages for the respective shells.

/etc/securetty   Identifies secure terminals, i.e., the terminals from which `root` is allowed to log in. Typically only the virtual consoles are listed, so that it becomes impossible (or at least harder) to gain superuser privileges by breaking into a system over a modem or a network.

/etc/shells   Lists trusted shells. The `chsh` command allows users to change their login shell only to shells listed in this file. `ftpd`, the server process that provides FTP services for a machine, will check that the user's shell is listed in /etc/shells and will not let people log in unles the shell is listed there.

/etc/termcap   The terminal capability database. Describes by what "escape sequences" various terminals can be controlled. Programs are written so that instead of directly outputting an escape sequence that only works on a particular brand of terminal, they look up the correct sequence to do whatever it is they want to do in /etc/termcap. As a result most programs work with most kinds of terminals. See the *termcap*, *curs_ termcap*, and *terminfo* manual pages for more information.

3.2.2 The /dev directory

The /dev directory contains the special device files for all the devices. The device files are named using special conventions; these are described in the Device list (see [?]). The device files are created during installation, and later with the /dev/MAKEDEV script. The /dev/MAKEDEV.local is a script written by the system administrator that creates local-only device files or links (i.e., those that are not part of the standard MAKEDEV, such as device files for some non-standard device driver).

3.3 The /usr filesystem

The /usr filesystem is often large, since all programs are installed there. All files in /usr usually come from a Linux distribution; locally installed programs and other stuff goes below /usr/local. This makes it possible to update the system from a new version of the distribution, or even a completely new distribution, without having to install all programs again. Some of the subdirectories of /usr are listed below (some of the less important directories have been dropped; see the FSSTND for more information).

/usr/X11R6   The X Window System, all files. To simplify the development and installation of X, the X files have not been integrated into the rest of the system. There is a directory tree below /usr/X11R6 similar to that below /usr itself.

/usr/X386   Similar to /usr/X11R6, but for X11 Release 5.

/usr/bin   Contains almost all user commands. Some user commands are in /bin or in /usr/local/bin.

/usr/sbin   System administration commands that are not needed on the root filesystem, e.g., most server programs.

/usr/man, /usr/info, /usr/doc   Manual pages, GNU Info documents, and miscellaneous other documentation files, respectively.

/usr/include   Header files for the C programming language. This should actually be below /usr/lib for consistency, but the tradition is overwhelmingly in support for this name.

/usr/lib   Unchanging data files for programs and subsystems, including some

site-wide configuration files. The name lib comes from library; originally libraries of programming subroutines were stored in /usr/lib.

/usr/local   The place for locally installed software and other files.

3.4   The /var filesystem

The /var contains data that is changed when the system is running normally. It is
specific for each system, i.e., not shared over the network with other computers.

/var/catman A cache for man pages that are formatted on demand. The source
for manual pages is usually stored in /usr/man/man*; some manual
pages might come with a pre-formatted version, which is stored in
/usr/man/cat*. Other manual pages need to be formatted when they
are first viewed; the formatted version is then stored in /var/man so
that the next person to view the same page won't have to wait for
it to be formatted. (/var/catman is often cleaned in the same way
temporary directories are cleaned.)

/var/lib   Files that change while the system is running normally.

/var/local Variable data for programs that are installed in /usr/local (i.e., programs that have been installed by the system administrator). Note that
even locally installed programs should use the other /var directories if
they are appropriate, e.g., /var/lock.

/var/lock   Lock files. Many programs follow a convention to create a lock file in
/var/lock to indicate that they are using a particular device or file.
Other programs will notice the lock file and won't attempt to use the
device or file.

/var/log   Log files from various programs, especially login (/var/log/wtmp,
which records all logins and logouts) and syslog (/var/log/messages,
where all kernel and system program message are usually stored). Files
in /var/log can often grow indefinitely, and may require cleaning at
regular intervals.

/var/run   Files that contain information about the system that is valid until the
system is next booted. For example, /var/run/utmp contains informa-

tion about people currently logged in.

/var/spool Directories for mail, news, printer queues, and other queued work. Each
            different spool has its own subdirectory below /var/spool, e.g., the
            mailboxes of the users are in /var/spool/mail.

/var/tmp   Temporary files that are large or that need to exist for a longer time
            than what is allowed for /tmp. (Although the system administrator
            might not allow very old files in /var/tmp either.)

3.5 The /proc filesystem

The /proc filesystem contains a illusionary filesystem. It does not exist on a disk.
Instead, the kernel creates it in memory. It is used to provide information about the
system (originally about processes, hence the name). Some of the more important
files and directories are explained below. The /proc filesystem is described in more
detail in the *proc* manual page.

/proc/1   A directory with information about process number 1. Each process has
                a directory below /proc with the name being its process identification
                number.

/proc/cpuinfo   Information about the processor, such as its type, make, model, and
                perfomance.

/proc/devices   List of device drivers configured into the currently running kernel.

/proc/dma   Shows which DMA channels are being used at the moment.

/proc/filesystems Filesystems configured into the kernel.

/proc/interrupts Shows which interrupts are in use, and how many of each there
                  have been.

/proc/ioports   Which I/O ports are in use at the moment.

/proc/kcore   An image of the physical memory of the system. This is exactly the
                same size as your physical memory, but does not really take up that
                much memory; it is generated on the fly as programs access it. (Re-
                member: unless you copy it elsewhere, nothing under /proc takes up

any disk space at all.)

/proc/kmsg Messages output by the kernel. These are also routed to syslog.

/proc/ksyms Symbol table for the kernel.

/proc/loadavg The 'load average' of the system; three meaningless indicators of how much work the system has to do at the moment.

/proc/meminfo Information about memory usage, both physical and swap.

/proc/modules Which kernel modules are loaded at the moment.

/proc/net Status information about network protocols.

/proc/self A symbolic link to the process directory of the program that is looking at /proc. When two processes look at /proc, they get different links. This is mainly a convenience to make it easier for programs to get at their process directory.

/proc/stat Various statistics about the system, such as the number of page faults since the system was booted.

/proc/uptime The time the system has been up.

/proc/version The kernel version.

Note that while the above files tend to be easily readable text files, they can sometimes be formatted in a way that is not easily digestable. There are many commands that do little more than read the above files and format them for easier understanding. For example, the free program reads /proc/meminfo and converts the amounts given in bytes to kilobytes (and adds a little more information, as well).

Chapter 4

Using Disks and Other Storage Media

On a clear disk you can seek forever.

When you install or upgrade your system, you need to do a fair amount of work on your disks. You have to make filesystems on your disks so that files can be stored on them and reserve space for the different parts of your system.

This chapter explains all these initial activities. Usually, once you get your system set up, you won't have to go through the work again, except for using floppies. You'll need to come back to this chapter if you add a new disk or want to fine-tune your disk usage.

The basic tasks in administering disks are:

- Format your disk. This does various things to prepare it for use, such as checking for bad sectors. (Formatting is nowadays not necessary for most hard disks.)

- Partition a hard disk, if you want to use it for several activities that aren't supposed to interfere with one another. One reason for partitioning is to store different operating systems on the same disk. Another reason is to keep user files separate from system files, which simplifies back-ups and helps protect the system files from corruption.

- Make a filesystem (of a suitable type) on each disk or partition. The disk means nothing to Linux until you make a filesystem; then files can be created and accessed on it.

- Mount different filesystems to form a single tree structure, either automatically,

245

or manually as needed. (Manually mounted filesystems usually need to be un-mounted manually as well.)

Chapter 5 contains information about virtual memory and disk caching, of which you also need to be aware when using disks.

This chapter explains what you need to know for hard disks, floppies, CD-ROM's, and tape drives.

4.1 Two kinds of devices

UNIX, and therefore Linux, recognizes two different kinds of device: random-access block devices (such as disks), and character devices (such as tapes and serial lines), some of which may be serial, and some random-access. Each supported device is represented in the filesystem as a **device file**. When you read or write a device file, the data comes from or goes to the device it represents. This way no special programs (and no special application programming methodology, such as catching interrupts or polling a serial port) are necessary to access devices; for example, to send a file to the printer, one could just say

```
$ cat filename > /dev/lp1
$
```

and the contents of the file are printed (the file must, of course, be in a form that the printer understands). However, since it is not a good idea to have several people cat their files to the printer at the same time, one usually uses a special program to send the files to be printed (usually `lpr`). This program makes sure that only one file is being printed at a time, and will automatically send files to the printer as soon as it finishes with the previous file. Something similar is needed for most devices. In fact, one seldom needs to worry about device files at all.

Since devices show up as files in the filesystem (in the /dev directory), it is easy to see just what device files exist, using `ls` or another suitable command. In the output of `ls -l`, the first column contains the type of the file and its permissions. For example, inspecting a serial device gives on my system

```
$ ls -l /dev/cua0
crw-rw-rw-   1 root      uucp      5,  64 Nov 30  1993 /dev/cua0
$
```

The first character in the first column, i.e., 'c' in `crw-rw-rw-` above, tells an informed user the type of the file, in this case a character device. For ordinary files, the first character is '-', for directories it is 'd', and for block devices 'b'; see the `ls` man page for further information.

Note that usually all device files exist even though the device itself might be not be installed. So just because you have a file `/dev/sda`, it doesn't mean that you really do have an SCSI hard disk. Having all the device files makes the installation programs simpler, and makes it easier to add new hardware (there is no need to find out the correct parameters for and create the device files for the new device).

4.2 Hard disks

This subsection introduces terminology related to hard disks. If you already know the terms and concepts, you can skip this subsection.

See figure 4.1 for a schematic picture of the important parts in a hard disk. A hard disk consists of one or more circular **platters**,[1] of which either or both **surfaces** are coated with a magnetic substance used for recording the data. For each surface, there is a **read-write head** that examines or alters the recorded data. The platters rotate on a common axis; a typical rotation speed is 3600 rotations per minute, although high-performance hard disks have higher speeds. The heads move along the radius of the platters; this movement combined with the rotation of the platters allows the head to access all parts of the surfaces.

The processor (CPU) and the actual disk communicate through a **disk controller**. This relieves the rest of the computer from knowing how to use the drive, since the controllers for different types of disks can be made to use the same interface towards the rest of the computer. Therefore, the computer can say just "hey disk, gimme what I want", instead of a long and complex series of electric signals to move the head to the proper location and waiting for the correct position to come under the head and doing all the other unpleasant stuff necessary. (In reality, the interface to the controller is still complex, but much less so than it would otherwise be.) The controller can also do some other stuff, such as caching, or automatic bad sector replacement.

The above is usually all one needs to understand about the hardware. There is also a bunch of other stuff, such as the motor that rotates the platters and moves the heads, and the electronics that control the operation of the mechanical parts, but that is mostly not relevant for understanding the working principle of a hard disk.

---

[1]The platters are made of a hard substance, e.g., aluminium, which gives the hard disk its name.

The surfaces are usually divided into concentric rings, called **tracks**, and these in turn are divided into **sectors**. This division is used to specify locations on the hard disk and to allocate disk space to files. To find a given place on the hard disk, one might say "surface 3, track 5, sector 7". Usually the number of sectors is the same for all tracks, but some hard disks put more sectors in outer tracks (all sectors are of the same physical size, so more of them fit in the longer outer tracks). Typically, a sector will hold 512 bytes of data. The disk itself can't handle smaller amounts of data than one sector.

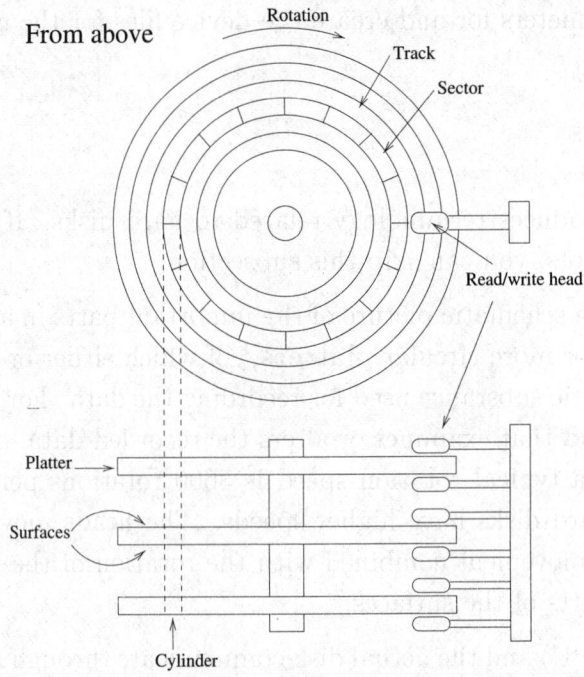

Figure 4.1: A schematic picture of a hard disk.

Each surface is divided into tracks (and sectors) in the same way. This means that when the head for one surface is on a track, the heads for the other surfaces are also on the corresponding tracks. All the corresponding tracks taken together are called a **cylinder**. It takes time to move the heads from one track (cylinder) to another, so by placing the data that is often accessed together (say, a file) so that it is within one cylinder, it is not necessary to move the heads to read all of it. This improves performance. It is not always possible to place files like this; files that are stored in several places on the disk are called **fragmented**.

The number of surfaces (or heads, which is the same thing), cylinders, and sectors vary a lot; the specification of the number of each is called the **geometry** of a hard disk. The geometry is usually stored in a special, battery-powered memory location called the **CMOS RAM**, from where the operating system can fetch it during bootup or driver initialization.

Unfortunately, the BIOS[2] has a design limitation, which makes it impossible to specify a track number that is larger than 1024 in the CMOS RAM, which is too little for a large hard disk. To overcome this, the hard disk controller lies about the geometry, and **translates the addresses** given by the computer into something that fits reality. For example, a hard disk might have 8 heads, 2048 tracks, and 35 sectors per track[3]. Its controller could lie to the computer and claim that it has 16 heads, 1024 tracks, and 35 sectors per track, thus not exceeding the limit on tracks, and translates the address that the computer gives it by halving the head number, and doubling the track number. The math can be more complicated in reality, because the numbers are not as nice as here (but again, the details are not relevant for understanding the principle). This translation distorts the operating system's view of how the disk is organized, thus making it impractical to use the all-data-on-one-cylinder trick to boost performance.

The translation is only a problem for IDE disks. SCSI disks use a sequential sector number (i.e., the controller translates a sequential sector number to a head, cylinder, and sector triplet), and a completely different method for the CPU to talk with the controller, so they are insulated from the problem. Note, however, that the computer might not know the real geometry of an SCSI disk either.

Since Linux often will not know the real geometry of a disk, its filesystems don't even try to keep files within a single cylinder. Instead, it tries to assign sequentially numbered sectors to files, which almost always gives similar performance. The issue is further complicated by on-controller caches, and automatic prefetches done by the controller.

Each hard disk is represented by a separate device file. There can (usually) be only two or four IDE hard disks. These are known as /dev/hda, /dev/hdb, /dev/hdc, and /dev/hdd, respectively. SCSI hard disks are known as /dev/sda, /dev/sdb, and so on. Similar naming conventions exist for other hard disk types; see [?] for more information. Note that the device files for the hard disks give access to the entire disk, with no regard to partitions (which will be discussed below), and it's easy to mess up the partitions or the data in them if you aren't careful. The disks' device files are usually used only to get access to the master boot record (which will also be

---

[2]The BIOS is some built-in software stored on ROM chips. It takes care, among other things, of the initial stages of booting.

[3]The numbers are completely imaginary.

discussed below).

4.3   Floppies

A floppy disk consists of a flexible membrane covered on one or both sides with similar magnetic substance as a hard disk. The floppy disk itself doesn't have a read-write head, that is included in the drive. A floppy corresponds to one platter in a hard disk, but is removable and one drive can be used to access different floppies, whereas the hard disk is one indivisible unit.

Like a hard disk, a floppy is divided into tracks and sectors (and the two corresponding tracks on either side of a floppy form a cylinder), but there are many fewer of them than on a hard disk.

A floppy drive can usually use several different types of disks; for example, a $3\frac{1}{2}$ inch drive can use both 720 kB and 1.44 MB disks. Since the drive has to operate a bit differently and the operating system must know how big the disk is, there are many device files for floppy drives, one per combination of drive and disk type. Therefore, /dev/fd0H1440 is the first floppy drive (fd0), which must be a $3\frac{1}{2}$ inch drive, using a $3\frac{1}{2}$ inch, high density disk (H) of size 1440 kB (1440), i.e., a normal $3\frac{1}{2}$ inch HD floppy. For more information on the naming conventions for the floppy devices, see [?].

The names for floppy drives are complex, however, and Linux therefore has a special floppy device type that automatically detects the type of the disk in the drive. It works by trying to read the first sector of a newly inserted floppy using different floppy types until it finds the correct one. This naturally requires that the floppy is formatted first. The automatic devices are called /dev/fd0, /dev/fd1, and so on.

The parameters the automatic device uses to access a disk can also be set using the program setfdprm. This can be useful if you need to use disks that do not follow any usual floppy sizes, e.g., if they have an unusual number of sectors, or if the autodetecting for some reason fails and the proper device file is missing.

Linux can handle many nonstandard floppy disk formats in addition to all the standard ones. Some of these require using special formatting programs. We'll skip these disk types for now, but in the mean time you can examine the /etc/fdprm file. It specifies the settings that setfdprm recognizes.

The operating system must know when a disk has been changed in a floppy drive, for example, in order to avoid using cached data from the previous disk. Unfortunately, the signal line that is used for this is sometimes broken, and worse, this won't always be noticeable when using the drive from within MS-DOS. If you are experiencing weird problems using floppies, this might be the reason. The only way to correct it is to repair the floppy drive.

4.4 CD-ROM's

A CD-ROM drive uses an optically read, plastic coated disk. The information is recorded on the surface of the disk[4] in small 'holes' aligned along a spiral from the center to the edge. The drive directs a laser beam along the spiral to read the disk. When the laser hits a hole, the laser is reflected in one way; when it hits smooth surface, it is reflected in another way. This makes it easy to code bits, and therefore information. The rest is easy, mere mechanics.

CD-ROM drives are slow compared to hard disks. Whereas a typical hard disk will have an average seek time less than 15 milliseconds, a fast CD-ROM drive can use tenths of a second for seeks. The actual data transfer rate is fairly high at hundreds of kilobytes per second. The slowness means that CD-ROM drives are not as pleasant to use instead of hard disks (some Linux distributions provide 'live' filesystems on CD-ROM's, making it unnecessary to copy the files to the hard disk, making installation easier and saving a lot of hard disk space), although it is still possible. For installing new software, CD-ROM's are very good, since it maximum speed is not essential during installation.

There are several ways to arrange data on a CD-ROM. The most popular one is specified by the international standard ISO 9660. This standard specifies a very minimal filesystem, which is even more crude than the one MS-DOS uses. On the other hand, it is so minimal that every operating system should be able to map it to its native system.

For normal UNIX use, the ISO 9660 filesystem is not usable, so an extension to the standard has been developed, called the Rock Ridge extension. Rock Ridge allows longer filenames, symbolic links, and a lot of other goodies, making a CD-ROM look more or less like any contemporary UNIX filesystem. Even better, a Rock Ridge filesystem is still a valid ISO 9660 filesystem, making it usable by non-UNIX systems as well. Linux supports both ISO 9660 and the Rock Ridge extensions; the extensions are recognized and used automatically.

The filesystem is only half the battle, however. Most CD-ROM's contain data that requires a special program to access, and most of these programs do not run under

---

[4]That is, the surface inside the disk, on the metal disk inside the plastic coating.

Linux (except, possibly, under dosemu, the Linux MS-DOS emulator).

A CD-ROM drive is accessed via the corresponding device file. There are several ways to connect a CD-ROM drive to the computer: via SCSI, via a sound card, or via EIDE. The hardware hacking needed to do this is outside the scope of this book, but the type of connection decides the device file. See [?] for enlightenment.

4.5   Tapes

A tape drive uses a tape, similar[5] to cassettes used for music. A tape is serial in nature, which means that in order to get to any given part of it, you first have to go through all the parts in between. A disk can be accessed randomly, i.e., you can jump directly to any place on the disk. The serial access of tapes makes them slow.

On the other hand, tapes are relatively cheap to make, since they do not need to be fast. They can also easily be made quite long, and can therefore contain a large amount of data. This makes tapes very suitable for things like archiving and backups, which do not require large speeds, but benefit from low costs and large storage capacities.

4.6   Formatting

Formatting is the process of writing marks on the magnetic media that are used to mark tracks and sectors. Before a disk is formatted, its magnetic surface is a complete mess of magnetic signals. When it is formatted, some order is brought into the chaos by essentially drawing lines where the tracks go, and where they are divided into sectors. The actual details are not quite exactly like this, but that is irrelevant. What is important is that a disk cannot be used unless it has been formatted.

The terminology is a bit confusing here: in MS-DOS, the word formatting is used to cover also the process of creating a filesystem (which will be discussed below). There, the two processes are often combined, especially for floppies. When the distinction needs to be made, the real formatting is called **low-level formatting**, while making the filesystem is called **high-level formatting**. In UNIX circles, the two are called formatting and making a filesystem, so that's what is used in this book as well.

For IDE and some SCSI disks the formatting is actually done at the factory and doesn't need to be repeated; hence most people rarely need to worry about it. In

---

[5]But completely different, of course.

fact, formatting a hard disk can cause it to work less well, for example because a disk might need to be formatted in some very special way to allow automatic bad sector replacement to work.

Disks that need to be or can be formatted often require a special program anyway, because the interface to the formatting logic inside the drive is different from drive to drive. The formatting program is often either on the controller BIOS, or is supplied as an MS-DOS program; neither of these can easily be used from within Linux.

During formatting one might encounter bad spots on the disk, called **bad blocks** or **bad sectors**. These are sometimes handled by the drive itself, but even then, if more of them develop, something needs to be done to avoid using those parts of the disk. The logic to do this is built into the filesystem; how to add the information into the filesystem is described below. Alternatively, one might create a small partition that covers just the bad part of the disk; this approach might be a good idea if the bad spot is very large, since filesystems can sometimes have trouble with very large bad areas.

Floppies are formatted with `fdformat`. The floppy device file to use is given as the parameter. For example, the following command would format a high density, $3\frac{1}{2}$ inch floppy in the first floppy drive:

```
$ fdformat /dev/fd0H1440
Double-sided, 80 tracks, 18 sec/track. Total capacity 1440 kB.
Formatting ... done
Verifying ... done
$
```

Note that if you want to use an autodetecting device (e.g., /dev/fd0), you *must* set the parameters of the device with `setfdprm` first. To achieve the same effect as above, one would have to do the following:

```
$ setfdprm /dev/fd0 1440/1440
$ fdformat /dev/fd0
Double-sided, 80 tracks, 18 sec/track. Total capacity 1440 kB.
Formatting ... done
Verifying ... done
$
```

It is usually more convenient to choose the correct device file that matches the type of the floppy. Note that it is unwise to format floppies to contain more information than what they are designed for.

fdformat will also validate the floppy, i.e., check it for bad blocks. It will try a bad
block several times (you can usually hear this, the drive noise changes dramatically).
If the floppy is only marginally bad (due to dirt on the read/write head, some errors
are false signals), fdformat won't complain, but a real error will abort the validation
process. The kernel will print log messages for each I/O error it finds; these will go
to the console or, if syslog is being used, to the file /usr/adm/messages. fdformat
itself won't tell where the error is (one usually doesn't care, floppies are cheap enough
that a bad one is automatically thrown away).

```
$ fdformat /dev/fd0H1440
Double-sided, 80 tracks, 18 sec/track. Total capacity 1440 kB.
Formatting ... done
Verifying ... read: Unknown error
$
```

The badblocks command can be used to search any disk or partition for bad
blocks (including a floppy). It does not format the disk, so it can be used to check
even existing filesystems. The example below checks a $3\frac{1}{2}$ inch floppy with two bad
blocks.

```
$ badblocks /dev/fd0H1440 1440
718
719
$
```

badblocks outputs the block numbers of the bad blocks it finds. Most filesystems can
avoid such bad blocks. They maintain a list of known bad blocks, which is initialized
when the filesystem is made, and can be modified later. The initial search for bad
blocks can be done by the mkfs command (which initializes the filesystem), but later
checks should be done with badblocks and the new blocks should be added with
fsck. We'll describe mkfs and fsck later.

Many modern disks automatically notice bad blocks, and attempt to fix them
by using a special, reserved good block instead. This is invisible to the operating
system. This feature should be documented in the disk's manual, if you're curious if
it is happening. Even such disks can fail, if the number of bad blocks grows too large,
although chances are that by then the disk will be so rotten as to be unusable.

4.7 Partitions

A hard disk can be divided into several **partitions**. Each partition functions as if it were a separate hard disk. The idea is that if you have one hard disk, and want to have, say, two operating systems on it, you can divide the disk into two partitions. Each operating system uses its partition as it wishes and doesn't touch the other one's. This way the two operating systems can co-exist peacefully on the same hard disk. Without partitions one would have to buy a hard disk for each operating system.

Floppies are not partitioned. There is no technical reason against this, but since they're so small, partitions would be useful only very rarely. CD-ROM's are usually also not partitioned, since it's easier to use them as one big disk, and there is seldom a need to have several operating systems on one.

4.7.1 The MBR, boot sectors and partition table

The information about how a hard disk has been partitioned is stored in its first sector (that is, the first sector of the first track on the first disk surface). The first sector is the **master boot record** (MBR) of the disk; this is the sector that the BIOS reads in and starts when the machine is first booted. The master boot record contains a small program that reads the partition table, checks which partition is active (that is, marked bootable), and reads the first sector of that partition, the partition's **boot sector** (the MBR is also a boot sector, but it has a special status and therefore a special name). This boot sector contains another small program that reads the first part of the operating system stored on that partition (assuming it is bootable), and then starts it.

The partitioning scheme is not built into the hardware, or even into the BIOS. It is only a convention that many operating systems follow. Not all operating systems do follow it, but they are the exceptions. Some operating systems support partitions, but they occupy one partition on the hard disk, and use their internal partitioning method within that partition. The latter type exists peacefully with other operating systems (including Linux), and does not require any special measures, but an operating system that doesn't support partitions cannot co-exist on the same disk with any other operating system.

As a safety precaution, it is a good idea to write down the partition table on a piece of paper, so that if it ever corrupts you don't have to lose all your files. (A bad partition table can be fixed with `fdisk`). The relevant information is given by the `fdisk -l` command:

```
$ fdisk -1 /dev/hda

Disk /dev/hda: 15 heads, 57 sectors, 790 cylinders
Units = cylinders of 855 * 512 bytes

    Device Boot  Begin  Start    End  Blocks   Id  System
  /dev/hda1          1      1     24   10231+  82  Linux swap
  /dev/hda2         25     25     48   10260   83  Linux native
  /dev/hda3         49     49    408  153900   83  Linux native
  /dev/hda4        409    409    790  163305    5  Extended
  /dev/hda5        409    409    744  143611+  83  Linux native
  /dev/hda6        745    745    790   19636+  83  Linux native
$
```

4.7.2 Extended and logical partitions

The original partitioning scheme for PC hard disks allowed only four partitions. This quickly turned out to be too little in real life, partly because some people want more than four operating systems (Linux, MS-DOS, OS/2, Minix, FreeBSD, NetBSD, or Windows/NT, to name a few), but primarily because sometimes it is a good idea to have several partitions for one operating system. For example, swap space is usually best put in its own partition for Linux instead of in the main Linux partition for reasons of speed (see below).

To overcome this design problem, **extended partitions** were invented. This trick allows partitioning a **primary partition** into sub-partitions. The primary partition thus subdivided is the extended partition; the subpartitions are **logical partitions**. They behave like primary[6] partitions, but are created differently. There is no speed difference between them.

The partition structure of a hard disk might look like that in figure 4.2. The disk is divided into three primary partitions, the second of which is divided into two logical partitions. Part of the disk is not partitioned at all. The disk as a whole and each primary partition has a boot sector.

---

[6]Illogical?

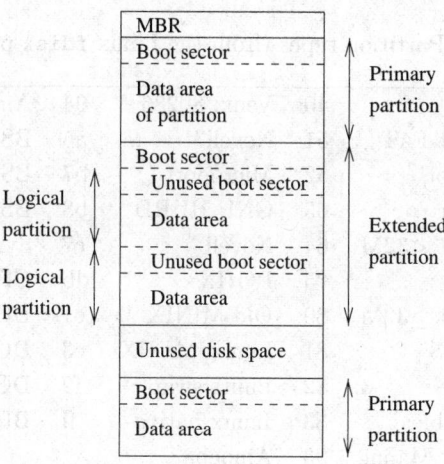

Figure 4.2: A sample hard disk partitioning.

4.7.3 Partition types

The partition tables (the one in the MBR, and the ones for extended partitions) contain one byte per partition that identifies the type of that partition. This attempts to identify the operating system that uses the partition, or what it uses it for. The purpose is to make it possible to avoid having two operating systems accidentally using the same partition. However, in reality, operating systems do not really care about the partition type byte; e.g., Linux doesn't care at all what it is. Worse, some of them use it incorrectly; e.g., at least some versions of DR-DOS ignore the most significant bit of the byte, while others don't.

There is no standardization agency to specify what each byte value means, but some commonly accepted ones are included in in table 4.1. The same list is available in the Linux fdisk program.

4.7.4 Partitioning a hard disk

There are many programs for creating and removing partitions. Most operating systems have their own, and it can be a good idea to use each operating system's own, just in case it does something unusual that the others can't. Many of the programs are called fdisk, including the Linux one, or variations thereof. Details on using the Linux fdisk are given on its man page. The cfdisk command is similar to fdisk, but has a nicer (full screen) user interface.

When using IDE disks, the boot partition (the partition with the bootable kernel

Table 4.1: Partition types (from the Linux `fdisk` program).

0	Empty	40	Venix 80286	94	Amoeba BBT
1	DOS 12-bit FAT	51	Novell?	a5	BSD/386
2	XENIX root	52	Microport	b7	BSDI fs
3	XENIX usr	63	GNU HURD	b8	BSDI swap
4	DOS 16-bit <32M	64	Novell	c7	Syrinx
5	Extended	75	PC/IX	db	CP/M
6	DOS 16-bit ≥32M	80	Old MINIX	e1	DOS access
7	OS/2 HPFS	81	Linux/MINIX	e3	DOS R/O
8	AIX	82	Linux swap	f2	DOS secondary
9	AIX bootable	83	Linux native	ff	BBT
a	OS/2 Boot Manag	93	Amoeba		

image files) must be completely within the first 1024 cylinders. This is because the disk is used via the BIOS during boot (before the system goes into protected mode), and BIOS can't handle more than 1024 cylinders. It is sometimes possible to use a boot partition that is only partly within the first 1024 cylinders. This works as long as all the files that are read with the BIOS are within the first 1024 cylinders. Since this is difficult to arrange, it is *a very bad idea* to do it; you never know when a kernel update or disk defragmentation will result in an unbootable system. Therefore, make sure your boot partition is completely within the first 1024 cylinders.

Some newer versions of the BIOS and IDE disks can, in fact, handle disks with more than 1024 cylinders. If you have such a system, you can forget about the problem; if you aren't quite sure of it, put it within the first 1024 cylinders.

Each partition should have an even number of sectors, since the Linux filesystems use a 1 kB block size, i.e., two sectors. An odd number of sectors will result in the last sector being unused. This won't result in any problems, but it is ugly, and some versions of `fdisk` will warn about it.

Changing a partition's size usually requires first backing up everything you want to save from that partition (preferably the whole disk, just in case), deleting the partition, creating new partition, then restoring everything to the new partition. If the partition is growing, you may need to adjust the sizes (and backup and restore) of the adjoining partitions as well.

Since changing partition sizes is painful, it is preferable to get the partitions right the first time, or have an effective and easy to use backup system. If you're installing from a media that does not require much human intervention (say, from CD-ROM, as opposed to floppies), it is often easy to play with different configuration at first. Since you don't already have data to back up, it is not so painful to modify partition sizes several times.

There is a program for MS-DOS, called `fips`, which resizes an MS-DOS partition without requiring the backup and restore, but for other filesystems it is still necessary.

4.7.5   Device files and partitions

Each partition and extended partition has its own device file. The naming convention for these files is that a partition's number is appended after the name of the whole disk, with the convention that 1–4 are primary partitions (regardless of how many primary partitions there are) and 5–8 are logical partitions (regardless of within which primary partition they reside). For example, `/dev/hda1` is the first primary partition on the first IDE hard disk, and `/dev/sdb7` is the third extended partition on the second SCSI hard disk. The device list in [?] gives more information.

4.8   Filesystems

4.8.1   What are filesystems?

A **filesystem** is the methods and data structures that an operating system uses to keep track of files on a disk or partition; that is, the way the files are organized on the disk. The word is also used to refer to a partition or disk that is used to store the files or the type of the filesystem. Thus, one might say "I have two filesystems" meaning one has two partitions on which one stores files, or that one is using the "extended filesystem", meaning the type of the filesystem.

The difference between a disk or partition and the filesystem it contains is important. A few programs (including, reasonably enough, programs that create filesystems) operate directly on the raw sectors of a disk or partition; if there is an existing file system there it will be destroyed or seriously corrupted. Most programs operate on a filesystem, and therefore won't work on a partition that doesn't contain one (or that contains one of the wrong type).

Before a partition or disk can be used as a filesystem, it needs to be initialized, and the bookkeeping data structures need to be written to the disk. This process is called **making a filesystem**.

Most UNIX filesystem types have a similar general structure, although the exact details vary quite a bit. The central concepts are **superblock**, **inode**, **data block**, **directory block**, and **indirection block**. The superblock contains information about the filesystem as a whole, such as its size (the exact information here depends on the filesystem). An inode contains all information about a file, except its name. The name is stored in the directory, together with the number of the inode. A directory entry consists of a filename and the number of the inode which represents the file. The inode contains the numbers of several data blocks, which are used to store the data in the file. There is space only for a few data block numbers in the inode, however, and if more are needed, more space for pointers to the data blocks is allocated dynamically. These dynamically allocated blocks are indirect blocks; the name indicates that in order to find the data block, one has to find its number in the indirect block first.

UNIX filesystems usually allow one to create a **hole** in a file (this is done with lseek; check the manual page), which means that the filesystem just pretends that at a particular place in the file there is just zero bytes, but no actual disk sectors are reserved for that place in the file (this means that the file will use a bit less disk space). This happens especially often for small binaries, Linux shared libraries, some databases, and a few other special cases. (Holes are implemented by storing a special value as the address of the data block in the indirect block or inode. This special address means that no data block is allocated for that part of the file, ergo, there is a hole in the file.)

Holes are moderately useful. On the author's system, a simple measurement showed a potential for about 4 MB of savings through holes of about 200 MB total used disk space. That system, however, contains relatively few programs and no database files. The measurement tool is described in appendix A.

4.8.2 Filesystems galore

Linux supports several types of filesystems. As of this writing the most important ones are:

minix   The oldest, presumed to be the most reliable, but quite limited in features (some time stamps are missing, at most 30 character filenames) and restricted in capabilities (at most 64 MB per filesystem).

xia   A modified version of the minix filesystem that lifts the limits on the filenames and filesystem sizes, but does not otherwise introduce new features. It is not very popular, but is reported to work very well.

ext2   The most featureful of the native Linux filesystems, currently also the most popular one. It is designed to be easily upwards compatible, so that new versions of the filesystem code do not require re-making the existing filesystems.

ext   An older version of `ext2` that wasn't upwards compatible. It is hardly ever used in new installations any more, and most people have converted to `ext2`.

In addition, support for several foreign filesystem exists, to make it easier to exchange files with other operating systems. These foreign filesystems work just like native ones, except that they may be lacking in some usual UNIX features, or have curious limitations, or other oddities.

msdos   Compatibility with MS-DOS (and OS/2 and Windows NT) FAT filesystems.

umsdos   Extends the `msdos` filesystem driver under Linux to get long filenames, owners, permissions, links, and device files. This allows a normal `msdos` filesystem to be used as if it were a Linux one, thus removing the need for a separate partition for Linux.

iso9660   The standard CD-ROM filesystem; the popular Rock Ridge extension to the CD-ROM standard that allows longer file names is supported automatically.

nfs   A networked filesystem that allows sharing a filesystem between many computers to allow easy access to the files from all of them.

hpfs   The OS/2 filesystem.

sysv   SystemV/386, Coherent, and Xenix filesystems.

The choice of filesystem to use depends on the situation. If compatibility or other reasons make one of the non-native filesystems necessary, then that one must be used. If one can choose freely, then it is probably wisest to use ext2, since it has all the features but does not suffer from lack of performance.

There is also the `proc` filesystem, usually accessible as the `/proc` directory, which is not really a filesystem at all, even though it looks like one. The `proc` filesystem makes it easy to access certain kernel data structures, such as the process list (hence the name). It makes these data structures look like a filesystem, and that filesystem can be manipulated with all the usual file tools. For example, to get a listing of all processes one might use the command

```
$  ls -l /proc
total 0
dr-xr-xr-x   4 root     root            0 Jan 31 20:37 1
dr-xr-xr-x   4 liw      users           0 Jan 31 20:37 63
dr-xr-xr-x   4 liw      users           0 Jan 31 20:37 94
dr-xr-xr-x   4 liw      users           0 Jan 31 20:37 95
dr-xr-xr-x   4 root     users           0 Jan 31 20:37 98
dr-xr-xr-x   4 liw      users           0 Jan 31 20:37 99
-r--r--r--   1 root     root            0 Jan 31 20:37 devices
-r--r--r--   1 root     root            0 Jan 31 20:37 dma
-r--r--r--   1 root     root            0 Jan 31 20:37 filesystems
-r--r--r--   1 root     root            0 Jan 31 20:37 interrupts
-r--------   1 root     root      8654848 Jan 31 20:37 kcore
-r--r--r--   1 root     root            0 Jan 31 11:50 kmsg
-r--r--r--   1 root     root            0 Jan 31 20:37 ksyms
-r--r--r--   1 root     root            0 Jan 31 11:51 loadavg
-r--r--r--   1 root     root            0 Jan 31 20:37 meminfo
-r--r--r--   1 root     root            0 Jan 31 20:37 modules
dr-xr-xr-x   2 root     root            0 Jan 31 20:37 net
dr-xr-xr-x   4 root     root            0 Jan 31 20:37 self
-r--r--r--   1 root     root            0 Jan 31 20:37 stat
-r--r--r--   1 root     root            0 Jan 31 20:37 uptime
-r--r--r--   1 root     root            0 Jan 31 20:37 version
$
```

(There will be a few extra files that don't correspond to processes, though. The above example has been shortened.)

Note that even though it is called a filesystem, no part of the proc filesystem touches any disk. It exists only in the kernel's imagination. Whenever anyone tries to look at any part of the proc filesystem, the kernel makes it look as if the part existed somewhere, even though it doesn't. So, even though there is a multi-megabyte /proc/kcore file, it doesn't take any disk space.

4.8.3   Which filesystem should be used?

There is usually little point in using many different filesystems. Currently, ext2fs is the most popular one, and it is probably the wisest choice. Depending on the overhead for bookkeeping structures, speed, (perceived) reliability, compatibility, and various other reasons, it may be advisable to use another file system. This needs to be decided on a case-by-case basis.

4.8.4   Creating a filesystem

Filesystems are created, i.e., initialized, with the `mkfs` command. There is actually a separate program for each filesystem type. `mkfs` is just a front end that runs the appropriate program depending on the desired filesystem type. The type is selected with the `-t fstype` option.

   The programs called by `mkfs` have slightly different command line interfaces. The common and most important options are summarized below; see the manual pages for more.

   `-t` *fstype* Select the type of the filesystem.

   `-c` Search for bad blocks and initialize the bad block list accordingly.

   `-l` *filename* Read the initial bad block list from the file *filename*.

To create an ext2 filesystem on a floppy, one would give the following commands:

```
$ fdformat -n /dev/fd0H1440
Double-sided, 80 tracks, 18 sec/track. Total capacity 1440 kB.
Formatting ... done
$ badblocks /dev/fd0H1440 1440 > bad-blocks
$ mkfs -t ext2 -l bad-blocks /dev/fd0H1440
mke2fs 0.5a, 5-Apr-94 for EXT2 FS 0.5, 94/03/10
360 inodes, 1440 blocks
72 blocks (5.00%) reserved for the super user
First data block=1
Block size=1024 (log=0)
Fragment size=1024 (log=0)
1 block group
8192 blocks per group, 8192 fragments per group
360 inodes per group
```

```
Writing inode tables: done
Writing superblocks and filesystem accounting information: done
$
```

First, the floppy was formatted (the **-n** option prevents validation, i.e., bad block checking). Then bad blocks were searched with **badblocks**, with the output redirected to a file, **bad-blocks**. Finally, the filesystem was created, with the bad block list initialized by whatever **badblocks** found.

The **-c** option could have been used with **mkfs** instead of **badblocks** and a separate file. The example below does that.

```
$ mkfs -t ext2 -c /dev/fd0H1440
mke2fs 0.5a, 5-Apr-94 for EXT2 FS 0.5, 94/03/10
360 inodes, 1440 blocks
72 blocks (5.00%) reserved for the super user
First data block=1
Block size=1024 (log=0)
Fragment size=1024 (log=0)
1 block group
8192 blocks per group, 8192 fragments per group
360 inodes per group


Checking for bad blocks (read-only test): done
Writing inode tables: done
Writing superblocks and filesystem accounting information: done
$
```

The **-c** is more convenient than a separate use of **badblocks**, but **badblocks** is necessary for checking after the filesystem has been created.

The process to prepare filesystems on hard disks or partitions is the same as for floppies, except that the formatting isn't needed.

4.8.5 Mounting and unmounting

Before one can use a filesystem, it has to be **mounted**. The operating system then does various bookkeeping things to make sure that everything works. Since all files in UNIX are in a single directory tree, the mount operation will make it look like the contents of the new filesystem are the contents of an existing subdirectory in some already mounted filesystem.

For example, figure 4.3 shows three separate filesystems, each with their own root directory. When the last two filesystems are mounted below /home and /usr, respectively, on the first filesystem, we can get a single directory tree, as in figure 4.4.

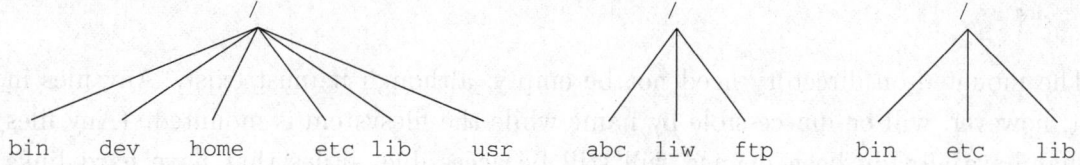

Figure 4.3: Three separate filesystems.

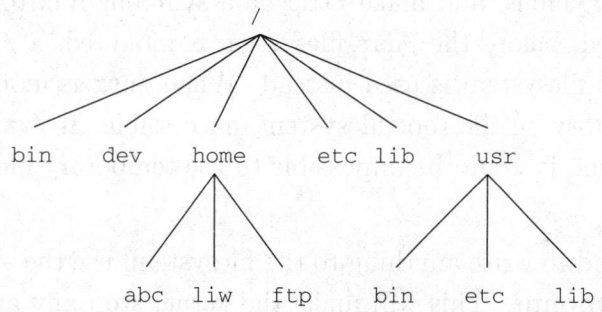

Figure 4.4: /home and /usr have been mounted.

The mounts could be done as in the following example:

```
$   mount /dev/hda2 /home
$   mount /dev/hda3 /usr
$
```

The **mount** command takes two arguments. The first one is the device file corresponding to the disk or partition containing the filesystem. The second one is the directory below which it will be mounted. After these commands the contents of the two filesystems look just like the contents of the /home and /usr directories, respectively. One would then say that "/dev/hda2 **is mounted on** /home", and similarly for /usr. To look at either filesystem, one would look at the contents of the directory on which it has been mounted, just as if it were any other directory. Note the difference between the device file, /dev/hda2, and the mounted-on directory, /home. The device file gives access to the raw contents of the disk, the mounted-on directory gives access to the files on the disk. The mounted-on directory is called the **mount point**.

Linux supports many filesystem types. mount tries to guess the type of the filesystem. You can also use the -t *fstype* option to specify the type directly; this is sometimes necessary, since the heuristics mount uses do not always work. For example, to mount an MS-DOS floppy, you could use the following command:

```
$   mount -t msdos /dev/fd0 /floppy
$
```

The mounted-on directory need not be empty, although it must exist. Any files in it, however, will be inaccessible by name while the filesystem is mounted. (Any files that have already been opened will still be accessible. Files that have hard links from other directories can be accessed using those names.) There is no harm done with this, and it can even be useful. For instance, some people like to have /tmp and /var/tmp synonymous, and make /tmp be a symbolic link to /var/tmp. When the system is booted, before the /usr filesystem is mounted, a /var/tmp directory residing on the root filesystem is used instead. When /usr is mounted, it will make the /var/tmp directory on the root filesystem inaccessible. If /var/tmp didn't exist on the root filesystem, it would be impossible to use temporary files before mounting /var.

If you don't intend to write anything to the filesystem, use the -r switch for mount to do a **readonly mount**. This will make the kernel stop any attempts at writing to the filesystem, and will also stop the kernel from updating file access times in the inodes. Read-only mounts are necessary for unwritable media, e.g., CD-ROM's.

The alert reader has already noticed a slight logistical problem. How is the first filesystem (called the **root filesystem**, because it contains the root directory) mounted, since it obviously can't be mounted on another filesystem? Well, the answer is that it is done by magic.[7] The root filesystem is magically mounted at boot time, and one can rely on it to always be mounted—if the root filesystem can't be mounted, the system does not boot. The name of the filesystem that is magically mounted as root is either compiled into the kernel, or set using LILO or rdev.

The root filesystem is usually first mounted readonly. The startup scripts will then run fsck to verify its validity, and if there are no problems, they will **re-mount** it so that writes will also be allowed. fsck must not be run on a mounted filesystem, since any changes to the filesystem while fsck is running *will* cause trouble. Since the root filesystem is mounted readonly while it is being checked, fsck can fix any problems without worry, since the remount operation will flush any metadata that the filesystem keeps in memory.

---

[7]For more information, see the kernel source or the Kernel Hackers' Guide.

On many systems there are other filesystems that should also be mounted automatically at boot time. These are specified in the **/etc/fstab** file; see the *fstab* man page for details on the format. The details of exactly when the extra filesystems are mounted depend on many factors, and can be configured by each administrator if need be. When the chapter on booting is finished, you may read all about it there.

When a filesystem no longer needs to be mounted, it can be unmounted with **umount**[8]. **umount** takes one argument: either the device file or the mount point. For example, to unmount the directories of the previous example, one could use the commands

```
$   umount /dev/hda2
$   umount /usr
$
```

See the man page for further instructions on how to use the command. It is imperative that you always unmount a mounted floppy. *Don't just pop the floppy out of the drive!* Because of disk caching, the data is not necessarily written to the floppy until you unmount it, so removing the floppy from the drive too early might cause the contents to become garbled. If you only read from the floppy, this is not very likely, but if you write, even accidentally, the result may be catastrophic.

Mounting and unmounting requires super user privileges, i.e., only **root** can do it. The reason for this is that if any user can mount a floppy on any directory, then it is rather easy to create a floppy with, say, a Trojan horse disguised as **/bin/sh**, or any other often used program. However, it is often necessary to allow users to use floppies, and there are several ways to do this:

- Give the users the **root** password. This is obviously bad security, but is the easiest solution. It works well if there is no need for security anyway, which is the case on many non-networked, personal systems.

- Use a program such as **sudo** to allow users to use mount. This is still bad security, but doesn't directly give super user privileges to everyone.[9]

- Make the users use **mtools**, a package for manipulating MS-DOS filesystems, without mounting them. This works well if MS-DOS floppies are all that is needed, but is rather awkward otherwise.

---

[8]It should of course be **unmount**, but the **n** mysteriously disappeared in the 70's, and hasn't been seen since. Please return it to Bell Labs, NJ, if you find it.

[9]It requires several seconds of hard thinking on the users' behalf.

- List the floppy devices and their allowable mount points together with the suitable options in `/etc/fstab`.

The last alternative can be implemented by adding a line like the following to the `/etc/fstab` file:

```
/dev/fd0 /floppy msdos user,noauto 0 0
```

The columns are: device file to mount, directory to mount on, filesystem type, options, backup frequency (used by `dump`), and `fsck` pass number (to specify the order in which filesystems should be checked upon boot; 0 means no check).

The `noauto` option stops this mount to be done automatically when the system is started (i.e., it stops `mount -a` from mounting it). The `user` option allows any user to mount the filesystem, and, because of security reasons, disallows execution of programs (normal or setuid) and interpretation of device files from the mounted filesystem. After this, any user can mount a floppy with an `msdos` filesystem with the following command:

```
$   mount /floppy
$
```

The floppy can (and needs to, of course) be unmounted with the corresponding `umount` command.

If you want to provide access to several types of floppies, you need to give several mount points. The settings can be different for each mount point. For example, to give access to both MS-DOS and ext2 floppies, you could have the following to lines in `/etc/fstab`:

```
/dev/fd0    /dosfloppy    msdos   user,noauto 0 0
/dev/fd0    /ext2floppy   ext2    user,noauto 0 0
```

For MS-DOS filesystems (not just floppies), you probably want to restrict access to it by using the `uid`, `gid`, and `umask` filesystem options, described in detail on the *mount* manual page. If you aren't careful, mounting an MS-DOS filesystem gives everyone at least read access to the files in it, which is not a good idea.

4.8.6   Checking filesystem integrity with `fsck`

Filesystems are complex creatures, and as such, they tend to be somewhat error-prone. A filesystem's correctness and validity can be checked using the `fsck` command. It can be instructed to repair any minor problems it finds, and to alert the user if there any unrepairable problems. Fortunately, the code to implement filesystems is debugged quite effectively, so there are seldom any problems at all, and they are usually caused by power failures, failing hardware, or operator errors; for example, by not shutting down the system properly.

Most systems are setup to run `fsck` automatically at boot time, so that any errors are detected (and hopefully corrected) before the system is used. Use of a corrupted filesystem tends to make things worse: if the data structures are messed up, using the filesystem will probably mess them up even more, resulting in more data loss. However, `fsck` can take a while to run on big filesystems, and since errors almost never occur if the system has been shut down properly, a couple of tricks are used to avoid doing the checks in such cases. The first is that if the file `/etc/fastboot` exists, no checks are made. The second is that the ext2 filesystem has a special marker in its superblock that tells whether the filesystem was unmounted properly after the previous mount. This allows `e2fsck` (the version of `fsck` for the ext2 filesystem) to avoid checking the filesystem if the flag indicates that the unmount was done (the assumption being that a proper unmount indicates no problems). Whether the `/etc/fastboot` trick works on your system depends on your startup scripts, but the ext2 trick works every time you use `e2fsck`—it has to be explicitly bypassed with an option to `e2fsck` to be avoided. (See the *e2fsck* man page for details on how.)

The automatic checking only works for the filesystems that are mounted automatically at boot time. Use `fsck` manually to check other filesystems, e.g., floppies.

If `fsck` finds unrepairable problems, you need either in-depth knowlege of how filesystems work in general, and the type of the corrupt filesystem in particular, or good backups. The latter is easy (although sometimes tedious) to arrange, the former can sometimes be arranged via a friend, the Linux newsgroups and mailing lists, or some other source of support, if you don't have the know-how yourself. I'd like to tell you more about it, but my lack of education and experience in this regard hinders me. The `debugfs` program by Theodore T'so should be useful.

`fsck` must only be run on unmounted filesystems, never on mounted filesystems (with the exception of the read-only root during startup). This is because it accesses the raw disk, and can therefore modify the filesystem without the operating system realizing it. There *will* be trouble, if the operating system is confused.

4.8.7 Checking for disk errors with `badblocks`

It can be a good idea to periodically check for bad blocks. This is done with the
`badblocks` command. It outputs a list of the numbers of all bad blocks it can find.
This list can be fed to `fsck` to be recorded in the filesystem data structures so that
the operating system won't try to use the bad blocks for storing data. The following
example will show how this could be done.

```
$ badblocks /dev/fd0H1440 1440 > bad-blocks
$ fsck -t ext2 -l bad-blocks /dev/fd0H1440
Parallelizing fsck version 0.5a (5-Apr-94)
e2fsck 0.5a, 5-Apr-94 for EXT2 FS 0.5, 94/03/10
Pass 1: Checking inodes, blocks, and sizes
Pass 2: Checking directory structure
Pass 3: Checking directory connectivity
Pass 4: Check reference counts.
Pass 5: Checking group summary information.

/dev/fd0H1440: ***** FILE SYSTEM WAS MODIFIED *****
/dev/fd0H1440: 11/360 files, 63/1440 blocks
$
```

If badblocks reports a block that was already used, `e2fsck` will try to move the block
to another place. If the block was really bad, not just marginal, the contents of the
file may be corrupted.

4.8.8 Fighting fragmentation

When a file is written to disk, it can't always be written in consecutive blocks. A
file that is not stored in consecutive blocks is **fragmented**. It takes longer to read
a fragmented file, since the disk's read-write head will have to move more. It is
desireable to avoid fragmentation, although it is less of a problem in a system with a
good buffer cache with read-ahead.

The ext2 filesystem attempts to keep fragmentation at a minimum, by keeping
all blocks in a file close together, even if they can't be stored in consecutive sectors.
Ext2 effectively always allocates the free block that is nearest to other blocks in a
file. For ext2, it is therefore seldom necessary to worry about fragmentation. There
is a program for defragmenting an ext2 filesystem, see [?] in the bibliography.

There are many MS-DOS defragmentation programs that move blocks around in the filesystem to remove fragmentation. For other filesystems, defragmentation must be done by backing up the filesystem, re-creating it, and restoring the files from backups. Backing up a filesystem before defragmening is a good idea for all filesystems, since many things can go wrong during the defragmentation.

4.8.9   Other tools for all filesystems

Some other tools are also useful for managing filesystems. `df` shows the free disk space on one or more filesystems; `du` shows how much disk space a directory and all its files contain. These can be used to hunt down disk space wasters.

`sync` forces all unwritten blocks in the buffer cache (see section 5.6) to be written to disk. It is seldom necessary to do this by hand; the daemon process `update` does this automatically. It can be useful in catastrophies, for example if `update` or its helper process `bdflush` dies, or if you must turn off power `now` and can't wait for `update` to run.

4.8.10   Other tools for the ext2 filesystem

In addition to the filesystem creator (`mke2fs`) and checker (`e2fsck`) accessible directly or via the filesystem type independent front ends, the ext2 filesystem has some additional tools that can be useful.

`tune2fs` adjusts filesystem parameters. Some of the more interesting parameters are:

- A maximal mount count. `e2fsck` enforces a check when filesystem has been mounted too many times, even if the clean flag is set. For a system that is used for developing or testing the system, it might be a good idea to reduce this limit.

- A maximal time between checks. `e2fsck` can also enforce a maximal time between two checks, even if the clean flag is set, and the filesystem hasn't been mounted very often. This can be disabled, however.

- Number of blocks reserved for `root`. Ext2 reserves some blocks for `root` so that if the filesystem fills up, it is still possible to do system administration without having to delete anything. The reserved amount is by default 5%, which on most disks isn't enough to be wasteful. However, for floppies there is no point in reserving any blocks.

```
dumpe2fs 0.5b, 11-Mar-95 for EXT2 FS 0.5a, 94/10/23
Filesystem magic number:  0xEF53
Filesystem state:         clean
Errors behavior:          Continue
Inode count:              360
Block count:              1440
Reserved block count:     72
Free blocks:              1133
Free inodes:              326
First block:              1
Block size:               1024
Fragment size:            1024
Blocks per group:         8192
Fragments per group:      8192
Inodes per group:         360
Last mount time:          Tue Aug  8 01:52:52 1995
Last write time:          Tue Aug  8 01:53:28 1995
Mount count:              3
Maximum mount count:      20
Last checked:             Tue Aug  8 01:06:31 1995
Check interval:           0
Reserved blocks uid:      0 (user root)
Reserved blocks gid:      0 (group root)

Group 0:
  Block bitmap at 3, Inode bitmap at 4, Inode table at 5
  1133 free blocks, 326 free inodes, 2 directories
  Free blocks: 307-1439
  Free inodes: 35-360
```

Figure 4.5: Sample output from dumpe2fs

See the *tune2fs* manual page for more information.

dumpe2fs shows information about an ext2 filesystem, mostly from the superblock. Figure 4.5 shows a sample output. Some of the information in the output is technical and requires understanding of how the filesystem works (see appendix **??**), but much of it is readily understandable even for layadmins.

debugfs is a filesystem debugger. It allows direct access to the filesystem data structures stored on disk and can thus be used to repair a disk that is so broken that fsck can't fix it automatically. It has also been known to be used to recover deleted files. However, debugfs very much requires that you understand what you're doing; a failure to understand can destroy all your data.

dump and restore can be used to back up an ext2 filesystem. They are ext2 specific

versions of the traditional UNIX backup tools. See chapter 10 for more information
on backups.

4.9 Disks without filesystems

Not all disks or partitions are used as filesystems. A swap partition, for example, will
not have a filesystem on it. Many floppies are used in a tape-drive emulating fashion,
so that a `tar` or other file is written directly on the raw disk, without a filesystem.
Linux boot floppies don't contain a filesystem, only the raw kernel.

Avoiding a filesystem has the advantage of making more of the disk usable, since
a filesystem always has some bookkeeping overhead. It also makes the disks more
easily compatible with other systems: for example, the `tar` file format is the same
on all systems, while filesystems are different on most systems. You will quickly get
used to disks without filesystems if you need them. Bootable Linux floppies also do
not necessarily have a filesystem, although that is also possible.

One reason to use raw disks is to make image copies of them. For instance, if the
disk contains a partially damaged filesystem, it is a good idea to make an exact copy
of it before trying to fix it, since then you can start again if your fixing breaks things
even more. One way to do this is to use `dd`:

```
$ dd if=/dev/fd0H1440 of=floppy-image
2880+0 records in
2880+0 records out
$ dd if=floppy-image of=/dev/fd0H1440
2880+0 records in
2880+0 records out
$
```

The first `dd` makes an exact image of the floppy to the file `floppy-image`, the second
one writes the image to the floppy. (The user has presumably switched the floppy
before the second command. Otherwise the command pair is of doubtful usefulness.)

4.10   Allocating disk space

4.10.1   Partitioning schemes

It is not easy to partition a disk in the best possible way. Worse, there is no universally correct way to do it; there are too many factors involved.

The traditional way is to have a (relatively) small root filesystem, which contains /bin, /etc, /dev, /lib, /tmp, and other stuff that is needed to get the system up and running. This way, the root filesystem (in its own partition or on its own disk) is all that is needed to bring up the system. The reasoning is that if the root filesystem is small and is not heavily used, it is less likely to become corrupt when the system crashes, and you will therefore find it easier to fix any problems caused by the crash. Then you create separate partitions or use separate disks for the directory tree below /usr, the users' home directories (often under /home), and the swap space. Separating the home directories (with the users' files) in their own partition makes backups easier, since it is usually not necessary to backup programs (which reside below /usr). In a networked environment it is also possible to share /usr among several machines (e.g., by using NFS), thereby reducing the total disk space required by several tens or hundreds of megabytes times the number of machines.

The problem with having many partitions is that it splits the total amount of free disk space into many small pieces. Nowadays, when disks and (hopefully) operating systems are more reliable, many people prefer to have just one partition that holds all their files. On the other hand, it can be less painful to back up (and restore) a small partition.

For a small hard disk (assuming you don't do kernel development), the best way to go is probably to have just one partition. For large hard disks, it is probably better to have a few large partitions, just in case something does go wrong. (Note that 'small' and 'large' are used in a relative sense here; your needs for disk space decide what the threshold is.)

If you have several disks, you might wish to have the root filesystem (including /usr) on one, and the users' home directories on another.

It is a good idea to be prepared to experiment a bit with different partitioning schemes (over time, not just while first installing the system). This is a bit of work, since it essentially requires you to install the system from scratch several times, but it is the only way to be sure you do it right.

4.10.2 Space requirements

The Linux distribution you install will give some indication of how much disk space you need for various configurations. Programs installed separately may also do the same. This will help you plan your disk space usage, but you should prepare for the future and reserve some extra space for things you will notice later that you need.

The amount you need for user files depends on what your users wish to do. Most people seem to need as much space for their files as possible, but the amount they will live happily with varies a lot. Some people do only light text processing and will survive nicely with a few megabytes, others do heavy image processing and will need gigabytes.

By the way, when comparing file sizes given in kilobytes or megabytes and disk space given in megabytes, it can be important to know that the two units can be different. Some disk manufacturers like to pretend that a kilobyte is 1000 bytes and a megabyte is 1000 kilobytes, while all the rest of the computing world uses 1024 for both factors. Therefore, my 345 MB hard disk is really a 330 MB hard disk.[10]

Swap space allocation is discusses in section 5.5.

4.10.3 Examples of hard disk allocation

I used to have a 109 MB hard disk. Now I am using a 330 MB hard disk. I'll explain how and why I partitioned these disks.

The 109 MB disk I partitioned in a lot of ways, when my needs and the operating systems I used changed; I'll explain two typical scenarios. First, I used to run MS-DOS together with Linux. For that, I needed about 20 MB of hard disk, or just enough to have MS-DOS, a C compiler, an editor, a few other utilities, the program I was working on, and enough free disk space to not feel claustrophobic. For Linux, I had a 10 MB swap partition, and the rest, or 79 MB, was a single partition with all the files I had under Linux. I experimented with having separate root, /usr, and /home partitions, but there was never enough free disk space in one piece to do much interesting.

When I didn't need MS-DOS anymore, I repartitioned the disk so that I had a 12 MB swap partition, and again had the rest as a single filesystem.

The 330 MB disk is partitioned into several partitions, like this:

---

[10]Sic transit discus mundi.

5 MB	root filesystem
10 MB	swap partition
180 MB	/usr filesystem
120 MB	/home filesystem
15 MB	scratch partition

The scratch partition is for playing around with things that require their own partition, e.g., trying different Linux distributions, or comparing speeds of filesystems. When not needed for anything else, it is used as swap space (I like to have a *lot* of open windows).

4.10.4 Adding more disk space for Linux

Adding more disk space for Linux is easy, at least after the hardware has been properly installed (the hardware installation is outside the scope of this book). You format it if necessary, then create the partitions and filesystem as described above, and add the proper lines to /etc/fstab so that it is mounted automatically.

4.10.5 Tips for saving disk space

The best tip for saving disk space is to avoid installing unnecessary programs. Most Linux distributions have an option to install only part of the packages they contain, and by analyzing your needs you might notice that you don't need most of them. This will help save a lot of disk space, since many programs are quite large. Even if you do need a particular package or program, you might not need all of it. For example, some on-line documentation might be unnecessary, as might some of the Elisp files for GNU Emacs, some of the fonts for X11, or some of the libraries for programming.

If you cannot uninstall packages, you might look into compression. Compression programs such as gzip or zip will compress (and uncompress) individual files or groups of files. The gzexe system will compress and uncompress programs invisibly to the user (unused programs are compressed, then uncompressed as they are used). The experimental DouBle system will compress all files in a filesystem, invisibly to the programs that use them. (If you are familiar with products such as Stacker for MS-DOS, the principle is the same.)

Chapter 5

Memory Management

Minnet, jag har tappat mitt minne,
är jag svensk eller finne
kommer inte ihåg...
(Bosse Österberg)

This section describes the Linux memory management features, i.e., virtual memory and the disk buffer cache. The purpose and workings and the things the system administrator needs to take into consideration are described.

5.1 What is virtual memory?

Linux supports **virtual memory**, that is, using a disk as an extension of RAM so that the effective size of usable memory grows correspondingly. The kernel will write the contents of a currently unused block of memory to the hard disk so that the memory can be used for another purpose. When the original contents are needed again, they are read back into memory. This is all made completely transparent to the user; programs running under Linux only see the larger amount of memory available and don't notice that parts of them reside on the disk from time to time. Of course, reading and writing the hard disk is slower (on the order of a thousand times slower) than using real memory, so the programs don't run as fast. The part of the hard disk that is used as virtual memory is called the **swap space**.

Linux can use either a normal file in the filesystem or a separate partition for swap space. A swap partition is faster, but it is easier to change the size of a swap file (there's no need to repartition the whole hard disk, and possibly install everything from scratch). When you know how much swap space you need, you should go for a swap partition, but if you are uncertain, you can use a swap file first, use the system for a while so that you can get a feel for how much swap you need, and then make a swap partition when you're confident about its size.

You should also know that Linux allows one to use several swap partitions and/or swap files at the same time. This means that if you only occasionally need an unusual amount of swap space, you can set up an extra swap file at such times, instead of keeping the whole amount allocated all the time.

A note on operating system terminology: computer science usually distinguishes between swapping (writing the whole process out to swap space) and paging (writing only fixed size parts, usually a few kilobytes, at a time). Paging is usually more efficient, and that's what Linux does, but traditional Linux terminology talks about swapping anyway.[1]

5.2   Creating a swap space

A swap file is an ordinary file; it is in no way special to the kernel. The only thing that matters to the kernel is that it has no holes, and that it is prepared for use with `mkswap`. It must reside on a local disk, however; it can't reside in a filesystem that has been mounted over NFS due to implementation reasons.

The bit about holes is important. The swap file reserves the disk space so that the kernel can quickly swap out a page without having to go through all the things that are necessary when allocating a disk sector to a file. The kernel merely uses any sectors that have already been allocated to the file. Because a hole in a file means that there are no disk sectors allocated (for that place in the file), it is not good for the kernel to try to use them.

One good way to create the swap file without holes is through the following command:

```
$ dd if=/dev/zero of=/extra-swap bs=1024 count=1024
1024+0 records in
1024+0 records out
$
```

---

[1]Thus quite needlessly annoying a number of computer scientists something horrible.

where /extra-swap is the name of the swap file and the size of is given after the count=. It is best for the size to be a multiple of 4, because the kernel writes out **memory pages**, which are 4 kilobytes in size. If the size is not a multiple of 4, the last couple of kilobytes may be unused.

A swap partition is also not special in any way. You create it just like any other partition; the only difference is that it is used as a raw partition, that is, it will not contain any filesystem at all. It is a good idea to mark swap partitions as type 82 (Linux swap); this will the make partition listings clearer, even though it is not strictly necessary to the kernel.

After you have created a swap file or a swap partition, you need to write a signature to its beginning; this contains some administrative information and is used by the kernel. The command to do this is mkswap, used like this:

```
$ mkswap /extra-swap 1024
Setting up swapspace, size = 1044480 bytes
$
```

Note that the swap space is still not in use yet: it exists, but the kernel does not use it to provide virtual memory.

You should be very careful when using mkswap, since it does not check that the file or partition isn't used for anything else. *You can easily overwrite important files and partitions with mkswap!* Fortunately, you should only need to use mkswap when you install your system.

The Linux memory manager limits the size of each swap space to about 127 MB (for various technical reasons, the actual limit is $(4096 - 10) \times 8 \times 4096 = 133890048$ bytes, or 127.6875 megabytes). You can, however, use up to 16 swap spaces simultaneously, for a total of almost 2 GB.[2]

5.3 Using a swap space

An initialized swap space is taken into use with swapon. This command tells the kernel that the swap space can be used. The path to the swap space is given as the argument, so to start swapping on a temporary swap file one might use the following command.

---

[2] A gigabyte here, a gigabyte there, pretty soon we start talking about real memory.

```
$ swapon /extra-swap
$
```

Swap spaces can be used automatically by listing them in the **/etc/fstab** file.

```
/dev/hda8        none         swap         sw      0     0
/swapfile        none         swap         sw      0     0
```

The startup scripts will run the command **swapon -a**, which will start swapping on all the swap spaces listed in **/etc/fstab**. Therefore, the **swapon** command is usually used only when extra swap is needed.

You can monitor the use of swap spaces with **free**. It will tell the total amount of swap space used.

```
$ free
                total      used      free     shared    buffers
Mem:            15152     14896       256      12404      2528
-/+ buffers:               12368      2784
Swap:           32452      6684     25768
$
```

The first line of output (**Mem:**) shows the physical memory. The total column does not show the physical memory used by the kernel, which is usually about a megabyte. The used column shows the amount of memory used (the second line does not count buffers). The free column shows completely unused memory. The shared column shows the amount of memory shared by several processes; the more, the merrier. The buffers column shows the current size of the disk buffer cache.

That last line (**Swap:**) shows similar information for the swap spaces. If this line is all zeroes, your swap space is not activated.

The same information is available via **top**, or using the **proc** filesystem in file **/proc/meminfo**. It is currently difficult to get information on the use of a specific swap space.

A swap space can be removed from use with **swapoff**. It is usually not necessary to do it, except for temporary swap spaces. Any pages in use in the swap space are swapped in first; if there is not sufficient physical memory to hold them, they will then be swapped out (to some other swap space). If there is not enough virtual memory to hold all of the pages Linux will start to thrash; after a long while it should recover, but meanwhile the system is unusable. You should check (e.g., with `free`) that there is enough free memory before removing a swap space from use.

All the swap spaces that are used automatically with `swapon -a` can be removed from use with `swapoff -a`; it looks at the file `/etc/fstab` to find what to remove. Any manually used swap spaces will remain in use.

Sometimes a lot of swap space can be in use even though there is a lot of free physical memory. This can happen for instance if at one point there is need to swap, but later a big process that occupied much of the physical memory terminates and frees the memory. The swapped-out data is not automatically swapped in until it is needed, so the physical memory may remain free for a long time. There is no need to worry about this, but it can be comforting to know what is happening.

5.4 Sharing swap spaces with other operating systems

Virtual memory is built into many operating systems. Since they each need it only when they are running, i.e., never at the same time, the swap spaces of all but the currently running one are being wasted. It would be more efficient for them to share a single swap space. This is possible, but can require a bit of hacking. The Tips-HOWTO contains some advice on how to implement this.

5.5 Allocating swap space

Some people will tell you that you should allocate twice as much swap space as you have physical memory, but this is a bogus rule. Here's how to do it properly:

1. Estimate your total memory needs. This is the largest amount of memory you'll probably need at a time, that is the sum of the memory requirements of all the programs you want to run at the same time. This can be done by running at the same time all the programs you are likely to ever be running at the same time.

   For instance, if you want to run X, you should allocate about 8 MB for it, gcc wants several megabytes (some files need an unusually large amount, up to tens of megabytes, but usually about four should do), and so on. The kernel will use about a megabyte by itself, and the usual shells and other small utilities perhaps a few hundred kilobytes (say a megabyte together). There is no need to try to be exact, rough estimates are fine, but you might want to be on the pessimistic side.

Remember that if there are going to be several people using the system at the same time, they are all going to consume memory. However, if two people run the same program at the same time, the total memory consumption is usually not double, since code pages and shared libraries exist only once.

The `free` and `ps` commands are useful for estimating the memory needs.

2. Add some security to the estimate in step 1. This is because estimates of program sizes will probably be wrong, because you'll probably forget some programs you want to run, and to make certain that you have some extra space just in case. A couple of megabytes should be fine. (It is better to allocate too much than too little swap space, but there's no need to over-do it and allocate the whole disk, since unused swap space is wasted space; see later about adding more swap.) Also, since it is nicer to deal with even numbers, you can round the value up to the next full megabyte.

3. Based on the computations above, you know how much memory you'll be needing in total. So, in order to allocate swap space, you just need to subtract the size of your physical memory from the total memory needed, and you know how much swap space you need. (On some versions of UNIX, you need to allocate space for an image of the physical memory as well, so the amount computed in step 2 is what you need and you shouldn't do the subtraction.)

4. If your calculated swap space is very much larger than your physical memory (more than a couple times larger), you should probably invest in more physical memory, otherwise performance will be too low.

It's a good idea to have at least some swap space, even if your calculations indicate that you need none. Linux uses swap space somewhat aggressively, so that as much physical memory as possible can be kept free. Linux will swap out memory pages that have not been used, even if the memory is not yet needed for anything. This avoids waiting for swapping when it is needed—the swapping can be done earlier, when the disk is otherwise idle.

Swap space can be divided among several disks. This can sometimes improve performance, depending on the relative speeds of the disks and the access patterns of the disks. You might want to experiment with a few schemes, but be aware that doing the experiments properly is quite difficult. You should not believe claims that any one scheme is superior to any other, since it won't always be true.

5.6   The buffer cache

Reading from a disk[3] is very slow compared to accessing (real) memory. In addition, it is common to read the same part of a disk several times during relatively short periods of time. For example, one might first read an e-mail message, then read the letter into an editor when replying to it, then make the mail program read it again when copying it to a folder. Or, consider how often the command `ls` might be run on a system with many users. By reading the information from disk only once and then keeping it in memory until no longer needed, one can speed up all but the first read. This is called **disk buffering**, and the memory used for the purpose is called the **buffer cache**.

Since memory is, unfortunately, a finite, nay, scarce resource, the buffer cache usually cannot be big enough (it can't hold all the data one ever wants to use). When the cache fills up, the data that has been unused for the longest time is discarded and the memory thus freed is used for the new data.

Disk buffering works for writes as well. On the one hand, data that is written is often soon read again (e.g., a source code file is saved to a file, then read by the compiler), so putting data that is written in the cache is a good idea. On the other hand, by only putting the data into the cache, not writing it to disk at once, the program that writes runs quicker. The writes can then be done in the background, without slowing down the other programs.

Most operating systems have buffer caches (although they might be called something else), but not all of them work according to the above principles. Some are **write-through**: the data is written to disk at once (it is kept in the cache as well, of course). The cache is called **write-back** if the writes are done at a later time. Write-back is more efficient than write-through, but also a bit more prone to errors: if the machine crashes, or the power is cut at a bad moment, or the floppy is removed from the disk drive before the data in the cache waiting to be written gets written, the changes in the cache are usually lost. This might even mean that the filesystem (if there is one) is not in full working order, perhaps because the unwritten data held important changes to the bookkeeping information.

Because of this, you should never turn off the power without using a proper shutdown procedure (see chapter 6), or remove a floppy from the disk drive until it has been unmounted (if it was mounted) or after whatever program is using it has signaled that it is finished and the floppy drive light doesn't shine anymore. The `sync`

---

[3]Except a RAM disk, for obvious reasons.

command **flushes** the buffer, i.e., forces all unwritten data to be written to disk, and can be used when one wants to be sure that everything is safely written. In traditional UNIX systems, there is a program called `update` running in the background which does a `sync` every 30 seconds, so it is usually not necessary to use `sync`. Linux has an additional daemon, `bdflush`, which does a more imperfect sync more frequently to avoid the sudden freeze due to heavy disk I/O that `sync` sometimes causes.

Under Linux, `bdflush` is started by `update`. There is usually no reason to worry about it, but if `bdflush` happens to die for some reason, the kernel will warn about this, and you should start it by hand (`/sbin/update`).

The cache does not actually buffer files, but blocks, which are the smallest units of disk I/O (under Linux, they are usually 1 kB). This way, also directories, super blocks, other filesystem bookkeeping data, and non-filesystem disks are cached.

The effectiveness of a cache is primarily decided by its size. A small cache is next to useless: it will hold so little data that all cached data is flushed from the cache before it is reused. The critical size depends on how much data is read and written, and how often the same data is accessed. The only way to know is to experiment.

If the cache is of a fixed size, it is not very good to have it too big, either, because that might make the free memory too small and cause swapping (which is also slow). To make the most efficient use of real memory, Linux automatically uses all free RAM for buffer cache, but also automatically makes the cache smaller when programs need more memory.

Under Linux, you do not need to do anything to make use of the cache, it happens completely automatically. Except for following the proper procedures for shutdown and removing floppies, you do not need to worry about it.

Chapter 6

Boots And Shutdowns

Start me up
Ah... you've got to... you've got to
Never, never never stop
Start it up
Ah... start it up, never, never, never
You make a grown man cry,
you make a grown man cry
(Rolling Stones)

This section explains what goes on when a Linux system is brought up and taken down, and how it should be done properly. If proper procedures are not followed, files might be corrupted or lost.

6.1 An overview of boots and shutdowns

The act of turning on a computer system and causing its operating system to be loaded[1] is called **booting**. The name comes from an image of the computer pulling itself up from its bootstraps, but the act itself slightly more realistic.

During bootstrapping, the computer first loads a small piece of code called the **bootstrap loader**, which in turn loads and starts the operating system. The bootstrap loader is usually stored in a fixed location on a hard disk or a floppy. The reason for this two step process is that the operating system is big and complicated, but the

---

[1] On early computers, it wasn't enough to merely turn on the computer, you had to manually load the operating system as well. These new-fangled thing-a-ma-jigs do it all by themselves.

first piece of code that the computer loads must be very small (a few hundred bytes), to avoid making the firmware unnecessarily complicated.

Different computers do the bootstrapping differently. For PC's, the computer (its BIOS) reads in the first sector (called the **boot sector**) of a floppy or hard disk. The bootstrap loader is contained within this sector. It loads the operating system from elsewhere on the disk (or from some other place).

After Linux has been loaded, it initializes the hardware and device drivers, and then runs `init`. `init` starts other processes to allow users to log in, and do things. The details of this part will be discussed below.

In order to shut down a Linux system, first all processes are told to terminate (this makes them close any files and do other necessary things to keep things tidy), then filesystems and swap areas are unmounted, and finally a message is printed to the console that the power can be turned off. If the proper procedure is not followed, terrible things can and will happen; most importantly, the filesystem buffer cache might not be flushed, which means that all data in it is lost and the filesystem on disk is inconsistent, and therefore possibly unusable.

6.2   The boot process in closer look

You can boot Linux either from a floppy or from the hard disk. The installation section in the Installation and Getting Started guide ([?]) tells you how to install Linux so you can boot it the way you want to.

When a PC is booted, the BIOS will do various tests to check that everything looks all right,[2] and will then start the actual booting. It will choose a disk drive (typically the first floppy drive, if there is a floppy inserted, otherwise the first hard disk, if one is installed in the computer; the order might be configurable, however) and will then read its very first sector. This is called the **boot sector**; for a hard disk, it is also called the **master boot record**, since a hard disk can contain several partitions, each with their own boot sectors.

The boot sector contains a small program (small enough to fit into one sector) whose responsibility is to read the actual operating system from the disk and start it. When booting Linux from a floppy disk, the boot sector contains code that just reads the first few hundred blocks (depending on the actual kernel size, of course) to a predetermined place in memory. On a Linux boot floppy, there is no filesystem, the

---

[2]This is called the **power on self test**, or **POST** for short.

kernel is just stored in consecutive sectors, since this simplifies the boot process. It is possible, however, to boot from a floppy with a filesystem, by using LILO, the LInux LOader.

When booting from the hard disk, the code in the master boot record will examine the partition table (also in the master boot record), identify the active partition (the partition that is marked to be bootable), read the boot sector from that partition, and then start the code in that boot sector. The code in the partition's boot sector does what a floppy disk's boot sector does: it will read in the kernel from the partition and start it. The details vary, however, since it is generally not useful to have a separate partition for just the kernel image, so the code in the partition's boot sector can't just read the disk in sequential order, it has to find the sectors wherever the filesystem has put them. There are several ways around this problem, but the most common way is to use LILO. (The details about how to do this are irrelevant for this discussion, however; see the LILO documentation for more information; it is most thorough.)

When booting with LILO, it will normally go right ahead and read in and boot the default kernel. It is also possible to configure LILO to be able to boot one of several kernels, or even other operating systems than Linux, and it is possible for the user to choose which kernel or operating system is to be booted at boot time. LILO can be configured so that if one holds down the `alt`, `shift`, or `ctrl` key at boot time (when LILO is loaded), LILO will ask what is to be booted and not boot the default right away. Alternatively, LILO can be configured so that it will always ask, with an optional timeout that will cause the default kernel to be booted.

With LILO, it is also possible to give a **kernel command line argument**, after the name of the kernel or operating system.

META: The are other boot loaders than LILO. Information about them will be added in some future version. loadlin.

Booting from floppy and from hard disk have both their advantages, but generally booting from the hard disk is nicer, since it avoids the hassle of playing around with floppies. It is also faster. However, it can be more troublesome to install the system to boot from the hard disk, so many people will first boot from floppy, then, when the system is otherwise installed and working well, will install LILO and start booting from the hard disk.

After the Linux kernel has been read into the memory, by whatever means, and is started for real, roughly the following things happen:

- The Linux kernel is installed compressed, so it will first uncompress itself. The beginning of the kernel image contains a small program that does this.

- If you have a super-VGA card that Linux recognizes and that has some special text modes (such as 100 columns by 40 rows), Linux asks you which mode you want to use. During the kernel compilation, it is possible to preset a video mode, so that this is never asked. This can also be done with LILO or rdev.

- After this, the kernel checks what other hardware there is (hard disks, floppies, network adapters...), and configures some of its device drivers appropriately; while it does this, it outputs messages about its findings. For example, when I boot, I it looks like this:

```
LILO boot:
Loading linux.
Console: colour EGA+ 80x25, 8 virtual consoles
Serial driver version 3.94 with no serial options enabled
tty00 at 0x03f8 (irq = 4) is a 16450
tty01 at 0x02f8 (irq = 3) is a 16450
lp_init: lp1 exists (0), using polling driver
Memory: 7332k/8192k available (300k kernel code, 384k reserved, 176k data)
Floppy drive(s): fd0 is 1.44M, fd1 is 1.2M
Loopback device init
Warning WD8013 board not found at i/o = 280.
Math coprocessor using irq13 error reporting.
Partition check:
   hda: hda1 hda2 hda3
VFS: Mounted root (ext filesystem).
Linux version 0.99.p19-1 (root@haven) 05/01/93 14:12:20
```

The exact texts are different on different systems, depending on the hardware, the version of Linux being used, and how it has been configured.

- Then the kernel will try to mount the root filesystem. The place is configurable at compilation time, or any time with rdev or LILO. The filesystem type is detected automatically. If the mounting of the root filesystem fails, for example because you didn't remember to include the corresponding filesystem driver in the kernel, the kernel panics and halts the system (there isn't much it can do, anyway).

The root filesystem is usually mounted read-only (this can be set in the same way as the place). This makes it possible to check the filesystem while it is mounted; it is not a good idea to check a filesystem that is mounted read-write.

- After this, the kernel starts the program init (located in /sbin/init) in the background (this will always become process number 1). init does various startup chores. The exact things it does depends on how it is configured; see chapter 7 for more information (not yet written). It will at least start some essential background daemons.

- `init` then switches to multi-user mode, and starts a `getty` for virtual consoles and serial lines. `getty` is the program which lets people log in via virtual consoles and serial terminals. `init` may also start some other programs, depending on how it is configured.

- After this, the boot is complete, and the system is up and running normally.

6.3   More about shutdowns

It is important to follow the correct procedures when you shut down a Linux system. If you fail do so, your filesystems probably will become trashed and the files probably will become scrambled. This is because Linux has a disk cache that won't write things to disk at once, but only at intervals. This greatly improves performance but also means that if you just turn off the power at a whim the cache may hold a lot of data and that what is on the disk may not be a fully working filesystem (because only some things have been written to the disk).

Another reason against just flipping the power switch is that in a multi-tasking system there can be lots of things going on in the background, and shutting the power can be quite disastrous. By using the proper shutdown sequence, you ensure that all background processes can save their data.

The command for properly shutting down a Linux system is `shutdown`. It is usually used in one of two ways.

If you are running a system where you are the only user, the usual way of using `shutdown` is to quit all running programs, log out on all virtual consoles, log in as `root` on one of them (or stay logged in as `root` if you already are, but you should change to the root directory, to avoid problems with unmounting), then give the command `shutdown -h now` (substitute `now` with a plus sign and a number in minutes if you want a delay, though you usually don't on a single user system).

If your system has many users, you can use the command `shutdown -h +`*time* *message*, where *time* is the time in minutes until the system is halted, and *message* is a short explanation of why the system is shutting down.

```
# shutdown -h +10 'We will install a new disk. System should
```

```
> be back on-line in three hours.'

#
```

This will warn everybody that the system will shut down in ten minutes, and that they'd better get lost or lose data. The warning is printed to every terminal on which someone is logged in, including all xterms:

```
Broadcast message from root (ttyp0) Wed Aug 2 01:03:25 1995...


We will install a new disk.  System should

be back on-line in three hours.

The system is going DOWN for system halt in 10 minutes !!
```

The warning is automatically repeated a few times before the boot, with shorter and shorter intervals as the time runs out.

When the real shutting down starts after any delays, all filesystems (except the root one) are unmounted, user processes (if anybody is still logged in) are killed, daemons are shut down, all filesystem are unmounted, and generally everything settles down. When that is done, init prints out a message that you can power down the machine. Then, *and only then*, should you move your fingers towards the power switch.

Sometimes, although rarely on any good system, it is impossible to shut down properly. For instance, if the kernel panics and crashes and burns and generally misbehaves, it might be completely impossible to give any new commands, hence shutting down properly is somewhat difficult, and just about everything you can do is hope that nothing has been too severely damaged and turn off the power. If the troubles are a bit less severe (say, somebody hit your keyboard with an axe), and the kernel and the update program still run normally, it is probably a good idea to wait a couple of minutes to give update a chance to flush the buffer cache, and only cut the power after that.

Some people like to shut down using the command sync[3] three times, waiting for the disk I/O to stop, then turn off the power. If there are no running programs, this is about equivalent to using shutdown. However, it does not unmount any filesystems and this can lead to problems with the ext2fs "clean filesystem" flag. The triple-sync method is *not recommended*.

(In case you're wondering: the reason for *three* syncs is that in the early days of UNIX, when the commands were typed separately, that usually gave sufficient time for most disk I/O to be finished.)

---

[3] sync flushes the buffer cache.

6.4   Rebooting

Rebooting means booting the system again. This can be accomplished by first shutting it down completely, turning power off, and then turning it back on. A simpler way is to ask `shutdown` to reboot the system, instead of merely halting it. This is accomplished by using the `-r` option to shutdown, for example, by giving the command `shutdown -r now`.

Most Linux systems run `shutdown -r now` when ctrl-alt-del is pressed on the keyboard. This reboots the system. The action on ctrl-alt-del is configurable, however, and it might be better to allow for some delay before the reboot on a multiuser machine. Systems that are physically accessible to anyone might even be configured to do nothing when ctrl-alt-del is pressed.

6.5   Single user mode

The shutdown command can also be used to bring the system down to single user mode, in which no one can log in, but `root` can use the console. This is useful for system administration tasks that can't be done while the system is running normally. Single user mode is discussed more thoroughly in chapter **??**.

6.6   Emergency boot floppies

It is not always possible to boot a computer from the hard disk. For example, if you make a mistake in configuring LILO, you might make your system unbootable. For these situations, you need an alternative way of booting that will always work (as long as the hardware works). For typical PC's, this means booting from the floppy drive.

Most Linux distributions allow one to create an **emergency boot floppy** during installation. It is a good idea to do this. However, some such boot disks contain only the kernel, and assume you will be using the programs on the distribution's installation disks to fix whatever problem you have. Sometimes those programs aren't enough; for example, you might have to restore some files from backups made with software not on the installation disks.

Thus, it might be necessary to create a custom root floppy as well. The *Bootdisk HOWTO* by Graham Chapman ([**?**]) contains instructions for doing this. You must, of course, remember to keep your emergency boot and root floppies up to date.

You can't use the floppy drive you use to mount the root floppy for anything else. This can be inconvenient if you only have one floppy drive. However, if you have enough memory, you can configure your boot floppy to load the root disk to a ramdisk (the boot floppy's kernel needs to be specially configured for this). Once the root floppy has been loaded into the ramdisk, the floppy drive is free to mount other disks.

Chapter 7

init

Uuno on numero yksi

This chapter describes the `init` process, which is the first user level process started by the kernel. `init` has many important duties, such as starting `getty` (so that users can log in), implementing run levels, and taking care of orphaned processes. This chapter explains how `init` is configured and how you can make use of the different run levels.

7.1   `init` comes first

`init` is one of those programs that are absolutely essential to the operation of a Linux system, but that you still can mostly ignore. A good Linux distribution will come with a configuration for `init` that will work for most systems, and on these systems there is nothing you need to do about `init`. Usually, you only need to worry about `init` if you hook up serial terminals, dial-in (not dial-out) modems, or if you want to change the default run level.

When the kernel has started itself (has been loaded into memory, has started running, and has initialized all device drivers and data structures and such), it finishes its own part of the boot process by starting a user level program, `init`. Thus, `init` is always the first process (its process number is always 1).

The kernel looks for `init` in a few locations that have been historically used for it, but the proper location for it (on a Linux system) is `/sbin/init`. If the kernel can't find `init`, it tries to run `/bin/sh`, and if that also fails, the startup of the system fails.

When init starts, it finishes the boot process by doing a number of administrative tasks, such as checking filesystems, cleaning up /tmp, starting various services, and starting a getty for each terminal and virtual console where users should be able to log in (see chapter 8).

After the system is properly up, init restarts getty for each terminal after a user has logged out (so that the next user can log in). init also adopts orphan processes: when a process starts a child process and dies before its child, the child immediately becomes a child of init. This is important for various technical reasons, but it is good to know it, since it makes it easier to understand process lists and process tree graphs.[1]

There are a few variants of init available. Most Linux distributions use sysvinit (written by Miquel van Smoorenburg), which is based on the System V init design. The BSD versions of Unix have a different init. The primary difference is run levels: System V has them, BSD does not (at least traditionally). This difference is not essential. We'll look at sysvinit only.

7.2 Configuring init to start getty: the /etc/inittab file

When it starts up, init reads the /etc/inittab configuration file. While the system is running, it will re-read it, if sent the HUP signal;[2] this feature makes it unnecessary to boot the system to make changes to the init configuration take effect.

The /etc/inittab file is a bit complicated. We'll start with the simple case of configuring getty lines. Lines in /etc/inittab consist of four colon-delimited fields:

id:runlevels:action:process

The fields are described below. In addition, /etc/inittab can contain empty lines, and lines that begin with a number sign ('#'); these are both ignored.

id   This identifies the line in the file. For getty lines, it specifies the termi-
            nal it runs on (the characters after /dev/tty in the device file name).
            For other lines, it doesn't matter (except for length restrictions), but it
            should be unique.

---

[1] init itself is not allowed to die. You can't kill init even with SIGKILL.
[2] Using the command kill -HUP 1 as root, for example

runlevels   The run levels the line should be considered for. The run levels are given as single digits, without delimiters. (Run levels are described in the next section.)

action   What action should be taken by the line, e.g., **respawn** to run the command in the next field again, when it exits, or **once** to run it just once.

process   The command to run.

To start a **getty** on the first virtual terminal (**/dev/tty1**), in all the normal multi-user run levels (2–5), one would write the following line:

```
1:2345:respawn:/sbin/getty 9600 tty1
```

The first field says that this is the line for **/dev/tty1**. The second field says that it applies to run levels 2, 3, 4, and 5. The third field means that the command should be run again, after it exits (so that one can log in, log out, and then log in again). The last field is the command that runs **getty** on the first virtual terminal.[3]

If you wanted to add terminals or dial-in modem lines to a system, you'd add more lines to **/etc/inittab**, one for each terminal or dial-in line. For more details, see the manual pages *init*(8), *inittab*(5), and *getty*(8).

If a command fails when it starts, and **init** is configured to **restart** it, it will use a lot of system resources: **init** starts it, it fails, **init** starts it, it fails, **init** starts it, it fails, and so on, ad infinitum. To prevent this, **init** will keep track of how often it restarts a command, and if the frequency grows to high, it will delay for five minutes before restarting again.

7.3 Run levels

A **run level** is a state of **init** and the whole system that defines what system services are operating. Run levels are identified by numbers, see table 7.1. There is no consensus of how to use the user defined run levels (2 through 5). Some system administrators use run levels to define which subsystems are working, e.g., whether X is running, whether the network is operational, and so on. Others have all subsystems always running or start and stop them individually, without changing run levels, since

---

[3]Different versions of **getty** are run differently. Consult your manual page—and make sure it is the correct manual page.

run levels are too coarse for controlling their systems. You need to decide for yourself, but it might be easiest to follow the way your Linux distribution does things.

Table 7.1: Run level numbers

0	Halt the system.
1	Single-user mode (for special administration).
2–5	Normal operation (user defined).
6	Reboot.

Run levels are configured in /etc/inittab by lines like the following:

```
12:2:wait:/etc/init.d/rc 2
```

The first field is an arbitrary label, the second one means that this applies for run level 2. The third field means that init should run the command in the fourth field once, when the run level is entered, and that init should wait for it to complete. The /etc/init.d/rc command runs whatever commands are necessary to start and stop services to enter run level 2.

The command in the fourth field does all the hard work of setting up a run level. It starts services that aren't already running, and stops services that shouldn't be running in the new run level any more. Exactly what the command is, and how run levels are configured, depends on the Linux distribution.

When init starts, it looks for a line in /etc/inittab that specifies the default run level:

```
id:2:initdefault:
```

You can ask init to go to a non-default run level at startup by giving the kernel a command line argument of single or emergency.[4] This allows you to choose the single user mode (run level 1), which is described in section 7.5.

While the system is running, the telinit command can change the run level. When the run level is changed, init runs the relevant command from /etc/inittab.

7.4 Special configuration in /etc/inittab

The /etc/inittab has some special features that allow init to react to special circumstances. These special features are marked by special keywords in the third

---

[4]Kernel command line arguments can be given via LILO, for example. See section 7.5.

field. Some examples:

powerwait   Allows init to shut the system down, when the power fails. This assumes the use of a UPS, and software that watches the UPS and informs init that the power is off.

ctrlaltdel   Allows init to reboot the system, when the user presses `control-alt-del` on the console keyboard. Note that the system administrator can configure the reaction to `C-A-D` to be something else instead, e.g., to be ignored, if the system is in a public location.[5]

sysinit   Command to be run when the system is booted. This command usually cleans up /tmp, for example.

The list above is not exhaustive. See your *inittab*(5) manual page for all possibilities, and for details on how to use the above ones.

7.5 Booting in single user mode

An important run level is **single user mode** (run level 1), in which only the system administrator is using the machine and as few system services—including logins—as possible are running. Single user mode is necessary for a few administrative tasks,[6] such as running fsck on a /usr partition—this requires that the partition be unmounted, and that can't happen, unless just about all system services are killed.

A running system can be taken to single user mode by using telinit to request run level 1. At bootup, it can be entered by giving the word single or emergency on the kernel command line: the kernel gives the command line to init as well, and init understands from that word that it shouldn't use the default run level. (The kernel command line is entered in a way that depends on how you boot the system.)

Booting into single user mode is sometimes necessary so that one can run fsck by hand, before anything mounts or otherwise touches a broken /usr partition (any activity on a broken filesystem is likely to break it more, so fsck should be run as soon as possible).

The bootup scripts init runs will automatically enter single user mode, if the automatic fsck at bootup fails. This is an attempt to prevent the system from using

---

[5]Or to start nethack.
[6]It probably shouldn't be used for playing nethack.

a filesystem that is so broken that `fsck` can't fix it automatically. Such breakage
is relatively rare, and usually involves a broken hard disk or an experimental kernel
release, but it's good to be prepared.

As a security measure, a properly configured system will ask for the `root` password
before starting the shell in single user mode. Otherwise, it would be simple to just
enter a suitable line to LILO to get in as `root`. (This will break if `/etc/passwd` has
been broken by filesystem problems, of course, and in that case you'd better have a
boot floppy handy.)

Chapter 8

Logging In And Out

This section describes what happens when a user logs in or out. The various inter-actions of background processes, log files, configuration files, and so on are described in some detail.

8.1   Logins via terminals

Figure 8.1 shows how logins happen via terminals. First, `init` makes sure there is a `getty` program for the terminal connection (or console). `getty` listens at the terminal and waits for the user to notify that he is ready to login in (this usually means that the user must type something). When it notices a user, `getty` outputs a welcome message (stored in `/etc/issue`), and prompts for the username, and finally runs the `login` program. `login` gets the username as a parameter, and prompts the user for the password. If these match, `login` starts the shell configured for the user; else it just exits and terminates the process (perhaps after giving the user another chance at entering the username and password). `init` notices that the process terminated, and starts a new `getty` for the terminal.

Note that the only new process is the one created by `init` (using the `fork` system call); `getty` and `login` only replace the program running in the process (using the `exec` system call).

A separate program, for noticing the user, is needed for serial lines, since it can be (and traditionally was) complicated to notice when a terminal becomes active. `getty` also adapts to the speed and other settings of the connection, which is important especially for dial-in connections, where these parameters may change from call to call.

There are several versions of `getty` and `init` in use, all with their good and bad points. It is a good idea to learn about the versions on your system, and also about the other versions (you could use the Linux Software Map to search them). If you don't have dial-in's, you probably don't have to worry about `getty`, but `init` is still important.

8.2   Logins via the network

Two computers in the same network are usually linked via a single physical cable. When they communicate over the network, the programs in each computer that take part in the communication are linked via a **virtual connection**, a sort of imaginary cable. As far as the programs at either end of the virtual connection are concerned, they have a monopoly on their own cable. However, since the cable is not real, only imaginary, the operating systems of both computers can have several virtual connections share the same physical cable. This way, using just a single cable, several programs can communicate without having to know of or care about the other communications. It is even possible to have several computers use the same cable; the virtual connections exist between two computers, and the other computers ignore those connections that they don't take part in.

That's a complicated and over-abstracted description of the reality. It might, however, be good enough to understand the important reason why network logins are somewhat different from normal logins. The virtual connections are established when there are two programs on different computers that wish to communicate. Since it is in principle possible to login from any computer in a network to any other computer, there is a huge number of potential virtual communications. Because of this, it is not practical to start a `getty` for each potential login.

There is a single process inetd (corresponding to `getty`) that handles *all* network logins. When it notices an incoming network login (i.e., it notices that it gets a new virtual connection to some other computer), it starts a new process to handle that single login. The original process remains and continues to listen for new logins.

To make things a bit more complicated, there is more than one communication protocol for network logins. The two most important ones are `telnet` and `rlogin`. In addition to logins, there are many other virtual connections that may be made (for

FTP, Gopher, HTTP, and other network services). It would be ineffective to have a separate process listening for a particular type of connection, so instead there is only one listener that can recognize the type of the connection and can start the correct type of program to provide the service. This single listener is called `inetd`; see the "Linux Network Administrators' Guide" for more information.

8.3 What `login` does

The `login` program takes care of authenticating the user (making sure that the username and password match), and of setting up an initial environment for the user by setting permissions for the serial line and starting the shell.

Part of the initial setup is outputting the contents of the file `/etc/motd` (short for message of the day) and checking for electronic mail. These can be disabled by creating a file called `.hushlogin` in the user's home directory.

If the file `/etc/nologin` exists, logins are disabled. That file is typically created by `shutdown` and relatives. `login` checks for this file, and will refuse to accept a login if it exists. If it does exist, `login` outputs its contents to the terminal before it quits.

`login` logs all failed login attempts in a system log file (via `syslog`). It also logs *all* logins by `root`. Both of these can be useful when tracking down intruders.

Currently logged in people are listed in `/var/run/utmp`. This file is valid only until the system is next rebooted or shut down; it is cleared when the system is booted. It lists each user and the terminal (or network connection) he is using, along with some other useful information. The `who`, `w`, and other similar commands look in `utmp` to see who are logged in.

All successful logins are recorded into `/var/log/wtmp`. This file will grow without limit, so it must be cleaned regularly, for example by having a weekly `cron` job to clear it.[1] The `last` command browses `wtmp`.

Both `utmp` and `wtmp` are in a binary format (see the *utmp* manual page); it is unfortunately not convenient to examine them without special programs.

8.4 X and xdm

META: X implements logins via xdm; also: xterm -ls

---

[1] Good Linux distributions do this out of the box.

8.5   Access control

The user database is traditionally contained in the /etc/passwd file. Some systems use **shadow passwords**, and have moved the passwords to /etc/shadow. Sites with many computers that share the accounts use NIS or some other method to store the user database; they might also automatically copy the database from one central location to all other computers.

The user database contains not only the passwords, but also some additional information about the users, such as their real names, home directories, and login shells. This other information needs to be public, so that anyone can read it. Therefore the password is stored encrypted. This does have the drawback that anyone with access to the encrypted password can use various cryptographical methods to guess it, without trying to actually log into the computer. Shadow passwords try to avoid this by moving the password into another file, which only **root** can read (the password is still stored encrypted). However, installing shadow passwords later onto a system that did not support them can be difficult.

With or without passwords, it is important to make sure that all passwords in a system are good, i.e., not easily guessable. The **crack** program can be used to crack passwords; any password it can find is by definition not a good one. While **crack** can be run by intruders, it can also be run by the system adminstrator to avoid bad passwords. Good passwords can also be enforced by the **passwd** program; this is in fact more effective in CPU cycles, since cracking passwords requires quite a lot of computation.

The user group database is kept in /etc/group; for systems with shadow passwords, there can be a /etc/shadow.group.

root usually can't login via most terminals or the network, only via terminals listed in the /etc/securetty file. This makes it necessary to get physical access to one of these terminals. It is, however, possible to log in via any terminal as any other user, and use the **su** command to become **root**.

8.6   Shell startup

When an interactive login shell starts, it automatically executes one or more predefined files. Different shells execute different files; see the documentation of each shell for further information.

Most shells first run some global file, for example, the Bourne shell (`/bin/sh`) and its derivatives execute `/etc/profile`; in addition, they execute `.profile` in the user's home directory. `/etc/profile` allows the system administrator to have set up a common user environment, especially by setting the PATH to include local command directories in addition to the normal ones. On the other hand, `.profile` allows the user to customize the environment to his own tastes by overriding, if necessary, the default environment.

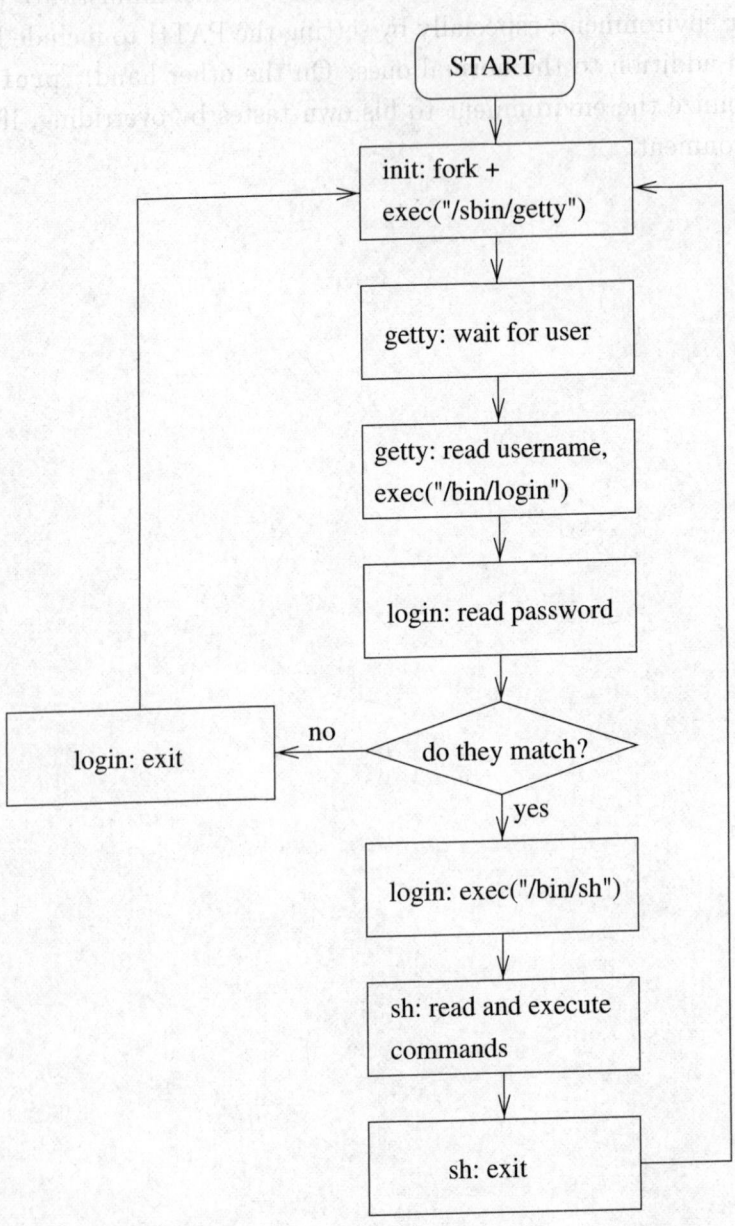

Figure 8.1: Logins via terminals: the interaction of init, getty, login, and the shell.

Chapter 9

Managing user accounts

The similarities of sysadmins and drug dealers:
both measure stuff in K's, and both have users.
(Old, tired computer joke.)

This chapter explains how to create new user accounts, how to modify the properties of those accounts, and how to remove the accounts. Different Linux systems have different tools for doing this.

9.1 What's an account?

When a computer is used by many people it is usually necessary to differentiate between the users, for example, so that their private files can be kept private. This is important even if the computer can only be used by a single person at a time, as with most microcomputers.[1] Thus, each user is given a unique username, and that name is used to log in.

There's more to a user than just a name, however. An **account** is all the files, resources, and information belonging to one user. The term hints at banks, and in a commercial system each account usually has some money attached to it, and that money vanishes at different speeds depending on how much the user stresses the system. For example, disk space might have a price per megabyte and day, and processing time might have a price per second.

---

[1]It might be quite embarrassing if my sister could read my love letters.

9.2   Creating a user

The Linux kernel itself treats users are mere numbers. Each user is identified by a unique integer, the **user id** or **uid**, because numbers are faster and easier for a computer to process than textual names. A separate database outside the kernel assigns a textual name, the **username**, to each user id. The database contains additional information as well.

To create a user, you need to add information about the user to the user database, and create a home directory for him. It may also be necessary to educate the user, and set up a suitable initial environment for him.

Most Linux distributions come with a program for creating accounts. There are several such programs available. Two command line alternatives are `adduser` and `useradd`; there may be a GUI tool as well. Whatever the program, the result is that there is little if any manual work to be done. Even if the details are many and intricate, these programs make everything seem trivial. However, section 9.2.4 describes how to do it by hand.

9.2.1   /etc/passwd and other informative files

The basic user database in a Unix system is the text file, `/etc/passwd` (called the **password file**), which lists all valid usernames and their associated information. The file has one line per username, and is divided into seven colon-delimited fields:

1. Username.

2. Password, in an encrypted form.

3. Numeric user id.

4. Numeric group id.

5. Full name or other description of account.

6. Home directory.

7. Login shell (program to run at login).

The format is explained in more detail in *passwd*(5).

Any user on the system may read the password file, so that they can, for example, learn the name of another user. This means that the password (the second field) is also available to everyone. The password file encrypts the password, so in theory there is no problem. However, the encryption is breakable, especially if the password is weak (e.g., it is short or it can be found in a dictionary). Therefore it is not a good idea to have the password in the password file.

Many Linux systems have **shadow passwords**. This is an alternative way of storing the password: the encrypted password is stored in a separate file, `/etc/shadow`, which only `root` can read. The `/etc/passwd` file only contains a special marker in the second field. Any program that needs to verify a user is setuid, and can therefore access the shadow password file. Normal programs, which only use the other fields in the password file, can't get at the password.[2]

9.2.2 Picking numeric user and group ids

On most systems it doesn't matter what the numeric user and group ids are, but if you use the Network filesystem (NFS), you need to have the same uid and gid on all systems. This is because NFS also identifies users with the numeric uids. If you aren't using NFS, you can let your account creation tool pick them automatically.

If you are using NFS, you'll have to be invent a mechanism for synchronizing account information. One alternative is to the NIS system (see [?]).

META: this is wrong place? However, you should try to avoid re-using numeric uid's (and textual usernames), because the new owner of the uid (or username) may get access to the old owner's files (or mail, or whatever).

9.2.3 Initial environment: `/etc/skel`

When the home directory for a new user is created, it is initialized with files from the `/etc/skel` directory. The system administrator can create files in `/etc/skel` that will provide a nice default environment for users. For example, he might create a `/etc/skel/.profile` that sets the EDITOR environment variable to some editor that is friendly towards new users.

However, it is usually best to try to keep `/etc/skel` as small as possible, since it will be next to impossible to update existing users' files. For example, if the name of the friendly editor changes, all existing users would have to edit their `.profile`. The system administrator could try to do it automatically, with a script, but that is almost certain going to break someone's file.

---

[2]Yes, this means that the password file has all the information about a user *except* his password. The wonder of development.

Whenever possible, it is better to put global configuration into global files, such as `/etc/profile`. This way it is possible to update it without breaking users' own setups.

9.2.4 Creating a user by hand

To create a new account manually, follow these steps:

1. Edit `/etc/passwd` with `vipw(8)` and add a new line for the new account. Be careful with the syntax. *Do not edit directly with an editor!* `vipw` locks the file, so that other commands won't try to update it at the same time. You should make the password field be '`*`', so that it is impossible to log in.

2. Similarly, edit `/etc/group` with `vigr`, if you need to create a new group as well.

3. Create the home directory of the user with `mkdir`.

4. Copy the files from `/etc/skel` to the new home directory.

5. Fix ownerships and permissions with `chown` and `chmod`. The `-R` option is most useful. The correct permissions vary a little from one site to another, but usually the following commands do the right thing:

   ```
   cd /home/newusername
   chown -R username.group .
   chmod -R go=u,go-w .
   chmod go= .
   ```

6. Set the password with `passwd(1)`.

After you set the password in the last step, the account will work. You shouldn't set it until everything else has been done, otherwise the user may inadvertently log in while you're still copying the files.

It is sometimes necessary to create dummy accounts[3] that are not used by people. For example, to set up an anonymous FTP server (so that anyone can download files from it, without having to get an account first), you need to create an account called `ftp`. In such cases, it is usually not necessary to set the password (last step above). Indeed, it is better not to, so that no-one can use the account, unless they first become `root`, since `root` can become any user.

---

[3]Surreal users?

9.3 Changing user properties

There are a few commands for changing various properties of an account (i.e., the relevant field in `/etc/passwd`):

chfn   Change the full name field.

chsh   Change the login shell.

passwd   Change the password.

The super-user may use these commands to change the properties of any account. Normal users can only change the properties of their own account. It may sometimes be necessary to disable these commands (with `chmod`) for normal users, for example in an environment with many novice users.

Other tasks need to be done by hand. For example, to change the username, you need to edit `/etc/passwd` directly (with `vipw`, remember). Likewise, to add or remove the user to more groups, you need to edit `/etc/group` (with `vigr`). Such tasks tend to be rare, however, and should be done with caution: for example, if you change the username, e-mail will no longer reach the user, unless you also create a mail alias.[4]

9.4 Removing a user

To remove a user, you first remove all his files, mailboxes, mail aliases, print jobs, `cron` and `at` jobs, and all other references to the user. Then you remove the relevant lines from `/etc/passwd` and `/etc/group` (remember to remove the username from all groups it's been added to). It may be a good idea to first disable the account (see below), before you start removing stuff, to prevent the user from using the account while it is being removed.

Remember that users may have files outside their home directory. The `find` command can find them:

```
find / -user username
```

However, note that the above command will take a *long* time, if you have large disks. If you mount network disks (see section 2.3.8), you need to be careful so that you won't trash the network or the server.

---

[4]The user's name might change due to marriage, for example, and he might want to have his username reflect his new name.

Some Linux distributions come with special commands to do this; look for `deluser` or `userdel`. However, it is easy to do it by hand as well, and the commands might not do everything.

9.5 Disabling a user temporarily

It is sometimes necessary to temporarily disable an account, without removing it. For example, the user might not have paid his fees, or the system administrator may suspect that a cracker has got the password of that account.

The best way to disable an account is to change its shell into a special program that just prints a message. This way, whoever tries to log into the account, will fail, and will know why. The message can tell the user to contact the system administrator so that any problems may be dealt with.

It would also be possible to change the username or password to something else, but then the user won't know what is going on. Confused users mean more work.[5]

A simple way to create the special programs is to write 'tail scripts':

```
#!/usr/bin/tail +2
This account has been closed due to a security breach.
Please call 555-1234 and wait for the men in black to arrive.
```

The first two characters ('#!') tell the kernel that the rest of the line is a command that needs to be run to interpret this file. The `tail` command in this case outputs everything except the first line to the standard output.

If `billg` is suspected of a security breach, the system administrator would do something like this:

```
# chsh -s /usr/local/lib/no-login/security billg
# su - tester
This account has been closed due to a security breach.
Please call 555-1234 and wait for the men in black to arrive.
#
```

The purpose of the `su` is to test that the change worked, of course.

Tail scripts should be kept in a separate directory, so that their names don't interfere with normal user commands.

---

[5]But they can be *so* fun, if you're a BOFH.

Chapter 10

Backups

> *Hardware is indeterministically reliable.*
> *Software is deterministically unreliable.*
> *People are indeterministically unreliable.*
> *Nature is deterministically reliable.*

This chapter explains about why, how, and when to make backups, and how to restore things from backups.

10.1   On the importance of being backed up

Your data is valuable. It will cost you time and effort re-create it, and that costs money or at least personal grief and tears; sometimes it can't even be re-created, e.g., if it is the results of some experiments. Since it is an investment, you should protect it and take steps to avoid losing it.

There are basically four reasons why you might lose data: hardware failures, software bugs, human action, or natural disasters.[1] Although modern hardware tends to be quite reliable, it can still break seemingly spontaneously. The most critical piece of hardware for storing data is the hard disk, which relies on tiny magnetic fields remaining intact in a world filled with electromagnetic noise. Modern software doesn't even tend to be reliable; a rock solid program is an exception, not a rule. Humans are quite unreliable, they will either make a mistake, or they will be malicious and destroy data on purpose. Nature might not be evil, but it can wreak havoc even when

---

[1] The fifth reason is "something else".

311

being good. All in all, it is a small miracle that anything works at all.

Backups are a way to protect the investment in data. By having several copies of the data, it does not matter as much if one is destroyed (the cost is only that of the restoration of the lost data from the backup).

It is important to do backups properly. Like everything else that is related to the physical world, backups will fail sooner or later. Part of doing backups well is to make sure they work; you don't want to notice that your backups didn't work.[2] Adding insult to injury, you might have a bad crash just as you're making the backup; if you have only one backup medium, it might destroyed as well, leaving you with the smoking ashes of hard work.[3] Or you might notice, when trying to restore, that you forgot to back up something important, like the user database on a 15 000 user site. Best of all, all your backups might be working perfectly, but the last known tape drive reading the kind of tapes you used was the one that now has a bucketful of water in it.

When it comes to backups, paranoia is in the job description.

10.2   Selecting the backup medium

The most important decision regarding backups is the choice of backup medium. You need to consider cost, reliability, speed, availability, and usability.

Cost is important, since you should preferably have several times more backup storage than what you need for the data. A cheap medium is usually a must.

Reliability is extremely important, since a broken backup can make a grown man cry. A backup medium must be able to hold data without corruption for years. The way you use the medium affects it reliability as a backup medium. A hard disk is typically very reliable, but as a backup medium it is not very reliable, if it is in the same computer as the disk you are backing up.

Speed is usually not very important, if backups can be done without interaction. It doesn't matter if a backup takes two hours, as long as it needs no supervision. On the other hand, if the backup can't be done when the computer would otherwise be idle, then speed is an issue.

Availability is obviously necessary, since you can't use a backup medium if it doesn't exist. Less obvious is the need for the medium to be available even in the

---

[2] Don't laugh. This has happened to several people.
[3] Been there, done that...

future, and on computers other than your own. Otherwise you may not be able to restore your backups after a disaster.

Usability is a large factor in how often backups are made. The easier it is to make backups, the better. A backup medium mustn't be hard or boring to use.

The typical alternatives are floppies and tapes. Floppies are very cheap, fairly reliable, not very fast, very available, but not very usable for large amounts of data. Tapes are cheap to somewhat expensive, fairly reliable, fairly fast, quite available, and—depending on the size of the tape—quite comfortable.

There are other alternatives. They are usually not very good on availability, but if that is not a problem, they can be better in other ways. For example, magneto-optical disks can have good sides of both floppies (they're random access, making restoration of a single file quick) and tapes (contain a lot of data).

10.3   Selecting the backup tool

There are many tools that can be used to make backups. The traditional UNIX tools used for backups are `tar`, `cpio`, and `dump`. In addition, there are large number of third party packages (both freeware and commercial) that can be used. The choice of backup medium can affect the choice of tool.

`tar` and `cpio` are similar, and mostly equivalent from a backup point of view. Both are capable of storing files on tapes, and retrieving files from them. Both are capable of using almost any media, since the kernel device drivers take care of the low level device handling and the devices all tend to look alike to user level programs. Some UNIX versions of `tar` and `cpio` may have problems with unusual files (symbolic links, device files, files with very long pathnames, and so on), but the Linux versions should handle all files correctly.

`dump` is different in that it reads the filesystem directly and not via the filesystem. It is also written specifically for backups; `tar` and `cpio` are really for archiving files, although they work for backups as well.

Reading the filesystem directly has some advantages. It makes it possible to back files up without affecting their time stamps; for `tar` and `cpio`, you would have to mount the filesystem read-only first. Directly reading the filesystem is also more effective, if everything needs to be backed up, since it can be done with much less disk head movement. The major disadvantage is that it makes the backup program specific to one filesystem type; the Linux `dump` program understands the ext2 filesystem only.

dump also directly supports backup levels (which we'll be discussing below); with tar and cpio this has to be implemented with other tools.

A comparison of the third party backup tools is beyond the scope of this book. The Linux Software Map lists many of the freeware ones.

10.4   Simple backups

A simple backup scheme is to back up everything once, then back up everything that has been modified since the previous backup. The first backup is called a **full backup**, the subsequent ones are **incremental backups**. A full backup is often more laborius than incremental ones, since there is more data to write to the tape and a full backup might not fit onto one tape (or floppy). Restoring from incremental backups can be many times more work than from a full one. Restoration can be optimized so that you always back up everything since the previous full backup; this way, backups are a bit more work, but there should never be a need to restore more than a full backup and an incremental backup.

If you want to make backups every day and have six tapes, you could use tape 1 for the first full backup (say, on a Friday), and tapes 2 to 5 for the incremental backups (Monday through Thursday). Then you make a new full backup on tape 6 (second Friday), and start doing incremental ones with tapes 2–5 again. You don't want to overwrite tape 1 with until you've got a new full backup, lest something happens while you're making the full backup. After you've made a full backup to tape 6, you want to keep tape 1 somewhere else, so that when your other backup tapes are destroyed in the fire, you still have at least something left. When you need to make the next full backup, you fetch tape 1 and leave tape 6 in its place.

If you have more than six tapes, you can use the extra ones for full backups. Each time you make a full backup, you use the oldest tape. This way you can have full backups from several previous weeks, which is good if you want to find an old, now deleted file, or an old version of a file.

10.4.1   Making backups with tar

A full backup can easily be made with tar:

```
# tar -create -file /dev/ftape /usr/src
tar: Removing leading / from absolute path names in the archive
```

```
#
```

The example above uses the GNU version of tar and its long option names. The traditional version of tar only understands single character options. The GNU version can also handle backups that don't fit on one tape or floppy, and also very long paths; not all traditional versions can do these things. (Linux only uses GNU tar.)

If your backup doesn't fit on one tape, you need to use the -multi-volume (-M) option:

```
# tar -cMf /dev/fd0H1440 /usr/src
tar: Removing leading / from absolute path names in the archive
Prepare volume #2 for /dev/fd0H1440 and hit return:
#
```

Note that you should format the floppies before you begin the backup, or else use another window or virtual terminal and do it when tar asks for a new floppy.

After you've made a backup, you should check that it is OK, using the -compare (-d) option:

```
# tar -compare -verbose -f /dev/ftape
usr/src/
usr/src/linux
usr/src/linux-1.2.10-includes/
....
#
```

Failing to check a backup means that you will not notice that your backups aren't working until after you've lost the original data.

An incremental backup can be done with tar using the -newer (-N) option:

```
# tar -create -newer '8 Sep 1995' -file /dev/ftape /usr/src -verbose
tar: Removing leading / from absolute path names in the archive
usr/src/
usr/src/linux-1.2.10-includes/
usr/src/linux-1.2.10-includes/include/
usr/src/linux-1.2.10-includes/include/linux/
usr/src/linux-1.2.10-includes/include/linux/modules/
usr/src/linux-1.2.10-includes/include/asm-generic/
```

```
usr/src/linux-1.2.10-includes/include/asm-i386/
usr/src/linux-1.2.10-includes/include/asm-mips/
usr/src/linux-1.2.10-includes/include/asm-alpha/
usr/src/linux-1.2.10-includes/include/asm-m68k/
usr/src/linux-1.2.10-includes/include/asm-sparc/
usr/src/patch-1.2.11.gz
#
```

Unfortunately, `tar` can't notice when a file's inode information has changed, for example, that it's permission bits have been changed, or when its name has been changed. This can be worked around using `find` and comparing current filesystem state with lists of files that have been previously backed up. Scripts and programs for doing this can be found on Linux ftp sites.

10.4.2   Restoring files with `tar`

The `-extract` (`-x`) option for `tar` extracts files:

```
# tar -extract -same-permissions -verbose -file /dev/fd0H1440
usr/src/
usr/src/linux
usr/src/linux-1.2.10-includes/
usr/src/linux-1.2.10-includes/include/
usr/src/linux-1.2.10-includes/include/linux/
usr/src/linux-1.2.10-includes/include/linux/hdreg.h
usr/src/linux-1.2.10-includes/include/linux/kernel.h
...
#
```

You also extract only specific files or directories (which includes all their files and subdirectories) by naming on the command line:

```
# tar xpvf /dev/fd0H1440 usr/src/linux-1.2.10-includes/include/linux/hdreg.h
usr/src/linux-1.2.10-includes/include/linux/hdreg.h
#
```

Use the `-list` (`-t`) option, if you just want to see what files are on a backup volume:

```
# tar -list -file /dev/fd0H1440
usr/src/
```

```
usr/src/linux
usr/src/linux-1.2.10-includes/
usr/src/linux-1.2.10-includes/include/
usr/src/linux-1.2.10-includes/include/linux/
usr/src/linux-1.2.10-includes/include/linux/hdreg.h
usr/src/linux-1.2.10-includes/include/linux/kernel.h
...
#
```

Note that `tar` always reads the backup volume sequentially, so for large volumes it is rather slow. It is not possible, however, to use random access database techniques when using a tape drive or some other sequential medium.

`tar` doesn't handle deleted files properly. If you need to restore a filesystem from a full and an incremental backup, and you have deleted a file between the two backups, it will exist again after you have done the restore. This can be a big problem, if the file has sensitive data that should no longer be available.

10.5 Multilevel backups

The simple backup method outlined in the previous section is often quite adequate for personal use or small sites. For more heavy duty use, multilevel backups are more appropriate.

The simple method has two backup levels: full and incremental backups. This can be generalized to any number of levels. A full backup would be level 0, and the different levels of incremental backups levels 1, 2, 3, ... At each incremental backup level you back up everything that has changed since the previous backup at the same or a previous level.

The purpose for doing this is that it allows a longer **backup history** cheaply. In the example in the previous section, the backup history went back to the previous full backup. This could be extended by having more tapes, but only a week per new tape, which might be too expensive. A longer backup history is useful, since deleted or corrupted files are often not noticed for a long time. Even a version of a file that is not very up to date is better than no file at all.

With multiple levels the backup history can be extended more cheaply. For example, if we buy ten tapes, we could use tapes 1 and 2 for monthly backups (first Friday each month), tapes 3 to 6 for weekly backups (other Fridays; note that there

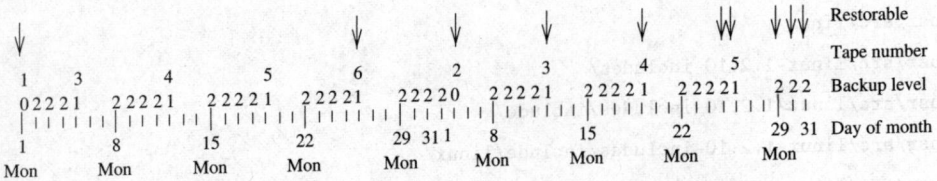

Figure 10.1: A sample multilevel backup schedule.

can be five Fridays in one month, so we need four more tapes), and tapes 7 to 10 for daily backups (Monday to Thursday). With only four more tapes, we've been able to extend the backup history from two weeks (after all daily tapes have been used) to two months. It is true that we can't restore every version of each file during those two months, but what we can restore is often good enough.

Figure 10.1 shows which backup level is used each day, and which backups can be restored from at the end of the month.

Backup levels can also be used to keep filesystem restoration time to a minimum. If you have many incremental backups with monotonously growing level numbers, you need to restore all of them if you need to rebuild the whole filesystem. Instead you can use level numbers that aren't monotonous, and keep down the number of backups to restore.

To minimize the number of tapes needed to restore, you could use a smaller level for each incremental tape. However, then the time to make the backups increases (each backup copies everything since the previous full backup). A better scheme is suggested by the dump manual page and described by the table 10.2. Use the following succession of backup levels: 3, 2, 5, 4, 7, 6, 9, 8, 9... This keeps both the backup and restore times low. The most you have to backup is two day's worth of work. The number of tapes for a restore depends on how long you keep between full backups, but it is less than in the simple schemes.

A fancy scheme can reduce the amount of labor needed, but it does mean there are more things to keep track of. You must decide if it is worth it.

dump has built-in support for backup levels. For tar and cpio it must be implemented with shell scripts.

Figure 10.2: Efficient backup scheme using many backup levels

Tape	Level	Backup (days)	Restore tapes
1	0	n/a	1
2	3	1	1, 2
3	2	2	1, 3
4	5	1	1, 2, 4
5	4	2	1, 2, 5
6	7	1	1, 2, 5, 6
7	6	2	1, 2, 5, 7
8	9	1	1, 2, 5, 7, 8
9	8	2	1, 2, 5, 7, 9
10	9	1	1, 2, 5, 7, 9, 10
11	9	1	1, 2, 5, 7, 9, 10, 11
...	9	1	1, 2, 5, 7, 9, 10, 11, ...

10.6   What to back up

You want to back up as much as possible. The major exception is software that can
be easily reinstalled,[4] but even they may have configuration files that it is important
to back up, lest you need to do all the work to configure them all over again. Another
major exception is the /proc filesystem; since that only contains data that the kernel
always generates automatically, it is *never* a good idea to back it up. Expecially the
/proc/kcore file is unnecessary, since it is just an image of your current physical
memory; it's pretty large as well.

Gray areas include the news spool, log files, and many other things in /var. You
must decide what you consider important.

The obvious things to back up are user files (/home) and system configuration files
(/etc, but possibly other things scattered all over the filesystem).

10.7   Compressed backups

Backups take a lot of space, which can cost quite a lot of money. To reduce the
space needed, the backups can be compressed. There are several ways of doing this.
Some programs have support for for compression built in; for example, the -gzip (-z)

---

[4]You get to decide what's easy. Some people consider installing from dozens of floppies easy.

option for GNU `tar` pipes the whole backup through the `gzip` compression program, before writing it to the backup medium.

Unfortunately, compressed backups can cause trouble. Due to the nature of how compression works, if a single bit is wrong, all the rest of the compressed data will be unusable. Some backup programs have some built in error correction, but no method can handle a large number of errors. This means that if the backup is compressed the way GNU `tar` does it, with the whole output compressed as a unit, a single error makes all the rest of the backup lost. Backups must be reliable, and this method of compression is not a good idea.

An alternative way is to compress each file separately. This still means that the one file is lost, but all other files are unharmed. The lost file would have been corrupted anyway, so this situation is not much worse than not using compression at all. The `afio` program (a variant of `cpio`) can do this.

Compression takes some time, which may make the backup program unable to write data fast enough for a tape drive.[5] This can be avoided by buffering the output (either internally, if the backup program if smart enough, or by using another program), but even that might not work well enough. This should only be a problem on slow computers.

_____

[5] If a tape drive doesn't data fast enough, it has to stop; this makes backups even slower, and can be bad for the tape and the drive.

Chapter 11

Keeping Time

Time is an illusion. Lunchtime double so.
(Douglas Adams.)

This chapter explains how a Linux system keeps time, and what you need to do to avoid causing trouble. Usually, you don't need to do anything about time, but it is good to understand it.

11.1 Time zones

Time measurement is based on mostly regular natural phenomena, such as alternating light and dark periods caused by the rotation of the planet. The total time taken by two successive periods is constant, but the lengths of the light and dark period vary. One simple constant is noon.

Noon is the time of the day when the Sun is at its highest position. Since the Earth is round,[1] noon happens at different times in different places. This leads to the concept of **local time**. Humans measure time in many units, most of which are tied to natural phenomena like noon. As long as you stay in the same place, it doesn't matter that local times differ.

As soon as you need to communicate with distant places, you'll notice the need for a common time. In modern times, most of the places in the world communicate with most other places in the world, so a global standard for measuring time has been defined. This time is called **universal time** (UT or UTC, formerly known as

---

[1] According to recent research.

Greenwich Mean Time or GMT, since it used to be local time in Greenwich, England). When people with different local times need to communicate, they can express times in universal time, so that there is no confusion about when things should happen.

Each local time is called a time zone. While geography would allow all places that have noon at the same time have the same time zone, politics makes it difficult. For various reasons, many countries use **daylight savings time**, that is, they move their clocks to have more natural light while they work, and then move the clocks back during winter. Other countries do not do this. Those that do, do not agree when the clocks should be moved, and they change the rules from year to year. This makes time zone conversions definitely non-trivial.

Time zones are best named by the location or by telling the difference between local and universal time. In the US and some other countries, the local time zones have a name and a three letter abbreviation. The abbreviations are not unique, however, and should not be used unless the country is also named. It is better to talk about the local time in, say, Helsinki, than about East European time, since not all countries in Eastern Europe follow the same rules.

Linux has a time zone package that knows about all existing time zones, and that can easily be updated when the rules change. All the system administrator needs to do is to select the appropriate time zone. Also, each user can set his own time zone—this is important since many people work with computers in different countries over the Internet. When the rules for daylight savings time change in your local time zone, make sure you'll upgrade at least that part of your Linux system. Other than setting the system time zone and upgrading the time zone data files, there is little need to bother about time.

11.2   The hardware and software clocks

A personal computer has a battery driven hardware clock. The battery ensures that the clock will work even if the rest of the computer is without electricity. The hardware clock can be set from the BIOS setup screen or from whatever operating system is running.

The Linux kernel keeps track of time independently from the hardware clock. During the boot, Linux sets its own clock to the same time as the hardware clock. After this, both clocks run independently. Linux maintains its own clock because looking at the hardware is slow and complicated.

The kernel clock always shows universal time. This way, the kernel does not need to know about time zones at all—the simplicity results in higher reliability and makes it easier to update the time zone information. Each process handles time zone conversions itself (using standard tools that are part of the time zone package).

The hardware clock can be in local time or in universal time. It is usually better to have it in universal time, because then you don't need to change the hardware clock when daylight savings time begins or ends (UTC does not have DST). Unfortunately, some PC operating systems—including MS-DOS, Windows, OS/2—assume the hardware clock shows local time. Linux can handle either, but if the hardware clock shows local time, then it must be modified when daylight savings time begins or ends (otherwise it wouldn't show local time).

11.3   Showing and setting time

In the Debian system, the system time zone is determined by the symbolic link `/etc/localtime`. This link points at a time zone data file that describes the local time zone. The time zone data files are stored in `/usr/lib/zoneinfo`. Other Linux distributions may do this differently.

A user can change his private time zone by setting the TZ environment variable. If it is unset, the system time zone is assumed. The syntax of the TZ variable is described in the *tzset*(3) manual page.

The `date` command shows the current date and time.[2] For example:

```
$ date
Sun Jul 14 21:53:41 EET DST 1996
$
```

That time is Sunday, 14th of July, 1996, at about ten before ten at the evening, in the time zone called "EET DST" (which might be East European Daylight Savings Time). `date` can also show the univeral time:

```
$ date -u
Sun Jul 14 18:53:42 UTC 1996
$
```

`date` is also used to set the kernel's software clock:

---

[2] Beware of the `time` command, which does *not* show the current time.

```
# date 07142157
Sun Jul 14 21:57:00 EET DST 1996
# date
Sun Jul 14 21:57:02 EET DST 1996
#
```

See the `date` manual page for more details—the syntax is a bit arcane. Only `root` can set the time. While each user can have his own time zone, the clock is the same for everyone.

   `date` only shows or sets the software clock. The `clock` commands syncronizes the hardware and software clocks. It is used when the system boots, to read the hardware clock and set the software clock. If you need to set both clocks, you first set the software clock with `date`, and then the hardware clock with `clock -w`.

   The `-u` option to `clock` tells it that the hardware clock is in universal time. You *must* use the `-u` option correctly. If you don't, your computer will be quite confused about what the time is.

   The clocks should be changed with care. Many parts of a Unix system require the clocks to work correctly. For example, the `cron` daemon runs commands periodically. If you change the clock, it can be confused of whether it needs to run the commands or not. On one early Unix system, someone set the clock twenty years into the future, and `cron` wanted to run all the periodic commands for twenty years all at once. Current versions of `cron` can handle this correctly, but you should still be careful. Big jumps or backward jumps are more dangeours than smaller or forward ones.

11.4   When the clock is wrong

The Linux software clock is not always accurate. It is kept running by a periodic **timer interrupt** generated by PC hardware. If the system has too many processes running, it may take too long to service the timer interrupt, and the software clock starts slipping behind. The hardware clock runs independently and is usually more accurate. If you boot your computer often (as is the case for most systems that aren't servers), it will usually keep fairly accurate time.

   If you need to adjust the hardware clock, it is usually simplest to reboot, go into the BIOS setup screen, and do it from there. This avoids all trouble that changing system time might cause. If doing it via BIOS is not an option, set the new time with `date` and `clock` (in that order), but be prepared to reboot, if some part of the system starts acting funny.

A networked computer (even if just over the modem) can check its own clock automatically, by comparing it to some other computer's time. If the other computer is known to keep very accurate time, then both computers will keep accurate time. This can be done by using the `rdate` and `netdate` commands. Both check the time of a remote computer (`netdate` can handle several remote computers), and set the local computer's time to that. By running one these commands regularly, your computer will keep as accurate time as the remote computer.

META: say something intelligent about NTP

Appendix A

Measuring Holes

This appendix contains the interesting part of the program used to measure the potential for holes in a filesystem. The source distribution of the book contains the full source code (sag/measure-holes/measure-holes.c).

```
int process(FILE *f, char *filename) {
        static char *buf = NULL;
        static long prev_block_size = -1;
        long zeroes;
        char *p;

        if (buf == NULL || prev_block_size != block_size) {
                free(buf);
                buf = xmalloc(block_size + 1);
                buf[block_size] = 1;
                prev_block_size = block_size;
        }
        zeroes = 0;
        while (fread(buf, block_size, 1, f) == 1) {
                for (p = buf; *p == '\0'; )
                        ++p;
                if (p == buf+block_size)
                        zeroes += block_size;
        }
        if (zeroes > 0)
                printf("%ld %s\n", zeroes, filename);
        if (ferror(f)) {
                errormsg(0, -1, "read failed for '%s'", filename);
                return -1;
        }
        return 0;
}
```

Appendix B

Glossary (DRAFT)

> *The Librarian of the Unseen University*
> *had unilaterally decided to aid comprehension*
> *by producing an Orang-utan/Human Dictionary.*
> *He'd been working on it for three months.*
>
> *It wasn't easy. He'd got as far as 'Oook.'*
>
> *(Terry Pratchett, "Men At Arms")*

This is a short list of word definitions for concepts relating to Linux and system administration. The page references are to the first or most important place where the word is used.

ambition The act of writing funny sentences in the hope of getting them into the Linux cookie file.

application program (p. 227) Software that does something useful. The results of using an application program is what the computer was bought for. See also system program, operating system.

daemon A process lurking in the background, usually unnoticed, until something triggers it into action. For example, the `update` daemon wakes up every thirty seconds or so to flush the buffer cache, and the `sendmail` daemon awakes whenever someone sends mail.

file system (p. 259) The methods and data structures that an operating system uses to keep track of files on a disk or partition; the way the files are organized on the disk. Also used about a partition or disk that is used to store the files or the type of the filesystem.

glossary A list of words and explanations of what they do. Not to be confused with a dictionary, which is also a list of words and explanations.

kernel (p. 227) Part of an operating system that implements the interaction with hardware and the sharing of resources. See also system program.

operating system (p. 227) Software that shares a computer system's resources (processor, memory, disk space, network bandwidth, and so on) between users and the application programs they run. Controls access to the system to provide security. See also kernel, system program, application program.

system call (p. 227) The services provided by the kernel to application programs, and the way in which they are invoked. See section 2 of the manual pages.

system program (p. 227) Programs that implement high level functionality of an operating system, i.e., things that aren't directly dependent on the hardware. May sometimes require special privileges to run (e.g., for delivering electronic mail), but often just commonly thought of as part of the system (e.g., a compiler). See also application program, kernel, operating system.

Linux Information Sheet

Michael K. Johnson <johnsonm@redhat.com>   v4.13, 24 October 1997

This document provides basic information about the Linux operating system, including an explanation of Linux, a list of features, some requirements, and some resources.

Contents

1   Introduction to Linux

Linux is a completely free reimplementation of the POSIX specification, with SYSV and BSD extensions (which means it looks like Unix, but does not come from the same source code base), which is available in both source code and binary form. Its copyright is owned by Linus Torvalds <torvalds@transmeta.com> and other contributors, and is freely redistributable under the terms of the GNU General Public License (GPL). A copy of the GPL is included with the Linux source; you can also get a copy from `<ftp://prep.ai.mit.edu/pub/gnu/COPYING>`

Linux is **not** public domain, nor is it 'shareware'. It is 'free' software, commonly called **freeware**, and you may give away or sell copies, but you must include the source code or make it available in the same way as any binaries you give or sell. If you distribute any modifications, you are legally bound to distribute the source for those modifications. See the GNU General Public License for details.

Linux is still free as of version 2.0, and will continue to be free. Because of the nature of the GPL to which Linux is subject, it would be illegal for it to be made not free. Note carefully: the 'free' part involves access to the source code rather than money; it is perfectly legal to charge money for distributing Linux, so long as you also distribute the source code. This is a generalization; if you want the fine points, read the GPL.

Linux runs on 386/486/Pentium machines with ISA, EISA, PCI and VLB busses. MCA (IBM's proprietary bus) is not well-supported in 2.0.x and earlier versions, but support has been added to the current development tree, 2.1.x. If you are interested, see `<http://glycerine.itsmm.uni.edu/mca>`

There is a port to multiple Motorola 680x0 platforms (currently running on some Amigas, Ataris, and VME machines), which now works quite well. It requires a 68020 with an MMU, a 68030, 68040, or a 68060, and also requires an FPU. Networking and X now work. See `<news:comp.os.linux.m68k>`

Linux runs well on DEC's Alpha CPU, currently supporting the "Jensen", "NoName", "Cabriolet", "Universal Desktop Box" (better known as the Multia), and many other platforms. For more information, see `<http://www.azstarnet.com/~axplinux/FAQ.html>`

Linux runs well on Sun SPARCs; most sun4c and sun4m machines now run Linux, with support for sun4 and sun4u in active development. Red Hat Linux is (as of this writing) the only Linux distribution available for SPARCs; see `<http://www.redhat.com/support/docs/rhl-sparc/>`

Linux is being actively ported to the PowerPC architecture, including PowerMac (Nubus and PCI), Motorola, IBM, and Be machines. See `<http://www.cs.nmt.edu/~linuxppc/>` and `<http://www.linuxppc.org/>`

Ports to other machines, including MIPS and ARM, are under way and showing various amounts of progress. Don't hold your breath, but if you are interested and able to contribute, you may well find other developers who wish to work with you.

Linux is no longer considered to be in beta testing, as version 1.0 was released on March 14, 1994. There are still bugs in the system, and new bugs will creep up and be fixed as time goes on. Because Linux follows the "open development model", all new versions will be released to the public, whether or not they are considered "production quality". However, in order to help people tell whether they are getting a stable version or not, the following scheme has been implemented: Versions 1.x.y, where x is an even number, are stable versions, and only bug fixes will be applied as y is incremented. So from version 1.2.2 to 1.2.3, there were only bug fixes, and no new features. Versions 1.x.y, where x is an odd number, are beta-quality releases for developers only, and may be unstable and may crash, and are having new features added to them all the time. From time to time, as the currect development kernel stabilizes, it will be frozen as the new "stable" kernel, and development will continue on a new development version of the kernel.

The current stable version is 2.0.31 (this will continue to change as new device drivers get added and bugs fixed), and development has also started on the experimental 2.1.x kernels. If 2.0.x is too new for you, you may want to stick with 1.2.13 for the time being. However, the latest releases of 2.0 have proved quite stable. Do note that in order to upgrade from 1.2 to 2.0, you need to upgrade some utilities as well; you may wish to upgrade to the latest version of your Linux distribution in order to obtain those utilities. The Linux kernel source code also contains a file, Documentation/Changes, which explains these changes and more.

Most versions of Linux, beta or not, are quite stable, and you can keep using those if they do what you need and you don't want to be on the bleeding edge. One site had a computer running version 0.97p1 (dating from the summer of 1992) for over 136 days without an error or crash. (It would have been longer if the backhoe operator hadn't mistaken a main power transformer for a dumpster...) Others have posted uptimes in excess of a year. One site still had a computer running Linux 0.99p15s over 600 days at last report.

One thing to be aware of is that Linux is developed using an open and distributed model, instead of a closed and centralized model like much other software. This means that the current development version is always public (with up to a week or two of delay) so that anybody can use it. The result is that whenever a version with new functionality is released, it almost always contains bugs, but it also results in a very rapid development so that the bugs are found and corrected quickly, often in hours, as many people work to fix them.

In contrast, the closed and centralized model means that there is only one person or team working on the project, and they only release software that they think is working well. Often this leads to long intervals between releases, long waiting for bug fixes, and slower development. The latest release of such software to the public is sometimes of higher quality, but the development speed is generally much slower.

As of October 24, 1997, the current stable version of Linux is 2.0.31, and the latest development version is 2.1.59.

2 Linux Features

- multitasking: several programs running at once.

- multiuser: several users on the same machine at once (and **no** two-user licenses!).

- multiplatform: runs on many different CPUs, not just Intel.

- multiprocessor: SMP support is available on the Intel and SPARC platforms (with work currently in progress on other platforms), and Linux is used in several loosely-coupled MP applications, including Beowulf systems (see <http://cesdis.gsfc.nasa.gov/linux-web/beowulf/beowulf.html>) and the Fujitsu AP1000+ SPARC-based supercomputer.

- runs in protected mode on the 386.

- has memory protection between processes, so that one program can't bring the whole system down.

- demand loads executables: Linux only reads from disk those parts of a program that are actually used.

- shared copy-on-write pages among executables. This means that multiple process can use the same memory to run in. When one tries to write to that memory, that page (4KB piece of memory) is copied somewhere else. Copy-on-write has two benefits: increasing speed and decreasing memory use.

- virtual memory using paging (not swapping whole processes) to disk: to a separate partition or a file in the filesystem, or both, with the possibility of adding more swapping areas during runtime (yes, they're still called swapping areas). A total of 16 of these 128 MB swapping areas can be used at once, for a theoretical total of 2 GB of useable swap space. It is simple to increase this if necessary, by changing a few lines of source code.

- a unified memory pool for user programs and disk cache, so that all free memory can be used for caching, and the cache can be reduced when running large programs.

- dynamically linked shared libraries (DLL's), and static libraries too, of course.

- does core dumps for post-mortem analysis, allowing the use of a debugger on a program not only while it is running but also after it has crashed.

- mostly compatible with POSIX, System V, and BSD at the source level.

- through an iBCS2-compliant emulation module, mostly compatible with SCO, SVR3, and SVR4 at the binary level.
- all source code is available, including the whole kernel and all drivers, the development tools and all user programs; also, all of it is freely distributable. Plenty of commercial programs are being provided for Linux without source, but everything that has been free, including the entire base operating system, is still free.
- POSIX job control.
- pseudoterminals (pty's).
- 387-emulation in the kernel so that programs don't need to do their own math emulation. Every computer running Linux appears to have a math coprocessor. Of course, if your computer already contains an FPU, it will be used instead of the emulation, and you can even compile your own kernel with math emulation removed, for a small memory gain.
- support for many national or customized keyboards, and it is fairly easy to add new ones dynamically.
- multiple virtual consoles: several independent login sessions through the console, you switch by pressing a hot-key combination (not dependent on video hardware). These are dynamically allocated; you can use up to 64.
- Supports several common filesystems, including minix, Xenix, and all the common system V filesystems, and has an advanced filesystem of its own, which offers filesystems of up to 4 TB, and names up to 255 characters long.
- transparent access to MS-DOS partitions (or OS/2 FAT partitions) via a special filesystem: you don't need any special commands to use the MS-DOS partition, it looks just like a normal Unix filesystem (except for funny restrictions on filenames, permissions, and so on). MS-DOS 6 compressed partitions do not work at this time without a patch (dmsdosfs). VFAT (WNT, Windows 95) support is available in Linux 2.0.
- special filesystem called UMSDOS which allows Linux to be installed on a DOS filesystem.
- read-only HPFS-2 support for OS/2 2.1
- HFS (Macintosh) file system support is available separately as a module.
- CD-ROM filesystem which reads all standard formats of CD-ROMs.
- TCP/IP networking, including ftp, telnet, NFS, etc.
- Appletalk server
- Netware client and server
- Lan Manager (SMB) client and server
- Many networking protocols: the base protocols available in the latest development kernels include TCP, IPv4, IPv6, AX.25, X.25, IPX, DDP (Appletalk), NetBEUI, Netrom, and others. Stable network protocols included in the stable kernels currently include TCP, IPv4, IPX, DDP, and AX.25.

3   Hardware Issues

3.1   Minimal configuration

The following is probably the smallest possible configuration that Linux will work on: 386SX/16, 1 MB RAM, 1.44 MB or 1.2 MB floppy, any supported video card (+ keyboards, monitors, and so on of course). This should allow you to boot and test whether it works at all on the machine, but you won't be able to do anything useful. See <http://rsphy1.anu.edu.au/~gpg109/mem.html> for minimal Linux configurations

In order to do something, you will want some hard disk space as well, 5 to 10 MB should suffice for a very minimal setup (with only the most important commands and perhaps one or two small applications installed, like, say, a terminal program). This is still very, very limited, and very uncomfortable, as it doesn't leave enough room to do just about anything, unless your applications are quite limited. It's generally not recommended for anything but testing if things work, and of course to be able to brag about small resource requirements.

3.2   Usable configuration

If you are going to run computationally intensive programs, such as gcc, X, and TeX, you will probably want a faster processor than a 386SX/16, but even that should suffice if you are patient.

In practice, you will want at least 4 MB of RAM if you don't use X, and 8 MB if you do. Also, if you want to have several users at a time, or run several large programs (compilations for example) at a time, you may want more than 4 MB of memory. It will still work with a smaller amount of memory (should work even with 2 MB), but it will use virtual memory (using the hard drive as **slow** memory) and that will be so slow as to be unusable. If you use many programs at once, 16 MB will reduce swapping considerably. If you don't want to swap appreciably under any normal load, 32 MB will probably suffice. Of course, if you run memory-hungry applications, you may want more.

The amount of hard disk you need depends on what software you want to install. The normal basic set of Unix utilities, shells, and administrative programs should be comfortable in less than 10 MB, with a bit of room to spare for user files. For a more complete system, get Red Hat, Debian, or another distribution, and assume that you will need 60 to 300 MB, depending on what you choose to install and what distribution you get. Add whatever space you want to reserve for user files to these totals. With today's prices on hard drives, if you are buying a new system, it makes no sense to buy a drive that is too small. Get at least 500 MB, preferably 1GB or more, and you will not regret it.

Add more memory, more hard disk, a faster processor and other stuff depending on your needs, wishes and budget to go beyond the merely usable. In general, one big difference from DOS is that with Linux, adding memory makes a large difference, whereas with DOS, extra memory doesn't make that much difference. This of course has something to do with DOS's 640KB limit, which is completely nonexistent under Linux.

3.3   Supported hardware

CPU:

Anything that runs 386 protected mode programs (all models of 386's 486's, 586's, and 686's should work. 286s and below may someday be supported on a smaller kernel called ELKS (Embeddable Linux Kernel Subset), but don't expect the same capabilities). A version for the 680x0 CPU (for $x = 2$ with external MMU, 3, 4, and 6) which runs on Amigas and Ataris can be found at tsx-11.mit.edu in the 680x0 directory. Many DEC Alphas, SPARCs, and PowerPC machines are supported. Ports are also being done to the ARM, StrongARM, and MIPS architectures. More details are available elsewhere.

Architecture:

ISA or EISA bus. MCA (mostly true blue PS/2's) support is incomplete but improving (see above). Local busses (VLB and PCI) work. Linux puts higher demands on hardware than DOS, Windows, and in fact most operating systems. This means that some marginal hardware that doesn't fail when running less demanding operating system may fail when running Linux. Linux is an excellent memory tester...

RAM:

Up to 1 GB on Intel; more on 64-bit platforms. Some people (including Linus) have noted that adding ram without adding more cache at the same time has slowed down their machine extremely, so if you add memory and find your machine slower, try adding more cache. Some machines can only cache certain amounts of memory regardless of how much RAM is installed (64 MB is the most one popular chipset can cache). Over 64 MB of memory will require a boot-time parameter, as the BIOS cannot report more than 64MB, because it is "broken as designed."

Data storage:

Generic AT drives (EIDE, IDE, 16 bit HD controllers with MFM or RLL, or ESDI) are supported, as are SCSI hard disks and CD-ROMs, with a supported SCSI adaptor. Generic XT controllers (8 bit controllers with MFM or RLL) are also supported. Supported SCSI adaptors: Advansys, Adaptec 1542, 1522, 1740, 27xx, and 29xx (with some exceptions) series, Buslogic MultiMaster and Flashpoint, NCR53c8xx-based controllers, DPT controllers, Qlogic ISP and FAS controllers, Seagate ST-01 and ST-02, Future Domain TMC-88x series (or any board based on the TMC950 chip) and TMC1660/1680, Ultrastor 14F, 24F and 34F, Western Digital wd7000, and others. SCSI, QIC-02, and some QIC-80 tapes are also supported. Several CD-ROM devices are also supported, including Matsushita/Panasonic, Mitsumi, Sony, Soundblaster, Toshiba, ATAPI (EIDE), SCSI, and others. For exact models, check the hardware compatibility HOWTO.

Video:

VGA, EGA, CGA, or Hercules (and compatibles) work in text mode. For graphics and X, there is support for (at least) normal VGA, some super-VGA cards (most of the cards based on ET3000, ET4000, Paradise, and some Trident chipsets), S3, 8514/A, ATI MACH8/32/64, and hercules. (Linux uses the Xfree86 X server, so that determines what cards are supported. A full list of supported chipsets alone takes over a page.)

Networking:

Ethernet support includes 3COM 503/509/579/589/595/905 (501/505/507 are supported but not recomended), AT&T GIS (neé NCR) WaveLAN, most WD8390-based cards, most WD80x3-based cards, NE1000/2000 and most clones, AC3200, Apricot 82596, AT1700, ATP, DE425/434/435/500, D-Link DE-600/620, DEPCA, DE100/101, DE200/201/202 Turbo, DE210, DE422, Cabletron E2100 (not recommended), Intel EtherExpress (not recommended), DEC EtherWORKS 3, HP LAN, HP PCLAN/plus, most AMD LANCE-based cards, NI5210, ni6510, SMC Ultra, DEC 21040 (tulip), Zenith Z-Note ethernet, All Zircom cards and all Cabletron cards other than the E2100 are unsupported, due to the manufacturers unwillingness to release programming information freely.

FDDI support currently includes the DEFxx cards from DEC.

Point-to-Point networking support include PPP, SLIP, CSLIP, and PLIP.

Limited Token Ring support is available.

Serial:

Most 16450 and 16550 UART-based boards, including AST Fourport, the Usenet Serial Card II, and others. Intelligent boards supported include Cyclades Cyclom series (supported by the manufacturer), Comtrol Rocketport series (supported by the manufacturer), Stallion (most boards; supported by the manufacturer), and Digi (some boards; supported by the manufacturer). Some ISDN, frame relay, and leased line hardware is supported.

Other hardware:

SoundBlaster, ProAudio Spectrum 16, Gravis Ultrasound, most other sound cards, most (all?) flavours of bus mice (Microsoft, Logitech, PS/2), etc.

4 An Incomplete List of Ported Programs and Other Software

Most of the common Unix tools and programs have been ported to Linux, including almost all of the GNU stuff and many X clients from various sources. Actually, ported is often too strong a word, since many programs compile out of the box without modifications, or only small modifications, because Linux tracks

POSIX quite closely. Unfortunately, there are not as many end-user applications yet as we would like, but this is changing rapidly. Contact the vendor of your favorite commercial Unix application and ask if they have ported it to Linux.

Here is an incomplete list of software that is known to work under Linux:

Basic Unix commands:

ls, tr, sed, awk and so on (you name it, Linux probably has it).

Development tools:

gcc, gdb, make, bison, flex, perl, rcs, cvs, prof.

Languages and Environments:

C, C++, Objective C, Java, Modula-3, Modula-2, Oberon, Ada95, Pascal, Fortran, ML, scheme, Tcl/tk, Perl, Python, Common Lisp, and many others.

Graphical environments:

X11R5 (XFree86 2.x), X11R6 (XFree86 3.x), MGR.

Editors:

GNU Emacs, XEmacs, MicroEmacs, jove, ez, epoch, elvis (GNU vi), vim, vile, joe, pico, jed, and others.

Shells:

bash (POSIX sh-compatible), zsh (includes ksh compatiblity mode), pdksh, tcsh, csh, rc, es, ash (mostly sh-compatible shell used as /bin/sh by BSD), and many more.

Telecommunication:

Taylor (BNU-compatible) UUCP, SLIP, CSLIP, PPP, kermit, szrz, minicom, pcomm, xcomm, term (runs multiple shells, redirects network activity, and allows remote X, all over one modem line), Seyon (popular X-windows communications program), and several fax and voice-mail (using ZyXEL and other modems) packages are available. Of course, remote serial logins are supported.

News and mail:

C-news, innd, trn, nn, tin, smail, elm, mh, pine, etc.

Textprocessing:

TeX, groff, doc, ez, LyX, Lout, Linuxdoc-SGML, and others.

Games:

Nethack, several Muds and X games, and lots of others. One of those games is looking through all the games available at tsx-11 and sunsite.

Suites:

AUIS, the Andrew User Interface System. ez is part of this suite.

All of these programs (and this isn't even a hundredth of what is available) are freely available. Commercial software is becoming widely available; ask the vendor of your favorite commercial software if they support Linux.

5 Who uses Linux?

Linux is freely available, and no one is required to register their copies with any central authority, so it is difficult to know how many people use Linux. Several businesses now survive solely on selling and supporting Linux (and relatively few Linux users purchase products from those businesses), and the Linux newsgroups are some of the most heavily read on the internet, so the number is likely in the millions, but firm numbers are hard to come by.

However, one brave soul, Harald T. Alvestrand <Harald.T.Alvestrand@uninett.no>, has decided to try. If you are willing to be counted as a Linux user, please use the web forms available at <http://counter.li.org/> Alternatively, you can send a message to linux-counter@uninett.no with one of the following subjects: 'I use Linux at home', 'I use Linux at work', or 'I use Linux at home and at work'. He will also accept 'third-party' registrations; ask him for details.

He posts his counts to <news:comp.os.linux.misc> each month; they are also available from <http://counter.li.org/>.

6   Getting Linux

6.1   Anonymous FTP

For freely-redistributable Linux documentation, see the Linux Documentation Project sites at <ftp://sunsite.unc.edu/pub/Linux/docs/LDP/> and <http://sunsite.unc.edu/LDP/>

Stay tuned to the <news:comp.os.linux.announce> newsgroup for further developments.

At least the following anonymous ftp sites carry Linux.

Textual name	Numeric address	Linux directory
===========================	===============	===============
tsx-11.mit.edu	18.172.1.2	/pub/linux
sunsite.unc.edu	152.2.22.81	/pub/Linux
ftp.funet.fi	128.214.248.6	/pub/Linux
net.tamu.edu	128.194.177.1	/pub/linux
ftp.mcc.ac.uk	130.88.203.12	/pub/linux
src.doc.ic.ac.uk	146.169.2.1	/packages/linux
fgb1.fgb.mw.tu-muenchen.de	129.187.200.1	/pub/linux
ftp.informatik.tu-muenchen.de	131.159.0.110	/pub/comp/os/linux
ftp.dfv.rwth-aachen.de	137.226.4.111	/pub/linux
ftp.informatik.rwth-aachen.de	137.226.225.3	/pub/Linux
ftp.Germany.EU.net	192.76.144.75	/pub/os/Linux
ftp.ibp.fr	132.227.60.2	/pub/linux
ftp.uu.net	137.39.1.9	/systems/unix/linux
wuarchive.wustl.edu	128.252.135.4	mirrors/linux
ftp.win.tue.nl	131.155.70.100	/pub/linux
ftp.stack.urc.tue.nl	131.155.2.71	/pub/linux
srawgw.sra.co.jp	133.137.4.3	/pub/os/linux
cair.kaist.ac.kr		/pub/Linux
ftp.denet.dk	129.142.6.74	/pub/OS/linux
NCTUCCCA.edu.tw	140.111.1.10	/Operating-Systems/Linux
nic.switch.ch	130.59.1.40	/mirror/linux
sunsite.cnlab-switch.ch	193.5.24.1	/mirror/linux
cnuce_arch.cnr.it	131.114.1.10	/pub/Linux
ftp.monash.edu.au	130.194.11.8	/pub/linux
ftp.dstc.edu.au	130.102.181.31	/pub/linux

ftp.sydutech.usyd.edu.au   129.78.192.2   /pub/linux

tsx-11.mit.edu and fgb1.fgb.mw.tu-muenchen.de are the official sites for Linux's GCC. Some sites mirror other sites. Please use the site closest (network-wise) to you whenever possible.

At least sunsite.unc.edu and ftp.informatik.tu-muenchen.de offer ftpmail services. Mail ftp-mail@sunsite.unc.edu or ftp@informatik.tu-muenchen.de for help.

If you are lost, try looking at `<ftp://sunsite.unc.edu/pub/Linux/distributions/>`, where several distributions are offered. Red Hat Linux and Debian appear to be the most popular distributions at the moment, at least in the U.S.

6.2 CDROM

Many people now install Linux from CDROM's. The distributions have grown to hundreds of MBs of Linux software, and downloading that over even a 28.8 modem takes a **long** time.

There are essentially two ways to purchase a Linux distribution on CDROM: as part of an archive of FTP sites, or directly from the manufacturer. If you purchase an archive, you will almost always get several different distributions to choose from, but usually support is not included. When you purchase a distribution directly from the vendor, you usually only get one distribution, but you usually get some form of support, usually installation support.

6.3 Other methods of obtaining Linux

There are many BBS's that have Linux files. A list of them is occasionally posted to comp.os.linux.announce. Ask friends and user groups, or order one of the commmercial distributions. A list of these is contained in the Linux distribution HOWTO, available as `<ftp://sunsite.unc.edu/pub/Linux/docs/HOWTO/distribution-HOWTO>`, and posted regularly to the `<news:comp.os.linux.announce>` newsgroup.

7 Getting started

As mentioned at the beginning, Linux is not centrally administered. Because of this, there is no "official" release that one could point at, and say "That's Linux." Instead, there are various "distributions," which are more or less complete collections of software configured and packaged so that they can be used to install a Linux system.

The first thing you should do is to get and read the list of Frequently Asked Questions (FAQ) from one of the FTP sites, or by using the normal Usenet FAQ archives (e.g. rtfm.mit.edu). This document has plenty of instructions on what to do to get started, what files you need, and how to solve most of the common problems (during installation or otherwise).

8 Legal Status of Linux

Although Linux is supplied with the complete source code, it is copyrighted software, not public domain. However, it is available for free under the GNU General Public License, sometimes referred to as the "copy-left". See the GPL for more information. The programs that run under Linux each have their own copyright, although many of them use the GPL as well. X uses the MIT X copyright, and some utilities are under the BSD copyright. In any case, all of the software on the FTP site is freely distributable (or else it shouldn't be there).

9   News About Linux

A monthly magazine, called *Linux Journal*, was launched over three years ago. It includes articles intended for almost all skill levels, and is intended to be helpful to all Linux users. One-year subscriptions are $22 in the U.S., $27 in Canada and Mexico, and $32 elsewhere, payable in US currency. Subscription inquiries can be sent via email to subs@ssc.com, or faxed to +1-206-782-7191, or phoned to +1-206-782-7733, or mailed to Linux Journal, PO Box 85867, Seattle, WA 98145-1867 USA. SSC has a PGP public key available for encrypting your mail to protect your credit card number; finger info@ssc.com to get the key.

There are several Usenet newsgroups for Linux discussion, and also several mailing lists. See the Linux FAQ for more information about the mailing lists (you should be able to find the FAQ either in the newsgroup or on the FTP sites).

The newsgroup <news:comp.os.linux.announce> is a moderated newsgroup for announcements about Linux (new programs, bug fixes, etc).

The newsgroup <news:comp.os.linux.answers> is a moderated newsgroup to which the Linux FAQ, HOWTO documents, and other documentation postings are made.

The newsgroup <news:comp.os.linux.admin> is an unmoderated newsgroup for discussion of administration of Linux systems.

The newsgroup <news:comp.os.linux.development.system> is an unmoderated newsgroup specifically for discussion of Linux **kernel** development. The only application development questions that should be discussed here are those that are intimately associated with the kernel. All other development questions are probably generic Unix development questions and should be directed to a comp.unix group instead, unless they are very Linux-specific applications questions, in which case they should be directed at comp.os.linux.development.apps.

The newsgroup <news:comp.os.linux.development.apps> is an unmoderated newsgroup specifically for discussion of Linux-related applications development. It is not for discussion of where to get applications for Linux, nor a discussion forum for those who would like to see applications for Linux.

The newsgroup <news:comp.os.linux.hardware> is for Linux-specific hardware questions.

The newsgroup <news:comp.os.linux.networking> is for Linux-specific networking development and setup questions.

The newsgroup <news:comp.os.linux.x> is for Linux-specific X Windows questions.

The newsgroup <news:comp.os.linux.misc> is the replacement for comp.os.linux, and is meant for any discussion that doesn't belong elsewhere.

In general, **do not** crosspost between the Linux newsgroups. The **only** crossposting that is appropriate is an occasional posting between one unmoderated group and <news:comp.os.linux.announce>. The whole point of splitting the old comp.os.linux group into many groups is to reduce traffic in each group. Those that do not follow this rule will be flamed without mercy...

Linux is on the web at the URL <http://sunsite.unc.edu/LDP/>

10   The Future

After Linux 1.0 was released, work was done on several enhancements. Linux 1.2 included disk access speedups, TTY improvements, virtual memory enhancements, multiple platform support, quotas, and more. Linux 2.0, the current stable version, has even more enhancements, including many performance improvements, several new networking protocols, one of the fastest TCP/IP implementations in the world, and far,

far more. Even higher performance, more networking protocols, and more device drivers will be available in Linux 2.2.

Even with over 3/4 million lines of code in the kernel, there is plenty of code left to write, and even more documentation. Please join the linux-doc@vger.rutgers.edu mailing list if you would like to contribute to the documentation. Send mail to majordomo@vger.rutgers.edu with a single line containing the word "help" in the body (**NOT** the subject) of the message.

11   This document

This document is maintained by Michael K. Johnson <johnsonm@redhat.com>. Please mail me with any comments, no matter how small. I can't do a good job of maintaining this document without your help. A more-or-less current copy of this document can always be found at <http://sunsite.unc.edu/LDP/>

12   Legalese

Trademarks are owned by their owners. There is no warranty about the information in this document. Use and distribute at your own risk. The content of this document is in the public domain, but please be polite and attribute any quotes.

Linux Meta-FAQ

Michael K. Johnson <johnsonm@redhat.com> v4.7, 25 October 1997

This is the Meta-FAQ for Linux. It is mainly a list of valuable sources of information. Check these sources out if you want to learn more about Linux, or have problems and need help.

1   Introduction

What is Linux?

Linux is an independent implementation of the POSIX operating system specification, with SYSV and BSD extensions, that has been written entirely from scratch (this means it looks and acts just like Unix). It has no proprietary code in it. Linux is freely distributable under the GNU General Public License.

Linux works on IBM PC compatibles with an ISA or EISA bus (including local bus variants VLB and PCI) and a 386 or higher processor. Some Amiga and Atari computers with MMU's are also supported. This means 68020 with an external MMU, 68030, 68040, or 68060. Support for the Digital Alpha is now stable. Red Hat and Craftworks have Alpha distributions of Linux. Support for Sparc is stable, and Red Hat Linux is available for Sparc. Support for PowerPC is in development for multiple platforms, including Nubus and PCI Macintosh, Motorola Powerstack, IBM 830 and 850, and other platforms. Support for ARM, StrongARM, and MIPS is in various stages of completion, but don't hold your breath. Read comp.os.linux.announce instead.

See the Linux INFO-SHEET for more technical information on these ports, and the Hardware Compatibility HOWTO for more exact hardware requirements.

The Linux kernel is written by Linus Torvalds <torvalds@transmeta.com> and other volunteers. Most of the programs running under Linux are generic Unix freeware, many of them from the GNU project.

The Linux INFO-SHEET

More specific technical information on Linux. Includes pointers to information on the various ports, a feature list, information about how to get Linux, and more.

The Linux HOWTO's

These are somewhat like FAQ's, but instead of answering common questions, they explain how to do common tasks, like ordering a release of Linux, setting up print services under Linux, setting up a basic UUCP feed, etc. See <http://sunsite.unc.edu/LDP/HOWTO/HOWTO-INDEX.html> or <ftp: //sunsite.unc.edu/pub/Linux/docs/HOWTO/> for the definitive versions of all the HOWTO's. Other sites with up-to-date copies of the HOWTOs are ftp.cc.gatech.edu and tsx-11.mit.edu.

In addition, there are many short, free-form documents called "mini-HOWTOs". These documents cover very specific subjects, such as BogoMIPS or Color-ls. These are available at <ftp: //sunsite.unc.edu/pub/Linux/docs/HOWTO/mini/> and at <http://sunsite.unc.edu/LDP/HOWTO/ HOWTO-INDEX.html>.

Linux newsgroups

There are several Usenet newsgroups for Linux. It is a good idea to follow at least comp.os.linux.announce if you use Linux. comp.os.linux.announce is moderated by Lars Wirzenius. To make submissions to the newsgroup, send mail to linux-announce@news.ornl.gov. You may direct questions about comp.os.linux.announce to Lars Wirzenius <wirzeniu@iki.fi>

The newsgroup comp.os.linux.announce is a moderated newsgroup for announcements about Linux (new programs, bug fixes, etc).

The newsgroup comp.os.linux.answers is a moderated newsgroup to which the Linux FAQ, HOWTO documents, and other documentation postings are made.

The newsgroup comp.os.linux.setup is an unmoderated newsgroup for discussion of issues and problems involved in setting up Linux systems.

The newsgroup comp.os.linux.admin is an unmoderated newsgroup for discussion of administration of Linux systems.

The newsgroup comp.os.linux.development.system is an unmoderated newsgroup specifically for discussion of Linux **kernel** development. The only application development questions that should be discussed here are those that are intimately associated with the kernel. All other development questions are probably generic Unix development questions and should be directed to a comp.unix group instead, unless they are very Linux-specific applications questions, in which case they should be directed at comp.os.linux.development.apps.

The newsgroup comp.os.linux.development.apps is an unmoderated newsgroup specifically for discussion of Linux-related applications development. It is not for discussion of where to get applications for Linux, nor a discussion forum for those who would like to see applications for Linux.

The newsgroup comp.os.linux.hardware is for Linux-specific hardware questions.

The newsgroup comp.os.linux.networking is for Linux-specific networking development and setup questions.

The newsgroup comp.os.linux.x is for Linux-specific X Windows questions.

The newsgroup comp.os.linux.misc is an unmoderated newsgroup for any Linux discussion that doesn't belong anywhere else.

In general, **do not** crosspost between the Linux newsgroups. The **only** crossposting that is appropriate is an occasional posting between one unmoderated group and comp.os.linux.announce. The whole point of splitting the old comp.os.linux group into many groups was to reduce traffic in each. Those that do not follow this rule will be flamed without mercy...

Other newsgroups

Do not assume that all your questions are appropriate for a Linux newsgroup just because you are running Linux. Is your question really about shell programming under any unix or unix clone? Then ask in comp.unix.shell. Is it about GNU Emacs? Then try asking in gnu.emacs.help. Also, if you don't know another group to ask in, but think there might be, politely ask in your post if there is another group that would be more appropriate for your question. At least the groups comp.unix.{questions,shell,programming,bsd,admin} and comp.windows.x.i386unix should be useful for a Linux user.

The World-Wide Web

Greg Hankins <gregh@cc.gatech.edu> maintains the home WWW page for the Linux project. The URL is <http://sunsite.unc.edu/LDP/>

Linux Journal

A magazine called *Linux Journal* was launched several years ago. It includes articles intended for almost all skill levels, and is intended to be helpful to all Linux users. Subscriptions are $22 in the U.S., $27 in Canada and Mexico, and $32 elsewhere around the world, all payable in U.S. funds. Subscription inquiries can be sent via email to subs@ssc.com or faxed to (U.S.) 1-206-782-7191 or mailed to Linux Journal, PO Box 85867, Seattle, WA 98145-1867 USA. SSC has a PGP public key if you wish to send your credit card number via encrypted email: finger info@ssc.com

The Linux Software Map

Information on free software available for Linux can be found in the Linux Software Map, which can be found at <http://www.execpc.com/~lsm/>

2 Getting Linux

2.1 Linux FTP sites

A more complete list of Linux FTP sites is in the Linux INFO-SHEET, which can always be found at <http://sunsite.unc.edu/LDP/HOWTO/INFO-SHEET.html> The most important sites are listed here; please see the INFO-SHEET for a site nearer to you (there are many mirrors).

```
textual name              numeric addr    Linux directory
======================    ==============  ===============
tsx-11.mit.edu            18.86.0.44      /pub/linux
sunsite.unc.edu           152.2.22.81     /pub/Linux
ftp.kernel.org            206.184.214.34  /pub/linux
```

These sites are the main "home" sites for Linux where most uploads take place. There are many mirror sites; please use the closest (network-wise) site to you.

2.2 Linux on physical media

Linux is distributed on physical media, mainly CD-ROM, by several commercial vendors. Please read the distribution HOWTO, posted regularly to comp.os.linux.announce, and available at <http://sunsite.unc.edu/LDP/HOWTO/Distribution-HOWTO.html>

2.3 AFS

Linux is available over AFS by mounting the volume project.linux from sipb.mit.edu

2.4 Commercial networks

Compu$erve has some Linux archives.

2.5 Mailservers and such

Sunsite offers ftp-mail service — mail <ftpmail@sunsite.unc.edu>.

3 Linux distributions

Linux is distributed by its author only as a kernel. Other people have put together "distributions" that pair the Linux kernel with utilities and application software to make a complete working package.

There are several distributions of Linux, which are available at various sites. Sunsite mirrors many of the distributions at <ftp://sunsite.unc.edu/pub/Linux/distributions/>. The most commonly-recommended freely-available distributions are Red Hat <http://www.redhat.com> and Debian <http://www.debian.org>. These are available for free over the internet, and are also sold on CD-ROM.

There are other distributions of Linux as well. Most commercial distributors of Linux advertise in *Linux Journal*.

4 Linux mailing-lists

Used mostly for discussion between developers of new features and testers of pre-release versions. See addresses in the FAQ. Send mail to majordomo@vger.rutgers.edu with the single word `help` in the body of the message , and you will get mail explaining how to subscribe to the many Linux mailing lists there. Save this mail, as it tells you how to unsubscribe from the lists, and if you post annoying messages to the list complaining about not being able to get off the list (because you didn't follow instructions and save the mail telling you how to unsubscribe), you will likely be flamed for wasting international bandwidth and money.

5 Documentation for various programs

Many programs come with some sort of documentation, often in a file called README or something similar. It is a VERY good idea to read them with care. It is boring to see (and answer) questions that are answered in the documentation. Most programs also have "man pages"; use the command `man programname` to get documentation on a program named `programname`. To get help using the man program, use `man man`.

Most distributions put other documentation about programs in the directory /usr/doc/; your distribution should include documentation on how to access that documentation.

6 More Documentation

The Linux Documentation Project is working on a lot of documentation. Already, over 3000 pages of book-style documentation has been released to the general public, and another 2000 or so printed pages of man pages have also been released, with more to follow. Check `<http://sunsite.unc.edu/LDP/>` for documents written by the LDP.

7 Keeping track of current releases

Important new releases, programs, and ports are usually announced in comp.os.linux.announce.

8 This Document

The latest version of this document should always be available from `<http://sunsite.unc.edu/LDP/HOWTO/META-FAQ.html>`

9 Legalese

Trademarks are owned by their owners. Satisfaction not guaranteed. No warranties about this document. Void where prohibited.

The content of this document is placed in the public domain, but if you quote it, please be polite and attribute your source.

Lars Wirzenius <wirzeniu@iki.fi> wrote the first version of this document; it is now maintained by Michael K. Johnson <johnsonm@redhat.com>. Mail me if you have any questions about this document.

The Linux Distribution HOWTO

Eric S. Raymond <esr@thyrsus.com>   v5.5, 8 February 1998

This document is intended to help new users choose a Linux distribution, and to help experienced users track the state of the Linux market.

Contents

1   Introduction

There is no single distribution of the Linux software. Instead, there are many such distributions, available both via anonymous FTP and by mail order on CD-ROM.

The purpose of this document is to provide short summaries of the English-language Linux distributions, and to provide pointers for the reader to find more information. A German Distributions HOWTO is maintained by Marco Budde at `<http://www.tu-harburg.de/~semb2204/dlhp/DE-Distribution-HOWTO.html>`. We are not aware of any distributions in languages other than English and German.

The information presented here is not complete; there are other Linux distributions than are listed here. If you are associated with a distribution we don't list, please see 4 (Submissions To This Document) near the end of this document for information on making a submission. It's easy and should take less then five minutes.

Disclaimer: We make absolutely *no* guarantee as to the correctness of the information, prices, and ordering details given in this document. Check the last-modified field of each to get an idea of its currency, then go to the vendor's web page for up-to-date information. Furthermore, unless otherwise stated the Linux software comes with *ABSOLUTELY NO WARRANTY*.

Your editor tries to stick to facts in most of this HOWTO, but he has some opinions on the state of the Linux market. If you care what they are, you can read them under 1.4 (Editorial Recommendations).

Disclosure: I (esr) have no financial connection to any Linux vendor, nor have I accepted any renumeration or perquisites from any vendor other than free product for review (and one T-shirt from Red Hat).

1.1   New versions of this document

This document will be posted monthly to the newsgroups `comp.os.linux.answers` . The document is archived on a number of Linux FTP sites, including `sunsite.unc.edu` in `pub/Linux/docs/HOWTO`.

You can also view the latest version of this HOWTO on the World Wide Web via the URL `<http://sunsite.unc.edu/mdw/HOWTO/Distribution-HOWTO.html>`.

Feel free to mail any questions or comments about this HOWTO to Eric S. Raymond, `esr@snark.thyrsus.com`. Please do *not* send me general Linux questions or requests for help in choosing a distribution unless you're willing to hire me at normal consulting rates; I don't have time to deal with them, and I try to put everything I know about choosing a distribution in this document.

1.2   Recent Changes

This HOWTO is much shorter than it used to be. In 1995-96 the Linux market underwent a serious shakeout, for reasons we discuss below.

Network distributions like the original Slackware no longer seem to be Linux's most important vector. Accordingly the General Information section and this HOWTO as a whole now focuses more on commercial CD distributions.

The old sections on re-packagers and miscellaneous related products have been trimmed and dropped. The information in them was old and hard to verify, and of rapidly decreasing value given recent changes in the Linux market.

1.3   Overview of the Linux Market

In the beginning (say, 1993), a Linux distribution was something you downloaded off the Internet onto floppies. Installation was a laborious process and repeated frustrations due to bad media were common.

Then came cheap CD-ROM drives and the CD-ROM, a medium ideally suited for shipping large volumes of operating-system software cheaply. There's a whole mini-industry now built around commercial CD-ROM Linuxes, and (because the vendors have actual cash flow to fund support and marketing) they increasingly dominate the Linux world. Debian is now the only significant non-commercial release, and even it seems to be propagated largely by shovelware CD-ROMs.

Most of the CD-ROM distributions (including Slackware, Yggdrasil and Red Hat) are still available for FTP from the home sites of their developers. But if you have a CD-ROM drive and a few dollars, you will have many more distributions and more support options to choose from (and you'll usually get some useful paper documentation). For more on the details of installation, see the Linux Installation HOWTO, <http://sunsite.unc.edu/mdw/HOWTO/Installation-HOWTO.html>.

Prices for CD-ROM distributions of Intel Linuxes start at $20 and top out at a whole $50 (and the extra few dollars can buy real value). Many vendors sell subscription deals that will lower your cost-per-CD for regular updates over the subscription period.

Price correlates with features and quality pretty well (as one would expect in a very competitive market). Your editor recommends paying the few extra dollars for a top-drawer original CD-ROM distribution; this will pay off in fewer installation and administration hassles down the road.

Making good choices is much simpler than it used to be. In 1995-96 the Linux market underwent a serious shakeout, with a very few commercial distributions emerging as leaders while weaker ones disappeared or stagnated. The toll among general-purpose non-commercial distributions has been even fiercer; essentially, only Debian survives in this role.

As a result, the three-tier structure of primary distribution builders, value-added repackagers, and bottom-feeding CD shovellers that used to define the market has nearly collapsed. To be competitive in 1997, a Linux outfit (whether commercial or noncommercial) has to offer reasonable support and behave like a primary distribution builder, whether it's really one or not. So as long as you look for a recent freeze date, it is pretty hard to get stuck with a dud distribution these days.

1.4   Editorial Recommendations

Last section, the facts. In this section, my opinions (for whatever they're worth – and remember the caveat about free advice). There is no substitute for doing your own evaluation based on experience and the data in this guide, and these are intended more to illuminate my possible biases than as a guide to what you should do.

From the beginnings of the Linux CD-ROM industry in 1993 to Fall 1995, Yggdrasil was the king of the hill – it essentially founded the CD-ROM market and then set the standard for everybody else. I used Yggdrasil, and I recommended it over commercial System V versions for its superior documentation, large collection of applications, and enlightened policy of sending free releases to freeware authors and dedicating part of the price of each CD-ROM to financially supporting free software. But Yggdrasil hasn't issued a new release in all 1996 (it's March '97 as I write) and they've perhaps been left behind by the market.

I now run Red Hat Linux and am quite satisfied with it. Red Hat's RPM technology currently gives it, IMO, a technical edge over any other vendor. They've made most of the right moves at the right times and I consider them the current market leader.

If you're ideologically wedded to using a non-commercial distribution, Debian seems to me to be the clear choice, the only one left with a serious support team behind it.

These opinions should certainly not be interpreted as an unconditional endorsement; different Linux distributions are optimized for different needs, and yours may well be best served by some other distribution (especially if, unlike me, you're mainly a DOS user and are looking for a distribution tuned for dual-boot systems and being launched from DOS).

Furthermore, industry standing is volatile. By the time you read this, Red Hat or Debian may well have fallen off their games and been displaced by hungrier newcomers.

2   American Linux Distributions

All these distributions are available on CD-ROM (some of the non-commercial ones only show up on network-archive snapshots). Most of these are available for free over the network (but the commercial ones won't support you if you buy this way). They are custom-assembled, rather than just being re-packagings of a pre-existing network release.

They are listed in alphabetical order.

2.1   Caldera OpenLinux

Distributor:

> Caldera, Inc.
> 633 South 550 East
> Provo, Utah 84606
>
> Net: *info@caldera.com* <mailto:info@caldera.com>
> WWW: <http://www.caldera.com>
> FTP: <ftp://ftp.caldera.com>
> Vox: (801)-377-7678
> Fax: (801)-377-8752

Provider's Description:

> Caldera is shipping OpenLinux 1.1 in a three-tiered family of products: OpenLinux Lite, OpenLinux Base, and OpenLinux Standard.
>
> OpenLinux Lite is a freely available evaluation of the OpenLinux product (it includes a 90-day evaluation of the Caldera integrated Desttop–the full licensed version of the desktop is included in the Base and Standard products). OpenLinxu Lite can be downloaded from Caldera's ftp site, or obtained on CD for the cost of shipping. It is also designed for use by book and software publishers to provide a commercially stable Linux offering with their books and software products.
>
> OpenLinux Base contains everything that is in Lite plus it is a complete, easy-to-install Linux operating system, with integrated Desktop, Internet client and server components, and Intranet connectivity. OpenLinux Base includes Netscape Navigator and full documentation.
>
> OpenLinux Standard includes what is in Base plus more high-end, name brand, commercial software components (such as Netscape FastTrack Web Server, Netscape Navigator Gold Web browser and authoring tools, ADABAS D database, StarOffice productivity suite, Caldera OpenDOS, and NetWare client and administration tools).
>
> All three tiers of the OpenLinux 1.1 release are currently available.
>
> With Caldera OpenLinux, you can see a whole world of powerful new computing, even the power of a UNIX workstation on your PC! By using a Linux kernel, OpenLinux gives you speed and stability that compare to systems costing thousands of dollars. Open Linux also gives you:

- Real multi-tasking runs many text or graphical applications at once; no application can cause another to crash, unlike less robust systems.

- The Linux 2.0 kernel gives super-fast TCP/IP access to the Internet, plus loadable device drivers, for the most efficient use of your system resources.

- Easy-to-follow, quick installation with menu-based choices and auto-detection of your hardware make installation a snap on most systems. The Getting Started Guide (included) provides a step-by-step illustrated procedure, with troubleshooting tips.

No other Linux system includes a complete, integrated desktop interface with configuration tools and graphical editor. Its powerful drag-and-drop capabilities come pre-configured with thousands of icons and application settings. The Desktop provides a convenient place where you can store your favorite programs and data files for instant access. The Desktop gives you:

- Drag-and-drop launching of programs with data files.

- An integrated graphical text editor.

- Easy access to an array of powerful system configuration tools.

- A configurable icon bar, custom layouts, and preference settings.

- Powerful file management using drag-and-drop or graphical dialogs.

Ordering:

By email with PGP key, by phone, by fax, or by conventional mail. Full ordering details are at <http://www.caldera.com/mpro/orinfo/orderinfo.html>.

Support:

Caldera is one of the only Linux distributers to offer E-mail and telephone support. OpenLinux Base (E-mail only) and Standard (Telephone and E-mail) users are fully supported (Standard users receive 5 free incident calls during the first 30 days). There is no technical support for the Lite product.

OpenLinux Base and Standard ship with full licensed versions of the Caldera Desktop, which do not expire. OpenLinux Lite ships with a 90-day evaluation version of the Desktop.

Last Freeze Date:

24 November 1996

Entry last modified:

12 August 1997

2.2 Craftworks Linux

Distributor:

Craftwork Solutions, Inc.
4320 Stevens Creek Blvd. #170
San Jose, CA 95129

Net: *info@craftwork.com* <mailto:info@craftwork.com>
WWW: <http://www.craftwork.com>
Vox: (408)-985-1878
Fax: (408)-985-1880

Provider's Description:

Craftworks Linux v2.2 is a commercial distribution of Linux for Intel and AXP (BeBox support is in the works). It is completely ELF, built one program at the time from the latest "stable" sources and organized using a methodology we call: CRAFT (Component Replacement And Fabrication Technology).

CRAFT accounts for each file in the system, groups them logically as true components which are filed into catalogs. For example from the 'System Install' catalog, the 'Main Operating System Component' which accounts for 3788 files (approx. 19MB), when combined with the 'Linux Standard Devices' component constitute an operational, network ready, GNU/Linux system.

CRAFT can now install RPM packages.

Security measures including shadow password are enforced throughout the distribution. Network information services (NYS) and domain name services (DNS) as provided, coexist to complement each other. Screen savers and a desktop environment are there for X Windows. Extensive use of kernel loadable modules including streaming tape (ftape) support have been utilized to minimize the need to provide various kernel configurations or requiring the end user to build one. These are some of the highlights, and the overall thought that went into this distribution, which provides a powerful modern UN*X environment for workstations and servers.

The Craftworks Linux v2.2 package includes:

- A boot/install floppy for installing on one or across multiple hard-disks from the CD-ROM media or via NFS (ethernet or PPP). Craftworks Genesis guides the user with panels and menus through a new install or upgrade.

- One CD-ROM with a live system (i.e. run directly from the CD-ROM) and all the sources as GNU zipped tar files. Supporting files such as a comprehensive list of CREDITS, the GNU Public License, etc. are also found on the CD-ROM media and copied as part of an install onto the hard-disk. Craftworks Sysadm (Main Operating System Component) provides for:

  - Security and User Account Management
  - System Maintenance (access to catalogs)
  - BRU Personal Edition backup utilities
  - X Window System Setup including Metro X enhanced server.
  - UPS Configuration
  - System Setup

- Reference and Installation Guide with chapters covering the installation and maintenance thereafter. Appendices on FAQs and hardware compatibility.

Internet Access:

Updates between releases are found in <ftp://ftp.craftwork.com/pub/v2.2>. FAQs and up-to-date product information <http://www.craftwork.com>.

Current upgrades bring the kernel to level 2.0.28.

Ordering:

Directly from Craftwork Solutions, Inc. or from distributors and stores. Suggested retail price $59.95 (Intel), $89.95 (AXP). Intel (80386/486/Pentium) version. Discounts available to dealers and educational institutions.

Support:

Craftwork Solutions, Inc. provides 30 days support with each copy. Longer term support as well as special projects support available on a contract or fee basis.

Miscellaneous:

The CRAFT-1.0 specification is available from <http://www.craftwork.com>. It includes a complete component listing for the distribution.

Last Freeze Date:

23 August 1996.

Entry last modified:

13 March 1997.

2.3   Debian Linux Distribution

Distributor:

> Debian Linux Association
> Software in the Public Interest
> P.O. Box 70152
> Pt. Richmond CA 94807-0152
> Net: *info@debian.org* <mailto:info@debian.org>
> WWW: <http://www.debian.org>
> FTP: <ftp://ftp.debian.org/debian>

Provider's Description:

> Debian Linux is the result of a volunteer effort to create a high-quality non-commercial Linux distribution. Debian Linux 1.3 is a complete and fully-functional Unix-compatible operating system for the personal computer. The system uses ELF executables, but also includes optional packages you can install to fully support development and maintenance of a.out programs. At present, Debian Linux is available for the IBM PC architecture (386/486/Pentium) with versions for Sparc, m68k and Alpha architectures well under way.
>
> Debian Linux is an easy-to-upgrade distribution that mostly consists of freely redistributable software from a number of different sources and systems. Support for shadow passwords is available, although it should be considered experimental in the 1.1 release. Non-free packages may also obtained, making Debian a well-rounded system.
>
> The benefits of Debian Linux are its upgradability, well-defined dependencies between packages, and its open development. It is the only distribution of Linux that is being developed co-operatively by many individuals through the Internet, in the same spirit as Linux and other open-source operating systems. More than 100 package maintainers are working on about 500 packages and improving Debian Linux. A sophisticated bug tracking system allows users to easily report bugs and security concerns which are quickly dealt with by the Debian community. A new release of the package will soon occur on well-known ftp archives.
>
> Debian Linux is a very dynamic distribution. Snap-shot releases are made about every three months, the ftp archives are updated daily.
>
> For more information about Debian Linux, please refer to the files at <ftp://ftp.debian.org/debian/doc/> or visit our World Wide Web page at <http://www.debian.org/>.
>
> If you're interested in joining this project you are invited to subscribe to either debian-user@lists.debian.org or debian-devel@lists.debian.org by sending a mail to debian-user-request@lists.debian.org (or debian-devel-request respectively) with the word "help" in the subject line.

Internet Access:

> Debian Linux is available via anonymous FTP from <ftp://ftp.debian.org/debian/> and on a *mirror* <http://www.debian.org/ftplist.html> near to you.

Last Freeze Date:

> 2 June 1997 (1.3)

Entry last modified:

> 13 March 1997

2.4   DOSLINUX

Distributor:

> Kent Robotti
>
> FTP: <ftp://ftp.sunsite.unc.edu/pub/Linux/distributions/doslinux>

Provider's Description:

A linux-elf slip/ppp networking system for use with DOS (formerly called 'DILINUX'). It can be dropped into a subdirectory of any DOS system and booted from DOS without messing with disk partitions. About 22 mbytes unzipped, 22 mbytes uncompressed. Noncommercial.

Internet Access:

By anonymous ftp or WWW from wauug.erols.com archives (see URL below).

WWW: <ftp://wauug.erols.com/pub/people/kent-robotti/doslinux/index.html>
FTP: <ftp://wauug.erols.com/pub/people/kent-robotti/doslinux>

Last Freeze Date:

2 Oct 1997

Entry last modified:

2 Oct 1997

Editor's comments:

As the author says, not a general-purpose release. Probably best suited to sites that primarily run DOS but want better networking tools for hooking up to an Internet service provider.

2.5   Linux Pro

Distributor:

WorkGroup Solutions, Inc.
P.O. Box 460190
Aurora, CO 80046-0190

Vox: (303)-699-7470
Fax: (303)-699-2793
Net: *info@wgs.com* <mailto:info@wgs.com> (orders)
FTP: <ftp://ftp.wgs.com/pub2/wgs>

Provider's Description:

The charter of the WGS Linux Pro CD is different from all other distributions currently on the market. We are actively pursuing penetration into the commercial marketplace for Linux. Everything we do is aimed at increasing the size of the Linux community, and helping Linux to become THE one true operating system, not just an operating system.

WGS Linux Pro consists of our Main "Stable" Linux CD, for which we select what we consider to be the best Linux distribution available. Then we make bug fixes & minor enhancements. This CD often contains software older than the latest, under the theory that "the latest is not always the greatest". Together with this approach we provide technical support as well as support agreements. For this reason WGS Linux Pro is considered a primary Linux distribution. Optionally, and in addition to our primary CD, we supply supplemental CDs containing all the latest Linux software (including current archives of the tsx-11, sunsite, and Red Hat sites). Virtually anything you will get with anyone's Linux product can be found on these supplemental CDs. We continually add more to these supplemental CDs as software becomes available. Even with all this, pricing on our product line is very favorable when correctly compared to other Linux distributions. Also optional (included with Linux Pro+) is a professionally produced and printed manual containing the Linux documentation project and more!

Current version is 4.0a; kernel is 1.2.13 with installable 2.0.x on the CD.

Internet Access:

Look in <http://www.wgs.com> for a list of WGS products, and latest information on the CD-ROM.

Ordering:

WGS Linux Pro is available on CD from dealers and distributors worldwide, and soon from our FTP site.

You may call, fax, email, or mail us, to purchase, or request additional information. We will be happy to respond to any question you have. We accept American Express, Visa, Discover, and MasterCard, or purchase orders with approval of credit.

Miscellaneous:

Complete information is available on our FTP site.

WGS publishes a free E-Mail newsletter on Linux and FlagShip to which you may subscribe by just emailing us your request.

In addition we carry Motif, FlagShip, A line of books, and other products to make your experience with Linux more complete and fulfilling. Check us out!

Last Freeze Date:

1 October 1996.

Entry last modified:

13 March 1997

Editor's comment:

They describe their current distribution as "Red Hat 3.03 plus".

2.6   Red Hat Linux

Distributor:

Red Hat Software
3201 Yorktown Rd, Suite 123 DeKalb Center
Durham, NC 27713

Vox: (800) 546-7274 or (919) 572-6500
Fax: (919) 572-6726
Net: *redhat@redhat.com* <mailto:redhat@redhat.com>
WWW: <http://www.redhat.com>
FTP: <ftp://ftp.redhat.com>

Provider's Description:

Red Hat 5.0 is based on the 2.0.31 kernel and is available for Intel, Sparc and Alpha platforms.

Four installation innovations make Red Hat the easiest Linux to install ever. Our graphical installation mode brings you straight up into X for most of the installation. Our boot disk creation script eases selection of the proper boot disk, and it saves your existing network configuration information and XF86Config so you don't have to configure TCP/IP or X! Our FTP install allows you to install simply by downloading 3 floppy disk images – the rest is done automatically! And finally, the installation includes seamless support for PCMCIA devices – install Red Hat on your laptop as easily as on your desktop machine!

After installing Red Hat Linux once, you will never need to reinstall Linux again! The new RPM packaging system is sophisticated enough to allow upgrading to new Red Hat releases without reinstalling your system - no partitioning, no backing up all your files, no headaches.

Ordering:

Available directly from Red Hat Software and most distributors of Linux related products. Please contact Red Hat Software for ordering details (on-line ordering is available through Red Hat's Web). Suggested retail price is for the Intel version is $49.95, for the Sparc and Alpha versions $99.95.

Last Freeze Date:

15 November 1997.

Entry last modified:

2 December 1997.

Editor's Comments:

The big selling point of this distribution is RPM, the Red Hat Package Manager. This piece of software is a remarkable advance; it allows you to cleanly install and de-install applications and operating-system components, including the kernel and OS base itself. Red Hat has issued this under GPL, which is a good thing for other distributors; it is the considered opinion of this editor that those who do not adopt it will shortly have their lunches eaten by those who do.

2.7 Trans-Ameritech Linuxware

Distributor:

Trans-Ameritech
2342A Walsh Avenue
Santa Clara, CA 95051

Net: *info@trans-am.com* <mailto:info@trans-am.com>
WWW: http://www.zoom.com/tae
Vox: (408)-727-3883
Fax: (408)-727-3882
BBS: (408)-980-9840

Provider's Description:

Trans-Ameritech has published 10 releases of Linux by early 1997. Traditionally, Trans-Ameritech has set new standards for combining ease of use and straightforward installation, even for a first-time user, with its line of LinuxWare CD-ROMs. This is a flexible, easy-to-install operating system geared toward those interested in learning Unix as well as technical people, students and home PC users.

- New Linux users will appreciate a Windows-based set up program from the CD.
- To minimize the possibility of hardware conflicts many extra kernels are provided for different configurations. They are usable for installation and normal operation.
- Many on-line documents are provided for quick reference, including the Linux Documentation Project files in source, dvi and ps formats.

Many applications are included:

- MS-Windows based X configuration program
- C/C++,Pascal and Ada compilers as well as converters fron Fortran
- TCP/IP networking, UUCP,SLIP,CSLIP,PPP
- Internet access with binaries and sources for FTP,Telnet,News and E-mail
- Multiple terminals and X-Windows environment
- Gnu and international versions of the ispell spell-cheker
- The communications apps:term,minicom,Seyon (X-Windows based)
- Editors:elvis(vi clone),joe,jove,Emacs
- PostScript clone ghostscript
- Object oriented GNU Smalltalk and the Smalltalk interface to X

- TCL/Tk (Powerful scripting language with Motif-like X interface)
- Programs for electrical engineers and ham enthusiasts
- Interviews libraries,include files and doc Word-processor and idraw drawing program
- Typesetting:TeX,LaTeX,xdvi,dvips,Metafont,groff
- Andrew multimedia word prodessor with hyperlinks
- FAX send and receive on either class 1 or class 2 fax modems
- DOOM for game enthusiasts

All the sources are available on the CD-ROM. The often needed sources are uncompressed and can be used directly from the CD-ROM.

An uncompressed Linux filesystem is available for references and disk space conversaion. You can run programs directly from the CD-ROM! There is a large info directory for on-line reference and many manpages.

For hacker's reference, uncompressed FreeBSD and netBSD sources are provided.

The latest upgrades and patches are always available through Trans-Ameritech Linux BBS:(408) 980 9840. It's free for all Trans-Ameritech customers.

Our distribution is targeted for Windows and DOS users who want an easy migration path upwards, rather than for UNIX experts.

Ordering:

Email orders are taken at *order@trans-am.com* `<mailto:order@trans-am.com>`

The price for our current release of LinuxWare 2.5 is $19.95

The price for a package order: LinuxWare 2.5,Supplement 5 and Supplement 4 (Ultimate LinuxWare Bundle) in one shipment is $30

If you order with a credit card (VISA, MC, AmEx, Discovery), please, indicate the card number, expiration date and your mailing address.

Shipping and handling in US: single CD-ROM or Ultimate LinuxWare Bundle is $5(first class US mail).

Overseas shipping is $8 for single CD-ROM , $12 for the bundle.

COD is available in the US only for $4.50. California residents, please add 7.75% sales tax.

Annual subscription (4 releases) is available for $80 plus S&H (note: there are 4 shipments in a subscription). Example: subscription in US is:$80+$5x4=$100. Subscription in Europe/Japan etc. $80 + $8x4 = $112.

Miscellaneous:

If you have any further questions,please contact us through E-mail: info@trans-am.com or order@trans-am.com.

Last Freeze Date:

January 1997 (Supplement 5)

Entry last modified:

13 March 1997

2.8   Slackware

Distributor:

Walnut Creek CDROM
4041 Pike Lane, Suite D

Concord, CA 94520

Net: *info@cdrom.com* <mailto:info@cdrom.com> (information), *order@cdrom.com* <mailto:order@ cdrom.com> (orders), *support@cdrom.com* <mailto:support@cdrom.com> (support).

Provider's Description:

Ftp.cdrom.com is the home of Slackware Linux. We are the publishers of the Official Slackware Linux CDROM. Our distribution is a 2-disc set with the current version being Slackware 96. The current disc is based on the 2.0.0 kernel.

Slackware Linux is a full featured distribution of the Linux operating system designed for 386/486 computers with a 3.5" floppy and CD-ROM drive.

Internet Access:

WWW: <http://www.cdrom.com/titles/os/slack96.htm>
FTP: <ftp:ftp.cdrom.com/pub/linux/slackware>

Ordering:

The cost of the CD-ROM set from Walnut Creek is $39.95.

Last Freeze Date:

August 1996.

Entry last modified:

13 March 1997.

2.9 Yggdrasil Plug-and-Play Linux CD-ROM and the Linux Bible

Distributor:

Yggdrasil Computing, Inc.
4880 Stevens Creek Blvd., Suite 205
San Jose, CA 95129-1034

Net: *info@yggdrasil.com* <mailto:info@yggdrasil.com>
WWW: <http://www.yggdrasil.com>
FTP: <http://ftp.yggdrasil.com>
Vox: (800) 261-6630, (408) 261-6630
Fax: (408) 261-6631

Provider's Description:

Yggdrasil Plug-and-Play Linux is a complete CD-ROM distribution of the Linux operating system. It includes a great deal of software—nearly every package that you would expect to find on a complete UNIX system is available. A complete file list is available via FTP from yggdrasil.com.

The Linux Bible is a compendium of Linux documentation, including 5 books from the Linux Documentation Project, The Yggdrasil installation manual, and the complete set of Linux HOWTO guides. We publish this and offer this separately from the CD-ROM distribution.

At the top of the sophistication hierarchy, programmers who want to explore or add the occasional feature know that Yggdrasil is the Linux distribution with a fully buildable source tree and with the ability to automatically trace installed files back to their sources.

Everybody, especially new users, will appreciate the Plug-and-Play operation for which Yggdrasil's product is named. Put the media in a computer with supported hardware, turn the computer on, and it's running everything, straight from the CDROM. (This is no longer unique to Yggdrasil, but Yggdrasil did it first.)

The login screen lists a number of preconfigured user names, including "install", which installs the system, giving paragraphs of explanation about every question that it asks the user. X windows configuration is automated too, prompting the user for configuration information the first time `xinit` is run.

From X windows, a graphical control panel allows simple "fill in the blanks" configuration of networking, SLIP, outgoing UUCP, the printer, NNTP, and many other features that previously required the knowledge of a system administrator to configure.

For more information, send mail to `info@yggdrasil.com`, surf to `www.yggdrasil.com`, FTP to `yggdrasil.com`, or contact us by any convenient method.

Ordering:

Plug-and-Play Linux costs $34.95 is and available directly from Yggdrasil or from your local computer, software or technical book store. If Plug-and-Play Linux is not available from your favorite reseller, help promote Linux by making it your mission to change that. Give your reseller our phone number and demand that they carry Plug-and-Play Linux.

Yggdrasil offers a $7 discount for upgrades or crossgrades. Send us your old Yggdrasil release and a check for $27.95 + $5 shipping and handling to upgrade. Or do the same, but send us a competing distribution such any version of SCO, Esix, minix, or one of the CD's with the slackware floppy images, and tell us where you got it, so that we can make sure that your favorite reseller carries our products too.

Miscellaneous:

Yggdrasil also sells OSF/Motif and The Linux Bible, a compilation of works from the Linux Documentation project. In addition to a copy of the Plug-and-Play Linux manual, The Linux Bible includes *Linux Installation and Getting Started*, *Network Administrator's Guide*, *System Administrator's Guide*, *Linux User's Guide*, and HOWTO guides on hardware compatibility, distributions, dos emulation, ethernet, floppy tape, installation, mail, networking version 2, MGR (an alternative to X windows), X windows, usenet news, printing, SCSI, serial communications, sound, and UUCP. The Linux Bible costs $39.95 and is printed on recycled paper. $1 from every copy sold is donated to the Linux Documentation Project. OSF/Motif costs $149.95, $5 of which is donated to the development of a free Motif clone.

Last Freeze Date:

Mid-August 1995. (Yes, 1995. They have a next release in pre-production but don't want to commit to a ship date yet.)

Entry last modified:

13 March 1997

Editor's Comments:

Yggdrasil includes lots of well-chosen stuff with their distribution; the CD-ROM-only demo mode is impressive; installation and administration are easy enough to live up to their "Plug And Play" name. The 167-page manual is very nice. Their previous problems in the installation scripts seem to have been fixed. Their only drawback is that they haven't yet adopted Red Hat's RPM technology or created an equivalent. They claim they're going to by RPM-compatible in their upcoming release.

3   Re-Packagers

This section lists re-packagers of the Linux distributions listed above. In other words, the people selling the software below probably do *not* maintain or support the software itself.

3.1   InfoMagic Developer's Resource CD-ROM kit

Distributor:

InfoMagic, Inc.
PO Box 30370. Flagstaff, AZ 86003-0370

Net: *info@infomagic.com* <mailto:info@infomagic.com>
WWW: <http://www.infomagic.com>
Vox: (800)-800-6613 (orders), (520)-526-9852 (tech support)
Fax: (520)-526-9573

Provider's Description:

The InfoMagic Linux Developer's Resource is a snapshot of the sunsite.unc.edu and tsx-11.mit.edu archives. It also includes the complete GNU software collection (in source form). The following Linux distributions are included on the discs: Red Hat, Slackware, Debian and JE (Japanese Extensions).

The Slackware distribution has been completely unpacked allowing many packages to be run directly from the disk. Sources for all the packages in Slackware are also included.

The Linux HOWTO documents have been formatted for use with the Microsoft Multimedia Viewer (which is included) to allow browsing and full-text search under Microsoft Windows. InfoMagic also includes complete archives of the linux mailing lists.

InfoMagic also distributes the "Installation and Getting Started Guide", by Matt Welsh as well as Linux T-Shirts (featuring the platypus logo).

Ordering:

The 5-CD set is $27.50/copy. Shipping within the US is $5 (USPS Priority Mail), outside the US $10 (International Airmail), FedEx and UPS on request. Orders may be placed via phone, fax, or email (a PGP key is available: finger info@InfoMagic.com). We accept Visa, Mastercard, and AMEX. 1-year subscriptions are available for $150 (within the US) and $175 (outside the US) including shipping. A 1 year subscription consists of 6 releases, one every two months or so.

Internet Access:

The contents of the CDs may be found at either <http://www.infomagic.com>, <ftp://ftp. infomagic.com>.

Support:

We provide unlimited email and FAX support. Telephone support is available via a 900 number at $2.00/minute. We also offer support contracts tailored to individual needs.

The CD-set includes a 30-page quick-start.

Last Freeze Date:

1st week of December 1996. Updates about every two months. The Slackware release is 3.1, Red Hat is 4.0

Entry last modified:

13 March 1997

4   Submissions To This Document

I encourage anyone and everyone who maintains a Linux distribution or mail order service, to submit information on their service to this HOWTO. It's easy and fun, and it's free advertising. This document is posted to many places and is archived (see the next section).

4.1   Types of Submissions

We are interested in submissions for:

- Complete distributions of Linux software, available either via anonymous FTP, UUCP, or mail order. By 'complete distribution' we mean any set of software which can be used to build a complete Linux system from scratch.

- Layered products or individual software packages available only via mail order. If your software package is available via anonymous FTP, chances are people can find it. Software products only available via mail-order include commercial things such as Motif, and any other commercial software ported to Linux.

- Any other *Linux-specific* goods available via mail order, such as Linux-specific books and documentation, T-shirts, and assorted paraphrenalia. Note: our interest in the latter categories is marginal – this is a Linux Distributions HOWTO, not a catalogue of cutesy Linux junk. Whatever you're selling will have to be (a) very useful, (b) very original, or (c) very funny, to get listed here.

If the number of submissions for services and layered products is large, I'll create a separate HOWTO for these items.

4.2   How to submit

To submit an entry to this HOWTO, please send mail to `esr@snark.thyrsus.com` with the following information. This format is not machine-parsable; any of the fields may be any length that you wish, but I'd like to keep each entry down to, say, 50 lines.

Name:

> *Name of service or distribution*

Distributor:

> *Name of company, person, etc. who distributes/maintains the service or distribution. Should include mail, email, phone contact information, and (if possible) a WWW reference.*

Provider's Description:

> *Description of the distribution or service that you provide. If this is a software distribution, please include information such as what software is included, versions, general overview of installation, requirements, and so on.*

Internet Access:

> *Where your service or distribution is available over the Internet; typically a WWW or FTP address.*

Ordering:

> *How to order your distribution or service, if applicable. Include prices, shipping information, methods of payment, etc.*

Support:

> Information on support terms and support contracts.

Miscellaneous:

> *Anything else that you find relevant.*

Last Freeze Date:

> Last freeze date of the current version(s). Also, your estimated update frequency.

4.3   Submission Guidelines

Please keep your entry as short as possible. If you need to include extensive information, please make a reference to where one can FTP or mail to get more information on your distribution; these entries are only meant to be *pointers* to where one can find information on your service or distribution.

If you provide more than one service or distribution, please use *separate entries* for each.

I may edit your entries for conciseness and brevity, if I find any irrelevant information, or if the entry is overly verbose. Otherwise the content should remain the same.

When making submissions to the Distribution-HOWTO, you grant implicit permission for me to use the entries in other materials, such as books from the LDP, and other online documents. For example, information from the Distribution-HOWTO may be included in a published Linux book. If you do not want me to include your entry in materials other than the Distribution-HOWTO, please say so.

5 Administrivia

5.1 Terms of Use

This document is copyright 1997 by Eric S. Raymond. You may use, disseminate, and reproduce it freely, provided you:

- Do not omit or alter this copyright notice.
- Do not omit or alter or omit the version number and date.
- Do not omit or alter the document's pointer to the current WWW version.
- Clearly mark any consdensed, altered or versions as such.

These restrictions are intended to protect potential readers from stale or mangled versions. If you think you have a good case for an exception, ask me.

5.2 Acknowledgements

This document was originated by Bill Riemers. Matt Welsh maintained the second version. Erik Troan then maintained the document to release 3.0.

In January 1995, Eric Raymond, while unaware of the existence of this document, began to develop a similar FAQ in the format of his now-discontinued "PC-clone UNIX Software Buyer's Guide", which had covered mainly System V UNIXes and BSD/OS.

In March 1995, Eric approached Erik about cooperating on a merged version. In early April 1995, Erik went to work for Red Hat Software, and (wishing to avoid a conflict of interest) handed the document to Eric. Eric merged in a lot of new information and added several new fields to the distribution entries.

Accordingly, this document has been a sort of serial collaboration. The editorial 'we' generally tags observations by all the maintainers; 'I' is Eric (the current one) speaking.

We are delighted to acknowledge the contributions of all the Linux users and Internet hackers who have contributed information and feedback.

The Linux Installation HOWTO

by Eric S. Raymond
v4.10, 1 February 1998

This document describes how to obtain and install Linux software. It is the first document which a new Linux user should read to get started.

Contents

1 Introduction

1.1 Purpose of this document

Linux is a freely-distributable implementation of Unix for inexpensive personal machines (it was developed on 386s, and now supports 486, 586, Pentium, PowerPC, Sun Sparc and DEC Alpha hardware). It supports a wide range of software, including X Windows, Emacs, TCP/IP networking (including SLIP), and many applications.

This document assumes that you have heard of and know about Linux, and now want to sit down and install it. It focuses on the Intel base version, which is the most popular, but much of the advice applies on Power PCs, Sparcs and Alphas as well.

1.2 Other sources of information

If you are new to Linux, there are several sources of basic information about the system. The best place to find these is at the Linux Documentation Project home page at `<http://sunsite.unc.edu/LDP/linux.html>`. You can find the latest, up-to-date version of this document there, as `<http://sunsite.unc.edu/LDP/HOWTO/Installation-HOWTO.html>`

You should probably start by browsing the resources under General Linux Information; the Linux *INFO-SHEET* `<http://sunsite.unc.edu/LDP/HOWTO/INFO-SHEET.html>` and the Linux *META-FAQ* `<http://sunsite.unc.edu/LDP/HOWTO/META-FAQ.html>`. The 'Linux Frequently Asked Questions' document contains many common questions (and answers!) about Linux—it is a "must read" for new users.

You can find help for common problems on the USENET newsgroups *comp.os.linux.help* `<news:comp.os.linux.help>` and *comp.os.linux.announce* `<news:comp.os.linux.announce>`.

The Linux Documentation Project is writing a set of manuals and books about Linux, all of which are freely distributable on the net and available from the LDP home page.

The book *"Linux Installation and Getting Started"* is a complete guide to getting and installing Linux, as well as how to use the system once you've installed it. It contains a complete tutorial to using and running the system, and much more information than is contained here. You can browse it, or download a copy, from the LDP home page.

Finally, there is a rather technical *Guide to x86 Bootstrapping* `<http://www.paranoia.com/~vax/boot.html>`. This document is NetBSD- rather than Linux-oriented, but contains useful material on disk configuration and boot managers for multi-OS setups.

1.3 New versions of this document

New versions of the Linux Installation HOWTO will be periodically posted to *comp.os.linux.help* `<news:comp.os.linux.help>` and `<news:comp.os.linux.announce>` and *news.answers* `<news:answers>`. They will also be uploaded to various Linux WWW and FTP sites, including the LDP home page.

You can also view the latest version of this on the World Wide Web via the URL `<http://sunsite.unc.edu/LDP/HOWTO/Installation-HOWTO.html>`.

1.4 Feedback and Corrections

If you have questions or comments about this document, please feel free to mail Eric S. Raymond, at *esr@thyrsus.com* `<mailto:esr@thyrsus.com>`. I welcome any suggestions or criticisms. If you find a mistake with this document, please let me know so I can correct it in the next version. Thanks.

Please do *not* mail me questions about how to solve hardware problems encountered during installation. Consult *"Linux Installation and Getting Started"*, bug your vendor, or consult the Linux newsgroup *comp.os.linux.setup* `<news:comp.os.linux.setup>`. This HOWTO is intended to be rapid, painless guide to *normal* installation – a separate HOWTO on hardware problems and diagnosis is in preparation.

2 Recent Changes

- Added indexing markup for the paper version.

3 Before You Begin

Before you can install Linux, you'll need to be sure your machine is Linux-capable, and choose a Linux to install.

3.1 Hardware requirements

What kind of system is needed to run Linux? This is a good question; the actual hardware requirements for the system change periodically. The Linux Hardware-HOWTO, `<http://sunsite.unc.edu/LDP/HOWTO/Hardware-HOWTO.html>`, gives a (more or less) complete listing of hardware supported by Linux. The Linux INFO-SHEET, `<http://sunsite.unc.edu/LDP/HOWTO/INFO-SHEET.html>`, provides another list.

For the Intel versions, a hardware configuration that looks like the following is required:

Any ISA, EISA, VESA Local Bus or PCI 80386, 80486, Pentium or Pentium Pro system will do. The MCA architecture (found on IBM PS/2 machines) is supported in the newest development (2.1.x) kernels, but may not be ready for prime time yet. Any CPU from the 386SX to the P-6 will work. You do not need a math coprocessor, although it is nice to have one.

You need at least 4 megabytes of memory in your machine. Technically, Linux will run with only 2 megs, but most installations and software require 4. The more memory you have, the happier you'll be. I suggest 8 or 16 megabytes if you're planning to use X-Windows.

Of course, you'll need a hard drive and an AT-standard drive controller. All MFM, RLL, and IDE drives and controllers should work. Many SCSI drives and adaptors are supported as well; the Linux SCSI-HOWTO contains more information on SCSI. If you are assembling a system from scratch to run Linux, the small additional cost of SCSI is well worth it for the extra performance and reliability it brings.

You will need a 3.5" floppy drive. While 5.25" floppies are supported under Linux, they are little-enough used that you should not count on disk images necessarily fitting on them. (A stripped-down Linux can actually run on a single floppy, but that's only useful for installation and certain troubleshooting tasks.)

You also need an MDA, Hercules, CGA, EGA, VGA, or Super VGA video card and monitor. In general, if your video card and monitor work under MS-DOS then it should work under Linux. However, if you wish to run X Windows, there are other restrictions on the supported video hardware. The Linux XFree86-HOWTO, <http://sunsite.unc.edu/LDP/HOWTO/XFree86-HOWTO.html>, contains more information about running X and its requirements.

You'll want a CD-ROM drive. If it's ATAPI, SCSI, or true IDE you should have no problem making it work (but watch for cheap drives advertising "IDE" interfaces that aren't true IDE). If your CD-ROM uses a proprietary interface card, it's possible the installation kernel you're going to boot from floppy won't be able to see it – and an inaccessible CD-ROM is a installation show-stopper. Also, CD-ROMs that attach to your parallel port won't work at all. If you're in doubt, consult the Linux CD-ROM HOWTO, <http://sunsite.unc.edu/LDP/HOWTO/CDROM-HOWTO.html> for a list and details of supported hardware.

So-called "Plug'n'Play" jumperless cards can be a problem. Support for these is under active development, but not there yet in the 2.0.25 kernel. Fortunately this is only likely to be a problem with sound or Ethernet cards.

If you're running on a box that uses one of the Motorola 68K processors (including Amiga, Atari, or VMEbus machines), see the Linux/m68k FAQ at <http://www.clark.net/pub/lawrencc/linux/faq/faq.html> for information on minimum requirements and the state of the port. The FAQ now says m68k Linux is as stable and usable as the Intel versions.

3.2   Space requirements and coexistence

You'll need free space for Linux on your hard drive. The amount of space needed depends on how much software you plan to install. Most installations require somewhere in the ballpark of 200 to 500 megs. This includes space for the software, swap space (used as virtual RAM on your machine), and free space for users, and so on.

It's conceivable that you could run a minimal Linux system in 80 megs or less (this used to be common when Linux distributions were smaller), and it's conceivable that you could use well over 500 megs or more for all of your Linux software. The amount varies greatly depending on the amount of software you install and how much space you require. More about this later.

Linux will co-exist with other operating systems, such as MS-DOS, Microsoft Windows, or OS/2, on your hard drive. (In fact you can even access MS-DOS files and run some MS-DOS programs from Linux.) In other words, when partitioning your drive for Linux, MS-DOS or OS/2 live on their own partitions, and Linux exists on its own. We'll go into more detail about such "dual-boot" systems later.

You do NOT need to be running MS-DOS, OS/2, or any other operating system to use Linux. Linux is a completely different, stand-alone operating system and does not rely on other OSs for installation and use.

In all, the minimal setup for Linux is not much more than is required for most MS-DOS or Windows 3.1 systems sold today (and it's a good deal less than the minimum for Windows 95!). If you have a 386 or 486 with at least 4 megs of RAM, then you'll be happy running Linux. Linux does not require huge amounts of diskspace, memory, or processor speed. Matt Welsh, the originator of this HOWTO, used to run Linux on a 386/16 MHz (the slowest machine you can get) with 4 megs of RAM, and was quite happy. The more you want to do, the more memory (and faster processor) you'll need. In our experience a 486 with 16 megabytes of RAM running Linux outdoes several models of expensive workstation.

3.3   Choosing a Linux distribution

Before you can install Linux, you need to decide on one of the "distributions" of Linux which are available. There is no single, standard release of the Linux software—there are many such releases. Each release has its own documentation and installation instructions.

Linux distributions are available both via anonymous FTP and via mail order on diskette, tape, and CD-ROM. The Linux Distribution HOWTO, <http://sunsite.unc.edu/LDP/HOWTO/Distribution-HOWTO. html>, includes descriptions of many Linux distributions available via FTP and mail order.

In the dim and ancient past when this HOWTO was first written (1992-93), most people got Linux by tortuous means involving long downloads off the Internet or a BBS onto their DOS machines, followed by an elaborate procedure which transferred the downloads onto multiple floppy disks. One of these disks would then be booted and used to install the other dozen. With luck (and no media failures) you'd finish your installation many hours later with a working Linux. Or maybe not.

While this path is still possible (and you can download any one of several disatributions from <http: //sunsite.unc.edu/pub/Linux/distributions/INDEX.html>), there are now much less strenuous ways. The easiest is to buy one of the high-quality commercial Linux distributions distributed on CD-ROM, such as Red Hat, Craftworks, Linux Pro, or WGS. These are typically available for less than $50 at your local bookstore or computer shop, and will save you many hours of aggravation.

You can also buy anthology CD-ROMs such as the InfoMagic Linux Developer's Resource set. These typically include several Linux distributions and a recent dump of major Linux archive sites, such as sunsite or tsx-11.

In the remainder of this HOWTO we will focus on the steps needed to install from an anthology CD-ROM, or one of the lower-end commercial Linuxes that doesn't include a printed installation manual. If your Linux includes a paper manual some of this HOWTO may provide useful background, but you should consult the manual for detailed installation instructions.

4   Installation Overview

4.1   Basic Installation Steps

The basic outline of Linux installation is simple:

1. Collect configuration information on your hardware.
2. Make installation floppies.
3. If you want to run a "dual-boot" system (Linux and DOS or Windows both), rearrange (repartition) your disk to make room for Linux.
4. Boot an installation mini-Linux from the floppies in order to get access to the CD-ROM.
5. Prepare the Linux filesystems. (If you didn't edit the disk partition table earlier, you will at this stage.)

6. Install a basic production Linux from the CD-ROM.

7. Boot Linux from the hard drive.

8. (Optional) Install more packages from CD-ROM.

4.2 Basic Parts of an Installation Kit

Here are the basic parts of an installable distribution:

1. The README and FAQ files. These will usually be located in the top-level directory of your CD-ROM and be readable once the hard disk has been mounted under Linux. (Depending on how the CD-ROM was generated, they may even be visible under DOS/Windows.) It is a good idea to read these files as soon as you have access to them, to become aware of important updates or changes.

2. A number of bootdisk images (often in a subdirectory). One of these is is the file that you will write to a floppy to create the boot disk. You'll select **one** of the above bootdisk images, depending on the type hardware that you have in your system.

The issue here is that some hardware drivers conflict with each other in strange ways, and instead of attempting to debug hardware problems on your system it's easier to use a boot floppy image with only the drivers you need enabled. (This will have the nice side effect of making your kernel smaller.)

- A rootdisk image (or perhaps two). This is a file that you will write to a floppy to create the installation disk(s). Nowadays the root disk or disks is generally independent of your hardware type; it will assume an EGA or better color screen.

- A rescue disk image. This is a disk containing a basic kernel and tools for disaster recovery in case something steps on the kernel or boot block of your hard disk.

- RAWRITE.EXE. This is an MS-DOS program that will write the contents of a file (such as a boot or rootdisk image) directly to a floppy, without regard to format.

You only need RAWRITE.EXE if you plan to create your boot and root floppies from an MS-DOS system. If you have access to a UNIX workstation with a floppy drive instead, you can create the floppies from there, using the 'dd' command. or possibly a vendor-provided build script. See the man page for dd(1) and ask your local UNIX gurus for assistance.

- The CD-ROM itself. The purpose of the boot disk is to get your machine ready to load the root or installation disks, which in turn are just devices for preparing your hard disk and copying portions of the CD-ROM to it.

5 Installation In Detail

5.1 Getting prepared for installation

Linux makes more effective use of PC hardware than MS-DOS, Windows or NT, and is accordingly less tolerant of misconfigured hardware. There are a few things you can do before you start that will lessen your chances of being stopped by this kind of problem.

First, collect any manuals you have on your hardware – motherboard, video card, monitor, modem, etc. – and put them within easy reach.

Second, gather detailed information on your hardware configuration. One easy way to do this, if you're running MS-DOS 5.0, or up, is to print a report from the Microsoft diagnostic utility msd.exe (you can leave out the TSR, driver, memory-map, environment-strings and OS-version parts). Among other things, this will guarantee you full and correct information on your video card and mouse type, which will be helpful in configuring X later on.

Third, check your machine for configuration problems with supported hardware that could cause an un-recoverable lockup during Linux installation.

- It is possible for a DOS/Windows system using IDE hard drive(s) and CD ROM to be functional even with the master/slave jumpers on the drives incorrectly set. Linux won't fly this way. If in doubt, check your master-slave jumpers!

- Is any of your peripheral hardware designed with neither configuration jumpers nor non-volatile configuration memory? If so, it may require boot-time initialization via an MS-DOS utility to start up, and may not be easily accessible from Linux. CD-ROMs, sound cards, Ethernet cards and low-end tape drives can have this problem. If so, you may be able to work around this with an argument to the boot prompt; see the Linux Boot Prompt HOWTO, <http://sunsite.unc.edu/LDP/HOWTO/ BootPrompt-HOWTO.html> for details).

- Some other operating systems will allow a bus mouse to share an IRQ with other devices. Linux doesn't support this; in fact, trying it may lock up your machine. If you are using a bus mouse, see the Linux Bus Mouse HOWTO, <http://sunsite.unc.edu/LDP/HOWTO/Busmouse-HOWTO.html>, for details.

If possible, get the telephone number of an experienced Linux user you can call in case of emergency. Nine times out of ten you won't need it, but it's comforting to have.

Budget time for installation. That will be about one hour on a bare system or one being converted to all-Linux operation. Or up to three hours for a dual-boot system (they have a much higher incidence of false starts and hangups).

5.2   Creating the boot and root floppies

Your Linux CD-ROM may come with installation aids that will take you through the process of building boot, root, and rescue disks with interactive prompts. These may be an MS-DOS installation program (such as the Red Hat redhat.exe program) or a Unix script, or both.

If you have such a program and can use it, you should read the rest of this subsection for information only. Run the program to do actual installation – its authors certainly knew more about the specific distribution than I, and you'll avoid many error-prone hand-entry steps.

More detailed information on making boot and root disks, see the Linux Bootdisk HOWTO at <http: //sunsite.unc.edu/LDP/HOWTO/Bootdisk-HOWTO.html>.

Your first step will be to select a boot-disk image to fit your hardware. If you must do this by hand, you'll generally find that either (a) the bootdisk images on your CD-ROM are named in a way that willl help you pick a correct one, or (b) there's an index file nearby describing each image.

Next, you must create floppies from the bootdisk image you selected, and from the root and rescue disk images. This is where the MS-DOS program RAWRITE.EXE comes into play.

Next, you must have two or three *high-density* MS-DOS formatted floppies. (They must be of the same type; that is, if your boot floppy drive is a 3.5" drive, both floppies must be high-density 3.5" disks.) You will use RAWRITE.EXE to write the boot and rootdisk images to the floppies.

Invoke it with no arguments, like this:

```
C:\> RAWRITE
```

Answer the prompts for the name of the file to write and the floppy to write it to (such as `A:`). RAWRITE will copy the file, block-by-block, directly to the floppy. Also use RAWRITE for the root disk image (such as COLOR144). When you're done, you'll have two floppies: one containing the boot disk, the other containing the root disk. Note that these two floppies will no longer be readable by MS-DOS (they are "Linux format" floppies, in some sense).

You can use the dd(1) commands on a UNIX system to do the same job. (For this, you will need a UNIX workstation with a floppy drive, of course.) For example, on a Sun workstation with the floppy drive on device */dev/rfd0*, you can use the command:

```
$ dd if=bare of=/dev/rfd0 obs=18k
```

You must provide the appropriate output block size argument (the 'obs' argument) on some workstations (e.g., Suns) or this will fail. If you have problems the man page for dd(1) may be be instructive.

Be sure that you're using brand-new, error-free floppies. The floppies must have no bad blocks on them.

Note that you do not need to be running Linux or MS-DOS in order to install Linux. However, running Linux or MS-DOS makes it easier to create the boot and root floppies from your CD-ROM. If you don't have an operating system on your machine, you can use someone else's Linux or MS-DOS just to create the floppies, and install from there.

5.3   Repartitioning your DOS/Windows drives

On most used systems, the hard drive is already dedicated to partitions for MS-DOS, OS/2, and so on. You'll need to resize these partitions in order to make space for Linux. If you're going to run a dual-boot system, it's strongly recommended that you read one or more of the following mini-HOWTOS, which describe different dual-boot configurations.

- The Linux+DOS+Win95 mini-HOWTO, `<http://sunsite.unc.edu/LDP/HOWTO/mini/Linux+DOS+Win95>`.

- The Linux+OS2+DOS mini-HOWTO, `<http://sunsite.unc.edu/LDP/HOWTO/mini/Linux+OS2+DOS>`.

- The DOS-Win95-OS2-Linux mini-HOWTO, `<http://sunsite.unc.edu/LDP/HOWTO/mini/Linux+DOS+Win95+OS2>`.

- The Linux+Win95 mini-HOWTO, `<http://sunsite.unc.edu/LDP/HOWTO/mini/Linux+Win95>`

- The Linux+WinNT-Loader mini-HOWTO, `<http://sunsite.unc.edu/LDP/HOWTO/mini/Linux+WinNT-Loader>`

Even if they are not directly applicable to your system, they will help you understand the issues involved.

NOTE: Some Linuxes will install to a directory on your MS-DOS partition. (This is different than installing FROM an MS-DOS partition.) Instead, you use the "UMSDOS filesystem", which allows you to treat a directory of your MS-DOS partition as a Linux filesystem. In this way, you don't have to repartition your drive.

I only suggest using this method if your drive already has four partitions and repartitioning would be more trouble than it's worth (it slows down your Linux due to filename translation overhead). Or, if you want to try out Linux before repartitioning, this is a good way to do so. But in most cases you should repartition, as described here. If you do plan to use UMSDOS, you are on your own—it is not documented in detail here. From now on, we assume that you are NOT using UMSDOS, and that you will be repartitioning.

A *partition* is just a section of the hard drive set aside for a particular operating system to use. If you only have MS-DOS installed, your hard drive probably has just one partition, entirely for MS-DOS. To use Linux, however, you'll need to repartition the drive, so that you have one partition for MS-DOS, and one (or more) for Linux.

Partitions come in three flavors: *primary*, *extended*, and *logical*. Briefly, primary partitions are one of the four main partitions on your drive. However, if you wish to have more than four partitions per drive, you need to create an extended partition, which can contain many logical partitions. You don't store data directly on an extended partition—it is used only as a container for logical partitions. Data is stored only on either primary or logical partitions.

To put this another way, most people use only primary partitions. However, if you need more than four partitions on a drive, you create an extended partition. Logical partitions are then created on top of the extended partition, and there you have it—more than four partitions per drive.

Note that you can easily install Linux on the second drive on your system (known as D: to MS-DOS). You simply specify the appropriate device name when creating Linux partitions. This is described in detail below.

Back to repartitioning your drive: The problem with resizing partitions is that there is no way to do it (easily) without deleting the data on those partitions. Therefore, you will need to make a full backup of your system before repartitioning. In order to resize a partition, we simply delete the partition(s), and re-create them with smaller sizes.

NOTE: There is a non-destructive disk repartitioner available for MS-DOS, called FIPS. Look at `<http://sunsite.unc.edu/pub/Linux/system/Install>`. With FIPS, a disk optimizer (such as Norton Speed Disk), and a little bit of luck, you should be able to resize MS-DOS partitions without destroying the data on them. It's still suggested that you make a full backup before attempting this.

If you're not using FIPS, however, the classic way to modify partitions is with the program FDISK. For example, let's say that you have an 80 meg hard drive, dedicated to MS-DOS. You'd like to split it in half—40 megs for MS-DOS and 40 megs for Linux. In order to do this, you run FDISK under MS-DOS, delete the 80 meg MS-DOS partition, and re-create a 40 meg MS-DOS partition in its place. You can then format the new partition and reinstall your MS-DOS software from backups. 40 megabytes of the drive is left empty. Later, you create Linux partitions on the unused portion of the drive.

In short, you should do the following to resize MS-DOS partitions with FDISK:

1. Make a full backup of your system.

2. Create an MS-DOS bootable floppy, using a command such as

   `FORMAT /S A:`

3. Copy the files `FDISK.EXE` and `FORMAT.COM` to this floppy, as well as any other utilities that you need. (For example, utilities to recover your system from backup.)

4. Boot the MS-DOS system floppy.

5. Run FDISK, possibly specifying the drive to modify (such as C: or D:).

6. Use the FDISK menu options to delete the partitions which you wish to resize. **This will destroy all data on the affected partitions.**

7. Use the FDISK menu options to re-create those partitions, with smaller sizes.

8. Exit FDISK and re-format the new partitions with the `FORMAT` command.

9. Restore the original files from backup.

Note that MS-DOS FDISK will give you an option to create a "logical DOS drive". A logical DOS drive is just a logical partition on your hard drive. You can install Linux on a logical partition, but you don't want to create that logical partition with MS-DOS fdisk. So, if you're currently using a logical DOS drive, and want to install Linux in its place, you should delete the logical drive with MS-DOS FDISK, and (later) create a logical partition for Linux in its place.

The mechanism used to repartition for OS/2 and other operating systems is similar. See the documentation for those operating systems for details.

5.4   Creating partitions for Linux

After repartitioning your drive, you need to create partitions for Linux. Before describing how to do that, we'll talk about partitions and filesystems under Linux.

5.4.1   Partition basics

Linux requires at least one partition, for the *root filesystem*, which will hold the Linux kernel and software itself.

You can think of a *filesystem* as a partition formatted for Linux. Filesystems are used to hold files. Every system must have a root filesystem, at least. However, many users prefer to use multiple filesystems—one for each major part of the directory tree. For example, you may wish to create a separate filesystem to hold all files under the */usr* directory. (Note that on UNIX systems, forward slashes are used to delimit directories, not backslashes as with MS-DOS.) In this case you have both a root filesystem, and a */usr* filesystem.

Each filesystem requires its own partition. Therefore, if you're using both root and */usr* filesystems, you'll need to create two Linux partitions.

In addition, most users create a *swap partition*, which is used for virtual RAM. If you have, say, 4 megabytes of memory on your machine, and a 10-megabyte swap partition, as far as Linux is concerned you have 14 megabytes of virtual memory.

When using swap space, Linux moves unused pages of memory out to disk, allowing you to run more applications at once on your system. However, because swapping is often slow, it's no replacement for real physical RAM. But applications that require a great deal of memory (such as the X Window System) often rely on swap space if you don't have enough physical RAM.

Nearly all Linux users employ a swap partition. If you have 4 megabytes of RAM or less, a swap partition is required to install the software. It is strongly recommended that you have a swap partition anyway, unless you have a great amount of physical RAM.

The size of your swap partition depends on how much virtual memory you need. It's often suggested that you have at least 16 megabytes of virtual memory total. Therefore, if you have 8 megs of physical RAM, you might want to create an 8-megabyte swap partition. Note that swap partitions can be no larger than 128 megabytes in size. Therefore, if you need more than 128 megs of swap, you must create multiple swap partitions. You may have up to 16 swap partitions in all.

You can find more on the theory of swap space layout and disk partitioning in the Linux Partition mini-HOWTO (<http://sunsite.unc.edu/LDP/HOWTO/mini/Partition>).

Note: it is possible, though a bit tricky, to share swap partitions between Linux and Windows 95 in a dual-boot system. For details, see the Linux Swap Space Mini-HOWTO, <http://sunsite.unc.edu/LDP/HOWTO/mini/Swap-Space>.

Gotcha #1: If you have an EIDE drive with a partition that goes above 504MB, your BIOS may not allow you to boot to a Linux installed there. So keep your root partition below 504MB. This shouldn't be a problem for SCSI drive controllers, which normally have their own drive BIOS firmware. For technical details, see the Large Disk Mini-HOWTO, <http://sunsite.unc.edu/LDP/HOWTO/mini/Large-Disk>.

Gotcha #2: Are you mixing IDE and SCSI drives? Then watch out. Your BIOS may not allow you to boot directly to a SCSI drive.

5.4.2 Sizing partitions

Besides your root and swap partitions, you'll want to set up one or more partitions to hold your software and home directories.

While, in theory, you could run everything off a single huge root partition, almost nobody does this. Having multiple partitions has several advantages:

- It often cuts down the time required for boot-time file-system checks.
- Files can't grow across partition boundaries. Therefore you can use partition boundaries as firebreaks against programs (like Usenet news) that want to eat huge amounts of disk, to prevent them from crowding out file space needed by your kernel and the rest of your applications.
- If you ever develop a bad spot on your disk, formatting and restoring a single partition is less painful than having to redo everything from scratch.

On today's large disks, a good basic setup is to have a small root partition (less than 80 meg), a medium-sized /usr partition (up to 300 meg or so) to hold system software, and a /home partition occupying the rest of your available space for home directories.

You can get more elaborate. If you know you're going to run Usenet news, for example, you may want to give it a partition of its own to control its maximum possible disk usage. Or create a /var partition for mail, news, and temporary files all together. But in today's regime of very cheap, very large hard disks these complications seem less and less necessary for your first Linux installation. For your first time, especially, keep it simple.

5.5 Booting the installation disk

The first step is to boot the bootdisk you generated. Normally you'll be able to boot hands-off; the boot kernel prompt will fill itself in after 10 seconds. But by giving arguments after the kernel name, you can specify various hardware parameters, such as your SCSI controller IRQ and address, or drive geometry, before booting the Linux kernel. This is necessary in case Linux does not detect your SCSI controller or hard drive geometry, for example.

In particular, many BIOS-less SCSI controllers require you to specify the port address and IRQ at boot time. Likewise, IBM PS/1, ThinkPad, and ValuePoint machines do not store drive geometry in the CMOS, and you must specify it at boot time. (Later on, you'll be able to configure your production system to supply such parameters itself.)

Watch the messages as the system boots. They will list and describe the hardware your installation Linux detects. In particular, f you have a SCSI controller, you should see a listing of the SCSI hosts detected. If you see the message

```
SCSI: 0 hosts
```

Then your SCSI controller was not detected, and you will have to figure out how to tell the kernel where it is.

Also, the system will display information on the drive partitions and devices detected. If any of this information is incorrect or missing, you will have to force hardware detection.

On the other hand, if all goes well and you hardware seems to be detected, you can skip to the following section, "Loading the root disk."

To force hardware detection, you must enter the appropriate parameters at the boot prompt, using the following syntax:

```
linux <parameters...>
```

There are a number of such parameters available; we list some of the most common below. Modern Linux boot disks will often give you the option to look at help screen describing kernel parameters before you boot.

- *hd=cylinders,heads,sectors* Specify the drive geometry. Required for systems such as the IBM PS/1, ValuePoint, and ThinkPad. For example, if your drive has 683 cylinders, 16 heads, and 32 sectors per track, enter

  ```
  linux hd=683,16,32
  ```

- *tmc8xx=memaddr,irq* Specify address and IRQ for BIOS-less Future Domain TMC-8xx SCSI controller. For example,

  ```
  linux tmc8xx=0xca000,5
  ```

  Note that the *0x* prefix must be used for all values given in hex. This is true for all of the following options.

- *st0x=memaddr,irq* Specify address and IRQ for BIOS-less Seagate ST02 controller.

- *t128=memaddr,irq* Specify address and IRQ for BIOS-less Trantor T128B controller.

- *ncr5380=port,irq,dma* Specify port, IRQ, and DMA channel for generic NCR5380 controller.

- *aha152x=port,irq,scsi_id,1* Specify port, IRQ, and SCSI ID for BIOS-less AIC-6260 controllers. This includes Adaptec 1510, 152x, and Soundblaster-SCSI controllers.

If you have questions about these boot-time options, please read the Linux *SCSI HOWTO*, which should be available on any Linux FTP archive site (or from wherever you obtained this document). The *SCSI HOWTO* explains Linux SCSI compatibility in much more detail.

5.6 Using the rootdisk

After booting the bootdisk, you will be prompted to enter the root disk or disks. At this point you should remove the bootdisk from the drive and insert the rootdisk. Then press *enter* to go on. You may have to load a second root disk.

What's actually happening here is this: the boot disk provides a miniature operating system which (because the hard drive isn't prepared) uses a portion of your RAM as a virtual disk (called, logically enough, a 'ramdisk').

The root disks loads onto the ramdisk a small set of files and installation tools which you'll use to prepare your hard drive and install a production Linux on it from your CD-ROM.

5.6.1 Choosing EGA or X installation

Older Linuxes (including Slackware) gave you a shell at this point and required you to enter installation commands by hand in a a prescribed sequence. This is still possible, but newer ones start by running a screen-oriented installation program which tries to interactively walk you through these steps, giving lots of help.

You will probably get the option to try to configure X right away so the installation program can go graphical. If you choose this route, the installation program will quiz you about your mouse and monitor type before getting to the installation proper. Once you get your production Linux installed, these settings will be saved for you. You will be able to tune your monitor's performance later, so at this stage it makes sense to settle for a basic 640x480 SVGA mode.

X isn't necessary for installation, but (assuming you can get past the mouse and monitor configuration) many people find the graphical interface easier to use. And you're going to want to bring up X anyway, so trying it early makes some sense.

Just follow the prompts in the program. It will take you through the steps necessary to prepare your disk, create initial user accounts, and install software packages off the CD-ROM.

In the following subsections we'll describe some of the tricky areas in the installation sequence as if you were doing them by hand. This should help you understand what the installation program is doing, and why.

5.6.2   Using fdisk and cfdisk

Your first installation step once the root-disk Linux is booted will be to create or edit the partition tables on your disks. Even if you used FDISK to set up partitions earlier, you'll need to go back to the partition table now and insert some Linux-specific information now.

To create or edit Linux partitions, we'll use the Linux version of the fdisk program, or its screen-oriented sibling cfdisk.

Generally the installation program will look for a preexisting partition table and offer to run fdisk or cfdisk on it for you. Of the two, cfdisk is definitely easier to use, but current versions of it are also less tolerant of a nonexistent or garbled partition table.

Therefore you may find (especially if you're installing on virgin hardware) that you need to start with fdisk to get to a state that cfdisk can deal with. Try running cfdisk; if it complains, run fdisk. (A good way to proceed if you're building an all-Linux system and cfdisk complains is to use fdisk to delete all the existing partions and then fire up cfdisk to edit the empty table.)

A few notes apply to both fdisk and cfdisk. Both take an argument which is the name of the drive that you wish to create Linux partitions on. Hard drive device names are:

- /dev/hda First IDE drive
- /dev/hdb Second IDE drive
- /dev/sda First SCSI drive
- /dev/sdb Second SCSI drive

For example, to create Linux partitions on the first SCSI drive in your system, you will use (or your installation program might generate from a menu choice) the command:

    cfdisk /dev/sda

If you use fdisk or cfdisk without an argument, it will assume /dev/hda.

To create Linux partitions on the second drive on your system, simply specify either /dev/hdb (for IDE drives) or /dev/sdb (for SCSI drives) when running fdisk.

Your Linux partitions don't all have to be on the same drive. You might want to create your root filesystem partition on */dev/hda* and your swap partition on */dev/hdb*, for example. In order to do so just run `fdisk` or `cfdisk` once for each drive.

In Linux, partitions are given a name based on the drive which they belong to. For example, the first partition on the drive */dev/hda* is */dev/hda1*, the second is */dev/hda2*, and so on. If you have any logical partitions, they are numbered starting with */dev/hda5*, */dev/hda6* and so on up.

NOTE: You should not create or delete partitions for operating systems other than Linux with Linux `fdisk` or `cfdisk`. That is, don't create or delete MS-DOS partitions with this version of `fdisk`; use MS-DOS's version of FDISK instead. If you try to create MS-DOS partitions with Linux `fdisk`, chances are MS-DOS will not recognize the partition and not boot correctly.

Here's an example of using `fdisk`. Here, we have a single MS-DOS partition using 61693 blocks on the drive, and the rest of the drive is free for Linux. (Under Linux, one block is 1024 bytes. Therefore, 61693 blocks is about 61 megabytes.) We will create just two partitions in this tutorial example, swap and root. You should probably extend this to four Linux partitions in line with the recommendations above: one for swap, one for the root filesystem, one for system software, and a home directory area.

First, we use the "p" command to display the current partition table. As you can see, */dev/hda1* (the first partition on */dev/hda*) is a DOS partition of 61693 blocks.

```
Command (m for help):   p
Disk /dev/hda: 16 heads, 38 sectors, 683 cylinders
Units = cylinders of 608 * 512 bytes


    Device Boot   Begin   Start    End  Blocks   Id  System
   /dev/hda1    *       1       1    203   61693    6  DOS 16-bit >=32M

Command (m for help):
```

Next, we use the "n" command to create a new partition. The Linux root partition will be 80 megs in size.

```
Command (m for help):  n
Command action
   e    extended
   p    primary partition (1-4)
p
```

Here we're being asked if we want to create an extended or primary partition. In most cases you want to use primary partitions, unless you need more than four partitions on a drive. See the section "Repartitioning", above, for more information.

```
Partition number (1-4): 2
First cylinder (204-683):   204
Last cylinder or +size or +sizeM or +sizeK (204-683): +80M
```

The first cylinder should be the cylinder AFTER where the last partition left off. In this case, */dev/hda1* ended on cylinder 203, so we start the new partition at cylinder 204.

As you can see, if we use the notation "+80M", it specifies a partition of 80 megs in size. Likewise, the notation "+80K" would specify an 80 kilobyte partition, and "+80" would specify just an 80 byte partition.

```
Warning: Linux cannot currently use 33090 sectors of this partition
```

If you see this warning, you can ignore it. It is left over from an old restriction that Linux filesystems could only be 64 megs in size. However, with newer filesystem types, that is no longer the case... partitions can now be up to 4 terabytes in size.

Next, we create our 10 megabyte swap partition, */dev/hda3*.

```
Command (m for help): n
Command action
   e   extended
   p   primary partition (1-4)
p
Partition number (1-4): 3
First cylinder (474-683):  474
Last cylinder or +size or +sizeM or +sizeK (474-683):  +10M
```

Again, we display the contents of the partition table. Be sure to write down the information here, especially the size of each partition in blocks. You need this information later.

```
Command (m for help): p
Disk /dev/hda: 16 heads, 38 sectors, 683 cylinders
Units = cylinders of 608 * 512 bytes
```

Device Boot	Begin	Start	End	Blocks	Id	System
/dev/hda1 *	1	1	203	61693	6	DOS 16-bit >=32M
/dev/hda2	204	204	473	82080	83	Linux native
/dev/hda3	474	474	507	10336	83	Linux native

Note that the Linux swap partition (here, */dev/hda3*) has type "Linux native". We need to change the type of the swap partition to "Linux swap" so that the installation program will recognize it as such. In order to do this, use the `fdisk` "t" command:

```
Command (m for help): t
Partition number (1-4): 3
Hex code (type L to list codes): 82
```

If you use "L" to list the type codes, you'll find that 82 is the type corresponding to Linux swap.

To quit `fdisk` and save the changes to the partition table, use the "w" command. To quit `fdisk` WITHOUT saving changes, use the "q" command.

After quitting `fdisk`, the system may tell you to reboot to make sure that the changes took effect. In general there is no reason to reboot after using `fdisk`—modern versions of `fdisk` and `cfdisk` are smart enough to update the partitions without rebooting.

5.6.3   Post-partition steps

After you've edited the partition tables, your installation program should look at them and offer to enable your swap partition for you. Tell it yes.

(This is made a question, rather than done automatically, on the off chance that you're running a dual-boot system and one of your non-Linux partitions might happen to look like a swap volume.)

Next the program will ask you to associate Linux filesystem names (such as /, /usr, /var, /tmp, /home, /home2, etc.) with each of the non-swap partitions you're going to use.

There is only one hard and fast rule for this. There must be a root filesystem, named /, and it must be bootable. You can name your other Linux partitions anything you like. But there are some conventions about how to name them which will probably simplify your life later on.

Earlier on I recommended a basic three-partition setup including a small root, a medium-sized system-software partition, and a large home-directory partition. Traditionally, these would be called /, /usr, and /home. The counterintuitive '/usr' name is a historical carryover from the days when (much smaller) Unix systems carried system software and user home directories on a single non-root partition. Some software depends on it.

If you have more than one home-directory area, it's conventional to name them /home, /home2, /home3, etc. This may come up if you have two physical disks. On my personal system, for example, the layout currently looks like this:

Filesystem	1024-blocks	Used	Available	Capacity	Mounted on
/dev/sda1	30719	22337	6796	77%	/
/dev/sda3	595663	327608	237284	58%	/usr
/dev/sda4	1371370	1174	1299336	0%	/home
/dev/sdb1	1000949	643108	306130	68%	/home2

The second disk (sdb1) isn't really all /home2; the swap partitions on sda and sdb aren't shown in this display. But you can see that /home is the large free area on sda and /home2 is the user area of sdb.

If you want to create an partition for scratch, spool, temporary, mail, and news files, call it /var. Otherwise you'll probably want to create a /usr/var and create a symbolic link named /var that points back to it (the installation program may offer to do this for you).

5.7   Installing software packages

Once you've gotten past preparing your partitions, the remainder of the installation should be almost automatic. Your installation program (whether EGA or X-based) will guide you through a series of menus which allow you to specify the CD-ROM to install from, the partitions to use, and so forth.

Here we're not going to document many of the specifics of this stage of installation. It's one of the parts that varies most between Linux distributions (vendors traditionally compete to add value here), but also the simplest part. And the installation programs are pretty much self-explanatory, with good on-screen help.

5.8   After package installations

After installation is complete, and if all goes well, the installation program will walk you through a few options for configuring your system before its first boot from hard drive.

5.8.1   LILO, the LInux LOader

LILO (which stands for LInux LOader) is a program that will allow you to boot Linux (as well as other operating systems, such as MS-DOS) from your hard drive.

You may be given the option of installing LILO on your hard drive. Unless you're running OS/2, answer 'yes'. OS/2 has special requirements; see 7.2 (Custom LILO Configuration) below.

Installing LILO as your primary loader makes a separate boot diskette unnecessary; instead, you can tell LILO at each boot time which OS to boot.

5.8.2   Making a production boot disk (optional)

You may also be given the chance to create a "standard boot disk", which you can use to boot your newly-installed Linux system. (This is an older and slightly less convenient method which assumes that you will normally boot DOS, but use the boot disk to start Linux.)

For this you will need a blank, high-density MS-DOS formatted diskette of the type that you boot with on your system. Simply insert the disk when prompted and a boot diskette will be created. (This is not the same as an installation bootdisk, and you can't substitute one for the other!)

5.8.3   Miscellaneous system configuration

The post-installation procedure may also take you through several menu items allowing you to configure your system. This includes specifying your modem and mouse device, as well as your time zone. Follow the menu options.

It may also prompt you to create user accounts or put a password on the root (administration) account. This is not complicated and you can usually just walk through the screen instructions.

6   Booting Your New System

If everything went as planned, you should now be able to boot Linux from the hard drive using LILO. Alternatively, you should be able to boot your Linux boot floppy (not the original bootdisk floppy, but the floppy created after installing the software). After booting, login as *root*. Congratulations! You have your very own Linux system.

If you are booting using LILO, try holding down *shift* or *control* during boot. This will present you with a boot prompt; press *tab* to see a list of options. In this way you can boot Linux, MS-DOS, or whatever directly from LILO.

7   After Your First Boot

You should now be looking at the login prompt of a new Linux, just booted from your hard drive. Congratulations!

7.1   Beginning System Administratration

Depending on how the installation phase went, you may need to create accounts, change your hostname, or (re)configure X at this stage. There are many more things you could set up and configure, including backup devices, SLIP/PPP links to an Internet Service Provider, etc.

A good book on UNIX systems administration should help. (I suggest *Essential Systems Administration* from O'Reilly and Associates.) You will pick these things up as time goes by. You should read various other

Linux HOWTOs, such as the *NET-2-HOWTO* and *Printing-HOWTO*, for information on other configuration tasks.

7.2   Custom LILO Configuration

LILO is a boot loader, which can be used to select either Linux, MS-DOS, or some other operating system at boot time. Chances are your distribution automatically configured LILO for you during the installation phase (unless you're using OS/2, this is what you should have done). If so, you can skip the rest of this section.

If you installed LILO as the *primary* boot loader, it will handle the first-stage booting process for all operating systems on your drive. This works well if MS-DOS is the only other operating system that you have installed. However, you might be running OS/2, which has its own Boot Manager. In this case, you want OS/2's Boot Manager to be the primary boot loader, and use LILO just to boot Linux (as the *secondary* boot loader).

An important gotcha for people using EIDE systems: due to a BIOS limitation, your boot sectors for any OS have to live on one of the first two physical disks. Otherwise LILO will hang after writing "LI", no matter where you run it from.

If you have to configure LILO manually, this will involve editing the file */etc/lilo.conf*. Below we present an example of a LILO configuration file, where the Linux root partition is on */dev/hda2*, and MS-DOS is installed on */dev/hdb1* (on the second hard drive).

```
# Tell LILO to install itself as the primary boot loader on /dev/hda.
boot = /dev/hda
# The boot image to install; you probably shouldn't change this
install = /boot/boot.b


# The stanza for booting Linux.
image = /vmlinuz        # The kernel is in /vmlinuz
  label = linux         # Give it the name "linux"
  root = /dev/hda2      # Use /dev/hda2 as the root filesystem
  vga = ask             # Prompt for VGA mode
  append = "aha152x=0x340,11,7,1"  # Add this to the boot options,
                                   # for detecting the SCSI controller


# The stanza for booting MS-DOS
other = /dev/hdb1       # This is the MS-DOS partition
  label = msdos         # Give it the name "msdos"
  table = /dev/hdb      # The partition table for the second drive
```

Once you have edited the */etc/lilo.conf* file, run */sbin/lilo* as *root*. This will install LILO on your drive. Note that you must rerun */sbin/lilo* anytime that you recompile your kernel in order to point the boot loader at it properly (something that you don't need to worry about just now, but keep it in mind).

Note how we use the *append* option in */etc/lilo.conf* to specify boot parameters as we did when booting the bootdisk.

You can now reboot your system from the hard drive. By default LILO will boot the operating system listed first in the configuration file, which in this case is Linux. In order to bring up a boot menu, in order to select another operating system, hold down *shift* or *ctrl* while the system boots; you should see a prompt such as

```
    Boot:
```

Here, enter either the name of the operating system to boot (given by the *label* line in the configuration file; in this case, either *linux* or *msdos*), or press *tab* to get a list.

Now let's say that you want to use LILO as the secondary boot loader; if you want to boot Linux from OS/2's Boot Manager, for example. In order to boot a Linux partition from OS/2 Boot Manager, unfortunately, you must create the partition using OS/2's *FDISK* (not Linux's), and format the partition as FAT or HPFS, so that OS/2 knows about it. (That's IBM for you.)

In order to have LILO boot Linux from OS/2 Boot Manager, you only want to install LILO on your Linux root filesystem (in the above example, */dev/hda2*). In this case, your LILO config file should look something like:

```
boot = /dev/hda2
install = /boot/boot.b
compact

image = /vmlinuz
  label = linux
  root = /dev/hda2
  vga = ask
```

Note the change in the *boot* line. After running */sbin/lilo* you should be able to add the Linux partition to Boot Manager. This mechanism should work for boot loaders used by other operating systems as well.

8 Administrivia

8.1 Terms of Use

This document is copyright 1996 by Eric S. Raymond. You may use, disseminate, and reproduce it freely, provided you:

- Do not omit or alter this copyright notice.
- Do not omit or alter or omit the version number and date.
- Do not omit or alter the document's pointer to the current WWW version.
- Clearly mark any condensed, altered or versions as such.

These restrictions are intended to protect potential readers from stale or mangled versions. If you think you have a good case for an exception, ask me.

8.2 Acknowledgements

My grateful acknowledgement to Matt D. Welsh, who originated this HOWTO. I removed much of the Slackware-specific content and refocused the remainder of the document on CD-ROM installation, but a substantial part of the content is still his.

The 4.1 version was substantially improved by some suggestions from David Shao <dshao@best.com>.

Configuration HOWTO

By Guido Gonzato, *guido@ibogfs.cineca.it* <mailto:guido@ibogfs.cineca.it>   v0.99.3, 4 November 1997

This HOWTO aims at making the fine-tuning of your newly installed Linux box quicker and easier. Here you will find a set of configurations for the most common applications, so you can start to work with a well-usable system.

Contents

1 Introduction

I have installed Linux on many PCs, and I've noted that current distributions are terrific, but often come with annoying lack of basic configuration. Most programs will work out of the box, but some won't. This is a shame: I don't see any reason why the newcomer should bear with the old and trite "backspace problem", or think that emacs doesn't have colours, or list directories contents in black and white.

To help myself remember what needs to be configured first, I wrote a summary that I later expanded to become this HOWTO. Here you will find a handful of configuration examples for the most common applications. These examples are based on my personal experience installing Red Hat-based Linux boxes, so if you use other distributions, be aware. Please don't take any tips in this work as gospel: they just happen to work for me. In any case, if you want to know more you'll have to read the package docs and one of more HOWTOs on the subject. This HOWTO is just a summary—hopefully, handy and useful.

There can be endless hardware configurations for a PC, but in my experience one is quite common: a PC fitted with a large HD split into three partitions (one for DOS/Windows, one for Linux, one for the swap), modem, CD-ROM drive, printer, mouse. This is the hardware I'll assume you want to configure, but it's easy to adapt the following tips to different configurations. It's implicitly assumed that you'll be root when editing/fixing/hacking.

And now, sleeves up.

2 General System Setup

2.1 Keyboard

First of all, how to configure the keyboard. If you missed this step during installation or have changed your keyboard, you'll have to:

- choose a suitable key table from `/usr/lib/kbd/keytables/`; for example, `it.map` selects the Italian keyboard

- edit the file /etc/sysconfig/keyboard so as it reads: `KEYTABLE="/usr/lib/kbd/keytables/it.map"`

- to set up the keyboard repeat rate and delay time, add this line to `/etc/profile` or to one of your rc files :

      /sbin/kbdrate -s -r 16 -d 500 # or whatever

- and finally, do this to get the permission to set up the keyboard:

      ~# chmod 666 /dev/port

Upon the next reboot, the keyboard will work fine.

2.2 Kernel

IMHO, the first thing to do next is build a kernel that best suits your system. It's very simple to do but, in any case, refer to the README file in /usr/src/linux/. Hints:

- consider carefully what your needs are. It's more productive to choose a suitable kernel and to apply patches once and for all, instead of reconfiguring and recompiling each month; this is especially true if your Linux box is a server. Don't forget to include support for all the hardware you might likely add in the future;
- if your PC is a Cyrix-based one, apply appropriate patches to improve performance. Information on *http://www.linuxhq.com/patch/20-p0591.html* <http://www.linuxhq.com/patch/20-p0591.html>;
- notebook users will want to improve legibility of their screen by applying the *noblink* <ftp://sunsite.unc.edu/pub/Linux/kernel/patches/console/noblink-1.7.tar.gz> patch;
- again for notebook users, if you plan to use a PCMCIA modem/fax *don't* compile serial support as a module; compile it in the kernel or your PCMCIA modem won't work.

2.3 Bootup Messages

If you want to customise the bootup messages, check whether your /etc/rc.d/rc.local overwrites /etc/issue and /etc/motd. If so, get your hands on your editor and go.

2.4 Hostname

Issuing the command hostname new_host_name is not enough. Edit /etc/sysconfig/network and change the hostname therein.

2.5 Sendmail Lock

On some systems, sendmail locks the machine at boot time. Make sure your /etc/hosts contains a line that reads

    127.0.0.1 localhost

2.6 Device Drivers

Devices in /dev (or better, links to the actual device drivers) may be missing. Check what devices your mouse, modem, and CD-ROM drive correspond to, then do what follows:

    ~# cd /dev
    /dev# ln -s /dev/cua0 mouse
    /dev# ln -s /dev/cua1 modem
    /dev# ln -s /dev/hdb cdrom

and, if you want, do chmod 666 to these devices to make them fully accessible by every user. Tip: in some laptops the mouse device is /dev/psaux: take this into account also when configuring X11.

In addition, you'll want to make the floppy accessible by non-root users with chmod 666 /dev/fd*. This is bound to cause security problems, but I don't know the details. Comments on this are welcome.

2.7 Mouse

gpm mouse services are useful to perform cut and paste in console and to use the mouse in some apps. Check that you have a file called /etc/sysconfig/mouse and that it reads:

```
MOUSETYPE="Microsoft"
XEMU3=yes
```

Moreover, you must have a file /etc/rc.d/init.d/gpm. Of course, make sure this configuration is right for your mouse type. Tip: in some laptops, MOUSETYPE is ``PS/2''.

2.8 Mount Points

It's handy to have mount points for the floppy, the CD-ROM, the DOS partition, and other devices. For example, you may do the following:

```
~# cd /mnt
/# mkdir a: ; mkdir floppy ; mkdir cdrom ; mkdir win ; mkdir zip
```

This creates mount points for an MS-DOS floppy, an ext2 floppy, the CD-ROM, the DOS partition, and the parallel port Zip drive.

Now edit the file /etc/fstab and add the following entries:

/dev/fd0	/mnt/a:	msdos	user,noauto 0 1
/dev/fd0	/mnt/floppy	ext2	user,noauto 0 1
/dev/cdrom	/mnt/cdrom	iso9660	ro,user,noauto 0 1
/dev/hda1	/mnt/dos	msdos	user,noauto 0 1
/dev/sda4	/mnt/zip	vfat	user,noauto 0 1

Obviously, you must use the correct device in the first field. To access Win95 long names, use **vfat** instead of msdos in the last line. This doesn't (yet) apply to vfat32, though.

2.9 LILO and Loadlin

Many users want their PC to run both Linux and DOS/Windows, and want to choose at boot time which os to use. Let's suppose that **/dev/hda1** contains DOS/Windows and that **/dev/hda2** contains Linux.

Do what follows:

```
~# fdisk
Using /dev/hda as default device!

Command (m for help):a
Partition number (1-4): 2

Command (m for help):w
~#
```

This makes the Linux partition bootable; this step ought to be carried out by **activate** when running LILO's `QuickInst`, but it won't work with my Red Hat.

Write this basic `/etc/lilo.conf` file:

```
boot = /dev/hda2
compact
delay = 50
# message = /boot/bootmesg.txt  # write your own
root = current
image = /boot/vmlinuz
  label = linux
other = /dev/hda1
  table = /dev/hda
  label = dos
```

Now issue `/sbin/lilo` and you're set. Being `LILO` a crucial part of your installation, you're strongly advised to read its documentation anyway.

To boot Linux from DOS without resetting, put `LOADLIN.EXE` in a directory (in the DOS partition!) included in the DOS path; then copy your kernel to, say, `C:\DOS\VMLINUZ`. The following `.BAT` file will boot linux:

```
rem    linux.bat
smartdrv /C
loadlin c:\dos\vmlinuz root=/dev/hda2 r
```

I you use Windows 95, set the properties of this `.BAT` so as it starts in MS-DOS mode.

2.10 Printer Configuration

Red Hat has a fine configuration tool that worked wonderfully for my HP DeskJet 400; if you don't use Red Hat, manual configuration follows.

Let's suppose you have a non-PostScript printer you want to use to print raw text (e.g., C source files) and PostScript files via GhostScript, which is assumed to be already installed.

Setting up the printer involves a few steps:

- check which one the parallel print device is: try

```
~# echo "hello, world" > /dev/lp0
~# echo "hello, world" > /dev/lp1
```

  and take note which one works.

- make two spool directories:

```
~# cd /var/spool/lpd
/var/spool/lpd/# mkdir raw ; mkdir postscript
```

- if your printer exibits the "staircase effect" (most inkjets do), you'll need a filter. Try printing two lines with

```
~# echo "first line" > /dev/lp1 ; echo "second line" > /dev/lp1
```

if the output is like

```
first line
          second line
```

then save this file as /var/spool/lpd/raw/filter:

```
#!/bin/sh
# This filter does away with the "staircase effect"
awk '{print $0, "\r"}'
```

and make it executable with chmod 755 /var/spool/lpd/raw/filter.

- make a filter for PostScript emulation. Write the following filter as /var/spool/lpd/postscript/filter:

```
#!/bin/sh

DEVICE=djet500
RESOLUTION=300x300
PAPERSIZE=a4
SENDEOF=

nenscript -TUS -ZB -p- |
if [ "$DEVICE" = "PostScript" ]; then
        cat -
else
        gs -q -sDEVICE=$DEVICE \
               -r$RESOLUTION \
               -sPAPERSIZE=$PAPERSIZE \
               -dNOPAUSE \
               -dSAFER \
               -sOutputFile=- -
fi

if [ "$SENDEOF" != "" ]; then
        printf "\004"
fi
```

(in this example an HP DeskJet printer is assumed. Fix it to suit your printer).

- finally, add the following entries in /etc/printcap:

```
# /etc/printcap
lp|ps|PS|PostScript|djps:\
        :sd=/var/spool/lpd/postscript:\
        :mx#0:\
        :lp=/dev/lp1:\
        :if=/var/spool/lpd/postscript/filter:\
```

```
                    :sh:
         raw:\
                    :sd=/var/spool/lpd/raw:\
                    :mx#0:\
                    :lp=/dev/lp1:\
                    :if=/var/spool/lpd/raw/filter:\
                    :sh:
```

For more complex or exotic printing configurations, the Printing-HOWTO awaits you.

For Red hat users: be aware that the GSDEVICE chosen by Printtool will work, but is not necessarily the best for your printer. You may consider fiddling a bit with the file `postscript.cfg`; for instance, I changed GSDEVICE from `cdj500` to `djet500` and now my prints come out much quicker.

3   Software Configuration

3.1   bash(1)

To tailor bash's behaviour, these are the files to edit:

- /etc/bashrc contains system wide aliases and functions;
- /etc/profile contains system wide environment stuff and startup programs;
- $HOME/.bashrc contains user's aliases and functions;
- $HOME/.bash_profile contains user's environment stuff and startup programs;
- $HOME/.bash_logout contains actions to be performed at logout;
- $HOME/.inputrc contains key bindings and other bits.

Examples of these files are shown below. First, the most important: /etc/profile. It's used to configure a lot of features in your Linux box, as you will see in the following sections.

```
# /etc/profile

# System wide environment and startup programs
# Functions and aliases go in /etc/bashrc

# This file sets the following features:
#
#   o path
#   o prompts
#   o a few environment variables
#   o colour ls
#   o less behaviour
#   o keyboard settings
#
# Users can override these settings and/or add others in their
# $HOME/.bash_profile

# set a decent path
```

```
echo $PATH | grep X11R6 > /dev/null
if [ $? = 1 ] ; then    # add entries to the path
  PATH="$PATH:/usr/X11R6/bin:$HOME/bin:."
fi


# notify the user: login or non-login shell. If login, the prompt is
# coloured in blue; otherwise in magenta. Root's prompt is red.


USER=`whoami`
if [ $LOGNAME = $USER ] ; then
  COLOUR=44
else
  COLOUR=45
fi

if [ $USER = 'root' ] ; then
  COLOUR=41
fi


# put a real escape character instead of ^[
PS1='^[[$COLOUR;37;1m$HOSTNAME:^[[37;40;1m\w\$ '
PS2="Continue> "


# no core dumps, please

ulimit -c 0

# set umask

if [ `id -gn` = `id -un` -a `id -u` -gt 14 ]; then
        umask 002
else
        umask 022
fi


# a few variables

USER=`id -un`
LOGNAME=$USER
MAIL="/var/spool/mail/$USER"
EDITOR=jed
HOSTNAME=`/bin/hostname`
HISTSIZE=1000
HISTFILESIZE=1000
export PATH PS1 PS2 USER LOGNAME MAIL EDITOR HOSTNAME HISTSIZE HISTFILESIZE


# enable colour ls

eval `dircolors /etc/DIR_COLORS -b`
export LS_OPTIONS='-F -s -T 0 --color=tty'


# customize less
```

```
LESS='-M-Q'
LESSEDIT="%E ?lt+%lt. %f"
LESSOPEN="| lesspipe.sh %s"
VISUAL=jed
LESSCHARSET=latin1
export LESS LESSEDIT LESSOPEN VISUAL LESSCHARSET

# customise the keyboard

/sbin/kbdrate -s -r 16 -d 500

for i in /etc/profile.d/*.sh ; do
        if [ -x $i ]; then
                . $i
        fi
done
```

This is /etc/bashrc:

```
# /etc/bashrc

# System wide functions and aliases
# Environment stuff goes in /etc/profile

alias which="type -path"
alias d="ls"
alias dir="d"
```

This is .bashrc:

```
# $HOME/.bashrc
# Source global definitions

if [ -f /etc/bashrc ]; then
        . /etc/bashrc
fi

# this is needed to notify the user that they are in non-login shell

COLOUR=45
# put a real escape character instead of ^[
PS1='^[[$COLOUR;37m$USER:^[[37;40m\w\$ '

# aliases

alias cp='cp -i'
alias l=less
alias lyx='lyx -width 900 -height 700'
alias mv='mv -i'
alias rm='rm -i'
alias x=startx
```

```
# A few useful functions

inst() # Install a .tar.gz archive in the current directory.
{ gzip -dc $1 | tar xvf - }

cz() # List the contents of a .zip archive.
{ unzip -l $* }

ctgz() # List the contents of a .tar.gz archive.
{
  for file in $* ; do
    gzip -dc ${file} | tar tf -
  done
}

tgz() # Create a .tgz archive a la zip.
{
  name=$1 ; tar -cvf $1 ; shift
  tar -rf ${name} $*
  gzip -S .tgz ${name}
}
```

This is .bash_profile:

```
# $HOME/.bash_profile

# User specific environment and startup programs
# This file contains user-defined settings that override
# those in /etc/profile

# Get aliases and functions
if [ -f ~/.bashrc ]; then
        . ~/.bashrc
fi

# re-get PS1 settings

if [ $USER = 'root' ] ; then
  COLOUR=41
else
  COLOUR=44
fi

# put a real escape character instead of ^[
PS1='^[[$COLOUR;37;1m$HOSTNAME:^[[37;40;1m\w\$ '

export PS1
```

This is .bash_logout:

```
# $HOME/.bash_logout
clear
```

This is .inputrc:

```
# $HOME/.inputrc

# key bindings

"\e[1~": beginning-of-line
"\e[3~": delete-char
"\e[4~": end-of-line
# (F1 .. F5) are "\e[[A" ... "\e[[E"
"\e[[A": "info \C-m"

set bell-style visible          # please don't beep
set meta-flag On                # allow 8-bit input (i.e, accented letters)
set convert-meta Off            # don't strip 8-bit characters
set output-meta On              # display 8-bit characters correctly
set horizontal-scroll-mode On
set show-all-if-ambiguous On
```

To make the backspace and delete keys work correctly in in **xterm** and other X11 applications, the following is also needed:

- put this in your .xinitrc:

      usermodmap=$HOME/.Xmodmap
      xmodmap $usermodmap

- put this in your .Xmodmap:

      keycode 22 = BackSpace
      keycode 107 = Delete

  this fixes the console. To fix **xterm**:

- put this in your .Xdefaults:

```
xterm*VT100.Translations: #override <Key>BackSpace: string(0x7F)\n\
        <Key>Delete:       string(0x1b) string("[3~")\n\
        <Key>Home:         string(0x1b) string("[1~")\n\
        <Key>End:          string(0x1b) string("[4~")\n\
        Ctrl<Key>Prior:    string(0x1b) string("[40~")\n\
        Ctrl<Key>Next:     string(0x1b) string("[41~")


nxterm*VT100.Translations: #override <Key>BackSpace: string(0x7F)\n\
        <Key>Delete:       string(0x1b) string("[3~")\n\
        <Key>Home:         string(0x1b) string("[1~")\n\
        <Key>End:          string(0x1b) string("[4~")\n\
        Ctrl<Key>Prior:    string(0x1b) string("[40~")\n\
        Ctrl<Key>Next:     string(0x1b) string("[41~")
```

More info in bash(1) and readline(3) man pages.

Don't expect every application to work correctly! If you run joe in xterm, for instance, some keys won't work; the same goes for rxvt. Rumour has it that it's a termcap problem.

3.2 ls(1)

ls can display directory listings using colours to highlight different file types. To enable this feature, add these lines to /etc/profile:

```
eval 'dircolors /etc/DIR_COLORS -b'
export LS_OPTIONS='-F -T 0 --color=tty'
```

This sets the environment variable LS_COLORS that contains the colour list set up in /etc/DIR_COLORS. Note: don't ask me why, but this won't work with some versions of rxvt; use some flavour of xterm instead. It looks like rxvt has a bug that prevents it from inheriting the environment correctly in some circumstances.

3.3 less(1)

With this excellent pager you can browse not only plain text files, but also gzip compressed, tar and zip archives, man pages, and so on. Its configuration involves a few steps:

- to use it with the movement keys, have this plain ASCII file .lesskey in your home directory:

```
^[[A    back-line
^[[B    forw-line
^[[C    right-scroll
^[[D    left-scroll
^[OA    back-line
^[OB    forw-line
^[OC    right-scroll
^[OD    left-scroll
^[[6~   forw-scroll
^[[5~   back-scroll
^[[1~   goto-line
^[[4~   goto-end
^[[7~   goto-line
^[[8~   goto-end
```

  then run the command lesskey. This creates a binary file .less containing the key bindings.

- write the following file as /usr/bin/lesspipe.sh:

```
#!/bin/sh
# This is a preprocessor for 'less'.  It is used when this environment
# variable is set:   LESSOPEN="|lesspipe.sh %s"

lesspipe() {
  case "$1" in
  *.tar) tar tf $1 2>/dev/null ;; # View contents of .tar and .tgz files
```

```
     *.tgz|*.tar.gz|*.tar.Z|*.tar.z) tar ztf $1 2>/dev/null ;;
     *.Z|*.z|*.gz) gzip -dc $1  2>/dev/null ;; # View compressed files correctly
     *.zip) unzip -l $1 2>/dev/null ;; # View archives
     *.arj) unarj -l $1 2>/dev/null ;;
     *.rpm) rpm -q -p -i -l $1 2>/dev/null ;;
     *.1|*.2|*.3|*.4|*.5|*.6|*.7|*.8|*.9|*.n|*.man) FILE=`file -L $1`
       FILE=`echo $FILE | cut -d ' ' -f 2`
       if [ "$FILE" = "troff" ]; then
         groff -s -p -t -e -Tascii -mandoc $1
       fi ;;
     *) FILE=`file -L $1` ; # Check to see if binary
       FILE1=`echo $FILE | cut -d ' ' -f 2`
       FILE2=`echo $FILE | cut -d ' ' -f 3`
       if [ "$FILE1" = "Linux/i386" -o "$FILE2" = "Linux/i386" \
           -o "$FILE1" = "ELF" -o "$FILE2" = "ELF" ]; then
         strings $1
       fi ;;
     esac
   }

   lesspipe $1
```

and remember to make it executable with `chmod 755 lesspipe.sh`.

- put these lines in /etc/profile:

```
   LESS="-M-Q"                       # long prompt, silent
   LESSEDIT="%E ?lt+%lt. %f"         # edit top line
   LESSOPEN="| lesspipe.sh %s"       # filter
   VISUAL=jed                        # default editor---insert your favourite
   LESSCHARSET=latin1                # display accented letters if needed
   export LESS LESSEDIT LESSOPEN VISUAL LESSCHARSET
```

The variable LESSCHARSET depends on the fact that I live in Italy and want to use the ISO 8859/1 character set. You fellow Americans, Japanese, Russians and so on had better not set it.

3.4 emacs(1)

Some emacs distributions don't come preconfigured for colours and syntax highlighting. Write this in your .emacs:

```
   (global-font-lock-mode t)
   (setq font-lock-maximum-decoration t)
```

This only works in X11. I'll leave it to you to peruse all of emacs' documentation to discover how to tailor it to your needs—potentially, it can take months of hacking...

3.5 joe(1)

Check in /usr/bin/ whether jmacs, jstar, and jpico are symlinks to joe or standalone binaries; in the latter case, you may turn them to symlinks to save some disk space:

```
~# cd /usr/bin
/usr/bin# ln -sf joe jmacs ; ln -sf joe jstar ; ln -sf joe jpico
```

Then, all you have to do is copy `/usr/lib/joe/joerc` to your home dir as `.joerc` and tailor it.

3.6 jed

This is my favourite editor: it does what I need, it's lighter and easier to configure than `emacs`, and IMHO emulates other editors quite better. Many users at my university want `jed` to emulate `EDT`, VMS' system editor.

The configuration files are `.jedrc` and `/usr/lib/jed/lib/*`; the former can be adapted from `jed.rc` in the latter directory.

- to make `jed` use some keys correctly, create `/usr/lib/jed/lib/defaults.sl` whose only line reads:

  ```
  () = evalfile("linux");
  ```

- edit `/usr/lib/jed/lib/linux.sl`; remove the comment from the line that reads `Info_Directory = "/usr/info"`; and add `/bin/mail` after `UCB_Mailer =`;

- configuring `jed` to make it emulate `EDT` (or other editors) is straightforward: you just have to edit a couple of lines in `.jedrc`. If you want to use the numeric keypad '+' to delete words instead of a single character, add this in `.jedrc`:

  ```
  unsetkey("\eOl");
  unsetkey("\eOP\eOl");
  setkey("edt_wdel", "\eOl");
  setkey("edt_uwdel", "\eOP\eOl");
  ```

  after the line that reads `() = evalfile("edt");`.

- making `xjed` use the numeric keypad for `EDT` emulation requires inserting the following in `.Xmodmap`:

  ```
  keycode 77  = KP_F1
  keycode 112 = KP_F2
  keycode 63  = KP_F3
  keycode 82  = KP_F4
  keycode 86  = KP_Separator
  ```

Moreover, make sure that your `/etc/X11/XF86Config` contains the following lines:

```
#    ServerNumLock  # must be commented out
     XkbDisable
```

This applies to XFree 3.2. Unless you use a standard American keyboard though, note that "XkbDisable" brings some little problems. You'll find out by yourself.

- colour customization for `xjed` is done adding lines like these in `.Xdefaults`:

  ```
  xjed*Geometry: 80x32+150+50
  xjed*font: 10x20
  xjed*background: midnight blue
  ```

More info in xjed.doc, included in the package.

3.7   TeX and Friends

I'll assume you have the TeTeX distribution. Just a couple of things here:

- To configure the hyphenation pattern for your language, edit the file `/usr/lib/texmf/texmf/tex/generic/config/language.dat`, then do:

    ```
    ~# texconfig init ; texconfig hyphen
    ```

- If you add a LaTeX package, after adding the files under `/usr/lib/texmf/texmf/tex/latex/` run the command `texhash` to make TeTeX recognise the new package.

- To tailor `dvips`, the file to edit is `/usr/lib/texmf/texmf/dvips/config/config.ps`. Be aware that the fields regarding the default resolution also affect `xdvi`'s behaviour; if you experience annoying attempts to create fonts each time you run it, put in `.Xdefault` the line

    ```
    XDvi*mfmode:
    ```

This should help.

3.8   PPP

I'll take it for granted that your kernel has PPP + TCP/IP support compiled in, that loopback is enabled, and that you already have the `pppd` package correctly installed. (These requirements should be there by default.) There are now two ways to get PPP to work: a) manual configuration, and b) using a program that automagically sees to it. First, the manual option.

Let's suppose that your ISP's specifications are the following:

- Phone number: 1234567
- Name server: 123.231.112.111
- Mail server: mbox.supernet.edu
- Domain: supernet.edu
- Remote hostname: www.supernet.edu
- Your username: John
- Your password: _Loo%ny

To configure manually your PPP connections, you'll do:

- write this file `/usr/local/bin/ppp-on`, which will be used to connect to your ISP:

    ```
    #!/bin/sh
    # ppp-on: script to connect to an ISP
    INIT=ATX3  # or whatever your modem wants
    PHONE=1234567
    /usr/sbin/pppd connect "/usr/sbin/chat '' $INIT OK ATDP$PHONE \
    CONNECT '' " user John
    ```

then make it executable with `chmod 755 /usr/local/bin/ppp-on`. If your ISP doesn't use the PAP protocol, the following script applies:

```
#!/bin/sh
# ppp-on: script to connect to an ISP
INIT=atx3  # or whatever your modem wants
PHONE=1234567
/usr/sbin/pppd connect "/usr/sbin/chat '' $INIT OK ATDT$PHONE \
CONNECT '' 'ogin' John 'word' _Loo%ny ''" /dev/modem 38400 \
modem defaultroute
```

- write this file /usr/local/bin/ppp-off, used to terminate a ppp session:

```
#!/bin/sh
# ppp-off
DEVICE=ppp0
if [ -r /var/run/$DEVICE.pid ]; then
  kill -INT `cat /var/run/$DEVICE.pid`
  if [ ! "$?" = "0" ]; then
    echo "removing stale $DEVICE pid file."
    rm -f /var/run/$DEVICE.pid ; exit 1
  fi
  echo "$DEVICE link terminated" ; exit 0
fi
# link not active
echo "$DEVICE link is not active" ; exit 1
```

  then make it executable with chmod 755 /usr/local/bin/ppp-off.

- write this file /etc/ppp/options:

```
# /etc/ppp/options
/dev/modem
38400
lock
crtscts
modem
asyncmap 0
remotename www.supernet.edu
defaultroute
```

- if your ISP uses the PAP protocol (most ISPs do), write the file /etc/ppp/pap-secrets:

```
# /etc/ppp/pap-secrets
# username      remotehost           secret
John            www.supernet.edu     _Loo%ny
```

- edit /etc/resolv.conf:

```
# /etc/resolv.conf
search supernet.edu
nameserver 123.231.112.111
```

- edit /etc/sendmail.cf. Look for the line starting with DS, and make it like the following:

         DSmbox.supernet.edu

Phew! If you're lucky, this should work. Otherwise, be prepared to study the PPP-HOWTO.

So much for manual configuration. There's a fine package that makes all this drudgery a thing of the past, though: it's called ezppp and you'll find it at *http://www.serv.net/~cameron/ezppp/index.html* <http://www.serv.net/cameron/ezppp/index.html> . Download it at once.

3.9 POP Client

To retrieve your mail from a POP server, use a POP client like fetchpop or fetchmail. The latter is probably the only option if your provider's PPP server has problems with the command LAST.

To configure these clients:

* fetchpop: the first time you run it, you'll be prompted for some information. Answer the questions and you're set.

* fetchmail: adapt this sample .fetchmailrc:

      # $HOME/.fetchmailrc
      poll mbox.supernet.edu with protocol pop3;
         user john there with password _Loo%ny is john here
         mda "/usr/bin/procmail -f fetchmail"

  The last line may not be required. You must set the permissions to this file with the command chmod 600 .fetchmailrc, otherwise fetchmail will rightly refuse to start.

3.10 X Window System

Once you've managed to make X work (right video card etc.), there are endless possibilities of configuration; it depends on the window manager you use. In any case, it's all down to editing one or more ASCII files in your home directory. As for the window manager:

* **fvwm**: copy /etc/X11/fvwm/system.fvwmrc to your home directory as .fvwmrc, browse it and start experimenting. This contributed system.fvwmrc is IMHO a wee bit too simple and doesn't do justice to fvwm.

* **fvwm95-2**: copy /etc/X11/fvwm95-2/fvwm2rc95 to your home as .fvwm2rc95, then edit it. The contributed example is quite good.

* **TheNextLevel**: this is rather harder to configure. Copy /etc/X11/TheNextLevel/.* to your home dir, browse them carefully, then try and tailor them. The first one to look at is .fvwm2rc.defines.

In addition, be sure you have a proper .xinitrc. An example:

    #!/bin/sh

    # $HOME/.xinitrc

    # set a few keys correctly

    usermodmap=$HOME/.Xmodmap

```
xmodmap $usermodmap

xset s noblank   # turn off the screen saver
xset s 300 2     # screen saver start after 5 min
xsetroot -solid "medium blue" &

# rxvt saves memory, but has a few bugs:
#   - home and end keys are not recognised;
#   - backspace and delete don't work as in console;
#   - colours are not properly inherited by the environment;
#   - problems with the environment in general;
# xterm is therefore better in many cases. However, rxvt is best
# for running some colour apps like mc.

xterm -ls -bg black -fg white -sb -sl 500 -j -ls -fn 10x20 -fb 10x20bold \
-title "Color xterm" -geometry 80x25+150+0 &


fvwm95-2
```

3.11   Fortran

In my experience, if you need Fortran a good alternative to g77 is the Fortran-to-C translator f2c and the front-end yaf77.

Get yaf77 from *ftp://sunsite.unc.edu/pub/Linux/devel/languages/fortran/yaf77-1.4.tgz* <ftp://sunsite. unc.edu/pub/Linux/devel/languages/fortran/yaf77-1.4.tgz> and its mirrors.

3.12   Users' Configurations

It's a good idea to let new users have a few configuration files ready when they first log in. Put the following files in /etc/skel: bashrc, bash_profile, bash_logout, inputrc, less, xinitrc, fvwmrc, fvwm2rc95, Xmodmap, Xdefaults, jedrc, joerc, emacs.

(Note: due to formatting problems, I had to remove the leading dot ('.') from each of these files.)

Note that .pinerc can't be fully tailored; make sure that at least the fields user-domain, smtp-server, and nntp-server are set up.

4   The End

4.1   Copyright

All translations, derivative works, or aggregate works incorporating any Linux HOWTO documents must be covered under this copyright notice. That is, you may not produce a derivative work from a HOWTO and impose additional restrictions on its distribution. Exceptions to these rules may be granted under certain conditions; please contact the Linux HOWTO coordinator at the address given below.

In short, we wish to promote dissemination of this information through as many channels as possible. However, we do wish to retain copyright on the HOWTO documents, and would like to be notified of any plans to redistribute the HOWTOs.

If you have questions, please contact Greg Hankins, the Linux HOWTO coordinator, at gregh@sunsite.unc.edu via email.

4.2   Feedback

Perhaps even more than other HOWTOs, this one needs and welcomes your suggestions, criticisms, and contributions. Not only is feedback welcome: it's necessary. If you think something is missing here, please email me. If you have a distribution other than Red Hat and your config files are different or placed in other directories, please tell me and I'll include your tips. My aim is making life with Linux as easy as possible.

Linux has a huge number of packages, so it's impossible to include directions for all of them. Please keep your requests/suggestions pertinent to the "most reasonable" programs—I'll leave it to your common sense.

4.3   Disclaimer

"Configuration HOWTO" was written by Guido Gonzato, *guido@ibogfs.cineca.it* <mailto:guido@ ibogfs.cineca.it>. Many thanks to all other HOWTO authors and man pages writers/maintainers, whose work I've cheeklessly pilfered.

This document is provided "as is". I put great effort into writing it as accurately as I could, but you use the information contained in it at your own risk. In no event shall I be liable for any damages resulting from the use of this work.

I hope you'll find this work useful. Whenever I install a new Linux box, I actually do...

Enjoy,

Guido =8-)

The Linux keyboard and console HOWTO

Andries Brouwer, aeb@cwi.nl   v2.7, 16 November 1997

This note contains some information about the Linux keyboard and console, and the use of non-ASCII characters. It describes Linux 2.0.

Contents

1 Copyright

LDP/COPYRIGHT.html> or *ftp://www.win.tue.nl/pub/linux/LDP/COPYRIGHT.txt* <ftp://www.win.tue.nl/pub/linux/LDP/COPYRIGHT.txt>.

2   Useful programs

The following packages contain keyboard or console related programs.

kbd-0.95.tar.gz contains loadkeys, dumpkeys, showkey, setmetamode, setleds, setfont, showfont, mapscrn, kbd_mode, loadunimap, chvt, resizecons, deallocvt, getkeycodes, setkeycodes.

util-linux-2.6 contains setterm, kbdrate. (Yes, the more in util-linux-2.6 dumps core due to a name conflict. Preserve your old copy, or use util-linux-2.5, or change 'savetty' to 'my_savetty' in more.c.)

sh-utils-1.12 contains stty.

open-1.4.tgz contains open (that should be renamed to openvt). (See also dynamic-vc-1.1.tar.gz.)

SVGATextMode-1.8.tar.gz contains SVGATextMode, a program that obsoletes resizecons.

The X distribution contains xmodmap, xset, kbd_mode. (See also X386keybd(1) for the situation under XFree86 1.3, and Xserver(1) for the XKEYBOARD extension under X11R6.)

termcap-2.0.8.tar.gz contains termcap, an old terminal capabilities data base. ncurses-1.9.9e.tar.gz contains the termlib data base which obsoletes termcap. (However, there are still many programs using termcap.)

See loadkeys(1), setleds(1) and setmetamode(1) for the codes generated by the various keys and the setting of leds when not under X. Under X, see xmodmap(1) and xset(1).

See setfont(8) for loading console fonts. Many people will want to load a font like iso01.f16 because the default font is the hardware font of the video card, and often is a 'Code Page 437' font missing accented characters and other Latin-1 symbols.

See setterm(1) and kbdrate(8) for properties such as foreground and background colors, screen blanking and character repeat rate when not under X. Under X, see xset(1), also for key click and bell volume.

The file /etc/termcap defines the escape sequences used by many programs addressing the console (or any other terminal). See termcap(5). A more modern version is found in /usr/lib/terminfo. See terminfo(5). Terminfo files are compiled by the terminfo compiler /usr/lib/terminfo/tic, see tic(1). Their contents can be examined using the program infocmp, see infocmp(1). The Linux console sequences are documented in console_codes(4).

3   Keyboard generalities

You press a key, and the keyboard controller sends scancodes to the kernel keyboard driver. Some keyboards can be programmed, but usually the scancodes corresponding to your keys are fixed. The kernel keyboard driver just transmits whatever it receives to the application program when it is in *scancode mode*, like when X is running. Otherwise, it parses the stream of scancodes into keycodes, corresponding to key press or key release events. (A single key press can generate up to 6 scancodes.) These keycodes are transmitted to the application program when it is in *keycode mode* (as used, for example, by showkey). Otherwise, these keycodes are looked up in the keymap, and the character or string found there is transmitted to the application, or the action described there is performed. (For example, if one presses and releases the a key, then the keyboard produces scancodes 0x1e and 0x9e, this is converted to keycodes 30 and 158, and then transmitted as 0141, the ASCII or latin-1 code for 'a'; if one presses and releases Delete, then the keyboard produces scancodes 0xe0 0x53 0xe0 0xd3, these are converted to keycodes 111 and 239, and then transmitted as the 4-symbol sequence ESC [3 ~, all assuming a US keyboard and a default keymap. An example of a key combination to which an action is assigned is Ctrl-Alt-Del.)

The translation between unusual scancodes and keycodes can be set using the utility `setkeycodes` - only very few people will need it. The translation between keycodes and characters or strings or actions, that is, the keymap, is set using the utilities `loadkeys` and `setmetamode`. For details, see getkeycodes(8), setkeycodes(8), dumpkeys(1), loadkeys(1), setmetamode(1). The format of the files output by `dumpkeys` and read by `loadkeys` is described in keytables(5).

Where it says 'transmitted to the application' in the above description, this really means 'transmitted to the terminal driver'. That is, further processing is just like that of text that comes in over a serial line. The details of this processing are set by the program `stty`.

4   Console generalities

Conversely, when you output something to the console, it first undergoes the standard tty processing, and then is fed to the console driver. The console driver emulates a VT100, and parses the input in order to recognize VT100 escape sequences (for cursor movement, clear screen, etc.). The characters that are not part of an escape sequence are first converted into Unicode, using one of four mapping tables if the console was not in UTF-8 mode to start with, then looked up in the table describing the correspondence between Unicode values and font positions, and the obtained 8- or 9-bit font indices are then written to video memory, where they cause the display of character shapes found in the video card's character ROM. One can load one's own fonts into character ROM using `setfont`, load the corresponding Unicode map with `loadunimap`, and load a user mapping table using `mapscrn`. More details will be given below.

There are many consoles (called *Virtual Consoles* or *Virtual Terminals*, abbreviated VCs or VTs) that share the same screen. You can use them as independent devices, either to run indendent login sessions, or just to send some output to, perhaps from `top`, or the tail of the system log or so. See below ('Console switching') on how to set them up and switch between them.

5   Resetting your terminal

There is garbage on the screen, or all your keystrokes are echoed as line drawing characters. What to do?

Many programs will redraw the screen when ^L is typed. This might help when there is some modem noise or broadcast message on your screen. The command `clear` will clear the screen.

The command `reset` will reset the console driver. This helps when the screen is full of funny graphic characters, and also if it is reduced to the bottom line. If you don't have this command, or if it does something else, make your own by putting the following two lines in an executable file `reset` in your PATH:

```
#!/bin/sh
echo -e \\033c
```

that is, you want to send the two characters ESC c to the console.

Why is it that the display sometimes gets confused and gives you a 24-line or 1-line screen, instead of the usual 25 lines? Well, the main culprit is the use of `TERM=vt100` (or some other entry with 24 lines) instead of `TERM=linux` when logged in remotely. If this happens on `/dev/tty2` then typing

```
% cat > /dev/tty2
^[c
^D
```

on some other VT (where 4 symbols are typed to cat: ESC, c, ENTER, Ctrl-D) and refreshing the screen on /dev/tty2 (perhaps using ^L) will fix things. Of course the permanent fix is to use the right termcap or terminfo entry.

Why is it that you sometimes get a lot of line-drawing characters, e.g., after catting a binary to the screen? Well, there are various character set changing escape sequences, and by accident your binary might contain some of these. The ESC c is a general reset, a cure for all, but if you know precisely what went wrong you can repair it without resetting other console attributes. For example, after

```
% cat
^N
^D
```

your shell prompt will be all line-drawing characters. Now do (typing blindly)

```
% cat
^O
^D
```

and all is well again. (Three symbols typed to each cat: ^N (or ^O), ENTER, Ctrl-D.) To understand what is happening, see 'The console character sets' below.

If you loaded some strange font, and want to return to the default,

```
% setfont
```

will do (provided you stored the default font in the default place). If this default font does not contain an embedded Unicode map (and gives the wrong symbols for accented characters), then say

```
% loadunimap
```

For example, if I do

```
% loadkeys de-latin1
```

then I have a German keyboard, and the key left of the Enter key gives me a-umlaut. This works, because the a-umlaut occurs on the CP437 code page and the kernel Unicode map is initialized to CP437, and my video card has a CP437 font built-in. If I now load an ISO 8859-1 font with

```
% setfont iso01.f16
```

then everything still works, because setfont invalidates the kernel Unicode map (if there is no Unicode map attached to the font), and without map the kernel goes directly to the font, and that is precisely correct for an ISO 8859-1 system with iso01.f16 font. But going back to the previous font with

```
% setfont
```

gives capital Sigma's instead of a-umlaut - all accented letters are mixed up because also this font has no embedded Unicode map. After

```
% loadunimap
```

which loads the default Unicode map (which is right for the default font) all works correctly again. Usually loadunimap is not invoked directly, but via setfont. Thus, the previous two commands may be replaced by

```
% setfont -u def
```

The Ethiopian fonts and the `lat1u*.psf` fonts have embedded Unicode code map. Most of the others don't.

On old terminals output involving tabs may require a delay, and you have to say

```
% stty tab3
```

(see stty(1)).

You can change the video mode using **resizecons** or **SVGATextMode**. This usually settles the output side. On the input side there are many things that might be wrong. If **X** or **DOOM** or some other program using raw mode crashed, your keyboard may still be in raw (or mediumraw) mode, and it is difficult to give commands. (See "How to get out of raw mode" below.) If you loaded a bad keymap, then

```
% loadkeys -d
```

loads the default map again, but it may well be difficult to type '-'! An alternative is

```
% loadkeys defkeymap
```

Sometimes even the letters are garbled. It is useful to know that there are four main types of keyboards: QWERTY, QWERTZ, AZERTY and DVORAK. The first three are named after the first six letter keys, and roughly represent the English, German and French speaking countries. Compared to QWERTY, the QWERTZ map interchanges Y and Z. Compared to QWERTY, the AZERTY map interchanges Q and A, W and Z, and has its M right of the L, at the semicolon position. DVORAK has an entirely different letter ordering.

5.1   Keyboard hardware reset

Things may be wrong on a lower level than Linux knows about. There are at least two distinct lower levels (keyboard and keyboard controller) where one can give the command "keyboard disable" to the keyboard hardware. Keyboards can often be programmed to use one out of three different sets of scancodes.

However, I do not know of cases where this turned out to be a problem.

Some keyboards have a remapping capability built in. Stormy Henderson (`stormy@Ghost.Net`) writes: 'If it's your keyboard accidently being reprogrammed, you can (on a Gateway AnyKey keyboard) press control-alt-suspend_macro to reset the keys to normal.'

6   Delete and Backspace

Getting Delete and Backspace to work just right is nontrivial, especially in a mixed environment, where you talk to console, to **X**, to **bash**, to **emacs**, login remotely, etc. You may have to edit several configuration files to tell all of the programs involved precisely what you want. On the one hand, there is the matter of which keys generate which codes (and how these codes are remapped by e.g. **kermit** or **emacs**), and on the other hand the question of what functions are bound to what codes.

People often complain 'my backspace key does not work', as if this key had a built-in function 'delete previous character'. Unfortunately, all this key, or any key, does is producing a code, and one only can hope that the kernel tty driver and all application programs can be configured such that the backspace key indeed does function as a 'delete previous character' key.

Most Unix programs get their tty input via the kernel tty driver in 'cooked' mode, and a simple `stty` command determines the erase character. However, programs like `bash` and `emacs` and X do their own input handling, and have to be convinced one-by-one to do the right thing.

6.1 How to tell Unix what character you want to use to delete the last typed character

```
% stty erase ^?
```

If the character is erased, but in a funny way, then something is wrong with your tty settings. If `echoprt` is set, then erased characters are enclosed between \ and /. If `echoe` is not set, then the erase char is echoed (which is reasonable when it is a printing character, like #). Most people will want `stty echoe -echoprt`. Saying `stty sane` will do this and more. Saying `stty -a` shows your current settings. How come this is not right by default? It is, if you use the right `getty`.

Note that many programs (like `bash`, `emacs` etc.) have their own keybindings (defined in `~/.inputrc`, `~/.emacs` etc.) and are unaffected by the setting of the erase character.

The standard Unix tty driver does not recognize a cursor, or keys (like the arrow keys) to move the current position, and hence does not have a command 'delete current character' either. But for example you can get `bash` on the console to recognize the Delete key by putting

```
set editing-mode emacs
"\e[3":delete-char
```

into `~/.inputrc`.

6.1.1 'Getty used to do the right thing with DEL and BS but is broken now?'

Earlier, the console driver would do BS Space BS (\010\040\010) when it got a DEL (\177). Nowadays, DEL's are ignored (as they should be, since the driver emulates a vt100). Get a better getty, i.e., one that does not output DEL.

6.1.2 'Login behaves differently at the first and second login attempts?'

At the first attempt, you are talking to `getty`. At the second attempt, you are talking to `login`, a different program.

6.2 How to tell Linux what code to generate when a key is pressed

On the console, or, more precisely, when not in (MEDIUM)RAW mode, use

```
% loadkeys mykeys.map
```

and under X use

```
% xmodmap mykeys.xmap
```

Note that (since XFree86-2.1) X reads the Linux settings of the keymaps when initialising the X keymap. Although the two systems are not 100% compatible, this should mean that in many cases the use of xmodmap has become superfluous.

For example, suppose that you would like the Backspace key to send a BackSpace (^H, octal 010) and the grey Delete key a DEL (octal 0177). Add the following to /etc/rc.local (or wherever you keep your local boot-time stuff):

```
/usr/bin/loadkeys << EOF
keycode 14 = BackSpace
keycode 111 = Delete
EOF
```

Note that this will only change the function of these keys when no modifiers are used. (You need to specify a keymaps line to tell which keymaps should be affected if you want to change bindings on more keymaps.) The Linux kernel default lets Ctrl-Backspace generate BackSpace - this is sometimes useful as emergency escape, when you find you can only generate DELs.

The left Alt key is sometimes called the Meta key, and by default the combinations AltL-X are bound to the symbol MetaX. But what character sequence is MetaX? That is determined (per-tty) by the Meta flag, set by the command setmetamode. The two choices are: ESC X or X or-ed with 0200.

6.2.1 'Why doesn't the Backspace key generate BackSpace by default?'

(i) Because the VT100 had a Delete key above the Enter key.

(ii) Because Linus decided so.

6.3 How to tell X to interchange Delete and Backspace

```
% xmodmap -e "keysym BackSpace = Delete" -e "keysym Delete = BackSpace"
```

Or, if you just want the Backspace key to generate a BackSpace:

```
% xmodmap -e "keycode 22 = BackSpace"
```

Or, if you just want the Delete key to generate a Delete:

```
% xmodmap -e "keycode 107 = Delete"
```

(but usually this is the default binding already).

6.4 How to tell emacs what to do when it receives a Delete or Backspace

Put in your .emacs file lines like

```
(global-set-key "\?" 'help-command)
(global-set-key "\C-h" 'delete-backward-char)
```

Of course you can bind other commands to other keys in the same way. Note that various major and minor modes redefine keybindings. For example, in incremental search mode one finds the code

```
(define-key map "\177" 'isearch-delete-char)
(define-key map "\C-h" 'isearch-mode-help)
```

This means that it may be a bad idea to use the above two global-set-key commands. There are too many places where there are built-in assumptions about ^H = help and DEL = delete. That doesn't mean that you have to setup keys so that Backspace generates DEL. But if it doesn't then it is easiest to remap them at the lowest possible level in emacs.

6.5 How to tell emacs to interchange Delete and Backspace

Put in your .emacs file lines

```
(setq keyboard-translate-table (make-string 128 0))
(let ((i 0))
   (while (< i 128)
      (aset keyboard-translate-table i i)
      (setq i (1+ i))))
(aset keyboard-translate-table ?\b ?\^?)
(aset keyboard-translate-table ?\^? ?\b)
```

Recent versions of emacs have a function **keyboard-translate** and one may simplify the above to

```
(keyboard-translate ?\C-h ?\C-?)
(keyboard-translate ?\C-? ?\C-h)
```

Note that under X emacs can distinguish between Ctrl-h and the Backspace key (regardless of what codes these produce on the console), and by default emacs will view the Backspace key as DEL (and do deletion things, as bound to that character, rather than help things, bound to ^H). One can distinguish Backspace and Delete, e.g. by

```
(global-unset-key [backspace] )
(global-set-key [backspace] 'delete-backward-char)
(global-unset-key [delete] )
(global-set-key [delete] 'delete-char)
```

6.6 How to tell kermit to interchange Delete and Backspace

Put in your .kermrc file the lines

```
set key \127 \8
set key \8 \127
```

6.7 How to tell xterm about your favourite tty modes

Normally xterm will inherit the tty modes from its invoker. Under xdm, the default erase and kill characters are # and @, as in good old Unix Version 6. If you don't like that, you might put something like

```
XTerm*ttymodes: erase ^? kill ^U intr ^C quit ^\ eof ^D \
                susp ^Z start ^Q stop ^S eol ^@
```

in /usr/lib/X11/app-defaults/XTerm or in $HOME/.Xresources, assuming that you have a line

          xrdb $HOME/.Xresources

in your $HOME/.xinitrc or $HOME/.xsession.

6.8   How to tell xmosaic that the Backspace key generates a DEL

Putting

```
        *XmText.translations: #override\n\
            <Key>osfDelete: delete-previous-character()
        *XmTextField.translations: #override\n\
            <Key>osfDelete: delete-previous-character()
```

in your $HOME/.Xresources helps.

The netscape FAQ, however, says:

> Why doesn't my Backspace key work in text fields?
> By default, Linux and XFree86 come with the Backspace and Delete keys
> misconfigured. All Motif programs (including, of course, Netscape
> Navigator) will malfunction in the same way.
>
> The Motif spec says that Backspace is supposed to delete the previous
> character and Delete is supposed to delete the following character.
> Linux and XFree86 come configured with both the Backspace and Delete
> keys generating Delete.
>
> You can fix this by using any one of the xmodmap, xkeycaps, or
> loadkeys programs to make the key in question generate the BackSpace
> keysym instead of Delete.
>
> You can also fix it by having a .motifbind file; see the man page
> for VirtualBindings(3).
>
> Note: Don't use the *XmText.translations or *XmTextField.translations
> resources to attempt to fix this problem. If you do, you will blow
> away Netscape Navigator's other text-field key bindings.

6.9   A better solution for Motif-using programs, like netscape

Ted Kandell (ted@tcg.net) suggests the following:

Somewhere in your .profile add the following:

```
    stty erase ^H
```

If you are using bash, add the following lines to your .inputrc:

```
    "\C-?": delete-char
    "\C-h": backward-delete-char
```

Add the following lines to your .xinitrc file:

```
xmodmap <<-EOF
keycode 22  =  BackSpace osfBackSpace
keycode 107 =  Delete
EOF

# start your window manager here,  for example:
#(fvwm) 2>&1 | tee /dev/tty /dev/console

stty sane
stty erase ^H
loadmap <<-EOF
keycode 14  = BackSpace
keycode 111 = Delete
EOF
```

This will definitely work for a PC 101 or 102 key keyboard with any Linux/XFree86 layout.

The important part to making Motif apps like Netscape work properly is adding osfBackSpace to keycode 22 in addition to BackSpace.

Note that there must be spaces on either side of the = sign.

6.10   What about termcap and terminfo?

When people have problems with backspace, they tend to look at their termcap (or terminfo) entry for the terminal, and indeed, there does exist a kb (or kbs) capability describing the code generated by the Backspace key. However, not many programs use it, so unless you are having problems with one particular program only, probably the fault is elsewhere. Of course it is a good idea anyway to correct your termcap (terminfo) entry. See also below under "The TERM variable".

7   The console character sets

The kernel first tries to figure out what symbol is meant by any given user byte, and next where this symbol is located in the current font.

The kernel knows about 5 translations of bytes into console-screen symbols. In Unicode (UTF-8) mode, the UTF-8 code is just converted directly into Unicode. The assumption is that almost all symbols one needs are present in Unicode, and for the cases where this does not hold the codes 0xff** are reserved for direct font access. When not in Unicode mode, one of four translation tables is used. The four tables are: a) Latin1 -> Unicode, b) VT100 graphics -> Unicode, c) PC -> Unicode, d) user-defined.

There are two character sets, called G0 and G1, and one of them is the current character set. (Initially G0.) Typing ^N causes G1 to become current, ^O causes G0 to become current.

These variables G0 and G1 point at a translation table, and can be changed by the user. Initially they point at tables a) and b), respectively. The sequences ESC (B and ESC (0 and ESC (U and ESC (K cause G0 to point at translation table a), b), c) and d), respectively. The sequences ESC) B and ESC) 0 and ESC) U and ESC) K cause G1 to point at translation table a), b), c) and d), respectively.

The sequence ESC c causes a terminal reset, which is what you want if the screen is all garbled. The oft-advised echo ^V^O will only make G0 current, but there is no guarantee that G0 points at table a). In some distributions there is a program reset(1) that just does echo ^[c. If your termcap entry for the console is correct (and has an entry :rs=\Ec:), then also setterm -reset will work.

The user-defined mapping table can be set using mapscrn(8). The result of the mapping is that if a symbol c is printed, the symbol s = map[c] is sent to the video memory. The bitmap that corresponds to s is found in the character ROM, and can be changed using setfont(8).

8   Console switching

By default, console switching is done using Alt-Fn or Ctrl-Alt-Fn. Under X (or recent versions of dosemu), only Ctrl-Alt-Fn works. Many keymaps will allow cyclic walks through all allocated consoles using Alt-RightArrow and Alt-LeftArrow.

XFree86 1.3 does not know that Alt is down when you switch to the X window. Thus, you cannot switch immediately to some other VT again but have to release Alt first. In the other direction this should work: the kernel always keeps track of the up/down status of all keys. (As far as possible: on some keyboards some keys do not emit a scancode when pressed (e.g.: the PFn keys of a FOCUS 9000) or released (e.g.: the Pause key of many keyboards)).

XFree86 1.3 saves the fonts loaded in the character ROMs when started, and restores it on a console switch. Thus, the result of setfont on a VT is wiped out when you go to X and back. Using setfont under X will lead to funny results.

One can change VT under program control using the chvt command.

8.1   Changing the number of Virtual Consoles

This question still comes up from time to time, but the answer is: you already have enough of them. Since kernel version 1.1.54, there are between 1 and 63 virtual consoles. A new one is created as soon as it is opened. It is removed by the utility deallocvt (but it can be removed only when no processes are associated to it anymore, and no text on it has been selected by programs like selection or gpm).

For older kernels, change the line

```
#define NR_CONSOLES     8
```

in include/linux/tty.h (don't increase this number beyond 63), and recompile the kernel.

If they do not exist yet, create the tty devices with MAKEDEV or mknod ttyN c 4 N where N denotes the tty number. For example,

```
for i in 9 10 11 12; do mknod /dev/tty$i c 4 $i; done
```

or, better (since it also takes care of owner and permissions),

```
for i in 9 10 11 12; do /dev/MAKEDEV tty$i; done
```

If you want the new VCs to run getty, add lines in /etc/inittab. (But it is much better to have only two getty's running, and to create more consoles dynamically as the need arises. That way you'll have more memory when you don't use all these consoles, and also more consoles, in case you really need them. Edit /etc/inittab and comment out all getty's except for the first two.)

When the consoles are allocated dynamically, it is usually easiest to have only one or two running `getty`. More are opened by `open -l -s bash`. Unused consoles (without associated processes) are deallocated using `deallocvt` (formerly `disalloc`). But, you say, I am involved in activities when I suddenly need more consoles, and do not have a bash prompt available to give the `open` command. Fortunately it is possible to create a new console upon a single keystroke, regardless of what is happening at the current console.

If you have `spawn_login` from `kbd-0.95.tar.gz` and you put

```
loadkeys << EOF
alt keycode 103 = Spawn_Console
EOF
spawn_login &
```

in `/etc/rc.local`, then typing Alt-UpArrow will create a fresh VC running `login` (and switch to it). With `spawn_console &` instead of `spawn_login &` you'll have bash running there. See also `open-1.4.tgz` and `dynamic-vc-1.1.tar.gz`.

What action should be taken upon this Spawn_Console keypress can also be set in `/etc/inittab` under `kbrequest`, if you have a recent `init`. See inittab(5).

(This action can be something entirely different - I just called the key Spawn_Console because that is what I used it for. When used for other purposes it is less confusing to use its synonym KeyboardSignal. For example, some people like to put the lines

```
kb::kbrequest:/sbin/shutdown -h now
```

in `/etc/inittab`, and

```
control alt keycode 79 = KeyboardSignal
control alt keycode 107 = KeyboardSignal
```

in their keymap. Now Ctrl-Alt-End will do a system shutdown.)

You can only login as "root" on terminals listed in `/etc/securetty`. There exist programs that read terminal settings from files `/etc/ttys` and `/etc/ttytype`. If you have such files, and create additional consoles, then it might be a good idea to also add entries for them in these files.

9   Ctrl-Alt-Del and other special key combinations

9.1   Ctrl-Alt-Del (Boot)

If you press Ctrl-Alt-Del (or whatever key was assigned the keysym Boot by loadkeys) then either the machine reboots immediately (without sync), or `init` is sent a SIGINT. The former behaviour is the default. The default can be changed by root, using the system call reboot(), see ctrlaltdel(8). Some `init`'s change the default. What happens when `init` gets SIGINT depends on the version of `init` used - often it will be determined by the pf entry in `/etc/inittab` (which means that you can run an arbitrary program in this case). In the current kernel Ctrl-AltGr-Del is no longer by default assigned to Boot.

9.2   Other combinations

```
Name           Default binding
-------------------------------
```

```
Show_Memory       Shift-Scrollock
Show_Registers    AltGr-ScrollLock
Show_State        Ctrl-ScrollLock
Console_n         Alt-Fn and Ctrl-Alt-Fn  (1 <= n <= 12)
Console_{n+12}    AltGr-Fn                (1 <= n <= 12)
Incr_Console      Alt-RightArrow
Decr_Console      Alt-LeftArrow
Last_Console      Alt[Gr]-PrintScreen
Scroll_Backward   Shift-PageUp
Scroll_Forward    Shift-PageDown
Caps_On                                   (CapsLock is a toggle; this key sets)
Compose           Ctrl-.
```

9.3 X Combinations

```
Ctrl-Alt-Fn       Switch to VT n
Ctrl-Alt-KP+      Next mode
Ctrl-Alt-KP-      Previous mode
Ctrl-Alt-Backspace    Kill X
```

On some motherboards, Ctrl-Alt-KP- and Ctrl-Alt-KP+ will be equivalent to pressing the Turbo button. That is, both will produce the scancodes 1d 38 4a ca b8 9d and 1d 38 4e ce b8 9d, and both will switch between Turbo (>= 25MHz) and non-Turbo (8 or 12 MHz). (Often these key combinations only function this way when enabled by jumpers on the motherboard.)

Perry F Nguyen (pfnguyen@netcom22.netcom.com) writes: AMI BIOS has a feature that locks up the keyboard and flashes the LED's if the Ctrl-Alt-Backspace combination is pressed while a BIOS password is enabled, until the CMOS/BIOS password is typed in.

9.4 Dosemu Combinations

```
Ctrl-Alt-Fn       Switch to VT n (from version 0.50; earlier Alt-Fn)
Ctrl-Alt-PgDn     Kill dosemu (when in RAW keyboard mode)
(and many other combinations - see the dosemu documentation)
```

9.5 Composing symbols

One symbol may be constructed using several keystrokes.

- LeftAlt-press, followed by a decimal number typed on the keypad, followed by LeftAlt-release, yields the symbol with code given by this number. (In Unicode mode this same mechanism, but then with 4 hexadecimal digits, may be used to define a Unicode symbol.)

- A dead diacritic followed by a symbol, yields that symbol adorned with that diacritic. If the combination is undefined, both keys are taken separately. Which keys are dead diacritics is user-settable; none is by default. Five (since 2.0.25 six) dead diacritics can be defined (using loadkeys(1)): dead_grave, dead_acute, dead_circumflex, dead_tilde, dead_diaeresis (and dead_cedilla). Precisely what this adorning means is also user-settable: dead-diacritic, symbol is equivalent to Compose + diacritic + symbol.

- Compose followed by two symbols yields a combination symbol. These combinations are user-settable. Today there are 68 combinations defined by default; you can see them by saying "dumpkeys | grep compose".

- Then there are 'Sticky' modifier keys (since 1.3.33). For example, one can type ^C as SControl, C and Ctrl-Alt-BackSpace as SControl, SAlt, BackSpace.

Note that there are at least three such composition mechanisms:

1. The Linux keyboard driver mechanism, used in conjunction with loadkeys.

2. The X mechanism - see X386keybd(1), later XFree86kbd(1). Under X11R6: edit `/usr/X11R6/lib/X11/locale/iso8859-1/Compose`.See also Andrew D. Balsa's comments at *http://wauug.erols.com/~balsa/linux/deadkeys/index.html* `<http://wauug.erols.com/~balsa/linux/deadkeys/index.html>`.

3. The emacs mechanism obtained by loading "iso-insert.el" or calling 'iso-accents-mode'.

For X the order of the two symbols is arbitrary: both Compose-,-c and Compose-c-, yield a c-cedilla; for Linux and emacs only the former sequence works by default. For X the list of compose combinations is fixed. Linux and emacs are flexible. The three default lists are somewhat similar, but the details are different.

10   How to get out of raw mode

If some program using K_RAW keyboard mode exits without restoring the keyboard mode to K_XLATE, then it is difficult to do anything - not even Ctrl-Alt-Del works. However, it is sometimes possible to avoid hitting the reset button. (And desirable as well: your users may get angry if you kill their Hack game by rebooting; you might also damage your file system.) Easy solutions involve logging in from another terminal or another machine and doing `kbd_mode -a`. The procedure below assumes that no X is running, that the display is in text mode, and that you are at your bash prompt, that you are using a US keyboard layout, and that your interrupt character is Ctrl-C.

Step 1. Start X. As follows: press 2 (and don't release), press F12 (and don't release) and immediately afterwards press = . This starts X. (Explanation: if a key press produces keycode K, then the key release produces keycode K+128. Probably your shell does not like these high characters, so we avoid generating them by not releasing any key. However, we have to be quick, otherwise key repeat starts. The digit 2 produces a Ctrl-C that discards previous junk, the F12 produces an X and the = a Return.) Probably your screen will be grey now, since no `.xinitrc` was specified. However, Ctrl-Alt-Fn will work and you can go to another VT. (Ctrl-Alt-Backspace also works, but that exits X, and gets you back into the previous state, which is not what you want.)

Step 2. Setup to change the keyboard mode. (For example, by `sleep 5; kbd_mode -a`.)

Step 3. Leave X again. Alt-Fx (often Alt-F7) brings you back to X, and then Ctrl-Alt-Backspace exits X. Within 5 seconds your keyboard will be usable again.

If you want to prepare for the occasion, then make `\215A\301` (3 symbols) an alias for `kbd_mode -a`. Now just hitting = F7 = (3 symbols) will return you to sanity.

11   The keyboard LEDs

1. There are per-tty keyboard flags: each VC has its own NumLock, CapsLock, ScrollLock. By default these keyboard flags are shown in the LEDs. The usual way to change them is by pressing the corresponding key. (Side remark: pressing the NumLock key when in application key mode will not change the NumLock status, but produce an escape sequence. If you want the NumLock key to always change the Numlock status, bind it to Bare_Num_Lock.)

2. Next, there are per-tty default keyboard flags, to initialize the keyboard flags when a reset occurs. Thus if you want NumLock on all the time, that is possible. The usual way to change them is by 'setleds -D ...'.

3. There is the possibility that the leds do not reflect the keyboard flags, but something else.

3A. This something else can be three bits somewhere in the kernel - which can be used if you want to monitor some hardware or software status bit(s). If you want this, edit the kernel source to call register_leds() somewhere.

3B. This something else can also be whatever some user program wants to show in the LEDs. Thus, people who like such things can make nice patterns of lights. If you want this, use the KDSETLED ioctl.

This latter use is not per-tty, but the choice between former and latter use is per-tty.

Summarizing: Each tty has a flag kbd->ledmode. If this has the value LED_SHOW_FLAGS then the keyboard flags (NumLock etc.) of that tty are shown. If this has the value LED_SHOW_MEM then three selected memory addresses are shown. If this has the value LED_SHOW_IOCTL then the leds show whatever value was last assigned to them using the KDSETLED ioctl.

One may add that X uses ioctl's to set the LEDs, but fails to reset its VT when it exits, so after using X there may be one VT that is not in the default LED_SHOW_FLAGS state. This can be fixed by doing 'setleds -L' on that VT. See setleds(1).

12 The TERM variable

Many programs use the TERM variable and the database /etc/termcap or /usr/lib/terminfo/* to decide which strings to send for clear screen, move cursor, etc., and sometimes also to decide which string is sent by the users backspace key, function keys etc. This value is first set by the kernel (for the console). Usually, this variable is re-set by getty, using /etc/ttytype or the argument specified in /etc/inittab. Sometimes, it is also set in /etc/profile.

Older systems use TERM=console or TERM=con80x25. Newer systems (with ncurses 1.8.6) use the more specific TERM=linux or TERM=linux-80x25. However, old versions of setterm test for TERM=con* and hence fail to work with TERM=linux.

Since kernel version 1.3.2, the kernel default for the console is TERM=linux.

If you have a termcap without entry for linux, add the word linux to the entry for the console:

        console|con80x25|linux:\

and make /usr/lib/terminfo/l/linux a copy of or symbolic link to /usr/lib/terminfo/c/console.

12.1 Terminfo

The terminfo entry for the linux console from ncurses 1.8.6 misses the entry kich1=\E[2~, needed by some programs. Edit the file and tic it.

13 How to make other programs work with non-ASCII chars

In the bad old days this used to be quite a hassle. Every separate program had to be convinced individually to leave your bits alone. Not that all is easy now, but recently a lot of gnu utilities have learned to react to LC_CTYPE=iso_8859_1 or LC_CTYPE=iso-8859-1. Try this first, and if it doesn't help look at the hints below.

Note that in recent versions of libc the routine setlocale() only works if you have installed the locale files (e.g. in /usr/lib/locale).

First of all, the 8-th bit should survive the kernel input processing, so make sure to have stty cs8 -istrip -parenb set.

A. For emacs the details strongly depend on the version. The information below is for version 19.34. Put lines

```
(set-input-mode nil nil 1)
(standard-display-european t)
(require 'iso-syntax)
```

into your $HOME/.emacs. The first line (to be precise: the final 1) tells emacs not to discard the 8-th bit from input characters. The second line tells emacs not to display non-ASCII characters as octal escapes. The third line specifies the syntactic properties and case conversion table for the Latin-1 character set These last two lines are superfluous if you have something like LC_CTYPE=ISO-8859-1 in your environment. (The variable may also be LC_ALL or even LANG. The value may be anything with a substring '88591' or '8859-1' or '8859_1'.)

This is a good start. On a terminal that cannot display non-ASCII ISO 8859-1 symbols, the command

```
(load-library "iso-ascii")
```

will cause accented characters to be displayed comme {,c}a. If your keymap does not make it easy to produce non-ASCII characters, then

```
(load-library "iso-transl")
```

will make the 2-character sequence Ctrl-X 8 a compose character, so that the 4-character sequence Ctrl-X 8 , c produces c-cedilla. Very inconvenient.
The command

```
(iso-accents-mode)
```

will toggle ISO-8859-1 accent mode, in which the six characters ', ', ", ^, ~, / are dead keys modifying the following symbol. Special combinations: ~c gives a c with cedilla, ~d gives an Icelandic eth, ~t gives an Icelandic thorn, "s gives German sharp s, /a gives a with ring, /e gives an a-e ligature, ~< and ~> give guillemots, ~! gives an inverted exclamation mark, ~? gives an inverted question mark, and " gives an acute accent. This is the default mapping of accents. The variable iso-languages is a list of pairs (language name, accent mapping), and a non-default mapping can be selected using

```
(iso-accents-customize LANGUAGE)
```

Here LANGUAGE can be one of "portuguese", "irish", "french", "latin-2", "latin-1".

Since the Linux default compose character is Ctrl-. it might be convenient to use that everywhere. Try

```
(load-library "iso-insert.el")
(define-key global-map [?\C-.] 8859-1-map)
```

The latter line will not work under xterm, if you use emacs -nw, but in that case you can put

```
XTerm*VT100.Translations:        #override\n\
     Ctrl <KeyPress> . : string("\0308")
```

in your `.Xresources`.)

B. For `less`, put `LESSCHARSET=latin1` in the environment. This is also what you need if you see `\255` or `<AD>` in `man` output: some versions of `less` will render the soft hyphen (octal 0255, hex 0xAD) this way when not given permission to output Latin-1.

C. For `ls`, give the option `-N`. (Probably you want to make an alias.)

D. For `bash` (version 1.13.*), put

```
        set meta-flag on
        set convert-meta off
```

and, according to the Danish HOWTO,

```
        set output-meta on
```

into your `$HOME/.inputrc`.

E. For `tcsh`, use

```
        setenv LANG      US_en
        setenv LC_CTYPE iso_8859_1
```

If you have nls on your system, then the corresponding routines are used. Otherwise `tcsh` will assume iso_8859_1, regardless of the values given to LANG and LC_CTYPE. See the section NATIVE LANGUAGE SYSTEM in tcsh(1). (The Danish HOWTO says: `setenv LC_CTYPE ISO-8859-1; stty pass8`)

F. For `flex`, give the option `-8` if the parser it generates must be able to handle 8-bit input. (Of course it must.)

G. For `elm`, set `displaycharset` to ISO-8859-1. (Danish HOWTO: `LANG=C` and `LC_CTYPE=ISO-8859-1`)

H. For programs using curses (such as `lynx`) David Sibley reports: The regular curses package uses the high-order bit for reverse video mode (see flag _STANDOUT defined in `/usr/include/curses.h`). However, `ncurses` seems to be 8-bit clean and does display iso-latin-8859-1 correctly.

I. For programs using `groff` (such as `man`), make sure to use `-Tlatin1` instead of `-Tascii`. Old versions of the program `man` also use `col`, and the next point also applies.

J. For `col`, make sure 1) that it is fixed so as to do `setlocale(LC_CTYPE,"")`; and 2) put `LC_CTYPE=ISO-8859-1` in the environment.

K. For `rlogin`, use option `-8`.

L. For `joe`, sunsite.unc.edu:/pub/Linux/apps/editors/joe-1.0.8-linux.tar.gz is said to work after editing the configuration file. Someone else said: joe: Put the `-asis` option in `/isr/lib/joerc` in the first column.

M. For LaTeX: `\documentstyle[isolatin]{article}`. For LaTeX2e: `\documentclass{article}\usepackage{isolatin}` where isolatin.sty is available from *ftp://ftp.vlsivie.tuwien.ac.at/pub/8bit* `<ftp://ftp.vlsivie.tuwien.ac.at/pub/8bit>`.

A nice discussion on the topic of ISO-8859-1 and how to manage 8-bit characters is contained in the file grasp.insa-lyon.fr:/pub/faq/fr/accents (in French). Another fine discussion (in English) can be found in *ftp.vlsivie.tuwien.ac.at:/pub/8bit/FAQ-ISO-8859-1* `<ftp.vlsivie.tuwien.ac.at:/pub/8bit/FAQ-ISO-8859-1>`, which is mirrored in *rtfm.mit.edu:pub/usenet-by-group/comp.answers/character-sets/iso-8859-1-faq* `<rtfm.mit.edu:pub/usenet-by-group/comp.answers/character-sets/iso-8859-1-faq>`.

If you need to fix a program that behaves badly with 8-bit characters, one thing to keep in mind is that if you have a signed char type then characters may be negative, and using them as an array index will fail. Several programs can be fixed by judiciously adding (unsigned char) casts.

14   What precisely does XFree86-2.1 do when it initializes its keymap?

Since version 2.1, XFree86 will initialize its keymap from the Linux keymap, as far as possible. However, Linux had 16 entries per key (one for each combination of the Shift, AltGr, Ctrl, Alt modifiers) and presently has 256 entries per key, while X has 4 entries per key (one for each combination of Shift, Mod), so some information is necessarily lost.

First X reads the Xconfig file, where definitions of the LeftAlt, RightAlt, RightCtl, ScrollLock keys as Meta, ModeShift, Compose, ModeLock or ScrollLock might be found - see X386keybd(1), later XFree86kbd(1).

For Mod the LeftAlt key is taken, unless RightCtl was defined as ModeShift or ModeLock, in which case RightCtl is taken, or RightAlt was so defined, in which case RightAlt is taken. This determines how the 4 XFree86 meanings of a key are selected from the 16 Linux meanings. Note that Linux today does not distinguish by default between the two Ctrl keys or between the two Shift keys. X does distinguish.

Now the kernel keymap is read and the usually obvious corresponding X bindings are made. The bindings for the "action keys" Show_Memory, Show_State, Show_Registers, Last_Console, Console_n, Scroll_Backward, Scroll_Forward, Caps_On and Boot are ignored, as are the dead diacriticals, and the locks (except for ShiftLock), and the "ASCII-x" keys.

Next, the definitions in the Xconfig file are used. (Thus, a definition of Compose in Xconfig will override its value as found in the Linux keymap.)

What happens to the strings associated with the function keys? Nothing, X does not have such a concept. (But it is possible to define strings for function keys in xterm - note however that the window manager gets the keys first.)

I don't know how to convince xterm that it should use the X keymap when Alt is pressed; it seems just to look at its resource eightBitInput, and depending on whether that is true or false either set the high order bit of the character, or generate an additional Escape character (just like setmetamode(1) does for the console).

15   Unusual keys and keyboards

The two keys PrintScrn/SysRq and Pause/Break are special in that they have two keycodes: the former has keycode 84 when Alt is pressed simultaneously, and keycode 99 otherwise; the latter has keycode 101 when Ctrl is pressed simultaneously, and keycode 119 otherwise. (Thus, it makes no sense to bind functions to Alt keycode 99 or Ctrl keycode 119.)

If you have strange keys, that do not generate any code under Linux (or generate messages like "unrecognized scancode"), and your kernel is 1.1.63 or later, then you can use setkeycodes(1) to tell the kernel about them. They won't work under X, however. Once they have gotten a keycode from setkeycodes, they can be assigned a function by loadkeys.

16   Examples of use of loadkeys and xmodmap

Switching Caps Lock and Control on the keyboard (assuming you use keymaps 0-15; check with dumpkeys | head -1)

```
% loadkeys
keymaps 0-15
```

```
keycode 58 = Control
keycode 29 = Caps_Lock
%
```

Switching them under X only:

```
% xmodmap .xmodmaprc
```

where .xmodmaprc contains lines

```
remove Lock = Caps_Lock
remove Control = Control_L
keysym Control_L = Caps_Lock
keysym Caps_Lock = Control_L
add Lock = Caps_Lock
add Control = Control_L
```

What is this about the key numbering? Backspace is 14 under Linux, 22 under X? Well, the numbering can best be regarded as arbitrary; the Linux number of a key can be found using showkey(1), and the X number using xev(1). Often the X number will be 8 more than the Linux number.

Something else people like to change are the bindings of the function keys. Suppose that you want to make F12 produce the string "emacs ". Then

```
% loadkeys
keycode 88 = F12
string F12 = "emacs "
%
```

will do this. More explicitly, the procedure is like this: (i) find the keycodes of the keys to be remapped, using showkey(1). (ii) save the current keymap, make a copy and edit that:

```
% dumpkeys > my_keymap
% cp my_keymap trial_keymap
% emacs trial_keymap
% loadkeys trial_keymap
%
```

The format of the table can be guessed by looking at the output of dumpkeys, and is documented in keytables(5). When the new keymap functions as desired, you can put an invocation

```
loadkeys my_new_keymap
```

in /etc/rc.local or so, to execute it automatically at boot-up. Note that changing modifier keys is tricky, and a newbie can easily get into a situation only an expert can get out of.

The default directory for keymaps is /usr/lib/kbd/keytables. The default extension for keymaps is .map. Thus, loadkeys uk would probably load /usr/lib/kbd/keytables/uk.map.

(On my machine) /dev/console is a symbolic link to /dev/tty0, and the kernel regards /dev/tty0 as a synonym for the current VT. XFree86 1.3 changes the owner of /dev/tty0, but does not reset this after finishing. Thus, loadkeys or dumpkeys might fail because someone else owns /dev/tty0; in such a case you might run X first. Note that you cannot change keyboard mappings when not at the console (and not superuser).

16.1 'I can use only one finger to type with'

"Can the Shift, Ctrl and Alt keys be made to behave as toggles?"

Yes, after saying

```
% loadkeys
keymaps 0-15
keycode 29 = Control_Lock
keycode 42 = Shift_Lock
keycode 56 = Alt_Lock
%
```

the left Control, Shift and Alt keys will act as toggles. The numbers involved are revealed by showkey (and usually are 29, 97, 42, 54, 56, 100 for left and right control, shift and alt, respectively), and the functions are Control_Lock, Shift_Lock, Alt_Lock, ALtGr_Lock.

"What about 'sticky' modifier keys?"

Since version 1.3.33, the kernel knows about 'sticky' modifier keys. These act on the next key pressed. So, where one earlier needed the 3-symbol sequence Shift_Lock a Shift_Lock to type 'A', one can now use the 2-symbol sequence SShift_Lock a. Versions of the kbd package older than 0.93 do not yet include code for these sticky modifiers, and have to invoke them using their hexadecimal codes. For example,

```
% loadkeys
keymaps 0-15
keycode 54 = 0x0c00
keycode 97 = 0x0c02
keycode 100 = 0x0c03
%
```

will make the right Shift, Ctrl, Alt sticky versions of the left ones. >From 0.93 on you can say

```
% loadkeys
keymaps 0-15
keycode 54 = SShift
keycode 97 = SCtrl
keycode 100 = SAlt
%
```

to obtain the same result. This will allow you to type Ctrl-Alt-Del in three keystrokes with one hand.

The keymaps line in these examples should cover all keymaps you have in use. You find what keymaps you have in use by

```
% dumpkeys | head -1
```

17 Changing the video mode

As far as I know there are 6 ways to change resolution:

1. At compile time: change the line

SVGA_MODE=   -DSVGA_MODE=NORMAL_VGA

in `/usr/src/linux/Makefile`.

1A. After compilation: use `rdev -v` - a terrible hack, but it exists.

2. At boot time: put `vga=ask` in the lilo config file, and lilo will ask you what video mode you want. Once you know, put `vga=mypreference`.

3. At run time: A. Use the `resizecons` command. (This is a very primitive wrapper around the VT_RESIZE ioctl.) B. Use the `SVGATextMode` command. (This is a less primitive wrapper around the VT_RESIZE ioctl.)

4. Not "on the console": Under `dosemu`, or with svgalib etc. you can change the hardware video mode without the console driver being aware of it. Sometimes this is useful in getting `resizecons` or `SVGATextMode` set up: use `dosemu` and some DOS program to get into the desired videomode, dump (say from another VT) the contents of all video hardware registers, and use that in the initialization that `resizecons` and `SVGATextMode` require. In some cases where the video mode has gotten into some unusable state, starting `dosemu`, relying on the BIOS to set up the video mode, and then killing `dosemu` (with `kill -9`), is the easiest way to get into shape again.

17.1   Instructions for the use of resizecons

Get svgalib and compile the program `restoretextmode`. Boot up your machine in all possible video modes (using `vga=ask` in the lilo config file), and write the video hardware register contents to files CxR (C=cols, R=rows), e.g., 80x25, 132x44, etc. Put these files in `/usr/lib/kbd/videomodes`. Now `resizecons 132x44` will change videomode for you (and send SIGWINCH to all processes that need to know about this, and load another font if necessary).

At present, `resizecons` only succeeds when there is memory enough for both the old and the new consoles at the same time.

18   Changing the keyboard repeat rate

At startup, the Linux kernel sets the repeat rate to its maximal value. For most keyboards this is reasonable, but for some it means that you can hardly touch a key without getting three copies of the corresponding symbol. Use the program kbdrate(8) to change the repeat rate, or, if that doesn't help, edit or remove the section

```
    ! set the keyboard repeat rate to the max

        mov     ax,#0x0305
        xor     bx,bx          ! clear bx
        int     0x16
```

of `/usr/src/linux/[arch/i386/]boot/setup.S`.

19   Scrolling

There are two ways to get a screen to scroll. The first, called 'hard scrolling', is to leave the text in video memory as it is, but change the viewing origin. This is very fast. The second, called 'soft scrolling', involves moving all screen text up or down. This is much slower. The kernel console driver will write text starting at the top of the video memory, continuing to the bottom, then copy the bottom part to the top again, and continue, all the time using hard scrolling to show the right part on the screen. You can scroll back until the top op the video memory by using Shift-PageUp (the grey PageUp) and scroll down again using Shift-PageDown (the grey PageDown), assuming a default keymap. The amount of scrollback is thus limited to the amount of video memory you happen to have and you cannot increase this amount. If you need more scrollback, use some program that buffers the text, like `less` or `screen` - by using a buffer on disk you can go back to what you did last week. (One can set the amount of scrollback for `xterm` by adding a line like `XTerm*saveLines:  2500` in `.Xresources`.)

Upon changing virtual consoles, the screen content of the old VT is copied to kernel memory, and the screen content of the new VT is copied from kernel memory to video memory. Only the visible screen is copied, not all of video memory, so switching consoles means losing the scrollback information.

Sometimes, hard scrolling is undesirable, for example when the hardware does not have the possibility to change viewing origin. The first example was a Braille machine that would render the top of video memory in Braille. There is a kernel boot-time option `no-scroll` to tell the console driver not to use hard scrolling. See bootparam(7).

20 Screensaving

`setterm -blank` *nn* will tell the console driver to blank the screen after *nn* minutes of inactivity. (With *nn* = 0, screensaving is turned off. In some old kernels this first took effect after the next keyboard interrupt.)

The s option of xset(1) will set the X screensaving parameters: `xset s off` turns off the screensaver, `xset s 10` blanks the screen after 10 minutes.

The video hardware powersaving modes can be enabled/disabled using the `setvesablank` program given in the starting comment of `/usr/src/linux/drivers/char/vesa_blank.c`.

21 Screen dumps

`setterm -dump` *N* will dump the contents of the screen of `/dev/tty`*N* to a file `screen.dump` in the current directory. See setterm(1).

The current contents of the screen of `/dev/tty`*N* can be accessed using the device `/dev/vcs`*N* (where 'vcs' stands for 'virtual console screen'). For example, you could have a clock program that displays the current time in the upper right hand corner of the console screen (see the program `vcstime` in `kbd-0.95.tar.gz`). Just dumping the contents goes with `cat /dev/vcs`*N*. These device files `/dev/vcs`*N* do not contain newlines, and do not contain attributes, like colors. From a program it is usually better to use `/dev/vcsa`*N* ('virtual console screen with attributes') instead - it starts with a header giving the number of rows and columns and the location of the cursor. See vcs(4).

22 Some properties of the VT100 - application key mode

: Sometimes my cursor keys or keypad keys produce strange codes?

When the terminal is in application cursor key mode the cursor keys produce Esc O x and otherwise Esc [x where x is one of A,B,C,D. Certain programs put the terminal in application cursor key mode; if you kill them with `kill -9`, or if they crash, then the mode will not be reset.

```
% echo -e '\033c'
```

resets all properties of the current VC. Just changing the cursor application key mode is done by

```
% echo -e '\033[?1h'
```

(set) and

```
% echo -e '\033[?1l'
```

(clear).

When the terminal is in application keypad key mode the keypad keys produce Esc O y and otherwise Esc [z ~ for certain y and z. Setting application keypad key mode is done by

```
% echo -e '\033='
```

and

```
% echo -e '\033>'
```

clears it again.

23   Hardware incompatibility

Several people have noticed that they lose typed characters when a floppy disk is active. It seems that this might be a problem with Uni-486WB motherboards. (Please mail me (`aeb@cwi.nl`) to confirm [yes, I have the same problem], deny [no, nothing wrong with my Uni-486WB], modify [My Xyzzy machine has the same problem].)

Tjalling Tjalkens (`tjalling@ei.ele.tue.nl`) reports very similar problems with "a no-brand GMB-486 UNP Vesa motherboard with AMD 486DX2-66 CPU" - during floppy activity some keystrokes are lost, during floppy tape streamer (Conner C 250 MQ) activity many keystrokes are lost.

Some people experience sporadic lockups - sometimes associated to hard disk activity or other I/O.

Ulf Tietz (`ulf@rio70.bln.sni.de`) wrote: 'I have had the same problems, when I had my motherboard tuned too fast. So I reset all the timings (CLK, wait statements etc) to more conventional values, and the problems are gone.'

Bill Hogan (`bhogan@crl.com`) wrote: 'If you have an AMI BIOS, you might try setting the Gate A20 emulation parameter to "chipset" (if you have that option). Whenever I have had that parameter set to any of the other options on my machine ("fast", "both", "disabled") I have had frequent keyboard lockups.'

Additions and corrections are welcome. Andries Brouwer - `aeb@cwi.nl`

The Linux Printing HOWTO

Grant Taylor <gtaylor+pht@picante.com>   v3.14, 23 September 1997

This is the Linux Printing HOWTO, a collection of information on how to generate, preview, print and fax anything under Linux (and other Unices in general).

Contents

1   Introduction

The Printing HOWTO should contain everything you need to know to help you set up printing services on your Linux box(en). As life would have it, it's a bit more complicated that in the point-and-click world of Microsoft and Apple, but it's also a bit more flexible and certainly easier to administer for large LANs.

This document is ordered such that most people will only need to read the first half or so. Much of the more obscure and situation-dependant information in here is in the last half, and can be easily located in the Table of Contents, whereas most of the information through section 9 or 10 is probably needed by most people.

Since version 3.x is a complete rewrite, much information from previous editions has been lost. This is by design, as the previous HOWTOs were so large as to be 60 typeset pages, and had the narrative flow of a dead turtle. If you do not find the answer here, you are encouraged to a) scan the previous version at *The PHT Home Page* <http://www.picante.com/~gtaylor/pht/> and b) drop me a note saying what ought to be here but isn't.

The *Printing HOWTO Home Page* <http://www.picante.com/~gtaylor/pht/> is a good place to find the latest version; it is also, of course, distributed from SunSite (`sunsite.unc.edu`) and your friendly local LDP mirror.

1.1   History

This is the third generation, which is to say the third complete rewrite, of the Printing HOWTO. The history of the PHT may be chronicled thusly:

1. I wrote the printing-howto in 1992 in response to too many printing questions in comp.os.linux, and posted it. This predated the HOWTO project by a few months and was thus the first FAQlet called a 'howto'. This edition was in plain ascii.

2. After joining the HOWTO project, the Printing-HOWTO was merged with an Lpd FAQ by Brian McCauley <`B.A.McCauley@bham.ac.uk`>; we continued to co-author the PHT for two years or so. At some point we incorporated the work of Karl Auer <`Karl.Auer@anu.edu.au`>. This generation of the PHT was in TeXinfo, and available in PS, HTML, Ascii, and Info.

3. After letting the PHT rot and decay for over a year, and an unsuccessful attempt at getting someone else to maintain it, this rewrite happened. This generation of the PHT is in Linuxdoc-SGML.

1.2   Copyright

This document is Copyright (c) 1997 by Grant Taylor. Please copy and distribute it widely, but do not modify the text or omit my name.

2   How to print

If you've already got lpd setup to print to your printer, or your system administrator already did so, or your vendor did so for you, then all you need to do is learn how to use the lpr command. The *Printing Usage HOWTO* <http://sunsite.unc.edu/LDP/HOWTO/Printing-Usage-HOWTO.html> covers this, and a few other queue manipulation commands you should probably know.

If, however, you have a new system or new printer, then you'll have to set up printing services one way or another before you can print. Read on!

3 Kernel printer devices

3.1 The lp device

The Linux kernel (<=2.1.32), assuming you have compiled in or loaded the lp device (the output of cat /proc/devices should include the device lp), provides one or more of /dev/lp0, /dev/lp1, and /dev/lp2. These are NOT assigned dynamically, rather, each corresponds to a specific hardware I/O address. This means that your first printer may be lp0 or lp1 depending on your hardware. Try both ;)

A few users have reported that their bidirectional lp ports aren't detected if they use an older unidirectional printer cable. Check that you've got a decent cable.

One cannot run the plip and lp drivers at the same time on any given port. You can, however, have one or the other driver loaded at any given time either manually, or by kerneld with version 2.x (and later 1.3.x) kernels. By carefully setting the interrupts and such, you can supposedly run plip on one port and lp on the other. One person did so by editing the drivers; I eagerly await a success report of someone doing so with only a clever command line.

There is a little utility called _tunelp_ <http://www.picante.com/~gtaylor/pht/man/tunelp.html> floating about with which you, as root, can tune the Linux lp device's interrupt usage, polling rate, and other options.

When built in to some 1.3.x and later kernels, the kernel will accept an lp= option to set interrupts and io addresses:

```
When the lp driver is built in to the kernel, you may use the
LILO/LOADLIN command line to set the port addresses and interrupts
that the driver will use.

Syntax:        lp=port0[,irq0[,port1[,irq1[,port2[,irq2]]]]]

For example:   lp=0x378,0    or    lp=0x278,5,0x378,7 **

Note that if this feature is used, you must specify *all* the ports
you want considered, there are no defaults.  You can disable a
built-in driver with lp=0.
```

When loaded as a module in version 2 and late-model 1.3.x kernels, it is possible to specify io addresses and interrupt lines on the insmod command line (or in /etc/conf.modules so as to affect kerneld) using the usual syntax. The parameters are io=port0,port1,port2 and irq=irq0,irq1,irq2. Read ye the man page for _insmod_ for more information on this.

**For those of you who (like me) can never find the standard port numbers when you need them, they are as in the second example above. The other port (lp0) is at 0x3bc. I've no idea what interrupt it usually uses.

The source code for the Linux parallel port driver is in /usr/src/linux/drivers/char/lp.c.

3.2 The parport device (kernels >= 2.1.33)

Beginning with kernel 2.1.33 (and available as a patch for kernel 2.0.30), the lp device is merely a client of the new parport device. The addition of the parport device corrects a number of the problems that plague the old lp device driver - it can share the port with other drivers, it dynamically assigns available parallel ports to device numbers rather than enforcing a fixed correspondence between I/O addresses and port numbers, and so forth.

I'll cover the parport driver more completely when I find myself using one, but in the meantime you can read the file *Documentation/parport.txt* <http://www.cyberelk.demon.co.uk/parport/parport.txt> in your kernel sources, or look at the *parport web site* <http://www.cyberelk.demon.co.uk/parport.html>.

3.3   Serial devices

Serial devices are usually called something like */dev/ttyS1* under Linux. The utility *stty* <http://www. picante.com/~gtaylor/pht/man/stty.html> will allow you to interactively view or set the settings for a serial port; *setserial* <http://www.picante.com/~gtaylor/pht/man/setserial.html> will allow you to control a few extended attributes and configure IRQs and I/O addresses for non-standard ports. Further discussion of serial ports under Linux may be found in the *Serial-HOWTO* <http://sunsite.unc.edu/mdw/ HOWTO/Serial-HOWTO.html>.

When using a slow serial printer with flow control, you may find that some of your print jobs get truncated. This may be due to the serial port, whose default behavior is to purge any untransmitted characters from its buffer 30 seconds after the port device is closed. The buffer can hold up to 4096 characters, and if your printer uses flow control and is slow enough that it can't accept all the data from the buffer within 30 seconds after printing software has closed the serial port, the tail end of the buffer's contents will be lost. If the command `cat file > /dev/ttyS2` produces complete printouts for short files but truncated ones for longer files, you may have this condition.

The 30 second interval can be adjusted through the "closing_wait" commandline option of setserial (version 2.12 and later). A machine's serial ports are usually initialized by a call to setserial in the rc.serial boot file. The call for the printing serial port can be modified to set the closing_wait at the same time as it sets that port's other parameters.

4   Supported Printers

The Linux kernel mostly supports any printer that you can plug into a serial or parallel port, but there are things to look out for, and printers that you won't be able to use, even though they can (electrically speaking) communicate with Linux. Primary among these incompatible printers are those that rely on the "Windows Printing System". (They're often vaguely labelled "for Windows".) These printers *do not work* with Linux. They haven't any "smarts" at all, and rely on the computer CPU to do much of the tasks that have been traditionally done by the printer's CPU. Unfortunately, these tasks can only be done by the vendor-supplied drivers, which only run under Windows. So don't buy one to use with Linux.

As for what printers *do* work with Linux, the best choice is to buy a printer with native PostScript support. Nearly all Unix software that produces printable output produces it in PostScript, so obviously it'd be nice to get a printer that supports PostScript directly. Unfortunately, PostScript support is scarce outside the laser printer domain.

Failing the (larger) budget necessary to buy a PostScript printer, you can use any printer supported by Ghostscript, the free PostScript interpreter used in lieu of actual printer PostScript support. The *Ghostscript Home Page* <http://www.cs.wisc.edu/~ghost/> has a list of supported printers and information on the status of new and experimental drivers. Please help improve the Ghostscript printer support page by reorting your successes and failures as it asks.

5   Which spooling software?

Until recently, the choice for Linux users was simple - everyone ran the same old lpd lifted mostly verbatim out of BSD's Net-2 code. Even today, most vendors ship this software. But this is beginning to change. SVR4-like systems including Sun's Solaris come with a completely different print spooling package, centered around lpsched. And there are signs that some Linux vendors will shift to providing LPRng, a far less ancient print spooling implementation that is freely available. LPRng is far easier to administer for large installations and has a less frightfully haphazard codebase than does stock lpd.

For the moment, even in light of the new options, lpd is probably fine for most Linux users. While it isn't the snazziest system, it works fine once set up, and it is well understood and extensively documented in third-party Unix books.

If you'd like more information on LPRng, check out *LPRng - An Enhanced Printer Spooler* <http://ltpwww.gsfc.nasa.gov/ltpcf/about/unix/Depotdoc/LPRng/>. Future versions of this HOWTO will include information on using both LPRng and regular lpd.

6   How it works, basic

In order to get printing working well, you need to understand how the lpd system works.

Lpd stands for Line Printer Daemon, and refers in different contexts to both the daemon and the whole collection of programs which run print spooling. These are:

lpd <http://www.picante.com/~gtaylor/pht/man/lpd.html>

> The spooling daemon. One of these runs to control everything on a machine, AND one is run per printer while the printer is printing.

lpr <http://www.picante.com/~gtaylor/pht/man/lpr.html>

> The user spooling command. Lpr contacts lpd and injects a new print job into the spool.

lpq <http://www.picante.com/~gtaylor/pht/man/lpq.html>

> Lists the jobs in a print queue.

lpc <http://www.picante.com/~gtaylor/pht/man/lpc.html>

> The Lpd system control command. With lpc you can stop, start, reorder, etc, the print queues.

lprm <http://www.picante.com/~gtaylor/pht/man/lprm.html>

> lprm will remove a job from the print spool.

So how does it fit together? Well, when the system boots, lpd is run. It scans the file */etc/printcap* to learn which printers it will be managing spools for. Each time someone runs lpr, lpr contacts lpd through the named socket */dev/printer*, and feeds lpd both the file to print and some information about who is printing and how to print it. Lpd then prints the file on the appropriate printer in turn.

The lp system was originally designed when most printers were line printers - that is, people mostly printed plain ascii. As it turns out, only a little extra scripting is needed to make lpd work quite well for today's print jobs, which are often in PostScript, or text, or dvi, or...

7   How to set things up, basic

7.1   Traditional lpd configuration

The minimal setup for lpd rsults in a system that can queue files and print them. It will not pay any attention to wether or not your printer will understand them, and will probably not let you produce attractive output. Nevertheless, it is the first step to understanding, so read on!

Basically, to add a print queue to lpd, you must add an entry in */etc/printcap*, and make the new spool directory under */var/spool/lpd*.

An entry in */etc/printcap* looks like:

```
# LOCAL djet500
lp|dj|deskjet:\
        :sd=/var/spool/lpd/dj:\
        :mx#0:\
        :lp=/dev/lp0:\
        :sh:
```

This defines a spool called *lp*, *dj*, or *deskjet*, spooled in the directory */var/spool/lpd/dj*, with no per-job maximum size limit, which prints to the device */dev/lp0*, and which does not have a banner page (with the name of the person who printed, etc) added to the front of the print job.

Go now and read the man page for printcap <http://www.picante.com/~gtaylor/pht/man/printcap.html>.

The above looks very simple, but there a catch - unless I send in files a DeskJet 500 can understand, this DeskJet will print strange things. For example, sending an ordinary Unix text file to a deskjet results in literally interpreted newlines, and gets me:

```
This is line one.
                This is line two.
                                This is line three.
```

ad nauseam. Printing a PostScript file to this spool would get a beautiful listing of the PostScript commands, printed out with this "staircase effect", but no useful output.

Clearly more is needed, and this is the purpose of filtering. The more observant of you who read the printcap man page might have noticed the spool attributes *if* and *of*. Well, *if*, or the input filter, is just what we need here.

If we write a small shell script called *filter* that adds carriage returns before newlines, the staircasing can be eliminated. So we have to add in an *if* line to our printcap entry above:

```
lp|dj|deskjet:\
        :sd=/var/spool/lpd/dj:\
        :mx#0:\
        :lp=/dev/lp0:\
        :if=/var/spool/lpd/dj/filter:\
        :sh:
```

A simple filter script might be:

```perl
#!perl
# The above line should really have the whole path to perl
# This script must be executable: chmod 755 filter
while(<STDIN>){chop $_; print "$_\r\n";};
# You might also want to end with a form feed: print "\f";
```

If we were to do the above, we'd have a spool to which we could print regular Unix text files and get meaningful results. (Yes, there are four million better ways to write this filter, but few so illustrative. You are encouraged to do this more efficiently.)

The only remaining problem is that printing plain text is really not too hot - surely it would be better to be able to print PostScript and other formatted or graphic types of output. Well, yes, it would, and it's easy to do. The method is simply an extention of the above linefeed-fixing filter. If you write a filter than can accept arbitrary file types as input and produce DeskJet-kosher output for each case, then you've got a clever print spooler indeed!

Such a filter is called a *magic* filter. Don't bother writing one yourself unless you print strange things - there are a good many written for you already on the net.

7.2   File Permissions

By popular demand, I include below a listing of the permissions on interesting files on my system. There are a number of better ways to do this, ideally using only SGID binaries and not making everything SUID root, but this is how my system came out of the box, and it works for me. (Quite frankly, if your vendor can't even ship a working lpd you're in for a rough ride).

```
-r-sr-sr-x   1 root    lp     /usr/bin/lpr*
-r-sr-sr-x   1 root    lp     /usr/bin/lprm*
-rwxr--r--   1 root    root   /usr/sbin/lpd*
-r-xr-sr-x   1 root    lp     /usr/sbin/lpc*
drwxrwxr-x   4 root    lp     /var/spool/lpd/
drwxr-xr-x   2 root    lp     /var/spool/lpd/lp/
```

Lpd must currently be run as root so that it can bind to the low-numbered lp service port. It should probably become UID lp.lp or something after binding, but I don't think it does. Bummer.

8   Getting Printing Software

Many prewritten filter packages (and other printer-related software) are available from *SunSite* <ftp:// sunsite.unc.edu/pub/Linux/system/printing/>. Such utilities as psutils, a2ps, mpage, dvitodvi, flpr, etc can all be found there.

8.1   Magicfilter

Magic filter is one of the fully-featured filter packages out there; it is designed to be installed in 10 minutes. I'm told it also includes special support for LPRng.

```
Title:        magicfilter
Version:      1.1b
```

```
Entered-date:   04APR95
Description:    A customizable, extensible automatic printer filter.
                Lets you automatically detect and print just about any
                data type you can find a conversion utility for.  This
                filter is written in C and is controlled completely
                from an external printer configuration file.
                This version adds automagic creation of configuration
                files based on the installed software on your system,
                courtesy of GNU Autoconf.
                This version is a bug fix from 1.1/1.1a; filters for
                non-ASCII capable PostScript printers have been added.
Author:         H. Peter Anvin <hpa@zytor.com>
Primary-site:   sunsite.unc.edu
                53000 /pub/Linux/system/printing/magicfilter-1.1b.tar.gz
Copying-policy: GPL
```

8.2   APS Filter

Another of the many magic filter packages is aps filter, by Andreas Klemm. The Linux Software Map entry
goes something like this:

```
Begin3
Title:          apsfilter
Version:        4.9.1
Entered-date:   Montag, 10. Juli 1995, 21:22:35 Uhr MET DST
Description:    magicfilter for lpd with auto filetype detection
Keywords:       lpd magicfilter aps apsfilter
Original-site:  sunsite.unc.edu
                /pub/Linux/system/printing/
                211KB aps-491.tgz
Platforms:      C-Compiler, gs Postscript emulator, pbmutils
Copying-policy: GPL
End
```

APS filter installs as an *if* filter for a print queue, and will translate from many common file types into your
printer's command set. It understands, for example, text, PostScript, dvi, gif, and others.

8.3   EZ-Magic

EZ-Magic is another filter package, written in bash, available on sunsite.

```
Title:          ez-magic printer filter
Version:        1.0.5
Entered-date:   January 26, 1997
Description:    ez-magic is a printer filter that supports 8 common file
                formats (txt,ps,gif,bmp,pcx,png,jpg,tif) for printing.
```

It can print over a network (SMB), or to a local printer.
Reads from a file, STDIN, or lpd. Simple to use and
configure. Just one script file, no huge manuals and
multibillion drivers. The only catch is that you need a
few common helper programs like netpbm and ghostscript.
Written in bash. Easy to add formats and code. Still more
bugs than I have appendages, but less than the number of
grams of fat in a hot dog. Pre-configured for HP DeskJet
870Cse over network. Comparable to apsfilter and others.

Keywords: magic filter, print, graphics, samba, network, smb,
ghostscript, postscript, gif, jpg, simple

Author: toby@eskimo.com (Toby Reed)

Maintained-by: toby@eskimo.com (Toby Reed)

Primary-site: http://www.eskimo.com/~toby/ez-magic-1.0.5.tar.gz
38 kb ez-magic-1.0.5.tar.gz

Alternate-site: sunsite.unc.edu /pub/Linux/system/printing
38 kb ez-magic-1.0.5.tar.gz

Copying-policy: Copyrighted, full manipulation rights, with one or two
restrictions.

9   Vendor Solutions

This section is, by definition, incomplete. Feel free to send in details of your favourite distribution.

9.1   Red Hat

Red Hat has a GUI printer administration tool which can add remote printers and printers on local devices. It lets you choose a ghostscript-supported printer type and Unix device file to print to, then installs a print queue in */etc/printcap* and writes a short PostScript-and-ascii magic filter based around gs and *nenscript* <http://www.picante.com/~gtaylor/pht/man/nenscript.html>. This solution works fairly well, and is trivial to setup for common cases.

9.2   Other Distributions

Please send me info on what other distributions do!

10   Ghostscript.

Ghostscript <http://www.cs.wisc.edu/~ghost/> is an incredibly significant program for Linux printing. Most printing software under Unix generates PostScript, which is typically a $100 option on a printer. Ghostscript, however, is free, and will generate the language of your printer from PostScript. When tied in with your lpd input filter, it gives you a virtual PostScript printer and simplifies life immensely.

Ghostscript is available in two forms. The commercial version of Ghostscript, called Aladdin Ghostscript, may be used freely for personal use but may not be distributed by commercial Linux distributions. It is generally a year or so ahead of the free Ghostscript; at the moment, for example, it supports Adobe Acrobat's Portable Document Format, while the older Ghostscripts do not.

The free version of Ghostscript is GNU Ghostscript, and is simply an aged version of Aladdin ghostscript kindly given to GNU. (Kudos to Aladdin for this arrangement; more software vendors should support free software in this way).

Whatever you do with *gs* <http://www.picante.com/~gtaylor/pht/man/gs.html>, be very sure to run it with the option for disabling file access (-dSAFER). PostScript is a fully functional language, and a bad PostScript program could give you quite a headache.

Speaking of PDF, Adobe's Portable Document Format is actually little more than organized PostScript in a compressed file. Ghostscript can handle PDF input just as it does PostScript. So you can be the first on your block with a PDF-capable printer.

10.1   Invoking Ghostscript

Typically, ghostscript will be run by whatever magic filter you settle upon, but for debugging purposes it's often handy to run it directly.

gs -help will give a brief informative listing of options and available drivers (note that this list is the list of drivers compiled in, not the master list of all available drivers).

You might run gs for testing purposes like: gs *options* -q -dSAFER -sOutputFile=/dev/lp1 test.ps.

10.2   Ghostscript output tuning

There are a number of things one can do if gs's output is not satisfactory (actually, you can do anything you darn well please, since you have the source).

10.2.1   Output location and size

The location, size, and aspect ratio of the image on a page is controlled by the printer-specific driver in ghostscript. If you find that your pages are coming out scrunched too short, or too long, or too big by a factor of two, you might want to look in your driver's source module and adjust whatever parameters jump out at you. Unfortunately, each driver is different, so I can't really tell you what to adjust, but most of them are reasonably well commented.

10.2.2   Gamma, dotsizes, etc.

Most non-laser printers suffer from the fact that their dots are rather large. This results in pictures coming out too dark. If you experience this problem you should use your own transfer function. Simply create the following file in the ghostscript lib-dir and add its name to the gs call just before the actual file. You may need to tweak the actual values to fit your printer. Lower values result in a brighter print. Especially if your driver uses a Floyd-Steinberg algorithm to rasterize colors, lower values (0.2 - 0.15) are probably a good choice.

```
    ---8<---- gamma.ps ----8<---
    %!
```

```
%transfer functions for cyan magenta yellow black
{0.3 exp} {0.3 exp} {0.3 exp} {0.3 exp} setcolortransfer
---8<------------------8<---
```

It is also possible to mend printers that have some kind of colour fault by tweaking these values. If you do that kind of thing, I recommend using the file colorcir.ps, that comes with ghostscript (in the examples/ subdir), as a test page.

11 How to print to a printer over the network

One of the features of lpd is that it supports printing over the network to printers physically connected to a different machine. With the careful combination of filter scripts and assorted utilities, you can make lpr print transparently to printers on all sorts of networks.

11.1 To a Unix/lpd host

To allow remote machines to print to your printer, you must list the machines in */etc/hosts.equiv* or */etc/hosts.lpd*. (Note that *hosts.equiv* has a host of other effects; be sure you know what you are doing if you list any machine there). You can allow only certain users on the other machines to print to your printer by usign the *rs* attribute; read the *lpd* <http://www.picante.com/~gtaylor/pht/man/lpd.html> man page for information on this.

11.1.1 With lpd

To print to another machine, you make an */etc/printcap* entry like this:

```
# REMOTE djet500
lp|dj|deskjet:\
        :sd=/var/spool/lpd/dj:\
        :rm=machine.out.there.com:\
        :rp=printername:\
        :lp=/dev/null:\
        :sh:
```

Note that there is still a spool directory on the local machine managed by lpd. If the remote machine is busy or offline, print jobs from the local machine wait in the spool area until they can be sent.

11.1.2 With rlpr

You can also use *rlpr* to send a print job directly to a queue on a remote machine without going through the hassle of configuring lpd to handle it. This is mostly useful in situations where you print to a variety of printers only occasionally. From the announcement for *rlpr*:

Rlpr uses TCP/IP to send print jobs to lpd servers anywhere on a network.

Unlike lpr, it *does not* require that the remote printers be explicitly known to the machine you wish to print from, (e.g. through */etc/printcap*) and thus is considerably more flexible and requires less administration.

rlpr can be used anywhere a traditional lpr might be used, and is backwards compatible with traditional BSD lpr.

The main power gained by rlpr is the power to print remotely *from anywhere to anywhere* without regard for how the system you wish to print from was configured. Can work as a filter just like traditional lpr so that clients executing on a remote machine like netscape, xemacs, etc, etc can print to your local machine with little effort.

Rlpr is available from *SunSite* `<ftp://sunsite.unc.edu/pub/Linux/system/printing/>`.

11.2   To a Win95, WinNT, LanManager, or Samba printer

There is a Printing to Windows mini-HOWTO out there which has more info than there is here.

It is possible to direct an lpd queue through the *smbclient* `<http://www.picante.com/~gtaylor/pht/man/smbclient.html>` program (part of the samba suite) to a TCP/IP based SMB print service. Samba includes a script to do this called smbprint. In short, you put a configuration file for the specific printer in question in the spool directory, and install the smbprint script as the *if*.

The */etc/printcap* entry goes like this:

```
lp|remote-smbprinter:\
    :lp=/dev/null:sh:\
    :sd=/var/spool/lpd/lp:\
    :if=/usr/local/sbin/smbprint:
```

You should read the documentation inside the smbprint script for more information on how to set this up.

You can also use smbclient to submit a file directly to an SMB printing service without involving lpd. See the man page.

11.3   To a NetWare Printer

The ncpfs suite includes a utility called nprint which provides the same functionality as smbprint but for NetWare. You can get ncpfs from *SunSite* `<ftp://sunsite.unc.edu/pub/Linux/system/filesystems/ncpfs/>`. From the LSM entry for version 0.16:

> With ncpfs you can mount volumes of your netware server under Linux. You can also print to netware print queues and spool netware print queues to the Linux printing system. You need kernel 1.2.x or 1.3.54 and above. ncpfs does NOT work with any 1.3.x kernel below 1.3.54.

To make nprint work via lpd, you write a little shell script to print stdin on the NetWare printer, and install that as the *if* for an lpd print queue. You'll get something like:

```
sub2|remote-NWprinter:\
        :lp=/dev/null:sh:\
        :sd=/var/spool/lpd/sub2:\
        :if=/var/spool/lpd/nprint-script:
```

The nprint-script might look approximately like:

```
#! /bin/sh
# You should try the guest account with no password first!
/usr/local/bin/nprint -S net -U name -P passwd -q printq-name -
```

11.4   To an EtherTalk (Apple) printer

The netatalk package includes something like nprint and smbclient. Others have documented the procedure for printing to and from an Apple network far better than I ever will; see the *Linux Netatalk-HOWTO* <http://thehamptons.com/anders/netatalk/>.

Obscure caveat of the week: Netatalk does not work with SMC Etherpower PCI Card with a DEC tulip chip.

11.5   To an HP or other ethernet printer

HPs and some other printers come with an ethernet interface which you can print to directly using lpd. You should follow the instructions that came with your printer or its network adaptor, but in general, such printers are "running" lpd, and provide one or more queues which you can print to. An HP, for example, might work with a printcap like:

```
lj-5|remote-hplj:\
        :lp=/dev/null:sh:\
        :sd=/var/spool/lpd/lj-5:\
        :rm=printer.name.com:rp=raw:
```

HP Laserjet printers with Jet Direct interfaces generally support two built in lpd queues - "raw" which accepts PCL (and possibly Postscript) and "text" which accepts straight ascii (and copes automatically with the staircase effect).

In a large scale environment, especially a large environment where some printers do not support PostScript, it may be useful to establish a dedicated print server to which all machines print and on which all ghostscript jobs are run.

This also allows your Linux box to act as a spool server for the printer so that your network users can complete their print jobs quickly and get on with things without waiting for the printer to print any other job that someone else has sent.

To do this, set up a queue on you linux box that points at the ethernet equipped HP LJ (as above). Now set up all the clients on your LAN to point at the Linux queue (eg lj-5 in the example above).

Some HP network printers apparently don't heed the banner page setting sent by clients; you can turn off their internally generated banner page by telnetting tot he printer, hitting return twice, typing "banner: 0" followed by "quit". There are other settings you can change this way, as well; type "?" to see a list.

11.5.1   To older HPs

Some printers (and printer networking "black boxes") support only a cheesy little non-protocol involving plain TCP connections. Notable in this category are early-model JetDirect (including some JetDirectEx) cards. Basically, to print to the printer, you must open a TCP connection to the printer on a specified port (typically 9100) and stuff your print job into it. This can be implemented, among other ways, in Perl:

```
#!/usr/bin/perl
# Thanks to Dan McLaughlin for writing the original version of this
# script (And to Jim W. Jones for sitting next to Dan when writing me
# for help ;)
```

```perl
$fileName = @ARGV[0];

open(IN,"$fileName") || die "Can't open file $fileName";

$dpi300    = "\x1B*t300R";
$dosCr     = "\x1B&k3G";
$ends = "\x0A";

$port =  9100 unless $port;
$them = "bach.sr.hp.com" unless $them;

$AF_INET = 2;
$SOCK_STREAM = 1;
$SIG{'INT'} = 'dokill';
$sockaddr = 'S n a4 x8';

chop($hostname = `hostname`);
($name,$aliases,$proto) = getprotobyname('tcp');
($name,$aliases,$port) = getservbyname($port,'tcp')
    unless $port =~ /^\d+$/;;
($name,$aliases,$type,$len,$thisaddr) =
        gethostbyname($hostname);
($name,$aliases,$type,$len,$thataddr) = gethostbyname($them);
$this = pack($sockaddr, $AF_INET, 0, $thisaddr);
$that = pack($sockaddr, $AF_INET, $port, $thataddr);

if (socket(S, $AF_INET, $SOCK_STREAM, $proto)) {
#    print "socket ok\n";
}
else {
    die $!;
}
# Give the socket an address.
if (bind(S, $this)) {
#    print "bind ok\n";
}
else {
    die $!;
}

# Call up the server.

if (connect(S,$that)) {
#    print "connect ok\n";
}
```

```
    else {
        die $!;
    }

    # Set socket to be command buffered.

    select(S); $| = 1; select(STDOUT);

    #    print S "@PJL ECHO Hi $hostname! $ends";
    #    print S "@PJL OPMSG DISPLAY=\"Job $whoami\" $ends";
    #    print S $dpi300;

    # Avoid deadlock by forking.

    if($child = fork) {
        print S $dosCr;
        print S $TimesNewR;

        while (<IN>) {
            print S;
        }
        sleep 3;
        do dokill();
    } else {
        while(<S>) {
            print;
        }
    }

    sub dokill {
        kill 9,$child if $child;
    }
```

11.6 Running an *if* for remote printers

One oddity of lpd is that the *if* is not run for remote printers. If you find that you need to run an *if*, you can do so by setting up a double queue and requeueing the job. As an example, consider this *printcap*:

```
lj-5:remote-hplj:\
        :lp=/dev/null:sh:\
        :sd=/var/spool/lpd/lj-5:\
        :if=/usr/lib/lpd/filter-lj-5:
lj-5-remote:lp=/dev/null:sh:rm=printer.name.com:\
        :rp=raw:sd=/var/spool/lpd/lj-5-raw:
```

in light of this filter-lj-5 script:

```
#!/bin/sh
gs <options> -q -dSAFER -sOutputFile=- - | \
        lpr -Plj-5-remote -U$5
```

The -*U* option to lpr only works if lpr is run as daemon, and it sets the submitter's name for the job in the resubmitted queue correctly. You should probably use a more robust method of getting the username, since in some cases it is not argument 5. See the man page for printcap <http://www.picante.com/~gtaylor/pht/man/printcap.html>.

11.7 From Windows.

Printing from a Windows (or presumably, OS/2) client to a Linux server is directly supported over SMB through the use of the SAMBA package, which also supports file sharing of your Linux filesystem to Windows clients.

Samba includes fairly complete documentation. You can either configure a magic filter on the Linux box and print PostScript to it, or run around installing printer-specific drivers on all the Windows machines and having a queue for them with no filters at all. Relying on the Windows drivers may in some cases produce better output, but is a bit more of an administrative hassle if there are many Windows boxen. So try PostScript first.

11.8 From an Apple.

Netatalk supports printing from Apple clients over EtherTalk. See the *Netatalk HOWTO Page* <http://thehamptons.com/anders/netatalk/> for more information.

11.9 From Netware.

There is some Netware service support available for Linux from or because of Caldera, but I have no idea if you can offer print services to Netware clients.

12 How to print to a fax machine.

12.1 Using a faxmodem

There are a number of fax programs out there that will let you fax and receive documents. One of the most complex is Sam Leffler's *HylaFax*, available from ftp.sgi.com. It supports all sorts of things from multiple modems to broadcasting.

Also available, and a better choice for most Linux boxen, is *efax* <http://www.picante.com/~gtaylor/pht/man/efax.html>, a simple program which sends faxes. The getty program mgetty can receive faxes (and even do voicemail on some modems!).

12.2 Using the Remote Printing Service

There is an experimental service offered that lets you send an email message containing something you'd like printed such that it will appear on a fax machine elsewhere. Nice formats like postscript are supported, so even though global coverage is spotty, this can still be a very useful service. For more information on printing via the remote printing service, see the *Remote Printing WWW Site* <http://www.tpc.int/>.

13 How to generate something worth printing.

Here we get into a real rat's-nest of software. Basically, Linux can run many types of binaries with varying degrees of success: Linux/x86, Linux/Alpha, Linux/Sparc, Linux/foo, iBCS, Win16/Win32s (with dosemu and, someday, with Wine), Mac/68k (with Executor), and Java. I'll just discuss native Linux and common Unix software, except to say that WordPerfect for SCO, and quite probably other commercial word processing software, runs fine under Linux's iBCS emulation, as does anything in pure Java (the Corel Office for Java Preview looked quite promising).

For Linux itself, choices are mostly limited to those available for Unix in general:

13.1 Markup languages

Most markup languages are more suitable for large or repetitive projects, where you want the computer to control the layout of the text to make things uniform. Trying to make a pretty sign in a markup language would probably hurt...

nroff

>   This was one of the first Unix markup languages. Man pages are the most common examples of things formatted in *roff macros; many people swear by them, but nroff has, to me at least, a more arcane syntax than needed, and probably makes a poor choice for new works. It is worth knowing, though, that you can typeset a man page directly into postscript with groff. Most man commands will do this for you with `man -t foo | lpr`.

TeX

>   TeX, and the macro package LaTeX, are one of the most widely used markup languages on Unix. Technical works are frequently written in LaTeX because it greatly simplifies the layout issues and is *still* one of the few text processing systems to support mathematics both completely and well. TeX's output format is `dvi`, and is converted to PostScript or Hewlett Packard's PCL with `dvips` or `dvilj`.

SGML

>   There is at least one free sgml parser available for Unix and Linux; it forms the basis of Linuxdoc-SGML's homegrown document system. It can support other DTD's, as well.

HTML

>   Someone suggested that for simple projects, it may suffice to write it in HTML and print it out using Netscape. I disagree, but YMMV.

13.2 WYSIWYG Word Processors

There is no longer any shortage of WYSIWYG word processing software. Several complete office suites are available, including one that's free for personal use (StarOffice).

StarOffice

>   A German company is distributing StarOffice 3.1 (as opposed to the newer version 4) on the net free for Linux. This full-blown office suite has all the features you'd expect, and you can't beat the price. There's a mini-HOWTO out there which describes how to obtain and install it. It generates PostScript or PCL, so should work with most any printer that works otherwise on Linux.

LyX

> LyX is a front-end to LaTeX which looks very promising. See the *LyX Homepage* <http://www-pu. informatik.uni-tuebingen.de/users/ettrich/> for more information.

The Andrew User Interface System

> AUIS includes ez, a WYSIWYG-style editor with most basic word processor features, HTML capabilities, and full MIME email and newsgroup support.

Commercial offerings

> At least Caldera and Red Hat ship packages containing the usual office apps like a WYSIWYGish word processor and a spreadsheet. I would assume they do a dandy job, but I've never used them. I think Caldera also ships Sun's WABI, so you could probably run something like MS Office under that if you had to integrate with other folks' files.

> Jeff Phillips <jeff@I_RATUS.org> uses Caldera's WordPerfect for Linux (on Slackware, of all things) and says that it works well. It apparently includes built-in printer support, as one would expect. Caldera should have info on <http://www.caldera.com/>.

> RedHat ships a suite called *Applixware*; you can find their web site at <http://www.redhat.com/>.

> Other vendors feel free to drop me a line with your offerings.

14 On-screen previewing of printable things.

Nearly anything you can print can be viewed on the screen, too.

14.1 PostScript

Ghostscript has an X11 driver best used under the management of the PostScript previewer *Ghostview* <http://www.picante.com/~gtaylor/pht/man/ghostview.html>. The latest versions of these programs should be able to view PDF files, as well.

14.2 TeX dvi

TeX DeVice Independant files may be previewed under X11 with *xdvi* <http://www.picante.com/~gtaylor/ pht/man/xdvi.html>. Modern versions of xdvi call ghostscript to render PostScript specials.

A VT100 driver exists as well. It's called dgvt. Tmview works with Linux and svgalib, if that's all you can do.

14.3 Adobe PDF

Adobe's Acrobat Reader is available for Linux; just download it form their web site <http://www.adobe. com/>.

You can also use xpdf, which is freeware and comes with source, and I should think Ghostview supports viewing PDF files with gs under X11 by now.

15   Serial printers under lpd

15.1   Setting up in printcap

Lpd provides five attributes which you can set in */etc/printcap* to control all the settings of the serial port a printer is on. Read the printcap <http://www.picante.com/~gtaylor/pht/man/printcap.html> man page and note the meanings of *br#*, *fc#*, *xc#*, *fs#* and *xs#*. The last four of these attributes are bitmaps indicating the settings for use the port. The *br#* atrribute is simply the baud rate, ie 'br#9600'.

It is very easy to translate from *stty* <http://www.picante.com/~gtaylor/pht/man/stty.html> settings to printcap flag settings. If you need to, see the man page for stty now.

Use stty to set up the printer port so that you can cat a file to it and have it print correctly. Here's what '*stty -a*' looks like for my printer port:

```
dina:/usr/users/andy/work/lpd/lpd# stty -a < /dev/ttyS2
speed 9600 baud; rows 0; columns 0; line = 0;
intr = ^C; quit = ^\; erase = ^?; kill = ^U; eof = ^D; eol = <undef>;
eol2 = <undef>; start = ^Q; stop = ^S; susp = ^Z; rprnt = ^R; werase = ^W;
lnext = ^V; min = 1; time = 0;
-parenb -parodd cs8 hupcl -cstopb cread -clocal -crtscts
-ignbrk -brkint -ignpar -parmrk -inpck -istrip -inlcr
-igncr -icrnl ixon -ixoff -iuclc -ixany -imaxbel
-opost -olcuc -ocrnl -onlcr -onocr -onlret -ofill -ofdel nl0 cr0 tab0
bs0 vt0 ff0
-isig -icanon -iexten -echo -echoe -echok -echonl -noflsh -xcase
-tostop -echoprt -echoctl -echoke
```

The only changes between this and the way the port is initialized at bootup are -clocal, -crtscts, and ixon. Your port may well be different depending on how your printer does flow control.

You actually use stty in a somewhat odd way. Since stty operates on the terminal connected to it's standard input, you use it to manipulate a given serial port by using the '<' character as above.

Once you have your stty settings right, so that '*cat file > /dev/ttyS2*' (in my case) sends the file to the printer, look at the file /usr/src/linux/include/asm-i386/termbits.h. This contains a lot of #defines and a few structs (You may wish to cat this file to the printer (you do have that working, right?) and use it as scratch paper). Go to the section that starts out

```
/* c_cflag bit meaning */
#define CBAUD    0000017
```

This section lists the meaning of the *fc#* and *fs#* bits. You will notice that the names there (after the baud rates) match up with one of the lines of stty output. Didn't I say this was going to be easy?

Note which of those settings are preceded with a - in your stty output. Sum up all those numbers (they are octal). This represents the bits you want to clear, so the result is your *fc#* capability. Of course, remember that you will be setting bits directly after you clear, so you can just use 'fc#0177777' (I do).

Now do the same for those settings (listed in this section) which do not have a - before them in your stty output. In my example the important ones are CS8 (0000060), HUPCL (0002000), and CREAD (0000200). Also note the flags for your baud rate (mine is 0000015). Add those all up, and in my example you get 0002275. This goes in your *fs#* capability ('fs#02275' works fine in my example).

Do the same with set and clear for the next section of the include file, "c_lflag bits". In my case I didn't have to set anything, so I just use 'xc#0157777' and 'xs#0'.

15.2 Older serial printers that drop characters

Jon Luckey points out that some older serial printers with ten-cent serial interfaces and small buffers *really* mean stop when they say so with flow control. He found that disabling the FIFO in his Linux box's 16550 serial port with *setserial* <http://www.picante.com/~gtaylor/pht/man/setserial.html> corrected the problem of dropped characters (you apparently just specify the uart type as an 8250 to do this).

16 Credits

The smbprint information is from an article by Marcel Roelofs <marcel@paragon.nl>.

The nprint information for using Netware printers was provided by Michael Smith <mikes@bioch.ox.ac.uk>.

The serial printers under lpd section is from Andrew Tefft <teffta@engr.dnet.ge.com>.

The blurb about gammas and such for gs was sent in by Andreas <quasi@hub-fue.franken.de>.

The two paragraphs about the 30 second closing_wait of the serial diver was contributed by Cris Johnson <cdj@netcom.com>.

Robert Hart sent a few excellent paragraphs about setting up a print server to networked HPs which I used verbatim.

And special thanks to the dozens upon dozens of you who've pointed out typos, bad urls, and errors in the document over the years.

The Linux Printing Usage HOWTO

by Mark Komarinski <markk@auratek.com>

v1.2.2, 6 February 1998

1 Introduction

This document describes how to use the line printer spooling system provided with the Linux operating system. This HOWTO is the supplementary document to the Linux Printing Setup HOWTO, which discusses the installation and setup of the Linux printing system. The material presented in this HOWTO should be equally relevent for all flavors of the BSD operating system in addition to the Linux operating system.

1.1 Linux Printing HOWTO History

Note from Mark Komarinski <markk@auratek.com>:

I'd like to thank Matt Foster for doing a lot of work in the re-write of this HOWTO. I'm keeping his style, and adding when necessary to keep everything updated.

Note from Matt Foster <mwf@engr.uark.edu>:

This version of the Linux Printing HOWTO is a complete rewrite of the one originally written by Grant Taylor <grant@god.tufts.edu> and Brian McCauley <B.A.McCauley@bham.ac.uk>. I have tried to keep with the coverage of material presented by Grant and Brian's HOWTO, but I have drastically modified the style of presentation and the depth of material covered. I feel that this makes the HOWTO more complete and easier to read. I can only hope that you agree.

1.2 Version History

v1.2.2

- Re-indexed, other changes to fit in the new RedHat docs. Thanks Ed!

v1.2.1

- updates, some changes for Dr. Linux publication

v1.2

- Windows Printers
- Changing max size of print files

v1.11

- new maintainter!
- Added lpc info
- Added some info for troubleshooting
- A start on printing graphics files!

v1.1

- revised some of the wording
- developed section on PostScript printing
- attempted to clarify some of the examples 8-)
- fleshed the discussion of the basic Linux printing utilities

v1.0

- initial public release of the Printing Usage HOWTO

1.3 Copyrights and Trademarks

Some names mentioned in this HOWTO are claimed as copyrights and/or trademarks of certain persons and/or companies. These names appear in full or initial caps in this HOWTO.

(c) 1995 Matt Foster (mwf@engr.uark.edu)
(c) 1996-1997 Mark F. Komarinski (markk@auratek.com)

All translations, derivative works, or aggregate works incorporating any Linux HOWTO documents must be covered under this copyright notice.

That is, you may not produce a derivative work from a HOWTO and impose additional restrictions on its distribution. Exceptions to these rules may be granted under certain conditions; please contact the Linux HOWTO coordinator at the address given below.

In short, we wish to promote dissemination of this information through as many channels as possible. However, we do wish to retain copyright on the HOWTO documents, and would like to be notified of any plans to redistribute the HOWTOs.

If you have questions, please contact Greg Hankins, the Linux HOWTO coordinator, at <gregh@sunsite.unc.edu>. You may finger this address for phone number and additional contact information.

1.4 Downloading the Linux Printing HOWTOs

I recommend that if you want to print a copy of this HOWTO that you download the PostScript version. It is formatted in a fashion that is aesthetically appealing and easier to read. You can get the PostScript version from one of the many Linux distribution sites (such as SunSITE `<ftp://sunsite.unc.edu/pub/Linux/docs/HOWTO/>`).

1.5 Feedback

Questions, comments, or corrections for this HOWTO may be directed to <markk@auratek.com>.

1.6 Acknowledgments

Thanks go out to all of the people who took the time to read the alpha version of this HOWTO and respond with many helpful comments and suggestions—some of you may see your comments reflected in the version.

I'd also like to thank Matt Foster who did the original re-write.

2 Printing Under Linux

This section discusses how to print files, examine the print queue, remove jobs from the print queue, format files before printing them, and configure your printing environment.

2.1 History of Linux Printing

The Linux printing system—the *lp* system—is a port of the source code written by the Regents of the University of California for the Berkeley Software Distribution version of the UNIX operating system.

2.2 Printing a File Using *lpr*

By far, the most simplistic way to print in the Linux operating system is to send the file to be printed directly to the printing device. One way to do this is to use the *cat* command. As the **root** user, one could do something like

```
# cat thesis.txt > /dev/lp
```

In this case, /dev/lp is a symbolic link to the actual printing device—be it a dot-matrix, laser printer, typesetter, or plotter. (See *ln*(1) for more information on symbolic links.)

For the purpose of security, only the **root** user and users in the same group as the print daemon are able to write directly to the printer. This is why commands such as *lpr*, *lprm*, and *lpq* have to be used to access the printer.

Because of this, users have to use *lpr* to print a file. The *lpr* command takes care of all the initial work needed to print the file, and then it hands control over to another program, *lpd*, the line printing daemon. The line printing daemon then tells the printer how to print the file.

When *lpr* is executed, it first copies the specified file to a certain directory (the spool directory) where the file remains until *lpd* prints it. Once *lpd* is told that there is a file to print, it will spawn a copy of itself (what we programmers call forking). This copy will print our file while the original copy waits for more requests. This allows for multiple jobs to be queued at once.

The syntax of *lpr*(1) is a very familiar one,

```
$ lpr [ options ] [ filename ... ]
```

If `filename` is not specified, *lpr* expects input to come from standard input (usually the keyboard, or another program's output). This enables the user to redirect a command's output to the print spooler. As such,

```
$ cat thesis.txt | lpr
```

or,

```
$ pr -l60 thesis.txt | lpr
```

The *lpr* command accepts several command-line arguments that allow a user to control how it works. Some of the most widely used arguments are: -P*printer* specifies the printer to use, -h suppresses printing of the burst page, -s creates a symbolic link instead of copying the file to the spool directory (useful for large files), and -#*num* specifies the number of copies to print. An example interaction with *lpr* might be something like

```
$ lpr -#2 -sP dj thesis.txt
```

This command will create a symbolic link to the file thesis.txt in the spool directory for the printer named *dj*, where it would be processed by *lpd*. It would then print a second copy of thesis.txt.

For a listing of all the options that *lpr* will recognize, see *lpr*(1).

2.3   Viewing the Print Queue with *lpq*

To view the contents of the print queue, use the *lpq* command. Issued without arguments, it returns the contents of the default printer's queue.

The returned output of *lpq* can be useful for many purposes.

```
$ lpq
lp is ready and printing
Rank    Owner     Job  Files              Total Size
active  mwf       31   thesis.txt         682048 bytes
```

2.4   Canceling a Print Job Using *lprm*

Another useful feature of any printing system is the ability to cancel a job that has been previously queued. To do this, use *lprm*.

```
$ lprm -
```

The above command cancels all of the print jobs that are owned by the user who issued the command. A single print job can be canceled by first getting the job number as reported by *lpq* and then giving that number to *lprm*. For example,

```
$ lprm 31
```

would cancel job 31 (thesis.txt) on the default printer.

2.5   Controlling the lpd program with *lpc*

The *lpc*(8) program is used to control the printers that lpd serves. you can enable or disable a printer or its queues, rearrange entries within a queue, and get a status report on the printers and their queues. Lpc is mostly used in a setup where there are multiple printers hanging off one machine.

```
$ lpc
```

The above will start the lpc program. By default, this enters you into an interactive mode, and you can begin issuing commands. The other option is to issue an lpc command on the command line.

```
$ lpc status all
```

A list of the available commands are in the *lpd* man page, but here are a few of the major commands you'll want to know about. Any commands marked with *option* can either be a printer name (lp, print, etc) or the keyword all, which means all printers.

- disable *option* - prevents any new printer job from being entered
- down *option* - disables all printing on the printer
- enable *option* - allow new jobs to enter the print queue
- quit (or exit) - leave lpc
- restart *option* - restarts lpd for that printer
- status *option* - print status of printer
- up *option* - enable everything and start a new lpd

2.6   The RedHat printtool

Just a quick note here on RedHat's amazing printtool program. It seems to do everything that a magicfilter would do. RedHat already installs many of the programs to do the filtering. Here's how I have my printer set up under RH 4.0 with an HP LJ 4L connected to my parallel port (should be the same for other versions of RH as well).

- Become root and fire up printtool (if you su'ed, you remembered to SETENV DISPLAY :0.0 and xhost +, right?)
- Click "Add", and hit "OK" for a local printer.
- Fill in the printer device (/dev/lp1 for me)
- Fill in the input filter - Select a printer type, resolution, and paper size (ljet4, 300x300, and letter)
- Hit "OK" all the way back, and restart the lpd.

Just like rolling an /etc/printcap file by hand, you can have multiple printer definitions for each physical printer. One for different paper sizes, resolutions, etc.

3   Printing files

This section covers printing the kinda of files that you'll run across in a Linux setup.

3.1   Printing graphics files

Printing graphics files through a printer usually depends on the kind of graphics you're converting, and the kind of printer you want to send to. Dot matrix is usually out of the question due to differences in the way dot-matrix handles graphics. Your best bet in this situation is to see if your printer is compatable with an Epson or an IBM ProPrinter, then convert the graphics file to PostScript, then use Ghostscript (see next section) to print the graphics.

If you have a laser printer, things are a bit easier since many are compatable with PCL. This now gives you a few options. Some programs may output directly in PCL. If not, programs like *NetPBM* can convert into PCL. Last option is to use ghostscript (see next section).

Your absolutely best option is to install packages like NetPBM and Ghostscript then installing a magic filter to process the graphics files automagically.

3.2   Printing PostScript files

Printing PostScript files on a printer that has a PostScript interpreter is simple; just use *lpr*, and the printer will take care of all of the details for you. For those of us that don't have printers with PostScript capabilities, we have to resort to other means. Luckily, there are programs available that can make sense of PostScript, and translate it into a language that most printers will understand. Probably the most well known of these programs is Ghostscript.

Ghostscript's responsibility is to convert all of the descriptions in a PostScript file to commands that the printer will understand. To print a PostScript file using Ghostscript, you might do something like

```
$ gs -dSAFER -dNOPAUSE -sDEVICE=deskjet -sOutputFile=\|lpr thesis.ps
```

Notice in the above example that we are actually piping the output of Ghostscript to the *lpr* command by using the **-sOutputFile** option.

Ghostview is an interface to Ghostscript for the X Window System. It allows you to preview a PostScript file before you print it. Ghostview and Ghostscript can both be swiped from `<ftp://prep.ai.mit.edu/pub/gnu/>`.

3.3   Printing PDF files

Adobe has released an Acrobat reader for Linux, and it's available on the Adobe home page `<http://www.adobe.com>`. Its predecessor, xpdf, is also available. Both should print to a postscript device.

3.4   Printing TeX files

One of the easiest ways to print TeX files is to convert them to PostScript and then print them using Ghostscript. To do this, you first need to convert them from TeX to a format known as DVI (which stands for device-independent). You can do this with the *tex*(1) command. Then you need to convert the DVI file to a PostScript file using *dvips*. All of this would look like the following when typed in.

```
$ tex thesis.tex
$ dvips thesis.dvi
```

Now you are ready to print the resulting PostScript file as described above.

3.5   Printing troff formatted files

```
$ groff -Tascii thesis.tr | lpr
```

or, if you prefer,

```
$ groff thesis.tr > thesis.ps
```

and then print the PostScript file as described above.

3.6 Printing man pages

```
$ man man | col -b | lpr
```

The man pages contain pre-formatted `troff` data, so we have to strip out any highlighting, underlines, etc. The 'col' program does this just nicely, and since we're piping data, the `man` program won't use `more`.

4 Miscellaneous Items

This covers topics not in any of the others.

4.1 Formatting Before Printing

Since most ASCII files are not formatted for printing, it is useful to format them in some way before they are actually printed. This may include putting a title and page number on each page, setting the margins, double spacing, indenting, or printing a file in multiple columns. A common way to do this is to use a print preprocessor such as *pr*.

```
$ pr +4 -d -h"Ph.D. Thesis, 2nd Draft" -l60 thesis.txt | lpr
```

In the above example, *pr* would take the file `thesis.txt` and skip the first three pages (+4), set the page length to sixty lines (-l60), double space the output (-d), and add the phrase "Ph.D. Thesis, 2nd Draft" to the top of each page (-h). *Lpr* would then queue *pr*'s output. See its on-line manual page for more information on using *pr*.

4.2 The PRINTER Environment Variables

All of the commands in the Linux printing system accept the **-P** option. This option allows the user to specify which printer to use for output. If a user doesn't specify which printer to use, then the default printer will be assumed as the output device.

Instead of having to specify a printer to use every time that you print, you can set the PRINTER environment variable to the name of the printer that you want to use. This is accomplished in different ways for each shell. For *bash* you can do this with

```
$ PRINTER="printer_name"; export PRINTER
```

and *csh*, you can do it with

```
% setenv PRINTER "printer_name"
```

These commands can be placed in your login scripts (.profile for *bash*, or .cshrc for *csh*), or issued on the command-line. (See *bash*(1) and *csh*(1) for more information on environment variables.)

5 Answers to Frequently Asked Questions

Q1. How do I prevent the staircase effect?

A1. The staircase effect is caused by the way some printers expect lines to be terminated. Some printers want lines that end with a carriage-return/line-feed sequence (DOS-style) instead of the line-feed sequence used for UNIX-type systems. The easiest way to fix this is to see if your printer can switch between the two styles somehow—either by flipping a DIP switch, or by sending an escape sequence at the start of each print job. To do the latter, you need to create a filter (see Q2).

A quick fix is to use a filter on the command-line. An example of this might be

```
$ cat thesis.txt | todos | lpr
```

Q2. What is a filter?

A2. A filter is a program that reads from standard input (*stdin*), performs some action on this input, and writes to standard output (*stdout*). Filters are used for a lot of things, including text processing.

Q3. What is a *magic* filter?

A3. A magic filter is a filter that performs an action based on a file's type. For example, if the file is a plain, text file, it would simply print the file using the normal methods. If the file is a PostScript file, or any other format, it would print it using another method (ghostscript). Two examples of this is magicfilter and APSfilter. One caveat of these filters is that the appropriate programs have to be installed before you install the filter.

The reason for this is that when the magicfilter gets installed, it queries your system for specific programs (such as ghostscript - if it finds it, then it knows it can handle PostScript data), then builds itself based on what it finds. To handle all the printer files, you should probably have at least the following installed:

- GhostScript
- TeX
- NetPBM
- jpeg utilities
- gzip

Q4. What about the Windows Printing System? Will Linux work with that?

A4. Maybe. Printers that accept only the WPS commands will not work with Linux. Printers that accept WPS and other commands (such as the Canon BJC 610) will work, as long as they're set to something other than WPS format. Other printers, such as some HP DeskJet 820Cxi/Cse, will *not* work with Linux. That being said, Linux can act as a print server (See Samba) for Win95 machines, since Win95 has drivers for those printers.

Q5. What kinda cheey system is this? I can't print more than 6 pages or else I get a "file too large" error.

A5. One of the options in the /etc/printcap file relates to the maximum size of a print file. The default is 1000 disk blocks (about 500k?). For PostScript files and the like, this will give you maybe 6-8 pages with graphics and all. Be sure to add the following line in the printer definition:

```
mx=0
```

The primary reason for this is to keep the spool partition from getting filled. There is another way to do it, by making lpr create a soft link from the spool directory to your print file. But you have to remember to add the -s option to lpr every time.

6 Troubleshooting

This section covers some common things that can go wrong with your printing system.

If your printer doesn't work:

- Do other print jobs work? (application problem?)
- Is lpd running? (check it using lpc) (print controller?)
- Can root send something directly to the printer? (print services?)
- Can you print from DOS? (cable/printer problem?)

Answering these questions can help find a solution.

Send other suggestions for this section to <markk@auratek.com>.

7 References

This is a section of references on the Linux printing system. I have tried to keep the references section of this HOWTO as focused as possible. If you feel that I have forgotten a significant reference work, please do not hesitate to contact me.

Before you post your question to a USENET group, consider the following:

- Is the printer accepting jobs? (Use *lpc*(8) to verify.)
- Is the answer to your question covered in this HOWTO or Grant Taylor's Printing HOWTO?

If any of the above are true, you may want to think twice before you post your question. And, when you do finally post to a newsgroup, try to include pertinent information. Try not to just say something like, "I'm having trouble with lpr, please help." These types of posts will most definitely be ignored by many. Also try to include the kernel version that you're running, how the error occured, and, if any, the specific error message that the system returned.

On-Line Manual Pages

- *cat*(1) concatenate and print files
- *dvips*(1) convert a TeX DVI file to PostScript
- *ghostview*(1) view PostScript documents using Ghostscript
- *groff*(1) front-end for the groff document formatting system
- *gs*(1) Ghostscript interpreter/viewer
- *lpc*(8) line printer control program
- *lpd*(8) line printer spooler daemon
- *lpq*(1) spool queue examination program
- *lpr*(1) off-line printer
- *lprm*(1) remove jobs from the line printer spooling queue
- *pr*(1) convert text files for printing
- *tex*(1) text formatting and typesetting

USENET newsgroups

- comp.os.linux.* a plethora of information on Linux
- comp.unix.* discussions relating to the UNIX operating system

The Linux Tips HOWTO

Paul Anderson, paul@geeky1.ebtech.net   v3.1, 26 December 1997

This HOWTO contains those hard to find hints and tweekings that make Linux a bit nicer.

Contents

1 Introduction

Welcome to the **Linux Tips HOWTO**, a list of neato tricks and optimizations that make Linux more fun. All I have in here right now are tips off of the top of my head, and tips from the old Tips-HOWTO(Why take out decent tips, right?). So send all your favorite hints and tips to me so I can put them in the next Tips-HOWTO.

Paul Anderson *Maintainer–Linux TIPS HOWTO*

`panderso@ebtech.net`

2 Short Tips

2.1 Handy Syslog Trick *Paul Anderson, Tips-HOWTO maintainer*

Edit your /etc/syslog.conf, and put in the following line:

```
# Dump everything on tty8
*.*                                      /dev/tty8
```

One caveat: *REMEMBER TO USE TABS!* syslog doesn't like spaces...

2.2 Script to view those compressed HOWTOs. *Didier Juges,* `dj@destin.nfds.net`

From a newbie to another, here is a short script that eases looking for and viewing howto documents. My howto's are in /usr/doc/faq/howto/ and are gzipped. The file names are XXX-HOWTO.gz, XXX being the subject. I created the following script called "howto" in the /usr/local/sbin directory:

```
#!/bin/sh
if [ "$1" = "" ]; then
    ls /usr/doc/faq/howto | less
else
    gunzip -c /usr/doc/faq/howto/$1-HOWTO.gz | less
fi
```

When called without argument, it displays a directory of the available howto's. Then when entered with the first part of the file name (before the hyphen) as an argument, it unzips (keeping the original intact) then displays the document.

For instance, to view the Serial-HOWTO.gz document, enter:

$ howto Serial

2.3   Is   there   enough   free   space???   *Hans   Zoebelein,* zocki@goldfish.cube.net

Here comes a short script which will check from time to time that there is enough free space available on anything which shows up in mount (disks, cdrom, floppy...)

If space runs out, a message is printed every X seconds to the screen and 1 mail message per filled device is fired up.

```sh
#!/bin/sh

#
# $Id: check_hdspace,v 1.18 1996/12/11 22:33:29 root Exp root $
#


#
# Since I got mysterious error messages during compile when
# tmp files filled up my disks, I wrote this to get a warning
# before disks are full.
#
# If this stuff saved your servers from exploding,
# send praising email to zocki@goldfish.cube.net.
# If your site burns down because of this, sorry but I
# warned you: no comps.
# If you really know how to handle sed, please forgive me :)
#


#
# Shoot and forget: Put 'check_hdspace &' in rc.local.
# Checks for free space on devices every $SLEEPTIME sec.
# You even might check your floppies or tape drives. :)
# If free space is below $MINFREE (kb), it will echo a warning
# and send one mail for each triggering device to $MAIL_TO_ME.
# If there is more free space than trigger limit again,
# mail action is also armed again.
#


# TODO: Different $MINFREE for each device.
# Free /*tmp dirs securely from old junk stuff if no more free space.
```

```
DEVICES='/dev/sda2 /dev/sda8 /dev/sda9'     # device; your put disks here
MINFREE=20480                               # kb; below this do warning
SLEEPTIME=10                                # sec; sleep between checks
MAIL_TO_ME='root@localhost'                 # fool; to whom mail warning


# ------- no changes needed below this line (hopefully :) -------


MINMB=0
ISFREE=0
MAILED=""
let MINMB=$MINFREE/1024        # yep, we are strict :)

while [ 1 ]; do
        DF="`/bin/df`"
                for DEVICE in $DEVICES ; do
                ISFREE=`echo $DF | sed s#.\*$DEVICE" "\*[0-9]\*""\*[0-9]\*" "\*## | sed s#" "

                if [ $ISFREE -le $MINFREE ] ; then
                        let ISMB=$ISFREE/1024
                        echo  "WARNING: $DEVICE only $ISMB mb free." >&2
                        #echo "more stuff here" >&2
                        echo -e "\a\a\a\a"

                        if [ -z  "`echo $MAILED | grep -w $DEVICE`" ] ; then
                                echo "WARNING: $DEVICE only $ISMB mb free.        (Trigger is s
                                | mail -s "WARNING: $DEVICE only $ISMB mb free!" $MAIL_TO_ME
                                MAILEDH="$MAILED $DEVICE"
                                MAILED=$MAILEDH
                                # put further action here like cleaning
                                # up */tmp dirs...
                        fi
                        elif [ -n  "`echo $MAILED | grep -w $DEVICE`" ] ; then
                                # Remove mailed marker if enough disk space
                                # again. So we are ready for new mailing action.
                                MAILEDH="`echo $MAILED  | sed s#$DEVICE##`"
                                MAILED=$MAILEDH
                        fi

                done
        sleep $SLEEPTIME

done
```

2.4 Util to clean up your logfiles. *Paul Anderson, Tips-HOWTO Maintainer>*

If you're like me, you have a list with 250 subscribers, plus 100+ messages per day coming in over UUCP. Well, what's a hacker to do with these huge logs? Install chklogs, that's what. Chklogs is written by Emilio Grimaldo, grimaldo@panama.iaehv.nl, and the current version 1.8 available from ftp.iaehv.nl:/pub/users/grimaldo/chklogs-1.8.tar.gz. It's pretty self explanatory to install(you will, of course, check out the info in the doc subdirectory). Once you've got it installed, add a crontab entry like this:

```
# Run chklogs at 9:00PM daily.
00 21 * * *        /usr/local/sbin/chklogs -m
```

While you're at it, mention to the author how nice a peice of software this is:)

2.5 Handy Script to Clean Up Corefiles. *Otto Hammersmith,* ohammers@cu-online.com

Create a file called rmcores(the author calls it handle-cores) with the following in it:

```
#!/bin/sh
USAGE="$0 <directory> <message-file>"


if [ $# != 2 ] ; then
        echo $USAGE
        exit
fi


 echo Deleting...
find $1 -name core -atime 7 -print -exec rm {} \;


echo e-mailing
for name in 'find $1 -name core -exec ls -l {} \; | cut -c16-24'
do
        echo $name
        cat $2 | mail $name
done
```

And have a cron job run it every so often.

2.6 Moving directories between filesystems. *Alan Cox,* A.Cox@swansea.ac.uk

Quick way to move an entire tree of files from one disk to another

```
(cd /source/directory && tar cf - . ) | (cd /dest/directory && tar xvfp -)
```

[Change from cd /source/directory; tar....etc. to prevent possibility of trashing directory in case of disaster. Thanks to Jim Dennis, jadestar@rahul.net, for letting me know. -Maint.]

2.7 Finding out which directories are the largest. *Mick Ghazey,* `mghazey@miso.lowdown.com`

Ever wondered which directories are the biggest on your computer? Here's how to find out.

```
du -S | sort -n
```

2.8 The Linux Gazette

Kudos go to John Fisk, creator of the Linux Gazette. This is an excellent e-zine plus, it's **FREE!!!** Now what more could you ask? Check it out at:

```
http://www.ssc.com/lg
```

BTW, It turns out that (1) LG is now out on a monthly basis, and (2) John Fisk no longer maintains it, the fellows at SSC do.

2.9 Pointer to patch for GNU Make 3.70 to change VPATH behavior. *Ted Stern,* `stern@amath.washington.edu`

I don't know if many people have this problem, but there is a "feature" of GNU make version 3.70 that I don't like. It is that VPATH acts funny if you give it an absolute pathname. There is an extremely solid patch that fixes this, which you can get from Paul D. Smith `<psmith@wellfleet.com>`. He also posts the documentation and patch after every revision of GNU make on the newsgroup "gnu.utils.bug" Generally, I apply this patch and recompile gmake on every system I have access to.

2.10 How do I stop my system from fscking on each reboot? *Dale Lutz,* `dal@wimsey.com`

Q: How do I stop e2fsck from checking my disk every time I boot up.

A: When you rebuild the kernel, the filesystem is marked as 'dirty' and so your disk will be checked with each boot. The fix is to run:

rdev -R /zImage 1

This fixes the kernel so that it is no longer convinced that the filesystem is dirty.

Note: If using lilo, then add `read-only` *to your linux setup in your lilo config file (Usually /etc/lilo.conf)*

2.11 How to avoid fscks caused by "device busy" at reboot time. *Jon Tombs,* `jon@gtex02.us.es`

If you often get device busy errors on shutdown that leave the filesystem in need of an fsck upon reboot, here is a simple fix:

To `/etc/rc.d/init.d/halt` or `/etc/rc.d/rc.0`, add the line

```
mount -o remount,ro /mount.dir
```

for all your mounted filesystems except /, before the call to umount -a. This means if, for some reason, shutdown fails to kill all processes and umount the disks they will still be clean on reboot. Saves a lot of time at reboot for me.

2.12   How to find the biggest files on your hard-drive.

Simon Amor, `simon@foobar.co.uk`

```
ls -l | sort +4n
```

Or, for those of you really scrunched for space this takes awhile but works great:

```
cd /
ls -lR | sort +4n
```

2.13   How to print pages with a margin for hole punching. *Mike Dickey,* `mdickey@thorplus.lib.purdue.edu`

```
#!/bin/sh
# /usr/local/bin/print
# a simple formatted printout, to enable someone to
# 3-hole punch the output and put it in a binder

cat $1 | pr -t -o 5 -w 85 | lpr
```

2.14   A way to search through trees of files for a particular regular expression. *Raul Deluth Miller,* `rockwell@nova.umd.edu`

I call this script 'forall'. Use it like this:

```
forall /usr/include grep -i ioctl
forall /usr/man grep ioctl
```

Here's forall:

```
#!/bin/sh
if [ 1 = `expr 2 \> $#` ]
then
        echo Usage: $0 dir cmd [optargs]
        exit 1
fi
dir=$1
shift
find $dir -type f -print | xargs "$@"
```

2.15 A script for cleaning up after programs that create autosave and backup files. *Barry Tolnas,* tolnas@nestor.engr.utk.edu

Here is a simple two-liner which recursively descends a directory hierarchy removing emacs auto-save (#) and backup (~) files, .o files, and TeX .log files. It also compresses .tex files and README files. I call it 'squeeze' on my system.

```
#!/bin/sh
#SQUEEZE removes unnecessary files and compresses .tex and README files
#By Barry tolnas, tolnas@sun1.engr.utk.edu
#
echo squeezing $PWD
find  $PWD \( -name \*~ -or -name \*.o -or -name \*.log -or -name \*\#\) -exec
rm -f {} \;
find $PWD \( -name \*.tex -or -name \*README\* -or -name \*readme\* \) -exec gzip -9 {} \;
```

2.16 How to find out what process is eating the most memory. *Simon Amor,* simon@foobar.co.uk

```
ps -aux | sort +4n
```

-OR-

```
ps -aux | sort +5n
```

2.17 Rigging vi for C programming, *Paul Anderson,*Tips-HOWTO Maintainer

I do a lot of C programming in my spare time, and I've taken the time to rig vi to be C friendly. Here's my .exrc:

```
set autoindent
set shiftwidth=4
set backspace=2
set ruler
```

What does this do? autoindent causes vi to automatically indent each line following the first one indented, shiftwidth sets the distance of ^T to 4 spaces, backspace sets the backspace mode, and ruler makes it display the line number. Remember, to go to a specific line number, say 20, use:

```
vi +20 myfile.c
```

2.18 Why does sendmail hang for 5 minutes on startup with RedHat? *Paul Anderson,* paul@geeky1.ebtech.net

This is a fairly common problem, almost to the point of being a FAQ. I don't know if RedHat has fixed this bug in their distribution, but you can repair it yourself. If you look in your /etc/hosts file, you will find it looks something like:

```
127.0.0.1          localhost          yourbox
```

When sendmail starts, it does a lookup on your hostname(in this example, yourbox). It then finds that the IP for yourbox is 127.0.0.1, sendmail doesn't like this, so it does the lookup again. It continues with this for a while until it eventually gives up and exits. Fixing the problem is extremely easy, edit your /etc/hosts file and change it to something like this:

```
127.0.0.1          localhost
10.56.142.1        yourbox
```

2.19 How do I configure RedHat for using color-ls? *Paul Anderson,* paul@geeky1.ebtech.net

RedHat's distribution comes with color-ls, however why they don't configure it for colour use by default is beyond me. Here's to fix it.

First, type eval 'DIRCOLORS'

Next, alias ls='ls --color=yes'

And put the 'alias.....' in your /etc/bashrc

2.20 How do I find which library in /usr/lib holds a certain function? *Pawel Veselow,* vps@unicorn.niimm.spb.su

What if you're compiling and you've missed a library that needed linking in? All gcc reports are function names... Here's a simple command that'll find what you're looking for:

```
for i in *; do echo $i:;nm $i|grep tgetnum 2>/dev/null;done
```

Where tgetnum is the name of the function you're looking for.

3 Detailed Tips

3.1 Sharing swap partitions between Linux and Windows. *Tony Acero,* ace3@midway.uchicago.edu

1. Format the partition as a dos partition, and create the Windows swap file on it, but don't run windows yet. (You want to keep the swap file completely empty for now, so that it compresses well).

2. Boot linux and save the partition into a file. For example if the partition was /dev/hda8:

   ```
   dd if=/dev/hda8 of=/etc/dosswap
   ```

3. Compress the dosswap file; since it is virtually all 0's it will compress very well

   ```
   gzip -9 /etc/dosswap
   ```

4. Add the following to the /etc/rc file to prepare and install the swap space under Linux:
   XXXXX is the number of blocks in the swap partition

```
mkswap /dev/hda8 XXXXX
swapon -av
```

Make sure you add an entry for the swap partition in your /etc/fstab file

5. If your init/reboot package supports /etc/brc or /sbin/brc add the following to /etc/brc, else do this by hand when you want to boot to dos|os/2 and you want to convert the swap partition back to the dos/windows version:

```
swapoff -av
zcat /etc/dosswap.gz | dd of=/dev/hda8 bs=1k count=100
```

Note that this only writes the first 100 blocks back to the partition. I've found empirically that this is sufficient

>> What are the pros and cons of doing this?

Pros: you save a substantial amount of disk space.

Cons: if step 5 is not automatic, you have to remember to do it by hand, and it slows the reboot process by a nanosecond :-)

3.2 Desperate Undelete. *Michael Hamilton,* michael@actrix.gen.nz

Here's a trick I've had to use a few times.

Desperate person's text file undelete.

If you accidentally remove a text file, for example, some email, or the results of a late night programming session, all may not be lost. If the file ever made it to disk, ie it was around for more than 30 seconds, its contents may still be in the disk partition.

You can use the grep command to search the raw disk partition for the contents of file.

For example, recently, I accidentally deleted a piece of email. So I immediately ceased any activity that could modify that partition: in this case I just refrained from saving any files or doing any compiles etc. On other occasions, I've actually gone to the trouble of bring the system down to single user mode, and unmounted the filesystem.

I then used the egrep command on the disk partition: in my case the email message was in /usr/local/home/michael/, so from the output from df, I could see this was in /dev/hdb5

```
sputnik3:~ % df
Filesystem         1024-blocks  Used Available Capacity Mounted on
/dev/hda3              18621     9759      7901      55%  /
/dev/hdb3             308852   258443     34458      88%  /usr
/dev/hdb5             466896   407062     35720      92%  /usr/local

sputnik3:~ % su
Password:
[michael@sputnik3 michael]# egrep -50 'ftp.+COL' /dev/hdb5 > /tmp/x
```

Now I'm ultra careful when fooling around with disk partitions, so I paused to make sure I understood the command syntax BEFORE pressing return. In this case the email contained the word 'ftp' followed by some text followed by the word 'COL'. The message was about 20 lines long, so I used -50 to get all the lines around the phrase. In the past I've used -3000 to make sure I got all the lines of some source code. I directed the output from the egrep to a different disk partition - this prevented it from over writing the message I was looking for.

I then used strings to help me inspect the output

```
strings /tmp/x | less
```

Sure enough the email was in there.

This method can't be relied on, all, or some, of the disk space may have already been re-used.

This trick is probably only useful on single user systems. On multi-users systems with high disk activity, the space you free'ed up may have already been reused. And most of use can't just rip the box out from under our users when ever we need to recover a file.

On my home system this trick has come in handy on about three occasions in the past few years - usually when I accidentally trash some of the days work. If what I'm working survives to a point where I feel I made significant progress, it get's backed up onto floppy, so I haven't needed this trick very often.

3.3 How to use the immutable flag. *Jim Dennis*, jadestar@rahul.net

Use the Immutable Flag

Right after you install and configure your system go through the /bin, /sbin/, /usr/bin, /usr/sbin and /usr/lib (and a few of the other usual suspects and make liberal use of the 'chattr +i command'. Also add that to the the kernel files in root. Now 'mkdir /etc/.dist/' copy everything from /etc/ on down (I do this in two steps using /tmp/etcdist.tar to avoid recursion) into that directory. (Optionally you can just create /etc/.dist.tar.gz) – and mark that as immutable.

The reason for all of this is to limit the damage that you can do when logged in as root. You won't overwrite files with a stray redirection operator, and you won't make the system unusable with a stray space in an 'rm -fr' command (you might still do alot of damage to your data – but your libs and bins will be safer).

This also makes a variety of security and denial of service exploits either impossible or more difficult (since many of them rely on overwriting a file through the actions of some SUID program that *isn't providing an arbitrary shell command*).

The only inconvenience of this is when building and doing your 'make install' on various sorts of system binaries. On the other hand it also prevents the 'make install' from over-writing the files. When you forget to read the Makefile and chattr -i the files that are to be overwritten (and the directories to which you want to add files) – the make fails, you just use the chattr command and rerun it. You can also take that opportunity to move your old bin's, libs, or whatever into a .old/ directory or rename or tar them or whatever.

3.4 A suggestion for where to put new stuff. *Jim Dennis*, jadestar@rahul.net

All new stuff starts under /usr/local! or /usr/local/'hostname'

If your distribution is one that leaves /usr/local empty then just create your /usr/local/src, /usr/local/bin etc and use that. If your distribution puts things in the /usr/local tree than you may want to 'mkdir /usr/local/'hostname'' and give the 'wheel' group +w to it (I also make it SUID and SGID to insure that each member of the wheel group can only mess with their own files thereunder, and that all files created will belong to the 'wheel' group.

Now discipline yourself to *ALWAYS! ALWAYS! ALWAYS!* put new packages under /usr/local/src/.from/$WHEREVER_I_GOT_IT/ (for the .tar or whatever files) and build them under /usr/local/src (or .../$HOSTNAME/src). Make sure that it installs under the local hierarchy. If it *absolutely must* be installed back in /bin or /usr/bin or somewhere else – put a symlink from the local heirarchy to each element that when anywhere else.

The reason for this – even though it's more work – is that it helps isolate what has to be backed up and restored or reinstalled in the event of a full re-install from the distribution medio (usually CD these days). By using a /usr/local/.from directory you also keep an informal log of where your sources are coming from – which helps when you're looking for new updates – and may be critical when monitoring the security announcement lists.

One of my systems at home (the one I'm calling from) was put together before I adopted these policies for myself. I still don't "know" all the ways that it differs from the stock "as installed" system. This is despite the fact that I've done very little with my home system's configuration and I'm the *only* person who ever uses it.

By contrast the systems I've set up at work (when I was thrust into the role of system administrator there) have all been configured this way – have been administered by many contractors and other MIS people, and have had a large number of upgrades and package installations. Nonetheless I have a very good idea which precise elements were put in *after* the initial installation and configuration.

3.5 Converting all files in a directory to lowercase. *Justin Dossey,* dossey@ou.edu

I noticed a few overly difficult or unnecessary procedures recommended in the 2c tips section of Issue 12. Since there is more than one, I'm sending it to you:

```
#!/bin/sh
       # lowerit
       # convert all file names in the current directory to lower case
       # only operates on plain files--does not change the name of directories
       # will ask for verification before overwriting an existing file
       for x in `ls`
         do
         if [ ! -f $x ]; then
           continue
           fi
         lc=`echo $x | tr '[A-Z]' '[a-z]'`
         if [ $lc != $x ]; then
           mv -i $x $lc
         fi
       done
```

Wow. That's a long script. I wouldn't write a script to do that; instead, I would use this command:

```
for i in * ; do [ -f $i ] && mv -i $i `echo $i | tr '[A-Z]' '[a-z]'`;
       done;
```

on the command line.

The contributor says he wrote the script how he did for understandability (see below).

On the next tip, this one about adding and removing users, Geoff is doing fine until that last step. Reboot? Boy, I hope he doesn't reboot every time he removes a user. All you have to do is the first two steps. What sort of processes would that user have going, anyway? An irc bot? Killing the processes with a simple

```
kill -9 `ps -aux |grep ^<username> |tr -s " " |cut -d " " -f2`
```

Example, username is foo

```
kill -9 `ps -aux |grep ^foo |tr -s " " |cut -d " " -f2`
```

That taken care of, let us move to the forgotten root password.

The solution given in the Gazette is the most universal one, but not the easiest one. With both LILO and loadlin, one may provide the boot parameter "single" to boot directly into the default shell with no login or password prompt. From there, one may change or remove any passwords before typing "init 3" to start multiuser mode. Number of reboots: 1 The other way Number of reboots: 2

Justin Dossey

3.6 Some tips for new sysadmins. *Jim Dennis,* jadestar@rahul.net

Create and maintain a /README.`hostname` and/or a /etc/README.`hostname` *[Or possibly /usr/local/etc/README.`hostname` -Maint.]*

Absolutely, from *day one* of administering a system take notes in an online log file. You might make "vi /README.$(hostname)" a line in root's /bash_logout. Another way to do this is to write an su or a sudo script that does something like:

```
function exit \
        { unset exit; exit; \
          cat ~/tmp/session.$(date +%y%m%d) \
          >> /README.$(hostname) && \
          vi /README.$(hostname)
          }
script -a ~/tmp/session.$(date +%y%m%d)
/bin/su.org -
```

(use the typescript command to create a session log and create a function to automate appending and updating the log).

I'll admit that I haven't implemented this automation of policy – I've just relied on self-discipline so far. However I have been toying with the idea (even to the point of prototyping the scripts and shell functions as you see them). One thing that holds me back on this is the 'script' command itself. I think I'll have to grab the sources and add a couple of command line parameters (to pause/stop the script recording from the command line) before I commit to using this).

My last suggestion (for this round):

Root's path should consist of 'PATH= /bin'

That's it. Nothing else on root's path. Everything root does is provided by a symlink from /bin or by an alias or shell function, or is a script or binary in /bin, or is typed out with an explicit path.

This makes anyone running as root aware (sometimes painfully so) of how he or she is trusting binaries. The wise admin of a multi-user host will periodically look through his or here /bin and /.*history files to look for patterns and loopholes.

The really motivated admin will spot sequences that can be automated, places where sanity checks can be inserted, and tasks for which "root" privileges should be temporarily eschewed (launching editors, MTA's and other large interactive programs with elaborate scripting features that *might* be embedded in transparent or data files – like the infamous vi ./.exrc and emacs ./.emacs and the even more insidious $EXINIT and the embedded header/footer macros). Naturally those sorts of commands can be run with something like:

```
cp $data $some_users_home/tmp
su -c $origcommand $whatever_switches
cp $some_users_home/tmp $data
```

(...where the specifics depend on the command).

Mostly these last sorts of precautions are overboard for the home or "single" user workstation – but they are very good policy the admin of a multi-user – particular a publicly exposed system (like the one's at netcom).

3.7 How to configure xdm's chooser for host selection. *Arrigo Triulzi,* a.triulzi@ic.ac.uk

1. Edit the file that launches xdm most likely /etc/rc/rc.6 or /etc/rc.local) so that it contains the following lines in the xdm startup section.

```
/usr/bin/X11/xdm
exec /usr/bin/X11/X -indirect hostname
```

2. Edit /usr/lib/X11/xdm/Xservers and comment out the line which starts the server on the local machine (i.e. starting 0:)
3. Reboot the machine and you're home and away.

I add this because when I was, desperately, trying to set it up for my own subnet over here it took me about a week to suss out all the problems.

Caveat: with old SLS (1.1.1) for some reason you can leave a -nodaemon after the xdm line – this does **NOT** work for later releases.

Colours with Linux terminals

Thorbjørn Ravn Andersen, ravn@dit.ou.dk   v1.4, 7 August 1997

Most Linux distributions have a 'ls' command for listing the contents of a directory that can visually enhance their output by using different colours, but configuring this to taste may not be a trivial task. This document explains the various aspects and approaches of altering the setup by configuring existing software, plus locations of alternative software usually not included with Slackware or RedHat, which may be used on most versions of Unix. The HTML version is also available from my own source at <http://www.mip.ou.dk/~ravn/colour-ls>.

Contents

1 Introduction

In recent years colour displays have become very common, and users are beginning to exploit this by using programs that utilizes colours to give quick visual feedback on e.g. reserved keywords in programming languages, or instant notification of misspelled words.

As the Linux text console supports colour, the original GNU ls was quickly modified to output colour information and included in Slackware around version 2.0. Improved versions of these patches have now migrated into the standard GNU distribution of ls, and should therefore be a part of all new Linux distributions by now.

This revision is an update on a major rewrite from the initial release, including information on xterms and kernel patching.

The information in this document has been confirmed on Redhat 4.1, and was originally compiled with the 2.0.2 release of Slackware, and the 1.1.54 kernel. The kernel patch information was retrieved on slackware 2.2.0 with the 1.2.13 kernel, and tcsh as the default shell, and later confirmed with a 2.0.27 kernel. If you use any other configuration, or unix version, I would appreciate a note stating your operating system and version, and whether colour support is available as standard.

2   Quickstart for the impatient

If you have a *new* distribution of Linux, do these modifications to these files in your home directory. They take effect after next login.

```
~/.bashrc:
    alias ls="ls --color"

~/.cshrc:
    alias ls 'ls --color'
```

That's it!

You may also want to do an "eval `dircolors $HOME/.colourrc`", to get your own colours. This file is created with "dircolors -p >$HOME/.colourrc" and is well commented for further editing.

3   Do I have it at all?

First of all you need to know if you have a version of ls which knows how to colourize properly. Try this command in a Linux text console (although an xterm will do):

```
% ls --color
```

(the % is a shell prompt):

If you get an error message indicating that ls does not understand the option, you need to install a new version of the GNU fileutils package. If you do not have an appropriate upgrade package for your distribution, just get the latest version from your GNU mirror and install directly from source.

If you do *not* get an error message, you have a ls which understands the command. Unfortunately, some of the earlier versions included previously with Slackware (and possible others) were buggy. The ls included with Redhat 4.1 is version 3.13 which is okay.

```
% ls --version
ls - GNU fileutils-3.13
```

If you ran the "ls -- color" command on a Linux textbased console, the output should have been colourized according to the defaults on the system, and you can now decide whether there is anything you want to change.

If you ran it in an xterm, you may or you may not have seen any colour changes. As with ls itself, the original xterm-program did not have any support of colour for the programs running inside of it, but recent versions do. If your xterm doesn't support colours, you should get a new version as described at the end of this document. In the meantime just switch to textmode and continue from there.

4   Which colours is there to choose from?

This shell script (thanks to the many who sent me bash versions) shows all standard colour combinations on the current console. If no colours appear, your console does not support ANSI colour selections.

```
#!/bin/bash
# Display ANSI colours.
#
esc="\033["
echo -n " _ _ _ _ _40 _ _ _ 41_ _ _ _42 _ _ _ 43"
echo "_ _ _ 44_ _ _ _45 _ _ _ 46_ _ _ _47 _"
for fore in 30 31 32 33 34 35 36 37; do
  line1="$fore  "
  line2="     "
  for back in 40 41 42 43 44 45 46 47; do
    line1="${line1}${esc}${back};${fore}m Normal  ${esc}0m"
    line2="${line2}${esc}${back};${fore};1m Bold    ${esc}0m"
  done
  echo -e "$line1\n$line2"
done
```

The foreground colour number is listed to the left, and the background number in the box. If you want bold characters you add a "1" to the parameters, so bright blue on white would be "37;44;1". The whole ANSI selection sequence is then

ESC [3 7 ; 4 4 ; 1 m

Note: The background currently cannot be bold, so you cannot have yellow (bold brown) as anything but foreground. This is a hardware limitation.

```
The colours are:
        0 - black    4 - blue        3# is foreground
        1 - red      5 - magenta     4# is background
        2 - green    6 - cyan
        3 - yellow   7 - white        ;1 is bold
```

5   How to configure colours with ls

If you wish to modify the standard colour set built into ls, you need your personal copy in your home directory, which you get with

```
cd ; dircolors -p > .coloursrc
```

After modifying this well-commented file you need to have it read into the environment string LS_COLORS, which is usually done with

```
eval `dircolors .colourrc`
```

You need to put this line in your .bashrc/.cshrc/.tcshrc (depending on your shell), to have it done at each login. See the dircolors(1) manual page for details.

6   How to change the text-mode default from white-on-black

You will need to tell the terminal driver code that you want another default. There exists no standard way of doing this, but in case of Linux you have the setterm program.

"setterm" uses the information in the terminal database to set the attributes. Selections are done like

```
setterm -foreground black -background white -store
```

where the "-store" besides the actual change makes it the default for the current console as well. This requires that the current terminal (TERM environment variable) is described "well enough" in the termcap database. If setterm for some reason does not work, here are some alternatives:

6.1   Xterm

One of these xterms should be available and at least one of them support colour.

```
xterm -fg white -bg blue4
color_xterm -fg white -bg blue4
color-xterm -fg white -bg blue4
nxterm -fg white -bg blue4
```

where 'color_xterm' supports the colour version of 'ls'. This particular choice resembles the colours used on an SGI.

6.2   Virtual console.

You may modify the kernel once and for all, as well as providing a run-time default for the virtual consoles with an escape sequence. I recommend the kernel patch if you have compiled your own kernel.

The kernel source file is **/usr/src/linux/drivers/char/console.c** around line 1940, where you should modify

```
def_color       = 0x07;    /* white */
ulcolor         = 0x0f;    /* bold white */
halfcolor       = 0x08;    /* grey */
```

as appropriate. I use white on blue with

```
        def_color      = 0x17;    /* white */
        ulcolor        = 0x1f;    /* bold white */
        halfcolor      = 0x18;    /* grey */
```

The numbers are the attribute codes used by the video card in hexadecimal: the most significant digit (the
"1" in the example colours above) is the background; the least significant the foreground. 0 = black, 1 =
blue, 2 = green, 3 = cyan, 4 = red, 5 = purple, 6 = brown/yellow, 7 = white. Add 8 to get "bright"
colours. Note that, in most cases, a bright background == blinking characters, dull background. (From
sjlam1@mda023.cc.monash.edu.au <mailto:sjlam1@mda023.cc.monash.edu.au>).

You may also supply a new run-time default for a virtual console, on a per-display basis with the non-standard
ANSI sequence (found by browsing the kernel sources)

```
        ESC [ 8 ]
```

which sets the default to the current fore- and background colours. Then the Reset Attributes string (ESC
[m) selects these colours instead of white on black.

You will need to actually echo this string to the console each time you reboot. Depending on what you use
your Linux box for, several places may be appropriate:

6.2.1 /etc/issue

This is where "Welcome to Linux xx.yy" is displayed under Slackware, and that is a good choice for standalone equipment (and probably be a pestilence for users logging in with telnet). This file is created at
boottime (Slackware in /etc/rc.d/rc.S; Redhat in /etc/rc.d/rc.local), and you should modify lines looking
somewhat like

```
        echo ""> /etc/issue
        echo Welcome to Linux '/bin/uname -a | /bin/cut -d\  -f3'. >> /etc/issue
```

to

```
        ESCAPE="<replace with a single escape character here>"
        echo "${ESCAPE}[H${ESCAPE}[37;44m${ESCAPE}[8]${ESCAPE}[2J"> /etc/issue
        echo Welcome to Linux '/bin/uname -a | /bin/cut -d\  -f3'. >> /etc/issue
```

This code will home the cursor, set the colour (here white on blue), save this selection and clean the rest
of the screen. The modification takes effect after the next reboot. Remember to insert the _literal_ escape
character in the file with C-q in emacs or control-v in vi, as apparently the sh used for executing this script
does not understand the /033 syntax.

6.2.2 /etc/profile or .profile

```
        if [ "$TERM" = "console" ]; then
            echo "\033[37;44m\033[8]" #
    # or use setterm.
            setterm -foreground white -background blue -store
        fi
```

6.2.3 /etc/login or .login

```
    if ( "$TERM" == "console" ) then
      echo "\033[37;44m\033[8]"
#  or use setterm.
        setterm -foreground white -background blue -store
    endif
```

6.3 Remote login

You should be able to use the setterm program as shown above. Again, this requires that the remote machine knows enough about your terminal, and that the terminal emulator providing the login supports colour. In my experience the best vt100 emulation currently available for other platforms are:

- MS-DOS: MS-Kermit (free, not a Microsoft product)
- Windows 95/NT: Kermit/95 (shareware)
- OS/2: Kermit/95 (shareware). Note though that the standard telnet understands colours and can be customized locally.

See <http://www.columbia.edu/kermit/> for details about Kermit.

7 Software

All the information described here is assuming a GNU/Linux installation. If you have something else (like e.g. a Sun running X or so) you can get and compile the actual software yourself.

The colour version of 'xterm' is based on the standard xterm source with a patch available from any X11R6 site. The xterm distributed with R6.3 is rumoured to have native colour support, but is untested by me.

```
ftp://ftp.denet.dk/pub/X11/contrib/utilities/color-xterm-R6pl5-patch.gz
```

See the documentation if you use an older version of X. *Note:* I haven't tried this myself!

'ls' is in the GNU fileutils package available from prep.mit.edu or one of the several mirrors. Get at least version 3.13.

```
ftp://ftp.denet.dk/pub/gnu/fileutils-3.XX.tar.gz
```

I have myself successfully compiled color-ls on Solaris, SunOS and Irix.

I would appreciate feedback on this text. My e-mail address is *ravn@dit.ou.dk* <mailto:ravn@dit.ou.dk>

—

Thorbjørn Ravn Andersen

Linux Ext2fs Undeletion mini-HOWTO

Aaron Crane, <*aaronc@pobox.com*> <mailto:aaronc@pobox.com>   v1.2, 4 August 1997

Picture this. You've spent the last three days with no sleep, no food, not even a shower. Your hacking compulsion has at last paid off: you've finished that program that will bring you world-wide fame and recognition. All that you still need to do is tar it up and put it on Sunsite. Oh, and delete all those Emacs backup files. So you say rm * ~. And too late, you notice the extra space in that command. You've just deleted your *magnum opus*! But help is at hand. This document presents a discussion of how to retrieve deleted files from a Second Extended File System. Just maybe, you'll be able to release that program after all...

Contents

1 Introduction

This mini-Howto attempts to provide hints on how to retrieve deleted files from an ext2 filesystem. It also contains a limited amount of discussion of how to avoid deleting files in the first place.

I intend it to be useful certainly for people who have just had, shall we say, a little accident with rm; however, I also hope that people read it anyway. You never know: one day, some of the information in here could save your bacon.

The text assumes a little background knowledge about UNIX filesystems in general; however, I hope that it will be accessible to most Linux users. If you are an outright beginner, I'm afraid that undeleting files under Linux *does* require a certain amount of technical knowledge and persistence, at least for the time being.

You will be unable to recover deleted files from an ext2 filesystem without at least read access to the raw device on which the file was stored. In general, this means that you must be root. You also need debugfs from the e2fsprogs package. This should have been installed by your distribution.

Why have I written this? It stems largely from my own experiences with a particularly foolish and disastrous rm -r command as root. I deleted about 97 JPEG files which I needed and could almost certainly not recover from other sources. Using some helpful tips (see section 15 (Credits and Bibliography)) and a great deal of persistence, I recovered 91 files undamaged. I managed to retrieve at least parts of five of the rest (enough to see what the picture was in each case). Only one was undisplayable, and even for this one, I am fairly sure that no more than 1024 bytes were lost (though unfortunately from the beginning of the file; given that I know nothing about the JFIF file format I had done as much as I could).

I shall discuss further below what sort of recovery rate you can expect for deleted files.

1.1 Revision history

The various publicly-released revisions of this document (and their publication dates) are as follows:

- v1.0 on 18 January 1997
- v1.1 on 23 July 1997 (see section 1.1.1 (Changes in v1.1))
- v1.2 on 4 August 1997 (see section 1.1.2 (Changes in v1.2))

1.1.1 Changes in version 1.1

What changes have been made in this version? First of all, the thinko in the example of file recovery has been fixed. Thankyou to all those who wrote to point out my mistaek; I hope I've learned to be more careful when making up program interaction.

Secondly, the discussion of UNIX filesystem layout has been rewritten to be, I hope, more understandable. I wasn't entirely happy with it in the first place, and some people's comments indicated that it wasn't clear.

Thirdly, the vast uuencoded gzipped tarball of `fsgrab` in the middle of the file has been removed. The program is now available on *my website* `<http://pobox.com/aaronc/tech/fsgrab-1.0.tar.gz>` and it should soon make its way onto *Sunsite* `<http://sunsite.unc.edu/pub/Linux/utils/disk-management/>` (and mirrors).

Fourthly, the document has been translated into the Linux Documentation Project SGML Tools content markup language. This markup language can be easily converted to any of a number of other markup languages (including HTML and LaTeX) for convenient display and printing. One benefit of this is that beautiful typography in paper editions is a much more achievable goal; another is that the document has cross-references and hyperlinks when viewed on the Web.

1.1.2   Changes in v1.2

This revision is very much an incremental change. It's here mainly to include changes suggested by readers, one of which is particularly important.

The first change was suggested by Egil Kvaleberg *<egil@kvaleberg.no>* `<mailto:egil@kvaleberg.no>`, who pointed out the `dump` command in `debugfs`. Thanks again, Egil.

The second change is to mention the use of `chattr` for avoiding deleting important files. Thanks to Herman Suijs *<H.P.M.Suijs@kub.nl>* `<mailto:H.P.M.Suijs@kub.nl>` for mentioning this one.

The abstract has been revised. URLs have been added for organisations and software. Various other minor changes have been made (including fixing typos and so on).

1.2   Canonical locations of this document

The latest public release of this document should always be available in plain text format on the *Linux Documentation Project site* `<http://sunsite.unc.edu/LDP/>` (and mirrors).

The latest release is also kept on *my website* `<http://pobox.com/aaronc/>` in several formats:

- *SGML source* `<http://pobox.com/aaronc/tech/e2-undel/howto.sgml>`. This is the source as I have written it, using the SGML Tools package.

- *HTML* `<http://pobox.com/aaronc/tech/e2-undel/html/>`. This is HTML, automatically generated from the SGML source.

- *Plain text* `<http://pobox.com/aaronc/tech/e2-undel/howto.txt>`. This is plain text, which is also automatically generated from the SGML source. Note that this file is identical to the one on Sunsite, so if you want the plain text, you are recommended to get it from your favourite LDP mirror (as it will probably be much faster).

2   How not to delete files

It is vital to remember that Linux is unlike MS-DOS when it comes to undeletion. For MS-DOS (and its bastard progeny Windows 95), it is generally fairly straightforward to undelete a file - the 'operating system' (I use the term loosely) even comes with a utility which automates much of the process. For Linux, this is not the case.

So. Rule number one (the prime directive, if you will) is:

KEEP BACKUPS

no matter what. I know, I'm a fine one to talk. I shall merely plead impoverishment (being a student must have *some* perks) and exhort all right-thinking Linux users to go out and buy a useful backup device, work out a decent backup schedule, and to *stick to it*. For more information on this, read Frisch (1995) (see section 15 (Bibliography and Credits)).

In the absence of backups, what then? (Or even in the presence of backups: belt and braces is no bad policy where important data is concerned.)

Try to set the permissions for important files to 440 (or less): denying yourself write access to them means that rm requires an explicit confirmation before deleting. (I find, however, that if I'm recursively deleting a directory with rm -r, I'll interrupt the program on the first or second confirmation request and reissue the command as rm -rf.)

A good trick for selected files is to create a hard link to them in a hidden directory. I heard a story once about a sysadmin who repeatedly deleted /etc/passwd by accident (thereby half-destroying the system). One of the fixes for this was to do something like the following (as root):

```
# mkdir /.backup
# ln /etc/passwd /.backup
```

It requires quite some effort to delete the file contents completely: if you say

```
# rm /etc/passwd
```

then

```
# ln /.backup/passwd /etc
```

will retrieve it. Of course, this does not help in the event that you overwrite the file, so keep backups anyway.

On an ext2 filesystem, it is possible to use ext2 attributes to protect things. These attributes are manipulated with the chattr command. There is an 'append-only' attribute: a file with this attribute may be appended to, but may not be deleted, and the existing contents of the file may not be overwritten. If a directory has this attribute, any files or directories within it may be modified as normal, but no files may be deleted. The 'append-only' attribute is set with

```
$ chattr +a FILE...
```

There is also an 'immutable' attribute, which can only be set or cleared by root. A file or directory with this attribute may not be modified, deleted, renamed, or (hard) linked. It may be set as follows:

```
# chattr +i FILE...
```

The ext2fs also provides the 'undeletable' attribute (+u in chattr). The intention is that if a file with that attribute is deleted, instead of actually being reused, it is merely moved to a 'safe location' for deletion at a later date. Unfortunately this feature has not yet been implemented in mainstream kernels. However, various kernel patches exist which provide the ability to do reversible deletion; see *<http://www.linuxhq.com/>* <http://www.linuxhq.com/> if you're interested in patching this facility into your kernel. The most recent patch I know of is by Rogier Wolff *<R.E.Wolff@BitWizard.nl>* <mailto:R.E.Wolff@BitWizard.nl>, Darren J Moffat *<darren@xarius.demon.co.uk>* <mailto:darren@xarius.demon.co.uk> and Kurt Huwig *<kurt@huwig.de>* <kurt@huwig.de>. I would point out though that while this patch implements the feature, it is not an 'undeletion solution' at the moment. Undeletable files are merely moved into another directory; there should be a daemon to periodically clean up that directory.

Some people advocate making `rm` a shell alias or function for `rm -i` (which asks for confirmation on *every* file you delete). Indeed, recent versions of the *Red Hat distribution* <http://www.redhat.com/> do this by default for all users, including root. Personally, I cannot stand software which won't run unattended, so I don't do that. There is also the problem that sooner or later, you'll be running in single-user mode, or using a different shell, or even a different machine, where your `rm` function doesn't exist. If you expect to be asked for confirmation, it is easy to forget where you are and to specify too many files for deletion. Likewise, the various scripts and programs that replace `rm` are, IMHO, very dangerous.

A slightly better solution is to start using a package which handles 'recyclable' deletion by providing a command not named `rm`. For details on these, see Peek, et al (1993) (see section 15 (Bibliography and Credits)).

3   What recovery rate can I expect?

That depends. Among the problems with recovering files on a high-quality, multi-tasking, multi-user operating system like Linux is that you never know when someone wants to write to the disk. So when the operating system is told to delete a file, it assumes that the blocks used by that file are fair game when it wants to allocate space for a new file. (This is a specific example of a general principle for Linux: the kernel and the associated tools assume that the users aren't idiots.) In general, the more usage your machine gets, the less likely you are to be able to recover files successfully.

Also, disk fragmentation can affect the ease of recovering files. If the partition containing the deleted files is very fragmented, you are unlikely to be able to read a whole file.

If your machine, like mine, is effectively a single-user workstation (mine doesn't even have a net connection yet; maybe next year), and you weren't doing anything disk-intensive at the fatal moment of deleting those files, I would expect a recovery rate in the same ball-park as detailed above. I retrieved nearly 94% of the files (and these were binary files, please note) undamaged. If you get 80% or better, you can feel pretty pleased with yourself, I should think.

4   So, how do I undelete a file?

The procedure principally involves finding the data on the raw partition device and making it visible again to the operating system. There are basically two ways of doing this: one is to modify the existing filesystem such that the deleted inodes have their 'deleted' flag removed, and hope that the data just magically falls back into place. The other method, which is safer but slower, is to work out where the data lies in the partition and write it out into a new file.

There are some steps you need to take before beginning to attempt your data recovery; see sections 5 (Unmounting the filesystem), 6 (Preparing to change inodes directly) and 7 (Preparing to write data elsewhere) for details. To find out how to actually retrieve your files, see sections 8 (Finding the deleted inodes), 9 (Obtaining the details of the inodes), 10 (Recovering data blocks) and 11 (Modifying inodes directly).

5   Unmounting the filesystem

Regardless of which method you choose, the first step is to unmount the filesystem containing the deleted files. I strongly discourage any urges you may have to mess around on a mounted filesystem. This step should be performed *as soon as possible* after you realise that the files have been deleted.

The simplest method is as follows: assuming the deleted files were in the `/usr` partition, say:

```
# umount /usr
```

You may, however, want to keep some things in /usr available. So remount it read-only:

```
# mount -o ro,remount /usr
```

If the deleted files were on the root partition, you'll need to add a -n option to prevent mount from trying to write to /etc/mtab:

```
# mount -n -o ro,remount /
```

Regardless of all this, it is possible that there will be another process using that filesystem (which will cause the unmount to fail with an error such as 'Resource busy'). There is a program which will send a signal to any process using a given file or mount point: fuser. Try this for the /usr partition:

```
# fuser -v -m /usr
```

This lists the processes involved. Assuming none of them are vital, you can say

```
# fuser -k -v -m /usr
```

to send each process a SIGKILL (which is guaranteed to kill it), or for example,

```
# fuser -k -TERM -v -m /usr
```

to give each one a SIGTERM (which will normally make the process exit cleanly).

6 Preparing to change inodes directly

My advice? Don't do it this way. I really don't think it's wise to play with a filesystem at a low enough level for this to work. There are also has problems in that you can only reliably recover the first 12 blocks of each file. So if you have any long files to recover, you'll have to use the other method anyway. (Although see section 12 (Will this get easier in future?) for additional information.)

If you feel you must do it this way, my advice is to copy the raw partition data to an image on a different partition, and then mount this using loopback:

```
# cp /dev/hda5 /root/working
# mount -t ext2 -o loop /root/working /mnt
```

This does, however, require a recent version of mount. (Although you should get version 2.6 or newer anyway, as all earlier versions have a major security bug which allows peons to get root access. The major distributions, that is, Debian, RedHat and Slackware, have all been updated with version 2.6 of mount.)

Using loopback means that when you completely destroy the filesystem (as you quite possibly will), all you have to do is copy the raw partition back and start again.

7   Preparing to write data elsewhere

You need to make sure you have a rescue partition somewhere. Hopefully, your system has several partitions on it: perhaps a root, a /usr, and a /home. With all these to choose from, you should have no problem: just create a new directory on one of these.

If you have only a root partition, and store everything on that (like me, until I can get around to repartitioning), things are slightly more awkward. Perhaps you have an MS-DOS or Windows partition you could use? Or you have the ramdisk driver in your kernel, maybe as a module? To use the ramdisk (assuming a kernel more recent than 1.3.48), say the following:

```
# dd if=/dev/zero of=/dev/ram0 bs=1k count=2048
# mke2fs -v -m 0 /dev/ram0 2048
# mount -t ext2 /dev/ram0 /mnt
```

This creates a 2MB ramdisk volume, and mounts it on /mnt.

A short word of warning: if you use kerneld to automatically load and unload kernel modules, then don't unmount the ramdisk until you've copied any files from it onto non-volatile storage. Once you unmount it, kerneld assumes it can unload the module (after the usual waiting period), and once this happens, the memory gets re-used by other parts of the kernel, losing all the painstaking hours you just spent recovering your data.

If you have any of the new 'superfloppy' removable devices, they're probably a good choice for a rescue partition location. Otherwise, you'll just have to stick with floppies.

The other thing you're likely to need is a program which can read the necessary data from the middle of the partition device. At a pinch, dd will do the job, but to read from, say, 600 MB into an 800 MB partition, dd insists on reading but ignoring the first 600 MB. This takes a not inconsiderable amount of time. My way round this was to write a program which will seek to the middle of the partition. It's called fsgrab; you can find the source package on *my website* <http://pobox.com/aaronc/tech/fsgrab-1.0.tar.gz> and it should soon make its way onto *Sunsite* <http://sunsite.unc.edu/pub/Linux/utils/disk-management/> (and mirrors). If you want to use this method, the rest of this mini-Howto assumes that you have fsgrab.

If none of the files you are trying to recover were more than 12 blocks long (where a block is usually one kilobyte), then you won't need fsgrab.

If you need to use fsgrab but don't want to, it is fairly straightforward to translate an fsgrab command-line to one for dd. If we have

```
fsgrab -c count -s skip device
```

then the corresponding dd command is

```
dd bs=1k if=device count=count skip=skip
```

I must warn you that, although fsgrab functioned perfectly for me, I can take no responsibility for how it performs. It was really a very quick and dirty kludge just to get things to work. For more details on the lack of warranty, see the 'No Warranty' section in the COPYING file included with it (the GNU General Public Licence).

8   Finding the deleted inodes

The next step is to ask the filesystem which inodes have recently been freed. This is a task you can accomplish with debugfs. Start debugfs with the name of the device on which the filesystem is stored:

```
# debugfs /dev/hda5
```

If you want to modify the inodes directly, add a `-w` option to enable writing to the filesystem:

```
# debugfs -w /dev/hda5
```

The `debugfs` command to find the deleted inodes is `lsdel`. So, type the command at the prompt:

```
debugfs:  lsdel
```

After much wailing and grinding of disk mechanisms, a long list is piped into your favourite pager (the value of `$PAGER`). Now you'll want to save a copy of this somewhere else. If you have `less`, you can type `-o` followed by the name of an output file. Otherwise, you'll have to arrange to send the output elsewhere. Try this:

```
debugfs:  quit
# echo lsdel | debugfs /dev/hda5 > lsdel.out
```

Now, based only on the deletion time, the size, the type, and the numerical permissions and owner, you must work out which of these deleted inodes are the ones you want. With luck, you'll be able to spot them because they're the big bunch you deleted about five minutes ago. Otherwise, trawl through that list carefully.

I suggest that if possible, you print out the list of the inodes you want to recover. It will make life a lot easier.

9 Obtaining the details of the inodes

`debugfs` has a `stat` command which prints details about an inode. Issue the command for each inode in your recovery list. For example, if you're interested in inode number 148003, try this:

```
debugfs:  stat <148003>
Inode: 148003   Type: regular   Mode:  0644   Flags: 0x0   Version: 1
User:   503   Group:   100   Size: 6065
File ACL: 0    Directory ACL: 0
Links: 0   Blockcount: 12
Fragment:  Address: 0    Number: 0    Size: 0
ctime: 0x31a9a574 -- Mon May 27 13:52:04 1996
atime: 0x31a21dd1 -- Tue May 21 20:47:29 1996
mtime: 0x313bf4d7 -- Tue Mar  5 08:01:27 1996
dtime: 0x31a9a574 -- Mon May 27 13:52:04 1996
BLOCKS:
594810 594811 594814 594815 594816 594817
TOTAL: 6
```

If you have a lot of files to recover, you'll want to automate this. Assuming that your `lsdel` list of inodes to recover in is in `lsdel.out`, try this:

```
# cut -c1-6 lsdel.out | grep "[0-9]" | tr -d " " > inodes
```

This new file `inodes` contains just the numbers of the inodes to recover, one per line. We save it because it will very likely come in handy later on. Then you just say:

```
# sed 's/^.*$/stat <\0>/' inodes | debugfs /dev/hda5 > stats
```

and `stats` contains the output of all the `stat` commands.

10   Recovering data blocks

This part is either very easy or distinctly less so, depending on whether the file you are trying to recover is more than 12 blocks long.

10.1   Short files

If the file was no more than 12 blocks long, then the block numbers of all its data are stored in the inode: you can read them directly out of the `stat` output for the inode. Moreover, `debugfs` has a command which performs this task automatically. To take the example we had before, repeated here:

```
debugfs:  stat <148003>
Inode: 148003   Type: regular   Mode:  0644   Flags: 0x0   Version: 1
User:    503   Group:    100   Size: 6065
File ACL: 0    Directory ACL: 0
Links: 0    Blockcount: 12
Fragment:  Address: 0     Number: 0    Size: 0
ctime: 0x31a9a574 -- Mon May 27 13:52:04 1996
atime: 0x31a21dd1 -- Tue May 21 20:47:29 1996
mtime: 0x313bf4d7 -- Tue Mar  5 08:01:27 1996
dtime: 0x31a9a574 -- Mon May 27 13:52:04 1996
BLOCKS:
594810 594811 594814 594815 594816 594817
TOTAL: 6
```

This file has six blocks. Since this is less than the limit of 12, we get `debugfs` to write the file into a new location, such as `/mnt/recovered.000`:

```
debugfs:  dump <148003> /mnt/recovered.000
```

Of course, this can also be done with `fsgrab`; I'll present it here as an example of using it:

```
# fsgrab -c 2 -s 594810 /dev/hda5 > /mnt/recovered.000
# fsgrab -c 4 -s 594814 /dev/hda5 >> /mnt/recovered.000
```

With either `debugfs` or `fsgrab`, there will be some garbage at the end of `/mnt/recovered.000`, but that's fairly unimportant. If you want to get rid of it, the simplest method is to take the `Size` field from the inode, and plug it into the `bs` option in a `dd` command line:

```
# dd count=1 if=/mnt/recovered.000 of=/mnt/resized.000 bs=6065
```

Of course, it is possible that one or more of the blocks that made up your file has been overwritten. If so, then you're out of luck: that block is gone forever. (But just imagine if you'd unmounted sooner!)

10.2   Longer files

The problems appear when the file has more than 12 data blocks. It pays here to know a little of how UNIX filesystems are structured. The file's data is stored in units called 'blocks'. These blocks may be numbered sequentially. A file also has an 'inode', which is the place where information such as owner, permissions, and type are kept. Like blocks, inodes are numbered sequentially, although they have a different sequence. A directory entry consists of the name of the file and an inode number.

But with this state of affairs, it is still impossible for the kernel to find the data corresponding to a directory entry. So the inode also stores the location of the file's data blocks, as follows:

- The block numbers of the first 12 data blocks are stored directly in the inode; these are sometimes referred to as the *direct block*s.

- The inode contains the block number of an *indirect block*. An indirect block contains the block numbers of 256 additional data blocks.

- The inode contains the block number of a *doubly indirect block*. A doubly indirect block contains the block numbers of 256 additional indirect blocks.

- The inode contains the block number of a *triply indirect block*. A triply indirect block contains the block numbers of 256 additional doubly indirect blocks.

Read that again: I know it's complex, but it's also important.

Now, the current kernel implementation (certainly for all versions up to and including 2.0.30) unfortunately zeroes all indirect blocks (and doubly indirect blocks, and so on) when deleting a file. So if your file was longer than 12 blocks, you have no guarantee of being able to find even the numbers of all the blocks you need, let alone their contents.

The only method I have been able to find thus far is to assume that the file was not fragmented: if it was, then you're in trouble. Assuming that the file was not fragmented, there are several layouts of data blocks, according to how many data blocks the file used:

0 to 12

> The block numbers are stored in the inode, as described above.

13 to 268

> After the direct blocks, count one for the indirect block, and then there are 256 data blocks.

269 to 65804

> As before, there are 12 direct blocks, a (useless) indirect block, and 256 blocks. These are followed by one (useless) doubly indirect block, and 256 repetitions of one (useless) indirect block and 256 data blocks.

65805 or more

> The layout of the first 65804 blocks is as above. Then follow one (useless) triply indirect block and 256 repetitions of a 'doubly indirect sequence'. Each doubly indirect sequence consists of a (useless) doubly indirect block, followed by 256 repetitions of one (useless) indirect block and 256 data blocks.

Of course, even if these assumed data block numbers are correct, there is no guarantee that the data in them is intact. In addition, the longer the file was, the less chance there is that it was written to the filesystem without appreciable fragmentation (except in special circumstances).

You should note that I assume throughout that your blocksize is 1024 bytes, as this is the standard value. If your blocks are bigger, some of the numbers above will change. Specifically: since each block number is 4 bytes long, blocksize/4 is the number of block numbers that can be stored in each indirect block. So every time the number 256 appears in the discussion above, replace it with blocksize/4. The 'number of blocks required' boundaries will also have to be changed.

Let's look at an example of recovering a longer file.

```
debugfs:  stat <1387>
Inode: 148004   Type: regular    Mode:  0644    Flags: 0x0   Version: 1
User:    503   Group:   100   Size: 1851347
File ACL: 0    Directory ACL: 0
Links: 0    Blockcount: 3616
Fragment:  Address: 0    Number: 0    Size: 0
ctime: 0x31a9a574 -- Mon May 27 13:52:04 1996
atime: 0x31a21dd1 -- Tue May 21 20:47:29 1996
mtime: 0x313bf4d7 -- Tue Mar  5 08:01:27 1996
dtime: 0x31a9a574 -- Mon May 27 13:52:04 1996
BLOCKS:
8314 8315 8316 8317 8318 8319 8320 8321 8322 8323 8324 8325 8326 8583
TOTAL: 14
```

There seems to be a reasonable chance that this file is not fragmented: certainly, the first 12 blocks listed in the inode (which are all data blocks) are contiguous. So, we can start by retrieving those blocks:

```
# fsgrab -c 12 -s 8314 /dev/hda5 > /mnt/recovered.001
```

Now, the next block listed in the inode, 8326, is an indirect block, which we can ignore. But we trust that it will be followed by 256 data blocks (numbers 8327 through 8582).

```
# fsgrab -c 256 -s 8327 /dev/hda5 >> /mnt/recovered.001
```

The final block listed in the inode is 8583. Note that we're still looking good in terms of the file being contiguous: the last data block we wrote out was number 8582, which is 8327 + 255. This block 8583 is a doubly indirect block, which we can ignore. It is followed by up to 256 repetitions of an indirect block (which is ignored) followed by 256 data blocks. So doing the arithmetic quickly, we issue the following commands. Notice that we skip the doubly indirect block 8583, and the indirect block 8584 immediately (we hope) following it, and start at block 8585 for data.

```
# fsgrab -c 256 -s 8585 /dev/hda5 >> /mnt/recovered.001
# fsgrab -c 256 -s 8842 /dev/hda5 >> /mnt/recovered.001
# fsgrab -c 256 -s 9099 /dev/hda5 >> /mnt/recovered.001
# fsgrab -c 256 -s 9356 /dev/hda5 >> /mnt/recovered.001
# fsgrab -c 256 -s 9613 /dev/hda5 >> /mnt/recovered.001
# fsgrab -c 256 -s 9870 /dev/hda5 >> /mnt/recovered.001
```

Adding up, we see that so far we've written $12 + (7 * 256)$ blocks, which is 1804. The 'stat' results for the inode gave us a 'blockcount' of 3616; unfortunately these blocks are 512 bytes long (as a hangover from UNIX), so we really want $3616/2 = 1808$ blocks of 1024 bytes. That means we need only four more blocks. The last data block written was number 10125. As we've been doing so far, we skip an indirect block (number 10126); we can then write those last four blocks.

```
# fsgrab -c 4 -s 10127 /dev/hda5 >> /mnt/recovered.001
```

Now, with some luck the entire file has been recovered successfully.

11 Modifying inodes directly

This method is, on the surface, much easier. However, as mentioned above, it cannot cope with files longer than 12 blocks.

For each inode you want to recover, you must set the usage count to one, and set the deletion time to zero. This is done with the mi (modify inode) command in debugfs. Some sample output, modifying inode 148003 from above:

```
debugfs:  mi <148003>
                        Mode    [0100644]
                     User ID    [503]
                    Group ID    [100]
                        Size    [6065]
               Creation time    [833201524]
           Modification time    [832708049]
                 Access time    [826012887]
               Deletion time    [833201524] 0
                  Link count    [0] 1
                 Block count    [12]
                  File flags    [0x0]
                   Reserved1    [0]
                    File acl    [0]
               Directory acl    [0]
            Fragment address    [0]
             Fragment number    [0]
               Fragment size    [0]
              Direct Block #0    [594810]
              Direct Block #1    [594811]
              Direct Block #2    [594814]
              Direct Block #3    [594815]
              Direct Block #4    [594816]
              Direct Block #5    [594817]
              Direct Block #6    [0]
              Direct Block #7    [0]
              Direct Block #8    [0]
              Direct Block #9    [0]
             Direct Block #10    [0]
             Direct Block #11    [0]
              Indirect Block    [0]
       Double Indirect Block    [0]
       Triple Indirect Block    [0]
```

That is, I set the deletion time to 0 and the link count to 1 and just pressed return for each of the other fields. Granted, this is a little unwieldy if you have a lot of files to recover, but I think you can cope. If you'd wanted chrome, you'd have used a graphical 'operating system' with a pretty 'Recycle Bin'.

By the way: the `mi` output refers to a 'Creation time' field in the inode. This is a lie! (Or misleading, anyway.) The fact of the matter is that you cannot tell on a UNIX filesystem when a file was created. The `st_ctime` member of a `struct stat` refers to the 'inode change time', that is, the last time when any inode details were changed. Here endeth today's lesson.

Note that more recent versions of `debugfs` than the one I'm using probably do not include some of the fields in the listing above (specifically, `Reserved1` and (some of?) the fragment fields).

Once you've modified the inodes, you can quit `debugfs` and say:

```
# e2fsck -f /dev/hda5
```

The idea is that each of the deleted files has been literally undeleted, but none of them appear in any directory entries. The `e2fsck` program can detect this, and will add a directory entry for each file in the `/lost+found` directory of the filesystem. (So if the partition is normally mounted on `/usr`, the files will now appear in `/usr/lost+found`.) All that still remains to be done is to work out the name of each file from its contents, and return it to its correct place in the filesystem tree.

When you run `e2fsck`, you will get some informative output, and some questions about what damage to repair. Answer 'yes' to everything that refers to 'summary information' or to the inodes you've changed. Anything else I leave up to you, although it's usually a good idea to say 'yes' to all the questions. When `e2fsck` finishes, you can remount the filesystem.

Actually, there's an alternative to having `e2fsck` leave the files in `/lost+found`: you can use `debugfs` to create a link in the filesystem to the inode. Use the `link` command in `debugfs` after you've modified the inode:

```
debugfs:  link <148003> foo.txt
```

This creates a file called `foo.txt` in what `debugfs` thinks is the current directory; `foo.txt` will be your file. You'll still need to run `e2fsck` to fix the summary information and block counts and so on.

12   Will this get easier in future?

Yes. In fact, I believe it already has. Kernels in the development 2.1.x series have not zeroed indirect blocks since more than six months ago. At the beginning of December 1996, there was some talk on the `linux-kernel` mailing-list of producing another 2.0.x production kernel that also leaves indirect blocks intact on deletion. Although as of the pre-released versions of kernel 2.0.31 this has not happened, I suspect that it is feasible. Once Linus and the other kernel hackers overcome this limitation in the production kernels, a lot of my objections to the technique of modifying inodes by hand will disappear. At the very latest, this should happen on the release of the 2.2.x kernel series, which (according to historical kernel development time-scales) should happen some time in the first quarter of 1998. When this wart is corrected, it will also be possible to use the `dump` command in `debugfs` on long files.

13   Are there any tools to automate this process?

As it happens, there are. Unfortunately, I believe that they suffer from the same problem as the manual inode modification technique: indirect blocks are unrecoverable. However, given the likelihood that this will shortly no longer be a problem, it's well worth looking these programs out now.

Someone on the net mentioned `lde` by Scott Heavner. To be honest, I wouldn't recommend this as a tool for automating file recovery. It's more like a full-screen `debugfs` than anything else, although it does have some features like the ability to scan for certain types of file or for certain file contents. It also works with the `xia` (does anyone actually use this any more?) and `minix` filesystems, which I guess is its major selling point these days. Version 2.3.4 is available on *Sunsite* `<ftp://sunsite.unc.edu/pub/Linux/system/ Filesystems/lde-2.3.4.tar.gz>` and mirrors (although it's possible there's a more recent version than this; I found that one on an 8-month-old CD-ROM archive). `lde` *does* have some fairly useful documentation on basic filesystem concepts, as well as a document on how to use it for recovering deleted files. Although I haven't used it, I suspect that my method above is better.

It sounds like the program that *really* works is the GNU Midnight Commander, `mc`. This is a full-screen file management tool, based AFAIK on a certain MS-DOS program commonly known as 'NC'. `mc` supports the mouse on the Linux console and in an xterm, and provides virtual filesystems which allow tricks like `cd`-ing to a tarfile. Among its virtual filesystems is one for ext2 undeletion. It all sounds very handy, although I must admit I've never used the program myself – I prefer good old-fashioned shell commands. Apparently one must configure the program with the `--with-ext2undel` option; you'll also need the development libraries and include files that come with the `e2fsprogs` package. I gather that once the program is built, you can tell it to `cd undel:dev/hda5/`, and get a 'directory listing' of deleted files.

The latest non-development version is probably 4.0; as with the kernel itself, development versions are *not* recommended to non-hackers. The list of (over 70) download sites is available on *the Midnight Commander 4 website* `<http://mc.blackdown.org/mc4/>`, or try the *official ftp site* `<ftp://ftp.nuclecu.unam.mx/linux/ local/mc-4.0.tar.gz>` (which if memory serves is rather slow).

14 Colophon

I intend to produce regular updates to this document as long as I have both enough time to do it, and something interesting to say. This means that I am eager to hear comments from readers. Could my writing be clearer?. Can you think of something that would make matters easier? Is there some new tool that does it all automatically? Who *did* kill JFK?

Whatever. If you have something to say, about this document or any other subject, drop me a line on *<aaronc@pobox.com>* `<mailto:aaronc@pobox.com>`.

15 Credits and Bibliography

> 'If I have seen farther than others, it is because I was standing on the shoulders of giants.'
> (Isaac Newton)

Much of this mini-Howto was derived from a posting in the `comp.os.linux.misc` `<news:comp.os.linux. misc>` newsgroup by Robin Glover *<swrglovr@met.rdg.ac.uk>* `<mailto:swrglovr@met.rdg.ac.uk>`. I would like to thank Robin for graciously allowing me to rework his ideas into this mini-Howto.

Some bibliographic references:

- **Frisch**, Æleen (1995), *Essential System Administration*, second edition, O'Reilly and Associates, Inc., ISBN: 1-56592-127-5.

- **Glover**, Robin (31 Jan 1996), *HOW-TO : undelete linux files (ext2fs/debugfs)*, comp.os.linux.misc Usenet posting.

- **Peek**, Jerry, Tim **O'Reilly**, Mike **Loukides** et al (1993), *UNIX Power Tools*, O'Reilly and Associates, Inc./Random House, Inc., ISBN: 0-679-79073-X.

16 Legalities

All trademarks are the property of their respective owners. Specifically:

- *MS-DOS* and *Windows* are trademarks of *Microsoft* <http://www.microsoft.com/>.
- *UNIX* is a trademark of *the Open Group* <http://www.open.org/>.
- The trademark status of the name *Linux* is currently being contested by lawyers. A certain Walter R. Della Croce has made an allegedly false trademark registration for the term. Further information on the Linux trademark issue is available from *the Linux Mall* <http://www.linuxmall.com/announce/>.

The Linux HOWTO Coordinator is Greg Hankins <*gregh@sunsite.unc.edu*> <mailto:gregh@sunsite.unc.edu>.

Linux Partition HOWTO

Kristan Koehntopp, kris@koehntopp.de $Id: howto.sgml,v 2.4 1997/11/03 06:27:22 kris Exp $

This Linux Mini-HOWTO teaches you how to plan and layout disk space for your Linux system. It talks about disk hardware, partitions, swap space sizing and positioning considerations. file systems, file system types and related topics. The intent is to teach some background knowledge, not procedures.

Contents

1 Introduction

1.1 What is this?

This is a Linux Mini-HOWTO text. A Mini-HOWTO is a small text explaining some business related to Linux installation and maintenance tutorial style. It's mini, because either the text or the topic it discusses are too small for a real HOWTO or even a book. A HOWTO is not a reference: that's what manual pages are for.

1.2   What is in it? and related HOWTO documents

This particular Mini-HOWTO teaches you how to plan and layout disk space for your Linux system. It talks about disk hardware, partitions, swap space sizing and positioning considerations, file systems, file system types and related topics. The intent is to teach some background knowlegde, so we are talking mainly principles and not tools in this text.

Ideally, this document should be read before your first installation, but this is somehow difficult for most people. First timers have other problems than disk layout optimization, too. So you are probably someone who just finished a Linux installation and is now thinking about ways to optimize this installation or how to avoid some nasty miscalculations in the next one. Well, expect some desire to tear down and rebuild your installation when you are finished with this text. :-)

This Mini-HOWTO limits itself to planning and layouting disk space most of the time. It does not discuss the usage of fdisk, LILO, mke2fs or backup programs. There are other HOWTOs that address these problems. Please see the Linux HOWTO Index for current information on Linux HOWTOs. There are instructions for obtaining HOWTO documents in the index, too.

To learn how to estimate the various size and speed requirements for different parts of the filesystem, see "Linux Multiple Disks Layout mini-HOWTO", by Gjoen Stein <gjoen@nyx.net>.

For instructions and considerations regarding disks with more than 1024 cylinders, see "Linux Large Disk mini-HOWTO", Andries Brouwer <aeb@cwi.nl>.

For instructions on limiting disk space usage per user (quotas), see "Linux Quota mini-HOWTO", by Albert M.C. Tam <bertie@scn.org>

Currently, there is no general document on disk backup, but there are several documents with pointers to specific backup solutions. See "Linux ADSM Backup mini-HOWTO", by Thomas Koenig <Thomas.Koenig@ciw.uni-karlsruhe.de> for instructions on integrating Linux into an IBM ADSM backup environment. See "Linux Backup with MSDOS mini-HOWTO", by Christopher Neufeld <neufeld@physics.utoronto.ca> for information about MS-DOS driven Linux backups.

For instructions on writing and submitting a HOWTO document, see the Linux HOWTO Index, by Greg Hankins <gregh@sunsite.unc.edu>.

Browsing through /usr/src/linux/Documentation can be very instructive, too. See ide.txt and scsi.txt for some background information on the properties of your disk drivers and have a look at the filesystems/ subdirectory.

2   What is a partition anyway?

When PC hard disks were invented people soon wanted to install multiple operating systems, even if their system had only one disk. So a mechanism was needed to divide a single physical disk into multiple logical disks. So that's what a partition is: A contiguous section of blocks on your hard disk that is treated like a completely seperate disk by most operating systems.

It is fairly clear that partitions must not overlap: An operating system will certainly not be pleased, if another operating system installed on the same machine were overwriting important information because of overlapping partitions. There should be no gap between adjacent partitions, too. While this constellation is not harmful, you are wasting precious disk space by leaving space between partitions.

A disk need not be partitioned completely. You may decide to leave some space at the end of your disk that is not assigned to any of your installed operating systems, yet. Later, when it is clear which installation is used by you most of the time, you can partition this left over space and put a file system on it.

Partitions can not be moved nor can they be resized without destroying the file system contained in it. So repartitioning usually involves backup and restore of all file systems touched during the repartitioning. In fact it is fairly common to mess up things completely during repartitioning, so you should back up anything on any disk on that particular machine before even touching things like fdisk.

Well, some partitions with certain file system types on them actually *can* be split into two without losing any data (if you are lucky). For example there is a program called "fips" for splitting MS-DOS partitions into two to make room for a Linux installation without having to reinstall MS-DOS. You are still not going to touch these things without carefully backing up everything on that machine, aren't you?

2.1 Backups are important

Tapes are your friend for backups. They are fast, reliable and easy to use, so you can make backups often, preferably automatically and without hassle.

Step on soapbox: And I am talking about real tapes, not that disk controller driven ftape crap. Consider buying SCSI: Linux does support SCSI natively. You don't need to load ASPI drivers, you are not losing precious HMA under Linux and once the SCSI host adapter is installed, you just attach additional disks, tapes and CD-ROMs to it. No more I/O addresses, IRQ juggling or Master/Slave and PIO-level matching.

Plus: Proper SCSI host adapters give you high I/O performance without much CPU load. Even under heavy disk activity you will experience good response times. If you are planning to use a Linux system as a major USENET news feed or if you are about to enter the ISP business, don't even think about deploying a system without SCSI. Climb of soapbox.

2.2 Device numbers and device names

The number of partitions on an Intel based system was limited from the very beginning: The original partition table was installed as part of the boot sector and held space for only four partition entries. These partitions are now called primary partitions. When it became clear that people needed more partitions on their systems, logical partitions were invented. The number of logical partitions is not limited: Each logical partition contains a pointer to the next logical partition, so you can have a potentially unlimited chain of partition entries.

For compatibility reasons, the space occupied by all logical partitions had to be accounted for. If you are using logical partitions, one primary partition entry is marked as "extended partition" and its starting and ending block mark the area occupied by your logical partitions. This implies that the space assigned to all logical partitions has to be contiguous. There can be only one extended partition: no fdisk program will create more than one extended partition.

Linux cannot handle more than a limited number of partitions per drive. So in Linux you have 4 primary partitions (3 of them useable, if you are using logical partitions) and at most 15 partitions altogether on an SCSI disk (63 altogether on an IDE disk).

In Linux, partitions are represented by device files. A device file is a file with type c (for "character" devices, devices that do not use the buffer cache) or b (for "block" devices, which go through the buffer cache). In Linux, all disks are represented as block devices only. Unlike other Unices, Linux does not offer "raw" character versions of disks and their partitions.

The only important thing with a device file are its major and minor device number, shown instead of the files size:

```
$ ls -l /dev/hda
brw-rw----   1 root      disk        3,    0 Jul 18  1994 /dev/hda
                                      ^    ^
                                      |    minor device number
```

When accessing a device file, the major number selects which device driver is being called to perform the input/output operation. This call is being done with the minor number as a parameter and it is entirely up to the driver how the minor number is being interpreted. The driver documentation usually describes how the driver uses minor numbers. For IDE disks, this documentation is in /usr/src/linux/Documentation/ide.txt. For SCSI disks, one would expect such documentation in /usr/src/linux/Documentation/scsi.txt, but it isn't there. One has to look at the driver source to be sure (/usr/src/linux/driver/scsi/sd.c:184-196). Fortunately, there is Peter Anvin's list of device numbers and names in /usr/src/linux/Documentation/devices.txt; see the entries for block devices, major 3, 22, 33, 34 for IDE and major 8 for SCSI disks. The major and minor numbers are a byte each and that is why the number of partitions per disk is limited.

By convention device files have certain names and many system programs have knowledge about these names compiled in. They expect your IDE disks to be named /dev/hd* and your SCSI disks to be named /dev/sd*. Disks are numbered a, b, c and so on, so /dev/hda is your first IDE disk and /dev/sda is your first SCSI disk. Both devices represent entire disks, starting at block one. Writing to these devices with the wrong tools will destroy the master boot loader and partition table on these disks, rendering all data on this disk unusable or making your system unbootable. Know what you are doing and, again, back up before you do it.

Primary partitions on a disk are 1, 2, 3 and 4. So /dev/hda1 is the first primary partition on the first IDE disk and so on. Logical partitions have numbers 5 and up, so /dev/sdb5 is the first logical partition on the second SCSI disk.

Each partition entry has a starting and an ending block address assigned to it and a type. The type is a numerical code (a byte) which designates a particular partition to a certain type of operating system. For the benefit of computing consultants partition type codes are not really unique, so there is always the probability of two operating systems using the same type code.

Linux reserves the type code 0x82 for swap partitions and 0x83 for "native" file systems (that's ext2 for almost all of you). The once popular, now outdated Linux/Minix file system used the type code 0x81 for partitions. OS/2 marks it's partitions with a 0x07 type and so does Windows NT's NTFS. MS-DOS allocates several type codes for its various flavors of FAT file systems: 0x01, 0x04 and 0x06 are known. DR-DOS used 0x81 to indicate protected FAT partitions, creating a type clash with Linux/Minix at that time, but neither Linux/Minix nor DR-DOS are widely used any more. The extended partition which is used as a container for logical partitions has a type of 0x05, by the way.

Partitions are created and deleted with the fdisk program. Every self respecting operating system program comes with an fdisk and traditionally it is even called fdisk (or FDISK.EXE) in almost all OSes. Some fdisks, noteable the DOS one, are somehow limited when they have to deal with other operating systems partitions. Such limitations include the complete inability to deal with anything with a foreign type code, the inability to deal with cylinder numbers above 1024 and the inability to create or even understand partitions that do not end on a cylinder boundary. For example, the MS-DOS fdisk can't delete NTFS partitions, the OS/2 fdisk has been known to silently "correct" partitions created by the Linux fdisk that do not end on a cylinder boundary and both, the DOS and the OS/2 fdisk, have had problems with disks with more than 1024 cylinders (see the "large-disk" Mini-Howto for details on such disks).

3   What Partitions do I need?

3.1   How many partitions do I need?

Okay, so what partitions do you need? Well, some operating systems do not believe in booting from logical partitions for reasons that are beyond the scope of any sane mind. So you probably want to reserve your primary partitions as boot partitions for your MS-DOS, OS/2 and Linux or whatever you are using. Remember that one primary partition is needed as an extended partition, which acts as a container for the rest of your disk with logical partitions.

Booting operating systems is a real-mode thing involving BIOSes and 1024 cylinder limitations. So you probably want to put all your boot partitions into the first 1024 cylinders of your hard disk, just to avoid problems. Again, read the "large-disk" Mini-Howto for the gory details.

To install Linux, you will need at least one partition. If the kernel is loaded from this partition (for example by LILO), this partition must be readable by your BIOS. If you are using other means to load your kernel (for example a boot disk or the LOADLIN.EXE MS-DOS based Linux loader) the partition can be anywhere. In any case this partition will be of type 0x83 "Linux native".

Your system will need some swap space. Unless you swap to files you will need a dedicated swap partition. Since this partition is only accessed by the Linux kernel and the Linux kernel does not suffer from PC BIOS deficiencies, the swap partition may be positioned anywhere. I recommed using a logical partition for it (/dev/?d?5 and higher). Dedicated Linux swap partitions are of type 0x82 "Linux swap".

These are minimal partition requirements. It may be useful to create more partitions for Linux. Read on.

3.2   How large should my swap space be?

If you have decided to use a dedicated swap partition, which is generally a Good Idea [tm], follow these guidelines for estimating its size:

- In Linux RAM and swap space add up (This is not true for all Unices). For example, if you have 8 MB of RAM and 12 MB swap space, you have a total of about 20 MB virtual memory.

- When sizing your swap space, you should have at least 16 MB of total virtual memory. So for 4 MB of RAM consider at least 12 MB of swap, for 8 MB of RAM consider at least 8 MB of swap.

- In Linux, a single swap partition can not be larger than 128 MB. That is, the partition may be larger than 128 MB, but excess space is never used. If you want more than 128 MB of swap, you have to create multiple swap partitions.

- When sizing swap space, keep in mind that too much swap space may not be useful at all.

  Every process has a "working set". This is a set of in-memory pages which will be referenced by the processor in the very near future. Linux tries to predict these memory accesses (assuming that recently used pages will be used again in the near future) and keeps these pages in RAM if possible. If the program has a good "locality of reference" this assumption will be true and prediction algorithm will work.

  Holding a working set in main memory does only work if there is enough main memory. If you have too many processes running on a machine, the kernel is forced to put pages on disk that it will reference again in the very near future (forcing a page-out of a page from another working set and then a page-in of the page referenced). Usually this results in a very heavy increase in paging activity and in a sustantial drop of performance. A machine in this state is said to be "thrashing" (For you german readers: That's "thrashing" ("dreschen", "schlagen", "haemmern") and not trashing ("muellen")).

  On a thrashing machine the processes are essentially running from disk and not from RAM. Expect performance to drop by approximately the ratio between memory access speed and disk access speed.

  A very old rule of thumb in the days of the PDP and the Vax was that the size of the working set of a program is about 25% of its virtual size. Thus it is probably useless to provide more swap than three times your RAM.

  But keep in mind that this is just a rule of thumb. It is easily possible to create scenarios where programs have extremely large or extremely small working sets. For example, a simulation program with a large data set that is accessed in a very random fashion would have almost no noticeable locality of reference in its data segment, so its working set would be quite large.

On the other hand, an xv with many simultaneously opened JPEGs, all but one iconified, would have a very large data segment. But image transformations are all done on one single image, most of the memory occupied by xv is never touched. The same is true for an editor with many editor windows where only one window is being modified at a time. These programs have - if they are designed properly - a very high locality of reference and large parts of them can be kept swapped out without too severe performance impact.

One could suspect that the 25% number from the age of the command line is no longer true for modern GUI programs editing multiple documents, but I know of no newer papers that try to verify these numbers.

So for a configuration with 16 MB RAM, no swap is needed for a minimal configuration and more than 48 MB of swap are probably useless. The exact amount of memory needed depends on the application mix on the machine (what did you expect?).

3.3   Where should I put my swap space?

- Mechanics are slow, electronics are fast.

  Modern hard disks have many heads. Switching between heads of the same track is fast, since it is purely electronic. Switching between tracks is slow, since it involves moving real world matter.

  So if you have a disk with many heads and one with less heads and both are identical in other parameters, the disk with many heads will be faster.

  Splitting swap and putting it on both disks will be even faster, though.

- Older disks have the same number of sectors on all tracks. With this disks it will be fastest to put your swap in the middle of the disks, assuming that your disk head will move from a random track towards the swap area.

- Newer disks use ZBR (zone bit recording). They have more sectors on the outer tracks. With a constant number of rpms, this yields a far greater performance on the outer tracks than on the inner ones. Put your swap on the fast tracks.

- Of course your disk head will not move randomly. If you have swap space in the middle of a disk between a constantly busy home partition and an almost unused archive partition, you would be better of if your swap were in the middle of the home partition for even shorter head movements. You would be even better off, if you had your swap on another otherwise unused disk, though.

Summary: Put your swap on a fast disk with many heads that is not busy doing other things. If you have multiple disks: Split swap and scatter it over all your disks or even different controllers.

Even better: Buy more RAM.

3.4   Some facts about file systems and fragmentation

Disk space is administered by the operating system in units of blocks and fragments of blocks. In ext2, fragments and blocks have to be of the same size, so we can limit our discussion to blocks.

Files come in any size. They don't end on block boundaries. So with every file a part of the last block of every file is wasted. Assuming that file sizes are random, there is approximately a half block of waste for each file on your disk. Tanenbaum calls this "internal fragmentation" in his book "Operating Systems".

You can guess the number of files on your disk by the number of allocated inodes on a disk. On my disk

```
# df -i
Filesystem              Inodes  IUsed  IFree  %IUsed Mounted on
```

/dev/hda3	64256	12234	52022	19%	/
/dev/hda5	96000	43058	52942	45%	/var

there are about 12000 files on / and about 44000 files on **/var**. At a block size of 1 KB, about $6+22 = 28$ MB of disk space are lost in the tail blocks of files. Had I chosen a block size of 4 KB, I had lost 4 times this space.

Data transfer is faster for large contiguous chunks of data, though. That's why ext2 tries to preallocate space in units of 8 contiguous blocks for growing files. Unused preallocation is released when the file is closed, so no space is wasted.

Noncontiguous placement of blocks in a file is bad for performance, since files are often accessed in a sequential manner. It forces the operating system to split a disk access and the disk to move the head. This is called "external fragmentation" or simply "fragmentation" and is a common problem with DOS file systems.

ext2 has several strategies to avoid external fragmentation. Normally fragmentation is not a large problem in ext2, not even on heavily used partitions such as a USENET news spool. While there is a tool for defragmentation of ext2 file systems, nobody ever uses it and it is not up to date with the current release of ext2. Use it, but do so on your own risk.

The MS-DOS file system is well known for its pathological managment of disk space. In conjunction with the abysmal buffer cache used by MS-DOS the effects of file fragmentation on performance are very noticeable. DOS users are accustomed to defragging their disks every few weeks and some have even developed some ritualistic beliefs regarding defragmentation. None of these habits should be carried over to Linux and ext2. Linux native file systems do not need defragmentation under normal use and this includes any condition with at least 5% of free space on a disk.

The MS-DOS file system is also known to lose large amounts of disk space due to internal fragmentation. For partitions larger than 256 MB, DOS block sizes grow so large that they are no longer useful (This has been corrected to some extent with FAT32).

ext2 does not force you to choose large blocks for large file systems, except for very large file systems in the 0.5 TB range (that's terabytes with 1 TB equaling 1024 GB) and above, where small block sizes become inefficient. So unlike DOS there is no need to split up large disks into multiple partitions to keep block size down. Use the 1 KB default block size if possible. You may want to experiment with a block size of 2 KB for some partitions, but expect to meet some seldom exercised bugs: Most people use the default.

3.5 File lifetimes and backup cycles as partitioning criteria

With ext2, Partitioning decisions should be governed by backup considerations and to avoid external fragmentation from different file lifetimes.

Files have lifetimes. After a file has been created, it will remain some time on the system and then be removed. File lifetime varies greatly throughout the system and is partly dependent on the pathname of the file. For example, files in /bin, /sbin, /usr/sbin, /usr/bin and similar directories are likely to have a very long lifetime: many months and above. Files in /home are likely to have a medium lifetime: several weeks or so. File in /var are usually short lived: Almost no file in /var/spool/news will remain longer than a few days, files in /var/spool/lpd measure their lifetime in minutes or less.

For backup it is useful if the amount of daily backup is smaller than the capacity of a single backup medium. A daily backup can be a complete backup or an incremental backup.

You can decide to keep your partition sizes small enough that they fit completely onto one backup medium (choose daily full backups). In any case a partition should be small enough that its daily delta (all modified files) fits onto one backup medium (choose incremental backup and expect to change backup media for the weekly/monthly full dump - no unattended operation possible).

Your backup strategy depends on that decision.

When planning and buying disk space, remember to set aside a sufficient amount of money for backup! Unbackuped data is worthless! Data reproduction costs are much higher than backup costs for virtually everyone!

For performance it is useful to keep files of different lifetimes on different partitions. This way the short lived files on the news partition may be fragmented very heavily. This has no impact on the performance of the / or /home partition.

4 An example

4.1 A recommended model for ambitious beginners

A common model creates /, /home and /var partitions as discussed above. This is simple to install and maintain and differentiates well enough to avoid adverse effects from different lifetimes. It fits well into a backup model, too: Almost noone bothers to backup USENET news spools and only some files in /var are worth backing up (/var/spool/mail comes to mind). On the other hand, / changes infrequently and can be backuped upon demand (after configuration changes) and is small enough to fit on most modern backup media as a full backup (plan 250 to 500 MB depending on the amount of installed software). /home contains valuable user data and should be backuped daily. Some installations have very large /homes and must use incremental backups.

Some systems put /tmp onto a seperate partition as well, others symlink it to /var/tmp to achieve the same effect (note that this can affect single user mode, where /var will be unavailable and the system will have no /tmp until you create one or mount /var manually) or put it onto a RAM disk (Solaris does this for example). This keeps /tmp out of /, a good idea.

This model is convenient for upgrades or reinstallations as well: Save your configuration files (or the entire /etc) to some /home directory, scrap your /, reinstall and fetch the old configurations from the save directory on /home.

5 How I did it on my machine

There was this old ISA bus 386/40 sitting on my shelf that I abandoned two years ago because it no longer cut it. I was planning to turn it into a small X-less server for my household LAN.

Here is how I did it: I took that 386 and put 16 MB RAM into it. Added a cheap EIDE disk, the smallest I could get (800 MB) and an ethernet card. Added an old Hercules because I still had a monitor for it. Installed Linux on it and there I have my local NFS, SMB, HTTP, LPD/LPR and NNTP server as well as my mail router and POP3 server. With an additional ISDN card the machine became my TCP/IP router and firewall, too.

Most of the disk space on this machine went into the /var directories, /var/spool/mail, /var/spool/news and /var/httpd/html. I put /var on a separate partition and made this one large. There will be almost no users on this machine, so I created no home partition and mounted /home from some other workstation via NFS.

Linux without X plus several locally installed utilities will be fine with a 250 MB partition as /. The machine has 16 MB of RAM, but it will be running many servers. 16 MB swap should be in order, 32 MB should be plenty. We are not short on disk space, so the machine will get 32 MB. Out of sentimentality a MS-DOS partition of some 20 MB is kept on it. I decided to import /home from another machine, so the remaining 500+ MB will end up as /var. This is more than sufficient for a household USENET news feed.

We get

Device	Mounted on	Size
/dev/hda1	/dos_c	25 MB
/dev/hda2	- (Swapspace)	32 MB
/dev/hda3	/	250 MB
/dev/hda4	- (Extended Container)	500 MB
/dev/hda5	/var	500 MB
homeserver:/home /home		1.6 GB

I am backing up this machine via the network using the tape in homeserver. Since everything on this machine has been installed from CD-ROM all I have to save are some configuration files from /etc, my customized locally installed *.tgz files from /root/Source/Installed and /var/spool/mail as well as /var/httpd/html. I copy these files into a dedicated directory /home/backmeup on homeserver every night, where the regular homeserver backup picks them up.

Upgrading Your linux Distribution mini-HOWTO

Greg Louis, glouis@dynamicro.on.ca

v1.11, 6 June 1996

Hints and tips on upgrading from one linux distribution to another.

Contents

1   IMPORTANT!!! Disclaimer and Copyright

The procedure to which this document attempts to be a guide is inherently dangerous to the programs and data stored in your computer. You carry out any such procedure entirely at your own risk. The steps described in this document worked for the author; there is no guarantee that they will work for you, nor that you can attempt to follow them without serious damage to your computer's programs and/or data. You are entirely on your own in any use you may make of the information presented herein, and the author shall not be liable in any way whatsoever for any damage or inconvenience of any kind that you may suffer in so doing.

This document is copyright 1996, Dynamicro Consulting Limited, and is released under the terms of the GNU General Public License. This basically means that you may copy and modify it at will, but may not prevent others from doing likewise.

Comments and questions may be directed to the author. Especially welcome, for use in future revisions, are accounts of successful upgrades of complex systems.

2   Changes since version 1.1

- Added this history section
- Added Zoltán Hidvégi's suggestion re mtime and ctime. Thanks, Zoltán!
- Added an Acknowledgements section

3   Introduction

3.1   How to slay and reincarnate your linux box!

The purpose of this document is to offer tips to help you through the destruction and reinstallation of a linux system. It's not a foolproof cookbook by any means; but I hope it will serve as some indication of what you need to think about, and of the order in which to do things. It would have been a help to me, if someone else had written something like this before I did my first upgrade; so I hope it will be a help to you, if you have a linux machine to rebuild.

Don't take it as gospel, though: your mileage will almost certainly vary. Even the directory names in this document may be different from the ones you need to use; some people have /usr/home instead of /home, for example; others call it /u, and some (delicate shudder :) even put all their users directly under /usr itself! I can't be specific about your system, so I've just used the names the way they are in mine.

You'll also notice that I use Slackware distributions, and that I assume you've enough RAM and hard disk space to install linux kernel source and build your own kernel. If your system is different, some of my recommendations won't apply; but I hope you'll still find the general outline to be of assistance in your rebuild project.

3.2 Why would anyone want to do that?

Good question! If it can possibly be avoided, don't do it! (That's the single most important recommendation in this whole guide!!!) But there are times when you may have to.

For example, I installed a 4Gb hard disk and then found out that Slackware 2.0 vintage linux didn't know a hard disk could have more than 2Gb, and it got horribly confused. So I had to upgrade to the then-current Slackware 2.3. That upgrade was a gruelling experience, and it's part of the reason I'm writing these notes. I did just about everything wrong, and only good luck and the fact that I had another running linux box beside me saved me from disaster.

As another example, I found that I just couldn't succeed in building a working a.out linux kernel in the 1.3 series, using an out-of-the-box Slackware 2.3 installation (another machine, not the one I botched before). I took the plunge, bought Slackware 3.0 on CDROM and converted to ELF. This time the reinstallation went better, thanks in part to the previous bitter experience, and it served as the source of most of the ideas I'm offering you here.

3.3 Do you have to "destroy and reinstall?"

It's safer, oddly enough. If you install over top of an existing linux system, chances are you'll have a mixture of old and new binaries, old and new configuration files, and generally a mess to try to administer. Wiping the system clean, and then putting back only what you know you need, is a drastic but effective way to get a clean result. (Of course we're talking about installing a whole new linux distribution here, not about upgrading one or two packages! The best way to avoid having to do a full reinstallation is, precisely, to keep the individual bits – especially gcc and its libraries, and binutils – current. If the stuff you use is reasonably up-to-date, and you can keep it so by bringing in, and if need be compiling, new code from time to time, then there's no need for a mass upgrade.)

As Patrick Volkerding points out (he too recommends the wipe-it-clean procedure for upgrades), installing ELF on top of a running a.out system is a recipe for disaster; at least, if you know enough to try it, you needn't read this guide!

Even without that complication, though, you're better to build from scratch.

3.4 How long will it take?

Depends, of course, on how complex your system is. But I figure that, for the successful upgrade (the other one? – don't ask! :) I spent about ten hours making backups, six hours rebuilding the system to the point where I could enable logins, and another half day or thereabouts restoring the less-crucial stuff. As time passes I keep discovering little things that still aren't exactly as I want them – I fix these as they're encountered – but in the main, twenty hours' work should suffice for a reasonably complex rebuilding job. Maybe less if you're reinstalling from hard disk (I used CDROM) or more if you need to install from floppies. Maybe less if you've got a fast Pentium, more if it's a 386. You get the idea.

So much for the introduction. Here's how to set about it, once you've decided it must be done. Arm yourself with fortitude and Jolt or whatever, and:

4 Write down everything you do.

It's extremely valuable to have a record of what you've done in the process of preparing for, and carrying out, the changeover. Especially important is a list of the backups you'll be making in preparation for the destruction of your existing system.

5 Make a full backup of the existing system.

Generally speaking, backups tend to be written on media that are sequentially accessed. That being so, you won't want to use this complete backup for restoring significant numbers of files; it's got too many files on it that you don't want. It's better to create small backups of individual segments that you know you're going to restore in their entirety. I'll list a bunch of examples later.

Why then should you start with a full backup? Two basic reasons: first, in the event of a catastrophic failure installing the new system, you'll have a way to get back to the starting point with minimum pain. Second, no matter how carefully you prepare for the new installation, there is a very large chance that one or two important files will be overlooked. In that case the clumsiness of restoring those one or two files from the full backup set will be preferable to the inconvenience of doing without them.

To save time and space, if you've still got the distribution medium for your old linux version, you might want to back up only those files the mtime or ctime of which is more recent than the date of the original installation.

6 Back up /etc and its subdirectories on one or more floppies.

This is the other extreme: you won't be restoring these files (for the most part, anyway); you'll be comparing them with the new ones that get created during installation. Why? Because the new ones may have data that the old ones didn't, or may express the old data in new ways. Changes in protocols, addition of new tools, or implementation of new features in existing tools may all dictate changes in the formats of the configuration files and startup scripts that the /etc tree contains, and you'll very likely have to edit your old data into these files so as to preserve the new formats and take advantage of the improvements.

7 Make separate backups of each group of files you want to preserve.

This is the most variable part of the job, and all I can really do to help is to describe what I did in my system, in the hope that it will serve as a rough guide. Basically, you want to look at every directory that contains any

- files that aren't part of your standard linux installation, or
- files that are actually newer than the ones you'll install when you do your new linux installation

and separate out only those files that you want to carry over.

(Another possible strategy is to back up all files with mtime or ctime more recent than the day of the previous linux installation, as mentioned above, and then restore from that. If you do that, you have to take into account that the new linux distribution may contain versions of some files that are newer still than the ones you saved.)

In my case, I ended up making a .tgz file on the backup medium for each of

- /usr/lib/rn
- /usr/lib/smail
- /usr/lib/trn (the rest of /usr/lib would be reinstalled)
- /usr/local/src
- /usr/local/bin
- /usr/local/lib
- /usr/local/lpfont
- /usr/local/man
- /usr/local/sbin
- /usr/local/thot (there were other /usr/local files I didn't need)
- /usr/openwin
- /usr/src/lilo-17 (because my new Slackware still had version 16)
- /usr/src/linux-1.2.13 (because I'd done some customizing)
- /usr/X11R6/lib/X11/app-defaults
- /usr/X11R6/lib/X11/initrc (the rest of Xfree86 was to be reinstalled)
- /var/named
- /var/openwin
- /var/texfonts

My machine was relatively easy in that there were no spool files to worry about. I don't run a news spool on this box, and since there are only two users, it was easiest just to get all the mail read before shutting down. Otherwise, /var/spool directories would have had to be backed up at the last minute. (And, of course, the news library and site directories!)

8   Prepare root and boot floppies for the new installation.

Details of how to do this will be found in the installation guide for your new distribution.

9   Format floppies for the temporary kernel and the final build.

You'll need two, one floppy for each.

After all that's done, you're ready for the Big Moment. The next step removes the system from production.

10   Inhibit logins and back up the /root and /home trees.

This is the last thing to be done on the old system before you destroy it, so as to carry forward the most current user and root information.

11   Boot from the new installation's boot and root floppies.

12   Delete the linux partitions with fdisk and recreate them.

The installation guide will explain how to set about doing this, which will destroy the old system. From now on you're dependent on the quality of the backups you made in the earlier steps! You have been warned!

13   Run the new linux installation.

There are already several good documents describing how to do this, so I'm not going into any detail. Continue from here when the new system can boot from its hard disk.

Along the way, be sure to make a floppy that you can boot as well, since the kernel that the linux setup installs has to be replaced and accidents can happen during that process. Be sure to install the development packages and the kernel source.

14   With the new linux system booted from the hard disk, edit /etc/fstab

and add your swap partition. Then run the command "swapon -a". I don't know why, but Slackware setup doesn't offer to do this for you if your swap partition exists already. Then, when you boot your new system and the rc.S script tries to turn swapping on, it can't find the partition in the fstab file and swapping doesn't get enabled. This step fixes it.

15   Restore configuration data to the /etc directory and sub-directories.

As described above, you can't just copy all of the old files back into /etc and expect things to work properly afterward. Some files you can do that with; for example, /etc/XF86Config (as long as you're using the same version of Xfree86 – and the same video hardware – in the new installation as you did in the old). For the most part, though, it's best to use diff to compare the old and new files before doing any copying. Watch out especially for significant changes in the files in /etc/rc.d, which may require you to reestablish your old configuration by hand editing, instead of by copying the old rc scripts from your backup. Once it's all done, reboot.

16   Configure and rebuild the linux kernel.

Even if you don't absolutely have to do this in order to get a kernel that supports your hardware, it's worth doing it in order to get a kernel that doesn't contain masses of drivers for stuff your machine doesn't have. For details, see the Kernel HOWTO. Install the rebuilt kernel on a floppy at first; once that boots ok, install on the hard disk, run lilo if you're using it, and reboot.

17　Restore the stuff from the backups you made earlier.

Some of the binaries may need to be reinstalled from the source directories; I had to do that with lilo, for example, since my version was newer than the one on the Slackware installation and I hadn't bothered to save the binary from /sbin. You'll want to check through your restored programs and confirm the existence and correctness of configuration files, libraries and so on. In some cases, you may have to restore things in a specific order; you did make notes during backup, didn't you? ;-)

18　Review security.

Check file permissions and directory permissions to be sure that access is neither too restricted nor too easy. I find that Slackware tends to lean toward a more open environment than I like, so I go around changing 755's to 711's for binaries in the .../bin directories and stuff like that. Or even 700's in the .../sbin ones. Especial care is needed if you've carried over an ftp server; but then, if you were running an ftp server, you probably thought of that already. :)

19　Enable logins.

You're up and running. Over the next little while, there'll probably be details to clean up; but the bulk of the work is done. Enjoy!

20　Sorry, but once again:

USE THIS INFORMATION AT YOUR OWN RISK!

(See the disclaimer at the start of this document.)

21　Acknowledgements

Thanks for contributing to the content of this mini-HOWTO are gratefully tendered to Zoltán Hidvégi.

PATH HOWTO

Esa Turtiainen etu@dna.fi   v0.4, 15 November 1997

Contents

1   Introduction

This document describes common tricks and problems with Unix / Linux environment variables, especially with PATH variable. PATH is a list of directories where commands are looked for. The details apply for Debian Linux 1.3 distribution.

Note! This document is in beta release status. Please send comments and corrections.

2   Copyright

3   General

All the Unix processes contain an "environment". This is a list of variables that contain name and value, both just strings that can contain most characters. All Unix processes have a parent process - the process that created this process as child. Child processes inherit environment from parent process. They can make some modifications to the environment before passing it in turn to their child processes.

One important environment variable is PATH, a list of directories separated by colons (':'). These directories are searched through to find commands. If you try to invoke command 'foo', all the directories in PATH (in that order) are searched for an executable file 'foo' (one with x-bit on). If a file is found, it is executed.

In this howto, I use term 'command' to refer executable program that is meant to be called with short names, using the path mechanism.

In Linux, even the low level operating system calls to start processes (the exec family of calls) searches through directories in the PATH variable: you can use the path mechanism anywhere where you try to execute a command. If exec operating system call gets a file name that does not contain '/', it evaluates the PATH environment variable. Even if there is no variable PATH in the environment, at least directories /bin and /usr/bin are looked for suitable commands.

In sh you use the 'export' command to set environment, in csh you use setenv command. For example:

sh:

```
PATH=/usr/local/bin:/usr/bin:/bin:/usr/bin/X11:/usr/games:.
```

csh:

```
setenv PATH /usr/local/bin:/usr/bin:/bin:/usr/bin/X11:/usr/games:.
```

C-programs can use setenv() library call to change environment. Perl has environment in an associative array %ENV, you can set PATH as $ENV{PATH}="/bin".

env command is the basic way of asking the current environment variables. It can be used to modify it as well.

More information of the basic environment mechanism can be found from manual pages 'environ', 'execl', 'setenv', info file 'env' and documentation of shells.

When Linux boots up, the first normal process that starts is the init process. It is a special process because it does not have parent. However, it is the ancestor of all the other processes. Init environment will remain as environment of all the processes if they do not touch it explicitly. Most processes do touch.

Init starts a group of processes. File /etc/inittab tells what processes the system starts. These processes work in the environment that is directly inherited from init - typically they are processes like 'getty', the program that writes 'login:' to console. If you start PPP connections here, you must remember that you are working in the init environment. The system initialization is often a script that is started here. In Debian 1.3 initialization script /etc/init.d/rc and it calls other initialization scripts in turn.

The system contains many running servers (daemons) that may or may not use the default environment. Most servers are started from the initialization scripts and thus they have the init environment.

When user logs in to the system, the environment is affected by the settings that are compiled into the programs, system wide initialization scripts and user initialization scripts. This is pretty complicated and the current situation is not completely satisfactory. It is totally different if user logs in from text console, XDM or from network.

4 Init

Init is a parent process for all the other processes of the system. Other processes inherit environment of the init process and the path is the init path in the rare case that no other path is set.

The 'init path' is fixed in the source of the init program and it is:

```
/usr/local/sbin:/sbin:/bin:/usr/sbin:/usr/bin
```

Note that init path does not contain /usr/local/bin.

All the programs that are started from /etc/inittab work in init environment, especially system initialization scripts in /etc/init.d (Debian 1.3).

Everything that is started from system initialization scripts has init environment as default environment. For example, syslogd, kerneld, pppd (when started from startup), gpm and most importantly lpd and inetd have init environment and they do not change it.

A group of programs are started from startup scripts but the PATH environment variable is explicitly set in the startup script. Examples are: atd, sendmail, apache and squid.

There are other programs that are started from boot scripts but they change the path completely. One such example is cron.

5 Login

In text console there is a getty program waiting for user login. It writes 'login:' and other messages. It is working in init environment. When getty gets user to log in to the system, it invokes the 'login' program. This program sets the user environment and invokes the shell.

Login program sets path as defined in /usr/include/paths.h. This 'login path' is different for root users and other users.

for common users (_PATH_DEFPATH):

        /usr/local/bin:/usr/bin:/bin:.

for root (_PATH_DEFPATH_ROOT):

        /sbin:/bin:/usr/sbin:/usr/bin

Common user's path does not contain any sbin directories. However, it contains the current directory, '.', which is considered dangerous for the root user. Not even /usr/local/bin is available for the root user.

Login path is often overwritten by shell initialization. However, it is possible to use other programs in /etc/passwd as user shells. For example, I have used the following line to start PPP when I log in using special user name. In this case, the pppd has exactly login path.

        etu-ppp:viYabVlxPwzDl:1000:1000:Esa Turtiainen, PPP:/:/usr/sbin/pppd

6 Shells

Often user processes are children processes of the shell mentioned in /etc/passwd for this user. Initialization files of shells often modify path.

In login, the name of the shell is preceded with '-', for example bash is called as '-bash'. This signals to the shell that it is a 'login' shell. In this case, the shell executes the 'login' initialization files. Otherwise some lighter initialization is performed. Additionally, the shell checks if it is interactive - are the commands coming from file or interactive tty. This modifies the shell initialization so that a non-interactive non-login shell is initialized very lightly - bash do not execute any initialization file in this case!

6.1   bash

As a normal login shell, bash 'sources' system-wide file /etc/profile, where the system environment and path can be set for bash users. However, it is not run when the system interprets the shell as non-interactive. The most important case is in rsh, where remote command is executed in the neighboring machine. The /etc/profile is not run and the path is inherited from rsh daemon.

bash receives command line arguments -login and -i that can be used to set the shell as a login shell or interactive shell respectively.

The user can overwrite values set in /etc/profile by creating a file ~/.bash_profile, ~/.bash_login or ~/.profile. Note that just the first one of these is executed thus differing of the logic of csh initialization. ~/.bash_login is not executed specially for login shells and if .bash_profile exists, it is not executed at all!

If bash is used with name sh instead of the name bash, it emulates original Bourne shell initialization: it sources just files /etc/profile and ~/.profile and just for login shells.

6.2   tcsh

As a login shell tcsh executes the following files in this order:

- /etc/csh.cshrc
- /etc/csh.login
- ~/.tcshrc
- ~/.cshrc (if .tcshrc is not found)
- ~/.history
- ~/.login
- ~/.cshdirs

tcsh can be compiled to execute login scripts before cshrc scripts. Beware!

Non-interactive shells execute just the *cshrc scripts. *login scripts can be used to set the path just once in the login.

7   Changing user ID

7.1   su

Command su sets a new user id to use. If no user id is given, root is used.

Normally su invokes a subshell with a different user id. With argument '-' (more recent synonyms -l or –login) su invokes shell like login shell. However, it does not use login program to do this but uses a yet another built-in path for login 'simulation' (term used in the source code). It is:

for normal users

        /usr/local/bin:/usr/bin:/bin:/usr/bin/X11:.

for root user

        /sbin:/bin:/usr/sbin:/usr/bin:/usr/bin/X11:/usr/local/sbin:/usr/local/bin

su makes many quite subtle environment changes as well.

7.2 sudo

There is a group of commands that make use of super user commands safer. They allow better logging, user-based restrictions and usage of individual passwords. Most widely used is sudo.

```
$ sudo env
```

executes command env as super user (if it is configured to allow it).

sudo command has again a different approach to path handling. It modifies the search path so that the current directory is always the last one. However, it does not modify PATH environment variable. 'sudo env' and 'env' give the same value for PATH variable. Sudo adds just couple of environment variables like SUDO_USER.

8 Network servers

Most network servers should not invoke subprocesses of any kind. For security reasons, their path should be minimal.

An important exception is all the services that allow logging in to the system from network. This section describes what is the environment in these cases. If the command is executed in the remote machine with rsh it gets different path than if it is executed with ssh. Similarly, logging in with rlogin, Telnet or ssh is different.

8.1 inetd

Most network servers do not have process of their own waiting for requests all the time. This work is delegated to an Internet super server called inetd. Inetd listens for all the defined network ports and starts the appropriate server when there is an incoming request. This behaviour is defined in /etc/inetd.conf.

inetd is started from system startup scripts. It inherits just path of init process. It does not modify it and all the servers started from inetd has init path. An example of such a server is imapd, the server of IMAP post office protocol.

Other examples of inetd processes are telnetd, rlogind, talkd, ftp, popd, many http servers and so on.

Often usage of inetd is still complicated by using a separate tcpd program to start the real server. It is a program that makes additional security checks before starting the real application. It does not affect the path (not verified).

8.2 rsh

rsh daemon sets the path from _PATH_DEFPATH (/usr/include/paths.h) that is the same path that login program uses for normal users. Root will get the same path than the normal user.

Actually, rshd executes the command it gets with the command line:

```
shell -c command-line
```

and shell is not a login shell. It is desirable that all the shells mentioned in /etc/passwd support -c option to give on the command line.

8.3   rlogin

Rlogin is invokes login to make the real login procedure. If you login with rlogin, you get the same path than in login. Most other ways to log in to a Linux computer do not use login. Note the difference with rsh.

The login command actually used is

```
login -p -h host-name user-name
```

-p preserves the environment except the variables HOME, PATH, SHELL, TERM, MAIL and LOGNAME. -h tells the remote host name for logging.

8.4   telnet

Telnet is similar than rlogin. It uses the login program and the command line to invoke it in a similar way.

8.5   ssh

ssh has a path setting of it's own. It has a fixed path where it adds the directory where ssh is. Often this means that /usr/bin is in the path twice:

```
/usr/local/bin:/usr/bin:/bin:.:/usr/bin
```

The path does not contain /usr/X11/bin and shell invoked by ssh command is not a login shell. Thus

```
ssh remotehost xterm
```

never works and anything in /etc/profile or /etc/csh.cshrc can change this. You must always use explicit path /usr/bin/X11/xterm.

ssh searches environment variables of form VAR=VALUE from file /etc/environment. Unfortunately this causes some problems with XFree86.

9   XFree86

9.1   XDM

XDM is the most common way to log in to a graphical terminal. It a bit looks like login but it is internally totally different.

In directory /etc/X11/xdm there are configuration files that are executed on different login phases. Xstartup (and Xstartup_0 specially for screen 0) contains commands to be run after the user has logged in (commands are run as user root).

The path that is set for users is in /etc/X11/xdm/xdm-config. There are lines:

```
DisplayManager*userPath: /usr/local/bin:/usr/bin:/bin:/usr/bin/X11:/usr/games
DisplayManager*systemPath: /usr/local/sbin:/usr/local/bin:/usr/sbin:\
                           /usr/bin:/sbin:/bin:/usr/bin/X11
```

(Ignore \ followed by newline in the above, if present it has been inserted to enable the example to fit in a printable line width.)

That will be a default path for normal and root users respectively. It is very important that /usr/bin/X11 is available for X users. If X user logs in to another machine to start and X client application, he should get /usr/bin/X11 to his path even he don't seem to come directly from X terminal.

After running Xstartup the XDM runs /etc/X11/Xsession that is run as the final user. Local configuration is meant to be done in /etc/environment that is sourced (included) from Xsession if available (Xsession is run with /bin/sh and thus /etc/environment must be a sh file). This clashes with ssh that supposes that /etc/environment is a file that contains just lines of form VAR=VALUE.

9.2   xterm -ls

By default the path for all the commands invoked from X window manager menus is the path inherited from XDM. To use something different it must be set explicitly. To start a terminal emulator with a path that is "normal" some special option must be used. In xterm the option -ls (login shell) must be used to get a login shell with path specified in shell login initialization files.

9.3   Window manager menus and buttons

Window manager inherits environment of XDM. All the programs started by the window manager inherit the environment of the window manager.

User shell environment does not affect the programs that are started from window manager buttons and menus. For example, if program is started from 'xterm -ls', it has the default environment of login shell but if it is started from menu, it has just environment of the window manager.

10   Delayed commands cron and at

10.1   cron

Cron is a command that executes commands periodically as specified in /etc/crontab and user-defined crontabs. In Debian 1.3 there is a standard mechanism to execute commands in /etc/cron.daily, /etc/cron.weekly and /etc/cron.monthly.

Cron is started from boot scripts but it seems to change it's PATH to a pretty strange one:

```
/usr/bin:/binn:/sbin:/bin:/usr/sbin:/usr/bin
```

THIS IS LIKELY A BUG IN CRON. This is the init path where there is /usr/bin:/bin written over the beginning without terminating 0! This bug does not exist in all the systems.

In crontab there can be PATH definition. In Debian 1.3 there is the following default line in the beginning of /etc/crontab:

```
PATH=/usr/local/sbin:/usr/local/bin:/sbin:/bin:/usr/sbin:/usr/bin
```

Because of this, the PATH of crond program is never used in user programs. All the scripts in /etc/cron.* directories get this path by default. This path is used even if a program is executed as non-root.

10.2 at

at is a command that can be used to run a one-time program at specific time.

atd is run using init path. However, the user programs are always run in the user environment using sh command. Therefore the usual shell overwrites apply. Look the chapter on bash.

11 Some examples

11.1 magicfilter

magicfilter is a common tool to manipulate files for printer. It analyzes the type of the file to be printed and invokes a filter script to make appropriate pretty-printing. These scripts are invoked from lpd that is started from /etc/init.d/lpd that is started from init. Thus, the path is that of init. That does not contain /usr/bin/X11!

You might want to insert printing of PDF files to magicfilter. It is possible to do this by using /usr/bin/X11/xpdf. Now you must remember to insert full directory path to the file name because magicfilter would not find it otherwise. Most programs used in magicfilter do not need full path, because they are on /bin or /usr/bin.

11.2 Printing from X applications

You may use PRINTER environment variable to show what is the printer that you are using. However, you may notice that in some cases in X applications it is sometimes lost.

You must remember that if the X session is started from XDM, the window manager has never evaluated your shell login scripts. All the X applications that you have started from xterm have your PRINTER variable. However, if the same application is started from menu or window manager button, it does not contain your PRINTER variable.

In some cases this can be inherited to an even lower layer: for example a Netscape helper application can have or have not your PRINTER definition.

12 Security concerns

The path is sometimes a big security problem. It is a very common way to hack into a system using some mistakes in path settings. It is easy to make Trojan horse attacks if hacker gets root or other users to execute his versions of commands.

A common mistake in the past (?) was to keep '.' in the root's path. Malicious hacker makes program 'ls' in his home directory. If root makes

```
# cd ~hacker
# ls
```

he executes ls command of hacker's.

Indirectly, this same applies to all the programs that are executed as root. Any of the important daemon processes should never execute anything that some other user can write into. In some systems, /usr/local/bin is allowed to contain programs with less strict security screening - it is just removed from the path of the root user. However, if it is known that some daemon executes 'foo' using path '/usr/local/bin/:...', it may be possible to cheat daemon to execute '/usr/local/bin/foo' instead of '/bin/foo'. Likely anybody who can write to '/usr/local/bin' is able to break into the system.

It is very important to consider in what order the directories are in the path. If /usr/local/bin is before /bin, it is a security risk - if it is after, it is not possible to overwrite command /bin/foo with some localized modification in /usr/local/bin/foo.

In Linux it should be remembered that the path evaluation is done in the operating system call level. Everywhere where an executable file path is given you can give a short name that is searched at least from /bin and /usr/bin - likely from many other places as well.

13 How to debug problems?

The basic command to read environment is /usr/bin/env.

It is possible to use /proc directory to find out path of any program. First you must know the process number - use ps command to get that. For example, if xterm is process number 1088, you can find it's environment with command

```
# more /proc/1088/environ
```

This does not work with daemon processes like xdm. To access environment of system processes or other user processes, root access is required.

To debug Netscape, you can create a script /tmp/test:

```
$ cat > /tmp/test
#!/bin/sh
/usr/bin/env > /tmp/env
^d
$ chmod +x /tmp/test
```

Then set some helper application, for example RealAudio, audio/x-pn-realaudio to call program "/tmp/test". When you try to browse some RealAudio link (something from http://www.realaudio.com/showcase), Netscape calls the dummy program that stores environment to /tmp/env.

14 Some strategies to get the same path for all the users

The most important settings is possible to set in the global shell initialization files for login shells: /etc/csh.login for tcsh and /etc/profile for bash.

Exceptions that do not get the right path from these files are rsh commands, ssh commands, menu items from X window manager that do not explicitly start login shell, commands invoked from inittab, cron jobs, daemons jobs like magic filters started from lprd, WWW CGI scripts, and so on.

If the path is set in /etc/csh.cshrc, the path is right even when rsh or ssh execute command in remote machine with account using tcsh/csh. However, it is not possible to set path if account uses bash/sh.

It is possible to combine path setting to one file, for example to a file /etc/environment-common. There we could write:

```
${EXPORT}PATH${EQ}/bin:/usr/bin:/usr/sbin:/usr/bin/X11:/usr/local/bin:/usr/games:.
```

This can be used from /etc/csh.login (for tcsh and csh)

```
set EQ=" " set EXPORT="setenv " source /etc/environment-common
```

And from /etc/profile (for bash, doesn't work for ordinary sh)

```
EQ='=' EXPORT="export " . /etc/environment-common
```

And from /etc/environment (for XDM)

```
EQ="=" EXPORT="export " . /etc/environment-common
```

This strategy works mostly but ssh will complain of the lines in /etc/environment (and defined environment variables EQ and EXPORT). And still, rsh commands executed with bash won't get this path.

15   Acknowledgements

One reason to start writing this document was the big frustration of Ari Mujunen. Juha Takala gave some valuable comments.

The Linux Bootdisk HOWTO

Tom Fawcett (`fawcett@croftj.net`) and Graham Chapman (`grahamc@zeta.org.au`)
3.1, 5 February 1998

This document describes how to design and build your own boot/root diskettes for Linux. These disks could be used as rescue disks or to test new system components. If you haven't read the Linux FAQ and related documents, such as the Linux Installation HOWTO and the Linux Install Guide, you should not be trying to build boot diskettes. If you just want a rescue disk to have for emergencies, see Appendix A.1 (Pre-made bootdisks).

Contents

1   Preface.

Note: This document may be outdated. If the date on the title page is more than six months ago, please check the Linux Documentation Project homepage `<http://sunsite.unc.edu/LDP/>` to see if a more recent version exists.

Although this document should be legible in its text and Info forms, it looks *much* better in Postscript (`.ps`) or HTML because of the typographical notation used. We encourage you to select one of these forms.

1.1   Version notes.

This document is intended for **Linux kernel 2.0 and later**. If you have an older kernel (1.2.xx or before), please consult previous versions of the Bootdisk-HOWTO archived on *Graham Chapman's homepage* `<http://www.zeta.org.au/~grahamc/linux.html>`.

This information is intended for Linux on the **Intel** platform. Much of this information may be applicable to Linux on other processors, but we have no first-hand experience or information about this. If anyone has experience with bootdisks on other platforms, please contact us.

1.2 Feedback and credits.

We welcome any feedback, good or bad, on the content of this document. We have done our best to ensure that the instructions and information herein are accurate and reliable. Please let us know if you find errors or omissions.

We thank the many people who assisted with corrections and suggestions. Their contributions have made it far better than we could ever have done alone.

Send comments, corrections and questions to the authors at the email addresses above. We don't mind answering questions, but please read section 7 (Troubleshooting) first.

1.3 Distribution policy.

Copyright © 1995,1996,1997 by Tom Fawcett and Graham Chapman. This document may be distributed under the terms set forth in the Linux Documentation Project License at `<http://sunsite.unc.edu/LDP/ COPYRIGHT.html>`. Please contact the authors if you are unable to get the license.

This is free documentation. It is distributed in the hope that it will be useful, but **without any warranty**; without even the implied warranty of **merchantability** or **fitness for a particular purpose**.

2 Introduction.

Linux boot disks are useful in a number of situations, such as:

- Testing a new kernel.
- Recovering from a disk failure — anything from a lost boot sector to a disk head crash.
- Fixing a disabled system. A minor mistake as root can leave your system unusable, and you may have to boot from diskette to fix it.
- Upgrading critical system files, such as `libc.so`.

There are several ways of obtaining boot disks:

- Use one from a distribution such as Slackware. This will at least allow you to boot.
- Use a rescue package to set up disks designed to be used as rescue disks.
- Learn what is required for each of the types of disk to operate, then build your own.

Some people choose the last option so they can do it themselves. That way, if something breaks, they can work out what to do to fix it. Plus it's a great way to learn about how a Linux system works.

This document assumes some basic familiarity with Linux system administration concepts. For example, you should know about directories, filesystems and floppy diskettes. You should know how to use `mount` and `df`. You should know what `/etc/$\{$passwd,fstab$\}$` files are for and what they look like. You should know that most of the commands in this HOWTO should be run as root.

Constructing your own bootdisk from scratch can be complicated. If you haven't read the Linux FAQ and related documents, such as the Linux Installation HOWTO and the Linux Install Guide, you should not be trying to build boot diskettes. If you just need a working bootdisk for emergencies, it is *much* easier to download a prefabricated one. See Appendix A.1 (Pre-made bootdisks), below, for where to find these.

3 Bootdisks and the boot process.

A bootdisk is basically a miniature, self-contained Linux system on a floppy diskette. It must perform many of the same functions that a complete full-size Linux system performs. Before trying to build one you should understand the basic Linux boot process. We present the basics here, which are sufficient for understanding the rest of this document. Many details and alternative options have been omitted.

3.1 The boot process.

All PC systems start the boot process by executing code in ROM (specifically, the BIOS) to load the sector from sector 0, cylinder 0 of the boot drive. The boot drive is usually the first floppy drive (designated "A:" in DOS and /dev/fd0 in Linux). The BIOS then tries to execute this sector. On most bootable disks, sector 0, cylinder 0 contains either:

- code from a boot loader such as LILO, which locates the kernel, loads it and executes it to start the boot proper.
- the start of an operating system kernel, such as Linux.

If a Linux kernel has been raw-copied to a diskette, the first sector of the disk will be the first sector of the Linux kernel itself. This first sector will continue the boot process by loading the rest of the kernel from the boot device.

Once the kernel is completely loaded, it goes through some basic device initialization. It then tries to load and mount a **root filesystem** from some device. A root filesystem is simply a filesystem that is mounted as "/". (the kernel is told where to look for the root filesystem; if it cannot find a loadable image there, it halts.)

In some boot situations — often when booting from a diskette — the root filesystem is loaded into a **ramdisk**, which is RAM accessed by the system as if it were a disk. There are two reasons why the system loads to ramdisk. First, RAM is several orders of magnitude faster than a floppy disk, so system operation is fast; and second, the kernel can load a **compressed filesystem** from the floppy and uncompress it onto the ramdisk, allowing many more files to be squeezed onto the diskette.

Once the root filesystem is loaded and mounted, you see a message like:

```
VFS: Mounted root (ext2 filesystem) readonly.
```

At this point the system finds the init program on the root filesystem (in /bin or /sbin) and executes it. init reads its configuration file /etc/inittab, looks for a line designated sysinit, and executes the named script . The sysinit script is usually something like /etc/rc or /etc/init.d/boot. This script is a set of shell commands that set up basic system services, such as:

- Running fsck on all the disks,
- Loading necessary kernel modules,
- Starting swapping,
- Initializing the network,
- Mounting disks mentioned in fstab.

This script often invokes various other scripts to do modular initialization. For example, in the common SysVinit structure, the directory `/etc/rc.d/` contains a complex structure of subdirectories whose files specify how to enable and shut down most system services. However, on a bootdisk the sysinit script is often very simple.

When the sysinit script finishes, control returns to `init`, which then enters the *default runlevel*. This runlevel is specified in `inittab` with the `initdefault` keyword. The runlevel line usually specifies a program like `getty`, which is responsible for handling commununications through the console and ttys. It is the `getty` program which prints the familiar "`login:`" prompt. The `getty` program in turn invokes the `login` program to handle login validation and to set up user sessions.

3.2 Disk types.

Having reviewed the basic boot process, we can now define various kinds of disks used in the process. We classify disks into four types. The discussion here and throughout this document uses the term "disk" to refer to floppy diskettes unless otherwise specified, though most of the discussion could apply equally well to hard disks.

boot

A disk containing a kernel which can be booted. The disk can be used to boot the kernel, which then may load a root file system on another disk. The kernel on a bootdisk usually must be told where to find its root filesystem.

Often a bootdisk loads a root filesystem from another diskette, but it is possible for a bootdisk to be set up to load a hard disk's root filesystem instead. This is commonly done when testing a new kernel. (in fact, "`make zdisk`" will create such a bootdisk automatically from the kernel source code).

root

A disk with a filesystem containing files required to run a Linux system. Such a disk does not necessarily contain either a kernel or a boot loader.

A root disk can be used to run the system independently of any other disks, once the kernel has been booted. Usually the root disk is automatically copied to a ramdisk. This makes root disk accesses much faster, and frees up the disk drive for a utility disk.

boot/root

A disk which contains both the kernel and a root filesystem. In other words, it contains everything necessary to boot and run a Linux system without a hard disk. The advantage of this type of disk is that is it compact — everything required is on a single disk. However, the gradually increasing size of everything means that it is increasingly difficult to fit everything on a single diskette, even with compression.

utility

A disk which contains a file system, but is not intended to be mounted as a root file system. It is an additional data disk. You would use this type of disk to carry additional utilities where you have too much to fit on your root disk.

In general, when we talk about "building a bootdisk" we mean creating both the boot (kernel) and root (files) portions. They may be either together (a single boot/root disk) or separate (boot + root disks). The most flexible approach for rescue diskettes is probably to use separate boot and root diskettes, and one or more utility diskettes to handle the overflow.

4   Building a root filesystem.

Creating the root filesystem involves selecting files necessary for the system to run. In this section we describe how to build a *compressed root filesystem*. A less common option is to build an uncompressed filesystem on a diskette that is directly mounted as root; this alternative is described in section 8.2 (Non-ramdisk Root Filesystem).

4.1   Overview.

A root filesystem must contain everything needed to support a full Linux system. To be able to do this, the disk must include the minimum requirements for a Linux system:

- The basic file system structure,
- Minimum set of directories: /dev, /proc, /bin, /etc, /lib, /usr, /tmp,
- Basic set of utilities: sh, ls, cp, mv, etc.,
- Minimum set of config files: rc, inittab, fstab, etc.,
- Devices: /dev/hd*, /dev/tty*, /dev/fd0, etc.,
- Runtime library to provide basic functions used by utilities.

Of course, any system only becomes useful when you can run something on it, and a root diskette usually only becomes useful when you can do something like:

- Check a file system on another drive, for example to check your root file system on your hard drive, you need to be able to boot Linux from another drive, as you can with a root diskette system. Then you can run fsck on your original root drive while it is not mounted.
- Restore all or part of your original root drive from backup using archive/compression utilities including cpio, tar, gzip and ftape.

We will describe how to build a *compressed* filesystem, so called because it is compressed on disk and, when booted, is uncompressed onto a ramdisk. With a compressed filesystem you can fit many files (approximately two megabytes) onto a standard 1440K diskette. Because the filesystem is much larger than a diskette, it cannot be built on the diskette. We have to build it elsewhere, compress it, then copy it to the diskette.

4.2   Creating the filesystem.

In order to build such a root filesystem, you need a spare device that is large enough. You will need a device capable of holding about four megabytes. There are several choices:

- Use a ramdisk (DEVICE = /dev/ram0). In this case, memory is used to simulate a disk drive. The ramdisk must be large enough to hold a filesystem of the appropriate size. If you use LILO, check your configuration file (/etc/lilo.conf) for a line like:

      RAMDISK_SIZE = nnn

  which determines how much RAM will be allocated. The default is 4096K, which should be sufficient. You should probably not try to use such a ramdisk on a machine with less than 8MB of RAM.

  Check to make sure you have a device like /dev/ram0,/dev/ram or /dev/ramdisk. If not, create /dev/ram0 with mknod (major number 1, minor 0).

- If you have an unused hard disk partition that is large enough (several megabytes), this is a good solution. If you have enough physical RAM you can turn off swapping and build the filesystem in your swap partition.

- Use a **loopback device**, which allows a disk file to be treated as a device. Using a loopback device you can create a three megabyte file on your hard disk and build the filesystem on it.

  In order to use loopback devices you need specially modified `mount` and `unmount` programs. You can find these at:

  > `ftp://ftp.win.tue.nl:/pub/linux/util/mount-2.5X.tar.gz`

  where X is the latest modification letter. (If you do not have a loop device (`/dev/loop0`, `/dev/loop1`, etc.) on your system, you will have to create one with `mknod /dev/loop0 b 7 0`.) One you've installed these special `mount` and `umount` binaries, create a temporary file on a hard disk with enough capacity (eg, `/tmp/fsfile`). You can use a command like

  > `dd if=/dev/zero of=/tmp/fsfile bs=1k count=`*nnn*

  to create an *nnn*-block file.

  Use the file name in place of DEVICE below. When you issue a mount command you must include the option "-o loop" to tell mount to use a loopback device. For example:

  > `mount -o loop -t ext2 /tmp/fsfile /mnt`

  will mount `/tmp/fsfile` (via a loopback device) at the mount point `/mnt`. A `df` will confirm this.

After you've chosen one of these options, prepare the DEVICE with:

> `dd if=/dev/zero of=DEVICE bs=1k count=3000`

This command zeroes out the device. This step is important because the filesystem on the device will be compressed later, so all unused portions should be filled with zeroes to achieve maximum compression.

Next, create the filesystem. The Linux kernel recognizes two file system types for root disks to be automatically copied to ramdisk. These are minix and ext2, of which ext2 is the preferred file system. If using ext2, you may find it useful to use the `-i` option to specify more inodes than the default; `-i 2000` is suggested so that you don't run out of inodes. Alternatively, you can save on inodes by removing lots of unnecessary `/dev` files. `mke2fs` will by default create 360 inodes on a 1.44Mb diskette. I find that 120 inodes is ample on my current rescue root diskette, but if you include all the devices in the `/dev` directory then you will easily exceed 360. Using a compressed root filesystem allows a larger filesystem, and hence more inodes by default, but you may still need to either reduce the number of files or increase the number of inodes.

So the command you use will look like:

> `mke2fs -m 0 -i 2000 DEVICE`

(If you're using a loopback device, the disk file you're using should be supplied in place of this DEVICE. In this case, `mke2fs` will ask if you really want to do this; say yes.)

The `mke2fs` command will automatically detect the space available and configure itself accordingly. The `-m 0` parameter prevents it from reserving space for root, and hence provides more usable space on the disk.

Next, mount the device:

> `mount -t ext2 DEVICE /mnt`

(You must create a mount point `/mnt` if it does not already exist.) In the remaining sections, all destination directory names are assumed to be relative to `/mnt`.

4.3   Populating the filesystem.

Here is a reasonable minimum set of directories for your root filesystem:

- /dev — Devices, required to perform I/O
- /proc — Directory stub required by the proc filesystem
- /etc — System configuration files
- /sbin — Critical system binaries
- /bin — Basic binaries considered part of the system
- /lib — Shared libraries to provide run-time support
- /mnt — A mount point for maintenance on other disks
- /usr — Additional utilities and applications

(The directory structure presented here is for root diskette use only. Real Linux systems have a more complex and disciplined set of policies, called the File System Standard, for determining where files should go.)

Three of these directories will be empty on the root filesystem, so they only need to be created with mkdir. The /proc directory is basically a stub under which the proc filesystem is placed. The directories /mnt and /usr are only mount points for use after the boot/root system is running. Hence again, these directories only need to be created.

The remaining four directories are described in the following sections.

4.3.1   /dev

A /dev directory containing a special file for all devices to be used by the system is mandatory for any Linux system. The directory itself is a normal directory, and can be created with mkdir in the normal way. The device special files, however, must be created in a special way, using the mknod command.

There is a shortcut, though — copy your existing /dev directory contents, and delete the ones you don't want. The only requirement is that you copy the device special files using -R option. This will copy the directory without attempting to copy the contents of the files. *Be sure to use an upper case R*. If you use lower case r, as in "-r", you will probably end up copying the entire contents of all of your hard disks — or at least as much of them as will fit on a diskette! Therefore, take care, and use the command:

```
cp -dpR /dev /mnt
```

assuming that the diskette is mounted at /mnt. The dp switches ensure that symbolic links are copied as links, rather than using the target file, and that the original file attributes are preserved, thus preserving ownership information.

Alternatively, you can use the cpio program with the -p option, because cpio handles device special files correctly, and will not try to copy the contents. For example, the commands:

```
cd /dev
find . -print | cpio -pmd /mnt/dev
```

will copy all device special files from /dev to /mnt/dev. In fact it will copy all files in the directory tree starting at /dev, and will create any required subdirectories in the target directory tree.

If you want to do it the hard way, use `ls -l` to display the major and minor device numbers for the devices you want, and create them on the diskette using `mknod`.

However the devices are copied, it is worth checking that any special devices you need have been placed on the rescue diskette. For example, `ftape` uses tape devices, so you will need to copy all of these if you intend to access your floppy tape drive from the bootdisk.

Note that one inode is required for each device special file, and inodes can at times be a scarce resource, especially on diskette filesystems. It therefore makes sense to remove any device special files that you don't need from the diskette `/dev` directory. Many devices are obviously unnecessary on specific systems. For example, if you do not have SCSI disks you can safely remove all the device files starting with "sd". Similarly, if you don't intend to use your serial port then all device files starting with "cua" can go.

Be sure to include the following files from this directory: `console`, `kmem`, `mem`, `null`, `ram`, `tty1`.

4.3.2   /etc

This directory must contain a number of configuration files. On most systems, these can be divided into three groups:

1. Required at all times, *e.g.* `rc`, `fstab`, `passwd`.
2. May be required, but no-one is too sure.
3. Junk that crept in.

Files which are not essential can be identified with the command:

```
ls -ltru
```

This lists files in reverse order of date last accessed, so if any files are not being accessed, they can be omitted from a root diskette.

On my root diskettes, I have the number of config files down to 15. This reduces my work to dealing with three sets of files:

1. The ones I must configure for a boot/root system:

    (a) `rc.d/*` — system startup and run level change scripts
    (b) `fstab` — list of file systems to be mounted
    (c) `inittab` — parameters for the `init` process, the first process started at boot time.

2. The ones I should tidy up for a boot/root system:

    (a) `passwd` — list of users, home directories, etc.
    (b) `group` — user groups.
    (c) `shadow` — passwords of users. You may not have this.

    If security is important, `passwd` and `shadow` should be pruned to avoid copying user passwords off the system, and so that when you boot from diskette, unwanted logins are rejected. However, there is a reason *not* to prune `passwd` and `group`. `tar` (and probably other archivers) stores user and group names with files. If you restore files to your hard disk from tape, the files will be restored with their original names. If these names do not exist in `passwd/group` when they are restored, the UIDs/GIDs will not be correct.

    Be sure that `passwd` contains at least `root`. If you intend other users to login, be sure their home directories and shells exist.

3. The rest. They work at the moment, so I leave them alone.

Out of this, I only really have to configure two files, and what they should contain is surprisingly small.

- rc should contain:

```
#!/bin/sh
/bin/mount -av
/bin/hostname Kangaroo
```

Be sure the directories are right. You don't really need to run hostname — it just looks nicer if you do.

- fstab should contain at least:

```
/dev/ram0       /              ext2    defaults
/dev/fd0        /              ext2    defaults
/proc           /proc          proc    defaults
```

You can copy entries from your existing fstab, but you should not automatically mount any of your hard disk partitions; use the noauto keyword with them. Your hard disk may be damaged or dead when the bootdisk is used.

Your inittab should be changed so that its sysinit line runs rc or whatever basic boot script will be used. Also, if you want to ensure that users on serial ports cannot login, comment out all the entries for getty which include a ttys or ttyS device at the end of the line. Leave in the tty ports so that you can login at the console.

A minimal inittab file looks like this:

```
id:2:initdefault:
si::sysinit:/etc/rc
1:2345:respawn:/sbin/getty 9600 tty1
2:23:respawn:/sbin/getty 9600 tty2
```

The inittab file defines what the system will run in various states including startup, move to multi-user mode, etc. A point to be careful of here is to carefully check that the commands entered in inittab refer to programs which are present and to the correct directory. If you place your command files on your rescue disk using Section C (Sample rootdisk directory listings). as a guide, and then copy your inittab to your rescue disk without checking it, the probability of failure will be quite high because half of the inittab entries will refer to missing programs or to the wrong directory.

Note that some programs cannot be moved elsewhere because other programs have hardcoded their locations. For example on my system, /etc/shutdown has hardcoded in it /etc/reboot. If I move reboot to /bin/reboot, and then issue a shutdown command, it will fail because it cannot find the reboot file.

For the rest, just copy all the text files in your /etc directory, plus all the executables in your /etc directory that you cannot be sure you do not need. As a guide, consult the sample listing in Section C (Sample rootdisk directory listings). Probably it will suffice to copy only those files, but systems differ a great deal, so you cannot be sure that the same set of files on your system is equivalent to the files in the list. The only sure method is to start with inittab and work out what is required.

Most systems now use an /etc/rc.d/ directory containing shell scripts for different run levels. The minimum is a single rc script, but it may be simpler just to copy inittab and the /etc/rc.d directory from your existing system, and prune the shell scripts in the rc.d directory to remove processing not relevent to a diskette system environment.

4.3.3 /bin and /sbin

bin directory sbin directory

The /bin directory is a convenient place for extra utilities you need to perform basic operations, utilities such as ls, mv, cat and dd. See Appendix C (Sample rootdisk directory listings) for an example list of files that go in a /bin and /sbin directories. It does not include any of the utilities required to restore from backup, such as cpio, tar and gzip. That is because I place these on a separate utility diskette, to save space on the boot/root diskette. Once the boot/root diskette is booted, it is copied to the ramdisk leaving the diskette drive free to mount another diskette, the utility diskette. I usually mount this as /usr.

Creation of a utility diskette is described below in the section Section 8.3 (Building a utility disk). It is probably desirable to maintain a copy of the same version of backup utilities used to write the backups so you don't waste time trying to install versions that cannot read your backup tapes.

Make sure you include the following programs: init, getty or equivalent, login, mount, some shell capable of running your rc scripts, a link from sh to the shell.

4.3.4 /lib

In /lib you place necessary shared libraries and loaders. If the necessary libraries are not found in your /lib directory then the system will be unable to boot. If you're lucky you may see an error message telling you why.

Nearly every program requires at least the libc library, libc.so.N, where N is the current version number. Check your /lib directory. libc.so.5 is usually a symlink to a filename with a complete version number:

```
% ls -l /lib/libc.so*
lrwxrwxrwx  1 root root      14 Nov  1 20:34 /lib/libc.so.5 -> libc.so.5.4.33*
-rwxr-xr-x  1 root root  573176 Jun 12 02:05 /lib/libc.so.5.4.33*
```

In this case, you want libc.so.5.4.33. To find other libraries you should go through all the binaries you plan to include and check their dependencies with the ldd command. For example:

```
% ldd /sbin/mke2fs
        libext2fs.so.2 => /lib/libext2fs.so.2
        libcom_err.so.2 => /lib/libcom_err.so.2
        libuuid.so.1 => /lib/libuuid.so.1
        libc.so.5 => /lib/libc.so.5
```

Each file on the right-hand side is required. Keep in mind that the libraries listed may be symbolic links.

In /lib you must also include a loader for the libraries. The loader will be either ld.so (for a.out libraries) or ld-linux.so (for ELF libraries). If you're not sure which you need, run the file command on the library. For example:

```
% file /lib/libc.so.5.4.33 /lib/libc.so.4.7.2
/lib/libc.so.4.7.2: Linux/i386 demand-paged executable (QMAGIC), stripped
/lib/libc.so.5.4.33: ELF 32-bit LSB shared object, Intel 386, version 1, stripped
```

The "QMAGIC" indicates that 4.7.2 is for a.out libraries, and "ELF" indicates that 5.4.33 is for ELF.

Copy the specific loader(s) you need to the root filesystem you're building. Libraries and loaders should be checked *carefully* against the included binaries. If the kernel cannot load a necessary library, the kernel will usually hang with no error message.

4.4   Modules.

If you have a modular kernel, you must consider which modules you may want to load from your bootdisk after booting. You might want to include `ftape` and `zftape` modules if your backup tapes are on floppy tape, modules for SCSI devices if you have them, and possibly modules for PPP or SLIP support if you want to access the net in an emergency.

These modules may be placed in `/lib/modules`. You should also include `insmod`, `rmmod` and `lsmod`. Depending on whether you want to load modules automatically, you might also include `modprobe`, `depmod` and `swapout`. If you use `kerneld`, include it along with `/etc/conf.modules`.

However, the main advantage to using modules is that you can move non-critical modules to a utility disk and load them when needed, thus using less space on your root disk. If you may have to deal with many different devices, this approach is preferable to building one huge kernel with many drivers built in.

Note that in order to boot a compressed ext2 filesystem, you must have ramdisk and ext2 support built-in. They cannot be supplied as modules.

4.5   Some final details.

Some system programs, such as `login`, complain if the file `/var/run/utmp` and the directory `/var/log` do not exist. So:

```
mkdir -p /mnt/var/{log,run}
touch /mnt/var/run/utmp
```

Finally, after you have set up all the libraries you need, run `ldconfig` to remake `/etc/ld.so.cache` on the root filesystem. The cache tells the loader where to find the libraries. To remake `ld.so.cache`, issue the following commands:

```
chdir /mnt; chroot /mnt /sbin/ldconfig
```

The `chroot` is necessary because `ldconfig` always remakes the cache for the root filesystem.

4.6   Wrapping it up.

Once you have finished constructing the root filesystem, unmount it, copy it to a file and compress it:

```
umount /mnt
dd if=DEVICE bs=1k | gzip -v9 > rootfs.gz
```

This may take several minutes. When it finishes you will have a file `rootfs.gz` that is your compressed root filesystem. You should check its size to make sure it will fit on a diskette; if it doesn't you'll have to go back and remove some files. Section 8.1 (Reducing root filesystem size) has some hints for reducing the size of the root filesystem.

5   Choosing a kernel.

At this point you have a complete compressed root filesystem. The next step is to build or select a kernel. In most cases it would be possible to copy your current kernel and boot the diskette from that. However, there may be cases where you wish to build a separate one.

One reason is size. If you are building a single boot/root diskette, the kernel will be one of the largest files on the diskette so you will have to reduce the size of the kernel as much as possible. If you are building a two-disk boot+root diskette, this is not a concern since the kernel will go on a separate disk.

To reduce kernel size, build it with the minumum set of facilities necessary to support the desired system. This means leaving out everything you don't need. Networking is a good thing to leave out, as well as support for any disk drives and other devices which you don't need when running your boot/root system. As stated before, your kernel *must* have ramdisk and ext2 support built into it.

Having worked out a minimum set of facilities to include in a kernel, you then need to work out what to add back in. Probably the most common uses for a boot/root diskette system would be to examine and restore a corrupted root file system, and to do this you may need kernel support. For example, if your backups are all held on tape using Ftape to access your tape drive, then, if you lose your current root drive and drives containing Ftape, then you will not be able to restore from your backup tapes. You will have to reinstall Linux, download and reinstall ftape, and then try to read your backups.

The point here is that, whatever I/O support you have added to your kernel to support backups should also be added into your boot/root kernel.

The procedure for actually building the kernel is described in the documentation that comes with the kernel. It is quite easy to follow, so start by looking in `/usr/src/linux`. Note that if you have trouble building a kernel, then you should probably not attempt to build boot/root systems anyway. Remember to compress the kernel with "`make zImage`".

6   Putting them together: Making the disk(s).

At this point you have a kernel and a compressed root filesystem. If you are making a boot/root disk, check their sizes to make sure they will both fit on one disk. If you are making a two disk boot+root set, check the root filesystem to make sure it will fit on a single diskette.

You should decide whether to use LILO to boot the bootdisk kernel. The alternative is to copy the kernel directly to the diskette and boot without LILO. The advantage of using LILO is that it enables you to supply some parameters to the kernel which may be necessary to initialize your hardware (Check the file `/etc/lilo.conf` on your system. If it exists and has a line like "`append=...`", you probably need this feature). The disadvantage of using LILO is that building the bootdisk is more complicated, and takes slightly more space. You will have to set up a small separate filesystem, which we shall call the **kernel filesystem**, where you transfer the kernel and a few other files that LILO needs.

If you are going to use LILO, read on; if you are going to transfer the kernel directly, skip ahead to the section 6.2 (Without using LILO).

6.1   Transferring the kernel with LILO.

The first thing you must do is create a small configuration file for LILO. It should look like this:

```
boot      =/dev/fd0
install   =/boot/boot.b
```

```
map        =/boot/map
read-write
backup     =/dev/null
compact
image      = KERNEL
label      = Bootdisk
root       =/dev/fd0
```

For an explanation of these parameters, see LILO's user documentation. You will probably also want to add an append=... line to this file from your hard disk's /etc/lilo.conf file.

Save this file as bdlilo.conf.

You now have to create a small filesystem, which we shall call a **kernel filesystem**, to distinguish it from the root filesystem.

First, figure out how large the filesystem should be. Take the size of your kernel in blocks (the size shown by "ls -l KERNEL" divided by 1024 and rounded up) and add 50. Fifty blocks is approximately the space needed for inodes plus other files. You can calculate this number exactly if you want to, or just use 50. If you're creating a two-disk set, you may as well overestimate the space since the first disk is only used for the kernel anyway. Call this number KERNEL_BLOCKS.

Put a floppy diskette in the drive (for simplicity we'll assume /dev/fd0) and create an ext2 kernel filesystem on it:

```
mke2fs -i 8192 -m 0 /dev/fd0 KERNEL_BLOCKS
```

The "-i 8192" specifies that we want one inode per 8192 bytes. Next, mount the filesystem, remove the lost+found directory, and create dev and boot directories for LILO:

```
mount /dev/fd0 /mnt
rm -rf /mnt/lost+found
mkdir /mnt/{boot,dev}
```

Next, create devices /dev/null and /dev/fd0. Instead of looking up the device numbers, you can just copy them from your hard disk using -R:

```
cp -R /dev/{null,fd0} /mnt/dev
```

LILO needs a copy of its boot loader, boot.b, which you can take from your hard disk. It is usually kept in the /boot directory.

```
cp /boot/boot.b /mnt/boot
```

Finally, copy in the LILO configuration file you created in the last section, along with your kernel. Both can be put in the root directory:

```
cp bdlilo.conf KERNEL /mnt
```

Everything LILO needs is now on the kernel filesystem, so you are ready to run it. LILO's -r flag is used for installing the boot loader on some other root:

```
        lilo -v -C bdlilo.conf -r /mnt
```

LILO should run without error, after which the kernel filesystem should look something like this:kernel
filesystem

```
total 361
  1 -rw-r--r--   1 root     root          176 Jan 10 07:22 bdlilo.conf
  1 drwxr-xr-x   2 root     root         1024 Jan 10 07:23 boot/
  1 drwxr-xr-x   2 root     root         1024 Jan 10 07:22 dev/
358 -rw-r--r--   1 root     root       362707 Jan 10 07:23 vmlinuz
boot:
total 8
  4 -rw-r--r--   1 root     root         3708 Jan 10 07:22 boot.b
  4 -rw-------   1 root     root         3584 Jan 10 07:23 map
dev:
total 0
  0 brw-r-----   1 root     root       2,   0 Jan 10 07:22 fd0
  0 crw-r--r--   1 root     root       1,   3 Jan 10 07:22 null
```

Do not worry if the file sizes are slightly different from yours.

Now leave the disk in the drive and go to section 6.3 (Setting the ramdisk word).

6.2   Transferring the kernel without LILO.

If you are *not* using LILO, transfer the kernel to the bootdisk with the **dd** command:

```
        % dd if=KERNEL of=/dev/fd0 bs=1k
        353+1 records in
        353+1 records out
```

In this example, **dd** wrote 353 complete records + 1 partial record, so the kernel occupies the first 354
blocks of the diskette. Call this number KERNEL_BLOCKS and remember it because you use it in the next
section.KERNEL_BLOCKS

Finally, set the root device to be the diskette itself, then set the root to be loaded read/write:

```
        rdev /dev/fd0 /dev/fd0
        rdev -R /dev/fd0 0
```

Be careful to use a capital -R in the second **rdev** command.

6.3   Setting the ramdisk word.

Inside the kernel image is the **ramdisk word** that specifies where the root filesystem is to be found, along
with other options. The word is defined in **/usr/src/linux/arch/i386/kernel/setup.c** and is interpreted
as follows:

```
          bits  0-10:     Offset to start of ramdisk, in 1024 byte blocks
          bits 11-13:     unused
          bit    14:      Flag indicating that ramdisk is to be loaded
          bit    15:      Flag indicating to prompt before loading rootfs
```

If bit 15 is set, on boot-up you will be prompted to place a new floppy diskette in the drive. This is necessary for a two-disk boot set.

There are two cases, depending on whether you are building a single boot/root diskette or a double "boot+root" diskette set.

1. If you are building a single disk, the compressed root filesystem will be placed right after the kernel, so the offset will be the first free block (which should be the same as KERNEL_BLOCKS). Bit 14 will be set to 1, and bit 15 will be zero.

2. If you are building a two-disk set, the root filesystem will begin at block zero of the second disk, so the offset will be zero. Bit 14 will be set to 1, and bit 15 will be 1.

After carefully calculating the value for the ramdisk word, set it with rdev -r. Be sure to use the *decimal* value. If you used LILO, the argument to rdev here should be the *mounted kernel path*, e.g. /mnt/vmlinuz; if you copied the kernel with dd, instead use the floppy device name (*e.g., /dev/fd0*).

```
          rdev -r KERNEL_OR_FLOPPY_DRIVE  VALUE
```

If you used LILO, unmount the diskette now.

6.4   Transferring the root filesystem.

The last step is to transfer the root filesystem.

- If the root filesystem will be placed on the *same* disk as the kernel, transfer it using dd with the seek option, which specifies how many blocks to skip:

```
          dd if=rootfs.gz of=/dev/fd0 bs=1k seek=KERNEL_BLOCKS
```

- If the root filesystem will be placed on a *second* disk, remove the first diskette, put the second diskette in the drive, then transfer the root filesystem to it:

```
          dd if=rootfs.gz of=/dev/fd0 bs=1k
```

Congratulations, you are done!

===== **You should always test a bootdisk before putting it aside for an emergency!** =====

7   Troubleshooting, or *The agony of defeat*.

When building bootdisks, the first few tries often will not boot. The general approach to building a root disk is to assemble components from your existing system, and try and get the diskette-based system to the point where it displays messages on the console. Once it starts talking to you, the battle is half over because you can see what it is complaining about, and you can fix individual problems until the system works smoothly. If the system just hangs with no explanation, finding the cause can be difficult. To get a system to boot to the stage where it will talk to you requires several components to be present and correctly configured. The recommended procedure for investigating the problem where the system will not talk to you is as follows:

- Check that the root disk actually contains the directories you think it does. It is easy to copy at the wrong level so that you end up with something like **/rootdisk/bin** instead of **/bin** on your root diskette.

- Check that there is a **/lib/libc.so** with the same link that appears in your **/lib** directory on your hard disk.

- Check that any symbolic links in your **/dev** directory in your existing system also exist on your root diskette filesystem, where those links are to devices which you have included in your root diskette. In particular, **/dev/console** links are essential in many cases.

- Check that you have included **/dev/tty1**, **/dev/null**, **/dev/zero**, **/dev/mem**, **/dev/ram** and **/dev/kmem** files.

- Check your kernel configuration — support for all resources required up to login point must be built in, not modules. So *ramdisk and ext2 support must be built-in.*

- Check that your kernel root device and ramdisk settings are correct.

Once these general aspects have been covered, here are some more specific files to check:

1. Make sure **init** is included as **/sbin/init** or **/bin/init**. Make sure it is executable.

2. Run **ldd init** to check init's libraries. Usually this is just **libc.so**, but check anyway. Make sure you included the necessary libraries and loaders.

3. Make sure you have the right loader for your libraries — **ld.so** for a.out or **ld-linux.so** for ELF.

4. Check the **/etc/inittab** on your bootdisk filesystem for the calls to **getty** (or some getty-like program, such as **agetty**, **mgetty** or **getty_ps**). Double-check these against your hard disk **inittab**. Check the man pages of the program you use to make sure these make sense. **inittab** is possibly the trickiest part because its syntax and content depend on the init program used and the nature of the system. The only way to tackle it is to read the man pages for **init** and **inittab** and work out exactly what your existing system is doing when it boots. Check to make sure **/etc/inittab** has a system initialisation entry. This should contain a command to execute the system initialization script, which must exist.

5. As with **init**, run **ldd** on your **getty** to see what it needs, and make sure the necessary library files and loaders were included in your root filesystem.

6. Be sure you have included a shell program (e.g., **bash** or **ash**) capable of running all of your rc scripts.

7. If you have a **/etc/ld.so.cache** file on your rescue disk, remake it.ld.so.cache

If **init** starts, but you get a message like:

        Id xxx respawning too fast: disabled for 5 minutes

it is coming from **init**, usually indicating that **getty** or **login** is dying as soon as it starts up. Check the **getty** and **login** executables and the libraries they depend upon. Make sure the invocations in **/etc/inittab** are correct. If you get strange messages from **getty**, it may mean the calling form in **/etc/inittab** is wrong. The options of the *getty* programs are variable; even different versions of **agetty** are reported to have different incompatible calling forms.

If you try to run some executable, such as **df**, which is on your rescue disk but you yields a message like: **df: not found**, check two things: (1) Make sure the directory containing the binary is in your PATH, and (2) make sure you have libraries (and loaders) the program needs.

8   Miscellaneous topics.

8.1   Reducing root filesystem size.

Sometimes a root filesystem is too large to fit on a diskette even after compression. Here are some ways to reduce the filesystem size:

Replace your shell

Some of the popular shells for Linux, such as `bash` and `tcsh`, are large and require many libraries. Light-weight alternatives exist, such as `ash`, `lsh`, `kiss` and `smash`, which are much smaller and require few (or no) libraries. Most of these replacement shells are available from <http://sunsite.unc.edu/pub/Linux/system/shells/>. Make sure any shell you use is capable of running commands in all the `rc` files you include on your bootdisk.

Strip libraries and binaries

Many libraries and binaries are typically unstripped (include debugging symbols). Running 'file' on these files will tell you 'not stripped' if so. When copying binaries to your root filesystem, it is good practice to use:

```
objcopy --strip-all FROM TO
```

When copying libraries, use:

```
objcopy --strip-debug FROM TO
```

Move non-critical files to a utility disk

If some of your binaries are not needed immediately to boot or login, you can move them to a utility disk. See section 8.3 (Building a utility disk) for details. You may also consider moving modules to a utility disk as well.

8.2   Non-ramdisk root filesystems.

Section 4 (Building a root filesystem) gave instructions for building a compressed root filesystem which is loaded to ramdisk when the system boots. This method has many advantages so it is commonly used. However, some systems with little memory cannot afford the RAM needed for this; for such cases a root filesystem can be built that is mounted directly instead of copied to ramdisk.

Such filesystems are actually easier to build than compressed root filesystems because they can be built on a diskette rather than on some other device, and they do not have to be compressed. We will outline the procedure as it differs from the instructions above. If you choose to do this, keep in mind that you will have *far less space* available.

1. Calculate how much space you will have available for root files.

   If you are building a single boot/root disk, you must fit all blocks for the kernel plus all blocks for the root filesystem on the one disk.

2. Using `mke2fs`, create a root filesystem on a diskette of the appropriate size.

3. Populate the filesystem as described above.

4. When done, unmount the filesystem and transfer it to a disk file but *do not compress it*.

5. Transfer the kernel to a floppy diskette, as described above. When calculating the ramdisk word, **set bit 14 to zero**, to indicate that the root filesystem is not to be loaded to ramdisk. Run the `rdev`'s as described.

6. Transfer the root filesystem as before.

There are several shortcuts you can take. If you are building a two-disk set, you can build the complete root filesystem directly on the second disk and you need not transfer it to a hard disk file and then back. Also, if you are building a single boot/root disk and using LILO, you can build a *single* filesystem on the entire disk, containing the kernel, LILO files and root files, and simply run LILO as the last step.

8.3   Building a utility disk.

Building a utility disk is relatively easy — simply create a filesystem on a formatted disk and copy files to it. To use it with a bootdisk, mount it manually after the system is booted.

In the instructions above, we mentioned that the utility disk could be mounted as /usr. In this case, binaries could be placed into a /bin directory on your utility disk, so that placing /usr/bin in your path will access them. Additional libraries needed by the binaries are placed in /lib on the utility disk.

There are several important points to keep in mind when designing a utility disk:

1. Do not place critical system binaries or libraries onto the utility disk, since it will not be mountable until after the system has booted.

2. You cannot access a floppy diskette and a floppy tape drive simultaneously. This means that if you have a floppy tape drive, you will not be able to access it while your utility disk is mounted.

3. Access to files on the utility disk will be slow.

Appendix D (Sample utility disk directory listing) shows a sample of files on a utility disk. Here are some ideas for files you may find useful: programs for examining and manipulating disks (format, fdisk) and filesystems (mke2fs, fsck, isofs.o), a lightweight text editor (elvis, jove), compression and archive utilities (gzip, tar, cpio, afio), tape utilities (mt, tob, taper), communications utilities (ppp.o, slip.o, minicom) and utilities for devices (setserial, mknod).

9   How the pros do it.

You may notice that the bootdisks used by major distributions such as Slackware, RedHat or Debian, seem more sophisticated than what is described in this document. Professional distribution bootdisks are based on the same principles outlined here, but employ various tricks because their bootdisks have additional requirements. First, they must be able to work with a wide variety of hardware, so they must be able to interact with the user and load various device drivers. Second, they must be prepared to work with many different installation options, with varying degrees of automation. Finally, distribution bootdisks usually combine installation and rescue capabilities.

Some bootdisks use a feature called **initrd** (**initial ramdisk**). This feature was introduced around 2.0.x and provides greater flexibility by allowing a kernel to boot in two phases. When the kernel first boots, it loads an initial ramdisk image from the boot disk. This initial ramdisk is a root filesystem containing a program that runs before the real root fs is loaded. This program usually inspects the environment and/or asks the user to select various boot options, such as the device from which to load the real rootdisk. It typically loads additional modules not built in to the kernel. When this initial program exits, the kernel loads the "real" root image and booting continues normally. For further information on initrd, see /usr/src/linux/Documentation/initrd.txt and <ftp://elserv.ffm.fgan.de/pub/linux/loadlin-1.6/initrd-example.tgz>

The following are summaries of how each distribution's installation disks seem to work, based on inspecting their filesystems and/or sourcecode. We do not guarantee that this information is completely accurate, or that they have not changed since the versions noted.

Slackware (v.3.1) uses a straightforward LILO boot similar to what is described in section 6.1 (Transferring the kernel with LILO). The Slackware bootdisk prints a bootup message ("Welcome to the Slackware Linux bootkernel disk!") using LILO's message parameter. This instructs the user to enter a boot parameter line if necessary. After booting, a root filesystem is loaded from a second disk. The user invokes a setup script which starts the installation. Instead of using a modular kernel, Slackware provides many different kernels and depends upon the user to select the one matching his or her hardware requirements.

RedHat (v.4.0) also uses a LILO boot. It loads a compressed ramdisk on the first disk, which runs a custom init program. This program queries for drivers, and loads additional files from a supplemental disk if necessary.

Debian (v.1.3) is probably the most sophisticated of the installation disk sets. It uses the SYSLINUX loader to arrange various load options, then uses an initrd image to guide the user through installation. It appears to use both a customized init and a customized shell.

10   Frequently asked question (FAQ) list.

Q. I boot from my boot/root disks and nothing happens. What do I do?

See section 7 (Troubleshooting), above.

Q. How does the Slackware/Debian/RedHat bootdisk work?

See section 9 (What the pros do), above.

Q. How can I make a boot disk with a XYZ driver?

The easiest way is to obtain a Slackware kernel from your nearest Slackware mirror site. Slackware kernels are generic kernels which atttempt to include drivers for as many devices as possible, so if you have a SCSI or IDE controller, chances are that a driver for it is included in the Slackware kernel.

Go to the a1 directory and select either IDE or SCSI kernel depending on the type of controller you have. Check the xxxxkern.cfg file for the selected kernel to see the drivers which have been included in that kernel. If the device you want is in that list, then the corresponding kernel should boot your computer. Download the xxxxkern.tgz file and copy it to your boot diskette as described above in the section on making boot disks.

You must then check the root device in the kernel, using the rdev command:

```
rdev zImage
```

rdev will then display the current root device in the kernel. If this is not the same as the root device you want, then use rdev to change it. For example, the kernel I tried was set to /dev/sda2, but my root SCSI partition is /dev/sda8. To use a root diskette, you would have to use the command:

```
rdev zImage /dev/fd0
```

If you want to know how to set up a Slackware root disk as well, that's outside the scope of this HOWTO, so I suggest you check the Linux Install Guide or get the Slackware distribution. See the section in this HOWTO titled "References".

Q. How do I update my boot diskette with a new kernel?

Just copy the kernel to your boot diskette using the dd command for a boot diskette without a filesystem, or the cp command for a boot/root disk. Refer to the section in this HOWTO titled "Boot" for details on creating a boot disk. The description applies equally to updating a kernel on a boot disk.

Q. How do I update my root diskette with new files?

The easiest way is to copy the filesystem from the rootdisk back to the DEVICE you used (from section 4.2 (Creating the filesystem), above). Then mount the filesystem and make the changes. You have to remember where your root filesystem started and how many blocks it occupied:

```
dd if=/dev/fd0 bs=1k skip=ROOTBEGIN count=BLOCKS | gunzip > DEVICE
mount -t ext2 DEVICE /mnt
```

After making the changes, proceed as before (in Section 4.6 (Wrapping it up)) and transfer the root filesystem back to the disk. You should not have to re-transfer the kernel or re-compute the ramdisk word if you do not change the starting position of the new root filesystem.

Q. How do I remove LILO so that I can use DOS to boot again?

This is not really a Bootdisk topic, but it is asked so often, so: the answer is, use the DOS command:

```
FDISK /MBR
```

MBR stands for Master Boot Record, and it replaces the boot sector with a clean DOS one, without affecting the partition table. Some purists disagree with this, but even the author of LILO, Werner Almesberger, suggests it. It is easy, and it works.

You can also use the dd command to copy the backup saved by LILO to the boot sector. Refer to the LILO documentation if you wish to do this.

Q. How can I boot if I've lost my kernel *and* my boot disk?

If you don't have a boot disk standing by, probably the easiest method is to obtain a Slackware kernel for your disk controller type (IDE or SCSI) as described above for "How do I make a boot disk with a XXX driver?". You can then boot your computer using this kernel, then repair whatever damage there is.

The kernel you get may not have the root device set to the disk type and partition you want. For example, Slackware's generic SCSI kernel has the root device set to /dev/sda2, whereas my root Linux partition happens to be /dev/sda8. In this case the root device in the kernel will have to be changed.

You can still change the root device and ramdisk settings in the kernel even if all you have is a kernel, and some other operating system, such as DOS.

rdev changes kernel settings by changing the values at fixed offsets in the kernel file, so you can do the same if you have a hex editor available on whatever systems you do still have running — for example, Norton Utilities Disk Editor under DOS. You then need to check and if necessary change the values in the kernel at the following offsets:

```
HEX      DEC    DESCRIPTION
0x01F8   504    Low byte of RAMDISK word
0x01F9   505    High byte of RAMDISK word
0x01FC   508    Root minor device number - see below
0X01FD   509    Root major device number - see below
```

The interpretation of the ramdisk word was described in Section 6.3 (Setting the ramdisk word), above.

The major and minor device numbers must be set to the device you want to mount your root filesystem on. Some useful values to select from are:

```
DEVICE          MAJOR MINOR
/dev/fd0          2     0   1st floppy drive
/dev/hda1         3     1   partition 1 on 1st IDE drive
/dev/sda1         8     1   partition 1 on 1st SCSI drive
/dev/sda8         8     8   partition 8 on 1st SCSI drive
```

Once you have set these values then you can write the file to a diskette using either Norton Utilities Disk Editor, or a program called rawrite.exe. This program is included in all distributions. It is a DOS program which writes a file to the "raw" disk, starting at the boot sector, instead of writing it to the file system. If you use Norton Utilities you must write the file to a physical disk starting at the beginning of the disk.

Q. How can I make extra copies of boot/root diskettes?

Because magnetic media may deteriorate over time, you should keep several copies of your rescue disk, in case the original is unreadable.

The easiest way of making copies of any diskettes, including bootable and utility diskettes, is to use the dd command to copy the contents of the original diskette to a file on your hard drive, and then use the same command to copy the file back to a new diskette. Note that you do not need to, and should not, mount the diskettes, because dd uses the raw device interface.

To copy the original, enter the command:

```
        dd if=DEVICENAME of=FILENAME
where   DEVICENAME is the device name of the diskette drive
and     FILENAME is the name of the (hard-disk) output file
```

Omitting the "count" parameter, as we have done here, means that the whole diskette of 2880 (for a high-density) blocks will be copied.

To copy the resulting file back to a new diskette, insert the new diskette and enter the reverse command:

```
        dd if=FILENAME of=DEVICENAME
```

Note that the above discussion assumes that you have only one diskette drive. If you have two of the same type, you can copy diskettes using a command like:

```
        dd if=/dev/fd0 of=/dev/fd1
```

Q. How can I boot without typing in "ahaxxxx=nn,nn,nn" every time?

Where a disk device cannot be autodetected it is necessary to supply the kernel with a command device parameter string, such as:

```
        aha152x=0x340,11,3,1
```

This parameter string can be supplied in several ways using LILO:

- By entering it on the command line every time the system is booted via LILO. This is boring, though.
- By using the LILO "lock" keyword to make it store the command line as the default command line, so that LILO will use the same options every time it boots.
- By using the append= statement in the LILO config file. Note that the parameter string must be enclosed in quotes.

For example, a sample command line using the above parameter string would be:

```
zImage  aha152x=0x340,11,3,1 root=/dev/sda1 lock
```

This would pass the device parameter string through, and also ask the kernel to set the root device to /dev/sda1 and save the whole command line and reuse it for all future boots.

A sample APPEND statement is:

```
APPEND = "aha152x=0x340,11,3,1"
```

Note that the parameter string must NOT be enclosed in quotes on the command line, but it MUST be enclosed in quotes in the APPEND statement.

Note also that for the parameter string to be acted on, the kernel must contain the driver for that disk type. If it does not, then there is nothing listening for the parameter string, and you will have to rebuild the kernel to include the required driver. For details on rebuilding the kernel, cd to **/usr/src/linux** and read the README, and read the Linux FAQ and Installation HOWTO. Alternatively you could obtain a generic kernel for the disk type and install that.

Readers are strongly urged to read the LILO documentation before experimenting with LILO installation. Incautious use of the "BOOT" statement can damage partitions.

Q. At boot time, I get error "A: cannot execute B". Why?

There are several cases of program names being hardcoded in various utilities. These cases do not occur everywhere, but they may explain why an executable apparently cannot be found on your system even though you can see that it is there. You can find out if a given program has the name of another hardcoded by using the **strings** command and piping the output through **grep**.

Known examples of hardcoding are:

- Shutdown in some versions has **/etc/reboot** hardcoded, so **reboot** must be placed in the **/etc** directory.

- **init** has caused problems for at least one person, with the kernel being unable to find **init**.

To fix these problems, either move the programs to the correct directory, or change configuration files (e.g. inittab) to point to the correct directory. If in doubt, put programs in the same directories as they are on your hard disk, and use the same **inittab** and **/etc/rc.d** files as they appear on your hard disk.

Q. My kernel has ramdisk support, but initializes ramdisks of 0K

Where this occurs, a kernel message like this will appear as the kernel is booting:

```
Ramdisk driver initialized : 16 ramdisks of 0K size
```

This is probably because the size has been set to 0 by kernel parameters at boot time. This could possibly be because of an overlooked LILO configuration file parameter:

```
ramdisk= 0
```

This was included in sample LILO configuration files in some older distributions, and was put there to override any previous kernel setting. If you have such a line, remove it.

Note that if you attempt to use a ramdisk which has been set to 0K the behaviour can be unpredictable, and can result in kernel panics.

A   Resources and pointers.

In this section, *vvv* is used in package names in place of the version, to avoid referring here to specific versions. When retrieving a package, always get the latest version unless you have good reasons for not doing so.

A.1   Pre-made bootdisks.

These are sources for distribution bootdisks. *Please use one of the mirror sites to reduce the load on these machines.*

- *Slackware bootdisks* <http://sunsite.unc.edu/pub/Linux/distributions/slackware/bootdsks. 144/> and *Slackware mirror sites* <http://sunsite.unc.edu/pub/Linux/distributions/slackware/ MIRRORS.TXT>

- *RedHat bootdisks* <http://sunsite.unc.edu/pub/Linux/distributions/redhat/current/i386/ images/> and *Red Hat mirror sites* <http://www.redhat.com/ftp.html>

- *Debian bootdisks* <ftp://ftp.debian.org/pub/debian/stable/disks-i386> and *Debian mirror sites* <ftp://ftp.debian.org/debian/README.mirrors>

In addition to the distribution bootdisks, the following rescue disk images are available.

- rescue02, by John Comyns, is a rescue disk using kernel 1.3.84, with support for IDE and Adaptec 1542 and NCR53C7,8xx. It uses ELF binaries but it has enough commands so that it can be used on any system. There are modules that can be loaded after booting for all other SCSI cards. It probably won't work on systems with 4 mb of ram since it uses a 3 mb ram disk. <http://sunsite.unc.edu/ pub/Linux/system/recovery/rescue02.zip>

- resque_disk-2.0.22, by Sergei Viznyuk, is a full-featured boot/root disk based on kernel 2.0.22 with built-in support for IDE, many difference SCSI controllers, and ELF/AOUT. Also includes many modules and useful utilities for repairing and restoring a hard disk. <http://sunsite.unc.edu/pub/ Linux/system/recovery/resque_disk-vvv.tar.gz>

- cramdisk images, based on the 2.0.23 kernel, available for 4 meg and 8 meg machines. They include math emulation and networking (PPP and dialin script, NE2000, 3C509), or support for the parallel port ZIP drive. These diskette images will boot on a 386 with 4MB RAM. MSDOS support is included so you can download from the net to a DOS partition. <http://sunsite.unc.edu/pub/ Linux/system/recovery/images/>

A.2   Rescue packages

Several packages for creating rescue disks are available on sunsite.unc.edu. With these packages you generally specify a set of files for inclusion and the software automates (to varying degrees) the creation of a bootdisk. See <http://sunsite.unc.edu/pub/Linux/system/recovery/!INDEX.html> for more information. **Check the file dates carefully** — some of these packages have not been updated in several years and will not support the creation of a compressed root filesystem loaded into ramdisk. To the best of our knowledge, Yard is the only package that will.

A.3   Graham Chapman's shell scripts

Graham Chapman has written a set of scripts that may be useful as examples of how to create bootdisks. In previous versions of this HOWTO the scripts appeared in an appendix, but they have been deleted from the documented and placed on a web page:

`<http://www.zeta.org.au/grahamc/linux.html>`

You may find it convenient to use these scripts, but if so, read the instructions carefully — for example, if you specify the wrong swap device, you will find your root filesystem has been throroughly and permanently erased. Be sure you have it correctly configured before you use it!

A.4   LILO — the Linux loader.

Written by Werner Almesberger. Excellent boot loader, and the documentation includes information on the boot sector contents and the early stages of the boot process.

Ftp from `<ftp://tsx-11.mit.edu/pub/linux/packages/lilo/lilo.vvv.tar.gz>`. It is also available on Sunsite and mirrors.

A.5   Linux FAQ and HOWTOs.

These are available from many sources. Look at the usenet newsgroups `news.answers` and `comp.os.linux.announce`.

The FAQ is available from `<http://sunsite.unc.edu/pub/Linux/docs/faqs/linux-faq>` and the HOW-TOs from `<http://sunsite.unc.edu/pub/Linux/docs/HOWTO>`.

Most documentation for Linux may be found at *The Linux Documentation Project homepage* `<http://sunsite.unc.edu/LDP/>`.

If desperate, send mail to `mail-server@rtfm.mit.edu` with the word "`help`" in the message, then follow the mailed instructions.

A.6   Ramdisk usage.

An excellent description of the how the new ramdisk code works may be found with the documentation supplied with the Linux kernel. See `/usr/src/linux/Documentation/ramdisk.txt`. It is written by Paul Gortmaker and includes a section on creating a compressed ramdisk.

A.7   The Linux boot process.

For more detail on the Linux boot process, here are some pointers:

- The Linux System Administrators' Guide has a section on booting, See `<http://sunsite.unc.edu/LDP/LDP/sag-0.5/node68.html>`

- The LILO "Technical overview" `<http://sunsite.unc.edu/pub/Linux/system/boot/lilo/lilo-t-20.ps.gz>` has the definitive technical, low-level description of the boot process, up to where the kernel is started.

- The source code is the ultimate guide. Below are some kernel files related to the boot process. If you have the Linux kernel source code, you can find these under `/usr/src/linux` on your machine; alternatively, Shigio Yamaguchi (shigio@wafu.netgate.net) has a very nice hypertext kernel browser at `<http://wafu.netgate.net/linux/>`.

  arch/i386/boot/bootsect.S,setup.S
       Contain assembly code for the bootsector.

arch/i386/boot/compressed/misc.c

Contains code for uncompressing the kernel.

arch/i386/kernel/

Directory containing kernel initialization code. `setup.c` contains the ramdisk word.

drivers/block/rd.c

Contains the ramdisk driver. The procedures `rd_load` and `rd_load_image` load blocks from a device into a ramdisk. The procedure `identify_ramdisk_image` determines what kind of filesystem is found and whether it is compressed.

B LILO boot error codes.

Questions about these errors are asked so often on Usenet that we include them here as a public service. This summary is excerpted from Werner Almsberger's LILO User Documentation, available at `<ftp:// lrcftp.epfl.ch:/pub/linux/local/lilo/lilo.u.19.ps.gz>`.

When LILO loads itself, it displays the word "LILO". Each letter is printed before or after performing some specific action. If LILO fails at some point, the letters printed so far can be used to identify the problem.

(nothing)

No part of LILO has been loaded. LILO either isn't installed or the partition on which its boot sector is located isn't active.

L

The first stage boot loader has been loaded and started, but it can't load the second stage boot loader. The two-digit error codes indicate the type of problem. (See also section "Disk error codes".) This condition usually indicates a media failure or a geometry mismatch (e.g. bad disk parameters)

LI

The first stage boot loader was able to load the second stage boot loader, but has failed to execute it. This can either be caused by a geometry mismatch or by moving /boot/boot.b without running the map installer.

LIL

The second stage boot loader has been started, but it can't load the descriptor table from the map file. This is typically caused by a media failure or by a geometry mismatch.

LIL?

The second stage boot loader has been loaded at an incorrect address. This is typically caused by a subtle geometry mismatch or by moving /boot/boot.b without running the map installer.

LIL-

The descriptor table is corrupt. This can either be caused by a geometry mismatch or by moving /boot/map without running the map installer.

LILO

All parts of LILO have been successfully loaded.

If the BIOS signals an error when LILO is trying to load a boot image, the respective error code is displayed. These codes range from `0x00` through `0xbb`. See the LILO User Guide for an explanation of these.

C Sample rootdisk directory listings.

Here are the contents of Graham's root and utility diskettes. These lists are provided as an example only of the files included to create a working system. Graham has added some explanatory notes where it seemed useful.

```
total 18
drwxr-xr-x   2 root    root      1024 Jul 29 21:16 bin/
drwxr-xr-x   2 root    root      9216 Jul 28 16:21 dev/
drwxr-xr-x   3 root    root      1024 Jul 29 20:25 etc/
drwxr-xr-x   2 root    root      1024 Jul 28 19:53 lib/
drwxr-xr-x   2 root    root      1024 Jul 24 22:47 mnt/
drwxr-xr-x   2 root    root      1024 Jul 24 22:47 proc/
drwxr-xr-x   2 root    root      1024 Jul 28 19:07 sbin/
drwxr-xr-x   2 root    root      1024 Jul 29 20:57 tmp/
drwxr-xr-x   4 root    root      1024 Jul 29 21:35 usr/
drwxr-xr-x   3 root    root      1024 Jul 28 19:52 var/

/bin:
total 713
-rwxr-xr-x   1 root    bin       7737 Jul 24 22:16 cat*
-rwxr-xr-x   1 root    bin       9232 Jul 24 22:48 chmod*
-rwxr-xr-x   1 root    bin       8156 Jul 24 22:48 chown*
-rwxr-xr-x   1 root    bin      19652 Jul 24 22:48 cp*
-rwxr-xr-x   1 root    root      8313 Jul 29 21:16 cut*
-rwxr-xr-x   1 root    bin      12136 Jul 24 22:48 dd*
-rwxr-xr-x   1 root    bin       9308 Jul 24 22:48 df*
-rwxr-xr-x   1 root    root      9036 Jul 29 20:24 dircolors*
-rwxr-xr-x   1 root    bin       9064 Jul 24 22:48 du*
-rwxr-x---   1 root    bin      69252 Jul 24 22:51 e2fsck*
-rwxr-xr-x   1 root    bin       5361 Jul 24 22:48 echo*
-rwxr-xr-x   1 root    bin       5696 Jul 24 22:16 hostname*
-rwxr-xr-x   1 root    bin       6596 Jul 24 22:49 kill*
-rwxr-xr-x   1 root    bin      10644 Jul 24 22:17 ln*
-rwxr-xr-x   1 root    bin      13508 Jul 24 22:17 login*
-rwxr-xr-x   1 root    bin      26976 Jul 24 22:17 ls*
-rwxr-xr-x   1 root    bin       7416 Jul 24 22:49 mkdir*
-rwxr-x---   1 root    bin      34596 Jul 24 22:51 mke2fs*
-rwxr-xr-x   1 root    bin       6712 Jul 24 22:49 mknod*
-rwxr-xr-x   1 root    bin      20304 Jul 24 22:17 more*
-rwxr-xr-x   1 root    bin      24704 Jul 24 22:17 mount*
-rwxr-xr-x   1 root    bin      12464 Jul 24 22:17 mv*
-rwxr-xr-x   1 root    bin      20829 Jul 24 22:50 ps*
-rwxr-xr-x   1 root    bin       9424 Jul 24 22:50 rm*
-rwxr-xr-x   1 root    bin       4344 Jul 24 22:50 rmdir*
-rwxr-xr-x   1 root    root    299649 Jul 27 14:12 sh*
```

```
-rwxr-xr-x   1 root   bin      9853 Jul 24 22:17 su*
-rwxr-xr-x   1 root   bin       380 Jul 27 14:12 sync*
-rwxr-xr-x   1 root   bin     13620 Jul 24 22:17 umount*
-rwxr-xr-x   1 root   root     5013 Jul 29 20:03 uname*

/dev:
total 0
lrwxrwxrwx   1 root   root         10 Jul 24 22:34 cdrom -> /dev/sbpcd
crw--w--w-   1 root   tty      4,   0 Jul 24 21:49 console
brw-rw----   1 root   floppy   2,   0 Apr 28  1995 fd0
lrwxrwxrwx   1 root   root          4 Jul 24 22:34 ftape -> rft0
crw-rw-rw-   1 root   sys     10,   2 Jul 18  1994 inportbm
crw-rw----   1 root   kmem     1,   2 Jul 28 16:21 kmem
crw-rw----   1 root   kmem     1,   1 Jul 18  1994 mem
lrwxrwxrwx   1 root   root          4 Jul 24 22:34 modem -> cua0
lrwxrwxrwx   1 root   root          4 Jul 24 22:34 mouse -> cua1
crw-rw-rw-   1 root   sys      1,   3 Jul 18  1994 null
brw-rw----   1 root   disk     1,   1 Jul 18  1994 ram
crw-rw----   1 root   disk    27,   0 Jul 18  1994 rft0
brw-rw----   1 root   disk    25,   0 Jul 19  1994 sbpcd
*** I have only included devices for the SCSI partitions I use.
*** If you use IDE, then use /dev/hdxx instead.
brw-rw----   1 root   disk     8,   0 Apr 29  1995 sda
brw-rw----   1 root   disk     8,   6 Apr 29  1995 sda6
brw-rw----   1 root   disk     8,   7 Apr 29  1995 sda7
brw-rw----   1 root   disk     8,   8 Apr 29  1995 sda8
lrwxrwxrwx   1 root   root          7 Jul 28 12:56 systty -> console
*** this link from tty to console is required
crw-rw-rw-   1 root   tty      5,   0 Jul 18  1994 tty
crw--w--w-   1 root   tty      4,   0 Jul 18  1994 tty0
crw--w----   1 root   tty      4,   1 Jul 24 22:33 tty1
crw--w----   1 root   tty      4,   2 Jul 24 22:34 tty2
crw--w--w-   1 root   root     4,   3 Jul 24 21:49 tty3
crw--w--w-   1 root   root     4,   4 Jul 24 21:49 tty4
crw--w--w-   1 root   root     4,   5 Jul 24 21:49 tty5
crw--w--w-   1 root   root     4,   6 Jul 24 21:49 tty6
crw-rw-rw-   1 root   tty      4,   7 Jul 18  1994 tty7
crw-rw-rw-   1 root   tty      4,   8 Jul 18  1994 tty8
crw-rw-rw-   1 root   tty      4,   9 Jul 19  1994 tty9
crw-rw-rw-   1 root   sys      1,   5 Jul 18  1994 zero

/etc:
total 20
-rw-r--r--   1 root   root     2167 Jul 29 20:25 DIR_COLORS
-rw-r--r--   1 root   root       20 Jul 28 12:37 HOSTNAME
```

```
-rw-r--r--    1 root   root        109 Jul 24 22:57 fstab
-rw-r--r--    1 root   root        271 Jul 24 22:21 group
-rw-r--r--    1 root   root       2353 Jul 24 22:27 inittab
-rw-r--r--    1 root   root          0 Jul 29 21:02 issue
-rw-r--r--    1 root   root       2881 Jul 28 19:38 ld.so.cache
*** Lots of things get upset at boot time if ld.so.cache is missing, but
*** make sure that ldconfig is included and run from rc.x to
*** update it.
-rw-r--r--    1 root   root         12 Jul 24 22:22 motd
-rw-r--r--    1 root   root        606 Jul 28 19:25 passwd
-rw-r--r--    1 root   root       1065 Jul 24 22:21 profile
drwxr-xr-x    2 root   root       1024 Jul 29 21:01 rc.d/
-rw-r--r--    1 root   root         18 Jul 24 22:21 shells
-rw-r--r--    1 root   root        774 Jul 28 13:43 termcap
-rw-r--r--    1 root   root        126 Jul 28 13:44 ttys
-rw-r--r--    1 root   root          0 Jul 24 22:47 utmp

/etc/rc.d:
total 5
*** I didn't bother with shutdown scripts - everthing runs on a
*** ramdisk, so there's not much point shutting it down.
-rwxr-xr-x    1 root   root       1158 Jul 24 22:23 rc.K*
-rwxr-xr-x    1 root   root       1151 Jul 28 19:08 rc.M*
-rwxr-xr-x    1 root   root        507 Jul 29 20:25 rc.S*

/lib:
total 588
*** I have an ELF system, so I include the ELF loader ld-linux.so. if
*** you are still on a.out, then you need ld.so. Use the file command to
*** see which libraries you should include.
lrwxrwxrwx    1 root   root         17 Jul 24 23:36 ld-linux.so.1 -> ld-linux.so.1.7.3*
-rwxr-xr-x    1 root   root      20722 Aug 15  1995 ld-linux.so.1.7.3*
lrwxrwxrwx    1 root   root         13 Jul 24 23:36 libc.so.5 -> libc.so.5.0.9*
-rwxr-xr-x    1 root   root     562683 May 19  1995 libc.so.5.0.9*
*** Must include libtermcap
lrwxrwxrwx    1 root   root         19 Jul 28 19:53 libtermcap.so.2 -> libtermcap.so.2.0.0*
-rwxr-xr-x    1 root   root      11360 May 19  1995 libtermcap.so.2.0.0*
nt:
al 0

/proc:
total 0

/sbin:
total 191
```

```
***  I use Slackware, which uses agetty. Many systems use getty.
***  Check your /etc/inittab to see which it uses. Note that you
***  need (a)getty and login to be able to start doing much.
-rwxr-xr-x   1 root   bin      11309 Jul 24 22:54 agetty*
-rwxr-xr-x   1 root   bin       5204 Jul 24 22:19 halt*
***  Must have this to boot
-rwxr-xr-x   1 root   bin      20592 Jul 24 22:19 init*
-rwxr-xr-x   1 root   root     86020 Jul 28 19:07 ldconfig*
-rwxr-xr-x   1 root   bin       5329 Jul 27 14:10 mkswap*
-rwxr-xr-x   1 root   root      5204 Jul 24 22:20 reboot*
-rwxr-xr-x   1 root   root      6024 Jul 24 22:20 rdev*
-rwxr-xr-x   1 root   bin      12340 Jul 24 22:20 shutdown*
-rwxr-xr-x   1 root   root      5029 Jul 24 22:20 swapoff*
-rwxr-xr-x   1 root   bin       5029 Jul 24 22:20 swapon*
-rwxr-xr-x   1 root   root     20592 Jul 27 18:18 telinit*
-rwxr-xr-x   1 root   root      7077 Jul 24 22:20 update*

/tmp:
total 0

/usr:
total 2
drwxr-xr-x   2 root   root      1024 Jul 29 21:00 adm/
drwxr-xr-x   2 root   root      1024 Jul 29 21:16 lib/

/usr/adm:
total 0

/usr/lib:
total 0

/var:
total 1
***  Several things complained until I included this and
***  the /etc/rc.S code to initialise /var/run/utmp, but this
***  won't necessarily apply to your system.
drwxr-xr-x   2 root   root      1024 Jul 28 19:52 run/

/var/run:
total 0
```

D   Sample utility disk directory listing.

```
total 579
```

```
-rwxr-xr-x   1 root   root     42333 Jul 28 19:05 cpio*
-rwxr-xr-x   1 root   root    103560 Jul 29 21:31 elvis*
-rwxr-xr-x   1 root   root     56401 Jul 28 19:06 find*
-rwxr-xr-x   1 root   root     29536 Jul 28 19:04 fdisk*
-rw-r--r--   1 root   root    128254 Jul 28 19:03 ftape.o
-rwxr-xr-x   1 root   root     17564 Jul 25 03:21 ftmt*
-rwxr-xr-x   1 root   root     64161 Jul 29 20:47 grep*
-rwxr-xr-x   1 root   root     45309 Jul 29 20:48 gzip*
-rwxr-xr-x   1 root   root     23560 Jul 28 19:04 insmod*
-rwxr-xr-x   1 root   root       118 Jul 28 19:04 lsmod*
lrwxrwxrwx   1 root   root         5 Jul 28 19:04 mt -> mt-st*
-rwxr-xr-x   1 root   root      9573 Jul 28 19:03 mt-st*
lrwxrwxrwx   1 root   root         6 Jul 28 19:05 rmmod -> insmod*
-rwxr-xr-x   1 root   root    104085 Jul 28 19:05 tar*
lrwxrwxrwx   1 root   root         5 Jul 29 21:35 vi -> elvis*
```

The Linux BootPrompt-HowTo

by Paul Gortmaker.   v1.14, 1 February 1998

This is the BootPrompt-Howto, which is a compilation of all the possible boot time arguments that can be passed to the Linux kernel at boot time. This includes all kernel and device parameters. A discussion of how the kernel sorts boot time arguments, along with an overview of some of the popular software used to boot Linux kernels is also included.

Contents

1   Introduction

The kernel has a limited capability to accept information at boot in the form of a 'command line', similar to an argument list you would give to a program. In general this is used to supply the kernel with information about hardware parameters that the kernel would not be able to determine on its own, or to avoid/override the values that the kernel would otherwise detect.

However, if you just copy a kernel image directly to a floppy, (e.g. `cp zImage /dev/fd0`) then you are not given a chance to specify any arguments to that kernel. So most Linux users will use software like *LILO* or *loadlin* that takes care of handing these arguments to the kernel, and then booting it.

IMPORTANT NOTE TO MODULE USERS: Boot Prompt arguments typically only apply to hardware drivers that are compiled directly into the kernel. They have *no effect* on drivers that are loaded as modules. Most distributions use modules. If you are unsure, then look at `man depmod` and `man modprobe` along with the contents of `/etc/conf.modules`.

This present revision covers kernels up to and including v2.0.33. Some features that are unique to development/testing kernels up to v2.1.84 are also documented.

The BootPrompt-Howto is by:

Paul Gortmaker, `gpg109@rsphy1.anu.edu.au`

[Please note that boot prompt arguments that are specific to the non-i386 ports and devices (esp. Atari/Amiga) are not currently documented.]

1.1   Disclaimer and Copyright

This document is *not* gospel. However, it is probably the most up to date info that you will be able to find. Nobody is responsible for what happens to your hardware but yourself. If your hardware goes up in smoke (...nearly impossible!) I take no responsibility. ie. THE AUTHOR IS NOT RESPONSIBLE FOR ANY DAMAGES INCURRED DUE TO ACTIONS TAKEN BASED ON THE INFORMATION INCLUDED IN THIS DOCUMENT.

This document is Copyright (C) 1995-1998 by Paul Gortmaker.

This document may be copied according to the conditions of the GNU General Public License, version 2, included herein by reference. See the file `linux/COPYING` that comes with the Linux kernel for full details.

If you are intending to incorporate this document into a published work, please contact me, and I will make an effort to ensure that you have the most up to date information available. In the past, out of date versions of the Linux howto documents have been published, which caused the developers undue grief from being plagued with questions that were already answered in the up to date versions.

1.2   Related Documentation

The most up-to-date documentation will always be the kernel source itself. Hold on! Don't get scared. You don't need to know any programming to read the comments in the source files. For example, if you were looking for what arguments could be passed to the AHA1542 SCSI driver, then you would go to the linux/drivers/scsi directory, and look at the file aha1542.c – and within the first 100 lines, you would find a plain english description of the boot time arguments that the 1542 driver accepts.

The next best thing will be any documentation files that are distributed with the kernel itself. There are now quite a few of these, and most of them can be found in the directory linux/Documentation and subdirectories from there. The linux directory is usually found in /usr/src/. Sometimes there will be README.foo files that can be found in the related driver directory (e.g. linux/drivers/XXX/, where XXX will be scsi, char, or net).

If you have figured out what boot-args you intend to use, and now want to know how to get that information to the kernel, then look at the documentation that comes with the software that you use to boot the kernel (e.g. LILO or loadlin). A brief overview is given below, but it is no substitute for the documentation that comes with the booting software.

1.3   The Linux Newsgroups

If you have questions about passing boot arguments to the kernel, please READ this document first. If this and the related documentation mentioned above does not answer your question(s) then you can try the Linux newsgroups. Of course you should try reading the group before blindly posting your question, as somebody else may have already asked it, or it may even be a Frequently Asked Question (a FAQ). A quick browse of the linux FAQ before posting is a *good* idea. You should be able to find the FAQ somewhere close to where you found this document.

General questions on how to configure your system should be directed to the comp.os.linux.setup newsgroup. We ask that you *please* respect this general guideline for content, and don't cross-post your request to other groups.

1.4   New Versions of this Document

New versions of this document can be retrieved via anonymous FTP from the site sunsite.unc.edu, in the directory /pub/Linux/docs/HOWTO/. Note that *SunSITE* is usually heavily loaded, and you are better advised to get the document from one of the Linux ftp mirror sites. Updates will be made as new information and/or drivers becomes available. If this copy that you are presently reading is more than a few months old, then you should probably check to see if a newer copy exists.

This document was produced by using a modified SGML system that was specifically set up for the Linux Howto project, and there are various output formats available, including, postscript, dvi, ascii, html, and soon TeXinfo. I would recommend viewing it in the html (via a WWW browser) or the Postscript/dvi format. Both of these contain cross-references that are lost in the ascii translation.

If you want to get the official copy off sunsite, here is URL.

BootPrompt-HOWTO <http://sunsite.unc.edu/mdw/HOWTO/BootPrompt-HOWTO.html>

2   Overview of Boot Prompt Arguments

This section gives some examples of software that can be used to pass kernel boot-time arguments to the kernel itself. It also gives you an idea of how the arguments are processed, what limitations there are on the boot args, and how they filter down to each appropriate device that they are intended for.

It is *important* to note that spaces should *not* be used in a boot argument, but only between separate arguments. A list of values that are for a single argument are to be separated with a comma between the values, and again without any spaces. See the following examples below.

```
ether=9,0x300,0xd0000,0xd4000,eth0  root=/dev/hda1        *RIGHT*
ether = 9, 0x300, 0xd0000, 0xd4000, eth0  root = /dev/hda1    *WRONG*
```

2.1   LILO (LInux LOader)

The LILO program (LInux LOader) written by Werner Almesberger is the most commonly used. It has the ability to boot various kernels, and stores the configuration information in a plain text file. Most distributions ship with LILO as the default boot-loader. LILO can boot DOS, OS/2, Linux, FreeBSD, etc. without any difficulties, and is quite flexible.

A typical configuration will have LILO stop and print `LILO:` shortly after you turn on your computer. It will then wait for a few seconds for any optional input from the user, and failing that it will then boot the default system. Typical system labels that people use in the LILO configuration files are `linux` and `backup` and `msdos`. If you want to type in a boot argument, you type it in here, after typing in the system label that you want LILO to boot from, as shown in the example below.

```
LILO: linux root=/dev/hda1
```

LILO comes with excellent documentation, and for the purposes of boot args discussed here, the LILO `append=` command is of significant importance when one wants to add a boot time argument as a permanent addition to the LILO config file. You simply add something like `append = "foo=bar"` to the `/etc/lilo.conf` file. It can either be added at the top of the config file, making it apply to all sections, or to a single system section by adding it inside an `image=` section. Please see the LILO documentation for a more complete description.

2.2   LoadLin

The other commonly used Linux loader is 'LoadLin' which is a DOS program that has the capability to launch a Linux kernel from the DOS prompt (with boot-args) assuming that certain resources are available. This is good for people that use DOS and want to launch into Linux from DOS.

It is also very useful if you have certain hardware which relies on the supplied DOS driver to put the hardware into a known state. A common example is 'SoundBlaster Compatible' sound cards that require the DOS driver to set a few proprietary registers to put the card into a SB compatible mode. Booting DOS with the supplied driver, and then loading Linux from the DOS prompt with `LOADLIN.EXE` avoids the reset of the card that happens if one rebooted instead. Thus the card is left in a SB compatible mode and hence is useable under Linux.

There are also other programs that can be used to boot Linux. For a complete list, please look at the programs available on your local Linux ftp mirror, under `system/Linux-boot/`.

2.3   The "rdev" utility

There are a few of the kernel boot parameters that have their default values stored in various bytes in the kernel image itself. There is a utility called `rdev` that is installed on most systems that knows where these values are, and how to change them. It can also change things that have no kernel boot argument equivalent, such as the default video mode used.

The rdev utility is usually also aliased to swapdev, ramsize, vidmode and rootflags. These are the five things that rdev can change, those being the root device, the swap device, the RAM disk parameters, the default video mode, and the readonly/readwrite setting of root device.

More information on `rdev` can be found by typing `rdev -h` or by reading the supplied man page (`man rdev`).

2.4   How the Kernel Sorts the Arguments

Most of the boot args take the form of:

```
name[=value_1][,value_2]...[,value_11]
```

---

where 'name' is a unique keyword that is used to identify what part of the kernel the associated values (if any) are to be given to. Multiple boot args are just a space separated list of the above format. Note the limit of 11 is real, as the present code only handles 11 comma separated parameters per keyword. (However, you can re-use the same keyword with up to an additional 11 parameters in unusually complicated situations, assuming the setup function supports it.) Also note that the kernel splits the list into a maximum of ten integer arguments, and a following string, so you can't really supply 11 integers unless you convert the 11th arg from a string to an int in the driver itself.

Most of the sorting goes on in `linux/init/main.c`. First, the kernel checks to see if the argument is any of the special arguments 'root=', 'ro', 'rw', or 'debug'. The meaning of these special arguments is described further on in the document.

Then it walks a list of setup functions (contained in the `bootsetups` array) to see if the specified argument string (such as 'foo') has been associated with a setup function (`foo_setup()`) for a particular device or part of the kernel. If you passed the kernel the line `foo=3,4,5,6,bar` then the kernel would search the `bootsetups` array to see if 'foo' was registered. If it was, then it would call the setup function associated with 'foo' (`foo_setup()`) and hand it the integer arguments 3, 4, 5 and 6 as given on the kernel command line, and also hand it the string argument `bar`.

2.5   Setting Environment Variables.

Anything of the form 'foo=bar' that is not accepted as a setup function as described above is then interpreted as an environment variable to be set. A (useless?) example would be to use 'TERM=vt100' as a boot argument.

2.6   Passing Arguments to the 'init' program

Any remaining arguments that were not picked up by the kernel and were not interpreted as environment variables are then passed onto process one, which is usually the `init` program. The most common argument that is passed to the `init` process is the word *single* which instructs `init` to boot the computer in single user mode, and not launch all the usual daemons. Check the manual page for the version of `init` installed on your system to see what arguments it accepts.

3 General Non-Device Specific Boot Args

These are the boot arguments that are not related to any specific device or peripheral. They are instead related to certain internal kernel parameters, such as memory handling, ramdisk handling, root file system handling and others.

3.1 Root Filesystem options

The following options all pertain to how the kernel selects and handles the root filesystem.

3.1.1 The 'root=' Argument

This argument tells the kernel what device is to be used as the root filesystem while booting. The default of this setting is the value of the root device of the system that the kernel was built on. For example, if the kernel in question was built on a system that used '/dev/hda1' as the root partition, then the default root device would be '/dev/hda1'. To override this default value, and select the second floppy drive as the root device, one would use 'root=/dev/fd1'.

Valid root devices are any of the following devices:

(1) /dev/hdaN to /dev/hddN, which is partition N on ST-506 compatible disk 'a to d'.

(2) /dev/sdaN to /dev/sdeN, which is partition N on SCSI compatible disk 'a to e'.

(3) /dev/xdaN to /dev/xdbN, which is partition N on XT compatible disk 'a to b'.

(4) /dev/fdN, which is floppy disk drive number N. Having N=0 would be the DOS 'A:' drive, and N=1 would be 'B:'.

(5) /dev/nfs, which is not really a device, but rather a flag to tell the kernel to get the root fs via the network.

The more awkward and less portable numeric specification of the above possible disk devices in major/minor format is also accepted. (e.g. /dev/sda3 is major 8, minor 3, so you could use root=0x803 as an alternative.)

This is one of the few kernel boot arguments that has its default stored in the kernel image, and which can thus be altered with the rdev utility.

3.1.2 The 'ro' Argument

When the kernel boots, it needs a root filesystem to read basic things off of. This is the root filesystem that is mounted at boot. However, if the root filesystem is mounted with write access, you can not reliably check the filesystem integrity with half-written files in progress. The 'ro' option tells the kernel to mount the root filesystem as 'readonly' so that any filesystem consistency check programs (fsck) can safely assume that there are no half-written files in progress while performing the check. No programs or processes can write to files on the filesystem in question until it is 'remounted' as read/write capable.

This is one of the few kernel boot arguments that has its default stored in the kernel image, and which can thus be altered with the rdev utility.

3.1.3 The 'rw' Argument

This is the exact opposite of the above, in that it tells the kernel to mount the root filesystem as read/write. The default is to mount the root filesystem as read/write anyway. Do not run any 'fsck' type programs on a filesystem that is mounted read/write.

The same value stored in the image file mentioned above is also used for this parameter, accessible via `rdev`.

3.2 Options Relating to RAM Disk Management

The following options all relate to how the kernel handles the RAM disk device, which is usually used for bootstrapping machines during the install phase, or for machines with modular drivers that need to be installed to access the root filesystem.

3.2.1 The 'ramdisk_start=' Argument

To allow a kernel image to reside on a floppy disk along with a compressed ramdisk image, the 'ramdisk_start=<offset>' command was added. The kernel can't be included into the compressed ramdisk filesystem image, because it needs to be stored starting at block zero so that the BIOS can load the bootsector and then the kernel can bootstrap itself to get going.

Note: If you are using an uncompressed ramdisk image, then the kernel can be a part of the filesystem image that is being loaded into the ramdisk, and the floppy can be booted with LILO, or the two can be separate as is done for the compressed images.

If you are using a two-disk boot/root setup (kernel on disk 1, ramdisk image on disk 2) then the ramdisk would start at block zero, and an offset of zero would be used. Since this is the default value, you would not need to actually use the command at all.

3.2.2 The 'load_ramdisk=' Argument

This parameter tells the kernel whether it is to try to load a ramdisk image or not. Specifying 'load_ramdisk=1' will tell the kernel to load a floppy into the ramdisk. The default value is zero, meaning that the kernel should not try to load a ramdisk.

Please see the file `linux/Documentation/ramdisk.txt` for a complete description of the new boot time arguments, and how to use them. A description of how this parameter can be set and stored in the kernel image via 'rdev' is also described.

3.2.3 The 'prompt_ramdisk=' Argument

This parameter tells the kernel whether or not to give you a prompt asking you to insert the floppy containing the ramdisk image. In a single floppy configuration the ramdisk image is on the same floppy as the kernel that just finished loading/booting and so a prompt is not needed. In this case one can use 'prompt_ramdisk=0'. In a two floppy configuration, you will need the chance to switch disks, and thus 'prompt_ramdisk=1' can be used. Since this is the default value, it doesn't really need to be specified. (Historical note: Sneaky people used to use the 'vga=ask' LILO option to temporarily pause the boot process and allow a chance to switch from boot to root floppy.)

Please see the file `linux/Documentation/ramdisk.txt` for a complete description of the new boot time arguments, and how to use them. A description of how this parameter can be set and stored in the kernel image via 'rdev' is also described.

3.2.4   The 'ramdisk_size=' Argument

While it is true that the ramdisk grows dynamically as required, there is an upper bound on its size so that it doesn't consume all available RAM and leave you in a mess. The default is 4096 (i.e. 4MB) which should be large enough for most needs. You can override the default to a bigger or smaller size with this boot argument.

Please see the file `linux/Documentation/ramdisk.txt` for a complete description of the new boot time arguments, and how to use them. A description of how this parameter can be set and stored in the kernel image via 'rdev' is also described.

3.2.5   The 'ramdisk=' Argument (obsolete)

(NOTE: This argument is obsolete, and should not be used except on kernels v1.3.47 and older. The commands that should be used for the ramdisk device are documented above.)

This specifies the size in kB of the RAM disk device. For example, if one wished to have a root filesystem on a 1.44MB floppy loaded into the RAM disk device, they would use:

```
ramdisk=1440
```

This is one of the few kernel boot arguments that has its default stored in the kernel image, and which can thus be altered with the `rdev` utility.

3.2.6   The 'noinitrd' (initial RAM disk) Argument

The v2.x and newer kernels have a feature where the root filesystem is initially a RAM disk, and the kernel executes `/linuxrc` on that RAM image. This feature is typically used to allow loading of modules needed to mount the real root filesystem (e.g. load the SCSI driver modules stored in the RAM disk image, and then mount the real root filesystem on a SCSI disk.)

The actual 'noinitrd' argument determines what happens to the initrd data after the kernel has booted. When specified, instead of converting it to a RAM disk, it is accessible via `/dev/initrd`, which can be read once before the RAM is released back to the system. For full details on using the initial RAM disk, please consult `linux/Documentation/initrd.txt`. In addition, the most recent versions of `LILO` and `LOADLIN` should have additional useful information.

3.3   Boot Arguments Related to Memory Handling

The following arguments alter how linux detects or handles the physical and virtual memory of your system.

3.3.1   The 'mem=' Argument

This argument has two purposes: The original purpose was to specify the amount of installed memory (or a value less than that if you wanted to limit the amount of memory available to linux). The second (and hardly used) purpose is to specify `mem=nopentium` which tells the linux kernel to not use the 4MB page table performance feature.

The original BIOS call defined in the PC specification that returns the amount of installed memory was only designed to be able to report up to 64MB. (Yes, another lack of foresight, just like the 1024 cylinder disks... sigh.) Linux uses this BIOS call at boot to determine how much memory is installed. If you have more than 64MB of RAM installed, you can use this boot argument to tell Linux how much memory you have. Here is a quote from Linus on usage of the `mem=` parameter.

"The kernel will accept any 'mem=xx' parameter you give it, and if it turns out that you lied to it, it will crash horribly sooner or later. The parameter indicates the highest addressable RAM address, so 'mem=0x1000000' means you have 16MB of memory, for example. For a 96MB machine this would be 'mem=0x6000000'.

NOTE NOTE NOTE: some machines might use the top of memory for BIOS cacheing or whatever, so you might not actually have up to the full 96MB addressable. The reverse is also true: some chipsets will map the physical memory that is covered by the BIOS area into the area just past the top of memory, so the top-of-mem might actually be 96MB + 384kB for example. If you tell linux that it has more memory than it actually does have, bad things will happen: maybe not at once, but surely eventually."

Note that the argument does not have to be in hex, and the suffixes 'k' and 'M' (case insensitive) can be used to specify kilobytes and Megabytes, respectively. (A 'k' will cause a 10 bit shift on your value, and a 'M' will cause a 20 bit shift.) The above warning still holds, in that a 96MB machine may work with `mem=97920k` but fail with either `mem=98304k` or `mem=96M`.

3.3.2   The 'swap=' Argument

This allows the user to tune some of the virtual memory (VM) parameters that are related to swapping to disk. It accepts the following eight parameters:

```
MAX_PAGE_AGE
PAGE_ADVANCE
PAGE_DECLINE
PAGE_INITIAL_AGE
AGE_CLUSTER_FRACT
AGE_CLUSTER_MIN
PAGEOUT_WEIGHT
BUFFEROUT_WEIGHT
```

Interested hackers are advised to have a read of `linux/mm/swap.c` and also make note of the goodies in `/proc/sys/vm`.

3.3.3   The 'buff=' Argument

Similar to the 'swap=' argument, this allows the user to tune some of the parameters related to buffer memory management. It accepts the following six parameters:

```
MAX_BUFF_AGE
BUFF_ADVANCE
BUFF_DECLINE
BUFF_INITIAL_AGE
BUFFEROUT_WEIGHT
BUFFERMEM_GRACE
```

Interested hackers are advised to have a read of `linux/mm/swap.c` and also make note of the goodies in `/proc/sys/vm`.

3.4   Boot Arguments for NFS Root Filesystem

Linux supports systems such as diskless workstations via having their root filesystem as NFS (Network FileSystem). These arguments are used to tell the diskless workstation which machine it is to get its system from. Also note that the argument `root=/dev/nfs` is required. Detailed information on using an NFS root fs is in the file `linux/Documentation/nfsroot.txt`. You should read that file, as the following is only a quick summary taken directly from that file.

3.4.1   The 'nfsroot=' Argument

This argument tells the kernel which machine, what directory and what NFS options to use for the root filesystem. The form of the argument is as follows:

---

    nfsroot=[<server-ip>:]<root-dir>[,<nfs-options>]

If the nfsroot parameter is not given on the command line, the default '/tftpboot/%s' will be used. The other options are as follows:

<server-ip> – Specifies the IP address of the NFS server. If this field is not given, the default address as determined by the nfsaddrs variable (see below) is used. One use of this parameter is for example to allow using different servers for RARP and NFS. Usually you can leave this blank.

<root-dir> – Name of the directory on the server to mount as root. If there is a '%s' token in the string, the token will be replaced by the ASCII-representation of the client's IP address.

<nfs-options> – Standard NFS options. All options are separated by commas. If the options field is not given, the following defaults will be used:

port	= as given by server portmap daemon
rsize	= 1024
wsize	= 1024
timeo	= 7
retrans	= 3
acregmin	= 3
acregmax	= 60
acdirmin	= 30
acdirmax	= 60
flags	= hard, nointr, noposix, cto, ac

3.4.2   The 'nfsaddrs=' Argument

This boot argument sets up the various network interface addresses that are required to communicate over the network. If this argument is not given, then the kernel tries to use RARP and/or BOOTP to figure out these parameters. The form is as follows:

---

    nfsaddrs=<my-ip>:<serv-ip>:<gw-ip>:<netmask>:<name>:<dev>:<auto>

<my-ip> – IP address of the client. If empty, the address will either be determined by RARP or BOOTP. What protocol is used de- pends on what has been enabled during kernel configuration and on the <auto> parameter. If this parameter is not empty, neither RARP nor BOOTP will be used.

<serv-ip> – IP address of the NFS server. If RARP is used to determine the client address and this parameter is NOT empty only replies from the specified server are accepted. To use different RARP and NFS server, specify your RARP server here (or leave it blank), and specify your NFS server in the nfsroot parameter (see above). If this entry is blank the address of the server is used which answered the RARP or BOOTP request.

<gw-ip> – IP address of a gateway if the server in on a different subnet. If this entry is empty no gateway is used and the server is assumed to be on the local network, unless a value has been received by BOOTP.

<netmask> – Netmask for local network interface. If this is empty, the netmask is derived from the client IP address, unless a value has been received by BOOTP.

<name> – Name of the client. If empty, the client IP address is used in ASCII-notation, or the value received by BOOTP.

<dev> – Name of network device to use. If this is empty, all devices are used for RARP requests, and the first one found for BOOTP. For NFS the device is used on which either RARP or BOOTP replies have been received. If you only have one device you can safely leave this blank.

<auto> – Method to use for autoconfiguration. If this is either 'rarp' or 'bootp' the specified protocol is being used. If the value is 'both' or empty, both protocols are used so far as they have been enabled during kernel configuration Using 'none' means no autoconfiguration. In this case you have to specify all necessary values in the fields before.

The <auto> parameter can appear alone as the value to the nfsaddrs parameter (without all the ':' characters before) in which case autoconfiguration is used. However, the 'none' value is not available in that case.

3.5   Other Misc. Kernel Boot Arguments

These various boot arguments let the user tune certain internal kernel parameters.

3.5.1   The 'debug' Argument

The kernel communicates important (and not-so important) messages to the operator via the `printk()` function. If the message is considered important, the `printk()` function will put a copy on the present console as well as handing it off to the `klogd()` facility so that it gets logged to disk. The reason for printing important messages to the console as well as logging them to disk is because under unfortunate circumstances (e.g. a disk failure) the message won't make it to disk and will be lost.

The threshold for what is and what isn't considered important is set by the `console_loglevel` variable. The default is to log anything more important than DEBUG (level 7) to the console. (These levels are defined in the include file `kernel.h`) Specifying `debug` as a boot argument will set the console loglevel to 10, so that *all* kernel messages appear on the console.

The console loglevel can usually also be set at run time via an option to the `klogd()` program. Check the man page for the version installed on your system to see how to do this.

3.5.2   The 'init=' Argument

The kernel defaults to starting the 'init' program at boot, which then takes care of setting up the computer for users via launching getty programs, running 'rc' scripts and the like. The kernel first looks for `/sbin/init`, then `/etc/init` (depreciated), and as a last resort, it will try to use `/bin/sh` (possibly on `/etc/rc`). If for example, your init program got corrupted and thus stopped you from being able to boot, you could simply use the boot prompt `init=/bin/sh` which would drop you directly into a shell at boot, allowing you to replace the corrupted program.

3.5.3 The 'no387' Argument

Some i387 coprocessor chips have bugs that show up when used in 32 bit protected mode. For example, some of the early ULSI-387 chips would cause solid lockups while performing floating point calculations, apparently due to a bug in the FRSAV/FRRESTOR instructions. Using the 'no387' boot argument causes Linux to ignore the math coprocessor even if you have one. Of course you must then have your kernel compiled with math emulation support! This may also be useful if you have one of those *really* old 386 machines that could use an 80287 FPU, as linux can't use an 80287.

3.5.4 The 'no-hlt' Argument

The i386 (and successors thereof) family of CPUs have a 'hlt' instruction which tells the CPU that nothing is going to happen until an external device (keyboard, modem, disk, etc.) calls upon the CPU to do a task. This allows the CPU to enter a 'low-power' mode where it sits like a zombie until an external device wakes it up (usually via an interrupt). Some of the early i486DX-100 chips had a problem with the 'hlt' instruction, in that they couldn't reliably return to operating mode after this instruction was used. Using the 'no-hlt' instruction tells Linux to just run an infinite loop when there is nothing else to do, and to *not* halt your CPU when there is no activity. This allows people with these broken chips to use Linux, although they would be well advised to seek a replacement through a warranty where possible.

3.5.5 The 'no-scroll' Argument

Using this argument at boot disables scrolling features that make it difficult to use Braille terminals.

3.5.6 The 'panic=' Argument

In the unlikely event of a kernel panic (i.e. an internal error that has been detected by the kernel, and which the kernel decides is serious enough to moan loudly and then halt everything), the default behaviour is to just sit there until someone comes along and notices the panic message on the screen and reboots the machine. However if a machine is running unattended in an isolated location it may be desirable for it to automatically reset itself so that the machine comes back on line. For example, using `panic=30` at boot would cause the kernel to try and reboot itself 30 seconds after the kernel panic happened. A value of zero gives the default behaviour, which is to wait forever.

Note that this timeout value can also be read and set via the `/proc/sys/kernel/panic` sysctl interface.

3.5.7 The 'profile=' Argument

Kernel developers can enable an option that allows them to profile how and where the kernel is spending its CPU cycles in an effort to maximize efficiency and performance. This option lets you set the profile shift count at boot. Typically it is set to two. You can also compile your kernel with profiling enabled by default. In either case, you need a tool such as `readprofile.c` that can make use of the `/proc/profile` output.

3.5.8 The 'reboot=' Argument

This option controls the type of reboot that Linux will do when it resets the computer (typically via `/sbin/init` handling a Control-Alt-Delete). The default as of late v2.0 kernels is to do a 'cold' reboot (i.e. full reset, BIOS does memory check, etc.) instead of a 'warm' reboot (i.e. no full reset, no memory check). It was changed to be cold by default since that tends to work on cheap/broken hardware that fails to reboot when a warm reboot is requested. To get the old behaviour (i.e. warm reboots) use `reboot=w` or in fact any word that starts with `w` will work.

Why would you bother? Some disk controllers with cache memory on board can sense a warm reboot, and flush any cached data to disk. Upon a cold boot, the card may be reset and the write-back data in your cache card's memory is lost. Others have reported systems that take a long time to go through the memory check, and/or SCSI BIOSes that take longer to initialize on a cold boot as a good reason to use warm reboots.

3.5.9 The 'reserve=' Argument

This is used to *protect* I/O port regions from probes. The form of the command is:

        reserve=iobase,extent[,iobase,extent]...

In some machines it may be necessary to prevent device drivers from checking for devices (auto-probing) in a specific region. This may be because of poorly designed hardware that causes the boot to *freeze* (such as some ethercards), hardware that is mistakenly identified, hardware whose state is changed by an earlier probe, or merely hardware you don't want the kernel to initialize.

The `reserve` boot-time argument addresses this problem by specifying an I/O port region that shouldn't be probed. That region is reserved in the kernel's port registration table as if a device has already been found in that region (with the name `reserved`). Note that this mechanism shouldn't be necessary on most machines. Only when there is a problem or special case would it be necessary to use this.

The I/O ports in the specified region are protected against device probes that do a `check_region()` prior to probing blindly into a region of I/O space. This was put in to be used when some driver was hanging on a NE2000, or misidentifying some other device as its own. A correct device driver shouldn't probe a reserved region, unless another boot argument explicitly specifies that it do so. This implies that `reserve` will most often be used with some other boot argument. Hence if you specify a `reserve` region to protect a specific device, you must generally specify an explicit probe for that device. Most drivers ignore the port registration table if they are given an explicit address.

For example, the boot line

---

        reserve=0x300,32   blah=0x300

---

keeps all device drivers except the driver for 'blah' from probing `0x300-0x31f`.

As usual with boot-time specifiers there is an 11 parameter limit, thus you can only specify 5 reserved regions per `reserve` keyword. Multiple `reserve` specifiers will work if you have an unusually complicated request.

3.5.10 The 'vga=' Argument

Note that this is not really a boot argument. It is an option that is interpreted by LILO and not by the kernel like all the other boot arguments are. However its use has become so common that it deserves a mention here. It can also be set via using `rdev -v` or equivalently `vidmode` on the vmlinuz file. This allows the setup code to use the video BIOS to change the default display mode before actually booting the Linux kernel. Typical modes are 80x50, 132x44 and so on. The best way to use this option is to start with `vga=ask` which will prompt you with a list of various modes that you can use with your video adapter before booting the kernel. Once you have the number from the above list that you want to use, you can later put it in place of the 'ask'. For more information, please see the file `linux/Documentation/svga.txt` that comes with all recent kernel versions.

Note that newer kernels (v2.1 and up) have the setup code that changes the video mode as an option, listed as *Video mode selection support* so you need to enable this option if you want to use this feature.

4 Boot Arguments for SCSI Peripherals.

This section contains the descriptions of the boot args that are used for passing information about the installed SCSI host adapters, and SCSI devices.

4.1 Arguments for Mid-level Drivers

The mid level drivers handle things like disks, CD-ROMs and tapes without getting into host adapter specifics.

4.1.1 Maximum Probed LUNs ('max_scsi_luns=')

Each SCSI device can have a number of 'sub-devices' contained within itself. The most common example is one of the new SCSI CD-ROMs that handle more than one disk at a time. Each CD is addressed as a 'Logical Unit Number' (LUN) of that particular device. But most devices, such as hard disks, tape drives and such are only one device, and will be assigned to LUN zero.

The problem arises with single LUN devices with bad firmware. Some poorly designed SCSI devices (old and unfortunately new) can not handle being probed for LUNs not equal to zero. They will respond by locking up, and possibly taking the whole SCSI bus down with them.

Newer kernels have the configuration option that allows you to set the maximum number of probed LUNs. The default is to only probe LUN zero, to avoid the problem described above.

To specify the number of probed LUNs at boot, one enters 'max_scsi_luns=n' as a boot arg, where n is a number between one and eight. To avoid problems as described above, one would use n=1 to avoid upsetting such broken devices

4.1.2 Parameters for the SCSI Tape Driver ('st=')

Some boot time configuration of the SCSI tape driver can be achieved by using the following:

```
st=buf_size[,write_threshold[,max_bufs]]
```

The first two numbers are specified in units of kB. The default buf_size is 32kB, and the maximum size that can be specified is a ridiculous 16384kB. The write_threshold is the value at which the buffer is committed to tape, with a default value of 30kB. The maximum number of buffers varies with the number of drives detected, and has a default of two. An example usage would be:

```
st=32,30,2
```

Full details can be found in the README.st file that is in the scsi directory of the kernel source tree.

4.2 Arguments for SCSI Host Adapters

General notation for this section:

iobase – the first I/O port that the SCSI host occupies. These are specified in hexidecimal notation, and usually lie in the range from 0x200 to 0x3ff.

irq – the hardware interrupt that the card is configured to use. Valid values will be dependent on the card in question, but will usually be 5, 7, 9, 10, 11, 12, and 15. The other values are usually used for common peripherals like IDE hard disks, floppies, serial ports, etc.

dma – the DMA (Direct Memory Access) channel that the card uses. Typically only applies to bus-mastering cards. PCI and VLB cards are native bus-masters, and do not require and ISA DMA channel.

scsi-id – the ID that the host adapter uses to identify itself on the SCSI bus. Only some host adapters allow you to change this value, as most have it permanently specified internally. The usual default value is seven, but the Seagate and Future Domain TMC-950 boards use six.

parity – whether the SCSI host adapter expects the attached devices to supply a parity value with all information exchanges. Specifying a one indicates parity checking is enabled, and a zero disables parity checking. Again, not all adapters will support selection of parity behaviour as a boot argument.

4.2.1   Adaptec aha151x, aha152x, aic6260, aic6360, SB16-SCSI ('aha152x=')

The aha numbers refer to cards and the aic numbers refer to the actual SCSI chip on these type of cards, including the Soundblaster-16 SCSI.

The probe code for these SCSI hosts looks for an installed BIOS, and if none is present, the probe will not find your card. Then you will have to use a boot argument of the form:

```
aha152x=iobase[,irq[,scsi-id[,reconnect[,parity]]]]
```

Note that if the driver was compiled with debugging enabled, a sixth value can be specified to set the debug level.

All the parameters are as described at the top of this section, and the reconnect value will allow device disconnect/reconnect if a non-zero value is used. An example usage is as follows:

```
aha152x=0x340,11,7,1
```

Note that the parameters must be specified in order, meaning that if you want to specify a parity setting, then you will have to specify an iobase, irq, scsi-id and reconnect value as well.

4.2.2   Adaptec aha154x ('aha1542=')

These are the aha154x series cards. The aha1542 series cards have an i82077 floppy controller onboard, while the aha1540 series cards do not. These are busmastering cards, and have parameters to set the "fairness" that is used to share the bus with other devices. The boot argument looks like the following.

```
aha1542=iobase[,buson,busoff[,dmaspeed]]
```

Valid iobase values are usually one of: 0x130, 0x134, 0x230, 0x234, 0x330, 0x334. Clone cards may permit other values.

The buson, busoff values refer to the number of microseconds that the card dominates the ISA bus. The defaults are 11us on, and 4us off, so that other cards (such as an ISA LANCE Ethernet card) have a chance to get access to the ISA bus.

The `dmaspeed` value refers to the rate (in MB/s) at which the DMA (Direct Memory Access) transfers proceed at. The default is 5MB/s. Newer revision cards allow you to select this value as part of the soft-configuration, older cards use jumpers. You can use values up to 10MB/s assuming that your motherboard is capable of handling it. Experiment with caution if using values over 5MB/s.

4.2.3   Adaptec aha274x, aha284x, aic7xxx ('aic7xxx=')

These boards can accept an argument of the form:

```
aic7xxx=extended,no_reset
```

The `extended` value, if non-zero, indicates that extended translation for large disks is enabled. The `no_reset` value, if non-zero, tells the driver not to reset the SCSI bus when setting up the host adaptor at boot.

4.2.4   AdvanSys SCSI Host Adaptors ('advansys=')

The AdvanSys driver can accept up to four i/o addresses that will be probed for an AdvanSys SCSI card. Note that these values (if used) do not effect EISA or PCI probing in any way. They are only used for probing ISA and VLB cards. In addition, if the driver has been compiled with debugging enabled, the level of debugging output can be set by adding an `0xdeb[0-f]` parameter. The `0-f` allows setting the level of the debugging messages to any of 16 levels of verbosity.

4.2.5   Always IN2000 Host Adaptor ('in2000=')

Unlike other SCSI host boot arguments, the IN2000 driver uses ASCII string prefixes for most of its integer arguments. Here is a list of the supported arguments:

ioport:addr – Where addr is IO address of a (usually ROM-less) card.

noreset – No optional args. Prevents SCSI bus reset at boot time.

nosync:x – x is a bitmask where the 1st 7 bits correspond with the 7 possible SCSI devices (bit 0 for device #0, etc). Set a bit to PREVENT sync negotiation on that device. The driver default is sync DISABLED on all devices.

period:ns – ns is the minimum # of nanoseconds in a SCSI data transfer period. Default is 500; acceptable values are 250 to 1000.

disconnect:x – x = 0 to never allow disconnects, 2 to always allow them. x = 1 does 'adaptive' disconnects, which is the default and generally the best choice.

debug:x If 'DEBUGGING_ON' is defined, x is a bitmask that causes various types of debug output to printed - see the DB_xxx defines in in2000.h

proc:x – If 'PROC_INTERFACE' is defined, x is a bitmask that determines how the /proc interface works and what it does - see the PR_xxx defines in in2000.h

Some example usages are listed below:

```
in2000=ioport:0x220,noreset
in2000=period:250,disconnect:2,nosync:0x03
in2000=debug:0x1e
in2000=proc:3
```

4.2.6 AMD AM53C974 based hardware ('AM53C974=')

Unlike other drivers, this one does not use boot parameters to communicate i/o, IRQ or DMA channels. (Since the AM53C974 is a PCI device, there shouldn't be a need to do so.) Instead, the parameters are used to communicate the transfer modes and rates that are to be used between the host and the target device. This is best described with an example:

```
AM53C974=7,2,8,15
```

This would be interpreted as follows: 'For communication between the controller with SCSI-ID 7 and the device with SCSI-ID 2, a transfer rate of 8MHz in synchronous mode with max. 15 bytes offset should be negotiated.' More details can be found in the file linux/drivers/scsi/README.AM53C974

4.2.7 BusLogic SCSI Hosts with v1.2 kernels ('buslogic=')

In older kernels, the buslogic driver accepts only one parameter, that being the I/O base. It expects that to be one of the following valid values: 0x130, 0x134, 0x230, 0x234, 0x330, 0x334.

4.2.8 BusLogic SCSI Hosts with v2.x kernels ('BusLogic=')

With v2.x kernels, the BusLogic driver accepts many parameters. (Note the case in the above; upper case B and L!!!). The following detailed description is taken directly from Leonard N. Zubkoff's driver as included in the v2.0 kernel.

For the BusLogic driver, a Kernel command line entry comprises the driver identifier "BusLogic=" optionally followed by a comma-separated sequence of integers and then optionally followed by a comma-separated sequence of strings. Each command line entry applies to one BusLogic Host Adapter. Multiple command line entries may be used in systems which contain multiple BusLogic Host Adapters.

The first integer specified is the I/O Address at which the Host Adapter is located. If unspecified, it defaults to 0 which means to apply this entry to the first BusLogic Host Adapter found during the default probe sequence. If any I/O Address parameters are provided on the command line, then the default probe sequence is omitted.

The second integer specified is the Tagged Queue Depth to use for Target Devices that support Tagged Queuing. The Queue Depth is the number of SCSI commands that are allowed to be concurrently presented for execution. If unspecified, it defaults to 0 which means to use a value determined automatically based on the Host Adapter's Total Queue Depth and the number, type, speed, and capabilities of the detected Target Devices. For Host Adapters that require ISA Bounce Buffers, the Tagged Queue Depth is automatically set to BusLogic_TaggedQueueDepth_BB to avoid excessive preallocation of DMA Bounce Buffer memory. Target Devices that do not support Tagged Queuing use a Queue Depth of BusLogic_UntaggedQueueDepth.

The third integer specified is the Bus Settle Time in seconds. This is the amount of time to wait between a Host Adapter Hard Reset which initiates a SCSI Bus Reset and issuing any SCSI Commands. If unspecified, it defaults to 0 which means to use the value of BusLogic_DefaultBusSettleTime.

The fourth integer specified is the Local Options. If unspecified, it defaults to 0. Note that Local Options are only applied to a specific Host Adapter.

The fifth integer specified is the Global Options. If unspecified, it defaults to 0. Note that Global Options are applied across all Host Adapters.

The string options are used to provide control over Tagged Queuing, Error Recovery, and Host Adapter Probing.

The Tagged Queuing specification begins with "TQ:" and allows for explicitly specifying whether Tagged Queuing is permitted on Target Devices that support it. The following specification options are available:

TQ:Default – Tagged Queuing will be permitted based on the firmware version of the BusLogic Host Adapter and based on whether the Tagged Queue Depth value allows queuing multiple commands.

TQ:Enable – Tagged Queuing will be enabled for all Target Devices on this Host Adapter overriding any limitation that would otherwise be imposed based on the Host Adapter firmware version.

TQ:Disable – Tagged Queuing will be disabled for all Target Devices on this Host Adapter.

TQ:<Per-Target-Spec> – Tagged Queuing will be controlled individually for each Target Device. <Per-Target-Spec> is a sequence of "Y", "N", and "X" characters. "Y" enabled Tagged Queuing, "N" disables Tagged Queuing, and "X" accepts the default based on the firmware version. The first character refers to Target Device 0, the second to Target Device 1, and so on; if the sequence of "Y", "N", and "X" characters does not cover all the Target Devices, unspecified characters are assumed to be "X".

Note that explicitly requesting Tagged Queuing may lead to problems; this facility is provided primarily to allow disabling Tagged Queuing on Target Devices that do not implement it correctly.

The Error Recovery Strategy specification begins with "ER:" and allows for explicitly specifying the Error Recovery action to be performed when ResetCommand is called due to a SCSI Command failing to complete successfully. The following specification options are available:

ER:Default – Error Recovery will select between the Hard Reset and Bus Device Reset options based on the recommendation of the SCSI Subsystem.

ER:HardReset – Error Recovery will initiate a Host Adapter Hard Reset which also causes a SCSI Bus Reset.

ER:BusDeviceReset – Error Recovery will send a Bus Device Reset message to the individual Target Device causing the error. If Error Recovery is again initiated for this Target Device and no SCSI Command to this Target Device has completed successfully since the Bus Device Reset message was sent, then a Hard Reset will be attempted.

ER:None – Error Recovery will be suppressed. This option should only be selected if a SCSI Bus Reset or Bus Device Reset will cause the Target Device to fail completely and unrecoverably.

ER:<Per-Target-Spec> – Error Recovery will be controlled individually for each Target Device. <Per-Target-Spec> is a sequence of "D", "H", "B", and "N" characters. "D" selects Default, "H" selects Hard Reset, "B" selects Bus Device Reset, and "N" selects None. The first character refers to Target Device 0, the second to Target Device 1, and so on; if the sequence of "D", "H", "B", and "N" characters does not cover all the possible Target Devices, unspecified characters are assumed to be "D".

The Host Adapter Probing specification comprises the following strings:

NoProbe – No probing of any kind is to be performed, and hence no BusLogic Host Adapters will be detected.

NoProbeISA – No probing of the standard ISA I/O Addresses will be done, and hence only PCI Host Adapters will be detected.

NoSortPCI – PCI Host Adapters will be enumerated in the order provided by the PCI BIOS, ignoring any setting of the AutoSCSI "Use Bus And Device # For PCI Scanning Seq." option.

4.2.9   EATA SCSI Cards ('eata=')

As of late v2.0 kernels, the EATA drivers will accept a boot argument to specify the i/o base(s) to be probed. It is of the form:

```
eata=iobase1[,iobase2][,iobase3]...[,iobaseN]
```

The driver will probe the addresses in the order that they are listed.

4.2.10 Future Domain TMC-8xx, TMC-950 ('tmc8xx=')

The probe code for these SCSI hosts looks for an installed BIOS, and if none is present, the probe will not find your card. Or, if the signature string of your BIOS is not recognized then it will also not be found. In either case, you will then have to use a boot argument of the form:

```
tmc8xx=mem_base,irq
```

The mem_base value is the value of the memory mapped I/O region that the card uses. This will usually be one of the following values: 0xc8000, 0xca000, 0xcc000, 0xce000, 0xdc000, 0xde000.

4.2.11 Future Domain TMC-16xx, TMC-3260, AHA-2920 ('fdomain=')

The driver detects these cards according to a list of known BIOS ROM signatures. For a full list of known BIOS revisions, please see linux/drivers/scsi/fdomain.c as it has a lot of information at the top of that file. If your BIOS is not known to the driver, you can use an override of the form:

```
fdomain=iobase,irq[,scsi_id]
```

4.2.12 IOMEGA Parallel Port / ZIP drive ('ppa=')

This driver is for the IOMEGA Parallel Port SCSI adapter which is embedded into the IOMEGA ZIP drives. It may also work with the original IOMEGA PPA3 device. The boot argument for this driver is of the form:

```
ppa=iobase,speed_high,speed_low,nybble
```

with all but iobase being optionally specified values. If you wish to alter any of the three optional parameters, you are advised to read linux/drivers/scsi/README.ppa for details of what they control.

4.2.13 NCR5380 based controllers ('ncr5380=')

Depending on your board, the 5380 can be either i/o mapped or memory mapped. (An address below 0x400 usually implies i/o mapping, but PCI and EISA hardware use i/o addresses above 0x3ff.) In either case, you specify the address, the IRQ value and the DMA channel value. An example for an i/o mapped card would be: ncr5380=0x350,5,3. If the card doesn't use interrupts, then an IRQ value of 255 (0xff) will disable interrupts. An IRQ value of 254 means to autoprobe. More details can be found in the file linux/drivers/scsi/README.g_NCR5380

4.2.14 NCR53c400 based controllers ('ncr53c400=')

The generic 53c400 support is done with the same driver as the generic 5380 support mentioned above. The boot argument is identical to the above with the exception that no DMA channel is used by the 53c400.

4.2.15   NCR53c406a based controllers ('ncr53c406a=')

This driver uses a boot argument of the form:

```
ncr53c406a=PORTBASE,IRQ,FASTPIO
```

where the IRQ and FASTPIO parameters are optional. An interrupt value of zero disables the use of interrupts. Using a value of one for the FASTPIO parameter enables the use of `insl` and `outsl` instructions instead of the single-byte `inb` and `outb` instructions. The driver can also use DMA as a compile-time option.

4.2.16   Pro Audio Spectrum ('pas16=')

The PAS16 uses a NCR5380 SCSI chip, and newer models support jumper-less configuration. The boot argument is of the form:

```
pas16=iobase,irq
```

The only difference is that you can specify an IRQ value of 255, which will tell the driver to work without using interrupts, albeit at a performance loss. The `iobase` is usually `0x388`.

4.2.17   Seagate ST-0x ('st0x=')

The probe code for these SCSI hosts looks for an installed BIOS, and if none is present, the probe will not find your card. Or, if the signature string of your BIOS is not recognized then it will also not be found. In either case, you will then have to use a boot argument of the form:

```
st0x=mem_base,irq
```

The `mem_base` value is the value of the memory mapped I/O region that the card uses. This will usually be one of the following values: `0xc8000`, `0xca000`, `0xcc000`, `0xce000`, `0xdc000`, `0xde000`.

4.2.18   Trantor T128 ('t128=')

These cards are also based on the NCR5380 chip, and accept the following options:

```
t128=mem_base,irq
```

The valid values for `mem_base` are as follows: `0xcc000`, `0xc8000`, `0xdc000`, `0xd8000`.

4.2.19   Ultrastor SCSI cards ('u14-34f=')

Note that there appears to be two independent drivers for this card, namely `CONFIG_SCSI_U14_34F` that uses `u14-34f.c` and `CONFIG_SCSI_ULTRASTOR` that uses `ultrastor.c`. It is the u14-34f one that (as of late v2.0 kernels) accepts a boot argument of the form:

```
u14-34f=iobase1[,iobase2][,iobase3]...[,iobaseN]
```

The driver will probe the addresses in the order that they are listed.

4.2.20   Western Digital WD7000 cards ('wd7000=')

The driver probe for the wd7000 looks for a known BIOS ROM string and knows about a few standard
configuration settings. If it doesn't come up with the correct values for your card, or you have an unrecognized
BIOS version, you can use a boot argument of the form:

```
wd7000=irq,dma,iobase
```

4.3   SCSI Host Adapters that don't Accept Boot Args

At present, the following SCSI cards do not make use of any boot-time parameters. In some cases, you can
hard-wire values by directly editing the driver itself, if required.

```
Adaptec aha1740 (EISA probing),
NCR53c7xx,8xx (PCI, both drivers)
Qlogic Fast (0x230, 0x330)
Qlogic ISP (PCI)
```

5   Hard Disks

This section lists all the boot args associated with standard MFM/RLL, ST-506, XT, and IDE disk drive
devices. Note that both the IDE and the generic ST-506 HD driver both accept the 'hd=' option.

5.1   IDE Disk/CD-ROM Driver Parameters

The IDE driver accepts a number of parameters, which range from disk geometry specifications, to support
for advanced or broken controller chips. The following is a summary of all the possible boot arguments. For
full details, you *really* should consult the file ide.txt in the linux/Documentation directory, from which
this summary was extracted.

```
"hdx=" is recognized for all "x" from "a" to "h", such as "hdc".
"idex=" is recognized for all "x" from "0" to "3", such as "ide1".

"hdx=noprobe"        : drive may be present, but do not probe for it
"hdx=none"           : drive is NOT present, ignore cmos and do not probe
"hdx=nowerr"         : ignore the WRERR_STAT bit on this drive
"hdx=cdrom"          : drive is present, and is a cdrom drive
"hdx=cyl,head,sect"  : disk drive is present, with specified geometry
"hdx=autotune"       : driver will attempt to tune interface speed
                       to the fastest PIO mode supported,
                       if possible for this drive only.
                       Not fully supported by all chipset types,
                       and quite likely to cause trouble with
                       older/odd IDE drives.

"idex=noprobe"       : do not attempt to access/use this interface
"idex=base"          : probe for an interface at the addr specified,
```

```
                              where "base" is usually 0x1f0 or 0x170
                              and "ctl" is assumed to be "base"+0x206
"idex=base,ctl"           : specify both base and ctl
"idex=base,ctl,irq"       : specify base, ctl, and irq number
"idex=autotune"           : driver will attempt to tune interface speed
                              to the fastest PIO mode supported,
                              for all drives on this interface.
                              Not fully supported by all chipset types,
                              and quite likely to cause trouble with
                              older/odd IDE drives.
"idex=noautotune"         : driver will NOT attempt to tune interface speed
                              This is the default for most chipsets,
                              except the cmd640.
"idex=serialize"          : do not overlap operations on idex and ide(x^1)
```

The following are valid ONLY on ide0, and the defaults for the base,ctl ports must not be altered.

```
"ide0=dtc2278"        : probe/support DTC2278 interface
"ide0=ht6560b"        : probe/support HT6560B interface
"ide0=cmd640_vlb"     : *REQUIRED* for VLB cards with the CMD640 chip
                        (not for PCI -- automatically detected)
"ide0=qd6580"         : probe/support qd6580 interface
"ide0=ali14xx"        : probe/support ali14xx chipsets (ALI M1439/M1445)
"ide0=umc8672"        : probe/support umc8672 chipsets
```

Everything else is rejected with a "BAD OPTION" message.

5.2   Standard ST-506 Disk Driver Options ('hd=')

The standard disk driver can accept geometry arguments for the disks similar to the IDE driver. Note however that it only expects three values (C/H/S) – any more or any less and it will silently ignore you. Also, it only accepts 'hd=' as an argument, i.e. 'hda=', 'hdb=' and so on are not valid here. The format is as follows:

```
hd=cyls,heads,sects
```

If there are two disks installed, the above is repeated with the geometry parameters of the second disk.

5.3   XT Disk Driver Options ('xd=')

If you are unfortunate enough to be using one of these old 8 bit cards that move data at a whopping 125kB/s then here is the scoop. The probe code for these cards looks for an installed BIOS, and if none is present, the probe will not find your card. Or, if the signature string of your BIOS is not recognized then it will also not be found. In either case, you will then have to use a boot argument of the form:

```
xd=type,irq,iobase,dma_chan
```

The `type` value specifies the particular manufacturer of the card, and are as follows: 0=generic; 1=DTC; 2,3,4=Western Digital, 5,6,7=Seagate; 8=OMTI. The only difference between multiple types from the same manufacturer is the BIOS string used for detection, which is not used if the type is specified.

The `xd_setup()` function does no checking on the values, and assumes that you entered all four values. Don't disappoint it. Here is an example usage for a WD1002 controller with the BIOS disabled/removed, using the 'default' XT controller parameters:

```
xd=2,5,0x320,3
```

6   CD-ROMs (Non-SCSI/ATAPI/IDE)

This section lists all the possible boot args pertaining to CD-ROM devices. Note that this does not include SCSI or IDE/ATAPI CD-ROMs. See the appropriate section(s) for those types of CD-ROMs.

Note that most of these CD-ROMs have documentation files that you *should* read, and they are all in one handy place: `linux/Documentation/cdrom`.

6.1   The Aztech Interface ('aztcd=')

The syntax for this type of card is:

```
aztcd=iobase[,magic_number]
```

If you set the `magic_number` to `0x79` then the driver will try and run anyway in the event of an unknown firmware version. All other values are ignored.

6.2   The CDU-31A and CDU-33A Sony Interface ('cdu31a=')

This CD-ROM interface is found on some of the Pro Audio Spectrum sound cards, and other Sony supplied interface cards. The syntax is as follows:

```
cdu31a=iobase,[irq[,is_pas_card]]
```

Specifying an IRQ value of zero tells the driver that hardware interrupts aren't supported (as on some PAS cards). If your card supports interrupts, you should use them as it cuts down on the CPU usage of the driver.

The 'is_pas_card' should be entered as 'PAS' if using a Pro Audio Spectrum card, and otherwise it should not be specified at all.

6.3   The CDU-535 Sony Interface ('sonycd535=')

The syntax for this CD-ROM interface is:

```
sonycd535=iobase[,irq]
```

A zero can be used for the I/O base as a 'placeholder' if one wishes to specify an IRQ value.

6.4   The GoldStar Interface ('gscd=')

The syntax for this CD-ROM interface is:

```
gscd=iobase
```

6.5   The ISP16 Interface ('isp16=')

The syntax for this CD-ROM interface is:

```
isp16=[port[,irq[,dma]]][[,]drive_type]
```

Using a zero for `irq` or `dma` means that they are not used. The allowable values for `drive_type` are `noisp16`, `Sanyo`, `Panasonic`, `Sony`, and `Mitsumi`. Using `noisp16` disables the driver altogether.

6.6   The Mitsumi Standard Interface ('mcd=')

The syntax for this CD-ROM interface is:

```
mcd=iobase,[irq[,wait_value]]
```

The `wait_value` is used as an internal timeout value for people who are having problems with their drive, and may or may not be implemented depending on a compile time `DEFINE`.

6.7   The Mitsumi XA/MultiSession Interface ('mcdx=')

At present this 'experimental' driver has a setup function, but no parameters are implemented yet (as of 1.3.15). This is for the same hardware as above, but the driver has extended features.

6.8   The Optics Storage Interface ('optcd=')

The syntax for this type of card is:

```
optcd=iobase
```

6.9 The Phillips CM206 Interface ('cm206=')

The syntax for this type of card is:

```
cm206=[iobase][,irq]
```

The driver assumes numbers between 3 and 11 are IRQ values, and numbers between 0x300 and 0x370 are I/O ports, so you can specify one, or both numbers, in any order. It also accepts 'cm206=auto' to enable autoprobing.

6.10 The Sanyo Interface ('sjcd=')

The syntax for this type of card is:

```
sjcd=iobase[,irq[,dma_channel]]
```

6.11 The SoundBlaster Pro Interface ('sbpcd=')

The syntax for this type of card is:

```
sbpcd=iobase,type
```

where type is one of the following (case sensitive) strings: 'SoundBlaster', 'LaserMate', or 'SPEA'. The I/O base is that of the CD-ROM interface, and *not* that of the sound portion of the card.

7 Other Hardware Devices

Any other devices that didn't fit into any of the above categories got lumped together here.

7.1 Ethernet Devices ('ether=')

Different drivers make use of different parameters, but they all at least share having an IRQ, an I/O port base value, and a name. In its most generic form, it looks something like this:

```
ether=irq,iobase[,param_1[,param_2,...param_8]]],name
```

The first non-numeric argument is taken as the name. The param_n values (if applicable) usually have different meanings for each different card/driver. Typical param_n values are used to specify things like shared memory address, interface selection, DMA channel and the like.

The most common use of this parameter is to force probing for a second ethercard, as the default is to only probe for one. This can be accomplished with a simple:

```
ether=0,0,eth1
```

Note that the values of zero for the IRQ and I/O base in the above example tell the driver(s) to autoprobe.

IMPORTANT NOTE TO MODULE USERS: The above will *not* force a probe for a second card if you are using the driver(s) as run time loadable modules (instead of having them complied into the kernel). Most Linux distributions use a bare bones kernel combined with a large selection of modular drivers. The `ether=` only applies to drivers compiled directly into the kernel.

The Ethernet-HowTo has complete and extensive documentation on using multiple cards and on the card/driver specific implementation of the `param_n` values where used. Interested readers should refer to the section in that document on their particular card for more complete information. *Ethernet-HowTo* <http://sunsite.unc.edu/mdw/HOWTO/Ethernet-HOWTO.html>

7.2   The Floppy Disk Driver ('floppy=')

There are many floppy driver options, and they are all listed in `README.fd` in `linux/drivers/block`. This information is taken directly from that file.

floppy=mask,allowed_drive_mask

Sets the bitmask of allowed drives to `mask`. By default, only units 0 and 1 of each floppy controller are allowed. This is done because certain non-standard hardware (ASUS PCI motherboards) mess up the keyboard when accessing units 2 or 3. This option is somewhat obsoleted by the cmos option.

floppy=all_drives

Sets the bitmask of allowed drives to all drives. Use this if you have more than two drives connected to a floppy controller.

floppy=asus_pci

Sets the bitmask to allow only units 0 and 1. (The default)

floppy=daring

Tells the floppy driver that you have a well behaved floppy controller. This allows more efficient and smoother operation, but may fail on certain controllers. This may speed up certain operations.

floppy=0,daring

Tells the floppy driver that your floppy controller should be used with caution.

floppy=one_fdc

Tells the floppy driver that you have only floppy controller (default)

floppy=two_fdc *or* floppy=address,two_fdc

Tells the floppy driver that you have two floppy controllers. The second floppy controller is assumed to be at address. If address is not given, 0x370 is assumed.

floppy=thinkpad

Tells the floppy driver that you have a Thinkpad. Thinkpads use an inverted convention for the disk change line.

floppy=0,thinkpad

Tells the floppy driver that you don't have a Thinkpad.

floppy=drive,type,cmos

Sets the cmos type of `drive` to `type`. Additionally, this drive is allowed in the bitmask. This is useful if you have more than two floppy drives (only two can be described in the physical cmos), or if your BIOS uses non-standard CMOS types. Setting the CMOS to 0 for the first two drives (default) makes the floppy driver read the physical cmos for those drives.

floppy=unexpected_interrupts

Print a warning message when an unexpected interrupt is received (default behaviour)

floppy=no_unexpected_interrupts *or* floppy=L40SX

Don't print a message when an unexpected interrupt is received. This is needed on IBM L40SX laptops in certain video modes. (There seems to be an interaction between video and floppy. The unexpected interrupts only affect performance, and can safely be ignored.)

7.3   The Sound Driver ('sound=')

The sound driver can also accept boot args to override the compiled in values. This is not recommended, as it is rather complex. It is (was?) described in the `Readme.Linux` file, in `linux/drivers/sound`. It accepts a boot arg of the form:

---

        sound=device1[,device2[,device3...[,device11]]]

---

where each `deviceN` value is of the following format `0xTaaaId` and the bytes are used as follows:

T - device type: 1=FM, 2=SB, 3=PAS, 4=GUS, 5=MPU401, 6=SB16, 7=SB16-MPU401

aaa - I/O address in hex.

I - interrupt line in hex (i.e 10=a, 11=b, ...)

d - DMA channel.

As you can see it gets pretty messy, and you are better off to compile in your own personal values as recommended. Using a boot arg of 'sound=0' will disable the sound driver entirely.

7.4   The Bus Mouse Driver ('bmouse=')

The busmouse driver only accepts one parameter, that being the hardware IRQ value to be used.

7.5   The MS Bus Mouse Driver ('msmouse=')

The MS mouse driver only accepts one parameter, that being the hardware IRQ value to be used.

7.6   The Printer Driver ('lp=')

As of kernels newer than 1.3.75, you can tell the printer driver what ports to use and what ports *not* to use. The latter comes in handy if you don't want the printer driver to claim all available parallel ports, so that other drivers (e.g. PLIP, PPA) can use them instead.

The format of the argument is multiple i/o, IRQ pairs. For example, `lp=0x3bc,0,0x378,7` would use the port at 0x3bc in IRQ-less (polling) mode, and use IRQ 7 for the port at 0x378. The port at 0x278 (if any) would not be probed, since autoprobing only takes place in the absence of a 'lp=' argument. To disable the printer driver entirely, one can use `lp=0`.

7.7   The ICN ISDN driver ('icn=')

This ISDN driver expects a boot argument of the form:

```
icn=iobase,membase,icn_id1,icn_id2
```

where `iobase` is the i/o port address of the card, `membase` is the shared memory base address of the card, and the two `icn_id` are unique ASCII string identifiers.

7.8   The PCBIT ISDN driver ('pcbit=')

This boot argument takes integer pair arguments of the form:

```
pcbit=membase1,irq1[,membase2,irq2]
```

where `membaseN` is the shared memory base of the N'th card, and `irqN` is the interrupt setting of the N'th card. The default is IRQ 5 and membase 0xD0000.

7.9   The Teles ISDN driver ('teles=')

This ISDN driver expects a boot argument of the form:

```
teles=iobase,irq,membase,protocol,teles_id
```

where `iobase` is the i/o port address of the card, `membase` is the shared memory base address of the card, `irq` is the interrupt channel the card uses, and `teles_id` is the unique ASCII string identifier.

7.10   The DigiBoard Driver ('digi=')

The DigiBoard driver accepts a string of six comma separated identifiers or integers. The 6 values in order are:

```
Enable/Disable this card
Type of card: PC/Xi(0), PC/Xe(1), PC/Xeve(2), PC/Xem(3)
Enable/Disable alternate pin arrangement
Number of ports on this card
I/O Port where card is configured (in HEX if using string identifiers)
Base of memory window (in HEX if using string identifiers)
```

An example of a correct boot prompt argument (in both identifier and integer form) is:

```
digi=E,PC/Xi,D,16,200,D0000
digi=1,0,0,16,512,851968
```

Note that the driver defaults to an i/o of 0x200 and a shared memory base of 0xD0000 in the absence of a `digi=` boot argument. There is no autoprobing performed. More details can be found in the file `linux/Documentation/digiboard.txt`.

7.11 The RISCom/8 Multiport Serial Driver ('riscom8=')

Up to four boards can be supported by supplying four unique i/o port values for each individual board installed. Other details can be found in the file linux/Documentation/riscom8.txt.

7.12 The Baycom Serial/Parallel Radio Modem ('baycom=')

The format of the boot argument for these devices is:

---

baycom=modem,io,irq,options[,modem,io,irq,options]

Using modem=1 means you have the ser12 device, modem=2 means you have the par96 device. Using options=0 means use hardware DCD, and options=1 means use software DCD. The io and irq are the i/o port base and interrupt settings as usual. There is more details in the file README.baycom which is currently in the /linux/drivers/char/ directory.

8 Closing

If you have found any glaring typos, or outdated info in this document, please let me know. It is easy to overlook stuff.

Thanks,

Paul Gortmaker, gpg109@rsphy1.anu.edu.au

Lilo mini-Howto

Cameron Spitzer (cls@truffula.sj.ca.us), Alessandro Rubini (rubini@linux.it).   v2.1, 9 January 1998

This file describes some typical LILO installations. It's intended as a supplement to the LILO User's Guide. I think examples are informative even if your setup isn't much like mine. I hope this saves you trouble. Since Lilo's own documentation is very good, who's interested in the details is referred to /usr/doc/lilo*

Contents

1   Introduction

Although the documentation found in Lilo's sources (the one installed in /usr/doc/lilo-version) is very comprehensive, most Linux users can find some difficulties in building their own /etc/lilo.conf file. This document is meant to support them by giving the minimal information and by showing five sample installations:

- The first example is the classical "Linux and other" installation.
- The next one shows how to install Lilo on a hard drive connected as /dev/hdc that will boot as /dev/hda. This is usually needed when you install a new Linux drive from your own running system.
- The third example shows how to boot a Linux system whose root partition can't be accessed by the BIOS.
- The next sample file is used to access huge disks, that neither the BIOS nor DOS can access easily (this one is somehow outdated).

- The last example shows how to restore a damaged disk (the damage in this case resulted from installing another operating system).

The last three examples are by Cameron Spitzer, cls@truffula.sj.ca.us, who wrote the original document. The current maintainer doesn't run anything but Linux, so I can't check if nor update them.

2   Background Information and Standard Installation

When Lilo boots the system, it can only load data sectors that can be accessed by the bios. Any pathname you put in /etc/lilo.conf is resolved at installation time (when you invoke *lilo*); this is when the program builds any table listing which sectors are used by the files. As a consequence, the files must live in a partition that can be accessed by the BIOS; moreover, you must reinstall the loader (i.e., you must reinvoke *lilo*) any time you modify the files. Whenever you recompile your kernel and overwrite your old image you must reinstall Lilo).

2.1   Where Should I Install Lilo?

The boot = directive in /etc/lilo.conf tells Lilo where it should put its primary boot loader. In general, you can either specify the master boot sector (/dev/hda) or the root partition of your Linux installation (is usually is /dev/hda1 or /dev/hda2).

If you have another operating system installed in your hard drive, you'd better install Lilo to the root partition. In this case, you must mark the partition as "bootable" (use the "a" command of *fdisk* or the "b" command of *cfdisk*. If you don't overwrite the master boot sector you'll find it easier to uninstall Linux and Lilo if needed.

2.2   How Should I Configure my IDE Hard Drives?

I personally don't use LBA or LARGE settings in the BIOS (but I only run Linux); they are horrible kludges forced on by design deficiencies in the PC world. This requires that the kernel lives in the first 1024 cylinders, but this is not a problem as long as you partition your hard drives and keep root small (as you should do anyways).

If your hard disk already carries another operating system, you won't be able to modify the BIOS settings, or the old system won't work any more. All recent Lilo distribution are able to deal with LBA and LARGE disk settings.

If you have more than one hard disk and some of them are only used by Linux, but are not used in booting, you can tell your BIOS that they are not installed. Your system will boot more quickly and Linux will autodetect all the disk in no time. I often connect extra disks to my system, but I never touch the BIOS configuration.

2.3   How Can I Interact at Boot Time?

When you see the Lilo prompt, you can hit the <Tab> key to show the list of possible choices. If Lilo is not configured to be interactive, press and hold the <Alt> or <Shift> key before the "LILO" message appears.

If you choose to boot a Linux kernel, you can add command-line arguments after the name of the system you choose. The kernel accepts many command-line arguments, and this is not the place to list them all. A few of them are particularly important, in my opinion:

- `root=`: you can tell the Linux kernel to mount as root a different partition from the one appearing in `lilo.conf`. For example, I have a tiny partition hosting a minimal Linux installation, and I've been able to boot the system after destroying my root partition by mistake.

- `init=`: verson 1.3.43 and newer of the Linux kernel accept the command-line specification of a program to execute in place of `/sbin/init`. If you experience bad problems during the boot process, you can access the bare system by specifying `init=/bin/sh` (when you are at the shell prompt you most likely will need to mount your disks: try "`/sbin/mount -w -n -o remount /; mount -a`", and remember to "`/sbin/umount -a`" before turning off the computer).

- A number: specifying a number on the kernel command line you instruct *init* to enter a specific run-level (the default is usually 3). Refer to the *init* documentation, to `/etc/inittab` and to `/etc/rc.d` to probe further.

2.4   How Can I Uninstall Lilo?

When Lilo overwrites a boot sector, it saves a backup copy in `/boot/boot.xxyy`, where *xxyy* are the major and minor numbers of the device, in hex. You can see the major and minor numbers of your disk or partition by running "`ls -l /dev/device`". For example, the first sector of `/dev/hda` (major 3, minor 0) will be saved in `/boot/boot.0300`, installing Lilo on `/dev/fd0` creates `/boot/boot.0200` and installing on `/dev/sdb3` (major 8, minor 19) creates `/boot/boot.0813`. Note that Lilo won't create the file if there is already one; you don't need to care about the backup copy whenever you reinstall Lilo (for example, after recompiling your kernel).

If you ever need to uninstall Lilo (for example, in the unfortunate case you need to uninstall Linux), you just need to restore the original boot sector. If Lilo is installed in `/dev/hda`, just do "`dd if=/boot/boot.0300 of=/dev/hda bs=446 count=1`" (I personally just do "`cat /boot/boot.0300 > /dev/hda`", but this is not safe, as this will restore the original partition table as well, which you might have modified in the meanwhile). This command is much easier to run than trying "`fdisk /mbr`" from a DOS shell: it allows you to cleanly remove Linux from a disk without ever booting anything else. After removing Lilo remember to run Linux' *fdisk* to destroy any Linux partition (DOS' *fdisk* is unable to remove non-dos partitions).

If you installed Lilo on your root partition (e.g., `/dev/hda2`), nothing special needs to be done to uninstall Lilo. Just run Linux' *fdisk* to remove Linux partitions from the partition table. You must also mark the DOS partition as bootable.

3   The Simple Configuration

Most Lilo installations use a configuration file like the following one:

```
boot = /dev/hda     # or your root partition
delay = 0           # or specify a delay in tenth of a second
vga = 0             # optional. Use "vga=1" to get 80x50

image = /boot/vmlinux # your zImage file
  root = /dev/hda1    # your root partition
  label = Linux       # or any fancy name
  read-only           # mount root read-only

other = /dev/hda4   # your dos partition, if any
  table = /dev/hda  # the current partition table
  label = dos       # or any non-fancy name
```

You can multiple "image" and "other" sections if you want. It's not uncommon to have several kernel images configured in your *lilo.conf*, at least if you keep up to dat with the developers.

4   Installing `hdc` to boot as `hda`

Lilo allows to map the kernel image from one disk and instruct the BIOS to retrieve it from another disk. For example, it's common for me to install Linux on a disk I connect to `hdc` (master disk of secondary controller) and boot it as a standalong system on the primary IDE controller of another computer. I copied the installation floppy to a tiny partition, so I can run *chroot* in a virtual console to install `hdc` while I use the system to do something else.

The *lilo.conf* file I use to install Lilo looks like:

```
# This file must be used from a system running from /dev/hdc
boot = /dev/hdc    # overwrite MBR of hdc
disk = /dev/hdc    # tell how hdc will look like:
   bios = 0x80     #  the bios will see it as first drive
delay = 0
vga = 0

image = /boot/vmlinux  # root partition is /dev/hdc1
   root = /dev/hda1         # hdc1 at boot will be hda1
   label = Linux
   read-only
```

This configuration file must be read by a Lilo running **off /dev/hdc1**. The Lilo maps that get written the boot sector (**/dev/hdc**) must rever the copies of **vmlinux** and to **/boot/boot.b** that will be available at boot time, i.e., the copies in `hdc`.

I call this configuration file **/mnt/etc/lilo.conf.hdc** and I install Lilo by invoking "`cd /mnt; chroot . sbin/lilo -C /etc/lilo.conf.hdc`" while **/dev/hdc1** is mounted under **/mnt**.

5   Using Lilo When the BIOS Can't See the Root Partition

I have two IDE drives, and a SCSI drive. The SCSI drive can't be seen from BIOS. The Linux Loader, Lilo, uses BIOS calls and can only see drives that BIOS can see. My stupid AMI BIOS will only boot from "A:" or "C:" My root file system is on a partition on the SCSI drive.

The solution consists in storing the kernel, map file, and chain loader in a Linux partition on the first IDE. Notice that it is not necessary to keep your kernel on your root partition.

The second partition on my first IDE (**/dev/hda2**, the Linux partition used to boot the system) is mounted on **/u2**. Here is the **/etc/lilo.conf** file I used.

```
#  Install LILO on the Master Boot Record
#  on the first IDE.
#
boot = /dev/hda
#  /sbin/lilo (the installer) copies the LILO boot record
#  from the following file to the MBR location.
install = /u2/etc/lilo/boot.b
```

```
#
#  I wrote a verbose boot menu.  LILO finds it here.
message = /u2/etc/lilo/message
#  The installer will build the following file. It tells
#  the boot-loader where the blocks of the kernels are.
map = /u2/etc/lilo/map
compact
prompt
#  Wait 10 seconds, then boot the 1.2.1 kernel by default.
timeout = 100
#  The kernel is stored where BIOS can see it by doing this:
#       cp -p /usr/src/linux/arch/i386/boot/zImage /u2/z1.2.1
image = /u2/z1.2.1
        label = 1.2.1
#  LILO tells the kernel to mount the first SCSI partition
#  as root.  BIOS does not have to be able to see it.
        root = /dev/sda1
#  This partition will be checked and remounted by /etc/rc.d/rc.S
        read-only
#  I kept an old Slackware kernel lying around in case I built a
#  kernel that doesn't work.  I actually needed this once.
image = /u2/z1.0.9
        label = 1.0.9
        root = /dev/sda1
        read-only
#  My DR-DOS 6 partition.
other = /dev/hda1
        loader=/u2/etc/lilo/chain.b
        label = dos
        alias = m
```

6   Accessing Huge Disks When the BIOS Can't

The system in my office has a 1GB IDE drive. The BIOS can only see the first 504 MB of the IDE. (Where MB means 2**10 bytes, not 10**6 bytes.) So I have MS-DOS on a 350 MB partition /dev/hda1 and my Linux root on a 120 MB partition /dev/hda2.

MS-DOS was unable to install itself correctly when the drive was fresh. Novell DOS 7 had the same problem. Luckily for me, "Options by IBM" forgot to put the "OnTrack" diskette in the box with the drive. The drive was supposed to come with a product called "OnTrack Disk Manager." If you only have MSDOS, I guess you have to use it.

So I made a partition table with Linux' fdisk. MSDOS-6.2 refused to install itself in /dev/hda1. It said something like "this release of MS-DOS is for new installations. Your computer already has MS-DOS so you need to get an upgrade release from your dealer." Actually, the disk was brand new.

What a crock! So I ran Linux' fdisk again and deleted partition 1 from the table. This satisfied MS-DOS 6.2 which proceeded to create the exact same partition 1 I had just deleted and installed itself. MS-DOS 6.2 wrote its Master Boot Record on the drive, but it couldn't boot.

Luckily I had a Slackware kernel on floppy (made by the Slackware installation program "setup"), so I booted Linux and wrote LILO over MS-DOS' broken MBR. This works. Here is the /etc/lilo.conf file I used:

```
boot = /dev/hda
map = /lilo-map
delay = 100
ramdisk = 0                    # Turns off ramdisk in Slackware kernel
timeout = 100
prompt
disk = /dev/hda                # BIOS only sees first 500 MB.
   bios = 0x80                 # specifies the first IDE.
   sectors = 63                # get the numbers from your drive's docs.
   heads = 16
   cylinders = 2100
image = /vmlinuz
   append = "hd=2100,16,63"
   root = /dev/hda2
   label = linux
   read-only
   vga = extended
other = /dev/hda1
   label = msdos
   table = /dev/hda
   loader = /boot/chain.b
```

After I installed these systems, I verified that the partition containing the zImage, boot.b, map, chain.b, and message files can use an msdos file system, as long as it is not "stackered" or "doublespaced." So I could have made the DOS partition on /dev/hda1 500 MB.

I have also learned that "OnTrack" would have written a partition table starting a few dozen bytes into the drive, instead of at the beginning, and it is possible to hack the Linux IDE driver to work around this problem. But installing would have been impossible with the precompiled Slackware kernel. Eventually, IBM sent me an "OnTrack" diskette. I called OnTrack's technical support. They told me Linux is broken because Linux doesn't use BIOS. I gave their diskette away.

7   Booting from a Rescue Floppy

Next, I installed Windows-95 on my office system. It blew away my nice LILO MBR, but it left my Linux partitions alone. Kernels take a long time to load from floppy, so I made a floppy with a working LILO setup on it, which could boot my kernel from the IDE.

I made the lilo floppy like so:

```
fdformat /dev/fd0H1440      # lay tracks on virgin diskette
mkfs -t minix /dev/fd0 1440 #  make file system of type minix
mount /dev/fd0 /mnt         #  mount in the standard tmp mount point
cp -p /boot/chain.b /mnt    #  copy the chain loader over
lilo -C /etc/lilo.flop      #  install LILO and the map on the diskette.
umount /mnt
```

Notice that the diskette **must be mounted when you run the installer** so that Lilo can write its map file properly.

This file is /etc/lilo.flop. It's almost the same as the last one:

```
#  Makes a floppy that can boot kernels from HD.
```

```
boot = /dev/fd0
map = /mnt/lilo-map
delay = 100
ramdisk = 0
timeout = 100
prompt
disk = /dev/hda        # 1 GB IDE, BIOS only sees first 500 MB.
   bios=0x80
   sectors = 63
   heads = 16
   cylinders = 2100
image = /vmlinuz
  append = "hd=2100,16,63"
  root = /dev/hda2
  label = linux
  read-only
  vga = extended
other = /dev/hda1
  label = msdos
  table = /dev/hda
  loader = /mnt/chain.b
```

Finally, I needed MS-DOS 6.2 on my office system, but I didn't want to touch the first drive. I added a SCSI controller and drive, made an msdos file system on it with Linux' mkdosfs, and Windows-95 sees it as "D:". But of course MSDOS will not boot off of D:. This is not a problem when you have LILO. I added the following to the lilo.conf in Example 2.

```
other = /dev/sda1
  label = d6.2
  table = /dev/sda
  loader = /boot/any_d.b
```

With this modification MSDOS-6.2 runs, and it thinks it is on C: and Windows-95 is on D:.

The Linux Kernel HOWTO

Brian Ward, bri@blah.math.tu-graz.ac.at

v0.80, 26 May 1997

This is a detailed guide to kernel configuration, compilation, upgrades, and troubleshooting for ix86-based systems.

Contents

1 Introduction

Should you read this document? Well, see if you've got any of the following symptoms:

- "Arg! This wizzo-46.5.6 package says it needs kernel release 1.8.193 and I still only have release 1.0.9!"
- There's a device driver in one of the newer kernels that you just gotta have
- You really have no idea at all how to compile a kernel
- "Is this stuff in the README *really* the whole story?"
- You came, you tried, it didn't work
- You need something to give to people who insist on asking you to install their kernels for them

1.1 Read this first! (I mean it)

Some of the examples in this document assume that you have GNU `tar`, `find`, and `xargs`. These are quite standard; this should not cause problems. It is also assumed that you know your system's filesystem structure; if you don't, it is critical that you keep a written copy of the `mount` command's output during normal system operation (or a listing of `/etc/fstab`, if you can read it). This information is important, and does not change unless you repartition your disk, add a new one, reinstall your system, or something similar.

The latest "production" kernel version at the time of this writing was 2.0.30, meaning that the references and examples correspond to that release. Even though I try to make this document as version-independent as possible, the kernel is constantly under development, so if you get a newer release, it will inevitably have some differences. Again, this should not cause major problems, but it may create some confusion.

There are two versions of the linux kernel source, "production" and "development." Production releases begin with 1.0.x and are currently the even-numbered releases; 1.0.x was production, 1.2.x is production, as well as 2.0.x. These kernels are considered to be the most stable, bug-free versions available at the time of release. The development kernels (1.1.x, 1.3.x, etc) are meant as testing kernels, for people willing to test out new and possibly very buggy kernels. You have been warned.

1.2   A word on style

`Text that looks like this` is either something that appears on your screen, a filename, or something that can be directly typed in, such as a command, or options to a command (if you're looking at a plain-text file, it doesn't look any different). Commands and other input are frequently quoted (with ' '), which causes the following classic punctuation problem: if such an item appears at the end of a sentence in quotes, people often type a '.' along with the command, because the American quoting style says to put the period inside of the quotation marks. Even though common sense (and unfortunately, this assumes that the one with the "common sense" is used to the so-called American style of quotation) should tell one to strip off the punctuation first, many people simply do not remember, so I will place it outside the quotation marks in such cases. In other words, when indicating that you should type "`make config`" I would write '`make config`', not '`make config.`'

2   Important questions and their answers

2.1   What does the kernel do, anyway?

The Unix kernel acts as a mediator for your programs and your hardware. First, it does (or arranges for) the memory management for all of the running programs (processes), and makes sure that they all get a fair (or unfair, if you please) share of the processor's cycles. In addition, it provides a nice, fairly portable interface for programs to talk to your hardware.

There is certainly more to the kernel's operation than this, but these basic functions are the most important to know.

2.2   Why would I want to upgrade my kernel?

Newer kernels generally offer the ability to talk to more types of hardware (that is, they have more device drivers), they can have better process management, they can run faster than the older versions, they could be more stable than the older versions, and they fix silly bugs in the older versions. Most people upgrade kernels because they want the device drivers and the bug fixes.

2.3   What kind of hardware do the newer kernels support?

See the Hardware-HOWTO. Alternatively, you can look at the '`config.in`' file in the linux source, or just find out when you try '`make config`'. This shows you all hardware supported by the standard kernel distribution, but not everything that linux supports; many common device drivers (such as the PCMCIA drivers and some tape drivers) are loadable modules maintained and distributed separately.

2.4   What version of gcc and libc do I need?

Linus recommends a version of gcc in the README file included with the linux source. If you don't have this version, the documentation in the recommended version of gcc should tell you if you need to upgrade your libc. This is not a difficult procedure, but it is important to follow the instructions.

2.5   What's a loadable module?

These are pieces of kernel code which are not linked (included) directly in the kernel. One compiles them separately, and can insert and remove them into the running kernel at almost any time. Due to its flexibility, this is now the preferred way to code certain kernel features. Many popular device drivers, such as the PCMCIA drivers and the QIC-80/40 tape driver, are loadable modules.

2.6   How much disk space do I need?

It depends on your particular system configuration. First, the compressed linux source is nearly 6 megabytes large at version 2.0.10. Most sites keep this even after unpacking. Uncompressed, it takes up 24 MB. But that's not the end – you need more to actually compile the thing. This depends on how much you configure into your kernel. For example, on one particular machine, I have networking, the 3Com 3C509 driver, and three filesystems configured, using close to 30 MB. Adding the compressed linux source, you need about 36 MB for this particular configuration. On another system, without network device support (but still with networking support), and sound card support, it consumes even more. Also, a newer kernel is certain to have a larger source tree than an older one, so, in general, if you have a lot of hardware, make sure that you have a big enough hard disk in that mess (and at today's prices, I cannot help but to recommend getting another disk space as an answer to your storage problems).

2.7   How long does it take?

For most people, the answer is "fairly long." The speed of your system and the amount of memory you have ultimately determines the time, but there is a small bit to do with the amount of stuff you configure into the kernel. On a 486DX4/100 with 16 MB of RAM, on a v1.2 kernel with five filesystems, networking support, and sound card drivers, it takes around 20 minutes. On a 386DX/40 (8 MB RAM) with a similar configuration, compilation lasts nearly 1.5 hours. It is a generally good recommendation to make a little coffee, watch some TV, knit, or whatever you do for fun while your machine compiles the kernel. You can have someone else with a faster machine compile it for you if you really have a slow machine.

3   How to actually configure the kernel

3.1   Getting the source

You can obtain the source via anonymous ftp from ftp.funet.fi in /pub/Linux/PEOPLE/Linus, a mirror, or other sites. It is typically labelled linux-x.y.z.tar.gz, where x.y.z is the version number. Newer (better?) versions and the patches are typically in subdirectories such as 'v1.1' and 'v1.2' The highest number is the latest version, and is usually a "test release," meaning that if you feel uneasy about beta or alpha releases, you should stay with a major release.

I *strongly* suggest that you use a mirror ftp site instead of ftp.funet.fi. Here is a short list of mirrors and other sites:

USA:	sunsite.unc.edu:/pub/Linux/kernel
USA:	tsx-11.mit.edu:/pub/linux/sources/system
UK:	sunsite.doc.ic.ac.uk:/pub/unix/Linux/sunsite.unc-mirror/kernel
Austria:	ftp.univie.ac.at:/systems/linux/sunsite/kernel
Germany:	ftp.Germany.EU.net:/pub/os/Linux/Local.EUnet/Kernel/Linus
Germany:	sunsite.informatik.rwth-aachen.de:/pub/Linux/PEOPLE/Linus
France:	ftp.ibp.fr:/pub/linux/sources/system/patches
Australia:	sunsite.anu.edu.au:/pub/linux/kernel

In general, a mirror of `sunsite.unc.edu` is a good place to look. The file `/pub/Linux/MIRRORS` contains a list of known mirrors. If you do not have ftp access, a list of BBS systems which carry linux is posted periodically to comp.os.linux.announce; try to obtain this.

If you were looking for general Linux information and distributions, try `http://www.linux.org`.

3.2   Unpacking the source

Log in as or su to 'root', and cd to /usr/src. If you installed kernel source when you first installed linux (as most do), there will already be a directory called 'linux' there, which contains the entire old source tree. If you have the disk space and you want to play it safe, preserve that directory. A good idea is to figure out what version your system runs now and rename the directory accordingly. The command 'uname -r' prints the current kernel version. Therefore, if 'uname -r' said '1.0.9', you would rename (with 'mv') 'linux' to 'linux-1.0.9'. If you feel mildly reckless, just wipe out the entire directory. In any case, make certain there is no 'linux' directory in /usr/src before unpacking the full source code.

Now, in /usr/src, unpack the source with 'tar zxpvf linux-x.y.z.tar.gz' (if you've just got a .tar file with no .gz at the end, 'tar xpvf linux-x.y.z.tar' works.). The contents of the source will fly by. When finished, there will be a new 'linux' directory in /usr/src. cd to linux and look over the README file. There will be a section with the label 'INSTALLING the kernel'. Carry out the instructions when appropriate – symbolic links that should be in place, removal of stale .o files, etc.

3.3   Configuring the kernel

Note: Some of this is reiteration/clarification of a similar section in Linus' README file.

The command 'make config' while in /usr/src/linux starts a configure script which asks you many questions. It requires bash, so verify that bash is /bin/bash, /bin/sh, or $BASH.

There are some alternatives to 'make config' and you may very well find them easier and more comfortable to use. For those "running X," you can try 'make xconfig' if you have Tk installed ('click-o-rama' - Nat). 'make menuconfig' is for those who have (n)curses and would prefer a text-based menu. These interfaces have one clear advantage: If you goof up and make a wrong choice during configuration, it is simple to go back and fix it.

You are ready to answer the questions, usually with 'y' (yes) or 'n' (no). Device drivers typically have an 'm' option. This means "module," meaning that the system will compile it, but not directly into the kernel, but as a loadable module. A more comical way to describe it is as "maybe." Some of the more obvious and non-critical options are not described here; see the section "Other configuration options" for short descriptions of a few others.

In 2.0.x and later, there is a '?' option, which provides a brief description of the configuration parameter. That information is likely to be the most up-to-date.

3.3.1 Kernel math emulation

If you don't have a math coprocessor (you have a bare 386 or 486SX), you must say 'y' to this. If you do have a coprocessor and you still say 'y', don't worry too much – the coprocessor is still used and the emulation ignored. The only consequence is that the kernel will be larger (costing RAM). I have been told that the math emulation is slow; although this does not have much to do with this section, it might be something to keep in mind when faced with sluggish X window system performance.

3.3.2 Normal (MFM/RLL) disk and IDE disk/cdrom support

You probably need to support this; it means that the kernel will support standard PC hard disks, which most people have. This driver does not include SCSI drives; they come later in the configuration.

You will then be asked about the "old disk-only" and "new IDE" drivers. You want to choose one of them; the main difference is that the old driver only supports two disks on a single interface, and the new one supports a secondary interface and IDE/ATAPI cdrom drives. The new driver is 4k larger than the old one and is also supposedly "improved," meaning that aside from containing a different number of bugs, it might improve your disk performance, especially if you have newer (EIDE-type) hardware.

3.3.3 Networking support

In principle, you would only say 'y' if your machine is on a network such as the internet, or you want to use SLIP, PPP, term, etc to dial up for internet access. However, as many packages (such as the X window system) require networking support even if your machine does not live on a real network, you should say 'y'. Later on, you will be asked if you want to support TCP/IP networking; again, say 'y' here if you are not absolutely sure.

3.3.4 Limit memory to low 16MB

There exist buggy 386 DMA controllers which have problems with addressing anything more than 16 MB of RAM; you want to say 'y' in the (rare) case that you have one.

3.3.5 System V IPC

One of the best definitions of IPC (Interprocess Communication) is in the Perl book's glossary. Not surprisingly, some Perl programmers employ it to let processes talk to each other, as well as many other packages (DOOM, most notably), so it is not a good idea to say n unless you know exactly what you are doing.

3.3.6 Processor type (386, 486, Pentium, PPro)

(in older kernels: Use -m486 flag for 486-specific optimizations)

Traditionally, this compiled in certain optimizations for a particular processor; the kernels ran fine on other chips, but the kernel was perhaps a bit larger. In newer kernels, however, this is no longer true, so you should enter the processor for which you are compiling the kernel. A "386" kernel will work on all machines.

3.3.7   SCSI support

If you have SCSI devices, say 'y'. You will be prompted for further information, such as support for CD-ROM, disks, and what kind of SCSI adapter you have. See the SCSI-HOWTO for greater detail.

3.3.8   Network device support

If you have a network card, or you would like to use SLIP, PPP, or a parallel port adapter for connecting to the Internet, say 'y'. The config script will prompt for which kind of card you have, and which protocol to use.

3.3.9   Filesystems

The configure script then asks if you wish to support the following filesystems:

Standard (minix) - Newer distributions don't create minix filesystems, and many people don't use it, but it may still be a good idea to configure this one. Some "rescue disk" programs use it, and still more floppies may have a minix filesystem, since the minix filesystem is less painful to use on a floppy.

Extended fs - This was the first version of the extended filesystem, which is no longer in widespread use. Chances are that you'll know it if you need it and that if you are doubt, you do not need it.

Second extended - This is widely used in new distributions. You probably have one of these, and need to say 'y'.

xiafs filesystem - At one time, this was not uncommon, but at the time of this writing, I did not know of anyone using it.

msdos - If you want to use your MS-DOS hard disk partitions, or mount MS-DOS formatted floppy disks, say 'y'.

umsdos - This filesystem expands an MS-DOS filesystem with usual Unix-like features such as long filenames. It is not useful for people (like me) who "don't do DOS."

/proc - Another one of the greatest things since powdered milk (idea shamelessly stolen from Bell Labs, I guess). One doesn't make a proc filesystem on a disk; this is a filesystem interface to the kernel and processes. Many process listers (such as 'ps') use it. Try 'cat /proc/meminfo' or 'cat /proc/devices' sometime. Some shells (rc, in particular) use /proc/self/fd (known as /dev/fd on other systems) for I/O. You should almost certainly say 'y' to this; many important linux tools depend on it.

NFS - If your machine lives on a network and you want to use filesystems which reside on other systems with NFS, say 'y'.

ISO9660 - Found on most CD-ROMs. If you have a CD-ROM drive and you wish to use it under Linux, say 'y'.

OS/2 HPFS - At the time of this writing, a read-only fs for OS/2 HPFS.

System V and Coherent - for partitions of System V and Coherent systems (These are other PC Unix variants).

But I don't know which filesystems I need!   Ok, type 'mount'. The output will look something like this:

```
blah# mount
/dev/hda1 on / type ext2 (defaults)
```

```
/dev/hda3 on /usr type ext2 (defaults)
none on /proc type proc (defaults)
/dev/fd0 on /mnt type msdos (defaults)
```

Look at each line; the word next to 'type' is the filesystem type. In this example, my / and /usr filesystems are second extended, I'm using /proc, and there's a floppy disk mounted using the msdos (bleah) filesystem.

You can try 'cat /proc/filesystems' if you have /proc currently enabled; it will list your current kernel's filesystems.

The configuration of rarely-used, non-critical filesystems can cause kernel bloat; see the section on modules for a way to avoid this and the "Pitfalls" section on why a bloated kernel is undesirable.

3.3.10 Character devices

Here, you enable the drivers for your printer (parallel printer, that is), busmouse, PS/2 mouse (many notebooks use the PS/2 mouse protocol for their built-in trackballs), some tape drives, and other such "character" devices. Say 'y' when appropriate.

Note: Selection is a program which allows the use of the mouse outside of the X window system for cut and paste between virtual consoles. It's fairly nice if you have a serial mouse, because it coexists well with X, but you need to do special tricks for others. Selection support was a configuration option at one time, but is now standard.

Note 2: Selection is now considered obsolete. "gpm" is the name of the new program. It can do fancier things, such translate mouse protocols, handle multiple mice, ..

3.3.11 Sound card

If you feel a great desire to hear biff bark, say 'y', and later on, another config program will compile and ask you all about your sound board. (A note on sound card configuration: when it asks you if you want to install the full version of the driver, you can say 'n' and save some kernel memory by picking only the features which you deem necessary.) I highly recommend looking at the Sound-HOWTO for more detail about sound support if you have a sound card.

3.3.12 Other configuration options

Not all of the configuration options are listed here because they change too often or fairly self-evident (for instance, 3Com 3C509 support to compile the device drive for this particular ethernet card). There exists a fairly comprehensive list of all the options (plus a way to place them into the Configure script) put together by Axel Boldt (axel@uni-paderborn.de) with the following URL:

```
http://math-www.uni-paderborn.de/~axel/config_help.html
```

or via anonymous FTP at:

```
ftp://sunsite.unc.edu/pub/Linux/kernel/config/krnl_cnfg_hlp.x.yz.tgz
```

where the x.yz is the version number.

For later (2.0.x and later) kernels, this has been integrated into the source tree.

3.3.13 Kernel hacking

>From Linus' README:

the "kernel hacking" configuration details usually result in a bigger or slower kernel (or both), and can even make the kernel less stable by configuring some routines to actively try to break bad code to find kernel problems (kmalloc()). Thus you should probably answer 'n' to the questions for a "production" kernel.

3.4 Now what? (The Makefile)

After you `make config`, a message tells you that your kernel has been configured, and to "check the top-level `Makefile` for additional configuration," etc.

So, look at the `Makefile`. You probably will not need to change it, but it never hurts to look. You can also change its options with the '`rdev`' command once the new kernel is in place.

4 Compiling the kernel

4.1 Cleaning and depending

When the configure script ends, it also tells you to '`make dep`' and (possibly) '`clean`'. So, do the '`make dep`'. This insures that all of the dependencies, such the include files, are in place. It does not take long, unless your computer is fairly slow to begin with. For older versions of the kernel, when finished, you should do a '`make clean`'. This removes all of the object files and some other things that an old version leaves behind. In any case, *do not* forget this step before attempting to recompile a kernel.

4.2 Compile time

After `depending` and `cleaning`, you may now '`make zImage`' or '`make zdisk`' (this is the part that takes a long time.). '`make zImage`' will compile the kernel, and leave a file in `arch/i386/boot` called '`zImage`' (among other things). This is the new compressed kernel. '`make zdisk`' does the same thing, but also places the new `zImage` on a floppy disk which you hopefully put in drive "A:". '`zdisk`' is fairly handy for testing new kernels; if it bombs (or just doesn't work right), just remove the floppy and boot with your old kernel. It can also be a handy way to boot if you accidentally remove your kernel (or something equally as dreadful). You can also use it to install new systems when you just dump the contents of one disk onto the other ("all this and more! NOW how much would you pay?").

All even halfway reasonably recent kernels are compressed, hence the '`z`' in front of the names. A compressed kernel automatically decompresses itself when executed.

4.3 Other "make"ables

'`make mrproper`' will do a more extensive '`clean`'ing. It is sometimes necessary; you may wish to do it at every patch. '`make mrproper`' will also delete your configuration file, so you might want to make a backup of it (`.config`) if you see it as valuable.

'`make oldconfig`' will attempt to configure the kernel from an old configuration file; it will run through the '`make config`' process for you. If you haven't ever compiled a kernel before or don't have an old config file, then you probably shouldn't do this, as you will most likely want to change the default configuration.

See the section on modules for a description of 'make modules'.

4.4   Installing the kernel

After you have a new kernel that seems to work the way you want it to, it's time to install it. Most people use LILO (Linux Loader) for this. 'make zlilo' will install the kernel, run LILO on it, and get you all ready to boot, BUT ONLY if lilo is configured in the following way on your system: kernel is /vmlinuz, lilo is in /sbin, and your lilo config (/etc/lilo.conf) agrees with this.

Otherwise, you need to use LILO directly. It's a fairly easy package to install and work with, but it has a tendency to confuse people with the configuration file. Look at the config file (either /etc/lilo/config for older versions or /etc/lilo.conf for new versions), and see what the current setup is. The config file looks like this:

```
image = /vmlinuz
    label = Linux
    root = /dev/hda1
    ...
```

The 'image =' is set to the currently installed kernel. Most people use /vmlinuz. 'label' is used by lilo to determine which kernel or operating system to boot, and 'root' is the / of that particular operating system. Make a backup copy of your old kernel and copy the zImage which you just made into place (you would say 'cp zImage /vmlinuz' if you use '/vmlinuz'). Then, rerun lilo – on newer systems, you can just run 'lilo', but on older stuff, you might have to do an /etc/lilo/install or even an /etc/lilo/lilo -C /etc/lilo/config.

If you would like to know more about LILO's configuration, or you don't have LILO, get the newest version from your favorite ftp site and follow the instructions.

To boot one of your old kernels off the hard disk (another way to save yourself in case you screw up the new kernel), copy the lines below (and including) 'image = xxx' in the LILO config file to the bottom of the file, and change the 'image = xxx' to 'image = yyy', where 'yyy' is the full pathname of the file you saved your backup kernel to. Then, change the 'label = zzz' to 'label = linux-backup' and rerun lilo. You may need to put a line in the config file saying 'delay=x', where x is an amount in tenths of a second, which tells LILO to wait that much time before booting, so that you can interrupt it (with the shift key, for example), and type in the label of the backup boot image (in case unpleasant things happen).

5   Patching the kernel

5.1   Applying a patch

Incremental upgrades of the kernel are distributed as patches. For example, if you have version 1.1.45, and you notice that there's a 'patch46.gz' out there for it, it means you can upgrade to version 1.1.46 through application of the patch. You might want to make a backup of the source tree first ('make clean' and then 'cd /usr/src; tar zcvf old-tree.tar.gz linux' will make a compressed tar archive for you.).

So, continuing with the example above, let's suppose that you have 'patch46.gz' in /usr/src. cd to /usr/src and do a 'zcat patch46.gz | patch -p0' (or 'patch -p0 < patch46' if the patch isn't compressed). You'll see things whizz by (or flutter by, if your system is that slow) telling you that it is trying to apply hunks, and whether it succeeds or not. Usually, this action goes by too quickly for you to read, and you're not too sure whether it worked or not, so you might want to use the -s flag to patch, which tells patch to only report error messages (you don't get as much of the "hey, my computer is actually doing something for a change!" feeling, but you may prefer this..). To look for parts which might not have gone smoothly, cd to /usr/src/linux and look for files with a .rej extension. Some versions of patch (older versions which may have been compiled with on an inferior filesystem) leave the rejects with a # extension. You can use 'find' to look for you;

```
find . -name '*.rej' -print
```

prints all files who live in the current directory or any subdirectories with a .rej extension to the standard output.

If everything went right, do a 'make clean', 'config', and 'dep' as described in sections 3 and 4.

There are quite a few options to the patch command. As mentioned above, patch -s will suppress all messages except the errors. If you keep your kernel source in some other place than /usr/src/linux, patch -p1 (in that directory) will patch things cleanly. Other patch options are well-documented in the manual page.

5.2   If something goes wrong

(Note: this section refers mostly to quite old kernels)

The most frequent problem that used to arise was when a patch modified a file called 'config.in' and it didn't look quite right, because you changed the options to suit your machine. This has been taken care of, but one still might encounter it with an older release. To fix it, look at the config.in.rej file, and see what remains of the original patch. The changes will typically be marked with '+' and '-' at the beginning of the line. Look at the lines surrounding it, and remember if they were set to 'y' or 'n'. Now, edit config.in, and change 'y' to 'n' and 'n' to 'y' when appropriate. Do a

```
patch -p0 < config.in.rej
```

and if it reports that it succeeded (no fails), then you can continue on with a configuration and compilation. The config.in.rej file will remain, but you can get delete it.

If you encounter further problems, you might have installed a patch out of order. If patch says 'previously applied patch detected: Assume -R?', you are probably trying to apply a patch which is below your current version number; if you answer 'y', it will attempt to degrade your source, and will most likely fail; thus, you will need to get a whole new source tree (which might not have been such a bad idea in the first place).

To back out (unapply) a patch, use 'patch -R' on the original patch.

The best thing to do when patches really turn out wrong is to start over again with a clean, out-of-the-box source tree (for example, from one of the linux-x.y.z.tar.gz files), and start again.

5.3   Getting rid of the .orig files

After just a few patches, the .orig files will start to pile up. For example, one 1.1.51 tree I had was once last cleaned out at 1.1.48. Removing the .orig files saved over a half a meg.

```
find . -name '*.orig' -exec rm -f {} ';'
```

will take care of it for you. Versions of patch which use # for rejects use a tilde instead of .orig.

There are better ways to get rid of the .orig files, which depend on GNU xargs:

```
find . -name '*.orig' | xargs rm
```

or the "quite secure but a little more verbose" method:

```
find . -name '*.orig' -print0 | xargs --null rm --
```

5.4 Other patches

There are other patches (I'll call them "nonstandard") than the ones Linus distributes. If you apply these, Linus' patches may not work correctly and you'll have to either back them out, fix the source or the patch, install a new source tree, or a combination of the above. This can become very frustrating, so if you do not want to modify the source (with the possibility of a very bad outcome), back out the nonstandard patches before applying Linus', or just install a new tree. Then, you can see if the nonstandard patches still work. If they don't, you are either stuck with an old kernel, playing with the patch or source to get it to work, or waiting (possibly begging) for a new version of the patch to come out.

How common are the patches not in the standard distribution? You will probably hear of them. I used to use the noblink patch for my virtual consoles because I hate blinking cursors (This patch is (or at least was) frequently updated for new kernel releases.). With most newer device drivers being developed as loadable modules, though, the frequecy of "nonstandard" patches is decreasing significantly.

6 Additional packages

Your linux kernel has many features which are not explained in the kernel source itself; these features are typically utilized through external packages. Some of the most common are listed here.

6.1 kbd

The linux console probably has more features than it deserves. Among these are the ability to switch fonts, remap your keyboard, switch video modes (in newer kernels), etc. The kbd package has programs which allow the user to do all of this, plus many fonts and keyboard maps for almost any keyboard, and is available from the same sites that carry the kernel source.

6.2 util-linux

Rik Faith (faith@cs.unc.edu) put together a large collection of linux utilities which are, by odd coincidence, called util-linux. These are now maintained by Nicolai Langfeldt (util-linux@math.uio.no). Available via anonymous ftp from sunsite.unc.edu in /pub/Linux/system/misc, it contains programs such as setterm, rdev, and ctrlaltdel, which are relevant to the kernel. As Rik says, *do not install without thinking;* you do not need to install everything in the package, and it could very well cause serious problems if you do.

6.3 hdparm

As with many packages, this was once a kernel patch and support programs. The patches made it into the official kernel, and the programs to optimize and play with your hard disk are distributed separately.

6.4 gpm

gpm stands for general purpose mouse. This program allows you to cut and paste text between virtual consoles and do other things with a large variety of mouse types.

7 Some pitfalls

7.1 make clean

If your new kernel does really weird things after a routine kernel upgrade, chances are you forgot to `make clean` before compiling the new kernel. Symptoms can be anything from your system outright crashing, strange I/O problems, to crummy performance. Make sure you do a `make dep`, too.

7.2 Huge or slow kernels

If your kernel is sucking up a lot of memory, is too large, and/or just takes forever to compile even when you've got your new 786DX6/440 working on it, you've probably got lots of unneeded stuff (device drivers, filesystems, etc) configured. If you don't use it, don't configure it, because it does take up memory. The most obvious symptom of kernel bloat is extreme swapping in and out of memory to disk; if your disk is making a lot of noise and it's not one of those old Fujitsu Eagles that sound like like a jet landing when turned off, look over your kernel configuration.

You can find out how much memory the kernel is using by taking the total amount of memory in your machine and subtracting from it the amount of "total mem" in /proc/meminfo or the output of the command 'free'. You can also find out by doing a 'dmesg' (or by looking at the kernel log file, wherever it is on your system). There will be a line which looks like this:

`Memory:  15124k/16384k available (552k kernel code, 384k reserved, 324k data)`

My 386 (which has slightly less junk configured) says this:

`Memory:  7000k/8192k available (496k kernel code, 384k reserved, 312k data)`

If you 'just gotta' have a big kernel but the system won't let you, you can try 'make bzimage'. You may very well have to install a new version of LILO if you do this.

7.3 Kernel doesn't compile

If it does not compile, then it is likely that a patch failed, or your source is somehow corrupt. Your version of gcc also might not be correct, or could also be corrupt (for example, the include files might be in error). Make sure that the symbolic links which Linus describes in the README are set up correctly. In general, if a standard kernel does not compile, something is seriously wrong with the system, and reinstallation of certain tools is probably necessary.

Or perhaps you're compiling a 1.2.x kernel with an ELF compiler (gcc 2.6.3 and higher). If you're getting a bunch of so-and-so undefined messages during the compilation, chances are that this is your problem. The fix is in most cases very simple. Add these lines to the top of arch/i386/Makefile:

```
AS=/usr/i486-linuxaout/bin/as
LD=/usr/i486-linuxaout/bin/ld -m i386linux
CC=gcc -b i486-linuxaout -D__KERNEL__ -I$(TOPDIR)/include
```

Then `make dep` and `zImage` again.

In rare cases, gcc can crash due to hardware problems. The error message will be something like "xxx exited with signal 15" and it will generally look very mysterious. I probably would not mention this, except that it happened to me once - I had some bad cache memory, and the compiler would occasionally barf at random. Try reinstalling gcc first if you experience problems. You should only get suspicious if your kernel compiles fine with external cache turned off, a reduced amount of RAM, etc.

It tends to disturb people when it's suggested that their hardware has problems. Well, I'm not making this up. There is an FAQ for it – it's at `http://www.bitwizard.nl/sig11/`.

7.4   New version of the kernel doesn't seem to boot

You did not run LILO, or it is not configured correctly. One thing that "got" me once was a problem in the config file; it said 'boot = /dev/hda1' instead of 'boot = /dev/hda' (This can be really annoying at first, but once you have a working config file, you shouldn't need to change it.).

7.5   You forgot to run LILO, or system doesn't boot at all

Ooops! The best thing you can do here is to boot off of a floppy disk and prepare another bootable floppy (such as 'make zdisk' would do). You need to know where your root (/) filesystem is and what type it is (e.g. second extended, minix). In the example below, you also need to know what filesystem your `/usr/src/linux` source tree is on, its type, and where it is normally mounted.

In the following example, / is `/dev/hda1`, and the filesystem which holds `/usr/src/linux` is `/dev/hda3`, normally mounted at `/usr`. Both are second extended filesystems. The working kernel image in `/usr/src/linux/arch/i386/boot` is called `zImage`.

The idea is that if there is a functioning `zImage`, it is possible to use that for the new floppy. Another alternative, which may or may not work better (it depends on the particular method in which you messed up your system) is discussed after the example.

First, boot from a boot/root disk combo or rescue disk, and mount the filesystem which contains the working kernel image:

```
mkdir /mnt
mount -t ext2 /dev/hda3 /mnt
```

If `mkdir` tells you that the directory already exists, just ignore it. Now, `cd` to the place where the working kernel image was. Note that

```
/mnt + /usr/src/linux/arch/i386/boot - /usr = /mnt/src/linux/arch/i386/boot
```

Place a formatted disk in drive "A:" (not your boot or root disk!), dump the image to the disk, and configure it for your root filesystem:

```
cd /mnt/src/linux/arch/i386/boot
dd if=zImage of=/dev/fd0
rdev /dev/fd0 /dev/hda1
```

`cd` to / and unmount the normal `/usr` filesystem:

```
cd /
umount /mnt
```

You should now be able to reboot your system as normal from this floppy. Don't forget to run lilo (or whatever it was that you did wrong) after the reboot!

As mentioned above, there is another common alternative. If you happened to have a working kernel image in / (/vmlinuz for example), you can use that for a boot disk. Supposing all of the above conditions, and that my kernel image is /vmlinuz, just make these alterations to the example above: change /dev/hda3 to /dev/hda1 (the / filesystem), /mnt/src/linux to /mnt, and if=zImage to if=vmlinuz. The note explaining how to derive /mnt/src/linux may be ignored.

Using LILO with big drives (more than 1024 cylinders) can cause problems. See the LILO mini-HOWTO or documentation for help on that.

7.6 It says 'warning: bdflush not running'

This can be a severe problem. Starting with a kernel release after 1.0 (around 20 Apr 1994), a program called 'update' which periodically flushes out the filesystem buffers, was upgraded/replaced. Get the sources to 'bdflush' (you should find it where you got your kernel source), and install it (you probably want to run your system under the old kernel while doing this). It installs itself as 'update' and after a reboot, the new kernel should no longer complain.

7.7 It says stuff about undefined symbols and does not compile

You probably have an ELF compiler (gcc 2.6.3 and up) and the 1.2.x (or earlier) kernel source. The usual fix is to add these three lines to the top of arch/i386/Makefile:

```
AS=/usr/i486-linuxaout/bin/as
LD=/usr/i486-linuxaout/bin/ld -m i386linux
CC=gcc -b i486-linuxaout -D__KERNEL__ -I$(TOPDIR)/include
```

This will compile a 1.2.x kernel with the a.out libraries.

7.8 I can't get my IDE/ATAPI CD-ROM drive to work

Strangely enough, lots of people cannot get their ATAPI drives working, probably because there are a number of things that can go wrong.

If your CD-ROM drive is the only device on a particular IDE interface, it must be jumpered as "master" or "single." Supposedly, this is the most common error.

Creative Labs (for one) has put IDE interfaces on their sound cards now. However, this leads to the interesting problem that while some people only have one interface to being with, many have two IDE interfaces built-in to their motherboards (at IRQ15, usually), so a common practice is to make the soundblaster interface a third IDE port (IRQ11, or so I'm told).

This causes problems with linux in that versions 1.2.x don't support a third IDE interface (there is support in starting somewhere in the 1.3.x series but that's development, remember, and it doesn't auto-probe). To get around this, you have a few choices.

If you have a second IDE port already, chances are that you are not using it or it doesn't already have two devices on it. Take the ATAPI drive off the sound card and put it on the second interface. You can then disable the sound card's interface, which saves an IRQ anyway.

If you don't have a second interface, jumper the sound card's interface (not the sound card's sound part) as IRQ15, the second interface. It should work.

If for some reason it absolutely has to be on a so-called "third" interface, or there are other problems, get a 1.3.x kernel (1.3.57 has it, for example), and read over `drivers/block/README.ide`. There is much more information here.

7.9 It says weird things about obsolete routing requests

Get new versions of the `route` program and any other programs which do route manipulation. `/usr/include/linux/route.h` (which is actually a file in `/usr/src/linux`) has changed.

7.10 Firewalling not working in 1.2.0

Upgrade to at least version 1.2.1.

7.11 "Not a compressed kernel Image file"

Don't use the `vmlinux` file created in `/usr/src/linux` as your boot image; `[..]/arch/i386/boot/zImage` is the right one.

7.12 Problems with console terminal after upgrade to 1.3.x

Change the word `dumb` to `linux` in the console termcap entry in `/etc/termcap`. You may also have to make a terminfo entry.

7.13 Can't seem to compile things after kernel upgrade

The linux kernel source includes a number of include files (the things that end with `.h`) which are referenced by the standard ones in `/usr/include`. They are typically referenced like this (where `xyzzy.h` would be something in `/usr/include/linux`):

```
#include <linux/xyzzy.h>
```

Normally, there is a link called `linux` in `/usr/include` to the `include/linux` directory of your kernel source (`/usr/src/linux/include/linux` in the typical system). If this link is not there, or points to the wrong place, most things will not compile at all. If you decided that the kernel source was taking too much room on the disk and deleted it, this will obviously be a problem. Another way it might go wrong is with file permissions; if your `root` has a umask which doesn't allow other users to see its files by default, and you extracted the kernel source without the `p` (preserve filemodes) option, those users also won't be able to use the C compiler. Although you could use the `chmod` command to fix this, it is probably easier to re-extract the include files. You can do this the same way you did the whole source at the beginning, only with an additional argument:

```
blah# tar zxvpf linux.x.y.z.tar.gz linux/include
```

Note: "make config" will recreate the /usr/src/linux link if it isn't there.

7.14 Increasing limits

The following few *example* commands may be helpful to those wondering how to increase certain soft limits imposed by the kernel:

```
echo 4096 > /proc/sys/kernel/file-max
echo 12288 > /proc/sys/kernel/inode-max
echo 300 400 500 > /proc/sys/vm/freepages
```

8 Note for upgrade to version 2.0.x

Kernel version 2.0.x introduced quite a bit of changes for kernel installation. The file Documentation/Changes in the 2.0.x source tree contains information that you should know when upgrading to version 2.0.x. You will most likely need to upgrade several key packages, such as gcc, libc, and SysVInit, and perhaps alter some system files, so expect this. Don't panic, though.

9 Modules

Loadable kernel modules can save memory and ease configuration. The scope of modules has grown to include filesystems, ethernet card drivers, tape drivers, printer drivers, and more.

9.1 Installing the module utilities

The module utilities are available from wherever you got your kernel source as modules-x.y.z.tar.gz; choose the highest patchlevel x.y.z that is equal to or below that of your current kernel. Unpack it with 'tar zxvf modules-x.y.z.tar.gz', cd to the directory it creates (modules-x.y.z), look over the README, and carry out its installation instructions (which is usually something simple, such as make install). You should now have the programs insmod, rmmod, ksyms, lsmod, genksyms, modprobe, and depmod in /sbin. If you wish, test out the utilities with the "hw" example driver in insmod; look over the INSTALL file in that subdirectory for details.

insmod inserts a module into the running kernel. Modules usually have a .o extension; the example driver mentioned above is called drv_hello.o, so to insert this, one would say 'insmod drv_hello.o'. To see the modules that the kernel is currently using, use lsmod. The output looks like this:

```
blah# lsmod
Module:        #pages:  Used by:
drv_hello         1
```

'drv_hello' is the name of the module, it uses one page (4k) of memory, and no other kernel modules depend on it at the moment. To remove this module, use 'rmmod drv_hello'. Note that rmmod wants a *module name*, not a filename; you get this from lsmod's listing. The other module utilities' purposes are documented in their manual pages.

9.2 Modules distributed with the kernel

As of version 2.0.30, most of everything is available as a loadable modules. To use them, first make sure that you don't configure them into the regular kernel; that is, don't say y to it during 'make config'. Compile a new kernel and reboot with it. Then, cd to /usr/src/linux again, and do a 'make modules'. This compiles all of the modules which you did not specify in the kernel configuration, and places links to them in /usr/src/linux/modules. You can use them straight from that directory or execute 'make modules_install', which installs them in /lib/modules/x.y.z, where x.y.z is the kernel release.

This can be especially handy with filesystems. You may not use the minix or msdos filesystems frequently. For example, if I encountered an msdos (shudder) floppy, I would insmod /usr/src/linux/modules/msdos.o, and then rmmod msdos when finished. This procedure saves about 50k of RAM in the kernel during normal operation. A small note is in order for the minix filesystem: you should *always* configure it directly into the kernel for use in "rescue" disks.

10 Other configuration options

This section contains descriptions of selected kernel configuration options (in make config) which are not listed in the configuration section. Most device drivers are not listed here.

10.1 General setup

Normal floppy disk support - is exactly that. You may wish to read over the file drivers/block/README.fd; this is especially important for IBM Thinkpad users.

XT harddisk support - if you want to use that 8 bit XT controller collecting dust in the corner.

PCI bios support - if you have PCI, you may want to give this a shot; be careful, though, as some old PCI motherboards could crash with this option. More information about the PCI bus under linux is found in the PCI-HOWTO.

Kernel support for ELF binaries - ELF is an effort to allow binaries to span architectures and operating systems; linux seems is headed in that direction and so you most likely want this.

Set version information on all symbols for modules - in the past, kernel modules were recompiled along with every new kernel. If you say y, it will be possible to use modules compiled under a different patchlevel. Read README.modules for more details.

10.2 Networking options

Networking options are described in the NET-3-HOWTO (or NET-something-HOWTO).

11 Tips and tricks

11.1 Redirecting output of the make or patch commands

If you would like logs of what those 'make' or 'patch' commands did, you can redirect output to a file. First, find out what shell you're running: 'grep root /etc/passwd' and look for something like '/bin/csh'.

If you use sh or bash,

```
(command) 2>&1 | tee (output file)
```

will place a copy of (command)'s output in the file '(output file)'.

For csh or tcsh, use

```
(command) |& tee (output file)
```

For rc (Note: you probably do not use rc) it's

```
(command) >[2=1] | tee (output file)
```

11.2 Conditional kernel install

Other than using floppy disks, there are several methods of testing out a new kernel without touching the old one. Unlike many other Unix flavors, LILO has the ability to boot a kernel from anywhere on the disk (if you have a large (500 MB or above) disk, please read over the LILO documentation on how this may cause problems). So, if you add something similar to

```
image = /usr/src/linux/arch/i386/boot/zImage
    label = new_kernel
```

to the end of your LILO configuration file, you can choose to run a newly compiled kernel without touching your old /vmlinuz (after running lilo, of course). The easiest way to tell LILO to boot a new kernel is to press the shift key at bootup time (when it says LILO on the screen, and nothing else), which gives you a prompt. At this point, you can enter 'new_kernel' to boot the new kernel.

If you wish to keep several different kernel source trees on your system at the same time (this can take up a *lot* of disk space; be careful), the most common way is to name them /usr/src/linux-x.y.z, where x.y.z is the kernel version. You can then "select" a source tree with a symbolic link; for example, 'ln -sf linux-1.2.2 /usr/src/linux' would make the 1.2.2 tree current. Before creating a symbolic link like this, make certain that the last argument to ln is not a real directory (old symbolic links are fine); the result will not be what you expect.

11.3 Kernel updates

Russell Nelson (nelson@crynwr.com) summarizes the changes in new kernel releases. These are short, and you might like to look at them before an upgrade. They are available with anonymous ftp from ftp.emlist.com in pub/kchanges or through the URL

```
http://www.crynwr.com/kchanges
```

12 Other relevant HOWTOs that might be useful

- Sound-HOWTO: sound cards and utilities
- SCSI-HOWTO: all about SCSI controllers and devices
- NET-2-HOWTO: networking
- PPP-HOWTO: PPP networking in particular

- PCMCIA-HOWTO: about the drivers for your notebook
- ELF-HOWTO: ELF: what it is, converting..
- Hardware-HOWTO: overview of supported hardware
- Module-HOWTO: more on kernel modules
- Kerneld mini-HOWTO: about kerneld
- BogoMips mini-HOWTO: in case you were wondering

13   Misc

13.1   Author

The author and maintainer of the Linux Kernel-HOWTO is Brian Ward (`bri@blah.math.tu-graz.ac.at`). Please send me any comments, additions, corrections (Corrections are, in particular, the most important to me.).

You can take a look at my 'home page' at one of these URLs:

```
http://www.math.psu.edu/ward/
http://blah.math.tu-graz.ac.at/~bri/
```

Even though I try to be attentive as possible with mail, please remember that I get a *lot* of it every day, so it may take a little time to get back to you. Especially when emailing me with a question, please try extra hard to be clear and detailed in your message. If you're writing about non-working hardware (or something like that), I need to know what your hardware configureation is. If you report an error, don't just say "I tried this but it gave an error;" I need to know what the error was. I would also like to know what versions of the kernel, gcc, and libc you're using. If you just tell me you're using this-or-that distribution, it won't tell me much at all. I don't care if you ask simple questions; remember, if you don't ask, you may never get an answer! I'd like to thank everyone who has given me feedback.

If you mailed me and did not get an answer within a resonable amount of time (three weeks or more), then chances are that I accidentally deleted your message or something (sorry). Please try again.

I get a lot of mail about thing which are actually hardware problems or issues. That's OK, but please try to keep in mind that I'm not familiar with all of the hardware in the world and I don't know how helpful I can be; I personally use machines with IDE and SCSI disks, SCSI CD-ROMs, 3Com and WD ethernet cards, serial mice, motherboards with PCI, NCR 810 SCSI controllers, AMD 386DX40 w/Cyrix copr., AMD 5x86, AMD 486DX4, and Intel 486DX4 processors (This is an overview of what I use and am familiar with, certainly not a recommendation, but if you want that, you're more than welcome to ask :-)).

Version -0.1 was written on October 3, 1994. This document is available in SGML, PostScript, TeX, roff, and plain-text formats.

13.2   To do

The "Tips and tricks" section is a little small. I hope to expand on it with suggestions from others.

So is "Additional packages."

More debugging/crash recovery info needed.

13.3   Contributions

A small part of Linus' README (kernel hacking options) is inclusive. (Thanks, Linus!)

uc@brian.lunetix.de (Ulrich Callmeier): patch -s and xargs.

quinlan@yggdrasil.com (Daniel Quinlan): corrections and additions in many sections.

nat@nat@nataa.fr.eu.org (Nat Makarevitch): mrproper, tar -p, many other things

boldt@math.ucsb.edu (Axel Boldt): collected descriptions of kernel configuration options on the net; then provided me with the list

lembark@wrkhors.psyber.com (Steve Lembark): multiple boot suggestion

kbriggs@earwax.pd.uwa.edu.au (Keith Briggs): some corrections and suggestions

rmcguire@freenet.columbus.oh.us (Ryan McGuire): makeables additions

dumas@excalibur.ibp.fr (Eric Dumas): French translation

simazaki@ab11.yamanashi.ac.jp (Yasutada Shimazaki): Japanese translation

jjamor@lml.ls.fi.upm.es (Juan Jose Amor Iglesias): Spanish translation

mva@sbbs.se (Martin Wahlen): Swedish translation

jzp1218@stud.u-szeged.hu (Zoltan Vamosi): Hungarian translation

bart@mat.uni.torun.pl (Bartosz Maruszewski): Polish translation

donahue@tiber.nist.gov (Michael J Donahue): typos, winner of the "sliced bread competition"

rms@gnu.ai.mit.edu (Richard Stallman): "free" documentation concept/distribution notice

dak@Pool.Informatik.RWTH-Aachen.DE (David Kastrup): NFS thing

esr@snark.thyrsus.com (Eric Raymond): various tidbits

The people who have sent me mail with questions and problems have also been quite helpful.

13.4   Copyright notice, License, and all that stuff

Large Disk HOWTO

Andries Brouwer, aeb@cwi.nl   v1.0, 26 July 1996

All about disk geometry and the 1024 cylinder limit for disks.

1   The problem

Suppose you have a disk with more than 1024 cylinders. Suppose moreover that you have an operating system that uses the BIOS. Then you have a problem, because the usual INT13 BIOS interface to disk I/O uses a 10-bit field for the cylinder on which the I/O is done, so that cylinders 1024 and past are inaccessible.

Fortunately, Linux does not use the BIOS, so there is no problem.

Well, except for two things:

(1) When you boot your system, Linux isn't running yet and cannot save you from BIOS problems. This has some consequences for LILO and similar boot loaders.

(2) It is necessary for all operating systems that use one disk to agree on where the partitions are. In other words, if you use both Linux and, say, DOS on one disk, then both must interpret the partition table in the same way. This has some consequences for the Linux kernel and for fdisk.

Below a rather detailed description of all relevant details. Note that I used kernel version 2.0.8 source as a reference. Other versions may differ a bit.

2   Booting

When the system is booted, the BIOS reads sector 0 (known as the MBR - the Master Boot Record) from the first disk (or from floppy), and jumps to the code found there - usually some bootstrap loader. These small bootstrap programs found there typically have no own disk drivers and use BIOS services. This means that a Linux kernel can only be booted when it is entirely located within the first 1024 cylinders.

This problem is very easily solved: make sure that the kernel (and perhaps other files used during bootup, such as LILO map files) are located on a partition that is entirely contained in the first 1024 cylinders of a disk that the BIOS can access - probably this means the first or second disk.

Another point is that the boot loader and the BIOS must agree as to the disk geometry. It may help to give LILO the 'linear' option. More details below.

3   Disk geometry and partitions

If you have several operating systems on your disks, then each uses one or more disk partitions. A disagreement on where these partitions are may have catastrophic consequences.

The MBR contains a *partition table* describing where the (primary) partitions are. There are 4 table entries, for 4 primary partitions, and each looks like

```
struct partition {
        char active;    /* 0x80: bootable, 0: not bootable */
```

```
        char begin[3];   /* CHS for first sector */
        char type;
        char end[3];     /* CHS for last sector */
        int start;       /* 32 bit sector number (counting from 0) */
        int length;      /* 32 bit number of sectors */
    };
```

(where CHS stands for Cylinder/Head/Sector).

Thus, this information is redundant: the location of a partition is given both by the 24-bit **begin** and **end** fields, and by the 32-bit **start** and **length** fields.

Linux only uses the **start** and **length** fields, and can therefore handle partitions of not more than 2^{32} sectors, that is, partitions of at most 2 TB. That is two hundred times larger than the disks available today, so maybe it will be enough for the next ten years or so.

Unfortunately, the BIOS INT13 call uses CHS coded in three bytes, with 10 bits for the cylinder number, 8 bits for the head number, and 6 bits for the track sector number. Possible cylinder numbers are 0-1023, possible head numbers are 0-255, and possible track sector numbers are 1-63 (yes, sectors on a track are counted from 1, not 0). With these 24 bits one can address 8455716864 bytes (7.875 GB), two hundred times larger than the disks available in 1983.

Even more unfortunately, the standard IDE interface allows 256 sectors/track, 65536 cylinders and 16 heads. This in itself allows access to $2^{37} = 137438953472$ bytes (128 GB), but combined with the BIOS restriction to 63 sectors and 1024 cylinders only 528482304 bytes (504 MB) remain addressable.

This is not enough for present-day disks, and people resort to all kinds of trickery, both in hardware and in software.

4 Translation and Disk Managers

Nobody is interested in what the 'real' geometry of a disk is. Indeed, the number of sectors per track often is variable - there are more sectors per track close to the outer rim of the disk - so there is no 'real' number of sectors per track. For the user it is best to regard a disk as just a linear array of sectors numbered 0, 1, ..., and leave it to the controller to find out where a given sector lives on the disk.

This linear numbering is known as LBA. The linear address belonging to (c,h,s) for a disk with geometry (C,H,S) is $c*H*S + h*S + (s-1)$. All SCSI controllers speak LBA, and some IDE controllers do.

If the BIOS converts the 24-bit (c,h,s) to LBA and feeds that to a controller that understands LBA, then again 7.875 GB is addressable. Not enough for all disks, but still an improvement. Note that here CHS, as used by the BIOS, no longer has any relation to 'reality'.

Something similar works when the controller doesn't speak LBA but the BIOS knows about translation. (In the setup this is often indicated as 'Large'.) Now the BIOS will present a geometry (C',H',S') to the operating system, and use (C,H,S) while talking to the disk controller. Usually S = S', C' = C/N and H' = H*N, where N is the smallest power of two that will ensure C' <= 1024 (so that least capacity is wasted by the rounding down in C' = C/N). Again, this allows access to up to 7.875 GB.

If a BIOS does not know about 'Large' or 'LBA', then there are software solutions around. Disk Managers like OnTrack or EZ-Drive replace the BIOS disk handling routines by their own. Often this is accomplished by having the disk manager code live in the MBR and subsequent sectors (OnTrack calls this code DDO: Dynamic Drive Overlay), so that it is booted before any other operating system. That is why one may have problems when booting from a floppy when a Disk Manager has been installed.

The effect is more or less the same as with a translating BIOS - but especially when running several different operating systems on the same disk, disk managers can cause a lot of trouble.

Linux does support OnTrack Disk Manager since version 1.3.14, and EZ-Drive since version 1.3.29. Some more details are given below.

5 Kernel disk translation for IDE disks

If the Linux kernel detects the presence of some disk manager on an IDE disk, it will try to remap the disk in the same way this disk manager would have done, so that Linux sees the same disk partitioning as for example DOS with OnTrack or EZ-Drive. However, NO remapping is done when a geometry was specified on the command line - so a 'hd=$cyls,heads,secs$' command line option might well kill compatibility with a disk manager.

The remapping is done by trying 4, 8, 16, 32, 64, 128, 255 heads (keeping H*C constant) until either C <= 1024 or H = 255.

The details are as follows - subsection headers are the strings appearing in the corresponding boot messages. Here and everywhere else in this text partition types are given in hexadecimal.

5.1 EZD

EZ-Drive is detected by the fact that the first primary partition has type 55. The geometry is remapped as described above, and the partition table from sector 0 is discarded - instead the partition table is read from sector 1. Disk block numbers are not changed, but writes to sector 0 are redirected to sector 1. This behaviour can be changed by recompiling the kernel with `#define FAKE_FDISK_FOR_EZDRIVE 0` in *ide.c*.

5.2 DM6:DDO

OnTrack DiskManager (on the first disk) is detected by the fact that the first primary partition has type 54. The geometry is remapped as described above and the entire disk is shifted by 63 sectors (so that the old sector 63 becomes sector 0). Afterwards a new MBR (with partition table) is read from the new sector 0. Of course this shift is to make room for the DDO - that is why there is no shift on other disks.

5.3 DM6:AUX

OnTrack DiskManager (on other disks) is detected by the fact that the first primary partition has type 51 or 53. The geometry is remapped as described above.

5.4 DM6:MBR

An older version of OnTrack DiskManager is detected not by partition type, but by signature. (Test whether the offset found in bytes 2 and 3 of the MBR is not more than 430, and the short found at this offset equals 0x55AA, and is followed by an odd byte.) Again the geometry is remapped as above.

5.5   PTBL

Finally, there is a test that tries to deduce a translation from the start and end values of the primary partitions: If some partition has start and end cylinder less than 256, and start and end sector number 1 and 63, respectively, and end heads 31, 63 or 127, then, since it is customary to end partitions on a cylinder boundary, and since moreover the IDE interface uses at most 16 heads, it is conjectured that a BIOS translation is active, and the geometry is remapped to use 32, 64 or 128 heads, respectively. (Maybe there is a flaw here, and *genhd.c* should not have tested the high order two bits of the cylinder number?) However, no remapping is done when the current idea of the geometry already has 63 sectors per track and at least as many heads (since this probably means that a remapping was done already).

6   Consequences

What does all of this mean? For Linux users only one thing: that they must make sure that LILO and fdisk use the right geometry where 'right' is defined for fdisk as the geometry used by the other operating systems on the same disk, and for LILO as the geometry that will enable successful interaction with the BIOS at boot time. (Usually these two coincide.)

How does fdisk know about the geometry? It asks the kernel, using the HDIO_GETGEO ioctl. But the user can override the geometry interactively or on the command line.

How does LILO know about the geometry? It asks the kernel, using the HDIO_GETGEO ioctl. But the user can override the geometry using the 'disk=' option. One may also give the linear option to LILO, and it will store LBA addresses instead of CHS addresses in its map file, and find out of the geometry to use at boot time (by using INT 13 Function 8 to ask for the drive geometry).

How does the kernel know what to answer? Well, first of all, the user may have specified an explicit geometry with a 'hd=*cyls*,*heads*,*secs*' command line option. And otherwise the kernel will ask the hardware.

6.1   IDE details

Let me elaborate. The IDE driver has four sources for information about the geometry. The first (G_user) is the one specified by the user on the command line. The second (G_bios) is the BIOS Fixed Disk Parameter Table (for first and second disk only) that is read on system startup, before the switch to 32-bit mode. The third (G_phys) and fourth (G_log) are returned by the IDE controller as a response to the IDENTIFY command - they are the 'physical' and 'current logical' geometries.

On the other hand, the driver needs two values for the geometry: on the one hand G_fdisk, returned by a HDIO_GETGEO ioctl, and on the other hand G_used, which is actually used for doing I/O. Both G_fdisk and G_used are initialized to G_user if given, to G_bios when this information is present according to CMOS, and to to G_phys otherwise. If G_log looks reasonable then G_used is set to that. Otherwise, if G_used is unreasonable and G_phys looks reasonable then G_used is set to G_phys. Here 'reasonable' means that the number of heads is in the range 1-16.

To say this in other words: the command line overrides the BIOS, and will determine what fdisk sees, but if it specifies a translated geometry (with more than 16 heads), then for kernel I/O it will be overridden by output of the IDENTIFY command.

6.2   SCSI details

The situation for SCSI is slightly different, as the SCSI commands already use logical block numbers, so a 'geometry' is entirely irrelevant for actual I/O. However, the format of the partition table is still the same, so fdisk has to invent some geometry, and also uses HDIO_GETGEO here - indeed, fdisk does not distinguish between IDE and SCSI disks. As one can see from the detailed description below, the various drivers each invent a somewhat different geometry. Indeed, one big mess.

If you are not using DOS or so, then avoid all extended translation settings, and just use 64 heads, 32 sectors per track (for a nice, convenient 1 MB per cylinder), if possible, so that no problems arise when you move the disk from one controller to another. Some SCSI disk drivers (aha152x, pas16, ppa, qlogicfas, qlogicisp) are so nervous about DOS compatibility that they will not allow a Linux-only system to use more than about 8 GB. This is a bug.

What is the real geometry? The easiest answer is that there is no such thing. And if there were, you wouldn't want to know, and certainly NEVER, EVER tell fdisk or LILO or the kernel about it. It is strictly a business between the SCSI controller and the disk. Let me repeat that: only silly people tell fdisk/LILO/kernel about the true SCSI disk geometry.

But if you are curious and insist, you might ask the disk itself. There is the important command READ CAPACITY that will give the total size of the disk, and there is the MODE SENSE command, that in the Rigid Disk Drive Geometry Page (page 04) gives the number of cylinders and heads (this is information that cannot be changed), and in the Format Page (page 03) gives the number of bytes per sector, and sectors per track. This latter number is typically dependent upon the notch, and the number of sectors per track varies - the outer tracks have more sectors than the inner tracks. The Linux program scsiinfo will give this information. There are many details and complications, and it is clear that nobody (probably not even the operating system) wants to use this information. Moreover, as long as we are only concerned about fdisk and LILO, one typically gets answers like C/H/S=4476/27/171 - values that cannot be used by fdisk because the partition table reserves only 10 resp. 8 resp. 6 bits for C/H/S.

Then where does the kernel HDIO_GETGEO get its information from? Well, either from the SCSI controller, or by making an educated guess. Some drivers seem to think that we want to know 'reality', but of course we only want to know what the DOS or OS/2 FDISK (or Adaptec AFDISK, etc) will use.

Note that Linux fdisk needs the numbers H and S of heads and sectors per track to convert LBA sector numbers into c/h/s addresses, but the number C of cylinders does not play a role in this conversion. Some drivers use $(C,H,S) = (1023,255,63)$ to signal that the drive capacity is at least $1023*255*63$ sectors. This is unfortunate, since it does not reveal the actual size, and will limit the users of most fdisk versions to about 8 GB of their disks - a real limitation in these days.

In the description below, M denotes the total disk capacity, and C, H, S the number of cylinders, heads and sectors per track. It suffices to give H, S if we regard C as defined by M / (H*S).

By default, H=64, S=32.

aha1740, dtc, g_NCR5380, t128, wd7000:

H=64, S=32.

aha152x, pas16, ppa, qlogicfas, qlogicisp:

H=64, S=32 unless C > 1024, in which case H=255, S=63, C = min(1023, M/(H*S)). (Thus C is truncated, and H*S*C is not an approximation to the disk capacity M. This will confuse most versions of fdisk.) The *ppa.c* code uses M+1 instead of M and says that due to a bug in *sd.c* M is off by 1.

advansys:

H=64, S=32 unless C > 1024 and moreover the '> 1 GB' option in the BIOS is enabled, in which case H=255, S=63.

aha1542:

Ask the controller which of two possible translation schemes is in use, and use either H=255, S=63 or H=64, S=32. In the former case there is a boot message "aha1542.c: Using extended bios translation".

aic7xxx:

H=64, S=32 unless C > 1024, and moreover either the "extended" boot parameter was given, or the 'extended' bit was set in the SEEPROM or BIOS, in which case H=255, S=63.

buslogic:

H=64, S=32 unless C >= 1024, and moreover extended translation was enabled on the controller, in which case if M < 2^22 then H=128, S=32; otherwise H=255, S=63. However, after making this choice for (C,H,S), the partition table is read, and if for one of the three possibilities (H,S) = (64,32), (128,32), (255,63) the value endH=H-1 is seen somewhere then that pair (H,S) is used, and a boot message is printed "Adopting Geometry from Partition Table".

fdomain:

Find the geometry information in the BIOS Drive Parameter Table, or read the partition table and use H=endH+1, S=endS for the first partition, provided it is nonempty, or use H=64, S=32 for M < 2^21 (1 GB), H=128, S=63 for M < 63*2^17 (3.9 GB) and H=255, S=63 otherwise.

in2000:

Use the first of (H,S) = (64,32), (64,63), (128,63), (255,63) that will make C <= 1024. In the last case, truncate C at 1023.

seagate:

Read C,H,S from the disk. (Horrors!) If C or S is too large, then put S=17, H=2 and double H until C <= 1024. This means that H will be set to 0 if M > 128*1024*17 (1.1 GB). This is a bug.

ultrastor and u14_34f:

One of three mappings ((H,S) = (16,63), (64,32), (64,63)) is used depending on the controller mapping mode.

If the driver does not specify the geometry, we fall back on an educated guess using the partition table, or using the total disk capacity.

Look at the partition table. Since by convention partitions end on a cylinder boundary, we can, given end = (endC,endH,endS) for any partition, just put H = endH+1 and S = endS. (Recall that sectors are counted from 1.) More precisely, the following is done. If there is a nonempty partition, pick the partition with the largest beginC. For that partition, look at end+1, computed both by adding start and length and by assuming that this partition ends on a cylinder boundary. If both values agree, or if endC = 1023 and start+length is an integral multiple of (endH+1)*endS, then assume that this partition really was aligned on a cylinder boundary, and put H = endH+1 and S = endS. If this fails, either because there are no partitions, or because they have strange sizes, then look only at the disk capacity M. Algorithm: put H = M/(62*1024) (rounded up), S = M/(1024*H) (rounded up), C = M/(H*S) (rounded down). This has the effect of producing a (C,H,S) with C at most 1024 and S at most 62.

Linux Hardware Compatibility HOWTO

Patrick Reijnen, <*patrickr@bart.nl* <mailto:patrickr@bart.nl>>   v98.1, 7 February 1998

This document lists most of the hardware supported by Linux and helps you locate any necessary drivers.

Contents

1 Introduction

1.1 Welcome

Welcome to the Linux Hardware Compatibility HOWTO. This document lists most of the hardware components (not computers with components build in) supported by Linux, so reading through this document you can choose the components for your own Linux computer. As the list of components supported by Linux is growing rapidly, this document will never be complete. So, when components are not mentioned in this HOWTO, the only reason will be that I don't know they are supported. I simply have not found support for the component and/or nobody has told me about support.

Subsections titled Others list hardware with alpha or beta drivers in varying degrees of usability or other drivers that aren't included in standard kernels. Note that some drivers only exist in alpha kernels, so if you see something listed as supported but isn't in your version of the Linux kernel, upgrade.

The latest version of this document can be found on <http://users.bart.nl/patrickr/hardware-howto/ Hardware-HOWTO.html>, SunSite and all the usual mirror sites. Translations of this and other Linux HOWTO's can be found at <http://sunsite.unc.edu/pub/Linux/docs/HOWTO/translations> and <ftp: //sunsite.unc.edu/pub/Linux/docs/HOWTO/translations>.

If you know of any Linux hardware (in)compatibilities not listed here please let me know, just send mail.

Still need some help selecting components after reading this document? Check the "Build Your Own PC" site at <http://www.verinet.com/pc/>.

1.2   Copyright

Copyright 1997, 1998 Patrick Reijnen

This HOWTO is free documentation; you can redistribute it and/or modify it under the terms of the GNU General Public License as published by the Free software Foundation; either version 2 of the license, or (at your option) any later version.

This document is distributed in the hope that it will be useful, but without any warranty; without even the implied warranty of merchantability or fitness for a particular purpose. See the GNU General Public License for more details. You can obtain a copy of the GNU General Public License by writing to the Free Software Foundation,, Inc., 675 Mass Ave, Cambridge, MA 02139, USA.

If you use this or any other Linux HOWTO's in a commercial distribution, it would be nice to send the authors a complimentary copy of your product.

1.3   System architectures

This document only deals with Linux for Intel platforms, for other platforms check the following:

- ARM Linux
  <http://www.arm.uk.linux.org/rmk92/armlinux.html>

- Linux/68k

- Linux/8086
  <http://www.linux.org.uk/Linux8086.html>

- Linux/Alpha
  <http://www.azstarnet.com/axplinux/>

- Linux/MIPS
  <http://www.fnet.fr/linux-mips/>

- Linux/PowerPC
  <http://www.linuxppc.org/>

- Linux for Acorn
  <http://www.ph.kcl.ac.uk/amb/linux.html>

- Linux for PowerMac
  <http://ftp.sunet.se/pub/os/Linux/mklinux/mkarchive/info/index.html>

2 Computers/Motherboards/BIOS

ISA, VLB, EISA, and PCI buses are all supported.

PS/2 and Microchannel (MCA) is supported in the standard kernel 2.0.7. There is support for MCA in kernel 2.1.16 and newer, but this code is still a little buggy. For more information you can always look at the Micro Channel Linux Home Page (<http://glycerine.itsmm.uni.edu/mca/>)

2.1 Specific systems

- IBM PS/2 MCA systems
  <ftp://ftp.dcrl.nd.edu/pub/misc/linux/>

Many new PCI boards are causing a couple of failure messages during boot time when "Probing PCI Hardware". The procedure presents the folowing message

```
Warning : Unknown PCI device (8086:7100).  Please read include/linux/pci.h
```

It tells you to read the pci.h file. From this file is the following quote

```
        PROCEDURE TO REPORT NEW PCI DEVICES
We are trying to collect information on new PCI devices, using
the standard PCI identification procedure. If some warning is
displayed at boot time, please report
        - /proc/pci
        - your exact hardware description. Try to find out
          which device is unknown. It may be you mainboard chipset.
          PCI-CPU bridge or PCI-ISA bridge.
        - If you can't find the actual information in your hardware
          booklet, try to read the references of the chip on the board.
        - Send all that to linux-pcisupport@cao-vlsi.ibp.fr,
          and I'll add your device to the list as soon as possible

BEFORE you send a mail, please check the latest linux releases
to be sure it has not been recently added.

        Thanks
                Frederic Potter.
```

Normally spoken you motherboard and the unknown PCI devices will function correctly.

2.2 Unsupported

- Supermicro P5MMA with BIOS versions 1.36, 1.37 and 1.4. Linux will not boot on this motherboard. A new (beta) release of the BIOS which makes Linux boot, is available at <ftp.supermicro.com/mma9051.zip>
- Supermicro P5MMA98. Linux will not boot on this motherboard. A new (beta) release of the BIOS which makes Linux boot, is available at <ftp.supermicro.com/a98905.zip>?

3   Laptops

For more information about Linux and laptops, the following site is a good starting point.

- Linux Laptop Homepage
  <http://www.cs.utexas.edu/users/kharker/linux-laptop/>

Other information related to laptops can be found at the following sites:

- Avanced Power Management
  <ftp://ftp.cs.unc.edu/pub/users/faith/linux/>
- Notebook battery status
  <ftp://sunsite.unc.edu/pub/Linux/system/power/>
- non-blinking cursor
  <ftp://sunsite.unc.edu/pub/Linux/kernel/patches/console/noblink-1.7.tar.gz>
- other general info
  <ftp://tsx-11.mit.edu/pub/linux/packages/laptops/>

3.1   Specific laptops

- Compaq Concerto (pen driver)
  <http://www.cs.nmsu.edu/pfeiffer/>
- Compaq Contura Aero
  <http://domen.uninett.no/hta/linux/aero-faq.html>
- IBM ThinkPad
  <http://peipa.essex.ac.uk/tp-linux/tp-linux.html>

- NEC Versa M and P
  <http://www.santafe.edu:80/nelson/versa-linux/>
- Tadpole P1000
  <http://www.tadpole.com/Support/linux.html>
- Tadpole P1000 (another one)

- TI TravelMate 4000M
  <ftp://ftp.biomath.jussieu.fr/pub/linux/TM4000M-mini-HOWTO.txt.Z>
- TI TravelMate 5100

- Toshiba Satellite Pro 400CDT
  <http://terra.mpikg-teltow.mpg.de/burger/T400CDT-Linux.html>

3.2   PCMCIA

- PCMCIA
  <http://hyper.stanford.edu/HyperNews/get/pcmcia/home.html>

PCMCIA drivers currently support all common PCMCIA controllers, including Databook TCIC/2, Intel i82365SL, Cirrus PD67xx, and Vadem VG-468 chipsets. Motorola 6AHC05GA controller used in some Hyundai laptops is not supported. See Appendix B for a list of supported PCMCIA cards.

4   CPU/FPU

Intel/AMD/Cyrix 386SX/DX/SL/DXL/SLC, 486SX/DX/SL/SX2/DX2/DX4 are supported. Intel Pentium, Pentium Pro and Pentium II (basically it's a Pentium Pro with MMX) also work. AMD K5 and K6 work good, although older versions of K6 should be avoided as they are buggy.

Linux has built-in FPU emulation if you don't have a math coprocessor.

Experimental SMP (multiple CPU) support is included in kernel 1.3.31 and newer. Check the Linux/SMP Project page for details and updates.

- Linux/SMP Project
  <http://www.linux.org.uk/SMP/title.html>

A few very early AMD 486DX's may hang in some special situations. All current chips should be okay and getting a chip swap for old CPU's should not be a problem.

ULSI Math*Co series has a bug in the FSAVE and FRSTOR instructions that causes problems with all protected mode operating systems. Some older IIT and Cyrix chips may also have this problem.

There are problems with TLB flushing in UMC U5S chips in very old kernels. (1.1.x)

- enable cache on Cyrix processors
  <ftp://sunsite.unc.edu/pub/Linux/kernel/patches/CxPatch030.tar.z>
- Cyrix software cache control
  <ftp://sunsite.unc.edu/pub/Linux/kernel/patches/linux.cxpatch>
- Cyrix 5x86 CPU register settings
  <ftp://sunsite.unc.edu/pub/Linux/kernel/patches/cx5x86mod_1.0c.tgz>

5   Memory

All memory like DRAM, EDO and SDRAM can be used with Linux. There is one thing you have to look at: normally the kernel is not supporting more than 64 Mb of memory. When you add more than 64 Mb of memory you have to add the following line to your LILO configuration file.

```
append="mem=<number of Mb>M"
```

So, when you have 96 Mb of memory this should become

```
append="mem=96M"
```

Don't type a number higher than the number Mb you really have. This can present unpredictable crashes.

6   Video cards

Linux will work with all video cards in text mode, VGA cards not listed below probably will still work with mono VGA and/or standard VGA drivers.

If you're looking into buying a cheap video card to run X, keep in mind that accelerated cards (ATI Mach, ET4000/W32p, S3) are MUCH faster than unaccelerated or partially accelerated (Cirrus, WD) cards.

"32 bpp" is actually 24 bit color aligned on 32 bit boundaries. It does NOT mean the cards are capable of 32 bit color, they still display 24 bit color (16,777,216 colors). 24 bit packed pixels modes are not supported in XFree86, so cards that can do 24 bit modes to get higher resolutions in other OS's are not able to do this in X using XFree86. These cards include Mach32, Cirrus 542x, S3 801/805/868/968, ET4000, and others.

6.1 Diamond video cards

Most currently available Diamond cards ARE supported by the current release of XFree86. Early Diamond cards may not be officially supported by XFree86, but there are ways of getting them to work. Diamond is now actively supporting the XFree86 Project.

6.2 SVGALIB (graphics for console)

- VGA
- EGA
- ARK Logic ARK1000PV/2000PV
- ATI VGA Wonder
- ATI Mach32
- Cirrus 542x, 543x
- OAK OTI-037/67/77/87
- S3 (limited support)
- Trident TVGA8900/9000
- Tseng ET3000/ET4000/W32

6.3 XFree86 3.3.1

6.3.1 Accelerated

- ARK Logic ARK1000PV/VL, ARK2000PV/MT
- ATI Mach8
- ATI Mach32 (16 bpp supported for cards with RAMDAC ATI68875, AT&T20C49x, BT481 and 2Mb video ram)
- ATI Mach64 (16/32 bpp supported for cards with RAMDAC ATI68860, ATI68875, CH8398, STG1702, STG1703, AT&T20C408, 3D Rage II, internal, IBM RGB514)
- Chips & Technologies 64200, 64300, 65520, 65525, 65530, 65535, 65540, 65545, 65546, 65548, 65550, 65554
- Cirrus Logic 5420, 542x/5430 (16 bpp), 5434 (16/32 bpp), 5436, 544x, 546x, 5480, 62x5, 754x
- IBM 8514/A
- IBM XGA-I, XGA-II
- IIT AGX-010/014/015/016 (16 bpp)
- Matrox MGA2064W (Millennium)
- Matrox MGA1064SG (Mystique)
- Number Nine Imagine I128

- Oak OTI-087
- S3 732 (Trio32), 764 (Trio64), Trio64V+, 801, 805, 864, 866, 868, 86C325 (ViRGE), 86C375 (ViRGE/DX), 86C385 (ViRGE/GX), 86C988 (ViRGE/VX), 911, 924, 928, 964, 968
    - see Appendix A for list of supported S3 cards
- SiS 86c201, 86c202, 86c205
- Trident 9440, 96xx, Cyber938x
- Tseng ET4000/W32/W32i/W32p, ET6000
- Weitek P9000 (16/32 bpp)
    - Diamond Viper VLB/PCI
    - Orchid P9000
- Western Digital WD90C24/24A/24A2/31/33

6.3.2   Unaccelerated

- Alliance AP6422, AT24
- ATI VGA Wonder series
- Avance Logic AL2101/2228/2301/2302/2308/2401
- Cirrus Logic 6420/6440, 7555
- Compaq AVGA
- DEC 21030
- Genoa GVGA
- MCGA (320x200)
- MX MX68000/MX68010
- NCR 77C22, 77C22E, 77C22E+
- NVidia NV1
- Oak OTI-037C, OTI-067, OTI-077
- RealTek RTG3106
- SGS-Thomson STG2000
- Trident 8800CS, 8200LX, 8900x, 9000, 9000i, 9100B, 9200CXr, 9320LCD, 9400CXi, 9420, 9420DGi, 9430DGi
- Tseng ET3000, ET4000AX
- VGA (standard VGA, 4 bit, slow)
- Video 7 / Headland Technologies HT216-32
- Western Digital/Paradise PVGA1, WD90C00/10/11/30

6.3.3   Monochrome

- Hercules mono
- Hyundai HGC-1280
- Sigma LaserView PLUS
- VGA mono

6.3.4 Others

- EGA (ancient, from c. 1992)
  `<ftp://ftp.funet.fi/pub/Linux/BETA/Xega/>`

6.4 S.u.S.E. X-Server

S.u.S.E. is building a serie of X-servers based on the XFree-86 code. These X-servers support new video cards and are bug fixe releases for XFree86 X-servers. S.u.S.E is building these X-servers together with The XFree86 Project, Inc. These X-Servers will be in the next XFree86 version. These X-servers can be found at `<http://www.suse.de/index.html>`. At this moment S.u.S.E. X-Servers are available for the following video cards.

- XSuSE Elsa GLoria X-Server
    - ELSA GLoria L, GLoria L/MX, Gloria S
- Video cards with the Alliance Semiconductor AT3D (also AT25) Chip
    - Hercules Stingray 128 3D
- XSuSE NVidia X-Server (PCI and AGP support, NV1 chipset and Riva128)
    - ASUS 3Dexplorer
    - Diamond Viper 330
    - ELSA VICTORY Erazor
    - STB Velocity 128
- XSuSE Matrox. Support for Mystique, Millennium, Millennium II and Millennium II AGP
- XSuSE Trident. Support for the 9685 (including ClearTV) and the latest Cyber chipset
- XSuSE Tseng. W32, W32i ET6100 and ET6300 support.

6.5 Commercial X servers

Commercial X servers provide support for cards not supported by XFree86, and might give better performances for cards that are supported by XFree86. In general they support many more cards than XFree86, so I'll onlys list cards that aren't supported by XFree86 here. Contact the vendors directly or check the Commercial HOWTO for more info.

6.5.1 Xi Graphics, Inc

Xi Graphics, Inc `<http://www.xig.com>` (formerly known as X Inside, Inc) is selling three X server products:

- Accelerated-X Display Server
- Laptop Accelerated-X Display Server
- Multi-head Accelerated-X Display Server

Next version of this HOWTO will contain lists of video cards supported by each server.

6.5.2   Metro-X 2.3

Metro Link <*sales@metrolink.com* <mailto:sales@metrolink.com>>

I don't have much more information about Metro-X as I can't seem to view the PostScript files they sent me. Mail them directly for more info.

The S3 ViRGE video card is said not to be supported by Metro-X.

7   Controllers (hard drive)

Linux will work with standard IDE, MFM and RLL controllers. When using MFM/RLL controllers it is important to use ext2fs and the bad block checking options when formatting the disk.

Enhanced IDE (EIDE) interfaces are supported. With up to two IDE interfaces and up to four hard drives and/or CD-ROM drives. Linux will detect these EIDE interfaces:

- CMD-640
- DTC 2278D
- FGI/Holtek HT-6560B
- RZ1000
- Triton I (82371FB) (with busmaster DMA)
- Triton II (82371SB) (with busmaster DMA)

ESDI controllers that emulate the ST-506 (MFM/RLL/IDE) interface will also work. The bad block checking comment also applies to these controllers.

Generic 8 bit XT controllers also work.

Starting with pre-patch-2.0.31-3 IDE/ATAPI is provided.

Other Controllers Supported:

- Tekram D690CD IDE PCI Cache Controller (with RAID level 1 Mirroring and caching)

8   Controllers (SCSI)

It is important to pick a SCSI controller carefully. Many cheap ISA SCSI controllers are designed to drive CD-ROM's rather than anything else. Such low end SCSI controllers are no better than IDE. See the SCSI HOWTO and look at performance figures before buying a SCSI card.

8.1   Supported

- AMI Fast Disk VLB/EISA (BusLogic compatible)
- Adaptec AVA-1505/1515 (ISA) (Adaptec 152x compatible)
- Adaptec AHA-1510/152x (ISA/VLB) (AIC-6260/6360)
- Adaptec AHA-154x (ISA) (all models)
- Adaptec AHA-174x (EISA) (in enhanced mode)

- Adaptec AHA-274x (EISA) / 284x (VLB) (AIC-7770)
- Adaptec AHA 2920
- Adaptec AHA-2940U/AU/UW, 3940 (PCI) (AIC-7870) (since 1.3.6)
- Adaptec AVA1502E (ISA/VLB) (AIC-6360). Use the AHA 152x driver
- Always IN2000
- BusLogic (ISA/EISA/VLB/PCI) (all models)
- DPT PM2001, PM2012A (EATA-PIO)
- DPT Smartcache/SmartRAID Plus,III,IV families (ISA/EISA/PCI)
  Take a look at <http://www.uni-mainz.de/neuffer/scsi/dpt/>(EATA-DMA)
  Cards in these families are PM2011, PM2021, PM2041, PM3021, PM2012B, PM2022, PM2122, PM2322, PM2042, PM3122, PM3222, PM3332, PM2024, PM2124, PM2044, PM2144, PM3224, PM3334
- DTC 329x (EISA) (Adaptec 154x compatible)
- Future Domain TMC-16x0, TMC-3260 (PCI)
- Future Domain TMC-8xx, TMC-950
- ICP-Vortex PCI-SCSI Disk Array Controllers (many RAID levels supported)
  Patches for Linux 1.2.13 and 2.0.29 are available at <ftp://icp-vortex.com/download/linux/>. The controllers GDT6111RP, GDT6121RP, GDT6117RP, GDT6127RP, GDT6511RP, GDT6521RP, GDT6517RP, GDT6527RP, GDT6537RP and GDT6557RP are supported. You can also use pre-patch-2.0.31-4 to pre-patch-2.0.31-9.
- ICP-Vortex EISA-SCSI Controllers (many RAID levels supported)
  Patches for Linux 1.2.13 and 2.0.29 are available at <ftp://icp-vortex.com/download/linux/>. The controllers GDT3000B, GDT3000A, GDT3010A, GDT3020A and GDT3050A are supported. You can also use pre-patch-2.0.31-4 to pre-patch-2.0.31-9.
- Media Vision Pro Audio Spectrum 16 SCSI (ISA)
- NCR 5380 generic cards
- NCR 53c400 (Trantor T130B) (use generic NCR 5380 SCSI support)
- NCR 53c406a (Acculogic ISApport / Media Vision Premium 3D SCSI)
- NCR 53c7x0, 53c8x0 (PCI)
- Qlogic / Control Concepts SCSI/IDE (FAS408) (ISA/VLB)
- Quantum ISA-200S, ISA-200MG
- Seagate ST-01/ST-02 (ISA)
- SoundBlaster 16 SCSI-2 (Adaptec 152x compatible) (ISA)
- Tekram DC-390, DC-390W/U/F
- Trantor T128/T128F/T228 (ISA)
- UltraStor 14F (ISA), 24F (EISA), 34F (VLB)
- Western Digital WD7000 SCSI

8.2 Others

- AMD AM53C974, AM79C974 (PCI) (Compaq, HP, Zeos onboard SCSI)
  <ftp://sunsite.unc.edu/pub/Linux/kernel/patches/scsi/AM53C974-0.3.tgz>
- Adaptec ACB-40xx SCSI-MFM/RLL bridgeboard
  <ftp://sunsite.unc.edu/pub/Linux/kernel/patches/scsi/adaptec-40XX.tar.gz>

- Always Technologies AL-500
  `<ftp://sunsite.unc.edu/pub/Linux/kernel/patches/scsi/al500-0.2.tar.gz>`
- BusLogic (ISA/EISA/VLB/PCI) (new beta driver)
  `<ftp://sunsite.unc.edu/pub/Linux/kernel/patches/scsi/BusLogic-1.3.0.tar.gz>`
- Iomega PC2/2B
  `<ftp://sunsite.unc.edu/pub/Linux/kernel/patches/scsi/iomega_pc2-1.1.x.tar.gz>`
- Qlogic (ISP1020) (PCI)
  `<ftp://sunsite.unc.edu/pub/Linux/kernel/patches/scsi/isp1020-0.5.gz>`
- Ricoh GSI-8
  `<ftp://tsx-11.mit.edu/pub/linux/ALPHA/scsi/gsi8.tar.gz>`

8.3 Unsupported

- Parallel port SCSI adapters
- Non Adaptec compatible DTC boards (327x, 328x)

9 Controllers (I/O)

Any standard serial/parallel/joystick/combo cards. Linux supports 8250, 16450, 16550, and 16550A UART's. Cards that support non-standard IRQ's (IRQ > 9) can be used.

See National Semiconductor's "Application Note AN-493" by Martin S. Michael. Section 5.0 describes in detail the differences between the NS16550 and NS16550A. Briefly, the NS16550 had bugs in the FIFO circuits, but the NS16550A (and later) chips fixed those. However, there were very few NS16550's produced by National, long ago, so these should be very rare. And many of the "16550" parts in actual modern boards are from the many manufacturers of compatible parts, which may not use the National "A" suffix. Also, some multiport boards will use 16552 or 16554 or various other multiport or multifunction chips from National or other suppliers (generally in a dense package soldered to the board, not a 40 pin DIP). Mostly, don't worry about it unless you encounter a very old 40 pin DIP National "NS16550" (no A) chip loose or in an old board, in which case treat it as a 16450 (no FIFO) rather than a 16550A. - Zhahai Stewart *<zstewart@hisys.com* `<mailto:zstewart@hisys.com>>`

10 Controllers (multiport)

10.1 Non-intelligent cards

10.1.1 Supported

- AST FourPort and clones (4 port)
- Accent Async-4 (4 port)
- Arnet Multiport-8 (8 port)
- Bell Technologies HUB6 (6 port)
- Boca BB-1004, 1008 (4, 8 port) - no DTR, DSR, and CD
- Boca BB-2016 (16 port)
- Boca IO/AT66 (6 port)

- Boca IO 2by4 (4 serial / 2 parallel, uses 5 IRQ's)

- Computone ValuePort (4, 6, 8 port) (AST FourPort compatible)

- DigiBoard PC/X (4, 8, 16 port)

- Comtrol Hostess 550 (4, 8 port)

- PC-COMM 4-port (4 port)

- SIIG I/O Expander 4S (4 port, uses 4 IRQ's)

- STB 4-COM (4 port)

- Twincom ACI/550

- Usenet Serial Board II (4 port)

Non-intelligent cards usually come in two varieties, one using standard com port addresses and use 4 IRQ's, and another that's AST FourPort compatible and uses a selectable block of addresses and a single IRQ. (Addresses and IRQ's are set using `setserial`.) If you're getting one of these cards, be sure to check which standard it conforms to, prices are no indication.

10.2 Intelligent cards

10.2.1 Supported

- Cyclades Cyclom-8Y/16Y (8, 16 port) (ISA/PCI)

- DigiBoard PC/Xe (ISA), PC/Xi (EISA) and PC/Xeve
  `<ftp://ftp.digibd.com/drivers/linux/>`

- Stallion EasyIO (ISA) / EasyConnection 8/32 (ISA/MCA)

- Stallion EasyConnection 8/64 / ONboard (ISA/EISA/MCA) / Brumby / Stallion (ISA)

10.2.2 Others

- Comtrol RocketPort (8/16/32 port)
  `<ftp://sunsite.unc.edu/pub/Linux/kernel/patches/serial/comtrol-1.04.tar.gz>`

- Computone IntelliPort II (4/8/16 port)
  contact Michael H. Warfield <*mhw@wittsend.com* `<mailto:mhw@wittsend.com>`>

- DigiBoard COM/Xi
  contact Simon Park (*si@wimpol.demon.co.uk* `<mailto:si@wimpol.demon.co.uk>`) or Mark Hatle (*fray@krypton.mankato.msus.edu* `<mailto:si@wimpol.demon.co.uk>`). NOTE: both email addresses seem not to exist any longer.

- Hayes ESP8
  contact Dennis Boylan <*dennis@lan.com* `<mailto:dennis@lan.com>`>

- Moxa C102, C104, C168, C218 (8 port), C320 (8/16/24/32 expandable) and C320T
  `<ftp://ftp.moxa.com.tw/drivers/linux/>`

- Specialix SIO/XIO (modular, 4 to 32 ports)
  `<ftp://sunsite.unc.edu/pub/Linux/kernel/patches/serial/sidrv.taz>`

11   Network adapters

Ethernet adapters vary greatly in performance. In general the newer the design the better. Some very old cards like the 3Com 3C501 are only useful because they can be found in junk heaps for $5 a time. Be careful with clones, not all are good clones and bad clones often cause erratic lockups under Linux. Read the Ethernet HOWTO, `<http://sunsite.unc.edu/LDP/HOWTO/>`, for detailed descriptions of various cards.

11.1   Supported

11.1.1   Ethernet

For ethernet cards with the DECchip DC21x4x family the "Tulip" driver is available. More information on this driver can be found at `<http://cesdis.gsfc.nasa.gov/linux/drivers/tulip.html>`.

- 3Com 3C501 - "avoid like the plague"
- 3Com 3C503, 3C505, 3C507, 3C509/3C509B (ISA) / 3C579 (EISA)
- 3Com Etherlink III Vortex Ethercards (3C590, 3c592, 3C595, 3c597) (PCI), 3Com Etherlink XL Boomerang Ethercards (3c900, 3c905) (PCI) and 3Com Fast EtherLink Ethercard (3c515) (ISA) Newer versions of this driver are available at `<http://cesdis.gsfc.nasa.gov/linux/drivers/vortex.html>` Avoid the 3c900 card when possible as the driver is not functioning well for this card.
- AMD LANCE (79C960) / PCnet-ISA/PCI (AT1500, HP J2405A, NE1500/NE2100)
- AT&T GIS WaveLAN
- Allied Telesis AT1700
- Allied Telesis LA100PCI-T
- Ansel Communications AC3200 EISA
- Apricot Xen-II / 82596
- Cabletron E21xx
- Cogent EM110
- Danpex EN-9400
- DEC DE425 (EISA) / DE434/DE435 (PCI) / DE450/DE500 (DE4x5 driver)
- DEC DE450/DE500-XA (Tulip driver)
- DEC DEPCA and EtherWORKS
- DEC EtherWORKS 3
- DEC QSilver's (Tulip driver)
- Fujitsu FMV-181/182/183/184
- HP PCLAN (27245 and 27xxx series)
- HP PCLAN PLUS (27247B and 27252A)
- HP 10/100VG PCLAN (J2577, J2573, 27248B, J2585) (ISA/EISA/PCI) More information at `<http://cesdis1.gsfc.nasa.gov:80/linux/drivers/100vg.html>`
- ICL EtherTeam 16i / 32 EISA
- Intel EtherExpress
- Intel EtherExpress Pro

- KTI ET16/P-D2, ET16/P-DC ISA (work jumperless and with hardware-configuration options)
- NE2000/NE1000 (be careful with clones)
- New Media Ethernet
- PureData PDUC8028, PDI8023
- SEEQ 8005
- SMC Ultra / EtherEZ (ISA)
- SMC 9000 series
- SMC PCI EtherPower 10/100 (Tulip driver)
- Schneider & Koch G16
- Western Digital WD80x3
- Zenith Z-Note / IBM ThinkPad 300 built-in adapter
- Znyx 312 etherarray (Tulip driver)

11.1.2 ISDN

- Linux ISDN WWW page
  <http://www.ix.de/ix/linux/linux-isdn.html>

- 3Com Sonix Arpeggio
  <ftp://sunsite.unc.edu/pub/Linux/kernel/patches/network/sonix.tgz>
- AVM A1
  <ftp://ftp.franken.de/pub/isdn4linux/>
- Combinet EVERYWARE 1000 ISDN
  <ftp://sunsite.unc.edu/pub/Linux/kernel/patches/network/combinet1000isdn-1.02.tar.gz>
- Creatix PnP S0
  <ftp://ftp.franken.de/pub/isdn4linux/>
- Elsa Microlink PCC-16, PCF, PCF-Pro, PCC-8
  <ftp://ftp.franken.de/pub/isdn4linux/>
- ELSA QuickStep 1000
  <ftp://ftp.franken.de/pub/isdn4linux/>
- ICN ISDN cards
  <ftp://ftp.franken.de/pub/isdn4linux/>
- ITK ix1-micro Rev.2
  <ftp://ftp.franken.de/pub/isdn4linux/>
- Octal PCBIT
  <ftp://ftp.franken.de/pub/isdn4linux/>
- Teles 8.0/16.0/16.3 and compatible ones
  <ftp://ftp.franken.de/pub/isdn4linux/>
- Teles S0
  <ftp://ftp.franken.de/pub/isdn4linux/>

ISDN cards that emulate standard modems or common Ethernet adapters don't need any special drivers to work.

11.1.3 Pocket and portable adapters

For more information on Linux and use of the parallel port, go to the Linux Parallel Port Home Page
<http://www.torque.net/linux-pp.html>

- Accton parallel port ethernet adapter
  <http://paradigm.uor.edu/harshman/linux/accton.html>
- AT-Lan-Tec/RealTek parallel port adapter
- D-Link DE600/DE620 parallel port adapter

11.1.4 Slotless

- SLIP/CSLIP/PPP (serial port)
- EQL (serial IP load balancing)
- PLIP (parallel port) - using "LapLink cable" or bi-directional cable

11.1.5 ARCnet

- Works with all ARCnet cards

11.1.6 Token Ring

- Any IBM token ring card not using DMA
- IBM Tropic chipset cards

11.1.7 FDDI

- DEC DEFEA (EISA) / DEFPA (PCI) (kernel 2.0.24 and later)

11.1.8 Amateur radio (AX.25)

- Gracilis PackeTwin
- Ottawa PI/PI2
- Most generic 8530 based HDLC boards

11.1.9 PCMCIA cards

- See Appendix B for complete list

11.2 Others

11.2.1 Ethernet

- Racal-Interlan NI5210 (i82586 Ethernet chip). Avoid this card. It is not functioning properly with the current driver.

- Racal-Interlan NI6510 (am7990 lance chip). Starting with kernel 1.3.66 more than 16Mb Ram is supported.
- Racal-Interlan PCI card (AMD PC net chip 97c970) ??

11.2.2 ISDN

- SpellCaster's Datacomute/BRI, Telecomute/BRI (ISA)
  `<ftp://ftp.franken.de/pub/isdn4linux/>`

11.2.3 ATM

- Efficient Networks ENI155P-MF 155 Mbps ATM adapter (PCI)
  `<http://lrcwww.epfl.ch/linux-atm/>`

11.2.4 Frame Relay

- Sangoma S502 56K Frame Relay card
  `<ftp://ftp.sovereign.org/pub/wan/fr/>`

11.2.5 Wireless

- Proxim RangeLan2 7100 (ISA) / 630x (OEM mini-ISA)
  `<http://www.komacke.com/distribution.html>`

11.3 Unsupported

- Xircom adapters (PCMCIA and parallel port)
- IBM PCI Token Ring cards (all of them)
- Sysconnect / Schneider & Koch Token Ring cards (all of them)

12 Sound cards

12.1 Supported

- 6850 UART MIDI
- Adlib (OPL2)
- Audio Excell DSP16
- Aztech Sound Galaxy NX Pro
- Crystal CS4232 (PnP) based cards
- ECHO-PSS cards (Orchid SoundWave32, Cardinal DSP16)
- Ensoniq SoundScape
- Gravis Ultrasound
- Gravis Ultrasound 16-bit sampling daughterboard

- Gravis Ultrasound MAX
- Logitech SoundMan Games (SBPro, 44kHz stereo support)
- Logitech SoundMan Wave (Jazz16/OPL4)
- Logitech SoundMan 16 (PAS-16 compatible)
- MediaTriX AudioTriX Pro
- Media Vision Premium 3D (Jazz16)
- Media Vision Pro Sonic 16 (Jazz)
- Media Vision Pro Audio Spectrum 16
- Microsoft Sound System (AD1848)
- OAK OTI-601D cards (Mozart)
- OPTi 82C925 cards. Use the MSS driver and the isapnp tools
- OPTi 82C928/82C929 cards (MAD16/MAD16 Pro/ISP16/Mozart)
- OPTi 82C931 cards. See <http://oto.dyn.ml.org/drees/opti931.html>
- Sound Blaster
- Sound Blaster Pro
- Sound Blaster 16
- Turtle Beach Wavefront cards (Maui, Tropez)
- Wave Blaster (and other daughterboards)
- Cards based on the ESS Technologies AudioDrive chips (688, 1688, 1868, etc)

- AWE32/64 supports is started in kernel series 2.1.x (check the SoundBlaster AWE mini-HOWTO by Marcus Brinkmann for installation details)
- MPU-401 MIDI

12.2   Others

- MPU-401 MIDI (intelligent mode)
  <ftp://sunsite.unc.edu/pub/Linux/kernel/sound/mpu401-0.2.tar.gz>
- PC speaker / Parallel port DAC
  <ftp://ftp.informatik.hu-berlin.de/pub/os/linux/hu-sound/>
- Turtle Beach MultiSound/Tahiti/Monterey
  <ftp://ftp.cs.colorado.edu/users/mccreary/archive/tbeach/multisound/>

12.3   Unsupported

The ASP chip on Sound Blaster 16 series is not supported. AWE32's onboard E-mu MIDI synthesizer is not supported.

Nathan Laredo < *laredo@gnu.ai.mit.edu* <mailto:laredo@gnu.ai.mit.edu>> is willing to write AWE32 drivers if you send him a complimentary card. He is also willing to write drivers for almost any hardware if you send him free samples of your hardware.

Sound Blaster 16's with DSP 4.11 and 4.12 have a hardware bug that causes hung/stuck notes when playing MIDI and digital audio at the same time. The problem can happen with either Wave Blaster daughterboards or MIDI devices attached to the MIDI port. There is no known fix.

13   Hard drives

All hard drives should work if the controller is supported.

(From the SCSI HOWTO) All direct access SCSI devices with a block size of 256, 512, or 1024 bytes should work. Other block sizes will not work (Note that this can often be fixed by changing the block and/or sector sizes using the MODE SELECT SCSI command).

Large IDE (EIDE) drives work fine with newer kernels. The boot partition must lie in the first 1024 cylinders due to PC BIOS limitations.

Some Conner CFP1060S drives may have problems with Linux and ext2fs. The symptoms are inode errors during e2fsck and corrupt file systems. Conner has released a firmware upgrade to fix this problem, contact Conner at 1-800-4CONNER (US) or +44-1294-315333 (Europe). Have the microcode version (found on the drive label, 9WA1.6x) handy when you call.

Certain Micropolis drives have problems with Adaptec and BusLogic cards, contact the drive manufacturers for firmware upgrades if you suspect problems.

- Multiple device driver (RAID-0, RAID-1)
  `<ftp://sweet-smoke.ufr-info-p7.ibp.fr/public/Linux/>`

14   Tape drives

14.1   Supported

- SCSI tape drives
  (From the SCSI HOWTO) Drives using both fixed and variable length blocks smaller than the driver buffer length (set to 32k in the distribution sources) are supported. Virtually all drives should work. (Send mail if you know of any incompatible drives.)

- QIC-02 drives

- Iomega DITTO internal (ftape 3.04c and newer)

14.2   Others

- QIC-117, QIC-40/80, QIC-3010/3020 (QIC-WIDE) drives
  Most tape drives using the floppy controller should work. Various dedicated controllers (Colorado FC-10/FC-20, Mountain Mach-2, Iomega Tape Controller II) are also supported
  `<ftp://sunsite.unc.edu/pub/Linux/kernel/tapes>`

- ATAPI tape drives
  For these an alpha driver (ide-tape.c) is available in the kernel. ATAPI tape drives supported are

  - Seagate TapeStor 8000

  - Conner CTMA 4000 IDE ATAPI Streaming tape drive

14.3   Unsupported

- Emerald and Tecmar QIC-02 tape controller cards - Chris Ulrich < *insom@math.ucr.edu* <mailto: insom@math.ucr.edu>>

- Drives that connect to the parallel port (eg: Colorado Trakker)

- Some high speed tape controllers (Colorado TC-15)
- Irwin AX250L/Accutrak 250 (not QIC-80)
- IBM Internal Tape Backup Unit (not QIC-80)
- COREtape Light

15   CD-ROM drives

For more information on CD-ROM drives check the CDROM-HOWTO at `<http://sunsite.unc.edu/LDP/HOWTO/>`.

15.1   Supported

Common CD-ROM drives

- SCSI CD-ROM drives
  (From the CD-ROM HOWTO) Any SCSI CD-ROM drive with a block size of 512 or 2048 bytes should work under Linux; this includes the vast majority of CD-ROM drives on the market.
- EIDE (ATAPI) CD-ROM drives (IDECD)
  Almost all double, quad and six speed drives are supported, including
    - Mitsumi FX400
    - Nec-260
    - Sony 55E

Proprietary CD-ROM drives

- Aztech CDA268-01A, Orchid CDS-3110, Okano/Wearnes CDD-110, Conrad TXC, CyCDROM CR520ie/CR540ie/CR940ie (AZTCD)
- Creative Labs CD-200(F) (SBPCD)
- Funai E2550UA/MK4015 (SBPCD)
- GoldStar R420 (GSCD)
- IBM External ISA (SBPCD)
- Kotobuki (SBPCD)
- Lasermate CR328A (OPTCD)
- LMS Philips CM 206 (CM206)
- Longshine LCS-7260 (SBPCD)
- Matsushita/Panasonic CR-521/522/523/562/563 (SBPCD)
- MicroSolutions Backpack parallel portdrive (BPCD)
- Mitsumi CR DC LU05S (MCD/MCDX)
- Mitsumi FX001D/F (MCD/MCDX)
- Optics Storage Dolphin 8000AT (OPTCD)
- Sanyo H94A (SJCD)
- Sony CDU31A/CDU33A (CDU31A)
- Sony CDU-510/CDU-515 (SOMYCD535)
- Sony CDU-535/CDU-531 (SONYCD535)
- Teac CD-55A SuperQuad (SBPCD)

15.2 Others

- LMS/Philips CM 205/225/202
  `<ftp://sunsite.unc.edu/pub/Linux/kernel/patches/cdrom/lmscd0.4.tar.gz>`
- NEC CDR-35D (old)
  `<ftp://sunsite.unc.edu/pub/Linux/kernel/patches/cdrom/linux-neccdr35d.patch>`
- Sony SCSI multisession CD-XA
  `<ftp://tsx-11.mit.edu/pub/linux/patches/sony-multi-0.00.tar.gz>`
- Parallel Port Driver
  `<http://www.torque.net/linux-pp.html>`

15.3 Notes

All CD-ROM drives should work similarly for reading data. There are various compatibility problems with audio CD playing utilities. (Especially with newer low-end NEC drives.) Some alpha drivers may not have audio support yet.

Early (single speed) NEC CD-ROM drives may have trouble with currently available SCSI controllers.

PhotoCD (XA) is supported. The hpcdtoppm program by Hadmut Danisch converts PhotoCD files to the portable pixmap format. The program can be obtained from `<ftp://ftp.gwdg.de/pub/linux/hpcdtoppm>` or as part of the PBM utilities.

Also, reading video CD is supported in kernel series 2.1.3x and later. A patch is available for kernel 2.0.30.

Finally, most IDE CD-ROM Changers are supported.

16 CD-Writers

Many CD-Writers are supported by Linux now. For an up to date list of CD-Writers supported check the CD-Writing mini-HOWTO at `<http://sunsite.unc.edu/LDP/HOWTO/mini/CD-Writing>` or check `<http://www.shop.de/cgi-bin/wini/lsc.pl>`. Cdwrite `<ftp://sunsite.unc.edu/pub/Linux/utils/disk-management/>` and cdrecord `<http://www.fokus.gmd.de/nthp/employees/schilling/cdrecord.html>` can be used for writing CD's. The X-CD-Roast package for Linux is a graphical front-end for using CD writers. The package can be found at `<ftp://sunsite.unc.edu/pub/Linux/utils/disk-management/xcdroast-0.96b.tar.gz>`.

- Grundig CDR 100 IPW
- HP CD-Writer+ 7100
- HP SureStore 4020i
- HP SureStore 6020es/i
- JVC XR-W2010
- Mitsubishi CDRW-225
- Mitsumi CR-2600TE
- Olympus CDS 620E
- Philips CDD-522/2000/2600/3610
- Pinnacle Micro RCD-5020/5040
- Plextor CDR PX-24CS

- Ricoh MP 1420C
- Ricoh MP 6200S/6201S
- Sanyo CRD-R24S
- Smart and Friendly Internal 2006 Plus 2.05
- Sony CDU 920S/924/926S
- Taiyo Yuden EW-50
- TEAC CD-R50S
- WPI(Wearnes) CDR-632P
- WPI(Wearnes) CDRW-622
- Yamaha CDR-100
- Yamaha CDR-200/200t/200tx
- Yamaha CDR-400t/400tx

17 Removable drives

All SCSI drives should work if the controller is supported, including optical (MO), WORM, floptical, Bernoulli, Zip, Jaz, SyQuest, PD, and others.

- Parallel port Zip drives
  `<ftp://gear.torque.net/pub/>`
- Parallel port Avatar Shark-250
  `<http://www.torque.net/shark.html>`

Removable drives work like hard disks and floppies, just `fdisk`/`mkfs` and mount the disks. Linux provides drive locking if your drives support it. `mtools` can also be used if the disks are in MS-DOS format.

CD-R drives require special software to work. Read the CD-R Mini-HOWTO.

Linux supports both 512 and 1024 bytes/sector disks. Starting with kernel 2.1.32 Linux also supports 2048 bytes/sector. A patch to kernel 2.0.30 is available at `<http://liniere.gen.u-tokyo.ac.jp/2048.html>`.

The 2048 bytes/sector support is needed for

- Fujitsu magneto-optical disk drives M2513

Starting with pre-patch-2.0.31-3 IDE/ATAPI internal Zip drives, flopticals and PD's are supported.

- LS-120 floptical
- PD-CD

18 Mice

18.1 Supported

- Microsoft serial mouse
- Mouse Systems serial mouse

- Logitech Mouseman serial mouse
- Logitech serial mouse
- ATI XL Inport busmouse
- C&T 82C710 (QuickPort) (Toshiba, TI Travelmate)
- Microsoft busmouse
- Logitech busmouse
- PS/2 (auxiliary device) mouse

18.2   Others

- Sejin J-mouse
  `<ftp://sunsite.unc.edu/pub/Linux/kernel/patches/console/jmouse.1.1.70-jmouse.tar.gz>`
- MultiMouse - use multiple mouse devices as single mouse
  `<ftp://sunsite.unc.edu/pub/Linux/system/misc/MultiMouse-1.0.tgz>`
- Microsoft Intellimouse

18.3   Notes

Touchpad devices like Alps Glidepoint also work, so long they're compatible with another mouse protocol.

Newer Logitech mice (except the Mouseman) use the Microsoft protocol and all three buttons do work. Eventhough Microsoft's mice have only two buttons, the protocol allows three buttons.

The mouse port on the ATI Graphics Ultra and Ultra Pro use the Logitech busmouse protocol. (See the Busmouse HOWTO for details.)

19   Modems

All internal modems or external modems connected to the serial port should work. Alas, some manufactures have created Windows 95 only modems. Check Appendix D for Linux incompatible hardware.

A small number of modems come with DOS software that downloads the control program at runtime. These can normally be used by loading the program under DOS and doing a warm boot. Such modems are probably best avoided as you won't be able to use them with non PC hardware in the future.

All PCMCIA modems should work with the PCMCIA drivers.

Fax modems need appropriated fax software to operate.

- Digicom Connection 96+/14.4+ - DSP code downloading program
  `<ftp://sunsite.unc.edu/pub/Linux/apps/serialcomm/smdl-linux.1.02.tar.gz>`
- ZyXEL U-1496 series - ZyXEL 1.4, modem/fax/voice control program
  `<http://www.pe1chl.demon.nl/ZyXEL/ZyXEL-1.6.tar.gz>`
- ZyXEL Elite 2864 series - modem/fax/voice control program
  `<http://www.pe1chl.demon.nl/ZyXEL/ZyXEL-1.6.tar.gz>`
- ZyXEL Omni TA 128 - modem/fax/voice control program
  `<http://www.pe1chl.demon.nl/ZyXEL/ZyXEL-1.6.tar.gz>`

20 Printers/Plotters

All printers and plotters connected to the parallel or serial port should work. Alas, some manufacturers have created Windows 95 only printers. Check Appendix D for Linux incompatible hardware.

- HP LaserJet 4 series - free-lj4, printing modes control program
  `<ftp://sunsite.unc.edu/pub/Linux/system/printing/free-lj4-1.1p1.tar.gz>`
- BiTronics parallel port interface
  `<ftp://sunsite.unc.edu/pub/Linux/kernel/patches/misc/bt-ALPHA-0.0.1.module.patch.gz>`

20.1 Ghostscript

Many Linux programs output PostScript files. Non-PostScript printers can emulate PostScript Level 2 using Ghostscript.

- Ghostscript
  `<ftp://ftp.cs.wisc.edu/pub/ghost/aladdin/>`

20.1.1 Ghostscript supported printers

- Apple Imagewriter
- C. Itoh M8510
- Canon BubbleJet BJ10e (bj10e)
- Canon BubbleJet BJ200, BJC-210 (B/W only), BJC-240 (B/W only) (bj200)
- Canon BubbleJet BJC-600, BJC-610, BJC-4000, BJC-4100, BJC-450, MultiPASS C2500, BJC-240, BJC-70 (bjc600)
- Canon BubbleJet BJC-800 (bjc800)
- Canon LBP-8II, LIPS III
- DEC LA50/70/75/75plus
- DEC LN03, LJ250
- Epson 9 pin, 24 pin, LQ series, AP3250
- Epson Stylus Color/Color II/500/800 (stcolor)
- HP 2563B
- HP DesignJet 650C
- HP DeskJet, Deskjet Plus (deskjet)
- HP Deskjet 500, Deskjet Portable (djet500)
- HP DeskJet 400/500C/540C/690C/693C (cdj500)
- HP DeskJet 550C/560C/600/660C/682C/683C/693C/850/870Cse (cdj550)
- HP DeskJet 850/870Cse/870Cxi/680 (cdj850)
- HP DeskJet 500C/510/520/5540C/693C printing black only (cdjmono)
- HP DeskJet 600 (lj4dith)
- HP DeskJet 600/870Cse, LaserJet 5/5L (ljet4)
- HP Deskjet 500/500C/510/520/540/550C/560C/850C/855C
  `<ftp:ftp.pdb.sni.de/pub/utilities/misc/hpdj-2.1.tar.gz>`

- HP PaintJet XL300, Deskjet 600/1200C/1600C (pjxl300)
- HP LaserJet/Plus/II/III/4
- HP PaintJet/XL
- IBM Jetprinter color
- IBM Proprinter
- Imagen ImPress
- Mitsubishi CP50 color
- NEC P6/P6+/P60
- Oki OL410ex LED (ljet4)
- Okidata MicroLine 182
- Ricoh 4081/6000 (r4081)
- SPARCprinter
- StarJet 48 inkjet printer
- Tektronix 4693d color 2/4/8 bit
- Tektronix 4695/4696 inkjet plotter
- Xerox XES printers (2700, 3700, 4045, etc.)

20.1.2   Others

- Canon BJC600/800 color printers
  `<ftp://petole.imag.fr/pub/postscript/ghostscript/bjc600/>`

21   Scanners

For scanner support there is the package SANE (Scanner Access Now Easy). Information can be found at `<http://www.mostang.com/sane/>`. It can be downloaded from `<ftp://ftp.mostang.com/pub/sane/>`. This is a universal scanner interface. It comes complete with documentation and several frontends and backends.

More information on handheld scanners can be found at `<http://swt-www.informatik.uni-hamburg.de/1willamo/scanner.html>`

21.1   Supported

- A4 Tech AC 4096 / AS 8000P
  `<ftp://ftp.informatik.hu-berlin.de/pub/local/linux/a4scan/a4scan.tgz>`
- Adara Image Star I
  `<http://fb4-1112.uni-muenster.de/ffwd/>`
  `<ftp://fb4-1112.uni-muenster.de/pub/ffwd/mtekscan-0.2.tar.gz>`
- Conrad Personal Scanner 64, P105 handheld scanners
  `<ftp://tsx-11.mit.edu/pub/linux/ALPHA/scanner/scan-driver-0.1.8.tar.gz>`
- Epson GT6000
  `<ftp://sunsite.unc.edu/pub/Linux/apps/graphics/capture/ppic0.5.tar.gz>`

- Fujitsu SCSI-2 scanners
  contact Dr. G.W. Wettstein <*greg@wind.rmcc.com* <mailto:greg@wind.rmcc.com>>

- Genius ColorPage-SP2
  <http://fb4-1112.uni-muenster.de/ffwd/>
  <ftp://fb4-1112.uni-muenster.de/pub/ffwd/mtekscan-0.2.tar.gz>

- Genius GS-B105G handheld scanner
  <ftp://tsx-11.mit.edu/pub/linux/ALPHA/scanner/gs105-0.0.1.tar.gz>

- Genius GeniScan GS4500, GS4500A handheld scanners
  <ftp://tsx-11.mit.edu/pub/linux/ALPHA/scanner/gs4500-2.0.tar.gz>

- HighScreen Greyscan 256 handheld scanner
  <ftp://tsx-11.mit.edu/pub/linux/ALPHA/scanner/gs4500-2.0.tar.gz>

- HP ScanJet II series SCSI
  <ftp://sunsite.unc.edu/pub/Linux/apps/graphics/capture/hpscanpbm-0.3a.tar.gz>

- HP ScanJet IIc, IIcx, IIp, 3c, 4c, 4p, 5p, 5pse, plus
  <http://www.tummy.com/xvscan/>

- Logitech Scanman+, Scanman 32, Scanman 256 handheld scanners
  <ftp://tsx-11.mit.edu/pub/linux/ALPHA/scanner/logiscan-0.0.4.tar.gz>

- Microtek ScanMaker E3, E6, II, IIXE, III and 35t models
  <http://fb4-1112.uni-muenster.de/ffwd/>
  <ftp://fb4-1112.uni-muenster.de/pub/ffwd/mtekscan-0.2.tar.gz>

- Mustek M105 handheld scanner
  <ftp://tsx-11.mit.edu/pub/linux/ALPHA/scanner/scan-driver-0.1.8.tar.gz>

- Mustek HT800 Turbo, Matador 105, Matador 256 handheld scanners
  <ftp://tsx-11.mit.edu/pub/linux/ALPHA/scanner/scan-driver-0.1.8.tar.gz>

- Mustek Paragon 6000CX
  <ftp://sunsite.unc.edu/pub/Linux/apps/graphics/capture/muscan-2.0.6.taz>

- Nikon Coolscan SCSI 35mm film scanner
  <ftp://sunsite.unc.edu/pub/Linux/apps/graphics/capture/coolscan-0.2.tgz>

- Pearl 256 handheld scanner
  <ftp://tsx-11.mit.edu/pub/linux/ALPHA/scanner/scan-driver-0.1.8.tar.gz>

- UMAX SCSI scanners
  <ftp://tsx-11.mit.edu/pub/linux/ALPHA/scanner/umax-0.5.5.tar.gz>

The Mustek drivers work only with GI1904 interface cards. Eric Chang *eric.chang@chrysalis.org* <mailto:eric.chang@chrysalis.org> has created a patch to use them with IF960 interface cards.

21.2   Others

- Genius GS-4000, ScanMate/32, ScanMate/GS handheld scanners
  <ftp://tsx-11.mit.edu/pub/linux/ALPHA/scanner/gs4500-2.0.tar.gz>

- Mustek HT105, M800 handheld scanners
  <ftp://tsx-11.mit.edu/pub/linux/ALPHA/scanner/scan-driver-0.1.8.tar.gz>

- Voelkner Personal Scanner 64 handheld scanner
  <ftp://tsx-11.mit.edu/pub/linux/ALPHA/scanner/scan-driver-0.1.8.tar.gz>

21.3 Unsupported

- Escom 256 (Primax Lector Premier 256) handheld scanner
- Genius ScanMate/256, EasyScan handheld scanners
- Mustek CG8000 handheld scanner
- Trust Ami Scan handheld scanner

22 Other hardware

22.1 VESA Power Savings Protocol (DPMS) monitors

Support for power savings is included in the Linux kernel. Just use `setterm` to enable support.

22.2 Touch screens

The Metro-X X-server is supporting the following touch screen:

- Carrol Touch serial touch screen. `<http://www.carrolltouch.com>`

22.3 Joysticks

Joystick support is in the latest XFree86 distributions (3.3.x) and in kernel versions 2.1.xx. For older kernels the links below are usefull.

- Joystick driver
  `<ftp://sunsite.unc.edu/pub/Linux/kernel/patches/console/joystick-0.8.0.tgz>`
- Joystick driver (module)
  `<ftp://sunsite.unc.edu/pub/Linux/kernel/patches/console/joyfixed.tgz>`

22.4 Video capture boards / Frame Grabbers / TV tuner

A couple of programs are available that support TV tuners. These are:

- BTTV `<http://www.thp.Uni-Koeln.DE/rjkm/linux/bttv.html>`
- Xawtv
- Xtvscreen

- Data Translation DT2803

- Data Translation DT2851 Frame Grabber
  `<ftp://sunsite.unc.edu/pub/Linux/apps/video/dt2851-2.01.tar.gz>`
- Data Translation DT3155
  `<http://krusty.eecs.umich.edu/people/ncowan/linux/welcome.html>`
- Diamond DTV2000 (based on BT848)

- Dipix XPG1000/FPG/PPMAPA (based on TI C40 DSP). Most add-on cards are supported.
  <http://www.thp.Uni-Koeln.DE/rjkm/linux/bttv.html>
- Epix SVM
- Epix Silicon Video MUX series of video frame grabbing boards
  <http://www.ssc.com/lj/issue13/npc13c.html>
- FAST Screen Machine II
  <ftp://sunsite.unc.edu/pub/Linux/apps/video/ScreenMachineII.2.0.tgz>
- Hauppage Wincast TV PCI (based on BT848)
  <http://www.thp.Uni-Koeln.DE/rjkm/linux/bttv.html>
- Imaging Technology ITI/IC-PCI
  <ftp://ftp.gom-online.de/pub/IC-PCI/icpci-0.3.2.tar.gz>
- ImageNation Cortex I
  <ftp://sunsite.unc.edu/pub/Linux/apps/video/cortex.drv.1.1.tgz>
- ImageNation CX100
  <ftp://sunsite.unc.edu/pub/Linux/apps/video/cxdrv-0.86.tar.gz>
- ImageNation PX500 (being worked on). Ask for current status
  rubini@linux.it <mailto:rubini@linux.it>
- Imaging Technology Inc. IC-PCI frame grabber board
  <ftp://gandalf.expmech.ing.tu-bs.de/pub/driver/icpci-0.2.0.tar.gz>
- Matrox Meteor
  <ftp://sunsite.unc.edu/pub/Linux/apps/video/meteor-1.4a.tgz>
- Matrox PIP-1024
  <http://www.powerup.com.au/sobeyp/pip_tar.gz>
- Miro PCTV (based on BT848)
  <http://www.thp.Uni-Koeln.DE/rjkm/linux/bttv.html>
- MuTech MV1000 PCI
  <ftp://sunsite.unc.edu/pub/Linux/apps/video/mv1000drv-0.33.tgz>
- MuTech MV200
  <http://www.powerup.com.au/sobeyp/mu_tar.gz>
- Philips PCA10TV (not in production anymore)
  <ftp://ftp.il.ft.hse.nl/pub/tv1000/pctv1000.02.tgz>
- Pro Movie Studio
  <ftp://sunsite.unc.edu/pub/Linux/apps/video/PMS-grabber.3.0.tgz>
- Quanta WinVision B&W video capture card
  <ftp://sunsite.unc.edu/pub/Linux/apps/video/fgrabber-1.0.tgz>
- Quickcam
  <ftp://sunsite.unc.edu/pub/Linux/apps/video/qcam-0.7c-5.tar.gz>
- Sensus 700
  <http://www.robots.com/s700.htm>
- Smart Video Recoder III (based on BT848)
  <http://www.thp.Uni-Koeln.DE/rjkm/linux/bttv.html>
- STB TV PCI Television Tuner (based on BT848)
  <http://www.thp.Uni-Koeln.DE/rjkm/linux/bttv.html>
- Video Blaster, Rombo Media Pro+
  <ftp://sunsite.unc.edu/pub/Linux/apps/video/vid_src-0.6.tgz>
- VT1500 TV cards
  <ftp://sunsite.unc.edu/pub/Linux/apps/video/vt1500-1.0.9.tar.gz>

22.5 Digital Camera

- HP Photo Smart Digital Camera
  <ftp://ftp.itojun.org/pub/digi-cam/>

22.6 UPS

Various other UPS's are supported, read the UPS HOWTO

- APC SmartUPS
  <ftp://sunsite.unc.edu/pub/Linux/system/ups/apcd-0.5.tar.gz>
- APC-BackUPS 400/600, APC-SmartUPS SU700/1400RM
  <ftp://sunsite.unc.edu/pub/Linux/system/ups/apcupsd-2.2.tar.gz>
- UPS's with RS-232 monitoring port (genpower package)
  <ftp://sunsite.unc.edu/pub/Linux/system/ups/genpower-1.0.1.tgz>
- MGE UPS's
  <http://www.mgeups.com/download/softlib.htm>   and   <http://www.mgeups.com/download/software/linux/upsp.tgz>
- A daemon to shut down and up computers connected to ups's. It's network aware and allows server- and client-mode
  <ftp://sunsite.unc.edu/pub/Linux/system/ups/powerd-2.0.tar.gz>

22.7 Multifunction boards

- Pro Audio Spectrum 16 SCSI / Sound interface card

22.8 Data acquisition

The Linux Lab Project site collects drivers for hardware dealing with data acquisition, they also maintain some mailing lists dealing with the subject. I have no experience with data acquisition so please check the site for more details.

- Linux Lab Project
  <http://www.llp.fu-berlin.de/>

- CED 1401
- DBCC CAMAC
- IEEE-488 (GPIB, HPIB) boards
- Keithley DAS-1200
- National Instruments AT-MIO-16F / Lab-PC+

- Analog Devices RTI-800/815 ADC/DAC board
  contact Paul Gortmaker <*gpg109@anu.edu.au* <mailto:gpg109@anu.edu.au>>

22.9 Watchdog timer interfaces

- ICS WDT500-P (<http://www.indcomp.src.com/products/data/html/wdt500-p.html>)
- ICS WDT501-P (with and without fan tachometer) (<http://www.indcomp.src.com/products/data/html/wdt500-p.html>)

22.10   Miscellaneous

- Mattel Powerglove

- AIMS Labs RadioTrack FM radio card
  <ftp://sunsite.unc.edu/pub/Linux/apps/sound/radio/radiotrack-1.1.tgz>

- Reveal FM Radio card
  <ftp://magoo.uwsuper.edu/docs/radio.html>

- Videotext cards
  <ftp://sunsite.unc.edu/pub/Linux/apps/video/videoteXt-0.6.tar.gz>

23   Related sources of information

- Cameron Spitzer's hardware FAQ archive (??)
  <ftp://ftp.rahul.net/pub/cameron/PC-info/>

- Computer Hardware and Software Vendor Phone Numbers
  <http://mtmis1.mis.semi.harris.com/comp_ph1.html>

- Guide to Computer Vendors
  <http://guide.sbanetweb.com/>

- System Optimization Information
  <http://www.dfw.net/sdw/>

24   Acknowledgments

Thanks to all the authors and contributors of other HOWTO's, many things here are shamelessly stolen from their works; to FRiC, Zane Healy and Ed Carp, the original authors of this HOWTO; and to everyone else who sent in updates and feedbacks. Special thanks to Eric Boerner and lilo (the person, not the program) for the sanity checks. And thanks to Dan Quinlan for the original SGML conversion.

25   Appendix A. S3 cards supported by XFree86 3.3.1.

CHIPSET	RAMDAC	CLOCKCHIP	BPP	CARD
801/805	AT&T 20C490		16	Actix GE 32 / 32+ 2Mb
				Orchid Fahrenheit 1280(+)
801/805	AT&T 20C490	ICD2061A	16	STB PowerGraph X.24
801/805				Del S3 805
				Miro Crystal 8S
				Orchid Fahrenheit VA
				VL-41
805	S3 GENDAC		16	Miro 10SD VLB/PCI
				SPEA Mirage VLB
801/805	SS2410	ICD2061A	8	Diamond Stealth 24 VLB/ISA
801/805	AT&T 20C490	Ch8391	16	JAX 8231/8241, SPEA Mirage
801/805	S3 GENDAC			Miro Crystal 10SD
805i				Actix GE 32i
				ELSA Winner 1000 ISA
928	AT&T 20C490		16	Actix Ultra
928	Sierra SC15025	ICD2061A	32	ELSA Winner 1000 ISA/VLB/EISA
928	Bt485	ICD2061A	32	STB Pegasus VL
928	Bt485	SC11412	16	SPEA(/V7) Mercury VLB
928	Bt485	ICD2061A	32	#9 GXE Level 10/11/12
928	Ti3020	ICD2061A	32	#9 GXE Level 14/16
928				928Movie
				Diamond Stealth Pro
				ELSA Winner 1000TwinBus
				ELSA Winner 1000VL
				ELSA Winner 2000
				Miro Crystal 16S
864		ICD2061A		Miro Crystal 20SD (BIOS 2.xx)
864	AT&T 20C498	ICS2494	32	Miro (Crystal) 20SD (BIOS 1.xx)
864	AT&T 20C498/	ICD2061A/	32	ELSA Winner 1000 PRO VLB/PCI
864	STG1700	ICS9161		MIRO 20SD (BIOS 2.x)
				ELAS Winner 1000 PRO
864	STG1700	ICD2061A	32	Actix GE 64 VLB
864	AT&T 20C498/	ICS2595	16	SPEA(/V7) Mirage P64 DRAM (BIOS 3.x)
	AT&T 21C498			
864	S3 86C716 SDAC		32	ELSA Winner 1000 PRO
				Miro 20SD (BIOS 3.x)
				SPEA Mirage P64 DRAM (BIOS 4.x)
				Diamond Stealth 64 DRAM
				Genoa Phantom 64i
				Miro Crystal 20SD VLB (BIOS 3.xx)
864	ICS5342	ICS5342	32	Diamond Stealth 64 DRAM (some)
864	SDAC			Diamond Stealth 64 Graphics 2001
864	AT&T 20C498-13	ICD2061A	32	#9 GXE64 PCI
864				ASUS Video Magic PCI V864
				VidTech FastMax P20

CHIPSET	RAMDAC	CLOCKCHIP	BPP	CARD
964				ELSA Winner 2000 PRO-2,4
				spider Tarantula 64
964	AT&T 20C505	ICD2061A	32	Miro Crystal 20SV PCI/40SV
964	Bt485	ICD2061A	32	Diamond Stealth 64
964	Bt9485	ICS9161A	32	SPEA Mercury 64
964	Ti3020	ICD2061A	8	ELSA Winner 2000 PRO PCI
964	Ti3025	Ti3025	32	#9 GXE64 Pro VLB/PCI
				Miro Crystal 40SV
964	IBM RGB		32	Hercules Graphite Terminator 64
868	S3 86C716 SDAC		32	ELSA Winner 1000AVI
				Miro Crystal 20SD PCI
868	AT&T 29C409			ELSA Winner 1000AVI
868				Diamond Stealth Video DRAM
				Diamond Stealth 64 Video 2120/2200
				ELSA Winner 1000PRO/X
				#9 FX Motion 531
				VideoLogic GrafixStar 500
968				Diamond Stealth 64 Video 3200
				ELSA Gloria-4/8
				ELSA Winner 2000AVI
				ELSA Winner 2000PRO/X-2/X-4/X-8
				Genoa VideoBlitz III AV
				Hercules Graphite Terminator Pro 64
				LeadTek WinFast S430
				LeadTek WinFast S510
				Miro Crystal 80SV
				Miro Crystal 20SV
				#9 FX Motion 771
				VideoLogic GrafixStar 700
				WinFast S430/S510
968	TVP3026		32	ELSA Winner 2000PRO/X
				Diamond Stealth 64 Video VRAM
968	IBM RGB		32	Genoa VideoBlitz III AVI
				Hercules Terminator Pro 64
				STB Velocity 64 Video
				#9 FX Motion 771
				Diamond Stealth 64 Video 3240/3400
968	TI RAMDAC			Diamond Stealth 64 Video 3240/3400
732	(Trio32)		32	Diamond Stealth 64 DRAM SE
				(all Trio32 based cards)
764	(Trio64)		32	SPEA Mirage P64 (BIOS 5.x)
				Diamond Stealth 64 DRAM
				Diamond Stealth 64 Graphics 2xx0
				#9 FX Vision 330
				STB PowerGraph 64
				(all Trio64 based cards)

CHIPSET	RAMDAC	CLOCKCHIP	BPP	CARD
	(Trio64V+)			DSV3326
				Diamond Stealth 64 Video 2001
				DataExpert DSV3365
				ExpertColor DSV3365
				MAXColor S3 Trio64V+
				ELSA Winner 1000TRIO/V
				Hercules Terminator 64/Video
				#9 FX Motion 331
				STB Powergraph 64 Video
				VideoLogic GrafixStar 400
	(Trio64V2)			ELSA Winner 1000/T2D
	(ViRGE)			Canopus Co. Power Window 3DV
				DSV3325
				DataExpert DSV3325
				Diamond Multimedia Stealth 3D 2000
				Diamond Multimedia Stealth 3D 2000 PRO
				Diamond Stealth 3D 2000
				Diamond Stealth 3D 2000 PRO
				Diamond Stealth 3D 3000
				ELSA Victory 3D
				ELSA Victory 3DX
				ELSA Winner 3000-S
				Expertcolor DSV3325
				Hercules Terminator 64/3D
				LeadTek WinFast 3D S600
				MELCO WGP-VG4S
				#9 FX Motion 332
				Orchid Tech. Fahrenheit Video 3D
				STB systems Powergraph 3D
				WinFast 3D S600
	(ViRGE/DX)			Hercules Terminator 3D/DX
	(ViRGE/GX)			STB Nitro 3D
	(ViRGE/VX)			ELSA Winner 2000AVI/3D
				ELSA Winner 3000
				ELSA Winner 3000-L-42/-M-22
				MELCO WGP-VX8
				STB Systems Velocity 3D
911/924				Diamond Stealth VRAM
924	SC1148 DAC			

NOTE: for the ViRGE/VX,DX,GX,GX2 chipsets you need XFree86 3.3.1. You should use the XF86_SVGA server.

26   Appendix B. Supported PCMCIA cards

These cards are supported by David Hinds' PCMCIA package and this list is taken from his web page.

26.1   Ethernet cards

- SMC, Megahertz and Ositech cards use the smc91c92_cs driver
- 3Com and Farallon cards use the 3c589_cs driver
- Fujitsu, TDK, RATOC, CONTEC, Eagle and Nextcom cards use the fmvj18x_cs driver

All other cards use the pcnet_cs driver. Other NE2000-compatible cards that are not on the list are also likely to work with pcnet_cs.

- 3Com 3c589, 3c589B, 3c589C, 3c589D
- Accton EN2212, EN2216 EtherCard
- Allied Telesis CentreCOM CE6001, LA-PCM
- Asante FriendlyNet
- AST 1082 Ethernet
- CeLAN EPCMCIA
- CNet CN30BC, CN40BC Ethernet
- Compex/ReadyLINK Ethernet Combo
- Compex Linkport Ethernet
- Connectware LANdingGear Adapter
- CONTEC C-NET(PC)C
- Danpex EN-6200P2 Ethernet
- Datatrek NetCard
- Dayna Communications CommuniCard E
- Digital DEPCM-AA Ethernet
- Digital EtherWORKS Turbo Ethernet
- D-Link DE-650, DE-660
- Eagle NE200 Ethernet
- Edimax Technology Ethernet Combo
- EFA InfoExpress 205, 207 Combo
- Eiger Labs EPX-ET10T2 Combo
- ELECOM Laneed LD-CDWA, LD-CDX, LD-CDNIA, LD-CDY
- EP-210 Ethernet
- Epson Ethernet
- EtherPRIME Ethernet
- Explorer NE-10000 Ethernet
- EZLink 4109 Ethernet
- Farallon Etherwave
- Fiberline FL-4680

- Fujitsu FMV-J181, FMV-J182, FMV-J182A
- Fujitsu Towa LA501
- Gateway 2000 Ethernet
- Genius ME3000II Ethernet
- Grey Cell Ethernet
- GVC NIC-2000P Ethernet Combo
- Hitachi HT-4840-11 EtherCard
- Hypertec HyperEnet
- IBM CreditCard Ethernet Adapter
- IC-Card Ethernet
- Infotel IN650ct Ethernet
- I-O Data PCLA/T
- Katron PE-520 Ethernet
- Kingston KNE-PCM/M, KNE-PC2
- LANEED Ethernet
- LanPro EP4000A
- Lantech Ethernet
- Linksys EtherCard
- Logitec LPM-LN10T, LPM-LN10BA Ethernet
- Longshine Ethernet
- Macnica ME-1 Ethernet
- Maxtech PCN2000 Ethernet
- Megahertz XJ10BT, XJ10BC, CC10BT Ethernet
- Melco LPC-TJ, LPC-TS
- Micronet Etherfast Adapter
- NDC Instant-Link
- Network General "Sniffer"
- New Media EthernetLAN
- New Media LiveWir (NOT the LiveWire+)
- New Media BASICS Ethernet
- NextCom NC5310
- Novell/National NE4100 InfoMover
- Ositech Four of Diamonds
- Panasonic CF-VEL211P-B
- Planet SmartCom 2000, 3500
- PreMax PE-200 Ethernet
- Proteon Ethernet
- Ratoc REX-9822, REX-5588A/W
- Relia RE2408T Ethernet
- RPTI EP400, EP401 Ethernet

- SCM Ethernet
- SMC 8020BT EtherEZ (not the EliteCard)
- Socket Communications Socket EA LAN Adapter
- SuperSocket RE450T
- Surecom Ethernet
- SVEC PN605C
- TDK LAC-CD02x, LAK-CD021, LAK-CD022A, LAK-CD021AX Ethernet
- Thomas-Conrad Ethernet
- Trust Ethernet Combo
- Volktek NPL-402CT Ethernet
- Xircom CreditCard CE2

26.2   Fast Ethernet (10/100baseT) adapters

- Linksys EtherFast 10/100
- Xircom CreditCard CE3

26.3   Token-ring adapters

You should at least have kernel 1.3.72

- IBM Token ring Adapter
- 3Com 3c689 TokenLink III

26.4   Wireless network adapters

- AT&T GIS / NCR WaveLAN version 2.0
- DEC RoamAbout/DS
- Xircom CreditCard Netwave

26.5   ISDN

- ELSA PCMCIA

26.6   Modem and serial cards

Virtually all modem cards, simple serial port cards, and digital cellular modems should work. Also ISDN modems that emulate a standard UART are supported.

- Advantech COMpad-32/85 dual serial
- Quatech, IOTech dual RS-232 cards
- Quatech quad RS-232 card
- Socket Communications dual RS-232 card

26.7 Memory cards

All SRAM cards should work. Unsupported flash cards can be read but not written.

- Epson 2MB SRAM
- IBM 8MB Flash
- Intel Series 2 and Series 2+ Flash
- Maxtor MobileMax 16MB Flash
- New Media SRAM
- TDK Flash Memory SFM20W/C 20MB

26.8 SCSI adapters

Be careful. Many vendors, particularly CD-ROM vendors, seem to switch controller chips at will. Generally, They will use a different product code, but not always: older (supported) New Media Bus Toaster cards are not easily distinguishable from the current (unsupported) Bus Toaster cards.

- Adaptec APA-1460, APA-1460A, APA-1450A SlimSCSI
- Digital SCSI II adapter
- Eiger Labs SCSI (Not the Eiger SS-1000)
- Future Domain SCSI2GO
- IBM SCSI
- Iomega ZIP Card
- IO-DATA PCSC-II, PCSC-II-L
- IO-DATA CDG-PX44/PCSC CD-ROM
- Logitec LPM-SCSI2
- Logitec LCD-601 CD-ROM
- MACNICA mPS110, mPS110-LP SCSI
- Melco IFC-SC2, IFC-DC
- NEC PC-9801N-J03R
- New Media Bus Toaster SCSI (older cards only)
- New Media Toast 'n Jam (SCSI only)
- Panasonic KXL-D740, KXL-DN740A, KXL-DN740A-NB 4X CD-ROM
- Pioneer PCP-PR1W CD-ROM
- Qlogic FastSCSI
- Raven CD-Note 4X
- RATOC REX-9530 SCSI-2
- Simple Technologies SCSI
- Sony CD-ROM Discman PRD-250
- Taxan ICD-400PN
- Toshiba NWB0107ABK, SCSC200B

26.9   ATA/IDE CD-ROM adapters

You should at least have kernel 1.3.72

- Argosy EIDE CD-ROM
- Caravelle CD-36N
- Creative Technology CD-ROM
- Digital Mobile Media CD-ROM
- EXP CD940 CD-ROM
- IO-DATA CDP-TX4/PCIDE, CDP-TX6/PCIDE, CDP-TX10/PCIDE, CDV-HDN6/PCIDE, MOP-230/PCIDE
- H45 Technologies Quick 2x CD-ROM

26.10   Multifunction cards

You should at least have kernel 1.3.73

- 3Com 3c562, 3c562B/C/D, 3c563B/C/D
- ActionTec Comnet EF336 modem 28.8 + ethernet 10Mb (only modem part works)
- IBM Home and Away Card
- Linksys LANmodem 28.8, 33.6
- Megahertz/U.S. Robotics EM1144, EM3288, EM3336
- Motorola Mariner
- Motorola Marquis
- Ositech Jack of Diamonds
- Xircom CreditCard CEM28, CEM33, CEM56

26.11   ATA/IDE card drives

These card drives are supported starting with kernel 1.3.72. Both Flash-ATA cards and rotating-media cards are supported.

26.12   Miscellaneous cards

- Trimble Mobile GPS (uses serial/modem driver)

26.13   Cards with separately distributed drivers

- IBM Smart Capture (Koji Okamura *oka@nanotsu.kobe-u.ac.jp* <mailto:oka@nanotsu.kobe-u.ac.jp>)

26.14 Working on ...

People are working on the following cards:

- Nat'l Inst DAQCard (Eric Gonzalez *root@colomsat.net.co* `<mailto:root@colomsat.net.co>`)
- Roland SCP-55 MIDI (Toshiaki Nakatsu *ir9k-nkt@asahi.net.or.jp* `<mailto:ir9k-nkt@asahi.net.or.jp>`)
- CyberRom CD-ROM (David Rowntree *rowntree@dircon.co.uk* `<mailto:rowntree@dircon.co.uk>`)
- IO DATA PCSC-II (Katayama Nobuhiro *kata-n@po.iijnet.or.jp* `<mailto:kata-n@po.iijnet.or.jp>`)
- Macnica mPS-1x0 (Katayama Nobuhiro *kata-n@po.iijnet.or.jp* `<mailto:kata-n@po.iijnet.or.jp>`)
- FORTEZZA encryption (Rex Riggins *rriggins@radium.ncsc.mil* `<mailto:rriggins@radium.ncsc.mil>`)
- Harris PRISM/AM79C930 (Mark Mathews *mark@mail.absoval.com* `<mailto:mark@mail.absoval.com>`)
- IBM Etherjet (Danilo Beuche *danili@cs.tu-berlin.de* `<mailto:danili@cs.tu-berlin.de>`). The driver can be found at `<http://www.first.gmd.de/danilo/pc-driver>`
- Teles PCMCIA
- Xircom CE3 (Werner Koch *werner.koch@guug.de* `<mailto:werner.koch@guug.de>`)

26.15 Unsupported

- ActionTec Comnet EF336 modem 28.8 + ethernet 10Mb (ethernet part not supported)
- Adaptec/Trantor APA-460 SlimSCSI
- CanonCompaq PCMCIA floppy drive
- New Media .WAVjammer and all other sound cards
- All 100baseT ethernet adapters
- Panasonic KXL-D720, KXL-D745
- SMC 8016 EliteCard
- Telxon/Aironet wireless adapter
- Xircom CE II Ethernet/Modem
- Xircom CE-10BT Ethernet

27 Appendix C. Plug and Play devices

For people having trouble getting Plug and Play devices to work, the ISA PnP utilities written by Peter Fox are available. Quote from the README:

```
These programs allow ISA Plug-And-Play devices to be configured
on a Linux machine.

This program is suitable for all systems, whether or not they
include a PnP BIOS.
```

Commands have been taken from the Plug and Play ISA specification Version 1.0a. (`<ftp://ftp.redhat.com/pub/pnp/docs/>`)

More information on ISA PnP utilities can be found on the website of Peter Fox: `<http://www.roestock.demon.co.uk/isapnptools/>`

Please let me know about hardware (not normally supported under Linux) which can be put to work with the aid of these utilities. A list of this hardware will be put in this appendix.

28   Appendix D. Linux incompatible Hardware

Some hardware manufacturers have created devices which are compatible with MS-Dos and Windows 95 only. They seem to emulate part of the normally available hardware in the devices by software packages sold together with the device. Specification on these devices are not presented to the world so it is almost impossible to write drivers for these devices. Below a list of devices reported as being Linux incompatible will be given.

Simply put, it is best to avoid hardware which states things like "Needs Windows" or "Windows only".

- Canon LBP-465 printer
- Hewlet Packard HP Deskjet 820xx printers
- Hewlet Packard HP Deskjet 722C printer
- Lexmark 1000 inkjet printer
- Sharp JX-9210 printer
- Boca Research 28.8 internal modem (model MV34AI)
- DSVD modem??
- Motorola ModemSURFR internal 56K??
- Multiwave Innovation CommWave V.34 modem (`<http://www.multiwave.com/>`)
- US Robotics WinModem series
- US Robotics Sportster Voice/Fax modem (X2 model 1785 internal PnP)
- Zoltrix 33.6 Win HSP Voice/Speaker Phone modem
- Compaq 192 PCMCIA modem/serial card
- New Media Winsurfer PCMCIA modem/serial card

29   Glossary

AGP

Accelerated Graphics Port. A bus interconnect mechanism designed to improve performance of 3D graphics applications. AGP is a dedicated bus from the graphics subsystem to the core-logic chipset. `<http://www.euro.dell.com/intl/euro/r+d/r+dnews/vectors/vect_2-1/v2-1_agp.htm>`

ATAPI

AT Attachment Packet Interface. A new protocol for controlling mass storage devices similar to SCSI protocols. It builds on the ATA (AT Attachment) interface, the official ANSI Standard name for the IDE interface developed for hard disk drives. ATAPI is commonly used for hard disks, CD-ROM drives, tape drives, and other devices.

ATM

Asynchronous Transfer Mode

CDDA

?? Capability of CD-ROM/Writer to read out audio tracks.

DMA

Direct Memory Access

EGA

Enhanced Graphics Adapter

EIDE

Enhanced IDE

EISA

Extended Industry System Architecture

FDDI

Fiber Distributed Data Interface. High-speed ring local area network.

IDE

Integrated Drive Electronics. Each drive has a built-in controller.

ISA

Industry System Architecture

ISDN

Integrated Services Digital Network

MCA

MicroChannel Architecture

MFM

Modified Frequency Modulation

MMX

Multimedia Extensions. Added to the newest generation of Intel Pentium Processors. It offers better audio and video quality

PCI

Pheripheral Component Interconnect

RAID

Redudant Arrays of Inexpensive Disks. The basic idea of RAID is to combinr multiple small, inexpensive disk drives into an array of disk drives which yields performance exceeding that of a single large expensive drive. There are five type of redundant array Architectures; RAID-1 through RAID-5. A non-redudant array of disk drives is referred to as RAID-0.
<http://www.uni-mainz.de/neuffer/scsi/what_is_raid.html>

RLL

Run Length Limited

SCSI

Small Computer Systems Interface. A standerd interface defined for all devices in a computer. It make it possible to use a single adapter for all devices.
<http://www.uni-mainz.de/neuffer/scsi/what_is_scsi.html>

SVGA

Super Video Graphics Adapter

UART
  Universal Asynchronous Receiver Transmitter
VGA
  Video Graphics Adapter
VLB
  VESA Local Bus
WORM
  Write Once Read Many

Linux PCI-HOWTO

by Michael Will, `Michael.Will@student.uni-tuebingen.de`   v0.6g, 30 March 1997

Information on what works with Linux and PCI-boards and what does not. Please get the latest version of this document at *The Linux Documentation Project* `<http://sunsite.unc.edu/LDP/linux.html>`

Contents

1   Introduction

Many people, including me, would like to run Linux on a PCI-based machine. Since it is not obvious which PCI motherboards and PCI cards will work with Linux and which do not, I conducted a survey and spent some hours to compile the information contained herein.

If you have information to add, please mail me. If you have questions, feel free to ask.

Help with my style/grammar/language is welcome as well. I am not a native- speaker of English and expect to make occasional mistakes.

Note: "on-board chip" refers to a SCSI chip integrated onto the motherboard rather than on a PCI expansion card.

Also, "quotes" herein may have slight context editing.

2 Why PCI?

2.1 General overview

The PC-architecture has several BUS-Systems to choose from:

ISA

> 16 or 8bit, cheap, slow (usually 8Mhz), standard, many cards available>

EISA

> 32bit, expensive, fast, few cards available, fading>

MCA

> 32 or 16bit ex-IBM-proprietary, fast, becoming rare>

VESA-Local-Bus

> 32bit, based on 486 architecture, cheap, fast, many cards available>

PCI-Local-Bus

> 32bit (64 bit coming), cheap, fast, many cards available, nowadays standard>

MCA worked fine, but never achieved much market, being used on only some early IBM PS/2 machines. There were very few cards.

EISA was reliable, but rather expensive, and intended more for servers, than for the average user. It has the next fewest cards available.

VESA-Local-Bus (VLB) had some problems with high bus-speeds, and was not very reliable, but mainly due to its low price and better-than-ISA performance, sold very well. Technically, it's almost a direct map of the 486 processor bus. Most VESA boards should be stable by now. At the beginning of 1996, many 486 motherboards still support VESA, but PCI is growing. VESA busses are tied directly to the speed of the memory bus for 486's, or half the speed for Pentiums.

PCI now has the advantage. Like EISA it is not proprietary. It is as faster than EISA or MCA, and cheaper. Most current Pentium motherboards use the PCI bus; VESA is fading. Virtualy all PCI motherboards and cards sold at the beginning of 1996 are 32 bit, and run at 0-33 MHz.

Currently, most Pentium motherboards run the PCI bus at 1/2 the memory speed (ie: 33 MHz for the 66 MHz memory bus on the P66,P100,P133,P166; 30 MHz for the 60 MHz memory bus on the P60,P90,P120,P150; and 25 Mhz on the 50 MHz memory bus of the P75). This is probably true of Cyrix 6x86 motherboards too. NexGen 5x86 implemention isn't known. The PCI spec does allow the PCI bus to be run asynchronously from the processor, (eg: 33 Mhz bus on P75), but this is not common yet.

PCI 2.1 has been defined, allowing 64 bit PCI, and/or 0-66 MHz operations, but no x86 chipsets yet support these options. 64 bit PCI will probably appear first, in 32/64 bit dual compatible versions. That is, you will be able to mix 32 and 64 bit cards. 66 MHz PCI will take longer, as it's technically demanding, can only support one or maybe two slots per bridge, and may not work well with 33 MHz cards.

PCI is not processor dependent like the VESA Local-Bus. This means you can use the winner-1000-PCI in an Alpha-driven-PCI computer as well as in a i486/Pentium-driven PCI computer, with the appropriate BIOS and software. Beside Intel and DEC Alpha platforms, PCI is used on some PowerPC's.

Some PCI variations to be aware of: some implementations support "Bus Master" cards in all PCI slots, some in only one slot, and some not at all; some implementations support "bridging" on cards and some do not.

2.2 Performance

taken from Craig Sutphin's early Pro-PCI-Propaganda

> Unlike some local buses, which are aimed at speeding up graphics alone, the PCI Local Bus is a total system solution, providing increased performance for networks, disk drives, full-motion video, graphics and the full range of high-speed peripherals. At 33 MHz, the synchronous PCI Local Bus transfers 32 bits of data at up to 132 Mbytes/sec. A transparent 64-bit extension of the 32-bit data and address buses can double the bus bandwidth (264 Mbytes/sec) and offer forward and backwards compatibility for 32 and 64-bit PCI Local Bus peripherals. Because it is processor-independent, the PCI Local Bus is optimized for I/O functions, enabling the local bus to operate concurrent with the processor/memory subsystem. For users of high-end desktop PC's, PCI makes high reliability, high performance and ease of use more affordable than ever before; no trivial task at 33 MHz bus-clock rates. Variable length linear or toggle mode bursting for both reads and writes improves write dependent graphics performance. By comprehending the loading and frequency requirements of the local bus at the component level, buffers and glue logic are eliminated.

See the chapter about Benchmarks for some crude (and perhaps meaningless) benchmarks on ASUS PCI Boards with 486 and 586.

2.3 The onboard-SCSI-II-chip NCR53c810

One very nice feature of some PCI mother boards is the NCR onboard-SCSI-II-chip, which is said to be as fast as the EISA-Adaptec-1742, but much cheaper. Drivers for DOS/OS2 are available. Drew Eckard has released his version of his NCR53c810-driver, which is in the standard kernel since v1.2.

This works so well I sold my adaptec-1542B-ISA soon after I bought the ASUS SP3-saturn-chipset II PCI board, and found the onboard NCR-SCSI controller to be much faster.

The NCR53c810-chip is onboard on some PCI-motherboards. There are add-on-boards available too, for about US$ 70.00.

There is only one thing I noticed did not work with the NCR-drivers when I tried them. Disconnect/Reconnect did not work, so using a SCSI-tape could be a pain, especially when using "mt erase" or the like blocks the whole SCSI-bus until it has finished. Since this was very unsatisfying for me, I bought one of these nice but expensive DPT PCI SCSI controller and had no such problems anymore.

People have reported this problem has been solved by Drew by now.

FreeBSD does support the NCR53c810 for quite a long time already, including Tagged Command Queues, FAST, WIDE and Disconnect for NCR 53c810, 815, 825. Drew said, it would be possible to adapt the FreeBSD driver to Linux. I somewhere saw some patches to do exactly this, any pointer to the location?

I personaly have the impression there are some important wheels invented more than once because of the differently evolving of FreeBSD and Linux. Some more cooperation could do both systems very well...

2.4 Drew Eckhardt on PCI-SCSI:

Drew said on end of March 95 about the SCSI on PCI: (slightly edited for clarity in context)

The Adaptec 2940, Buslogic BT946, BT946W, DPT PCI boards, Future Domain 3260, NCR53c810, NCR53c815, NCR53c820, and NCR53c825 all work for some definition of the word works.

- The Adaptec 2940 suffers from the same cabling sensitivity that plagues all recent boards, but otherwise works fine.

- The Future Domain boards are not busmasters, and the driver doesn't support multiple simultaenous commands. If you don't (currently) need multiple simultaneous commands, get a NCR board, which will be cheaper and is busmastering. If you need multiple simultaneous commands, get a Buslogic.

- The Buslogic BT956W will do WIDE SCSI with the Linux drivers (although you can't use targets 8-15), the Adaptec 2940W (with one line patch to the 2940 driver) won't, nor will the NCR53c820 and NCR53c825.

- The NCR boards are dirt cheap (< $ 70 US), are generally quite fast, but the driver currently doesn't support multiple simultaenous commands. Alpha which do neat things like disconnect/reconnect and synchronous transfer are now publicly available, see below.

- Emulux, Forex, and other unmentioned PCI SCSI controllers will not work.

2.5 New Alpha Version of the NCR driver

Well, this is not exactly *that* new anymore, please try to he versions which are in the kernel by version 2.0.x before going for this entry.

Alpha versions of the NCR driver which do neat things like disconnect/reconnect and synchronous transfers are now publically available. Any one interested in playing with them should

- Join the NCR mailing list, by sending mail to majordomo@colorado.edu with subscribe ncr53c810 in the text.

- Get all of the readmes, and latest diffs file from ftp://tsx-11.mit.edu/pub/ALPHA/linux/SCSI/ncr53c810

2.6 The EATA-DMA driver and the PCI SCSI controllers from DPT

The EATA-DMA scsi driver has undergone extensive changes and now also supports PCI SCSI controllers, multiple controllers and all SCSI channels on the multichannel SmartCache/Raid boards in all combinations of WIDE, FAST-20 (ULTRA) and DIFFERENTIAL.

The driver supports all EATA-DMA Protocol (CAM document CAM/89-004 rev. 2.0c) compliant SCSI controllers and has been tested with many of those controllers in mixed combinations.

```
Those are:              (ISA)   (EISA) (PCI)
   DPT Smartcache: PM2011 PM2012B
   Smartcache III: PM2021  PM2022 PM2024
                           PM2122 PM2124
                           PM2322
   Smartcache IV:  PM2041  PM2042 PM2044
                           PM2142 PM2144
                           PM2322
   SmartRAID     : PM3021  PM3122
                           PM3222 PM3224
                                  PM3334
   and some controllers from NEC, AT&T, SNI, AST, Olivetti and Alphatronix.
```

On a "base" DPT card (no caching or RAID module), a MC680x0 controls the bus-mastering DMA chip(s) and the SCSI controller chip. The DPT SCSI card almost works like a SCSI coprocessor.

The DPT card also will emulate an IDE controller/drive (ST506 interface), which enables you to use it with all operating systems even if they don't have an EATA driver.

On a card with the caching module, the 680x0 maintains and manages the on-board cacheing. The DPT card supports up to 64 MB RAM for disk-cacheing.

On a card with the RAID module, the 680x0 also performs the management of the RAID, doing the mirroring on RAID-1, doing the striping and ECC info generation on RAID-5, etc.

The entry level boards utilize a Motorola 68000, the high-end, more raid specific DPT cards use a 68020, 68030 or 68040/40MHz processor.

Official list prices range from $ 265 to $1.645 (January 18, 1996)

Since I've been asked numerous times where you can buy those boards in Europe, I asked DPT to send me a list of their official European distributors. Here is a small excerpt:

```
Austria: Macrotron GmbH           Tel:+43 1 408 15430  Fax:+43 1 408 1545
Denmark: Tallgrass Technologies A/S Tel:+45 86 14 7000  Fax:+45 86 14 7333
Finland: Computer 2000 Finnland OY Tel:+35 80 887 331   Fax:+35 80 887 333 43
France : Chip Technologies        Tel:+33 1 49 60 1011  Fax:+33 1 49 599350
Germany: Akro Datensysteme GmbH   Tel:+49 (0)89 3178701 Fax:+49 (0)89 31787299
Russia : Soft-tronik             Tel:+7 812 315 92 76   Fax:+7 812 311 01 08
U.K.   : Ambar Systems Ltd.      Tel:+44 1296 311 300   Fax:+44 296 479 461
```

"IMHO, the DPT cards are the best-designed SCSI cards available for a PC. And I've written code for just about every type of SCSI card for the PC. (Although, in retrospect, I don't know why!) ;-)" Jon R. Taylor (jtaylor@magicnet.net) President, Visionix, Inc.

The latest version of the EATA-DMA driver and a Slackware bootdisk is available on: ftp.i-Connect.Net:/pub/Local/EATA

Since patchlevel 1.1.81 the driver is included in the standard kernel distribution.

The author can be reached under these addresses: neuffer@mail.uni-mainz.de or mike@i-Connect.Net

2.7   BT-946C fully supported with kernel 1.3.x and newer

There is a driver in the 1.3.x kernels (available as a patch for the 1.2.13 kernel) written by someone associated with buslogic that fully supports the 946C and ALL of it's features including strict round robin, tagged queueing, multiple scatter/gather, multiple mailboxes, IRQ sharing, and yes, 15 devices on Fast/Wide. It is no longer necessary to use any ISA emulation with the driver (no DMA channel, no ISA address), and the driver is /fast/ and /stable/ (it's out of BETA and into full release).

The driver is available on ftp.dandelion.com (the newest version can always be got by doing "get BusLogic*"). It supports ALL BusLogic controllers with the exception of the FlashPoint LT, which uses a different interface. The driver is included in the 1.3.x kernels as standard for BusLogic devices.

2.8   Future Domain TMC-3260 PCI SCSI

Rik Faith (faith@cs.unc.edu) informed me on Wed, 1 Feb 1995 about the Future Domain TMC-3260 PCI SCSI card being supported by the Future Domain 16x0 SCSI driver. Newer information might be contained in the SCSI-HOWTO.

- Detection is not done well, and does not use standard PCI BIOS detection methods (someone who has a PCI board needs to send me patches to fix this problem). So, you might have to fiddle with the detection routine in the kernel to get it detected.

- The driver still does not support multiple outstanding commands, so your system will hang while your tape rewinds.

- The driver does not support the enhanced pseudo-32bit transfer mode supported by recent Future Domain chips, so you will not get transfer rates as high as under DOS.

- The driver only supports the SCSI-I protocol, so your really fast hard disks will not get used at the highest possible throughput. (Again, fixes for all these problems are solicited – no one is working on them at this time.)

2.9 other thoughts on scsi

James Soutter (J.K.Soutter1@lut.ac.uk) asked me to add the following information on Fast-Wide-SCSI-2:

Fast Wide SCSI-2 is sometimes incorrectly called SCSI-3. It differs from the normal Fast SCSI-2 (like the Adapted 1542B?) because it uses a 16 bit data bus rather than the more usual 8 bit bus. This improves the maximum transfer rate from 10 MB/s to 20 MB/s but requires the use of special Fast Wide SCSI-2 drives. The added performance of Fast Wide SCSI-2 will not necessarily improve the speed of your system. Most hard disk drives have a maximum internal transfer rate of less than 10 MB/s and so one drive alone can not flood a FAST SCSI-2 bus.

In Seagate's Oct 1993 product overview, only one Fast Wide SCSI-2 drive has an internal transfer rate of more than 10 MB/s (the ST12450W). Most of the drives have a maximum internal transfer rate of 6 MB/s or less, although the ST12450W is not the only exception to the rule. In conclusion, Fast Wide SCSI is designed for the file server market and will not necessarily benefit a single user workstation style system.

Rather than buying a PCI system with a SCSI interface on the motherboard, or rather than waiting for the NCR driver, you could purchase a separate PCI based SCSI card. According to Drew, the only PCI SCSI option that stands a chance of working is the Buslogic 946. It purports to be Adaptec 1540 compatible, like the EISA/VESA/ISA boards in the series.

Drew commented that other PCI based SCSI controllers are unlikely to be supported under Linux or the BSD's because the NCR based controllers are cheaper and more prevalent.

I definitly recommend reading the SCSI HOWTO in regards to newer information about PCI SCSI drivers.

Ernst Kloecker (ernst@cs.tu-berlin.de) wrote: (edited)

Talus Corporation has finished a NS/FIP driver for PCI boards with NCR SCSI. It will be shipping very soon, might even be free because a third party might pay for the work and donate the driver to NeXT.

Not every PCI-Board has got the chip. The old ASUS do, and one of the J-Bond boards does, too. (Most of the boards nowadays (6/95) do expect you to buy the NCR53c810 seperately.) Some vendors provide an alternative as you can read in Drew's text...

The NCR-Chip is clever enough to work with drives formatted by other controllers, and should be no problem.

3 ASUS-Boards

3.1 ASUS and the NMI (Parity) – impact on Gravis-Ultrasound

The newer trition PCI-Mainboards in 1995 did not seem to support parity-SIMMS anymore. Since I usualy took the cheaper nonparity-SIMMS anyway, I did not consider this a problem until I put the Gravis-Ultrasound into my machine. Under DOS the SBOS-Driver and Setup/Test utility does complain about "nmi procedure disabled on this p.c.". The manual says I'd better get a better mainboard in that case, not very helpful.

The gravis-ultrasound did work nice in the ASUS-SP3 and ASUS-SP4, inspite of this, but the gravis-ultrasound-max I have here got gmod to kernel panic on both boards, and sometimes when playing au-files via /dev/audio did strange things, like playing the rest of an older, previously played sound after the new one. The sounddriver does recommend a buffer of 65536 with the GUS Max instead of the small one like the GUS - why I do not know. I do not have such a problem with the newer ASUS TP4 XE boards, though. Both are equipped with 1M DRAM onboard. These problems are probably not related to the NMI-problem, but because of the sounddriver?

I heard not only ASUS but most of the newer PCI-Mainboards are lacking in parity/NMI-support.

Strange enough - the ASUS-TP4 (Trition Chipset) does work with the GUS Max - it does load the SBOS-Driver. I have to admit, I am confused.

3.2 Various types of ASUS Boards

3.2.1 ASUS SP3 with saturn chipset I (rev. 2) for 486,

- 2 x rs232 with 16550
- NCR53c810 onboard,
- slightly broken saturn-chipset I (rev. 2)

3.2.2 ASUS SP3G with saturn chipset II (rev. 4) for 486,

like SP3, but less buggy saturn chipset

3.2.3 ASUS SP3-SiS chipset, for 486

like AP4, but newer, SiS chipset, green functions and all the EIDE, rs232 with 2 16550 and centronics. Only 2 SIMM Slots, Does seem to work with AMD486DX4/120, but was not very reliably on NCR53c810 and various operating systems (Windows-NT, Windows95, OS2), after upgrading to a PentiumBoard ASUS SP4, all the problems vanished, so it must have been the board. Still does seem to work nice for Linux, though.

3.2.4 ASUS AP4, for 486, with PCI/ISA/VesaLocalbus

green functions, 1VL, 3 ISA, 4 PCI slots, only EIDE onboard, no fd-controller, no rs232/centronics. Very small size.

does recognice AMD486DX2/66 as DX4/100 only. This can be corrected with soldering one pin (which?) to ground, but I would not recommend a board like this anyway.

The one I tested was broken for OS2 and Linux, but people are said to use it for both.

The VesaLocalbus-Slot is expected to be slower than the normal vesa-localbus boards because of the PCI2VL bridge, but without penalty to the PCI section.

3.2.5 ASUS SP4-SiS, for Pentium90, PCI/ISA

like SP3-SiS, but for Pentium90/100.

3.2.6 ASUS TP4 with Triton chipset and EDO-Support

has the Triton-Chipset for better performance and supports normal PS2-Simms as well as Fast-Page-Mode and EDO modules.

3.2.7 ASUS TP4XE with Triton chipset and additional SRAM/EDORAM support

supports the new EDORAM and upcoming SRAM standards. At least SRAM is said to considerably increase performance. Did for some reason not accept the 8M PS2-SIMMS working ok in ASUS SP4, after changing them against others, bigger looking ones, (16 chips instead of 8 if I remember right) it worked ok. Has been tested with P90 and P100.

3.2.8 ...and many others now.

if you have new information on problems with them, please report.

3.3 Benchmarks on ASUS Mainboards

I tried to compare the speed of CPUs in two ASUS Mainboards: for 486 I tested the SP3 SiS (the one with one vesa-local-bus slot) and for 586 I tested the ASUS TP4/XE, each with 16M RAM, always the same unloaded system with another CPU, with whetstone and dhrystone.

I must admit, I have not read the benchmarks-faq yet, and will probably edit the section a loot soon. If you have any comments, please mail me.

I am especially confused about the amd486DX4/100 being faster on dhrystones than the DX4/120 version? I did not see that kind of inconsistency on comparing the P90 and P100.

Perhaps this was at fault: when I plugged in the amdDX4-100, I had the board jumpered for DX2-66. While the BIOS did report it as an DX4-100, the board might have used the wrong clockspeeds... but since DX2-66 uses 33Mhz * 2 and DX4 uses 33Mhz * 3, this would have been correct?

The board running with DX4-120 is jumpered to 40Mhz * 3 = 120 Mhz.

Another thing I wonder about is why the whetstones-result does yield so even numbers on some machines?

3.3.1 ASUS SP3 with amd486DX4-100

- Dhrystone time for 500000 passes = 7 by 63559 dhrystones/second
- Whetstone time for 1000 passes = 5 by 200.0000 Whetstones/second

3.3.2   ASUS SP3 with amd486DX4-120

- Dhrystone time for 500000 passes = 8 by 56074 dhrystones/second
- Whetstone time for 1000 passes = 4 by 250.0000 Whetstones/second

3.3.3   ASUS SP3 with intel486DX2-66

- Dhrystone time for 500000 passes = 9 by 50761 dhrystones/second
- Whetstone time for 1000 passes = 7 by 142.8571 Whetstones/second

3.3.4   ASUS TP4/XE with intel586-90

- Dhrystone time for 500000 passes = 4 by 101010 dhrystones/second
- Whetstone time for 1000 passes = 3 by 333.3333 Whetstones/second

3.3.5   ASUS TP4/XE with intel586-100

- Dhrystone time for 500000 passes = 4 by 102040 dhrystones/second
- Whetstone time for 1000 passes = 2 by 500.0000 Whetstones/second

3.4   Detailed information on the old ASUS PCI-I-SP3 with saturn chipset from heinrich@zsv.gmd.de:

- 3 PCI, 4 ISA Slots (3x16, 1x8 Bit)
- ZIF Socket for the CPU
- room for 4 72pin-SIMMs (max. 128M)
- Award BIOS in Flash-Eprom
- Onboard: NCR-SCSI, 1par, 2ser (with FIFO), AT-Bus, Floppy

The board does like most in that price class – write-through cache, no write-back. This should not be significant, maybe 3% of performance.

The BIOS supports scsi-drives under DOS/Windows without additional drivers, but with the board come additional drivers which are said to give better performance, for DOS/Windows(ASPI), OS2, Windows-NT, SCO-Unix, Netware (3.11 and 4, if interpreted correctly)

Gert Doering (gert@greenie.muc.de) was saying the SCO-Unix-driver for the onboard-SCSI-Chip was not working properly. After two or three times doing: "time dd if=/dev/rhd20 of=/dev/null bs=100k count=500" it kernel-paniced...

The trouble some people experienced with this board might be due to them using an outboard Adaptec-SCSI-Controller with "sync negotiation" turned on. (This predates the NCR driver release; hence the use of the Adaptec.) Please check that in the BIOS-Setup of the Adaptec-1542C if you use one and have problems with occasional hangups!

There is a new version of the ASUS-Board which should have definitely less problems. It is called ASUS-PCI-I/SP3G, the G is important. It has the new Saturn-chipset rev. 4 and the bugs should be gone. They use the Saturn-ZX-variant and the new SP3G has fully PCI conforming level-triggered (thus shareable), BIOS-configurable interrupts. It has an on-board PS/2-mouseport, EPA-power-saving-modes and DX4-support, too. It performs excellently. If you can get the German computer magazine C't from July (?), you will find a test report where the ASUS-Board is the best around.

Latest information about ASUS-SP3-G: You might experience crashes when using PCI-to-Memory-Posting. If you disable this, all works perfect. jw@peanuts.informatik.uni-tuebingen.de said he believed it to be a problem of the current Linux-kernel rather than the hardware, because part of the system still works when crashing, looking like a deadlock in the swapper, and OS2/DOS/WINDOZE don't crash at all.

Someone else with a very old ASUS-SP3 (saturn-I chipset) reported crashes with using XFree86, which went away when he installed the very latest betaversion which seems to work around a bit of the problems.

3.5 Pat Dowler (dowler@pt1B1106.FSH.UVic.CA) with ASUS SP3G

- ASUS SP3G board (it is rev.4 == saturn II)
- AMD DX4-100 CPU (need to set jumper 36 to 1&2 rather than 2&3, otherwise it's set the same as other 486DXn chips)
- 256K cache (comes with 15ns cache :-)
- 16meg RAM (2x8meg)
- ET4000 ISA video card
- quantum IDE hard drive
- SMC Elitel16 combo ethernet card

Unlike some other reports, I find the mouse pointer moves very smoothy under X (just like the ol' 386) - it is jumpy under some, but not all, DOS games though...

Performance is great!! I ran some large floating point tests and found the performance in 3x33 (100MHz) mode to be almost 1.5x that in 2x (66MHz) mode (large being 500x500 doubles - 4meg or so)... I was a little dubious about clock-tripling but I seem to be getting full benefit :-)

The heavily configurable energy star stuff doesn't work with the current AMD DX4 chips - you need an SL chip

I really need a SCSI disk and a PCI video card :-)

(I had a phonecall by a person who had this problem with the buggy SMC FIFO chipset, after using X-window they hung.)

4 confusion about saturn chipsets

Pat Duffy (duffy@theory.chem.ubc.ca) said:

```
Saturn I:  these are revisions 1 and 2 of the Saturn chipsets.
Saturn II: This is also called rev. 4 of the Saturn chipsets.

As far as I know, rev. 3 never actually shipped, and (from a few people who
have it) the SP3G now has rev. 4 (or Saturn II) in it.

Confused?  Well, the only real definitive answer is to get ahold of the board
and run the debug script in the PCI chipset list on it.  As far as I know,
though, the SP3G board is indeed shipping with rev. 4 (Saturn II).
```

5   Video-Cards

Linux people have successfully used # 9 XGE Level 12, ELSA Winner 1000, and S3-928 video cards. The XFree86(tm)-3.1.1 does support boards with the tseng et4000/w32 in accelerated mode, as well as S3 Vision 864 and 964 chipsets including boards like the ELSA Winner 1000Pro and 2000Pro, Number Nine GXE64 and GXE64Pro, Miro Crystal 20SV). Support in the S3 Server for the Chrontel8391 clock chip has been added.

Trio32 and Trio64 S3 Boards like the SPEA V7 Mirage P64 PCI and MIRO Crystal 40SV, are also supported, the Mach32 and Mach64 are supported in accelerated mode, too.

The SVGA Driver

16bpp mode (65K colors instead of the usual 256) support for Mach32 boards as well as 32bpp for some S3 boards and the P9000 boards has been added.

tldraben@teleport.com reported:

- Diamond Stealth W32 (et4000/W32) – Text mode works, X11 suffered from "pixel dust", unbearable never got it to work and returned it.

- # 9GXE L12 – Works, virtual consoles corrupted when switched, fixed this with disabling the "fast dram mode" feature in his BIOS. Does not get a dot clock above 85, though.

Genoa Phantom 8900PCI card seems to work well. Genoa Phantom/W32 2MB does not work in an ASUS-Board. Tseng 3000/W32i chipset seems to work well. Spea-v7 mercury-lite works perfectly since XFree86(tm)-2.1.

Spea V7 Mirage P64 PCI 2M with Trio64 works nice since XFree86(tm)-3.1.1

ATI Graphics Ultra Pro for PCI with 2MB VRAM and an ATI68875C DAC run well as dem@skyline.dayton.oh.us tells us: "It's humming right along at 1280x1024 w/256 colors @74Hz non-interlaced. Looks great."

Paradise WD90C33 PCI did lock up on screensaver/X - this has been solved in the newer versions of the kernel. jbauer@badlands.NoDak.edu (John Edward Bauer)

miroChrystal 8S/PCI (1MB) S3 - no problem.

Stephen Tweedie reported his Cirrus Logics 5434 PCI card works well. It is a 64bit with 2M and runs perfectly with the SVGA driver in 8, 16 and 32 bit per pixel.

6   Ethernet Cards

Of course the ISA-ethernet-cards still work, but people are asking for PCI-based ones. The author of many (if not most) ethernet- drivers said the following some time ago (unfortunately I have not managed to contact him about new information):

> From: Donald Becker (becker@cesdis.gsfc.nasa.gov) Subject: PCI ethernet cards supported? The LANCE code has been extended to handle the PCI version. I hope to get the PCI probe code (about a dozen extra lines in the LANCE driver) into the next kernel version. I'm working on the 32 bit mode code. I haven't yet started the 21040 code.
>
> I'll write drivers for the PCnet32 mode and the DEC 21040. That will cover most of the PCI ethercard market.
>
> file://cesdis.gsfc.nasa.gov/pub/people/becker/whoiam.html

In the new testkernels of 1.1.50 and above, the AMD-singlechip ethernetadapters are supported. With a pentium, they ought to then see 900K/second ftps +(assuming an NCR PCI scsi controller) at about 20% cpu load. (AMD Lance).

Anything based on the AMD PCnet/PCI chip should work at the time being. In the US the Boca board costs under US$ 70

Geoffry Coram reported in the news that he got his 3com 590 TPO to work. He had to get the alpha driver from http://cesdis.gsfc.nasa.gov/linux/drivers. Other drivers would be there as well. Note http://cesdis.gsfc.nasa.gov/linux/drivers/vortex.html

Donald Holmgren said he successfully attached his DEC DE435 (PCI) card to the local network on thin coax (BNC). The DE435 driver checks the twisted pair connection first, then switches to the alternate port (jumper selectable as AUI or BNC) if the 10BaseT port fails.

Jim Cusick uses the Boca BEN 1PI card on a thin coax network. It works just fine. You might want to check out: http://cesdis.gsfc.nasa.gov/linux/misc/boca-failure.html for details on the early failures of this card. My second card, after sending one back for replacement, was marked "PN 4186". The old one that did not work was "PN 4185". Mandate this newer model when you order from you vendor. At $ 70, the card is a good deal.

Dave Platt recommends to stay off the Boca BEN1PI card at all costs. It would be unreliable due to design flaws, and Boca seems unable to really fix the problem. The 3Com 3c590 "Vortex" PCI card is available in a combo version (10BaseT, thin coax, and AUI). The Linux driver for this card is not yet part of the release kernel, but is available from http://cesdis.gsfc.nasa.gov/linux/drivers/vortex.html and can be patched into the later 1.2.x kernels (as well as 1.3.x) without much difficulty. The Linux driver does not support the interface autodetect feature of this card - you must use the DOS utility to configure the card for the interface you wish to use (thin coax in this case). Once you've done that, the Linux driver will use the correct interface.

He has been using a 3c590 for several weeks, and it is working fine.

Dave Kennedy said he got two of the above Boca boards and they work fine under light load, but under heavy work like ftping two 16M files into both directions, they failed. He sent the boards back to Boca for a hardwarefix. After they soldered a couple of things (diodes/resistors) onto the card and sent them back, the cards worked fine regardless of load. The two cards have been in 7/24 use in two P90 systems without problems for 6 months now.

Craig does not recommend it since Boca seems not to follow the AMD specs but he has been running them for 2 weeks without problems. He tested his NFS performance and has been moving large files to and from server (16M, 8M). He also tried to do all his workin localy using his data files mounted by NFS and has had no problems. Performance seems to be 100 percent better (wrt to NFS performance) over his NE2000 ISA board. (editors note: but so would probably have been the ISA SMC Elite Ultra?)

6.1 3com-3c590-tpo

Someone on usenet mentioned ht used the 3Com-3C590-TPO (EtherLink III - PCI). He had to get the "3c59x.c" driver and "vortex.patch" to make it work with his 1.2.8 Linux kernel.

6.2 DEC435 PCI NIC

The DEC435 PCI NIC is said to work great with the drivers included in the Slackwaredistribution - I'd say they are in the standard-kernel?

7   Motherboards

The people who answered were using the following boards:

7.1   ASUS

- Ruediger.Funck@Physik.TU-Muenchen.DE - successful.
- strauss@dagoba.escape.de - half-successful, works, but...
- krypton@netzservice.de (Ulrich Teichert), - successful.
- heinrich@zsv.gmd.de - successful
- CARSTEN@AWORLD.aworld.de - successful
- egooch@mc.com - successful - but trouble with the serial port
- archie@CS.Berkeley.EDU and his friend - successful after solving IDE-puzzle
- Lars Heinemann (lars@uni-paderborn.de) successful
- Michael Will (Michael.Will@student.uni-tuebingen.de) - successful.

7.2   Micronics P54i-90

root@intellibase.gte.com succesful bill.foster@mccaw.com successful karpens@ncssm-server.ncssm.edu successful

7.3   SA486P AIO-II

ah@doc.ic.ac.uk successful

7.4   Sirius SPACE

hi86@rz.uni-karlsruhe.de - successful

7.5   Gateway-2000

kenf@clark.net - no problems except the soundcard he tries to swap dmarples@comms.eee.strathclyde.ac.uk - successful, but... robert logan (rl@de-montfort.ac.uk) - flawless. James D. Levine (jdl@netcom.com) - flawless.

7.6   Intel-Premiere

grif@cs.ucr.edu - successful jeromem@amiserv.xnet.com - successful demarest@rerf.or.jp - successful (Premier-II)

7.7 DELL Poweredge SP4100 gbelow@pmail.sams.ch - successful

7.8 DELL OptiPlex Gl+ 575 torsten@videonetworks.com - successful when turning off plug and play

7.9 Comtrade Best Buy PCI / PCI48X MB Rev 1.0

tldraben@Teleport.Com - "Works, I believe it has buggy Saturn chipset. I would also like to add: I strongly recommend not buying from Contrade. Their service is horrible. "

7.10 IDeal PCI / PCI48X MB Rev 1.0

tldraben@Teleport.Com - "Did not work with PCI48X motherboard"

7.11 CMD Tech. PCI IDE / CSA-6400C

tldraben@TelePort.com - "Works"

7.12 GA-486iS (Gigabyte)

Stefan.Dalibor@informatik.uni-erlangen.de - success with problems.

7.13 GA-586-ID (Gigabyte) 90 Mhz Pentium PCI/EISA Board

kkeyte@esoc.bitnet - succesful

7.14 ESCOM 486dx2/66 - which board?

Works perfect except the ftape-streamer (archive)

7.15 J-Bond with i486dx2/66

Drew Eckhardt (drew@kinglear.cs.Colorado.EDU) uses Diamond Stealth 64 VRAM with 4M of memory (964 based). It works great, he usualy runs it at 1024x768 72hz in 32bpp; 16 and 8bpp also work. He needed to get the X311u2S3.tgz server from ftp.xfree86.org; people with 968 based Diamond boards will definately need to do this.

7.16 super micro 011895 03:50 SUPER P54CI-PCI rev 1.3 (Opti)

Manuel de Vega Barreiro

- board super micro 011895 03:50 SUPER P54CI-PCI rev 1.3
- Opti chipset: 82c557,82c556,82c558,82c621.

- 4 PCI, 4 ISA Slots (4x16 Bit)
- ZIF Socket for CPU (120,100,90,75 mHz)
- 4 72 pin-SIMMs (max 128Mb)
- cache 256,512,1024 Kb L2-cache
- Ami WinBIOS in Flash-Eprom (101094-VIPER-P)
- onboard: EIDE for 4 drives
- Pentium with 90Mhz, 8M (now 16M) RAM and 256K L2-cache.
- 1 maxtor 540 Mb, 1 st3122A 1Gb
- Number Nine 9GXE64pro with 2Mb
- Sound blaster 16 + cdrom Matsushita
- 17" microscan 5ep ADI monitor

I run linux 1.1.57 (now 1.2.1) without problems. dosemu0.53 work fine (com. software like kermit and xtalk) XFree86 3.1 at 1024x768 resolution

8   reports on success

8.1   GigaByte GA486-AM with AMD Am5x86-133-WB @ 160MHz (40MHz PCI)

GigaByte GA486-AM

- AMD Am5x86-133-WB @ 160MHz (40MHz PCI)
- BIOS as of 11/07/95 (Rev.A)
- 256KB 2nd level cache (15ns)
- 48MB RAM (Mixed 60/70ns)

Hercules Terminator 64/VIDEO (S3 765 or "Trio 64V+")

Sound Blaster 16

- Panasonic CR563 CD-ROM drive

Silicon 4Ser/3Par I/O

- Mouse
- Terminal
- Terminal
- Modem (14k4)
- HP Laserjet III

Mitsumi CD-ROM controller

- FX001D drive

Longshine 1MBit Floppy controller

- IOMega Tape Insider 250
- 3,5" Floppy
- 5,25" Floppy

No Network card, because the 4 ISA slots are full, and I don't have a PCI card. I (now) use kernel 2.0.22 with APM enabled, and the hard drives power down and up properly without panics. The system is 24hrs up a day and still running. Kernel compilation takes between 5 and 7 minutes, depending on options.

8.2 California Graphics - Sunray II Pro

Guido Trentalancia (guido@gulliver.unian.it) reported the California Graphics - Sunray II Pro with Triton chipset to work well with Pentium100, Hd: Conner cfs420a, Conner cfs210a, crunching numbers at 147492 dhrystones/second.

8.3 Micronics P54i-90 (root@intellibase.gte.com)

Pentium with 90Mhz, 32M RAM and 512K L2-cache. Works extremely well (a kernel recompile takes 10 minutes :-).

The board includes:

- UART - two 16550A high speed UARTS
- ECP - one enhanced parallel port
- Onboard IDE controller
- Onboard floppy controller

Pros: Currently, I'm using it with an Adaptec 1542CF and a 1G Seagate drive, No problems. Graphics is ATI Graphics Pro Turbo (PCI). Very fast. The serial ports can keep up with a TeleBit T3000 modem (38400) without overruns. Caching above 16M does occur. There are 3 banks of SIMM slots (2 SIMM's per bank), with each bank capable of 64M each (2 32M 72-pin SIMM's). Each bank must be filled completely to be used (I'm only using bank 0 with 2 16Mx72-pin SIMM's). The CPU socket is a ZIF type socket. The BIOS is Phoenix, FLASH type.

Drawbacks: RAM is expandable to 192M, but the L2 cache is maxed at 512K. While the graphics are very fast, there is currently no XF86 server for the Mach64 (well, actually there is, but it doesn't use any of the accelerator features; it's just an SVGA server). I don't know if the onboard IDE hard drive controller works; I'm prejudiced against a standard that won't allow my peripherals to operate across platforms, so I didn't buy an IDE disk; instead, I got a Seagate 31200N and a NEC 3Xi.

Mitch

8.4 Angelo Haritsis (ah@doc.ic.ac.uk) about SA486P AIO-II:

The motherboard I eventually bought (in the UK) is one supporting 486 SX/DX/DX2/DX4 chips. It is called SA486P AIO-II. Features include:

- Intel Saturn v2 chipset
- Phoenix BIOS (flash eprom option)
- NCR scsi BIOS v 3.04.00

- 256K 15ns cache (max 512) write back and write through
- 4 72-pin SIMM slots in 2 banks
- 3 PCI slots, 4 ISA
- On-board NCR 53c810 scsi controller
- On-board IDE / floppy / 2 x 16550A uarts / enhanced parallel

I bought it from a company (UK) called ICS, (note I have no connections whatsoever with the company, just a happy customer). I use a 486/DX2-66 CPU.

Before I had a VLB 486 m/board with a buslogic BT-445S controller that I was borrowing. I have 2 scsi devices: 1 barracuda 2.1GB ST12550N disk and a Wangtek 5525ES tape drive. I was expecting a lot of adventures by switching to the new motherboard, esp after hearing all these non-success stories on the net. To my surprise everything worked flawlessly on the 1st boot! (1.1.50). And it has been doing so for about a month now. I did not even have to repartition the disk: apparently the disk geometry bios translation of the 2 controllers is the same. Linux has had no problems at all. SCSI is visibly much faster as well (sorry, I have no actual performance measurements).

The only problems (related to Drew's linux ncr53c7,810 scsi driver - thanks for the good work Drew!) are:

- no synchronous transfers are yet supported => performance hit
- disconnect/reconnect is disabled => disk scsi ops "hold" during certain slow scsi device opeartions (eg tape rewind)
- tagged queuing is not there (?) => performance hit

If you get Windows complainingg about 32-bit disk driver problems, just disable 32-bit disk access via Control Panel. This should not hurt performance. (What I did is remove the WDCTRL driver from my SYSTEM.INI).

All else is fine. I tried the serial ports with some dos/windows s/w and worked ok. The IDE/floppy work ok as well. I have not tried the parallel yet. The motherboard is quite fast and so far I am very pleased with the upgrade. I have not yet tried a PCI graphics board. I will later on. I am using an old ISA S3 which is fine at the moment.

PS: the NCR drivers in the 2.0.x kernels should have no problems of that kind anymore. please consult the SCSI-HOWTO for further and hopefully more uptodate information.

8.5   bill.foster@mccaw.com about his Micronics M5Pi

Micronics M5Pi motherboard with 60 MHz Pentium, PCI bus having the following components:

```
16Mb RAM/512k cache
onboard IDE, parallel, 16550A UARTS
2 X 340MB Maxtor IDE Hard Drives
Soundblaster 16 SCSI-II
Toshiba 3401B SCSI CD-ROM
Archive Viper 525MB SCSI Tape Drive
Viewsonic 17 monitor
Cardex Challenger PCI video card (ET4000/W32P)
A4-Tech Serial Mouse
```

Everything works great, Slackware installation was very easy, I can run Quicken 7 for DOS under DOSEMU. I run X at 1152x900 resolution at 67Hz.

8.6 Simon Karpen (karpens@ncssm-server.ncssm.edu) with Micronics M54pi

I have had no problems with the above board, the on-board PCI IDE (hopefully soon will also have SCSI), and an ATI Mach32 (GUP) with 2MB of VRAM.

8.7 Goerg von Below (gbelow@pmail.sams.ch) about DELL Poweredge

```
- Intel 486DX4/100
- 16 MB RAM
- DELL SCSI array (DSA) with Firmware A07, DSA-Manager 1.7
- 1 GB SCSI HD DIGITAL
- NEC SCSI CD-ROM
- 2 GB internal SCSI streamer
- 3-Com C579 EISA Ethernet card
- ATI 6800AX PCI VGA subsystem, 1024 MB RAM

CAVE! DELL SCSI Array controller (DSA) runs only with firmware Rev. A07 !
A06 is buggy, impossible to reboot !
To get it: ftp dell.com , file is /dellbbs/dsa/dsaman17.zip
```

Apart from this firmware-problem there where no problems for the last 2 months, running with linux 1.1.42 as primary nameserver, newsserver and www-server on internet.

8.8 zenon@resonex.com about Gateway2000 P-66

Gateway2000's P5-66 system with Intel's PCI motherboard, with 5 ISA slots and 3 PCI slots. The only PCI card I am using is the # 9 GXe level 12 PCI card (2 MB VRAM and 1 MB DRAM). This card was bought from Dell. Under Linux I am using the graphics in the 80x25 mode only (I am waiting for some XFree86 refinements before using it in 1280x1024 resolution), but under DOS/Windows I have used the card in 1280x1024x256 mode without problems. Etherlink 3C509 Ethernet card, Mitsumi bus-interface card, Adaptec 1542C SCSI interface card and additional serial/parallel ports card (which makes the total of serial ports 3).

I have total of 32 MB RAM (recognized and used by both Linux and DOS). There is also a bus mouse (Microsoft in the PS2 mode).

No problems so far.

8.9 James D. Levine (jdl@netcom.com) with Gateway2000

Gateway 2000 P5-60 with an Intel Mercury motherboard, AMI-Flash-BIOS, (1.00.03.AF1, (c)'92) 16M RAM, on-board IDE controller and an ATI AX0 (Mach32 Ultra XLR) PCI display adapter. He had absolutely no problems with the hardware so far but has not tried anything fancy, such as accelerated IDE drivers or SCSI support.

8.10 hi86@rz.uni-karlsruhe.de with SPACE

SPACE-board, 8MB RAM, S3 805 1MB DRAM PCI 260MB Seagate IDE-hard disk because of lack of NCR53c810-Driver, 0.99pl15d, does seem to work well.

8.11 grif@cs.ucr.edu with INTEL

17 machines running a 60Mhz-i586 on Intel-Premier-PCI-Board

8.12 Jermoe Meyers (jeromem@amiserv.xnet.com) with Intel Premiere

Motherboard - Intel Premiere Plato-babyAT 90mhz with Buslogic bt946c w/4.86 mcode w/4.22 autoSCSI firmware, (note, mine came with 4.80 mcode and 4.17 autoSCSI firmware. (interrupt pins A,B,C conform to respective PCI slots!) ATI Xpression (Mach64) - using driver from sunsite, (running AcerView 56L monitor).

The motherboard has 4 IDE drives, Linux (Slackware 2.0) sees the first two and everything on the Buslogic as it emulates an adaptec 1542. Uh, yes, Dos sees them all. Buslogic is VERY accomodating in regards to shipping upgraded chips (you will have to know how to change PLCC (plastic leaded chip carrier) chips, 3 of them. Though, don't let that scare you :-) it's not that tough. Get a low end PLCC removal tool, and your in business. You also might want to "flash upgrade your system bios from Intel's IPAN BBS, a trivial process. Whats even more interesting is I also have a Sound Blaster SCSI-2 running a scsi CDROM drive off it's adaptech 1522 onboard controller. So thats 4 IDE drives (2 under Linux) and 2 SCSI-2 controllers.

I hope this helps others who are struggling with PCI technology use Linux! Jerry (jeromem@xnet.com)

8.13 Timothy Demarest (demarest@rerf.or.jp) Intel Plato Premiere II

My system is configured as follows: 16Mb 60ns RAM, 3Com Etherlink-III 53C809 ethernet card (using 10base2), ATI Mach 64 2Mb VRAM, Toshiba 2x SCSI CDROM, NCR 53c810 PCI SCSI, Syquest 3270 270Mb Cartridge Drive, Viewsonic 17 monitor, Pentium-90 (FDIV Bug Free). Running Slackware 2.1.0, Kernel 1.2.0, with other misc patches/upgrades.

Everything is functioning flawlessly. I dont recommend the Syquest drives. I have used the 3105 and the 3270 and both a very, very fragile. Also, the cartridges are easily damaged and I have had frequent problems with them. I am in the process of looking for alternative removable storage (MO, Zip, Minidisc, etc).

Some information you might need:

8.13.1 Flash Bios upgrades

Flash Bios updates can be ftp'd from wuarchive.wustl.edu:/pub/MSDOS_UPLOADS/plato. The current version is 1.00.12.AX1. The BIOS upgrades *must* be done in order. 1.00.03.AZ1 to 1.00.06.AX1 to 1.00.08.AX1 to 1.00.10.AX1 to 1.00.12.AX1. The Flash BIOS updates can also be downloaded from the Intel BBS. I do not have that number right now.

8.13.2 NCR 53c810 BIOSless PCI SCSI

If you are using an NCR 53c810 BIOSless PCI SCSI card in the Plato, you may have trouble getting the card to be recognized. I had to change one of the jumpers on the NCR card: the jumper that controls whether there is 1 or 2 NCR SCSI cards in your system must be set to "2". I dont know why, but this is how I got it to work. The other jumper controls the INT setting (A,B,C,D). I left mine at A (the default).

8.13.3   apart from that - plug and play!

There are no settings in the motherboard BIOS for setting the NCR 53c810. Dont worry - once the card is jumpered correctly, it will be recognized! So much for PCI Plug-n-Play!

8.14   heinrich@zsv.gmd.de with ASUS

ASUS-PCI-Board (SP3) having:

- – Asus PCI-Board with AMD 486/dx2-66 and 16M RAM
- – Fujitsu 2196ESA 1G SCSI-II
- – Future Domain 850MEX Controller (cheap-SCSI-Controller, almost a clone to Seagate's ST01... want's to use ncr53c810 as soon as the driver comes out
- – ATI Graphics Ultra (the older one with Mach-8 Chip, ISA-Bus)
- – Slackware 1.1.1

He just exchanged the boards, plugged his cards in, connected the cables, and it worked perfect. He does not use any PCI-Cards yet, though.

8.15   CARSTEN@AWORLD.aworld.de with ASUS

ASUS-PCI-Board with 486DX66/2, miro-crystal 8s PCI driven by the S3-drivers of XFree86-2.0, using the onboard SCSI-Chip. No problems with compatibility at all.

8.16   Lars Heinemann (lars@uni-paderborn.de) with ASUS

ASUS PCI/I-486SP3 Motherboard w/ 486DX2/66 and 16M RAM (2x8), miroChrystal 8S/PCI (1MB) S3, Soundblaster PRO, Adaptec 1542b (3.20 ROM) SCSI host adapter with two hard disks (Fujitsu M2694ESA u. Quantum LPS52) and a QIC-150 Streamer attached. No problems at all!

8.17   Ruediger.Funck@Physik.TU-Muenchen.DE with ASUS

ASUS PCI/I-486SP3 / i486DX2-66 / 8 MB PS/2 70 ns BIOS: Award v 4.50 CPU TO DRAM write buffer: enabled CPU TO PCI write buffer: enabled PCI TO DRAM write buffer: disabled, unchangeable CPU TO PCI burst write: enabled Miro Crystal 8s PCI - S3 P86C805 - 1MB DRAM

Quantum LPS 540S SCSI-Harddisk on NCR53c810-controller.

8.18   robert logan (rl@de-montfort.ac.uk with GW/2000)

Gateway 2000 4DX2-66P 16 Megs RAM, PCI ATI AX0 2MB DRAM (ATI GUP). WD 2540 Hard Disk (528 Megs) CrystalScan 1776LE 17inch. (Runs up to 1280x1024) Slackware 1.1.2 (0.99pl15f)

It is giving no problems. He uses SLIP for networking and an Orchid-Soundwave-32 for niceties, awaiting the NCR-Driver. The only problem he has is that the IDE-Drive could be much faster on the PCI-IDE. It is one of the new Western Digital fast drives and in DOS/WfW it absolutely screams - on Linux it is just as slow as a good IDE-Drive.

8.19   archie@CS.Berkeley.EDU and his friend use ASUS

Archie and his friend have rather similar configurations:

- ASUS PCI-SP3 board (4 ISA, 3 PCI)
- Intel 486DX2/66
- Genoa Phantom 8900PCI card (friend: Tseng 3000/W32i chipset)
- Maxtor 345 MB IDE hard drive
- Supra 14.4 internal modem
- ViewSonic 6e monitor (Archie)
- NEC Multisync 4fge (friend)
- Slackware 1.2.0

The onboard-SCSI is disabled. First there were problems with the IDE-drive: "on the board there's a jumper which selects whether IRQ14 comes from the ISA bus or the PCI bus. The manual has an example where they show connecting it to PCI INT-A. Well, we did that just like the example... but then later our IDE drive would not work (the IDE controller is on board). Had to take it back. The guys at NCA were puzzled, then traced it back to this jumper. I guess the IDE controller uses IRQ14 or something? That's not documented anywhere in the manual. Other than that, seems to be kicking ass nicely now. Running X, modeming, etc. (for the Supra you have to explicitly tell the kernel that the COM port has a 16550A using setserial (in Slackware /etc/rc.d/rc.serial))".

8.20   Michael Will with ASUS-SP3 486 (the old one)

used the following:

- ASUS PCI-SP3-Board with 486dx2/66 and 16M RAM
- NCR53c810-SCSI-II chip driving a 1GB-Seagate-SCSI-II disk and a Wangtec-tape
- ATI-GUP PCI Mach32 Graphics card with 2M VRAM running perfectly with XFree86(tm)-3.1 8bpp and 16bpp
- Linux kernel 1.1.69

It runs perfectly and I am content with the speed, the ATI-GUP-PCI (Mach32) does not give as good benchmarks as expected, though. Since I got the money by now, I got me an ASUS-SP4 with P90 which gives me better throughput on Mach32-PCI... If I had even more money I'd get me another 16M of RAM and a Mach64-PCI with 4M RAM, though... I still keep on dreaming :-)

8.21   Mike Frisch (mfrisch@saturn.tlug.org) Giga-Byte 486IM

- Motherboard: Giga-Byte 486IM
- Configuration: 4 ISA slots (2 double as VLB) and 4 PCI slots

- CPU: Intel 486DX/33
- BIOS: Award 4.50G
- PCI EIDE Disk Controller: Giga-Byte GA-107 (CMD 640x PCI Multi-I/O)
- PCI Video card: ATI Graphics eXpression PCI 2MB DRAM
- Linux Kernel: 1.2.9
- Linux Dist'n: Highly modified Slackware 2.2.0

I have been running this board 24 hours a day for the past 5-6 months. It has worked flawlessly for me under DOS/Windows, OS/2 Warp, and Linux (with Linux being run usually 24 hours a day).

8.22 Karl Keyte (kkeyte@esoc.bitnet) Gigabyte GA586 Pentium

- PCI/EISA Board Gigabyte GA586-ID 90MHz Pentium (dual processor, one fitted)
- 32M RAM
- SCSI - no scsi-NCR-chip on-board, using Adaptec 1542C,
- PCI ATI GUP 2M VRAM
- Adaptec 1742 EISA SCSI controller
- Soundblaster 16
- usual I/O

Everything under DOS AND Linux works perfectly. No problem whatsoever. A VERY fast machine! BYTE Unix benchmarks place it about the same as a Sun SuperSPARC-20 running Solaris 2.3. The PC is faster for integer arithmetic and process stuff (including context switching). The SPARC is faster for floating point and one of the disk benchmarks.

8.23 kenf@clark.net with G/W 2000

He uses a Gateway 2000 with no problems, except the soundcard (which one?). He is trading it in for a genuine soundblaster in hopes that will help.

8.24 Joerg Wedeck (jw@peanuts.informatik.uni-tuebingen.de) / ESCOM

originaly buyed a 486 DX2/66 from ESCOM (which board?) with onboard IDE and without (!) onboard NCR-SCSI-chip. ISA-adaptec 1542cf scsi-controller instead spea v7 mercury lite (s3, PCI, 1MB), ISA-Soundblaster-16, mitsumi-cdrom (the slower one). Everything except the archive-streamer works with no problems. The spea-v7 works perfectly since XFree86-2.1

He abandoned the Intel-board in favour of an ASUS-SP3-g and has some problems with PCI-to-Memory burstmode which is crashing only on Linux, "looking like a deadlock in the swapper". If you have any information on this, please eMail the maintainer of the PCI-HOWTO.

After turning off the PCI-to-Memory posting feature it just works perfect.

Rather than sending him mail please read his http-homepage at "http://wsiserv.informatik.uni-tuebingen.de/ jw" where he keeps information about his PCI-system, too.

8.25   Ulrich Teichert / ASUS

ASUS-PCI board with AMD486dx40 (but actually running at 33Mhz?!) His ISA-ET3000 Optima 1024A ISA works nice. No problems with Quantum540S SCSI Harddisk attached to the onboard NCR53c810.

9   Reports of problems

9.1   Compaq PCI systems, especially Presarios

Patrick Yaner (p_yaner@eos.ncsu.edu) reported a Compaq-speciality to me. It seems they are mapping the PCI BIOS data area to an obscure area of memory, one that Linux (or OS2) cannot access. It can usually find it, but it can't get in, and gives a message on startup (something like "pcibios_init: entry in high memory area, unable to access"). Although this is alright with the display (which is on the PCI bus) and the IDE controller (also PCI), it means any other PCI devices – such as an Ethernet card – cannot be detected by Linux.

Compaq offers a driver for DOS at ftp://ftp.compaq.com/pub/softpaq/Drivers/SP1116.ZIP

but using this with linux would mean using the program that boots linux from DOS, instead of LILO. Note that Compaq occasionally updates the software in this archive, so the file ftp://ftp.compaq.com/pub/softpaq/allfiles.html (also available as allfiles.txt) might be handy in checking to see that they haven't upgraded.

Oddly, this information can also be found in the SCSI HOWTO, although the Pressarios come with IDE built in.

9.2   VLSI Wildcat PCI chipset like in Zeos P120 box

Paul Bame (bame@sde.hp.com) reported:

The Wildcat PCI chipset works fine in late 1.3 and all 2.0 kernels.

9.3   dmarples@comms.eee.strathclyde.ac.uk G/W 2000

Gateway 2000 G/W 2000 4DX2/66 PCI ATI-Graphics-Ultra-Pro IDE of indeterminate make

It works well - only the IDE-Card runs in ISA-compatibility-mode, and works a lot faster when switched into PCI-Mode by a DOS-program... thus it's not that fast in Linux, and a patch would be nice.

9.4   cip574@wpax01.physik.uni-wuerzburg.de (Frank Hofmann) / ASUS

He uses the ASUS-board with 16MB-RAM, ISA-based S3/928, and the onboard-IDE-controller with a Seagate ST4550A harddisk. He's had no trouble with the newer Linux-kernels.

His problem:

```
using X, my mouse is not responding the way I was used to before.  It's sometimes
behind movement and makes jumps if moved quickly.  I think this was discussed In
a Linux newsgroup before (I don't know which one) and is due to the use of 16550
serial chips for the onboard serial interfaces.  After two weeks, I got used to
it :-)
```

Reducing the threshold of the 16550 should help. There should be a patch to setserial available somewhere, but I do not know where.

9.5 axel@avalanche.cs.tu-berlin.de (Axel Mahler) / ASUS

ASUS PCI/I-486SP3 Motherboard (Award BIOS 4.50), 16 MB RAM the on-Board NCR Chip is disabled, he had the Genoa Phantom/W32 2MB for PCI and a Adaptec AHA-1542CF (BIOS v2.01) connected to:

- an IBM 1.05 GB Harddisk
- a Toshiba CD-ROM (XM4101-B)
- a HP DAT-Streamer (2GB)

when creating the filesystems, 'mke2fs' (0.4, v. 1.11.93) hung and installation was impossible. After replacing the Genoa Phantom/W32 2MB PCI with an ELSA Winner 1000 2MB PCI it worked perfectly. He tested it with an old Eizo VGA-ISA and it worked as well, so the problem was in the Genoa-PCI-card.

9.6 Frank Strauss (strauss@dagoba.escape.de) / ASUS

ASUS SP3 Board i486DX2/66 NCR53c810 disabled Adaptec 1542B in ISA Slot with 2 hard drives (200MB Maxtor, 420MB Fijutsu), SyQuest 88MB and Tandberg Streamer ELSA Winner 1000 PCI, 1MB-VRAM Soundblaster Pro in ISA Slot at IRQ 5 Onboard IDE disabled Onboard serial, parallel, FD enabled

After a reset, the machine sometimes 'hangs' (soft and hard-reset the same) - this is probably not related to the Adaptec and the Soundcard, because even without these the system sometimes fails to come up. But if it runs, (and the ELSA-WINNER-1000-PCI-message appears) it runs ok.

The two serial ports are detected as 16550 as they should, but at some mailbox-sessions there was heavy data-loss at V42bis... The problem seems to be in the hardware...

CPU>-PCI-Burst seems to work well with DOS/MS-Windows

CPU->PCI-Burst does not work properly with linux0.99p15, Messing up when switching the virtual-consoles, crashing completely when calling big apps like ghostview, or xdvi, leaving the SCSI-LED on (!).

(I suspect these apps would be using a lot of CPU->PCI-burst because of the big heap of data to transmit to the PCI-Winner-1000)

After disabling CPU->PCI-Burst, it works well, the Winner-1000 at 1152x846 (not much font cache with 1MB) does 93k xstones. OpaqueMove with twm is more than just endureable :-)

He has got a SATURN.EXE which he loads under DOS before starting Linux, helping to turn on burst without hangs...

Someone stated that these problems might go away when turning off "sync negotiation" on the Adaptec - I do not know if this is possible with the adaptec1542B too? But I guess so.

With CPU->PCI-Burst it yielded 95k xstones, so he considers it as not too grave to do without. His only problem is that he would like to run his Winner-1000 at 1152x900 which fails because it seems to take any x-resolution higher than 1024pixels as a 1280pixel-resolution, thus wasting a lot end resulting in a y-resolution of 816pixels... but this is probably no PCI-related problem. It should have gone away with XFree86-2.1

9.7 egooch@mc.com / ASUS

- BOARD ASUS PCI/I-486 SP3 RAM: 16MB (4x4M-SIMM)

- CPU 486DX33 CPU
- BIOS Ver. 4.50 (12/30/93)
- Floppy Two floppy drives (1.2 and 1.44), using ASUS on-board floppy controller
- SCSI tried both WD7000 SCSI controller and Adaptec 1542CF and worked.
- Two SCSI 320M hard drives
- SCSI NEC84 CDROM drive
- SCSI QIC150 Archive tape drive
- Video - Tseng ET4000 ISA graphics card
- Sound PAS16 sound card
- Printer attached to on-board ASUS parallel port

He has nothing in the PCI-Slots yet, but wants to buy a PCI-Video-Card, currently uses WD7000 SCSI controller but will switch to the NCR-Chip onboard as soon as the driver is out.

Everything works perfectly - the first serial port which has a 14.4K-Modem attached does hang occasionally when reconnecting with the modem after having used it previously. He says that would not be unique to ASUS but rather a bug in the SMC-LSI device with its 16550UART. The logitech-serial-mouse on the second port works fine. Setting down the threshold of the 16550 for the mouseport would definitely help, one does seem to need a special patched setserial for that? I have not got the information yet, please contact me if you know more!

9.8   Stefan.Dalibor@informatik.uni-erlangen.de / GigaByte

- Board - GA-486iS from Gigabyte w/ 256Kb 2L-Cache, i486-DX2
- Bios - AMI, 93/8
- SCSI - no scsi-NCR-chip on-board, using Adaptec 1542C,
- Video - ELSA Winner 1000
- Linux 0.99pl14 + SCSI-Clustering-Patches / Slackware 1.1.1

All seems to go well, but he has not tried neither networking, printing or a streamer yet. Before applying the clustering- patches he had some problems with hangs triggered by "find", but this no longer is the case - perhaps it was an older kernel-bug.

The ELSA-Winner-1000 sometimes hangs, with very strange patterns on the screen resolved only by rebooting... The dealer has told him it was a bug in the ELSA-Card, but the manufacturer claims it had solved the problem. The bug is not reproducible so he does not plan to take any action at the moment.

All in all the machine seems to work very well under heavy text processing (emacs, LaTeX, xfig, ghostview) usage. Interaction is surprisingly responsive, little difference between it and the 3-4X as expensive Sun he works on...

CPU->PCI-Burst is still disabled because the bios does not support the PCI-things well?

A problem with his new modem (v32 terbo) arose: it looses characters. Especially when using SLIP it complains a lot about RX and TX errors. As soon as he runs X it gets unusable. He said he activated FIFO and RTS/CTS with stty, but to no avail...

9.9   Steve Durst (sdurst@burns.rl.af.mil) with UMC 8500 mainboard

Running Linux 1.2.12 on the UMC8500-100Mhz motherboard with the dreaded CMD PCIO640B (E)IDE controller, when booting the screen wiggles a few seconds, as if the Diamond Stealth64-DRAM (S3 864) has to warm up first, but he can live with that.

9.10 Tom Drabenstott (tldraben@Teleport.Com) with Comtrade / PCI48IX

PCI48IX Motherboard Rev. 1.0. Made by ??? documentation copyrighted by "exrc". The BIOS says not very much about PCI.

His E-315E Super IDE UMC (863+865) ISA-Controller-card does have problems. (It is a multifunction controller-card). It seems to work well under DOS/OS2 but not under Linux.

10 General tips for PCI-Motherboard + Linux NCR PCI SCSI

This was compiled by Angelo Haritsis (ah@doc.ic.ac.uk) from various people's postings:

10.1 DON'Ts:

Do *NOT* go for combination VLB/PCI motherboards. They usually have a lot of problems. Get a plain PCI version (with ISA slots as well of course). A lot of bad things have been heard about OPTI chipset PCI motherboards. Someone hints: "Avoid the OPTi (82C596/82C597/82C822) chipset based motherboards like the TMC PCI54PV".

(I know of at least one person having no problems with his TMC PCI54PV motherboard. He just had to put the NCR53c810 addonboard into slot-A which is the only slot capable of busmastering as it seems.)

Rumours say that Intel chipset PCI motherboards will have problems with more than one bus-mastering PCI board. I have not tried this one yet on mine and have nothing to suggest. I also heard that the Saturn II chipset is problematic, but this is the one I use and it is perfectly ok! Advice: Try to negotiate a 1-2 week money back agreement with your supplier, in case the motherboard you get has problems with the use you plan for it.

10.2 SIMM slots

Go for 72-pin only SIMMs for speed: Some (all?) of the mainboards which take 30 pin SIMMs use a 32 bit main memory interface, and will be significantly slower than the Intel based boards which all use a 64 bit or permantly interleaved memory interface. You might want to keep that in mind.

10.3 Praised PCI Pentium motherboard

The P90 Intel motherboard with the Intel Premiere II chipset (aka Plato). Get the latest BIOS which has concatenated NCR scsi BIOS 3.04.00. Otherwise DOS won't see your scsi disk(s) if you use a BIOS-less 53c810 based controller. NCR SCSI BIOS exists in the AMI BIOS of the plato after version 1.00.08 (or maybe verion 1.00.06). This BIOS is FLASH upgradeable so you should be able to get the upgrade on a floppy from your supplier. The current version is 1.00.10 and has all early problems fixed.

(Bios files should be available at ftp.demon.co.uk:/pub/ibmpc/intel, but I did not check that myself. the Autor.)

10.4   irq-lines

The value in the interrupt line PCI configuration register is usually set manually (for compatability with legacy ISA boards) in the extended CMOS setup screens on a per-slot or per-device basis. Older PCI mainboards also force you to set jumpers for each PCI slot/device which select how PCI INTA and perhaps INTB, INTC, and INTD are mapped to an 8259 IRQ line, Obviously, if these jumpers exist on your board, they must match the settings in the extended CMOS setup. Also note that some boards (notably Viglens) have silkscreens and instruction manuals which disagree with the wiring, and some experimentation may be in order.

10.5   Info about the different NCR 8xx family scsi chips:

All NCR 8XX Chips are dircet connect PCI bus mastering devices, that have no preformance difference wether on motherboard or add in option card. All devices comply with PCI 2.0 Specification, and can burst 32 bit data at the full 33 MHz (133Mbytes/Sec)

10.5.1   53C810

53C810 = 8 bit Fast SCSI-2 (10 MB/Sec) Single ended only Requires Integrated Mother board BIOS 100 pin Quad Flat Pack (PQFP) Worlds first PCI SCSI Chip, Volumes make it the most inexpensive.

10.5.2   53C815

53C815 = 8 bit Fast SCSI-2 (10 MB/Sec) Single Ended only Support ROM BIOS interface, which makes it ideal for add-in card Designs. 128 Pin QFP

10.5.3   53C825

53C825 = 8 bit Fast SCSI-2, Single ended or Differential 16 bit Fast SCSI-2 (20 MB/Sec), Single ended or Differetial Also has support for external Rom, making it a good candidate for add in cards. 160 pin QFP Not supported by linux yet. (See section below on news about the 825). Must have devices with wide or differential scsi to use these features.

10.6   future of 53c8xx

There are 4 new devices planned for announcement late this year and into early next year. Footprint compitible with 810 and 825 with some new features.

All the Chips require a BIOS in DOS/Intel applications. The 810 is the only chip that needs it resident on the motherboard. Latest NCR SCSI BIOS version: 3.04.00 The bios supports disks >1GB, indeed up to 8G under MS-LOSS.

10.7   Performance of the 53c810

C't magazine's DOS benchmarks showed that it was significantly faster than the Buslogic BT-946, one user noted a 10-15% performance increase versus an Adaptec 2940, and with a very fast disk it may be 2.5X as fast as an Adaptec 1540.

10.8   News about NCR53c825 support

works. period.

10.9   Frederic POTTER (Frederic.Potter@masi.ibp.fr) about Pentium+NCR+Strap_bug

On some Intel Plato board, the NCR bios doesn't recognize the board, because it needs to see the board as a "secondary SCSI controller", and because on most SCSI board the jumper to select between primary/secondary has been ironed to primary (to spare 1 cent, presumably).

Solution:

```
near the NCR chip, they are 3 via ( kind of holes ) with a strap like
that
            O--O  O

        this mean primary is selected as default setting. For the Plato Intel
        Mainboard, it should be like that

            O  O--O

        The best solution is to get rid of the strap and to put a 2 position
        jumper instead.
```

10.10   PCIprobe in the latest Linux Kernels by Frederic Potter

Frederic Potter has added a PCI-Probe into the latest kernels. If you do a "cat /proc/pci" it should list all your cards. If you own cards which are not properly recogniced, please contact him via mail as "Frederic.Potter@masi.ibp.fr".

See arch/i386/kernel/bios32.c and include/linux/pci.h in the kernel source for more information on PCI-Probe-Stuff.

10.11   Other PCI Devices

What other PCI-cards are supported? Apart from various graphicscards, I would like to know about other cards like ethernet, framegrabber, or the TSET boards Cyclades is about to beta-test at the moment:

10.11.1   Cyclades: a 16-port PCI RISC-based multiport card.

The product is called Cyclom-Ye, and has the following characteristics:

- PCI host card based on the PLX chip-set. This host card supports 8 to 32 serial ports, utilizing 8 or 16-port external boxes.

- SCSI II cable.

- 8 or 16-port external boxes with RJ45 or DB25 connectors (your choice). You can start with 8 ports and expand to 32, by just adding more boxes. Each external box contains 2 or 4 CD-1400 RISC Serial controllers (each CD-1400 controls 4 serial ports).

- Up to 4 Host cards can be installed in the PC system, allowing a maximum of 128 serial ports per system.

The product is being in the beta-test phase at July the 26th, 1995, and should be available by Octobre or something. eMail them at sales@cyclades.com.

11 Conclusion

If you have some moneny to put into your machine, you'd be well off with a Pentium90, ASUS-SP4, which is what I use at the moment. If you can afford 32M RAM that would be much better than 16M RAM.

Real soon now the upcoming standard will be the Triton Chipset with support for special SIMMS called EDODRAM, and SRAM. Both will be more expensive than PS2-RAM, and at the time of writing (28-June-1995) SRAM is not available. While EDO-DRAM is more expensive, this is not because of the production costs, they are said to be the same.

For a highperformance system I would still choose an ASUS-TP4/XE with EDO-DRAM, but if you do not need to use it at the moment, I d rather wait some more.

For Graphic-boards I'd say the best cheap board fitting perfectly on a good Multisync-15 like the Samsung SyncMaster 15Gli, is the SPEA V7 Mirage P64 with Trio64 Chipset and 2M DRAM. For more sophisticated Display like the Iiyama-IDEK 8617A-T I think the PCI Mach64 ATI-GUP-Turbo (not the cheaper GUP-Turbo-Windows) would be a good choice, with 4M RAM you can have truecolor in higher resolutions. It is well supported in the XFree86(tm)-3.1.1, and there are commercial X-Servers available of which I'd recommend Accelerated/X by Roell, which supports the Mach64 very well and fast.

For SCSI I'd take the DPT rather than the (much cheaper and very fast) NCR53c810 in case you plan to use SCSI-Tapes a lot. The NCR53c810 driver on Linux does lack disconnect/reconnect support, thus blocking the SCSIbus on operations like "mt rewind", "mt fsf" etc. It bears a performance penalty on tar-operations - but check out Drews new alpha drivers before making a decision, perhaps it does solve all the problems.

For building servers, the DPT would be the controller of choice anyway because of all the nifty hardware cache (with elevator sorting on accesses, so cache it is not a silly thing even in a Linux enviroment where the OS does the caching) and RAID-Support up to raid level 5.

If you do not want to spend that much money on computer equipment (e.g.: you are having a life) you might go for an ASUS-SP3-SiS with AMD-DX2/66 or DX4/100. The SPEA V7 Mirage P64 PCI with 2M DRAM would be a good choice, since it uses the Trio64 S3 Chip, which is well supported by XFree86(tm)-3.1.1, quite cheap to buy and fast, too.

Another fine card since XFree86(tm)-3.1 is the fast and cheap et4000/w32-PCI-card.

12 Thanks

I want to thank the following people for supporting this document:

- David Lesher (wb8foz@netcom.com) for extensive help with the english language
- Nathanael MAKAREVITCH (nat@nataa.frmug.fr.net) for translating into french
- Jun Morimoto (morimoto@lab.imagica.co.jp) for translating into japanese
- Marco Melgazzi (marco@vcldec1.polito.it) for translating into italian
- Donald Becker (becker@cesdis.gsfc.nasa.gov) for ethernet-informations
- Drew Eckhardt (drew@kinglear.cs.Colorado.EDU) for SCSI-informations

- Zhahai Stewart (zhahai@hisys.com) for help with the intro section

and many more peole adding information mostly by mail and by posts, some of them will be named here:

```
CARSTEN@AWORLD.aworld.de,
dmarples@comms.eee.strathclyde.ac.uk,
drew@kinglear.cs.Colorado.EDU (Working at the PCI-NCR53c810-Driver),
duncan@spd.eee.strathclyde.ac.uk,
fm3@irz.inf.tu-dresden.de,
grif@ucrengr.ucr.edu,
heinrich@zsv.gmd.de,
hm@ix.de (iX-Magazine),
hm@seneca.ix.de,
kebsch.pad@sni.de,
kenf@clark.net,
matthias@penthouse.boerde.de,
ortloff@omega.informatik.uni-dortmund.de,
preberle@cip.informatik.uni-erlangen.de,
rob@me62.lbl.gov,
rsi@netcom.com,
sk001sp@unidui.uni-duisburg.de,
strauss@dagoba.escape.de,
strauss@dagoba.priconet.de,
hi86@rz.uni-karlsruhe.de,
Ulrich Teichert, krypton@netzservice.de,
Stefan.Dalibor@informatik.uni-erlangen.de,
tldraben@teleport.com
mundkur@eagle.ece.uci.edu,
ooch@jericho.mc.com,
Gert Doering (gert@greenie.muc.de),
James D. Levine (jdl@netcom.com),
Georg von Below (gbelow@pmail.sams.ch),
Jerome Meyers (jeromem@quake.xnet.com),
Angelo Haritsis (ah@doc.ic.ac.uk),
archie@CS.Berkeley.EDU and his friend kenf@clark.net.
```

13   copyright/legalese

If you sell this HOWTO on a CD or in a book I would be happy to have a copy for reference.

(Michael.Will@student.uni-tuebingen.de)

Contact me, either via eMail or call +49-7071-969063.

For german users I am offering tested, preinstalled / preconfigured and supported Linux-PCI-machines. Call me at 07071-969063.

14   GPL - Gnu Public License

GNU GENERAL PUBLIC LICENSE
Version 2, June 1991

Copyright (C) 1989, 1991 Free Software Foundation, Inc.
                    675 Mass Ave, Cambridge, MA 02139, USA
Everyone is permitted to copy and distribute verbatim copies
of this license document, but changing it is not allowed.

                              Preamble

  The licenses for most software are designed to take away your
freedom to share and change it. By contrast, the GNU General Public
License is intended to guarantee your freedom to share and change free
software--to make sure the software is free for all its users. This
General Public License applies to most of the Free Software
Foundation's software and to any other program whose authors commit to
using it. (Some other Free Software Foundation software is covered by
the GNU Library General Public License instead.) You can apply it to
your programs, too.

  When we speak of free software, we are referring to freedom, not
price. Our General Public Licenses are designed to make sure that you
have the freedom to distribute copies of free software (and charge for
this service if you wish), that you receive source code or can get it
if you want it, that you can change the software or use pieces of it
in new free programs; and that you know you can do these things.

  To protect your rights, we need to make restrictions that forbid
anyone to deny you these rights or to ask you to surrender the rights.
These restrictions translate to certain responsibilities for you if you
distribute copies of the software, or if you modify it.

  For example, if you distribute copies of such a program, whether
gratis or for a fee, you must give the recipients all the rights that
you have. You must make sure that they, too, receive or can get the
source code. And you must show them these terms so they know their
rights.

  We protect your rights with two steps: (1) copyright the software, and
(2) offer you this license which gives you legal permission to copy,
distribute and/or modify the software.

  Also, for each author's protection and ours, we want to make certain
that everyone understands that there is no warranty for this free
software. If the software is modified by someone else and passed on, we
want its recipients to know that what they have is not the original, so
that any problems introduced by others will not reflect on the original
authors' reputations.

  Finally, any free program is threatened constantly by software
patents. We wish to avoid the danger that redistributors of a free

program will individually obtain patent licenses, in effect making the
program proprietary. To prevent this, we have made it clear that any
patent must be licensed for everyone's free use or not licensed at all.

   The precise terms and conditions for copying, distribution and
modification follow.

GNU GENERAL PUBLIC LICENSE
TERMS AND CONDITIONS FOR COPYING, DISTRIBUTION AND MODIFICATION

   0. This License applies to any program or other work which contains
a notice placed by the copyright holder saying it may be distributed
under the terms of this General Public License. The "Program", below,
refers to any such program or work, and a "work based on the Program"
means either the Program or any derivative work under copyright law:
that is to say, a work containing the Program or a portion of it,
either verbatim or with modifications and/or translated into another
language. (Hereinafter, translation is included without limitation in
the term "modification".) Each licensee is addressed as "you".

Activities other than copying, distribution and modification are not
covered by this License; they are outside its scope. The act of
running the Program is not restricted, and the output from the Program
is covered only if its contents constitute a work based on the
Program (independent of having been made by running the Program).
Whether that is true depends on what the Program does.

   1. You may copy and distribute verbatim copies of the Program's
source code as you receive it, in any medium, provided that you
conspicuously and appropriately publish on each copy an appropriate
copyright notice and disclaimer of warranty; keep intact all the
notices that refer to this License and to the absence of any warranty;
and give any other recipients of the Program a copy of this License
along with the Program.

You may charge a fee for the physical act of transferring a copy, and
you may at your option offer warranty protection in exchange for a fee.

   2. You may modify your copy or copies of the Program or any portion
of it, thus forming a work based on the Program, and copy and
distribute such modifications or work under the terms of Section 1
above, provided that you also meet all of these conditions:

   a) You must cause the modified files to carry prominent notices
   stating that you changed the files and the date of any change.

   b) You must cause any work that you distribute or publish, that in
   whole or in part contains or is derived from the Program or any
   part thereof, to be licensed as a whole at no charge to all third
   parties under the terms of this License.

   c) If the modified program normally reads commands interactively
   when run, you must cause it, when started running for such
   interactive use in the most ordinary way, to print or display an

announcement including an appropriate copyright notice and a
notice that there is no warranty (or else, saying that you provide
a warranty) and that users may redistribute the program under
these conditions, and telling the user how to view a copy of this
License. (Exception: if the Program itself is interactive but
does not normally print such an announcement, your work based on
the Program is not required to print an announcement.)

These requirements apply to the modified work as a whole. If
identifiable sections of that work are not derived from the Program,
and can be reasonably considered independent and separate works in
themselves, then this License, and its terms, do not apply to those
sections when you distribute them as separate works. But when you
distribute the same sections as part of a whole which is a work based
on the Program, the distribution of the whole must be on the terms of
this License, whose permissions for other licensees extend to the
entire whole, and thus to each and every part regardless of who wrote it.

Thus, it is not the intent of this section to claim rights or contest
your rights to work written entirely by you; rather, the intent is to
exercise the right to control the distribution of derivative or
collective works based on the Program.

In addition, mere aggregation of another work not based on the Program
with the Program (or with a work based on the Program) on a volume of
a storage or distribution medium does not bring the other work under
the scope of this License.

 3. You may copy and distribute the Program (or a work based on it,
under Section 2) in object code or executable form under the terms of
Sections 1 and 2 above provided that you also do one of the following:

    a) Accompany it with the complete corresponding machine-readable
    source code, which must be distributed under the terms of Sections
    1 and 2 above on a medium customarily used for software interchange; or,

    b) Accompany it with a written offer, valid for at least three
    years, to give any third party, for a charge no more than your
    cost of physically performing source distribution, a complete
    machine-readable copy of the corresponding source code, to be
    distributed under the terms of Sections 1 and 2 above on a medium
    customarily used for software interchange; or,

    c) Accompany it with the information you received as to the offer
    to distribute corresponding source code. (This alternative is
    allowed only for noncommercial distribution and only if you
    received the program in object code or executable form with such
    an offer, in accord with Subsection b above.)

The source code for a work means the preferred form of the work for
making modifications to it. For an executable work, complete source
code means all the source code for all modules it contains, plus any
associated interface definition files, plus the scripts used to
control compilation and installation of the executable. However, as a

special exception, the source code distributed need not include anything that is normally distributed (in either source or binary form) with the major components (compiler, kernel, and so on) of the operating system on which the executable runs, unless that component itself accompanies the executable.

If distribution of executable or object code is made by offering access to copy from a designated place, then offering equivalent access to copy the source code from the same place counts as distribution of the source code, even though third parties are not compelled to copy the source along with the object code.

4. You may not copy, modify, sublicense, or distribute the Program except as expressly provided under this License. Any attempt otherwise to copy, modify, sublicense or distribute the Program is void, and will automatically terminate your rights under this License. However, parties who have received copies, or rights, from you under this License will not have their licenses terminated so long as such parties remain in full compliance.

5. You are not required to accept this License, since you have not signed it. However, nothing else grants you permission to modify or distribute the Program or its derivative works. These actions are prohibited by law if you do not accept this License. Therefore, by modifying or distributing the Program (or any work based on the Program), you indicate your acceptance of this License to do so, and all its terms and conditions for copying, distributing or modifying the Program or works based on it.

6. Each time you redistribute the Program (or any work based on the Program), the recipient automatically receives a license from the original licensor to copy, distribute or modify the Program subject to these terms and conditions. You may not impose any further restrictions on the recipients' exercise of the rights granted herein. You are not responsible for enforcing compliance by third parties to this License.

7. If, as a consequence of a court judgment or allegation of patent infringement or for any other reason (not limited to patent issues), conditions are imposed on you (whether by court order, agreement or otherwise) that contradict the conditions of this License, they do not excuse you from the conditions of this License. If you cannot distribute so as to satisfy simultaneously your obligations under this License and any other pertinent obligations, then as a consequence you may not distribute the Program at all. For example, if a patent license would not permit royalty-free redistribution of the Program by all those who receive copies directly or indirectly through you, then the only way you could satisfy both it and this License would be to refrain entirely from distribution of the Program.

If any portion of this section is held invalid or unenforceable under any particular circumstance, the balance of the section is intended to apply and the section as a whole is intended to apply in other circumstances.

It is not the purpose of this section to induce you to infringe any
patents or other property right claims or to contest validity of any
such claims; this section has the sole purpose of protecting the
integrity of the free software distribution system, which is
implemented by public license practices. Many people have made
generous contributions to the wide range of software distributed
through that system in reliance on consistent application of that
system; it is up to the author/donor to decide if he or she is willing
to distribute software through any other system and a licensee cannot
impose that choice.

This section is intended to make thoroughly clear what is believed to
be a consequence of the rest of this License.

 8. If the distribution and/or use of the Program is restricted in
certain countries either by patents or by copyrighted interfaces, the
original copyright holder who places the Program under this License
may add an explicit geographical distribution limitation excluding
those countries, so that distribution is permitted only in or among
countries not thus excluded. In such case, this License incorporates
the limitation as if written in the body of this License.

 9. The Free Software Foundation may publish revised and/or new versions
of the General Public License from time to time. Such new versions will
be similar in spirit to the present version, but may differ in detail to
address new problems or concerns.

Each version is given a distinguishing version number. If the Program
specifies a version number of this License which applies to it and "any
later version", you have the option of following the terms and conditions
either of that version or of any later version published by the Free
Software Foundation. If the Program does not specify a version number of
this License, you may choose any version ever published by the Free Software
Foundation.

 10. If you wish to incorporate parts of the Program into other free
programs whose distribution conditions are different, write to the author
to ask for permission. For software which is copyrighted by the Free
Software Foundation, write to the Free Software Foundation; we sometimes
make exceptions for this. Our decision will be guided by the two goals
of preserving the free status of all derivatives of our free software and
of promoting the sharing and reuse of software generally.

NO WARRANTY

 11. BECAUSE THE PROGRAM IS LICENSED FREE OF CHARGE, THERE IS NO WARRANTY
FOR THE PROGRAM, TO THE EXTENT PERMITTED BY APPLICABLE LAW. EXCEPT WHEN
OTHERWISE STATED IN WRITING THE COPYRIGHT HOLDERS AND/OR OTHER PARTIES
PROVIDE THE PROGRAM "AS IS" WITHOUT WARRANTY OF ANY KIND, EITHER EXPRESSED
OR IMPLIED, INCLUDING, BUT NOT LIMITED TO, THE IMPLIED WARRANTIES OF
MERCHANTABILITY AND FITNESS FOR A PARTICULAR PURPOSE. THE ENTIRE RISK AS
TO THE QUALITY AND PERFORMANCE OF THE PROGRAM IS WITH YOU. SHOULD THE
PROGRAM PROVE DEFECTIVE, YOU ASSUME THE COST OF ALL NECESSARY SERVICING,

REPAIR OR CORRECTION.

12. IN NO EVENT UNLESS REQUIRED BY APPLICABLE LAW OR AGREED TO IN WRITING
WILL ANY COPYRIGHT HOLDER, OR ANY OTHER PARTY WHO MAY MODIFY AND/OR
REDISTRIBUTE THE PROGRAM AS PERMITTED ABOVE, BE LIABLE TO YOU FOR DAMAGES,
INCLUDING ANY GENERAL, SPECIAL, INCIDENTAL OR CONSEQUENTIAL DAMAGES ARISING
OUT OF THE USE OR INABILITY TO USE THE PROGRAM (INCLUDING BUT NOT LIMITED
TO LOSS OF DATA OR DATA BEING RENDERED INACCURATE OR LOSSES SUSTAINED BY
YOU OR THIRD PARTIES OR A FAILURE OF THE PROGRAM TO OPERATE WITH ANY OTHER
PROGRAMS), EVEN IF SUCH HOLDER OR OTHER PARTY HAS BEEN ADVISED OF THE
POSSIBILITY OF SUCH DAMAGES.

END OF TERMS AND CONDITIONS

Appendix: How to Apply These Terms to Your New Programs

If you develop a new program, and you want it to be of the greatest
possible use to the public, the best way to achieve this is to make it
free software which everyone can redistribute and change under these terms.

To do so, attach the following notices to the program. It is safest
to attach them to the start of each source file to most effectively
convey the exclusion of warranty; and each file should have at least
the "copyright" line and a pointer to where the full notice is found.

    <one line to give the program's name and a brief idea of what it does.>
    Copyright (C) 19yy (name of author)

    This program is free software; you can redistribute it and/or modify
    it under the terms of the GNU General Public License as published by
    the Free Software Foundation; either version 2 of the License, or
    (at your option) any later version.

    This program is distributed in the hope that it will be useful,
    but WITHOUT ANY WARRANTY; without even the implied warranty of
    MERCHANTABILITY or FITNESS FOR A PARTICULAR PURPOSE. See the
    GNU General Public License for more details.

    You should have received a copy of the GNU General Public License
    along with this program; if not, write to the Free Software
    Foundation, Inc., 675 Mass Ave, Cambridge, MA 02139, USA.

Also add information on how to contact you by electronic and paper mail.

If the program is interactive, make it output a short notice like this
when it starts in an interactive mode:

    Gnomovision version 69, Copyright (C) 19yy name of author
    Gnomovision comes with ABSOLUTELY NO WARRANTY; for details type 'show w'.
    This is free software, and you are welcome to redistribute it
    under certain conditions; type 'show c' for details.

The hypothetical commands 'show w' and 'show c' should show the appropriate
parts of the General Public License. Of course, the commands you use may

be called something other than 'show w' and 'show c'; they could even be
mouse-clicks or menu items--whatever suits your program.

You should also get your employer (if you work as a programmer) or your
school, if any, to sign a "copyright disclaimer" for the program, if
necessary. Here is a sample; alter the names:

  Yoyodyne, Inc., hereby disclaims all copyright interest in the program
  'Gnomovision' (which makes passes at compilers) written by James Hacker.

  (signature of Ty Coon), 1 April 1989
  Ty Coon, President of Vice

This General Public License does not permit incorporating your program into
proprietary programs. If your program is a subroutine library, you may
consider it more useful to permit linking proprietary applications with the
library. If this is what you want to do, use the GNU Library General
Public License instead of this License.

HOWTO: Multi Disk System Tuning

Stein Gjoen, sgjoen@nyx.net   v0.17, 3 February 1998

This document describes how best to use multiple disks and partitions for a Linux system. Although some of this text is Linux specific the general approach outlined here can be applied to many other multi tasking operating systems.

Contents

1 Introduction

For strange and artistic reasons this brand new release is code named the **Daybreak** release.

New code names will appear as per industry standard guidelines to emphasize the state-of-the-art-ness of this document.

This document was written for two reasons, mainly because I got hold of 3 old SCSI disks to set up my Linux system on and I was pondering how best to utilise the inherent possibilities of parallelizing in a SCSI system. Secondly I hear there is a prize for people who write documents...

This is intended to be read in conjunction with the Linux Filesystem Structure Standard (FSSTND). It does not in any way replace it but tries to suggest where physically to place directories detailed in the FSSTND, in terms of drives, partitions, types, RAID, file system (fs), physical sizes and other parameters that should be considered and tuned in a Linux system, ranging from single home systems to large servers on the Internet.

Even though it is now more than a year since last release of the FSSTND work is still continuing, under a new name, and will encompass more than Linux, fill in a few blanks hinted at in FSSTND version 1.2 as well as other general improvements. The development mailing list is currently private but a general release is hopefully in the near future. The new issue will be named Filesystem Hierarchy Standard (FHS) and will cover more than Linux alone. Very recently FHS version 2.0 was released but there are still a few issues to be dealt with and even longer before this new standard will have an impact on actual distribusions.

It is also a good idea to read the Linux Installation guides thoroughly and if you are using a PC system, which I guess the majority still does, you can find much relevant and useful information in the FAQs for the newsgroup comp.sys.ibm.pc.hardware especially for storage media.

This is also a learning experience for myself and I hope I can start the ball rolling with this HOWTO and that it perhaps can evolve into a larger more detailed and hopefully even more correct HOWTO.

First of all we need a bit of legalese. Recent development shows it is quite important.

1.1 Copyright

This HOWTO is copyrighted 1996 Stein Gjoen.

electronic, as long as this copyright notice is retained on all copies. Commercial redistribution is allowed and encouraged; however, the author would like to be notified of any such distributions.

All translations, derivative works, or aggregate works incorporating any Linux HOWTO documents must be covered under this copyright notice. That is, you may not produce a derivative work from a HOWTO and impose additional restrictions on its distribution. Exceptions to these rules may be granted under certain conditions; please contact the Linux HOWTO coordinator at the address given below.

In short, we wish to promote dissemination of this information through as many channels as possible. However, we do wish to retain copyright on the HOWTO documents, and would like to be notified of any plans to redistribute the HOWTOs.

If you have questions, please contact Greg Hankins, the Linux HOWTO coordinator, at gregh@sunsite.unc.edu via email.

1.2   Disclaimer

Use the information in this document at your own risk. I disavow any potential liability for the contents of this document. Use of the concepts, examples, and/or other content of this document is entirely at your own risk.

All copyrights are owned by their owners, unless specifically noted otherwise. Use of a term in this document should not be regarded as affecting the validity of any trademark or service mark.

Naming of particular products or brands should not be seen as endorsements.

You are strongly recommended to take a backup of your system before major installation and backups at regular intervals.

1.3   News

The most recent news is that FHS version 2.0 is released and the work is picing up momentum. No linux distributions using FHS has been announced yet but when that happens there will have to be a few rewrites to this HOWTO. And speaking of HOWTO, I have now dropped all pretenses and removed the 'mini' prefix, as this was becoming something of a joke.

A recent addition is a new section on how best to get help should you find yourself unable to solve your problems as well as more suggestion on maintenance.

Due to an enormous amount of spam I have been forced to mangle all e-mail addresses herein in order to fool the e-mail harvesters that scan through the net for victims to be put on the lists. Feedbeck tells me some damage has already happened, this is very unfortunate. Mangiling is done by replacing the @ character with (at)

A number of pointers to relevant mailing lists are also added.

Since the 0.14 version was released there have been too many changes to list here. I have received much input and a substantial patch from kris (at) koentopp.de that adds many new details. The document has grown a lot, actually beyond expectations.

I have also upgraded my system to Debian 1.2.6 and have replaced the old Slackware values with the Debian values for disk space requirements for the various directory. I will use Debian as a base for discussions and examples here, though the HOWTO is equally applicable to other distributions, even other operating systems. At the time of writing this Debian 1.3 is out in beta and will soon be used as the test bench for further versions of this document.

More news: there has been a fair bit of interest in new kinds of file systems in the comp.os.linux newsgroups, in particular logging, journaling and inherited file systems. Watch out for updates. Projects on volume management is also under way. The old defragmentation program for `ext2fs` is being updated and there is continuing interests for compression.

The latest version number of this document can be gleaned from my plan entry if you *finger* `<finger: sgjoen@nox.nyx.net>` my Nyx account.

Also, the latest version will be available on my web space on nyx: *The Multi Disk System Tuning HOWTO Homepage* `<http://www.nyx.net/sgjoen/disk.html>`.

A text-only version as well as the SGML source can also be downloaded there. A nicely formatted postscript version is also available now. In order to save disk space and bandwidth it has been compressed using gzip.

Also planned is a series of URLs to helpful software referred to in this document. A mirror in Europe will be announced soon.

I have very recently changed jobs, address etc so there will be a few delays in updates before I get the time for a more systematic updates.

From version 0.15 onward this document is primarily handled as an SGML document which means future printouts should look nicer than the old text based version. This also means that it has more or less grown into a full HOWTO. With respect to size it must be admitted it is a long time since there was anything "mini" about it.

1.4   Credits

In this version I have the pleasure of acknowledging even more people who have contributed in one way or another:

```
ronnej (at ) ucs.orst.edu
cm (at) kukuruz.ping.at
armbru (at) pond.sub.org
R.P.Blake (at) open.ac.uk
neuffer (at) goofy.zdv.Uni-Mainz.de
sjmudd (at) redestb.es
nat (at) nataa.fr.eu.org
sundbyk (at) horten.geco-prakla.slb.com
gjoen (at) sn.no
mike (at) i-Connect.Net
roth (at) uiuc.edu
phall (at) ilap.com
szaka (at) mirror.cc.u-szeged.hu
CMckeon (at) swcp.com
kris (at) koentopp.de
edick (at) idcomm.com
pot (at) fly.cnuce.cnr.it
earl (at) sbox.tu-graz.ac.at
ebacon (at) oanet.com
vax (at) linkdead.paranoia.com
```

Special thanks go to `nakano (at) apm.seikei.ac.jp` for doing the *Japanese translation* `<http://jf.linux.or.jp/JF/JF-ftp/other-formats/Disk-HOWTO/html/Disk-HOWTO.html>`, general contributions as well as contributing an example of a computer in an academic setting, which is included at the end of this document.

Not many still, so please read through this document, make a contribution and join the elite. If I have forgotten anyone, please let me know.

New in this version is an appendix with a few tables you can fill in for your system in order to simplify the design process.

Any comments or suggestions can be mailed to my mail address on nyx: *sgjoen@nyx.net* `<mailto:sgjoen@nyx.net/>`.

So let's cut to the chase where `swap` and `/tmp` are racing along hard drive...

2   Structure

As this type of document is supposed to be as much for learning as a technical reference document I have rearranged the structure to this end. For the designer of a system it is more useful to have the information presented in terms of the goals of this exercise than from the point of view of the logical layer structure of the devices themselves. Nevertheless this document would not be complete without such a layer structure the computer field is so full of, so I will include it here as an introduction to how it works.

It is a long time since the *mini* in mini-HOWTO could be defended as proper but I am convinced that this document is as long as it needs to be in order to make the right design decisions, and not longer.

2.1   Logical structure

This is based on how each layer access each other, traditionally with the application on top and the physical layer on the bottom. It is quite useful to show the interrelationship between each of the layers used in controlling drives.

```
        ----------------------------------------------------------
        |__    File structure       ( /usr /tmp etc)          __|
        |__    File system          (ext2fs, vfat etc)        __|
        |__    Volume management     (AFS)                    __|
        |__    RAID, concatenation   (md)                     __|
        |__    Device driver         (SCSI, IDE etc)          __|
        |__    Controller            (chip, card)             __|
        |__    Connection            (cable, network)         __|
        |__    Drive                 (magnetic, optical etc)  __|
        ----------------------------------------------------------
```

In the above diagram both volume management and RAID and concatenation are optional layers. The 3 lower layers are in hardware. All parts are discussed at length later on in this document.

2.2   Document structure

Most users start out with a given set of hardware and some plans on what they wish to achieve and how big the system should be. This is the point of view I will adopt in this document in presenting the material, starting out with hardware, continuing with design constraints before detailing the design strategy that I have found to work well. I have used this both for my own personal computer at home, a multi purpose server at work and found it worked quite well. In addition my Japanese co-worker in this project have applied the same strategy on a server in an academic setting with similar success.

Finally at the end I have detailed some configuration tables for use in your own design. If you have any comments regarding this or notes from your own design work I would like to hear from you so this document can be upgraded.

3   Drive technologies

A far more complete discussion on drive technologies for IBM PCs can be found at the home page of *The Enhanced IDE/Fast-ATA FAQ* <http://thef-nym.sci.kun.nl/pieterh/storage.html> which is also regularly posted on Usenet News. Here I will just present what is needed to get an understanding of the technology and get you started on your setup.

3.1   Drives

This is the physical device where your data lives and although the operating system makes the various types seem rather similar they can in actual fact be very different. An understanding of how it works can be very useful in your design work. Floppy drives fall outside the scope of this document, though should there be a big demand I could perhaps be persuaded to add a little here.

3.2   Geometry

Physically disk drives consists of one or more platters containing data that is read in and out using sensors mounted on movable heads that are fixed with respects to themselves. Data transfers therefore happens across all surfaces simultaneously which defines a cylinder of tracks. The drive is also divided into sectors containing a number of data fields.

Drives are therefore often specified in terms of its geometry: the number of Cylinders, Heads and Sectors (CHS).

For various reasons there is now a number of translations between

- the physical CHS of the drive itself
- the logical CHS the drive reports to the BIOS or OS
- the logical CHS used by the OS

Basically it is a mess and a source of much confusion. For more information you are strongly recommended to read the *Large Disk mini-HOWTO*

3.3   Media

The media technology determines important parameters such as read/write rates, seek times, storage size as well as if it is read/write or read only.

3.3.1   Magnetic Drives

This is the typical read-write mass storage medium, and as everything else in the computer world, comes in many flavours with different properties. Usually this is the fastest technology and offers read/write capability. The platter rotates with a constant angular velocity (CAV) with a variable physical sector density for more efficient magnetic media area utilisation. In other words, the number of bits per unit length is kept roughly constant by increasing the number of logical sectors for the outer tracks.

Typical values for rotational speeds are 4500 and 5400 rpm, though 7200 is also used. Very recently also 10000 rpm has entered the mass market. Seek times are around 10ms, transfer rates quite variable from one type to another but typically 4-40 MB/s. With the extreme high performance drives you should remember that performance costs more electric power which is dissipated as heat, see the point on 16.6 (Power and Heating).

Note that there are several kinds of transfers going on here, and that these are quoted in different units. First of all there is the platter-to-drive cache transfer, usually quoted in Mbits/s. Typical values here is about 50-250 Mbits/s. The second stage is from the built in drive cache to the adapter, and this is typically quoted in MB/s, and typical quoted values here is 3-40 MB/s. Note, however, that this assumed data is already in the cache and hence for maximum readout speed from the drive the effective transfer rate will decrease dramatically.

3.3.2   Optical drives

Optical read/write drives exist but are slow and not so common. They were used in the NeXT machine but the low speed was a source for much of the complaints. The low speed is mainly due to the thermal nature of the phase change that represents the data storage. Even when using relatively powerful lasers to induce the phase changes the effects are still slower than the magnetic effect used in magnetic drives.

Today many people use CD-ROM drives which, as the name suggests, is read-only. Storage is about 650 MB, transfer speeds are variable, depending on the drive but can exceed 1.5 MB/s. Data is stored on a spiraling single track so it is not useful to talk about geometry for this. Data density is constant so the drive uses constant linear velocity (CLV). Seek is also slower, about 100ms, partially due to the spiraling track. Recent, high speed drives, use a mix of CLV and CAV in order to maximize performance. This also reduces access time caused by the need to reach correct rotational speed for readout.

A new type (DVD) is on the horizon, offering up to about 18 GB on a single disk.

3.3.3   Solid State Drives

This is a relatively recent addition to the available technology and has been made popular especially in portable computers as well as in embedded systems. Containing no movable parts they are very fast both in terms of access and transfer rates. The most popular type is flash RAM, but also other types of RAM is used. A few years ago many had great hopes for magnetic bubble memories but it turned out to be relatively expensive and is not that common.

In general the use of RAM disks are regarded as a bad idea as it is normally more sensible to add more RAM to the motherboard and let the operating system divide the memory pool into buffers, cache, program and data areas. Only in very special cases, such as real time systems with short time margins, can RAM disks be a sensible solution.

Flash RAM is today available in several 10's of megabytes in storage and one might be tempted to use it for fast, temporary storage in a computer. There is however a huge snag with this: flash RAM has a finite life time in terms of the number of times you can rewrite data, so putting `swap`, `/tmp` or `/var/tmp` on such a device will certainly shorten its lifetime dramatically. Instead, using flash RAM for directories that are read often but rarely written to, will be a big performance win.

In order to get the optimum life time out of flash RAM you will need to use special drivers that will use the RAM evenly and minimize the number of block erases.

This example illustrates the advantages of splitting up your directory structure over several devices.

Solid state drives have no real cylinder/head/sector addressing but for compatibility reasons this is simulated by the driver to give a uniform interface to the operating system.

3.4 Interfaces

There is a plethora of interfaces to chose from widely ranging in price and performance. Most motherboards today include IDE interface or better, Intel supports it through the Triton PCI chip set which is very popular these days. Many motherboards also include a SCSI interface chip made by NCR and that is connected directly to the PCI bus. Check what you have and what BIOS support you have with it.

3.4.1 MFM and RLL

Once upon a time this was the established technology, a time when 20 MB was awesome, which compared to todays sizes makes you think that dinosaurs roamed the Earth with these drives. Like the dinosaurs these are outdated and are slow and unreliable compared to what we have today. Linux does support this but you are well advised to think twice about what you would put on this. One might argue that an emergency partition with a suitable vintage of DOS might be fitting.

3.4.2 ESDI

Actually, ESDI was an adaptation of the very widely used SMD interface used on "big" computers to the cable set used with the ST506 interface, which was more convenient to package than the 60-pin + 26-pin connector pair used with SMD. The ST506 was a "dumb" interface which relied entirely on the controller and host computer to do everything from computing head/cylinder/sector locations and keeping track of the head location, etc. ST506 required the controller to extract clock from the recovered data, and control the physical location of detailed track features on the medium, bit by bit. It had about a 10-year life if you include the use of MFM, RLL, and ERLL/ARLL modulation schemes. ESDI, on the other hand, had intelligence, often using three or four separate microprocessors on a single drive, and high-level commands to format a track, transfer data, perform seeks, and so on. Clock recovery from the data stream was accomplished at the drive, which drove the clock line and presented its data in NRZ, though error correction was still the task of the controller. ESDI allowed the use of variable bit density recording, or, for that matter, any other modulation technique, since it was locally generated and resolved at the drive. Though many of the techniques used in ESDI were later incorporated in IDE, it was the increased popularity of SCSI which led to the demise of ESDI in computers. ESDI had a life of about 10 years, though mostly in servers and otherwise "big" systems rather than PC's.

3.4.3 IDE and ATA

Progress made the drive electronics migrate from the ISA slot card over to the drive itself and Integrated Drive Electronics was borne. It was simple, cheap and reasonably fast so the BIOS designers provided the kind of snag that the computer industry is so full of. A combination of an IDE limitation of 16 heads together with the BIOS limitation of 1024 cylinders gave us the infamous 504 MB limit. Following the computer industry traditions again, the snag was patched with a kludge and we got all sorts of translation schemes and BIOS bodges. This means that you need to read the installation documentation very carefully and check up on what BIOS you have and what date it has as the BIOS has to tell Linux what size drive you have. Fortunately with Linux you can also tell the kernel directly what size drive you have with the drive parameters, check the documentation for LILO and Loadlin, thoroughly. Note also that IDE is equivalent to ATA, AT Attachment. IDE uses CPU-intensive Programmed Input/Output (PIO) to transfer data to and from the drives and has no capability for the more efficient Direct Memory Access (DMA) technology. Highest transfer rate is 8.3 MB/s.

3.4.4   EIDE, Fast-ATA and ATA-2

These 3 terms are roughly equivalent, fast-ATA is ATA-2 but EIDE additionally includes ATAPI. ATA-2 is what most use these days which is faster and with DMA. Highest transfer rate is increased to 16.6 MB/s.

3.4.5   Ultra-ATA

A new, faster DMA mode that is approximately twice the speed of EIDE PIO-Mode 4 (33 MB/s). Disks with and without Ultra-ATA can be mixed on the same cable without speed penalty for the faster adapters. The Ultra-ATA interface is electrically identical with the normal Fast-ATA interface, including the maximum cable length.

3.4.6   ATAPI

The ATA Packet Interface was designed to support CD-ROM drives using the IDE port and like IDE it is cheap and simple.

3.4.7   SCSI

The Small Computer System Interface is a multi purpose interface that can be used to connect to everything from drives, disk arrays, printers, scanners and more. The name is a bit of a misnomer as it has traditionally been used by the higher end of the market as well as in work stations since it is well suited for multi tasking environments.

The standard interface is 8 bits wide and can address 8 devices. There is a wide version with 16 bit that is twice as fast on the same clock and can address 16 devices. The host adapter always counts as a device and is usually number 7. It is also possible to have 32 bit wide busses but this usually requires a double set of cables to carry all the lines.

The old standard was 5 MB/s and the newer fast-SCSI increased this to 10 MB/s. Recently ultra-SCSI, also known as Fast-20, arrived with 20 MB/s transfer rates for an 8 bit wide bus.

The higher performance comes at a cost that is usually higher than for (E)IDE. The importance of correct termination and good quality cables cannot be overemphasized. SCSI drives also often tend to be of a higher quality than IDE drives. Also adding SCSI devices tend to be easier than adding more IDE drives: Often it is only a matter of plugging or unplugging the device; some people do this without powering down the system. This feature is most convenient when you have multiple systems and you can just take the devices from one system to the other should one of them fail for some reason.

There is a number of useful documents you should read if you use SCSI, the SCSI HOWTO as well as the SCSI FAQ posted on Usenet News.

SCSI also has the advantage you can connect it easily to tape drives for backing up your data, as well as some printers and scanners. It is even possible to use it as a very fast network between computers while simultaneously share SCSI devices on the same bus. Work is under way but due to problems with ensuring cache coherency between the different computers connected, this is a non trivial task.

3.5 Cabling

I do not intend to make too many comments on hardware but I feel I should make a little note on cabling. This might seem like a remarkably low technological piece of equipment, yet sadly it is the source of many frustrating problems. At todays high speeds one should think of the cable more of a an RF device with its inherent demands on impedance matching. If you do not take your precautions you will get a much reduced reliability or total failure. Some SCSI host adapters are more sensitive to this than others.

Shielded cables are of course better than unshielded but the price is much higher. With a little care you can get good performance from a cheap unshielded cable.

- For Fast-ATA and Ultra-ATA, the maximum cable length is specified as 45cm (18"). The data lines of both IDE channels are connected on many boards, though, so they count as **one** cable. In any case EIDE cables should be as short as possible. If there are mysterious crashes or spontaneous changes of data, it is well worth investigating your cabling. Try a lower PIO mode or disconnect the second channel and see if the problem still occurs.

- Use as short cable as possible, but do not forget the 30 cm minimum separation for ultra SCSI.

- Avoid long stubs between the cable and the drive, connect the plug on the cable directly to the drive without an extension.

- Use correct termination for SCSI devices and at the correct position: the end of the SCSI chain.

- Do not mix shielded or unshielded cabling, do not wrap cables around metal, try to avoid proximity to metal parts along parts of the cabling. Any such discontinuities can cause impedance mismatching which in turn can cause reflection of signals which increases noise on the cable. This problems gets even more severe in the case of multi channel controllers. Recently someone suggested wrapping bubble plastic around the cables in order to avoid too close proximity to metal, a real problem inside crowded cabinets.

3.6 Host Adapters

This is the other end of the interface from the drive, the part that is connected to a computer bus. The speed of the computer bus and that of the drives should be roughly similar, otherwise you have a bottleneck in your system. Connecting a RAID 0 disk-farm to a ISA card is pointless. These days most computers come with 32 bit PCI bus capable of 132 MB/s transfers which should not represent a bottleneck for most people in the near future.

As the drive electronic migrated to the drives the remaining part that became the (E)IDE interface is so small it can easily fit into the PCI chip set. The SCSI host adapter is more complex and often includes a small CPU of its own and is therefore more expensive and not integrated into the PCI chip sets available today. Technological evolution might change this.

Some host adapters come with separate caching and intelligence but as this is basically second guessing the operating system the gains are heavily dependent on which operating system is used. Some of the more primitive ones, that shall remain nameless, experience great gains. Linux, on the other hand, have so much smarts of its own that the gains are much smaller.

Mike Neuffer, who did the drivers for the DPT controllers, states that the DPT controllers are intelligent enough that given enough cache memory it will give you a big push in performance and suggests that people who have experienced little gains with smart controllers just have not used a sufficiently intelligent caching controller.

3.7   Multi Channel Systems

In order to increase throughput it is necessary to identify the most significant bottlenecks and then eliminate them. In some systems, in particular where there are a great number of drives connected, it is advantageous to use several controllers working in parallel, both for SCSI host adapters as well as IDE controllers which usually have 2 channels built in. Linux supports this.

Some RAID controllers feature 2 or 3 channels and it pays to spread the disk load across all channels. In other words, if you have two SCSI drives you want to RAID and a two channel controller, you should put each drive on separate channels.

3.8   Multi Board Systems

In addition to having both a SCSI and an IDE in the same machine it is also possible to have more than one SCSI controller. Check the SCSI-HOWTO on what controllers you can combine. Also you will most likely have to tell the kernel it should probe for more than just a single SCSI or a single IDE controller. This is done using kernel parameters when booting, for instance using LILO. Check the HOWTOs for SCSI and LILO for how to do this.

3.9   Speed Comparison

The following tables are given just to indicate what speeds are possible but remember that these are the theoretical maximum speeds. All transfer rates are in MB per second and bus widths are measured in bits.

3.9.1   Controllers

```
IDE           :      8.3 - 16.7
Ultra-ATA     :      33


SCSI          :

                     Bus width (bits)

Bus Speed (MHz)      |      8      16      32
-------------------------------------------------
 5                   |      5      10      20
10  (fast)           |     10      20      40
20  (fast-20 / ultra)|     20      40      80
40  (fast-40 / ultra-2) |  40      80      --
-------------------------------------------------
```

3.9.2   Bus types

```
ISA           :      8-12
EISA          :      33
VESA          :      40      (Sometimes tuned to 50)
```

```
PCI
                        Bus width (bits)


Bus Speed (MHz)        |      32      64
-----------------------------------------------------
33                     |     132     264
66                     |     264     528
-----------------------------------------------------
```

3.10 Benchmarking

This is a very, very difficult topic and I will only make a few cautious comments about this minefield. First of all, it is more difficult to make comparable benchmarks that have any actual meaning. This, however, does not stop people from trying...

Instead one can use benchmarking to diagnose your own system, to check it is going as fast as it should, that is, not slowing down. Also you would expect a significant increase when switching from a simple file system to RAID, so a lack of performance gain will tell you something is wrong.

When you try to benchmark you should not hack up your own, instead look up `iozone` and `bonnie` and read the documentation very carefully. More information about this is coming soon.

3.11 Comparisons

SCSI offers more performance than EIDE but at a price. Termination is more complex but expansion not too difficult. Having more than 4 (or in some cases 2) IDE drives can be complicated, with wide SCSI you can have up to 15 per adapter. Some SCSI host adapters have several channels thereby multiplying the number of possible drives even further.

RLL and MFM is in general too old, slow and unreliable to be of much use.

3.12 Future Development

SCSI-3 is under way and will hopefully be released soon. Faster devices are already being announced, most recently an 80 MB/s monster specification has been proposed. This is based around the ultra-2 standard (which used a 40MHz clock) combined with a 16 bit cable.

Some manufacturers already announce SCSI-3 devices but this is currently rather premature as the standard is not yet firm. As the transfer speeds increase the saturation point of the PCI bus is getting closer. Currently the 64 bit version has a limit of 264 MB/s. The PCI transfer rate will in the future be increased from the current 33MHz to 66MHz, thereby increasing the limit to 528 MB/s.

Another trend is for larger and larger drives. I hear it is possible to get 55 GB on a single drive though this is rather expensive. Currently the optimum storage for your money is about 6.4 GB but also this is continuously increasing. The introduction of DVD will in the near future have a big impact, with nearly 20 GB on a single disk you can have a complete copy of even major FTP sites from around the world. The only thing we can be reasonably sure about the future is that even if it won't get any better, it will definitely be bigger.

Addendum: soon after I first wrote this I read that the maximum useful speed for a CD-ROM was 20x as mechanical stability would be too great a problem at these speeds. About one month after that again the first commercial 24x CD-ROMs were available...

3.13   Recommendations

My personal view is that EIDE is the best way to start out on your system, especially if you intend to use DOS as well on your machine. If you plan to expand your system over many years or use it as a server I would strongly recommend you get SCSI drives. Currently wide SCSI is a little more expensive. You are generally more likely to get more for your money with standard width SCSI. There is also differential versions of the SCSI bus which increases maximum length of the cable. The price increase is even more substantial and cannot therefore be recommended for normal users.

In addition to disk drives you can also connect some types of scanners and printers and even networks to a SCSI bus.

Also keep in mind that as you expand your system you will draw ever more power, so make sure your power supply is rated for the job and that you have sufficient cooling. Many SCSI drives offer the option of sequential spin-up which is a good idea for large systems. See also the point on 16.6 (Power and Heating).

4   Considerations

The starting point in this will be to consider where you are and what you want to do. The typical home system starts out with existing hardware and the newly converted Linux user will want to get the most out of existing hardware. Someone setting up a new system for a specific purpose (such as an Internet provider) will instead have to consider what the goal is and buy accordingly. Being ambitious I will try to cover the entire range.

Various purposes will also have different requirements regarding file system placement on the drives, a large multiuser machine would probably be best off with the /home directory on a separate disk, just to give an example.

In general, for performance it is advantageous to split most things over as many disks as possible but there is a limited number of devices that can live on a SCSI bus and cost is naturally also a factor. Equally important, file system maintenance becomes more complicated as the number of partitions and physical drives increases.

4.1   File system features

The various parts of FSSTND have different requirements regarding speed, reliability and size, for instance losing root is a pain but can easily be recovered. Losing /var/spool/mail is a rather different issue. Here is a quick summary of some essential parts and their properties and requirements. Note that this is just a guide, there can be binaries in etc and lib directories, libraries in bin directories and so on.

4.1.1   Swap

Speed

Maximum! Though if you rely too much on swap you should consider buying some more RAM. Note, however, that on many PC motherboards the cache will not work on RAM above 128 MB.

Size

Similar as for RAM. Quick and dirty algorithm: just as for tea: 16 MB for the machine and 2 MB for each user. Smallest kernel run in 1 MB but is tight, use 4 MB for general work and light applications, 8 MB for X11 or GCC or 16 MB to be comfortable. (The author is known to brew a rather powerful cuppa tea...)

Some suggest that swap space should be 1-2 times the size of the RAM, pointing out that the locality of the programs determines how effective your added swap space is. Note that using the same algorithm as for 4BSD is slightly incorrect as Linux does not allocate space for pages in core.

Also remember to take into account the type of programs you use. Some programs that have large working sets, such as finite element modeling (FEM) have huge data structures loaded in RAM rather than working explicitly on disk files. Data and computing intensive programs like this will cause excessive swapping if you have less RAM than the requirements.

Other types of programs can lock their pages into RAM. This can be for security reasons, preventing copies of data reaching a swap device or for performance reasons such as in a real time module. Either way, locking pages reduces the remaining amount of swappable memory and can cause the system to swap earlier then otherwise expected.

In `man 8 mkswap` it is explained that each swap partition can be a maximum of just under 128 MB in size.

Reliability

Medium. When it fails you know it pretty quickly and failure will cost you some lost work. You save often, don't you?

Note 1

Linux offers the possibility of interleaved swapping across multiple devices, a feature that can gain you much. Check out "man 8 swapon" for more details. However, software raiding `swap` across multiple devices adds more overheads than you gain.

Thus the `/etc/fstab` file might look like this:

```
/dev/sda1        swap          swap      pri=1            0        0
/dev/sdc1        swap          swap      pri=1            0        0
```

Remember that the `fstab` file is *very* sensitive to the formatting used, read the man page carefully and do *not* just cut and paste the lines above.

Note 2

Some people use a RAM disk for swapping or some other file systems. However, unless you have some very unusual requirements or setups you are unlikely to gain much from this as this cuts into the memory available for caching and buffering.

4.1.2   Temporary storage (/tmp and /var/tmp)

Speed

Very high. On a separate disk/partition this will reduce fragmentation generally, though `ext2fs` handles fragmentation rather well.

Size

Hard to tell, small systems are easy to run with just a few MB but these are notorious hiding places for stashing files away from prying eyes and quota enforcements and can grow without control on larger machines. Suggested: small home machine: 8 MB, large home machine: 32 MB, small server: 128 MB, and large machines up to 500 MB (The machine used by the author at work has 1100 users and a 300 MB `/tmp` directory). Keep an eye on these directories, not only for hidden files but also for old files. Also be prepared that these partitions might be the first reason you might have to resize your partitions.

Reliability

> Low. Often programs will warn or fail gracefully when these areas fail or are filled up. Random file errors will of course be more serious, no matter what file area this is.

Files

> Mostly short files but there can be a huge number of them. Normally programs delete their old `tmp` files but if somehow an interruption occurs they could survive. Many distributions have a policy regarding cleaning out `tmp` files at boot time, you might want to check out what your setup is.

Note

> In FSSTND there is a note about putting `/tmp` on RAM disk. This, however, is not recommended for the same reasons as stated for swap. Also, as noted earlier, do not use flash RAM drives for these directories. One should also keep in mind that some systems are set to automatically clean `tmp` areas on rebooting.

(* That was 50 lines, I am home and dry! *)

4.1.3 Spool areas (`/var/spool/news` and `/var/spool/mail`)

Speed

> High, especially on large news servers. News transfer and expiring are disk intensive and will benefit from fast drives. Print spools: low. Consider RAID0 for news.

Size

> For news/mail servers: whatever you can afford. For single user systems a few MB will be sufficient if you read continuously. Joining a list server and taking a holiday is, on the other hand, not a good idea. (Again the machine I use at work has 100 MB reserved for the entire **/var/spool**)

Reliability

> Mail: very high, news: medium, print spool: low. If your mail is very important (isn't it always?) consider RAID for reliability.

Files

> Usually a huge number of files that are around a few KB in size. Files in the print spool can on the other hand be few but quite sizable.

Note

> Some of the news documentation suggests putting all the `.overview` files on a drive separate from the news files, check out all news FAQs for more information.

4.1.4 Home directories (`/home`)

Speed

> Medium. Although many programs use `/tmp` for temporary storage, others such as some news readers frequently update files in the home directory which can be noticeable on large multiuser systems. For small systems this is not a critical issue.

Size

> Tricky! On some systems people pay for storage so this is usually then a question of finance. Large systems such as *nyx.net* <http://www.nyx.net/> (which is a free Internet service with mail, news and WWW services) run successfully with a suggested limit of 100 KB per user and 300 KB as enforced maximum. Commercial ISPs offer typically about 5 MB in their standard subscription packages.
>
> If however you are writing books or are doing design work the requirements balloon quickly.

Reliability

Variable. Losing /home on a single user machine is annoying but when 2000 users call you to tell you their home directories are gone it is more than just annoying. For some their livelihood relies on what is here. You do regular backups of course?

Files

Equally tricky. The minimum setup for a single user tends to be a dozen files, 0.5 - 5 KB in size. Project related files can be huge though.

Note1

You might consider RAID for either speed or reliability. If you want extremely high speed and reliability you might be looking at other operating system and hardware platforms anyway. (Fault tolerance etc.)

Note2

Web browsers often use a local cache to speed up browsing and this cache can take up a substantial amount of space and cause much disk activity. There are many ways of avoiding this kind of performance hits, for more information see the sections on 8.6.1 (Home Directories) and 8.6.3 (WWW).

Note3

Users often tend to use up all available space on the /home partition. The Linux Quota subsystem is capable of limiting the number of blocks and the number of inode a single user ID can allocate on a per-filesystem basis. See the *Linux Quota mini-HOWTO* <http://sunsite.unc.edu/LDP/mini> by *Albert M.C. Tam* <mailto:bertie(at)scn.org> for details on setup.

4.1.5   Main binaries (/usr/bin and /usr/local/bin)

Speed

Low. Often data is bigger than the programs which are demand loaded anyway so this is not speed critical. Witness the successes of live file systems on CD ROM.

Size

The sky is the limit but 200 MB should give you most of what you want for a comprehensive system. A big system, for software development or a multi purpose server should perhaps reserve 500 MB both for installation and for growth.

Reliability

Low. This is usually mounted under root where all the essentials are collected. Nevertheless losing all the binaries is a pain...

Files

Variable but usually of the order of 10 - 100 kB.

4.1.6   Libraries (/usr/lib and /usr/local/lib)

Speed

Medium. These are large chunks of data loaded often, ranging from object files to fonts, all susceptible to bloating. Often these are also loaded in their entirety and speed is of some use here.

Size

Variable. This is for instance where word processors store their immense font files. The few that have given me feedback on this report about 70 MB in their various lib directories. A rather complete Debian 1.2 installation can take as much as 250 MB which can be taken as an realistic upper limit. The following ones are some of the largest disk space consumers: GCC, Emacs, TeX/LaTeX, X11 and perl.

Reliability

Low. See point 4.1.5 (Main binaries).

Files

Usually large with many of the order of 100 kB in size.

Note

For historical reasons some programs keep executables in the lib areas. One example is GCC which have some huge binaries in the **/usr/lib/gcc/lib** hierarchy.

4.1.7 Root

Speed

Quite low: only the bare minimum is here, much of which is only run at startup time.

Size

Relatively small. However it is a good idea to keep some essential rescue files and utilities on the root partition and some keep several kernel versions. Feedback suggests about 20 MB would be sufficient.

Reliability

High. A failure here will possibly cause a fair bit of grief and you might end up spending some time rescuing your boot partition. With some practice you can of course do this in an hour or so, but I would think if you have some practice doing this you are also doing something wrong.

Naturally you do have a rescue disk? Of course this is updated since you did your initial installation? There are many ready made rescue disks as well as rescue disk creation tools you might find valuable. Presumably investing some time in this saves you from becoming a root rescue expert.

Note 1

If you have plenty of drives you might consider putting a spare emergency boot partition on a separate physical drive. It will cost you a little bit of space but if your setup is huge the time saved, should something fail, will be well worth the extra space.

Note 2

For simplicity and also in case of emergencies it is not advisable to put the root partition on a RAID level 0 system. Also if you use RAID for your boot partition you have to remember to have the md option turned on for your emergency kernel.

4.1.8 DOS etc.

At the danger of sounding heretical I have included this little section about something many reading this document have strong feelings about. Unfortunately many hardware items come with setup and maintenance tools based around those systems, so here goes.

Speed

Very low. The systems in question are not famed for speed so there is little point in using prime quality drives. Multitasking or multi-threading are not available so the command queueing facility found in SCSI drives will not be taken advantage of. If you have an old IDE drive it should be good enough. The exception is to some degree Win95 and more notably NT which have multi-threading support which should theoretically be able to take advantage of the more advanced features offered by SCSI devices.

Size

The company behind these operating systems is not famed for writing tight code so you have to be prepared to spend a few tens of MB depending on what version you install of the OS or Windows. With an old version of DOS or Windows you might fit it all in on 50 MB.

Reliability

Ha-ha. As the chain is no stronger than the weakest link you can use any old drive. Since the OS is more likely to scramble itself than the drive is likely to self destruct you will soon learn the importance of keeping backups here.

Put another way: "Your mission, should you choose to accept it, is to keep this partition working. The warranty will self destruct in 10 seconds..."

Recently I was asked to justify my claims here. First of all I am not calling DOS and Windows sorry excuses for operating systems. Secondly there are various legal issues to be taken into account. Saying there is a connection between the last two sentences are merely the ravings of the paranoid. Surely. Instead I shall offer the esteemed reader a few key words: DOS 4.0, DOS 6.x and various drive compression tools that shall remain nameless.

4.2 Explanation of terms

Naturally the faster the better but often the happy installer of Linux has several disks of varying speed and reliability so even though this document describes performance as 'fast' and 'slow' it is just a rough guide since no finer granularity is feasible. Even so there are a few details that should be kept in mind:

4.2.1 Speed

This is really a rather woolly mix of several terms: CPU load, transfer setup overhead, disk seek time and transfer rate. It is in the very nature of tuning that there is no fixed optimum, and in most cases price is the dictating factor. CPU load is only significant for IDE systems where the CPU does the transfer itself but is generally low for SCSI, see SCSI documentation for actual numbers. Disk seek time is also small, usually in the millisecond range. This however is not a problem if you use command queueing on SCSI where you then overlap commands keeping the bus busy all the time. News spools are a special case consisting of a huge number of normally small files so in this case seek time can become more significant.

There are two main parameters that are of interest here:

Seek

is usually specified in the average time take for the read/write head to seek from one track to another. This parameter is important when dealing with a large number of small files such as found in spool files. There is also the extra seek delay before the desired sector rotates into position under the head. This delay is dependent on the angular velocity of the drive which is why this parameter quite often is quoted for a drive. Common values are 4500, 5400 and 7200 rpm (rotations per minute). Higher rpm reduces the seek time but at a substantial cost. Also drives working at 7200 rpm have been known to be noisy and to generate a lot of heat, a factor that should be kept in mind if you are building a large array or "disk farm". Very recently drives working at 10000 rpm has entered the market and here the cooling requirements are even stricter and minimum figures for air flow are given.

Transfer

is usually specified in megabytes per second. This parameter is important when handling large files that have to be transferred. Library files, dictionaries and image files are examples of this. Drives featuring a high rotation speed also normally have fast transfers as transfer speed is proportional to angular velocity for the same sector density.

It is therefore important to read the specifications for the drives very carefully, and note that the maximum transfer speed quite often is quoted for transfers out of the on board cache (burst speed) and *not* directly from the platter (sustained speed). See also section on 16.6 (Power and Heating).

4.2.2   Reliability

Naturally no-one would want low reliability disks but one might be better off regarding old disks as unreliable. Also for RAID purposes (See the relevant information) it is suggested to use a mixed set of disks so that simultaneous disk crashes become less likely.

So far I have had only one report of total file system failure but here unstable hardware seemed to be the cause of the problems.

4.2.3   Files

The average file size is important in order to decide the most suitable drive parameters. A large number of small files makes the average seek time important whereas for big files the transfer speed is more important. The command queueing in SCSI devices is very handy for handling large numbers of small files, but for transfer EIDE is not too far behind SCSI and normally much cheaper than SCSI.

4.3   Technologies

In order to decide how to get the most of your devices you need to know what technologies are available and their implications. As always there can be some tradeoffs with respect to speed, reliability, power, flexibility, ease of use and complexity.

4.3.1   RAID

This is a method of increasing reliability, speed or both by using multiple disks in parallel thereby decreasing access time and increasing transfer speed. A checksum or mirroring system can be used to increase reliability. Large servers can take advantage of such a setup but it might be overkill for a single user system unless you already have a large number of disks available. See other documents and FAQs for more information.

For Linux one can set up a RAID system using either software (the `md` module in the kernel), a Linux compatible controller card (PCI-to-SCSI) or a SCSI-to-SCSI controller. Check the documentation for what controllers can be used. A hardware solution is usually faster, and perhaps also safer, but comes at a significant cost.

SCSI-to-SCSI controllers are usually implemented as complete cabinets with drives and a controller that connects to the computer with a second SCSI bus. This makes the entire cabinet of drives look like a single large, fast SCSI drive and requires no special RAID driver. The disadvantage is that the SCSI bus connecting the cabinet to the computer becomes a bottleneck.

PCI-to-SCSI are as the name suggests, connected to the high speed PCI bus and is therefore not suffering from the same bottleneck as the SCSI-to-SCSI controllers. These controllers require special drivers but you also get the means of controlling the RAID configuration over the network which simplifies management.

Currently the only supported SCSI RAID controller cards are the SmartCache I/III/IV and SmartRAID I/III/IV controller families from DPT. These controllers are supported by the EATA-DMA driver in the standard kernel. This company also has an informative *home page* <http://www.dpt.com> which also describes various general aspects of RAID and SCSI in addition to the product related information.

More information from the author of the DPT controller drivers (EATA* drivers) can be found at his pages on *SCSI* <http://www.uni-mainz.de/neuffer/scsi> and *DPT* <http://www.uni-mainz.de/neuffer/scsi/dpt>.

SCSI-to-SCSI-controllers are small computers themselves, often with a substantial amount of cache RAM. To the host system they mask themselves as a gigantic, fast and reliable SCSI disk whereas to their disks they look like the computer's SCSI host adapter. Some of these controllers have the option to talk to multiple hosts simultaneously. Since these controllers look to the host as a normal, albeit large SCSI drive they need no special support from the host system. Usually they are configured via the front panel or with a vt100 terminal emulator connected to their on-board serial interface.

Very recently I have heard that Syred also makes SCSI-to-SCSI controllers that are supported under Linux. I have no more information about this yet but will come back with more information soon. In the mean time check out their *home* <http://www.syred.com> pages for more information.

RAID comes in many levels and flavours which I will give a brief overview of this here. Much has been written about it and the interested reader is recommended to read more about this in the RAID FAQ.

- RAID *0* is not redundant at all but offers the best throughput of all levels here. Data is striped across a number of drives so read and write operations take place in parallel across all drives. On the other hand if a single drive fail then everything is lost. Did I mention backups?

- RAID *1* is the most primitive method of obtaining redundancy by duplicating data across all drives. Naturally this is massively wasteful but you get one substantial advantage which is fast access. The drive that access the data first wins. Transfers are not any faster than for a single drive, even though you might get some faster read transfers by using one track reading per drive.

  Also if you have only 2 drives this is the only method of achieving redundancy.

- RAID *2* and *4* are not so common and are not covered here.

- RAID *3* uses a number of disks (at least 2) to store data in a striped RAID 0 fashion. It also uses an additional redundancy disk to store the XOR sum of the data from the data disks. Should the redundancy disk fail, the system can continue to operate as if nothing happened. Should any single data disk fail the system can compute the data on this disk from the information on the redundancy disk and all remaining disks. Any double fault will bring the whole RAID set off-line.

  RAID 3 makes sense only with at least 2 data disks (3 disks including the redundancy disk). Theoretically there is no limit for the number of disks in the set, but the probability of a fault increases with the number of disks in the RAID set. Usually the upper limit is 5 to 7 disks in a single RAID set.

  Since RAID 3 stores all redundancy information on a dedicated disk and since this information has to be updated whenever a write to any data disk occurs, the overall write speed of a RAID 3 set is limited by the write speed of the redundancy disk. This, too, is a limit for the number of disks in a RAID set. The overall read speed of a RAID 3 set with all data disks up and running is that of a RAID 0 set with that number of data disks. If the set has to reconstruct data stored on a failed disk from redundant information, the performance will be severely limited: All disks in the set have to be read and XOR-ed to compute the missing information.

- RAID *5* is just like RAID 3, but the redundancy information is spread on all disks of the RAID set. This improves write performance, because load is distributed more evenly between all available disks.

There are also hybrids available based on RAID 1 and one other level. Many combinations are possible but I have only seen a few referred to. These are more complex than the above mentioned RAID levels.

RAID *0/1* combines striping with duplication which gives very high transfers combined with fast seeks as well as redundancy. The disadvantage is high disk consumption as well as the above mentioned complexity.

RAID *1/5* combines the speed and redundancy benefits of RAID5 with the fast seek of RAID1. Redundancy is improved compared to RAID 0/1 but disk consumption is still substantial. Implementing such a system would involve typically more than 6 drives, perhaps even several controllers or SCSI channels.

4.3.2   AFS, Veritas and Other Volume Management Systems

Although multiple partitions and disks have the advantage of making for more space and higher speed and reliability there is a significant snag: if for instance the /tmp partition is full you are in trouble even if the news spool is empty, as it is not easy to retransfer quotas across partitions. Volume management is a system that does just this and AFS and Veritas are two of the best known examples. Some also offer other file systems like log file systems and others optimised for reliability or speed. Note that Veritas is not available (yet) for Linux and it is not certain they can sell kernel modules without providing source for their proprietary code, this is just mentioned for information on what is out there. Still, you can check their *home page* <http://www.veritas.com> to see how such systems function.

Derek Atkins, of MIT, ported AFS to Linux and has also set up the *Linux AFS mailing List* <mailto:linux-afs@mit.edu> for this which is open to the public. Requests to join the list should go to *Request* <mailto:linux-afs-request@mit.edu> and finally bug reports should be directed to *Bug Reports* <mailto:linux-afs-bugs@mit.edu>.

Important: as AFS uses encryption it is restricted software and cannot easily be exported from the US. AFS is now sold by Transarc and they have set up a www site. The directory structure there has been reorganized recently so I cannot give a more accurate URL than just the *Transarc Home Page* <http://www.transarc.com> which lands you in the root of the web site. There you can also find much general information as well as a FAQ.

The is now also development based on the last free sources of AFS.

Volume management is for the time being an area where Linux is lacking. Someone has recently started a virtual partition system project that will reimplement many of the volume management functions found in IBM's AIX system.

4.3.3 Linux md Kernel Patch

There is however one kernel project that attempts to do some of this, md, which has been part of the kernel distributions since 1.3.69. Currently providing spanning and RAID it is still in early development and people are reporting varying degrees of success as well as total wipe out. Use with caution.

Currently it offers linear mode and RAID levels 0,1,4,5; all in various stages of development and reliability with linear mode and RAID levels 0 and 1 being the most stable. It is also possible to stack some levels, for instance mirroring (RAID 1) two pairs of drives, each pair set up as striped disks (RAID 0), which offers the speed of RAID 0 combined with the reliability of RAID 1.

Think very carefully what drives you combine so you can operate all drives in parallel, which gives you better performance and less wear. Read more about this in the documentation that comes with md.

4.3.4 General File System Consideration

In the Linux world ext2fs is well established as a general purpose system. Still for some purposes others can be a better choice. News spools lend themselves to a log file based system whereas high reliability data might need other formats. This is a hotly debated topic and there are currently few choices available but work is underway. Log file systems also have the advantage of very fast file checking. Mail servers in the 100 GB class can suffer file checks taking several days before becoming operational after rebooting.

The Minix file system is the oldest one, used in some rescue disk systems but otherwise very little used these days. At one time the Xiafs was a strong contender to the standard for Linux but seems to have fallen behind these days.

Adam Richter from Yggdrasil posted recently that they have been working on a compressed log file based system but that this project is currently on hold. Nevertheless a non-working version is available on their FTP server. Check out *the Yggdrasil ftp server* <ftp://ftp.yggdrasil.com/private/adam> where special patched versions of the kernel can be found. Hopefully this will be rolled into the mainstream kernel in the near future.

As of July, 23th 1997 *Hans Reiser* `<mailto:reiser(at)RICOCHET.NET>` has put up the source to his tree based *reiserfs* `<http://idiom.com/beverly/reiserfs.html>` on the web. While his filesystem has some very interesting features and is much faster than `ext2fs`, it is still very experimental and difficult to integrate with the standard kernel. Expect some interesting developments in the future - this is different from your "average log based file system for Linux" project, because Hans already has working code.

There is room for access control lists (ACL) and other unimplemented features in the existing `ext2fs`, stay tuned for future updates.

There is also an encrypted file system available but again as this is under export control from the US, make sure you get it from a legal place.

File systems is an active field of academic and industrial research and development, the results of which are quite often freely available. Linux has in many cases been a development tool in such activities so you can expect a lot of continuous work in this field, stay tuned for the latest development.

4.3.5 CD-ROM File Systems

There has been a number of file systems available for use on CD-ROM systems and one of the earliest one was the *High Sierra* format, supposedly named after the hotel where the final agreement took place. This was the precursor to the *ISO 9660* format which is supported by Linux. Later there were the *Rock Ridge* extensions which added file system features such as long filenames, permissions and more.

The Linux iso9660 file system supports both High Sierra as well as Rock Ridge extensions.

However, once again Microsoft decided it should create another standard and their latest effort here is called *Joliet* and offers some internationalisation features. This is at the time of writing not yet available in the standard kernel releases but exists in beta versions. Hopefully this should soon work its way into the standard kernel.

In a recent Usenet News posting hpa (at) transmeta.com (H. Peter Anvin) writes the following the following interesting piece of trivia:

```
Actually, Joliet is a city outside Chicago; best known for being the
site of the prison where Elwood was locked up in the movie "Blues
Brothers."  Rock Ridge (the UNIX extensions to ISO 9660) is named
after the (fictional) town in the movie "Blazing Saddles."
```

4.3.6 Compression

Disk versus file compression is a hotly debated topic especially regarding the added danger of file corruption. Nevertheless there are several options available for the adventurous administrators. These take on many forms, from kernel modules and patches to extra libraries but note that most suffer various forms of limitations such as being read-only. As development takes place at neck breaking speed the specs have undoubtedly changed by the time you read this. As always: check the latest updates yourself. Here only a few references are given.

- DouBle features file compression with some limitations.
- Zlibc adds transparent on-the-fly decompression of files as they load.
- there are many modules available for reading compressed files or partitions that are native to various other operating systems though currently most of these are read-only.
- dmsdos (currently in version 0.8.0a) offer many of the compression options available for DOS and Windows. It is not yet complete but work is ongoing and new features added regularly.

- e2compr is a package that extends `ext2fs` with compression capabilities. It is still under testing and will therefore mainly be of interest for kernel hackers but should soon gain stability for wider use. Check the *e2compr homepage* `<http://netspace.net.au/~reiter/e2compr.html>` for more information. I have reports of speed and good stability which is why it is mentioned here.

4.3.7   Other filesystems

Also there is the user file system (`userfs`) that allows FTP based file system and some compression (`arcfs`) plus fast prototyping and many other features. The `docfs` is based on this filesystem.

Recent kernels feature the loop or loopback device which can be used to put a complete file system within a file. There are some possibilities for using this for making new file systems with compression, tarring, encryption etc.

Note that this device is unrelated to the network loopback device.

There is a number of other ongoing file system projects, but these are in the experimental stage and fall outside the scope of this HOWTO.

4.3.8   Physical Track Positioning

This trick used to be very important when drives were slow and small, and some file systems used to take the varying characteristics into account when placing files. Although higher overall speed, on board drive and controller caches and intelligence has reduced the effect of this.

Nevertheless there is still a little to be gained even today. As we know, "*world dominance*" is soon within reach but to achieve this "*fast*" we need to employ all the tricks we can use   `<finger:linus@linux.cs. helsinki.fi>`.

To understand the strategy we need to recall this near ancient piece of knowledge and the properties of the various track locations. This is based on the fact that transfer speeds generally increase for tracks further away from the spindle, as well as the fact that it is faster to seek to or from the central tracks than to or from the inner or outer tracks.

Most drives use disks running at constant angular velocity but use (fairly) constant data density across all tracks. This means that you will get much higher transfer rates on the outer tracks than on the inner tracks; a characteristics which fits the requirements for large libraries well.

Newer disks use a logical geometry mapping which differs from the actual physical mapping which is transparently mapped by the drive itself. This makes the estimation of the "middle" tracks a little harder.

In most cases track 0 is at the outermost track and this is the general assumption most people use. Still, it should be kept in mind that there are no guarantees this is so.

Inner
> tracks are usually slow in transfer, and lying at one end of the seeking position it is also slow to seek to.
> This is more suitable to the low end directories such as DOS, root and print spools.

Middle
> tracks are on average faster with respect to transfers than inner tracks and being in the middle also on average faster to seek to.
> This characteristics is ideal for the most demanding parts such as `swap`, `/tmp` and `/var/tmp`.

Outer

tracks have on average even faster transfer characteristics but like the inner tracks are at the end of the seek so statistically it is equally slow to seek to as the inner tracks.

Large files such as libraries would benefit from a place here.

Hence seek time reduction can be achieved by positioning frequently accessed tracks in the middle so that the average seek distance and therefore the seek time is short. This can be done either by using `fdisk` or `cfdisk` to make a partition on the middle tracks or by first making a file (using `dd`) equal to half the size of the entire disk before creating the files that are frequently accessed, after which the dummy file can be deleted. Both cases assume starting from an empty disk.

The latter trick is suitable for news spools where the empty directory structure can be placed in the middle before putting in the data files. This also helps reducing fragmentation a little.

This little trick can be used both on ordinary drives as well as RAID systems. In the latter case the calculation for centring the tracks will be different, if possible. Consult the latest RAID manual.

5 Other Operating Systems

Many Linux users have several operating systems installed, often necessitated by hardware setup systems that run under other operating systems, typically DOS or some flavour of Windows. A small section on how best to deal with this is therefore included here.

5.1 DOS

Leaving aside the debate on weather or not DOS qualifies as an operating system one can in general say that it has little sophistication with respect to disk operations. The more important result of this is that there can be severe difficulties in running various versions of DOS on large drives, and you are therefore strongly recommended in reading the *Large Drives mini-HOWTO*. One effect is that you are often better off placing DOS on low track numbers.

Having been designed for small drives it has a rather unsophisticated file system (*FAT*) which when used on large drives will allocate enormous block sizes. It is also prone to block fragmentation which will after a while cause excessive seeks and slow effective transfers.

One solution to this is to use a defragmentation program regularly but it is strongly recommended to back up data and verify the disk before defragmenting. All versions of DOS have `chkdsk` that can do some disk checking, newer versions also have `scandisk` which is somewhat better. There are many defragmentation programs available, some versions have one called `defrag`. Norton Utilities have a large suite of disk tools and there are many others available too.

As always there are snags, and this particular snake in our drive paradise is called *hidden files*. Some vendors started to use these for copy protection schemes and would not take kindly to being moved to a different place on the drive, even if it remained in the same place in the directory structure. The result of this was that newer defragmentation programs will not touch any hidden file, which in turn reduces the effect of defragmentation.

Being a single tasking, single threading and single most other things operating system there is very little gains in using multiple drives unless you use a drive controller with built in RAID support of some kind.

There are a few utilities called `join` and `subst` which can do some multiple drive configuration but there is very little gains for a lot of work. Some of these commands have been removed in newer versions.

In the end there is very little you can do, but not all hope is lost. Many programs need fast, temporary storage, and the better behaved ones will look for environment variables called `TMPDIR` or `TEMPDIR` which you can set to point to another drive. This is often best done in `autoexec.bat`.

```
SET TMPDIR=E:/TMP
```

Not only will this possibly gain you some speed but also it can reduce fragmentation.

There have been reports about difficulties in removing multiple primary partitions using the `fdisk` program that comes with DOS. Should this happen you can instead use a Linux rescue disk with Linux `fdisk` to repair the system.

5.2   Windows

Most of the above points are valid for Windows too, with the exception of Windows95 which apparently has better disk handling, which will get better performance out of SCSI drives.

A useful thing is the introduction of long filenames, to read these from Linux you will need the `vfat` file system for mounting these partitions.

The most important thing is the introduction of the new file system `FAT32` which is better suited to large drives. The snag is that there is very little support for this today, not even in NT 4.0 or many drive utility systems. A stable driver for Linux is coming soon but is not yet ready for prime time. Stay tuned for updates.

Disk fragmentation is still a problem. Some of this can be avoided by doing a defragmentation immediately before and immediately after installing large programs or systems. I use this scheme at work and have found it to work quite well. Purging unused files and emptying the waste basket first can improve defragmentation further.

Windows also use swap drives, redirecting this to another drive can give you some performance gains. There are several mini-HOWTOs telling you how best to share swap space between various operating systems.

Very recently someone started a project supporting `ext2fs` support for Win95 which you can read about at this *web site* <http://www.globalxs.nl/home/p/pvs/>.

The trick of setting `TEMPDIR` can still be used but not all programs will honour this setting. Some do, though. To get a good overview of the settings in the control files you can run `sysedit` which will open a number of files for editing, one of which is the `autoexec` file where you can add the `TEMPDIR` settings.

Much of the temporary files are located in the `/windows/temp` directory and changing this is more tricky. To achieve this you can use `regedit` which is rather powerful and quite capable of rendering your system in a state you will not enjoy, or more precisely, in a state much les enjoyable than windows in general. Registry database error is a message that means seriously bad news. Also you will see that many programs have their own private temporary directories scattered around the system.

Setting the swap file to a separate partition is a better idea and much less risky. Keep in mind that this partition cannot be used for anything else, even if there should appear to be space left there.

5.3   OS/2

The only special note here is that you can get a file system driver for OS/2 that can read an `ext2fs` partition.

5.4   NT

This is a more serious system featuring most buzzwords known to marketing. It is well worth noting that it features software striping and other more sophisticated setups. Check out the drive manager in the control panel. I do not have easy access to NT, more details on this can take a bit of time.

One important snag was recently reported by acahalan at cs.uml.edu : (reformatted from a Usenet News posting)

NT DiskManager has a serious bug that can corrupt your disk when you have several (more than one?) extended partitions. Microsoft provides an emergency fix program at their web site. See the *knowledge base* <http://www.microsoft.com/kb/> for more. (This affects Linux users, because Linux users have extra partitions)

5.5   Sun OS

There is a little bit of confusion in this area between Sun OS vs. Solaris. Strictly speaking Solaris is just Sun OS 5.x packaged with Openwindows and a few other things. If you run Solaris, just type `uname -a` to see your version. Parts of the reason for this confusion is that Sun Microsystems used to use an OS from the BSD family, albeight with a few bits and pieces from elsewhere as well as things made by themselves. This was the situation up to Sun OS 4.x.y when they did a "strategic roadmap decision" and decided to switch over to the official Unix, System V, Release 4 (aka SVR5), and Sun OS 5 was created. This made a lot of people unhappy. Also this was bundled with other things and marketed under the name Solaris, which currently stands at release 2.6 .

5.5.1   Sun OS 4

This is quite familiar to most Linux users. Note however that the file system structure is quite different and does not conform to FSSTND so any planning must be based on the traditional structure. You can get some information by the man page on this: `man hier`. This is, like most manpages, rather brief but should give you a good start. If you are still confused by the structure it will at least be at a higher level.

5.5.2   Sun OS 5 (aka Solaris)

This comes with a snazzy installation system that runs under Openwindows, it will help you in partitioning and formatting the drives before installing the system from CD-ROM. It will also fail if your drive setup is too far out, and as it takes a complete installation run from a full CD-ROM in a 1x only drive this failure will dawn on you after too long time. That is the experience we had where I used to work. Instead we installed everything onto one drive and then moved directories across.

The default settings are sensible for most things, yet there remains a little oddity: swap drives. Even though the official manual recommends multiple swap drives (which are used in a similar fashion as on Linux) the default is to use only a single drive. It is recommended to change this as soon as possible.

Sun OS 5 offers also a file system especially designed for temporary files, `tmpfs`. This is a kind of souped up RAM disk, and like ordinary RAM disks the contents is lost when the power goes. If space is scarce parts of the pseudo drive is swapped out, so in effect you store temporary files on the swap partition. Linux does not have such a file system; it has been discussed in the past but opinions were mixed. I would be interested in hearing comments on this.

The only comment so far is: don't! Under Solaris 2.0 it seem that creating too big files in `/tmp` can cause a out of swap space kernel panic trap. As the evidence of what has happened is as lost as any data on a RAMdisk after powering down it can be hard to find out what has happened. What is worse, it seems that user space processes can cause this kernel panic and unless this problem is taken care of it is best not to use `tmpfs`.

Also see the note on 16.1 (Combining swap and /tmp).

Trivia: There is a movie also called Solaris, a science fiction movie that is very, very long, slow and incomprehensible. This was often pointed out at the time Solaris (the OS) appeared...

6 Clusters

In this section I will briefly touch on the ways machines can be connected together but this is so big a topic it could be a separate HOWTO in its own right, hint, hint. Also, strictly speaking, this section lies outside the scope of this HOWTO, so if you feel like getting fame etc. *you* could contact me and take over this part and turn it into a new document.

These days computers gets outdated at an incredible rate. There is however no reason why old hardware could not be put to good use with Linux. Using an old and otherwise outdated computer as a network server can be both useful in its own right as well as a valuable educational exercise. Such a local networked cluster of computers can take on many forms but to remain within the charter of this HOWTO I will limit myself to the disk strategies. Nevertheless I would hope someone else could take on this topic and turn it into a document on its own.

This is an exciting area of activity today, and many forms of clustering is available today, ranging from automatic workload balancing over local network to more exotic hardware such as Scalable Coherent Interface (SCI) which gives a tight integration of machines, effectively turning them into a single machine. Various kinds of clustering has been available for larger machines for some time and the VAXcluster is perhaps a well known example of this. Clustering is done usually in order to share resources such as disk drives, printers and terminals etc, but also processing resources equally transparently between the computational nodes.

There is no universal definition of clustering, in here it is taken to mean a network of machines that combine their resources to serve users. Admittedly this is a rather loose definition but this will change later.

These days also Linux offers some clustering features but for a starter I will just describe a simple local network. It is a good way of putting old and otherwise unusable hardware to good use, as long as they can run Linux or something similar.

One of the best ways of using an old machine is as a network server in which case the effective speed is more likely to be limited by network bandwidth rather than pure computational performance. For home use you can move the following functionality off to an older machine used as a server:

- news
- mail
- web proxy
- printer server
- modem server (PPP, SLIP, FAX, Voice mail)

You can also NFS mount drives from the server onto your workstation thereby reducing drive space requirements. Still read the FSSTND to see what directories should *not* be exported. The best candidates for exporting to all machines are /usr and /var/spool and possibly /usr/local but probably not /var/spool/lpd.

Most of the time even slow disks will deliver sufficient performance. On the other hand, if you do processing directly on the disks on the server or have very fast networking, you might want to rethink your strategy and use faster drives. Searching features on a web server or news database searches are two examples of this.

Such a network can be an excellent way of learning system administration and building up your own toaster network, as it often is called. You can get more information on this in other HOWTOs but there are two important things you should keep in mind:

- Do not pull IP numbers out of thin air. Configure your inside net using IP numbers reserved for private use, and use your network server as a router that handles this IP masquerading.

- Remember that if you additionally configure the router as a firewall you might not be able to get to your own data from the outside, depending on the firewall configuration.

The *nyx* network provides an example of a cluster in the sense defined here. It consists of the following machines:

nyx

    is one of the two user login machines and also provides some of the networking services.

nox

    (aka nyx10) is the main user login machine and is also the mail server.

noc

    is a dedicated news server. The news spool is made accessible through NFS mounting to nyx and nox.

arachne

    (aka www) is the web server. Web pages are written by NFS mounting onto nox.

There are also some more advanced clustering projects going, notably

- *The Beowolf Project* <http://cesdis.gsfc.nasa.gov/linux/beowulf/beowulf.html>
- *The Genoa Active Message Machine (GAMMA)* <http://www.disi.unige.it/project/gamma/>

High-tech clustering requires high-tech interconnect, and SCI is one of them. To find out more you can either look up the home page of *Dolphin Interconnect Solutions* <http://www.dolphinics.no/> which is one of the main actors in this field, or you can have a look at *scizzl* <http://www.scizzl.com/>.

7 Mount Points

In designing the disk layout it is important not to split off the directory tree structure at the wrong points, hence this section. As it is highly dependent on the FSSTND it has been put aside in a separate section, and will most likely have to be totally rewritten when FHS is released. Nobody knows when that will happen, and at the time of writing this a debate of near-religious qualities is taking place on the mailing list. In the meanwhile this will do.

Remember that this is a list of where a separation *can* take place, not where it *has* to be. As always, good judgement is always required.

Again only a rough indication can be given here. The values indicate

```
0=don't separate here
1=not recommended
  ...
4=useful
5=recommended
```

In order to keep the list short, the uninteresting parts are removed.

Directory   Suitability

```
/
|
+-bin        0
+-boot       0
+-dev        0
+-etc        0
+-home       5
+-lib        0
+-mnt        0
+-proc       0
+-root       0
+-sbin       0
+-tmp        5
+-usr        5
| \
| +-X11R6    3
| +-bin      3
| +-lib      4
| +-local    4
| | \
| | +bin     2
| | +lib     4
| +-src      3
|
+-var        5
   \
    +-adm        0
    +-lib        2
    +-lock       1
    +-log        1
    +-preserve   1
    +-run        1
    +-spool      4
    | \
    | +-mail     3
    | +-mqueue   3
    | +-news     5
    | +-smail    3
    | +-uucp     3
    +-tmp        5
```

There is of course plenty of adjustments possible, for instance a home user would not bother with splitting off the /var/spool hierarchy but a serious ISP should. The key here is *usage*.

8   Disk Layout

With all this in mind we are now ready to embark on the layout. I have based this on my own method developed when I got hold of 3 old SCSI disks and boggled over the possibilities.

The tables in the appendices are designed to simplify the mapping process. They have been designed to help you go through the process of optimizations as well as making an useful log in case of system repair. A few examples are also given.

8.1   Selection for partitioning

Determine your needs and set up a list of all the parts of the file system you want to be on separate partitions and sort them in descending order of speed requirement and how much space you want to give each partition.

The table in Appendix A (section 17 ( )) is a useful tool to select what directories you should put on different partitions. It is sorted in a logical order with space for your own additions and notes about mounting points and additional systems. It is therefore NOT sorted in order of speed, instead the speed requirements are indicated by bullets ('o').

If you plan to RAID make a note of the disks you want to use and what partitions you want to RAID. Remember various RAID solutions offers different speeds and degrees of reliability.

(Just to make it simple I'll assume we have a set of identical SCSI disks and no RAID)

8.2   Mapping partitions to drives

Then we want to place the partitions onto physical disks. The point of the following algorithm is to maximise parallelizing and bus capacity. In this example the drives are A, B and C and the partitions are 987654321 where 9 is the partition with the highest speed requirement. Starting at one drive we 'meander' the partition line over and over the drives in this way:

```
A : 9 4 3
B : 8 5 2
C : 7 6 1
```

This makes the 'sum of speed requirements' the most equal across each drive.

Use the table in Appendix B (section 18 ( )) to select what drives to use for each partition in order to optimize for parallelicity.

Note the speed characteristics of your drives and note each directory under the appropriate column. Be prepared to shuffle directories, partitions and drives around a few times before you are satisfied.

8.3   Sorting partitions on drives

After that it is recommended to select partition numbering for each drive.

Use the table in Appendix C (section 19 ( )) to select partition numbers in order to optimize for track characteristics. At the end of this you should have a table sorted in ascending partition number. Fill these numbers back into the tables in appendix A and B.

You will find these tables useful when running the partitioning program (`fdisk` or `cfdisk`) and when doing the installation.

8.4   Optimizing

After this there are usually a few partitions that have to be 'shuffled' over the drives either to make them fit or if there are special considerations regarding speed, reliability, special file systems etc. Nevertheless this gives what this author believes is a good starting point for the complete setup of the drives and the partitions. In the end it is actual use that will determine the real needs after we have made so many assumptions. After commencing operations one should assume a time comes when a repartitioning will be beneficial.

For instance if one of the 3 drives in the above mentioned example is very slow compared to the two others a better plan would be as follows:

```
A : 9 6 5
B : 8 7 4
C : 3 2 1
```

8.4.1   Optimizing by characteristics

Often drives can be similar in apparent overall speed but some advantage can be gained by matching drives to the file size distribution and frequency of access. Thus binaries are suited to drives with fast access that offer command queueing, and libraries are better suited to drives with larger transfer speeds where IDE offers good performance for the money.

8.4.2   Optimizing by drive parallelising

Avoid drive contention by looking at tasks: for instance if you are accessing `/usr/local/bin` chances are you will soon also need files from `/usr/local/lib` so placing these at separate drives allows less seeking and possible parallel operation and drive caching. It is quite possible that choosing what may appear less than ideal drive characteristics will still be advantageous if you can gain parallel operations. Identify common tasks, what partitions they use and try to keep these on separate physical drives.

Just to illustrate my point I will give a few examples of task analysis here.

Office software
   such as editing, word processing and spreadsheets are typical examples of low intensity software both in terms of CPU and disk intensity. However, should you have a single server for a huge number of users you should not forget that most such software have auto save facilities which cause extra traffic, usually on the home directories. Splitting users over several drives would reduce contention.

News
   readers also feature auto save features on home directories so ISPs should consider separating home directories

   News spools are notorious for their deeply nested directories and their large number of very small files. Loss of a news spool partition is not a big problem for most people, too, so they are good candidates for a RAID 0 setup with many small disks to distribute the many seeks among multiple spindles. It is recommended in the manuals and FAQs for the INN news server to put news spool and `.overview` files on separate drives for larger installations.

   There is also a web page dedicated to *INN optimising* `<http://www.spinne.com/usenet/inn-perf.html>` well worth reading.

Database
   applications can be demanding both in terms of drive usage and speed requirements. The details are naturally application specific, read the documentation carefully with disk requirements in mind. Also consider RAID both for performance and reliability.

E-mail

reading and sending involves home directories as well as in- and outgoing spool files. If possible keep home directories and spool files on separate drives. If you are a mail server or a mail hub consider putting in- and outgoing spool directories on separate drives.

Losing mail is an extremely bad thing, if you are and ISP or major hub. Think about RAIDing your mail spool and consider frequent backups.

Software development

can require a large number of directories for binaries, libraries, include files as well as source and project files. If possible split as much as possible across separate drives. On small systems you can place /usr/src and project files on the same drive as the home directories.

Web browsing

is becoming more and more popular. Many browsers have a local cache which can expand to rather large volumes. As this is used when reloading pages or returning to the previous page, speed is quite important here. If however you are connected via a well configured proxy server you do not need more than typically a few megabytes per user for a session. See also the sections on 8.6.1 (Home Directories) and 8.6.3 (WWW).

8.5   Usage requirements

When you get a box of 10 or so CD-ROMs with a Linux distribution and the entire contents of the big FTP sites it can be tempting to install as much as your drives can take. Soon, however, one would find that this leaves little room to grow and that it is easy to bite over more than can be chewed, at least in polite company. Therefore I will make a few comments on a few points to keep in mind when you plan out your system. Comments here are actively sought.

Testing

Linux is simple and you don't even need a hard disk to try it out, if you can get the boot floppies to work you are likely to get it to work on your hardware. If the standard kernel does not work for you, do not forget that often there can be special boot disk versions available for unusual hardware combinations that can solve your initial problems until you can compile your own kernel.

Learning

about operating system is something Linux excels in, there is plenty of documentation and the source is available. A single drive with 50 MB is enough to get you started with a shell, a few of the most frequently used commands and utilities.

Hobby

use or more serious learning requires more commands and utilities but a single drive is still all it takes, 500 MB should give you plenty of room, also for sources and documentation.

Serious

software development or just serious hobby work requires even more space. At this stage you have probably a mail and news feed that requires spool files and plenty of space. Separate drives for various tasks will begin to show a benefit. At this stage you have probably already gotten hold of a few drives too. Drive requirements gets harder to estimate but I would expect 2-4 GB to be plenty, even for a small server.

Servers

come in many flavours, ranging from mail servers to full sized ISP servers. A base of 2 GB for the main system should be sufficient, then add space and perhaps also drives for separate features you will offer. Cost is the main limiting factor here but be prepared to spend a bit if you wish to justify the "S" in ISP. Admittedly, not all do it.

8.6   Servers

Big tasks require big drives and a separate section here. If possible keep as much as possible on separate drives. Some of the appendices detail the setup of a small departmental server for 10-100 users. Here I will present a few consideration for the higher end servers. In general you should not be afraid of using RAID, not only because it is fast and safe but also because it can make growth a little less painful. All the notes below come as additions to the points mentioned earlier.

Popular servers rarely just happens, rather they grow over time and this demands both generous amounts of disk space as well as a good net connection. In many of these cases it might be a good idea to reserve entire SCSI drives, in singles or as arrays, for each task. This way you can move the data should the computer fail. Note that transferring drives across computers is not simple and might not always work, especially in the case of IDE drives. Drive arrays require careful setup in order to reconstruct the data correctly, so you might want to keep a paper copy of your `fstab` file as well as a note of SCSI IDs.

8.6.1   Home directories

Estimate how many drives you will need, if this is more than 2 I would recommend RAID, strongly. If not you should separate users across your drives dedicated to users based on some kind of simple hashing algorithm. For instance you could use the first 2 letters in the user name, so `jbloggs` is put on `/u/j/b/jbloggs` where `/u/j` is a symbolic link to a physical drive so you can get a balanced load on your drives.

8.6.2   Anonymous FTP

This is an essential service if you are serious about service. Good servers are well maintained, documented, kept up to date, and immensely popular no matter where in the world they are located. The big server `ftp.funet.fi` is an excellent example of this.

In general this is not a question of CPU but of network bandwidth. Size is hard to estimate, mainly it is a question of ambition and service attitudes. I believe the big archive at ftp.cdrom.com is a *BSD machine with 50 GB disk. Also memory is important for a dedicated FTP server, about 256 MB RAM would be sufficient for a very big server, whereas smaller servers can get the job done well with 64 MB RAM. Network connections would still be the most important factor.

8.6.3   WWW

For many this is the main reason to get onto the Internet, in fact many now seem to equate the two. In addition to being network intensive there is also a fair bit of drive activity related to this, mainly regarding the caches. Keeping the cache on a separate, fast drive would be beneficial. Even better would be installing a caching proxy server. This way you can reduce the cache size for each user and speed up the service while at the same time cut down on the bandwidth requirements.

With a caching proxy server you need a fast set of drives, RAID0 would be ideal as reliability is not important here. Higher capacity is better but about 2 GB should be sufficient for most. Remember to match the cache period to the capacity and demand. Too long periods would on the other hand be a disadvantage, if possible try to adjust based on the URL. For more information check up on the most used servers such as `Harvest`, *Squid* `<http://www.nlanr.net/Squid>` and the one from Netscape.

8.6.4 Mail

Handling mail is something most machines do to some extent. The big mail servers, however, come into a class of their own. This is a demanding task and a big server can be slow even when connected to fast drives and a good net feed. In the Linux world the big server at `vger.rutgers.edu` is a well known example. Unlike a news service which is distributed and which can partially reconstruct the spool using other machines as a feed, the mail servers are centralised. This makes safety much more important, so for a major server you should consider a RAID solution with emphasize on reliability. Size is hard to estimate, it all depends on how many lists you run as well as how many subscribers you have.

8.6.5 News

This is definitely a high volume task, and very dependent on what news groups you subscribe to. On Nyx there is a fairly complete feed and the spool files consume about 17 GB. The biggest groups are no doubt in the `alt.binary.*` hierarchy, so if you for some reason decide not to get these you can get a good service with perhaps 12 GB. Still others, that shall remain nameless, feel 2 GB is sufficient to claim ISP status. In this case news expires so fast I feel the spelling IsP is barely justified. A full newsfeed means a traffic of a few GB every day and this is an ever growing number.

8.6.6 Others

There are many services available on the net and even though many have been put somewhat in the shadows by the web. Nevertheless, services like *archie*, *gopher* and *wais* just to name a few, still exist and remain valuable tools on the net. If you are serious about starting a major server you should also consider these services. Determining the required volumes is hard, it all depends on popularity and demand. Providing good service inevitably has its costs, disk space is just one of them.

8.7 Pitfalls

The dangers of splitting up everything into separate partitions are briefly mentioned in the section about volume management. Still, several people have asked me to emphasize this point more strongly: when one partition fills up it cannot grow any further, no matter if there is plenty of space in other partitions.

In particular look out for explosive growth in the news spool (`/var/spool/news`). For multi user machines with quotas keep an eye on `/tmp` and `/var/tmp` as some people try to hide their files there, just look out for filenames ending in gif or jpeg...

In fact, for single physical drives this scheme offers very little gains at all, other than making file growth monitoring easier (using 'df') and physical track positioning. Most importantly there is no scope for parallel disk access. A freely available volume management system would solve this but this is still some time in the future. However, when more specialised file systems become available even a single disk could benefit from being divided into several partitions.

8.8 Compromises

One way to avoid the aforementioned pitfalls is to only set off fixed partitions to directories with a fairly well known size such as swap, `/tmp` and `/var/tmp` and group together the remainders into the remaining partitions using symbolic links.

Example: a slow disk (`slowdisk`), a fast disk (`fastdisk`) and an assortment of files. Having set up swap and tmp on `fastdisk`; and `/home` and root on `slowdisk` we have (the fictitious) directories `/a/slow`, `/a/fast`,

/b/slow and /b/fast left to allocate on the partitions /mnt.slowdisk and /mnt.fastdisk which represents the remaining partitions of the two drives.

Putting /a or /b directly on either drive gives the same properties to the subdirectories. We could make all 4 directories separate partitions but would lose some flexibility in managing the size of each directory. A better solution is to make these 4 directories symbolic links to appropriate directories on the respective drives.

Thus we make

```
/a/fast point to /mnt.fastdisk/a/fast    or    /mnt.fastdisk/a.fast
/a/slow point to /mnt.slowdisk/a/slow    or    /mnt.slowdisk/a.slow
/b/fast point to /mnt.fastdisk/b/fast    or    /mnt.fastdisk/b.fast
/b/slow point to /mnt.slowdisk/b/slow    or    /mnt.slowdisk/b.slow
```

and we get all fast directories on the fast drive without having to set up a partition for all 4 directories. The second (right hand) alternative gives us a flatter files system which in this case can make it simpler to keep an overview of the structure.

The disadvantage is that it is a complicated scheme to set up and plan in the first place and that all mount point and partitions have to be defined before the system installation.

9   Implementation

Having done the layout you should now have a detailed description on what goes where. Most likely this will be on paper but hopefully someone will make a more automated system that can deal with everything from the design, through partitioning to formatting and installation. This is the route one will have to take to realise the design.

Modern distributions come with installation tools that will guide you through partitioning and formatting and also set up /etc/fstab for you automatically. For later modifications, however, you will need to understand the underlying mechanisms.

9.1   Drives and Partitions

When you start DOS or the like you will find all partitions labeled C: and onwards, with no differentiation on IDE, SCSI, network or whatever type of media you have. In the world of Linux this is rather different. During booting you will see partitions described like this:

```
Dec  6 23:45:18 demos kernel: Partition check:
Dec  6 23:45:18 demos kernel:  sda: sda1
Dec  6 23:45:18 demos kernel:  hda: hda1 hda2
```

SCSI drives are labelled sda, sdb, sdc etc, and (E)IDE drives are labelled hda, hdb, hdc etc. There are also standard names for all devices, full information can be found in /dev/MAKEDEV and /usr/src/linux/Documentation/devices.txt.

Partitions are labelled numerically for each drive hda1, hda2 and so on. On SCSI drives there can be 15 partitions per drive, on EIDE drives there can be 63 partitions per drive. Both limits exceed what is currently useful for most disks.

These are then mounted according to the file /etc/fstab before they appear as a part of the file system.

9.2 Partitioning

First you have to partition each drive into a number of separate partitions. Under Linux there are two main methods, `fdisk` and the more screen oriented `cfdisk`. These are complex programs, read the manual *very* carefully. Under DOS there are other choices, mainly the version of `fdisk` that is bundled with for instance DOS, or `fips`. The latter has the unique advantage here that it can repartition a drive without necessarily damaging existing data, unlike all the other partitioning programs.

In order to get the most out of `fips` you should first defragment your drive. This way you can allocate more space to other partitions.

Nevertheless, it is important you do a full backup of all your valued data before partitioning.

Partitions come in 3 flavours, `primary`, `extended` and `logical`. You have to use `primary` partitions for booting, but there is a maximum of 4 primary partitions. If you want more you have to define an `extended` partition within which you define your `logical` partitions.

Each partition has an identifier number which tells the operating system what it is, for Linux the types `swap` and `ext2fs` are the ones you will need to know.

There is a readme file that comes with `fdisk` that gives more in-depth information on partitioning.

Someone has just made a *Partitioning HOWTO* which contains excellent, in depth information on the nitty-gritty of partitioning. Rather than repeating it here and bloating this document further, I will instead refer you to it instead.

9.3 Multiple devices (`md`)

Being in a state of flux you should make sure to read the latest documentation on this kernel feature. It is not yet stable, beware.

Briefly explained it works by adding partitions together into new devices `md0`, `md1` etc. using `mdadd` before you activate them using `mdrun`. This process can be automated using the file `/etc/mdtab`.

Then you then treat these like any other partition on a drive. Proceed with formatting etc. as described below using these new devices.

There is now also a HOWTO in development for RAID using `md` you should read.

9.4 Formatting

Next comes partition formatting, putting down the data structures that will describe the files and where they are located. If this is the first time it is recommended you use formatting with verify. Strictly speaking it should not be necessary but this exercises the I/O hard enough that it can uncover potential problems, such as incorrect termination, before you store your precious data. Look up the command `mkfs` for more details.

Linux can support a great number of file systems, rather than repeating the details you can read the manpage for `fs` which describes them in some details. Note that your kernel has to have the drivers compiled in or made as modules in order to be able to use these features. When the time comes for kernel compiling you should read carefully through the file system feature list. If you use `make menuconfig` you can get online help for each file system type.

Note that some rescue disk systems require `minix`, `msdos` and `ext2fs` to be compiled into the kernel.

Also swap partitions have to be prepared, and for this you use `mkswap`.

9.5 Mounting

Data on a partition is not available to the file system until it is mounted on a mount point. This can be done manually using `mount` or automatically during booting by adding appropriate lines to `/etc/fstab`. Read the manual for `mount` and pay close attention to the tabulation.

10 Maintenance

It is the duty of the system manager to keep an eye on the drives and partitions. Should any of the partitions overflow, the system is likely to stop working properly, no matter how much space is available on other partitions, until space is reclaimed.

Partitions and disks are easily monitored using `df` and should be done frequently, perhaps using a cron job or some other general system management tool.

Do not forget the swap partitions, these are best monitored using one of the memory statistics programs such as `free`, `procinfo` or `top`.

Drive usage monitoring is more difficult but it is important for the sake of performance to avoid contention - placing too much demand on a single drive if others are available and idle.

It is important when installing software packages to have a clear idea where the various files go. As previously mentioned GCC keeps binaries in a library directory and there are also other programs that for historical reasons are hard to figure out, X11 for instance has an unusually complex structure.

When your system is about to fill up it is about time to check and prune old logging messages as well as hunt down core files. Proper use of `ulimit` in global shell settings can help saving you from having core files littered around the system.

10.1 Backup

The observant reader might have noticed a few hints about the usefulness of making backups. Horror stories are legio about accidents and what happened to the person responsible when the backup turned out to be non-functional or even non existent. You might find it simpler to invest in proper backups than a second, secret identity.

There are many options and also a mini-HOWTO (`Backup-With-MSDOS`) detailling what you need to know. In addition to the DOS specifics it also contains general information and further leads.

In addition to making these backups you should also make sure you can restore the data. Not all systems verify that the data written is correct and many administrators have started restoring the system after an accident happy in the belief that everything is working, only to discover to their horror that the backups were useless. Be careful.

10.2 Defragmentation

This is very dependent on the file system design, some suffer fast and nearly debilitating fragmentation. Fortunately for us, `ext2fs` does not belong to this group and therefore there has been very little talk about making a defragmentation tool.

If for some reason you feel this is necessary, the quick and easy solution is to do a backup and a restore. If only a small area is affected, for instance the home directories, you could `tar` it over to a temporary area on another partition, *verify* the archive, delete the original and then untar it back again.

10.3 Deletions

Quite often disk space shortages can be remedied simply by deleting unnecessary files that accumulate around the system. Quite often programs that terminate abnormally cause all kinds of mess lying around the oddest places. Normally a core dump results after such an incident and unless you are going to debug it you can simply delete it. These can be found everywhere so you are advised to do a global search for them now and then.

Unexpected termination can also cause all sorts of temporary files remaining in places like /tmp or /var/tmp, files that are automatically removed when the program ends normally. Rebooting cleans up some of these areas but not necessary all and if you have a long uptime you could end up with a lot of old junk. If space is short you have to delete with care, make sure the file is not in active use first. Utilities like `file` can often tell you what kind of file you are looking at.

Many things are logged when the system is running, mostly to files in the /var/log area. In particular the file /var/log/messages tends to grow until deleted. It is a good idea to keep a small archive of old log files around for comparison should the system start to behave oddly.

If the mail or news system is not working properly you could have excessive growth in their spool areas, /var/spool/mail and /var/spool/news respectively. Beware of the overview files as these have a leading dot which makes them invisible to `ls -l`, it is always better to use `ls -Al` which will reveal them.

User space overflow is a particularly tricky topic. Wars have been waged between system administrators and users. Tact, diplomacy and a generous budget for new drives is what is needed. Make use of the message-of-the-day feature, information displayed during login from the /etc/motd file to tell users when space is short. Setting the default shell settings to prevent core files being dumped can save you a lot of work too.

Certain kinds of people try to hide files around the system, usually trying to take advantage of the fact that files with a leading dot in the name are invisible to the `ls` command. One common example are files that look like ... that normally either are not seen, or, when using `ls -al` disappear in the noise of normal files like . or .. that are in every directory. There is however a countermeasure to this, use `ls -Al` that suppresses . or .. but shows all other dot-files.

10.4 Upgrades

No matter how large your drives, time will come when you will find you need more. As technology progresses you can get ever more for your money. At the time of writing this, it appears that 6.4 GB drives gives you the most bang for your bucks.

Note that with IDE drives you might have to remove an old drive, as the maximum number supported on your mother board is normally only 2 or some times 4. With SCSI you can have up to 7 for narrow (8-bit) SCSI or up to 15 for wide (15 bit) SCSI, per channel. Some host adapters can support more than a single channel and in any case you can have more than one host adapter per system. My personal recommendation is that you will most likely be better off with SCSI in the long run.

The question comes, where should you put this new drive? In many cases the reason for expansion is that you want a larger spool area, and in that case the fast, simple solution is to mount the drive somewhere under /var/spool. On the other hand newer drives are likely to be faster than older ones so in the long run you might find it worth your time to do a full reorganizing, possibly using your old design sheets.

If the upgrade is forced by running out of space in partitions used for things like /usr or /var the upgrade is a little more involved. You might consider the option of a full re-installation from your favourite (and hopefully upgraded) distribution. In this case you will have to be careful not to overwrite your essential setups. Usually these things are in the /etc directory. Proceed with care, fresh backups and working rescue disks. The other possibility is to simply copy the old directory over to the new directory which is mounted on a temporary mount point, edit your /etc/fstab file, reboot with your new partition in place and check that it works. Should it fail you can reboot with your rescue disk, re-edit **/etc/fstab** and try again.

Until volume management becomes available to Linux this is both complicated and dangerous. Do not get too surprised if you discover you need to restore your system from a backup.

The Tips-HOWTO gives the following example on how to move an entire directory structure across:

```
(cd /source/directory; tar cf - . ) | (cd /dest/directory; tar xvfp -)
```

While this approach to moving directory trees is portable among many Unix systems, it is inconvenient to remember. Also, it fails for deeply nested directory trees when pathnames become to long to handle for tar (GNU tar has special provisions to deal with long pathnames).

If you have access to GNU cp (which is always the case on Linux systems), you could as well use

```
cp -av /source/directory /dest/directory
```

GNU cp knows specifically about symbolic links, FIFOs and device files and will copy them correctly.

11 Advanced Issues

Linux and related systems offer plenty of possibilities for fast, efficient and devastating destruction. This document is no exception. With power comes dangers and the following sections describe a few more esoteric issues that should not be attempted before reading and understanding the documentation, the issues and the dangers. You should also make a backup. Also remember to try to restore the system from scratch from your backup at least once. Otherwise you might not be the first to be found with a perfect backup of your system and no tools available to reinstall it (or, even more embarrassing, some critical files missing on tape).

The techniques described here are rarely necessary but can be used for very specific setups. Think very clearly through what you wish to accomplish before playing around with this.

11.1 Hard Disk Tuning

The hard drive parameters can be tuned using the **hdparms** utility. Here the most interesting parameter is probably the read-ahead parameter which determines how much prefetch should be done in sequential reading.

If you want to try this out it makes most sense to tune for the characteristic file size on your drive but remember that this tuning is for the *entire* drive which makes it a bit more difficult. Probably this is only of use on large servers using dedicated news drives etc.

For safety the default hdparm settings are rather conservative. The disadvantage is that this mean you can get lost interrupts if you have a high frequency of IRQs as you would when using the serial port and an IDE disk as IRQs from the latter would mask other IRQs. THis would be noticable as less then ideal performance when downloading data from the net to disk. Setting **hdparm -u1 device** would prevent this masking and either improve your performance or, depending on hardware, corrupt the data on your disk. Experiment with caution and fresh backups.

11.2 File System Tuning

Most file systems come with a tuning utility and for `ext2fs` there is the `tune2fs` utility. Several parameters can be modified but perhaps the most useful parameter here is what size should be reserved and who should be able to take advantage of this which could help you getting more useful space out of your drives, possibly at the cost of less room for repairing a system should it crash.

11.3 Spindle Synchronizing

This should not in itself be dangerous, other than the peculiar fact that the exact details of the connections remain unclear for many drives. The theory is simple: keeping a fixed phase difference between the different drives in a RAID setup makes for less waiting for the right track to come into position for the read/write head. In practice it now seems that with large read-ahead buffers in the drives the effect is negligible.

Spindle synchronisation should not be used on RAID0 or RAID 0/1 as you would then lose the benefit of having the read heads over different areas of the mirrored sectors.

12 Further Information

There is wealth of information one should go through when setting up a major system, for instance for a news or general Internet service provider. The FAQs in the following groups are useful:

12.1 News groups

Some of the most interesting news groups are:

- *Storage* <news:comp.arch.storage>.
- *PC storage* <news:comp.sys.ibm.pc.hardware.storage>.
- *AFS* <news:alt.filesystems.afs>.
- *SCSI* <news:comp.periphs.scsi>.
- *Linux setup* <news:comp.os.linux.setup>.

Most newsgroups have their own FAQ that are designed to answer most of your questions, as the name Frequently Asked Questions indicate. Fresh versions should be posted regularly to the relevant newsgroups. If you cannot find it in your news spool you could go directly to the *FAQ main archive FTP site* <ftp://rtfm.mit.edu>. The WWW versions can be browsed at *FAQ main archive WWW site* <http://www.cis.ohio-state.edu/hypertext/faq/usenet/FAQ-List.html>.

Some FAQs have their own home site, of particular interest here are

- *SCSI FAQ* <http://www.paranoia.com/filipg/HTML/LINK/F_SCSI.html> and
- *comp.arch.storage FAQ* <http://alumni.caltech.edu/rdv/comp_arch_storage/FAQ-1.html>.

12.2 Mailing lists

These are low noise channels mainly for developers. Think twice before asking questions there as noise delays the development. Some relevant lists are `linux-raid`, `linux-scsi` and `linux-ext2fs`. Many of the most useful mailing lists run on the `vger.rutgers.edu` server but this is notoriously overloaded, so try to find a mirror. There are some lists mirrored at *The Redhat Home Page* `<http://www.redhat.com>`. Many lists are also accessible at *linuxhq* `<http://www.linuxhq.com/lnxlists>`, and the rest of the web site is a gold mine of useful information.

If you want to find out more about the lists available you can send a message with the line `lists` to the *list server at vger.rutgers.edu* `<mailto:majordomo@vger.rutgers.edu>`. If you need help on how to use the mail server just send the line `help` to the same address. Due to the popularity of this server it is likely it takes a bit to time before you get a reply or even get messages after you send a `subscribe` command.

There is also a number of other majordomo list servers that can be of interest such as the *EATA driver list* `<mailto:linux-eata@mail.uni-mainz.de>` and the *Intelligent IO list* `<mailto:linux-i2o@dpt.com>`.

Mailing lists are in a state of flux but you can find links to a number of interesting lists from the *Linux Documentation Homepage* `<http://sunsite.unc.edu/LDP>`.

12.3   HOWTO

These are intended as the primary starting points to get the background information as well as show you how to solve a specific problem. Some relevant HOWTOs are `Bootdisk`, `Installation`, `SCSI` and `UMSDOS`. The main site for these is the *LDP archive* `<http://sunsite.unc.edu/LDP>` at Sunsite.

There is a a new HOWTO out that deals with setting up a DPT RAID system, check out the *DPT RAID HOWTO homepage* `<http://www.ram.org/computing/linux/dpt_raid.html>`.

12.4   Mini-HOWTO

These are the smaller free text relatives to the HOWTOs.   Some relevant mini-HOWTOs are `Backup-With-MSDOS`, `Diskless`, `LILO`, `Linux+DOS+Win95+OS2`, `Linux+OS2+DOS`, `Linux+Win95`, `NFS-Root`, `Win95+Win+Linux`, `ZIP Drive` . You can find these at the same place as the HOWTOs, usually in a sub directory called `mini`. Note that these are scheduled to be converted into SGML and become proper HOWTOs in the near future.

The   old   `Linux Large IDE mini-HOWTO`   is   no   longer   valid,   instead   read `/usr/src/linux/drivers/block/README.ide` or `/usr/src/linux/Documentation/ide.txt`.

12.5   Local resources

In most distributions of Linux there is already a document directory already, have a look in the *document archive* `<file:///usr/doc>` where most packages store their main documentation and README files etc. Also you will here find the *HOWTO archive* `<file:///usr/doc/HOWTO>` of ready formatted HOWTOs and also the *mini-HOWTO archive* `<file:///usr/doc/HOWTO/mini>` of plain text documents.

Many of the configuration files mentioned earlier can be found in the *etc* `<file:///etc>` directory.   In particular you will want to work with the *fstab* `<file:///etc/fstab>` file that sets up the mounting of partitions and possibly also *mdtab* `<file:///etc/mdtab>` file that is used for the `md` system to set up RAID.

The *kernel source* `<file:///usr/src/linux>` is, of course, the ultimate documentation.   In other words, *use the source, Luke*.   It should also be pointed out that the kernel comes not only with source code which is even commented (well, partially at least) but also an informative *documentation directory* `<file:///usr/src/linux/Documentation>`. If you are about to ask any questions about the kernel you should read this first, it will save you and many others a lot of time and possibly embarrassment.

Also have a look in your *system log file* `<file:///var/log/messages>` to see what is going on and in particular how the booting went if too much scrolled off your screen. Using `tail -f /var/log/messages` in a separate window or screen will give you a continuous update of what is going on in your system.

You can also take advantage of the */proc* `<file:///proc>` file system that is a window into the inner workings of your system. Use `cat` rather than `more` to view the files as they are reported as being zero length.

Much of the work here is based on the Filesystem Structure Standard (FSSTND). It has changed name to File Hierarchy Standard (FHS) and is less Linux specific. The maintainer has set up a *home page* `<http://www.pathname.com/fhs>` which tells you how to join the currently private mailing list, where the development takes place.

12.6 Web pages

There is a huge number of informative web pages out there and by their very nature they change quickly so don't be too surprised if these links become quickly outdated.

A good starting point is of course the Sunsite *LDP archive* `<http://sunsite.unc.edu/LDP/>` that is a information central for documentation, project pages and much, much more.

- Mike Neuffer, the author of the DPT caching RAID controller drivers, has some interesting pages on *SCSI* `<http://www.uni-mainz.de/neuffer/scsi>` and *DPT* `<http://www.uni-mainz.de/neuffer/scsi/dpt>`.

- Software RAID 1 development information can be found at *RAID 1 development page* `<http://www.nuclecu.unam.mx/miguel/raid>`.

- Disk related information on benchmarking, RAID, reliability and much, much more can be found at *Linas Vepstas* `<http://linas.org>` project page.

- There is also information available on how to *RAID the root partition* `<ftp://ftp.bizsystems.com/pub/raid/Root-RAID-HOWTO.html>` and what software packages are needed to achieve this.

- In depth documentation on *ext2fs* `<http://step.polymtl.ca/ldd/ext2fs/ext2fs_toc.html>` is also available.

- Mark D. Roth has information on *VPS* `<http://www.uiuc.edu/ph/www/roth>`

- A similar kind of project on an *Enhanced File System* `<http://www.virtual.net.au/rjh/enh-fs.html>`

- People who are awaiting support for VFAT32 and Joliet could have a look at the *development page* `<http://bmrc.berkeley.edu/people/chaffee/index.html>` for a preview. These drivers are now entering the 2.1.x kernel development series.

- There is an ongoing compression project that integrates in `ext2fs` and is called e2compr. For more information check out the *e2compr homepage* `<http://netspace.net.au/~reiter/e2compr.html>`.

- For more information on booting and also some BSD information have a look at *booting information* `<http://www.paranoia.com/~vax/boot.html>` page.

For diagrams and information on all sorts of disk drives, controllers etc. both for current and discontinued lines *The Ref* `<http://theref.c3d.rl.af.mil>` is the site you need. There is a lot of useful information here, a real treasure trove. You can also download the database using *FTP* `<ftp://theref.c3d.rl.af.mil/public>`.

Please let me know if you have any other leads that can be of interest.

12.7 Search engines

Remember you can also use the web search engines and that some, like

- *Altavista* <http://www.altavista.digital.com>
- *Excite* <http://www.excite.com>
- *Hotbot* <http://www.hotbot.com>

can also search usenet news.

Also remember that *Dejanews* <http://www.dejanews.com> is a dedicated news searcher that keeps a news spool from early 1995 and onwards.

If you have to ask for help you are most likely to get help in the `comp.os.linux.setup` news group. Due to large workload and a slow network connection I am not able to follow that newsgroup so if you want to contact me you have to do so by e-mail.

13 Getting Help

In the end you might find yourself unable to solve your problems and need help from someone else. The most efficient way is either to ask someone local or in your nearest Linux user group, search the web for the nearest one.

Another possibility is to ask on Usenet News in one of the many, many newsgroups available. The problem is that these have such a high volume and noise (called low signal-to-noise ratio) that your question can easily fall through unanswered.

No matter where you ask it is important to ask well or you will not be taken seriously. Saying just *my disk does not work* is not going to help you and instead the noise level is increased even further and if you are lucky someone will ask you to clarify.

Instead you are recommended to describe your problems in some detail that will enable people to help you. The problem could lie somewhere you did not expect. Therefore you are advised to list up the following information on your system:

Hardware

- Processor
- Chip set (Triton, Saturn etc)
- Bus (ISA, VESA, PCI etc)
- Expansion cards used (Disk controllers, video, io etc)

Software

- BIOS (On motherboard and possibly SCSI host adapters)
- LILO, if used
- Linux kernel version as well as possible modifications and patches
- Kernel parameters, if any
- Software that shows the error (with version number or date)

Peripherals

- Type of disk drives with manufacturer name, version and type
- Other relevant peripherals connected to the same busses

As an example of how interrelated these problems are: an old chip set caused problems with a certain combination of video controller and SCSI host adapter.

Remember that booting text is logged to /var/log/messages which can answer most of the questions above. Obviously if the drives fail you might not be able to get the log saved to disk but you can at least scroll back up the screen using the SHIFT and PAGE UP keys. It may also be useful to include part of this in you request for help but do not go overboard, keep it *brief* as a complete log file dumped to Usenet News is more than a little annoying.

14 Concluding Remarks

Disk tuning and partition decisions are difficult to make, and there are no hard rules here. Nevertheless it is a good idea to work more on this as the payoffs can be considerable. Maximizing usage on one drive only while the others are idle is unlikely to be optimal, watch the drive light, they are not there just for decoration. For a properly set up system the lights should look like Christmas in a disco. Linux offers software RAID but also support for some hardware base SCSI RAID controllers. Check what is available. As your system and experiences evolve you are likely to repartition and you might look on this document again. Additions are always welcome.

14.1 Coming Soon

There are a few more important things that are about to appear here. In particular I will add more example tables as I am about to set up two fairly large and general systems, one at work and one at home. These should give some general feeling on how a system can be set up for either of these two purposes. Examples of smooth running existing systems are also welcome.

There is also a fair bit of work left to do on the various kinds of file systems and utilities.

There will be a big addition on drive technologies coming soon as well as a more in depth description on using fdisk or cfdisk. The file systems will be beefed up as more features become available as well as more on RAID and what directories can benefit from what RAID level.

Recently I received an information pack from DPT, who made the first hardware RAID supported by Linux. Their leaflets now carry the familiar penguin logo to show they support Linux. More in-depth information will come soon.

There is some minor overlapping with the Linux Filesystem Structure Standard that I hope to integrate better soon, which will probably mean a big reworking of all the tables at the end of this document. When the new version is released there will be a substantial rewrite of some of the sections in this HOWTO but no release date has been announced yet.

When the new standard appear various details such as directory names, sizes and file placements will be changed.

I have made the assumption that the first partition starts at track 0 and that this track is the innermost track. That, however, is looking more and more like an unwarranted assumption, and not only because of the logical re-mapping that takes place. More on this when information becomes available.

As more people start reading this I should get some more comments and feedback. I am also thinking of making a program that can automate a fair bit of this decision making process and although it is unlikely to be optimum it should provide a simpler, more complete starting point.

14.2   Request for Information

It has taken a fair bit of time to write this document and although most pieces are beginning to come together there are still some information needed before we are out of the beta stage.

- More information on swap sizing policies is needed as well as information on the largest swap size possible under the various kernel versions.
- How common is drive or file system corruption? So far I have only heard of problems caused by flaky hardware.
- References to speed and drives is needed.
- Are any other Linux compatible RAID controllers available?
- Leads to file system, volume management and other related software is welcome.
- What relevant monitoring, management and maintenance tools are available?
- General references to information sources are needed, perhaps this should be a separate document?
- Usage of /tmp and /var/tmp has been hard to determine, in fact what programs use which directory is not well defined and more information here is required. Still, it seems at least clear that these should reside on different physical drives in order to increase parallelicity.

14.3   Suggested Project Work

Now and then people post on comp.os.linux.*, looking for good project ideas. Here I will list a few that comes to mind that are relevant to this document. Plans about big projects such as new file systems should still be posted in order to either find co-workers or see if someone is already working on it.

Planning tools
   that can automate the design process outlines earlier would probably make a medium sized project, perhaps as an exercise in constraint based programming.

Partitioning tools
   that take the output of the previously mentioned program and format drives in parallel and apply the appropriate symbolic links to the directory structure. It would probably be best if this were integrated in existing system installation software. The drive partitioning setup used in Solaris is an example of what it can look like.

Surveillance tools
   that keep an eye on the partition sizes and warn before a partition overflows.

Migration tools
   that safely lets you move old structures to new (for instance RAID) systems. This could probably be done as a shell script controlling a back up program and would be rather simple. Still, be sure it is safe and that the changes can be undone.

15   Questions and Answers

This is just a collection of what I believe are the most common questions people might have. Give me more feedback and I will turn this section into a proper FAQ.

- Q:How many physical disk drives (spindles) does a Linux system need? A: Linux can run just fine on one drive (spindle). Having enough RAM (around 32 MB, and up to 64 MB) to support swapping is a better price/performance choice than getting a second disk. (E)IDE disk is usually cheaper (but a little slower) than SCSI.

- Q: I have a single drive, will this HOWTO help me? A: Yes, although only to a minor degree. Still, the section on 4.3.8 (Physical Track Positioning) will offer you some gains.

- Q: Are there any disadvantages in this scheme? A: There is only a minor snag: if even a single partition overflows the system might stop working properly. The severity depends of course on what partition is affected. Still this is not hard to monitor, the command df gives you a good overview of the situation. Also check the swap partition(s) using free to make sure you are not about to run out of virtual memory.

- Q: OK, so should I split the system into as many partitions as possible for a single drive? A: No, there are several disadvantages to that. First of all maintenance becomes needlessly complex and you gain very little in this. In fact if your partitions are too big you will seek across larger areas than needed. This is a balance and dependent on the number of physical drives you have.

- Q: Does that mean more drives allows more partitions? A: To some degree, yes. Still, some directories should not be split off from root, check out the file system standard (soon released under the name File Hierarchy Standard) for more details.

- Q: What if I have many drives I want to use? A: If you have more than 3-4 drives you should consider using RAID of some form. Still, it is a good idea to keep your root partition on a simple partition without RAID, see the section on 4.3.1 (RAID) for more details.

- Q: I have installed the latest Windows95 but cannot access this partition from within the Linux system, what is wrong? A: Most likely you are using FAT32 in your windows partition. It seems that Microsoft decided we needed yet another format, and this was introduced in their latest version of Windows95, called OSR2. The advantage is that this format is better suited to large drives. Unfortunately there is no stable driver for Linux out *yet* . A test version is out but not yet in the standard kernel.

  You might also be interested to hear that Microsoft NT 4.0 does not support it yet either.

  Until a stable version is available you can avoid this problem by installing Windows95 over an existing FAT16 partition, made for instance by an older installation of DOS. This forces the Windows95 to use FAT16 which *is* supported by Linux.

- Q: I cannot get the disk size and partition sizes to match, something is missing. What has happened? A:It is possible you have mounted a partition onto a mount point that was not an empty directory. Mount points are directories and if it is not empty the mounting will mask the contents. If you do the sums you will see the amount of disk space used in this directory is missing from the observed total.

  To solve this you can boot from a rescue disk and see what is hiding behind your mount points and remove or transfer the contents by mounting th offending partition on a temporary mounting point. You might find it useful to have "spare" emergency mounting points ready made.

- Q: What is this nyx that is mentioned several times here? A: It is a large free Unix system with currently about 10000 users. I use it for my web pages for this HOWTO as well as a source of ideas for a setup of large Unix systems. It has been running for many years and has a quite stable setup. For more information you can view the *Nyx homepage* <http://www.nyx.net> which also gives you information on how to get your own free account.

16 Bits and Pieces

This is basically a section where I stuff all the bits I have not yet decided where should go, yet that I feel is worth knowing about. It is a kind of transient area.

16.1 Combining swap and /tmp

Recently there have been discussions in the various linux related news groups about specialized file systems for temporary storage. This is partly inspired by the tmpfs on *BSD* and Solaris, as well as swapfs on the NeXT machines.

The rationale is that these are temporary storage that normally does not require much space, yet in normal systems you need to reserve a certain amount of space for these. Elementary statistical knowledge tells you (very simplified) that when you sum a number of variables the relative statistical uncertainty decreases. So combining swap and /tmp you do not need to reserve as much space as you otherwise would need.

This specialized file system is nothing more than a swappable RAM disk that are swapped out to disk when and only when space is limited, thus effectively putting temporary files on the swap partition.

There is, however, a snag. This scheme prevents you from getting parallel activity on swap and /tmp drives so under heavy activity the system takes a bigger performance hit. Put another way, you trade speed to get space. Interleaving across multiple drives reduces this somewhat.

16.2   Interleaved swap drives.

This is not striping across several drives, instead drives are accessed in a round robin fashion in order to spread the load in a crude fashion. In Linux you additionally have a priority parameter you can adjust for tuning your system, especially useful if your disks differs significantly in speed. Check man 8 swapon as well as man 2 swapon for more information.

16.3   Swap partition: to use or not to use

In many cases you do not need a swap partition, for instance if you have plenty of RAM, say, more than 64 MB, and you are the sole user of the machine. In this case you can experiment running without a swap partition and check the system logs to see if you ran out of virtual memory at any point.

Removing swap partitions have two advantages:

- you save disk space (rather obvious really)
- you save seek time as swap partitions otherwise would lie in the middle of your disk space.

In the end, having a swap partition is like having a heated toilet: you do not use it very often, but you sure appreciate it when you require it.

16.4   Mount point and /mnt

In an earlier version of this document I proposed to put all permanently mounted partitions under /mnt. That, however, is not such a good idea as this itself can be used as a mount point, which leads to all mounted partitions becoming unavailable. Instead I will propose mounting straight from root using a meaningful name like /mnt.descriptive-name.

Lately I have become aware that some Linux distributions use mount points at subdirectories *under* /mnt, such as /mnt/floppy and /mnt/cdrom, which just shows how confused the whole issue is. Hopefully FHS should clarify this.

16.5   SCSI id numbers and names

Partitions are labeled in the order they are found, *not* depending on the SCSI id number. This means that if you add a drive with an id number inserted in the previous order of numbers, or change id number in any other way, the partition names will be messed up. This is important if you use removable media. In order to save yourself from some unpleasant experiences, you are recommended to use low numbers for fixed media and reserve the last number(s) for removable media drives.

Many have been bitten by this misfeature and there is a strong call for something to be done about it. Nobody knows how soon this will be fixed so in the meantime it is wise to take this into consideration when you design your system. For instance it may be a good idea to use the lowest SCSI id number for you root disk so that it has the least probability of being renumbered should one drive fail.

16.6 Power and Heating

Not many years ago a machine with the equivalent power of a modern PC required 3-phase power and cooling, usually by air conditioning the machine room but some times also by water cooling. Technology has progressed very quickly giving not only high speed but also low power components. Still, there is a definite limit to the technology, something one should keep in mind as the system is expanded with yet another disk drive or PCI card. When the power supply is running at full rated power, keep in mind that all this energy is going somewhere, mostly into heat. Unless this is dissipated using fans you will get a serious heating inside the cabinet followed by a reduced reliability and also life time of the electronics. Manufacturers state minimum cooling requirements for their drives, usually in terms of cubic feet per minute (CFM). You are well advised to take this serious.

Keep air flow passages open, clean out dust and check the temperature of your system running. If it is too hot to touch it is probably running too hot.

If possible use sequential spin up for the drives. It is during spin up, when the drive platters accelerate up to normal speed, that a drive consumes maximum power and if all drives start up simultaneously you could go beyond the rated power maximum of your power supply.

16.7 Dejanews

This is an Internet system that no doubt most of you are familiar with. It searches and serves *Usenet News* articles from 1995 and to the latest postings and also offers a web based reading and posting interface. There is a lot more, check out *Dejanews* <http://www.dejanews.com> for more information.

What perhaps is less known, is that they use about 20 Linux SMP computers each of which uses the md module to manage between 4 and 24 Gig of disk space (over 150 Gig altogether) for this service. The system is continuously growing but at the time of writing they use mostly dual Pentium Pro 200MHz systems with 256 MB RAM.

A production machine normally has 1 disk for the operating system and between 4 and 6 disks managed by the md module where the articles are archived. The drives are connected to BusLogic Model BT-946C PCI SCSI adapters, usually two to a machine.

Just in case: this is not an advertisement, it is stated as an example of how much is required for what is a major Internet service.

16.8 File system structure

There are many file system structures in existence, differing with FSSTND (and soon FHS) to varying degree both in terms of philosophy, strategy and implementation. It is not possible to detail all here, instead the interested reader should read the relevant manual page, man hier which is available on many platforms and implementations.

16.9   Track numbering and optimizing schemes

In the old days the file system used to take advantage of knowing the physical drive parameters in order
to optimize transfers, for instance by endeavouring to keep a file within a single track if possible which
saves track-to-track seek time. These days with logical drive parameters, drive cache and schemes to map
out bad sectors, such optimizations become meaningless and might even cost more than it would gain. As
most Linux installations use modern file systems these schemes are not used, however, some other operating
systems have retained such schemes.

17   Appendix A: Partitioning layout table: mounting and linking

The following table is designed to make layout a simpler paper and pencil exercise. It is probably best to
print it out (using NON PROPORTIONAL fonts) and adjust the numbers until you are happy with them.

Mount point is what directory you wish to mount a partition on or the actual device. This is also a good
place to note how you plan to use symbolic links.

The size given corresponds to a fairly big Debian 1.2.6 installation. Other examples are coming later.

Mainly you use this table to select what structure and drives you will use, the partition numbers and letters
will come from the next two tables.

Directory	Mount point	speed	seek	transfer	size	SIZE
swap	----------	ooooo	ooooo	ooooo	32	----
/	----------	o	o	o	20	----
/tmp	----------	oooo	oooo	oooo		----
/var	----------	oo	oo	oo	25	----
/var/tmp	----------	oooo	oooo	oooo		----
/var/spool	----------					----
/var/spool/mail	----------	o	o	o		----
/var/spool/news	----------	ooo	ooo	oo		----
/var/spool/____	----------	----	----	----		----
/home	----------	oo	oo	oo		----
/usr	----------				500	----
/usr/bin	----------	o	oo	o	250	----
/usr/lib	----------	oo	oo	ooo	200	----
/usr/local	----------					----
/usr/local/bin	----------	o	oo	o		----
/usr/local/lib	----------	oo	oo	ooo		----
/usr/local/____	----------					----

```
/usr/src      _____    o      oo      o         50       ____

DOS           _____    o      o       o                  ____
Win           _____    oo     oo      oo                 ____
NT            _____    ooo    ooo     ooo                ____

/mnt._____  _____   ____   ____   ____              ____
/mnt._____  _____   ____   ____   ____              ____
/mnt._____  _____   ____   ____   ____              ____
/_____    _____   ____   ____   ____              ____
/_____    _____   ____   ____   ____              ____
/_____    _____   ____   ____   ____              ____
```

Total capacity:

18 Appendix B: Partitioning layout table: numbering and sizing

This table follows the same logical structure as the table above where you decided what disk to use. Here you select the physical tracking, keeping in mind the effect of track positioning mentioned earlier in 4.3.8 (Physical Track Positioning).

The final partition number will come out of the table after this.

```
    Drive       sda    sdb    sdc    hda    hdb    hdc    ___

SCSI ID        | __  | __  | __  |

Directory
swap           |     |     |     |     |     |     |

/              |     |     |     |     |     |     |

/tmp           |     |     |     |     |     |     |

/var           :     :     :     :     :     :     :
/var/tmp       |     |     |     |     |     |     |
/var/spool     :     :     :     :     :     :     :
/var/spool/mail|     |     |     |     |     |     |
/var/spool/news:     :     :     :     :     :     :
/var/spool/____|     |     |     |     |     |     |

/home          |     |     |     |     |     |     |
```

```
/usr          |      |      |      |      |      |      |
/usr/bin      :      :      :      :      :      :      :
/usr/lib      |      |      |      |      |      |      |
/usr/local    :      :      :      :      :      :      :
/usr/local/bin |     |      |      |      |      |      |
/usr/local/lib :     :      :      :      :      :      :
/usr/local/____ |    |      |      |      |      |      |
/usr/src      :      :      :      :

DOS           |      |      |      |      |      |      |
Win           :      :      :      :      :      :      :
NT            |      |      |      |      |      |      |

/mnt.___/_____  |    |      |      |      |      |      |
/mnt.___/_____  :    :      :      :      :      :      :
/mnt.___/_____  |    |      |      |      |      |      |
/_____  :     :      :      :      :      :      :
/_____  |     |      |      |      |      |      |
/_____  :     :      :      :      :      :      :


    Total capacity:
```

19   Appendix C: Partitioning layout table: partition placement

This is just to sort the partition numbers in ascending order ready to input to fdisk or cfdisk. Here you take physical track positioning into account when finalizing your design. Unless you get specific information otherwise, you can assume track 0 is the outermost track.

These numbers and letters are then used to update the previous tables, all of which you will find very useful in later maintenance.

In case of disk crash you might find it handy to know what SCSI id belongs to which drive, consider keeping a paper copy of this.

```
           Drive :   sda     sdb     sdc     hda     hdb     hdc     ___

Total capacity: |   ___  |   ___  |   ___  |   ___  |   ___  |   ___  |   ___
SCSI ID         |   __   |   __   |   __   |

Partition

1                   |       |       |       |       |       |       |
2                   :       :       :       :       :       :       :
```

```
3     |     |     |     |     |     |     |
4     :     :     :     :     :     :     :
5     |     |     |     |     |     |     |
6     :     :     :     :     :     :     :
7     |     |     |     |     |     |     |
8     :     :     :     :     :     :     :
9     |     |     |     |     |     |     |
10    :     :     :     :     :     :     :
11    |     |     |     |     |     |     |
12    :     :     :     :     :     :     :
13    |     |     |     |     |     |     |
14    :     :     :     :     :     :     :
15    |     |     |     |     |     |     |
16    :     :     :     :     :     :     :
```

20   Appendix D: Example: Multipurpose server

The following table is from the setup of a medium sized multipurpose server where I work. Aside from being a general Linux machine it will also be a network related server (DNS, mail, FTP, news, printers etc.) X server for various CAD programs, CD ROM burner and many other things. The files reside on 3 SCSI drives with a capacity of 600, 1000 and 1300 MB.

Some further speed could possibly be gained by splitting /usr/local from the rest of the /usr system but we deemed the further added complexity would not be worth it. With another couple of drives this could be more worthwhile. In this setup drive sda is old and slow and could just a well be replaced by an IDE drive. The other two drives are both rather fast. Basically we split most of the load between these two. To reduce dangers of imbalance in partition sizing we have decided to keep /usr/bin and /usr/local/bin in one drive and /usr/lib and /usr/local/lib on another separate drive which also affords us some drive parallelizing.

Even more could be gained by using RAID but we felt that as a server we needed more reliability than was then afforded by the md patch and a dedicated RAID controller was out of our reach.

21   Appendix E: Example: mounting and linking

Directory	Mount point	speed	seek	transfer	size	SIZE
swap	sdb2, sdc2	ooooo	ooooo	ooooo	32	2x64
/	sda2	o	o	o	20	100
/tmp	sdb3	oooo	oooo	oooo		300
/var	----------	oo	oo	oo		----
/var/tmp	sdc3	oooo	oooo	oooo		300
/var/spool	sdb1					436

Directory	Device					
/var/spool/mail	_____	o	o	o		____
/var/spool/news	_____	ooo	ooo	oo		____
/var/spool/____	_____	____	____	____		____
/home	sda3	oo	oo	oo		400
/usr	sdb4				230	200
/usr/bin	_____	o	oo	o	30	____
/usr/lib	-> libdisk	oo	oo	ooo	70	____
/usr/local	_____					____
/usr/local/bin	_____	o	oo	o		____
/usr/local/lib	-> libdisk	oo	oo	ooo		____
/usr/local/____	_____					____
/usr/src	->/home/usr.src	o	oo	o	10	____
DOS	sda1	o	o	o		100
Win	_____	oo	oo	oo		____
NT	_____	ooo	ooo	ooo		____
/mnt.libdisk	sdc4	oo	oo	ooo		226
/mnt.cd	sdc1	o	o	oo		710

Total capacity: 2900 MB

22   Appendix F: Example: numbering and sizing

Here we do the adjustment of sizes and positioning.

Directory	sda	sdb	sdc
swap	|	| 64 |	64 |
/	| 100 |	|	|
/tmp	|	| 300 |	|
/var	:	:	:	:
/var/tmp	|	|	| 300 |
/var/spool	:	: 436	:	:
/var/spool/mail	|	|	|	|
/var/spool/news	:	:	:	:
/var/spool/____	|	|	|	|

```
/home              |  400  |       |       |

/usr               |       |  200  |       |
/usr/bin           :       :       :       :
/usr/lib           |       |       |       |
/usr/local         :       :       :       :
/usr/local/bin     |       |       |       |
/usr/local/lib     :       :       :       :
/usr/local/____    |       |       |       |
/usr/src           :       :       :       :

DOS                |  100  |       |       |
Win                :       :       :       :
NT                 |       |       |       |

/mnt.libdisk       |       |       |  226  |
/mnt.cd            :       :       :  710  :
/mnt.___/_____     |       |       |       |


Total capacity:  |  600  | 1000  | 1300  |
```

23 Appendix G: Example: partition placement

This is just to sort the partition numbers in ascending order ready to input to fdisk or cfdisk. Remember to optimize for physical track positioning (not done here).

```
            Drive :   sda     sdb     sdc

Total capacity:  |  600  | 1000  | 1300  |

Partition


1                |  100  |  436  |  710  |
2                :  100  :   64  :   64  :
3                |  400  |  300  |  300  |
4                :       :  200  :  226  :
```

24 Appendix H: Example II

The following is an example of a server setup in an academic setting, and is contributed by nakano (at) apm.seikei.ac.jp. I have only done minor editing to this section.

`/var/spool/delegate` is a directory for storing logs and cache files of an WWW proxy server program, "delegated". Since I don't notice it widely, there are 1000–1500 requests/day currently, and average disk usage is 15–30% with expiration of caches each day.

`/mnt.archive` is used for data files which are big and not frequently referenced such a s experimental data (especially graphic ones), various source archives, and Win95 backups (growing very fast...).

`/mnt.root` is backup root file system containing rescue utilities. A boot floppy is also prepared to boot with this partition.

```
=================================================
Directory               sda     sdb     hda

swap                 |   64 |   64 |        |
/                    |      |      |      | 20 |
/tmp                 |      |      |      | 180 |


/var                 :  300 :        :        :
/var/tmp             |      |  300 |        |
/var/spool/delegate  |  300 |        |        |


/home                |      |      |      | 850 |
/usr                 |  360 |        |        |
/usr/lib             -> /mnt.lib/usr.lib
/usr/local/lib       -> /mnt.lib/usr.local.lib


/mnt.lib             |      |  350 |        |
/mnt.archive         :      : 1300 :        :
/mnt.root            |      |   20 |        |

Total capacity:        1024   2034   1050



=================================================
        Drive :         sda    sdb    hda
Total capacity:      | 1024 | 2034 | 1050 |

Partition
1                    |  300 |   20 |   20 |
2                    :   64 : 1300 :  180 :
3                    |  300 |   64 |  850 |
4                    :  360 :  ext :        :
5                    |      |  300 |        |
6                    :      :  350 :        :


Filesystem        1024-blocks  Used  Available  Capacity  Mounted on
```

/dev/hda1	19485	10534	7945	57%	/
/dev/hda2	178598	13	169362	0%	/tmp
/dev/hda3	826640	440814	343138	56%	/home
/dev/sda1	306088	33580	256700	12%	/var
/dev/sda3	297925	47730	234807	17%	/var/spool/delegate
/dev/sda4	363272	170872	173640	50%	/usr
/dev/sdb5	297598	2	282228	0%	/var/tmp
/dev/sdb2	1339248	302564	967520	24%	/mnt.archive
/dev/sdb6	323716	78792	228208	26%	/mnt.lib

Apparently /tmp and /var/tmp is too big. These directories shall be packed together into one partition when disk space shortage comes.

/mnt.lib is also seemed to be, but I plan to install newer TeX and ghostscript archives, so /usr/local/lib may grow about 100 MB or so (since we must use Japanese fonts!).

Whole system is backed up by Seagate Tapestore 8000 (Travan TR-4, 4G/8G).

25 Appendix I: Example III: SPARC Solaris

The following section is the basic design used at work for a number of Sun SPARC servers running Solaris 2.5.1 in an industrial development environment. It serves a number of database and cad applications in addition to the normal services such as mail.

Simplicity is emphasized here so /usr/lib has not been split off from /usr.

This is the basic layout, planned for about 100 users.

Drive:	SCSI 0		SCSI 1	
Partition	Size (MB)	Mount point	Size (MB)	Mount point
0	160	swap	160	swap
1	100	/tmp	100	/var/tmp
2	400	/usr		
3	100	/		
4	50	/var		
5				
6	remainder	/local0	remainder	/local1

Due to specific requirements at this place it is at times necessary to have large partitions available on a short notice. Therefore drive 0 is given as many tasks as feasible, leaving a large /local1 partition.

This setup has been in use for some time now and found satisfactorily.

For a more general and balanced system it would be better to swap /tmp and /var/tmp and then move /var to drive 1.

ftape-HOWTO

Kevin Johnson, <*kjj@pobox.com*> <mailto:kjj@pobox.com>   v2.0, 15 March 1997

This HOWTO discusses essential do's and dont's for the ftape driver under Linux. The ftape driver interfaces to QIC-40, QIC-80, QIC-3010 and QIC-3020 compatible drives. The QIC-3010 and QIC-3020 standards
are also known as 'Travan' (TR-2 and TR-3). These drives connects via the floppy disk controller (FDC). It
does not cover SCSI or QIC-02 tape drives. DAT tape drives usually (always?) connect to a SCSI controller.
This is but one of the Linux HOWTO documents. You can get an index of the HOWTOs from *the Linux
HOWTO index* <http://sunsite.unc.edu/mdw/HOWTO>, while the real HOWTO's can be fetched (using ftp)
from sunsite.unc.edu:pub/Linux/doc/HOWTO (this is the "official" place) or via the World Wide Web from
the Linux Documentation Project home page <http://sunsite.unc.edu/mdw/linux.html>.

Contents

1 Legalese

Linux ftape-HOWTO may be reproduced and distributed in whole or in part, subject to the following conditions:

If you have questions or comments, please contact the author at kjj@pobox.com.

2 Revision History

version 2.0 (March 15, 1997)

- Updated to ftape v2.11 and v3.xx
- Lots of updates.

version 1.9 (September 20, 1996)

- New maintainers of ftape and the HOWTO.
- A few minor formatting and spelling fixes.
- Updated for Linux v2.0.
- Started to integrate some of Andrew Martin's ftape info.

version 1.8 (May 22, 1996)

- Copyright policy changed to GNU GPL v2
- The maintainer's email address has changed.
- Updated to ftape-2.08
- ftape is now a part of the kernel distribution.

version 1.7.1 (February 13, 1996)

- Updated to ftape-2.06b

version 1.7 (January 28, 1996)

- Updated to ftape-2.06 and modules-1.3.57

version 1.6.2 (January 23, 1996)

- Connor TST3200R drive added
- Updated 2Mbps fdc information.

version 1.6.1 (January 16, 1996)

- minor corrections

version 1.6 (January 10, 1996)

- New maintainer of ftape
- updated to v2.05
- added new drives

3   The preliminaries

The maintainer of the source for ftape is Claus Heine <*claus@momo.math.rwth-aachen.de*> <mailto:claus@momo.math.rwth-aachen.de>. He has a web page at *http://samuel.math.rwth-aachen.de/~LBFM/claus/ftape/ftape-page.html* <http://samuel.math.rwth-aachen.de/~LBFM/claus/ftape/ftape-page.html>.

If you have a problem or questions about ftape, try posting to the linux.dev.tape newsgroups. This is a Usenet group that mirrors the traffic on the mailing list linux-tape@vger.rutger.edu (see 4.3 (Following the ftape development) below). It is recommended that the newsgroup be used in preference to the mailing list, since the vger machine is overburdened with the load of the Linux mailing lists.

I use ftape (it is my sole means of backing up on my linux box :-). I hesitate to make recommendations on what hardware to buy. I use an Iomega Ditto Tape Insider 3200 and it seems to work OK for me, but I won't even try to tell you not to buy something else. See the section 6.1 (Supported drives) and 6.3 (Unsupported drives) for a list of supported and unsupported drives.

You should try to post a summary of your problems and its solution(s), after you've got it working, even if you only got it partially working. Please also send me (<kjj@pobox.com>) a copy of your solution or post it to the linux.dev.tape newsgroup so that I can add it to the HOWTO.

I generally read my mail several times a week, I try to respond to everyone, but I cannot guarantee that I will respond immediately. I usually read the newsgroups (linux.dev.tape and the kernel list).

If you receive this as part of a printed distribution or on a CD-ROM, please check out *the Linux Documentation home page* <http://sunsite.unc.edu/mdw/linux.html> or ftp to <ftp://sunsite.unc.edu:/pub/Linux/doc/HOWTO> to see if there exists a more recent version. This could potentially save you a lot of trouble.

If you email me, please include the string ftape in the subject line. This will help ensure the mail doesn't inadvertently get buried.

3.1   What is ftape

ftape is a driver program that controls various low-cost tape drives that connect to the floppy controller.

ftape is not a backup program as such; it is a device driver, which allows you to use the tape drive (just like the SoundBlaster 16 driver let you use your sound card) through the device files /dev/[n]rft[0-3].

ftape was originally written by Bas Laarhoven <bas@vimec.nl>, with "a little help from his friends" to sort out the ECC (Error Correcting Code) stuff. ftape is copyrighted by Bas under the GNU General Public License, which basically says: "go ahead and share this with the world, just don't disallow other people from copying it further".

ftape is quite stable, and has been that for some time now. It is reliable enough for critical backups (but it's always a good idea to check your backups, so you won't get a nasty surprise some day).

ftape supports drives that conform to the QIC-117 and one of the QIC-80, QIC-40, QIC-3010, and QIC-3020 standards.

ftape supports neither QIC-02, IDE (ATAPI), nor SCSI tape drives. SCSI drives are accessed as /dev/[n]st[0-7] and are supported by the kernel through the SCSI drivers. If you look for help on SCSI tape drives, you should read the SCSI-howto. ATAPI tape drives are supported by the kernel since 1.3.46. See section 6.1 (Supported drives) and 6.3 (Unsupported drives) for a list of supported and unsupported drives.

4   Getting and installing `ftape`

4.1   Getting `ftape`

The v2.0.X versions of the kernel have version 2.08 of `ftape` already. I recommend, however, that you grab the latest version of the full source code package for `ftape`. It is a newer version, includes files that are not included in the kernel distribution, and includes much better documentation about how to install `ftape`.

Version 2.11a or newer of `ftape` is available from *http://samuel.math.rwth-aachen.de/~LBFM/claus/ftape/ftape-page.html* `<http://samuel.math.rwth-aachen.de/~LBFM/claus/ftape/ftape-page.html>`. At the time of writing this version of the HOWTO document, v3.xx is available. I recommend sticking with v2.xx unless you are ready, willing, and able to use a development release with bugs.

4.2   Installing the driver

The following sections provide some useful information to get you going with the installation of v2.11a.

Once you've downloaded the source code (probably `ftape-2.11a.tar.gz`), untar it. You can do this by determining what directory you want the source code to be located in. I recommend `/usr/src/` or `~/src`. When the tar file is extracted, it will dump everything into a `ftape-2.11a` subdirectory, so that you'll end up, in the example I've given, with something like `/usr/src/ftape-2.11a` or `~/src/ftape-2.11a`. It is possible to drop the entire ftape distribution into the `/usr/src/linux/drivers/char/ftape` directory, but untar the file into a location like I've suggested first, read through the documentation, then decide how you want to proceed.

Read the `README` file. The `README` is required reading. It's the top of the tree, so to speak. If there are specific files that the `README` tells you to read then read them. It will make the process much less complicated.

Do NOT proceed with compiling the package until you have read the appropriate `README` files and the `Install-guide`.

The `README` mentions that the `linux-tape` mailing list. I recommend subscribing to the `linux.dev.tape` newsgroup instead. The machine serving the mailing list is overburdened.

There are two ways that `ftape` support can be added to the kernel.

- Compile it directly into the kernel.
- Compile it as a kernel module.

Of these two methods, the first has fewer potential problems. The second has the benefit of only consuming memory while the driver is loaded. The original author of `ftape` (Bas Laarhoven) has pointed out that `ftape` was not originally designed to be used with modules.

I compile `ftape` directly into the kernel on my computer. In general, fewer difficulties or complications are reported when it is done this way. A good rule of thumb is to compile it into the kernel unless you both have a good reason not to and are willing to accept any of the complications that can arise from doing otherwise. If you do compile it into the kernel, please keep in mind that you cannot use `zftape` instead of `ftape` because the two use the same major device number.

If you are compiling the driver directly into the kernel, you can generally ignore the instructions regarding modules.

If you have a v1.2 kernel, you should use the modules-1.3.57 package, not the modules-1.2.8 package (Bjørn Ekwall, maintainer of the modules package, encourages this).

If you are using v1.3.x of the kernel, you should consider moving to v2.0.x. v1.3.x was the development release prior to the production release v2.0.x.

4.3 Following the development of the `ftape` driver

If you want to follow the development of the `ftape` driver, you should read the Usenet newsgroup `linux.dev.tape`. This is really gatewayed from the mailing list `linux-tape@vger.rutgers.edu`, but since `vger` is brought to it's knees due to the load of the various Linux mailing lists, I recommend everyone to read the newsgroup instead.

If you are unable to read news, you can subscribe to the TAPE mailing list by sending a mail saying 'subscribe linux-tape' (*in the body*) to `majordomo@vger.rutgers.edu`. When you subscribe, you will be sent a greeting mail, which will tell you how to submit real mails and how to get off the list again.

Please note that I do not, repeat **DO NOT**, have any special powers with regard to this mailing list. If you're stuck on the list, don't bother to tell me that. I can only shrug and send you my sympathy (but that won't get you off the list).

4.4 Mixing `ftape` and floppies

Since both the floppy driver and `ftape` needs the FDC (and IRQ6), they cannot run concurrently. Thus, if you have mounted a floppy and then try to access the tape drive, `ftape` will complain that it cannot grab IRQ6 and then die. This is especially a problem when designing a emergency disk for use with ftape. This solution is to either load the boot/root disk into a ramdisk and then unmount the floppy, or have two floppy drive controllers.

5 The Care and Feeding of Tape and Tape Drives

5.1 Formatting

Before a tape can be used, it must be formatted. The formatting process lays out sector information onto the tape. Other tape interfaces don't typically require formatting. The reason floppy tapes do is that they need to look like a floppy (kinda gross, but what the hey - it works :-).

5.1.1 Can I format my tapes under Linux?

Not yet, but it's being worked on.

Until formatting becomes available under Linux, you'll have to use MessyDOS (arghhh!) instead or buy preformatted tapes. However, some of the preformatted tapes are *not* checked for bad sectors!. If the `ftape` driver encounters a tape with no bad blocks, it will issue a warning. If `ftape` barfs at your preformatted tapes, try out your DOS software. If both the DOS software *and* `ftape` barfs on your tapes, a reformat will very probably cure the problem.

Note that to be able to use your newly formatted tapes under ftape, you must *erase* the tape first:

```
# mt -f /dev/nftape erase
```

5.1.2 Which formatting programs can I use under DOS?

The following are known to work:

- Colorado Memory System's software (`tape.exe`)
- Conner Backup Basics v1.1 and all Windows versions
- Norton Backup
- QICstream version 2
- Tallgrass FileSecure v1.52
- Escom Powerstream 3.0 (`qs3.exe` – QICstream v3?)

These programs are known to be more or less buggy:

- Conner Backup Basics 1.0
- Colorado Windows tape program
- CP Backup (wastes tape space, but is OK apart from that)

As a general rule, most software under DOS should work. The Conner Backup Basics v1.0 has a parameter off by one (someone could not read the QIC-80 specs right!), which is corrected in version 1.1. However, `ftape` detects this, and will work around it. Dennis T. Flaherty (`<dennisf@denix.elk.miles.com>`) report that Conner C250MQ owners can obtain the new v1.1, by calling Conner at 1-800-4Conner (in the US) and ask for an upgrade (for a nominal fee for the floppy). The Windows versions should work fine. Some versions of Colorado's tape program for windows, has an off-by-one error in the number of segments. `ftape` also detect and work around that bug.

Central Point Backup can be used, but it wastes precious tape space when it encounters a bad spot on the tape.

NOTE: If you are running a formatting software under DOS, which is not mentioned here, please mail the relevant info to me (`<kjj@pobox.com>` `<mailto:kjj@pobox.com>`), so I can update the list.

5.2 Retensioning

QIC tapes are particularly sensitive to tape stretch. The reason is that floppy tapes are pre-formatted with sector information, whereas other tape types have their sync information written as the data is written to the tape. If the floppy tape stretches and the sync fields get out of sync the result will be read errors. The problem is worse with longer tapes.

It is a good idea to retension new tapes a few times before using them and before formatting them. You should also try retensioning the tape if you are start getting read errors. It might also be a good idea retension the tape before a backup.

5.3 Drive Cleaning

The coating on the tape is an oxide compound. As the tape is dragged across the tape head it has a tendency to leave tiny amounts of residue on the head. You should periodically use a tape cleaner - following the specs for the drive in question. Tape cleaners should be available from any distributer of tapes.

One more additional note about tape cleaning. You might want to clean the drive after the first use of a brand new tape. A brand new tape will typically leave quite a bit of residue the first time it's used.

Thanks to *Neal Friedman* `<mailto:nealf@rcs.ee.washington.edu>` for the explanation and suggestion that this information be included in the HOWTO.

6   Hardware support

6.1   Supported tape drives

All drives that are both QIC-117 compatible *and* one of the QIC-40, 80, 3010, and 3020 standards should work. QIC-WIDE and Travan drives are also supported (TR-1 is just QIC-80 with 8mm tapes, while TR-2 and TR-3 is a.k.a QIC-3010 and 3020 respectively).

Currently, the list of drives that are known to work with `ftape` is:

Alloy Retriever 250

Archive 5580i, XL9250i

Colorado DJ-10, DJ-20 (aka: Jumbo 120, Jumbo 250)

Colorado 1400

<kosowsky@bellini.harvard.edu> reported a problem doing a 1G backup using taper.

HP Colorado T1000

Works with 3M Travan 400M (TR-1) tapes with 120M tapes. Also reported that mt dies, but with backups using tar it works ok. With cpio, ftape is recommended rather than zftape. (<millner@millner.bevc.blacksburg.va.us>)

Problems have been reported with the drive continually stopping and starting with zftape (<75104.1756@compuserve.com>). This appears to be a problem with the tape going too fast for the computer; the DMA buffers are getting flushed beforee getting filled again. Newer versions of zftape don't do this any more is a suitably fast backup program or large DMA buffers are used (<millner@millner.bevc.blacksburg.va.us>).

Conner C250MQ(T)

The 250Q is reported to generate write error and frequent repositioning. (Frank Stuess at Nacamar Data Communications)

Conner TSM420R, TSM850R

The 400 and 800 models only work with TR-1 tapes.

Conner TST3200R

Works with TR-3 tapes at 1Mbps (ie. 1600M capacity only). Wirks with QIC-WIDE 400M tapes (Sony 5122's?) (<chris@cs.wmich.edu>). Works with TR3, QIC-3010, and QIC-3020 tapes. Comes with a 2MB FDC which the Promise 2300+ 1Mbps controller works (<kjh@pollux.usc.edu>). Works with ftape 2.05; NOTE: ftape 2.03, 2.04, and zftape 1.03 don't work. Booting problems reported with ftape-2.06 and QIC-3020 with the CTC-2MB controller (<merkel@def.gmpt.gmeds.com>).

Supposedly works fine with ftape 2.06 using a fast controller to support QIC-3020. Reported that the floppy disk can no longer read low-density floppies. May have to fiddle with IRQ/ports/dms channels (<chris@yakkocs.wmich.edu>).

Conner TST800R

The TST800R works with TR-1, Sony QW5122F (210M) and DC2120 tapes. Reported to work with ftape 2.02e (not 2.03b). It works with ftape 2.05 (<khp@pip.dknet.dk>). Requires the length patch. Reported that you may need to nodify the Makefile to ensure ftape talks to the PRIMARY floppy drive controller (>jzc@primenet.com>). Also, a "Timer expired" error reported (using TR-1 tapes with ftape 2.05-2.07) (<les@amc.uva.nl>).

Conner CTT3200

The CTT3200 is supposedly identical to the Iomega Ditto 3200. It works with the supplised 2Mbps controller (but at 1Mbps), but reported not to work under DOS on some machines. (<jmorris@dtx.net>)

Conner 1.7G Tapestor (TSM1700R)

Works with QIC-WIDE tapes (<pschmidt@slip.net>). Partially works with QIS-3200. Using the HSC-2 controller, the DMA channel needs to be changed (incremented by 1, channel2?, Modify the Makefile). You then need to modify the ftape Makefile to reflect this change. However, ftape seems to be a bit flaky with this (no version number supplied) (<ttait@tiac.net>). It may not work at 2Mbps (QIC-3020) with the HSC controller. The tape died with a messages like "dumb tape stop" and has since been unreliable (<ttait@tiac.net>).

Escom or Archive (Hornet) 31250Q

Exabyte EXB-1500

Work with QIC-3010 tapes. Requires the length patch.

Exabyte TR-3

Irwin 80SX, Insight 80Mb

Iomega 250

Iomega Ditto Tape Insider 420, 1700

Iomega Ditto Tape Insider 3200

This is the unit, that I use. The default jumper settings don't work. Leave the irq and ioport address at the default (6 and 0x370, respectfully), but change the DMA from 3 to 2.

May require the having {0x08882, 80, wake_up_colorado, "Iomega 3200"}, added to vendors.h on older versions of ftape.

Problems reported with ftape 2.07 and kernel 1.12.13. With all sorts of combinations of accelerator, etc, the drive may (on some systems) only be accessed once (<erwin@box.nl>). Also, after the first access, the next use of the tape says it is write protected (<erwin@box.nl>, <M.J.Ammerlaan@dutiwy.twi.tudelft.nl>).

There has been one report of a problem where the tape got wound off the end of the spool.

Another problem has been reported with writing archives (with dd) to the tape. It may start fine, but when the driver catches up with dd, it stops the tape and rewinds it to the beginning. Then it starts winding on through the tape ad infinitum. It appears to occur when the driver asks the tape to pause which should cause the tape to move back by 3 segments, but instead is moves back to the beginning of the tape. A bug fix submitted is reported to not solve the solve the problem.

Iomega Ditto 800 Insider

Work with Travan TR1, TR2, or DC2120 tapes (<klein@informatik.uni-rostock.de>). Requires the length patch.

Mountain FS8000

Reveal TB1400

Reported not to work with kernel 1.3.79 and ftape (no version given) or with kernel 1.2.13 and zftape 1.04 (<colin@colina.demon.co.uk>).

Summit SE 150, SE 250

Tallgrass FS300

If you have a Tallgrass FS300 and an AHA1542B, you need to increase the bus-on / bus-off time of the 1542B. Antti Virjo (<klanvi@uta.fi>), says that changing CMD_BUSON_TIME to 4 and CMD_BUSOFF_CMD to 12 in linux/drivers/scsi/aha1542.c will do the trick.

Teac 800

Memorex tape drive backup system

Wangtek 3040F, 3080F

You can always check out the newest list of drives that are recognized by `ftape`, by looking in the file `vendors.h` in the `ftape` distribution.

Although I do not want to endorse one drive type over another, it has been reported that the Colorado DJ-20 drive is rather noisy, when compared to, say, a Conner C250MQ drive ('tis said that the Colorado is 5-10 times as noisy as the Conner drive. Since I have neither, I can't tell for sure).

NOTE: If you have a drive that works fine, but it is not listed here, or if you have corrections to the above information, please send a mail to the HOWTO maintainer (<kjj@pobox.com>).

6.2   Supported special controllers

These dedicated high-speed tape controllers are supported by `ftape`:

- Colorado FC-10, FC-20
- Mountain MACH-2
- Iomega Tape Accelerator II
- 2Mbps controllers (using the i82078-1 fdc)

Support for the FC-10 controller has been merged into the `ftape` driver in version 1.12. See the `RELEASE-NOTES` and the `Makefile` files in the `ftape` distribution. Since of version 2.03 of `ftape`, the FC-20 controller will work (but do check the Release notes!).

The support for the MACH-2 controller was added in `ftape-1.14d`.

To use the Iomega Tape Accelerator II, use `-DMACH2`, and set the right settings for I/O base, IRQ and DMA. This works (by the empirical testing of Scott Bailey *<sbailey@xcc.mc.xerox.com>* <mailto:sbailey@xcc. mc.xerox.com>), with at least `ftape-2.02`.

6.2.1   Iomega Ditto Dash and other 2Mbps controllers

The Iomega Ditto Dash, and all other known 2Mbps controllers, use the Intel 82078-1 chip, which can run at 2Mbps. Support for the 82078-1 is currently under development. It is hoped that the support will be completed during January or February.

Current status is that it will work at 1Mbps, with 2Mbps support coming soon (I hope!).

6.3   Unsupported tape drives

- All drives that connect to the parallel port (eg: Colorado Trakker)
- Irwin AX250L / Accutrak 250. (not a QIC-80 drive)
- IBM Internal Tape Backup Unit (identical to the Irwin AX250L drive)
- COREtape light

Generally, ALL drives that connect to the parallel port are NOT supported. This is because these drives uses (different) proprietary interfaces, that are very much different from the QIC-117 standard.

The Irwin AX250L (and the IBM Internal Tape Backup Unit) does not work the `ftape`. This is because they only support QIC-117, but not the QIC-80 standard (they use Irwin's proprietary "servoe (Rhomat)" format). I know nothing about the Rhomat format, nor where to get any info on it. Sorry.

The COREtape light does not accept the initialisation commands, we're feeding it. This pretty much leaves the drive unusable.

The Iomega 2GB Ditto drive does not work with ftape. That particular tape uses a proprietary format that the Claus has not been able to get information on.

6.4 Using an external tape drive with `ftape`

If you have a floppy controller which has a female DB37 connector on the bracket (and some means of delivering power to the drive), you can use it with **ftape**. OK, that sentence was not very obvious. Let's try it this way: Some FDC's (the very ancient one's), have a DB37 connector on the bracket, for connecting to external floppy drives.

If you make a suitable cable from the DB37 connector (on the FDC) to your external tape drive, you can get **ftape** to control your tape drive.

This is because that from a program's view there is no difference between the internal and the external connectors. So, from **ftape**'s point of view, they are identical.

- Pins 20-37: GROUND
- 1: +12 Volt (POWER)
- 2: +12 Volt return (GROUND)
- 3: +5 Volt return (GROUND)
- 4: +5 Volt (POWER)
- 5: 2
- 6: 8
- 7: 10
- 8: 12
- 9: 14
- 10: 16
- 11: 18
- 12: 20
- 13: 22
- 14: 24
- 15: 26
- 16: 28
- 17: 30
- 18: 32
- 19: 34

The power connector is of the "mini" type, sitting on 3.5" floppy drives. The idea appears to be that you plug one of the power connectors from the PSU to this connector on the board. If you want to use just a single cable, you might want to get a 50 wire cable, and use multiple wires for the power lines (and ground, for that matter).

I have received no confirmation from anyone that this works. Let me know your results if you try it.

6.5   PCI motherboards and `ftape`

Unfortunately, some PCI motherboards cause problems when running `ftape`. Some people have experienced that `ftape` would not run in a PCI based box, but ran flawlessly in a normal ISA based 386DX machine. If you have such a problem, please read the `README.PCI` file in the `ftape` distribution.

7   Backing up and restoring data

This section describes some simple uses of `tar` and `mt`.

7.1   Writing an archive to a tape

You can use 'tar', 'dd', 'cpio', and 'afio'. You will need to use 'mt' to get the full potential of your tapes and the `ftape` driver. For a start I'd recommend using 'tar', as it can archive lots of directories and let you pick out separate files from an archive. `cpio` creates smaller archives and is more generally more flexible than `tar`, but is missing some features like volume labels. 'afio' creates backups where each file is compressed individually and then concatenated. This will allow you to access the files "after" the point of the error. If you use gzipped `tar` files, all data after the point of the error is lost! (to me, this is a pretty good reason for NOT using compression on backups). The choice of which is most appropriate depends on the situation and the features and malfeatures of each of the packages. I recommend taking a look at each package at reviewing the options that each provides. It's possible that this HOWTO may provide more detail on this subject at some point in the future.

To make a backup of your kernel source tree using `tar`, do this (assuming you have the sources in `/usr/src/linux`):

```
# cd /usr/src
# tar cf /dev/ftape linux
```

This will not compress the files, but gives you a smoother tape run. If you want the compression (and you've got `tar` 1.11.2), you just include the -z flag(*), eg: 'tar czf /dev/ftape linux'

For further instructions on how to use `tar`, `dd` and `mt` look at the man pages and the texinfo files that comes with the respective distributions.

(*) `tar` assumes that the first argument is options, so the '-' is not necessary, i.e. these two commands are the same: 'tar xzf /dev/ftape' and 'tar -xzf /dev/ftape'

7.2   Restoring an archive

OK, let us restore the backup of the kernel source you made in section 7.1 (Writing an archive to a tape) above. To do this you simply say

```
tar xf /dev/ftape
```

If you used compression, you will have to say

```
tar xzf /dev/ftape
```

When you use compression, `gzip` will complain about trailing garbage after the very end of the archive (and this will lead to a 'broken pipe' message). This can be safely ignored.

For the other utilities, please read the man page.

7.3 Testing the archive

tar has an option (`-d`) for detecting differences between two archives. To test your backup of the kernel source say

```
tar df /dev/ftape
```

If you do not have the man page for `tar`, you are not lost (yet); tar has a built-in option list: try '`tar --help 2>&1 | less`'

7.4 Putting more than one backup on a tape

To put more than one backup on a tape you must have the `mt` utility. You will probably have it already, if you got one of the mainline distributions (eg. Slackware or Debian).

Programs like `tar` and `cpio` generate a single Tape ARchive and know nothing about multiple files or positioning of a tape, it just reads or writes from/to a device. `mt` knows everything about moving the tape back and forth, but nothing about reading the data off the tape. As you might have guessed, combining `tar` or `cpio` with `mt` does the trick.

By using the `nrft[0-3]` (`nftape`) device, you can use '`mt`' to position the tape the correct place ('`mt -f /dev/nftape fsf 2`' means step over two "file marks", i.e. `tar` files) and then use `tar` or `cpio` to read or write the relevant data.

The most common use of the non-rewinding device is to append another backup to an existing tape. Here are the specific steps with a little explanation thrown in for good measure.

- Insert a tape into the drive. On some devices this may cause the tape to be rewound.
- Issue an End-of-Tape command to the NON-rewinding device.

```
mt -f /dev/n???? eof
```

   The tape should now be positioned at the End-of-Tape (EOT), which is actually between to End-of-File (EOF) marks. The tape won't move unless a program opens the device, closes the rewinding device, removes the device driver from kernel memory (rmmod) or ejects the tape. Using '`mt eof`' may be faster on QIC tapes.

- The next tape operation will start at the End-of-Tape (EOF) mark. If you perform a write, it will append a new 'file'. If you perform a read it will fail with EOF. The EOT mark on mast tape formats is actually two consecutive EOF marks. When appending to a tape the second EOF mark is overwritten with new data, leaving a normal EOF. If the second EOF is present, it is interpreted as a logical EOF. Writing the EOF marks is handled by either the device driver or the hardware when a close() is performed.

- Here's where you write the actual data to the tape.

- Here's the important part. **Now rewind the tape.** Both `ftape` and `zftape` cache some information that belongs in the header segments on the tape and update those header segments **only when the tape is rewound.** This caching is necessary because rewinding the tape and updating the header segments takes a conspicious amount of time. The drawback of this caching is that you will lose information if you have written to the tape and not rewound the device.

7.5   Appending files to an archive

"Is there a way to extend an archive – put a file on the tape, then later, add more to the tape?"

No. The `tar` documentation will tell you to use '`tar -Ar`', but it does not work. This is a limitation of the current `ftape` driver.

7.6   Mount/unmounting tapes

Since a tape does not have a "filesystem" on it, you do not mount / unmount the tape. To backup, you just insert the tape and run your '`tar`' command (or whatever you use to access the tape with).

8   Creating an emergency boot floppy for `ftape`

This section was written by Claus Tøndering <ct@login.dknet.dk>.

Once you are the happy owner of a tape drive and several tapes full of backups, you will probably ask yourself this question: "If everything goes wrong, and I completely lose my hard disk, how do I restore my files from tape?"

What you need is an emergency floppy disk that contains enough files to enable you to boot Linux and restore your hard disk from tape.

The first thing you should do is to read "The Linux Bootdisk HOWTO" written by Graham Chapman <*grahamc@zeta.org.au*> <mailto:grahamc@zeta.org.au>. That document tells you almost everything you need to know about making an emergency floppy boot kit. The paragraphs below contain a few extra pieces of information that will make your life a bit easier when you follow Graham Chapman's procedures:

- You don't really need /etc/init, /etc/inittab, /etc/getty, and /etc/rc.d/* on your floppy disk. If Linux doesn't find /etc/init, it will start /bin/sh on your console, which is fine for restoring your system. Deleting these files gives you extra space on your floppy, which you will probably need.

- Find a small version of /bin/sh. They are frequently available on the boot floppies that come with a Linux distribution. This again will give you extra space. I'd suggest `ash`, which is extremely small (approx 62Kbytes), and yet very `bash` compatible.

- The /etc/fstab you include on your floppy disk should look something like this:

  ```
  /dev/fd0        /           minix    defaults
  none            /proc       proc     defaults
  /dev/hda        /mnt        ext2     defaults
  ```

  Once you have booted from your floppy, give the command:

  ```
  mount -av
  ```

- Make sure your floppy drive is not mounted when you access the streamer tape! Otherwise you may get the following error message:

  ```
  Unable to grab IRQ6 for ftape driver
  ```

This means that you **MUST** load the floppy into a RAMDISK.

This has the unfortunate consequence that the programs needed to restore the files from the tape can not be located on a separate floppy disk. You have two options here:

1. You place `tar` (or `cpio` or `afio` or whatever other backup program you use) on your root floppy disk. (This is where you'll need all the extra space created in the steps above.)

2. Before you start restoring from tape, copy `tar` (or `cpio` or `afio` or whatever) to your hard disk and load it from there.

- Apart from your backup program, you will probably need `mt` on your root floppy as well.
- Make sure your ftape device (typically `/dev/nrft0`) is present on your boot floppy.
- Finally: **TRY IT OUT!** Of course, I don't recommend that you destroy your hard disk contents to see if you are able to restore everything. What I do recommend, however, is that you try booting from your emergency disks and make sure that you can at least make a file listing of the contents of your backup tape.

9 Frequently Asked Questions

This is a collection of questions that get asked once in a while, which could fall into the category of FAQ's. If you feel that there is some question that ought to be added to the list, please feel free to mail me (but do include an answer, thanks!).

9.1 Does `ftape` support the Iomega 2GB tape drive?

Sorry, no, it doesn't. Iomega uses a proprietary data format on their 'Ditto 2GB' tape cartridges. The maintainer of `ftape` has been unable to get the necessary information to include support from the vendor.

9.2 How fast is `ftape`?

You can achieve quite respectable backup and restore speeds with `ftape`: a Colorado DJ-20 and an Adaptec 1542CF controller, has been measured at 4.25Mbyte/min sustained data transfer rate (no compression) across a 70Mbyte tar archive, while comparing the archive on the tape with data on an IDE disk. The speed of `ftape` is mostly dependent on the data transfer rate of your FDC: The AHA1542CF has a "post-1991 82077" FDC, and it will push 1Mbit/sec at the tape drive. If you have an FDC which can only deliver 500Kbit/sec data rates, you will see half the transfer rate (well, roughly).

9.3 How do I change the trace-level?

There are three ways you can do this (in order of personal preference).

While we're at it, here are the meanings of the various trace levels.

- 0 Bugs
- 1 + Errors
- 2 + Warnings
- 3 + Information
- 4 + More information

- 5 + Program flow
- 6 + FDC/DMA info
- 7 + Data flow
- 8 + Everything else

9.3.1 Using insmod to change trace-level

If you are using the modules mechanism to load the ftape driver, you can specify the tracing level as an option to the insmod command.

```
/sbin/insmod ftape.o tracing=<tracing-level>
```

9.3.2 Using mt to change trace-level

The ftape driver has a hack in it that allows the fsr option in mt to be used to set the tracing level. zftape does not have this hack.

```
mt -f /dev/ftape fsr <tracing-level>
```

The use of the fsr command in mt is a *hack*, and will probably disappear or change with time.

9.3.3 Recompiling to change trace-level

The file tracing.c contains a line int tracing = 3;. Change the 3 to whatever is appropriate and recompile.

9.4 Can I exchange tapes with someone using DOS?

No. The DOS software conforms to the QIC-80 specs about the layout of the DOS filesystem, and it should(?) be a small problem to write a program that can read/write the DOS format. In fact, I'd bet that creating a nice user interface would be a bigger problem.

9.5 How do I '....' with tar?

These are really tar questions: Please read the man page and the info page. If you have not got it either, try 'tar --help 2>&1 | less'.

If your version of tar is v1.11.1 or earlier, consider upgrading to v1.11.8 - This version can call GNU zip directly (i.e.: it supports the -z option) and has an elaborate help included. Also, it compiles right out of the box on Linux.

9.6 ftape DMA transfers gives ECC errors

Sadly to say there are some SVGA cards and Ethernet cards that do not decode their addresses correct. This typically happens when the ftape buffers are in the range 0x1a0000 to 0x1c0000. Somehow, the DMA write cycles get clobbered and every other byte written gets a bad value (0xff). These problems are reported to happen with both SVGA and Ethernet cards. We know of at least one (bad?) ATI 16bit VGA card that caused this.

The easiest solution is to put the card in an 8bit slot (it is often not enough to reconfigure the card to 8bit transfers). Moving the `ftape` buffer away from the VGA range is only a partial solution; All DMA buffers used in Linux can have this problem! Let us make this one clear: This has nothing to do with the `ftape` software.

9.7 `insmod` says the kernel version is wrong

The `insmod` program can check the kernel version against the version that `ftape` was compiled for in two ways: It can directly compare the kernel version number recorded in the ftape module against the version of the running kernel, or, if both the kernel and `ftape` is compiled with versioned symbols, compare the version of the used kernel symbols.

If you have upgraded your version of GCC to v2.7.0 or later, you must recompile the modules utilities with gcc v2.7.x.

Newer versions of `insmod` allows you to "force" insertion of a module into the kernel, even though the version string is incorrect.

9.8 What is this versioned symbols stuff anyway?

When you say 'yes' to CONFIG_MODVERSIONS during '`make config`', all the symbols exported by the kernel, i.e: the symbols that the loadable modules can "see", are augmented to include a checksum across the types of the call/return parameters. This allows `insmod` to detect whether the definition of a variable or function in the kernel has changed since the time when `ftape` was compiled.

This ensures a high degree of safety, such that you do not crash the kernel because you used an outdated module with your kernel.

If you enable CONFIG_MODVERSIONS in the kernel, make sure you have '-DMODVERSIONS -include /usr/include/linux/modversions.h' uncommented in the MODULE_OPT line in the `ftape` Makefile. Conversely, if you do not have CONFIG_MODVERSIONS enabled, make sure you have it commented out.

9.9 `insmod` says that kernel 1.2.0 and 1.2.0 differ

Did you remember to apply the `ksyms.c` patch to the kernel? If not, read the `README.linux-1.2` file in the source distribution.

9.10 `ftape` says "This tape has no 'Linux raw format'"

You get this complaint if you haven't *erased* your freshly formatted tape. This is because `ftape` expect a "magic header" on the tape, to be able that it is allowed to interpret the header segment in its own way (eg: file marks). To remove the problem, say '`mt -f /dev/nftape erase`'

9.11 Where can I find the `tar/mt/cpio/dd` binaries/sources/manpages?

All of these tools have been developed by the GNU project, and the source (and man page) can be fetched from just-about any ftp site in the world (including `ftp.funet.fi`, `tsx-11.mit.edu`, and `sunsite.unc.edu`).

In any case they can be fetched from the official GNU home site: prep.ai.mit.edu [18.71.0.38]:/pub/gnu.
The latest versions (as of September 12 1996) are:

cpio:	2.4.2 (cpio-2.4.2.tar.gz)
dd:	3.13 (fileutils-3.13.tar.gz)
mt:	2.4.2 (cpio-2.4.2.tar.gz)
tar:	1.11.8 (tar-1.11.8.tar.gz)
gzip:	1.2.4 (gzip-1.2.4.tar.gz)

They all compile out of the box on Linux v1.0.4 / libc v4.5.19 / gcc v2.5.8.

9.12   Where can I obtain the QIC standards?

If you wish to help developing ftape, or add some utility (e.g. a tape formatting program), you will need that appropriate QIC standards. The standard(s) to get is: QIC-80, -117, -3010, and 3020. QIC-117 describes how commands are sent to the tape drive (including timing etc), so you would probably never need it. QIC-80/3010/3020 describes higher level part, such as tape layout, ECC code, standard filesystem. You can get the QIC standards from the following address:

```
Quarter Inch Cartridge Drive Standards, Inc.
311 East Carrillo Street
Santa Barbara, California 93101
Phone: (805) 963-3853
Fax:   (805) 962-1541
```

Note: They are registered as 'Freeman Associates, Inc' in the phone book.

9.13   What block-size should I use with tar

When using compression, and in all general, it can be a benefit to specify to tar, that it should block the output into chunks. Since ftape cuts things into 29Kbyte blocks, saying '-b58' should be optimum.

"Why 29Kbyte?", I hear you cry. Well, the QIC-80 standard specifies that all data should be protected by an Error Correcting Code (ECC) code. The code specified in the QIC-80 standard is known as a Reed-Solomon (R-S) code. The R-S code takes 29 data bytes and generates 3 parity bytes. To increase the performance of the ECC code, the parity bytes are generated across 29 1Kbyte sectors. Thus, ftape takes 29Kbytes of data, adds 3Kbytes of ECC parity, and writes 32Kbytes to the tape at a time. For this reason, ftape will always read and write 32K byte blocks to be able to detect (and correct) data errors.

If you are curious, and wish to know more, look in the ecc.c and ecc.h files, for an explanation of the code and a reference to a textbook on Reed-Solomon codes.

9.14   ftape detects more bad sectors than DOS on QIC-3020 tapes

If you look at the difference, you will notice that ftape always detects 2784 sectors more than DOS.

The number that ftape reports is correct (of course :-). Each correctly formatted QIC-3020 tape has 2784 sectors at fixed positions that are marked in the bad sector map. To quote from the specs:

"Tracks 5,7,9,11,13,15,17,19,21,23,25 and 27 within 4 segments of either EOT or BOT are prone to increased error rates due to hole imprints. Therefore, these regions shall be mapped as bad at format time and entered in the bad sector map by indicating that all sectors within the identified segments are bad."

This gives 12 tracks * 2 * 4 segments * 29 sectors == 2784 sectors.

So ftape choose to report the real number of sectors that cannot be used on the tape, while DOS gives a more optimistic number giving a better indication of tape quality. (ftape's behavior might change in the future to detect correct formatting and display the separate numbers. It has rather low priority though).

QIC-3010 are alike QIC-3020 tapes regarding this.

9.15 Syslogd works overtime when running ftape

The compile-time options NO_TRACE and NO_TRACE_AT_ALL in ftape control the amount of system logging. Add whichever is appropriate to the FTAPE_OPT line in the Makefile and recompile.

9.16 'Shoeshining'

There been a few reports of 'shoeshining'. This is when the tape just seems to run back and forth endlessly. This has been seen on a Jumbo 250 (74407.3051@compuserve.com) and on an Iomega 250 Ditto Insider (tom@opus.cais.com). In the latter case it has been narrowed own to using an ELF Linux and running off a SCSI hard disk (connected to an Adaptec 1542cf). Please contact me if you have an update to this problem.

9.17 Trying to compile `ftape` gives me the error '"modversions.h: no such file or directory'

The `modversions.h` file is created when the kernel is compiled with the configuration item `CONFIG_MODVERSIONS` turned on. With this option enabled, the file will be created during the `make dep` step.

One more handy tip is that a `make mrproper` will remove `/usr/include/linux/modversions.h`. You will need to reconfig the kernel and do a `make dep` to get the file back.

9.18 How does 'mt eom' work when you've started overwriting a tape in the middle?

(EOM is "End Of recorded Media", the position right after all data already recorded to the tape)

One cannot use tape "files" like files on an ordinary file system.

In principle, a tape doesn't allow anything but appending new data at EOM. However, if one positiones just in the middle of the already recorded data AND starts writing, then the driver first deletes all following files (thus moving the EOM to the actual position) and then starts writing.

Thus, the new EOM after finishing the write process, is then after the newly recorded data.

One of the consequences of the above is, of course, that writing to the tape in the middle of the already recorded area, is destructive in the sense, that it not only overwrites the "file" the tape is positioned at, but also deletes all following files.

9.19   Help! I'm getting 'dmaalloc() failed' in my syslog file.

You should only see this is you are trying to insmod the `ftape.o` module. Try running `swapout` first. It is provided with the standalone `ftape` source. It doesn't appear in the `ftape` source that's provided with the kernel.

Here's an example of how you can set your rc.local file to use it.

```
# Install the Floppy Tape Driver
if [ -f /boot/modules/'uname -r'/misc/ftape.o ]; then
    echo Installing ftape for Linux 'uname -r'
    swapout
    insmod /boot/modules/'uname -r'/misc/ftape.o
fi
```

Please note that you won't have this type of problem if you compile the `ftape` driver into the kernel.

9.20   Is it ok that I'm not hearing the tape move when I do a fsf or a bsf with mt?

Yes. The driver merely updates an internal counter when those commands are issues. The tape should move to the proper location on the next read or write access to the tape drive.

10   Debugging the `ftape` driver

10.1   The kernel/`ftape` crashes on me when I do '...' - is that a bug?

No, that is a feature ;-)

Seriously, reliable software do not crash. Especially kernels do not or rather **should** not crash. If the kernel crashes upon you when you are running `ftape`, and you can show that it is `ftape` that is messing things up, regard it as a Bug That Should Be Fixed. Mail the details to the maintainer (<kjj@pobox.com>) and to the tape list.

10.2   OK, it's a bug ...ehhh... feature - How do I submit a report?

First, make sure you can reproduce the problem. Spurious errors are a pain in the ass, since they are just about impossible to hunt down :-/ This is a quick check list:

- Kernel version, and patches applied
- `ftape` version
- tape drive model / manufacturer
- Expansion bus type (EISA, ISA, PCI, or VL-bus)
- What you did to expose the problem
- What went wrong on your system.

- Do not delete the kernel and the `ftape.o` file. I might want you run try some patches out or run a different test on your system.

Increase the tracing level to 7 (just below maximum tracing) and run the offending command again. Get the tracing data from the kernel log or `/proc/kmsg`, depending on where you harvest your error messages. Try to look at what `ftape` spews out at you. It may look in-comprehensible to you at first, but you can get valuable information from the logfile. Most messages have a function name prepended, to make it easier to locate the problem. Look through the source, don't just cry "WOLF!", without giving it a try. If your version of the kernel (or `ftape` for that matter), is "old", when compared to the newest version of the kernel, try to get a newer (or even the newest) kernel and see if the problem goes away under the new kernel. When you post your problem report, include the information about ftape version, kernel version, expansion bus type (ISA, VL-bus, PCI or EISA), bus speed, floppy controller, and tape drive. State exactly what you did, and what happened on your system. Some people have experienced that `ftape` would not run in a PCI based box, but ran flawlessly in a normal ISA based 386DX machine (see section 6.5 (Getting PCI motherboards to work with <tt/ftape/) on PCI machines above)

Also, please think of the poor souls who actually *pay* the their Internet access (like me): avoid posting a (huge) log from the `ftape` run, without reason. Instead, you could describe the problem, and offer to send the log to the interested parties.

Send your bug report to <linux-tape@vger.rutgers.edu>. You might also want to mail the bug to <claus@momo.math.rwth-aachen.de>.

11   Contributions

The following is a list of notable folks that have contributed to `ftape` and it's HOWTO document. This is a recent addition added by someone coming in midstream. My sincerest apologies if I've inadvertently left someone important off the list.

Kai Harrekilde-Petersen <khp@dolphinics.no>: The previous maintainer of `ftape` and the HOWTO.

Andrew Martin <martin@biochemistry.ucl.ac.uk>: Many additions to the HOWTO.

Bas Laarhoven <bas@vimec.nl>: The original author of `ftape`.

The Linux SCSI HOWTO

Drew Eckhardt,<drew@PoohSticks.ORG> (transformed to linuxdoc-sgml format by Dieter Faulbaum), <faulbaum@bii.bessy.de>

v2.30, 30 August 1996

Contents

1   Introduction

This documentation is free documentation; you can redistribute it and/or modify it under the terms of the GNU General Public License as published by the Free Software Foundation; either version 2 of the License, or (at your option) any later version.

This documentation is distributed in the hope that it will be useful, but WITHOUT ANY WARRANTY; without even the implied warranty of MERCHANTABILITY or FITNESS FOR A PARTICULAR PUR-POSE. See the GNU General Public License for more details.

You should have received a copy of the GNU General Public License along with this documentation; if not, write to the Free Software Foundation, Inc., 675 Mass Ave, Cambridge, MA 02139, USA.

That said, I'd appreciate it if people would ask me <drew@PoohSticks.ORG> if there's a newer version available before they publish it. When people publish outdated versions, I get questions from users that are answered in newer versions, and it reflects poorly on the publisher. I'd also prefer that all references to free distribution sites, and possibly competing distributions/products be left intact.

IMPORTANT :

BUG REPORTS OR OTHER REQUESTS FOR HELP WHICH FAIL TO FOLLOW THE PROCEDURES OUTLINED IN THE 3 (REPORTING BUGS) SECTION WILL BE IGNORED.

This HOWTO covers the Linux SCSI subsystem, as implemented in Linux kernel revision 1.2.10 and newer alpha code. Earlier revisions of the SCSI code are _unsupported_, and may differ significantly in terms of the drivers implemented, performance, and options available.

For additional information, you may wish to join the linux-scsi mailing list by mailing major-domo@vger.rutgers.edu with the line

    subscribe linux-scsi

in the text. You can unsubscribe by sending mail to the same address and including

    unsubscribe linux-scsi

in the text.

Once you're subscribed, you can send mail to the list at

    linux-scsi@vger.rutgers.edu

I'm aware that this document isn't the most user-friendly, and that there may be inaccuracies and oversights. If you have constructive comments on how to rectify the situation you're free to mail me about it.

2   Common Problems

This section lists some of the common problems that people have. If there is not anything here that answers your questions, you should also consult the sections for your host adapter and the devices in that are giving you problems.

2.1   General Flakiness

If you experience random errors, the most likely causes are cabling and termination problems.

Some products, such as those built around the newer NCR chips, feature digital filtering and active signal negation, and aren't very sensitive to cabling problems.

Others, such as the Adaptec 154xC, 154xCF, and 274x, are _extremely_ sensitive and may fail with cables that work with other systems.

I reiterate : some host adapters are _extremely_ sensitive to cabling and termination problems and therefore, cabling and termination should be the first things checked when there are problems.

To minimize your problems, you should use cables which

1. Claim SCSI-II compliance
2. Have a characteristic impedance of 132 ohms
3. All come from the same source to avoid impedance mismatches
4. Come from a reputable vendor such as Amphenol

Termination power should be provided by _all_ devices on the SCSI bus, through a diode to prevent current backflow, so that sufficient power is available at the ends of the cable where it is needed. To prevent damage if the bus is shorted, TERMPWR should be driven through a fuse or other current limiting device.

If multiple devices, external cables, or FAST SCSI 2 are used, active or forced perfect termination should be used on both ends of the SCSI bus.

See the Comp.Periphs.Scsi FAQ (available on tsx-11 in pub/linux/ALPHA/scsi) for more information about active termination.

2.2   The kernel command line

Other parts of the documentation refer to a "kernel command line".

The kernel command line is a set of options you may specify from either the LILO : prompt after an image name, or in the append field in your LILO configuration file (LILO .14 and newer use /etc/lilo.conf, older versions use /etc/lilo/config).

Boot your system with LILO, and hit one of the alt, control, or shift keys when it first comes up to get a prompt. LILO should respond with

        :

At this prompt, you can select a kernel image to boot, or list them with ?. Ie

    :?

    ramdisk floppy harddisk

To boot that kernel with the command line options you have selected, simply enter the name followed by a white space delimited list of options, terminating with a return.

Options take the form of

```
variable=valuelist
```

Where valuelist may be a single value or comma delimited list of values with no whitespace. With the exception of root device, individual values are numbers, and may be specified in either decimal or hexadecimal.

Ie, to boot linux with an Adaptec 1520 clone not recognized at bootup, you might type

```
:floppy aha152x=0x340,11,7,1
```

If you don't care to type all of this at boot time, it is also possible to use the LILO configuration file "append" option with LILO .13 and newer.

Ie,

```
append="aha152x=0x340,11,7,1"
```

2.3   A SCSI device shows up at all possible IDs

If this is the case, you have strapped the device at the same address as the controller (typically 7, although some boards use other addresses, with 6 being used by some Future Domain boards).

Please change the jumper settings.

2.4   A SCSI device shows up at all possible LUNs

The device has buggy firmware.

As an interim solution, you should try using the kernel command line option

```
max_scsi_luns=1
```

If that works, there is a list of buggy devices in the kernel sources in drivers/scsi/scsi.c in the variable blacklist. Add your device to this list and mail the patch to Linus Torvalds <Linus.Torvalds@cs.Helsinki.FI>.

2.5   You get sense errors when you know the devices are error free

Sometimes this is caused by bad cables or improper termination.

See section 2.1 (General Flakiness)

2.6   A kernel configured with networking does not work

The auto-probe routines for many of the network drivers are not passive, and will interfere with operation with some of the SCSI drivers.

2.7   Device detected, but unable to access

A SCSI device is detected by the kernel, but you are unable to access it - ie mkfs /dev/sdc, tar xvf /dev/rst2, etc fails.

You don't have a special file in /dev for the device.

Unix devices are identified as either block or character (block devices go through the buffer cache, character devices do not) devices, a major number (ie which driver is used - block major 8 corresponds to SCSI disks) and a minor number (ie which unit is being accessed through a given driver - ie character major 4, minor 0 is the first virtual console, minor 1 the next, etc). However, accessing devices through this separate namespace would break the unix/Linux metaphor of "everything is a file," so character and block device special files are created under /dev. This lets you access the raw third SCSI disk device as /dev/sdc, the first serial port as /dev/ttyS0, etc.

The preferred method for creating a file is using the MAKEDEV script - cd /dev

and run MAKEDEV (as root) for the devices you want to create - ie

```
./MAKEDEV sdc
```

wildcards "should" work - ie

```
./MAKEDEV sd\*
```

"should" create entries for all SCSI disk devices (doing this should create /dev/sda through /dev/sdp, with fifteen partition entries for each)

```
./MAKEDEV sdc\*
```

"should" create entries for /dev/sdc and all fifteen permissible partitions on /dev/sdc, etc.

I say "should" because this is the standard unix behavior - the MAKEDEV script in your installation may not conform to this behavior, or may have restricted the number of devices it will create.

If MAKEDEV won't do the right magic for you, you'll have to create the device entries by hand with the mknod command.

The block/character type, major, and minor numbers are specified for the various SCSI devices in section 6.3 (Device Files) in the appropriate section.

Take those numbers, and use (as root)

```
mknod /dev/device b|c major minor
```

ie -

```
mknod /dev/sdc b 8 32
mknod /dev/rst0 c 9 0
```

2.8   SCSI System Lockups

This could be one of a number of things. Also see the section for your specific host adapter for possible further solutions.

There are cases where the lockups seem to occur when multiple devices are in use at the same time. In this case, you can try contacting the manufacturer of the devices and see if firmware upgrades are available which would correct the problem. If possible, try a different scsi cable, or try on another system. This can also be caused by bad blocks on disks, or by bad handling of DMA by the motherboard (for host adapters that do DMA). There are probably many other possible conditions that could lead to this type of event.

Sometimes these problems occur when there are multiple devices in use on the bus at the same time. In this case, if your host adapter driver supports more than one outstanding command on the bus at one time, try reducing this to 1 and see if this helps. If you have tape drives or slow cdrom drives on the bus, this might not be a practical solution.

2.9   Configuring and building the kernel

Unused SCSI drivers eat up valuable memory, aggravating memory shortage problems on small systems because kernel memory is unpagable.

So, you will want to build a kernel tuned for your system, with only the drivers you need installed.

```
cd to /usr/src/linux
```

If you are using a root device other than the current one, or something other than 80x25 VGA, and you are writing a boot floppy, you should edit the makefile, and make sure the

```
ROOT_DEV =
```

and

```
SVGA_MODE =
```

lines are the way you want them.

If you've installed any patches, you may wish to guarantee that all files are rebuilt. If this is the case, you should type

```
make mrproper
```

Irregardless of weather you ran make mrproper, type

```
make config
```

and answer the configuration questions. Then run

```
make depend
```

and finally

```
make
```

Once the build completes, you may wish to update the lilo configuration, or write a boot floppy. A boot floppy may be made by running

```
make zdisk
```

2.10   LUNS other than 0 don't work

Many SCSI devices are horrendously broken, lock the SCSI bus up solid, and do other bad things when you attempt to talk to them at a logical unit someplace other than zero.

So, by default recent versions of the Linux kernel will not probe luns other than 0. To work around this, you need to the max_scsi_luns command line option, or recompile the kernel with the CONFIG_SCSI_MULTI_LUN option.

Usually, you'll put

```
max_scsi_luns=8
```

on your LILO command line.

If your multi-LUN devices still aren't detected correctly after trying one of these fixes (as the case will be with many old SCSI->MFM, RLL, ESDI, SMD, and similar bridge boards), you'll be thwarted by this piece of code

```
/* Some scsi-1 peripherals do not handle lun != 0.
   I am assuming that scsi-2 peripherals do better */
if((scsi_result[2] & 0x07) == 1 &&
   (scsi_result[3] & 0x0f) == 0) break;
```

in scan_scsis() in drivers/scsi/scsi.c. Delete this code, and you should be fine.

3   Reporting Bugs

The Linux SCSI developers don't necessarily maintain old revisions of the code due to space constraints. So, if you are not running the latest publically released Linux kernel (note that many of the Linux distributions, such as MCC, SLS, Yggdrasil, etc. often lag one or even twenty patches behind this) chances are we will be unable to solve your problem. So, before reporting a bug, please check to see if it exists with the latest publically available kernel.

If after upgrading, and reading this document thoroughly, you still believe that you have a bug, please mail a bug report to the SCSI channel of the mailing list where it will be seen by many of the people who've contributed to the Linux SCSI drivers.

In your bug report, please provide as much information as possible regarding your hardware configuration, the exact text of

all of the messages that Linux prints when it boots, when the error condition occurs, and where in the source code the error is. Use the procedures outlined in 3.1 (Capturing messages) and 3.2 (Locating the source of a panic()).

Failure to provide the maximum possible amount of information may result in misdiagnosis of your problem, or developers deciding that there are other more interesting problems to fix.

The bottom line is that if we can't reproduce your bug, and you can't point at us what's broken, it won't get fixed.

3.1   Capturing messages

If you are not running a kernel message logging system :

Insure that the /proc filesystem is mounted.

```
grep proc /etc/mtab
```

If the /proc filesystem is not mounted, mount it

```
mkdir /proc
chmod 755 /proc
mount -t proc /proc /proc
```

Copy the kernel revision and messages into a log file

```
cat /proc/version > /tmp/log
cat /proc/kmsg >> /tmp/log
```

Type CNTRL-C after a second or two.

If you are running some logger, you'll have to poke through the appropriate log files (/etc/syslog.conf should be of some use in locating them), or use dmesg.

If Linux is not yet bootstrapped, format a floppy diskette under DOS. Note that if you have a distribution which mounts the root diskette off of floppy rather than RAM drive, you'll have to format a diskette readable in the drive not being used to mount root or use their ramdisk boot option.

Boot Linux off your distribution boot floppy, preferably in single user mode using a RAM disk as root.

```
mkdir /tmp/dos
```

Insert the diskette in a drive not being used to mount root, and mount it. Ie

```
mount -t msdos /dev/fd0 /tmp/dos
```

or

```
mount -t msdos /dev/fd1 /tmp/dos
```

Copy your log to it

```
cp /tmp/log /tmp/dos/log
```

Unmount the DOS floppy

```
umount /tmp/dos
```

And shutdown Linux

```
shutdown
```

Reboot into DOS, and using your favorite communications software include the log file in your trouble mail.

3.2   Locating the source of a panic()

Like other unices, when a fatal error is encountered, Linux calls the kernel panic() function. Unlike other unices, Linux doesn't dump core to the swap or dump device and reboot automatically. Instead, a useful summary of state information is printed for the user to manually copy down. Ie :

```
Unable to handle kernel NULL pointer dereference at virtual address c0000004
current->tss,cr3 = 00101000, %cr3 = 00101000
*pde = 00102027
*pte = 00000027
Oops: 0000
EIP:     0010:0019c905
EFLAGS: 00010002
eax: 0000000a   ebx: 001cd0e8   ecx: 00000006   edx: 000003d5
esi: 001cd0a8   edi: 00000000   ebp: 00000000   esp: 001a18c0
ds: 0018   es: 0018   fs: 002b   gs: 002b   ss: 0018
Process swapper (pid: 0, process nr: 0, stackpage=001a09c8)
Stack: 0019c5c6 00000000 0019c5b2 00000000 0019c5a5 001cd0a8 00000002 00000000
       001cd0e8 001cd0a8 00000000 001cdb38 001cdb00 00000000 001ce284 0019d001
       001cd004 0000e800 fbfff000 0019d051 001cd0a8 00000000 001a29f4 00800000
Call Trace: 0019c5c6 0019c5b2 0018c5a5 0019d001 0019d051 00111508 00111502
            0011e800 0011154d 00110f63 0010e2b3 0010ef55 0010ddb7
Code: 8b 57 04 52 68 d2 c5 19 00 e8 cd a0 f7 ff 83 c4 20 8b 4f 04
Aiee, killing interrupt handler
kfree of non-kmalloced memory: 001a29c0, next= 00000000, order=0
task[0] (swapper) killed: unable to recover
Kernel panic: Trying to free up swapper memory space
In swapper task - not syncing
```

Take the hexadecimal number on the EIP: line, in this case 19c905, and search through /usr/src/linux/zSystem.map for the highest number not larger than that address. Ie,

```
0019a000 T _fix_pointers
0019c700 t _intr_scsi
0019d000 t _NCR53c7x0_intr
```

That tells you what function its in. Recompile the source file which defines that function file with debugging enabled, or the whole kernel if you prefer by editing /usr/src/linux/Makefile and adding a "-g" to the CFLAGS definition.

```
#
# standard CFLAGS
#
```

Ie,

```
CFLAGS = -Wall -Wstrict-prototypes -O2 -fomit-frame-pointer -pipe
```

becomes

```
CFLAGS = -g -Wall -Wstrict-prototypes -O2 -fomit-frame-pointer -pipe
```

Rebuild the kernel, incrementally or by doing a

```
make clean
make
```

Make the kernel bootable by creating an entry in your /etc/lilo.conf for it

```
image = /usr/src/linux/zImage
label = experimental
```

and re-running LILO as root, or by creating a boot floppy

```
make zImage
```

Reboot and record the new EIP for the error.

If you have script installed, you may want to start it, as it will log your debugging session to the typescript file.

Now, run

```
gdb /usr/src/linux/tools/zSystem
```

and enter

```
info line *<your EIP>
```

Ie,

```
info line *0x19c905
```

To which GDB will respond something like

```
(gdb) info line *0x19c905
Line 2855 of "53c7,8xx.c" starts at address 0x19c905 <intr_scsi+641&>
    and ends at 0x19c913 <intr_scsi+655>.
```

Record this information. Then, enter

```
list <line number>
```

Ie,

```
(gdb) list 2855
2850    /*      printk("scsi%d : target %d lun %d unexpected disconnect\n",
2851            host->host_no, cmd->cmd->target, cmd->cmd->lun); */
2852            printk("host : 0x%x\n", (unsigned) host);
2853            printk("host->host_no : %d\n", host->host_no);
```

```
2854            printk("cmd : 0x%x\n", (unsigned) cmd);
2855            printk("cmd->cmd : 0x%x\n", (unsigned) cmd->cmd);
2856            printk("cmd->cmd->target : %d\n", cmd->cmd->target);
2857            if (cmd) {;
2858                abnormal_finished(cmd, DID_ERROR << 16);
2859            }
2860            hostdata->dsp = hostdata->script + hostdata->E_schedule /
2861                sizeof(long);
2862            hostdata->dsp_changed = 1;
2863    /* SCSI PARITY error */
2864    }
2865
2866    if (sstat0_sist0 & SSTAT0_PAR) {
2867        fatal = 1;
2868        if (cmd && cmd->cmd) {
2869            printk("scsi%d : target %d lun %d parity error.\n",
```

Obviously, quit will take you out of GDB.

Record this information too, as it will provide a context in case the developers' kernels differ from yours.

4   Modules

This section gives specific details regarding the support for loadable kernel modules and how it relates to SCSI.

4.1   General Information

Loadable modules are a means by which the user or system administrator can load files into the kernel's memory in such a way that the kernel's capabilities are expanded. The most common usages of modules are for drivers to support hardware, or to load filesytems.

There are several advantages of modules for SCSI. One is that a system administrator trying to maintain a large number of machines can use a single kernel image for all of the machines, and then load kernel modules to support hardware that is only present on some machines.

It is also possible for someone trying to create a distribution to use a script on the bootable floppy to query for which modules to be loaded. This saves memory that would otherwise be wasted on unused drivers, and it would also reduce the possibility that a probe for a non-existent card would screw up some other card on the system.

Modules also work out nicely on laptops, which tend to have less memory than desktop machines, and people tend to want to keep the kernel image as small as possible and load modules as required. Also, modules makes supporting PCMCIA SCSI cards on laptops somewhat easier, since you can load and unload the driver as the card is inserted/removed. [Note: currently the qlogic and 152x drivers support PCMCIA].

Finally, there is the advantage that kernel developers can more easily debug and test their drivers, since testing a new driver does not require rebooting the machine (provided of course that the machine has not completely crashed as a result of some bug in the driver).

Although modules are very nice, there is one limitation. If your root disk partition is on a scsi device, you will not be able to use modularized versions of scsi code required to access the disk. This is because the system must be able to mount the root partition before it can load any modules from disk. There are people thinking about ways of fixing the loader and the kernel so that the kernel can self-load modules prior to attempting to mount the root filesystem, so at some point in the future this limitation may be lifted.

4.2   Module support in the 1.2.N kernel

In the 1.2.N series of kernels, there is partial support for SCSI kernel modules. While none of the high level drivers (such as disk, tape, etc) can be used as modules, most of the low level drivers (i.e. 1542, 1522) can be loaded and unloaded as required. Each time you load a low-level driver, the driver first searches for cards that can be driven. Next, the bus is scanned for each card that is found, and then the internal data structures are set up so as to make it possible to actually use the devices attached to the cards that the driver is managing.

When you are through with a low-level driver, you can unload it. You should keep in mind that usage counts are maintained based upon mounted filesystems, open files, etc, so that if you are still using a device that the driver is managing, the rmmod utility will tell you that the device is still busy and refuse to unload the driver. When the driver is unloaded, all of the associated data structures are also freed so that the system state should be back to where it was before the module was loaded. This means that the driver could be reloaded at a later time if required.

4.3   Module support in the 1.3.N kernel

In the 1.3 series of kernels, the scsi code is completely modularized. This means that you can start with a kernel that has no scsi support whatsoever, and start loading modules and you will eventually end up with complete support.

If you wish, you can compile some parts of the SCSI code into the kernel and then load other parts later - it is all up to you how much gets loaded at runtime and how much is linked directly into the kernel.

If you are starting with a kernel that has no support whatsoever for SCSI, then the first thing you will need to do is to load the scsi core into the kernel - this is in a module called "scsi_mod". You will not be able to load any other scsi modules until you have this loaded into kernel memory. Since this does not contain any low-level drivers, the act of loading this module will not scan any busses, nor will it activate any drivers for scsi disks, tapes, etc. If you answered 'Y' to the CONFIG_SCSI question when you built your kernel, you will not need to load this module.

At this point you can add modules in more or less any order to achieve the desired functionality. Usage counts are interlocks are used to prevent unloading of any component which might still be in use, and you will get a message from rmmod if a module is still busy.

The high level drivers are in modules named "sd_mod", "sr_mod", "st", and "sg", for disk, cdrom, tape, and scsi generics support respectively. When you load a high level driver, the device list for all attached hosts is examined for devices which the high level driver can drive, and these are automatically activated.

The use of modules with low level drivers were described in the section of the 4.2 (modules under 1.2 kernels). When a low-level driver is loaded, the bus is scanned, and each device is examined by each of the high level drivers to see if they recognize it as something that they can drive - anything recognized is automatically attached and activated.

5 Hosts

This section gives specific information about the various host adapters that are supported in some way or another under linux.

5.1 Supported and Unsupported Hardware

Drivers in the distribution kernel :

Adaptec 152x, Adaptec 154x (DTC 329x boards usually work, but are unsupported), Adaptec 174x, Adaptec 274x/284x (294x support requires a newer version of the driver), BusLogic MultiMaster Host Adapters, EATA-DMA and EATA-PIO protocol compilant boards (DPT PM2001, PM2011, PM2012A, PM2012B, PM2021, PM2022, PM2024, PM2122, PM2124, PM2322, PM2041, PM2042, PM2044, PM2142, PM2144, PM2322, PM3021, PM3122, PM3222, PM3224, PM3334 some boards from NEC, AT&T, SNI, AST, Olivetti, and Alphatronix), Future Domain 850, 885, 950, and other boards in that series (but not the 840, 841, 880, and 881 boards unless you make the appropriate patch), Future Domain 16x0 with TMC-1800, TMC-18C30, or TMC-18C50 chips, NCR53c8xx,PAS16 SCSI ports, Seagate ST0x, Trantor T128/T130/T228 boards, Ultrastor 14F, 24F, and 34F, and Western Digital 7000.

MCA :

MCA boards which are compatible with a supported board (ie, Adaptec 1640 and BusLogic 640) will work.

Alpha drivers :

Many ALPHA drivers are available at

        ftp://tsx-11.mit.edu/pub/linux/ALPHA/scsi

Drivers which will work with modifications
NCR53c8x0/7x0:

        A NCR53c8xx driver has been developed, but currently will not work
    with NCR53c700, NCR53c700-66, NCR53c710, and NCR53c720 chips. A list
    of changes needed to make each of these chips work follows, as well
    as a summary of the complexity.

    NCR53c720 (trivial) - detection changes, initialization changes, change
        fixup code to translate '810 register addresses to
        '7xx mapping.

    NCR53c710 (trivial) - detection changes, initialization changes,
        of assembler, change fixup code to translate '810 register
        addresses to '7xx mapping, change interrupt handlers to treat
        IID interrupt from INTFLY instruction to emulate it.

    NCR53c700, NCR53c700-66 (very messy) - detection changes,
        initialization changes, modification of NCR code to not use DSA,
        modification of Linux code to handle context switches.

SCSI hosts that will not work :

All parallel->SCSI adapters, Rancho SCSI boards, and Grass Roots SCSI boards. BusLogic FlashPoint boards, such as the BT-930/932/950, are currently unsupported.

SCSI hosts that will NEVER work :

Non Adaptec compatible, non NCR53c8xx DTC boards (including the 3270 and 3280).

CMD SCSI boards.

Acquiring programming information requires a non-disclosure agreement with DTC/CMD. This means that it would be impossible to distribute a Linux driver if one were written, since complying with the NDA would mean distributing no source, in violation of the GPL, and complying with the GPL would mean distributing source, in violation of the NDA.

If you want to run Linux on some other unsupported piece of hardware, your options are to either write a driver yourself (Eric Youngdale and I are usually willing to answer technical questions concerning the Linux SCSI drivers) or to commission a driver (Normal consulting rates mean that this will not be a viable option for personal use).

5.1.1   Multiple host adapters

With some host adapters (see 10.7 (Buyers' Guide : Feature Comparison)), you can use multiple host adapters of the same type in the same system. With multiple adapters of the same type in the same system, generally the one at the lowest address will be scsi0, the one at the next address scsi1, etc.

In all cases, it is possible to use multiple host adapters of different types, provided that none of their addresses conflict. SCSI controllers are scanned in the order specified in the builtin_scsi_hosts[] array in drivers/scsi/hosts.c, with the order currently being

> BusLogic, Ultrastor 14/34F, Ultrastor 14F,, Adaptec 151x/152x, Adaptec 154x, Adaptec 174x, AIC7XXX, AM53C974, Future Domain 16x0, Always IN2000, Generic NCR5380, QLOGIC, PAS16, Seagate, Trantor T128/T130, NCR53c8xx, EATA-DMA, WD7000, debugging driver.

In most cases (ie, you aren't trying to use both BusLogic and Adaptec drivers), this can be changed to suit your needs (ie, keeping the same devices when new SCSI devices are added to the system on a new controller) by moving the individual entries.

5.2   Common Problems

5.2.1   SCSI timeouts

Make sure interrupts are enabled correctly, and there are no IRQ, DMA, or address conflicts with other boards.

5.2.2   Failure of autoprobe routines on boards that rely on BIOS for autoprobe.

If your SCSI adapter is one of the following :

> Adaptec 152x, Adaptec 151x, Adaptec AIC-6260, Adaptec AIC-6360, Future Domain 1680, Future Domain TMC-950, Future Domain TMC-8xx, Trantor T128, Trantor T128F, Trantor T228F, Seagate ST01, Seagate ST02, or a Western Digital 7000

and it is not detected on bootup, ie you get a

```
scsi : 0 hosts
```

message or a

```
    scsi%d : type
```

message is not printed for each supported SCSI adapter installed in the system, you may have a problem
with the autoprobe routine not knowing about your board.

Autodetection will fail for drivers using the BIOS for autodetection if the BIOS is disabled. Double check
that your BIOS is enabled, and not conflicting with any other peripherial BIOSes.

Autodetection will also fail if the board's "signature" and/or BIOS address don't match known ones.

If the BIOS is installed, please use DOS and DEBUG to find a signature that will detect your board -

Ie, if your board lives at 0xc8000, under DOS do

```
    debug
    d c800:0
    q
```

and send a message to the SCSI channel of the mailing list with the ASCII message, with the length and
offset from the base address (ie, 0xc8000). Note that the EXACT text is required, and you should provide
both the hex and ASCII portions of the text.

If no BIOS is installed, and you are using an Adaptec 152x, Trantor T128, or Seagate driver, you can use
command line or compile time overrides to force detection.

Please consult the appropriate subsection for your SCSI board as well as section 2.1 (General Flakiness).

5.2.3   Failure of boards using memory mapped I/O

(This include the Trantor T128 and Seagate boards, but not the Adaptec, Generic NCR5380, PAS16, and
Ultrastor drivers)

This is often caused when the memory mapped I/O ports are incorrectly cached. You should have the
board's address space marked as uncachable in the XCMOS settings.

If this is not possible, you will have to disable cache entirely.

If you have manually specified the address of the board, remember that Linux needs the actual address of
the board, and not the 16 byte segment the documentation may refer to.

Ie, 0xc8000 would be correct, 0xc800 would not work and could cause memory corruption.

5.2.4   "kernel panic : cannot mount root device" when booting an ALPHA driver
boot floppy

You'll need to edit the binary image of the kernel (before or after writing it out to disk), and modify a few
two byte fields (little endian) to guarantee that it will work on your system.

1. default swap device at offset 502, this should be set to 0x00 0x00

2. ram disk size at offset 504, this should be set to the size of the boot floppy in K - ie, 5.25" = 1200,
   3.5" = 1440.

```
      This means the bytes are

   3.5"  : 0xA0 0x05
   5.25" : 0xB0 0x04
```

3. root device offset at 508, this should be 0x00 0x00, ie the boot device.

dd or rawrite the file to a disk. Insert the disk in the first floppy drive, wait until it prompts you to insert the root disk, and insert the root floppy from your distribution.

5.2.5 Installing a device driver not included with the distribution kernel

You need to start with the version of the kernel used by the driver author. This revision may be alluded to in the documentation included with the driver.

Various recent kernel revisions can be found at

```
   nic.funet.fi:/pub/OS/Linux/PEOPLE/Linus
```

as linux-version.tar.gz

They are also mirrored at tsx-11.mit.edu and various other sites.

```
   cd to /usr/src.
```

Remove your old Linux sources, if you want to keep a backup copy of them

```
   mv linux linux-old
```

Untar the archive

```
   gunzip < linux-0.99.12.tar.gz | tar xvfp -
```

Apply the patches. The patches will be relative to some directory in the filesystem. By examining the output file lines in the patch file (grep for ^—), you can tell where this is - ie patches with these lines

```
   --- ./kernel/blk_drv/scsi/Makefile
```

```
   --- ./config.in Wed Sep  1 16:19:33 1993
```

would have the files relative to /usr/src/linux.

Untar the driver sources at an appropriate place - you can type

```
   tar tfv patches.tar
```

to get a listing, and move files as necessary (The SCSI driver files should live in /usr/src/linux/kernel/drivers/scsi)

Either cd to the directory they are relative to and type

```
   patch -p0 < patch_file
```

or tell patch to strip off leading path components. Ie, if the files started with

```
--- linux-new/kernel/blk_drv/scsi/Makefile
```

and you wanted to apply them while in /usr/src/linux, you could cd to /usr/src/linux and type

```
patch -p1 < patches
```

to strip off the "linux-new" component.

After you have applied the patches, look for any patch rejects, which will be the name of the rejected file with a # suffix appended.

```
find /usr/src/linux/ -name "*#" -print
```

If any of these exist, look at them. In some cases, the differences will be in RCS identifiers and will be harmless, in other cases, you'll have to manually apply important parts. Documentation on diff files and patch is beyond the scope of this document.

See also 2.9 (Configuring and building the kernel).

5.2.6   Installing a driver that has no patches

In some cases, a driver author may not offer patches with the .c and .h files which comprise his driver, or the patches may be against an older revision of the kernel and not go in cleanly.

1. Copy the .c and .h files into /usr/src/linux/drivers/scsi

2. Add the configuration option
   Edit /usr/src/linux/config.in, and add a line in the

   ```
   *
   * SCSI low-level drivers
   *
   ```

   section, add a boolean configuration variable for your driver. Ie,

   ```
   bool 'Always IN2000 SCSI support' CONFIG_SCSI_IN2000 y
   ```

3. Add the makefile entries
   Edit /usr/src/linux/drivers/scsi/Makefile, and add an entry like

   ```
   ifdef CONFIG_SCSI_IN2000
   SCSI_OBS := $(SCSI_OBJS) in2000.o
   SCSI_SRCS := $(SCSI_SRCS) in2000.c
   endif
   ```

   before the

   ```
   scsi.a: $(SCSI_OBJS)
   ```

   line in the makefile, where the .c file is the .c file you copied in, and the .o file is the basename of the .c file with a .o suffixed.

4. Add the entry points
   Edit /usr/src/linux/drivers/scsi/hosts.c, and add a #include for the header file, conditional on the CONFIG_SCSI preprocessor define you added to the configuration file. Ie, after

```
#ifdef CONFIG_SCSI_GENERIC_NCR5380
#include "g_NCR5380.h"
#endif
```

you might add

```
#ifdef CONFIG_SCSI_IN2000
#include "in2000.h"
#endif
```

You will also need to add the Scsi_Host_Template entry into the scsi_hosts[] array. Take a look into the .h file, and you should find a #define that looks something like this :

```
#define IN2000 {"Always IN2000", in2000_detect, \
     in2000_info, in2000_command,     \
     in2000_queuecommand,             \
     in2000_abort,                    \
     in2000_reset,                    \
     NULL,                            \
     in2000_biosparam,                \
     1, 7, IN2000_SG, 1, 0, 0}
```

the name of the preprocessor define, and add it into the scsi_hosts[] array, conditional on definition of the preprocessor symbol you used in the configuration file.
Ie, after

```
#ifdef CONFIG_SCSI_GENERIC_NCR5380
        GENERIC_NCR5380,
#endif
```

you might add

```
#ifdef CONFIG_SCSI_IN2000
        IN2000,
#endif
```

See also 2.9 (Configuring and building the kernel).

5.2.7   Failure of a PCI board in a Compaq System

A number of Compaq systems map the 32-bit BIOS extensions used to probe for PCI devices into memory which is inaccessible to the Linux kernel due to the memory layout. If Linux is unable to detect a supported PCI SCSI board, and the kernel tells you something like

```
pcibios_init: entry in high memory, unable to access
```

Grab

```
ftp://ftp.compaq.com/pub/softpaq/Software-Solutions/sp0921.zip
```

which is a self-extracting archive of a program which will relocate the BIOS32 code.

5.2.8 A SCSI system with PCI boards hangs after the %d Hosts message

Some PCI systems have broken BIOSes which disable interrupts and fail to reenable them before returning control to the caller. The following patch fixes this

```
--- bios32.c.orig        Mon Nov 13 22:35:31 1995
+++ bios32.c     Thu Jan 18 00:15:09 1996
@@ -56,6 +56,7 @@
 #include <linux/pci.h>

 #include <asm/segment.h>
+#include <asm/system.h>

 #define PCIBIOS_PCI_FUNCTION_ID        0xb1XX
 #define PCIBIOS_PCI_BIOS_PRESENT       0xb101
@@ -125,7 +126,9 @@
        unsigned long address;          /* %ebx */
        unsigned long length;           /* %ecx */
        unsigned long entry;            /* %edx */
+       unsigned long flags;

+       save_flags(flags);
        __asm__("lcall (%%edi)"
                : "=a" (return_code),
                  "=b" (address),
@@ -134,6 +137,7 @@
                : "0" (service),
                  "1" (0),
                  "D" (&bios32_indirect));
+       restore_flags(flags);

        switch (return_code) {
                case 0:
@@ -161,11 +165,13 @@
        unsigned char present_status;
        unsigned char major_revision;
        unsigned char minor_revision;
+       unsigned long flags;
        int pack;

        if ((pcibios_entry = bios32_service(PCI_SERVICE))) {
                pci_indirect.address = pcibios_entry;

+               save_flags(flags);
                __asm__("lcall (%%edi)\n\t"
                        "jc 1f\n\t"
```

```
                                       "xor %%ah, %%ah\n"
@@ -176,6 +182,7 @@

                               : "1" (PCIBIOS_PCI_BIOS_PRESENT),
                                 "D" (&pci_indirect)
                               : "bx", "cx");
+               restore_flags(flags);

                   present_status = (pack >> 16) & 0xff;
                   major_revision = (pack >> 8) & 0xff;
@@ -210,7 +217,9 @@
 {
       unsigned long bx;
       unsigned long ret;
+       unsigned long flags;

+       save_flags(flags);
       __asm__ ("lcall (%%edi)\n\t"
               "jc 1f\n\t"
               "xor %%ah, %%ah\n"
@@ -221,6 +230,7 @@
                   "c" (class_code),
                   "S" ((int) index),
                   "D" (&pci_indirect));
+       restore_flags(flags);
       *bus = (bx >> 8) & 0xff;
       *device_fn = bx & 0xff;
       return (int) (ret & 0xff00) >> 8;
@@ -232,7 +242,9 @@
 {
       unsigned short bx;
       unsigned short ret;
+       unsigned long flags;

+       save_flags(flags);
       __asm__("lcall (%%edi)\n\t"
               "jc 1f\n\t"
               "xor %%ah, %%ah\n"
@@ -244,6 +256,7 @@
                   "d" (vendor),
                   "S" ((int) index),
                   "D" (&pci_indirect));
+       restore_flags(flags);
       *bus = (bx >> 8) & 0xff;
       *device_fn = bx & 0xff;
       return (int) (ret & 0xff00) >> 8;
```

```
@@ -254,7 +267,9 @@
 {
        unsigned long ret;
        unsigned long bx = (bus << 8) | device_fn;
+       unsigned long flags;

+       save_flags (flags);
        __asm__("lcall (%%esi)\n\t"
                "jc 1f\n\t"
                "xor %%ah, %%ah\n"
@@ -273,7 +288,9 @@
 {
        unsigned long ret;
        unsigned long bx = (bus << 8) | device_fn;
+       unsigned long flags;

+       save_flags(flags);
        __asm__("lcall (%%esi)\n\t"
                "jc 1f\n\t"
                "xor %%ah, %%ah\n"
@@ -292,7 +309,9 @@
 {
        unsigned long ret;
        unsigned long bx = (bus << 8) | device_fn;
+       unsigned long flags;

+       save_flags(flags);
        __asm__("lcall (%%esi)\n\t"
                "jc 1f\n\t"
                "xor %%ah, %%ah\n"
@@ -303,6 +322,7 @@
                  "b" (bx),
                  "D" ((long) where),
                  "S" (&pci_indirect));
+       restore_flags(flags);
        return (int) (ret & 0xff00) >> 8;
 }

@@ -311,7 +331,9 @@
 {
        unsigned long ret;
        unsigned long bx = (bus << 8) | device_fn;
+       unsigned long flags;

+       save_flags(flags);
```

```
            __asm__("lcall (%%esi)\n\t"
                    "jc 1f\n\t"
                    "xor %%ah, %%ah\n"
@@ -322,6 +344,7 @@
                      "b" (bx),
                      "D" ((long) where),
                      "S" (&pci_indirect));
+       restore_flags(flags);
        return (int) (ret & 0xff00) >> 8;
 }


@@ -330,7 +353,9 @@
 {
        unsigned long ret;
        unsigned long bx = (bus << 8) | device_fn;
+       unsigned long flags;

+       save_flags(flags);
        __asm__("lcall (%%esi)\n\t"
                "jc 1f\n\t"
                "xor %%ah, %%ah\n"
@@ -341,6 +366,7 @@
                      "b" (bx),
                      "D" ((long) where),
                      "S" (&pci_indirect));
+       restore_flags(flags);
        return (int) (ret & 0xff00) >> 8;
 }


@@ -349,7 +375,9 @@
 {
        unsigned long ret;
        unsigned long bx = (bus << 8) | device_fn;
+       unsigned long flags;

+       save_flags(flags);
        __asm__("lcall (%%esi)\n\t"
                "jc 1f\n\t"
                "xor %%ah, %%ah\n"
@@ -360,6 +388,7 @@
                      "b" (bx),
                      "D" ((long) where),
                      "S" (&pci_indirect));
+       restore_flags(flags);
        return (int) (ret & 0xff00) >> 8;
```

```
    }
```

5.3   Adaptec 152x, 151x, 1505, 282x, Sound Blaster 16 SCSI, SCSI Pro, Gigabyte, and other AIC 6260/6360 based products (Standard)

Supported Configurations :

```
    BIOS addresses : 0xd8000, 0xdc000, 0xd0000, 0xd4000, 0xc8000, 0xcc000, 0xe0000,
                     0xe4000.
    Ports          : 0x140, 0x340
    IRQs           : 9, 10, 11, 12
    DMA            : not used
    IO             : port mapped
```

Autoprobe :

```
    Works with many boards with an installed BIOS.  All
    other boards, including the Adaptec 1510, and Sound Blaster16 SCSI
    must use a kernel command line or compile time override.
```

Autoprobe Override :

Compile time :

```
    Define PORTBASE, IRQ, SCSI_ID, RECONNECT, PARITY as appropriate, see Defines
```

kernel command line :

```
    aha152x=<PORTBASE>[,<IRQ>[,<SCSI-ID>[,<RECONNECT>[,<PARITY>]]]]
```

SCSI-ID is the SCSI ID of the HOST adapter, not of any devices you have installed on it. Usually, this should be 7.

To force detection at 0x340, IRQ 11, at SCSI-ID 7, allowing disconnect/reconnect, you would use the following command line option :

```
    aha152x=0x340,11,7,1
```

Antiquity Problems, fix by upgrading :

1. The driver fails with VLB boards. There was a timing problem in kernels older than revision 1.0.5.

Defines :

```
    AUTOCONF      : use configuration the controller reports (only 152x)
    IRQ           : override interrupt channel (9,10,11 or 12) (default 11)
    SCSI_ID       : override SCSI ID of AIC-6260 (0-7) (default 7)
    RECONNECT     : override target disconnect/reselect (set to non-zero to
                    allow, zero to disable)
    DONT_SNARF    : Don't register ports (pl12 and below)
    SKIP_BIOSTEST : Don't test for BIOS signature (AHA-1510 or disabled BIOS)
    PORTBASE      : Force port base. Don't try to probe
```

5.4   Adaptec 154x, AMI FastDisk VLB, DTC 329x (Standard)

Supported Configurations :

```
Ports         : 0x330 and 0x334
IRQs          : 9, 10, 11, 12, 14, 15
DMA channels  : 5, 6, 7
IO            : port mapped, bus master
```

Autoprobe :

```
will detect boards at 0x330 and 0x334 only.
```

Autoprobe override :

```
aha1542=<PORTBASE>[,<BUSON>,<BUSOFF>[,<DMASPEED>]]
```

Notes:

1. BusLogic makes a series of boards that are software compatible with the Adaptec 1542, and these come in ISA, VLB, EISA, and PCI flavors.

2. No-suffix boards, and early 'A' suffix boards do not support scatter/gather, and thus don't work. However, they can be made to work for some definition of the word works if AHA1542_SCATTER is changed to 0 in drivers/scsi/aha1542.h.

Antiquity Problems, fix by upgrading :

1. Linux kernel revisions prior to .99.10 don't support the 'C' revision.

2. Linux kernel revisions prior to .99.14k don't support the 'C' revision options for

   - BIOS support for the extended mapping for disks > 1G
   - BIOS support for > 2 drives
   - BIOS support for autoscanning the SCSI bus

3. Linux kernel revisions prior to .99.15e don't support the 'C' with the BIOS support for > 2 drives turned on and the BIOS support for the extended mapping for disks > 1G turned off.

4. Linux kernel revisions prior to .99.14u don't support the 'CF' revisions of the board.

5. Linux kernel revisions prior to 1.0.5 have a race condition when multiple devices are accessed at the same time.

Common problems :

1. There are unexpected errors with a 154xC or 154xCF board,
   Early examples of the 154xC boards have a high slew rate on one of the SCSI signals, which results in signal reflections when cables with the wrong impedance are used. Newer boards aren't much better, and also suffer from extreme cabling and termination sensitivity.
   See also Common Problems 2 (#2) and 3 (#3) and 5.2 (Common Problems), 2.1 (General Flakiness).

2. There are unexpected errors with a 154xC or 154x with both internal and external devices connected.

   This is probably a termination problem. In order to use the software option to disable host adapter termination, you must turn switch 1 off.

   See also Common Problems 1 (#1) and 3 (#3) and 5.2 (Common Problems), 2.1 (General Flakiness).

3. The SCSI subsystem locks up completely.

   There are cases where the lockups seem to occur when multiple devices are in use at the same time. In this case, you can try contacting the manufacturer of the devices and see if firmware upgrades are available which would correct the problem. As a last resort, you can go into aha1542.h and change AHA1542_MAILBOX to 1. This will effectively limit you to one outstanding command on the scsi bus at one time, and may help the situation. If you have tape drives or slow cdrom drives on the bus, this might not be a practical solution.

   See also Common Problems 1 (#1) and 2 (#2) and 5.2 (Common Problems), 2.8 (Common Problems : SCSI System Lockups).

4. An "Interrupt received, but no mail" message is printed on bootup and your SCSI devices are not detected.

   Disable the BIOS options to support the extended mapping for disks > 1G, support for > 2 drives, and for autoscanning the bus. Or, upgrade to Linux .99.14k or newer.

5. If infinite timeout errors occur on 'C' revision boards, you may need to go into the Adaptec setup program and enable synchronous negotiation.

6. Linux 1.2.x gives the message

   Unable to determine Adaptec DMA priority. Disabling board.

   This is due to a conflict on some systems with the obsolete BusLogic driver. Either rebuild your kernel without it, or give the BusLogic driver a command line option telling it to look somewhere other than where your controller is configured. Ie, if you have an Adaptec board at port 0x334, and nothing at 0x330, use a command line option like

   ```
   buslogic=0x330
   ```

7. The system locks up with simultaneous access to multiple devices on a 1542C or 1540C and disconnection enabled

   Some Adaptec firmware revisions have bugs. Upgrading to BIOS v2.11 purportedly fixes these problems.

5.5   Adaptec 174x

Supported Configurations :

```
Slots         : 1-8
Ports         : EISA board, not applicable
IRQs          : 9, 10, 11, 12, 14, 15
DMA Channels  : EISA board, not applicable
IO            : port mapped, bus master
```

Autoprobe :

```
works with all supported configurations
```

Autoprobe override :

```
none
```

Note:

1. This board has been discontinued by Adaptec.

Common Problems :

1. If the Adaptec 1740 driver prints the message "aha1740: Board detected, but EBCNTRL = %x, so disabled it." your board was disabled because it was not running in enhanced mode. Boards running in standard 1542 mode are not supported.

5.6 Adaptec 274x, 284x (Standard) 294x (ALPHA)

A newer version which also supports the Adaptec 294x boards is available at

```
ftp://ftp.ims.com/pub/Linux/aic7xxx
```

Supported Configurations :

	274x	284x	294x
EISA Slots :	1-12	N/A	N/A
Ports :	N/A	ALL	ALL
IRQs :	ALL	ALL	ALL
DMA Channels :	N/A	ALL	N/A
IO	: port mapped, bus master		

Autoprobe Override :

kernel command line :

```
aha274x=extended
(to force extended mapping)
```

Notes:

1. BIOS MUST be enabled
2. The B channel on 2742AT boards is ignored.
3. CONFIG_PCI must be set if you are using a PCI board.

5.7 Always IN2000 (Standard)

Supported Configurations :

```
Ports    : 0x100, 0x110, 0x200, 0x220
IRQs     : 10, 11, 14, 15
DMA      : not used
IO       : port mapped
```

Autoprobe :

    `BIOS not required`

Autoprobe override :

    `none`

Common Problems :

    1. There are known problems in systems with IDE drives and with swapping.

5.8   BusLogic MultiMaster Host Adapters

(this section Copyright 1995 by Leonard N. Zubkoff <lnz@dandelion.com>) (see README.BusLogic for more complete BusLogic driver documentation)

```
              BusLogic MultiMaster SCSI Driver for Linux

                   Version 1.2.2 for Linux 1.2.13
                   Version 1.3.2 for Linux 1.3.88


              ftp://ftp.dandelion.com/BusLogic-1.2.2.tar.gz
              ftp://ftp.dandelion.com/BusLogic-1.3.2.tar.gz


                         16 April 1996


                    Leonard N. Zubkoff
                    Dandelion Digital
                    lnz@dandelion.com


BusLogic, Inc. designs and manufactures a variety of high performance SCSI host
adapters which share a common programming interface across a diverse collection
of bus architectures by virtue of their MultiMaster ASIC technology.  This
driver supports all present BusLogic MultiMaster Host Adapters, and should
support any future MultiMaster designs with little or no modification.  Host
adapters based on the new FlashPoint architecture are not supported by this
driver; consult the README.FlashPoint file for information about a program to
upgrade Linux users from the unsupported FlashPoint LT to the supported BT-948.

My primary goals in writing this completely new BusLogic driver for Linux are
to achieve the full performance that BusLogic SCSI Host Adapters and modern
SCSI peripherals are capable of, and to provide a highly robust driver that can
be depended upon for high performance mission critical applications.  All of
the major performance and error recovery features can be configured from the
Linux kernel command line, allowing individual installations to tune driver
performance and error recovery to their particular needs.

BusLogic has been an excellent company to work with and I highly recommend
their products to the Linux community.  In November 1995, I was offered the
opportunity to become a beta test site for their latest MultiMaster product,
the BT-948 PCI Ultra SCSI Host Adapter, and then again for the BT-958 PCI Wide
```

Ultra SCSI Host Adapter in January 1996. This was mutually beneficial since
BusLogic received a degree and kind of testing that their own testing group
cannot readily achieve, and the Linux community has available high performance
host adapters that have been well tested with Linux even before being brought
to market. This relationship has also given me the opportunity to interact
directly with their technical staff, to understand more about the internal
workings of their products, and in turn to educate them about the needs and
potential of the Linux community. Their interest and support is greatly
appreciated.

Unlike some other vendors, if you contact BusLogic Technical Support with a
problem and are running Linux, they will not tell you that your use of their
products is unsupported. Their latest product marketing literature even states
"BusLogic SCSI host adapters are compatible with all major operating systems
including: ... Linux ...".

BusLogic, Inc. is located at 4151 Burton Drive, Santa Clara, California, 95054,
USA and can be reached by Voice at 408/492-9090 or by FAX at 408/492-1542.
BusLogic maintains a World Wide Web site at http://www.buslogic.com, an
anonymous FTP site at ftp.buslogic.com, and a BBS at 408/492-1984. BusLogic
Technical Support can be reached by electronic mail at techsup@buslogic.com, by
Voice at 408/654-0760, or by FAX at 408/492-1542. Contact information for
offices in Europe and Japan is available on the Web site.

SUPPORTED HOST ADAPTERS

The following list comprises the supported BusLogic SCSI Host Adapters as of
the date of this document. It is recommended that anyone purchasing a BusLogic
Host Adapter not in the following table contact the author beforehand to verify
that it is or will be supported.

"W" Series Host Adapters:

```
BT-948      PCI     Ultra Fast Single-ended SCSI-2
BT-958      PCI     Ultra Wide Single-ended SCSI-2
BT-958D     PCI     Ultra Wide Differential SCSI-2
```

"C" Series Host Adapters:

```
BT-946C     PCI     Fast Single-ended SCSI-2
BT-956C     PCI     Fast Wide Single-ended SCSI-2
BT-956CD    PCI     Fast Wide Differential SCSI-2
BT-445C     VLB     Fast Single-ended SCSI-2
BT-747C     EISA    Fast Single-ended SCSI-2
BT-757C     EISA    Fast Wide Single-ended SCSI-2
BT-757CD    EISA    Fast Wide Differential SCSI-2
BT-545C     ISA     Fast Single-ended SCSI-2
BT-540CF    ISA     Fast Single-ended SCSI-2
```

"S" Series Host Adapters:

```
BT-445S     VLB     Fast Single-ended SCSI-2
BT-747S     EISA    Fast Single-ended SCSI-2
BT-747D     EISA    Fast Differential SCSI-2
```

```
BT-757S        EISA      Fast Wide Single-ended SCSI-2
BT-757D        EISA      Fast Wide Differential SCSI-2
BT-545S        ISA       Fast Single-ended SCSI-2
BT-542D        ISA       Fast Differential SCSI-2
BT-742A        EISA      Single-ended SCSI-2 (742A revision H)
BT-542B        ISA       Single-ended SCSI-2 (542B revision H)
```

"A" Series Host Adapters:

```
BT-742A        EISA      Single-ended SCSI-2 (742A revisions A - G)
BT-542B        ISA       Single-ended SCSI-2 (542B revisions A - G)
```

AMI FastDisk Host Adapters that are true BusLogic clones are supported by this
driver.

BT-948/958/958D INSTALLATION NOTES

The BT-948/958/958D PCI Ultra SCSI Host Adapters have some features which may
require attention in some circumstances when installing Linux.

o PCI I/O Port Assignments

  When configured to factory default settings, the BT-948/958/958D will only
  recognize the PCI I/O port assignments made by the motherboard's PCI BIOS.
  The BT-948/958/958D will not respond to any of the ISA compatible I/O ports
  that previous BusLogic SCSI Host Adapters respond to. This driver supports
  the PCI I/O port assignments, so this is the preferred configuration.
  However, if the obsolete BusLogic driver must be used for any reason, such as
  a Linux distribution that does not yet use this driver in its boot kernel,
  BusLogic has provided an AutoSCSI configuration option to enable a legacy ISA
  compatible I/O port.

  To enable this backward compatibility option, invoke the AutoSCSI utility via
  Ctrl-B at system startup and select "Adapter Configuration", "View/Modify
  Configuration", and then change the "ISA Compatible Port" setting from
  "Disable" to "Primary" or "Alternate". Once this driver has been installed,
  the "ISA Compatible Port" option should be set back to "Disable" to avoid
  possible future I/O port conflicts. The older BT-946C/956C/956CD also have
  this configuration option, but the factory default setting is "Primary".

o PCI Slot Scanning Order

  In systems with multiple BusLogic PCI Host Adapters, the order in which the
  PCI slots are scanned may appear reversed with the BT-948/958/958D as
  compared to the BT-946C/956C/956CD. For booting from a SCSI disk to work
  correctly, it is necessary that the host adapter's BIOS and the kernel agree
  on which disk is the boot device, which requires that they recognize the PCI
  host adapters in the same order. The motherboard's PCI BIOS provides a
  standard way of enumerating the PCI host adapters, which is used by the Linux
  kernel. Some PCI BIOS implementations enumerate the PCI slots in order of
  increasing bus number and device number, while others do so in the opposite
  direction.

  Unfortunately, Microsoft decided that Windows 95 would always enumerate the
```
```

PCI slots in order of increasing bus number and device number regardless of
the PCI BIOS enumeration, and requires that their scheme be supported by the
host adapter's BIOS to receive Windows 95 certification. Therefore, the
factory default settings of the BT-948/958/958D enumerate the host adapters
by increasing bus number and device number. To disable this feature, invoke
the AutoSCSI utility via Ctrl-B at system startup and select "Adapter
Configuration", "View/Modify Configuration", press Ctrl-F10, and then change
the "Use Bus And Device # For PCI Scanning Seq." option to OFF.

This driver will interrogate the setting of the PCI Scanning Sequence option
so as to recognize the host adapters in the same order as they are enumerated
by the host adapter's BIOS.

BUSLOGIC ANNOUNCEMENTS MAILING LIST

The BusLogic Announcements Mailing List provides a forum for informing Linux
users of new driver releases and other announcements regarding Linux support
for BusLogic SCSI Host Adapters. To join the mailing list, send a message to
"BusLogic-announce-request@dandelion.com" with the line "subscribe" in the
message body.

5.9   BusLogic FlashPoint Host Adapters

(this section Copyright 1995 by Leonard N. Zubkoff <lnz@dandelion.com>)

There are no Linux drivers for the FlashPoint LT/DL/LW (BT-930/932/950)
available and it is not clear when or if there will be any. The FlashPoint
boards have a different architecture from the MultiMaster boards and have no
onboard CPU, only a SCSI sequencer engine. They are positioned as a desktop
workstation product, and are not particularly well suited for a high
performance multitasking operating system like Linux.

The MultiMaster BT-948/958 have an onboard CPU and the mailbox programming
interface allows for parallelism and pipelining between the host operating
system and the host adapter, whereas the FlashPoint boards require frequent
host CPU intervention. As interrupt latencies rise in a loaded multitasking
system, the BT-948/958 should maintain excellent performance whereas the
FlashPoint's performance will likely drop quite rapidly. Furthermore, the
firmware on the BT-948/958 contains the low level knowledge for proper
interaction with the SCSI bus, whereas with a sequencer engine the Linux driver
must contain some or all of this information, and it often takes quite a long
time to get all the kinks worked out. Given the relatively small difference in
the street price of these products, the BT-948 or BT-958 is clearly the better
choice for Linux.

ANNOUNCEMENT
BusLogic FlashPoint/BT-948 Upgrade Program
1 February 1996

Ever since its introduction last October, the BusLogic FlashPoint LT has

been problematic for members of the Linux community, in that no Linux
drivers have been available for this new Ultra SCSI product. Despite it's
officially being positioned as a desktop workstation product, and not being
particularly well suited for a high performance multitasking operating
system like Linux, the FlashPoint LT has been touted by computer system
vendors as the latest thing, and has been sold even on many of their high
end systems, to the exclusion of the older MultiMaster products. This has
caused grief for many people who inadvertently purchased a system expecting
that all BusLogic SCSI Host Adapters were supported by Linux, only to
discover that the FlashPoint was not supported and would not be for quite
some time, if ever.

After this problem was identified, BusLogic contacted its major OEM
customers to make sure the BT-946C/956C MultiMaster cards would still be
made available, and that Linux users who mistakenly ordered systems with
the FlashPoint would be able to upgrade to the BT-946C. While this helped
many purchasers of new systems, it was only a partial solution to the
overall problem of FlashPoint support for Linux users. It did nothing to
assist the people who initially purchased a FlashPoint for a supported
operating system and then later decided to run Linux, or those who had
ended up with a FlashPoint LT, believing it was supported, and were unable
to return it.

In the middle of December, I asked to meet with BusLogic's senior
management to discuss the issues related to Linux and free software support
for the FlashPoint. Rumors of varying accuracy had been circulating
publicly about BusLogic's attitude toward the Linux community, and I felt
it was best that these issues be addressed directly. I sent an email
message after 11pm one evening, and the meeting took place the next
afternoon. Unfortunately, corporate wheels sometimes grind slowly,
especially when a company is being acquired, and so it's taken until now
before the details were completely determined and a public statement could
be made.

BusLogic is not prepared at this time to release the information necessary
for third parties to write drivers for the FlashPoint. The only existing
FlashPoint drivers have been written directly by BusLogic Engineering, and
there is no FlashPoint documentation sufficiently detailed to allow outside
developers to write a driver without substantial assistance. While there
are people at BusLogic who would rather not release the details of the
FlashPoint architecture at all, that debate has not yet been settled either
way. In any event, even if documentation were available today it would
take quite a while for a usable driver to be written, especially since I'm
not convinced that the effort required would be worthwhile.

However, BusLogic does remain committed to providing a high performance
SCSI solution for the Linux community, and does not want to see anyone left
unable to run Linux because they have a Flashpoint LT. Therefore, BusLogic
has put in place a direct upgrade program to allow any Linux user worldwide
to trade in their FlashPoint LT for the new BT-948 MultiMaster PCI Ultra
SCSI Host Adapter. The BT-948 is the Ultra SCSI successor to the BT-946C
and has all the best features of both the BT-946C and FlashPoint LT,
including smart termination and a flash PROM for easy firmware updates, and
is of course compatible with the present Linux driver. The price for this

upgrade has been set at US $45, and the upgrade program will be
administered through BusLogic Technical Support, which can be reached by
electronic mail at techsup@BusLogic.com, by Voice at +1 408 654-0760, or by
FAX at +1 408 492-1542.

I was a beta test site for the BT-948 and versions 1.2.1 and 1.3.1 of my
BusLogic driver already include latent support for the BT-948. Additional
cosmetic support for the Ultra SCSI MultiMaster cards will be added in a
subsequent release. As a result of this cooperative testing process,
several firmware bugs were found and corrected (make sure you have firmware
version 5.05R or later). My heavily loaded Linux test system provided an
ideal environment for testing error recovery processes that are much more
rarely exercised in production systems, but are crucial to overall system
stability. It was especially convenient being able to work directly with
their firmware engineer in demonstrating the problems under control of the
firmware debugging environment; things sure have come a long way since the
last time I worked on firmware for an embedded system. I am presently
working on some performance testing and expect to have some data to report
in the not too distant future.

BusLogic asked me to send this announcement since a large percentage of the
questions regarding support for the FlashPoint have either been sent to me
directly via email, or have appeared in the Linux newsgroups in which I
participate. To summarize, BusLogic is offering Linux users an upgrade
from the unsupported FlashPoint LT (BT-930) to the supported BT-948 for US
$45. Contact BusLogic Technical Support at techsup@BusLogic.com or +1 408
654-0760 to take advantage of their offer.

                    Leonard N. Zubkoff
                    lnz@dandelion.com

<end quotation>

5.10 EATA: DPT SmartCache, SmartCache Plus, SmartCache III, SmartCache IV and SmartRAID (Standard)

Supported boards: all, that support the EATA-DMA protocol.

Among them are:

```
DPT Smartcache (Plus) family:
PM2011     ISA      Fast Single-ended SCSI-2
PM2012B    EISA     Fast Single-ended SCSI-2

DPT Smartcache III family:
PM2021     ISA      Fast Single-ended SCSI-2
PM2021W    ISA      Wide Single-ended SCSI-2
PM2022     EISA     Fast Single-ended SCSI-2
PM2022W    EISA     Wide Single-ended SCSI-2
PM2024     PCI      Fast Single-ended SCSI-2
PM2024W    PCI      Wide Single-ended SCSI-2
PM2122     EISA     Fast Single-ended SCSI-2
```

```
PM2122W     EISA    Wide Single-ended SCSI-2
PM2124      PCI     Fast Single-ended SCSI-2
PM2124W     PCI     Wide Single-ended SCSI-2
PM2322      EISA    Fast Single-ended SCSI-2
PM2322W     EISA    Wide Single-ended SCSI-2

DPT Smartcache VI family:
PM2041W     ISA     Wide Single-ended SCSI-2
PM2041UW    ISA     Ultra Wide Single-ended SCSI-2
PM2042W     EISA    Wide Single-ended SCSI-2
PM2042UW    EISA    Ultra Wide Single-ended SCSI-2
PM2044W     PCI     Wide Single-ended SCSI-2
PM2044UW    PCI     Ultra Wide Single-ended SCSI-2
PM2142W     EISA    Wide Single-ended SCSI-2
PM2142UW    EISA    Ultra Wide Single-ended SCSI-2
PM2144W     PCI     Wide Single-ended SCSI-2
PM2144UW    PCI     Ultra Wide Single-ended SCSI-2
PM2322W     EISA    Wide Single-ended SCSI-2
PM2322UW    EISA    Ultra Wide Single-ended SCSI-2

DPT SmartRAID family:
PM3021      ISA     Fast Single-ended SCSI-2
PM3021W     ISA     Wide Single-ended SCSI-2
PM3122      EISA    Fast Single-ended SCSI-2
PM3122W     EISA    Wide Single-ended SCSI-2
PM3222      EISA    Fast Single-ended SCSI-2
PM3222W     EISA    Wide Single-ended SCSI-2
PM3224      PCI     Fast Single-ended SCSI-2
PM3224W     PCI     Wide Single-ended SCSI-2
PM3334W     PCI     Wide Single-ended SCSI-2
PM3334UW    PCI     Ultra Wide Single-ended SCSI-2
```

also the differential versions of the above controllers.

and some controllers from:

NEC, AT&T, SNI, AST, Olivetti, Alphatronix.

Supported Configurations :

```
Slots          : ALL
Ports          : ALL
IRQs           : ALL level & edge triggered
DMA Channels   : ISA ALL, EISA/PCI not applicable
IO             : port mapped, bus master
SCSI Channels  : ALL
```

Autoprobe :

```
works with all supported configurations
```

The latest version of the EATA-DMA driver is available on:

```
ftp.i-Connect.Net:/pub/Local/EATA/
```

Mailinglist: The EATA Mailing List provides a forum to Linux users of the EATA-DMA and EATA-PIO driver for discussions and announcements of new releases and other announcements. To join the mailing list, send a message to "linux-eata-request@i-connect.net" with the line "subscribe" in the message body.

/proc/scsi support: To get advanced command statistics, do the following: echo "eata_dma latency" >/proc/scsi/eata_dma/<driver_no> and to switch it off again: echo "eata_dma nolatency" >/proc/scsi/eata_dma/<driver_no>

Common Problems :

1. Slackware doesn't find the controller. Solution: Use one of the ascsi* bootdisks.

2. The IDE driver can detect the ST-506 interface of the EATA board in old kernels (<v1.3).

   (a) This will look like similar to one of the following 2 examples:

   ```
   hd.c: ST-506 interface disk with more than 16 heads detected,
       probably due to non-standard sector translation.  Giving up.
   (disk %d: cyl=%d, sect=63, head=64)
   ```

   ```
   hdc: probing with STATUS instead of ALTSTATUS
   hdc: MP0242 A, 0MB w/128KB Cache, CHS=0/0/0
   hdc: cannot handle disk with 0 physical heads
   hdd: probing with STATUS instead of ALTSTATUS
   hdd: MP0242 A, 0MB w/128KB Cache, CHS=0/0/0
   hdd: cannot handle disk with 0 physical heads
   ```

   If the IDE driver gets into trouble because of this, ie. you can't access your (real) IDE hardware, change the IO Port and/or the IRQ of the EATA board.

   (b) If the IDE driver finds hardware it can handle ie. harddisks with a capacity <=504MB, it will allocate the IO Port and IRQ, so that the eata driver can't utilize them. In this case also change IO Port and IRQ (!= 14,15).

3. Some old SK2011 boards have a broken firmware. Please contact DPT's customer support for an update.

Notes:

1. CONFIG_PCI must be set if you are using a PCI board.

5.11 Future Domain 16x0 with TMC-1800, TMC-18C30, TMC-18C50, or TMC-36C70 chip

Supported Configurations :

```
BIOSs          : 2.0, 3.0, 3.2, 3.4, 3.5
BIOS Addresses : 0xc8000, 0xca000, 0xce000, 0xde000
Ports          : 0x140, 0x150, 0x160, 0x170
IRQs           : 3, 5, 10, 11, 12, 14, 15
DMA            : not used
IO             : port mapped
```

Autoprobe :

works with all supported configurations, requires installed BIOS

Autoprobe Override :

Antiquity Problems, fix by upgrading :

1. Old versions do not support the TMC-18C50 chip, and will fail with newer boards.

2. Old versions will not have the most current BIOS signatures for autodetection.

3. Versions prior to the one included in Linux 1.0.9 and 1.1.6 don't support the new SCSI chip or 3.4 BIOS.

Notes :

1. The Future Domain BIOS often scans for SCSI-devices from highest ID to 0, in reverse order of other SCSI BIOSes. sda will be the last "drive letter" (ie, D: rather than C:). You may also need to use a a disktab override for LILO.

5.12   Generic NCR5380 / T130B (Standard)

Supported and Unsupported Configurations :

```
Ports          : all
IRQs           : all
DMA channels   : DMA is not used
IO             : port mapped
```

Autoprobe :

Autoprobe Override :

```
Compile time : Define GENERIC_NCR5380_OVERRIDE to be an array of tuples
with port, irq, dma, board type - ie
#define GENERIC_NCR5380_OVERRIDE {{0x330, 5, DMA_NONE, BOARD_NCR5380}}

for a NCR5380 board at port 330, IRQ 5.

#define GENERIC_NCR5380_OVERRIDE {{0x350, 5, DMA_NONE, BOARD_NCR53C400}}

for a T130B at port 0x350.

Older versions of the code eliminate the BOARD_* entry.

The symbolic IRQs IRQ_NONE and IRQ_AUTO may be used.
```

kernel command line :

```
ncr5380=port,irq
ncr5380=port,irq,dma
ncr53c400=port,irq
```

255 may be used for no irq, 254 for irq autoprobe.

Common Problems :

1. Using the T130B board with the old (pre public release 6) generic NCR5380 driver which doesn't support the ncr53c400 command line option. The NCR5380 compatible registers are offset eight from the base address. So, if your address is 0x350, use

   ```
   ncr5380=0x358,254
   ```

   on the kernel command line.

Antiquity problems, fix by upgrading :

1. The kernel locks up during disk access with T130B or other NCR53c400 boards. Pre-public release 6 versions of the Generic NCR5380 driver didn't support interrupts on these boards. Upgrade.

Notes :

1. the generic driver doesn't support DMA yet, and pseudo-DMA isn't supported in the generic driver.

5.13 NCR53c8xx (Standard)

Supported and Unsupported Configurations :

```
Base addresses : ALL
IRQs           : ALL
DMA channels   : PCI, not applicable
IO             : port mapped, busmastering
```

Autoprobe :

```
requires PCI BIOS, uses PCI BIOS routines to
search for devices and read configuration space
```

The driver uses the pre-programmed values in some registers for initialization, so a BIOS must be installed.

Antiquity Problems, fix by upgrading :

1. Older versions of Linux had a problem with swapping See6.2.7 (Disks : System Hangs When Swapping)
2. Older versions of Linux didn't recognize '815 and '825 boards.
3. Distribution kernels include release 4 or 5 of the driver, which does not support useful things like disconnect/reconnect (the most noticeable effect of this being attempts to retension/rewind/file space a tape lock you out of all SCSI devices), multiple host adapters, and BIOSless operation. The latest release of the driver is available at

   ```
   ftp://tsx-11.mit.edu/pub/linux/ALPHA/scsi/ncr53c810
   ```

Currently, this is a 1.2.10 and newer patch, although the next release will be 1.3.x exclusively. These patches are NOT entirely clean due to some ELF and other patches which were in the baseline revision of my source tree, and if you can't manually correct the (four) problems you should get, you shouldn't use them. Note that only the newest patch is needed; these are not incremental.

If you wish to run the newer NCR driver with a 1.3.x kernel before then, Harald Evensen <Harald.Evensen@pvv.unit.no> has adapted the patches for 1.3.x

```
ftp://ftp.pvv.unit.no/pub/Linux/ALPHA/ncr
```

These patches should be clean.

Please see all of the READMEs in these directories. You should also join the NCR mailing list if you are interested in running the ALPHA code, since interim bug fixes and announcements of the next release are posted to this list.

To subscribe, send mail to majordomo@colorado.edu with

```
subscribe ncr53c810
```

in the text. You can unsubscribe by sending mail to the same address and including

```
unsubscribe ncr53c810
```

in the text.

Common Problems :

1. Many people have encountered problems where the chip worked fine under DOS, but failed under Linux with a timeout on test 1 due to a lost interrupt. This is often due to a mismatch between the IRQ hardware jumper for a slot or mainboard device and the value set in the CMOS setup. DOUBLE CHECK

   - The IRQ you are using is used only by your onboard NCR chip, or the slot an NCR board is installed in
   - Any main board jumpers selecting the IRQ for the onboard chip or slot match your CMOS setup.a
   - Some PCI mainboards have an "auto" assignment feature, which will not work.

   It may also be due to PCI INTB, INTC, or INTD being selected on a PCI board in a system which only supports PCI INTA. If you are using an NCR board which has jumpers to select between PCI interrupt lines, make sure you are using INTA.

   Finally, PCI should be using level-sensitive rather than edge triggered interrupts. Check that your board is jumpered for level-sensitive, and if that fails try edge-triggered because your system may be broken.

   This problem is especially common with Viglen some Viglen motherboards, where the mainboard IRQ jumper settings are NOT as documented in the manual. I've been told that what claims to be IRQ5 is really IRQ9, your mileage will vary.

2. Lockups / other problems occur when using an S3 928, or Tseng ET4000W32 PCI video board.

   There are hardware bugs in at least some revisions of these chips. Don't use them.

3. You get a message on boot up indicating that the I/O mapping was disabled because base address 0 bits 0..1 indicated a non I/O mapping

   This is due to a BIOS bug in some machines which results in dword reads of configuration registers returning the high and low 16 bit words swapped.

4. Some systems have problems if PCI write posting, or CPU-> PCI buffering are enabled. If you have problems, disable these options.

5. Some systems with the NCR SDMS software in an onboard BIOS
ROM and in the system BIOS are unable to boot DOS. Disabling the image in one place should rectify this problem.

6. If you encounter the message

```
"scsi%d: IRQ0 not free, detaching"
```

or

```
"scsi%d: IRQ255 not free, detaching"
```

The NCR chip had all 0 or 1 bits stored in the PCI configuration register. Either you have configuration problems (see 1 (Common Problem 1)), or you have a defective mainboard BIOS.

As a work around, you could edit drivers/scsi/ncr53c7,8xx.c, and change pci_init() so that you have

```
irq = my_irq;
```

before

```
return normal_init (tpnt, board, chip, (int) base,
        (int) io_port, (int) irq, DMA_NONE, 1, bus, device_fn,
        options);
```

7. Some systems have hideous, broken, BIOS chips. Don't make any bug reports until you've made sure you have the newest ROM from your vendor.

8. The command line overrides ncr53c810=xxx, etc. don't work.

In stock kernels, this is because their entry points are not included in init/main.c, which is quite intentional :

The driver makes no attempt to avoid autoprobing for a board where a command line override was used, so if an override is used where the board actually showed up to the PCI configuration routines, you'll have big problems.

The only reason you would need an override would be if the PCI hardware + BIOS were broken, in which case certain error recovery routines wouldn't work, rendering the override less than useful.

Finally, nearly all of people who _think_ they need a command line override do because they get configuration or other error messages from the driver. If the driver says you have a configuration problem, you have a broken system or a configuration problem and no override is going to fix this.

If some one has gone and added the appropriate entry points to init/main.c for command line overrides, they are totally unsupported and may not work.

9. Certain NCR boards (most notably Nexstor) which don't use an NCR BIOS get timeouts. Some of these ROMs handle synchronous and transfers, negotiate for sync. transfers on power up, and leave the drives in an unknown state. When the distribution Linux NCR driver attempts to talk with them, it gets timeouts and cannot recover because it won't do a bus reset or renegotiate.

If you run into this problem, you can either disable synchronous transfers in the board's setup program, or upgrade to a newer ALPHA release of the NCR driver which will do synchronous negotiation.

10. Tyan S1365 '825 boards have problems with timeouts, especially when disconnects are enabled. Some of these boards have the documentation regarding the termination enable jumper reversed - so that termination is off when you need it, and on when it shouldn't be.

Try reversing the position of the jumper.

Notes:

1. CONFIG_PCI must be set

5.14   Seagate ST0x/Future Domain TMC-8xx/TMC-9xx (Standard)

Supported and Unsupported Configurations :

```
Base addresses : 0xc8000, 0xca000, 0xcc000, 0xce000, 0xdc000, 0xde000
IRQs           : 3, 5
DMA channels   : DMA is not used
IO             : memory mapped
```

Autoprobe :

```
probes for address only, IRQ is assumed to be 5, requires installed BIOS.
```

Autoprobe Override :

Compile time :

```
Define OVERRIDE to be the base address, CONTROLLER to
FD or SEAGATE as appropriate, and IRQ to the IRQ.
```

kernel command line :

```
st0x=address,irq or tmc8xx=address,irq (only works for .99.13b and newer)
```

Antiquity Problems, fix by upgrading :

1. Versions prior to the one in the Linux .99.12 kernel had a problem handshaking with some slow devices, where This is what happens when you write data out to the bus

    (a) Write byte to data register, data register is asserted to bus

    (b) time_remaining = 12us

    (c) wait while time_remaining > 0 and REQ is not asserted

    (d) if time_remaining > 0, assert ACK

    (e) wait while time remaining > 0 and REQ is asserted

    (f) deassert ACK

   The problem was encountered in slow devices that do the command processing as they read the command, where the REQ/ACK handshake takes over 12us - REQ didn't go false when the driver expected it to, so the driver ended up sending multiple bytes of data for each REQ pulse.

2. With Linux .99.12, a bug was introduced when I fixed the arbitration code, resulting in failed selections on some systems. This was fixed in .99.13.

Common Problems :

1. There are command timeouts when Linux attempts to read the partition table or do other disk access. The board ships with the defaults set up for MSDOS, ie interrupts are disabled. To jumper the board for interrupts, on the Seagate use jumper W3 (ST01) or JP3 (ST02) and short pins F-G to select IRQ 5.

2. The driver can't handle some devices, particularly cheap SCSI tapes and CDROMs.

The Seagate ties the SCSI bus REQ/ACK handshaking into the PC bus IO CHANNEL READY and (optionally) 0WS signals. Unfortunately, it doesn't tell you when the watchdog timer runs out, and you have no way of knowing for certain that REQ went low, and may end up seeing one REQ pulse as multiple REQ pulses.

Dealing with this means using a tight loop to look for REQ to go low, with a timeout incase you don't catch the transition due to an interrupt, etc. This results in a performance decrease, so it would be undesirable to apply this to all SCSI devices. Instead, it is selected on a per-device basis with the "broken" field for the given SCSI device in the scsi_devices array. If you run into problems, you should try adding your device to the list of devices for which broken is not reset to zero (currently, only the TENEX CDROM drives).

3. A future domain board (specific examples include the 840, 841, 880, and 881) doesn't work.

A few of the Future domain boards use the Seagate register mapping, and have the MSG and CD bits of the status register flipped.

You should edit seagate.h, swapping the definitions for STAT_MSG and STAT_CD, and recompile the kernel with CONTROLLER defined to SEAGATE and an appropriate IRQ and OVERRIDE specified.

4. When attempting to fdisk your drive, you get error messages indicating that the HDIO_REQ or HDIO_GETGEO ioctl failed, or

```
You must set heads sectors and cylinders.
You can do this from the extra functions menu.
```

See 6.4 (Disks Partitioning)

5. After manually specifying the drive geometry, subsequent attempts to read the partition table result in partition boundary not on a cylinder boundary, physical and logical boundaries don't match, etc. error messages.

See 6.4 (Disks Partitioning)

6. Some systems which worked prior to .99.13 fail with newer versions of Linux. Older versions of Linux assigned the CONTROL and DATA registers in an order different than that outlined in the Seagate documentation, which broke on some systems. Newer versions make the assignment in the correct way, but this breaks other systems.

The code in seagate.c looks like this now :

```
cli();
DATA = (unsigned char) ((1 << target) | (controller_type == SEAGATE ? 0x80 : 0x40));
CONTROL = BASE_CMD | CMD_DRVR_ENABLE | CMD_SEL |
          (reselect ? CMD_ATTN : 0);
sti();
```

Changing this to

```
cli();
CONTROL = BASE_CMD | CMD_DRVR_ENABLE | CMD_SEL |
          (reselect ? CMD_ATTN : 0);
DATA = (unsigned char) ((1 << target) | (controller_type == SEAGATE ? 0x80 : 0x40));
sti();
```

may fix your problem.

Defines :

```
FAST or FAST32 will use blind transfers where possible

ARBITRATE will cause the host adapter to arbitrate for the
         bus for better SCSI-II compatibility, rather than just
         waiting for BUS FREE and then doing its thing.  Should
         let us do one command per Lun when I integrate my
         reorganization changes into the distribution sources.

SLOW_HANDSHAKE will allow compatibility with broken devices that don't
         handshake fast enough (ie, some CD ROM's) for the Seagate
         code.

SLOW_RATE=x, x some number will let you specify a default
         transfer rate if handshaking isn't working correctly.
```

5.15   PAS16 SCSI (Standard)

Supported and Unsupported Configurations :

```
Ports         : 0x388, 0x384, 0x38x, 0x288
IRQs          : 10, 12, 14, 15
    IMPORTANT : IRQ MUST be different from the IRQ used for the sound
                portion of the board.
DMA           : is not used for the SCSI portion of the board
IO            : port mapped
```

Autoprobe :

```
does not require BIOS
```

Autoprobe Override :

```
Compile time : Define PAS16_OVERRIDE to be an array of port, irq
tuples.  Ie

#define PAS16_OVERRIDE {{0x388, 10}}

for a board at port 0x388, IRQ 10.
```

kernel command line :

```
pas16=port,irq
```

Defines :

```
AUTOSENSE - if defined, REQUEST SENSE will be performed automatically
for commands that return with a CHECK CONDITION status.
```

PSEUDO_DMA - enables PSEUDO-DMA hardware, should give a 3-4X performance
increase compared to polled I/O.

PARITY - enable parity checking. Not supported

SCSI2 - enable support for SCSI-II tagged queuing. Untested

UNSAFE - leave interrupts enabled during pseudo-DMA transfers. You
        only really want to use this if you're having a problem with
        dropped characters during high speed communications, and even
        then, you're going to be better off twiddling with transfersize.

USLEEP - enable support for devices that don't disconnect. Untested.

Common problems :

1. Command timeouts, aborts, etc. You should install the NCR5380 patches that I posted to the net some time ago, which should be integrated into some future alpha release. These patches fix a race condition in earlier NCR5380 driver cores, as well as fixing support for multiple devices on NCR5380 based boards.

   If that fails, you should disable the PSEUDO_DMA option by changing the #define PSEUDO_DMA line in drivers/scsi/pas16.c to #undef PSEUDO_DMA.

   Note that the later should be considered a last resort, because there will be a severe performance degradation.

5.16   Trantor T128/T128F/T228 (Standard)

Supported and Unsupported Configurations :

```
Base addresses :  0xcc000, 00xc8000, 0xdc000, 0xd8000
IRQs           : none, 3, 5, 7 (all boards)
                 10, 12, 14, 15 (T128F only)
DMA            : not used.
IO             : memory mapped
```

Autoprobe :

works for all supported configurations, requires installed BIOS.

Autoprobe Override :

```
Compile time : Define T128_OVERRIDE to be an array of address, irq
tuples.  Ie

#define T128_OVERRIDE {{0xcc000, 5}}
```

for a board at address 0xcc000, IRQ 5.

The symbolic IRQs IRQ_NONE and IRQ_AUTO may be used.

kernel command line :

    t128=address,irq
    -1 may be used for no irq, -2 for irq autoprobe.

Defines :

    AUTOSENSE - if defined, REQUEST SENSE will be performed automatically
    for commands that return with a CHECK CONDITION status.

    PSEUDO_DMA - enables PSEUDO-DMA hardware, should give a 3-4X performance
    increase compared to polled I/O.

    PARITY - enable parity checking. Not supported

    SCSI2 - enable support for SCSI-II tagged queuing. Untested

    UNSAFE - leave interrupts enabled during pseudo-DMA transfers. You
             only really want to use this if you're having a problem with
             dropped characters during high speed communications, and even
             then, you're going to be better off twiddling with transfersize.

    USLEEP - enable support for devices that don't disconnect. Untested.

Common Problems :

1. Command timeouts, aborts, etc.
   You should install the NCR5380 patches that I posted to the net some time ago, which should be
   integrated into some future alpha release. These patches fix a race condition in earlier NCR5380
   driver cores, as well as fixing support for multiple devices on NCR5380 based boards. If that
   fails, you should disable the PSEUDO_DMA option by changing the #define PSEUDO_DMA line
   in drivers/scsi/pas16.c to #undef PSEUDO_DMA.
   Note that the later should be considered a last resort, because there will be a severe performance
   degradation.

5.17 Ultrastor 14f (ISA), 24f (EISA), 34f (VLB) (Standard)

Supported Configurations :

    Ports   : 0x130, 0x140, 0x210, 0x230, 0x240, 0x310, 0x330, 0x340
    IRQs   : 10, 11, 14, 15
    DMA channels : 5, 6, 7
    IO   : port mapped, bus master

Autoprobe :

    `does not work for boards at port 0x310, BIOS not required.`

Autoprobe override :

    `compile time only, define PORT_OVERRIDE`

Common Problems :

1. The address 0x310 is not supported by the autoprobe code, and may cause conflicts if networking is enabled.

   Please use a different address.

2. Using an Ultrastor at address 0x330 may cause the system to hang when the sound drivers are autoprobing.

   Please use a different address.

3. Various other drivers do unsafe probes at various addresses, if you are having problems with detection or the system is hanging at boot time, please try a different address.

   0x340 is recommended as an address that is known to work.

4. Linux detects no SCSI devices, but detects your SCSI hard disk on an Ultrastor SCSI board as a normal hard disk, and the hard disk driver refuses to support it. Note that when this occurs, you will probably also get a message

   hd.c: ST-506 interface disk with more than 16 heads detected, probably due to non-standard sector translation. Giving up. (disk %d: cyl=%d, sect=63, head=64)

   If this is the case, you are running the Ultrastor board in WD1003 emulation mode. You have

   (a) Switch the Ultrastor into native mode. This is the recommended action, since the SCSI driver can be significantly faster than the IDE driver, especially with the clustered read/write patches installed. Some users have sustained in excess of 2M/sec through the file system using these patches.

      Note that this will be necessary if you wish to use any non- hard disk, or more than two hard disk devices on the Ultrastor.

   (b) Use the kernel command line switch

          `hd=cylinders,heads,sectors`

      to override the default setting to bootstrap yourself, keeping number of cylinders <= 2048, number of heads <= 16, and number of sectors <= 255 such that cylinders * heads * sectors is the same for both mappings.

      You'll also have to manually specify the disk geometry when running fdisk under Linux. Failure to do so will result in incorrect partition entries being written, which will work correctly with Linux but fail under MSDOS which looks at the cylinder/head/sector entries in the table.

      Once Linux is up, you can avoid the inconvenience of having to boot by hand by recompiling the kernel with an appropriately defined HD_TYPE macro in include/linux/config.h.

5.18 Western Digital 7000 (Standard)

Supported Configurations :

```
BIOS Addresses : 0xce000
Ports          : 0x350
IRQs           : 15
DMA Channels   : 6
IO             : port mapped, bus master
```

Autoprobe :

```
requires installed BIOS
```

Common Problems :

1. There are several revisions of the chip and firmware. Supposedly, revision 3 boards do not work, revision 5 boards do, chips with no suffix do not work, chips with an 'A' suffix do.

2. The board supports a few BIOS addresses which aren't on the list of supported addresses. If you run into this situation, please use one of the supported addresses and submit a bug report as outlined in 3 (Bug Reports).

5.19   AM53/79C974 (ALPHA)

ftp://tsx-11.mit.edu/pub/linux/ALPHA/scsi/AM53C974-0.3.tar.gz

Supported Configurations :

```
Ports          : all
IRQs           : all
DMA Channels   : 6
IO             : port mapped, bus master (unintelligent)
```

5.20   qlogic (Standard)

Hey Drew, where is this section (I (D.F.) saw it only in the toc ;-)?

6   Disks

This section gives information that is specific to disk drives.

6.1   Supported and Unsupported Hardware

All direct access SCSI devices with a block size of 256, 512, or 1024 bytes should work. Other block sizes will not work (Note that this can often be fixed by changing the block and/or sector sizes using the MODE SELECT SCSI command)

Sector size refers to the number of data bytes allocated per sector on a device, ie CDROMs use a 2048 byte sector size.

Block size refers to the size of the logical blocks used to interface with the device. Although this is usually identical to sector size, some devices map multiple smaller physical sectors (ie, 256 bytes in the case of 55M Syquest drives) to larger logical blocks or vice versa (ie, 512 byte blocks on SUN compatible CDROM drives).

Removable media devices, including Bernoulis, flopticals, MO drives, and Syquests.

In theory, drives up to a terabyte in size should work. There is definitely no problem with tiny 9G drives.

6.2 Common Problems

6.2.1 Cylinder > 1024 message

When partitioning, you get a warning message about "cylinder > 1024" or you are unable to boot from a partition including a logical cylinder past logical cylinder 1024.

This is a BIOS limitation.

See Disk 6.5 (Geometry) and 6.4 (Partitioning) for an explanation.

6.2.2 You are unable to partition "/dev/hd*"

/dev/hd* aren't SCSI devices, /dev/sd* are.

See 6.3 (Device Files) and Disk 6.5 (Geometry) and 6.4 (Partitioning) for the correct device names and partitioning procedure.

6.2.3 Unable to eject media from a removable media drive

Linux attempts to lock the drive door when a piece of media is mounted to prevent filesystem corruption due to an inadvertent media change.

Please unmount your disks before ejecting them.

6.2.4 Unable to boot using LILO from a SCSI disk

In some cases, the SCSI driver and BIOS will disagree over the correct BIOS mapping to use, and will result in LILO hanging after 'LI' at boot time and/or other problems.

To workaround this, you'll have to determine your BIOS geometry mapping used under DOS, and make an entry for your disk in /etc/lilo/disktab.

Alternatively, you may be able to use the "linear" configuration jfile option.

6.2.5 Fdisk responds with

    You must set heads sectors and cylinders.
    You can do this from the extra functions menu.

and disk geometry is not 'remembered' when fdisk is rerun.

See 6.4 (Partitioning)

6.2.6   Only one drive is detected on a bridge board with multiple drives connected.

Linux won't search LUNs past zero on SCSI devices which predate ANSI SCSI revision 1. If you wish devices on alternate LUNs to be recognized, you will have to modify drivers/scsi/scsi.c:scan_scsis().

6.2.7   System hangs when swapping

We think this has been fixed, try upgrading to 1.1.38.

6.2.8   Connor CFP1060S disks get corrupted

This is due to a microcode bug in the read-ahead and caching code.

>From Soenke Behrens of Conner tech. support :

```
During the past few weeks, we got several calls from customers stating
that they had severe problems with Conner CFP1060x 1GB SCSI drives
using the Linux operating system. Symptoms were corrupt filesystems
(damaged inodes) reported by e2fsck on each system boot and similar
errors.

There is now a fix available for customers with a CFP1060x (microcode
revisions 9WA1.62/1.66/1.68) and Linux. To apply the upgrade, you
will need a DOS boot disk and ASPI drivers that can access the hard
drive. The upgrade downloads new queuing and lookahead code into the
non-volatile SCSI RAM of the drive.

If you are experiencing problems with a disk that has microcode
revision 9WA1.60, you will have to contact your nearest Conner service
centre to get the disk upgraded. The microcode revision can be found
on the label of the drive and on the underside of the drive on a label
on one of the ICs.

If you are confident that you can perform the upgrade yourself, please
contact Conner Technical Support and have your microcode revision
ready. Conner Technical Support Europe can be reached on +44-1294-315333,
Conner Technical Support in the USA can be reached on 1-800-4CONNER.

Regards
Soenke Behrens
European Technical Support
```

6.3   Device Files

SCSI disks use block device major 8, and there are no "raw" devices ala BSD.

16 minor numbers are allocated to each SCSI disk, with minor % 16 == 0 being the whole disk, minors $1 <=$ (minor % 16) $<= 4$ the four primary partitions, minors $5 <=$ (minor % 16) $<= 15$ any extended partitions.

Ie, a configuration may work out like this (with one host adapter)

```
Device                      Target, Lun      SCSI disk
84M Seagate                    0       0      /dev/sda
SCSI->SMD bridge disk 0 3              0      /dev/sdb
SCSI->SMD bridge disk 1 3              1      /dev/sdc
Wangtek tape                   4       0      none
213M Maxtor                    6       0      /dev/sdd
```

Etc.

The standard naming convention is

/dev/sd{letter} for the entire disk device ((minor % 16) == 0) /dev/sd{letter}{partition} for the partitions on that device (1 <= (minor % 16) <= 15)

Ie

```
/dev/sda        block device major 8 minor 0
/dev/sda1       block device major 8 minor 1
/dev/sda2       block device major 8 minor 2
/dev/sdb        block device major 8 minor 16
```

etc.

6.4 Partitioning

You can partition your SCSI disks using the partitioning program of your choice, under DOS, OS/2, Linux or any other operating system supporting the standard partitioning scheme.

The correct way to run the Linux fdisk program is by specifying the device on the command line. Ie, to partition the first SCSI disk,

```
fdisk /dev/sda
```

If you don't explicitly specify the device, the partitioning program may default to /dev/hda, which isn't a SCSI disk.

In some cases, fdisk will respond with

```
You must set heads sectors and cylinders.
You can do this from the extra functions menu.

Command (m for help):
```

and/or give a message to the effect that the HDIO_REQ or HDIO_GETGEO ioctl failed. In these cases, you must manually specify the disk geometry as outlined in 6.5 (Disk Geometry) when running fdisk, and also in /etc/disktab if you wish to boot kernels off that disk with LILO.

If you have manually specified the disk geometry, subsequent attempts to run fdisk will give the same error message. This is normal, since PCs don't store the disk geometry information in the partition table. In and of itself, will cause _NO PROBLEMS_, and you will have no problems accessing partitions you created on the drive with Linux. Some vendors' poor installation code will choke on this, in which case you should contact your vendor and insist that they fix the code.

In some cases, you will get a warning message about a partition ending past cylinder 1024. If you create one of these partitions, you will be unable to boot Linux kernels off of that partition using LILO. Note, however, that this restriction does not preclude the creation of a root partition partially or entirely above the 1024 cylinder mark, since it is possible to create a small /boot partition below the 1024 cylinder mark or to boot kernels off existing partitions.

6.5   Disk Geometry

Under Linux, each disk is viewed as the SCSI host adapter sees it : N blocks, numbered from 0 to N-1, all error free, where as DOS/BIOS predate intelligent disks and apply an arbitrary head / cylinder / sector mapping to this linear addressing.

This can pose a problem when you partition the drives under Linux, since there is no portable way to get DOS/BIOS's idea of the mapped geometry. In most cases, a HDIO_GETGEO ioctl() can be implemented to return this mapping. Unfortunately, when the vendor (ie Seagate) has chosen a perverse, non-standard, and undocumented mapping, this is not possible and geometry must be manually specified

If manual specification of the is required, you have one of several options :

1. If you don't care about using DOS, or booting kernels from the drive with LILO, create a translation such that heads * cylinders * sectors * 512 < size of your drive in bytes (a megabyte is defined as 2^20 bytes).

   ```
   1 <= heads <= 256
   1 <= cylinders <= 1024
   1 <= sectors <= 63
   ```

2. Use the BIOS mapping. In some cases, this will mean reconfiguring the disk so that it is at SCSI ID 0, and disabling the second IDE drive (if you have one).

You can either use a program like NU, or you can use the following program :

```
begin 664 dparam.com
MBAZ''##_B+^^!'+N!'(H'OSP@=/D\,'5:@#]X='6'/UAU4(!_'3AU2H!_'P!U
M1(I7'H#J,(#Z'7<Y@,,*'M'C-$PCD=3-14HC()#\PY.@R'.@J'%J(\/['.3H
M)0#H#H'0!8AL2Q!M+LQ07'+K"';')S2'#NIP!ZR"ZQO'K&[K+K5'>L6N]T!-=*Y
M"@#W\8#",$N,#E(%PG'=>^)VK0)S2'#=7-A9V4Z(&1P87)A;2!P>#@P#L@("!0
L<B'@9'!A<F%M(#!X.#$.#$$-"B1R;:8C#@('D$#OHD(""^"'D'D'1
'
end
```

When run it prints the sectors, heads, and cylinders of the drive whose BIOS address was specified on the command line (0x80 is the first disk, 0x81 the second).

Ie, dparam 0x80

```
60       17       1007
```

Would mean that C: had 60 sectors, 17 heads, and 1007 cylinders.

7   CD ROMs

This section gives information that is specific to cdrom drives.

7.1 Supported and Unsupported Hardware

SCSI CDs with a block size of 512 or 2048 bytes should work. Other block sizes will not work.

7.2 Common Problems

7.2.1 Unable to mount cdrom

The correct syntax to mount an ISO-9660 CDROM is

```
mount -t iso9660 /dev/sr0 /mount_point -o ro
```

Note that for this to work, you must have the kernel configured with support for SCSI, your host adapter, the SCSI CDROM driver, and the iso9660 filesystem.

Note that as of Linux 1.1.32, read-only devices such as CDROMs CANNOT be mounted with the default read/write options.

7.2.2 Unable to eject cdrom

Linux attempts to lock the drive door when a piece of media is mounted to prevent filesystem corruption due to an inadvertent media change.

7.2.3 Unable to play audio

The programs Workman or xcdplayer will do this for you.

7.2.4 Workman or Xcdplayer do not work

The functions to control audio functions are part of the SCSI-II command set, so any drive that is not SCSI-II will probably not work here. Also, many SCSI-I and some SCSI-II CDROM drives use a proprietary command set for accessing audio functions instead of the SCSI-II command set. For NEC drives, there is a version of xcdplayer specially adapted to use this command set floating around - try looking on tsx-11.mit.edu in pub/linux/BETA/cdrom.

These programs may work with some of the non-SCSI cdrom drives if the driver implements the same ioctls as the scsi drivers.

7.2.5 Additional drives on CD ROM changers do not work

Most CD changers assign each disc to a logical unit. Insure that you have special files made for each platter (see 6.3 (Device Files)) and see 2.10 (LUNS other than 0 don't work).

7.3 Device Files

SCSI CD ROMs use major 11.

Minors are allocated dynamically (See 6 (Disks), 6.3 (Device Files) for an example) with the first CDROM found being minor 0, the second minor 1, etc.

The standard naming convention is

/dev/sr{digit}, although some distributions have used /dev/scd{digit}, with examples being

```
/dev/sr0        /dev/scd0
/dev/sr1        /dev/scd1
```

8   Tapes

This section gives information that is specific to scsi tape drives.

8.1   Supported and Unsupported Hardware

Drives using both fixed and variable length blocks smaller than the the driver buffer length (set to 32K in the distribution sources) are supported.

Parameters (block size, buffering, density) are set with ioctls (usually with the mt program), and remain in effect after the device is closed and reopened.

Virtually all drives should work, including :

- Archive Viper QIC drives, including the 150M and 525M models
- Exabyte 8mm drives
- Wangtek 5150S drives
- Wangdat DAT drives

8.2   Common Problems

8.2.1   Tape drive not recognized at boot time

Try booting with a tape in the drive.

8.2.2   Tapes with multiple files cannot be read properly

When reading a tape with multiple files, the first tar is successful, a second tar fails silently, and retrying the second tar is successful.

User level programs, such as tar, don't understand file marks. The first tar reads up until the end of the file. The second tar attempts to read at the file mark, gets nothing, but the tape spaces over the file mark. The third tar is successful since the tape is at the start of the next file.

Use mt on the no-rewind device to space forward to the next file.

8.2.3   Decompression fails

Decompressing programs cannot handle the zeros padding the last block of the file.

To prevent warnings and errors, wrap your compressed files in a .tar file - ie, rather than doing

        tar cfvz /dev/nrst0 file.1 file.2 ...

do

        tar cfvz tmp.tar.z file.1 file.2 ...

        tar cf /dev/nrst0 tmp.tar.z

8.2.4   Problems taking tapes to/from other systems

You can't read a tape made with another operating system or another operating system can't read a tape written in Linux.

Different systems often use different block sizes. On a tape device using a fixed blocksize, you will get errors when reading blocks written using a different block size.

To read these tapes, you must set the blocksize of the tape driver to match the blocksize used when the tape was written, or to variable.

NOTE : this is the hardware block size, not the blocking factor used with tar, dump, etc.

You can do this with the mt command -

        mt setblk <size>

or

        mt setblk 0

to get variable block length support.

Note that these mt flags are NOT supported under the GNU version of mt which is included with some Linux distributions. Instead, you must use the BSD derived Linux SCSI mt command. Source should be available from

        tsx-11.mit.edu:/pub/linux/ALPHA/scsi

Also note that by default, ST_BUFFER_BLOCKS (defined in /usr/src/linux/drivers/scsi/st_options.h in newer kernels, st.c in older kernels) is set to allow for a 32K maximum buffer size; you'll need to edit the source to use larger blocks.

8.2.5   "No such device" error message

All attempts to access the tape result in a

"No such device"

or similar error message. Check the type of your tape device - it MUST be a character device with major and minor numbers matching those specified in 6.3 (Device Files).

8.2.6 Tape reads at a given density work, writes fail

Many tape drives support reading at lower densities for compatibility with older hardware, but will not write at those same densities.

This is especially the case with QIC drives, which will read old 60M tapes but only write new 120, 150, 250, and 525M formats.

8.2.7 Repositioning the tape locks out access to all SCSI devices

This is most common with SCSI drivers which only support one outstanding command at a time (see 10.5 (Multiple devices) for an explanation, and 10.7 (Driver feature comparison) to see which drivers suffer from this limitation), although there may be a few tape drives out there which refuse to disconnect.

In either case, you can work around the problem by editing drivers/scsi/st.c and adding a

```
#define ST_NOWAIT
```

at the top and rebuilding the kernel.

Note that this will defer error condition reporting until the next SCSI command is executed. For this reason, you may want to do something like a

```
mt status
```

after a mt file positioning command so you don't overwrite tape files if the positioning command failed.

You may also wish to consider changing to a better-supported SCSI board or newer tape drive if you need to use this workaround and are writing multiple files to tapes.

8.3 Device Files

SCSI tapes use character device major 9.

Due to constraints imposed by Linux's use of a sixteen bit dev_t with only eight bits allocated to the minor number, the SCSI tape minor numbers are assigned dynamically starting with the lowest SCSI HOST/ID/LUN.

Rewinding devices are numbered from 0 - with the first SCSI tape, /dev/rst0 being c 9 0, the second /dev/rst1 c 9 1, etc. Non-rewinding devices have the high bit set in the minor number, ie /dev/nrst0 is c 9 128.

The standard naming convention is

```
/dev/nst{digit}          for non-rewinding devices
/dev/st{digit}           for rewinding devices
```

9 Generic

This information gives information that is specific to the generic scsi driver.

9.1 Supported Hardware

The Generic SCSI device driver provides an interface for sending SCSI commands to all SCSI devices - disks, tapes, CDROMs, media changer robots, etc.

Everything electrically compatible with your SCSI board should work.

9.2 Common Problems

None :-).

9.3 Device Files

SCSI generic devices use character major 21. Due to constraints imposed by Linux's use of a 16 bit dev_t, minor numbers are dynamically assigned from 0, one per device, with

/dev/sg0

corresponding to the lowest numerical target/lun on the first SCSI board.

10 Buyers' Guide

A frequent question is:

"Linux supports quite a number of different boards, so which scsi host adapter should I get."

The answer depends upon how much performance you expect or need, motherboard, and the scsi peripherals that you plan on attaching to your machine.

10.1 Transfer types

The biggest factor affecting performance (in terms of throughput and interactive response time during SCSI I/O) is the transfer type used. The table below lists the various transfer types, the effects they have on performance, and some recommendations as to their use.

Transfer type
> Description / Performance / Recommendations

Pure Polled
> A pure polled I/O board will use the CPU to handle all of the SCSI processing, including the REQ/ACK handshaking.
>
> Even a fast CPU will be slower handling the REQ/ACK handshake sequence than a simple finite state machine, resulting in peak transfer rates of about 150K/sec on a fast machine, perhaps 60K/sec on a slow machine (through the filesystem).
>
> The driver also must sit in a tight loop as long as the SCSI bus is busy, resulting in near 100% CPU utilization and extremely poor responsiveness during SCSI I/O. Slow CDROMs which don't disconnect/reconnect will kill interactive performance with these boards.
>
> Not recommended.

Interlocked Polled

Boards using interlocked polled I/O are essentially the same as pure polled I/O boards, only the SCSI REQ/ACK handshaking signals are interlocked with the PC bus handshaking signals. All SCSI processing beyond the handshaking is handled by the CPU.

Peak transfer rates of 500-600K/sec through the filesystem are possible on these boards.

As with pure polled I/O boards, the driver must sit in a tight loop as long as the SCSI bus is busy, resulting in CPU utilization dependent on the transfer rates of the devices, and when they disconnect/reconnect. CPU utilization may vary between 25% for single speed CDs which handle disconnect/reconnect properly to 100% for faster drives or broken CD ROMs which fail to disconnect/reconnect.

On my 486-66, with a T128, I use 90% of my CPU time to sustain a throughput of 547K/sec on a drive with a headrate of 1080K/sec with a T128 board.

Sometimes acceptable for slow tapes and CDROMs when low cost is essential.

FIFO Polled

Boards using FIFO polled I/O put a small (typically 8K) buffer between the CPU and the SCSI bus, and often implement some amount of intelligence. The net effect is that the CPU is only tied up when it is transferring data at top speed to the FIFO and when it's handling the rest of the interrupt processing for FIFO empty conditions, disconnect/reconnect, etc.

Peak transfer rates should be sufficient to handle most SCSI devices, and have been measured at up to 4M/sec using raw SCSI commands to read 64K blocks on a fast Seagate Baracuda with an Adaptec 1520.

CPU utilization is dependent on the transfer rates of the devices, with faster devices generating more interrupts per unit time which require more CPU processing time. Although CPU usage may be high (perhaps 75%) with fast devices, the system usually remains usable. These boards will provide excellent interactive performance with broken devices which don't disconnect/reconnect (typically cheap CDROM drives)

Recommended for persons on a budget.

Slave DMA

Drivers for boards using slave DMA program the PC's DMA controller for a channel when they do a data transfer, and return control to the CPU.

Peak transfer rates are usually handicapped by the poor DMA controller used on PCs, with one such 8-bit board having problems going faster than 140-150K/sec with one mainboard.

CPU utilization is very reasonable, slightly less than what is seen with FIFO polled I/O boards. These boards are very tolerant of broken devices which don't disconnect/reconnect (typically cheap CSG limitDROM drives).

Acceptable for slow CDROM drives, tapes, etc.

Busmastering DMA

These boards are intelligent. Drivers for these boards throw a SCSI command, the destination target and lun, and where the data should end up in a structure, and tell the board "Hey, I have a command for you." The driver returns control to various running programs, and eventually the SCSI board gets back and says that it's done.

Since the intelligence is in the host adapter firmware and not the driver, drivers for these boards typically support more features - synchronous transfers, tagged queuing, etc.

With the clustered read/write patches, peak transfer rates through the file system approach 100% of head rate writing, 75% reading.

CPU utilization is minimal, irregardless of I/O load, with a measured 5% CPU usage while accessing a double speed CDROM on an Adaptec 1540 and 20% while sustaining a 1.2M/sec transfer rate on a SCSI disk.

Recommended in all cases where money is not extremely tight, the main board is not broken (some broken main boards do not work with bus masters), and applications where time to data is more important than throughput are not being run (bus master overhead may hit 3-4ms per command).

10.2 Scatter/gather

The second most important driver/hardware feature with respect to performance is support for scatter/gather I/O. The overhead of executing a SCSI command is significant - on the order of milliseconds. Intelligent bus masters like the Adaptec 1540 may take 3-4ms to process a SCSI command before the target even sees it. On unbuffered devices, this overhead is always enough to slip a revolution, resulting in a transfer rate of about 60K/sec (assuming a 3600RPM drive) per block transfered at a time. So, to maximize performance, it is necessary to minimize the number of SCSI commands needed to transfer a given amount of data by transferring more data per command. Due to the design of the Linux buffer cache, contiguous disk blocks are not contiguous in memory. With the clustered read/write patches, 4K worth of buffers are contiguous. So, the maximum amount of data which can be transfered per SCSI command is going to be 1K * # of scatter/gather regions without the clustered read/write patches, 4K * # of regions with. Experimentally, we've determined that 64K is a reasonable amount to transfer with a single SCSI command - meaning 64 scatter/gather buffers with clustered read/write patches, 16 without. With the change from 16K to 64K transfers, we saw an improvement from 50% of headrate, through the filesystem, reading and writing, to 75% and 100% respectively using an Adaptec 1540 series board.

10.3 Mailbox vs. non-mailbox

A number of intelligent host adapters, such as the Ultrastor, WD7000, Adaptec 1540, 1740, and BusLogic boards have used a mailbox-metaphor interface, where SCSI commands are executed by putting a SCSI command structure in a fixed memory location (mailbox), signaling the board (ie, raising the outgoing mail flag), and waiting for a return (incoming mail). With this high level programming interface, users can often upgrade to a newer board revision to take advantage of new features, such as FAST + WIDE SCSI, without software changes. Drivers tend to be simpler to implement, may implement a larger feature set, and may be more stable.

Other intelligent host adapters, such as the NCR53c7/8xx family, and Adaptec AIC-7770/7870 chips (including the 274x, 284x, and 2940 boards) use a lower level programming interface. This may prove faster since processing can be shifted between the board's processor and faster host CPU, allow better flexibility in implementing certain features (ie, target mode for arbitrary devices), and these boards can be built for less money (In some cases, this is passed on to the consumer (ie, most NCR boards)). On the down side, drivers tend to be more complex (read : there is more potential for bugs), and must be modified to take advantage of the features present on newer chips.

10.4 Bus types

Bus type is the next thing to consider, with choices including ISA, EISA, VESA, and PCI. Marketing types often spout of absurd bandwidth numbers based on burst transfer rates and fiction, which isn't very useful. Instead, I've chosen to state "real-world" numbers based on measured performance with various peripherals.

Bus

> Bandwidth, description,

ISA

> Bandwidth is slightly better than 5M/sec for busmastering devices. With an ISA bus, arbitration for busmasters is performed by the venerable 8237 third party DMA controller, resulting in relatively high bus acquisition times. Interrupt drivers are tri-state and edge triggered, meaning interrupts cannot be shared. Generally, ISA is unbuffered, meaning the host/memory bus is tied up whenever a transfer is occuring. No mechanism is provided to prevent bus-hogging.

VESA

Bandwidth is about 30M/sec. Some VESA systems run the bus out of spec, rendering them incompatible with some boards, so this should be taken into consideration before purchasing hardware without a return guarantee. Generally, VESA is unbuffered, meaning meaning the host/memory bus is tied up whenever a transfer is occuring.

EISA

Bandwidth is about 30M/sec, with busmastering operations generally being faster than VESA. Some EISA systems buffer the bus, allowing burst transfers to the faster host/memory bus and minimizing impact on CPU performance. EISA interrupt drivers may be either tri-state edge-triggered or open collector level-active, allowing interrupt sharing with drivers that support it. Since EISA allocates a separate address space for each board, it is usually less prone to resource conflicts than ISA or VESA.

PCI

Bandwidth is about 60M/sec. Most PCI systems implement write posting buffers on the host bridge, allowing speed mismatches on either side to have a minimum impact on bus/CPU performance. PCI interrupt drivers are open collector level-active, allowing interrupt sharing with drivers that support it. Mechanisms are provided to prevent bus hogging, and for both master and slave to suspend a bus-mastering operation.

Since PCI provides a plug-n-play mechanism with writeable configuration registers on every board, in a separate address space, a properly implemented PCI system is plug-and play.

PCI is extremely strict as to trace length, loading, mechanical specifications, etc. and ultimately should be more reliable than VESA or ISA.

In summary, PCI is the best PC bus, although it does have its dark side. PCI is still in its infancy, and although most manufacturers have ironed out the problems, there is still stock of older, buggy PCI hardware and broken main BIOSes. For this reason, I _strongly_ recommend a return guarantee on the hardware. While the latest PCI mainboards are truly plug-and-play, older PCI boards may require the user to set options with both jumpers and in software (ie, interrupt assignments). Although many users have resolved their PCI problems, it has taken time and for this reason I cannot recommend a PCI purchase if having the system operational is extremely time critical.

For many slower SCSI devices, such as disks with head rates around 2M/sec or less, CDROMs, and tapes, there will be little difference in throughputs with the different PC bus interfaces. For faster contemporary SCSI drives (Typical high end multi-gigabyte drives have a head rate of 4-5M/sec, and at least one company is currently ALPHA testing a parallel head unit with a 14M/sec head rate), throughput will often be significantly better with controllers on faster busses, with one user noting a 2.5 fold performance improvement when going from an Adaptec 1542 ISA board to a NCR53c810 PCI board.

With the exception of situations where PCI write-posting or a similar write-buffering mechanism is being used, when one of the busses in your system is busy, all of the busses will be unaccessible. So, although bus saturation may not be interfering with SCSI performance, it may have a negative effect on interactive performance. Ie, if you have a 4M/sec SCSI disk under ISA, you'll have lost 80% of your bandwidth, and in an ISA/VESA system would only be able to bitblt at 6M/sec. In most cases, a similar impact on processing jobs in the background would also be felt.

Note that having over 16M of memory does not preclude using an ISA busmastering SCSI board. Unlike various broken operating systems, Linux will double buffer when using a DMA with an ISA controller and a transfer is ultimately destined for an area above 16M. Performance on these transfers only suffers by about 1.5%, ie not noticeably.

Finally, the price difference between bus masters offered with the different bus interfaces is often minimal.

With all that in mind, based on your priorities you will have certain bus preferences

```
        Stability, time critical installations,          EISA ISA VESA PCI
                  and poor return policies
        Performance, and typical hobbiest                 PCI EISA VESA ISA
```

installations

As I pointed out earlier, bus mastering versus other transfer modes is going to have a bigger impact on total system performance, and should be considered more important than bus type when purchasing a SCSI controller.

10.5   Multiple devices

If will you have multiple devices on your SCSI bus, you may want to see whether the host adapter/driver that you are considering supports more than one outstanding command at one time. This is almost essential if you'll be running a tape drive, and very desirable if you are mixing devices of different speeds, like a CD ROM and a disk drive. If the linux driver only supports one outstanding command, you may be locked out of your disk drive while a tape in the tape drive is rewinding or seeking to end of media (perhaps for half an hour). With two disk drives, the problem will not be as noticeable, although throughput would approach the average of the two transfer rates rather than the sum of the two transfer rates.

10.6   SCSI-I, SCSI-II, SCSI-III FAST and WIDE options, etc.

Over the years, SCSI has evolved, with new revisions of the standard introducing higher transfer rates, methods to increase throughput, standardized commands for new devices, and new commands for previously supported devices.

In and of themselves, the revision levels don't really mean anything. Excepting minor things like SCSI-II not allowing the single initiator option of SCSI-I, SCSI is backwards compatible, with new features being introduced as options and not mandatory. So, the decision to call a SCSI adapter SCSI, SCSI-II, or SCSI-III is almost entirely a marketing one.

10.7   Driver feature comparison

Driver feature comparison (supported chips are listed in parenthesis)

Driver	Transfer mode	Simultaneous Commands total/LUN	SG limit	> 1 Boards
AM53C974	Busmastering DMA	12s/1s	255s	Y
aha152x (AIC6260, AIC6360)	FIFO(8k) Polled	7s/1s	255s	N
aha1542	Busmastering DMA	8s/1s	16	Y
aha1740	Busmastering DMA	32s	16	N
aha274x	Busmastering DMA	4s/1s	255s	Y
BusLogic	Busmastering DMA	192/31	128s, 8192h	Y
(values are for BT-948/958/958D, older boards support fewer commands)				
eata_dma	Busmastering DMA	64s-8192h/2-64	512s, 8192h	Y
fdomain (TMC1800, TMC18c30, TMC18c50, TMC36c70)	FIFO(8k) Polled except TMC18c30 with 2k FIFO	1s	64s	N

in2000*	FIFO(2k) Polled	1s	255s	N
g_NCR5380	Pure Polled	16s/2s	255s	Y
(NCR5380,				
NCR53c80,				
NCR5381,				
NCR53c400)				
gsi8*	Slave DMA	16s/2s	255s	
(NCR5380)				
PAS16	Pure Polled	16s/2s	255s	Y
(NCR5380)	or Interlocked Polled			
	(fails on some systems!)			
seagate	Interlocked Polled	1s/1s	255s	Y
wd7000	Busmastering DMA	16s/1s	16	Y
t128	Interlocked Polled	16s	255s	Y
(NCR5380)				
qlogic	Interlocked Polled	1s/1s	255s	Y
ultrastor	Busmastering DMA	16s/2s	32	Y
53c7,8xx	Busmastering DMA			
(NCR53c810,				
NCR53c815,				
NCR53c820,				
NCR53c825)				
rel5		1s/1s	127s	N
rel10		8s/1s	127s	Y

Notes :

1. drivers flagged with an '*' are not included with the distribution kernel, and binary boot images may be unavailable.

2. numbers suffixed with an 's' are arbitrary limits set in software which may be changed with a compile time define.

3. hardware limits are indicated by an 'h' suffix, and may differ from the software limits currently imposed by the Linux drivers.

4. unsuffixed numbers may indicate either hard or soft limits.

5. rel5 of the NCR53c810 driver is included in the stock 1.2.x and 1.3.x kernels; rel10 is available via anonymous FTP.

6. With the exception of the AM53C974, the busmastering DMA boards are intelligent; with the NCR executing microcode from main memory, the AIC7770 executing microcode from on-chip RAM, and the rest using a mailbox-style interface.

10.8 Board comparison

Board	Driver	Bus	Price	Notes
Adaptec AIC-6260	aha152x	ISA		chip, not board
Adaptec AIC-6360	aha152x	VLB		chip, not board
(Used in most				
VESA/ISA multi-IO				
boards with SCSI,				
Zenon mainboards)				
Adaptec 1520	aha152x	ISA		
Adaptec 1522	aha152x	ISA	$80	1520 w/FDC

Adaptec 1510	aha152x	ISA		1520 w/out boot ROM, won't autoprobe.
Adaptec 1540C	aha1542	ISA		
Adaptec 1542C	aha1542	ISA		1540C w/FDC
Adaptec 1540CF	aha1542	ISA		FAST SCSI-II
Adaptec 1542CF	aha1542	ISA	$200	1540CF w/FDC
Adaptec 1640	aha1542	MCA		
Adaptec 1740	aha1740	EISA		discontinued
Adaptec 1742	aha1740	EISA		discontinued, 1740 w/FDC
Adaptec 2740	aha274x	EISA		
Adaptec 2742	aha274x	EISA		w/FDC
Adaptec 2840	aha274x	VLB		
Adaptec 2842	aha274x	VLB		w/FDC
Adaptec 2940	aha274x	PCI		
Always IN2000	in2000	ISA		
BusLogic BT-948	BusLogic	PCI	$180	Ultra SCSI
BusLogic BT-958	BusLogic	PCI	$230	Wide Ultra SCSI

(see the section 5.8 (BusLogic MultiMaster Host Adapters) for additional BusLogic board descriptions)

DPT	PM2011	eata_dma	ISA	FAST SCSI-II
	PM2012A	eata_dma	EISA	FAST SCSI-II
	PM2012B	eata_dma	EISA	FAST SCSI-II
	PM2021	eata_dma	ISA	FAST SCSI-II
	PM2022	eata_dma	EISA	FAST SCSI-II
	PM2024	eata_dma	PCI	FAST SCSI-II
	PM2122	eata_dma	EISA	FAST SCSI-II
	PM2322	eata_dma	EISA	FAST SCSI-II
	PM2124	eata_dma	PCI	FAST SCSI-II
	PM2124	eata_dma	PCI	FAST SCSI-II
	PM2124	eata_dma	PCI	FAST SCSI-II
	PM2124	eata_dma	PCI	FAST SCSI-II
	PM2124	eata_dma	PCI	FAST SCSI-II
	PM2124	eata_dma	PCI	FAST SCSI-II
	PM2041W	eata_dma	ISA	Wide Single-ended SCSI-II
	PM2041UW	eata_dma	ISA	Ultra Wide Single-ended
	PM2042W	eata_dma	EISA	Wide Single-ended
	PM2042UW	eata_dma	EISA	Ultra Wide Single-ended
	PM2044W	eata_dma	PCI	Wide Single-ended
	PM2044UW	eata_dma	PCI	Ultra Wide Single-ended
	PM2142W	eata_dma	EISA	Wide Single-ended
	PM2142UW	eata_dma	EISA	Ultra Wide Single-ended
	PM2144W	eata_dma	PCI	Wide Single-ended
	PM2144UW	eata_dma	PCI	Ultra Wide Single-ended
	PM3021	eata_dma	ISA	multichannel raid/simm sockets
	PM3122	eata_dma	EISA	multichannel/raid
	PM3222	eata_dma	EISA	multichannel raid/simm sockets
	PM3224	eata_dma	PCI	multichannel

				raid/simm sockets
PM3334	eata_dma	PCI		Wide Ultra SCSI multichannel raid/simm sockets
DTC 3290	aha1542	EISA		Although it should work, due to documentation release polcies, DTC hardware is unsupported
DTC 3130	53c7,8xx	PCI		'810
DTC 3130B	53c7,8xx	PCI		'815
DTC 3292	aha1542	EISA		3290 w/FDC
DTC 3292	aha1542	EISA		3290 w/FDC
Future Domain 1680	fdomain	ISA		FDC
Future Domain 3260	fdomain	PCI		
NCR53c810 (boards sold by FIC, Chaintech, Nextor, Gigabyte, etc. Mainboards with chip by AMI, ASUS, J-Bond, etc. Common in DEC PCI systems)	53c7,8xx	PCI	$60 (board)	chip, not board. Boards don't include BIOS, although most non-NCR equipped main boards have the SDMS BIOS
NCR53c815 (Intel PCISCSIKIT, NCR8150S, etc)	53c7,8xx	PCI	$100	NCR53c810 plus bios
NCR53c825	53c7,8xx	PCI	$120	Wide variant of NCR53c815. Note that the current Linux driver does not negotiate for wide transfers.
Pro Audio Spectrum 16	pas16	ISA		Sound board w/SCSI
Seagate ST01	seagate	ISA	$20	BIOS only works with some drives
Seagate ST02	seagate	ISA	$40	ST01 w/FDC
Sound Blaster 16 SCSI	aha152x	ISA		Sound board w/SCSI
Western Digital 7000	wd7000	ISA		w/FDC
Trantor T128	t128	ISA		
Trantor T128F	t128	ISA		T128 w/FDC and support for high IRQs
Trantor T130B	g_NCR5380	ISA		
Ultrastor 14F	ultrastor	ISA		w/FDC
Ultrastor 24F	ultrastor	EISA		w/FDC
Ultrastor 34F	ultrastor	VLB		

Notes :

1. Trantor was recently purchased by Adaptec, and some products are being sold under the Adaptec name.

2. Ultrastor recently filed for Chapter 11 Bankruptcy, so technical support is non-existent at this time.

3. The price for the busmastering NCR53c810 boards is not a typo, includes the standard ASPI/CAM driver package for DOS, OS/2 and Windows (32 bit access), and other drivers are available for free download.

Some people have had luck with the following companies :

    SW (swt@netcom.com) (214) 907-0871 fax (214) 907-9339

As of 23 Dec 1995, their price was $53 on '810 boards.

4. Adaptec's recent SCSI chips show an unusual sensitivity to cabling and termination problems. For this reason, I cannot recommend the Adaptec 154x C and CF revisions or the 2xxx series.

    Note that the reliability problems do not apply to the older 154x B revision boards, 174x A revision boards, or to my knowledge AIC-6360/AIC-6260 based boards (1505, 1510, 1520, etc).

    Also, the quality of their technical support has slipped markedly, with long delays becoming more common, and their employees being ignorant (suggesting there were non-disclosure policies affecting certain literature when there were none), and hostile (ie, refusing to pass questions on to some one else when they couldn't answer them).

    If users desire handholding, or wish to make a political statement, they should take this point into consideration. Otherwise, the Adaptec 152x/1510/1505 are nicer than the other ISA boards in the same price range, and there are some excellent deals on used and surplus 154x B revision boards and 1742 boards which IMHO outweigh the support problems.

5. All DPT boards can be upgraded with cache and raid modules, most of the boards are also available in Wide and/or Differential versions.

6. The various NCR boards are not entirely equivalent. Ie, while the ASUS SC200 uses active termination, many other NCR53c810 boards use passive termination. Most '825 boards use active termination, but some use a ROM for BIOS and others have a FLASH ROM. Most '825 boards have a WIDE external connector, WIDE internal connector, and narrow internal connector, although a few (ie, CSC's less expensive model) lack the narrow internal connector.

10.9   Summary

Most ISA, EISA, VESA, and PCI users will probably be served best by a BusLogic MultiMaster board, due to its performance, features such as active termination, and Adaptec 1540 compatibility. There are a number of models available with EISA, ISA, PCI, and VESA local bus interfaces, in single ended and differential, and 8/16 bit SCSI bus widths. The most recent Ultra SCSI PCI models, the BT-948/958/958D, also include Flash ROM for easy firmware updates, as well as automatic "smart" termination.

People with the need for the highest possible IO performance at their fingertips should consider the boards from DPT, which are the only ones that support RAID, caching and more than one SCSI channel.

People with PCI systems should consider NCR53c8xx based boards. These are bus mastering SCSI controllers, '810s are available quantity one for $53 (ie, cheaper than the Adaptec 1520). C't magazine benchmarked the boards as faster than both the Adaptec 2940 and BusLogic BT-946C (under DOS), and they get reasonable performance under Linux (up to 6M/sec through the file system). The disadvantages of these boards versus the BusLogics are that they aren't Adaptec 1540 compatible, may or may not come with active termination, you'll need the latest driver revision (standard in 1.3.5x, also available via anonymous FTP for 1.2.x) to make full use of the hardware, and are more likely to have problems than with a mailbox interface board like a BusLogic or DPT.

Where everything working right on the first try is imperative, a BusLogic MultiMaster or DPT board is probably optimal due to the complexity and potential for problems in non-mailbox interface boards like the NCR53c8xx and Adaptec AIC7xxx .

People wanting non-PCI SCSI on a limited budget will probably be happiest finding a surplus or used Adaptec 154x B revision or 174x A revision, or an Adaptec 1520 clone of some sort (about $80) if they want new hardware. These boards offer reasonable throughput and interactive performance at a modest price.

11   Assignment of minor numbers

Due to constraints imposed by Linux's use of a sixteen bit dev_t with only eight bits allocated to the minor number, SCSI disk, tape, CDROM, and generic minor numbers are assigned dynamically. according to the following procedure :

```
For all SCSI host adapters, from scsi0 through scsiN
  For all SCSI IDs on this bus, from 0 through 7, except for
    this host adapter's ID
    For all logical units, from 0 through max_scsi_luns
      - Probe the bus, target, and LUN combination by
        issuing a TEST UNIT READY command.  If we don't
        think a unit was here, don't probe any more LUNs
        on this bus + SCSI ID.
      - Send an INQUIRY command to determine what we've
        found; including the device type, vendor, model,
        firmware revision, etc.
      - Pass the results of this to a special recognition
        function for each high level driver present (i.e. disk,
        tape, etc).  Attach this device to the next available
        unit for any drivers that are willing to drive this.
        The generic device will attach to all devices.
      - If it was SCSI-I, or in a list of devices known
        not to handle multiple LUNs, don't probe any more
        LUNs on this bus + SCSI ID.
      - If it is a device known to have multiple LUNs, then
        a scan of the full LUN spectrum is forced, overriding
        max_scsi_luns.
```

There are frequently problems with this approach because if you have a system where some devices are only present some of the time, then the minor numbers for a given device will depend upon which devices were present at boot time. This can present problem, because rc scripts or the file /etc/fstab might contain instructions for mounting specific partitions which fails when the disk appears with a different minor number.

This problem has not yet been fully solved. There is a program which can be found on tsx-11 that creates a /dev/scsi hierarchy based upon host number, id and lun. This is a bit clumsy, but it would help to alleviate some of the problems.

A better solution will probably come out of the /proc/scsi pseudo directory. This is currently a work in progress, so at present we cannot say exactly the form of the solution, but at the time of this writing this appears to be a promising approach for resolving some of these issues.

The 3 Button Serial Mouse mini-HOWTO

Geoff Short, *geoff@kipper.york.ac.uk* <mailto:geoff@kipper.york.ac.uk> v1.32, 4 November 1997

How to get a 3 button serial mouse working properly under Linux.

Contents

1 Disclaimer

The following document is offered in good faith as comprising only safe programming and procedures. No responsibility is accepted by the author for any loss or damage caused in any way to any person or equipment, as a direct or indirect consequence of following these instructions.

2   Introduction

The most recent version of this document can always be found at *http://kipper.york.ac.uk/mouse.html* <http://kipper.york.ac.uk/mouse.html>

There is a Japanese translation at *http://jf.gee.kyoto-u.ac.jp/JF/JF-ftp/euc/3-Button-Mouse.euc* <http://jf.gee.kyoto-u.ac.jp/JF/JF-ftp/euc/3-Button-Mouse.euc>

Most X applications are written with the assumption that the user will be working with a 3 button mouse. Serial mice are commonly used on computers and are cheap to buy. Many of these mice have 3 buttons and claim to use the Microsoft protocol, which in theory means they are ideal for the X windows setup. (The record for the cheapest working 3 button mouse currently stands at $1.14!)

Most dual-protocol mice will work in two modes:

- 2-button Microsoft mode.
- 3-button MouseSystems mode.

This document leads you through the different steps needed to configure your mouse in these two different modes, especially the steps needed to use the more useful 3-button mode.

3   Serial Ports

The first thing to do is to make sure the software can find the mouse. Work out which serial port your mouse is connected to - usually this will be **/dev/ttyS0** (COM1 under DOS) or **/dev/ttyS1** (COM2). (**ttyS0** is usually the 9 pin socket, **ttyS1** the 25 pin socket, but of course there is no hard and fast rule about these things.) There are also an equivalent number of **/dev/cua** devices, which are almost the same as the **ttyS** ones, but their use is now discouraged. For convenience make a new link **/dev/mouse** pointing at this port. For instance, for **ttyS0**:

```
ln -s /dev/ttyS0 /dev/mouse
```

4   Switched Mice

Some mice, not usually the cheapest ones, have a switch on the bottom marked '2/3'. Sometimes this may be 'PC/MS'. In this case the '2' setting is for 2 button Microsoft mode, and the '3' for 3 button MouseSystems mode. The 'PC/MS' switch is a bit more complicated. You will probably find the 'MS' setting is for Microsoft, and the 'PC' is for MouseSystems. You may find the 'PC' setting described as ps/2 mode, but it should do MouseSystems as well. If you have such a mouse, you can switch the switch to '3' or 'PC', put the MouseSystems settings in your XConfigs (see below) and the mouse should work perfectly in 3-button mode.

5   Normal Mice

If you don't have any switches, and no instructions, then a little bit of experimentation is needed. The first thing to try is to assume the mouse maker is telling the truth, and the mouse is full Microsoft. Set up your Xconfigs to expect a Microsoft mouse (see the 9 (Xconfig section)) and give it a try.

If the mouse didn't work at all, then you don't have a Microsoft mouse, or there is some other problem. Try the other protocols in the configs, the man page for the config file is the best place to start looking. Also look in the 11 (Miscellaneous Problems) section below.

What you will probably find is that when you run X, the mouse works fine but only the outer two buttons do anything. You can of course accept this, and emulate the third button (press both buttons at once to click the middle one) like you do with a two button mouse. To do this, change your Xconfig file as shown in the *Xconfig example* <config> section below. This may mean you have bought a 3 button mouse for no good reason, and you are certainly no further forward. So, now you need to look at your hardware.

6 Switching a Mouse to 3-Button Mode

Even cheap mice can also work under the Mouse Systems protocol, with all three buttons working. The trick is to get the mouse to think it's a Mouse Systems one, something you rarely see in your instructions.

- Before you power up your computer, hold down the left mouse button (and keep it held down until it has booted to be on the safe side).

When the mouse first gets power, if the left button is held down it switches into Mouse Systems mode. A simple fact, but not always publicised. Note that a soft reboot of your computer may not cut the mouse power and therefore may not work. There are a number of other ways of switching the mode, which may or may not work with your particular mouse. Some of these are less drastic than rebooting your computer, two are more so!

- If your computer is get-at-able you can unplug the mouse and plug it back in with the button held down (although you shouldn't normally plug things in to a live computer, the RS232 spec says it is OK).

- You may be able to reset the mouse by typing echo "*n" > /dev/mouse, which should have the same effect as unplugging it. Hold the left button down for Mouse Systems mode, not for Microsoft. You could put this in whatever script you use to start X up.

- Bob Nichols (rnichols@interaccess.com) has written a small c program to do the same thing, which may work if echo "*n" does not (and vice versa). You can find a copy of his source code at *http://kipper.york.ac.uk/src/fix-mouse.c* <http://kipper.york.ac.uk/src/fix-mouse.c>

- Someone has reported that the 'ClearDTR' line in the Xconfig is enough to switch their mouse into Mouse Systems mode.

- If you are brave enough, open the mouse up (remember that this will invalidate your warranty) and have a look inside. In some cases, the mouse may have a switch inside, for some strange reason known only to the manufacturer. More likely on the cheap mice is a jumper which you can move. The switch or jumper may have the same effect as a 'MS/PC' switch described in the 4 (Switched Mice section) above. You may find that the circuit board is designed for a switch between 2 & 3 buttons, but it hasn't been fitted. It will look something like:

```
          ------------
          | o | o | o |  SW1
          ------------
            1   2   3
```

Try linking pins 1-2 or 2-3, and see if it changes the behaviour of the mouse. If it does, you can either fit a small switch, or solder across the contacts for a quick and permanent solution.

- Another soldering solution which might be a last-resort for mice which don't understand MouseSystems at all, from Peter Benie (*pjb1008@chiark.chu.cam.ac.uk* <mailto:pjb1008@chiark.chu.cam.ac.uk>). If the middle button's switch is double-pole, connect one side of the switch to the left button's switch, and the other side to right button's switch. If it's not a double pole switch then use diodes rather than wire. Now, the middle button pushes the left and right buttons down together. Select ChordMiddle in the XF86Config and you have a working middle button.

- The ultimate recourse with the soldering iron was first described to me by Brian Craft (*bcboy@pyramid.bio.brandeis.edu* <mailto:bcboy@pyramid.bio.brandeis.edu>). Two common generic mouse chips are the 16 pin **Z8350**, and the 18 pin **HM8350A**. On each of these chips, one pin controls the mode of the chip, as follows.

```
Pin 3   Mode
-----   ----
Open    Default Microsoft. Mouse Systems if a button is held on power-up.
GND     Always Mouse Systems.
Vdd     Always Microsoft.
```

(Pins are numbered as follows:)

```
         ----
pin1  -| \/ |-
pin2  -|    |-
pin3  -|    |-
      -|    |-
      -|    |-
      -|    |-
      -|    |-
pin8  -|____|-
```

(This info comes courtesy of Hans-Christoph Wirth, and Juergen Exner, who posted it to de.comp.os.linux.hardware) You can solder a link between pin 3 and gnd, which will fix the mouse into MouseSystems mode.

  - Peter Fredriksson (*peterf@lysator.liu.se* <mailto:peterf@lysator.liu.se>) has tried the SYSGRATION **SYS2005** chip, and found that linking Pin 3 to Gnd forced Mouse System mode.

  - Uli Drescher (*ud@digi.ruhr.de* <mailto:ud@digi.ruhr.de>) confirms it works on an **HN8348A** chip.

  - Urban Widmark (*ubbe@ts.umu.se* <mailto:ubbe@ts.umu.se>) says the same applies to the **EC3567A1** chip, where Pin 8 is ground. I've tried it as well and it works fine.

  - Timo T Metsala (*metsala@cc.helsinki.fi* <mailto:metsala@cc.helsinki.fi>) has found that on the **HT6510A** chip pin 3 is mode select, pin 9 is Gnd. The same works for the **HT6513A** chip. Holtek also make **HT6513B** and **HT6513F** chips - on these, pin 8 is Gnd.

  - Robert Romanowski (*robin@cs.tu-berlin.de* <mailto:robin@cs.tu-berlin.de>) says pin 3 - pin 8 (Gnd) works on an **EM83701BP** chip too.

  - Robert Kaiser (*rkaiser@sysgo.de* <mailto:rkaiser@sysgo.de>) confirms that pin 3 - Gnd works on a **EC3576A1** chip too.

- As an alternative to the above soldering methods, you can get the mouse to hold it's own button down when booting: this circuit from *Mathias Katzer* <mailto:mkatzer@TechFak.Uni-Bielefeld.DE>.

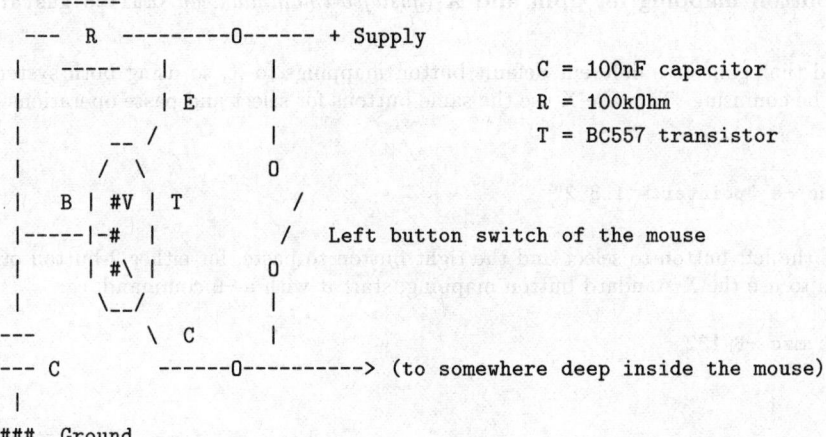

```
                 -----
         --- R ---------0------ + Supply
        |  -----  |        |              C = 100nF capacitor
        |        | E |     |              R = 100kOhm
        |     __ /         |              T = BC557 transistor
        |    /  \         0
       .| B | #V | T        /
       |-----|-# |          /  Left button switch of the mouse
       |     | #\ |        0
       |      \__/         |
       ---           \  C  |
       --- C         ------0----------> (to somewhere deep inside the mouse)
       |
       ### Ground
```

The test mouse was a no-name model MUS2S - whether this works in other mice depends on the circuit of the mouse; if the switch is connected to ground and not to +Supply, an npn-transistor like the BC547 should work; R and C have to be swapped then, too.

So there you have it, the choice is yours. Stick with the default Microsoft two buttons, or work out how to switch the mode and set X up to take advantage of this.

7 Using gpm to Switch Mouse Modes

gpm is the program that lets you use the mouse in console mode. It is usually included in linux distributions, and can be started from the command line or in the startup script /etc/rc.d/rc.local. gpm is the cause of much problem to people using bus mice, since it locks the mouse and stops X from using it - those of us using serial mice don't have this problem.

The main modes for serial mice under gpm are:

```
gpm -t ms
gpm -t msc
gpm -t help
```

for Microsoft or MouseSystems modes, or to probe the mouse for you and tell you what it found. To run gpm in MouseSystems mode, you may need a -3 flag, and possibly a DTR option, using the -o dtr flag:

```
gpm -3 -o dtr -t msc
```

gpm is often able to recognise all three buttons of the mouse even in Microsoft mode. And newer versions (Version 1.0 and later (?)) can then make this information available to other programs. For this to work, you need to run gpm with the -R tag, like this:

```
gpm -R -t ms
```

This will make gpm re-export the mouse data to a new device, called /dev/gpmdata, which looks like a mouse to any other program. Note that this device **always** uses the MouseSystems protocol. You can then set your Xconfig to use this instead of /dev/mouse as shown below, but of course you must ensure gpm is always running when you use X. Some people have reported that some middle-button events are not correctly interpreted by X using this technique, this may be down to an individual mouse setup.

Changing button mapping for gpm and X (*gustafso@math.utah.edu* <mailto:gustafso@math.utah.edu>)

You may find that gpm uses different default button mappings to X, so using both systems on the same machine can be confusing. To make X use the same buttons for select and paste operations as gpm, use the X command

```
xmodmap -e "pointer = 1 3 2"
```

which causes the left button to select and the right button to paste, for either 2-button or 3-button mice. To force gpm to use the X standard button mapping, start it with a -B command, eg:

```
gpm -t msc -B 132
```

8   Using two mice

In some cases, for instance a laptop with a built-in pointing device, you may wish to use a serial mouse as a second device. In most cases the built-in device uses the PS/2 protocol, and can be ignored if you don't wish to use it. Simply configure gpm or X to use **/dev/ttyS0** (or whatever) as usual.

To use both at once, you can use **gpm -M** to re-export the devices. More details in the gpm man page.

9   XF86Config and Xconfig file examples

The location of your configuration file for X depends on the particular release and distribution you have. It will probably be either **/etc/Xconfig**, **/etc/XF86Config** or **/usr/X11/lib/X11/XF86Config**. You should see which one it is when you start X - it will be echoed to the screen before all the options are displayed. The syntax is slightly different between the XF86Config and Xconfig files, so both are given.

Microsoft Serial Mouse

- XF86config:

```
Section "Pointer"
    Protocol "microsoft"
    Device "/dev/mouse"
EndSection
```

- Xconfig:

```
#
# Mouse definition and related parameters
#
Microsoft       "/dev/mouse"
```

Microsoft Serial Mouse with Three Button Emulation

- XF86config:

```
        Section "Pointer"
            Protocol "microsoft"
            Device "/dev/mouse"
            Emulate3Buttons
        EndSection
```

- Xconfig:

```
        #
        # Mouse definition and related parameters
        #
        Microsoft       "/dev/mouse"
        Emulate3Buttons
```

MouseSystems Three Button Serial Mouse

- XF86config:

```
        Section "Pointer"
            Protocol "mousesystems"
            Device "/dev/mouse"
            ClearDTR              # These two lines probably won't be needed,
            ClearRTS              # try without first and then just the DTR
        EndSection
```

- Xconfig:

```
        #
        # Mouse definition and related parameters
        #
        MouseSystems    "/dev/mouse"
        ClearDTR                  # These two lines probably won't be needed,
        ClearRTS                  # try without first and then just the DTR
```

Microsoft Serial Mouse with gpm -R

- XF86config:

```
        Section "Pointer"
            Protocol "MouseSystems"
            Device "/dev/gpmdata"
        EndSection
```

- Xconfig:

```
        #
        # Mouse definition and related parameters
        #
        MouseSystems    "/dev/gpmdata"
```

10   Cables, extensions and adaptors

The only wires needed in a mouse cable are as follows: TxD and RxD for data transfer, RTS and/or DTR for power sources, and ground. Translated into pin numbers, they are:

	9-pin port	25-pin port
TxD	3	2
RxD	2	3
RTS	7	4
DTR	4	20
Gnd	5	7

The above table may be of use if you wish to make adaptors between 9- and 25-pin plugs, or extension cables.

11   Miscellaneous Problems and Setups

- If you have trouble with your mouse in X or console mode, check you are not running a getty on the serial line, or anything else such as a modem for that matter. Also check for IRQ conflicts.

- It is possible that you need to hold down the left button when booting X windows. Some systems may send some sort of signal or spike to the mouse when X starts.

- Problems with serial devices may be due to the serial port not being initialised correctly at boot. This is done by the `setserial` command, run from the start-up script `/etc/rc.d/rc.serial`. Check the man page for `setserial` and the Serial-HOWTO for more details. It may be worth a little experimentation with types, for instance try `setserial /dev/mouse uart 16550` or `16550a` regardless of what port you actually have. (For instance, mice don't like the 16c550AF).

- The `ClearDTR` flag may not work properly on some systems, unless you disable the RTS/CTS hand-shaking with the command:

      stty -crtscts < /dev/mouse

  (Tested on UART 16450/Pentium by Vladimir Geogjaev *geogjaev@wave.sio.rssi.ru* <mailto: geogjaev@wave.sio.rssi.ru>)

- Logitech mice may require the line `ChordMiddle` to enable the middle of the three buttons to work. This line replaces `Emulate3Buttons` or goes after the `/dev/mouse` line in the config file. You may well need the `ClearDTR` and `ClearRTS` lines in your Xconfig. Some Logitech mice positively do not need the `ChordMiddle` line - one symptom of this problem is that menus seem to move with the mouse instead of scrolling down. (From: *chang@platform.com* <mailto:chang@platform.com>)

- Swapping buttons: use the `xmodmap` command to change which physical button registers as each mouse click. eg: `xmodmap -e "pointer = 3 2 1"` will turn round the buttons for use in the left hand. If you only have a two-button mouse then it's just numbers 1 & 2.

- Acceleration: use the `xset m` command to change the mouse settings. eg `xset m 2` will set the acceleration to 2. Look at the manpage for full details.

- Pointer offset: If the click action appears to be coming from the left or right of where the cursor is, it may be that your screen is not aligned. This is a problem with the S3 driver, which you may be able to fix using xvidtune. Try `Invert_VCLK/InvertVCLK`, or `EarlySC`. This info from Bill Lavender (*lavender@MCS.COM* <mailto:lavender@MCS.COM>) and Simon Hargrave. In the XF86Config, it might look like this:

```
            Subsection "Display"
                Modes       "1024x768" "800x600" "640x480" "1280x1024"
                Invert_VCLK "*" 1
                ...
```

- If you are getting 'bouncing' of the mouse buttons, ie two clicks when you only wanted one, there may be something wrong with the mouse. This problem has been solved for Logitech mice by Bob Nichols (*rnichols@interaccess.com* <mailto:rnichols@interaccess.com>) and involves soldering some resistors and a chip in the mouse to debounce the microswitches.

- If some users cannot get the mouse to work but some (eg root) can, it is possible that the users are not running exactly the same thing - for instance a different version of X or a different Xconfig. Check the X start-up messages carefully to make sure.

- If you find the mouse pointer is erasing things from your screen, you have a server config problem. Try adding the option linear, or maybe nolinear to the graphics card section, or if it is a PCI board, the options tgui_pci_write_off and tgui_pci_read_off. (This seems to be a Trident Card problem.)

- If the mouse cursor doesn't show up on the screen, but otherwise seems to be working, try the option "sw_cursor" in the Device section of the config file.

- If your mouse stops working when its sunny or when you turn a light on, it may be that the sensors are being swamped by light getting through the case. You could try painting the inside of the case black, or putting some card in the top.

- Microsoft Brand mice are often a cause of problems. The newest "Microsoft Serial Mouse 2.1A" has been reported not to work on many systems, although unplugging it and plugging it in again may help. The "Microsoft Intellimouse" also causes problems, although it should now be supported by XFree version 3.3 and later.

12   Models Tested

There are a lot of different mice out there, and I cannot honestly say that you should go out and buy one rather than the other. What I can do is give a list of what I think these mice do, based on experience and heresay. Even with this information you should be a little cautious - we had two identical mice in our office on two computers, some things worked on one and not t'other! Any additions to this list would be welcome.

Mouse Systems optical mouse, serial version
Works well (as you might expect from the name!) without ClearDTR or ClearRTS in the config.
WiN mouse, as sold by Office World for eight quid.
Standard dual-mode Microsoft/MouseSystems.
Agiler Mouse 2900
Standard dual-mode Microsoft/MouseSystems. SYSGRATION SYS2005 chip is solderable.
Sicos mouse,
Works ok, needs ClearDTR & Clear RTS in config.
Index sell a mouse for 10 quid,
Doesn't work in 3 button mode, but does have nice instructions :-)
Artec mouse
Usual dual-protocol mouse, needs 'ClearDTR' set in config, NOT 'ClearRTS'
DynaPoint 3 button serial mouse.
Usual dual-protocol mouse, needs 'ClearDTR' AND 'ClearRTS' in Xconfig.
Genius Easymouse 3 button mouse
Works fine with Mouseman protocol without the ChordMiddle parameter set. From Roderick Johnstone (*rmj@ast.cam.ac.uk* <mailto:rmj@ast.cam.ac.uk>)
Truemouse, made in Taiwan

Works OK, needs 'ClearDTR' in config. (From *Tim MacEachern* `<http://ccn.cs.dal.ca/ae721/Profile.html>`)

Champ brand mouse

Needs to have switch in PC mode, which enables MouseSystems protocol also. (From tnugent@gucis.cit.gu.edu.au)

MicroSpeed mouse

Usual dual-protocol mouse.

Venus brand ($7)

Has a jumper inside to switch between 2 and 3 button mode. (From *mhoward@mth.com* `<mailto:mhoward@mth.com>`)

Saturn

Switched mouse, works OK as MouseSystems in 3-button position. (From *grant@oj.rsmas.miami.edu* `<mailto:grant@oj.rsmas.miami.edu>`.)

Manhattan mouse.

Switch for 'MS AM' / 'PC AT' modes, MS mode works fine with the `gpm -R` method. (From *komanec@umel.fee.vutbr.cz* `<mailto:komanec@umel.fee.vutbr.cz>`).

Inland mouse.

Switch for 'PC/MS' modes, works fine. (From *http://ptsg.eecs.berkeley.edu/~venkates* `<http://ptsg.eecs.berkeley.edu/venkates/>`).

qMouse (3-button), FCC ID E6qmouse X31.

Sells in the USA for about $10. Works with 'gpm -t msc -r 20'. No jumpers or switches for MouseSystems 3-button mode. Unreliable in X. Does not respond to `echo "*n"` > `/dev/mouse`.

Mitsumi Mouse (2-button), FCC ID EW4ECM-S3101.

Sells in the USA for about $12. Reliable in X and under gpm, smooth double-button. (These two from *gustafso@math.utah.edu* `<mailto:gustafso@math.utah.edu>`)

PC Accessories mouse that i got from CompUSA for under $10.

Has PC/MS switch on bottom. Works OK. (From *steveb@communique.net* `<mailto:steveb@communique.net>`)

First Mouse - seriously cheap at 7.79 pounds at Tempo.

Dual Microsoft/MouseSystems, mode set by button depress at power-up. No switches, no links. Four wire connection, echo '*n' doesn't work. 'gpm -R' works a treat. (From *peterk@henhouse.demon.co.uk* `<mailto:peterk@henhouse.demon.co.uk>`)

Trust 3-button mouse.

Dual-mode with switch, works OK as MouseSystems in 'PC' mode. gpm doesn't like the Microsoft mode.

Chic 410

Works perfectly when kept in ms mode and used with the gpm -R command. From Stephen M. Weiss (*steve@esc.ie.lehigh.edu* `<mailto:steve@esc.ie.lehigh.edu>`)

KeyMouse 3-button mouse.

Works OK with ClearDTR and ClearRTS in Xconfig; '-o dtr' needed with gpm. (From *EZ4PHIL@aol.com* `<mailto:EZ4PHIL@aol.com>`)

Qtronix keyboard 'Scorpio 60'

All three buttons work in MouseSystems protocol. (From *hwe@uebemc.siemens.de* `<mailto:hwe@uebemc.siemens.de>`)

Tecra 720 laptop

The glidepoint is on /dev/cua0; the stick is on /dev/psaux. (From *apollo@anl.gov* `<mailto:apollo@anl.gov>`)

Anubis mouse

Works fine, need to hold down left button whenever switching to the X virtual console. (From *Joel Crisp* `<mailto:Joel.Crisp@bristol.ac.uk>`)

Yakumo No.1900 mouse

Works with `gpm -R -t ms` exporting to X. (From *Oliver Schwank* `<mailto:flinx.nbg.sub.org!oli@flinx.nbg.sub.org>`)

Genius 'Easy Trak' Trackball

Is not Microsoft compatible, use `Mouseman` in the Xconfig and it will work fine. (From *VTanger@aol.com*

`<mailto:VTanger@aol.com>`.)
Highscreen Mouse Pro
'Works fine' says *alfonso@univaq.it* `<mailto:alfonso@univaq.it>`.
Logitech CA series
Works in X using MMseries protocol, at 2400 Baud, 150 SampleRate. (Should also apply to Logitech CC, CE, C7 & C9 mice). (From *vkochend@nyx.net* `<mailto:vkochend@nyx.net>`.)
A4-Tech mouse
Works OK, needs `DTR` line under both X and gpm. (From *deane@gooroos.com* `<mailto:deane@gooroos.com>`)
Vertech mouse
Normal Microsoft/Mousesystems behaviour, can be soldered for a permenant fix. (From *duncan@fs3.ph.man.ac.uk* `<mailto:duncan@fs3.ph.man.ac.uk>`.)
Boeder M-7 "Bit Star" (and other M series apart from M13)
Switches to Mousesystems protocol by holding any button down at power-on. (From *mailto:sjt@tappin.force9.co.uk* `<mailto:sjt@tappin.force9.co.uk>`.)
Mouse Systems "Scroll" Mouse (four buttons and a roller/button)
Has a 2/3 switch - in mode 3 functions as a three button MouseSystems mouse, ignoring extra button & wheel. Doesn't need `ClearDTS/DTR`. (From *parker1@airmail.net* `<mailto:parker1@airmail.net>`.)
Radio Shack 3-button Serial Mouse
Model 26-8432, available in Tandy for about 20 quid. Works as Mousesystems with ClearDTR. (From *Sherilyn@sidaway.demon.co.uk* `<mailto:Sherilyn@sidaway.demon.co.uk>`.)

13 Further Information

- Mouse Systems has a web site at *http://www.mousesystems.com/* `<http://www.mousesystems.com/>`. They have a Windows driver if you need one.

- The Linux Serial HOWTO is available from mirrors of sunsite around the world. If you don't know where your nearest mirror is, start at *http://sunsite.unc.edu/mdw/linux.html* `<http://sunsite.unc.edu/mdw/linux.html>`

- There is a very good explanation of how mice work at `<http://box.argonet.co.uk/users/4qd/faq/meece.html>`.

- Fuller details of the Xconfig and XF86Config files are found on the relevant man pages, and in the documentation about installing X windows such as the Xfree86 HOWTO. Also, see the XFree86 FAQ at a mirror of *http://www.XFree86.org/* `<http://www.XFree86.org/>`.

- Information about gpm can be found on the man page, also try the web page of Darin Ernst at *http://www.castle.net/X-notebook/mouse.txt* `<http://www.castle.net/X-notebook/mouse.txt>`.

- Lots of information on mice hardware and software can be found at `<http://www.hut.fi/Misc/Electronics/pc/interface.html>`

14 Mouse Tail

Much of the information for this document has been trawled from the various linux newsgroups. I am sorry I did not keep a record of everyone who has indirectly contributed by this route, thank you all very much.

So, to sum up:

- Even cheap 3 button Microsoft mice can be made to work.
- Configure your copy of X to expect a Mouse Systems mouse.
- Hold down the left button at power-on to switch the mouse to MouseSystems mode.

- You might need to hold the left button down when starting X.
- Mice are more intelligent than you think.

The Clock Mini-HOWTO

Ron Bean, *rbean@execpc.com* <mailto:rbean@execpc.com> Dec. 1996

How to set and keep your computer clock on time.

Contents

1   Introduction

The real-time-clock chips used on PC motherboards (and even expensive workstations) are notoriously inaccurate. Linux provides a simple way to correct for this in software, making the clock potentially *very* accurate even without an external time source. But most people don't seem to know about it, for several reasons:

1. It's not mentioned in most of the general "how to set up linux" documentation, and it would be difficult to set up automatically at install time (although not impossible in theory, if you have a modem).

2. If you check "man clock" you'll get clock(3), which is not what you want. (try "man 8 clock").

3. Most people don't seem to care what time it is anyway.

4. Those few who do care often want to use the xntpd package from louie.udel.edu to sync to an external time source, such as a network time server or radio clock.

This mini-HOWTO describes the low-tech approach. If you're at all interested in this sort of thing, I highly recommend that you spend some time at <http://www.eecis.udel.edu/ntp/> which includes all kinds of interesting stuff, including complete info on xntpd and links to NIST and USNO (I have a few more comments on xntpd at the end.)

Note

> If you run more than one OS on your machine, you should only let one of them reset the CMOS clock, so they don't confuse each other. If you regularly run both Linux and Windows on the same machine, you may want to check out some of the shareware clock programs that are available for Windows instead (follow the links from the URL above).

2 Using the "clock" program

Everything you need to know is in the clock(8) man page, but this mini-HOWTO will walk you through the process.

Note
> You must be **root** to run "clock", or any other program that affects either the system time or the CMOS clock.

2.1 Checking your installation

Check your system startup files for a command like "clock -a" or "clock -ua". Depending on which distribution you're using, it might be in /etc/rc.local, or /etc/rc.d/rc.sysinit, or some similar place.

If it says "clock -s" or "clock -us", change the "s" to an "a", and then check to see if you have the file /etc/adjtime, which contains a single line that looks something like this:

    0.000000 842214901 0.000000

These numbers are the correction factor (in seconds per day), the time the clock was last corrected (in seconds since Jan 1, 1970), and the partial second that was rounded off last time. If you don't have this file, login as **root** and create it, with a single line that looks like this (all zeros):

    0.0 0 0.0

Then run "clock -a" or "clock -ua" manually from the shell to update the 2nd number (use the "u" if your clock is set to Universal instead of local time).

2.2 Measuring your clock's drift rate

First, you need to know what time it is :-). Your local time of day number may or may not be accurate. My favorite method is to call WWV's voice announcment at (303)499-7111 (this is a toll call). If you have access to a network time server, you can use the **ntpdate** program from the **xntpd** package (use the -b flag to keep the kernel from messing with the CMOS clock). Otherwise use "date -s hh:mm:ss" to set the kernel time by hand, and then "clock -w" to set the CMOS clock from the kernel clock. You'll need to remember when you last set the clock, so write down the date someplace where you won't lose it. If you used **ntpdate**, do "date +%s" and write down the number of seconds since Jan 1,1970.

Then come back some days or weeks later and see how far the clock has drifted. If you're setting the clock by hand, I'd recommend waiting at least two weeks, and only calculate the drift rate to the nearest .1 sec/day. After several months you could get to the nearest .01 sec/day (some people claim more accuracy than that, but I'm being conservative here). If you use **ntpdate** you shouldn't have to wait that long, but in any case you can always fine-tune it later.

You can have cron run "clock -a" at regular intervals to keep the system time in line with the (corrected) CMOS time. This command will also be run from your startup file every time you boot the system, so if you do that often (as some of us do), that may be enough for your purposes.

Note that certain programs may complain if the system time jumps by more than one second at a time, or if it jumps backwards. If you have this problem, you can use **xntpd** or **ntpdate** to correct the time more gradually.

2.3 Example

2.3.1 To set time

Login as **root**. Dial (303)499-7111 (voice), listen for time announcement. Then type:

    date -s hh:mm:ss

but don't press enter until you hear the beep. (You could use "**ntpdate**" here instead of "**date**", and skip
the phone call) This sets the "kernel time". Then type:

    clock -w

This sets the CMOS time to match the kernel time. Then type:

    date +%j

(or "**date +%s**" if you used "**ntpdate**" instead of "**date**" above) and write down the number it gives you for
next time.

2.3.2 To reset time and check drift rate

Find the date you wrote down last time. Login as **root** Then type:

    clock -a

This sets the kernel time to match the current CMOS time. Dial (303)499-7111 (voice), listen for announcement. Then type:

    date

and press enter when you hear the beep, but while you're waiting, write down the time they announce, and
don't hang up yet. This tells you what time your machine thought it was, when it should have been exactly
on the minute. Now type in

    date hh:mm:00

using the minute *after* the one that was just announced, and press enter when you hear the beep again
(now you can hang up). For **hh** use the local hour. This sets the "kernel time". Then type:

    clock -w

which writes the new (correct) time to the CMOS clock. Now type:

    date +%j

(or "**date +%s**" if that's what you used before)

You now have three numbers (two dates and a time) that will allow you to calculate the drift rate.

2.3.3   Calculating the correction factor

When you ran "`date`" on the minute, was your machine slow or fast? If it was fast, you'll have to subtract some number of seconds, so write it down as a negative number. If it was slow, you have to add some seconds, so write it down as positive.

Now subtract the two dates. If you used "`date +%j`", the numbers represent the day-of-year (1-365, or 1-366 in leap years). If you've passed Jan 1 since you last set the clock you'll have to add 365 (or 366) to the 2nd number. If you used "`date +%s`" then your number is in seconds, and you'll have to divide it by 86400 to get days.

If you already had a correction factor in `/etc/adjtime`, you'll have to account for the number of seconds you've already corrected. If you've overcorrected, this number will have the opposite sign of the one you just measured; if you've undercorrected it will have the same sign. Multiply the old correction factor by the number of days, and then add the new number of seconds (signed addition– if the two numbers have the same sign, you'll get a larger number, if they have opposite signs, you'll get a smaller number).

Then divide the total number of seconds by the number of days to get the new correction factor, and put it in `/etc/adjtime` in place of the old one. Write down the new date (in seconds or days) for next time.

Here's what my `/etc/adjtime` looks like:

```
-9.600000 845082716 -0.250655
```

(note 9.6 seconds per day is nearly five minutes per month!)

3   A few words about xntpd

Your system actually has two clocks– the battery powered "real time clock" that keeps track of time when the system is turned off (also known as the "CMOS clock", "Hardware clock", or "RTC") and the "kernel time" (sometimes called the "software clock" or "system clock") which is based on the timer interrupt and is initialized from the CMOS clock at boot time. The two will drift at different rates, so they will gradually drift apart from each other, and also away from the "real" time.

All references to "the clock" in the `xntpd` documentation refer to the "kernel clock". When you run `xntpd` or `timed` (or any other program that uses the `adjtimex` system call), the linux kernel assumes that the kernel clock is more accurate than the CMOS clock, and resets the CMOS time every 11 minutes from then on (until you reboot the machine). This means that "`clock`" no longer knows when the CMOS clock was last reset, so you can't use the correction factor in `/etc/adjtime`. You can use `ntpdate` in your startup file to initially set the clock from a timeserver before starting `xntpd`. If you don't always have access to an accurate time source when you boot the machine, this can be a bit awkward– `xntpd` isn't really designed to be used in situations like that.

`Xntpd` includes drivers for many radio clocks, and can also be set to call NIST's dial-up time service at regular intervals (be sure to calculate the effect on your phone bill when setting the interval between calls). It can also apply a correction factor to the kernel clock if it loses contact with its other sources for an extended period of time.

Most radio clocks cost $3-4K, but you can get plans for an inexpensive "**gadget box**" (actually a 300 baud modem) that sits between your computer and any shortwave radio tuned to Canada's CHU time station (see <ftp://ftp.udel.edu/pub/ntp/gadget.tar.Z>). The Heathkit WWV receiver (the "Most Accurate Clock") is also still available (although not as a kit), and costs around $4-500. GPS signals also contain time information, and some GPS recievers can connect to a serial port. This may become the low cost solution in the near future.

In theory, someone could write a program to use NIST's dial up time service to calculate the drift rate of both the CMOS clock and the kernel clock automatically. I am not aware of any stand-alone program to do this, but most of the code could probably be borrowed from xntpd.

The Linux Serial Programming HOWTO

by Peter H. Baumann, *Peter.Baumann@dlr.de* <mailto:Peter.Baumann@dlr.de>   v1.0 January 22, 1998

This document describes how to program communications with devices over a serial port on a Linux box.

Contents

1 Introduction

This is the Linux Serial Programming HOWTO. All about how to program communications with other devices / computers over a serial line under Linux. Different techniques are explained: Canonical I/O (only complete lines are transmitted/received), asyncronous I/O, and waiting for input from multiple sources.

This document does not describe how to set up serial ports, because this has been described by Greg Hankins in the Serial-HOWTO.

I have to emphasize that I am not an expert in this field, but have had problems with a project that involved such communication. The code examples presented here were derived from the miniterm code available from the LDP programmers guide (`ftp://sunsite.unc.edu/pub/Linux/docs/LDP/programmers-guide/lpg-0.4.tar.gz` and mirrors) in the examples directory.

Since I wrote this document in June 1997, I have moved to WinNT to satisfy customers need, so I have not built up more in depth knowledge. If anybody has any comments, I will gladly incorporate them into this document (see sect. Feedback). If someone would like to take over and do a better job, please e-mail me.

All examples were tested using a i386 Linux Kernel 2.0.29.

1.1   Copyright

The Linux Serial-Programming-HOWTO is copyright (C) 1997 by Peter Baumann. Linux HOWTO documents may be reproduced and distributed in whole or in part, in any medium physical or electronic, as long as this copyright notice is retained on all copies. Commercial redistribution is allowed and encouraged; however, the author would *like* to be notified of any such distributions.

All translations, derivative works, or aggregate works incorporating any Linux HOWTO documents must be covered under this copyright notice. That is, you may not produce a derivative work from a HOWTO and impose additional restrictions on its distribution. Exceptions to these rules may be granted under certain conditions; please contact the Linux HOWTO coordinator at the address given below.

In short, we wish to promote dissemination of this information through as many channels as possible. However, we do wish to retain copyright on the HOWTO documents, and would *like* to be notified of any plans to redistribute the HOWTOs.

If you have questions, please contact Greg Hankins, the Linux HOWTO coordinator, at *gregh@sunsite.unc.edu* <mailto:gregh@sunsite.unc.edu> via email.

1.2   New Versions Of This Document

New versions of the Serial-Programming-HOWTO will be available at
ftp://sunsite.unc.edu:/pub/Linux/docs/HOWTO/Serial-Programming-HOWTO <ftp://sunsite.unc.edu:/pub/Linux/docs/HOWTO/Serial-Programming-HOWTO> and mirror sites. There are other formats, such as PostScript and DVI versions in the `other-formats` directory. The Serial-Programming-HOWTO is also available at *http://sunsite.unc.edu/LDP/HOWTO/Serial-Programming-HOWTO.html* <http://sunsite.unc.edu/LDP/HOWTO/Serial-Programming-HOWTO.html> and will be posted to *comp.os.linux.answers* <news:comp.os.linux.answers> monthly.

1.3   Feedback

Please send me any corrections, questions, comments, suggestions, or additional material. I would like to improve this HOWTO! Tell me exactly what you don't understand, or what could be clearer. You can reach me at *Peter.Baumann@dlr.de* <mailto:Peter.Baumann@dlr.de> via email. Please include the version number of the Serial-Programming-HOWTO when writing, this is version 0.3.

2   Getting started

2.1   Debugging

The best way to debug your code is to set up another Linux box, and connect the two computers via a null-modem cable. Use miniterm (available from the LDP programmers guide (`ftp://sunsite.unc.edu/pub/Linux/docs/LDP/programmers-guide/lpg-0.4.tar.gz` in the examples directory) to transmit characters to your Linux box. Miniterm can be compiled very easily and will transmit all keyboard input raw over the serial port. Only the define statement `#define MODEMDEVICE "/dev/ttyS0"` has to be checked. Set it to `ttyS0` for COM1, `ttyS1` for COM2, etc.. It is essential for testing, that *all* characters are transmitted raw (without output processing) over the line. To test your connection, start miniterm on both computers and just type away. The characters input on one computer should appear on the other computer and vice versa. The input will not be echoed to the attached screen.

To make a null-modem cable you have to cross the TxD (transmit) and RxD (receive) lines. For a description of a cable see sect. 7 of the Serial-HOWTO.

It is also possible to perform this testing with only one computer, if you have two unused serial ports. You can then run two miniterms off two virtual consoles. If you free a serial port by disconnecting the mouse, remember to redirect /dev/mouse if it exists. If you use a multiport serial card, be sure to configure it correctly. I had mine configured wrong and everything worked fine as long as I was testing only on my computer. When I connected to another computer, the port started loosing characters. Executing two programs on one computer just isn't fully asynchronous.

2.2   Port Settings

The devices `/dev/ttyS*` are intended to hook up terminals to your Linux box, and are configured for this use after startup. This has to be kept in mind when programming communication with a raw device. E.g. the ports are configured to echo characters sent from the device back to it, which normally has to be changed for data transmission.

All parameters can be easily configured from within a program. The configuration is stored in a structure `struct termios`, which is defined in <asm/termbits.h>:

```
#define NCCS 19
struct termios {
        tcflag_t c_iflag;               /* input mode flags */
        tcflag_t c_oflag;               /* output mode flags */
        tcflag_t c_cflag;               /* control mode flags */
        tcflag_t c_lflag;               /* local mode flags */
        cc_t c_line;                    /* line discipline */
        cc_t c_cc[NCCS];                /* control characters */
};
```

This file also includes all flag definitions. The input mode flags in `c_iflag` handle all input processing, which means that the characters sent from the device can be processed before they are read with `read`. Similarly `c_oflag` handles the output processing. `c_cflag` contains the settings for the port, as the baudrate, bits per character, stop bits, etc.. The local mode flags stored in `c_lflag` determine if characters are echoed, signals are sent to your program, etc.. Finally the array `c_cc` defines the control characters for end of file, stop, etc.. Default values for the control characters are defined in <asm/termios.h>. The flags are described in the manual page `termios(3)`. The structure `termios` contains the `c_line` (line discipline) element, which is not used in POSIX compliant systems.

2.3 Input Concepts for Serial Devices

Here three different input concepts will be presented. The appropriate concept has to be chosen for the intended application. Whenever possible, do not loop reading single characters to get a complete string. When I did this, I lost characters, whereas a **read** for the whole string did not show any errors.

2.3.1 Canonical Input Processing

This is the normal processing mode for terminals, but can also be useful for communicating with other dl input is processed in units of lines, which means that a **read** will only return a full line of input. A line is by default terminated by a NL (ASCII LF), an end of file, or an end of line character. A CR (the DOS/Windows default end-of-line) will not terminate a line with the default settings.

Canonical input processing can also handle the erase, delete word, and reprint characters, translate CR to NL, etc..

2.3.2 Non-Canonical Input Processing

Non-Canonical Input Processing will handle a fixed amount of characters per read, and allows for a character timer. This mode should be used if your application will always read a fixed number of characters, or if the connected device sends bursts of characters.

2.3.3 Asynchronous Input

The two modes described above can be used in synchronous and asynchronous mode. Synchronous is the default, where a **read** statement will block, until the read is satisfied. In asynchronous mode the **read** statement will return immediatly and send a signal to the calling program upon completion. This signal can be received by a signal handler.

2.3.4 Waiting for Input from Multiple Sources

This is not a different input mode, but might be useful, if you are handling multiple devices. In my application I was handling input over a TCP/IP socket and input over a serial connection from another computer quasi-simultaneously. The program example given below will wait for input from two different input sources. If input from one source becomes available, it will be processed, and the program will then wait for new input.

The approach presented below seems rather complex, but it is important to keep in mind that Linux is a multi-processing operating system. The **select** system call will not load the CPU while waiting for input, whereas looping until input becomes available would slow down other processes executing at the same time.

3 Program Examples

All examples have been derived from **miniterm.c**. The type ahead buffer is limited to 255 characters, just like the maximum string length for canonical input processing (<linux/limits.h> or <posix1_lim.h>).

See the comments in the code for explanation of the use of the different input modes. I hope that the code is understandable. The example for canonical input is commented best, the other examples are commented only where they differ from the example for canonical input to emphasize the differences.

The descriptions are not complete, but you are encouraged to experiment with the examples to derive the best solution for your application.

Don't forget to give the appropriate serial ports the right permissions (e. g.: `chmod a+rw /dev/ttyS1`)!

3.1 Canonical Input Processing

```
#include <sys/types.h>
#include <sys/stat.h>
#include <fcntl.h>
#include <termios.h>
#include <stdio.h>

/* baudrate settings are defined in <asm/termbits.h>, which is
included by <termios.h> */
#define BAUDRATE B38400
/* change this definition for the correct port */
#define MODEMDEVICE "/dev/ttyS1"
#define _POSIX_SOURCE 1 /* POSIX compliant source */

#define FALSE 0
#define TRUE 1

volatile int STOP=FALSE;

main()
{
  int fd,c, res;
  struct termios oldtio,newtio;
  char buf[255];
/*
  Open modem device for reading and writing and not as controlling tty
  because we don't want to get killed if linenoise sends CTRL-C.
*/
  fd = open(MODEMDEVICE, O_RDWR | O_NOCTTY );
  if (fd <0) {perror(MODEMDEVICE); exit(-1); }

  tcgetattr(fd,&oldtio); /* save current serial port settings */
  bzero(&newtio, sizeof(newtio)); /* clear struct for new port settings */

/*
  BAUDRATE: Set bps rate. You could also use cfsetispeed and cfsetospeed.
  CRTSCTS : output hardware flow control (only used if the cable has
            all necessary lines. See sect. 7 of Serial-HOWTO)
  CS8     : 8n1 (8bit,no parity,1 stopbit)
  CLOCAL  : local connection, no modem contol
```

```
   CREAD   : enable receiving characters
*/
 newtio.c_cflag = BAUDRATE | CRTSCTS | CS8 | CLOCAL | CREAD;


/*
   IGNPAR  : ignore bytes with parity errors
   ICRNL   : map CR to NL (otherwise a CR input on the other computer
             will not terminate input)
   otherwise make device raw (no other input processing)
*/
 newtio.c_iflag = IGNPAR | ICRNL;


/*
 Raw output.
*/
 newtio.c_oflag = 0;


/*
   ICANON  : enable canonical input
   disable all echo functionality, and don't send signals to calling program
*/
 newtio.c_lflag = ICANON;


/*
   initialize all control characters
   default values can be found in /usr/include/termios.h, and are given
   in the comments, but we don't need them here
*/
 newtio.c_cc[VINTR]    = 0;     /* Ctrl-c */
 newtio.c_cc[VQUIT]    = 0;     /* Ctrl-\ */
 newtio.c_cc[VERASE]   = 0;     /* del */
 newtio.c_cc[VKILL]    = 0;     /* @ */
 newtio.c_cc[VEOF]     = 4;     /* Ctrl-d */
 newtio.c_cc[VTIME]    = 0;     /* inter-character timer unused */
 newtio.c_cc[VMIN]     = 1;     /* blocking read until 1 character arrives */
 newtio.c_cc[VSWTC]    = 0;     /* '\0' */
 newtio.c_cc[VSTART]   = 0;     /* Ctrl-q */
 newtio.c_cc[VSTOP]    = 0;     /* Ctrl-s */
 newtio.c_cc[VSUSP]    = 0;     /* Ctrl-z */
 newtio.c_cc[VEOL]     = 0;     /* '\0' */
 newtio.c_cc[VREPRINT] = 0;     /* Ctrl-r */
 newtio.c_cc[VDISCARD] = 0;     /* Ctrl-u */
 newtio.c_cc[VWERASE]  = 0;     /* Ctrl-w */
 newtio.c_cc[VLNEXT]   = 0;     /* Ctrl-v */
 newtio.c_cc[VEOL2]    = 0;     /* '\0' */
```

```
/*
  now clean the modem line and activate the settings for the port
*/
tcflush(fd, TCIFLUSH);
tcsetattr(fd,TCSANOW,&newtio);

/*
  terminal settings done, now handle input
  In this example, inputting a 'z' at the beginning of a line will
  exit the program.
*/
while (STOP==FALSE) {        /* loop until we have a terminating condition */
/* read blocks program execution until a line terminating character is
    input, even if more than 255 chars are input. If the number
    of characters read is smaller than the number of chars available,
    subsequent reads will return the remaining chars. res will be set
    to the actual number of characters actually read */
    res = read(fd,buf,255);
    buf[res]=0;                  /* set end of string, so we can printf */
    printf(":%s:%d\n", buf, res);
    if (buf[0]=='z') STOP=TRUE;
}
/* restore the old port settings */
tcsetattr(fd,TCSANOW,&oldtio);
}
```

3.2   Non-Canonical Input Processing

In non-canonical input processing mode, input is not assembled into lines and input processing (erase, kill, delete, etc.) does not occur. Two parameters control the behavior of this mode: c_cc[VTIME] sets the character timer, and c_cc[VMIN] sets the minimum number of characters to receive before satisfying the read.

If MIN > 0 and TIME = 0, MIN sets the number of characters to receive before the read is satisfied. As TIME is zero, the timer is not used.

If MIN = 0 and TIME > 0, TIME serves as a timeout value. The read will be satisfied if a single character is read, or TIME is exceeded (t = TIME *0.1 s). If TIME is exceeded, no character will be returned.

If MIN > 0 and TIME > 0, TIME serves as an inter-character timer. The read will be satisfied if MIN characters are received, or the time between two characters exceeds TIME. The timer is restarted every time a character is received and only becomes active after the first character has been received.

If MIN = 0 and TIME = 0, read will be satisfied immediately. The number of characters currently available, or the number of characters requested will be returned. According to Antonino (see contributions), you could issue a fcntl(fd, F_SETFL, FNDELAY); before reading to get the same result.

By modifying newtio.c_cc[VTIME] and newtio.c_cc[VMIN] all modes described above can be tested.

```
#include <sys/types.h>
#include <sys/stat.h>
#include <fcntl.h>
#include <termios.h>
#include <stdio.h>

#define BAUDRATE B38400
#define MODEMDEVICE "/dev/ttyS1"
#define _POSIX_SOURCE 1 /* POSIX compliant source */
#define FALSE 0
#define TRUE 1

volatile int STOP=FALSE;

main()
{
  int fd,c, res;
  struct termios oldtio,newtio;
  char buf[255];

  fd = open(MODEMDEVICE, O_RDWR | O_NOCTTY );
  if (fd <0) {perror(MODEMDEVICE); exit(-1); }

  tcgetattr(fd,&oldtio); /* save current port settings */

  bzero(&newtio, sizeof(newtio));
  newtio.c_cflag = BAUDRATE | CRTSCTS | CS8 | CLOCAL | CREAD;
  newtio.c_iflag = IGNPAR;
  newtio.c_oflag = 0;

  /* set input mode (non-canonical, no echo,...) */
  newtio.c_lflag = 0;

  newtio.c_cc[VTIME]    = 0;   /* inter-character timer unused */
  newtio.c_cc[VMIN]     = 5;   /* blocking read until 5 chars received */

  tcflush(fd, TCIFLUSH);
  tcsetattr(fd,TCSANOW,&newtio);

  while (STOP==FALSE) {          /* loop for input */
    res = read(fd,buf,255);    /* returns after 5 chars have been input */
    buf[res]=0;                /* so we can printf... */
    printf(":%s:%d\n", buf, res);
    if (buf[0]=='z') STOP=TRUE;
```

```
  }
  tcsetattr(fd,TCSANOW,&oldtio);
}
```

3.3   Asynchronous Input

```
#include <termios.h>
#include <stdio.h>
#include <unistd.h>
#include <fcntl.h>
#include <sys/signal.h>
#include <sys/types.h>


#define BAUDRATE B38400
#define MODEMDEVICE "/dev/ttyS1"
#define _POSIX_SOURCE 1 /* POSIX compliant source */
#define FALSE 0
#define TRUE 1


volatile int STOP=FALSE;


void signal_handler_IO (int status);    /* definition of signal handler */
int wait_flag=TRUE;                      /* TRUE while no signal received */

main()
{
  int fd,c, res;
  struct termios oldtio,newtio;
  struct sigaction saio;                 /* definition of signal action */
  char buf[255];

  /* open the device to be non-blocking (read will return immediatly) */
  fd = open(MODEMDEVICE, O_RDWR | O_NOCTTY | O_NONBLOCK);
  if (fd <0) {perror(MODEMDEVICE); exit(-1); }

  /* install the signal handler before making the device asynchronous */
  saio.sa_handler = signal_handler_IO;
  saio.sa_mask = 0;
  saio.sa_flags = 0;
  saio.sa_restorer = NULL;
  sigaction(SIGIO,&saio,NULL);

  /* allow the process to receive SIGIO */
  fcntl(fd, F_SETOWN, getpid());
  /* Make the file descriptor asynchronous (the manual page says only
```

```
      O_APPEND and O_NONBLOCK, will work with F_SETFL...) */
    fcntl(fd, F_SETFL, FASYNC);

    tcgetattr(fd,&oldtio); /* save current port settings */
    /* set new port settings for canonical input processing */
    newtio.c_cflag = BAUDRATE | CRTSCTS | CS8 | CLOCAL | CREAD;
    newtio.c_iflag = IGNPAR | ICRNL;
    newtio.c_oflag = 0;
    newtio.c_lflag = ICANON;
    newtio.c_cc[VMIN]=1;
    newtio.c_cc[VTIME]=0;
    tcflush(fd, TCIFLUSH);
    tcsetattr(fd,TCSANOW,&newtio);

    /* loop while waiting for input. normally we would do something
       useful here */
    while (STOP==FALSE) {
      printf(".\n");usleep(100000);
      /* after receiving SIGIO, wait_flag = FALSE, input is available
         and can be read */
      if (wait_flag==FALSE) {
        res = read(fd,buf,255);
        buf[res]=0;
        printf(":%s:%d\n", buf, res);
        if (res==1) STOP=TRUE; /* stop loop if only a CR was input */
        wait_flag = TRUE;      /* wait for new input */
      }
    }
    /* restore old port settings */
    tcsetattr(fd,TCSANOW,&oldtio);
}

/***************************************************************************
* signal handler. sets wait_flag to FALSE, to indicate above loop that    *
* characters have been received.                                          *
***************************************************************************/

void signal_handler_IO (int status)
{
  printf("received SIGIO signal.\n");
  wait_flag = FALSE;
}
```

3.4   Waiting for Input from Multiple Sources

This section is kept to a minimum. It is just intended to be a hint, and therefore the example code is kept short. This will not only work with serial ports, but with any set of file descriptors.

The select call and accompanying macros use a fd_set. This is a bit array, which has a bit entry for every valid file descriptor number. select will accept a fd_set with the bits set for the relevant file descriptors and returns a fd_set, in which the bits for the file descriptors are set where input, output, or an exception occurred. All handling of fd_set is done with the provided macros. See also the manual page select(2).

```
#include <sys/time.h>
#include <sys/types.h>
#include <unistd.h>

main()
{
    int     fd1, fd2;  /* input sources 1 and 2 */
    fd_set readfs;     /* file descriptor set */
    int     maxfd;     /* maximum file desciptor used */
    int     loop=1;    /* loop while TRUE */

    /* open_input_source opens a device, sets the port correctly, and
       returns a file descriptor */
    fd1 = open_input_source("/dev/ttyS1");   /* COM2 */
    if (fd1<0) exit(0);
    fd2 = open_input_source("/dev/ttyS2");   /* COM3 */
    if (fd2<0) exit(0);
    maxfd = MAX (fd1, fd2)+1;  /* maximum bit entry (fd) to test */

    /* loop for input */
    while (loop) {
      FD_SET(fd1, &readfs);  /* set testing for source 1 */
      FD_SET(fd2, &readfs);  /* set testing for source 2 */
      /* block until input becomes available */
      select(maxfd, &readfs, NULL, NULL, NULL);
      if (FD_ISSET(fd1))         /* input from source 1 available */
        handle_input_from_source1();
      if (FD_ISSET(fd2))         /* input from source 2 available */
        handle_input_from_source2();
    }

}
```

The given example blocks indefinitely, until input from one of the sources becomes available. If you need to timeout on input, just replace the select call by:

```
int res;
struct timeval Timeout;
```

```
/* set timeout value within input loop */
Timeout.tv_usec = 0;  /* milliseconds */
Timeout.tv_sec  = 1;  /* seconds */
res = select(maxfd, &readfs, NULL, NULL, &Timeout);
if (res==0)
/* number of file descriptors with input = 0, timeout occurred. */
```

This example will timeout after 1 second. If a timeout occurs, select will return 0, but beware that `Timeout` is decremented by the time actually waited for input by `select`. If the timeout value is zero, select will return immediatly.

4 Other Sources of Information

- The Linux Serial-HOWTO describes how to set up serial ports and contains hardware information.
- *Serial Programming Guide for POSIX Compliant Operating Systems* <http://www.easysw.com/~mike/serial>, by Michael Sweet. This link is obsolete and I could not find a new location for it. Does somebody know where we can find it again? It was a well prepared document!
- The manual page `termios(3)` describes all flags for the `termios` structure.

5 Contributions

As mentioned in the introduction, I am no expert in this field, but had problems myself, and found a solution with the help of others. Thanks for the help from Mr. Strudthoff from the European Transonic Windtunnel, Cologne, Michael Carter (mcarter@rocke.electro.swri.edu, and Peter Waltenberg (p.waltenberg@karaka.chch.cri.nz)

Antonino Ianella (antonino@usa.net wrote the Serial-Port-Programming Mini HOWTO, at the same time I prepared this document. Greg Hankins asked me to incorporate Antonino's Mini-HOWTO into this document.

The structure of this document and SGML formatting was derived from the Serial-HOWTO by Greg Hankins. Thanks also for various corrections made by : Dave Pfaltzgraff (Dave_Pfaltzgraff@patapsco.com), Sean Lincolne (slincol@tpgi.com.au), Michael Wiedmann (mw@miwie.in-berlin.de), and Adrey Bonar (andy@tipas.lt).

Linux I/O port programming mini-HOWTO

Author: Riku Saikkonen <Riku.Saikkonen@hut.fi>   Last modified: Dec 28 1997

This HOWTO document describes programming hardware I/O ports and waiting for small periods of time in user-mode Linux programs running on the Intel x86 architecture.

Contents

1 Introduction

This HOWTO document describes programming hardware I/O ports and waiting for small periods of time in user-mode Linux programs running on the Intel x86 architecture. This document is a descendant of the very small IO-Port mini-HOWTO by the same author.

This document is Copyright 1995-1997 Riku Saikkonen. See the *Linux HOWTO copyright* <http://sunsite.unc.edu/pub/Linux/docs/HOWTO/COPYRIGHT> for details.

If you have corrections or something to add, feel free to e-mail me (Riku.Saikkonen@hut.fi)...

Changes from the previous released version (Mar 30 1997):

- Clarified things regarding inb_p/outb_p and port 0x80.
- Removed information about udelay(), since nanosleep() provides a cleaner way of using it.
- Converted to Linuxdoc-SGML, and reorganised somewhat.
- Lots of minor additions and modifications.

2 Using I/O ports in C programs

2.1 The normal method

Routines for accessing I/O ports are in /usr/include/asm/io.h (or linux/include/asm-i386/io.h in the kernel source distribution). The routines there are inline macros, so it is enough to #include <asm/io.h>; you do not need any additional libraries.

Because of a limitation in gcc (present at least in 2.7.2.3 and below) and in egcs (all versions), you *have to* compile any source code that uses these routines with optimisation turned on (gcc -O1 or higher), or alternatively #define extern to be empty before you #include <asm/io.h>.

For debugging, you can use gcc -g -O (at least with modern versions of gcc), though optimisation can sometimes make the debugger behave a bit strangely. If this bothers you, put the routines that use I/O port access in a separate source file and compile only that with optimisation turned on.

Before you access any ports, you must give your program permission to do so. This is done by calling the ioperm() function (declared in unistd.h, and defined in the kernel) somewhere near the start of your program (before any I/O port accesses). The syntax is ioperm(from, num, turn_on), where from is the first port number to give access to, and num the number of consecutive ports to give access to. For example, ioperm(0x300, 5, 1) would give access to ports 0x300 through 0x304 (a total of 5 ports). The last argument is a Boolean value specifying whether to give access to the program to the ports (true (1)) or to remove access (false (0)). You can call ioperm() multiple times to enable multiple non-consecutive ports. See the ioperm(2) manual page for details on the syntax.

The ioperm() call requires your program to have root privileges; thus you need to either run it as the root user, or make it setuid root. You can drop the root privileges after you have called ioperm() to enable the ports you want to use. You are not required to explicitly drop your port access privileges with ioperm(..., 0) at the end of your program; this is done automatically as the process exits.

A setuid() to a non-root user does not disable the port access granted by ioperm(), but a fork() does (the child process does not get access, but the parent retains it).

ioperm() can only give access to ports 0x000 through 0x3ff; for higher ports, you need to use iopl() (which gives you access to all ports at once). Use the level argument 3 (i.e., iopl(3)) to give your program access to *all* I/O ports (so be careful — accessing the wrong ports can do all sorts of nasty things to your computer). Again, you need root privileges to call iopl(). See the iopl(2) manual page for details.

Then, to actually accessing the ports... To input a byte (8 bits) from a port, call `inb(port)`, it returns the byte it got. To output a byte, call `outb(value, port)` (please note the order of the parameters). To input a word (16 bits) from ports x and x+1 (one byte from each to form the word, using the assembler instruction `inw`), call `inw(x)`. To output a word to the two ports, use `outw(value, x)`. If you're unsure of which port instructions (byte or word) to use, you probably want `inb()` and `outb()` — most devices are designed for bytewise port access. Note that all port access instructions take at least about a microsecond to execute.

The `inb_p()`, `outb_p()`, `inw_p()`, and `outw_p()` macros work otherwise identically to the ones above, but they do an additional short (about one microsecond) delay after the port access; you can make the delay about four microseconds with `#define REALLY_SLOW_IO` before you `#include <asm/io.h>`. These macros normally (unless you `#define SLOW_IO_BY_JUMPING`, which is probably less accurate) use a port output to port 0x80 for their delay, so you need to give access to port 0x80 with `ioperm()` first (outputs to port 0x80 should not affect any part of the system). For more versatile methods of delaying, read on.

There are man pages for `ioperm(2)`, `iopl(2)`, and the above macros in reasonably recent releases of the Linux manual page collection.

2.2   An alternate method: `/dev/port`

Another way to access I/O ports is to `open()` `/dev/port` (a character device, major number 1, minor 4) for reading and/or writing (the stdio `f*()` functions have internal buffering, so avoid them). Then `lseek()` to the appropriate byte in the file (file position 0 = port 0x00, file position 1 = port 0x01, and so on), and `read()` or `write()` a byte or word from or to it.

Naturally, for this to work your program needs read/write access to `/dev/port`. This method is probably slower than the normal method above, but does not need compiler optimisation nor `ioperm()`. It doesn't need root access either, if you give a non-root user or group access to `/dev/port` — but this is a very bad thing to do in terms of system security, since it is possible to hurt the system, perhaps even gain root access, by using `/dev/port` to access hard disks, network cards, etc. directly.

3   Interrupts (IRQs) and DMA access

You cannot use IRQs or DMA directly from a user-mode process. You need to write a kernel driver; see *The Linux Kernel Hacker's Guide* <http://www.redhat.com:8080/HyperNews/get/khg.html> for details and the kernel source code for examples.

Also, you cannot disable interrupts from within a user-mode program.

4   High-resolution timing

4.1   Delays

First of all, I should say that you cannot guarantee user-mode processes to have exact control of timing because of the multi-tasking nature of Linux. Your process might be scheduled out at any time for anything from about 10 milliseconds to a few seconds (on a system with very high load). However, for most applications using I/O ports, this does not really matter. To minimise this, you may want to nice your process to a high-priority value (see the `nice(2)` manual page) or use real-time scheduling (see below).

If you want more precise timing than normal user-mode processes give you, there are some provisions for user-mode 'real time' support. Linux 2.x kernels have soft real time support; see the manual page for sched_setscheduler(2) for details. There is a special kernel that supports hard real time; see <http://luz.cs.nmt.edu/rtlinux/> for more information on this.

4.1.1 Sleeping: sleep() and usleep()

Now, let me start with the easier timing calls. For delays of multiple seconds, your best bet is probably to use sleep(). For delays of at least tens of milliseconds (about 10 ms seems to be the minimum delay), usleep() should work. These functions give the CPU to other processes ("sleep"), so CPU time isn't wasted. See the manual pages sleep(3) and usleep(3) for details.

For delays of under about 50 milliseconds (depending on the speed of your processor and machine, and the system load), giving up the CPU takes too much time, because the Linux scheduler (for the x86 architecture) usually takes at least about 10-30 milliseconds before it returns control to your process. Due to this, in small delays, usleep(3) usually delays somewhat more than the amount that you specify in the parameters, and at least about 10 ms.

4.1.2 nanosleep()

In the 2.0.x series of Linux kernels, there is a new system call, nanosleep() (see the nanosleep(2) manual page), that allows you to sleep or delay for short times (a few microseconds or more).

For delays <= 2 ms, if (and only if) your process is set to soft real time scheduling (using sched_setscheduler()), nanosleep() uses a busy loop; otherwise it sleeps, just like usleep().

The busy loop uses udelay() (an internal kernel function used by many kernel drivers), and the length of the loop is calculated using the BogoMips value (the speed of this kind of busy loop is one of the things that BogoMips measures accurately). See /usr/include/asm/delay.h) for details on how it works.

4.1.3 Delaying with port I/O

Another way of delaying small numbers of microseconds is port I/O. Inputting or outputting any byte from/to port 0x80 (see above for how to do it) should wait for almost exactly 1 microsecond independent of your processor type and speed. You can do this multiple times to wait a few microseconds. The port output should have no harmful side effects on any standard machine (and some kernel drivers use it). This is how {in|out}[bw]_p() normally do the delay (see asm/io.h).

Actually, a port I/O instruction on most ports in the 0-0x3ff range takes almost exactly 1 microsecond, so if you're, for example, using the parallel port directly, just do additional inb()s from that port to delay.

4.1.4 Delaying with assembler instructions

If you know the processor type and clock speed of the machine the program will be running on, you can hard-code shorter delays by running certain assembler instructions (but remember, your process might be scheduled out at any time, so the delays might well be longer every now and then). For the table below, the internal processor speed determines the number of clock cycles taken; e.g., for a 50 MHz processor (e.g. 486DX-50 or 486DX2-50), one clock cycle takes 1/50000000 seconds (=200 nanoseconds).

Instruction	i386 clock cycles	i486 clock cycles
nop	3	1
xchg %ax,%ax	3	3
or %ax,%ax	2	1

```
        mov %ax,%ax              2              1
        add %ax,0                2              1
```

(Sorry, I don't know about Pentiums; probably close to the i486. I cannot find an instruction which would use one clock cycle on an i386. Use the one-clock-cycle instructions if you can, otherwise the pipelining used in modern processors may shorten the times.)

The instructions `nop` and `xchg` in the table should have no side effects. The rest may modify the flags register, but this shouldn't matter since gcc should detect it. `nop` is a good choice.

To use these, call `asm("instruction")` in your program. The syntax of the instructions is as in the table above; if you want multiple instructions in a single `asm()` statement, separate them with semicolons. For example, `asm("nop ; nop ; nop ; nop")` executes four `nop` instructions, delaying for four clock cycles on i486 or Pentium processors (or 12 clock cycles on an i386).

`asm()` is translated into inline assembler code by gcc, so there is no function call overhead.

Shorter delays than one clock cycle are impossible in the Intel x86 architecture.

4.1.5 `rdtsc` for Pentiums

For Pentiums, you can get the number of clock cycles elapsed since the last reboot with the following C code:

```
extern __inline__ unsigned long long int rdtsc()
{
    unsigned long long int x;
    __asm__ volatile (".byte 0x0f, 0x31" : "=A" (x));
    return x;
}
```

You can poll this value to delay for as many clock cycles as you want.

4.2 Measuring time

For times accurate to one second, it is probably easiest to use `time()`. For more accurate times, `gettimeofday()` is accurate to about a microsecond (but see above about scheduling). For Pentiums, the `rdtsc` code fragment above is accurate to one clock cycle.

If you want your process to get a signal after some amount of time, use `setitimer()` or `alarm()`. See the manual pages of the functions for details.

5 Other programming languages

The description above concentrates on the C programming language. It should apply directly to C++ and Objective C. In assembler, you have to call `ioperm()` or `iopl()` as in C, but after that you can use the I/O port read/write instructions directly.

In other languages, unless you can insert inline assembler or C code into the program or use the system calls mentioned above, it is probably easiest to write a simple C source file with functions for the I/O port accesses or delays that you need, and compile and link it in with the rest of your program. Or use `/dev/port` as described above.

6   Some useful ports

Here is some programming information for common ports that can be directly used for general-purpose TTL (or CMOS) logic I/O.

If you want to use these or other common ports for their intended purpose (e.g., to control a normal printer or modem), you should most likely use existing drivers (which are usually included in the kernel) instead of programming the ports directly as this HOWTO describes. This section is intended for those people who want to connect LCD displays, stepper motors, or other custom electronics to a PC's standard ports.

If you want to control a mass-market device like a scanner (that has been on the market for a while), look for an existing Linux driver for it. The *Hardware-HOWTO* <http://sunsite.unc.edu/pub/Linux/docs/HOWTO/Hardware-HOWTO> is a good place to start.

<http://www.hut.fi/Misc/Electronics/> is a good source for more information on connecting devices to computers (and on electronics in general).

6.1   The parallel port

The parallel port's base address (called "BASE" below) is 0x3bc for /dev/lp0, 0x378 for /dev/lp1, and 0x278 for /dev/lp2. If you only want to control something that acts like a normal printer, see the *Printing-HOWTO* <http://sunsite.unc.edu/pub/Linux/docs/HOWTO/Printing-HOWTO>.

In addition to the standard output-only mode described below, there is an 'extended' bidirectional mode in most parallel ports. For information on this and the newer ECP/EPP modes (and the IEEE 1284 standard in general), see <http://www.fapo.com/> and <http://www.senet.com.au/cpeacock/parallel.htm>. Remember that since you cannot use IRQs or DMA in a user-mode program, you will probably have to write a kernel driver to use ECP/EPP; I think someone is writing such a driver, but I don't know the details.

The port BASE+0 (Data port) controls the data signals of the port (D0 to D7 for bits 0 to 7, respectively; states: 0 = low (0 V), 1 = high (5 V)). A write to this port latches the data on the pins. A read returns the data last written in standard or extended write mode, or the data in the pins from another device in extended read mode.

The port BASE+1 (Status port) is read-only, and returns the state of the following input signals:

- Bits 0 and 1 are reserved.
- Bit 2 IRQ status (not a pin, I don't know how this works)
- Bit 3 ERROR (1=high)
- Bit 4 SLCT (1=high)
- Bit 5 PE (1=high)
- Bit 6 ACK (1=high)
- Bit 7 -BUSY (0=high)

(I'm not sure about the high and low states.)

The port BASE+2 (Control port) is write-only (a read returns the data last written), and controls the following status signals:

- Bit 0 -STROBE (0=high)
- Bit 1 AUTO_FD_XT (1=high)
- Bit 2 -INIT (0=high)

- Bit 3 SLCT_IN (1=high)
- Bit 4 enables the parallel port IRQ (which occurs on the low-to-high transition of ACK) when set to 1.
- Bit 5 controls the extended mode direction (0 = write, 1 = read), and is completely write-only (a read returns nothing useful for this bit).
- Bits 6 and 7 are reserved.

(Again, I am not sure about the high and low states.)

Pinout (a 25-pin female D-shell connector on the port) (i=input, o=output):

```
1io -STROBE, 2io D0, 3io D1, 4io D2, 5io D3, 6io D4, 7io D5, 8io D6,
9io D7, 10i ACK, 11i -BUSY, 12i PE, 13i SLCT, 14o AUTO_FD_XT,
15i ERROR, 16o -INIT, 17o SLCT_IN, 18-25 Ground
```

The IBM specifications say that pins 1, 14, 16, and 17 (the control outputs) have open collector drivers pulled to 5 V through 4.7 kiloohm resistors (sink 20 mA, source 0.55 mA, high-level output 5.0 V minus pullup). The rest of the pins sink 24 mA, source 15 mA, and their high-level output is min. 2.4 V. The low state for both is max. 0.5 V. Non-IBM parallel ports probably deviate from this standard. For more information on this, see <http://www.hut.fi/Misc/Electronics/circuits/lptpower.html>.

Finally, a warning: Be careful with grounding. I've broken several parallel ports by connecting to them while the computer is turned on. It might be a good thing to use a parallel port not integrated on the motherboard for things like this. (You can usually get a second parallel port for your machine with a cheap standard 'multi-I/O' card; just disable the ports that you don't need, and set the parallel port I/O address on the card to a free address. You don't need to care about the parallel port IRQ, since it isn't normally used.)

6.2   The game (joystick) port

The game port is located at port addresses 0x200-0x207. For controlling normal joysticks, there is a kernel-level joystick driver, see <ftp://sunsite.unc.edu/pub/Linux/kernel/patches/>, filename joystick-*.

Pinout (a 15-pin female D-shell connector on the port):

- 1,8,9,15: +5 V (power)
- 4,5,12: Ground
- 2,7,10,14: Digital inputs BA1, BA2, BB1, and BB2, respectively
- 3,6,11,13: "Analog" inputs AX, AY, BX, and BY, respectively

The +5 V pins seem to often be connected directly to the power lines in the motherboard, so they should be able to source quite a lot of power, depending on the motherboard, power supply and game port.

The digital inputs are used for the buttons of the two joysticks (joystick A and joystick B, with two buttons each) that you can connect to the port. They should be normal TTL-level inputs, and you can read their status directly from the status port (see below). A real joystick returns a low (0 V) status when the button is pressed and a high (the 5 V from the power pins through an 1 Kohm resistor) status otherwise.

The so-called analog inputs actually measure resistance. The game port has a quad one-shot multivibrator (a 558 chip) connected to the four inputs. In each input, there is a 2.2 Kohm resistor between the input pin and the multivibrator output, and a 0.01 uF timing capacitor between the multivibrator output and the ground. A real joystick has a potentiometer for each axis (X and Y), wired between +5 V and the appropriate input pin (AX or AY for joystick A, or BX or BY for joystick B).

The multivibrator, when activated, sets its output lines high (5 V) and waits for each timing capacitor to reach 3.3 V before lowering the respective output line. Thus the high period duration of the multivibrator is proportional to the resistance of the potentiometer in the joystick (i.e., the position of the joystick in the appropriate axis), as follows:

$$R = (t - 24.2) / 0.011,$$

where R is the resistance (ohms) of the potentiometer and t the high period duration (seconds).

Thus, to read the analog inputs, you first activate the multivibrator (with a port write; see below), then poll the state of the four axes (with repeated port reads) until they drop from high to low state, measuring their high period duration. This polling uses quite a lot of CPU time, and on a non-realtime multitasking system like (normal user-mode) Linux, the result is not very accurate because you cannot poll the port constantly (unless you use a kernel-level driver and disable interrupts while polling, but this wastes even more CPU time). If you know that the signal is going to take a long time (tens of ms) to go down, you can call usleep() before polling to give CPU time to other processes.

The only I/O port you need to access is port 0x201 (the other ports either behave identically or do nothing). Any write to this port (it doesn't matter what you write) activates the multivibrator. A read from this port returns the state of the input signals:

- Bit 0: AX (status (1=high) of the multivibrator output)
- Bit 1: AY (status (1=high) of the multivibrator output)
- Bit 2: BX (status (1=high) of the multivibrator output)
- Bit 3: BY (status (1=high) of the multivibrator output)
- Bit 4: BA1 (digital input, 1=high)
- Bit 5: BA2 (digital input, 1=high)
- Bit 6: BB1 (digital input, 1=high)
- Bit 7: BB2 (digital input, 1=high)

6.3   The serial port

If the device you're talking to supports something resembling RS-232, you should be able to use the serial port to talk to it. The Linux serial driver should be enough for almost all applications (you shouldn't have to program the serial port directly, and you'd probably have to write a kernel driver to do it); it is quite versatile, so using non-standard bps rates and so on shouldn't be a problem.

See the `termios(3)` manual page, the serial driver source code (`linux/drivers/char/serial.c`), and `<http://www.easysw.com/mike/serial/index.html>` for more information on programming serial ports on Unix systems.

7   Hints

If you want good analog I/O, you can wire up ADC and/or DAC chips to the parallel port (hint: for power, use the game port connector or a spare disk drive power connector wired to outside the computer case, unless you have a low-power device and can use the parallel port itself for power, or use an external power supply), or buy an AD/DA card (most of the older/slower ones are controlled by I/O ports). Or, if you're satisfied with 1 or 2 channels, inaccuracy, and (probably) bad zeroing, a cheap sound card supported by the Linux sound driver should do (and it's quite fast).

With accurate analog devices, improper grounding may generate errors in the analog inputs or outputs. If you experience something like this, you could try electrically isolating your device from the computer with optocouplers (on *all* signals between the computer and your device). Try to get power for the optocouplers from the computer (spare signals on the port may give enough power) to achieve better isolation.

If you're looking for printed circuit board design software for Linux, there is a free X11 application called Pcb that should do a nice job, at least if you aren't doing anything very complex. It is included in many Linux distributions, and available in `<ftp://sunsite.unc.edu/pub/Linux/apps/circuits/>` (filename `pcb-*`).

8 Troubleshooting

Q1.

I get segmentation faults when accessing ports.

A1.

Either your program does not have root privileges, or the `ioperm()` call failed for some other reason. Check the return value of `ioperm()`. Also, check that you're actually accessing the ports that you enabled with `ioperm()` (see Q3). If you're using the delaying macros (`inb_p()`, `outb_p()`, and so on), remember to call `ioperm()` to get access to port 0x80 too.

Q2.

I can't find the `in*()`, `out*()` functions defined anywhere, and gcc complains about undefined references.

A2.

You did not compile with optimisation turned on (`-O`), and thus gcc could not resolve the macros in `asm/io.h`. Or you did not `#include <asm/io.h>` at all.

Q3.

`out*()` doesn't do anything, or does something weird.

A3.

Check the order of the parameters; it should be `outb(value, port)`, not `outportb(port, value)` as is common in MS-DOS.

Q4.

I want to control a standard RS-232 device/parallel printer/joystick...

A4.

You're probably better off using existing drivers (in the Linux kernel or an X server or somewhere else) to do it. The drivers are usually quite versatile, so even slightly non-standard devices usually work with them. See the information on standard ports above for pointers to documentation for them.

9 Example code

Here's a piece of simple example code for I/O port access:

```
/*
 * example.c: very simple example of port I/O
 *
 * This code does nothing useful, just a port write, a pause,
 * and a port read. Compile with 'gcc -O2 -o example example.c',
 * and run as root with './example'.
```

```
*/

#include <stdio.h>
#include <unistd.h>
#include <asm/io.h>

#define BASEPORT 0x378 /* lp1 */

int main()
{
  /* Get access to the ports */
  if (ioperm(BASEPORT, 3, 1)) {perror("ioperm"); exit(1);}

  /* Set the data signals (D0-7) of the port to all low (0) */
  outb(0, BASEPORT);

  /* Sleep for a while (100 ms) */
  usleep(100000);

  /* Read from the status port (BASE+1) and display the result */
  printf("status: %d\n", inb(BASEPORT + 1));

  /* We don't need the ports anymore */
  if (ioperm(BASEPORT, 3, 0)) {perror("ioperm"); exit(1);}

  exit(0);
}


/* end of example.c */
```

10   Credits

Too many people have contributed for me to list, but thanks a lot, everyone. I have not replied to all the contributions that I've received; sorry for that, and thanks again for the help.

The Linux CD-ROM HOWTO

Jeff Tranter, *tranter@pobox.com* <mailto:tranter@pobox.com>   v1.13, 23 January 1998

This document describes how to install, configure, and use CD-ROM drives under Linux. It lists the supported hardware and answers a number of frequently asked questions. The intent is to bring new users up to speed quickly and reduce the amount of traffic in the Usenet news groups and mailing lists.

Contents

1 Introduction

This is the Linux CD-ROM HOWTO. It is intended as a quick reference covering everything you need to know to install and configure CD-ROM hardware under Linux. Frequently asked questions related to CD-ROM are answered, and references are given to other sources of information related to CD-ROM applications and technology.

1.1 Acknowledgments

Much of this information came from the documentation and source files provided with the Linux kernel, the Internet *alt.cdrom* <news:alt.cd-rom> newsgroup FAQ, and input from Linux users.

Thanks to the *SGML Tools* <ftp://sunsite.unc.edu/pub/Linux/utils/text/sgml-tools-0.99.0.tar.gz> package, this HOWTO is available in several formats, all generated from a common source file.

1.2 Revision History

Version 1.0

First version made publicly available

Version 1.1

CDU33A is explicitly supported as of 1.1.20 kernel; notes on Reveal FX; info on reading audio tracks; info on some alpha drivers; added troubleshooting section; a few other minor additions

Version 1.2

ISO-9660 file systems must be mounted read-only starting with 1.1.33 kernel; clarified that SB16 SCSI is supported and newer Aztech drives are not supported; references to photocd and xpcd programs; note on new SBPCD auto eject feature

Version 1.3

Minor change to the way SBPCD eject feature is disabled starting with the 1.1.49 kernel; added info on XA discs and how to identify them

Version 1.4

HOWTO now available in other languages; IBM and Longshine drives now supported by SBPCD; alpha driver for Aztech drives; CDU-33 driver no longer auto-probes, supports PhotoCD and audio; more than 2 SCSI drives are supported; new driver for IDE; reminder to check drive jumpers; can now set SBPCD auto-eject with IOCTL; list drivers with multisession support; question on flashing light on CDU-33

Version 1.5

A long overdue update (I've been busy); document placed under GPL; info on many new kernel drivers; more info on configuration and troubleshooting; lots of HTML links added; many other minor changes

Version 1.6

Added link to eject program; question on file permission patch; link to Creative Labs Web site; reference to ATA/EIDE FAQ and FTP site; note that many Creative Labs and Mitsumi drives are now EIDE; mention Supermount; drives listed as supporting digital data are obsolete, refer to cdda2wav; more info on writing CDs; multi-disc EIDE drive info; a few typos fixed

Version 1.7

new kernel version; most README files moved to `/usr/src/linux/Documentation`; some drivers are no longer experimental; a few more supported drives; emphasize that most drives are now IDE/ATAPI; added questions on Plug and Play support and identifying drive speed; vger mailing lists being shut down; other miscellaneous minor changes

Version 1.8

question on why CD-ROM stops working after install; aztcd driver now supports two CyCDROM drives; more pleading not to use SBPCD driver with IDE drives; some ATAPI multi-disc changer support; note on (lack of) support for parallel port drives; latest stable kernel is 2.0; other miscellaneous minor changes

Version 1.9

removed some questions that were very old and now obsolete; new e-mail address for author; Chinese translation available; fixed some links to point to latest software packages; more information on multimedia book; minor spelling and grammatical changes

Version 1.10

clarify that new Aztech drives are ATAPI; added CDU31A options for modular driver; mount option for reading hidden files; added six month "best before" date; new URL to web page for book; minor spelling and grammatical changes

Version 1.11

added reference for parallel port drives; added info on bpcd driver; new URL for Chinese version; alternate CR-56x driver; info on bootable CDs; answered question on CD-ROM API; Linux Multimedia Guide is now available in French and Japanese

Version 1.12

added link to Polish translation; CD Writing is no longer a mini-HOWTO; added two questions related to Joliet filesystem

Version 1.13

added index entries; placed under LDP license rather than GPL; SuperProbe replaced by reference to kernel based automounter

1.3 New Versions Of This Document

New versions of this document will be periodically posted to the *comp.os.linux.answers* `<news:comp.os.linux.answers>` newsgroup. They will also be uploaded to various anonymous ftp sites that archive such information including `<ftp://sunsite.unc.edu/pub/Linux/docs/HOWTO/>`.

Hypertext versions of this and other Linux HOWTOs are available on many World-Wide-Web sites, including `<http://sunsite.unc.edu/LDP/HOWTO/>`. Most Linux CD-ROM distributions include the HOWTOs, often under the `/usr/doc` directory, and you can also buy printed copies from several vendors. Sometimes the HOWTOs available from CD-ROM vendors, ftp sites, and printed format are out of date. If the date on this HOWTO is more than six months in the past, then a newer copy is probably available on the Internet.

A French translation of this document, by Bruno Cornec (*cornec@stna7.stna.dgac.fr* `<mailto:cornec@stna7.stna.dgac.fr>`) is available at `<ftp://ftp.ibp.fr/pub2/linux/french/docs/HOWTO/>`.

A Japanese translation by Itsushi Minoura (*minoura@uni.zool.s.u-tokyo.ac.jp* `<mailto:minoura@uni.zool.s.u-tokyo.ac.jp>`) is available from `<http://jf.linux.or.jp/JF/JF.html/>`.

A Chinese translation (BIG-5 encoding) by Yung-kang Wu (*yorkwu@ms4.hinet.net* <mailto:yorkwu@ms4.hinet.net>) is available from <http://linux.ntcic.edu.tw/~yorkwu/linux/howto/cdrom/>.

A Polish translation by Bartosz Maruszewski (*b.maruszewski@zsmeie.torun.pl* <mailto:b.maruszewski@zsmeie.torun.pl>) is available from <http://www.jtz.org.pl/Html/CDROM-HOWTO.pl.html>.

Most translations of this and other Linux HOWTOs can also be found at <http://sunsite.unc.edu/pub/Linux/docs/HOWTO/translations/> and <ftp://sunsite.unc.edu/pub/Linux/docs/HOWTO/translations/>.

If you make a translation of this document into another language, let me know and I'll include a reference to it here.

1.4   Feedback

I rely on you, the reader, to make this HOWTO useful. If you have any suggestions, corrections, or comments, please send them to me, *tranter@pobox.com* <mailto:tranter@pobox.com>, and I will try to incorporate them in the next revision.

I am also willing to answer general questions on CD-ROM under Linux, as best I can. Before doing so, please read all of the information in this HOWTO, and then send me detailed information about the problem. Please do not ask me about using CD-ROM drives under operating systems other than Linux.

If you publish this document on a CD-ROM or in hardcopy form, a complimentary copy would be appreciated; mail me for my postal address. Also consider making a donation to the Linux Documentation Project to help support free documentation for Linux. Contact the Linux HOWTO coordinator, Greg Hankins (*gregh@sunsite.unc.edu* <mailto:gregh@sunsite.unc.edu>), for more information.

1.5   Distribution Policy

Copyright (c) 1995-1998 by Jeff Tranter. This document may be distributed under the terms set forth in the LDP license at <http://sunsite.unc.edu/LDP/COPYRIGHT.html>.

2   CD-ROM Technology

```
"CD-ROM is read-only memory, and audio compact disc system is
available as package-media of digital data for those purpose. For
playing audio CD, please insert Head-phone jack."
--- from a CD-ROM instruction manual
```

Don't Panic! The world of CD-ROM technology is not as confusing as your instruction manual.

CD-ROM stands for *Compact Disc Read-Only Memory*, a mass storage medium utilizing an optical laser to read microscopic pits on the aluminized layer of a polycarbonate disc. The same format is used for audio Compact Discs. Because of its high storage capacity, reliability, and low cost, CD-ROM has become an increasingly popular storage media.

The storage capacity of a CD-ROM disc is approximately 650 megabytes, equivalent to over 500 high density 3.5" floppy disks or roughly 250,000 typed pages.

First generation drives (known as *single speed*), provided a transfer rate of approximately 150 kilobytes per second. Hardware manufacturers then introduced double speed (300 kB/sec), quad speed (600 kB/sec), and higher. As I write this, 24 times (24X) drives are readily available and affordable.

Most CD-ROM drives use either the Small Computer Systems Interface (SCSI), ATAPI enhanced IDE interface, or a vendor proprietary interface. They also typically support playing audio CDs via an external headphone jack or line level output. Some CDs also allow reading the frames of data from audio CDs in digital form.

CD-ROMs are usually formatted with an ISO-9660 (formerly called *High Sierra*) file system. This format restricts filenames to the MS-DOS style (8+3 characters). The *Rock Ridge Extensions* use undefined fields in the ISO-9660 standard to support longer filenames and additional Unix style information (e.g. file ownership, symbolic links, etc.).

PhotoCD is a standard developed by Kodak for storing photographic images as digital data on a CD-ROM. With appropriate software, you can view the images on a computer, manipulate them, or send them to a printer. Information can be added to a PhotoCD at a later date; this is known as *multi-session* capability.

CD recorders (CD-R) are also available and are becoming increasingly affordable. They use a different media and specialized equipment for recording, but the resulting disc can be read by any CD-ROM drive.

In the future CD-ROM drive vendors are expected to offer new technologies that will increase storage capacity by an order of magnitude.

3   Supported Hardware

This section lists the CD-ROM drivers and interfaces that are currently supported under Linux. The information here is based on the latest stable Linux kernel, which at time of writing was version 2.0.33. A development kernel (2.1.x versions) is also available but is not guaranteed to be stable.

This information is only valid for Linux on the Intel platform. Much of it should be applicable to Linux on other processor architectures, but I have no first hand experience or information.

3.1   ATAPI CD-ROM Drives

ATAPI (ATA Packet Interface) is a protocol for controlling mass storage devices. It builds on the ATA (AT Attachment) interface, the official ANSI standard name for the IDE interface developed for hard disk drives. ATAPI is commonly used for hard disks, CD-ROM drives, tape drives, and other devices. Currently the most popular type of interface, it offers most of the functionality of SCSI, without the need for an expensive controller or cables.

The Linux kernel has a device driver that should work with any ATAPI compliant CD-ROM drive. Vendors shipping compatible drives include Aztech, Mitsumi, NEC, Sony, Creative Labs, and Vertos. If you have recently purchased a CD-ROM drive, especially if it is quad speed or faster, it is almost guaranteed to be IDE/ATAPI.

3.2   SCSI CD-ROM Drives

SCSI (Small Computer Systems Interface) is a popular format for CD-ROM drives. Its chief advantages are a reasonably fast transfer rate, multi-device capability, and support on a variety of computer platforms. Some disadvantages of SCSI are the need for a relatively expensive controller card and cables.

Any SCSI CD-ROM drive with a block size of 512 or 2048 bytes should work under Linux; this includes the vast majority of CD-ROM drives on the market.

You will also need a supported SCSI controller card; see the *SCSI HOWTO* <http://sunsite.unc.edu/ LDP/HOWTO/SCSI-HOWTO.html> for more information on interface hardware.

Note that some CD-ROMs include a proprietary controller with a modified interface that is not fully SCSI compatible (e.g. it may not support adding other SCSI devices on the bus). These will most likely *not* work under Linux.

3.3   Proprietary CD-ROM Drives

Several CD-ROM drives using proprietary interfaces are available; the interface is often provided on a sound card. Simple interface cards equivalent to that provided on the sound card are also available. These drives generally tend to be lower in cost and smaller than SCSI drives. Their disadvantages are the lack of standardization and expandability.

Note that proprietary interfaces are sometimes erroneously referred to as IDE interfaces, because like IDE hard disks, they use a simple interface based on the PC/AT bus. To add to the confusion, some vendors, most notably Creative Labs, have shipped many different types of CD-ROM drives and have offered proprietary, SCSI, and ATAPI interfaces on their sound cards.

The table below lists the proprietary CD-ROM drives that are known to be supported under Linux. Drivers for additional devices may be available in the latest development kernels or as kernel patches. The latter can most often be found at <ftp://sunsite.unc.edu/pub/Linux/kernel/patches/cdrom/>. Also check the README files included with the kernel distribution, usually installed in /usr/src/linux/Documentation/ cdrom, for the latest information.

Proprietary CD-ROM Drives

Vendor	Model	Kernel Driver	Notes
Panasonic	CR-521	sbpcd	Note 1
Panasonic	CR-522	sbpcd	Note 1
Panasonic	CR-523	sbpcd	Note 1
Panasonic	CR-562	sbpcd	Note 1
Panasonic	CR-563	sbpcd	Note 1
Creative Labs	CD-200	sbpcd	
IBM	External ISA	sbpcd	Note 2
Longshine	LCS-7260	sbpcd	
Teac	CD-55A	sbpcd	
Sony	CDU-31A	cdu31a	
Sony	CDU-33A	cdu31a	
Sony	CDU-535	sonycd535	Note 3
Sony	CDU-531	sonycd535	
Aztech	CDA268-01A	aztcd	Note 4
Orchid	CDS-3110	aztcd	
Okano/Wearnes	CDD110	aztcd	
Conrad	TXC	aztcd	
CyCDROM	CR520ie	aztcd	
CyCDROM	CR940ie	aztcd	
GoldStar	R420	gscd	Note 5
Philips/LMS	CM206	cm206	Note 6
Mitsumi	CRMC LU005S	mcd/mcdx	Note 7, 8
Mitsumi	FX001	mcd/mcdx	Note 7, 8
Optics Storage	Dolphin 8000AT	optcd	
Lasermate	CR328A	optcd	
Sanyo	H94A	sjcd	
various	various	isp16	Note 9

```
MicroSolutions Backpack        bpcd
```

Notes:

1. These drives may be sold under the names Creative Labs, Panasonic, Matsushita, or Kotobuki.

2. This drive is the same as a Panasonic CR-562.

3. May also be sold under the Procomm name.

4. This driver is for the CDA268-01A only. Other models, including the CDA268-03I and CDA269-031SE are not proprietary and should use the IDECD (ATAPI) kernel driver.

5. May also be sold as part of a Reveal Multimedia Kit.

6. The Philips CM205 is not supported by this driver, but there is a separate alpha release driver available from ftp://sunsite.unc.edu in /pub/Linux/kernel/patches/cdrom/lmscd0.4.tar.gz

7. May also be sold under the Radio Shack name.

8. There are two drivers available. "mcd" is the original one, and "mcdx" is a newer driver with more features (but possibly less stable).

9. This driver works with CD-ROM drives that are attached to the interface on an ISP16, MAD16 or Mozart sound card.

If a drive listed here is not supported by your kernel, you probably need to upgrade to a newer version.

If your drive is not one of the models listed here, particularly if it was bought recently and is quad speed or faster, it probably uses the IDE/ATAPI interface listed in a previous section. *The single most common error among Linux CD-ROM users is to assume that any drive connected to a SoundBlaster card should use the SBPCD driver*. Creative Labs and most other vendors are no longer selling proprietary interface drives, they are following the standard ATAPI/IDE interface.

3.4   Parallel Port Drives

Some vendors sell CD-ROM drives that attach via a parallel port. The only drive of this type that is currently supported in the Linux kernel is the MicroSolutions Backpack.

Linux kernel drivers for several more of these drives are available separately as kernel patches or loadable modules. For the latest information check <http://www.torque.net/linux-pp.html>.

3.5   Alternate Drivers

There is an alternate kernel driver available for Panasonic/Matsushita CR-56x drives written by Zoltan Vorosbaranyi. It can be found at <ftp://ftp.tarki.hu/pub/linux/pcd/pcd-0.29.tar.gz>.

4   Installation

Installation of a CD-ROM under Linux consists of these steps:

1. Installing the hardware.

2. Configuring and building the Linux kernel.

3. Creating device files and setting boot time parameters

4. Booting the Linux kernel.

5. Mounting the media.

The next sections will cover each of these steps in detail.

4.1   Installing the Hardware

Follow the manufacturer's instructions for installing the hardware or have your dealer perform the installation. The details will vary depending on whether the drive is internal or external and on the type of interface used. There are no special installation requirements for Linux. You may need to set jumpers on the drive and/or interface card for correct operation; some of the kernel drivers include README files that include this information.

As explained in the file ide-cd, ATAPI CD-ROMS should be jumpered as "single" or "master", and not "slave" when only one IDE device is attached to an interface (although this restriction is no longer enforced with recent kernels).

4.2   Configuring and Building the Kernel

When initially installing Linux from CD-ROM you will likely be using a boot and/or root disk provided as part of a Linux distribution. If possible, you should choose a boot disk with the kernel driver for your CD-ROM device type. If you cannot find a boot disk with the necessary CD-ROM driver, you have several options:

1. Install over a network

2. Boot DOS, and install the Linux files onto your hard disk

3. Boot DOS, and create a set of floppies to install Linux

4. Find someone who can build you a boot disk with the needed CD-ROM driver

The *Linux Installation HOWTO* <http://sunsite.unc.edu/LDP/HOWTO/Installation-HOWTO.html> has more information on installing Linux. If you purchased Linux on CD-ROM, it likely also came with some installation instructions (that little booklet inside the jewel case, and/or files on the CD).

Once Linux has initially been installed, most users will want to compile their own kernel, usually for one of these reasons:

- to support a CD-ROM drive or other hardware

- to upgrade to a newer kernel release

- to free up memory resources by minimizing the size of the kernel

The *Linux Kernel HOWTO* <http://sunsite.unc.edu/LDP/HOWTO/Kernel-HOWTO.html> should be consulted for the details of building a kernel. I will just mention here some issues that are specific to CD-ROM drives.

Obviously, you need to compile in support for your CD-ROM drive when you do a "make config".

If you have an ATAPI CD-ROM drive, you need to answer **yes** to the questions:

```
Enhanced IDE/MFM/RLL disk/cdrom/tape support (CONFIG_BLK_DEV_IDE) [Y/n/?]
Include IDE/ATAPI CDROM support (CONFIG_BLK_DEV_IDECD) [Y/n/?]
```

For SCSI CD-ROM drives, enable these options:

```
SCSI support (CONFIG_SCSI) [Y/n/m/?]
SCSI CD-ROM support (CONFIG_BLK_DEV_SR) [Y/n/m/?]
```

Also enable support for your SCSI host adapter when prompted, e.g.

```
Adaptec AHA152X support (CONFIG_SCSI_AHA152X) [Y/n/m/?]
```

For proprietary interface CD-ROM drives, enable the appropriate driver. You can use the table listed previously to determine the driver to use for your model.

Virtually all CD-ROMs use the ISO-9660 file system, so you must also enable:

```
ISO9660 cdrom filesystem support (CONFIG_ISO9660_FS) [Y/n/m/?]
```

Although not needed for CD-ROM operation, if you have a sound card that is supported under Linux you might want to enable and configure the kernel sound driver at this time as well. The *Sound HOWTO* <http://sunsite.unc.edu/LDP/HOWTO/Sound-HOWTO.html> can be a useful reference here.

You should then follow the usual procedure for building the kernel and installing it. Don't boot with the new kernel until you create the device files and set up any boot time parameters as described in the next section.

The ISO-9660 filesystem and almost all of the CD-ROM drivers can be built as loadable kernel modules. This scheme allows the kernel drivers to be loaded and unloaded without rebooting the kernel, freeing up memory. I recommend you get your CD-ROM installation running using compiled-in drivers first. How to use modules is described in the modules documentation and the *Kernel HOWTO* <http://sunsite.unc.edu/LDP/HOWTO/Kernel-HOWTO.html>.

If a drive type listed here is not supported by your kernel, you likely need to upgrade to a newer version.

It is possible that you need to use a driver that is distributed separately from the kernel source code. This usually involves patching the kernel. Again, the *Kernel HOWTO* <http://sunsite.unc.edu/LDP/HOWTO/Kernel-HOWTO.html> explains how to do this.

Note that there is a menu-based kernel configuration program invoked by "make menuconfig" and an X11-based graphical configuration invoked as "make xconfig". All three configuration methods offer on-line help.

4.3   Creating Device Files and Setting Boot Time Parameters

The kernel uses device files to identify which device driver to use. If you are running a standard Linux distribution you may have created the necessary device files during installation. Under Slackware Linux, for example, there is a menu-based **setup** tool that includes CD-ROM setup, and most systems have a /dev/MAKEDEV script. If you don't use these methods, you can use the more manual procedure listed in this section. Even if you use either of these methods, it is recommended that you at least verify the device files against the information in this section.

You create the device file by running the shell commands indicated for your drive type. This should be done as user **root**. Note that some Linux distributions may use slightly different CD-ROM device names from those listed here.

It is recommended that you also create a symbolic link to the CD-ROM device to make it easier to remember. For example, for an IDE CD-ROM drive that is the second device on the secondary interface, the link would be created using

```
# ln -s /dev/hdd /dev/cdrom
```

If you want to play audio CDs, you will need to set the protection on the device file (the real file, not the symbolic link to it) to allow all users to read, e.g.

```
# chmod 664 /dev/hdd
# ls -l /dev/hdd
brw-rw-r--   1 root      disk      22,  64 Feb  4  1995 /dev/hdd
```

When booting Linux, the device drivers attempt to determine whether the appropriate devices are present, typically by probing specific addresses. Many of the drivers auto-probe at several addresses, but because of differences in configuration, possible device conflicts, and hardware limitations, the drivers sometimes need help identifying the addresses and other parameters. Most drivers support an option on the kernel command line to pass this information to the device driver. This can be done interactively, or more commonly, configured into your boot loader. With LILO, for example, you would add an `append` command such as the following to your `/etc/lilo.conf` file:

```
append = "sbpcd=0x230,SoundBlaster"
```

See the LILO documentation for more information.

In the next section I discuss issues specific to individual device drivers, including device files, boot parameters, and the capabilities of the different drivers. You probably only need to read the section relevant to your drive type. The README files are usually found in the directory **/usr/src/linux/Documentation/cdrom**.

4.3.1 Sbpcd Driver

```
        Principal author: Eberhard Moenkeberg (emoenke@gwdg.de)
   Multi-session support: yes (but not all drives)
  Multiple drive support: yes
Loadable module support: yes
   Reading audio frames: yes (CR-562, CR-563, CD-200 only)
            Auto-probing: yes
             Device file: /dev/sbpcd, major 25
      Configuration file: sbpcd.h
   Kernel config option: Matsushita/Panasonic CDROM support?
             README file: sbpcd
```

This driver accepts a kernel command line of the form:

```
sbpcd=<io-address>,<interface-type>
```

where the first parameter is the base address of the device (e.g. 0x230), and <interface-type> is one of "SoundBlaster", "LaserMate", or "SPEA". See the file `sbpcd.h` for hints on what interface type to use. Using `sbpcd=0` disables auto-probing, disabling the driver.

The device file can be created using:

```
# mknod /dev/sbpcd b 25 0
```

Up to four drives per controller are supported. The next three drives on the first controller would use minor device numbers 1 through 3. If you have more than one controller, create devices with major numbers 26, 27, and 28, up to a maximum of 4 controllers (this is 16 CD-ROM drives in total; hopefully enough for most users :-).

See the file sbpcd for more information on this driver.

If you recently bought a CD-ROM drive, don't assume that if it connects to a SoundBlaster card it should use this kernel driver. Most CD-ROM drives being sold by Creative Labs are now EIDE/ATAPI drives.

4.3.2   Sonycdu535 Driver

```
        Principal author: Ken Pizzini (ken@halcyon.com)
   Multi-session support: no
  Multiple drive support: no
Loadable module support: yes
    Reading audio frames: no
            Auto-probing: no
             Device file: /dev/sonycd535, major 24
      Configuration file: sonycd535.h
     Kernel config option: Sony CDU535 CDROM support?
             README file: sonycd535
```

This driver accepts a kernel command line of the form:

```
    sonycd535=<io-address>
```

where <io-address> is the base address of the controller (e.g. 0x320). Alternatively you can set the address in the file sonycd535.h and compile it in.

The device file can be created using:

```
    # mknod /dev/sonycd535 b 24 0
```

Some Linux distributions use /dev/sonycd for this device. Older versions of the driver used major device number 21; make sure your device file is correct.

This driver was previously distributed as a patch but is now part of the standard kernel. See the file sonycd535 for more information on this driver.

4.3.3   Cdu31a Driver

```
        Principal author: Corey Minyard (minyard@-rch.cirr.com)
   Multi-session support: yes
  Multiple drive support: no
Loadable module support: yes
    Reading audio frames: yes
            Auto-probing: no
             Device file: /dev/cdu31a, major 15
      Configuration file: cdu31a.h
     Kernel config option: Sony CDU31A/CDU33A CDROM support?
             README file: cdu31a
```

This driver accepts a kernel command line of the form:

```
cdu31a=<io-address>,<interrupt>,PAS
```

The first number is the I/O base address of the card (e.g. 0x340). The second is the interrupt number to use (0 means to use polled i/o). The optional third parameter should be "PAS" if the drive is connected to a Pro-Audio Spectrum 16 sound card, otherwise left blank.

If the driver is loaded as a module, it uses a slightly different format. When loading the driver using the modprobe or insmod command, the parameters take the form:

```
cdu31a_port=<io-address> cdu31a_irq=<interrupt>
```

The base io-address is required while the interrupt number is optional.

The device file can be created using:

```
# mknod /dev/cdu31a b 15 0
```

See the file cdu31a for more information on this driver.

Also see the Web page put together by Jeffrey Oxenreider (*zureal@infinet.com* <mailto:zureal@infinet. com>) that covers a lot of common problems with these drives. It can be found at <http://www.infinet. com/~zureal/cdu31a.html>.

4.3.4   Aztcd Driver

```
         Principal author: Werner Zimmermann (zimmerma@rz.fht-esslingen.de)
   Multi-session support: yes
 Multiple drive support: no
Loadable module support: yes
   Reading audio frames: no
            Auto-probing: no
             Device file: /dev/aztcd0, major 29
      Configuration file: aztcd.h
   Kernel config option: Aztech/Orchid/Okano/Wearnes (non IDE) CDROM support?
             README file: aztcd
```

This driver accepts a kernel command line of the form:

```
aztcd=<io-address>
```

where the parameter is the I/O base address of the card (e.g. 0x340).

The device file can be created using:

```
# mknod /dev/aztcd0 b 29 0
```

Note that this driver is for the CDA268-01A only. Other models, including the CDA268-03I and CDA269-031SE are not proprietary and should use the IDECD (ATAPI) kernel driver.

See the file aztcd for more information on this driver.

4.3.5   Gscd Driver

```
        Principal author: Oliver Raupach (raupach@nwfs1.rz.fh-hannover.de)
  Multi-session support: no
 Multiple drive support: no
Loadable module support: yes
   Reading audio frames: no
           Auto-probing: no
            Device file: /dev/gscd0, major 16
     Configuration file: gscd.h
   Kernel config option: Goldstar R420 CDROM support?
            README file: gscd
```

This driver accepts a kernel command line of the form:

```
    gscd=<io-address>
```

specifying the I/O base address of the card (e.g. 0x340).

The device file can be created using:

```
    # mknod /dev/gscd0 b 16 0
```

See the file gscd and the World-Wide Web site <http://linux.rz.fh-hannover.de/~raupach/> for more information on this driver.

4.3.6   Mcd Driver

```
        Principal author: Martin  (martin@bdsi.com)
   Multi-session support: no
 Multiple drive support: no
Loadable module support: yes
   Reading audio frames: no
           Auto-probing: no
            Device file: /dev/mcd, major 23
     Configuration file: mcd.h
   Kernel config option: Standard Mitsumi CDROM support?
            README file: mcd
```

This is the older driver for Mitsumi drivers that has been available for some time. You might want to try the newer mcdx driver, which has some new features but is possibly less stable.

This driver accepts a kernel command line of the form:

```
    mcd=<io-address>,<irq>
```

specifying the I/O base address of the card (e.g. 0x340) and the IRQ request number used.

The device file can be created using:

```
    # mknod /dev/mcd b 23 0
```

See the file mcd for more information on this driver.

4.3.7   Mcdx Driver

```
          Principal author: Heiko Schlittermann
    Multi-session support: yes
  Multiple drive support: yes
 Loadable module support: yes
    Reading audio frames: no (not supported by hardware)
            Auto-probing: no
             Device file: /dev/mcdx0, major 20
      Configuration file: mcdx.h
     Kernel config option: Experimental Mitsumi support?
             README file: mcdx
```

This is a newer driver for Mitsumi drivers. The older and possibly more stable mcd driver is still available.

This driver accepts a kernel command line of the form:

```
    mcdx=<io-address>,<irq>
```

specifying the I/O base address of the card (e.g. 0x340) and the IRQ request number used.

The device file can be created using:

```
    # mknod /dev/mcdx0 b 20 0
```

If you recently bought a Mitsumi CD-ROM drive, don't assume that it should use this kernel driver. Some Mitsumi models are now EIDE/ATAPI drives and should use the idecd kernel driver.

See the file mcdx for more information on this driver.

4.3.8   Cm206 Driver

```
          Principal author: David A. van Leeuwen (david@tm.tno.)
    Multi-session support: yes
  Multiple drive support: no
 Loadable module support: yes
    Reading audio frames: no
            Auto-probing: yes
             Device file: /dev/cm206cd, major 32
      Configuration file: cm206.h
     Kernel config option: Philips/LMS CM206 CDROM support?
             README file: cm206
```

The driver accepts a kernel command line of the form:

```
    cm206=<io-address>,<interrupt>
```

where the first number is the I/O base address of the card (e.g. 0x340). The second is the interrupt channel.

The device file can be created using:

```
    # mknod /dev/cm206cd b 32 0
```

See the file cm206 for more information on this driver.

4.3.9   Optcd Driver

```
        Principal author: Leo Spiekman (spiekman@dutette.et.tudelft.nl)
   Multi-session support: yes
 Multiple drive support: no
Loadable module support: yes
   Reading audio frames: no
           Auto-probing: no
            Device file: /dev/optcd0, major 17
     Configuration file: optcd.h
    Kernel config option: Experimental Optics Storage ... CDROM support?
            README file: optcd
```

The driver accepts a kernel command line of the form

```
    optcd=<io-address>
```

to specify the I/O base address of the card (e.g. 0x340).

The device file can be created using:

```
    # mknod /dev/optcd0 b 17 0
```

See the file optcd for more information on this driver.

4.3.10   Sjcd Driver

```
        Principal author: Vadim V. Model (vadim@rbrf.msk.su)
   Multi-session support: no
 Multiple drive support: no
Loadable module support: yes
   Reading audio frames: no
           Auto-probing: no
            Device file: /dev/sjcd, major 18
     Configuration file: sjcd.h
    Kernel config option: Experimental Sanyo H94A CDROM support?
            README file: sjcd
```

The driver accepts a kernel command line of the form:

```
    sjcd=<io-address>,<interrupt>,<dma>
```

indicating the base address, interrupt, and DMA channel to be used (e.g. sjcd=0x340,10,5).

The device file can be created using:

```
    # mknod /dev/sjcd b 18 0
```

See the file sjcd for more information on this driver.

4.3.11   Bpcd Driver

```
       Principal author: Grant R. Guenther (grant@torque.net)
   Multi-session support: unknown
  Multiple drive support: no
 Loadable module support: yes
     Reading audio frames: no
            Auto-probing: yes
             Device file: /dev/bpcd, major 41
      Configuration file: bpcd.h
    Kernel config option: MicroSolutions backpack CDROM support?
            README file: bpcd
```

The driver accepts a kernel command line of the form:

```
    bpcd=<io-address>
```

indicating the base address to be used (e.g. bpcd=0x3bc).

The device file can be created using:

```
    # mknod /dev/bpcd b 41 0
```

This driver is included with the 2.1 kernel source distribution. See the file bpcd for more information on this driver.

4.3.12   SCSI Driver

```
       Principal author: David Giller
   Multi-session support: yes (depending on drive)
  Multiple drive support: yes
 Loadable module support: yes
     Reading audio frames: no
            Auto-probing: yes
             Device file: /dev/scd0, major 11
      Configuration file: cdrom.h
    Kernel config option: SCSI CDROM support?
            README file: none
```

There are kernel command line option specific to each type of SCSI controller. See the *SCSI HOWTO* <http://sunsite.unc.edu/LDP/HOWTO/SCSI-HOWTO.html> for more information.

Multiple drives are supported (up to the limit of the maximum number of devices on the SCSI bus). Create device files with major number 11 and minor numbers starting at zero:

```
    # mknod /dev/scd0 b 11 0
    # mknod /dev/scd1 b 11 1
```

While the kernel driver itself does not support reading digital audio frames, some SCSI drives have the capability and will work with the cdda2wav program (which uses the generic SCSI kernel interface).

4.3.13 IDECD Driver

```
      Principal author: Scott Snyder (snyder@fnald0.fnal.gov)
  Multi-session support: yes
Multiple drive support: yes
Loadable module support: no
   Reading audio frames: yes (on supported drives)
           Auto-probing: yes
            Device file: /dev/hd{a,b,c,d},  major 22
     Configuration file: cdrom.h
    Kernel config option: Include support for IDE/ATAPI CDROMs?
            README file: ide-cd
```

This is the driver for ATAPI CD-ROMS. The driver accepts a kernel command line of the form

```
    hdx=cyls,heads,sects,wpcom,irq
      or
    hdx=cdrom
```

where hdx can be any of {hda,hdb,hdc,hdd}, or simply hd, for the "next" drive in sequence. Only the first three parameters are required (cyls,heads,sects). For example hdc=1050,32,64 hdd=cdrom.

Getting the IDE driver to recognize your CD-ROM drive can be tricky, especially if you have more than 2 devices or more than one IDE controller. Usually all that is required is to pass the right command line options from LILO. The file /usr/src/linux/Documentation/ide-cd explains how to do this. Read it carefully.

Recent Linux kernels have better support for multiple IDE devices. If you have problems with an older kernel, upgrading may help.

Some IDE controllers have hardware problems which the kernel driver can work around. You may need to pass additional parameters to the driver to enable this. See the documentation for details.

4.4 Booting the Linux Kernel

You can now reboot with the new kernel. Watch for a message such as the following indicating that the CD-ROM has been found by the device driver (the message will vary depending on the drive type):

```
    hdd: NEC CD-ROM DRIVE:282, ATAPI CDROM drive
```

If the bootup messages scroll by too quickly to read, you should be able to retrieve them using dmesg or tail /var/adm/messages.

If the drive is not found, then a problem has occurred, See the section on troubleshooting.

4.5 Mounting, Unmounting, and Ejecting Devices

To mount a CD-ROM, insert a disc in the drive, and run the mount command as root (this assumes you created a symbolic link to your device file as recommended above and that an empty directory /mnt/cdrom exists):

```
    # mount -t iso9660 -r /dev/cdrom /mnt/cdrom
```

The CD can now be accessed under the directory /mnt/cdrom.

There are other options to the mount command that you may wish to use; see the mount(8) man page for details.

You can add an entry to /etc/fstab to automatically mount a CD-ROM when Linux boots or to specify parameters to use when it is mounted; see the fstab(5) man page.

Note that to play audio CDs you should *not* try to mount them.

To unmount a CD-ROM, use the umount command as root:

```
# umount /mnt/cdrom
```

The disc can only be unmounted if no processes are currently accessing the drive (including having their default directory set to the mounted drive). You can then eject the disc. Most drives have an eject button; there is also a standalone *eject* <ftp://sunsite.unc.edu/pub/Linux/utils/disk-management/eject-1.4. tar.gz> program that allows ejecting CD-ROMs under software control.

Note that you should not eject a disc while it is mounted (this may or may not be possible depending on the type of drive). Some CD-ROM drivers can automatically eject a CD-ROM when it is unmounted and insert the CD tray when a disc is mounted (you can turn this feature off when compiling the kernel or by using a software command).

Its possible that after playing an audio CD you may not be able to mount a CD-ROM. You need to send a CD audio "stop" command (using a CD player program) before trying the mount. This problem only appears to occur with the SBPCD driver.

Recent 2.0 and 2.1 kernels support a kernel-based automounter which provides transparent mounting of removable media including CD-ROM. You can find the tools needed to use it at <ftp.kernel.org:/pub/ linux/daemons/autofs/>.

4.6   Troubleshooting

If you still encounter problems after following the instructions in the HOWTO, here are some things to check. The checks are listed in increasing order of complexity. If a check fails, solve the problem before moving to the next stage.

4.6.1   Step 1: Make sure you are really running the kernel you compiled

You can check the date stamp on the kernel to see if you are running the one that you compiled with CD-ROM support. You can do this with the uname command:

```
% uname -a
Linux fizzbin 2.0.18 #1 Fri Sep 6 10:10:54 EDT 1996 i586
```

or by displaying the file /proc/version:

```
% cat /proc/version
Linux version 2.0.18 (root@fizzbin) (gcc version 2.7.2) #1 Fri Sep 6 10:10:54 EDT 1996
```

If the date stamp doesn't seem to match when you compiled the kernel, then you are running an old kernel. Did you really reboot? If you use LILO, did you re-install it (typically by running /sbin/lilo)? If booting from floppy, did you create a new boot floppy and use it when booting?

4.6.2 Step 2: Make sure the proper kernel drivers are compiled in

You can see what drivers are compiled in by looking at /proc/devices:

```
% cat /proc/devices
Character devices:
  1 mem
  2 pty
  3 ttyp
  4 ttyS
  5 cua
  7 vcs

Block devices:
  3 ide0
 22 ide1
```

First look for your CD-ROM device driver. These are all block devices, in this case we can see that the idecd driver with major number 22 was present.

Also make sure that ISO-9660 filesystem support was compiled in, by looking at /proc/filesystems:

```
% cat /proc/filesystems
        ext2
        msdos
nodev   proc
        iso9660
```

You can also see what i/o port addresses are being used by a driver with the file /proc/ioports:

```
howto % cat /proc/ioports
...
0230-0233 : sbpcd
...
```

If any of the drivers you thought you compiled in are not displayed, then something went wrong with the kernel configuration or build. Start the installation process again, beginning with configuration and building of the kernel.

4.6.3 Step 3: Did the kernel detect your drive during booting?

Make sure that the CD-ROM device was detected when the kernel booted. You should have seen a message on bootup. If the messages scrolled off the screen, you can usually recall them using the dmesg command:

```
% dmesg
```

or

```
% tail /var/adm/messages
```

If your drive was not found then something is wrong. Make sure it is powered on and all cables are connected. If your drive has hardware jumpers for addressing, check that they are set correctly (e.g. drive 0 if you have only one drive). ATAPI CD-ROMS must be jumpered as "single" or "master", and not "slave" when only one IDE device is attached to an interface. If the drive works under DOS then you can be reasonably confident that the hardware is working.

Many kernel drivers using auto-probing, but some do not, and in any case the probing is not always reliable. Use the kernel command line option listed for your kernel driver type. You may want to try several different values if you are not sure of the i/o address or other parameters. LILO can be (and usually is) configured to allow you to enter the parameters manually when booting.

Another possibility is that you used the wrong kernel driver for your CD-ROM driver. Some documentation may refer to proprietary interfaces as IDE, leading some to mistakenly believe they are ATAPI drives.

Another possibility is that your drive (or interface card) is one of the "compatible" type that requires initialization by the DOS driver. Try booting DOS and loading the vendor supplied DOS device driver. Then soft boot Linux using `Control-Alt-Delete`.

If your drive is not listed in this document, it is possible that there are no drivers for it available under Linux. You can check with some of the references listed at the end of this document for assistance.

4.6.4   Step 4: Can you read data from the drive?

Try reading from the CD-ROM drive. Typing the following command should cause the drive activity light (if present) to come on and no errors should be reported. Use whatever device file is appropriate for your drive and make sure a CD-ROM is inserted; use Control-C to exit.

```
# dd if=/dev/cdrom of=/dev/null bs=2048
^C
124+0 records in
124+0 records out
```

If this works, then the kernel is communicating with the drive and you can move on to step 5.

If not, then a possible cause is the device file. Make sure than the device file in the `/dev` directory has the correct major and minor numbers as listed previously for your drive type. Check that the permissions on the device file allow reading and writing.

A remote possibility is a hardware problem. Try testing the drive under DOS, if possible, to determine if this could be the case.

4.6.5   Step 5: Can you mount the drive?

If you can read from the drive but cannot mount it, first verify that you compiled in ISO-9660 file system support by reading /proc/filesystems, as described previously.

Make sure you are mounting the drive with the "-t iso9660" and "-r" options and that a known good ISO-9660 CD-ROM (not Audio CD) is inserted in the drive. You normally must mount drives as user `root`.

Make sure that the mount point exists and is an empty directory.

If you are automatically mounting the CD-ROM on bootup, make sure that you have correct entries in the `/etc/fstab` file.

If you are running the syslog daemon, there may be error messages from the kernel that you are not seeing. Try using the "dmesg" command:

```
% dmesg
SBPCD: sbpcd_open: no disk in drive
```

There may also be errors logged to files in **/var/adm**, depending on how your system is configured.

4.6.6 Debugging Audio Problems

If the drive works with CD-ROMs, but not for playing audio CDs, here are some possible solutions.

You need an application program to play audio CDs. Some applications may be broken or may not be compatible with your drive. Try other applications and/or try recompiling them yourself. A good place to look for software is **<ftp://sunsite.unc.edu/pub/Linux/apps/sound/cdrom/>**.

A few of the CD-ROM drivers do not support playing Audio CDs. Check the README file or source code to see if that is the case.

Check if the audio can be played through the headphone jack. If so, then the problem is likely related to your sound card. Use a mixer program to set the input device and volume levels. Make sure you have installed an audio cable from the CD-ROM drive to the sound card. Make sure that the kernel sound card driver is installed and working (see the *Sound HOWTO* **<http://sunsite.unc.edu/LDP/HOWTO/Sound-HOWTO.html>**).

4.6.7 When All Else Fails

If you still have problems, here are some final suggestions for things to try:

- carefully re-read this HOWTO document
- read the references listed at the end of this document, especially the relevant kernel source README files
- post a question to one of the **comp.os.linux** or other usenet newsgroups
- send a question to the Linux mailing list
- try using the latest Linux kernel
- contact your computer dealer
- contact the CD-ROM manufacturer
- send mail to the maintainer of the relevant kernel driver (look in the file **/usr/src/linux/MAINTAINERS**)
- send mail to me
- fire up emacs and type **Esc-x doctor** :-)

5 Applications

This section briefly lists some of the key applications related to CD-ROM that are available under Linux. Check the Linux Software Map for the latest versions and archive sites.

5.1 Audio CD Players

Several programs are available for playing audio CDs, either through a headphone jack or an attached sound card.

Workman

a graphical player running under X11 and supporting a CD database and many other features

WorkBone

an interactive text-mode player

xcdplayer

a simple X11 based player

cdplayer

a very simple command line based player

Xmcd

an X11/Motif based player

xmitsumi

another X11 based player for Mitsumi drives

xplaycd

another X11 based player, bundled with sound mixer and VU meter programs

cdtool

command line tools for playing audio CDs

Some of these programs are coded to use a specific device file for the CD-ROM (e.g. `/dev/cdrom`). You may be able to pass the correct device name as a parameter, or you can create a symbolic link in the `/dev` directory. If sending the CD output to a sound card, you may wish to use a mixer program to set volume settings or select the CD-ROM input for recording.

5.2   PhotoCD

PhotoCDs use an ISO-9660 file system containing image files in a proprietary format. Not all CD-ROM drives support reading PhotoCDs.

The `hpcdtoppm` program by Hadmut Danisch converts PhotoCD files to the portable pixmap format. It can be obtained from `<ftp://ftp.gwdg.de/pub/linux/hpcdtoppm>` or as part of the PBM (portable bit map) utilities, available on many archive sites (look for "pbm" or "netpbm").

The `photocd` program by Gerd Knorr *kraxel@cs.tu-berlin.de* `<mailto:kraxel@cs.tu-berlin.de>` can convert PhotoCD images into Targa or Windows and OS/2 bitmap files.

The same author has written the program `xpcd`, an X11-based program for handling PhotoCD images. You can select the images with a mouse, preview the image in a small window, and load the image with any of the five possible resolutions. You can also mark a part of the Image and load only the selected part. Look for these packages at `<ftp://ftp.cs.tu-berlin.de/pub/linux/Local/misc/>`.

The ImageMagick image file manipulation program also supports PhotoCD files. It is available from `<ftp://ftp.x.org/contrib/applications/ImageMagick/>`.

5.3   Mkisofs

Eric Youngdale's `mkisofs` package allows creating an ISO-9660 file system on a hard disk partition. This can then be used to assist in creating and testing CD-ROM file systems before mastering discs.

The tools for actually writing data to writable CD-ROM drives tend to be vendor specific. They also require writing the data with no interruptions, so a multitasking operating system like Linux is not particularly well suited.

5.4 ISO-9660 Utilities

These are some utilities for verifying the format of ISO-9660 formatted discs; you may find them useful for testing suspect CDs. The package can be found at `<ftp://ftp.cdrom.com/pub/unixfreeware/archive/>`. They were written by Bill Siegmund and Rich Morin.

6 Answers to Frequently Asked Questions

6.1 How can a non-root user mount and unmount discs?

Most `mount` commands support the *user* option. If you make an entry such as the following in `/etc/fstab`:

```
/dev/sbpcd   /mnt/cdrom   iso9660       user,noauto,ro
```

then an ordinary user will be allowed to mount and unmount the drive using these commands:

```
% mount /mnt/cdrom
% umount /mnt/cdrom
```

The disc will be mounted with some options that help enforce security (e.g. programs cannot executed, device files are ignored); in some cases this may be too restrictive.

Another method is to get the `usermount` package which allows non-root users to mount and unmount removable devices such as floppies and CD-ROMs, but restricts access to other devices (such as hard disk partitions). It is available on major archive sites.

The archive site `ftp.cdrom.com` has the source file `mount.c` which allows mounting an unmounting of CD-ROMs (only) by normal users. It runs as a setuid executable.

6.2 Why do I get device is busy when unmounting a CD-ROM?

The disc cannot be unmounted if any processes are accessing the drive, including having their default directory set to the mounted filesystem. If you cannot identify the processes using the disc, you can use the `fuser` command, as shown in the following example.

```
% umount /cdrom
umount: /dev/hdd: device is busy
% fuser -v /cdrom
                    USER      PID ACCESS COMMAND
/mnt/cdrom          tranter   133 ..c.. bash
```

On some systems you may need to be root when running the `fuser` command in order to see the processes of other users.

6.3 How do I export a CD-ROM to other hosts over NFS?

You need to add an entry to the `/etc/exports` file. Users on other machines will then be able to mount the device. See the `exports(5)` man page for details.

6.4   Can I boot Linux from a CD-ROM?

When initially installing Linux the most common method is to use a boot floppy. Some distributions allow booting a Linux kernel on CD directly from DOS.

Michael Fulbright (*msf@redhat.com* `<mailto:msf@redhat.com>`) reports that with the right CD-ROM, ROM BIOS, and ATAPI CD-ROM drive it is possible to boot directly from CD. The latest version of `mkisofs` also supports creating such disks. He has added some patches to support the El Torito standard for bootable CDs.

6.5   How can I read digital data from audio CDs?

Heiko Eissfeldt (*heiko@colossus.escape.de* `<mailto:heiko@colossus.escape.de>`) and Olaf Kindel have written a utility that reads audio data and saves it as `.wav` format sound files. The package is called `cdda2wav.tar.gz` and can be found on `sunsite.unc.edu`.

Because CD-ROM drives are changing very quickly, it is difficult to list which models support reading digital data. You best bet is to get the latest `cdda2wav` package and read the documentation.

For more information on this subject, see the web site *http://www.tardis.ed.ac.uk/~psyche/cdda/* `<http://www.tardis.ed.ac.uk/~psyche/cdda/>` and the alt.cd-rom FAQ listed in the references section.

6.6   Why doesn't the find command work properly?

On ISO-9660 formatted discs without the Rock Ridge Extensions, you need to add the `-noleaf` option to the `find` command. See the find(1) man page for details.

(In my experience virtually all recent Linux CDs use the Rock Ridge extensions, so this problem should occur very rarely.)

6.7   Does Linux support any recordable CD-ROM drives?

The X-CD-Roast package for Linux is a graphical front-end for using CD writers. The package can be found at sunsite.unc.edu in /pub/Linux/utils/disk-management/xcdroast-0.95.tar.gz

Also see the Linux CD-Writing HOWTO document, found at `<ftp://sunsite.unc.edu/pub/Linux/docs/HOWTO/CD-Writing.html>` or `<http://sunsite.unc.edu/LDP/HOWTO/CD-Writing.html>`.

6.8   Why do I get mount: Read-only file system when mounting a CD-ROM?

CD-ROM is a read-only media. With some early kernels you could mount a CD-ROM for read/write; attempts to write data to the CD would simple be ignored. As of kernel version 1.1.33 this was corrected so that CD-ROMs must be mounted read only (e.g. using the -r option to mount).

6.9   Why does the disc tray open when I shut down the system?

As of the 1.1.38 kernel, the sbpcd driver ejects the CD when it is unmounted. If you shut down the system, a mounted CD will be unmounted, causing it to eject.

This feature is for convenience when changing discs. If the tray is open when you mount or read a CD, it will also automatically be closed.

I found that this caused problems with a few programs (e.g. cdplay and workbone). As of the 1.1.60 kernel you can control this feature under software control. A sample program is included in the sbpcd documentation file (or use the *eject* `<ftp://sunsite.unc.edu/pub/Linux/utils/disk-management/eject-1.4.tar.gz>` program).

6.10   I have a "special" CD that can't be mounted

The "special" CD is likely an XA disc (like all Photo CDs or "one-offs" created using CD-R drives). Most of the Linux kernel CD-ROM drivers do not support XA discs, although you may be able to find a patch to add support on one of the archive sites.

The sbpcd driver *does* support XA. If you are using this driver you can determine if the disc is XA using the following procedure: go into the file sbpcd.c and enable the display of the "Table of Contents" (DBG_TOC). Build and install the new kernel and boot from it. During each mount the TOC info will be written (either to the console or to a log file). If the first displayed value in the TOC header line is "20", then it is an XA disc. That byte is "00" with normal disks. If the TOC display shows different tracks, that is also a sign that it is an XA disc.

(thanks to Eberhard Moenkeberg for the above information)

Other possibilities for unreadable CDs are:

1. The disc doesn't use an ISO-9660 file system (e.g. some use SunOS or HFS)
2. It is an audio CD
3. The CD is damaged or defective
4. You put it in the drive upside down :-)

6.11   Do multi-platter CD-ROM drives work with Linux?

Several users have reported success with SCSI multi-disc CD-ROM changers. You probably need to enable the "Probe all LUNs on each SCSI device" kernel configuration option. At least one user also had to increase a SCSI timeout value in the kernel driver. The Nakamichi MBR-7 7 disc changer and Pioneer 12 disc changer have been reported to work.

EIDE/ATAPI multi-disc changers are also available. The 2.0 kernel has rudimentary support for some drives using the CDROM_SELECT_DISC ioctl function. The IDE-CD kernel driver documentation file includes source code for a program to select changer slots, or you can use a recent version of the `eject` program described earlier.

6.12   I get "/cdrom: Permission denied" errors

Some CDs have root directory file permissions that only allow user `root` to read them. The March 1995 InfoMagic CD set is one example. This is a real inconvenience.

The following patch, courtesy of Christoph Lameter (*clameter@waterf.org* `<mailto:clameter@waterf.org>`) patches the kernel to get around this problem.

```
From: clameter@waterf.org (Christoph Lameter)
Newsgroups: comp.os.linux.setup
```

```
Subject: InfoMagic Developers Set: Fix for CD-ROM permissions
Date: 12 Apr 1995 20:32:03 -0700
Organization: The Water Fountain - Mining for streams of Living Water
NNTP-Posting-Host: waterf.org
X-Newsreader: TIN [version 1.2 PL2]
```

The March 1995 Edition of the InfoMagic Developers CD-ROM Set has
problems because the information stored in the root directory
permissions is causing the following problems with using the CDs

1. Disc1 will always have the owner/group of 5101/51 and has write
access allowed (?)

2. Disc2 and 3 have rwx set for root and no rights at all for any
other group/user. These discs cannot be accessed from any user other
than root! I run a BBS and I need to make them accessible for download
by others.

I have seen several fixes to this problem already floating
around. Trouble is that these fixes usually change the rights for ALL
directories on the CD. This fix here changes ONLY the rights for the
root directory of the CD-ROM. If you want to run parts of Linux
directly off the CD you might run into trouble if all directories are
readable for everyone and if they are all owned by root.

This fix will set the rights for the root directory to r-xr-xr-x and
the owner/group to the values indicated in the uid and gid options to
the mount command.

```
To apply:
 cd /usr/src/linux/fs/isofs
 patch <**THIS MESSAGE**
```

and recompile kernel (you may have to fix up the patch by hand
depending on your kernel version).

This fix should probably be incorporated into the kernel. What business
does data on a CD have to mess around with the permissions/owners of the
mount-point anyways?

```
--- inode.c.ORIG       Wed Apr 12 17:24:36 1995
+++ inode.c    Wed Apr 12 17:59:12 1995
@@ -552,7 +552,15 @@
    these numbers in the inode structure. */

        if (!high_sierra)
-          parse_rock_ridge_inode(raw_inode, inode);
+        { parse_rock_ridge_inode(raw_inode, inode);
+           /* check for access to the root directory rights/owner CL */
+           if((inode->i_sb->u.isofs_sb.s_firstdatazone) == inode->i_ino)
+            { /* Change owner/rights to the ones demanded by the mount command */
+               inode->i_uid = inode->i_sb->u.isofs_sb.s_uid;
+               inode->i_gid = inode->i_sb->u.isofs_sb.s_gid;
+               inode->i_mode = S_IRUGO | S_IXUGO | S_IFDIR;
```

```
+           }
+        }

#ifdef DEBUG
        printk("Inode: %x extent: %x\n",inode->i_ino, inode->u.isofs_i.i_first_extent);
@@ -805,4 +813,3 @@
 }


 #endif
-
```

Note that the above patch is somewhat old and probably won't apply cleanly against recent 2.0 kernels. Also see the related question on hidden files later in this document.

6.13   How do I interpret IDE CD kernel error messages?

What does it mean when I get a kernel message from the IDE CD-ROM driver like "hdxx: code: xx key: x asc: xx ascq: x"?

This is an status/error message from the IDE CD-ROM drive. By default the IDECD driver prints out the raw information instead of wasting kernel space with error messages. You can change the default to display the actual error messages by going into /usr/src/linux/drivers/block/ide-cd.c, changing the value of VERBOSE_IDE_CD_ERRORS to 1, and recompiling the kernel.

6.14   How can I tell what speed CD-ROM I have?

Here's one way. This command measures how long is takes to read 1500K of data from CD:

```
% time -p dd if=/dev/cdrom of=/dev/null bs=1k count=1500
1500+0 records in
1500+0 records out
real 5.24
user 0.03
sys 5.07
```

The transfer rate of single speed drives is 150 kilobytes per second, which should take about 10 seconds. At double speed it would take five seconds, quad speed would take 2.5, etc...

The "real" time above is probably the best number to look at – in this case it indicates a double speed drive. You can increase the amount of data transferred to get a more accurate value (in case you were wondering, the data does not get cached). You should probably run the command a few times and take the average.

6.15   My CD-ROM stopped working after Linux was installed

The usual symptom is that the boot disk used to initially install Linux recognized your CD-ROM drive, but after Linux was installed on the hard drive or floppy and rebooted it no longer recognizes the CD-ROM.

The most common reason for this problem is that with some Linux distributions the kernel that is installed on your hard drive (or floppy) is not necessarily the same one that was on your boot disk. You selected a boot disk that matched your CD-ROM hardware, while the kernel you installed is a "generic" kernel that is lacking CD-ROM support. You can verify this by following the troubleshooting guidelines discussed previously in this document (e.g. start by checking /proc/devices).

The solution is to recompile the kernel, ensuring that the drivers for your CD-ROM drive and any others that are needed (e.g. SCSI controller, ISO-9660 file system) are included. See the *Kernel HOWTO* <http://sunsite.unc.edu/LDP/HOWTO/Kernel-HOWTO.html> if you don't know how to do this.

If you passed any command line options to the boot disk (e.g. "hdc=cdrom") you need to add these to your boot program configuration file (typically /etc/lilo.conf).

6.16   There are "hidden" files on a CD which I can't read

Some CDs have files with the "hidden" bit set on them. Normally these files are not visible. If you mount the CD with the "unhide" option then the files should be accessible (this doesn't seem to be documented anywhere).

6.17   Where is the CD-ROM API documented?

If you want to write your own application, such as an audio CD player program, you will need to understand the application programming interface (API) provided by Linux.

Originally the CD-ROM kernel drivers used their own ioctl() functions to support features specific to each drive. Header files such as /usr/include/linux/sbpcd.h describe these. Because many of the drivers were based on other drivers, the interfaces, while not identical, have a lot in common.

More recently there has been an initiative headed by David van Leeuwen (*david@tm.tno.nl* <mailto:david@tm.tno.nl>) to standardize the API for CD-ROM drives, putting common code in one place and ensuring that all drivers exhibit the same behaviour. This is documented in the file /usr/src/linux/Documentation/cdrom/cdrom-standard.tex. Several kernel drivers support this. I expect that by the next major kernel release (3.0?) all CD-ROM drivers will conform to this API.

My book, *Linux Multimedia Guide*, goes into quite a bit of detail on how to program CD-ROM drives, especially for audio functions. See the end of the References section.

6.18   Why don't I see long filenames on this Windows CD-ROM?

If you have a CD-ROM which has long filenames under Windows but not under Linux, it may be formatted using Microsoft's proprietary Joliet filesystem. See the next question for a solution.

6.19   Is Microsoft's Joliet filesystem supported?

Microsoft has created an extension to the ISO CD-ROM format called Joliet. At the time of writing, support for Joliet was in progress and patches were available from <http://www-plateau.cs.berkeley.edu/people/chaffee/joliet.html> or <ftp://www-plateau.cs.berkeley.edu/pub/multimedia/linux/joliet/>.

7   References

I have already mentioned the README files, typically installed in /usr/src/linux/Documentation/cdrom. These can be a gold mine of useful information.

The following Usenet FAQs are posted periodically to *news.answers* <news:news.answers> and archived at
Internet FTP sites such as <ftp://rtfm.mit.edu/>:

- alt.cd-rom FAQ
- comp.periphs.scsi FAQ
- Enhanced IDE/Fast-ATA/ATA-2 FAQ

Several other Linux HOWTOs have useful information relevant to CD-ROM:

- *SCSI HOWTO* <http://sunsite.unc.edu/LDP/HOWTO/SCSI-HOWTO.html>
- *Hardware Compatibility HOWTO* <http://sunsite.unc.edu/LDP/HOWTO/Hardware-HOWTO.html>
- *Sound HOWTO* <http://sunsite.unc.edu/LDP/HOWTO/Sound-HOWTO.html>
- *Kernel HOWTO* <http://sunsite.unc.edu/LDP/HOWTO/Kernel-HOWTO.html>
- *Distribution HOWTO* <http://sunsite.unc.edu/LDP/HOWTO/Distribution-HOWTO.html>
- *CD Writing HOWTO* <http://sunsite.unc.edu/LDP/HOWTO/CD-Writing.html>

At least a dozen companies sell Linux distributions on CD-ROM; most of them are listed in the Distribution
HOWTO.

The following Usenet news groups cover CD-ROM related topics:

- *comp.publish.cdrom.hardware* <news:comp.publish.cdrom.hardware>
- *comp.publish.cdrom.multimedia* <news:comp.publish.cdrom.multimedia>
- *comp.publish.cdrom.software* <news:comp.publish.cdrom.software>
- *comp.sys.ibm.pc.hardware.cd-rom* <news:comp.sys.ibmpc.hardware.cd-rom>
- *alt.cd-rom* <news:alt.cd-rom>
- *alt.cd-rom.reviews* <news:alt.cd-rom.reviews>

The comp.os.linux newsgroups are also good sources of Linux specific information.

There is a large archive of CD-ROM information and software at <ftp://ftp.cdrom.com/pub/cdrom/>.

A FAQ document on IDE and ATA devices can be found at <ftp://rtfm.mit.edu/pub/usenet/news.
answers/pc-hardware-faq/enhanced-IDE/> and at <http://www.seagate.com/techsuppt/faq/faqlist.
html>.

Western Digital, the company that started the IDE protocol, has information available on the IDE protocol
available on their FTP site at <ftp://fission.dt.wdc.com/pub/standards/atapi/>.

A Web site dedicated to multimedia can be found at <http://viswiz.gmd.de/MultimediaInfo/>. Creative
Labs has a Web site at <http://www.creaf.com/>.

The Linux Documentation Project has produced several books on Linux, including *Linux Installation and
Getting Started*. These are freely available by anonymous FTP from major Linux archive sites or can be
purchased in hardcopy format.

The *Linux Software Map* (LSM) is an invaluable reference for locating Linux software. The LSM can be
found on various anonymous FTP sites, including <ftp://sunsite.unc.edu/pub/Linux/docs/LSM/>.

The Linux mailing list has a number of "channels" dedicated to different topics. To find out how to join,
send a mail message with the word "help" as the message body to *majordomo@vger.rutgers.edu* <mailto:
majordomo@vger.rutgers.edu> (Note: at time of writing these mailing lists were severely overloaded and a
replacement was being sought).

Finally, a shameless plug: If you want to learn a lot more about multimedia under Linux (especially CD-ROM and sound card applications and programming), check out my book *Linux Multimedia Guide*, ISBN 1-56592-219-0, published by O'Reilly and Associates. As well as the original English version, French and Japanese translations are now in print. For details, call 800-998-9938 in North America or check the Web page <http://www.ora.com/catalog/multilinux/noframes.html> or my home page <http://www.pobox.com/~tranter/>.

CD-Writing HOWTO

Winfried Trümper <winni@xpilot.org>   v2.4.1, 16 December 1997

This document deals with the process of writing CDs under Linux.

Contents

1 Introduction

My first experience with CD Writers was guided by the "Linux CD Writer mini-HOWTO" by Matt Cutts <cutts@cs.unc.edu>. Thanks Matt!

Although my intention was only to upgrade his document, I rewrote it from the scratch after I realized how much changed since 1994.

1.1 Disclaimer

I (Winfried Truemper) **DISCLAIM ALL WARRANTIES WITH REGARD TO THIS DOC-UMENT, INCLUDING ALL IMPLIED WARRANTIES OF MERCHANTABILITY AND FITNESS FOR A CERTAIN PURPOSE; IN NO EVENT SHALL I BE LIABLE FOR ANY SPECIAL, INDIRECT OR CONSEQUENTIAL DAMAGES OR ANY DAMAGES WHAT-SOEVER RESULTING FROM LOSS OF USE, DATA OR PROFITS, WHETHER IN AN ACTION OF CONTRACT, NEGLIGENCE OR OTHER TORTIOUS ACTION, ARISING OUT OF OR IN CONNECTION WITH THE USE OF THIS DOCUMENT.** Short: read and use at your own risk.

1.2 Suggested readings

The *CD-R FAQ* <http://www.cd-info.com/CDIC/Technology/CD-R/FAQ.html> is a general FAQ about compact-disk recordables (CD-R).

The *Linux CD-ROM HOWTO* explains everything one should know about CD-ROM drives under Linux. As a supplement, you may want to take a look at the *Linux SCSI HOWTO* and the *Linux Kernel HOWTO*.

1.3   Terminology ... lasers at maximum ... fire!

CD-ROM stands for *Compact Disc Read Only Memory*, a storage medium utilizing an optical laser to sense microscopic pits on a silver shimmering disk. (The silver shimmering comes from an aluminized layer which is the carrier.) The pits represent the bits of the information (in some way) and are so petite that some billions of them fit on the disc. Thus a CD is a mass-storage medium.

The Term *CD-R* is a short form of *CD-ROM recordable* and refers to a CD that doesn't have those "microscopic pits" on it's surface... thus it's empty.

Instead of the aluminium layer (silver) a CD-R has a special film (colored) into which "microscopic pits" can be burned in. This is done by giving the laser which normally only senses the pits a little bit more power so he burns the pits. This action can only be taken **once** on a CD-R.

You can leave out some areas for later writing, though, creating a so called multi-session CD.

This mini-HOWTO deals with the task of writing a CD-R. Welcome on board, captain.

1.4   Supported CD-Writers

The detailed list of models which have been reported (not) to work successfully is available from

<http://www.shop.de/cgi-bin/winni/lsc.pl>

The list will be included in future versions of this mini-HOWTO. Most SCSI cd-writers are supported and the newest version of cdrecord even supports ATAPI cd-writers.

If your hardware isn't supported you can still use Linux to create an image of the later CD but then you have to use DOS-Software to write the image to the CD-R. [You may wish to do so because most DOS-software cannot deal with long filenames available in Linux.]

In this case you can skip all hardware-related sections (those about *generic SCSI devices* and cdwrite/cdrecord).

1.5   Supported "features"

Currently the software for burning CDs under Linux does support the following main features:

```
Feature          cdwrite-2.1      cdrecord-1.7
-----------------------------------------------
ATAPI support    no               yes
Multisession     only partial     yes

RockRidge        yes (mkisofs)    yes (mkisofs)
El Torito        yes (mkisofs)    yes (mkisofs)
HFS              yes (mkhybrid)   yes (mkhybrid)
Joliet           yes (mkhybrid)   yes (mkhybrid)
```

RockRidge is an extension to allow longer filenames and a deeper directory hierarchy. *El Torito* can be used to produce bootable CDs. Please see the accompanied documentation for further details upon this special features. *HFS* lets a macintosh read the CD-ROM as if it were an HFS volume. *Joliet* brings long filenames (among other things) to some variants of Windows (95, NT).

Section 2.8 lists the availability of the mentioned software.

1.6 Mailinglists

If you want to join the development team (with the intention to actively _help_ them), send e-mail to

> cdwrite-request@pixar.com

and put the word subscribe in body of the message.

1.7 Availability

The newest version of this document is always available from

> `<http://www.shop.de/~winni/linux/cdr/>`

2 Prepare your Linux-box for writing CD-ROMs

Before November 1997, the software for Linux didn't support ATAPI cd-writers. As a result, the current release of the HOWTO concentrates on dealing with SCSI devices.

The good news is, that dealing with ATAPI devices is much easier and you can still use this HOWTO if you just forget about the "generic SCSI devices". To find out how to address ATAPI devices you can issue the command cdrecord -scanbus.

Future versions of this HOWTO will contain more details of dealing with ATAPI cd-writers.

2.1 Set up the hardware

Shut down your computer, switch it off and hook CD writer to the SCSI-bus.

Make sure the SCSI-bus is properly terminated and choose a free SCSI-ID for the writer. Look at the Linux SCSI-HOWTO if you're not sure. If you're completely clueless, ask an expert.

Switch the power on again and check the messages that the BIOS of the SCSI-controller prints immediatly after switching the power on. If it doesn't recognize you writer, go back to step (b). You should see a message like

[missing picture; has anyone a screenshot of it?]

2.2 A note on writing CDs under Linux

In contrast to other rumors, the Linux-kernel does _not_ require a patch in order to write to CDs. Although the file drivers/scsi/scsi.c from the kernel-sources contains the lines

```
case TYPE_WORM:
case TYPE_ROM:
 SDpnt->writeable = 0;
```

this does only mean that that CDs and WORMs are not writeable through the standard-devices /dev/sda-/dev/sdh - which is ok.

Instead of using these devices the writing of CDs is done through the so called *generic SCSI-devices* which permit nearly everything - even writing to CDs.

2.3 Create the generic devices

The *Linux SCSI-HOWTO* says about generic SCSI-devices:

> The Generic SCSI device driver provides an interface for sending SCSI commands to all SCSI devices - disks, tapes, CDROMs, media changer robots, etc.

Speaking of the generic devices as *interfaces* means that they provide an alternate way of accessing SCSI-hardware than through the standard devices.

This alternate way is required because the standard devices are designed to read data block-wise from a disk, tape or cd-rom. Compared to this, driving a cd-writer (or a scanner) is more exotic, e.g commands to position the laser must be transmitted. To have a clean (and therefore fast) implementation of standard-devices, all such exotic actions must be done through the generic SCSI devices.

As everthing can be done to SCSI-hardware through the generic devices they are not fixed to a certain purpose - therefore the name *generic*.

Goto the /dev-directory and check for generic SCSI devices; ls-command should show sga-sgh:

```
bash> cd /dev
bash> ls -l sg*
crw-------    1 root    sys     21,    0 Jan  1  1970 sga
crw-------    1 root    sys     21,    1 Jan  1  1970 sgb
crw-------    1 root    sys     21,    2 Jan  1  1970 sgc
crw-------    1 root    sys     21,    3 Jan  1  1970 sgd
crw-------    1 root    sys     21,    4 Jan  1  1970 sge
crw-------    1 root    sys     21,    5 Jan  1  1970 sgf
crw-------    1 root    sys     21,    6 Jan  1  1970 sgg
crw-------    1 root    sys     21,    7 Jan  1  1970 sgh
```

If you don't have those device-files then create them by using the /dev/MAKEDEV-script:

```
bash> cd /dev/
bash> ./MAKEDEV sg
```

Now the device-files should show up.

2.4   Enable usage of the *generic SCSI* and *loopback* devices

The Linux-kernel needs a module that lends it the ability to deal with generic SCSI devices. If your running kernel has this feature, it should be listed in the pseudo-file /proc/devices:

```
bash> cat /proc/devices
Character devices:
 1 mem
 2 pty
 3 ttyp
 4 ttyp
 5 cua
 7 vcs
21 sg           <----- stands for "SCSI Generic device"

30 socksys

Block devices:
 2 fd
 7 loop         <----- we even can use the loop-devices
 8 sd
11 sr           <----- stands for "SCSI cd-Rom"
```

Maybe you have to issue the commands insmod sg, insmod loop or insmod sr_mod to load the modules into the kernel. Check again after you've tried this.

If one of them doesn't succeed, you must re-configure your kernel and re-compile it.

```
bash> cd /usr/src/linux
bash> make config

[..]
*
* Additional Block Devices
*
Loopback device support (CONFIG_BLK_DEV_LOOP) [M/n/y/?] M

[..]
*
* SCSI support
*
SCSI support (CONFIG_SCSI) [Y/m/n/?] Y
*
* SCSI support type (disk, tape, CD-ROM)
*
SCSI disk support (CONFIG_BLK_DEV_SD) [Y/m/n/?] Y
SCSI tape support (CONFIG_CHR_DEV_ST) [M/n/y/?] M
```

```
SCSI CD-ROM support (CONFIG_BLK_DEV_SR) [M/n/y/?] M
SCSI generic support (CONFIG_CHR_DEV_SG) [M/n/y/?] M

[..]
ISO9660 cdrom filesystem (CONFIG_ISO9660_FS) [Y/m/n/?] M
```

Please note that I omitted the not-so-important questions.

2.5 Build and install the kernel

If you have questions regarding to this the Linux Kernel-HOWTO is the suggested reading. Furthermore your Linux-distribution should ship with some documentation about this issue.

[Hint: while re-compiling, you can continue with steps 2.7-2.9]

2.6 Reboot the computer for the changes to take effect.

Don't panic if the Linux-kernel prints the messages faster than you can read them, at least the initialization of SCSI-devices can be re-displayed with the command **dmesg**:

```
scsi0 : NCR53c{7,8}xx (rel 17)
scsi : 1 host.
scsi0 : target 0 accepting period 100ns offset 8 10.00MHz
scsi0 : setting target 0 to period 100ns offset 8 10.00MHz

   Vendor: FUJITSU   Model: M1606S-512     Rev: 6226
   Type:   Direct-Access                   ANSI SCSI
Detected scsi disk sda at scsi0, channel 0, id 0, lun 0

   Vendor: NEC       Model: CD-ROM DRIVE:84  Rev: 1.0a
   Type:   CD-ROM                          ANSI SCSI
Detected scsi CD-ROM sr0 at scsi0, channel 0, id 4, lun 0

scsi : detected 1 SCSI disk total.
SCSI device sda: hdwr sector= 512 bytes. Sectors= 2131992
```

Shown above is only that part of the initialization-messages that report the detection of physically present SCSI-devices.

2.7 Create *loopback devices*

Goto the /dev-directory and check for *loopback devices*. It's not critical if you don't have those devices, but it's convenient if you do (see 3.5). If you already have them, the ls-command should show loop0-loop7:

```
bash> cd /dev
bash> ls -l loop*
```

```
brw-rw----   1 root   disk   7,   0 Sep 23 17:15 loop0
brw-rw----   1 root   disk   7,   1 Sep 23 17:15 loop1
brw-rw----   1 root   disk   7,   2 Sep 23 17:15 loop2
brw-rw----   1 root   disk   7,   3 Sep 23 17:15 loop3
brw-rw----   1 root   disk   7,   4 Sep 23 17:15 loop4
brw-rw----   1 root   disk   7,   5 Sep 23 17:15 loop5
brw-rw----   1 root   disk   7,   6 Sep 23 17:15 loop6
brw-rw----   1 root   disk   7,   7 Sep 23 17:15 loop7
```

If you don't have those device-files, then create them by using the /dev/MAKEDEV-script:

```
bash> cd /dev/
bash> ./MAKEDEV loop
```

The last command only succeeds if you have the loop-module in your kernel (see 2.4 for handling of modules). If insmod loop does not help, you must wait until the new kernel is properly installed (see 2.5).

2.8   Get the user-software for burning CDs

2.8.1   Command line utilities

The following package is required to generate prototypes of CD-Rs:

<ftp://tsx-11.mit.edu/pub/linux/packages/mkisofs/> (mkisofs) <ftp://ftp.ge.ucl.ac.uk/pub/mkhfs> (mkhybrid)

Depending on the model of your cd-writer (see 1.3), one of the following software for writing prototypes to CD-Rs is required:

<ftp://ftp.fokus.gmd.de/pub/unix/cdrecord/> (cdrecord)   <ftp://sunsite.unc.edu/pub/Linux/utils/disk-management/> (cdwrite)

Please use the nearest mirrors of these ftp-Servers or get them from a CD.

Be absolutely sure you have version 2.0 of cdwrite or newer. No older version and especially no beta-versions will work properly! Don't trust the man-page of (old) mkisofs which states you need version 1.5 of cdwrite.

For information about ports of cdwrite to Irix and AIX visit the URL

<http://lidar.ssec.wisc.edu/~forrest/>

If you are using a kernel prior to release 2.0.31, you may want to patch mkisofs to get along a bug in the Linux filesystem code. The Debian-Distribution ships a patch for release 1.05 of mkisofs (1.11 should work, too) of mkisofs that adds the option '-K' to it (see 3.4); it's available from

<ftp://ftp.debian.org/pub/debian/bo/source/otherosfs/mkisofs_1.11-1.diff.gz>

This patch is only necassary if you want to mount the CD-image via the loopback-device (see 3.5.).

2.8.2 A graphical user interface (optional)

X-CD-Roast is full X based CD-Writer-Program, and it is the successor of the `cdwtools-0.93`. It's available from

> `<http://www.fh-muenchen.de/home/ze/rz/services/projects/xcdroast/e_overview.html>`

Currently X-CD-Roast is based on a patched version of cdwrite-2.0 and thus comes with exactly the same features (see 1.4). Future versions may be based on the alternate cdrecord software.

3   Burning your CDs

"If to smoke you turn I shall not cease to fiddle while you burn." (Emperor Nero about burning his own classic CDs, AD64. He misunderstood it completely.)

Usally the writing of a CD under Linux is done in 2 steps:

- packaging the desired software into one big file using the `mkisofs/mkhybrid`-utility
- writing the big file to the CD-R with `cdwrite` or `cdrecord`

It is also possible to combine the 2 steps into one via a pipe but that is discouraged because it's not reliable. See below.

3.1   Determine which generic scsi device the writer is attached to

[Please note: the current scheme for naming scsi devices under Linux is unnecessary complicated and not reliable enough. The fact that I describe it in greater detail here should not be misinterpreted as a confirmation of this scheme. People with an ATAPI cd-writer can try "cdrecord -scanbus" to detect the right device and skip the rest of this section.]

After following all steps of the second chapter your system should be able to deal with the task of writing CDs. This section can be used as a proof that everything works as intended.

Issue the command `dmesg`. It should report the messages of the Linux-kernel including those printed while booting (limitation: only the last 200) and contain some information about the CD-Writer connected to the SCSI-bus.

Simple example:

```
Vendor: YAMAHA   Model: CDR100      Rev: 1.11
Type:    WORM                        ANSI SCSI revision: 02
Detected scsi CD-ROM sr1 at scsi0, channel 0, id 3, lun 0
```

This machine has 4 SCSI-devices connected to it (you can't see it so I tell you), with SCSI-id's from 0 to 3. The writer is the 4th physically present SCSI-device and therefore connected to **/dev/sgd** (the fourth generic SCSI-device when counting is started with the letter a). In this case the command

```
cdwrite  --eject  --device /dev/sgd
```

opens the tray and is a test if everything is set up properly. A more complicated example:

```
scsi0 : AdvanSys SCSI 1.5: ISA (240 CDB)
scsi1 : Adaptec 1542
scsi : 2 hosts.


  Vendor: HP      Model: C4324/C4325  Rev: 1.20
  Type:   CD-ROM                      ANSI SCSI revision: 02
Detected scsi CD-ROM sr0 at scsi0, channel 0, id 2, lun 0


  Vendor: IBM     Model: DPES-31080   Rev: S31Q
  Type:   Direct-Access              ANSI SCSI revision: 02
Detected scsi disk sda at scsi1, channel 0, id 0, lun 0


scsi : detected 1 SCSI cdrom 1 SCSI disk total.
SCSI device sda: hdwr sector= 512 bytes.
```

In this example two SCSI-controllers host 1 SCSI-device each. What a waste (they are able to host up to 7 devices each). It's not my setup so stop asking if I have too much money ... Anyway for the purpose of being an overlookable example this setup is just excellent. :-)

In the above example the CD-Writer has SCSI-id 2 but it is associated with the first generic SCSI-device /dev/sga because it's the first physically present SCSI-device which Linux has detected. Hopefully this shows clearly that the SCSI-id of a device has nothing to do with the associated generic device.

Two questions are left: what happens if you catch the wrong device? If you neither specify the option "–<MANUFACTURER>" nor write any data to the device, usally a warning message is printed and nothing bad happens:

```
bash> cdwrite  --eject  --device /dev/sgb


Unknown CD-Writer; if this model is compatible with any
supported type, please use the appropriate command line
flag.


Manufacturer:  IBM
Model:         DPES-31080
Revision:      S31Q
```

In this case the device /dev/sbg is a SCSI harddisk (from IBM).

If you write data to the wrong device, you overwrite the original content of it and probably irrecoverable damage your system. Be careful, it already happened to me by accident.

3.2   Collect software

Usally this takes up longer than one expects. Remember that missing files cannot be added once the CD is written. :-)

Also keep in mind that a certain amount of the free space of a CD is used for storing the information of the iso9660-filesystem (usally a few MB).

3.3   Storing data on a CD.

The term *iso9660* refers to the format in which data is organised on the CD. To be more precise: it's the filesystem on the CD.

Of course the appearance of files stored in this format is unified by the Linux-kernel as for every other filesystem, too. So if you mount a CD into the directory tree, you cannot distinguish it's files from other files ... beside the fact that they are not writeable ... even not for root. :-) (The mechanism used to unify the appearance of files is called *virtual filesystem*, short *VFS*.)

The features of the iso9660 filesystem are not so rich compared to those of the extended-2 filesystem which is normally used under Linux. On the other hand, the CD is only writable once and some features make no sense anyway. The limitations of the iso9660-filesystem are:

- only 8 levels of sub-directories allowed (counted from the top-level directory of the CD) (use RockRidge Extensions to enlarge this number)
- maximum length for filenames: 32 characters
- 650 MB capacity

3.4   Create an iso9660 filesystem

Before any storage medium (e.g. floppy disk, harddisk or CD) can be used, it must get a filesystem (DOS speak: get formatted). This filesystem is responsible for organising and incorporating the files that should be stored on the medium.

Well, a writable CD is only writable once so if we would write an empty filesystem to it, it would get formated - but remain completely empty forever. :-)

So what we need is a tool that creates the filesystem while copying the files to the CD. This tool is called mkisofs. A sample usage looks as follows:

```
mkisofs  -r  -o cd_image   private_collection/
            '---------'    '-----------------'
                 |                  |
           write output to   take directory as input
```

The option '-r' sets the permissions of all files to be public readable on the CD and enables Rock Ridge extensions. That is what one usually wants and use of this option is recommended until you know what you're doing (hint: without '-r' the mount-point gets the permissions of private_collection!).

If you are running a Linux kernel prior to 2.0.31, you should add the option '-K' to work around a bug in the filesystem code. You need the patched version of mkisofs for it. This option is equivalent to the option '-P' of cdwrite. Please see the manual-page of mkisofs for details. Users of a more recent version of Linux have to worry about neither.

mkisofs will try to map all filenames to the 8.3-format used by DOS to ensure highest possible compatibility. In case of naming conflicts (different files have the same 8.3-name), numbers are used in the filenames and information about the chosen filename is printed via STDERR (usually the screen).

DON'T PANIC:

> Under Linux you will never see these 8.3 filenames because Linux makes use of the Rock Ridge extensions which contain the original file-information (permissions, filename, etc.).

Now you may wonder why the output of `mkisofs` is not directly sent to the writer-device. This has two reasons:

- `mkisofs` knows nothing about driving CD-writers (see section 2.3.)
- It would not be reliable (see section 4.)

Because the timing of the CD-writer is a critical point, we don't feed it directly from `mkisofs` (remember Linux is not a real-time operating system and tasks can be timed badly). Instead it is recommended to store the output of `mkisofs` in a separate file on the harddisk. This file is then an 1:1-image of the later CD and is actually written to the CD with the tool `cdwrite` in a second step.

The 1:1-image gets stored in a huge file so you need the same amount of free disk space that your collected software already eats up. That's a drawback.

One could think of creating an extra partition for that and writing the image to that partition instead to a file. I vote against such a strategy because if you write to the wrong partition (due to a typo), you can lose your complete Linux-system. Furthermore, it's a waste of disk-space because the CD-image is temporary data that can be deleted after writing the CD.

3.5   Test the CD-image

Linux has the ability to mount files as if they were disk-partitions. This feature is useful to check the directory layout of the CD-image is ok. To mount the file `cd_image` created above on the directory `/cdrom`, give the command

```
mount -t iso9660 -o ro,loop=/dev/loop0 cd_image /cdrom
```

Now you can inspect the files under `/cdrom` - they appear exactly as they were on a real CD. To umount the CD-image, just say `umount /cdrom`. Warning: If you did not use the option '-K' for mkisofs then the last file on `/cdrom` may not be fully readable.

Note:

some ancient versions of `mount` are not able to deal with loopback-devices. If you have such an old version of `mount` it is a hint to upgrade your Linux-system.Several people already suggested to put information about how to get the newest mount-utilities into this mini-HOWTO. I always refuse this. If your Linux-Distribution ships with an ancient `mount`: report it as a bug. If your Linux-Distribution is not easily upgradable: report it as a bug.

If I included all the information that is necessary to work around bugs in bad designed Linux-Distributions, this mini-HOWTO would be a lot bigger and harder to read.

3.6   Remarks on the blank CD-Recordable discs

The german computer magazine "c't" has a list of tips regarding the blank CDs in their november 1996 issue:

- "no-name" discs are generally not of highest quality and should better not be used
- if a recordable CD is defective, this is likely to apply to the whole batch (if you bought more then one at a time); maybe you are lucky and can at least use the first 500MB of such CDs ...
- don't touch the CDs at their shimmering side before writing

3.7 Write the CD-image to a CD

Not much more left to do. Before showing you the last command, let me warn you that CD-writers want to be fed with a constant stream of data because they have only small data-buffers. So the process of writing the CD-image to the CD mustn't be interupted or a corrupt CD will be the result.

To be sure nothing can interupt this process, throw all users of the system and unplug the ethernet-cable ... Read the *Bastard operator from hell* to learn about the right attitude to do so. ;-)

If you are mentally prepared, dress up in a black robe, multiply the SCSI-id of the CD-writer with it's SCSI-revision and light as many candles, speak two verses of the ASR-FAQ and finally type

```
cdwrite  --device /dev/sgd  cd_image
or
cdrecord -v speed=2 dev=4,0 cd_image
```

depending on which software you want to use. Of course you have to replace the example SCSI device with the device your writer is connected to.

Please note that no writer can re-position it's laser and can't continue at the original spot on the CD when it gets disturbed. Therefore any strong vibrations or even a shock will completely destroy the CD you are writing.

3.8 If something goes wrong ...

... remember you can still use corrupt CDs as coasters. :-)

4 Frequently asked questions with answers

4.1 "How sensitive is the burning process?"

Answer: that depends on your writer. Modern ones should have a data-buffer of 1MB or such and can live 1-2 seconds without data. See the manuals or ask your manufacturer if you want to know the details.

Regardless of the size of those data-buffers you must guarantee a constant throughput of 300kb/s or 600kb/s in the long time run.

Disk intensive processes such as updating the *locate*-database lower the maximum flow-rate will surely corrupt the CD; you better check such processes are not started via cron, at or anacron while you burn CD-Rs.

On the other hand, people reported that they compiled a kernel while burning a CD without a glitch. Of course you need a fast machine for such experiments.

4.2 "Has fragmentation a bad impact on the throughput?"

Fragmentation is usally so low that it's impact isn't noticed.

If you're uncertain than look at the messages printed while booting, the percentage of fragmentation is reported while checking the filesystems. You can check for this value with the very dangerous command

```
bash> e2fsck -n  /dev/sda5          # '-n' is important!
[stuff deleted - ignore any errors]
/dev/sda5: 73/12288 files (12.3% non-contiguous)
```

In this example the fragmentation seems to be very high - but there are only 73 very small files on this filesystem (used as /tmp) so the value is _not_ alarming.

4.3 "Is it possible to store the CD-image on an UMSDOS-filesystem?"

Yes. The only filesystem that isn't reliable and fast enough for writing CDs from is the *network filesystem* (*NFS*).

I'm using UMSDOS myself to share the disk-space between Linux and DOS/Win on a PC (486/66) dedicated for writing CDs.

4.4 "Isn't there some way to get around the iso9660 limitations?"

Yes. You can put any filesystem you like on the CD. But other operating systems than Linux won't be able to deal with this CD.

Here goes the recipe:

- Create an empty file of 650MB size.

  ```
  dd if=/dev/zero of="empty_file" bs=1024k count=650
  ```

- Create an extended-2 filesystem on this file

  ```
  bash> /sbin/mke2fs  empty_file
  empty_file is not a block special device.
  Proceed anyway? (y,n) y
  ```

- Mount this empty file through the loopback-devices

  ```
  mount -t ext2 -o loop=/dev/loop1 empty_file /mnt
  ```

- Copy files to /mnt and umount it afterwards.
- Use cdwrite or cdrecord on empty_file (which is no longer empty) as if it were an iso9660-image.

If you want to make an entry in /etc/fstab for such a CD, disable the checking of it, e.g.:

```
/dev/cdrom  /cdrom  ext2  defaults,ro  0 0
```

The first 0 means "don't include in dumps", the second (=important) one means "don't check for errors on startup" (fsck will fail to check the CD for errors).

4.5 "How to read and write audio CDs?"

Please get the packages "cdda2wav" and "sox", available from sunsite and it's mirrors:

```
<ftp://sunsite.unc.edu/pub/Linux/apps/sound/cdrom/cdda2wav0.71.src.tar.gz>
<ftp://sunsite.unc.edu/pub/Linux/apps/sound/convert/sox-11gamma-cb3.tar.gz>
```

cdda2wav enables you to get a specific interval (or a whole track) from your audio CD and converts it into a .wav-file. sox converts the wav-files back into the (audio-CD) cdda-format so it can be written to the CD-R using cdwrite.

4.6 "How to probe for SCSI-devices after boot?"

The file drivers/scsi/scsi.c contains the information

```
/*
 * Usage: echo "scsi add-single-device 0 1 2 3" >/proc/scsi/scsi
 * with  "0 1 2 3" replaced by your "Host Channel Id Lun".
 * Consider this feature BETA.
 *    CAUTION: This is not for hotplugging your peripherals. As
 *    SCSI was not designed for this you could damage your
 *    hardware !
 * However perhaps it is legal to switch on an
 * already connected device. It is perhaps not
 * guaranteed this device doesn't corrupt an ongoing data transfer.
 */
```

4.7 "Is it possible to make a 1:1 copy of a data CD?"

Yes. But you should be aware of the fact that any errors while reading the original (due to dust or scratches) will result in a defective copy.

First case: you have a CD-writer and a seperate CD-ROM drive. By issuing the command

```
cdwrite -v -D /dev/sgc --pad -b $(isosize /dev/scd0) /dev/scd0
or
cdrecord -v dev=3,0 speed=2 -isosize /dev/scd0
```

you read the data stream from the CD-ROM drive attached as /dev/scd0 and write it directly through /dev/sgc to the CD-R.

Second case: you don't have a seperate CD-ROM drive. You have to use the writer to read out the CD-ROM in this case:

```
dd if=/dev/scd0 of=cdimage bs=1c count=`isosize /dev/scd0`
```

This command is equivalent to the result of mkisofs, so you should procede as described in chapter 3. Please note that this method will fail on audio CDs!

4.8 "Can Linux read Joliet CDs?"

Yes. But you need to patch the kernel and recompile it. For further details see

<http://www-plateau.cs.berkeley.edu/people/chaffee/joliet.html>

4.9 "How do I read/mount CD-ROMs with the CD-writer?"

Just as you do with regular CD-ROM drives. No tricks at all. Note that you have to use the scd-devices (SCSI CD-ROM) to mount CDs for reading. Example-entry for /etc/fstab:

```
/dev/scd0  /cdrom  iso9660  ro,user,noauto  0  0
```

5 Troubleshooting

5.1 It doesn't work: under Linux

Please check first if the writer works under other operating systems. Concretely:

- Does the controller recognize the writer as a SCSI device?
- Does the driver software recognize the writer?
- Is it possible to make a CD using the accompanied software?

If "it doesn't work" even under other operating systems you have a hardware conflict or defective hardware.

5.2 It doesn't work: under DOS and friends

Try to use Linux. Installation and configuration of SCSI-drivers for DOS is the hell. Linux is too complicated? Ha!

5.3 SCSI errors during the burning phase

Most likely those errors are caused by

- missing dis-/reconnect feature on the SCSI bus
- unsufficiently cooled hardware
- defektive hardware (should be detected by 5.1.)

Under various circumstances SCSI devices dis- and reconnect themselves (electronically) from the SCSI bus. If this feature is not available (check controller and kernel parameters) some writers run into trouble during burning or fixating the CD-R.

Especially the NCR 53c7,8xx SCSI driver has the feature disabled by default, so you might want to check it first:

```
NCR53c7,8xx SCSI support                     [N/y/m/?] y
    always negotiate synchronous transfers [N/y/?] (NEW) n
    allow FAST-SCSI [10MHz]                 [N/y/?] (NEW) y
    allow DISCONNECT                        [N/y/?] (NEW) y
```

6 Credits

Andreas Erdmann <erdmann@zpr.uni-koeln.de>
  provided the example with the YAMAHA-writer

Art Stone <stone@math.ubc.ca>
  had the idea to put non-iso9660 filesystems on a CD

Bartosz Maruszewski <B.Maruszewski@zsmeie.torun.pl>
  reported spelling mistakes

Bernhard Gubanka <beg@ipp-garching.mpg.de>
  noticed the need of a recent version of mount to utilize the loopback device

Brian H. Toby
  polished the wording.

Bruce Perens <bruce@pixar.com>
  gave information about the cdwrite-mailinglist

Dale Scheetz <dwarf@polaris.net>
  helped improving the section about creating the cdimage.

"Don H. Olive" <don@andromeda.campbellsvil.edu>
  URL of the mkhybrid tool

Edwin H. Kribbs
  reported that '-K' requires a patch for mkisofs

Gerald C Snyder <gcsnyd@loop.com>
  tested writing of an ext2 CD-ROM (see 4.4)

Ingo Fischenisch <ingo@mi.uni-koeln.de>
  provided the example with 2 controllers hosting 2 devices

Janne Himanka <shem@oyt.oulu.fi>
  pointer to kernel patch to read Joliet CDs

Joerg Schilling <schilling@fokus.gmd.de>
  information about cdrecord

Jos van Geffen <jos@tnj.phys.tue.nl>
  noted the problem in 4.9.

Markus Dickebohm <m.dickebohm@uni-koeln.de>

Pierre Pfister <pp@uplift.fr>
  helped to develop the recipe on 1:1 copies.

Rick Cochran <rick@msc.cornell.edu>
  hint about dis-/reconnect disabled by default in the ncr driver

Stephan Noy <stnoy@mi.uni-koeln.de>
  information and experience about writing audio-CDs

Stephen Harris <sweh@mpn.com>
  contributed hint about writing audio-CDs

The Sheepy One <kero@escape.com>
  suggested using defective CDs as coasters for drinks

Volker Kuhlmann <kuhlmav@elec.canterbury.ac.nz>
  noticed that the "cdwrite"-package does not contain mkisofs

End of the Linux CD-Writing mini-HOWTO

The Linux Sound HOWTO

Jeff Tranter, *tranter@pobox.com* <mailto:tranter@pobox.com>   v1.19, 23 January 1998

This document describes sound support for Linux. It lists the supported sound hardware, describes how to configure the kernel drivers, and answers frequently asked questions. The intent is to bring new users up to speed more quickly and reduce the amount of traffic in the Usenet news groups and mailing lists.

Contents

6 Answers To Frequently Asked Questions

1 Introduction

This is the Linux Sound HOWTO. It is intended as a quick reference covering everything you need to know to install and configure sound support under Linux. Frequently asked questions about sound under Linux are answered, and references are given to some other sources of information on a variety of topics related to computer generated sound and music.

The scope is limited to the aspects of sound cards pertaining to Linux. See the other documents listed in the *References* section for more general information on sound cards and computer sound and music generation.

1.1 Acknowledgments

Much of this information came from the documentation provided with the sound driver source code, by Hannu Savolainen (*hannu@voxware.pp.fi* <mailto:hannu@voxware.pp.fi>). Thanks go to Hannu and the many other people who developed the Linux kernel sound drivers and utilities.

Thanks to the *SGML Tools* <ftp://sunsite.unc.edu/pub/Linux/utils/text/sgml-tools-0.99.0.tar.gz> package, this HOWTO is available in several formats, all generated from a common source file.

1.2 Revision History

Version 1.1

first version; posted to SOUND channel of Linux activists mailing list only

Version 1.2

minor updates; first version available on archive sites

Version 1.3

converted to SGML; now available in several formats using Matt Welsh's Linuxdoc-SGML tools; appearance changed due to new format, only minor changes to content

Version 1.4

minor tweaking of SGML; added answer on PAS16 and Adaptec1542A SCSI adaptor incompatibilities

Version 1.5

2.5a sound driver is now in 1.1 kernel distribution; note on GUS-MAX support; other minor updates

Version 1.6

added info on "no space on device" error; added note that Hacker's Guide is in a "hidden" directory; added question on bidirectional mode; info on "device busy" errors; other minor changes

Version 1.7

added info on ASP and AWE32; VoxWare 2.9 is available; answer to question on using IRQ2; references to Sound and SCSI HOWTOs

Version 1.8

added question on errors under DOS; many minor things updated to match the version 2.90 sound driver; info on DOOM; answer on reducing noise

Version 1.9

> questions on recording and clone cards

Version 1.10

> mentioned that HOWTO is available on WWW, as printed copies, and translations; info on DMA conflict with QIC tape driver; info on Sound Galaxy NX Pro and Logitech BusMouse

Version 1.11

> A long overdue update (I've been busy); document placed under GPL; brought up to date with version 3.0 sound driver; info on many new supported sound card drivers; more info on configuration and troubleshooting; lots of HTML links added; brought in line with format of CD-ROM HOWTO

Version 1.12

> new sound drivers in 1.3.34 kernel; new sound device names; 1542 address is 334 not 333; clarify status of Creative Labs Emu and ASP; pointer to Creative Labs and MediaTrix Web sites

Version 1.13

> note on the name VoxWare; updated to reflect latest supported sound cards and configuration options; question on Plug and Play support; question on block size problem; new xconfig and menuconfig options; modutils has sound device support; vger mailing list going away; emphasize author's Web site; other miscellaneous minor changes

Version 1.14

> Audio Excell DSP16 is not currently supported (should be working again in a few months); changes to configure program; Italian version of HOWTO available; trick for setting mixer gains when loading sound module; latest stable kernel is now 2.0; new name for sound driver; question on root permissions on sound device files

Version 1.15

> removed some questions that were very old and now obsolete; new e-mail address for author; fixed some links to point to latest software packages; more information on multimedia book; minor spelling and grammatical changes

Version 1.16

> many updates and corrections from Hannu Savolainen; added six month "best before" date; new URL to web page for book; added link to Spanish translation; minor spelling and grammatical changes

Version 1.17

> Chinese version available; alternate GUS driver; packet radio modem; Linux Multimedia guide is now available in French and Japanese; references to a couple of relevant mini-HOWTOs; pointer for IBM ThinkPad

Version 1.18

> Korean translation available; more information on status of sound on MIPS; updated info on multiple sound card support; should be root when running fuser

Version 1.19

> added index entries; placed under LDP license rather than GPL

1.3   New versions of this document

New versions of this document will be periodically posted to the *comp.os.linux.answers* <news:comp.os.linux.answers> newsgroup. They will also be uploaded to various anonymous ftp sites that archive such information including <ftp://sunsite.unc.edu/pub/Linux/docs/HOWTO/>.

Hypertext versions of this and other Linux HOWTOs are available on many World-Wide-Web sites, including <http://sunsite.unc.edu/LDP/>. Most Linux CD-ROM distributions include the HOWTOs, often under the /usr/doc directory, and you can also buy printed copies from several vendors. Sometimes the HOWTOs available from CD-ROM vendors, ftp sites, and printed format are out of date. If the date on this HOWTO is more than six months in the past, then a newer copy is probably available on the Internet.

A French translation of this document is available at <ftp://ftp.ibp.fr/pub2/linux/french/docs/HOWTO/>.

A Japanese translation is available from <http://yebisu.ics.es.osaka-u.ac.jp/linux/>.

An Italian translation is available from <http://www.psy.unipd.it/ildp/docs/HOWTO/Sound-HOWTO.html>.

A Spanish translation is available from <http://www.insflug.nova.es/howtos/online/sonido/sonido-COMO.html>.

A Chinese translation is available from <http://linux.ntcic.edu.tw/~yorkwu/linux/howto/sound/>.

A Hangul (Korean) translation is available from <http://members.iWorld.net/mangchi/HOWTO/Sound-HOWTO.html>.

Most translations of this and other Linux HOWTOs can also be found at <http://sunsite.unc.edu/pub/Linux/docs/HOWTO/translations/> and <ftp://sunsite.unc.edu/pub/Linux/docs/HOWTO/translations/>.

If you make a translation of this document into another language, let me know and I'll include a reference to it here.

1.4   Feedback

I rely on you, the reader, to make this HOWTO useful. If you have any suggestions, corrections, or comments, please send them to me, *tranter@pobox.com* <mailto:tranter@pobox.com>, and I will try to incorporate them in the next revision.

I am also willing to answer general questions on sound cards under Linux, as best I can. Before doing so, please read all of the information in this HOWTO, and send me detailed information about the problem. Please do not ask me about using sound cards under operating systems other than Linux.

If you publish this document on a CD-ROM or in hardcopy form, a complimentary copy would be appreciated. Mail me for my postal address. Also consider making a donation to the Linux Documentation Project to help support free documentation for Linux. Contact the Linux HOWTO coordinator, Greg Hankins <mailto:gregh@sunsite.unc.edu>, for more information.

1.5   Distribution Policy

Copyright (c) 1995-1998 by Jeff Tranter. This document may be distributed under the terms set forth in the LDP license at <http://sunsite.unc.edu/LDP/COPYRIGHT.html>.

2   Sound Card Technology

This section gives a *very* cursory overview of computer audio technology, in order to help you understand the concepts used later in the document. You should consult a book on digital audio or digital signal processing in order to learn more.

Sound is an *analog* property; it can take on any value over a continuous range. Computers are *digital*; they like to work with discrete values. Sound cards use a device known as an *Analog to Digital Converter* (A/D or ADC) to convert voltages corresponding to analog sound waves into digital or numeric values which can be stored in memory. Similarly, a *Digital to Analog Converter* (D/A or DAC) converts numeric values back to an analog voltage which can in turn drive a loudspeaker, producing sound.

The process of analog to digital conversion, known as sampling, introduces some error. Two factors are key in determining how well the sampled signal represents the original. *Sampling rate* is the number of samples made per unit of time (usually expresses as samples per second or Hertz). A low sampling rate will provide a less accurate representation of the analog signal. Sample size is the range of values used to represent each sample, usually expressed in bits. The larger the sample size, the more accurate the digitized signal will be.

Sound cards commonly use 8 or 16 bit samples at sampling rates from about 4000 to 44,000 samples per second. The samples may also be contain one channel (mono) or two (stereo).

FM Synthesis is an older technique for producing sound. It is based on combining different waveforms (e.g. sine, triangle, square). FM synthesis is simpler to implement in hardware that D/A conversion, but is more difficult to program and less flexible. Many sound cards provide FM synthesis for backward compatibility with older cards and software. Several independent sound generators or *voices* are usually provided.

Wavetable Synthesis combines the flexibility of D/A conversion with the multiple channel capability of FM synthesis. With this scheme digitized voices can be downloaded into dedicated memory, and then played, combined, and modified with little CPU overhead. State of the art sound cards all support wavetable synthesis.

Most sound cards provide the capability of *mixing*, combining signals from different input sources and controlling gain levels.

MIDI stands for Musical Instrument Digital Interface, and is a standard hardware and software protocol for allowing musical instruments to communicate with each other. The events sent over a MIDI bus can also be stored as MIDI files for later editing and playback. Many sound cards provide a MIDI interface. Those that do not can still play MIDI files using the on-board capabilities of the sound card.

MOD files are a common format for computer generated songs. As well as information about the musical notes to be played, the files contain digitized samples for the instruments (or voices). MOD files originated on the Amiga computer, but can be played on other systems, including Linux, with suitable software.

3   Supported Hardware

This section lists the sound cards and interfaces that are currently supported under Linux. The information here is based on the latest Linux kernels, at time of writing.

The sound driver has its own version numbering. The latest stable Linux kernel release was version 2.0.33, using sound driver version 3.5.4-960630.

The author of the sound driver, Hannu Savolainen, typically also makes available newer beta releases of the sound driver before they are included as part of the standard Linux kernel distribution. The most up to date list of supported cards is available at <http://www.4front-tech.com/ossfree/new_cards.html> (USA) or <http://personal.eunet.fi/pp/voxware/new_cards.html> (Europe). These pages indicate which sound driver version is required for a given type of sound card or if support for it is still under development. The file /usr/src/linux/drivers/sound/Readme.cards distributed with the kernel sound driver contains information on supported cards but it is not always up to date.

The information in this HOWTO is valid for Linux on the Intel platform.

The sound driver should also work with most sound cards on the Alpha platform. However, some cards may conflict with I/O ports of other devices on Alpha systems even though they work perfectly on i386 machines, so in general it's not possible to tell if a given card will work or not without actually trying it.

At the time of writing the sound driver was not yet working on the PowerPC version of Linux, but it should be supported in future.

Sound can be configured into the kernel under the MIPs port of Linux, and some MIPs machines have EISA slots and/or built in sound hardware. I'm told the Linux-MIPs group is interested in adding sound support in the future.

The Linux kernel includes a separate driver for the Atari and Amiga versions of Linux that implements a compatible subset of the sound driver on the Intel platform using the built-in sound hardware on these machines.

The SPARC port of Linux does not currently have sound support. Like the Amiga and Atari, SPARC machines have built in sound hardware, so it could be done with a new driver (this is somewhat ironic, as under Linux /dev/dsp emulates the SunOS sound device).

3.1 Sound Cards

The following sound cards are supported by the Linux kernel sound driver:

- ATI Stereo F/X (no longer manufactured)
- AdLib (no longer manufactured)
- Ensoniq SoundScape (and compatibles made by Reveal and Spea)
- Gravis Ultrasound
- Gravis Ultrasound ACE
- Gravis Ultrasound Max
- Gravis Ultrasound with 16 bit sampling option
- Logitech Sound Man 16
- Logitech SoundMan Games
- Logitech SoundMan Wave
- MAD16 Pro (OPTi 82C928, 82C929, 82C930, 82C924 chipsets)
- Media Vision Jazz16
- MediaTriX AudioTriX Pro
- Microsoft Windows Sound System (MSS/WSS)
- Mozart (OAK OTI-601)
- Orchid SW32
- Personal Sound System (PSS)
- Pro Audio Spectrum 16
- Pro Audio Studio 16
- Pro Sonic 16
- Roland MPU-401 MIDI interface
- Sound Blaster 1.0
- Sound Blaster 16
- Sound Blaster 16ASP
- Sound Blaster 2.0
- Sound Blaster AWE32

- Sound Blaster Pro
- TI TM4000M notebook
- ThunderBoard
- Turtle Beach Tropez ("classic" but not Plus)
- Turtle Beach Maui
- Yamaha FM synthesizers (OPL2, OPL3 and OPL4)
- 6850 UART MIDI Interface

It should be noted that Plug and Play (PnP) sound cards are not fully compatible with the older non-PnP models of the same device. For example, the SoundBlaster16 PnP is not fully compatible with the original SoundBlaster16. The same is true for the Soundscape PnP and GUS PnP cards. More information related to Plug and Play is found later in this document.

The following cards are *not* supported, either because they are obsolete or because the vendor will not release the programming information needed to write a driver:

- Pro Audio Spectrum (original)
- Pro Audio Spectrum+
- older (Sierra Aria based) sound cards made by Diamond

Other sound cards that are claimed to be compatible with one of the supported sound cards *may* work if they are hardware (i.e. register level) compatible.

Even though most sound cards are claimed to be "SoundBlaster compatible", very few currently sold cards are compatible enough to work with the Linux SoundBlaster driver. These cards usually work better using the MSS/WSS or MAD16 driver. Only real SoundBlaster cards made by Creative Labs, which use Creative's custom chips (e.g. SoundBlaster16 Vibra), MV Jazz16 and ESS688/1688 based cards generally work with the SoundBlaster driver. Trying to use a "SoundBlaster Pro compatible 16 bit sound card" with the SoundBlaster driver is usually just a waste of time.

The Linux kernel supports the SCSI port provided on some sound cards (e.g. ProAudioSpectrum 16) and the proprietary interface for some CD-ROM drives (e.g. Soundblaster Pro). See the Linux *SCSI HOWTO* <http://sunsite.unc.edu/LDP/HOWTO/SCSI-HOWTO.html> and *CDROM HOWTO* <http://sunsite.unc.edu/LDP/HOWTO/CDROM-HOWTO.html> documents for more information.

A loadable kernel module to support joystick ports, including those provided on some sound cards, is also available.

Note that the kernel SCSI, CD-ROM, joystick, and sound drivers are completely independent of each other.

For the latest information on the sound card driver check Hannu Savolainen's World-Wide Web site listed in the References section.

3.2 Alternate Sound Drivers

There are some "unofficial" sound drivers available, not included in the standard Linux kernel distribution, and used in place of the standard sound driver.

A commercial version of the Linux sound driver is sold by 4Front Technologies. It offers a number of additional features over the free version included in the Linux kernel. For more information see the 4Front Technologies Web page at <http://www.4front-tech.com/>.

Markus Mummert (*mum@mmk.e-technik.tu-muenchen.de* <mailto:mum@mmk.e-technik.tu-muenchen.de>) has written a driver package for the Turtle Beach MultiSound (classic), Tahiti, and Monterey sound cards. The documentation states:

"It is designed for high quality hard disk recording/playback without losing sync even on a busy system. Other features such as wave synthesis, MIDI and digital signal processor (DSP) cannot be used. Also, recording and playback at the same time is not possible. It currently replaces VoxWare and was tested on several kernel versions ranging from 1.0.9 to 1.2.1. Also, it is installable on UN*X SysV386R3.2 systems."

It can be found at `<http://www.cs.colorado.edu/~mccreary/tbeach>`.

Kim Burgaard (*burgaard@daimi.aau.dk* `<mailto:burgaard@daimi.aau.dk>`) has written a device driver and utilities for the Roland MPU-401 MIDI interface. The Linux software map entry gives this description:

"A device driver for true Roland MPU-401 compatible MIDI interfaces (including Roland SCC-1 and RAP-10/ATW-10). Comes with a useful collection of utilities including a Standard MIDI File player and recorder.

Numerous improvements have been made since version 0.11a. Among other things, the driver now features IRQ sharing policy and complies with the new kernel module interface. Metronome functionality, possibility for synchronizing e.g. graphics on a per beat basis without losing precision, advanced replay/record/overdub interface and much, much more."

It can be found at `<ftp://sunsite.unc.edu/pub/Linux/kernel/sound/mpu401-0.2.tar.gz>`.

Jaroslav Kysela and others have written an alternate sound driver for the Gravis UltraSound Card. Information can be found at `<http://romeo.pf.jcu.cz/~perex/ultra>`, the home page of the Linux UltraSound Project.

Another novel use for a sound card under Linux is as a modem for amateur packet radio. The recent 2.1.x kernels include a driver that works with SoundBlaster and Windows Sound System compatible sound cards to implement 1200 bps AFSK and 9600 bps FSK packet protocols. See the Linux AX25 HOWTO for details (I'm a ham myself, by the way – callsign VE3ICH).

3.3 PC Speaker

An alternate sound driver is available that requires no additional sound hardware; it uses the internal PC speaker. It is mostly software compatible with the sound card driver, but, as might be expected, provides much lower quality output and has much more CPU overhead. The results seem to vary, being dependent on the characteristics of the individual loudspeaker. For more information, see the documentation provided with the release.

The current version is 1.1, and can be found at `<ftp://ftp.informatik.hu-berlin.de/pub/os/linux/hu-sound/>`

3.4 Parallel Port

Another option is to build a digital to analog converter using a parallel printer port and some additional components. This provides better sound quality than the PC speaker but still has a lot of CPU overhead. The PC sound driver package mentioned above supports this, and includes instructions for building the necessary hardware.

4 Installation

Configuring Linux to support sound involves the following steps:

1. Installing the sound card.
2. Configuring and building the kernel for sound support.
3. Creating the device files.
4. Booting the Linux kernel and testing the installation.

The next sections will cover each of these steps in detail.

4.1 Installing the Sound Card

Follow the manufacturer's instructions for installing the hardware or have your dealer perform the installation.

Older sound cards usually have switch or jumper settings for IRQ, DMA channel, etc; note down the values used. If you are unsure, use the factory defaults. Try to avoid conflicts with other devices (e.g. ethernet cards, SCSI host adaptors, serial and parallel ports) if possible.

Usually you should use the same I/O port, IRQ, and DMA settings that work under DOS. In some cases though (particularly with PnP cards) you may need to use different settings to get things to work under Linux. Some experimentation may be needed.

4.2 Configuring the Kernel

When initially installing Linux you likely used a precompiled kernel. These kernels usually do not provide sound support. It is best to recompile the kernel yourself with the drivers you need. You may also want to recompile the kernel in order to upgrade to a newer version or to free up memory resources by minimizing the size of the kernel.

The *Linux Kernel HOWTO* <http://sunsite.unc.edu/LDP/HOWTO/Kernel-HOWTO.html> should be consulted for the details of building a kernel. I will just mention here some issues that are specific to sound cards.

If you have never configured the kernel for sound support before it is a good idea to read *all* of the Readme files included with the kernel sound drivers, particularly information specific to your card type. The following documentation files can be found in the kernel sound driver directory, usually installed in /usr/src/linux/ drivers/sound:

```
CHANGELOG            - description of changes in each release
COPYING              - copying and copyright restrictions
Readme               - latest and most important news
Readme.aedsp16       - information about Audio Excel DSP 16 sound card
Readme.cards         - notes on configuring specific cards
Readme.linux         - notes on installing separately release sound drivers
Readme.modules       - how to build driver as a loadable kernel module
Readme.v30           - new features in version 3.0 sound driver
experimental.txt     - notes on experimental features
```

Follow the usual procedure for building the kernel. There are currently three interfaces to the configuration process. A graphical user interface that runs under X11 can be invoked using "make xconfig". A menu-based system that only requires text displays is available as "make menuconfig". The original method, using "make config", offers a simple text-based interface.

Special care must be taken when using "make xconfig" or "make menuconfig". All Yes/No questions must be examined carefully. The default answer provided by these commands is always No which is not the proper one in all cases. In particular the "/dev/dsp and /dev/audio support" (CONFIG_AUDIO) option should usually be enabled.

In this document I will assume that you use the traditional command line configuration process invoked using "make config", although the process is similar in each case.

There are also two different ways to configure sound. The first is the "old" way (the only one offered prior to the 2.0.0 kernels). It uses a standalone configuration program that is part of the sound driver. This method works with most sound cards except the rare few that require additional "low level" drivers (miroSOUND, AWE32, and AEDSP16 cards).

The second is the "new" method which is better integrated with the menu-based configuration used for the rest of the kernel. This one doesn't work with sound cards that require a firmware download file. This includes the PSS, SM Wave, AudioTrix Pro and TurtleBeach Tropez/Maui cards. With these cards the old method has to be used.

The "new" method is always used by "make xconfig". When using "make menuconfig" you can select between the "old" and "new" methods in the sound subscreen. When using "make config" you get the "old" method by default. However if you have used the "new" method once, it will be used by "make config" too. You can switch back to the "old" method by running "make menuconfig" and by selecting the "old" one.

The recommended method is to use "make menuconfig" together with the "old" sound config method. Many sound configuration problems are caused (at least partly) by incorrect use of the "new" method.

It is also possible to build the sound driver as a kernel loadable module. I recommend initially building the driver into the kernel. Once it is tested and working you can explore using the kernel module option.

When you run `make config`, enable sound support by answering "y" to the question

```
    Sound card support (CONFIG_SOUND) [M/n/y/?]
```

At the end of the configuration questions a sound configuration program will be compiled, run, and will then ask you what sound card options you want. Be careful when answering these questions since answering a question incorrectly may prevent some later ones from being asked. For example, don't answer "yes" to the first question (PAS16) if you don't really have a PAS16. Don't enable more cards than you really need, since they just consume memory. Also some drivers (like MPU-401) may conflict with your SCSI controller and prevent the kernel from booting.

I list here a brief description of each of the configuration dialog options. Answer "y" (yes) or "n" (no) to each question. The default answer is shown so that "[Y/n/?]" means "y" by default and "[N/y/?]" means the default is "n". To use the default value, just hit Enter, but remember that the default value isn't necessarily correct.

Entering a question mark ("?") will produce a short descriptive message describing that configuration option.

Note also that all questions may not be asked. The configuration program may disable some questions depending on the earlier choices. It may also select some options automatically as well.

Old configuration exists in /etc/soundconf. Use it [Y/n/?]

If you have previously compiled the kernel for sound support, then the previous configuration can be saved. If you want to use the previous setup, answer "y". If you are trying a different configuration or have upgraded to a newer kernel, you should answer "n" and go through the configuration process.

ProAudioSpectrum 16 support [Y/n/?]

Answer "y" *only* if you have a Pro Audio Spectrum *16*, ProAudio Studio 16 or Logitech SoundMan 16. Don't answer 'y' if you have some other card made by Media Vision or Logitech since they are not PAS16 compatible.

SoundBlaster support [Y/n/?]

Answer "y" if you have an original SoundBlaster card made by Creative Labs or a 100% hardware compatible clone (like the Thunderboard or SM Games). If your card was in the list of supported cards look at the card specific instructions in the `Readme.cards` file before answering this question. For an unknown card you may answer "y'"if the card claims to be SoundBlaster compatible.

Gravis Ultrasound support [Y/n/?]

Answer "y" if you have a GUS or GUS MAX. Answer "n" if you don't have a GUS since the driver consumes a lot of memory.

MPU-401 support (NOT for SB16) [Y/n/?]

Be careful with this question. The MPU-401 interface is supported by almost all sound cards. However, some natively supported cards have their own driver for MPU-401. Enabling the MPU-401 option with these cards will cause a conflict. Also enabling MPU-401 on a system that doesn't really have a MPU-401 could cause some trouble. If your card was in the list of supported cards, look at the card specific instructions in the `Readme.cards` file. It's safe to answer "y" if you have a true MPU-401 MIDI interface card.

6850 UART Midi support [Y/n/?]

It's safe to answer "n" to this question in all cases. The 6850 UART interface is very rarely used.

PSS (ECHO-ADI2111) support [Y/n/?]

Answer "y" only if you have Orchid SW32, Cardinal DSP16 or some other card based on the PSS chipset (AD1848 codec + ADSP-2115 DSP chip + Echo ESC614 ASIC CHIP).

16 bit sampling option of GUS (*not* GUS MAX) [Y/n/?]

Answer "y" if you have installed the 16 bit sampling daughtercard on your GUS. Answer "n" if you have a GUS MAX. Enabling this option disables GUS MAX support.

GUS MAX support [Y/n/?]

Answer "y" only if you have a GUS MAX.

Microsoft Sound System support [Y/n/?]

Again think carefully before answering "y" to this question. It's safe to answer "y" if you have the original Windows Sound System card made by Microsoft or Aztech SG 16 Pro (or NX16 Pro). Also you may answer "y" in case your card was not listed earlier in this file. For cards having native support in VoxWare, consult the card specific instructions in `Readme.cards`. Some drivers have their own MSS support and enabling this option will cause a conflict.

Ensoniq Soundscape support [Y/n/?]

Answer "y" if you have a sound card based on the Ensoniq SoundScape chipset. Such cards are being manufactured at least by Ensoniq, Spea and Reveal (Reveal makes other cards also).

MediaTriX AudioTriX Pro support [Y/n/?]

Answer "y" if you have the AudioTriX Pro.

Support for MAD16 and/or Mozart based cards?

Answer "y" if your card has a Mozart (OAK OTI-601) or MAD16 (OPTi 82C928 or 82C929) audio interface chip. These chips are currently quite common so it's possible that many no-name cards have one of them. In addition the MAD16 chip is used in some cards made by known manufacturers such as Turtle Beach (Tropez), Reveal (some models) and Diamond (latest ones).

Support for Crystal CS4232 based (PnP) cards [Y/n/?]

Answer "y" if you have a card based on the Crystal CS4232 chip set.

Support for Turtle Beach Wave Front (Maui, Tropez) synthesizers [Y/n/?]

Answer "y" if you have any of these cards.

SoundBlaster Pro support [Y/n/?]

Enable this option if your card is a SoundBlaster Pro or SoundBlaster 16. Enable it also with any SoundBlaster Pro clones. Answering "n" saves some memory but "y" is the safe alternative.

SoundBlaster 16 support [Y/n/?]

Enable if you have a SoundBlaster 16 (including the AWE32).

Audio Excel DSP 16 initialization support [Y/n/?]

Enable this if you have an Audio Excel DSP16 card. See the file Readme.aedsp16 for more information.

The configuration program then asks some questions about the higher level services. It's recommended to answer "y" to each of these questions. Answer "n" only if you know you will not need the option.

/dev/dsp and /dev/audio support (usually required) [Y/n/?]

Answering "n" disables /dev/dsp and /dev/audio, the A/D and D/A converter devices. Answer "y".

MIDI interface support [Y/n/?]

Answering "n" disables /dev/midixx devices and access to any MIDI ports using /dev/sequencer and /dev/music. This option also affects any MPU-401 and/or General MIDI compatible devices.

FM synthesizer (YM3812/OPL-3) support [Y/n/?]

Answer "y" here.

/dev/sequencer support [Y/n/?]

Answering "n" disables /dev/sequencer and /dev/music

Do you want support for the mixer of SG NX Pro ?

Answer "y" if you have a Sound Galaxy NX Pro sound card and want support for its extended mixer functions.

Do you want support for the MV Jazz16 (ProSonic etc.) ?

Answer "y" if you have an MV Jazz16 sound card.

Do you have a Logitech SoundMan Games [Y/n/?]

Answer "y" if you have a Logitech SoundMan Games sound card.

After the above questions the configuration program prompts for the card specific configuration information. Usually just a set of I/O address, IRQ and DMA numbers are asked. With some cards the program asks for some files to be used during initialization of the card. These are used by cards which have a DSP chip or microprocessor which must be initialized by downloading a program (microcode) file to the card. In some cases this file is written to a .h file by the config program and then included to the driver during compile. Again, read the information in the file Readme.cards pertaining to your card type.

At the end you will be prompted:

```
The sound driver is now configured.
Save copy of this configuration to /etc/soundconf [Y/n/?]
```

Normally you would enter "y" so that if you later need to recompile the kernel you have the option of using the same sound driver configuration.

If you are upgrading from an older sound driver, make sure that the files /usr/include/sys/soundcard.h and /usr/include/sys/ultrasound.h are symbolic links to the corresponding files in /usr/include/linux, or that they simply contain the lines #include <linux/soundcard.h> and #include <linux/ultrasound.h>, respectively.

You are now ready to compile and install the new kernel.

4.3   Creating the Device Files

For proper operation, device file entries must be created for the sound devices. These are normally created for you during installation of your Linux system. A quick check can be made using the command listed below. If the output is as shown (the date stamp will vary) then the device files are almost certainly okay.

```
% ls -l /dev/sndstat
crw-rw-rw-   1 root      root      14,   6 Apr 25  1995 /dev/sndstat
```

Note that having the right device files there doesn't guarantee anything on its own. The kernel driver must also be loaded or compiled in before the devices will work (more on that later).

In rare cases, if you believe the device files are wrong, you can recreate them using the short shell script from the end of the file `Readme.linux` in the directory `/usr/src/linux/drivers/sound`, running it as user `root`. Alternatively, most Linux distributions have a /dev/MAKEDEV script which can be used for this purpose.

If you are using the PC speaker sound driver, read the documentation that came with the package to determine if any device files need to be created.

4.4   Booting Linux and Testing the Installation

You should now be ready to boot the new kernel and test the sound drivers. Follow your usual procedure for installing and rebooting the new kernel (keep the old kernel around in case of problems, of course).

During booting, check for a message such as the following on powerup (if they scroll by too quickly to read, you may be able to retrieve them with the `dmesg` command):

```
Sound initialization started
<Sound Blaster 16 (4.13)> at 0x220 irq 5 dma 1,5
<Sound Blaster 16> at 0x330 irq 5 dma 0
<Yamaha OPL3 FM> at 0x388
Sound initialization complete
```

This should match your sound card type and jumper settings (if any).

Note that the above messages are not displayed when using loadable sound driver module (unless you enable it, e.g. using "insmod sound trace_init=1).

When the sound driver is linked into the kernel, the "Sound initialization started" and "Sound initialization complete" messages should be displayed. If they are not printed, it means that there is no sound driver present in the kernel. In this case you should check that you actually installed the kernel you compiled when enabling the sound driver.

If nothing is printed between the "Sound initialization started" and the "Sound initialization complete" lines, it means that no sound devices were detected. Most probably it means that you don't have the correct driver enabled, the card is not supported, the I/O port is bad or that you have a PnP card that has not been configured.

The driver may also display some error messages and warnings during boot. Watch for these when booting the first time after configuring the sound driver.

Next you should check the device file `/dev/sndstat`. Reading the sound driver status device file should provide additional information on whether the sound card driver initialized properly. Sample output should look something like this:

```
% cat /dev/sndstat
Sound Driver:3.5.4-960630 (Sat Jan 4 23:56:57 EST 1997 root,
Linux fizzbin 2.0.27 #48 Thu Dec 5 18:24:45 EST 1996 i586)
Kernel: Linux fizzbin 2.0.27 #48 Thu Dec 5 18:24:45 EST 1996 i586
Config options: 0

Installed drivers:
Type 1: OPL-2/OPL-3 FM
Type 2: Sound Blaster
Type 7: SB MPU-401

Card config:
Sound Blaster at 0x220 irq 5 drq 1,5
SB MPU-401 at 0x330 irq 5 drq 0
OPL-2/OPL-3 FM at 0x388 drq 0

Audio devices:
0: Sound Blaster 16 (4.13)

Synth devices:
0: Yamaha OPL-3

Midi devices:
0: Sound Blaster 16

Timers:
0: System clock

Mixers:
0: Sound Blaster
```

The command above can report some error messages. "No such file or directory" indicates that you need to create the device files (see section 4.3). "No such device" means that sound driver is not loaded or linked into kernel. Go back to section 4.2 to correct this.

If lines in the "Card config:" section of /dev/sndstat are listed inside parentheses (such as "(SoundBlaster at 0x220 irq 5 drq 1,5)"), it means that this device was configured but not detected.

Now you should be ready to play a simple sound file. Get hold of a sound sample file, and send it to the sound device as a basic check of sound output, e.g.

```
% cat endoftheworld >/dev/dsp
% cat crash.au >/dev/audio
```

(Make sure you don't omit the ">" in the commands above).

Note that, in general, using cat is not the proper way to play audio files, it's just a quick check. You'll want to get a proper sound player program (described later) that will do a better job.

This command will work only if there is at least one device listed in the audio devices section of /dev/sndstat. If the audio devices section is empty you should check why the device was not detected.

If the above commands return "I/O error", you should look at the end of the kernel messages listed using the "dmesg" command. It's likely that an error message is printed there. Very often the message is "Sound: DMA (output) timed out - IRQ/DRQ config error?". The above message means that the driver didn't get the expected interrupt from the sound card. In most cases it means that the IRQ or the DMA channel configured to the driver doesn't work. The best way to get it working is to try with all possible DMAs and IRQs supported by the device.

Another possible reason is that the device is not compatible with the device the driver is configured for. This is almost certainly the case when a supposedly "SoundBlaster (Pro/16) compatible" sound card doesn't work with the SoundBlaster driver. In this case you should try to find out the device your sound card is compatible with (by posting to the comp.os.linux.hardware newsgroup, for example).

Some sample sound files can be obtained from `<ftp://tsx-11.mit.edu/pub/linux/packages/sound/snd-data-0.1.tar.Z>`

Now you can verify sound recording. If you have sound input capability, you can do a quick test of this using commands such as the following:

```
# record 4 seconds of audio from microphone
EDT% dd bs=8k count=4 </dev/audio >sample.au
4+0 records in
4+0 records out
# play back sound
% cat sample.au >/dev/audio
```

Obviously for this to work you need a microphone connected to the sound card and you should speak into it. You may also need to obtain a mixer program to set the microphone as the input device and adjust the recording gain level.

If these tests pass, you can be reasonably confident that the sound D/A and A/D hardware and software are working. If you experience problems, refer to the next section of this document.

4.5 Troubleshooting

If you still encounter problems after following the instructions in the HOWTO, here are some things to check. The checks are listed in increasing order of complexity. If a check fails, solve the problem before moving to the next stage.

4.5.1 Step 1: Make sure you are really running the kernel you compiled.

You can check the date stamp on the kernel to see if you are running the one that you compiled with sound support. You can do this with the uname command:

```
% uname -a
Linux fizzbin 2.0.0 #1 Tue Jun 4 16:57:55 EDT 1996 i386
```

or by displaying the file /proc/version:

```
% cat /proc/version
Linux version 2.0.0 (root@fizzbin) (gcc version 2.7.0) #1 Tue Jun 4 16:57:55 EDT 1996
```

If the date stamp doesn't seem to match when you compiled the kernel, then you are running an old kernel. Did you really reboot? If you use LILO, did you re-install it (typically by running /etc/lilo/install)? If booting from floppy, did you create a new boot floppy and use it when booting?

4.5.2 Step 2: Make sure the kernel sound drivers are compiled in.

The easiest way to do this is to check the output of "dev/sndstat" as described earlier. If the output is not as expected then something went wrong with the kernel configuration or build. Start the installation process again, beginning with configuration and building of the kernel.

4.5.3 Step 3: Did the kernel detect your sound card during booting?

Make sure that the sound card was detected when the kernel booted. You should have seen a message on bootup. If the messages scrolled off the screen, you can usually recall them using the dmesg command:

```
% dmesg
```

or

```
% tail /var/adm/messages
```

If your sound card was not found then something is wrong. Make sure it really is installed. If the sound card works under DOS then you can be reasonably confident that the hardware is working, so it is likely a problem with the kernel configuration. Either you configured your sound card as the wrong type or wrong parameters, or your sound card is not compatible with any of the Linux kernel sound card drivers.

One possibility is that your sound card is one of the "compatible" type that requires initialization by the DOS driver. Try booting DOS and loading the vendor supplied sound card driver. Then soft boot Linux using Control-Alt-Delete. Make sure that card I/O address, DMA, and IRQ settings for Linux are the same as used under DOS. Read the Readme.cards file from the sound driver source distribution for hints on configuring your card type.

If your sound card is not listed in this document, it is possible that the Linux drivers do not support it. You can check with some of the references listed at the end of this document for assistance.

4.5.4 Step 4: Can you read data from the dsp device?

Try reading from the /dev/audio device using the dd command listed earlier in this document. The command should run without errors.

If it doesn't work, then chances are that the problem is an IRQ or DMA conflict or some kind of hardware incompatibility (the device is not supported by Linux or the driver is configured for a wrong device).

A remote possibility is broken hardware. Try testing the sound card under DOS, if possible, to eliminate that as a possibility.

4.5.5 When All Else Fails

If you still have problems, here are some final suggestions for things to try:

- carefully re-read this HOWTO document

- read the references listed at the end of this document, especially Hannu Savolainen's web pages and the relevant kernel source Readme files
- post a question to one of the `comp.os.linux` or other Usenet newsgroups (comp.os.linux.hardware is a good choice; because of the high level of traffic in these groups it helps to put the string "sound" in the subject header for the article so the right experts will see it)
- Using a Web/Usenet search engine with an intelligently selected search criteria can give very good results quickly. One such choice is `<http://www.altavista.digital.com>`
- try using the latest Linux kernel (but only as a last resort, the latest development kernels can be unstable)
- send mail to the author of the sound driver
- send mail to the author of the Sound HOWTO
- fire up emacs and type `Esc-x doctor` :-)

5 Applications Supporting Sound

I give here a sample of the types of applications that you likely want if you have a sound card under Linux. You can check the Linux Software Map, Internet archive sites, and/or files on your Linux CD-ROM for more up to date information.

As a minimum, you will likely want to obtain the following sound applications:

- audio file format conversion utility (e.g. `Sox`)
- mixer utility (e.g. `aumix` or `xmix`)
- digitized file player/recorder (e.g. `play` or `wavplay`)
- MOD file player (e.g. `tracker`)
- MIDI file player (e.g. `playmidi`)

There are text-based as well as GUI-based versions of most of these tools. There are also some more esoteric applications (e.g. speech synthesis and recognition) that you may wish to try.

6 Answers To Frequently Asked Questions

This section answers some of the questions that have been commonly asked on the Usenet news groups and mailing lists.

Answers to more questions can also be found at the OSS sound driver web page.

6.1 What are the various sound device files?

These are the most "standard" device file names, some Linux distributions may use slightly different names.

/dev/audio
> normally a link to /dev/audio0

/dev/audio0
> Sun workstation compatible audio device (only a partial implementation, does not support Sun ioctl interface, just u-law encoding)

/dev/audio1

second audio device (if supported by sound card or if more than one sound card installed)

/dev/dsp

normally a link to **/dev/dsp0**

/dev/dsp0

first digital sampling device

/dev/dsp1

second digital sampling device

/dev/mixer

normally a link to **/dev/mixer0**

/dev/mixer0

first sound mixer

/dev/mixer1

second sound mixer

/dev/music

high-level sequencer interface

/dev/sequencer

low level MIDI, FM, and GUS access

/dev/sequencer2

normally a link to **/dev/music**

/dev/midi00

1st raw MIDI port

/dev/midi01

2nd raw MIDI port

/dev/midi02

3rd raw MIDI port

/dev/midi03

4th raw MIDI port

/dev/sndstat

displays sound driver status when read

The PC speaker driver provides the following devices:

/dev/pcaudio

equivalent to /dev/audio

/dev/pcsp

equivalent to /dev/dsp

/dev/pcmixer

equivalent to /dev/mixer

6.2   How can I play a sound sample?

Sun workstation (.au) sound files can be played by sending them to the **/dev/audio** device. Raw samples can be sent to **/dev/dsp**. This will generally give poor results though, and using a program such as **play** is preferable, as it will recognize most file types and set the sound card to the correct sampling rate, etc.

Programs like wavplay or vplay (in the snd-util package) will give best results with WAV files. However they don't recognize Microsoft ADPCM compressed WAV files. Also older versions of play (from the Lsox package) doesn't work well with 16 bit WAV files.

The splay command included in the snd-util package can be used to play most sound files if proper parameters are entered manually in the command line.

6.3   How can I record a sample?

Reading **/dev/audio** or **/dev/dsp** will return sampled data that can be redirected to a file. A program such as **vrec** makes it easier to control the sampling rate, duration, etc. You may also need a mixer program to select the appropriate input device.

6.4   Can I have more than one sound card?

With the current sound driver it's possible to have several SoundBlaster, SoundBlaster/Pro, SoundBlaster16, MPU-401 or MSS cards at the same time on the system. Installing two SoundBlasters is possible but requires defining the macros SB2_BASE, SB2_IRQ, SB2_DMA and (in some cases) SB2_DMA2 by editing **local.h** manually. It's also possible to have a SoundBlaster at the same time as a PAS16.

With the newer 2.0.x kernels that configure sound using make config, instead of **local.h**, you need to edit the file **/usr/include/linux/autoconf.h**. After the section containing the lines:

```
#define SBC_BASE 0x220
#define SBC_IRQ (5)
#define SBC_DMA (1)
#define SB_DMA2 (5)
#define SB_MPU_BASE 0x0
#define SB_MPU_IRQ (-1)
```

add these lines (with values appropriate for your system):

```
#define SB2_BASE 0x330
#define SB2_IRQ (7)
#define SB2_DMA (2)
#define SB2_DMA2 (2)
```

The following drivers don't permit multiple instances:

- GUS (driver limitation)
- MAD16 (hardware limitation)
- AudioTrix Pro (hardware limitation)
- CS4232 (hardware limitation)

6.5   Error: No such file or directory for sound devices

You need to create the sound driver device files. See the section on creating device files. If you do have the device files, ensure that they have the correct major and minor device numbers (some older CD-ROM distributions of Linux may not create the correct device files during installation).

6.6   Error: No such device for sound devices

You have not booted with a kernel containing the sound driver or the I/O address configuration doesn't match your hardware. Check that you are running the newly compiled kernel and verify that the settings entered when configuring the sound driver match your hardware setup.

6.7   Error: No space left on device for sound devices

This can happen if you tried to record data to `/dev/audio` or `/dev/dsp` without creating the necessary device file. The sound device is now a regular file, and has filled up your disk partition. You need to run the script described in the *Creating the Device Files* section of this document.

This may also happen with Linux 2.0 and later if there is not enough free RAM on the system when the device is opened. The audio driver requires at least two pages (8k) of contiguous physical RAM for each DMA channel. This happens sometimes in machines with less than 16M of RAM or which have been running for very long time. It may be possible to free some RAM by compiling and running the following C program before trying to open the device again:

```
main() {
  int i;
  char mem[500000];
  for (i = 0; i < 500000; i++)
    mem[i] = 0;
  exit(0);
}
```

6.8   Error: Device busy for sound devices

Only one process can open a given sound device at one time. Most likely some other process is using the device in question. One way to determine this is to use the `fuser` command:

```
% fuser -v /dev/dsp
/dev/dsp:              USER        PID ACCESS COMMAND
                       tranter     265 f....  tracker
```

In the above example, the `fuser` command showed that process 265 had the device open. Waiting for the process to complete or killing it will allow the sound device to be accessed once again. You should run the `fuser` command as root in order to report usage by users other than yourself.

6.9   I still get device busy errors!

According to Brian Gough, for the SoundBlaster cards which use DMA channel 1 there is a potential conflict with the QIC-02 tape driver, which also uses DMA 1, causing "device busy" errors. If you are using FTAPE, you may have this driver enabled. According to the FTAPE-HOWTO the QIC-02 driver is not essential for the use of FTAPE; only the QIC-117 driver is required. Reconfiguring the kernel to use QIC-117 but not QIC-02 allows FTAPE and the sound-driver to coexist.

6.10   Partial playback of digitized sound file

The symptom is usually that a sound sample plays for about a second and then stops completely or reports an error message about "missing IRQ" or "DMA timeout". Most likely you have incorrect IRQ or DMA channel settings. Verify that the kernel configuration matches the sound card jumper settings and that they do not conflict with some other card.

Another symptom is sound samples that "loop". This is usually caused by an IRQ conflict.

6.11   There are pauses when playing MOD files

Playing MOD files requires considerable CPU power. You may have too many processes running or your computer may be too slow to play in real time. Your options are to:

- try playing with a lower sampling rate or in mono mode
- eliminate other processes
- buy a faster computer
- buy a more powerful sound card (e.g. Gravis UltraSound)

If you have a Gravis UltraSound card, you should use one of the mod file players written specifically for the GUS (e.g. gmod).

6.12   Compile errors when compiling sound applications

The version 1.0c and earlier sound driver used a different and incompatible ioctl() scheme. Obtain newer source code or make the necessary changes to adapt it to the new sound driver. See the sound driver Readme file for details.

Also ensure that you have used the latest version of soundcard.h and ultrasound.h when compiling the application. See the installation instructions at beginning of this text.

6.13   SEGV when running sound binaries that worked previously

This is probably the same problem described in the previous question.

6.14   What known bugs or limitations are there in the sound driver?

See the Readme and CHANGELOG files included with the sound driver kernel source.

6.15   Where are the sound driver ioctls() etc. documented?

These are partially documented in the *Hacker's Guide to VoxWare*, currently available in draft form. The latest version is draft 2, and can be found on `<ftp://nic.funet.fi/pub/Linux/ALPHA/sound/>`. Note that this directory is "hidden" and will not appear in directory listings. If you "cd" to the directory and use the FTP "dir" command, the files *are* there.

At time of writing new documentation was becoming available on the 4Front Technologies Web site.

Another source of information is the Linux Multimedia Guide, described in the references section.

6.16   What CPU resources are needed to play or record without pauses?

There is no easy answer to this question, as it depends on:

- whether using PCM sampling or FM synthesis
- sampling rate and sample size
- which application is used to play or record
- Sound Card hardware
- disk I/O rate, CPU clock speed, cache size, etc.

In general, any 386 machine should be able to play samples or FM synthesized music on an 8 bit sound card with ease.

Playing MOD files, however, requires considerable CPU resources. Some experimental measurements have shown that playing at 44kHz requires more than 40% of the speed of a 486/50 and a 386/25 can hardly play faster than 22 kHz (these are with an 8 bit card sound such as a SoundBlaster). A card such as the Gravis UltraSound card performs more functions in hardware, and will require less CPU resources.

These statements assume the computer is not performing any other CPU intensive tasks.

Converting sound files or adding effects using a utility such as `sox` is also much faster if you have a math coprocessor (or CPU with on board FPU). The kernel driver itself does not do any floating point calculations, though.

6.17   Problems with a PAS16 and an Adaptec 1542 SCSI host adaptor

(the following explanation was supplied by `seeker@indirect.com`)

Linux only recognizes the 1542 at address 330 (default) or 334, and the PAS only allows the MPU-401 emulation at 330. Even when you disable the MPU-401 under software, something still wants to conflict with the 1542 if it's at its preferred default address. Moving the 1542 to 334 makes everyone happy.

Additionally, both the 1542 and the PAS-16 do 16-bit DMA, so if you sample at 16-bit 44 KHz stereo and save the file to a SCSI drive hung on the 1542, you're about to have trouble. The DMAs overlap and there isn't enough time for RAM refresh, so you get the dread "PARITY ERROR - SYSTEM HALTED" message, with no clue to what caused it. It's made worse because a few second-party vendors with QIC-117 tape drives recommend setting the bus on/off times such that the 1542 is on even longer than normal. Get the SCSISEL.EXE program from Adaptec's BBS or several places on the internet, and reduce the BUS ON time or increase the BUS OFF time until the problem goes away, then move it one notch or more further. SCSISEL changes the EEPROM settings, so it's more permanent than a patch to the DOS driver line in CONFIG.SYS, and will work if you boot right into Linux (unlike the DOS patch). Next problem solved.

Last problem - the older Symphony chipsets drastically reduced the timing of the I/O cycles to speed up bus accesses. None of various boards I've played with had *any* problem with the reduced timing except for the PAS-16. Media Vision's BBS has SYMPFIX.EXE that's supposed to cure the problem by twiddling a diagnostic bit in Symphony's bus controller, but it's not a hard guarantee. You may need to:

- get the motherboard distributor to replace the older version bus chip,
- replace the motherboard, or
- buy a different brand of sound card.

Young Microsystems will upgrade the boards they import for around $30 (US); other vendors may be similar if you can figure out who made or imported the motherboard (good luck). The problem is in ProAudio's bus interface chip as far as I'm concerned; *nobody* buys a $120 sound card and sticks it in a 6MHz AT. Most of them wind up in 25-40MHz 386/486 boxes, and should be able to handle *at least* 12MHz bus rates if the chips are designed right. Exit soapbox (stage left).

The first problem depends on the chipset used on your motherboard, what bus speed and other BIOS settings, and the phase of the moon. The second problem depends on your refresh option setting (hidden or synchronous), the 1542 DMA rate and (possibly) the bus I/O rate. The third can be determined by calling Media Vision and asking which flavor of Symphony chip is incompatible with their slow design. Be warned, though - 3 of 4 techs I talked to were brain damaged. I would be very leery of trusting *anything* they said about someone else's hardware, since they didn't even know their own very well.

6.18 Is it possible to read and write samples simultaneously?

Due to hardware limitations, this is not possible with most sound cards. Some newer cards do support it. See the section on "bidirectional mode" in the *Hacker's Guide to Voxware* for more information.

6.19 My SB16 is set to IRQ 2, but configure does not allow this value.

On '286 and later machines, the IRQ 2 interrupt is cascaded to the second interrupt controller. It is equivalent to IRQ 9.

6.20 Are the SoundBlaster AWE32 or SoundBlaster16 ASP supported?

In the past, Creative Labs was not willing to release programming information for these cards. They have since changed their policy and an AWE driver is now included in the Linux 2.1.x kernels.

6.21 If I run Linux, then boot DOS, I get errors and/or sound applications do not work properly.

This happens after a soft reboot to DOS. Sometimes the error message misleadingly refers to a bad CONFIG. SYS file.

Most of the current sound cards have software programmable IRQ and DMA settings. If you use different settings between Linux and MS-DOS/Windows, this may cause problems. Some sound cards don't accept new parameters without a complete reset (i.e. cycle the power or use the hardware reset button).

The quick solution to this problem it to perform a full reboot using the reset button or power cycle rather than a soft reboot (e.g. Ctrl-Alt-Del).

The correct solution is to ensure that you use the same IRQ and DMA settings with MS-DOS and Linux (or not to use DOS :-).

6.22   Problems running DOOM under Linux

Users of the port of ID software's game DOOM for Linux may be interested in these notes.

For correct sound output you need version 2.90 or later of the sound driver; it has support for the real-time "DOOM mode".

The sound samples are 16-bit. If you have an 8-bit sound card you can still get sound to work using one of several programs available in `<ftp://sunsite.unc.edu/pub/Linux/games/doom>`.

If performance of DOOM is poor on your system, disabling sound (by renaming the file `sndserver`) may improve it.

By default DOOM does not support music (as in the DOS version). The program `musserver` will add support for music to DOOM under Linux. It can be found at `<ftp://pandora.st.hmc.edu/pub/linux/musserver.tgz>`.

6.23   How can I reduce noise picked up by my sound card?

Using good quality shielded cables and trying the sound card in different slots may help reduce noise. If the sound card has a volume control, you can try different settings (maximum is probably best).

Using a mixer program you can make sure that undesired inputs (e.g. microphone) are set to zero gain.

Some sound cards are simply not designed with good shielding and grounding and are prone to noise pickup.

Finally, on my system I found that the kernel command line option `no-hlt` reduces the noise level. This tells the kernel not to use the halt instruction when running the idle process loop. You can try this manually when booting, or set it up using the command `append="no-hlt"` in your LILO configuration file.

6.24   I can play sounds, but not record.

If you can play sound but not record, try these steps:

- use a mixer program to select the appropriate device (e.g. microphone)
- use the mixer to set the input gains to maximum
- If you can, try to test sound card recording under MS-DOS to determine if there is a hardware problem

Sometimes a different DMA channel is used for recording than for playback. In this case the most probable reason is that the recording DMA is set up incorrectly.

6.25   My "compatible" sound card only works if I first initialize under MS-DOS.

In most cases a "SoundBlaster compatible" card will work better under Linux if configured with a driver other than the SoundBlaster one. Most sound cards claim to be compatible (e.g. "16 bit SB Pro compatible" or "SB compatible 16 bit") but usually this SoundBlaster mode is just a "hack" provided for DOS games compatibility. Most cards have a 16 bit native mode which is likely to be supported by recent Linux versions (2.0.1 and later).

Only with some (usually rather old) cards is it necessary to try to get them to work in the SoundBlaster mode. The only newer cards that are the exception to this rule are the Mwave-based cards.

6.26 My 16-bit SoundBlaster "compatible" sound card only works in 8-bit mode under Linux.

16-bit sound cards described as SoundBlaster compatible are really only compatible with the 8-bit Sound-Blaster Pro. They typically have a 16-bit mode which is not compatible with the SoundBlaster 16 and not compatible with the Linux sound driver.

You may be able to get the card to work in 16-bit mode by using the MAD16 or MSS/WSS driver.

6.27 Where can I find sound applications for Linux?

Here are some good archive sites to search for Linux specific sound applications:

- `<ftp://sunsite.unc.edu:/pub/Linux/kernel/sound/>`
- `<ftp://sunsite.unc.edu:/pub/Linux/apps/sound/>`
- `<ftp://tsx-11.mit.edu:/pub/linux/packages/sound/>`
- `<ftp://nic.funet.fi:/pub/Linux/util/sound/>`
- `<ftp://nic.funet.fi:/pub/Linux/xtra/snd-kit/>`
- `<ftp://nic.funet.fi:/pub/Linux/ALPHA/sound/>`

6.28 Can the sound driver be compiled as a loadable module?

With recent kernels the sound driver is supported as a kernel loadable module.

See the files `/usr/src/linux/drivers/sound/Readme.modules` and `/usr/src/linux/Documentation/modules.txt` (or `/usr/src/linux/README`) for details.

6.29 Can I use a sound card to replace the system console beep?

Try the `oplbeep` program, found at `<ftp://sunsite.unc.edu/pub/Linux/apps/sound/oplbeep-alpha.tar.gz>`

Another variant is the `beep` program found at `<ftp://sunsite.unc.edu/pub/Linux/kernel/patches/misc/modreq_beep.tgz>`

The `modutils` package has an example program and kernel patch that supports calling an arbitrary external program to generate sounds when requested by the kernel.

Alternatively, with some sound cards you can connect the PC speaker output to the sound card so that all sounds come from the sound card speakers.

6.30   What is VoxWare?

The kernel sound drivers support several different Intel-based Unix compatible operating systems, and can be obtained as a package separate from the Linux kernel. Up until February 1996 the author had called the software "VoxWare". Unfortunately this name has been registered by *VoxWare Incorporated* <http://www.voxware.com/>, and can not be used. The new name of the driver is OSS/Free.

The Open Sound System (OSS) is a commercially available kernel sound driver for various Unix systems, sold by 4Front Technologies. The free version, known as OSS/Free will continue to be made freely available for Linux systems.

Other names you may come across that have been used in the past to refer to the same sound driver are TASD (Temporarily Anonymous Sound Driver) and USS (Unix Sound System).

For more information see the 4Front Technologies Web page at <http://www.4front-tech.com/>. I wrote a review of OSS/Linux in the June 1997 issue of *Linux Journal* <http://www.ssc.com/lj/>.

6.31   Are Plug and Play sound card supported?

Full Plug and Play support should be coming in Linux version 2.1. In the mean time there are a number of workarounds for getting Plug and Play sound cards to work.

If you have a newer Pentium system with a Plug and Play BIOS, it should take care of configuring the cards for you. Make sure that you configure the Linux sound driver to use the same I/O address, IRQ, and DMA channel parameters as the BIOS.

There is a package of Plug and Play tools for Linux that can be used to set up the card. It can be found at Red Hat's Web site <http://www.redhat.com/> (it may also be included in your Linux distribution).

If you use the card under Windows95, you can use the device manager to set up the card, then soft boot into Linux using the LOADLIN program. Make sure Windows95 and Linux use the same card setup parameters.

If you use the card under DOS, you can use the `icu` utility that comes with SoundBlaster16 PnP cards to configure it under DOS, then soft boot into Linux using the LOADLIN program. Again, make sure DOS and Linux use the same card setup parameters.

The commercial OSS sound driver has support for the SoundBlaster16 PnP sound card. You can purchase this driver from 4Front Technologies.

6.32   Sox/Play/Vplay reports "invalid block size 1024"

A change to the sound driver in version 1.3.67 broke some sound player programs which (incorrectly) checked that the result from the SNDCTL_DSP_GETBLKSIZE ioctl was greater than 4096. The utilities included in the latest snd-util-3.x.tar.gz package (at <ftp://ftp.4front-tech.com/ossfree>.) now handle this properly. The latest sound driver versions have also been fixed to avoid allocating fragments shorter than 4096 bytes which solves this problem with old utilities.

6.33   Why does the sound driver have its own configuration program?

The sound driver supports many different configuration parameters. The `configure` program included with the sound driver checks for many dependencies between parameters. The tools used to configure the kernel don't support this level of functionality.

That said, the latest kernels do optionally allow using the standard kernel configuration tools with the sound driver (see the earlier section on "Configuring the Kernel".

6.34 The mixer settings are reset whenever I load the sound driver module

You can build the sound driver as a loadable module and use `kerneld` to automatically load and unload it. This can present one problem - whenever the module is reloaded the mixer settings go back to their default values. For some sound cards this can be too loud (e.g. SoundBlaster16) or too quiet. Markus Gutschke (`gutschk@uni-muenster.de`) found this solution. Use a line in your `/etc/conf.modules` file such as the following:

```
options sound dma_buffsize=65536 && /usr/bin/setmixer igain 0 ogain 0 vol 75
```

This causes your mixer program (in this case `setmixer`) to be run immediately after the sound driver is loaded. The `dma_buffsize` parameter is just a dummy value needed because the option command requires a command line option. Change the line as needed to match your mixer program and gain settings.

If you have compiled the sound driver into your kernel and you want to set the mixer gains at boot time you can put a call to your mixer program in a system startup file such as `/etc/rc.d/rc.local`.

6.35 Only user root can record sound

By default the script in Readme.linux that creates the sound device files only allows the devices to be read by user `root`. This is to plug a potential security hole. In a networked environment, external users could conceivably log in remotely to a Linux PC with a sound card and microphone and eavesdrop. If you are not worried about this, you can change the permissions used in the script.

With the default setup, users can still play sound files. This is not a security risk but is a potential for nuisance.

6.36 Is the sound hardware on the IBM ThinkPad supported?

Information on how to use the mwave sound card on an IBM ThinkPad laptop computer under Linux can be found at `<http://www.screamin.demon.co.uk/>`.

7 References

If you have a sound card that supports a CD-ROM or SCSI interface, the Linux *SCSI HOWTO* `<http://sunsite.unc.edu/LDP/HOWTO/SCSI-HOWTO.html>` and the Linux *CD-ROM HOWTO* `<http://sunsite.unc.edu/LDP/HOWTO/CDROM-HOWTO.html>` have additional information that may be useful to you.

The *Sound Playing HOWTO* `<http://sunsite.unc.edu/LDP/HOWTO/Sound-Playing-HOWTO.html>` describes how to play various types of sound and music files under Linux.

The *Ultrasound Plug'n'play Mini-HOWTO* `<http://sunsite.unc.edu/LDP/HOWTO/mini/Gravis-UltraSound>` describes how to get a plug and play Gravis Ultrasound card working under Linux.

The *Linux SoundBlaster 16 PnP Mini-HOWTO* `<http://sunsite.unc.edu/LDP/HOWTO/mini/Soundblaster-16>` describes how to get a plug and play SoundBlaster 16 card working under Linux.

The *Linux SoundBlaster AWE64 PnP Mini-HOWTO* `<http://sunsite.unc.edu/LDP/HOWTO/mini/Soundblaster-AWE64>` describes how to get a plug and play SoundBlaster AWE64 card working under Linux.

There is an old document called the *Hacker's Guide to VoxWare*, available from `<ftp://nic.funet.fi/pub/Linux/ALPHA/sound/>`. Most of the information in there has been superseded by the documents at `<http://www.4front-tech.com/pguide>`, but the section on `/dev/sequencer` may still be useful.

The following FAQs are regularly posted to the Usenet newsgroup *news.announce* `<news:news.announce>` as well as being archived at `<ftp://rtfm.mit.edu/pub/usenet/news.answers>`:

- PCsoundcards/generic-faq (Generic PC Soundcard FAQ)
- PCsoundcards/soundcard-faq (comp.sys.ibm.pc.soundcard FAQ)
- PCsoundcards/gravis-ultrasound/faq (Gravis UltraSound FAQ)
- audio-fmts/part1 (Audio file format descriptions)
- audio-fmts/part2 (Audio file format descriptions)

The FAQs also list several product specific mailing lists and archive sites. The following Usenet news groups discuss sound and/or music related issues:

- *alt.binaries.sounds.** `<news:alt.binaries.sounds>` (various groups for posting sound files)
- *alt.binaries.multimedia* `<news:alt.binaries.multimedia>` (for posting Multimedia files)
- *alt.sb.programmer* `<news:alt.sb.programmer>` (Soundblaster programming topics)
- *comp.multimedia* `<news:comp.multimedia>` (Multimedia topics)
- *comp.music* `<news:comp.music>` (Computer music theory and research)
- *comp.sys.ibm.pc.soundcard.** `<news:comp.sys.ibm.pc.soundcard>` (various IBM PC sound card groups)

A Web site dedicated to multimedia can be found at `<http://viswiz.gmd.de/MultimediaInfo/>`. Creative Labs has a Web site at `<http://www.creaf.com/>`. MediaTrix has a Web site at `<http://www.mediatrix.com/>`.

The Linux mailing list has a number of "channels" dedicated to different topics, including sound. To find out how to join, send a mail message with the word "help" as the message body to *majordomo@vger.rutgers.edu* `<mailto:majordomo@vger.rutgers.edu>`. These mailing lists are not recommended for questions on sound card setup etc., they are intended for development related discussion.

As mentioned several times before, the kernel sound driver includes a number of `Readme` files containing useful information about the sound card driver. These can typically be found in the directory `/usr/src/linux/drivers/sound`.

The author of the kernel sound driver, Hannu Savolainen, can be contacted by email at *hannu@voxware.pp.fi* `<mailto:hannu@voxware.pp.fi>`. He also has a World-Wide Web site at `<http://personal.eunet.fi/pp/voxware>`. The Web site is the best source for finding out the latest status of supported sound cards, known problems, and bug fixes.

Information on OSS, the commercial sound driver for Linux and other Unix compatible operating systems, can be found on the 4Front Technologies Web page at `<http://www.4front-tech.com/>`.

The *Linux Software Map* (LSM) is an invaluable reference for locating Linux software. Searching the LSM for keywords such as *sound* is a good way to identify applications related to sound hardware. The LSM can be found on various anonymous FTP sites, including `<ftp://sunsite.unc.edu/pub/Linux/docs/LSM/>`.

The Linux Documentation Project has produced several books on Linux, including *Linux Installation and Getting Started*. These are freely available by anonymous FTP from major Linux archive sites or can be purchased in hardcopy format.

Finally, a shameless plug: If you want to learn a lot more about multimedia under Linux (especially CD-ROM and sound card applications and programming), check out my book *Linux Multimedia Guide*, ISBN

1-56592-219-0, published by O'Reilly and Associates. As well as the original English version, French and Japanese translations are now in print. For details, call 800-998-9938 in North America or check the Web page <http://www.ora.com/catalog/multilinux/noframes.html> or my home page <http://www.pobox.com/~tranter>.

The Linux Sound Playing HOWTO

Yoo C. Chung <http://laplace.snu.ac.kr/wacko/>, wacko@laplace.snu.ac.kr   v1.5b, 2 February 1998

This document lists applications for Linux that play various sound formats.

Contents

1   Introduction

This is the Sound Playing HOWTO. It lists the many sound formats and the applications that can be used to play them. It also lists some hacks and advice on using these applications. There are also some other interesting applications related to sound not directly related to playback. However, this document does *not* describe how one can setup a Linux system for sound support. Refer to the Linux Sound HOWTO by *Jeff Tranter* <mailto:jeff_tranter@pobox.com> for instructions on setting up a Linux system for sound support and the supported sound hardware.

This deals with normal user sound applications. That is, it is only concerned about what the average user needs to know on the application side of sound, not exotic stuff like speech synthesis, or hardware stuff which is dealt in the Sound HOWTO.

1.1   Copyright of this document

This document can be freely distributed and modified (I would appreciate it if I were notified of any modifications), as long as this copyright notice is preserved. However, it cannot be placed under any further restrictions, and a modified document must have the same copyright as this one. Also, credit must be given where due.

1.2   Copyright of the listed applications

If there is no mention of any copyright, then the application is under the GNU General Public License.

1.3   Where to get this document

The most recent official version of this document can be obtained from the *Linux Documentation Project* `<http://sunsite.unc.edu/LDP/>`. The most recent unofficial version of this document can be obtained from `<http://laplace.snu.ac.kr/wacko/howto/>`.

A Korean version of this document (very outdated) is available at `<http://laplace.snu.ac.kr/wacko/howto/Sound-Playing-HOWTO.ks>`.

A Japanese version of this document is available at `<http://jf.gee.kyoto-u.ac.jp/JF/JF-ftp/euc/Sound-Playing-HOWTO.euc>`.

1.4   Feedback

I am not omniscient, and I don't use all the applications in here (a few I can't even try), so there are bound to be mistakes. Also, programs usually continuously evolve, so documentation tends to get out of date. Therefore, if you find anything wrong, please *send me* `<mailto:wacko@laplace.snu.ac.kr>` any corrections. Suggestions or additions to this document are welcome, too.

1.5   Acknowledgments

All the authors of the applications in this HOWTO. Also, Hannu Savolainen for the great sound driver and Linus Torvalds for the great underlying OS.

I'd also like to thank Raymond Nijssen (`raymond@es.ele.tue.nl`), Jeroen Rutten (`jeroen@es.ele.tue.nl`), Antonio Perez (`aperez@arrakis.es`), Ian Jackson (`ijackson@gnu.org`), and Peter Amstutz (`amstpi@freenet.tlh.fl.us`) for their information and help.

2   Playing Various Sound Formats

There are many kinds of sound formats (WAV, MIDI, MPEG etc.). Below, we list the various formats and the applications that can be used to play them.

2.1   MIDI

MIDI stands for Musical Instrument Device Interface. MIDI files usually have the extension `.mid`. They contain sequencing information, that is, information on when to play what instrument in what way, etc. Depending on your hardware (and maybe the software you use to play them), the sound might be awesome, or it might be downright crappy.

2.1.1   The adagio package

This package includes `mp` (a command-line MIDI file player) and `xmp` (an XView based MIDI file player, not to be confused with the module player also called `xmp`). You will need the SlingShot extensions to use `xmp`. It also contains other programs for playing Adagio scores.

If you have a GUS, `mp` can also play MOD files (see section 2.2 (Modules) for more information on modules).

One little annoying bug (as of version 0.5 on some hardware) is that the sound breaks at the end. Namely, instead of ending the sound the way the MIDI file specifies, it ends by playing the note right before the last one in a long interval. It hasn't stopped me from using mp, but it might prevent someone from using it for 'real' work. It also starts up relatively slowly.

The package does not mention any copyright (at least none that I can find), so I assume it can be freely redistributed and modified. (By a strict interpretation of copyright law, nothing gives one the right to do these things, but I somehow doubt that this was the intention of the author.)

It is a port of the CMU MIDI Toolkit to Linux (though there was enough added to make this questionable) by Greg Lee (`lee@uhunix.uhcc.hawaii.edu`).

It can be obtained by *anonymous FTP* <`ftp://tsx-11.mit.edu/pub/linux/packages/sound/adagio05.tar.gz`> from `tsx-11.mit.edu` at `/pub/linux/packages/sound/adagio05.tar.gz`. The binaries included here are in a.out format (linked with ancient libraries), and the `xmp` binary segfaults in a X11R6 environment (XFree86 3.1.1, libc 4.7.2). The `mp` binary works fine in an `a.out` environment.

You will need a bit of hackery to compile it. Actually, it's not much of a hackery. All you have to do is to include the `-lfl` switch at the end of `SHROBJ` and `XMPOBJ` in the Makefile. This is to link in the `flex` library, which is not linked in by default. Then follow the installation instructions. And don't forget to have XView and the SlingShot extensions installed if you want to compile `xmp`.

2.1.2 TiMidity

Some people recommend this *experimental* program because of good sound quality (which is very true, it's much better than mp on a Sound Blaster 16, though it probably won't be much different on soundcards with wavetable synthesis like the GUS). However, it suffers from high CPU loads. It plays MIDI by first converting MIDI to WAV and then plays the WAV (you can also convert a MIDI file to a WAV file without playing if you want). This is the reason for its CPU intensive nature.

It also has an optional ncurses, SLang, Tcl/Tk or Motif interface.

You need Gravis Ultrasound patch files to use this. Look into the FAQ included with TiMidity for more information.

The author is Tuukka Toivonen (`tt@cgs.fi`).

The latest version of TiMidity can be found at the *TiMidity home page* <`http://www.cgs.fi/tt/timidity/`>. This page also contains a link to a small library of GUS patches.

2.1.3 playmidi

This is a MIDI player that plays to FM, GUS, and external MIDI. It is supposed to have a faster startup time compared to other MIDI players. It is also able to play Creative Music Files, Microsoft RIFF files, and large MIDI archives from games such as Ultima 7.

It has an X interface and a SVGA interface. It also has an option for real time playback with tracking all the notes on each channel and the current playback clock (included automatically with `xplaymidi` and `splaymidi`).

You should do something like

```
$ splaymidi foo.mid; stty sane
```

if you are going to use the SVGA interface, since it doesn't reset the terminal tty mode properly. The SVGA interface may be removed in the near future.

It was written by Nathan Laredo (`laredo@gnu.org` or `laredo@ix.netcom.com`).

It can be obtained by *anonymous FTP* `<ftp://sunsite.unc.edu/pub/Linux/apps/sound/players/playmidi-2.3.tar.gz>` from `sunsite.unc.edu` at `/pub/Linux/apps/sound/players/playmidi-2.3.tar.gz`.

2.2   Modules

Modules (in computer music) are digital music files, made up of a set of samples and sequencing information, telling the player when to play which sample (instrument) on which track at what pitch, optionally performing an effect, like vibrato for example.

An advantage it has over MIDI is that it can include almost any kind of sound (including human voices). Another is that it sounds just about the same on any platform, because the samples are in the module. A disadvantage it has is that it has a much larger file size compared to MIDI. Another one is that it has no real standard format (the only 'real' one is the ProTracker, which many modules aren't quite compatible with). It originated on the Amiga.

The most common format has the extension `.mod`. There are many other extensions depending on what format they are in.

2.2.1   tracker

This very portable program (it has been ported to many platforms) plays Soundtracker and Protracker music modules. It uses 16 bit stereo output, and I consider the quality to be very good. If you need a simple way to reduce CPU load use the `-mono` option.

This is a giftware program (quoting the author). It is by Marc Espie (`Marc.Espie@ens.fr`).

A version of this with the Makefile already tweaked for Linux can be obtained by *anonymous FTP* `<ftp://sunsite.unc.edu/pub/Linux/apps/sound/players/tracker-4.3-linux.tar.gz>` from `sunsite.unc.edu` at `/pub/Linux/apps/sound/players/tracker-4.3-linux.tar.gz`.

2.2.2   gmod

This is a music module player for the Gravis Ultrasound card. 4/6/8 channel MOD, 8 channel 669, Multi-Tracker (MTM), UltraTracker (ULT), FastTracker (XM), and ScreamTracker III (S3M) are the supported formats.

It requires a version 3.0 or later sound driver. And a GUS, of course. You may need to modify the kernel to make volume control work the way you want.

This has an X interface. It uses the QT toolkit (needs version 0.99 or greater). Check the *QT toolkit homepage* `<http://www.troll.no/>` for information on QT.

This can be freely distributed. It was originally written by Hannu Savolainen, and now maintained by Andrew J. Robinson (`robinson@cnj.digex.net`).

It can be obtained by *anonymous FTP* `<ftp://sunsite.unc.edu/pub/Linux/apps/sound/players/gmod-3.1.tar.gz>` from `sunsite.unc.edu` at `/pub/Linux/apps/sound/players/gmod-3.1.tar.gz`.

2.2.3   MikMod

This portable module player plays XM, ULT, STM, S3M, MTM, MOD and UNI formats. (The UNI format is an internal format used by MikMod.) It has support for zipped module files. It uses 16 bit stereo for the sound output. Use the `-m` option (for mono output) if you need a simple way to lower the CPU load.

The Unix version can either use ncurses or Tcl/Tk for its interface. It can also be used as a library, not just an independent program.

It was originally written by Jean-Paul Mikkers (`mikmak@via.nl`). It is now maintained by Jake Stine (`dracoirs@epix.net`). This is shareware that has to be registered if you want to use it commercially. You also need permission to redistribute it commercially (non-commercial redistribution does not need such permission).

This can be found at the *MikMod home page* `<http://www.aics.net/amstutz/mikmod.html>`.

2.2.4   xmp

This is a module player (not to be confused with Adagio's `xmp`) which can play MOD, S3M, MTM, PTR, STM, 669, and XM modules (other formats are also supported, but still experimental or incomplete). If you have soundcards with wavetable synthesis (GUS or SoundBlaster 32AWE), then you can use this feature of the soundcard to lower the load on the CPU.

An X frontend to `xmp` is also available.

This was written by Claudio Matsuoka (`claudio@lobo.inf.ufpr.br`) and H. Carraro Jr.

This can found at the *xmp home page* `<http://www.merdre.net/claudio/xmp/>`.

2.2.5   s3mod

This plays 4/6/8 track MOD modules and Scream Tracker 3 modules. It uses 8 bit mono output with a sampling rate of 22000 Hz by default. You can use the option `-s` to enable stereo, `-b` to enable 16 bit output, and `-f` to set the sampling frequency. However, the sound output is worse than tracker (some noise), so I recommend using `tracker` instead of `s3mod` for playing ordinary MOD files (unless you have an underpowered machine). It has a much smaller CPU load compared to tracker.

It is copyrighted by Daniel Marks and David Jeske (`jeske@uiuc.edu`), but you can do anything you want with it (except that you can't claim you wrote it).

It can be obtained by *anonymous FTP* `<ftp://sunsite.unc.edu/pub/Linux/apps/sound/players/s3mod-v1.09.tar.gz>` from `sunsite.unc.edu` at `/pub/Linux/apps/sound/players/s3mod-v1.09.tar.gz`.

2.2.6   mod

This *beta* program plays MODs (15/31-instrument, up to 32 voices), MTMs, ULTs and S3Ms on the Gravis Ultrasound card. It can also use packed modules if you have `gzip`, `lharc`, `unzip`, and `unarj` installed. It cannot play Powerpacked modules or modules packed with some Amiga composers ("PACK" signature).

This requires at least version 3.0 of the sound driver. It *won't* work with the 2.90-2 or earlier version of the sound driver. The text interface requires ncurses. There is also an X interface included, which uses Tcl/Tk.

It was written by Mikael Nordqvist (`mech@df.lth.se` or `d91mn@efd.lth.se`).

It can be obtained by *anonymous FTP* `<ftp://sunsite.unc.edu/pub/Linux/apps/sound/players/mod-v0.81.tgz>` from `sunsite.unc.edu` at `/pub/Linux/apps/sound/players/mod-v0.81.tgz`.

2.2.7   nspmod

This is an *alpha* module player which can play MTM, S3M, and MOD modules. It is intended to be a module player for soundcards without a DSP (not to be confused with what Creative Labs calls a DSP). It has a CPU load somewhat similar compared to `tracker`.

It has a feature which lets modules loop if they want to. The number of loops can be limited by the `-l` option. It uses only 8 bit sound output (as of version 0.1).

This was written by Toru Egashira (`toru@jms.jeton.or.jp`).

It can be obtained by *anonymous FTP* <`ftp://sunsite.unc.edu/pub/Linux/apps/sound/players/nspmod-0.1.tar.gz`> from `sunsite.unc.edu` at `/pub/Linux/apps/sound/players/nspmod-0.1.tar.gz`.

2.2.8   yampmod

This *alpha* program was designed to play 4-channel modules using the minimum of CPU resources. It was *not* designed to produce high quality sound. So the only sound output it produces is 22 kHz mono output. Also, the output isn't as clean as it should be, reflecting its alpha status.

It was written by David Groves (`djg@djghome.demon.co.uk`).

It can be obtained by *anonymous FTP* <`ftp://sunsite.unc.edu/pub/Linux/apps/sound/players/yampmod-0.1.tar.gz`> from `sunsite.unc.edu` at `/pub/Linux/apps/sound/players/yampmod-0.1.tar.gz`.

2.3   MPEG audio streams

MPEG is a standard specifying the coding of video and the associated audio for digital storage. MPEG is usually associated with video, but the audio part of the standard can be used separately. The audio part of the MPEG standard defines three layers, layer I, II, and III. Players that can decode higher layers can also decode lower layers (e.g. layer III players can play layer II files). Layer I MPEG audio files usually have the extension `.mpg` (so if there is a file with this extension that can't be played by a MPEG video player, it's probably an audio stream), layer II usually have the extension `.mp2`, and layer III usually have the extension `.mp3`. The audio compression is pretty good. A two megabyte layer II MPEG audio file will probably take up 25 megabytes for a raw PCM sample file with the same quality.

2.3.1   mpg123

This *beta* program is an efficient MPEG audio stream player, which has support for layers I, II, and III. It is based on code from many sources. It is able to play in real time streams that are read by HTTP (i.e. one can play an MPEG audio stream directly over the World Wide Web).

The main author is Michael Hipp (`Michael.Hipp@student.uni-tuebingen.de`). It may be used and distributed in unmodified form freely for non-commercial purposes. Inclusion in a collection of free software (such as CD-ROM images of FTP servers) is explicitly allowed.

The latest version can be obtained from *Oliver Fromme's mpg123 page* <`http://www.heim3.tu-clausthal.de/olli/mpg123/`>.

2.3.2   maplay 1.2

This MPEG audio stream player only has support for layer I and layer II streams, and lacks support for layer III streams. It supports 16 bit sound cards on Linux.

It is pretty CPU intensive, taking up to about 55% CPU time on a 60MHz Pentium. The output is intolerable on a 66MHz 486 because the CPU just can't catch up with the sound. If this happens to you, try playing only one side of the audio stream (with the `-l` or `-r` option), instead of the default stereo.

A slight change in one of the files may be necessary in order to compile it. Namely, you may need to add the following line to the beginning of the file **configuration.sh**.

```
#! /bin/sh
```

The author is Tobias Bading (**bading@cs.tu-berlin.de**). maplay 1.2 can be obtained by *anonymous FTP* **<ftp://ftp.cs.tu-berlin.de/pub/multimedia/maplay1.2/maplay1_2.tar>** from **ftp.cs.tu-berlin.de** at **/pub/multimedia/maplay1.2/maplay1_2.tar**.

2.3.3   maplay 1.3b

This is an unofficial modification (i.e. not by the original author) of **maplay** 1.2, so that it can run with a much lower load on the CPU. It accomplishes this mainly by making u-law output actually work on other platforms besides the SPARC. Note that it uses u-law output by default, so the sound quality is lower.

The modifications were made by Orlando Andico (**orly@gibson.eee.upd.edu.ph**).

This can be obtained by *anonymous FTP* **<ftp://sunsite.unc.edu/pub/Linux/apps/sound/players/ maplay-1.3b-Linux.tar.gz>** from **sunsite.unc.edu** at **/pub/Linux/apps/sound/players/maplay-1. 3b-Linux.tar.gz**.

2.3.4   maplay3

This is another derivative of **maplay** 1.2. It adds support for MPEG Layer 3 audio streams. Currently it seems to have some bugs in its playback (you may hear some screeching noises). You may have to twiddle with the options to solve this.

The modifications were made by Timo Jantunen (**timo.jantunen@hut.fi** or **jeti@cc.hut.fi**). It says that it can be used freely, but making money off of it is not allowed. However, I'm not entirely sure about the validity of this copyright, since the original **maplay** is under the GNU General Public License, which does not allow derivative works to have a different copyright.

This can be obtained by *anonymous FTP* **<ftp://sunsite.unc.edu/pub/Linux/apps/sound/players/ maplay3.tar.gz>** from **sunsite.unc.edu** at **/pub/Linux/apps/sound/players/maplay3.tar.gz**.

2.3.5   splay

This *beta* player is another derivative of **maplay** 1.2 (actually, it is a derivative of **maplay** 1.2+, which is a MS Windows only derivative of **maplay** 1.2). It adds support for MPEG Layer 3 audio streams. It is also able to play WAV files. It can also play audio streams received over an HTTP connection.

Another feature of **splay** is that it can be used as a library (under the LGPL), so that it can be used in other programs. It also tries to improve performance by using threading (you need **pthread** to use this feature) and a little inline assembly.

splay uses a command line interface and an optional X interface (which uses QT).

If after compiling it doesn't work (e.g. it segmentation faults), try compiling it again without threading.

This is by Jung Woo-jae (**jwj95@eve.kaist.ac.kr**).

It can be obtained from *splay's home page* **<http://adam.kaist.ac.kr/jwj95/>**.

2.3.6   Sajber Jukebox

This program is a MPEG audio player with a graphical user interface. It is based on `splay`, so it includes support for MPEG audio layers up to III. It is also able to play MPEG audio streams in real time with the stream being fed by HTTP. It is also easy to configure.

It uses the *QT toolkit* <http://www.troll.no/> (at least version 1.2 is required). It also uses the *LinuxThreads* <http://pauillac.inria.fr/~xleroy/linuxthreads/> library (the included binary only works with version 0.5).

The author is Joel Lindholm (`wizball@kewl.campus.luth.se`).

The latest version can be obtained by *anonymous FTP* <ftp://kewl.campus.luth.se/pub/jukebox> from `kewl.campus.luth.se` in /pub/jukebox.

2.3.7   amp

This *beta* MPEG audio player only has support for MPEG Layer 3 audio streams. It is able to play directly to the soundcard, and it can output to raw PCM or WAV files. This also gives quite a load on the CPU (about 60% on a 133MHz Pentium).

This was written by Tomislav Uzelac (`tuzelac@rasip.fer.hr`). It can be freely used and distributed, as long as it is not sold commercially without permission (including it in CD-ROMs that contain free software is explicitly permitted, though).

It can be obtained by *anonymous FTP* <ftp://ftp.rasip.fer.hr/pub/mpeg/amp-0.7.3.tgz> from `ftp.rasip.fer.hr` at /pub/mpeg/amp-0.7.3.tgz.

2.3.8   XAudio

This *alpha* library was written to be a fast implementation of an MPEG audio decoding library to be used by various GUI front-ends. It supports MPEG audio layers I, II, and III. It is capable of random access to bitstreams. A command-line interface is included. A Motif (Lesstif) front-end is also included in the Linux version.

This is by Gilles Boccon-Gibod, Alain Jobart and others. The front-ends to the libary can be freely downloaded. The library itself must be licensed to be used (a source and binary license is available).

The front-ends to the library can be obtained from *XAudio home page* <http://www.mpeg.org/xaudio/>.

2.3.9   Layer 3 Shareware Encoder/Decoder

This is actually a converter that converts MPEG Layer 3 audio streams to WAV, AIFF, SND, AIFC, or just raw PCM sample files. The Linux version does not directly output the sound to the soundcard. One has to first convert it to some other format.

However, when you try to play a converted file using `sox`, you'll probably just get noise because the word order in the PCM samples is not right (at least on Intel platforms). You need to give `sox` the option `-x` to solve this problem. But there are some players that don't have to be told that the word order is wrong, so you might not have to worry about this.

If you have a really fast computer (probably at least a 100Mhz Pentium), then you can try to play MPEG Layer 3 streams directly without having to first convert the audio file to another format like in the following example (this example assumes that you're using `sox` and playing a 44.1 kHz stereo sample).

```
$ l3dec foo.mp3 -sto | play -t raw -x -u -w -c 2 -r 44100 -
```

The number after `-r` is the sample rate of the audio stream, and the number after `-c` depends on whether it is mono or stereo (or even quad). If this looks too complicated, you can use something like a shell script or an alias.

This is shareware copyrighted by Fraunhofer-IIS. A demo version for Linux on x86 systems can be obtained by *anonymous FTP* `<ftp://ftp.fhg.de/pub/layer3>` from `ftp.fhg.de` in `/pub/layer3`. The demo version only converts layer III audio streams.

2.4   WAV

Quote from the `sox` man page:

> These appear to be very similar to IFF files, but not the same. They are the native sound file format of Windows 3.1. Obviously, Windows 3.1 is of such incredible importance to the computer industry that it just had to have its own sound file format.

These usually have the extension `.wav`.

Also see section 2.5.1 (sox) and 2.5.2 (bplay) for other WAV players besides the ones listed here.

2.4.1   wavplay

This program supports playing and recording with the WAV format. It uses locking so that only one sound may be played at a time. Its locking capabilities can also be used separately from its sound playing capabilities.

In addition to a command-line interface, it also has a Motif interface, which can be used with Lesstif.

It was originally written by Andre Fuechsel (`af1@irz.inf.tu-dresden.de`), but was evolved to the point of being completely rewritten by Warren W. Gay (`bx249@freenet.toronto.on.ca` or `wwg@ica.net`).

It can be obtained by *anonymous FTP* `<ftp://sunsite.unc.edu/pub/Linux/apps/sound/players/wavplay-1.0.tar.gz>` from `sunsite.unc.edu` at `/pub/Linux/apps/sound/players/wavplay-1.0.tar.gz`.

2.5   Other stuff

This section lists stuff that play sound formats that don't deserve a separate section (i.e. formats that have only one player available), or players that play more than one format.

2.5.1   sox

This program is actually a converter, that is, it converts one sound format to another. However, some versions of `sox`, when invoked as `play`, plays the sound (the `play` application in the Sound HOWTO probably refers to this). It supports raw (no header) binary and textual data, IRCAM Sound Files, Sound Blaster `.voc`, SPARC `.au` (w/header), Mac HCOM, PC/DOS `.sou`, Sndtool, and Sounder, NeXT `.snd`, Windows 3.1 RIFF/WAV, Turtle Beach `.smp`, CD-R, and Apple/SGI AIFF and 8SVX formats

Since somewhere in the 1.3.6x kernels, you might have to make a small change in one file to make it play the sound directly. Namely, you may have to change line 179 in `sbdsp.c` from

```
      if (abuf_size < 4096 || abuf_size > 65536) {
```

to

```
      if (abuf_size < 1 || abuf_size > 65536) {
```

But then again, you may not have to do this. But doing this won't break anything.

It is written and copyrighted by many people, and can be used for any purpose.

It can be obtained by *anonymous FTP* `<ftp://sunsite.unc.edu/pub/Linux/apps/sound/convert/Lsox-linux.tar.gz>` from `sunsite.unc.edu` at `/pub/Linux/apps/sound/convert/Lsox-linux.tar.gz`.

A more recent version by Chris Bagwell (`cbagwell@sprynet.com`) (based on the latest gamma version of the original sox, and includes the above fix) can be obtained by *anonymous FTP* `<ftp://sunsite.unc.edu/pub/Linux/apps/sound/convert/sox-11gamma-cb3.tar.gz>` from `sunsite.unc.edu` at `/pub/Linux/apps/sound/convert/sox-11gamma-cb3.tar.gz`.

2.5.2 bplay

This *beta* program plays raw audio, WAV, and VOC files. It's also able to record to these files. It uses a variety of techniques to get the highest speed possible so that it can run acceptably even on slow machines. One of these techniques require that the installed programs be setuid root. The paranoid hoping to use this may want to use the Debian package by Ian Jackson (`ijackson@gnu.org`), which disables the feature that needs the setuid bit.

The author is David Monro (`davidm@gh.cs.usyd.edu.au`).

It can be obtained by *anonymous FTP* `<ftp://sunsite.unc.edu/pub/Linux/apps/sound/players/bplay-0.96.tar.gz>` from `sunsite.unc.edu` at `/pub/Linux/apps/sound/players/bplay-0.96.tar.gz`.

2.5.3 SIDPLAY

This program emulates the Sound Interface Device chip (MOS 6581, commonly called SID) and the Micro Processor Unit (MOS 6510) of the Commodore 64. Therefore it is able to load and execute C64 machine code programs which produce music or sound. In general these are independent fragments of code and data which have been ripped from games and demonstration programs and have been transferred directly from the C64.

It uses a command line interface by default. There are also Tk and QT interfaces available separately from the main package.

It is maintained by Michael Schwendt (`sidplay@geocities.com`).

It can be obtained from *SIDPLAY's home page* `<http://www.geocities.com/SiliconValley/Lakes/5147/>`.

2.5.4 RealAudio Player

This lets you listen to sound, which is stored in a proprietary format, in real time over the Internet without downloading the whole sound file first. It could be used stand alone, but it is really intended to be used along with a web browser (the explicitly supported ones are Mosaic and Netscape). It cannot be used without X (you wouldn't be able to get it working with Lynx in a text console).

This is by Progressive Networks, Inc. This cannot be redistributed, modified etc. Look at the license for exact details on what you can do. It can be obtained by registering with no cost at the *RealAudio home page* <http://www.realaudio.com/>.

2.5.5 cat

One might think what `cat`, the sometimes overused concatenating utility, has to do with playing sounds. I'll show a use of it through an example.

```
$ cat sample.voc > /dev/dsp
$ cat sample.wav > /dev/dsp
$ cat sample.au > /dev/audio
```

Doing a `cat` of an `.au` file to `/dev/audio` will usually work, and if you're lucky enough that the file has the correct byte order (for your platform) etc., a `cat` of a sound file that uses PCM samples (like `.wav` or `.voc`) to `/dev/dsp` might even sound right.

This isn't a totally useless use of `cat`. It might be useful, for example, if you have a sound file that none of your programs recognize, and you know that it uses PCM samples, then you might be able to get a very approximate idea on how it sounds like this way (if you're lucky).

3 Other useful sound utilities

This section has nothing to do with the actual playing of sound files. Rather, it is a collection of some sound utilities that one might find useful.

3.1 volume

This is a simple command line interface for controlling the volume (what else could it be?). It also has a separate program with a Tcl/Tk interface included in the package for controlling the volume and playing .au sound files. A very simple Tcl/Tk CD player is also included.

This is Freeware and it is written by Sam Lantinga (slouken@cs.ucdavis.edu).

It can be obtained by *anonymous FTP* <ftp://sunsite.unc.edu/pub/Linux/apps/sound/soundcard/volume-2.1.tar.gz> from sunsite.unc.edu at /pub/Linux/apps/sound/soundcard/volume-2.1.tar.gz.

3.2 Sound Studio

This is a Tcl/Tk application that supports playback, recording, and editing of digital sound using `sox`. It includes `sox` in the distribution to avoid compatibility problems.

This was written by Paul Sharpe and N. J. Bailey (N.J.Bailey@leeds.ac.uk). It may be freely used and redistributed if a postcard is sent.

It can be found at *Sound Studio's home page* <http://www.elec-eng.leeds.ac.uk/staff/een6njb/Software/Studio/screens.html>.

3.3 *Tickle Music*

This *beta* Tcl/Tk program is a music file browser that allows you to play various sound formats as long as an appropriate program to play it is on your system. By default `gmod` is used for playing MOD files and `mp` for playing MIDI files (you can change the source to use other programs).

It is written and copyrighted by Shannon Hendrix (`shendrix@pcs.cnu.edu` or `shendrix@escape.widomaker.com`).

It can be obtained by *anonymous FTP* `<ftp://sunsite.unc.edu/pub/Linux/apps/sound/players/tmusic-1.0.tar.gz>` from `sunsite.unc.edu` at `/pub/Linux/apps/sound/players/tmusic-1.0.tar.gz`.

4 References

1. The documentation included with the applications in this document.
2. The Linux Sound HOWTO. It can be found at the *Linux Documentation Project* `<http://sunsite.unc.edu/LDP/>`.
3. *The Linux MIDI and Sound Pages* `<http://www.digiserve.com/ar/linux-snd/>`
4. *MPEG Audio Layer 3 FAQ* `<http://www.iis.fhg.de/departs/amm/layer3/sw/>`
5. *Programmer's Guide to OSS* `<http://www.4front-tech.com/pguide/>`
6. *SoX home page* `<http://www.spies.com/Sox/>`

The Linux 3Dfx HOWTO

Bernd Kreimeier (*bk@gamers.org* <mailto:bk@gamers.org>)   v1.16 6. February 1998

This document describes 3Dfx graphics accelerator chip support for Linux. It lists some supported hardware, describes how to configure the drivers, and answers frequently asked questions.

Contents

1 Introduction

This is the Linux 3Dfx HOWTO document. It is intended as a quick reference covering everything you need to know to install and configure 3Dfx support under Linux. Frequently asked questions regarding the 3Dfx support are answered, and references are given to some other sources of information on a variety of topics related to computer generated, hardware accelerated 3D graphics.

This information is only valid for Linux on the Intel platform. Some information may be applicable to other processor architectures, but I have no first hand experience or information on this. It is only applicable to boards based on 3Dfx technology, any other graphics accelerator hardware is beyond the scope of this document.

1.1 Contributors and Contacts

This document would not have been possible without all the information contributed by other people - those involved in the Linux Glide port and the beta testing process, in the development of Mesa and the Mesa

Voodoo drivers, or rewieving the document on behalf of 3Dfx and Quantum3D. Some of them contributed entire sections to this document.

Daryll Strauss *daryll@harlot.rb.ca.us* `<mailto:DaryllStrauss<daryll@harlot.rb.ca.us>>` did the port, Paul J. Metzger *pjm@rbd.com* `<mailto:PaulJ.Metzger<pjm@rbd.com>>` modified the Mesa Voodoo driver (written by David Bucciarelli *tech.hmw@plus.it* `<mailto:DavidBucciarelli<tech.hmw@plus.it>>`) for Linux, Brian Paul *brianp@RA.AVID.COM* `<mailto:BrianPaul<brianp@RA.AVID.COM>>` integrated it with his famous Mesa library. With respect to Voodoo Graphics (tm) accelerated Mesa, additional thanks has to go to Henri Fousse, Gary McTaggart, and the maintainer of the 3Dfx Mesa for DOS, Charlie Wallace *Charlie.Wallace@unistudios.com* `<mailto:CharlieWallace<Charlie.Wallace@unistudios.com>>`. The folks at 3Dfx, notably Gary Sanders, Rod Hughes, and Marty Franz, provided valuable input, as did Ross Q. Smith of Quantum3D. The pages on the Voodoo Extreme and Operation 3Dfx websites provided useful info as well, and in some case I relied on the 3Dfx local Newsgroups. The Linux glQuake2 port that uses Linux Glide and Mesa is maintained by Dave Kirsch *zoid@idsoftware.com* `<mailto:DaveKirsch<zoid@idsoftware.com>>`. Thanks to all those who sent e-mail regarding corrections and updates, and special thanks to Mark Atkinson for reminding me of the dual cable setup.

Thanks to the SGML-Tools package (formerly known as Linuxdoc-SGML), this HOWTO is available in several formats, all generated from a common source file. For information on SGML-Tools see its homepage at *pobox.com/~cg/sgmltools* `<http://pobox.com/~cg/sgmltools>`.

1.2 Acknowledgments

3Dfx, the 3Dfx Interactive logo, Voodoo Graphics (tm), and Voodoo Rush (tm) are registered trademarks of 3Dfx Interactive, Inc. Glide, TexUS, Pixelfx and Texelfx are trademarks of 3Dfx Interactive, Inc. OpenGL is a registered trademark of Silicon Graphics. Obsidian is a trademark of Quantum3D. Other product names are trademarks of the respective holders, and are hereby considered properly acknowledged.

1.3 Revision History

Version 1.03
First version for public release.

Version 1.16
Current version v1.16 6. February 1998.

1.4 New versions of this document

You will find the most recent version of this document at *www.gamers.org/dEngine/xf3D/* `<http://www.gamers.org/dEngine/xf3D/>`.

New versions of this document will be periodically posted to the *comp.os.linux.answers* `<news:comp.os.linux.answers>` newsgroup. They will also be uploaded to various anonymous ftp sites that archive such information including *ftp://sunsite.unc.edu/pub/Linux/docs/HOWTO/* `<ftp://sunsite.unc.edu/pub/Linux/docs/HOWTO/>`.

Hypertext versions of this and other Linux HOWTOs are available on many World-Wide-Web sites, including *sunsite.unc.edu/LDP/* `<http://sunsite.unc.edu/LDP/>`. Most Linux CD-ROM distributions include the HOWTOs, often under the `/usr/doc/` directory, and you can also buy printed copies from several vendors.

If you make a translation of this document into another language, let me know and I'll include a reference to it here.

1.5   Feedback

I rely on you, the reader, to make this HOWTO useful. If you have any suggestions, corrections, or comments, please send them to me (*bk@gamers.org* `<mailto:bk@gamers.org>`), and I will try to incorporate them in the next revision. Please add `HOWTO 3Dfx` to the Subject-line of the mail, so procmail will dump it in the appropriate folder.

Before sending bug reports or questions, *please read all of the information in this HOWTO*, and *send detailed information about the problem.*

If you publish this document on a CD-ROM or in hardcopy form, a complimentary copy would be appreciated. Mail me for my postal address. Also consider making a donation to the Linux Documentation Project to help support free documentation for Linux. Contact the Linux HOWTO coordinator, Greg Hankins (*gregh@sunsite.unc.edu* `<mailto:gregh@sunsite.unc.edu>`), for more information.

1.6   Distribution Policy

Copyright (c) 1997, 1998 by Bernd Kreimeier. This document may be distributed under the terms set forth in the LDP license at *sunsite.unc.edu/LDP/COPYRIGHT.html* `<http://sunsite.unc.edu/LDP/COPYRIGHT.html>`.

This HOWTO is free documentation; you can redistribute it and/or modify it under the terms of the LDP license. This document is distributed in the hope that it will be useful, but **without any warranty**; without even the implied warranty of **merchantability** or **fitness for a particular purpose**. See the LDP license for more details.

2   Graphics Accelerator Technology

2.1   Basics

This section gives a *very* cursory overview of computer graphics accelerator technology, in order to help you understand the concepts used later in the document. You should consult e.g. a book on OpenGL in order to learn more.

2.2   Hardware configuration

Graphics accelerators come in different flavors: either as a separate PCI board that is able to pass through the video signal of a (possibly 2D or video accelerated) VGA board, or as a PCI board that does both VGA and 3D graphics (effectively replacing older VGA controllers). The 3Dfx boards based on the Voodoo Graphics (tm) belong to the former category. We will get into this again later.

If there is no address conflict, any 3D accelerator board could be present under Linux without interfering, but in order to access the accelerator, you will need a driver. A combined 2D/3D accelerator might behave differently.

2.3   A bit of Voodoo Graphics (tm) architecture

Usually, accessing texture memory and frame/depth buffer is a major bottleneck. For each pixel on the screen, there are at least one (nearest), four (bi-linear), or eight (tri-linear mipmapped) read accesses to texture memory, plus a read/write to the depth buffer, and a read/write to frame buffer memory.

The Voodoo Graphics (tm) architecture separates texture memory from frame/depth buffer memory by introducing two separate rendering stages, with two corresponding units (Pixelfx and Texelfx), each having a separate memory interface to dedicated memory. This gives an above-average fill rate, paid for restrictions in memory management (e.g. unused framebuffer memory can not be used for texture caching).

Moreover, a Voodoo Graphics (tm) could use two TMU's (texture management or texelfx units), and finally, two Voodoo Graphics (tm) could be combined with a mechanism called Scan-Line Interleaving (SLI). SLI essentially means that each Pixelfx unit effectively provides only every other scanline, which decreases bandwidth impact on each Pixelfx' framebuffer memory.

3 Installation

Configuring Linux to support 3Dfx accelerators involves the following steps:

1. Installing the board.
2. Installing the Glide distribution.
3. Compiling, linking and/or running the application.

The next sections will cover each of these steps in detail.

3.1 Installing the board

Follow the manufacturer's instructions for installing the hardware or have your dealer perform the installation. It should not be necessary to select settings for IRQ, DMA channel, either Plug&Pray (tm) or factory defaults should work. The add-on boards described here are memory mapped devices and do not use IRQ's. The only kind of conflict to avoid is memory overlap with other devices.

As 3Dfx does not develop or sell any boards, do not contact them on any problems.

3.1.1 Troubleshooting the hardware installation

To check the installation and the memory mapping, do `cat /proc/pci`. The output should contain something like

```
Bus  0, device  12, function  0:
  VGA compatible controller: S3 Inc. Vision 968 (rev 0).
    Medium devsel.  IRQ 11.
    Non-prefetchable 32 bit memory at 0xf4000000.

Bus  0, device  9, function  0:
  Multimedia video controller: Unknown vendor Unknown device (rev 2).
    Vendor id=121a. Device id=1.
    Fast devsel.  Fast back-to-back capable.
    Prefetchable 32 bit memory at 0xfb000000.
```

for a Diamond Monster 3D used with a Diamond Stealth-64. Additionally a `cat /proc/cpuinfo /proc/meminfo` might be helpfull for tracking down conflicts and/or submitting a bug report.

With current kernels, you will probably get a boot warning like

```
Jun 12 12:31:52 hal kernel: Warning : Unknown PCI device (121a:1).
Please read include/linux/pci.h
```

which could be safely ignored. If you happen to have a board not very common, or have encountered a new revision, you should take the time to follow the advice in /usr/include/linux/pci.h and send all necessary information to *linux-pcisupport@cao-vlsi.ibp.fr* <mailto:linux-pcisupport@cao-vlsi.ibp.fr>.

If you experience any problems with the board, you should try to verify that DOS and/or Win95 or NT support works. You will probably not receive any useful response from a board manufacturer on a bug report or request regarding Linux. Having dealt with the Diamond support e-mail system, I would not expect useful responses for other operating systems either.

3.1.2   Configuring the kernel

There is no kernel configuration necessary, as long as PCI support is enabled. The *Linux Kernel HOWTO* <http://sunsite.unc.edu/mdw/HOWTO/Kernel-HOWTO.html> should be consulted for the details of building a kernel.

3.1.3   Configuring devices

The current drivers do not (yet) require any special devices. This is different from other driver developments (e.g. the sound drivers, where you will find a /dev/dsp and /dev/audio). The driver uses the /dev/mem device which should always be available. In consequence, you need to use setuid or root privileges to access the accelerator board.

3.2   Setting up the Displays

There are two possible setups with add-on boards. You could either pass-through the video signal from your regular VGA board via the accelerator board to the display, or you could use two displays at the same time. Rely to the manual provided by the board manufacturer for details. Both configurations have been tried with the Monster 3D board.

3.2.1   Single screen display solution

This configuration allows you to check basic operations of the accelerator board - if the video signal is not transmitted to the display, hardware failure is possible.

Beware that the video output signal might deteoriate significantly if passed through the video board. To a degree, this is inevitable. However, reviews have complained about below-average of the cables provided e.g. with the Monster 3D, and judging from the one I tested, this has not changed.

There are other pitfalls in single screen configurations. Switching from the VGA display mode to the accelerated display mode will change resolution and refresh rate as well, even if you are using 640x480 e.g. with X11, too. Moreover, if you are running X11, your application is responsible for demanding all keyboard and mouse events, or you might get stuck because of changed scope and exposure on the X11 display (that is effectively invisible when the accelerated mode is used) You could use SVGA console mode instead of X11.

If you are going to use a single screen configuration and switch modes often, remember that your monitor hardware might not enjoy this kind of use.

3.2.2 Single screen dual cable setup

Some high end monitors (e.g. the EIZO F-784-T) come with two connectors, one with 5 BNC connectors for RGB, HSync, VSync, the other e.g. a regular VGA or a 13W3 Sub-D VGA. These displays usually also feature a front panel input selector to safely switch from one to the other. It is thus possible to use e.g. a VGA-to-BNC cable with your high end 2D card, and a VGA-to-13W3 Sub-D cable with your 3Dfx, and effectively run dual screen on one display.

3.2.3 Dual screen display solution

The accelerator board does not need the VGA input signal. Instead of routing the common video output through the accelerator board, you could attach a second monitor to its output, and use both at the same time. This solution is more expensive, but gives best results, as your main display will still be hires and without the signal quality losses involved in a pass-through solution. In addition, you could use X11 and the accelerated full screen display in parallel, for development and debugging.

A common problem is that the accelerator board will not provide any video signal when not used. In consequence, each time the graphics application terminates, the hardware screensave/powersave might kick in depending on your monitors configuration. Again, your hardware might not enjoy being treated like this. You should use

```
setenv SST_DUALSCREEN 1
```

to force continued video output in this setup.

3.3 Installing the Glide distribution

The Glide driver and library are provided as a single compressed archive. Use `tar` and `gzip` to unpack, and follow the instructions in the README and INSTALL accompanying the distribution. Read the install script and run it. Installation puts everything in /usr/local/glide/include,lib,bin and sets the ld.conf to look there. Where it installs and setting ld.conf are independent actions. If you skip the ld.conf step then you need the LD_LIBRARY_PATH.

You will need to install the header files in a location available at compile time, if you want to compile your own graphics applications. If you do not want to use the installation as above (i.e. you insist on a different location), make sure that any application could access the shared libary at runtime, or you will get a response like `can't load library 'libglide.so'`.

3.3.1 Using the detect program

There is a `bin/detect` program in the distribution (the source is not available). You have to run it as root, and you will get something like

slot	vendorId	devId	baseAddr0	command	description
00	0x8086	0x122d	0x00000000	0x0006	Intel:430FX (Triton)
07	0x8086	0x122e	0x00000000	0x0007	Intel:ISA bridge
09	0x121a	0x0001	0xfb000008	0x0002	3Dfx:video multimedia adapter
10	0x1000	0x0001	0x0000e401	0x0007	???:SCSI bus controller
11	0x9004	0x8178	0x0000e001	0x0017	Adaptec:SCSI bus controller
12	0x5333	0x88f0	0xf4000000	0x0083	S3:VGA-compatible display co.

as a result. If you do not have root privileges, the program will bail out with

```
Permission denied: Failed to change I/O privilege. Are you root?
```

output might come handy for a bug report as well.

3.3.2   Using the test programs

Within the Glide distribution, you will find a folder with test programs. Note that these test programs are under 3Dfx copyright, and are legally available for use only if you have purchased a board with a 3Dfx chipset. See the LICENSE file in the distribution, or their web site *www.3dfx.com* <http://www.3dfx.com/> for details.

It is recommend to compile and link the test programs even if there happen to be binaries in the distribution. Note that some of the programs will requires some files like `alpha.3df` from the distribution to be available in the same folder. All test programs use the 640x480 screen resolution. Some will request a variety of single character inputs, others will just state `Press A Key To Begin Test`. Beware of loss of input scope if running X11 on the same screen at the same time.

See the README.test for a list of programs, and other details.

4   Answers To Frequently Asked Questions

The following section answers some of the questions that (will) have been asked on the Usenet news groups and mailing lists. The FAQ has been subdivided into several parts for convenience, namely

- FAQ: Requirements?
- FAQ: Voodoo Graphics (tm)? 3Dfx?
- FAQ: Glide?
- FAQ: Glide and SVGA?
- FAQ: Glide and XFree86?
- FAQ: Glide versus OpenGL/Mesa?
- FAQ: But Quake?
- FAQ: Troubleshooting?

Each section lists several questions and answers, which will hopefully address most problems.

5   FAQ: Requirements?

5.1   What are the system requirements?

A Linux PC, PCI 2.1 compliant, a monitor capable of 640x480, and a 3D accelerator board based on the 3Dfx Voodoo Graphics (tm). It will work on a P5 or P6, with or without MMX. The current version does not use MMX, but it has some optimized code paths for P6.

At one point, some 3Dfx statements seemed to imply that using Linux Glide required using a RedHat distribution. Note that while Linux Glide has originally been ported in a RedHat 4.1 environment, it has been used and tested with many other Linux distributions, including homebrew, Slackware, and Debian 1.3.1.

5.2   Does it work with Linux-Alpha?

There is currently no Linux Glide distribution available for any platform besides i586. As the Glide sources are not available for distribution, you will have to wait for the binary. Quantum3D has DEC Alpha support announced for 2H97. Please contact Daryll Strauss if you are interested in supporting this.

There is also the issue of porting the the assembly modules. While there are alternative C paths in the code, the assembly module in Glide (essentially triangle setup) offered significant performance gains depending on the P5 CPU used.

5.3   Which 3Dfx chipsets are supported?

Currently, the 3Dfx Voodoo Graphics (tm) chipset is supported under Linux. The Voodoo Rush (tm) chipset is not yet supported.

5.4   Is the Voodoo Rush (tm) supported?

The current port of Glide to Linux does not support the Voodoo Rush (tm). An update is in the works.

The problem is that at one point the Voodoo Rush (tm) driver code in Glide depended on Direct Draw. There was an SST96 based DOS portion in the library that could theoretically be used for Linux, as soon as all portions residing in the 2D/Direct Draw/D3D combo driver are replaced.

Thus Voodoo Rush (tm) based boards like the *Hercules Stingray 128/3D* or *Intergraph Intense Rush* are not supported yet.

5.5   Which boards are supported?

There are no officially supported boards, as 3Dfx does not sell any boards. This section does not attempt to list all boards, it will just give an overview, and will list only boards that have been found to cause trouble.

It is important to recognize that Linux support for a given board does not only require a driver for the 3D accelerator component. If a board features its own VGA core as well, support by either Linux SVGA or XFree86 is required as well (see section about Voodoo Rush (tm) chipset). Currently, an add-on solution is recommended, as it allows you to choose a regular graphics board well supported for Linux. There are other aspects discussed below.

All Quantum3D Obsidian boards, independend of texture memory, frame buffer memory, number of Pixelfx and Texelfx units, and SLI should work. Same for all other Voodoo Graphics (tm) based boards, like Orchid Righteous 3D, Canopus Pure 3D, Flash 3D, and Diamond Monster 3D. Voodoo Rush (tm) based boards are not yet supported.

Boards that are not based on 3Dfx chipsets (e.g. manufactured by S3, Matrox, 3Dlabs, Videologic) do *not* work with the 3Dfx drivers and are beyond the scope of this document.

5.6   How do boards differ?

As the board manufacturers are using the same chipset, any differences are due to board design. Examples are quality of the pass-through cable and connectors (reportedly, Orchid provided better quality than Diamond), availability of a TV-compliant video signal output (Canopus Pure 3D), and, most notably, memory size on board.

Most common were boards for games with 2MB texture cache and 2 MB framebuffer memory, however, the Canopus Pure3D comes with a maximal 4 MB texture cache, which is an advantage e.g. with games using dynamically changed textures, and/or illumation textures (Quake, most notably). The memory architecture of a typical Voodoo Graphics (tm) board is described below, in a separate section.

Quantum 3D offers the widest selection of 3Dfx-based boards, and is probably the place to go if you are looking for a high end Voodoo Graphics (tm) based board configuration. Quantum 3D is addressing the visual simulation market, while most of the other vendors are only targetting the consumer-level PC-game market.

5.7   What about AGP?

There is no Voodoo Graphics (tm) or Voodoo Rush (tm) AGP board that I am aware of. I am not aware of AGP support under Linux, and I do not know whether upcmong AGP boards using 3Dfx technology might possibly be supported with Linux.

6   FAQ: Voodoo Graphics (tm)? 3Dfx?

6.1   Who is 3Dfx?

3Dfx is a San Jose based manufacturer of 3D graphics accelerator hardware for arcade games, game consoles, and PC boards. Their official website is *www.3dfx.com* <http://www.3dfx.com/>. 3Dfx does not sell any boards, but other companies do, e.g. Quantum3D.

6.2   Who is Quantum3D?

Quantum3D started as a 3Dfx spin-off, manufacturing high end accelerator boards based on 3Dfx chip technology for consumer and business market, and supplying arcade game technology. See their home page at *www.quantum3d.com* <http://www.quantum3d.com/> for additional information. For general inquiries regarding Quantum3D, please send mail to *info@quantum3d* <mailto:info@quantum3d>.

6.3   What is the Voodoo Graphics (tm)?

The Voodoo Graphics (tm) is a chipset manufactured by 3Dfx. It is used in hardware acceleration boards for the PC. See the HOWTO section on supported hardware.

6.4   What is the Voodoo Rush (tm)?

The Voodoo Rush (tm) is a derivate of the Voodoo Graphics (tm) that has an interface to cooperate with a 2D VGA video accelerator, effectively supporting accelerated graphics in windows. This combo is currently not supported with Linux.

6.5   What is the Voodoo 2 (tm)?

The Voodoo 2 (tm) is the successor of the Voodoo Graphics (tm) chipset, featuring several improvements. It is announced for late March 1998, and annoucements of Voodoo 2 (tm) based boards have been published e.g. by Quantum 3D, by Creative Labs, Orchid Technologies, and Diamond Multimedia.

The Voodoo 2 (tm) is supposed to be backwards compatible. However, a new version of Glide will have to be ported to Linux.

6.6   What is VGA pass-though?

The Voodoo Graphics (tm) (but not the Voodoo Rush (tm)) boards are add-on boards, meant to be used with a regular 2D VGA video accelerator board. In short, the video output of your regular VGA board is used as input for the Voodoo Graphics (tm) based add-on board, which by default passes it through to the display also connected to the Voodoo Graphics (tm) board. If the Voodoo Graphics (tm) is used (e.g. by a game), it will disconnect the VGA input signal, switch the display to a 640x480 fullscreen mode with the refresh rate configured by SST variables and the application/driver, and generate the video signal itself. The VGA doesn't need to be aware of this, and won't be.

This setup has several advantages: free choice of 2D VGA board, which is an issue with Linux, as XFree86 drivers aren't available for all chipsets and revisions, and a cost effective migration path to accelerated 3D graphics. It also has several disadvantages: an application using the Voodoo Graphics (tm) might not re-enable video output when crashing, and regular VGA video signal deteoriates in the the pass-through process.

6.7   What is Texelfx or TMU?

Voodoo Graphics (tm) chipsets have two units. The first one interfaces the texture memory on the board, does the texture mapping, and ultimately generates the input for the second unit that interfaces the frame-buffer. This one is called Texelfx, aka Texture Management Unit, aka TMU. The neat thing about this is that a board can use two Texelfx instead of only one, like some of the Quantum3D Obsidian boards did, effectively doubling the processing power in some cases, depending on the application.

As each Texelfx can address 4MB texture memory, a dual Texelfx setup has an effective texture cache of up to 8MB. This can be true even if only one Texelfx is actually needed by a particular application, as textures can be distributed to both Texelfx, which are used depending on the requested texture. Both Texelfx are used together to perform certain operations as trilinear filtering and illumination texture/lightmap passes (e.g. in glQuake) in a single pass instead of the two passes that are required with only one Texelfx. To actually exploit the theoretically available speedup and cache size increase, a Glide application has to use both Texelfx properly.

The two Texelfx can not be used separately to each draw a textured triangle at the same time. A triangle is always drawn using whatever the current setup is, which can be to use both Texelfx for a single pass operation combining two textures, or one Texelfx for only a single texture. Each Texelfx can only access its own memory.

6.8   What is a Pixelfx unit?

Voodoo Graphics (tm) chipsets have two units. The second one interfaces the framebuffer and ultimately generates the depth buffer and pixel color updates. This one is called Pixelfx. The neat thing here is that two Pixelfx units can cooperate in SLI mode, like with some of the Quantum3D Obsidian boards, effectively doubling the frame rate.

6.9   What is SLI mode?

SLI means "Scanline Interleave". In this mode, two Pixelfx are connected and render in alternate turns, one handling odd, the other handling even scanlines of the actual output. Inthis mode, each Pixelfx stores only half of the image and half of the depth buffer data in its own local framebuffer, effectively doubling the number of pixels.

The Pixelfx in question can be on the same board, or on two boards properly connected. Some Quantum3D Obsidian boards support SLI with Voodoo Graphics (tm).

As two cards can decode the same PCI addresses and receive the same data, there is not necessarily additional bus bandwidth required by SLI. On the other hand, texture data will have to be replicated on both boards, thus the amount of texture memory effectively stays the same.

6.10   Is there a single board SLI setup?

There are now two types of Quantum3D SLI boards. The intial setup used two boards, two PCI slots, and an interconnect (e.g. the Obsidian 100-4440). The later revision which performs identically is contained on one full-length PCI board (e.g. Obsidian 100-4440SB). Thus a single board SLI solution is possible, and has been done.

6.11   How much memory? How many buffers?

The most essential difference between different boards using the Voodoo Graphics (tm) chipset is the amount and organization of memory. Quantum3D used a three digit scheme to descibe boards. Here is a slightly modifed one (anticipating Voodoo 2 (tm)). Note that if you use more than one Texelfx, they need the same amount of texture cache memory each, and if you combine two Pixelfx, each needs the same amount of frame buffer memory.

```
"SLI / Pixelfx / Texelfx1 / Texelfx2 "
```

It means that a common 2MB+2MB board would be a 1/2/2/0 solution, with the minimally required total 4Mb of memory. A Canopus Pure 3D would be 1/2/4/0, or 6MB. An Obsidian-2220 board with two Texelfx would be 1/2/2/2, and an Obsidian SLI-2440 board would be 2/2/4/4. A fully featured dual board solution (2 Pixelfx, each with 2 Texelfx and 4MB frame buffer, each Texelfx 4 MB texture cache) would be 2/4/4/4, and the total amount of memory would be SLI*(Pixelfx+Texelfx1+Texelfx2), or 24 MB.

So there.

6.12   Does the Voodoo Graphics (tm) do 24 or 32 bit color?

No. The Voodoo Graphics (tm) architecture uses 16bpp internally. This is true for Voodoo Graphics (tm), Voodoo Rush (tm) and Voodoo 2 (tm) alike. Quantum3D claims to implement 22-bpp effective color depth with an enhanced 16-bpp frame buffer, though.

6.13   Does the Voodoo Graphics (tm) store 24 or 32 bit z-buffer per pixel?

No. The Voodoo Graphics (tm) architecture uses 16bpp internally for the depth buffer, too. This again is true for Voodoo Graphics (tm), Voodoo Rush (tm) and Voodoo 2 (tm) alike. Again, Quantum3D claims that using the floating point 16-bits per pixel (bpp) depth buffering provides 22-bpp effective Z-buffer precision.

6.14   What resolutions does the Voodoo Graphics (tm) support?

The Voodoo Graphics (tm) chipset supports up to 4 MB frame buffer memory. Presuming double buffering and a depth buffer, a 2MB framebuffer will support a resolution of 640x480. With 4 MB frame buffer, 800x600 is possible.

Unfortunately 960x720 is not supported. The Voodoo Graphics (tm) chipset requires that the amount of memory for a particular resolution must be such that the vertical and horizontal resolutions must be evenly divisible by 32. The video refresh controller, though can output any particular resolution, but the "virtual" size required for the memory footprint must be in dimensions evenly divisible by 32. So, 960x720 actually requires 960x736 amount of memory, and 960x736x2x3 = 4.04MBytes.

However, using two boards with SLI, or a dual Pixelfx SLI board means that each framebuffer will only have to store half of the image. Thus 2 times 4 MB in SLI mode are good up to 1024x768, which is the maximum because of the overall hardware design. You will be able to do 1024x768 tripled buffered with Z, but you will not be able to do e.g. 1280x960 with double buffering.

Note that triple buffering (no VSync synchonization required by the application), stereo buffering (for interfacing LCD shutters) and other more demanding setups will severely decrease the available resolution.

6.15   What texture sizes are supported?

The maximum texture size for the Voodoo Graphics (tm) chipset is 256x256, and you have to use powers of two. Note that for really small textures (e.g. 16x16) you are better off merging them into a large texture, and adjusting your effective texture coordinates appropriately.

6.16   Does the Voodoo Graphics (tm) support paletted textures?

The Voodoo Graphics (tm) hardware and Glide support the palette extension to OpenGL. The most recent version of Mesa does support the `GL_EXT_paletted_texture` and `GL_EXT_shared_texture_palette` extensions.

6.17   What about overclocking?

If you want to put aside considerations about warranty and overheating, and want to do overclocking to boost up performance even further, there is related info out on the web. The basic mechanism is to use Glide environment variables to adjust the clock.

Note that the actual recommended clock is board dependend. While the default clock speed is 50 Mhz, the Diamond Monster 3D property sheet lets you set up a clock of 57 MHz. It all comes down to the design of a specific board, and which components are used with the Voodoo Graphics (tm) chipset - most notably access speed of the RAM in question. If you exceed the limits of your hardware, rendering artifacts will occur to say the least. Reportedly, 57 MHz usually works, while 60 MHz or more is already pushing it.

Increasing the clock frequency also means increasing the waste heat disposed in the chips, in a nonlinear dependency (10% increase in frequency means a lot larger increase in heating). In consequence, for permanent overclocking you might want to educate yourself about ways to add cooling fans to the board in a way that does not affect warranty. A very recommendable source is the "3Dfx Voodoo Heat Report" by Eric van Ballegoie, available on the web.

6.18   Where could I get additional info on Voodoo Graphics (tm)?

There is a FAQ by 3Dfx, which should be available at their *web site* <http://www.3dfx.com/voodoo/faq. html>. You will find retail information at the following locations: *www.3dfx.com* <http://www.3dfx.com/ voodoo/sale/> and *www.quantum3d.com* <http://www.quantum3d.com/>.

Inofficial sites that have good info are "Voodoo Extreme" at *www.ve3d.com* <http://www.ve3d.com/>, and "Operation 3Dfx" at *www.ve3d.com* <http://www.ve3d.com/>.

7   FAQ: Glide? TexUS?

7.1   What is Glide anyway?

Glide is a proprietary API plus drivers to access 3D graphics accelerator hardware based on chipsets manufactured by 3Dfx. Glide has been developed and implemented for DOS, Windows, and Macintosh, and has been ported to Linux by Daryll Strauss.

7.2   What is TexUS?

In the distribution is a `libtexus.so`, which is the 3Dfx Interactive Texture Utility Software. It is an image processing libary and utility program for preparing images for use with the 3Dfx Interactive Glide library. Features of TexUS include file format conversion, MIPmap creation, and support for 3Dfx Interactive Narrow Channel Compression textures.

The TexUS utility program `texus` reads images in several popular formats (TGA, PPM, RGT), generates MIPmaps, and writes the images as 3Dfx Interactive textures files (see e.g. alpha.3df, as found in the distribution) or as an image file for inspection. For details on the parameters for `texus`, and the API, see the TexUS documentation.

7.3   Is Glide freeware?

Nope. Glide is neither GPL'ed nor subject to any other public license. See LICENSE in the distribution for any details. Effectively, by downloading and using it, you agree to the End User License Agreement (EULA) on the 3Dfx web site. Glide is provided as binary only, and you should neither use nor distribute any files but the ones released to the public, if you have not signed an NDA. The Glide distribution including the test program sources are copyrighted by 3Dfx.

The same is true for all the sources in the Glide distribution. In the words of 3Dfx: These are not public domain, but they can be freely distributed to owners of 3Dfx products only. No card, No code!

7.4 Where do I get Glide?

The entire 3Dfx SDK is available for download off their public web-site located at *www.3dfx.com/software/download_glide.html* <http://www.3dfx.com/software/download_glide.html>. Anything else 3Dfx publicly released by 3Dfx is nearby on their website, too.

There is also an FTP site, *ftp.3dfx.com* <ftp://ftp.3dfx.com/>. The FTP has a longer timeout, and some of the larger files have been broken into 3 files (approx. 3MB each).

7.5 Is the Glide source available?

Nope. The Glide source is made available only based on a special agreement and NDA with 3Dfx.

7.6 Is Linux Glide supported?

Currently, Linux Glide is unsupported. Basically, it is provided under the same disclaimers as the 3Dfx GL DLL (see below).

However, 3Dfx definitely wants to provide as much support as possible, and is in the process of setting up some prerequisites. For the time being, you will have to rely on the 3Dfx newsgroup (see below).

In addition, the Quantum3D web page claims that Linux support (for Obsidian) is planned for both Intel and AXP architecture systems in 2H97.

7.7 Where could I post Glide questions?

There are newsgroups currently available only on the NNTP server *news.3dfx.com* <news://news.3dfx.com/> run by 3Dfx. This USENET groups are dedicated to 3Dfx and Glide in general, and will mainly provide assistance for DOS, Win95, and NT. The current list includes:

```
3dfx.events
3dfx.games.glquake
3dfx.glide
3dfx.glide.linux
3dfx.products
3dfx.test
```

---

and the `3dfx.oem.products.*` group for specific boards, eg. `3dfx.oem.products.quantum3d.obsidian`. Please use *news.3dfx.com/3dfx.glide.linux* <news://news.3dfx.com/3dfx.glide.linux> for all Lnux Glide related questions.

A mailing list dedicated to Linux Glide is in preparation for 1Q98. Send mail to *majordomo@gamers.org* <mailto:majordomo@gamers.org>, no subject, body of the message `info linux-3dfx` to get information about the posting guidelines, the hypermail archive and how to subscribe to the list or the digest.

7.8   Where to send bug reports?

Currently, you should rely on the newsgroup (see above), that is *news.3dfx.com/3dfx.glide.linux* <news:
//news.3dfx.com/3dfx.glide.linux>. There is no official support e-mail set up yet. For questions not
specific to Linux Glide, make sure to use the other newsgroups.

7.9   Who is maintaining it?

3Dfx will appoint an official maintainer soon. Currently, inofficial maintainer of the Linux Glide port is
Daryll Strauss. Please post bug reports in the newsgroup (above). If you are confident that you found a bug
not previously reported, please mail to Daryll at *daryll@harlot.rb.ca.us* <mailto:daryll@harlot.rb.ca.us>

7.10   How can I contribute to Linux Glide?

You could submit precise bug reports. Providing sample programs to be included in the distribution is
another possibility. A major contribution would be adding code to the Glide based Mesa Voodoo driver
source. See section on Mesa Voodoo below.

7.11   Do I have to use Glide?

Yes. As of now, there is no other Voodoo Graphics (tm) driver available for Linux. At the lowest level, Glide
is the only interface that talks directly to the hardware. However, you can write OpenGL code without
knowing anything about Glide, and use Mesa with the Glide based Mesa Voodoo driver. It helps to be
aware of the involvement of Glide for recognizing driver limitations and bugs, though.

7.12   Should I program using the Glide API?

That depends on the application you are heading for. Glide is a proprietary API that is partly similar to
OpenGL or Mesa, partly contains features only available as EXTensions to some OpenGL implementations,
and partly contains features not available anywhere but within Glide.

If you want to use the OpenGL API, you will need Mesa (see below). Mesa, namely the Mesa Voodoo driver,
offers an API resembling the well documented and widely used OpenGL API. However, the Mesa Voodoo
driver is in early alpha, and you will have to accept performance losses and lack of support for some features.

In summary, the decision is up to you - if you are heading for maximum performance while accepting potential
problems with porting to non-3dfx hardware, Glide is not a bad choice. If you care about maintenance,
OpenGL might be the best bet in the long run.

7.13   What is the Glide current version?

The current version of Linux Glide is 2.4. The next version will probably be identical to the current version
for DOS/Windows, which is 2.4.3, which comes in two distributions. Right now, various parts of Glide
are different for Voodoo Rush (tm) (VR) and Voodoo Graphics (tm) (VG) boards. Thus you have to pick
up separate distributions (under Windows) for VR and VG. The same will be true for Linux. There will
possibly be another chunk of code and another distribution for Voodoo 2 (tm) (V2) boards.

There is also a Glide 3.0 in preparation that will extend the API for use of triangle fans and triangle strips,
and provide better state change optimization. Support for fans and strips will in some situations significantly

reduce the amount of data sent ber triangle, and the Mesa driver will benefit from this, as the OpenGL API has separate modes for this. For a detailed explanation on this see e.g. the OpenGL documentation.

7.14   Does it support multiple Texelfx already?

Multiple Texelfx/TMU's can be used for single pass trilinear mipmapping for improvement image quality without performance penalty in current Linux Glide already. You will need a board with two Texelfx (that is, one of the appropriate Quantum3D Obsidian boards). The application needs to specify the use of both Texelfx accordingly, it does not happen automatically.

Note that because most applications are implemented for consumer boards with a single Texelfx, they might not query the presence of a second Texelfx, and thus not use it. This is not a flaw of Glide but of the application.

7.15   Is Linux Glide identical to DOS/Windows Glide?

The publicly available version of Linux Glide should be identical to the respective DOS/Windows versions. Delays in releasing the Linux port of newer DOS/Windows releases are possible.

7.16   Where to I get information on Glide?

There is exhaustive information available from 3Dfx. You could download it from their home page at *www.3dfx.com/software/download_glide.html* <http://www.3dfx.com/software/download_glide.html>. These are for free, presuming you bought a 3Dfx hardware based board. Please read the licensing regulations.

Basically, you should look for some of the following:

- *Glide Release Notes*
- *Glide Programming Guide*
- *Glide Reference Manual*
- *Glide Porting Guide*
- *TexUs Texture Utility Software*
- *ATB Release Notes*
- *Installing and Using the Obsidian*

These are available as Microsoft Word documents, and part of the Windows Glide distribution, i.e. the self-extracting archive file. Postscript copies for separate download should be available at *www.3dfx.com* <http://www.3dfx.com/software/download_glide.html> as well. Note that the release numbers are not always in sync with those of Glide.

7.17   Where to get some Glide demos?

You will find demo sources for Glide within the distribution (test programs), and on the 3dfx home page. The problem with the latter is that some require ATB. To port these demos to Linux, the event handling has to be completely rewritten.

In addition, you might find useful some of the OpenGL demo sources accompanying Mesa and GLUT. While the Glide API is different from the OpenGL API, they target the same hardware rendering pipeline.

7.18   What is ATB?

Some of the 3Dfx demo programs for Glide depend not only on Glide but also on 3Dfx's proprietary Arcade Toolbox (ATB), which is available for DOS and Win32, but has not been ported for Linux. If you are a devleoper, the sources are available within the Total Immersion program, so porting ATB to Linux would be possible.

8   FAQ: Glide and XFree86?

8.1   Does it run with XFree86?

Basically, the Voodoo Graphics (tm) hardware does not care about X. The X server will not even notice that the video signal generated by the VGA hardware does not reach the display in single screen configurations. If your application is not written X aware, Glide switching to full screen mode might cause problems (see troubleshooting section). If you do not want the overhead of writing an X11-aware application, you might want to use SVGA console mode instead.

So yes, it does run with XFree86, but no, it is not cooperating if you don't write your application accordingly. You can use the Mesa "window hack", which will be significantly slower than fullscreen, but still a lot faster than software rendering (see section below).

8.2   Does it only run full screen?

See above. The Voodoo Graphics (tm) hardware is not window environment aware, neither is Linux Glide. Again, the experimental Mesa "window hack" covered below will allow for pasting the Voodoo Graphics (tm) board framebuffer's content into an X11 window.

8.3   What is the problem with AT3D/Voodoo Rush (tm) boards?

There is an inherent problem when using Voodoo Rush (tm) boards with Linux: Basically, these boards are meant to be VGA 2D/3D accelerator boards, either as a single board solution, or with a Voodoo Rush (tm) based daughterboard used transparently. The VGA component tied to the Voodoo Rush (tm) is a Alliance Semiconductor's ProMotion-AT3D multimedia accelerator. To use this e.g. with XFree86 at all, you need a driver for the AT3D chipset.

There is a mailing list on this, and a web site with FAQ at *www.frozenwave.com/linux-stingray128* <http: //www.frozenwave.com/linux-stingray128>. Look there for most current info. There is a SuSE maintained driver at *ftp.suse.com/suse_update/special/xat3d.tgz* <ftp://ftp.suse.com/suse_update/special/xat3d. tgz>. Reportedly, the XFree86 SVGA server also works, supporting 8, 16 and 32 bpp. Official support will probably be in XFree86 4.0. XFree86 decided to prepare an intermediate XFree86 3.3.2 release as well, which might already address the issues.

The following `XF86Config` settings reportedly work.

```
# device section settings
Chipset "AT24"
Videoram 4032

# videomodes tested by Oliver Schaertel
```

```
#  25.18  28.32  for 640 x 480   (70hz)
#  61.60         for 1024 x 786  (60hz)
#  120           for 1280 x 1024 (66hz)
```

In summary, there is nothing prohibiting this except for the fact that the drivers in XFree86 are not yet finished.

If you want a more technical explanation: Voodoo Rush (tm) support requires X server changes to support grabbing a buffer area in the video memory on the AT3D board, as the Voodoo Rush (tm) based boards need to store their back buffer and z buffer there. This memory allocation and locking requirement is not a 3Dfx specific problem, it is also needed e.g. for support of TV capture cards, and is thus under active development for XFree86. This means changes at the device dependend X level (thus XAA), which are currently implemented as an extension to XFree86 DGA (Direct Graphics Access, an X11 extension proposal implemented in different ways by Sun and XFree86, that is not part of the final X11R6.1 standard and thus not portable). It might be part of an XFree86 GLX implementation later on. The currently distributed X servers assume they have full control of the framebuffer, and use anything that is not used by the visual region of the framebuffer as pixmap cache, e.g. for caching fonts.

8.4   What about GLX for XFree86?

There are a couple of problems.

The currently supported Voodoo Graphics (tm) hardware and the available revision of Linux Glide are full screen only, and not set up to share a framebuffer with a window environment. Thus GLX or other integration with X11 is not yet possible.

The Voodoo Rush (tm) might be capable of cooperating with XFree86 (that is, an SVGA compliant board will work with the XFree86 SVGA server), but it is not yet supported by Linux Glide, nor do S3 or other XFree86 servers support these boards yet.

In addition, GLX is tied to OpenGL or, in the Linux case, to Mesa. The XFree86 team is currently working on integrating Mesa with their X Server. GLX is in beta, XFree86 3.3 has the hooks for GLX. See Steve Parker's GLX pages at *www.cs.utah.edu/~sparker/xfree86-3d/* <http://www.cs.utah.edu/~sparker/xfree86-3d/> for the most recent information. Moreover, there is a joint effort by XFree86 and SuSe, which includes a GLX, see *www.suse.de/~sim/* <http://www.suse.de/~sim/>. Currently, Mesa still uses its GLX emulation with Linux.

8.5   Glide and commerical X Servers?

I have not received any mail regarding use of Glide and/or Mesa with commercial X Servers. I would be interested to get confirmation on this, especially on Mesa and Glide with a commercial X Server that has GLX support.

8.6   Glide and SVGA?

You should have no problems running Glide based applications either single or dual screen using VGA modes. It might be a good idea to set up the 640x480 resolution in the SVGA modes, too, if you are using a single screen setup.

8.7   Glide and GGI?

A GGI driver for Glide is under development by Jon M. Taylor, but has not officially been released and was put on hold till completion of GGI 0.0.9. For information about GGI see *synergy.caltech.edu/~ggi/* <http://synergy.caltech.edu/~ggi/>. If you are adventurous, you might find the combination of XGGI (a GGI based X Server for XFree86) and GGI for Glide an interesting prospect. There is also a GGI driver interfacing the OpenGL API; tested with unaccelerated Mesa. Essentially, this means X11R6 running on a Voodoo Graphics (tm), using either Mesa or Glide directly.

9   FAQ: OpenGL/Mesa?

9.1   What is OpenGL?

OpenGL is an immediate mode graphics programming API originally developed by SGI based on their previous proprietary Iris GL, and became in industry standard several years ago. It is defined and maintained by the Architectural Revision Board (ARB), an organization that includes members as SGI, IBM, and DEC, and Microsoft.

OpenGL provides a complete feature set for 2D and 3D graphics operations in a pipelined hardware accelerated architecture for triangle and polygon rendering. In a broader sense, OpenGL is a powerful and generic toolset for hardware assisted computer graphics.

9.2   Where to get additional information on OpenGL?

The official site for OpenGL maintained by the members of the ARB, is *www.opengl.org* <http://www.opengl.org/>,

A most recommended site is Mark Kilgard's Gateway to OpenGL Info at *reality.sgi.com/mjk_asd/opengl-links.html* <http://reality.sgi.com/mjk_asd/opengl-links.html>: it provides pointers to book, online manual pages, GLUT, GLE, Mesa, ports to several OS, tons of demos and tools.

If you are interested in game programming using OpenGL, there is the OpenGL-GameDev-L@fatcity.com at Listserv@fatcity.com. Be warned, this is a high traffic list with very technical content, and you will probably prefer to use procmail to handle the 100 messages per day coming in. You cut down bandwidth using the SET OpenGL-GameDev-L DIGEST command. It is also not appropriate if you are looking for introductions. The archive is handled by the ListServ software, use the INDEX OpenGL-GameDev-L and GET OpenGL-GameDev-L "filename" commands to get a preview before subscribing.

9.3   Is Glide an OpenGL implementation?

No, Glide is a proprietary 3Dfx API which several features specific to the Voodoo Graphics (tm) and Voodoo Rush (tm). A 3Dfx OpenGL is in preparation (see below). Several Glide features would require EXTensions to OpenGL, some of which already found in other implementations (e.g. paletted textures).

The closest thing to a hardware accelerated Linux OpenGL you could currently get is Brian Paul's Mesa along with David Bucciarelli's Mesa Voodoo driver (see below).

9.4 Is there an OpenGL driver from 3Dfx?

Both the 3Dfx website and the Quantum3D website announced OpenGL for Voodoo Graphics (tm) to be available 4Q97. The driver is currently in Beta, and accessible only to registered deverloper's under written Beta test agreement.

A linux port has not been announced yet.

9.5 Is there a commercial OpenGL for Linux and 3Dfx?

I am not aware of any third party commercial OpenGL that supports the Voodoo Graphics (tm). Last time I paid attention, neither MetroX nor XInside OpenGL did.

9.6 What is Mesa?

Mesa is a free implementation of the OpenGL API, designed and written by Brian Paul, with contributions from many others. Its performance is competitive, and while it is not officially certified, it is an almost fully compliant OpenGL implementation conforming to the ARB specifications - more complete than some commercial products out, actually.

9.7 Does Mesa work with 3Dfx?

The latest Mesa MesaVer; release works with Linux Glide 2.4. In fact, support was included in earlier versions, however, this driver is still under development, so be prepared for bugs and less than optimal performance. It is steadily improving, though, and bugs are usually fixed very fast.

You will need to get the Mesa library archive from the *iris.ssec.wisc.edu FTP site* <ftp://iris.ssec.wisc.edu/>. It is recommended to subscribe to the mailing list as well, especially when trying to track down bugs, hardware, or driver limitations. Make sure to get the most recent distribution. A Mesa-3.0 is in preparation.

9.8 How portable is Mesa with Glide?

It is available for Linux and Win32, and any application based on Mesa will only have the usual system specific code, which should usually mean XWindows vs. Windows, or GLX vs. WGL. If you use e.g. GLUT or Qt, you should get away with any system specifics at all for virtually most applications. There are only a few issues (like sampling relative mouse movement) that are not adressed by the available portable GUI toolkits.

Mesa/Glide is also available for DOS. The port which is 32bit DOS is maintained by Charlie Wallace and kept up to date with the main Mesa base. See *www.geocities.com/~charlie_x/* <http://www.geocities.com/~charlie_x/>.for the most current releases.

9.9 Where to get info on Mesa?

The Mesa home page is at *www.ssec.wisc.edu/~brianp/Mesa.html* <http://www.ssec.wisc.edu/~brianp/Mesa.html>. There is an archive of the Mesa mailing list. at *www.iqm.unicamp.br/mesa/* <http://www.iqm.unicamp.br/mesa/>. This list is not specific to 3Dfx and Glide, but if you are interested in using 3Dfx hardware to accelerate Mesa, it is a good place to start.

9.10   Where to get information on Mesa Voodoo?

For latest information on the Mesa Voodoo driver maintained by David Bucciarelli *tech.hmw@plus.it* <mailto:tech.hmw@plus.it> see the home page at *www-hmw.caribel.pisa.it/fxmesa/* <http://www-hmw. caribel.pisa.it/fxmesa/index.shtml>.

9.11   Does Mesa support multitexturing?

Not yet (as of Mesa 2.6), but it is on the list. In Mesa you will probably have to use the OpenGL `EXT_multitexture` extension once it is available. There is no final specification for multitextures in OpenGL, which is supposed to be part of the upcoming OpenGL 1.2 revision. There might be a Glide driver specific implementation of the extension in upcoming Mesa releases, but as long as only certain Quantum3D Obsidian boards come with multiple TMU's, it is not a top priority. This will surely change once Voodoo 2 (tm) based boards are in widespread use.

9.12   Does Mesa support single pass trilinear mipmapping?

Multiple TMU's should be used for single pass trilinear mipmapping for improvement image quality without performance penalty in current Linux Glide already. Mesa support is not yet done (as of Mesa 2.6), but is in preparation.

9.13   What is the Mesa "Window Hack"?

The most recent revisions of Mesa contain an experimental feature for Linux XFree86. Basically, the GLX emulation used by Mesa copies the contents of the Voodoo Graphics (tm) board's most recently finished framebuffer content into video memory on each `glXSwapBuffers` call. This feature is also available with Mesa for Windows.

This obviously puts some drain on the PCI, doubled by the fact that this uses X11 MIT SHM, not XFree86 DGA to access the video memory. The same approach could theoretically be used with e.g. SVGA. The major benefit is that you could use a Voodoo Graphics (tm) board for accelerated rendering into a window, and that you don't have to use the VGA passthrough mode (video output of the VGA board deteoriates in passing through, which is very visible with high end monitors like e.g. EIZO F784-T).

Note that this experimental feature is *NOT* Voodoo Rush (tm) support by any means. It applies only to the Voodoo Graphics (tm) based boards. Moreover, you need to use a modified GLUT, as interfacing the window management system and handling the events appropriately has to be done by the application, it is not handled in the driver.

Make really sure that you have enabled the following environment variables:

```
export SST_VGA_PASS=1        # to stop video signal switching
export SST_NOSHUTDOWN=1      # to stop video signal switching
export MESA_GLX_FX="window"  # to initiate Mesa window mode
```

If you manage to forget one of the SST variables, your VGA board will be shut off, and you will loose the display (but not the actual X). It is pretty hard to get that back being effectively blind.

Finally, note that the libMesaGL.a (or .so) library can contain multiple client interfaces. I.e. the GLX, OSMesa, and fxMesa (and even SVGAMesa) interfaces call all be compiled into the same libMesaGL.a. The client program can use any of them freely, even simultaneously if it's careful.

9.14   How about GLUT?

Mark Kilgard's GLUT distribution is a very good place to get sample applications plus a lot of useful utilities. You will find it at *reality.sgi.com/mjk_asd/glut3/* <http://reality.sgi.com/mjk_asd/glut3/glut3.html>, and you should get it anyway. The current release is GLUT 3.6, and discussion on a GLUT 3.7 (aka GameGLUT) has begun. Note that Mark Kilgard has left SGI recently, so the archive might move some time this year - for the time being it will be kept at SGI.

There is also a GLUT mailing list, `glut@perp.com`. Send mail to *majordomo@perp.com* <mailto:Majordomo@ perp.com>, with the (on of the) following in the body of your email message:

```
help
info glut
subscribe glut
end
```

As GLUT handles double buffers, windows, events, and other operations closely tied to hardware and operating system, using GLUT with Voodoo Graphics (tm) requires support, which is currently in development within GLX for Mesa. It already works for most cases.

10   FAQ: But Quake?

10.1   What about that 3Dfx GL driver for Quake?

The 3Dfx Quake GL, aka mini-driver, aka miniport, aka Game GL, aka 3Dfx GL alpha, implemented only a Quake-specific subset of OpenGL (see *http://www.cs.unc.edu/~martin/3dfx.html* <http://www.cs.unc.edu/ ~martin/3dfx.html> for an inofficial list of supported code paths). It is not supported, and not updated anymore. It was a Win32 DLL (`opengl32.dll`) released by 3Dfx and was available for Windows only. This DLL is not, and will not be ported to Linux.

10.2   Is there a 3Dfx based glQuake for Linux?

Yes. A Quake linuxquake v0.97 binary has been released based on Mesa with Glide. The Quake2 q2test binary for Linux and Voodoo Graphics (tm) has been made available as well. A full Quake2 for Linux was released in January 1998, with linuxquake2-3.10. Dave "Zoid" Kirsch is the official maintainer of all Linux ports of Quake, Quakeworld, and Quake2, including all the recent Mesa based ports. Note that all Linux ports, including the Mesa based ones, are not officially supported by id Software.

See *ftp.idsoftware.com/idstuff/quake/unix/* <ftp://ftp.idsoftware.com/idstuff/quake/unix/> for the latest releases.

10.3   Does glQuake run in an XFree86 window?

A revision of Mesa and the Mesa-based Linux glQuake is in preparation. Mesa already does support this by GLX, but Linux glQuake does not use GLX.

10.4   Known Linux Quake problems?

Here is an excerpt, as of January 7th, 1998. I omitted most stuff not specific to &3Dfx; hardware.

- You really should run Quake2 as root when using the SVGALib and/or GL renders. You don't have to run as root for the X11 refresh, but the modes on the mouse and sound devices must be read/writable by whatever user you run it as. Dedicated server requires no special permissions.

- X11 has some garbage on the screen when 'loading'. This is normal in 16bit color mode. X11 doesn't work in 24bit (TrueColor). It would be very slow in any case.

- Some people are experiencing crashes with the GL renderer. Make sure you install the libMesa that comes with Quake2! Older versions of libMesa don't work properly.

- If you are experience video 'lag' in the GL renderer (the frame rate feels like it's lagging behind your mouse movement) type "gl_finish 1" in the console. This forces update on a per frame basis.

- When running the GL renderer, make sure you have killed selection and/or gpm or the mouse won't work as they won't "release" it while Quake2 is running in GL mode.

10.5   Know Linux Quake security problems?

As Dave Kirsch posted on January 28th, 1998: an exploit for Quake2 under Linux has been published. Quake2 is using shared libraries. While the READMRE so far does not specifically mention it, note that Quake2 should not be `setuid`.

If you want to use the `ref_soft` and `ref_gl` renderers, you should run Quake2 as root. Do not make the binary setuid. You can only run both those renderers at the console only, so being root is not that much of an issue.

The X11 render does not need any root permissions (if `/dev/dsp` is writable by others for sound). The dedicated server mode does not need to be root either, obviously.

Problems such as root requirements for games has been sort of a sore spot in Linux for a number of years now. This is one of the goals that e.g. GGI is targetting to fix. A `ref_ggi` might be supported in the near future.

10.6   Does LinuxQuake use multitexturing?

To my understadnding, glQuake will use a multitexture EXTension if the OpenGL driver in question offers it. The current Mesa implementation and the Glide driver for Linux do not yet support this extension, so for the time being the answer is no. See section on Mesa and multitexturing for details.

10.7   Where can I get current information on Linux glQuake?

Try some of these sites: the "The Linux Quake Resource" at *linuxquake.telefragged.com* <http://linuxquake.telefragged.com/>, or the "Linux Quake Page" at *www.planetquake.com/threewave/linux/* <http://www.planetquake.com/threewave/linux/>. Alternatively, you could look for Linux Quake sites in the "SlipgateCentral" database at *www.slipgatecentral.com* <http://www.slipgatecentral.com/>.

11 FAQ: Troubleshooting?

11.1 Has this hardware been tested?

See hardware requirements list above. I currently do not maintain a conclusive list of vendors and boards, as no particular board specific problems have been verified. Currently, only 3Dfx and Quantum3D provide boards for testing to the developers, so Quantum3D consumer boards are a safe bet. Every other Voodoo Graphics (tm) based board should work, too. I have reports regarding the Orchid Righteous 3D, Guillemot Maxi 3D Gamer, and Diamond Monster 3D.

If you are a board manufacturer who wants to make sure his Voodoo Graphics (tm), Voodoo Rush (tm) or Voodoo 2 (tm) boards work with upcoming releases of Linux, Xfree86, Linux Glide and/or Mesa, please contact me, and I will happily forward your request to the persons maintaining the drivers in question. If you are interested in support for Linux Glide on other then the PC platfrom, e.g. DEC Alpha, please contact the maintainer of Linux Glide Daryll Strauss, at *daryll@harlot.rb.ca.us* `<mailto:daryll@harlot.rb.ca.us>`

11.2 Failed to change I/O privilege?

You need to be root, or `setuid` your application to run a Glide based application. For DMA, the driver accesses `/dev/mem`, which is not writeable for anybody but root, with good reasons. See the README in the Glide distribution for Linux.

11.3 Does it work without root privilege?

There are compelling case where the setuid requirement is a problem, obviously. There are currently solutions in preparation, which require changes to the library internals itself.

11.4 Displayed images looks awful (single screen)?

If you are using the analog pass through configuration, the common SVGA or X11 display might look pretty bad. You could try to get a better connector cable than the one provided with the accelerator board (the ones delivered with the Diamond Monster 3D are reportedly worse then the one accompanying the Orchid Righteous 3D), but up to a degree there will inevitably be signal loss with an additional transmission added.

If the 640x480 full screen image created by the accelerator board does look awful, this might indicate a real hardware problem. You will have to contact the board manufacturer, not 3Dfx for details, as the quality of the video signal has nothing to do with the accelerator - the board manufacturer chooses the RAMDAC, output drivers, and other components responsible.

11.5 The last frame is still there (single or dual screen)?

You terminated your application with Ctrl-C, or it did not exit normally. The accelerator board will dutifully provide the current content of the framebuffer as a video signal unless told otherwise.

11.6 Powersave kicks in (dual screen)?

When you application terminates in dual screen setups, the accelerator board does not provide video output any longer. Thus powersave kicks each time. To avoid this, use

```
setenv SST_DUALSCREEN 1
```

11.7   My machine seem to lock (X11, single screen)?

If you are running X when calling a Glide application, you probably moved the mouse out of the window, and the keyboard inputs do not reach the application anymore.

If you application is supposed to run concurrently with X11, it is recommend to expose a full screen window, or use the `XGrabPointer` and `XGrabServer` functions to redirect all inputs to the application while the X server cannot access the display. Note that grabbing all input with `XGrabPointer` and `XGrabServer` does not qualify as well-behaved application, and that your program might block the entire system.

If you experience this problem without running X, be sure that there is no hardware conflict (see below).

11.8   My machine locks (single or dual screen)?

If the system definitely does not respond to any inputs (you are running two displays and know about the loss of focus), you might experience a more or less subtle hardware conflict. See installation troubleshooting section for details.

If there is no obvious address conflict, there might still be other problems (below). If you are writing your own code the most common reason for locking is that you didn't snap your vertices. See the section on snapping in the Glide documentation.

11.9   My machine locks (used with S3 VGA board)?

It is possible you have a problem with memory region overlap specific to S3. There is some info and a patch to the so-called S3 problem in the 3Dfx web site, but these apply to Windows only. To my understanding, the cause of the problem is that some S3 boards (older revisions of Diamond Stealth S3 968) reserve more memory space than actually used, thus the Voodoo Graphics (tm) has to be mapped to a different location. However, this has not been reported as a problem with Linux, and might be Windows-specific.

11.10   No address conflict, but locks anyway?

If you happen to use a motherboard with non-standard or incomplete PCI support, you could try to shuffle the boards a bit. I am running an ASUS TP4XE that has that non-standard modified "Media Slot", i.e. PCI slot4 with additional connector for ASUS-manufactured SCSI/Sound combo boards, and I experienced severe problems while running a Diamond Monster 3D in that slot. The system operates flawlessly since I put the board in one of the regular slots.

11.11   Mesa runs, but does not access the board?

Be sure that you recompiled all the libraries (including the toolkits the demo programs use - remember that GLUT does not yet support Voodoo Graphics (tm)), and that you removed the older libraries, run `ldconfig`, and/or set your `LD_LIBRARY_PATH` properly. Mesa supports several drivers in parallel (you could use X11 SHM, off screen rendering, and Mesa Voodoo at the same time), and you might have to create and switch contexts explicitly (see `MakeCurrent` function) if the Voodoo Graphics (tm) isn't chosen by default.

11.12 Resetting dual board SLI?

If a Quantum 3D Obsidian board using in an SLI setup exits abruptly (i.e., the application crashes, or is aborted by user), the boards are left in an undefined state. With the dual-board set, you can run a program called `resetsli` to reset them. Until you run the `resetsli` program, you will not be able to re-initialize the Obsidian board.

11.13 Resetting single board SLI?

The `resetsli` program mentioned above does not yet work with a single board Obsidian SLI (e.g. the Obsidian 100-4440SB). You will have to reboot your system by reset in order to reset the board.

Battery Powered Linux Mini-HOWTO

Hanno Mueller, *hanno@lava.de* <mailto:hanno@lava.de> *http://www.lava.de/~hanno/* <http://www.lava.de/~hanno/>
Dec 21, 1997

This document describes how to reduce a Linux system's power consumption by tweaking some of its configuration settings. This will be helpful for everyone who runs Linux on a portable computer system. There is also some general information about how to take care of your battery. If you are using Linux on a desktop system, you probably don't need to read all this.

1 Introduction

"Ages 6 and up. Batteries included."

1.1 Before you ask

This document does not describe how to install Linux on laptops, but how to optimize a ready-configured Linux for use on laptops. Please read the *Installation-HOWTO* or your distributor's handbook for help with installing Linux.

This document does not describe how to use an uninterruptable power supply and the **powerd** daemon, either (even though a ups is a big battery). Read the *UPS-HOWTO* for details about that subject.

1.2 What this document is about

More and more people own portable computers these days and in turn, more and more people install Linux on such machines.

Installing and using Linux on a laptop is usually no problem at all, so go ahead and give it a try. Unlike some other operating systems, Linux still supports and runs well on even very old hardware, so you might give your outdated portable a new purpose in life by installing Linux on it.

If you need help with installing Linux on a laptop or if you have questions about laptop hardware, you can check the excellent *Linux Laptop webpage* at *http://www.cs.utexas.edu/users/kharker/linux-laptop/* <http://www.cs.utexas.edu/users/kharker/linux-laptop/> where you will find a lot of useful information and detailed help. The Linux Laptop page describes hardware configuration for specific laptop models and chipsets.

This HOWTO however will focus on the one problem that is common to all portable systems: *Power consumption*.

Yet, I have not found a Linux distribution that comes with a configuration *optimized* for laptops. Since I could not find this kind of information anywhere else, I have started to collect a few simple but effective tricks that will help you save battery power and in turn increase your system's uptime while running on battery.

(Sidenote. I received a complaint by a reader that these tips were not very effective with his laptop. So does all this really work? Yes, but don't expect miracles. I was able to increase my laptop's battery time from 90 minutes to more than 120 minutes.)

1.3 Roadmap

If you are a laptop pro, you can probably skip the 2 (General Information) section. If you are a Linux pro, what you really want to know can be found in the 4 (Changing some general system settings) section. If you are a Linux distributor, please read 5.1 (A message to Linux distributors).

1.4 Feedback

Your feedback is welcome. Please send comments to *hanno@lava.de* <mailto:hanno@lava.de>. Did it work on your system? Do you have new tips? Are there any outdated links or addresses in this text?

I am sorry, but I will not be able to help you with questions about specific laptop models. I don't claim to be a laptop guru, I just happen to own one laptop myself and I simply want to share the information I collected. Please check the Linux Laptop webpage first, probably someone else has already written a page dedicated to your model. Ask your manufacturer's technical support. Or go the the laptop newsgroup *comp.sys.laptops* <news:comp.sys.laptops> and ask there.

1.5 Disclaimer

All methods described here were tested by me and worked fine on my laptop, unless noted otherwise. However, I cannot guarantee that any of this won't crash or seriously damage your system. Life is dangerous, so keep backup copies of your important files before playing with your Linux configuration. If things go wrong, I do not take any responsibility for your data loss. In other words: Don't sue me. Thank you.

1.6 Copyright

This document shall be distributed under the standard HOWTO-copyright notice, found in the HOWTO folder at *http://sunsite.unc.edu/mdw/linux.html* <http://sunsite.unc.edu/mdw/linux.html>.

2 General information

This section describes a few technical things about laptop batteries and some general power saving tips. This information is not Linux-specific and if you are experienced with laptops, you might already know all this.

2.1 Be kind to your battery

(Please note the 5.2 (credits) for this section.)

There are currently three types of batteries commonly used for portable computers.

- *NiCd* batteries were the standard technology for years, but today they are out of date and new laptops don't use them anymore. They are heavy and very prone to the "memory effect". When recharging a NiCd battery that has not been fully discharged, it "remembers" the old charge and continues there the next time you use it.

  The memory effect is caused by crystallization of the battery's substances and can permanently reduce your battery's lifetime, even make it useless. To avoid it, you should completely discharge the battery and then fully recharge it again at least once every few weeks.

(A sidenote about the memory effect. James Youngman knows of a rather drastic method to - uhm - "repair" batteries: "If your NiCd battery is suffering from the memory effect, remove it from your computer, hold it about 30cm above a desk or the floor, and drop it (make sure it lands flat)." He says that this will break the whiskers that have formed in the battery and that are the cause of the memory effect if your battery is already affected by it. "I don't know if this works for non-NiCd batteries or not.")

Cadmium is a very hazardous poison, but if returned to your dealer, the material can almost be fully recycled.

Just in case you might be interested, here are some specs for NiCd:

```
Cell voltage: 1,2 V
Energy / mass: 40 Wh/kg
Energy / volume: 100 Wh/l
max. Energy: 20 Wh
Charge temp.: 10 to 35 C (50 to 95 F)
Discharge temp.: -20 to 50 C (-5 to 120 F)
Storage temp.: 0 to 45 C (30 to 115 F)
```

- *NiMh* batteries are the current standard used in most low price laptops to date. They can be made smaller and are less affected by the memory effect than NiCd.

  However, they have problems at very high or low room temperatures. And even though they use less hazardous and non-poisonous substances, they cannot be fully recycled yet (but this will probably change in the future).

  NiMh specs:

```
Cell voltage: 1,2 V
Energy / mass: 55 Wh/kg
Energy / volume: 160 Wh/l
max. Energy: 35 Wh
Charge temp.: 10 to 35 C (50 to 95 F)
Discharge temp.: 0 to 45 C (30 to 115 F)
Storage temp.: 0 to 30 C (30 to 85 F)
```

- The new high performance batteries use *LiIon* technology. In theory, there is no memory effect at all with these batteries, but on occasion, they seem to have similar problems. Their substances are non-hazardous to the enviroment, but they should be returned for recycling as well.

  LiIon specs:

```
Cell voltage: 3,6 V
Energy / mass: 100 Wh/kg
Energy / volume: 230 Wh/l
max. Energy: 60 Wh
Charge temp.: 0 to 45 C (30 to 115 F)
Discharge temp.: -20 to 60 C (-5 to 140 F)
Storage temp.: -20 to 60 C (-5 to 140 F)
```

Even if the battery case looks the same, you cannot just upgrade to another battery technology. The recharging process is different for the kind of battery you use.

Some manufacturers integrate the recharging circuit inside the laptop's external ac adapter, so you might just get away with buying a new power supply to upgrade. A good indication for an external recharging unit is when your ac adapter uses a proprietary connector with a lot of power lines.

Other manufacturers put the recharging unit inside the laptop case where users cannot simply replace it with a newer technology. If your ac adapter only uses two power lines to connect to the computer (just like mine), the recharging unit is probably inside the laptop.

When in doubt, ask your manufacturer if your laptop supports a more modern battery.

A battery that is not used for a long time will slowly discharge itself. And even with greatest care, a battery needs to be replaced after 500 to 1000 recharges. But still it is not recommended to run a laptop without the battery while on ac power - the battery often serves as a big capacitor to protect against voltage peaks from your ac outlet.

As the manufacturers change the shapes of their batteries every few months, you might have problems to find a new battery for your laptop in a few years from now. Buy a spare battery now - before it's out of stock.

2.2 Power saving - The obvious stuff

There are some obvious things that you can do to reduce your system's power consumption. Well, maybe not so obvious, since not very many people follow these rules...

- Decrease or turn off your display's backlight when you don't need it. By the way, tft displays use more power than dstn (so now you have a fine excuse why you bought the cheaper laptop...).

  (David Bateman tells me that using a crt screen while on battery and turning off the laptop display will extend battery time by about 30%: "Not that this is a very useful piece of knowledge though, if you've got the crt plugged in then why not the laptop too.")

- How much processing power do you really need? I doubt that you will be doing very much more than text editing when on the road (well, at least I don't compile linux kernels then). While on battery, reducing the cpu clock speed will decrease power consumption, too. Quite a few laptops offer a cpu clock selector that will toggle between normal and slow speed.

- Turn off the cpu cooler (if you have one). Many recent laptops offer a bios option called "cooling control". If your system's cpu is becoming too hot, this option allows you to have it cooled by a tiny fan (setting "performance") or to have its cpu clock slowed down (setting "silence"). To increase your uptime while on battery, use "silence".

- Avoid using external devices (printer, crt screen, zip drive, portable camera etc.) with your computer while on battery. When connected to a standard ink jet printer, my laptop's battery time is reduced from up to 120 minutes down to 20 minutes.

- Avoid using any built in device unless necessairy: Diskette drive, harddisk, cd-rom. Especially cd-rom access will dramatically decrease your battery time.

- Pcmcia cards can also consume a lot of power, so don't leave your modem or network adapter plugged in when it is not in use. But this is different between the various pcmcia manufacturers, so check the product specs before you buy (e. g. some cards never turn themselves off even when not in use).

  (By the way, I recently read that pcmcia cards are the biggest problem for windows ce palmtops - they drain so much power that the tiny machines' little batteries have to be replaced within minutes...)

- Use simple software. A full blown multimedia application will create a lot more system load and harddisk / cd-rom activity than a small simple word processor.

- Grant Taylor has a tip for those of us who want to upgrade their system: "Newer versions of some upgradable components consume less power. For example, IBM's Travelstar 2.5 inch 1.6 gigabyte ide harddisk drive consumes 20 percent less than the 500 megabyte toshiba harddisk my laptop came with."

- If you are yet about to buy a laptop - don't buy a laptop with a 2nd level cache if battery uptime is important. A computer with 2nd level cache is about 10% to 20% faster and it will be a lot better with multimedia applications and number crunching, but it consumes a lot of power. Bjoern Kriews tells me that he has two almost identical laptops and the one without cache ram runs 4h30 compared to 2h30 with cache.

If you already have 2nd level cache installed, turning it off will probably not help you very much. Give it a try and write me about your experience.

- Another tip for those still buying a laptop - don't buy the latest, fastest cpu type. Usually, the older generations are optimized by the manufacturer after some time without notice. The "new" versions of old cpu types often create less heat and consume less power than the product's premiere version.

  There are also frankenstein laptops available that use cpus not optimized for portable systems. As I wrote this in May 97, the newest generation pentium-200 laptops ran about 20 minutes on battery and became so hot that they burnt your lap. When writing the second revision in Oct 97, pentium-233 laptops run two hours or longer without ac power. Go figure.

Well, you get the idea. Most of these are restrictions that will probably stop you from doing any serious work with your Linux system. (The best way to save power while on battery is... not to do anything at all. That increases my laptop's battery uptime by almost 100 percent.)

So let's go ahead to some other, more useful measures that will save power without disturbing your work.

3   Advanced Power Management

Portable systems in general, but even many desktop computers come equipped with support for apm, the "advanced power management" scheme. This section describes how to activate apm support in your Linux kernel. People who are experienced with Linux may find this section rather boring and want to skip to the next.

3.1   What APM can do for you

I won't describe it in detail here, check the *Linux APM drivers page* at *http://www.cs.utexas.edu/users/kharker/linux-laptop/apm.html* <http://www.cs.utexas.edu/users/kharker/linux-laptop/apm.html> for more information. All that you need to know is that with the help of apm, the cpu can tell the bios when there's nothing really exciting going on so that the bios can take care of some power saving by itself - e. g. reducing the cpu clock, turning off the harddisk, turning off the display's backlight etc.

Apm is also responsible for the "system suspend" (or "sleep") mode and for the "suspend to disk" (or "hiberntation") mode. And yet another cool, though not very important feature is that with the help of apm, shutdown -h will not just halt your system, but also turn it off.

(By the way, most Linux systems put a shutdown -r in their /etc/inittab and map it to pressing control-alt-delete. I prefer having shutdown -h there, so when pressing the famous key combination, my laptop simply turns itself off.)

Not all manufacturers implement a correct apm bios, so some laptops have trouble with the Linux apm drivers (if your machine has trouble with apm, it will most likely either lock up at Linux' boot up or after returning from suspend). If you are not sure, check the Linux laptop page for your specific model.

3.2   How to activate APM support in Linux

It's easy - just recompile the Linux kernel. Check the Kernel-HOWTO if you don't know how to do that.

When the configuration script reaches the "character devices" section, the default setting for full apm bios support in kernel version 2.0.30 or higher is:

```
Advanced Power Management BIOS support: Yes
Ignore USER SUSPEND: No
Enable PM at boot time: Yes
Make CPU Idle calls when idle: Yes
Enable console blanking using APM: Yes
Power off on shutdown: Yes
```

Please read the configuration script's help texts. They explain in detail what each option does, so I won't repeat them here.

If your system does not fully support the apm bios standard, some of those options might crash your system. Test all apm features with the new kernel to make sure that everything works as it should.

(A sidenote about console blanking: David Bateman tells me that you should not enable it because it can cause problems with the current version of XFree 3.2: "The symptoms are that the screen will be blank when X starts, and it can be fixed usually by just hitting a key. It's a small but annoying problem. The next relase of XFree, will have pretty good DPMS support for a lot of laptop chipset, which should include code to turn off the LCD. Check out the manpage for xset in XFree 3.2A." David also notes that the lifetime of your display's backlight is determined by the number of times it's switched on and off: "So its a compromise, lifetime of the battery versus lifetime of the backlight.")

(*Update:* With XFree 3.3, this problem still remained on my laptop. I am told that this will be fixed in a future kernel version.)

3.3   APM support and the PCMCIA drivers

After recompiling the kernel, don't forget to recompile the linux pcmcia drivers as well.

The precompiled pcmcia drivers that come with most linux distribution have apm support disabled, so that the bios can't instruct your card adapters to turn off.

Also, you must recompile the drivers if you upgrade to a new kernel version and your old kernel was compiled with module version information turned on (this option is found in the "loadable module support" section of the kernel configuration).

Read the PCMCIA-HOWTO for detailed instructions on how to compile the drivers or go to the *Linux PCMCIA drivers homepage* at *http://hyper.stanford.edu/HyperNews/get/pcmcia/home.html* <http://hyper.stanford.edu/HyperNews/get/pcmcia/home.html>.

3.4   The apmd package

Now that you have APM support installed, go and get the apmd package from the *Linux APM drivers page*. You don't really need it, but it is a very useful collection of programs. The apmd daemon logs your battery's behaviour and it will send out a warning if you are on low power. The apm command will suspend your system with a shell command and xapm shows the current state of your battery.

(BTW, if you have problems with pcmcia cards after returning from suspend, you can check out an alternative apmd package at *http://www.cut.de/bkr/linux/apmd/apmd.html* <http://www.cut.de/bkr/linux/apmd/apmd.html>. It unloads the pcmcia driver module before going to suspend and reloads the module on resume.)

Grant Taylor has been playing a little with the apmd package and came up with helpful tips.

He found that his laptop's harddisk forgets its hdparm -S standby period when returning from suspend: "I modified apmd to reset this setting on each resume. This may be system-specific; but it's an important thing to do..."

(Note: On my own laptop, the bios takes care of the harddisk standby period and resets the value on resuming. So I could not test if this little problem is system-specific. If it happens to you as well, send me a message.)

Grant also had a nice trick for screen blanking with 4.7 (the XFree86 package) and the help of the apmd package, you'll find it there.

3.5   And if my laptop does not support APM?

If your computer's bios does not offer any power saving settings (even the old ones without apm should at least allow to set harddisk and display standby), you can use hdparm -S to define your harddisk's standby period. This will already help a lot, since harddisk activity consumes a lot of power. Your system should have hdparm installed, so read man hdparm for the command syntax.

4   Changing some general system settings

After I got Linux up and running on my laptop, I found it accessing the harddisk every few seconds, even when there was no user logged in to the system. The harddisk could never enter its power saving mode. Reducing harddisk activity can greatly increase the battery runtime, so this is why I collected the following recipes.

I tested all this with RedHat 4.1, the locations of some configuration settings may be different for your distribution. (If so, please let me know.)

4.1   The crond daemon and atrun

Check your /etc/crontab file if it starts a process every minute. You will often find atrun there.

With the at command, you can spool commands that must be invoked some time in the future. Some Linux systems use a dedicated atd daemon to take care of this, others (e. g. RedHat) let the crond daemon run atrun once every minute.

This is not really necessairy on most systems, since at commands rarely depend upon being invoked on exact time. So if you find a line like this in your /etc/crontab:

```
# Run any at jobs every minute
* * * * * root [ -x /usr/sbin/atrun ] && /usr/sbin/atrun
```

Then you can safely change this to:

```
# Run any at jobs every hour
00 * * * * root [ -x /usr/sbin/atrun ] && /usr/sbin/atrun
```

Read man 5 crontab for details. Some folks can even work fine without the crond daemon, so if you know what you are doing, you might want to consider disabling it completely.

4.2   The update / bdflush daemon

Linux deals with a lot of open file buffers at any given moment, so the system must make sure that file changes are saved to the harddisk as soon possible. Otherwise, those changes will be lost after a system crash.

The update / bdflush daemon takes care of this. (These are two names for the same program, so you can use either name to start the daemon). The default settings will make this daemon call flush every 5 seconds and sync every 30 seconds.

With my Fujitsu disk this caused non-stop access. (It seems that this harddisk flushes its ram cache even when nothing has changed. But this depends on your harddisk's firmware: Other people told me that their harddisk does enter its power saving mode even without the following modification.)

Since Linux does not crash very often anymore, I have changed both values to 3600 seconds (= one hour). This caused no problems at all and the constant disk access has stopped. (But if my system crashes now, there will be more broken files, of course.)

RedHat 4.1: In /etc/inittab, change the update call to:

```
ud::once:/sbin/update -s 3600 -f 3600
```

Suse 4.4.1: update is called in /sbin/init.d/boot.

Slackware: update is called in /etc/rc.d/rc.S.

See man update for details.

4.3   The syslogd daemon

The syslogd daemon is responsible for the various Linux system log files that are found in the /var/log/ directory. By default syslogd will sync the log file each time after logging a system message.

You can turn that off by preceding the filename with a dash in /etc/syslog.conf. Here's an example as found in my system's syslog.conf:

```
# Log anything (except mail) of level info or higher.
# Don't log private authentication messages!
*.info;mail.none;authpriv.none                    -/var/log/messages
```

This again means that if the system crashes, the message that reported the problem may not have been stored to disk. Dilemma...

4.4   The init command

During the bootup, the initial processes and daemons will be started using the init command. This command (yet again) calls sync before each process it creates.

You can change this by removing the sync() call in the source code and recompiling the command.

To avoid problems with lost file buffers, you should add a call to sync in your system's /etc/rc.d/init.d/halt script, right before the script unmounts the file systems.

4.5   The swap partition

The Linux swap partition is used to increase the physical ram space with virtual memory. This again is a possible reason for harddisk access. If your laptop already has a lot of ram or if the applications that you use are quite simple (think of vi), you might want to consider turning it off.

This of course depends on what you plan to do. 4 to 8 megs are not enough, you must use a swap partition then. With 8 to 16 megs, text console applications will work fine and if you can avoid using a lot of multitasking features, you can safely disable swap. The X-Windows enviroment requires a lot of ram and you should not use it without a swap partition unless you really have a lot more than 16 megs.

(Sidenote: My laptop with 16 megs and disabled swap partition can run an emacs session, four bash shells and compile a kernel without running out of memory. That's enough for me.)

If you already have installed a swap partition, you can disable it by preceding the swapon command that is called in /etc/rc.d/rc.sysinit with a hash mark. If you don't want to make it a permanent move, let the system ask during boot if you want to use the swap partition. In /etc/rc.d/rc.sysinit (RedHat 4.1) or /sbin/init.d/boot (Suse 4.4.1):

```
echo "Should the system use swap?"
echo "  0: No."
echo "  1: Yes."
/bin/echo "Your choice: \c"
read SWAPCHOICE

case "$SWAPCHOICE" in
    0)
        # Do nothing.
        echo "(Swap partitions disabled)"
        ;;
    *)
        # Start up swapping.
        echo "Activating swap partitions"
        swapon -a
esac
```

Then you can use the swap partition while on ac power and drop it while on battery.

4.6   The apache httpd webserver daemon

I am using my laptop to develop and test cgi scipts for websites, that is why I am running a local webserver on it. The standard configuration is a bit too much if all you want to do is just test a script or check a page from time to time.

In httpd.conf, just change the values of MinSpareServers and StartServers to 1. This will be enough for a local test site.

If you wish to turn off the webserver's logging, you must recompile the httpd daemon. Read the documentation for details.

Grant Taylor recompiled apache's logging and found that this "didn't make it stop churning the disk. So I used another, IMHO better, solution: I configured apache to run from inetd instead of standalone." Read man inetd for details.

4.7 The XFree86 package

Configuring XFree86 for laptops is a story of its own. And yet again, I have to refer you to the Linux Laptop page where you will find a lot of help on this.

X's console blanking only turns the screen black, but does not turn it off. As mentioned in the 3.2 (sidenote about console blanking), you can use xset's dpms option to change this. However, this feature depends on your laptop's graphics chipset and bios.

Grant Taylor uses the following setup to send his laptop to sleep with the help of apmd and the screensaver:

```
# Run xscreensaver with APM program
xscreensaver -timeout 5 \
             -xrm xscreensaver.programs:apm_standby \
             -xrm xscreensaver.colorPrograms:apm_standby &
```

Where "apm_standby is a suid perl script that allows only certain people to run apm -S."

4.8 The emacs editor

Ok, emacs is not an editor, but a way of life. Here's a tip from Florent Chabaud: "If you use emacs, perhaps you have noticed that the editor makes some automatic saves. This is of course useful and should *not* be disabled, but the default parameters can be adjusted to a laptop use.

I have put in the file /usr/share/emacs/site-lisp/site-start.el the two following lines:

```
(setq auto-save-interval 2500)
(setq auto-save-timeout nil)
```

This disables auto-saving based on time, and makes the auto-saving be done every 2500 keyboard actions. Of course if you are typing a text this last parameter should be reduced, but for programming it is sufficient. Since every action (up, down, left, backspace, paste, etc...) is counted, 2500 actions are reached very rapidly."

4.9 How to find more ways to optimize

If your Linux system still seems to access the harddisk too often, you can find out what is going on inside by using the ps ax command. This will show all running processes and their full name, sometimes it also reveals the command line arguments of each process.

Now read the man page of each process to find out what it does and how to change its behaviour. With this method, you will most likely find the process that is responsible. You may also find strace helpful.

Please send me an email if you found something new.

5 Appendix

5.1 A message to Linux distributors

If you happen to be a Linux distributor, thank you for reading all this. Laptops are becoming more and more popular, but still most Linux distributions are not very well prepared for portable computing. Please make this document obsolete and change this for your distribution.

- The installation routine should include a configuration, optimized for laptops. The "mimimal install" is often not lean enough. There are a lot of things that a laptop user does not need on the road. Just a few examples. There is no need for three different versions of vi (as found in Suse Linux). Most portable systems do not need printing support (they will never be connected to a printer, printing is usually done with the desktop system at home). Quite a few laptops do not need any network support at all.
- Don't forget to describe laptop-specific installation problems, e. g. how to install your distribution without a cd-rom drive or how to setup the plip network driver.
- Add better power management and seamless pcmcia support to your distribution. Add a precompiled kernel and an alternative set of pcmcia drivers with apm support that the user can install on demand. Include a precompiled apmd package with your distribution.
- Add support for dynamically switching network configurations. Most Linux laptops travel between locations with different network settings (e. g. the network at home, the network at the office and the network at the university) and have to change the network id very often. Changing a Linux system's network id is a pain with most distributions.

Please mail me if your distribution is optimized for portable computing and what kind of features you added for that. Future versions of this HOWTO will include a section where you can advertise your distribution's laptop features.

5.2   Credits

- The information about battery technology is mostly based on the article "Stromkonserve" by Michael Reiter, published in "c't Magazin fuer Computertechnik" (Heise Verlag Hannover, Germany), edition 10/96, page 204. Used by permission. Visit their website at *http://www.heise.de/* <http://www.heise.de/>.
- The following people contributed to this document:

```
Frithjof Anders <anders@goethe.ucdavis.edu>
David Bateman <dbateman@ee.uts.edu.au>
Florent Chabaud <chabaud@celar.fr>
Markus Gutschke <gutschk@uni-muenster.de>
Kenneth E. Harker <kharker@cs.utexas.edu>
Bjoern Kriews <bkr@rrz.uni-hamburg.de>
R. Manmatha <manmatha@bendigo.cs.umass.edu>
Juergen Rink <jr@ct.heise.de>
Grant Taylor <gtaylor@picante.com>
James Youngman <JYoungman@vggas.com>
```

5.3   About this document

This text mentions batteries 53 times.

The current version of this and many other HOWTOs, most of them a lot more useful than this one, can be found at the main Linux documentation site *http://sunsite.unc.edu/mdw/linux.html* <http://sunsite.unc.edu/mdw/linux.html> or at one of its many mirror sites.

Most of this text was written during my trips between Hamburg and Hannover on German rail. (The new ice-2 coaches have power outlets for laptops, yeah!).

And now hum along with me: "...on the road again..."

Linux PCMCIA HOWTO

David Hinds, dhinds@hyper.stanford.edu   v2.3, 4 February 1998

This document describes how to install and use PCMCIA Card Services for Linux, and answers some frequently asked questions. The latest version of this document can always be found at <ftp://hyper.stanford.edu/pub/pcmcia/doc>. An HTML version is at <http://hyper.stanford.edu/HyperNews/get/pcmcia/home.html>.

Contents

1   General information and hardware requirements

1.1   Introduction

Card Services for Linux is a complete PCMCIA support package. It includes a set of loadable kernel modules that implement a version of the PCMCIA Card Services applications program interface, a set of client drivers for specific cards, and a card manager daemon that can respond to card insertion and removal events, loading and unloading drivers on demand. It supports "hot swapping" of PCMCIA cards, so cards can be inserted and ejected at any time.

This software is continually under development. It probably contains bugs, and should be used with caution. I'll do my best to fix problems that are reported to me, but if you don't tell me, I may never know. If you use this code, I hope you will send me your experiences, good or bad!

If you have any suggestions for how this document could be improved, please let me know (dhinds@hyper.stanford.edu).

1.2   Copyright notice and disclaimer

1.3   What is the latest version, and where can I get it?

The current major release of Card Services is version 3.0, and minor updates or bug fixes are numbered 3.0.1, 3.0.2, and so on.

Source code for the latest version is available from hyper.stanford.edu in the /pub/pcmcia directory, as pcmcia-cs-3.0.?.tar.gz. There will usually be several versions here. I generally only keep the latest minor release for a given major release. New major releases may contain relatively untested code, so I also keep the latest version of the previous major release as a relatively stable fallback; the current fallback is 2.9.12.

It is up to you to decide which version is more appropriate, but the CHANGES file will summarize the most important differences.

hyper.stanford.edu is mirrored at sunsite.unc.edu (and all sunsite mirror sites) in /pub/Linux/kernel/pcmcia.

If you do not feel up to compiling the PCMCIA drivers from scratch, pre-compiled drivers are included with current releases of most of the major Linux distributions, including Slackware, Red Hat, Caldera, and Yggdrasil, among others.

1.4 What systems are supported?

This code should run on almost any Linux-capable laptop. All common PCMCIA controllers are supported, including Intel, Cirrus, Vadem, VLSI, Ricoh, and Databook chips. Custom controllers used in IBM and Toshiba laptops are also supported. PCMCIA card docks for desktop systems should work as long as they are the type that plugs directly into the ISA bus, rather than SCSI-to-PCMCIA or IDE-to-PCMCIA adapters.

CardBus bridge controllers that conform to the "Yenta" register specification (including TI, Cirrus, SMC, and Ricoh chips) are supported, though support for 32-bit CardBus cards is still somewhat experimental. Drivers prior to version 3.0 only support 16-bit cards in CardBus sockets.

The Motorola 6AHC05GA controller used in some Hyundai laptops is not supported. The custom PCMCIA controller in the HP Omnibook 600 is unsupported.

1.5 What PCMCIA cards are supported?

The current release includes drivers for a variety of ethernet cards, a driver for modem and serial port cards, several SCSI adapter drivers, a driver for ATA/IDE drive cards, and memory card drivers that should support most SRAM cards and some flash cards. The SUPPORTED.CARDS file included with each release of Card Services lists all cards that are known to work in at least one actual system.

The likelihood that a card not on the supported list will work depends on the type of card. Essentially all modems should work with the supplied driver. Some network cards may work if they are OEM versions of supported cards. Other types of IO cards (frame buffers, sound cards, etc) will not work until someone writes the appropriate drivers.

1.6 When will my new card be supported?

Unfortunately, they usually don't pay me to write device drivers, so if you would like to have a driver for your favorite card, you are probably going to have to do at least some of the work. Ideally, I'd like to work towards a model like the Linux kernel, where I would be responsible mainly for the "core" PCMCIA code and other authors would contribute and maintain drivers for specific cards. The SUPPORTED.CARDS file mentions some cards for which driver work is currently in progress. I will try to help where I can, but be warned that debugging kernel device drivers by email is not particularly effective.

Manufacturers interested in helping provide Linux support for their products can contact me about consulting arrangements.

1.7 Mailing lists and other information sources

I used to maintain a database and mailing list of Linux PCMCIA users. More recently, I've turned my web page for Linux PCMCIA information into a "HyperNews" site, with a set of message lists for Linux PCMCIA issues. There are lists for installation and configuration issues, for different types of cards, and for PCMCIA programming and debugging. The Linux PCMCIA information page is at <http://hyper.stanford.edu/HyperNews/get/pcmcia/home.html>. Users can request email notification of new responses to particular questions, or notification for all new messages in a given category. I hope that this will become a useful repository of information, for questions that go beyond the scope of the HOWTO.

There is a Linux mailing list devoted to laptop issues, the "linux-laptop" list. For more information, send a message containing the word "help" to majordomo@vger.rutgers.edu. To subscribe, send a message containing "subscribe linux-laptop" to the same address. This mailing list might be a good forum for discussion of Linux PCMCIA issues.

The Linux Laptop Home Page at <http://www.cs.utexas.edu/users/kharker/linux-laptop> has links to many sites that have information about configuring specific types of laptops for Linux (and PCMCIA). There is also a searchable database of system configuration information.

1.8 Why don't you distribute PCMCIA binaries?

For me, distributing binaries would be a significant hassle. It is complicated because some features can only be selected at compile time, and because the PCMCIA modules are somewhat dependent on having the "right" kernel configuration. So, I would probably need to distribute precompiled modules along with matching kernels. Beyond this, the greatest need for precompiled modules is when installing Linux on a clean system. This typically requires setting up PCMCIA so that it can be used in the installation process for a particular Linux distribution. Each Linux distribution has its own procedures, and it is not feasible for me to provide boot and root disks for even just the common combinations of drivers and distributions.

PCMCIA is now a part of many of the major Linux distributions, including Red Hat, Caldera, Slackware, Yggdrasil, Craftworks, and Nascent Technology.

1.9 Why is the PCMCIA package so darned big?

Well, first of all, it isn't actually that large. All the driver modules together take up about 200K of disk space. The utility programs add up to about 70K, and the stuff in /etc/pcmcia is about 30K. When running, the core PCMCIA modules take up 48K of system memory. The cardmgr daemon will generally be swapped out except when cards are inserted or removed. The total package size is not much different from DOS Card Services implementations.

Compared to DOS "point enablers", this may still seem like a lot of overhead, especially for people that don't plan on using many of the features of PCMCIA, such as power management or hot swapping. Point enablers can be tiny because they generally support only one or a small set of cards, and also generally support a restricted set of PCMCIA controllers. If someone were to write a genuinely "generic" modem enabler, it would end up incorporating much of the functionality of Card Services, to handle cards from different vendors and the full range of PCMCIA controller variants.

2 Compilation and installation

2.1 Prerequisites and kernel setup

Before starting, you should think about whether you really need to compile the PCMCIA package yourself. All common Linux distributions come with pre-compiled PCMCIA driver packages. Generally, you only need to install the drivers from scratch if you need a new feature of the current drivers, or if you've updated and/or reconfigured your kernel in a way that is incompatible with the drivers included with your Linux distribution. While compiling the PCMCIA package is not technically difficult, it does require some general Linux familiarity.

The following things should be installed on your system before you start installing PCMCIA:

- A 2.0.* or 2.1.* series kernel source tree.

- An appropriate set of module utilities.

- (Optional) the "Forms" X11 user interface toolkit.

The current driver package actually works with most kernel versions back to 1.2.8. However, use with older kernels is deprecated, and backwards compatibility with very old kernels may go away at any time.

You need to have a complete linux source tree for your kernel, not just an up-to-date kernel image, to compile the PCMCIA package. The PCMCIA modules contain some references to kernel source files. While you may want to build a new kernel to remove unnecessary drivers, installing PCMCIA does not require you to do so.

Current "stable" kernel sources and patches are available from `<ftp://sunsite.unc.edu/pub/Linux/kernel/v2.0>`, or from `<ftp://tsx-11.mit.edu/pub/linux/sources/system/v2.0>`. Development kernels can be found in the corresponding v2.1 subdirectories. Current module utilities can be found in the same locations.

In the Linux source tree for 2.0 and 2.1 kernels, the `Documentation/Changes` file describes the versions of all sorts of other system components that are required for that kernel release. You may want to check through this and verify that your system is up to date, especially if you have updated your kernel. If you are using a 2.1 kernel, be sure that you are using the right combination of shared libraries and module tools.

When configuring your kernel, if you plan on using a PCMCIA ethernet card, you should turn on networking support but turn off the normal Linux network card drivers, including the "pocket and portable adapters". The PCMCIA network card drivers are all implemented as loadable modules. Any drivers compiled into your kernel will only waste space.

If you want to use SLIP, PPP, or PLIP, you do need to either configure your kernel with these enabled, or use the loadable module versions of these drivers. There is an unfortunate deficiency in the kernel config process in 1.2.X kernels, in that it is not possible to set configuration options (like SLIP compression) for a loadable module, so it is probably better to just link SLIP into the kernel if you need it.

In order to use a PCMCIA token ring adapter, your kernel should be configured with "Token Ring driver support" (`CONFIG_TR`) enabled, though you should leave `CONFIG_IBMTR` off.

If you want to use a PCMCIA IDE adapter, your kernel should be configured with `CONFIG_BLK_DEV_IDE_PCMCIA` enabled, for 1.3.72 through 2.1.7 kernels. Older kernels do not support removeable IDE devices; newer kernels do not require a special configuration setting.

If you will be using a PCMCIA SCSI adapter, you should enable `CONFIG_SCSI` when configuring your kernel. Also, enable any top level drivers (SCSI disk, tape, cdrom, generic) that you expect to use. All low-level drivers for particular host adapters should be disabled, as they will just take up space.

If you want to modularize a driver that is needed for a PCMCIA device, you must modify /etc/pcmcia/config to specify what modules need to be loaded for what card types. For example, if the serial driver is modularized, then the serial device definition should be:

```
device "serial_cs"
    class "serial" module "misc/serial", "serial_cs"
```

This package includes an X-based card status utility called cardinfo. This utility is based on a freely distributed user interface toolkit called the Forms Library, which you will need to install before building cardinfo. A binary distribution is at <ftp://hyper.stanford.edu/pub/pcmcia/extras>: there are both a.out and ELF versions of the library. You will also need to have all the normal X header files and libraries installed.

2.2   Installation

Here is a synopsis of the installation process:

- Unpack pcmcia-cs-3.0.?.tar.gz in /usr/src.
- Run "make config" in the new pcmcia-cs-3.0.? directory.
- Run "make all", then "make install".
- Customize the PCMCIA startup script and the option files in /etc/pcmcia for your site.

If you plan to install any contributed client drivers not included in the core PCMCIA distribution, unpack each of them in the top-level directory of the PCMCIA source tree. Then follow the normal build instructions. The extra drivers will be compiled and installed automatically.

Running "make config" prompts for a few configuration options, and checks out your system to verify that it satisfies all prerequisites for installing PCMCIA support. In most cases, you'll be able to just accept all the default configuration options. Be sure to carefully check the output of this command in case there are problems.

If you are compiling the PCMCIA package for installation on another machine, specify an alternate target directory when prompted by the configure script. This should be an absolute path. All the PCMCIA tools will be installed relative to this directory. You will then be able to tar this directory tree and copy to your target machine, and unpack relative to its root directory to install everything in the proper places.

If you are cross compiling on another machine, you may want to specify alternate names for the compiler and linker. This may also be helpful on mixed a.out and ELF systems. The script will also prompt for additional compiler flags for debugging.

Some of the support utilities (cardctl and cardinfo) can be compiled either in "safe" or "trusting" forms. The "safe" forms prevent non-root users from modifying card configurations. The "trusting" forms permit ordinary users to issue commands to suspend and resume cards, reset cards, and change the current configuration scheme. The configuration script will ask if you want the utilities compiled as safe or trusting: the default is to be safe.

There are a few kernel configuration options that affect the PCMCIA tools. The configuration script can deduce these from the running kernel (the most common case). Alternatively, if you are compiling for installation on another machine, it can read the configuration from a kernel source tree, or each option can be set interactively.

Running "make all" followed by "make install" will build and then install the kernel modules and utility programs. Kernel modules are installed under /lib/modules/<version>/pcmcia. The cardmgr and cardctl programs are installed in /sbin. If cardinfo is built, it is installed in /usr/bin/X11.

Configuration files will be installed in the /etc/pcmcia directory. If you are installing over an older version, your old config scripts will be backed up before being replaced. The saved scripts will be given extensions like *.~1~, *.~2~, and so on.

If you don't know what kind of PCMCIA controller chip you have, you can use the probe utility in the cardmgr/ subdirectory to determine this. There are two major types: the Databook TCIC-2 type and the Intel i82365SL-compatible type.

In a few cases, the probe command will be unable to determine your controller type automatically. If you have a Halikan NBD 486 system, it has a TCIC-2 controller at an unusual location: you'll need to edit rc.pcmcia to load the tcic module, and also set the PCIC_OPTS parameter to "tcic_base=0x02c0".

On some systems using Cirrus controllers, including the NEC Versa M, the BIOS puts the controller in a special suspended state at system startup time. On these systems, the probe command will fail to find any known PCMCIA controller. If this happens, edit rc.pcmcia and set PCIC to i82365, and PCIC_OPTS to "wakeup=1".

2.3   Post-installation for systems using BSD init scripts

Some Linux distributions, including Slackware, use a BSD arrangement for system startup scripts. If /etc/rc.d/rc.M exists, your system is in this group. The script rc.pcmcia, installed in /etc/rc.d, controls starting up and shutting down the PCMCIA system. "make install" will use the probe command to determine your controller type and modify rc.pcmcia appropriately. You should add a line to your system startup file /etc/rc.d/rc.M to invoke the PCMCIA startup script, like:

        /etc/rc.d/rc.pcmcia start

It does not really matter where you insert this line, as long as the PCMCIA drivers are started after syslogd.

2.4   Post-installation for systems using System V init scripts

Red Hat, Caldera, and Debian Linux have a System V-ish arrangement for system startup files. If you have a directory called /etc/init.d or /etc/rc.d/init.d, then your system is in this group. The rc.pcmcia script will be installed as /etc/rc.d/init.d/pcmcia, or /etc/init.d/pcmcia, as appropriate. There is no need to edit any of the startup scripts to enable PCMCIA: it will happen automatically.

If the /etc/sysconfig directory exists, then a separate configuration file, /etc/sysconfig/pcmcia, will be created for startup options. If you need to change any module options (like the PCIC= or PCIC_OPTS= settings), edit this config file rather than the actual PCMCIA startup script. This file will not be overwritten by subsequent installs.

Some previous releases used the /etc/sysconfig/pcmcia-scripts directory in place of /etc/pcmcia on these platforms. The current release instead uses /etc/pcmcia for all systems, and will move an existing /etc/sysconfig/pcmcia-scripts to /etc/pcmcia.

2.5   Socket driver options

Some PCMCIA controllers have optional features that may or may not be implemented in a particular system. In some cases, it is impossible for the socket driver to detect if these features are implemented. Check the man page for your socket driver to see what optional features may be present for your controller.

The low level socket drivers, tcic and i82365, have numerous bus timing parameters that may need to be adjusted for systems with particularly fast processors. Symptoms of timing problems include card recognition problems, lock-ups under heavy loads, high error rates, or poor device performance. Check the corresponding man pages for more details, but here is a brief summary:

- Cirrus controllers have numerous configurable timing parameters. The most important seems to be the `cmd_time` flag, which determines the length of PCMCIA bus cycles. Fast 486 systems (i.e., DX4-100) seem to often benefit from increasing this from 6 (the default) to 12 or 16.

- The Cirrus PD6729 PCI controller has the `fast_pci` flag, which should be set if the PCI bus speed is greater than 25 MHz.

- For Vadem VG-468 controllers and Databook TCIC-2 controllers, the `async_clock` flag changes the relative clocking of PCMCIA bus and host bus cycles. Setting this flag adds extra wait states to some operations. However, I have yet to hear of a laptop that needs this.

- The `pcmcia_core` module has the `cis_speed` parameter for changing the memory speed used for accessing a card's Card Information Structure (CIS). On some systems with fast bus clocks, increasing this parameter (i.e., slowing down card accesses) may be beneficial for card recognition problems.

- This isn't a timing issue, but if you have more than one ISA-to-PCMCIA controller in your system or extra sockets in a docking station, the `i82365` module should be loaded with the `extra_sockets` parameter set to 1. This should not be necessary for PCI-to-PCMCIA or PCI-to-CardBus bridges

All these options should be configured by modifying the top of /etc/rc.d/rc.pcmcia. For example:

```
# Should be either i82365 or tcic
PCIC=i82365
# Put socket driver timing parameters here
PCIC_OPTS="cmd_time=12"
# Put pcmcia_core options here
CORE_OPTS="cis_speed=500"
```

Here are some timing settings for specific systems:

- On the ARM Pentium-90 or Midwest Micro Soundbook Plus, use "freq_bypass=1 cmd_time=8".
- On a Midwest Micro Soundbook Elite, use "cmd_time=12".
- On a Gateway Liberty, try "cmd_time=16".

2.6 System resource settings

Card Services should automatically avoid allocating IO ports and interrupts already in use by other standard devices. It will also attempt to detect conflicts with unknown devices, but this is not completely reliable. In some cases, you may need to explicitly exclude resources for a device in /etc/pcmcia/config.opts.

Here are some resource settings for specific laptop types.

- On the AMS SoundPro, exclude irq 10.
- On some AMS TravelPro 5300 models, use memory 0xc8000-0xcffff.
- On the BMX 486DX2-66, exclude irq 5, irq 9.
- On the Chicony NB5, use memory 0xda000-0xdffff.
- On the Compaq Presario 1020, exclude port 0x2f8-0x2ff, irq 3, irq 5.
- On the HP Omnibook 4000C, exclude port 0x300-0x30f.
- On the Micron Millenia Transport, exclude irq 5, irq 9.

- On the NEC Versa M, exclude irq 9, port 0x2e0-2ff.
- On the NEC Versa P/75, exclude irq 5, irq 9.
- On the NEC Versa S, exclude irq 9, irq 12.
- On the NEC Versa 6000 series, exclude port 0x300-0x33f, irq 9, irq 10.
- On the ProStar 9200, Altima Virage, and Acquiline Hurricane DX4-100, exclude irq 5, port 0x330-0x35f. Maybe use memory 0xd8000-0xdffff.
- On the Siemens Nixdorf SIMATIC PG 720C, use memory 0xc0000-0xcffff, port 0x300-0x3bf.
- On the TI TravelMate 5000, use memory 0xd4000-0xdffff.
- On the Toshiba T4900 CT, exclude irq 5, port 0x2e0-0x2e8, port 0x330-0x338.
- On the Twinhead 5100, HP 4000, Sharp PC-8700 and PC-8900, exclude irq 9 (sound), irq 12.
- On an MPC 800 Series, exclude irq 5, port 0x300-0x30f for the CD-ROM.

3 Resolving installation and configuration problems

3.1 Base PCMCIA kernel modules do not load

Symptoms:

- Kernel version mismatch errors are reported when the PCMCIA startup script runs.
- After startup, lsmod does not show any PCMCIA modules.
- cardmgr reports "no pcmcia driver in /proc/devices" in the system log.

Kernel modules contain version information that is checked against the current kernel when a module is loaded. The type of checking depends on the setting of the CONFIG_MODVERSIONS kernel option. If this is false, then the kernel version number is compiled into each module, and insmod checks this for a match with the running kernel. If CONFIG_MODVERSIONS is true, then each symbol exported by the kernel is given a sort of checksum. These codes are all compared against the corresponding codes compiled into a module. The intent was for this to make modules less version-dependent, because the checksums would only change if a kernel interface changed, and would generally stay the same across minor kernel updates. In practice, the checksums have turned out to be even more restrictive, because many kernel interfaces depend on compile-time kernel option settings. Also, the checksums turned out to be an excessively pessimistic judge of compatibility.

Some of the PCMCIA modules require kernel services that may or may not be present, depending on kernel configuration. For instance, the SCSI card drivers require that the kernel be configured with SCSI support, and the network drivers require a networking kernel. If a kernel lacks a necessary feature, insmod may report undefined symbols and refuse to load a module.

The practical upshot of this is that kernel modules are closely tied to both the kernel version, and the setting of many kernel configuration options. Generally, a set of modules compiled for one 2.0.31 kernel will not load against some other 2.0.31 kernel unless special care is taken to ensure that the two were built with similar configurations. This makes distribution of precompiled kernel modules a tricky business.

You have several options:

- If you obtained precompiled drivers as part of a Linux distribution, verify that you are using an unmodified kernel as supplied with that distribution. If you intend to use precompiled modules, you generally must stick with the corresponding kernel.
- If you have reconfigured or upgraded your kernel, you will probably need to compile and install the PCMCIA package from scratch. This is easily done if you already have the kernel source tree installed. See the PCMCIA-HOWTO for detailed instructions.

- In some cases, incompatibilities in other system components can prevent correct loading of kernel modules. If you have upgraded your own kernel, pay attention to the "minimal requirements" for module utilities and binutils listed in the **Documentation/Changes** file in the kernel source code tree.

3.2 Interrupt scan failures

Symptoms:

- The system locks up when the PCMCIA drivers are loaded, even with no cards present.
- The system log shows a successful PCMCIA controller probe just before the lock-up, but does not show interrupt probe results.

After identifying the PCMCIA controller, the socket driver probes for free interrupts. The probe involves programming the controller for each apparently free interrupt, then generating a "soft" interrupt, to see if the interrupt can be detected correctly. In some cases, probing a particular interrupt can interfere with another system device.

The reason for the probe is to identify interrupts which appear to be free (i.e., are not reserved by any other Linux device driver), yet are either not physically wired to the PCMCIA controller, or are connected to another device that does not have a driver.

There are two ways to proceed:

- The interrupt probe can be restricted to a list of interrupts using the `irq_list` parameter for the socket drivers. For example, "`irq_list=5,9,10`" would limit the scan to three interrupts. All PCMCIA devices will be restricted to using these interrupts (assuming they pass the probe). You may need to use trial and error to find out which interrupts can be safely probed.
- The interrupt probe can be disabled entirely by loading the socket driver with the "do_scan=0" option. In this case, a default interrupt list will be used, which avoids interrupts already allocated for other devices.

In either case, the probe options can be specified using the `PCIC_OPTS` definition in the PCMCIA startup script, for example:

```
PCIC_OPTS="irq_list=5,9,10"
```

3.3 Memory probe failures

Symptoms:

- The core drivers load correctly when no cards are present, with no errors in the system log.
- The system freezes and/or reboots as soon as any card is inserted, before any beeps are heard.

Or alternately:

- All card insertions generate a high beep followed by a low beep.
- All cards are identified as "anonymous memory cards".
- The system log reports that various memory ranges have been excluded.

The core modules perform a memory scan at the time of first card insertion. This scan can potentially interfere with other memory mapped devices. Also, pre-3.0.0 driver packages perform a more aggressive scan than more recent drivers. The memory window is defined in `/etc/pcmcia/config.opts`. The default window is large, so it may help to restrict the scan to a narrower range. Reasonable ranges to try include 0xd0000-0xdffff, 0xc0000-0xcffff, 0xc8000-0xcffff, or 0xd8000-0xdffff.

If you have DOS or Windows PCMCIA drivers, you may be able to deduce what memory region those drivers use. Note that DOS memory addresses are often specified in "segment" form, which leaves off the final hex digit (so an absolute address of 0xd0000 might be given as 0xd000). Be sure to add the extra digit back when making changes to `/etc/pcmcia/config.opts`.

3.4   Failure to detect card insertions and removals

Symptoms:

- Cards are detected and configured properly if present at boot time.
- The drivers do not respond to insertion and removal events, either by recording events in the system log, or by beeping.

In most cases, the socket driver (`i82365` or `tcic`) will automatically probe and select an appropriate interrupt to signal card status changes. The automatic interrupt probe doesn't work on some Intel-compatible controllers, including Cirrus chips and the chips used in some IBM ThinkPads. If a device is inactive at probe time, its interrupt may also appear to be available. In these cases, the socket driver may pick an interrupt that is used by another device.

With the `i82365` and `tcic` drivers, the `irq_list` option can be used to limit the interrupts that will be tested. This list limits the set of interrupts that can be used by PCMCIA cards as well as for monitoring card status changes. The `cs_irq` option can also be used to explicitly set the interrupt to be used for monitoring card status changes.

If you can't find an interrupt number that works, there is also a polled status mode: both `i82365` and `tcic` will accept a `poll_interval=100` option, to poll for card status changes once per second. This option should also be used if your system has a shortage of interrupts available for use by PCMCIA cards. Especially for systems with more than one PCMCIA controller, there is little point in dedicating interrupts for monitoring card status changes.

All these options should be set in the `PCIC_OPTS=` line in either `/etc/rc.d/rc.pcmcia` or `/etc/sysconfig/pcmcia`, depending on your site setup.

3.5   Resource conflict between two cards

Symptoms:

- Two cards each work fine when used separately.
- When both cards are inserted, only one works.

This usually indicates a resource conflict with a system device that Linux does not know about. PCMCIA devices are dynamically configured, so, for example, interrupts are allocated as needed, rather than specifically assigned to particular cards or sockets. Given a list of resources that appear to be available, cards are assigned resources in the order they are configured. In this case, the card configured last is being assigned a resource that in fact is not free.

Check the system log to see what resources are used by the non-working card. Exclude these in `/etc/pcmcia/config.opts`, and restart the `cardmgr` daemon to reload the resource database.

3.6   Device configuration does not complete

Symptoms:

- When a card is inserted, exactly one high beep is heard.
- Subsequent card insertions and removals may be ignored.

This indicates that the card was identified successfully, however, `cardmgr` has been unable to complete the configuration process for some reason. The most likely reason is that a step in the card setup script has blocked. A good example would be the network script blocking if a network card is inserted with no actual network hookup present.

To pinpoint the problem, you can manually run a setup script to see where it is blocking. The scripts are in the `/etc/pcmcia` directory. They take two parameters: a device name, and an action. The `cardmgr` daemon records the configuration commands in the system log. For example, if the system log shows that the command "./network start eth0" was the last command executed by `cardmgr`, the following commands would trace the script:

```
cd /etc/pcmcia
sh -x ./network start eth0
```

4   Usage and features

4.1   Tools for configuring and monitoring PCMCIA devices

If the modules are all loaded correctly, the output of the `lsmod` command should look like the following, when no cards are inserted:

```
Module          Size  Used by
ds              5640  2
i82365         15452  2
pcmcia_core    30012  3  [ds i82365]
```

The system log should also include output from the socket driver describing the host controller(s) found and the number of sockets detected.

4.1.1   The cardmgr configuration daemon

The `cardmgr` daemon is responsible for monitoring PCMCIA sockets, loading client drivers when needed, and running user-level scripts in response to card insertions and removals. It records its actions in the system log, but also uses beeps to signal card status changes. The tones of the beeps indicate success or failure of particular configuration steps. Two high beeps indicate that a card was identified and configured successfully. A high beep followed by a low beep indicates that a card was identified, but could not be configured for some reason. One low beep indicates that a card could not be identified.

`Cardmgr` records device information for each socket in `/var/run/stab`. Here is a sample `/var/run/stab` listing:

```
Socket 0: Adaptec APA-1460 SlimSCSI
0     scsi     aha152x_cs     0     sda     8     0
```

```
0        scsi    aha152x_cs    1      scd0    11    0
Socket 1: Serial or Modem Card
1        serial  serial_cs     0      ttyS1   5     65
```

For the lines describing devices, the first field is the socket, the second is the device class, the third is the driver name, the fourth is used to number multiple devices associated with the same driver, the fifth is the device name, and the final two fields are the major and minor device numbers for this device (if applicable).

The cardmgr daemon configures cards based on a database of known card types kept in /etc/pcmcia/config. This file describes the various client drivers, then describes how to identify various cards, and which driver(s) belong with which cards. The format of this file is described in the pcmcia(5) man page.

4.1.2 The cardctl and cardinfo utilities

The cardctl command can be used to check the status of a socket, or to see how it is configured. It can also be used to alter the configuration status of a card. Here is an example of the output of the "cardctl config" command:

```
Socket 0:
Socket 1:
  Vcc = 5.0, Vpp1 = 0.0, Vpp2 = 0.0
  Card type is memory and I/O
  IRQ 3 is dynamic shared, level mode, enabled
  Speaker output is enabled
  Function 0:
    Config register base = 0x0800
      Option = 0x63, status = 0x08
    I/O window 1: 0x0280 to 0x02bf, auto sized
    I/O window 2: 0x02f8 to 0x02ff, 8 bit
```

The "cardctl suspend" and "cardctl resume" commands can be used to shut down a card without unloading its associated drivers. The "cardctl reset" command attempts to reset and reconfigure a card. "cardctl insert" and "cardctl eject" mimic the actions performed when a card is physically inserted or ejected, including loading or unloading drivers, and configuring or shutting down devices.

If you are running X, the cardinfo utility produces a graphical display showing the current status of all PCMCIA sockets, similar in content to "cardctl config". It also provides a graphical interface to most other cardctl functions.

4.1.3 Inserting and ejecting cards

In theory, you can insert and remove PCMCIA cards at any time. However, it is a good idea not to eject a card that is currently being used by an application program. Kernels older than 1.1.77 would often lock up when serial/modem cards were ejected, but this should be fixed now.

4.1.4 Card Services and Advanced Power Management

Card Services can be compiled with support for APM (Advanced Power Management) if you've installed this package on your system. APM is incorporated into 1.3.46 and later kernels. It is currently being maintained by Rick Faith (faith@cs.unc.edu), and APM tools can be obtained from `<ftp://ftp.cs.unc.edu/pub/users/faith/linux>`. The PCMCIA modules will automatically be configured for APM if a compatible version is detected on your system.

Without resorting to APM, you can do "`cardctl suspend`" before suspending your laptop, and "`cardctl resume`" after resuming, to properly shut down and restart your PCMCIA cards. This will not work with a PCMCIA modem that is in use, because the serial driver isn't able to save and restore the modem operating parameters.

APM seems to be unstable on some systems. If you experience trouble with APM and PCMCIA on your system, try to narrow down the problem to one package or the other before reporting a bug.

Some drivers, notably the PCMCIA SCSI drivers, cannot recover from a suspend/resume cycle. When using a PCMCIA SCSI card, use "`cardctl eject`" prior to suspending the system.

4.1.5 Shutting down the PCMCIA system

To unload the entire PCMCIA package, invoke `rc.pcmcia` with:

```
/etc/rc.d/rc.pcmcia stop
```

This script will take several seconds to run, to give all client drivers time to shut down gracefully. If a PCMCIA device is currently in use, the shutdown will be incomplete, and some kernel modules may not be unloaded. To avoid this, use "`cardctl eject`" to shut down all sockets before invoking `rc.pcmcia`. The exit status of the `cardctl` command will indicate if any sockets could not be shut down.

4.2 Overview of the PCMCIA configuration scripts

Each PCMCIA device has an associated "class" that describes how it should be configured and managed. Classes are associated with device drivers in `/etc/pcmcia/config`. There are currently five IO device classes (network, SCSI, cdrom, fixed disk, and serial) and two memory device classes (memory and FTL). For each class, there are two scripts in `/etc/pcmcia/config`: a main configuration script (i.e., `/etc/pcmcia/scsi` for SCSI devices), and an options script (i.e., `/etc/pcmcia/scsi.opts`). The main script for a device will be invoked to configure that device when a card is inserted, and to shut down the device when the card is removed. For cards with several associated devices, the script will be invoked for each device.

The config scripts start by extracting some information about a device from `/var/run/stab`. Each script constructs a "device address", that uniquely describes the device it has been asked to configure, in the `ADDRESS` shell variable. This is passed to the `*.opts` script, which should return information about how a device at this address should be configured. For some devices, the device address is just the socket number. For others, it includes extra information that may be useful in deciding how to configure the device. For example, network devices pass their hardware ethernet address as part of the device address, so the `network.opts` script could use this to select from several different configurations.

The first part of all device addresses is the current PCMCIA "scheme". This parameter is used to support multiple sets of device configurations based on a single external user-specified variable. One use of schemes would be to have a "home" scheme, and a "work" scheme, which would include different sets of network configuration parameters. The current scheme is selected using the "`cardctl scheme`" command. The default if no scheme is set is "default".

As a general rule, when configuring Linux for a laptop, PCMCIA devices should only be configured from the PCMCIA device scripts. Do not try to configure a PCMCIA device the same way you would configure a permanently attached device. However, some Linux distributions provide PCMCIA packages that are hooked into those distributions' own device configuration tools. In that case, some of the following sections may not apply; ideally, this will be documented in the distribution.

4.3   PCMCIA network adapters

Linux ethernet-type network interfaces normally have names like eth0, eth1, and so on. Token-ring adapters are handled similarly, however they are named tr0, tr1, and so on. The ifconfig command is used to view or modify the state of a network interface. A peculiarity of Linux is that network interfaces do not have corresponding device files under /dev, so do not be surprised when you do not find them.

When a PCMCIA ethernet card is detected, it will be assigned the first free interface name, which will probably be eth0. Cardmgr will run the /etc/pcmcia/network script to configure the interface.

Do not configure your PCMCIA ethernet card in /etc/rc.d/rc.inet1, since the card may not be present when this script is executed. Comment out everything except the loopback stuff in rc.inet1. Instead, edit the /etc/pcmcia/network.opts file to match your local network setup. The network and network.opts scripts will be executed only when your ethernet card is actually present. If your system has an automatic network configuration procedure, it may or may not be PCMCIA-aware. Consult the documentation of your Linux distribution to determine if PCMCIA network devices should be configured with the automatic tools, or by editing network.opts.

The device address passed to network.opts consists of four comma-separated fields: the scheme, the socket number, the device instance, and the card's hardware ethernet address. The device instance is used to number devices for cards that have several network interfaces, so it will usually be 0. If you have several network cards used for different purposes, one option would be to configure the cards based on socket position, as in:

```
case "$ADDRESS" in
*,0,*,*)
    # definitions for network card in socket 0
    ;;
*,1,*,*)
    # definitions for network card in socket 1
    ;;
esac
```

Alternatively, they could be configured using their hardware addresses, as in:

```
case "$ADDRESS" in
*,*,*,00:80:C8:76:00:B1)
    # definitions for a D-Link card
    ;;
*,*,*,08:00:5A:44:80:01)
    # definitions for an IBM card
esac
```

To automatically mount and unmount NFS filesystems, first add all these filesystems to /etc/fstab, but include noauto in the mount options. In network.opts, list the filesystem mount points in the MOUNTS variable. It is especially important to use either cardctl or cardinfo to shut down a network card when NFS mounts are configured this way. It is not possible to cleanly unmount NFS filesystems if a network card is simply ejected without warning.

In addition to the usual network configuration parameters, the network.opts script can specify extra actions to be taken after an interface is configured, or before an interface is shut down. If network.opts defines a shell function called start_fn, it will be invoked by the network script after the interface is configured, and the interface name will be passed to the function as its first (and only) argument. Similarly, if it is defined, stop_fn will be invoked before shutting down an interface.

4.3.1 Transceiver selection

The transceiver type can be selected in `network.opts` using the `IF_PORT` setting. This can either be a numeric value as in previous PCMCIA releases, or a keyword identifying the transceiver type. All the network drivers default to either autodetect the interface if possible, or 10baseT otherwise. The `ifport` command can be used to check or set the current transceiver type. For example:

```
# ifport eth0 10base2
#
# ifport eth0
eth0    2 (10base2)
```

Current releases of the 3c589 driver attempt to autodetect the network connection, but this doesn't seem to be completely functional yet. For autodetection to work, the network cable should be connected to the card when the card is configured. Alternatively, once the network is connected, you can force the driver to check the connection with:

```
ifconfig eth0 down up
```

4.3.2 Comments about specific cards

- With IBM CCAE and Socket EA cards, you need to pick the transceiver type (10base2, 10baseT, AUI) when the network device is configured. Make sure that the transceiver type reported in the system log matches your connection.

- The drivers for SMC, Megahertz, Ositech, and 3Com cards should autodetect the attached network type (10base2 or 10baseT). Setting the transceiver type when the driver is loaded serves to define the card's "first guess".

- The Farallon EtherWave is actually based on the 3Com 3c589, with a special transceiver. Though the EtherWave uses 10baseT-style connections, its transceiver requires that the 3c589 be configured in 10base2 mode.

- If you have trouble with an IBM CCAE, NE4100, Thomas Conrad, or Kingston adapter, try increasing the memory access time with the `mem_speed=#` option to the `pcnet_cs` module. An example of how to do this is given in the standard `config.opts` file. Try speeds of up to 1000 (in nanoseconds).

- For the New Media Ethernet adapter, on some systems, it may be necessary to increase the IO port access time with the `io_speed=#` option when the `pcmcia_core` module is loaded. Edit `CORE_OPTS` in the startup script to set this option.

- The multicast support in the New Media Ethernet driver is incomplete. The latest driver will function with multicast kernels, but will ignore multicast packets. Promiscuous mode should work properly.

- The driver used by the IBM and 3Com token ring adapters seems to behave very badly if the cards are not connected to a ring when they get initialized. Always connect these cards to the net before they are powered up. This driver also requires free IO ports in the range of 0xa20-0xa27. On some systems, the automatic IO port conflict checker will incorrectly determine that this port range is unavailable. In that case, the port check can be disabled by loading the `pcmcia_core` module with `probe_io=0`.

- Newer Linksys and D-Link cards have a unique way of selecting the transceiver type that isn't handled by the Linux drivers. One workaround is to boot DOS and use the vendor-supplied utility to select the transceiver, then warm boot Linux. I am looking for beta testers for a Linux utility to perform this function.

- For WaveLAN wireless network adapters, Jean Tourrilhes (`jt@hplb.hpl.hp.com`) has put together a wireless HOWTO at `<http://www-uk.hpl.hp.com/people/jt/Linux/Wavelan.html>`.

4.3.3   Diagnosing problems with network adapters

- Is your card recognized as an ethernet card? Check the system log and make sure that `cardmgr` identifies the card correctly and starts up one of the network drivers. If it doesn't, your card might still be usable if it is compatible with a supported card. This will be most easily done if the card claims to be "NE2000 compatible".

- Is the card configured properly? If you are using a supported card, and it was recognized by `cardmgr`, but still doesn't work, there might be an interrupt or port conflict with another device. Find out what resources the card is using (from the system log), and try excluding these in `/etc/pcmcia/config.opts` to force the card to use something different.

- If your card seems to be configured properly, but sometimes locks up, particularly under high load, you may need to try changing your socket driver timing parameters. See section 2.5 (2.3) for more information.

- If you get messages like "network unreachable" when you try to access the network, then you have probably set up `/etc/pcmcia/network.opts` incorrectly. On the other hand, mis-configured cards will usually fail silently.

- To diagnose problems in `/etc/pcmcia/network.opts`, start by trying to ping other systems on the same subnet using their IP addresses. Then try to ping your gateway, and then machines on other subnets. Ping machines by name only after trying these simpler tests.

- Make sure your problem is really a PCMCIA one. It may help to see see if the card works under DOS with the vendor's drivers. Double check your modifications to the `/etc/pcmcia/network.opts` script. Make sure your drop cable, "T" jack, terminator, etc are working.

4.4   PCMCIA serial and modem devices

Linux serial devices are accessed via the `/dev/cua*` and `/dev/ttyS*` special device files. The `ttyS*` devices are for incoming connections, such as directly connected terminals. The `cua*` devices are for outgoing connections, such as modems. Each physical serial port has both a `ttyS` and a `cua` device file: it is up to you to pick the appropriate device for your application. The configuration of a serial device can be examined and modified with the `setserial` command.

When a PCMCIA serial or modem card is detected, it will be assigned to the first available serial device slot. This will usually be `/dev/ttyS1` (cua1) or `/dev/ttyS2` (cua2), depending on the number of built-in serial ports. The `ttyS*` device is the one reported in `/var/run/stab`. The default serial device option script, `/etc/pcmcia/serial.opts`, will link the corresponding `cua*` device file to `/dev/modem` as a convenience.

Do not try to use `/etc/rc.d/rc.serial` to configure a PCMCIA modem. This script should only be used to configure non-removable devices. Modify `/etc/pcmcia/serial.opts` if you want to do anything special to set up your modem. Also, do not try to change the IO port and interrupt settings of a PCMCIA serial device using `setserial`. This would tell the serial driver to look for the device in a different place, but would not change how the card hardware is actually configured. The serial configuration script allows you to specify other `setserial` options, as well as whether a line should be added to `/etc/inittab` for this port.

The device address passed to `serial.opts` has three comma-separated fields: the first is the scheme, the second is the socket number, and the third is the device instance. The device instance may take several values for cards that support multiple serial ports, but for single-port cards, it will always be 0. If you commonly use more than one PCMCIA modem, you may want to specify different settings based on socket position, as in:

```
case "$ADDRESS" in
*,0,*)
    # Options for modem in socket 0
```

```
        LINK=/dev/modem0
        ;;
    *,1,*)
        # Options for modem in socket 1
        LINK=/dev/modem1
        ;;
    esac
```

If a PCMCIA modem is already configured when Linux boots, it may be incorrectly identified as an ordinary built-in serial port. This is harmless, however, when the PCMCIA drivers take control of the modem, it will be assigned a different device slot. It is best to either parse **/var/run/stab** or use **/dev/modem**, rather than expecting a PCMCIA modem to always have the same device assignment.

If you configure your kernel to load the basic Linux serial port driver as a module, you must edit **/etc/pcmcia/config** to indicate that this module must be loaded. Edit the serial device entry to read:

```
    device "serial_cs"
      class "serial" module "misc/serial", "serial_cs"
```

4.4.1 Diagnosing problems with serial devices

- Is your card recognized as a modem? Check the system log and make sure that **cardmgr** identifies the card correctly and starts up the **serial_cs** driver. If it doesn't, you may need to add a new entry to your **/etc/pcmcia/config** file so that it will be identified properly. See section 6.1 (3.6) for details.

- Is the modem configured successfully by serial_cs? Again, check the system log and look for messages from the serial_cs driver. If you see "register_serial() failed", you may have an I/O port conflict with another device. Another tip-off of a conflict is if the device is reported to be an 8250; most modern PCMCIA modems should be identified as 16550A UART's. If you think you're seeing a port conflict, edit **/etc/pcmcia/config.opts** and exclude the port range that was allocated for the modem.

- Is there an interrupt conflict? If the system log looks good, but the modem just doesn't seem to work, try using **setserial** to change the irq to 0, and see if the modem works. This causes the serial driver to use a slower polled mode instead of using interrupts. If this seems to fix the problem, it is likely that some other device in your system is using the interrupt selected by serial_cs. You should add a line to **/etc/pcmcia/config.opts** to exclude this interrupt.

- If the modem seems to work only very, very slowly, this is an almost certain indicator of an interrupt conflict.

- Make sure your problem is really a PCMCIA one. It may help to see if the card works under DOS with the vendor's drivers. Also, don't test the card with something complex like SLIP or PPP until you are sure you can make simple connections. If simple things work but SLIP does not, your problem is most likely with SLIP, not with PCMCIA.

- If you get kernel messages indicating that the serial_cs module cannot be loaded, it means that your kernel does not have serial device support. If you have compiled the serial driver as a module, you must modify **/etc/pcmcia/config** to indicate that the **serial** module should be loaded before **serial_cs**.

4.5 PCMCIA SCSI adapters

All the currently supported PCMCIA SCSI cards are work-alikes of one of the following ISA bus cards: the Qlogic, the Adaptec AHA-152X, or the Future Domain TMC-16x0. The PCMCIA drivers are built by linking some PCMCIA-specific code (in `qlogic_cs.c`, `toaster_cs.c`, or `fdomain_cs.c`) with the normal Linux SCSI driver.

When a new SCSI host adapter is detected, the SCSI drivers will probe for devices. Check the system log to make sure your devices are detected properly. New SCSI devices will be assigned to the first available SCSI device files. The first SCSI disk will be `/dev/sda`, the first SCSI tape will be `/dev/st0`, and the first CD-ROM will be `/dev/scd0`.

With 1.3.X and later kernels, the PCMCIA core drivers are able to find out from the kernel which SCSI devices are connected to a card. They will be listed in `/var/run/stab`, and the SCSI configuration script, `/etc/pcmcia/scsi`, will be called once for each attached device, to either configure or shut down that device. The default script does not take any actions to configure SCSI devices, but will properly unmount filesystems on SCSI devices when a card is removed.

With 1.2.X kernels, the PCMCIA drivers cannot automatically deduce which devices are associated with a particular SCSI adapter. Instead, if you have one normal SCSI device configuration, you may list these devices in `/etc/pcmcia/scsi.opts`. For example, if you normally have a SCSI disk and a CD-ROM, you would use:

```
# For 1.2 kernels: list of attached devices
SCSI_DEVICES="sda scd0"
```

The device addresses passed to `scsi.opts` are complicated, because of the variety of things that can be attached to a SCSI adapter. Addresses consist of either six or seven comma-separated fields: the current scheme, the device type, the socket number, the SCSI channel, ID, and logical unit number, and optionally, the partition number. The device type will be "sd" for disks, "st" for tapes, "sr" for CD-ROM devices, and "sg" for generic SCSI devices. For most setups, the SCSI channel and logical unit number will be 0. For disk devices with several partitions, `scsi.opts` will first be called for the whole device, with a five-field address. The script should set the `PARTS` variable to a list of partitions. Then, `scsi.opts` will be called for each partition, with the longer seven-field addresses. For example, here is a script for configuring a disk device at SCSI ID 3, with two partitions, and a CD-ROM at SCSI ID 6:

```
case "$ADDRESS" in
*,sd,*,0,3,0)
    # This device has two partitions...
    PARTS="1 2"
    ;;
*,sd,*,0,3,0,1)
    # Options for partition 1:
    #  update /etc/fstab, and mount an ext2 fs on /usr1
    DO_FSTAB="y" ; DO_FSCK="y" ; DO_MOUNT="y"
    FSTYPE="ext2"
    OPTS=""
    MOUNTPT="/usr1"
    ;;
*,sd,*,0,3,0,2)
    # Options for partition 2:
    #  update /etc/fstab, and mount an MS-DOS fs on /usr2
    DO_FSTAB="y" ; DO_FSCK="y" ; DO_MOUNT="y"
    FSTYPE="msdos"
    OPTS=""
```

```
        MOUNTPT="/usr2"
        ;;
    *,sr,*,0,6,0)
        # Options for CD-ROM at SCSI ID 6
        PARTS=""
        DO_FSTAB="y" ; DO_FSCK="n" ; DO_MOUNT="y"
        FSTYPE="iso9660"
        OPTS="ro"
        MOUNTPT="/cdrom"
        ;;
    esac
```

If your kernel does not have a top-level driver (disk, tape, etc) for a particular SCSI device, then the device will not be configured by the PCMCIA drivers. As a side effect, the device's name in /var/run/stab will be something like "sd#nnnn" where "nnnn" is a four-digit hex number. This happens when cardmgr is unable to translate a SCSI device ID into a corresponding Linux device name.

It is possible to modularize the top-level SCSI drivers so that they are only loaded when a PCMCIA SCSI adapter is detected. To do so, you need to edit /etc/pcmcia/config to tell cardmgr which extra modules need to be loaded when your adapter is configured. For example:

```
    device "aha152x_cs"
        class "scsi" module "scsi/scsi_mod", "scsi/sd_mod", "aha152x_cs"
```

would say to load the core SCSI module and the top-level disk driver module before loading the regular PCMCIA driver module. The PCMCIA Configure script will not automatically detect modularized SCSI modules, so you will need use the manual configure option to enable SCSI support.

Always turn on SCSI devices before powering up your laptop, or before inserting the adapter card, so that the SCSI bus is properly terminated when the adapter is configured. Also be very careful about ejecting a SCSI adapter. Be sure that all associated SCSI devices are unmounted and closed before ejecting the card. The best way to ensure this is to use either cardctl or cardinfo to request card removal before physically ejecting the card. For now, all SCSI devices should be powered up before plugging in a SCSI adapter, and should stay connected until after you unplug the adapter and/or power down your laptop.

There is a potential complication when using these cards that does not arise with ordinary ISA bus adapters. The SCSI bus carries a "termination power" signal that is necessary for proper operation of ordinary passive SCSI terminators. PCMCIA SCSI adapters do not supply termination power, so if it is required, an external device must supply it. Some external SCSI devices may be configured to supply termination power. Others, such as the Zip Drive and the Syquest EZ-Drive, use active terminators that do not depend on it. In some cases, it may be necessary to use a special terminator block such as the APS SCSI Sentry 2, which has an external power supply. When configuring your SCSI device chain, be aware of whether or not any of your devices require or can provide termination power.

The Adaptec APA-460 SlimSCSI adapter is not supported. This card was originally sold under the Trantor name, and when Adaptec merged with Trantor, they continued to sell the Trantor card with an Adaptec label. The APA-460 is not compatible with any existing Linux driver. I'm not sure how hard it would be to write a driver; I don't think anyone has been able to obtain the technical information from Adaptec.

The (unsupported) Trantor SlimSCSI can be identified by the following:

```
    Trantor / Adaptec APA-460 SlimSCSI
    FCC ID: IE8T460
    Shipped with SCSIworks! driver software
```

The (supported) Adaptec SlimSCSI can be identified by the following:

```
Adaptec APA-1460 SlimSCSI
FCC ID: FGT1460
P/N: 900100
Shipped with EZ-SCSI driver software
```

4.5.1   Diagnosing problems with SCSI adapters

- With the aha152x_cs driver (used by Adaptec, New Media, and a few others), it seems that SCSI disconnect/reconnect support is a frequent source of trouble with tape drives. To disable this "feature," add the following to /etc/pcmcia/config.opts:

      ```
      module "aha152x_cs" opts "reconnect=0"
      ```

- If you have compiled SCSI support as modules (CONFIG_SCSI is "m"), when configuring PCMCIA, you must explicitly specify that you want the SCSI drivers to be built. You must also modify /etc/pcmcia/config to load the SCSI modules before the appropriate *_cs driver is loaded.

- If you get "aborting command due to timeout" messages when the SCSI bus is probed, you almost certainly have an interrupt conflict.

4.6   PCMCIA memory cards

The memory_cs driver handles all types of memory cards, as well as providing direct access to the PCMCIA memory address space for cards that have other functions. When loaded, it creates a combination of character and block devices. See the man page for the module for a complete description of the device naming scheme. Block devices are used for disk-like access (creating and mounting filesystems, etc). The character devices are for "raw" unbuffered reads and writes at arbitrary locations.

The device address passed to memory.opts consists of two fields: the scheme, and the socket number. The options are applied to the first common memory partition on the corresponding memory card. Here is an example of a script that will automatically mount memory cards based on which socket they are inserted into:

```
case "$ADDRESS" in
*,0,0)
    # Mount filesystem, but don't update /etc/fstab
    DO_FSTAB="n" ; DO_FSCK="y" ; DO_MOUNT="y"
    FSTYPE="ext2" ; OPTS=""
    MOUNTPT="/mem0"
    ;;
*,1,0)
    # Mount filesystem, but don't update /etc/fstab
    DO_FSTAB="n" ; DO_FSCK="y" ; DO_MOUNT="y"
    FSTYPE="ext2" ; OPTS=""
    MOUNTPT="/mem1"
    ;;
esac
```

Some older memory cards, and most simple static RAM cards, lack a "Card Information Structure" (CIS), which is the scheme PCMCIA cards use to identify themselves. Normally, cardmgr will assume that any card that lacks a CIS is a simple memory card, and load the memory_cs driver. Thus, a common side effect of a general card identification problem is that other types of cards may be misdetected as memory cards.

The memory_cs driver uses a heuristic to guess the capacity of these cards. The heuristic does not work for write protected cards, and may make mistakes in some other cases as well. If a card is misdetected, its size should then be explicitly specified when using commands such as dd or mkfs.

4.6.1   Using flash memory cards

The device address passed to ftl.opts consists of three or four fields: the scheme, the socket number, the region number, and optionally, the partition number. Most flash cards have just one flash memory region, so the region number will generally always be zero.

To use a flash memory card as an ordinary disk-like block device, first create an FTL, or "flash translation layer", partition on the device with the ftl_format command. This layer hides the device-specific details of flash memory programming and make the card look like a simple block device. For example:

```
ftl_format -i /dev/mem0c0c
```

Note that this command accesses the card through the "raw" memory card interface. Once formatted, the card can be accessed as an ordinary block device via the ftl_cs driver. For example:

```
mke2fs /dev/ftl0c0
mount -t ext2 /dev/ftl0c0 /mnt
```

Device naming for FTL devices is tricky. Minor device numbers have three parts: the card number, the region number on that card, and optionally, the partition within that region. A region can either be treated as a single block device with no partition table (like a floppy), or it can be partitioned like a hard disk device. The "ftl0c0" device is card 0, common memory region 0, the entire region. The "ftl0c0p1" through "ftl0c0p4" devices are primary partitions 1 through 4 if the region has been partitioned.

There are two major formats for flash memory cards: the FTL style, and the Microsoft Flash File System. The FTL format is generally more flexible because it allows any ordinary high-level filesystem (ext2, ms-dos, etc) to be used on a flash card as if it were an ordinary disk device. The FFS is a completely different filesystem type. Linux cannot currently handle cards formated with FFS.

4.7   PCMCIA ATA/IDE card drives

ATA/IDE drive support requires a 1.3.72 or higher kernel. The PCMCIA-specific part of the driver is fixed_cs. Be sure to use cardctl or cardinfo to shut down an ATA/IDE card before ejecting it, as the driver has not been made "hot-swap-proof".

The device addresses passed to fixed.opts consist of either three or four fields: the current scheme, the socket number, the drive's serial number, and an optional partition number. As with SCSI devices, fixed.opts is first called for the entire device. If fixed.opts returns a list of partitions in the PARTS variable, the script will then be called for each partition.

Here is an example fixed.opts file to mount the first partition of any ATA/IDE card on /mnt.

```
case "$ADDRESS" in
*,*,*)
```

```
        PARTS="1"
        ;;
    *,*,*,1)
        DO_FSTAB="y" ; DO_FSCK="y" ; DO_MOUNT="y"
        FSTYPE="msdos"
        OPTS=""
        MOUNTPT="/mnt"
        ;;
    esac
```

Note that the default `fixed.opts` file has these lines but they are commented out. If you wish, you can have separate configurations for specific cards based on their serial numbers. To find out a drive's serial number, use the `ide_info` utility. Then, part of `fixed.opts` might look like:

```
    case "$ADDRESS" in
    *,*,Z4J60542)
        # This is my DOS stuff
        PARTS="1"
        ;;
    *,*,Z4J60542,1)
        DO_FSTAB="y" ; DO_FSCK="y" ; DO_MOUNT="y"
        FSTYPE="msdos"
        OPTS=""
        MOUNTPT="/mnt"
        ;;
    esac
```

4.7.1 Diagnosing problems with ATA/IDE adapters

- Some IDE drives violate the PCMCIA specification by requiring a longer time to spin up than the maximum allowed card setup time. To use these cards, load the `pcmcia_core` module with:

  ```
      CORE_OPTS="unreset_delay=400"
  ```

- To use an ATA/IDE CD-ROM device, your kernel must be compiled with `CONFIG_BLK_DEV_IDECD` enabled. This will normally be the case for standard kernels, however it is something to be aware of if you compile a custom kernel.

4.8 Multifunction cards

Starting with the 1.3.73 Linux kernel, a single interrupt can be shared by several drivers, such as the serial driver and an ethernet driver. When using a multifunction card under a newer kernel, all card functions can be used without loading and unloading drivers.

Simultaneous use of two card functions is "tricky" and various hardware vendors have implemented interrupt sharing in their own incompatible (and sometimes proprietary) ways. The drivers for some cards (Ositech Jack of Diamonds, 3Com 3c562, Linksys) properly support simultaneous access, but others (Megahertz in particular) do not.

Earlier kernels do not support interrupt sharing between different device drivers, so it is not possible for the PCMCIA drivers to configure this card for simultaneous ethernet and modem access. The ethernet and serial drivers are both loaded automatically. However, the ethernet driver "owns" the card interrupt by default. To use the modem, you can unload the ethernet driver and reconfigure the serial port by doing something like:

```
ifconfig eth0 down
rmmod 3c589_cs
setserial /dev/modem autoconfig auto_irq
setserial /dev/modem
```

The second `setserial` should verify that the port has been configured to use the interrupt previously used by the ethernet driver.

5   Advanced topics

5.1   Resource allocation for PCMCIA devices

In theory, it should not really matter which interrupt is allocated to which device, as long as two devices are not configured to use the same interrupt. In `/etc/pcmcia/config.opts` you'll find a place for excluding interrupts that are used by non-PCMCIA devices.

Similarly, there is no way to directly specify the I/O addresses for a PCMCIA card to use. The `/etc/pcmcia/config.opts` file allows you to specify ranges of ports available for use by all PCMCIA devices, or to exclude ranges that conflict with other devices.

After modifying `/etc/pcmcia/config.opts`, you can restart `cardmgr` with "`kill -HUP`".

The interrupt used to monitor card status changes is chosen by the low-level socket driver module (`i82365` or `tcic`) before `cardmgr` parses `/etc/pcmcia/config`, so it is not affected by changes to this file. To set this interrupt, use the `cs_irq=` option when the socket driver is loaded, by setting the `PCIC_OPTS` variable in `/etc/rc.d/rc.pcmcia`.

All the client card drivers have a parameter called `irq_list` for specifying which interrupts they may try to allocate. These driver options should be set in your `/etc/pcmcia/config` file. For example:

```
device "serial_cs"
  module "serial_cs" opts "irq_list=8,12"
  ...
```

would specify that the serial driver should only use irq 8 or irq 12. Regardless of `irq_list` settings, Card Services will never allocate an interrupt that is already in use by another device, or an interrupt that is excluded in the config file.

5.2   How can I have separate device setups for home and work?

This is fairly easy using PCMCIA "scheme" support. Use two configuration schemes, called "home" and "work". Here is an example of a `network.opts` script with scheme-specific settings:

```
case "$ADDRESS" in
```

```
    work,*,*,*)
        # definitions for network card in work scheme
        ...
        ;;
    home,*,*,*|default,*,*,*)
        # definitions for network card in home scheme
        ...
        ;;
    esac
```

The first part of a PCMCIA device address is always the configuration scheme. In this example, the second "case" clause will select for both the "home" and "default" schemes. So, if the scheme is unset for any reason, it will default to the "home" setup.

Now, to choose between the two sets of settings, run either:

```
    cardctl scheme home
```

or

```
    cardctl scheme work
```

The `cardctl` command does the equivalent of shutting down all your cards and restarting them. The command can be safely executed whether or not the PCMCIA system is loaded, but the command may fail if you are using other PCMCIA devices at the time (even if their configurations are not explicitly dependant on the scheme setting).

To find out the current PCMCIA scheme setting, run:

```
    cardctl scheme
```

5.3   Booting from a PCMCIA device

Having the root filesystem on a PCMCIA device is tricky because the Linux PCMCIA system is not designed to be linked into the kernel. Its core components, the loadable kernel modules and the user mode cardmgr daemon, depend on an already running system. The kernel's "initrd" facility works around this requirement by allowing Linux to boot using a temporary ram disk as a minimal root image, load drivers, and then re-mount a different root filesystem. The temporary root can configure PCMCIA devices and then re-mount a PCMCIA device as root.

The initrd image absolutely must reside on a bootable device: this generally cannot be put on a PCMCIA device. This is a BIOS limitation, not a kernel limitation. It is useful here to distinguish between "boot-able" devices (i.e., devices that can be booted), and "root-able" devices (i.e., devices that can be mounted as root). "Boot-able" devices are determined by the BIOS, and are generally limited to internal floppy and hard disk drives. "Root-able" devices are any block devices that the kernel supports once it has been loaded. The initrd facility makes more devices "root-able", not "boot-able".

Some Linux distributions will allow installation to a device connected to a PCMCIA SCSI adapter, as an unintended side-effect of their support for installs from PCMCIA SCSI CD-ROM devices. However, at present, no Linux installation tools support configuring an appropriate "initrd" to boot Linux with a PCMCIA root filesystem. Setting up a system with a PCMCIA root thus requires that you use another Linux system to create the "initrd" image. If another Linux system is not available, another option would be to temporarily install a minimal Linux setup on a non-PCMCIA drive, create an initrd image, and then reinstall to the PCMCIA target.

The Linux Bootdisk-HOWTO has some general information about setting up boot disks but nothing specific to initrd. The main initrd document is included with recent kernel source code distributions, in `linux/Documentation/initrd.txt`. Before beginning, you should read this document. A familiarity with `lilo` is also helpful. Using initrd also requires that you have a kernel compiled with `CONFIG_BLK_DEV_RAM` and `CONFIG_BLK_DEV_INITRD` enabled.

This is an advanced configuration technique, and requires a high level of familiarity with Linux and the PCMCIA system. Be sure to read all the relevant documentation before starting. The following cookbook instructions should work, but deviations from the examples will quickly put you in uncharted and "unsupported" territory, and you will be on your own.

This method absolutely requires that you use a PCMCIA driver release of 2.9.5 or later. Older PCMCIA packages or individual components will not work in the initrd context. Do not mix components from different releases.

5.3.1   The pcinitrd helper script

The `pcinitrd` script creates a basic initrd image for booting with a PCMCIA root partition. The image includes a minimal directory heirarchy, a handful of device files, a few binaries, shared libraries, and a set of PCMCIA driver modules. When invoking `pcinitrd`, you specify the driver modules that you want to be included in the image. The core PCMCIA components, `pcmcia_core` and `ds`, are automatically included.

As an example, say that your laptop uses an i82365-compatible PCMCIA host controller, and you want to boot Linux with the root filesystem on a hard drive attached to an Adaptec SlimSCSI adapter. You could create an appropriate initrd image with:

```
pcinitrd -v initrd pcmcia/i82365.o pcmcia/aha152x_cs.o
```

To customize the initrd startup sequence, you could mount the image using the "loopback" device with a command like:

```
mount -o loop -t ext2 initrd /mnt
```

and then edit the `linuxrc` script. The PCMCIA configuration files will be installed under `/etc` in the image, and can also be customized. See the man page for `pcinitrd` for more information.

5.3.2   Creating an initrd boot floppy

After creating an image with `pcinitrd`, you can create a boot floppy by copying the kernel, the compressed initrd image, and a few support files for `lilo` to a clean floppy. In the following example, we assume that the desired PCMCIA root device is `/dev/sda1`:

```
mke2fs /dev/fd0
mount /dev/fd0 /mnt
mkdir /mnt/etc /mnt/boot /mnt/dev
cp -a /dev/fd0 /dev/sda1 /mnt/dev
cp [kernel-image] /mnt/vmlinuz
gzip < [initrd-image] > /mnt/initrd
```

Create `/mnt/etc/lilo.conf` with the contents:

```
boot=/dev/fd0
compact
image=/vmlinuz
    label=linux
    initrd=/initrd
    read-only
    root=/dev/sda1
```

Finally, invoke lilo with:

```
lilo -r /mnt
```

When `lilo` is invoked with `-r`, it performs all actions relative to the specified alternate root directory. The reason for creating the device files under `/mnt/dev` was that `lilo` will not be able to use the files in `/dev` when it is running in this alternate-root mode.

5.3.3 Installing an initrd image on a non-Linux drive

One common use of the initrd facility would be on systems where the internal hard drive is dedicated to another operating system. The Linux kernel and initrd image can be placed in a non-Linux partition, and `lilo` or `LOADLIN` can be set up to boot Linux from these images.

Assuming that you have a kernel has been configured for the appropriate root device, and an initrd image created on another system, the easiest way to get started is to boot Linux using `LOADLIN`, as:

```
LOADLIN <kernel> initrd=<initrd-image>
```

Once you can boot Linux on your target machine, you could then install `lilo` to allow booting Linux directly. For example, say that `/dev/hda1` is the non-Linux target partition and `/mnt` can be used as a mount point. First, create a subdirectory on the target for the Linux files:

```
mount /dev/hda1 /mnt
mkdir /mnt/linux
cp [kernel-image] /mnt/linux/vmlinuz
cp [initrd-image] /mnt/linux/initrd
```

In this example, say that `/dev/sda1` is the desired Linux root partition, a SCSI hard drive mounted via a PCMCIA SCSI adapter. To install `lilo`, create a `lilo.conf` file with the contents:

```
boot=/dev/hda
map=/mnt/linux/map
compact
image=/mnt/linux/vmlinuz
        label=linux
        root=/dev/sda1
        initrd=/mnt/linux/initrd
        read-only
```

```
other=/dev/hda1
        table=/dev/hda
        label=windows
```

The `boot=` line says to install the boot loader in the master boot record of the specified device. The `root=` line identifies the desired root filesystem to be used after loading the initrd image, and may be unnecessary if the kernel image is already configured this way. The `other=` section is used to describe the other operating system installed on `/dev/hda1`.

To install `lilo` in this case, use:

```
lilo -C lilo.conf
```

Note that in this case, the `lilo.conf` file uses absolute paths that include `/mnt`. I did this in the example because the target filesystem may not support the creation of Linux device files for the `boot=` and `root=` options.

6   Dealing with unsupported cards

6.1   Configuring unrecognized cards

Assuming that your card is supported by an existing driver, all that needs to be done is to add an entry to `/etc/pcmcia/config` to tell `cardmgr` how to identify the card, and which driver(s) need to be linked up to this card. Check the man page for `pcmcia` for more information about the config file format. If you insert an unknown card, `cardmgr` will normally record some identification information in the system log that can be used to construct the config entry.

Here is an example of how cardmgr will report an unsupported card in `/usr/adm/messages`.

```
cardmgr[460]: unsupported card in socket 1
cardmgr[460]: version info: "MEGAHERTZ", "XJ2288", "V.34 PCMCIA MODEM"
```

The corresponding entry in `/etc/pcmcia/config` would be:

```
card "Megahertz XJ2288 V.34 Fax Modem"
  version "MEGAHERTZ", "XJ2288", "V.34 PCMCIA MODEM"
  bind "serial_cs"
```

You can use "*" to match strings that don't need to match exactly, like version numbers. When making new config entries, be careful to copy the strings exactly, preserving case and blank spaces. Also be sure that the config entry has the same number of strings as are reported in the log file.

Beware that you can specify just about any driver for a card, but if you're just shooting in the dark, there is not much reason to expect this to be productive. You may get lucky and find that your card is supported by an existing driver. However, the most likely outcome is that the driver won't work, and may have unfortunate side effects like locking up your system. Unlike most ordinary device drivers, which probe for an appropriate card, the probe for a PCMCIA device is done by `cardmgr`, and the driver itself may not do much validation before attempting to communicate with the device.

After editing `/etc/pcmcia/config`, you can signal `cardmgr` to reload the file with:

```
kill -HUP `cat /var/run/cardmgr.pid`
```

If you do set up an entry for a new card, please send me a copy so that I can include it in the standard config file.

6.2 Adding support for an NE2000-compatible ethernet card

First, see if the card is already recognized by `cardmgr`. Some cards not listed in `SUPPORTED.CARDS` are actually OEM versions of cards that are supported. If you find a card like this, let me know so I can add it to the list.

If your card is not recognized, follow the instructions in section 6.1 (3.6) to create a config entry for your card, and bind the card to the `pcnet_cs` driver. Restart `cardmgr` to use the updated config file.

If the `pcnet_cs` driver says that it is unable to determine your card's hardware ethernet address, then edit your new config entry to bind the card to the memory card driver, `memory_cs`. Restart `cardmgr` to use the new updated config file. You will need to know your card's hardware ethernet address. This address is a series of six two-digit hex numbers, often printed on the card itself. If it is not printed on the card, you may be able to use a DOS driver to display the address. In any case, once you know it, run:

```
dd if=/dev/mem0a count=20 | od -Ax -t x1
```

and search the output for your address. Only the even bytes are defined, so ignore the odd bytes in the dump. Record the hex offset of the first byte of the address. Now, edit `modules/pcnet_cs.c` and find the `hw_info` structure. You'll need to create a new entry for your card. The first field is the memory offset. The next three fields are the first three bytes of the hardware address. The final field contains some flags for specific card features; to start, try setting it to 0.

After editing `pcnet_cs.c`, compile and install the new module. Edit `/etc/pcmcia/config` again, and change the card binding from `memory_cs` to `pcnet_cs`. Follow the instructions for reloading the config file, and you should be all set. Please send me copies of your new `hw_info` and config entries.

If you can't find your card's hardware address in the hex dump, as a method of last resort, it is possible to "hard-wire" the address when the `pcnet_cs` module is initialized. Edit `/etc/pcmcia/config.opts` and add a `hw_addr=` option, like so:

```
module "pcnet_cs" opts "hw_addr=0x00,0x80,0xc8,0x01,0x02,0x03"
```

Substitute your own card's hardware address in the appropriate spot, of course. Beware that if you've gotten this far, it is very unlikely that your card is genuinely NE2000 compatible. In fact, I'm not sure if there are *any* cards that are not handled by one of the first two methods.

6.3 PCMCIA floppy interface cards

The PCMCIA floppy interface used in the Compaq Aero and a few other laptops is not yet supported by this package. The snag in supporting the Aero floppy is that the Aero seems to use a customized PCMCIA controller to support DMA to the floppy. Without knowing exactly how this is done, there isn't any way to implement support under Linux.

If the floppy adapter card is present when an Aero is booted, the Aero BIOS will configure the card, and Linux will identify it as a normal floppy drive. When the Linux PCMCIA drivers are loaded, they will notice that the card is already configured and attached to a Linux driver, and this socket will be left alone. So, the drive can be used if it is present at boot time, but the card is not hot swappable.

6.4 What's up with support for Xircom cards?

A driver for Xircom ethernet and ethernet/modem cards is included in the current PCMCIA package, thanks to the work of Werner Koch. I've set up a HyperNews forum specifically for discussion of Xircom driver development, at <http://hyper.stanford.edu/HyperNews/get/pcmcia/xircom.html>.

For a long time, Xircom cards were not supported because Xircom had a company policy of not disclosing technical information about their cards. However, they have relaxed their rules, and now, they do distribute driver information.

7 Debugging tips and programming information

7.1 Submitting useful bug reports

The best way to submit bug reports is to use the HyperNews message lists on the Linux PCMCIA information site. That way, other people can see current problems (and fixes or workarounds, if available). Here are some things that should be included in all bug reports:

- Your system type, and the output of the probe command.
- What PCMCIA cards you are using.
- Your Linux kernel version, and PCMCIA driver version.
- Any changes you have made to the startup files in /etc/pcmcia, or to the PCMCIA startup script.
- All PCMCIA-related messages in your system log file.

All the PCMCIA modules and the cardmgr daemon send status messages to the system log. This will usually be something like /var/log/messages or /usr/adm/messages. This file should be the first place to look when tracking down a problem. When submitting a bug report, always include the contents of this file. If you are having trouble finding your system messages, check /etc/syslogd.conf to see how different classes of messages are handled.

Before submitting a bug report, please check to make sure that you are using an up-to-date copy of the driver package. While it is somewhat gratifying to read bug reports for things I've already fixed, it isn't a particularly constructive use of my time.

If your problem involves a kernel fault, the register dump from the fault is only useful if you can track down the fault address, EIP. If it is in the main kernel, look up the address in System.map to identify the function at fault. If the fault is in a loadable module, it is a bit harder to trace. With the current module tools, "ksyms -m" will report the base address of each loadable module. Pick the module that contains the EIP address, and subtract its base address from EIP to get an offset inside that module. Then, run gdb on that module, and look up the offset with the list command. This will only work if you've compiled that module with -g to include debugging information.

If you do not have web access, bug reports can be sent to me at dhinds@hyper.stanford.edu. However, I prefer that bug reports be posted to my web site, so that they can be seen by others.

7.2 Low level PCMCIA debugging aids

The PCMCIA modules contain a lot of conditionally-compiled debugging code. Most of this code is under control of the PCMCIA_DEBUG preprocessor define. If this is undefined, debugging code will not be compiled. If set to 0, the code is compiled but inactive. Larger numbers specify increasing levels of verbosity. Each module built with PCMCIA_DEBUG defined will have an integer parameter, pc_debug, that controls the verbosity of its output. This can be adjusted when the module is loaded, so output can be controlled on a per-module basis without recompiling.

There are a few debugging tools in the debug_tools/ subdirectory of the PCMCIA distribution. The dump_tcic and dump_i365 utilities generate complete register dumps of the PCMCIA controllers, and decode a lot of the register information. They are most useful if you have access to a datasheet for the corresponding controller chip. The dump_tuples utility lists a card's CIS (Card Information Structure), and decodes some of the important bits. And the dump_cisreg utility displays a card's local configuration registers.

The memory_cs memory card driver is also sometimes useful for debugging. It can be bound to any PCMCIA card, and does not interfere with other drivers. It can be used to directly access any card's attribute memory or common memory.

7.3   Writing Card Services drivers for new cards

The Linux PCMCIA Programmer's Guide is the best documentation for the Linux PCMCIA interface. The latest version is always available from hyper.stanford.edu in /pub/pcmcia/doc, or on the web at <http://hyper.stanford.edu/HyperNews/get/pcmcia/home.html>.

For devices that are close relatives of normal ISA devices, you'll probably be able to use parts of existing Linux drivers. In some cases, the biggest stumbling block will be modifying an existing driver so that it can handle adding and removing devices after boot time. Of the current drivers, the memory card driver is the only "self-contained" driver that does not depend on other parts of the Linux kernel to do most of the dirty work.

In many cases, the largest barrier to supporting a new card type is obtaining technical information from the manufacturer. It may be difficult to figure out who to ask, or to explain exactly what information is needed. However, with a few exceptions, it is very difficult if not impossible to implement a driver for a card without technical information from the manufacturer.

I've written a skeleton driver with lots of comments that explains a lot of how a driver communicates with Card Services; you'll find this in the PCMCIA source distribution in modules/skeleton.c.

7.4   Guidelines for PCMCIA client driver authors

I have decided that it is not really feasible for me to distribute all PCMCIA client drivers as part of the PCMCIA package. Each new driver makes the main package incrementally harder to maintain, and including a driver inevitably transfers some of the maintenance work from the driver author to me. Instead, I will decide on a case by case basis whether or not to include contributed drivers, based on user demand as well as maintainability. For drivers not included in the core package, I suggest that driver authors adopt the following scheme for packaging their drivers for distribution.

Driver files should be arranged in the same directory scheme used in the PCMCIA source distribution, so that the driver can be unpacked on top of a complete PCMCIA source tree. A driver should include source files (in ./modules/), a man page (in ./man/), and configuration files (in ./etc/). The top level directory should also include a README file.

The top-level directory should include a makefile, set up so that "make -f ... all" and "make -f ... install" compile the driver and install all appropriate files. If this makefile is given an extension of .mk, then it will automatically be invoked by the top-level Makefile for the all and install targets. Here is an example of how such a makefile could be constructed:

```
# Sample Makefile for contributed client driver
```

```
        FILES = sample_cs.mk README.sample_cs \
                modules/sample_cs.c modules/sample_cs.h \
                etc/sample etc/sample.opts man/sample_cs.4
        all:
                $(MAKE) -C modules MODULES=sample_cs.o
        install:
                $(MAKE) -C modules install-modules MODULES=sample_cs.o
                $(MAKE) -C etc install-clients CLIENTS=sample
                $(MAKE) -C man install-man4 MAN4=sample_cs.4
        dist:
                tar czvf sample_cs.tar.gz $(FILES)
```

This makefile uses install targets defined in 2.9.10 and later versions of the PCMCIA package. This makefile also includes a "dist" target for the convenience of the driver author. You would probably want to add a version number to the final package filename (for example, `sample_cs-1.5.tar.gz`). A complete distribution could look like:

```
        sample_cs.mk
        README.sample_cs
        modules/sample_cs.c
        modules/sample_cs.h
        etc/sample
        etc/sample.opts
        man/sample_cs.4
```

With this arrangement, when the contributed driver is unpacked, it becomes essentially part of the PCMCIA source tree. It can make use of the PCMCIA header files, as well as the machinery for checking the user's system configuration, and automatic dependency checking, just like a "normal" client driver.

I will accept client drivers prepared according to this specification and place them in the `/pub/pcmcia/contrib` directory on my FTP server, `hyper.stanford.edu`. The README in this directory will describe how to unpack a contributed driver.

The PCMCIA client driver interface has not changed much over time, and has almost always preserved backwards compatibility. A client driver will not normally need to be updated for minor revisions in the main PCMCIA package. I will try to notify authors of contributed drivers of changes that require updates to their drivers.

7.5   Guidelines for Linux distribution maintainers

If your distribution has system configuration tools that you would like to be PCMCIA-aware, please use the `*.opts` files in `/etc/pcmcia` for your "hooks." These files will not be modified if a user compiles and installs a new release of the PCMCIA package. If you modify the main configuration scripts, then a fresh PCMCIA install will silently overwrite your custom scripts and break the connection with your configuration tools. Contact me if you are not sure how to write an appropriate option script.

It is helpful for users (and for me) if you can document how your distribution deviates from the PCMCIA package as described in this document. In particular, please document changes to the startup script and configuration scripts.

When building PCMCIA for distribution, you should consider including contributed drivers that are not part of the main PCMCIA package. For reasons of maintainability, I am trying to limit the core package size, by only adding new drivers if I think they are of particularly broad interest. Other drivers will be distributed separately, as described in the previous section. The split between integral and separate drivers is somewhat arbitrary and partly historical, and should not imply a difference in quality.

Pilot HOWTO

by David H. Silber *pilot@orbits.com* <mailto:pilot@orbits.com>   v0.5, 17 August 1997

This HOWTO document explains how to use your Pilot with a linux system. Although HOWTO documents are targeted towards use with the linux operating system, this one is not dependent on the version of unix used.

Contents

1   Introduction

The Pilot comes with software to synchronize its memory with data on a Microsoft Windows system. There is optional software you can buy to synchronize with an Apple Macintosh. The linux/unix community has been ignored by the manufacturers of the Pilot. Fortunately, a suite of free software has been developed to fill this need. This document describes this software, where to get it, and how to install and use it.

1.1   This Document

The latest version of this document can be read at *http://www.orbits.com/Pilot/Pilot-HOWTO.html* <http://www.orbits.com/Pilot/Pilot-HOWTO.html>, and is part of the Linux Documentation Project (LDP). See *http://sunsite.unc.edu/LDP/* <http://sunsite.unc.edu/LDP/> for further information about the LDP and other HOWTO documents.

Future versions will cover more unix tools for writing application programs to run on the Pilot and conduits to transfer data between the unix system and the Pilot.

If you find anything in this document which needs to be corrected or better explained, please send me e-mail at the address above and specify which version of this document you are referring to.

This document is Copyright © 1997 by David H. Silber. It is released under the copyright terms in the LDP HOWTO-INDEX document.

1.2   Mailing List

The pilot-unix mailing list is maintained by *Matthew Cravit* <mailto:pilot-unix-owner@lists.best.com>. Its mandate is:

```
The pilot-unix mailing list is for discussion and idea-sharing for those
interested in using the US Robotics Pilot PDAs with UNIX systems. This
includes people who are interested in helping to develop tools to allow the
Pilot to operate with UNIX, and possibly to develop an SDK for the Pilot
for Unix.
```

For more information, including how to subscribe to the list, send mail containing the word "**INFO**" to *pilot-unix-request@lists.best.com* <mailto:pilot-unix-request@lists.best.com>. The subject line does not matter.

1.3   Mailing List Archives

An archive of the pilot-unix mailing list can be found at *http:///www.acm.rpi.edu/~albert/pilot/* <http:///www.acm.rpi.edu/albert/pilot/>. It is maintained by *Chris Stevens* <mailto:albert@acm.rpi.edu>.

1.4   FTP Site

An FTP site containing an archive of Pilot tools for use on unix systems is located at *ftp://ryeham.ee.ryerson.ca/pub/PalmOS/* <ftp://ryeham.ee.ryerson.ca/pub/PalmOS/>. It is maintained by *Jeff Dionne* <mailto:jeff@ryeham.ee.ryerson.ca>.

2   General Information

2.1   What is a Pilot?

The Pilot is a small pen-based Personal Digital Assistant (PDA). It is made by U. S. Robotics, now part of 3Com.

For those of you unfamiliar with the term, a *Personal Digital Assistant* is one of those small electronic devices which typically contain various types of personal information, such as addresses and telephone numbers, a calendar, checkbook registry, lists of reminders and/or memos and is designed to be conveniently carried so as to be handy when the information is needed.

The more adaptable PDAs, such as the Pilot, allow for the data stored on the PDA to be backed up to another computer and for data and new programs to be loaded onto the PDA from another computer.

2.2   Different types of Pilots

There are four versions of the Pilot. The earlier two, the *1000* and the *5000* have 128k and 512k of RAM, respectively.

The more recent two, the *PalmPilot Personal* and the *PalmPilot Professional* have 512k and 1 Meg of RAM, respectively. They also have a backlighting feature for the LCD panel and version 2.0 of the operating system. The *Professional* also comes with a TCP/IP stack and a few extra programs built-in.

It is possible to upgrade any Pilot by swapping out the memory card, which includes both RAM & ROM. Of course, this doesn't get you backlighting for the older pilots.

2.3   Hardware Installation

Pilots come with a "cradle" for exchanging data with the desktop computer. This device is actually a serial cable with a custom holder for the Pilot end and a 'HotSync' button. Plug your cradle into a spare serial port on your computer. When you run each of the stand-alone programs, you will need to place your Pilot in the cradle and push the 'HotSync' button so the Pilot knows that it has to communicate. If the Pilot happens to be off when the button is pushed, it will turn itself on.

For convenience, create a device, `/dev/pilot` which will be an alternate name for the serial port to which your Pilot cradle is connected. As the root user, enter the following at the shell prompt:

```
ln /dev/cua0 /dev/pilot
```

Replace cua0 with the name of the port to which you connected your Pilot's cradle.

3   Sharing Pilot Data with your Linux System

3.1   The pilot-link software

The pilot-link suite of software tools allows you to download programs onto your Pilot, and transfer data for the Pilot's various built-in programs between the linux system and the Pilot. While these programs are not quite as seamless as the desktop software that comes with the Pilot, they do allow you to copy your data in both directions. In general, each separate program in the `pilot-link` suite manages one type of data.

The PilotManager software is built on top of `pilot-link` and provides a more integrated solution, which typically includes full synchronization of the various types of data.

3.1.1 Installing the pilot-link software

The prepackaged versions will inevitably lag slightly behind the master distribution, but will be easier to install and not require configuration. The master distribution might be a better choice in those rare occasions when you have been waiting for a particular feature or bug fix.

You can get the *Debian Linux* port of *pilot-link* version 0.7.2 from *ftp://ftp.debian.org/pub/debian/hamm/hamm/binary-i386/otherosfs/pilot-link_0.7.2-1.deb* <ftp://ftp.debian.org/pub/debian/hamm/hamm/binary-i386/otherosfs/pilot-link_0.7.2-1.deb>. Install this file in the normal manner and skip to *Using the pilot-link software*.

You can get the *RedHat Linux* port of *pilot-link* version 0.7.6 from *ftp://ftp.redhat.com/pub/contrib/i386/pilot-link-0.7.6-2.i386.rpm* <ftp://ftp.redhat.com/pub/contrib/i386/pilot-link-0.7.6-2.i386.rpm>. Install this file in the normal manner and skip to *Using the pilot-link software*.

For other versions of linux or unix, download the version 0.8.2 of pilot-link from *ftp://ryeham.ee.ryerson.ca/pub/PalmOS/pilot-link.0.8.2.tar.gz* <ftp://ryeham.ee.ryerson.ca/pub/PalmOS/pilot-link.0.8.2.tar.gz>. The version number is likely to change, but new versions should end up in the same location with a similar name.

Once you have the software distribution, unpack it with:

```
tar -xvzf pilot-link.0.8.2.tar.gz
```

This will create a directory (`pilot-link.0.8.2`) containing the source.

Run `./configure`. This will search through your system for information needed to compile the software. `configure` will set things up to be installed in `/usr/local` by default. If you want to change it, run `./configure --prefix=DIR`, where `DIR` is replaced with the name of the directory to which the software will be installed.

Run `make`. This will compile the software. The software will not be installed until later, so that you have a chance to try it out first. (If you are replacing an older version with a newer release, you may wish to check and make sure that no functionality that you need has been broken. Generally, this is not a problem.)

As the root user, run `make install`. This will copy the software into directories under `/usr/local` (or wherever you specified with the `--prefix` option). If you can not log in as root, you can install the software to some directory where you have write access.

Don't forget to add any new directories of executables to your search path.

3.1.2 Using the pilot-link software

Most of the programs in the `pilot-link` suite are *conduits*, that is they transfer data into or out of your Pilot.

Each time you use of one of these programs, press the HotSync button on your Pilot's cradle. This will initiate the Pilot side of the data transfer. Note that not all of these programs prompt you to press the 'HotSync' button, so you may have to remember to do it yourself.

For more details, and other options to these programs, view the corresponding manual page. For the `pilot-xfer` program, for example, type `man pilot-xfer` at your unix shell prompt.

If you are going to use `PilotManager`, you may not need to bother learning to use these (more primitive) tools.

pilot-xfer   Possibly the most useful program in the pilot-link suite, `pilot-xfer` allows you to install programs on your Pilot, make a backup, and restore that backup.

To install a program:

```
pilot-xfer /dev/pilot -i program.prc
```

To backup your Pilot:

```
pilot-xfer /dev/pilot -b backup-directory
```

This will copy all of the databases on your Pilot, (including programs?) to a directory called "backup-directory", creating it if it does not already exist.

To restore data to Pilot:

```
pilot-xfer /dev/pilot -r backup-directory
```

Generally, you will only need to do this if your Pilot loses power or if you have to do a hard reset.

To list the programs on your Pilot:

```
pilot-xfer /dev/pilot -l
```

install-memo   Install a linux file onto the Pilot as a memo.

To install a memo into your (already existing) *project* category:

```
install-memo /dev/pilot -c project project.memo
```

The name of the file will be inserted into the memo as its first line and will appear in the directory of memos on your Pilot.

memos   This program grabs each memo from the Pilot and prints it out in standard mailbox format.

To view your memos:

```
memos /dev/pilot
```

pilot-addresses   `pilot-addresses` Transfer the address database to or from the Pilot.

To write your address data to a linux file from your Pilot:

```
pilot-addresses /dev/pilot -w storage.file
```

To read your address data from a linux file onto your Pilot:

```
pilot-addresses /dev/pilot -r storage.file
```

3.2   MakeDoc

One short-coming of the Pilot's built-in memo program is that it does not deal well with large documents. To compensate for this, *Rick Bram* <mailto:rbram@concentric.net> wrote *Doc*, a document reader for the Pilot. (See *http://www.concentric.net/~rbram/doc.shtml* <http://www.concentric.net/rbram/doc.shtml>). Documents can be converted to the Doc format with MakeDoc, by *Pat Beirne* <mailto:pat.beirne@sympatico.ca>.

3.2.1   Installing MakeDoc

MakeDoc can be downloaded from *http://www.concentric.net/~rbram/makedoc7.cpp* <http://www.concentric.net/rbram/makedoc7.cpp>. Compile it with your C++ compiler and install the resulting executable as "makedoc" in a directory in your search path. There seems to be a small bug in makedoc (version 0.7a) in that it does not output a newline as the last character displayed to the user. This does not seem to affect the resulting document file, but it is annoying.

There is a new version out, but it requires Java. Take a look at Pat Beirne's MakeDoc web page at *http://cpu563.adsl.sympatico.ca/MakeDocJ.htm* <http://cpu563.adsl.sympatico.ca/MakeDocJ.htm>.

3.2.2   Using MakeDoc

Use MakeDoc as follows:

```
makedoc data.txt data.prc "Data to display with Doc"
```

This will create a file data.prc, which can be installed on your Pilot with pilot-xfer. The text *"Data to display with Doc"* will be displayed in the directory of documents that *Doc* manages.

The syntax for MakeDoc is as follows:

```
makedoc [-n] [-b] <text-file> <prc-file> <story-name>
or
makedoc -d [-b] <prc-file> <text-file>
```

<text-file>
    The file that you wish to convert.
<prc-file>
    The name of the resulting file. (End the name with ".prc".)
<story-name>
    The name you want displayed in the Doc or Jdoc directory of documents.

There are also options to decode the resulting .prc file and manage various compression options.

3.3   PilotManager

PilotManager is a generalized tool which allows multiple databases to be synchronized in a single HotSync session.

I have not been able to build and install PilotManager in time to write about it for this version of the Pilot-HOWTO.

A few links that might be helpful:

- The PilotManager package: *http://playground.sun.com/˜bharat/pilotmgr.html* <http://playground.sun.com/bharat/pilotmgr.html>
- A patch: *ftp://ftp.orbits.com/pub/Pilot/pilotmgr,v1.009-BETA-3.patch* <ftp://ftp.orbits.com/pub/Pilot/pilotmgr,v1.009-BETA-3.patch>

This patch for PilotManager is only intended for use with PilotManager version 1.009 Beta 3 when used with pilot-link version 0.8.0. Install the PilotManager source and apply the patch with the commands:

```
tar -xvzf pilotmgr,v1.009-BETA-3.dev.tar.gz
cd pilotmgr,v1.009-BETA-3
patch -p1 < ../pilotmgr,v1.009-BETA-3.patch
```

I hope to be able to install this software soon and report about it in a future version of this document.

4   Tools for Developing Pilot Software

4.1   prc-tools

The prc-tools package is a complete development environment built from the FSF GNU utilities, compiler and debugger with the addition of a few special tools.

There is not much in the way of documentation, but you might want to look at the *Pilot Software Development* web page at *http://www.massena.com/darrin/pilot/* <http://www.massena.com/darrin/pilot/>.

4.1.1   Installing prc-tools

Download the most recent version of prc-tools from *ftp://ryeham.ee.ryerson.ca/pub/PalmOS* <ftp://ryeham.ee.ryerson.ca/pub/PalmOS>. The GNU tools can be retrieved from *ftp://prep.ai.mit.edu/pub/gnu* <ftp://prep.ai.mit.edu/pub/gnu>. Get binutils-2.7.tar.gz, gcc-2.7.2.2.tar.gz and gdb-4.16.tar.gz. The version numbers specified for the GNU tools are correct as of prc-tools release 0.5.0. Later releases of *prc-tools* may require newer versions of the GNU tools.

Put all of the distribution packages in one directory. Unpack only the prc-tools distribution. The prc-tools Makefile will take care of the other packages. By default, prc-tools will be installed in /usr/local/gnu. If you want them installed somewhere else, you need to change the value of INSTALLDIR in Makefile. The steps are:

```
tar -xvzf prc-tools.0.5.0.tar.gz
cd prc-tools-0.5.0
(Edit Makefile, if necessary.)
make doeverything
```

4.1.2   Using prc-tools

One good reference for general use of prc-tools is the example directory, particularly the Makefile. Documentation for PilRC is provided in the file pilrc1.5/doc/pilrc.htm included as part of prc-tool version 0.5.0.

A People

Kenneth Albanowski <mailto:kjahds@kjahds.com> Maintains the pilot-link suite of tools.

Donnie Barnes <mailto:djb@redhat.com> Packaged pilot-link suite as Red Hat RPM files.

Rick Bram <mailto:rbram@concentric.net> Author of Doc.

Matthew Cravit <mailto:pilot-unix-owner@lists.best.com> List owner for the *pilot-unix* mailing list.

Jeff Dionne <mailto:jeff@ryeham.ee.ryerson.ca> Original author of the pilot-link suite of tools. Manages the FTP area for the UNIX PalmOS/Pilot development project.

Mark W. Eichin <mailto:eichen@kitten.gen.ma.us> Ported pilot-link suite to Debian Linux.

David H. Silber <mailto:pilot@orbits.com> Author of this document.

Chris Stevens <mailto:albert@acm.rpi.edu> Maintains the pilot-unix mailing list archives.

DNS HOWTO

Nicolai Langfeldt `janl@math.uio.no`   v1.4.2, 1 January 1998

HOWTO become a totally small time DNS admin.

Contents

1 Preamble

Keywords: DNS, bind, named, dialup, ppp, slip, Internet, domain, name, hosts, resolving

1.1 Legal stuff

(C)opyright 1995 Nicolai Langfeldt. Do not modify without amending copyright, distribute freely but retain copyright message.

1.2 Credits and request for help.

I want to thank Arnt Gulbrandsen who read the drafts to this work countless times and provided many useful suggestions. I also want to thank the people that have e-mailed suggestions, and thank you notes.

This will never be a finished document, please send me mail about your problems and successes, it can make this a better HOWTO. So please send money, comments and/or questions to janl@math.uio.no. If you send e-mail and want an answer please show the simple courtecy of *making sure* that the return address is correct and working. Also, **please** read the 9 (FAQ) section before mailing me.

If you want to translate this HOWTO please notify me so I can keep track of what languages I have been published in :-).

1.3 Dedication

This HOWTO is dedicated to Anne Line Norheim Langfeldt. Though she will probably never read it since she's not that kind of girl.

2 Introduction.

What this is and isn't.

For starters, DNS is is the Domain Name System. The rules that name machines and software that maps those names to IP numbers. This HOWTO documents how to define such mappings using a Linux system. A mapping i simply a association between two things, in this case a machine name, like ftp.linux.org, and the machines IP number, 199.249.150.4.

DNS is, to the uninitiated (you ;-), one of the more opaque areas of network administration. This HOWTO will try to make a few things clearer. It describes how to set up a *simple* DNS name server. Starting with a caching only server and going on to setting up a primary DNS server for a domain. For more complex setups you can check the 9 (FAQ) section of this document. If it's not described there you will need to *read* the Real Documentation. I'll get back to what this Real Documentation consists of in 10 (the last chapter).

Before you start on this you should configure your machine so that you can telnet in and out of it, and make successfully make all kinds of connections to the net, and you should especially be able to do `telnet 127.0.0.1` and get your own machine (test it now!). You also need a good `/etc/host.conf` (or `/etc/nsswitch.conf`), `/etc/resolv.conf` and `/etc/hosts` files as a starting point, since I will not explain their function here. If you don't already have all this set up and working the networking/NET-2 HOWTO explains how to set it up. Read it.

If you're using SLIP or PPP you need that working. Read the PPP HOWTO if it's not.

When I say 'your machine' I mean the machine you are trying to set up DNS on. Not any other machine you might have that's involved in your networking effort.

I assume you're not behind any kind of firewall that blocks name queries. If you are you will need a special configuration, see the section on 9 (FAQ).

Name serving on Unix is done by a program called **named**. This is a part of the bind package which is coordinated by Paul Vixie for The Internet Software Consortium. **Named** is included in most Linux distributions and is usually installed as **/usr/sbin/named**. If you have a named you can probably use it; if you don't have one you can get a binary off a Linux ftp site, or get the latest and greatest source from *ftp.isc.org:/isc/bind/src/cur/* <ftp://ftp.isc.org/isc/bind/src/cur/> This howto is about bind version 4. If you install version 8 you're almost on your own. There is a section later to help you a bit though.

DNS is a net-wide database. Take care about what you put into it. If you put junk into it, you, and others will get junk out of it. Keep your DNS tidy and consistent and you will get good service from it. Learn to use it, admin it, debug it and you will be another good admin keeping the net from falling to it's knees overloaded by mismanagement.

In this document I state flatly a couple of things that are not completely true (they are at least half truths though). All in the interest of simplification. Things will (probably ;-) work if you believe what I say.

Tip: Make backup copies of all the files I instruct you to change if you already have them, so if after going through this nothing works you can get it back to your old, working state.

3 A caching only name server.

A first stab at DNS config, very useful for dialup users.

A caching only name server will find the answer to name queries and remember the answer the next time you need it.

First you need a file called **/etc/named.boot**. This is read when named starts. For now it should simply contain:

```
; Boot file for caching only name server
;
directory /var/named
;
; type          domain                          source file or host
cache           .                               root.cache
primary         0.0.127.in-addr.arpa            pz/127.0.0
```

VERY IMPORTANT: In some versions of this document the file contents listed here will have a couple of spaces or a tab before the first non blank character. These are not supposed to be in the file. **Delete any leading space** in the files you cut and paste from this HOWTO.

The 'directory' line tells named where to look for files. All files named subsequently will be relative to this. **/var/named** is the right directory according to the *Linux File system Standard*. Thus **pz** is a directory under **/var/named**, i.e., **/var/named/pz**.

The file named **/var/named/root.cache** is named in this. **/var/named/root.cache** should contain this:

```
.       518400  NS      D.ROOT-SERVERS.NET.
.       518400  NS      E.ROOT-SERVERS.NET.
.       518400  NS      I.ROOT-SERVERS.NET.
```

```
.        518400   NS      F.ROOT-SERVERS.NET.
.        518400   NS      G.ROOT-SERVERS.NET.
.        518400   NS      A.ROOT-SERVERS.NET.
.        518400   NS      H.ROOT-SERVERS.NET.
.        518400   NS      B.ROOT-SERVERS.NET.
.        518400   NS      C.ROOT-SERVERS.NET.
;
D.ROOT-SERVERS.NET.      3600000  A      128.8.10.90
E.ROOT-SERVERS.NET.      3600000  A      192.203.230.10
I.ROOT-SERVERS.NET.      3600000  A      192.36.148.17
F.ROOT-SERVERS.NET.      3600000  A      192.5.5.241
G.ROOT-SERVERS.NET.      3600000  A      192.112.36.4
A.ROOT-SERVERS.NET.      3600000  A      198.41.0.4
H.ROOT-SERVERS.NET.      3600000  A      128.63.2.53
B.ROOT-SERVERS.NET.      3600000  A      128.9.0.107
C.ROOT-SERVERS.NET.      3600000  A      192.33.4.12
```

Remember what I said about leading spaces!

The file describes the root name servers in the world. This changes over time and *must* be maintained. See the 6 (maintenance section) for how to keep it up to date. This file is described in the named man page, but it is, IMHO, best suited for people that already understand named.

The next line in `named.boot` is the `primary` line. I will explain its use in a later chapter, for now just make this a file named `127.0.0` in the subdirectory `pz`:

```
@       IN      SOA     ns.linux.bogus. hostmaster.linux.bogus. (
                        ; Serial
                        28800   ; Refresh
                        7200    ; Retry
                        604800  ; Expire
                        86400)  ; Minimum TTL
        NS      ns.linux.bogus.
1       PTR     localhost.
```

Next, you need a `/etc/resolv.conf` looking something like this:

```
search subdomain.your-domain.edu your-domain.edu
nameserver 127.0.0.1
```

The 'search' line specifies what domains should be searched for any host names you want to connect to. The 'nameserver' line specifies the address of your nameserver at, in this case your own machine since that is where your named runs. If you want to list several name servers put in one 'nameserver' line for each. (Note: Named never reads this file, the resolver that uses named does.)

To illustrate what this file does: If a client tries to look up `foo`, `foo.subdomain.your-domain.edu` is tried first, then `foo.your-fomain.edu`, finally `foo`. If a client tries to look up `sunsite.unc.edu`, `sunsite.unc.edu.subdomain.your-domain.edu` is tried first (yes, it's silly, but that's the way it's gotta be) , then `sunsite.unc.edu.your-domain.edu`, and finally `sunsite.unc.edu`. You may not want to put in too many domains in the search line, it takes time to search them.

The example assumes you belong in the domain `subdomain.your-domain.edu`, your machine then, is probably called `your-machine.subdomain.your-domain.edu`. The search line should not contain your TLD (Top

Level Domain, 'edu' in this case). If you frequently need to connect to hosts in another domain you can add that domain to the search line like this:

```
search subdomain.your-domain.edu your-domain.edu other-domain.com
```

and so on. Obviously you need to put real domain names in instead. Please note the lack of periods at the end of the domain names.

Next, depending on your libc version you either need to fix `/etc/nsswitch.conf` or `/etc/host.conf`. If you already have `nsswitch.conf` that's what we'll fix, if not, we'll fix `host.conf`.

/etc/nsswitch.conf

This is a long file specifying where to get different kinds of data types, from what file or database. It usually contains helpful comments at the top, which you should consider reading, now. After that find the line starting with 'hosts:', it should read

```
hosts:      files dns
```

If there is no line starting with 'hosts:' then put in the one above. It says that programs should first look in the /etc/hosts file, then check DNS according to `resolv.conf`.

/etc/host.conf

It probably contains several lines, one should starting with `order` and it should look like this:

```
order hosts,bind
```

If there is no 'order' line you should stick one in. It tells the host name resolving routines to first look in /etc/hosts, then ask the name server (which you in `resolv.conf` said is at 127.0.0.1) These two latest files are documented in the resolv(8) man page (do 'man 8 resolv') in most Linux distributions. That man page is IMHO readable, and everyone, especially DNS admins, should read it. Do it now, if you say to yourself "I'll do it later" you'll never get around to it.

3.1 Starting named

After all this it's time to start named. If you're using a dialup connection connect first. Type 'ndc start', and press return, no options. If that back-fires try '/usr/sbin/ndc start' instead. If that back-fires see the 9 (FAQ) section. Now you can test your setup. If you view your syslog message file (usually called /var/adm/messages, but another directory to look in is /var/log and another file to look in is syslog) while starting named (do `tail -f /var/adm/messages`) you should see something like:

```
Jun 30 21:50:55 roke named[2258]: starting. \
        named 4.9.4-REL Sun Jun 30 21:29:03 MET DST 1996 \
        janl@roke.slip.ifi.uio.no:/var/tmp/bind/named
Jun 30 21:50:55 roke named[2258]: cache zone "" loaded (serial 0)
Jun 30 21:50:55 roke named[2258]: primary zone "0.0.127.in-addr.arpa" \
        loaded (serial 1)
```

(Ignore the he backspace-newlines, they have been inserted to fit the above on a print page.)

If there are any messages about errors then there is a mistake. Named will name the file it is in (one of named.boot and root.cache I hope :-) Kill named and go back and check the file.

Now it's time to start nslookup to examine your handywork.

```
$ nslookup
Default Server:  localhost
Address:  127.0.0.1


>
```

If that's what you get it's working. We hope. Anything else, go back and check everything. Each time you change the **named.boot** file you need to restart named using the **ndc restart** command.

Now you can enter a query. Try looking up some machine close to you. **pat.uio.no** is close to me, at the University of Oslo:

```
> pat.uio.no
Server:  localhost
Address:  127.0.0.1

Name:     pat.uio.no
Address:  129.240.2.50
```

nslookup now asked your named to look for the machine **pat.uio.no**. It then contacted one of the name server machines named in your **root.cache** file, and asked its way from there. It might take tiny while before you get the result as it searches all the domains you named in **/etc/resolv.conf**.

If you try again you get this:

```
> pat.uio.no
Server:  localhost
Address:  127.0.0.1

Non-authoritative answer:
Name:     pat.uio.no
Address:  129.240.2.50
```

Note the 'Non-authoritative answer:' line we got this time around. That means that named did not go out on the network to ask this time, it instead looked in it's cache and found it there. But the cached information *might* be out of date (stale). So you are informed of this (very slight) danger by it saying 'Non-authoritative answer:'. When nslookup says this the second time you ask for a host it's a sure sign it named caches the information and that it's working. You exit **nslookup** by giving the command '**exit**'.

If you're a dialup (ppp, slip) user please read the 8 (section on dialup connections), there is some advice there for you.

Now you know how to set up a caching named. Take a beer, milk, or whatever you prefer to celebrate it.

4 A *simple* domain.

How to set up your own domain.

4.1 But first some dry theory

Before we *really* start this section I'm going to serve you some theory on how DNS works. And you're going to read it because it's good for you. If you don't 'wanna' you should at least skim it very quickly. Stop skimming when you get to what should go in your **named.boot** file.

DNS is a hierarchical system. The top is written '.' and pronounced 'root'. Under . there are a number of Top Level Domains (TLDs), the best known ones are ORG, COM, EDU and NET, but there are many more.

When looking for a machine the query proceeds recursively into the hierarchy starting at the top. If you want to find out the address of **prep.ai.mit.edu** your name server has to find a name server that serves edu. It asks a . server (it already knows the . servers, that's what the **root.cache** file is for), the . server gives a list of edu servers:

```
$ nslookup
Default Server:  localhost
Address:  127.0.0.1
```

Start asking a root server.

```
> server c.root-servers.net.
Default Server:  c.root-servers.net
Address:  192.33.4.12
```

Set the Query type to NS (name server records).

```
> set q=ns
```

Ask about edu.

```
> edu.
```

The trailing . here is significant, it tells the server we're asking that edu is right under . (this narrows the search somewhat).

```
edu        nameserver = A.ROOT-SERVERS.NET
edu        nameserver = H.ROOT-SERVERS.NET
edu        nameserver = B.ROOT-SERVERS.NET
edu        nameserver = C.ROOT-SERVERS.NET
edu        nameserver = D.ROOT-SERVERS.NET
edu        nameserver = E.ROOT-SERVERS.NET
edu        nameserver = I.ROOT-SERVERS.NET
edu        nameserver = F.ROOT-SERVERS.NET
edu        nameserver = G.ROOT-SERVERS.NET
A.ROOT-SERVERS.NET        internet address = 198.41.0.4
```

```
H.ROOT-SERVERS.NET          internet address = 128.63.2.53
B.ROOT-SERVERS.NET          internet address = 128.9.0.107
C.ROOT-SERVERS.NET          internet address = 192.33.4.12
D.ROOT-SERVERS.NET          internet address = 128.8.10.90
E.ROOT-SERVERS.NET          internet address = 192.203.230.10
I.ROOT-SERVERS.NET          internet address = 192.36.148.17
F.ROOT-SERVERS.NET          internet address = 192.5.5.241
G.ROOT-SERVERS.NET          internet address = 192.112.36.4
```

This tells us that *.root-servers.net serves edu., so we can go on asking c. Now we want to know who
serves the next level of the domain name: mit.edu.:

```
> mit.edu.
Server:  c.root-servers.net
Address:  192.33.4.12


Non-authoritative answer:
mit.edu nameserver = STRAWB.mit.edu
mit.edu nameserver = W20NS.mit.edu
mit.edu nameserver = BITSY.mit.edu


Authoritative answers can be found from:
STRAWB.mit.edu  internet address = 18.71.0.151
W20NS.mit.edu   internet address = 18.70.0.160
BITSY.mit.edu   internet address = 18.72.0.3
```

steawb, w20ns and bitsy serves mit, select one and inquire about ai.mit.edu:

```
> server W20NS.mit.edu.
```

Host names are not case sensitive, but I use my mouse to cut and paste so it gets copied as-is from the
screen.

```
Server:  W20NS.mit.edu
Address:  18.70.0.160

> ai.mit.edu.
Server:  W20NS.mit.edu
Address:  18.70.0.160


Non-authoritative answer:
ai.mit.edu      nameserver = WHEATIES.AI.MIT.EDU
ai.mit.edu      nameserver = ALPHA-BITS.AI.MIT.EDU
ai.mit.edu      nameserver = GRAPE-NUTS.AI.MIT.EDU
ai.mit.edu      nameserver = TRIX.AI.MIT.EDU
ai.mit.edu      nameserver = MUESLI.AI.MIT.EDU
```

```
         Authoritative answers can be found from:
         AI.MIT.EDU        nameserver = WHEATIES.AI.MIT.EDU
         AI.MIT.EDU        nameserver = ALPHA-BITS.AI.MIT.EDU
         AI.MIT.EDU        nameserver = GRAPE-NUTS.AI.MIT.EDU
         AI.MIT.EDU        nameserver = TRIX.AI.MIT.EDU
         AI.MIT.EDU        nameserver = MUESLI.AI.MIT.EDU
         WHEATIES.AI.MIT.EDU    internet address = 128.52.32.13
         WHEATIES.AI.MIT.EDU    internet address = 128.52.35.13
         ALPHA-BITS.AI.MIT.EDU  internet address = 128.52.32.5
         ALPHA-BITS.AI.MIT.EDU  internet address = 128.52.37.5
         GRAPE-NUTS.AI.MIT.EDU  internet address = 128.52.32.4
         GRAPE-NUTS.AI.MIT.EDU  internet address = 128.52.36.4
         TRIX.AI.MIT.EDU internet address = 128.52.32.6
         TRIX.AI.MIT.EDU internet address = 128.52.38.6
         MUESLI.AI.MIT.EDU      internet address = 128.52.32.7
         MUESLI.AI.MIT.EDU      internet address = 128.52.39.7
```

So `weaties.ai.mit.edu` is a nameserver for `ai.mit.edu`:

```
         > server WHEATIES.AI.MIT.EDU.
         Default Server:  WHEATIES.AI.MIT.EDU
         Addresses:  128.52.32.13, 128.52.35.13
```

Now I change query type, we've found the name server so now we're going to ask about everything wheaties knows about `prep.ai.mit.edu`.

```
         > set q=any
         > prep.ai.mit.edu.
         Server:  WHEATIES.AI.MIT.EDU
         Addresses:  128.52.32.13, 128.52.35.13
```

```
         prep.ai.mit.edu CPU = dec/decstation-5000.25    OS = unix
         prep.ai.mit.edu
               inet address = 18.159.0.42, protocol = tcp
               #21 #23 #25 #79
         prep.ai.mit.edu preference = 1, mail exchanger = life.ai.mit.edu
         prep.ai.mit.edu internet address = 18.159.0.42
         ai.mit.edu        nameserver = alpha-bits.ai.mit.edu
         ai.mit.edu        nameserver = wheaties.ai.mit.edu
         ai.mit.edu        nameserver = grape-nuts.ai.mit.edu
         ai.mit.edu        nameserver = mini-wheats.ai.mit.edu
         ai.mit.edu        nameserver = trix.ai.mit.edu
         ai.mit.edu        nameserver = muesli.ai.mit.edu
         ai.mit.edu        nameserver = count-chocula.ai.mit.edu
         ai.mit.edu        nameserver = life.ai.mit.edu
         ai.mit.edu        nameserver = mintaka.lcs.mit.edu
```

```
life.ai.mit.edu internet address = 128.52.32.80
alpha-bits.ai.mit.edu    internet address = 128.52.32.5
wheaties.ai.mit.edu      internet address = 128.52.35.13
wheaties.ai.mit.edu      internet address = 128.52.32.13
grape-nuts.ai.mit.edu    internet address = 128.52.36.4
grape-nuts.ai.mit.edu    internet address = 128.52.32.4
mini-wheats.ai.mit.edu   internet address = 128.52.32.11
mini-wheats.ai.mit.edu   internet address = 128.52.54.11
mintaka.lcs.mit.edu      internet address = 18.26.0.36
```

So starting at . we found the successive name servers for the next level in the domain name. If you had used your own DNS server instead of using all those other servers, your named would of-course cache all the information it found while digging this out for you, and it would not have to ask again for a while.

A much less talked about, but just as important domain is in-addr.arpa. It too is nested like the 'normal' domains. in-addr.arpa allows us to get the hosts name when we have it's address. A important thing here is to note that ip#s are written in reverse order in the in-addr.arpa domain. If you have the address of a machine: 192.128.52.43 named proceeds just like for the prep.ai.mit.edu example: find arpa. servers. Find in-addr.arpa. servers, find 192.in-addr.arpa. servers, find 128.192.in-addr.arpa. servers, find 52.128.192.in-addr.arpa. servers. Find needed records for 43.52.128.192.in-addr.arpa. Clever huh? (Say 'yes'.) The reversion of the numbers can be confusing the first 2 years.

I have just told a lie. DNS does not work literally the way I just told you. But it's close enough.

4.2   Our own domain

Now to define our own domain. We're going to make the domain *linux.bogus* and define machines in it. I use a totally bogus domain name to make sure we disturb no-one Out There.

We've already started this part with this line in named.boot:

```
primary          0.0.127.in-addr.arpa            pz/127.0.0
```

Please note the lack of '.' at the end of the domain names in this file. The first line names the file pz/127.0.0 as defining 0.0.127.in-addr.arpa. We've already set up this file, it reads:

```
@           IN    SOA    ns.linux.bogus. hostmaster.linux.bogus. (
                         1       ; Serial
                         28800   ; Refresh
                         7200    ; Retry
                         604800  ; Expire
                         86400)  ; Minimum TTL
            NS    ns.linux.bogus.
1           PTR    localhost.
```

Please note the '.' at the end of all the full domain names in this file, in contrast to the named.boot file above. Some people like to start each zone file with a $ORIGIN directive, but this is superfluous. The origin (where in the DNS hierarchy it belongs) of a zone file is specified in the 'domain' column of the named.boot file, in this case it's 0.0.127.in-addr.arpa.

This 'zone file' contains 3 'resource records' (RRs): A SOA RR. A NS RR and a PTR RR. SOA is short for Start Of Authority. The '@' is a special notation meaning the origin, and since the 'domain' column for this file says 0.0.127.in-addr.arpa the first line really means

```
0.0.127.IN-ADDR.ARPA. IN      SOA ...
```

NS is the Name Server RR, it tells DNS what machine is the name server of the domain 0.0.127.in-addr.arpa, it is ns.linux.bogus. And finally the PTR record says that 1 (equals 1.0.0.127.in-addr.arpa, i.e. 127.0.0.1) is named `localhost`.

The SOA record is the preamble to *all* zone files, and there should be exactly one in each zone file, the very first record. It describes the zone, where it comes from (a machine called `linux.bogus`), who is responsible for its contents (`hostmaster@linux.bogus`), what version of the zone file this is (serial: 1), and other things having to do with caching and secondary DNS servers. For the rest of the fields ,refresh, retry, expire and minimum use the numbers used in this HOWTO and you should be safe.

Now restart your named (the command is `ndc restart`) and use nslookup to examine what you've done:

```
$ nslookup

Default Server:  localhost
Address:  127.0.0.1

> 127.0.0.1
Server:  localhost
Address:  127.0.0.1

Name:    localhost
Address:  127.0.0.1
```

so it manages to get `localhost` from 127.0.0.1, good. Now for our main task, the `linux.bogus` domain, insert a new primary line in `named.boot`:

```
primary             linux.bogus             pz/linux.bogus
```

Note the continued lack of ending '.' on the domain name in the `named.boot` file.

In the linux.bogus zone file we'll put some totally bogus data:

```
;
; Zone file for linux.bogus
;
; Mandatory minimum for a working domain
;
@       IN      SOA     ns.linux.bogus. hostmaster.linux.bogus. (
                        199511301       ; serial, todays date + todays serial #
                        28800           ; refresh, seconds
                        7200            ; retry, seconds
                        3600000         ; expire, seconds
                        86400 )         ; minimum, seconds
                NS      ns.linux.bogus.
```

```
            NS      ns.friend.bogus.
            MX      10 mail.linux.bogus   ; Primary Mail Exchanger
            MX      20 mail.friend.bogus. ; Secondary Mail Exchanger

localhost   A       127.0.0.1
ns          A       127.0.0.2
mail        A       127.0.0.4
```

Two things must be noted about the SOA record. ns.linux.bogus *must* be a actual machine with a A record. It is not legal to have a CNAME record for he machine mentioned in the SOA record. It's name need not be 'ns', it could be any legal host name. Next, hostmaster.linux.bogus should be read as hostmaster@linux.bogus, this should be a mail alias, or a mailbox, where the person(s) maintaining DNS should read mail frequently. Any mail regarding the domain will be sent to the address listed here. The name need not be 'hostmaster', it can be any legal e-mail address, but the e-mail address 'hostmaster' *is* expected to work as well.

There is one new RR type in this file, the MX, or Mail eXchanger RR. It tells mail systems where to send mail that is addressed to someone@linux.bogus, namely too mail.linux.bogus or mail.friend.bogus. The number before each machine name is that MX RRs priority. The RR with the lowest number (10) is the one mail should be sent to primarily. If that fails it can be sent to one with a higher number, a secondary mail handler, i.e. mail.friend.bogus which has priority 20 here.

Restart named by running ndc restart. Examine the results with nslookup:

```
$ nslookup
> set q=any
> linux.bogus
Server:  localhost
Address:  127.0.0.1

linux.bogus
        origin = linux.bogus
        mail addr = hostmaster.linux.bogus
        serial = 199511301
        refresh = 28800 (8 hours)
        retry  = 7200 (2 hours)
        expire = 604800 (7 days)
        minimum ttl = 86400 (1 day)
linux.bogus     nameserver = ns.linux.bogus
linux.bogus     nameserver = ns.friend.bogus
linux.bogus     preference = 10, mail exchanger = mail.linux.bogus.linux.bogus
linux.bogus     preference = 20, mail exchanger = mail.friend.bogus
linux.bogus     nameserver = ns.linux.bogus
linux.bogus     nameserver = ns.friend.bogus
ns.linux.bogus  internet address = 127.0.0.2
mail.linux.bogus        internet address = 127.0.0.4
```

Upon careful examination you will discover a bug. The line

```
        linux.bogus     preference = 10, mail exchanger = mail.linux.bogus.linux.bogus
```

is all wrong. It should be

        linux.bogus   preference = 10, mail exchanger = mail.linux.bogus

I deliberately made a mistake so you could learn from it :-) Looking in the zone file we find that the line

      @   MX   10 mail.linux.bogus   ; Primary Mail Exchanger

is missing a period. Or has a 'linux.bogus' too many. If a machine name does not end in a period in a zone file the origin is added to it's end. So either

```
@               MX       10 mail.linux.bogus.     ; Primary Mail Exchanger
```

or

```
@               MX       10 mail                  ; Primary Mail Exchanger
```

is correct. I prefer the latter form, it's less to type. In a zone file the domain should either be written out and ended with a '.' or it should not be included at all, in which case it defaults to the origin. Others have strong opinions going in the other direction.

I must stress that in the named.boot file there should *not* be '.'s after the domain names. You have no idea how many times a '.' too many or few have fouled up things and confused the h*ll out of people.

So having made my point here is the new zone file, with some extra information in it as well:

```
;
; Zone file for linux.bogus
;
; Mandatory minimum for a working domain
;
@       IN      SOA     ns.linux.bogus. hostmaster.linux.bogus. (
                        199511301       ; serial, todays date + todays serial #
                        28800           ; refresh, seconds
                        7200            ; retry, seconds
                        604800          ; expire, seconds
                        86400 )         ; minimum, seconds

                NS      ns              ; Inet Address of name server
                NS      ns.friend.bogus.
                MX      10 mail         ; Primary Mail Exchanger
                MX      20 mail.friend.bogus. ; Secondary Mail Exchanger

localhost       A       127.0.0.1
ns              A       127.0.0.2
mail            A       127.0.0.4
;
; Extras
;
@               TXT     "Linux.Bogus, your DNS consultants"
```

```
ns              MX      10 mail
                MX      20 mail.friend.bogus.
                HINFO   "Pentium" "Linux 1.2"
                TXT     "RMS"
richard         CNAME   ns
www             CNAME   ns

donald          A       127.0.0.3
                MX      10 mail
                MX      20 mail.friend.bogus.
                HINFO   "i486"   "Linux 1.2"
                TXT     "DEK"

mail            MX      10 mail
                MX      20 mail.friend.bogus.
                HINFO   "386sx" "Linux 1.0.9"

ftp             A       127.0.0.5
                MX      10 mail
                MX      20 mail.friend.bogus.
                HINFO   "P6" "Linux 1.3.59"
```

You might want to move the first three A records so that they're placed next to their respective other records, instead on top like that.

There are a number of new RRs here: HINFO (Host INFOrmation) has two parts, it's a good habit to quote each. The first part is the hardware or CPU on the machine, and the second part the software or OS on the machine. ns has a Pentium CPU and runs Linux 1.2. The TXT record is a free text record that you can use for anything you like. CNAME (Canonical NAME) is a way to give each machine several names. So richard and www is a alias for ns. It's important to note that A MX, CNAME and SOA record should *never* refer to a CNAME record, they should only refer to something with a A record, so it would wrong to have

```
foobar  CNAME   richard                 ; NO!
```

but correct to have

```
foobar  CNAME   ns                      ; Yes!
```

It's also important to note that a CNAME is not a legal host name for a e-mail address: `webmaster@www.linux.bogus` is an illegal e-mail address given the setup above. You can expect quite a few mail admins Out There to enforce this rule even if it works for you. The way to avoid this is to use A records (and perhaps some others too, like a MX record) instead:

```
www     A       127.0.0.2
```

Paul Vixie, the primary named wizard, recommends *not* using CNAME. So consider not using it *very* seriously.

Load the new database by running **ndc reload**, this causes named to read its files again.

```
$ nslookup
Default Server:  localhost
Address:  127.0.0.1


> ls -d linux.bogus
```

This means that all records should be listed.

```
[localhost]
linux.bogus.                     SOA   ns.linux.bogus hostmaster.linux.bogus.
                                       (199511301 28800 7200 604800 86400)

linux.bogus.                     NS    ns.linux.bogus
linux.bogus.                     NS    ns.friend.bogus
linux.bogus.                     MX    10   mail.linux.bogus
linux.bogus.                     MX    20   mail.friend.bogus
linux.bogus.                     TXT   "Linux.Bogus, your DNS consultants"
localhost                        A     127.0.0.1
mail                             A     127.0.0.4
mail                             MX    10   mail.linux.bogus
mail                             MX    20   mail.friend.bogus
mail                             HINFO 386sx       Linux 1.0.9
donald                           A     127.0.0.3
donald                           MX    10   mail.linux.bogus
donald                           MX    20   mail.friend.bogus
donald                           HINFO i486        Linux 1.2
donald                           TXT   "DEK"
www                              CNAME ns.linux.bogus
richard                          CNAME ns.linux.bogus
ftp                              A     127.0.0.5
ftp                              MX    10   mail.linux.bogus
ftp                              MX    20   mail.friend.bogus
ftp                              HINFO P6          Linux 1.3.59
ns                               A     127.0.0.2
ns                               MX    10   mail.linux.bogus
ns                               MX    20   mail.friend.bogus
ns                               HINFO Pentium     Linux 1.2
ns                               TXT   "RMS"
linux.bogus.                     SOA   ns.linux.bogus hostmaster.linux.bogus.
                                       (199511301 28800 7200 604800 86400)
```

That's good. Let's check what it says for www alone:

```
> set q=any
> www.linux.bogus.
Server:  localhost
Address:  127.0.0.1
```

```
www.linux.bogus canonical name = ns.linux.bogus
```

...In other words, the real name of `www.linux.bogus` is `ns.linux.bogus`

```
linux.bogus      nameserver = ns.linux.bogus
linux.bogus      nameserver = ns.friend.bogus
ns.linux.bogus   internet address = 127.0.0.2
```

and ns.linux.bogus has the address 127.0.0.2. Looks good too.

4.3   Winding down

Of course, this domain is highly bogus, and so are all the addresses in it, and it is perhaps, unfortunately a bit confusing. For a real example of a real domain see the next section.

5   A real domain example

Where we list some *real* zone files

Users have suggested that I include a real example of a working domain as my explanation of what the differences between a working domain and the bogus example was was a bit unclear.

One thing about this example: Do *not* enter it into your name servers! Use it only to read for reference. If you want to experiment do that with the bogus example. I use this example with permission from David Bullock of LAND-5. These files were current 24th of September 1996, and might differ from what you find if you query LAND-5's name servers now. Also, keep in mind: delete the leading spaces ;-)

5.1   /etc/named.boot (or /var/named/named.boot)

Here we find primary lines for the two reverse zones needed: the 127.0.0 net, as well as LAND-5's 206.6.177 subnet. And a primary line for land-5's forward zone land-5.com. Also note that instead of stuffing the files in a directory called **pz**, as I do in this HOWTO, he puts them in a directory called **zone**.

```
;  Boot file for LAND-5 name server
;
directory /var/named
;
; type          domain                          source file or host
cache           .                               root.cache
primary         0.0.127.in-addr.arpa            zone/127.0.0
primary         177.6.206.in-addr.arpa          zone/206.6.177
primary         land-5.com                      zone/land-5.com
```

5.2 /var/named/root.cache

Keep in mind that this file is dynamic, and the one listed here is old. You're better off using one produced now, with dig.

```
; <<>> DiG 2.1 <<>>
;; res options: init recurs defnam dnsrch
;; got answer:
;; ->>HEADER<<- opcode: QUERY, status: NOERROR, id: 6
;; flags: qr rd ra; Ques: 1, Ans: 9, Auth: 0, Addit: 9
;; QUESTIONS:
;;      ., type = NS, class = IN

;; ANSWERS:
.               518357  NS      H.ROOT-SERVERS.NET.
.               518357  NS      B.ROOT-SERVERS.NET.
.               518357  NS      C.ROOT-SERVERS.NET.
.               518357  NS      D.ROOT-SERVERS.NET.
.               518357  NS      E.ROOT-SERVERS.NET.
.               518357  NS      I.ROOT-SERVERS.NET.
.               518357  NS      F.ROOT-SERVERS.NET.
.               518357  NS      G.ROOT-SERVERS.NET.
.               518357  NS      A.ROOT-SERVERS.NET.

;; ADDITIONAL RECORDS:
H.ROOT-SERVERS.NET.     165593  A       128.63.2.53
B.ROOT-SERVERS.NET.     165593  A       128.9.0.107
C.ROOT-SERVERS.NET.     222766  A       192.33.4.12
D.ROOT-SERVERS.NET.     165593  A       128.8.10.90
E.ROOT-SERVERS.NET.     165593  A       192.203.230.10
I.ROOT-SERVERS.NET.     165593  A       192.36.148.17
F.ROOT-SERVERS.NET.     299616  A       192.5.5.241
G.ROOT-SERVERS.NET.     165593  A       192.112.36.4
A.ROOT-SERVERS.NET.     165593  A       198.41.0.4

;; Total query time: 250 msec
;; FROM: land-5 to SERVER: default ---- 127.0.0.1
;; WHEN: Fri Sep 20 10:11:22 1996
;; MSG SIZE  sent: 17  rcvd: 312
```

5.3 /var/named/zone/127.0.0

Just the basics, the obligatory SOA record, and a record that maps 127.0.0.1 to localhost. Both are required. No more should be in this file. It will probably never need to be updated, unless your nameserver or hostmaster address changes.

```
@               IN      SOA     land-5.com. root.land-5.com. (
                                199609203       ; Serial
                                28800   ; Refresh
                                7200    ; Retry
                                604800  ; Expire
```

```
                        86400)  ; Minimum TTL
                NS      land-5.com.

1               PTR     localhost.
```

5.4   /var/named/zone/land-5.com

Here we see the mandatory SOA record, the needed NS records. We can see that he has a secondary name server at ns2.psi.net. This is as it should be, *always* have a off site secondary server as backup. We can also see that he as a master host called land-5 which takes care of all the different services, and that he's done it with CNAMEs (a alternative is using A records).

As you see from the SOA record, the zone file originates at land-5.com, the contact person is root@land-5.com. hostmaster is another oft used address for the contact person. The serial number is in the customary yyyymmdd format with todays serial number appended; this is probably the sixth version of zone file on the 20th of September 1996. Remember that the serial number *must* increase monotonically, here there is only *one* digit for todays serial#, so after 9 edits he has to wait until tomorrow before he can edit the file again. Consider using two digits.

```
@       IN      SOA     land-5.com. root.land-5.com. (
                        199609206       ; serial, todays date + todays serial #
                        10800           ; refresh, seconds
                        7200            ; retry, seconds
                        10800           ; expire, seconds
                        86400 )         ; minimum, seconds
                NS      land-5.com.
                NS      ns2.psi.net.
                MX      10 land-5.com.  ; Primary Mail Exchanger

localhost       A       127.0.0.1

router          A       206.6.177.1

land-5.com.     A       206.6.177.2
ns              CNAME   land-5.com.
ftp             CNAME   land-5.com.
www             CNAME   land-5.com.
mail            CNAME   land-5.com.
news            CNAME   land-5.com.

funn            A       206.6.177.3
illusions       CNAME   funn.land-5.com.
@               TXT     "LAND-5 Corporation"

;
;       Workstations
;
ws_177200       A       206.6.177.200
                MX      10 land-5.com.    ; Primary Mail Host
ws_177201       A       206.6.177.201
                MX      10 land-5.com.    ; Primary Mail Host
ws_177202       A       206.6.177.202
```

```
              MX       10 land-5.com.    ; Primary Mail Host
ws_177203     A        206.6.177.203
              MX       10 land-5.com.    ; Primary Mail Host
ws_177204     A        206.6.177.204
              MX       10 land-5.com.    ; Primary Mail Host
ws_177205     A        206.6.177.205
              MX       10 land-5.com.    ; Primary Mail Host
; {Many repetitive definitions deleted - SNIP}
ws_177250     A        206.6.177.250
              MX       10 land-5.com.    ; Primary Mail Host
ws_177251     A        206.6.177.251
              MX       10 land-5.com.    ; Primary Mail Host
ws_177252     A        206.6.177.252
              MX       10 land-5.com.    ; Primary Mail Host
ws_177253     A        206.6.177.253
              MX       10 land-5.com.    ; Primary Mail Host
ws_177254     A        206.6.177.254
              MX       10 land-5.com.    ; Primary Mail Host
```

Another thing to note is that the workstations don't have individual names, but rather a prefix followed by the two last parts of the IP numbers. Using such a convention can simplify maintenance significantly, but can be a bit impersonal, and, in fact, be a source of disgruntlement among your customers.

5.5   /var/named/zone/206.6.177

I'll comment on this file after it.

```
@             IN    SOA    land-5.com. root.land-5.com. (
                          199609206        ; Serial
                          28800     ; Refresh
                          7200      ; Retry
                          604800    ; Expire
                          86400)    ; Minimum TTL
                    NS     land-5.com.
                    NS     ns2.psi.net.
;
;       Servers
;
1       PTR    router.land-5.com.
2       PTR    land-5.com.
3       PTR    funn.land-5.com.
;
;       Workstations
;
200     PTR    ws_177200.land-5.com.
201     PTR    ws_177201.land-5.com.
202     PTR    ws_177202.land-5.com.
203     PTR    ws_177203.land-5.com.
204     PTR    ws_177204.land-5.com.
205     PTR    ws_177205.land-5.com.
; {Many repetitive definitions deleted - SNIP}
```

250	PTR	ws_177250.land-5.com.
251	PTR	ws_177251.land-5.com.
252	PTR	ws_177252.land-5.com.
253	PTR	ws_177253.land-5.com.
254	PTR	ws_177254.land-5.com.

The reverse zone is the bit of the setup that seems to cause the most grief. It is used to find the host name if you have the IP number of a machine. Example: you are an irc server and accept connections from irc clients. However you are a Norwegian irc server and so you only want to accept connections from clients in Norway and other Scandinavian countries. When you get a connection from a client the C library is able to tell you the IP number of the connecting machine because the IP number of the client is contained in all the packets that are passed over the network. Now you can call a function called gethostbyaddr that looks up the name of a host given the IP number. Gethostbyaddr will ask a DNS server, which will then traverse the DNS looking for the machine. Supposing the client connection is from ws_177200.land-5.com. The IP number the C library provides to the irc server is 206.6.177.200. To find out the name of that machine we need to find 200.177.6.206.in-addr.arpa. The DNS server will first find the arpa. servers, then find in-addr.arpa. servers, following the reverse trail through 206, then 6 and at last finding the server for the 177.6.206.in-addr.arpa zone at land-5. From which it will finally get the answer that for 200.177.6.206.in-addr.arpa we have a 'PTR ws_177200.land-5.com' record, meaning that the name that goes with 206.6.177.200 is ws_177200.land-5.com. As with the explanation of how prep.ai.mit.edu is looked up, this is slightly fictitious.

Getting back to the irc server example. The irc server only accepts connections from the Scandinavian countries, i.e., *.no, *.se, *.dk, the name ws_177200.land-5.com clearly does not match any of those, and the server will deny the connection. If there was *no* reverse mapping of 206.2.177.200 through the in-addr.arpa zone the server would have been unable to find the name at all and would have to settle to comparing 206.2.177.200 with *.no, *.se and *.dk, none of which will match.

Some people will tell you that reverse lookup mappings are only important for servers, or not important at all. Not so: Many ftp, news, irc and even some http (WWW) servers will *not* accept connections from machines that they are not able to find the name of. So reverse mappings for machines are in fact *mandatory*.

6 Maintenance

Keeping it working.

There is one maintenance task you have to do on nameds, other than keeping them running. That's keeping the root.cache file updated. The easiest way is using dig, first run dig with no arguments, you will get the root.cache according to your own server. Then ask one of the listed root servers with **dig @rootserver . ns**. You will note that the output looks terribly like a root.cache file except for a couple of extra numbers. Those numbers are harmless. Save it to a file (**dig @e.root-servers.net . ns >root.cache.new**) and replace the old root.cache with it.

Remember to restart named after replacing the cache file.

Al Longyear sent me this script that can be run automatically to update root.cache, install a crontab entry to run it once a month and forget it. The script assumes you have mail working and that the mail-alias 'hostmaster' is defined. You must hack it to suit your setup.

```
#!/bin/sh
#
# Update the nameserver cache information file once per month.
# This is run automatically by a cron entry.
#
```

```
(
echo "To: hostmaster <hostmaster>"
echo "From: system <root>"
echo "Subject: Automatic update of the named.boot file"
echo

export PATH=/sbin:/usr/sbin:/bin:/usr/bin:
cd /var/named

dig @rs.internic.net . ns >root.cache.new

echo "The named.boot file has been updated to contain the following
information:"
echo
cat root.cache.new

chown root.root root.cache.new
chmod 444 root.cache.new
rm -f root.cache.old
mv root.cache root.cache.old
mv root.cache.new root.cache
ndc restart
echo
echo "The nameserver has been restarted to ensure that the update is complete."
echo "The previous root.cache file is now called
/var/named/root.cache.old."
) 2>&1 | /usr/lib/sendmail -t
exit 0
```

Some of you might have picked up that the root.cache file is also available by ftp from Internic. Please *don't* use ftp to update root.cache, the above method is much more friendly to the net.

7   Bind version 8

Bind version 8 is the latest in bind technology. I haven't tried to use it, but David E. Smith (dave@bureau42.ml.org) has. He's written the rest of this section.

There's not much to it. Except for using named.conf instead of named.boot, everything is identical. And bind8 comes with a perl script that converts old-style files to new. Example named.boot (old style) for a cache-only name server:

```
directory /var/named
cache    .                            root.hint
primary 0.0.127.IN-ADDR.ARPA          127.0.0.zone
primary localhost                     localhost.zone
```

On the command line, in the bind8/src/bin/named directory, type:

```
named-bootconf.pl < named.boot > named.conf
```

Which creates named.conf:

```
// generated by named-bootconf.pl

options {
        directory "/var/named";
};

zone "." {
        type hint;
        file "root.hint";
};

zone "0.0.127.IN-ADDR.ARPA" {
        type master;
        file "127.0.0.zone";
};

zone "localhost" {
        type master;
        file "localhost.zone";
};
```

It works for everything that can go into a named.boot file, although it doesn't add all of the new enhancements and configuration options that bind8 allows. Here's a more complete named.conf that does the same things, but a little more efficiently.

```
// This is a configuration file for named (from BIND 8.1 or later).
// It would normally be installed as /etc/named.conf.
// The only change made from the 'stock' named.conf (aside from this
// comment :) is that the directory line was uncommented, since I
// already had the zone files in /var/named.

options {
        directory "/var/named";
        check-names master warn;                    /* default. */
        datasize 20M;
};

zone "localhost" IN {
        type master;
        file "localhost.zone";
        check-names fail;
        allow-update { none; };
        allow-transfer { any; };
};

zone "0.0.127.in-addr.arpa" IN {
        type master;
        file "127.0.0.zone";
```

```
        check-names fail;
        allow-update { none; };
        allow-transfer { any; };
};

zone "." IN {
        type hint;
        file "root.hint";
};
```

bind8/src/bin/named/test has this, and copies of the zone files, that many people can just drop in and use instantly.

The formats for zone files and root.hint (root.cache) files are identical, as are the commands for updating them.

8   Automatic setup for dialup connections.

This section explains how I have set things up to automate everything. My way might not suit you at all, but you might get a idea from something I've done. Also, I use ppp for dialup, while many use slip or cslip, so almost everything in your setup can be different from mine. But slip's dip program should be able to do many of the things I do.

Normally, when I'm not connected to the net I have a `resolv.conf` file simply containing the line

```
    domain uio.no
```

This ensures I don't have to wait for the host name resolving library to try to connect to a nameserver that can't help me. But when I connect I want to start my named and have a `resolv.conf` looking like the one described above. I have solved this by keeping two `resolv.conf` 'template' files named `resolv.conf.local` and `resolv.conf.connected`. The latter looks like the `resolv.conf` described before in this document.

To automatically connect to the net I run a script called 'ppp-on':

```
#!/bin/sh
echo calling...
pppd
```

pppd has a file called `options` that tells it the particulars of how to get connected. Once my ppp connection is up the pppd starts a script called `ip-up` (this is described in the pppd man page). This is parts of the script:

```
#!/bin/sh
interface="$1"
device="$2"
speed="$3"
myip="$4"
upip="$5"
 ...
cp -v /etc/resolv.conf.connected /etc/resolv.conf
 ...
/usr/sbin/named
```

I.e. I start my named there. When ppp is disconnected pppd runs a script called `ip-down`:

```
#!/bin/sh
cp /etc/resolv.conf.local /etc/resolv.conf
read namedpid </var/run/named.pid
kill $namedpid
```

So this gets things configured and up when connecting and Dis-configured and down when disconnecting.

Some programs, irc and talk come to mind, make a few too many assumptions, and for irc the dcc features and talk to work right you have to fix your hosts file. I insert have this in my `ip-up` script:

```
cp /etc/hosts.ppp /etc/hosts
echo $myip      roke >>/etc/hosts
```

`hosts.ppp` simply contains

```
127.0.0.1      localhost
```

and the echo thing inserts the ip# i have received for my host name (roke). You should use the name your host knows itself by instead. This can be found with the `hostname` command.

It is probably not smart to run named when you are not connected to the net, this is because named will try to send queries to the net and it has a long timeout, and you have to wait for this timeout every time some program tries to resolve a name. If you're using dialup you should start named when connecting and kill it when disconnecting. But please see the 9 (FAQ) section for a tip.

Some people like to use a forwarders directive on slow connections. If your internet provider has DNS servers at 1.2.3.4 and 1.2.3.5 you can insert the line

```
forwarders 1.2.3.4 1.2.3.5
```

in the `named.boot` file. That will decrease the amount of IP traffic your host originates, any possibly speed things up. This especially important if you're paying pr. byte that goes over the wire. This has the added value of letting you off the one maintenance duty you have as a caching named maintainer; you don't have to update a empty `root.cache` file.

9 FAQ

In this section I list some of the most frequently asked questions related to DNS and this HOWTO. And the answers :-) Please read this section before mailing me.

1. How do use DNS from inside a firewall?
   A couple of hints: 'forwarders', 'slave', and have a look in the literature list at the end of this HOWTO.

2. How do I make DNS rotate through the available addresses for a service, say www.busy.site to obtain a load balancing effect, or similar?

Make several **A** records for www.busy.site and use bind 4.9.3 or later. Then bind will round-robin the answers. It will *not* work with earlier versions of bind.

3. I want to set up DNS on a (closed) intranet. What do I do?

You drop the cache file and just do zone files. That also means you don't have to get new cache files all the time.

4. My system does not have the ndc program. What do I do?

Your system then has an old, somewhat obsolete, bind installed. If security is important to you: upgrade bind at once. If not, you can live with it. And instead of running `ndc start` you run `named`. `ndc reload` becomes `named.reload` and `ndc restart` becomes `named.restart`. All of those programs are most likely in `/usr/sbin`.

5. How do I set up a secondary name server?

If the primary server has address 127.0.0.1 you put a line like this in the named.boot file of your secondary:

```
secondary      linux.bogus              127.0.0.1        sz/linux.bogus
```

6. I want bind running when I'm disconnected from the net.

I have received this mail from Ian Clark <ic@deakin.edu.au> where he explains his way of doing this:

```
I run named on my 'Masquerading' machine here. I have
two root.cache files, one called root.cache.real which contains
the real root server names and the other called root.cache.fake
which contains...


--------------
; root.cache.fake
; this file contains no information
--------------


When I go off line I copy the root.cache.fake file to root.cache and
restart named.

When I go online I copy root.cache.real to root.cache and restart
named.

This is done from ip-down & ip-up respectively.

The first time I do a query off line on a domain name named doesn't
have details for it puts an entry like this in messages..

Jan 28 20:10:11 hazchem named[10147]: No root nameserver for class IN

which I can live with.
```

> It certainly seems to work for me. I can use the nameserver for
> local machines while off the 'net without the timeout delay for
> external domain names and I while on the 'net queries for external
> domains work normally

7. Where does the caching name server store it's cache? Is there any way I can control the size of the cache?

   The cache is completely stored in memory, it is *not* written to disk at any time. Every time you kill named the cache is lost. The cache is *not* controllable in any way. named manages it according to some simple rules and that is it. You cannot control the cache or the cache size in any way for any reason. If you want to you can "fix" this by hacking named. This is however not recommended.

8. Does named save the cache between restarts? Can I make it save it?

   No, named does *not* save the cache when it dies. That means that the cache must be built anew each time you kill and restart named. There is *no* way to make named save the cache in a file. If you want you can "fix" this by hacking named. This is however not recommended.

10   How to become a bigger time DNS admin.

Documentation and tools.

Real Documentation exists. Online and in print. The reading of several of these is required to make the step from small time DNS admin to a big time one. In print the standard book is *DNS and BIND* by C. Liu and P. Albitz from O'Reilly & Associates, Sebastopol, CA, ISBN 0-937175-82-X. I read this, it's excellent. There is also a section in on DNS in *TCP/IP Network Administration*, by Craig Hunt from O'Reilly..., ISBN 0-937175-82-X. Another must for Good DNS administration (or good anything for that matter) is *Zen and the Art of Motorcycle Maintenance* by Robert M. Prisig :-) Available as ISBN 0688052304 and others.

Online you will find stuff on `<http://www.dns.net/dnsrd/>`, `<http://www.isc.org/bind.html>`; A FAQ, a reference manual (BOG; Bind Operations Guide) as well as papers and protocol definitions and DNS hacks (these, and most, if not all, of the rfcs mentioned below, are also contained in the bind distribution). I have not read most of these, but then I'm not a big-time DNS admin either. Arnt Gulbrandsen on the other hand has read BOG and he's ecstatic about it :-). The newsgroup *comp.protocols.tcp-ip.domains* `<news:comp.protocols.tcp-ip.domains>` is about DNS. In addition there are a number of RFCs about DNS, the most important are probably these:

RFC 2052

   A. Gulbrandsen, P. Vixie, *A DNS RR for specifying the location of services (DNS SRV)*, October 1996

RFC 1918

   Y. Rekhter, R. Moskowitz, D. Karrenberg, G. de Groot, E. Lear, *Address Allocation for Private Internets*, 02/29/1996.

RFC 1912

   D. Barr, *Common DNS Operational and Configuration Errors*, 02/28/1996.

RFC 1713

   A. Romao, *Tools for DNS debugging*, 11/03/1994.

RFC 1712

   C. Farrell, M. Schulze, S. Pleitner, D. Baldoni, *DNS Encoding of Geographical Location*, 11/01/1994.

RFC 1183

   R. Ullmann, P. Mockapetris, L. Mamakos, C. Everhart, *New DNS RR Definitions*, 10/08/1990.

RFC 1035

P. Mockapetris, *Domain names - implementation and specification*, 11/01/1987.

RFC 1034

P. Mockapetris, *Domain names - concepts and facilities*, 11/01/1987.

RFC 1033

M. Lottor, *Domain administrators operations guide*, 11/01/1987.

RFC 1032

M. Stahl, *Domain administrators guide*, 11/01/1987.

RFC 974

C. Partridge, *Mail routing and the domain system*, 01/01/1986.

Linux Ethernet-Howto

by Paul Gortmaker   v2.65, 1 February 1998

This is the Ethernet-Howto, which is a compilation of information about which ethernet devices can be used for Linux, and how to set them up. It hopefully answers all the frequently asked questions about using ethernet cards with Linux. Note that this Howto is focused on the hardware and low level driver aspect of the ethernet cards, and does not cover the software end of things like `ifconfig` and `route`. See the Network Howto for that stuff.

Contents

1 Introduction

The Ethernet-Howto covers what cards you should and shouldn't buy; how to set them up, how to run more than one, and other common problems and questions. It contains detailed information on the current level of support for all of the most common ethernet cards available.

It does *not* cover the software end of things, as that is covered in the NET-2 Howto. Also note that general non-Linux specific questions about Ethernet are not (or at least they should not be) answered here. For those types of questions, see the excellent amount of information in the *comp.dcom.lans.ethernet* FAQ. You can FTP it from `rtfm.mit.edu` just like all the other newsgroup FAQs.

This present revision covers distribution kernels up to and including 2.0.33. Some information pertaining to development kernels up to version 2.1.82 is also included.

The Ethernet-Howto is by:

       Paul Gortmaker, `gpg109@rsphy1.anu.edu.au`

The primary source of information for the initial ASCII-only version of the Ethernet-Howto was:

       Donald J. Becker, `becker@cesdis.gsfc.nasa.gov`

who we should thank for writing the vast majority of ethernet card drivers that are presently available for Linux. He also is the original author of the NFS server too. Thanks Donald!

Net-surfers may wish to check out the following URL:

Donald Becker `<http://cesdis.gsfc.nasa.gov/pub/people/becker/whoiam.html>`

Please see the Disclaimer and Copying information at the end of this document for information about redistribution of this document and the usual 'we are not responsible for what you do...' legal type mumblings.

1.1 New Versions of this Document

New versions of this document can be retrieved via anonymous FTP from:

Sunsite HOWTO Archive `<ftp://sunsite.unc.edu/pub/Linux/docs/HOWTO/>`

and various Linux ftp mirror sites. Updates will be made as new information and/or drivers becomes available. If this copy that you are reading is more than 6 months old, it is either out of date, or it means that I have been lazy and haven't updated it.

If you have sent me an update and it is not included in the next release, it probably means I've lost it amongst the ton of junk e-mail I get. Please re-send it (along with an abusive message) and I will try and make sure it gets included in the next release.

This document was produced by using the SGML system that was specifically set up for the Linux Howto project, and there are various output formats available, including, postscript, dvi, ascii, html, and soon TeXinfo.

I would recommend viewing it in the html (via a WWW browser) or the Postscript/dvi format. Both of these contain cross-references that are lost in the ascii translation.

If you want to get the official copy off sunsite, here is URL.

Ethernet-HOWTO <http://sunsite.unc.edu/mdw/HOWTO/Ethernet-HOWTO.html>

1.2   Using the Ethernet-Howto

As this guide is getting bigger and bigger, you probably don't want to spend the rest of your afternoon reading the whole thing. And the good news is that you don't *have* to read it all.

Chances are you are reading this document beacuse you can't get things to work and you don't know what to do or check. The next section (1.3 (HELP - It doesn't work!)) is aimed at newcomers to linux and will point you in the right direction.

Typically the same problems and questions are asked *over and over* again by different people. Chances are your specific problem or question is one of these frequently asked questions, and is answered in the FAQ portion of this document . (3 (The FAQ section)). Everybody should have a look through this section before posting for help.

If you haven't got an ethernet card, then you will want to start with deciding on a card. (2 (What card should I buy...))

If you have already got an ethernet card, but are not sure if you can use it with Linux, then you will want to read the section which contains specific information on each manufacturer, and their cards. (5 (Vendor Specific...))

If you are interested in some of the technical aspects of the Linux device drivers, then you can have a browse of the section with this type of information. (8 (Technical Information))

1.3   HELP - It doesn't work!

Okay, don't panic. This will lead you through the process of getting things working, even if you have no prior background in linux or ethernet hardware.

First thing you need to do is figure out what model your card is so you can determine if Linux has a driver for that particular card. Different cards typically have different ways of being controlled by the host computer, and the linux driver (if there is one) contains this control information in a format that allows linux to use the card. If you don't have any manuals or anything of the sort that tell you anything about the card model, then you can try the section on helping with mystery cards (reference section: 5.39 (Identifying an Unknown Card)).

Now that you know what type of card you have, read through the details of your particular card in the card specific section (reference section: 5 (Vendor Specific...)) which lists in alphabetical order, card manufacturers, individual model numbers and whether it has a linux driver or not. If it lists it as 'Not Supported' you can pretty much give up here. If you can't find your card in that list, then check to see if your card manual lists it as being 'compatible' with another known card type. For example there are hundreds, if not thousands of different cards made to be compatible with the original Novell NE2000 design.

Assuming you have found out that your card does have a linux driver, you now need to go back to the CD-ROM or whatever you installed from, and find the list of pre-built kernels that comes with it. The kernel is the core operating system that is first loaded at boot, and contains drivers for various pieces of hardware, among other things. Just because linux has a driver for your card does *not* mean that it is built into every kernel. Depending on who made the CD-ROM, there may be only a few pre-built kernels, and a whole bunch of drivers as smaller separate modules, or there may be a whole lot of kernels, covering a vast combination of built-in driver combinations. Hopefully there will also be a text file with them that lists what drivers are included into which kernels. Try and find a kernel that is listed as having the driver you need as built into it, or try and find a module with the name of the driver you need.

If you found a pre-built kernel that has your driver in it, you will want to boot that kernel instead of the one you are presently using. Most linux systems use LILO to boot, and will have installed the LILO documentation on your system. Follow the instructions in that for booting another kernel, as they are beyond the scope of this document.

If you instead found a small module that contains the driver, you will need to attach this module to the kernel after it has booted up. See the information that came with your distribution on installing and using modules, along with the module section in this document. (10.2 (Using the Ethernet Drivers as Modules))

If you didn't find either a pre-built kernel with your driver, or a module form of the driver, chances are you have a typically uncommon card, and you will have to build your own kernel with that driver included. Once you have linux installed, building a custom kernel is not difficult at all. You essentially answer yes or no to what you want the kernel to contain, and then tell it to build it. There is a Kernel-HowTo that will help you along.

At this point you should have somehow managed to be booting a kernel with your driver built in, or be loading it as a module. About half of the problems people have are related to not having driver loaded one way or another, so you may find things work now.

If it still doesn't work, then you need to verify that the kernel is indeed detecting the card. To do this, you need to type `dmesg | more` when logged in after the system has booted and all modules have been loaded. This will allow you to review the boot messages that the kernel scrolled up the screen during the boot process. If the card has been detected, you should see somewhere in that list a message from your card's driver that starts with `eth0`, mentions the driver name and the hardware parameters (interrupt setting, input/output port address, etc) that the card is set for. If you don't see a message like this, then the driver didn't detect your card, and that is why things aren't working. See the FAQ (3 (The FAQ Section)) for what to do if your card is not detected. If you have a NE2000 compatible, there is also some NE2000 specific tips on getting a card detected in the FAQ section as well.

If the card is detected, but the detection message reports some sort of error, like a resource conflict, then the driver probably won't have initialized properly and the card still wont be useable. Most common error messages of this sort are also listed in the FAQ section, along with a solution.

If the detection message seems okay, then double check the card resources reported by the driver against those that the card is physically set for (either by little black jumpers on the card, or by a software utility supplied by the card manufacturer.) These must match exactly. For example, if you have the card jumpered or configured to IRQ 15 and the driver reports IRQ 10 in the boot messages, things will not work. The FAQ section discusses the most common cases of drivers incorrectly detecting the configuration information of various cards.

At this point, you have managed to get you card detected with all the correct parameters, and hopefully everything is working. If not, then you either have a software configuration error, or a hardware configuration error. A software configuration error is not setting up the right network addresses for the `ifconfig` and `route` commands, and details of how to do that are fully described in the Network HowTo and the 'Network Administrator's Guide' which both probably came on the CD-ROM you installed from.

A hardware configuration error is when some sort of resource conflict or mis-configuration (that the driver didn't detect at boot) that stops the card from working properly. This typically can be observed in one of three different ways. (1) You get an error message when `ifconfig` tries to open the device for use, such as "SIOCSFFLAGS: Try again". (2) The driver reports `eth0` error messages (viewed by `dmesg | more`) or strange inconsistencies for each time it tries to send or receive data. (3) Typing `cat /proc/net/dev` shows non-zero numbers in one of the errs, drop, fifo, frame or carrier columns for `eth0`. Most of the typical hardware configuration errors are also discussed in the FAQ section.

Well, if you have got to this point and things still aren't working, read the FAQ section of this document, read the vendor specific section detailing your particular card, *and if it still doesn't work* then you may have to resort to posting to an appropriate newsgroup for help. If you do post, please detail all relevant information in that post, such as the card brand, the kernel version, the driver boot messages, the output from `cat /proc/net/dev`, a clear description of the problem, and of course what you have already tried to do in an effort to get things to work.

You would be surprised at how many people post useless things like "Can someone help me? My ethernet doesn't work." and nothing else. Readers of the newsgroups tend to ignore such silly posts, whereas a detailed and informational problem description may allow a 'linux-guru' to spot your problem right away.

2   What card should I buy for Linux?

The answer to this question depends heavily on exactly what you intend on doing with your net connection, and how much traffic it will see.

If you only expect a single user to be doing the occasional ftp session or WWW connection, then an old 8 bit card will probably keep you happy.

If you intend to set up a server, and you require the CPU overhead of Rx'ing and Tx'ing ether packets to be kept at a minimum, you probably want to look at one of the newer PCI cards with the DEC 21040 chip, or the AMD PCnet-PCI chip.

If you fall somewhere in the middle of the above, then any one of the 16 bit ISA cards with stable drivers will do the job for you.

2.1   So What Drivers are Stable?

Of the 16 bit ISA cards, the following drivers are very mature, and you shouldn't have any problems if you buy a card that uses these drivers.

SMC-Ultra/EtherEZ, WD80x3, 3c509, 3c503/16, Lance, NE2000.

This is not to say that all the other drivers are unstable. It just happens that the above are the oldest and most used of all the linux drivers, making them the safest choice.

Note that some el-cheapo motherboards can have trouble with the bus-mastering that the lance cards do, and some el-cheapo NE2000 clones can have trouble getting detected at boot.

As for PCI cards, the PCnet-PCI cards that use the lance driver are a safe choice (except for the Boca cards as they have hardware flaws). The Allied Telsyn AT2450 is a PCnet-PCI implementation that is known to work well.

The DEC 21040 'tulip' driver and the 3c59x 'vortex' driver are relatively new drivers, but have proven themselves to be quite stable already.

2.2   Eight bit vs 16 bit Cards

You probably can't buy a new 8 bit ISA ethercard anymore, but you will find lots of them turning up at computer swap meets and the like for the next few years, at very low prices. This will make them popular for "home-ethernet" systems.

Some 8 bit cards that will provide adequate performance for light to average use are the wd8003, the 3c503 and the ne1000. The 3c501 provides poor performance, and these poor 12 year old relics of the XT days should be avoided.

The 8 bit data path doesn't hurt performance that much, as you can still expect to get about 500 to 800kB/s ftp download speed to an 8 bit wd8003 card (on a fast ISA bus) from a fast host. And if most of your net-traffic is going to remote sites, then the bottleneck in the path will be elsewhere, and the only speed difference you will notice is during net activity on your local subnet.

2.3 32 Bit / VLB / PCI Ethernet Cards

There aren't many 32 bit ethercard device drivers because there aren't that many 32 bit ethercards. There aren't many 32 bit ethercards out there because a 10Mbs network doesn't justify spending a large price increment for the 32 bit interface. Now that 100Mbs networks are becoming more common, this is changing though.

See 2.6 (Programmed I/O vs. ...) as to why having a 10Mbps ethercard on an 8MHz ISA bus is really not a bottleneck. Even though having the ethercard on a fast bus won't necessarily mean faster transfers, it will usually mean reduced CPU overhead, which is good for multi-user systems.

AMD has the 32 bit PCnet-VLB and PCnet-PCI chips. See 5.4.2 (AMD PCnet-32) for info on the 32 bit versions of the LANCE / PCnet-ISA chip.

The DEC 21040 PCI chip is another option (see 5.17.4 (DEC 21040)) for power-users. Many manufacturers produce cards that use this chip, and the prices of such no-name cards is usually quite cheap.

3Com's 'Vortex' and 'Boomerang' PCI cards are also another option, and the price is quite cheap if you can get one under their evaluation deal while it lasts. (see 5.1.14 (3c590/3c595))

Various clone manufacturers have started making PCI ne2000 clones based on a RealTek or Winbond chip. These cards are also supported by the linux ne2000 driver for v2.0.31 and newer kernels. However you only benefit from the faster bus interface, as the card is still using the age-old ne2000 driver interface.

2.4 Available 100Mbs Cards and Drivers

The present list of supported 100Mbs hardware is as follows: cards with the DEC 21140 chip; the 3c595/3c90x Vortex cards; and the HP 100VG ANY-LAN. The drivers for the first two are quite stable, but feedback on the HP driver has been low so far.

The EtherExpressPro10/100B now also has a driver in the current v2.0 kenrel. For updates and/or support, see the relevant section in this document.

The 21140 100Base-? chip is supported with the same driver as its 10Mbs counterpart, the 21040. SMC's 100Mbs EtherPower PCI card uses this chip. As with the 21040, you have a choice of two drivers to pick from.

Also have a look at the information on Donald's WWW site, at the following URL:

100Mbs Ethernet <http://cesdis.gsfc.nasa.gov/linux/misc/100mbs.html>

Donald had done a fair bit of work with the SMC EtherPower-10/100 cards, and reported getting about 4.6MB/s application to application with TCP on P5-100 Triton machines.

(See 5.1.14 (3c595) and 5.17.4 (DEC 21140) for more details.)

For 100VG information, see the following section, and this URL on Donald's Site:

Donald's 100VG Page <http://cesdis.gsfc.nasa.gov/linux/drivers/100vg.html>

You may also be interested in looking at:

Dan Kegel's Fast Ethernet Page <http://alumni.caltech.edu/dank/fe/>

2.5 100VG versus 100BaseT

The following blurb from yet another one of Donald's informative comp.os.linux postings summarizes the situation quite well:

"For those not in the know, there are two competing 100Mbs ethernet standards, 100VG (aka 100baseVG and 100VG-AnyLAN) and 100baseT (with 100baseTx, 100baseT4 and 100baseFx cable types).

100VG was on the market first, and I feel that it is better engineered than 100baseTx. I was rooting for it to win, but it clearly isn't going to. HP et al. made several bad choices:

1) Delaying the standard so that they could accommodate IBM and support token ring frames. It 'seemed like a good idea at the time', since it would enable token ring shops to upgrade without the managers having to admit they made a very expensive mistake committing to the wrong technology. But there was nothing to be gained, as the two frame types couldn't coexist on a network, token ring is a morass of complexity, and IBM went with 100baseT anyway.

2) Producing only ISA and EISA cards. (A PCI model was only recently announced.) The ISA bus is too slow for 100mbs, and relatively few EISA machines exist. At the time VLB was common, fast, and cheap with PCI a viable choice. But "old-timer" wisdom held that servers would stay with the more expensive EISA bus.

3) Not sending me a databook. Yes, this action was the real reason for the 100VGs downfall :-). I called all over for programming info, and all I could get was a few page color glossy brochure from AT&T describing how wonderful the Regatta chipset was."

2.6 Programmed I/O vs. Shared Memory vs. DMA

Ethernet is 10Mbs. (Don't be pedantic, 3Mbs and 100Mbs don't count.) If you can already send and receive back-to-back packets, you just can't put more bits over the wire. Every modern ethercard can receive back-to-back packets. The Linux DP8390 drivers (wd80x3, SMC-Ultra, 3c503, ne2000, etc) come pretty close to sending back-to-back packets (depending on the current interrupt latency) and the 3c509 and AT1500 hardware have no problem at all automatically sending back-to-back packets.

The ISA bus can do 5.3MB/sec (42Mb/sec), which sounds like more than enough. You can use that bandwidth in several ways, listed below.

2.6.1 Programmed I/O (e.g. NE2000, 3c509)

Pro: Doesn't use any constrained system resources, just a few I/O registers, and has no 16M limit.

Con: Usually the slowest transfer rate, the CPU is waiting the whole time, and interleaved packet access is usually difficult to impossible.

2.6.2 Shared memory (e.g. WD80x3, SMC-Ultra, 3c503)

Pro: Simple, faster than programmed I/O, and allows random access to packets. The linux drivers compute the checksum of incoming IP packets as they are copied off the card, resulting in a further reduction of CPU usage vs. an equivalent PIO card.

Con: Uses up memory space (a big one for DOS users, essentially a non-issue under Linux), and it still ties up the CPU.

2.6.3 Slave (normal) Direct Memory Access (e.g. none for Linux!)

Pro: Frees up the CPU during the actual data transfer.

Con: Checking boundary conditions, allocating contiguous buffers, and programming the DMA registers makes it the slowest of all techniques. It also uses up a scarce DMA channel, and requires aligned low memory buffers.

2.6.4 Bus Master Direct Memory Access (e.g. LANCE, DEC 21040)

Pro: Frees up the CPU during the data transfer, can string together buffers, can require little or no CPU time lost on the ISA bus.

Con: Requires low-memory buffers and a DMA channel. Any bus-master will have problems with other bus-masters that are bus-hogs, such as some primitive SCSI adaptors. A few badly-designed motherboard chipsets have problems with bus-masters. And a reason for not using *any* type of DMA device is using a 486 processor designed for plug-in replacement of a 386: these processors must flush their cache with each DMA cycle. (This includes the Cx486DLC, Ti486DLC, Cx486SLC, Ti486SLC, etc.)

2.7 Type of cable that your card should support

If you are setting up a small "personal" network, you will probably want to use thinnet or thin ethernet cable. This is the style with the standard BNC connectors. See 6 (Cables, Coax...) for other concerns with different types of ethernet cable.

Most ethercards also come in a 'Combo' version for only $10-$20 more. These have both twisted pair and thinnet transceiver built-in, allowing you to change your mind later.

The twisted pair cables, with the RJ-45 (giant phone jack) connectors is technically called 10BaseT. You may also hear it called UTP (Unsheilded Twisted Pair).

The thinnet, or thin ethernet cabling, (RG-58 coaxial cable) with the BNC (metal push and turn-to-lock) connectors is technically called 10Base2.

The older thick ethernet (10mm coaxial cable) which is only found in older installations is called 10Base5.

Large corporate installations will most likely use 10BaseT instead of 10Base2. 10Base2 does not offer an easy upgrade path to the new upcoming 100Base-whatever.

3 Frequently Asked Questions

Here are some of the more frequently asked questions about using Linux with an Ethernet connection. Some of the more specific questions are sorted on a 'per manufacturer basis'. However, since this document is basically 'old' by the time you get it, any 'new' problems will not appear here instantly. For these, I suggest that you make efficient use of your newsreader. For example, nn users would type

```
nn -xX -s'3c'
```

to get all the news articles in your subscribed list that have '3c' in the subject. (ie. 3com, 3c509, 3c503, etc.) The moral: Read the man page for your newsreader.

3.1   Alpha Drivers – Getting and Using them

I heard that there is an updated or alpha driver available for my card. Where can I get it?

The newest of the 'new' drivers can be found on Donald's ftp site: `cesdis.gsfc.nasa.gov` in the `/pub/linux/` area. Things change here quite frequently, so just look around for it. Alternatively, it may be easier to use a WWW browser on:

Don's Linux Home Page `<http://cesdis.gsfc.nasa.gov/pub/linux/linux.html>`

to locate the driver that you are looking for. (Watch out for WWW browsers that silently munge the source by replacing TABs with spaces and so on - use ftp, or at least an FTP URL for downloading if unsure.)

Now, if it really is an alpha, or pre-alpha driver, then please treat it as such. In other words, don't complain because you can't figure out what to do with it. If you can't figure out how to install it, then you probably shouldn't be testing it. Also, if it brings your machine down, don't complain. Instead, send us a well documented bug report, or even better, a patch!

Note that some of the 'useable' experimental/alpha drivers have been included in the standard kernel source tree. When running `make config` one of the first things you will be asked is whether to "Prompt for development and/or incomplete code/drivers". You will have to answer 'Y' here to get asked about including any alpha/experiemntal drivers.

3.2   Using More than one Ethernet Card per Machine

What needs to be done so that Linux can run two ethernet cards?

The hooks for multiple ethercards are all there. However, note that at the moment only *one* ethercard is auto-probed for by default. This helps to avoid possible boot time hangs caused by probing sensitive cards.

There are two ways that you can enable auto-probing for the second (and third, and...) card. The easiest method is to pass boot-time arguments to the kernel, which is usually done by LILO. Probing for the second card can be achieved by using a boot-time argument as simple as `ether=0,0,eth1`. In this case `eth0` and `eth1` will be assigned in the order that the cards are found at boot. Say if you want the card at `0x300` to be `eth0` and the card at `0x280` to be `eth1` then you could use

```
LILO: linux ether=5,0x300,eth0 ether=15,0x280,eth1
```

The `ether=` command accepts more than the IRQ + i/o + name shown above. Please have a look at 10.1 (Passing Ethernet Arguments...) for the full syntax, card specific parameters, and LILO tips.

These boot time arguments can be made permanent so that you don't have to re-enter them every time. See the LILO configuration option '`append`' in the LILO manual.

The second way (not recommended) is to edit the file `Space.c` and replace the `0xffe0` entry for the i/o address with a zero. The `0xffe0` entry tells it not to probe for that device – replacing it with a zero will enable autoprobing for that device.

Note that if you are intending to use Linux as a gateway between two networks, you will have to re-compile a kernel with IP forwarding enabled. Usually using an old AT/286 with something like the 'kbridge' software is a better solution.

If you are viewing this while *net-surfing*, you may wish to look at a mini-howto Donald has on his WWW site. Check out *Multiple Ethercards* `<http://cesdis.gsfc.nasa.gov/linux/misc/multicard.html>`.

For module users with 8390 based cards, you can have a single module control multiple cards of the same brand. Please see 10.2.1 (8390 Based Cards as Modules) for module specific information about using multiple cards.

3.3   Poor NE2000 Clones

Here is a list of some of the NE-2000 clones that are known to have various problems. Most of them aren't fatal. In the case of the ones listed as 'bad clones' – this usually indicates that the cards don't have the two NE2000 identifier bytes. NEx000-clones have a Station Address PROM (SAPROM) in the packet buffer memory space. NE2000 clones have `0x57,0x57` in bytes `0x0e,0x0f` of the SAPROM, while other supposed NE2000 clones must be detected by their SA prefix.

This is not a comprehensive list of all the NE2000 clones that don't have the `0x57,0x57` in bytes `0x0e,0x0f` of the SAPROM. There are probably hundreds of them. If you get a card that causes the driver to report an 'invalid signature' then you will have to add your cards signature to the driver. The process for doing this is described below.

Accton NE2000 – might not get detected at boot, see below.

Artisoft LANtastic AE-2 – OK, but has flawed error-reporting registers.

AT-LAN-TEC NE2000 – clone uses Winbond chip that traps SCSI drivers

ShineNet LCS-8634 – clone uses Winbond chip that traps SCSI drivers

Cabletron E10**, E20**, E10**-x, E20**-x – bad clones, but the driver checks for them. See 5.11.1 (E10**).

D-Link Ethernet II – bad clones, but the driver checks for them. See 5.15.1 (DE-100 / DE-200).

DFI DFINET-300, DFINET-400 – bad clones, but the driver checks for them. See 5.16.1 (DFI-300 / DFI-400)

EtherNext UTP8, EtherNext UTP16 – bad clones, but the driver checks for them.

3.4   Problems with NE1000 / NE2000 cards (and clones)

Problem: PCI NE2000 clone card is not detected at boot with v2.0.x.

Reason: The `ne.c` driver up to v2.0.30 only knows about the PCI ID number of RealTek 8029 based clone cards. Since then, Winbond and Compex have also released PCI NE2000 clone cards, with different PCI ID numbers, and hence the driver doesn't detect them.

Solution: The easiest solution is to upgrade to a v2.0.31 (or newer) version of the linux kernel. It knows the ID numbers of about five different NE2000-PCI chips, and will detect them automatically at boot or at module loading time.

Alternatively, after booting, you can get the I/O address (and interrupt) that the card will use from a "`cat /proc/pci`". Say for example it reports IRQ 9 and I/O at `0xffe0`, then at the LILO boot prompt you can add `ether=9,0xffe0,eth0` which will point the driver right at your card and avoid the PCI based probing altogether. (Future v2.1+ kernels will know about the PCI IDs of Winbond and Compex NE2000 clones as well, so this won't be necessary then.)

Problem: PCI NE2000 clone card is reported as an ne1000 (8 bit card!) at boot or when I load the ne.o module for v2.0.x, and hence doesn't work.

Reason: Some PCI clones don't implement byte wide access (and hence are not truly 100% NE2000 compatible). This causes the probe to think they are NE1000 cards if the PCI probing wasn't used (which it isn't when an explicit I/O address is given with the module or at boot.)

Solution: You can upgrade to v2.0.31 (or newer) as described above, or manually make the following change to `drivers/net/ne.c`:

```
-        if (pci_irq_line)
+        if (pci_irq_line || ioaddr >= 0x400)
             wordlength = 2;   /* Catch broken PCI cards mentioned above. */
```

and then recompile the module (or the kernel). Note that v2.0.31 and recent v2.1.x revisons do not require an I/O address for detecting most PCI cards at boot or with the ne.o module - it is best to let it autodetect the card with these versions.

Problem: PCI NE2000 card gets terrible performance, even when reducing the window size as described in the Performance Tips section.

Reason: The spec sheets for the original 8390 chip, desgined and sold over ten years ago, noted that a dummy read from the chip was required before the write operation for maximum reliablity. The driver has the facility to do this but it has been disabled by default since the v1.2 days, once the real problem causing the crashes back then was located. One user has reported that re-enabling this 'mis-feature' helped their performance with a cheap PCI NE2000 clone card.

Solution: Since it has only been reported as a solution by one person, don't get your hopes up. Re-enabling the read before write fix is done by simply editing the file `linux/drivers/net/ne.c`, uncommenting the line containing `NE_RW_BUGFIX` and then rebuilding the kernel or module as appropriate. Please send an e-mail describing the performance difference and type of card/chip you have if this helps you.

Problem: NE*000 card hangs machine, sometimes with a 'DMA conflict' message, sometimes completely silently.

Reason: There were some bugs in the driver and the upper networking layers that caused this. They have been fixed long ago, in kernels v1.2.9 and above. Upgrade your kernel.

Problem: NE*000 card hangs machine during NE probe, or can not read station address properly.

Reason: Kernels previous to v1.3.7 did not fully reset the card after finding it at boot. Some cheap cards are not left in a reasonable state after power-up and need to be fully reset before any attempt is made to use them. Also, a previous probe may have upset the NE card prior to the NE probe taking place. In that case, look in to using the "reserve=" boot keyword to protect the card from other probes.

Problem: NE*000 driver reports 'not found (no reset ack)' during boot probe.

Reason: This is related to the above change. After the initial verification that an 8390 is at the probed i/o address, the reset is performed. When the card has completed the reset, it is supposed to acknowedge that the reset has completed. Your card doesn't, and so the driver assumes that no NE card is present.

Solution: You can tell the driver that you have a bad card by using an otherwise unused mem_end hexidecimal value of 0xbad at boot time. You *have* to also supply a non-zero i/o base for the card when using the 0xbad override. For example, a card that is at 0x340 that doesn't ack the reset would use something like:

```
    LILO: linux ether=0,0x340,0,0xbad,eth0
```

This will allow the card detection to continue, even if your card doesn't ACK the reset. If you are using the driver as a module, then you can supply the option `bad=0xbad` just like you supply the I/O address. Note that v2.0.x modules won't understand the `bad=` option, as it was added during the v2.1 development.

Problem: NE*000 card hangs machine at first network access.

Reason: This problem has been reported for kernels as old as 1.1.57 to the present. It appears confined to a few software configurable clone cards. It appears that they expect to be initialized in some special way.

Solution: Several people have reported that running the supplied DOS software config program and/or the supplied DOS driver prior to warm booting (i.e. loadlin or the 'three-finger-salute') into linux allowed the card to work. This would indicate that these cards need to be initialized in a particular fashion, slightly different than what the present Linux driver does.

Problem: NE*000 ethercard at `0x360` doesn't get detected anymore.

Reason: Recent kernels (> 1.1.7X) have more sanity checks with respect to overlapping i/o regions. Your NE2000 card is `0x20` wide in i/o space, which makes it hit the parallel port at `0x378`. Other devices that could be there are the second floppy controller (if equipped) at `0x370` and the secondary IDE controller at `0x376--0x377`. If the port(s) are already registered by another driver, the kernel will not let the probe happen.

Solution: Either move your card to an address like `0x280`, `0x340`, `0x320` or compile without parallel printer support.

Problem: Network 'goes away' every time I print something (NE2000)

Reason: Same problem as above, but you have an older kernel that doesn't check for overlapping i/o regions. Use the same fix as above, and get a new kernel while you are at it.

Problem: NE*000 ethercard probe at 0xNNN: 00 00 C5 ... not found. (invalid signature yy zz)

Reason: First off, do you have a NE1000 or NE2000 card at the addr. 0xNNN? And if so, does the hardware address reported look like a valid one? If so, then you have a poor NE*000 clone. All NE*000 clones are supposed to have the value `0x57` in bytes 14 and 15 of the SA PROM on the card. Yours doesn't – it has 'yy zz' instead.

Solution: There are two ways to get around this. The easiest is to use an `0xbad` mem_end value as described above for the 'no reset ack' problem. This will bypass the signature check, as long as a non-zero i/o base is also given. This way no recompilation of the kernel is required.

The second method involves changing the driver itself, and then recompiling your kernel. The driver (/usr/src/linux/drivers/net/ne.c) has a "Hall of Shame" list at about line 42. This list is used to detect poor clones. For example, the DFI cards use 'DFI' in the first 3 bytes of the PROM, instead of using `0x57` in bytes 14 and 15, like they are supposed to.

You can determine what the first 3 bytes of your card PROM are by adding a line like:

```
printk("PROM prefix: %2.2x %2.2x %2.2x\n",SA_prom[0],SA_prom[1],SA_prom[2]);
```

into the driver, right after the error message you got above, and just before the "return ENXIO" at line 227.

Reboot with this change in place, and after the detection fails, you will get the three bytes from the PROM like the DFI example above. Then you can add your card to the bad_clone_list[] at about line 43. Say the above line printed out:

```
PROM prefix:  0x3F 0x2D 0x1C
```

after you rebooted. And say that the 8 bit version of your card was called the "FOO-1k" and the 16 bit version the "FOO-2k". Then you would add the following line to the bad_clone_list[]:

```
{"FOO-1k", "FOO-2k", {0x3F, 0x2D, 0x1C,}},
```

Note that the 2 name strings you add can be anything – they are just printed at boot, and not matched against anything on the card. You can also take out the "printk()" that you added above, if you want. It shouldn't hit that line anymore anyway. Then recompile once more, and your card should be detected.

Problem: Errors like `DMA address mismatch`

Is the chip a real NatSemi 8390? (DP8390, DP83901, DP83902 or DP83905)? If not, some clone chips don't correctly implement the transfer verification register. MS-DOS drivers never do error checking, so it doesn't matter to them. (Note: The DMA address check is not done by default as of v1.2.4 for performance reasons. Enable it with the 'NE_SANITY' define in `ne.c` if you want the check done.)

Are most of the messages off by a factor of 2? If so: Are you using the NE2000 in a 16 bit slot? Is it jumpered to use only 8 bit transfers?

The Linux driver expects a NE2000 to be in a 16 bit slot. A NE1000 can be in either size slot. This problem can also occur with some clones, notably older D-Link 16 bit cards, that don't have the correct ID bytes in the station address PROM.

Are you running the bus faster than 8Mhz? If you can change the speed (faster or slower), see if that makes a difference. Most NE2000 clones will run at 16MHz, but some may not. Changing speed can also mask a noisy bus.

What other devices are on the bus? If moving the devices around changes the reliability, then you have a bus noise problem – just what that error message was designed to detect. Congratulations, you've probably found the source of other problems as well.

Problem: The machine hangs during boot right after the '8390...' or 'WD....' message. Removing the NE2000 fixes the problem.

Solution: Change your NE2000 base address to something like 0x340. Alternatively, you can use the "reserve=" boot argument in conjunction with the "ether=" argument to protect the card from other device driver probes.

Reason: Your NE2000 clone isn't a good enough clone. An active NE2000 is a bottomless pit that will trap any driver autoprobing in its space. Changing the NE2000 to a less-popular address will move it out of the way of other autoprobes, allowing your machine to boot.

Problem: The machine hangs during the SCSI probe at boot.

Reason: It's the same problem as above, change the ethercard's address, or use the reserve/ether boot arguments.

Problem: The machine hangs during the soundcard probe at boot.

Reason: No, that's really during the silent SCSI probe, and it's the same problem as above.

Problem: NE2000 not detected at boot - no boot messages at all

Solution: There is no 'magic solution' as there can be a number of reasons why it wasn't detected. The following list should help you walk through the possible problems.

1) Build a new kernel with only the device drivers that you need. Verify that you are indeed booting the fresh kernel. Forgetting to run lilo, etc. can result in booting the old one. (Look closely at the build time/date reported at boot.) Sounds obvious, but we have all done it before. Make sure the driver is in fact included in the new kernel, by checking the `System.map` file for names like `ne_probe`.

2) Look at the boot messages carefully. Does it even ever mention doing a ne2k probe such as 'NE*000 probe at 0xNNN: not found (blah blah)' or does it just fail silently. There is a big difference. Use `dmesg|more` to review the boot messages after logging in, or hit Shift-PgUp to scroll the screen up after the boot has completed and the login prompt appears.

3) After booting, do a `cat /proc/ioports` and verify that the full iospace that the card will require is vacant. If you are at 0x300 then the ne2k driver will ask for 0x300-0x31f. If any other device driver has registered even one port anywhere in that range, the probe will not take place at that address and will silently continue to the next of the probed addresses. A common case is having the lp driver reserve 0x378 or the second IDE channel reserve 0x376 which stops the ne driver from probing 0x360-0x380.

4) Same as above for `cat /proc/interrupts`. Make sure no other device has registered the interrupt that you set the ethercard for. In this case, the probe will happen, and the ether driver will complain loudly at boot about not being able to get the desired IRQ line.

5) If you are still stumped by the silent failure of the driver, then edit it and add some printk() to the probe. For example, with the ne2k you could add/remove lines (marked with a '+' or '-') in net/ne.c like:

```
      int reg0 = inb_p(ioaddr);

+     printk("NE2k probe - now checking %x\n",ioaddr);
-     if (reg0 == 0xFF)
+     if (reg0 == 0xFF) {
+         printk("NE2k probe - got 0xFF (vacant i/o port)\n");
          return ENODEV;
+     }
```

Then it will output messages for each port address that it checks, and you will see if your card's address is being probed or not.

6) You can also get the ne2k diagnostic from Don's ftp site (mentioned in the howto as well) and see if it is able to detect your card after you have booted into linux. Use the '-p 0xNNN' option to tell it where to look for the card. (The default is 0x300 and it doesn't go looking elsewhere, unlike the boot-time probe.) The output from when it finds a card will look something like:

```
Checking the ethercard at 0x300.
  Register 0x0d (0x30d) is 00
  Passed initial NE2000 probe, value 00.
8390 registers: 0a 00 00 00 63 00 00 00 01 00 30 01 00 00 00 00
SA PROM  0: 00 00 00 00 c0 c0 b0 b0 05 05 65 65 05 05 20 20
SA PROM 0x10: 00 00 07 07 0d 0d 01 01 14 14 02 02 57 57 57 57

        NE2000 found at 0x300, using start page 0x40 and end page 0x80.
```

Your register values and PROM values will probably be different. Note that all the PROM values are doubled for a 16 bit card, and that the ethernet address (00:00:c0:b0:05:65) appears in the first row, and the double 0x57 signature appears at the end of the PROM.

The output from when there is no card installed at 0x300 will look something like this:

```
Checking the ethercard at 0x300.
  Register 0x0d (0x30d) is ff
  Failed initial NE2000 probe, value ff.
8390 registers: ff ff ff ff ff ff ff ff ff ff ff ff ff ff ff ff
SA PROM       0: ff ff ff ff ff ff ff ff ff ff ff ff ff ff ff ff
SA PROM 0x10: ff ff ff ff ff ff ff ff ff ff ff ff ff ff ff ff

  Invalid signature found, wordlength 2.
```

The 0xff values arise because that is the value that is returned when one reads a vacant i/o port. If you happen to have some other hardware in the region that is probed, you may see some non 0xff values as well.

7) Try warm booting into linux from a DOS boot floppy (via loadlin) after running the supplied DOS driver or config program. It may be doing some extra (i.e. non-standard) "magic" to initialize the card.

8) Try Russ Nelson's ne2000.com packet driver to see if even it can see your card – if not, then things do not look good. Example:

```
A:> ne2000 0x60 10 0x300
```

The arguments are software interrupt vector, hardware IRQ, and i/o base. You can get it from any msdos archive in pktdrv11.zip – The current version may be newer than 11.

3.5   Problems with SMC Ultra/EtherEZ and WD80*3 cards

Problem: You get messages such as the following:

```
eth0: bogus packet size: 65531, status=0xff, nxpg=0xff
```

Reason: There is a shared memory problem.

Solution: The most common reason for this is PCI machines that are not configured to map in ISA memory devices. Hence you end up reading the PC's RAM (all `0xff` values) instead of the RAM on the card that contains the data from the received packet.

Other typical problems that are easy to fix are board conflicts, having cache or 'shadow ROM' enabled for that region, or running your ISA bus faster than 8Mhz. There are also a surprising number of memory failures on ethernet cards, so run a diagnostic program if you have one for your ethercard.

Problem: SMC EtherEZ doesn't work in non-shared memory (PIO) mode.

Reason: Older versions of the Ultra driver only supported the card in the shared memory mode of operation.

Solution: The driver in kernel version 2.0 and above also supports the programmed i/o mode of operation. Upgrade to v2.0, or get the drop-in replacement for kernel v1.2.13 from Donald's ftp/www site.

Problem: Old wd8003 and/or jumper-settable wd8013 always get the IRQ wrong.

Reason: The old wd8003 cards and jumper-settable wd8013 clones don't have the EEPROM that the driver can read the IRQ setting from. If the driver can't read the IRQ, then it tries to auto-IRQ to find out what it is. And if auto-IRQ returns zero, then the driver just assigns IRQ 5 for an 8 bit card or IRQ 10 for a 16 bit card.

Solution: Avoid the auto-IRQ code, and tell the kernel what the IRQ that you have jumpered the card to is via a boot time argument. For example, if you are using IRQ 9, using the following should work.

```
LILO: linux ether=9,0,eth0
```

Problem: SMC Ultra card is detected as wd8013, but the IRQ and shared memory base is wrong.

Reason: The Ultra card looks a lot like a wd8013, and if the Ultra driver is not present in the kernel, the wd driver may mistake the ultra as a wd8013. The ultra probe comes before the wd probe, so this usually shouldn't happen. The ultra stores the IRQ and mem base in the EEPROM differently than a wd8013, hence the bogus values reported.

Solution: Recompile with only the drivers you need in the kernel. If you have a mix of wd and ultra cards in one machine, and are using modules, then load the ultra module first.

3.6   Problems with 3Com cards

Problem: The 3c503 picks IRQ N, but this is needed for some other device which needs IRQ N. (eg. CD ROM driver, modem, etc.) Can this be fixed without compiling this into the kernel?

Solution: The 3c503 driver probes for a free IRQ line in the order {5, 9/2, 3, 4}, and it should pick a line which isn't being used. The driver chooses when the card is `ifconfig`'ed into operation.

If you are using a modular driver, you can use module parameters to set various things, including the IRQ value.

The following selects IRQ9, base location 0x300, <ignored value>, and if_port #1 (the external transceiver).

```
io=0x300 irq=9 xcvr=1
```

Alternately, if the driver is compiled into the kernel, you can set the same values at boot by passing parameters via LILO.

    LILO: linux ether=9,0x300,0,1,eth0

The following selects IRQ3, probes for the base location, <ignored value>, and the default if_port #0 (the internal transceiver)

    LILO: linux ether=3,0,0,0,eth0

Problem: 3c503: configured interrupt X invalid, will use autoIRQ.

Reason: The 3c503 card can only use one of IRQ{5, 2/9, 3, 4} (These are the only lines that are connected to the card.) If you pass in an IRQ value that is not in the above set, you will get the above message. Usually, specifying an interrupt value for the 3c503 is not necessary. The 3c503 will autoIRQ when it gets ifconfig'ed, and pick one of IRQ{5, 2/9, 3, 4}.

Solution: Use one of the valid IRQs listed above, or enable autoIRQ by not specifying the IRQ line at all.

Problem: The supplied 3c503 drivers don't use the AUI (thicknet) port. How does one choose it over the default thinnet port?

Solution: The 3c503 AUI port can be selected at boot-time for in-kernel drivers, and at module insertion for modular drivers. The selection is overloaded onto the low bit of the currently-unused dev->rmem_start variable, so a boot-time parameter of:

    LILO: linux ether=0,0,0,1,eth0

should work for in-kernel drivers.

To specify the AUI port when loading as a module, just append xcvr=1 to the module options line along with your i/o and irq values.

3.7 FAQs Not Specific to Any Card.

3.7.1 Ethercard is Not Detected at Boot.

The usual reason for this is that people are using a kernel that does not have support for their particular card built in. For a modular kernel, it usually means that the required module has not been requested for loading, or that an I/O address needs to be specified as a module option.

If you are using a modular based kernel, such as those installed by most of the linux distributions, then try and use the configuration utility for the distribution to select the module for your card. For ISA cards, it is a good idea to determine the I/O address of the card and add it as an option (e.g. io=0x340) if the configuration utility asks for any options. If there is no configuration utility, then you will have to add the correct module name (and options) to /etc/conf.modules – see man modprobe for more details.

If you are using a pre-compiled kernel that is part of a distribution set, then check the documentation to see which kernel you installed, and if it was built with support for your particular card. If it wasn't, then your options are to try and get one that has support for your card, or build your own.

It is usually wise to build your own kernel with only the drivers you need, as this cuts down on the kernel size (saving your precious RAM for applications!) and reduces the number of device probes that can upset sensitive hardware. Building a kernel is not as complicated as it sounds. You just have to answer yes or no to a bunch of questions about what drivers you want, and it does the rest.

The next main cause is having another device using part of the i/o space that your card needs. Most cards are 16 or 32 bytes wide in i/o space. If your card is set at 0x300 and 32 bytes wide, then the driver will ask for 0x300-0x31f. If any other device driver has registered even one port anywhere in that range, the probe will not take place at that address and the driver will silently continue to the next of the probed addresses. So, after booting, do a `cat /proc/ioports` and verify that the full iospace that the card will require is vacant.

Another problem is having your card jumpered to an i/o address that isn't probed by default. There is a list 8.1 (probed addresses) for each card in this document. Even if the i/o setting of your card is not in the list of porbed addresses, you can supply it at boot (for in-kernel drivers) with the `ether=` command as described in 10.1 (Passing Ethernet Arguments...) Modular drivers can make use of the `io=` option to specify an address that isn't probed by default.

3.7.2 `ifconfig` reports the wrong i/o address for the card.

No it doesn't. You are just interpreting it incorrectly. This is *not* a bug, and the numbers reported are correct. It just happens that some 8390 based cards (wd80x3, smc-ultra, etc) have the actual 8390 chip living at an offset from the first assigned i/o port. This is the value stored in `dev->base_addr`, and is what `ifconfig` reports. If you want to see the full range of ports that your card uses, then try `cat /proc/ioports` which will give the numbers you expect.

3.7.3 PCI machine detects card but driver fails probe.

Newer PCI BIOSes may not enable all PCI cards at power-up, especially if the BIOS option 'PNP OS' is enabled. This mis-feature is to support the next release of Windows which still uses some real-mode drivers. Either disable this option, or try and upgrade to a newer driver which has the code to enable a disabled card.

3.7.4 Shared Memory ISA cards in PCI Machine dont work (0xffff)

This will usually show up as reads of lots of `0xffff` values. No shared memory cards of any type will work in a PCI machine unless you have the PCI ROM BIOS/CMOS SETUP configuration set properly. You have to set it to allow shared memory access from the ISA bus for the memory region that your card is trying to use. If you can't figure out which settings are applicable then ask your supplier or local computer guru. For AMI BIOS, there is usually a "Plug and Play" section where there will be an "ISA Shared Memory Size" and "ISA Shared Memory Base" settings. For cards like the wd8013 and SMC Ultra, change the size from the default of 'Disabled' to 16kB, and change the base to the shared memory address of your card.

3.7.5 NexGen machine gets 'mismatched read page pointers' errors.

A quirk of the NexGen CPU caused all users with 8390 based cards (wd80x3, 3c503, SMC Ultra/EtherEZ, ne2000, etc.) to get these error messages. Kernel versions 2.0 and above do not have these problems. Upgrade your kernel.

3.7.6 Asynchronous Transfer Mode (ATM) Support

Werner Almesberger has been working on ATM support for linux. He has been working with the Efficient Networks ENI155p board (*Efficient Networks* <http://www.efficient.com/>) and the Zeitnet ZN1221 board (*Zeitnet* <http://www.zeitnet.com/>).

Werner says that the driver for the ENI155p is rather stable, while the driver for the ZN1221 is presently unfinished.

Check the latest/updated status at the following URL:

Linux ATM Support <http://lrcwww.epfl.ch/linux-atm/>

3.7.7 Gigabyte Ethernet Support

Is there any gigabyte ethernet support for Linux?

A driver for the Packet Engines G-NIC PCI Gigabit Ethernet adapter is due to be added into the upcoming release of kernel v2.0.34. For more details, support, and driver updates, see:

http://cesdis.gsfc.nasa.gov/linux/drivers/yellowfin.html

3.7.8 FDDI Support

Is there FDDI support for Linux?

Yes. Larry Stefani has written a driver for v2.0 with Digital's DEFEA (FDDI EISA) and DEFPA (FDDI PCI) cards. This was included into the v2.0.24 kernel. Currently no other cards are supported though.

3.7.9 Full Duplex Support

Will Full Duplex give me 20MBps? Does Linux support it?

Cameron Spitzer writes the following about full duplex 10Base-T cards: "If you connect it to a full duplex switched hub, and your system is fast enough and not doing much else, it can keep the link busy in both directions. There is no such thing as full duplex 10BASE-2 or 10BASE-5 (thin and thick coax). Full Duplex works by disabling collision detection in the adapter. That's why you can't do it with coax; the LAN won't run that way. 10BASE-T (RJ45 interface) uses separate wires for send and receive, so it's possible to run both ways at the same time. The switching hub takes care of the collision problem. The signalling rate is 10 Mbps."

So as you can see, you still will only be able to receive or transmit at 10Mbps, and hence don't expect a 2x performance increase. As to whether it is supported or not, that depends on the card and possibly the driver. Some cards may do auto-negotiation, some may need driver support, and some may need the user to select an option in a card's EEPROM configuration. Only the serious/heavy user would notice the difference between the two modes anyway.

3.7.10 Ethernet Cards for Linux on Alpha/AXP PCI Boards

As of v2.0, only the 3c509, depca, de4x5 lance32, and all the 8390 drivers (wd, smc-ultra, ne, 3c503, etc.) have been made 'architecture independent' so as to work on the DEC Alpha CPU based systems.

Note that the changes that are required aren't that complicated. You only need to do the following:

-multiply all `jiffies` related values by HZ/100 to account for the different HZ value that the Alpha uses. (i.e `timeout=2;` becomes `timeout=2*HZ/100;`)

-replace any i/o memory (640k to 1MB) pointer dereferences with the appropriate readb() writeb() readl() writel() calls, as shown in this example.

```
-       int *mem_base = (int *)dev->mem_start;
-       mem_base[0] = 0xba5eba5e;
+       unsigned long mem_base = dev->mem_start;
+       writel(0xba5eba5e, mem_base);
```

-replace all memcpy() calls that have i/o memory as source or target destinations with the appropriate one of memcpy_fromio() or memcpy_toio().

Details on handling memory accesses in an architecture independent fashion are documented in the file linux/Documentation/IO-mapping.txt that comes with recent kernels.

3.7.11   Linking 10BaseT without a Hub

Can I link 10BaseT (RJ45) based systems together without a hub?

You can link 2 machines easily, but no more than that, without extra devices/gizmos. See 6.2 (Twisted Pair) – it explains how to do it. And no, you can't hack together a hub just by crossing a few wires and stuff. It's pretty much impossible to do the collision signal right without duplicating a hub.

3.7.12   SIOCSIFxxx: No such device

I get a bunch of 'SIOCSIFxxx: No such device' messages at boot, followed by a 'SIOCADDRT: Network is unreachable' What is wrong?

Your ethernet device was not detected at boot/module insertion time, and when ifconfig and route are run, they have no device to work with. Use dmesg | more to review the boot messages and see if there are any messages about detecting an ethernet card.

3.7.13   SIOCSFFLAGS: Try again

I get 'SIOCSFFLAGS: Try again' when I run 'ifconfig' – Huh?

Some other device has taken the IRQ that your ethercard is trying to use, and so the ethercard can't use the IRQ. You don't necessairly need to reboot to resolve this, as some devices only grab the IRQs when they need them and then release them when they are done. Examples are some sound cards, serial ports, floppy disk driver, etc. You can type cat /proc/interrupts to see which interrupts are presently *in use*. Most of the Linux ethercard drivers only grab the IRQ when they are opened for use via 'ifconfig'. If you can get the other device to 'let go' of the required IRQ line, then you should be able to 'Try again' with ifconfig.

3.7.14   Using 'ifconfig' and Link UNSPEC with HW-addr of 00:00:00:00:00:00

When I run ifconfig with no arguments, it reports that LINK is UNSPEC (instead of 10Mbs Ethernet) and it also says that my hardware address is all zeros.

This is because people are running a newer version of the 'ifconfig' program than their kernel version. This new version of ifconfig is not able to report these properties when used in conjunction with an older kernel. You can either upgrade your kernel, 'downgrade' ifconfig, or simply ignore it. The kernel knows your hardware address, so it really doesn't matter if ifconfig can't read it.

You may also get strange information if the ifconfig program you are using is a lot older than the kernel you are using.

3.7.15   Huge Number of RX and TX Errors

When I run ifconfig with no arguments, it reports that I have a huge error count in both rec'd and transmitted packets. It all seems to work ok – What is wrong?

Look again. It says RX packets *big number* **PAUSE** errors 0 **PAUSE** dropped 0 **PAUSE** overrun 0. And the same for the TX column. Hence the big numbers you are seeing are the total number of packets that your machine has rec'd and transmitted. If you still find it confusing, try typing cat /proc/net/dev instead.

3.7.16   Entries in /dev/ for Ethercards

I have /dev/eth0 as a link to /dev/xxx. Is this right?

Contrary to what you have heard, the files in /dev/* are not used. You can delete any **/dev/wd0**, **/dev/ne0** and similar entries.

3.7.17   Linux and "trailers"

Should I disable trailers when I 'ifconfig' my ethercard?

You can't disable trailers, and you shouldn't want to. 'Trailers' are a hack to avoid data copying in the networking layers. The idea was to use a trivial fixed-size header of size 'H', put the variable-size header info at the end of the packet, and allocate all packets 'H' bytes before the start of a page. While it was a good idea, it turned out to not work well in practice. If someone suggests the use of '-trailers', note that it is the equivalent of sacrificial goats blood. It won't do anything to solve the problem, but if problem fixes itself then someone can claim deep magical knowledge.

3.7.18   Access to the raw Ethernet Device

How do I get access to the raw ethernet device in linux, without going through TCP/IP and friends?

```
int s=socket(AF_INET,SOCK_PACKET,htons(ETH_P_ALL));
```

This gives you a socket receiving every protocol type. Do recvfrom() calls to it and it will fill the sockaddr with device type in sa_family and the device name in the sa_data array. I don't know who originally invented SOCK_PACKET for Linux (its been in for ages) but its superb stuff. You can use it to send stuff raw too via sendto() calls. You have to have root access to do either of course.

4   Performance Tips

Here are some tips that you can use if you are suffering from low ethernet throughput, or to gain a bit more speed on those ftp transfers.

The ttcp.c program is a good test for measuring raw throughput speed. Another common trick is to do a ftp> get large_file /dev/null where large_file is > 1MB and residing in the buffer cache on the Tx'ing machine. (Do the 'get' at least twice, as the first time will be priming the buffer cache on the Tx'ing machine.) You want the file in the buffer cache because you are not interested in combining the file access speed from the disk into your measurement. Which is also why you send the incoming data to /dev/null instead of onto the disk.

4.1   General Concepts

Even an 8 bit card is able to receive back-to-back packets without any problems. The difficulty arises when the computer doesn't get the Rx'd packets off the card quick enough to make room for more incoming packets. If the computer does not quickly clear the card's memory of the packets already received, the card will have no place to put the new packet.

In this case the card either drops the new packet, or writes over top of a previously received packet. Either one seriously interrupts the smooth flow of traffic by causing/requesting re-transmissions and can seriously degrade performance by up to a factor of 5!

Cards with more onboard memory are able to "buffer" more packets, and thus can handle larger bursts of back-to-back packets without dropping packets. This in turn means that the card does not require as low a latency from the the host computer with respect to pulling the packets out of the buffer to avoid dropping packets.

Most 8 bit cards have an 8kB buffer, and most 16 bit cards have a 16kB buffer. Most Linux drivers will reserve 3kB of that buffer (for two Tx buffers), leaving only 5kB of receive space for an 8 bit card. This is room enough for only three full sized (1500 bytes) ethernet packets.

4.2   ISA Bus Speed

As mentioned above, if the packets are removed from the card fast enough, then a drop/overrun condition won't occur even when the amount of Rx packet buffer memory is small. The factor that sets the rate at which packets are removed from the card to the computer's memory is the speed of the data path that joins the two – that being the ISA bus speed. (If the CPU is a dog-slow 386sx-16, then this will also play a role.)

The recommended ISA bus clock is about 8MHz, but many motherboards and peripheral devices can be run at higher frequencies. The clock frequency for the ISA bus can usually be set in the CMOS setup, by selecting a divisor of the mainboard/CPU clock frequency.

For example, here are some receive speeds as measured by the TTCP program on a 40MHz 486, with an 8 bit WD8003EP card, for different ISA bus speeds.

ISA Bus Speed (MHz)	Rx TTCP (kB/s)
6.7	740
13.4	970
20.0	1030
26.7	1075

You would be hard pressed to do better than 1075kB/s with *any* 10Mb/s ethernet card, using TCP/IP. However, don't expect every system to work at fast ISA bus speeds. Most systems will not function properly at speeds above 13MHz. (Also, some PCI systems have the ISA bus speed fixed at 8MHz, so that the end user does not have the option of increasing it.)

In addition to faster transfer speeds, one will usually also benefit from a reduction in CPU usage due to the shorter duration memory and i/o cycles. (Note that hard disks and video cards located on the ISA bus will also usually experience a performance increase from an increased ISA bus speed.)

Be sure to back up your data prior to experimenting with ISA bus speeds in excess of 8MHz, and thouroughly test that all ISA peripherals are operating properly after making any speed increases.

4.3 Setting the TCP Rx Window

Once again, cards with small amounts of onboard RAM and relatively slow data paths between the card and the computer's memory run into trouble. The default TCP Rx window setting is 32kB, which means that a fast computer on the same subnet as you can dump 32k of data on you without stopping to see if you received any of it okay.

Recent versions of the `route` command have the ability to set the size of this window on the fly. Usually it is only for the local net that this window must be reduced, as computers that are behind a couple of routers or gateways are 'buffered' enough to not pose a problem. An example usage would be:

```
route add <whatever> ... window <win_size>
```

where `win_size` is the size of the window you wish to use (in bytes). An 8 bit 3c503 card on an ISA bus operating at a speed of 8MHz or less would work well with a window size of about 4kB. Too large a window will cause overruns and dropped packets, and a drastic reduction in ethernet throughput. You can check the operating status by doing a `cat /proc/net/dev` which will display any dropped or overrun conditions that occurred.

4.4 Increasing NFS performance

Some people have found that using 8 bit cards in NFS clients causes poorer than expected performance, when using 8kB (native Sun) NFS packet size.

The possible reason for this could be due to the difference in on board buffer size between the 8 bit and the 16 bit cards. The maximum ethernet packet size is about 1500 bytes. Now that 8kB NFS packet will arrive as about 6 back to back maximum size ethernet packets. Both the 8 and 16 bit cards have no problem Rx'ing back to back packets. The problem arises when the machine doesn't remove the packets from the cards buffer in time, and the buffer overflows. The fact that 8 bit cards take an extra ISA bus cycle per transfer doesn't help either. What you *can* do if you have an 8 bit card is either set the NFS transfer size to 2kB (or even 1kB), or try increasing the ISA bus speed in order to get the card's buffer cleared out faster. I have found that an old WD8003E card at 8MHz (with no other system load) can keep up with a large receive at 2kB NFS size, but not at 4kB, where performance was degraded by a factor of three.

5 Vendor/Manufacturer/Model Specific Information

The following lists many cards in alphabetical order by vendor name and then product identifier. Beside each product ID, you will see either 'Supported', 'Semi-Supported' or 'Not Supported'.

Supported means that a driver for that card exists, and many people are happily using it and it seems quite reliable.

Semi-Supported means that a driver exists, but at least one of the following descriptions is true: (1) The driver and/or hardware are buggy, which may cause poor performance, failing connections or even crashes. (2) The driver is new or the card is fairly uncommon, and hence the driver has seen very little use/testing and the driver author has had very little feedback. Obviously (2) is preferable to (1), and the individual description of the card/driver should make it clear which one holds true. In either case, you will probably have to answer 'Y' when asked "Prompt for development and/or incomplete code/drivers?" when running `make config`.

Not Supported means there is not a driver currently available for that card. This could be due to a lack of interest in hardware that is rare/uncommon, or because the vendors won't release the hardware documentation required to write a driver.

Note that the difference between 'Supported' and 'Semi-Supported' is rather subjective, and is based on user feedback observed in newsgroup postings and mailing list messages. (After all, it is impossible for one person to test all drivers with all cards for each kernel version!!!) So be warned that you may find a card listed as semi-supported works perfectly for you (which is great), or that a card listed as supported gives you no end of troubles and problems (which is not so great).

5.1   3Com

If you are not sure what your card is, but you think it is a 3Com card, you can probably figure it out from the assembly number. 3Com has a document 'Identifying 3Com Adapters By Assembly Number' (ref 24500002) that would most likely clear things up. See 8.6 (Technical Information from 3Com) for info on how to get documents from 3Com.

Also note that 3Com has a FTP site with various goodies: `ftp.3Com.com` that you may want to check out.

For those of you browsing this document by a WWW browser, you can try 3Com's WWW site as well.

5.1.1   3c501

Status – *Semi-Supported*

Too brain-damaged to use. Available surplus from many places. Avoid it like the plague. Again, do not purchase this card, even as a joke. It's performance is horrible, and it breaks in many ways.

For those not yet convinced, the 3c501 can only do one thing at a time – while you are removing one packet from the single-packet buffer it cannot receive another packet, nor can it receive a packet while loading a transmit packet. This was fine for a network between two 8088-based computers where processing each packet and replying took 10's of msecs, but modern networks send back-to-back packets for almost every transaction.

AutoIRQ works, DMA isn't used, the autoprobe only looks at `0x280` and `0x300`, and the debug level is set with the third boot-time argument.

Once again, the use of a 3c501 is *strongly discouraged*! Even more so with a IP multicast kernel, as you will grind to a halt while listening to *all* multicast packets. See the comments at the top of the source code for more details.

5.1.2   3c503, 3c503/16

Status – *Supported*

If you have a 3c503/16 you may be interested to know that as of 1.3.37 the driver has the facility to use the full 16kB RAM on your card. Previous versions treated the 16bit cards as 8bit cards, and only used half of the available RAM. This update also detects the newer 3Com prefix found on newly manufactured cards mentioned below.

Recently made 3c503/16 cards have a new base hardware address because 3Com ran out of numbers (they made too many cards!) The cards used to start with `02 60 8C` and the newer ones use `00 20 AF`. Up to 1.3.37, the driver will only check for the old address, and skip over the newer cards. You can upgrade to a kernel newer than 1.3.37, or change the numbers in 3c503.c for older kernels.

These cards should be about the same speed as the same bus width WD80x3, but turn out to be actually a bit slower. The 3c503 does not have "EEPROM setup", so a diagnostic/setup program isn't needed before running the card with Linux. The shared memory address of the 3c503 is set using jumpers that are shared with the boot PROM address. This is confusing to people familiar with other ISA cards, where you always leave the jumper set to "disable" unless you have a boot PROM.

These shared-memory ethercards also have a programmed I/O mode that doesn't use the 8390 facilities (their engineers found too many bugs!) The Linux 3c503 driver can also work with the 3c503 in programmed-I/O mode, but this is slower and less reliable than shared memory mode. Also, programmed-I/O mode is not as well tested when updating the drivers. You shouldn't use the programmed-I/O mode unless you need it for MS-DOS compatibility.

The 3c503's IRQ line is set in software, with no hints from an EEPROM. Unlike the MS-DOS drivers, the Linux driver has capability to autoIRQ: it uses the first available IRQ line in {5,2/9,3,4}, selected each time the card is ifconfig'ed. (Older driver versions selected the IRQ at boot time.) The ioctl() call in 'ifconfig' will return EAGAIN if no IRQ line is available at that time.

Some common problems that people have with the 503 are discussed in 3.6 (Problems with...).

If you intend on using this driver as a loadable module you should probably see 10.2 (Using the Ethernet Drivers as Modules) and also 10.2.1 (8390 Based Cards as Modules) for module specific information.

5.1.3   3c505

Status – *Semi-Supported*

This is a driver that was written by Craig Southeren geoffw@extro.ucc.su.oz.au. These cards also use the i82586 chip. There are not that many of these cards about. It is included in the standard kernel, but it is classed as an alpha driver. See 3.1 (Alpha Drivers) for important information on using alpha-test ethernet drivers with Linux.

There is also the file /usr/src/linux/drivers/net/README.3c505 that you should read if you are going to use one of these cards. It contains various options that you can enable/disable. Technical information is available in 8.5 (Programming the Intel chips).

5.1.4   3c507

Status – *Semi-Supported*

This card uses one of the Intel chips, and the development of the driver is closely related to the development of the Intel Ether Express driver. The driver is included in the standard kernel release, but as an alpha driver.

See 3.1 (Alpha Drivers) for important information on using alpha-test ethernet drivers with Linux. Technical information is available in 8.5 (Programming the Intel chips).

5.1.5   3c509 / 3c509B

Status – *Supported*

This card is fairly inexpensive and has good performance for a non-bus-master design. The drawbacks are that the original 3c509 requires very low interrupt latency. The 3c509B shouldn't suffer from the same problem, due to having a larger buffer. (See below.) These cards use PIO transfers, similar to a ne2000 card, and so a shared memory card such as a wd8013 will be more efficient in comparison.

The original 3c509 has a small packet buffer (4kB total, 2kB Rx, 2kB Tx), causing the driver to occasionally drop a packet if interrupts are masked for too long. To minimize this problem, you can try unmasking interrupts during IDE disk transfers (see `man hdparm`) and/or increasing your ISA bus speed so IDE transfers finish sooner.

The newer model 3c509B has 8kB on board, and the buffer can be split 4/4, 5/3 or 6/2 for Rx/Tx. This setting is changed with the DOS configuration utility, and is stored on the EEPROM. This should alleviate the above problem with the original 3c509.

3c509B users should use the supplied DOS utility to disable the *plug and play* support, *and* to set the output media to what they require. The linux driver currently does *not* support the Autodetect media setting, so you *have* to select 10Base-T or 10Base-2 or AUI. With regards to the media detection features, Cameron said: "Autoselect is a feature of the commercial drivers for 3C509(B). AFAIK nobody ever claimed the Linux driver attempts it. When drivers/net/3c509.c recognizes my 3C509B at boot time, it says: `eth0: 3c509 at 0x300 tag 1, 10baseT port,` ... revealing that the card is configured for 10BASE-T. It finds that out by reading the little EEPROM, which IMHO is the Right Way To Do It."

As for the plug-and-pray stuff, Cameron adds: "The 3C509B has 3Com's relocatable I/O port scheme, and Microsoft[tm] Plug-and-play ("PnP"). You can't use them both at the same time. Some (broken, IMHO) BIOSes begin a PnP sequence by writing to the PnP address (0x279 ?), which causes PnP adapters like 3C509B to enter the PnP state, but then they (these funny BIOSes) never come back to finish the job. The 3C509Bs hang there in the middle of the PnP ID Sequence, where they have no idea you didn't mean it and you're going to use the 3Com ID sequence after all. 3C5X9CFG /PNPRST clears this hang. Disable PnP if your drivers (eg., Linux) don't use it.

It was a marketing decision to turn PnP on as a factory default setting. If it caused you a hassle, or not, please take the time to say so when you mail in your warranty card. The more info they have, the better decisions they can make. Also, check with your motherboard supplier to see if you need a BIOS upgrade."

It has been reported that you have to do a hard reset after doing the '3C5X9CFG /PNPRST' for the change to take effect.

Some people ask about the "Server or Workstation" and "Highest Modem Speed" settings presented in the DOS configuration utility. Donald writes "These are only hints to the drivers, and the Linux driver does not use these parameters: it always optimizes for high throughput rather than low latency ('Server'). Low latency was critically important for old, non-windowed, IPX throughput. To reduce the latency the MS-DOS driver for the 3c509 disables interrupts for some operations, blocking serial port interrupts. Thus the need for the 'modem speed' setting. The Linux driver avoids the need to disable interrupts for long periods by operating only on whole packets e.g. by not starting to transmit a packet until it is completely transferred to the card."

Note that the ISA card detection uses a different method than most cards. Basically, you ask the cards to respond by sending data to an ID_PORT (port 0x100). This detection method means that a particular card will *always* get detected first in a multiple ISA 3c509 configuration. The card with the lowest hardware ethernet address will *always* end up being `eth0`. This shouldn't matter to anyone, except for those people who want to assign a 6 byte hardware address to a particular interface. If you have multiple 3c509 cards, it is best to append `ether=0,0,ethN` commands without the i/o port specified (i.e. use i/o=zero) and allow the probe to sort out which card is first, otherwise it may not detect all your cards.

If this really bothers you, have a look at Donald's latest driver, as you may be able to use a `0x3c509` value in the unused mem address fields to order the detection to suit.

5.1.6   3c515

Status – *Not Supported*

This is 3Com's farily recent ISA 100Mbps offering, codenamed "CorkScrew". Donald is working on support for these cards, and it will probably appear in the near future on his WWW driver page. The driver will be incorporated into the 3c59x/3c90x driver, so you should probably expect to look for it on the Vortex page:

Vortex <http://cesdis.gsfc.nasa.gov/linux/drivers/vortex.html>

5.1.7   3c523

Status – *Semi-Supported*

This MCA bus card uses the i82586, and Chris Beauregard has modified the ni52 driver to work with these cards. The driver for it can be found in the v2.1 kernel source tree.

More details can be found on the MCA-Linux page at http://glycerine.cetmm.uni.edu/mca/

5.1.8   3c527

Status – *Not Supported*

Yes, another MCA card. No, not too much interest in it. Better chances with the 3c529 if you are stuck with MCA.

5.1.9   3c529

Status – *Semi-Supported*

This card actually uses the same chipset as the 3c509. Donald actually put hooks into the 3c509 driver to check for MCA cards after probing for EISA cards, and before probing for ISA cards. But it hasn't evolved much further than that. Donald writes:

"I don't have access to a MCA machine (nor do I fully understand the probing code) so I never wrote the mca_adaptor_select_mode() or mca_adaptor_id() routines. If you can find a way to get the adaptor I/O address that assigned at boot time, you can just hard-wire that in place of the commented-out probe. Be sure to keep the code that reads the IRQ, if_port, and ethernet address."

Darrell Frappier (aa822@detroit.freenet.org) reports that you can get the i/o address from running the PS/2 reference diskette, and once you put that directly into the driver, it does actually work.

The required MCA probe code will probably appear in the driver in a development kernel sometime soon, now that MCA support is in the kernel.

More details can be found on the MCA-Linux page at http://glycerine.cetmm.uni.edu/mca/

5.1.10   3c562

Status – *Supported*

This PCMCIA card is the combination of a 3c589B ethernet card with a modem. The modem appears as a standard modem to the end user. The only difficulty is getting the two separate linux drivers to share one interrupt. There are a couple of new registers and some hardware interrupt sharing support. You need to use a v2.0 or newer kernel that has the support for interrupt sharing.

As a side note, the modem part of the card has been reported to be not well documented for the end user (the manual just says 'supports the AT command set') and it may not connect as well as other name brand modems. The recommendation is to buy a 3c589B instead, and then get a PCMCIA modem card from a company that specializes in modems.

Thanks again to Cameron for getting a sample unit and documentation sent off to David Hinds. Look for support in David's PCMCIA package release.

See 9.3 (PCMCIA Support) for more info on PCMCIA chipsets, socket enablers, etc.

5.1.11   3c575

Status – *Not Supported*

A driver for this PCMCIA card is under development and hopefully will be included in David's PCMCIA package within a few months.

5.1.12   3c579

Status – *Supported*

The EISA version of the 509. The current EISA version uses the same 16 bit wide chip rather than a 32 bit interface, so the performance increase isn't stunning. Make sure the card is configured for EISA addressing mode. Read the above 3c509 section for info on the driver.

5.1.13   3c589 / 3c589B

Status – *Semi-Supported*

Many people have been using this PCMCIA card for quite some time now. Note that support for it is not (at present) included in the default kernel source tree. You will also need a supported PCMCIA controller chipset. There are drivers available on Donald's ftp site:

        cesdis.gsfc.nasa.gov:/pub/linux/pcmcia/README.3c589
        cesdis.gsfc.nasa.gov:/pub/linux/pcmcia/3c589.c
        cesdis.gsfc.nasa.gov:/pub/linux/pcmcia/dbether.c

Or for those that are *net-surfing* you can try:

Don's PCMCIA Stuff <http://cesdis.gsfc.nasa.gov/linux/pcmcia.html>

You will still need a PCMCIA socket enabler as well.

See 9.3 (PCMCIA Support) for more info on PCMCIA chipsets, socket enablers, etc.

The "B" in the name means the same here as it does for the 3c509 case.

5.1.14   3c590 / 3c595

Status – *Supported*

These "Vortex" cards are for PCI bus machines, with the '590 being 10Mbps and the '595 being 3Com's 100Mbs offering. Also note that you can run the '595 as a '590 (i.e. in a 10Mbps mode). The driver is included in the v2.0 kernel source, but is also continually being updated. If you have problems with the driver in the v2.0 kernel, you can get an updated driver from the following URL:

Vortex <http://cesdis.gsfc.nasa.gov/linux/drivers/vortex.html>

Note that there are two different 3c590 cards out there, early models that had 32kB of on-board memory, and later models that only have 8kB (eeccch!) of memory. Chances are you won't be able to buy a new 3c59x for much longer, as it is being replaced with the 3c90x card. If you are buying a used one off somebody, try and get the 32kB version. The 3c595 cards have 64kB, as you can't get away with only 8kB RAM at 100Mbps!

A thanks to Cameron Spitzer and Terry Murphy of 3Com for sending cards and documentation to Donald so he could write the driver.

Donald has set up a mailing list for Vortex driver support. To join the list, just do:

```
echo subscribe | /bin/mail linux-vortex-request@cesdis.gsfc.nasa.gov
```

5.1.15   3c592 / 3c597

Status – *Supported*

These are the EISA versions of the 3c59x series of cards. The 3c592/3c597 (aka Demon) should work with the vortex driver discussed above.

5.1.16   3c900 / 3c905

Status – *Supported*

These cards (aka 'Boomerang', aka EtherLink III XL) have been recently released to take over the place of the 3c590/3c595 cards. Cameron Spitzer of 3Com writes that the "3C900 has a scatter gather bus master controlled by a descriptor ring in main memory. Aside from that, it's a lot like 3C590."

You may still be able to get a couple of these cards at a reduced price through one of 3Com's evaluation deals, if you are quick.

To use this card with v2.0 kernels, you must obtain the updated 3c59x.c driver from Donald's site at:

Vortex-Page <http://cesdis.gsfc.nasa.gov/linux/drivers/vortex.html>

This updated 3c59x driver allows you to use the 3c900 in a 3c59x compatible mode, and has been reported to be quite stable. Note that this updated driver may be snuck into the v2.0 source tree at a later date.)

On the same WWW page, you will also find the experimental boomerang.c driver which uses some of the enhancements of the 3c900 over that which is available on the 3c59x cards. Since this is a new/experimental driver, you may be better off in using the updated 3c59x.c if system stability is a primary concern.

Donald has set up a mailing list for Vortex driver support announcements and etc. To join the list, just do:

```
echo subscribe | /bin/mail linux-vortex-request@cesdis.gsfc.nasa.gov
```

5.2   Accton

5.2.1   Accton MPX

Status – *Supported*

Don't let the name fool you. This is still supposed to be a NE2000 compatible card. The MPX is supposed to stand for MultiPacket Accelerator, which, according to Accton, increases throughput substantially. But if you are already sending back-to-back packets, how can you get any faster...

5.2.2   Accton EN1203, EN1207, EtherDuo-PCI

Status – *Supported*

This is another implementation of the DEC 21040 PCI chip. The EN1207 card has the 21140, and also has a 10Base-2 connector, which has proved troublesome for some people in terms of selecting that media. Using the card with 10Base-T and 100Base-T media have worked for others though. So as with all purchases, you should try and make sure you can return it if it doesn't work for you.

See 5.17.4 (DEC 21040) for more information on these cards, and the present driver situation.

5.2.3   Accton EN2209 Parallel Port Adaptor (EtherPocket)

Status – *Semi-Supported*

A driver for these parallel port adapters is available but not yet part of the 2.0 or 2.1 kernel source. You have to get the driver from:

`http://www.unix-ag.uni-siegen.de/~nils/accton_linux.html`

5.2.4   Accton EN2212 PCMCIA Card

Status – *Semi-Supported*

David Hinds has been working on a driver for this card, and you are best to check the latest release of his PCMCIA package to see what the present status is.

5.3   Allied Telesyn/Telesis

5.3.1   AT1500

Status –*Supported*

These are a series of low-cost ethercards using the 79C960 version of the AMD LANCE. These are bus-master cards, and hence one of the faster ISA bus ethercards available.

DMA selection and chip numbering information can be found in 5.4.1 (AMD LANCE).

More technical information on AMD LANCE based Ethernet cards can be found in 8.7 (Notes on AMD...).

5.3.2   AT1700

Status – *Supported*

Note that to access this driver during `make config` you still have to answer 'Y' when asked "Prompt for development and/or incomplete code/drivers?" at the first. This is simply due to lack of feedback on the driver stability due to it being a relatively rare card. This will probably be changed for v2.1 kernels.

The Allied Telesis AT1700 series ethercards are based on the Fujitsu MB86965. This chip uses a programmed I/O interface, and a pair of fixed-size transmit buffers. This allows small groups of packets to be sent back-to-back, with a short pause while switching buffers.

A unique feature is the ability to drive 150ohm STP (Shielded Twisted Pair) cable commonly installed for Token Ring, in addition to 10baseT 100ohm UTP (unshielded twisted pair). A fibre optic version of the card (AT1700FT) exists as well.

The Fujitsu chip used on the AT1700 has a design flaw: it can only be fully reset by doing a power cycle of the machine. Pressing the reset button doesn't reset the bus interface. This wouldn't be so bad, except that it can only be reliably detected when it has been freshly reset. The solution/work-around is to power-cycle the machine if the kernel has a problem detecting the AT1700.

Some production runs of the AT1700 had another problem: they are permanently wired to DMA channel 5. This is undocumented, there are no jumpers to disable the "feature", and no driver dares use the DMA capability because of compatibility problems. No device driver will be written using DMA if installing a second card into the machine breaks both, and the only way to disable the DMA is with a knife.

5.3.3 AT2450

Status – *Supported*

This is the PCI version of the AT1500, and it doesn't suffer from the problems that the Boca 79c970 PCI card does. Allied Telsyn was still 'beta testing' the card in early/mid 1995, so it may not have spread to various retailers yet (but it doesn't hurt to ask.)

DMA selection and chip numbering information can be found in 5.4.1 (AMD LANCE).

More technical information on AMD LANCE based Ethernet cards can be found in 8.7 (Notes on AMD...).

5.4 AMD / Advanced Micro Devices

Carl Ching of AMD was kind enough to provide a very detailed description of all the relevant AMD ethernet products which helped clear up this section.

5.4.1 AMD LANCE (7990, 79C960/961/961A, PCnet-ISA)

Status – *Supported*

There really is no AMD ethernet card. You are probably reading this because the only markings you could find on your card said AMD and the above number. The 7990 is the original 'LANCE' chip, but most stuff (including this document) refer to all these similar chips as 'LANCE' chips. (...incorrectly, I might add.)

These above numbers refer to chips from AMD that are the heart of many ethernet cards. For example, the Allied Telesis AT1500 (see 5.3.1 (AT1500)) and the NE1500/2100 (see 5.26.4 (NE1500)) use these chips.

The 7990/79c90 have long been replaced by newer versions. The 79C960 (a.k.a. PCnet-ISA) essentially contains the 79c90 core, along with all the other hardware support required, which allows a single-chip ethernet solution. The 79c961 (PCnet-ISA+) is a jumperless Plug and Play version of the '960. The final chip in the ISA series is the 79c961A (PCnet-ISA II), which adds full duplex capabilities. All cards with one of these chips should work with the lance.c driver, with the exception of very old cards that used the original 7990 in a shared memory configuration. These old cards can be spotted by the lack of jumpers for a DMA channel.

One common problem people have is the 'busmaster arbitration failure' message. This is printed out when the LANCE driver can't get access to the bus after a reasonable amount of time has elapsed (50us). This usually indicates that the motherboard implementation of bus-mastering DMA is broken, or some other device is hogging the bus, or there is a DMA channel conflict. If your BIOS setup has the 'GAT option' (for Guaranteed Access Time) then try toggling/altering that setting to see if it helps.

Also note that the driver only looks at the addresses: 0x300, 0x320, 0x340, 0x360 for a valid card, and any address supplied by an `ether=` boot argument is silently ignored (this will be fixed) so make sure your card is configured for one of the above I/O addresses for now.

The driver will still work fine, even if more than 16MB of memory is installed, since low-memory 'bounce-buffers' are used when needed (i.e. any data from above 16MB is copied into a buffer below 16MB before being given to the card to transmit.)

The DMA channel can be set with the low bits of the otherwise-unused dev->mem_start value (a.k.a. PARAM_1). (see 10.1.1 (PARAM_1)) If unset it is probed for by enabling each free DMA channel in turn and checking if initialization succeeds.

The HP-J2405A board is an exception: with this board it's easy to read the EEPROM-set values for the IRQ, and DMA.

See 8.7 (Notes on AMD...) for more info on these chips.

5.4.2   AMD 79C965 (PCnet-32)

Status – *Supported*

This is the PCnet-32 – a 32 bit bus-master version of the original LANCE chip for VL-bus and local bus systems. chip. While these chips can be operated with the standard `lance.c` driver, a 32 bit version (`lance32.c`) is also available that does not have to concern itself with any 16MB limitations associated with the ISA bus.

5.4.3   AMD 79C970/970A (PCnet-PCI)

Status – *Supported*

This is the PCnet-PCI – similar to the PCnet-32, but designed for PCI bus based systems. Please see the above PCnet-32 information. This means that you need to build a kernel with PCI BIOS support enabled. The '970A adds full duplex support along with some other features to the original '970 design.

Note that the Boca implementation of the 79C970 fails on fast Pentium machines. This is a hardware problem, as it affects DOS users as well. See the Boca section for more details.

5.4.4   AMD 79C971 (PCnet-FAST)

Status – *Supported*

This is AMD's 100Mbit chip for PCI systems, which also supports full duplex operation. It was introduced in June 1996.

5.4.5   AMD 79C974 (PCnet-SCSI)

Status – *Supported*

This is the PCnet-SCSI – which is basically treated like a '970 from an Ethernet point of view. Also see the above information. Don't ask if the SCSI half of the chip is supported – this is the *Ethernet-HowTo*, not the *SCSI-HowTo*.

5.5 Ansel Communications

5.5.1 AC3200 EISA

Status – *Semi-Supported*

Note that to access this driver during `make config` you still have to answer 'Y' when asked "Prompt for development and/or incomplete code/drivers?" at the first. This is simply due to lack of feedback on the driver stability due to it being a relatively rare card.

This driver is included in the present kernel as an alpha test driver. It is based on the common NS8390 chip used in the ne2000 and wd80x3 cards. Please see 3.1 (Alpha Drivers) in this document for important information regarding alpha drivers.

If you use it, let one of us know how things work out, as feedback has been low, even though the driver has been in the kernel since v1.1.25.

If you intend on using this driver as a loadable module you should probably see 10.2 (Using the Ethernet Drivers as Modules) and also 10.2.1 (8390 Based Cards as Modules) for module specific information.

5.6 Apricot

5.6.1 Apricot Xen-II On Board Ethernet

Status – *Supported*

This on board ethernet uses an i82596 bus-master chip. It can only be at i/o address `0x300`. The author of this driver is Mark Evans. By looking at the driver source, it appears that the IRQ is hardwired to 10.

Earlier versions of the driver had a tendency to think that anything living at `0x300` was an apricot NIC. Since then the hardware address is checked to avoid these false detections.

5.7 Arcnet

Status – *Supported*

With the very low cost and better performance of ethernet, chances are that most places will be giving away their Arcnet hardware for free, resulting in a lot of home systems with Arcnet.

An advantage of Arcnet is that all of the cards have identical interfaces, so one driver will work for everyone. It also has built in error handling so that it supposedly never loses a packet. (Great for UDP traffic!)

Avery Pennarun's arcnet driver has been in the default kernel sources since 1.1.80. The arcnet driver uses 'arc0' as its name instead of the usual 'eth0' for ethernet devices. Bug reports and success stories can be mailed to:

`apenwarr@foxnet.net`

There are information files contained in the standard kernel for setting jumpers and general hints.

Supposedly the driver also works with the 100Mbs ARCnet cards as well!

5.8   AT&T

Note that AT&T's StarLAN is an orphaned technology, like SynOptics LattisNet, and can't be used in a
standard 10Base-T environment, without a hub that 'speaks' both.

5.8.1   AT&T T7231 (LanPACER+)

Status – *Not Supported*

These StarLAN cards use an interface similar to the i82586 chip.   At one point, Matthijs Melchior
(`matthijs.n.melchior@att.com`) was playing with the 3c507 driver, and almost had something useable
working. Haven't heard much since that.

5.9   AT-Lan-Tec / RealTek

5.9.1   AT-Lan-Tec / RealTek Pocket adaptor

Status – *Supported*

This is a generic, low-cost OEM pocket adaptor being sold by AT-Lan-Tec, and (likely) a number of other
suppliers. A driver for it is included in the standard kernel. Note that there is substantial information
contained in the driver source file 'atp.c'.

Note that the device name that you pass to `ifconfig` is *not* `eth0` but `atp0` for this device.

5.9.2   RealTek 8029

Status – *Supported*

This is a PCI single chip implementation of a NE2000 clone. Various vendors are now selling cards with this
chip. See 5.26.2 (NE2000-PCI) for information on using any of these cards.

5.9.3   RealTek 8129/8139

Status – *Semi-Supported*

Another PCI single chip ethernet solution from RealTek. A driver for cards based upon this chip is due to
be included in the v2.0.34 release of linux. For more information, see:

`http://cesdis.gsfc.nasa.gov/linux/drivers/rtl8139.html`

5.10   Boca Research

Yes, they make more than just multi-port serial cards. :-)

5.10.1   Boca BEN (PCI, VLB)

Status – *Supported*

These cards are based on AMD's PCnet chips. Perspective buyers should be warned that many users have had endless problems with these cards. Owners of fast Pentium systems have been especially hit. Note that this is not a driver problem, as it hits DOS/Win/NT users as well. Boca's technical support number is (407) 241-8088, and you can also reach them at 75300.2672@compuserve.com.

Donald did a comparitive test with the above Boca PCI card and a similar Allied Telsyn PCnet/PCI implementation, which showed that the problem lies in Boca's implementation of the PCnet/PCI chip. These test results can be accessed on Don's www server.

Linux at CESDIS <http://cesdis.gsfc.nasa.gov/linux/>

Boca is offering a 'warranty repair' for affected owners, which involves adding one of the missing capacitors, but it appears that this fix doesn't work 100 percent for most people, although it helps some.

If you are *still* thinking of buying one of these cards, then at least try and get a 7 day unconditional return policy, so that if it doesn't work properly in your system, you can return it.

More general information on the AMD chips can be found in 5.4.1 (AMD LANCE).

More technical information on AMD LANCE based Ethernet cards can be found in 8.7 (Notes on AMD...).

5.11 Cabletron

Donald writes: 'Yes, another one of these companies that won't release its programming information. They waited for months before actually confirming that all their information was proprietary, deliberately wasting my time. Avoid their cards like the plague if you can. Also note that some people have phoned Cabletron, and have been told things like 'a D. Becker is working on a driver for linux' – making it sound like I work for them. This is NOT the case.'

If you feel like asking them why they don't want to release their low level programming info so that people can use their cards, write to support@ctron.com. Tell them that you are using Linux, and are disappointed that they don't support open systems. And no, the usual driver development kit they supply is useless. It is just a DOS object file that you are supposed to link against. Which you aren't allowed to even reverse engineer.

5.11.1 E10**, E10**-x, E20**, E20**-x

Status – *Semi-Supported*

These are NEx000 almost-clones that are reported to work with the standard NEx000 drivers, thanks to a ctron-specific check during the probe. If there are any problems, they are unlikely to be fixed, as the programming information is unavailable.

5.11.2 E2100

Status – *Semi-Supported*

Again, there is not much one can do when the programming information is proprietary. The E2100 is a poor design. Whenever it maps its shared memory in during a packet transfer, it maps it into the *whole 128K region!* That means you **can't** safely use another interrupt-driven shared memory device in that region, including another E2100. It will work most of the time, but every once in a while it will bite you. (Yes, this problem can be avoided by turning off interrupts while transferring packets, but that will almost certainly lose clock ticks.) Also, if you mis-program the board, or halt the machine at just the wrong moment, even the reset button won't bring it back. You will *have* to turn it off and *leave* it off for about 30 seconds.

Media selection is automatic, but you can override this with the low bits of the dev->mem_end parameter. See 10.1.1 (PARAM_2). Module users can specify an `xcvr=N` value on the `insmod` command line to do the same.

Also, don't confuse the E2100 for a NE2100 clone. The E2100 is a shared memory NatSemi DP8390 design, roughly similar to a brain-damaged WD8013, whereas the NE2100 (and NE1500) use a bus-mastering AMD LANCE design.

There is an E2100 driver included in the standard kernel. However, seeing as programming info isn't available, don't expect bug-fixes. Don't use one unless you are already stuck with the card.

If you intend on using this driver as a loadable module you should probably see 10.2 (Using the Ethernet Drivers as Modules) and also 10.2.1 (8390 Based Cards as Modules) for module specific information.

5.11.3   E22**

Status – *Semi-Supported*

According to information in a Cabletron Tech Bulletin, these cards use the standard AMD PC-Net chipset (see 5.4.1 (AMD PC-Net)) and should work with the generic lance driver.

5.12   Cogent

Here is where and how to reach them:

```
Cogent Data Technologies, Inc.
175 West Street, P.O. Box 926
Friday Harbour, WA 98250, USA.

Cogent Sales
15375 S.E. 30th Place, Suite 310
Bellevue, WA 98007, USA.

Technical Support:
Phone (360) 378-2929 between 8am and 5pm PST
Fax (360) 378-2882
Compuserve GO COGENT
Bulletin Board Service (360) 378-5405
Internet: support@cogentdata.com
```

5.12.1   EM100-ISA/EISA

Status – *Semi-Supported*

These cards use the SMC 91c100 chip and may work with the SMC 91c92 driver, but this has yet to be verified.

5.12.2   Cogent eMASTER+, EM100-PCI, EM400, EM960, EM964

Status – *Supported*

These are yet another DEC 21040 implementation that should hopefully work fine with the standard 21040 driver.

The EM400 and the EM964 are four port cards using a DEC 21050 bridge and 4 21040 chips.

See 5.17.4 (DEC 21040) for more information on these cards, and the present driver situation.

5.13   Compaq

Compaq aren't really in the business of making ethernet cards, but a lot of their systems have embedded ethernet controllers on the motherboard.

5.13.1   Compaq Deskpro / Compaq XL (Embedded AMD Chip)

Status – *Supported*

Machines such as the XL series have an AMD 79c97x PCI chip on the mainboard that can be used with the standard LANCE driver. But before you can use it, you have to do some trickery to get the PCI BIOS to a place where Linux can see it. Frank Maas was kind enough to provide the details:

" The problem with this Compaq machine however is that the PCI directory is loaded in high memory, at a spot where the Linux kernel can't (won't) reach. Result: the card is never detected nor is it usable (sideline: the mouse won't work either) The workaround (as described thoroughly in http://www-c724.uibk.ac.at/XL/) is to load MS-DOS, launch a little driver Compaq wrote and then load the Linux kernel using LOADLIN. Ok, I'll give you time to say 'yuck, yuck', but for now this is the only working solution I know of. The little driver simply moves the PCI directory to a place where it is normally stored (and where Linux can find it)."

More general information on the AMD chips can be found in 5.4.1 (AMD LANCE).

5.14   Danpex

5.14.1   Danpex EN9400

Status – *Supported*

Yet another card based on the DEC 21040 chip, reported to work fine, and at a relatively cheap price.

See 5.17.4 (DEC 21040) for more information on these cards, and the present driver situation.

5.15   D-Link

5.15.1   DE-100, DE-200, DE-220-T, DE-250

Status – *Supported*

Some of the early D-Link cards didn't have the 0x57 PROM signature, but the ne2000 driver knows about them. For the software configurable cards, you can get the config program from www.dlink.com. The DE2** cards were the most widely reported as having the spurious transfer address mismatch errors with early versions of linux. Note that there are also cards from Digital (DEC) that are also named DE100 and DE200, but the similarity stops there.

5.15.2 DE-520

Status – *Supported*

This is a PCI card using the PCI version of AMD's LANCE chip. DMA selection and chip numbering information can be found in 5.4.1 (AMD LANCE).

More technical information on AMD LANCE based Ethernet cards can be found in 8.7 (Notes on AMD...).

5.15.3 DE-530

Status – *Supported*

This is a generic DEC 21040 PCI chip implementation, and is reported to work with the generic 21040 tulip driver.

See 5.17.4 (DEC 21040) for more information on these cards, and the present driver situation.

5.15.4 DE-600

Status – *Supported*

Laptop users and other folk who might want a quick way to put their computer onto the ethernet may want to use this. The driver is included with the default kernel source tree. Bjorn Ekwall `bj0rn@blox.se` wrote the driver. Expect about 180kb/s transfer speed from this via the parallel port. You should read the README.DLINK file in the kernel source tree.

Note that the device name that you pass to `ifconfig` is *now* eth0 and not the previously used dl0.

If your parallel port is *not* at the standard 0x378 then you will have to recompile. Bjorn writes: "Since the DE-620 driver tries to sqeeze the last microsecond from the loops, I made the irq and port address constants instead of variables. This makes for a usable speed, but it also means that you can't change these assignments from e.g. lilo; you _have_ to recompile..." Also note that some laptops implement the on-board parallel port at 0x3bc which is where the parallel ports on monochrome cards were/are.

5.15.5 DE-620

Status – *Supported*

Same as the DE-600, only with two output formats. Bjorn has written a driver for this model, for kernel versions 1.1 and above. See the above information on the DE-600.

5.15.6 DE-650

Status – *Semi-Supported*

Some people have been using this PCMCIA card for some time now with their notebooks. It is a basic 8390 design, much like a NE2000. The LinkSys PCMCIA card and the IC-Card Ethernet (available from Midwest Micro) are supposedly DE-650 clones as well. Note that at present, this driver is *not* part of the standard kernel, and so you will have to do some patching.

See 9.3 (PCMCIA Support) in this document, and if you can, have a look at:

Don's PCMCIA Stuff `<http://cesdis.gsfc.nasa.gov/linux/pcmcia.html>`

5.16 DFI

5.16.1 DFINET-300 and DFINET-400

Status – *Supported*

These cards are now detected (as of 0.99pl15) thanks to Eberhard Moenkeberg emoenke@gwdg.de who noted that they use 'DFI' in the first 3 bytes of the prom, instead of using 0x57 in bytes 14 and 15, which is what all the NE1000 and NE2000 cards use. (The 300 is an 8 bit pseudo NE1000 clone, and the 400 is a pseudo NE2000 clone.)

5.17 Digital / DEC

5.17.1 DEPCA, DE100/1, DE200/1/2, DE210, DE422

Status – *Supported*

As of linux v1.0, there is a driver included as standard for these cards. It was written by David C. Davies. There is documentation included in the source file 'depca.c', which includes info on how to use more than one of these cards in a machine. Note that the DE422 is an EISA card. These cards are all based on the AMD LANCE chip. See 5.4.1 (AMD LANCE) for more info. A maximum of two of the ISA cards can be used, because they can only be set for 0x300 and 0x200 base I/O address. If you are intending to do this, please read the notes in the driver source file depca.c in the standard kernel source tree.

This driver will also work on Alpha CPU based machines, and there are various ioctl()s that the user can play with.

5.17.2 Digital EtherWorks 3 (DE203, DE204, DE205)

Status – *Supported*

Included into kernels v1.1.62 and above is this driver, also by David C. Davies of DEC. These cards use a proprietary chip from DEC, as opposed to the LANCE chip used in the earlier cards like the DE200. These cards support both shared memory or programmed I/O, although you take about a 50%performance hit if you use PIO mode. The shared memory size can be set to 2kB, 32kB or 64kB, but only 2 and 32 have been tested with this driver. David says that the performance is virtually identical between the 2kB and 32kB mode. There is more information (including using the driver as a loadable module) at the top of the driver file ewrk3.c and also in README.ewrk3. Both of these files come with the standard kernel distribution.

The standard driver has a number of interesting ioctl() calls that can be used to get or clear packet statistics, read/write the EEPROM, change the hardware address, and the like. Hackers can see the source code for more info on that one.

David has also written a configuration utility for this card (along the lines of the DOS program NICSETUP.EXE) along with other tools. These can be found on sunsite.unc.edu in the directory /pub/Linux/system/Network/management – look for the file ewrk3tools-X.XX.tar.gz.

The next release of this driver (v0.40) will have Alpha CPU support like depca.c does and is available from David now if you require it.

5.17.3 DE425 (EISA), DE434, DE435, DE500

Status – *Supported*

These cards are based on the 21040 chip mentioned below. Included into kernels v1.1.86 and above is this driver, also by David C. Davies of DEC. It sure is nice to have support from someone on the inside ;-) The DE500 uses the newer 21140 chip to provide 10/100Mbs ethernet connections. Have a read of the 21040 section below for extra info.

Note that as of 1.1.91, David has added a compile time option that will allow non-DEC cards to work with this driver. Have a look at `README.de4x5` for details.

All the Digital cards will autoprobe for their media (except, temporarily, the DE500 due to a patent issue).

This driver is also ALPHA CPU ready and supports being loaded as a module. Users can access the driver internals through ioctl() calls - see the 'ewrk3' tools and the de4x5.c sources for information about how to do this.

5.17.4   DEC 21040, 21041, 2114x, Tulip

Status – *Supported*

The DEC 21040 is a bus-mastering single chip ethernet solution from Digital, similar to AMD's PCnet chip. The 21040 is specifically designed for the PCI bus architecture. SMC's new EtherPower PCI card uses this chip.

You have a choice of *two* drivers for cards based on this chip. There is the DE425 driver discussed above, and the generic 21040 driver that Donald has written.

Warning: Even though your card may be based upon this chip, *the drivers may not work for you*. David C. Davies writes:

"There are no guarantees that either 'tulip.c' OR 'de4x5.c' will run any DC2114x based card other than those they've been written to support. WHY?? You ask. Because there is a register, the General Purpose Register (CSR12) that (1) in the DC21140A is programmable by each vendor and they all do it differently (2) in the DC21142/3 this is now an SIA control register (a la DC21041). The only small ray of hope is that we can decode the SROM to help set up the driver. However, this is not a guaranteed solution since some vendors (e.g. SMC 9332 card) don't follow the Digital Semiconductor recommended SROM programming format."

In non-technical terms, this means that if you aren't sure that an unknown card with a DC2114x chip will work with the linux driver(s), then make sure you can return the card to the place of purchase *before* you pay for it.

The updated 21041 chip is also found in place of the 21040 on most of the later SMC EtherPower cards. The 21140 is for supporting 100Base-? and works with the Linux drivers for the 21040 chip. To use David's `de4x5` driver with non-DEC cards, have a look at `README.de4x5` for details.

Donald has used SMC EtherPower-10/100 cards to develop the 'tulip' driver. Note that the driver that is in the standard kernel tree at the moment is not the most up to date version. If you are having trouble with this driver, you should get the newest version from Donald's ftp/WWW site.

Tulip Driver <http://cesdis.gsfc.nasa.gov/linux/drivers/tulip.html>

The above URL also contains a (non-exhaustive) list of various cards/vendors that use the 21040 chip.

Also note that the tulip driver is still considered an *alpha* driver (see 3.1 (Alpha Drivers)) at the moment, and should be treated as such. To use it, you will have to edit `arch/i386/config.in` and uncomment the line for `CONFIG_DEC_ELCP` support.

Donald has even set up a mailing list for tulip driver support announcements, etc. To join it just type:

```
echo subscribe | /bin/mail linux-tulip-request@cesdis.gsfc.nasa.gov
```

5.18   Farallon

Farallon sells EtherWave adaptors and transceivers. This device allows multiple 10baseT devices to be daisy-chained.

5.18.1   Farallon Etherwave

Status – *Supported*

This is reported to be a 3c509 clone that includes the EtherWave transceiver. People have used these successfully with Linux and the present 3c509 driver. They are too expensive for general use, but are a great option for special cases. Hublet prices start at $125, and Etherwave adds $75-$100 to the price of the board – worth it if you have pulled one wire too few, but not if you are two network drops short.

5.19   Hewlett Packard

The 272** cards use programmed I/O, similar to the NE*000 boards, but the data transfer port can be 'turned off' when you aren't accessing it, avoiding problems with autoprobing drivers.

Thanks to Glenn Talbott for helping clean up the confusion in this section regarding the version numbers of the HP hardware.

5.19.1   27245A

Status – *Supported*

8 Bit 8390 based 10BaseT, not recommended for all the 8 bit reasons. It was re-designed a couple years ago to be highly integrated which caused some changes in initialization timing which only affected testing programs, not LAN drivers. (The new card is not 'ready' as soon after switching into and out of loopback mode.)

If you intend on using this driver as a loadable module you should probably see 10.2 (Using the Ethernet Drivers as Modules) and also 10.2.1 (8390 Based Cards as Modules) for module specific information.

5.19.2   HP PC Lan+ (27247, 27252A)

Status – *Supported*

The HP PC Lan+ is different to the standard HP PC Lan card. This driver was added to the list of drivers in the standard kernel during the v1.1.x development cycle. It can be operated in either a PIO mode like a ne2000, or a shared memory mode like a wd8013.

The 47B is a 16 Bit 8390 based 10BaseT w/AUI, and the 52A is a 16 Bit 8390 based ThinLAN w/AUI. These cards have 32K onboard RAM for Tx/Rx packet buffering instead of the usual 16KB, and they both offer LAN connector autosense.

If you intend on using this driver as a loadable module you should probably see 10.2 (Using the Ethernet Drivers as Modules) and also 10.2.1 (8390 Based Cards as Modules) for module specific information.

5.19.3   HP-J2405A

Status – *Supported*

These are lower priced, and slightly faster than the 27247/27252A, but are missing some features, such as AUI, ThinLAN connectivity, and boot PROM socket. This is a fairly generic LANCE design, but a minor design decision makes it incompatible with a generic 'NE2100' driver. Special support for it (including reading the DMA channel from the board) is included thanks to information provided by HP's Glenn Talbott.

More technical information on LANCE based cards can be found in 8.7 (Notes on AMD...)

5.19.4   HP-Vectra On Board Ethernet

Status – *Supported*

The HP-Vectra has an AMD PCnet chip on the motherboard. Earlier kernel versions would detect it as the HP-J2405A but that would fail, as the Vectra doesn't report the IRQ and DMA channel like the J2405A. Get a kernel newer than v1.1.53 to avoid this problem.

DMA selection and chip numbering information can be found in 5.4.1 (AMD LANCE).

More technical information on LANCE based cards can be found in 8.7 (Notes on AMD...)

5.19.5   HP 10/100 VG Any Lan Cards (27248B, J2573, J2577, J2585)

Status – *Supported*

As of early 1.3.x kernels, this driver was made available by Jaroslav Kysela, (perex@pf.jcu.cz). Due to the newness of the driver and the relatively small number of VG cards in use, feedback on this driver has been low.

Donald has also written a driver for these cards. Unlike the above, it is not presently in the standard kernel source tree. Check out the following URL for more information on Donald's 100VG work.

Donald's 100VG Page <http://cesdis.gsfc.nasa.gov/linux/drivers/100vg.html>

5.20   IBM / International Business Machines

5.20.1   IBM Thinkpad 300

Status – *Supported*

This is compatible with the Intel based Zenith Z-note. See 5.37.1 (Z-note) for more info.

Supposedly this site has a comprehensive database of useful stuff for newer versions of the Thinkpad. I haven't checked it out myself yet.

Thinkpad-info <http://peipa.essex.ac.uk/html/linux-thinkpad.html>

For those without a WWW browser handy, try `peipa.essex.ac.uk:/pub/tp750/`

5.20.2   IBM Credit Card Adaptor for Ethernet

Status – *Semi-Supported*

People have been using this PCMCIA card with Linux as well. Similar points apply, those being that you need a supported PCMCIA chipset on your notebook, and that you will have to patch the PCMCIA support into the standard kernel.

See 9.3 (PCMCIA Support) in this document, and if you can, have a look at:

Don's PCMCIA Stuff <http://cesdis.gsfc.nasa.gov/linux/pcmcia.html>

5.20.3 IBM Token Ring

Status – *Semi-Supported*

To support token ring requires more than only writing a device driver, it also requires writing the source routing routines for token ring. It is the source routing that would be the most time comsuming to write.

Peter De Schrijver has been spending some time on Token Ring lately. and has worked with IBM ISA and MCA token ring cards.

The present token ring code has been included into the first of the 1.3.x series kernels.

Peter says that it was originally tested on an MCA 16/4 Megabit Token Ring board, but it should work with other Tropic based boards.

5.21 ICL Ethernet Cards

5.21.1 ICL EtherTeam 16i/32

Status – *Supported*

Mika Kuoppala (miku@pupu.elt.icl.fi) wrote this driver, and it was included into early 1.3.4x kernels. It uses the Fujitsu MB86965 chip that is also used on the at1700 cards.

5.22 Intel Ethernet Cards

5.22.1 Ether Express

Status – *Supported*

This card uses the intel i82586. (Surprise, huh?) Earlier versions of this driver (in v1.2 kernels) were classed as alpha-test, as it didn't work well for most people. The driver in the v2.0 kernel seems to work much better for those who have tried it. The comments at the top of the driver source list some of the problems associated with these cards.

There is also some technical information available on the i82586 in 8.5 (Programming the Intel Chips) and also in the source code for the driver 'eexpress.c'. Don't be afraid to read it. ;-)

5.22.2 Ether Express PRO/10

Status – *Supported*

Bao Chau Ha has written a driver for these cards that has been included into early 1.3.x kernels. It may also work with some of the Compaq built-in ethernet systems that are based on the i82595 chip.

5.22.3 Ether Express PRO/10 PCI (EISA)

Status – *Semi-Supported*

John Stalba (stalba@ultranet.com) has written a driver for the PCI version. These cards the PLX9036 PCI interface chip with the Intel i82596 LAN controller chip. If your card has the i82557 chip, then you *don't* have this card, but rather the "+" version discussed next, and hence want the EEPro100 driver instead.

You can get the alpha driver for the PRO/10 PCI card, along with instructions on how to use it at:

EEPro10 Driver <http://www.ultranet.com/~stalba/eep10pci.html>

If you have the EISA card, you will probably have to hack the driver a bit to account for the different (PCI vs. EISA) detection mechanisms that are used in each case.

5.22.4   Ether Express PRO/10+

Status – *Supported*

A slight change in name (from the above) but a different design. This card uses the i82557 chip, and hence uses the eepro100 driver described below.

5.22.5   Ether Express PRO 10/100B

Status – *Supported*

A driver for this card is included in the v2.0 kernel source tree, so you may no longer have to get it separately. Note that this driver will *not* work with the older 100A cards.

For driver updates and/or driver support, have a look at:

EEPro-100B Page <http://cesdis.gsfc.nasa.gov/linux/drivers/eepro100.html>

Apparently Donald had to sign a non-disclosure agreement that stated he could actually disclose the driver source code! How is that for sillyness on intel's part?

This driver will be included into the v2.1 source tree sometime in the future. There is also a mailing list for driver announcements. To join it, just do:

```
echo subscribe | /bin/mail linux-eepro100-request@cesdis.gsfc.nasa.gov
```

5.23   LinkSys

LinkSys make a handful of different NE2000 clones, some straight ISA cards, some ISA plug and play and some even ne2000-PCI clones based on one of the supported ne2000-PCI chipsets. There are just too many models to list here.

Linux gets a mention in their WWW support page. Have a look at:

http://www.linksys.com/support/solution/nos/linux.htm

if you are having trouble using one of their cards with linux.

5.23.1   LinkSys Etherfast 10/100 Cards.

Status – *Supported*

Beware with these cards - apparently some use the DEC chipset, and some use a proprietary PNIC chipset. The drivers for the DEC chips will *not* work with the PNIC cards. Thanks to Blake Wright for reporting this useful bit of information.

5.23.2 LinkSys Pocket Ethernet Adapter Plus (PEAEPP)

Status – *Supported*

This is supposedly a DE-620 clone, and is reported to work well with that driver. See 5.15.5 (DE-620) for more information.

5.23.3 LinkSys PCMCIA Adaptor

Status – *Supported*

This is supposed to be a re-badged DE-650. See 5.15.6 (DE-650) for more information.

5.24 Microdyne

5.24.1 Microdyne Exos 205T

Status – *Semi-Supported*

Another i82586 based card. Dirk Niggemann dabn100@hermes.cam.ac.uk has written a driver that he classes as "pre-alpha" that he would like people to test. Mail him for more details.

5.25 Mylex

Mylex can be reached at the following numbers, in case anyone wants to ask them anything.

```
MYLEX CORPORATION, Fremont
Sales:  800-77-MYLEX, (510) 796-6100
FAX:    (510) 745-8016.
```

They also have a web site: *Mylex WWW Site* <http://www.mylex.com>

5.25.1 Mylex LNE390A, LNE390B

Status – *Semi-Supported*

These are fairly old EISA cards that make use of a shared memory implementation similar to the wd80x3. If you are interested in testing a driver for this card, contact me (pg).

5.25.2 Mylex LNP101

Status – *Supported*

This is a PCI card that is based on DEC's 21040 chip. It is selectable between 10BaseT, 10Base2 and 10Base5 output. The LNP101 card has been verified to work with the generic 21040 driver.

See the section on the 21040 chip (5.17.4 (DEC 21040)) for more information.

5.25.3 Mylex LNP104

Status – *Semi-Supported*

The LNP104 uses the DEC 21050 chip to deliver *four* independent 10BaseT ports. It should work with recent 21040 drivers that know how to share IRQs, but nobody has reported trying it yet (that I am aware of).

5.26 Novell Ethernet, NExxxx and associated clones.

The prefix 'NE' came from Novell Ethernet. Novell followed the cheapest NatSemi databook design and sold the manufacturing rights (spun off?) Eagle, just to get reasonably-priced ethercards into the market. (The now ubiquitous NE2000 card.)

5.26.1 NE1000, NE2000

Status – *Supported*

NOTE: If you are using a kernel that is older than v1.2.9, it is *strongly* recommended that you upgrade to a newer version. There was an important bugfix made to the ne driver in 1.2.7, and another important bugfix made to the upper layers (dev.c) in 1.2.9. Both of these bugs can cause a ne2000 card to hang your computer.

The ne2000 is now a generic name for a bare-bones design around the NatSemi 8390 chip. They use programmed I/O rather than shared memory, leading to easier installation but slightly lower performance and a few problems. Again, the savings of using an 8 bit NE1000 over the NE2000 are only warranted if you expect light use. Some problems can arise with poor NE2000 clones. You should see 3.4 (Problems with...), and 3.3 (Poor NE2000 Clones)

Some recently introduced NE2000 clones use the National Semiconductor 'AT/LANTic' 83905 chip, which offers a shared memory mode similar to the wd8013 and EEPROM software configuration. The shared memory mode will offer less CPU usage (i.e. more efficient) than the programmed i/o mode.

In general it is not a good idea to put a NE2000 clone at I/O address 0x300 because nearly *every* device driver probes there at boot. Some poor NE2000 clones don't take kindly to being prodded in the wrong areas, and will respond by locking your machine. Also 0x320 is bad because SCSI drivers probe into 0x330.

Donald has written a NE2000 diagnostic program (ne2k.c) for all ne2000 cards. See 7.2 (Diagnostic Programs) for more information.

If you intend on using this driver as a loadable module you should probably see 10.2 (Using the Ethernet Drivers as Modules) and also 10.2.1 (8390 Based Cards as Modules) for module specific information.

5.26.2 NE2000-PCI (RealTek/Winbond/Compex)

Status – *Supported*

Yes, believe it or not, people are making PCI cards based on the ten year old interface design of the ne2000. At the moment nearly all of these cards are based on the RealTek 8029 chip, or the Winbond 89c940 chip. The Compex, KTI, VIA and Netvin cards apparently also use these chips, but have a different PCI ID. The linux kernel v2.0.33 has support to automatically detect all these cards and use them. (If you are using a kernel v2.0.30 or older, you should upgrade to ensure your card will be detected.)

Note that you have to say 'Y' to the 'Other ISA cards' option when running `make config` as you are actually using the same NE2000 driver as the ISA cards use. (That should also give you a hint that these cards aren't anywhere as intelligent as say a DEC 21040 card...) In the future, a PCI-only NE2000 driver will be included in the kernel source for these cards. The driver is currently available for testing at:

`http://cesdis.gsfc.nasa.gov/linux/drivers/ne2k-pci.html`

Some newer motherboards don't enable all the PCI cards at power-up, and this generally causes the card to be detected, but to fail the probe. Code to enable such cards is due to be added to the v2.0.34 `ne.c` driver, based on that which is in the above PCI-only driver.

If you have a NE2000 PCI card that is *not* detected by the driver, please contact the maintainer of the NE2000 driver as listed in `/usr/src/linux/MAINTAINERS` along with the output from a `cat /proc/pci` and `dmesg` so that support for your card can also be added to the driver.

5.26.3   NE-10/100

Status – *Not Supported*

These are ISA 100Mbps cards based on the National Semiconductor DP83800 and DP83840 chips. There is currently no driver support, nor has anyone reported that they are working on a driver.

5.26.4   NE1500, NE2100

Status – *Supported*

These cards use the original 7990 LANCE chip from AMD and are supported using the Linux lance driver. Newer NE2100 clones use the updated PCnet/ISA chip from AMD.

Some earlier versions of the lance driver had problems with getting the IRQ line via autoIRQ from the original Novell/Eagle 7990 cards. Hopefully this is now fixed. If not, then specify the IRQ via LILO, and let us know that it still has problems.

DMA selection and chip numbering information can be found in 5.4.1 (AMD LANCE).

More technical information on LANCE based cards can be found in 8.7 (Notes on AMD...)

5.26.5   NE3200

Status – *Not Supported*

This card uses a lowly 8MHz 80186, and hence you are better off using a cheap NE2000 clone. Even if a driver was available, the NE2000 card would most likely be faster.

5.26.6   NE5500

Status – *Supported*

These are just AMD PCnet-PCI cards ('970A) chips. More information on LANCE/PCnet based cards can be found in 5.4.1 (AMD LANCE).

5.27 Proteon

5.27.1 Proteon P1370-EA

Status – *Supported*

Apparently this is a NE2000 clone, and works fine with Linux.

5.27.2 Proteon P1670-EA

Status – *Supported*

This is yet another PCI card that is based on DEC's Tulip chip. It has been reported to work fine with Linux.

See the section on the 21040 chip (5.17.4 (DEC 21040)) for more driver information.

5.28 Pure Data

5.28.1 PDUC8028, PDI8023

Status – *Supported*

The PureData PDUC8028 and PDI8023 series of cards are reported to work, thanks to special probe code contributed by Mike Jagdis `jaggy@purplet.demon.co.uk`. The support is integrated with the WD driver.

5.29 Racal-Interlan

Racal Interlan can be reached via WWW at `www.interlan.com`. I believe they were also known as MiCom-Interlan at one point in the past.

5.29.1 ES3210

Status – *Semi-Supported*

This is an EISA 8390 based shared memory card. An experimetal driver for v2.0 is available (from me, pg). It is reported to work fine, but the EISA IRQ and shared memory address detection appears not to work with (at least) the early revision cards. In that case, you have to supply them at boot; e.g. `ether=5,0,0xd0000,eth0` for IRQ 5 and shared memory at `0xd0000`. The i/o base is automatically detected and hence a value of zero should be used.

This driver will appear in the v2.1 kernels at some time in the near future.

5.29.2 NI5010

Status – *Semi-Supported*

This driver, by Jan-Pascal van Best (jvbest@qv3pluto.leidenuniv.nl) supports the old 8 bit MiCom-Interlan cards. You can get the driver from:

NI5010 Driver <http://qv3pluto.leidenuniv.nl/jvbest/ni5010/ni5010.html>

Jan-Pascal has got very little feedback on this driver and would appreciate it if you dropped him a note saying if it worked or not.

5.29.3 NI5210

Status – *Semi-Supported*

Michael Hipp has written a driver for this card. It is included in the standard kernel as an 'alpha' driver. Michael would like to hear feedback from users that have this card. See 3.1 (Alpha Drivers) for important information on using alpha-test ethernet drivers with Linux.

Michael says that "the internal sysbus seems to be slow. So we often lose packets because of overruns while receiving from a fast remote host."

This card also uses one of the Intel chips. See 8.5 (Programming the Intel Chips) for more technical information.

5.29.4 NI6510 (not EB)

Status – *Semi-Supported*

There is also a driver for the LANCE based NI6510, and it is also written by Michael Hipp. Again, it is also an 'alpha' driver. For some reason, this card is not compatible with the generic LANCE driver. See 3.1 (Alpha Drivers) for important information on using alpha-test ethernet drivers with Linux.

5.29.5 EtherBlaster (aka NI6510EB)

Status – *Supported*

As of kernel 1.3.23, the generic LANCE driver had a check added to it for the `0x52, 0x44` NI6510EB specific signature. Others have reported that this signature is not the same for all NI6510EB cards however, which will cause the lance driver to not detect your card. If this happens to you, you can change the probe (at about line 322 in lance.c) to printk() out what the values are for your card and then use them instead of the `0x52, 0x44` defaults.

The cards should probably be run in 'high-performance' mode and not in the NI6510 compatible mode when using the lance driver.

5.30 Sager

5.30.1 Sager NP943

Status – *Semi-Supported*

This is just a 3c501 clone, with a different S.A. PROM prefix. I assume it is equally as brain dead as the original 3c501 as well. Kernels 1.1.53 and up check for the NP943 I.D. and then just treat it as a 3c501 after that. See 5.1.1 (3Com 3c501) for all the reasons as to why you really don't want to use one of these cards.

5.31   Schneider & Koch

5.31.1   SK G16

Status – *Supported*

This driver was included into the v1.1 kernels, and it was written by PJD Weichmann and SWS Bern. It appears that the SK G16 is similar to the NI6510, in that it is based on the first edition LANCE chip (the 7990). Once again, it appears as though this card won't work with the generic LANCE driver.

5.32   SEEQ

5.32.1   SEEQ 8005

Status – *Supported*

This driver was included into early 1.3.x kernels, and was written by Hamish Coleman. There is little information about the card included in the driver, and hence little information to be put here. If you have a question, you are probably best off e-mailing hamish@zot.apana.org.au

5.33   SMC (Standard Microsystems Corp.)

Please see 5.35 (Western Digital) for information on SMC cards. (SMC bought out Western Digital's network card section quite a while ago.)

5.34   Thomas Conrad

5.34.1   Thomas Conrad TC-5048

This is yet another PCI card that is based on DEC's 21040 chip.

See the section on the 21040 chip (5.17.4 (DEC 21040)) for more information.

5.35   Western Digital / SMC

The ethernet part of Western Digital has been bought out by SMC. One common mistake people make is that the relatively new SMC Elite Ultra is the same as the older SMC Elite16 models – this is **not** the case. They have separate drivers.

Here is how to contact SMC (not that you should need to.)

SMC / Standard Microsystems Corp., 80 Arkay Drive, Hauppage, New York, 11788, USA.

Technical Support via phone:

```
800-992-4762  (USA)
800-433-5345  (Canada)
516-435-6250  (Other Countries)
```

Literature requests:

```
800-SMC-4-YOU (USA)
800-833-4-SMC (Canada)
516-435-6255  (Other Countries)
```

Technical Support via E-mail:

```
techsupt@ccmail.west.smc.com
```

FTP Site:

```
ftp.smc.com
```

WWW Site: *SMC* <http://www.smc.com>

5.35.1   WD8003, SMC Elite

Status – *Supported*

These are the 8-bit versions of the card. The 8 bit 8003 is slightly less expensive, but only worth the savings for light use. Note that some of the non-EEPROM cards (clones with jumpers, or old *old* old wd8003 cards) have no way of reporting the IRQ line used. In this case, auto-irq is used, and if that fails, the driver silently assings IRQ 5. You can get the SMC setup/driver disks from SMC's ftp site. Note that some of the newer SMC 'SuperDisk' programs will fail to detect the real old EEPROM-less cards. The file SMCDSK46.EXE seems to be a good all-round choice. Also the jumper settings for all their cards are in an ascii text file in the aforementioned archive. The latest (greatest?) version can be obtained from ftp.smc.com.

As these are basically the same as their 16 bit counterparts (WD8013 / SMC Elite16), you should see the next section for more information.

5.35.2   WD8013, SMC Elite16

Status – *Supported*

Over the years the design has added more registers and an EEPROM. (The first wd8003 cards appeared about ten years ago!) Clones usually go by the '8013' name, and usually use a non-EEPROM (jumpered) design. Late model SMC cards will have the SMC 83c690 chip instead of the original Nat Semi DP8390 found on earlier cards. The shared memory design makes the cards a bit faster than PIO cards, especially with larger packets. More importantly, from the driver's point of view, it avoids a few bugs in the programmed-I/O mode of the 8390, allows safe multi-threaded access to the packet buffer, and it doesn't have a programmed-I/O data register that hangs your machine during warm-boot probes.

Non-EEPROM cards that can't just read the selected IRQ will attempt auto-irq, and if that fails, they will silently assign IRQ 10. (8 bit versions will assign IRQ 5)

Cards with a non standard amount of memory on board can have the memory size specified at boot (or at 'insmod' time if using modules). The standard memory size is 8kB for an 8bit card and 16kB for a 16bit card. For example, the older WD8003EBT cards could be jumpered for 32kB memory. To make full use of that RAM, you would use something like (for i/o=0x280 and IRQ 9):

```
LILO: linux ether=9,0x280,0xd0000,0xd8000,eth0
```

Also see 3.5 (8013 problems) for some of the more common problems and frequently asked questions that pop up often.

If you intend on using this driver as a loadable module you should probably see 10.2 (Using the Ethernet Drivers as Modules) and also 10.2.1 (8390 Based Cards as Modules) for module specific information.

5.35.3 SMC Elite Ultra

Status – *Supported*

This ethercard is based on a new chip from SMC, the 83c790, which has a few new features. While it has a mode that is similar to the older SMC ethercards, it's not entirely compatible with the old WD80*3 drivers. However, in this mode it shares most of its code with the other 8390 drivers, while operating slightly faster than a WD8013 clone.

Since part of the Ultra *looks like* an 8013, the Ultra probe is supposed to find an Ultra before the wd8013 probe has a chance to mistakenly identify it.

Donald mentioned that it is possible to write a separate driver for the Ultra's 'Altego' mode which allows chaining transmits at the cost of inefficient use of receive buffers, but that will probably not happen.

Bus-Master SCSI host adaptor users take note: In the manual that ships with Interactive UNIX, it mentions that a bug in the SMC Ultra will cause data corruption with SCSI disks being run from an aha-154X host adaptor. This will probably bite aha-154X compatible cards, such as the BusLogic boards, and the AMI-FastDisk SCSI host adaptors as well.

SMC has acknowledged the problem occurs with Interactive, and older Windows NT drivers. It is a hardware conflict with early revisions of the card that can be worked around in the driver design. The current Ultra driver protects against this by only enabling the shared memory during data transfers with the card. Make sure your kernel version is at least 1.1.84, or that the driver version reported at boot is at least `smc-ultra.c:v1.12` otherwise you are vulnerable.

If you intend on using this driver as a loadable module you should probably see 10.2 (Using the Ethernet Drivers as Modules) and also 10.2.1 (8390 Based Cards as Modules) for module specific information.

5.35.4 SMC Elite Ultra32 EISA

Status – *Semi-Supported*

This EISA card shares a lot in common with its ISA counterpart. A working (and stable) driver is available for v2.0 kernels upon request from the author of this document. Thanks go to Leonard Zubkoff for purchasing some of these cards so that Leonard and myself could add linux support for them. The driver will be included with a future release of the v2.1.x linux kernel as well.

5.35.5 SMC EtherEZ (8416)

Status – *Supported*

This card uses SMC's 83c795 chip and supports the Plug 'n Play specification. It also has an *SMC Ultra* compatible mode, which allows it to be used with the Linux Ultra driver. Be sure to set your card for this compatibility mode. See the above information for notes on the Ultra driver.

For v1.2 kernels, the card had to be configured for shared memory operation. However v2.0 kernels can use the card in shared memory or programmed i/o mode. Shared memory mode will be slightly faster, and use considerably less CPU resources as well.

Note that the EtherEZ specific checks were added to the SMC Ultra driver in 1.1.84, and hence earlier kernel versions will not detect or handle these cards correctly.

5.35.6   SMC EtherPower PCI (8432)

Status – *Supported*

NB: The EtherPower II is an entirely different card. See below! These cards are a basic DEC 21040 implementation, i.e. one big chip and a couple of transceivers. Donald has used one of these cards for his development of the generic 21040 driver (aka `tulip.c`). Thanks to Duke Kamstra, once again, for supplying a card to do development on.

Some of the later revisons of this card use the newer DEC 21041 chip, which may cause problems with older versions of the tulip driver. If you have problems, make sure you are using the latest driver release, which may not yet be included in the current kernel source tree.

See 5.17.4 (DEC 21040) for more details on using one of these cards, and the current status of the driver.

Apparently, the latest revision of the card, the EtherPower-II uses the 9432 chip. It is unclear at the moment if this one will work with the present driver. As always, if unsure, check that you can return the card if it doesn't work with the linux driver *before* paying for the card.

5.35.7   SMC EtherPower II PCI (9432)

Status – *Semi-Supported*

These cards, based upon the SMC 83c170 chip, are entirely different than the Tulip based cards. A new alpha-test driver named `epic100.c` is due to be included in kernel v2.0.34 to support these cards. For more details, see:

```
http://cesdis.gsfc.nasa.gov/linux/drivers/epic100.html
```

5.35.8   SMC 3008

Status – *Not Supported*

These 8 bit cards are based on the Fujitsu MB86950, which is an ancient version of the MB86965 used in the Linux at1700 driver. Russ says that you could probably hack up a driver by looking at the at1700.c code and his DOS packet driver for the Tiara card (tiara.asm). They are not very common.

5.35.9   SMC 3016

Status – *Not Supported*

These are 16bit i/o mapped 8390 cards, much similar to a generic NE2000 card. If you can get the specifications from SMC, then porting the NE2000 driver would probably be quite easy. They are not very common.

5.35.10   SMC-9000 / SMC 91c92/4

Status – *Supported*

The SMC9000 is a VLB card based on the 91c92 chip. The 91c92 appears on a few other brand cards as well, but is fairly uncommon. Erik Stahlman (erik@vt.edu) has written this driver which is in v2.0 kernels, but not in the older v1.2 kernels. You may be able to drop the driver into a v1.2 kernel source tree with minimal difficulty.

5.35.11   SMC 91c100

Status – *Semi-Supported*

The SMC 91c92 driver is supposed to work for cards based on this 100Base-T chip, but at the moment this is unverified.

5.36   Xircom

For the longest time, Xircom wouldn't release the programming information required to write a driver, unless you signed your life away. Apparently enough linux users have pestered them for driver support (they claim to support all popular networking operating systems...) so that they have changed their policy to allow documentation to be released without having to sign a non-disclosure agreement, and apparently they will release the source code to the SCO driver as well. If you want to verify that this is the case, you can reach Xircom at 1-800-874-7875, 1-800-438-4526 or +1-818-878-7600.

However, at the moment nobody has rushed forth offering to write any drivers, so all their products are still unsupported.

5.36.1   PE1, PE2, PE3-10B*

Status – *Not Supported*

Not to get your hopes up, but if you have one of these parallel port adaptors, you may be able to use it in the DOS emulator with the Xircom-supplied DOS drivers. You will have to allow DOSEMU access to your parallel port, and will probably have to play with SIG (DOSEMU's Silly Interrupt Generator).

5.37   Zenith

5.37.1   Z-Note

Status – *Supported*

The built-in Z-Note network adaptor is based on the Intel i82593 using *two* DMA channels. There is an (alpha?) driver available in the present kernel version. As with all notebook and pocket adaptors, it is under the 'Pocket and portable adaptors' section when running `make config`. See 8.5 (Programming the Intel chips) for more technical information. Also note that the IBM ThinkPad 300 is compatible with the Z-Note.

5.38 Znyx

5.38.1 Znyx ZX342 (DEC 21040 based)

Status – *Supported*

You have a choice of *two* drivers for cards based on this chip. There is the DE425 driver written by David, and the generic 21040 driver that Donald has written.

Note that as of 1.1.91, David has added a compile time option that may allow non-DEC cards (such as the Znyx cards) to work with this driver. Have a look at README.de4x5 for details.

See 5.17.4 (DEC 21040) for more information on these cards, and the present driver situation.

5.39 Identifying an Unknown Card

Okay, so your uncle's cousin's neighbour's friend had a brother who found an old ISA ethernet card in the AT case he was using as a cage for his son's pet hampster. Somehow you ended up with the card and want to try and use it with linux, but nobody has a clue what the card is and there isn't any documentation.

First of all, look for any obvious model numbers that might give a clue. Any model number that contains 2000 will most likely be a NE2000 clone. Any cards with 8003 or 8013 on them somewhere will be Western/Digital WD80x3 cards or SMC Elite cards or clones of them.

5.39.1 Identifying the Network Interface Controller

Look for the biggest chip on the card. This will be the network controller (NIC) itself, and most can be identified by the part number. If you know which NIC is on the card, the following might be able to help you figure out what card it is.

Probably still the most common NIC is the National Semiconductor DP8390 aka NS32490 aka DP83901 aka DP83902 aka DP83905 aka DP83907. And those are just the ones made by National! Other companies such as Winbond and UMC make DP8390 and DP83905 clone parts, such as the Winbond 89c904 (DP83905 clone) and the UMC 9090. If the card has some form of 8390 on it, then chances are it is a ne1000 or ne2000 clone card. The second most common 8390 based card are wd80x3 cards and clones. Cards with a DP83905 can be configured to be an ne2000 *or* a wd8013. Never versions of the genuine wd80x3 and SMC Elite cards have an 83c690 in place of the original DP8390. The SMC Ultra cards have an 83c790, and use a slightly different driver than the wd80x3 cards. The SMC EtherEZ cards have an 83c795, and use the same driver as the SMC Ultra. All BNC cards based on some sort of 8390 or 8390 clone will usually have an 8392 (or 83c692, or XXX392) 16 pin DIP chip very close to the BNC connector.

Another common NIC found on older cards is the Intel i82586. Cards having this NIC include the 3c505, 3c507, 3c523, Intel EtherExpress-ISA, Microdyne Exos-205T, and the Racal-Interlan NI5210.

The original AMD LANCE NIC was numbered AM7990, and newer revisions include the 79c960, 79c961, 79c965, 79c970, and 79c974. Most cards with one of the above will work with the Linux LANCE driver, with the exception of the old Racal-Interlan NI6510 cards that have their own driver.

Newer PCI cards having a DEC 21040, 21041, 21140, or similar number on the NIC should be able to use the linux tulip or de4x5 driver.

Other PCI cards having a big chip marked RTL8029 are ne2000 clone cards, and the ne driver in linux version v2.0 and up should automatically detect these cards at boot.

5.39.2   Identifying the Ethernet Address

Each ethernet card has its own six byte address that is unique to that card. The first three bytes of that address are the same for each card made by that particular manufacturer. For example all SMC cards start with `00:00:c0`. The last three are assigned by the manufacturer uniquely to each individual card as they are produced.

If your card has a sticker on it giving all six bits of its address, you can look up the vendor from the first three. However it is more common to see only the last three bytes printed onto a sticker attached to a socketed PROM, which tells you nothing.

You can determine which vendors have which assigned addresses from RFC-1340. Apparently there is a more up to date listing available in various places as well. Try a WWW or FTP search for `EtherNet-codes` or `Ethernet-codes` and you will find something.

5.39.3   Tips on Trying to Use an Unknown Card

If you are still not sure what the card is, but have at least narrowed it down some, then you can build a kernel with a whole bunch of drivers included, and see if any of them autodetect the card at boot.

If the kernel doesn't detect the card, it may be that the card is not configured to one of the addresses that the driver probes when looking for a card. In this case, you might want to try getting `scanport.tar.gz` from your local linux ftp site, and see if that can locate where your card is jumpered for. It scans ISA i/o space from 0x100 to 0x3ff looking for devices that aren't registered in `/proc/ioports`. If it finds an unknown device starting at some particular address, you can then explicity point the ethernet probes at that address with an `ether=` boot argument.

If you manage to get the card detected, you can then usually figure out the unknown jumpers by changing them one at a time and seeing at what i/o base and IRQ that the card is detected at. The IRQ settings can also usually be determined by following the traces on the back of the card to where the jumpers are soldered through. Counting the 'gold fingers' on the backside, from the end of the card with the metal bracket, you have IRQ 9, 7, 6, 5, 4, 3, 10, 11, 12, 15, 14 at fingers 4, 21, 22, 23, 24, 25, 34, 35, 36, 37, 38 respectively. Eight bit cards only have up to finger 31.

Jumpers that appear to do nothing usually are for selecting the memory address of an optional boot ROM. Other jumpers that are located near the BNC or RJ-45 or AUI connectors are usually to select the output media. These are also typically near the 'black box' voltage converters marked YCL, Valor, or Fil-Mag.

A nice collection of jumper settings for various cards can be found at the following URL: *Ethercard Settings* `<http://www.syd.dit.csiro.au/staff/ken/personal/NIC/>`

5.40   Drivers for Non-Ethernet Devices

There are a few other drivers that are in the linux source that present an *ethernet-like* device to network programs, while not really being ethernet. These are briefly listed here for completeness.

`dummy.c` - The purpose of this driver is to provide a device to point a route through, but not to actually transmit packets.

`eql.c` - Load Equalizer, enslaves multiple devices (usually modems) and balances the Tx load across them while presenting a single device to the network programs.

`ibmtr.c` - IBM Token Ring, which is not really ethernet. Broken-Ring requires source routing and other uglies.

`loopback.c` - Loopback device, for which all packets from you machine and destined for your own machine go. It essentially just moves the packet off the Tx queue and onto the Rx queue.

`pi2.c` - Ottawa Amateur Radio Club PI and PI2 interface.

`plip.c` - Parallel Line Internet Protocol, allows two computers to send packets to each other over two joined parallel ports in a point-to-point fashion.

`ppp.c` - Point-to-Point Protocol (RFC1331), for the Transmission of Multi-protocol Datagrams over a Point-to-Point Link (again usually modems).

`slip.c` - Serial Line Internet Protocol, allows two computers to send packets to each other over two joined serial ports (usually via modems) in a point-to-point fashion.

`tunnel.c` - Provides an IP tunnel through which you can tunnel network traffic transparently across subnets

`wavelan.c` - An Ethernet-like radio transceiver controlled by the Intel 82586 coprocessor which is used on other ethercards such as the Intel EtherExpress.

6   Cables, Coax, Twisted Pair

If you are starting a network from scratch, it's considerably less expensive to use thin ethernet, RG58 co-ax cable with BNC connectors, than old-fashioned thick ethernet, RG-5 cable with N connectors, or 10baseT, twisted pair telco-style cables with RJ-45 eight wire 'phone' connectors. See 2.7 (Type of cable...) for an introductory look at cables.

Also note that the FAQ from *comp.dcom.lans.ethernet* has a lot of useful information on cables and such. Look in *Usenet FAQs* `<ftp://rtfm.mit.edu/pub/usenet-by-hierarchy/>` for the FAQ for that newsgroup.

6.1   Thin Ethernet (thinnet)

Thin ethernet is the 'ether of choice'. The cable is inexpensive. If you are making your own cables solid-core RG58A is $0.27/m. and stranded RG58AU is $0.45/m. Twist-on BNC connectors are < $2 ea., and other misc. pieces are similarly inexpensive. It is essential that you properly terminate each end of the cable with 50 ohm terminators, so budget $2 ea. for a pair. It's also vital that your cable have no 'stubs' – the 'T' connectors must be attached directly to the ethercards.

The only drawback is that if you have a big loop of machines connected together, and some bonehead breaks the loop by taking one cable off the side of his tee, the whole network goes down because it sees an infinite impedance (open circuit) instead of the required 50 ohm termination. Note that you can remove the tee piece from the card itself without killing the whole subnet, as long as you don't remove the cables from the tee itself. Of course this will disturb the machine that you pull the actual tee off of. 8-) And if you are doing a small network of two machines, you *still* need the tees and the 50 ohm terminators – you *can't* just cable them together!

Note that there are a few cards out there with 'on-board termination'. These cards have a jumper which when closed, puts a 50 ohm resistor across the BNC input. With these cards, you can use a BNC T and terminator like normal, or put the cable directly onto the card and close the jumper to enable the on-board termination.

There are also some fancy cable systems which *look like* a single lead going to the card, but the lead is actually a loop, with the two runs of cable laying side-by-side covered by an outer sheath, giving the lead an oval shaped cross-section. At the turnaround point of the loop, a BNC connector is spliced in which connects to your card. So you have the equivalent of two runs of cable and a BNC T, but in this case, it is impossible for the user to remove a cable from one side of the T and disturb the network.

6.2   Twisted Pair

Twisted pair networks require active hubs, which start around $200, and the raw cable cost can actually be higher than thinnet. They are usually sold using the claim that you can use your existing telephone wiring, but it's a rare installation where that turns out to be the case. The claim that you can upgrade to higher speeds is also suspect, as most proposed schemes use higher-grade (read $$) cable and more sophisticated termination ($$$) than you would likely install on speculation.

New gizmos are floating around which allow you to daisy-chain machines together, and the like. For example, Farallon sells EtherWave adaptors and transceivers. This device allows multiple 10baseT devices to be daisy-chained. They also sell a 3c509 clone that includes the EtherWave transceiver. The drawback is that it's more expensive and less reliable than a cheap ($100-$150) mini-hub and another ethercard. You probably should either go for the hub approach or switch over to 10base2 thinnet.

On the other hand, hubs are rapidly dropping in price, all 100Mb/sec ethernet proposals use twisted pair, and most new business installations use twisted pair. (This is probably to avoid the problem with idiots messing with the BNC's as described above.)

Also, Russ Nelson adds that 'New installations should use Category 5 wiring. Anything else is a waste of your installer's time, as 100Base-whatever is going to require Cat 5.'

If you are only connecting two machines, it is possible to avoid using a hub, by swapping the Rx and Tx pairs (1-2 and 3-6).

If you hold the RJ-45 connector facing you (as if you were going to plug it into your mouth) with the lock tab on the top, then the pins are numbered 1 to 8 from left to right. The pin usage is as follows:

```
Pin Number        Assignment
----------        ----------
1                 Output Data (+)
2                 Output Data (-)
3                 Input Data (+)
4                 Reserved for Telephone use
5                 Reserved for Telephone use
6                 Input Data (-)
7                 Reserved for Telephone use
8                 Reserved for Telephone use
```

If you want to make a cable, the following should spell it out for you. Differential signal pairs must be on the same twisted pair to get the required minimal impedance/loss of a UTP cable. If you look at the above table, you will see that 1+2 and 3+6 are the two sets of differential signal pairs. Not 1+3 and 2+6 !!!!!! At 10MHz, with short lengths, you *may* get away with such errors, if it is only over a short length. Don't even think about it at 100MHz.

For a normal patch cord, with ends 'A' and 'B', you want straight through pin-to-pin mapping, with the input and output each using a pair of twisted wires (for impedance issues). That means 1A goes to 1B, 2A goes to 2B, 3A goes to 3B and 6A goes to 6B. The wires joining 1A-1B and 2A-2B must be a twisted pair. Also the wires joining 3A-3B and 6A-6B must be another twisted pair.

Now if you don't have a hub, and want to make a 'null cable', what you want to do is make the input of 'A' be the output of 'B' and the output of 'A' be the input of 'B', without changing the polarity. Tha means connecting 1A to 3B (out+ A to in+ B) and 2A to 6B (out- A to in- B). These two wires must be a twisted pair. They carry what card/plug 'A' considers output, and what is seen as input for card/plug 'B'. Then connect 3A to 1B (in+ A to out+ B) and also connect 6A to 2B (in- A to out- B). These second two must also be a twisted pair. They carry what card/plug 'A' considers input, and what card/plug 'B' considers output.

So, if you consider a normal patch cord, chop one end off of it, swap the places of the Rx and Tx twisted pairs into the new plug, and crimp it down, you then have a 'null' cable. Nothing complicated. You just want to feed the Tx signal of one card into the Rx of the second and vice versa.

Note that before 10BaseT was ratified as a standard, there existed other network formats using RJ-45 connectors, and the same wiring scheme as above. Examples are SynOptics's LattisNet, and AT&T's StarLAN. In some cases, (as with early 3C503 cards) you could set jumpers to get the card to talk to hubs of different types, but in most cases cards designed for these older types of networks will not work with standard 10BaseT networks/hubs. (Note that if the cards also have an AUI port, then there is no reason as to why you can't use that, combined with an AUI to 10BaseT transceiver.)

6.3   Thick Ethernet

Thick ethernet is mostly obsolete, and is usually used only to remain compatible with an existing implementation. You can stretch the rules and connect short spans of thick and thin ethernet together with a passive \$3 N-to-BNC connector, and that's often the best solution to expanding an existing thicknet. A correct (but expensive) solution is to use a repeater in this case.

7   Software Configuration and Card Diagnostics

In most cases, if the configuration is done by software, and stored in an EEPROM, you will usually have to boot DOS, and use the supplied DOS program to set the cards IRQ, I/O, mem_addr and whatnot. Besides, hopefully it is something you will only be setting once. If you don't have the DOS software for your card, try looking on the WWW site of your card manufacturer. If you don't know the site name, take a guess at it, i.e. 'www.my_vendor.com' where 'my_vendor' is the name of your card manufacturer. This works for SMC, 3Com, and many *many* other manufacturers.

There are some cards for which Linux versions of the config utils exist, and they are listed here. Donald has written a few small card diagnostic programs that run under Linux. Most of these are a result of debugging tools that he has created while writing the various drivers. Don't expect fancy menu-driven interfaces. You will have to read the source code to use most of these. Even if your particular card doesn't have a corresponding diagnostic, you can still get some information just by typing `cat /proc/net/dev` – assuming that your card was at least detected at boot.

In either case, you will have to run most of these programs as root (to allow I/O to the ports) and you probably want to shut down the ethercard before doing so by typing `ifconfig eth0 down` (Note: replace `eth0` with `atp0` or whatever when appropriate.)

7.1   Configuration Programs for Ethernet Cards

7.1.1   WD80x3 Cards

For people with wd80x3 cards, there is the program `wdsetup` which can be found in `wdsetup-0.6a.tar.gz` on Linux ftp sites. I am not sure if it is being actively maintained or not, as it has not been updated for quite a while. If it works fine for you then great, if not, use the DOS version that you should have got with your card. If you don't have the DOS version, you will be glad to know that the SMC setup/driver disks are available at SMC's ftp site. Of course, you *have* to have an EEPROM card to use this utility. Old, *old* wd8003 cards, and some wd8013 clones use jumpers to set up the card instead.

7.1.2   Digital / DEC Cards

The Digital EtherWorks 3 card can be configured in a similar fashion to the DOS program NICSETUP.EXE. David C. Davies wrote this and other tools for the EtherWorks 3 in conjunction with the driver. Look on sunsite.unc.edu in the directory /pub/linux/system/Network/management for the file that is named ewrk3tools-X.XX.tar.gz.

7.1.3   NE2000+ or AT/LANTIC Cards

Some Nat Semi DP83905 implementations (such as the AT/LANTIC and the NE2000+) are software configurable. (Note that these cards can also emulate a wd8013 card!) You can get the file /pub/linux/setup/atlantic.c from Donald's ftp server, cesdis.gsfc.nasa.gov to configure this card. In addition, the configuration programs for the Kingston DP83905 cards seem to work with all cards, as they don't check for a vendor specific address before allowing you to use them. Follow the following URL: *Kingston Software* <http://www.kingston.com/download/etherx/etherx.htm> and get 20XX12.EXE and INFOSET.EXE.

Be careful when configuring NE2000+ cards, as you can give them bad setting values which can cause problems. A typical example is accidentally enabling the boot ROM in the EEPROM (even if no ROM is installed) to a setting that conflicts with the VGA card. The result is a computer that just beeps at you (AMI beep eight times for VGA failure) when you turn it on and nothing appears on the screen.

You can typically recover from this by doing the following: Remove the card from the machine, and then boot and enter the CMOS setup. Change the 'Display Adapter' to 'Not Installed' and change the default boot drive to 'A:' (your floppy drive). Also change the 'Wait for F1 if any Error' to 'Disabled'. This way, the computer should boot without user intervention. Now create a bootable DOS floppy ('format a: /s /u') and copy the program default.exe from the 20XX12.EXE archive above onto that floppy. Then type echo default > a:autoexec.bat so that the program to set the card back to sane defaults will be run automatically when you boot from this floppy. Shut the machine off, re-install the ne2000+ card, insert your new boot floppy, and power it back up. It will still probably beep at you, but eventually you should see the floppy light come on as it boots from the floppy. Wait a minute or two for the floppy to stop, indicating that it has finished running the default.exe program, and then power down your computer. When you then turn it on again, you should hopefully have a working display again, allowing you to change your CMOS settings back, and to change the card's EEPROM settings back to the values you want.

Note that if you don't have DOS handy, you can do the whole method above with a linux boot disk that automatically runs Donald's atlantic program (with the right command line switches) instead of a DOS boot disk that automatically runs the default.exe program.

7.1.4   3Com Cards

The 3Com Etherlink III family of cards (i.e. 3c5x9) can be configured by using another config utility from Donald. You can get the file /pub/linux/setup/3c5x9setup.c from Donald's ftp server, cesdis.gsfc.nasa.gov to configure these cards. (Note that the DOS 3c5x9B config utility may have more options pertaining to the new "B" series of the Etherlink III family.)

7.2   Diagnostic Programs for Ethernet Cards

Any of the diagnostic programs that Donald has written can be obtained from this URL.

Ethercard Diagnostics <http://cesdis.gsfc.nasa.gov/pub/linux/diag/diagnostic.html>

Allied Telesis AT1700 – look for the file /pub/linux/diag/at1700.c on cesdis.gsfc.nasa.gov.

Cabletron E21XX – look for the file /pub/linux/diag/e21.c on cesdis.gsfc.nasa.gov.

HP PCLAN+ – look for the file /pub/linux/diag/hp+.c on cesdis.gsfc.nasa.gov.

Intel EtherExpress – look for the file /pub/linux/diag/eexpress.c on cesdis.gsfc.nasa.gov.

NE2000 cards – look for the file /pub/linux/diag/ne2k.c on cesdis.gsfc.nasa.gov. There is also a PCI version for the now common NE2000-PCI clones.

RealTek (ATP) Pocket adaptor – look for the file /pub/linux/diag/atp-diag.c on cesdis.gsfc.nasa.gov.

All Other Cards – try typing cat /proc/net/dev and dmesg to see what useful info the kernel has on the card in question.

8   Technical Information

For those who want to play with the present drivers, or try to make up their own driver for a card that is presently unsupported, this information should be useful. If you do not fall into this category, then perhaps you will want to skip this section.

8.1   Probed Addresses

While trying to determine what ethernet card is there, the following addresses are autoprobed, assuming the type and specs of the card have not been set in the kernel. The file names below are in /usr/src/linux/drivers/net/

3c501.c	0x280, 0x300
3c503.c:	0x300, 0x310, 0x330, 0x350, 0x250, 0x280, 0x2a0, 0x2e0
3c505.c:	0x300, 0x280, 0x310
3c507.c:	0x300, 0x320, 0x340, 0x280
3c509.c:	Special ID Port probe
apricot.c	0x300
at1700.c:	0x300, 0x280, 0x380, 0x320, 0x340, 0x260, 0x2a0, 0x240
atp.c:	0x378, 0x278, 0x3bc
depca.c	0x300, 0x200
de600.c:	0x378
de620.c:	0x378
eexpress.c:	0x300, 0x270, 0x320, 0x340
hp.c:	0x300, 0x320, 0x340, 0x280, 0x2C0, 0x200, 0x240
hp-plus.c	0x200, 0x240, 0x280, 0x2C0, 0x300, 0x320, 0x340
lance.c:	0x300, 0x320, 0x340, 0x360
ne.c:	0x300, 0x280, 0x320, 0x340, 0x360
ni52.c	0x300, 0x280, 0x360, 0x320, 0x340
ni65.c	0x300, 0x320, 0x340, 0x360
smc-ultra.c:	0x200, 0x220, 0x240, 0x280, 0x300, 0x340, 0x380
wd.c:	0x300, 0x280, 0x380, 0x240

There are some NE2000 clone ethercards out there that are waiting black holes for autoprobe drivers. While many NE2000 clones are safe until they are enabled, some can't be reset to a safe mode. These dangerous ethercards will hang any I/O access to their 'dataports'. The typical dangerous locations are:

Ethercard jumpered base	Dangerous locations (base + 0x10 - 0x1f)
0x300 *	0x310-0x317
0x320	0x330-0x337
0x340	0x350-0x357
0x360	0x370-0x377

* The 0x300 location is the traditional place to put an ethercard, but it's also a popular place to put other devices (often SCSI controllers). The 0x320 location is often the next one chosen, but that's bad for for the AHA1542 driver probe. The 0x360 location is bad, because it conflicts with the parallel port at 0x378. If you have two IDE controllers, or two floppy controlers, then 0x360 is also a bad choice, as a NE2000 card will clobber them as well.

Note that kernels > 1.1.7X keep a log of who uses which i/o ports, and will not let a driver use i/o ports registered by an earlier driver. This may result in probes silently failing. You can view who is using what i/o ports by typing `cat /proc/ioports` if you have the proc filesystem enabled.

To avoid these lurking ethercards, here are the things you can do:

- Probe for the device's BIOS in memory space. This is easy and always safe, but it only works for cards that always have BIOSes, like primary SCSI controllers.

- Avoid probing any of the above locations until you think you've located your device. The NE2000 clones have a reset range from <base>+0x18 to <base>+0x1f that will read as 0xff, so probe there first if possible. It's also safe to probe in the 8390 space at <base>+0x00 - <base>+0x0f, but that area will return quasi-random values

- If you must probe in the dangerous range, for instance if your target device has only a few port locations, first check that there isn't an NE2000 there. You can see how to do this by looking at the probe code in /usr/src/linux/net/inet/ne.c

- Use the 'reserve' boot time argument to protect volatile areas from being probed. See the information on using boot time arguments with LILO in 10.1.2 (The reserve command)

8.2 Writing a Driver

The only thing that one needs to use an ethernet card with Linux is the appropriate driver. For this, it is essential that the manufacturer will release the technical programming information to the general public without you (or anyone) having to sign your life away. A good guide for the likelihood of getting documentation (or, if you aren't writing code, the likelihood that someone else will write that driver you really, really need) is the availability of the Crynwr (nee Clarkson) packet driver. Russ Nelson runs this operation, and has been very helpful in supporting the development of drivers for Linux. *Net-surfers* can try this URL to look up Russ' software.

Russ Nelson's Packet Drivers <http://www.crynwr.com/crynwr/home.html>

Given the documentation, you can write a driver for your card and use it for Linux (at least in theory). Keep in mind that some old hardware that was designed for XT type machines will not function very well in a multitasking environment such as Linux. Use of these will lead to major problems if your network sees a reasonable amount of traffic.

Most cards come with drivers for MS-DOS interfaces such as NDIS and ODI, but these are useless for Linux. Many people have suggested directly linking them in or automatic translation, but this is nearly impossible. The MS-DOS drivers expect to be in 16 bit mode and hook into 'software interrupts', both incompatible with the Linux kernel. This incompatibility is actually a feature, as some Linux drivers are considerably better than their MS-DOS counterparts. The '8390' series drivers, for instance, use ping-pong transmit buffers, which are only now being introduced in the MS-DOS world.

(Ping-pong Tx buffers means using at least 2 max-size packet buffers for Tx packets. One is loaded while the card is transmitting the other. The second is then sent as soon as the first finished, and so on. In this way, most cards are able to continuously send back-to-back packets onto the wire.)

OK. So you have decided that you want to write a driver for the Foobar Ethernet card, as you have the programming information, and it hasn't been done yet. (...these are the two main requirements ;-) You should start with the skeleton network driver that is provided with the Linux kernel source tree. It can be found in the file /usr/src/linux/drivers/net/skeleton.c in all recent kernels. Also have a look at the Kernel Hackers Guide, at the following URL: *KHG* <http://www.redhat.com:8080/HyperNews/get/khg.html>

8.3 Driver interface to the kernel

Here are some notes on the functions that you would have to write if creating a new driver. Reading this in conjunction with the above skeleton driver may help clear things up.

8.3.1 Probe

Called at boot to check for existence of card. Best if it can check un-obtrsively by reading from memory, etc. Can also read from i/o ports. Initial writing to i/o ports in a probe is *not good* as it may kill another device. Some device initialization is usually done here (allocating i/o space, IRQs,filling in the dev->??? fields etc.) You need to know what io ports/mem the card can be configured to, how to enable shared memory (if used) and how to select/enable interrupt generation, etc.

8.3.2 Interrupt handler

Called by the kernel when the card posts an interrupt. This has the job of determining why the card posted an interrupt, and acting accordingly. Usual interrupt conditions are data to be rec'd, transmit completed, error conditions being reported. You need to know any relevant interrupt status bits so that you can act accordingly.

8.3.3 Transmit function

Linked to dev->hard_start_xmit() and is called by the kernel when there is some data that the kernel wants to put out over the device. This puts the data onto the card and triggers the transmit. You need to know how to bundle the data and how to get it onto the card (shared memory copy, PIO transfer, DMA?) and in the right place on the card. Then you need to know how to tell the card to send the data down the wire, and (possibly) post an interrupt when done. When the hardware can't accept additional packets it should set the dev->tbusy flag. When additional room is available, usually during a transmit-complete interrupt, dev->tbusy should be cleared and the higher levels informed with mark_bh(INET_BH).

8.3.4 Receive function

Called by the kernel interrupt handler when the card reports that there is data on the card. It pulls the data off the card, packages it into a sk_buff and lets the kernel know the data is there for it by doing a netif_rx(sk_buff). You need to know how to enable interrupt generation upon Rx of data, how to check any relevant Rx status bits, and how to get that data off the card (again sh mem, PIO, DMA, etc.)

8.3.5   Open function

linked to dev->open and called by the networking layers when somebody does `ifconfig eth0 up` - this puts the device on line and enables it for Rx/Tx of data. Any special initialization incantations that were not done in the probe sequence (enabling IRQ generation, etc.) would go in here.

8.3.6   Close function (optional)

This puts the card in a sane state when someone does `ifconfig eth0 down`. It should free the IRQs and DMA channels if the hardware permits, and turn off anything that will save power (like the transceiver).

8.3.7   Miscellaneous functions

Things like a reset function, so that if things go south, the driver can try resetting the card as a last ditch effort. Usually done when a Tx times out or similar. Also a function to read the statistics registers of the card if so equipped.

8.4   Interrupts and Linux

There are two kinds of interrupt handlers in Linux: fast ones and slow ones. You decide what kind you are installing by the flags you pass to irqaction(). The fast ones, such as the serial interrupt handler, run with _all_ interrupts disabled. The normal interrupt handlers, such as the one for ethercard drivers, runs with other interrupts enabled.

There is a two-level interrupt structure. The 'fast' part handles the device register, removes the packets, and perhaps sets a flag. After it is done, and interrupts are re-enabled, the slow part is run if the flag is set.

The flag between the two parts is set by:

```
mark_bh(INET_BH);
```

Usually this flag is set within dev_rint() during a received-packet interrupt, and set directly by the device driver during a transmit-complete interrupt.

You might wonder why all interrupt handlers cannot run in 'normal mode' with other interrupts enabled. Ross Biro uses this scenario to illustrate the problem:

- You get a serial interrupt, and start processing it. The serial interrupt is now masked.
- You get a network interrupt, and you start transferring a maximum-sized 1500 byte packet from the card.
- Another character comes in, but this time the interrupts are masked!

The 'fast' interrupt structure solves this problem by allowing bounded-time interrupt handlers to run without the risk of leaving their interrupt lines masked by another interrupt request.

There is an additional distinction between fast and slow interrupt handlers – the arguments passed to the handler. A 'slow' handler is defined as

```
static void
handle_interrupt(int reg_ptr)
{
```

```
                    int irq = -(((struct pt_regs *)reg_ptr)->orig_eax+2);
                    struct device *dev = irq2dev_map[irq];
        ...
```

While a fast handler gets the interrupt number directly

```
            static void
            handle_fast_interrupt(int irq)
            {
        ...
```

A final aspect of network performance is latency. The only board that really addresses this is the 3c509, which allows a predictive interrupt to be posted. It provides an interrupt response timer so that the driver can fine-tune how early an interrupt is generated.

8.5   Programming the Intel chips (i82586 and i82593)

These chips are used on a number of cards, namely the 3c507 ('86), the Intel EtherExpress 16 ('86), Microdyne's exos205t ('86), the Z-Note ('93), and the Racal-Interlan ni5210 ('86).

Russ Nelson writes: 'Most boards based on the 82586 can reuse quite a bit of their code. More, in fact, than the 8390-based adapters. There are only three differences between them:

- The code to get the Ethernet address,
- The code to trigger CA on the 82586, and
- The code to reset the 82586.

The Intel EtherExpress 16 is an exception, as it I/O maps the 82586. Yes, I/O maps it. Fairly clunky, but it works.

Garrett Wollman did an AT&T driver for BSD that uses the BSD copyright. The latest version I have (Sep '92) only uses a single transmit buffer. You can and should do better than this if you've got the memory. The AT&T and 3c507 adapters do; the ni5210 doesn't.

The people at Intel gave me a very big clue on how you queue up multiple transmit packets. You set up a list of NOP-> XMIT-> NOP-> XMIT-> NOP-> XMIT-> beginning) blocks, then you set the 'next' pointer of all the NOP blocks to themselves. Now you start the command unit on this chain. It continually processes the first NOP block. To transmit a packet, you stuff it into the next transmit block, then point the NOP to it. To transmit the next packet, you stuff the next transmit block and point the previous NOP to *it*. In this way, you don't have to wait for the previous transmit to finish, you can queue up multiple packets without any ambiguity as to whether it got accepted, and you can avoid the command unit start-up delay.'

8.6   Technical information from 3Com

If you are interested in working on drivers for 3Com cards, you can get technical documentation from 3Com. Cameron has been kind enough to tell us how to go about it below:

3Com's Ethernet Adapters are documented for driver writers in our 'Technical References' (TRs). These manuals describe the programmer interfaces to the boards but they don't talk about the diagnostics, installation programs, etc that end users can see.

The Network Adapter Division marketing department has the TRs to give away. To keep this program efficient, we centralized it in a thing called 'CardFacts.' CardFacts is an automated phone system. You call it with a touch-tone phone and it faxes you stuff. To get a TR, call CardFacts at 408-727-7021. Ask it for Developer's Order Form, document number 9070. Have your fax number ready when you call. Fill out the order form and fax it to 408-764-5004. Manuals are shipped by Federal Express 2nd Day Service.

After you get a manual, if you still can't figure out how to program the board, try our 'CardBoard' BBS at 1-800-876-3266, and if you can't do that, write Andy_Chan@3Mail.3com.com and ask him for alternatives. If you have a real stumper that nobody has figured out yet, the fellow who needs to know about it is Steve_Lebus@3Mail.3com.com.

There are people here who think we are too free with the manuals, and they are looking for evidence that the system is too expensive, or takes too much time and effort. That's why it's important to try to use CardFacts *before* you start calling and mailing the people I named here.

There are even people who think we should be like Diamond and Xircom, requiring tight 'partnership' with driver writers to prevent poorly performing drivers from getting written. So far, 3Com customers have been really good about this, and there's no problem with the level of requests we've been getting. We need your continued cooperation and restraint to keep it that way.

```
Cameron Spitzer, 408-764-6339
3Com NAD
Santa Clara
work: camerons@nad.3com.com
home: cls@truffula.sj.ca.us
```

8.7   Notes on AMD PCnet / LANCE Based cards

The AMD LANCE (Local Area Network Controller for Ethernet) was the original offering, and has since been replaced by the 'PCnet-ISA' chip, otherwise known as the 79C960. A relatively new chip from AMD, the 79C960, is the heart of many new cards being released at present. Note that the name 'LANCE' has stuck, and some people will refer to the new chip by the old name. Dave Roberts of the Network Products Division of AMD was kind enough to contribute the following information regarding this chip:

'As for the architecture itself, AMD developed it originally and reduced it to a single chip – the PCnet(tm)-ISA – over a year ago. It's been selling like hotcakes ever since.

Functionally, it is equivalent to a NE1500. The register set is identical to the old LANCE with the 1500/2100 architecture additions. Older 1500/2100 drivers will work on the PCnet-ISA. The NE1500 and NE2100 architecture is basically the same. Initially Novell called it the 2100, but then tried to distinguish between coax and 10BASE-T cards. Anything that was 10BASE-T only was to be numbered in the 1500 range. That's the only difference.

Many companies offer PCnet-ISA based products, including HP, Racal-Datacom, Allied Telesis, Boca Research, Kingston Technology, etc. The cards are basically the same except that some manufacturers have added 'jumperless' features that allow the card to be configured in software. Most have not. AMD offers a standard design package for a card that uses the PCnet-ISA and many manufacturers use our design without change. What this means is that anybody who wants to write drivers for most PCnet-ISA based cards can just get the data-sheet from AMD. Call our literature distribution center at (800)222-9323 and ask for the Am79C960, PCnet-ISA data sheet. It's free.

A quick way to understand whether the card is a 'stock' card is to just look at it. If it's stock, it should just have one large chip on it, a crystal, a small IEEE address PROM, possibly a socket for a boot ROM, and a connector (1, 2, or 3, depending on the media options offered). Note that if it's a coax card, it will have some transceiver stuff built onto it as well, but that should be near the connector and away from the PCnet-ISA.'

There is also some info regarding the LANCE chip in the file lance.c which is included in the standard kernel.

A note to would-be card hackers is that different LANCE implementations do 'restart' in different ways. Some pick up where they left off in the ring, and others start right from the beginning of the ring, as if just initialised. This is a concern when setting the multicast list.

8.8 Multicast and Promiscuous Mode

Another one of the things Donald has worked on is implementing multicast and promiscuous mode hooks. All of the *released* (i.e. **not** ALPHA) ISA drivers now support promiscuous mode.

Donald writes: 'At first I was planning to do it while implementing either the /dev/* or DDI interface, but that's not really the correct way to do it. We should only enable multicast or promiscuous modes when something wants to look at the packets, and shut it down when that application is finished, neither of which is strongly related to when the hardware is opened or released.

I'll start by discussing promiscuous mode, which is conceptually easy to implement. For most hardware you only have to set a register bit, and from then on you get every packet on the wire. Well, it's almost that easy; for some hardware you have to shut the board (potentially dropping a few packet), reconfigure it, and then re-enable the ethercard. This is grungy and risky, but the alternative seems to be to have every application register before you open the ethercard at boot-time.

OK, so that's easy, so I'll move on something that's not quite so obvious: Multicast. It can be done two ways:

1. Use promiscuous mode, and a packet filter like the Berkeley packet filter (BPF). The BPF is a pattern matching stack language, where you write a program that picks out the addresses you are interested in. Its advantage is that it's very general and programmable. Its disadvantage is that there is no general way for the kernel to avoid turning on promiscuous mode and running every packet on the wire through every registered packet filter. See 8.9 (The Berkeley Packet Filter) for more info.

2. Using the built-in multicast filter that most etherchips have.

I guess I should list what a few ethercards/chips provide:

```
Chip/card   Promiscuous  Multicast filter
-----------------------------------------
Seeq8001/3c501 Yes       Binary filter (1)
3Com/3c509     Yes       Binary filter (1)
8390           Yes       Autodin II six bit hash (2) (3)
LANCE          Yes       Autodin II six bit hash (2) (3)
i82586         Yes       Hidden Autodin II six bit hash (2) (4)
```

1. These cards claim to have a filter, but it's a simple yes/no 'accept all multicast packets', or 'accept no multicast packets'.

2. AUTODIN II is the standard ethernet CRC (checksum) polynomial. In this scheme multicast addresses are hashed and looked up in a hash table. If the corresponding bit is enabled, this packet is accepted. Ethernet packets are laid out so that the hardware to do this is trivial – you just latch six (usually) bits from the CRC circuit (needed anyway for error checking) after the first six octets (the destination address), and use them as an index into the hash table (six bits – a 64-bit table).

3. These chips use the six bit hash, and must have the table computed and loaded by the host. This means the kernel must include the CRC code.

4. The 82586 uses the six bit hash internally, but it computes the hash table itself from a list of multicast addresses to accept.

Note that none of these chips do perfect filtering, and we still need a middle-level module to do the final filtering. Also note that in every case we must keep a complete list of accepted multicast addresses to recompute the hash table when it changes.

My first pass at device-level support is detailed in the outline driver skeleton.c

It looks like the following:

```
#ifdef HAVE_MULTICAST
static void set_multicast_list(struct device *dev, int num_addrs,
              void *addrs);
#endif
.
.

ethercard_open() {
...
#ifdef HAVE_MULTICAST
        dev->set_multicast_list = &set_multicast_list;
#endif
...


#ifdef HAVE_MULTICAST
/* Set or clear the multicast filter for this adaptor.
   num_addrs -- -1     Promiscuous mode, receive all packets
   num_addrs -- 0      Normal mode, clear multicast list
   num_addrs > 0       Multicast mode, receive normal and
        MC packets, and do best-effort filtering.
 */
static void
set_multicast_list(struct device *dev, int num_addrs, void *addrs)
{
...
```

Any comments, criticism, etc. are welcome.'

8.9   The Berkeley Packet Filter (BPF)

The general idea of the developers is that the BPF functionality should not be provided by the kernel, but should be in a (hopefully little-used) compatibility library.

For those not in the know: BPF (the Berkeley Packet Filter) is an mechanism for specifying to the kernel networking layers what packets you are interested in. It's implemented as a specialized stack language interpreter built into a low level of the networking code. An application passes a program written in this language to the kernel, and the kernel runs the program on each incoming packet. If the kernel has multiple BPF applications, each program is run on each packet.

The problem is that it's difficult to deduce what kind of packets the application is really interested in from the packet filter program, so the general solution is to always run the filter. Imagine a program that registers a BPF program to pick up a low data-rate stream sent to a multicast address. Most ethernet cards have a hardware multicast address filter implemented as a 64 entry hash table that ignores most unwanted multicast packets, so the capability exists to make this a very inexpensive operation. But with the BFP the kernel must switch the interface to promiscuous mode, receive _all_ packets, and run them through this filter. This is work, BTW, that's very difficult to account back to the process requesting the packets.

9   Networking with a Laptop/Notebook Computer

There are currently only a few ways to put your laptop on a network. You can use the SLIP code (and run at serial line speeds); you can buy one of the few laptops that come with a NE2000-compatible ethercard; you can get a notebook with a supported PCMCIA slot built-in; you can get a laptop with a docking station and plug in an ISA ethercard; or you can use a parallel port Ethernet adapter such as the D-Link DE-600.

9.1   Using SLIP

This is the cheapest solution, but by far the most difficult. Also, you will not get very high transmission rates. Since SLIP is not really related to ethernet cards, it will not be discussed further here. See the NET-2 Howto.

9.2   Built in NE2000

This solution severely limits your laptop choices and is fairly expensive. Be sure to read the specifications carefully, as you may find that you will have to buy an additional non-standard transceiver to actually put the machine on a network. A good idea might be to boot the notebook with a kernel that has ne2000 support, and make sure it gets detected and works before you lay down your cash.

9.3   PCMCIA Support

As this area of Linux development is fairly young, I'd suggest that you join the LAPTOPS mailing channel. See 10.3 (Mailing lists...) which describes how to join a mailing list channel.

Try and determine exactly what hardware you have (ie. card manufacturer, PCMCIA chip controller manufacturer) and then ask on the LAPTOPS channel. Regardless, don't expect things to be all that simple. Expect to have to fiddle around a bit, and patch kernels, etc. Maybe someday you will be able to type 'make config' 8-)

At present, the two PCMCIA chipsets that are supported are the Databook TCIC/2 and the intel i82365.

There is a number of programs on tsx-11.mit.edu in /pub/linux/packages/laptops/ that you may find useful. These range from PCMCIA Ethercard drivers to programs that communicate with the PCMCIA controller chip. Note that these drivers are usually tied to a specific PCMCIA chip (ie. the intel 82365 or the TCIC/2)

For NE2000 compatible cards, some people have had success with just configuring the card under DOS, and then booting linux from the DOS command prompt via `loadlin`.

For those that are *net-surfing* you can try:

Don's PCMCIA Stuff <http://cesdis.gsfc.nasa.gov/linux/pcmcia.html>

Anyway, the PCMCIA driver problem isn't specific to the Linux world. It's been a real disaster in the MS-DOS world. In that world people expect the hardware to work if they just follow the manual. They might not expect it to interoperate with any other hardware or software, or operate optimally, but they do expect that the software shipped with the product will function. Many PCMCIA adaptors don't even pass this test.

Things are looking up for Linux users that want PCMCIA support, as substantial progress is being made. Pioneering this effort is David Hinds. His latest PCMCIA support package can be obtained from `cb-iris.stanford.edu` in the directory `/pub/pcmcia/`. Look for a file like `pcmcia-cs-X.Y.Z.tgz` where X.Y.Z will be the latest version number. This is most likely uploaded to `tsx-11.mit.edu` as well.

Note that Donald's PCMCIA enabler works as a user-level process, and David Hinds' is a kernel-level solution. You may be best served by David's package as it is much more widely used.

9.4   ISA Ethercard in the Docking Station.

Docking stations for laptops typically cost about $250 and provide two full-size ISA slots, two serial and one parallel port. Most docking stations are powered off of the laptop's batteries, and a few allow adding extra batteries in the docking station if you use short ISA cards. You can add an inexpensive ethercard and enjoy full-speed ethernet performance.

9.5   Pocket / parallel port adaptors.

The 'pocket' ethernet adaptors may also fit your need. Until recently they actually costed more than a docking station and cheap ethercard, and most tie you down with a wall-brick power supply. At present, you can choose from the D-Link, or the RealTek adaptor. Most other companies treat the programming information as a trade secret, so support will likely be slow in coming. (if ever!) Xircom (see 5.36 (Xircom)) apparently are now releasing their specs, but nobody is currently working on a driver.

Note that the transfer speed will not be all that great (perhaps 200kB/s tops?) due to the limitations of the parallel port interface.

See 5.15.4 (DE-600 / DE-620) and 5.9.1 (RealTek) for supported pocket adaptors.

You can sometimes avoid the wall-brick with the adaptors by buying or making a cable that draws power from the laptop's keyboard port. (See 5.9.1 (keyboard power))

10   Miscellaneous.

Any other associated stuff that didn't fit in anywhere else gets dumped here. It may not be relevant, and it may not be of general interest but it is here anyway.

10.1   Passing Ethernet Arguments to the Kernel

Here are two generic kernel commands that can be passed to the kernel at boot time. This can be done with LILO, loadlin, or any other booting utility that accepts optional arguments.

For example, if the command was 'blah' and it expected 3 arguments (say 123, 456, and 789) then, with LILO, you would use:

```
LILO: linux blah=123,456,789
```

Note: PCI cards have their i/o and IRQ assigned by the BIOS at boot. This means that any boot time arguments for a PCI card's IRQ or i/o ports are usually ignored.

For more information on (and a complete list of) boot time arguments, please see the *BootPrompt-HOWTO* <http://sunsite.unc.edu/mdw/HOWTO/BootPrompt-HOWTO.html>

10.1.1 The `ether` command

In its most generic form, it looks something like this:

```
ether=IRQ,BASE_ADDR,PARAM_1,PARAM_2,NAME
```

All arguments are optional. The first non-numeric argument is taken as the NAME.

IRQ: Obvious. An IRQ value of '0' (usually the default) means to autoIRQ. It's a historical accident that the IRQ setting is first rather than the base_addr – this will be fixed whenever something else changes.

BASE_ADDR: Also obvious. A value of '0' (usually the default) means to probe a card-type-specific address list for an ethercard.

PARAM_1: It was orginally used as an override value for the memory start for a shared-memory ethercard, like the WD80*3. Some drivers use the low four bits of this value to set the debug message level. 0 – default, 1-7 – level 1..7, (7 is maximum verbosity) 8 – level 0 (no messages). Also, the LANCE driver uses the low four bits of this value to select the DMA channel. Otherwise it uses auto-DMA.

PARAM_2: The 3c503 driver uses this to select between the internal and external transceivers. 0 – default/internal, 1 – AUI external. The Cabletron E21XX card also uses the low 4 bits of PARAM_2 to select the output media. Otherwise it detects automatically.

NAME: Selects the network device the values refer to. The standard kernel uses the names 'eth0', 'eth1', 'eth2' and 'eth3' for bus-attached ethercards, and 'atp0' for the parallel port 'pocket' ethernet adaptor. The arcnet driver uses 'arc0' as its name. The default setting is for a single ethercard to be probed for as 'eth0'. Multiple cards can only be enabled by explicitly setting up their base address using these LILO parameters. The 1.0 kernel has LANCE-based ethercards as a special case. LILO arguments are ignored, and LANCE cards are always assigned 'eth<n>' names starting at 'eth0'. Additional non-LANCE ethercards must be explicitly assigned to 'eth<n+1>', and the usual 'eth0' probe disabled with something like 'ether=0,-1,eth0'. (Yes, this is bug.)

10.1.2 The `reserve` command

This next lilo command is used just like 'ether=' above, ie. it is appended to the name of the boot select specified in lilo.conf

```
reserve=IO-base,extent{,IO-base,extent...}
```

In some machines it may be necessary to prevent device drivers from checking for devices (auto-probing) in a specific region. This may be because of poorly designed hardware that causes the boot to *freeze* (such as some ethercards), hardware that is mistakenly identified, hardware whose state is changed by an earlier probe, or merely hardware you don't want the kernel to initialize.

The `reserve` boot-time argument addresses this problem by specifying an I/O port region that shouldn't be probed. That region is reserved in the kernel's port registration table as if a device has already been found in that region. Note that this mechanism shouldn't be necessary on most machines. Only when there is a problem or special case would it be necessary to use this.

The I/O ports in the specified region are protected against device probes. This was put in to be used when some driver was hanging on a NE2000, or misidentifying some other device as its own. A correct device driver shouldn't probe a reserved region, unless another boot argument explicitly specifies that it do so.

This implies that `reserve` will most often be used with some other boot argument. Hence if you specify a `reserve` region to protect a specific device, you must generally specify an explicit probe for that device. Most drivers ignore the port registration table if they are given an explicit address.

For example, the boot line

```
LILO: linux reserve=0x300,32 ether=0,0x300,eth0
```

keeps all device drivers except the ethercard drivers from probing 0x300-0x31f.

As usual with boot-time specifiers there is an 11 parameter limit, thus you can only specify 5 reserved regions per `reserve` keyword. Multiple `reserve` specifiers will work if you have an unusually complicated request.

10.2   Using the Ethernet Drivers as Modules

See the `insmod`(8) manual page for information on passing arguments to the module as it is being loaded. The command `lsmod` will show you what modules are loaded, and `rmmod` will remove them.

At present, all the modules are put in the subdirectory `modules` in your Linux kernel source tree (usually in the form of symbolic links). To actually generate the modules, you have to type `make modules` after you have finished building the kernel proper. Earlier kernels built them automatically, which wasn't fair to those compiling on 4MB 386sx-16 machines.

Most modules accept parameters like `io=0x340` and `irq=12` on the `insmod` command line. It is *STRONGLY ADVISED* that you supply these parameters to avoid probing for the card. Unlike PCI and EISA devices, there is no real safe way to do auto-probing for ISA devices, and so it should be avoided when using drivers as modules.

A list of all the parameters that each module accepts can be found in the file:

`/usr/src/linux/Documentation/networking/net-modules.txt`

It is recommended that you read that to find out what options you can use for your particular card.

Once you have figured out the arguments/options you are going to use, you can insert the module by typing as root:

```
insmod mod_name.o [io=val1[,val2,...]] [irq=val7[,val8,...]]
```

The comma separated value lists are used for modules that have the capability to handle multiple devices from a single module, such as all the 8390 drivers, and the PLIP driver.

Once a module is inserted, then you can use it just like normal, and give `ifconfig` commands. If you set up your networking at boot, then make sure your `/etc/rc*` files run the `insmod` command(s) before getting to the `ifconfig` command.

Also note that a *busy* module can't be removed. That means that you will have to `ifconfig eth0 down` (shut down the ethernet card) before you can remove the module(s).

10.2.1   8390 Based Cards as Modules

The present list of 8390 based drivers is: 3c503, ac3200, e2100, hp, hp-plus, ne, smc-ultra and wd. These cards were not supported as modules for kernel versions prior to 1.3.42. (This does not include some of the separately distributed PCMCIA drivers (e.g. de-650) that are also 8390 based, that have had module support for quite some time now.)

If you have an 8390 based card, you may have to insert *two* modules, 8390.o and then the module for your card. If 8390 support has been built into your kernel, then you will not need to insert the 8390 module. (8390 support is built in whenever an 8390 based card is selected to be built into the kernel.) Doing a `cat /proc/ksyms | grep 8390` will tell you if 8390 support is in your kernel.

For an 8390 based card, you will have to remove the card module before removing the 8390 module, as the 8390 module is used by the card module, and thus marked as *busy*.

The 8390 series of network drivers now support multiple card systems without reloading the same module multiple times (memory efficient!) This is done by specifying multiple comma separated values, such as:

```
insmod 3c503.o io=0x280,0x300,0x330,0x350 xcvr=0,1,0,1
```

The above would have the one module controlling four 3c503 cards, with card 2 and 4 using external transcievers.

It is *STRONGLY RECOMMENDED* that you supply "io=" instead of autoprobing. If an "io=" argument is not supplied, then the ISA 8390 drivers will complain about autoprobing being not recommended, and begrudgingly autoprobe for a *SINGLE CARD ONLY* – if you want to use multiple cards you *have* to supply an "io=0xNNN,0xQQQ,..." argument.

The ne module is an exception to the above. A NE2000 is essentially an 8390 chip, some bus glue and some RAM. Because of this, the ne probe is more invasive than the rest, and so at boot we make sure the ne probe is done last of all the 8390 cards (so that it won't trip over other 8390 based cards) With modules we can't ensure that all other non-ne 8390 cards have already been found. Because of this, the ne module *REQUIRES* an io=0xNNN argument passed in via insmod. It will *refuse* to autoprobe.

It is also worth noting that auto-IRQ probably isn't as reliable during the flurry of interrupt activity on a running machine. Cards such as the ne2000 that can't get the IRQ setting from an EEPROM or configuration register are probably best supplied with an `irq=M` argument as well. The file

`/usr/src/linux/Documentation/networking/net-modules.txt`

also lists how the interrupt settings are determined for the various cards if an `irq=N` value is not given.

10.3 Mailing Lists and the Linux Newsgroups

If you have questions about your ethernet card, please READ this document first. You may also want to join the NET channel of the Linux mailing lists by sending mail to majordomo@vger.rutgers.edu to get help with what lists are available, and how to join them.

Furthermore keep in mind that the NET channel is for development discussions only. General questions on how to configure your system should be directed to comp.os.linux.setup unless you are actively involved in the development of part of the networking for Linux. We ask that you *please* respect this general guideline for content.

Also, the news groups *comp.sys.ibm.pc.hardware.networking* and *comp.dcom.lans.ethernet* should be used for questions that are not Linux specific.

10.4 Related Documentation

Much of this info came from saved postings from the comp.os.linux groups, which shows that it is a valuable resource of information. Other useful information came from a bunch of small files by Donald himself. Of course, if you are setting up an Ethernet card, then you will want to read the NET-2 Howto so that you can actually configure the software you will use. Also, if you fancy yourself as a bit of a hacker, you can always scrounge some additional info from the driver source files as well. There is usually a paragraph or two in there describing any important points before any actual code starts..

For those looking for information that is not specific in any way to Linux (i.e. what is 10BaseT, what is AUI, what does a hub do, etc.) I strongly recommend the **Ethernet-FAQ** that is posted regularly to the newsgroup *comp.dcom.lans.ethernet*. You can grab it from RTFM which holds all the newsgroup FAQs at the following URL:

Usenet FAQs <ftp://rtfm.mit.edu/pub/usenet-by-hierarchy/>

You can also have a look at the 'Ethernet-HomePage' so to speak, which is at the following URL:

Ethernet-HomePage <http://wwwhost.ots.utexas.edu/ethernet/ethernet-home.html>

10.5   Contributors

Other people who have contributed (directly or indirectly) to the Ethernet-Howto are, in alphabetical order:

```
        Ross Biro              <bir7@leland.stanford.edu>
        Alan Cox               <iialan@www.linux.org.uk>
        David C. Davies        <davies@wanton.enet.dec.com>
        Bjorn Ekwall           <bj0rn@blox.se>
        David Hinds            <dhinds@allegro.stanford.edu>
        Michael Hipp           <mhipp@student.uni-tuebingen.de>
        Mike Jagdis            <jaggy@purplet.demon.co.uk>
        Duke Kamstra           <kamstra@ccmail.west.smc.com>
        Russell Nelson         <nelson@crynwr.com>
        Cameron Spitzer        <camerons@NAD.3Com.com>
        Dave Roberts           <david.roberts@amd.com>
        Glenn Talbott          <gt@hprnd.rose.hp.com>
```

These mail addresses are intentionally not 'mailto' links so as to protect these people from WWW 'spam-bot' filters. Many thanks to the above people, and all the other unmentioned testers out there.

10.6   Disclaimer and Copyright

This document is *not* gospel. However, it is probably the most up to date info that you will be able to find. Nobody is responsible for what happens to your hardware but yourself. If your ethercard or any other hardware goes up in smoke (...nearly impossible!) we take no responsibility. ie. THE AUTHORS ARE NOT RESPONSIBLE FOR ANY DAMAGES INCURRED DUE TO ACTIONS TAKEN BASED ON THE INFORMATION INCLUDED IN THIS DOCUMENT.

This document is Copyright (c) 1993-1997 by Paul Gortmaker. Permission is granted to make and distribute verbatim copies of this manual provided the copyright notice and this permission notice are preserved on all copies.

Permission is granted to copy and distribute modified versions of this document under the conditions for verbatim copying, provided that this copyright notice is included exactly as in the original, and that the entire resulting derived work is distributed under the terms of a permission notice identical to this one.

Permission is granted to copy and distribute translations of this document into another language, under the above conditions for modified versions.

If you are intending to incorporate this document into a published work, please make contact (vai e-mail) so that you can be supplied with the most up to date information available. In the past, out of date versions of the Linux HowTo documents have been published, which caused the developers undue grief from being plagued with questions that were already answered in the up to date versions.

10.7 Closing

If you have found any glaring typos, or outdated info in this document, please send an e-mail. It's getting big, and it is easy to overlook stuff. If you have e-mailed about a change, and it hasn't been included in the next version, please don't hesitate to send it again, as it might have got lost amongst the usual sea of SPAM and junk mail.

Thanks!

Firewalling and Proxy Server HOWTO

Mark Grennan, markg@netplus.net   v0.4, 8 November 1996

This document is designed to teach the basics of firewall systems and give you some detail on setting up both a filtering and proxy firewall on a Linux based PC. An HTML version of this document is available at *http://okcforum.org/~markg/Firewall-HOWTO.html*

Contents

1 Introduction

This original Firewall-HOWTO was written by David Rudder, **drig@execpc.com**. I'd like to thank him for allowing me to update his work.

Firewalls have gained great fame recently as the ultimate in Internet Security. Like most things that gain fame, with that fame has come misunderstanding. This HOWTO will go over the basics of what a firewall is, how to set one up, what proxy servers are, how to set up proxy servers, and the applications of this technology outside of the security realm.

1.1 Feedback

Any feedback is very welcome. **PLEASE REPORT ANY INACCURACIES IN THIS PAPER!!!** I am human, and prone to making mistakes. If you find any, fixing them is of my highest interest. I will try to answer all e-mail, but I am busy, so don't get insulted if I don't.

*My email address is **markg@netplus.net***

1.2   Disclaimer

I AM NOT RESPONSIBLE FOR ANY DAMAGES INCURRED DUE TO ACTIONS TAKEN BASED ON THIS DOCUMENT. This document is meant as an introduction to how firewalls and proxy servers work. I am not, nor do I pretend to be, a security expert. I am just some guy who has read to much and likes computers more than most people. Please, I am writing this to help get people acquainted with this subject, and I am not ready to stake my life on the accuracy of what is in here.

1.3   Copyright

Unless otherwise stated, Linux HOWTO documents are copyrighted by their respective authors. Linux HOWTO documents may be reproduced and distributed in whole or in part, in any medium physical or electronic, as long as this copyright notice is retained on all copies. Commercial redistribution is allowed and encouraged; however, the author would like to be notified of any such distributions.

All translations, derivative works, or aggregate works incorporating any Linux HOWTO documents must be covered under this copyright notice. That is, you may not produce a derivative work from a HOWTO and impose additional restrictions on its distribution. Exceptions to these rules may be granted under certain conditions; please contact the Linux HOWTO coordinator.

In short, we wish to promote dissemination of this information through as many channels as possible. However, we do wish to retain copyright on the HOWTO documents, and would like to be notified of any plans to redistribute the HOWTOs.

If you have any questions, please contact Mark Grennan at <markg@netplus.net>.

1.4   My Reasons for Writing This

Even though there were a lot of discussions on comp.os.linux.* over the past year about firewalling, I found it difficult to find the information I needed to setup a firewall. The original version of this HOWTO was helpful but still lacking. I hope this beefed up version of David Rudder's Firewall HOWTO will give everyone the information they need to create a functioning firewall in hours, not weeks.

I also feel I should return something to the Linux community.

1.5   TODO

- Give some instructions on how to setup the clients
- Find a good UDP proxy server that works with Linux

1.6   Further Readings

- The NET-2 HOWTO
- The Ethernet HOWTO
- The Multiple Ethernet Mini HOWTO
- Networking with Linux
- The PPP HOWTO

- TCP/IP Network Administrator's Guide by O'Reilly and Associates
- The Documentation for the TIS Firewall Toolkit

Trusted Information System's (TIS) web site has a great collection of documentation on firewalls and related meterial. **http://www.tis.com/**

Also, I am working on a security project called I am calling *Secure Linux*. On the *Secure Linux* web site I am gathering all the information, documemtation and programs you need to create a trusted Linux system. Email me if you would like information.

2   Understanding Firewalls

A firewall is a term used for a part of a car. In cars, firewalls are physical objects that separate the engine from the passengers. They are meant to protect the passenger in case the car's engine catches fire while still providing the driver access to the engine's controls.

A firewall in computers is a device that protects a private network from the public part (the internet as a whole).

The firewall computer, from now on named "firewall", can reach both the protected network and the internet. The protected network can't reach the internet, and the internet can not reach the protected network.

For someone to reach the internet from inside the protected network, they must telnet to firewall, and use the internet from there.

The simplest form of a firewall is a dual homed system. (a system with two network connections) If you can TRUST ALL your users, you can simple setup a Linux (compile it with IP forwarding/gatewaying turned OFF!) and give everyone accounts on it. The can then login to this system and telnet, FTP, read mail, and use any other service you provided. With this setup, the only computer on your private network that knows anything about the outside world is the firewall. The other system on your protected network dont even need a default route.

This needs re-stating. For the above firewall to work **YOU MUST TRUST ALL YOUR USERS!** I don't recommend it.

2.1   Drawbacks with Firewalls

The problem with filtering firewalls are they inhibit the access to your network from the internet. Only services on systems that have pass filters can be accessed. With a proxy server users can login to the firewall and then access any system within the private network they have access to.

Also, new types of network clients and servers a coming out almost daily. When they do you must find a new way to allow controled access before these services can be used.

2.2   Types of Firewalls

There are two types of firewalls.

1. IP or Filtering Firewalls - that block all but selected network traffic.
2. Proxy Servers - that make the network connections for you.

2.2.1   IP Filtering Firewalls

An IP filtering firewall works at the packet level. It is designed to control the flow of packets based the source, destination, port and packet type information contained in each packet.

This type of firewall is very secure but lacks any sort of useful logging. It can block people from accessing private system but it will not tell you who accessed your public systems or who accessed the internet from the inside.

Filtering firewalls are absolute filters. Even if you want to give someone on outside access to your private servers you can not without giving everyone access to the servers.

Linux has included packet filtering software in the kernel starting with version 1.3.x.

2.2.2   Proxy Servers

Proxy servers allow indirect internet access through the firewall. The best example of how this works is a person telneting to a system and then telneting from there to another. Only with a proxy server the process is automatic. When you connect to a proxy server with your client software, the proxy server starts it's client (proxy) software and passes you the data.

Because proxy servers are duplicating all the communications they can log every thing they do.

The great thing about proxy servers is that they are completely secure, when configured correctly. They will not allow someone in through them. There are no direct IP routes.

3   Setting up the Firewall

3.1   Hardware requirements

For our example, the computer is a 486-DX66 with 16 meg of memory and a 500 meg Linux partition. This system has two network cards one connected to our private LAN and the other connected to the a lan we will call the de-militarized zone (DMZ). The DMZ has a router connected to it with a connection to the internet.

This is a pretty standard setup for a business. You could use one network card and a modem with PPP to the internet. The point is, the firewall must have two IP network numbers.

I know a lot of people have small LANs at home with two or three computers on them. Something you might consider is putting all your modems in on Linux box (maybe an old 386) and connecting all of them to the internet with load balancing. With this setup when only one person was pulling data they would get both modems doubling the throughput. :-)

4   Firewalling Software

4.1   Available packages

If all you want is a filtering firewall, you only need Linux and the basic networking packages. One package that might not come with your distribution is the IP Firewall Administration tool.

(IPFWADM) Comes from **http://www.xos.nl/linux/ipfwadm/**

If you want to setup a poxy server you will need one of these packages.

1. SOCKS

2. TIS Firewall Toolkit (FWTK)

4.2 The TIS Firewall Toolkit vs SOCKS

Trusted Information System (**http://www.tis.com**) has put out a collection of programs designed to facilitate firewalling. The programs do basically the same thing as the SOCKS package, but with a different design strategy. Where Socks has one program that covers all Internet transactions, TIS has provided one program for each utility that wishes to use the firewall.

To contrast the two, let's use the example of world wide web and Telnet access. With SOCKS, you set up one configuration file and one daemon. Through this file and daemon, both telnet and WWW are enabled, as well as any other service that you have not disabled.

With the TIS toolkit, you set up one daemon for each WWW and telnet, as well as configuration files for each. After you have done this, other internet access is still prohibited until explicitly set up. If a daemon for a specific utility has not been provided (like talk), there is a "plug-in" daemon, but it is neither as flexible, nor as easy to set up, as the other tools.

This might seem a minor, but it makes a major difference. SOCKS allows you to be sloppy. With a poorly set up SOCKS server, someone from the inside could gain more access to the internet than was originally intended. With the TIS toolkit, the people on the inside have only the access the system administrator wants them to have.

SOCKS is easier to set up, easier to compile and allows for greater flexibility. The TIS toolkit is more secure if you want to regulate the users inside the protected network. Both provide absolute protection from the outside.

I will cover the installation and setup of both.

5 Preparing the Linux system

5.1 Compiling the Kernel

Start with a clean installation of your Linux distribution. (I used RedHat 3.0.3 and the examples here are based on this distribution.) The less software you have loaded the less holes, backdoors and/or bugs there will be to introduce security problems in your system, so load only a minimal set of applications.

Pick a stable kernel. I used the Linux 2.0.14 kernel for my system. So this documentation is based on it's settings.

You well need to recompile the Linux kernel with the appropriate options. At this point, you should look at the Kernel HOWTO, the Ethernet HOWTO, and the NET-2 HOWTO if you haven't done this before.

Here are the network related setting I know work in 'make config'

1. Under General setup

    (a) Turn Networking Support ON

2. Under Networking Options

    (a) Turn Network firewalls ON

(b) Turn TCP/IP Networking ON

(c) Turn IP forwarding/gatewaying OFF (UNLESS you wish to use IP filtering)

(d) Turn IP Firewalling ON

(e) Turn IP firewall packet loggin ON (this is not required but it is a good idea)

(f) Turn IP: masquerading OFF (I am not covering this subject here.)

(g) Turn IP: accounting ON

(h) Turn IP: tunneling OFF

(i) Turn IP: aliasing OFF

(j) Turn IP: PC/TCP compatibility mode OFF

(k) Turn IP: Reverse ARP OFF

(l) Turn Drop source routed frames ON

3. Under Network device support

(a) Turn Network device support ON

(b) Turn Dummy net driver support ON

(c) Turn Ethernet (10 or 100Mbit) ON

(d) Select your network card

Now you can recompile, reinstall the kernel and reboot. Your network card/s should show up in the boot-up sequence. If not, go over the other HOWTOs again until it is working.

5.2 Configuring two network cards

If you have two network cards in your computer, you most likely will need to add an append statement to your /etc/lilo.conf file to describe the IRQ and address of both cards. My lilo append statement looks like this:

```
append="ether=12,0x300,eth0 ether=15,0x340,eth1"
```

5.3 Configuring the Network Addresses

This is the real interesting part. Now you have a few decisions to make. Since we don't want the internet to have access to any part of the private network, we do not need to use real addresses. There are a number of internet addresses set aside for private networks. Because everyone needs more addresses and because these addresses can not cross the Internet they are a good choice.

Of these, 192.168.2.xxx, is set aside and we will use it in our examples.

Your proxy firewall will be a member of both networks and so it can pass the data through to and from the private network.

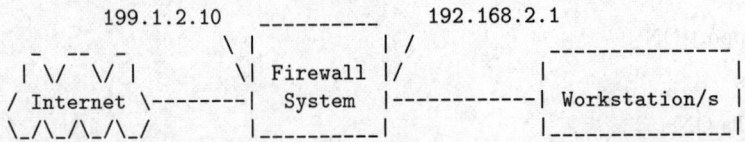

```
           199.1.2.10    _____    192.168.2.1
   _  __  _       \ |            | /       _____
  | \/  \/ |       \| Firewall  |/       |               |
  / Internet \--------| System  |------------| Workstation/s |
  \_/\_/\_/\_/       |_____|            |_____|
```

If your going to use a filtering firewall you can still use these numbers. You will need to use IP masquerading to make this happen. With this process the firewall will forward packets and translate them into "REAL " " IP address to travel on the Internet.

You must assign the real IP address to the network card on the Internet (out) side. And, assign 192.168.2.1 to the Ethernet card on inside. This will be your proxy/gateway IP address. You can assign all the other machines in the protected network some number in that 192.168.2.xxx range. (192.168.2.2 through 192.168.2.254)

Since I use RedHat Linux (Hey guys, want to give me a copy for the plugs? ;-) to configure the network at boot time I added a 'ifcfg-eth1' file in the /etc/sysconfig/network-scripts directory. This file is read during the boot process to set your network and routing tables.

Here is what my ifcfg-eth1 looks like;

```
#!/bin/sh
#>>>Device type: ethernet
#>>>Variable declarations:
DEVICE=eth1
IPADDR=192.168.2.1
NETMASK=255.255.255.0
NETWORK=192.168.2.0
BROADCAST=192.168.2.255
GATEWAY=199.1.2.10
ONBOOT=yes
#>>>End variable declarations
```

You can also use these scripts to automatically connect by modem to your provider. Look at the ipup-ppp script.

If your going to use a modem for your internet connection your outside IP address will be assigned for you by your provider at connect time.

5.4 Testing your network

Start by checking ifconfig and route. If you have two network cards your ifconfig should look something like:

```
#ifconfig
lo        Link encap:Local Loopback
          inet addr:127.0.0.0  Bcast:127.255.255.255  Mask:255.0.0.0
          UP BROADCAST LOOPBACK RUNNING  MTU:3584  Metric:1
          RX packets:1620 errors:0 dropped:0 overruns:0
          TX packets:1620 errors:0 dropped:0 overruns:0

eth0      Link encap:10Mbps Ethernet  HWaddr 00:00:09:85:AC:55
          inet addr:199.1.2.10  Bcast:199.1.2.255  Mask:255.255.255.0
          UP BROADCAST RUNNING MULTICAST  MTU:1500  Metric:1
          RX packets:0 errors:0 dropped:0 overruns:0
          TX packets:0 errors:0 dropped:0 overruns:0
          Interrupt:12 Base address:0x310

eth1      Link encap:10Mbps Ethernet  HWaddr 00:00:09:80:1E:D7
          inet addr:192.168.2.1  Bcast:192.168.2.255  Mask:255.255.255.0
          UP BROADCAST RUNNING MULTICAST  MTU:1500  Metric:1
```

```
                RX packets:0 errors:0 dropped:0 overruns:0
                TX packets:0 errors:0 dropped:0 overruns:0
                Interrupt:15 Base address:0x350
```

and your route table sould look like:

```
#route -n
Kernel routing table
Destination    Gateway        Genmask          Flags MSS     Window Use Iface
199.1.2.0      *              255.255.255.0    U     1500     0      15 eth0
192.168.2.0    *              255.255.255.0    U     1500     0       0 eth1
127.0.0.0      *              255.0.0.0        U     3584     0       2 lo
default        199.1.2.10     *                UG    1500     0      72 eth0
```

Note: 199.1.2.0 is the Internet side of this firewall and 192.168.2.0 is the private side.

Now try to ping the internet from the firewall. I used to use nic.ddn.mil as my test point. It's still a good test, but has proven to be less reliable than I had hoped. If it doesn't work at first, try pinging a couple other places that are not connected to your LAN. If this doesn't work, then your PPP is incorrectly setup. Reread the Net-2 HOWTO, and try again.

Next, try pinging a host within the protected network from the firewall. All the computers should be able to ping each other. If not, go over the NET-2 HOWTO again and work on the network some more.

Then, try to ping the outside address of firewall from inside the protected network. (NOTE: this is not any of the 192.168.2.xxx IP numbers.) If you can, then you have not turned off IP Forwarding. Make sure this is the way you want it. If you leave it turned on you will have to go through the IP filtering section of this document as well.

Now try pinging the internet from behind your firewall. Use the same address that worked for you before. (I.E. nic.ddn.mil) Again, if you have IP Forwarding turned off, this should not work. But, if you have it turned on, it should.

If have IP Forwarding turned on and your using a "REAL" (not 192.168.2.*) IP address for your private network, and you can't ping the internet but you can ping the internet side your firewall, check if the next router up stream is routing packets for your private network address. (Your provider may have to do this for you.)

If you have assigned your protected network to 192.168.2.*, then no can packets can be routed to it anyway. If you have skipped ahead and you already have IP masquerading turn on, this test should work.

Now, you have your basic system setup.

5.5 Securing the Firewall

A firewall isn't any good if it is left wide open to attacks through a unused service. A "bad guy" could gain access to the firewall and modify it for their own needs.

Start by turning off any unneeded services. Look at /etc/inetd.conf file. This file controls what are called the "super server". It controls a bunch of the server daemons and starts them as they are requested.

Definitely turn off netstat, systat, tftp, bootp, and finger. To turn a service off, put # as the first character of the service line. When your done, send a SIG-HUP to the process by typing **"kill -HUP <pid>"**, where <pid> is the process number of inetd. This will make inetd re-read its configuration file (inetd.conf) and restart.

Test it out by telneting to port 15 on firewall, the netstat port. If you get an output of netstat, you have not restarted it correctly.

6   IP filtering setup (IPFWADM)

To start, you should have IP Forwarding turned on in your kernel and your system should be up and forwarding everything you send it. Your routing tables should be in place and you should be able to access everything, both from the inside out and from the outside in.

But, we're building a firewall so we need to start chocking down what everyone has access to.

In my system I created a couple of scripts to set the firewall forwarding policy and accounting policy. I call theses scripts from the /etc/rc.d scripts so my system is configured at boot time.

By default the IP Forwarding system in the Linux kernel forwards everything. Because of this, your firewall script should start by denying access to everything and flushing any ipfw rules in place from the last time it was run. This script will do the trick.

```
#
# setup IP packet Accounting and Forwarding
#
#    Forwarding
#
# By default DENY all services
ipfwadm -F -p deny
# Flush all commands
ipfwadm -F -f
ipfwadm -I -f
ipfwadm -O -f
```

Now we have the ultimate firewall. Nothing can get through. No doubt you have some services you need to forward so here are a few examples you should find useful.

```
# Forward email to your server
ipfwadm -F -a accept -b -P tcp -S 0.0.0.0/0 1024:65535 -D 192.1.2.10 25

# Forward email connections to outside email servers
ipfwadm -F -a accept -b -P tcp -S 196.1.2.10 25 -D 0.0.0.0/0 1024:65535

# Forward Web connections to your Web Server
/sbin/ipfwadm -F -a accept -b -P tcp -S 0.0.0.0/0 1024:65535 -D 196.1.2.11 80

# Forward Web connections to outside Web Server
/sbin/ipfwadm -F -a accept -b -P tcp -S 196.1.2.* 80 -D 0.0.0.0/0 1024:65535

# Forward DNS traffic
/sbin/ipfwadm -F -a accept -b -P udp -S 0.0.0.0/0 53 -D 196.1.2.0/24
```

You might also be interested in accounting for traffic going through your firewall. This script will count ever packet. You could add a line or to to account for packets going to just a single system.

```
# Flush the current accounting rules
ipfwadm -A -f
# Accounting
/sbin/ipfwadm -A -f
```

```
/sbin/ipfwadm -A out -i -S 196.1.2.0/24 -D 0.0.0.0/0
/sbin/ipfwadm -A out -i -S 0.0.0.0/0 -D 196.1.2.0/24
/sbin/ipfwadm -A in -i -S 196.1.2.0/24 -D 0.0.0.0/0
/sbin/ipfwadm -A in -i -S 0.0.0.0/0 -D 196.1.2.0/24
```

If all you wanted was a filtering firewall you can stop here. Enjoy :-)

7   Installing the TIS Proxy server

7.1   Getting the software

The TIS FWTK is avaible at **ftp://ftp.tis.com/**.

Don't make the mistake I did. When you ftp files from TIS, READ THE README's. The TIS fwtk is locked up in a hidden directory on their server. TIS requires you **send email to fwtk-request@tis.com** with only the word **SEND** in the body of the message to learn the name of this hidden directory. No subject is needed in the message. Their system will then mails you back the directory name (good for 12 hours) to download the source.

As I'm writing this TIS is releasing version 2.0 (beta) of the FWTK. This version seems to compile well (with a few exceptions) and everything is working for me. This is the version I will be covering here. When they release the final code I'll update the HOWTO.

To install the FWTK, create a fwtk-2.0 directory in your /usr/src directory. Move your copy of the FWTK (fwtk-2.0.tar.gz) to your this directory and untar it (tar zxf fwtk-2.0.tar.gz).

The FWTK does not proxy SSL web documents but there is an addon for it written by Jean-Christophe Touvet. It is avaible at **ftp://ftp.edelweb.fr/pub/contrib/fwtk/ssl-gw.tar.Z**. Touvet does not support this code.

I am using a modified version that includes access to Netscape secure news servers written by Eric Wedel. It is available at **ftp://mdi.meridian-data.com/pub/tis.fwtk/ssl-gw/ssl-gw2.tar.Z**.

In our example I will use Eric Wedel's version.

To install it, simply create a ssl-gw directory in your /usr/src/fwtk-2.0 directory and put the files in it.

When I installed this gateway it required a few changes before it would compile with the rest of the toolkit.

The first change was to the ssl-gw.c file. I found it didn't include a needed include file.

```
#if defined(__linux)
#include        <sys/ioctl.h>
#endif
```

Second it didn't come with a Makefile. I copied one out of the other gateway directories and replaced the gateway's name with ssl-gw.

7.2   Compiling the TIS FWTK

Version 2.0 of the FWTK compiles much easier then any of the older versions. I still found a couple of things that needed to be changed before the BETA version would compile cleanly. Hopefully these changes will be make in the final version.

To fix it up, start by changing to the /usr/src/fwtk/fwtk directory and coping the Makefile.config.linux file over the Makefile.config file.

DON'T RUN FIXMAKE. The instructions tell you to run this. If you do it will break the makefiles in each directory.

I do have a fix for fixmake. The problem is the sed script add a '.' and " to the include line of ever Makefile. This sed script works.

```
sed 's/^include[        ]*\([^ ].*\)/include \1/' $name .proto > $name
```

Next we need to edit the Makefile.config file. There are two changes you may need to make.

The author set the source directory to his home directory. We are compiling our code in /usr/src so you should changed the FWTKSRCDIR variable to reflect this.

```
FWTKSRCDIR=/usr/src/fwtk/fwtk
```

Second, at least some Linux system us the gdbm database. The Makefile.config is using dbm. You might need to change this. I had to for RedHat 3.0.3.

```
DBMLIB=-lgdbm
```

The last fix is in the x-gw. The bug in the BETA version is in the socket.c code. To fix it remove these lines of code.

```
#ifdef SCM_RIGHTS  /* 4.3BSD Reno and later */
                   + sizeof(un_name->sun_len) + 1
#endif
```

If you added the ssl-gw to your FWTK source directory you will need to add it to the list of directory in the Makefile.

```
DIRS=   smap smapd netacl plug-gw ftp-gw tn-gw rlogin-gw http-gw x-gw ssl-gw
```

Now run **make**.

7.3   Installing the TIS FWTK

Run **make install**.

The default installation directory is /usr/local/etc. You could change this (I didn't) to a more secure directory. I chose to change the access to this directory to 'chmod 700'.

All last is left now is to configure the firewall.

7.4   Configuring the TIS FWTK

Now the fun realy begins. We must teach the system to call theses new services and create the tables to control them.

I'm not going to try to re-write the TIS FWTK manual here. I will show you the setting I found worked and explain the problems I ran into and how I got around them.

There are three files that make up these controls.

- /etc/services

  - Tells the system what ports a services is on.

- /etc/inetd.conf

  - Tells inetd what program to call when someone knocks on a service port.

- /usr/local/etc/netperm-table

  - Tells the FWTK services who to allow and deny service to.

To get the FWTK functioning, you should edit these files from the bottom up. Editing the services file without the inetd.conf or netperm-table file set correctly could make your system inaccessible.

7.4.1   The netperm-table file

This file controls who can access the services of the TIS FWTK. You should think about the traffic using the firewall from both sides. People outside your network should identify themselves before gaining access, but the people inside your network might be allowed to just pass through.

So people can identify themselves, the firewall uses a program called **authsrv** to keep a database of user IDs and passwords. The authentication section of the netperm-table controls where the database is keep and who can access it.

I had some trouble closing the access to this service. Note the premit-hosts line I show uses a '*' to give everyone access. The correct setting for this line is " **authsrv: premit-hosts localhost** if you can get it working.

```
#
# Proxy configuration table
#
# Authentication server and client rules
authsrv:        database /usr/local/etc/fw-authdb
authsrv:        permit-hosts *
authsrv:        badsleep 1200
authsrv:        nobogus true
# Client Applications using the Authentication server
*:              authserver 127.0.0.1 114
```

To initialize the database, su to root, and run **./authsrv** in the /var/local/etc directory to create the administrative user record. Here is a sample session.

Read the FWTK documentation to learn how to add users and groups.

```
#
# authsrv
authsrv# list
authsrv# adduser admin "Auth DB admin"
ok - user added initially disabled
authsrv# ena admin
enabled
authsrv# proto admin pass
changed
authsrv# pass admin "plugh"
Password changed.
authsrv# superwiz admin
set wizard
authsrv# list
Report for users in database
user    group  longname           ok?    proto   last
------  ------ ------------------ -----  ------  -----
admin          Auth DB admin      ena    passw   never
authsrv# display admin
Report for user admin (Auth DB admin)
Authentication protocol: password
Flags: WIZARD
authsrv# ^D
EOT
#
```

The telnet gateway (tn-gw) controls are straight forward and the first you should set up.

In my example, I premit host from inside the private network to pass through without authenticating themselves. (permit-hosts 19961.2.* -passok) But, any other user must enter their user ID and password to use the proxy. (permit-hosts * -auth)

I also allow one other system (196.1.2.202) to access the firewall directly without going through the firewall at all. The two inetacl-in.telnetd lines do this. I will explain how these lines are called latter.

The Telnet timeout should be keep short.

```
# telnet gateway rules:
tn-gw:                  denial-msg      /usr/local/etc/tn-deny.txt
tn-gw:                  welcome-msg     /usr/local/etc/tn-welcome.txt
tn-gw:                  help-msg        /usr/local/etc/tn-help.txt
tn-gw:                  timeout 90
tn-gw:                  permit-hosts 196.1.2.* -passok -xok
tn-gw:                  permit-hosts * -auth
# Only the Administrator can telnet directly to the Firewall via Port 24
netacl-in.telnetd: permit-hosts 196.1.2.202 -exec /usr/sbin/in.telnetd
```

The r-commands work the same way as telnet.

```
# rlogin gateway rules:
rlogin-gw:   denial-msg     /usr/local/etc/rlogin-deny.txt
rlogin-gw:   welcome-msg    /usr/local/etc/rlogin-welcome.txt
rlogin-gw:   help-msg       /usr/local/etc/rlogin-help.txt
rlogin-gw:   timeout 90
```

```
rlogin-gw:    permit-hosts 196.1.2.* -passok -xok
rlogin-gw:    permit-hosts * -auth -xok
# Only the Administrator can telnet directly to the Firewall via Port
netacl-rlogind: permit-hosts 196.1.2.202 -exec /usr/libexec/rlogind -a
```

You shouldn't have anyone accessing your firewall directly and that includes FTP so don't put an FTP, server on you firewall.

Again, the permit-hosts line allows anyone in the protected network free access to the Internet and all others must authenticate themselves. I included logging of every file sent and received to my controls. (-log { retr stor })

The ftp timeout controls how long it will take to drop a bad connections as well as how long a connection will stay open with out activity.

```
# ftp gateway rules:
ftp-gw:                denial-msg     /usr/local/etc/ftp-deny.txt
ftp-gw:                welcome-msg    /usr/local/etc/ftp-welcome.txt
ftp-gw:                help-msg       /usr/local/etc/ftp-help.txt
ftp-gw:                timeout 300
ftp-gw:                permit-hosts 196.1.2.* -log { retr stor }
ftp-gw:                permit-hosts * -authall -log { retr stor }
```

Web, gopher and browser based ftp are contorted by the http-gw. The first two lines create a directory to store ftp and web documents as they are passing through the firewall. I make these files owned by root and put the in a directory accessible only by root.

The Web connection should be kept short. It controls how long the user will wait on a bad connections.

```
# www and gopher gateway rules:
http-gw:     userid      root
http-gw:     directory   /jail
http-gw:     timeout 90
http-gw:     default-httpd   www.afs.net
http-gw:     hosts       196.1.2.* -log { read write ftp }
http-gw:     deny-hosts  *
```

The ssl-gw is really just a pass anything gateway. Be carefull with it. In this example I allow anyone inside the protected network to connect to any server outside the network except the addresses 127.0.0.* and 192.1.1.* and then only on ports 443 through 563. Ports 443 through 563 are known SSL ports.

```
# ssl gateway rules:
ssl-gw:      timeout 300
ssl-gw:      hosts       196.1.2.* -dest { !127.0.0.* !192.1.1.* *:443:563 }
ssl-gw:      deny-hosts  *
```

Here is an example of how to use the plug-gw to allow connections to a news server. In this example I allow anyone inside the protected network to connect to only one system and only to it's news port.

The seconded line allows the news server to pass its data back to the protected network.

Because most clients expect to stay connected while the user read news, the timeout for a news server should be long.

```
# NetNews Pluged gateway
plug-gw:          timeout 3600
plug-gw: port nntp 196.1.2.* -plug-to 199.5.175.22 -port nntp
plug-gw: port nntp 199.5.175.22 -plug-to 196.1.2.* -port nntp
```

The finger gateway is simple. Anyone inside the protected network must login first and then we allow them to use the finger program on the firewall. Anyone else just gets a message.

```
# Enable finger service
netacl-fingerd: permit-hosts 196.1.2.* -exec /usr/libexec/fingerd
netacl-fingerd: permit-hosts * -exec /bin/cat /usr/local/etc/finger.txt
```

I haven't setup the Mail and X-windows services so I'm not including examples. If anyone has a working example, please send me email.

7.4.2   The inetd.conf file

Here is a complete /etc/inetd.conf file. All un-needed services have been commented out. I have included the complete file to show what to turn off, as well as how to setup the new firewall services.

```
#echo    stream  tcp  nowait  root        internal
#echo    dgram   udp  wait    root        internal
#discard         stream tcp nowait root        internal
#discard         dgram  udp wait   root        internal
#daytime         stream tcp nowait root        internal
#daytime         dgram  udp wait   root        internal
#chargen         stream tcp nowait root        internal
#chargen         dgram  udp wait   root        internal
# FTP firewall gateway
ftp-gw       stream tcp nowait.400  root  /usr/local/etc/ftp-gw  ftp-gw
# Telnet firewall gateway
telnet  stream tcp nowait     root  /usr/local/etc/tn-gw /usr/local/etc/tn-gw
# local telnet services
telnet-a    stream tcp nowait     root  /usr/local/etc/netacl in.telnetd
# Gopher firewall gateway
gopher  stream tcp nowait.400  root  /usr/local/etc/http-gw /usr/local/etc/http-gw
# WWW firewall gateway
http    stream tcp nowait.400  root  /usr/local/etc/http-gw /usr/local/etc/http-gw
# SSL firewall gateway
ssl-gw  stream tcp     nowait root /usr/local/etc/ssl-gw   ssl-gw
# NetNews firewall proxy (using plug-gw)
nntp    stream tcp     nowait root  /usr/local/etc/plug-gw plug-gw nntp
#nntp   stream tcp     nowait root  /usr/sbin/tcpd  in.nntpd
# SMTP (email) firewall gateway
#smtp   stream tcp     nowait root  /usr/local/etc/smap smap
#
# Shell, login, exec and talk are BSD protocols.
#
#shell  stream tcp     nowait root  /usr/sbin/tcpd  in.rshd
```

```
#login  stream  tcp     nowait  root    /usr/sbin/tcpd  in.rlogind
#exec   stream  tcp     nowait  root    /usr/sbin/tcpd  in.rexecd
#talk   dgram   udp     wait    root    /usr/sbin/tcpd  in.talkd
#ntalk  dgram   udp     wait    root    /usr/sbin/tcpd  in.ntalkd
#dtalk  stream  tcp     waut    nobody  /usr/sbin/tcpd  in.dtalkd
#
# Pop and imap mail services et al
#
#pop-2  stream  tcp nowait  root    /usr/sbin/tcpd      ipop2d
#pop-3  stream  tcp nowait  root    /usr/sbin/tcpd      ipop3d
#imap   stream  tcp nowait  root    /usr/sbin/tcpd      imapd
#
# The Internet UUCP service.
#
#uucp   stream  tcp nowait  uucp /usr/sbin/tcpd  /usr/lib/uucp/uucico -l
#
# Tftp service is provided primarily for booting.  Most sites
# run this only on machines acting as "boot servers." Do not uncomment
# this unless you *need* it.
#
#tftp   dgram   udp     wait    root    /usr/sbin/tcpd  in.tftpd
#bootps dgram   udp     wait    root    /usr/sbin/tcpd  bootpd
#
# Finger, systat and netstat give out user information which may be
# valuable to potential "system crackers."  Many sites choose to disable
# some or all of these services to improve security.
#
# cfinger is for GNU finger, which is currently not in use in RHS Linux
#
finger stream  tcp nowait  root    /usr/sbin/tcpd  in.fingerd
#cfinger        stream  tcp nowait  root    /usr/sbin/tcpd  in.cfingerd
#systat stream  tcp nowait  guest   /usr/sbin/tcpd  /bin/ps -auwwx
#netstat        stream  tcp nowait  guest   /usr/sbin/tcpd  /bin/netstat -f inet
#
# Time service is used for clock syncronization.
#
#time   stream  tcp nowait  root    /usr/sbin/tcpd  in.timed
#time   dgram   udp wait    root    /usr/sbin/tcpd  in.timed
#
# Authentication
#
auth           stream  tcp wait    root    /usr/sbin/tcpd  in.identd -w -t120
authsrv stream  tcp nowait  root    /usr/local/etc/authsrv authsrv
#
# End of inetd.conf
```

7.4.3   The /etc/services file

This is where it all begins. When a client connects to the firewall it connects on a known port (less then 1024). For example telnet connects on port 23. The inetd deamon hears this connection and looks up the name of these service in the /etc/services file. It then calls the program assigned to the name in the /etc/inetd.conf file.

Some of the services we are creating are not normally in the /etc/services file. You can assign some of them
to any port you want. For example, I have assigned the administrator's telnet port (telnet-a) to port 24.
You could assign it to port 2323 if you wished. For the administrator (YOU) to connect directly to the
firewall you will need to telnet to port 24 not 23 and if you setup your netperm-table file, like I did, you will
only be able to to this from one system inside your protected network.

```
telnet-a        24/tcp
ftp-gw          21/tcp                  # this named changed
auth            113/tcp     ident       # User Verification
ssl-gw          443/tcp
```

8   The SOCKS Proxy Server

8.1   Setting up the Proxy Server

The SOCKS proxy server available from `<ftp://sunsite.unc.edu/pub/Linux/system/Network/misc/`
`socks-linux-src.tgz>`. There is also an example config file in that directory called "socks-conf". Un-
compress and untar the files into a directory on your system, and follow the instructions on how to make it.
I had a couple problems when I made it. Make sure that your Makefiles are correct.

One important thing to note is that the proxy server needs to be added to /etc/inetd.conf. You must add
a line:

```
socks   stream  tcp  nowait  nobody  /usr/local/etc/sockd  sockd
```

to tell the server to run when requested.

8.2   Configuring the Proxy Server

The SOCKS program needs two separate configuration files. One to tell the access allowed, and one to route
the requests to the appropriate proxy server. The access file should be housed on the server. The routing file
should be housed on every Un*x machine. The DOS and, presumably, Macintosh computers will do their
own routing.

8.2.1   The Access File

With socks4.2 Beta, the access file is called "sockd.conf". It should contain 2 lines, a permit and a deny
line. Each line will have three entries:

- The Identifier (permit/deny)
- The IP address
- The address modifier

The identifier is either permit or deny. You should have both a permit and a deny line.

The IP address holds a four byte address in typical IP dot notation. I.E. 192.168.2.0.

The address modifier is also a typical IP address four byte number. It works like a netmask. Envision this number to be 32 bits (1s or 0s). If the bit is a 1, the corresponding bit of the address that it is checking must match the corresponding bit in the IP address field. For instance, if the line is:

```
permit 192.168.2.23 255.255.255.255
```

it will permit only the IP address that matches every bit in 192.168.2.23, eg, only 192.168.2.3. The line:

```
permit 192.168.2.0 255.255.255.0
```

will permit every number within group 192.168.2.0 through 192.168.2.255, the whole C Class domain. One should not have the line:

```
permit 192.168.2.0 0.0.0.0
```

as this will permit every address, regardless.

So, first permit every address you want to permit, and then deny the rest. To allow everyone in the domain 192.168.2.xxx, the lines:

```
permit 192.168.2.0 255.255.255.0
deny 0.0.0.0 0.0.0.0
```

will work nicely. Notice the first "0.0.0.0" in the deny line. With a modifier of 0.0.0.0, the IP address field does not matter. All 0's is the norm because it is easy to type.

More than one entry of each is allowed.

Specific users can also be granted or denied access. This is done via ident authentication. Not all systems support ident, including Trumpet Winsock, so I will not go into it here. The documentation with socks is quite adequate on this subject.

8.2.2 The Routing File

The routing file in SOCKS is poorly named "socks.conf". I say "poorly named" because it is so close to the name of the access file that it is easy to get the two confused.

The routing file is there to tell the SOCKS clients when to use socks and when not to. For instance, in our network, 192.168.2.3 will not need to use socks to talk with 192.168.2.1, firewall. It has a direct connection in via Ethernet. It defines 127.0.0.1, the loopback, automatically. Of course you do not need SOCKS to talk to yourself. There are three entries:

- deny
- direct
- sockd

Deny tells SOCKS when to reject a request. This entry has the same three fields as in sockd.conf, identifier, address and modifier. Generally, since this is also handled by sockd.conf, the access file, the modifier field is set to 0.0.0.0. If you want to preclude yourself from calling any place, you can do it here.

The direct entry tells which addresses to not use socks for. These are all the addresses that can be reached without the proxy server. Again we have the three fields, identifier, address and modifier. Our example would have

```
direct 192.168.2.0 255.255.255.0
```

Thus going direct for any on our protected network.

The sockd entry tells the computer which host has the socks server daemon on it. The syntax is:

```
sockd @=<serverlist> <IP address> <modifier>
```

Notice the @= entry. This allows you to set the IP addresses of a list of proxy servers. In our example, we only use one proxy server. But, you can have many to allow a greater load and for redundancy in case of failure.

The IP address and modifier fields work just like in the other examples. You specify which addresses go where through these. 6.2.3. DNS from behind a Firewall

Setting up Domain Name service from behind a firewall is a relatively simple task. You need merely to set up the DNS on the firewalling machine. Then, set each machine behind the firewall to use this DNS.

8.3 Working With a Proxy Server

8.3.1 Unix

To have your applications work with the proxy server, they need to be "sockified". You will need two different telnets, one for direct communication, one for communication via the proxy server. SOCKS comes with instructions on how to SOCKify a program, as well as a couple pre-SOCKified programs. If you use the SOCKified version to go somewhere direct, SOCKS will automatically switch over to the direct version for you. Because of this, we want to rename all the programs on our protected network and replace them with the SOCKified programs. "Finger" becomes "finger.orig", "telnet" becomes "telnet.orig", etc. You must tell SOCKS about each of these via the include/socks.h file.

Certain programs will handle routing and sockifying itself. Netscape is one of these. You can use a proxy server under Netscape by entering the server's address (192.168.2.1 in our case) in the SOCKs field under Proxies. Each application will need at least a little messing with, regardless of how it handles a proxy server.

8.3.2 MS Windows with Trumpet Winsock

Trumpet Winsock comes with built in proxy server capabilities. In the "setup" menu, enter the IP address of the server, and the addresses of all the computers reachable directly. Trumpet will then handle all outgoing packets.

8.3.3 Getting the Proxy Server to work with UDP Packets

The SOCKS package works only with TCP packets, not UDP. This makes it quite a bit less useful. Many useful programs, such as talk and Archie, use UDP. There is a package designed to be used as a proxy server for UDP packets called UDPrelay, by Tom Fitzgerald <fitz@wang.com>. Unfortunately, at the time of this writing, it is not compatible with Linux.

8.4 Drawbacks with Proxy Servers

The proxy server is, above all, a `security device`. Using it to increase internet access with limited IP addresses will have many drawbacks. A proxy server will allow greater access from inside the protected network to the outside, but will keep the inside completely unaccessible from the outside. This means no servers, talk or archie connections, or direct mailing to the inside computers. These drawbacks might seem slight, but think of it this way:

- You have left a report you are doing on your computer inside a firewall protected network. You are at home, and decide that you would like to go over it. You can not. You can not reach your computer because it is behind the firewall. You try to log into `firewall` first, but since everyone has proxy server access, no one has set up an account for you on it.

- Your daughter goes to college. You want to email her. You have some private things to talk about, and would rather have your mail sent directly to your machine. You trust your systems administrator completely, but still, this is private mail.

- The inability to use UDP packets represents a big drawback with the proxy servers. I imagine UDP capabilities will be coming shortly.

FTP causes another problem with a proxy server. When getting or doing an `ls`, the FTP server opens a socket on the client machine and sends the information through it. A proxy server will not allow this, so FTP doesn't particularly work.

And, proxy servers run slow. Because of the greater overhead, almost any other means of getting this access will be faster.

Basically, if you have the IP addresses, and you are not worried about security, do not use a firewall and/or proxy servers. If you do not have the IP addresses, but you are also not worried about security, you might also want to look into using an IP emulator, like Term, Slirp or TIA. Term is available from `ftp://sunsite.unc.edu`, Slirp is available from `ftp://blitzen.canberra.edu.au/pub/slirp`, and TIA is available from marketplace.com. These packages will run faster, allow better connections, and provide a greater level of access to the inside network from the internet. Proxy servers are good for those networks which have a lot of hosts that will want to connect to the internet on the fly, with one setup and little work after that.

9 Advanced Configurations

There is one configuration I would like to go over before wrapping this document up. The one I have just outlined will probably suffice for most people. However, I think the next outline will show a more advanced configuration that can clear up some questions. If you have questions beyond what I have just covered, or are just interested in the versatility of proxy servers and firewalls, read on.

9.1 A large network with emphasis on security

Say, for instance, you are the leader of millisha and you wish to network your site. You have 50 computers and a subnet of 32 (5 bits) IP numbers. You need various levels of access within your network because you tell your followers different things. Therefore, you'll need to protect certain parts of the network from the rest.

The levels are:

1. The external level. This is the level that gets shown to everybody. This is where you rant and rave to get new volunteers.

2. **Troop** This is the level of people who have gotten beyond the external level. Here is where you teach them about the evail goverment and how to make bombs.

3. **Mercenary** Here is where the *real* plans are keep. In this level is stored all the information on how the 3rd world goverment is going to take over the world, your plans involving Newt Gingrich, Oklahoma City, lown care products and what realy is stored in that hangers at area 51.

9.1.1 The Network Setup

The IP numbers are arranged as:

- 1 number is 192.168.2.255, which is the broadcast address and is not usable.
- 23 of the 32 IP addresses are allocated to 23 machines that will be accessible to the internet.
- 1 extra IP goes to a linux box on that network
- 1 extra goes to a different linux box on that network.
- 2 IP #'s go to the router
- 4 are left over, but given domain names paul, ringo, john, and george, just to confuse things a bit.
- The protected networks both have the addresses 192.168.2.xxx

Then, two separate networks are built, each in different rooms. They are routed via infrared Ethernet so that they are completely invisible to the outside room. Luckily, infrared ethernet works just like normal ethernet.

These networks are each connected to one of the linux boxes with an extra IP address.

There is a file server connecting the two protected networks. This is because the plans for taking over the world involves some of the higher Troops. The file server holds the address 192.168.2.17 for the Troop network and 192.168.2.23 for the Mercenary network. It has to have different IP addresses because it has to have different Ethernet cards. IP Forwarding on it is turned off.

IP Forwarding on both Linux boxes is also turned off. The router will not forward packets destined for 192.168.2.xxx unless explicitly told to do so, so the internet will not be able to get in. The reason for turning off IP Forwarding here is so that packets from the Troop's network will not be able to reach the Mercenary network, and vica versa.

The NFS server can also be set to offer different files to the different networks. This can come in handy, and a little trickery with symbolic links can make it so that the common files can be shared with all. Using this setup and another ethernet card can offer this one file server for all three networks.

9.1.2 The Proxy Setup

Now, since all three levels want to be able to monitor the network for their own devious purposes, all three need to have net access. The external network is connected directly into the internet, so we don't have to mess with proxy servers here. The Mercenary and Troop networks are behind firewalls, so it is necessary to set up proxy servers here.

Both networks will be setup very similarly. They both have the same IP addresses assigned to them. I will throw in a couple of parameters, just to make things more interesting though.

1. No one can use the file server for internet access. This exposes the file server to viruses and other nasty things, and it is rather important, so its off limits.

2. We will not allow troop access to the World Wide Web. They are in training, and this kind of information retrieval power might prove to be damaging.

So, the sockd.conf file on the Troop's linux box will have this line:

```
deny 192.168.2.17 255.255.255.255
```

and on the Mercenary machine:

```
deny 192.168.2.23 255.255.255.255
```

And, the Troop's linux box will have this line

```
deny 0.0.0.0 0.0.0.0 eq 80
```

This says to deny access to all machines trying to access the port equal (eq) to 80, the http port. This will still allow all other services, just deny Web access.

Then, both files will have:

```
permit 192.168.2.0 255.255.255.0
```

to allow all the computers on the 192.168.2.xxx network to use this proxy server except for those that have already been denied (ie. the file server and Web access from the Troop network).

The Troop's sockd.conf file will look like:

```
deny 192.168.2.17 255.255.255.255
deny 0.0.0.0 0.0.0.0 eq 80
permit 192.168.2.0 255.255.255.0
```

and the Mercenary file will look like:

```
deny 192.168.2.23 255.255.255.255
permit 192.168.2.0 255.255.255.0
```

This should configure everything correctly. Each network is isolated accordingly, with the proper amount of interaction. Everyone should be happy.

Now, take over the world!

Linux NET-3-HOWTO, Linux Networking.

Terry Dawson, VK2KTJ, terry@perf.no.itg.telstra.com.au   v1.2, 20 August 1997

The Linux Operating System boasts kernel based networking support written almost entirely from scratch. The performance of the tcp/ip implementation in recent kernels makes it a worthy alternative to even the best of its peers. This document aims to describe how to install and configure the Linux networking software and associated tools.

Contents

1   Changes from the previous version

```
Additions:
        Reference to PLIP-mini-HOWTO - thanks Claes
        IP NAT - Network Address Translation

Corrections/Updates:
        Many corrections from Alessandro Rubini - thanks!
        Updated Larry Stefani's email address - thanks Larry
        Corrected ftp.linux.uk.org nettools location - thanks Ron
        Corrected incorrect route command - thanks John
        More broken route commands! - thanks Jean-Pierre
        IPv6 addresses are 16 bytes not 32, oops - thanks Erez

ToDo:
        Add traffic shaper
        Describe new routing algorithm
        Add IPv6 kernel compile options
        Describe /proc/sys/net/* entries.
        WanRouter device
```

2   Introduction.

The original NET-FAQ was written by Matt Welsh and I to answer frequently asked questions about networking for Linux at a time before the Linux Documentation Project had formally started. It covered the very early development versions of the Linux Networking Kernel. The NET-2-HOWTO superceded the NET-FAQ and was one of the original LDP HOWTO documents, it covered what was called version 2 and later version 3 of the Linux kernel Networking software. This document in turn supercedes it and relates only to version 3 of the Linux Networking Kernel.

Previous versions of this document became quite large because of the enormous amount of material that fell within its scope. To help reduce this problem a number of HOWTO's dealing with specific networking topics have been produced. This document will provide pointers to them where relevant and cover those areas not yet covered by other documents.

2.1 Feedback

I always appreciate feedback and especially value contributions. Please direct any feedback or contributions to me by *email* <mailto:terry@perf.no.itg.telstra.com.au>.

3 How to use this HOWTO document (NET-3-HOWTO-HOWTO ?).

The format of this document is differs from earlier versions. I've now regrouped the sections so that there is informative material at the beginning which you can skip if you are not interested, generic material next which you must ensure you understand before proceeding to the technology specific sections in the rest of the document.

Read the generic sections
> These sections apply to every, or nearly every, technology described later and so are very important for you to understand.

Consider your network
> You should know how your network is, or will be, designed and exactly what hardware and technology types you will be implementing.

Read the technology specific sections related to your requirements
> When you know what you want you can address each component in turn. These sections cover only details specific to a particular technology.

Do the configuration work
> You should actually try to configure your network and take careful note of any problems you have.

Look for further help if needed
> If you experience problems that this document does not help you to resolve then read the section related to where to get help or where to report bugs.

Have fun!
> Networking is fun, enjoy it.

4 General Information about Linux Networking.

4.1 A brief history of Linux Networking Kernel Development.

Developing a brand new kernel implementation of the tcp/ip protocol stack that would perform as well as existing implementations was not an easy task. The decision not to port one of the existing implementations was made at a time when there was some uncertainty as to whether the existing implementations may become encumbered by restrictive copyrights because of the court case put by U.S.L. and when there was a lot of fresh enthusiasm for doing it differently and perhaps even better than had already been done.

The original volunteer to lead development of the kernel network code was Ross Biro <biro@yggdrasil.com>. Ross produced a simple and incomplete but mostly usable implementation set of routines that were complemented by an ethernet driver for the WD-8003 network interface card. This was enough to get many people testing and experimenting with the software and some people even managed to connect machines in this configuration to live internet connections. The pressure within the Linux community driving development for networking support was building and eventually the cost of a combination of some unfair pressure applied to Ross and his own personal commitments outweighed the benefit he was deriving and he stepped down as lead developer. Ross's efforts in getting the project started and accepting the responsibility for actually producing something useful in such controversial circumstances were what catalysed all future work and were therefore an essential component of the success of the current product.

Orest Zborowski <obz@Kodak.COM> produced the original BSD socket programming interface for the Linux kernel. This was a big step forward as it allowed many of the existing network applications to be ported to linux without serious modification.

Somewhere about this time Laurence Culhane <loz@holmes.demon.co.uk> developed the first drivers for Linux to support the SLIP protocol. These enabled many people who did not have access to Ethernet networking to experiment with the new networking software. Again, some people took this driver and pressed it into service to connect them to the Internet. This gave many more people a taste of the possibilities that could be realised if Linux had full networking support and grew the number of users actively using and experimenting with the networking software that existed.

One of the people that had also been actively working on the task of building networking support was Fred van Kempen <waltje@uwalt.nl.mugnet.org>. After a period of some uncertainty following Ross's resignation from the lead developer position Fred offered his time and effort and accepted the role essentially unopposed. Fred had some ambitious plans for the direction that he wanted to take the Linux networking software and he set about progressing in those directions. Fred produced a series of networking code called the 'NET-2' kernel code (the 'NET' code being Ross's) which many people were able to use pretty much usefully. Fred formally put a number of innovations on the development agenda, such as the dynamic device interface, Amateur Radio AX.25 protocol support and a more modularly designed networking implementation. Fred's NET-2 code was used by a fairly large number of enthusiasts, the number increasing all the time as word spread that the software was working. The networking software at this time was still a large number of patches to the standard release of kernel code and was not included in the normal release. The NET-FAQ and subsequent NET-2-HOWTO's described the then fairly complex procedure to get it all working. Fred's focus was on developing innovations to the standard network implementations and this was taking time. The community of users was growing impatient for something that worked reliably and satisfied the 80% of users and, as with Ross, the pressure on Fred as lead developer rose.

Alan Cox <iialan@www.uk.linux.org> proposed a solution to the problem designed to resolve the situation. He proposed that he would take Fred's NET-2 code and debug it, making it reliable and stable so that it would satisfy the impatient user base while relieving that pressure from Fred allowing him to continue his work. Alan set about doing this, with some good success and his first version of Linux networking code was called 'Net-2D(ebugged)'. The code worked reliably in many typical configurations and the user base was happy. Alan clearly had ideas and skills of his own to contribute to the project and many discussions relating to the direction the NET-2 code was heading ensued. There developed two distinct schools within the Linux networking community, one that had the philosophy of 'make it work first, then make it better' and the other of 'make it better first'. Linus ultimately arbitrated and offered his support to Alan's development efforts and included Alan's code in the standard kernel source distribution. This placed Fred in a difficult position. Any continued development would lack the large user base actively using and testing the code and this would mean progress would be slow and difficult. Fred continued to work for a short time and eventually stood down and Alan came to be the new leader of the Linux networking kernel development effort.

Donald Becker <becker@cesdis.gsfc.nasa.gov> soon revealed his talents in the low level aspects of networking and produced a huge range of ethernet drivers, nearly all of those included in the current kernels were developed by Donald. There have been other people that have made significant contributions, but Donald's work is prolific and so warrants special mention.

Alan continued refining the NET-2-Debugged code for some time while working on progressing some of the matters that remained unaddressed on the 'TODO' list. By the time the Linux 1.3.* kernel source had grown its teeth the kernel networking code had migrated to the NET-3 release on which current versions are based. Alan worked on many different aspects of the networking code and with the assistance of a range of other talented people from the Linux networking community grew the code in all sorts of directions.

Alan produced dynamic network devices and the first standard AX.25 and IPX implementations. Alan has continued tinkering with the code, slowly restructuring and enhancing it to the state it is in today.

PPP support was added by Michael Callahan <callahan@maths.ox.ac.uk> and Al Longyear <longyear@netcom.com> this too was critical to increasing the number of people actively using linux for networking.

Jonathon Naylor <jsn@cs.nott.ac.uk> has contributed by significantly enhancing Alan's AX.25 code, adding NetRom and Rose protocol support. The AX.25/NetRom/Rose support itself is quite significant, because no other operating system can boast standard native support for these protocols beside Linux.

There have of course been hundreds of other people who have made significant contribution to the development of the Linux networking software. Some of these you will encounter later in the technology specific sections, other people have contributed modules, drivers, bug-fixes, suggestions, test reports and moral support. In all cases each can claim to have played a part and offered what they could. The Linux kernel networking code is an excellent example of the results that can be obtained from the Linux style of anarchic development, if it hasn't yet surprised you, it is bound to soon enough, the development hasn't stopped.

4.2 Where to get other information about Linux Networking.

There are a number of places where you can find good information about Linux networking.

Alan Cox, the current maintainer of the Linux kernel networking code maintains a world wide web page that contains highlights of current and new developments in linux Networking at: *www.uk.linux.org* <http://www.uk.linux.org/NetNews.html>.

Another good place is a book written by Olaf Kirch entitled the **Network Administrators Guide**. It is a work of the *Linux Documentatation Project* <http://sunsite.unc.edu/LDP/> and you can read it interactively at *Network Administrators Guide HTML version* <http://sunsite.unc.edu/LDP/LDP/nag/nag.html> or you can obtain it in various formats by ftp from the *sunsite.unc.edu LDP ftp archive* <ftp://sunsite.unc.edu/pub/Linux/docs/LDP/network-guide/>. Olaf's book is quite comprehensive and provides a good high level overview of network configuration under linux.

There is a newsgroup in the Linux news heirarchy dedicated to networking and related matters, it is: *comp.os.linux.networking* <news:comp.os.linux.networking>

There is a mailing list to which you can subscribe where you may ask questions relating to Linux networking. To subscribe you should send a mail message:

```
To: majordomo@vger.rutgers.edu
Subject: anything at all
Message:

subscribe linux-net
```

On the various IRC networks there are often #linux channels on which people will be able to answer questions on linux networking.

Please remember when reporting any problem to include as much relevant detail about the problem as you can. Specifically you should specify the versions of software that you are using, especially the kernel version, the version of tools such as *pppd* or *dip* and the exact nature of the problem you are experiencing. This means taking note of the exact syntax of any error messages you receive and of any commands that you are issuing.

4.3   Where to get some non-linux-specific network information.

If you are after some basic tutorial information on tcp/ip networking generally, then I recommend you take a look at the following documents:

tcp/ip introduction

> this document comes as both a *text version* <ftp://athos.rutgers.edu/runet/tcp-ip-intro.doc> and a *postscript version* <ftp://athos.rutgers.edu/runet/tcp-ip-intro.ps>.

tcp/ip administration

> this document comes as both a *text version* <ftp://athos.rutgers.edu/runet/tcp-ip-admin.doc> and a *postscript version* <ftp://athos.rutgers.edu/runet/tcp-ip-admin.ps>.

If you are after some more detailed information on tcp/ip networking then I highly recommend:

> ```
> "Internetworking with TCP/IP"
> by Douglas E. Comer
>
>
> ISBN 0-13-474321-0
> Prentice Hall publications.
> ```

If you are wanting to learn about how to write network applications in a Unix compatible environment then I also highly recommend:

> ```
> "Unix Network Programming"
> by W. Richard Stevens
>
>
> ISBN 0-13-949876-1
> Prentice Hall publications.
> ```

You might also try the *comp.protocols.tcp-ip* <news:comp.protocols.tcp-ip> newsgroup.

An important source of specific technical information relating to the Internet and the tcp/ip suite of protocols are RFC's. RFC is an acronym for 'Request For Comment' and is the standard means of submitting and documenting Internet protocol standards. There are many RFC repositories. Many of these sites are ftp sites and other provide World Wide Web access with an associated search engine that allows you to search the RFC database for particular keywords.

One possible source for RFC's is at: *Nexor RFC database* <http://pubweb.nexor.co.uk/public/rfc/index/rfc.html>.

5   Generic Network Configuration Information.

The following subsections you will pretty much need to know and understand before you actually try to configure your network. They are fundamental principles that apply regardless of the exact nature of the network you wish to deploy.

5.1   What do I need to start ?

Before you start building or configuring your network you will need some things. The most important of these are:

5.1.1 Current Kernel source.

Because the kernel you are running now might not yet have support for the network types or cards that you wish to use you will probably need the kernel source so that you can recompile the kernel with the appropriate options.

You can always obtain the latest kernel source from: *ftp.funet.fi* `<ftp://ftp.funet.fi/pub/Linux/PEOPLE/Linus/v2.0>`.

Normally the kernel source will be untarred into the `/usr/src/linux` directory. For information on how to apply patches and build the kernel you should read the *Kernel-HOWTO* `<Kernel-HOWTO.html>`. For information on how to configure kernel modules you should read the *Module-HOWTO* `<Module-HOWTO.html>`.

Unless specifically stated otherwise, I recommend you stick with the standard kernel release (the one with the even number as the second digit in the version number). Development release kernels (the ones with the odd second digit) may have structural or other changes that may cause problems working with the other software on your system. If you are uncertain that you could resolve those sorts of problems in addition to the potential for there being other software errors, then don't use them.

5.1.2 Current Network tools.

The network tools are the programs that you use to configure linux network devices. These tools allow you to assign addresses to devices and configure routes for example.

Most modern linux distributions are supplied with the network tools, so if you have installed from a distribution and haven't yet installed the network tools then you should do so.

If you haven't installed from a distribution then you will need to source and compile the tools yourself. This isn't difficult.

The network tools are now maintained by Bernd Eckenfels and are available at: *ftp.inka.de* `<ftp://ftp.inka.de/pub/comp/Linux/networking/NetTools/>` and are mirrored at: *ftp.uk.linux.org* `<ftp://ftp.uk.linux.org/pub/linux/Networking/base/>`.

Be sure to choose the version that is most appropriate for the kernel you wish to use and follow the instructions in the package to install.

To install and configure the version current at the time of the writing you need do the following:

```
#
# cd /usr/src
# tar xvfz net-tools-1.33.tar.gz
# cd net-tools-1.33
# make config
# make
# make install
#
```

Additionally, if you intend configuring a firewall or using the IP masquerade feature you will require the *ipfwadm* command. The latest version of it may be obtained from: *ftp.xos.nl* `<ftp:/ftp.xos.nl/pub/linux/ipfwadm>`. Again there are a number of versions available. Be sure to pick the version that most closely matches your kernel.

To install and configure the version current at the time of the writing you need do the following:

```
#
# cd /usr/src
```

```
# tar xvfz ipfwadm-2.3.0.tar.gz
# cd ipfwadm-2.3.0
# make
# make install
#
```

5.1.3   Network Application Programs.

The network application programs are programs such as *telnet* and *ftp* and their respective server programs. David Holland <dholland@hcs.harvard.edu> now manages a distribution of the most common of these. You may obtain it from: *ftp.uk.linux.org* <ftp://ftp.uk.linux.org/pub/linux/Networking/base>.

To install and configure the version current at the time of the writing you need do the following:

```
#
# cd /usr/src
# tar xvfz /pub/net/NetKit-B-0.08.tar.gz
# cd NetKit-B-0.08
# more README
# vi MCONFIG
# make
# make install
#
```

5.1.4   Addresses.

Internet Protocol Addresses are composed of four bytes. The convention is to write addresses in what is called 'dotted decimal notation'. In this form each byte is converted to a decimal number (0-255) dropping any leading zero's unless the number is zero and written with each byte seperated by a '.' character. By convention each interface of a host or router has an IP address. It is legal for the same IP address to be used on each interface of a single machine in some circumstances but usually each interface will have its own address.

Internet Protocol Networks are contiguous sequences of IP addresses. All addresses within a network have a number of digits within the address in common. The portion of the address that is common amongst all addresses within the network is called the 'network portion' of the address. The remaining digits are called the 'host portion'. The number of bits that are shared by all addresses within a network is called the netmask and it is role of the netmask to determine which addresses belong to the network it is applied to and which don't. For example, consider the following:

```
-----------------   ---------------
Host Address        192.168.110.23
Network Mask        255.255.255.0
Network Portion     192.168.110.
Host portion                  .23
-----------------   ---------------
Network Address     192.168.110.0
Broadcast Address   192.168.110.255
-----------------   ---------------
```

Any address that is 'bitwise anded' with its netmask will reveal the address of the network it belongs to. The network address is therefore always the lowest numbered address within the range of addresses on the network and always has the host portion of the address coded all zeroes.

The broadcast address is a special address that every host on the network listens to in addition to its own unique address. This address is the one thhat datagrams are sent to if every host on the network is meant to receive it. Certain types of data like routing information and warning messages are transmitted to the broadcast address so that every host on the network can receive it simultaneously. There are two commonly used standards for what the broadcast address should be. The most widely accepted one is to use the highest possible address on the network as the broadcast address. In the example above this would be 192.168.110.255. For some reason other sites have adopted the convention of using the network address as the broadcast address. In practice it doesn't matter very much which you use but you must make sure that every host on the network is configured with the same broadcast address.

For administrative reasons some time early in the development of the IP protocol some arbitrary groups of addresses were formed into networks and these networks were grouped into what are called classes. These classes provide a number of standard size networks that could be allocated. The ranges allocated are:

```
-------------------------------------------------------------
| Network | Netmask       | Network Addresses              |
| Class   |               |                                |
-------------------------------------------------------------
|    A    | 255.0.0.0     | 0.0.0.0    - 127.255.255.255   |
|    B    | 255.255.0.0   | 128.0.0.0  - 191.255.255.255   |
|    C    | 255.255.255.0 | 192.0.0.0  - 223.255.255.255   |
|Multicast| 240.0.0.0     | 224.0.0.0  - 239.255.255.255   |
-------------------------------------------------------------
```

What addresses you should use depends on exactly what it is that you are doing. You may have to use a combination of the following activities to get all the addresses you need:

Installing a linux machine on an existing IP network

If you wish to install a linux machine onto an existing IP network then you should contact whoever administers the network and ask them for the following information:

- Host IP Address
- IP network address
- IP broadcast address
- IP netmask
- Router address
- Domain Name Server Address

You should then configure your linux network device with those details. You can not make them up and expect your configuration to work.

Building a brand new network that will never connect to the Internet

If you are building a private network and you never intend that network to be connected to the Internet then you can choose whatever addresses you like. However, for safety and consistency reasons there have been some IP network addresses that have been reserved specifically for this purpose. These are specified in RFC1597 and are as follows:

```
-------------------------------------------------------------
|         RESERVED PRIVATE NETWORK ALLOCATIONS             |
-------------------------------------------------------------
| Network | Netmask       | Network Addresses              |
| Class   |               |                                |
-------------------------------------------------------------
```

```
|   A   | 255.0.0.0     | 10.0.0.0    - 10.255.255.255  |
|   B   | 255.255.0.0   | 172.16.0.0  - 172.31.255.255  |
|   C   | 255.255.255.0 | 192.168.0.0 - 192.168.255.255 |
------------------------------------------------------------
```

You should first decide how large you want your network to be and then choose as many of the addresses as you require.

5.2   Where should I put the configuration commands ?

There are a few different approaches to Linux system boot procedures. After the kernel boots, it always executes a program called '*init*'. The *init* program then reads its configuration file called /etc/inittab and commences the boot process. There are a few different flavours of *init* and it is this variation that is the largest cause of variation between distributions or machines.

Usually the /etc/inittab file contains an entry looking something like:

```
si::sysinit:/etc/init.d/boot
```

This line specifies the name of the shell script file that actually manages the boot sequence. This file is somewhat equivalent to the AUTOEXEC.BAT file in MS-DOS.

There are usually other scripts that are called by the boot script and often the network is configured within one of many of these.

The following table may be used as a guide for your system:

```
----------------------------------------------------------------------------
Distrib. |Interface Config/Routing                |Server Initialisation
----------------------------------------------------------------------------
Debian   |/etc/init.d/network                     |/etc/init.d/netbase
         |                                         |/etc/init.d/netstd_init
         |                                         |/etc/init.d/netstd_nfs
         |                                         |/etc/init.d/netstd_misc
----------------------------------------------------------------------------
Slackware|/etc/rc.d/rc.inet1                       |/etc/rc.d/rc.inet2
----------------------------------------------------------------------------
RedHat   |/etc/sysconfig/network-scripts/ifup-<ifname>|/etc/rc.d/init.d/network
----------------------------------------------------------------------------
```

Most modern distributions include a program that will allow you to configure many of the common sorts of network interfaces. If you have one of these then you should see if it will do what you want before attempting a manual configuration.

```
-------------------------------------------
Distrib  | Network configuration program
-------------------------------------------
RedHat   | /sbin/netcfg
Slackware | /sbin/netconfig
-------------------------------------------
```

5.3   Creating your network interfaces.

In many Unix operating systems the network devices have appearances in the */dev* directory. This is not so in Linux. In Linux the network devices are created dynamically in software and thus do not require device files to be present.

In the majority of cases the network devices is automatically created by the device driver while it is initialising and has located your hardware. For example, the ethernet device driver creates `eth[0..n]` interfaces sequentially as it locates your ethernet hardware. The first ethernet card found becomes `eth0`, the second `eth1` etc.

In some cases though, notably *slip* and *ppp*, the network devices are created through the action of some user program. The same sequential device numbering applies, but the devices are not created automatically at boot time. The reason for this is that unlike ethernet devices, the number of active *slip* or *ppp* devices may vary during the uptime of the machine. These cases will be covered in more detail in later sections.

5.4   Configuring a network interface.

When you have all of the programs you need and your address and network information you can configure your network interfaces. When we talk about configuring a network interface we are talking about the process of assigning appropriate addresses to a network device and to setting appropriate values for other configurable paramaters of a network device. The program most commonly used to do this is the *ifconfig* (interface configure) command.

Typically you would use a command similar to the following:

```
# ifconfig eth0 192.168.0.1 netmask 255.255.255.0 up
```

In this case I'm configuring an ethernet interface 'eth0' with the IP address '192.168.0.1' and a network mask of '255.255.255.0'. The 'up' that trails the command tells the interface that it should become active.

The kernel assumes certain defaults when configuring interfaces. For example, you may specify the network address and broadcast address for an interface, but if you don't, as in my example above, then the kernel will make reasonable guesses as to what they should be based on the netmask you supply and if you don't supply a netmask then on the network class of the IP address configured. In my example the kernel would assume that it is a class-C network being configured on the interface and configure a network address of '192.168.0.0' and a broadcast address of '192.168.0.255' for the interface.

There are many other options to the *ifconfig* command. The most important of these are:

up

> this option activates an interface.

down

> this option deactivates an interface.

[- arp]

> this option enables or disables use of the address resolution protocol on this interface

[- allmulti]

> this option enables or disables the reception of all hardware multicast packets. Hardware multicast enables groups of hosts to receive packets addressed to special destinations. This may be of importance if you are using applications like desktop videoconferencing but is normally not used.

mtu N

> this parameter allows you to set the *MTU* of this device.

netmask addr

> this parameter allows you to set the network mask of the network this device belongs to.

irq addr

> this parameter only works on certain types of hardware and allows you to set the IRQ of the hardware of this device.

[- broadcast [addr]]

> this parameter allows you to enable and set the accepting of datagrams destined to the broadcast address, or to disable reception of these datagrams.

[- pointopoint [addr]]

> this parameter allows you to set the address of the machine at the remote end of a point to point link such as for *slip* or *ppp*.

hw <type> <addr>

> this parameter allows you to set the hardware address of certain types of network devices. This is not often useful for ethernet, but is useful for other network types such as AX.25.

You may use the *ifconfig* command on any network interface. Some user programs such as *pppd* and *dip* automatically configure the network devices as they create them, so manual use of *ifconfig* is unnecessary.

5.5   Configuring your Name Resolver.

The '*Name Resolver*' is a part of the linux standard library. Its prime function is to provide a service to convert human-friendly hostnames like '`ftp.funet.fi`' into machine friendly IP addresses such as `128.214.248.6`.

5.5.1   What's in a name ?

You will probably be familiar with the appearance of Internet host names, but may not understand how they are constructed, or deconstructed. Internet domain names are heirarchial in nature, that is, they have a tree-like structure. A '*domain*' is a family, or group of names. A '*domain*' may be broken down into '*subdomain*'. A '*toplevel domain*' is a domain that is not a subdomain. The Top Level Domains are specified in RFC-920. Some examples of the most common top level domains are:

COM

> Commercial Organisations

EDU

> Educational Organisations

GOV

> Government Organisations

MIL

> Millitary Organisations

ORG

> Other organisations

Country Designator

> these are two letters codes that represent a particular country.

Each of these top level domains has subdomains. The top level domains based on country name are used next broken down into subdomains based on the `com`, `edu`, `gov`, `mil` and `org` domains. So for example you end up with: `com.au` and `gov.au` for commercial and government organisations in Australia. For historical reasons most domains belonging to one of the non-country based top level domains are for organisations within the United States, although the United States also has its own country code '`.us`'.

The next level of division usually represents the name of the organisation. Further subdomains vary in nature, often the next level of subdomain is based on the departmental structure of the organisation but it may be based on any criterion considered reasonable and meaningful by the network adminstrators for the organisation.

The very left-most portion of the name is always the unique name assigned to the host machine and is called the '*hostname*', the portion of the name to the right of the hostname is called the '*domainname*' and the complete name is called the '*Fully Qualified Domain Name*'.

To use my own email host as an example, the fully qualified domain name is '`perf.no.itg.telstra.com.au`'. This means that the host name is '`perf`' and the domain name is '`no.itg.telstra.com.au`'. The domain name is based on a top level domain based on my country, Australia and as my email address belongs to a commercial organisation we have '`.com`' as the next level domain. The name of the company is (was) '`telstra`' and our internal naming structure is based on organisational structure, in my case, my machine belongs to the Information Technology Group, Network Operations section.

5.5.2   What information you will need.

You will need to know what domain your hosts name will belong to. The name resolver software provides this name translation service by making requests to a '*Domain Name Server*', so you will need to know the IP address of a local nameserver that you can use.

There are three files you need to edit, I'll cover each of these in turn.

5.5.3   /etc/resolv.conf

The `/etc/resolv.conf` is the main configuration file for the name resolver code. Its format is quite simple. It is a text file with one keyword per line. There are three keywords typically used, they are:

domain
:   this keyword specifies the local domain name.

search
:   this keyword specifies a list of alternate domain names to search for a hostname

nameserver
:   this keyword, which may be used many times, specifies an IP address of a domain name server to query when resolving names

An example `/etc/resolv.conf` might look something like:

```
domain maths.wu.edu.au
search maths.wu.edu.au wu.edu.au
nameserver 192.168.10.1
nameserver 192.168.12.1
```

This example specifies that the default domain name to append to unqualified names (ie hostnames supplied without a domain) is `maths.wu.edu.au` and that if the host is not found in that domain to also try the `wu.edu.au` domain directly. Two nameservers entry are supplied, each of which may be called upon by the name resolver code to resolve the name.

5.5.4 /etc/host.conf

The /etc/host.conf file is where you configure some items that govern the behaviour of the name resolver code. The format of this file is described in detail in the 'resolv+' man page. In nearly all circumstances the following example will work for you:

```
order hosts,bind
multi on
```

This configuration tells the name resolver to check the /etc/hosts file before attempting to query a name-server and to return all valid addresses for a host found in the /etc/hosts file instead of just the first.

5.5.5 /etc/hosts

The /etc/hosts file is where you put the name and IP address of local hosts. If you place a host in this file then you do not need to query the domain name server to get its IP Address. The disadvantage of doing this is that you must keep this file up to date yourself if the IP address for that host changes. In a well managed system the only hostnames that usually appear in this file are an entry for the loopback interface and the local hosts name.

```
# /etc/hosts
127.0.0.1       localhost loopback
192.168.0.1     this.host.name
```

You may specify more than one host name per line as demonstrated by the first entry, which is a standard entry for the loopback interface.

5.6 Configuring your loopback interface.

The 'loopback' interface is a special type of interface that allows you to make connections to yourself. There are various reasons why you might want to do this, for example, you may wish to test some network software without interfering with anybody else on your network. By convention the IP address '127.0.0.1' has been assigned specifically for loopback. So no matter what machine you go to, if you open a telnet connection to 127.0.0.1 you will always reach the local host.

Configuring the loopback interface is simple and you should ensure you do.

```
# ifconfig lo 127.0.0.1
# route add -host 127.0.0.1 lo
```

We'll talk more about the *route* command in the next section.

5.7 Routing.

Routing is a big topic. It is easily possible to write large volumes of text about it. Most of you will have fairly simple routing requirements, some of you will not. I will cover some basic fundamentals of routing only. If you are interested in more detailed information then I suggest you refer to the references provided at the start of the document.

Let's start with a definition. What is IP routing ? Here is one that I'm using:

IP Routing is the process by which a host with multiple network connections decides where to deliver IP datagrams it has received.

It might be useful to illustrate this with an example. Imagine a typical office router, it might have a PPP link off the Internet, a number of ethernet segments feeding the workstations and another PPP link off to another office. When the router receives a datagram on any of its network connections, routing is the mechanism that it uses to determine which interface it should send the datagram to next. Simple hosts also need to route, all Internet hosts have two network devices, one is the loopback interface described above and the other is the one it uses to talk to the rest of the network, perhaps an ethernet, perhaps a PPP or SLIP serial interface.

Ok, so how does routing work ? Each host keeps a special list of routing rules, called a routing table. This table contains rows which typically contain at least three fields, the first is a destination address, the second is the name of the interface to which the datagram is to be routed and the third is optionally the IP address of another machine which will carry the datagram on its next step through the network. In linux you can see this table by using the following command:

```
# cat /proc/net/route
```

or by using either of the following commands:

```
# /sbin/route -n
# /bin/netstat -r
```

The routing process is fairly simple: an incoming datagram is received, the destination address (who it is for) is examined and compared with each entry in the table. The entry that best matches that address is selected and the datagram is forwarded to the specified interface. If the gateway field is filled then the datagram is forwarded to that host via the specified interface, otherwise the destination address is assumed to be on the network supported by the interface.

To manipulate this table a special command is used. This command takes command line arguments and converts them into kernel system calls that request the kernel to add, delete or modify entries in the routing table. The command is called '*route*'.

A simple example. Imagine you have an ethernet network. You've been told it is a class-C network with an address of 192.168.1.0. You've been supplied with an IP address of 192.168.1.10 for your use and have been told that 192.168.1.1 is a router connected to the Internet.

The first step is to configure the interface as described earlier. You would use a command like:

```
# ifconfig eth0 192.168.1.10 netmask 255.255.255.0 up
```

You now need to add an entry into the routing table to tell the kernel that datagrams for all hosts with addresses that match 192.168.1.* should be sent to the ethernet device. You would use a command similar to:

```
# route add -net 192.168.1.0 netmask 255.255.255.0 eth0
```

Note the use of the '-net' argument to tell the route program that this entry is a network route. Your other choice here is a '-host' route which is a route that is specific to one IP address.

This route will enable you to establish IP connections with all of the hosts on your ethernet segment. But what about all of the IP hosts that aren't on your ethernet segment ?

It would be a very difficult job to have to add routes to every possible destination network, so there is a special trick that is used to simplify this task. The trick is called the '**default**' route. The default route matches every possible destination, but poorly, so that if any other entry exists that matches the required address it will be used instead of the `default` route. The idea of the `default` route is simply to enable you to say "and everything else should go here". In the example I've contrived you would use an entry like:

```
# route add default gw 192.168.1.1 eth0
```

The 'gw' argument tells the route command that the next argument is the IP address, or name, of a gateway or router machine which all datagrams matching this entry should be directed to for further routing.

So, your complete configuration would look like:

```
# ifconfig eth0 192.168.1.10 netmask 255.255.255.0 up
# route add -net 192.168.1.0 netmask 255.255.255.0 eth0
# route add default gw 192.168.1.1 eth0
```

If you take a close look at your network 'rc' files you will find that at least one of them looks very similar to this. This is a very common configuration.

Let's now look at a slightly more complicated routing configuration. Let's imagine we are configuring the router we looked at earlier, the one supporting the PPP link to the Internet and the lan segments feeding the workstations in the office. Lets imagine the router has three ethernet segments and one PPP link. Our routing configuration would look something like:

```
# route add -net 192.168.1.0 netmask 255.255.255.0 eth0
# route add -net 192.168.2.0 netmask 255.255.255.0 eth1
# route add -net 192.168.3.0 netmask 255.255.255.0 eth2
# route add default ppp0
```

Each of the workstations would use the simpler form presented above, only the router needs to specify each of the network routes seperately because for the workstations the `default` route mechanism will capture all of them letting the router worry about splitting them up appropriately. You may be wondering why the default route presented doesn't specify a 'gw'. The reason for this is simple, serial link protocols such as PPP and slip only ever have two hosts on their network, one at each end. To specify the host at the other end of the link as the gateway is pointless and redundant as there is no other choice, so you do not need to specify a gateway for these types of network connections. Other network types such as ethernet, arcnet or token ring do require the gateway to be specified as these networks support large numbers of hosts on them.

5.7.1   So what does the *routed* program do ?

The routing configuration described above is best suited to simple network arrangements where there are only ever single possible paths to destinations. When you have a more complex network arrangement things get a little more complicated. Fortunately for most of you this won't be an issue.

The big problem with 'manual routing' or 'static routing' as described, is that if a machine or link fails in your network then the only way you can direct your datagrams another way, if another way exists, is by manually intervening and executing the appopriate commands. Naturally this is clumsy, slow, impractical and hazard prone. Various techniques have been developed to automatically adjust routing tables in the event of network failures where there are alternate routes, all of these techniques are loosely grouped by the term 'dynamic routing protocols'.

You may have heard of some of the more common dynamic routing protocols. The most common are probably RIP (Routing Information Protocol) and OSPF (Open Shortest Path First Protocol). The Routing Information Protocol is very common on small networks such as small-medium sized corporate networks or building networks. OSPF is more modern and more capable at handling large network configurations and better suited to environments where there is a large number of possible paths through the network. Common implementations of these protocols are: '*routed*' - RIP and '*gated*' - RIP, OSPF and others. The '*routed*' program is normally supplied with your Linux distribution or is included in the 'NetKit' package detailed above.

An example of where and how you might use a dynamic routing protocol might look something like the following:

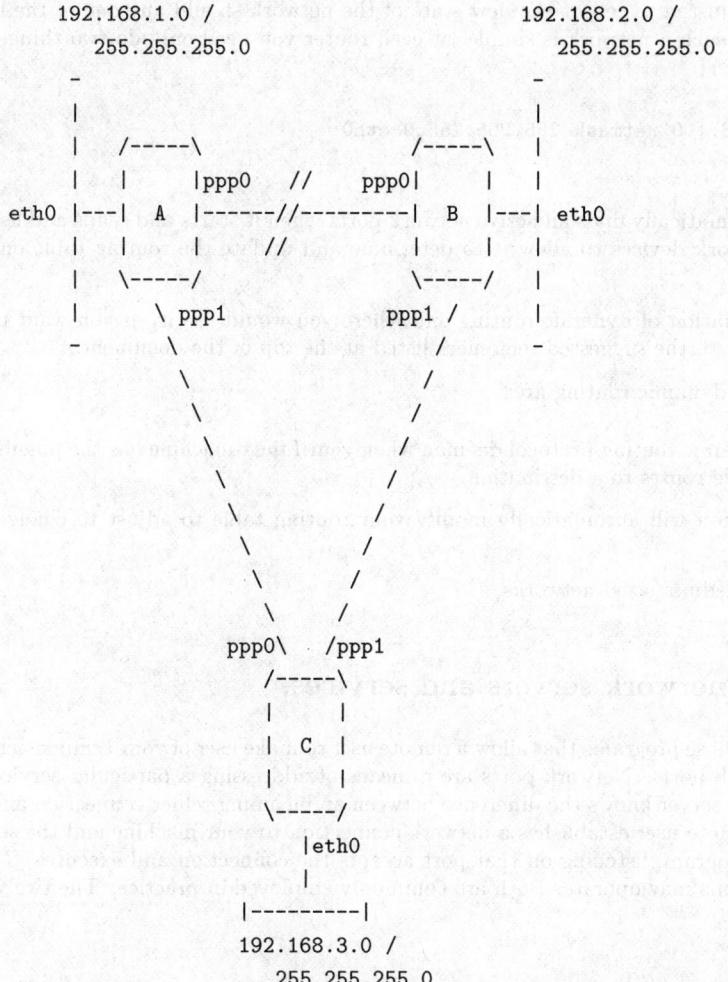

We have three routers A, B and C. Each supports one ethernet segment with a Class C IP network (netmask 255.255.255.0). Each router also has a PPP link to each of the other routers. The network forms a triangle.

It should be clear that the routing table at router A could look like:

```
# route add -net 192.168.1.0 netmask 255.255.255.0 eth0
# route add -net 192.168.2.0 netmask 255.255.255.0 ppp0
# route add -net 192.168.3.0 netmask 255.255.255.0 ppp1
```

This would work just fine until the link between router A and B should fail. If that link failed then with the routing entry shown above hosts on the ethernet segment of A could not reach hosts on the ethernet segment on B because their datagram would be directed to router A's ppp0 link which is broken. They could still continue to talk to hosts on the ethernet segment of C and hosts on the C's ethernet segment could still talk to hosts on B's ethernet segment because the link between B and C is still intact.

But wait, if A can talk to C and C can still talk to B, why shouldn't A route its datagrams for B via C and let C send them to B ? This is exactly the sort of problem that dynamic routing protocols like RIP were designed to solve. If each of the routers A, B and C were running a routing daemon then their routing tables would be automatically adjusted to reflect the new state of the network should any one of the links in the network fail. To configure such a network is simple, at each router you need only do two things. In this case for Router A:

```
# route add -net 192.168.1.0 netmask 255.255.255.0 eth0
# /usr/sbin/routed
```

The 'routed' routing daemon automatically finds all active network ports when it starts and sends and listens for messages on each of the network devices to allow it to determine and update the routing table on the host.

This has been a very brief explanation of dynamic routing and where you would use it. If you want more information then you should refer to the suggested references listed at the top of the document.

The important points relating to dynamic routing are:

1. You only need to run a dynamic routing protocol daemon when your Linux machine has the possibility of selecting multiple possible routes to a destination.

2. The dynamic routing daemon will automatically modify your routing table to adjust to changes in your network.

3. RIP is suited to small to medium sized networks.

5.8   Configuring your network servers and services.

Network servers and services are those programs that allow a remote user to make user of your Linux machine. Server programs listen on network ports. Network ports are a means of addressing a particular service on any particular host and are how a server knows the difference between an incoming telnet connection and an incoming ftp connection. The remote user establishes a network connection to your machine and the server program, the network daemon program, listening on that port accepts the connection and executes. There are two ways that network daemons may operate. Both are commonly employed in practice. The two ways are:

standalone

> the network daemon program listens on the designated network port and when an incoming connection is made it manages the network connection itself to provide the service.

slave to the *inetd* server

> the *inetd* server is a special network daemon program that specialises in managing incoming network connections. It has a configuration file which tells it what program needs to be run when an incoming connection is received. Any service port may be configured for either of the tcp or udp protcols. The ports are described in another file that we will talk about soon.

There are two important files that we need to configure. They are the `/etc/services` file which assigns names to port numbers and the `/etc/inetd.conf` file which is the configuration file for the *inetd* network daemon.

5.8.1 /etc/services

The /etc/services file is a simple database that associates a human friendly name to a machine friendly service port. Its format is quite simple. The file is a text file with each line representing and entry in the database. Each entry is comprised of three fields seperated by any number of whitespace (tab or space) characters. The fields are:

```
name        port/protocol        aliases        # comment
```

name

> a single word name that represents the service being described.

port/protocol

> this field is split into two subfields.

> **port**

>> a number that specifies the port number the named service will be available on. Most of the common services have assigned service numbers. These are described in RFC-1340.

> **protocol**

>> this subfield may be set to either tcp or udp.

> It is important to note that an entry of 18/tcp is very different from an entry of 18/udp and that there is no technical reason why the same service needs to exist on both. Normally common sense prevails and it is only if a particular service is available via both tcp and udp that you will see an entry for both.

aliases

> other names that may be used to refer to this service entry.

Any text appearing in a line after a '#' character is ignored and treated as a comment.

An example /etc/services file. All modern linux distributions provide a good /etc/services file. Just in case you happen to be building a machine from the ground up, here is a copy of the /etc/services file supplied with the *Debian* <http://www.debian.org/> distribution.

```
# /etc/services:
# $Id: NET-3-HOWTO.sgml,v 1.2 1998/02/16 04:35:11 esr Exp $
#
# Network services, Internet style
#
# Note that it is presently the policy of IANA to assign a single well-known
# port number for both TCP and UDP; hence, most entries here have two entries
# even if the protocol doesn't support UDP operations.
# Updated from RFC 1340, ``Assigned Numbers'' (July 1992).  Not all ports
# are included, only the more common ones.


tcpmux          1/tcp                           # TCP port service multiplexer
echo            7/tcp
echo            7/udp
discard         9/tcp           sink null
discard         9/udp           sink null
```

```
systat        11/tcp      users
daytime       13/tcp
daytime       13/udp
netstat       15/tcp
qotd          17/tcp      quote
msp           18/tcp                      # message send protocol
msp           18/udp                      # message send protocol
chargen       19/tcp      ttytst source
chargen       19/udp      ttytst source
ftp-data      20/tcp
ftp           21/tcp
ssh           22/tcp                      # SSH Remote Login Protocol
ssh           22/udp                      # SSH Remote Login Protocol
telnet        23/tcp
# 24 - private
smtp          25/tcp      mail
# 26 - unassigned
time          37/tcp      timserver
time          37/udp      timserver
rlp           39/udp      resource        # resource location
nameserver    42/tcp      name            # IEN 116
whois         43/tcp      nicname
re-mail-ck    50/tcp                      # Remote Mail Checking Protocol
re-mail-ck    50/udp                      # Remote Mail Checking Protocol
domain        53/tcp      nameserver      # name-domain server
domain        53/udp      nameserver
mtp           57/tcp                      # deprecated
bootps        67/tcp                      # BOOTP server
bootps        67/udp
bootpc        68/tcp                      # BOOTP client
bootpc        68/udp
tftp          69/udp
gopher        70/tcp                      # Internet Gopher
gopher        70/udp
rje           77/tcp      netrjs
finger        79/tcp
www           80/tcp      http            # WorldWideWeb HTTP
www           80/udp                      # HyperText Transfer Protocol
link          87/tcp      ttylink
kerberos      88/tcp      kerberos5 krb5  # Kerberos v5
kerberos      88/udp      kerberos5 krb5  # Kerberos v5
supdup        95/tcp
# 100 - reserved
hostnames     101/tcp     hostname        # usually from sri-nic
iso-tsap      102/tcp     tsap            # part of ISODE.
```

```
csnet-ns        105/tcp     cso-ns          # also used by CSO name server
csnet-ns        105/udp     cso-ns
rtelnet         107/tcp                     # Remote Telnet
rtelnet         107/udp
pop-2           109/tcp     postoffice      # POP version 2
pop-2           109/udp
pop-3           110/tcp                     # POP version 3
pop-3           110/udp
sunrpc          111/tcp     portmapper      # RPC 4.0 portmapper TCP
sunrpc          111/udp     portmapper      # RPC 4.0 portmapper UDP
auth            113/tcp     authentication tap ident
sftp            115/tcp
uucp-path       117/tcp
nntp            119/tcp     readnews untp   # USENET News Transfer Protocol
ntp             123/tcp
ntp             123/udp                     # Network Time Protocol
netbios-ns      137/tcp                     # NETBIOS Name Service
netbios-ns      137/udp
netbios-dgm     138/tcp                     # NETBIOS Datagram Service
netbios-dgm     138/udp
netbios-ssn     139/tcp                     # NETBIOS session service
netbios-ssn     139/udp
imap2           143/tcp                     # Interim Mail Access Proto v2
imap2           143/udp
snmp            161/udp                     # Simple Net Mgmt Proto
snmp-trap       162/udp     snmptrap        # Traps for SNMP
cmip-man        163/tcp                     # ISO mgmt over IP (CMOT)
cmip-man        163/udp
cmip-agent      164/tcp
cmip-agent      164/udp
xdmcp           177/tcp                     # X Display Mgr. Control Proto
xdmcp           177/udp
nextstep        178/tcp     NeXTStep NextStep       # NeXTStep window
nextstep        178/udp     NeXTStep NextStep       # server
bgp             179/tcp                     # Border Gateway Proto.
bgp             179/udp
prospero        191/tcp                     # Cliff Neuman's Prospero
prospero        191/udp
irc             194/tcp                     # Internet Relay Chat
irc             194/udp
smux            199/tcp                     # SNMP Unix Multiplexer
smux            199/udp
at-rtmp         201/tcp                     # AppleTalk routing
at-rtmp         201/udp
at-nbp          202/tcp                     # AppleTalk name binding
```

```
        at-nbp          202/udp
        at-echo         204/tcp                          # AppleTalk echo
        at-echo         204/udp
        at-zis          206/tcp                          # AppleTalk zone information
        at-zis          206/udp
        z3950           210/tcp         wais             # NISO Z39.50 database
        z3950           210/udp         wais
        ipx             213/tcp                          # IPX
        ipx             213/udp
        imap3           220/tcp                          # Interactive Mail Access
        imap3           220/udp                          # Protocol v3
        ulistserv       372/tcp                          # UNIX Listserv
        ulistserv       372/udp
        #
        # UNIX specific services
        #
        exec            512/tcp
        biff            512/udp         comsat
        login           513/tcp
        who             513/udp         whod
        shell           514/tcp         cmd              # no passwords used
        syslog          514/udp
        printer         515/tcp         spooler          # line printer spooler
        talk            517/udp
        ntalk           518/udp
        route           520/udp         router routed    # RIP
        timed           525/udp         timeserver
        tempo           526/tcp         newdate
        courier         530/tcp         rpc
        conference      531/tcp         chat
        netnews         532/tcp         readnews
        netwall         533/udp                          # -for emergency broadcasts
        uucp            540/tcp         uucpd            # uucp daemon
        remotefs        556/tcp         rfs_server rfs   # Brunhoff remote filesystem
        klogin          543/tcp                          # Kerberized 'rlogin' (v5)
        kshell          544/tcp         krcmd            # Kerberized 'rsh' (v5)
        kerberos-adm    749/tcp                          # Kerberos 'kadmin' (v5)
        #
        webster         765/tcp                          # Network dictionary
        webster         765/udp
        #
        # From ''Assigned Numbers'':
        #
        #> The Registered Ports are not controlled by the IANA and on most systems
        #> can be used by ordinary user processes or programs executed by ordinary
```

```
#> users.
#
#> Ports are used in the TCP [45,106] to name the ends of logical
#> connections which carry long term conversations.  For the purpose of
#> providing services to unknown callers, a service contact port is
#> defined.  This list specifies the port used by the server process as its
#> contact port.  While the IANA can not control uses of these ports it
#> does register or list uses of these ports as a convienence to the
#> community.
#
ingreslock          1524/tcp
ingreslock          1524/udp
prospero-np         1525/tcp                    # Prospero non-privileged
prospero-np         1525/udp
rfe                 5002/tcp                    # Radio Free Ethernet
rfe                 5002/udp                    # Actually uses UDP only
bbs                 7000/tcp                    # BBS service
#
#
# Kerberos (Project Athena/MIT) services
# Note that these are for Kerberos v4 and are unofficial.  Sites running
# v4 should uncomment these and comment out the v5 entries above.
#
kerberos4           750/udp     kdc             # Kerberos (server) udp
kerberos4           750/tcp     kdc             # Kerberos (server) tcp
kerberos_master     751/udp                     # Kerberos authentication
kerberos_master     751/tcp                     # Kerberos authentication
passwd_server       752/udp                     # Kerberos passwd server
krb_prop            754/tcp                     # Kerberos slave propagation
krbupdate           760/tcp     kreg            # Kerberos registration
kpasswd             761/tcp     kpwd            # Kerberos "passwd"
kpop                1109/tcp                    # Pop with Kerberos
knetd               2053/tcp                    # Kerberos de-multiplexor
zephyr-srv          2102/udp                    # Zephyr server
zephyr-clt          2103/udp                    # Zephyr serv-hm connection
zephyr-hm           2104/udp                    # Zephyr hostmanager
eklogin             2105/tcp                    # Kerberos encrypted rlogin
#
# Unofficial but necessary (for NetBSD) services
#
supfilesrv          871/tcp                     # SUP server
supfiledbg          1127/tcp                    # SUP debugging
#
# Datagram Delivery Protocol services
#
```

```
rtmp            1/ddp               # Routing Table Maintenance Protocol
nbp             2/ddp               # Name Binding Protocol
echo            4/ddp               # AppleTalk Echo Protocol
zip             6/ddp               # Zone Information Protocol
#
# Debian GNU/Linux services
rmtcfg          1236/tcp            # Gracilis Packeten remote config server
xtel            1313/tcp            # french minitel
cfinger         2003/tcp            # GNU Finger
postgres        4321/tcp            # POSTGRES
mandelspawn     9359/udp    mandelbrot      # network mandelbrot


# Local services
```

5.8.2 /etc/inetd.conf

The /etc/inetd.conf file is the configuration file for the *inetd* server daemon. Its function is to tell *inetd* what to do when it receives a connection request for a particular service. For each service that you wish to accept connections for you must tell *inetd* what network server daemon to run and how to run it.

Its format is also fairly simple. It is a text file with each line describing a service that you wish to provide. Any text in a line following a '#' is ignored and considered a comment. Each line contains seven fields seperated by any number of whitespace (tab or space) characters. The general format is as follows:

```
service  socket_type  proto  flags  user  server_path  server_args
```

service

is the service relevant to this configuration as taken from the **/etc/services** file.

socket_type

this field describes the type of socket that this entry will consider relevant, allowable values are: **stream**, **dgram**, **raw**, **rdm**, or **seqpacket**. This is a little technical in nature, but as a rule of thumb nearly all **tcp** based services use **stream** and nearly all **udp** based services use **dgram**. It is only very special types of server daemons that would use any of the other values.

proto

the protocol to considered valid for this entry. This should match the appropriate entry in the /etc/services file and will typically be either **tcp** or **udp**. Sun RPC (Remote Procedure Call) based servers will use **rpc/tcp** or **rpc/udp**.

flags

there are really only two possible settings for this field. This field setting tells *inetd* whether the network server program frees the socket after it has been started and therefore whether *inetd* can start another one on the next connection request, or whether *inetd* should wait and assume that any server daemon already running will handle the new connection request. Again this is a little tricky to work out, but as a rule of thumb all **tcp** servers should have this entry set to **nowait** and most **udp** servers should have this entry set to **wait**. Be warned there are some notable exceptions to this, so let the example guide you if you are not sure.

user

this field describes which user account from **/etc/passwd** will be set as the owner of the network daemon when it is started. This is often useful if you want to safeguard against security risks. You can set the user of an entry to the **nobody** user so that if the network server security is breached the possible damage is minimised. Typically this field is set to **root** though, because many servers require root priveledges in order to function correctly.

server_path

this field is pathname to the actual server program to execute for this entry.

server_args

this field comprises the rest of the line and is optional. This field is where you place any command line arguments that you wish to pass to the server daemon program when it is launched.

An example /etc/inetd.conf   As for the /etc/services file all modern distributions will include a good /etc/inetd.conf file for you to work with. Here, for completeness is the /etc/inetd.conf file from the *Debian* <http://www.debian.org/> distribution.

```
# /etc/inetd.conf:  see inetd(8) for further informations.
#
# Internet server configuration database
#
#
# Modified for Debian by Peter Tobias <tobias@et-inf.fho-emden.de>
#
# <service_name> <sock_type> <proto> <flags> <user> <server_path> <args>
#
# Internal services
#
#echo            stream  tcp     nowait  root    internal
#echo            dgram   udp     wait    root    internal
discard         stream  tcp     nowait  root    internal
discard         dgram   udp     wait    root    internal
daytime         stream  tcp     nowait  root    internal
daytime         dgram   udp     wait    root    internal
#chargen         stream  tcp     nowait  root    internal
#chargen         dgram   udp     wait    root    internal
time            stream  tcp     nowait  root    internal
time            dgram   udp     wait    root    internal
#
# These are standard services.
#
telnet  stream  tcp     nowait  root    /usr/sbin/tcpd  /usr/sbin/in.telnetd
ftp     stream  tcp     nowait  root    /usr/sbin/tcpd  /usr/sbin/in.ftpd
#fsp     dgram   udp     wait    root    /usr/sbin/tcpd  /usr/sbin/in.fspd
#
# Shell, login, exec and talk are BSD protocols.
#
shell   stream  tcp     nowait  root    /usr/sbin/tcpd  /usr/sbin/in.rshd
login   stream  tcp     nowait  root    /usr/sbin/tcpd  /usr/sbin/in.rlogind
#exec    stream  tcp     nowait  root    /usr/sbin/tcpd  /usr/sbin/in.rexecd
talk    dgram   udp     wait    root    /usr/sbin/tcpd  /usr/sbin/in.talkd
```

```
ntalk   dgram   udp      wait    root    /usr/sbin/tcpd  /usr/sbin/in.ntalkd
#
# Mail, news and uucp services.
#
smtp    stream  tcp      nowait  root    /usr/sbin/tcpd  /usr/sbin/in.smtpd
#nntp   stream  tcp      nowait  news    /usr/sbin/tcpd  /usr/sbin/in.nntpd
#uucp   stream  tcp      nowait  uucp    /usr/sbin/tcpd  /usr/lib/uucp/uucico
#comsat dgram   udp      wait    root    /usr/sbin/tcpd  /usr/sbin/in.comsat
#
# Pop et al
#
#pop-2  stream  tcp      nowait  root    /usr/sbin/tcpd  /usr/sbin/in.pop2d
#pop-3  stream  tcp      nowait  root    /usr/sbin/tcpd  /usr/sbin/in.pop3d
#
# 'cfinger' is for the GNU finger server available for Debian.  (NOTE: The
# current implementation of the 'finger' daemon allows it to be run as 'root'.)
#
#cfinger stream tcp      nowait  root    /usr/sbin/tcpd  /usr/sbin/in.cfingerd
#finger stream  tcp      nowait  root    /usr/sbin/tcpd  /usr/sbin/in.fingerd
#netstat        stream   tcp     nowait  nobody  /usr/sbin/tcpd  /bin/netstat
#systat stream  tcp      nowait  nobody  /usr/sbin/tcpd  /bin/ps -auwwx
#
# Tftp service is provided primarily for booting.  Most sites
# run this only on machines acting as "boot servers."
#
#tftp   dgram   udp      wait    nobody  /usr/sbin/tcpd  /usr/sbin/in.tftpd
#tftp   dgram   udp      wait    nobody  /usr/sbin/tcpd  /usr/sbin/in.tftpd /boot
#bootps dgram   udp      wait    root    /usr/sbin/bootpd         bootpd -i -t 120
#
# Kerberos authenticated services (these probably need to be corrected)
#
#klogin  stream tcp nowait root /usr/sbin/tcpd  /usr/sbin/in.rlogind -k
#eklogin stream tcp nowait root /usr/sbin/tcpd  /usr/sbin/in.rlogind -k -x
#kshell stream  tcp nowait root /usr/sbin/tcpd  /usr/sbin/in.rshd -k
#
# Services run ONLY on the Kerberos server (these probably need to be corrected)
#
#krbupdate      stream tcp      nowait  root    /usr/sbin/tcpd  /usr/sbin/registerd
#kpasswd        stream tcp      nowait  root    /usr/sbin/tcpd  /usr/sbin/kpasswdd
#
# RPC based services
#
#mountd/1       dgram   rpc/udp wait    root    /usr/sbin/tcpd  /usr/sbin/rpc.mountd
#rstatd/1-3     dgram   rpc/udp wait    root    /usr/sbin/tcpd  /usr/sbin/rpc.rstatd
#rusersd/2-3    dgram   rpc/udp wait    root    /usr/sbin/tcpd  /usr/sbin/rpc.rusersd
```

```
#walld/1         dgram  rpc/udp wait    root     /usr/sbin/tcpd /usr/sbin/rpc.rwalld
#
# End of inetd.conf.
ident           stream  tcp     nowait nobody /usr/sbin/identd       identd -i
```

5.9 Other miscellaneous network related configuration files.

There are a number of miscellaneous files relating to network configuration under linux that you might be
interested in. You may never have to modify these files, but it is worth describing them so you know what
they contain and what they are for.

5.9.1 /etc/protocols

The /etc/protocols file is a database that maps protocol id numbers against protocol names. This is used
by programmers to allow them to specify protocols by name in their programs and also by some programs
such as *tcpdump* to allow them to display names instead of numbers in their output. The general syntax of
the file is:

```
protocolname  number  aliases
```

The /etc/protocols file supplied with the *Debian* <http://www.debian.org/> distribution is as follows:

```
# /etc/protocols:
# $Id: NET-3-HOWTO.sgml,v 1.2 1998/02/16 04:35:11 esr Exp $
#
# Internet (IP) protocols
#
#       from: @(#)protocols      5.1 (Berkeley) 4/17/89
#
# Updated for NetBSD based on RFC 1340, Assigned Numbers (July 1992).

ip        0     IP            # internet protocol, pseudo protocol number
icmp      1     ICMP          # internet control message protocol
igmp      2     IGMP          # Internet Group Management
ggp       3     GGP           # gateway-gateway protocol
ipencap   4     IP-ENCAP      # IP encapsulated in IP (officially ``IP'')
st        5     ST            # ST datagram mode
tcp       6     TCP           # transmission control protocol
egp       8     EGP           # exterior gateway protocol
pup       12    PUP           # PARC universal packet protocol
udp       17    UDP           # user datagram protocol
hmp       20    HMP           # host monitoring protocol
xns-idp   22    XNS-IDP       # Xerox NS IDP
rdp       27    RDP           # "reliable datagram" protocol
iso-tp4   29    ISO-TP4       # ISO Transport Protocol class 4
xtp       36    XTP           # Xpress Tranfer Protocol
ddp       37    DDP           # Datagram Delivery Protocol
```

```
idpr-cmtp     39      IDPR-CMTP       # IDPR Control Message Transport
rspf    73    RSPF              # Radio Shortest Path First.
vmtp    81    VMTP              # Versatile Message Transport
ospf    89    OSPFIGP           # Open Shortest Path First IGP
ipip    94    IPIP              # Yet Another IP encapsulation
encap   98    ENCAP             # Yet Another IP encapsulation
```

5.9.2 /etc/networks

The /etc/networks file has a similar function to that of the /etc/hosts file. It provides a simple database of network names against network addresses. Its format differs in that there may be only two fields per line and that the fields are coded as:

```
networkname networkaddress
```

An example might look like:

```
loopnet    127.0.0.0
localnet   192.168.0.0
amprnet    44.0.0.0
```

When you use commands like the *route* command, if a destination is a network and that network has an entry in the /etc/networks file then the route command will display that network name instead of its address.

5.10   Network Security and access control.

Let me start this section by warning you that securing your machine and network against malicious attack is a complex art. I do not consider myself an expert in this field at all and while the following mechanisms I describe will help, if you are serious about security then I recommend you do some research of your own into the subject. There are many good references on the Internet relating to the subject.

An important rule of thumb is: '**Don't run servers you don't intend to use**'. Many distributions come configured with all sorts of services configured and automatically started. To ensure even a minimum level of safety you should go through your /etc/inetd.conf file and comment out (*place a '#' at the start of the line*) any entries for services you don't intend to use. Good candidates are services such as: shell, login, exec, uucp, ftp and informational services such as finger, netstat and systat.

There are all sorts of security and access control mechanisms, I'll describe the most elementary of them.

5.10.1   /etc/ftpusers

The /etc/ftpusers file is a simple mechanism that allows you to deny certain users from logging into your machine via ftp. The /etc/ftpusers file is read by the ftp daemon program (*ftpd*) when an incoming ftp connection is received. The file is a simple list of those users who are disallowed from logging in. It might looks something like:

```
# /etc/ftpusers - users not allowed to login via ftp
root
uucp
```

```
        bin
        mail
```

5.10.2 /etc/securetty

The `/etc/securetty` file allows you to specify which `tty` devices `root` is allowed to login on. The `/etc/securetty` file is read by the login program (usually */bin/login*). Its format is a list of the tty devices names allowed, on all others `root` login is disallowed:

```
        # /etc/securetty - tty's on which root is allowed to login
        tty1
        tty2
        tty3
        tty4
```

5.10.3 The *tcpd* hosts access control mechanism.

The *tcpd* program you will have seen listed in the same `/etc/inetd.conf` provides logging and access control mechanisms to services it is configured to protect.

When it is invoked by the *inetd* program it reads two files containing access rules and either allows or denies access to the server it is protecting accordingly.

It will search the rules files until the first match is found. If no match is found then it assumes that access should be allowed to anyone. The files it searches in sequence are: `/etc/hosts.allow`, `/etc/hosts.deny`. I'll describe each of these in turn. For a complete description of this facility you should refer to the appopriate *man* pages (`hosts_access(5)` is a good starting point).

/etc/hosts.allow The `/etc/hosts.allow` file is a configuration file of the */usr/sbin/tcpd* program. The `hosts.allow` file contains rules describing which hosts are *allowed* access to a service on your machine.

The file format is quite simple:

```
        # /etc/hosts.allow
        #
        # <service list>: <host list> [: command]
```

service list
> is a comma delimited list of server names that this rule applies to. Example server names are: `ftpd`, `telnetd` and `fingerd`.

host list
> is a comma delimited list of host names. You may also use IP addresses here. You may additionally specify hostnames or addresses using wildcard characters to match groups of hosts. Examples include: `gw.vk2ktj.ampr.org` to match a specific host, `.uts.edu.au` to match any hostname ending in that string, `44.` to match any IP address commencing with those digits. There are some special tokens to simplify configuration, some of these are: `ALL` matches every host, `LOCAL` matches any host whose name does not contain a '.' ie is in the same domain as your machine and `PARANOID` matches any host whose name does not match its address (name spoofing). There is one last token that is also useful. The `EXCEPT` token allows you to provide a list with exceptions. This will be covered in an example later.

command
:   is an optional parameter. This parameter is the full pathname of a command that would be executed everytime this rule is matched. It could for example run a command that would attempt to identify who is logged onto the connecting host, or to generate a mail message or some other warning to a system administrator that someone is attempting to connect. There are a number of expansions that may be included, some common examples are: %h expands to the name of the connecting host or address if it doesn't have a name, %d the daemon name being called.

An example:

```
# /etc/hosts.allow
#
# Allow mail to anyone
in.smtpd: ALL
# All telnet and ftp to only hosts within my domain and my host at home.
telnetd, ftpd: LOCAL, myhost.athome.org.au
# Allow finger to anyone but keep a record of who they are.
fingerd: ALL: (finger @%h | mail -s "finger from %h" root)
```

/etc/hosts.deny   The /etc/hosts.deny file is a configuration file of the /usr/sbin/tcpd program. The hosts.deny file contains rules describing which hosts are *disallowed* access to a service on your machine.

A simple sample would look something like this:

```
# /etc/hosts.deny
#
# Disallow all hosts with suspect hostnames
ALL: PARANOID
#
# Disallow all hosts.
ALL: ALL
```

The PARANOID entry is really redundant because the other entry traps everything in any case. Either of these entry would make a reasonable default depending on your particular requirement.

Having an ALL: ALL default in the /etc/hosts.deny and then specifically enabling on those services and hosts that you want in the /etc/hosts.allow file is the safest configuration.

5.10.4   /etc/hosts.equiv

The hosts.equiv file is used to grant certain hosts and users access rights to accounts on your machine without having to supply a password. This is useful in a secure environment where you control all machines, but is a security hazard otherwise. Your machine is only as secure as the least secure of the trusted hosts. To maximise security, don't use this mechanism and encourage your users not to use the .rhosts file as well.

5.10.5   Configure your *ftp* daemon properly.

Many sites will be interested in running an anonymous *ftp* server to allow other people to upload and download files without requiring a specific userid. If you decide to offer this facility make sure you configure the *ftp* daemon properly for anonymous access. Most *man* pages for `ftpd(8)` describe in some length how to go about this. You should always ensure that you follow these instructions. An important tip is to not use a copy of your `/etc/passwd` file in the anonymous account `/etc` directory, make sure you strip out all account details except those that you must have, otherwise you will be vulnerable to brute force password cracking techniques.

5.10.6   Network Firewalling.

Not allowing datagrams to even reach your machine or servers is an excellent means of security. This is covered in depth in the *Firewall-HOWTO* `<Firewall-HOWTO.html>`.

5.10.7   Other suggestions.

Here are some other, potentially religious suggestions for you to consider.

sendmail

> despite its popularity the *sendmail* daemon appears with frightening regularity on security warning announcements. Its up to you, but I choose not to run it.

NFS and other Sun RPC services

> be wary of these. There are all sorts of possible exploits for these services. It is difficult finding an option to services like NFS, but if you configure them, make sure you are careful with who you allow mount rights to.

6   Network Technology Specific Information.

The following subsections are specific to particular network technologies. The information contained in these sections does not necessarily apply to any other type of network technology.

6.1   ARCNet

ARCNet device names are 'arc0e', 'arc1e', 'arc2e' etc. or 'arc0s', 'arc1s', 'arc2s' etc. The first card detected by the kernel is assigned 'arc0e' or 'arc0s' and the rest are assigned sequentially in the order they are detected. The letter at the end signifies whether you've selected ethernet encapsulation packet format or RFC1051 packet format.

Kernel Compile Options:

```
Network device support   --->
    [*] Network device support
    <*> ARCnet support
    [ ]     Enable arc0e (ARCnet "Ether-Encap" packet format)
    [ ]     Enable arc0s (ARCnet RFC1051 packet format)
```

Once you have your kernel properly built to support your ethernet card then configuration of the card is easy.

Typically you would use something like:

```
# ifconfig arc0e 192.168.0.1 netmask 255.255.255.0 up
# route add -net 192.168.0.0 netmask 255.255.255.0 arc0e
```

Please refer to the `/usr/src/linux/Documentation/networking/arcnet.txt` and `/usr/src/linux/Documentation/networking/arcnet-hardware.txt` files for further information.

ARCNet support was developed by Avery Pennarun, `apenwarr@foxnet.net`.

6.2   Appletalk (`AF_APPLETALK`)

The Appletalk support has no special device names as it uses existing network devices.

Kernel Compile Options:

```
Networking options  --->
    <*> Appletalk DDP
```

Appletalk support allows your Linux machine to interwork with Apple networks. An important use for this is to share resources such as printers and disks between both your Linux and Apple computers. Additional software is required, this is called *netatalk*. Wesley Craig `netatalk@umich.edu` represents a team called the 'Research Systems Unix Group' at the University of Michigan and they have produced the *netatalk* package which provides software that implements the Appletalk protocol stack and some useful utilities. The *netatalk* package will either have been supplied with your Linux distribution, or you will have to ftp it from its home site at the *University of Michigan* `<ftp://terminator.rs.itd.umich.edu/unix/netatalk/>`

To build and install the package do something like:

```
# cd /usr/src
# tar xvfz .../netatalk-1.4b2.tar.Z
- You may want to edit the 'Makefile' at this point, specifically to change
  the DESTDIR variable which defines where the files will be installed later.
  The default of /usr/local/atalk is fairly safe.
# make
- as root:
# make install
```

6.2.1   Configuring the Appletalk software.

The first thing you need to do to make it all work is to ensure that the appropriate entries in the `/etc/services` file are present. The entries you need are:

```
rtmp    1/ddp   # Routing Table Maintenance Protocol
nbp     2/ddp   # Name Binding Protocol
echo    4/ddp   # AppleTalk Echo Protocol
zip     6/ddp   # Zone Information Protocol
```

The next step is to create the Appletalk configuration files in the `/usr/local/atalk/etc` directory (or wherever you installed the package).

The first file to create is the `/usr/local/atalk/etc/atalkd.conf` file. Initially this file needs only one line that gives the name of the network device that supports the network that your Apple machines are on:

```
eth0
```

The Appletalk daemon program will add extra details after it is run.

6.2.2 Exporting a Linux filesystems via Appletalk.

You can export filesystems from your linux machine to the network so that Apple machine on the network can share them.

To do this you must configure the `/usr/local/atalk/etc/AppleVolumes.system` file. There is another configuration file called `/usr/local/atalk/etc/AppleVolumes.default` which has exactly the same format and describes which filesystems users connecting with guest priveledges will receive.

Full details on how to configure these files and what the various options are can be found in the *afpd* man page.

A simple example might look like:

```
/tmp Scratch
/home/ftp/pub "Public Area"
```

Which would export your `/tmp` filesystem as AppleShare Volume 'Scratch' and your ftp public directory as AppleShare Volume 'Public Area'. The volume names are not mandatory, the daemon will choose some for you, but it won't hurt to specify them anyway.

6.2.3 Sharing your Linux printer across Appletalk.

You can share your linux printer with your Apple machines quite simply. You need to run the *papd* program which is the Appletalk Printer Access Protocol Daemon. When you run this program it will accept requests from your Apple machines and spool the print job to your local line printer daemon for printing.

You need to edit the `/usr/local/atalk/etc/papd.conf` file to configure the daemon. The syntax of this file is the same as that of your usual `/etc/printcap` file. The name you give to the definition is registered with the Appletalk naming protocol, NBP.

A sample configuration might look like:

```
TricWriter:\
    :pr=lp:op=cg:
```

Which would make a printer named 'TricWriter' available to your Appletalk network and all accepted jobs would be printed to the linux printer 'lp' (as defined in the `/etc/printcap` file) using *lpd*. The entry 'op=cg' says that the linux user 'cg' is the operator of the printer.

6.2.4 Starting the appletalk software.

Ok, you should now be ready to test this basic configuration. There is an *rc.atalk* file supplied with the *netatalk* package that should work ok for you, so all you should have to do is:

```
# /usr/local/atalk/etc/rc.atalk
```

and all should startup and run ok. You should see no error messages and the software will send messages to the console indicating each stage as it starts.

6.2.5   Testing the appletalk software.

To test that the software is functioning properly, go to one of your Apple machines, pull down the Apple menu, select the Chooser, click on AppleShare, and your Linux box should appear.

6.2.6   Caveats of the appletalk software.

- You may need to start the Appletalk support before you configure your IP network. If you have problems starting the Appletalk programs, or if after you start them you have trouble with your IP network, then try starting the Appletalk software before you run your `/etc/rc.d/rc.inet1` file.

- The *afpd* (Apple Filing Protocol Daemon) severely messes up your hard disk. Below the mount points it creates a couple of directories called `.AppleDesktop` and `Network Trash Folder`. Then, for each directory you access it will create a `.AppleDouble` below it so it can store resource forks, etc. So think twice before exporting `/`, you will have a great time cleaning up afterwards.

- The *afpd* program expects clear text passwords from the Macs. Security could be a problem, so be very careful when you run this daemon on a machine connected to the Internet, you have yourself to blame if somebody nasty does something bad.

- The existing diagnostic tools such as *netstat* and *ifconfig* don't support Appletalk. The raw information is available in the `/proc/net/` directory if you need it.

6.2.7   More information.

For a much more detailed description of how to configure Appletalk for Linux refer to Anders Brownworth *Linux Netatalk-HOWTO* page at *thehamptons.com* `<http://thehamptons.com/anders/netatalk/>`.

6.3   ATM

Werner Almesberger `<werner.almesberger@lrc.di.epfl.ch>` is managing a project to provide Asynchronous Transfer Mode support for Linux. Current information on the status of the project may be obtained from: *lrcwww.epfl.ch* `<http://lrcwww.epfl.ch/linux-atm/>`.

6.4   AX25 (`AF_AX25`)

AX.25 device names are 'sl0', 'sl1', etc. in `2.0.*` kernels or 'ax0', 'ax1', etc. in `2.1.*` kernels.

Kernel Compile Options:

```
Networking options  --->
    [*] Amateur Radio AX.25 Level 2
```

The AX25, Netrom and Rose protocols are covered by the *AX25-HOWTO* `<AX25-HOWTO.html>`. These protocols are used by Amateur Radio Operators world wide in packet radio experimentation.

Most of the work for implementation of these protocols has been done by Jonathon Naylor, `jsn@cs.nott.ac.uk`.

6.5   DECNet

Support for DECNet is currently being worked on. You should expect it to appear in a late `2.1.*` kernel.

6.6   EQL - multiple line traffic equaliser

The EQL device name is 'eql'. With the standard kernel source you may have only one EQL device per machine. EQL provides a means of utilising multiple point to point lines such as PPP, slip or plip as a single logical link to carry tcp/ip. Often it is cheaper to use multiple lower speed lines than to have one high speed line installed.

Kernel Compile Options:

```
Network device support  --->
    [*] Network device support
    <*> EQL (serial line load balancing) support
```

To support this mechanism the machine at the other end of the lines must also support EQL. Linux, Livingstone Portmasters and newer dial-in servers support compatible facilities.

To configure EQL you will need the eql tools which are available from: *sunsite.unc.edu* <ftp://sunsite.unc.edu/pub/linux/system/Serial/eql-1.2.tar.gz>.

Configuration is fairly straightforward. You start by configuring the eql interface. The eql interface is just like any other network device. You configure the IP address and mtu using the *ifconfig* utility, so something like:

```
ifconfig eql 192.168.10.1 mtu 1006
```

Next you need to manually initiate each of the lines you will use. These may be any combination of point to point network devices. How you initiate the connections will depend on what sort of link they are, refer to the appropriate sections for further information.

Lastly you need to associate the serial link with the EQL device, this is called 'enslaving' and is done with the *eql_enslave* command as shown:

```
eql_enslave eql sl0 28800
eql_enslave eql ppp0 14400
```

The '*estimated speed*' parameter you supply *eql_enslave* doesn't do anything directly. It is used by the EQL driver to determine what share of the datagrams that device should receive, so you can fine tune the balancing of the lines by playing with this value.

To disassociate a line from an EQL device you use the *eql_emancipate* command as shown:

```
eql_emancipate eql sl0
```

You add routing as you would for any other point to point link, except your routes should refer to the eql device rather than the actual serial devices themselves, typically you would use:

```
route add default eql
```

The EQL driver was developed by Simon Janes, simon@ncm.com.

6.7   Ethernet

Ethernet device names are 'eth0', 'eth1', 'eth2' etc. The first card detected by the kernel is assigned 'eth0' and the rest are assigned sequentially in the order they are detected.

To learn how to make your ethernet card working under Linux you should refer to the *Ethernet-HOWTO*
`<Ethernet-HOWTO.html>`.

Once you have your kernel properly built to support your ethernet card then configuration of the card is
easy.

Typically you would use something like:

```
# ifconfig eth0 192.168.0.1 netmask 255.255.255.0 up
# route add -net 192.168.0.0 netmask 255.255.255.0 eth0
```

Most of the ethernet drivers were developed by Donald Becker, `becker@CESDIS.gsfc.nasa.gov`.

6.8   FDDI

FDDI device names are 'fddi0', 'fddi1', 'fddi2' etc. The first card detected by the kernel is assigned 'fddi0'
and the rest are assigned sequentially in the order they are detected.

Lawrence V. Stefani, `larry_stefani@us.newbridge.com`, has developed a driver for the Digital Equipment
Corporation FDDI EISA and PCI cards.

Kernel Compile Options:

```
Network device support  --->
    [*] FDDI driver support
    [*] Digital DEFEA and DEFPA adapter support
```

When you have your kernel built to support the FDDI driver and installed, configuration of the FDDI
interface is almost identical that for an ethernet interface. You just specify the appropraite FDDI interface
name in the *ifconfig* and *route* comands.

6.9   Frame Relay

The Frame Relay device names are 'dlci00', 'dlci01' etc for the DLCI encapsulation devices and 'sdla0',
'sdla1' etc for the FRAD(s).

Frame Relay is a new networking technology that is designed to suit data communications traffic that is of a
'bursty' or intermittent nature. You connect to a Frame Relay network using a Frame Relay Access Device
(FRAD). The Linux Frame Relay supports IP over Frame Relay as described in RFC-1490.

Kernel Compile Options:

```
Network device support  --->
    <*> Frame relay DLCI support (EXPERIMENTAL)
    (24)    Max open DLCI
    (8)     Max DLCI per device
    <*>     SDLA (Sangoma S502/S508) support
```

Mike McLagan, `mike.mclagan@linux.org`, developed the Frame Relay support and configuration tools.

Currently the only FRAD supported are the *Sangoma Technologies* `<http://www.sangoma.com/>` S502A,
S502E and S508.

To configure the FRAD and DLCI devices after you have rebuilt your kernel you will need the Frame Relay
configuration tools. These are available from *ftp.invlogic.com* `<ftp://ftp.invlogic.com/pub/linux/fr/`

`frad-0.15.tgz>`. Compiling and installing the tools is straightforward, but the lack of a top level Makefile makes it a fairly manual process:

```
# cd /usr/src
# tar xvfz .../frad-0.15.tgz
# cd frad-0.15
# for i in common dlci frad; make -C $i clean; make -C $i; done
# mkdir /etc/frad
# install -m 644 -o root -g root bin/*.sfm /etc/frad
# install -m 700 -o root -g root frad/fradcfg /sbin
# install -m 700 -o root -g root dlci/dlcicfg /sbin
```

After installing the tools you need to create an `/etc/frad/router.conf` file. You can use this template, which is a modified version of one of the example files:

```
# /etc/frad/router.conf
# This is a template configuration for frame relay.
# All tags are included. The default values are based on the code
# supplied with the DOS drivers for the Sangoma S502A card.
#
# A '#' anywhere in a line constitutes a comment
# Blanks are ignored (you can indent with tabs too)
# Unknown [] entries and unknown keys are ignored
#

[Devices]
Count=1                 # number of devices to configure
Dev_1=sdla0             # the name of a device
#Dev_2=sdla1            # the name of a device

# Specified here, these are applied to all devices and can be overriden for
# each individual board.
#
Access=CPE
Clock=Internal
KBaud=64
Flags=TX
#
# MTU=1500              # Maximum transmit IFrame length, default is 4096
# T391=10               # T391 value    5 - 30, default is 10
# T392=15               # T392 value    5 - 30, default is 15
# N391=6                # N391 value    1 - 255, default is 6
# N392=3                # N392 value    1 - 10, default is 3
# N393=4                # N393 value    1 - 10, default is 4

# Specified here, these set the defaults for all boards
# CIRfwd=16             # CIR forward   1 - 64
```

```
# Bc_fwd=16              # Bc forward     1 - 512
# Be_fwd=0               # Be forward     0 - 511
# CIRbak=16              # CIR backward   1 - 64
# Bc_bak=16              # Bc backward    1 - 512
# Be_bak=0               # Be backward    0 - 511


#
#
# Device specific configuration
#
#


#
# The first device is a Sangoma S502E
#
[sdla0]
Type=Sangoma            # Type of the device to configure, currently only
                        # SANGOMA is recognised
#
# These keys are specific to the 'Sangoma' type
#
# The type of Sangoma board - S502A, S502E, S508
Board=S502E
#
# The name of the test firmware for the Sangoma board
# Testware=/usr/src/frad-0.10/bin/sdla_tst.502
#
# The name of the FR firmware
# Firmware=/usr/src/frad-0.10/bin/frm_rel.502
#
Port=360                # Port for this particular card
Mem=C8                  # Address of memory window, A0-EE, depending on card
IRQ=5                   # IRQ number, do not supply for S502A
DLCIs=1                 # Number of DLCI's attached to this device
DLCI_1=16               # DLCI #1's number, 16 - 991
# DLCI_2=17
# DLCI_3=18
# DLCI_4=19
# DLCI_5=20
#
# Specified here, these apply to this device only,
# and override defaults from above
#
# Access=CPE             # CPE or NODE, default is CPE
```

```
# Flags=TXIgnore,RXIgnore,BufferFrames,DropAborted,Stats,MCI,AutoDLCI
# Clock=Internal        # External or Internal, default is Internal
# Baud=128              # Specified baud rate of attached CSU/DSU
# MTU=2048              # Maximum transmit IFrame length, default is 4096
# T391=10               # T391 value   5 - 30, default is 10
# T392=15               # T392 value   5 - 30, default is 15
# N391=6                # N391 value   1 - 255, default is 6
# N392=3                # N392 value   1 - 10, default is 3
# N393=4                # N393 value   1 - 10, default is 4

#
# The second device is some other card
#
# [sdla1]
# Type=FancyCard        # Type of the device to configure.
# Board=                # Type of Sangoma board
# Key=Value             # values specific to this type of device


#
# DLCI Default configuration parameters
# These may be overridden in the DLCI specific configurations
#
CIRfwd=64               # CIR forward    1 - 64
# Bc_fwd=16             # Bc forward     1 - 512
# Be_fwd=0              # Be forward     0 - 511
# CIRbak=16             # CIR backward   1 - 64
# Bc_bak=16             # Bc backward    1 - 512
# Be_bak=0              # Be backward    0 - 511

#
# DLCI Configuration
# These are all optional. The naming convention is
# [DLCI_D<devicenum>_<DLCI_Num>]
#

[DLCI_D1_16]
# IP=
# Net=
# Mask=
# Flags defined by Sangoma: TXIgnore,RXIgnore,BufferFrames
# DLCIFlags=TXIgnore,RXIgnore,BufferFrames
# CIRfwd=64
# Bc_fwd=512
# Be_fwd=0
```

```
# CIRbak=64
# Bc_bak=512
# Be_bak=0

[DLCI_D2_16]
# IP=
# Net=
# Mask=
# Flags defined by Sangoma: TXIgnore,RXIgnore,BufferFrames
# DLCIFlags=TXIgnore,RXIgnore,BufferFrames
# CIRfwd=16
# Bc_fwd=16
# Be_fwd=0
# CIRbak=16
# Bc_bak=16
# Be_bak=0
```

When you've built your `/etc/frad/router.conf` file the only step remaining is to configure the actual devices themselves. This is only a little trickier than a normal network device configuration, you need to remember to bring up the FRAD device before the DLCI encapsulation devices.

```
# Configure the frad hardware and the DLCI parameters
/sbin/fradcfg /etc/frad/router.conf || exit 1
/sbin/dlcicfg file /etc/frad/router.conf
#
# Bring up the FRAD device
ifconfig sdla0 up
#
# Configure the DLCI encapsulation interfaces and routing
ifconfig dlci00 192.168.10.1 pointopoint 192.168.10.2 up
route add -net 192.168.10.0 netmask 255.255.255.0 dlci00
#
ifconfig dlci01 192.168.11.1 pointopoint 192.168.11.2 up
route add -net 192.168.11.0 netmask 255.255.255.0 dlci00
#
route add default dev dlci00
#
```

6.10   IP Accounting

The IP accounting features of the Linux kernel allow you to collect and analyse some network usage data. The data collected comprises the number of packets and the number of bytes accumulated since the figures were last reset. You may specify a variety of rules to categorise the figures to suit whatever purpose you may have.

Kernel Compile Options:

```
Networking options   --->
    [*] IP: accounting
```

After you have compiled and installed the kernel you need to use the *ipfwadm* command to configure IP accounting. There are many different ways of breaking down the accounting information that you might choose. I've picked a simple example of what might be useful to use, you should read the *ipfwadm* man page for more information.

Scenario: You have a ethernet network that is linked to the internet via a PPP link. On the ethernet you have a machine that offers a number of services and that you are interested in knowing how much traffic is generated by each of telnet, rlogin, ftp and world wide web traffic.

You might use a command set that looks like the following:

```
#
# Flush the accounting rules
ipfwadm -A -f
#
# Add rules for local ethernet segment
ipfwadm -A in -a -P tcp -D 44.136.8.96/29 20
ipfwadm -A out -a -P tcp -S 44.136.8.96/29 20
ipfwadm -A in -a -P tcp -D 44.136.8.96/29 23
ipfwadm -A out -a -P tcp -S 44.136.8.96/29 23
ipfwadm -A in -a -P tcp -D 44.136.8.96/29 80
ipfwadm -A out -a -P tcp -S 44.136.8.96/29 80
ipfwadm -A in -a -P tcp -D 44.136.8.96/29 513
ipfwadm -A out -a -P tcp -S 44.136.8.96/29 513
ipfwadm -A in -a -P tcp -D 44.136.8.96/29
ipfwadm -A out -a -P tcp -D 44.136.8.96/29
ipfwadm -A in -a -P udp -D 44.136.8.96/29
ipfwadm -A out -a -P udp  -D 44.136.8.96/29
ipfwadm -A in -a -P icmp -D 44.136.8.96/29
ipfwadm -A out -a -P icmp -D 44.136.8.96/29
#
# Rules for default
ipfwadm -A in -a -P tcp -D 0/0 20
ipfwadm -A out -a -P tcp -S 0/0 20
ipfwadm -A in -a -P tcp -D 0/0 23
ipfwadm -A out -a -P tcp -S 0/0 23
ipfwadm -A in -a -P tcp -D 0/0 80
ipfwadm -A out -a -P tcp -S 0/0 80
ipfwadm -A in -a -P tcp -D 0/0 513
ipfwadm -A out -a -P tcp -S 0/0 513
ipfwadm -A in -a -P tcp -D 0/0
ipfwadm -A out -a -P tcp -D 0/0
ipfwadm -A in -a -P udp -D 0/0
ipfwadm -A out -a -P udp  -D 0/0
ipfwadm -A in -a -P icmp -D 0/0
```

```
ipfwadm -A out -a -P icmp -D 0/0
#
# List the rules
ipfwadm -A -l -n
#
```

The last command lists each of the Accounting rules and displays the collected totals.

An important point to note when analysing IP accounting is that **totals for all rules that match will be incremented** so that to obtain differential figures you need to perform appropriate maths. For example if I wanted to know how much data was not ftp, telnet, rlogin or www I would substract the individual totals from the rule that matches all ports.

```
# ipfwadm -A -l -n
IP accounting rules
 pkts bytes dir prot source              destination          ports
    0     0 in  tcp  0.0.0.0/0           44.136.8.96/29       * -> 20
    0     0 out tcp  44.136.8.96/29      0.0.0.0/0            20 -> *
    0     0 in  tcp  0.0.0.0/0           44.136.8.96/29       * -> 23
    0     0 out tcp  44.136.8.96/29      0.0.0.0/0            23 -> *
   10  1166 in  tcp  0.0.0.0/0           44.136.8.96/29       * -> 80
   10   572 out tcp  44.136.8.96/29      0.0.0.0/0            80 -> *
  242  9777 in  tcp  0.0.0.0/0           44.136.8.96/29       * -> 513
  220 18198 out tcp  44.136.8.96/29      0.0.0.0/0            513 -> *
  252 10943 in  tcp  0.0.0.0/0           44.136.8.96/29       * -> *
  231 18831 out tcp  0.0.0.0/0           44.136.8.96/29       * -> *
    0     0 in  udp  0.0.0.0/0           44.136.8.96/29       * -> *
    0     0 out udp  0.0.0.0/0           44.136.8.96/29       * -> *
    0     0 in  icmp 0.0.0.0/0           44.136.8.96/29       *
    0     0 out icmp 0.0.0.0/0           44.136.8.96/29       *
    0     0 in  tcp  0.0.0.0/0           0.0.0.0/0            * -> 20
    0     0 out tcp  0.0.0.0/0           0.0.0.0/0            20 -> *
    0     0 in  tcp  0.0.0.0/0           0.0.0.0/0            * -> 23
    0     0 out tcp  0.0.0.0/0           0.0.0.0/0            23 -> *
   10  1166 in  tcp  0.0.0.0/0           0.0.0.0/0            * -> 80
   10   572 out tcp  0.0.0.0/0           0.0.0.0/0            80 -> *
  243  9817 in  tcp  0.0.0.0/0           0.0.0.0/0            * -> 513
  221 18259 out tcp  0.0.0.0/0           0.0.0.0/0            513 -> *
  253 10983 in  tcp  0.0.0.0/0           0.0.0.0/0            * -> *
  231 18831 out tcp  0.0.0.0/0           0.0.0.0/0            * -> *
    0     0 in  udp  0.0.0.0/0           0.0.0.0/0            * -> *
    0     0 out udp  0.0.0.0/0           0.0.0.0/0            * -> *
    0     0 in  icmp 0.0.0.0/0           0.0.0.0/0            *
    0     0 out icmp 0.0.0.0/0           0.0.0.0/0            *
#
```

6.11 IP Aliasing

There are some applications where being able to configure multiple IP addresses to a single network device is useful. Internet Service Providers often use this facility to provide a 'customised' to their World Wide Web and ftp offerings for their customers.

Kernel Compile Options:

```
Networking options --->
    ....
    [*] Network aliasing
    ....
    <*> IP: aliasing support
```

After compiling and installing your kernel with IP_Alias support configuration is very simple. The aliases are added to virtual network devices associated with the actual network device. A simple naming convention applies to these devices being <devname>:<virtual dev num>, e.g. eth0:0, ppp0:10 etc.

For example, assume you have an ethernet network that supports two different IP subnetworks simultaneously and you wish your machine to have direct access to both, you could use something like:

```
#
# ifconfig eth0:0 192.168.1.1 netmask 255.255.255.0 up
# route add -net 192.168.1.0 netmask 255.255.255.0 eth0:0
#
# ifconfig eth0:1 192.168.10.1 netmask 255.255.255.0 up
# route add -net 192.168.10.0 netmask 255.255.255.0 eth0:0
#
```

To delete an alias you simply add a '-' to the end of its name and refer to it and is as simple as:

```
# ifconfig eth0:0- 0
```

All routes associated with that alias will also be deleted automatically.

6.12 IP Firewall

IP Firewall and Firewalling issues are covered in more depth in the *Firewall-HOWTO* <Firewall-HOWTO.html>. IP Firewalling allows you to secure your machine against unauthorised network access by filtering or allowing datagrams from or to IP addresses that you nominate. There are three different classes of rules, incoming filtering, outgoing filtering and forwarding filtering. Incoming rules are applied to datagrams that are received by a network device. Outgoing rules are applied to datagrams that are to be transmitted by a network device. Forwarding rules are applied to datagrams that are received and are not for this machine, ie datagrams that would be routed.

Kernel Compile Options:

```
Networking options --->
    [*] Network firewalls
    ....
    [*] IP: forwarding/gatewaying
```

```
    ....
    [*] IP: firewalling
    [ ] IP: firewall packet logging
```

Configuration of the IP firewall rules is performed using the *ipfwadm* command. As I mentioned earlier, security is not something I am expert at, so while I will present an example you can use, you should do your own research and develop your own rules if security is important to you.

Probably the most common use of IP firewall is when you are using your linux machine as a router and firewall gateway to protect your local network from unauthorised access from outside your network.

The following configuration is based on a contribution from Arnt Gulbrandsen, <agulbra@troll.no>.

The example describes the configuration of the firewall rules on the Linux firewall/router machine illustrated in this diagram:

```
  _                                 _
   \                              |  172.16.37.0
    \                             |  /255.255.255.0
     \          ---------         |
     | 172.16.174.30 | Linux |    |
 NET ================| f/w  |------|    ..37.19
     |     PPP       | router|    |   --------
    /                 ---------    |--| Mail |
   /                               |  | /DNS |
  /                                |   --------
  _                                 _
```

The following commands would normally be placed in an rc file so that they were automatically started each time the system boots. For maximum security they would be performed after the network interfaces are configured, but before the interfaces are actually brought up to prevent anyone gaining access while the firewall machine is rebooting.

```
#!/bin/sh

# Flush the 'Forwarding' rules table
# Change the default policy to 'accept'
#
/sbin/ipfwadm -F -f
/sbin/ipfwadm -F -p accept
#
# .. and for 'Incoming'
#
/sbin/ipfwadm -I -f
/sbin/ipfwadm -I -p accept


# First off, seal off the PPP interface
# I'd love to use '-a deny' instead of '-a reject -y' but then it
# would be impossible to originate connections on that interface too.
# The -o causes all rejected datagrams to be logged. This trades
```

```
# disk space against knowledge of an attack of configuration error.
#
/sbin/ipfwadm -I -a reject -y -o -P tcp -S 0/0 -D 172.16.174.30

# Throw away certain kinds of obviously forged packets right away:
# Nothing should come from multicast/anycast/broadcast addresses
#
/sbin/ipfwadm -F -a deny -o -S 224.0/3 -D 172.16.37.0/24
#
# and nothing coming from the loopback network should ever be
# seen on a wire
#
/sbin/ipfwadm -F -a deny -o -S 127.0/8 -D 172.16.37.0/24

# accept incoming SMTP and DNS connections, but only
# to the Mail/Name Server
#
/sbin/ipfwadm -F -a accept -P tcp -S 0/0 -D 172.16.37.19 25 53
#
# DNS uses UDP as well as TCP, so allow that too
# for questions to our name server
#
/sbin/ipfwadm -F -a accept -P udp -S 0/0 -D 172.16.37.19 53
#
# but not "answers" coming to dangerous ports like NFS and
# Larry McVoy's NFS extension.  If you run squid, add its port here.
#
/sbin/ipfwadm -F -a deny -o -P udp -S 0/0 53 \
        -D 172.16.37.0/24 2049 2050

# answers to other user ports are okay
#
/sbin/ipfwadm -F -a accept -P udp -S 0/0 53 \
        -D 172.16.37.0/24 53 1024:65535

# Reject incoming connections to identd
# We use 'reject' here so that the connecting host is told
# straight away not to bother continuing, otherwise we'd experience
# delays while ident timed out.
#
/sbin/ipfwadm -F -a reject -o -P tcp -S 0/0 -D 172.16.37.0/24 113

# Accept some common service connections from the 192.168.64 and
# 192.168.65 networks, they are friends that we trust.
#
```

```
/sbin/ipfwadm -F -a accept -P tcp -S 192.168.64.0/23 \
        -D 172.16.37.0/24 20:23


# accept and pass through anything originating inside
#
/sbin/ipfwadm -F -a accept -P tcp -S 172.16.37.0/24 -D 0/0


# deny most other incoming TCP connections and log them
# (append 1:1023 if you have problems with ftp not working)
#
/sbin/ipfwadm -F -a deny -o -y -P tcp -S 0/0 -D 172.16.37.0/24


# ... for UDP too
#
/sbin/ipfwadm -F -a deny -o -P udp -S 0/0 -D 172.16.37.0/24
```

Good firewall configurations are a little tricky. This example should be a reasonable starting point for you. The *ipfwadm* manual page offers some assistance in how to use the tool. If you intend to configure a firewall, be sure to ask around and get as much advice from sources you consider reliable and get someone to test/sanity check your configuration from the outside.

6.13   IPIP Encapsulation

Why would you want to encapsulate IP datagrams within IP datagrams? It must seem an odd thing to do if you've never seen an application of it before. Ok, here are a couple of common places where it is used: Mobile-IP and IP-Multicast. What is perhaps the most widely spread use of it though is also the least well known, Amateur Radio.

Kernel Compile Options:

```
Networking options  --->
    [*] TCP/IP networking
    [*] IP: forwarding/gatewaying
    ....
    <*> IP: tunneling
```

IP tunnel devices are called 'tunl0', 'tunl1' etc.

"But why ?". Ok, ok. Conventional IP routing rules mandate that an IP network comprises a network address and a network mask. This produces a series of contiguous addresses that may all be routed via a single routing entry. This is very convenient, but it means that you may only use any particular IP address while you are connected to the particular piece of network to which it belongs. In most instances this is ok, but if you are a mobile netizen then you may not be able to stay connected to the one place all the time. IP/IP encapsulation (IP tunneling) allows you to overcome this restriction by allowing datagrams destined for your IP address to be wrapped up and redirected to another IP address. If you know that you're going to be operating from some other IP network for some time you can set up a machine on your home network to accept datagrams to your IP address and redirect them to the address that you will actually be using temporarily.

6.13.1 A tunneled network configuration.

As always, I believe a diagram will save me lots of confusing text, so here is one:

```
      192.168.1/24                          192.168.2/24

       _                                      _
      |        ppp0 =            ppp0 =        |
      |   aaa.bbb.ccc.ddd   fff.ggg.hhh.iii    |
      |                                        |
      |   /-----\                 /-----\      |
      |   |     |        //       |     |      |
      |---| A   |------//---------| B   |---|
      |   |     |        //       |     |      |
      |   \-----/                 \-----/      |
      |                                        |
       _                                      _
```

The diagram illustrates another possible reason to use IPIP encapsulation, virtual private networking. This example presupposes that you have two machines each with a simple dial up internet connection. Each host is allocated just a single IP address. Behind each of these machines are some private local area networks configured with reserved IP network addresses. Suppose that you want to allow any host on network A to connect to any host on network B, just as if they were properly connected to the Internet with a network route. IPIP encapsulation will allow you to do this. Note, encapsulation does not solve the problem of how you get the hosts on networks A and B to talk to any other on the Internet, you still need tricks like IP Masquerade for that. Encapsulation is normally performed by machine functioning as routers.

Linux router 'A' would be configured with:

```
#
PATH=/sbin:/usr/sbin
#
# Ethernet configuration
ifconfig eth0 192.168.1.1 netmask 255.255.255.0 up
route add -net 192.168.1.0 netmask 255.255.255.0 eth0
#
# ppp0 configuration (start ppp link, set default route)
pppd
route add default ppp0
#
# Tunnel device configuration
ifconfig tunl0 192.168.1.1 up
route add -net 192.168.2.0 netmask 255.255.255.0 gw fff.ggg.hhh.iii tunl0
```

Linux router 'B' would be configured with:

```
#
PATH=/sbin:/usr/sbin
#
```

```
# Ethernet configuration
ifconfig eth0 192.168.2.1 netmask 255.255.255.0 up
route add -net 192.168.2.0 netmask 255.255.255.0 eth0
#
# ppp0 configuration (start ppp link, set default route)
pppd
route add default ppp0
#
# Tunnel device configuration
ifconfig tunl0 192.168.2.1 up
route add -net 192.168.1.0 netmask 255.255.255.0 gw aaa.bbb.ccc.ddd tunl0
```

The command:

```
route add -net 192.168.1.0 netmask 255.255.255.0 gw aaa.bbb.ccc.ddd tunl0
```

reads: 'Send any datagrams destined for 192.168.1.0/24 inside an IPIP encap datagram with a destination address of aaa.bbb.ccc.ddd'.

Note that the configurations are reciprocated at either end. The tunnel device uses the 'gw' in the route as the *destination* of the IP datagram in which it will place the datagram it has received to route. That machine must know how to decapsulate IPIP datagrams, that is, it must also be configured with a tunnel device.

6.13.2 A tunneled host configuration.

It doesn't have to be a whole network you route. You could for example route just a single IP address. In that instance you might configure the tunl device on the 'remote' machine with its home IP address and at the A end just use a host route (and Proxy Arp) rather than a network route via the tunnel device. Let's redraw and modify our configuration appropriately. Now we have just host 'B' which to want to act and behave as if it is both fully connected to the Internet and also part of the remote network supported by host 'A':

192.168.1/24

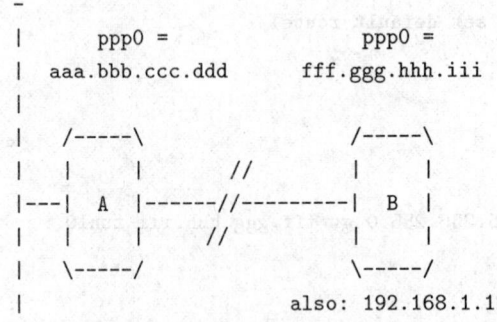

Linux router 'A' would be configured with:

```
#
PATH=/sbin:/usr/sbin
#
# Ethernet configuration
ifconfig eth0 192.168.1.1 netmask 255.255.255.0 up
route add -net 192.168.1.0 netmask 255.255.255.0 eth0
#
# ppp0 configuration (start ppp link, set default route)
pppd
route add default ppp0
#
# Tunnel device configuration
ifconfig tun0 192.168.1.1 up
route add -host 192.168.1.12 gw fff.ggg.hhh.iii tun0
#
# Proxy ARP for the remote host
arp -s 192.168.1.12 xx:xx:xx:xx:xx:xx pub
```

Linux host 'B' would be configured with:

```
#
PATH=/sbin:/usr/sbin
#
# ppp0 configuration (start ppp link, set default route)
pppd
route add default ppp0
#
# Tunnel device configuration
ifconfig tun0 192.168.1.12 up
route add -net 192.168.1.0 netmask 255.255.255.0 gw aaa.bbb.ccc.ddd tun0
```

This sort of configuration is more typical of a Mobile-IP application. Where a single host wants to roam around the Internet and maintain a single usable IP address the whole time. You should refer to the Mobile-IP section for more information on how that is handled in practice.

6.14 IPX (AF_IPX)

The IPX protocol is most commonly utilised in Novell NetWare(tm) local area network environments. Linux includes support for this protocol and may be configured to act as a network endpoint, or as a router for IPX.

Kernel Compile Options:

```
Networking options  --->
     [*] The IPX protocol
     [ ] Full internal IPX network
```

The IPX protocol and the NCPFS are covered in greater depth in the *IPX-HOWTO* <IPX-HOWTO.html>.

6.15   IPv6

Just when you thought you were beginning to understand IP networking the rules get changed! IPv6 is the shorthand notation for version 6 of the Internet Protocol. IPv6 was developed primarily to overcome the concerns in the Internet community that there would soon be a shortage of IP addresses to allocate. IPv6 addresses are 16 bytes long (128 bits). IPv6 incorporates a number of other changes, mostly simplifications, that will make IPv6 networks more managable than IPv4 networks.

Linux already has a working, but not completed, IPv6 implementation in the 2.1.* series kernels.

If you wish to experiment with this next generation Internet technology, or have a requirement for it, then you should read the IPv6-FAQ which is available from *www.terra.net* <http://www.terra.net/ipv6/>.

6.16   ISDN

The Integrated Services Digital Network (ISDN) is a series of standards that specify a general purpose switched digital data network. An ISDN 'call' creates a synchronous point to point data service to the destination. ISDN is generally delivered on a high speed link that is broken down into a number of discrete channels. There are two different types of channels, the 'B Channels' which will actually carry the user data and a single channel called the 'D channel' which is used to send control information to the ISDN exchange to establish calls and other functions. In Australia for example, ISDN may be delivered on a 2Mbps link that is broken into 30 discreet 64kbps B channels with one 64kbps D channel. Any number of channels may be used at a time and in any combination. You could for example establish 30 seperate calls to 30 different destinations at 64kbps each, or you could establish 15 calls to 15 different destinations at 128kbps each (two channels used per call), or just a small number of calls and leave the rest idle. A channel may be used for either incoming or outgoing calls. The original intention of ISDN was to allow Telecommunications companies to provide a single data service which could deliver either telephone (via digitised voice) or data services to your home or business without requiring you to make any special configuration changes.

There are a few different ways to connect your computer to an ISDN service. One way is to use a device called a 'Terminal Adaptor' which plugs into the Network Terminating Unit that you telecommunications carrier will have installed when you got your ISDN service and presents a number of serial interfaces. One of those interfaces is used to enter commands to establish calls and configuration and the others are actually connected to the network devices that will use the data circuits when they are established. Linux will work in this sort of configuration without modification, you just treat the port on the Terminal Adaptor like you would treat any other serial device. Another way, which is the way the kernel ISDN support is designed for allows you to install an ISDN card into your Linux machine and then has your Linux software handle the protocols and make the calls itself.

Kernel Compile Options:

```
ISDN subsystem  --->
        <*> ISDN support
        [ ] Support synchronous PPP
        [ ] Support audio via ISDN
        < > ICN 2B and 4B support
        < > PCBIT-D support
        < > Teles/NICCY1016PC/Creatix support
```

The Linux implementation of ISDN support a number of different types of internal ISDN cards. These are those listed in the kernel configuration options:

- ICN 2B and 4B

- Octal PCBIT-D
- Teles ISDN-cards and compatibles

Some of these cards require software to be downloaded to them to make them operational. There is a seperate utility to do this with.

Full details on how to configure the Linux ISDN support is available from the /usr/src/linux/Documentation/isdn/ directory and an FAQ dedicated to *isdn4linux* is available at *www.lrz-muenchen.de* <http://www.lrz-muenchen.de/~ui161ab/www/isdn/>. (You can click on the english flag to get an english version).

A note about PPP. The PPP suite of protocols will operate over either asynchronous or synchronous serial lines. The commonly distributed PPP daemon for Linux '*pppd*' supports only asynchronous mode. If you wish to run the PPP protocols over your ISDN service you need a specially modified version. Details of where to find it are available in the documentation referred to above.

6.17 IP Masquerade

Many people have a simple dialup account to connect to the Internet. Nearly everybody using this sort of configuration is allocated a single IP address by the Internet Service Provider. This is normally enough to allow only one host full access to the network. IP Masquerade is a clever trick that enables you to have many machines make use of that one IP address, by causing the other hosts to look like, hence the term masquerade, the machine supporting the dialup connection. There is a small caveat and that is that the masqerade function nearly always works only in one direction, that is the masqueraded hosts can make calls out, but they cannot accept or receive network connections from remote hosts. This means that some network services do not work such as *talk* and others such as *ftp* must be configured to operate in passive (PASV) mode to operate. Fortunately the most common network services such as *telnet*, World Wide Web and *irc* do work just fine.

Kernel Compile Options:

```
    Code maturity level options   --->
        [*] Prompt for development and/or incomplete code/drivers
    Networking options   --->
        [*] Network firewalls
        ....
        [*] TCP/IP networking
        [*] IP: forwarding/gatewaying
        ....
        [*] IP: masquerading (EXPERIMENTAL)
```

Normally you have your linux machine supporting a slip or PPP dialup line just as it would if it were a standalone machine. Additionally it would have another network device configured, perhaps an ethernet, configured with one of the reserved network addresses. The hosts to be masqueraded would be on this second network. Each of these hosts would have the IP address of the ethernet port of the linux machine set as their default gateway or router.

A typical configuration might look something like this:

```
    -                        -
     \                        | 192.168.1.0
      \                       | /255.255.255.0
```

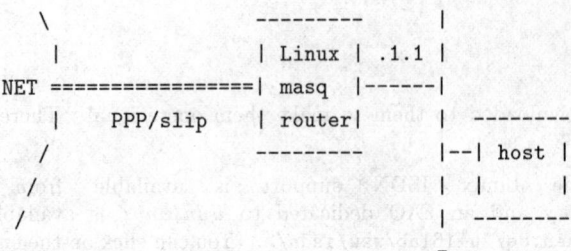

```
    \                    ---------       |
    |                    | Linux | .1.1 |
NET =================| masq  |------|
    |    PPP/slip     | router|      |  --------
    /                    ---------       |--| host |
   /                                    | |     |
  /                                     | --------
 _                                      _
```

The most relevant commands for this configuration are:

```
# Network route for ethernet
route add -net 192.168.1.0 netmask 255.255.255.0 eth0
#
# Default route to the rest of the internet.
route add default ppp0
#
# Cause all hosts on the 192.168.1/24 network to be masqueraded.
ipfwadm -F -a m -S 192.168.1.0/24 -D 0.0.0.0/0
```

You can get more information on the Linux IP Masquerade feature from the *IP Masquerade Resource Page*
<http://www.hwy401.com/achau/ipmasq/>

6.18   IP Transparent Proxy

IP transparent proxy is a feature that enables you to redirect servers or services destined for another machine
to those services on this machine. Typically this would be useful where you have a linux machine as a router
and also provides a proxy server. You would redirect all connections destined for that service remotely to
the local proxy server.

Kernel Compile Options:

```
Code maturity level options   --->
        [*] Prompt for development and/or incomplete code/drivers
Networking options   --->
        [*] Network firewalls
        ....
        [*] TCP/IP networking
        ....
        [*] IP: firewalling
        ....
        [*] IP: transparent proxy support (EXPERIMENTAL)
```

Configuration of the transparent proxy feature is performed using the *ipfwadm* command.

An example that might be useful is as follows:

```
ipfwadm -I -a accept -D 0/0 80 -r 8080
```

This example will cause any connection attempts to port 80 (www) on any host to be redirected to port 8080 on this host. This could be used to ensure that all WWW traffic from your network is automatically directed to a local WWW cache program.

6.19   Mobile IP

The term "IP mobility" describes the ability of a host that is able to move its network connection from one point on the Internet to another without changing its IP address or losing connectivity. Usually when an IP host changes its point of connectivity it must also change its IP address. IP Mobility overcomes this problem by allocating a fixed IP address to the mobile host and using IP encapsulation (tunneling) with automatic routing to ensure that datagrams destined for it are routed to the actual IP address it is currently using.

A project is underway to provide a complete set of IP mobility tools for Linux. The Status of the project and tools may be obtained from the: *Linux Mobile IP Home Page* <http://anchor.cs.binghamton.edu/~mobileip/>.

6.20   Multicast

IP Multicast allows an arbitrary number of IP hosts on disparate IP networks to have IP datagrams simultaneously routed to them. This mechanism is exploited to provide Internet wide "broadcast" material such as audio and video transmissions and other novel applications.

Kernel Compile Options:

```
Networking options  --->
        [*] TCP/IP networking
        ....
        [*] IP: multicasting
```

A suite of tools and some minor network configuration is required. One source of information on how to install and configure these for Linux is provided at *www.teksouth.com* <http://www.teksouth.com/linux/multicast/>.

6.21   NAT - Network Address Translation

The IP Network Address Translation facility is pretty much the standardised big brother of the Linux IP Masquerade facility. It is specified in some detail in RFC-1631 at your nearest RFC archive. NAT provides features that IP-Masquerade does not that make it eminently more suitable for use in corporate firewall router designs and larger scale installations.

An alpha implementation of NAT for Linux 2.0.29 kernel has been developed by Michael.Hasenstein, `Michael.Hasenstein@informatik.tu-chemnitz.de`. Michaels documentation and implementation are available from:

Linux IP Network Address Web Page <http://www.csn.tu-chemnitz.de/HyperNews/get/linux-ip-nat.html>

Newer Linux 2.1.* kernels also include some NAT functionality in the routing algorithm.

6.22   NetRom (AF_NETROM)

NetRom device names are 'nr0', 'nr1', etc.

Kernel Compile Options:

```
Networking options  --->
    [*] Amateur Radio AX.25 Level 2
    [*] Amateur Radio NET/ROM
```

The AX25, Netrom and Rose protocols are covered by the *AX25-HOWTO* <AX25-HOWTO.html>. These protocols are used by Amateur Radio Operators world wide in packet radio experimentation.

Most of the work for implementation of these protocols has been done by Jonathon Naylor, jsn@cs.nott.ac.uk.

6.23   PLIP

PLIP device names are 'plip0', 'plip1 and plip2.

Kernel Compile Options:

```
Networking options  --->
    <*> PLIP (parallel port) support
```

plip (Parallel Line IP), is like SLIP, in that it is used for providing a *point to point* network connection between two machines, except that it is designed to use the parallel printer ports on your machine instead of the serial ports (a cabling diagram in included in the cabling diagram section later in this document). Because it is possible to transfer more than one bit at a time with a parallel port, it is possible to attain higher speeds with the *plip* interface than with a standard serial device. In addition, even the simplest of parallel ports, printer ports, can be used in lieu of you having to purchase comparatively expensive 16550AFN UART's for your serial ports. PLIP uses a lot of CPU compared to a serial link and is most certainly not a good option if you can obtain some cheap ethernet cards, but it will work when nothing else is available and will work quite well. You should expect a data transfer rate of about 20 kilobytes per second when a link is running well.

The PLIP device drivers competes with the parallel device driver for the parallel port hardware. If you wish to use both drivers then you should compile them both as modules to ensure that you are able to select which port you want to use for PLIP and which ports you want for the printer driver. Refer to the *Modules-HOWTO* <Modules-HOWTO.html> for more information on kernel module configuration.

Please note that some laptops use chipsets that will not work with PLIP because they do not allow some combinations of signals that PLIP relies on, that printers don't use.

The Linux *plip* interface is compatible with the *Crynwyr Packet Driver PLIP* and this will mean that you can connect your Linux machine to a DOS machine running any other sort of tcp/ip software via *plip*.

In the 2.0.* series kernel the plip devices are mapped to i/o port and IRQ as follows:

```
device  i/o    IRQ
------  -----  ---
plip0   0x3bc  5
plip1   0x378  7
plip2   0x278  2
```

If your parallel ports don't match any of the above combinations then you can change the IRQ of a port using the *ifconfig* command using the 'irq' parameter. Be sure to enable IRQ's on your printer ports in your ROM BIOS if it supports this option.

In late 2.1.* series kernel with Plug'n'Play support the plip devices are allocated sequentially as they are detected just like the ethernet devices with plip0 being the first allocated.

When compiling the kernel, there is only one file that might need to be looked at to configure *plip*. That file is /usr/src/linux/driver/net/CONFIG and it contains *plip* timers in milliseconds. The defaults are probably ok in most cases. You will probably need to increase them if you have an especially slow computer, in which case the timers to increase are actually on the **other** computer. A program called *plipconfig* exists that allows you to change these timer settings without recompiling your kernel. It is supplied with many Linux distributions.

To configure a *plip* interface, you will need to **add** the following lines to your network **rc** file:

```
#
# Attach a PLIP interface
#
#  configure first parallel port as a plip device
/sbin/ifconfig plip0 IPA.IPA.IPA.IPA pointopoint IPR.IPR.IPR.IPR up
#
# End plip
```

Where:

IPA.IPA.IPA.IPA

represents your IP address.

IPR.IPR.IPR.IPR

represents the IP address of the remote machine.

The *pointopoint* parameter has the same meaning as for SLIP, in that it specifies the address of the machine at the other end of the link.

In almost all respects you can treat a *plip* interface as though it were a *SLIP* interface, except that neither *dip* nor *slattach* need be, nor can be, used.

Further information on PLIP may be obtained from the *PLIP-mini-HOWTO* <mini/PLIP>

6.24 PPP

PPP devices names are 'ppp0', 'ppp1', etc. Devices are numbered sequentially with the first device configured receiving '0'.

Kernel Compile Options:

```
Networking options  --->
    <*> PPP (point-to-point) support
```

PPP configuration is covered in detail in the *PPP-HOWTO* <PPP-HOWTO.html>.

6.24.1 Maintaining a permanent connection to the net with *pppd*.

If you are fortunate enough to have a semi permanent connection to the net and would like to have your machine automatically redial your PPP connection if it is lost then here is a simple trick to do so.

Configure PPP such that it can be started by the `root` user by issuing the command:

```
# pppd
```

Be sure that you have the '-detach' option configured in your `/etc/ppp/options` file. Then, insert the following line into your `/etc/inittab` file, down with the *getty* definitions:

```
pd:23:respawn:/usr/sbin/pppd
```

This will cause the *init* program to spawn and monitor the *pppd* program and automatically restart it if it dies.

6.25 Rose protocol (AF_ROSE)

Rose device names are 'rs0', 'rs1', etc. in 2.1.* kernels. Rose is available in the 2.1.* kernels.

Kernel Compile Options:

```
Networking options  --->
    [*] Amateur Radio AX.25 Level 2
    <*> Amateur Radio X.25 PLP (Rose)
```

The AX25, Netrom and Rose protocols are covered by the *AX25-HOWTO* `<AX25-HOWTO.html>`. These protocols are used by Amateur Radio Operators world wide in packet radio experimentation.

Most of the work for implementation of these protocols has been done by Jonathon Naylor, jsn@cs.nott.ac.uk.

6.26 SAMBA - 'NetBEUI', 'NetBios' support.

SAMBA is an implementation of the Session Management Block protocol. Samba allows Microsoft and other systems to mount and use your disks and printers.

SAMBA and its configuration are covered in detail in the *SMB-HOWTO* `<SMB-HOWTO.html>`.

6.27 SLIP client

SLIP devices are named 'sl0', 'sl1' etc. with the first device configured being assigned '0' and the rest incrementing sequentially as they are configured.

Kernel Compile Options:

```
Network device support  --->
    [*] Network device support
    <*> SLIP (serial line) support
    [ ] CSLIP compressed headers
    [ ] Keepalive and linefill
```

[ ] Six bit SLIP encapsulation

SLIP (Serial Line Internet Protocol) allows you to use tcp/ip over a serial line, be that a phone line with a dialup modem, or a leased line of some sort. Of course to use SLIP you need access to a *SLIP-server* in your area. Many universities and businesses provide SLIP access all over the world.

Slip uses the serial ports on your machine to carry IP datagrams. To do this it must take control of the serial device. Slip device names are named *sl0*, *sl1* etc. How do these correspond to your serial devices ? The networking code uses what is called an *ioctl* (i/o control) call to change the serial devices into SLIP devices. There are two programs supplied that can do this, they are called *dip* and *slattach*

6.27.1 dip

dip (Dialup IP) is a smart program that is able to set the speed of the serial device, command your modem to dial the remote end of the link, automatically log you into the remote server, search for messages sent to you by the server and extract information for them such as your IP address and perform the *ioctl* necessary to switch your serial port into SLIP mode. *dip* has a powerful scripting ability and it is this that you can exploit to automate your logon procedure.

You can find it at: *sunsite.unc.edu* <ftp://sunsite.unc.edu/pub/Linux/system/Network/serial/dip/dip337o-uri.tgz>.

To install it, try the following:

```
#
# cd /usr/src
# gzip -dc dip337o-uri.tgz | tar xvf -
# cd dip-3.3.7o

<edit Makefile>

# make install
#
```

The Makefile assumes the existence of a group called *uucp*, but you might like to change this to either *dip* or *SLIP* depending on your configuration.

6.27.2 slattach

slattach as contrasted with *dip* is a very simple program, that is very easy to use, but does not have the sophistication of *dip*. It does not have the scripting ability, all it does is configure your serial device as a SLIP device. It assumes you have all the information you need and the serial line is established before you invoke it. *slattach* is ideal to use where you have a permanent connection to your server, such as a physical cable, or a leased line.

6.27.3 When do I use which ?

You would use *dip* when your link to the machine that is your SLIP server is a dialup modem, or some other temporary link. You would use *slattach* when you have a leased line, perhaps a cable, between your machine and the server and there is no special action needed to get the link working. See section 'Permanent Slip connection' for more information.

Configuring SLIP is much like configuring an Ethernet interface (read section 'Configuring an ethernet device' above). However there are a few key differences.

First of all, SLIP links are unlike ethernet networks in that there is only ever two hosts on the network, one at each end of the link. Unlike an ethernet that is available for use as soon are you are cabled, with SLIP, depending on the type of link you have, you may have to initialize your network connection in some special way.

If you are using *dip* then this would not normally be done at boot time, but at some time later, when you were ready to use the link. It is possible to automate this procedure. If you are using *slattach* then you will probably want to add a section to your *rc.inet1* file. This will be described soon.

There are two major types of SLIP servers: Dynamic IP address servers and static IP address servers. Almost every SLIP server will prompt you to login using a username and password when dialing in. *dip* can handle logging you in automatically.

6.27.4   Static SLIP server with a dialup line and DIP.

A static SLIP server is one in which you have been supplied an IP address that is exclusively yours. Each time you connect to the server, you will configure your SLIP port with that address. The static SLIP server will answer your modem call, possibly prompt you for a username and password, and then route any datagrams destined for your address to you via that connection. If you have a static server, then you may want to put entries for your hostname and IP address (since you know what it will be) into your `/etc/hosts`. You should also configure some other files such as: `rc.inet2`, `host.conf`, `resolv.conf`, `/etc/HOSTNAME` and `rc.local`. Remember that when configuring `rc.inet1`, you don't need to add any special commands for your SLIP connection since it is *dip* that does all of the hard work for you in configuring your interface. You will need to give *dip* the appropriate information and it will configure the interface for you after commanding the modem to establish the call and logging you into your SLIP server.

If this is how your SLIP server works then you can move to section 'Using Dip' to learn how to configure *dip* appropriately.

6.27.5   Dynamic SLIP server with a dialup line and DIP.

A *dynamic* SLIP server is one which allocates you an IP address randomly, from a pool of addresses, each time you logon. This means that there is no guarantee that you will have any particular address each time, and that address may well be used by someone else after you have logged off. The network administrator who configured the SLIP server will have assigned a pool of address for the SLIP server to use, when the server receives a new incoming call, it finds the first unused address, guides the caller through the login process and then prints a welcome message that contains the IP address it has allocated and will proceed to use that IP address for the duration of that call.

Configuring for this type of server is similar to configuring for a static server, except that you must add a step where you obtain the IP address that the server has allocated for you and configure your SLIP device with that.

Again, *dip* does the hard work and new versions are smart enough to not only log you in, but to also be able to automatically read the IP address printed in the welcome message and store it so that you can have it configure your SLIP device with it.

If this is how your SLIP server works then you can move to section 'Using Dip' to learn how to configure *dip* appropriately.

6.27.6 Using DIP.

As explained earlier, *dip* is a powerful program that can simplify and automate the process of dialing into the SLIP server, logging you in, starting the connection and configuring your SLIP devices with the appropriate *ifconfig* and *route* commands.

Essentially to use *dip* you'll write a 'dip script', which is basically a list of commands that *dip* understands that tell *dip* how to perform each of the actions you want it to perform. See `sample.dip` that comes supplied with *dip* to get an idea of how it works. *dip* is quite a powerful program, with many options. Instead of going into all of them here you should look at the *man* page, README and sample files that will have come with your version of *dip*.

You may notice that the `sample.dip` script assumes that you're using a static SLIP server, so you know what your IP address is beforehand. For dynamic SLIP servers, the newer versions of *dip* include a command you can use to automatically read and configure your SLIP device with the IP address that the dynamic server allocates for you. The following sample is a modified version of the `sample.dip` that came supplied with *dip337j-uri.tgz* and is probably a good starting point for you. You might like to save it as `/etc/dipscript` and edit it to suit your configuration:

```
#
# sample.dip    Dialup IP connection support program.
#
#              This file (should show) shows how to use the DIP
#       This file should work for Annex type dynamic servers, if you
#       use a static address server then use the sample.dip file that
#       comes as part of the dip337-uri.tgz package.
#
#
# Version:      @(#)sample.dip  1.40    07/20/93
#
# Author:       Fred N. van Kempen, <waltje@uWalt.NL.Mugnet.ORG>
#


main:
# Next, set up the other side's name and address.
# My dialin machine is called 'xs4all.hacktic.nl' (== 193.78.33.42)
get $remote xs4all.hacktic.nl
# Set netmask on sl0 to 255.255.255.0
netmask 255.255.255.0
# Set the desired serial port and speed.
port cua02
speed 38400


# Reset the modem and terminal line.
# This seems to cause trouble for some people!
reset


# Note! "Standard" pre-defined "errlevel" values:
#  0 - OK
```

```
#  1 - CONNECT
#  2 - ERROR
#
# You can change those grep'ping for "addchat()" in *.c...

# Prepare for dialing.
send ATQOV1E1X4\r
wait OK 2
if $errlvl != 0 goto modem_trouble
dial 555-1234567
if $errlvl != 1 goto modem_trouble

# We are connected.  Login to the system.
login:
sleep 2
wait ogin: 20
if $errlvl != 0 goto login_trouble
send MYLOGIN\n
wait ord: 20
if $errlvl != 0 goto password_error
send MYPASSWD\n
loggedin:

# We are now logged in.
wait SOMEPROMPT 30
if $errlvl != 0 goto prompt_error

# Command the server into SLIP mode
send SLIP\n
wait SLIP 30
if $errlvl != 0 goto prompt_error

# Get and Set your IP address from the server.
#   Here we assume that after commanding the SLIP server into SLIP
#   mode that it prints your IP address
get $locip remote 30
if $errlvl != 0 goto prompt_error

# Set up the SLIP operating parameters.
get $mtu 296
# Ensure "route add -net default xs4all.hacktic.nl" will be done
default

# Say hello and fire up!
done:
```

```
       print CONNECTED $locip ---> $rmtip
       mode CSLIP
       goto exit

       prompt_error:
       print TIME-OUT waiting for sliplogin to fire up...
       goto error

       login_trouble:
       print Trouble waiting for the Login: prompt...
       goto error

       password:error:
       print Trouble waiting for the Password: prompt...
       goto error

       modem_trouble:
       print Trouble occurred with the modem...
       error:
       print CONNECT FAILED to $remote
       quit

       exit:
       exit
```

The above example assumes you are calling a *dynamic* SLIP server, if you are calling a *static* SLIP server, then the `sample.dip` file that comes with *dip337j-uri.tgz* should work for you.

When *dip* is given the *get $local* command it searches the incoming text from the remote end for a string that looks like an IP address, ie strings numbers separated by '.' characters. This modification was put in place specifically for *dynamic* SLIP servers, so that the process of reading the IP address granted by the server could be automated.

The example above will automatically create a default route via your SLIP link, if this is not what you want, you might have an ethernet connection that should be your default route, then remove the *default* command from the script. After this script has finished running, if you do an *ifconfig* command, you will see that you have a device *sl0*. This is your SLIP device. Should you need to, you can modify its configuration manually, after the *dip* command has finished, using the *ifconfig* and *route* commands.

Please note that *dip* allows you to select a number of different protocols to use with the `mode` command, the most common example is *cSLIP* for SLIP with compression. Please note that both ends of the link must agree, so you should ensure that whatever you select agrees with what your server is set to.

The above example is fairly robust and should cope with most errors. Please refer to the *dip* man page for more information. Naturally you could, for example, code the script to do such things as redial the server if it doesn't get a connection within a prescribed period of time, or even try a series of servers if you have access to more than one.

6.27.7   Permanent SLIP connection using a leased line and slattach.

If you have a cable between two machines, or are fortunate enough to have a leased line, or some other permanent serial connection between your machine and another, then you don't need to go to all the trouble of using *dip* to set up your serial link. *slattach* is a very simple to use utility that will allow you just enough functionality to configure your connection.

Since your connection will be a permanent one, you will want to add some commands to your `rc.inet1` file. In essence all you need to do for a permanent connection is ensure that you configure the serial device to the correct speed and switch the serial device into SLIP mode. *slattach* allows you to do this with one command. **Add** the following to your `rc.inet1` file:

```
#
# Attach a leased line static SLIP connection
#
#  configure /dev/cua0 for 19.2kbps and cslip
/sbin/slattach -p cslip -s 19200 /dev/cua0 &
/sbin/ifconfig sl0 IPA.IPA.IPA.IPA pointopoint IPR.IPR.IPR.IPR up
#
# End static SLIP.
```

Where:

IPA.IPA.IPA.IPA

> represents your IP address.

IPR.IPR.IPR.IPR

> represents the IP address of the remote end.

slattach allocates the first unallocated SLIP device to the serial device specified. *slattach* starts with *sl0*. Therefore the first *slattach* command attaches SLIP device *sl0* to the serial device specified and *sl1* the next time, etc.

slattach allows you to configure a number of different protocols with the `-p` argument. In your case you will use either *SLIP* or *cSLIP* depending on whether you want to use compression or not. Note: both ends must agree on whether you want compression or not.

6.28   SLIP server.

If you have a machine that is perhaps network connected, that you'd like other people be able to dial into and provide network services, then you will need to configure your machine as a server. If you want to use SLIP as the serial line protocol, then currently you have three options as to how to configure your Linux machine as a SLIP server. My preference would be to use the first presented, *sliplogin*, as it seems the easiest to configure and understand, but I will present a summary of each, so you can make your own decision.

6.28.1   Slip Server using *sliplogin*.

sliplogin is a program that you can use in place of the normal login shell for SLIP users that converts the terminal line into a SLIP line. It allows you to configure your Linux machine as either a *static address server*, users get the same address everytime they call in, or a *dynamic address server*, where users get an address allocated for them which will not necessarily be the same as the last time they called.

The caller will login as per the standard login process, entering their username and password, but instead of being presented with a shell after their login, *sliplogin* is executed which searches its configuration file (`/etc/slip.hosts`) for an entry with a login name that matches that of the caller. If it locates one, it configures the line as an 8bit clean line, and uses an *ioctl* call to convert the line discipline to SLIP. When this process is complete, the last stage of configuration takes place, where *sliplogin* invokes a shell script which configures the SLIP interface with the relevant ip address, netmask and sets appropriate routing in place. This script is usually called `/etc/slip.login`, but in a similar manner to *getty*, if you have certain callers that require special initialisation, then you can create configuration scripts called `/etc/slip.login.loginname` that will be run instead of the default specifically for them.

There are either three or four files that you need to configure to get *sliplogin* working for you. I will detail how and where to get the software and how each is configured in detail. The files are:

- `/etc/passwd`, for the dialin user accounts.

- `/etc/slip.hosts`, to contain the information unique to each dial-in user.

- `/etc/slip.login`, which manages the configuration of the routing that needs to be performed for the user.

- `/etc/slip.tty`, which is required only if you are configuring your server for *dynamic address allocation* and contains a table of addresses to allocate

- `/etc/slip.logout`, which contains commands to clean up after the user has hung up or logged out.

Where to get *sliplogin* You may already have the *sliplogin* package installed as part of your distribution, if not then *sliplogin* can be obtained from: *sunsite.unc.edu* <ftp://sunsite.unc.edu/pub/linux/system/Network/serial/sliplogin-2.1.1.tar.gz>. The tar file contains both source, precompiled binaries and a *man* page.

To ensure that only authorised users will be able to run *sliplogin* program, you should add an entry to your `/etc/group` file similar to the following:

```
    . .
    slip::13:radio,fred
    . .
```

When you install the *sliplogin* package, the `Makefile` will change the group ownership of the *sliplogin* program to `slip`, and this will mean that only users who belong to that group will be able to execute it. The example above will allow only users `radio` and `fred` to execute *sliplogin*.

To install the binaries into your `/sbin` directory and the *man* page into section 8, do the following:

```
    # cd /usr/src
    # gzip -dc .../sliplogin-2.1.1.tar.gz | tar xvf -
    # cd sliplogin-2.1.1
    # <..edit the Makefile if you don't use shadow passwords..>
    # make install
```

If you want to recompile the binaries before installation, add a `make clean` before the `make install`. If you want to install the binaries somewhere else, you will need to edit the `Makefile` *install* rule.

Please read the `README` files that come with the package for more information.

Configuring /etc/passwd **for Slip hosts.** Normally you would create some special logins for Slip callers in your /etc/passwd file. A convention commonly followed is to use the *hostname* of the calling host with a capital 'S' prefixing it. So, for example, if the calling host is called radio then you could create a /etc/passwd entry that looked like:

        Sradio:FvKurok73:1427:1:radio SLIP login:/tmp:/sbin/sliplogin

It doesn't really matter what the account is called, so long as it is meaningful to you.

Note: the caller doesn't need any special home directory, as they will not be presented with a shell from this machine, so /tmp is a good choice. Also note that *sliplogin* is used in place of the normal login shell.

Configuring /etc/slip.hosts The /etc/slip.hosts file is the file that *sliplogin* searches for entries matching the login name to obtain configuration details for this caller. It is this file where you specify the ip address and netmask that will be assigned to the caller and configured for their use. Sample entries for two hosts, one a static configuration for host radio and another, a dynamic configuration for user host albert might look like:

        #
        Sradio   44.136.8.99   44.136.8.100   255.255.255.0   normal   -1
        Salbert   44.136.8.99   DYNAMIC   255.255.255.0   compressed 60
        #

The /etc/slip.hosts file entries are:

1. the login name of the caller.

2. ip address of the server machine, ie this machine.

3. ip address that the caller will be assigned. If this field is coded DYNAMIC then an ip address will be allocated based on the information contained in your /etc/slip.tty file discussed later. **Note:** you must be using at least version 1.3 of sliplogin for this to work.

4. the netmask assigned to the calling machine in dotted decimal notation eg 255.255.255.0 for a Class C network mask.

5. the slip mode setting which allows you to enable/disable compression and slip other features. Allowable values here are "normal" or "compressed".

6. a timeout parameter which specifies how long the line can remain idle (no datagrams received) before the line is automatically disconnected. A negative value disables this feature.

7. optional arguments.

Note: You can use either hostnames or IP addresses in dotted decimal notation for fields 2 and 3. If you use hostnames then those hosts must be resolvable, that is, your machine must be able to locate an ip address for those hostnames, otherwise the script will fail when it is called. You can test this by trying trying to telnet to the hostname, if you get the '*Trying nnn.nnn.nnn...*' message then your machine has been able to find an ip address for that name. If you get the message '*Unknown host*', then it has not. If not, either use ip addresses in dotted decimal notation, or fix up your name resolver configuration (See section **Name Resolution**).

The most common slip modes are:

normal
        to enable normal uncompressed SLIP.

compressed

> to enable van Jacobsen header compression (cSLIP)

Naturally these are mutually exclusive, you can use one or the other. For more information on the other options available, refer to the *man* pages.

Configuring the /etc/slip.login file. After *sliplogin* has searched the /etc/slip.hosts and found a matching entry, it will attempt to execute the /etc/slip.login file to actually configure the SLIP interface with its ip address and netmask.

The sample /etc/slip.login file supplied with the *sliplogin* package looks like this:

```
#!/bin/sh -
#
#       @(#)slip.login  5.1 (Berkeley) 7/1/90
#
# generic login file for a SLIP line.  sliplogin invokes this with
# the parameters:
#       $1         $2        $3     $4, $5, $6 ...
#    SLIPunit ttyspeed    pid    the arguments from the slip.host entry
#
/sbin/ifconfig $1 $5 pointopoint $6 mtu 1500 -trailers up
/sbin/route add $6
arp -s $6 <hw_addr> pub
exit 0
#
```

You will note that this script simply uses the *ifconfig* and *route* commands to configure the SLIP device with its ipaddress, remote ip address and netmask and creates a route for the remote address via the SLIP device. Just the same as you would if you were using the *slattach* command.

Note also the use of *Proxy ARP* to ensure that other hosts on the same ethernet as the server machine will know how to reach the dial-in host. The <hw_addr> field should be the hardware address of the ethernet card in the machine. If your server machine isn't on an ethernet network then you can leave this line out completely.

Configuring the /etc/slip.logout file. When the call drops out, you want to ensure that the serial device is restored to its normal state so that future callers will be able to login correctly. This is achieved with the use of the /etc/slip.logout file. It is quite simple in format and is called with the same argument as the /etc/slip.login file.

```
#!/bin/sh -
#
#               slip.logout
#
/sbin/ifconfig $1 down
arp -d $6
exit 0
#
```

All it does is 'down' the interface which will delete the manual route previously created. It also uses the *arp* command to delete any proxy arp put in place, again, you don't need the *arp* command in the script if your server machine does not have an ethernet port.

Configuring the /etc/slip.tty file. If you are using dynamic ip address allocation (have any hosts configured with the DYNAMIC keyword in the /etc/slip.hosts file, then you must configure the /etc/slip.tty file to list what addresses are assigned to what port. You only need this file if you wish your server to dynamically allocate addresses to users.

The file is a table that lists the *tty* devices that will support dial-in SLIP connections and the ip address that should be assigned to users who call in on that port.

Its format is as follows:

```
# slip.tty    tty -> IP address mappings for dynamic SLIP
# format: /dev/tty?? xxx.xxx.xxx.xxx
#
/dev/ttyS0      192.168.0.100
/dev/ttyS1      192.168.0.101
#
```

What this table says is that callers that dial in on port /dev/ttyS0 who have their remote address field in the /etc/slip.hosts file set to DYNAMIC will be assigned an address of 192.168.0.100.

In this way you need only allocate one address per port for all users who do not require an dedicated address for themselves. This helps you keep the number of addresses you need down to a minimum to avoid wastage.

6.28.2   Slip Server using *dip*.

Let me start by saying that some of the information below came from the *dip* man pages, where how to run Linux as a SLIP server is briefly documented. Please also beware that the following has been based on the *dip3370-uri.tgz* package and probably will not apply to other versions of *dip*.

dip has an input mode of operation, where it automatically locates an entry for the user who invoked it and configures the serial line as a SLIP link according to information it finds in the /etc/diphosts file. This input mode of operation is activated by invoking *dip* as *diplogin*. This therefore is how you use *dip* as a SLIP server, by creating special accounts where *diplogin* is used as the login shell.

The first thing you will need to do is to make a symbolic link as follows:

```
# ln -sf /usr/sbin/dip /usr/sbin/diplogin
```

You then need to add entries to both your /etc/passwd and your /etc/diphosts files. The entries you need to make are formatted as follows:

To configure Linux as a SLIP server with *dip*, you need to create some special SLIP accounts for users, where *dip* (in input mode) is used as the login shell. A suggested convention is that of having all SLIP accounts begin with a capital 'S', eg 'Sfredm'.

A sample /etc/passwd entry for a SLIP user looks like:

```
Sfredm:ij/SMxiTlGVCo:1004:10:Fred:/tmp:/usr/sbin/diplogin

  |          |           |   |   |    |      \__ diplogin as login shell
```

```
|          |         |      |    |  _____  Home directory
|          |         |      |    _____  User Full Name
|          |         |      _____  User Group ID
|          |         _____  User ID
|          _____  Encrypted User Password
_____  Slip User Login Name
```

After the user logs in, the *login* program, if it finds and verifies the user ok, will execute the *diplogin* command. *dip*, when invoked as *diplogin* knows that it should automatically assume that it is being used a login shell. When it is started as *diplogin* the first thing it does is use the *getuid()* function call to get the userid of whoever has invoked it. It then searches the /etc/diphosts file for the first entry that matches either the userid or the name of the *tty* device that the call has come in on and configures itself appropriately. By judicious decision as to whether to give a user an entry in the diphosts file, or whether to let the user be given the default configuration you can build your server in such a way that you can have a mix of static and dynamically assigned address users.

dip will automatically add a 'Proxy-ARP' entry if invoked in input mode, so you do not need to worry about manually adding such entries.

Configuring /etc/diphosts /etc/diphosts is used by *dip* to lookup preset configurations for remote hosts. These remote hosts might be users dialing into your linux machine, or they might be for machines that you dial into with your linux machine.

The general format for /etc/diphosts is as follows:

```
  ..
  Suwalt::145.71.34.1:145.71.34.2:255.255.255.0:SLIP uwalt:CSLIP,1006
  ttyS1::145.71.34.3:145.71.34.2:255.255.255.0:Dynamic ttyS1:CSLIP,296
  ..
```

The fields are:

1. login name: as returned by getpwuid(getuid()) or tty name.
2. unused: compat. with passwd
3. Remote Address: IP address of the calling host, either numeric or by name
4. Local Address: IP address of this machine, again numeric or by name
5. Netmask: in dotted decimal notation
6. Comment field: put whatever you want here.
7. protocol: Slip, CSlip etc.
8. MTU: decimal number

An example /etc/net/diphosts entry for a remote SLIP user might be:

```
  Sfredm::145.71.34.1:145.71.34.2:255.255.255.0:SLIP uwalt:SLIP,296
```

which specifies a SLIP link with remote address of 145.71.34.1 and MTU of 296, or:

```
  Sfredm::145.71.34.1:145.71.34.2:255.255.255.0:SLIP uwalt:CSLIP,1006
```

which specifies a cSLIP-capable link with remote address 145.71.34.1 and MTU of 1006.

Therefore, all users who you wish to be allowed a statically allocated dial-up IP access should have an entry in the /etc/diphosts. If you want users who call a particular port to have their details dynamically allocated then you must have an entry for the tty device and do not configure a user based entry. You should remember to configure at least one entry for each tty device that your dialup users use to ensure that a suitable configuration is available for them regardless of which modem they call in on.

When a user logs in they will receive a normal login and password prompt at which they should enter their SLIP-login userid and password. If these verify ok then the user will see no special messages and they should just change into SLIP mode at their end. The user should then be able to connect ok and be configured with the relevant parameters from the diphosts file.

6.28.3   SLIP server using the *dSLIP* package.

Matt Dillon <dillon@apollo.west.oic.com> has written a package that does not only dial-in but also dial-out SLIP. Matt's package is a combination of small programs and scripts that manage your connections for you. You will need to have *tcsh* installed as at least one of the scripts requires it. Matt supplies a binary copy of the *expect* utility as it too is needed by one of the scripts. You will most likely need some experience with *expect* to get this package working to your liking, but don't let that put you off.

Matt has written a good set of installation instructions in the README file, so I won't bother repeating them.

You can get the *dSLIP* package from its home site at:

apollo.west.oic.com

        /pub/linux/dillon_src/dSLIP203.tgz

or from:

sunsite.unc.edu

        /pub/Linux/system/Network/serial/dSLIP203.tgz

Read the README file and create the /etc/passwd and /etc/group entries **before** doing a make install.

6.29   STRIP support (Starmode Radio IP)

STRIP device names are 'st0', 'st1', etc.

Kernel Compile Options:

```
Network device support  --->
        [*] Network device support
        ....
        [*] Radio network interfaces
        < > STRIP (Metricom starmode radio IP)
```

STRIP is a protocol designed specifically for a range of Metricom radio modems for a research project being conducted by Stanford University called the *MosquitoNet Project* <http://mosquitonet.Stanford. EDU/mosquitonet.html>. There is a lot of interesting reading here, even if you aren't directly interested in the project.

The Metricom radios connect to a serial port, employ spread spectrum technology and are typically capable of about 100kbps. Information on the Metricom radios is available from the: *Metricom Web Server* <http://www.metricom.com/>.

At present the standard network tools and utilities do not support the STRIP driver, so you will have to download some customised tools from the MosquitoNet web server. Details on what software you need is available at the: *MosquitoNet STRIP Page* <http://mosquitonet.Stanford.EDU/strip.html>.

A summary of configuration is that you use a modified *slattach* program to set the line discipline of a serial tty device to STRIP and then configure the resulting 'st[0-9]' device as you would for ethernet with one important exception, for technical reasons STRIP does not support the ARP protocol, so you must manually configure the ARP entries for each of the hosts on your subnet. This shouldn't prove too onerous.

6.30 Token Ring

Token ring device names are 'tr0', 'tr1' etc. Token Ring is an IBM standard LAN protocol that avoids collisions by providing a mechanism that allows only one station on the LAN the right to transmit at a time. A 'token' is held by one station at a time and the station holding the token is the only station allowed to transmit. When it has transmitted its data it passes the token onto the next station. The token loops amongst all active stations, hence the name 'Token Ring'.

Kernel Compile Options:

```
Network device support  --->
        [*] Network device support
        ....
        [*] Token Ring driver support
        < > IBM Tropic chipset based adaptor support
```

Configuration of token ring is identical to that of ethernet with the exception of the network device name to configure.

6.31 X.25

X.25 is a circuit based packet switching protocol defined by the C.C.I.T.T. (a standards body recognised by Telecommunications companies in most parts of the world). An implementation of X.25 and LAPB are being worked on and recent 2.1.* kernels include the work in progress.

Jonathon Naylor jsn@cs.nott.ac.uk is leading the development and a mailing list has been established to discuss Linux X.25 related matters. To subscribe send a message to: majordomo@vger.rutgers.edu with the text "subscribe linux-x25" in the body of the message.

Early versions of the configuration tools may be obtained from Jonathon's ftp site at *ftp.cs.nott.ac.uk* <ftp://ftp.cs.nott.ac.uk/jsn/>.

6.32 WaveLan Card

Wavelan device names are 'eth0', 'eth1', etc.

Kernel Compile Options:

```
Network device support  --->
```

```
[*] Network device support
....
[*] Radio network interfaces
....
<*> WaveLAN support
```

The WaveLAN card is a spread spectrum wireless lan card. The card looks very like an ethernet card in practice and is configured in much the same way.

You can get information on the Wavelan card from *Wavelan.com* <http://www.wavelan.com/>.

7 Cables and Cabling

Those of you handy with a soldering iron may want to build your own cables to interconnect two linux machines. The following cabling diagrams should assist you in this.

7.1 Serial NULL Modem cable

Not all NULL modem cables are alike. Many null modem cables do little more than trick your computer into thinking all the appropriate signals are present and swap transmit and receive data. This is ok but means that you must use software flow control (XON/XOFF) which is less efficient than hardware flow control. The following cable provides the best possible signalling between machines and allows you to use hardware (RTS/CTS) flow control.

```
Pin Name  Pin                                      Pin
Tx Data   2   -----------------------------  3
Rx Data   3   -----------------------------  2
RTS       4   -----------------------------  5
CTS       5   -----------------------------  4
Ground    7   -----------------------------  7
DTR       20  -\---------------------------  8
DSR       6   -/
RLSD/DCD  8   ---------------------------/-  20
                                         \-  6
```

7.2 Parallel port cable (PLIP cable)

If you intend to use the PLIP protocol between two machines then this cable will work for you irrespective of what sort of parallel ports you have installed.

```
Pin Name   pin          pin
STROBE     1*
D0->ERROR  2   ----------- 15
D1->SLCT   3   ----------- 13
D2->PAPOUT 4   ----------- 12
D3->ACK    5   ----------- 10
```

```
D4->BUSY      6  ----------- 11
D5            7*
D6            8*
D7            9*
ACK->D3       10 ----------- 5
BUSY->D4      11 ----------- 6
PAPOUT->D2    12 ----------- 4
SLCT->D1      13 ----------- 3
FEED          14*
ERROR->D0     15 ----------- 2
INIT          16*
SLCTIN        17*
GROUND        25 ----------- 25
```

Notes:

- Do not connect the pins marked with an asterisk '*'.
- Extra grounds are 18,19,20,21,22,23 and 24.
- If the cable you are using has a metallic shield, it should be connected to the metallic DB-25 shell at **one end only**.

Warning: A miswired PLIP cable can destroy your controller card. Be very careful and double check every connection to ensure you don't cause yourself any unnecessary work or heartache.

While you may be able to run PLIP cables for long distances, you should avoid it if you can. The specifications for the cable allow for a cable length of about 1 metre or so. Please be very careful when running long plip cables as sources of strong electromagnetic fields such as lightning, power lines and radio transmitters can interfere with and sometimes even damage your controller. If you really want to connect two of your computers over a large distance you really should be looking at obtaining a pair of thin-net ethernet cards and running some coaxial cable.

7.3   10base2 (thin coax) Ethernet Cabling

10base2 is an ethernet cabling standard that specifies the use of 52 ohm coaxial cable with a diameter of about 5 millimetres. There are a couple of important rules to remember when interconnecting machines with 10base2 cabling. The first is that you must use terminators at **both ends** of the cabling. A terminator is a 52 ohm resistor that helps to ensure that the signal is absorbed and not reflected when it reaches the end of the cable. Without a terminator at each end of the cabling you may find that the ethernet is unreliable or doesn't work at all. Normally you'd use 'T pieces' to interconnect the machines, so that you end up with something that looks like:

```
|==========T=============T=============T==========T=========|
           |             |             |          |
           |             |             |          |
         -----         -----         -----      -----
        |  |          |  |          |  |        |  |
         -----         -----         -----      -----
```

where the '|' at either end represents a terminator, the '======' represents a length of coaxial cable with BNC plugs at either end and the 'T' represents a 'T piece' connector. You should keep the length of cable between the 'T piece' and the actual ethernet card in the PC as short as possible, ideally the 'T piece' will be plugged directly into the ethernet card.

7.4   Twisted Pair Ethernet Cable

If you have only two twisted pair ethernet cards and you wish to connect them you do not require a hub. You can cable the two cards directly together. A diagram showing how to do this is included in the *Ethernet-HOWTO* `<Ethernet-HOWTO.html>`

8   Glossary of Terms used in this document.

The following is a list of some of the most important terms used in this document.

ARP

> This is an acronym for the *Address Resolution Protocol* and this is how a network machine associates an IP Address with a hardware address.

ATM

> This is an acronym for *Asynchronous Transfer Mode*. An ATM network packages data into standard size blocks which it can convey efficiently from point to point. ATM is a circuit switched packet network technology.

client

> This is usually the piece of software at the end of a system where the user is. There are exceptions to this, for example, in the X11 window system it is actually the server with the user and the client runs on the remote machine. The client is the program or end of a system that is receiving the service provided by the server. In the case of *peer to peer* systems such as *slip* or *ppp* the client is taken to be the end that initiates the connection and the remote end, being called, is taken to be the server.

datagram

> A datagram is a discrete package of data and headers which contain addresses, which is the basic unit of transmission across an IP network. You might also hear this called a 'packet'.

DLCI

> The DLCI is the Data Link Connection Identifier and is used to identify a unique virtual point to point connection via a Frame Relay network. The DLCI's are normally assigned by the Frame Relay network provider.

Frame Relay

> Frame Relay is a network technology ideally suited to carrying traffic that is of bursty or sporadic nature. Network costs are reduced by having many Frame Relay customer sharing the same network capacity and relying on them wanting to make use of the network at slightly different times.

Hardware address

> This is a number that uniquely identifies a host in a physical network at the media access layer. Examples of this are *Ethernet Addresses* and *AX.25 Addresses*.

ISDN

> This is an acronym for *Integrated Services Digital Network*. ISDN provides a standardised means by which Telecommunications companies may deliver either voice or data information to a customers premises. Technically ISDN is a circuit switched data network.

ISP

> This is an acronym of Internet Service Provider. These are organisations or companies that provide people with network connectivity to the Internet.

IP address

> This is a number that uniquely identifies a TCP/IP host on the network. The address is 4 bytes long and is usually represented in what is called the "dotted decimal notation", where each byte is represented in decimal from with dots '.' between them.

MSS

> The Maximum Segment Size (*MSS*) is the largest quantity of data that can be transmitted at one time. If you want to prevent local fragmentation MSS would equal MTU-IP header.

MTU

> The Maximum Transmission Unit (*MTU*) is a parameter that determines the largest datagram than can be transmitted by an IP interface without it needing to be broken down into smaller units. The MTU should be larger than the largest datagram you wish to transmit unfragmented. Note, this only prevents fragmentation locally, some other link in the path may have a smaller MTU and the datagram will be fragmented there. Typical values are 1500 bytes for an ethernet interface, or 576 bytes for a SLIP interface.

route

> The *route* is the path that your datagrams take through the network to reach their destination.

server

> This is usually the piece of software or end of a system remote from the user. The server provides some service to one or many clients. Examples of servers include *ftp*, *Networked File System*, or *Domain Name Server*. In the case of *peer to peer* systems such as *slip* or *ppp* the server is taken to be the end of the link that is called and the end calling is taken to be the client.

window

> The *window* is the largest amount of data that the receiving end can accept at a given point in time.

9   Linux for an ISP ?

If you are interested in using Linux for ISP purposes the I recommend you take a look at the *Linux ISP homepage* <http://www.anime.net/linuxisp/> for a good list of pointers to information you might need and use.

10   Acknowledgements

I'd like to thank the following people for their contributions to this document (in no particular order): Axel Boldt, Arnt Gulbrandsen, Gary Allpike, Cees de Groot, Alan Cox, Jonathon Naylor, Claes Ensson, Ron Nessim, John Minack, Jean-Pierre Cocatrix, Erez Strauss.

A special thanks to Alessandro Rubini for his excellent feedback and contributed corrections.

11   Copyright.

The NET-3-HOWTO, information on how to install and configure networking support for Linux. Copyright (c) 1997 Terry Dawson.

This program is free software; you can redistribute it and/or modify it under the terms of the GNU General Public License as published by the Free Software Foundation; either version 2 of the License, or (at your option) any later version.

This program is distributed in the hope that it will be useful, but WITHOUT ANY WARRANTY; without even the implied warranty of MERCHANTABILITY or FITNESS FOR A PARTICULAR PURPOSE. See the GNU General Public License for more details.

You should have received a copy of the GNU General Public License along with this program; if not, write to the:

Free Software Foundation, Inc., 675 Mass Ave, Cambridge, MA 02139, USA.

NFS HOWTO

Nicolai Langfeldt `janl@math.uio.no`   v0.7, 3 November 1997

HOWTO set up NFS clients and servers.

Contents

1 Preamble

1.1 Legal stuff

(C)opyright 1997 Nicolai Langfeldt. Do not modify without amending copyright, distribute freely but retain this paragraph. The FAQ section is based on a NFS FAQ compiled by Alan Cox. The Checklist section is based on a mount problem checklist compiled by the IBM Corporation.

1.2 Other stuff

This will never be a finished document, please send me mail about your problems and successes, it can make this a better HOWTO. Please send money, comments and/or questions to janl@math.uio.no. If you send E-mail please *make sure* that the return address is correct and working, I get *a lot* of E-mail and figuring out your e-mail address can be a lot of work. Please.

If you want to translate this HOWTO please notify me so I can keep track of what languages I have been published in :-).

Curses and Thanks to Olaf Kirch who got me to write this and then gave good suggestions for it :-)

This HOWTO covers NFS in the 2.0 versions of the kernel. There are significant enhancements, and changes, of NFS in the 2.1 versions of the kernel.

1.3 Dedication

This HOWTO is dedicated to Anne Line Norheim Langfeldt. Though she will probably never read it since she's not that kind of girl.

2 README.first

NFS, the Network File System has three important characteristics:

- It makes sharing of files over a network possible.
- It mostly works well enough.
- It opens a can of security risks that are well understood by crackers, and easily exploited to get access (read, write and delete) to all your files.

I'll say something on both issues in this HOWTO. Please make sure you read the security section of this HOWTO, and you will be vulnerable to fewer silly security risks. The passages about security will at times be pretty technical and require some knowledge about IP networking and the terms used. If you don't recognize the terms you can either go back and check the networking HOWTO, wing it, or get a book about TCP/IP network administration to familiarize yourself with TCP/IP. That's a good idea anyway if you're administrating UNIX/Linux machines. A very good book on the subject is *TCP/IP Network Administration* by Craig Hunt, published by O'Reilly & Associates, Inc. And after you've read it and understood it you'll have higher value on the job market, you can't loose ;-)

There are two sections to help you troubleshoot NFS, called *Mount Checklist* and *FAQs*. Please refer to them if something doesn't work as advertized.

3 Setting up a NFS server

3.1 Prerequisites

Before you continue reading this HOWTO you will need to be able to telnet back and forth between the machine you're using as server and the client. If that does not work you need to check the networking/NET-2 HOWTO and set up networking properly.

3.2 First step

Before we can do anything else we need a NFS server set up. If you're part of a department or university network there are likely numerous NFS servers already set up. If they will let you get access to them, or indeed, if you're reading this HOWTO to get access to one of them you obviously don't need to read this section and can just skip ahead to the section on 4 (setting up a NFS client)

If you need to set up a non-Linux box as server you will have to read the system manual(s) to discover how to enable NFS serving and export of file systems through NFS. There is a separate section in this HOWTO on how to do it on many different systems. After you have figured all that out you can continue reading the next section of this HOWTO. Or read more of this section since some of the things I will say are relevant no matter what kind of machine you use as server.

Those of you still reading will need to set up a number of programs.

3.3 The portmapper

The portmapper on Linux is called either `portmap` or `rpc.portmap`. The man page on my system says it is a "DARPA port to RPC program number mapper". It is the first security holes you'll open reading this HOWTO. Description of how to close one of the holes is in the 6 (security section). Which I, again, urge you to read.

Start the portmapper. It's either called `portmap` or `rpc.portmap` and it should live in the `/usr/sbin` directory (on some machines it's called rpcbind). You can start it by hand now, but it will need to be started every time you boot your machine so you need to make/edit the rc scripts. Your rc scripts are explained more closely in the init man page, they usually reside in `/etc/rc.d`, `/etc/init.d` or `/etc/rc.d/init.d`. If there is a script called something like `inet` it's probably the right script to edit. But, what to write or do is outside the scope of this HOWTO. Start portmap, and check that it lives by running `ps aux`. It does? Good.

3.4 Mountd and nfsd

The next programs we need running are mountd and nfsd. But first we'll edit another file. `/etc/exports` this time. Say I want the file system `/mn/eris/local` which lives on the machine `eris` to be available to the machine called `apollon`. Then I'd put this in `/etc/exports` on eris:

```
/mn/eris/local   apollon(rw)
```

The above line gives apollon read/write access to `/mn/eris/local`. Instead of `rw` it could say `ro` which means read only (if you put nothing it defaults to read only). There are other options you can give it, and I will discuss some security related ones later. They are all enumerated in the `exports` man page which you should have read at least once in your life. There are also better ways than listing all the hosts in the exports file. You can for example use net groups if you are running NIS (or NYS) (NIS was known as YP), and always specify domain wild cards and IP-subnets as hosts that are allowed to mount something. But you should consider who can get access to the server in unauthorized ways if you use such blanket authorizations.

Note: This exports file is not the same syntax that other Unixes use. There is a separate section in this HOWTO about other Unixes `exports` files.

Now we're set to start mountd (or maybe it's called `rpc.mountd` and then nfsd (which could be called `rpc.nfsd`). They will both read the exports file.

If you edit `/etc/exports` you will have to make sure nfsd and mountd knows that the files have changed. The traditonal way is to run `exportfs`. Many Linux distributions lack a exportfs program. If you're exportfs-less you can install this script on your machine:

```
#!/bin/sh
killall -HUP /usr/sbin/rpc.mountd
killall -HUP /usr/sbin/rpc.nfsd
echo re-exported file systems
```

Save it in, say, `/usr/sbin/exportfs`, and don't forget to `chmod a+rx` it. Now, whenever you change your exports file, you run exportfs after, as root.

Now you should check that mountd and nfsd are running properly. First with `rpcinfo -p`. It should show something like this:

---

program	vers	proto	port	
100000	2	tcp	111	portmapper
100000	2	udp	111	portmapper
100005	1	udp	745	mountd
100005	1	tcp	747	mountd
100003	2	udp	2049	nfs
100003	2	tcp	2049	nfs

As you see the portmapper has announced it's services, and so has mountd and nfsd.

If you get `rpcinfo: can't contact portmapper: RPC: Remote system error - Connection refused` or something similar instead then the portmapper isn't running. Fix it. If you get `No remote programs registered.` then either the portmapper doesn't want to talk to you, or something is broken. Kill nfsd, mountd, and the portmapper and try the ignition sequence again.

After checking that the portmapper reports the services you can check with ps too. The portmapper will continue to report the services even after the programs that extend them have crashed. So a ps check can be smart if something seems broken.

Of course, you will need to modify your system rc files to start mountd and nfsd as well as the portmapper when you boot. It is very likely that the scripts already exist on your machine, you just have to uncomment the critical section or activate it for the correct init run levels.

Man pages you should be familiar with now: portmap, mountd, nfsd, and exports.

Well, if you did everything exactly like I said you should you're all set to start on the NFS client.

4   Setting up a NFS client

First you will need a kernel with the NFS file system either compiled in or available as a module. This is configured before you compile the kernel. If you have never compiled a kernel before you might need to check the kernel HOWTO and figure it out. If you're using a very cool distribution (like Red Hat) and you've never fiddled with the kernel or modules on it (and thus ruined it ;-), nfs is likely automagicaly available to you.

You can now, at a root prompt, enter a appropriate mount command and the file system will appear. Continuing the example in the previous section we want to mount /mn/eris/local from eris. This is done with this command:

```
mount -o rsize=1024,wsize=1024 eris:/mn/eris/local /mnt
```

(We'll get back to the rsize and wsize options.) The file system is now available under /mnt and you can cd there, and ls in it, and look at the individual files. You will notice that it's not as fast as a local file system, but a lot more convenient than ftp. If, instead of mounting the file system, mount produces a error message like mount: eris:/mn/eris/local failed, reason given by server: Permission denied then the exports file is wrong, or you forgot to run exportfs after editing the exports file. If it says mount clntudp_create: RPC: Program not registered it means that nfsd or mountd is not running on the server.

To get rid of the file system you can say

```
umount /mnt
```

To make the system mount a nfs file system upon boot you edit /etc/fstab in the normal manner. For our example a line such as this is required:

```
# device        mountpoint     fs-type     options            dump fsckorder
...
eris:/mn/eris/local  /mnt       nfs         rsize=1024,wsize=1024 0    0
...
```

That's all there is too it, almost. Read on please.

4.1   Mount options

There are some options you should consider adding at once. They govern the way the NFS client handles a server crash or network outage. One of the cool things about NFS is that it can handle this gracefully. If you set up the clients right. There are two distinct failure modes:

soft

> The NFS client will report and error to the process accessing a file on a NFS mounted file system. Some programs can handle this with composure, most won't. I cannot recommend using this setting.

hard

> The program accessing a file on a NFS mounted file system will hang when the server crashes. The process cannot be interrupted or killed unless you also specify `intr`. When the NFS server is back online the program will continue undisturbed from where it were. This is probably what you want. I recommend using `hard,intr` on all NFS mounted file systems.

Picking up the previous example, this is now your fstab entry:

```
# device        mountpoint      fs-type     options                       dump fsckorder
...
eris:/mn/eris/local  /mnt       nfs         rsize=1024,wsize=1024,hard,intr 0 0
...
```

4.2   Optimizing NFS

Normally, if no rsize and wsize options are specified NFS will read and write in chunks of 4096 or 8192 bytes. Some combinations of Linux kernels and network cards cannot handle that large blocks, and it might not be optimal, anyway. So we'll want to experiment and find a rsize and wsize that works and is as fast as possible. You can test the speed of your options with some simple commands. Given the mount command above and that you have write access to the disk you can do this to test the sequential write performance:

```
time dd if=/dev/zero of=/mnt/testfile bs=16k count=4096
```

This creates a 64Mb file of zeroed bytes (which should be large enough that caching is no significant part of any performance perceived, use a larger file if you have a lot of memory). Do it a couple (5-10?) of times and average the times. It is the 'elapsed' or 'wall clock' time that's most interesting in this connection. Then you can test the read performance by reading back the file:

```
time dd if=/mnt/testfile of=/dev/null bs=16k
```

do that a couple of times and average. Then umount, and mount again with a larger rsize and wsize. They should probably be multiples of 1024, and not larger than 16384 bytes since that's the maximum size in NFS version 2. Directly after mounting with a larger size cd into the mounted file system and do things like ls, explore the fs a bit to make sure everything is as it should. If the rsize/wsize is too large the symptoms are *very* odd and not 100% obvious. A typical symptom is incomplete file lists when doing 'ls', and no error messages. Or reading files failing mysteriously with no error messages. After establishing that the given rsize/wsize works you can do the speed tests again. Different server platforms are likely to have different optimal sizes. SunOS and Solaris is reputedly a lot faster with 4096 byte blocks than with anything else.

Newer Linux kernels (since 1.3 sometime) perform read-ahead for rsizes larger or equal to the machine page size. On Intel CPUs the page size is 4096 bytes. Read ahead will *significantly* increase the NFS read performance. So on a Intel machine you will want 4096 byte rsize if at all possible.

Remember to edit `/etc/fstab` to reflect the rsize/wsize you found.

A trick to increase NFS write performance is to disable synchronous writes on the server. The NFS specification states that NFS write requests shall not be considered finished before the data written is on a non-volatile medium (normally the disk). This restricts the write performance somewhat, asynchronous writes will speed NFS writes up. The Linux nfsd has never done synchronous writes since the Linux file system implementation does not lend itself to this, but on non-Linux servers you can increase the performance this way with this in your exports file:

```
/dir    -async,access=linuxbox
```

---

or something similar. Please refer to the exports man page on the machine in question. Please note that this increases the risk of data loss.

5 NFS over slow lines

Slow lines include Modems, ISDN and quite possibly other long distance connections.

This section is based on knowledge about the used protocols but no actual experiments. My home computer has been down for 6 months (bad HD, low on cash) and so I have had no modem connection to test this with. Please let me hear from you if try this :-)

The first thing to remember is that NFS is a slow protocol. It has high overhead. Using NFS is almost like using kermit to transfer files. It's *slow*. Almost anything is faster than NFS. FTP is faster. HTTP is faster. rcp is faster. ssh is faster.

Still determined to try it out? Ok.

NFS' default parameters are for quite fast, low latency, lines. If you use these default parameters over high latency lines it can cause NFS to report errors, abort operations, pretend that files are shorter than they really are, and act mysteriously in other ways.

The first thing to do is *not* to use the `soft` mount option. This will cause timeouts to return errors to the software, which will, most likely not handle the situation at all well. This is a good way to get for mysterious failures. Instead use the `hard` mount option. When `hard` is active timeouts causes infinite retries instead of aborting whatever it was the software wanted to do. This is what you want. Really.

The next thing to do is to tweak the timeo and retrans mount options. They are described in the nfs(5) man page, but here is a copy:

```
       timeo=n        The  value  in  tenths  of  a second before
                      sending the first retransmission  after  an
                      RPC timeout.  The default value is 7 tenths
                      of a second.  After the first timeout,  the
                      timeout  is  doubled  after each successive
                      timeout until a maximum timeout of 60  sec-
                      onds  is  reached or the enough retransmis-
                      sions have occured to cause a  major  time-
                      out.   Then,  if  the  filesystem  is  hard
                      mounted, each new timeout cascade  restarts
                      at  twice  the initial value of the previous
                      cascade, again doubling at each retransmis-
                      sion.   The  maximum  timeout  is always 60
                      seconds.  Better overall performance may be
                      achieved  by  increasing  the  timeout when
                      mounting  on  a  busy  network,  to  a  slow
                      server,  or  through  several routers or gate-
```

ways.

retrans=n   The number of minor timeouts and retrans-
missions that must occur before a major
timeout occurs. The default is 3 timeouts.
When a major timeout occurs, the file operation is either aborted or a "server not
responding" message is printed on the console.

In other words: If a reply is not received within the 0.7 second (700ms) timeout the NFS client will repeat the request and double the timeout to 1.4 seconds. If the reply does not appear within the 1.4 seconds the request is repeated again and the timeout doubled again, to 2.8 seconds.

A lines speed can be measured with ping with the same packet size as your rsize/wsize options.

```
$ ping -s 8192 lugulbanda
PING lugulbanda.uio.no (129.240.222.99): 8192 data bytes
8200 bytes from 129.240.222.99: icmp_seq=0 ttl=64 time=15.2 ms
8200 bytes from 129.240.222.99: icmp_seq=1 ttl=64 time=15.9 ms
8200 bytes from 129.240.222.99: icmp_seq=2 ttl=64 time=14.9 ms
8200 bytes from 129.240.222.99: icmp_seq=3 ttl=64 time=14.9 ms
8200 bytes from 129.240.222.99: icmp_seq=4 ttl=64 time=15.0 ms

--- lugulbanda.uio.no ping statistics ---
5 packets transmitted, 5 packets received, 0% packet loss
round-trip min/avg/max = 14.9/15.1/15.9 ms
```

The time here is how long the ping packet took to get back and forth to lugulbanda. 15ms is quite fast. Over a 28.000 bps line you can expect something like 4000-5000ms, and if the line is otherwise loaded this time will be even higher, easily double. When this time is high we say that there is 'high latency'. Generally, for larger packets and for more loaded lines the latency will tend to increase. Increase timeo suitably for your line and load. And since the latency increases when you use the line for other things: If you ever want to use FTP and NFS at the same time you should try measuring ping times while using FTP to transfer files.

6   Security and NFS

I am by no means a computer security expert. But I do have a *little* advice for the security conscious. But be warned: This is by no means a complete list of NFS related problems and if you think you're safe once you're read and implemented all this I have a bridge I want to sell you.

This section is probably of no concern if you are on a *closed* network where you trust all the users, and no-one you don't trust can get access to machines on the network. I.e., there should be no way to dial into the network, and it should in no way be connected to other networks where you don't trust everyone using it as well as the security. Do you think I sound paranoid? I'm not at all paranoid. This is just *basic* security advice. And remember, the things I say here is just the start of it. A *secure* site needs a diligent and knowledgeable admin that knows where to find information about current and potential security problems.

NFS has a basic problem in that the client, if not told otherwise, will trust the NFS server and vice versa. This can be bad. It means that if the server's root account is broken into it can be quite easy to break into the client's root account as well. And vice versa. There are a couple of coping strategies for this, which we'll get back to.

Something you should read is the CERT advisories on NFS, most of the text below deals with issues CERT has written advisories about. See *ftp.cert.org/01-README* <ftp://ftp.cert.org/01-README> for a up to date list of CERT advisories. Here are some NFS related advisories:

```
CA-91:21.SunOS.NFS.Jumbo.and.fsirand                        12/06/91
     Vulnerabilities concerning Sun Microsystems, Inc. (Sun) Network
     File System (NFS) and the fsirand program.  These vulnerabilities
     affect SunOS versions 4.1.1, 4.1, and 4.0.3 on all architectures.
     Patches are available for SunOS 4.1.1.  An initial patch for SunOS
     4.1 NFS is also available. Sun will be providing complete patches
     for SunOS 4.1 and SunOS 4.0.3 at a later date.

CA-94:15.NFS.Vulnerabilities                                12/19/94
     This advisory describes security measures to guard against several
     vulnerabilities in the Network File System (NFS). The advisory was
     prompted by an increase in root compromises by intruders using tools
     to exploit the vulnerabilities.

CA-96.08.pcnfsd                                             04/18/96
     This advisory describes a vulnerability in the pcnfsd program (also
     known as rpc.pcnfsd). A patch is included.
```

6.1   Client Security

On the client we can decide that we don't want to trust the server too much a couple of ways with options to mount. For example we can forbid suid programs to work off the NFS file system with the `nosuid` option. This is a good idea and you should consider using this with all NFS mounted disks. It means that the server's root user cannot make a suid-root program on the file system, log in to the client as a normal user and then use the suid-root program to become root on the client too. We could also forbid execution of files on the mounted file system altogether with the `noexec` option. But this is more likely to be impractical than `nosuid` since a file system is likely to at least contain *some* scripts or programs that needs to be executed. You enter these options in the options column, with the `rsize` and `wsize`, separated by commas.

6.2   Server security: nfsd

On the server we can decide that we don't want to trust the client's root account. We can do that by using the root_squash option in exports:

```
/mn/eris/local apollon(rw,root_squash)
```

Now, if a user with UID 0 on the client attempts to access (read, write, delete) the file system the server substitutes the UID of the servers 'nobody' account. Which means that the root user on the client can't access or change files that only root on the server can access or change. That's good, and you should probably use `root_squash` on all the file systems you export. "But the root user on the client can still use 'su' to become any other user and access and change that users files!" say you. To which the answer is: Yes, and that's the way it is, and has to be with Unix and NFS. This has one important implication: All important binaries and files should be owned by `root`, and not `bin` or other non-root account, since the only account the clients root user cannot access is the servers root account. In the NFSd man page there are several other squash options listed so that you can decide to mistrust whomever you (don't) like on the clients. You also have options to squash any UID and GID range you want to. This is described in the Linux NFSd man page.

root_squash is in fact the default with the Linux NFSd, to grant root access to a filesystem use no_root_squash.

Another important thing is to ensure that nfsd checks that all it's requests comes from a privileged port. If it accepts requests from any old port on the client a user with no special privileges can run a program that's is easy to obtain over the Internet. It talks nfs protocol and will claim that the user is anyone the user wants to be. Spooky. The Linux nfsd does this check by default, on other OSes you have to enable this check yourself. This should be described in the nfsd man page for the OS.

Another thing. Never export a file system to 'localhost' or 127.0.0.1. Trust me.

6.3   Server security: the portmapper

The basic portmapper, in combination with nfsd has a design problem that makes it possible to get to files on NFS servers without any privileges. Fortunately the portmapper Linux uses is relatively secure against this attack, and can be made more secure by configuring up access lists in two files.

First we edit /etc/hosts.deny. It should contain the line

```
portmap: ALL
```

which will deny access to *everyone*. That's a bit drastic perhaps, so we open it again by editing /etc/hosts.allow. But first we need to figure out what to put in it. It should basically list all machines that should have access to your portmapper. On a run of the mill Linux system there are very few machines that need any access for any reason. The portmapper administrates nfsd, mountd, ypbind/ypserv, pcnfsd, and 'r' services like ruptime and rusers. Of these only nfsd, mountd, ypbind/ypserv and perhaps pcnfsd are of any consequence. All machines that needs to access services on your machine should be allowed to do that. Let's say that your machines address is 129.240.223.254 and that it lives on the subnet 129.240.223.0 should have access to it (those are terms introduced by the networking HOWTO, go back and refresh your memory if you need to). Then we write

```
portmap: 129.240.223.0/255.255.255.0
```

in hosts.allow. This is the same as the network address you give to route and the subnet mask you give to ifconfig. For the device eth0 on this machine ifconfig should show

```
...
eth0      Link encap:10Mbps Ethernet  HWaddr 00:60:8C:96:D5:56
          inet addr:129.240.223.254  Bcast:129.240.223.255  Mask:255.255.255.0
          UP BROADCAST RUNNING MULTICAST  MTU:1500  Metric:1
          RX packets:360315 errors:0 dropped:0 overruns:0
          TX packets:179274 errors:0 dropped:0 overruns:0
          Interrupt:10 Base address:0x320
...
```

and netstat -rn should show

```
Kernel routing table
Destination     Gateway        Genmask          Flags Metric Ref Use     Iface
...
129.240.223.0   0.0.0.0        255.255.255.0    U     0      0   174412  eth0
...
```

(Network address in first column).

The `hosts.deny` and `hosts.allow` files are described in the manual pages of the same names.

IMPORTANT: Do *not* put *anything* but *IP NUMBERS* in the portmap lines of these files. Host name lookups can indirectly cause portmap activity which will trigger host name lookups which can indirectly cause portmap activity which will trigger...

The above things should make your server tighter. The only remaining problem (Yeah, right!) is someone breaking root (or boot MS-DOS) on a trusted machine and using that privilege to send requests from a secure port as any user they want to be.

6.4 NFS and firewalls

It's a very good idea to firewall the nfs and portmap ports in your router or firewall. The nfsd operates at port 2049, both udp and tcp protocols. The portmapper at port 111, tcp and udp, and mountd at port 745 and and 747, tcp and udp. Normally. You should check the ports with the `rpcinfo -p` command.

If on the other hand you want NFS to go through a firewall there are options for newer NFSds and mountds to make them use a specific (nonstandard) port which can be open in the firewall.

6.5 Summary

If you use the hosts.allow/deny, root_squash, nosuid and privileged port features in the portmapper/nfs software you avoid many of the presently known bugs in nfs and can almost feel secure about *that* at least. But still, after all that: When an intruder has access to your network, s/he can make strange commands appear in your `.forward` or mailbox file when `/home` or `/var/spool/mail` are mounted over NFS. For the same reason, you should never access your PGP private key over nfs. Or at least you should know the risk involved. And now you know a bit of it.

NFS and the portmapper makes up a complex subsystem and therefore it's not totally unlikely that new bugs will be discovered, either in the basic design or the implementation we use. There might even be holes known now, which someone is abusing. But that's life. To keep abreast of things like this you should at least read the newsgroups *comp.os.linux.announce* <news:comp.os.linux.announce> and *comp.security.announce* <news:comp.security.announce> at a absolute minimum.

7 Mount Checklist

This section is based on IBM Corp. NFS mount problem checklist. My thanks to them for making it available for this HOWTO. If you experience a problem mounting a NFS filesystem please refer to this list before posting your problem. Each item describes a failure mode and the fix.

1. File system not exported, or not exported to the client in question.

   Fix: Export it

2. Name resolution doesn't jibe with the exports list.

   e.g.: export list says export to `johnmad` but `johnmad`'s name is resolved as `johnmad.austin.ibm.com`. mount permission is denied.

   Fix: Export to both forms of the name.

   It can also happen if the client has 2 interfaces with different names for each of the two adapters and the export only specifies one.

   Fix: export both interfaces.

   This can also happen if the server can't do a lookuphostbyname or lookuphostbyaddr (these are library functions) on the client. Make sure the client can do `host <name>`; `host <ip_addr>`; and that both shows the same machine.

   Fix: straighten out name resolution.

3. The file system was mounted after NFS was started (on that server). In that case the server is exporting underlying mount point, not the mounted filesystem.

   Fix: Shut down NFSd and then restart it.

   Note: The clients that had the underlying mount point mounted will get problems accessing it after the restart.

4. The date is wildly off on one or both machines (this can mess up make)

   Fix: Get the date set right.

   The HOWTO author recommends using NTP to synchronize clocks. Since there are export restrictions on NTP in the US you have to get NTP for debian, redhat or slackware from ftp://ftp.hacktic.nl/pub/replay/pub/linux or a mirror.

5. The server can not accept a mount from a user that is in more than 8 groups.

   Fix: decrease the number of groups the user is in or mount via a different user.

8 FAQs

This is the FAQ section. Most of it was written by Alan Cox.

1. I get a lot of 'stale nfs handle' errors when using Linux as a nfs server.

   This is caused by a bug in some oldish nfsd versions. It is fixed in nfs-server2.2beta16 and later.

2. When I try to mount a file system I get

   ```
   can't register with portmap: system error on send
   ```

   You are probably using a Caldera system. There is a bug in the rc scripts. Please contact Caldera to obtain a fix.

3. Why can't I execute a file after copying it to the NFS server?

   The reason is that nfsd caches open file handles for performance reasons (remember, it runs in user space). While nfsd has a file open (as is the case after writing to it), the kernel won't allow you to execute it. Nfsds newer than spring 95 release open files after a few seconds, older ones would cling to them for days.

4. My NFS files are all read only

   The Linux NFS server defaults to read only. RTFM the "exports" and nfsd manual pages. You will need to alter /etc/exports.

5. I mount from a linux nfs server and while ls works I can't read or write files.

   On older versions of Linux you must mount a NFS servers with `rsize=1024,wsize=1024`.

6. I mount from a Linux NFS server with a block size of between 3500-4000 and it crashes the Linux box regularly

   Basically don't do it then.

7. Can Linux do NFS over TCP

   No, not at present.

8. I get loads of strange errors trying to mount a machine from a Linux box.

   Make sure your users are in 8 groups or less. Older servers require this.

9. When I reboot my machine it sometimes hangs when trying to unmount a hung NFS server.

   Do **not** unmount NFS servers when rebooting or halting, just ignore them, it will not hurt anything if you don't unmount them. The command is `umount -avt nonfs`.

10. Linux NFS clients are very slow when writing to Sun and BSD systems

    NFS writes are normally synchronous (you can disable this if you don't mind risking losing data). Worse still BSD derived kernels tend to be unable to work in small blocks. Thus when you write 4K of data from a Linux box in the 1K packets it uses BSD does this

    ```
    read 4K page
    alter 1K
    write 4K back to physical disk
    read 4K page
    alter 1K
    write 4K page back to physical disk
    etc..
    ```

9 Exporting filesystems

The way to export filesytems with NFS is not completely consistent across platforms of course. In this case Linux and Solaris 2 are the deviants. This section lists, superficially the way to do it on most systems. If the kind of system you have is not covered you must check your OS man-pages. Keywords are: nfsd, system administration tool, rc scripts, boot scripts, boot sequence, /etc/exports, exportfs. I'll use one example throughout this section: How to export /mn/eris/local to apollon read/write.

9.1 IRIX, HP-UX, Digital-UNIX, Ultrix, SunOS 4 (Solaris 1), AIX

These OSes use the traditional Sun export format. In **/etc/exports** write:

```
/mn/eris/local -rw=apollon
```

The complete documentation is in the `exports` man page. After editing the file run `exportfs -av` to export the filesystems.

How strict the exportfs command is about the syntax varies. On some OSes you will find that previously entered lines reads:

```
/mn/eris/local apollon
```

or even something degenerate like:

```
/mn/eris/local rw=apollon
```

I recommend being formal. You risk that the next version of `exportfs` if much stricter and then suddenly everything will stop working.

9.2 Solaris 2

Sun completely re-invented the wheel when they did Solaris 2. So this is completely different from all other OSes. What you do is edit the file **/etc/dfs/dfstab**. In it you place share commands as documented in the share(1M) man page. Like this:

```
share -o rw=apollon -d "Eris Local" /mn/eris/local
```

After editing run the program `shareall` to export the filesystems.

10 PC-NFS

You should not run PC-NFS. You should run samba.

Sorry: I don't know anything about PC-NFS. If someone feels like writing something about it please do and I'll include it here.

The Linux NIS(YP)/NYS/NIS+ HOWTO

Thorsten Kukuk   v0.10, 6 February 1998

This document describes how to configure Linux as NIS(YP) or NIS+ client and how to install as NIS server.

Contents

1   Introduction

More and more, Linux machines are installed as part of a network of computers. To simplify network administration, most networks (mostly Sun-based networks) run the Network Information Service. Linux machines can take full advantage of existing NIS service or provide NIS service themselves. Linux machines can also act as full NIS+ clients, this support is in beta stage.

This document tries to answer questions about setting up NIS(YP) and NIS+ on your Linux machine. Don't forget to read the section about 5 (the RPC Portmapper)

The NIS-Howto is edited and maintained by:

> Thorsten Kukuk, kukuk@vt.uni-paderborn.de

The primary source of the information for the initial NIS-Howto was from:

> Andrea Dell'Amico   <adellam@ZIA.ms.it>
> Mitchum DSouza   <Mitch.DSouza@NetComm.IE>
> Erwin Embsen   <erwin@nioz.nl>
> Peter Eriksson   <peter@ifm.liu.se>

who we should thank for writing the first versions of this document.

1.1   New versions of this document

New versions of this document will be posted periodically to the newsgroups *comp.os.linux.help* <news:comp.os.linux.help> and *comp.os.linux.announce* <news:comp.os.linux.announce>. They will also be uploaded to various Linux WWW and FTP sites, including the LDP home page.

You can always view the latest version of this on the World Wide Web via the URL *http://sunsite.unc.edu/mdw/HOWTO/NIS-HOWTO.html*   <http://sunsite.unc.edu/mdw/HOWTO/NIS-HOWTO.html>.

1.2 Disclaimer

Although this document has been put together to the best of our knowledge it may, and probably does contain errors. Please read any README files that are bundled with any of the various pieces of software described in this document for more detailed and accurate information. We will attempt to keep this document as error free as possible.

1.3 Feedback and Corrections

If you have questions or comments about this document, please feel free to mail Thorsten Kukuk, at *kukuk@vt.uni-paderborn.de* <mailto:kukuk@vt.uni-paderborn.de>. I welcome any suggestions or criticisms. If you find a mistake with this document, please let me know so I can correct it in the next version. Thanks.

Please do *not* mail me questions about special problems with your Linux distributions! I don't know every Linux Distribution. But I will try to add every solution you send me.

1.4 Acknowledgements

We would like to thank all the people who have contributed (directly or indirectly) to this document. In alphabetical order:

```
Byron A Jeff              <byron@cc.gatech.edu>
Miquel van Smoorenburg    <miquels@cistron.nl>
```

Theo de Raadt <deraadt@theos.com> is responsible for the original yp-clients code. Swen Thuemmler <swen@uni-paderborn.de> ported the yp-clients code to Linux and also ported the yp-routines in libc (again based on Theo's work). Thorsten Kukuk has written the NIS(YP) and NIS+ routines for GNU libc 2.x from scratch.

2 Glossary and General Information

2.1 Glossary of Terms

In this document a lot of acronyms are used. Here are the most important acronyms and a brief explanation:

DBM

DataBase Management, a library of functions which maintain key-content pairs in a data base.

DLL

Dynamically Linked Library, a library linked to an executable program at run-time.

domainname

A name "key" that is used by NIS clients to be able to locate a suitable NIS server that serves that domainname key. Please note that this does not necessarily have anything at all to do with the DNS "domain" (machine name) of the machine(s).

FTP

File Transfer Protocol, a protocol used to transfer files between two computers.

libnsl

Name services library, a library of name service calls (getpwnam, getservbyname, etc...) on SVR4 Unixes. GNU libc uses this for the NIS (YP) and NIS+ functions.

libsocket

Socket services library, a library for the socket service calls (socket, bind, listen, etc...) on SVR4 Unixes.

NIS

Network Information Service, a service that provides information, that has to be known throughout the network, to all machines on the network. There is support for NIS in Linux's standard libc library, which in the following text is referred to as "traditional NIS".

NIS+

Network Information Service (Plus :-), essentially NIS on steroids. NIS+ is designed by Sun Microsystems Inc. as a replacement for NIS with better security and better handling of _large_ installations.

NYS

This is the name of a project and stands for NIS+, YP and Switch and is managed by Peter Eriksson <peter@ifm.liu.se>. It contains among other things a complete reimplementation of the NIS (= YP) code that uses the Name Services Switch functionality of the NYS library.

NSS

Name Service Switch. The /etc/nsswitch.conf file determines the order of lookups performed when a certain piece of information is requested.

RPC

Remote Procedure Call. RPC routines allow C programs to make procedure calls on other machines across the network. When people talk about RPC they most often mean the Sun RPC variant.

YP

Yellow Pages(tm), a registered trademark in the UK of British Telecom plc.

TCP-IP

Transmission Control Protocol/Internet Protocol. It's the data communication protocol most often used on Unix machines.

2.2   Some General Information

The next four lines are quoted from the Sun(tm) System & Network Administration Manual:

```
"NIS was formerly known as Sun Yellow Pages (YP) but
 the name Yellow Pages(tm) is a registered trademark
 in the United Kingdom of British Telecom plc and may
 not be used without permission."
```

NIS stands for Network Information Service. Its purpose is to provide information, that has to be known throughout the network, to all machines on the network. Information likely to be distributed by NIS is:

- login names/passwords/home directories (/etc/passwd)
- group information (/etc/group)

So, for example, if your password entry is recorded in the NIS passwd database, you will be able to login on all machines on the net which have the NIS client programs running.

Sun is a trademark of Sun Microsystems, Inc. licensed to SunSoft, Inc.

3 NIS or NIS+ ?

The choice between NIS and NIS+ is easy - use NIS if you don't have to use NIS+ or have severe security needs. NIS+ is _much_ more problematic to administer (it's pretty easy to handle on the client side, but the server side is horrible). Another problem is that the support for NIS+ under Linux is still under developement - you need the latest glibc snapshot for it or have to wait for glibc 2.1. There is a port of the glibc NIS+ support for libc5 as drop in replacement.

3.1 libc 4/5 with traditional NIS or NYS ?

The choice between "traditional NIS" or the NIS code in the NYS library is a choice between laziness and maturity vs. flexibility and love of adventure.

The "traditional NIS" code is in the standard C library and has been around longer and sometimes suffers from it's age and slight inflexibility.

The NIS code in the NYS library requires you to recompile the libc library to include the NYS code into the libc library (or maybe you can go get a precompiled version of libc from someone who has already done it).

Another difference is that the traditional NIS code has some support for NIS Netgroups, which the NYS code doesn't (yet). On the other hand the NYS code allows you to handle Shadow Passwords in a transparent way. The "traditonal NIS" code doesn't support Shadow Passwords over NIS.

Forgot this all if you use the new GNU C Library 2.x (aka libc6). It supports NSS (name switch service), which makes it very flexible, and contains support for the following NIS/NIS+ maps: aliases, ethers, group, hosts, netgroups, networks, protocols, publickey, passwd, rpc, services and shadow.

4 How it works

4.1 How NIS(YP) works

Within a network there must be at least one machine acting as a NIS server. You can have multiple NIS servers, each serving different NIS "domains" - or you can have cooperating NIS servers, where one is said to be the master NIS server, and all the other are so-called slave NIS servers (for a certain NIS "domain", that is!) - or you can have a mix of them...

Slave servers only have copies of the NIS databases and receive these copies from the master NIS server whenever changes are made to the master's databases. Depending on the number of machines in your network and the reliability of your network, you might decide to install one or more slave servers. Whenever a NIS server goes down or is too slow in responding to requests, a NIS client connected to that server will try to find one that is up or quicker.

NIS databases are in so-called DBM format, derived from ASCII databases. For example, the files /etc/passwd and /etc/group can be directly converted to DBM format using ASCII-to-DBM translation software ("makedbm", it's included with the server software). The master NIS server should have both, the ASCII databases and the DBM databases.

Slave servers will be notified of any change to the NIS maps, (via the "yppush" program), and automatically retrieve the necessary changes in order to synchronize their databases. NIS clients do not need to do this since they always talk to the NIS server to read the information stored in it's DBM databases.

The author of the YP clients for linux has informed us that the newest ypbind (ypbind-3.3.tar.gz) is able to get the server from a configuration file - thus no need to broadcast (which is insecure - due to the fact that anyone may install a NIS server and answer the broadcast queries...)

4.2   How NIS+ works

NIS+ is a new version of the network information nameservice from Sun. The biggest difference between NIS and NIS+ is, that NIS+ has support for data encryption and authentication over secure RPC.

The naming model of NIS+ is based upon a tree structure. Each node in the tree corresponds to an NIS+ object, from which we have six types: directory, entry, group, link, table and private.

The NIS+ directory that forms the root of the NIS+ namespace is called the root directory. There are two special NIS+ directories: org_dir and groups_dir. The org_dir directory consists of all administration tables, such as passwd, hosts, and mail_aliases. The groups_dir directory consists of NIS+ group objects which are used for access control. The collection of org_dir, groups_dir and their parent directory is referred to as an NIS+ domain.

5   The RPC Portmapper

To run any of the software mentioned below you will need to run the program /usr/sbin/portmap. Some Linux distributions already have the code in the /etc/rc.d/ files to start up this daemon. All you have to do is to activate it and reboot your Linux machine. Read your Linux Distribution Documentation how to do this.

The RPC portmapper (portmap(8)) is a server that converts RPC program numbers into TCP/IP (or UDP/IP) protocol port numbers. It must be running in order to make RPC calls (which is what the NIS/NIS+ client software does) to RPC servers (like a NIS or NIS+ server) on that machine. When an RPC server is started, it will tell portmap what port number it is listening to, and what RPC program numbers it is prepared to serve. When a client wishes to make an RPC call to a given program number, it will first contact portmap on the server machine to determine the port number where RPC packets should be sent.

Normally, standard RPC servers are started by inetd(8), so portmap must be started before inetd is invoked.

For secure RPC, the portmapper needs the Time Service. Make sure, that the Time Service is enabled in /etc/inetd.conf on all hosts:

```
#
# Time service is used for clock syncronization.
#
time    stream  tcp    nowait  root    internal
time    dgram   udp    wait    root    internal
```

IMPORTANT: Don't forget to restart inetd after changes on this file !

6   What do you need to set up NIS?

6.1   Determine whether you are a Server, Slave or Client.

To answer this question you have to consider two cases:

1. Your machine is going to be part of a network with existing NIS servers

2. You do not have any NIS servers in the network yet

In the first case, you only need the client programs (ypbind, ypwhich, ypcat, yppoll, ypmatch). The most important program is ypbind. This program must be running at all times, that is, it should always appear in the list of processes. It's a so-called daemon process and needs to be started from the system's startup file (eg. /etc/rc.local, /etc/init.d/nis, /etc/rc.d/init.d/ypbind). As soon as ypbind is running, your system has become a NIS client.

In the second case, if you don't have NIS servers, then you will also need a NIS server program (usually called ypserv). Section 8 describes how to set up a NIS server on your Linux machine using the "ypserv" implementation by Peter Eriksson and Thorsten Kukuk. Note that from version 0.14 this implementation supports the master-slave concept talked about in section 4.1.

There is also another free NIS server available, called "yps", written by Tobias Reber in Germany which does support the master-slave concept, but has other limitations and isn't supported any longer.

6.2 The Software

The system library "/usr/lib/libc.a" (version 4.4.2 and better) or the shared library "/lib/libc.so.x" contain all necessary system calls to succesfully compile the NIS client and server software. For glibc 2.x, you also need /lib/libnsl.so.1.

Some people reported that NIS only works with "/usr/lib/libc.a" version 4.5.21 and better so if you want to play it safe don't use older libc's. The NIS client software can be obtained from:

Site	Directory	File Name
ftp.uni-paderborn.de	/linux/local/yp	yp-clients-2.2.tar.gz
ftp.uni-paderborn.de	/linux/local/yp	ypbind-3.3.tar.gz
ftp.kernel.org	/pub/linux/utils/net/NIS	yp-tools-1.4.1.tar.gz
ftp.kernel.org	/pub/linux/utils/net/NIS	ypbind-3.3.tar.gz
sunsite.unc.edu	/pub/Linux/system/Network/admin	yp-clients-2.2.tar.gz

Once you obtained the software, please follow the instructions which come with the software. yp-clients 2.2 are for use with libc4 and libc5 until 5.4.20. libc 5.4.21 and glibc 2.x needs yp-tools 1.4.1. Since there was some bugs in the NIS code, you shouldn't use libc 5.4.21-5.4.35. Use libc 5.4.36 or later instead. ypbind 3.3 will work with all libraries. You should never use the ypbind from yp-clients 2.2.

6.3 The ypbind daemon

Assuming you have succesfully compiled the software you are now ready to install the software. A suitable place for the ypbind daemon is the directory /usr/sbin. Some people may tell you, that you don't need ypbind on a system with NYS. This is wrong, ypwhich and ypcat need it.

You'll need to do this as root of course. The other binaries (ypwhich, ypcat, yppoll, ypmatch) should go in a directory accessible by all users, normally /usr/bin.

The ypbind process has a configuration file called /etc/yp.conf. You can hardcode a NIS server there - for more info see the manual page for ypbind(8). You also need this file for NYS. An example:

```
ypserver voyager
ypserver ds9
```

If the system could resolv the hostnames without NIS, you could use the name, else you have to use the IP address.

It might be a good idea to test ypbind before incorporating it in the /etc/rc.d/ files. To test ypbind do the following:

- Make sure you have your domain name set. If it is not set then issue the command:

  /bin/domainname nis.domain

  where nis.domain should be some string, _NOT_ normally associated with the domain name of your machine! The reason for this is that it makes it a little harder for external crackers to retreive the password database from your NIS servers. If you don't know what the NIS domain name is on your network, ask your system/network administrator.
- Start up "/usr/sbin/portmap" if it is not already running.
- Create the directory "/var/yp" if it does not exist.
- Start up "/usr/sbin/ypbind"
- Use the command "rpcinfo -p localhost" to check if ypbind was able to register its service with the portmapper. The rpcinfo should produce something like:

```
program vers proto  port
100000   2   tcp   111  portmapper
100000   2   udp   111  portmapper
100007   2   udp   637  ypbind
100007   2   tcp   639  ypbind
300019   1   udp   660
```

- You may also run "rpcinfo -u localhost ypbind". This command should produce something like:

  program 100007 version 2 ready and waiting

At this point you should be able to use NIS client programs like ypcat, etc... For example, "ypcat passwd" will give you the entire NIS password database.

IMPORTANT: If you skipped the test procedure then make sure you have set the domain name, and created the directory:

  /var/yp

This directory MUST exist for ypbind to start up succesfully.

If the test worked you may now want to change the files in /etc/rc.d/ on your system so that ypbind will be started up at boot time and your system will act as a NIS client. Make sure, that the domainname will be set at boot time.

Well, that's it. Reboot the machine and watch the boot messages to see if ypbind is actually started.

6.4   Setting up a NIS Client using Traditional NIS

For host lookups you must set (or add) "nis" to the lookup order line in your /etc/host.conf file. Please read the manpage "resolv+.8" for more details.

Add the following line to /etc/passwd on your NIS clients:

```
+:::::::
```

You can also use the + and - characters to include/exclude or change users. If you want to exclude the user guest just add -guest to your /etc/passwd file. You want to use a different shell (e.g. ksh) for the user "linux"? No problem, just add "+linux:::::::/bin/ksh" (without the quotes) to your /etc/passwd. Fields that you don't want to change have to be left empty. You could also use Netgroups for user control.

For example, to only allow login-access to miquels, dth and ed, and all members of the sysadmin netgroup, but to have the account data of all other users available:

```
+miquels:::::::
+ed:::::::
+dth:::::::
+@sysadmins:::::::
-ftp
+:*:::::::/etc/NoShell
```

Note that in Linux you can also override the password field, as we did in this example. In this example, we also remove the login "ftp", so it isn't known any longer, and anonymous ftp will not work.

The netgroup would be look like

```
sysadmins (-,software,) (-,kukuk,)
```

IMPORTANT: Note that the netgroup feature is implemented starting from libc 4.5.26. But if you have a version of libc earlier than 4.5.26, every user in the NIS password database can access your linux machine if you run "ypbind".

6.5 Setting up a NIS Client using NYS

All that is required is that the NIS configuration file (/etc/yp.conf) points to the correct server(s) for its information. Also, the Name Services Switch configuration file (/etc/nsswitch.conf) must be correctly set up.

You should install ypbind. It isn't needed by the libc, but the NIS(YP) tools need it.

If you wish to use the include/exclude user feature (+/-guest/+@admins), you have to use "passwd: compat" and "group: compat". Note, that there is no "shadow: compat" ! You have to use "shadow: files nis" in this case.

The NYS sources are part of the libc 5 sources. When run configure, say the first time "NO" to the "Values correct" question, then say "YES" to "Build a NYS libc from nys".

6.6 Setting up a NIS Client using glibc 2.x

The glibc uses "traditional NIS", so you need to start ypbind. The Name Services Switch configuration file (/etc/nsswitch.conf) must be correctly set up. If you use the compat mode for passwd, shadow or group, you have to add the "+" at the end of this files, and you could use the include/exclude user feature. The configuration is excatly the same as under Solaris 2.x.

6.7   The nsswitch.conf File

The Network Services switch file /etc/nsswitch.conf determines the order of lookups performed when a certain piece of information is requested, just like the /etc/host.conf file which determines the way host lookups are performed. For example, the line

```
        hosts: files nis dns
```

specifies that host lookup functions should first look in the local /etc/hosts file, followed by a NIS lookup and finally thru the domain name service (/etc/resolv.conf and named), at which point if no match is found an error is returned.

A first version of a manual page for nsswitch.conf could be found at *http://www-vt.uni-paderborn.de/~kukuk/linux/misc.html* <http://www-vt.uni-paderborn.de/~kukuk/linux/misc.html>.

A good /etc/nsswitch.conf file for NIS is:

```
#
# /etc/nsswitch.conf
#
# An example Name Service Switch config file. This file should be
# sorted with the most-used services at the beginning.
#
# The entry '[NOTFOUND=return]' means that the search for an
# entry should stop if the search in the previous entry turned
# up nothing. Note that if the search failed due to some other reason
# (like no NIS server responding) then the search continues with the
# next entry.
#
# Legal entries are:
#
#       nisplus               Use NIS+ (NIS version 3)
#       nis                   Use NIS (NIS version 2), also called YP
#       dns                   Use DNS (Domain Name Service)
#       files                 Use the local files
#       db                    Use the /var/db databases
#       [NOTFOUND=return]     Stop searching if not found so far
#

passwd:     compat
group:      compat
shadow:     compat

passwd_compat: nis
group_compat: nis
shadow_compat: nis

hosts:      nis files dns
```

```
        services:    nis [NOTFOUND=return] files
        networks:    nis [NOTFOUND=return] files
        protocols:   nis [NOTFOUND=return] files
        rpc:         nis [NOTFOUND=return] files
        ethers:      nis [NOTFOUND=return] files
        netmasks:    nis [NOTFOUND=return] files
        netgroup:    nis
        bootparams:  nis [NOTFOUND=return] files
        publickey:   nis [NOTFOUND=return] files
        automount:   files
        aliases:     nis [NOTFOUND=return] files
```

passwd_compat, group_compat and shadow_compat are only supported by glibc 2.x. If there are no shadow rules in /etc/nsswitch.conf, glibc will use the passwd rule for lookups. There are some more lookup module for glibc like hesoid. For more information, read the glibc documentation.

7   What do you need to set up NIS+ ?

7.1   The Software

The Linux NIS+ client code was developed for the GNU C library 2. There is also a port for Linux libc5, since all commercial Applicatons are linked against this library, and you couldn't recompile them for using glibc. There are problems with libc5 + NIS+: You couldn't link static programs with it, and programs compiled with this library will not work with other libc5 versions.

You need to retrieve and compile the latest GNU C library 2 snapshot. And you need a glibc based system like RedHat 5.0 or the unstable Debian. But be warned: This are all beta Software ! Read the Docs about glibc snapshots and from the Distributions ! glibc 2.0.x doesn't contain the NIS+ support, and will never contain it. The first public version with NIS+ support will be 2.1.

The NIS+ client software can be obtained from:

Site	Directory	File Name
ftp.kernel.org	/pub/software/libs/glibc	libc-*, glibc-crypt-*,
		glibc-linuxthreads-*
ftp.kernel.org	/pub/linux/utils/net/NIS+	nis-tools-1.4.tar.gz
ftp.kernel.org	/pub/linux/utils/net/NIS+	pam_keylogin-1.1.tar.gz

Distributions based on glibc can be fetched from:

Site	Directory
ftp.redhat.com	/pub/redaht/mustang
ftp.debian.org	/pub/debian/hamm

For compilation of the GNU C Library, please follow the instructions which come with the software. Here you could find the patched libc5, based on NYS and the glibc sources as drop in replacement for the standart libc5:

Site	Directory	File Name
ftp.kernel.org	/pub/linux/utils/net/NIS+	libc-5.4.38-nsl-0.4.6.tar.gz

You should also look at *http://www-vt.uni-paderborn.de/~kukuk/linux/nisplus.html* <http://www-vt.uni-paderborn.de/~kukuk/linux/nisplus.html> for more information and the latest sources.

7.2 Setting up a NIS+ client

IMPORTANT: For setting up a NIS+ client, read your Solaris NIS+ docs what to do on the server side ! This document only describes what to do on the client side !

After installing the new libc and nis-tools, create the credentials for the new client on the NIS+ server. Then run

```
domainname nisplus.domain.
nisinit -c -H <NIS+ server>
```

to initialize the cold Start File. Read the nisinit man page for more options. Make sure, that the domainname will always be set after a reboot. If you don't know what the NIS+ domain name is on your network, ask your system/network administrator.

Now you should change your /etc/nsswitch.conf file. Make sure, that the only service after publickey is nisplus ("publickey: nisplus"), and nothing else !

After this, start keyserv and make sure, that it will always be started at boot time. Run

```
keylogin -r
```

to store the root secretkey on your system. (I hope you have added the publickey for the new host on the NIS+ Server ?).

"niscat passwd.org_dir" should now show you all entries in the passwd database.

7.3 NIS+, keylogin, login and PAM

When the user logs in, he need to set his secretkey to keyserv. This is done by calling "keylogin". The login from the shadow package will do this for the user. For a PAM aware login, you have to install pam_keylogin-1.1.tar.gz and change the /etc/pam.d/login file to use pam_unix_auth, not pwdb, which doesn't support NIS+. An example:

```
#%PAM-1.0
auth       required     /lib/security/pam_securetty.so
auth       required     /lib/security/pam_keylogin.so
auth       required     /lib/security/pam_unix_auth.so
auth       required     /lib/security/pam_nologin.so
account    required     /lib/security/pam_unix_acct.so
password   required     /lib/security/pam_unix_passwd.so
session    required     /lib/security/pam_unix_session.so
```

7.4 The nsswitch.conf File

The Network Services switch file /etc/nsswitch.conf determines the order of lookups performed when a certain piece of information is requested, just like the /etc/host.conf file which determines the way host lookups are performed. For example, the line

```
        hosts: files nisplus dns
```

specifies that host lookup functions should first look in the local /etc/hosts file, followed by a NIS+ lookup and finally thru the domain name service (/etc/resolv.conf and named), at which point if no match is found an error is returned.

A first version of a manual page for nsswitch.conf could be found at *http://www-vt.uni-paderborn.de/~kukuk/linux/misc.html* <http://www-vt.uni-paderborn.de/~kukuk/linux/misc.html>.

A good /etc/nsswitch.conf file for NIS+ is:

```
#
# /etc/nsswitch.conf
#
# An example Name Service Switch config file. This file should be
# sorted with the most-used services at the beginning.
#
# The entry '[NOTFOUND=return]' means that the search for an
# entry should stop if the search in the previous entry turned
# up nothing. Note that if the search failed due to some other reason
# (like no NIS server responding) then the search continues with the
# next entry.
#
# Legal entries are:
#
#       nisplus              Use NIS+ (NIS version 3)
#       nis                  Use NIS (NIS version 2), also called YP
#       dns                  Use DNS (Domain Name Service)
#       files                Use the local files
#       db                   Use the /var/db databases
#       [NOTFOUND=return]    Stop searching if not found so far
#


passwd:     compat
# for libc5: passwd: files nisplus
group:      compat
# for libc5: group: files nisplus
shadow:     compat
# for libc5: shadow: files nisplus

passwd_compat: nisplus
group_compat:  nisplus
shadow_compat: nisplus
```

```
hosts:       nisplus files dns

services:    nisplus [NOTFOUND=return] files
networks:    nisplus [NOTFOUND=return] files
protocols:   nisplus [NOTFOUND=return] files
rpc:         nisplus [NOTFOUND=return] files
ethers:      nisplus [NOTFOUND=return] files
netmasks:    nisplus [NOTFOUND=return] files
netgroup:    nisplus
bootparams:  nisplus [NOTFOUND=return] files
publickey:   nisplus
automount:   files
aliases:     nisplus [NOTFOUND=return] files
```

8 Setting up a NIS Server

8.1 The Server Program ypserv

This document only describes how to set up the "ypserv" NIS server.

The NIS server software can be found on:

Site	Directory	File Name
ftp.kernel.org	/pub/linux/utils/net/NIS	ypserv-1.2.8.tar.gz
waaug.erols.com	/pub/net/nis	ypserv-1.2.8.tar.gz

You could also look at *http://www-vt.uni-paderborn.de/~kukuk/linux/nis.html* `<http://www-vt.uni-paderborn.de/~kukuk/linux/nis.html>` for more information and the latest sources.

The server setup is the same for both traditional NIS and NYS.

Compile the software to generate the "ypserv" and "makedbm" programs. If you run your server as master, determine what files you require to be available via NIS and then add or remove the appropriate entries to the `/var/yp/Makefile`.

Now edit /var/yp/securenets and /etc/ypserv.conf. For more information, read the ypserv(8) and ypserv.conf(5) manual pages.

Make sure the portmapper (portmap(8)) is running, and start the server "ypserv". The command

```
% rpcinfo -u localhost ypserv
```

should output something like

```
program 100004 version 2 ready and waiting
```

Now generate the NIS (YP) database. On the master, run

        % /usr/lib/yp/ypinit -m

on a slave, make sure that ypwhich -m works. Then run

        % /usr/lib/yp/ypinit -s masterhost

That's it, your server is up and running.

You might want to edit root's crontab *on the slave* server and add the following lines:

        20 *   * * *   /usr/lib/yp/ypxfr_1perhour
        40 6   * * *   /usr/lib/yp/ypxfr_1perday
        55 6,18 * * *   /usr/lib/yp/ypxfr_2perday

This will ensure that most NIS maps are kept up-to-date, even if an update is missed because the slave was down at the time the update was done on the master.

If you want to restrict access to your NIS server, you'll have to setup the NIS server as a client as well by running ypbind and adding the plus-entries to /etc/passwd _halfway_ the password file. The library functions will ignore all normal entries after the first NIS entry, and will get the rest of the info through NIS. This way the NIS access rules are maintained. example:

        root:x:0:0:root:/root:/bin/bash
        daemon:*:1:1:daemon:/usr/sbin:
        bin:*:2:2:bin:/bin:
        sys:*:3:3:sys:/dev:
        sync:*:4:100:sync:/bin:/bin/sync
        games:*:5:100:games:/usr/games:
        man:*:6:100:man:/var/catman:
        lp:*:7:7:lp:/var/spool/lpd:
        mail:*:8:8:mail:/var/spool/mail:
        news:*:9:9:news:/var/spool/news:
        uucp:*:10:50:uucp:/var/spool/uucp:
        nobody:*:65534:65534:noone at all,,,,:/dev/null:
        +miquels::::::
        +:*:::::/etc/NoShell
        [All normal users AFTER this line!]
        tester:*:299:10:Just a test account:/tmp:
        miquels:1234567890123:101:10:Miquel van Smoorenburg:/home/miquels:/bin/zsh

The user tester will exist, but have a shell of /etc/NoShell. miquels will have normal access.

Alternatively, you could edit the /var/yp/Makefile file and set NIS to use another source password file. On big systems, the NIS password and group files are usually stored in /var/yp/ypfiles/. If you do this the normal tools to administrate the password file such as "passwd", "chfn", "adduser" will not work anymore and you will need special homemade tools for this.

However yppasswd, ypchsh and ypchfn will work ofcourse.

8.2   The Server Program yps

To set up the "yps" NIS server please refer to the previous paragraph. The "yps" server setup is similar, _but_ not exactly the same so beware if you try to apply the "ypserv" instructions to "yps"! "yps" is not supported by any author, and contains some security leaks. You shouldn't really use it !

The "yps" NIS server software can be found on:

```
        Site                Directory                         File Name

        ftp.kernel.org      /pub/linux/utils/net/NIS          yps-0.21.tar.gz
        ftp.lysator.liu.se  /pub/NYS/servers                  yps-0.21.tar.gz
```

8.3   The Program rpc.yppasswdd

Whenever users change their passwords, the NIS password database and probably other NIS databases, which depend on the NIS password database, should be updated. The program "rpc.yppasswdd" is a server that handles password changes and makes sure that the NIS information will be updated accordingly. rpc.yppasswdd is now integrated in ypserv 1.2.8. You don't need the older, separate yppasswd-0.9.tar.gz or yppasswd-0.10.tar.gz, and you shouldn't use them any longer. The rpc.yppasswdd in ypserv 1.2.8 has full shadow support. yppasswd is now part of yp-tools-1.4.1.tar.gz,

You need to start rpc.yppasswdd only on the NIS master server. By default, users are not allowed to change their full name or the login shell. You could allow this with the -e chfn or -e chsh option.

9   Verifying the NIS/NYS Installation

If everything is fine (as it should be), you should be able to verify your installation with a few simple commands. Assuming, for example, your passwd file is being supplied by NIS, the command

```
        % ypcat passwd
```

should give you the contents of your NIS passwd file. The command

```
        % ypmatch userid passwd
```

(where userid is the login name of an arbitrary user) should give you the user's entry in the NIS passwd file. The "ypcat" and "ypmatch" programs should be included with your distribution of traditional NIS or NYS.

If a user couldn't log in, run the following program on the client:

```
#include <stdio.h>
#include <pwd.h>
#include <sys/types.h>

int
main(int argc, char *argv[])
{
  struct passwd *pwd;
```

```
if(argc != 2)
  {
    fprintf(stderr,"Usage: getwpnam username\n");
    exit(1);
  }

pwd=getpwnam(argv[1]);

if(pwd != NULL)
  {
    printf("name.....: [%s]\n",pwd->pw_name);
    printf("password.: [%s]\n",pwd->pw_passwd);
    printf("user id..: [%d]\n", pwd->pw_uid);
    printf("group id.: [%d]\n",pwd->pw_gid);
    printf("gecos....: [%s]\n",pwd->pw_gecos);
    printf("directory: [%s]\n",pwd->pw_dir);
    printf("shell....: [%s]\n",pwd->pw_shell);
  }
else
  fprintf(stderr,"User \"%s\" not found!\n",argv[1]);

exit(0);
}
```

Running this program with the username as parameter, will print all the information the getpwnam function will give back for this user. This should show you, which entry is incorrect. The most common problem is, that the password field is overwritten with a "*".

10 Common Problems and Troubleshooting NIS

Here are some common problems reported by various users:

1. The libraries for 4.5.19 are broken. NIS won't work with it.

2. If you upgrade the libraries from 4.5.19 to 4.5.24 then the su command breaks. You need to get the su command from the slackware 1.2.0 distribution. Incidentally that's where you can get the updated libraries.

3. You could run into trouble with NIS and DNS on the same machine using an old a.out distribution. The DNS server occasionally will not bring up NIS.

4. When a NIS server goes down and comes up again ypbind starts complaining with messages like:

```
yp_match: clnt_call:
            RPC: Unable to receive; errno = Connection refused
```

and logins are refused for those who are registered in the NIS database. Try to login as root and if you succeed, then kill ypbind and start it up again. An update to ypbind 3.3 or higher should also help.

5. After upgrade the libc to a version greater then 5.4.20, the YP tools will not work any longer. You need yp-tools 1.2 or later for libc $>=$ 5.4.21 and glibc 2.x and yp-clients 2.2. for earlier versions.

6. In libc 5.4.21 - 5.4.35 yp_maplist is broken, you need 5.4.36 or later for yp-tools 1.x.

7. libc 5 with traditional NIS doesn't support shadow passwords over NIS. You need libc5 + NYS or glibc 2.x.

11   Frequently Asked Questions

Most of your questions should be answered by now. If there are still questions unanswered you might want to post a message to

           comp.os.linux.help

or

           comp.os.linux.networking

or contact one of the authors of this HOWTO.

Bridging mini-Howto

Christopher Cole, *cole@lynkmedia.com* <mailto:cole@lynkmedia.com> v1.10, 13 November 1997

This document describes how to setup an ethernet bridge. What is an ethernet bridge? An ethernet bridge is a device that controls data packets within a subnet in an attempt to cut down the amount of traffic. A bridge is usually placed between two separate groups of computers that talk within themselves, but not so much with the computers in the other group. A good example of this is to consider a cluster of Macintoshes and a cluster of Unix machines. Both of these groups of machines tend to be quite chatty amongst themselves, and the traffic they produce on the network causes collisions for the other machines who are trying to speak to one another. A bridge would be placed between these groups of computers. The job of the bridge is then to examine the destination of the data packets one at a time and decide whether or not to pass the packets to the other side of the ethernet segment. The result is a faster, quieter network with less collisions.

Contents

1 Setup

1. Get "Bridge Config":

   <ftp://shadow.cabi.net/pub/Linux/BRCFG.tgz>

2. Obtain and read the "Multiple ethernet" HOWTO:

   <ftp://sunsite.unc.edu/pub/Linux/docs/HOWTO/mini/Multiple-Ethernet>

3. Enable multiple ethernet devices on your machine by adding this to your /etc/lilo.conf, and re-run lilo:

   ```
   append = "ether=0,0,eth1"
   ```

   If you have three interfaces on your bridge, use this line instead:

   ```
   append = "ether=0,0,eth1 ether=0,0,eth2"
   ```

   More interfaces can be found by adding more ether statements. By default a stock Linux kernel probes for a single ethercard, and once one is found the probe ceases. The above append statement tells the kernel to keep probing for more ethernet devices after the first one is found.

   Alternatively, the boot parameter can be used instead:

   ```
   linux ether=0,0,eth1
   ```

   Or, with 3 interfaces, use:

```
linux ether=0,0,eth1 ether=0,0,eth2
```

4. Recompile the kernel with BRIDGING enabled.

5. A bridge should not have an IP address. It CAN, but a plain bridge doesn't need one. To remove the IP address from your bridge, go to /etc/sysconfig/network-scripts/ (for a RedHat system) and copy ifcfg-lo0 to ifcfg-eth0 & ifcfg-eth1. In these 2 eth files, change the line containing "DEVICE=lo" to "DEVICE=eth0" and "DEVICE=eth1". Other distributions may deviate from this, do what you need to do! If there are more than 2 interfaces to this bridge, be sure to make the corresponding configurations to those, as well.

6. Reboot, so you are running the new kernel with bridging in it, and also to make sure that an IP addresses are not bound to the network interfaces.

7. Once the system is back up, put the ethernet cards into promiscuous mode, so they will look at every packet that passes by its interface:

```
ifconfig promisc eth0 ; ifconfig promisc eth1
```

All interfaces which are connected to network segments to be bridged are to be put into promiscuous mode.

8. Turn bridging ON using the brcfg program:

```
brcfg -ena
```

9. Verify that there is different traffic on each interface:

```
tcpdump -i eth0     (in one window)
tcpdump -i eth1     (in another window)
```

10. Run a sniffer or tcpdump on another machine to verify the bridge is separating the segment correctly.

2   Common problems

1. **Question**

   I get the message

   ```
   ioctl(SIOCGIFBR) failed: Package not installed
   ```

   What does this mean?

   Answer

   You don't have bridging capability in your kernel. Get a 2.0 or greater kernel, and recompile with the BRIDGING option enabled.

2. **Question**

   Machines on one side cannot ping the other side!

   Answer

   - Did you enable bridging using "brcfg -ena"? (brcfg should say "bridging is ENABLED")
   - Did you put the interfaces into promiscuous mode? (issue the "ifconfig" command. The "PROMISC" flag should be on for both interfaces.)

- If using multiple-media interface adapters, make sure that the correct one is enabled. You may need to use the config/setup program that came with the network interface card.

3. **Question**

I cannot `telnet/ftp` from the bridge! Why?

Answer

This is because there is no IP address bound to any of bridge interfaces. A bridge is to be a transparent part of a network.

4. **Question**

What do I need to set up in the way of routing?

Answer

Nothing! All routing intelligence is handled by the bridging code in the kernel. To see the ethernet addresses as they are learned by the bridge, use the `brcfg` program in debug mode:

```
brcfg -deb
```

5. **Question**

The bridge appears to work, but why doesn't "traceroute" show the bridge as a part of the path?

Answer

Due to the nature of a bridge, a "traceroute" should NOT show the bridge as a part of the path. A bridge is to be a transparent component of the network.

6. **Question**

Is it necessary to compile `IP_FORWARD` into the kernel?

Answer

No. The bridging code in the kernel takes care of the packet transport. `IP_FORWARD` is for a gateway which has IP addresses bound to its interfaces.

7. **Question**

Why are the physical ethernet addresses for port 1 and port 2 the same according to the "`brcfg`" program? Shouldn't they be different?

Answer

No. Every port on a bridge intentionally is assigned the same physical ethernet address by the bridging code.

8. **Question**

Bridging does not appear to be an option when performing a make config on the kernel. How does one enable it?

Answer

During the kernel config, answer 'Y' to the question, "Prompt for development and/or incomplete code/drivers (CONFIG_EXPERIMENTAL) [Y/n/?]".

9. **Question**

Too many hubs (4 or more) chained one after another (in series) cause timing problems on an ethernet. What effect does a bridge have in a subnet that is layered with hubs?

Answer

A bridge resets the 3/4/5 hubs rule. A bridge does not deal with packets the way a hub does, and is therefore not a contributor to timing problems on a network.

10. **Question**

Can a bridge interface to both 10Mb and 100Mb ethernet segments? Will such a configuration slow down the rest of the traffic on the high speed side?

Answer

Yes, a bridge can tie together a 10Mb segment with a 100Mb segment. As long as the network card on the fast network side of the bridge

is 100Mb capable, TCP will take care of the rest. While it is true

that the packets from a host in the 100Mb network communicating to

a host in the 10Mb network are moving at only 10Mb/s, the rest of

the traffic on the fast ethernet is not slowed down.

Linux Bridge+Firewall Mini-HOWTO version 1.2.0

Peter Breuer (*ptb@it.uc3m.es* <mailto:ptb@it.uc3m.es>)

Dec. 19 1997

Contents

1   Introduction

You should look at the original *Bridging mini-HOWTO* <ftp://sunsite.unc.edu/pub/Linux/docs/HOWTO/
mini/Bridge> by Chris Cole for a different perspective on this. He is *chris@polymer.uakron.edu* <mailto:
chris@polymer.uakron.edu>. The version of his HOWTO that I have based this document on (alternatively,
ripped off) is 1.03 dated Aug 23 1996.

2   What and Why (and How?)

2.1   What

A bridge is an intelligent connecting wire betwen two network cards. A firewall is an intelligent insulator.

2.2   Why

You might want a bridge if you have several computers:

1. to save the price of a new hub when you just happen to have an extra ethernet card available.
2. to save the bother of learning how to do IP-forwarding and other tricks when you _have_ two cards in
   your computer.
3. to avoid maintenance work in the future when things change around!

"Several computers" might be as few as three if those are routing or bridging or just moving around the
room from time to time! You also might want a bridge just for the fun of finding out what it does. 2 (2)
was what I wanted a bridge for.

If you are really interested in 1 (1), you have to be one of the very few. Check the *NET-2-HOWTO* <ftp:
//sunsite.unc.edu/pub/Linux/docs/HOWTO/NET-2-HOWTO> and the *Serial-HOWTO* <ftp://sunsite.unc.
edu/pub/Linux/docs/HOWTO/Serial-HOWTO> for better tricks.

You want a firewall if

1. you are trying to protect your network from external accesses, or
2. you are trying to deny access to the world outside from your network.

Curiously, I needed 2 (2) here too. Policy at my university presently is that we should not act as internet
service providers to undergraduates.

2.3   How?

I started out bridging the network cards in a firewalling machine and ended up firewalling without having
cut the bridge. It seems to work and is more flexible than either configuration alone. I can take down the
firewall and keep bridging or take down the bridge when I want to be more circumspect.

I would guess that the bridge code lives just above the physical device layer and the firewalling code lives
one layer higher up, so that the bridging and firewalling configurations effectively act as though they are
running connected together "in sequence" and not "in parallel" (ouch!). Diagram:

```
   -> Bridge-in -> Firewall-in -> Kernel -> Firewall-out -> Bridge-out ->
```

There is no other way to explain how one machine can be a "conductor" and an "insulator" at the same time. There are a few caveats but I'll come to those later. Basically you must route packets that you want to firewall. Anyway, it all seems to work together nicely for me. Here is what you do ...

3 BRIDGING

3.1 Software

Get the *bridge configuration utility* `<ftp://shadow.cabi.net/pub/Linux/BRCFG.tgz>` from Alan Cox's home pages. This is the same reference as in Chris' document. I just didn't realize that it was an ftp and not an http URL ...

3.2 Prior Reading.

Read the *Multiple Ethernet HOWTO* `<ftp://sunsite.unc.edu/pub/Linux/docs/HOWTO/mini/Multiple-Ethernet>` for some advice on getting more than one network card recognized and configured.

Yet more details of the kind of boot magic that you may need are in the *Boot Prompt HOWTO* `<ftp://sunsite.unc.edu/pub/Linux/docs/HOWTO/BootPrompt-HOWTO>`.

You may be able to get away without the *NET-2 HOWTO* `<ftp://sunsite.unc.edu/pub/Linux/docs/HOWTO/NET-2-HOWTO>`. It is a good long read and you will have to pick from it the details you need.

3.3 Boot configuration

The reading material above will tell you that you need to prepare the kernel to recognize a second ethernet device at boot up by adding this to your **/etc/lilo.conf**, and then re-run **lilo**:

```
append = "ether=0,0,eth1"
```

Note the "eth1". "eth0" is the first card. "eth1" is the second card. You can always add the boot parameters in your response to the line that lilo offers you. This is for three cards:

```
linux ether=0,0,eth1 ether=0,0,eth2
```

I use **loadlin** to boot my kernel from DOS:

```
loadlin.exe c:\vmlinuz root=/dev/hda3 ro ether=0,0,eth1 ether=0,0,eth2
```

Note that this trick makes the kernel probe at bootup. That will not happen if you load the ethernet drivers as **modules** (for safety since the probe order can't be determined) so if you use modules you will have to add the appropriate IRQ and port parameters for the driver in your **/etc/conf.modules**. I have at least

```
alias eth0 3c509
alias eth1 de620
options 3c509 irq=5 io=0x210
options de620 irq=7 bnc=1
```

You can tell if you use modules by using "ps -aux" to see if **kerneld** is running and checking that there are .o files in a subdirectory of your **/lib/modules** directory. You want the directory named with what uname -r tells you. If you have kerneld and/or you have a foo.o then edit **/etc/conf.modules** and read the man page for depmod carefully.

Note also that until recently (kernel 2.0.25) the **3c509** driver could not be used for more than one card if used as a module. I have seen a patch floating around that fixes the oversight. It may be in the kernel when you read this.

3.4   Kernel configuration

Recompile the kernel with bridging enabled.

```
CONFIG_BRIDGE=y
```

I also compiled with firewalling and IP-forwarding and -masquerading and the rest enabled. Only if you want firewalling too ...

```
CONFIG_FIREWALL=y
CONFIG_NET_ALIAS=y
CONFIG_INET=y
CONFIG_IP_FORWARD=y
CONFIG_IP_MULTICAST=y
CONFIG_IP_FIREWALL=y
CONFIG_IP_FIREWALL_VERBOSE=y
CONFIG_IP_MASQUERADE=y
```

You don't need all of this. What you do need apart from this is the standard net configuration:

```
CONFIG_NET=y
```

and I do not think you need worry about any of the other networking options. I have any options that I did not actually compile into the kernel available through kernel modules that I can add in later.

Install the new kernel in place, rerun lilo and reboot with the new kernel. Nothing should have changed at this point!

3.5   Network addresses

Chris says that a bridge should not have an IP address but that is not the setup to be described here.

You are going to want to use the machine for connecting to the net so you need an address and you need to make sure that you have the loopback device configured in the normal way so that your software can talk to the places they expect to be able to talk to. If loopback is down the name resolver or other net sevices might fail. See the NET-2-HOWTO, but your standard configuration should already have done this bit:

```
ifconfig lo 127.0.0.1 route add -net 127.0.0.0
```

You will have to give addresses to your network cards. I altered the /etc/rc.d/rc.inet1 file in my slackware (3.x) to setup two cards and you should also essentially just look for your net configuration file and double or treble the number of instructions in it. Suppose that you already have an address at

192.168.2.100

(that is in the private net reserved address space, but never mind - it won't hurt anybody if you use this address by mistake) then you probably already have a line like

```
ifconfig eth0 192.168.2.100 netmask 255.255.255.0 metric 1
```

in your configuration. The first thing you are going to probably want to do is cut the address space reached by this card in half so that you can eventually bridge or firewall the two halves. So add a line which reduces the mask to address a smaller number of machines:

```
ifconfig eth0 netmask 255.255.255.128
```

Try it too. That restricts the card to at most the address space between .0 and .127.

Now you can set your second card up in the other half of the local address space. Make sure that nobody already has the address. For symmetry I set it at 228=128+100 here. Any address will do so long as it is not in the other card's mask, and even then, well, maybe. Avoid special addresses like .0, .1, .128 etc. unless you really know what you are doing.

```
ifconfig eth1 192.168.2.228 netmask 255.255.255.128 metric 1
```

That restricts the second card to addresses between .128 and .255.

3.6 Network routing

This is where I have to announce the caveats in the bridging + firewalling scheme: you cannot firewall packets which are not routed. No routes, no firewall. At least this appears to be true in the 2.0.30 and more recent kernels. The firewalling filters are closely involved with the ip-forwarding code.

That does not mean that you cannot bridge. You can bridge between two cards and firewall them from a third. You can have only two cards and firewall both of them against an outside IP such as a nearby router, provided that the router is routed by you to exactly one of the cards.

In other words, since I will be doing firewalling, so I want to precisely control the physical destination of some packets.

I have the small net of machines attached to a hub hanging off eth0, so I configure a net there:

```
route add -net 192.168.2.128 netmask 255.255.255.128 dev eth0
```

The 128 would be 0 if I had a full class C network there. I don't, by definition, since I just halved the address space. The "dev eth0" is not necessary here because the cards address falls within the mask, but it may be necessary for you. One might need more than one card holding up this subnet (127 machines on one segment, oh yeah) but those cards would be being bridged under the same netmask so that they appear as one to the routing code.

On the other card I have a line going straight through to a big router that I trust.

```
                                      client 129
                                          |
        --                                       --
client 1  \    .0                    .128      |  /   net 1
client 2 --- Hub - eth0 - Kernel - eth1 - Hub - Router --- net 2
client 3 __/       .100              .228       .2 |  \__ net 3
                                          |
                                      client 254
```

I attach the address of the router to that card as a fixed ("static") route because it would otherwise fall within the first cards netmask and the kernel would be thinking wrongly about how to send packets to the big router. I will want to firewall these packets and that is another reason fow wanting to route them specifically.

```
route add 192.168.2.2 dev eth1
```

I don't need it, since I don't have any more machines in that half of the address space, but I declare a net also on the second card. Separating my interfaces into two sets via routing will allow me to do very tight firewalling eventually , but you can get away with far less routing than this.

```
route add -net 192.168.2.128 netmask 255.255.255.128 dev eth1
```

I also need to send all non-local packets out to the world so I tell the kernel to send them to the big router

```
route add default gw 192.168.2.2
```

3.7   Card configuration

So much was standard networking setup, but we are bridging so we also have to listen on both (?) cards for packets that are not aimed at us. The following should go into the network configuration file.

```
ifconfig promisc eth0 ifconfig promisc eth1
```

The man page says allmulti=promisc, but it didn't work for me.

3.8   Additional routing

One thing that I noticed was that I had to put at least the second card into a mode where it would respond to the big router's questions about which machines I was hiding in my local net.

```
ifconfig arp eth1
```

For good measure I did this to the other card too.

```
ifconfig arp eth0.
```

3.9   Bridge Configuration

Put bridging enabling on and into your configuration file:

```
brcfg -enable
```

You should have been trying this out in real time all along, of course! The bridge configure will bring up some numbers. You can experiment with turning on and off the ports one at a time

```
brcfg -port 0 -disable/-enable
 brcfg -port 1 -disable/-enable
```

You get status reports anytime by just running

```
brcfg
```

without any parameters. You will see that the bridge listens,learns, and then does forwarding. (I don't understand why the code repeats the same hardware addresses for both my cards, but never mind .. Chris' howto say that is OK)

3.10 Try it out

If you are still up and running as things are, try out your configuration script for real by taking down both cards and then executing it:

```
ifconfig eth0 down ifconfig eth1 down /etc/rc.d/rc.inet1
```

With any luck the various subsystems (**nfs**, **ypbind**, etc.) won't notice. *Do not try this unless you are sitting at the keyboard!*

If you want to be more careful than this, you should take down as many daemons as possible beforehand, and unmount nfs directories. The worst that can happen is that you have to reboot in single-user mode (the **"single"** parameter to **lilo** or **loadlin**), and take out your changes before rebooting with things the way they were before you started.

3.11 Checks

Verify that there is different traffic on each interface:

```
tcpdump -i eth0
```

(in one window)

```
tcpdump -i eth1
```

(in another window)

You should get used to using **tcpdump** to look for things that should not be happening or that are happening and should not.

For instance look for packets that have gone through the bridge to the second card from the internal net. Here I am looking for packets from the machine with address .22:

```
tcpdump -i eth1 -e host 192.168.2.22
```

Then send a ping from the .22 host to the router. You should see the packet reported by tcpdump.

At this stage you should have a bridge ready that also has two network addresses. Test that you can ping them from outside and inside your local net, and that you can telnet and ftp around between inside and outside too.

4 FIREWALLING

4.1 Software and reading

You should read the *Firewall-HOWTO* <ftp://sunsite.unc.edu/pub/Linux/docs/HOWTO/Firewall-HOWTO>.

That will tell you where to get **ipfwadm** if you don't already have it. There are other tools you can get but I made no progress until I tried **ipfwadm**. It is nice and low level! You can see exactly what it is doing.

4.2 Preliminary checks

You have compiled IP-forwarding and masquerading into the kernel so you will want to check that the firewall is in its default (accepting) state with

```
ipfwadm -I -l ipfwadm -O -l ipfwadm -F -l
```

That is respectively, "display the rules affecting the .." incoming or outgoing or forwarding (masquerading) ".. sides of the firewall". The "-l" means "list".

You might have compiled in accounting too:

```
ipfwadm -A -l
```

You should see that there are no rules defined and that the default is to accept every packet. You can get back to this working state anytime with

```
ipfwadm -I -f
ipfwadm -O -f
ipfwadm -F -f
```

The "-f" means "flush". You may need to use that.

4.3 Default rule

I want to cut the world off from my internal net and do nothing else, so I will want to give as a last (default) rule that the firewall should ignore any packets coming in from the internal net and directed to outside. I put all the rules (in this order) into **/etc/rc.d/rc.firewall** and execute it from **/etc/rc.d/rc.local** at bootup.

```
ipfwadm -I -a reject -S 192.168.2.0/255.255.255.128 -D 0.0.0.0/0.0.0.0
```

The "-S" is the source address/mask. The "-D" is the destination address/mask.

This format to is rather long-winded. **Ipfwadm** is intelligent about network names and some common abbreviations. Check the man pages.

It is possibly more convenient to put some or all of these rules on the outgoing half of the firewall by using "-O" instead of "-I", but I'll state the rules here all formulated for the incoming half.

4.4 Holes per address

Before that default rule, I have to place some rules that serve as exceptions to this general denial of external services to internal clients.

I want to treat the firewall machines address on the internal net specially. I will stop people logging in to the firewall machine unless they have special permission, but once they are there they should be allowed to talk to the world.

```
ipfwadm -I -i accept -S 192.168.2.100/255.255.255.255 \
   -D 0.0.0.0/0.0.0.0
```

I also want the internal clients to be able to talk to the firewalling machine. Maybe they can persuade it to let them get out!

```
ipfwadm -I -i accept -S 192.168.2.0/255.255.255.128 \
   -D 192.168.2.100/255.255.255.255
```

Check at this point that you can get in to the clients from outside the firewall via **telnet**, but that you cannot get out. That should mean that you can just about make first contact, but the clients cannot send you any prompts. You should be able to get all the way in if you use the firewall machine as a staging post. Try **rlogin** and **ping** too, with **tcpdump** running on one card or the other. You should be able to make sense of what you see.

4.5 Holes per protocol

I went on to relax the rules protocol by protocol. I want to allow pings from the outside to the inside to get an echo back, for instance, so I inserted the rule:

```
ipfwadm -I -i accept -P icmp -S 192.168.2.0/255.255.255.128 \
   -D 0.0.0.0/0.0.0.0
```

The "-P icmp" works the protocol-specific magic.

Until I get hold of an **ftp** proxy I am also allowing ftp calls out with port-specific relaxations. This targets ports 20 21 and 115 on outside machines.

```
ipfwadm -I -i accept -P tcp -S 192.168.2.0/255.255.255.128 \
   -D 0.0.0.0/0.0.0.0 20 21 115
```

I could not make **sendmail** between the local clients work without a nameserver. Rather than set up a nameserver right then on the firewall, I just lifted the firewall for tcp domain service queries precisely aimed at the nearest existing nameserver and put its address in the clients **/etc/resolv.conf** ("nameserver 123.456.789.31" on a separate line).

```
ipfwadm -I -i accept -P tcp -S 192.168.2.0/255.255.255.128 \
   -D 123.456.789.31/255.255.255.255 54
```

You can find which port number and protocol a service requires with **tcpdump**. Trigger the service with a an **ftp** or a **telnet** or whatever to or from the internal machine and then watch for it on the input and output ports of the firewall with **tcpdump**:

```
tcpdump -i eth1 -e host client04
```

for example. The /etc/services file is another important source of clues. To let **telnet** and **ftp** IN to the firewall from outside, you have to allow the local clients to call OUT on a specific port. I understand why this is necessary for **ftp** - it's the server that establishes the data stream in the end - but I am not sure why **telnet** also needs this.

```
ipfwadm -I -i accept -P tcp -S 192.168.2.0/255.255.255.128 ftp telnet \
-D 0.0.0.0/0.0.0.0
```

There is a particular problem with some daemons that look up the hostname of the firewalling machine in order to decide what is their networking address. **Rpc.yppasswdd** is the one I had trouble with. It insists on broadcasting information that says it is outside the firewall (on the second card). That means the clients inside can't contact it.

Rather than start IP aliasing or change the daemon code, I mapped the name to the inside card address on the clients in their /etc/hosts.

4.6   Checks

You want to test that you can still **telnet**, **rlogin** and **ping** from the outside. From the inside you should be able to **ping** out. You should also be able to **telnet** to the firewall machine from the inside and the latter should be able to do anything.

That is it. At this point you probably want to learn about **rpc/Yellow Pages** and the interaction with the password file. The firewalled network wants to run without its unprivileged users being able to log on to the firewall - and thus get out. Some other HOWTO!

The Linux Intranet Server HOWTO

Pramod Karnad, *karnad@indiamail.com* <mailto:karnad@indiamail.com>   v2.11, 7 August 1997

This document describes how to setup an Intranet using Linux as the server which binds Unix, Netware, NT and Windows together. Hence by just establishing the connection to the Linux box you are provided transparent access to all the various platforms. Detailed explanations are provided for setting up HTTP using the NCSA server and connect to it using TCP/IP clients from Novell, Microsoft under Windows3.1, WFWG,Win95 and WinNT and MacTCP on the Apple PowerMac.

Contents

1   Introduction

In simple terms, the **Intranet** is the descriptive term being used for the implementation of Internet technologies within a corporate organisation, rather than for external connection to the global Internet. This implementation is performed in such a way as to transparently deliver the immense informational resources of an organisation to each individual's desktop with minimal cost, time and effort. This document attempts to explain in simple terms how to setup an Intranet using tools which are readily available and are generally costing little or are free.

This document assumes that you already know how to install TCP/IP on your Linux server and connect it physically to your LAN using an Ethernet network card. This also assumes you have some basic knowledge of Netware, WinNT and Mac systems. The configuration of the Netware server has been shown using version 3.1x as the basis. You can also use INETCFG to achieve the same result. On the client side the discussion is with respect to Windows 3.1x, Windows for Workgroups and Win95, WinNT and the Apple PowerMac.

I am using the private network addresses (RFC-1918) of 172.16.0.0 and 172.17.0.0 only as examples. You may choose suitable addresses depending on your configuration.

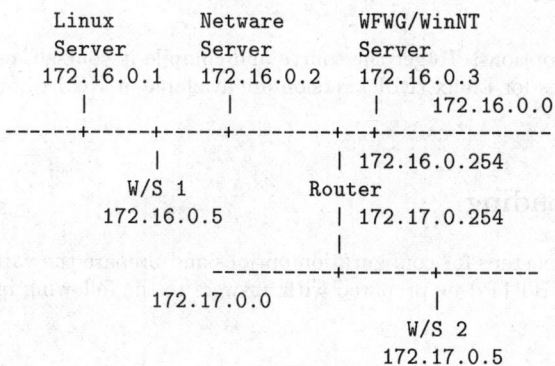

```
        Linux        Netware        WFWG/WinNT
        Server       Server         Server
        172.16.0.1   172.16.0.2     172.16.0.3
          |            |              |      172.16.0.0
   ------+-----+-----+--------+--+---------------
          |                   |  172.16.0.254
        W/S 1           Router
        172.16.0.5          |  172.17.0.254
                            |
          ----------+-------+--------
        172.17.0.0            |
                            W/S 2
                            172.17.0.5
```

1.1 What is required

You will need the following software before attempting the installation.

- the HTTP server software which can be downloaded from OneStep NCSA HTTPd Downloader at *http://hoohoo.ncsa.uiuc.edu/docs/setup/OneStep.html* `<http://hoohoo.ncsa.uiuc.edu/docs/setup/OneStep.html>` page.

- The Novell Netware Client available from *HTTP://support.novell.com/* `<HTTP://support.novell.com/>` (The TCP/IP files are included with the client).

- The Microsoft TCP/IP client available from *HTTP://www.microsoft.com/* `<HTTP://www.microsoft.com/>`

- The Apple MacTCP client available from *HTTP://www.apple.com/* `<HTTP://www.apple.com/>`

- WWW Browsers like Netscape at *HTTP://home.netscape.com/* `<HTTP://home.netscape.com/>` or MS Internet Explorer at *HTTP://www.microsoft.com/* `<HTTP://www.microsoft.com/>` or NCSA Mosaic from *http://www.ncsa.uiuc.edu/SDG/Software/Mosaic/NCSAMosaicHome.html* `<http://www.ncsa.uiuc.edu/SDG/Software/Mosaic/NCSAMosaicHome.html>`

1.2 New versions of this document

New versions of the Linux Intranet Server HOWTO will be periodically posted to comp.os.linux.announce and comp.os.linux.help. They will also be uploaded to various Linux FTP sites, including sunsite.unc.edu.

The Latest version of this document is available in HTML format at *http://www.inet.co.th/cyberclub/karnadp/http.html* `<http://www.inet.co.th/cyberclub/karnadp/http.html>`

1.3 Feedback

If you have questions or comments about this document, please feel free to mail Pramod Karnad, at *karnad@indiamail.com* `<mailto:karnad@indiamail.com>`. Suggestions, criticism and mail are always welcome. If you find a mistake with this document, please let me know so I can correct it in the next version. Thanx.

2   Install the HTTP server

When you download the server you have two options: To get the source and compile it yourself, or get the precompiled binaries. The precompiled binaries for Linux (ELF) version are available at NCSA but not the older versions.

2.1   Preparation before downloading

The server at NCSA will guide you through the steps for configuration options and prepare the various files for you. But before you attempt to download HTTPd be prepared with answers to the following questions

2.1.1   The Operating System

First, you must choose whether to download the source or a pre-compiled version of the software. If your particular system doesn't appear in the menu, then you will have to get the default source, and compile it yourself.

To check the version of your Linux go to the command prompt on your Linux machine and type

```
    linux:~$  uname -a
```

which will respond with a line which looks similar to this

```
    linux:~$  uname -a
    Linux linux 2.0.29 #4 Tue Sep 13 04:05:51 CDT 1994 i586
    linux:~$
```

The version of Linux is 2.0.29.

The remaining parameters can be specified before downloading or configured later by modifying the file srm.conf in the /usr/local/etc/httpd/conf directory. The names of the actual directives that appear in the file httpd.conf are shown in brackets. The only exception is the directive DocumentRoot which appears in the file srm.conf

2.1.2   Process type (ServerType)

This specifies how your machine will run your HTTPd server. The preferred method is "standalone". This makes the HTTP daemon to be running constantly. If you choose to load HTTPd under "inetd", the server binary will be reloaded into memory for every request, which may slow your server down.

2.1.3   Binding Port (Port)

This specifies which port of your machine that the HTTPd daemon will bind to and listen for HTTP requests. If you can login as "root", use the default setting of 80. Otherwise choose a setting between 1025 and 65535.

2.1.4   Server user identity (User)

This is the user id the server will change to when answering requests and acting on files.This question needs to be answered only if you are running the server as "standalone". If you are someone without root permissions, just use your own login name. If you are system administrator, you might want to create a special user so you can control file permissions.

2.1.5   Server group identity (Group)

This is the group id the server will change to when answering requests and acting on files. This is similar to Server User identity and is applicable only if you are running the server as standalone.

If you do not have root permissions, just use the name of your primary group. You can find out your group by typing **groups** at the Linux command prompt.

2.1.6   Server administrator email address (ServerAdmin)

This is the email address that the user should send an email message to when reporting a problem with the server. You can put your personal e-mail address.

2.1.7   Location of server directory (ServerRoot)

This is where the server resides on your system. If you have root permissions leave it in its recommended location /usr/local/etc/httpd. If you cannot login as root, choose a subdirectory in your home path. You can find out the path of your home directory with the **pwd** command.

2.1.8   Location of HTML files (DocumentRoot)

This is where the HTML files to be served are located. The default location is /usr/local/etc/httpd/htdocs. You could however set it to be the home directory of the special user you chose in Server user identity, or a subdirectory in your home directory if you can't login as root.

When in doubt, use the default settings. Now that you have answers to the above questions you can Download NCSA HTTPd at *http://hoohoo.ncsa.uiuc.edu/docs/setup/OneStep.html* <http:// hoohoo.ncsa.uiuc.edu/docs/setup/OneStep.html>. You should read the HTTPd Documentation at *http://hoohoo.ncsa.uiuc.edu/docs/* <http://hoohoo.ncsa.uiuc.edu/docs/> before you attempt installation. If you are planning to compile the code then you need to modify the makefiles in each of the th ree directories support, src, cgi-src. If your version of Linux is already supported then you just have to type **make linux** at the top level directory (i.e. /usr/local/etc/httpd)

2.2   Compiling HTTPd

Compiling is simple, just type make linux at the prompt in the server root directory. **Note:** Users of pre-ELF Linux have to uncomment #define NO_PASS in file portability.h and set DBM_LIBS= -ldbm in the Makefile before compiling HTTPd.

3   Testing HTTPd

After you have installed HTTPd, login as root and start it by typing **httpd &** . (assuming you have installed as standalone) You should now be able to see it in the list generated by **ps**. The simplest way to test HTTPd is by Telnet. At the Linux command prompt type

```
linux:~$ telnet 172.16.0.1 80
```

where 80 is the default port for HTTP. If you have configured "Port" as something different then type that number instead. You should get a response which looks like this

```
Trying 172.16.0.1...
Connected to linux.mydomain.
Escape character is '^]'.
```

Now if you type in any character and press Enter you should get a response similar to the one shown below.

```
HTTP/1.0 400 Bad Request
Date: Wed, 10 Jan 1996 10:24:37 GMT
Server: NCSA/1.5
Content-type: text/html

<HEAD><TITLE>400 Bad Request < /TITLE> < /HEAD>
<BODY><H1>400 Bad Request < /H1>
Your client sent a query that this server could
not understand.<P>
Reason: Invalid or unsupported method.<P>
< /BODY>
```

Now we are ready to connect to this server using another PC and a WWW Browser.

4   Connecting to the Linux Server

Please refer to the diagram shown in the chapter 1 (Introduction) for the addressing scheme used. Workstation 1 (W/S1) is on network 172.16.0.0 and can access the Linux server directly whereas Workstation 2 (W/S2) is on network 172.17.0.0 and needs to use the gateway (router) 172.17.0.254 to access the Linux box. This gateway information needs to be provided while configuring the clients only on W/S2. Netware refers to the gateway as 'ip_router'.

I am using W/S2 to illustrate the client setup. To setup W/S1 just change the address 172.17.0.5 to 172.16.0.5 and ignore all references to the gateway/router.

If you do not have a router you can skip the next section and proceed to

- 4.2 (Setup Netware Server) if you use a Netware server.
- 4.4 (Setup MS Windows Client) if you use the Microsoft Client.

4.1   Setup the Linux server

You may skip this section if you do not have a router.

You have to configure the Linux server to recognise the router thus allowing Workstation 2 to connect to the Web server. In order to setup the Linux server you should login as root. At the server prompt type

```
route add gw default 172.16.0.254
```

To use this gateway everytime you boot the Linux server edit the file **/etc/rc.d/rc.inet1** and change the line containing the gateway definition to `GATEWAY = "172.16.0.254"`. Make sure the line for adding the gateway is not commented out.

ALT: You can add routes to the networks on the other side of the router. This would be done as

```
route add -net 172.17.0.0 gw 172.16.0.254
```

To add this route everytime you boot Linux add the command to your **/etc/rc.d/rc.local** file.

4.2 Setup the Netware server

In order to setup the Netware server you should have Supervisor permissions or atleast Console operator permissions. If these cannot be got, try asking your Network Administrator to help you with the setup. At the Server enable the Ethernet_II frame type on the LAN by typing these commands or include them in the AUTOEXEC.ncf file.

```
load NE2000 frame=Ethernet_II name=IPNET
load TCPIP
bind IP to IPNET addr=172.16.0.2 mask=FF.FF.FF.0
```

You might have to specify the slot or board number while loading the NE2000 driver depending on your machine configuration. (eg: load NE2000 slot=3 frame=.....)

4.3 Setup the Netware Client

On the PC you have the choice of Win3.1,WFWG or Win95. The installation procedure differs between Win95 and the older windows if you are using the 32bit client from Microsoft or Novell. If you are going to use the 16bit client, the procedure is the same and you can refer to the Windows 3.x installation instructions. For installing the 32bit client for Win95 skip to 4.3.2 (Windows 95 installation).

4.3.1 Windows 3.x

If you are using Win3.1 or WFWG you can install the Netware Client (VLMs) and some additional files which are provided with the TCP/IP diskette, namely

TCPIP.exe, VTCPIP.386, WINSOCK.dll and WLIBSOCK.dll

Note that the WINSOCK.dll file is different from the ones provided with Win95 and Trumpet. Install the Netware Client with the support for windows. Copy VTCPIP.386, WINSOCK.dll and WLIBSOCK.dll to the SYSTEM directory and TCPIP.exe to the NWCLIENT directory. Now modify the STARTNET.bat in the NWCLIENT directory to

```
lsl
ne2000        ---> your network card driver
c:\windows\odihlp.exe      ---->if you are using WFWG
ipxodi
tcpip         ---> add this line
nwip          ---> if you use Netware/IP
vlm
```

Create a subdirectory (say) \NET\TCP and copy the files HOSTS, NETWORKS, PROTOCOLS and SER-
VICES from /etc on your Linux server or the directory SYS:ETC on your Netware server. Edit the copied
HOSTS file to add the line for your new Linux server. This will enable you to refer to the Linux server as
http://linux.mydomain/ instead of http://172.16.0.1/in your WWW browser

```
        127.0.0.1          localhost
        172.16.0.1         linux.mydomain
```

Edit the NET.cfg file in NWCLIENT directory

```
        Link Driver NE2000
            port 300
            int 3
            MEM D0000
            FRAME Ethernet_802.2

    ; ---- add these lines ----

            FRAME Ethernet_II

        Protocol TCPIP
            PATH TCP_CFG C:\NET\TCP
            ip_address   172.17.0.5
            ip_netmask   255.255.255.0
            ip_router    172.17.0.254     ---> add the address of your gateway only
                                          ---> if you have to use this
                                          ---> gateway to reach your HTTP server

        Link Support
            MemPool 6192       ---> the minimum is 1024. Try with different values
            Buffers 10 1580    ---> this again can be fine tuned


    ;---------------------------------
    ; You may need to add lines like these if you are using Netware/IP
    ;
        NWIP
            NWIP_DOMAIN_NAME   mydomain
            NSQ_BROADCAST      ON
            NWIP1_1 COMPATIBILITY   OFF
            AUTORETRIES        1
            AUTORETRY SECS   10
```

Edit the SYSTEM.ini file in the WINDOWS directory and add this entry for VTCPIP.386

```
        [386Enh]
        .....
        network=*vnetbios, vipx.386, vnetware.386, VTCPIP.386
```

. . . . .

Reboot your PC, run STARTNET.bat and you can now use your favorite WWW browser to access your Web pages. You need not login to Netware and you don't have to run TCPMAN (if you use Trumpet Winsock).

4.3.2 Windows 95

This section explains how to install the 32bit client on Win95. Firstly you must install the following

```
Client for Netware Networks (from Microsoft or Novell)
Microsoft TCP/IP Protocol
Network Adapter
```

To install these items, click on My Computer, Control Panel, Networks. Click Add. You will now be in a window that displays Client, Adapter, Protocol and Service. To install the Client for Netware Networks:

```
1. DoubleClick on Client
2. Click on Microsoft or Novell
3. DoubleClick on Client for Netware Networks
```

To install the TCP/IP Protocol:

```
1. DoubleClick on Protocol
2. Click on Microsoft
3. DoubleClick on TCP/IP
```

Windows 95 by default installs several other protocols automatically. Remove them by clicking on them and clicking the Remove button. Typically Win95 installs the Microsoft NetBeui protocol, and IPX/SPX compatible protocol. You can delete the NetBEUI protocol, but you will need the IPX/SPX protocol if you wish to login to the Netware Server.

To setup TCP/IP click on TCP/IP, click on Properties, click on the tab IP address

```
Enter your IP address in the "Specify an IP address "
                box as 172.17.0.5
In the Subnet Mask box enter 255.255.255.0
```

select the tab Gateway

```
Enter your gateway (router) address in the box New gateway
    as 172.17.0.254
Click the Add button
```

The gateway address should now appear under the installed gateways box. Now Click OK.

You should get a message to reboot. Do so. You should now be able to use the Browser to connect to your HTTP Server.

4.4 Setup Microsoft Client

If you are using the Microsoft Client for accessing your network, then this section details how to install TCP/IP for

- 4.4.1 (Windows for Workgroups (WFWG))
- 4.4.2 (Windows 95)
- 4.4.3 (Windows NT 4.0)

Note: To enable you to refer to the Linux server as `http://linux.mydomain/` instead of `http://172.16.0.1/` in the WWW browser and all your intranet commands you need to edit the `hosts` file. You can add more entries for each of your other hosts (Netware, Unix, WinNT) as well. The Windows family keeps its HOSTS file in `\WINDOWS` or in `\WINDOWS\SYSTEM` depending on the version. Edit this file and add a line for your Linux server as:

```
127.0.0.1      localhost
172.16.0.1     linux.mydomain

172.16.0.2     netware.mydomain
172.16.0.3     winNT.mydomain
172.16.0.5     ws_1
```

4.4.1   Windows for Workgroups

This section explains how to install the 32bit client on WFWG. Firstly you must download the TCP/IP drivers for Windows from Microsoft. The current version is 3.11b and is available at *ftp://ftp.microsoft.com* `<ftp://ftp.microsoft.com>` or other sites as `tcp32b.exe`. Make sure that you have load Win32s before trying to load the TCP/IP-32bit driver.

Having expanded the TCP/IP files into a temporary directory (say `C:\TEMP`), check your `\WINDOWS\SYSTEM` directory for copies of `OEMSETUP.INF`. If there are any, rename them. Now copy the `OEMSETUP.INF` file from the TEMP directory to the `\WINDOWS\SYSTEM` directory. If you have loaded any other TCP/IP stacks on your system, please remove them before you proceed.

Start Network Setup or Windows Setup/Change Network settings

```
Click the Networks button
Click Install Microsoft Windows Network.
  Choose support for additional networks (if required)
Click OK
```

You should be prompted for your network adapter - select the appropriate one. If you are not prompted, then

```
Click the Adapter button
    select an adapter (say NE2000)
    Click OK
Click the Protocol button
    select the MS TCP/IP-32 protocol
    click OK
```

You will now be prompted to configure the TCP/IP protocol stack. You can always reconfigure this by highlighting the TCP/IP protocol shown in the box Adapters and clicking the Setup button.

```
In the IP address box enter 172.17.0.5
In the Subnet Mask box enter 255.255.255.0
```

> Enter your gateway (router) address in the box default gateway
> as 172.17.0.254

Click OK. The computer will ask you to restart. Do so. You should now be able to use the Browser to connect to your HTTP Server.

4.4.2 Windows 95

This section explains how to install the 32bit client for Microsoft on Win95. Firstly you must install the following

> Client for Microsoft Networks
> Microsoft TCP/IP Protocol
> Network Adapter

To install these items, click on My Computer, Control Panel, Networks. Click Add. You will now be in a window that displays Client, Adapter, Protocol and Service. To install the Client for Microsoft Networks:

> 1. DoubleClick on Client
> 2. Click on Microsoft
> 3. DoubleClick on Client for Microsoft Networks

To install the TCP/IP Protocol:

> 1. DoubleClick on Protocol
> 2. Click on Microsoft
> 3. DoubleClick on TCP/IP

Windows 95 by default installs several protocols automatically. Remove them by clicking on them and clicking the Remove button. Typically Win95 installs the Microsoft NetBeui protocol.

To setup TCP/IP click on TCP/IP, click on Properties, click on the tab IP address

> Enter your IP address in the "Specify an IP address "
> box as 172.17.0.5
> In the Subnet Mask box enter 255.255.255.0

select the tab Gateway

> Enter your gateway (router) address in the box New gateway
> as 172.17.0.254
> Click the Add button

The gateway address should now appear under the installed gateways box. Now Click OK.

You should get a message to reboot. Do so. You should now be able to use the Browser to connect to your HTTP Server.

4.4.3 Windows NT

This section details how to Install the TCP/IP client for WinNT 4.0. Start Control Panel/ Network

```
Select the Adapter tab.
    Click Add to add a new adapter (if you don't have one)
```

You should be prompted for your network adapter - select the appropriate one. To add the protocols.

```
Select the Protocols tab
    Click Add
    Select the TCP/IP protocol
    Click OK
```

You will now be prompted to configure the TCP/IP protocol stack. You can always reconfigure this by highlighting the TCP/IP protocol and clicking the Properties button.

```
Select the tab IP Address
    Mark the checkbox 'Specify an IP address'
    In the IP address box enter 172.17.0.5
    In the Subnet Mask box enter 255.255.255.0
    Enter your gateway (router) address in the box Default Gateway
        as 172.17.0.254
```

Click OK. The computer will ask you to restart. You can now use any Browser to connect to your HTTP Server.

4.5 Setup TCP/IP on Macintosh

If you are using the Macintosh for accessing your network, then this section details how to install MacTCP for the PowerMacs.

Note: To enable you to refer to the Linux server as `http://linux.mydomain/` instead of `http://172.16.0.1/` in the WWW browser and all your intranet commands you need to edit the `hosts` file. The format of the hosts file is different from the one used in Unix. The Mac hosts file is based on RFC-1035. You can add more entries for each of your other hosts (Netware, Unix, WinNT) as well. The MacOS keeps its HOSTS file in the `Preferences folder` under the `System folder`. Edit this file and add a line for your Linux server as:

```
linux.mydomain     A   172.16.0.1

netware.mydomain   A   172.16.0.2
winNT.mydomain     A   172.16.0.3
ws_1               A   172.16.0.5
```

4.5.1 MacTCP

This section explains how to install MacTCP. Firstly you must download the MacTCP files from Apple or install it from the Internet Connection CD. To configure MacTCP, click the Apple Menu/ Control Panels/ TCP/IP. In the screen change the setting for 'Connect via:' to 'Ethernet'

Change the 'Configure' setting to 'Manually'

```
In the IP address box enter 172.17.0.5
```

In the Subnet Mask box enter 255.255.255.0

Enter your gateway (router) address in the box

Router address as 172.17.0.254

Click OK. You should now be able to use the Browser to connect to your HTTP Server.

5 Setting up the Intranet

An Intranet cannot be complete without sharing the resources on the different platforms. You will need support for other filesystems, so that you can access the data available on them. This document provides instructions to connect Linux to the following popular filesystems.

- 5.1 (NCP filesystem for Netware)
- 5.2 (SMB filesystem for Windows)
- 5.3 (NFS filesystem for Unix)

These filesystems can be compiled into the Linux kernel or added as modules, depending on the version of Linux. If you are not familiar with compiling the kernel you can refer to the Kernel HOWTO *http://sunsite.unc.edu/mdw/HOWTO/Kernel-HOWTO.html* <http://sunsite.unc.edu/mdw/ HOWTO/Kernel-HOWTO.html> and the Module HOWTO *http://sunsite.unc.edu/mdw/HOWTO/Module-HOWTO.html* <http://sunsite.unc.edu/mdw/HOWTO/Module-HOWTO.html> for compiling the kernel with modules.

5.1 NCPFS

To share the files on the Netware server you will need support for NCP (ncpfs). NCPFS works with kernel version 1.2.x and 1.3.71 upwards. It does not work with any earlier 1.3.x kernel. It cannot access the NDS database in Netware 4.x, but can make use of the bindery. If you are using Netware 4.x you can enable bindery support for specific containers using the command **Set Bindery Context** at the console as:

set Bindery Context = CORP.MYDOM;WEBUSER.MYDOM

In the above example two containers have bindery support enabled.

You will need to download the NCP filesystem utilities using the URL *ftp://sunsite.unc.edu/pub/Linux/system/filesystems/ncpfs/ncpfs.tgz* <ftp://sunsite.unc.edu/pub/ Linux/system/filesystems/ncpfs/ncpfs.tgz> (currently ncpfs-2.0.10) from Sunsite.

5.1.1 Installation

To install the ncpfs utilities, type

zcat ncpfs.tgz | tar xvf -

to expand the files into its own directory. In this case you will get a directory ncpfs-2.0.10 Change your directory to this ncpfs directory before proceeding with the installation. Read the README and edit the Makefile if necessary.

The installation of ncpfs depends on the kernel version you are using. For kernel 1.2, you should simply type 'make'. Subsequently typing 'make install' will install the executables and man pages.

If you use Kernel 1.3.71 or later, you might have to recompile your kernel. With these kernels, the kernel part of ncpfs is already included in the main source tree. To check if the kernel needs to be recompiled type

```
cat /proc/filesystems
```

It should show you a line saying that the kernel knows ncpfs.

If ncpfs is not there, you can either recompile the kernel or add ncpfs as a module. For recompiling the kernel you should type 'make config' and when it asks you for

```
The IPX protocol (CONFIG_IPX) [N/y/?]
```

simply answer 'y'. Probably you do not need the full internal net that you are asked for next. Once the kernel is successfully installed, reboot, check /proc/filesystems and if everything is OK proceed with the installation of the ncpfs utilities. Change directory to the location holding your downloaded ncpfs files, and type 'make'. After the compilation is finished type 'make install' to install the various utilities and man pages.

5.1.2   Mounting NCPFS

To check the installation type

```
ipx_configure --auto_interface=on --auto_primary=on
```

```
....wait for 10 seconds and type
```

```
slist
```

You should be able to see a list of your Netware servers. Now we are ready to share files from the Netware server.

Suppose we need to access HTML files from directory \home\htmldocs on volume VOL1: on the server MYDOM_NW, I recommend that you create a new user (say) 'EXPORT' with password 'EXP123' on this server to whom you grant appropriate access rights to this directory using SYSCON or NWADMIN.

On the Linux machine create a new directory /mnt/MYDOM_NW. Now type the command

```
ncpmount -S MYDOM_NW -U EXPORT -P EXP123 /mnt/MYDOM_NW
```

to mount the netware file system. Typing the command

```
ls /mnt/MYDOM_NW/vol1/home/htmldocs
```

will show you a list of all the files in MYDOM_NW/VOL1:\HOME\HTMLDOCS (using Netware file notation). If you have any problems please read the IPX HOWTO at *http://sunsite.unc.edu/mdw/HOWTO/IPX-HOWTO.html* <http://sunsite.unc.edu/mdw/HOWTO/IPX-HOWTO.html> for more insights into the IPX system.

5.2   SMBFS

To share the files on the Windows server you will need support for SMB (smbfs).

You will need to download the SMB filesystem utilities from `<ftp://sunsite.unc.edu/pub/Linux/system/` `filesystems/smbfs/smbfs.tgz>` (currently smbfs-2.0.1) from Sunsite.

5.2.1   Installation

To install the smbfs utilities, type

```
zcat smbfs.tgz | tar xvf -
```

to expand the files into its own directory. In this case you will get a directory `smbfs-2.0.1` Change your directory to this smbfs directory before proceeding with the installation. Read the README and edit the Makefile if necessary.

The installation of smbfs depends on the kernel version you are using. For kernel 1.2, you should simply type 'make'. Subsequently typing 'make install' will install the executables and man pages.

If you use Kernel 2.0 or later, you might have to recompile your kernel. With these kernels, the kernel part of smbfs is already included in the main source tree. To check if the kernel needs to be recompiled type

```
cat /proc/filesystems
```

It should show you a line saying that the kernel knows smbfs.

If smbfs is not there, you can either recompile the kernel or add smbfs as a module. For recompiling the kernel you should type 'make config' and when it asks you for adding SMB filesystem support simply answer yes. Once the kernel is successfully installed, reboot, check `/proc/filesystems` and if everything is OK proceed with the installation of the smbfs utilities. Change directory to the location holding your downloaded smbfs files, and type 'make'. After the compilation is finished type 'make install' to install the various utilities and man pages.

5.2.2   Mounting SMBFS

In our example let us assume that the WinNT server is called 'MYDOM_NT' and is sharing its directory `C:\PUB\HTMLDOCS` with a share name of 'HTMLDOCS' without a password. On the Linux machine create a new directory `/mnt/MYDOM_NT`. Now type the command

```
smbmount //MYDOM_NT/HTMLDOCS /mnt/MYDOM_NT -n
```

to mount the SMB (windows share) file system. If this does not work try

```
smbmount //MYDOM_NT/COMMON /mnt/MYDOM_NT -n -I 172.16.0.3
```

Typing the command

```
ls /mnt/MYDOM_NT
```

will show you a list of all the files in `bsol;bsol;MYDOM_NT\PUB\HTMLDOCS` (using Windows file notation).

5.3   NFS

First you will need a kernel with the NFS file system either compiled in or available as a module.

Suppose you have a Unix host running NFS with the name MYDOM_UNIX and an IP address of 172.16.0.4. You can check the directories that are being exported (shared) by this host by typing the command

```
showmount -e 172.16.0.4
```

Once we know the exported directories you can mount them by entering a appropriate mount command. I recommend that you create a subdirectory under '/mnt' (say) 'MYDOM_UNIX' and use that as your mount point.

```
mount -o rsize=1024,wsize=1024 172.16.0.4:/pub/htmldocs /mnt/MYDOM_UNIX
```

The rsize and wsize may have to be changed depending on your environment.

If you have any problems please read the NFS HOWTO at *http://sunsite.unc.edu/mdw/HOWTO/NFS-HOWTO.html* <http://sunsite.unc.edu/mdw/HOWTO/NFS-HOWTO.html> for more insights into the NFS system.

6   Accessing the Web

Now that we have setup the HTTP server, the clients and interconnected the Linux server with the other servers, we need to make some small adjustments on the Linux server to be able to access these mounted filesystems from the Web Browser.

6.1   Accessing the mounted filesystems

To access the mounted directories in your HTML pages you have two methods:

- Create a link in DocumentRoot (/usr/local/etc/httpd/htdocs) to refer to the mounted directory as

```
ln -s /mnt/MYDOM_NW/vol1/home/htmldocs netware
```
                                     or

```
ln -s /mnt/MYDOM_NT    winNT
```
                                     or

```
ln -s /mnt/MYDOM_UNIX    unix
```

- to edit the file srm.conf in your /usr/local/etc/httpd/conf directory and add a new alias.

```
# Alias fakename realname
Alias /icons/     /usr/local/etc/httpd/icons/

# alias for netware server
Alias /netware/   /mnt/MYDOM_NW/vol1/home/htmldocs/
Alias /winNT/     /mnt/MYDOM_NT/
Alias /unix/      /mnt/MYDOM_UNIX
```

And restart your HTTPd. You can access the documents on the netware server by referring to them as http://linux.mydomain/netware/index.htm for the netware files and similar notations for the others.

6.2   Connecting to the Internet

You can finally connect your Intranet to the Internet to access E-Mail and all the wonderful information out there. I propose to write a brief note on how to do this in a future revision. Detailed explanations are available in the ISP Hookup HOWTO from *http://sunsite.unc.edu/mdw/HOWTO/ISP-Hookup-HOWTO.html* <http://sunsite.unc.edu/mdw/HOWTO/ISP-Hookup-HOWTO.html> and Diald mini HOWTO at *http://sunsite.unc.edu/mdw/HOWTO/mini/Diald* <http://sunsite.unc.edu/mdw/HOWTO/mini/Diald> for setting up these connections.

6.3   Other uses

The HTTP server can be used in the office to provide transparent access to information residing on different servers, at several locations and directories. The data can be simple documents in Word, Lotus spreadsheets, or complex databases.

The application of this technology is being typically used as follows:-

- Publishing corporate documentsThese documents can include newsletters, annual reports, maps, company facilities, price lists, product information literature, and any document which is of value within the corporate entity.

- Access into searchable directoriesRapid access to corporate phone books and the like. This data can be mirrored at a Web site or, via CGI scripts, the Web server can serve as a gateway to backend pre-existing or new applications. This means that, using the same standard access mechanisms, information can be made more widely available and in a simpler manner. This means that it can be used to create an interface with RDBMS like ORACLE and SYBASE for generating real-time information. Here is a list of links to such sites on the Web.
  -    Web   Access   -   *http://cscsun1.larc.nasa.gov/~beowulf/db/web_access.html*   <http://cscsun1.larc.nasa.gov/~beowulf/db/web_access.html>   -   CGI   gateways   -   *HTTP://www.w3.org/hypertext/WWW/RDBGate/Overview.html* <HTTP://www.w3.org/hypertext/WWW/RDBGate/Overview.html>

- Corporate/Department/Individual pagesAs cultures change within organistions to the point where even each department moves towards their own individual mission statements, the Intranet technology provides the ideal medium to communicate current information to the Department or Individual. Powerful search engines provide the means for people to find the group or individual who has the answers to the continuous questions which arise in the normal day-to-day course of doing business.

- Simple Groupware applicationsWith HTML forms support, sites can provide sign-up sheets, surveys and simple scheduling.

- Software distributionAdministrators can use the Intranet to deliver software and up-dates 'on-demand' to users across the corporate network . This can be done with 'Java' which allows the creation and transparent distribution of objects on-demand rather than just data or applications. This is indeed possible more easily with the newer versions of Linux which has builtin support for Java.

- MailWith the move to the use of Intranet mail products with standard and simple methods for attachment of documents, sound, vision and other multimedia between individuals, mail is being pushed further forward as a simple, de facto communications method. Mail is essentially individual to individual, or individual to small group, communication. Several utilities are available on the Linux platform to setup an E-mail system like **sendmail, pop3d, imapd**.

- User InterfaceThe Intranet technology is evolving so rapidly that the tools available, in particular HTML, can be used to dramatically change the way we interface with systems. With HTML you can build an Interface which is only limited by the creator's imagination. The beauty about using Intranet technologies for this is that it is so simple. Clicking a hyperlink from HTML can take you to another page, it could ring an alarm, run a yearend procedure or anything else that a computer program can do.

7 More things to do

Here is a list of other interesting things to do with your Linux Intranet server. All the software mentioned below is freeware or shareware.

- Browse the Linux server using Network Neighbourhood in Win95/ NT; Setup a WINS like NBT server. Check out the SAMBA Web page at *http://lake.canberra.edu.au/pub/samba/samba.html* `<http://lake.canberra.edu.au/pub/samba/samba.html>`

- Implement a search engine on your Intranet. Connect to ht://Dig at *http://htdig.sdsu.edu/* `<http://htdig.sdsu.edu/>`

- Use CUSeeMe by setting up a local reflector. Refer to their page at Cornell *http://cu-seeme.cornell.edu/* `<http://cu-seeme.cornell.edu/>`

- Setup Web Conferencing. Use COW from *http://thecity.sfsu.edu/COW/* `<http://thecity.sfsu.edu/COW/>`

- Deploy a SQL database. Refer to the mSQL Home page at *http://Hughes.com.au/* `<http://Hughes.com.au/>`

- Setup FTP,Gopher,Finger,Bootp servers on the Netware server. Get them at *http://mft.ucs.ed.ac.uk/* `<http://mft.ucs.ed.ac.uk/>`

- Emulate a Netware server. Check out the NCP Utilities at *ftp://sunsite.unc.edu/pub/Linux/system/filesystems/ncpfs/* `<ftp://sunsite.unc.edu/pub/Linux/system/filesystems/ncpfs/>`

If you find other interesting things to do with your Linux Intranet server, please feel free to mail me.

8 Credits and Legalities

8.1 Thanks

Thanks to the people at NCSA for providing such excellent documentation, David Anderson and all others for trying out this HOWTO and sending in their comments. The details on Netware/IP are courtesy Romel Flores (rom@mnl.sequel.net).

8.2 Copyright information

This document is copyrighted © 1996,1997 Pramod Karnad and distributed under the following terms:

Linux IP Masquerade mini HOWTO

Ambrose Au, *ambrose@writeme.com* <mailto:ambrose@writeme.com>   v1.20, 10 November 1997

This document describes how to enable IP masquerade feature on a Linux host, allowing connected computers that do not have registered Internet IP addresses to connect to the Internet through your Linux box.

Contents

1   Introduction

1.1   Introduction

This document describes how to enable IP masquerade feature on a Linux host, allowing connected computers that do not have registered Internet IP addresses to connect to the Internet through your Linux box. It is possible to connect your machines to the Linux host with ethernet, as well as other kinds of connection such as a dialup ppp link. This document will emphasize on ethernet connection, since it should be the most likely case.

> **This document is intended for users using kernels 2.0.x. Development kernels 2.1.x are NOT covered.**

1.2   Foreword, Feedback & Credits

I find it very confusing as a new user setting up IP masquerade on a newer kernel, i.e. 2.x kernel. Although there is a FAQ and a mailing list, there is no document dedicates on that; and there are some requests on the mailing list for such a HOWTO. So, I decided to write this up as a starting point for new users, and possibly a building block for knowledgeable users to build on for documentation. If you think I'm not doing a good job, feel free to tell me so that I can make it better.

This document is heavily based on the original FAQ by Ken Eves , and numerous helpful messages in the IP Masquerade mailing list. And a special thanks to Mr. Matthew Driver whose mailing list message inspired me to set up IP Masquerade and eventually writing this.

Please feel free to send any feedback or comments to *ambrose@writeme.com* <mailto:ambrose@writeme.com> if I'm mistaken on any information, or if any information is missing. Your invaluable feedback will certainly be influencing the future of this HOWTO!

This HOWTO is meant to be a quick guide to get your IP Masquerade working in the shortest time. As I am not a technical writer, you may find the information in this document not as general and objective as it can be. The latest news and information can be found at the *IP Masquerade Resource* <http://ipmasq.home.ml.org/> web page that I maintained. If you have any technical questions on IP Masquerade, please join the IP Masquerade Mailing List instead of sending email to me since I have limited time, and the developers of IP_Masq are more capable of answering your questions.

The latest version of this document can be found at the *IP Masquerade Resource* <http://ipmasq.home. ml.org/>, which also contains the HTML and postscript version:

- *http://ipmasq.home.ml.org/* <http://ipmasq.home.ml.org/>
- Please refer to *IP Masquerade Resource Mirror Sites Listing* <http://ipmasq.home.ml.org/index. html##mirror> for other mirror sites available.

1.3 Copyright & Disclaimer

This document is copyright(c) 1996 Ambrose Au, and it's a free document. You can redistribute it under the terms of the GNU General Public License.

The information and other contents in this document are to the best of my knowledge. However, IP Masquerade is *experimental*, and there is chance that I make mistakes as well; so you should determine if you want to follow the information in this document.

Nobody is responsible for any damage on your computers and any other losses by using the information on this document. i.e.

THE AUTHOR IS NOT RESPONSIBLE FOR ANY DAMAGES INCURRED DUE TO ACTIONS TAKEN BASED ON THE INFORMATION IN THIS DOCUMENT.

2 Background Knowledge

2.1 What is IP Masquerade?

IP Masquerade is a developing networking function in Linux. If a Linux host is connected to the Internet with IP Masquerade enabled, then computers connecting to it (either on the same LAN or connected with modems) can reach the Internet as well, even though they have *no official assigned IP addresses*.

This allows a set of machines to *invisibly* access the Internet hidden behind a gateway system, which appears to be the only system using the Internet. Breaking the security of a well set-up masquerading system should be considerably more difficult than breaking a good packet filter based firewall (assuming there are no bugs in either).

2.2 Current Status

IP Masquerade is still at its experimental stages. However, kernels since 1.3.x had built-in support already. Many individuals and even companies are using it, with satisfactory results.

Browsing web pages and telnet are reported to work well over IP Masquerade. FTP, IRC and listening to Real Audio are working with certain modules loaded. Other network streaming audio such as True Speech and Internet Wave work too. Some fellow users on the mailing list even tried video conferencing software. Ping is now working, with the newly available ICMP patch

Please refer to section 4.3 for a more complete listing of software supported.

IP Masquerade works well with 'client machines' on several different OS and platforms. There are successful cases with systems using Unix, Windows 95, Windows NT, Windows for Workgroup(with TCP/IP package), OS/2, Macintosh System's OS with Mac TCP, Mac Open Transport, DOS with NCSA Telnet package, VAX, Alpha with Linux, and even Amiga with AmiTCP or AS225-stack.

2.3   Who Can Benefit From IP Masquerade?

- If you have a Linux host connected to the Internet, and
- if you have some computers running TCP/IP connected to that Linux box on a local subnet, and/or
- if your Linux host has more than one modem and acts as a PPP or SLIP server connecting to others, which
- those **OTHER** machines do not have official assigned IP addresses. (these machines are represented by **OTHER** machines hereby)
- And of course, if you want those **OTHER** machines to make it onto the Internet without spending extra bucks :)

2.4   Who Doesn't Need IP Masquerade?

- If your machine is a stand-alone Linux host connected to the Internet, then it is pointless to have IP Masquerade running, or
- if you already have assigned addresses for your **OTHER** machines, then you don't need IP Masquerade,
- and of course, if you don't like the idea of a 'free ride'.

2.5   How IP Masquerade Works?

From IP Masquerade FAQ by Ken Eves:

```
Here is a drawing of the most simple setup:

SLIP/PPP          +------------+                              +------------+
to provider       | Linux      |        SLIP/PPP              | Anybox     |
<---------- modem1|            |modem2 ----------- modem |            |
 111.222.333.444  |            |         192.168.1.100 |            |
                  +------------+                              +------------+
```

In the above drawing a Linux box with ip_masquerading installed and running is connected to the Internet via SLIP/or/PPP using modem1. It has an assigned IP address of 111.222.333.444. It is setup that modem2 allows callers to login and start a SLIP/or/PPP connection.

The second system (which doesn't have to be running Linux) calls into the Linux box and starts a SLIP/or/PPP connection. It does NOT have an assigned IP address on the Internet so it uses 192.168.1.100. (see below)

With ip_masquerade and the routing configured properly the machine
Anybox can interact with the Internet as if it was really connected (with a
few exceptions).

Quoting Pauline Middelink:
Do not forget to mention the ANYBOX should have the Linux box
as its gateway (whether is be the default route or just a subnet
is no matter). If the ANYBOX can not do this, the Linux machine
should do a proxy arp for all routed address, but the setup of
proxy arp is beyond the scope of the document.

The following is an excerpt from a post on comp.os.linux.networking which
has been edited to match the names used in the above example:
  o I tell machine ANYBOX that my slipped linux box is its gateway.
  o When a packet comes into the linux box from ANYBOX, it will assign it
    new source port number, and slap its own ip address in the packet
    header, saving the originals. It will then send the modified packet
    out over the SLIP/or/PPP interface to the Internet.
  o When a packet comes from the Internet to the linux box, if the port
    number is one of those assigned above, it will get the original
    port and ip address, put them back in the packet header, and send the
    packet to ANYBOX.
  o The host that sent the packet will never know the difference.

An IP Masquerading Example

typical example is given in the diagram below:-

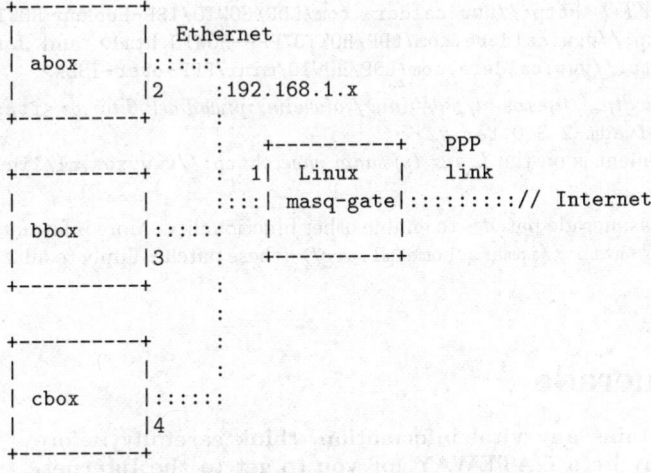

```
+----------+
|          |  Ethernet
|  abox    |::::::::
|          |2     :192.168.1.x
+----------+      :
                  :   +----------+  PPP
+----------+      :  1|  Linux   |  link
|          |      ::::| masq-gate|:::::::::// Internet
|  bbox    |::::::    |          |
|          |3     :   +----------+
+----------+      :
                  :
+----------+      :
|          |      :
|  cbox    |::::::
|          |4
+----------+


<-Internal Network->
```

In this example there are 4 computer systems that we are concerned about (there is presumably also something on the far right that your IP connection to the internet comes through, and there is something (far off the page) on the internet that you are interested in exchanging information with). The Linux system masq-gate is the masquerading gateway for the internal network of machines abox, bbox and cbox to get to the internet. The internal network uses one of the assigned private network addresses, in this case the class C network 192.168.1.0, with the linux box having address 192.168.1.1 and the other systems having addresses on that network.

The three machines abox, bbox and cbox (which can, by the way, be running any operating system as long as they can speak IP - such as **Windows 95**, **Macintosh MacTCP** or even another linux box) can connect to other machines on the internet, however the masquerading system masq-gate converts all of their connections so that they appear to originate from masq-gate, and arranges that data coming back in to a masqueraded connection is relayed back to the originating system - so the systems on the internal network see a direct route to the internet and are unaware that their data is being masqueraded.

2.6   Requirements for Using IP Masquerade on Linux 2.x

** Please refer to *IP Masquerade Resource* <http://ipmasq.home.ml.org/> for the latest information, since it is difficult to update the HOWTO frequently. **

- Kernel 2.0.x source available from *ftp://ftp.funet.fi/pub/Linux/kernel/src/v2.0/* <ftp://ftp.funet.fi/pub/Linux/kernel/src/v2.0/>
  (Yes, you'll have to compile your kernel with certain supports.... The latest stable kernel is recommended)
- Loadable   kernel   modules,   preferably   2.0.0   or   newer   available   from
  http://www.pi.se/blox/modules/modules-2.0.0.tar.gz <http://www.pi.se/blox/modules/modules-2.0.0.tar.gz>
  (modules-1.3.57 is the minimal requirement)
- A well set up TCP/IP network
  covered in *Linux NET-2 HOWTO* <http://www.caldera.com/LDP/HOWTO/NET-2-HOWTO.html> and
  the *Network Administrator's Guide* <http://linuxwww.db.erau.edu/NAG/>
- Connectivity to Internet for your Linux host
  covered in *Linux ISP Hookup HOWTO* <http://www.caldera.com/LDP/HOWTO/ISP-Hookup-HOWTO.html>, *Linux PPP HOWTO* <http://www.caldera.com/LDP/HOWTO/PPP-HOWTO.html> and *Linux PPP-over-ISDN mini-HOWTO* <http://www.caldera.com/LDP/HOWTO/mini/PPP-over-ISDN>
- Ipfwadm 2.3 or newer available from *ftp://ftp.xos.nl/pub/linux/ipfwadm/ipfwadm-2.3.tar.gz* <ftp://ftp.xos.nl/pub/linux/ipfwadm/ipfwadm-2.3.0.tar.gz>
  more information on version requirement is on the *Linux Ipfwadm page* <http://www.xos.nl/linux/ipfwadm/>
- You can optionally apply some IP Masquerade patches to enable other functionality. More information availabe on *IP Masquerade Resources* <http://ipmasq.home.ml.org/> (these patches apply to all 2.0.x kernels)

3   Setting Up IP Masquerade

If your private network contains any vital information, think carefully before using IP Masquerade. This may be a GATEWAY for you to get to the Internet, and vice versa for someone on the other side of the world to get into your network.

3.1   Compiling the Kernel for IP Masquerade Support

** Please refer to *IP Masquerade Resource* <http://ipmasq.home.ml.org/> for the latest information, since it is difficult to update the HOWTO frequently. **

- First of all, you need the kernel source (preferably stable kernel version 2.0.0 or above)
- If this is your first time compiling the kernel, don't be scared. In fact, it's rather easy and it's covered in *Linux Kernel HOWTO* <http://www.caldera.com/LDP/HOWTO/Kernel-HOWTO.html>.
- Unpack the kernel source to /usr/src/ with a command: `tar xvzf linux-2.0.x.tar.gz -C` /usr/src, where x is the patch level beyond 2.0
  (make sure there is a directory or symbolic link called `linux`)
- Apply appropriate patches. Since new patches are coming out, details will not be included here. Please refer to *IP Masquerade Resources* <http://ipmasq.home.ml.org/> for up-to-date information.
- Refer to the Kernel HOWTO and the README file in the kernel source directory for further instructions on compiling a kernel
- Here are the options that you need to compile in: Say *YES* to the following,

```
* Prompt for development and/or incomplete code/drivers
  CONFIG_EXPERIMENTAL
  - this will allow you to select experimental IP Masquerade code compiled
    into the kernel

* Enable loadable module support
  CONFIG_MODULES
  - allows you to load modules

* Networking support
  CONFIG_NET

* Network firewalls
  CONFIG_FIREWALL

* TCP/IP networking
  CONFIG_INET

* IP: forwarding/gatewaying
  CONFIG_IP_FORWARD

* IP: firewalling
  CONFIG_IP_FIREWALL

* IP: masquerading (EXPERIMENTAL)
  CONFIG_IP_MASQUERADE
  - although it is experimental, it is a *MUST*

* IP: ipautofw masquerade support (EXPERIMENTAL)
  CONFIG_IP_MASQUERADE_IPAUTOFW
  -recommended

* IP: ICMP masquerading
  CONFIG_IP_MASQUERADE_ICMP
```

- support for masquerading ICMP packets, optional.

```
* IP: always defragment
  CONFIG_IP_ALWAYS_DEFRAG
  - highly recommended

* Dummy net driver support
  CONFIG_DUMMY
  - recommended
```

NOTE: These are just the component you need for IP Masquerade, select whatever other options you need for your specific setup.

- After compiling the kernel, you should compile and install the modules:

      make modules; make modules_install

- Then you should add a few lines into your /etc/rc.d/rc.local file (or any file you think is appropriate) to load the required modules reside in /lib/modules/2.0.x/ipv4/ automatically during each reboot:

```
              .
              .
              .

/sbin/depmod -a
/sbin/modprobe ip_masq_ftp
/sbin/modprobe ip_masq_raudio
/sbin/modprobe ip_masq_irc
(and other modules such as ip_masq_cuseeme, ip_masq_vdolive
 if you have applied the patches)
              .
              .
              .
```

Note: You can also load it manually before using ip_masq, but DON'T use kerneld for this, it will NOT work!

3.2 Assigning Private Network IP Address

Since all **OTHER** machines do not have official assigned addressees, there must be a right way to allocate address to those machines.

From IP Masquerade FAQ:

There is an RFC (#1597) on which IP addresses are to be used on a non-connected network. There are 3 blocks of numbers set aside specifically for this purpose. One which I use is 255 Class-C subnets at 192.168.1.n to 192.168.255.n .

```
From RCF 1597:


Section 3: Private Address Space
```

The Internet Assigned Numbers Authority (IANA) has reserved the
following three blocks of the IP address space for private networks:

```
        10.0.0.0      -    10.255.255.255
        172.16.0.0    -    172.31.255.255
        192.168.0.0   -    192.168.255.255
```

We will refer to the first block as "24-bit block", the second as
"20-bit block", and to the third as "16-bit" block". Note that the
first block is nothing but a single class A network number, while the
second block is a set of 16 contiguous class B network numbers, and
third block is a set of 255 contiguous class C network numbers.

So, if you're using a class C network, you should name your machines as 192.168.1.1, 1.92.168.1.2, 1.92.168.1.3, ..., 192.168.1.x

192.168.1.1 is usually the gateway machine, which is your Linux host connecting to the Internet. Notice that 192.168.1.0 and 192.168.1.255 are the Network and Broadcast address respectively, which are reserved. Avoid using these addresses on your machines.

3.3 Configuring the OTHER machines

Besides setting the appropriate IP address for each machine, you should also set the appropriate gateway. In general, it is rather straight forward. You simply enter the address of your Linux host (usually 192.168.1.1) as the gateway address.

For the Domain Name Service, you can add in any DNS available. The most apparent one should be the one that your Linux is using. You can optionally add any domain search suffix as well.

After you have reconfigured those IP addresses, remember to restart the appropriate services or reboot your systems.

The following configuration instructions assume that you are using a Class C network with 192.168.1.1 as your Linux host's address. Please note that 192.168.1.0 and 192.168.1.255 are reserved.

3.3.1 Configuring Windows 95

1. If you haven't installed your network card and adapter driver, do so now.

2. Go to *'Control Panel'/'Network'*.

3. Add *'TCP/IP protocol'* if you don't already have it.

4. In *'TCP/IP properties'*, goto *'IP Address'* and set IP Address to 192.168.1.x, ($1 < x < 255$), and then set Subnet Mask to 255.255.255.0

5. Add 192.168.1.1 as your gateway under *'Gateway'*.

6. Under *'DNS Configuration'/'DNS Server search order'* add your the DNS that your Linux host uses (usually find in /etc/resolv.conf). Optionally, you can add the appropriate domain search suffix.

7. Leave all the other settings as they are unless you know what you're doing.

8. Click *'OK'* on all dialog boxes and restart system.

9. Ping the linux box to test the network connection: *'Start/Run'*, type: `ping 192.168.1.1`
   (This is only a LAN connection testing, you can't `ping` the outside world yet.)

10. You can optionally create a `HOSTS` file in the windows directory so that you can use hostname of the machines on your LAN. There is an example called `HOSTS.SAM` in the windows directory.

3.3.2   Configuring Windows for Workgroup 3.11

1. If you haven't installed your network card and adapter driver, do so now.

2. Install the TCP/IP 32b package if you don't have it already.

3. In *'Main'/'Windows Setup'/'Network Setup'*, click on *'Drivers'*.

4. Highlight *'Microsoft TCP/IP-32 3.11b'* in the *'Network Drivers'* section, click *'Setup'*.

5. Set IP Address to 192.168.1.x (1 < x < 255), then set Subnet Mask to 255.255.255.0 and Default Gateway to 192.168.1.1

6. Do not enable *'Automatic DHCP Configuration'* and put anything in those *'WINS Server'* input areas unless you're in a Windows NT domain and you know what you're doing.

7. Click *'DNS'*, fill in the appropriate information mentioned in STEP 6 of section 3.3.1, then click *'OK'* when you're done with it.

8. Click *'Advanced'*, check *'Enable DNS for Windows Name Resolution'* and *'Enable LMHOSTS lookup'* if you're using a look up host file, similar to the one mentioned in STEP 10 of section 3.3.1

9. Click *'OK'* on all dialog boxes and restart system.

10. Ping the linux box to test the network connection: *'File/Run'*, type: `ping 192.168.1.1`
    (This is only a LAN connection testing, you can't `ping` the outside world yet.)

3.3.3   Configuring Windows NT

1. If you haven't installed your network card and adapter driver, do so now.

2. Go to *'Main'/'Control Panel'/'Network'*

3. Add the TCP/IP Protocol and Related Component from the *'Add Software'* menu if you don't have TCP/IP service installed already.

4. Under *'Network Software and Adapter Cards'* section, highlight *'TCP/IP Protocol'* in the *'Installed Network Software'* selection box.

5. In *'TCP/IP Configuration'*, select the appropriate adapter, e.g. `[1]Novell NE2000 Adapter`. Then set the IP Address to 192.168.1.x (1 < x < 255), then set Subnet Mask to 255.255.255.0 and Default Gateway to 192.168.1.1

6. Do not enable *'Automatic DHCP Configuration'* and put anything in those *'WINS Server'* input areas unless you're in a Windows NT domain and you know what you're doing.

7. Click *'DNS'*, fill in the appropriate information mentioned in STEP 6 of section 3.3.1, then click *'OK'* when you're done with it.

8. Click *'Advanced'*, check *'Enable DNS for Windows Name Resolution'* and *'Enable LMHOSTS lookup'* if you're using a look up host file, similar to the one mentioned in STEP 10 of section 3.3.1

9. Click *'OK'* on all dialog boxes and restart system.

10. Ping the linux box to test the network connection: *'File/Run'*, type: `ping 192.168.1.1`
    (This is only a LAN connection testing, you can't `ping` the outside world yet.)

3.3.4 Configuring UNIX Based Systems

1. If you haven't installed your network card and recompile your kernel with the appropriate adapter driver, do so now.

2. Install TCP/IP networking, such as the nettools package, if you don't have it already.

3. Set *IPADDR* to 192.168.1.x (1 < x < 255), then set *NETMASK* to 255.255.255.0, *GATEWAY* to 192.168.1.1, and *BROADCAST* to 192.168.1.255
   For example, you can edit the `/etc/sysconfig/network-scripts/ifcfg-eth0` file on a Red Hat Linux system, or simply do it through the Control Panel.
   (it's different in SunOS, BSDi, Slackware Linux, etc...)

4. Add your domain name service (DNS) and domain search suffix in `/etc/resolv.conf`

5. You may want to update your `/etc/networks` file depending on your settings.

6. Restart the appropriate services, or simply restart your system.

7. Issue a `ping` command: `ping 192.168.1.1` to test the connection to your gateway machine.
   (This is only a LAN connection testing, you can't `ping` the outside world yet.)

3.3.5 Configuring DOS using NCSA Telnet package

1. If you haven't installed your network card, do so now.

2. Load the appropriate packet driver. For an NE2000 card, issue `nwpd 0x60 10 0x300`, with your network card set to IRQ 10 and hardware address at 0x300

3. Make a new directory, and then unpack the NCSA Telnet package: `pkunzip tel2308b.zip`

4. Use a text editor to open the `config.tel` file

5. Set `myip=192.168.1.x` (1 < x < 255), and netmask=255.255.255.0

6. In this example, you should set `hardware=packet, interrupt=10, ioaddr=60`

7. You should have at least one individual machine specification set as the gateway, i.e. the Linux host:

   ```
   name=default
   host=yourlinuxhostname
   hostip=192.168.1.1
   gateway=1
   ```

8. Have another specification for a domain name service:

   ```
   name=dns.domain.com ; hostip=123.123.123.123; nameserver=1
   ```

   Note: substitute the appropriate information about the DNS that your Linux host uses

9. Save your `config.tel` file

10. Telnet to the linux box to test the network connection: `telnet 192.168.1.1`

3.3.6 Configuring MacOS Based System Running MacTCP

1. If you haven't installed the appropriate driver software for your Ethernet adapter, now would be a very good time to do so.

2. Open the *MacTCP control panel*. Select the appropriate network driver (Ethernet, NOT EtherTalk) and click on the *'More...'* button.

3. Under *'Obtain Address:'*, click *'Manually'*.

4. Under *'IP Address:'*, select *class C* from the popup menu. Ignore the rest of this section of the dialog box.

5. Fill in the appropriate information under *'Domain Name Server Information:'*.

6. Under *'Gateway Address:'*, enter 192.168.1.1

7. Click *'OK'* to save the settings. In the main window of the *MacTCP control panel*, enter the IP address of your Mac (192.168.1.x, 1 < x < 255) in the *'IP Address:'* box.

8. Close the *MacTCP control panel*. If a dialog box pops up notifying you to do so, restart the system.

9. You may optionally ping the Linux box to test the network connection. If you have the freeware program *MacTCP Watcher*, click on the *'Ping'* button, and enter the address of your Linux box (192.168.1.1) in the dialog box that pops up. (This is only a LAN connection testing, you can't ping the outside world yet.)

10. You can optionally create a `Hosts` file in your System Folder so that you can use the hostnames of the machines on your LAN. The file should already exist in your System Folder, and should contain some (commented-out) sample entries which you can modify according to your needs.

3.3.7   Configuring MacOS Based System Running Open Transport

1. If you haven't installed the appropriate driver software for your Ethernet adapter, now would be a very good time to do so.

2. Open the *TCP/IP Control Panel* and choose *'User Mode ...'* from the *Edit* menu. Make sure the user mode is set to at least *'Advanced'* and click the *'OK'* button.

3. Choose *'Configurations...'* from the *File* menu. Select your *'Default'* configuration and click the *'Duplicate...'* button. Enter 'IP Masq' (or something to let you know that this is a special configuration) in the *'Duplicate Configuration'* dialog, it will probably say something like *'Deafault copy'*. Then click the *'OK'* button, and the *'Make Active'* button

4. Select *'Ethernet'* from the *'Connect via:'* pop-up.

5. Select the appropriate item from the *'Configure:'* pop-up. If you don't know which option to choose, you probably should re-select your *'Default'* configuration and quit. I use *'Manually'*.

6. Enter the IP address of your Mac (192.168.1.x, 1 < x < 255) in the *'IP Address:'* box.

7. Enter 255.255.255.0 in the *'Subnet mask:'* box.

8. Enter 192.168.1.1 in the *'Router address:'* box.

9. Enter the IP addresses of your domain name servers in the *'Name server addr.:'* box.

10. Enter the name of your Internet domain (e.g. 'microsoft.com') in the *'Starting domain name'* box under *'Implicit Search Path:'*.

11. The following procedures are optional. Incorrect values may cause erratic behavior. If your not sure, it's probably better to leave them blank, unchecked and/or un- selected. Remove any information from those fields, if necessary. As far as I know there is no way through the TCP/IP dialogs, to tell the system not to use a previously select alternate "Hosts" file. If you know, I would be interested. Check the *'802.3'* if your network requires 802.3 frame types.

12. Click the *'Options...'* button to make sure that the TCP/IP is active. I use the *'Load only when needed'* option. If you run and quit TCP/IP applications many times without rebooting your machine, you may find that unchecking the *'Load only when needed'* option will prevent/reduce the effects on your machines memory management. With the item unchecked the TCP/IP protocol stacks are always loaded and available for use. If checked, the TCP/IP stacks are automatically loaded when needed and un- loaded when not. It's the loading and unloading process that can cause your machines memory to become fragmented.

13. You may ping the Linux box to test the network connection. If you have the freeware program *MacTCP Watcher*, click on the *'Ping'* button, and enter the address of your Linux box (192.168.1.1) in the dialog box that pops up. (This is only a LAN connection testing, you can't ping the outside world yet.)

14. You can create a `Hosts` file in your System Folder so that you can use the hostnames of the machines on your LAN. The file may or may not already exist in your System Folder. If so, it should contain some (commented-out) sample entries which you can modify according to your needs. If not, you can get a copy of the file from a system running MacTCP, or just create your own (it follows a subset of the Unix /etc/hosts file format, described on page 33 of RFC 1035). Once you've created the file, open the *TCP/IP control panel*, click on the *'Select Hosts File...'* button, and open the `Hosts` file.

15. Click the close box or choose *'Close'* or *'Quit'* from the *File* menu, and then click the *'Save'* button to save the changes you have made.

16. The changes take effect immediately, but rebooting the system won't hurt.

3.3.8 Configuring Novell network using DNS

1. If you haven't installed the appropriate driver software for your Ethernet adapter, now would be a very good time to do so.

2. Downloaded tcpip16.exe from **<ftp.novell.com/pub/updates/unixconn/lwp5>**

3. edit c:\nwclient\startnet.bat

   : (here is a copy of mine)

```
SET NWLANGUAGE=ENGLISH
LH LSL.COM
LH KTC2000.COM
LH IPXODI.COM
LH tcpip
LH VLM.EXE
F:
```

4. edit c:\nwclient\net.cfg

   : (change link driver to yours i.e. NE2000)

```
Link Driver KTC2000
        Protocol IPX 0 ETHERNET_802.3
        Frame ETHERNET_802.3
        Frame Ethernet_II
        FRAME Ethernet_802.2

NetWare DOS Requester
        FIRST NETWORK DRIVE = F
        USE DEFAULTS = OFF
        VLM = CONN.VLM
        VLM = IPXNCP.VLM
        VLM = TRAN.VLM
        VLM = SECURITY.VLM
        VLM = NDS.VLM
        VLM = BIND.VLM
        VLM = NWP.VLM
        VLM = FIO.VLM
        VLM = GENERAL.VLM
        VLM = REDIR.VLM
```

```
               VLM = PRINT.VLM
               VLM = NETX.VLM

    Link Support
          Buffers 8 1500
          MemPool 4096


    Protocol TCPIP
          PATH SCRIPT      C:\NET\SCRIPT
          PATH PROFILE     C:\NET\PROFILE
          PATH LWP_CFG     C:\NET\HSTACC
          PATH TCP_CFG     C:\NET\TCP
          ip_address       xxx.xxx.xxx.xxx
          ip_router        xxx.xxx.xxx.xxx
```

5. and finally created

   ```
   c:\bin\resolv.cfg
   ```

   :

   ```
   SEARCH DNS HOSTS SEQUENTIAL
   NAMESERVER 207.103.0.2
   NAMESERVER 207.103.11.9
   ```

6. I hope this helps some people get their Novell Nets online, BTW this can be done using Netware 3.1x
   or 4.x

3.3.9   Configuring OS/2 Warp

1. If you haven't installed the appropriate driver software for your Ethernet adapter, now would be a
   very good time to do so.

2. Install the TCP/IP protocoll if you don't have it already.

3. Go to *Programms/TCP/IP (LAN) / TCP/IP* Settings

4. In *'Network'* add your TCP/IP Address and set your Netmask (255.255.255.0)

5. Under *'Routing'* press *'Add'*. Set the *Type* to *'default'* and type the IP Address of your Linux Box in
   the Field *'Router Address'*. (192.168.1.1).

6. Set the same DNS (Nameserver) Address that your Linux host uses in *'Hosts'*.

7. Close the TCP/IP control panel. Say yes to the following question(s).

8. Reboot your system

9. You may ping the Linux box to test the network configuration. Type `'ping 192.168.1.1'` in a 'OS/2
   Command prompt Window'. When ping packets are received all is ok.

3.3.10   Configuring Other Systems

They should be following the same theory for setup. Check the sections above. If you're interested in
writing about any of these systems, please send a detail setup instruction to *ambrose@writeme.com* <mailto:
ambrose@writeme.com>.

3.4 Configuring IP Forwarding Policies

At this point, you should have your kernel and other required packages installed, as well as your modules loaded. Also, the IP addresses, gateway, and DNS should be all set on the **OTHER** machines.

Now, the only thing left to do is to use ipfwadm to forward appropriate packets to the appropriate machine:

> ** This can be accomplished in many different ways. The following suggestions
> and examples worked for me, but you may have different ideas, please refer to
> section 4.4 and the ipfwadm manpages for more detail. **

```
ipfwadm -F -p deny
ipfwadm -F -a m -S yyy.yyy.yyy.yyy/x -D 0.0.0.0/0
```

where x is one of the following numbers according to the class of your subnet, and yyy.yyy.yyy.yyy is your network address.

```
netmask          | x  | Subnet
~~~~~~~~~~~~~~~~~~|~~~~|~~~~~~~~~~~~~~~~
255.0.0.0        | 8  | Class A
255.255.0.0      | 16 | Class B
255.255.255.0    | 24 | Class C
255.255.255.255  | 32 | Point-to-point
```

For example, if I'm on a class C subnet, I would have entered:

```
ipfwadm -F -p deny
ipfwadm -F -a m -S 192.168.1.0/24 -D 0.0.0.0/0
```

Since bootp request packets comes without valid IP's once the client knows nothing about it, for people with a bootp server in the masquerade/firewall machine it is necessary to use the following before the deny command:

```
ipfwadm -I -a accept -S 0/0 68 -D 0/0 67 -W bootp_clients_net_if_name -P udp
```

You can also do it on a per machine basis. For example, if I want 192.168.1.2 and 192.168.1.8 to have access to the Internet, but not the other machines, I would have entered:

```
ipfwadm -F -p deny
ipfwadm -F -a m -S 192.168.1.2/32 -D 0.0.0.0/0
ipfwadm -F -a m -S 192.168.1.8/32 -D 0.0.0.0/0
```

Alternately, you can type the netmask instead of the value, e.g. 192.168.1.0/255.255.255.0

What appears to be a common mistake is to make the first command be this

```
ipfwadm -F -p masquerade
```

Do **not** make your default policy be masquerading - otherwise someone who can manipulate their routing will be able to tunnel straight back through your gateway, using it to masquerade their identity!

Again, you can add these lines to the /etc/rc.local files, one of the rc files you prefer, or do it manually every time you need IP Masquerade.

Please read section 4.4 for a detail guide on Ipfwadm

3.5   Testing IP Masquerade

It's time to give it a try, after all these hard work. Make sure the connection of your Linux hosts to the Internet is okay.

You can try browsing some 'INTERNET!!!' web sites on your **OTHER** machines, and see if you get it. I recommend using an IP address rather than a hostname on your first try, because your DNS setup may not be correct.

For example, you can access the Linux Documentation Project site http://sunsite.unc.edu/mdw/linux.html with an entry of *http://152.2.254.81/mdw/linux.html* <http://152.2.254.81/mdw/linux.html>

If you see that nice sailboat, then congratulations! It's working! You may then try one with hostname entry, and then telnet, ftp, Real Audio, True Speech, whatever supported by IP Masquerade.....

So far, I have no trouble with the above settings, and it's full credit to the people who spend their time making this wonderful feature working.

4   Other IP Masquerade Issues and Software Support

4.1   Problems with IP Masquerade

Some protocols will not currently work with masquerading because they either assume things about port numbers, or encode data in their data stream about addresses and ports - these latter protocols need specific proxies built into the masquerading code to make them work.

4.2   Incoming services

Masquerading cannot handle incoming services at all. There are a few ways of allowing them, but they are completely separate from masquerading, and are really part of standard firewall practice.

If you do not require high levels of security then you can simply redirect ports. There are various ways of doing this - I use a modified redir program (which I hope will be available from sunsite and mirrors soon). If you wish to have some level of authorisation on incoming connections then you can either use TCP wrappers or Xinetd on top of redir (0.7 or above) to allow only specific IP addresses through, or use some other tools. The TIS Firewall Toolkit is a good place to look for tools and information.

More details can be found at *IP Masquerade Resource* <http://ipmasq.home.ml.org>.

4.3   Supported Client Software and Other Setup Note

> **** The following list is not being maintained anymore. Please refer to *this page*** <http://masqapps.home.ml.org> **on applications that work thru Linux IP masquerading and *IP Masquerade Resource* <http://ipmasq.home.ml.org/> for more detail. ****

Generally, application that uses TCP and UDP should work. If you have any suggestion, hints, or questions about applications with IP Masquerade, please visit this page on *applications that work thru Linux IP masquerading* <http://masqapps.home.ml.org> by Lee Nevo.

4.3.1 Clients that Work

General Clients

HTTP
all supported platforms, surfing the web

POP & SMTP
all supported platforms, email client

Telnet
all supported platforms, remote session

FTP
all supported platforms, with ip_masq_ftp.o module (not all sites work with certain clients; e.g. some sites cannot be reached using ws_ftp32 but works with netscape)

Archie
all supported platforms, file searching client (not all archie clients are supported)

NNTP (USENET)
all supported platforms, USENET news client

VRML
Windows(possibly all supported platforms), virtual reality surfing

traceroute
mainly UNIX based platforms, some variations may not work

ping
all platforms, with ICMP patch

anything based on IRC
all supported platforms, with ip_masq_irc.o modules

Gopher client
all supported platforms

WAIS client
all supported platforms

Multimedia Clients

Real Audio Player
Windows, network streaming audio, with ip_masq_raudio module loaded

True Speech Player 1.1b
Windows, network streaming audio

Internet Wave Player
Windows, network streaming audio

Worlds Chat 0.9a
Windows, Client-Server 3D chat program

Alpha Worlds
Windows, Client-Server 3D chat program

Internet Phone 3.2
Windows, Peer-to-peer audio communications, people can reach you only if you initiate the call, but people cannot call you

Powwow

   Windows, Peer-to-peer Text audio whiteboard communications, people can reach you only if you initiate the call, but people cannot call you

CU-SeeMe

   all supported platforms, with cuseeme modules loaded, please see *IP Masquerade Resource* `<http://ipmasq.home.ml.org/>` for detail

VDOLive

   Windows, with vdolive patch

Note: Some clients such as IPhone and Powwow may work even if you're not the one who initiate the call by using *ipautofw package* (refer to section 4.6)

Other Clients

NCSA Telnet 2.3.08

   DOS, a suite containing telnet, ftp, ping, etc.

PC-anywhere for windows 2.0

   MS-Windows, Remotely controls a PC over TCP/IP, only work if it is a client but not a host

Socket Watch

   uses ntp - network time protocol

Linux net-acct package

   Linux, network administration-account package

4.3.2   Clients that do not Work

Intel Internet Phone Beta 2

   Connects but voice travels one way (out) Traffic only

Intel Streaming Media Viewer Beta 1

   Cannot connect to server

Netscape CoolTalk

   Cannot connect to opposite side

talk,ntalk

   will not work - requires a kernel proxy to be written.

WebPhone

   Cannot work at present (it makes invalid assumptions about addresses).

X

   Untested, but I think it cannot work unless someone builds an X proxy, which is probably an external program to the masquerading code. One way of making this work is to use **ssh** as the link and use the internal X proxy of that to make things work!

4.3.3   Platforms/OS Tested as on OTHER machines

- Linux
- Solaris
- Windows 95
- Windows NT (both workstation and server)

- Windows For Workgroup 3.11 (with TCP/IP package)
- Windows 3.1 (with Chameleon package)
- Novel 4.01 Server
- OS/2 (including Warp v3)
- Macintosh OS (with MacTCP or Open Transport)
- DOS (with NCSA Telnet package, DOS Trumpet works partially)
- Amiga (with AmiTCP or AS225-stack)
- VAX Stations 3520 and 3100 with UCX (TCP/IP stack for VMS)
- Alpha/AXP with Linux/Redhat
- SCO Openserver (v3.2.4.2 and 5)
- IBM RS/6000 running AIX
- (Anyone tried other platforms?)

4.4   IP Firewall Administration (ipfwadm)

This section provides a more in-depth guide on using ipfwadm.

This is a setup for a firewall/masquerade system behind a PPP link with a static PPP address follows. Trusted interface is 192.168.255.1, PPP interface has been changed to protect the guilty :). I listed each incoming and outgoing interface individually to catch IP spoofing as well as stuffed routing and/or masquerading. Also anything not explicitly allowed is forbidden!

```
#!/bin/sh
#
# /etc/rc.d/rc.firewall, define the firewall configuration, invoked from
# rc.local.
#

PATH=/sbin:/bin:/usr/sbin:/usr/bin

# testing, wait a bit then clear all firewall rules.
# uncomment following lines if you want the firewall to automatically
# disable after 10 minutes.
# (sleep 600; \
# ipfwadm -I -f; \
# ipfwadm -I -p accept; \
# ipfwadm -O -f; \
# ipfwadm -O -p accept; \
# ipfwadm -F -f; \
# ipfwadm -F -p accept; \
# ) &

# Incoming, flush and set default policy of deny. Actually the default policy
# is irrelevant because there is a catch all rule with deny and log.
ipfwadm -I -f
ipfwadm -I -p deny
# local interface, local machines, going anywhere is valid
ipfwadm -I -a accept -V 192.168.255.1 -S 192.168.0.0/16 -D 0.0.0.0/0
# remote interface, claiming to be local machines, IP spoofing, get lost
```

```
ipfwadm -I -a deny -V your.static.PPP.address -S 192.168.0.0/16 -D 0.0.0.0/0 -o
# remote interface, any source, going to permanent PPP address is valid
ipfwadm -I -a accept -V your.static.PPP.address -S 0.0.0.0/0 -D
your.static.PPP.address/32
# loopback interface is valid.
ipfwadm -I -a accept -V 127.0.0.1 -S 0.0.0.0/0 -D 0.0.0.0/0
# catch all rule, all other incoming is denied and logged. pity there is no
# log option on the policy but this does the job instead.
ipfwadm -I -a deny -S 0.0.0.0/0 -D 0.0.0.0/0 -o

# Outgoing, flush and set default policy of deny. Actually the default policy
# is irrelevant because there is a catch all rule with deny and log.
ipfwadm -O -f
ipfwadm -O -p deny
# local interface, any source going to local net is valid
ipfwadm -O -a accept -V 192.168.255.1 -S 0.0.0.0/0 -D 192.168.0.0/16
# outgoing to local net on remote interface, stuffed routing, deny
ipfwadm -O -a deny -V your.static.PPP.address -S 0.0.0.0/0 -D 192.168.0.0/16 -o
# outgoing from local net on remote interface, stuffed masquerading, deny
ipfwadm -O -a deny -V your.static.PPP.address -S 192.168.0.0/16 -D 0.0.0.0/0 -o
# outgoing from local net on remote interface, stuffed masquerading, deny
ipfwadm -O -a deny -V your.static.PPP.address -S 0.0.0.0/0 -D 192.168.0.0/16 -o
# anything else outgoing on remote interface is valid
ipfwadm -O -a accept -V your.static.PPP.address -S your.static.PPP.address/32 -D
0.0.0.0/0
# loopback interface is valid.
ipfwadm -O -a accept -V 127.0.0.1 -S 0.0.0.0/0 -D 0.0.0.0/0
# catch all rule, all other outgoing is denied and logged. pity there is no
# log option on the policy but this does the job instead.
ipfwadm -O -a deny -S 0.0.0.0/0 -D 0.0.0.0/0 -o

# Forwarding, flush and set default policy of deny. Actually the default policy
# is irrelevant because there is a catch all rule with deny and log.
ipfwadm -F -f
ipfwadm -F -p deny
# Masquerade from local net on local interface to anywhere.
ipfwadm -F -a masquerade -W ppp0 -S 192.168.0.0/16 -D 0.0.0.0/0
# catch all rule, all other forwarding is denied and logged. pity there is no
# log option on the policy but this does the job instead.
ipfwadm -F -a deny -S 0.0.0.0/0 -D 0.0.0.0/0 -o
```

You can block traffic to a particular site using the -I, -O or -F. Remember that the set of rules are scanned top to bottom and -a means "append" to the existing set of rules so any restrictions need to come before global rules. For example (and untested) :-

Using -I rules. Probably the fastest but it only stops the local machines, the firewall itself can still access the "forbidden" site. Of course you might want to allow that combination.

```
... start of -I rules ...
# reject and log local interface, local machines going to 204.50.10.13
ipfwadm -I -a reject -V 192.168.255.1 -S 192.168.0.0/16 -D 204.50.10.13/32 -o
# local interface, local machines, going anywhere is valid
ipfwadm -I -a accept -V 192.168.255.1 -S 192.168.0.0/16 -D 0.0.0.0/0
... end of -I rules ...
```

Using -O rules. Slowest because the packets go through masquerading first but this rule even stops the firewall accessing the forbidden site.

```
... start of -O rules ...
# reject and log outgoing to 204.50.10.13
ipfwadm -O -a reject -V your.static.PPP.address -S your.static.PPP.address/32 -D
204.50.10.13/32 -o
# anything else outgoing on remote interface is valid
ipfwadm -O -a accept -V your.static.PPP.address -S your.static.PPP.address/32 -D
0.0.0.0/0
... end of -O rules ...
```

Using -F rules. Probably slower than -I and this still only stops masqueraded machines (i.e. internal), firewall can still get to forbidden site.

```
... start of -F rules ...
# Reject and log from local net on PPP interface to 204.50.10.13.
ipfwadm -F -a reject -W ppp0 -S 192.168.0.0/16 -D 204.50.10.13/32 -o
# Masquerade from local net on local interface to anywhere.
ipfwadm -F -a masquerade -W ppp0 -S 192.168.0.0/16 -D 0.0.0.0/0
... end of -F rules ...
```

No need for a special rule to allow 192.168.0.0/16 to go to 204.50.11.0, it is covered by the global rules.

There is more than one way of coding the interfaces in the above rules. For example instead of -V 192.168.255.1 you can code -W eth0, instead of -V your.static.PPP.address you can use -W ppp0. Personal choice and documentation more than anything.

4.5 IP Masquerade and Demand-Dial-Up

1. If you would like to setup your network to automatically dial up the Internet, the *diald* demand dial-up package will be of great utility.

2. To setup the diald, please check out the *Setting Up Diald for Linux Page* <http://home.pacific.net.sg/harish/diald.config.html>

3. Once diald and IP masq have been setup, you can go to any of the client machines and initiate a web, telnet or ftp session.

4. Diald will detect the incoming request, then dial up your ISP and establish the connection.

5. There is a timeout that will occur with the first connection. This is inevitable if you are using analog modems. The time taken to establish the modem link and the PPP connections will cause your client program to timeout. This can be avoided if you are using an ISDN connection. All you need to do is to terminate the current process on the client and restart it.

4.6 IPautofw Packet Fowarder

IPautofw <ftp://ftp.netis.com/pub/members/rlynch/ipautofw.tar.gz> is a generic forwarder of TCP and UDP for Linux masquerading. Generally to utilize a package which requires UDP, a specific ip_masq module needs to be loaded; ip_masq_raudio, ip_masq_cuseeme, ... Ipautofw acts in a more generic manner, it will forward any type of traffic including those which the application specific modules will not forward. This may create a security hole if not administered correctly.

5   Miscellaneous

5.1   Getting Help

**   ** Please TRY NOT TO send me email for IP Masquerade problems or questions. Due to personal work load, I cannot promise a reply for all non-website related questions. Please post your questions to the *IP Masquerade mailing list* `<http://ipmasq.home.ml.org/index.html##mailinglist>` instead (and I think this is the best source for help). Sorry about this, but I don't want to get you a reply after weeks.**

- *IP Masquerade Resource page* `<http://ipmasq.home.ml.org/>` should have enough information for setting up IP Masquerade

- Joining IP masquerade mailing list (recommended)
  To subscribe, send a mail with subject "subscribe" (no quote) to *masq-request@indyramp.com* `<mailto:masq-request@indyramp.com>`
  To unsubscribe, send a mail with subject "unsubscribe" (no quote) to *masq-request@indyramp.com* `<mailto:masq-request@indyramp.com>`
  To get help on using the mailing list, send a mail with subject "archive help" or "archive dir" (no quote) to *masq-request@indyramp.com* `<mailto:masq-request@indyramp.com>`

- *IP masquerade mailing list archive* `<http://www.indyramp.com/masq/list/>` contains all the past messages sent to the mailing list.

- This *Linux IP Masquerade mini HOWTO* `<http://ipmasq.home.ml.org/ipmasq-HOWTO.html>` for kernel 2.x (if you're using a 1.3.x or 2.x kernel)

- *IP Masquerade HOWTO for kernel 1.2.x* `<http://ipmasq.home.ml.org/ipmasq-HOWTO-1.2.x.txt>` if you're using an older kernel

- *IP masquerade FAQ* `<http://www.indyramp.com/masq/ip_masquerade.txt>` has some general information

- *X/OS Ipfwadm page* `<http://www.xos.nl/linux/ipfwadm/>` contains sources, binaries, documentation, and other information about the `ipfwadm` package

- A page on *applications that work thru Linux IP masquerading* `<http://masqapps.home.ml.org>` by Lee Nevo provides tips and tricks on getting applications to work with IP Masquerade.

- *LDP Network Administrator's Guide* `<http://linuxwww.db.erau.edu/NAG/>` is a must for beginners trying to set up a network

- *Linux NET-2 HOWTO* `<http://www.caldera.com/LDP/HOWTO/NET-2-HOWTO.html>` also has lots of useful information about Linux networking

- *Linux ISP Hookup HOWTO* `<http://www.caldera.com/LDP/HOWTO/ISP-Hookup-HOWTO.html>` and *Linux PPP HOWTO* `<http://www.caldera.com/LDP/HOWTO/PPP-HOWTO.html>` gives you information on how to connect your Linux host to the Internet

- *Linux Ethernet-Howto* `<http://www.caldera.com/LDP/HOWTO/Ethernet-HOWTO.html>` is a good source of information about setting up a LAN running ethernet

- You may also be interested in *Linux Firewalling and Proxy Server HOWTO* `<http://www.caldera.com/LDP/HOWTO/Firewall-HOWTO.html>`

- *Linux Kernel HOWTO* `<http://www.caldera.com/LDP/HOWTO/Kernel-HOWTO.html>` will guide you through the kernel compilation process

- Other *Linux HOWTOs* `<http://www.caldera.com/LDP/HOWTO/HOWTO-INDEX-3.html>` such as Kernel HOWTO

- Posting to the USENET newsgroup: *comp.os.linux.networking* `<news:comp.os.linux.networking>`

5.2   Thanks to

- Gabriel Beitler, gbeitler@aciscorp.com
  on providing section 3.3.8 (setting up Novel)

- Ed Doolittle, dolittle@math.toronto.edu
  on suggestion to -V option in `ipfwadm` command for improved security

- Matthew Driver, mdriver@cfmeu.asn.au
  on helping extensively on this HOWTO, and providing section 3.3.1 (setting up Windows 95)

- Ken Eves, ken@eves.com
  on the FAQ that provides invaluable information for this HOWTO

- Ed. Lott, edlott@neosoft.com
  for a long list of tested system and software

- Nigel Metheringham, Nigel.Metheringham@theplanet.net
  on contributing his version of IP Packet Filtering and IP Masquerading HOWTO, which make this
  HOWTO a better and technical in-depth document
  section 4.1, 4.2, and others

- Keith Owens, kaos@ocs.com.au
  on providing an excellent guide on ipfwadm section 4.2
  on correction to `ipfwadm -deny` option which avoids a security hole, and clarified the status of `ping`
  over IP Masquerade

- Rob Pelkey, rpelkey@abacus.bates.edu
  on providing section 3.3.6 and 3.3.7 (setting up MacTCP and Open Transport)

- Harish Pillay, h.pillay@ieee.org
  on providing section 4.5 (dial-on-demand using diald)

- Mark Purcell, purcell@rmcs.cranfield.ac.uk
  on providing section 4.6 (IPautofw)

- Ueli Rutishauser, rutish@ibm.net
  on providing section 3.3.9 (setting up OS/2 Warp)

- John B. (Brent) Williams, forerunner@mercury.net
  on providing section 3.3.7 (setting up Open Transport)

- Enrique Pessoa Xavier, enrique@labma.ufrj.br
  on the bootp setup suggestion

- developers of IP Masquerade for this great feature

  - Delian Delchev, delian@wfpa.acad.bg
  - Nigel Metheringham, Nigel.Metheringham@theplanet.net
  - Keith Owens, kaos@ocs.com.au
  - Jeanette Pauline Middelink, middelin@polyware.iaf.nl
  - David A. Ranch, trinity@value.net
  - Miquel van Smoorenburg, miquels@q.cistron.nl
  - Jos Vos, jos@xos.nl
  - And more who I may have failed to mention here (please let me know)

- all users sending feedback and suggestion to the mailing list, especially the ones who reported errors
  in the document and the clients that are supported and not supported

- I appologize if I have not included information that some fellow users sent me. There are many
  suggestions and ideas sent to me, but I just do not have enough time to verify or I lost track of them.
  I am trying my best to incorporate all the information sent to me into the HOWTO. I thank you for
  the effort, and I hope you understand my situation.

5.3   Reference

- IP masquerade FAQ by Ken Eves
- IP masquerade mailing list archive by Indyramp Consulting
- Ipfwadm page by X/OS
- Various networking related Linux HOWTOs

IP Sub-Networking Mini-Howto

Robert Hart, hartr@interweft.com.au   v1.0, 31 March 1997

This document describes why and how to subnetwork an IP network - that is using a single A, B or C Class network number to function correctly on several interconnected networks.

1   Copyright

2   Introduction

With available IP network numbers rapidly becoming an endangered species, efficient use of this increasingly scarce resource is important.

This document describes how to split a single IP network number up so that it can be used on several different networks.

This document concentrates on C Class IP network numbers - but the principles apply to A and B class networks as well.

2.1   Other sources of information

There are a number of other sources of information that are of relevance for both detailed and background information on IP numbers. Those recommended by the author are:-

- *The Linux Network Administrators Guide* <http://sunsite.unc.edu/LDP/LDP/nag/nag.html>.
- *The Linux System Administration Guide* <http://linuxwww.db.erau.edu/SAG/>.
- *TCP/IP Network Administration by Craig Hunt, published by O'Reilly and Associates* <http://www.ora.com/catalog/tcp/noframes.html>.

3   The Anatomy of IP numbers

Before diving into the delight of sub-networking, we need to establish some IP number basics.

3.1   IP numbers belong to Interfaces - NOT hosts!

First of all, let's clear up a basic cause of misunderstanding - IP numbers are **not** assigned to hosts. IP numbers are assigned to network interfaces on hosts.

Eh - what's that?

Whilst many (if not most) computers on an IP network will possess a single network interface (and have a single IP number as a consequence), this is not the only way things happen. Computers and other devices can have several (if not many) network interfaces - and each interface has its own IP number.

So a device with 6 active interfaces (such as a router) will have 6 IP numbers - one for each interface to each network to which it is connected. The reason for this becomes clear when we look at an IP network!

Despite this, most people refer to *host addresses* when referring to an IP number. Just remember, this is simply shorthand for *the IP number of this particular interface on this host*. Many (if not the majority) of devices on the Internet have only a single interface and thus a single IP number.

3.2 IP Numbers as "Dotted Quads"

In the current (IPv4) implementation of IP numbers, IP numbers consist of 4 (8 bit) bytes - giving a total of 32 bits of available information. This results in numbers that are rather large (even when written in decimal notation). So for readability (and organisational reasons) IP numbers are usually written in the 'dotted quad' format. The IP number

```
192.168.1.24
```

is an example of this - 4 (decimal) numbers separated by (.) dots.

As each one of the four numbers is the decimal representation of an 8 bit byte, each of the 4 numbers can range from 0 to 255 (that is take on 256 unique values - remember, zero is a value too).

In addition, part of the IP number of a host identifies the network on which the host resides, the remaining 'bits' of the IP number identify the host (oops - network interface) itself. Exactly how many bits are used by the network ID and how many are available to identify hosts (interfaces) on that network is determined by the network 'class'.

3.3 Classes of IP Networks

There are three classes of IP numbers

- Class A IP network numbers use the leftmost 8 bits (the leftmost of the dotted quads) to identify the network, leaving 24 bits (the remaining three dotted quads) to identify host interfaces on that network.
  Class A addresses **always** have the leftmost bit of the leftmost byte a zero - that is a decimal value of 0 to 127 for the first dotted quad. So there are a maximum of 128 class A network numbers available, with each one containing up to 33,554,430 possible interfaces.

  However, the networks 0.0.0.0 (known as the default route) and 127.0.0.0 (the loop back network) have special meanings and are not available for use to identify networks. So there are only 126 *available* A class network numbers.

- Class B IP network numbers use the leftmost 16 bits (the leftmost two dotted quads) to identify the network, leaving 16 bits (the last two dotted quads) to identify host interfaces. Class B addresses always have the leftmost 2 bits of the leftmost byte set to 1 0. This leaves 14 bits left to specify the network address giving 32767 available B class networks. B Class networks thus have a range of 128 to 191 for the first of the dotted quads, with each network containing up to 32,766 possible interfaces.

- Class C IP network numbers use the leftmost 24 bits (the leftmost three bytes) to identify the network, leaving 8 bits (the rightmost byte) to identify host interfaces. Class C addresses always start with the leftmost 3 bits set to 1 1 0 or a range of 192 to 255 for the leftmost dotted quad. There are thus 4,194,303 available C class network numbers, each containing 254 interfaces. (C Class networks with the first byte greater than 223 are however reserved and unavailable for use).

In summary:

```
        Network class    Usable range of first byte values (decimal)
              A                      1 to 126
              B                    128 to 191
              C                    192 to 254
```

There are also special addresses that are reserved for 'unconnected' networks - that is networks that use IP but are not connected to the Internet, These addresses are:-

- One A Class Network
  10.0.0.0
- 16 B Class Networks
  172.16.0.0 - 172.31.0.0
- 256 C Class Networks 192.168.0.0 - 192.168.255.0

You will note that this document uses these sequences throughout to avoid confusion with 'real' networks and hosts.

3.4   Network numbers, interface addresses and broadcast addresses

IP numbers can have three possible meanings:-

- the address of an IP network (a group of IP devices sharing common access to a transmission medium - such as all being on the same Ethernet segment). A network number will always have the interface (host) bits of the address space set to 0 (unless the network is sub-networked - as we shall see);
- the broadcast address of an IP network (the address used to 'talk', simultaneously, to all devices in an IP network). Broadcast addresses for a network always have the interface (host) bits of the the address space set to 1 (unless the network is sub-networked - again, as we shall see).
- the address of an interface (such as an Ethernet card or PPP interface on a host, router, print server etc). These addresses can have any value in the host bits **except** all zero or all 1 - because with the host bits all 0, the address is a network address and with the host bits all 1 the address is the broadcast address.

In summary and to clarify things

```
        For an A class network...
        (one byte of network address space followed by three bytes of host
        address space)

                10.0.0.0 is an A Class  network number  because all the host
                        bits of the address space are 0
                10.0.1.0 is a host address on this network
```

```
          10.255.255.255.255 is the broadcast address of this network
                because all the host bits of the address space are 1
```

For a B class network...
(two bytes of network address space followed by two bytes of host
address space)

```
          172.17.0.0 is a B Class network number
          172.17.0.1 is a host address on this network
          172.17.255.255 is the network broadcast address
```

For a C Class network...
(three bytes of network address space followed by one byte of host
address space)

```
          192.168.3.0 is a C Class network number
          192.168.3.42 is a host address on this network
          192.168.3.255 is the network broadcast address
```

Almost all IP network numbers remaining available for allocation at present are C Class addresses.

3.5   The network mask

The network mask is more properly called the subnetwork mask. However, it is generally referred to as the network mask.

It is the network mask and its implications on how IP addresses are interpreted *locally* on an IP network segment that concerns us most here, as this determines what (if any) sub-networking occurs.

The standard (sub-) network mask is all the network bits in an address set to '1' and all the host bits set to '0'. This means that the standard network masks for the three classes of networks are:-

- A Class network mask: 255.0.0.0
- B Class network mask: 255.255.0.0
- C Class network mask: 255.255.255.0

There are two important things to remember about the network mask:-

- The network mask affects only the **local** interpretation of **local** IP numbers (where local means on this particular network segment);
- The network mask is **not** an IP number - it is used to modify how local IP numbers are interpreted locally.

4   What are subnets?

A subnet is a way of taking a single IP network address and **locally** splitting it up so that this single network IP address can actually be used on several interconnected local networks. Remember, a single IP network number can only be used on a single network.

The important word here is **locally**: as far as the world outside the machines and physical networks covered by the sub-netted IP network are concerned, nothing whatsoever has changed - it is still just a single IP network. This is important - sub-networking is a **local** configuration and is invisible to the rest of the world.

5 Why subnetwork?

The reasons behind sub-networking date back to the early specification of IP - where just a few sites were running on Class A network numbers, which allow for millions of connected hosts.

It is obviously a huge traffic and administration problem if all IP computers at a large site need to be connected to the same network: trying to manage such a huge beast would be a nightmare and the network would (almost certainly) collapse under the load of its own traffic (saturate).

Enter sub-networking: the A class IP network address can be split up to allow its distribution across several (if not many) separate networks. The management of each separate network can easily be delegated as well.

This allows small, manageable networks to be established - quite possibly using different networking technologies. Remember, you cannot mix Ethernet, Token Ring, FDDI, ATM etc on the same physical network - they can be interconnected, however!

Other reasons for sub-networking are:-

- Physical site layout can create restrictions (cable run lengths) in terms of the how the physical infrastructure can be connected, requiring multiple networks. Sub-networking allows this to be done in an IP environment using a single IP network number.

  This is in fact now very commonly done by ISPs who wish to give their permanently connected clients with local networks static IP numbers.
- Network traffic is sufficiently high to be causing significant slow downs. By splitting the network up using subnetworks, traffic that is local to a network segment can be kept local - reducing overall traffic and speeding up network connectivity without requiring more actual network bandwidth;
- Security requirements may well dictate that different classes of users do not share the same network - as traffic on a network can always be intercepted by a knowledgeable user. Sub-networking provides a way to keep the marketing department from snooping on the R & D network traffic (or students from snooping on the administration network)!
- You have equipment which uses incompatible networking technologies and need to interconnect them (as mentioned above).

6 How to subnetwork a IP network number

Having decided that you need to subnetwork your IP network number, how do you go about it? The following is an overview of the steps which will then be explained in detail:-

- Set up the physical connectivity (network wiring and network interconnections - such as routers;
- Decide how big/small each subnetwork needs to be in terms of the number of devices that will connect to it - ie how many usable IP numbers are required for each individual segment.
- Calculate the appropriate network mask and network addresses;
- Give each interface on each network its own IP address and the appropriate network mask;
- Set up the routes on the routers and the appropriate gateways, routes and/or default routes on the networked devices;

- Test the system, fix problems and then relax!

For the purpose of this example, we will assume we are sub-networking a single C class network number: 192.168.1.0

This provides for a maximum of 254 connected interfaces (hosts), plus the obligatory network number (192.168.1.0) and broadcast address (192.168.1.255).

6.1 Setting up the physical connectivity

You will need to install the correct cabling infrastructure for all the devices you wish to interconnect designed to meet your physical layout.

You will also need a mechanism to interconnect the various segments together (routers, media converters etc.).

A detailed discussion of this is obviously impossible here. Should you need help, there are network design/installation consultants around who provide this sort of service. Free advice is also available on a number of Usenet news groups (such as comp.os.linux.networking).

6.2 Subnetwork sizing

There is a play off between the number of subnetworks you create and 'wasted' IP numbers.

Every individual IP network has two addresses unusable as interface (host) addresses - the network IP number itself and the broadcast address. When you subnetwork, each subnetwork requires its own, unique IP network number and broadcast address - and these have to be valid addresses from within the range provided by the IP network that you are sub-networking.

So, by sub-networking an IP network into two separate subnetworks, there are now **two** network addresses and **two** broadcast addresses - increasing the 'unusable' interface (host) addresses; creating 4 subnetworks creates **eight** unusable interface (host) addresses and so on.

In fact the smallest usable subnetwork consists of 4 IP numbers:-

- Two usable IP interface numbers - one for the router interface on that network and one for the single host on that network.
- One network number.
- One broadcast address.

Quite why one would want to create such a small network is another question! With only a single host on the network, any network communication must go out to another network. However, the example does serve to show the law of diminishing returns that applies to sub-networking.

In principle, you can only divide your IP network number into 2^n (where n is one less that the number of host bits in your IP network number) equally sized subnetworks (you can subnetwork a subnetwork and combine subnetworks however).

So be realistic about designing your network design - you want the **minimum** number of separate local networks that is consistent with management, physical, equipment and security constraints!

6.3 Calculating the subnetwork mask and network numbers

The network mask is what performs all the **local** magic of dividing an IP network into subnetworks.

The network mask for an un-sub-networked IP network number is simply a dotted quad which has all the 'network bits' of the network number set to '1' and all the host bits set to '0'.

So, for the three classes of IP networks, the standard network masks are:-

- Class A (8 network bits) : 255.0.0.0
- Class B (16 network bits): 255.255.0.0
- Class C (24 network bits): 255.255.255.0

The way sub-networking operates is to *borrow* one or more of the available host bits and make then make interfaces **locally** interpret these borrowed bits as part of the network bits. So to divide a network number into two subnetworks, we would borrow one host bit by setting the appropriate bit in the network mask of the first (normal) host bit to '1'.

For a C Class address, this would result in a netmask of
11111111.11111111.11111111.10000000
or 255.255.255.128

For our C Class network number of 192.168.1.0, these are some of the sub-networking options you have:-

No of subnets	No of Hosts/net	netmask	
2	126	255.255.255.128	(11111111.11111111.11111111.10000000)
4	62	255.255.255.192	(11111111.11111111.11111111.11000000)
8	30	255.255.255.224	(11111111.11111111.11111111.11100000)
16	14	255.255.255.240	(11111111.11111111.11111111.11110000)
32	6	255.255.255.248	(11111111.11111111.11111111.11111000)
64	2	255.255.255.252	(11111111.11111111.11111111.11111100)

In principle, there is absolutely no reason to follow the above way of subnetworking where network mask bits are added from the most significant host bit to the least significant host bit. However, if you do not do it this way, the resulting IP numbers will be in a *very* odd sequence! This makes it extremely difficult for us humans to decide to which subnetwork an IP number belongs as we are not too good at thinking in binary (computers on the other hand are and will use whatever scheme you tell them with equal equanimity).

Having decided on the appropriate netmask, you then need to work out what the various Network and broadcast addresses are - and the IP number range for each of these networks. Again, considering only a C Class IP Network number and listing only the *final* (host part) we have:-

Netmask	Subnets	Network	B'cast	MinIP	MaxIP	Hosts	Total Hosts
128	2	0	127	1	126	126	
		128	255	129	254	126	252
192	4	0	63	1	62	62	
		64	127	65	126	62	
		128	191	129	190	62	
		192	255	193	254	62	248
224	8	0	31	1	30	30	
		32	63	33	62	30	
		64	95	65	94	30	
		96	127	97	126	30	

128	159	129	158	30	
160	191	161	190	30	
192	223	193	222	30	
224	255	225	254	30	240

As can be seen, there is a very definite sequence to these numbers, which make them fairly easy to check. The 'downside' of sub-networking is also visible in terms of the reducing total number of available host addresses as the number of subnetworks increases.

With this information, you are now in a position to assign host and network IP numbers and netmasks.

7 Routing

If you are using a Linux PC with two network interfaces to route between two (or more) subnets, you need to have IP Forwarding enabled in your kernel. Do a

```
cat /proc/ksyms | grep ip_forward
```

You should get back something like...

```
00141364 ip_forward_Rf71ac834
```

If you do not, then you do not have IP-Forwarding enabled in your kernel and you need to recompile and install a new kernel.

For the sake of this example, let us assume that you have decided to subnetwork you C class IP network number 192.168.1.0 into 4 subnets (each of 62 usable interface/host IP numbers). However, two of these subnets are being combined into a larger single network, giving three physical networks.

These are :-

Network	Broadcast	Netmask	Hosts
192.168.1.0	192.168.1.63	255.255.255.192	62
192.168.1.64	192.168.1.127	255.255.255.192	62
182.168.1.128	192.168.1.255	255.255.255.126	124 (see note)

Note: the reason the last network has only 124 usable network addresses (not 126 as would be expected from the network mask) is that it is really a 'super net' of two subnetworks. Hosts on the other two networks will interpret 192.168.1.192 as the *network* address of the 'non-existent' subnetwork. Similarly, they will interpret 192.168.1.191 as the broadcast address of the 'non-existent' subnetwork.

So, if you use 192.168.1.191 or 192 as host addresses on the third network, then machines on the two smaller networks will not be able to communicate with them.

This illustrates an important point with subnetworks - the usable addresses are determined by the **SMALLEST** subnetwork in that address space.

7.1   The routing tables

Let us assume that a computer running Linux is acting as a router for this network. It will have three network interfaces to the local LANs and possibly a fourth interface to the Internet (which would be its default route.

Let us assume that the Linux computer uses the lowest available IP address in each subnetwork on its interface to that network. It would configure its network interfaces as

Interface	IP Address	Netmask
eth0	192.168.1.1	255.255.255.192
eth1	192.168.1.65	255.255.255.192
eth2	192.168.1.129	255.255.255.128

The routing it would establish would be

Destination	Gateway	Genmask	Iface
192.168.1.0	0.0.0.0	255.255.255.192	eth0
192.168.1.64	0.0.0.0	255.255.255.192	eth1
192.168.1.128	0.0.0.0	255.255.255.128	eth2

On each of the subnetworks, the hosts would be configured with their own IP number and net mask (appropriate for the particular network). Each host would declare the Linux PC as its gateway/router, specifying the Linux PCs IP address for its interface on to that particular network.

Robert Hart Melbourne, Australia March 1997.

Using Term to Pierce an Internet Firewall

Barak Pearlmutter, bap@cs.unm.edu   15-Jul-1996

Directions for using "term" to do network stuff through a TCP firewall that you're not supposed to be able to.

Contents

1 Disclaimer

!!! READ THIS IMPORTANT SECTION !!!

I hereby disclaim all responsibility for this hack. If it backfires on you in any way whatsoever, that's the breaks. Not my fault. If you don't understand the risks inherent in doing this, don't do it. If you use this hack and it allows vicious hackers to break into your company's computers and costs you your job and your company millions of dollars, well that's just tough nuggies. Don't come crying to me.

2 Copyright

Unless otherwise stated, Linux HOWTO documents are copyrighted by their respective authors. Linux HOWTO documents may be reproduced and distributed in whole or in part, in any medium physical or electronic, as long as this copyright notice is retained on all copies. Commercial redistribution is allowed and encouraged; however, the author would like to be notified of any such distributions.

All translations, derivative works, or aggregate works incorporating any Linux HOWTO documents must be covered under this copyright notice. That is, you may not produce a derivative work from a HOWTO and impose additional restrictions on its distribution. Exceptions to these rules may be granted under certain conditions; please contact the Linux HOWTO coordinator at the address given below.

In short, we wish to promote dissemination of this information through as many channels as possible. However, we do wish to retain copyright on the HOWTO documents, and would like to be notified of any plans to redistribute the HOWTOs.

If you have questions, please contact Greg Hankins, the Linux HOWTO coordinator, at gregh@sunsite.unc.edu via email, or at +1 404 853 9989.

3 Introduction

The "term" program is normally used over a modem or serial line, to allow various host-to-host services to flow along this simple serial connection. However, sometimes it is useful to establish a term connection between two machines that communicate via telnet. The most interesting instance of this is for connecting two hosts which are separated by ethernet firewalls or SOCKS servers. Such firewalls provides facilities for establishing a telnet connection through the firewall, typically by using the SOCKS protocol to allow inside machines to get connections out, and requiring outside users to telnet first to a gateway machine which requires a one-time password. These firewalls make it impossible to, for instance, have X clients on an inside machine communicate with an X server on an outside machine. But, by setting up a term connection, these restrictions can all be bypassed quite conveniently, at the user level.

4 The basic procedure

Setting up a term connection over a telnet substrate is a two-phase process. First your usual telnet client is used to set up a telnet connection and log in. Next, the telnet client is paused and control of the established telnet connection is given to term.

5 Detailed directions

In detail, the process goes like this.

First, from a machine inside the firewall, telnet to a target machine outside the firewall and log in.

Unless you are under linux and will be using the proc filesystem (see below) make sure your shell is an sh style shell. Ie if your default shell is a csh variant, invoke telnet by

```
(setenv SHELL /bin/sh; telnet machine.outside)
```

After logging in, on the remote (outside) machine invoke the command

```
term -r -n off telnet
```

Now break back to the telnet prompt on the local (inside) machine, using ^] or whatever, and use the telnet shell escape command ! to invoke term,

```
telnet> ! term -n on telnet >&3 <&3
```

Et voila!!!

(If you have a variant telnet, you might have to use some other file descriptor than 3; easy to check using strace. But three seems to work on all bsd descendent telnet clients I've tried, under both SunOS 4.x and the usual linux distributions.)

Some telnet clients do not have the ! shell escape command. Eg the telnet client distributed with Slackware 3.0 is one such client. The sources that the Slackware telnet client is supposedly built from,

```
ftp://ftp.cdrom.com:/pub/linux/slackware-3.0/source/n/tcpip/NetKit-B-0.05.tar.gz
```

have the shell escape command. A simple solution is therefore to obtain these sources and recompile them. This unfortunately is a task I have had no luck with. Plus, if you are running from inside a SOCKS firewall, you will need a SOCKSified telnet client anyway. To that end, I was able to compile a SOCKSified telnet client from

```
ftp://ftp.nec.com/pub/security/socks.cstc/socks.cstc.4.2.tar.gz
```

or if you're outside the USA,

```
ftp://ftp.nec.com/pub/security/socks.cstc/export.socks.cstc.4.2.tar.gz
```

Alternatively, under linux kernels up to 1.2.13, you can pause the telnet with ^]^z, figure out its pid, and invoke

```
term -n on -v /proc/<telnetpid>/fd/3 telnet
```

This doesn't work with newer 1.3.x kernels, which closed some mysterious security hole by preventing access to these fd's by processes other than the owner process and its children.

6   Multiple term sockets

It is a good idea to give the term socket an explicit name. This is the "telnet" argument in the invocations of term above. Unless you have the TERMSERVER environment variable set to telnet as appropriate, you invoke term clients with the -t switch, e.g. "trsh -t telnet".

7   The ~/.term/termrc.telnet init file

I have checked line clarity using linecheck over this medium. I expected it to be completely transparent, but it is not. However, the only bad character seems to be 255. The ~/.term/termrc.telnet I use (the .telnet is the name of the term connection, see above) contains:

```
baudrate off
escape 255
ignore 255
timeout 600
```

Perhaps it could be improved by diddling, I am getting a throughput of only about 30k cps over a long-haul connection through a slow firewall. Ftp can move about 100k cps over the same route. A realistic baudrate might avoid some timeouts.

8 Direction

Obviously, if you are starting from outside the firewall and zitching in using a SecureID card or something, you will want to reverse the roles of the remote vs local servers given above. (If you don't understand what this means, perhaps you are not familiar enough with term to use the trick described in this file responsibly.)

9 Security

This is not much more of a vulnerability than the current possibility of having a telnet connection hijacked on an unsecured outside machine. The primary additional risk comes from people being able to use the term socket you set up without you even being aware of it. So be careful out there. (Personally, I do this with an outside machine I know to be pretty secure, namely a linux laptop I maintain myself that does not accept any incoming connections.)

Another possibility is to add "socket off" to the remote ~/.term/termrc.telnet, or add "-u off" to invocation of term. This prevents the socket from being hijacked from the remote end, with only a minor loss of functionality.

10 Telnet mode

Be sure the remote telnetd is not in some nasty seven-bit mode. Or if it is, you have to tell term about it when you invoke term, by adding the -a switch at both ends. (I sometimes use "^] telnet> set outbin" or "set bin" or invoke telnet with a -8 switch to put the connection into eight-bit mode.)

11 Bugs and term wish list

The linecheck program has some problems checking telnet connections sometimes. This is sometimes because it doesn't check the return code of the read() call it makes. For network connections, this call to read() can return -1 with an EINTR (interrupted) or EAGAIN (try again) error code. Obviously this should be checked for.

There are a number of features that could ease the use of term over telnet. These primarily relate to an assumption that influenced the design of term, namely that the connection is low bandwidth, low latency, and somewhat noisy.

A telnet connection is in general high bandwidth, high latency, and error free. This means that the connection could be better utilized if (a) the maximum window size was raised, well above the limit imposed by term's

N_PACKETS/2=16, (b) there was an option to turn off sending and checking packet checksums, and (c) larger packets were permitted when appropriate.

Also, to enhance security, it would be nice to have a term option to log all connections through the socket it monitors to a log file, or to stderr, or both. This would allow one to see if one's term connection is being subverted by nasty hackers on the outside insecure machine.

12   Tricks that don't seem to work

Some telnet clients and servers agree to encrypt their communications, to prevent evesdropping on the connection. Unfortunately, the hack used above (using the network connection that the telnet client has set up while the telnet client is idle) won't work in that case. Instead, one really must go through the telnet client itself, so it can do its encryption. It seems like that requires a simple hack to the telnet client itself, to add a command that runs a process with its stdin and stdout are connected to the live telnet connection. This would also be useful for various 'bots, so perhaps someone has already hacked it up.

13   Related resources

A vaguely related trick is to SOCKSify one's Term library. Details, including patches to SOCKS, are available from Steven Danz <danz@wv.mentorg.com>.

14   Acknowledgments

Thanks for valuable suggestions from:

- Gary Flake <flake@scr.siemens.com>
- Bill Riemers <bcr@physics.purdue.edu>
- Greg Louis <glouis@dynamicro.on.ca>

Extra copy of IMPORTANT DISCLAIMER — BELIEVE IT!!!

I hereby disclaim all responsibility for this hack. If it backfires on you in any way whatsoever, that's the breaks. Not my fault. If you don't understand the risks inherent in doing this, don't do it. If you use this hack and it allows vicious hackers to break into your company's computers and costs you your job and your company millions of dollars, well that's just tough nuggies. Don't come crying to me.

Virtual Services Howto

Brian Ackerman, `brian@nycrc.net`   v1.2, 4 November 1997

This document came about to satisfy the ever increasing need to know how to virtualize a service.

Contents

1   Introduction

1.1   Knowledge Required

Creating a virtual services machine is not all that difficult. However, more than fundamental knowledge is required. And this document is not a primer to how to fully configure a Linux machine.

In order to understand this HOWTO document it is assumed that you are thoroughly familiar with the following:

- Compiling a Linux kernel and adding IP aliasing support *IP alias mini-HOWTO* `<http://sunsite.unc.edu/mdw/HOWTO/mini/IP-Alias>`

- Setting up and configuring of network devices *NET-3 HOWTO* `<http://sunsite.unc.edu/mdw/HOWTO/NET-3-HOWTO.html>`

- Setting up of inetd *NET-3 HOWTO* `<http://sunsite.unc.edu/mdw/HOWTO/NET-3-HOWTO.html>`

- Compiling and installing various network packages like *Sendmail Site* `<http://www.sendmail.org>` *Apache Site* `<http://www.apache.org>` *Wu-Ftpd FAQ* `<http://www.cetis.hvu.nl/~koos/wu-ftpd-faq.html>`

- Setting up DNS *DNS HOWTO* `<http://sunsite.unc.edu/mdw/HOWTO/DNS-HOWTO.html>`

If you are uncertain of how to proceed with any of the above it is STRONGLY recommended that you use the links provided to familiarize yourself with all packages. I will NOT reply to any mail reguarding any of the above. Please direct any questions to the appropriate author of the HOWTO.

1.2   Purpose

The purpose of virtual services is to allow a single machine to recognize multiple IP addresses without multiple network cards. IP aliasing is a kernel option that allows you to assign each network device more than one IP address. The kernel then multiplexes (swaps between them very fast) in the background and to the user it appears like you have more than one network card.

This multiplexing allows multiple domains (www.domain1.com, www.domain2.com, etc.) to be hosted by the same machine for the same cost as hosting one domain. Unfortunately, most services (ftp, web, mail) were not designed to handle muliple domains. In order to make them work properly you must modify both configuration files and source code. This document describes how to make these modifications in the setting up of a virtual machine.

A deamon is also required in order to make virtual services function. The source for this daemon (virtuald) is provided later in this document.

1.3 Feedback

This document will expand as packages are updated and source or configuration modifications change. If there are any portions of this document that are unclear please feel free to email me with your suggestions or questions. So that I do not have to go searching through the entire HOWTO please make certain that all comments are as specific as possible and include the section where the uncertainty lies. It is important that all mail be addressed with VIRTSERVICES HOWTO in the subject line. Any other mail will be considered personal and all my friends know that I do not ever read my personal mail so it will probably get discarded with theirs.

Please note that my examples are just that, examples and should not be copied verbatim. You may have to insert your own values. If you are having trouble, send me mail, with all the pertinent configuration files and the error messages you get when installing, and I will look them over and mail my suggestions back.

1.4 Revision History

V1.0 Initial version

V1.1 Fixed error in Virtual Web Section

V1.2 Fixed the date

1.5 Copyright/Distribution

This document is Copyright (c) 1997 by The Computer Resource Center Inc.

A verbatim copy may be reproduced or distributed in any medium physical or electronic without permission of the author. Translations are similiarly permitted without express permission if it includes a notice on who translated it. Commercial redistribution is allowed and encouraged; however please notify *Computer Resource Center* <mailto:brian@nycrc.net> of any such distributions.

Excerpts from the document may be used without prior consent provided that the derivative work contains the verbatim copy or a pointer to a verbatim copy.

Permission is granted to make and distribute verbatim copies of this document provided the copyright notice and this permission notice are preserved on all copies.

In short, we wish to promote dissemination of this information through as many channels as possible. However, I do wish to retain copyright on this HOWTO document, and would like to be notified of any plans to redistribute this HOWTO.

2 IP aliasing

IP aliasing is a kernel option that needs to be set up in order to run a virtual hosting machine. There is already a mini-HOWTO on *IP aliasing* <http://sunsite.unc.edu/mdw/HOWTO/mini/IP-Alias>. Consult that for any questions on how to set it up.

3   Virtuald

3.1   How it works

Every network connection is made up of two IP address/port pairs. The API (Applications Program Interface) for network programming is called the Sockets API. The socket acts like an open file and by reading/writing to it you can send data over a network connection. There is a function call `getsockname` that will return the IP address of the local socket. Virtuald uses `getsockname` to determine which IP on the local machine is being accessed. Virtuald reads a config file to retrieve the directory associated with that IP. It will `chroot` to that directory and hand the connection off to the service. `Chroot` resets / or the root directory to a new point so everything higher in the directory tree is cut off from the running program. Therefore, each IP address gets their own virtual filesystem. To the network program this is transparent and the program will behave like nothing happened. Virtuald in conjunction with a program like inetd can then be used to virtualize any service.

3.2   inetd

Inetd is a network super server that listens at multiple ports and when it receives a connection (for example, an incoming pop request), inetd performs the network negotiation and hands the network connection off to the specified program. This prevents servers from running idly when they are not needed.

A standard /etc/inetd.conf file looks like this:

```
ftp   stream tcp nowait root /usr/sbin/tcpd wu.ftpd -l -a
pop-3 stream tcp nowait root /usr/sbin/tcpd in.qpop -s
```

A virtual /etc/inetd.conf file looks like this:

```
ftp   stream tcp nowait root /usr/bin/virtuald virtuald /virtual/conf.ftp wu.ftpd -l -a
pop-3 stream tcp nowait root /usr/bin/virtuald virtuald /virtual/conf.pop in.qpop -s
```

3.3   virtual.conf

Each service gets a conf file that will control what IPs and directories are allowed for that service. You can have one master conf file or several conf files if you want each service to get a different list of domains. A virtual.conf file looks like this:

```
# This is a comment and so are blank lines

# Format IP <SPACE> dir <NOSPACES>
10.10.10.129 /virtual/foo.bar.com
10.10.10.130 /virtual/bar.foo.com
10.10.10.157 /virtual/boo.la.com
```

3.4   The source (virtuald)

```
#include <netinet/in.h>
#include <sys/socket.h>
```

```
#include <arpa/inet.h>
#include <stdarg.h>
#include <string.h>
#include <syslog.h>
#include <stdio.h>

#define BUFSIZE 8192

main(int argc,char **argv)
{
        char buffer[BUFSIZE];
        char *ipaddr,*dir;

        logit("Virtuald Starting: $Revision: 1.2 $");
        if (!argv[1])
        {
                logit("invalid arguments: no conf file");
                quitting_virtuald(0);
        }
        if (!argv[2])
        {
                logit("invalid arguments: no program to run");
                quitting_virtuald(0);
        }
        if (getipaddr(&ipaddr))
        {
                logit("getipaddr failed");
                quitting_virtuald(0);
        }
        sprintf(buffer,"Incoming ip: %s",ipaddr);
        logit(buffer);
        if (iptodir(&dir,ipaddr,argv[1]))
        {
                logit("iptodir failed");
                quitting_virtuald(0);
        }
        if (chroot(dir)<0)
        {
                logit("chroot failed: %m");
                quitting_virtuald(0);
        }
        sprintf(buffer,"Chroot dir: %s",dir);
        logit(buffer);
        if (chdir("/")<0)
        {
                logit("chdir failed: %m");
                quitting_virtuald(0);
        }
        if (execvp(argv[2],argv+2)<0)
        {
                logit("execvp failed: %m");
                quitting_virtuald(0);
        }
}
```

```
int logit(char *buf)
{
        openlog("virtuald",LOG_PID,LOG_DAEMON);
        syslog(LOG_ERR,buf);
        closelog();
        return 0;
}

int quitting_virtuald(int retval)
{
        exit(retval);
        return 0;
}

int getipaddr(char **ipaddr)
{
        struct sockaddr_in virtual_addr;
        static char ipaddrbuf[BUFSIZE];
        int virtual_len;
        char *ipptr;

        virtual_len=sizeof(virtual_addr);
        if (getsockname(0,(struct sockaddr *)&virtual_addr,&virtual_len)<0)
        {
                logit("getipaddr: getsockname failed: %m");
                return -1;
        }
        if (!(ipptr=inet_ntoa(virtual_addr.sin_addr)))
        {
                logit("getipaddr: inet_ntoa failed: %m");
                return -1;
        }
        strncpy(ipaddrbuf,ipptr,sizeof(ipaddrbuf)-1);
        *ipaddr=ipaddrbuf;
        return 0;
}

int iptodir(char **dir,char *ipaddr,char *filename)
{
        char buffer[BUFSIZE],*bufptr;
        static char dirbuf[BUFSIZE];
        FILE *fp;

        if (!(fp=fopen(filename,"r")))
        {
                logit("iptodir: fopen failed: %m");
                return -1;
        }
        *dir=NULL;
        while(fgets(buffer,BUFSIZE,fp))
        {
                buffer[strlen(buffer)-1]=0;
                if (*buffer=='#' || *buffer==0)
```

```
                                continue;
                        if (!(bufptr=strchr(buffer,' ')))
                        {
                                logit("iptodir: strchr failed");
                                return -1;
                        }
                        *bufptr++=0;
                        if (!strcmp(buffer,ipaddr))
                        {
                                strncpy(dirbuf,bufptr,sizeof(dirbuf)-1);
                                *dir=dirbuf;
                                break;
                        }
                }
        if (fclose(fp)==EOF)
        {
                logit("iptodir: fclose failed: %m");
                return -1;
        }
        if (!*dir)
        {
                logit("iptodir: ip not found in conf file");
                return -1;
        }
        return 0;
}
```

4   Virt scripts

4.1   virtfs

Each domain should get their own directory structure. Since you are using chroot   you will require duplicate copies of the shared libraries, binaries, conf files, etc. I use /virtual/domain.com for each domain that I create. I realize that you are taking up more disk space but it is cheaper than a whole new machine and network cards. If you really want to preserve space you can link the files together so only one copy of each binary exists.

Here is a sample virtfs script:

```
#!/bin/bash

echo '$Revision: 1.2 $'

echo -n "Enter the domain name: "
read domain

if [ "$domain" = "" ]
then
        echo Nothing entered: aborting
        exit 0
fi
```

```
leadingdir=/virtual

echo -n "Enter leading dir: (Enter for default: $leadingdir): "
read ans

if [ "$ans" != "" ]
then
        leadingdir=$ans
fi

newdir=$leadingdir/$domain

if [ -d "$newdir" ]
then
        echo New directory: $newdir: ALREADY exists
        exit 0
else
        echo New directory: $newdir
fi

echo Create $newdir
mkdir -p $newdir

echo Create bin
cp -pdR /bin $newdir

echo Create dev
cp -pdR /dev $newdir

echo Create dev/log
ln -f /virtual/log $newdir/dev/log

echo Create etc
mkdir -p $newdir/etc
for i in /etc/*
do
        if [ -d "$i" ]
        then
                continue
        fi
        cp -pd $i $newdir/etc
done

echo Create etc/skel
mkdir -p $newdir/etc/skel

echo Create home
for i in a b c d e f g h i j k l m n o p q r s t u v w x y z
do
        mkdir -p $newdir/home/$i
done

echo Create home/c/crc
```

```
mkdir -p $newdir/home/c/crc
chown crc.users $newdir/home/c/crc

echo Create lib
mkdir -p $newdir/lib
for i in /lib/*
do
        if [ -d "$i" ]
        then
                continue
        fi
        cp -pd $i $newdir/lib
done

echo Create proc
mkdir -p $newdir/proc

echo Create sbin
cp -pdR /sbin $newdir

echo Create tmp
mkdir -p -m 0777 $newdir/tmp
chmod +t $newdir/tmp

echo Create usr
mkdir -p $newdir/usr

echo Create usr/bin
cp -pdR /usr/bin $newdir/usr

echo Create usr/lib
mkdir -p $newdir/usr/lib

echo Create usr/lib/locale
cp -pdR /usr/lib/locale $newdir/usr/lib

echo Create usr/lib/terminfo
cp -pdR /usr/lib/terminfo $newdir/usr/lib

echo Create usr/lib/zoneinfo
cp -pdR /usr/lib/zoneinfo $newdir/usr/lib

echo Create usr/lib/\*.so\*
cp -pdR /usr/lib/*.so* $newdir/usr/lib

echo Create usr/sbin
cp -pdR /usr/sbin $newdir/usr

echo Linking usr/tmp
ln -s /tmp $newdir/usr/tmp

echo Create var
mkdir -p $newdir/var
```

```
echo Create var/lock
cp -pdR /var/lock $newdir/var

echo Create var/log
mkdir -p $newdir/var/log

echo Create var/log/wtmp
cp /dev/null $newdir/var/log/wtmp

echo Create var/run
cp -pdR /var/run $newdir/var

echo Create var/run/utmp
cp /dev/null $newdir/var/run/utmp

echo Create var/spool
cp -pdR /var/spool $newdir/var

echo Linking var/tmp
ln -s /tmp $newdir/var/tmp

echo Create var/www/html
mkdir -p $newdir/var/www/html
chown webmast.www $newdir/var/www/html
chmod g+s $newdir/var/www/html

echo Create var/www/master
mkdir -p $newdir/var/www/master
chown webmast.www $newdir/var/www/master

echo Create var/www/server
mkdir -p $newdir/var/www/server
chown webmast.www $newdir/var/www/server

exit 0
```

4.2   virtexec

To execute commands in a virtual environment you have to **chroot** to that directory and then run the command. I have written a special shell script called virtexec that handles this for any command:

```
#!/bin/sh

echo '$Revision: 1.2 $'

BNAME=`basename $0`
FIRST4CHAR=`echo $BNAME | cut -c1-4`
REALBNAME=`echo $BNAME | cut -c5-`

if [ "$BNAME" = "virtexec" ]
then
        echo Cannot run virtexec directly: NEED a symlink
```

```
        exit 0
fi

if [ "$FIRST4CHAR" != "virt" ]
then
        echo Symlink not a virt function
        exit 0
fi

list=""
num=1
for i in /virtual/*
do
        if [ ! -d "$i" ]
        then
                continue
        fi
        if [ "$i" = "/virtual/lost+found" ]
        then
                continue
        fi
        list="$list $i $num"
        num='expr $num + 1'
done

if [ "$list" = "" ]
then
        echo No virtual environments exist
        exit 0
fi

dialog --clear --title 'Virtexec' --menu Pick 20 70 12 $list 2> /tmp/menu.$$
if [ "$?" = "0" ]
then
        newdir='cat /tmp/menu.$$'
else
        newdir=""
fi
tput clear
rm -f /tmp/menu.$$

echo '$Revision: 1.2 $'

if [ ! -d "$newdir" ]
then
        echo New directory: $newdir: NOT EXIST
        exit 0
else
        echo New directory: $newdir
fi

echo bname: $BNAME

echo realbname: $REALBNAME
```

```
if [ "$*" = "" ]
then
        echo args: none
else
        echo args: $*
fi

echo Changing to $newdir
cd $newdir

echo Running program $REALBNAME

chroot $newdir $REALBNAME $*

exit 0
```

Please note that you must have the `dialog` program installed on your system for this to work. To use virtexec just symlink a program to it. For example,

```
ln -s /usr/bin/virtexec /usr/bin/virtpasswd
ln -s /usr/bin/virtexec /usr/bin/virtvi
ln -s /usr/bin/virtexec /usr/bin/virtpico
ln -s /usr/bin/virtexec /usr/bin/virtemacs
ln -s /usr/bin/virtexec /usr/bin/virtmailq
```

Then if you type virtvi or virtpasswd or virtmailq it will allow you to vi a program, change a user's password or check the mail queue on your virtual system. You can create as many virtexec symlinks as you want. However, note that if your program requires a shared library it has to be in the virtual filesystem. The binary has to exist on the virtual filesystem also.

4.3   Notes on virtfs and virtexec

I install all the scripts in /usr/bin. Anything that I do not want to put on the virtual filesystem I put in /usr/local. The script does not touch anything in there for copying. Any files that are important to not cross virtual filesystems should be removed. For example, ssh is installed on my system and I did not want the private key for the server available on all the virtual filesystems so I remove it from each virtual filesystem after I run virtfs. I also change resolv.conf and remove anything that has the name of another domain on it for legal reasons. For example, /etc/hosts and /etc/HOSTNAME.

The programs that I symlink to virtexec are:

- virtpasswd – change a user password
- virtadduser – create a user
- virtdeluser – delete a user
- virtsmbstatus – see samba status
- virtvi – edit a file
- virtmailq – check out the mailq
- virtnewaliases – rebuild alias tables

5 DNS

You can configure DNS normally. The beauty of this system is that all services will behave normally like they are on separate machines. There is a HOWTO on *DNS* <http://sunsite.unc.edu/mdw/HOWTO/DNS-HOWTO.html>.

6 Syslog

6.1 Problem

Syslog is the system logging utility commonly used on UNIX systems. Syslog is a daemon that opens a special file called a FIFO. A FIFO is a special file that is like a pipe. Anything that is written to the write side will come out the read side. The syslog daemon waits for data from the read side. There are C functions that write to the write side. If you write your program with these C functions your output will go to syslog. Remember that we have used a `chroot` environment and the FIFO /dev/log is not in the virtual environment. That means all the virtual environments will not log to syslog. We cannot simply copy the file since the programs use /dev/log instead of the new one we would create.

Beware that certain versions of syslog use a udp socket instead of the FIFO. However, this is usually not the case.

6.2 Solution

Syslog can look to a different FIFO if you tell it on the command line so run syslog with the argument:

```
syslog -p /virtual/log
```

Then link /dev/log to /virtual/log by (Note it is a SYMLINK):

```
ln -sf /virtual/log /dev/log
```

Then link all the /dev/log copies to this file by running (Note it is a hard link and NOT a symlink):

```
ln /virtual/log /virtual/domain.com/dev/log
```

The virtfs script above already does this. Since /virtual is one contiguous disk and the /dev/log's are linked they have the same inode number and point to the same data. The `chroot` cannot stop this so all your virtual /dev/log's will now function. Note that all the messages from all the environments will be logged in one place. However, you can write separate programs to filter out the data. If you do not want to write a program and require separate log files you can use a separate syslog for each virtual filesystem by running:

```
syslog -p /virtual/domain1.com/dev/log
syslog -p /virtual/domain2.com/dev/log
```

However that wastes process id's so I do not recommend it. This version of the syslog.init file relinks the /dev/log's each time you start it in case they have been improperly set up. Here is a modified syslog.init file:

```sh
#!/bin/sh

# Source function library.
. /etc/rc.d/init.d/functions

case "$1" in
  start)
        echo -n "Starting dev log: "
        ln -sf /virtual/log /dev/log
        echo done
        echo -n "Starting system loggers: "
        daemon syslogd -p /virtual/log
        daemon klogd
        echo
        echo -n "Starting virtual dev log: "
        for i in /virtual/*
        do
                if [ ! -d "$i" ]
                then
                        continue
                fi
                if [ "$i" = "/virtual/lost+found" ]
                then
                        continue
                fi
                ln -f /virtual/log $i/dev/log
                echo -n "."
        done
        echo " done"
        touch /var/lock/subsys/syslog
        ;;
  stop)
        echo -n "Shutting down system loggers: "
        killproc syslogd
        killproc klogd
        echo
        rm -f /var/lock/subsys/syslog
        ;;
  *)
        echo "Usage: syslog {start|stop}"
        exit 1
esac

exit 0
```

Note that you do not have to put all the virtual filesystems on one disk. However, you will have to run a different syslog for each partition that has virtual filesystems on it.

7   Virtual FTP

Wu-ftpd comes with built in support to make it virtual. However, you cannot maintain separate password files for each domain. For example, if bob@domain1.com and bob@domain2.com both want an account you would have to make one of them bob2 or have one of the users choose a different user name. Since you now have a virtual filesystem for each domain you have separate password files and this problem goes away. Just create a virtnewuser script and virtpasswd script in the way mentioned above and you are all set. You can also have anonymous ftp in each virtual environment as that would be unaffected by the virtual filesystem as well.

The inetd.conf entries for wu-ftp:

```
ftp stream tcp nowait root /usr/bin/virtuald virtuald /virtual/conf.ftp wu.ftpd -l -a
```

8   Virtual Web

Apache has their own support for virtual domains. This is the only program I recommend using the internal virtual domain mechanism. When you run something through inetd there is a cost. The program now has to start up each time you run it. That means slower response times which is unacceptable for web service. Apache also has a mechanism for stopping connections when too many come in.

However, if you did want to run Apache through inetd then add the following to your inetd.conf file as a single line (line breaks have been inserted here to fit the example on a standard-width page):

```
www stream tcp nowait www
    /usr/bin/virtuald virtuald /virtual/conf.www
    httpd -f /var/www/conf/httpd.conf
```

In the /var/www/conf/httpd.conf file you have to specify:

```
ServerType inetd
```

Then configure each instance of the Apache server like you would normally for single domain use.

At the time of this writing there is no virtual web HOWTO. However, I am under the impression one is coming. Eventually I will just refer to that HOWTO and have some notes on it. If it does not come soon and I get enough requests I will write a small section on how to configure the Apache virthost directive.

9   Virtual Mail/Pop

9.1   Qmail Notice

This section applies to sendmail only. A section for qmail will be added in the next version of this HOWTO document.

9.2   Problem

Virtual mail support is in ever increasing demand. Sendmail says it supports virtual mail. What it does support is listening for incoming mail from different domains. You can then specify to have the mail forwarded somewhere. However, if you forward it to the local machine and have incoming mail to bob@domain1.com and bob@domain2.com they will go to the same mail folder. This is a problem since both bob's are different people with different mail.

9.3   Bad Solution

You can make sure that each user name is unique by using a numbering scheme: bob1, bob2, etc or prepending a few characters to each username dom1bob, dom2bob, etc. You could also hack mail and pop to do these conversions behind the scenes but that can get messy. Outgoing mail also has the banner maindomain.com and you want each subdomain's outgoing mail banner to be different.

9.4   Good Solution

Each virtual filesystem gives a domain its own /etc/passwd. This means that bob@domain1.com and bob@domain2.com are different users in different /etc/passwds so mail will be no problem. They also have their own spool directories so the mail folders will be different files on different virtual filesystems.

However, sendmail requires one minor source code modification. Sendmail has a file called /etc/sendmail.cw and it contains all machine names that sendmail will deliver mail to locally rather than forwarding to another machine. Sendmail does internal checking of all the devices on the machine to initialize this list with the local IPs. This presents a problem if you are mailing between virtual domains on the same machine. Sendmail will be fooled into thinking another virtual domain is a local address and spool the mail locally. For example, bob@domain1.com sends mail to fred@domain2.com. Since domain1.com's sendmail thinks domain2.com is local, it will spool the mail on domain1.com and never send it to domain2.com. You have to modify sendmail (I did this on v8.8.5 without a problem):

```
vi v8.8.5/src/main.c # Approximately Line 494
It should say:

load_if_names();

Replace it with:

/* load_if_names(); Commented out since hurts virtual */
```

Note only do this if you need to send mail between virtual domains which I think is probable.

This will fix the problem. However, the main ethernet device eth0 is not removed. Therefore, if you send mail from a virtual IP to the one on eth0 on the same box it will delivery locally. Therefore, I just use this as a dummy IP virtual1.domain.com (10.10.10.157). I never send mail to this host so neither will the virtual domains. This is also the IP I would use to ssh into the box to check if the system is ok.

Edit /etc/sendmail.cw with the local hostnames.

```
vi /etc/sendmail.cw
mail.domain1.com
domain1.com
domain1
localhost
```

Create /etc/sendmail.cf like you would normally through m4. I used:

```
divert(0)dnl
VERSIONID('@(#)tcpproto.mc      8.5 (Berkeley) 3/23/96')
OSTYPE(linux)
FEATURE(redirect)
```

```
FEATURE(always_add_domain)
FEATURE(use_cw_file)
FEATURE(local_procmail)
MAILER(local)
MAILER(smtp)
```

Edit /etc/sendmail.cf to respond as your virtual domain:

```
vi /etc/sendmail.cf # Approximately Line 86
It should say:
```

```
#Dj$w.Foo.COM
```

Replace it with:

```
Djdomain1.com
```

Sendmail cannot be started stand alone anymore so you have to run it through inetd. This is inefficient and will result in lower start up time but if you had such a high hit site you would not share it on a virtual box with other domains. Note that you are NOT running with the -bd flag. Also note that you need a sendmail -q running for each domain to queue up undelivered mail. The new sendmail.init file:

```
#!/bin/sh

# Source function library.
. /etc/rc.d/init.d/functions

case "$1" in
  start)
        echo -n "Starting sendmail: "
        daemon sendmail -q1h
        echo
        echo -n "Starting virtual sendmail: "
        for i in /virtual/*
        do
                if [ ! -d "$i" ]
                then
                        continue
                fi
                if [ "$i" = "/virtual/lost+found" ]
                then
                        continue
                fi
                chroot $i sendmail -q1h
                echo -n "."
        done
        echo " done"
        touch /var/lock/subsys/sendmail
        ;;
  stop)
        echo -n "Stopping sendmail: "
        killproc sendmail
```

```
        echo
        rm -f /var/lock/subsys/sendmail
        ;;
  *)
        echo "Usage: sendmail {start|stop}"
        exit 1
esac

exit 0
```

Pop should install normally with no extra effort. It will just need the inetd entry for it with the virtuald part added. The inetd.conf entries for sendmail and pop:

```
pop-3 stream tcp nowait root /usr/bin/virtuald virtuald /virtual/conf.pop in.qpop -s
smtp stream tcp nowait root /usr/bin/virtuald virtuald /virtual/conf.mail sendmail -bs
```

10 Virtual other

Any other service should be a similar procedure.

- Add the binary and the libraries to the virtual filesystem.
- Add it to /etc/inetd.conf.
- Create a /virtual/conf.service file.
- Create any virtual scripts that need to be made.

I have experimented with both the samba package and have written a virtual poppassd through Eudora. Both work without any problems. If there is enough interest, I will add a section on installing virtual samba.

11 Conclusion

Those are all the steps you need. I hope that this article meets with a positive response. Again mail any responses to *Computer Resource Center* <mailto:brian@nycrc.net>. If you have a question or an update to the document let me know and I will add it.

12 FAQ

Q1. Why are there no questions in this FAQ?

A1. Because nobody has asked any yet.

ISP-Hookup-HOWTO

Egil Kvaleberg, egil@kvaleberg.no   v1.24, 14 February 1997

This document describes how to use Linux to connect to an Internet Service Provider via a dial-up modem connection. As well as the basic dial-up procedure and IP establishment, email and news handling is covered.

Contents

1   Introduction

This description has been made to answer a few questions about how dial-up ISP (Internet Service Provider) subscribers may configure and use Linux.

To aid those who will connect their Linux based machines to an ISP for the first time, an attempt has been made to cover most issues encountered. This quite unavoidably will create a certain degree of overlap with other Linux Howto-documents and LDP books. Reference should be made to these documents to provide better understanding and detail.

Much of the existing documentation is targeted towards users with a certain degree of experience, and first time users will often have trouble sorting out the relevant information.

To simplify, the examples given will assume the following:

- User name: `dirk`
- Password: `PrettySecret`
- Internet service provider: `acme.net`
- Email server: `mail.acme.net`
- News server: `news.acme.net`
- Name server: `193.212.1.0`
- Phone number: `12345678`

Our `dirk` will be calling his machine `roderick`.

All references in the table above should naturally be replaced by whatever is valid for the ISP one is using. Often, just a minimum of changes will otherwise be required for users with different ISPs. I would like to be informed about what problems you encounter on this account.

1.1   New versions of this document

New versions of this document will be periodically posted to *comp.os.linux.answers*. They will also be added to the various anonymous FTP sites who archive such information, including:

ftp://sunsite.unc.edu/pub/Linux/docs/HOWTO <ftp://sunsite.unc.edu/pub/Linux/docs/HOWTO>

In addition, you should generally be able to find this document on the Linux Documentation Project page via:

http://sunsite.unc.edu/LDP/ <http://sunsite.unc.edu/LDP/>

Finally, the very latest version of this document should also be available in various formats from:

ftp://ftp.sn.no/user/egilk/ISP-Hookup-HOWTO.txt <ftp://ftp.sn.no/user/egilk/ ISP-Hookup-HOWTO.txt>

ftp://ftp.sn.no/user/egilk/ISP-Hookup-HOWTO.ps.gz <ftp://ftp.sn.no/user/egilk/ ISP-Hookup-HOWTO.ps.gz>

ftp://ftp.sn.no/user/egilk/ISP-Hookup-HOWTO.tar.gz <ftp://ftp.sn.no/user/egilk/ ISP-Hookup-HOWTO.tar.gz>

http://home.sn.no/home/egilk/ISP-Hookup-HOWTO.html <http://home.sn.no/home/egilk/ ISP-Hookup-HOWTO.html>

1.2 Feedback

All comments, error reports, additional information and criticism of all sorts should be directed to:

egil@kvaleberg.no <mailto:egil@kvaleberg.no>

http://home.sn.no/home/egilk/ <http://home.sn.no/home/egilk/>

1.3 Disclaimer

No liability for the contents of this documents can be accepted. Use the concepts, examples and other content at your own risk. Additionally, this is an early version, with many possibilities for inaccuracies and errors.

One of many possible setups will be described. In the Linux world, there is usually a number of ways in which to accomplish things. Paragraphs containing hints to alternatives are marked by **ALT:** Please also note that FTP-references often will change slightly as new versions of programs arrive.

As far as I know, only programs that under certain terms may be used or evaluated for personal purposes will be described. Most of the programs will be available complete with source under GNU-like terms.

1.4 Copyright information

This document is copyrighted (c)1996 Egil Kvaleberg and distributed under the following terms:

2   How do I connect to the rest of the world?

It will be assumed that we have installed the essential networking software modules (e.g. essential parts of the Slackware N-series), and that you have set up which serial port that is to be used for the /dev/modem.

The default configuration will usually only allow direct access to /dev/modem as user root.

To connect to ISP shell accounts directly, and to experiment with connection sequences, you may use the minicom program. It is pretty straight forward to use.

2.1   The basic configuration

Configuration of the machine for use on the net should be done as user `root`. Before proceeding any further, ensure that the file `/etc/hosts.deny` contains the following line:

```
ALL: ALL
```

You would normally want to allow yourself, so add the following line to `/etc/hosts.allow`:

```
ALL: LOCAL
```

Or if you insist:

```
ALL: 127.0.0.1
```

For the following, note that it is meant for those connected via PPP and with a dynamic IP address. If you have the benefit of a fixed connection, there will be some differences.

It is nice to have a name connected to the machine, a name that the dynamic IP user really can select as he or she pleases. Put the name in `/etc/HOSTNAME`:

```
roderick
```

The next step is to set up the name server in `/etc/resolv.conf`:

```
search .
nameserver 193.212.1.0
```

The name server must be specified by a numeric IP address, and will be different from ISP to ISP. If required, you can have up to three different servers, each on a separate line. They will be requested in the sequence in which they are listed.

If you want to be able to use names like `somemachine` as an abbreviation for `somemachine.acme.net`, you must replace the first line with:

```
search acme.net
```

A certain minimum of configuration will also be required in `/etc/hosts`. Most users will be able to manage with:

```
127.0.0.1 localhost
0.0.0.0   roderick
```

Those with a fixed IP-address will obviously replace 0.0.0.0 with this.

Likewise, a minimum `/etc/networks` is:

```
loopback  127.0.0.0
localnet  0.0.0.0
```

You should also set your external mail domain in `/etc/mailname`:

```
acme.net
```

The username and password at the ISP must be specified in `/etc/ppp/pap-secrets` dirk * PrettySecret

For those ISPs using CHAP instead of PAP, the filename is `/etc/ppp/chap-secrets`.

Finally, the nitty gritty regarding the connection procedure itself must be specified before PPP can be initiated. This is done in `/etc/ppp/chatscript`:

```
TIMEOUT 5
"" ATZ
OK ATDT12345678
ABORT "NO CARRIER"
ABORT BUSY
ABORT "NO DIALTONE"
ABORT WAITING
TIMEOUT 45
CONNECT ""
TIMEOUT 5
"name:" ppp
```

Details here may have to be tuned somewhat. The phone number in the third line must of course be set as required. Some users may need to replace the `ATZ` modem initialization string with something more tailored for the modem being used. The last line specifies that one is expecting the prompt `name:`, and that the response should be `ppp` when it arrives. Other systems may have other login procedures.

To actually initiate a call, the PPP-protocol may be initiated by issuing the following command:

```
exec pppd connect \
     'chat -v -f /etc/ppp/chatscript' \
     -detach crtscts modem defaultroute \
     user dirk \
     /dev/modem 38400
```

We should now be on-air, and stay up until the program is killed by typing a Ctrl-C. Any messages concerning the connection will be appended to the system logs. To read them, try:

```
tail /var/adm/messages
```

As long as PPP is up, you will have direct access to the Internet, and may use programs like ftp, ncftp, rlogin, telnet, finger etc. All these programs should be part of the network package.

Further information concerning PPP is also available from:

/usr/lib/ppp/README.linux <file:/usr/lib/ppp/README.linux>

/usr/lib/ppp/README.linux-chat <file:/usr/lib/ppp/README.linux-chat>

Finally, an additional word about safety. The file `/etc/inetd.conf` lists all services that your machine will offer externally. With the `/etc/hosts.deny` file we have made, no external access will be allowed. For those who need it, access must be allowed explicitly in `/etc/hosts.allow`. Local traffic may be allowed by:

```
ALL: LOCAL
```

See also `man 5 hosts_access`.

A final small issue: A certain confusion exists regarding the names of the POP-protocols. A definition in `/etc/services` compatible with just about everything is:

```
pop2        109/tcp    pop-2            # PostOffice V.2
pop3        110/tcp    pop-3 pop # PostOffice V.3
```

ALT: Instead of `chatscript`, one might use the much more flexible `dip`. But not in connection with `diald`.

ALT: Those fortunate enough to have a permanent TCP/IP connection via e.g. an Ethernet may safely ignore anything about PPP, and rather start concentrating about setting up their network card.

ALT: Others may not have the possibility of using PPP, but may be able to use SLIP instead, for which there is support in much the same manner as for PPP. Another possibility is UUCP. Others again may have to rely on exchange of news and email be means of SOUP. A description for the latter case may be found in:

ftp://ftp.sn.no/user/bjorn/Linux-offline.tgz <ftp://ftp.sn.no/user/bjorn/Linux-offline.tgz>

The TERM program is also an option. Refer to the *Term-HOWTO*.

3   How do I *surf*?

If you think that text is the most important, you might want to use the Lynx Web-browser. It is available from:

ftp://sunsite.unc.edu/pub/Linux/system/Network/info-systems/lynx-2.3.bin2.tar.gz <ftp://sunsite.unc.edu/pub/Linux/system/Network/info-systems/lynx-2.3.bin2.tar.gz>

If you have installed X-windows, you can also use one of the many graphical browsers. Chimera may be found at:

ftp://sunsite.unc.edu/pub/Linux/system/Network/info-systems/chimera-1.65.bin.ELF.tar.gz <ftp://sunsite.unc.edu/pub/Linux/system/Network/info-systems/chimera-1.65.bin.ELF.tar.gz>

http://www.unlv.edu/chimera/ <http://www.unlv.edu/chimera/>

Mosaic:

ftp://sunsite.unc.edu/pub/Linux/system/Network/info-systems/Mosaic-2.7b1-aout.tgz <ftp://sunsite.unc.edu/pub/Linux/system/Network/info-systems/Mosaic-2.7b1-aout.tgz>

ftp://ftp.NCSA.uiuc.edu/Web/Mosaic/Unix/binaries/2.6 <ftp://ftp.NCSA.uiuc.edu/Web/Mosaic/Unix/binaries/2.6>

Mozilla (Netscape):

ftp://sunsite.unc.edu/pub/Linux/system/Network/info-systems/netscape-v11b3.tar.gz <ftp://sunsite.unc.edu/pub/Linux/system/Network/info-systems/netscape-v11b3.tar.gz>

ftp://ftp.cs.uit.no/pub/www/netscape <ftp://ftp.cs.uit.no/pub/www/netscape>

These browsers are constantly available in new and in various ways *exciting* versions.

Use and evaluation of these programs is subject to certain terms. Please observe them.

4   How do I send and receive email?

First of all, ensure that `sendmail` is installed. Sendmail sorts internal and out-bound mail, and will buffer out-bound mail until such time it is possible to forward it.

Sendmail is based on a configuration found in `/etc/sendmail.cf`. An example suitable for ISP users can be found in:

ftp://ftp.sn.no/user/egilk/sendmail.cf <ftp://ftp.sn.no/user/egilk/sendmail.cf> This is based on *procmail* as a delivery agent, but may easily be changed to use *deliver*.

It is if course required to have an **official** domain address for out-bound mail, something which is specified in /etc/sendmail.cf:

```
# who I masquerade as (null for no masquerading)
DMacme.net
```

This assumes that you have the same user name locally as you have at your ISP. Sendmail is now configured for sending **directly** to the recipient. To avoid long and repeated connections in those cases where the connection to the receiving end is slow and irregular, is is usually nice to use ones ISP as a buffer store. This can be specified by the DS specification:

```
# "Smart" relay host (may be null)
DSmail.acme.net
```

Beware that sendmail is somewhat sensitive to handling of tab stop characters in sendmail.cf. You might want to use the vi editor to ensure that these tab characters are retained unchanged.

Email reception can often be performed via the POP3 protocol, which can be initiated every time the connection is brought up. A script for testing this is:

```
sendmail -q
popclient -3 -v mail.acme.net -u dirk -p "PrettySecret" \
        -k -o /usr/spool/mail/dirk
```

This script may be started after PPP connection has been established. Beware that this script is just for testing, so ensure that the local mailbox is left untouched while it runs. The -k option means that the mail is **kept** in the ISP mailbox, and you are simply given a copy of the mail. You would of course want to remove this option once you are confident that your setup is working.

Beware that the password will show on the command line. This really should be fixed ASAP.

A safe and better version of this script may be found at:

ftp://ftp.sn.no/user/egilk/pop-script.tar.gz <ftp://ftp.sn.no/user/egilk/pop-script.tar.gz>

This version of the script requires that procmail is installed, but that is something you'll never regret anyway:

ftp://sunsite.unc.edu/pub/Linux/system/Mail/mailhandlers/procmail-3.10-2.tar.gz <ftp://sunsite.unc.edu/pub/Linux/system/Mail/mailhandlers/procmail-3.10-2.tar.gz>

Procmail is a simple and flexible tool that can sort incoming email based on a large range of criteria. In addition to being able to handle automated tasks like vacation messages and such.

Note that when we use procmail directly as in this case, the situation is somewhat different from what is described in the procmail documentation. A .forward is **not** required, and we also don't need a .procmailrc. The latter is only required if we want to sort the mail.

The user interface for reading and sending of email can be found in programs like Pine or Elm.

ALT: Fetchmail has recently become a most interesting alternative to popclient. The latest version is available from:

ftp://ftp.ccil.org/pub/esr/fetchmail/fetchmail-3.3.tar.gz <ftp://ftp.ccil.org/pub/esr/fetchmail/fetchmail-3.3.tar.gz>

ALT: For an ordinary dial-up ISP user it is not really necessary to have the sendmail daemon active. To reduce the resource usage, one may thus comment out any startup of sendmail, as is usually found in `/etc/rc.d/rc.M`.

ALT: In place of sendmail one might use the simpler **smail**. You'll find a good description of it (as well as most other things mentioned here) in the *Linux Network Administrator's Guide*.

ALT: There is also an m4 macro package for making a fresh `sendmail.cf`. For a simple installation it might be just as well to modify an existing configuration.

ALT: There are also simpler although less flexible alternatives. Pine may run stand-alone as long as it is configured properly, for instance. It might even be possible to use newer versions of some web-browsers.

ALT: Many are very enthusiastic regarding the Emacs companion Gnus as an email and news handler. Further information can be found at:

http://www.ifi.uio.no/~larsi/ <http://www.ifi.uio.no/~larsi/>

ALT: An alternative to popclient is pop-perl5. It is available from:

ftp://sunsite.unc.edu/pub/Linux/System/Mail/pop-perl5-1.1.tar.gz <ftp://sunsite.unc.edu/pub/Linux/System/Mail/pop-perl5-1.1.tar.gz>

5   News

5.1   How do I set up an online news-reader?

As long as PPP is active, it will be possible to read news **online**. There are lots of available programs. Two simple alternatives are rtin and trn.

To start reading news, the only thing required in terms of configuration in most cases is to do (usually once and for all in the file `.profile`):

```
export NNTPSERVER=news.acme.net
```

To get the *From*-address correct in postings, some programs *may* require:

```
export NNTP_INEWS_DOMAIN=acme.net
```

5.2   How do I set up an offline news-reader?

To be able to read news while offline, and thus reduce phone bills and give greater flexibility, one must set up a local news-spool of one sort or the other. This requires some configuration, and there will also be a certain amount of disk space involved. After initial setup, things should run more or less by themselves, with only some attention needed from time to time.

Two different solutions will be described here.

5.3   How do I set up C News?

The solution described here is based on the news-server **C News** and the NNTP protocol. C News was originally targeted towards another sort of configuration, but is flexible enough to handle our situation too.

One might also use the more recent **INN** news server, but it might require a bit more in terms of resources. Any way, be careful **not** to install both; they don't live together easily.

It is crucial that all maintenance of news is done while logged in as user `news`, and that all configuration files is placed in `/usr/lib/news`. One way of handling this is, while logged in as `root` to write `su news; cd`.

The most important files in the configuration are:

- `active` is an overview over active newsgroups. It is updated as required by the command addgroup, e.g. addgroup `comp.os.linux.networking y`.

- `organization` should simply contain whatever you want in the *Organization:* header field, in our case:

  `Dirk Gently's Holistic Detective Agency`

- `mailname` should in our case be set to `acme.net`.

- `whoami` is set to the name of your `site` in the *Path:* thread. In a setup as described here, using **NewsX**, this name will never leave the machine, so you can set this to whatever you like as long as you are pretty sure it is unique. In this case `roderick`.

- `sys` controls fetching and further distribution of news. We will assume the ISP in our case adds `acme.net` to the Path, and that this is the only news source we have. The example given really tells that we will accept everything that arrives, and that we will only post news to `acme.net` that it hasn't seen before, and is originally posted at our own site. In this simplified setup we assume that the all groups will come from a single source. `/all` specifies the distribution, and **must** be included. The letter F says that (pointers to) outgoing news articles will be collected in a file.

  `ME:all/all::`
  `acme/acme.net:all,!junk/all:FL:`

- A subdirectory for the outgoing news must be created, in our case:

  `mkdir /var/spool/news/out.going/acme`

- `mailpaths` controls posting in moderated groups, although this task may usually be left to the ISP.

C News needs a certain degree of daily maintenance, but this can be specified once and for all via the command `crontab -e` issued as user `news`. A suggested setup follows; it can be tuned as required:

```
# maintain incoming and outgoing batches
10,40 *  * * * /usr/lib/newsbin/input/newsrun

# expire C News, once a day
30 0  * * * /usr/lib/newsbin/expire/doexpire

# monitor and report if needed
00 2  * * sat /usr/lib/newsbin/maint/addmissing
40 3  * * * /usr/lib/newsbin/maint/newswatch
50 3  * * * /usr/lib/newsbin/maint/newsdaily
```

newsrun moves articles in and out (twice every hour), doexpire will delete articles as they get old (every night at 00:30), and the three last commands does various supervisory and error correcting tasks.

One should also ensure that things are cleaned up when starting the machine. As user root, add the following line to `/etc/rc.d/rc.local`:

```
su news -c /usr/lib/newsbin/maint/newsboot
```

News may be collected via the program **NewsX**, picking news from an NNTP-server. The program can be found at:

ftp://sunsite.unc.edu/pub/Linux/system/news/transport/newsx-0.9.tar.gz <ftp://sunsite.unc. edu/pub/Linux/system/news/transport/newsx-0.9.tar.gz> Or:

ftp://ftp.sn.no/user/egilk/newsx-0.9.tar.gz <ftp://ftp.sn.no/user/egilk/newsx-0.9.tar.gz>

Setting up NewsX is quite simple. Installation is a classic case of:

```
make
su
make install
exit
```

With the setup outlined here, all you have to do is to create the groups you want to read using the "addgroup" command.

To fetch articles, user news issues the following commands (assuming communication via PPP or similar is up):

```
newsrun
newsx acme news.acme.net
newsrun
```

The option -d gives continuous printout to the screen. Refer to the NewsX documentation for further information.

NewsX will also take care of posting of outgoing news.

To control disposal of articles as they get old, a file **explist** is required. The comments in this example should explain what we want to do:

```
# hold onto history lines 14 days, nobody gets >120 days
/expired/          x    14    -
/bounds/           x    0-1-120 -

# retain these for 2 months
comp.sources,comp.os.linux.all    x    60    -

# noise gets thrown away fast
junk,control       x    2     -

# default:  14 days, no archive
all                x    14    -
```

ALT: In a small news-spool, one will often not need the newsgroup **control**. The traffic is **huge** compared to the usefulness. The main point is that articles will be canceled, and that groups may be created automatically. To ensure that control messages containing **newgroup** not shall mess up things for us, a file called **newgroupperm** specifies what we will allow:

```
comp.os.linux   tale@uunet.com yv
all        any        nq
```

In this example, all proper groups under comp.os.linux will be created (y), and the user **news** will be notified (v). Everything else will be silently (q) ignored (n). The last line is sufficient if you want to create all groups manually.

ALT: Alternatives to NewsX are `suck`, or `slurp` combined with `postit`. Slurp uses the NNTP NEWNEWS which will put severe loads on many news server.

5.4   How do I set up Leafnode?

A different solution altogether is to install the integrated package `leafnode`. This will handle all tasks required for a personal news spool, and is easy to configure. It is available via:

http://www.troll.no/freebies/leafnode.html <http://www.troll.no/freebies/leafnode.html>

As for C News, all news maintenance should be performed as user **news**.

The home directory for leafnode is in **/usr/lib/leafnode**. To install, write:

```
cd /usr/lib/leafnode
tar -xzvf leafnode-0.8.tgz
cd leafnode-0.8
make
su
make install
```

While still being logged in as **root**, change the line that controls NNTP in **/etc/inetd.conf**:

```
nntp  stream  tcp  nowait  news  /usr/sbin/tcpd /usr/local/sbin/leafnode
```

Activate it by:

```
killall -HUP inetd
```

Return to user **news** by writing **exit**. In **/usr/lib/leafnode/config** change the line that defines the NNTP server. In our case:

```
server = news.acme.net
```

Leafnode will look after itself by adding the following command via **crontab -e** as user **news**:

```
# expire Leafnode, once a day
0 4 * * * /usr/local/sbin/texpire
```

The news exchange is also done as user **news** by the following command (assuming PPP is up and running):

```
/usr/local/sbin/fetch
```

Users who wants to read news should then use the recipe in *How do I set up an online news-reader?*, except that they configure for the local machine, i.e:

```
export NNTPSERVER=localhost
```

That should be all there is to it. The first `fetch` will transfer a list of available newsgroups. Leafnode will then monitor what groups the users are requesting, and adapt to this the **next** time it is activated.

ALT: An alternative to `leafnode` is `nntpcache`, available from:

ftp://ftp.suburbia.net/pub/nntpcache/nntpcache.tgz <ftp://ftp.suburbia.net/pub/nntpcache/nntpcache.tgz>

6   How do I automate the connection procedure?

Automated handling of news and email is quite easy to implement in Linux.

First and foremost one should make a `/usr/lib/ppp/ppp-on` that initiates the ISP connection. Often, this file will simply contain the following:

```
/usr/sbin/pppd
```

Further specification will be performed in `/etc/ppp/options`:

```
connect "/usr/lib/ppp/chat -v -f /etc/ppp/chatscript"
crtscts
modem
defaultroute
asyncmap 00000000
user dirk
/dev/modem 38400
```

To end a connection, use the supplied version of `/usr/lib/ppp/ppp-off`.

Having tested the functionality of these two scripts, one must then write scripts that perform the various tasks. The script to collect email has been described before, and we will here assume it is located at `/home/dirk/pop`.

A script for exchange of email can then be produced in `/root/mail`:

```
#! /bin/sh
#
# exchange mail
# 10 minutes timeout:
TIMEOUT=600
DT=10

# kick sendmail:
sendmail -q &

# retrieve mail:
su dirk -c /home/dirk/pop

# wait for sendmail to terminate:
t=0
while ! mailq | grep -q "Mail queue is empty"; do
```

```
        t=$[$t+$DT]
        if [ $t -gt $TIMEOUT ] ; then
         echo "sendmail -q timeout ($TIMEOUT).."
         exit 1
        fi
        sleep $DT
    done


    exit 0
```

The script to exchange news may be placed in **/usr/lib/news/news**:

```
    #!/bin/sh
    #
    # exchange news
    # must be run as news:
    cd /usr/lib/news

    #update the outgoing batch (C News):
    /usr/lib/newsbin/input/newsrun < /dev/null

    #exchange news:
    /usr/lib/newsbin/newsx acme news.acme.net

    #and flush the incoming batch:
    /usr/lib/newsbin/input/newsrun < /dev/null
```

A script to connect the various bits and pieces remains, and can be placed in **/root/news+mail**:

```
    #!/bin/sh
    #
    # exchange news and email
    # must be run as root
    #
    if ! /usr/lib/ppp/ppp-on; then
        exit 1
    fi
    trap "/usr/lib/ppp/ppp-off" 1 2 3 15

    #exchange news+mail:
    /root/mail &
    su news -c ~news/news
    wait

    #disconnect..
    /usr/lib/ppp/ppp-off
```

```
#update the incoming batch (C News):
su news -c /usr/lib/newsbin/input/newsrun < /dev/null &

exit 0
```

It is quite easy to make an extension to the above that only will establish a connection if outgoing email and news is present. Lets call it `/root/news+mail.cond`, and keep in mind that the name of the outgoing news-spool must be updated to suit:

```
#!/bin/sh
#
# exchange news and email, only if outgoing news or mail
# (C News spool)
if [ -s /var/spool/news/out.going/acme/togo ] ||
    ! ( mailq | grep -q "Mail queue is empty"); then
     /root/news+mail
fi
```

The only thing remaining is to specify when all this is going to happen. This is done using the command `crontab -e` as root. Let us assume that we always want to exchange news and mail at 07:00 in the morning, and after that every 4th hour assuming there are outgoing email and news:

```
00 7       * * *      /root/news+mail
00 11,15,19,23 * * *    /root/news+mail.cond
```

Ensure that every component is tested well before you connect them together. One may later add several other tasks, such as adjustment of the time of day (using ntpdate), and automatic update (mirroring) of locally maintained WWW and FTP files up to the ISP (using make and ftp).

ALT: Depending on ones preferences, it is also possible to turn the process upside down. Every time a PPP link is initiated, the script `/etc/ppp/ip-up` will be started. One may here add whatever magic is required to start exchange of email and news. See `man pppd` for further detail.

ALT: It is also possible to automatically connect PPP whenever network traffic is detected. This is in many ways the more elegant solution, but it is quite dependent on a good configuration to avoid frequent (and costly) connections being made. More information can be found at:

http://www.dna.lth.se/~erics/diald.html <http://www.dna.lth.se/~erics/diald.html>

The `diald` utility is available from:

ftp://sunsite.unc.edu/pub/Linux/system/network/serial/diald-0.16.tar.gz <ftp://sunsite.unc.edu/pub/Linux/system/network/serial/diald-0.16.tar.gz>

At the same location one will also find other variations on the theme PPP connections.

7   Final words

7.1   Other things I should know about?

- Various error messages in the system will normally be issued as internal email. To ensure that these will actually be read, one should create an `/etc/aliases`. Remember the command `newaliases` every time you change this. An example that should cover most eventualities is:

```
        PostMaster: root
        ftp: root
        news: root
        usenet: root
        FaxMaster: root
        fax: root
        WebMaster: root
        MAILER.DAEMON: root
```

- Many programs for Linux may be found at **Sunsite**, which is usually quite busy. But there are many mirrors, and every time there is a reference to `ftp://sunsite.unc.edu/pub/Linux/..` one should try to use a mirror close to home, e.g. `ftp://ftp.nvg.unit.no/pub/linux/sunsite/...`

- If you happen to be migrating from Yarn, it should be possible to convert these to standard folders using the `yarn2mf` available at:

ftp://ftp.sn.no/user/egilk/yarn2mf.zip <ftp://ftp.sn.no/user/egilk/yarn2mf.zip>

8   ISP specific information

More specific information for certain ISPs is available from a variety of sources:

Demon Internet (demon.co.uk)

ftp://ftp.demon.co.uk/pub/unix/linux/Demon/slack3.0.help.tgz <ftp://ftp.demon.co.uk/pub/unix/linux/Demon/slack3.0.help.tgz>

Easynet TBA

Netcom http://www.netcom.com/bin/webtech/NetCruiser/Operating_Systems/Linux/linux.cfg.html

PowerTech, Schibstednett, Telenor Online

http://home.sn.no/home/egilk/no-isp.html <http://home.sn.no/home/egilk/no-isp.html>

Primenet TBA

Stanford

http://www-leland.stanford.edu/~wkn/Linux/network/network.html <http://www-leland.stanford.edu/~wkn/Linux/network/network.html>

If you know of ISP specific information not listed here, please get in touch.

8.1   How do I learn more?

The *Linux Documentation Project* book called *Linux Network Administrator's Guide* by Olaf Kirch is pretty mandatory for anyone that will set up and maintain anything involving TCP/IP and Internet:

ftp://sunsite.unc.edu/pub/Linux/docs/linux-doc-project/network-guide/nag-1.0.ascii.tar.gz <ftp://sunsite.unc.edu/pub/Linux/docs/linux-doc-project/network-guide/nag-1.0.ascii.tar.gz>

The documentation that follows each software package will normally give you all the detailed information you need, if not always the overview. The man-pages will be the first place to look. Try for instance:

```
        man pppd
```

You will also find some documentation about certain programs in the `/usr/doc` tree, although this is not always well structured.

The following HOWTOs will be highly relevant:

- **Installation-HOWTO** will get the basics sorted.
- **NET-2-HOWTO** is a very thorough description of installation and setup of the NET code. Much of this should already have been done if you use a standard Linux distribution (e.g. Slackware, Red Hat, Debian). But many sections on setup and troubleshooting will be very worthwhile.
- **Mail-HOWTO** explains how to configure various tools. Again, much of this will already have been done for you when you install a standard Linux distribution.
- **News-HOWTO** is for setting up a (conventional) news spool.
- **Tiny-News** covers yet another alternative for collecting news.
- **PPP-HOWTO** is a good description of problems you may encounter when setting up a PPP connection.
- **Serial-HOWTO** contains everything you need to know about setting up serial ports.
- **Mail-Queue** tells you how to send up *sendmail* to always queue remote mail but deliver local mail at once.

Red Hat has a mailing list for PPP issues; to join send an email to

redhat-ppp-list-request `<mailto:redhat-ppp-list-request>` with the subject line

     subscribe

8.2   Thanks to

Information here is collected from many sources. Thanks to the following that either indirectly or directly have contributed:

```
Adam Holt <holt@graphics.lcs.mit.edu>
Arne Coucheron <arneco@oslonett.no>
Arne Riiber <riiber@oslonett.no>
Arnt Gulbrandsen <agulbra@troll.no>
Bjorn Steensrud <bjornst@powertech.no>
Gisle Hannemyr <gisle@a.sn.no>
Hans Amund Rosbach <haro@sesam.dnv.no>
Hans Peter Verne <hpv@ulrik.uio.no>
Harald T Alvestrand <Harald.T.Alvestrand@uninett.no>
Harald Terkelsen  <Harald.Terkelsen@adm.hioslo.no>
Haavard Engum <hobbes@interlink.no>
James Youngman <JYoungman@vggas.com>
Johan S. Seland <johanss@sn.no>
John Phillips <john@linux.demon.co.uk>
Jorn Lokoy <jorn@oslonett.no>
Kenneth Tjostheim <kenneth.tjostheim@asplanviak.no>
Kjell M. Myksvoll <kjell.myksvoll@fou.telenor.no>
Kjetil T. Homme <kjetilho@math.uio.no>
```

Michael Meissner <meissner@cygnus.com>
N J Bailey <N.J.Bailey@leeds.ac.uk>
Nicolai Langfeldt <janl@math.uio.no>
Ove Ruben R Olsen <Ove.R.Olsen@ub.uib.no>
R. Bardarson <ronb@powernet.net>
Steinar Fremme <steinar@fremme.no>
Sverre H. Huseby <sverrehu@ifi.uio.no>
Trond Eivind Glomsrod <teg@stud.imf.unit.no>
Tommy Larsen <tommy@mix.hive.no>

Linux PPP HOWTO

Robert Hart, hartr@interweft.com.au   v3.0, 31 March 1997

This document shows how to connect your Linux PC to a PPP server, how to use PPP to link two LANs together and provides one method of setting up your Linux computer as a PPP server. The document also provides help in debugging non-functional PPP connections.

Contents

Copyright

This document is distributed under the terms of the GPL (GNU Public License).

Distribution

This document will be posted to comp.os.linux.answers as new versions of the document are produced. It is also available in HTML format at:-

- *Linux Howto Index* <http://sunsite.unc.edu/mdw/linux.html##howto>

- *PPP-HOWTO* <http://www.interweft.com.au/other/ppp-howto/ppp-howto.html>

Other formats (SGML, ASCII, postscript, DVI) are available from *Howtos - other formats* `<ftp://sunsite.unc.edu/pub/Linux/docs/HOWTO/other-formats>`.

As sunsite.unc.edu carries a very heavy load, please use an appropriate mirror site close to you.

Acknowledgements

A growing number of people have provided me with assistance in preparing this document. Special thanks go to Al Longyear for the guidance on PPP itself (if there are mistakes here, they are mine not his), Greg Hankins (maintainer of the Linux Howto system)and Debi Tackett (of MaximumAccess.com) for many helpful suggestions on style, content order, logic and clarity of explanations.

Finally, to the many people who have contacted me by email offering comments - my thanks. As with all HOWTO authors, the satisfaction of helping is all the payment we receive and it is enough. By writing this HOWTO I am repaying in a small way the debt I - and all other Linux users - owe to the people who write and maintain our OS of choice.

1 Introduction

PPP (the Point to Point Protocol) is a mechanism for creating and running IP (the Internet Protocol) and other network protocols over a serial link - be that a direct serial connection (using a null-modem cable), over a telnet established link or a link made using modems and telephone lines (and of course using digital lines such as ISDN).

Using PPP, you can connect your Linux PC to a PPP server and access the resources of the network to which the server is connected (almost) as if you were directly connected to that network.

You can also set up your Linux PC as a PPP server, so that other computers can dial into your computer and access the resources on your local PC and/or network.

As PPP is a peer-to-peer system, you can also use PPP on two Linux PCs to link together two networks (or a local network to the Internet), creating a Wide Area Network (WAN).

One major difference between PPP and an Ethernet connection is of course speed - a standard Ethernet connection operates at 10 Mbs (Mega - million bits per second) maximum theoretical throughput, whereas an analogue modem operates at speeds up to 56 kbps (kilo - thousand bits per second).

Also, depending on the type of PPP connection, there may be some limitations in usage of some applications and services.

1.1 Clients and Servers

PPP is strictly a **peer to peer** protocol; there is (technically) no difference between the machine that dials in and the machine that is dialed into. However, for clarity's sake, it is useful to think in terms of **servers** and **clients**.

When you dial into a site to establish a PPP connection, you are a **client**. The machine to which you connect is the **server**.

When you are setting up a Linux box to receive and handle dial in PPP connections, you are setting up a PPP **server**.

Any Linux PC can be both a PPP server and client - even simultaneously if you have more than one serial port (and modem if necessary). As stated above, there is no real difference between clients and servers as far as PPP is concerned, once the connection is made.

This document refers to the machine that initiates the call (that dials in) as the **CLIENT**, whilst the machine that answers the telephone, checks the authentication of the dial in request (using user names, passwords and possibly other mechanisms) is referred to as the **SERVER**.

The use of PPP as a client to link one or more machines at a location into the Internet is, probably, the one in which most people are interested - that is using their Linux PC as a client.

The procedure described in this document will allow you to establish and automate your Internet connection.

This document will also give you guidance in setting up your Linux PC as a PPP **server** and in linking two LANs together (with full routing) using PPP (this is frequently characterised as establishing a WAN - wide area network - link).

1.2 Differences between Linux distributions

There are many different Linux distributions and they all have their own idiosyncrasies and ways of doing things.

In particular, there are two different ways a Linux (and Unix) computer actually starts up, configures its interfaces and so forth.

These are **BSD system initialisation** and **System V system initialisation**. If you dip into some of the Unix news groups, you will find occasional religious wars between proponents of these two systems. If that sort of thing amuses you, have fun burning bandwidth and join in!

Possibly the most widely used distributions are

- Slackware
  which uses BSD style system initialisation
- Red Hat (and its former associate Caldera)
  which use SysV system initialisation (although in a slightly modified form)
- Debian
  which uses SysV system initialisation

BSD style initialisation typically keeps its initialisation files in `/etc/...` and these files are:-

```
/etc/rc
/etc/rc.local
/etc/rc.serial
        (and possibly other files)
```

Of recent times, some BSD system initialisation schemes use a `/etc/rc.d...` directory to hold the start up file rather than putting everything into `/etc`.

System V initialisation keeps its initialisation files in directories under `/etc/...` or `/etc/rc.d/...` and a number of subdirectories under there:-

```
drwxr-xr-x   2 root      root        1024 Jul  6 15:12 init.d
-rwxr-xr-x   1 root      root        1776 Feb  9 05:01 rc
-rwxr-xr-x   1 root      root         820 Jan  2  1996 rc.local
-rwxr-xr-x   1 root      root        2567 Jul  5 20:30 rc.sysinit
drwxr-xr-x   2 root      root        1024 Jul  6 15:12 rc0.d
drwxr-xr-x   2 root      root        1024 Jul  6 15:12 rc1.d
```

```
drwxr-xr-x    2 root    root        1024 Jul  6 15:12 rc2.d
drwxr-xr-x    2 root    root        1024 Jul 18 18:07 rc3.d
drwxr-xr-x    2 root    root        1024 May 27  1995 rc4.d
drwxr-xr-x    2 root    root        1024 Jul  6 15:12 rc5.d
drwxr-xr-x    2 root    root        1024 Jul  6 15:12 rc6.d
```

If you are trying to track down where your Ethernet interface and associated network routes are actually configured, you will need to track through these files to actually find where the commands are that do this.

1.3   Distribution specific PPP configuration tools

On some installations (for example Red Hat and Caldera), there is a X Windows configured PPP dial up system. This HOWTO does not cover these distribution specific tools. If you are having problems with them, contact the distributors directly!

For Red Hat 4.x users, there is now a *Red Hat PPP-TIP* <http://www.interweft.com.au> in the Linux resources area and also from *Red Hat Software* <http://www.redhat.com> in the support area.

2   IP Numbers

Every device that connects to the Internet must have its own, unique IP number. These are assigned centrally by a designated authority for each country.

If you are connecting a local area network (LAN) to the Internet, **YOU MUST** use an IP number from your own assigned network range for all the computers and devices you have on your LAN. You **MUST NOT** pick IP numbers out of the air and use these whilst connecting to another LAN (let alone the Internet). At worst this will simply not work at all and could cause total havoc as your 'stolen' IP number starts interfering with the communications of another computer that is already using the IP number you have picked out of the air.

Please note that the IP numbers used throughout this document (with some exceptions) are from the 'unconnected network numbers' series that are reserved for use by networks that are not (ever) connected to the Internet.

There are IP numbers that are specifically dedicated to LANs that do not connect to the Internet. The IP number sequences are:-

- One A Class Network Address
  10.0.0.0 (netmask 255.0.0.0)
- 16 B Class Network Addresses
  172.16.0.0 - 172.31.0.0 (netmask 255.255.0.0)
- 256 C Class Network Addresses
  192.168.0.0 - 192.168.255.0 (netmask 255.255.255.0)

If you have a LAN for which you have **not** been allocated IP numbers by the responsible authority in your country, you should use one of the network numbers from the above sequences for your machines.

These numbers should **never** be used on the Internet.

However, they can be used for the local Ethernet on a machine that is connecting to the Internet. This is because IP numbers are actually allocated to a network interface, not to a computer. So whilst your Ethernet interface may use 10.0.0.1 (for example), when you hook onto the Internet using PPP, your PPP interface will be given another (and valid) IP number by the server. Your PC will have Internet connectivity, but the other computers on your LAN will not.

However, using Linux and the IP Masquerade (also known as NAT - Network address Translation) capabilities of the Linux and the ipfwadm software, you can connect your LAN to the Internet (with some restriction of services), even if you do not have valid IP numbers for the machines on your Ethernet.

For more information on how to do this see the IP Masquerade mini-HOWTO at *Linux IP Masquerade mini HOWTO* <http://sunsite.unc.edu/mdw/HOWTO/mini/IP-Masquerade>

For most users, who are connecting a single machine to an Internet service provider via PPP, obtaining an IP number (or more accurately, a network number) will not be necessary.

If you wish to connect a small LAN to the Internet, many Internet Service Providers (ISPs) can provide you with a dedicated subnet (a specific sequence of IP numbers) from their existing IP address space. Alternatively, use IP Masquerading.

For users, who are connecting a single PC to the Internet via an ISP, most providers use **dynamic** IP number assignment. That is, as part of the connection process, the PPP service you contact will tell your machine what IP number to use for the PPP interface during the current session. This number will not be the same every time you connect to your ISP.

With dynamic IP numbers, you are **not** given the same IP number each time you connect. This has implications for server type applications on your Linux machine such as sendmail, ftpd, httpd and so forth. These services are based on the premise that the computer offering the service is accessible at the same IP number all the time (or at least the same fully qualified domain name - FQDN - and that DNS resolution of the name to IP address is available).

The limitations of service due to dynamic IP number assignment (and ways to work around these, where possible) are discussed later in the document.

3 Aims of this Document

3.1 Setting up a PPP Client

This document provides guidance to people who wish to use Linux and PPP to dial into a PPP server and set up an IP connection using PPP. It assumes that PPP has been compiled and installed on your Linux machine (but does briefly cover reconfiguring/recompiling your kernel to include PPP support).

Whilst DIP (the standard way of creating a SLIP connection) can be used to set up a PPP connection, DIP scripts are generally quite complex. For this reason, this document does NOT cover using DIP to set up a PPP connection.

Instead, this document describes the standard Linux PPP software (chat/pppd).

3.2 Linking two LANs or a LAN to the Internet using PPP

This document provides (basic) information on linking two LANs or a LAN to the Internet using PPP.

3.3 Setting up a PPP server

This document provides guidance on how to configure your Linux PC as a PPP server (allowing other people to dial into your Linux PC and establish a PPP connection).

You should note that there are a myriad of ways of setting up Linux as a PPP server. This document gives one method - that used by the author to set up several small PPP servers (each of 16 modems).

This method is known to work well. However, it is not necessarily the best method.

3.4   Using PPP over a direct null modem connection

This document provides a brief overview of using PPP to link two Linux PCs via a null modem cable. It is possible to link other OS's to Linux this way as well. To do so, you will need to consult the documentation for the operating system you are interested in.

3.5   This document at present does NOT cover...

- Compiling the PPP daemon software
  See the documentation that comes with the version of pppd you are using.
- Connecting and configuring a modem to Linux (in detail)
  See the Serial-HOWTO and for modem specific initialisation, see *Modem Setup Information* <http://www.in.net/info/modems/index.html> for information that may help you to configure your modem.
- Using DIP to make PPP connections
  Use chat instead...
- Using socks or IP Masquerade
  There are perfectly good documents already covering these two packages.
- Using `diald` to set up an automated connection
  See the `diald` documentation for information on this.
- Using EQL to gang together two modems into a single PPP link.
- Distribution specific PPP connection methods (such as the Red Hat 4.x network configuration tool.
  See the distribution for documentation on the methods used.
- The growing number of tools available to automate PPP set up
  See the appropriate documentation.

4   Software versions covered

This HOWTO assumes that you are using a Linux 1.2.x kernel with the PPP 2.1.2 software or Linux 1.3.X/2.0.x and PPP 2.2.

At the time of writing, the latest official version of PPP available for Linux is ppp-2.2f. The new version (ppp-2.3) is still in beta.

It is possible to use PPP 2.2.0 with kernel 1.2.13. This requires kernel patches. It is recommended that version 1.2.13 kernel users move up to ppp-2.2 as it includes several bug fixes and enhancements.

Also, you should particularly note that you cannot use the PPP 2.1.2 software with Linux kernel version 2.0.X.

Please note that this document does **NOT** cover problems arising from the use of loadable modules for Linux kernel 2.0.x. Please see the kerneld mini-HOWTO and the kernel/module 2.0.x documentation (in the Linux 2.0.x source tree at `/usr/src/linux/Documentation/...`).

As this document is designed to assist new users, it is highly recommended that you use a version of the Linux kernel and the appropriate PPP version that are known to be stable together.

5 Other Useful/Important Documents

Users are advised to read :-

- the documentation that comes with the PPP package;
- the pppd and chat man pages;
  (use `man chat` and `man pppd` to explore these)
- the Linux Network Administration Guide (NAG);
  see *The Network Administrators' Guide* <http://sunsite.unc.edu/mdw/LDP-books/nag-1.0/nag.html>
- the Net-2/3 HOWTO;
  see *Linux NET-2/3-HOWTO* <http://sunsite.unc.edu/mdw/HOWTO/NET-2-HOWTO.html>
- Linux kernel documentation installed in `/usr/src/linux/Documentation` when you install the Linux source code;
- The modem setup information page - see *Modem Setup Information* <http://www.in.net/info/modems/index.html>
- The excellent Unix/Linux books published by O'Reilly and Associates. See (*O'Reilly and Associates On-Line Catalogue* <http://www.ora.com/>). If you are new to Unix/Linux, **run** (don't walk) to your nearest computer book shop and invest in a number of these immediately!
- The PPP-FAQ maintained by Al Longyear, available from *Linux PPP-FAQ* <ftp://sunsite.unc.edu/pub/Linux/docs/faqs>.
  This contains a great deal of useful information in question/answer format that is very useful when working out why PPP is not working (properly).
- The growing number of Linux books from various publishing houses and authors;
  You are actively encouraged to check the currency of these books. Linux development and distributions tend to evolve fairly rapidly, whilst the revision of books move (generally) much more slowly! Buying an excellent book (and there are many) that is now out of date will cause new users considerable confusion and frustration.

The best general starting point for Linux documentation is *The Linux Documentation Project Home Page* <http://sunsite.unc.edu/mdw/>. The HOWTO's tend to be revised reasonably regularly.

Whilst you can use this document to create your PPP link without reading any of these documents, you will have a far better understanding of what is going on if you do so! You will also be able to address problems yourself (or at least ask more intelligent questions on the comp.os.linux... newsgroups or Linux mailing lists).

These documents (as well as various others, including the relevant RFCs) provide additional and more detailed explanation than is possible in this HOWTO.

If you are connecting a LAN to the Internet using PPP, you will need to know a reasonable amount about TCP/IP networking. In addition to the documents above, you will find the O'Reilly books "TCP/IP Network Administration" and "Building Internet Firewalls" of considerable benefit!

5.1 Useful Linux Mailing Lists

There are many Linux mailing lists that operate as a means of communication between users of many levels of ability. By all means subscribe to those that interest you and contribute your expertise and views.

A word to the wise: some lists are specifically aimed at "high powered" users and/or specific topics. Whilst no-one will complain if you 'lurk' (subscribe but don't post messages), you are likely to earn heated comments (if not outright flames) if you post 'newbie' questions to inappropriate lists.

This is not because guru level users hate new users, but because these lists are there to handle the specific issues at particular levels of difficulty.

By all means join the lists that offer open subscription, but keep your comments relevant to the subject of the list!

A good starting point for Linux mailing lists is *Linux Mailing List Directory* `<http://summer.snu.ac.kr/~djshin/linux/mail-list/index.shtml>`

6   Overview of what has to be done to get PPP working as a client

This document contains a great deal of information - and with each version it grows!

As a consequence, this section aims to provide a concise overview of the actions you will need to take to get your Linux system connected as a client to a PPP server.

6.1   Obtaining/Installing the software

If your Linux distribution does not include the PPP software, you will need to obtain this from *the Linux PPP daemon* `<ftp://sunsite.unc.edu/pub/Linux/system/Network/serial/ppp/ppp-2.2.0f.tar.gz>`.

This is the latest official version at the time of writing. However, choose the latest version available from this site (ppp-2.3 is in beta at the time of writing and should be released soon).

The PPP package contains instructions on how to compile and install the software **so this HOWTO does not!**

6.2   Compiling PPP support into the kernel

Linux PPP operations come in two parts

- the PPP daemon mentioned above
- kernel support for PPP

Many distributions seem to provide PPP kernel support in their default installation kernels, but others do not.

If at boot your kernel reports messages like

```
PPP Dynamic channel allocation code copyright 1995 Caldera, Inc.
PPP line discipline registered.
```

---

your kernel does have PPP support compiled in.

That said, you will probably want to compile your own kernel whatever your distribution to provide the most efficient use of system resources given your particular hardware configuration. It is worth remembering that the kernel cannot be swapped out of memory and so keeping the kernel as small as possible has advantages on a memory limited machine.

This document provides minimal kernel re-compilation instructions at section 7 (Configuring your Linux Kernel).

For greater detail, see the Kernel-HOWTO at *The Linux Kernel HOWTO* `<http://sunsite.unc.edu/mdw/ HOWTO/Kernel-HOWTO.html>`

6.3 Obtaining information from your ISP

There are an almost infinite number of ways in which a PPP server can be set up. In order to connect to your ISP (or corporate PPP server to access your intranet), you will need to obtain information on how the PPP server operates.

Because you are using Linux, you may have some difficulty with some ISP help desks (and work site based PPP intranet servers) which know only about MS Windows clients.

However, a rapidly growing number of ISPs use Linux to provide their service - and Linux is also penetrating the corporate environment as well, so you may be lucky if you do strike problems.

Section 8 (Getting the Information you need about the PPP server) tells you what you need to know about the PPP server to which you are going to connect - and how to find out the information you need to know.

6.4 Configuring your modem and serial port

In order to connect to a PPP server and to obtain the best possible data transfer rate, your modem needs to be configured correctly.

Similarly, the serial ports on your modem and computer need to be set up correctly.

Section 9 (Configuring your modem and serial port) provides information on this.

6.5 Setting up Name to Address Resolution (DNS)

In addition to the files that run PPP and perform the automated log in to the PPP server, there are a number of text configuration files that have to be set up for your computer to be able to resolve names like `www.interweft.com.au` to the IP address that is actually used to contact that computer. These are:-

- `/etc/resolv.conf`
- `/etc/host.conf`

Section 10 (Setting up Name to Address Resolution) for details on setting this up.

In particular, you do **NOT** need to run a name server on your Linux PC in order to connect to the Internet (although you may wish to). All you need is to know the IP number of at least one name server that you can use (preferably one at your ISPs site).

6.6 PPP and root Privileges

As establishing a PPP link between you Linux computer and another PPP server requires manipulation of network devices (the PPP interface is a network interface) and the kernel routing table, pppd requires root privileges.

For details on this, see section 11 (Using PPP and root privileges).

6.7 Checking your distribution PPP Files and setting up the PPP Options

There are a number of configuration and dialer files that need to be set up to get PPP operational. There are examples as part of the PPP distribution and this section shows what files you should have:-

```
/etc/ppp/options
/etc/ppp/scripts/ppp-on
/etc/ppp/scripts/ppp-on-dialer
/etc/ppp/options.tpl
```

You may need to create some additional files depending on exactly what you are aiming to achieve with PPP:-

```
/etc/ppp/options.ttyXX
/etc/ppp/ip-up
/etc/ppp/pap-secrets
/etc/ppp/chap-secrets
```

In addition, the PPP daemon can use a large number of command line options and it is important to use the right ones; so this section takes you through the standard PPP options and helps you choose the options you should use.

For details on this, see 12 (Setting up the PPP connection files).

6.8 If your PPP server uses PAP (Password Authentication Protocol)

Many ISPs and corporate PPP servers use PAP. If your server does **not** require you to use PAP (if you can log in manually and receive the standard user name/password text based prompts it does not use PAP), you can safely ignore this section.

Instead of logging into such a server using a user name and password when prompted to enter them by the server, a PPP server using PAP does not require a text based login.

The user authentication information instead is exchanged as part of the link control protocol (LCP) which is the first part of establishing a PPP link.

Section 13 (If your PPP server uses PAP (Password Authentication Protocol)) provides information on the files you need to set up to establish a PPP link using PAP.

6.9 Connecting to the PPP server by hand

Having set up the basic files, it is a good idea to test these by connecting (using minicom or seyon) and starting pppd on your Linux PC by hand.

See Section 14 (Setting up the PPP connection manually) for full details of setting this up.

6.10   Automating your PPP Connection

Once you are able to log in by hand, you can now move to setting up a set of scripts that will automate the establishment of the connection.

Section 15 (Automating your connections - Creating the connection scripts) covers setting up the necessary scripts, with considerable attention paid to `chat` and scripting the login process to the PPP server.

This section discusses scripts for user name/password authentication as well as scripts for PAP/CHAP authenticating servers.

6.11   Shutting down the link

Once your link is up and working, you need to be able to deactivate the link.

This is covered in Section 17 (Shutting down the PPP link).

6.12   If you have problems

Many people have problems getting PPP to work straight away. The variation in PPP servers and how they require you to set up the connection is enormous. Similarly, there are many options to PPP - and some combinations of these just do not work together, ever.

In addition to the problems of logging in and starting the PPP service, there are problems with the modems and the actual telephone lines as well!

Section 18 (Fixing problems) provides some basic information about common errors, how to isolate these and fix them.

This is **NOT** intended to provide more than just the basics. Al Longyear maintains the PPP-FAQ which contains much more information on this topic!

6.13   After the link comes up

Once a PPP link is operational (specifically, once the IP layer is operational), Linux PPP can automatically run (as the root user), a script to perform **any** function you can write a script to accomplish.

Section 23 (After the link comes up) provides information on the `/etc/ppp/ip-up` script, the parameters it receives from PPP and how to use it to do things like acquire your email from your ISP account, send any queued email waiting transmission on your machine and such.

6.14   Problems with standard IP services on a Dynamic IP number PPP link

As noted in the introduction, dynamic IP numbers affect the ability of your Linux PC to act as a server on the Internet.

Section 21 (Problems with standard IP services on a Dynamic IP number PPP link) provides information on the (main) services affected and what you can do (if anything) to overcome this.

7   Configuring your Linux Kernel

In order to use PPP, your Linux kernel must be compiled to include PPP support. Obtain the Linux source code for your kernel if you do not already have this - it belongs in `/usr/src/linux` on Linux's standard file system.

Check out this directory - many Linux distributions install the source tree (the files and subdirectories) as part of their installation process.

At bootup, your Linux kernel prints out a great deal of information. Amongst this is information about PPP support if the kernel includes this. To view this information, look at your syslog file or use `dmesg | less` to display the information to the screen. If your kernel includes PPP support, you will see lines like

```
PPP Dynamic channel allocation code copyright 1995 Caldera, Inc.
PPP line discipline registered.
```

(this is for the Linux 2.0.x kernel series).

Linux kernel sources can be obtained by ftp from `sunsite.unc.edu` or its mirror sites.

7.1   Installing the Linux Kernel source

The following are brief instructions for obtaining and installing the Linux kernel sources. Full information can be obtained from *The Linux Kernel HOWTO* <http://sunsite.unc.edu/mdw/HOWTO/Kernel-HOWTO.html>.

In order to install and compile the Linux kernel, you need to be logged in as root.

1. Change directory to the `/usr/src` directory
   `cd /usr/src`

2. Check in `/usr/src/linux` to see if you already have the sources installed.

3. If you don't have the sources, get them from *Linux kernel source directory* <ftp://sunsite.unc.edu/pub/Linux/kernel/v2.0> or your nearest mirror.
   If you are looking for earlier versions of the kernel (such as 1.2.X), these are kept in *Old Linux kernel source directory* <ftp://sunsite.unc.edu/pub/Linux/kernel/old>.

4. Choose the appropriate kernel - usually the most recent one available is what you are looking for. Retrieve this and put the source tar file in `/usr/src`.
   Note: a 'tar' file is an archive - possibly compressed (as are the Linux kernel source tar files) containing many files in a number of directories. It is the Linux equivalent of a DOS multi-directory zip file.

5. If you already have the Linux sources installed but are upgrading to a new kernel, you must remove the old sources. Use the command
   `rm -rf /usr/src/linux`

6. Now uncompress and extract the sources using the command
   `tar xzf linux-2.0.XX.tar.gz`

7. Now, `cd /usr/src/linux` and read the README file. This contains an excellent explanation of how to go about configuring and compiling a new kernel. Read this file (it's a good idea to print it out and have a copy handy whilst you are compiling until you have done this enough times to know your way around).

7.2   Knowing your hardware

You **MUST** know what cards/devices you have inside your PC if you are going to recompile your kernel!!!
For some devices (such as sound cards) you will also need to know various settings (such as IRQ's, I/O
addresses and such).

7.3   Kernel compilation - the Linux 1.2.13 kernel

To start the configuration process, follow the instructions in the README file to properly install the sources.
You start the kernel configuration process with

```
make config
```

In order to use PPP, you must configure the kernel to include PPP support (PPP requires BOTH pppd
AND kernel support for PPP).

```
PPP (point-to-point) support (CONFIG_PPP) [n] y
```

Answer the other make config questions according to the hardware in your PC and the features of the Linux
operating system you want. Then continue to follow the README to compile and install your new kernel.

The 1.2.13 kernel creates only 4 PPP devices. For multi- port serial cards, you will need to edit the kernel
PPP sources to obtain more ports. (See the README.linux file that comes as part of the PPP-2.1.2
distribution for full details of the simple edits you need to make).

Note: the 1.2.13 configuration dialogue does NOT allow you to go backwards - so if you make a mistake in
answering one of the questions in the `make config` dialogue, exit by typing CTRL C and start again.

7.4   Kernel compilation - the Linux 1.3.x and 2.0.x kernels

For Linux 1.3.x and 2.0.x, you can use a similar process as for Linux 1.2.13. Again, follow the instructions
in the README file to properly install the sources. You start the kernel configuration process with

```
make config
```

However, you also have the choice of

```
make menuconfig
```

This provides a menu based configuration system with online help that allows you to move backwards and
forwards in the configuration process.

There is also a highly recommended X windows based configuration interface

```
make xconfig
```

You can compile PPP support directly into your kernel or as a loadable module.

If you only use PPP some of the time that your Linux machine is operating, then compiling PPP support
as a loadable module is recommended. Using 'kerneld', your kernel will automatically load the module(s)
required to provide PPP support when you start your PPP link process. This saves valuable memory space:

no part of the kernel can be swapped out of memory, but loadable modules are automatically removed if they are not in use.

To do this, you need to enable loadable module support:-

```
Enable loadable module support (CONFIG_MODULES) [Y/n/?] y
```

To add PPP kernel support, answer the following question:-

```
PPP (point-to-point) support (CONFIG_PPP) [M/n/y/?]
```

For a PPP loadable module, answer **M**, otherwise for PPP compiled in as part of the kernel, answer **Y**.

Unlike kernel 1.2.13, kernel 2.0.x creates PPP devices on the fly as needed and it is not necessary to hack the sources to increase available PPP device numbers at all.

7.5   Note on PPP-2.2 and /proc/net/dev

If you are using PPP-2.2, you will find that a side effect of the 'on the fly' creation of the PPP devices is that no devices show up if you look in the **/proc/net** file system until a device is created by starting up pppd:-

```
[hartr@archenland hartr]$ cat /proc/net/dev
Inter-|   Receive                           |  Transmit
 face |packets errs drop fifo frame|packets errs drop fifo colls carrier
    lo: 92792    0    0    0     0   92792    0    0    0     0    0
  eth0: 621737   13   13    0    23  501621    0    0    0  1309    0
```

Once you have one (or more) ppp services started, you will see entries such as this (from a ppp server):-

```
[root@kepler /root]# cat /proc/net/dev
Inter-|   Receive                           |  Transmit
 face |packets errs drop fifo frame|packets errs drop fifo colls carrier
    lo: 428021    0    0    0     0  428021    0    0    0     0    0
  eth0:4788257  648  648  319   650 1423836    0    0    0  4623    5
  ppp0:  2103    3    3    0     0    2017     0    0    0     0    0
  ppp1: 10008    0    0    0     0    8782     0    0    0     0    0
  ppp2:   305    0    0    0     0     297     0    0    0     0    0
  ppp3:  6720    7    7    0     0    7498     0    0    0     0    0
  ppp4:118231  725  725    0     0  117791     0    0    0     0    0
  ppp5: 38915    5    5    0     0   28309     0    0    0     0    0
```

7.6   General kernel config considerations for PPP

If you are setting up your Linux PC as a PPP server, you must compile in IP forwarding support. This is also necessary if you want to use Linux to link to LANs together or your LAN to the Internet.

If you are linking a LAN to the Internet (or linking together two LANs), you should be concerned about security. Adding support for IP fire walls to the kernel is probably a MUST!

You will also need this if you want to use IP masquerade to connect a LAN that uses any of the above mentioned 'unconnected' IP network numbers.

To enable IP Masquerade and IP fire walling, you **MUST** answer yes to the first question in the `make config` process:-

---

```
Prompt for development and/or incomplete code/drivers (CONFIG_EXPERIMENTAL)?
```

Whilst this may sound a bit off-putting to new users, many users are actively using the IP Masquerade and IP fire walling features of the Linux 2.0.XX kernel with no problems.

Once you have installed and rebooted your new kernel, you can start configuring and testing your PPP link(s).

8   Getting the Information you need about the PPP server

Before you can establish a PPP connection with a server, you need to obtain the following information (from the sysadmin/user support people of the PPP server):-

- The telephone number(s) to dial for the service
  If you are behind a PABX, you also need the PABX number that gives you an outside dial tone - this is frequently digit zero (0) or nine (9).
- Does the server use DYNAMIC or STATIC IP numbers?
  If the server uses STATIC IP numbers, then you may need to know what IP number to use for your end of the PPP connection. If your ISP is providing you with a subnet of valid IP numbers, you will need to know the IP numbers you can use and the network mask (netmask).

  Most Internet Service Providers use DYNAMIC IP numbers. As mentioned above, this has some implications in terms of the services you can use.

  However, even if you are using STATIC IP numbers, most PPP servers will never (for security reasons) allow the client to specify an IP number as this is a security risk. You **do** still need to know this information!

- What are the IP numbers of the ISPs Domain Name Servers?
  There should be at least two although only one is needed.

  There could be a problem here. The MS Windows 95 PPP setup allows the DNS address to be passed to the client as part of its connection process. So your ISP (or corporate help desk) may well tell you you don't need the IP address of the DNS server(s).

  For Linux, you **DO** need the address of at least one DNS. The linux implementation of PPP does not allow the setting of the DNS IP number dynamically at connection time - and quite possibly will never do so.

Note: whilst Linux (as a PPP client) cannot accept the DNS address from a server, it can, when acting as a server, pass this information to clients using the `dns-addr` pppd option.

- Does the server require the use of PAP/CHAP?
If this is the case you need to know the "id" and "secret" you are to use in connecting. (These are probably your user name and password at your ISP).

- Does the server automatically start PPP or do you need to issue any commands to start PPP on the server once you are logged in?
If you must issue a command to start PPP, what is it?

- Is the server a Microsoft Windows NT system and, if so, is it using the MS PAP/CHAP system? Many corporate LANs seem to use MS Windows NT this way for increased security.

Carefully note down this information - you are going to use it!

9   Configuring your modem and serial port

You should make sure that your modem is correctly set up and that you know which serial port it is connected to.

Remember:-

- DOS com1: = Linux /dev/cua0 (and /dev/ttyS0)
- DOS com2: = Linux /dev/cua1 (and /dev/ttyS1)
et cetera

It is also worth remembering that if you have 4 serial ports, the standard PC set up is to have com1 and com3 share IRQ4 and com2 and com4 share IRQ3.

If you have devices on standard serial ports that share an IRQ with your modem you are going to have problems. You need to make sure that your modem serial port is on its own, unique IRQ. Many modern serial cards (and better quality motherboard serial ports) allow you to move the IRQ of the serial ports around.

If you are running Linux kernel 2, you can check the in-use IRQs using `cat /proc/interrupts`, which will produce output like

```
 0:   6766283    timer
 1:     91545    keyboard
 2:         0    cascade
 4:    156944  + serial
 7:    101764    WD8013
10:    134365  + BusLogic BT-958
13:         1    math error
15:   3671702  + serial
```

This shows a serial port on IRQ4 (a mouse) and a serial port on IRQ15 (the permanent modem based PPP link to the Internet. (There is also a serial port on com2, IRQ3 and com4 is on IRQ14, but as they are not in use, they do not show up).

Be warned - you need to know what you are doing if you are going to play with your IRQs! Not only do you have to open up you computer, pull out cards and play with jumpers, but you need to know what is on which IRQ. In my case, this is a totally SCSI based PC, and so I can disable the on motherboard IDE interfaces that normally use IRQ14 and 15!

You should also remember that if your PC boots other operating systems, moving IRQs around may well mean that OS cannot boot properly - or at all!

If you do move your serial ports to non-standard IRQs, then you need to tell Linux which IRQ each port is using. This is done using `setserial` and is best done as part of the boot process in `rc.local` or `rc.serial` which is called from `rc.local` or as part of the SysV initialisation. For the machine illustrated above, the commands used are

```
/bin/setserial -b /dev/ttyS2 IRQ 11
/bin/setserial -b /dev/ttyS3 IRQ 15
```

However, if you are using serial modules dynamically loaded when required by the `kerneld` process, you cannot set and forget the IRQ etc once at boot time. This is because if the serial module is unloaded, Linux forgets the special settings.

So, if you are loading the serial module on demand, you will need to reconfigure the IRQs etc each time the module is loaded.

9.1   A note about serial ports and speed capabilities

If you are using a high speed (external) modem (14,400 Baud or above), your serial port needs to be capable of handling the throughput that such a modem is capable of producing, particularly when the modems are compressing the data.

This requires your serial port to use a modern UART (Universal Asynchronous Receiver Transmitter) such as a 16550(A). If you are using an old machine (or old serial card), it is quite possible that your serial port has only an 8250 UART, which will cause you considerable problems when used with a high speed modem.

Use the command

```
setserial -a /dev/ttySx
```

to get Linux to report to you the type of UART you have. If you do not have a 16550A type UART, invest in a new serial card (available for under $50). When you purchase a new card, make sure you can move the IRQs around on it!

Note: the first versions of the 16550 UART chip had an error. This was rapidly discovered and a revision of the chip was released - the 16550A UART. A relatively small number of the faulty chips did however get into circulation. It is unlikely that you will encounter one of these but you should look for a response that says 16550A, particularly on serial cards of some vintage.

9.2   Serial Port Names

Historically, Linux used `cuaX` devices for dial out and `ttySx` devices for dial in.

The kernel code that required this was changed in kernel version 2.0.x and you should now use `ttySx` for both dial in and dial out. I understand that the `cuaX` device names may well disappear in future kernel versions.

9.3   Configuring your modem

You will need to configure your modem correctly for PPP - to do this **READ YOUR MODEM MANUAL**! Most modems come with a **factory default setting** that selects the options required for PPP. The minimum configuration specifies:-

- Hardware flow control (RTS/CTS) (&K3 on many Hayes modems)

Other settings (in standard Hayes commands) you should investigate are:-

- E1 Command/usr/src/linux-2.0.27/include/linux/serial.h Echo ON (required for chat to operate)
- Q0 Report result codes (required for chat to operate)
- S0=0 Auto Answer OFF (unless you want your modem to answer the phone)
- &C1 Carrier Detect ON only after connect
- &S0 Data Set Ready (DSR) always ON
- (depends) Data Terminal Ready

There is a site offering modem setups for a growing variety of modem makes and models at *Modem setup information* <http://www.in.net/info/modems/index.html> which may assist you in this.

It is also worth while investigating how the modem's serial interface between your computer and modem operates. Most modern modems allow you to run the serial interface at a FIXED speed whilst allowing the telephone line interface to change its speed to the highest speed it and the remote modem can both handle.

This is known as split speed operation. If your modem supports this, lock the modem's serial interface to its highest available speed (usually 115,200 baud but maybe 38,400 baud for 14,400 baud modems).

Use your communications software (e.g. minicom or seyon) to find out about your modem configuration and set it to what is required for PPP. Many modems report their current settings in response to AT&V, but you should consult your modem manual.

If you completely mess up the settings, you can return to sanity (usually) by issuing an AT&F - return to factory settings. (For most modem modems I have encountered, the factory settings include all you need for PPP - but you should check).

Once you have worked out the modem setup string required write it down. You now have a decision: you can store these settings in your modem non-volatile memory so they can be recalled by issuing the appropriate AT command. Alternatively you can pass the correct settings to your modem as part of the PPP dialing process.

If you only use your modem from Linux to call into your ISP or corporate server, the simplest set up will have you save your modem configuration in non-volatile RAM.

If on the other hand, you modem is used by other applications and operating systems, it is safest to pass this information to the modem as each call is made so that the modem is guaranteed to be in the correct state for the call. (This has the added advantage also of recording the modem setup string in case the modem looses the contents of its NV-RAM, which can indeed happen).

9.4   Note on Serial Flow Control

When data is traveling on serial communication lines, it can happen that data arrives faster than a computer can handle it (the computer may be busy doing something else - remember, Linux is a multi-user, multi-tasking operating system). In order to ensure that data is not lost (data does not over run in the input buffer and hence get lost), some method of controlling the flow of data is necessary.

There are two ways of doing this on serial lines:-

- Using hardware signals (Clear To Send/Request to Send - CTS/RTS)
- Using software signals (control S and control Q, also known as XON/XOFF).

Whilst the latter may be fine for a terminal (text) link, data on a PPP link uses all 8 bits - and it is quite probable that somewhere in the data there will be data bytes that translate as control S and control Q. So, if a modem is set up to use software flow control, things can rapidly go berserk!

For high speed links using PPP (which uses 8 bits of data) hardware flow control is vital and it is for this reason that you must use hardware flow control.

9.5   Testing your modem for dial out

Now that you have sorted out the serial port and modem settings it is a good idea to make sure that these setting do indeed work by dialing you ISP and seeing if you can connect.

Using you terminal communications package (such as minicom), set up the modem initialisation required for PPP and dial into the PPP server you want to connect to with a PPP session.

(Note: at this stage we are **NOT** trying to make a PPP connection - just establishing that we have the right phone number and also to find out **exactly** what the server sends to us in order to get logged in and start PPP).

During this process, either capture (log to a file) the entire login process or carefully (*very carefully*) write down **exactly** what prompts the server gives to let you know it is time to enter your user name and password (and any other commands needed to establish the PPP connection).

If your server uses PAP, you should not see a login prompt, but should instead see the (text representation) of the link control protocol (which looks like garbage) starting on your screen.

A few words of warning:-

- some servers are quite intelligent: you can log in using text based user name/passwords OR using PAP. So if your ISP or corporate site uses PAP but you do not see the garbage start up immediately, this may not mean you have done something wrong.
- some servers require you to enter some text initially and *then* start a standard PAP sequence.
- Some PPP servers are passive - that is they simply sit there sending nothing until the client that is dialing in sends them a valid lcp packet. If the ppp server you are connecting to operates in passive mode, you will never see the garbage!
- Some servers do not start PPP until you press ENTER - so it is worth trying this if you correctly log in and do not see the garbage!

It is worth dialing in at least twice - some servers change their prompts (e.g. with the time!) every time you log in. The two critical prompts your Linux box needs to be able to identify every time you dial in are:-

- the prompt that requests you to enter your user name;
- the prompt that requests you to enter your password;

If you have to issue a command to start PPP on the server, you will also need to find out the prompt the server gives you once you are logged in to tell you that you can now enter the command to start ppp.

If your server automatically starts PPP, once you have logged in, you will start to see garbage on your screen - this is the PPP server sending your machine information to start up and configure the PPP connection.

This should look something like this :-

```
~y}#.!}!}!} }8}!}$}%U}"}&} } } } }%}& ...}'}"}(}"} .~~y}
```

(and it just keeps on coming!)

On some systems PPP must be explicitly started on the server. This is usually because the server has been set up to allow PPP logins and shell logins using the same user name/password pair. If this is the case, issue this command once you have logged in. Again, you will see the garbage as the server end of the PPP connection starts up.

If you do not see this immediately after connecting (and logging in and starting the PPP server if required), press **Enter** to see if this starts the PPP server...

At this point, you can hang up your modem (usually, type +++ quickly and then issue the ATHO command once your modem responds with OK).

If you can't get your modem to work, read your modem manual, the man pages for your communications software and the Serial HOWTO! Once you have this sorted out, carry on as above.

10   Setting up Name to Address Resolution (DNS)

Whilst we humans like to give names to things, computers really like numbers. On a TCP/IP network (which is what the Internet is), we call machines by a particular name - and every machine lives in a particular "domain". For example, my Linux workstation is called **archenland** and it resides in the **interweft.com.au** domain. Its human readable address is thus archenland.interweft.com.au (which is known as the FQDN - fully qualified domain name).

However, for this machine to be found by other computers on the Internet, it is actually known by its IP number when computers are communicating across the Internet.

Translating (resolving) machine (and domain) names into the numbers actually used on the Internet is the business of machines that offer the Domain Name Service.

What happens is this:-

- your machine needs to know the IP address of a particular computer. The application requiring this information asks the 'resolver' on your Linux PC to provide this information;
- the resolver queries the local host file (/etc/hosts and/or the domain name servers it knows about (the exact behaviour of the resolver is determined by /etc/host.conf);
- if the answer is found in the host file, this answer is returned;
- if a domain name server is specified, your PC queries this machine;
- if the DNS machine already knows the IP number for the required name, it returns it. If it does not, it queries other name servers across the Internet to find the information. The name server than passes this information back to the requesting resolver - which gives the information to the requesting application.

When you make a PPP connection, you need to tell your Linux machine where it can get host name to IP number (address resolution) information so that **you** can use the machine names but your **computer** can translate these to the IP numbers it needs to do its work.

One way is to enter every host that you want to talk to into the **/etc/hosts** file (which is in reality totally impossible if you are connecting to the Internet); another is to use the machine IP numbers as opposed to the names (an impossible memory task for all but the smallest LANs).

The best way is to set up Linux so that it knows where to go to get this name to number information - automatically. This service is provided by the Domain Name Server (DNS) system. All that is necessary is to enter the IP number(s) for the domain name servers into your /etc/resolv.conf file.

10.1   The /etc/resolv.conf file

Your PPP server sysadmin/user support people should provide you with two DNS IP numbers (only one is necessary - but two gives some redundancy in the event of failure).

As previously mentioned, Linux cannot set its name server IP number in the way that MS Windows 95 does. So you must **insist** (politely) that your ISP provide you with this information!

Your /etc/resolv.conf should look something like :-

```
domain your.isp.domain.name
nameserver 10.25.0.1
nameserver 10.25.1.2
```

Edit this file (creating it if necessary) to represent the information that your ISP has provided. It should have ownership and permissions as follows :-

```
    -rw-r--r--    1 root      root          73 Feb 19 01:46 /etc/resolv.conf
```

If you have already set up a /etc/resolv.conf because you are on a LAN, simply add the IP numbers of the PPP DNS servers to your existing file.

10.2   The /etc/host.conf file

You should also check that your /etc/host.conf file is correctly set up. This should look like

```
order hosts,bind
multi on
```

This tells the resolver to use information in the host file before it sends queries to the DNS for resolution.

11   Using PPP and root privileges

Because PPP needs to set up networking devices, change the kernel routing table and so forth, it requires root privileges to do this.

If users other than root are to set up PPP connections, the pppd program should be setuid root :-

```
    -rwsr-xr-x   1 root      root       95225 Jul 11 00:27 /usr/sbin/pppd
```

If /usr/sbin/pppd is not set up this way, then **as root** issue the command:-

```
    chmod u+s /usr/sbin/pppd
```

What this does is make pppd run with root privileges **even** if the binary is run by an ordinary user. This allows a normal user to run pppd with the necessary privileges to set up the network interfaces and the kernel routing table.

Programs that run 'set uid root' are potential security holes and you should be extremely cautious about making programs 'suid root'. A number of programs (including pppd) have been carefully written to minimise the danger of running suid root, so you should be safe with this one (but no guarantees).

Depending on how you want your system to operate - specifically if you want ANY user on your system to be able to initiate a PPP link, you should make your ppp-on/off scripts world read/execute. (This is probably fine if your PC is used ONLY by you).

However, if you do NOT want just anyone to be able to start up a PPP connection (for example, your children have accounts on your Linux PC and you do not want them hooking into the Internet without your supervision), you will need to establish a PPP group (as root, edit /etc/group) and :-

- Make pppd suid root, owned by user root and group PPP, with the 'other' permissions on this file empty. It should then look like

```
   -rwsr-x---  1 root      PPP        95225 Jul 11 00:27 /usr/sbin/pppd
```
- Make the ppp-on/off scripts owned by user root and group PPP
- Make the ppp-on/off scripts read/executable by group PPP

```
   -rwxr-x---  1 root      PPP          587 Mar 14  1995 /usr/sbin/ppp-on
   -rwxr-x---  1 root      PPP          631 Mar 14  1995 /usr/sbin/ppp-off
```
- Make the other access rights for ppp-on/off nill.
- add the users who will be firing up PPP to the PPP group in /etc/group

Even if you do this, ordinary users will STILL not be able to shut down the link under software control! Running the `ppp-off` script requires root privileges. However, any user can just turn off the modem (or disconnect the telephone line from an internal modem).

An alternative (and better method) to this set up is to use the `sudo` program. This offers superior security and will allow you to set things up so that any (authorised) user can activate/deactivate the link using the scripts. Using `sudo` will allow an authorised user to activate/deactivate the PPP link cleanly and securely.

12   Setting up the PPP connection files

You now need to be logged in as **root** to create the directories and edit the files needed to set up PPP, even if you want PPP to be accessible to all users.

PPP uses a number of files to connect and set up a PPP connection. These differ in name and location between PPP 2.1.2 and 2.2.

For PPP 2.1.2 the files are:-

```
/usr/sbin/pppd            # the PPP binary
/usr/sbin/ppp-on          # the dialer/connection script
/usr/sbin/ppp-off         # the disconnection script
/etc/ppp/options          # the options pppd uses for all connections
/etc/ppp/options.ttyXX    # the options specific to a connection on this port
```

For PPP 2.2 the files are:-

```
/usr/sbin/pppd                   # the PPP binary
/etc/ppp/scripts/ppp-on          # the dialer/connection script
/etc/ppp/scripts/ppp-on-dialer   # part 1 of the dialer script
/etc/ppp/scripts/ppp-off         # the actual chat script itself
/etc/ppp/options                 # the options pppd uses for all connections
/etc/ppp/options.ttyXX           # the options specific to a connection on this port
```

Red Hat Linux users should note that the standard Red Hat 4.X installation places these scripts in /usr/doc/ppp-2.2.0f-2/scripts.

In your /etc directory there should be a ppp directory:-

```
drwxrwxr-x   2 root      root        1024 Oct  9 11:01 ppp
```

If it does not exist - create it with these ownerships and permissions.

If the directory already existed, it should contain a template options file called **options.tpl**. This file is included below in case it does not.

Print it out as it contains an explanation of nearly all the PPP options (these are useful to read in conjunction with the pppd man pages). Whilst you can use this file as the basis of your /etc/ppp/options file, it is probably better to create your own options file that does not include all the comments in the template - it will be much shorter and easier to read/maintain.

If you have multiple serial lines/modems (typically the case for PPP servers), create a general /etc/ppp/options file containing the options that are common for all the serial ports on which you are supporting dial in/out and set up individual option files for each serial line on which you will be establishing a PPP connection with the individual settings required for each port.

These port specific option files are named **options.ttyx1**, **options.ttyx2** and so forth (where x is the appropriate letter for your serial ports).

However, for a single PPP connection, you can happily use the /etc/ppp/options file. Alternatively, you can put all the options as arguments in the pppd command itself.

It is easier to maintain a setup that uses /etc/ppp/options.ttySx files. If you use PPP to connect to a number of different sites, you can create option files for each site in /etc/ppp/options.site and then specify the option file as a parameter to the PPP command as you connect (using the **file** **option-file** pppd option to pppd on the command line).

12.1 The supplied options.tpl file

Some distributions of PPP seem to have lost the options.tpl file, so here is the complete file. I suggest that you do NOT edit this file to create your /etc/ppp/options file(s). Rather, copy this to a new file and then edit that. If you mess up your edits, you can then go back to the original and start again.

```
# /etc/ppp/options -*- sh -*- general options for pppd
# created 13-Jul-1995 jmk
# autodate: 01-Aug-1995
# autotime: 19:45

# Use the executable or shell command specified to set up the serial
# line.  This script would typically use the "chat" program to dial the
# modem and start the remote ppp session.
```

```
#connect "echo You need to install a connect command."

# Run the executable or shell command specified after pppd has
# terminated the link.  This script could, for example, issue commands
# to the modem to cause it to hang up if hardware modem control signals
# were not available.
#disconnect "chat -- \d+++\d\c OK ath0 OK"

# async character map -- 32-bit hex; each bit is a character
# that needs to be escaped for pppd to receive it.  0x00000001
# represents '\x01', and 0x80000000 represents '\x1f'.
#asyncmap 0

# Require the peer to authenticate itself before allowing network
# packets to be sent or received.
#auth

# Use hardware flow control (i.e. RTS/CTS) to control the flow of data
# on the serial port.
#crtscts

# Use software flow control (i.e. XON/XOFF) to control the flow of data
# on the serial port.
#xonxoff

# Add a default route to the system routing tables, using the peer as
# the gateway, when IPCP negotiation is successfully completed.  This
# entry is removed when the PPP connection is broken.
#defaultroute

# Specifies that certain characters should be escaped on transmission
# (regardless of whether the peer requests them to be escaped with its
# async control character map).  The characters to be escaped are
# specified as a list of hex numbers separated by commas.  Note that
# almost any character can be specified for the escape option, unlike
# the asyncmap option which only allows control characters to be
# specified.  The characters which may not be escaped are those with hex
# values 0x20 - 0x3f or 0x5e.
#escape 11,13,ff

# Don't use the modem control lines.
#local

# Specifies that pppd should use a UUCP-style lock on the serial device
# to ensure exclusive access to the device.
#lock

# Use the modem control lines.  On Ultrix, this option implies hardware
# flow control, as for the crtscts option.  (This option is not fully
# implemented.)
#modem

# Set the MRU [Maximum Receive Unit] value to <n> for negotiation.  pppd
# will ask the peer to send packets of no more than <n> bytes.  The
```

```
# minimum MRU value is 128.  The default MRU value is 1500.  A value of
# 296 is recommended for slow links (40 bytes for TCP/IP header + 256
# bytes of data).
#mru 542


# Set the interface netmask to <n>, a 32 bit netmask in "decimal dot"
# notation (e.g. 255.255.255.0).
#netmask 255.255.255.0


# Disables the default behaviour when no local IP address is specified,
# which is to determine (if possible) the local IP address from the
# hostname. With this option, the peer will have to supply the local IP
# address during IPCP negotiation (unless it specified explicitly on the
# command line or in an options file).
#noipdefault


# Enables the "passive" option in the LCP.  With this option, pppd will
# attempt to initiate a connection; if no reply is received from the
# peer, pppd will then just wait passively for a valid LCP packet from
# the peer (instead of exiting, as it does without this option).
#passive


# With this option, pppd will not transmit LCP packets to initiate a
# connection until a valid LCP packet is received from the peer (as for
# the "passive" option with old versions of pppd).
#silent


# Don't request or allow negotiation of any options for LCP and IPCP
# (use default values).
#-all


# Disable Address/Control compression negotiation (use default, i.e.
# address/control field disabled).
#-ac


# Disable asyncmap negotiation (use the default asyncmap, i.e. escape
# all control characters).
#-am


# Don't fork to become a background process (otherwise pppd will do so
# if a serial device is specified).
#-detach


# Disable IP address negotiation (with this option, the remote IP
# address must be specified with an option on the command line or in an
# options file).
#-ip


# Disable magic number negotiation.  With this option, pppd cannot
# detect a looped-back line.
#-mn


# Disable MRU [Maximum Receive Unit] negotiation (use default, i.e.
# 1500).
```

```
#-mru

# Disable protocol field compression negotiation (use default, i.e.
# protocol field compression disabled).
#-pc

# Require the peer to authenticate itself using PAP.
# This requires TWO WAY authentication - do NOT use this for a standard
# PAP authenticated link to an ISP as this will require the ISP machine
# to authenticate itself to your machine (and it will not be able to).
#+pap

# Don't agree to authenticate using PAP.
#-pap

# Require the peer to authenticate itself using CHAP [Cryptographic
# Handshake Authentication Protocol] authentication.
# This requires TWO WAY authentication - do NOT use this for a standard
# CHAP authenticated link to an ISP as this will require the ISP machine
# to authenticate itself to your machine (and it will not be able to).
#+chap

# Don't agree to authenticate using CHAP.
#-chap

# Disable negotiation of Van Jacobson style IP header compression (use
# default, i.e. no compression).
#-vj

# Increase debugging level (same as -d).  If this option is given, pppd
# will log the contents of all control packets sent or received in a
# readable form.  The packets are logged through syslog with facility
# daemon and level debug. This information can be directed to a file by
# setting up /etc/syslog.conf appropriately (see syslog.conf(5)).  (If
# pppd is compiled with extra debugging enabled, it will log messages
# using facility local2 instead of daemon).
#debug

# Append the domain name <d> to the local host name for authentication
# purposes.  For example, if gethostname() returns the name porsche,
# but the fully qualified domain name is porsche.Quotron.COM, you would
# use the domain option to set the domain name to Quotron.COM.
#domain <d>

# Enable debugging code in the kernel-level PPP driver.  The argument n
# is a number which is the sum of the following values: 1 to enable
# general debug messages, 2 to request that the contents of received
# packets be printed, and 4 to request that the contents of transmitted
# packets be printed.
#kdebug n

# Set the MTU [Maximum Transmit Unit] value to <n>. Unless the peer
# requests a smaller value via MRU negotiation, pppd will request that
# the kernel networking code send data packets of no more than n bytes
```

```
# through the PPP network interface.
#mtu <n>

# Set the name of the local system for authentication purposes to <n>.
# This will probably have to be set to your ISP user name if you are
# using PAP/CHAP.
#name <n>

# Set the user name to use for authenticating this machine with the peer
# using PAP to <u>.
# Do NOT use this if you are using 'name' above!
#user <u>

# Enforce the use of the host name as the name of the local system for
# authentication purposes (overrides the name option).
#usehostname

# Set the assumed name of the remote system for authentication purposes
# to <n>.
#remotename <n>

# Add an entry to this system's ARP [Address Resolution Protocol]
# table with the IP address of the peer and the Ethernet address of this
# system.
#proxyarp

# Use the system password database for authenticating the peer using
# PAP.
#login

# If this option is given, pppd will send an LCP echo-request frame to
# the peer every n seconds. Under Linux, the echo-request is sent when
# no packets have been received from the peer for n seconds. Normally
# the peer should respond to the echo-request by sending an echo-reply.
# This option can be used with the lcp-echo-failure option to detect
# that the peer is no longer connected.
#lcp-echo-interval <n>

# If this option is given, pppd will presume the peer to be dead if n
# LCP echo-requests are sent without receiving a valid LCP echo-reply.
# If this happens, pppd will terminate the connection.  Use of this
# option requires a non-zero value for the lcp-echo-interval parameter.
# This option can be used to enable pppd to terminate after the physical
# connection has been broken (e.g., the modem has hung up) in
# situations where no hardware modem control lines are available.
#lcp-echo-failure <n>

# Set the LCP restart interval (retransmission timeout) to <n> seconds
# (default 3).
#lcp-restart <n>

# Set the maximum number of LCP terminate-request transmissions to <n>
# (default 3).
#lcp-max-terminate <n>
```

```
# Set the maximum number of LCP configure-request transmissions to <n>
# (default 10).
# Some PPP servers are slow to start up. You may need to increase this
# if you keep getting 'serial line looped back' errors and your are SURE
# that you have logged in correctly and PPP should be starting on the server.
#lcp-max-configure <n>

# Set the maximum number of LCP configure-NAKs returned before starting
# to send configure-Rejects instead to <n> (default 10).
#lcp-max-failure <n>

# Set the IPCP restart interval (retransmission timeout) to <n>
# seconds (default 3).
#ipcp-restart <n>

# Set the maximum number of IPCP terminate-request transmissions to <n>
# (default 3).
#ipcp-max-terminate <n>

# Set the maximum number of IPCP configure-request transmissions to <n>
# (default 10).
#ipcp-max-configure <n>

# Set the maximum number of IPCP configure-NAKs returned before starting
# to send configure-Rejects instead to <n> (default 10).
#ipcp-max-failure <n>

# Set the PAP restart interval (retransmission timeout) to <n> seconds
# (default 3).
#pap-restart <n>

# Set the maximum number of PAP authenticate-request transmissions to
# <n> (default 10).
#pap-max-authreq <n>

# Set the CHAP restart interval (retransmission timeout for
# challenges) to <n> seconds (default 3).
#chap-restart <n>

# Set the maximum number of CHAP challenge transmissions to <n>
# (default 10).
#chap-max-challenge

# If this option is given, pppd will re-challenge the peer every <n>
# seconds.
#chap-interval <n>

# With this option, pppd will accept the peer's idea of our local IP
# address, even if the local IP address was specified in an option.
#ipcp-accept-local

# With this option, pppd will accept the peer's idea of its (remote) IP
# address, even if the remote IP address was specified in an option.
```

```
#ipcp-accept-remote
```

12.2 What options should I use? (No PAP/CHAP)

Well, as in all things that depends (sigh). The options specified here should work with most servers.

However, if it does NOT work, READ THE TEMPLATE FILE (/etc/ppp/options.tpl) and the pppd man pages and speak to the sysadmin/user support people who run the server to which you are connecting.

You should also note that the connect scripts presented here also use some command line options to pppd to make things a bit easier to change.

```
# /etc/ppp/options (NO PAP/CHAP)
#
# Prevent pppd from forking into the background
-detach
#
# use the modem control lines
modem
# use uucp style locks to ensure exclusive access to the serial device
lock
# use hardware flow control
crtscts
# create a default route for this connection in the routing table
defaultroute
# do NOT set up any "escaped" control sequences
asyncmap 0
# use a maximum transmission packet size of 552 bytes
mtu 552
# use a maximum receive packet size of 552 bytes
mru 552
#
#-------END OF SAMPLE /etc/ppp/options (no PAP/CHAP)
```

13 If your PPP server uses PAP (Password Authentication Protocol)

If the server to which you are connecting requires PAP or CHAP authentication, you have a little bit more work.

To the above options file, add the following lines

```
#
# force pppd to use your ISP user name as your 'host name' during the
# authentication process
name <your ISP user name>        # you need to edit this line
#
# If you are running a PPP *server* and need to force PAP or CHAP
# uncomment the appropriate one of the following lines. Do NOT use
```

```
# these is you are a client connecting to a PPP server (even if it uses PAP
# or CHAP) as this tells the SERVER to authenticate itself to your
# machine (which almost certainly can't do - and the link will fail).
#+chap
#+pap
#
# If you are using ENCRYPTED secrets in the /etc/ppp/pap-secrets
# file, then uncomment the following line.
# Note: this is NOT the same as using MS encrypted passwords as can be
# set up in MS RAS on Windows NT.
#+papcrypt
```

13.1   Using MSCHAP

Microsoft Windows NT RAS can be set up to use a variation on CHAP (Challenge/Handshake Authentication Protocol). In your PPP sources tar ball, you will find a file called README.MSCHAP80 that discusses this.

You can determine if the server is requesting authentication using this protocol by enabling debugging for pppd. If the server is requesting MS CHAP authentication, you will see lines like

```
rcvd [LCP ConfReq id=0x2 <asyncmap 0x0> <auth chap 80> <magic 0x46a3>]
```

The critical information here is **auth chap 80**.

In order to use MS CHAP, you will need to recompile pppd to support this. Please see the instructions in the README.MSCHAP80 file in the PPP source file for instructions on how to compile and use this variation.

You should note that at present this code supports only Linux PPP clients connecting to an MS Windows NT server. It does **NOT** support setting up a Linux PPP server to use MSCHAP80 authentication from clients.

13.2   The PAP/CHAP secrets file

If you are using pap or chap authentication, then you also need to create the secrets file. These are:

```
/etc/ppp/pap-secrets
/etc/ppp/chap-secrets
```

They must be owned by user root, group root and have file permissions 740 for security.

The first point to note about PAP and CHAP is that they are designed to authenticate **computer systems** not **users**.

"Huh? What's the difference?" I hear you ask.

Well now, once your computer has made its PPP connection to the server, **ANY** user on your system can use that connection - not just you. This is why you can set up a WAN (wide area network) link that joins two LANs (local area networks) using PPP.

PAP can (and for CHAP **DOES**) require **bidirectional** authentication - that is a valid name and secret is required on each computer for the other computer involved. However, this is **NOT** the way most PPP servers offering dial up PPP PAP-authenticated connections operate.

That being said, your ISP will probably have given you a user name and password to allow you to connect to their system and thence the Internet. Your ISP is not interested in your computer's name at all, so you will probably need to use the user name at your ISP as the name for your computer.

This is done using the `name user name` option to pppd. So, if you are to use the user name given you by your ISP, add the line

---

```
name your_user name_at_your_ISP
```

---

to your `/etc/ppp/options` file.

Technically, you should really use `user our_user name_at_your_ISP` for PAP, but pppd is sufficiently intelligent to interpret `name` as `user` if it is required to use PAP. The advantage of using the `name` option is that this is also valid for CHAP.

As PAP is for authenticating **computers**, technically you need also to specify a remote computer name. However, as most people only have one ISP, you can use a wild card (*) for the remote host name in the secrets file.

It is also worth noting that many ISPs operate multiple modem banks connected to different terminal servers - each with a different name, but ACCESSED from a single (rotary) dial in number. It can therefore be quite difficult in some circumstances to know ahead of time what the name of the remote computer is, as this depends on which terminal server you connect to!

13.3   The PAP secrets file

The `/etc/ppp/pap-secrets` file looks like

```
# Secrets for authentication using PAP
# client        server        secret        acceptable_local_IP_addresses
```

The four fields are white space delimited and the last one can be blank (which is what you want for a dynamic and probably static IP allocation from your ISP).

Suppose your ISP gave you a user name of `fred` and a password of `flintstone` you would set the `name fred` option in `/etc/ppp/options[.ttySx]` and set up your `/etc/ppp/pap-secrets` file as follows

---

```
# Secrets for authentication using PAP
# client        server  secret          acceptable local IP addresses
fred            *       flintstone
```

This says for the local machine name `fred` (which we have told pppd to use even though it is not our local machine name) and for **ANY** server, use the password (secret) of `flintstone`.

Note that we do not need to specify a local IP address, unless we are required to FORCE a particular local, static IP address. Even if you try this, it is unlikely to work as most PPP servers (for security reasons) do not allow the remote system to set the IP number they are to be given.

13.4   The CHAP secrets file

This requires that you have mutual authentication methods - that is you must allow for both your machine to authenticate the remote server **AND** the remote server to authenticate your machine.

So, if your machine is `fred` and the remote is `barney`, your machine would set `name fred remotename barney` and the remote machine would set `name barney remotename fred` in their respective `/etc/ppp/options.ttySx` files.

The `/etc/chap-secrets` file for fred would look like

```
# Secrets for authentication using CHAP
# client        server  secret          acceptable local IP addresses
fred            barney  flintstone
barney          fred    wilma
```

and for barney

```
# Secrets for authentication using CHAP
# client        server  secret          acceptable local IP addresses
barney          fred    flintstone
fred            barney  wilma
```

Note in particular that both machines must have entries for bidirectional authentication. This allows the local machine to authenticate itself to the remote **AND** the remote machine to authenticate itself to the local machine.

13.5   Handling multiple PAP-authenticated connections

Some users have more than one server to which they connect that use PAP. Provided that your user name is different on each machine to which you want to connect, this is not a problem.

However, many users have the same user name on two (or more - even all) systems to which they connect. This then presents a problem in correctly selecting the appropriate line from `/etc/ppp/pap-secrets`.

As you might expect, PPP provides a mechanism for overcoming this. PPP allows you to set an 'assumed name' for the remote (server) end of the connection using the **remotename** option to pppd.

Let us suppose that you connect to two PPP servers using the username fred. You set up your `/etc/ppp/pap-secrets` something like

```
fred    pppserver1      barney
fred    pppserver2      wilma
```

Now, to set connect to pppserver1 you would use `name fred remotename pppserver1` in your ppp-options and for pppserver2 `name fred remotename pppserver2`.

As you can select the ppp options file to use with pppd using the `file filename` option, you can set up a script to connect to each of your PPP servers, correctly picking the options file to use and hence selecting the right `remotename` option.

14   Setting up the PPP connection manually

Now that you have created your `/etc/ppp/options` and `/etc/resolv.conf` files (and, if necessary, the `/etc/ppp/pap|chap-secrets` file), you can test the settings by manually establishing a PPP connection. (Once we have the manual connection working, we will automate the process).

To do this, your communications software must be capable of quitting WITHOUT resetting the modem. Minicom can do this - ALT Q (or in older version of minicom CTRL A Q)

Make sure you are logged in as root.

Fire up you communications software (such as minicom), dial into the PPP server and log in as normal. If you need to issue a command to start up PPP on the server, do so. You will now see the garbage you saw before.

If you are using pap or chap, then merely connecting to the remote system should start ppp on the remote and you will see the garbage without logging in (although this may not happen for some servers - try pressing **Enter** and see if the garbage starts up).

Now quit the communications software *without resetting the modem* (ALT Q or CTL A Q in minicom) and at the Linux prompt (as root) type

```
pppd -d -detach /dev/ttySx 38400 &
```

The -d option turns on debugging - the ppp connection start up conversation will be logged to your system log - which is useful if you are having trouble.

Your modem lights should now flash as the PPP connection is established. It will take a short while for the PPP connection to be made.

At this point you can look at the PPP interface, by issuing the command

```
ifconfig
```

In addition to any Ethernet and loop back devices you have, you should see something like :-

```
ppp0      Link encap:Point-Point Protocol
          inet addr:10.144.153.104  P-t-P:10.144.153.51 Mask:255.255.255.0
          UP POINTOPOINT RUNNING  MTU:552  Metric:1
          RX packets:0 errors:0 dropped:0 overruns:0
          TX packets:0 errors:0 dropped:0 overruns:0
```

Where

- inet addr:10.144.153.10 is the IP number of your end of the link.
- P-t-P:10.144.153.5 is the SERVER's IP number.

(Naturally, ifconfig will not report these IP numbers, but the ones used by your PPP server.)

Note: ifconfig also tells you that the link is UP and RUNNING!

If you get no ppp device listed or something like

```
ppp0        Link encap:Point-Point Protocol
            inet addr:0.0.0.0  P-t-P:0.0.0.0  Mask:0.0.0.0
            POINTOPOINT  MTU:1500  Metric:1
            RX packets:0 errors:0 dropped:0 overruns:0
            TX packets:0 errors:0 dropped:0 overruns:0
```

Your PPP connection has not been made...see the later section on debugging!

You should also be able to see a route to the the remote host (and beyond). To do this, issue the command

```
route -n
```

You should se something like:-

```
Kernel routing table
Destination     Gateway         Genmask          Flags MSS  Window Use Iface
10.144.153.3    *               255.255.255.255  UH    1500  0       1 ppp0
127.0.0.0       *               255.0.0.0        U     3584  0      11 lo
10.0.0.0        *               255.0.0.0        U     1500  0      35 eth0
default         10.144.153.3    *                UG    1500  0       5 ppp0
```

Of particular importance here, notice we have TWO entries pointing to our ppp interface.

The first is a HOST route (indicated by the H flag) and that allows us to see the host to which we are connected to - but no further.

The second is the default route (established by giving pppd the option **defaultroute**. This is the route that tells our Linux PC to send any packets NOT destined for the local Ethernet(s) - to which we have specific network routes - to the PPP server itself. The PPP server then is responsible for routing our packets out onto the Internet and routing the return packets back to us.

If you do not see a routing table with two entries, something is wrong. In particular if your syslog shows a message telling you pppd is not replacing an existing default route, then you have a default route pointing at your Ethernet interface - which **MUST** be replaced by a specific network route: **YOU CAN ONLY HAVE ONE DEFAULT ROUTE!!!**

You will need to explore your system initialisation files to find out where this default route is being set up (it will use a **route add default...** command). Change this command to something like **route add net....**

Now test the link by 'pinging' the server at its IP number as reported by the ifconfig output, i.e.

```
ping 10.144.153.51
```

You should receive output like

```
PING 10.144.153.51 (10.144.153.51): 56 data bytes
64 bytes from 10.144.153.51: icmp_seq=0 ttl=255 time=328.3 ms
64 bytes from 10.144.153.51: icmp_seq=1 ttl=255 time=190.5 ms
64 bytes from 10.144.153.51: icmp_seq=2 ttl=255 time=187.5 ms
64 bytes from 10.144.153.51: icmp_seq=3 ttl=255 time=170.7 ms
```

This listing will go on for ever - to stop it press CTRL C, at which point you will receive some more information :-

```
--- 10.144.153.51 ping statistics ---
4 packets transmitted, 4 packets received, 0% packet loss
round-trip min/avg/max = 170.7/219.2/328.3 ms
```

So far so good.

Now try pinging a host by name (not the name of the PPP server itself) but a host at another site that you KNOW is probably going to be up and running...). For example

```
ping sunsite.unc.edu
```

This time there will be a bit of a pause as Linux obtains the IP number for the fully qualified host name you have 'ping'ed from the DNS you specified in /etc/resolv.conf - so don't worry (but you will see your modem lights flash). Shortly you will receive output like

```
 PING sunsite.unc.edu (152.2.254.81): 56 data bytes
64 bytes from 152.2.254.81: icmp_seq=0 ttl=254 time=190.1 ms
64 bytes from 152.2.254.81: icmp_seq=1 ttl=254 time=180.6 ms
64 bytes from 152.2.254.81: icmp_seq=2 ttl=254 time=169.8 ms
64 bytes from 152.2.254.81: icmp_seq=3 ttl=254 time=170.6 ms
64 bytes from 152.2.254.81: icmp_seq=4 ttl=254 time=170.6 ms
```

Again, stop the output by pressing CTRL C and get the statistics...

```
--- sunsite.unc.edu ping statistics ---
5 packets transmitted, 5 packets received, 0% packet loss
round-trip min/avg/max = 169.8/176.3/190.1 ms
```

If you don't get any response, try pinging the IP address of the DNS server at your ISP's site. If you get a result from this, then it looks like you have a problem with /etc/resolv.conf.

If this doesn't work, you have a routing problem, or your ISP has a problem routing packets back to you. Check your routing table as shown above and if that is OK, contact your ISP. A good test of the ISP is to use another operating system to connect. If you can get beyond your ISP with that, then the problem is at your end.

If everything works, shut down the connection by typing

```
ppp-off
```

After a short pause, the modem should hang itself up.

If that does not work, either turn off your modem or fire up your communications software and interrupt the modem with +++ and then hang up with ATH0 when you receive the modem's OK prompt.

You may also need to clean up the lock file created by pppd

```
rm -f /var/lock/LCK..ttySx
```

15   Automating your connections - Creating the connection scripts

Whilst you can continue to log in by hand as shown above, it is much neater to set up some scripts to do this automatically for you.

A set of scripts automates the log in and PPP start up so all you have to do (as root or as a member of the PPP group) is issue a single command to fire up your connection.

15.1   Connection scripts for User name/Password Authentication

If your ISP does NOT require the use of PAP/CHAP, these are the scripts for you!

If the ppp package installed correctly, you should have two example files. For PPP 2.1.2 they are in `/usr/sbin` and for PPP 2.2 they are in `/etc/ppp/scripts`. They are called

for PPP-2.1.2

```
ppp-on
ppp-off
```

and for PPP-2.2

```
ppp-off
ppp-on
ppp-on-dialer
```

Now, if you are using PPP 2.1.2, I strongly urge you to delete the sample files. There are potential problems with these - and don't tell me they work fine - I used them for ages too (and recommended them in the first version of this HOWTO)!

For the benefit of PPP 2.1.2 users, here are BETTER template versions, taken from the PPP 2.2 distribution. I suggest you copy and use these scripts **instead of** the old PPP-2.1.2 scripts.

15.2   The ppp-on script

This is the first of a PAIR of scripts that actually fire up the connection.

```sh
#!/bin/sh
#
# Script to initiate a PPP connection. This is the first part of the
# pair of scripts. This is not a secure pair of scripts as the codes
# are visible with the 'ps' command.  However, it is simple.
#
# These are the parameters. Change as needed.
TELEPHONE=555-1212        # The telephone number for the connection
ACCOUNT=george            # The account name for logon (as in 'George Burns')
PASSWORD=gracie           # The password for this account (and 'Gracie Allen')
LOCAL_IP=0.0.0.0          # Local IP address if known. Dynamic = 0.0.0.0
REMOTE_IP=0.0.0.0         # Remote IP address if desired. Normally 0.0.0.0
```

```
NETMASK=255.255.255.0    # The proper netmask if needed
#
# Export them so that they will be available to 'ppp-on-dialer'
export TELEPHONE ACCOUNT PASSWORD
#
# This is the location of the script which dials the phone and logs
# in.  Please use the absolute file name as the $PATH variable is not
# used on the connect option.  (To do so on a 'root' account would be
# a security hole so don't ask.)
#
DIALER_SCRIPT=/etc/ppp/ppp-on-dialer
#
# Initiate the connection
#
#
exec /usr/sbin/pppd debug /dev/ttySx 38400 \
        $LOCAL_IP:$REMOTE_IP \
        connect $DIALER_SCRIPT
```

Here is the ppp-on-dialer script:-

```
#!/bin/sh
#
# This is part 2 of the ppp-on script. It will perform the connection
# protocol for the desired connection.
#
/usr/sbin/chat -v                                          \
        TIMEOUT         3                          \
        ABORT           '\nBUSY\r'                 \
        ABORT           '\nNO ANSWER\r'            \
        ABORT           '\nRINGING\r\n\r\nRINGING\r'  \
        ''              \rAT                       \
        'OK-+++\c-OK'   ATHO                       \
        TIMEOUT         30                         \
        OK              ATDT$TELEPHONE             \
        CONNECT         ''                         \
        ogin:--ogin:    $ACCOUNT                   \
        assword:        $PASSWORD
```

For PPP-2.2, the ppp-off script looks like:-

```
#!/bin/sh
######################################################################
#
# Determine the device to be terminated.
#
if [ "$1" = "" ]; then
        DEVICE=ppp0
else
        DEVICE=$1
fi
```

```
####################################################################
#
# If the ppp0 pid file is present then the program is running. Stop it.
if [ -r /var/run/$DEVICE.pid ]; then
        kill -INT `cat /var/run/$DEVICE.pid`
#
# If the kill did not work then there is no process running for this
# pid. It may also mean that the lock file will be left. You may wish
# to delete the lock file at the same time.
        if [ ! "$?" = "0" ]; then
                rm -f /var/run/$DEVICE.pid
                echo "ERROR: Removed stale pid file"
                exit 1
        fi
#
# Success. Let pppd clean up its own junk.
        echo "PPP link to $DEVICE terminated."
        exit 0
fi
#
# The ppp process is not running for ppp0
echo "ERROR: PPP link is not active on $DEVICE"
exit 1
```

15.3   Editing the supplied PPP startup scripts

As the new scripts come in two parts, we will edit them in turn.

15.3.1   The ppp-on script

You will need to edit the script to reflect YOUR user name at your ISP, YOUR password at your ISP, the telephone number of your ISP.

Each of the lines like TELEPHONE= actually set up shell variables that contain the information to the right of the '=' (excluding the comments of course). So edit each of these lines so it is correct for your ISP and connection.

Also, as you are setting the IP number (if you need to) in the /etc/ppp/options file, DELETE the line that says

```
$LOCAL_IP:$REMOTE_IP \
```

Also, make sure that the shell variable DIALER_SCRIPT points at the full path and name of the dialer script that you are actually going to use. So, if you have moved this or renamed the script, make sure you edit this line correctly in the ppp-on script!

15.3.2   The ppp-on-dialer script

This is the second of the scripts that actually brings up our ppp link.

Note: a chat script is normally all on one line. the backslashes are used to allow line continuations across several physical lines (for human readability) and do not form part of the script itself.

However, it is very useful to look at it in detail so that we understand what it is actually (supposed) to be doing!

15.4   What a Chat script means...

A chat script is a sequence of "expect string" "send string" pairs. In particular, note that we **ALWAYS** expect **something** before we send something.

If we are to send something **WITHOUT** receiving anything first, we must use an empty expect string (indicated by "") and similarly for expecting something without sending anything! Also, if a string consists of several words, (e.g. NO CARRIER), you must quote the string so that it is seen as a single entity by chat.

The chat line in our template is:-

```
exec /usr/sbin/chat -v
```

Invoke chat, the -v tells chat to copy ALL its I/O into the system log (usually /var/log/messages). Once you are happy that the chat script is working reliably, edit this line to remove the -v to save unnecessary clutter in your syslog.

```
TIMEOUT        3
```

This sets the timeout for the receipt of expected input to three seconds. You may need to increase this to say 5 or 10 seconds if you are using a really slow modem!

```
ABORT          '\nBUSY\r'
```

If the string BUSY is received, abort the operation.

```
ABORT          '\nNO ANSWER\r'
```

If the string NO ANSWER is received, abort the operation

```
ABORT          '\nRINGING\r\n\r\nRINGING\r'
```

If the (repeated) string RINGING is received, abort the operation. This is because someone is ringing your phone line!

```
"              \rAT
```

Expect nothing from the modem and send the string AT.

```
OK-+++\c-OK    ATH0
```

This one is a bit more complicated as it uses some of chat's error recovery capabilities.

What is says is...Expect OK, if it is NOT received (because the modem is not in command mode) then send +++ (the standard Hayes-compatible modem string that returns the modem to command mode) and expect OK. Then send ATH0 (the modem hang up string). This allows your script to cope with the situation of your modem being stuck on-line!

```
TIMEOUT        30
```

Set the timeout to 30 seconds for the remainder of the script. If you experience trouble with the chat script aborting due to timeouts, increase this to 45 seconds or more.

```
OK             ATDT$TELEPHONE
```

Expect OK (the modem's response to the ATH0 command) and dial the number we want to call.

```
CONNECT        ''
```

Expect CONNECT (which our modem sends when the remote modem answers) and send nothing in reply.

```
ogin:--ogin:   $ACCOUNT
```

Again, we have some error recovery built in here. Expect the login prompt (...ogin:) but if we don't receive it by the timeout, send a return and then look for the login prompt again. When the prompt is received, send the username (stored in the shell variable $ACCOUNT).

```
assword:       $PASSWORD
```

Expect the password prompt and send our password (again, stored in a shell variable).

This chat script has reasonable error recovery capability. Chat has considerably more features than demonstrated here. For more information consult the chat manual page (`man 8 chat`).

15.4.1 Starting PPP at the server end

Whilst the ppp-on-dialer script is fine for servers that automatically start pppd at the server end once you have logged in, some servers require that you explicitly start PPP on the server.

If you need to issue a command to start up PPP on the server, you DO need to edit the ppp-on-dialer script.

At the END of the script (after the password line) add an additional **expect send** pair - this one would look for your login prompt (beware of characters that have a special meaning in the Bourne shell - such as $ and [or] (open and close square brackets).

Once chat has found the shell prompt, chat must issue the ppp start up command required for your ISPs PPP server.

In my case, my PPP server uses the standard Linux Bash prompt

```
[hartr@kepler hartr]$
```

and requires that I type

```
PPP
```

to start up PPP on the server.

It is a good idea to allow for a bit of error recovery here, so in my case I use

```
hartr--hartr     ppp
```

This says, if we don't receive the prompt within the timeout, send a carriage return and looks for the prompt again.

Once the prompt is received, then send the string `ppp`.

Note: don't forget to add a \ to the end of the previous line so chat still thinks the entire chat script is on one line!

Unfortunately, some servers produce a very variable set of prompts! You may need to log in several times using minicom to understand what is going on and pick the stable "expect" strings.

15.5   A chat script for PAP/CHAP authenticated connections

If your ISP is using PAP/CHAP, then your chat script is much simpler. All your chat script needs to do is dial the telephone, wait for a connect and then let pppd handle the logging in!

```
#!/bin/sh
#
# This is part 2 of the ppp-on script. It will perform the connection
# protocol for the desired connection.
#
exec /usr/sbin/chat -v                                          \
      TIMEOUT        3                                          \
      ABORT          '\nBUSY\r'                                 \
      ABORT          '\nNO ANSWER\r'                            \
      ABORT          '\nRINGING\r\n\r\nRINGING\r'               \
      ''             \rAT                                       \
      'OK-+++\c-OK'  ATHO                                       \
      TIMEOUT        30                                         \
      OK             ATDT$TELEPHONE                             \
      CONNECT        ''                                         \
```

15.6   The pppd `debug` and `file` option_file options

As we have already seen, you can turn on debug information logging with the -d option to pppd. The 'debug' option is equivalent to this.

As we are establishing a new connection with a new script, leave in the debug option for now. (Warning: if your disk space is tight, logging pppd exchanges can rapidly extend your syslog file and run you into trouble - but to do this you must fail to connect and keep on trying for quite a few minutes).

Once you are happy that all is working properly, then you can remove this option.

If you have called your ppp options file anything other than **/etc/ppp/options** or **/etc/ppp/options.ttySx**, specify the file name with the `file` option to pppd - e.g.

```
exec /usr/sbin/pppd debug file options.myserver /dev/ttyS0 38400 \
```

16   Testing your connection script

Open a new root Xterm (if you are in X) or open a new virtual console and log in as root.

In this new session, issue the command

```
tail -f /var/log/messages
```

(or whatever your system log file is).

In the first window (or virtual console) issue the command

```
ppp-on &
```

(or whatever name you have called your edited version of /usr/sbin/ppp- on). If you do not put the script into the background by specifying & at the end of the command, you will not get your terminal prompt back until ppp exits (when the link terminates).

Now switch back to the window that is tracking your system log.

You will see something like the following (provided you specified -v to chat and -d to pppd)....this is the chat script and responses being logged to the system log file followed by the start up information for pppd :-

```
Oct 21 16:09:58 hwin chat[19868]: abort on (NO CARRIER)
Oct 21 16:09:59 hwin chat[19868]: abort on (BUSY)
Oct 21 16:09:59 hwin chat[19868]: send (ATZ^M)
Oct 21 16:09:59 hwin chat[19868]: expect (OK)
Oct 21 16:10:00 hwin chat[19868]: ATZ^M^M
Oct 21 16:10:00 hwin chat[19868]: OK -- got it
Oct 21 16:10:00 hwin chat[19868]: send (ATDT722298^M)
Oct 21 16:10:00 hwin chat[19868]: expect (CONNECT)
Oct 21 16:10:00 hwin chat[19868]: ^M
Oct 21 16:10:22 hwin chat[19868]: ATDT722298^M^M
Oct 21 16:10:22 hwin chat[19868]: CONNECT -- got it
Oct 21 16:10:22 hwin chat[19868]: send (^M)
Oct 21 16:10:22 hwin chat[19868]: expect (ogin:)
Oct 21 16:10:23 hwin chat[19868]: kepler login: -- got it
```

```
Oct 21 16:10:23 hwin chat[19868]: send (hartr^M)
Oct 21 16:10:23 hwin chat[19868]: expect (ssword:)
Oct 21 16:10:23 hwin chat[19868]:  hartr^M
Oct 21 16:10:23 hwin chat[19868]: Password: -- got it
Oct 21 16:10:23 hwin chat[19868]: send (??????^M)
Oct 21 16:10:23 hwin chat[19868]: expect (hartr)
Oct 21 16:10:24 hwin chat[19868]: [hartr -- got it
Oct 21 16:10:24 hwin chat[19868]: send (ppp^M)
Oct 21 16:10:27 hwin pppd[19872]: pppd 2.1.2 started by root, uid 0
Oct 21 16:10:27 hwin pppd[19873]: Using interface ppp0
Oct 21 16:10:27 hwin pppd[19873]: Connect: ppp0 <--> /dev/cua1
Oct 21 16:10:27 hwin pppd[19873]: fsm_sdata(LCP): Sent code 1, id 1.
Oct 21 16:10:27 hwin pppd[19873]: LCP: sending Configure-Request, id 1
Oct 21 16:10:27 hwin pppd[19873]: fsm_rconfreq(LCP): Rcvd id 1.
Oct 21 16:10:27 hwin pppd[19873]: lcp_reqci: rcvd MRU
Oct 21 16:10:27 hwin pppd[19873]: (1500)
Oct 21 16:10:27 hwin pppd[19873]:  (ACK)
Oct 21 16:10:27 hwin pppd[19873]: lcp_reqci: rcvd ASYNCMAP
Oct 21 16:10:27 hwin pppd[19873]: (0)
Oct 21 16:10:27 hwin pppd[19873]:  (ACK)
Oct 21 16:10:27 hwin pppd[19873]: lcp_reqci: rcvd MAGICNUMBER
Oct 21 16:10:27 hwin pppd[19873]: (a098b898)
Oct 21 16:10:27 hwin pppd[19873]:  (ACK)
Oct 21 16:10:27 hwin pppd[19873]: lcp_reqci: rcvd PCOMPRESSION
Oct 21 16:10:27 hwin pppd[19873]:  (ACK)
Oct 21 16:10:27 hwin pppd[19873]: lcp_reqci: rcvd ACCOMPRESSION
Oct 21 16:10:27 hwin pppd[19873]:  (ACK)
Oct 21 16:10:27 hwin pppd[19873]: lcp_reqci: returning CONFACK.
Oct 21 16:10:27 hwin pppd[19873]: fsm_sdata(LCP): Sent code 2, id 1.
Oct 21 16:10:27 hwin pppd[19873]: fsm_rconfack(LCP): Rcvd id 1.
Oct 21 16:10:27 hwin pppd[19873]: fsm_sdata(IPCP): Sent code 1, id 1.
Oct 21 16:10:27 hwin pppd[19873]: IPCP: sending Configure-Request, id 1
Oct 21 16:10:27 hwin pppd[19873]: fsm_rconfreq(IPCP): Rcvd id 1.
Oct 21 16:10:27 hwin pppd[19873]: ipcp: received ADDR
Oct 21 16:10:27 hwin pppd[19873]: (10.144.153.51)
Oct 21 16:10:27 hwin pppd[19873]:  (ACK)
Oct 21 16:10:27 hwin pppd[19873]: ipcp: received COMPRESSTYPE
Oct 21 16:10:27 hwin pppd[19873]: (45)
Oct 21 16:10:27 hwin pppd[19873]:  (ACK)
Oct 21 16:10:27 hwin pppd[19873]: ipcp: returning Configure-ACK
Oct 21 16:10:28 hwin pppd[19873]: fsm_sdata(IPCP): Sent code 2, id 1.
Oct 21 16:10:30 hwin pppd[19873]: fsm_sdata(IPCP): Sent code 1, id 1.
Oct 21 16:10:30 hwin pppd[19873]: IPCP: sending Configure-Request, id 1
Oct 21 16:10:30 hwin pppd[19873]: fsm_rconfreq(IPCP): Rcvd id 255.
Oct 21 16:10:31 hwin pppd[19873]: ipcp: received ADDR
Oct 21 16:10:31 hwin pppd[19873]: (10.144.153.51)
Oct 21 16:10:31 hwin pppd[19873]:  (ACK)
Oct 21 16:10:31 hwin pppd[19873]: ipcp: received COMPRESSTYPE
Oct 21 16:10:31 hwin pppd[19873]: (45)
Oct 21 16:10:31 hwin pppd[19873]:  (ACK)
Oct 21 16:10:31 hwin pppd[19873]: ipcp: returning Configure-ACK
Oct 21 16:10:31 hwin pppd[19873]: fsm_sdata(IPCP): Sent code 2, id 255.
Oct 21 16:10:31 hwin pppd[19873]: fsm_rconfack(IPCP): Rcvd id 1.
Oct 21 16:10:31 hwin pppd[19873]: ipcp: up
```

```
Oct 21 16:10:31 hwin pppd[19873]: local  IP address 10.144.153.104
Oct 21 16:10:31 hwin pppd[19873]: remote IP address 10.144.153.51
```

(Note - I am using STATIC IP numbers - hence my machine sent that to the PPP server - you won't see this if you are using DYNAMIC IP numbers.) Also, this server requires a specific command to start ppp at its end.

This looks OK - so test it out as before with pings to IP numbers and host names.

Fire up you web browser or whatever and go surfing - you are connected!

17   Shutting down the PPP link

When you have finished with the PPP link, use the standard ppp-off command to shut it down (remember - you need to be root or a member of the PPP group!).

In your system log you will see something like:-

```
Oct 21 16:10:45 hwin pppd[19873]: Interrupt received: terminating link
Oct 21 16:10:45 hwin pppd[19873]: ipcp: down
Oct 21 16:10:45 hwin pppd[19873]: default route ioctl(SIOCDELRT): Bad address
Oct 21 16:10:45 hwin pppd[19873]: fsm_sdata(LCP): Sent code 5, id 2.
Oct 21 16:10:46 hwin pppd[19873]: fsm_rtermack(LCP).
Oct 21 16:10:46 hwin pppd[19873]: Connection terminated.
Oct 21 16:10:46 hwin pppd[19873]: Exit.
```

Don't worry about the SIOCDELRT - this is just pppd noting that it is terminating and is nothing to worry about.

18   Debugging

There are any number of reasons that your connection does not work - chat has failed to complete correctly, you have a dirty line, etc. So check your syslog for indications.

18.1   I have compiled PPP support into the kernel, but...

A very common problem is that people compile PPP support into the kernel and yet when they try to run pppd, the kernel complains that it does not support ppp! There are a variety of reasons this can occur.

18.1.1   Are you booting the right kernel? Whilst you have recompiled your kernel to support ppp, you are not booting the new kernel. This can happen if you do not update /etc/lilo.conf and rerun lilo.

A good check on the kernel can be obtained by issuing the command uname -a, which should produce a line like

```
Linux archenland 2.0.28 #2 Thu Feb 13 12:31:37 EST 1997 i586
```

This gives the kernel version and the date on which this kernel was compiled - which should give you a pretty good idea of what is going on.

18.1.2   Did you compile ppp kernel support as a module?

If you compiled your kernel ppp support as a module, but did not make and install the modules, then you can get this error. Check the kernel-HOWTO and the README file in `/usr/src/linux`!

Another module connected possibility is that you are expecting required modules to be automatically loaded, but are not running the `kerneld` daemon (which auto-loads and unloads modules on the fly). Check the kerneld mini-HOWTO for information on setting up kerneld.

18.1.3   Are you using the correct version of PPP for your kernel?

You **must** use ppp-2.2 with kernel version 2.0.x. You can use ppp-2.2 with kernel version 1.2.x (if you patch the kernel) otherwise you must use ppp-2.1.2.

18.1.4   Are you running pppd as root?

If you are not running pppd as the root user (and pppd is not suid to root), you can receive this message.

18.2   My modem connects but ppp never starts up

There are innumerable variations on this (take a look in comp.os.linux...).

A **VERY** common mistake is that you have mistyped something in your scripts. The only thing to do here is to make sure you are logging the chat conversation between you Linux PC and the server into your syslog (/var/log/messages) and then go through this *line by line* to make. You may need to dial into the ppp server manually to check things out again.

You need to check the log against the actual prompts very carefully - and bear in mind that we humans have a tendency to read what we THINK we have typed - not what is actually there!

18.3   The syslog says "serial line is not 8 bit clean..."

There are variations on this too - such as `serial line looped back` etc., and the cause can be one (or a sequence) of a number of things.

To understand what is going on here, it is necessary to grasp a bit of what is going on behind the scenes in pppd itself.

When pppd starts up, it sends LCP (link control protocol) packets to the remote machine. If it receives a valid response it then goes on to the next stage (using IPCP - IP control protocol packets) and only when this negotiation completes is the actual IP layer started so that you can use the PPP link.

If there is no ppp server operating at the remote end when your PC sends lcp packets, these get reflected by the login process at the far end. As these packets use 8 bits, reflecting them strips the 8th bit (remember, ASCII is a 7 bit code). PPP sees this and complains accordingly.

There are several reasons this reflection can occur.

18.3.1 You are not correctly logging into the server

When your chat script completes, pppd starts on your PC. However, if you have not completed the log in process to the server (including sending any command required to start PPP on the server), PPP will not start.

So, the lcp packets are reflected and you receive this error.

You need to carefully check and correct (if necessary) your chat script (see above).

18.3.2 You are not starting PPP on the server

Some PPP servers require you to enter a command and/or a RETURN after completing the log in process before the remote end starts ppp.

Check your chat script (see above).

If you log in manually and find you need to send a RETURN after this to start PPP, simply add a blank expect/send pair to the end of your chat script (an empty send string actually sends a RETURN).

18.3.3 The remote PPP process is slow to start

This one is a bit tricksy!

By default, your Linux pppd is compiled to send a maximum of 10 lcp configuration requests. If the server is a bit slow to start up, all 10 such requests can be sent before the remote PPP is ready to receive them.

On your machine, pppd sees all 10 requests reflected back (with the 8th bit stripped) and exits.

There are two ways round this:-

Add `lcp-max-configure` 30 to your ppp options. This increases the maximum number of lcp configure packets pppd sends before giving up. For really slow server, you may need even more than this.

Alternatively, you can get a bit tricksy in return. You may have noticed that when you logged in by hand to the PPP server and PPP started there, the **first** character of the ppp garbage that appears was always the tilde character (˜).

Using this knowledge we can add a new **expect/send** pair to the end of the chat script which expects a tilde and sends nothing. This would look like:-

---

\˜   ''

Note: as the tilde character has a special meaning in the shell, it must be escaped (and hence the leading backslash).

18.4 Default route not set

If pppd refuses to set up a default route, it is because (quite correctly) it refuses remove/replace an existing default route.

The usual reason that this error occurs is that some distributions set up a default route via your Ethernet card as opposed to setting up a specific network route.

See the Linux NAG and the Net2/3 HOWTOs for information on correctly setting up your Ethernet card and associated routes.

An alternative to this is that your LAN uses a gateway/router already and your routing table has been set up to point the default route at this.

Fixing up this last situation can require a fair bit of IP networking knowledge and is beyond the scope of this HOWTO. It is suggested you obtain some expert advice (via the news groups of from someone locally you can ask).

18.5   Other Problems

There are many reasons apart from these that ppp fails to connect and/or operate properly.

Look in the PPP FAQ (which is really a series of questions and answers). This is a very comprehensive document and the answers ARE there! From my own (sad) experience, if the answer to your problems is not there, the problem is NOT ppp's fault! In my case I was using an ELF kernel that I had not upgraded to the appropriate kernel modules. I only wasted about 2 days (and most of one night) cursing what had been a perfect PPP server before the light dawned!

19   Getting Help when totally stuck

If you can't get your PPP link to work, go back through this document and check everything - in conjunction with the output created by "chat-v..." and "pppd -d" in you system log.

Also consult the PPP documentation and FAQ plus the other documents mention herein!

If you are still stuck, try the comp.os.linux.misc and comp.os.linux.networking newsgroups are reasonably regularly scanned by people that can help you with PPP as is comp.protocols.ppp

You can try sending me personal email, but I do have a day job (and a life) and I do not guarantee to respond quickly (if at all) as this depends on my current work load and the state of my private life!

In particular - **DO NOT POST REAMS OF DEBUGGING OUTPUT TO THE NEWS GROUPS NOR SEND IT TO ME BY EMAIL** - the former wastes huge amounts of network bandwidth and the latter will be consigned to /dev/null (unless I have specifically requested it).

20   Common Problems once the link is working

One problem you will find is that many service providers will only support the connection software package that they distribute to new accounts. This is (typically) for Microsoft Windows :-(- and many service provider help desks seem to know nothing about Unix (or Linux). So, be prepared for limited assistance from them!

You could of course do the individual a favour and educate then about Linux (any ISP help desk person should be reasonably 'with it' in Internet terms and that means they should have a home Linux box - of course it does)!

20.1   I can't see beyond the PPP server I connect to

OK - your PPP connection is up and running and you can ping the PPP server by IP number (the second or "remote" IP number shown by `ifconfig ppp0`), but you can't reach anything beyond this.

First of all, try pinging the IP numbers you have specified in /etc/resolv.conf as name servers. If this works, you **can** see beyond your PPP server (unless this has the same IP number as the "remote" IP number of your connection). So now try pinging the full Internet name of your service provider - eg

```
ping my.provider.net.au
```

If this does NOT work, you have a problem with the name resolution. This is probably because of a typo in your /etc/resolv.conf file. Check this carefully against the information you acquired by ringing your service provider. If all looks OK, ring your service provider and check that you wrote down the IP numbers correctly.

If it STILL doesn't work (and your service provider confirms that his name servers are up and running), you have a problem somewhere else - and I suggest you check carefully through your Linux installation (looking particularly for file permissions).

If you STILL can't ping your service provider's IP name servers by IP number, either they are down (give them a voice call and check) or there is a routing problem at your service provider's end. Again, ring them and check this out.

One possibility is that the "remote end" is a Linux PPP server where the IP forwarding option has not been specified in the kernel!

A good general test is to try connecting to your service provider using the software that most supply for (gulp) Microsoft Windows. If everything works from another operating system to exactly the same account, then the problem is with your Linux system and NOT your service provider.

20.2   I can send email, but not receive it

If you are using dynamic IP numbers, this is perfectly normal. See "Setting up Services" below.

20.3   Why can't people finger, WWW, gopher, talk etc to my machine?

Again, if you are using dynamic IP numbers, this is perfectly normal. See "Setting up Services" below.

21   Using Internet services with Dynamic IP numbers

If you are using dynamic IP numbers (and many service providers will only give you a dynamic IP number unless you pay significantly more for your connection), then you have to recognise the limitations this imposes.

First of all, outbound service requests will work just fine. That is, you can send email using sendmail (provided you have correctly set up sendmail), ftp files from remote sites, finger users on other machines, browse the web etc.

In particular, you can answer email that you have brought down to your machine whilst you are off line. Mail will simply sit in your mail queue until you dial back into your ISP.

However, your machine is NOT connected to the Internet 24 hours a day, nor does it have the same IP number every time it is connected. So it is impossible for you to receive email directed to your machine, and very difficult to set up a web or ftp server that your friends can access! As far as the Internet is concerned your machine does not exist as a unique, permanently contactable machine as it does not have a unique IP number (remember - other machines will be using the IP number when they are allocated it on dial in).

If you set up a WWW (or any other server), it is totally unknown by any user on the Internet UNLESS they know that your machine is connected AND its actual (current) IP number. There are a number of ways they can get this info, ranging from you ringing them, sending them email to tell them or cunning use of ".plan" files on a shell account at your service provider (assuming that your provider allows shell and finger access).

Now, for most users, this is not a problem - all that most people want is to send and receive email (using your account on your service provider) and make outbound connections to WWW, ftp and other servers on the Internet. If you MUST have inbound connections to your server, you should really get a static IP number. Alternatively you can explore the methods hinted at above...

21.1 Setting up email

Even for dynamic IP numbers, you can certainly configure sendmail on your machine to send out any email that you compose locally. Configuration of sendmail can be obscure and difficult - so this document does not attempt to tell you how to do this. However, you should probably configure sendmail so that your Internet service provider is designated as your "smart relay" host (the **sendmail.cf DS** option). (For more sendmail configuration info, see the sendmail documents - and look at the m4 configurations that come with sendmail. There is almost certain to be one there that will meet your needs).

There are also excellent books on Sendmail (notably the 'bible' from O'Reilly and Associates), but these are almost certainly overkill for most users!

Once you have sendmail configured, you will probably want to have sendmail dispatch any messages that have been sitting in the outbound mail queue as soon as the PPP connection comes up. To do this, add the command

```
sendmail -q &
```

to your /etc/ppp/ip-up script (see below).

Inbound email is a problem for dynamic IP numbers. The way to handle this is to:-

- configure your mail user agent so that all mail is sent out with a "reply to" header giving your email address at your Internet Service provider.
  If you can, you should also set your FROM address to be your email address at your ISP as well.

- use the popclient, fetchmail programs to retrieve your email from your service provider. Alternatively, if your ISP is using IMAP, use an IMAP enabled mail user agent (such as pine).

You can automate this process at dial up time by putting the necessary commands in the /etc/ppp/ip-up script (see below).

21.2 Setting Up a local Name server

Whilst you can quite happily use the domain name servers located at your ISP, you can also set up a local caching only (secondary) name server that is brought up by the ip-up script. The advantage of running a local (caching only) name server is that it will save you time (and bandwidth) if you frequently contact the same sites during a long on-line session.

DNS configuration for a caching only nameserver (that uses a "forwarders' line in the named.boot file pointing at your ISPs DNS) is relatively simple. The O'Reilly book (DNS and Bind) explains all you want to know about this.

There is also a DNS-HOWTO available.

If you are running a small LAN that can access the Internet through you Linux PC (using IP Masquerade for example), it is probably a good idea to run a local name server (with a forwarders directive) whilst the link is up as this will minimise the bandwidth and delays associated with name resolution.

One point of Nettiquette: ask permission from your ISP before you start using a secondary, caching only name server in your ISP's domain. Properly configured, your DNS will not cause any problems to your ISP at all, but if you get things wrong, it can cause problems.

22 Linking two networks using PPP

There is basically no difference between linking a single Linux PC to a PPP server and linking two LANs using PPP on a machine on each LAN. Remember, PPP is a **peer to peer** protocol.

However, you **DEFINITELY** need to understand about how routing is established. Read the NET-2 howto and the Linux Network Administrator Guide (NAG). You will also find " TCP/IP Network Administration" (published by O'Reilly and Assoc - ISBN 0-937175-82-X) to be of invaluable assistance.

If you are going to be sub networking an IP network number on either side of the link, you will also find the Linux (draft) sub networking mini-howto) to be of use. This is available at *Linux Sub networking mini-HOWTO* <http://www.interweft.com.au/other/>.

In order to link two LANs, you **must** be using different IP network numbers (or subnets of the same network number) and you will need to use static IP numbers - or use IP masquerade. If you want to use IP masquerade, see the IP masquerade mini-howto for instructions on setting that up.

22.1 Setting up the IP numbers

Arrange with the network administrator of the other LAN the IP numbers that will be used for each end of the PPP interface. If you are using static IP numbers, this will also probably require you to dial into a specific telephone number.

Now edit the appropriate /etc/ppp/options[.ttyXX] file - it's a good idea to have a specific modem and port at your end for this connection. This may well require you to change your /etc/ppp/options file - and create appropriate options.ttyXX files for any other connections!

Specify the IP numbers for your end of the PPP link in the appropriate options file exactly as shown above for static IP numbers.

22.2 Setting up the routing

You must arrange that packets on your local LAN are routed across the interface that the PPP link establishes. This is a two stage process.

First of all, you need to establish a route from the machine running the PPP link to the network(s) at the far end of the link. If the link is to the Internet, this can be handled by a default route established by pppd itself at your end of the connection using the 'defaultroute' option to pppd.

If however, the link is only linking two LANs, then a specific network route must be added for each network that is accessible across the link. This is done using a 'route' command for each network in the /etc/ppp/ip-up script (see After the link comes up...) for instructions on doing this.

The second thing you need to do is to tell the other computers on your LAN that your Linux computer is actually the 'gateway' for the network(s) at the far end of the ppp link.

Of course, the network administrator at the other end of the link has to do all this too! However, as s/he will be routing packets to your specific networks, a **specific network route** will be required, not a default route (unless the LANs at the far and of the link are linking into you to access the Internet across your connection).

22.3   Network security

If you are linking you LAN to the Internet using PPP - or even just to a "foreign" LAN, you need to think about security issues. I strongly urge you to think about setting up a firewall!

You should also speak to the LAN administrator at your site **BEFORE** you start linking to foreign LANs or the Internet this way. Failure to do so could earn you anything from no reaction to really serious trouble!

23   After the link comes up - the /etc/ppp/ip-up script

Once the PPP link is established, pppd looks for **/etc/ppp/ip-up**. If this script exists and is executable, the PPP daemon executes the script. This allows you to automate any special routing commands that may be necessary and any other actions that you want to occur every time the PPP link is activated.

This is just a shell script and can do anything that a shell script can do (i.e. virtually anything you want).

For example, you can get sendmail to dispatch any waiting outbound messages in the mail queue.

Similarly, you can insert the commands into ip-up to collect (using pop) any email waiting for you at your ISP.

There are restrictions on **/etc/ppp/ip-up**:-

- It runs in a deliberately restricted environment to enhance security. This means you must give a full path to binaries etc.

- Technically, **/etc/ppp/ip-up** is a *program* not a script. This means it can be directly executed - and hence it requires the standard file magic (**#!/bin/bash**) at the start of the first line and must be readable and executable by root.

23.1   Special routing

If you are linking two LANs, you will need to set up specific routes to the 'foreign' LANs. This is easily done using the **/etc/ppp/ip-up** script. The only difficulty arises if your machine handles multiple PPP links.

This is because the **/etc/ppp/ip-up** is executed for EVERY ppp connection that comes up, so you need to carefully execute the correct routing commands for the particular link that comes up - and not when any other link comes up!

23.2   Handling email queues

When the link between two LANs comes up, you may well want to make sure that email that is queued at either end is *flushed* - sent out to its destination. This is done by adding the appropriate `sendmail` invocation.

Using the bash 'case' statement on an appropriate parameter that pppd passes into the script accomplishes this. For example, this is the `/etc/ppp/ip-up` script I use to handle our WAN links and the link to my home Ethernet (also handled on the same ppp server).

23.3   A sample `/etc/ppp/ip-up` script

The example below provides a variety of example uses.

```
#!/bin/bash
#
# Script which handles the routing issues as necessary for pppd
# Only the link to Newman requires this handling.
#
# When the ppp link comes up, this script is called with the following
# parameters
#        $1       the interface name used by pppd (e.g. ppp3)
#        $2       the tty device name
#        $3       the tty device speed
#        $4       the local IP address for the interface
#        $5       the remote IP address
#        $6       the parameter specified by the 'ipparam' option to pppd
#
case "$5" in
# Handle the routing to the Newman Campus server
        202.12.126.1)
                /sbin/route add -net 202.12.126.0 gw 202.12.126.1
# and flush the mail queue to get their email there asap!
                /usr/sbin/sendmail -q &
                ;;
        139.130.177.2)
# Our Internet link
# When the link comes up, start the time server and synchronise to the world
# provided it is not already running
                if [ ! -f /var/lock/subsys/xntpd ]; then
                        /etc/rc.d/init.d/xntpd.init start &
                fi
# Start the news server (if not already running)
                if [ ! -f /var/lock/subsys/news ]; then
                        /etc/rc.d/init.d/news start &
                fi
                ;;
        203.18.8.104)
# Get the email down to my home machine as soon as the link comes up
# No routing is required as my home Ethernet is handled by IP
# masquerade and proxyarp routing.
                /usr/sbin/sendmail -q &
```

```
            ;;
      *)
esac
exit 0
```

As a result of bringing up the ppp link to our Newman campus and this script, we end up with the following
routing table entries (this machine also is our general dial up PPP server AND handles our Internet link).
I have interspersed comments in the output to help explain what each entry is) :-

```
[root@kepler /root]# route -n
Kernel routing table
Destination     Gateway         Genmask         Flags MSS   Window Use Iface
# the HOST route to our remote internet gateway
139.130.177.2   *               255.255.255.255 UH    1500  0      134 ppp4
# the HOST route to our Newman campus server
202.12.126.1    *               255.255.255.255 UH    1500  0       82 ppp5
# the HOST route to my home ethernet
203.18.8.104    *               255.255.255.255 UH    1500  0       74 ppp3
# two of our general dial up PPP lines
203.18.8.64     *               255.255.255.255 UH    552   0        0 ppp2
203.18.8.62     *               255.255.255.255 UH    552   0        1 ppp1
# the specific network route to the Newman campus LAN
202.12.126.0    202.12.126.1    255.255.255.0   UG    1500  0        0 ppp5
# the route to our local Ethernet (super-netting two adjacent C classes)
203.18.8.0      *               255.255.254.0   U     1500  0     1683 eth0
# the route to the loop back device
127.0.0.0       *               255.0.0.0       U     3584  0      483 lo
# the default route to the Internet
default         139.130.177.2   *               UG    1500  0     3633 ppp4
```

23.4 Handling email

The previous section shows how to handle the outgoing mail - simply by flushing the mail queue once the
link is up.

If you are running a WAN link, you can arrange with the network administrator of the remote LAN to do
exactly the same thing. For example, at the Newman Campus end of our WAN link, the /etc/ppp/ip-up
script looks like :-

```
#!/bin/bash
#
# Script which handles the routing issues as necessary for pppd
# Only the link to Hedland requires this handling.
#
# When the ppp link comes up, this script is called with the following
# parameters
#     $1      the interface name used by pppd (e.g. ppp3)
#     $2      the tty device name
#     $3      the tty device speed
#     $4      the local IP address for the interface
#     $5      the remote IP address
```

```
#        $6       the parameter specified by the 'ipparam' option to pppd
#
case "$5" in
        203.18.8.4)
                /usr/sbin/sendmail -q
                ;;
        *)
esac
exit 0
```

If however you have only a dynamic IP PPP link to your ISP, you need to get your email from the account on your ISPs machine. This is usually done using the POP (Post Office Protocol). This process can be handled using the 'popclient' program - and the ip-up script can automate this process for you too!

Simply create a **/etc/ppp/ip-up** script that contains the appropriate invocation of popclient. For my laptop that runs Red Hat Linux (which I take on any travels), this is

```
popclient -3 -c -u hartr -p <password> kepler.hedland.edu.au |formail -s procmail
```

You could use slurp or whatever to do the same for news, and so forth. Remember, the ip-up script is just a standard bash script and so can be used to automate ANY function that needs to be accomplished every time the appropriate PPP link comes up.

24   Using /etc/ppp/ip-down

You can create a script that will be executed once the link has been terminated. This is stored in /etc/ppp/ip-down. It can be used to undo anything special that you did in the corresponding /etc/ppp/ip-up script.

25   Routing issues on a LAN

If you are connected to a LAN but still want to use PPP on your personal Linux machine , you need to address some issues of the routes packets need to take from your machine to reach your LAN (through your Ethernet interface) and also to the remote PPP server and beyond.

This section does NOT attempt to teach you about routing - it deals only with a simple, special case of (static) routing!

I strongly urge you to read the Linux Network Administrator Guide (NAG) if you are NOT familiar with routing. Also the O'Reilly book "TCP/IP Network Administration" covers this topic in a very understandable form.

The basic rule of static routing is that the DEFAULT route should be the one that points to the MOST number of network addresses. For other networks, enter specific routes to the routing table.

The ONLY situation I am going to cover here is where your Linux box is on a LAN that is not connected to the Internet - and you want to dial out to the Internet for personal use whilst still connected to the LAN.

First of all, make sure that your Ethernet route is set up to the specific network addresses available across your LAN - NOT set to the default route!

Check this by issuing a route command, you should see something like the following:-

```
[root@hwin /root]# route -n
Kernel routing table
Destination   Gateway        Genmask         Flags MSS    Window Use Iface
loopback      *              255.255.255.0   U     1936    0       50 lo
10.0.0.0      *              255.255.255.0   U     1436    0      565 eth0
```

If your Ethernet interface (eth0) is pointing at the default route, (the first column will show "default" in the eth0 line) you need to change your Ethernet initialisation scripts to make it point at the specific network numbers rather than the default route (consult the Net2 HOWTO and NAG).

This will allow pppd to set up your default route as shown below:-

```
[root@hwin /root]# route -n
Kernel routing table

Destination     Gateway        Genmask         Flags MSS    Window Use Iface
10.144.153.51   *              255.255.255.255 UH    488     0        0 ppp0
127.0.0.0       *              255.255.255.0   U     1936    0       50 lo
10.1.0.0        *              255.255.255.0   U     1436    0      569 eth0
default         10.144.153.51  *               UG    488     0        3 ppp0
```

As you can see, we have a host route to the PPP server (10.144.153.51) via ppp0 and also a default network route that uses the PPP server as its gateway.

If your set up needs to be more complex than this - read the routing documents already mentioned and consult an expert at your site!

If your LAN already has routers on it, you will already have gateways established to the wider networks available at your site. You should STILL point your default route at the PPP interface - and make the other routes specific to the networks they serve.

25.1   Note on Security

When you set up a Linux box on an existing LAN to link into the Internet, you are potentially opening your entire LAN to the Internet - and the hackers that reside there. Before you do this, I strongly urge you to consult your network administrator and site security policy. If your PPP connection to the Internet is used to successfully attack your site, you will at the very least earn the intense anger of your fellow users, network and system administrators. You may also find yourself in very much more serious trouble!

Before you connect a LAN to the Internet, you should consider the security implications of even a DYNAMIC connection - hence the earlier reference to the O'Reilly "Building Internet Firewalls"!

26   Setting up a PPP server

As already mentioned, there are many ways to do this. What I present here is the way I do it (using a Cyclades multi-port serial card) and a rotary dial in set of telephone lines.

If you don't like the method I present here, please feel free to go your own way. I would however, be pleased to include additional methods in future versions of the HOWTO. So, please send me your comments and methods!

Please note, this section only concerns setting up Linux as a PPP server. I do not (ever) intend to include information on setting up special terminal servers and such.

Also, I have yet to experiment with shadow passwords (but will be doing so sometime). Information currently presented does NOT therefore include any bells and whistles that are required by the shadow suite.

26.1   Kernel compilation

All the earlier comments regarding kernel compilation and kernel versions versus pppd versions apply. This section assumes that you have read the earlier sections of this document!

For a PPP server, you **MUST** include IP forwarding in your kernel. You may also wish to include other capabilities (such as IP fire walls, accounting etc etc).

If you are using a multi-port serial card, then you must obviously include the necessary drivers in your kernel too!

26.2   Overview of the server system

We offer dial up PPP (and SLIP) accounts and shell accounts using the same user name/password pair. This has the advantages (for us) that a user requires only one account and can use it for all types of connectivity.

As we are an educational organisation, we do not charge our staff and students for access, and so do not have to worry about accounting and charging issues.

We operate a firewall between our site and the Internet, and this restricts some user access as the dial up lines are inside our (Internet) firewall (for fairly obvious reasons, details of our other internal fire walls are not presented here and are irrelevant in any case).

The process a user goes through to establish a PPP link to our site (once they have a valid account of course) is :-

- Dial into our rotary dialer (this is a single phone number that connects to a bank of modems - the first free modem is then used).

- Log in using a valid user name and password pair.

- At the shell prompt, issue the command **ppp** to start PPP on the server.

- Start PPP on their PC (be it running Windows, DOS, Linux MAC OS or whatever - that is their problem).

The server uses individual **/etc/ppp/options.ttyXX** files for each dial in port that set the remote IP number for dynamic IP allocation. The server users proxyarp routing for the remote clients (set via the appropriate option to pppd). This obviates the need for routed or gated.

When the user hangs up at their end, pppd detects this and tells the modem to hang up, bringing down the PPP link at the same time.

26.3   Getting the software together

You will need the following software:-

- Linux, properly compiled to include the necessary options.

- The appropriate version of pppd for your kernel.

- A 'getty' program that intelligently handles modem communications.
  We use getty_ps2.0.7h, but mgetty is highly thought of. I understand that mgetty can detect a call that is using pap/chap (pap is the standard for Windows95) and invoke pppd automatically, but I have yet to explore this.

- An operational domain name server (DNS) that is accessible to your dial up users.
  You should really be running your own DNS if possible...

26.4 Setting up standard (shell access) dialup.

Before you can set up your PPP server, your Linux box must be capable of handling standard dial up access.

This howto does NOT cover setting this up. Please see the documentation of the getty of your choice and serial HOWTO for information on this.

26.5 Setting up the PPP options files

You will need to set up the overall /etc/ppp/options with the common options for all dial up ports. The options we use are:-

```
asyncmap 0
netmask 255.255.254.0
proxyarp
lock
crtscts
modem
```

Note - we do NOT use any (obvious) routing - and in particular there is no defaultroute option. The reason for this is that all you (as a PPP server) are required to do is to route packets **from** the ppp client out across your LAN/Internet and route packets **to** the client from your LAN and beyond.

All that is necessary for this is a host route to the client machine and the use of the 'proxyarp' option to pppd.

The 'proxyarp' option sets up (surprise) a proxy ARP entry in the PPP server's ARP table that basically says 'send all packets destined for the PPP client to me'. This is the easiest way to set up routing to a single PPP client - but you cannot use this if you are routing between two LANs - you must add proper network routes which can't use proxy ARP.

You will almost certainly wish to provide dynamic IP number allocation to your dial up users. You can accomplish this by allocating an IP number to each dial up port. Now, create a /etc/ppp/options.ttyXX for each dial up port.

In this, simply put the local (server) IP number and the IP number that is to be used for that port. For example

```
kepler:slip01
```

In particular, note that you can use valid host names in this file (I find that I only remember the IP numbers of critical machines and devices on my networks - names are more meaningful)!

26.6   Setting pppd up to allow users to (successfully) run it

As starting a ppp link implies configuring a kernel device (a network interface) and manipulating the kernel routing tables, special privileges are required - in fact full root privileges.

Fortunately, pppd has been designed to be 'safe' to run set uid to root. So you will need to

```
chmod u+s /usr/sbin/pppd
```

When you list the file, it should then appear as

```
-rwsr-xr-x   1 root     root        74224 Apr 28 07:17 /usr/sbin/pppd
```

If you do not do this, users will be unable to set up their ppp link.

26.7   Setting up the global alias for pppd

In order to simplify things for our dial up PPP users, we create a global alias (in /etc/bashrc) so that one simple command will start ppp on the server once they are logged in.

This looks like

```
alias ppp="exec /usr/sbin/pppd -detach"
```

What this does is

- exec : this means replace the running program (in this case the shell) with the program that is run.
- pppd -detach : start up pppd and do NOT fork into the background. This ensures that when pppd exits there is no process hanging around.

When a user logs in like this, they will appear in the output of 'w' as

```
  6:24pm  up 3 days,  7:00,  4 users,  load average: 0.05, 0.03, 0.00
User     tty       login@ idle   JCPU   PCPU  what
hartr    ttyC0     3:05am 9:14                -
```

And that is it...I told you this was a simple, basic PPP server system!

27   Using PPP across a null modem (direct serial) connection

This is very simple - there is no modem in the way so things are much simpler.

First of all, choose one of the machines as a 'server', setting up a getty on the serial port so you can test that you do have connectivity using minicom to access the serial port on the 'client'.

Once you have this functioning, you can remove the getty UNLESS you want to make sure that the connection is validated using user name/password pairs as for a dial up connection. As you have 'physical control' of both machines, I will presume that you do NOT want to do this.

Now, on the server, remove the getty and make sure that you have the serial ports on both machines configured correctly using 'setserial'.

All you need to do now is to start pppd on both systems. I will assume that the connection uses /dev/ttyS34 on both machines. So, on both machines execute the command:-

```
pppd -detach crtscts lock <local IP>:<remote IP> /dev/ttyS3 38400 &
```

This will bring up the link - but as yet you have no routing specified. You can test the link by pinging to and fro to each machine. If this works, bring down the link by killing one of the pppd processes.

The routing you need will of course depend on exactly what you are trying to do. Generally, one of the machines will be connected to an Ethernet (and beyond) and so the routing required is exactly the same as for a PPP server and client.

So on the Ethernet equipped machine, the pppd command would be

```
pppd -detach crtscts lock proxyarp <local IP>:<remote IP> /dev/ttyS3 38400 &
```

and on the other machine

```
pppd -detach crtscts lock defaultroute <local IP>:<remote IP> /dev/ttyS3 38400 &
```

If you are linking two networks (using a serial link!) or have more complex routing requirements, you can use /etc/ppp/ip-up in exactly the same way as mentioned earlier in this document.

Robert Hart
Port Hedland, Western Australia
Melbourne, Victoria, Australia August/October 1996 January/March 1997

ISP-Connectivity-mini-HOWTO

Michael Strates, `mstrates@croftj.net` v2.0, 6 November 1997

This document describes how to setup PPP, connect up to your ISP, configure mail and news, get a permanent IP (if available), get a domain name, and have a bonda fide system running in a little over thirty minutes.

Contents

1 Introduction

The main goal of this document obviously is to make the new user friendly with the many terms of connecting your Linux PC up to the Internet, obtaining IP addresses, domain names, and setting things up. This guide is intended for the intermediate user in mind, although intelligent newbies shouldn't have any problems.

1.1 New versions of this document

New versions of this document will be periodically posted to *comp.os.linux.answers*. They will also be added to the various anonymous FTP sites who archive such information, including:

ftp://sunsite.unc.edu/pub/Linux/docs/HOWTO `<ftp://sunsite.unc.edu/pub/Linux/docs/HOWTO>`

In addition, you should generally be able to find this document on the Linux Documentation Project page via:

http://sunsite.unc.edu/LDP/ `<http://sunsite.unc.edu/LDP/>`

1.2 Feedback

I certaintly welcome any feedback about this HOWTO, spelling mistakes, how it all worked out, thankyou notes and critisisms. I hope I helped a few people with this HOWTO, and if I did, I'd be really happy to hear from you.

mstrates@croftj.net <mailto:mstrates@croftj.net>

http://linloft.home.ml.org/ <http://linloft.home.ml.org/>

1.3 Standard Disclaimer

No liability for the contents of this documents can be accepted. Use the concepts, examples and other content at your own risk. As this is a new edition of this document, there may be errors and inaccuracies, that may of course be damaging to your system. Proceed with caution, and although this is highly unlikely, I don't take any responsibility for that.

Naturally, there are probably better and easier ways to do things in this document. There will always be another way in the Linux World. This is the way I've done things, and that's the way I'll be presenting them in this HOWTO.

1.4 Copyright Information

This document is copyrighted (c)1997 Michael Strates and distributed under the following terms:

- Linux HOWTO documents may be reproduced and distributed in whole or in part, in any medium physical or electronic, as long as this copyright notice is retained on all copies. Commercial redistribution is allowed and encouraged; however, the author would like to be notified of any such distributions.
- All translations, derivative works, or aggregate works incorporating any Linux HOWTO documents must be covered under this copyright notice. That is, you may not produce a derivative work from a HOWTO and impose additional restrictions on its distribution. Exceptions to these rules may be granted under certain conditions; please contact the Linux HOWTO coordinator at the address given below.
- If you have questions, please contact Greg Hankins, the Linux HOWTO coordinator, at

gregh@sunsite.unc.edu <mailto:gregh@sunsite.unc.edu> Finger for phone number and snail mail address.

2 Connecting to the Outside World

In this document, we'll explain how to do this using PPP (Point to Point Protocol), a popular protocol nearly always used over the Internet. It allows your modem to **speak** to the outside world. This is what applications like Trumpet Winsock in Windows 3.x did, and many other programs that you've probably have never seen.

In Linux, we use a thing called chat to do the dialing up to the ISP and then use a utility called pppd to 'use' the connection. In a sense, chat is your dialer, and pppd is your protocol. We'll describe how to setup both below.

2.1 Talking and Communicating with pppd and chat

Probably the easiest way to go about things is to make a shell script in root's home directory called **ppp-connect** and involke the script whenever you wish to make your connection. We'll discuss this method.

Open up your favourite editor as root on /ppp-connect. You'll then have to decide on your parameters.

pppd connect 'chat -v "" "your_init_string" "" ATDTisp_number CONNECT "" ogin: your_username word: your_passwd' /dev/tty(0/1/2) speed modem

pppd involkes /usr/sbin/pppd on my system, then loads up chat to do the dialing. Chat sends *your_init_string* to the modem, then dials *isp_number*. It then waits for CONNECT, then waits for ogin: (l removed as the first character is sometimes lost), sends *your_passwd*, chat then terminates and hands the show over to pppd.

The last of the command specifies your modem port (mine's /dev/ttyS1). In most cases it will be ttyS1 (COM2: in DOS), ttyS0 (COM1: in DOS), or if your using Slackware, cua1 or cua0. The speed is the speed of the modem. I use 115200 for my modem (a 33.6k). If you have got a fairly recent computer (one with a 16550 UART), then I wouldn't go any lower than 57600. Otherwise, for 14.4k 38400. Modem just tells pppd that it's a serial/modem based connection. Remove the -v option if you don't want verbose logging to your logfiles.

The scenario below is one of a person who dials up an ISP that automatically starts PPP for them, ie; they don't have a shell that actually starts. This is his command in his /ppp-connect:

pppd connect 'chat "" "ATZ" "" ATDT555-1800 CONNECT "" ogin: johnny word: blackjak' /dev/ttyS1 115200 modem

But for some people, they're ISP starts up a shell and doesn't automatically start PPP this may be a problem. Luckily, chat can deal with that too. You just add another command to your chat script. For example, below this johnny character is using an ISP that just dumps him to a shell, requiring him to type ppp to get a ppp connection. His shell prompt ends with a $. *pppd connect 'chat "" "ATZ" "" ATDT555-1800 CONNECT "" ogin: johnny word: blackjak $ ppp' /dev/ttyS1 115200 modem*

If it's more than one word, ensure you quote it. I hope you can see the drift of this, and are able to create your own script up to suit your connection. Simply modify either the first johnny or the second johnny script to suit your taste, port, server, etc and save the file.

Now you've made your file, ensure that only root can execute, read or write to it. This is extreemly important. Also make sure nobody can read your logfiles, if you decide to leave the -v option in, as your password is seen in cleartext in the logs (I don't see much need for -v, if you don't know what I'm talking about, leave -v out).

2.2   IP's, Domain Names and Subnets

For most people using the options above, a changing IP address won't bother them. These people include basic, easy going users, that just have dialup accounts, and aren't very technically minded. For those people, skim read this section, I'll come to important things you need to do to setup your system properly. Newbies, skip the sections dealing with permanent IP, Domain Names, Subnets, and just read the last bit of this section.

Getting a permanent IP address might be free for your ISP, so if in doubt ask them. Personally, I'd pay for a permanent IP address. It lets you send e-mail to and from using a unique IP or domain, etc. If you want to get yourself a permanent IP, write an e-mail to root@yourisp.com, and ask him nicely if he can arrange a permanent IP for you.

When you get your permanent IP address, grep through your /etc directory to find where your old IP addresses are. I had to change files in my sendmail directory and /etc/hosts. There are some other key files that you will only discover with grepping. Open up /etc/hosts, and add your new IP address in the standard format. Reboot your computer, and you should be ready to go.

You'll now need to change your chat script to reflect your new settings. If you are forced into PPP as soon as you start your connection, you'll need to tell your System Administrator of your ISP to ensure their PPP system recognises that you have a permanent IP address and allocates you that instead of a changing one. If you get dumped at a shell prompt, and you need to type ppp or something to start the connection, instead of typing that, change your /ppp-connect script to send this instead of just ppp or whatever when it sees $ or whatever your shell prompt is.

/usr/sbin/pppd :Your_IP_Address

Substitute your IP address for the IP address your ISP gave to you. Be sure you encapsulate the thing in " " marks when you put it into your chat script. If this doesn't work, consult your ISP where your PPP daemon is located, and ask him for the command to give. You could just try leaving it as is and seeing if the server will recognise you and give you your rightful address.

The next thing probably to do is to get yourself a domain name. I know that in Australia, .asn.au and .org.au are free. In the United States, you can get a .us domain for free, but they tend to be long. If your in Australia, you must go to *http://www.aunic.net/* <http://www.aunic.net/> to register your domains. In the United States, it is *http://www.internic.net/* <http://www.internic.net/> .

To register domains you need to be able to provide DNS services, and gorey stuff like that. If your ISP can't provide these, throw out an official .asn.au or whatever domain out the window, and get a Monolith Internet Domain.

Monolith offer free domains to anybody and anyone all around the world. Everything is done without human interaction, via a web forms interface with your browser. Your domain comes in the form of Your_Choice.ml.org. Monolith will then host the DNS locally for you. If you want to send and receive mail from that domain, ask your ISP to become a mail exchanger for you.

Go to *http://www.ml.org/* <http://www.ml.org/> and fill out an application, enter the NIC with your username and password, and make a FREED domain. You'll need to enter your IP address, so have that ready. Your domain will be in the DNS in a couple of days.

Okay now, we'll move onto the newbies section, or for those people who can't get a permanent IP address or a domain name. All you have to do is edit /etc/hosts as root, call your site something that won't clash, give it a 10.10.10 or something for an IP address and reboot your computer.

There you go, you've just setup your computer with pppd and chat in just ten minutes. Now let's move onto the next section, which deals with Electronic Mail.

3   Electronic Mail on your Linux Box

One of the most important aspects of the Internet, is it's fasinating capaiblity to transfer mail to and from countries, or more locally perhaps. Linux is extreemly strong in easy mail packages for the console. The one we're going to document today is called Pine (Program for Internet Mail and News), made by the University of Washington, and to download the mail, a program called Fetchmail, made by Eric S. Raymond. Both should be included in your Linux distribution.

Fetchmail is a program that downloads your e-mail from your server using POP, transfers the mail onto your computer and then deletes it off the server, much like programs like Eudora or Microsoft Internet Mail/Exchange do. To configure and automate fetchmail, you use a file in your home directory called .fetchmailrc. Simply open up /.fetchmailrc (Remember: your doing this bit as yourself, not as root) with your favourite editor and observe the command lin eoptions below:

poll mail.yourisp.com proto pop3 user login_name password your_passwd

user login_name with pass your_passwd is login_name here

All you have to do is replace *mail.yourisp.com* with the name of the mail server of your ISP, *your_passwd* with your password, and *login_name* with your login name.

An important thing to note. For Pine and this procedure to work correctly, your login name must corrospond with the login name you use on your ISP. That is your local login name must match the one you use on your server, and your e-mail address.

Next, ensure that .fetchmailrc has the correct permissions (user read/write only) and your laughing. Fetchmail can be started in two ways, in standard mode (where it'll fetch messages from the server and terminate), or in daemon mode (where it will stay active, and check/download mail every X seconds). To use daemon mode, type *fetchmail -a -d(Seconds between Polls)*. -a ensures it downloads all mail. To use the standard mode, just type *fetchmail -a*.

Next, you need to setup Pine. Open up Pine, by typing pine at your prompt, choose Setup - Configuration. Setup your userdomain as the domain in your e-mail address, for example jack@linux.org, would be linux.org. Next, setup smtp-server as your POP mail server (the same you used in the fetchmail setup). So we enter www.linux.org. If you want news, setup your nntp server to your ISP's news server.

So there you have it folks, everything should be working now. To connect up to your ISP, just run /ppp-connect as root. Then, to get your e-mail run fetchmail -a as yourself. To browse your e-mail and news, use Pine. Install a text-based browser such as Lynx to browse the web if you like.

Send any comments questions and suggestions to mstrates@croftj.net

Linux Mail-Queue mini-HOWTO

Leif Erlingsson, leif@lege.com, Jan P Tietze, jptietze@mail.hh.provi.de   v2.02, 03 September 1997, sendmail 8.8.7

Queue Remote Mail + Deliver Local Mail The Configuration Changes Neccessary to Make Sendmail Deliver Local Mail ***Now*** While Stashing Remote Mail in The Queue Until "I Say So".

Contents

1 Introduction

The document is written by two authors. The NON dial-on-demand solutions part (oldest part) is written by Leif Erlingsson <leif@lege.com>, and the newer dial-on-demand solutions part is written by Jan P Tietze <jptietze@mail.hh.provi.de>.

2 NON dial-on-demand solutions PART

Written by Leif Erlingsson <leif@lege.com>.

The original version of this part contained a lot of unnecessary stuff. This is all it takes, really...

2.1 Starting sendmail

Slackware et al: /etc/rc.d/rc.M:

```
echo "Starting sendmail daemon (/usr/sbin/sendmail -bd -os) [queue only mode]..."
/usr/sbin/sendmail -bd -os        # NOT "-bd -q 15m", the "standard" flags!
```

RedHat et al: /etc/rc.d/init.d/sendmail.init:

```
echo -n "Starting sendmail: [queue only mode]"
daemon sendmail -bd -os           # NOT daemon sendmail -bd -q1h
```

The -os is not really essential, all it does is this:

```
SuperSafe [s] Be super-safe when running things, i.e.,
        always instantiate the queue file, even if
        you are going to attempt immediate delivery.
        Sendmail always instantiates the queue file
        before returning control the client under
        any circumstances. This should really
        always be set.
```

This should already be configured in the default sendmail.cf anyway.

2.2 Configuring sendmail

Serious sendmail users use the m4 source for this. I recommend this solution if you ever plan on upgrading sendmail and also make anything but trivial changes to sendmail.cf.

If you never intend to fix sendmail so envelope return headers et al works even though you might be on dynamic dial in IP or something, then you may not need to get the m4 source.

2.2.1 Configuring sendmail.cf directly, for trivial configurations

This way of doing things is extremeley version dependent vs. sendmail.cf versions. The following solution is *only* valid for sendmail-8.8.x.

Edit /etc/sendmail.cf:

```
# avoid connecting to "expensive" mailers on initial submission?
O HoldExpensive=True
```

... later ...

```
#####  @(#)smtp.m4      8.33 (Berkeley) 7/9/96  #####

Msmtp,        P=[IPC], F=mDFMuXe, S=11/31, R=21, E=\r\n, L=990,
              T=DNS/RFC822/SMTP,
              A=IPC $h

Mesmtp,       P=[IPC], F=mDFMuXae, S=11/31, R=21, E=\r\n, L=990,
              T=DNS/RFC822/SMTP,
              A=IPC $h

Msmtp8,       P=[IPC], F=mDFMuX8e, S=11/31, R=21, E=\r\n, L=990,
              T=DNS/RFC822/SMTP,
              A=IPC $h

Mrelay,       P=[IPC], F=mDFMuXa8e, S=11/31, R=61, E=\r\n, L=2040,
              T=DNS/RFC822/SMTP,
              A=IPC $h
```

The important flag above is "e". Don't fuss if the other flags look different in your file. Keep your flags as-is, only add "e" to your flags according to the above examples, unless it's there already. "e" marks the mailers as "expensive".

2.2.2   Configuring sendmail.cf using m4 source

In the following I will, for simplicity, assume that the sendmail version is 8.8.7. If you have a different version, replace 8.8.7 with that version number below! Also, the instructions will not work for older versions of sendmail. Get the latest sendmail!

Download the sendmail source. Try "http://WWW.Sendmail.ORG" or possibly "ftp.sendmail.org".

I also recommend that you obtain my patch for allowing envelope sender reverse aliasing and other nice stuff to really make you take control over your mail environment.

Write to "Sendmail Patch <sendmail@lege.com>", Subject: "sendmail-8.8.7", if 8.8.7 is your sendmail version.

They are also available from "http://www.lege.com", as is the sgml source of this mini-HOWTO!

You don't have to get my patches in order to get "Queue Remote Mail + Deliver Local Mail" to work. My patches solve other things. But I just thought this would be a nice place to mention them, as many Linux users will find them extremely useful. (They will even give you properly working virtual domains, if you like. The virtual domains don't have to be "local". They will give you "xaliases", or in other words "reverse aliasing".)

Unpack the sendmail source. You may get /usr/src/sendmail-8.8.7/. cd /usr/src/sendmail-8.8.7/cf

Now overlay my patch, if you want it, otherwise skip this step: If you don't want to use procmail as Local Delivery Agent, save away your /usr/src/sendmail-8.8.7/cf/ostype/linux.m4 before doing this... Save my patch to "/tmp/sendmail-8.8.7-cf-cpio-idcmu.gz", then...

```
cd /usr/src/sendmail-8.8.7/cf
gzip -dc < /tmp/sendmail-8.8.7-cf-cpio-idcmu.gz | cpio -idcmu
```

If you didn't want to use procmail, write back the saved copy of /usr/src/sendmail-8.8.7/cf/ostype/linux.m4 again.

And regardless of if you applied my patch or not, you must make sure these lines or very similar ones are added to /usr/src/sendmail-8.8.7/cf/cf/yourhostname.smtp.mc (but if you applied my patch you may want to investigate filenames containing the word "elijah", under /usr/src/sendmail-8.8.7/cf):

```
dnl # Defer Delivery to "expensive" mailers until next time the
dnl # queue is processed using "O HoldExpensive=True" and make
dnl # sure smtp mailers are "expensive".
dnl # (See original "sendmail" book Chapter 30: Options,
dnl # "Oc - Don't connect to expensive mailers", or
dnl # 2nd Edition "sendmail" book Chapter 34.8.29,
dnl # "HoldExpensive (c), Queue for expensive mailers".)
dnl #                          / Leif Erlingsson <leif@lege.com>
define('confCON_EXPENSIVE', 'True')
define(SMTP_MAILER_FLAGS, e)
MAILER(local)dnl
MAILER(smtp)dnl
```

2.3   Menu support suggestions

The 1.x versions of this document contained Menu support suggestions for /var/X11R6/lib/fvwm/system.fvwmrc. I have dropped those in the current version, but they are available on request:

Write to "Menu support suggestions <fvwmrc@lege.com>", Subject: "Menu support suggestions"

3   Dial-on-demand solutions PART

Written by Jan P Tietze <jptietze@mail.hh.provi.de>.

Many Linux users access the Internet through a dialup line, and many have decided to implement dial-on-demand facilities on their system. That is, whenever an IP packet of some sort has to leave the local network or the local host, the link to an Internet Service Provider (ISP) will automatically be established. The link will be dropped after some period of time that no packet has travelled across.

Although this is very comfortable and cost effective, there is one special case in which this is neither comfortable (as the time to bring up a "traditional" modem dialup is very noticeable) nor cost effective, and this is sending e-mail. E-Mail is commonly sent by SMTP, either delivered by your own system or through a SMTP host on the Internet that usually resides in your ISP's network.

With dialup lines, every time you send a message the link will have to be brought up. This is quite okay if you send only one message, but if you happen to create and send multiple messages, bringing up the line more than once can be tedious and cost ineffective. Also, if your ISP imposes limits as to what times you are allowed to login, this would also restrict you to postpone messages at certain times of the day, and you would have to manually send them later.

Section 1 of this document will solve the situation, however in situations where an external DNS lookup would cause the link up, the link will still be established even if e-mail is just being queued. The reason is that sendmail wishes to "canonify" host names.

The solution to this problem is twofold: First, we'll have to moderately change sendmail.cf. And then we have to define the process of actual mail delivery. Personally, I prefer to have cron do the job for me and describe the necessary changes below.

3.1 Configuring sendmail.cf

For the reasons stated in [1.2], I recommend modifying the m4 sources instead of editing sendmail.cf directly. It will actually save you a lot of hassle and make configuration changes more verbose.

First, perform all the changes described in the first part of this document. Then go through the dial-on-demand specific stuff.

3.1.1 Configuring sendmail.cf directly, for trivial configurations

Configuring directly is highly impractical and anything but verbose, but obviously, this is your decision.

Close to very bottom of your sendmail.cf should be a line that reads:

```
R$* < @ $* $P > $*                    $: $1 < @ $[ $2 $3 $] > $4
```

Precede that line with a "#" so that it reads

```
#R$* < @ $* $P > $*                   $: $1 < @ $[ $2 $3 $] > $4
```

3.1.2 Configuring sendmail.cf using the m4 source.

Add the following line to /usr/src/sendmail-8.8.7/cf/cf/yourhostname.smtp.mc:

```
FEATURE(nocanonify)dnl
```

Your final sendmail.cf can then be built by issuing the following commands. Remember to always back up your old /etc/sendmail.cf before installing the new one:

```
cp /etc/sendmail.cf /etc/sendmail.cf.bak
cd /usr/src/sendmail-8.8.7/cf/cf
m4 yourhostname.smtp.mc > /etc/sendmail.cf
```

3.2 Adding dial delay

It is oftentimes useful, especially when using modem lines, to have a dial delay installed. This means that if sendmail tries to initiate a connection in an attempt to send an e-mail (and this causes the line to go up) but the link actually takes more time to get established than what sendmail thinks should be a reasonable timeout, sendmail will simply wait some seconds and then retry.

3.2.1 Configuring sendmail.cf directly

Somewhere in your sendmail.cf could be a line that would read:

```
#O DialDelay=10s
```

(or very similar). Delete the "#". If there's no "#" at the beginning of the line, things should be considered okay (it just means this had already been enabled before).

If there is no such line in your sendmail.cf, add one (it is a wise thing to do to add this in the "options" part of the file):

```
O DialDelay=10s
```

Now change the "10s" part to the number of seconds you deem suitable.

3.2.2   Configuring sendmail.cf using m4 source

Add the following line to /usr/src/sendmail-8.8.7/cf/cf/yourhostname.smtp.mc:

```
define('confDIAL_DELAY','10s')
```

Now change the "10s" part to the number of seconds you deem suitable.

Your final sendmail.cf can then be built by issuing the following commands. Remember to always back up your old /etc/sendmail.cf before installing the new one:

```
cp /etc/sendmail.cf /etc/sendmail.cf.bak
cd /usr/src/sendmail-8.8.7/cf/cf
m4 yourhostname.smtp.mc > /etc/sendmail.cf
```

4   Delivering e-mail

E-Mail delivery can be invoked by issuing the command "sendmail -q". For those who are interested in what sendmail actually does, "sendmail -q -v" will give a more verbose version of the delivery process.

It is very convenient to automate the process of e-mail delivery. A tool commonly used for this process is cron.

4.1   How to have e-mail delivered at special times.

Edit your crontab:

```
crontab -e
```

Add lines of the form:

```
05 18-23,0-7    * * Mon,Tue,Wed,Thu,Fri /usr/sbin/sendmail -q
05 *            * * Sat,Sun             /usr/sbin/sendmail -q
```

Please refer to the crontab man page (available through "man 5 \ crontab") for further information. I think the format is pretty obvious. The example crontab entries shown above send e-mail (if, and only if, e-mail is available from the queue) 5 minutes after an hour on weekdays, starting at 6:05 pm, and stopping at 7:05 am. On weekends, e-mail is delivered 5 minutes after an hour, starting at 12:05 pm on Saturday, and stopping 11:05 pm on Sunday.

As a dial-on-demand user, it is sometimes desirable to have your system collect your e-mail via the POP3 protocol at certain times of the day. You could therefore add an entry similar to the following to your crontab:

```
0 21           * * * popclient -3 -u <your pop3 user name
goes here> -p <put your password here> -o /var/spool/mail/<the user
on your system that should receive the collected e-mail>
<mailhost.somedomain.com>
```

Of course, this should all go on a single line.

Then, save the file and leave the editor. The crontab should now be installed.

Linux WWW HOWTO

by Wayne Leister, *n3mtr@qis.net* <mailto:n3mtr@qis.net>   v0.82, 19 November 1997

This document contains information about setting up WWW services under Linux (both server and client). It tries not to be a in detail manual but an overview and a good pointer to further information.

Contents

1   Introduction

Many people are trying Linux because they are looking for a really good *Internet capable* operating system. Also, there are institutes, universities, non-profits, and small businesses which want to set up Internet sites on a small budget. This is where the WWW-HOWTO comes in. This document explains how to set up clients and servers for the largest part of the Internet - *The World Wide Web*.

All prices in this document are stated in US dollars. This document assumes you are running Linux on an Intel platform. Instructions and product availability my vary from platform to platform. There are many links for downloading software in this document. Whenever possible use a mirror site for faster downloading and to keep the load down on the main server.

The US government forbids US companies from exporting encryption stronger than 40 bit in strength. Therefore US companies will usually have two versions of software. The import version will usually support 128 bit, and the export only 40 bit. This applies to web browsers and servers supporting secure transactions. Another name for secure transactions is Secure Sockets Layer (SSL). We will refer to it as SSL for the rest of this document.

1.1   Copyright

This document is Copyright (c) 1997 by Wayne Leister. The original author of this document was Peter Dreuw.(All versions prior to 0.8)

This document is distributed in the hope that it will be useful, but without any warranty; without even the implied warranty of merchantability or fitness for a particular purpose. See the GNU General Public License for more details.

You can obtain a copy of the GNU General Public License by writing to the Free Software Foundation, Inc., 675 Mass Ave, Cambridge, MA 02139, USA.

Trademarks are owned by there respective owners.

1.2 Feedback

Any feedback is welcome. I do not claim to be an expert. Some of this information was taken from badly written web sites; there are bound to be errors and omissions. But make sure you have the latest version before you send corrections; It may be fixed in the next version (see the next section for where to get the latest version). Send feedback to *n3mtr@qis.net* `<mailto:n3mtr@qis.net>`.

1.3 New versions of this Document

New versions of this document can be retrieved in text format from Sunsite at `<http://sunsite.unc.edu/pub/Linux/docs/HOWTO/WWW-HOWTO>` and almost any Linux mirror site. You can view the latest HTML version on the web at `<http://sunsite.unc.edu/LDP/HOWTO/WWW-HOWTO.html>`. There are also HTML versions available on Sunsite in a tar archive.

2 Setting up WWW client software

The following chapter is dedicated to the setting up web browsers. Please feel free to contact me, if your favorite web browser is not mentioned here. In this version of the document only a few of the browsers have there own section, but I tried to include all of them (all I could find) in the overview section. In the future those browsers that deserve there own section will have it.

The overview section is designed to help you decide which browser to use, and give you basic information on each browser. The detail section is designed to help you install, configure, and maintain the browser.

Personally, I prefer the Netscape; it is the only browser that keeps up with the latest things in HTML. For example, Frames, Java, Javascript, style sheets, secure transactions, and layers. Nothing is worse than trying to visit a web site and finding out that you can't view it because your browser doesn't support some new feature.

However I use Lynx when I don't feel like firing up the X-windows/Netscape monster.

2.1 Overview

5 (Navigator/Communicator)

Netscape Navigator is the only browser mentioned here, which is capable of advanced HTML features. Some of these features are frames, Java, Javascript, automatic update, and layers. It also has news and mail capability. But it is a resource hog; it takes up lots of CPU time and memory. It also sets up a separate cache for each user wasting disk space. Netscape is a commercial product. Companies have a 30 day trial period, but there is no limit for individuals. I would encourage you to register anyway to support Netscape in there efforts against Microsoft (and what is a measly $40US). My guess is if Microsoft wins, we will be forced to use MS Internet Explorer on a Windows platform :(

3 (Lynx)

Lynx is the one of the smallest web browsers. It is the king of text based browsers. It's free and the source code is available under the GNU public license. It's text based, but it has many special features.

Kfm

Kfm is part of the K Desktop Environment (KDE). KDE is a system that runs on top of X-windows. It gives you many features like drag an drop, sounds, a trashcan and a unified look and feel. Kfm is the K File Manager, but it is also a web browser. Don't be fooled by the name, for a young product it is very usable as a web browser. It already supports frames, tables, ftp downloads, looking into tar files, and more. The current version of Kfm is 1.39, and it's free. Kfm can be used without KDE, but you still need the librarys that come with KDE. For more information about KDE and Kfm visit the KDE website at `<http://www.kde.org>`.

4 (Emacs)

Emacs is the one program that does everything. It is a word processor, news reader, mail reader, and web browser. It has a steep learning curve at first, because you have to learn what all the keys do. The X-windows version is easier to use, because most of the functions are on menus. Another drawback is that it's mostly text based. (It can display graphics if you are running it under X-windows). It is also free, and the source code is available under the GNU public license.

NCSA Mosaic

Mosaic is an X-windows browser developed by the National Center for Supercomputing Applications (NCSA) at the University of Illinois. NCSA spent four years on the project and has now moved on to other things. The latest version is 2.6 which was released on July 7, 1995. Source code is available for non-commercial use. *Spyglass Inc.* `<http://www.spyglass.com>` has the commercial rights to Mosaic. Its a solid X-windows browser, but it lacks the new HTML features. For more info visit the NCSA Mosaic home page at `<http://www.ncsa.uiuc.edu/SDG/Software/Mosaic/>`. The software can be downloaded from `<ftp://ftp.ncsa.uiuc.edu/Mosaic/Unix/binaries/2.6/Mosaic-linux-2.6.Z>`.

Arena

Arena was a X-windows concept browser for the W3C (World Wide Web Consortium) when they were testing HTML 3.0. Hence it supports all the HTML 3.0 standards such as style sheets and tables. Development was taken over by Yggdrasil Computing, with the idea to turn it into a full fledge free X-windows browser. However development has stopped in Feb 1997 with version 0.3.11. Only part of the HTML 3.2 standard has been implemented. The source code is released under the GNU public licence. For more information see the web site at `<http://www.yggdrasil.com/Products/Arena/>`. It can be downloaded from `<ftp://ftp.yggdrasil.com/pub/dist/web/arena/>`.

Amaya

Amaya is the X-windows concept browser for the W3C for HTML 3.2. Therefore it supports all the HTML 3.2 standards. It also supports some of the features of HTML 4.0. It supports tables, forms, client side image maps, put publishing, gifs, jpegs, and png graphics. It is both a browser and authoring tool. The latest public release is 1.0 beta. Version 1.1 beta is in internal testing and is due out soon. For more information visit the Amaya web site at `<http://www.w3.org/Amaya/>`. It can be downloaded from `<ftp://ftp.w3.org/pub/Amaya-LINUX-ELF-1.0b.tar.gz>`.

Red Baron

Red Baron is an X-windows browser made by Red Hat Software. It is bundled with The Official Red Hat Linux distribution. I could not find much information on it, but I know it supports frames, forms and SSL. If you use Red Baron, please help me fill in this section. For more information visit the Red Hat website at `<http://www.redhat.com>`

Chimera

Chimera is a basic X-windows browser. It supports some of the features of HTML 3.2. The latest release is 2.0 alpha 6 released August 27, 1997. For more information visit the Chimera website at `<http://www.unlv.edu/chimera/>`. Chimera can be downloaded from `<ftp://ftp.cs.unlv.edu/pub/chimera-alpha/chimera-2.0a6.tar.gz>`.

Qweb

Qweb is yet another basic X-windows browser. It supports tables, forms, and server site image maps. The latest version is 1.3. For more information visit the Qweb website at `<http://sunsite.auc.dk/qweb/>` The source is available from `<http://sunsite.auc.dk/qweb/qweb-1.3.tar.gz>` The binaries are available in a Red Hat RPM from `<http://sunsite.auc.dk/qweb/qweb-1.3-1.i386.rpm>`

Grail

Grail is an X-windows browser developed by the Corporation for National Research Initiatives (CNRI). Grail is written entirely in Python, a interpreted object-oriented language. The latest version is 0.3 released on May 7, 1997. It supports forms, bookmarks, history, frames, tables, and many HTML 3.2 things.

Internet Explorer

There are rumors, that Microsoft is going to port the Internet Explorer to various Unix platforms - maybe Linux. If its true they are taking their time doing it. If you know something more reliable, please drop me an e-mail.

In my humble opinion most of the above software is unusable for serious web browsing. I'm not trying to discredit the authors, I know they worked very hard on these projects. Just think, if all of these people had worked together on one project, maybe we would have a free browser that would rival Netscape and Internet Explorer.

In my opinion out of all of the broswers, Netscape and Lynx are the best. The runners up would be Kfm, Emacs-W3 and Mosaic.

3 Lynx

Lynx is one of the smaller (around 600 K executable) and faster web browsers available. It does not eat up much bandwidth nor system resources as it only deals with text displays. It can display on any console, terminal or xterm. You will not need an *X Windows system* or additional system memory to run this little browser.

3.1 Where to get

Both the Red Hat and Slackware distributions have Lynx in them. Therefore I will not bore you with the details of compiling and installing Lynx.

The latest version is 2.7.1 and can be retrieved from `<http://www.slcc.edu/lynx/fote/>` or from almost any friendly Linux FTP server like *ftp://sunsite.unc.edu under /pub/Linux/apps/www/broswers/* `<ftp://sunsite.unc.edu/pub/Linux/apps/www/browsers/>` or mirror site.

For more information on Lynx try these locations:

Lynx Links

`<http://www.crl.com/~subir/lynx.html>`

Lynx Pages

`<http://lynx.browser.org>`

Lynx Help Pages

`<http://www.crl.com/~subir/lynx/lynx_help/lynx_help_main.html>` (the same pages you get from lynx –help and typing ? in lynx)

Note: The Lynx help pages have recently moved. If you have an older version of Lynx, you will need to change your lynx.cfg (in /usr/lib) to point to the new address(above).

I think the most special feature of Lynx against all other web browsers is the capability for batch mode retrieval. One can write a shell script which retrieves a document, file or anything like that via *http*, *FTP*, *gopher*, *WAIS*, *NNTP* or *file://* - url's and save it to disk. Furthermore, one can fill in data into HTML forms in batch mode by simply redirecting the standard input and using the *-post_data* option.

For more special features of Lynx just look at the help files and the man pages. If you use a special feature of Lynx that you would like to see added to this document, let me know.

4   Emacs-W3

There are several different flavors of Emacs. The two most popular are GNU Emacs and XEmacs. GNU Emacs is put out by the Free Software Foundation, and is the original Emacs. It is mainly geared toward text based terminals, but it does run in X-Windows. XEmacs (formerly Lucid Emacs) is a version that only runs on X-Windows. It has many special features that are X-Windows related (better menus etc).

4.1   Where to get

Both the Red Hat and Slackware distributions include GNU Emacs.

The most recent GNU emacs is 19.34. It doesn't seem to have a web site. The FTP site is at `<ftp://ftp.gnu.ai.mit.edu/pub/gnu/>`.

The latest version of XEmacs is 20.2. The XEmacs FTP site is at `<ftp://ftp.xemacs.org/pub/xemacs>`. For more information about XEmacs goto see its web page at `<http://www.xemacs.org>`.

Both are available from the Linux archives at *ftp://sunsite.unc.edu under /pub/Linux/apps/editors/emacs/* `<ftp://sunsite.unc.edu/pub/Linux/apps/editors/emacs/>`

If you got GNU Emacs or XEmacs installed, you probably got the W3 browser running to.

The Emacs W3 mode is a nearly fully featured web browser system written in the Emacs Lisp system. It mostly deals with text, but can display graphics, too - at least - if you run the emacs under the X Window system.

To get XEmacs in to W3 mode, goto the apps menu and select browse the web.

I don't use Emacs, so if someone will explain how to get it into the W3 mode I'll add it to this document. Most of this information was from the original author. If any information is incorrect, please let me know. Also let me know if you think anything else should be added about Emacs.

5   Netscape Navigator/Communicator

5.1   Different versions and options.

Netscape Navigator is the King of WWW browsers. Netscape Navigator can do almost everything. But on the other hand, it is one of the most memory hungry and resource eating program I've ever seen.

There are 3 different versions of the program:

Netscape Navigator includes the web browser, netcaster (push client) and a basic mail program.

Netscape Communicator includes the web browser, a web editor, an advanced mail program, a news reader, netcaster (push client), and a group conference utility.

Netscape Communicator Pro includes everything Communicator has plus a group calendar, IBM terminal emulation, and remote administration features (administrators can update thousands of copies of Netscape from their desk).

In addition to the three versions there are two other options you must pick.

The first is full install or base install. The full install includes everything. The base install includes enough to get you started. You can download the additional components as you need them (such as multimedia support and netcaster). These components can be installed by the Netscape smart update utility (after installing goto help->software updates). At this time the full install is not available for Linux.

The second option is import or export. If you are from the US are Canada you have the option of selecting the import version. This gives you the stronger 128 bit encryption for secure transactions (SSL). The export version only has 40 bit encryption, and is the only version allowed outside the US and Canada.

The latest version of the Netscape Navigator/Communicator/Communicator Pro is 4.03. There are two different versions for Linux. One is for the old 1.2 series kernels and one for the new 2.0 kernels. If you don't have a 2.0 kernel I suggest you upgrade; there are many improvements in the new kernel.

Beta versions are also available. If you try a beta version, they usually expire in a month or so!

5.2   Where to get

The best way to get Netscape software is to go through their web site at `<http://www.netscape.com/ download/>`. They have menu's to guide you through the selection. When it ask for the Linux version, it is referring to the kernel (most people should be using 2.0 by now). If your not sure which version kernel you have run 'cat /proc/version'. Going through the web site is the only way to get the import versions.

If you want an export version you can download them directly from the Netscape FTP servers. The FTP servers are also more up to date. For example when I first wrote this the web interface did not have the non-beta 4.03 for Linux yet, but it was on the FTP site. Here are the links to the export Linux 2.0 versions:

Netscape Navigator 4.03 is at `<ftp://ftp.netscape.com/pub/communicator/4.03/shipping/english/ unix/linux20/navigator_standalone/navigator-v403-export.x86-unknown-linux2.0.tar.gz>`

Netscape Communicator 4.03 for Linux 2.0 (kernel) is at `<ftp://ftp.netscape.com/pub/communicator/4. 03/shipping/english/unix/linux20/base_install/communicator-v403-export.x86-unknown-linux2. 0.tar.gz>`

Communicator Pro 4.03 for Linux was not available at the time I wrote this.

These url's will change as new versions come out. If these links break you can find them by fishing around at the FTP site `<ftp://ftp.netscape.com/pub/communicator/>`.

These servers are heavily loaded at times. Its best to wait for off peak hours or select a mirror site. Be prepared to wait, these archives are large. Navigator is almost 8megs, and Communicator base install is 10megs.

5.3   Installing

This section explains how to install version 4 of Netscape Navigator, Communicator, and Communicator Pro.

First unpack the archive to a temporary directory. Then run the `ns-install` script (type `./ns-install`). Then make a symbolic link from the `/usr/local/netscape/netscape` binary to `/usr/local/bin/netscape` (type `ln -s /usr/local/netscape/netscape /usr/local/bin/netscape`). Finally set the system wide environment variable `$MOZILLA_HOME` to `/usr/local/netscape` so Netscape can find its files. If you are using bash for your shell edit your `/etc/profile` and add the lines:

```
MOZILLA_HOME="/usr/local/netscape"
export MOZILLA_HOME
```

After you have it installed the software can automatically update itself with smart update. Just run Netscape as root and goto help->software updates. If you only got the base install, you can also install the Netscape components from there.

Note: This will not remove any old versions of Netscape, you must manually remove them by deleting the Netscape binary and Java class file (for version 3).

6   Setting up WWW server systems

This section contains information on different http server software packages and additional server side tools like script languages for CGI programs etc. There are several dozen web servers, I only covered those that are fully functional. As some of these are commercial products, I have no way of trying them. Most of the information in the overview section was pieced together from various web sites. If there is any incorrect or missing information please let me know.

For a technical description on the http mechanism, take a look at the RFC documents mentioned in the chapter "For further reading" of this HOWTO.

I prefer to use the Apache server. It has almost all the features you would ever need and its free! I will admit that this section is heavily biased toward Apache. I decided to concentrate my efforts on the Apache section rather than spread it out over all the web servers. I may cover other web servers in the future.

6.1   Overview

Cern httpd

This was the first web server. It was developed by the European Laboratory for Particle Physics (CERN). CERN httpd is no longer supported. The CERN httpd server is reported to have some ugly bugs, to be quite slow and resource hungry. The latest version is 3.0. For more information visit the CERN httpd home page at `<http://www.w3.org/Daemon/Status.html>`. It is available for download at `<ftp://sunsite.unc.edu/pub/Linux/apps/www/servers/httpd-3.0.term.tpz>` (no it is not a typo, the extension is actually .tpz on the site; probably should be .tgz)

NCSA HTTPd

The NCSA HTTPd server is the father to Apache (The development split into two different servers). Therefore the setup files are very similar. NCSA HTTPd is free and the source code is available. This server not covered in this document, although reading the Apache section may give you some help. The NCSA server was once popular, but most people are replacing it with Apache. Apache is a drop in replacement for the NCSA server(same configuration files), and it fixes several shortcomings of the NCSA server. NCSA HTTPd accounts for 4.9% (and falling) of all web servers. (source September 1997 *Netcraft survey* `<http://www.netcraft.com/survey/>`). The latest version is 1.5.2a. For more information see the NCSA website at `<http://hoohoo.ncsa.uiuc.edu>`.

7 (Apache)

Apache is the king of all web servers. Apache and its source code is free. Apache is modular, therefore it is easy to add features. Apache is very flexible and has many, many features. Apache and its derivatives makes up 44% of all web domains (50% if you count all the derivatives). There are over 695,000 Apache servers in operation (source November 1997 *Netcraft survey* `<http://www.netcraft.com/survey/>`).

The official Apache is missing SSL, but there are two derivatives that fill the gap. Stronghold is a commercial product that is based on Apache. It retails for $995; an economy version is available for $495 (based on an old version of Apache). Stronghold is the number two secure server behind Netscape (source *C2 net* `<http://www.c2.net/products/stronghold>` and *Netcraft survey* `<http://www.netcraft.com/survey/>`). For more information visit the Stronghold website at `<http://www.c2.net/products/stronghold/>`. It was developed outside the US, so it is available with 128 bit SSL everywhere.

Apache-SSL is a free implementation of SSL, but it is not for commercial use in the US (RSA has US patents on SSL technology). It can be used for non-commercial use in the US if you link with the free RSAREF library. For more information see the website at `<http://www.algroup.co.uk/Apache-SSL/>`.

Netscape Fast Track Server

Fast Track was developed by Netscape, but the Linux version is put out by Caldera. The Caldera site lists it as Fast Track for OpenLinux. I'm not sure if it only runs on Caldera OpenLinux or if any Linux distribution will do (E-mail me if you have the answer). Netscape servers account for 11.5% (and falling) of all web servers (source September 1997 `<http://www.netcraft.com/survey/>`). The server sells for $295. It is also included with the Caldera OpenLinux Standard distribution which sells for $399 ($199.50 educational). The web pages tell of a nice administration interface and a quick 10 minute setup. The server has support for 40-bit SSL. To get the full 128-bit SSL you need Netscape Enterprise Server. Unfortunately that is not available for Linux :(The latest version available for Linux is 2.0 (Version 3 is in beta, but its not available for Linux yet). To buy a copy goto the Caldera web site at `<http://www.caldera.com/products/netscape/netscape.html>` For more information goto the Fast Track page at `<http://www.netscape.com/comprod/server_central/product/fast_track/>`

WN

WN has many features that make it attractive. First it is smaller than the CERN, NCSA HTTPd, an Apache servers. It also has many built-in features that would require CGI's. For example site searches, enhanced server side includes. It can also decompress/compress files on the fly with its filter feature. It also has the ability to retrieve only part of a file with its ranges feature. It is released under the GNU public license. The current version is 1.18.3. For more information see the WN website at `<http://hopf.math.nwu.edu/>`.

AOLserver

AOLserver is made by America Online. I'll admit that I was surprised by the features of a web server coming from AOL. In addition to the standard features it supports database connectivity. Pages can query a database by Structured Query Language (SQL) commands. The database is access through Open Database Connectivity (ODBC). It also has built-in search engine and TCL scripting. If that is not enough you can add your own modules through the c Application Programming Interface (API). I almost forgot to mention support for 40 bit SSL. And you get all this for free! For more information visit the AOLserver site at `<http://www.aolserver.com/server/>`

Zeus Server

Zeus Server was developed by Zeus Technology. They claim that they are the fastest web server (using WebSpec96 benchmark). The server can be configured and controlled from a web browser! It can limit processor and memory resources for CGI's, and it executes them in a secure environment (whatever that means). It also supports unlimited virtual servers. It sells for $999 for the standard version. If you want the secure server (SSL) the price jumps to $1699. They are based outside the US so 128 bit SSL is available everywhere. For more information visit the Zeus Technology website at `<http://www.zeus.co.uk>`. The US website is at `<http://www.zeus.com>`. I'll warn you they are cocky about the fastest web server thing. But they don't even show up under top web servers in the Netcraft Surveys.

CL-HTTP

CL-HTTP stands for Common Lisp Hypermedia Server. If you are a Lisp programmer this server is for you. You can write your CGI scripts in Lisp. It has a web based setup function. It also supports all the standard server features. CL-HTTP is free and the source code is available. For more information visit the CL-HTTP website at `<http://www.ai.mit.edu/projects/iiip/doc/cl-http/home-page.html>` (could they make that url any longer?).

If you have a commercial purpose (company web site, or ISP), I would strongly recommend that you use Apache. If you are looking for easy setup at the expense of advanced features then the Zeus Server wins hands down. I've also heard that the Netscape Server is easy to setup. If you have an internal use you can be a bit more flexible. But unless one of them has a feature that you just have to use, I would still recommend using one of the three above.

This is only a partial listing of all the servers available. For a more complete list visit Netcraft at `<http://www.netcraft.com/survey/servers.html>` or Web Compare at `<http://webcompare.internet.com>`.

7 Apache

The current version of Apache is 1.2.4. Version 1.3 is in beta testing. The main Apache site is at `<http://www.apache.org/>`. Another good source of information is Apacheweek at `<http://www.apacheweek.com/>`. The Apache documentation is ok, so I'm not going to go into detail in setting up apache. The documentation is on the website and is included with the source (in HTML format). There are also text files included with the source, but the HTML version is better. The documentation should get a whole lot better once the Apache Documentation Project gets under way. Right now most of the documents are written by the developers. Not to discredit the developers, but they are a little hard to understand if you don't know the terminology.

7.1 Where to get

Apache is included in the Red Hat, Slackware, and OpenLinux distributions. Although they may not be the latest version, they are very reliable binaries. The bad news is you will have to live with their directory choices (which are totally different from each other and the Apache defaults).

The source is available from the Apache web site at `<http://www.apache.org/dist/>` Binaries are are also available at apache at the same place. You can also get binaries from sunsite at `<ftp://sunsite.unc.edu/pub/Linux/apps/www/servers/>`. And for those of us running Red Hat the latest binary RPM file can usually be found in the contrib directory at `<ftp://ftp.redhat.com/pub/contrib/i386/>`

If your server is going to be used for commercial purposes, it is highly recommended that you get the source from the Apache website and compile it yourself. The other option is to use a binary that comes with a major distribution. For example Slackware, Red Hat, or OpenLinux distributions. The main reason for this is security. An unknown binary could have a back door for hackers, or an unstable patch that could crash your system. This also gives you more control over what modules are compiled in, and allows you to set the default directories. It's not that difficult to compile Apache, and besides you not a real Linux user until you compile your own programs ;)

7.2 Compiling and Installing

First untar the archive to a temporary directory. Next change to the src directory. Then edit the Configuration file if you want to include any special modules. The most commonly used modules are already included. There is no need to change the rules or makefile stuff for Linux. Next run the Configure shell script (`./Configure`). Make sure it says Linux platform and gcc as the compiler. Next you may want to edit the httpd.h file to change the default directories. The server home (where the config files are kept) default is **/usr/local/etc/httpd/**, but you may want to change it to just **/etc/httpd/**. And the server root (where the HTML pages are served from) default is **/usr/local/etc/httpd/htdocs/**, but I like the directory **/home/httpd/html** (the Red Hat default for Apache). If you are going to be using su-exec (see special features below) you may want to change that directory too. The server root can also be changed from the config files too. But it is also good to compile it in, just encase Apache can't find or read the config file. Everything else should be changed from the config files. Finally run make to compile Apache.

If you run in to problems with include files missing, check the following things. Make sure you have the kernel headers (include files) installed for your kernel version. Also make sure you have these symbolic links in place:

```
/usr/include/linux should be a link to /usr/src/linux/include/linux
/usr/include/asm should be a link to /usr/src/linux/include/asm
/usr/src/linux should be a link to the Linux source directory (ex.linux-2.0.30)
```

Links can be made with `ln -s`, it works just like the cp command except it makes a link (`ln -s source-dir destination-link`)

When make is finished there should be an executable named httpd in the directory. This needs to be moved in to a bin directory. **/usr/sbin** or **/usr/local/sbin** would be good choices.

Copy the conf, logs, and icons sub-directories from the source to the server home directory. Next rename 3 of the files files in the conf sub-directory to get rid of the **-dist** extension (ex. **httpd.conf-dist** becomes **httpd.conf**)

There are also several support programs that are included with Apache. They are in the **support** directory and must be compiled and installed separately. Most of them can be make by using the makefile in that directory (which is made when you run the main **Configure** script). You don't need any of them to run Apache, but some of them make the administrators job easier.

7.3 Configuring

Now you should have four files in your **conf** sub-directory (under your server home directory). The **httpd.conf** sets up the server daemon (port number, user, etc). The **srm.conf** sets the root document tree, special handlers, etc. The **access.conf** sets the base case for access. Finally **mime.types** tells the server what mime type to send to the browser for each extension.

The configuration files are pretty much self-documented (plenty of comments), as long as you understand the lingo. You should read through them thoroughly before putting your server to work. Each configuration item is covered in the Apache documentation.

The **mime.types** file is not really a configuration file. It is used by the server to translate file extensions into mime-types to send to the browser. Most of the common mime-types are already in the file. Most people should not need to edit this file. As time goes on, more mime types will be added to support new programs. The best thing to do is get a new mime-types file (and maybe a new version of the server) at that time.

Always remember when you change the configuration files you need to restart Apache or send it the SIGHUP signal with **kill** for the changes to take effect. Make sure you send the signal to the parent process and not any of the child processes. The parent usually has the lowest process id number. The process id of the parent is also in the **httpd.pid** file in the log directory. If you accidently send it to one of the child processes the child will die and the parent will restart it.

I will not be walking you through the steps of configuring Apache. Instead I will deal with specific issues, choices to be made, and special features.

I highly recommend that all users read through the security tips in the Apache documentation. It is also available from the Apache website at `<http://www.apache.org/docs/mics/security_tips.html>`.

7.4   Hosting virtual websites

Virtual Hosting is when one computer has more than one domain name. The old way was to have each virtual host have its own IP address. The new way uses only one IP address, but it doesn't work correctly with browsers that don't support HTTP 1.1.

My recommendation for businesses is to go with the IP based virtual hosting until most people have browsers that support HTTP 1.1 (give it a year or two). This also gives you a more complete illusion of virtual hosting. While both methods can give you virtual mail capabilities (can someone confirm this?), only IP based virtual hosting can also give you virtual FTP as well.

If it is for a club or personal page, you may want to consider shared IP virtual hosting. It should be cheaper than IP based hosting and you will be saving precious IP addresses.

You can also mix and match IP and shared IP virtual hosts on the same server. For more information on virtual hosting visit Apacheweek at `<http://www.apacheweek.com/features/vhost>`.

7.4.1   IP based virtual hosting

In this method each virtual host has its own IP address. By determining the IP address that the request was sent to, Apache and other programs can tell what domain to serve. This is an incredible waste of IP space. Take for example the servers where my virtual domain is kept. They have over 35,000 virtual accounts, that means 35,000 IP addresses. Yet I believe at last count they had less than 50 servers running.

Setting this up is a two part process. The first is getting Linux setup to accept more than one IP address. The second is setting up apache to serve the virtual hosts.

The first step in setting up Linux to accept multiple IP addresses is to make a new kernel. This works best with a 2.0 series kernel (or higher). You need to include IP networking and IP aliasing support. If you need help with compiling the kernel see the *kernel howto* `<http://sunsite.unc.edu/LDP/HOWTO/Kernel-HOWTO.html>`.

Next you need to setup each interface at boot. If you are using the Red Hat Distribution then this can be done from the control panel. Start X-windows as root, you should see a control panel. Then double click on network configuration. Next goto the interfaces panel and select your network card. Then click alias at the bottom of the screen. Fill in the information and click done. This will need to be done for each virtual host/IP address.

If you are using other distributions you may have to do it manually. You can just put the commands in the `rc.local` file in `/etc/rc.d` (really they should go in with the networking stuff). You need to have a `ifconfig` and `route` command for each device. The aliased addresses are given a sub device of the main one. For example eth0 would have aliases eth0:0, eth0:1, eth0:2, etc. Here is an example of configuring a aliased device:

```
ifconfig eth0:0 192.168.1.57
route add -host 192.168.1.57 dev eth0:0
```

You can also add a broadcast address and a netmask to the ifconfig command. If you have alot of aliases you may want to make a for loop to make it easier. For more information see the *IP alias mini howto* `<http://sunsite.unc.edu/LDP/HOWTO/mini/IP-Alias.html>`.

Then you need to setup your domain name server (DNS) to serve these new domains. And if you don't already own the domain names, you need to contact the *Internic* <http://www.internic.net> to register the domain names. See the DNS-howto for information on setting up your DNS.

Finally you need to setup Apache to server the virtual domain correctly. This is in the `httpd.conf` configuration file near the end. They give you an example to go by. All commands specific to that virtual host are put in between the `virtualhost` directive tags. You can put almost any command in there. Usually you set up a different document root, script directory, and log files. You can have almost unlimited number of virtual hosts by adding more `virtualhost` directive tags.

In rare cases you may need to run separate servers if a directive is needed for a virtual host, but is not allowed in the virtual host tags. This is done using the bindaddress directive. Each server will have a different name and setup files. Each server only responds to one IP address, specified by the bindaddress directive. This is an incredible waste of system resources.

7.4.2 Shared IP virtual hosting

This is a new way to do virtual hosting. It uses a single IP address, thus conserving IP addresses for real machines (not virtual ones). In the same example used above those 30,000 virtual hosts would only take 50 IP addresses (one for each machine). This is done by using the new HTTP 1.1 protocol. The browser tells the server which site it wants when it sends the request. The problem is browsers that don't support HTTP 1.1 will get the servers main page, which could be setup to provide a menu of virtual hosts available. That ruins the whole illusion of virtual hosting. The illusion that you have your own server.

The setup is much simpler than the IP based virtual hosting. You still need to get your domain from the Internic and setup your DNS. This time the DNS points to the same IP address as the original domain. Then Apache is setup the same as before. Since you are using the same IP address in the virtualhost tags, it knows you want Shared IP virtual hosting.

There are several work arounds for older browsers. I'll explain the best one. First you need to make your main pages a virtual host (either IP based or shared IP). This frees up the main page for a link list to all your virtual hosts. Next you need to make a back door for the old browsers to get in. This is done using the `ServerPath` directive for each virtual host inside the `virtualhost` directive. For example by adding `ServerPath /mysite/` to www.mysite.com old browsers would be able to access the site by www.mysite.com/mysite/. Then you put the default page on the main server that politely tells them to get a new browser, and lists links to all the back doors of all the sites you host on that machine. When an old browser accesses the site they will be sent to the main page, and get a link to the correct page. New browsers will never see the main page and will go directly to the virtual hosts. You must remember to keep all of your links relative within the web sites, because the pages will be accessed from two different URL's (www.mysite.com and www.mysite.com/mysite/).

I hope I didn't lose you there, but its not an easy workaround. Maybe you should consider IP based hosting after all. A very similar workaround is also explained on the apache website at <http://www.apache.org/manual/host.html>.

If anyone has a great resource for Shared IP hosting, I would like to know about it. It would be nice to know what percent of browsers out there support HTTP 1.1, and to have a list of which browsers and versions support HTTP 1.1.

7.5   CGI scripts

There are two different ways to give your users CGI script capability. The first is make everything ending in `.cgi` a CGI script. The second is to make script directories (usually named `cgi-bin`). You could also use both methods. For either method to work the scripts must be world executable (`chmod 711`). By giving your users script access you are creating a big security risk. Be sure to do your homework to minimize the security risk.

I prefer the first method, especially for complex scripting. It allows you to put scripts in any directory. I like to put my scripts with the web pages they work with. For sites with allot of scripts it looks much better than having a directory full of scripts. This is simple to setup. First uncomment the `.cgi` handler at the end of the `srm.conf` file. Then make sure all your directories have the `option ExecCGI` or `All` in the `access.conf` file.

Making script directories is considered more secure. To make a script directory you use the ScriptAlias directive in the `srm.conf` file. The first argument is the Alias the second is the actual directory. For example `ScriptAlias /cgi-bin/ /usr/httpd/cgi-bin/` would make `/usr/httpd/cgi-bin` able to execute scripts. That directory would be used whenever someone asked for the directory `/cgi-bin/`. For security reasons you should also change the properties of the directory to `Options none, AllowOverride none` in the `access.conf` (just uncomment the example that is there). Also do not make your script directories subdirectories of your web page directories. For example if you are serving pages from `/home/httpd/html/`, don't make the script directory `/home/httpd/html/cgi-bin`; Instead make it `/home/httpd/cgi-bin`.

If you want your users to have there own script directories you can use multiple `ScriptAlias` commands. Virtual hosts should have there `ScriptAlias` command inside the `virtualhost` directive tags. Does anyone know a simple way to allow all users to have a cgi-bin directory without individual ScriptAlias commands?

7.6   Users Web Directories

There are two different ways to handle user web directories. The first is to have a subdirectory under the users home directory (usually `public_html`). The second is to have an entirely different directory tree for web directories. With both methods make sure set the access options for these directories in the `access.conf` file.

The first method is already setup in apache by default. Whenever a request for `/~bob/` comes in it looks for the `public_html` directory in bob's home directory. You can change the directory with the `UserDir` directive in the `srm.conf` file. This directory must be world readable and executable. This method creates a security risk because for Apache to access the directory the users home directory must be world executable.

The second method is easy to setup. You just need to change the `UserDir` directive in the `srm.conf` file. It has many different formats; you may want to consult the Apache documentation for clarification. If you want each user to have their own directory under `/home/httpd/`, you would use `UserDir /home/httpd`. Then when the request `/~bob/` comes in it would translate to `/home/httpd/bob/`. Or if you want to have a subdirectory under bob's directory you would use `UserDir /home/httpd/*/html`. This would translate to `/home/httpd/bob/html/` and would allow you to have a script directory too (for example `/home/httpd/bob/cgi-bin/`).

7.7   Daemon mode vs. Inetd mode

There are two ways that apache can be run. One is as a daemon that is always running (Apache calls this standalone). The second is from the inetd super-server.

Daemon mode is far superior to inetd mode. Apache is setup for daemon mode by default. The only reason to use the inetd mode is for very low use applications. Such as internal testing of scripts, small company Intranet, etc. Inetd mode will save memory because apache will be loaded as needed. Only the inetd daemon will remain in memory.

If you don't use apache that often you may just want to keep it in daemon mode and just start it when you need it. Then you can kill it when you are done (be sure to kill the parent and not one of the child processes).

To setup inetd mode you need to edit a few files. First in **/etc/services** see if http is already in there. If its not then add it:

```
http    80/tcp
```

Right after 79 (finger) would be a good place. Then you need to edit the **/etc/inetd.conf** file and add the line for Apache:

```
http    stream  tcp     nowait  root    /usr/sbin/httpd httpd
```

Be sure to change the path if you have Apache in a different location. And the second httpd is not a typo; the inet daemon requires that. If you are not currently using the inet daemon, you may want to comment out the rest of the lines in the file so you don't activate other services as well (FTP, finger, telnet, and many other things are usually run from this daemon).

If you are already running the inet deamon (**inetd**), then you only need to send it the SIGHUP signal (via kill; see kill's man page for more info) or reboot the computer for changes to take effect. If you are not running **inetd** then you can start it manually. You should also add it to your init files so it is loaded at boot (the **rc.local** file may be a good choice).

7.8   Allowing put and delete commands

The newer web publishing tools support this new method of uploading web pages by http (instead of FTP). Some of these products don't even support FTP anymore! Apache does support this, but it is lacking a script to handle the requests. This script could be a big security hole, be sure you know what you are doing before attempting to write or install one.

If anyone knows of a script that works let me know and I'll include the address to it here.

For more information goto Apacheweek's article at **<http://www.apacheweek.com/features/put>**.

7.9   User Authentication/Access Control

This is one of my favorite features. It allows you to password protect a directory or a file without using CGI scripts. It also allows you to deny or grant access based on the IP address or domain name of the client. That is a great feature for keeping jerks out of your message boards and guest books (you get the IP or domain name from the log files).

To allow user authentication the directory must have **AllowOverrides AuthConfig** set in the **access.conf** file. To allow access control (by domain or IP address) AllowOverrides Limit must be set for that directory.

Setting up the directory involves putting an **.htaccess** file in the directory. For user authentication it is usually used with an **.htpasswd** and optionally a **.htgroup** file. Those files can be shared among multiple **.htaccess** files if you wish.

For security reasons I recommend that everyone use these directives in there access.conf file:

```
<files ~ "/\.ht">
order deny,allow
deny from all
</files>
```

If you are not the administrator of the system you can also put it in your .htaccess file if AllowOverride Limit is set for your directory. This directive will prevent people from looking into your access control files (.htaccess, .htpasswd, etc).

There are many different options and file types that can be used with access control. Therefore it is beyond the scope of this document to describe the files. For information on how to setup User Authentication see the Apacheweek feature at `<http://www.apacheweek.com/features/userauth>` or the NCSA pages at `<http://hoohoo.ncsa.uiuc.edu/docs-1.5/tutorials/user.html>`.

7.10   su-exec

The su-exec feature runs CGI scripts as the user of the owner. Normally it is run as the user of the web server (usually nobody). This allows users to access there own files in CGI scripts without making them world writable (a security hole). But if you are not careful you can create a bigger security hole by using the su-exec code. The su-exec code does security checks before executing the scripts, but if you set it up wrong you will have a security hole.

The su-exec code is not for amateurs. Don't use it if you don't know what you are doing. You could end up with a gaping security hole where your users can gain root access to your system. Do not modify the code for any reason. Be sure to read all the documentation carefully. The su-exec code is hard to setup on purpose, to keep the amateurs out (everything must be done manually, no make file no install scripts).

The su-exec code resides in the **support** directory of the source. First you need to edit the **suexec.h** file for your system. Then you need to compile the su-exec code with this command:

```
gcc suexec.c -o suexec
```

Then copy the suexec executable to the proper directory. The Apache default is **/usr/local/etc/httpd/sbin/**. This can be changed by editing **httpd.h** in the Apache source and recompiling Apache. Apache will only look in this directory, it will not search the path. Next the file needs to be changed to user root (**chown root suexec**) and the suid bit needs to be set (**chmod 4711 suexec**). Finally restart Apache, it should display a message on the console that su-exec is being used.

CGI scripts should be set world executable like normal. They will automaticaly be run as the owner of the CGI script. If you set the SUID (set user id) bit on the CGI scripts they will not run. If the directory or file is world or group writable the script will not run. Scripts owned by system users will not be run (root, bin, etc.). For other security conditions that must be met see the su-exec documentation. If you are having problems see the su-exec log file named **cgi.log**.

Su-exec does not work if you are running Apache from inetd, it only works in daemon mode. It will be fixed in the next version because there will be no inetd mode. If you like playing around in source code, you can edit the http_main.c. You want to get rid of the line where Apache announces that it is using the su-exec wrapper (It wrongly prints this in front of the output of everything).

Be sure and read the Apache documentation on su-exec. It is included with the source and is available on the Apache web site at `<http://www.apache.org/docs/suexec.html>`

7.11   Imagemaps

Apache has the ability to handle server side imagemaps. Imagemaps are images on webpages that take users to different locations depending on where they click. To enable imagemaps first make sure the imagemap module is installed (its one of the default modules). Next you need to uncomment the **.map** handler at the end of the **srm.conf** file. Now all files ending in **.map** will be imagemap files. Imagemap files map different areas on the image to separate links. Apache uses map files in the standard NCSA format. Here is an example of using a map file in a web page:

```
<a href="/map/mapfile.map">
<img src="picture.gif" ISMAP>
</a>
```

In this example `mapfile.map` is the mapfile, and `picture.gif` is the image to click on.

There are many programs that can generate NCSA compatible map files or you can create them yourself. For a more detailed discussion of imagemaps and map files see the Apacheweek feature at `<http://www.apacheweek.com/features/imagemaps>`.

7.12   SSI/XSSI

Server Side Includes (SSI) adds dynamic content to otherwise static web pages. The includes are embedded in the web page as comments. The web server then parses these includes and passes the results to the web server. SSI can add headers and footers to documents, add date the document was last updated, execute a system command or a CGI script. With the new eXtended Server Side Includes (XSSI) you can do a whole lot more. XSSI adds variables and flow control statements (if, else, etc). Its almost like having an programming language to work with.

Parsing all HTML files for SSI commands would waste allot of system resources. Therefore you need to distinguish normal HTML files from those that contain SSI commands. This is usually done by changing the extension of the SSI enhanced HTML files. Usually the `.shtml` extension is used.

To enable SSI/XSSI first make sure that the includes module is installed. Then edit `srm.conf` and uncomment the `AddType` and `AddHandler` directives for `.shtml` files. Finally you must set `Options Includes` for all directories where you want to run SSI/XSSI files. This is done in the `access.conf` file. Now all files with the extension `.shtml` will be parsed for SSI/XSSI commands.

Another way of enabling includes is to use the `XBitHack` directive. If you turn this on it looks to see if the file is executable by user. If it is and `Options Includes` is on for that directory, then it is treated as an SSI file. This only works for files with the mime type text/html (`.html .htm` files). This is not the preferred method.

There is a security risk in allowing SSI to execute system commands and CGI scripts. Therefore it is possible to lock that feature out with the `Option IncludesNOEXEC` instead of Option Includes in the `access.conf` file. All the other SSI commands will still work.

For more information see the Apache mod_includes documentation that comes with the source. It is also available on the website at `<http://www.apache.org/docs/mod/mod_include.html>`.

For a more detailed discussion of SSI/XSSI implementation see the Apacheweek feature at `<http://www.apacheweek.com/features/ssi>`.

For more information on SSI commands see the NCSA documentation at `<http://hoohoo.ncsa.uiuc.edu/docs/tutorials/includes.html>`.

For more information on XSSI commands goto `<ftp://pageplus.com/pub/hsf/xssi/xssi-1.1.html>`.

7.13   Module system

Apache can be extended to support almost anything with modules. There are allot of modules already in existence. Only the general interest modules are included with Apache. For links to existing modules goto the

Apache Module Registry at `<http://www.zyzzyva.com/module_registry/>`.

For module programming information goto `<http://www.zyzzyva.com/module_registry/reference/>`

8   Web Server Add-ons

Sorry this section has not been written yet.

Coming soon: mSQL, PHP/FI, cgiwrap, Fast-cgi, MS frontpage extentions, and more.

9   FAQ

There aren't any frequent asked questions - yet...

10   For further reading

10.1   O'Reilly & Associates Books

In my humble opinion O'Reilly & Associates make the best technical books on the planet. They focus mainly on Internet, Unix and programming related topics. They start off slow with plenty of examples and when you finish the book your an expert. I think you could get by if you only read half of the book. They also add some humor to otherwise boring subjects.

They have great books on HTML, PERL, CGI Programming, Java, JavaScript, C/C++, Sendmail, Linux and much much more. And the fast moving topics (like HTML) are updated and revised about every 6 months or so. So visit the *O'Reilly & Associates* <http://www.ora.com/> web site or stop by your local book store for more info.

And remember if it doesn't say O'Reilly & Associates on the cover, someone else probably wrote it.

10.2   Internet Request For Comments (RFC)

- RFC1866 written by T. Berners-Lee and D. Connolly, "Hypertext Markup Language - 2.0", 11/03/1995
- RFC1867 writtenm by E. Nebel and L. Masinter, "Form-based File Upload in HTML", 11/07/1995
- RFC1942 written by D. Raggett, "HTML Tables", 05/15/1996
- RFC1945 by T. Berners-Lee, R. Fielding, H. Nielsen, "Hypertext Transfer Protocol – HTTP/1.0", 05/17/1996.
- RFC1630 by T. Berners-Lee, "Universal Resource Identifiers in WWW: A Unifying Syntax for the Expression of Names and Addresses of Objects on the Network as used in the World-Wide Web", 06/09/1994
- RFC1959 by T. Howes, M. Smith, "An LDAP URL Format", 06/19/1996

A mSQL and perl Web Server Mini HOWTO

Oliver Corff, `corff@zedat.fu-berlin.de`   v0.1, 17 September 1997

This Mini HOWTO, highly inspired by Michael Schilli's article *Gebunkert: Datenbankbedienung mit Perl und CGI*, published in the german computer magazine iX 8/1997, describes how to build a SQL client/server database using WWW and HTML for the user interface.

Contents

1   About this Document

1.1   Intended Audience

Everybody who wants to install a web server database but does not know which software is necessary and how it is installed should benefit from reading this text. This text provides all information necessary to get a SQL database for a web server going; it does *not* go into any detail of CGI programming, nor does it explain the SQL database language. Excellent books are available on both topics, and it is the intention of this text to provide a working platform based on which a user can then study CGI programming and SQL.

For getting a small scale SQL system running (not the notorious example of a major airline booking system, or space mission management database) it will be sufficient to have the software described in this text and the documentation accompanying it. The user manual of msql (a database introduced in this text) provides sufficient information on SQL for building your own database.

The reader of this text should have a working knowledge of how to obtain files via `ftp` if he has no access to CD-ROMs, and a basic understanding of how to build binaries from sources. Anyway, all steps explained in this text were tested on a real life system and should also work on the reader's system.

1.2   Conventions used in this text

A user command:

```
# make install
```

Screen output from a program:

```
    Program installed. Read README for details on how to start.
```

Sample code of a file:

```
# My comment
char letter;
```

2   Introduction

It can be safely assumed that databases with a high volume of data or a complicated relational setup (like, perhaps, a lexical database for a living language) must be accessible to many users and operators at the same time. Ideally, it should be possible to use existing different hardware and software platforms that can be combined into the actual system. In order to reduce the implementation cost, only one system, the database server, needs to be powerful; the user stations typically just display data and accept user commands, but the processing is done on one machine only which led to the name client-server database. In addition, the user interface should be easy to maintain and should require as little as possible on the client side.

A system which meets these criteria can be built around the following items of protocols, concepts and software:

Linux

> supplies the operating system. It is a stable Unix implementation providing true multi-user multi-tasking services with full network (TCP/IP e. a.) support. Except from the actual media and transmission cost, it is available free of charge and comes in form of so-called distributions which usually include everything needed from the basic OS to text processing, scripting, software development, interface builders, etc.

HTML

> is the Hypertext Markup Language used to build interfaces to network systems like Intranets and the WWW, the World Wide Web. HTML is very simple and can be produced with any ASCII-capable text editor.

Browsers

> are text-based (e. g. Lynx) or graphical (e. g. Mosaic, Netscape, Arena etc.) applications accepting, evaluating and displaying HTML documents. They are the only piece of software which is directly operated by the database user. Using browsers, it is possible to display various types of data (text, possibly images) and communicate with http servers (see next) on about every popular computer model for which a browser has been made available.

http servers

> provide access to the area of a host computer where data intended for public use in a network are stored. They understand the http protocol and procure the information the user requests.

SQL

> Structured Query Language is a language for manipulating data in relational databases. It has a very simple grammar and is a standard with wide industry support. SQL-based databases have become the core of the classical client/server database concept. There are many famous SQL systems available, like Oracle, Informix etc., and then there is also msql which comes with a very low or even zero price tag if it is used in academical and educational environments.

CGI

> Common Gateway Interface is the programming interface between the system holding the data (in our case an SQL-based system) and the network protocol (HTML, of course). CGIs can be built around many programming languages, but a particularly popular language is perl.

perl

> is an extremely powerful scripting language which combines all merits of C, various shell languages, and stream manipulation languages like awk and sed. Perl has a lot of modularized interfaces and can be used to control SQL databases, for example.

3   Installation Procedure

3.1   Hardware Requirements

No general statement can be made about the hardware requirements of a database server. Too much depends on the expected number of users, the kind of application, the network load etc. In a small environment with only a few users and little network traffic a i486-equivalent machine with 16 MB of RAM can be completely sufficient. Linux, the operating system, is very efficient in terms of resources, and can supply enough horsepower for running a broad variety of applications at the same time. Of course, faster processors and more RAM mean more speed, but much more important than the processor is the amount of RAM. The more RAM the system has the less it is forced to swap memory intensive processes to disk in case a bottleneck occurs.

Given anything like 32 MB RAM and a PCI bus, searches and sorting operations can be done without much resorting to swap files etc., resulting in lightening fast speed.

The model installation described in this article was made on a IBM 686 (133Mhz) with 32 MB RAM and a 1.2 GB IDE hard disk. Assuming that the installation process starts from scratch, here is a list of the necessary steps.

3.2   Software Requirements

The software described in this article is available from the Internet or from CD-ROM. The following products were used:

- Red Hat Linux PowerTools: 6 CD's Complete Easy-to-Use Red Hat 4.2, Summer '97; alternatively from http://www.redhat.com;
- msql SQL database server: it is now available in two versions. The versions have differences in the number of transactions they can handle, the administration interface, etc. The elder version, 1.0.16, is available from Sunsite mirrors. The ELF executable can be found at sunsite:apps/database/sql/msql-1.0.16 or on CD-ROM (here: disc 4 of InfoMagic Linux Developer's Resource, 6-CD set, December 1996) or alternatively from the following URL: http://www.infomagic.com.
  The newer version, 2.0.1, can be directly obtained from Hughes' homepage in Australia (http://www.hughes.com.au) or from numerous mirror sites around the world;
- perl from CPAN: The Comprehensive Perl Archive Network. Walnut Creek CDROM, ISBN 1-57176-077-6, May 1997;
- Michael Schilli's CGI example program from computer journal iX 8/1997, pages 150–152, available via ftp from ftp.uni-paderborn.de:/doc/magazin/iX;

3.3   Installing the Operating System

Linux is installed in form of the Red Hat Linux Distribution 4.2. In order to install successfully, the machine must either have a DOS-accessible CD-ROM drive, a bootable CD-ROM drive, or else a boot disk must be made following the instructions on the Linux CD.

During installation the user has the choice to select and configure numerous software packages. It is convenient to select the following items now:

- TCP/IP network support,
- the http server Apache, and

- the scripting language perl, and
- the X Window System, as well as
- the browsers Arena (graphical) and Lynx (text-based).

All these packages are provided with the Linux distribution. If you do not install these packages now you still have the chance to do this later with the assistance of glint, the graphical and intuitive software package installation manager. Be sure to be root when installing these packages.

It is beyond the scope of this article to describe the network installation and initialization procedure. Please consult the online (manpages, HTML, texinfo) and printed (Linux Bible, etc. etc.) documentation.

The installation procedure of Red Hat is very mature and requires only little user attention besides the usual choices (like providing host names, etc.). Once the installation ends successfully, the system is basically ready to go.

Installing the X Window System is not mandatory for a pure server but it makes local access and testing much easier. The X installation procedure is done by any of several programs; XF86Setup offers the most extensive self-testing facilities and needs the least handling of hairy details (like video clock programming, etc.). The only requirement is that the software can detect the video adapter. A cheap accelerated graphics adapter (like Trio S64 based cards prior to S64UV+) usually works "out of the box".

At this point we assume that our system is up and running and that Apache, Perl and the X Window System have been successfully installed. We further assume that all standard structures like the file and directory structure are kept as they are defined in the installation. Last but not least we leave the host name as it is, and do at this moment accept the name localhost. We'll use this name for testing the installation; once the whole system works the true name can be added. Please note that the network setup also requires editing the files /etc/hosts, among others. Ideally this should be done with the administration tools provided to user root.

3.4   The http Server

The http server supplied with Linux is known as Apache to humans and as httpd to the system. The manpage (man httpd) explains how to install and start the http daemon (hence http*d*) but, as mentioned, if the installation went without problems then the server should be running. You can verify the directory tree: there must be a directory /home/httpd/ with three subdirectories: ../cgi-bin/, ../html/ and ../icons/. In ../html/ there must be a file index.html. Later we will manipulate or replace this file by our own index.html. All configuration information is stored in/etc/httpd/conf/. The system is well preconfigured and does not need further setup provided the installation went without error.

3.5   The Browsers

There are essentially three types of browsers available for Linux: pure text-based systems like Lynx, experimental and simple ones like Arena (free!) and commercial ones like Netscape (shareware!) with Java support. While Lynx and Arena come with Linux, Netscape must be procured from other sources. Netscape is available as a precombiled binary for Linux on ix86 architectures and will run "out of the box" as soon as the archive is unpacked.

3.5.1   Configuring Lynx

Once Lynx is started it will look for a 'default URL' which is usually not very meaningful if the system does not have permanent Internet access. In order to change the default URL (and lots of other configuration details) the system administrator should edit /usr/lib/lynx.cfg. The file is big, around 57000 bytes and contains occasionally contradicting information. It states its own home as /usr/local/lib/. Not far from top is a line beginning with STARTFILE. We replace this line by the following entry: STARTFILE:http://localhost and make sure that no spacing etc. is inserted:

```
# STARTFILE:http://www.nyu.edu/pages/wsn/subir/lynx.html
STARTFILE:http://localhost
```

After saving the file, Lynx should now reveal our index.html document if started without arguments.

3.5.2 Configuring Arena

Arena first looks for its own default URL when started without arguments. This URL is hard-wired into the executable but can be overrun by the environment variable WWW_HOME. The system administrator can place a line saying WWW_HOME="http://localhost" in /etc/profile. The variable must then be exported, either by a separate statement (export WWW_HOME) or by appending WWW_HOME to the existing export statement:

```
WWW_HOME="http://localhost"
export WWW_HOME
```

After relaunching a login shell, the new default URL is now system-wide known to Arena.

3.5.3 Installing and Configuring Netscape

Netscape is a commercial product and thus not included with the Linux distributions. It is either downloadable from the Internet or available from software collections on CDROM. Netscape comes in form of precompiled binaries for every important hardware platform. For installation purposes, it is useful to create a directory /usr/local/Netscape/ where the archive is unpacked. The files can be kept in place (except for the Java library: follow the instructions in the README file that comes with the Netscape binary), and it is sufficient to create a soft link in /usr/local/bin/ by issuing the command

```
# ln -s /usr/local/Netscape/netscape .
```

from within /usr/local/bin/.

Netscape is now ready for use and can be configured via the "Options" menu. In "General Preferences" there is a card "Appearance" with the entry "Home Page Location". Enter http://localhost here and do not forget to save the options (via "Options" — "Save Options") before exiting Netscape. At the next startup, Netscape will now show the Apache 'homepage'.

3.6 Cooperation of Apache and Browsers

You can now conduct the first real test of both the browser and the http server: simply start any of the available browsers and the Apache: Red Hat Linux Web Server page will pop up. This page shows the file locations and other basics of http server installation. If this page is not displayed please check whether the files mentioned above are in place and whether the browser configuration is correct. Close edited configuration files before you start the browser again. If all files are in place and the browsers seem to be configured correctly then examine the network setup of your machine. Either the host name is different from what was entered in the configuration, or the network setup as such is not correct. It is utterly important that /etc/hosts contains at least a line like

```
127.0.0.1                    localhost localhost.localdomain
```

which implies that you can connect locally to your machine. One can verify this by issuing any network-sensitive command requiring a host name as argument, like `telnet localhost` (provided `telnet` is installed). If that does not work then the network setup must be verified before continuing with the main task.

3.7   The Database Engine and its Installation

Installing the database requires only little more preparation than the previous installation steps. There are a few SQL database engines available with different runtime and administrative requirements, and possibly one of the most straightforward systems is msql, or "Mini-SQL" by David Hughes. msql is shareware. Depending on the version used, commercial sites are charged USD 250.00 and more, private users are charged USD 65.00 and more, and only educational institutions and registered non-profit organizations can use this software free of charge. Please note that the exact figures are provided in the licence notes of the database documentation. The figures given here serve as a rough indicator only.

A few words are in place here why the author chose msql. First of all, there is personal experience. While searching for a database engine the author found msql to be about the easiest to install and maintain, and it provides enough coverage of the SQL language to meet general needs. Only when writing these lines, the author discovered the following words of praise in Alligator Descartes' DBI FAQ (perl database interface FAQ):

> From the current author's point of view, if the dataset is relatively small, being tables of less than 1 million rows, and less than 1000 tables in a given database, then mSQL is a perfectly acceptable solution to your problem. This database is extremely cheap, is wonderfully robust and has excellent support. [...]

Msql is available in two versions now, msql-1.0.16 and msql-2.0.1, which differ in performance (not noticeable in small scale projects) and accompanying software (the newer version comes with more tools, its own scripting language, etc.). We will describe both versions of msql since their installion differs in a few points.

3.7.1   Installing msql-1.0.16

msql is available as source and as compiled executable with ELF support. Using the ELF binaries makes installation easy since the archive file `msql-1.0.16.ELF.tgz` contains a complete absolute directory tree so that all directories are generated properly when unpacked from /.

If you decide to compile msql-1.0.16 yourself and are going to use the MsqlPerl package rather than the DBI interface (see a detailed discussion on the difference between these two further down) then be prepared that MsqlPerl might complain during the test suites that some instruction inside msql failed. In this case a patch may be necessary which is described in the MsqlPerl documentation (file `patch.lost.tables`). Notably, this demands including three lines in `msqldb.c` after line 1400 which says `entry->def = NULL;`:

```
*(entry->DB) = 0;
*(entry->table) = 0;
entry->age = 0;
```

The code fragment should now look like

```
        freeTableDef(entry->def);
        safeFree(entry->rowBuf);
        safeFree(entry->keyBuf);
        entry->def = NULL;
        *(entry->DB) = 0;
        *(entry->table) = 0;
        entry->age = 0;
```

Compiling msql involves several steps. After unpacking the source archive, it is necessary to build a target directory. This is done by saying

```
# make target
```

If successful, the system will then answer with

```
        Build of target directory for Linux-2.0.30-i486 complete
```

You must now change into this newly created directory and run a

```
# ./setup
```

command first. The ./ sequence is necessary to make sure that really the command **setup** in this directory and not another command which happens to have the same name is executed. You will then be asked questions on the location of the source directory and whether a root installation is desired. These questions answered, the system should then run a number of tests checking for available software (compilers, utilities etc.) and finally say

```
        Ready to build mSQL.


        You may wish to check "common/site.h" although the defaults should be
        fine.  When you're ready, type  "make all" to build the software
```

We say

```
# make all
```

If everything went as intended, we'll read:

```
        make[2]: Leaving directory '/usr/local/Minerva/src/msql'
        <-- [msql] done

        Make of mSQL complete.
        You should now mSQL using make install

        NOTE : mSQL cannot be used free of charge at commercial sites.
               Please read the doc/License file to see what you have to do.


        make[1]: Leaving directory '/usr/local/Minerva/src'
```

All binaries must then be made visible to the search paths by creating soft links in **/usr/local/bin/**. Change to that directory and issue the command

```
# ln -s /usr/local/Minerva/bin/* .
```

after which the links will be properly set.

3.7.2   Testing msql-1

After the installation it is now possible to test whether the database works. Before anything else is done, the server daemon must be started. The system administrator holding root privileges issues the command

```
# msqld &
```

(do not forget to add the &, otherwise msql won't run in the background.) after which the following screen message appears:

```
mSQL Server 1.0.16 starting ...

Warning : Couldn't open ACL file: No such file or directory
Without an ACL file global access is Read/Write
```

This message tells us that everything so far worked since we did not set up any access restrictions. For the moment it is sufficient to start the msql daemon from within a shell but later we may want to have the system startup automatically execute this command for us. The command must then be mentioned in a suitable rc.d script. Only now the administrator can issue the first genuine database command:

```
# msqladmin create inventur
```

msql replies by saying Database "inventur" created.. As a further proof, we find that the directory /usr/local/Minerva/msqldb/ contains now the empty subdirectory ../inventur/. We could manipulate the newly created database with the administration tools; these procedures are all covered in detail in the msql documentation.

3.7.3   Installing msql-2.0.1

There is now a newer, more powerful version of Hughes' mSQL server available the installation of which is different in a few points. Installing msql-2 from scratch involves the following steps. Copy the archive to your extraction point, e. g. /usr/local/msql-2/, then untar the archive:

```
# tar xfvz msql-2.0.1.tar.gz
```

Change to the root direction of the install tree and issue a

```
# make target
```

Change to targets and look for your machine type. There should be a new subdirectory Linux-*(your version)-(your cpu)/*. Change to that directory and start the setup facility located here:

```
# ./setup
```

There is also a file `site.mm` which can be edited. Maybe you have got used to the directory name `/usr/local/Minerva/` and want to preserve it? In this case change the `INST_DIR=...` line to your desired target directory. Otherwise, leave everything as it is.

Now you can start building the database:

```
# make
# make install
```

If everything went successfully, we'll see a message like:

```
[...]

Installation of mSQL-2 complete.

*********
**    This is the commercial, production release of mSQL-2.0
**    Please see the README file in the top directory of the
**    distribution for license information.
*********
```

After all is installed properly we have to take care of the administration details. Here, the real differences from msql-1 begin. First, a user `msql` is created which is responsible for database administration.

```
# adduser msql
```

Then we have to change all ownerships in the mSQL directory to `msql` by saying:

```
# cd /usr/local/Minerva
# chown -R msql:msql *
```

Then we create soft links for all database binaries in `/usr/local/bin/` by saying:

```
# ln -s /usr/local/Minerva/bin/* .
```

3.7.4   Testing msql-2

We can now start the database server by issuing the command `msql2d &` and should get a response similar to this one:

```
Mini SQL Version 2.0.1
Copyright (c) 1993-4 David J. Hughes
Copyright (c) 1995-7 Hughes Technologies Pty. Ltd.
All rights reserved.


        Loading configuration from '/usr/local/Minerva/msql.conf'.
        Server process reconfigured to accept 214 connections.
        Server running as user 'msql'.
        Server mode is Read/Write.
```

```
    Warning : No ACL file.  Using global read/write access.
```

That looks perfect. The database is compiled and in place, and we can now continue with the perl modules since these rely partially on the presence of a working database server for testing.

Accidentally, this is also a good moment to print the complete manual that comes with msql-2.0.1:

```
# gzip -d manual.ps.gz
# lpr manual.ps
```

We can proceed to building the interfaces now, but it is a good idea to keep the newly created SQL server up and running since that makes testing the interface libraries somewhat simpler.

3.8   Choice of Interfaces: DBI/mSQL, MsqlPerl, and Lite

A frequently quoted saying in the Camel Book (the authorative perl documentation) states that there is more than one way to achieve a result when using perl. This, alas, holds true for our model application, too. Basically there are three ways to access an msql database via CGI. First of all the question is whether or not perl shall be used. If we use perl (on which this article focuses) then we still have the choice between two completely different interface models. Besides using perl, we can also employ msql's own scripting language, called Lite, which is reasonably simple and a close clone of C.

3.8.1   DBI and DBD-mSQL

By the time of this writing, using perl's generic database interface called DBI is the method of choice. DBI has a few advantages: It provides unified access control to a number of commercial databases with a single command set. The actual database in use on a given system is then contacted through a driver which effectively hides the pecularities of that database from the programmer. Being such, using DBI provides for a smooth transition between different databases by different makers. In one single script it is even possible to contact several different databases. Please refer to the DBI-FAQ for details. There is, however, one drawback: The DBI interface is still under development and shows rapidly galloping version numbers (sometimes with updates taking place within less than a month). Similarly, the individual database drivers are also frequently updated and may rely on specific versions of the database interface. Users making first-time installations should stick to the version numbers given in this article since other versions may cause compilation and testing problems the trouble shooting of which is nothing for the faint-hearted.

3.8.2   MsqlPerl

MsqlPerl is a library for directly accessing msql from perl scripts. It bypasses the DBI interface and is fairly compact. Though it works fine with both versions of msql, its usage is not promoted anymore in favour of the generalized DBI interface. Nonetheless, in a given installation it may prove to be the interface of choice since it is small and easy to install. Notably, it has less version dependencies than revealed by the interaction of DBI and particular database drivers.

3.8.3   msql's own scripting language: Lite

Last but not least msql-2 comes with its own scripting language: Lite. The language is a close relative of C stripped of its oddities with additional shell-like features (in a way, something like a very specialized version of perl). Lite is a simple language and is well documented in the msql-2 manual. The msql-2 package also comes with a sample application sporting Lite.

We will not describe Lite here because it is well documented but fairly specific to msql-2, and because it is assumed that the readers of this article have a basic interest in and a basic understanding of perl. Nonetheless it is highly recommended to have a closer look at Lite: it may well be the case that Lite offers the solution of choice in an exclusive msql-2 environment (implying no other databases are involved) due to its simplicity and straightforward concept.

3.9   Going the generic way: DBI and DBD-msql

We assume that perl was installed during the system setup or via the package manager mentioned above. No further details will be given here. Nonetheless we first test whether our version of perl is up to date:

```
# perl -v
```

perl should respond with the following message:

```
This is perl, version 5.003 with EMBED
        Locally applied patches:
            SUIDBUF - Buffer overflow fixes for suidperl security

        built under linux at Apr 22 1997 10:04:46
        + two suidperl security patches

Copyright 1987-1996, Larry Wall
[...]
```

So far, everything is fine. The next step includes installing the perl libraries for databases in general (DBI), the msql driver (DBD-mSQL) and CGI. The CGI driver is necessary in any case. The following archives are necessary:

1. DBI-0.81.tar.gz
2. DBD-mSQL-0.65.tar.gz
3. CGI.pm-2.31.tar.gz (or higher)

A caveat is necessary here for beginners: the test installation described here works fine using software with *exactly* these version numbers, and combinations of other versions failed in one or the other way. Debugging flawed version combinations is nothing for those who are not very familiar with the intimate details of the calling conventions etc. of the interfaces. Sometimes only a method is renamed while performing the same task, but sometimes the internal structure changes significantly. So, again, stick with these version numbers if you want to be on the safe side even if you discover that version numbers have increased in the meantime. Frequent updates of these interfaces are the rule rather than the exception, so you should really anticipate problems when installing other versions than those indicated here.

It is very important that the database driver for mSQL (DBD-mSQL) is installed *after* the generic interface DBI.

We start by creating the directory **/usr/local/PerlModules/** as it is very important to keep the original perl directory tree untouched. We could also choose a different directory name since the name is completely uncritical, and unfortunately that is not really mentioned in the README files of the verious perl modules. Having copied the above-mentioned archives to **/usr/local/PerlModules/** we unpack them saying

```
# tar xzvf [archive-file]
```

for every single of the three archives. Do not forget to supply the real archive name to `tar`. The installation process for the three modules is essentially stardardized; only the screen messages showing important steps of individual packages are reproduced here.

3.9.1 Installing perl's Database Interface DBI

The database interface must always be installed before installing the specific database driver. Unpacking the DBI archive creates the directory `/usr/local/PerlModules/DBI-0.81/`. Change to that directory. There are a `README` file (you should read it) and a perl-specific makefile. Now issue the command

```
# perl Makefile.PL
```

The system should answer with a lengthy message of which the most important part is shown here::

```
[...]
MakeMaker (v5.34)
Checking if your kit is complete...
Looks good
        NAME => q[DBI]
        PREREQ_PM => {  }
        VERSION_FROM => q[DBI.pm]
        clean => { FILES=>q[$(DISTVNAME)/] }
        dist => { DIST_DEFAULT=>q[clean distcheck disttest [...]
Using PERL=/usr/bin/perl

WARNING! By default new modules are installed into your 'site_lib'
directories. Since site_lib directories come after the normal library
directories you MUST delete old DBI files and directories from your
'privlib' and 'archlib' directories and their auto subdirectories.

Writing Makefile for DBI
```

This looks good, as the program says, and we can proceed with the next step:

```
# make
```

If no error message occurs (the detailed protocol dumped on screen is *not* an error message) we test the newly installed library with the command

```
# make test
```

Watch the output for the following lines (you can always scroll back with [Shift]-[PgUp]):

```
[...]
t/basics...........ok
t/dbidrv...........ok
```

```
        t/examp.............ok
        All tests successful.
        [...]
        DBI test application $Revision: 1.20 $
        Switch: DBI-0.81 Switch by Tim Bunce, 0.81
        Available Drivers: ExampleP, NullP, Sponge
        ExampleP: testing 2 sets of 5 connections:
        Connecting... 1 2 3 4 5
        Disconnecting...
        Connecting... 1 2 3 4 5
        Disconnecting...
        Made 10 connections in  0 secs ( 0.00 usr  0.00 sys =  0.00 cpu)

        test.pl done
```

The final step is to install all files in their proper directories. The following command will take care of it:

```
# make install
```

No more duties are left. If for some reason the installation failed and you want to redo it do not forget to issue

```
# make realclean
```

first. This will remove stale leftovers of the previous installation. You can also remove the files which were installed by copying the screen contents (shown abbreviated)

```
        Installing /usr/lib/perl5/site_perl/i386-linux/./auto/DBI/DBIXS.h
        Installing /usr/lib/perl5/site_perl/i386-linux/./auto/DBI/DBI.so
        Installing /usr/lib/perl5/site_perl/i386-linux/./auto/DBI/DBI.bs
        [...]
        Writing /usr/lib/perl5/site_perl/i386-linux/auto/DBI/.packlist
        Appending installation info to /usr/lib/perl5/i386-linux/5.003/perllocal.pod
```

into a file, replacing every `Installing` with `rm`. Provided you named the file `uninstall` you can then say

```
# . uninstall
```

which will remove the recently installed files.

3.9.2 perl's msql Driver DBD-mSQL

The msql driver can only be installed *after* a successful installation of perl's generic database interface.

The basic steps are the same as above; so first go through

```
# perl Makefile.PL
```

Here, the system should answer with an urgent warning to read the accompanying documentation. It will then detect where msql resides, and asks which version you use:

```
$MSQL_HOME not defined. Searching for mSQL...
Using mSQL in /usr/local/Hughes

  -> Which version of mSQL are you using [1/2]?
```

State your correct version number. Quite a few lines of text will follow. Watch for the following ones:

```
Splendid! Your mSQL daemon is running. We can auto-detect your configuration!

I've auto-detected your configuration to be running on port: 1114
```

You can now test the driver by saying

```
# make test
```

Again, a lengthy output follows. If it ends with

```
Testing: $cursor->func( '_ListSelectedFields' ). This will fail.
      ok: not a SELECT in msqlListSelectedFields!
Re-testing: $dbh->do( 'DROP TABLE testaa' )
      ok
*** Testing of DBD::mSQL complete! You appear to be normal! ***
```

you are on the safe side of life and can install your driver by saying

```
# make install
```

You are now ready to go and can skip the next paragraph.

3.10   The MsqlPerl Interface

If you decide to use the exclusive MsqlPerl interface then no generic database driver is needed, only MsqlPerl-1.15.tar.gz, since, as mentioned earlier, MsqlPerl provides a direct interface between perl and the database server without using the DBI interface. Installing and testing is straightforward.

After saying `perl Makefile.PL` the make utility can be started. First you have to answer the question where mSQL resides. If it resides in `/usr/local/Minerva/` the default answer can be confirmed.

Then do a `make test`. Before doing so you must ensure that you have a database named `test` and that you have read and write permissions for it. This can be done by

```
# msqladmin create test
```

3.11   perl's CGI library

Installing perl's CGI part is the simplest of the three steps. Execute the following commands in the given order and everything is done:

```
# perl Makefile.PL
# make
# make install
```

Unlike the previous drivers this interface does not have a test option (**# make test**) whereas the other modules *should* be tested in any case.

A subdirectory with CGI example scripts is also created. You can copy the contents of this directory into `/home/http/cgi-bin/` and use the browser to experiment with the scripts.

3.12 Installation Checklist

We went through the following steps, in this order:

1. Install Linux with networking support
2. Install a http server, e. g. Apache
3. Install a browser, e. g. Arena, lynx or Netscape
4. Install an SQL server, e. g. msql
5. Install a suitable perl SQL interface
6. Install the CGI files

Finally, you can do some clean-up. All source trees for msql and the perl modules can be safely deleted (however, you should not delete your archive files!) since the binaries and documentation are now based in different directories.

4   Running an Example Database

After completing the system installation we can now finally run a model application. Depending on the version of msql installed and the perl database interface used, we have to modify the sample programs in a few points.

First however, the file `index.html` residing in `/home/httpd/html/` must be modified to allow calling a sample database application. We can place our database (which we call `database.cgi` or `inventur.cgi` here despite its archive name `perl.lst.ck`) in `/home/httpd/html/test/`.

We add one line (of course, depending on your installation choices) similar to the following to `index.html`:

```
<LI>Test the <A HREF="test/database.cgi">Database, DBI:DBD-mSQL style!</A>
<LI>Test the <A HREF="test/inventur.cgi">Database, MsqlPerl style!</A>
```

Usually you should only pick one of these two choices but if you have both types of database interface installed you can leave both lines here as they are. You can then compare performance, etc.

4.1 Adapting the sample script for MsqlPerl

Our sample script has to be told to use the MsqlPerl interface. The modification takes place in several locations. First, near the beginning of the file, we change the **use** clause:

```
#
# use DBI;              # Generisches Datenbank-Interface
use Msql;
```

Then, near line 27, the MsqlPerl syntax does not require the mentioning of a specific driver:

```
# $dbh = DBI->connect($host, $database, '', $driver) ||
$dbh = Msql->connect($host, $database) ||
```

Then, from line 33 onward throughout the whole script, we have to change all instances of do against query:

```
# $dbh->do("SELECT * FROM hw") || db_init($dbh);
$dbh->query("SELECT * FROM hw") || db_init($dbh);
```

Finally, in MsqlPerl speak, line 207 can be commented out:

```
# $sth->execute || msg("SQL Error:", $sth->errstr);
```

In addition, it may become necessary to swap all errstr calls like the one in the preceding code fragment against errmsg. This is also version dependent.

After these modifications, the script should run smoothly.

4.2 Adapting the sample script for msql-2

The SQL syntax was redefined during the development of mslq-2. The original script will fail to execute the table initialization statements in lines 45 – 58. The **primary key** modifier is no longer supported by msql-2, and should simply be skipped:

```
    $dbh->do(<<EOT) || die $dbh->errstr; # Neue Personen-Tabelle
        create table person (
# We do not need the 'primary key' modifier anymore in msql-2!
#        pn          int primary key,   # Personalnummer
         pn          int,               # Personalnummer
         name        char(80),          # Nachname, Vorname
         raum        int                # Raumnummer
    )
EOT
    $dbh->do(<<EOT) || die $dbh->errstr; # Neue Hardware-Tabelle
        create table hw (
# We do not need the 'primary key' modifier anymore in msql-2!
#        asset int primary key,         # Inventurnummer
         asset int,                     # Inventurnummer
         name    char(80),              # Bezeichnung
         person int                     # Besitzer
    )
EOT
```

Unfortunately, this specific script will then accept new entries with identical personnel numbers; the msql-1 modifier **primary key** intends to prevent exactly this behaviour. The msql-2 documentation shows how to use the CREATE INDEX clause to create unique entries.

5 Conclusion and Outlook

If you have installed msql-2 on your system then you can have a look at the sample programs written in Lite, msql-2's own scripting language.

Either version of msql comes with a basic set of administration tools which allow the user to create and drop tables (`msqladmin`) and examine database structures (`relshow`).

The second generation msql (i.e. msql-2) has a few more genuinely useful utilities: `msqlimport` and `msqlexport`. These allow the dumping of flat line data files into and out of the SQL database. They can be used for loading quantities of existing data *d'un coup* into existing tables, or extract flat data from tables, and the user does not have to deal with writing a *single* line of perl or SQL or whatever code for this task.

If you want to write your own perl scripts dealing with databases you'll find sufficient support in the example files and the extensive on-line documentation that comes with the DBI module.

Anyway, you are now ready to go and present your data to the users of your own network, or even the WWW.

The Linux Public Web Browser mini-HOWTO

Donald B. Marti Jr., dmarti@best.com   v0.3, 5 January 1998

The basic idea here is to give web access to people who wander by, while limiting their ability to mess anything up.

Contents

1   Copyright and Disclaimer

This document currently contains information for Netscape Navigator only, but I plan to add notes for other browsers too as I get the necessary information. If you try this with a different browser, please let me know.

2   Introduction

The basic idea here is to give web access to people who wander by, while limiting their ability to mess anything up.

This setup was originally intended for trade shows, but it might be applicable other places you want to have a web browser going without having to babysit a computer.

Following these instructions does **not** make your system bulletproof or idiot-proof.

3   Before you begin

3.1   You need a graphical browser

This document assumes that you already have a running graphical web browser, such as Netscape Navigator, on your system. You should have permission to use your graphical web browser. If you want to use Netscape Navigator in a commercial setting, you can buy a copy with appropriate license through Caldera.

3.2   You need to be able to add an account

If you don't have the right to be **root**, get the system administrator to add the "**guest**" account and give you ownership of **guest**'s home directory. Skip to the "Create or edit the following files" step (5 (Create or edit the following files in /home/guest)) when he or she is done.

3.3   You need `httpd` **for a stand-alone web browsing station**

If you are setting up a web browsing station to run stand-alone, without a network connection, you should have `httpd` working and the web documents installed. To tell if this is the case, enter:

```
lynx -dump http://localhost/
```

You should get the text of the home page on your system.

4   Add the guest account

As **root**, run `adduser` to add a user named **guest**. Then enter

```
passwd guest
```

to set the password for the **guest** account. This should be something easy to remember, like "**guest**". You will be telling people this password. Don't make it the same as your own password.

Then make **guest**'s home directory owned by you. Enter

```
chown me.mygroup /home/guest
```

Replace "**me**" with your regular username and "**mygroup**" with your group name. (On Red Hat Linux, these will be the same, since every user has his or her own group.)

You should now exit and do the rest of the steps as yourself, not **root**.

5   Create or edit the following files in /home/guest

5.1   File name: .bash_login

```
exec startx
```

This means that when **guest** logs in, the login shell will start up the X Window System right away.

5.2   File name: .Xclients

```
netscape
```

This means that when X starts, **guest** just gets the web browser, no window manager. If you prefer another web browser, do something else.

The file **.Xclients** should be executable by **guest**. Enter

```
    chmod 755 /home/guest/.Xclients
```

to make it so.

5.3   File name: .xsession

```
#!/bin/sh
netscape
```

If you use **xdm(1)** to log people in, this file should make guest get the web browser as if he or she had logged in normally. The file **.xsession** should be executable by **guest**. Enter

```
    chmod 755 /home/guest/.xsession
```

to make it so.

5.4   File name: .Xdefaults

```
! Disable drag-to-select.
*hysteresis:                        3000


! Make visited and unvisited links the same color by default
*linkForeground:                    #0000EE
*vlinkForeground:                   #0000EE


Netscape.Navigator.geometry: =NETSCAPE_GEOMETRY

! Disable some of the keyboard commands.
*globalTranslations:

! Mouse bindings: make all mouse buttons do the same thing.
*drawingArea.translations:              #replace                  \
<Btn1Down>:              ArmLink()                           \n\
```

```
        <Btn2Down>:             ArmLink()                       \n\
        <Btn3Down>:             ArmLink()                       \n\
        ~Shift<Btn1Up>:         ActivateLink()                  \
                                DisarmLink()                    \n\
        ~Shift<Btn2Up>:         ActivateLink()                  \
                                DisarmLink()                    \n\
        ~Shift<Btn3Up>:         ActivateLink()                  \
                                DisarmLink()                    \n\
        Shift<Btn1Up>:          ActivateLink()                  \
                                DisarmLink()                    \n\
        Shift<Btn2Up>:          ActivateLink()                  \
                                DisarmLink()                    \n\
        Shift<Btn3Up>:          ActivateLink()                  \
                                DisarmLink()                    \n\
        <Btn1Motion>:           DisarmLinkIfMoved()             \n\
        <Btn2Motion>:           DisarmLinkIfMoved()             \n\
        <Btn3Motion>:           DisarmLinkIfMoved()             \n\
        <Motion>:               DescribeLink()                  \n\
```

This file disables blink tags, drag-to-select, and some of the keyboard commands. It also makes all mouse buttons do the same thing, hides the menu bar, and makes visited and unvisited links the same colour, so each visitor gets nice clean blue links, not ones that other people have been thumbing through and staining purple.

You should replace the NETSCAPE_GEOMETRY in this file with an X geometry that looks like this: XxY+0-0, where X is the width of your screen and Y is the height of your screen + 32. This will position the Netscape menu bar off the top of the screen, so the user won't be distracted. For example, if your screen is 800x600, the geometry should be 800x632+0-0.

6   Make a .netscape directory for guest

Enter

```
mkdir /home/guest/.netscape
chmod 777 /home/guest/.netscape
```

to create guest's .netscape directory and make it world-writable.

7   Try it

Log out, then log in as guest.

8   Changing preferences

Since you won't be able to use the menu bar as guest, you should edit guest's preferences manually if you need to change them, or change your own preferences to what you want guest's to be and copy the preferences file.

The Linux XFree86 HOWTO

by Eric S. Raymond   v5.3, 2 December 1997

This document describes how to obtain, install, and configure version 3.3 of the XFree86 version of the X Window System (X11R6) for Linux systems. It is a step-by-step guide to configuring XFree86 on your system.

Contents

1 Introduction

The X Window System is a large and powerful (some might say excessively large and overly complex) graphics environment for UNIX systems. The original X Window System code was developed at MIT; commercial vendors have since made X the industry standard for UNIX platforms. Virtually every UNIX workstation in the world runs some variant of the X Window system.

A freely redistributable port of the MIT X Window System version 11, release 6 (X11R6) for 80386/80486/Pentium UNIX systems has been developed by a team of programmers originally headed by David Wexelblat <*dwex@XFree86.org*> <mailto:dwex@XFree86.org>. The release, known as XFree86, is available for System V/386, 386BSD, and other x86 UNIX implementations, including Linux. It includes all of the required binaries, support files, libraries, and tools.

Complete information on XFree86 is available at the XFree86 web site, <http://www.XFree86.org>.

In this document, we'll give a step-by-step description of how to install and configure XFree86 for Linux, but you will have to fill in some of the details yourself by reading the documentation released with XFree86 itself. (This documentation is discussed below.) However, using and customizing the X Window System is far beyond the scope of this document—for this purpose you should obtain one of the many good books on using the X Window System.

1.1   Other sources of information

If you have never heard of Linux before, there are several sources of basic information about the system. The best place to find these is at the Linux Documentation Project home page at `<http://sunsite.unc.edu/LDP>`. You can find the latest, up-to-date version of this document there, as `<http://sunsite.unc.edu/LDP/HOWTO/XFree86-HOWTO.html>`

1.2   New versions of this document

New versions of the Linux XFree86 HOWTO will be periodically posted to *comp.os.linux.help* `<news:comp.os.linux.help>` and `<news:comp.os.linux.announce>` and *news.answers* `<news:news.answers>`. They will also be uploaded to various Linux WWW and FTP sites, including the LDP home page.

You can always view the latest version of this on the World Wide Web via the URL `<http://sunsite.unc.edu/LDP/HOWTO/XFree86-HOWTO.html>`.

1.3   Feedback and Corrections

If you have questions or comments about this document, please feel free to mail Eric S. Raymond, at *esr@thyrsus.com* `<mailto:esr@thyrsus.com>`. I welcome any suggestions or criticisms. If you find a mistake with this document, please let me know so I can correct it in the next version. Thanks.

Please do *not* mail me questions about how to make your video card and monitor work with X. This HOWTO is intended to be a rapid, painless guide to *normal* installation using the new interactive configurator. If you run into problems, browse the XFree86 Video Timings HOWTO, `<http://sunsite.unc.edu/LDP/HOWTO/XFree86-Video-Timings-HOWTO.html>`. (This is the up-to-date HTML version of XFree86's 'Videomodes.doc' file.) That document tells everything I know about configuration troubleshooting. If it can't help you, I can't either.

2   Hardware requirements

As of XFree86 version 3.3 the following video chipsets are supported. The documentation included with your video adaptor should specify the chipset used. If you are in the market for a new video card, or are buying a new machine that comes with a video card, have the vendor find out exactly what the make, model, and chipset of the video card is. This may require the vendor to call technical support on your behalf; in general vendors will be happy to do this. Many PC hardware vendors will state that the video card is a "standard SVGA card" which "should work" on your system. Explain that your software (mention Linux and XFree86!) does not support all video chipsets and that you must have detailed information.

You can also determine your videocard chipset by running the `SuperProbe` program included with the XFree86 distribution. This is covered in more detail below.

The following standard SVGA chipsets are supported:

- Tseng ET3000, ET4000AX, ET4000/W32, ET6000

- Western Digital/Paradise PVGA1

- Western Digital WD90C00, WD90C10, WD90C11, WD90C24, WD90C30, WD90C31, WD90C33

- Genoa GVGA

- Trident TVGA8800CS, TVGA8900B, TVGA8900C, TVGA8900CL, TVGA9000, TVGA9000i, TVGA9100B, TVGA9200CX, TVGA9320, TVGA9400CX, TVGA9420, TGUI9420DGi, TGUI9430DGi, TGUI9440AGi, TGUI9660XGi, TGUI9680

- ATI 18800, 18800-1, 28800-2, 28800-4, 28800-5, 28800-6, 68800-3, 68800-6, 68800AX, 68800LX, 88800GX-C, 88800GX-D, 88800GX-E, 88800GX-F, 88800CX, 264CT, 264ET, 264VT, 264VT2, 264GT

- NCR 77C22, 77C22E, 77C22E+

- Cirrus Logic CLGD5420, CLGD5422, CLGD5424, CLGD5426, CLGD5428, CLGD5429, CLGD5430, CLGD5434, CLGD5436, CLGD5440, CLGD5446, CLGD5462, CLGD5464, CLGD6205, CLGD6215, CLGD6225, CLGD6235, CLGD6410, CLGD6412, CLGD6420, CLGD6440

- OAK OTI067, OTI077, OTI087

- Avance Logic ALG2101, ALG2228, ALG2301, ALG2302, ALG2308, ALG2401

- Chips & Technologies 65520, 65530, 65540, 65545, 65520, 65530, 65540, 65545, 65546, 65548, 65550, 65554

- MX MX68000, MX680010

- Video 7/Headland Technologies HT216-32

- SiS 86C201, 86C202, 86C205

- ARK Logic ARK1000PV, ARK1000VL, ARK2000PV, ARK2000MT

- RealTek RTG3106

- Alliance AP6422

- Matrox MGA2064W and Mystique cards

- NVidia/SGS Thomson NV1, STG2000

The following SVGA chipsets with accelerated features are also supported:

- 8514/A (and true clones)

- ATI Mach8, Mach32, Mach64

- Cirrus CLGD5420, CLGD5422, CLGD5424, CLGD5426, CLGD5428, CLGD5429, CLGD5430, CLGD5434, CLGD5436, CLGD5440, CGLD5446, CLGD5462, CLGD5464.

- S3 86C911, 86C924, 86C801, 86C805, 86C805i, 86C928, 86C864, 86C964, 86C732, 86C764, 86C765, 86C868, 86C968, 86C325, 86C988

- Western Digital WD90C31, WD90C33, WD90C24A

- Weitek P9000

- IIT AGX-014, AGX-015, AGX-016

- IBM XGA-2

- Tseng ET4000/W32, ET4000/W32i, ET4000/W32p, ET6000

- Ark Logic ARK1000PV, ARK1000VL, ARK2000PV, ARK2000MT

- MGA2064W

Video cards using these chipsets are supported on all bus types, including VLB and PCI.

All of the above are supported in both 256 color and monochrome modes, with the exception of the Avance Logic, MX and Video 7 chipsets, which are only supported in 256 color mode. If your video card has enough DRAM installed, many of the above chipsets are supported in 16 and 32 bits-per-pixel mode (specifically, some Mach32, P9000, S3 and Cirrus boards). The usual configuration is 8 bits per pixel (that is, 256 colors).

The monochrome server also supports generic VGA cards, the Hercules monochrome card, the Hyundai HGC1280, Sigma LaserView, and Apollo monochrome cards. On the Compaq AVGA, only 64k of video memory is supported for the monochrome server, and the GVGA has not been tested with more than 64k.

This list will undoubtedly expand as time passes. The release notes for the current version of XFree86 should contain the complete list of supported video chipsets.

One problem faced by the XFree86 developers is that some video card manufacturers use non-standard mechanisms for determining clock frequencies used to drive the card. Some of these manufacturers either don't release specifications describing how to program the card, or they require developers to sign a non-disclosure statement to obtain the information. This would obviously restrict the free distribution of the XFree86 software, something that the XFree86 development team is not willing to do. For a long time, this has been a problem with certain video cards manufactured by Diamond, but as of release 3.1 of XFree86, Diamond has started to work with the development team to release free drivers for these cards.

The suggested setup for XFree86 under Linux is a 486 or better with at least 8 megabytes of RAM, and a video card with a chipset listed above. For optimal performance, we suggest using an accelerated card, such as an S3-chipset card. You should check the documentation for XFree86 and verify that your particular card is supported before taking the plunge and purchasing expensive hardware.

Farrel McKay compiles benchmark ratings comparisons for various video cards under XFree86. These are posted routinely to the USENET newsgroups *comp.windows.x.i386unix* <news:comp.windows.x.i386unix>, *comp.os.linux.x* <news:comp.os.linux.x>, <comp.benchmarks>, <comp.sys.ibm.pc.hardware.video>. They are available on the Web at <http://www.goof.com/xbench>.

As a side note, the personal Linux system of Matt Welsh (this FAQ's originator) was a 486DX2-66, 20 megabytes of RAM, equipped with a VLB S3-864 chipset card with 2 megabytes of DRAM. He ran X benchmarks on this machine as well as on Sun Sparc IPX workstations. The Linux system was roughly 7 times faster than the Sparc IPX (for the curious, XFree86-3.1 under Linux, with this video card, runs at around 171,000 xstones; the Sparc IPX at around 24,000). In general, XFree86 on a Linux system with an accelerated SVGA card will give you much greater performance than that found on commercial UNIX workstations (which usually employ simple framebuffers for graphics).

Your machine will need at least 4 megabytes of physical RAM, and 16 megabytes of virtual RAM (for example, 8 megs physical and 8 megs swap). Remember that the more physical RAM that you have, the less that the system will swap to and from disk when memory is low. Because swapping is inherently slow (disks are very slow compared to memory), having 8 megabytes of RAM or more is necessary to run XFree86 comfortably. 16 is better. A system with 4 megabytes of physical RAM could run *much* (up to 10 times) more slowly than one with 8 megs or more.

3   Installing XFree86

It's quite likely that you obtained XFree86 as part of a Linux distribution, in which case downloading the software separately is not necessary. In that case you can skip this section.

The Linux binary distribution of XFree86 can be found on a number of FTP sites. On the XFree86 site it's at <ftp://ftp.xfree86.org/pub/XFree86/current/binaries/Linux-ix86> (As of the time of this writing, the current version is 3.2A; newer versions are released periodically).

Before doing anything else, download and run the 'preinst.sh' shell script first. This may tell you about prerequisites you'll need to have in place before contibuing your installation.

If you are downloading XFree86 directly, this table lists the files in the XFree86-3.3 distribution.

One of the following servers is required:

X338514.tgz
>   Server for 8514-based boards.

X33AGX.tgz
>   Server for AGX-based boards.

X33I128.tgz
>   Server for the Number Nine Imagine 128.

X33Mach32.tgz
>   Server for Mach32-based boards.

X33Mach64.tgz
>   Server for Mach64-based boards.

X33Mach8.tgz
>   Server for Mach8-based boards.

X33Mono.tgz
>   Server for monochrome video modes.

X33P9K.tgz
>   Server for P9000-based boards.

X33S3.tgz
>   Server for S3-based boards.

X33S3V.tgz
>   Server for the S3 ViRGE and ViRGE/VX (considered beta)

X33SVGA.tgz
>   Server for Super VGA-based boards.

X33W32.tgz
>   Server for ET4000/W32-based boards.

If you don't know which one to take, take the VGA16 server, X33VGA16.tgz. You want to download this one anyway, because you'll need it to run the auto-configuration utility in the next step.

All of the following files are required:

preinst.sh
>   Pre-installation script

postinst.sh
>   Post-installation script

X33bin.tgz
>   The rest of the X11R6 binaries.

X33cfg.tgz
>   Config files for `xdm`, `xinit` and `fs`.

X33doc.tgz
>   Documentation.

X33man.tgz

　　Manual pages.

X33fnts.tgz

　　75dpi, misc and PEX fonts

X33lib.tgz

　　Shared X libraries and support files.

X33set.tgz

　　XF86Setup utility

X33VG16.tgz

　　Server for VGA/EGA-based boards.

The following files are optional:

X33f100.tgz

　　100dpi fonts

X33fcyr.tgz

　　Cyrillic fonts

X33fnon.tgz

　　Other fonts (Chinese, Japanese, Korean, Hebrew)

X33fscl.tgz

　　Scalable fonts (Speedo and Type1)

X33fsrv.tgz

　　Font server and config files

X33prog.tgz

　　X header files, config files and compile-time libs

X33lkit.tgz

　　X server LinkKit

X33lk98.tgz

　　PC98 X server LinkKit

X33nest.tgz

　　Nested X server

X33prt.tgz

　　X print server

X33vfb.tgz

　　Virtual framebuffer X server

X33ps.tgz

　　PostScript version of the documentation

X33html.tgz

　　HTML version of the documentation

The XFree86 directory should contain release notes for the current version in **RELNOTES**. Consult those for installation details

All that is required to install XFree86 is to obtain the above files, create the directory **/usr/X11R6** (as **root**), and unpack the files from **/usr/X11R6** with a command such as:

```
gzip -dc X33bin.tgz | tar xfB -
```

Remember that these tar files are packed relative to `/usr/X11R6`, so it's important to unpack the files there.

You need to make sure that `/usr/X11R6/bin` is on your path. This can be done by editing your system default `/etc/profile` or `/etc/csh.login` (based on the shell that you, or other users on your system, use). Or you can simply add the directory to your personal path by modifying `/etc/.bashrc` or `/etc/.cshrc`, based on your shell.

You also need to make sure that `/usr/X11R6/lib` can be located by `ld.so`, the runtime linker. To do this, add the line

```
/usr/X11R6/lib
```

to the file `/etc/ld.so.conf`, and run `/sbin/ldconfig`, as `root`.

4   Configuring XFree86

4.1   Normal Configuration

Configuring XFree86 to use your mouse, keyboard, monitor, and video card correctly used to be something of a black art, requiring extensive hand-hacking of a complex configuration file. No more; the 3.2/3.3 released made the process nearly trivial. All you do is fire up the program `XF86Setup`.

This program depends on the fact that all new PC hardware these days ships with EGA/VGA capable monitors. It invokes the SVGA16 server and uses it to bring up X in a lowest-common-denominator 640x480 mode. Then it runs an interactive program that walks you through a series of five configuration panels – mouse, keyboard, (video) card, monitor, and 'other' (miscellaneous server options). The whole process is quite painless.

One minor point to keep in mind is that, if you're like most people using current PC, your keyboard is actually what XF86Setup calls 'Generic 102-key PC (intl)' rather than the default 'Generic 101-key PC'. If you pick the default (101) the key cluster on the extreme right of your keyboard (numeric keypad and friends) may stop working.

If you're not sure of your monitor type, you can try the listed ones in succession. Work your way from top down (upper choices involve lower dot-clock speeds and are less demanding on the hardware). Back off if you get hash or a seriously distorted picture. Minor distortions (picture slightly too large, slightly too small, or slightly off-center) are no problem; you'll get a chance to correct those immediately by fine-tuning the mode.

And, when the program brings up `xvidtune` to allow you to tweak your video mode, don't let the initial warning box make you nervous. Modern multisync monitors (unlike their fixed-frequency predecessors) are not easy to damage this way.

XF86Config may assume that your mouse device is `/dev/mouse`. If you find this doesn't work, you may need to link `/dev/mouse` to whatever `/dev/ca[01]` the mouse is on. If you find that XFree86 gives you a "mouse busy" error when

---

gpm

---

is running, you may need to link to `/dev/ttyS[01]` instead.

4.2 Troubleshooting

Occasionally, something will not be quite right when you initially fire up the X server. This is almost always caused by a problem in your configuration file. Usually, the monitor timing values are off, or the video card dot clocks set incorrectly. Minor problems can be fixed with **xvidtune**; a really garbled screen usually means you need to go back into XF86Setup and choose a less capable monitor type.

If your display seems to roll, or the edges are fuzzy, this is a clear indication that the monitor timing values or dot clocks are wrong. Also be sure that you are correctly specifying your video card chipset, as well as other options for the **Device** section of **XF86Config**. Be absolutely certain that you are using the right X server and that **/usr/X11R6/bin/X** is a symbolic link to this server.

If all else fails, try to start X "bare"; that is, use a command such as:

```
X > /tmp/x.out 2>&1
```

You can then kill the X server (using the **ctrl-alt-backspace** key combination) and examine the contents of **/tmp/x.out**. The X server will report any warnings or errors—for example, if your video card doesn't have a dot clock corresponding to a mode supported by your monitor.

Remember that you can use **ctrl-alt-numeric +** and **ctrl-alt-numeric -** to switch between the video modes listed on the **Modes** line of the **Screen** section of **XF86Config**. If the highest resolution mode doesn't look right, try switching to lower resolutions. This will let you know, at least, that those parts of your X configuration are working correctly.

Also, check the vertical and horizontal size/hold knobs on your monitor. In many cases it is necessary to adjust these when starting up X. For example, if the display seems to be shifted slightly to one side, you can usually correct this using the monitor controls.

The USENET newsgroup **comp.windows.x.i386unix** is devoted to discussions about XFree86, as is **comp.os.linux.x**. It might be a good idea to watch that newsgroup for postings relating to your video configuration—you might run across someone with the same problems as your own.

4.3 Custom Configuration

You will need to hand-hack your X configuration to get optimal performance if your monitor can support 1600x1200 – the highest canned resolution XF86Setup supports is 1280x1024.

If you want to hand-hack your video configuration for this or any other reason, go see the LDP's XFree86 Video Timings HOWTO, **<http://sunsite.unc.edu/LDP/HOWTO/video-modes.html>**. (This is the up-to-date HTML version of XFree86's 'Videomodes.doc' file.)

4.4 Using 16-bit Color

By default, X uses 8-bit color depth giving 256 colors. To circumvent this restriction, many applications allocate their own colormaps, resulting in sudden color jumps when the cursor moves between two windows each having a color map of its own. The Arena WWW browser does it this way.

If you want to use advanced graphic applications 256 colors may be not sufficient. You may need to go to 16-bit color depth (65,536 colors). But beware, not all applications will work with 16bit colors.

You can use 16bit color depth with 65K different colors simply by starting X with

```
startx -- -bpp 16
```

or putting

```
exec X :0 -bpp 16
```

into your .xserverrc file. In order for this to work, however, you need to have a

screen

section in your XF86Config with

```
DefaultColorDepth 16
```

If you're using xdm, you nay need to change the **Xservers** file, which is probably located in **/etc/X11/xdm/**. A typical configuration has just one uncommented line, looking something like

```
:0 local /usr/X11R6/bin/X
```

Add

```
-bpp 16
```

to the startup options:

```
:0 local /usr/X11R6/bin/X -bpp 16
```

Also, you'll need to add to the "screen" section of your

More colors makes your video card transfer more data during the same time. If your video card cannot cope, then either the resolution has or the refresh rate has to be reduced. By default, XFree reduces the resolution. If you want to keep the resolution and reduce the refresh rate, you must insert a new appropriate Modeline into your XF86Config file which defines that resolution with a lower refresh rate. For instance replace the old value

```
Modeline "1024x768"  75  1024 1048 1184 1328 768 771 777 806 -hsync -vsync
```

with

```
Modeline "1024x768"  65  1024 1032 1176 1344 768 771 777 806 -hsync -vsync.
```

The magic numbers 75 and 65 are the respective clock rates which you find reported by X in your .X.err file. Consult the monitors file in the XF86 documentation for Modelines suitable to the maximum clock rate your video card can deliver under 16bit color depth.

5   Running XFree86

With your `XF86Config` file configured, you're ready to fire up the X server and give it a spin. First, be sure that `/usr/X11R6/bin` is on your path.

The command to start up XFree86 is

```
startx
```

This is a front-end to `xinit` (in case you're used to using `xinit` on other UNIX systems).

This command will start the X server and run the commands found in the file `.xinitrc` in your home directory. `.xinitrc` is just a shell script containing X clients to run. If this file does not exist, the system default `/usr/X11R6/lib/X11/xinit/xinitrc` will be used.

A standard `.xinitrc` file looks like this:

```
#!/bin/sh

xterm -fn 7x13bold -geometry 80x32+10+50 &
xterm -fn 9x15bold -geometry 80x34+30-10 &
oclock -geometry 70x70-7+7 &
xsetroot -solid midnightblue &

exec twm
```

This script will start up two `xterm` clients, an `oclock`, and set the root window (background) color to `midnightblue`. It will then start up `twm`, the window manager. Note that `twm` is executed with the shell's `exec` statement; this causes the `xinit` process to be replaced with `twm`. Once the `twm` process exits, the X server will shut down. You can cause `twm` to exit by using the root menus: depress mouse button 1 on the desktop background—this will display a pop up menu which will allow you to `Exit Twm`.

Be sure that the last command in `.xinitrc` is started with `exec`, and that it is not placed into the background (no ampersand on the end of the line). Otherwise the X server will shut down as soon as it has started the clients in the `.xinitrc` file.

Alternately, you can exit X by pressing `ctrl-alt-backspace` in combination. This will kill the X server directly, exiting the window system.

The above is a very, very simple desktop configuration. Many wonderful programs and configurations are available with a bit of work on your `.xinitrc` file. For example, the `fvwm` window manager will provide a virtual desktop, and you can customize colors, fonts, window sizes and positions, and so forth to your heart's content.

If you are new to the X Window System environment, we strongly suggest picking up a book such as *The X Window System: A User's Guide*. Using and configuring X is far too in-depth to cover here. See the man pages for `xterm`, `oclock`, and `twm` for clues on getting started.

5.1   Terms of Use

This document is copyright 1996 by Eric S. Raymond. You may use, disseminate, and reproduce it freely, provided you:

- Do not omit or alter this copyright notice.
- Do not omit or alter or omit the version number and date.

- Do not omit or alter the document's pointer to the current WWW version.
- Clearly mark any condsensed, altered or versions as such.

These restrictions are intended to protect potential readers from stale or mangled versions. If you think you have a good case for an exception, ask me.

5.2 Acknowledgements

This document was originated by Matt Welsh in the dim and backward abysm of time. Thanks, Matt!

XFree86 Video Timings HOWTO

Eric S. Raymond <esr@thyrsus.com>   v3.1, 31 October 1997

How to compose a mode line for your card/monitor combination under XFree86. The XFree86 distribution now includes good facilities for configuring most standard combinations; this document is mainly useful if you are tuning a custom mode line for a high-performance monitor or very unusual hardware. It may also help you in using xvidtune to tweak a standard mode that is not quite right for your monitor.

Contents

1   Disclaimer

You use the material herein SOLELY AT YOUR OWN RISK. It is possible to harm both your monitor and yourself when driving it outside the manufacturer's specs. Read 11 (Overdriving Your Monitor) for detailed cautions. Any damages to you or your monitor caused by overdriving it are your problem.

The most up-to-date version of this HOWTO can be found at the *Linux Documentation Project* `<http://sunsite.unc.edu/LDP>` web page.

Please direct comments, criticism, and suggestions for improvement to *esr@snark.thyrsus.com* `<mailto:esr@thyrsus.com>`. Please do *not* send email pleading for a magic solution to your special monitor problem, as doing so will only burn up my time and frustrate you – everything I know about the subject is already in here.

2   Introduction

The XFree86 server allows users to configure their video subsystem and thus encourages best use of existing hardware. This tutorial is intended to help you learn how to generate your own timing numbers to make optimum use of your video card and monitor.

We'll present a method for getting something that works, and then show you how you can experiment starting from that base to develop settings that optimize for your taste.

Starting with XFree86 3.2, XFree86 provides an **XF86Setup**(1) program that makes it easy to generate a working monitor mode interactively, without messing with video timing number directly. So you shouldn't actually need to calculate a base monitor mode in most cases. Unfortunately, **XF86Setup**(1) has some limitations; it only knows about standard video modes up to 1280x1024. If you have a very high-performance monitor capable of 1600x1200 or more you will still have to compute your base monitor mode yourself.

Recent versions of XFree86 provide a tool called **xvidtune**(1) which you will probably find quite useful for testing and tuning monitor modes. It begins with a gruesome warning about the possible consequences of mistakes with it. If you pay careful attention to this document and learn what is behind the pretty numbers in xvidtune's boxes, you will become able to use xvidtune effectively and with confidence.

If you already have a mode that almost works (in particular, if one of predefined VESA modes gives you a stable display but one that's displaced right or left, or too small, or too large) you can go straight to the section on 14 (Fixing Problems with the Image). This will enlighten you on ways to tweak the timing numbers to achieve particular effects.

If you have **xvidtune**(1), you'll be able to test new modes on the fly, without modifying your X configuration files or even rebooting your X server. Otherwise, XFree86 allows you to hot-key between different modes defined in Xconfig (see XFree86.man for details). Use this capabilty to save yourself hassles! When you want to test a new mode, give it a unique mode label and add it to the *end* of your hot-key list. Leave a known-good mode as the default to fall back on if the test mode doesn't work.

3   How Video Displays Work

Knowing how the display works is essential to understanding what numbers to put in the various fields in the file Xconfig. Those values are used in the lowest levels of controlling the display by the XFree86 server.

The display generates a picture from a series of dots. The dots are arranged from left to right to form lines. The lines are arranged from top to bottom to form the picture. The dots emit light when they are struck by the electron beam inside the display. To make the beam strike each dot for an equal amount of time, the beam is swept across the display in a constant pattern.

The pattern starts at the top left of the screen, goes across the screen to the right in a straight line, and stops temporarily on the right side of the screen. Then the beam is swept back to the left side of the display, but down one line. The new line is swept from left to right just as the first line was. This pattern is repeated until the bottom line on the display has been swept. Then the beam is moved from the bottom right corner of the display to the top left corner, and the pattern is started over again.

There is one variation of this scheme known as interlacing: here only every second line is swept during one half-frame and the others are filled in in during a second half-frame.

Starting the beam at the top left of the display is called the beginning of a frame. The frame ends when the beam reaches the the top left corner again as it comes from the bottom right corner of the display. A frame is made up of all of the lines the beam traced from the top of the display to the bottom.

If the electron beam were on all of the time it was sweeping through the frame, all of the dots on the display would be illuminated. There would be no black border around the edges of the display. At the edges of the display the picture would become distorted because the beam is hard to control there. To reduce the distortion, the dots around the edges of the display are not illuminated by the beam even though the beam may be pointing at them. The viewable area of the display is reduced this way.

Another important thing to understand is what becomes of the beam when no spot is being painted on the visible area. The time the beam would have been illuminating the side borders of the display is used for sweeping the beam back from the right edge to the left and moving the beam down to the next line. The time the beam would have been illuminating the top and bottom borders of the display is used for moving the beam from the bottom-right corner of the display to the top-left corner.

The adapter card generates the signals which cause the display to turn on the electron beam at each dot to generate a picture. The card also controls when the display moves the beam from the right side to the left and down a line by generating a signal called the horizontal sync (for synchronization) pulse. One horizontal sync pulse occurs at the end of every line. The adapter also generates a vertical sync pulse which signals the display to move the beam to the top-left corner of the display. A vertical sync pulse is generated near the end of every frame.

The display requires that there be short time periods both before and after the horizontal and vertical sync pulses so that the position of the electron beam can stabilize. If the beam can't stabilize, the picture will not be steady.

In a later section, we'll come back to these basics with definitions, formulas and examples to help you use them.

4   Basic Things to Know about your Display and Adapter

There are some fundamental things you need to know before hacking an Xconfig entry. These are:

- your monitor's horizontal and vertical sync frequency options
- your video adapter's driving clock frequency, or "dot clock"
- your monitor's bandwidth

The monitor sync frequencies:

The horizontal sync frequency is just the number of times per second the monitor can write a horizontal scan line; it is the single most important statistic about your monitor. The vertical sync frequency is the number of times per second the monitor can traverse its beam vertically.

Sync frequencies are usually listed on the specifications page of your monitor manual. The vertical sync frequency number is typically calibrated in Hz (cycles per second), the horizontal one in KHz (kilocycles per second). The usual ranges are between 50 and 150Hz vertical, and between 31 and 135KHz horizontal.

If you have a multisync monitor, these frequencies will be given as ranges. Some monitors, especially lower-end ones, have multiple fixed frequencies. These can be configured too, but your options will be severely limited by the built-in monitor characteristics. Choose the highest frequency pair for best resolution. And be careful — trying to clock a fixed-frequency monitor at a higher speed than it's designed for can easily damage it.

Earlier versions of this guide were pretty cavalier about overdriving multisync monitors, pushing them past their nominal highest vertical sync frequency in order to get better performance. We have since had more reasons pointed out to us for caution on this score; we'll cover those under 11 (Overdriving Your Monitor) below.

The card driving clock frequency:

Your video adapter manual's spec page will usually give you the card's dot clock (that is, the total number of pixels per second it can write to the screen). If you don't have this information, the X server will get it for you. Even if your X locks up your monitor, it will emit a line of clock and other info to standard output. If you redirect this to a file, it should be saved even if you have to reboot to get your console back. (Recent versions of the X servers allsupport a –probeonly option that prints out this information and exits without actually starting up X or changing the video mode.)

Your X startup message should look something like one of the following examples:

If you're using XFree86:

```
Xconfig: /usr/X11R6/lib/X11/Xconfig
(**) stands for supplied, (--) stands for probed/default values
(**) Mouse: type: MouseMan, device: /dev/ttyS1, baudrate: 9600
Warning: The directory "/usr/andrew/X11fonts" does not exist.
          Entry deleted from font path.
(**) FontPath set to "/usr/lib/X11/fonts/misc/,/usr/lib/X11/fonts/75dpi/"
(--) S3: card type: 386/486 localbus
(--) S3: chipset:   924
          ---
    Chipset -- this is the exact chip type; an early mask of the 86C911

(--) S3: chipset driver: s3_generic
(--) S3: videoram:  1024k
          -----
```

```
            Size of on-board frame-buffer RAM

(**) S3: clocks:   25.00   28.00   40.00    3.00   50.00   77.00   36.00   45.00
(**) S3: clocks:    0.00    0.00   79.00   31.00   94.00   65.00   75.00   71.00
                  -------------------------------------------------------------
                      Possible driving frequencies in MHz

(--) S3: Maximum allowed dot-clock: 110MHz
                  ------
                      Bandwidth
(**) S3: Mode "1024x768": mode clock =   79.000, clock used =   79.000
(--) S3: Virtual resolution set to 1024x768
(--) S3: Using a banksize of 64k, line width of 1024
(--) S3: Pixmap cache:
(--) S3: Using 2 128-pixel 4 64-pixel and 8 32-pixel slots
(--) S3: Using 8 pages of 768x255 for font caching
```

If you're using SGCS or X/Inside X:

```
WGA: 86C911 (mem: 1024k clocks: 25 28 40 3 50 77 36 45 0 0 79 31 94 65 75 71)
---  ------    -----  ---------------------------------------------
 |     |          |            Possible driving frequencies in MHz
 |     |          +-- Size of on-board frame-buffer RAM
 |     +-- Chip type
 +-- Server type
```

Note: do this with your machine unloaded (if at all possible). Because X is an application, its timing loops can collide with disk activity, rendering the numbers above inaccurate. Do it several times and watch for the numbers to stabilize; if they don't, start killing processes until they do. SVr4 users: the mousemgr process is particularly likely to mess you up.

In order to avoid the clock-probe inaccuracy, you should clip out the clock timings and put them in your Xconfig as the value of the Clocks property — this suppresses the timing loop and gives X an exact list of the clock values it can try. Using the data from the example above:

```
wga
        Clocks   25 28 40 3 50 77 36 45 0 0 79 31 94 65 75 71
```

On systems with a highly variable load, this may help you avoid mysterious X startup failures. It's possible for X to come up, get its timings wrong due to system load, and then not be able to find a matching dot clock in its config database — or find the wrong one!

4.1   The monitor's video bandwidth:

If you're running XFree86, your server will probe your card and tell you what your highest-available dot clock is.

Otherwise, your highest available dot clock is approximately the monitor's video bandwidth. There's a lot of give here, though — some monitors can run as much as 30% over their nominal bandwidth. The risks here have to do with exceeding the monitor's rated vertical-sync frequency; we'll discuss them in detail below.

Knowing the bandwidth will enable you to make more intelligent choices between possible configurations. It may affect your display's visual quality (especially sharpness for fine details).

Your monitor's video bandwidth should be included on the manual's spec page. If it's not, look at the monitor's higest rated resolution. As a rule of thumb, here's how to translate these into bandwidth estimates (and thus into rough upper bounds for the dot clock you can use):

640x480	25
800x600	36
1024x768	65
1024x768 interlaced	45
1280x1024	110
1600x1200	185

BTW, there's nothing magic about this table; these numbers are just the lowest dot clocks per resolution in the standard XFree86 Modes database (except for the last, which I interpolated). The bandwidth of your monitor may actually be higher than the minimum needed for its top resolution, so don't be afraid to try a dot clock a few MHz higher.

Also note that bandwidth is seldom an issue for dot clocks under 65MHz or so. With an SVGA card and most hi-res monitors, you can't get anywhere near the limit of your monitor's video bandwidth. The following are examples:

Brand	Video Bandwidth
NEC 4D	75Mhz
Nano 907a	50Mhz
Nano 9080i	60Mhz
Mitsubishi HL6615	110Mhz
Mitsubishi Diamond Scan	100Mhz
IDEK MF-5117	65Mhz
IOCOMM Thinksync-17 CM-7126	136Mhz
HP D1188A	100Mhz
Philips SC-17AS	110Mhz
Swan SW617	85Mhz
Viewsonic 21PS	185Mhz

Even low-end monitors usually aren't terribly bandwidth-constrained for their rated resolutions. The NEC Multisync II makes a good example — it can't even display 800x600 per its spec. It can only display 800x560. For such low resolutions you don't need high dot clocks or a lot of bandwidth; probably the best you can do is 32Mhz or 36Mhz, both of them are still not too far from the monitor's rated video bandwidth of 30Mhz.

At these two driving frequencies, your screen image may not be as sharp as it should be, but definitely of tolerable quality. Of course it would be nicer if NEC Multisync II had a video bandwidth higher than, say, 36Mhz. But this is not critical for common tasks like text editing, as long as the difference is not so significant as to cause severe image distortion (your eyes would tell you right away if this were so).

4.2   What these control:

The sync frequency ranges of your monitor, together with your video adapter's dot clock, determine the ultimate resolution that you can use. But it's up to the driver to tap the potential of your hardware. A superior hardware combination without an equally competent device driver is a waste of money. On the other hand, with a versatile device driver but less capable hardware, you can push the hardware's envelope a little. This is the design philosophy of XFree86.

5   Interpreting the Basic Specifications

This section explains what the specifications above mean, and some other things you'll need to know. First, some definitions. Next to each in parens is the variable name we'll use for it when doing calculations

horizontal sync frequency (HSF)

> Horizontal scans per second (see above).

vertical sync frequency (VSF)

> Vertical scans per second (see above). Mainly important as the upper limit on your refresh rate.

dot clock (DCF)

> More formally, 'driving clock frequency'; The frequency of the crystal or VCO on your adaptor — the maximum dots-per-second it can emit.

video bandwidth (VB)

> The highest frequency you can feed into your monitor's video input and still expect to see anything discernible. If your adaptor produces an alternating on/off pattern, its lowest frequency is half the DCF, so in theory bandwidth starts making sense at DCF/2. For tolerately crisp display of fine details in the video image, however, you don't want it much below your highest DCF, and preferably higher.

frame length (HFL, VFL)

> Horizontal frame length (HFL) is the number of dot-clock ticks needed for your monitor's electron gun to scan one horizontal line, *including the inactive left and right borders*. Vertical frame length (VFL) is the number of scan lines in the *entire* image, including the inactive top and bottom borders.

screen refresh rate (RR)

> The number of times per second your screen is repainted (this is also called "frame rate"). Higher frequencies are better, as they reduce flicker. 60Hz is good, VESA-standard 72Hz is better. Compute it as

> $$RR = DCF / (HFL * VFL)$$

Note that the product in the denominator is *not* the same as the monitor's visible resolution, but typically somewhat larger. We'll get to the details of this below.

The rates for which interlaced modes are usually specified (like 87Hz interlaced) are actually the half-frame rates: an entire screen seems to have about that flicker frequency for typical displays, but every single line is refreshed only half as often.

For calculation purposes we reckon an interlaced display at its full-frame (refresh) rate, i.e. 43.5Hz. The quality of an interlaced mode is better than that of a non-interlaced mode with the same full-frame rate, but definitely worse then the non-interlaced one corresponding to the half-frame rate.

5.1   About Bandwidth:

Monitor makers like to advertise high bandwidth because it constrains the sharpness of intensity and color changes on the screen. A high bandwidth means smaller visible details.

Your monitor uses electronic signals to present an image to your eyes. Such signals always come in in wave form once they are converted into analog form from digitized form. They can be considered as combinations of many simpler wave forms each one of which has a fixed frequency, many of them are in the Mhz range, eg, 20Mhz, 40Mhz, or even 70Mhz. Your monitor video bandwidth is, effectively, the highest-frequency analog signal it can handle without distortion.

For our purposes, video bandwidth is mainly important as an approximate cutoff point for the highest dot clock you can use.

5.2   Sync Frequencies and the Refresh Rate:

Each horizontal scan line on the display is just the visible portion of a frame-length scan. At any instant there is actually only one dot active on the screen, but with a fast enough refresh rate your eye's persistence of vision enables you to "see" the whole image.

Here are some pictures to help:

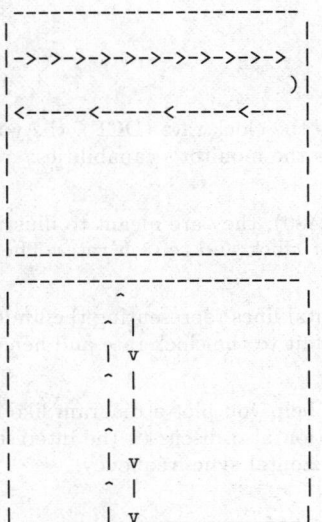

```
 ----------------------
|                      |       The horizontal sync frequency
|->->->->->->->->->->  |       is the number of times per
|                    )| |       second that the monitor's
|<-----<-----<-----<---|       electron beam can trace
|                      |       a pattern like this
|                      |
|                      |
|_____|

 ----------------------
|        ^            |       The vertical sync frequency
|      ^ |            |       is the number of times per
|      | v            |       second that the monitor's
|      ^ |            |       electron beam can trace
|      | |            |       a pattern like this
|      ^ |            |
|      | v            |
|      ^ |            |
|_____|_v_____|
```

Remember that the actual raster scan is a very tight zigzag pattern; that is, the beam moves left-right and at the same time up-down.

Now we can see how the dot clock and frame size relates to refresh rate. By definition, one hertz (hz) is one cycle per second. So, if your horizontal frame length is HFL and your vertical frame length is VFL, then to cover the entire screen takes (HFL * VFL) ticks. Since your card emits DCF ticks per second by definition, then obviously your monitor's electron gun(s) can sweep the screen from left to right and back and from bottom to top and back DCF / (HFL * VFL) times/sec. This is your screen's refresh rate, because it's how many times your screen can be updated (thus *refreshed*) per second!

You need to understand this concept to design a configuration which trades off resolution against flicker in whatever way suits your needs.

For those of you who handle visuals better than text, here is one:

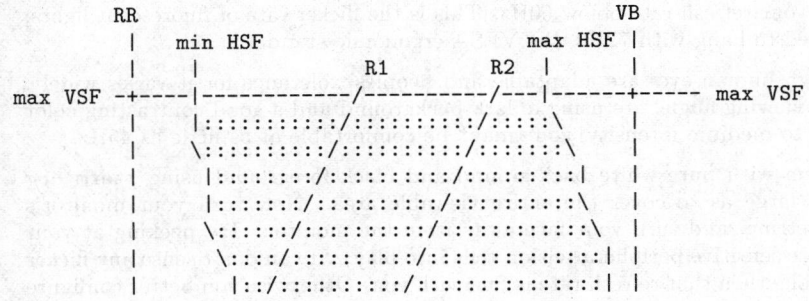

```
        RR                                          VB
         |    min HSF                         max HSF |
         |     |              R1        R2    |        |
max VSF -+----|------------/----------/---|------+----- max VSF
         |    |::::::::::/:::::::::::/:::::\       |
         |    \:::::::::/:::::::::::/::::::\       |
         |    |::::::::/:::::::::::/::::::::|       |
         |    |:::::::/:::::::::::/:::::::::\       |
         |    \::::::/:::::::::::/::::::::::\       |
         |     \::::/:::::::::::/::::::::::::|       |
         |     |::/:::::::::::/:::::::::::::|       |
```

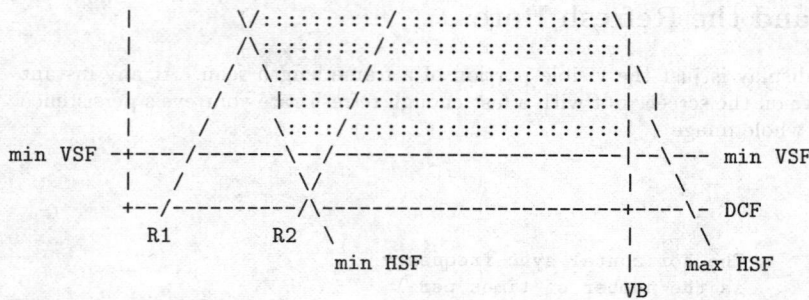

```
         |         \/::::::::::/:::::::::::::::::\|
         |          /\:::::::::/:::::::::::::::::|
         |       /  \::::::::/::::::::::::::::::|\
         |      /    |:::::/:::::::::::::::::::| |
         |     /      \::::/:::::::::::::::::::| \
min VSF -+----/-------\--/-------------------|--\--- min VSF
         | /           \/                    |   \
         +--/----------/\--------------------+----\- DCF
         R1          R2  \                   |     \
                     min HSF                 |   max HSF
                                             VB
```

This is a generic monitor mode diagram. The x axis of the diagram shows the clock rate (DCF), the y axis represents the refresh rate (RR). The filled region of the diagram describes the monitor's capabilities: every point within this region is a possible video mode.

The lines labeled 'R1' and 'R2' represent a fixed resolutions (such as 640x480); they are meant to illustrate how one resolution can be realized by many different combinations of dot clock and refresh rate. The R2 line would represent a higher resolution than R1.

The top and bottom boundaries of the permitted region are simply horizontal lines representing the limiting values for the vertical sync frequency. The video bandwidth is an upper limit to the clock rate and hence is represented by a vertical line bounding the capability region on the right.

Under 15 (Plotting Monitor Capabilities)) you'll find a program that will help you plot a diagram like this (but much nicer, with X graphics) for your individual monitor. That section also discusses the interesting part; the derivation of the boundaries resulting from the limits on the horizontal sync frequency.

6   Tradeoffs in Configuring your System

Another way to look at the formula we derived above is

$$DCF = RR * HFL * VFL$$

That is, your dot clock is fixed. You can use those dots per second to buy either refresh rate, horizontal resolution, or vertical resolution. If one of those increases, one or both of the others must decrease.

Note, though, that your refresh rate cannot be greater than the maximum vertical sync frequency of your monitor. Thus, for any given monitor at a given dot clock, there is a minimum product of frame lengths below which you can't force it.

In choosing your settings, remember: if you set RR too low, you will get mugged by screen flicker.

You probably do not want to pull your refresh rate below 60Hz. This is the flicker rate of fluorescent lights; if you're sensitive to those, you need to hang with 72Hz, the VESA ergonomic standard.

Flicker is very eye-fatiguing, though human eyes are adaptable and peoples' tolerance for it varies widely. If you face your monitor at a 90% viewing angle, are using a dark background and a good contrasting color for foreground, and stick with low to medium intensity, you *may* be comfortable at as little as 45Hz.

The acid test is this: open a xterm with pure white back-ground and black foreground using xterm -bg white -fg black and make it so large as to cover the entire viewable area. Now turn your monitor's intensity to 3/4 of its maximum setting, and turn your face away from the monitor. Try peeking at your monitor sideways (bringing the more sensitive peripheral-vision cells into play). If you don't sense any flicker or if you feel the flickering is tolerable, then that refresh rate is fine with you. Otherwise you better configure a higher refresh rate, because that semi-invisible flicker is going to fatigue your eyes like crazy and give you headaches, even if the screen looks OK to normal vision.

For interlaced modes, the amount of flicker depends on more factors such as the current vertical resolution and the actual screen contents. So just experiment. You won't want to go much below about 85Hz half frame rate, though.

So let's say you've picked a minimum acceptable refresh rate. In choosing your HFL and VFL, you'll have some room for maneuver.

7   Memory Requirements

Available frame-buffer RAM may limit the resolution you can achieve on color or gray-scale displays. It probably isn't a factor on displays that have only two colors, white and black with no shades of gray in between.

For 256-color displays, a byte of video memory is required for each visible dot to be shown. This byte contains the information that determines what mix of red, green, and blue is generated for its dot. To get the amount of memory required, multiply the number of visible dots per line by the number of visible lines. For a display with a resolution of 800x600, this would be 800 x 600 = 480,000, which is the number of visible dots on the display. This is also, at one byte per dot, the number of bytes of video memory that are necessary on your adapter card.

Thus, your memory requirement will typically be (HR * VR)/1024 Kbytes of VRAM, rounded up. If you have more memory than strictly required, you'll have extra for virtual-screen panning.

However, if you only have 512K on board, then you can't use this resolution. Even if you have a good monitor, without enough video RAM, you can't take advantage of your monitor's potential. On the other hand, if your SVGA has one meg, but your monitor can display at most 800x600, then high resolution is beyond your reach anyway (see 12 (Using Interlaced Modes) for a possible remedy).

Don't worry if you have more memory than required; XFree86 will make use of it by allowing you to scroll your viewable area (see the Xconfig file documentation on the virtual screen size parameter). Remember also that a card with 512K bytes of memory really doesn't have 512,000 bytes installed, it has 512 x 1024 = 524,288 bytes.

If you're running SGCS X (now called X/Inside) using an S3 card, and are willing to live with 16 colors (4 bits per pixel), you can set depth 4 in Xconfig and effectively double the resolution your card can handle. S3 cards, for example, normally do 1024x768x256. You can make them do 1280x1024x16 with depth 4.

8   Computing Frame Sizes

Warning: this method was developed for multisync monitors. It will probably work with fixed-frequency monitors as well, but no guarantees!

Start by dividing DCF by your highest available HSF to get a horizontal frame length.

For example; suppose you have a Sigma Legend SVGA with a 65MHz dot clock, and your monitor has a 55KHz horizontal scan frequency. The quantity (DCF / HSF) is then 1181 (65MHz = 65000KHz; 65000/55 = 1181).

Now for our first bit of black magic. You need to round this figure to the nearest multiple of 8. This has to do with the VGA hardware controller used by SVGA and S3 cards; it uses an 8-bit register, left-shifted 3 bits, for what's really an 11-bit quantity. Other card types such as ATI 8514/A may not have this requirement, but we don't know and the correction can't hurt. So round the usable horizontal frame length figure down to 1176.

This figure (DCF / HSF rounded to a multiple of 8) is the minimum HFL you can use. You can get longer HFLs (and thus, possibly, more horizontal dots on the screen) by setting the sync pulse to produce a lower HSF. But you'll pay with a slower and more visible flicker rate.

As a rule of thumb, 80% of the horizontal frame length is available for horizontal resolution, the visible part of the horizontal scan line (this allows, roughly, for borders and sweepback time – that is, the time required for the beam to move from the right screen edge to the left edge of the next raster line). In this example, that's 944 ticks.

Now, to get the normal 4:3 screen aspect ratio, set your vertical resolution to 3/4ths of the horizontal resolution you just calculated. For this example, that's 708 ticks. To get your actual VFL, multiply that by 1.05 to get 743 ticks.

The 4:3 is not technically magic; nothing prevents you from using a non-Golden-Section ratio if that will get the best use out of your screen real estate. It does make figuring frame height and frame width from the diagonal size convenient, you just multiply the diagonal by by 0.8 to get width and 0.6 to get height.

So, HFL=1176 and VFL=743. Dividing 65MHz by the product of the two gives us a nice, healthy 74.4Hz refresh rate. Excellent! Better than VESA standard! And you got 944x708 to boot, more than the 800 by 600 you were probably expecting. Not bad at all!

You can even improve the refresh rate further, to almost 76 Hz, by using the fact that monitors can often sync horizontally at 2khz or so higher than rated, and by lowering VFL somewhat (that is, taking less than 75% of 944 in the example above). But before you try this "overdriving" maneuver, if you do, make *sure* that your monitor electron guns can sync up to 76 Hz vertical. (the popular NEC 4D, for instance, cannot. It goes only up to 75 Hz VSF). (See 11 (Overdriving Your Monitor) for more general discussion of this issue.)

So far, most of this is simple arithmetic and basic facts about raster displays. Hardly any black magic at all!

9   Black Magic and Sync Pulses

OK, now you've computed HFL/VFL numbers for your chosen dot clock, found the refresh rate acceptable, and checked that you have enough VRAM. Now for the real black magic – you need to know when and where to place synchronization pulses.

The sync pulses actually control the horizontal and vertical scan frequebcies of the monitor. The HSF and VSF you've pulled off the spec sheet are nominal, approximate maximum sync frequencies. The sync pulse in the signal from the adapter card tells the monitor how fast to actually run.

Recall the two pictures above? Only part of the time required for raster-scanning a frame is used for displaying viewable image (ie. your resolution).

9.1   Horizontal Sync:

By previous definition, it takes HFL ticks to trace the a horizontal scan line. Let's call the visible tick count (your horizontal screen resolution) HR. Then Obviously, HR < HFL by definition. For concreteness, let's assume both start at the same instant as shown below:

```
|___ __ __ __ __ __ __ __ __ __ __ __ __ __
|_ _ _ _ _ _ _ _ _ _ _ _ _        |
```

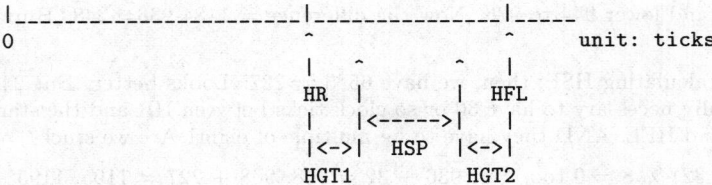

```
|_____|_____|_____
0                          ^        ^        ^            unit: ticks
                           |        ^        ^ |
                           HR |             | HFL
                           |  |<----->|        |
                           |<->|  HSP  |<->|
                           HGT1           HGT2
```

Now, we would like to place a sync pulse of length HSP as shown above, ie, between the end of clock ticks for display data and the end of clock ticks for the entire frame. Why so? because if we can achieve this, then your screen image won't shift to the right or to the left. It will be where it supposed to be on the screen, covering squarely the monitor's viewable area.

Furthermore, we want about 30 ticks of "guard time" on either side of the sync pulse. This is represented by HGT1 and HGT2. In a typical configuration HGT1 != HGT2, but if you're building a configuration from scratch, you want to start your experimentation with them equal (that is, with the sync pulse centered).

The symptom of a misplaced sync pulse is that the image is displaced on the screen, with one border excessively wide and the other side of the image wrapped around the screen edge, producing a white edge line and a band of "ghost image" on that side. A way-out-of-place vertical sync pulse can actually cause the image to roll like a TV with a mis-adjusted vertical hold (in fact, it's the same phenomenon at work).

If you're lucky, your monitor's sync pulse widths will be documented on its specification page. If not, here's where the real black magic starts...

You'll have to do a little trial and error for this part. But most of the time, we can safely assume that a sync pulse is about 3.5 to 4.0 microsecond in length.

For concretness again, let's take HSP to be 3.8 microseconds (which btw, is not a bad value to start with when experimenting).

Now, using the 65Mhz clock timing above, we know HSP is equivalent to 247 clock ticks (= 65 * 10**6 * 3.8 * 10^-6) [recall M=10^6, micro=10^-6]

Some makers like to quote their horizontal framing parameters as timings rather than dot widths. You may see the following terms:

active time (HAT)
> Corresponds to HR, but in milliseconds. HAT * DCF = HR.

blanking time (HBT)
> Corresponds to (HFL - HR), but in milliseconds. HBT * DCF = (HFL - HR).

front porch (HFP)
> This is just HGT1.

sync time
> This is just HSP.

back porch (HBP)
> This is just HGT2.

9.2   Vertical Sync:

Going back to the picture above, how do we place the 247 clock ticks as shown in the picture?

Using our example, HR is 944 and HFL is 1176. The difference between the two is 1176 - 944=232 < 247! Obviously we have to do some adjustment here. What can we do?

The first thing is to raise 1176 to 1184, and lower 944 to 936. Now the difference = 1184-936= 248. Hmm, closer.

Next, instead using 3.8, we use 3.5 for calculating HSP; then, we have 65*3.5=227. Looks better. But 248 is not much higher than 227. It's normally necessary to have 30 or so clock ticks between HR and the start of SP, and the same for the end of SP and HFL. AND they have to be multiple of eight! Are we stuck?

No. Let's do this, 936 % 8 = 0, (936 + 32) % 8 = 0 too. But 936 + 32 = 968, 968 + 227 = 1195, 1195 + 32 = 1227. Hmm.. this looks not too bad. But it's not a multiple of 8, so let's round it up to 1232.

But now we have potential trouble, the sync pulse is no longer placed right in the middle between h and H any more. Happily, using our calculator we find 1232 - 32 = 1200 is also a multiple of 8 and (1232 - 32) - 968 = 232 corresponding using a sync pulse of 3.57 micro second long, still reasonable.

In addition, 936/1232   0.76 or 76%, still not far from 80%, so it should be all right.

Furthermore, using the current horizontal frame length, we basically ask our monitor to sync at 52.7khz (= 65Mhz/1232) which is within its capability. No problems.

Using rules of thumb we mentioned before, 936*75%=702, This is our new vertical resolution. 702 * 1.05 = 737, our new vertical frame length.

Screen refresh rate = 65Mhz/(737*1232)=71.6 Hz. This is still excellent.

Figuring the vertical sync pulse layout is similar:

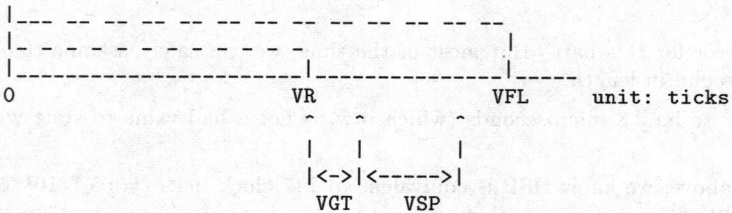

We start the sync pulse just past the end of the vertical display data ticks. VGT is the vertical guard time required for the sync pulse. Most monitors are comfortable with a VGT of 0 (no guard time) and we'll use that in this example. A few need two or three ticks of guard time, and it usually doesn't hurt to add that.

Returning to the example: since by the defintion of frame length, a vertical tick is the time for tracing a complete HORIZONTAL frame, therefore in our example, it is 1232/65Mhz=18.95us.

Experience shows that a vertical sync pulse should be in the range of 50us and 300us. As an example let's use 150us, which translates into 8 vertical clock ticks (150us/18.95us 8).

Some makers like to quote their vertical framing parameters as timings rather than dot widths. You may see the following terms:

active time (VAT)
> Corresponds to VR, but in milliseconds. VAT * VSF = VR.

blanking time (VBT)
> Corresponds to (VFL - VR), but in milliseconds. VBT * VSF = (VFL - VR).

front porch (VFP)
> This is just VGT.

sync time
> This is just VSP.

back porch (VBP)
> This is like a second guard time after the vertical sync pulse. It is often zero.

10 Putting it All Together

The Xconfig file Table of Video Modes contains lines of numbers, with each line being a complete specification for one mode of X-server operation. The fields are grouped into four sections, the name section, the clock frequency section, the horizontal section, and the vertical section.

The name section contains one field, the name of the video mode specified by the rest of the line. This name is referred to on the "Modes" line of the Graphics Driver Setup section of the Xconfig file. The name field may be omitted if the name of a previous line is the same as the current line.

The dot clock section contains only the dot clock (what we've called DCF) field of the video mode line. The number in this field specifies what dot clock was used to generate the numbers in the following sections.

The horizontal section consists of four fields which specify how each horizontal line on the display is to be generated. The first field of the section contains the number of dots per line which will be illuminated to form the picture (what we've called HR). The second field of the section indicates at which dot the horizontal sync pulse will begin. The third field indicates at which dot the horizontal sync pulse will end. The fourth field specifies the toal horzontal frame length (HFL).

The vertical section also contains four fields. The first field contains the number of visible lines which will appear on the display (VR). The second field indicates the line number at which the vertical sync pulse will begin. The third field specifies the line number at which the vertical sync pulse will end. The fourth field contains the total vertical frame length (VFL).

Example:

```
#Modename    clock  horizontal timing  vertical timing

"752x564"    40     752 784  944 1088   564 567 569 611
             44.5   752 792  976 1240   564 567 570 600
```

(Note: stock X11R5 doesn't support fractional dot clocks.)

For Xconfig, all of the numbers just mentioned - the number of illuminated dots on the line, the number of dots separating the illuminated dots from the beginning of the sync pulse, the number of dots representing the duration of the pulse, and the number of dots after the end of the sync pulse - are added to produce the number of dots per line. The number of horizontal dots must be evenly divisible by eight.

Example horizontal numbers: 800 864 1024 1088

This sample line has the number of illuminated dots (800) followed by the number of the dot when the sync pulse starts (864), followed by the number of the dot when the sync pulse ends (1024), followed by the number of the last dot on the horizontal line (1088).

Note again that all of the horizontal numbers (800, 864, 1024, and 1088) are divisible by eight! This is not required of the vertical numbers.

The number of lines from the top of the display to the bottom form the frame. The basic timing signal for a frame is the line. A number of lines will contain the picture. After the last illuminated line has been displayed, a delay of a number of lines will occur before the vertical sync pulse is generated. Then the sync pulse will last for a few lines, and finally the last lines in the frame, the delay required after the pulse, will be generated. The numbers that specify this mode of operation are entered in a manner similar to the following example.

Example vertical numbers: 600 603 609 630

This example indicates that there are 600 visible lines on the display, that the vertical sync pulse starts with the 603rd line and ends with the 609th, and that there are 630 total lines being used.

Note that the vertical numbers don't have to be divisible by eight!

Let's return to the example we've been working. According to the above, all we need to do from now on is to write our result into Xconfig as follows:

```
<name>   DCF    HR  SH1 SH2   HFL   VR  SV1 SV2 VFL
```

where SH1 is the start tick of the horizontal sync pulse and SH2 is its end tick; similarly, SV1 is the start tick of the vertical sync pulse and SV2 is its end tick.

```
#name     clock    horizontal timing    vertical timing    flag
936x702   65       936 968 1200 1232    702 702 710 737
```

No special flag necessary; this is a non-interlaced mode. Now we are really done.

11   Overdriving Your Monitor

You should absolutely *not* try exceeding your monitor's scan rates if it's a fixed-frequency type. You can smoke your hardware doing this! There are potentially subtler problems with overdriving a multisync monitor which should be aware of.

Having a pixel clock higher than the monitor's maximum bandwidth is rather harmless, in contrast. (Note: the theoretical limit of discernable features is reached when the pixel clock reaches double the monitor's bandwidth. This is a straightforward application of Nyquist's Theorem: consider the pixels as a spatially distributed series of samples of the drive signals and you'll see why.)

It's exceeding the rated maximum sync frequencies that's problematic. Some modern monitors might have protection circuitry that shuts the monitor down at dangerous scan rates, but don't rely on it. In particular there are older multisync monitors (like the Multisync II) which use just one horizontal transformer. These monitors will not have much protection against overdriving them. While you necessarily have high voltage regulation circuitry (which can be absent in fixed frequency monitors), it will not necessarily cover every conceivable frequency range, especially in cheaper models. This not only implies more wear on the circuitry, it can also cause the screen phosphors to age faster, and cause more than the specified radiation (including X-rays) to be emitted from the monitor.

Another importance of the bandwidth is that the monitor's input impedance is specified only for that range, and using higher frequencies can cause reflections probably causing minor screen interferences, and radio disturbance.

However, the basic problematic magnitude in question here is the slew rate (the steepness of the video signals) of the video output drivers, and that is usually independent of the actual pixel frequency, but (if your board manufacturer cares about such problems) related to the maximum pixel frequency of the board.

So be careful out there...

12   Using Interlaced Modes

(This section is largely due to David Kastrup <dak@pool.informatik.rwth-aachen.de>)

At a fixed dot clock, an interlaced display is going to have considerably less noticable flicker than a non-interlaced display, if the vertical circuitry of your monitor is able to support it stably. It is because of this that interlaced modes were invented in the first place.

Interlaced modes got their bad repute because they are inferior to their non-interlaced companions at the same vertical scan frequency, VSF (which is what is usually given in advertisements). But they are definitely superior at the same horizontal scan rate, and that's where the decisive limits of your monitor/graphics card usually lie.

At a fixed *refresh rate* (or half frame rate, or VSF) the interlaced display will flicker more: a 90Hz interlaced display will be inferior to a 90Hz non-interlaced display. It will, however, need only half the video bandwidth and half the horizontal scan rate. If you compared it to a non-interlaced mode with the same dot clock and the same scan rates, it would be vastly superior: 45Hz non-interlaced is intolerable. With 90Hz interlaced, I have worked for years with my Multisync 3D (at 1024x768) and am very satisfied. I'd guess you'd need at least a 70Hz non-interlaced display for similar comfort.

You have to watch a few points, though: use interlaced modes only at high resolutions, so that the alternately lighted lines are close together. You might want to play with sync pulse widths and positions to get the most stable line positions. If alternating lines are bright and dark, interlace will *jump* at you. I have one application that chooses such a dot pattern for a menu background (XCept, no other application I know does that, fortunately). I switch to 800x600 for using XCept because it really hurts my eyes otherwise.

For the same reason, use at least 100dpi fonts, or other fonts where horizontal beams are at least two lines thick (for high resolutions, nothing else will make sense anyhow).

And of course, never use an interlaced mode when your hardware would support a non-interlaced one with similar refresh rate.

If, however, you find that for some resolution you are pushing either monitor or graphics card to their upper limits, and getting dissatisfactorily flickery or outwashed (bandwidth exceeded) display, you might want to try tackling the same resolution using an interlaced mode. Of course this is useless if the VSF of your monitor is already close to its limits.

Design of interlaced modes is easy: do it like a non-interlaced mode. Just two more considerations are necessary: you need an odd total number of vertical lines (the last number in your mode line), and when you specify the "interlace" flag, the actual vertical frame rate for your monitor doubles. Your monitor needs to support a 90Hz frame rate if the mode you specified looks like a 45Hz mode apart from the "Interlace" flag.

As an example, here is my modeline for 1024x768 interlaced: my Multisync 3D will support up to 90Hz vertical and 38kHz horizontal.

```
ModeLine "1024x768" 45 1024 1048 1208 1248 768 768 776 807 Interlace
```

Both limits are pretty much exhausted with this mode. Specifying the same mode, just without the "Interlace" flag, still is almost at the limit of the monitor's horizontal capacity (and strictly speaking, a bit under the lower limit of vertical scan rate), but produces an intolerably flickery display.

Basic design rules: if you have designed a mode at less than half of your monitor's vertical capacity, make the vertical total of lines odd and add the "Interlace" flag. The display's quality should vastly improve in most cases.

If you have a non-interlaced mode otherwise exhausting your monitor's specs where the vertical scan rate lies about 30% or more under the maximum of your monitor, hand-designing an interlaced mode (probably with somewhat higher resolution) could deliver superior results, but I won't promise it.

13 Questions and Answers

Q. The example you gave is not a standard screen size, can I use it?

A. Why not? There is NO reason whatsover why you have to use 640x480, 800x600, or even 1024x768. The XFree86 servers let you configure your hardware with a lot of freedom. It usually takes two to three tries to come up the right one. The important thing to shoot for is high refresh rate with reasonable viewing area. not high resolution at the price of eye-tearing flicker!

Q. It this the only resolution given the 65Mhz dot clock and 55Khz HSF?

A. Absolutely not! You are encouraged to follow the general procedure and do some trial-and-error to come up a setting that's really to your liking. Experimenting with this can be lots of fun. Most settings may just give you nasty video hash, but in practice a modern multi-sync monitor is usually not damaged easily. Be sure though, that your monitor can support the frame rates of your mode before using it for longer times.

Beware fixed-frequency monitors! This kind of hacking around can damage them rather quickly. Be sure you use valid refresh rates for *every* experiment on them.

Q. You just mentioned two standard resolutions. In Xconfig, there are many standard resolutions available, can you tell me whether there's any point in tinkering with timings?

A. Absolutely! Take, for example, the "standard" 640x480 listed in the current Xconfig. It employes 25Mhz driving frequency, frame lengths are 800 and 525 => refresh rate   59.5Hz. Not too bad. But 28Mhz is a commonly available driving frequency from many SVGA boards. If we use it to drive 640x480, following the procedure we discussed above, you would get frame lengths like 812 and 505. Now the refresh rate is raised to 68Hz, a quite significant improvement over the standard one.

Q. Can you summarize what we have discussed so far?

A. In a nutshell:

1. for any fixed driving frequency, raising max resolution incurs the penalty of lowering refresh rate and thus introducing more flicker.

2. if high resolution is desirable and your monitor supports it, try to get a SVGA card that provides a matching dot clock or DCF. The higher, the better!

14   Fixing Problems with the Image.

OK, so you've got your X configuration numbers. You put them in Xconfig with a test mode label. You fire up X, hot-key to the new mode, ... and the image doesn't look right. What do you do? Here's a list of common video image distortions and how to fix them.

(Fixing these minor distortions is where **xvidtune**(1) really shines.)

You *move* the image by changing the sync pulse timing. You *scale* it by changing the frame length (you need to move the sync pulse to keep it in the same relative position, otherwise scaling will move the image as well). Here are some more specific recipes:

The horizontal and vertical positions are independent. That is, moving the image horizontally doesn't affect placement vertically, or vice-versa. However, the same is not quite true of scaling. While changing the horizontal size does nothing to the vertical size or vice versa, the total change in both may be limited. In particular, if your image is too large in both dimensions you will probably have to go to a higher dot clock to fix it. Since this raises the usable resolution, it is seldom a problem!

14.1   The image is displaced to the left or right

To fix this, move the horizontal sync pulse. That is, increment or decrement (by a multiple of 8) the middle two numbers of the horizontal timing section that define the leading and trailing edge of the horizontal sync pulse.

If the image is shifted left (right border too large, you want to move the image to the right) decrement the numbers. If the image is shifted right (left border too large, you want it to move left) increment the sync pulse.

14.2 The image is displaced up or down

To fix this, move the vertical sync pulse. That is, increment or decrement the middle two numbers of the vertical timing section that define the leading and trailing edge of the vertical sync pulse.

If the image is shifted up (lower border too large, you want to move the image down) decrement the numbers. If the image is shifted down (top border too large, you want it to move up) increment the numbers.

14.3 The image is too large both horizontally and vertically

Switch to a higher card clock speed. If you have multiple modes in your clock file, possibly a lower-speed one is being activated by mistake.

14.4 The image is too wide (too narrow) horizontally

To fix this, increase (decrease) the horizontal frame length. That is, change the fourth number in the first timing section. To avoid moving the image, also move the sync pulse (second and third numbers) half as far, to keep it in the same relative position.

14.5 The image is too deep (too shallow) vertically

To fix this, increase (decrease) the vertical frame length. That is, change the fourth number in the second timing section. To avoid moving the image, also move the sync pulse (second and third numbers) half as far, to keep it in the same relative position.

Any distortion that can't be handled by combining these techniques is probably evidence of something more basically wrong, like a calculation mistake or a faster dot clock than the monitor can handle.

Finally, remember that increasing either frame length will decrease your refresh rate, and vice-versa.

15 Plotting Monitor Capabilities

To plot a monitor mode diagram, you'll need the gnuplot package (a freeware plotting language for UNIX-like operating systems) and the tool `modeplot`, a shell/gnuplot script to plot the diagram from your monitor characteristics, entered as command-line options.

Here is a copy of `modeplot`:

```
#!/bin/sh
#
# modeplot -- generate X mode plot of available monitor modes
#
# Do 'modeplot -?' to see the control options.
#
```

```
# ($Id: video-modes.sgml,v 1.4 1997/10/31 13:51:07 esr Exp $)

# Monitor description. Bandwidth in MHz, horizontal frequencies in kHz
# and vertical frequencies in Hz.
TITLE="Viewsonic 21PS"
BANDWIDTH=185
MINHSF=31
MAXHSF=85
MINVSF=50
MAXVSF=160
ASPECT="4/3"
vesa=72.5          # VESA-recommended minimum refresh rate

while [ "$1" != "" ]
do
        case $1 in
        -t) TITLE="$2"; shift;;
        -b) BANDWIDTH="$2"; shift;;
        -h) MINHSF="$2" MAXHSF="$3"; shift; shift;;
        -v) MINVSF="$2" MAXVSF="$3"; shift; shift;;
        -a) ASPECT="$2"; shift;;
        -g) GNUOPTS="$2"; shift;;
        -?) cat <<EOF
modeplot control switches:

-t "<description>"      name of monitor            defaults to "Viewsonic 21PS"
-b <nn>                 bandwidth in MHz           defaults to 185
-h <min> <max>          min & max HSF (kHz)        defaults to 31 85
-v <min> <max>          min & max VSF (Hz)         defaults to 50 160
-a <aspect ratio>       aspect ratio               defaults to 4/3
-g "<options>"          pass options to gnuplot

The -b, -h and -v options are required, -a, -t, -g optional.  You can
use -g to pass a device type to gnuplot so that (for example) modeplot's
output can be redirected to a printer.  See gnuplot(1) for  details.

The modeplot tool was created by Eric S. Raymond <esr@thyrsus.com> based on
analysis and scratch code by Martin Lottermoser <Martin.Lottermoser@mch.sni.de>

This is modeplot $Revision: 1.4 $
EOF
                exit;;
        esac
        shift
done

gnuplot $GNUOPTS <<EOF
set title "$TITLE Mode Plot"

# Magic numbers.  Unfortunately, the plot is quite sensitive to changes in
# these, and they may fail to represent reality on some monitors.  We need
# to fix values to get even an approximation of the mode diagram.  These come
# from looking at lots of values in the ModeDB database.
F1 = 1.30        # multiplier to convert horizontal resolution to frame width
```

```
F2 = 1.05         # multiplier to convert vertical resolution to frame height

# Function definitions (multiplication by 1.0 forces real-number arithmetic)
ac = (1.0*$ASPECT)*F1/F2
refresh(hsync, dcf) = ac * (hsync**2)/(1.0*dcf)
dotclock(hsync, rr) = ac * (hsync**2)/(1.0*rr)
resolution(hv, dcf) = dcf * (10**6)/(hv * F1 * F2)


# Put labels on the axes
set xlabel 'DCF (MHz)'
set ylabel 'RR (Hz)' 6  # Put it right over the Y axis


# Generate diagram
set grid
set label "VB" at $BANDWIDTH+1, ($MAXVSF + $MINVSF) / 2 left
set arrow from $BANDWIDTH, $MINVSF to $BANDWIDTH, $MAXVSF nohead
set label "max VSF" at 1, $MAXVSF-1.5
set arrow from 0, $MAXVSF to $BANDWIDTH, $MAXVSF nohead
set label "min VSF" at 1, $MINVSF-1.5
set arrow from 0, $MINVSF to $BANDWIDTH, $MINVSF nohead
set label "min HSF" at dotclock($MINHSF, $MAXVSF+17), $MAXVSF + 17 right
set label "max HSF" at dotclock($MAXHSF, $MAXVSF+17), $MAXVSF + 17 right
set label "VESA $vesa" at 1, $vesa-1.5
set arrow from 0, $vesa to $BANDWIDTH, $vesa nohead # style -1
plot [dcf=0:1.1*$BANDWIDTH] [$MINVSF-10:$MAXVSF+20] \
  refresh($MINHSF, dcf) notitle with lines 1, \
  refresh($MAXHSF, dcf) notitle with lines 1, \
  resolution(640*480,   dcf) title "640x480  " with points 2, \
  resolution(800*600,   dcf) title "800x600  " with points 3, \
  resolution(1024*768,  dcf) title "1024x768 " with points 4, \
  resolution(1280*1024, dcf) title "1280x1024" with points 5, \
  resolution(1600*1280, dcf) title "1600x1200" with points 6

pause 9999
EOF
```

Once you know you have modeplot and the gnuplot package in place, you'll need the following monitor
characteristics:

- video bandwidth (VB)
- range of horizontal sync frequency (HSF)
- range of vertical sync frequency (VSF)

The plot program needs to make some simplifying assumptions which are not necessarily correct. This is
the reason why the resulting diagram is only a rough description. These assumptions are:

1. All resolutions have a single fixed aspect ratio AR = HR/VR. Standard resolutions have AR = 4/3
   or AR = 5/4. The modeplot programs assumes 4/3 by default, but you can override this.
2. For the modes considered, horizontal and vertical frame lengths are fixed multiples of horizontal and
   vertical resolutions, respectively:

$$HFL = F1 * HR$$
$$VFL = F2 * VR$$

As a rough guide, take F1 = 1.30 and F2 = 1.05 (see 8 () "Computing Frame Sizes").

Now take a particular sync frequency, HSF. Given the assumptions just presented, every value for the clock rate DCF already determines the refresh rate RR, i.e. for every value of HSF there is a function RR(DCF). This can be derived as follows.

The refresh rate is equal to the clock rate divided by the product of the frame sizes:

```
RR = DCF / (HFL * VFL)            (*)
```

On the other hand, the horizontal frame length is equal to the clock rate divided by the horizontal sync frequency:

```
HFL = DCF / HSF                   (**)
```

VFL can be reduced to HFL be means of the two assumptions above:

```
VFL = F2 * VR
    = F2 * (HR / AR)
    = (F2/F1) * HFL / AR          (***)
```

Inserting (**) and (***) into (*) we obtain:

```
RR = DCF / ((F2/F1) * HFL**2 / AR)
   = (F1/F2) * AR * DCF * (HSF/DCF)**2
   = (F1/F2) * AR * HSF**2 / DCF
```

For fixed HSF, F1, F2 and AR, this is a hyperbola in our diagram. Drawing two such curves for minimum and maximum horizontal sync frequencies we have obtained the two remaining boundaries of the permitted region.

The straight lines crossing the capability region represent particular resolutions. This is based on (*) and the second assumption:

```
RR = DCF / (HFL * VFL) = DCF / (F1 * HR * F2 * VR)
```

By drawing such lines for all resolutions one is interested in, one can immediately read off the possible relations between resolution, clock rate and refresh rate of which the monitor is capable. Note that these lines do not depend on monitor properties, but they do depend on the second assumption.

The `modeplot` tool provides you with an easy way to do this. Do `modeplot -?` to see its control options. A typical invocation looks like this:

```
modeplot -t "Swan SW617" -b 85 -v 50 90 -h 31 58
```

The -b option specifies video bandwidth; -v and -h set horizontal and vertical sync frequency ranges.

When reading the output of `modeplot`, always bear in mind that it gives only an approximate description. For example, it disregards limitations on HFL resulting from a minimum required sync pulse width, and it can only be accurate as far as the assumptions are. It is therefore no substitute for a detailed calculation (involving some black magic) as presented in 10 (Putting it All Together). However, it should give you a better feeling for what is possible and which tradeoffs are involved.

16 Credits

The original ancestor of this document was by Chin Fang <fangchin@leland.stanford.edu>.

Eric S. Raymond <esr@snark.thyrsus.com> reworked, reorganized, and massively rewrote Chin Fang's original in an attempt to understand it. In the process, he merged in most of a different how-to by Bob Crosson <crosson@cam.nist.gov>.

The material on interlaced modes is largely by David Kastrup <dak@pool.informatik.rwth-aachen.de>

Martin Lottermoser <Martin.Lottermoser@mch.sni.de> contributed the idea of using gnuplot to make mode diagrams and did the mathematical analysis behind `modeplot`. The distributed `modeplot` was redesigned and generalized by ESR from Martin's original gnuplot code for one case.

Linux XFree-to-Xinside mini-HOWTO

by Marco Melgazzi, marco@techie.com   version 1.3 / 1997 September

How to convert an XFree86 modeline into an XInside/XiGraphics one

Contents

1 Introduction

During the spring of 1996 I've seen a lot of posts in comp.os.linux.x asking how to convert video modes between XFree86 and one of its commercial alternatives: XInside (now named XiGraphics, note anyway that in this document I'll use the old product name, since I will mainly refer to that version)

I had evaluated before the product and had this evaluation version still floating on my hard disk: since I like problem solving, I've decided to give it a try and, after a couple of hours of fiddling and calculating, I came up with a supposedly informative article that was promptly posted.

The discussions about how to convert suddendly vanished and I received 1 (one) mail thanking me for the article so, since maybe somebody else could need this information in the future, I decided to transform that post in the mini-HOWTO you are reading.

Let me state something first: I do NOT work for XInside and I only had access to the evaluation 1.2 version for Linux. I know that nowadays (May 97) AccelX has reached revision 3.1, but I do think that the information included in this document, if not verbatim, is still applicable.

Due to the fact that this HOWTO has been written with the help of a pretty old Xinside version, it may well happen that some of the information contained here is not completely accurate: as you will read later, thanks to the birth of XFree 3.2, I haven't bought this commercial server, so if you have, and if you notice any incorrect information here please take the time to email me.

Notice anyway that fiddling with monitor timings can be hazardous and, for this reason, I absolutely make no guarantees. If it works for you , fine, if you blow up your computer I shall not be held responsible for it.

As you may have noticed from may name, I'm not a native speaker of English so you will probably find some errors here and there, I apologize for them and I ask you to please avoid flooding my mailbox with language-related flames. Thanks !

2   Why should I need it ?

I think that the Xinside policy of not giving you an utility to tweak your video modes (like xvidtune) and/or to import your existing XFree ones in the evaluation (and AFAIK commercial) version is incomprehensible. I've spent about three hours putting this together (hint: I've compared the VESA 1024x768@70Hz entry in the two formats (and I'm nearly an electronic engineer ;-)) while an Xinside programmer could have written a comparable article in a fraction of this time...

I haven't downloaded any evaluation version from 1.3 onwards and I really hope they have fixed this. Well, if they have, this mini-HOWTO could be considered useless but, alas, if you read it you will learn something more about how everything works...

3   Let's go

Let's suppose that you have your oh-so-tweaked XFree86 mode and you want to evaluate Xinside in the same conditions: follow the steps described below and you should be able to do it; we will use my default video mode as a real-life example and I will explain what you will have to do to convert it.

An Xfree86 entry looks like this:

```
Modeline "blahblah" DOTCLK  A B C D  a b c d
```

Every one of the A-D and a-d numbers has a meaning: if you want you can search for it in the 'The Hitchhiker's Guide to X386/XFree86 Video Timing' (/usr/lib/X11/doc/VideoModes.doc) but you don't need to know the theory behind all this to perform a succesful conversion...

My modeline in /usr/lib/X11/XF86Config is:

```
Modeline "1168x876" 105   1168 1256 1544 1640  876 877 891 900
                      |      |    |    |    |    |   |   |   |
                    DOT_CLK  A    B    C    D    a   b   c   d
```

In Xinside, you have to add an entry in the Xtimings file, which should be located in etc/ (from now on we suppose you are in the top Xaccel directory that should be something like /usr/X11/lib/X11/AcceleratedX)

```
!    Somewhere in the file, put here the name you want

[PREADJUSTED_TIMING]
    PreadjustedTimingName = "1168x876 @ 72Hz";

!

!    These four are obvious
```

```
    !
        HorPixel        = 1168;              // pixels
        VerPixel        = 876;               // lines
        PixelWidthRatio = 4;
        PixelHeightRatio = 3;

    !
    ! hsync: DOT_CLK / D * 1000 [KHz]
    !
    ! hsync = 105 / 1640 * 1000 = 64.024 KHz
    !
    ! vsync: ( 1 / (( D / DOT_CLK ) * d) ) * 1,000,000 [Hz]
    !
    ! vsync: ( 1 / (( 1640 / 105 ) * 900) ) * 1,000,000
    !        ( 1 / 14057.1428571 ) * 1,000,000 = 71.138 Hz
    !

        HorFrequency    = 64.180;            // kHz
        VerFrequency    = 71.138;            // Hz

    ! Obvious

        ScanType        = NONINTERLACED;

    !
    ! Put here the +/-hsync +/-vsync XFree86 options
    !
        HorSyncPolarity = POSITIVE;
        VerSyncPolarity = POSITIVE;

    ! Shouldn't change

        CharacterWidth  = 8;                 // pixels

    ! DOT_CLK here

        PixelClock      = 105.000;           // MHz
    !
    !
    ! horizontal timings section: [usec]
    !
        HorTotalTime  = D / DOT_CLK                      = 15.619;
        HorAddrTime   = A / DOT_CLK                      = 11.124;
        HorBlankStart = A / DOT_CLK                      = 11.124;
        HorBlankTime  = HorTotalTime - HorBlankStart =  4.495;
```

```
        HorSyncStart  = B / DOT_CLK                 =  11.962;
        HorSyncTime   = C / DOT_CLK - HorSyncStart  =   2.743;


   !
   !  vertical timings section:     [msec]
   !

        VerTotalTime  = ( HorTotalTime * d ) / 1000 = 14.057;
        VerAddrTime   = ( HorTotalTime * a ) / 1000 = 13.682;
        VerBlankStart = ( HorTotalTime * a ) / 1000 = 13.682;
        VerBlankTime  = VerTotalTime - VerBlankStart =  0.375;
        VerSyncStart  = ( HorTotalTime * b ) / 1000 = 13.698;
        VerSyncTime   = ( HorTotalTime * ( c - b ) ) / 1000
                                                    =  0.219


   ! Finished !
```

Now you have to put this newly created mode in the files shown below in the appropriate place.

4   Fixing up things

In the excerpts shown below the -> sign tells you what was modified: do NOT include it in your files!

Monitor entry (mine is monitors/mfreq/mfreq64.vda)

```
        [ESTABLISHED_TIMINGS]
             "640x480 @ 60Hz",
             "640x480 @ 72Hz",
             "640x480 @ 75Hz",
             "800x600 @ 56Hz",
             "800x600 @ 60Hz",
             "800x600 @ 72Hz",
             "800x600 @ 75Hz",
             "1024x768 Interlaced",
             "1024x768 @ 60Hz",
             "1024x768 @ 70Hz",
             "1024x768 @ 75Hz",
          "1152x900 Interlaced",
             "1152x900 @ 60Hz",
             "1152x900 @ 67Hz",
   ->        "1168x876 @ 72Hz",
             "1280x1024 Interlaced",
             "1280x1024 @ 60Hz",
          "1600x1200 Interlaced";
```

Board info file (mine is boards/s3/764-2.xqa , I wonder why they have nearly all the Hercules boards but not MINE: Terminator 64/Dram)

```
[VISUAL]
    BitsPerPixel    = 8;
    MemoryModel     = Packed;
    ColorModel      = Indexed;
    BitsRGB         = 6;
    NumberOfColors = 256;

    [RESOLUTIONS]
    640x480,
    800x600,
    1024x768,
->  1168x876,
    1152x900,
    1280x1024

    [DESKTOPS]
    640x480,
    800x600,
    1024x768,
    1152x900,
->  1168x876,
    1280x1024,
    1600x1200
```

If the dot clock is low enough (NOT in this case for my board) you can put the entry even in the 16bpp and 32bpp sec- tions.

The /etc/Xaccel.ini will look something like this

```
----------------------------------------------------------------
    Board   = "s3/764-2.xqa";
    Monitor = "mfreq/mfreq64.vda";
    Depth   = 8;
->  Desktop = 1168x876;

    [RESOLUTIONS]
->      1168x876,
        1024x768;
```

The actual Xinside mode entry in etc/Xtimings

```
----------------------------------------------------------------
[PREADJUSTED_TIMING]
    PreadjustedTimingName = "1168x876 @ 72Hz";
```

```
HorPixel            = 1168;           // pixels
VerPixel            = 876;            // lines
PixelWidthRatio     = 4;
PixelHeightRatio    = 3;
HorFrequency        = 64.024;         // kHz
VerFrequency        = 71.138;         // Hz
ScanType            = NONINTERLACED;
HorSyncPolarity     = POSITIVE;
VerSyncPolarity     = POSITIVE;
CharacterWidth      = 8;              // pixels
PixelClock          = 105.000;        // MHz
HorTotalTime        = 15.619;         // (usec) =  205 chars
HorAddrTime         = 11.124;         // (usec) =  146 chars
HorBlankStart       = 11.124;         // (usec) =  146 chars
HorBlankTime        =  4.495;         // (usec) =   59 chars
HorSyncStart        = 11.962;         // (usec) =  157 chars
HorSyncTime         =  2.743;         // (usec) =   36 chars
VerTotalTime        = 14.057;         // (msec) =  900 lines
VerAddrTime         = 13.682;         // (msec) =  876 lines
VerBlankStart       = 13.682;         // (msec) =  876 lines
VerBlankTime        =  0.375;         // (msec) =   24 lines
VerSyncStart        = 13.698;         // (msec) =  877 lines
VerSyncTime         =  0.219;         // (msec) =   14 lines
```

You can check your conversion by running the vgaset program with no parameters while running the Xinside server: it will output an XFree-like line and, if everything went OK, this line will be equal to the line you started from (except if b and c are equal, I haven't been able to reproduce this situation in Xinside: the best case was c=b+1).

5   The end...

That's all folks ! I hope this will be useful to you. I don't think I'll buy the XiGraphics server in the near future for one simple reason: the release of XFree86 3.2 solved all of the text speed problems I was having on my humble Trio 64 video board ;)

It seems anyway that the XiGraphics server supports a much wider array of chipsets and video boards than XFree, so it may well happen that the commercial 'alternative' is the only viable one for you. If this is the case, and you bought the XiGraphics server, I would really like to hear from you to know if the information presented here has been useful to you, or if you found it too complex or whatever.

6   Automating the process

This small script automates most of the work. Be very careful with the ScanType and with the two Polarity lines: the script do not set them and, if you are too lazy to correct them, the risks of blowing up your monitor increase quite a lot.

Notice that I don't know if the 'Doublescan' flag has meaning in XInside: if you try to convert a low-res doublescan mode BE CAREFUL, you can easily kill your monitor since the refresh rate that you get is doubled (in fact my 400x300@72Hz became a 400x300@144Hz !).

```sh
#!/bin/sh
#######################################################################
# XF2XInside
#
# This script converts modelines from XF86Config format to XInside
# format as needed for the etc/Xtiming file.
#
# This is a quick hack, so don't expect much error checking (not to
# speak of anything like user friendlyness).
#
# If you call it without arguments it should tell you what to do.
#
#                               ( July 1996, hcz@tazlwurm.bb.bawue.de)
#
# Btw: New modes created as described in the HOWTO work, but don't
# show up in Xsetup's menu. Anybody who knows why?
#
#######################################################################
#---------------------------------------------- Here we go:
# Change this if your modeline file lives somewhere else:
XF=/usr/X11/lib/X11/XF86Config
if [ $# -ne 1 ] ; then
  echo "usage: ${0##*/} <mode>"
  echo " example: ${0##*/} 1024x764"
  echo -e " function: converts $XF modeline entry into\n Xinside Format (stdout)"
  exit 1
fi
egrep -i "^[\t ]*modeline.+\"$1\""  /usr/X11/lib/X11/XF86Config |
gawk '
NF < 11  { print "! invalid Modeline:\n! " $0 "\n!"; next }
{
  print "//", $0  ":"
  name = $2
  DOT_CLK = $3;
  A = $4;
  B = $5;
  C = $6;
  D = $7;
  a = $8;
  b = $9;
  c = $10;
  d = $11;
```

```
     VerFrequency =  1000000 / ((D / DOT_CLK) * d)
     print "[PREADJUSTED_TIMING]"
     printf "  PreadjustedTimingName = \"%dx%d @ %.0dHz\";\n", A, a, VerFrequency
     print "  HorPixel\t\t= " A ";"
     print "  VerPixel\t\t= " a ";"
     print "  PixelWidthRatio\t= 4;\n  PixelHeightRatio\t= 3;"
     print "  HorFrequency\t\t= " DOT_CLK / D * 1000 ";\t// kHz"
     print "  VerFrequency\t\t= " VerFrequency  ";\t// Hz"
     print "  ScanType\t\t= NONINTERLACED;\t\t// *CHECK*"
     print "  HorSyncPolarity\t= NEGATIVE;\t\t\t// *CHECK*"
     print "  VerSyncPolarity\t= NEGATIVE;\t\t\t// *CHECK*"
     print "  CharacterWidth\t= 8;"
     print "  PixelClock\t\t= " DOT_CLK ";"
 HorTotalTime = D / DOT_CLK
     print "  HorTotalTime\t\t= " HorTotalTime ";"
     print "  HorAddrTime \t\t= " A / DOT_CLK ";"
     print "  HorBlankStart\t\t= " A / DOT_CLK ";"
     print "  HorBlankTime\t\t= " D / DOT_CLK - A / DOT_CLK ";"
     print "  HorSyncStart\t\t= " B / DOT_CLK ";"
     print "  HorSyncTime\t\t= " C / DOT_CLK - B / DOT_CLK ";"
 VerTotalTime  = ( HorTotalTime * d ) / 1000
     print "  VerTotalTime\t\t= " VerTotalTime ";"
     print "  VerAddrTime\t\t= " ( HorTotalTime * a ) / 1000 ";"
 VerBlankStart = ( HorTotalTime * a ) / 1000
     print "  VerBlankStart\t\t= " VerBlankStart ";"
     print "  VerBlankTime\t\t= " VerTotalTime - VerBlankStart ";"
     print "  VerSyncStart\t\t= " ( HorTotalTime * b ) / 1000 ";"
     print "  VerSyncTime\t\t= " ( HorTotalTime * ( c - b ) ) / 1000
     print ""
 }'
```

7   Thanks to

- Heike Claudia Zimmerer *hcz@tazlwurm.bb.bawue.de* `<mailto:hcz@tazlwurm.bb.bawue.de>` for pointing out a small inconsistency and for sending me a script that automates most of the work.

- Bartosz Maruszewski *B.Maruszewski@zsmeie.torun.pl* `<mailto:B.Maruszewski@zsmeie.torun.pl>` for translating this mini HOWTO in Polish and for pointing out a small typo.

8   Copyright/legalese

The LBX Mini-HOWTO

Paul D. Smith, *psmith@baynetworks.com* <mailto:psmith@baynetworks.com>   v1.04, 11 Dec 1997

LBX (Low Bandwidth X) is an X server extension which performs compression on the X protocol. It is meant to be used in conjunction with X applications and an X server which are separated by a slow network connection, to improve display and response time.

Contents

1 Introduction

Low-Bandwidth X (LBX) attempts to recognize that in this day and age, not everyone will be a fast LAN hop or two away from the system that they are running their applications on.

The X protocol can generate an extraordinary amount of traffic, especially for simple-seeming things such as creating new windows. As anyone who has tried to use X over a dial-in modem at 28.8 or even higher can attest, creating new X windows can involve an excruciating wait.

LBX is fundamentally a compression and caching scheme designed to minimize the amount of X traffic generated between two systems.

2   What's The Status Of LBX?

As of the X Consortium's release of X11R6.3 in December, 1996, LBX is a full extension to the X protocol. For XFree86 folks, that's XFree86 version 3.3.

3   Who Can Benefit From LBX?

If you use a modem to dial into a service provider, then run X applications on remote machines with their DISPLAYs set to your local machine (or vice versa), LBX will speed up that connection. Also if you set DISPLAYs from systems across WANs (other countries, for example) or other slow links, LBX can help.

4   Who Doesn't Need LBX?

LBX is useless, of course, if you're only running applications locally, or if you're not running X at all.

Also, if you're running on a fast LAN, LBX won't be much help. Some people say "if LBX cuts down on network traffic, wouldn't it be good to use even on fast LANs?" It might be, if your goal is to reduce network traffic. But if your goal is to get better response time LBX probably isn't what you want. Although it does introduce caching and compression, that comes at a cost on both ends (extra memory for caching, and extra CPU for decompression). If your link is fairly speedy LBX will probably result in an overall slowdown.

5   How Does LBX Work?

LBX works by introducing a *proxy server* at the client side, which performs caching and compression. The X server knows that the client is using a proxy server, and decompresses accordingly.

Here's a normal setup for remote X clients. In our discussion, LOCAL is always the workstation sitting in front of you, whose monitor you're looking at, and REMOTE is the remote workstation, where the actual application is running.

```
        REMOTE                                     LOCAL
        +-----+                                    +-----+
        | APP |-\        Network        +----------+ |    |\
        +-----+  \----------------------->| X SERVER |=>|    ||
        +-----+  /        (X Protocol)   +----------+ +-----+\
        | APP |-/                                    /_____//
        +-----+
```

When using LBX, a proxy server (`lbxproxy`) is introduced on the remote side, and the applications talk to that process instead of directly to the LOCAL server. That process then performs the caching and compression of X requests and forwards them. It looks like this:

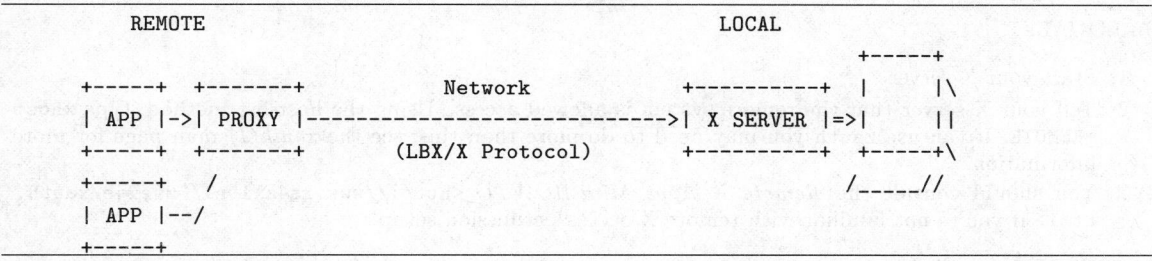

```
          REMOTE                                    LOCAL
                                                           +-----+
 +-----+  +-------+       Network         +----------+  |     |\
 | APP |->| PROXY |---------------------->| X SERVER |=>|     ||
 +-----+  +-------+     (LBX/X Protocol)   +----------+  +-----+\
 +-----+     /                                          /_____//
 | APP |--/
 +-----+
```

Details on exactly what caching and compression LBX does is beyond the scope of this document.

6   What Do I Need To Use LBX?

You need an X server on your LOCAL system which has the LBX extension compiled in. Unless you explicitly told it not to when building it, X11R6.3 servers automatically enable LBX. Also, all XFree86 3.3 servers have LBX enabled by default.

You can use the xdpyinfo command to see if your server has the LBX extension: run xdpyinfo and look at the list just under "number of extensions"; you should see "LBX" listed there.

Next, you need to get an `lbxproxy` program compiled for the REMOTE system. This is the tricky part. If the remote system is not the same type as your local system, the `lbxproxy` on your local system will do you no good, of course.

There is unfortunately no "broken out" distribution of `lbxproxy`, so you will have to either (a) get and build most, if not all, of X11R6.3 for the remote system, or (b) find someplace to get a pre-compiled `lbxproxy` binary for your system. The latter is much simpler of course.

The `lbxproxy` is simply a single executable. There are no configuration files, resource files, etc. associated with it.

7   What Don't I Need To Use LBX?

The REMOTE system **does not** need a new X server (as always, the REMOTE system doesn't need *any* X server running).

The application you want to run **does not** need to be linked with any special version of X, or any special libraries; I regularly use commercial X11R5 apps over LBX with no trouble.

You **do not** need root or other privileged access on the REMOTE system; the `lbxproxy` process runs under your normal access permissions. Further, you can run it right from your home directory: it does not have to be installed anywhere.

8   How Do I Start LBX?

OK, here it is... after all that it's actually quite simple. Replace LOCAL and REMOTE below with the hostnames of your local workstation and remote system, respectively (don't get them mixed up!)

On LOCAL:

1. Start your X server.
2. Tell your X server that the remote system is allowed access. Using the host-list method, type `xhost +REMOTE`. If you use `xauth` you may need to do more than this; see the *xauth(1)* man page for more information.

   You should consult the *Remote X Apps Mini-HOWTO* <http://www.xs4all.nl/~zweije/xauth.html> if you're not familiar with remote X access permission setup.

On REMOTE:

1. Start `lbxproxy` and tell it to forward to the LOCAL X server, like this:

   ```
   $ lbxproxy -display LOCAL:0 :1 &
   ```

   This tells `lbxproxy` to use display :1 on the REMOTE system; if that system has >1 display already you can use :2 or whatever instead.
2. Set your DISPLAY environment variable to point to the display that `lbxproxy` is providing, instead of the normal display:

   ```
   $ DISPLAY=:1
   $ export DISPLAY
   ```

   Or, if you use csh or clones:

   ```
   % setenv DISPLAY :1
   ```
3. If you're using `xauth` you will need to ensure that your cookie is available locally. See the *Remote X Apps Mini-HOWTO* <http://www.xs4all.nl/~zweije/xauth.html> for more information on this.
4. Start your X applications!

That's it; all X apps that are started up pointing to :1 will use LBX. Of course, there's no reason you couldn't also start X apps pointing to `LOCAL:0` and have both running at the same time.

9   Problems

Here are some common problems:

Q)

    `lbxproxy` exits with an "access denied" error.

A)

    This means the LOCAL system isn't accepting connections from the REMOTE system due to permissions errors. See the *Remote X Apps Mini-HOWTO* <http://www.xs4all.nl/~zweije/xauth.html> for details on these issues.

    As a simple trouble-shooting measure, try running a simple X app like `xclock` on REMOTE and have it display on the local system without using `lbxproxy`:

```
$ xclock -display LOCAL:0
```

If that doesn't work, it's `xhost` or some other basic X problem, not LBX.

10   Documentation

The only documentation available in a standard X distribution may be the *lbxproxy(1)* man page.

If you have access to the X source tree, then very interesting information on LBX is available there:

- xc/doc/specs/Xext/lbx.mif (Framemaker MIF)
- xc/doc/hardcopy/Xext/lbx.PS.Z (Compressed Postscript)
- xc/doc/hardcopy/Xext/lbxTOC.html (HTML)

More detailed discussion of specific LBX algorithms is available here:

- xc/doc/specs/Xext/lbxalg.mif (Framemaker MIF)
- xc/doc/specs/Xext/lbxalg.PS.Z (Compressed Postscript)

If you don't have access to the X11 source, you can obtain these files from *the X Consortium's FTP site* <ftp://ftp.x.org/pub/R6.3/xc/doc/>.

11   Alternatives

If you don't like lbxproxy for some reason: you're not satisfied with the performance, it doesn't work for you, you don't want to hassle with creating an lbxproxy for the remote host, or you simply are interested in trying other options, there is at least one other package for X protocol compression (anyone have others?)

11.1   dxpc - The Differential X Protocol Compressor

- Original Author: *Brian Pane <brianp@cnet.com>* <mailto:brianp@cnet.com>
- Current Maintainer: *Zachary Vonler <lightborn@mail.utexas.edu>* <mailto:lightborn@mail.utexas.edu>

dxpc <http://ccwf.cc.utexas.edu/~zvonler/dxpc/> works in essentially the same way as LBX. However, to avoid having to implement an X extension and modify the X server code, dxpc uses two proxies: one that runs on the REMOTE host, like lbxproxy, and one that runs on the LOCAL host.

The REMOTE host proxy communicates between the X clients and the LOCAL host proxy, and the LOCAL host proxy communicates between the X server and the REMOTE host proxy.

So, to *both* the X clients and the X server, it looks like X protocol as usual.

11.1.1   Advantages

- Since it's a completely separate application that does not require any X internals, it's *much* simpler to compile and install.
- It's maintained separately, so you don't have to wait for the OSF to release new X versions for enhancements or fixes.
- It provides more and better compression information and statistics than lbxproxy.

11.1.2 Disadvantages

- It is not a standard part of X; you must obtain and build it separately.
- It is slightly more complex to set up, since it requires a LOCAL-side proxy as well as the REMOTE proxy.

11.1.3 Where Can I Get dxpc?

The source for dxpc is available at *ftp.x.org* `<ftp://ftp.x.org/contrib/utilities/>`.

There is a WWW homepage for dxpc that gives a lot of good information, including pointers to the dxpc mailing list, access to the source code, and a number of pre-built binaries for various platforms:

`<http://ccwf.cc.utexas.edu/~zvonler/dxpc/>`

11.2 Ssh (Secure Shell)

Ken Chase <*lbxhowto@sizone.org*> `<mailto:lbxhowto@sizone.org>` notes that *ssh* `<http://www.cs.hut.fi/ssh/>` can be used for compression. Although its main purpose is to provide security, it also compresses the data it sends.

Thus, if you run X over a `ssh` link you will automatically obtain some amount of compression.

11.3 Which Is Better?

I don't know. Both LBX and `dxpc` are certainly better at raw compression than `ssh`. Of course, `ssh` provides the added advantage of security. And of course, there's no reason you can't use both `ssh` and one of the other two, to get good compression and security.

It shouldn't be hard to run some benchmarking against these options and get both subjective and statistical measurings of performance. But I haven't done this, and I don't know of anyone who has.

Assembly HOWTO

François-René Rideau rideau@ens.fr

v0.4l, 16 November 1997

This is the Linux Assembly HOWTO. This document describes how to program in assembly using *FREE* programming tools, focusing on development for or from the Linux Operating System on i386 platforms. Included material may or may not be applicable to other hardware and/or software platforms. Contributions about these would be gladly accepted. *keywords*: assembly, assembler, free, macroprocessor, preprocessor, asm, inline asm, 32-bit, x86, i386, gas, as86, nasm

Contents

1 INTRODUCTION

1.1 Legal Blurp

Copyright © 1996,1997 by François-René Rideau. This document may be distributed under the terms set forth in the LDP license at `<http://sunsite.unc.edu/LDP/COPYRIGHT.html>`.

1.2 IMPORTANT NOTE

This is expectedly the last release I'll make of this document. There's one candidate new maintainer, but until he really takes the HOWTO over, I'll accept feedback.

You are especially invited to ask questions, to answer to questions, to correct given answers, to add new FAQ answers, to give pointers to other software, to point the current maintainer to bugs or deficiencies in the pages. If you're motivated, you could even *TAKE OVER THE MAINTENANCE OF THE FAQ*. In one word, contribute!

To contribute, please contact whoever appears to maintain the Assembly-HOWTO. Current maintainers are *François-René Rideau* `<mailto:rideau@clipper.ens.fr>` and now *Paul Anderson* `<mailto:paul@geeky1.ebtech.net>`.

1.3 Foreword

This document aims at answering frequently asked questions of people who program or want to program 32-bit x86 assembly using *free* assemblers, particularly under the Linux operating system. It may also point to other documents about non-free, non-x86, or non-32-bit assemblers, though such is not its primary goal.

Because the main interest of assembly programming is to build to write the guts of operating systems, interpreters, compilers, and games, where a C compiler fails to provide the needed expressivity (performance is more and more seldom an issue), we stress on development of such software.

1.3.1 How to use this document

This document contains answers to some frequently asked questions. At many places, Universal Resource Locators (URL) are given for some software or documentation repository. Please see that the most useful repositories are mirrored, and that by accessing a nearer mirror site, you relieve the whole Internet from unneeded network traffic, while saving your own precious time. Particularly, there are large repositories all over the world, that mirror other popular repositories. You should learn and note what are those places near you (networkwise). Sometimes, the list of mirrors is listed in a file, or in a login message. Please heed the advice. Else, you should ask archie about the software you're looking for...

The most recent version for this documents sits in

`<http://www.eleves.ens.fr:8080/home/rideau/Assembly-HOWTO>` or `<http://www.eleves.ens.fr:8080/home/rideau/Assembly-HOWTO.sgml>`

but what's in Linux HOWTO repositories *should* be fairly up to date, too (I can't know):

`<ftp://sunsite.unc.edu/pub/Linux/docs/HOWTO/>` (?)

A french translation of this HOWTO can be found around

`<ftp://ftp.ibp.fr/pub/linux/french/HOWTO/>`

1.3.2 Other related documents

- If you don't know what *free* software is, please do read *carefully* the GNU General Public License, which is used in a lot of free software, and is a model for most of their licenses. It generally comes in a file named `COPYING`, with a library version in a file named `COPYING.LIB`. Litterature from the FSF (free software foundation) might help you, too.

- Particularly, the interesting kind of free software comes with sources that you can consult and correct, or sometimes even borrow from. Read your particular license carefully, and do comply to it.

- There is a FAQ for comp.lang.asm.x86 that answers generic questions about x86 assembly programming, and questions about some commercial assemblers in a 16-bit DOS environment. Some of it apply to free 32-bit asm programming, so you may want to read this FAQ...
  `<http://www2.dgsys.com/raymoon/faq/asmfaq.zip>`

- FAQs and docs exist about programming on your favorite platform, whichever it is, that you should consult for platform-specific issues not directly related to programming in assembler.

1.4 History

Each version includes a few fixes and minor corrections, which needs not be repeatedly mentionned every time.

Version 0.1 23 Apr 1996

Francois-Rene "Faré" Rideau <rideau@ens.fr> creates and publishes the first mini-HOWTO, because "I'm sick of answering ever the same questions on comp.lang.asm.x86"

Version 0.2 4 May 1996
*

Version 0.3c 15 Jun 1996
*

Version 0.3f 17 Oct 1996

found -fasm option to enable GCC inline assembler w/o -O optimizations

Version 0.3g 2 Nov 1996

Created the History. Added pointers in cross-compiling section. Added section about I/O programming under Linux (particularly video).

Version 0.3h 6 Nov 1996

more about cross-compiling – See on sunsite: devel/msdos/

Version 0.3i 16 Nov 1996

   NASM is getting pretty slick

Version 0.3j 24 Nov 1996

   point to french translated version

Version 0.3k 19 Dec 1996

   What? I had forgotten to point to terse???

Version 0.3l 11 Jan 1997

   *

Version 0.4pre1 13 Jan 1997

   text mini-HOWTO transformed into a full linuxdoc-sgml HOWTO, to see what the SGML tools are like.

Version 0.4 20 Jan 1997

   first release of the HOWTO as such.

Version 0.4a 20 Jan 1997

   CREDITS section added

Version 0.4b 3 Feb 1997

   NASM moved: now is before AS86

Version 0.4c 9 Feb 1997

   Added section "DO YOU NEED ASSEMBLY?"

Version 0.4d 28 Feb 1997

   Vapor announce of a new Assembly-HOWTO maintainer.

Version 0.4e 13 Mar 1997

   Release for DrLinux

Version 0.4f 20 Mar 1997

   *

Version 0.4g 30 Mar 1997

   *

Version 0.4h 19 Jun 1997

   still more on "how not to use assembly"; updates on NASM, GAS.

Version 0.4i 17 July 1997

   info on 16-bit mode access from Linux.

Version 0.4j 7 September 1997

   *

Version 0.4k 19 October 1997

   *

Version 0.4l 16 November 1997

   release for LSL 6th edition.

   This is yet another last-release-by-Faré-before-new-maintainer-takes-over (?)

1.5   Credits

I would like to thanks the following persons, by order of appearance:

- *Linus Torvalds* `<mailto:buried.alive@in.mail>` for Linux
- *Bruce Evans* `<mailto:bde@zeta.org.au>` for bcc from which as86 is extracted
- *Simon Tatham* `<mailto:anakin@poboxes.com>` and *Julian Hall* `<mailto:jules@earthcorp.com>` for NASM
- *Jim Neil* `<mailto:jim-neil@digital.net>` for Terse
- *Greg Hankins* `<mailto:gregh@sunsite.unc.edu>` for maintaining HOWTOs
- *Raymond Moon* `<mailto:raymoon@moonware.dgsys.com>` for his FAQ
- *Eric Dumas* `<mailto:dumas@excalibur.ibp.fr>` for his translation of the mini-HOWTO into french (sad thing for the original author to be french and write in english)
- *Paul Anderson* `<mailto:paul@geeky1.ebtech.net>` and *Rahim Azizarab* `<mailto:rahim@megsinet. net>` for helping me, if not for taking over the HOWTO.
- All the people who have contributed ideas, remarks, and moral support.

2   DO YOU NEED ASSEMBLY?

Well, I wouldn't want to interfere with what you're doing, but here are a few advice from hard-earned experience.

2.1   Pros and Cons

2.1.1   The advantages of Assembly

Assembly can express very low-level things:

- you can access machine-dependent registers and I/O.
- you can control the exact behavior of code in critical sections that might involve hardware or I/O lock-ups
- you can break the conventions of your usual compiler, which might allow some optimizations (like temporarily breaking rules about GC, threading, etc).
- get access to unusual programming modes of your processor (e.g. 16 bit code for startup or BIOS interface on Intel PCs)
- you can build interfaces between code fragments using incompatible conventions (e.g. produced by different compilers, or separated by a low-level interface).
- you can produce reasonably fast code for tight loops to cope with a bad non-optimizing compiler (but then, there are free optimizing compilers available!)
- you can produce hand-optimized code that's perfectly tuned for your particular hardware setup, though not to anyone else's.
- you can write some code for your new language's optimizing compiler (that's something few will ever do, and even they, not often).

2.1.2 The disadvantages of Assembly

Assembly is a very low-level language (the lowest above hand-coding the binary instruction patterns). This means

- it's long and tedious to write initially,
- it's very bug-prone,
- your bugs will be very difficult to chase,
- it's very difficult to understand and modify, i.e. to maintain.
- the result is very non-portable to other architectures, existing or future,
- your code will be optimized only for a certain implementation of a same architecture: for instance, among Intel-compatible platforms, each CPU design and variation (bus width, relative speed and size of CPU/caches/RAM/Bus/disks presence of FPU, MMX extensions, etc) implies potentially completely different optimization techniques. CPU designs already include Intel 386, 486, Pentium, PPro, Pentium II; Cyrix 5x86, 6x86; AMD K5, K6. New designs keep appearing, so don't expect either this listing or your code to be up-to-date.
- your code might also be unportable accross different OS platforms on the same architecture, by lack of proper tools. (well, GAS seems to work on all platforms; NASM seems to work or be workable on all intel platforms).
- you spend more time on a few details, and can't focus on small and large algorithmic design, that are known to bring the largest part of the speed up. [e.g. you might spend some time building very fast list/array manipulation primitives in assembly; only a hash table would have sped up your program much more; or, in another context, a binary tree; or some high-level structure distributed over a cluster of CPUs]
- a small change in algorithmic design might completely invalidate all your existing assembly code. So that either you're ready (and able) to rewrite it all, or you're tied to a particular algorithmic design;
- On code that ain't too far from what's in standard benchmarks, commercial optimizing compilers outperform hand-coded assembly (well, that's less true on the x86 architecture than on RISC architectures, and perhaps less true for widely available/free compilers; anyway, for typical C code, GCC is fairly good);
- And in any case, as says moderator John Levine on comp.compilers, "compilers make it a lot easier to use complex data structures, and compilers don't get bored halfway through and generate reliably pretty good code." They will also *correctly* propagate code transformations throughout the whole (huge) program when optimizing code between procedures and module boundaries.

2.1.3 Assessment

All in all, you might find that though using assembly is sometimes needed, and might even be useful in a few cases where it is not, you'll want to:

- minimize the use of assembly code,
- encapsulate this code in well-defined interfaces
- have your assembly code automatically generated from patterns expressed in a higher-level language than assembly (e.g. GCC inline-assembly macros).
- have automatic tools translate these programs into assembly code
- have this code be optimized if possible
- All of the above, i.e. write (an extension to) an optimizing compiler back-end.

Even in cases when Assembly is needed (e.g. OS development), you'll find that not so much of it is, and that the above principles hold.

See the sources for the Linux kernel about it: as little assembly as needed, resulting in a fast, reliable, portable, maintainable OS. Even a successful game like DOOM was almost massively written in C, with a tiny part only being written in assembly for speed up.

2.2 How to NOT use Assembly

2.2.1 General procedure to achieve efficient code

As says Charles Fiterman on comp.compilers about human vs computer-generated assembly code,

"The human should always win and here is why.

- First the human writes the whole thing in a high level language.
- Second he profiles it to find the hot spots where it spends its time.
- Third he has the compiler produce assembly for those small sections of code.
- Fourth he hand tunes them looking for tiny improvements over the machine generated code.

The human wins because he can use the machine."

2.2.2 Languages with optimizing compilers

Languages like ObjectiveCAML, SML, CommonLISP, Scheme, ADA, Pascal, C, C++, among others, all have free optimizing compilers that'll optimize the bulk of your programs, and often do better than hand-coded assembly even for tight loops, while allowing you to focus on higher-level details, and without forbidding you to grab a few percent of extra performance in the above-mentionned way, once you've reached a stable design. Of course, there are also commercial optimizing compilers for most of these languages, too!

Some languages have compilers that produce C code, which can be further optimized by a C compiler. LISP, Scheme, Perl, and many other are suches. Speed is fairly good.

2.2.3 General procedure to speed your code up

As for speeding code up, you should do it only for parts of a program that a profiling tool has consistently identified as being a performance bottleneck.

Hence, if you identify some code portion as being too slow, you should

- first try to use a better algorithm;
- then try to compile it rather than interpret it;
- then try to enable and tweak optimization from your compiler;
- then give the compiler hints about how to optimize (typing information in LISP; register usage with GCC; lots of options in most compilers, etc).
- then possibly fallback to assembly programming

Finally, before you end up writing assembly, you should inspect generated code, to check that the problem really is with bad code generation, as this might really not be the case: compiler-generated code might be better than what you'd have written, particularly on modern multi-pipelined architectures! Slow parts of a program might be intrinsically so. Biggest problems on modern architectures with fast processors are due to delays from memory access, cache-misses, TLB-misses, and page-faults; register optimization becomes useless, and you'll more profitably re-think data structures and threading to achieve better locality in memory access. Perhaps a completely different approach to the problem might help, then.

2.2.4 Inspecting compiler-generated code

There are many reasons to inspect compiler-generated assembly code. Here are what you'll do with such code:

- check whether generated code can be obviously enhanced with hand-coded assembly (or by tweaking compiler switches)
- when that's the case, start from generated code and modify it instead of starting from scratch
- more generally, use generated code as stubs to modify, which at least gets right the way your assembly routines interface to the external world
- track down bugs in your compiler (hopefully rarer)

The standard way to have assembly code be generated is to invoke your compiler with the -S flag. This works with most Unix compilers, including the GNU C Compiler (GCC), but YMMV. As for GCC, it will produce more understandable assembly code with the -fverbose-asm command-line option. Of course, if you want to get good assembly code, don't forget your usual optimization options and hints!

3 ASSEMBLERS

3.1 GCC Inline Assembly

The well-known GNU C/C++ Compiler (GCC), an optimizing 32-bit compiler at the heart of the GNU project, supports the x86 architecture quite well, and includes the ability to insert assembly code in C programs, in such a way that register allocation can be either specified or left to GCC. GCC works on most available platforms, notably Linux, *BSD, VSTa, OS/2, *DOS, Win*, etc.

3.1.1 Where to find GCC

The original GCC site is the GNU FTP site <ftp://prep.ai.mit.edu/pub/gnu/> together with all the released application software from the GNU project. Linux-configured and precompiled versions can be found in <ftp://sunsite.unc.edu/pub/Linux/GCC/> There exists a lot of FTP mirrors of both sites. everywhere around the world, as well as CD-ROM copies.

GCC development has split in two branches recently. See more about the experimental version, egcs, at <http://www.cygnus.com/egcs/>

Sources adapted to your favorite OS, and binaries precompiled for it, should be found at your usual FTP sites.

For most popular DOS port of GCC is named DJGPP, and can be found in directories of such name in FTP sites. See:

<http://www.delorie.com/djgpp/>

There is also a port of GCC to OS/2 named EMX, that also works under DOS, and includes lots of unix-emulation library routines. See around:

<http://www.leo.org/pub/comp/os/os2/gnu/emx+gcc/>

<http://warp.eecs.berkeley.edu/os2/software/shareware/emx.html>

<ftp://ftp-os2.cdrom.com/pub/os2/emx09c/>

3.1.2   Where to find docs for GCC Inline Asm

The documentation of GCC includes documentation files in texinfo format. You can compile them with tex and print then result, or convert them to .info, and browse them with emacs, or convert them to .html, or nearly whatever you like. convert (with the right tools) to whatever you like, or just read as is. The .info files are generally found on any good installation for GCC.

The right section to look for is: `C Extensions::Extended Asm::`

Section `Invoking GCC::Submodel Options::i386 Options::` might help too. Particularly, it gives the i386 specific constraint names for registers: abcdSDB correspond to %eax, %ebx, %ecx, %edx, %esi, %edi, %ebp respectively (no letter for %esp).

The DJGPP Games resource (not only for game hackers) has this page specifically about assembly:

<http://www.rt66.com/brennan/djgpp/djgpp_asm.html>

Finally, there is a web page called, "DJGPP Quick ASM Programming Guide", that covers URLs to FAQs, AT&T x86 ASM Syntax, Some inline ASM information, and converting .obj/.lib files:

<http://remus.rutgers.edu/avly/djasm.html>

GCC depends on GAS for assembling, and follow its syntax (see below); do mind that inline asm needs percent characters to be quoted so they be passed to GAS. See the section about GAS below.

Find *lots* of useful examples in the `linux/include/asm-i386/` subdirectory of the sources for the Linux kernel.

3.1.3   Invoking GCC to have it properly inline assembly code ?

Be sure to invoke GCC with the -O flag (or -O2, -O3, etc), to enable optimizations and inline assembly. If you don't, your code may compile, but not run properly!!! Actually (kudos to Tim Potter, timbo@moshpit.air.net.au), it is enough to use the -fasm flag (and perhaps -finline-functions) which is part of all the features enabled by -O. So if you have problems with buggy optimizations in your particular implementation/version of GCC, you can still use inline asm. Similarly, use -fno-asm to disable inline assembly (why would you?).

More generally, good compile flags for GCC on the x86 platform are

```
gcc -O2 -fomit-frame-pointer -m386 -Wall
```

-O2 is the good optimization level. Optimizing besides it yields code that is a lot larger, but only a bit faster; such overoptimizationn might be useful for tight loops only (if any), which you may be doing in assembly anyway; if you need that, do it just for the few routines that need it.

-fomit-frame-pointer allows generated code to skip the stupid frame pointer maintenance, which makes code smaller and faster, and frees a register for further optimizations. It precludes the easy use of debugging tools (gdb), but when you use these, you just don't care about size and speed anymore anyway.

-m386 yields more compact code, without any measurable slowdown, (note that small code also means less disk I/O and faster execution) but perhaps on the above-mentioned tight loops; you might appreciate -mpentium for special pentium-optimizing GCC targetting a specifically pentium platform.

-Wall enables all warnings and helps you catch obvious stupid errors.

To optimize even more, option -mregparm=2 and/or corresponding function attribute might help, but might pose lots of problems when linking to foreign code...

Note that you can add make these flags the default by editing file /usr/lib/gcc-lib/i486-linux/2.7.2.2/specs or wherever that is on your system (better not add -Wall there, though).

3.2 GAS

GAS is the GNU Assembler, that GCC relies upon.

3.2.1 Where to find it

Find it at the same place where you found GCC, in a package named binutils.

3.2.2 What is this AT&T syntax

Because GAS was invented to support a 32-bit unix compiler, it uses standard "AT&T" syntax, which resembles a lot the syntax for standard m68k assemblers, and is standard in the UNIX world. This syntax is no worse, no better than the "Intel" syntax. It's just different. When you get used to it, you find it much more regular than the Intel syntax, though a bit boring.

Here are the major caveats about GAS syntax:

- Register names are prefixed with %, so that registers are %eax, %dl and suches instead of just eax, dl, etc. This makes it possible to include external C symbols directly in assembly source, without any risk of confusion, or any need for ugly underscore prefixes.

- The order of operands is source(s) first, and destination last, as opposed to the intel convention of destination first and sources last. Hence, what in intel syntax is mov ax,dx (move contents of register dx into register ax) will be in att syntax mov %dx, %ax.

- The operand length is specified as a suffix to the instruction name. The suffix is b for (8-bit) byte, w for (16-bit) word, and l for (32-bit) long. For instance, the correct syntax for the above instruction would have been movw %dx,%ax. However, gas does not require strict att syntax was, so the suffix is optional when length can be guessed from register operands, and else defaults to 32-bit (with a warning).

- Immediate operands are marked with a $ prefix, as in addl $5,%eax (add immediate long value 5 to register %eax).

- No prefix to an operand indicates it is a memory-address; hence movl $foo,%eax puts the *address* of variable foo in register %eax, but movl foo,%eax puts the contents of variable foo in register %eax.

- Indexing or indirection is done by enclosing the index register or indirection memory cell address in parentheses, as in testb $0x80,17(%ebp) (test the high bit of the byte value at offset 17 from the cell pointed to by %ebp).

A program exists to help you convert programs from TASM syntax to AT&T syntax. See

<ftp://x2ftp.oulu.fi/pub/msdos/programming/convert/ta2asv08.zip>

GAS has comprehensive documentation in TeXinfo format, which comes at least with the source distribution. Browse extracted .info pages with Emacs or whatever. There used to be a file named gas.doc or as.doc around the GAS source package, but it was merged into the TeXinfo docs. Of course, in case of doubt, the ultimate documentation is the sources themselves! A section that will particularly interest you is `Machine Dependencies::i386-Dependent::`

Again, the sources for Linux (the OS kernel), come in as good examples; see under linux/arch/i386, the following files: `kernel/*.S, boot/compressed/*.S, mathemu/*.S`

If you are writing kind of a language, a thread package, etc you might as well see how other languages (OCaml, gforth, etc), or thread packages (QuickThreads, MIT pthreads, LinuxThreads, etc), or whatever, do it.

Finally, just compiling a C program to assembly might show you the syntax for the kind of instructions you want. See section 2 (Do you need Assembly?) above.

3.2.3   Limited 16-bit mode

GAS is a 32-bit assembler, meant to support a 32-bit compiler. It currently has only limited support for 16-bit mode, which consists in prepending the 32-bit prefixes to instructions, so you write 32-bit code that runs in 16-bit mode on a 32 bit CPU. In both modes, it supports 16-bit register usage, but what is unsupported is 16-bit addressing. Use the directive `.code16` and `.code32` to switch between modes. Note that an inline assembly statement `asm(".code16\n")` will allow GCC to produce 32-bit code that'll run in real mode!

I've been told that most code needed to fully support 16-bit mode programming was added to GAS by Bryan Ford (please confirm?), but at least, it doesn't show up in any of the distribution I tried, up to binutils-2.8.1.x ... more info on this subject would be welcome.

A cheap solution is to define macros (see below) that somehow produce the binary encoding (with `.byte`) for just the 16-bit mode instructions you need (almost nothing if you use code16 as above, and can safely assume the code will run on a 32-bit capable x86 CPU). To find the proper encoding, you can get inspiration from the sources of 16-bit capable assemblers for the encoding.

3.3   GASP

GASP is the GAS Preprocessor. It adds macros and some nice syntax to GAS.

3.3.1   Where to find GASP

GASP comes together with GAS in the GNU binutils archive.

3.3.2   How it works

It works as a filter, much like cpp and the like. I have no idea on details, but it comes with its own texinfo documentation, so just browse them (in .info), print them, grok them. GAS with GASP looks like a regular macro-assembler to me.

3.4   NASM

The Netwide Assembler project is producing yet another assembler, written in C, that should be modular enough to eventually support all known syntaxes and object formats.

3.4.1 Where to find NASM

<http://www.cryogen.com/Nasm>

Binary release on your usual sunsite mirror in `devel/lang/asm/` Should also be available as .rpm or .deb in your usual RedHat/Debian distributions' contrib.

3.4.2 What it does

At the time this HOWTO is written, the current NASM version is 0.96.

The syntax is Intel-style. Some macroprocessing support is integrated.

Supported object file formats are `bin`, `aout`, `coff`, `elf`, `as86`, (DOS) `obj`, `win32`, (their own format) `rdf`.

NASM can be used as a backend for the free LCC compiler (support files included).

Surely NASM evolves too fast for this HOWTO to be kept up to date. Unless you're using BCC as a 16-bit compiler (which is out of scope of this 32-bit HOWTO), you should use NASM instead of say AS86 or MASM, because it is actively supported online, and runs on all platforms.

Note: NASM also comes with a disassembler, NDISASM.

Its hand-written parser makes it much faster than GAS, though of course, it doesn't support three bazillion different architectures. For the x86 target, it should be the assembler of choice...

3.5 AS86

AS86 is a 80x86 assembler, both 16-bit and 32-bit, part of Bruce Evans' C Compiler (BCC). It has mostly Intel-syntax, though it differs slightly as for addressing modes.

3.5.1 Where to get AS86

A completely outdated version of AS86 is distributed by HJLu just to compile the Linux kernel, in a package named bin86 (current version 0.4), available in any Linux GCC repository. But I advise no one to use it for anything else but compiling Linux. This version supports only a hacked minix object file format, which is not supported by the GNU binutils or anything, and it has a few bugs in 32-bit mode, so you really should better keep it only for compiling Linux.

The most recent versions by Bruce Evans (bde@zeta.org.au) are published together with the FreeBSD distribution. Well, they were: I could not find the sources from distribution 2.1 on :(Hence, I put the sources at my place:

<http:///www.eleves.ens.fr:8080/home/rideau/files/bcc-95.3.12.src.tgz>

The Linux/8086 (aka ELKS) project is somehow maintaining bcc (though I don't think they included the 32-bit patches). See around <http://www.linux.org.uk/Linux8086.html> <ftp://linux.mit.edu/>.

Among other things, these more recent versions, unlike HJLu's, supports Linux GNU a.out format, so you can link you code to Linux programs, and/or use the usual tools from the GNU binutil package to manipulate your data. This version can co-exist without any harm with the previous one (see according question below).

BCC from 12 march 1995 and earlier version has a misfeature that makes all segment pushing/popping 16-bit, which is quite annoying when programming in 32-bit mode. A patch is published in the Tunes project <http://www.eleves.ens.fr:8080/home/rideau/Tunes/> subpage `files/tgz/tunes.0.0.0.25.src.tgz` in unpacked subdirectory `LLL/i386/` The patch should also be in available directly from <http://www.eleves.

`ens.fr:8080/home/rideau/files/as86.bcc.patch.gz>` Bruce Evans accepted this patch, so if there is a more recent version of bcc somewhere someday, the patch should have been included...

3.5.2   How to invoke the assembler?

Here's the GNU Makefile entry for using bcc to transform `.s` asm into both GNU a.out `.o` object and `.l` listing:

```
%.o %.l:          %.s
        bcc -3 -G -c -A-d -A-l -A$*.l -o $*.o $<
```

Remove the `%.l`, `-A-l`, and `-A$*.l`, if you don't want any listing. If you want something else than GNU a.out, you can see the docs of bcc about the other supported formats, and/or use the objcopy utility from the GNU binutils package.

3.5.3   Where to find docs

The docs are what is included in the bcc package. Man pages are also available somewhere on the FreeBSD site. When in doubt, the sources themselves are often a good docs: it's not very well commented, but the programming style is straightforward. You might try to see how as86 is used in Tunes 0.0.0.25...

3.5.4   What if I can't compile Linux anymore with this new version ?

Linus is buried alive in mail, and my patch for compiling Linux with a Linux a.out as86 didn't make it to him (!). Now, this shouldn't matter: just keep your as86 from the bin86 package in /usr/bin, and let bcc install the good as86 as /usr/local/libexec/i386/bcc/as where it should be. You never need explicitly call this "good" as86, because bcc does everything right, including conversion to Linux a.out, when invoked with the right options; so assemble files exclusively with bcc as a frontend, not directly with as86.

3.6   OTHER ASSEMBLERS

These are other, non-regular, options, in case the previous didn't satisfy you (why?), that I don't recommend in the usual (?) case, but that could prove quite useful if the assembler must be integrated in the software you're designing (i.e. an OS or development environment).

3.6.1   Win32Forth assembler

Win32Forth is a *free* 32-bit ANS FORTH system that successfully runs under Win32s, Win95, Win/NT. It includes a free 32-bit assembler (either prefix or postfix syntax) integrated into the FORTH language. Macro processing is done with the full power of the reflective language FORTH; however, the only supported input and output contexts is Win32For itself (no dumping of .obj file – you could add that yourself, of course). Find it at `<ftp://ftp.forth.org/pub/Forth/win32for/>`

3.6.2   Terse

Terse is a programming tool that provides *THE* most compact assembler syntax for the x86 family! See
<http://www.terse.com>. It is said that there was a free clone somewhere, that was abandonned after
worthless pretenses that the syntax would be owned by the original author, and that I invite you to take
over, in case the syntax interests you.

3.6.3   Non-free and/or Non-32bit x86 assemblers.

You may find more about them, together with the basics of x86 assembly programming, in Raymond Moon's
FAQ for comp.lang.asm.x86 <http://www2.dgsys.com/raymoon/faq/asmfaq.zip>

Note that all DOS-based assemblers should work inside the Linux DOS Emulator, as well as other similar
emulators, so that if you already own one, you can still use it inside a real OS. Recent DOS-based assemblers
also support COFF and/or other object file formats that are supported by the GNU BFD library, so that
you can use them together with your free 32-bit tools, perhaps using GNU objcopy (part of the binutils) as
a conversion filter.

4   METAPROGRAMMING/MACROPROCESSING

Assembly programming is a bore, but for critical parts of programs.

You should use the appropriate tool for the right task, so don't choose assembly when it's not fit; C, OCAML,
perl, Scheme, might be a better choice for most of your programming.

However, there are cases when these tools do not give a fine enough control on the machine, and assembly is
useful or needed. In those case, you'll appreciate a system of macroprocessing and metaprogramming that'll
allow recurring patterns to be factored each into a one indefinitely reusable definition, which allows safer
programming, automatic propagation of pattern modification, etc. A "plain" assembler is often not enough,
even when one is doing only small routines to link with C.

4.1   What's integrated into the above

Yes I know this section does not contain much useful up-to-date information. Feel free to contribute what
you discover the hard way...

4.1.1   GCC

GCC allows (and requires) you to specify register constraints in your "inline assembly" code, so the optimizer
always know about it; thus, inline assembly code is really made of patterns, not forcibly exact code.

Then, you can make put your assembly into CPP macros, and inline C functions, so anyone can use it in
as any C function/macro. Inline functions resemble macros very much, but are sometimes cleaner to use.
Beware that in all those cases, code will be duplicated, so only local labels (of 1: style) should be defined
in that asm code. However, a macro would allow the name for a non local defined label to be passed as
a parameter (or else, you should use additional meta-programming methods). Also, note that propagating
inline asm code will spread potential bugs in them, so watch out doubly for register constraints in such inline
asm code.

Lastly, the C language itself may be considered as a good abstraction to assembly programming, which
relieves you from most of the trouble of assembling.

Beware that some optimizations that involve passing arguments to functions through registers may make those functions unsuitable to be called from external (and particularly hand-written assembly) routines in the standard way; the "asmlinkage" attribute may prevent a routine to be concerned by such optimization flag; see the linux kernel sources for examples.

4.1.2 GAS

GAS has some macro capability included, as detailed in the texinfo docs. Moreover, while GCC recognizes .s files as raw assembly to send to GAS, it also recognizes .S files as files to pipe through CPP before to feed them to GAS. Again and again, see Linux sources for examples.

4.1.3 GASP

It adds all the usual macroassembly tricks to GAS. See its texinfo docs.

4.1.4 NASM

NASM has some macro support, too. See according docs. If you have some bright idea, you might wanna contact the authors, as they are actively developing it. Meanwhile, see about external filters below.

4.1.5 AS86

It has some simple macro support, but I couldn't find docs. Now the sources are very straightforward, so if you're interested, you should understand them easily. If you need more than the basics, you should use an external filter (see below).

4.1.6 OTHER ASSEMBLERS

- Win32FORTH: CODE and END-CODE are normal that do not switch from interpretation mode to compilation mode, so you have access to the full power of FORTH while assembling.

- TUNES: it doesn't work yet, but the Scheme language is a real high-level language that allows arbitrary meta-programming.

4.2 External Filters

Whatever is the macro support from your assembler, or whatever language you use (even C !), if the language is not expressive enough to you, you can have files passed through an external filter with a Makefile rule like that:

```
%.s:    %.S other_dependencies
        $(FILTER) $(FILTER_OPTIONS) < $< > $@
```

4.2.1 CPP

CPP is truly not very expressive, but it's enough for easy things, it's standard, and called transparently by GCC.

As an example of its limitations, you can't declare objects so that destructors are automatically called at the end of the declaring block; you don't have diversions or scoping, etc.

CPP comes with any C compiler. If you could make it without one, don't bother fetching CPP (though I wonder how you could).

4.2.2 M4

M4 gives you the full power of macroprocessing, with a Turing equivalent language, recursion, regular expressions, etc. You can do with it everything that CPP cannot.

See macro4th/This4th from `<ftp://ftp.forth.org/pub/Forth/>` in Reviewed/ ANS/ (?), or the Tunes 0.0.0.25 sources as examples of advanced macroprogramming using m4.

However, its disfunctional quoting and unquoting semantics force you to use explicit continuation-passing tail-recursive macro style if you want to do *advanced* macro programming (which is remindful of TeX – BTW, has anyone tried to use TeX as a macroprocessor for anything else than typesetting ?). This is NOT worse than CPP that does not allow quoting and recursion anyway.

The right version of m4 to get is GNU m4 1.4 (or later if exists), which has the most features and the least bugs or limitations of all. m4 is designed to be slow for anything but the simplest uses, which might still be ok for most assembly programming (you're not writing million-lines assembly programs, are you?).

4.2.3 Macroprocessing with yer own filter

You can write your own simple macro-expansion filter with the usual tools: perl, awk, sed, etc. That's quick to do, and you control everything. But of course, any power in macroprocessing must be earned the hard way.

4.2.4 Metaprogramming

Instead of using an external filter that expands macros, one way to do things is to write programs that write part or all of other programs.

For instance, you could use a program outputting source code

- to generate sine/cosine/whatever lookup tables,
- to extract a source-form representation of a binary file,
- to compile your bitmaps into fast display routines,
- to extract documentation, initialization/finalization code, description tables, as well as normal code from the same source files,
- to have customized assembly code, generated from a perl/shell/scheme script that does arbitrary processing,
- to propagate data defined at one point only into several cross-referencing tables and code chunks.
- etc.

Think about it!

Backends from existing compilers Compilers like SML/NJ, Objective CAML, MIT-Scheme, etc, do have their own generic assembler backend, which you might or not want to use, if you intend to generate code semi-automatically from the according languages.

The New-Jersey Machine-Code Toolkit There is a project, using the programming language Icon, to build a basis for producing assembly-manipulating code. See around `<http://www.cs.virginia.edu/nr/toolkit/>`

Tunes The Tunes OS project is developing its own assembler as an extension to the Scheme language, as part of its development process. It doesn't run at all yet, though help is welcome.

The assembler manipulates symbolic syntax trees, so it could equally serve as the basis for a assembly syntax translator, a disassembler, a common assembler/compiler back-end, etc. Also, the full power of a real language, Scheme, make it unchallenged as for macroprocessing/metaprograming.

`<http://www.eleves.ens.fr:8080/home/rideau/Tunes/>`

5   CALLING CONVENTIONS

5.1   Linux

5.1.1   Linking to GCC

That's the preferred way. Check GCC docs and examples from Linux kernel `.S` files that go through gas (not those that go through as86).

32-bit arguments are pushed down stack in reverse syntactic order (hence accessed/popped in the right order), above the 32-bit near return address. `%ebp`, `%esi`, `%edi`, `%ebx` are callee-saved, other registers are caller-saved; `%eax` is to hold the result, or `%edx:%eax` for 64-bit results.

FP stack: I'm not sure, but I think it's result in `st(0)`, whole stack caller-saved.

Note that GCC has options to modify the calling conventions by reserving registers, having arguments in registers, not assuming the FPU, etc. Check the i386 .info pages.

Beware that you must then declare the `cdecl` attribute for a function that will follow standard GCC calling conventions (I don't know what it does with modified calling conventions). See in the GCC info pages the section: `C Extensions::Extended Asm::`

5.1.2   ELF vs a.out problems

Some C compilers prepend an underscore before every symbol, while others do not.

Particularly, Linux a.out GCC does such prepending, while Linux ELF GCC does not.

If you need cope with both behaviors at once, see how existing packages do. For instance, get an old Linux source tree, the Elk, qthreads, or OCAML...

You can also override the implicit C->asm renaming by inserting statements like

```
void foo asm("bar") (void);
```

to be sure that the C function foo will be called really bar in assembly.

Note that the utility objcopy, from the binutils package, should allow you to transform your a.out objects into ELF objects, and perhaps the contrary too, in some cases. More generally, it will do lots of file format conversions.

5.1.3 Direct Linux syscalls

This is specifically *NOT* recommended, because the conventions change from time to time or from kernel flavor to kernel flavor (cf L4Linux), plus it's not portable, it's a burden to write, it's redundant with the libc effort, AND it precludes fixes and extensions that are made to the libc, like, for instance the zlibc package, that does on-the-fly transparent decompression of gzip-compressed files. The standard, recommended way to call Linux system services is, and will stay, to go through the libc.

Shared objects should keep your stuff small. And if you really want smaller binaries, do use #! stuff, with the interpreter having all the overhead you want to keep out of your binaries.

Now, if for some reason, you don't want to link to the libc, go get the libc and understand how it works! After all, you're pretending to replace it, ain't you?

You might also take a look at how my *eforth 1.0c* <ftp://ftp.forth.org/pub/Forth/Linux/linux-eforth-1.0c.tgz> does it.

The sources for Linux come in handy, too, particularly the asm/unistd.h header file, that describes how to do system calls...

Basically, you issue an int $0x80, with the __NR_syscallname number (from asm/unistd.h) in %eax, and parameters (up to five) in %ebx, %ecx, %edx, %esi, %edi respectively. Result is returned in %eax, with a negative result being an error whose opposite is what libc would put in errno. The user-stack is not touched, so you needn't have a valid one when doing a syscall.

5.1.4 I/O under Linux

If you want to do direct I/O under Linux, either it's something very simple that needn't OS arbitration, and you should see the IO-Port-Programming mini-HOWTO; or it needs a kernel device driver, and you should try to learn more about kernel hacking, device driver development, kernel modules, etc, for which there are other excellent HOWTOs and documents from the LDP.

Particularly, if what you want is Graphics programming, then do join the GGI project: <http://synergy.caltech.edu/ggi/> <http://sunserver1.rz.uni-duesseldorf.de/becka/doc/scrdrv.html>

Anyway, in all these cases, you'll be better off using GCC inline assembly with the macros from linux/asm/*.h than writing full assembly source files.

5.1.5 Accessing 16-bit drivers from Linux/i386

Such thing is theoretically possible (proof: see how DOSEMU can selectively grant hardware port access to programs),and I've heard rumors that someone somewhere did actually do it (in the PCI driver? Some VESA access stuff? ISA PnP? dunno). If you have some more precise information on that, you'll be most welcome. Anyway, good places to look for more information are the Linux kernel sources, DOSEMU sources (and other programs in the *DOSEMU repository* <ftp://tsx-11.mit.edu/pub/linux/ALPHA/dosemu/>), and sources for various low-level programs under Linux... (perhaps GGI if it supports VESA).

Basically, you must either use 16-bit protected mode or vm86 mode.

The first is simpler to setup, but only works with well-behaved code that won't do any kind of segment arithmetics or absolute segment addressing (particularly addressing segment 0), unless by chance it happens that all segments used can be setup in advance in the LDT.

The later allows for more "compatibility" with vanilla 16-bit environments, but requires more complicated handling.

In both cases, before you can jump to 16-bit code, you must

- mmap any absolute address used in the 16-bit code (such as ROM, video buffers, DMA targets, and memory-mapped I/O) from /dev/mem to your process' address space,
- setup the LDT and/or vm86 mode monitor.
- grab proper I/O permissions from the kernel (see the above section)

Again, carefully read the source for the stuff contributed to the DOSEMU repository above, particularly these mini-emulators for running ELKS and/or simple .COM programs under Linux/i386.

5.2   DOS

Most DOS extenders come with some interface to DOS services. Read their docs about that, but often, they just simulate int $0x21 and such, so you do "as if" you were in real mode (I doubt they have more than stubs and extend things to work with 32-bit operands; they most likely will just reflect the interrupt into the real-mode or vm86 handler).

Docs about DPMI and such (and much more) can be found on   <ftp://x2ftp.oulu.fi/pub/msdos/programming/>

DJGPP comes with its own (limited) glibc derivative/subset/replacement, too.

It is possible to cross-compile from Linux to DOS, see the devel/msdos/ directory of your local FTP mirror for sunsite.unc.edu Also see the MOSS dos-extender from the Flux project in utah.

Other documents and FAQs are more DOS-centered. We do not recommend DOS development.

5.3   Winblows and suches

Hey, this document covers only free software. Ring me when Winblows becomes free, or when there are free dev tools for it!

Well, after all there is: *Cygnus Solutions* <http://www.cygnus.com> has developped the cygwin32.dll library, for GNU programs to run on MacroShit platforms. Thus, you can use GCC, GAS, all the GNU tools, and many other Unix applications. Have a look around their homepage. I (Faré) don't intend to expand on Losedoze programming, but I'm sure you can find lots of documents about it everywhere...

5.4   Yer very own OS

Control being what attract many programmers to assembly, want of OS development is often what leads to or stems from assembly hacking. Note that any system that allows self-development could be qualified an "OS" even though it might run "on top" of an underlying system that multitasking or I/O (much like Linux over Mach or OpenGenera over Unix), etc. Hence, for easier debugging purpose, you might like to develop your "OS" first as a process running on top of Linux (despite the slowness), then use the *Flux OS kit* <http://ww.cs.utah.edu/projects/flux/> (which grants use of Linux and BSD drivers in yer own OS) to make it standalone. When your OS is stable, it's still time to write your own hardware drivers if you really love that.

This HOWTO will not itself cover topics such as Boot loader code & getting into 32-bit mode, Handling Interrupts, The basics about intel "protected mode" or "V86/R86" braindeadness, defining your object format and calling conventions. The main place where to find reliable information about that all is source code of existing OSes and bootloaders. Lots of pointers lie in the following WWW page: `<http://www.eleves.ens.fr:8080/home/rideau/Tunes/Review/OSes.html>`

6   TODO & POINTERS

- fill incomplete sections
- add more pointers to software and docs
- add simple examples from real life to illustrate the syntax, power, and limitations of each proposed solution.
- ask people to help with this HOWTO
- find someone who has got some time to takeover the maintenance
- perhaps give a few words for assembly on other platforms?
- A few pointers (in addition to those already in the rest of the HOWTO)

  - *pentium manuals* `<http://www.intel.com/design/pentium/manuals/>`
  - *cpu bugs in the x86 family* `<http://www.xs4all.nl/feldmann>`
  - *hornet.eng.ufl.edu for assembly coders* `<http://www.eng.ufl.edu/ftp>`
  - *ftp.luth.se* `<ftp://ftp.luth.se/pub/msdos/demos/code/>`
  - *PM FAQ* `<ftp://zfja-gate.fuw.edu.pl/cpu/protect.mod>`
  - *80x86 Assembly Page* `<http://www.fys.ruu.nl/faber/Amain.html>`
  - *Courseware* `<http://www.cit.ac.nz/smac/csware.htm>`
  - *game programming* `<http://www.ee.ucl.ac.uk/phart/gameprog.html>`
  - *experiments with asm-only linux programming* `<http://bewoner.dma.be/JanW>`

- And of course, do use your usual Internet Search Tools to look for more information, and tell me anything interesting you find!

Authors' .sig:

```
--   ,                                     ,      _ v  ^  --
-- Fare -- rideau@clipper.ens.fr -- Francois-Rene Rideau -- +)ang-Vu Ban --
--                                    ,                 /.          --
Join the TUNES project for a computing system based on computing freedom !
                TUNES is a Useful, Not Expedient System
WWW page at URL: http://www.eleves.ens.fr:8080/home/rideau/Tunes/
```

The Linux GCC HOWTO

Daniel Barlow <dan@detached.demon.co.uk>   v1.17, 28 February 1996

This document covers how to set up the GNU C compiler and development libraries under Linux, and gives an overview of compiling, linking, running and debugging programs under it. Most of the material in it has been taken from Mitch D'Souza's GCC-FAQ, which it replaces, or the ELF-HOWTO, which it will eventually largely replace. This is the first publically released version (despite the version number; that's an artifact of RCS). Feedback is welcomed.

1 Preliminaries

1.1 ELF vs. a.out

Linux development is in a state of flux right now. Briefly, there are two formats for the binaries that Linux knows how to execute, and depending on how your system is put together, you may have either. When reading this HOWTO, it helps to know which.

How to tell? Use the 'file' utility (eg `file /bin/bash`). For an ELF program it will say something with ELF in, for an a.out program it will say something involving `Linux/i386`.

The differences between ELF and a.out are covered (extensively) later in this document. ELF is the newer format, and generally accepted as better.

1.2 Administrata

The copyright information and like legalese can be found at the *end* of this document, together with the statutory warnings about asking dumb questions on Usenet, revealing your ignorance of the C language by reporting bugs which aren't, and picking your nose while chewing gum.

1.3 Typography

If you're reading this in Postscipt, dvi, or html format, you get to see a little more font variation than people with the plain text version. In particular, filenames, commands, command output and source code excerpts are set in some form of `typewriter` font, whereas 'variables' and random things that need emphasizing are *empasized*.

You also get a usable index. In dvi or postscript, the numbers in the index are section numbers. In HTML they're just sequentially assigned numbers that you can click on. In the plain text version, they really are just numbers. Get an upgrade!

The Bourne (rather than C) shell syntax is used in examples. C shell users will want to use

```
% setenv FOO bar
```

where I have written

```
$ FOO=bar; export FOO
```

If the prompt shown is **#** rather than **$**, the command shown will probably only work as root. Of course, I accept no responsibility for anything that happens to your system as a result of trying these examples. Have a nice day :-)

2   Where to get things

2.1   This document

This document is one of the Linux HOWTO series, so is available from all Linux HOWTO repositories, such as `<http://sunsite.unc.edu/pub/linux/docs/HOWTO/>`. The HTML version can also be found (possibly in a slightly newer version) from `<http://ftp.linux.org.uk/~barlow/howto/gcc-howto.html>`.

2.2   Other documentation

The official documentation for gcc is in the source distribution (see below) as texinfo files, and as `.info` files. If you have a fast network connection, a cdrom, or a reasonable amount of patience, you can just untar it and copy the relevant bits into `/usr/info`. If not, you may find them at *tsx-11* `<ftp://tsx-11.mit.edu:/pub/linux/packages/GCC/>`, but not necessarily always the latest version.

There are two source of documentation for libc. GNU libc comes with info files which describe Linux libc fairly accurately except for stdio. Also, the *manpages* `<ftp://sunsite.unc.edu/pub/Linux/docs/>` archive are written for Linux and describe a lot of system calls (section 2) and libc functions (section 3).

2.3   GCC

There are two answers.

(a) The official Linux GCC distribution can always be found in binary (ready-compiled) form at `<ftp://tsx-11.mit.edu:/pub/linux/packages/GCC/>`. At the time of writing, 2.7.2 (`gcc-2.7.2.bin.tar.gz`) is the latest version.

(b) The latest source distribution of GCC from the Free Software Foundation can be had from *GNU archives* `<ftp://prep.ai.mit.edu/pub/gnu/>`. This is not necessarily always the same version as above, though it is just now. The Linux GCC maintainer(s) have made it easy for you to compile the latest version available yourself — the `configure` script should set it all up for you. Check *tsx-11* `<ftp://tsx-11.mit.edu:/pub/linux/packages/GCC/>` as well, for patches which you may want to apply.

To compile anything non-trivial (and quite a few trivial things also) you will also need the

2.4   C library and header files

What you want here depends on (i) whether your system is ELF or a.out, and (ii) which you want it to be. If you're upgrading from libc 4 to libc 5, you are recommended to look at the ELF-HOWTO from approximately the same place as you found this document.

These are available from *tsx-11* `<ftp://tsx-11.mit.edu:/pub/linux/packages/GCC/>` as above:

`libc-5.2.18.bin.tar.gz`
   — ELF shared library images, static libraries and include files for the C and maths libraries.

`libc-5.2.18.tar.gz`

— Source for the above. You will also need the `.bin.` package for the header files. If you are deliberating whether to compile the C library yourself or use the binaries, the right answer in nearly all cases is to use the binaries. You will however need to roll your own if you want NYS or shadow password support.

`libc-4.7.5.bin.tar.gz`

— a.out shared library images and static libraries for version 4.7.5 of the C library and friends. This is designed to coexist with the libc 5 package above, but is only really necessary if you wish to keep using/developing a.out format programs.

2.5 Associated tools (as, ld, ar, strings etc)

From *tsx-11* `<ftp://tsx-11.mit.edu:/pub/linux/packages/GCC/>`, just like everything else so far. The current version is `binutils-2.6.0.2.bin.tar.gz`.

Note that the binutils are only available in ELF, the current libc version is in ELF and the a.out libc is happiest when used in conjunction with an ELF libc. C library development is moving emphatically ELFwards, and unless you have really good reasons for needing a.out things you're encouraged to follow suit.

3 GCC installation and setup

3.1 GCC versions

You can find out what GCC version you're running by typing `gcc -v` at the shell prompt. This is also a fairly reliable way to find out whether you are set up for ELF or a.out. On my system it does

```
$ gcc -v
Reading specs from /usr/lib/gcc-lib/i486-box-linux/2.7.2/specs
gcc version 2.7.2
```

The key things to note here are

- `i486`. This indicates that the gcc you are using was built for a 486 processor — you might have 386 or 586 instead. All of these chips can run code compiled for each of the others; the difference is that the 486 code has added padding in some places so runs faster on a 486. This has no detrimental performance effect on a 386, but does make the binaries slightly larger.

- `box`. This is *not* at all important, and may say something else (such as `slackware` or `debian`) or nothing at all (so that the complete directory name is `i486-linux`). If you build your own gcc, you can set this at build time for cosmetic effect. Just like I did :-)

- `linux`. This may instead say `linuxelf` or `linuxaout`, and, confusingly, the meaning of each varies according to the version that you are using.

  - `linux` means ELF if the version is 2.7.0 or newer, a.out otherwise.

  - `linuxaout` means a.out. It was introduced as a target when the definition of `linux` was changed from a.out to ELF, so you won't see any `linuxaout` gcc older than 2.7.0.

  - `linuxelf` is obsolete. It is generally a version of gcc 2.6.3 set to produce ELF executables. Note that gcc 2.6.3 has known bugs when producing code for ELF — an upgrade is advisable.

- 2.7.2 is the version number.

So, in summary, I have gcc 2.7.2 producing ELF code. Quelle surprise.

3.2   Where did it go?

If you installed gcc without watching, or if you got it as part of a distribution, you may like to find out where it lives in the filesystem. The key bits are

- /usr/lib/gcc-lib/*target*/*version*/ (and subdirectories) is where most of the compiler lives. This includes the executable programs that do actual compiling, and some version-specific libraries and include files.

- /usr/bin/gcc is the compiler driver — the bit that you can actually run from the command line. This can be used with multiple versions of gcc provided that you have multiple compiler directories (as above) installed. To find out the default version it will use, type **gcc -v**. To force it to another version, type **gcc -V** *version*. For example

```
# gcc -v
Reading specs from /usr/lib/gcc-lib/i486-box-linux/2.7.2/specs
gcc version 2.7.2
# gcc -V 2.6.3 -v
Reading specs from /usr/lib/gcc-lib/i486-box-linux/2.6.3/specs
gcc driver version 2.7.2 executing gcc version 2.6.3
```

- /usr/*target*/(bin|lib|include)/. If you have multiple targets installed (for example, a.out and elf, or a cross-compiler of some sort, the libraries, binutils (**as**, **ld** and so on) and header files for the non-native target(s) can be found here. Even if you only have one kind of gcc installed you might find anyway that various bits for it are kept here. If not, they're in /usr/(bin|lib|include).

- /lib/,/usr/lib and others are library directories for the native system. You will also need /lib/cpp for many applications (X makes quite a lot of use of it) — either copy it from /usr/lib/gcc-lib/*target*/*version*/ or make a symlink pointing there.

3.3   Where are the header files?

Apart from whatever you install yourself under /usr/local/include, there are three main sources of header files in Linux:

- Most of /usr/include/ and its subdirectories are supplied with the libc binary package from H J Lu. I say 'most' because you may also have files from other sources (**curses** and **dbm** libraries, for example) in here, especially if you are using the newest libc distribution (which doesn't come with curses or dbm, unlike the older ones).

- /usr/include/linux and /usr/include/asm (for the files <linux/*.h> and <asm/*.h>) should be symbolic links to the directories linux/include/linux and linux/include/asm in the kernel source distribution. You need to install these if you plan to do *any* non-trivial development; they are not just there for compiling the kernel.

  You might find also that you need to do **make config** in the kernel directory after unpacking the sources. Many files depend on <linux/autoconf.h> which otherwise may not exist, and in some kernel versions asm is a symbolic link itself and only created at **make config** time.

  So, if you unpack your kernel sources under /usr/src/linux, that's

```
$ cd /usr/src/linux
$ su
# make config
[answer the questions.  Unless you're going to go on and build the kernel
it doesn't matter _too_ much what you say]
# cd /usr/include
# ln -s ../src/linux/include/linux .
# ln -s ../src/linux/include/asm .
```

- Files such as <float.h>, <limits.h>, <varargs.h>, <stdarg.h> and <stddef.h> vary according to the compiler version, so are found in /usr/lib/gcc-lib/i486-box-linux/2.7.2/include/ and places of that ilk.

3.4 Building cross compilers

3.4.1 Linux as the target platform

Assuming you have obtained the source code to gcc, usually you can just follow the instructions given in the INSTALL file for GCC. A configure --target=i486-linux --host=XXX on platform XXX followed by a make should do the trick. Note that you will need the Linux includes, the kernel includes, and also to build the cross assembler and cross linker from the sources in <ftp://tsx-11.mit.edu/pub/linux/packages/GCC/>.

3.4.2 Linux as the source platform, MSDOS as the target

Ugh. Apparently this is somewhat possible by using the "emx" package or the "go" extender. Please look at <ftp://sunsite.unc.edu/pub/Linux/devel/msdos>.

I have not tested this and cannot vouch for its abilities.

4 Porting and Compiling

4.1 Automatically defined symbols

You can find out what symbols your version of gcc defines automatically by running it with the -v switch. For example, mine does:

```
$ echo 'main(){printf("hello world\n");}' | gcc -E -v -
Reading specs from /usr/lib/gcc-lib/i486-box-linux/2.7.2/specs
gcc version 2.7.2
 /usr/lib/gcc-lib/i486-box-linux/2.7.2/cpp -lang-c -v -undef
-D__GNUC__=2 -D__GNUC_MINOR__=7 -D__ELF__ -Dunix -Di386 -Dlinux
-D__ELF__ -D__unix__ -D__i386__ -D__linux__ -D__unix -D__i386
-D__linux -Asystem(unix) -Asystem(posix) -Acpu(i386)
-Amachine(i386) -D__i486__ -
```

If you are writing code that uses Linux-specific features, it is a good idea to enclose the nonportable bits in

```
#ifdef __linux__
/* ... funky stuff ... */
#endif /* linux */
```

Use __linux__ for this purpose, *not* linux. Although the latter is defined, it is not POSIX compliant.

4.2   Compiler invocation

The documentation for compiler switches is the gcc info page (in Emacs, use C-h i then select the 'gcc' option). Your distributor may not have packed this with your system, or you may have an old version; the best thing to do in this case is to download the gcc source archive from <ftp://prep.ai.mit.edu/pub/gnu> or one of its mirrors, and copy them out of it.

The gcc manual page (gcc.1) is, generally speaking, out of date. It will warn you of this when you try to look at it.

4.2.1   Compiler flags

gcc can be made to optimize its output code by adding -On to its command line, where n is an optional small integer. Meaningful values of n, and their exact effect, vary according to the exact version, but typically it ranges from 0 (no optimization) to 2 (lots) or 3 (lots and lots).

Internally, gcc translates these to a series of -f and -m options. You can see exactly which -O levels map to which options by running gcc with the -v flag and the (undocumented) -Q flag. For example, for -O2, mine says

```
enabled: -fdefer-pop -fcse-follow-jumps -fcse-skip-blocks
-fexpensive-optimizations
        -fthread-jumps -fpeephole -fforce-mem -ffunction-cse -finline
        -fcaller-saves -fpcc-struct-return -frerun-cse-after-loop
        -fcommon -fgnu-linker -m80387 -mhard-float -mno-soft-float
        -mno-386 -m486 -mieee-fp -mfp-ret-in-387
```

Using an optimization level higher than your compiler supports (e.g. -O6) will have exactly the same effect as using the highest level that it *does* support. Distributing code which is set to compile this way is a poor idea though — if further optimisations are incorporated into future versions, you (or your users) may find that they break your code.

Users of gcc 2.7.0 thru 2.7.2 should note that there is a bug in -O2 on these. Specifically, strength reduction doesn't work. A patch can be had to fix this if you feel like recompiling gcc, otherwise make sure that you always compile with -fno-strength-reduce

Processor-specific   There are other -m flags which aren't turned on by any variety of -O but are nevertheless useful. Chief among these are -m386 and -m486, which tell gcc to favour the 386 or 486 respectively. Code compiled with one of these will still work on the other; 486 code is bigger, but otherwise not slower on the 386.

There is currently no -mpentium or -m586. Linus suggests using -m486 -malign-loops=2 -malign-jumps=2 -malign-functions=2, to get 486 code optimisations but without the big gaps for alignment (which the pentium doesn't need). Michael Meissner (of Cygnus) says

My hunch is that `-mno-strength-reduce` also results in faster code on the x86 (note, I'm not talking about the strength reduction bug, which is another issue). This is because the x86 is rather register starved (and GCC's method of grouping registers into spill registers vs. other registers doesn't help either). Strength reduction typically results in using additional registers to replace multiplications with addition. I also suspect `-fcaller-saves` may also be a loss.

Another hunch is that `-fomit-frame-pointer` might or might not be a win. On the one hand, it can mean that another register is available for allocation. On the other hand, the way the x86 encodes its instruction set, means that stack relative addresses take more space instead of frame relative addresses, which means slightly less Icache availble to the program. Also, `-fomit-frame-pointer`, means that the compiler has to constantly adjust the stack pointer after calls, while with a frame, it can let the stack accumulate for a few calls.

The final word on this subject is from Linus again:

Note that if you want to get optimal performance, don't believe me: test. There are lots of gcc compiler switches, and it may be that a particular set gives the best optimizations for you.

4.2.2 Internal compiler error: `cc1 got fatal signal 11`

Signal 11 is SIGSEGV, or 'segmentation violation'. Usually it means that the program got its pointers confused and tried to write to memory it didn't own. So, it could be a gcc bug.

gcc is however, a well tested and reliable piece of software, for the most part. It also uses a large number of complex data structures, and an awful lot of pointers. In short, it's the pickiest RAM tester commonly available. If you *can't duplicate the bug* — if it doesn't stop in the same place when you restart the compilation — it's almost certainly a problem with your hardware (CPU, memory, motherboard or cache). **Don't** claim it as a bug because your computer passes the power-on checks or runs Windows ok or whatever; these 'tests' are commonly and rightly held to be worthless. And don't claim it's a bug because a kernel compile always stops during '`make zImage`' — of course it will! '`make zImage`' is probably compiling over 200 files; we're looking for a slightly *smaller* place than that.

If you can duplicate the bug, and (better) can produce a short program that exhibits it, you can submit it as a bug report to the FSF, or to the linux-gcc mailing list. See the gcc documentation for details of exactly what information they need.

4.3 Portability

It has been said that, these days, if something hasn't been ported to Linux then it is not worth having :-)

Seriously though, in general only minor changes are needed to the sources to get over Linux's 100% POSIX compliance. It is also worthwhile passing back any changes to authors of the code such that in the future only 'make' need be called to provide a working executable.

4.3.1 BSDisms (including `bsd_ioctl`, `daemon` and `<sgtty.h>`)

You can compile your program with `-I/usr/include/bsd` and link it with `-lbsd` (i.e. add `-I/usr/include/bsd` to `CFLAGS` and `-lbsd` to the `LDFLAGS` line in your Makefile). There is *no* need to add `-D__USE_BSD_SIGNAL` any more if you want BSD type signal behavior, as you get this automatically when you have `-I/usr/include/bsd` and include `<signal.h>`.

4.3.2 'Missing' signals (SIGBUS, SIGEMT, SIGIOT, SIGTRAP, SIGSYS etc)

Linux is POSIX compliant. These are not POSIX-defined signals — ISO/IEC 9945-1:1990 (IEEE Std 1003.1-1990), paragraph B.3.3.1.1 sez:

> "The signals SIGBUS, SIGEMT, SIGIOT, SIGTRAP, and SIGSYS were omitted from POSIX.1 because their behavior is implementation dependent and could not be adequately categorized. Conforming implementations may deliver these signals, but must document the circumstances under which they are delivered and note any restrictions concerning their delivery."

The cheap and cheesy way to fix this is to redefine these signals to SIGUNUSED. The *correct* way is to bracket the code that handles them with appropriate #ifdefs:

```
#ifdef SIGSYS
/* ... non-posix SIGSYS code here .... */
#endif
```

4.3.3 K & R Code

GCC is an ANSI compiler; much existing code is not ANSI. There's really not much that can be done about this, except to add -traditional to the compiler flags. There is a certain amount of finer-grained control over which varieties of brain damage to emulate; consult the gcc info page.

Note that -traditional has effects beyond just changing the language that gcc accepts. For example, it turns on -fwritable-strings, which moves string constants into data space (from text space, where they cannot be written to). This increases the memory footprint of the program.

4.3.4 Preprocessor symbols conflict with prototypes in the code

One of the most frequent problems is that some common functions are defined as macros in Linux's header files and the preprocessor will refuse to parse similar prototype definitions in the code. Common ones are atoi() and atol().

4.3.5 sprintf()

Something to be aware of, especially when porting from SunOS, is that sprintf(string, fmt, ...) returns a pointer to string on many unices, whereas Linux (following ANSI) returns the number of characters which were put into the string.

4.3.6 fcntl and friends. Where are the definitions of FD_* stuff ?

In <sys/time.h>. If you are using fcntl you probably want to include <unistd.h> too, for the actual prototype.

Generally speaking, the manual page for a function lists the necessary #includes in its SYNOPSIS section.

4.3.7 The select() timeout. Programs start busy-waiting.

Once upon a time, the timeout parameter to select() was used read-only. Even then, manual pages warned:

> select() should probably return the time remaining from the original timeout, if any, by modifying the time value in place. This may be implemented in future versions of the system. Thus, it is unwise to assume that the timeout pointer will be unmodified by the select() call.

The future has arrived! At least, it has here. On return from a select(), the timeout argument will be set to the remaining time that it would have waited had data not arrived. If no data had arrived, this will be zero, and future calls using the same timeout structure will immediately return.

To fix, put the timeout value into that structure every time you call select(). Change code like

```
struct timeval timeout;
timeout.tv_sec = 1; timeout.tv_usec = 0;
while (some_condition)
        select(n,readfds,writefds,exceptfds,&timeout);
```

to, say,

```
struct timeval timeout;
while (some_condition) {
        timeout.tv_sec = 1; timeout.tv_usec = 0;
        select(n,readfds,writefds,exceptfds,&timeout);
}
```

Some versions of Mosaic were at one time notable for this problem. The speed of the spinning globe animation was inversely related to the speed that the data was coming in from the network at!

4.3.8 Interrupted system calls.

Symptom: When a program is stopped using Ctrl-Z and then restarted - or in other situations that generate signals: Ctrl-C interruption, termination of a child process etc. - it complains about "interrupted system call" or "write: unknown error" or things like that.

Problem: POSIX systems check for signals a bit more often than some older unices. Linux may execute signal handlers —

- asynchronously (at a timer tick)
- on return from any system call
- during the execution of the following system calls: select(), pause(), connect(), accept(), read() on terminals, sockets, pipes or files in /proc, write() on terminals, sockets, pipes or the line printer, open() on FIFOs, PTYs or serial lines, ioctl() on terminals, fcntl() with command F_SETLKW, wait4(), syslog(), any TCP or NFS operations.

For other operating systems you may have to include the system calls creat(), close(), getmsg(), putmsg(), msgrcv(), msgsnd(), recv(), send(), wait(), waitpid(), wait3(), tcdrain(), sigpause(), semop() to this list.

If a signal (that the program has installed a handler for) occurs during a system call, the handler is called. When the handler returns (to the system call) it detects that it was interrupted, and immediately returns with -1 and errno = EINTR. The program is not expecting that to happen, so bottles out.

You may choose between two fixes.

(1) For every signal handler that you install, add SA_RESTART to the sigaction flags. For example, change

```
        signal (sig_nr, my_signal_handler);
```

to

```
        signal (sig_nr, my_signal_handler);
        { struct sigaction sa;
          sigaction (sig_nr, (struct sigaction *)0, &sa);
#ifdef SA_RESTART
          sa.sa_flags |= SA_RESTART;
#endif
#ifdef SA_INTERRUPT
          sa.sa_flags &= ~ SA_INTERRUPT;
#endif
          sigaction (sig_nr, &sa, (struct sigaction *)0);
        }
```

Note that while this applies to most system calls, you must still check for EINTR yourself on read(), write(), ioctl(), select(), pause() and connect(). See below.

(2) Check for EINTR explicitly, yourself:

Here are two examples for read() and ioctl(),

Original piece of code using read()

```
        int result;
        while (len > 0) {
          result = read(fd,buffer,len);
          if (result < 0) break;
          buffer += result; len -= result;
        }
```

becomes

```
        int result;
        while (len > 0) {
          result = read(fd,buffer,len);
          if (result < 0) { if (errno != EINTR) break; }
          else { buffer += result; len -= result; }
        }
```

and a piece of code using ioctl()

```
    int result;
    result = ioctl(fd,cmd,addr);
```

becomes

```
    int result;
    do { result = ioctl(fd,cmd,addr); }
    while ((result == -1) && (errno == EINTR));
```

Note that in some versions of BSD Unix the default behaviour is to restart system calls. To get system calls interrupted you have to use the SV_INTERRUPT or SA_INTERRUPT flag.

4.3.9 Writable strings (program seg faults randomly)

GCC has an optimistic view of its users, believing that they intend string constants to be exactly that — constant. Thus, it stores them in the text (code) area of the program, where they can be paged in and out from the program's disk image (instead of taking up swapspace), and any attempt to rewrite them will cause a segmentation fault. This is a feature!

It may cause a problem for old programs that, for example, call mktemp() with a string constant as argument. mktemp() attempts to rewrite its argument in place.

To fix, either (a) compile with -fwritable-strings, to get gcc to put constants in data space, or (b) rewrite the offending parts to allocate a non-constant string and strcpy the data into it before calling.

4.3.10 Why does the execl() call fail?

Because you're calling it wrong. The first argument to execl is the program that you want to run. The second and subsequent arguments become the argv array of the program you're calling. Remember: argv[0] is traditionally set even when a program is run with 'no' arguments. So, you should be writing

```
    execl("/bin/ls","ls",NULL);
```

not just

```
    execl("/bin/ls", NULL);
```

Executing the program with no arguments at all is construed as an invitation to print out its dynamic library dependencies, at least using a.out. ELF does things differently.

(If you want this library information, there are simpler interfaces; see the section on dynamic loading, or the manual page for ldd).

5 Debugging and Profiling

5.1 Preventative maintenance (lint)

There is no widely-used lint for Linux, as most people are satisfied with the warnings that gcc can generate. Probably the most useful is the -Wall switch — this stands for 'Warnings, all' but probably has more mnemonic value if thought of as the thing you bang your head against.

There is a public domain lint available from `<ftp://larch.lcs.mit.edu/pub/Larch/lclint>`. I don't know how good it is.

5.2 Debugging

5.2.1 How do I get debugging information into a program ?

You need to compile and link all its bits with the `-g` switch, and without the `-fomit-frame-pointer` switch. Actually, you don't need to recompile all of it, just the bits you're interested in debugging.

On a.out configurations the shared libraries are compiled with `-fomit-frame-pointer`, which gdb won't get on with. Giving the `-g` option when you link should imply static linking; this is why.

If the linker fails with a message about not finding libg.a, you don't have `/usr/lib/libg.a`, which is the special debugging-enabled C library. It may be supplied in the libc binary package, or (in newer C library versions) you may need to get the libc source code and build it yourself. You don't actually *need* it though; you can get enough information for most purposes simply by symlinking it to `/usr/lib/libc.a`

How do I get it out again?   A lot of GNU software comes set up to compile and link with `-g`, causing it to make very big (and often static) executables. This is not really such a hot idea.

If the program has an autoconf generated `configure` script, you can usually turn off debugging information by doing `./configure CFLAGS=` or `./configure CFLAGS=-O2`. Otherwise, check the Makefile. Of course, if you're using ELF, the program is dynamically linked regardless of the `-g` setting, so you can just `strip` it.

5.2.2 Available software

Most people use **gdb**, which you can get in source form from *GNU archive sites* `<ftp://prep.ai.mit.edu/pub/gnu>`, or as a binary from *tsx-11* `<ftp://tsx-11.mit.edu/pub/linux/packages/GCC>` or sunsite. **xxgdb** is an X debugger based on this (i.e. you need gdb installed first). The source may be found at `<ftp://ftp.x.org/contrib/xxgdb-1.08.tar.gz>`

Also, the **UPS** debugger has been ported by Rick Sladkey. It runs under X as well, but unlike xxgdb, it is not merely an X front end for a text based debugger. It has quite a number of nice features, and if you spend any time debugging stuff, you probably should check it out. The Linux precompiled version and patches for the stock UPS sources can be found in `<ftp://sunsite.unc.edu/pub/Linux/devel/debuggers/>`, and the original source at `<ftp://ftp.x.org/contrib/ups-2.45.2.tar.Z>`.

Another tool you might find useful for debugging is '**strace**', which displays the system calls that a process makes. It has a multiplicity of other uses too, including figuring out what pathnames were compiled into binaries that you don't have the source for, exacerbating race conditions in programs that you suspect contain them, and generally learning how things work. The latest version of strace (currently 3.0.8) can be found at `<ftp://ftp.std.com/pub/jrs/>`.

5.2.3 Background (daemon) programs

Daemon programs typically execute `fork()` early, and terminate the parent. This makes for a short debugging session.

The simplest way to get around this is to set a breakpoint for `fork`, and when the program stops, force it to return 0.

```
(gdb) list
1        #include <stdio.h>
2
3        main()
4        {
5          if(fork()==0) printf("child\n");
6          else printf("parent\n");
7        }
(gdb) break fork
Breakpoint 1 at 0x80003b8
(gdb) run
Starting program: /home/dan/src/hello/./fork
Breakpoint 1 at 0x400177c4

Breakpoint 1, 0x400177c4 in fork ()
(gdb) return 0
Make selected stack frame return now? (y or n) y
#0  0x80004a8 in main ()
    at fork.c:5
5          if(fork()==0) printf("child\n");
(gdb) next
Single stepping until exit from function fork,
which has no line number information.
child
7        }
```

5.2.4 Core files

When Linux boots it is usually configured not to produce core files. If you like them, use your shell's builtin command to re-enable them: for C-shell compatibles (e.g. tcsh) this is

```
% limit core unlimited
```

while Bourne-like shells (sh, bash, zsh, pdksh) use

```
$ ulimit -c unlimited
```

If you want a bit more versatility in your core file naming (for example, if you're trying to conduct a post-mortem using a debugger that's buggy itself) you can make a simple mod to your kernel. Look for the code in fs/binfmt_aout.c and fs/binfmt_elf.c (in newer kernels, you'll have to grep around a little in older ones) that says

```
        memcpy(corefile,"core.",5);
#if 0
        memcpy(corefile+5,current->comm,sizeof(current->comm));
#else
        corefile[4] = '\0';
#endif
```

and change the 0s to 1s.

5.3   Profiling

Profiling is a way to examine which bits of a program are called most often or run for longest. It is a good way to optimize code and look at where time is being wasted. You must compile all object files that you require timing information for with -p, and to make sense of the output file you will also need gprof (from the binutils package). See the gprof manual page for details.

6   Linking

Between the two incompatible binary formats, the static vs shared library distinction, and the overloading of the verb 'link' to mean both 'what happens after compilation' and 'what happens when a compiled program is invoked' (and, actually, the overloading of the word 'load' in a comparable but opposite sense), this section is complicated. Little of it is much more complicated than that sentence, though, so don't worry too much about it.

To alleviate the confusion somewhat, we refer to what happens at runtime as 'dynamic loading' and cover it in the next section. You will also see it described as 'dynamic linking', but not here. This section, then, is exclusively concerned with the kind of linking that happens at the end of a compilation.

6.1   Shared vs static libraries

The last stage of building a program is to 'link' it; to join all the pieces of it together and see what is missing. Obviously there are some things that many programs will want to do — open files, for example, and the pieces that do these things are provided for you in the form of libraries. On the average Linux system these can be found in /lib and /usr/lib/, among other places.

When using a static library, the linker finds the bits that the program modules need, and physically copies them into the executable output file that it generates. For shared libraries, it doesn't — instead it leaves a note in the output saying 'when this program is run, it will first have to load this library'. Obviously shared libraries tend to make for smaller executables; they also use less memory and mean that less disk space is used. The default behaviour of Linux is to link shared if it can find the shared libraries, static otherwise. If you're getting static binaries when you want shared, check that the shared library files (*.sa for a.out, *.so for ELF) are where they should be, and are readable.

On Linux, static libraries have names like libname.a, while shared libraries are called libname.so.x.y.z where x.y.z is some form of version number. Shared libraries often also have links pointing to them, which are important, and (on a.out configurations) associated .sa files. The standard libraries come in both shared and static formats.

You can find out what shared libraries a program requires by using ldd (List Dynamic Dependencies)

```
$ ldd /usr/bin/lynx
        libncurses.so.1 => /usr/lib/libncurses.so.1.9.6
        libc.so.5 => /lib/libc.so.5.2.18
```

This shows that on my system the WWW browser 'lynx' depends on the presence of libc.so.5 (the C library) and libncurses.so.1 (used for terminal control). If a program has no dependencies, ldd will say 'statically linked' or 'statically linked (ELF)'.

6.2   Interrogating libraries ('which library is `sin()` in?')

nm *libraryname* should list all the symbols that *libraryname* has references to. It works on both static and shared libraries. Suppose that you want to know where `tcgetattr()` is defined: you might do

```
$ nm libncurses.so.1 |grep tcget
         U tcgetattr
```

The `U` stands for 'undefined' — it shows that the ncurses library uses but does not define it. You could also do

```
$ nm libc.so.5 | grep tcget
00010fe8 T __tcgetattr
00010fe8 W tcgetattr
00068718 T tcgetpgrp
```

The 'W' stands for 'weak', which means that the symbol is defined, but in such a way that it can be overridden by another definition in a different library. A straightforward 'normal' definition (such as the one for `tcgetpgrp`) is marked by a 'T'

The short answer to the question in the title, by the way, is `libm.(so|a)`. All the functions defined in `<math.h>` are kept in the maths library; thus you need to link with `-lm` when using any of them.

6.3   Finding files

`ld:   Output file requires shared library 'libfoo.so.1'`

The file search strategy of ld and friends varies according to version, but the only default you can reasonably assume is `/usr/lib`. If you want libraries elsewhere to be searched, specify their directories with the `-L` option to gcc or ld.

If that doesn't help, check that you have the right file in that place. For a.out, linking with `-lfoo` makes ld look for `libfoo.sa` (shared stubs), and if unsuccessful then for `libfoo.a` (static). For ELF, it looks for `libfoo.so` then `libfoo.a`. `libfoo.so` is usually a symbolic link to `libfoo.so.x`.

6.4   Building your own libraries

6.4.1   Version control

As any other program, libraries tend to have bugs which get fixed over time. They also may introduce new features, change the effect of existing ones, or remove old ones. This could be a problem for programs using them; what if it was depending on that old feature?

So, we introduce library versioning. We categorise the changes that might be made to a library as 'minor' or 'major', and we rule that a 'minor' change is not allowed to break old programs that are using the library. You can tell the version of a library by looking at its filename (actually, this is, strictly speaking, a lie for ELF; keep reading to find out why) : `libfoo.so.1.2` has major version 1, minor version 2. The minor version number can be more or less anything — libc puts a 'patchlevel' in it, giving library names like `libc.so.5.2.18`, and it's also reasonable to put letters, underscores, or more or less any printable ASCII in it.

One of the major differences between ELF and a.out format is in building shared libraries. We look at ELF first, because it's simpler.

6.4.2   ELF? What is it then, anyway?

ELF (Executable and Linking Format) is a binary format originally developed by USL (UNIX System Laboratories) and currently used in Solaris and System V Release 4. Because of its increased flexibility over the older a.out format that Linux was using, the GCC and C library developers decided last year to move to using ELF as the Linux standard binary format also.

Come again?   This section is from the document '/news-archives/comp.sys.sun.misc'.

> ELF ("Executable Linking Format) is the "new, improved" object file format introduced in SVR4. ELF is much more powerful than straight COFF, in that it *is* user-extensible. ELF views an object-file as an arbitarily long list of sections (rather than an array of fixed size entities), these sections, unlike in COFF, do not HAVE to be in a certain place and do not HAVE to come in any specific order etc. Users can add new sections to object-files if they wish to capture new data. ELF also has a far more powerful debugging format called DWARF (Debugging With Attribute Record Format) - not currently fully supported on linux (but work is underway). A linked list of DWARF DIEs (or Debugging Information Entries) forms the .debug section in ELF. Instead of being a collection of small, fixed-size information records, DWARF DIEs each contain an arbitrarily long list of complex attributes and are written out as a scope-based tree of program data. DIEs can capture a large amount of information that the COFF .debug section simply couldn't (like C++ inheritance graphs etc.).

> ELF files are accessed via the SVR4 (Solaris 2.0 ?) ELF access library, which provides an easy and fast interface to the more gory parts of ELF. One of the major boons in using the ELF access library is that you will never need to look at an ELF file qua. UNIX file, it is accessed as an Elf *, after an elf_open() call and from then on, you perform elf_foobar() calls on its components instead of messing about with its actual on-disk image (something many COFFers did with impunity).

The case for/against ELF, and the necessary contortions to upgrade an a.out system to support it, are covered in the ELF-HOWTO and I don't propose to cut/paste them here. The HOWTO should be available in the same place as you found this one.

ELF shared libraries   To build libfoo.so as a shared library, the basic steps look like this:

```
$ gcc -fPIC -c *.c
$ gcc -shared -Wl,-soname,libfoo.so.1 -o libfoo.so.1.0 *.o
$ ln -s libfoo.so.1.0 libfoo.so.1
$ ln -s libfoo.so.1 libfoo.so
$ LD_LIBRARY_PATH=`pwd`:$LD_LIBRARY_PATH ; export LD_LIBRARY_PATH
```

This will generate a shared library called libfoo.so.1.0, and the appropriate links for ld (libfoo.so) and the dynamic loader (libfoo.so.1) to find it. To test, we add the current directory to LD_LIBRARY_PATH.

When you're happpy that the library works, you'll have to move it to, say, /usr/local/lib, and recreate the appropriate links. The link from libfoo.so.1 to libfoo.so.1.0 is kept up to date by ldconfig, which on most systems is run as part of the boot process. The libfoo.so link must be updated manually. If you are scrupulous about upgrading all the parts of a library (e.g. the header files) at the same time, the simplest thing to do is make libfoo.so -> libfoo.so.1, so that ldconfig will keep both links current for you. If you *aren't*, you're setting yourself up to have *all kinds of weird things* happen at a later date. Don't say you weren't warned.

```
$ su
# cp libfoo.so.1.0 /usr/local/lib
# /sbin/ldconfig
# ( cd /usr/local/lib ; ln -s libfoo.so.1 libfoo.so )
```

Version numbering, sonames and symlinks   Each library has a *soname*. When the linker finds one of these in a library it is searching, it embeds the soname into the binary instead of the actual filename it is looking at. At runtime, the dynamic loader will then search for a file with the name of the soname, not the library filename. Thus a library called `libfoo.so` could have a soname `libbar.so`, and all programs linked to it would look for `libbar.so` instead when they started.

This sounds like a pointless feature, but it is key to understanding how multiple versions of the same library can coexist on a system. The de facto naming standard for libraries in Linux is to call the library, say, `libfoo.so.1.2`, and give it a soname of `libfoo.so.1`. If it's added to a 'standard' library directory (e.g. `/usr/lib`), `ldconfig` will create a symlink `libfoo.so.1 -> libfoo.so.1.2` so that the appropriate image is found at runtime. You also need a link `libfoo.so -> libfoo.so.1` so that ld will find the right soname to use at link time.

So, when you fix bugs in the library, or add new functions (any changes that won't adversely affect existing programs), you rebuild it, keeping the soname as it was, and changing the filename. When you make changes to the library that would break existing binaries, you simply increment the number in the soname — in this case, call the new version `libfoo.so.2.0`, and give it a soname of `libfoo.so.2`. Now switch the `libfoo.so` link to point to the new version and all's well with the world again.

Note that you don't *have* to name libraries this way, but it's a good convention. ELF gives you the flexibility to name libraries in ways that will confuse the pants off people, but that doesn't mean you have to use it.

Executive summary: supposing that you observe the tradition that major upgrades may break compatibility, minor upgrades may not, then link with

```
gcc -shared -Wl,-soname,libfoo.so.major -o libfoo.so.major.minor
```

and everything will be all right.

6.4.3   a.out. Ye olde traditional format

The ease of building shared libraries is a major reason for upgrading to ELF. That said, it's still possible in a.out. Get `<ftp://tsx-11.mit.edu/pub/linux/packages/GCC/src/tools-2.17.tar.gz>` and read the 20 page document that you will find after unpacking it. I hate to be so transparently partisan, but it should be clear from context that I never bothered myself :-)

ZMAGIC vs QMAGIC   QMAGIC is an executable format just like the old a.out (also known as ZMAGIC) binaries, but which leaves the first page unmapped. This allows for easier NULL dereference trapping as no mapping exists in the range 0-4096. As a side effect your binaries are nominally smaller as well (by about 1K).

Obsolescent linkers support ZMAGIC only, semi-obsolescent support both formats, and current versions support QMAGIC only. This doesn't actually matter, though, as the kernel can still run both formats.

Your 'file' command should be able to identify whether a program is QMAGIC.

File Placement   An a.out (DLL) shared library consists of two real files and a symlink. For the 'foo' library used throughout this document as an example, these files would be `libfoo.sa` and `libfoo.so.1.2`; the symlink would be `libfoo.so.1` and would point at the latter of the files. What are these for?

At compile time, `ld` looks for `libfoo.sa`. This is the 'stub' file for the library, and contains all exported data and pointers to the functions required for run time linking.

At run time, the dynamic loader looks for `libfoo.so.1`. This is a symlink rather than a real file so that libraries can be updated with newer, bugfixed versions without crashing any application that was using the library at the time. After the new version — say, `libfoo.so.1.3` — is completely there, running ldconfig will switch the link to point to it in one atomic operation, leaving any program which had the old version still perfectly happy.

DLL libraries (I know that's a tautology — so sue me) often appear bigger than their static counterparts. They reserve space for future expansion in the form of 'holes' which can be made to take no disk space. A simple `cp` call or using the program `makehole` will achieve this. You can also strip them after building, as the addresses are in fixed locations. **Do not attempt to strip ELF libraries**.

"libc-lite"?   A libc-lite is a light-weight version of the libc library built such that it will fit on a floppy and suffice for all of the most menial of UNIX tasks. It does *not* include curses, dbm, termcap etc code. If your `/lib/libc.so.4` is linked to a lite lib, you are advised to replace it with a full version.

6.4.4   Linking: common problems

Send me your linking problems! I probably won't do anything about them, but I will write them up if I get enough ...

Programs link static when you wanted them shared

Check that you have the right links for `ld` to find each shared library. For ELF this means a `libfoo.so` symlink to the image, for a.out a `libfoo.sa` file. A lot of people had this problem after moving from ELF binutils 2.5 to 2.6 — the earlier version searched more 'intelligently' for shared libraries, so they hadn't created all the links. The intelligent behaviour was removed for compatibility with other architectures, and because quite often it got its assumptions wrong and caused more trouble than it solved.

The DLL tool 'mkimage' fails to find libgcc, or

As of `libc.so.4.5.x` and above, libgcc is no longer shared. Hence you must replace occurrences of '`-lgcc`' on the offending line with '`gcc -print-libgcc-file-name`' (complete with the backquotes). Also, delete all `/usr/lib/libgcc*` files. This is important.

_NEEDS_SHRLIB_libc_4 multiply defined messages

are another consequence of the same problem.

"Assertion failure" message when rebuilding a DLL ?

This cryptic message most probably means that one of your jump table slots has overflowed because too little space has been reserved in the original `jump.vars` file. You can locate the culprit(s) by running the '`getsize`' command provided in the tools-2.17.tar.gz package. Probably the only solution, though, is to bump the major version number of the library, forcing it to be backward incompatible.

ld: output file needs shared library libc.so.4

This usually happens when you are linking with libraries other than libc (e.g. X libraries), and use the `-g` switch on the link line without also using `-static`.

The `.sa` stubs for the shared libraries usually have an undefined symbol _NEEDS_SHRLIB_libc_4 which gets resolved from the `libc.sa` stub. However with `-g` you end up linking with `libg.a` or `libc.a` and thus this symbol never gets resolved, leading to the above error message.

In conclusion, add -static when compiling with the -g flag, or don't link with -g. Quite often you can get enough debugging information by compiling the individual files with -g, and linking *without* it.

7 Dynamic Loading

This section is a tad short right now; it will be expanded over time as I gut the ELF howto

7.1 Concepts

Linux has shared libraries, as you will by now be sick of hearing if you read the whole of the last section at a sitting. Some of the matching-names-to-places work which was traditionally done at link time must be deferred to load time.

7.2 Error messages

Send me your link errors! I won't do anything about them, but I might write them up ...

`can't load library:  /lib/libxxx.so, Incompatible version`

> (a.out only) This means that you don't have the correct major version of the xxx library. No, you can't just make a symlink to another version that you do have; if you are lucky this will cause your program to segfault. Get the new version. A similar situation with ELF will result in a message like

> `ftp: can't load library 'libreadline.so.2'`

`warning using incompatible library version xxx`

> (a.out only) You have an older minor version of the library than the person who compiled the program used. The program will still run. Probably. An upgrade wouldn't hurt, though.

7.3 Controlling the operation of the dynamic loader

There are a range of environment variables that the dynamic loader will respond to. Most of these are more use to ldd than they are to the average user, and can most conveniently be set by running ldd with various switches. They include

- LD_BIND_NOW — normally, functions are not 'looked up' in libraries until they are called. Setting this flag causes all the lookups to happen when the library is loaded, giving a slower startup time. It's useful when you want to test a program to make sure that everything is linked.

- LD_PRELOAD can be set to a file containing 'overriding' function definitions. For example, if you were testing memory allocation strategies, and wanted to replace 'malloc', you could write your replacement routine, compile it into **malloc.o** and then

    ```
    $ LD_PRELOAD=malloc.o; export LD_PRELOAD
    $ some_test_program
    ```

    LD_ELF_PRELOAD and LD_AOUT_PRELOAD are similar, but only apply to the appropriate type of binary. If LD_*something*_PRELOAD and LD_PRELOAD are set, the more specific one is used.

- LD_LIBRARY_PATH is a colon-separated list of directories in which to look for shared libraries. It does *not* affect ld; it only has effect at runtime. Also, it is disabled for programs that run setuid or setgid. Again, LD_ELF_LIBRARY_PATH and LD_AOUT_LIBRARY_PATH can also be used to direct the search differently for different flavours of binary. LD_LIBRARY_PATH shouldn't be necessary in normal operation; add the directories to /etc/ld.so.conf/ and rerun ldconfig instead.

- LD_NOWARN applies to a.out only. When set (e.g. with LD_NOWARN=true; export LD_NOWARN) it stops the loader from issuing non-fatal warnings (such as minor version incompatibility messages).

- LD_WARN applies to ELF only. When set, it turns the usually fatal "Can't find library" messages into warnings. It's not much use in normal operation, but important for ldd.

- LD_TRACE_LOADED_OBJECTS applies to ELF only, and causes programs to think they're being run under ldd:

```
$ LD_TRACE_LOADED_OBJECTS=true /usr/bin/lynx
        libncurses.so.1 => /usr/lib/libncurses.so.1.9.6
        libc.so.5 => /lib/libc.so.5.2.18
```

7.4   Writing programs with dynamic loading

This is very close to the way that Solaris 2.x dynamic loading support works, if you're familiar with that. It is covered extensively in H J Lu's ELF programming document, and the dlopen(3) manual page, which can be found in the ld.so package. Here's a nice simple example though: link it with -ldl

```
#include <dlfcn.h>
#include <stdio.h>

main()
{
  void *libc;
  void (*printf_call)();

  if(libc=dlopen("/lib/libc.so.5",RTLD_LAZY))
  {
    printf_call=dlsym(libc,"printf");
    (*printf_call)("hello, world\n");
  }

}
```

8   Contacting the developers

8.1   Bug reports

Start by **narrowing the problem down**. Is it specific to Linux, or does it happen with gcc on other systems? Is it specific to the kernel version? Library version? Does it go away if you link static? Can you trim the program down to something **short** that demonstrates the bug?

Having done that, you'll know what program(s) the bug is in. For GCC, the bug reporting procedure is explained in the info file. For ld.so or the C or maths libraries, send mail to `linux-gcc@vger.rutgers.edu`. If possible, include a short and self-contained program that exhibits the bug, and a description both of what you want it to do, and what it actually does.

8.2 Helping with development

If you want to help with the development effort for GCC or the C library, the first thing to do is join the `linux-gcc@vger.rutgers.edu` mailing list. If you just want to see what the discussion is about, there are list archives at `<http://homer.ncm.com/linux-gcc/>`. The second and subsequent things depend on what you want to do!

9 The Remains

9.1 The Credits

> Only presidents, editors, and people with tapeworms have the right to use the editorial "we".

(Mark Twain)

This HOWTO is based very closely on Mitchum DSouza's GCC-FAQ; most of the information (not to mention a reasonable amount of the text) in it comes directly from that document. Instances of the first person pronoun in this HOWTO could refer to either of us; generally the ones that say "I have not tested this; don't blame me if it toasts your hard disk/system/spouse" apply to both of us.

Contributors to this document have included (in ASCII ordering by first name) Andrew Tefft, Axel Boldt, Bill Metzenthen, Bruce Evans, Bruno Haible, Daniel Barlow, Daniel Quinlan, David Engel, Dirk Hohndel, Eric Youngdale, Fergus Henderson, H.J. Lu, Jens Schweikhardt, Kai Petzke, Michael Meissner, Mitchum DSouza, Olaf Flebbe, Paul Gortmaker, Rik Faith, Steven S. Dick, Tuomas J Lukka, and of course Linus Torvalds, without whom the whole exercise would have been pointless, let alone impossible :-)

Please do not feel offended if your name has not appeared here and you have contributed to this document (either as HOWTO or as FAQ). Email me and I will rectify it.

9.2 Translations

At this time, there are no known translations of this work. If you wish to produce one, please go right ahead, but do tell me about it! The chances are (sadly) several hundred to one against that I speak the language you wish to translate to, but that aside I am happy to help in whatever way I can.

9.3 Feedback is welcomed. Mail me at *dan@detached.demon.co.uk* `<mailto:dan@detached.demon.co.uk>`. My PGP public key (ID 5F263625) is available from my *web pages* `<http://ftp.linux.org.uk/~barlow/>`, if you feel the need to be secretive about things.

9.4 Legalese

All trademarks used in this document are acknowledged as being owned by their respective owners.

This document is copyright (C) 1996 Daniel Barlow <dan@detached.demon.co.uk> It may be reproduced and distributed in whole or in part, in any medium physical or electronic, as long as this copyright notice is retained on all copies. Commercial redistribution is allowed and encouraged; however, the author would like to be notified of any such distributions.

All translations, derivative works, or aggregate works incorporating any Linux HOWTO documents must be covered under this copyright notice. That is, you may not produce a derivative work from a HOWTO and impose additional restrictions on its distribution. Exceptions to these rules may be granted under certain conditions; please contact the Linux HOWTO coordinator at the address given below.

In short, we wish to promote dissemination of this information through as many channels as possible. However, we do wish to retain copyright on the HOWTO documents, and would like to be notified of any plans to redistribute the HOWTOs.

If you have questions, please contact Greg Hankins, the Linux HOWTO coordinator, at gregh@sunsite.unc.edu via email.

10 Index

Entries starting with a non-alphabetical character are listed in ASCII order.

- -fwritable-strings 4.3.3 (39) 4.3.9 (56)
- /lib/cpp 3.2 (16)
- a.out 1.1 (1)
- ar 2.5 (10)
- as 2.5 (8)
- <asm/*.h> 3.3 (19)
- atoi() 4.3.4 (40)
- atol() 4.3.4 (41)
- binaries too big 5.2.1 (63) 6.1 (65) 6.4.4 (77)
- chewing gum 1.2 (3)
- cos() 6.2 (68)
- debugging 5.2 (59)
- dlopen() 7.4 (82)
- dlsym() 7.4 (83)
- documentation 2.2 (4)
- EINTR 4.3.8 (52)
- elf 1.1 (0) 6.4.2 (71)
- execl() 4.3.10 (57)
- fcntl 4.3.6 (47)
- FD_CLR 4.3.6 (44)
- FD_ISSET 4.3.6 (45)
- FD_SET 4.3.6 (43)
- FD_ZERO 4.3.6 (46)
- file 1.1 (2)

Java CGI HOWTO

by David H. Silber *dhs@orbits.com* <mailto:dhs@orbits.com>   v0.4, 18 November 1996

This HOWTO document explains how to set up your server to allow CGI programs written in Java and how to use Java to write CGI programs. Although HOWTO documents are targetted towards use with the Linux operating system, this particular one is not dependant on the particular version of unix used.

Contents

1   Introduction

Because of the way that Java is designed the programmer does not have easy access to the system's environment variables. Because of the way that the Java Development Kit (JDK) is set up, it is necessary to use
multiple tokens to invoke a program, which does not mesh very well with the standard HTML forms/CGI
manner of operations. There are ways around these limitations, and I have implemented one of them. Read
further for details.

1.1   Prior Knowledge

I am assuming that you have a general knowledge of HTML and CGI concepts and at least a minimal
knowledge of your HTTP server. You should also know how to program in Java, or a lot of this will not
make sense.

1.2   This Document

The latest version of this document can be read at *http://www.orbits.com/software/Java_CGI.html* `<http: //www.orbits.com/software/Java_CGI.html>`.

1.3   The Package

The latest version of the package described here can be accessed via anonymous FTP at
ftp://ftp.orbits.com/pub/software/java_cgi-0.4.tgz `<ftp://ftp.orbits.com/pub/software/java_cgi-0.4. tgz>`. The package distribution includes SGML source for this document.

The package is distributed under the terms of the GNU Library General Public License. This document can be distributed under the terms of the Linux HOWTO copyright notice.

If you use this software, please make some reference to *http://www.orbits.com/software/Java_CGI.html* <http://www.orbits.com/software/Java_CGI.html>, so that others will be able to find the Java CGI classes.

1.4   Shameless Plug

This document is brought to you courtesy of **Stellar Orbits Technology Services**. (Visit us at *http://www.orbits.com/* <http://www.orbits.com/> to see what we do.)

2   Setting Up Your Server to Run Java CGI Programs (With Explanations)

This section will lead you through installing my *Java CGI* package with copious explanations so that you know what the effects of your actions will be. If you just want to install the programs and don't care about the whys & wherefores, skip to 3 (Setting Up Your Server to Run Java CGI Programs (The Short Form)).

2.1   System Requirements

This software should work on any unix-like web server that has the Java Development Kit installed. I am using it on a *Debian Linux* system running *apache* as the HTTP daemon. If you find that it does not run on your server, please contact me at *dhs@orbits.com* <mailto:dhs@orbits.com>.

Unfortunaly, the Java run-time interpreter seems to be something of a memory hog – you may want to throw another few megabytes of RAM onto your server if you will be using Java CGI programs a lot.

2.2   Java CGI Add-On Software

The software that I wrote to aid in this is called *Java CGI*. You can get it from *ftp://www.orbits.com/pub/software/java_cgi-0.4.tgz* <ftp://www.orbits.com/pub/software/java_cgi-0. 4.tgz>. (The version number may have changed.)

2.3   Unpacking the Source

Find a convenient directory to unpack this package into. (If you don't already have a standard place to put packages, I suggest that you use /usr/local/src.) Unpack the distribution with this command:

```
gzip -dc java_cgi-0.4.tgz | tar -xvf -
```

This will create a directory called java_cgi-0.4. In there you will find the files referenced in the rest of this document. (If the version number has changed, use the instructions from within that distribution from this point on.)

2.4   Decide On Your Local Path Policies

You need to decide where you want your Java CGI programs to live. Generally, you will want to put them in a directory in parallel with your `cgi-bin` directory. My *apache* server came configured to use `/var/web/cgi-bin` as the `cgi-bin` directory, so I use `/var/web/javacgi` as the directory to put Java CGI programs in. You probably do not want to put your Java CGI programs into one of the existing `CLASSPATH` directories. Edit the Makefile to reflect your system configuration. Make sure that you are logged in as the root user and run `make install`. This will compile the Java programs, modify the `java.cgi` script to fit in with your system and install the programs in the appropriate places. If you want the HTML version of this documentation and an HTML test document in addition, run `make all` instead.

2.5   Testing your installation.

Installed from the distribution are HTML documents called `javacgitest.html`, `javaemailtest.html` and `javahtmltest.html`. If you installed `all` in the previous section, it will be in the directory you specified for WEBDIR in the `Makefile`. If you didn't, you can run `make test` to build them from `javacgitest.html-dist`, `javaemailtest.html-dist` and `javahtmltest.html-dist`.

When you are sure that your installation is working correctly, you may wish to remove `CGI_Test.class`, `Email_Test.class` and `HTML_Test.class` from your JAVACGI directory and `javacgitest.html`, `javaemailtest.html` and `javahtmltest.html` from your WEBDIR directory as they show the user information that is normally only available to the server.

3   Setting Up Your Server to Run Java CGI Programs (The Short Form)

- Get the *Java CGI* package from *ftp://www.orbits.com/pub/software/java_cgi-0.4.tgz* <ftp://www.orbits.com/pub/software/java_cgi-0.4.tgz>. (The version number may have changed.)
- Unpack the distribution with this command:

  ```
  gzip -dc java_cgi-0.4.tgz | tar -xvf -
  ```

  (If the version number has changed, use the instructions from within that distribution from this point on.)
- Edit the `Makefile` you will find in the newly created directory `java_cgi-0.4` as appropriate to your system.
- As root, run `make install`. This will compile the Java programs, apply your system-specific information and install the various files. If you want the HTML version of this documentation and an HTML test document, run `make all` instead.
- You should be ready to go.

4   Executing a Java CGI Program

4.1   Obstacles to Running Java Programs Under the CGI Model

There are two main problems in running a Java program from a web server:

4.1.1   You can't run Java programs like ordinary executables.

You need to run the Java run-time interpreter and provide the initial class (program to run) on the command-line. With an HTML form, there is no provision for sending a command-line to the web server.

4.1.2   Java does not have general access to the environment.

Every environment variable that will be needed by the Java program must be explicitly passed in. There is no method similar to the **C getenv()** function.

4.2   Overcoming Problems in Running Java CGI Programs

To deal with these obstacles, I wrote a shell CGI program that provides the information needed by the Java interpreter.

4.2.1   The java.cgi script.

This shell script manages the interaction between the HTTP daemon and the Java CGI program that you wish to use. It extracts the name of the program that you want to run from the server-provided data. It collects all of the environment data into a temporary file. Then, it runs the Java run-time interpreter with the name of the file of environment information and the program name added to the command-line.

The java.cgi script was configured and installed in 2.4 (Decide On Your Local Path Policies).

4.2.2   Invoking java.cgi from an HTML form.

My forms that use Java CGI programs specify a form action as follows:

```
<form action="/cgi-bin/java.cgi/CGI_Test" method="POST">
```

Where /cgi-bin/ is your local CGI binary directory, java.cgi is the Java front-end that allows us to run Java programs over the web and CGI_Test is an example of the name of the Java program to run.

5   Using the Java CGI Classes.

There are currently three main classes supported – 5.1 (CGI), 5.3 (Email) and 5.5 (HTML). I am considering adding classes to deal with MIME-formatted input and output – MIMEin & MIMEout, respectively.

There are also a few support and test classes. 5.2 (CGI_Test), 5.4 (Email_Test) and 5.4 (HTML_Test) are intended to be used to test your installation. They can also be used as a starting-point for your own Java programs which use this class library. The 5.7 (Text) class is the superclass for both the Email and the HTML classes.

5.1 CGI

5.1.1 Class Syntax

`public class CGI`

5.1.2 Class Description

The CGI class holds the "CGI Information" – Environment variables set by the web server and the name/value sent from a form when its **submit** action is selected. All information is stored in a `Properties` class object.

This class is in the "Orbits.net" package.

5.1.3 Member Summary

```
CGI()           //  Constructor.
getNames()      //  Get the list of names.
getValue()      //  Get form value by specifying name.
```

5.1.4 See Also

`CGI_Test`.

5.1.5 CGI()

Purpose

Constructs an object which contains the available CGI data.

Syntax

`public CGI()`

Description

When a CGI object is constructed, all available CGI information is sucked-up into storage local to the new object.

5.1.6 getNames()

Purpose

List the names which are defined to have corresponding values.

Syntax

`public Enumeration getKeys ()`

Description

Provides the full list of names for which coresponding values are defined.

Returns

An `Enumeration` of all the names defined.

5.1.7   getValue()

Purpose

Retrieves the **value** associated with the **name** specified.

Syntax

    public String getValue (String name)

Description

This method provides the corespondence between the **names** and **values** sent from an HTML form.

Parameter

name

The key by which values are selected.

Returns

A String containing the value.

5.2   CGI_Test

This class provides both an example of how to use the CGI class and a test program which can be used to confirm that the *Java CGI* package is functioning correctly.

5.2.1   Member Summary

    main()   // Program main().

5.2.2   See Also

CGI.

5.2.3   main()

Purpose

Provide a main() method.

Syntax

    public static void main(String argv[])

Description

This is the entry point for a CGI program which does nothing but return a list of the available name/value pairs and their current values.

Parameter

argv[ ]

Arguments passed to the program by the java.cgi script. Currently unused.

5.3   Email

5.3.1   Class Syntax

    public class Email extends Text

5.3.2   Class Description

Messages are built up with the `Text` class `add*()` methods and the e-mail-specific methods added by this class. When complete, the message is sent to its destination.

This class is in the "Orbits.net" package.

5.3.3   Member Summary

```
Email()      //  Constructor.
send()       //  Send the e-mail message.
sendTo()     //  Add a destination for message.
subject()    //  Set the Subject: for message.
```

5.3.4   See Also

Email_Test, Text.

5.3.5   Email()

Purpose

Constructs an object which will contain an email message.

Syntax

```
public Email()
```

Description

Sets up an empty message to be completed by the Email methods.

See Also

Text.

5.3.6   send()

Purpose

Send the e-mail message.

Syntax

```
public void send ()
```

Description

This formats and sends the message. If no destination address has been set, there is no action taken.

5.3.7   sendTo()

Purpose

Add a destination for this message.

Syntax

```
public String sendTo ( String address )
```

Description

Add `address` to the list of destinations for this method. There is no set limit to the number of destinations an e-mail message may have. I'm sure that if you build up the list large enough, you can exceed the size of the parameter list that the *Mail Transport Agent* can accept or use up your memory.

Parameter/

address

A destination to send this message to.

5.3.8 subject()

Purpose

Set the subject for this message.

Syntax

```
public void subject ( String subject )
```

Description

This method sets the text for the e-mail's `Subject:` line. If called more than once, the latest subject set is the one that is used.

Parameter

subject

The text of this message's `Subject:` line.

5.4 Email_Test

This class provides both an example of how to use the `Email` class and a test program which can be used to confirm that the *Java CGI* package is functioning correctly.

5.4.1 Member Summary

```
main()        //  Program main().
```

5.4.2 See Also

`Email`.

5.4.3 main()

Purpose

Provide a `main()` method.

Syntax

```
public static void main( String argv[] )
```

Description

This is the entry point for a CGI program which returns a list of the available name/value pairs and their current values. It will also send this list to the address specified in the `Email` variable.

Parameter

argv[ ]

Arguments passed to the program by the `java.cgi` script. Currently unused.

5.5   HTML

5.5.1   Class Syntax

`public class HTML extends Text`

5.5.2   Class Description

Messages are built up with the `Text` class `add*()` methods and the HTML-specific methods added by this class. When complete, the message is sent to its destination.

Currently, there is no error checking to confirm that the list-building methods are being used in a correct order, so the programmer must take pains not to violate HTML syntax.

This class is in the "Orbits.net" package.

5.5.3   Member Summary

```
HTML()                   // Constructor.
author()                 // Set the name of the document author.
definitionList()         // Start a definition list.
definitionListTerm()     // Add a term to a definition list.
endList()                // End a list.
listItem()               // Add an entry to a list.
send()                   // Send the HTML message.
title()                  // Set the text for the document title.
```

5.5.4   See Also

`HTML_Test, Text.`

5.5.5   HTML()

Purpose

    Constructs an object which will contain an HTML message.

Syntax

    `public HTML()`

Description

    Sets up an empty message to be completed by the HTML methods.

See Also

    `Text.`

5.5.6   author()

Purpose

    Set the name of the document author.

Syntax

    `public void author ( String author )`

Description

Set the name of the document author to `author`.

Parameter/

author

The text to use as the author of this message.

See Also

`title()`.

5.5.7   definitionList()

Purpose

Start a definition list.

Syntax

`public void definitionList ()`

Description

Start a definition list. A *definition list* is a list specialized so that each entry in the list is a *term* followed by the definition *text* for that term. The start of a definition list should be followed by the creation of (at least) one term/text pair and a call to the `endList()` method. *Note that, currently, lists cannot be nested.*

See Also

`definitionListTerm()`, `endList()`, `listItem()`.

5.5.8   definitionListTerm()

Purpose

Add a term to a definition list.

Syntax

`public void definitionListTerm ()`

Description

Add a term to a definition list. The text for the term part of the current list entry should be appended to the message after this method is called and before a corresponding `listItem` method is called.

See Also

`definitionList()`, `listItem()`.

5.5.9   endList()

Purpose

End a list.

Syntax

`public void endList ()`

Description

End a list. This method closes out a list. *Note that, currently, lists cannot be nested.*

See Also

`definitionList()`.

5.5.10 listItem()

Purpose

Add an entry to a list.

Syntax

```
public void listItem ()


public void listItem ( String item )


public boolean listItem ( String term, String item )
```

Description

Add an entry to a list. If the first form is used, the text for the current list item should be appended to the message after this method is called and before any other list methods are called. In the second and third forms, the `item` text is specified as a parameter to the method instead of (or in addition to) being appended to the message. The third form is specific to definition lists and provides both the term and the definition of the list entry.

Parameters

    item

        The text of this list entry.

    term

        The text of this definition list entry's term part.

See Also

    definitionList(), definitionListTerm(), endList().

5.5.11 send()

Purpose

Send the HTML message.

Syntax

```
public void send ()
```

Description

Send the HTML message.

5.5.12 title()

Purpose

Set the text for the document title.

Syntax

```
public void title ( String title )
```

Description

Set the text for the document title.

Parameter

    title

        The text of this message's title.

See Also

    author().

5.6   HTML_Test

This class provides both an example of how to use the **HTML** class and a test program which can be used to confirm that the *Java CGI* package is functioning correctly.

5.6.1   Member Summary

```
main()       //  Program main().
```

5.6.2   See Also

HTML.

5.6.3   main()

Purpose

Provide a main() method.

Syntax

```
public static void main( String argv[] )
```

Description

This is the entry point for a CGI program which returns a list of the available name/value pairs in an HTML document, with each name/value pair displayed in a definition list element.

Parameter

argv[ ]

Arguments passed to the program by the **java.cgi** script. Currently unused.

5.7   Text

5.7.1   Class Syntax

```
public abstract class Text
```

5.7.2   Class Description

This class is the superclass of the **Email** and **HTML** classes. Messages are built up with the methods in this class and completed and formatted with the methods in subclasses.

This class is in the "Orbits.text" package.

5.7.3   Member Summary

```
Text()           //  Constructor.
add()            //  Add text to this object.
addLineBreak()   //  Add a line break.
addParagraph()   //  Add a paragraph break.
```

5.7.4 See Also

Email, HTML.

5.7.5 add()

Purpose

Add text to this item.

Syntax

public void add (char addition)

public void add (String addition)

public void add (StringBuffer addition)

Description

Add addition to the contents of this text item.

Parameter

addition

Text to be added to the text item.

See Also

addLineBreak(), addParagraph().

5.7.6 addLineBreak()

Purpose

Force a line break at this point in the text.

Syntax

public void addLineBreak ()

Description

Add a line break to the text at the current point.

See Also

add(), addParagraph().

5.7.7 addParagraph()

Purpose

Start a new paragaph.

Syntax

public void add ()

Description

Start a new paragraph at this point in the text flow.

See Also

add(), addLineBreak().

6   Future Plans

- Add to the Email class:

  Email(int capacity)
  > Used when we know how much space the message will need to have allocated.

  sendTo(String [address)]
  > Add a list of primary destinations to the e-mail message.

  sendCc(String address)
  > Add a Carbon-Copy destination to the e-mail message.

  sendCc(String [address)]
  > Add a list of Carbon-Copy destinations to the e-mail message.

  sendBcc(String address)
  > Add a Blind Carbon-Copy destination to the e-mail message.

  sendBcc(String [address)]
  > Add a list of Blind Carbon-Copy destinations to the e-mail message.

- Add to the HTML class:

  HTML(int capacity)
  > Used when we know how much space the message will need to have allocated.

  public void unorderedList()
  > Start an unordered list.

  public void orderedList()
  > Start an ordered list.

  public void directoryList()
  > Start a directory list.

  public void menuList()
  > Start a menu list.

  void anchor(String anchorName)
  > Specify an anchor.

  void link(String url, String text)
  > Specify a link.

  void applet(String url, String altText)
  > Specify an applet link.

- Allow HTML lists to be nested.
- Add error checking code to enforce correct ordering of HTML list formatting codes.
- The location of the file of environment data should be configurable from the `Makefile`.
- Get rid of the spurious empty name/value pair that appears in the list when we are dealing with the GET method of data transfer.
- Consider having CGI implement the java.util.Enumeration interface to successively provide variable names.
- Add a `Test` class, which would use every method in this package.
- Document how `CGI_Test`, `Email_Test` and `HTML_Test` build on each other to provide incremental tests for debugging purposes.
- Document how Test uses every feature available in this package.

7 Changes

7.1 Changes from 0.3 to 0.4

- Fleshed out the HTML class to provide minimal functionality.
- Wrote the HTML_Test class and javahtmltest.html-dist.
- Added the HTML methods to deal with a definition list.

7.2 Changes from 0.2 to 0.3

- Added the Text and Email classes. HTML was also added, but it is merely a stub at this point.
- Put the various classes into packages. The main classes are in `Orbits.net.*`, the support class `Text` is in `Orbits.text.Text`.
- Changed `CGItest` to `CGI_Test`.
- Added the `Email_Test` class.

7.3 Changes from 0.1 to 0.2

- The environment variables are put into a temporary file instead of being crammed into the Java inperpreter command-line. The `CGI` class and `java.cgi` had to be modified.
- The `javacgitest.html` document is made part of the distribution.
- The text files which are modified by `make` upon installation are provided with names that end with *-dist*.

RPM HOWTO (RPM at Idle)

Donnie Barnes, djb@redhat.com   v2.0, 8 April 1997

Contents

1 Introduction

RPM is the Red Hat Package Manager. While it does contain Red Hat in the name, it is completely intended to be an open packaging system available for anyone to use. It allows users to take source code for new software and package it into source and binary form such that binaries can be easily installed and tracked and source can be rebuilt easily. It also maintains a database of all packages and their files that can be used for verifying packages and querying for information about files and/or packages.

Red Hat Software encourages other distribution vendors to take the time to look at RPM and use it for their own distributions. RPM is quite flexible and easy to use, though it provides the base for a very extensive system. It is also completely open and available, though we would appreciate bug reports and fixes. Permission is granted to use and distribute RPM royalty free under the GPL.

More complete documentation is available on RPM in the book by Ed Bailey, *Maximum RPM*. That book is available for download or purchase at *www.redhat.com* <http://www.redhat.com>.

2 Overview

First, let me state some of the philosophy behind RPM. One design goal was to allow the use of "pristine" sources. With RPP (our former packaging system of which *none* of RPM is derived), our source packages were the "hacked" sources that we built from. Theoretically, one could install a source RPP and then `make` it with no problems. But the sources were not the original ones, and there was no reference as to what changes we had to make to get it to build. One had to download the pristine sources separately. With RPM, you have the pristine sources along with a patch that we used to compile from. We see this as a big advantage. Why? Several reasons. For one, if a new version of a program comes out, you don't necessarily have to start from scratch to get it to compile under RHL. You can look at the patch to see what you *might* need to do. All the compile-in defaults are easily visible this way.

RPM is also designed to have powerful querying options. You can do searches through your entire database for packages or just certain files. You can also easily find out what package a file belongs to and where it came from. The RPM files themselves are compressed archives, but you can query individual packages easily and *quickly* because of a custom binary header added to the package with everything you could possibly need to know contained in uncompressed form. This allows for *fast* querying.

Another powerful feature is the ability to verify packages. If you are worried that you deleted an important file for some package, just verify it. You will be notified of any anomalies. At that point, you can reinstall the package if necessary. Any config files that you had are preserved as well.

We would like to thank the folks from the BOGUS distribution for many of their ideas and concepts that are included in RPM. While RPM was completely written by Red Hat Software, its operation is based on code written by BOGUS (PM and PMS).

3 General Information

3.1 Acquiring RPM

The best way to get RPM is to install Red Hat Linux. If you don't want to do that, you can still get and use RPM. It can be acquired from *ftp.redhat.com* `<ftp://ftp.redhat.com/pub/redhat/code/rpm>`.

3.2 RPM Requirements

The main requirement to run RPM is cpio 2.4.2 or greater. While this system is intended for use with Linux, it may very well be portable to other Unix systems. It has, in fact, been compiled on SunOS, Solaris, AIX, Irix, AmigaOS, and others. Be warned, the binary packages generated on a different type of Unix system will not be compatible.

Those are the minimal requirements to install RPMs. To build RPMs from source, you also need everything normally required to build a package, like `gcc`, `make`, etc.

4 Using RPM

In its simplest form, RPM can be used to install packages:

```
rpm -i foobar-1.0-1.i386.rpm
```

The next simplest command is to uninstall a package:

```
rpm -e foobar
```

One of the more complex but *highly* useful commands allows you to install packages via FTP. If you are connected to the net and want to install a new package, all you need to do is specify the file with a valid URL, like so:

```
rpm -i ftp://ftp.pht.com/pub/linux/redhat/rh-5.0/RPMS/foobar-1.0-1.i386.rpm
```

Please note, that RPM will now query and/or install via FTP.

While these are simple commands, rpm can be used in a multitude of ways as seen from the `Usage` message:

```
RPM version 2.3.9
Copyright (C) 1997 - Red Hat Software
This may be freely redistributed under the terms of the GNU Public License

usage: rpm {--help}
       rpm {--version}
       rpm {--initdb}   [--dbpath <dir>]
       rpm {--install -i} [-v] [--hash -h] [--percent] [--force] [--test]
                     [--replacepkgs] [--replacefiles] [--root <dir>]
```

```
                   [--excludedocs] [--includedocs] [--noscripts]
                   [--rcfile <file>] [--ignorearch] [--dbpath <dir>]
                   [--prefix <dir>] [--ignoreos] [--nodeps]
                   [--ftpproxy <host>] [--ftpport <port>]
                   file1.rpm ... fileN.rpm
  rpm {--upgrade -U} [-v] [--hash -h] [--percent] [--force] [--test]
                   [--oldpackage] [--root <dir>] [--noscripts]
                   [--excludedocs] [--includedocs] [--rcfile <file>]
                   [--ignorearch]  [--dbpath <dir>] [--prefix <dir>]
                   [--ftpproxy <host>] [--ftpport <port>]
                   [--ignoreos] [--nodeps] file1.rpm ... fileN.rpm
  rpm {--query -q} [-afpg] [-i] [-l] [-s] [-d] [-c] [-v] [-R]
                   [--scripts] [--root <dir>] [--rcfile <file>]
                   [--whatprovides] [--whatrequires] [--requires]
                   [--ftpuseport] [--ftpproxy <host>] [--ftpport <port>]
                   [--provides] [--dump] [--dbpath <dir>] [targets]
  rpm {--verify -V -y} [-afpg] [--root <dir>] [--rcfile <file>]
                   [--dbpath <dir>] [--nodeps] [--nofiles] [--noscripts]
                   [--nomd5] [targets]
  rpm {--setperms} [-afpg] [target]
  rpm {--setugids} [-afpg] [target]
  rpm {--erase -e} [--root <dir>] [--noscripts] [--rcfile <file>]
                   [--dbpath <dir>] [--nodeps] [--allmatches]
                   package1 ... packageN
  rpm {-b|t}[plciba] [-v] [--short-circuit] [--clean] [--rcfile  <file>]
                   [--sign] [--test] [--timecheck <s>] specfile
  rpm {--rebuild} [--rcfile <file>] [-v] source1.rpm ... sourceN.rpm
  rpm {--recompile} [--rcfile <file>] [-v] source1.rpm ... sourceN.rpm
  rpm {--resign} [--rcfile <file>] package1 package2 ... packageN
  rpm {--addsign} [--rcfile <file>] package1 package2 ... packageN
  rpm {--checksig -K} [--nopgp] [--nomd5] [--rcfile <file>]
                   package1 ... packageN
  rpm {--rebuilddb} [--rcfile <file>] [--dbpath <dir>]
  rpm {--querytags}
```

You can find more details on what those options do in the RPM man page.

5   Now what can I *really* do with RPM?

RPM is a very useful tool and, as you can see, has several options. The best way to make sense of them is to look at some examples. I covered simple install/uninstall above, so here are some more examples:

- Let's say you delete some files by accident, but you aren't sure what you deleted. If you want to verify your entire system and see what might be missing, you would do:

  ```
  rpm -Va
  ```

- Let's say you run across a file that you don't recognize. To find out which package owns it, you would do:

      rpm -qf /usr/X11R6/bin/xjewel

  The output would be:

      xjewel-1.6-1

- You find a new koules RPM, but you don't know what it is. To find out some information on it, do:

      rpm -qpi koules-1.2-2.i386.rpm

  The output would be:

```
Name        : koules              Distribution: Red Hat Linux Colgate
Version     : 1.2                       Vendor: Red Hat Software
Release     : 2                     Build Date: Mon Sep 02 11:59:12 1996
Install date: (none)               Build Host: porky.redhat.com
Group       : Games                Source RPM: koules-1.2-2.src.rpm
Size        : 614939
Summary     : SVGAlib action game with multiplayer, network, and sound support
Description :
This arcade-style game is novel in conception and excellent in execution.
No shooting, no blood, no guts, no gore.  The play is simple, but you
still must develop skill to play.  This version uses SVGAlib to
run on a graphics console.
```

- Now you want to see what files the koules RPM installs. You would do:

      rpm -qpl koules-1.2-2.i386.rpm

  The output is:

```
/usr/doc/koules
/usr/doc/koules/ANNOUNCE
/usr/doc/koules/BUGS
/usr/doc/koules/COMPILE.OS2
/usr/doc/koules/COPYING
/usr/doc/koules/Card
/usr/doc/koules/ChangeLog
/usr/doc/koules/INSTALLATION
/usr/doc/koules/Icon.xpm
/usr/doc/koules/Icon2.xpm
/usr/doc/koules/Koules.FAQ
/usr/doc/koules/Koules.xpm
/usr/doc/koules/README
/usr/doc/koules/TODO
/usr/games/koules
/usr/games/koules.svga
/usr/games/koules.tcl
/usr/man/man6/koules.svga.6
```

These are just several examples. More creative ones can be thought of really easy once you are familiar with RPM.

6   Building RPMs

Building RPMs is fairly easy to do, especially if you can get the software you are trying to package to build on its own.

The basic procedure to build an RPM is as follows:

- Make sure your **/etc/rpmrc** is setup for your system.
- Get the source code you are building the RPM for to build on your system.
- Make a patch of any changes you had to make to the sources to get them to build properly.
- Make a spec file for the package.
- Make sure everything is in its proper place.
- Build the package using RPM.

Under normal operation, RPM builds both binary and source packages.

6.1   The rpmrc File

Right now, the only configuration of RPM is available via the **/etc/rpmrc** file. An example one looks like:

```
require_vendor: 1
distribution: I roll my own!
require_distribution: 1
topdir: /usr/src/me
vendor: Mickiesoft
packager:  Mickeysoft Packaging Account <packages@mickiesoft.com>

optflags: i386 -O2 -m486 -fno-strength-reduce
optflags: alpha -O2
optflags: sparc -O2

signature: pgp
pgp_name: Mickeysoft Packaging Account
pgp_path: /home/packages/.pgp

tmppath: /usr/tmp
```

The **require_vendor** line causes RPM to require that it find a vendor line. This can come from the **/etc/rpmrc** or from the header of the spec file itself. To turn this off, change the number to 0. The same holds true for the **require_distribution** and **require_group** lines.

The next line is the **distribution** line. You can define that here or later in the header of the spec file. When building for a particular distribution, it's a good idea to make sure this line is correct, even though it is not required. The **vendor** line works much the same way, but can be anything (ie. Joe's Software and Rock Music Emporium).

RPM also now has support for building packages on multiple architectures. The **rpmrc** file can hold an "optflags" variable for building things that require architecture specific flags when building. See later sections for how to use this variable.

In addition to the above macros, there are several more. You can use:

```
rpm --showrc
```

to find out how your tags are set and what all the available flags are.

6.2   The Spec File

We'll begin with discussion of the spec file. Spec files are required to build a package. The spec file is a description of the software along with instructions on how to build it and a file list for all the binaries that get installed.

You'll want to name your spec file according to a standard convention. It should be the package name-dash-version number-dash-release number-dot-spec.

Here is a small spec file (vim-3.0-1.spec):

```
Summary: ejects ejectable media and controls auto ejection
Name: eject
Version: 1.4
Release: 3
Copyright: GPL
Group: Utilities/System
Source: sunsite.unc.edu:/pub/Linux/utils/disk-management/eject-1.4.tar.gz
Patch: eject-1.4-make.patch
Patch1: eject-1.4-jaz.patch
%description
This program allows the user to eject media that is autoejecting like
CD-ROMs, Jaz and Zip drives, and floppy drives on SPARC machines.

%prep
%setup
%patch -p1
%patch1 -p1

%build
make RPM_OPT_FLAGS="$RPM_OPT_FLAGS"

%install
install -s -m 755 -o 0 -g 0 eject /usr/bin/eject
install -m 644 -o 0 -g 0 eject.1 /usr/man/man1

%files
%doc README COPYING ChangeLog
```

```
/usr/bin/eject
/usr/man/man1/eject.1
```

6.3   The Header

The header has some standard fields in it that you need to fill in. There are a few caveats as well. The fields must be filled in as follows:

- `Summary:` This is a one line description of the package.
- `Name:` This must be the name string from the rpm filename you plan to use.
- `Version:` This must be the version string from the rpm filename you plan to use.
- `Release:` This is the release number for a package of the same version (ie. if we make a package and find it to be slightly broken and need to make it again, the next package would be release number 2).
- `Icon:` This is the name of the icon file for use by other high level installation tools (like Red Hat's "glint"). It must be a gif and resides in the SOURCES directory.
- `Source:` This line points at the HOME location of the pristine source file. It is used if you ever want to get the source again or check for newer versions. Caveat: The filename in this line MUST match the filename you have on your own system (ie. don't download the source file and change its name). You can also specify more than one source file using lines like:

  ```
  Source0: blah-0.tar.gz
  Source1: blah-1.tar.gz
  Source2: fooblah.tar.gz
  ```

  These files would go in the SOURCES directory. (The directory structure is discussed in a later section, "The Source Directory Tree".)

- `Patch:` This is the place you can find the patch if you need to download it again. Caveat: The filename here must match the one you use when you make YOUR patch. You may also want to note that you can have multiple patch files much as you can have multiple sources.] You would have something like:

  ```
  Patch0: blah-0.patch
  Patch1: blah-1.patch
  Patch2: fooblah.patch
  ```

  These files would go in the SOURCES directory.

- `Copyright:` This line tells how a package is copyrighted. You should use something like GPL, BSD, MIT, public domain, distributable, or commercial.
- `BuildRoot:` This line allows you to specify a directory as the "root" for building and installing the new package. You can use this to help test your package before having it installed on your machine.
- `Group:` This line is used to tell high level installation programs (such as Red Hat's "glint") where to place this particular program in its hierarchical structure. The group tree currently looks something like this:

  ```
  Applications
      Communications
      Editors
          Emacs
      Engineering
  ```

```
            Spreadsheets
            Databases
            Graphics
            Networking
            Mail
            Math
            News
            Publishing
                TeX
    Base
        Kernel
    Utilities
        Archiving
        Console
        File
        System
        Terminal
        Text
Daemons
Documentation
X11
    XFree86
        Servers
        Applications
            Graphics
            Networking
        Games
            Strategy
            Video
        Amusements
        Utilities
        Libraries
        Window Managers
    Libraries
    Networking
        Admin
        Daemons
        News
        Utilities
    Development
        Debuggers
        Libraries
            Libc
        Languages
            Fortran
```

- **%description** It's not really a header item, but should be described with the rest of the header. You need one description tag per package and/or subpackage. This is a multi-line field that should be used to give a comprehensive description of the package.

6.4   Prep

This is the second section in the spec file. It is used to get the sources ready to build. Here you need to do anything necessary to get the sources patched and setup like they need to be setup to do a **make**.

One thing to note: Each of these sections is really just a place to execute shell scripts. You could simply make an **sh** script and put it after the **%prep** tag to unpack and patch your sources. We have made macros to aid in this, however.

The first of these macros is the **%setup** macro. In its simplest form (no command line options), it simply unpacks the sources and **cd**'s into the source directory. It also takes the following options:

- **-n name** will set the name of the build directory to the listed **name**. The default is **$NAME-$VERSION**. Other possibilities include **$NAME**, **${NAME}${VERSION}**, or whatever the main tar file uses. (Please note that these "$" variables are *not* real variables available within the spec file. They are really just used here in place of a sample name. You need to use the real name and version in your package, not a variable.)

- **-c** will create and cd to the named directory *before* doing the untar.

- **-b #** will untar Source# *before* cd'ing into the directory (and this makes no sense with **-c** so don't do it). This is only useful with multiple source files.

- **-a #** will untar Source# *after* cd'ing into the directory.

- **-T** This option overrides the default action of untarring the Source and requires a **-b 0** or **-a 0** to get the main source file untarred. You need this when there are secondary sources.

- **-D** Do *not* delete the directory before unpacking. This is only useful where you have more than one setup macro. It should *only* be used in setup macros *after* the first one (but never in the first one).

The next of the available macros is the **%patch** macro. This macro helps automate the process of applying patches to the sources. It takes several options, listed below:

- **#** will apply Patch# as the patch file.

- **-p #** specifies the number of directories to strip for the patch(1) command.

- **-P** The default action is to apply Patch (or Patch0). This flag inhibits the default action and will require a 0 to get the main source file untarred. This option is useful in a second (or later) **%patch** macro that required a different number than the first macro.

- You can also do **%patch#** instead of doing the real command: **%patch # -P**

That should be all the macros you need. After you have those right, you can also do any other setup you need to do via **sh** type scripting. Anything you include up until the **%build** macro (discussed in the next section) is executed via **sh**. Look at the example above for the types of things you might want to do here.

6.5 Build

There aren't really any macros for this section. You should just put any commands here that you would need to use to build the software once you had untarred the source, patched it, and cd'ed into the directory. This is just another set of commands passed to `sh`, so any legal `sh` commands can go here (including comments). **Your current working directory is reset in each of these sections to the toplevel of the source directory**, so keep that in mind. You can `cd` into subdirectories if necessary.

6.6 Install

There aren't really any macros here, either. You basically just want to put whatever commands here that are necessary to install. If you have `make install` available to you in the package you are building, put that here. If not, you can either patch the makefile for a `make install` and just do a `make install` here, or you can hand install them here with `sh` commands. You can consider your current directory to be the toplevel of the source directory.

6.7 Optional pre and post Install/Uninstall Scripts

You can put scripts in that get run before and after the installation and uninstallation of binary packages. A main reason for this is to do things like run `ldconfig` after installing or removing packages that contain shared libraries. The macros for each of the scripts is as follows:

- `%pre` is the macro to do pre-install scripts.
- `%post` is the macro to do post-install scripts.
- `%preun` is the macro to do pre-uninstall scripts.
- `%postun` is the macro to do post-uninstall scripts.

The contents of these sections should just be any `sh` style script, though you do *not* need the `#!/bin/sh`.

6.8 Files

This is the section where you *must* list the files for the binary package. RPM has no way to know what binaries get installed as a result of `make install`. There is *NO* way to do this. Some have suggested doing a `find` before and after the package install. With a multiuser system, this is unacceptable as other files may be created during a package building process that have nothing to do with the package itself.

There are some macros available to do some special things as well. They are listed and described here:

- `%doc` is used to mark documentation in the source package that you want installed in a binary install. The documents will be installed in `/usr/doc/$NAME-$VERSION-$RELEASE`. You can list multiple documents on the command line with this macro, or you can list them all separately using a macro for each of them.
- `%config` is used to mark configuration files in a package. This includes files like sendmail.cf, passwd, etc. If you later uninstall a package containing config files, any unchanged files will be removed and any changed files will get moved to their old name with a `.rpmsave` appended to the filename. You can list multiple files with this macro as well.
- `%dir` marks a single directory in a file list to be included as being owned by a package. By default, if you list a directory name *WITHOUT* a `%dir` macro, *EVERYTHING* in that directory is included in the file list and later installed as part of that package.

- `%files -f <filename>` will allow you to list your files in some arbitrary file within the build directory of the sources. This is nice in cases where you have a package that can build it's own filelist. You then just include that filelist here and you don't have to specifically list the files.

The biggest caveat in the file list is listing directories. If you list `/usr/bin` by accident, your binary package will contain *every* file in `/usr/bin` on your system.

6.9   Building It

6.9.1   The Source Directory Tree

The first thing you need is a properly configured build tree. This is configurable using the `/etc/rpmrc` file. Most people will just use `/usr/src`.

You may need to create the following directories to make a build tree:

- `BUILD` is the directory where all building occurs by RPM. You don't have to do your test building anywhere in particular, but this is where RPM will do it's building.

- `SOURCES` is the directory where you should put your original source tar files and your patches. This is where RPM will look by default.

- `SPECS` is the directory where all spec files should go.

- `RPMS` is where RPM will put all binary RPMs when built.

- `SRPMS` is where all source RPMs will be put.

6.9.2   Test Building

The first thing you'll probably want to to is get the source to build cleanly without using RPM. To do this, unpack the sources, and change the directory name to $NAME.orig. Then unpack the source again. Use this source to build from. Go into the source directory and follow the instructions to build it. If you have to edit things, you'll need a patch. Once you get it to build, clean the source directory. Make sure and remove any files that get made from a `configure` script. Then `cd` back out of the source directory to its parent. Then you'll do something like:

    diff -uNr dirname.orig dirname > ../SOURCES/dirname-linux.patch

This will create a patch for you that you can use in your spec file. Note that the "linux" that you see in the patch name is just an identifier. You might want to use something more descriptive like "config" or "bugs" to describe *why* you had to make a patch. It's also a good idea to look at the patch file you are creating before using it to make sure no binaries were included by accident.

6.9.3   Generating the File List

Now that you have source that will build and you know how to do it, build it and install it. Look at the output of the install sequence and build your file list from that to use in the spec file. We usually build the spec file in parallel with all of these steps. You can create the initial one and fill in the easy parts, and then fill in the other steps as you go.

6.9.4 Building the Package with RPM

Once you have a spec file, you are ready to try and build your package. The most useful way to do it is with a command like the following:

```
rpm -ba foobar-1.0.spec
```

There are other options useful with the -b switch as well:

- p means just run the prep section of the specfile.
- l is a list check that does some checks on %files.
- c do a prep and compile. This is useful when you are unsure of whether your source will build at all. It seems useless because you might want to just keep playing with the source itself until it builds and then start using RPM, but once you become accustomed to using RPM you will find instances when you will use it.
- i do a prep, compile, and install.
- b prep, compile, install, and build a binary package only.
- a build it all (both source and binary packages).

There are several modifiers to the -b switch. They are as follows:

- --short-circuit will skip straight to a specified stage (can only be used with c and i).
- --clean removes the build tree when done.
- --keep-temps will keep all the temp files and scripts that were made in /tmp. You can actually see what files were created in /tmp using the -v option.
- --test does not execute any real stages, but does keep-temp.

6.10 Testing It

Once you have a source and binary rpm for your package, you need to test it. The easiest and best way is to use a totally different machine from the one you are building on to test. After all, you've just done a lot of make install's on your own machine, so it should be installed fairly well.

You can do an rpm -u packagename on the package to test, but that can be deceiving because in building the package, you did a make install. If you left something out of your file list, it will not get uninstalled. You'll then reinstall the binary package and your system will be complete again, but your rpm still isn't. Make sure and keep in mind that just because you do a rpm -ba package, most people installing your package will just be doing the rpm -i package. Make sure you don't do anything in the build or install sections that will need to be done when the binaries are installed by themselves.

6.11 What to do with your new RPMs

Once you've made your own RPM of something (assuming its something that hasn't already been RPM'ed), you can contribute your work to others (also assuming you RPM'ed something freely distributable). To do so, you'll want to upload it to *ftp.redhat.com* <ftp://ftp.redhat.com>.

6.12   What Now?

Please see the above sections on Testing and What to do with new RPMs. We want all the RPMs available we can get, and we want them to be good RPMs. Please take the time to test them well, and then take the time to upload them for everyone's benefit. Also, *please* make sure you are only uploading *freely available software*. Commercial software and shareware should *not* be uploaded unless they have a copyright expressly stating that this is allowed. This includes Netscape software, ssh, pgp, etc.

7   Multi-architectural RPM Building

RPM can now be used to build packages for the Intel i386, the Digital Alpha running Linux, and the Sparc. It has been reported to work on SGI's and HP workstations as well. There are several features that make building packages on all platforms easy. The first of these is the "optflags" directive in the /etc/rpmrc. It can be used to set flags used when building software to architecture specific values. Another feature is the "arch" macros in the spec file. They can be used to do different things depending on the architecture you are building on. Another feature is the "Exclude" directive in the header.

7.1   Sample spec File

The following is part of the spec file for the "fileutils" package. It is setup to build on both the Alpha and the Intel.

```
Summary: GNU File Utilities
Name: fileutils
Version: 3.16
Release: 1
Copyright: GPL
Group: Utilities/File
Source0: prep.ai.mit.edu:/pub/gnu/fileutils-3.16.tar.gz
Source1: DIR_COLORS
Patch: fileutils-3.16-mktime.patch

%description
These are the GNU file management utilities.  It includes programs
to copy, move, list, etc, files.

The ls program in this package now incorporates color ls!

%prep
%setup

%ifarch alpha
%patch -p1
autoconf
%endif
%build
```

```
configure --prefix=/usr --exec-prefix=/
make CFLAGS="$RPM_OPT_FLAGS" LDFLAGS=-s

%install
rm -f /usr/info/fileutils*
make install
gzip -9nf /usr/info/fileutils*
```

7.2 Optflags

In this example, you see how the "optflags" directive is used from the **/etc/rpmrc**. Depending on which architecture you are building on, the proper value is given to **RPM_OPT_FLAGS**. You must patch the Makefile for your package to use this variable in place of the normal directives you might use (like −m486 and −O2). You can get a better feel for what needs to be done by installing this source package and then unpacking the source and examine the Makefile. Then look at the patch for the Makefile and see what changes must be made.

7.3 Macros

The **%ifarch** macro is very important to all of this. Most times you will need to make a patch or two that is specific to one architecture only. In this case, RPM will allow you to apply that patch to just one architecture only.

In the above example, fileutils has a patch for 64 bit machines. Obviously, this should only be applied on the Alpha at the moment. So, we add an **%ifarch** macro around the 64 bit patch like so:

```
%ifarch axp
%patch1 -p1
%endif
```

This will insure that the patch is not applied on any architecture except the alpha.

7.4 Excluding Architectures from Packages

So that you can maintain source RPMs in one directory for all platforms, we have implemented the ability to "exclude" packages from being built on certain architectures. This is so you can still do things like

```
rpm --rebuild /usr/src/SRPMS/*.rpm
```

and have the right packages build. If you haven't yet ported an application to a certain platform, all you have to do is add a line like:

```
ExcludeArch: axp
```

to the header of the spec file of the source package. Then rebuild the package on the platform that it does build on. You'll then have a source package that builds on an Intel and can easily be skipped on an Alpha.

7.5   Finishing Up

Using RPM to make multi-architectural packages is usually easier to do than getting the package itself to build both places. As more of the hard packages get built this is getting much easier, however. As always, the best help when you get stuck building an RPM is to look a similar source package.

8   Copyright Notice

RPM+Slackware Mini-Howto

Dave Whitinger, `wolf@redhat.com` v1.0, 29 August 1997

This document describes how to get RPM installed and working properly under Slackware. The information contained herein, however, is probably applicable to any Linux distribution.

Contents

1 Introduction

I've been asked many many times how to use RPM under Slackware. Enough was enough, so today I decided that creating this document might be a good idea.

RPM is the "Red Hat Package Manager" and is the heart of the Red Hat Linux distribution. It's most basic functionality is to install and de-install packages. Check out the RPM-HOWTO, or get a copy of "Maximum RPM" for more information on using RPM.

This document is geared toward installing RPM on a Slackware system using an Intel processor, but the information contained herein can easily be applied to any distribution using any processor type.

2 Obtaining the software

The newest release of RPM is always available from:

> `ftp.rpm.org/pub/rpm/dist/latest`

As of this writing, the latest version was

> `rpm-2.4.5-1.i386.tar.gz`

Notice the .i386 section. This means that it is a binary package for the Intel architecture, ready to untar and run. Make sure that the file you download has the i386 in the filename, otherwise the following instructions will not work.

3 Installing the software

You must be root to accomplish the next steps.

You must then untar the package from the root directory. Here are the instructions for doing so:

```
cd /
tar zxvpf /home/wolf/rpm-2.4.5-1.i386.tar.gz
```

Of course, replace the /home/wolf with the correct path for the filename.

Next, you have to create a directory called "rpm" under the /var/lib tree.

mkdir /var/lib/rpm

Now type 'rpm –initdb' to initialize the rpm database.

If everything has gone correctly up to this point, you will have a rpm-capable system! Test it out by grabbing any rpm file and installing it with 'rpm -Uvh filename.rpm'

The RCS MINI-HOWTO

Robert Kiesling   · $Id: RCS-HOWTO.sgml,v 1.4 1997/08/14 15:09:56 rak Exp rak $

This document covers basic installation and usage of RCS, the GNU Revision Control System, under Linux. It also covers the installation of the diff(1) and diff3(1) utilities, which are necessary for RCS to operate. This document may be reproduced freely, in whole or in part, provided that any usage of this document conforms to the general copyright notice of the HOWTO series of the Linux Documentation Project. See the file COPYRIGHT for details. Send all complaints, suggestions, errata, and any miscellany to *kiesling@terracom.net* <mailto: kiesling@terracom.net>, so I can keep this document as complete and up to date as possible.

Contents

1 Overview of RCS.

RCS, the revision control system, is a suite of programs that tracks changes in text files and controls shared access to files in work group situations. It is generally used to maintain source code modules. It lends itself to tracking revisions of document files as well.

RCS was written by Walter F. Tichy and Paul Eggert. The latest version which has been ported to Linux is RCS Version 5.7. There is also a semi-official, threaded version available. Much of the information in this HOWTO is taken from the RCS man pages.

RCS includes the rcs(1) program, which controls RCS archive file attributes, ci(1) and co(1), which check files in and out of RCS archives, ident(1), which searches RCS archives by keyword identifiers, rcsclean(1), a program to clean up files that are not being worked on or haven't changed, rcsdiff(1), which runs diff(1) to compare the revisions, rcsmerge(1), which merges two RCS branches into a single working file, and rlog(1), which prints RCS log messages.

Files archived by RCS may be text of any format, or binary if the diff program used to generate change files handles 8-bit data. Files may optionally include identification strings to aid in tracking by ident(1).

RCS uses the utilities diff(1) and diff3(3) to generate the change files between revisions. A RCS archive consists of the initial revision of a file, which is version 1.1, and a series of change files, one for each revision. Each time a file is checked out of an archive with co(1), edited, and checked back into the archive with ci(1), the version number is increased, for example, to 1.2, 1.3, 1.4, and so on for successive revisions.

The archives themselves commonly reside in a ./RCS subdirectory, although RCS has other options for archive storage.

For an overview of RCS, see the rcsintro(1) manual page.

2   System requirements.

RCS needs diff(1) and diff3(3) to generate the context diff files between revisions. The diff utilities suite needs to be installed on your system, and when you install RCS, the software will check for its presence.

Precompiled diffutils binaries are available at:

ftp://sunsite.unc.edu/pub/Linux/utils/text/diffutils-2.6.bin.ELF.tar.gz

and its mirror sites. If you need to compile diff(1), et al., from source, it is located at:

ftp://prep.ai.mit.edu/pub/gnu/diffutils-2.7.tar.gz

and its mirror sites.

You will also need to have the ELF libraries installed on your system if you want to install pre-built binaries. See the ELF-HOWTO for further details.

3   Compiling RCS from Source.

Get the source distribution of RCS Version 5.7. It is available at

ftp://sunsite.unc.edu/pub/Linux/devel/vc/rcs-5.7.src.tar.gz

and its mirrors. After you have unpacked the archive into your source tree, you need to configure RCS for your system. This is done via the configure script in the source directory, which you need to execute first. This will generate a Makefile and the appropriate conf.sh for your system. You can then type

make install

which will build the binaries. At some point you may need to su to root so the binaries can be installed in the correct directories.

4   Creating and maintaining archives.

The program rcs(1) does the work or creating archives and modifying their attributes. A summary of rcs(1) options may be found in the rcs(1) manual page.

The easiest way to create an archive is first to mkdir RCS in the current directory, then initialize the archive with the

```
rcs -i name_of_work_file
```

command. This creates and archive with the name `./RCS/name_of_work_file,v` and requests a text message describing the archive, but it does not deposit any revisions in the archive. You can turn on or off strict archive locking with the commands

```
rcs -L name_of_work_file
```

and

```
rcs -U name_of_work_file
```

respectively. There are other options for controlling access to the archive, setting its format, and setting revision numbers, which are covered in the `rcs(1)` manual page.

5   ci(1) **and** co(1).

ci(1) and co(1) are the commands used to check files in and out of their RCS archives. The ci(1) command may also be used to a check a file both in and out of an archive. In their simplest forms, ci(1) and co(1) take only the name of the working file.

```
ci name_of_work_file
```

and

```
co name_of_work_file
```

The command form

```
ci -l name_of_work_file
```

checks in the file with locking enabled, and

```
co -l name_of_work_file
```

is performed automatically. That is, ci -l checks the file out again with locking enabled.

```
ci -u name_of_work_file
```

checks the file into the archive, and checks it out again with locking disabled. In all cases, the user is prompted for a log message.

ci(1) will also create a RCS archive if one does not exist already.

If you don't specify a revision, ci(1) increments the version number of the last revision locked in the archive, and appends the revised working file to it. If you specify a revision on an existing branch, it must be higher than the existing revision numbers. ci(1) will also create a new branch if you specify the revision of a branch which does not exist. See the ci(1) and co(1) man pages for details.

ci(1) and co(1) have various options for interactive and non-interactive use. Again, see the ci(1) and co(1) man pages for details.

6   Revision histories.

The `rlog(1)` program provides information about the archive file and the logs of each revision stored in it. A command like

```
rlog work_file_name
```

will print the version history of the file, each revision's creation date and **userids** of author and the person who locked the file. You can specify archive attributes and revision parameters to view.

7   Including RCS data in working files.

`co(1)` maintains a list of keywords of the RCS database which are expanded when the working file is checked out. The keyword `$Id$` in a document will expand to a string which contains the file name, revision number, the date checked out, the author, the revision status, and the locker, if any. Including the keyword `$Log$` will expand to the document's revision history log.

These and other keywords may be used as search criteria of the RCS archive. See the `ident(1)` man page for further details.

8   RCS and `emacs(1)` Version Control.

The Version Control facility of `emacs(1)` works as a front end to RCS. This information applies specifically to Version 19.34 of GNU Emacs, which is provided with the major Linux distributions. When editing a file with `emacs(1)` which is registered with RCS, the command `vc-toggle-read-only` (bound to `C-x C-q` by default) will check a file in to the emacs's Version Control, and then into RCS. Emacs will open a buffer where you can type a log message to be included in the RCS log. When you are finished typing a log entry, type `C-c C-c` to terminate your input and proceed with the check-in process.

If you have selected strict locking for the file with RCS, you must re-lock the file for editing by `emacs(1)`. You can check the file out for emacs's Version Control with the command `%` in buffer-menu mode.

For more information, see the GNU Emacs Manual and the Emacs info pages.

Linux Commercial HOWTO

Martin   Michlmayr,   *tbm@cyrius.com*   <mailto:tbm@cyrius.com>,   *http://www.cyrius.com/tbm*
<http://www.cyrius.com/tbm>

v5.10rh, 8 February 1998

This document contains a listing of commercial software and applications which are offered for Linux. It is maintained by *Martin Michlmayr* <http://www.cyrius.com/tbm> <*tbm@cyrius.com*> <mailto:tbm@cyrius.com>.

Contents

1   About this document

This is the Linux Commercial HOWTO. It contains a listing of commercial software which is available for Linux. The Linux Commercial HOWTO doesn't contain any information on Linux distributions – this is covered by the Distribution HOWTO.

If you contact any companies or purchase any products listed in this document, please mention the Linux Commercial HOWTO.

This document was originated by Harald Milz <*Harald.Milz@Linux.org*> <mailto:Harald.Milz@Linux. org>. It is now maintained by *Martin Michlmayr* <http://www.cyrius.com/tbm> <*tbm@cyrius.com*> <mailto:tbm@cyrius.com>.

If you need to know more about the *Linux Documentation Project* <http://sunsite.unc.edu/mdw/linux. html> or about Linux HOWTO's, feel free to contact the supervisor *Greg Hankins* <http://www.cc.gatech. edu/staff/h/Greg.Hankins> <*gregh@sunsite.unc.edu*> <mailto:gregh@sunsite.unc.edu>.

Greg Hankins will post the listing to several national and international newsgroups on a monthly basis. In addition, the Linux Commercial HOWTO can be found on the World Wide Web at *http://commercial.cyrius.com/redhat.html* <http://commercial.cyrius.com/redhat.html>, or can be requested by sending a blank message to *commercial+redhat@howto.cyrius.com* <mailto:commercial+redhat@ howto.cyrius.com>.

The Linux Commercial HOWTO is not a forum for product announcements or marketing hype; it is a service for potential customers and the whole Linux community. Resellers will not be listed; the list is for companies who produce their software themselves. Two main goals are being aimed at:

- It shall help companies who want to run Linux to find software solutions and applications. The international distribution of this list will enhance the contact opportunity.
- It is meant to prove the commercial useability of Linux and thus to encourage other vendors to port their software as well.

Companies and developers who are offering their products for Linux and interested in joining the Linux Commercial HOWTO are invited to fill out the following form and contact me at *tbm@cyrius.com* <mailto: tbm@cyrius.com>.

This HOWTO contains tabular entries for each product (example follows). The entry format is similar to the Linux Software Map (LSM) entry (field/stanza lengths are arbitrary). If you want me to add your entry please *keep short*, otherwise I'll have to shorten your data. Furthermore, please send me plain ASCII data; no HTML, and no PostScript.

```
Category:

        Databases, Data Visualisation, Development tools, Financial
        Software, Mathematics, Multimedia, Network Management, Text
        Processing, X Windows or Other Software.

Name:

The name of your application.

Description:

Short description of the package, just the basic functionality.

Distribution media:

Licensing policy:

Whatever applies.  Is there a free demo or shareware version available
via FTP or WWW?  Where?

OS provisions:

Kernel version, XFree86 version, Motif version, RAM, harddisk usage, etc.

Documentation:

Printed documentation, page number, online help, language.

Extra features and add-Ons:

(and their prices)

Price range:

Whatever it costs.

Vendor:

Address:
Phone: (U.S. and Canada: if you like to be reachable internationally,
        please don't enter only a +1 800 or +1 900 number)
Fax:
```

```
EMail:
URL:
Contact:
```

2 Copyright Information

This HOWTO is Copyright © 1996, 1997, 1998 by *Martin Michlmayr* <http://www.cyrius.com/tbm>.

A verbatim copy may be reproduced or distributed in any medium physical or electronic without permission of the author. Translations are similarly permitted without express permission if it includes a notice on who translated it.

Short quotes may be used without prior consent by the author. Derivative work and partial distributions of the Linux Commercial HOWTO must be accompanied with either a verbatim copy of this file or a pointer to the verbatim copy.

Commercial redistribution is allowed and encouraged; however, the author would like to be notified of any such distributions.

In short, we wish to promote dissemination of this information through as many channels as possible. However, we do wish to retain copyright on the HOWTO documents, and would like to be notified of any plans to redistribute the HOWTOs.

We further want that *all* information provided in the HOWTOs is disseminated. If you have questions, please contact Greg Hankins, the Linux HOWTO coordinator, at *gregh@sunsite.unc.edu* <mailto:gregh@ sunsite.unc.edu>.

3 Disclaimer

This HOWTO is not actually a HOWTO in the sense of the *Linux Documentation Project* <http://sunsite. unc.edu/pub/Linux/docs/HOWTO/INDEX.html>. Instead, it is an instrument to investigate the commercial Linux opportunity and to list applications which were already ported and marketed in a native Linux version. As a software vendor, you probably know that you can alternatively offer Linux users a statically linked SCO version of your application which would probably run under the iBCS2 emulator (albeit with a small performance penalty and higher memory requirements). Such applications will not be listed here.

I will not select nor deselect any particular product. Instead, everyone who wants to have her product included will be serviced. However, I reserve the right to shorten individual entries to keep things in shape.

If you don't find a particular product or vendor in this list, this is probably due to one of the following reasons:

- I never heard of that product or vendor and thus didn't try to get in contact.
- I did get in contact, but the vendor didn't answer yet.
- I did get in contact, but the vendor stated positively that he doesn't sell his product for Linux (yet).

In any case, please get in contact if you feel someone's missing; also if you discover any errors in the file.

Sometimes two vendor's addresses are mentioned in the "Vendor:" field. In these cases I received the information from the German subsidiary/distributor. The original manufacturer's address is always mentioned first.

4   Related Information

There's another document which covers commercial Linux software. It is maintained by Alan Cox <*Alan.Cox@Linux.org*> <mailto:Alan.Cox@Linux.org> and can be found at *http://www.uk.linux.org/LxCommercial.html* <http://www.uk.linux.org/LxCommercial.html>.

In addition, feel free to visit the Linux Mall at http://www.LinuxMall.com/cgi-bin/weblead.cgi/?0000001036 where you can order most products presented in this HOWTO.

5   Linux for the Commercial Market?

Copyright © 1996 iX Multiuser Multitasking Magazin
Courtesy of iX Multiuser Multitasking Magazin!

People keep asking me "When is Linux going to be ready for the *commercial market*". I guess the first thing to discuss is what is meant by "commercial" in this context.

Some CD-ROM vendors have put the word "commercial" in their name, only to have the technical people think their product is good only for use by banks and insurance companies. Other people look at their product with disdain and say that "Linux is not *commercial quality*", because it is missing some feature they need, or they feel it is unstable (usually without ever trying it even one time).

To me, the word "commercial" has lost as much meaning in the marketplace as some of the other buzzwords:

- "Open" vs "Proprietary" (People are now saying UNIX is "Proprietary")
- "Workstation" vs "PC" (What is a workstation, anyway?)

In the old days of computing the commercial market was banks, insurance companies and business-oriented facilities where the use of COBOL or RPG was the mainstream. The technical market was scientific, engineering and manufacturing where FORTRAN and assembly language was used. Somewhere along the way the term "commercial" seems to have gotten twisted around to mean "ready for the mass market", versus "ready for hackers".

For the purpose of this article I will take the second meaning, and address whether I think Linux is ready for commercial purposes rather than the hobbyist and hacker market, and ready for the mass market rather than limited markets.

For those of you who hate reading long articles, or who are short on time, let me give you my conclusion right now. Then you can go out and drink beer or other fun activities:

"Yes, Linux is ready for the commercial market...in some cases".

In order for an operating system to be ready for the mass market it must have several attributes:

- have lots of applications
- be relatively easy to install
- have lots of applications
- be relatively easy to maintain
- have lots of applications
- be relatively easy to use
- have lots of applications
- not crash (much)

- have lots of applications
- be economical
- have lots of applications

But you can eliminate all of these considerations in today's mass market if only one thing is true:

You have lots of applications.

after all, there would not be 170,000,000 DOS systems in the world if any of the others *had* to be true.

I almost added that is has to be economical, but history has actually proven me wrong on that. If people added up the total cost of ownership, then Apple would certainly have won over the PC. But people ignore the human costs of someone else (or even themselves) beating their head against the wall trying to get something to work, or the system crashing repeatedly, or the fact that the one keystroke they can hit the easiest (through practice) is

<CTRL><ALT><DEL>

In the old days people were content to spend several hundreds of dollars on a simple ASCII text editor, or deal with a simple spreadsheet. And it took an act of mangement to get them, with lots of Purchase Orders. Today, they want multi-media integrated with their operating system, and have all the applications available that their neighbor (or boss, or compatriot) has available on *their* system. And they want to get these applications easily, certainly no harder than to call up on the phone to order them through a catalog, or go down to their corner store to get them.

Now what causes this plethora of applications for an operating system? Ease of programming? Good software development tools? Features inside the operating system? Stability of the interfaces over time?

The answer is "none of these". While all these attributes may help convince an application developer to port, the one overriding issue is volume of the operating system platform. Again, if MSDOS were compared to MacOS, or even to UNIX and volume were not taken into account, we know which two operating systems would have the most applications, and they would not be from Microsoft.

While it is true that several Linux vendors are working on getting these applications for the mass market (read this " your mother and father"), the number of applications that run on Microsoft platforms have been estimated as high as 35,000. SunOS has an estimated 10,000 applications, with other 'commercial UNIX" systems (including Solaris 2.x) much lower in number. It will take the Linux vendors a long time to get the number of applications necessary to hit the really large mass market, particularly if they did not depend on iBCS2 and DOS/Windows compatibility (which could supply a fair number of current applications), but depended on "native" Linux applications.

So applications are king (and queen) for the mass market, and installed base (volume) or the promise of explosive growth (volume) is the key to these. But is the mass market the only "commercial" market? The answer is "no". The mass market is a subset (albeit very large one) of the commercial market. So let's look at what the rest of the commercial market needs. We will look at this by segmenting the market into:

- turnkey systems
- large end-user customers
- specialized markets

5.1 Turnkey systems

When I speak of turnkey systems I typically mean a computer system that has one specific (or not so specific) application that runs on it. Examples of turnkey systems are point-of-sale terminals, reservation systems, CAD systems, etc. But in a larger sense, other applications such as Web servers, nameservers (such as

BIND), etc. could also be considered "turnkey", since they have only a few necessary programs that have to run on the system.

Usually turnkey systems are ones that an Independent Software Vendor (ISV) or Value Added Reseller (VAR) will chose a hardware system, an operating system, port an application to it, then duplicate that system 500 to 1000 times without change to the basic application. These ISVs and VARs will try to chose the lowest cost solution to fit their customer's needs.

Linux is perfect for these types of applications. The operating system is stable enough for the developer to port their application and test the application fully. Once it is fully tested and stable, the entire package is "frozen" and duplicated any number of times for the end customer.

Since the operating system may be freely copied, and it runs on inexpensive hardware, their variable costs are minimal. Even a developer who is not familiar with the Linux system (so they need help getting it running on a platform) will quickly pay back the porting and system programmer costs they accrue by not paying $200-$500. per license for the operating system. Plus they have all the source code for the entire system, in case they run into trouble later on. You can buy a lot of Linux support for $200-$500K.

As I said before, I include Internet Service Providers (ISPs) as part of this "turnkey" environment, for both external internet and internal internet. Why overload your expensive, high-powered, highly complex general-purpose server to do Web serving when a smaller, simpler box can offload it? Why not run your NIS slaves on a Linux box? Or perhaps your BIND server?

In the early days of Digital UNIX (known then as DEC OSF/1) we did not have very many applications. In fact we had none. The marketing staff came to me with sad faces asking if it was possible to sell an operating system that had no applications. I invented a term called "Turbocharging", which allowed a Digital UNIX system using the speed and power of the Alpha processor (as well as the throughput of our networking devices) to offload NIS, NFS, BIND and other services from people's overloaded, slower SPARC machines. We also showed people how they could use the rsh(1) command to allow the Alpha to do a portion of their very CPU intensive processing while delivering the result back to the SPARCs on their desk. This allowed the SPARCs to work more on applications and less on the other "system administration" tasks that they were performing. We sold lots of Digital UNIX systems based solely on executing those tasks. Today, of course, Digital UNIX has a lot more applications, and particularly very large memory databases that are extremely fast. But the same principle applies. The database engine runs on the Alpha system, supplying data to the slower SPARC engines as a "Turbocharger". I could see Linux systems headed in the same direction, following the same path.

5.2   Large end-user customers

Very large customers often have their own home-grown applications which they need to deploy across a wide network of people. Or they can have management dictate a certain suite of applications, which then can be ported to Linux. Since these customers are so large, their operating system costs are huge, and utilizing the savings using the Linux operating system they may completely cover the expenses of porting their software.

Or these very large customers may "influence" their layered product providers to port to the Linux platform. Finally, they may even change some of their computing habits (to use existing programs) if the cost savings are enough to warrant it.

Companies like Caldera are creating a suite of applications and approaching these very large customers to show them the operating system savings that they can achieve if they switch to Linux. While it is true that every application the customer could ever conceive of running may not run on Linux, by using the native applications, the iBCS2 applications, the DOSEMU applications, and applications that run under WABI, a nice suite of applications could be built to solve their needs.

5.3   Specialized markets

Finally there are what I call "specialized markets". Markets that might buy Linux simply because it is Linux, and not because of the application suites that it provides.

In the education field there are three main markets:

- administrative
- "campus computing"
- computer science education

The administrative part is the "business" aspect of the market. They are looking for easy-to-use systems that can also handle complex administrative tasks that might cover a community the size of a small city.

The "campus computing" is the supply of computing power and service for majors of all types, web services and research into non-computer science (for example, molecular modeling) research.

Finally there is computer science education, both on the undergraduate and graduate level, as well as research into computer science.

While the administrative sub-market typically relies more on shrink-wrapped applications, the other two rely on them to a lesser extent (with the computer science education market relying the least). The other two markets can utilize a lot more of the freeware and shareware applications that are already ported to Linux. This gives them a very low-cost (from a software perspective) platform while allowing them to see and (often) modify the source code for the applications they use.

More importantly, in the computer science research area, the results of the research can be freely distributed to others working in the field, or even published as source code to illustrate the results. This can not be done with "commercial" operating systems.

Some universities are utilizing Linux more and more to run their campus. From a "commercial" standpoint, their needs are the same as many large businesses. Students graduating from college will know about Linux, and bring the word to their future employers.

Finally, there is the computer hobbyist and software developer market. I relate this market to the amateur radio market. In the amateur radio market the radio is often used to simply talk to other people, but at the same time the users investigate new ways of using radio, and improving it. Many electrical engineers started out as amateur radio users. So it can be with Linux, since for the first time both the prices of the hardware and the prices of the operating system source code are within the reach of mortal people.

In conclusion, I feel that Linux does have the items needed for several types of "commercial" uses:

- stability and quality
- low variable costs for turnkey applications
- explosive growth in volume to attract ISVs

What Linux really needs is for the "commercial" community to understand what is going on, and to embrace it where it will be useful. This will increase the volume numbers even more, which will attract more applications.

Along these lines I would like to "advertise" a joint effort of USENIX and Linux International to happen in January of 1997 in Anaheim, California of the United States. There will be a joint USENIX/Linux development conference, and while a certain part of the Linux conference will be oriented towards the development of the Linux operating system, the bulk of the conference will be oriented towards application developers and marketing people, to better understand the Linux operating system and how to sell their applications and services into the Linux market. We hope to show ISVs, VARs, resellers and distributors how they can make money by selling their applications and services on top of the Linux operating system.

5.4   Biography

Jon "maddog" Hall is a Senior Leader in the Digital Equipment Corporation UNIX group. He has been in the computer industry for twenty-five years, UNIX for sixteen years and has guided the emergence of six operating systems, including Alpha Linux. He has an MS in Computer Science.

6   Website Development

6.1   ASWedit, HTML editor

Description:

ASWedit is a commercial, comprehensive and easy to use HTML and text editor for X Window System and Motif. It offers three independent modes: a plain text editing mode and two context-sensitive, validating modes for authoring of HTML documents as used on the Internet and Intranets. The two HTML modes are: standard and experimental.

Distribution media:

3.5" diskettes, 4-mm DAT, 1/4" and 8mm tapes, Internet (FTP).

Licensing policy:

Per machine basis. The number of users that can run the software on the licensed computer is unlimited.

A version of the program, called asWedit, is available for free for students and staff in education and charitable non-profit organizations, and for free evaluation by individuals and commercial organizations. It is available via FTP from many archives. See *http://www.advasoft.com/asWedit.html* <http://www.advasoft.com/asWedit.html> for details.

OS provisions:

Linux 1.2.13 or higher (ELF), X11R6, Motif 2.0 (not required if the statically linked version is used), 5 MB of RAM, 1.5-3.5 MB hard disk usage.

Documentation:

Printed documentation, online help, language: User's Guide (44 pages), HTML 3.2 extended, Reference Manual (89 pages), HTML 3.2 experimental, Reference Manual (106 pages). Online, context sensitive, hypertext help - 560 KB. Localized resource files are available for the following languages: English (default), Czech, Danish, Dutch, French, German, Polish, Portuguese, Spanish and Swedish. Commands and messages are localized for each language but the online help and documentation are only available in English.

Product support:

The license includes free product upgrades by FTP for a period of one year.

Extra features and add-ons:

Can work with external Unix filters. Highly customizable. Supports four different browsers for previewing.

Available since:

July, 1995.

Countries with distribution:

World wide.

Price range:

US$149. Quantity discounts are available.

Vendor:

AdvaSoft Ltd.

    30 Hatch Road
    London SW16 4PN
    England

Phone:

+44 181 251 0033

Fax:

+44 181 251 0011

EMail:

as@advasoft.com `<mailto:as@advasoft.com>`

URL:

http://www.advasoft.com `<http://www.advasoft.com>`

Contact:

Andre Stochniol

6.2 Empress DataWEB

Description:

Empress DataWEB allows users to easily and rapidly build dynamic, interactive, database-fed web applications. No special programming language needs to be learned; developers of applications simply can use HTML with the Empress extensions for accessing the RDBMS.

Distribution media:

CD-ROM.

Licensing policy:

Please contact vendor for evaluation copies.

OS provisions:

16 MB of RAM; 60 MB harddisk space (additional requirements: web browser required).

Documentation:

Online help.

Product support:

Full technical support available, priced separately.

Extra features and add-ons:

Extra features such as an HTTP server and other tools to facilitate the creation of web applications come with the software package.

Available since:

April, 1996.

Countries with distribution:

World wide.

Price range:

Please contact vendor.

Vendor:

Empress Software Inc.

6401 Golden Triangle Drive
Greenbelt, MD 20770
U.S.A.

3100 Steeles Avenue East
Markham, ON L3R 8T3
Canada

Phone:

+1 301 220 1919 (USA), +1 905 513 8888 (Canada)

Fax:

+1 301 220 1919 (USA), +1 905 513 1668 (Canada)

EMail:

sales@empress.com `<mailto:sales@empress.com>`

URL:

http://www.empress.com `<http://www.empress.com>`

Contact:

Dick Naedel

6.3 EZ-EDIT

Description:

EZ-EDIT is an online HTML editor, which allows users to completly manage their web site through a web browser (edit, create, upload, rename/move/copy, create and remove directories)! EZ-EDIT is the only editor which features the "File Filter" which allows you to specify what file types are allowed on your system. Create the look you want by editing EZ-EDIT's 16 template files with over 80 tags. Also allows you to set disk space limits! Supports form based file uploads, also includes a Java page creater. All administration is also done through a web browser.

Distribution media:

3.5" diskettes, Internet (FTP and WWW).

Licensing policy:

A free demo is available from our *web site* `<http://www.relative-web.com/dynamic/ez-edit>`. Demo version is unlocked to full version with registration key.

OS provisions:

Linux/Intel.

Documentation:

Online HTML user and admin manuals (English only).

Product support:

Update service, support (via EMail).

Available since:

September 17, 1997.

Countries with distribution:

World wide.

Price range:

US$149.95.

Vendor:

Relative Web

    P. O. Box 351
    Saylorsburg, PA 18353-0351
    U.S.A.

Phone:

+1 610 381 3072

Fax:

+1 610 381 3072

EMail:

ez-edit@relative-web.com `<mailto:ez-edit@relative-web.com>`

URL:

http://www.relative-web.com/dynamic/ez-edit/   `<http://www.relative-web.com/dynamic/`
`ez-edit/>`

Contact:

John Bergeron

6.4   LinkScan

Description:

LinkScan operates on Unix an NT servers on both Internets and Intranets, LinkScan can test over 40,000 links per hour because it is the only link checker that uses multi-threaded simultaneous processing. LinkScan has been tested on web sites with over 45,000 pages and more than 80,000 links. LinkScan also produces two revolutionary types of maps of web sites. LinkScan's SiteMap enables the user to produce a site map that includes every link on a web site arranged in a hierarchical format that resembles a book's table of contents. LinkScan's TapMap is an expandable and collapsible site map that allows viewers to tap down through the various and multiple levels of a web site to quickly and easily navigate and explore the web site by tapping on a few control icons.

Distribution media:

Internet (WWW).

Licensing policy:

A license is required for each server on which the product is used. Free evaluation copies of LinkScan may be downloaded from our *web site* `<http://www.elsop.com>`.

OS provisions:

Requires Perl 5 or higher.

Documentation:

Complete documentation and a comprehensive FAQ may be read at our web site and/or downloaded.

Product support:

This product is continuously updated and maintained. Prompt responses to all inquiries and problems via EMail or telephone as required. No fees for support.

Available since:

January 7, 1997.

Countries with distribution:

World wide.

Price range:

US$495.

Vendor:

Electronic Software Publishing Corporation

        1504 #8-00200 Main Street
        Gardnerville, NV 89410-5273
        U.S.A.

EMail:

ken@elsop.com <mailto:ken@elsop.com>

URL:

http://www.elsop.com <http://www.elsop.com>

Contact:

Ken Churilla

6.5   TalentSoft Web+ (WebPlus)

Description:

TalentSoft Web+ is a development tool dedicated to developing web-based client/server applications without writing low level CGI programs. Web+ enables rapid and easy creation of highly functional web pages which integrates with databases, file systems, EMail, Java applets, your legacy applications (EXEs, DLLs), and communicates with other TCP/IP applications using sockets. Web+ works with all popular web severs, databases, and operating systems and integrates closely with Netscape web servers via NSAPI and CGI. Web+ also acts as a multi-threaded web middleware that integrates the web servers with databases, EMail, TCP/IP sockets, and other applications. Please check out the "Teach Me Web+" link on our *web site* <http://www.TalentSoft.com> for the coolest interactive tutorial with hands on exercises. We are proud to be the first to provide dynamic code interpretation on the Internet! Now you may start writing and running your own web application without buying or installing Web+.

Distribution media:

3.5" diskettes, CD-ROM and Internet (FTP and WWW).

Licensing policy:

Free evluation copy available at *http://www.TalentSoft.com* <http://www.TalentSoft.com>. Trial out version notices displayed by will not time out.

OS provisions:

16 MB RAM, 5 MB HD.

Documentation:

Both printed documentation (about 200 pages) and HTML online help. English only.

Product support:

Free EMail, web+ conference, and phone support. Training available for a fee.

Available since:

May 1, 1997.

Countries with distribution:

USA, UK, Hong Kong, China, Singapore.

Price range:

US$195 to $1295.

Vendor:

TalentSoft / Talent Information Management, LLC.

> ```
> 900 Nicollet Mall, Suite 700
> Minneapolis, MN 55402
> U.S.A.
> ```
>
> ```
> P.O. Box 2997
> Minneapolis, MN 55402
> U.S.A.
> ```

Phone:

+1 612 338 8900

Fax:

+1 612 904 0010

EMail:

info@TalentSoft.com `<mailto:info@TalentSoft.com>`

URL:

http://www.TalentSoft.com `<http://www.TalentSoft.com>`

Contact:

Victor Tong, Ian Gorrie, Jeff Persche, Tony Tong

6.6 VirtuFlex 1.1

Description:

VirtuFlex 1.1 is a web application builder for adding dynamic functionality to a web site. VirtuFlex provides the power to transform web sites into live applications by integrating databases, fax, EMail and pagers with the web. VirtuFlex provides sophisticated functionality that can be added to web sites by any HTML developer. VirtuFlex is reusable, modular, easy to use, high performance and provides DB connectivity almost any database. The componenets of VirtuFlex are a macro language, macro processor, DB server and pre-built template packs.

Distribution media:

Internet (WWW).

Licensing policy:

VirtuFLex is licensed on a per domain basis. A free evaluation copy is available on our *web site* `<http://www.virtuflex.com>`.

OS provisions:

Linux ELF binary format (1.2.x kernels or higher). VirtuFlex runs on standard Unix workstations with 8 MB of RAM minimum, 16 MB recommended.

Documentation:

Available for download from our web site, English.

Product support:

Basic support four hours. Other support options available - call for details.

Extra features and add-ons:

Pre-built Template-Paks come free with VirtuFlex for shopping carts, threaded discussion groups, database application builder, quizzes and surveys, web spiders and banner rotators. Additional Template-Paks are added on a regular basis.

Available since:

   1996.

Countries with distribution:

   World wide through UniDirect, Soft Export and the Internet.

Price range:

   US$995, educational discounts available.

Vendor:

   VirtuFlex Software Corp.

   ```
   930 Massachusetts Ave.
   Cambridge, MA 02139
   U.S.A.
   ```

Phone:

   +1 617 497 8006

Fax:

   +1 617 492 0486

EMail:

   comments@virtuflex.com `<mailto:comments@virtuflex.com>`

URL:

   http://www.virtuflex.com `<http://www.virtuflex.com>`

Contact:

   Dan Housman

6.7   Visual prolog

Description:

   One of the worlds strongest prolog development environments.

Distribution media:

   CD-ROM and Internet (WWW).

Documentation:

   Manuals supplied on CD-ROM, online help and intro.html lots of examples.

Product support:

   EMail based.

Available since:

   1984.

Countries with distribution:

   World wide.

Vendor:

   Prolog Development Center

   ```
   H.J. Holstvej 3-5A
   DK-2605 Broendby
   Dankmark
   ```

Phone:

+45 36 72 10 22

Fax:

+45 36 72 02 69

EMail:

sales@pdc.dk <mailto:sales@pdc.dk>

URL:

http://www.pdc.dk <http://www.pdc.dk>

Contact:

Claus Witfelt <*witfelt@pdc.dk*> <mailto:witfelt@pdc.dk>

6.8   Web Crossing

Description:

Online conferencing server for the Intranet and Extranet and world wide web providing discussion forums and chat rooms. Web Crossing is a groupware application server, accessible with any web browser, via most web servers. It makes communication more efficient and productive than newsgroups or EMail mailing lists.

Distribution media:

Internet.

Licensing policy:

commercial; fully-functional demo available.

Price range:

US$995, unlimited users.

Vendor:

Lundeen & Associates

        P.O. Box 2900
        Alameda, CA 94501
        U.S.A.

Phone:

+1 510 521 5855

Fax:

+1 510 522 6647

EMail:

sales@lundeen.com <mailto:sales@lundeen.com>

URL:

http://webcrossing.com <http://webcrossing.com>

6.9   ThreadTrack and WebTailor from Webthreads.

Description:

ThreadTrack and WebTailor are lightweight browser and server independent CGI script packages, developed under Linux, that add state to web servers. ThreadTrack is used for tracking the activity of individual visitors to a web site, and WebTailor is used to dynamically modify the content of a web site in response to a visitor's profile or actions.

WebTailor uses a simple server-side scripting language to modify the site's content. The language, targeted to non-technical web designers, is easy to learn and use. For the more technical, the CGI interface has been expanded to enable parameter passing on a per visitor basis between scripts running on different pages.

ThreadTrack tags individual visitors to a web site with a unique identifier that remains with them for their visit. Each visitor's session is recorded click-by-click, so a database of aggregate and individual activity is available for reports. Comprehensive reporting is included, and the data (dBase III) is easily transferrable to custom reporting packages.

Distribution media:

Internet (WWW).

Licensing policy:

30 Day fully functional eval available from *http://www.webthreads.com* <http://www.webthreads.com>

OS provisions:

Any version of Linux on x86, a.out and ELF.

Documentation:

Web site and online provided with the package.

Product support:

EMail support.

Extra features and add-ons:

Msql interface. Registration site management addition.

Available since:

June, 1996.

Countries with distribution:

World wide.

Price range:

ThreadTrack starts at US$295. WebTailor starts at US$895.

Vendor:

Webthreads, L.L.C.

        1919 Gallows Road, 10th floor
        Vienna, VA 22182
        U.S.A.

Phone:

+1 703 848 9027

Fax:

+1 703 848 2444

EMail:

info@webthreads.com <mailto:info@webthreads.com>

URL:

http://www.webthreads.com <http://www.webthreads.com>

Contact:

Gavin Sutcliffe

7   Databases

7.1   c-tree Plus

Description:

Based on advanced B+tree (balanced) algorithm, c-tree Plus API handles all aspects of database I/O. Program single user or multi-user non-server applications royalty free and migrate existing c-tree Plus applications to the FairCom Server by recompiling.

Distribution media:

3.5" diskettes and CD-ROM.

Licensing policy:

c-tree Plus is licensed on a per programmer basis. Single-user, multi-user and multi-user non-server royalty-free distribution. Contact FairCom for possible restrictions: general purpose database and application development systems prohibited.

OS provisions:

3 MB hard drive space; 128 KB of RAM.

Documentation:

Printed manuals distributed with product; full online documentation with CD-ROM, available in English and Japanese.

Product support:

Three months of full technical support from purchase date. Unlimited technical support and product updates available thereafter with c-tree Plus maintenance program.

Available since:

October, 1995.

Countries with distribution:

World wide.

Price range:

US$895 includes source.

Vendor:

FairCom

> 4006 W. Broadway
> Columbia, MO 65203-0100
> U.S.A.

Phone:

+1 573 445 6833

Fax:

+1 573 445 9698

EMail:

Faircom@faircom.com `<mailto:Faircom@faircom.com>`

URL:

http://www.faircom.com `<http://www.faircom.com>`

Contact:

Tamra Brown *<tami@faircom.com>* `<mailto:tami@faircom.com>`

Vendor:

FairCom Europe

      Via Patrioti 6
      I-24021 Albino
      Italy

Phone:

+39 35 773 464

Fax:

+39 35 773 806

EMail:

Europe@faircom.com <mailto:Europe@faircom.com>

Vendor:

FairCom Japan

      Ikeda Bldg. #3 4F, 112-5
      Komei-chou, Tsu-city MIE 514
      Japan

Phone:

+81 059 229 7504

Fax:

+81 059 249 723

Vendor:

FairCom do Brasil Ltda.

Phone:

+55 14 224 1610

Fax:

+55 14 234 6462

EMail:

Brazil@faircom.com <mailto:Brazil@faircom.com>

7.2 Empress

Description:

Empress for Linux is a multimedia RDBMS for members of the rapidly growing Linux developer community. Key components of the package include the powerful Empress RDBMS as well as dynamic SQL, Empress 4GL, Empress GUI Builder for rapidly developing graphical front-ends to Empress applications, a WWW HTML toolkit, and a grahical point and click interface to the Empress RDBMS development environment. A streamlined, single-user version of this product, Personal Empress for Linux, is available also.

Distribution media:

3.5" diskettes.

Licensing policy:

Free demos are available via FTP. Must contact vendor.

OS provisions:

Empress GUI Builder requires OSF Motif version 1.2.4 or 2.0. 16 MB RAM. 80 MB Disk Space. 486 CPU or better.

Documentation:

Printed documentation.

Product support:

Full technical support available, priced separately.

Extra features and add-ons:

Other features which are components of the package include shared libraries, shared memory, math library functions and a C language interface.

Available since:

December, 1995.

Countries with distribution:

World wide.

Price range:

Product is priced by number of concurrent users. Please contact vendor.

Vendor:

Empress Software Inc.

    6401 Golden Triangle Drive
    Greenbelt, MD 20770
    U.S.A.

    3100 Steeles Avenue East
    Markham, ON L3R 8T3
    Canada

Phone:

+1 301 220 1919 (USA), +1 905 513 8888 (Canada)

Fax:

+1 301 220 1919 (USA), +1 905 513 1668 (Canada)

EMail:

sales@empress.com <mailto:sales@empress.com>

URL:

http://www.empress.com <http://www.empress.com>

Contact:

Dick Naedel

7.3   Essentia

Description:

Database Engine.

Some Features: Remote databases, client/server, automatic consistency check, incremental backup, mirroring, shadowing, distributable database, journaling, versions, RISE, object oriented DBMS, implements relational model three tier client/server architecture, cooperative servers, language independent user-configurable (English, Spanish, Portuguese).

Distribution media:

4/8 mm. DAT, 150/525 MB tape. Academic version available from:

- *ftp://ftp.inter-soft.com* `<ftp://ftp.inter-soft.com>`
- *http://www.inter-soft.com/html/products/essentia*   `<http://www.inter-soft.com/html/ products/essentia>`

Licensing policy:

Commercial. Free version for Linux available.

OS provisions:

10 MB disk space.

Documentation:

Available in PostScript and HTML.

Product support:

Contact *essentia-info@inter-soft.com* `<mailto:essentia-info@inter-soft.com>` for more information.

Extra features and add-ons:

SQL Server, ODBC Interface for Windows, JDBC Interface, User servers.

Available since:

1993.

Countries with distribution:

Argentina, Brazil, Russia, Mexico, Venezuela and USA.

Price range:

Linux version for free (with some restrictions). Other prices available on request.

Vendor:

InterSoft Argentina S.A.

```
Córdoba 883 9th. Floor
Capital Federal (1054)
Argentina
```

Phone:

+54 1 318 8900

Fax:

+54 1 318 8997

EMail:

info@inter-soft.com `<mailto:info@inter-soft.com>`

URL:

http://www.inter-soft.com `<http://www.inter-soft.com>`

7.4   FairCom Server

Description:

High-performance, multi-threaded, transaction processing server. Features include: industrial quality transaction processing, including full commit and rollback; intermediate save points and complete logging; automatic log management; restart/disaster recovery; user passwords; access security and online administration; deadlock detection/resolution; read/write locks at the record/individual key level; more.

Distribution media:

3.5" diskettes and CD-ROM.

Licensing policy:

The FairCom Server is licensed on a per machine basis. Contact FairCom for specific licensing questions.

OS provisions:

2 MB of RAM.

Documentation:

Printed manuals distributed with product; full online documentation with CD-ROM, available in English and Japanese.

Product support:

Three months of full technical support from purchase date. Unlimited technical support and product updates available thereafter with Server maintenance program.

Available since:

October, 1995.

Countries with distribution:

World wide.

Price range:

US$445-$6795 depending upon platform and number of users. Special licensing and OEM agreements available.

Vendor:

FairCom

```
4006 W. Broadway
Columbia, MO 65203-0100
U.S.A.
```

Phone:

+1 573 445 6833

Fax:

+1 573 445 9698

EMail:

Faircom@faircom.com `<mailto:Faircom@faircom.com>`

URL:

http://www.faircom.com `<http://www.faircom.com>`

Contact:

Tamra Brown *<tami@faircom.com>* `<mailto:tami@faircom.com>`

Vendor:

FairCom Europe

```
Via Patrioti 6
I-24021 Albino
Italy
```

Phone:

+39 35 773 464

Fax:

+39 35 773 806

EMail:

Europe@faircom.com <mailto:Europe@faircom.com>

Vendor:

FairCom Japan

        Ikeda Bldg. #3 4F, 112-5
        Komei-chou, Tsu-city MIE 514
        Japan

Phone:

+81 059 229 7504

Fax:

+81 059 249 723

Vendor:

FairCom do Brasil Ltda.

Phone:

+55 14 224 1610

Fax:

+55 14 234 6462

EMail:

Brazil@faircom.com <mailto:Brazil@faircom.com>

7.5 Just Logic/SQL

Description:

Relational Database Management System

Distribution media:

3.5" diskettes.

Licensing policy:

Unlimited runtime included.

Documentation:

Printed manual, examples.

Product support:

EMail, fax or phone.

Extra features and add-ons:

- client-server option: lets run applications on several computers running Windows or Linux, that access a central database on a Linux system.

- web-enabling option: passthrough between an HTTP Web server and a Just Logic/SQL database. No C or Perl required. SQL commands are embedded directly within HTML files. Compatible with Netscape, Apache, NCSA and all other CGI-compliant HTTP servers.

Available since:

1993.

Countries with distribution:

World wide.

Price range:

US$149-$395.

Vendor:

Just Logic Technologies

> P.O. Box 63050, 40 Commerce St.
> Nun's Island, Montreal, QC H3E 1V6
> Canada

Phone:

+1 514 761 6887

Fax:

+1 514 642 6480

EMail:

sales@justlogic.com <mailto:sales@justlogic.com>

URL:

http://www.justlogic.com <http://www.justlogic.com>

Contact:

Luc Vallieres

7.6 KE Texpress

Description:

KE Texpress is a high-speed client server database engine that supports object-oriented, relational and free text data structures and operations. It is particularly suited to applications with large data sets, complex operations and large numbers of concurrent users. KE Texpress is used for a wide variety WWW database applications. Vertical applications include collections management, library systems, vital statistics, archives, text retrieval and records management.

Distribution media:

Internet (FTP and WWW) and tape.

Licensing policy:

Commercial product licensed by number of concurrent users. A 30 day free trial is available at our *web site* <http://www.kesoftware.com>.

OS provisions:

Linux ELF and a.out libraries. Requires about 30 MB disk space. Runs on over 20 other varieties of Unix and Windows NT.

Documentation:

Printed and HTML documentation is available.

Product support:

Annual technical support (EMail, fax and phone) and software maintenance contracts.

Extra features and add-ons:

- Texhtml WWW module - publish KE Texpress databases on the web
- Texql - SQL-like structured query language

- TexAPI - applications programming interface with client libraries for Windows (C, C++ and VB), Unix and Macintosh System 7
- TexODBC - ODBC drivers for Windows

KE Software has an extensive consulting service assisting clients to develop KE Texpress database applications.

Available since:

1984.

Countries with distribution:

USA, Canada, Australia, Hong Kong, Japan and Malaysia.

Price range:

US$2,000 to $100,000+.

Vendor:

KE Software Inc.

```
303-601 West Broadway
Vancouver, BC V5Z 4C2
Canada
```

Phone:

+1 604 877 1960

Fax:

+1 604 877 1961

EMail:

info@kesoftware.com <mailto:info@kesoftware.com>

URL:

http://www.kesoftware.com <http://www.kesoftware.com>

Contact:

Andrzej Kowalski

7.7   Qddb

Description:

Qddb is fast, powerful and flexible database software that runs on Unix. Some of its features include: Tcl/Tk programming interface, easy to use, you can have a DB application completely up and, running in about 5 minutes, using nxqddb. CGI interface for quick and easy online databases and guestbooks. Fast, and powerful searching capability. Report generator. Barcharts and graphs. Mass mailings with EMail, letters and postcards.

Distribution media:

3.5" diskettes, tape and Internet (FTP and WWW).

Licensing policy:

GNU and Commercial versions available.

OS provisions:

GNU version comes with source code.   Binary packages available for Linux, FreeBSD, and BSD/OS(BSDI) — RPM and buildkit format.

Documentation:

Online documentation and PostScript files available. Printed manuals also available upon request.

Product support:

User and programmer support available along with upgrade contracts.

Extra features and add-ons:

Tcl/Tk programming interface, CGI interface, report generator, many useful free and commercial applications built with Qddb.

Available since:

1996.

Countries with distribution:

World wide.

Price range:

See *http://www.hsdi.com/orders* `<http://www.hsdi.com/orders>`

Vendor:

Herrin Software Development, Inc.

```
41 South Highland Avenue
Prestonsburg, KY 41653
U.S.A.
```

Phone:

+1 606 886 8202

Fax:

+1 606 277 3239

EMail:

info@hsdi.com `<mailto:info@hsdi.com>`

URL:

http://www.hsdi.com `<http://www.hsdi.com>`

Contact:

Eric Herrin

7.8   Raima Database Manager++

Description:

Low-level high performance database engine with C API and C++ class library, for embedding in applications. This database is used in thousands of leading commercial applications. Includes source for C++ class library that encapsulates database navigation and object storage and retrieval into C++ classes, adding an object-oriented interface. Supports multiple database models, including relational, network model, and combined.

Distribution media:

3.5" diskettes and tape.

Licensing policy:

Pay for development license, distribute runtime copies freely.

Documentation:

Extensive documentation available from Raima Corporation, dealing with all aspects of database, C API and C++ class library.

Product support:

Available from Raima Corporation on annual basis, raining available.

Extra features and add-ons:

Windows GUI Report Writer.

Available since:

1984, originally called db_VISTA.

Countries with distribution:

Direct in the USA, use distributors internationally - Germany, England, France, Italy, Spain, Netherlands, Russia, Estonia, Argentina, Columbia, Singapore, Malaysia, Australia, Finland, Taiwan, other countries.

Price range:

RDM++ Database Module is US$995 for single user, US$2,395 for multi-user. System is US$1,395 for single user, US$3,395 for multi-user (System includes RDM++ database, QUERY SQL query tool and REVISE database restructuring tool). All versions available with source code for extra cost.

Depends on machine class; lowest is US$3,995 without system utilities; US$6,195 with system utilities.

Vendor:

Raima Corporation

```
    4800 Columbia Center
    701 5th Avenue
    Seattle, WA 98104
```

Phone:

+1 800 327 2462, +1 206 515 9477

Fax:

+1 206 748 5200

EMail:

sales@raima.com <mailto:sales@raima.com>

URL:

http://www.raima.com <http://www.raima.com>

Contact:

Dave Morse

7.9 Empress Embedded RDBMS

Description:

The Empress Embedded RDBMS is an embedded systems developer's toolkit. The RDBMS engine is fast, compact and easy-to-embed. Additionally, this package possesses superior bulk object handling capabilities. Embedded Empress RDBMS is Internet ready with a JDBC/ODBC bridge available.

Distribution media:

3.5" diskettes.

Licensing policy:

Please contact vendor for evaluations copies.

OS provisions:

32 MB of RAM, 60 MB disk disk space.

Documentation:

Printed documentation.

Product support:

Full technical support available, priced separately.

Extra features and add-ons:

Extra features included with the toolkit are Empress Report Writer and enhanced Internet capabilities (ability to use Java applets, etc.) via the HTML toolkit.

Available since:

January, 1997.

Countries with distribution:

World wide.

Price range:

Starting at US$1000 for PCs, US$4000 for typical workstations, US$16,000 for mid-range servers.

Vendor:

Empress Software Inc.

```
6401 Golden Triangle Drive
Greenbelt, MD 20770
U.S.A.

3100 Steeles Avenue East
Markham, ON L3R 8T3
Canada
```

Phone:

+1 301 220 1919 (USA), +1 905 513 8888 (Canada)

Fax:

+1 301 220 1919 (USA), +1 905 513 1668 (Canada)

EMail:

sales@empress.com `<mailto:sales@empress.com>`

URL:

http://www.empress.com `<http://www.empress.com>`

Contact:

Dick Naedel

7.10 SOLID Server

Description:

SOLID Server is a database engine for new applications and products. It is extremely easy to set up, and has a small footprint. SOLID Server is standards-compliant and full of power. It is perfectly suited for distributed use in countless copies. Its maintenance is care-free, requiring minimal or no administrator attention.

Distribution media:

3.5" diskettes and Internet (FTP and WWW).

Licensing policy:

Copy-protected.

OS provisions:

At least 2 MB RAM, recommended are 8 MB; harddisk about 3-4 MB.

Documentation:

English manuals and online help. WWW.

Product support:

Available.

Available since:

1994.

Countries with distribution:

World wide.

Price range:

SOLID Desktop US$99, SOLID Server US$199/seat, SOLID Web Engine US$495.

Vendor:

Solid Information Technology Ltd

        Huovitie 3
        FIN-00400 Helsinki
        Finland

Phone:

+358 9 477 4730

Fax:

+358 9 477 47 390

EMail:

info@solidtech.com `<mailto:info@solidtech.com>`

URL:

http://www.solidtech.com `<http://www.solidtech.com>`

7.11   Velocis Database Server

Description:

Velocis Database Server is designed for database application developers who are looking for a high performance client/server or web database engine. Velocis is a scaleable SQL client/server database engine that provides a rich set of architectural choices and APIs including ANSI SQL, SQL C-API, low-level C-API, C++ class libraries, and support for custom APIs. Unlike typical relational client/server database products, Velocis supports both relational and pointer-based network model databases in any combination as well as processing on either side of the client/server equation. The choices of multiple operating platforms, APIs, processing locality (client or server), and database model can be mixed and combined to satisfy the performance requirements of virtually any application.

Distribution media:

3.5" diskettes and tape.

Licensing policy:

Pay for development license. Runtimes are requires to distribute applications.

Documentation:

Extensive documentation available from Raima Corporation, dealing with all aspects of database, C API and C++ class library.

Product support:
Available from Raima Corporation on annual basis, raining available.

Extra features and add-ons:
Windows GUI Report Writer, Raima Object Manager.

Available since:
1993, originally called Raima Database Server.

Countries with distribution:
World wide.

Price range:
1-8 users: US$1,995, 1-25 users: US$3,995, unlimited: US$8,995.

Vendor:
Raima Corporation

> 4800 Columbia Center
> 701 5th Avenue
> Seattle, WA 98104

Phone:
+1 800 327 2462, +1 206 515 9477

Fax:
+1 206 748 5200

EMail:
sales@raima.com <mailto:sales@raima.com>

URL:
http://www.raima.com <http://www.raima.com>

Contact:
Dave Morse

7.12   Yard SQL

Description:
The YARD company offers the following products:

- YARD-SQL – Relational SQL client/server database with compliance to X/Open XPG4 and ANSI SQL 92 including network support for accessing remote databases
- YARD-ESQLC – Embedded SQL for C
- YARD-ODBC – ODBC interface for MS Windows clients
- YARD-X – Motif client for database access (No development tool)
- YARD-JDBC – Java Interface

Distribution media:
CD-ROM and Internet (FTP).

Licensing policy:
License number and activation key for each product and installation with user dependent licenses. A Private Edition (limited to 1 user and 5 MB database) for non commercial private use and for evaluation is available at *ftp://ftp.yard.de* <ftp://ftp.yard.de>.

OS provisions:

Linux ELF version; RAM usage: 1 MB (minimum) for shared memory, 500 KB per user. Disk usage: YARD-SQL 10 MB, YARD-ESQLC 1 MB, YARD-ODBC 1.5 MB and YARD-X 5 MB.

Documentation:

Printed 600 pages reference and users guide in German. English documentation is available only as PostScript file.

Product support:

Upon request.

Extra features and add-ons:

All products also available for other widely distributed Unix systems (e.g. SCO Unix, SPARC Solaris, IBM, HP, SGI).

Available since:

January, 1994.

Countries with distribution:

Contact YARD Software GmbH for information about resellers.

Price range:

Upon request.

Vendor:

YARD Software GmbH

```
Wikingerstr. 18
D-51107 Köln
Germany
```

Fax:

+49 221 98664 99

EMail:

yard@yard.de `<mailto:yard@yard.de>`

URL:

http://www.yard.de `<http://www.yard.de>`

FTP:

ftp://ftp.yard.de `<ftp://ftp.yard.de>`

Contact:

Thomas Schonhoven *<thomass@yard.de>* `<mailto:thomass@yard.de>`

8 Data Visualisation and CAD

8.1 IDL (Interactive Data Language)

Description:

IDL is powerful software for data analysis, visualization, and application development. IDL's features include flexible I/O, object-oriented programming, 2D plotting, 3D graphics, volume rendering, image processing, mathematics, statistics, a cross-platform GUI toolkit, plus a high-level, array-oriented programming language. Use IDL for visual data analysis, rapid prototyping, or application development.

IDL programs, including their graphical user interfaces, are portable across Linux, Windows 3.11, Windows 95, Windows NT, Mac, PowerMac, Unix and VMS.

The IDL-Student Version is a functionality-limited version of IDL 5.0. It is designed to compliment IDL-teaching lab environments and give students access to software specifically designed for technical curriculums including physics, astronomy, engineering, earth sciences, medical sciences and computer science. For more information or to place an order, visit our *web site* `<http://www.rsinc.com>`.

Distribution media:

CD-ROM and Internet (FTP).

Licensing policy:

Free demo CD-ROM available or download via FTP.

OS provisions:

IDL 5.0 for Linux is built using the Linux 2.0.18 kernel and the Red Hat version 4.0 Linux distribution.

Documentation:

3000+ pages of documentation on paper and hypertext online help.

Product support:

Customer support service, maintenance/update service, training and consulting are available. In addition, a *Usenet group* `<news:comp.lang.idl-pvwave>` is devoted to IDL.

Extra features and add-ons:

ENVI: remote sensing image processing application, DataMiner: ODBC database access, HDF, CDF, netCDF support, animation, volume slicer, high resolution mapping.

Available since:

May, 1997.

Countries with distribution:

Ask vendor.

Price range:

Contact vendor/distributor.

Vendor:

Research Systems, Inc.

> 2995 Wilderness Place
> Boulder, CO 80301
> U.S.A.

Phone:

+1 303 786 9900

Fax:

+1 303 786 9909

EMail:

info@rsinc.com `<mailto:info@rsinc.com>`

URL:

http://www.rsinc.com `<http://www.rsinc.com>`

FTP:

ftp://ftp.rsinc.com `<ftp://ftp.rsinc.com>`

8.2   Megahedron

Description:

A flexible and powerful 3D graphics engine controlled by a high-level interpreted language called SMPL. With it, you can learn about 3D, write your own interactive simulations, animations, and ray-tracings. You can even write your own shaders, customize procedural objects and motions, and use up to 64 computers at once for net rendering. Includes executables for Windows 95, Windows NT x86 and Alpha, SGI Irix and Linux.

Distribution media:

CD-ROM, ISO-9660 and Rock Ridge.

Licensing policy:

Very flexible. The owner is allowed to run as many copies as they can, on any platforms. Demo version, full documentation and sample images and scripts available on our *web site* <http://www.threedee.com>.

OS provisions:

Supports kernel 1.2.8 or 1.3.15. Non-ELF, a.out executable (QMAGIC). 16 MB of RAM minimum recommended. 7 MB free disk space recommended.

Documentation:

In HTML on CDROM.

Product support:

Private news server, EMail. Patches on web site.

Extra features and add-ons:

Everything included on one CD-ROM.

Available since:

August, 1996.

Countries with distribution:

World wide, direct and through dealers.

Price range:

US$99

Vendor:

Syndesis Corporation

        235 South Main Street
        Jefferson, WI 53549
        U.S.A.

Phone:

+1 414 674 5200

Fax:

+1 414 674 6363

EMail:

syndesis@threedee.com <mailto:syndesis@threedee.com>

URL:

http://www.threedee.com <http://www.threedee.com>

Contact:

John Foust <*jfoust@threedee.com*> <mailto:jfoust@threedee.com>

8.3 Tecplot 7.0

Description:

Tecplot is interactive data visualization software for XY plotting, 2D and 3D mesh, contour, vector, scatter, and shade plots. For more information, see the Amtec Engineering *web site* <http://www.amtec.com>.

Distribution media:

CD-ROM and Internet (FTP).

Licensing policy:

Either personal licenses (node locked) or network licenses. Evaluation copies available on CD-ROM or by anonymous FTP.

OS provisions:

12 MB minimum, Linux 1.2 or newer (available in both statically linked and dynamically linked versions). Use the statically linked version if your system does not have Motif 1.2 or newer installed. 32 MB RAM is recommended.

Documentation:

Printed User's and Reference Manuals, full online help. English.

Product support:

Update and technical support included with license for first three months. Extra charge (ask for EUSS) after that. Training courses available.

Available since:

V7 since September 1996, V6 since August 1993.

Countries with distribution:

Many, see Amtec *web site* <http://www.amtec.com>.

Price range:

US$1795 for personal license, US$2395 for single-user network license, US$1795 for each additional user. All prices the USA and Canada only.

Vendor:

Amtec Engineering, Inc

```
PO Box 3633
Bellevue, WA 98009-3633
U.S.A.
```

Phone:

+1 800 676 7568, +1 425 827 3304

Fax:

+1 425 827 3989

EMail:

tecplot@amtec.com <mailto:tecplot@amtec.com>

URL:

http://www.amtec.com <http://www.amtec.com>

8.4   VARKON

Description:

A high level development tool for CAD and Product modeling applications. Interactive parametric modelling in 2D and 3D with object oriented database. High level CAD and modelling language MBS included.

Distribution media:

Internet (WWW).

Licensing policy:

Free binary for Linux.

OS provisions:

Requires X but not Motif. Needs 3 MB of harddisk for basic installation and 3MB of RAM to run.

Documentation:

400 pages of documentation included in the free version for Linux.

Product support:

Service with continous updates and free consultation available for US $75/month.

Extra features and add-ons:

Additional plotterdrivers available free of charge.

Available since:

July, 1996.

Countries with distribution:

World wide.

Price range:

Linux version is free of charge.

Vendor:

Microform AB

```
        Henningsholmsgatan 4
        S-703 69 Orebro
        Sweden
```

Phone:

+46 19314932

Fax:

+46 19314969

EMail:

info@microform.se <mailto:info@microform.se>

URL:

http://www.microform.se <http://www.microform.se>

Contact:

Johan Kjellander

8.5 XVScan

Description:

Image scanning and manipulation software for HP ScanJet scanners.

Distribution media:

Internet (EMail and FTP). 4mm DDS2 DAT tape or 3.5 diskettes (additional US$15 in the USA, US$25 international).

Licensing policy:

XVScan is based on XV and is not available in demo version due to licensing restrictions. Distributed with full source code.

OS provisions:

Linux, tested with 1.2.x and 2.0.x, requires a recent generic SCSI driver support to be built in (no earlier than 1.1.79). Motif is not required. Any XFree version (X11R5, X11R6).

Documentation:

Online, *WWW* <http://www.tummy.com/xvscan>, English.

Product support:

Updates free for first year.

Extra features and add-ons:

Also available for HP-UX, BSD/OS 2.2 and 3.0, SunOS 4.1.x, Solaris 2.x, and FreeBSD.

Available since:

May, 1995.

Countries with distribution:

World wide.

Price range:

US$50 for FTP or EMail shipping. Additional US$15 for media in the United States, US$15, internationally. Mastercard, Visa and Discover, and American Express Credit Cards accepted.

Vendor:

tummy.com, ltd.

> 3506 Stratton Drive
> Fort Collins, CO 80525-2722
> U.S.A.

Phone:

+1 970 223 8215

Fax:

+1 408 490 2728

EMail:

xvscan@tummy.com <mailto:xvscan@tummy.com>

URL:

http://www.tummy.com/xvscan <http://www.tummy.com/xvscan>

Contact:

Sean Reifschneider *<jafo@tummy.com>* <mailto:jafo@tummy.com> or Evelyn Mitchell *<efm@tummy.com>* <mailto:efm@tummy.com>

9 Development Tools

9.1 ACUCOBOL-GT

Description:

ACUCOBOL-GT is an ANSI-85 COBOL development system with compiler, runtime, debugger, support utilities and documentation. It offers single source hardware independence, GUI COBOL, client/server capabilities, multithreading support, and data source flexibility. Additionally, ACUCOBOL-GT is year 2000 compliant.

Distribution media:

currently 3,5" Diskettes (A CD-ROM is planned for 2Q/98).

Licensing policy:

Runtime license for each installed application including license fees for all products free of charge 30 day evaluation copy available on our *web site* <http://www.acucobol.com>.

OS provisions:

Linux a.out and ELF. Tested on Red Hat Linux 4.1 with kernel version 2.0.30.

Documentation:

Printed documentation for all products (english), online documentation for web evaluation copy.

Product support:

Update service (annual fee is 20% of product list price), training courses for core products (DM 600/day at scheduled dates), technical support included in update service.

Available since:

February, 1995.

Countries with distribution:

World wide.

Price range:

US$1.500 for single user development system (Linux), US$300 for each additional developer, runtime fees on request (price is depending on contract form).

Vendor (Germany):

Acucobol Deutschland GmbH

```
Otto-Hahn-Str. 9
D-61381 Friedrichsdorf
Germany
```

Phone:

+49 6175 93310

Fax:

+49 6175 1429

EMail:

aschmidt@acucobol.de <mailto:aschmidt@acucobol.de>

Contact:

Annette Schmidt

Vendor (USA):

Acucobol, Inc.

7950 Silverton Avenue, Suite #201
San Diego, CA 92126
U.S.A.

Phone:

+1 800 COBOL 85, +1 619 6897220

Fax:

+1 619 566 3071

EMail:

info@acucobol.com <mailto:info@acucobol.com>

URL:

http://www.acucobol.com <http://www.acucobol.com>

Contact:

Jeff Freedman

9.2   Amzi! Prolog & Logic Server

Description:

Amzi! enables the easy integration of intelligent components with conventional applications allowing you to add logic-bases that give advice, configure and tune systems, diagnose problems, apply business rules, monitor processes and parse documents. Your applications access a logic-base of rules just as a database server accesses records. The rules are expressed in Prolog which has powerful, built-in search and pattern matching capabilities. The Amzi! Logic Server is encapsulated as a C++ Class and C API Interface. You can add your own Prolog functions in C/C++. Includes: compiler, listener, debugger, linker, EXE, generator, call-in/call-out Logic Server API, full documentation, comprehensive Prolog tutorial and lots of sample code.

Distribution media:

Internet.

Licensing policy:

The Professional Edition includes an unlimited, royalty-free license. The Personal Edition is limited to distributing applications for non-commercial use only.

OS provisions:

About 350 KB of RAM for typical small application, 3-4 MB disk.

Documentation:

HTML format, includes full Prolog tutorial.

Product support:

Subscription Plus service provides automatic updates for a full year, $198. Custom development services available.

Linux Support:

No Linux system included. For Amzi! software, free tech support for registered users by phone, fax and EMail.

Available since:

November 3, 1995.

Countries with distribution:

World wide.

Price range:

Personal (Shareware), $49. Professional, $298.

Vendor:

Amzi! inc.

        40 Samuel Prescott Drive
        Stow, MA 01775
        U.S.A.

Phone:

+1 508 897 7332

Fax:

+1 508 897 2784

EMail:

info@amzi.com <mailto:info@amzi.com>

URL:

http://www.amzi.com <http://www.amzi.com>

Contact:

Mary Kroening

9.3   Basmark QuickBASIC

Description:

The Basmark QuickBASIC Compiler is a multi-user IBM-PC BASICA, MBASIC and Microsoft Quick-BASIC Compiler designed to provide performance and consistency across a variety of machines (e.g. i386 and i486, Pentium, SPARC, RS/6000, HP PA-RISC) under Unix, AIX, SunOS, Linux, HP-UX and Xenix.

Distribution media:

Internet.

Licensing policy:

Per machine, no run-time restrictions.

OS provisions:

GNU GAS and LD must be installed.

Documentation:

400+ page manual, release and installation notes available in hardcopy form for an additional US$50 (plus shipping).

Product support:

Updates available for US$139 less shipping. Maintenance contracts available.

Extra features and add-ons:

C-ISAM (Informix Inc.) Interface in C source code form. Cost is US$35.

Available since:

December, 1993.

Countries with distribution:

World wide.

Price range:

US$195.

Vendor:

Basmark Corporation

P.O. Box 40450
Cleveland, OH 44140
U.S.A.

Phone:

+1 216 871 8855

Fax:

+1 216 871 9011

EMail:

jgo@basmark.com <mailto:jgo@basmark.com> (for orders)

URL:

http://www.basmark.com <http://www.basmark.com>

Contact:

Joseph O'Toole (for orders)

9.4 Critical Mass CM3

Description:

Systems development compiler and runtime.

Distribution media:

Internet (WWW).

Licensing policy:

Commercial with library source, evaluation licenses available for download at *http://www.cmass.com/cm3* <http://www.cmass.com/cm3>.

OS provisions:

Linux/ELF.

Documentation:

Online.

Product support:

Optional.

Extra features and add-ons:

See *http://www.cmass.com/cm3* <http://www.cmass.com/cm3>

Available since:

May, 1996.

Countries with distribution:

USA.

Price range:

US$479/seat.

Vendor:

Critical Mass, Inc.

```
Critical Mass, Inc.
225R Concord Avenue
Cambridge, MA 02138
U.S.A.
```

Phone:

+1 617 354 6277

Fax:

+1 617 354 5027

EMail:

info@cmass.com `<mailto:info@cmass.com>`

URL:

http://www.cmass.com `<http://www.cmass.com>`

9.5   Dynace

Description:

Dynace (pronounced like "dynasty" without the "t") is a preprocessor, include files and a library which extends the C language with advanced object oriented capabilities, automatic garbage collection and multiple threads. Dynace is designed to solve many of the problems associated with C++ while being easier to learn and containing more flexable object oriented facilities. Dynace is able to add facilities previously only available in languages such as Smalltalk and CLOS without all the overhead normally associated with those environments.

Distribution media:

Internet (WWW); including full C source code.

Licensing policy:

One license per programmer; Applications are royalty free.   Full system is on *http://www.edge.net/algorithms* `<http://www.edge.net/algorithms>`.   Free for non-commercial use.

OS provisions:

Any Linux.

Documentation:

310 pages; in Postscript, HP PCL, or TeX DVI.

Product support:

Dynace-support@edge.net `<mailto:Dynace-support@edge.net>`

Extra features and add-ons:

Complete Windows development system.

Available since:

December, 1993.

Price range:

US$599.

Vendor:

Algorithms Corporation

```
3020 Liberty Hills Drive
Franklin, TN 37067
U.S.A.
```

Phone:

+1 800 566 8991, +1 615 791 1636

Fax:

+1 615 791 7736

EMail:

blake@edge.net `<mailto:blake@edge.net>`

URL:

http://www.edge.net/algorithms `<http://www.edge.net/algorithms>`

Contact:

Blake McBride

9.6   Absoft Fortran 77

Description:

VAX/VMS compatible ANSI Fortran 77 compiler and debugger.

Distribution media:

3.5" diskettes.

Licensing policy:

Single user license; multi-user packages also available.

OS provisions:

Linux 1.2.13.

Documentation:

300+ pages hard copy documentation.

Product support:

No-charge technical support.

Available since:

March, 1996.

Countries with distribution:

World wide.

Price range:

US$525-$2,000.

Vendor:

Absoft Corporation

```
2781 Bond Street
Rochester Hills, MI 48309
U.S.A.
```

Phone:

+1 248 853 0050

Fax:

+1 248 853 0108

EMail:

sales@absoft.com `<mailto:sales@absoft.com>`

URL:

http://www.absoft.com `<http://www.absoft.com>`

Contact:

Wood Lotz

9.7   Finesse

Description:

OSF/Motif GUI for shell scripts.

Distribution media:

Internet (FTP).

Licensing policy:

Finesse is a fully commercial product for other Unixes where nodelocked licenses are possible. The Linux version is freely available via *FTP* `<ftp://ftp.science-computing.de/pub/finesse>`. Floppy medium is DM 90.

OS provisions:

ELF Libraries. X11R6. No Motif required.

Documentation:

PostScript File.

Product support:

No support for free version.

Available since:

May, 1995.

Countries with distribution:

World wide.

Price range:

Free demo. Commercial version with support on request.

Vendor:

science + computing GmbH

        Hagellocher Weg 71
        D-72070 Tübingen
        Germany

Phone:

+49 7071 9457 0

Fax:

+49 7071 9457 27

EMail:

info@science-computing.de `<mailto:info@science-computing.de>`

URL:

http://www.science-computing.de `<http://www.science-computing.de>`

FTP:

ftp://ftp.science-computing.de/pub/finesse `<ftp://ftp.science-computing.de/pub/finesse>`.

Contact:

Olaf Flebbe

9.8 ISE Eiffel

Description:

ISE Eiffel is a seamless object-oriented development environment. ISE Eiffel provides an integrated solution for software developers through pure object-oriented methods, from analysis and design through code generation, maintenance, and reverse engineering.

The components of ISE Eiffel include EiffelBench, EiffelBase, EiffelBuild, EiffelVision, EiffelLex, EiffelParse, EiffelNet, EiffelStore, ObjEdit, EiffelCase, EiffelMath, EiffelWeb, DLE (Dynamic Linking in Eiffel) and SCOOP (Distribution/Concurrency mechanism).

Distribution media:

CD-ROM and Internet (FTP and WWW)

Licensing policy:

No run-time fees are required for products, commercial or otherwise, developed with ISE's technology. In the case of commercial products we simply require the product and its documentation to acknowledge ISE Eiffel clearly. The copyright holder must acknowledge the product's use/incorporation of ISE Eiffel by (a) Featuring "ISE Eiffel" prominently in product documentation, and (b) Featuring an "ISE Eiffel" software window or pop-up message clearly visible during the copyrighted product's installation process.

OS provisions:

Linux ELF or a.out.

Documentation:

Printed documentation. Additional online help.

Product support:

Update service, maintenance, training available.

Available since:

August, 1994.

Countries with distribution:

World wide.

Price range:

Starting at US$99.

Vendor:

Interactive Software Engineering, Inc.

```
ISE Building
270 Storke Road, 2nd Floor
Goleta, CA 93117
U.S.A.
```

Phone:

+1 805 685 1006

Fax:

+1 805 685 6869

EMail:

info@eiffel.com `<mailto:info@eiffel.com>`

URL:

http://www.eiffel.com `<http://www.eiffel.com>`

9.9 EiffelBench

Description:

Object-oriented CASE Workbench.

Distribution media:

CD-ROM and Internet (FTP and WWW).

Licensing policy:

No run-time fees are required for products, commercial or otherwise, developed with ISE's technology. In the case of commercial products we simply require the product and its documentation to acknowledge ISE Eiffel clearly. The copyright holder must acknowledge the product's use/incorporation of ISE Eiffel by (a) Featuring "ISE Eiffel" prominently in product documentation, and (b) Featuring an "ISE Eiffel" software window or pop-up message clearly visible during the copyrighted product's installation process.

OS provisions:

Linux ELF or a.out.

Documentation:

Eiffel: The Environment. Language References.

Product support:

Update service, maintenance, training available.

Available since:

August, 1994.

Countries with distribution:

World wide.

Price range:

Starting at US$99.

Vendor:

Interactive Software Engineering, Inc.

        ISE Building
        270 Storke Road, 2nd Floor
        Goleta, CA 93117
        U.S.A.

Phone:

+1 805 685 1006

Fax:

+1 805 685 6869

EMail:

info@eiffel.com <mailto:info@eiffel.com>

URL:

http://www.eiffel.com <http://www.eiffel.com>

9.10   IdeaFix

Description:

The InterSoft Development Environment for Applications in Unix, or IdeaFix, is a set of programming tools and utilities designed to provide an integrated environment for programmers as well as end-users. The aim of IdeaFix is to maximize performance and productivity for both.

For the end-user, IdeaFix offers a user-friendly interface and an online help system. IdeaFix provides the developer with tools to simplify development of such design criteria as relational databases and modular structured programming.

Distribution media:

4/8 mm. DAT, 150/525 MB tape. Academic version available from:

- *ftp://ftp.inter-soft.com/pub/ideafix* `<ftp://ftp.inter-soft.com/pub/ideafix>`
- *http://www.inter-soft.com/html/products/ideafix*   `<http://www.inter-soft.com/html/ products/ideafix>`

Licensing policy:

Commercial.

OS provisions:

20 MB disk space, and GNU C/C++ compiler.

Documentation:

Available in PostScript.

Product support:

Contact *ideafix-info@inter-soft.com* `<mailto:ideafix-info@inter-soft.com>` for more information.

Extra features and add-ons:

SQL server, Dali - Development Environment, Cracker for Windows.

Available since:

1986.

Countries with distribution:

Argentina, Brazil, Russia, Mexico, Venezuela and USA.

Price range:

Linux version for free (with some restrictions). Other prices available on request.

Vendor:

InterSoft Argentina S.A.

```
Córdoba 883 9th. Floor
Capital Federal (1054)
Argentina
```

Phone:

+54 1 318 8900

Fax:

+54 1 318 8997

EMail:

info@inter-soft.com `<mailto:info@inter-soft.com>`

URL:

http://www.inter-soft.com `<http://www.inter-soft.com>`

9.11   j-tree

Description:

Harness the power of Java clients while maintaining a legacy database on wide variety of O/S. Java API with c-tree Plus' ISAM functionality gives Java functionality through native methods/RMI. j-tree utilizes the power/flexibility of FairCom's full line of database Servers.

Distribution media:

3.5" diskettes.

Licensing policy:

A licensed copy of c-tree Plus, thereafter royalty free.

OS provisions:

2 MB of RAM.

Documentation:

Full online documentation with CD-ROM, available in English and Japanese.

Product support:

Three months of full technical support from purchase date.

Available since:

August, 1997.

Countries with distribution:

World wide.

Price range:

Upon request.

Vendor:

FairCom

```
      4006 W. Broadway
      Columbia, MO 65203-0100
      U.S.A.
```

Phone:

+1 573 445 6833

Fax:

+1 573 445 9698

EMail:

Faircom@faircom.com <mailto:Faircom@faircom.com>

URL:

http://www.faircom.com <http://www.faircom.com>

Contact:

Tamra Brown <*tami@faircom.com*> <mailto:tami@faircom.com>

Vendor:

FairCom Europe

```
      Via Patrioti 6
      I-24021 Albino
      Italy
```

Phone:

+39 35 773 464

Fax:

+39 35 773 806

EMail:

Europe@faircom.com <mailto:Europe@faircom.com>

Vendor:

FairCom Japan

Ikeda Bldg. #3 4F, 112-5
Komei-chou, Tsu-city MIE 514
Japan

Phone:

+81 059 229 7504

Fax:

+81 059 249 723

Vendor:

FairCom do Brasil Ltda.

Phone:

+55 14 224 1610

Fax:

+55 14 234 6462

EMail:

Brazil@faircom.com <mailto:Brazil@faircom.com>

9.12 KAI C++

Description:

The KAI C++ compiler provides conformance to the latest draft standard, high performance, low abstraction penalty, identical syntax and libraries on all supported platforms and superior customer support. No other compiler is as close to the draft standard.

Distribution media:

Internet (FTP and WWW).

Licensing policy:

Commercial. 30 day free trial available at *http://www.kai.com/kcc_howto.shtml* <http://www.kai.com/kcc_howto.shtml>

OS provisions:

Red Hat Linux 2.1 or later. Other Software: gcc 2.7.2.1. Disk space: 15 MB.

Documentation:

Complete online documentation is supplied.

Product support:

No-charge technical support. Annual Support service provides automatic updates for a full year, US$79.

Available since:

> May, 1997.

Countries with distribution:

> World wide.

Price range:

> US$395 single processor; US$545 multiprocessor.

Vendor:

> Kuck & Associates, Inc.
>
> > 1906 Fox Drive
> > Champaign, IL   61820-7345
> > U.S.A.

Phone:

> +1 217 356 2288

Fax:

> +1 217 356 5199

EMail:

> *kai@kai.com* <mailto:kai@kai.com>

URL:

> *http://www.kai.com/kcc_howto.shtml* <http://www.kai.com/kcc_howto.shtml>

Contact:

> Bruce Leasure *<bruce@kai.com>* <mailto:bruce@kai.com>

9.13   Khoros Pro 2.1

Description:

> Khoros Pro 2.2 is a software development environment with extensive image processing, software development, and data visualization capabilities.

Distribution media:

> CD-ROM.

Licensing policy:

> Single user license comes with Khoros Pro CD-ROM. For software developers, independent software developer licenses are available.

OS provisions:

> Linux 2.0.18, gcc 2.7.2, Fortran compiler f2c 19951025+ AT&T Bell Labs.

Documentation:

> Printed documentation; Installation Guide and User's Guide come with the CD-ROM. Five volume Developer's Manual set available from KRI.

Product support:

> Training in Software Development and Digital Image Processing scheduled through 1998.   See *http://www.khoral.com/training/training.html* <http://www.khoral.com/training/training.html>. Maintenance, technical and engineering support may be purchased from KRI on a negotiated basis.

Available since:

> August, 1996.

Countries with distribution:

World wide. Addison Wesley selling to educational market.

Price range:

Single user Khoros Pro 2.2 is US$549. Independent software developer licenses start at US$5,000 and go up depending on platforms and organization structure. Royalty agreements can be negotiated.

Vendor:

Khoral Research Inc.

> 6001 Indian School NE Suite 200
> Albuquerque, NM 87110
> U.S.A.

Phone:

+1 505 837 6500

Fax:

+1 505 881 3842

EMail:

info@khoral.com `<mailto:info@khoral.com>`

URL:

http://www.khoral.com `<http://www.khoral.com>`

FTP:

ftp://ftp.khoral.com `<ftp://ftp.khoral.com>`

Contact:

Annie MacFarlane *<annie@khoral.com>* `<mailto:annie@khoral.com>`

9.14   MetaCard

Description:

MetaCard is a GUI development and multimedia authoring tool compatible with Apple Corporation's HyperCard. Anyone can use MetaCard to build GUI applications and hypermedia documents using a powerful, direct manipulation editor and an easy-to-learn scripting language.

MetaCard goes beyond HyperCard by including support for color controls and images, vector graphics, scrollbars, and dialog boxes. MetaCard's scripting language has support for arrays, custom (user defined) object properties, and is based on high-perforance "virtual compiler" technology. Stacks developed with MetaCard are portable among all popular Unix platforms and Windows 95/NT and can be distributed with without licensing fees or royalties.

Distribution media:

3.5" diskettes and Internet (FTP and EMail).

Licensing policy:

MetaCard can be licensed to a single, named individual, but can be used on any machine or combination of machines by that user. Multiple user packages are also available.

The save-disabled distribution is available via anonymous FTP from *ftp://ftp.metacard.com/MetaCard* `<ftp://ftp.metacard.com/MetaCard>` and *ftp://ftp.uu.net/vendor/MetaCard* `<ftp://ftp.uu.net/vendor/MetaCard>`.

OS provisions:

The Linux engine is built on a 1.2.13 ELF system. Minumum 8 MB RAM for runtime, 16MB RAM for development. Minimum 640x480x8 screen resolution for runtime, 800x600x8 for development. Development system requires about 5MB disk space. GUI is Motif-compliant, but does not require Motif libraries.

Documentation:

Complete online documentation is supplied. Printed documentation is an extra-cost option.

Product support:

Free EMail technical support, phone support available at extra cost.

Extra features and add-ons:

A library version of MetaCard that can be linked directly to C programs (Embedded MetaCard) is available at extra cost.

Available since:

June, 1992.

Countries with distribution:

World wide.

Price range:

US$995 for single-user all-platform development license.

Vendor:

MetaCard Corporation

```
4710 Shoup pl.
Boulder, CO 80303
U.S.A.
```

Phone:

+1 303 447 3936

Fax:

+1 303 499 9855

EMail:

info@metacard.com `<mailto:info@metacard.com>`

URL:

http://www.metacard.com `<http://www.metacard.com>`

9.15   ObjectManual Release 3.0

Description:

Automated documentation generator from C++ programs. Generates doucmentation in various formats including HTML, RTF, MIF along with Java classes.

Distribution media:

Internet (FTP and WWW).

Licensing policy:

Single, Multiple, Site and Floating Licenses.

OS provisions:

Linux ELF.

Documentation:

Provided in PostScript along with the distribution.

Product support:

Free for 30 days. Then a contract based on six month to a one year cycle.

Extra features and add-ons:

New release are released every quarter.

Available since:

1995.

Countries with distribution:

USA.

Price range:

US$2295 for most flavours of Unix. Free of charge for Linux users that work in a non-commercial environment.

Vendor:

ObjectSoftware, Inc.

```
3519 Misty Meadow Dr.
Dallas, TX 75287
U.S.A.
```

Phone:

+1 214 373 2021

Fax:

+1 972 662 0756

EMail:

objsoft@netcom.com <mailto:objsoft@netcom.com>

URL:

http://www.obsoft.com <http://www.obsoft.com>

Contact:

Bobby Sardana

9.16   Critical Mass Reactor

Description:

Distributed application development environment.

Distribution media:

CD-ROM.

Licensing policy:

Commercial with library source, evaluation licenses available for purchase.

OS provisions:

Linux/ELF.

Documentation:

Extensive documentation included (printed and online)

Product support:

Optional.

Extra features and add-ons:

See *http://www.cmass.com/reactor/overview/index.html#reactor_features* <http://www.cmass.com/reactor/overview/index.html##reactor_features>

Available since:

May, 1996.

Countries with distribution:

USA.

Price range:

US$479-$3500/seat. Discounts are available for non-commercial and academic use.

Vendor:

Critical Mass, Inc.

```
Critical Mass, Inc.
225R Concord Avenue
Cambridge, MA 02138
U.S.A.
```

Phone:

+1 617 354 6277

Fax:

+1 617 354 5027

EMail:

info@cmass.com `<mailto:info@cmass.com>`

URL:

http://www.cmass.com `<http://www.cmass.com>`

9.17   Resource Standard Metrics

Description:

A source code metrics and quality analysis tool for C and C++. This creates standard metrics like Lines of Code, Cylcomatic complexity and functional analysis. This tool is portable across most all popular operating systems. The quality analysis checks for semantic errors that most compilers miss and enforces stardard software development standards.

Distribution media:

Software can be downloaded *http://207.92.81.101/rsm.htm* `<http://207.92.81.101/rsm.htm>` or EMailed or shipped on floppy disk in ZIP and tar format.

Licensing policy:

Shareware licensing for the demo version which processes one file. Commercial single user and network licenses will process any number of files of any size from wild cards at the command line, from a list or recursively descend a directory tree.

OS provisions:

Linux 1.2.

Documentation:

Comes with full online documentation or printed text file. English language only.

Product support:

1 Email support. 1 year software maintenance available.

Extra features and add-ons:

Some license come with unmodifiable source code for compiling on your specific OS. Each license comes with a pretty printing utility and a DOS to Unix conversion utility.

Available since:

March, 1997.

Countries with distribution:

World wide.

Price range:

US$99.99 for single user non-source code version to US$999.95 for the network source code license.

Vendor:

M Squared Technolgies

        2128 Hidden Pine Lane
        Apopka, FL 32712
        U.S.A.

Phone:

+1 407 880 2627

Fax:

+1 407 880 2627

EMail:

m2tech@reachus.com `<mailto:m2tech@reachus.com>`

URL:

http://207.92.81.101/rsm.htm `<http://207.92.81.101/rsm.htm>`

9.18 r-tree

Description:

r-tree report generator in C source code.

Provides complex, multi-line reports by handling virtually every aspect of report generation. The only programming requirement is to call the r-tree report function, which reads c-tree data files, performs calculations, monitors control breaks and accumulators and produces a formatted report. Complete with C source code. Requires c-tree Plus.

Distribution media:

3.5" diskettes and CD-ROM.

Licensing policy:

r-tree Plus is licensed on a per programmer basis. Royalty-free distribution. Contact FairCom for possible restrictions.

Documentation:

Printed manuals distributed with product; full online documentation with CD-ROM, available in English and Japanese.

Product support:

Three months of full technical support from purchase date. Unlimited technical support and product updates available thereafter with r-tree maintenance program.

Available since:

October, 1995.

Countries with distribution:

World wide.

Price range:
US$445.

Vendor:
FairCom

4006 W. Broadway
Columbia, MO 65203-0100
U.S.A.

Phone:
+1 573 445 6833

Fax:
+1 573 445 9698

EMail:
Faircom@faircom.com `<mailto:Faircom@faircom.com>`

URL:
http://www.faircom.com `<http://www.faircom.com>`

Contact:
Tamra Brown *<tami@faircom.com>* `<mailto:tami@faircom.com>`

Vendor:
FairCom Europe

Via Patrioti 6
I-24021 Albino
Italy

Phone:
+39 35 773 464

Fax:
+39 35 773 806

EMail:
Europe@faircom.com `<mailto:Europe@faircom.com>`

Vendor:
FairCom Japan

Ikeda Bldg. #3 4F, 112-5
Komei-chou, Tsu-city MIE 514
Japan

Phone:
+81 059 229 7504

Fax:
+81 059 249 723

Vendor:
FairCom do Brasil Ltda.

Phone:
+55 14 224 1610

Fax:
+55 14 234 6462

EMail:
Brazil@faircom.com `<mailto:Brazil@faircom.com>`

9.19   sdoc (Source Documenter)

Description:

This program helps to create a complete, indexed documentation from your sources (C, tcl, Perl currently available, other will follow soon).

You add documentation information to your scripts using pod (Plain old documentation), the documentation format also used in Perl. The documentation options provided by pod are simple and easy to learn but powerfull enough to create nice and good looking documents.

sdoc uses this information to create a pod-document which in turn may be transformed to HTML, LaTeX (and PostScript), nroff or just plain text.

The preview function of tdoc lets you create documentation interactively - add or modify your documentation to the source file and check the output for correctness.

Here are some highlights:

- Documentation is included in source file, no separate files needed
- Powerfull formatting options combined with easy learning
- Good looking documentation can be created without hassle
- Automated indexing
- Output may be in HTML, PostScript and a lot of other formats (have a look at the perlpod manual page or at available pod converters).

The Tcl Documenter is also available as a commercial version. This version adds the following features:

- Significantly faster
- May optionally use Netscape to display preview pages.
- Includes the package concept to further automate file selection.
- Direct connection to emacs for file editing
- Direct creation of postscript output
- Full support, upgrades
- Complete documentation

Distribution media:

3.5" diskettes and Internet (EMail and WWW).

Licensing policy:

You can download the public domain version of sdoc from the neosoft tcl archive:

- *http://www.neosoft.com/tcl/ftparchive/sorted/development*   `<http://www.neosoft.com/tcl/ftparchive/sorted/development>`
- *ftp://ftp.neosoft.com/pub/tcl/sorted/development* `<ftp://ftp.neosoft.com/pub/tcl/sorted/development>`

OS provisions:

You need an ELF based system with X11.

Documentation:

Context sensitive help and complete documentation in Pod format. Available as PostScript on request.

Product support:

Installation support included, additional support available.

Available since:

July, 1996.

Countries with distribution:

World wide.

Price range:

Contact softWorks for pricing details. Discounts for students and educational institutions available.

Vendor:

softWorks, Richard Schwaninger

```
Theodor-Körnerstr. 173
A-8010 Graz
Austria
```

Phone:

+43 316 686590

Fax:

+43 316 686590

EMail:

risc@ping.at <mailto:risc@ping.at>

URL:

http://members.ping.at/risc <http://members.ping.at/risc>

Contact:

Richard Schwaninger

9.20 SEDIT, S/REXX

Description:

SEDIT is a powerful Unix text editor patterned after IBM's XEDIT editor. It operates with a GUI under X windows or in character mode from a tty device. S/REXX is a full Unix implementation of IBM's SAA procedural language except that the numeric digit specification is limited to 15 digits. S/REXX functions as an imbedded macro language for SEDIT as well as providing a powerful modern programming language alternative to shell scripting languages. SEDIT and S/REXX may be purchased in a bundle or individually. See our *web site* <http://www.sedit.com> for more information including pricing for Linux, etc. For additional information, please contact one of the local distributors listed on the web site or mail us at *sedit@dialup.FranceNet.fr* <mailto:sedit@dialup.FranceNet.fr>

Distribution media:

4mm, 8mm, 1/4" or 3.5" diskettes and Internet (FTP).

Licensing policy:

SEDIT and S/REXX are licensed products. See the above WWW site for details. For demo purposes, a short term license key will be provided on request to anyone who obtains the product via ftp.

OS provisions:

We believe these products will work with any recent stable Linux kernel since 1.1.18 supporting a.out format. Motif is fully bound with SEDIT and SEDIT is distributed with XFree86 3.1 shared libraries for use if your system is not at that level.

Documentation:

Documentation is furnished in PostScript form, in extensive online help files, and in optional printed manuals.

Product support:

Technical support is available for all licensed users. For maintenance, see the above URLs.

Extra features and add-ons:

A REXX interactive graphical debugger is available as an optional feature as are printed manuals, physical media, and on going maintenance. See the above URLs.

Available since:

The original Linux version has been available since 3rd quarter 1995.

Countries with distribution:

SEDIT and S/REXX are available worldwide. The URLs should be consulted for current information.

Price range:

Pricing information should be requested from the local distributor responsible for your country. An economical 2 user license is available for Linux without media or printed documentation with other options for more users, S/REXX, hardcopy manuals, etc.

Vendor:

Benaroya

31 Rue de Constantinople
F-75008 Paris
France

Phone:

+33 1 47 22 22 13

Fax:

+33 1 47 22 06 17

EMail:

sedit@dialup.FranceNet.fr <mailto:sedit@dialup.FranceNet.fr>

URL:

http://www.sedit.com <http://www.sedit.com>

Contact:

Robert Benaroya

9.21 SNiFF+

Description:

SNiFF+ is an open, scalable and multiplatform programming environment for C/C++, Java, CORBA IDL and Fortran. The main goal in developing SNiFF+ was to create an efficient and portable programming environment with a comfortable user interface and special support for object oriented programming.

Distribution media:

CD-ROM and Internet (FTP).

Licensing policy:

Trial license avialable.

OS provisions:

Linux 1.2 or 2.0.

Documentation:

Printed documentation and HTML version.

Extra features and add-ons:

Extensions for other programming languages available.

Vendor:

TakeFive Software GmbH

Jakob-Haringer-Straße 8
A-5020 Salzburg
Austria

Phone:

+43 662 4579150

Fax:

+43 662 4579156

EMail:

info@takefive.co.at <mailto:info@takefive.co.at>

URL:

http://www.takefive.co.at <http://www.takefive.co.at>

9.22   ST/X (Smalltalk/X)

Description:

ST/X is a complete implementation of the Smalltalk programming language with development environment providing all of the advantages you would expect from Smalltalk: a fully object oriented programming language, a graphical development environment with editors, browsers, symbolic debugger, incremental compiler and just-in-time compilation to machine code as well as an extensive class library.

Distribution media:

CD-ROM.

Licensing policy:

There are non-commercial, evaluation and commercial licences available. There is also demo version on the Internet, although it is quite old, this should be updated at some time in 1997.

OS provisions:

ST/X requires 32 MB or more of memory and 100 MB hard disk space.

Documentation:

The ST/X documentation is available online as hypertext (HTML).

Product support:

eXept Software AG provides mentoring, training, and consulting. Onsite support is also available. For the commercial licence there is an update service and maintenance support.

Extra features and add-ons:

ST/X includes a supplementary stand-alone machine code compiler and the possibility to embed C code directly into Smalltalk methods. This allows the exploitation and use of existing C libraries or a performance improvement in the speed of time critical operations. An integral part of ST/X is an HTML browser which is fully implemented in Smalltalk. It supports network loadable Smalltalk applets and smalltalk scripts embedded in HTML pages. This allows the development of Internet and Intranet applications analogous to Java.

Available since:

ST/X has been available as a beta version on the Internet for quite a while. eXept Software AG has been further developing and marketing ST/X since 1996. Claus Gittinger (the developer from ST/X) is a founding member of eXept.

Countries with distribution:
World wide.

Price range:
There are non-commercial, evaluation and commercial licences available. The commercial licence costs US$3,500. A six month evaluation licence costs US$350. The non-commercial license is available for US$150 plus shipping and handling.

Vendor:
eXept Software AG

```
Besigheimerstr. 1
D-74369 Löchgau
Germany
```

Phone:
+49 7143 870045

Fax:
+49 7143 870048

EMail:
info@exept.de <mailto:info@exept.de>

URL:
http://home.t-online.de/home/exept <http://home.t-online.de/home/exept>

Contact:
David Queeney

9.23   tdb (Tcl Debugger)

Description:
This is a debugger for tcl scripts. It allows interactive debugging of tcl/tk programs and speeds up your development cycle.

Here are some highlights:

- Step by step execution with breakpoints
- Display and manipulation of local and global variables
- On-the-fly source code modifications and fast programm restarts
- Graphical user interface, easy use
- Easy configuration and installation

The commercial version adds the following features:

- Full screen context display
- Hot link to editor (currently emacs)
- Scripting and user extensibility (tcl)
- Plugin support (script, popup)
- A lot faster
- Full support, upgrades
- Complete documentation

Distribution media:

3.5" diskettes and Internet (EMail and WWW)

Licensing policy:

You can download the public domain version of tdb from the neosoft archive:

- *http://www.neosoft.com/tcl/ftparchive/sorted/development*   `<http://www.neosoft.com/tcl/ftparchive/sorted/development>`

- *ftp://ftp.neosoft.com/pub/tcl/sorted/development* `<ftp://ftp.neosoft.com/pub/tcl/sorted/development>`

OS provisions:

ELF based system with X11.

Note that tdb requires changes to the base tcl C-libraries and also depends on dynamic loading. Please check out the info package for further details. You don' need tcl installed to use the debugger, all necessary code is included.

The commercial version may be purchased in source form and support for porting to other platforms is available. Please contact softWorks for details.

Documentation:

Context sensitive help and complete documentation in HTML format. Available as PostScript on request.

Product support:

Installation support included, additional support available.

Extra features and add-ons:

Debugger-PlugIns for speacialized debug tasks (e.g. to debug tk widget hierarchies are also available).

Available since:

July, 1996.

Countries with distribution:

World wide.

Price range:

US$450 for a binary version, US$750 for the source code, with a 10% discount for students and educational institutions.

Vendor:

softWorks, Richard Schwaninger

```
Theodor-Körnerstr. 173
A-8010 Graz
Austria
```

Phone:

+43 316 686590

Fax:

+43 316 686590

EMail:

risc@ping.at `<mailto:risc@ping.at>`

URL:

http://members.ping.at/risc `<http://members.ping.at/risc>`

Contact:

Richard Schwaninger

9.24 tprof (Tcl Profiler)

Description:

This is a profiler for tcl scripts. It allows the creation of profiling data from your tcl programms and later analysis and detailed inspection through a graphical frontend.

This tool is especially well suited if you encounter performance problems with your tcl scripts. Instead of rewriting the whole application in C you can isolate time-critical procedures and speed them up (if necessary using C).

Here are some highlights:

- Call flow display
- Barcharts for number of calls, cpu time and real time
- Tabular display of profiling data set
- Analyse both tcl procs and commands written in C
- Graphical user interface, easy use
- Simple aquisition of profiling data
- Easy configuration and installation

tprof is available both as a public domain and as a commercial version. The commercial version adds the following features:

- *Zoom in* on interesting subsets of the data
- Printout of data sets
- PostScript (eps) images of charts and tables
- Merging of multiple data sets
- Exporting data sets in different formats to inspect them further (eg. sc/xspread, Wingz, DBase, text)
- A lot faster
- Full support, upgrades
- Complete documentation

Distribution media:

3.5" diskettes, Internet (EMail and WWW).

Licensing policy:

You can download the public domain version of tprof from sunsite.unc.edu and it's mirrors.

OS provisions:

You need an ELF based system with X11.

Documentation:

Context sensitive help and complete documentation in HTML format. Available as PostScript on request.

Product support:

Installation support included, additional support available.

Available since:

October, 1996.

Countries with distribution:

World wide.

Price range:

Contact softWorks for details and discounts.

Vendor:

softWorks, Richard Schwaninger

        Theodor-Körnerstr. 173
        A-8010 Graz
        Austria

Phone:

+43 316 686590

Fax:

+43 316 686590

EMail:

risc@ping.at <mailto:risc@ping.at>

URL:

http://members.ping.at/risc <http://members.ping.at/risc>

Contact:

Richard Schwaninger

9.25 View Designer/X (VDX)

Description:

Motif interface builder that generates C and C++ code. VDX provides WYSIWYG view, widget tree browser, resource editor, widget templates and more tools to design user interfaces.

Distribution media:

Internet (WWW).

Licensing policy:

Free demo version. Purchase of license key that removes restrictions of the demo version. Three types of licenses are available: company license, host license, student license.

OS provisions:

Linux, ELF, X11R6, Libc.5, 5 MB on harddisk.

Documentation:

Online help, English. PostScript manual, English. A German version of the manual is available.

Product support:

Minor update (1.x to 1.x) free. Free EMail support.

Available since:

December, 1996.

Countries with distribution:

World wide.

Price range:

DM 800 (approximately US$470), Major update (1.x to 2.x) DM 500 (approximately US$295).

Vendor:

Bredex GmbH

```
          Fallersleber-Tor-Wall 23
          D-38100 Braunschweig
          Germany
```

Phone:

+49 531 24 33 00

Fax:

+49 531 24 33 099

EMail:

info@bredex.de <mailto:info@bredex.de>

URL:

http://www.bredex.de <http://www.bredex.de>

Contact:

Regina Heine

9.26   XBasic

Description:

XBasic is a comprehensive visual program development environment that integrates a powerful editor, advanced 32/64-bit BASIC compiler, debugger, GuiDesigner and GraphicsDesigner. XBasic is written entirely in XBasic.

Distribution media:

Internet (FTP).

Licensing policy:

Each copy is licensed on a per machine basis.

OS provisions:

Linux (ELF 1.2.13 or higher).

Documentation:

300+ page electronic manual (Word format).

Product support:

US$3 per minute.

Available since:

January, 1996.

Countries with distribution:

World wide,

Price range:

US$195.

Vendor:

Basmark Corporation

```
          P.O. Box 40450
          Cleveland, OH 44140
          U.S.A.
```

Phone:

+1 216 871 8855

Fax:

+1 216 871 9011

EMail:

jgo@basmark.com <mailto:jgo@basmark.com>

URL:

http://www.basmark.com <http://www.basmark.com>

Contact:

Joseph G. O'Toole

9.27   XMove 4.0 for Linux

Description:

XMove is a software package for design, prototyping and testing the graphic user interface of a software system dealing dynamically changing values. This conception shall be partially reflected in the name XMove, which is also the abbreviation of "X Window System Meter Object Visualization and Editing Tool".

X Window System: XMove is based completely on the standard X Windows System. XMove was specifically designed to support this standard for graphics user interfaces. In many applications XMove can be used complementary to OSF/Motif.

Meter Object: Meter Object is the reference to the dynamic features of XMove. Using XMove the user can provide dynamic attributes for any graphics object in addition to the definition of static behavior.

Visualizing: means that the displaying and managing of the application-specific graphics, which can be designed interactively usign XMove, is done by XMove during of the application.

Editing Tool: stands for the interactive possibilities of creating the static and dynamic parts of an application-specific graphyc usign the XMove editors.

XMove generate the necesary C++ code for X Windows System to develop the application in a very sample way. XMove is an object oriented graphics developing system.

Distribution media:

CD-ROM, Internet (EMail and WWW).

Documentation:

PostScript manuals are included with the package.

Available since:

March, 1997.

Countries with distribution:

World wide.

Price range (Europe, Asia, Australia):

- US$6,000 (including the editor and libraries).
- US$3,500 (only the editor).
- US$3,500 (only the library).

Price range (America):

- US$5,000 (including the editor and libraries).
- US$3,000 (only the editor).
- US$3,000 (only the library).

Vendor:

Future Technologies

> Via B. Cairoli, 1
> I-33170 Pordenone
> Italy

Phone:

+39 434 20 91 07

Fax:

+39 434 20 95 10

EMail:

info@futuretg.com <mailto:info@futuretg.com>

URL:

http://www.futuretg.com <http://www.futuretg.com>

Contact:

Giovanni A. Orlando

10   Emulation

10.1   Emulus

Description:

Emulus is an X-Windows/Motif application which uses TCP/IP to establish a connection to an IBM mainframe host, emulating a 3270 terminal. Emulus supports mainframe graphics, including 3270 graphics datastream extension used by mainframe SAS Software. Other features include customization through dialogs, a scripting facility to record and playback host interaction, EasyPads (customized windows of buttons), and cut and paste between Emulus and other X applications. Emulus also comes with Helplus, an hypertext help viewer modeled after WinHelp. It is used to provide online help for Emulus, but can also be used to develop Help for other X applications.

Distribution media:

CD-ROM.

Licensing policy:

Licensing is per CPU.

OS provisions:

Linux 1.2 or higher, 8-16 MB RAM, 5 MB hard disk; Motif statically linked.

Documentation:

Printed book, man pages, online help, English.

Product support:

Technical Support from SAS Institute.

Price range:

US$99; includes hardcopy documentation, and Technical Support for one year.

Vendor:

SAS Institute Inc.

SAS Campus Drive
Cary, NC 27513
U.S.A.

Phone:

+1 919 677 8000

Fax:

+1 919 677 8166

EMail:

saspjh@unx.sas.com `<mailto:saspjh@unx.sas.com>`

URL:

http://www.sas.com `<http://www.sas.com>`

Contact:

Phil Herold

10.2 Executor 2

Description:

Executor 2 allows your Linux system to run many Macintosh applications, including commercial software like Adobe Photoshop and Illustrator, Quark XPress, Microsoft Word and Excel and Quicken, as well as lots of Macintosh shareware, freeware and demoware. A compatibility database is available at our *web site* `<http://www.ardi.com>`. Executor 2 also allows you to read and write Macintosh formatted media without losing important meta-data information like the file type and file creator.

Distribution media:

CD-ROM.

Licensing policy:

Commercial software with a time limited demo available from our *web site* `<http://www.ardi.com>`.

OS provisions:

Linux/X and Linux/SVGAlib.

Documentation:

30 page mini-manual in CD-ROM jewel-box case, additional tutorial information available on our web site and in the Usenet group comp.emulators.mac.executor.

Extra features and add-ons:

Each Executor 2 CD-ROM contains Executor/DOS and Executor/Linux. You can switch between them, but are allowed to only run one at a time.

Price range:

Suggested Retail: US$249. Educational Institutions: US$149, Full-time Students: US$65.

Vendor:

ARDI

Suite 4-101
1650 University Blvd., NE
Albuquerque, NM 87102
U.S.A.

Phone:

+1 505 766 9115

Fax:

+1 505 766 5153

EMail:

questions@ardi.com `<mailto:questions@ardi.com>`

URL:

http://www.ardi.com `<http://www.ardi.com>`

10.3   Wabi 2.2 for OpenLinux

Description:

Caldera licensed and ported SunSoft's Wabi technology to enable end users to run popular Windows 3.1 applications on Linux-based system software. Channel Partners and customers can utilize Caldera Wabi 2.2 for Linux running on Caldera OpenLinux, an open source environment, to remotely manage Windows 3.1 applications at home, in the office or on the road. Channel Partners who create customized turn-key solutions based on environments like SCOR OpenServer 5 or Windows NT can now use the Wabi/COL solution to increase revenues by lowering overall cost and system requirements. The suggested retail price for Wabi 2.2 for Linux is US$199. The product requires Linux on a 386 (or higher) Intel-based processor, 16 MB RAM (24 MB recommended), VGA-quality video and 10 MB disk space.

Distribution media:

CD-ROM.

Licensing policy:

One user per licensed copy. No shareware or FTP.

OS provisions:

Runs on Caldera Network Desktop and OpenLinux.

Documentation:

Online and printed manual.

Product support:

30-days installation support via EMail and phone.

Available since:

November 18, 1996.

Countries with distribution:

47 countries worldwide; see our *web site* `<http://www.caldera.com>` for local reseller.

Price range:

US$199 with additional licenses at US$179. Educational pricing is US$149 with additional licenses at US$129.

Vendor:

Caldera, Inc.

        633 S. 550 E.
        Provo, UT 84606
        U.S.A.

Phone:

+1 800 850 7779, +1 801 377 7687

Fax:

+1 801 377 8752

EMail:

orders@caldera.com <mailto:orders@caldera.com>

URL:

http://www.caldera.com <http://www.caldera.com>

Contact:

Nathan Hatch

11   Financial Software

11.1   BB Stock Pro and BB Stock Tool

Description:

BB Stock Pro and BB Stock Tool are powerful stock charting, tracking and analysis tools for investors. Features include stock charting, technical analysis, market timing, portfolio management. In addition, it has customized alerts, automatic stock split detection and management, stock screening, most active issues and big price movers, personalized watch list, Auto-Run, and builtin Easy Stock Update via Internet with either direct connection or behind firewall via proxy server.

Distribution media:

Internet (FTP and WWW).

Licensing policy:

Per machine license. 30 day free trial is available at our *web site* <http://www.falkor.com>.

OS provisions:

Linux 2.0 ELF.

Documentation:

Context sensitive online help, and User's Guide in HTML, viewed with web browser.

Product support:

Free technical support. Frequently asked questions and answers available at our web site.

Available since:

Sun SPARC version available since December 1993. Linux version available since April 1995.

Countries with distribution:

USA, Canada, Sweden, Germany, Singapore, Malaysia, Taiwan.

Price range:

Linux version is US$99.

Vendor:

Falkor Technologies

```
P.O. Box 14201
Fremont, CA 94539
U.S.A.
```

Phone:

+1 510 505 0700

EMail:

skyline@falkor.com `<mailto:skyline@falkor.com>`

URL:

http://www.falkor.com `<http://www.falkor.com>`

Contact:

Henry Chen

11.2   TimeClock

Description:

Employee time and attendance package for small to medium sized businesses. Includes custom report module, interface to barcode/magnetic card readers (Employee ID), and data export module.

Distribution media:

3.5" diskettes.

Licensing policy:

One CPU, unlimited users.

Documentation:

Printed manual and online HTML manual included with software.

Product support:

Free, usually 20 minute response time.

Extra features and add-ons:

Barcode/magnetic card interface.

Available since:

1992 XENIX and MS-DOS version, 1994 AIX version, October 1996 Linux version.

Countries with distribution:

USA.

Price range:

US$149.99.

Vendor:

Quality Software Solutions, Inc.

```
1322 Dodds Ave.
Chattanooga, TN 37404
U.S.A.
```

Phone:

+1 888 423 5757, +1 423 821 5757

Fax:

+1 423 629 0744

EMail:

dbryson@tclock.com `<mailto:dbryson@tclock.com>`

URL:

http://www.tclock.com `<http://www.tclock.com>`

Contact:

Donald Bryson

12   Libraries

12.1   FontScope

Description:

Type 1 Font Rasterizer Library. Allows users to arbitrarily scale, skew or rotate characters in Type 1 fonts and get back either a bitmap or an outline. Product includes full sources.

Distribution media:

3.5" diskettes.

Licensing policy:

Single user license with product. Since product includes full sources and our resources are limited, it is sold with *no warranty* and *no support*. Support contracts may be purchased at additional cost. OEM licenses, site licenses and enterprise-wide licenses available.

Documentation:

A manual, nicely typeset in 2-column format, is available with the distribution as a PostScript file.

Product support:

Support contracts may be purchased at additional cost.

Available since:

October 15, 1997.

Countries with distribution:

World wide.

Price range:

US$39.95. California residents subject to sales tax. Price subject to change without notice.

Vendor:

CurveSoft, Inc.

```
2053 Grant Road, Suite 555
Los Altos, CA 94024
U.S.A.
```

Phone:

+1 800 563 0843, +1 510 843 6485 (Sales only)

Fax:

+1 650 254 0900

EMail:

info@curvesoft.com <mailto:info@curvesoft.com>

URL:

http://www.curvesoft.com <http://www.curvesoft.com>

Contact:

Munagala V. S. Ramanath

12.2   INTERACTER

Description:

INTERACTER is a portable user-interface and graphics subroutine library for Fortran software developers. INTERACTER-based programs are portable to a wide range of Fortran compilers running on Unix, VMS, Windows, DOS. The Linux version supports f2c and g77 (ELF). Functions include menus, text windows, forms, graphics primitives, presentation graphics, hardcopy (many formats) and operating system interface.

Distribution media:

3.5" diskettes and 4mm DAT.

Licensing policy:

INTERACTER-based programs can be distributed royalty free. Linux demo program available at *http://www.demon.co.uk/issltd* <http://www.demon.co.uk/issltd>.

OS provisions:

Linux version supports X Windows (via Xlib), graphics terminals or Linux console (colour text-mode). Requires g77 or f2c.

Documentation:

Two-volume English language printed manual.

Product support:

Free lifetime technical support. New releases every six months. Chargeable software updates.

Extra features and add-ons:

Optional INTERACTER Toolkit provides form designer, graphics file viewer, online help, hardcopy post-processor and set-up file editor.

Available since:

October, 1995.

Countries with distribution:

Distributors in North America, Europe and Australia.

Price range:

Linux version: US$675 (UK £450).

Vendor:

Interactive Software Services Ltd.

```
Westwood House
Littleton Drive
Huntington
Staffs WS12 4TS
United Kingdom
```

Phone:

+44 1543 503611

Fax:

+44 1543 574566

EMail:

support@issltd.demon.co.uk <mailto:support@issltd.demon.co.uk>

URL:

http://www.demon.co.uk/issltd <http://www.demon.co.uk/issltd>

12.3 Matrix<LIB> - C++ Math Matrix Library

Description:

Matrix<LIB> is a Matlab Compatible C++ Matrix Class Library, designed for development of advanced scientific high-level C++ code. Our main design objective was to keep the C++ source code clear and similar to the equivalent Matlab code, making your shift from Matlab to C++ easier. If you know how to program Matlab, you already know how to use our Matrix<LIB> C++ Math Library. The code was carefully optimized for maximal performance, too. Matrix<LIB> is also included in the MATCOM V2 distribution.

The library includes complex math, binary and unary operators, powerful indexing capabilities, signal processing, file I/O, linear algebra, string operations and graphics. Over 300 mathematical functions are included in Matrix<LIB>.

MS Windows and many Unix platform are supported with a variety of C++ compilers. An evaluation version (fully functional, 30 days limited) is available for free download from our *web site* <http://www.mathtools.com>.

Distribution media:

Internet (WWW).

Licensing policy:

From single license to site license. Contact The MathTools for details.

OS provisions:

Linux 1.2, gcc 2.6.3 or later, 8 MB of RAM, 15 MB on disk.

Documentation:

Users manual and library reference in various formats (MS Word, MS Write, plain text, PostScript).

Product support:

A fast product support is given by EMail only. The support section in the web page give immediate access to a wealth of resources, technical support, answers to frequently asked questions, technical documents and more.

Extra features and add-ons:

MathTools Accelerator: provides significant performance gains for Matrix<LIB> programs using Linear Algebra and matrix multiplication, on a Pentium with the Visuall C++ compiler.

Available since:

November, 1996.

Countries with distribution:

World wide.

Price range:

US$499 (US$249 for academic institutes).

Vendor:

MathTools, Ltd.

```
P.O. Box 855
Horsham, PA 19044-0855
U.S.A.
```

Phone:

+1 212 208 4476

Fax:

+1 888 628 4866, +1 215 957 1719

EMail:

   info@mathtools.com `<mailto:info@mathtools.com>`

URL:

   http://www.mathtools.com `<http://www.mathtools.com>`

Contact:

   Robert G. Ford

12.4   PKWARE Data Compression Library for Linux

Description:

   The library does lossless compression and consists of compression, an extraction, and an error checking routine. To maintain flexibility and keep the library's code size at a minimum, the PKWARE Data Compression Library does not create .ZIP compatible archives.

Distribution media:

   3.5" diskettes.

Licensing policy:

   Per machine with no runtime royalties.

OS provisions:

   Intel x86, 36 KB RAM for compressing and 13 KB RAM for uncompressing, 1 MB on hard disk.

Documentation:

   Printed 33 page manual and separate installation notes in English. Example code provided on disk.

Product support:

   No-charge. Technical support via phone, fax or EMail.

Extra features and add-ons:

   Also compatible with FreeBSD.

Available since:

   September 14, 1995.

Countries with distribution:

   Australia, Brazil, France, Germany, India, Italy, Germany, The Netherlands, Japan, and the UK.

Price range:

   US$450. Educational discount available.

Vendor:

   PKWARE, Inc.

```
9025 N. Deerwood Drive
Brown Deer, WI 53223-2480
U.S.A.
```

Phone:

   +1 414 354 8699

Fax:

   +1 414 354 8559

EMail:

   info@pkware.com `<mailto:info@pkware.com>`

URL:

   http://www.pkware.com `<http://www.pkware.com>`

Contact:

   Bob Gorman

12.5   SIMLIB IG

Description:

SIMLIB IG is a C library. It enables the user to communicate with an Evans & Sutherland image generator (Liberty and ESIG Systems) using a very efficient raw Ethernet protocol. There is no need for using opcodes, since SIMLIB IG provides an API to the functionality of the image generators.

Distribution media:

4mm DAT tar format and 3.5" diskettes.

Licensing policy:

Commercial.

OS provisions:

Linux 2.0.

Documentation:

Printed manual in English, source code examples on media.

Price range:

US$2,500.

Vendor:

KNIENIEDER Simulationstechnik

```
Technologiezentrum Tirol
Eduard Bodemgasse 5
A-6020 Innsbruck
Austria
```

Phone:

+43 512 390415 650

Fax:

+43 512 364000 20, +43 512 364000 30

EMail:

office@knienieder.co.at <mailto:office@knienieder.co.at>

Contact:

Stephan Haidacher

13   Mathematics

13.1   Maple V Release 4 - The Power Edition

Description:

Maple V Release 4 is the powerful computer algebra system used by mathematicians, engineers, and scientists for teaching and research. Maple V lets you perform a wide range of symbolic and numeric computations quickly and accurately. It includes more than 2500 built-in math functions, 2D and 3D graphics, animation, and more. New features in Release 4 include outlining, styles, and hyperlinking, typeset math notation in input, output, and text, full text search of Help Database and new computational and plotting facilities.

Distribution media:

CD-ROM.

Licensing policy:

License for unlimited use in time of the bought version, floating license with user based pricing.

OS provisions:

Linux kernel 2.0.0 or above, X11 R6.1 or above (for running X11 GUI components), 12 MB of RAM suggested. The binaries are available in ELF format only.

Documentation:

3 books: "Maple V - Learning Guide", "Maple V - Programming Guide", "The Maple V Handbook". Also available in German: "Einführung in Maple V" und "Programmieren mit Maple V".

Documentation and help in English, a variety of books available in different languages.

Product support:

Updates/maintenance depending on license, please call the distributor or WMSI.

Extra features and add-ons:

Share library via EMail and FTP. Free mailing list available (maple_group@daisy.waterloo.edu).

Available since:

September, 1994.

Countries with distribution:

USA/Canada, Europe and Asia.

Vendor:

Waterloo Maple Inc.

```
450 Phillip Street
Waterloo, ON N2L 5J2
Canada
```

Phone:

+1 519 747 2373

Fax:

+1 519 747 5284

EMail:

info@maplesoft.com `<mailto:info@maplesoft.com>`

Vendor in Germany:

Scientific Computers GmbH

```
Franzstr. 106
D-52064 Aachen
Germany
```

Phone:

+49 241 47075 0

Fax:

+49 241 44983

EMail:

maple@scientific.de `<mailto:maple@scientific.de>`

Contact:

Andreas Himmeldorf

13.2 MATCOM and MATCOM MATH LIBRARY

Description:

MATCOM is a Matlab to C++ compiler and C++ MATRIX MATH LIBRARY. MATCOM compiles Matlab source files (M-Files) to C++ source code. The resulting code is linked with the supplied C++ Matrix class library to create standalone executables or MEX files.

The C++ code and library can be integrated in products, royalty free, saving the need to translate the algorithm prototype.

Compiled code runs significantly faster than the original interpreted source.

Matrices of doubles, floats, ints and chars are supported, providing lower memory usage for many applications, especially signal and image processing.

MS Windows and many Unix platform are supported with a variety of C++ compilers. An evaluation version (fully functional, 30 days limited) is available for free download from our *web site* <http://www.mathtools.com>.

Distribution media:

Internet (WWW).

Licensing policy:

From single license to site license. Contact The MathTools for details.

OS provisions:

Linux 1.2, gcc 2.6.3 or later, 8 MB of RAM, 15 MB on disk.

Documentation:

Users manual and library reference in various formats (MS Word, MS Write, plain text, PostScript).

Product support:

A fast product support is given by EMail only. The support section in the web page give immediate access to a wealth of resources, technical support, answers to frequently asked questions, technical documents and more.

Extra features and add-ons:

MathTools Accelerator: provides significant performance gains for MATCOM programs using Linear Algebra and matrix multiplication, on a Pentium with the Visuall C++ compiler.

Available since:

May, 1995.

Countries with distribution:

World wide.

Price range:

US$499 ($249 for academic institutes).

Vendor:

MathTools, Ltd.

```
P.O. Box 855
Horsham, PA 19044-0855
U.S.A.
```

Phone:

+1 212 208 4476

Fax:

+1 888 628 4866, +1 215 957 1719

EMail:

info@mathtools.com `<mailto:info@mathtools.com>`

URL:

http://www.mathtools.com `<http://www.mathtools.com>`

Contact:

Robert G. Ford

13.3 Mathematica 3.0

Description:

Mathematica 3.0–Known for delivering quick, accurate numeric and symbolic solutions, Mathematica is ideal for creating interactive technical reports and presentations that include text, active formulas, graphics, and customizable buttons and palettes. Breakthrough new features, such as an innovative typesetting system that can do math, now make Mathematica even easier to use.

Distribution media:

CD-ROM.

Licensing policy:

Commercial, 30 day fully functional demo CD-ROM.

OS provisions:

Kernel 1.2 or higher.

Documentation:

The Mathematica Book 1400 pages. Complete book and additional help files online.

Product support:

Three service levels, see *http://www.wolfram.com/service* `<http://www.wolfram.com/service>` for details.

Extra features and add-ons:

About 15 application packages.

Available since:

October, 1996.

Countries with distribution:

World wide.

Price range:

US$1295, academic and student discounts, site licenses available.

Vendor:

Wolfram Research, Inc.

```
100 Trade Center Drive
Champaign, IL 61820
U.S.A.
```

Phone:

+1 800 441 6284, +1 217 398 0700

Fax:

+1 217 398 0747

EMail:

info@wolfram.com `<mailto:info@wolfram.com>`

URL:

http://www.wolfram.com `<http://www.wolfram.com>`

13.4   MATLAB and Simulink

Description:

MATLAB is a high-performance language for technical computing. It integrates computation, visualization, and programming in an easy-to-use environment where problems and solutions are expressed in familiar mathematical notation. MATLAB supports the development of large complex applications. Features include the M-file Performance Profiler for algorithm optimization, the integrated visual editor and debugger, and powerful interactive tools for signal processing and control system design.

Simulink is a powerful, interactive software package for modeling, analyzing, and simulating dynamic systems. It provides extremely accurate simulations of nonlinear continuous-time systems and systems with multiple modes of operation. Features include support for conditionally executed subsystems; state-of-the-art solvers; usability improvements such as signal and port labeling; and new blocks.

Distribution media:

CD-ROM and Internet (FTP).

Licensing policy:

Using GlobeTrotter (FLEXlm) CPU locked or floating network options. Contact The MathWorks for details.

OS provisions:

Linux 2.0.18, 32 MB of RAM, 40 MB disk space (60 MB to include all help files and documentation).

Documentation:

Printed documentation, online help, MATLAB Reference Guide (HTML).

Product support:

The MathWorks supports a variety of Internet-based services to provide product information and services 24 hours a day. These services give immediate access to a wealth of resources, product data sheets, technical support, answers to frequently asked questions, user-contributed materials, open-forum discussions, and more.

Extra features and add-ons:

MATLAB Extensions: MATLAB Compiler, MATLAB C/C++ Math Library.

Toolboxes: Fuzzy Logic, Signal Processing, Image Processing, Spline, Symbolic Math, Neural Network, Control System, Robust Control, Mu-Analysis & Synthesis, System Identification, Optimization, Statistics, Financial, Frequency Domain System Identification, Higher-Order Spectral Analysis, Communication, LMI Control, Model Predicitve Control, NAG Foundation, Neural Network, Partial Differential Equation, QFT Control Design, Symbolic Math and Extended Symbolic Math, Wavelet.

Simulink Extensions: Simulink Accelerator, Real-Time Workshop.

Blocksets: Fixed-Point, DSP, Nonlinear Control Design.

Available since:

June, 1995.

Countries with distribution:

World wide.

Price range:

Upon request.

Vendor:

The MathWorks, Inc.

```
24 Prime Park Way
Natick, MA 01760
U.S.A.
```

Phone:

+1 508 647 7000 x7322

Fax:

+1 508 647 7002

EMail:

efroio@mathworks.com `<mailto:efroio@mathworks.com>`, *brian@mathworks.com* `<mailto:brian@mathworks.com>`

URL:

http://www.mathworks.com `<http://www.mathworks.com>`

Contact:

Enza Froio (Marketing), Brian Bourgault (Technical)

14   Multimedia

14.1   Peter Lipa and his Journeys

Description:

This is a multimedia CD-ROM about world-known jazzman Peter Lipa. It is the first product from edition Journeys of Groups and Singers from KDK Company to contain Linux version of the program directly on the CD-ROM. The CD-ROM contains more than 8 hours of near-CD quality music (101 songs in full length), more than 30 minutes of videos, 2 hours of spoken word, more than 120 photos, 10 karaoke songs and a lot of other information (Bratislava Jazz Days, various performances all over the world, TV and theatre performances, ...). The CD-ROM is multilingual: English, German and Slovak.

Distribution media:

CD-ROM.

Licensing policy:

Program is free, data licensed per CPU.

OS provisions:

Linux kernel 2.0.27 or higher (may work with 1.2), XFree86 3.2 (may work with older X11R6 versions), 16 MB of RAM, 10-30 MB of disk space, no Motif, Intel Linux ELF.

Documentation:

On-line and short description of controls in CD-ROM booklet (English, German and Slovak).

Available since:

October 14, 1997.

Countries with distribution:

World wide.

Price range:

US$30 plus shipping, includes unlimited free program upgrades (via FTP).

Vendor:

KDK Company, Ltd.

```
Vodna 8
040 01 Kosice
Slovakia
```

Phone:

+421 95 6233335

Fax:

+421 95 6233336

EMail:

linux@kdk.sk <mailto:linux@kdk.sk>

URL:

http://www.kdk.sk <http://www.kdk.sk>, *http://obchod.kdk.sk* <http://obchod.kdk.sk> (virtual store).

Contact:

Ivan Schreter

14.2   Lucka Vondrackova and her Journeys

Description:

This is a multimedia CD-ROM about Lucka Vondrackova, young Czech singer and actress. This CD-ROM is multilingual: English, Slovak and Czech. The product does not yet contain Linux version of the program directly on the CD-ROM (The Linux version of the program is supplied on an extra diskette or can be downloaded via FTP). The CD-ROM contains more than three hours of music (all Lucka's songs in full length), 9 videoclips, all lyrics to Lucka's songs with notes and guitar accords, more than 130 photos, a lot of interesting interviews, 10 karaoke songs and a lot of other information about Lucka.

Distribution media:

Multimedia data on CD-ROM, program on diskette or via FTP.

Licensing policy:

Program is free, data licensed per CPU.

OS provisions:

Linux kernel 2.0.27 or higher (may work with 1.2), XFree86 3.2 (may work with older X11R6 versions), 16 MB of RAM, 10-30 MB of disk space, no Motif, Intel Linux ELF.

Documentation:

On-line and short description of controls in CD-ROM booklet (English and Slovak).

Available since:

October 14, 1997.

Countries with distribution:

World wide.

Price range:

US$34 plus shipping, includes unlimited free program upgrades (via FTP).

Vendor:

KDK Company, Ltd.

        Vodna 8
        040 01 Kosice
        Slovakia

Phone:

+421 95 6233335

Fax:

+421 95 6233336

EMail:

linux@kdk.sk `<mailto:linux@kdk.sk>`

URL:

http://www.kdk.sk `<http://www.kdk.sk>`, *http://obchod.kdk.sk* `<http://obchod.kdk.sk>` (virtual store).

Contact:

Ivan Schreter

14.3 MpegTV Player 1.0

Description:

Real-time MPEG Video player (with audio) and Video-CD player.

Distribution media:

Internet.

Licensing policy:

Shareware for personal and non-profit use. Commercial licenses required for commercial and governmental use.

Documentation:

Online help and HTML manual on web site.

Extra features and add-ons:

Can stream video from networks.

Price range:

Shareware registration fee is US$10. Commercial licenses: please contact MpegTV at *sales@mpegtv.com* `<mailto:sales@mpegtv.com>`.

Vendor:

MpegTV LLC

        90 Divisadero Str, #15
        San Francisco, CA 94117
        U.S.A.

Phone:

+1 415 864 6466

EMail:

info@mpegtv.com `<mailto:info@mpegtv.com>`

URL:

http://www.mpegtv.com `<http://www.mpegtv.com>`

Contact:

Tristan Savatier

14.4   Peter Nagy and his Journeys

Description:

This is a multimedia CD-ROM about Peter Nagy, Slovak pop singer. This CD-ROM is available in Slovak only and does not yet contain the Linux version of the program directly on the CD-ROM (The Linux version of the program is supplied on an extra diskette or can be downloaded via FTP). The CD-ROM contains more than four hours of music (154 song samples, 38 songs in full length), 9 videoclips, 222 song lyrics, 93 song notes with guitar accords, 120 photos, 8 interviews, citations from the book Musicross, information about all albums of Peter Nagy and a lot of other information.

Distribution media:

Multimedia data on CD-ROM, program on diskette or via FTP.

Licensing policy:

Program is free, data licensed per CPU.

OS provisions:

Linux kernel 2.0.27 or higher (may work with 1.2), XFree86 3.2 (may work with older X11R6 versions), 16 MB of RAM, 10-30 MB of disk space, no Motif, Intel Linux ELF.

Documentation:

On-line and short description of controls in CD-ROM booklet (Slovak only).

Available since:

October 14, 1997.

Countries with distribution:

World wide.

Price range:

US$34 plus shipping, includes unlimited free program upgrades (via FTP).

Vendor:

KDK Company, Ltd.

```
Vodna 8
040 01 Kosice
Slovakia
```

Phone:

+421 95 6233335

Fax:

+421 95 6233336

EMail:

linux@kdk.sk `<mailto:linux@kdk.sk>`

URL:

http://www.kdk.sk `<http://www.kdk.sk>`, *http://obchod.kdk.sk* `<http://obchod.kdk.sk>` (virtual store).

Contact:

Ivan Schreter

14.5 Xaudio

Description:

MP3 Player.

Distribution media:

Internet.

Licensing policy:

Free for personal and non-profit use. Commercial licenses required for commercial and governmental use.

Documentation:

Online help and HTML manual on web site.

Extra features and add-ons:

Can stream CD-quality audio from networks.

Price range:

Free for personal and non-profit use. Commercial licenses: please contact MpegTV at *sales@mpegtv.com* `<mailto:sales@mpegtv.com>`.

Vendor:

MpegTV LLC

```
90 Divisadero Str, #15
San Francisco, CA 94117
U.S.A.
```

Phone:

+1 415 864 6466

EMail:

xaudio@mpegtv.com `<mailto:xaudio@mpegtv.com>`

URL:

http://www.xaudio.com `<http://www.xaudio.com>`

Contact:

Gilles Boccon-Gibod

15 Network Servers

15.1 Aventail Internet Policy Manager

Description:

Commerical sOCKS5 server for Linux, easily extensible authentication and encryption modules.

Distribution media:

CD-ROM and Internet (FTP).

Licensing policy:

Commercial, free demo availalbe from *http://www.aventail.com/download.html* `<http://www.aventail.com/download.html>`

OS provisions:

Linux 2.0, 16 MB of RAM, amdinistration tool requires X11R5 or later. Approximately 14 MB of hard disk space required (less if you have Perl 5.003 and Perl/Tk installed).

Documentation:

English documentation available in PDF or Microsoft Word format.

Product support:

90 days free technical support. Yearly maintenance is 20% of initial purchase price. Maintenance includes product upgrades.

Extra features and add-ons:

Various plugins to add functionality at run-time. Authentication and filtering plugins, and encryption/VPN plugins (both domestic and exportable versions).

Available since:

November, 1996.

Countries with distribution:

World wide. VPN products avaiable only in 40 bit encryption strength outside of the USA or Canada due to export restrictions.

Price range:

IPM starting at US$6.495. VPN starting at US$7.995.

Vendor:

Aventail Corporation

```
117 South Main, Suite 400
Seattle, WA 98104
U.S.A.
```

Phone:

+1 888 762 5785, +1 206 777 5600

Fax:

+1 206 777 5656

EMail:

info@aventail.com `<mailto:info@aventail.com>`

URL:

http://www.aventail.com `<http://www.aventail.com>`

15.2   Aventail MobileVPN and PartnerVPN

Description:

Aventail MobileVPN and Aventail PartnerVPN are client/server software solutions that allow organizations to privately communicate and exchange data over the Internet. By implementing Aventail's Virtual Private Network (VPN) systems, companies can create a secure channel for use by mobile or remote employees, customers, suppliers, or business partners.

Aventail's VPN solutions work with any dial-up or direct network connection to the Internet. Privacy is ensured because the communication channel between the client and server is strongly authenticated and completely encrypted. Aventail MobileVPN and PartnerVPN support all of the popular authentication and encryption methods such as SSL, Kerberos, SecureID, DES, Triple DES, CHAP, RC4, MD4, MD5 and RADIUS. Aventail's solutions also include granular access controls that allow IS managers to specify access based on destination, source, IP address, application/services, and user ID. In addition to these comprehensive security features, Aventail MobileVPN and PartnerVPN include management tools such as protocol/content filtering, reporting, and logging.

Distribution media:

CD-ROM.

Licensing policy:

60 day evaluation period; pricing based on server connections and quantity of clients.

Product support:

All products ship with an automatic 90 day warranty and dial-up telephone technical support. To extend your coverage, you may purchase the Annual Support Program. The Support Program is 20% of your total license cost, annually renewable.

Available since:

May, 1997.

Countries with distribution:

World wide.

Price range:

Starts at US$4,995; Pricing based on connections.

Vendor:

Aventail Corporation

```
117 South Main Street, 4th Floor
Seattle, WA 98104
U.S.A.
```

Phone:

+1 206 777 5600

Fax:

+1 206 777 5656

EMail:

info@aventail.com `<mailto:info@aventail.com>`

URL:

http://www.aventail.com `<http://www.aventail.com>`

Contact:

Deanna Leung

15.3   Critical Angle X.500 Enabler

Description:

The Critical Angle X.500 Enabler allows an LDAP-only directory server to be integrated into an X.500 directory service, such as the PARADISE international white pages directory or an enterprise messaging directory service. It supports all X.500(88) operations, including authentication.

Distribution media:

Internet (WWW).

Licensing policy:

Licensed per server.

OS provisions:

Reference platform is Red Hat Linux 3 or later for Intel.

Documentation:

English documentation is included.

Product support:

An upgrade subscription is also available.

Countries with distribution:

World wide.

Price range:

A single server license is US$495.

There is also (in 1997) a special version, PARADISE X.500 Enabler, exclusively for universities. This version does not include the support for authentication or modification operations; it is intended only for searching public information. A single server license of PARADISE X.500 Enabler is currently US$95.

Vendor:

Critical Angle Inc.

```
4815 W. Braker Lane #502-385
Austin TX 78759
U.S.A.
```

EMail:

info@critical-angle.com `<mailto:info@critical-angle.com>`

URL:

http://www.critical-angle.com `<http://www.critical-angle.com>`

Contact:

Mark Wahl

15.4   DNEWS News Server

Description:

DNEWS is an advanced, full featured NNTP based news server. It is suitable for ISP's and Corporate Intranets. DNEWS can be used as a replacement for INN or cnews and will generally result in improved performance and much lower administration. Features include: easy installation and management, flexible expire settings, flexible access restrictions, EMail confirmation of posts, XOVER extentions implemented, streaming extentions built in, dynamic sucking feeds option, news to web gateway included.

Distribution media:

Internet (WWW).

Licensing policy:

Commercial, DNEWS is try before you buy software and can be downloaded from our *web site* `<http://netwinsite.com>` for free trial.

OS provisions:

No special requirements

Documentation:

A user manual is provided in HTML format. Online help included.

Product support:

Supported by Netwin LTD.

Extra features and add-ons:

DNEWSWEB - A news to web gateway. Allows local and Usenet news groups to be added to ordinary HTML pages and allows users to read and post to local and Usenet news groups directly using any web browser.

Available since:

1995.

Countries with distribution:

World wide.

Price range:

US$485 (Free registration for schools and universities).

Vendor:

Netwin LTD

```
P.O Box 27574
MT Roskill
Auckland
New Zealand
```

Fax:

+64 9 6300 689

EMail:

netwin@netwinsite.com `<mailto:netwin@netwinsite.com>`

URL:

http://netwinsite.com `<http://netwinsite.com>`

Contact:

Stephen Pugmire

15.5   Zeus Web Server

Description:

Scalable web application server for ISP hosting, Ontranets and secure e-Commerce. Full Frontpage support, 128 bit SSL3 world wide, Apache compatibility, web-centric delegatable management interface.

Application development in ISAPI, Java-Servlets and CGI. Distributed server-side Java gives high-performance database connectivity.

Unlimited virtual servers with groupable configuration, real-time statistics, bandwidth throttling and extensive logging.

Distribution media:

Internet (WWW).

Licensing policy:

One License per machine running the software. Free 30 day evaluations are available from the site.

Documentation:

Online help, available in Germany and Spanish.

Price range:

Academic: £50. Commercial: £999.

Vendor:

Zeus Technology Limited

    St Johns Innovation Centre, Cowley Road
    Cambridge, CB4 4WS
    UK

Phone:

+44 1223 42 17 27

Fax:

+44 1223 42 17 31

EMail:

sales@zeustech.net <mailto:sales@zeustech.net>

URL:

http://www.zeustech.net <http://www.zeustech.net>

Contact:

Bryan Amesbury *<bames@zeustech.net>* <mailto:bames@zeustech.net>

16   Office Tools

16.1   The American Heritage Dictionary Deluxe

Description:

This long-awaited release is ideal for technical writers, authors, and researchers. Previously available only on PC's, the product offers the ultimate reference tool for Linux users, with full definitions for well over 200,000 words, plus pronunciations, derivations, proper usage, idioms and sample sentences. The world reknowned Roget's 500,000 word Thesarus is fully integrated with the AHD. Browse, word and topic search, anagrams and more. Single user, network, academic and site licenses are available for Linux and key Unix platforms.

Distribution media:

CD-ROM, tapes, Internet (FTP and WWW).

Licensing policy:

Single user node locked or server license (shared). A free unclockable demo is available at our *web site* <http://www.dux.com>.

OS provisions:

Motif GUI, 8-16 MB RAM, 15 MB harddisk or run from the CD-ROM.

Documentation:

Documentation as a help text file. English language.

Product support:

Maintenance available. Call DUX for details.

Extra features and add-ons:

Addlitional reference volumes and additional language support to be announced.

Available since:

February, 1997.

Countries with distribution:

Currently sold in the USA and Germany. However, sales are made internationally via unclockable FTP/WWW copies and sold with authorized major credit card.

Price range:

US$49.95 for node lock single user. Call DUX or an authorized reseller for sliding scale or site license pricing.

Vendor:

DUX Software Corporation

> 425 Sherman Ave. Ste 330
> Palo Alto, CA 94306
> U.S.A.

Phone:

+1 800 543 4999, +1 415 473 1800

Fax:

+1 415 462 8723

EMail:

sales@dux.com <mailto:sales@dux.com>

URL:

http://www.dux.com <http://www.dux.com>

Contact:

Bob Adams, Rob DuFrane

16.2   Applixware Office Suite for Linux

Description:

Fully-graphical, fully-integrated office suite for Linux. Includes word processor, spreadsheet, presentation graphics, mail and HTML authoring software. Also ships with a version of Red Hat Linux. The Developer's version includes all of the above and the builder (rapid application development) program.

Distribution media:

CD-ROM.

Licensing policy:

Per machine license.

OS provisions:

Kernel 1.2.13 or better, XFree86 3.1.2 or better, 16 MB RAM, 150 MB hard disk.

Documentation:

Printed docs approximately 750 pages, online docs approximately 3000 pages, English.

Product support:

Installation support for 60 days by EMail or fax. Additional support based on number of users, etc. Contact Red Hat Software. Upgrades are offered at discounted prices to registered users. Applixware users can subscribe to applixware-list@redhat.com and archives of FAQs on web site.

Extra features and add-ons:

Add-on documentation.

Available since:

July, 1996.

Countries with distribution:

North America, Europe, Japan, Australia.

Price range:

US$79.95 (student version) to $495 (developer's version).

Vendor:

Red Hat Software, Inc.

```
4201 Research Commons, Suite 100
79 TW Alexander Drive, P.O. Box 13588
Research Triangle Park, NC 27709
U.S.A.
```

Phone:

+1 888 REDHAT 1, +1 919 572 6500

Fax:

+1 919 572 6726

EMail:

redhat@redhat.com `<mailto:redhat@redhat.com>`

URL:

http://www.redhat.com `<http://www.redhat.com>`

Contact:

Lisa Sullivan *<sulli@redhat.com>* `<mailto:sulli@redhat.com>`

16.3   D.M.S. Document Management System

Description:

The system collects documents in Tiff-g4, PostScript and JPEG and organizes them in folders with record information like names and descriptions. The system can be access using any web broswer: viewing, modify, full text retrieval and faxing are provided by a web interface. New documents are made by printing to printer spooler.

Licensing policy:

The system is installed by vendor on your Linux box with a server licence, unlimited clients, unlimited document number.

OS provisions:

Linux 2.0.

Documentation:

HTML.

Extra features and add-ons:

SQL server integrationm, print capture from accounting software.

Price range:

Upon request.

Vendor:

Studio LEADER Pro

```
Via Pietrastretta, 76
I-38100 Trento
Italy
```

Phone:

+39 461 828229

Fax:

+39 461 829826, +39 461 829877

EMail:

DMS@leader.it `<mailto:DMS@leader.it>`

URL:

http://www.leader.it `<http://www.leader.it>`

Contact:

Guido Brugnara *<brugnara@leader.it>* `<mailto:brugnara@leader.it>`

16.4   HotWire EasyFAX

Description:

Fully functional GUI Fax Management Program.

Distribution media:

Internet (WWW).

Licensing policy:

Free fully functional eval from WWW site..

OS provisions:

5.5 MB Disk, 4 MB RAM.

Documentation:

Online context-sensitive help.

Product support:

Via EMail and Usenet only.

Available since:

January 1, 1997.

Countries with distribution:

USA/Canada (Unisource Systems, Inc.), Germany/Europe (Delix Computer, GmbH).

Price range:

US$99.

Vendor:

Unisource Systems, Inc.

```
1409 N. Cove Blvd.
Longwood, FL 32750
U.S.A.
```

Phone:

+1 407 834 1973

Fax:

+1 407 834 8013

EMail:

sales@unisrc.com `<mailto:sales@unisrc.com>`

URL:

http://www.unisrc.com `<http://www.unisrc.com>`

Contact:

Gary Heller

16.5   NExS, the Network Extensible Spreadsheet

Description:

NExS is a full-featured graphical spreadsheet package which is designed to take advantage of the advanced features of Unix and the X Window system. It includes more than 230 computational functions and 13 2D and 3D graph types for engineering, scientific and business applications. NExS is extensible through a network aware API that allows user-defined "plug-ins" to add new features and functions in a variety of programming languages. NExS software plug-in bus includes 63 "slots" for remote processes to connect and extend NExS' basic functionality, allowing for the development of sophisticated networked applications.

Distribution media:

Internet (FTP and WWW).

Licensing policy:

The NExS Personal Edition license is for a single user and single platform type. The owner may use the license on multiple machines. The Professional Edition license is a floating network license which allows a pool of licenses to be used on any supported platform in your network. Without a license, NExS runs in "demo mode" with limited functionality.

OS provisions:

NExS runs on Linux kernels which support ELF binaries. There are two flavors for Linux, one which requires Motif 2.0 shared libraries, and one which includes Motif 2.0 statically linked.

Documentation:

The NExS User Guide is available in PostScript (letter format, 431 pages, or A4 format, 403 pages), and in HTML. API and tclNExS documentation are available separate from the User Guide, also in PostScript and HTML format. Printed documentation is also available. All documentation is in English.

Product support:

EMail support is standard at no cost. Phone-in support is available for a charge. Bug fix and minor version releases (e.g., 1.2.x -> 1.3.0) are no cost. Major releases are substantially discounted for existing licensees.

Extra features and add-ons:

NExS plug-ins and user-contributed code are available at *http://www.xess.com/plugins.html* `<http://www.xess.com/plugins.html>`.

Available since:

1994.

Countries with distribution:

World wide.

Price range:

- US$149 ($99 academic) for Personal Edition
- US$249 ($125 academic) for Professional Edition

Vendor:

X Engineering Software Systems (XESS) Corp.

```
P.O. Box 33091
Raleigh, NC 27636
U.S.A.
```

Phone:

+1 800 961 7840, +1 919 387 0076

Fax:

+1 919 387 1302

EMail:

info@xess.com <mailto:info@xess.com>

URL:

http://www.xess.com <http://www.xess.com>

FTP:

ftp://ftp.vnet.net/pub/users/xess/NExS <ftp://ftp.vnet.net/pub/users/xess/NExS>

Contact:

Dave Van den Bout <*devb@xess.com*> <mailto:devb@xess.com>

16.6   Axene Office

Description:

Axene Office suite includes Xclamation (Desktop Publishing), XQuad (Spreadsheet), XAllWrite (Word Processor) and XMayday (HTML Documentation browser). Available in English, French, German and Spanish.

Distribution media:

CD-ROM, tape, Internet (FTP).

Licensing policy:

Workstation or floating licenses. Downloadable demo version by FTP.

OS provisions:

8-16 MB RAM, 10 MB harddisk or run from the CD-ROM. a.out or ELF version.

Documentation:

Online HTML help and printed documentation.

Available since:

1998.

Countries with distribution:

World wide.

Price range:

US$49.

Vendor:

AXENE, Inc.

    30 Montgomery street, suite 604
    Jersey City, NJ 07302-3821
    U.S.A.

Phone:

+1 201 434 4244

EMail:

info@axene.com <mailto:info@axene.com>

URL:

http://www.axene.com/english/showroom.html <http://www.axene.com/english/showroom.html>

FTP:

ftp://ftp.axene.com/pub <ftp://ftp.axene.com/pub>

16.7   Axene XAllWrite

Description:

> The word-processing application Axene XAllWrite permits the user to create excellent quality documents with ease, whether a simple letter or a large, complex publication. It features tools for multi-document management, bitmap or line-art image integration, various font capabilities, and HTML format exportation. Available in English, French, German and Spanish.

Distribution media:

> CD-ROM, tape, Internet (FTP).

Licensing policy:

> Workstation or floating licenses. Downloadable demo version by FTP.

OS provisions:

> 8-16 MB RAM, 10 MB harddisk or run from the CD-ROM. a.out or ELF version.

Documentation:

> Online HTML help and printed documentation.

Available since:

> 1998.

Countries with distribution:

> World wide.

Price range:

> US$25.

Vendor:

> AXENE, Inc.
>
>> 30 Montgomery street, suite 604
>> Jersey City, NJ 07302-3821
>> U.S.A.

Phone:

> +1 201 434 4244

EMail:

> *info@axene.com* <mailto:info@axene.com>

URL:

> *http://www.axene.com/english/xallwrite.html* <http://www.axene.com/english/xallwrite.html>

FTP:

> *ftp://ftp.axene.com/pub* <ftp://ftp.axene.com/pub>

16.8   Axene Xclamation

Description:

> Xclamation has multidocument capabilities, multi-column and gutters capabilities, magnetic ruler marks, integration of text, bitmap or vectorized images within polymorphous frames, complex editing operations on frames (including logical, zooming, outlining, rotation, background transparency, etc.), and text exportation in HTML format. Available in English, French, Spanish and German.

Distribution media:

> CD-ROM, tape, Internet (FTP).

Licensing policy:

Workstation or floating licenses. Downloadable demo version by FTP.

OS provisions:

8-16 MB RAM, 10 MB harddisk or run from the CD-ROM. a.out or ELF version.

Documentation:

Online HTML help and printed documentation.

Available since:

1996.

Countries with distribution:

World wide.

Price range:

US$25.

Vendor:

AXENE, Inc.

```
30 Montgomery street, suite 604
Jersey City, NJ 07302-3821
U.S.A.
```

Phone:

+1 201 434 4244

EMail:

info@axene.com `<mailto:info@axene.com>`

URL:

http://www.axene.com/english/xclamation.html   `<http://www.axene.com/english/xclamation.html>`

FTP:

ftp://ftp.axene.com/pub `<ftp://ftp.axene.com/pub>`

16.9   Axene XQuad

Description:

XQuad features all the necessary functions for scientific and financial calculations and for graphical presentation of numerical data, including over 100 mathematical, logical, and string manipulation functions, various types of graphs (from histograms to radar), importation of external data files (text, Excel, etc.), production tools which allow text in cells to have automatic effect on graphical presentation. Available in English, French, German and Spanish.

Distribution media:

CD-ROM, tape, Internet (FTP).

Licensing policy:

Workstation or floating licenses. Downloadable demo version by FTP.

OS provisions:

8-16 MB RAM, 10 MB harddisk or run from the CD-ROM. a.out or ELF version.

Documentation:

Online HTML help and printed documentation.

Available since:

1996.

Countries with distribution:

World wide.

Price range:

US$25.

Vendor:

AXENE, Inc.

> 30 Montgomery street, suite 604
> Jersey City, NJ 07302-3821
> U.S.A.

Phone:

+1 201 434 4244

EMail:

info@axene.com <mailto:info@axene.com>

URL:

http://www.axene.com/english/xquad.html <http://www.axene.com/english/xquad.html>

FTP:

ftp://ftp.axene.com/pub <ftp://ftp.axene.com/pub>

17   Text Processing

17.1   Edith Pro for X11

Description:

Edith Pro is a powerful and easy-to-use text editing package, for editing plain text such as EMail messages, HTML, LaTeX and programming languages. It is aimed at people who want a flexible editing tool but who are not prepared to spend much time into learning and configuring their application. It includes a fast text-only web browser with access to the system manual and info.

Distribution media:

Internet (WWW).

Licensing policy:

You are only allowed to download Edith from the ZFC web pages for *personal use*. Without a licence, Edith will regularly issue messages stressing that the copy used is not licenced. Personal use without a licence is allowed, but organizations are required to buy a licence.

OS provisions:

ELF binary. 1MB is sufficient for editing normally sized text.

Documentation:

Online HTML help covers the printed manual completely. The printed manual contains illustrations not in the online help.

Product support:

Free updates can be downloaded from the ZFC web pages. Licence holders will be notified of updates. Licence holders can contact ZFC by EMail for immediate support.

Available since:

January 1, 1997.

Countries with distribution:

World wide directly from ZFC.

Price range:

NLG 70 (approximately US$35) single host, NLG 400 (approximately US$200) full site licence. 50%50 discount for educational organizations and students.

Vendor:

ZFC

      P.O. Box 15813
      1001 NH Amsterdam
      The Netherlands

Phone:

+31 20 4 208 248

EMail:

zfc@zfc.nl `<mailto:zfc@zfc.nl>`

URL:

http://www.zfc.nl `<http://www.zfc.nl>`

Contact:

Annius V. Groenink

17.2   TeraSpell 97 for Emacs

Description:

TeraSpell 97 for Emacs is the user-friendly spell checker for Emacs which incorporates visual highlights for misspelled words and on-the-fly spell checking. TeraSpell 97 for Emacs sets a new standard of quality in spelling correction software by providing the technically most advanced spelling correction system available on the market.

TeraSpell eliminates the traditional tedious spelling dialog and speeds up the process of spell checking your documents. Visual highlights let you efficiently identify all spelling errors in your documents at once and ignore all non-words that you may have used in your document. TeraSpell can spell check your document as you type. As soon as you type an incorrect word, it becomes highlighted. By clicking right on a highlighted word, a menu of suggestions appears.

Distribution media:

Internet (EMail anf WWW).

Licensing policy:

Evaluation version available for free from our *web site* `<http://www.teragram.com>`. Single user license, 3, 5, 10, 20 users license. Site-wide and University wide licenses,

OS provisions:

Emacs 19.29.1 or higher. XEmacs 19.14 or higher.

Documentation:

Online documentation.

Product support:

EMmail support. WWW Updates. FAQs on WWW.

Extra features and add-ons:
>   Additional languages available.

Available since:
>   August, 1997.

Countries with distribution:
>   World wide.

Price range:
>   US$29.99 single user student Linux license. US$89 single user Linux, Solaris, Irix, HPUX.

Vendor:
>   Teragram Corporation

>    ```
   236 Huntington Avenue
   Boston MA 02115-4701
   U.S.A.
   ```

**Phone:**
>    +1 617 369 0100

**Fax:**
>    +1 617 369 0101

**EMail:**
>    *info@teragram.com* `<mailto:info@teragram.com>`

**URL:**
>    *http://www.teragram.com* `<http://www.teragram.com>`

**Contact:**
>    Yves Schabes

# 18   System Administration Tools

## 18.1   Host Factory

**Description:**
>    Host Factory is a system to control the entire software contents of deployed Unix machines. Host Factory lets you customize one prototype Unix system and use it to build hundreds of similar systems. You can deliver incremental changes to running systems and roll them back if they fail. Changes are tracked in a version-control filesystem integral to the product. Host Factory provides an environment to do configuration management and version control of complete hosts.

**Licensing policy:**
>    Commercial and GPL.

**Documentation:**
>    Printed documentation.

**Product support:**
>    EMail.

**Available since:**
>    1996.
   ```

Countries with distribution:

World wide.

Price range:

Upon request. Special prices for educational institutions.

Vendor:

Working Version

> 31 Shea Road
> Cambridge, MA 02140
> U.S.A.

EMail:

bb@wv.com `<mailto:bb@wv.com>`

URL:

http://www.wv.com `<http://www.wv.com>`

Contact:

Brian Bartholomew

18.2 PerfectBACKUP+

Description:

PerfectBACKUP+ is the Unix/Linux world's premier Backup/Restore utility. It is the worlds fastest backup/restore for Unix and has been since 1985. Previously sold in the US as FASTBACK PLUS for Unix, the counterpart to the DOS FASTBACK PLUS, it now has character and Motif interfaces, networking support, compression, the best verification and recovery, scheduling and is compatible with both tar and cpio. Backs up all files, devices, partitions etc. and can backup Windows, Netware and Windows NT drives too.

Distribution media:

3.5" diskettes, Internet (WWW), 4/8mm DAT and soon CD-ROM.

Licensing policy:

Free evaluation copy from our *web site* `<http://www.unisrc.com>`. Free online manual from same the same address. Price per CPU, unlimited users.

OS provisions:

Kernels 1.2.x and 2.0.x, X11R6, Motif 1.2, 3 MB of RAM, 3 MB disk.

Documentation:

Printed (188 pages), PostScript online, and online help. English language documentation, but help by phone and EMail also avilable in Spanish.

Product support:

Unlimited free EMail support and phone support.

Extra features and add-ons:

Comes with free PC program to read tar/cpio diskettes onto PC. AutoChanger add-on with tape recycling for high-end shops.

Available since:

1996.

Countries with distribution:

USA, Canada, Germay, UK, Switzerland, Singapore, Malaysia, Germany.

Price range:

UD$79 to US$499. Linux off the net (no media) is US$79 and HP/UX is US$499. Always full product.

Vendor:

Unisource Systems, Inc.

```
1409 North Cove Blvd.
Longwood, FL 32750
U.S.A.
```

Phone:

+1 407 834 1973

Fax:

+1 407 834 1973

EMail:

sales@unisrc.com `<mailto:sales@unisrc.com>`

URL:

http://www.unisrc.com `<http://www.unisrc.com>`

Contact:

Gary Heller

18.3   Venus

Description:

Venus is an distributed administration tool for any network built of Unix workstations from different hardware vendors. A Venus network presents itselfs to the user as a homogeneous computer system and guarantees transparent access to any network resource. It provides software tools for major cluster management tasks: configuration management, software distribution, user and filesystem administration.

Licensing policy:

Commercial.

OS provisions:

Currently build on top of the S.u.S.E distribution.

Documentation:

Printed doumentation, online help.

Product support:

Hotline, EMail, courses.

Available since:

1994.

Countries with distribution:

World wide.

Price range:

Upon request. Special prices for educational institutions.

Vendor:

science + computing GmbH

```
        Hagellocher Weg 71
        D-72070 Tübingen
        Germany
```

Phone:

+49 7071 9457 0

Fax:

+49 7071 9457 27

EMail:

info@science-computing.de `<mailto:info@science-computing.de>`

URL:

http://www.science-computing.de `<http://www.science-computing.de>`

Contact:

Olaf Flebbe

19   X Windows Related Products

19.1   Accelerated-X Display Server

Description:

Commercial grade X display server with workstation-class features like multiple visuals, overlays, and gamma correction for FreeBSD, and Linux. The AcceleratedX server drives the most popular graphics hardware, including the latest cards from ATI, Diamond, Matrox, NeoMagic, Number 9, and S3. In all, more than 490 different cards are supported.

Distribution media:

CD-ROM.

Licensing policy:

Per CPU.

OS provisions:

No known problems with any Linux distribution.

Documentation:

A 100 page perfect bound manual is included.

Product support:

Unlimited support in included.

Available since:

1994.

Countries with distribution:

World wide.

Price range:

Contact your local reseller, or Xi Graphics.

Vendor:

Xi Graphics

> 1801 Broadway, Suite 1710
> Denver, CO 80202
> U.S.A.

Phone:

> +1 303 298 7478

Fax:

> +1 303 298 1406

EMail:

> *sales@xig.com* <mailto:sales@xig.com>

URL:

> *http://www.xig.com* <http://www.xig.com>

Contact:

> Kyle Fink

19.2   BXwidgets

Description:

> BXwidgets is a supplementary widget set to develop especially commercial Motif applications. It includes special widgets for tabulars, masks, formatted input field and the full support for a complete help system. All has Motif look and feel and is platform independent.

Distribution media:

> 3.5" diskettes.

Licensing policy:

> Source code licence.

OS provisions:

> Any kernel, X11R5 or X11R6, Motif 1.1 or Motif 1.2.

Documentation:

> About 250 pages of documenation with examples. Several demo programs.

Product support:

> Support and update service is available (DM 1200; approximately US$750)

Available since:

> 1992.

Countries with distribution:

> Germany, UK and USA.

Price range:

> DM 1600 (approximately US$1000) for a full source code licence.

Vendor:

> BREDEX GmbH

> Fallersleber-Tor-Wall 23
> D-38100 Braunschweig
> Germany

Phone:

> +49 531 24 33 0 0

Fax:

+49 531 24 33 0 99

EMail:

info@bredex.de <mailto:info@bredex.de>

URL:

http://www.bredex.de <http://www.bredex.de>

19.3   BXwidgets/DB

Description:

BXwidgets/DB is a supplementary widget set to access relational databases. Data can be automatically queried form the database, displayed in various forms, changed and stored in the database. All applications built with BXwidgets/DB are database independent. The database access is performed by transaction-servers. Transaction-Server and database may reside on other hotsts in the network.

Distribution media:

CD-ROM.

Licensing policy:

Per OS license, no run-time restrictions. Evaluation license available.

OS provisions:

X11R5 and Motif 1.2 must be installed.

Documentation:

Printed manual in English.

Product support:

Support and update service is available.

Available since:

1996.

Price range:

DM 4900 (approximately US$2900).

Vendor:

BREDEX GmbH

Fallersleber-Tor-Wall 23
D-38100 Braunschweig
Germany

Phone:

+49 531 24 33 0 0

Fax:

+49 531 24 33 0 99

EMail:

info@bredex.de <mailto:info@bredex.de>

URL:

http://www.bredex.de <http://www.bredex.de>

19.4 Laptop, Accelerated-X Display Server

Description:

Commercial grade X display server with workstation-class features like multiple visuals, overlays, and gamma correction for FreeBSD and Linux. The AcceleratedX server drives the most popular laptop hardware, including the latest cards from Dell, IBM, Toshiba, and Neo Magic.

Distribution media:

CD-ROM.

Licensing policy:

Per CPU.

OS provisions:

No known problems with any Linux distribution.

Documentation:

A 100 page perfect bound manual is included.

Product support:

Unlimited support in included.

Available since:

1994.

Countries with distribution:

World wide.

Price range:

Contact your local reseller, or Xi Graphics.

Vendor:

Xi Graphics

```
        1801 Broadway, Suite 1710
        Denver, CO 80202
        U.S.A.
```

Phone:

+1 303 298 7478

Fax:

+1 303 298 1406

EMail:

sales@xig.com <mailto:sales@xig.com>

URL:

http://www.xig.com <http://www.xig.com>

Contact:

Kyle Fink

19.5 MaXimum cde Developer's Edition v1.0

Description:

A complete networked desktop that enables administrators to integrate industry-standard PCs into existing Unix networks with better internationalization and the same functionality as more expensive workstations. Also includes developer's tools.

Distribution media:

CD-ROM.

Licensing policy:

Per CPU.

OS provisions:

No known problems with any Linux distribution.

Documentation:

A 100 page perfect bound manual the Accelerated-X server and a 300 page perfect bound manual for CDE is included.

Product support:

Unlimited support in included.

Available since:

1997.

Countries with distribution:

World wide.

Price range:

Contact your local reseller, or Xi Graphics.

Vendor:

Xi Graphics

```
1801 Broadway, Suite 1710
Denver, CO 80202
U.S.A.
```

Phone:

+1 303 298 7478

Fax:

+1 303 298 1406

EMail:

sales@xig.com <mailto:sales@xig.com>

URL:

http://www.xig.com <http://www.xig.com>

Contact:

Kyle Fink

19.6 Multi-headed, Accelerated-X Display Server

Description:

Commercial grade X display server with workstation-class features like multiple visuals, overlays, and gamma correction for FreeBSD and Linux. The AcceleratedX server drives the most popular graphics hardware, including the latest cards from Colorgraphics, STB, and Matrox. In all, more than 10 different cards are supported.

Distribution media:

CD-ROM.

Licensing policy:
> Per CPU.

OS provisions:
> No known problems with any Linux distribution.

Documentation:
> A 100 page perfect bound manual is included.

Product support:
> Installation support in included.

Available since:
> 1994.

Countries with distribution:
> World wide.

Price range:
> Contact your local reseller, or Xi Graphics.

Vendor:
> Xi Graphics

>>   1801 Broadway, Suite 1710
>>   Denver, CO 80202
>>   U.S.A.

Phone:
> +1 303 298 7478

Fax:
> +1 303 298 1406

EMail:
> *sales@xig.com* <mailto:sales@xig.com>

URL:
> *http://www.xig.com* <http://www.xig.com>

Contact:
> Kyle Fink

19.7   OpenGL, Accelerated-X Display Server

Description:
> Commercial grade X display server with workstation-class features like multiple visuals, overlays, and gamma correction for FreeBSD and Linux. The AcceleratedX server drives the most popular graphics hardware, including the latest cards from ATI, Diamond, Matrox, NeoMagic, Number 9, and S3. The lastest version of OpenGL from Silicon Graphics Inc. In all, more than 450 different cards are supported.

Distribution media:
> CD-ROM.

Licensing policy:
> Per CPU.

OS provisions:

No known problems with any Linux distribution.

Documentation:

A 100 page perfect bound manual is included.

Product support:

Installation support in included.

Available since:

1994.

Countries with distribution:

World wide.

Price range:

Contact your local reseller, or Xi Graphics.

Vendor:

Xi Graphics

```
1801 Broadway, Suite 1710
Denver, CO 80202
U.S.A.
```

Phone:

+1 303 298 7478

Fax:

+1 303 298 1406

EMail:

sales@xig.com <mailto:sales@xig.com>

URL:

http://www.xig.com <http://www.xig.com>

Contact:

Kyle Fink

19.8   OSF-Certified Motif

Description:

A complete OSF-Certified Motif runtime and development environment.

Distribution media:

CD-ROM.

Licensing policy:

Per CPU.

OS provisions:

No known problems with any Linux distribution.

Documentation:

Release note that include references to well-written commerical reference manuals.

Product support:

Installation support in included.

Available since:

    1995.

Countries with distribution:

    World wide.

Price range:

    Contact your local reseller, or Xi Graphics.

Vendor:

    Xi Graphics

        1801 Broadway, Suite 1710
        Denver, CO 80202
        U.S.A.

Phone:

    +1 303 298 7478

Fax:

    +1 303 298 1406

EMail:

    sales@xig.com <mailto:sales@xig.com>

URL:

    http://www.xig.com <http://www.xig.com>

Contact:

    Kyle Fink

19.9   Red Hat Motif

Description:

    Red Hat Motif is the full OSF/Motif development system. Red Hat Motif will turn your Linux PC into a Motif development workstation. This product is available for Intel, Alpha and SPARC platforms. For developers, Motif 2.0.1 makes creation of software applications and custom widgets simple. The many toolkit enhancements, new widgets, and UIL improvements provide uncomplicated application portability across a variety of platforms. For end users, Red Hat Motif 2.0.1 improves their interface performance. The virtual screen support unclutters their workspace by providing alternate locations for chosen windows, while providing greater consistency with PC environments.

Distribution media:

    CD-ROM.

Licensing policy:

    Single user license.

OS provisions:

    Red Hat's Motif for Linux is compatible with all major Linux distributions, including Red Hat, Slackware, Debian, Caldera and others. Compatible with ELF: libc 5.0.9, 5.2.18+, xpm 3.4f, XFree86 3.1x+, 8 MB RAM, 15 MB hard disk space, CD-ROM drive.

Documentation:

    Red Hat Motif 2.0.1 comes with a 120 page manual and online documentation.

Product support:

    EMail installation support provided for thirty days after registering the product. Motif users can access FAQs at our *web site* <http://www.redhat.com>.

Available since:

December, 1995.

Countries with distribution:

World wide.   For specific locations, see our *web site* `<http://www.redhat.com/redhat/reseller-list.phtml?table=reseller>`.

Price range:

US$149.

Vendor:

Red Hat Software, Inc.

```
4201 Research Commons, Suite 100
79 TW Alexander Drive, P.O. Box 13588
Research Triangle Park, NC 27709
U.S.A.
```

Phone:

+1 888 REDHAT 1, +1 919 547 0012

Fax:

+1 919 547 0024

EMail:

sales@redhat.com `<mailto:sales@redhat.com>`

URL:

http://www.redhat.com `<http://www.redhat.com>`

20   Other Software

20.1   Clustor

Description:

Clustor is a program for managing large computational tasks. Clustor greatly simplifies a common computationally intensive activity - running the same program code numerous times with different inputs. Clustor provides increased performance by distributing jobs over a network of computers and improved task management through a friendly user interface.

Targeted at users who run computationally demanding tasks, Clustor supports all phases of running such a task: task preparation, job generation and job execution. With Clustor, users who do not have extensive knowledge of programming parallel applications, such as scientists, engineers, researchers, are able to utilize the power of networked computers.

Distribution media:

Internet (WWW). Optional CD-ROM.

Licensing policy:

A free demo licenses with limited functionality, 30 days evaluation licenses with complete functionality from our *web site* `<http://www.activetools.com>`.

OS provisions:

Linux 1.2 or higher.

Documentation:

Web site, optional printed documentation.

Product support:

EMail support.

Extra features and add-ons:

Features for load monitoring and resource sharing, network installation program.

Available since:

February, 1997.

Countries with distribution:

World wide

Price range:

Starting at US$495.

Vendor:

Active Tools Inc.

```
246 First St, Suite 310
San Francisco, CA 94105
U.S.A.
```

Phone:

+1 415 882 7062

Fax:

+1 415 680 2369

EMail:

info@activetools.com `<mailto:info@activetools.com>`

URL:

http://www.activetools.com `<http://www.activetools.com>`

Contact:

Rok Sosic, Sergij Foski

20.2 FootPrints

Description:

The first web-based helpdesk software system. Tracks problems/solutions, trouble tickets – whatever information you need to manage – and makes it available via the World Wide Web to your customers or users. Resides on Unix or NT Web server; platform independent access using any web browser.

Distribution media:

Internet (FTP and WWW). Also available: 3.5" diskettes and tape.

Licensing policy:

Free eval available from *http://www.unipress.com/cgi-bin/free_evals* `<http://www.unipress.com/cgi-bin/free_evals>` or *ftp://ftp.unipress.com/pub/free_evals* `<ftp://ftp.unipress.com/pub/free_evals>`.

Pricing is on a per-user basis.

OS provisions:

Runs with any Linux running a web server.

Documentation:

Online manual/help.

Product support:

15% of software purchase price charged for maintenance and updates. Technical support via web and phone is free.

Available since:

January 1, 1997.

Countries with distribution:

World wide.

Price range:

US$1995 per starter pack (server software plus 3 user licenses). Licenses may be Group (a number of users can access your helpdesk, e.g. all your customers use one Group license) or Individual (helpdesk engineers and administrators would each require one Individual license).

Vendor:

UniPress Software, Inc.

```
2025 Lincoln Highway
Edison, NJ 08817
U.S.A.
```

Phone:

+1 800 222 0550, +1 732 287 2100

Fax:

+1 732 287 4929

EMail:

info@unipress.com `<mailto:info@unipress.com>`

URL:

http://www.unipress.com/footprints `<http://www.unipress.com/footprints>`

Contact:

Sue Glassberg *<sue@unipress.com>* `<mailto:sue@unipress.com>`

20.3   Aladdin Ghostscript

Description:

PostScript, PDF, PCL5e (2Q97), PCL5c (2Q97), and PCL XL interpreter. Provides X Windows previewing, conversion to half a dozen raster file formats, and output to dozens of printers. Runs in all OS environments, not just Linux, and on any processor (32- or 64-bit) with a C compiler. Can drive black-and-white, RGB, and CMYK devices, both bilevel and continuous-tone. For more information, see *http://www.cs.wisc.edu/~ghost/index.html* `<http://www.cs.wisc.edu/ghost/index.html>`. Note that Aladdin Ghostscript is an OEM product only: end-user licensing is not available (and not necessary, since the product is free for end users), nor is end-user support.

Distribution media:

3.5" diskettes.

Licensing policy:

Normally per-CPU. License normally includes source code, upgrades, and support.

OS provisions:

X11R5 or later is required for X Windows previewing. OS-specific modules are available for Unix (including Linux), VMS, MS Windows (including Windows NT), OS/2, and Macintosh. Porting to other OSs is simple: all OS dependencies are segregated in a single file of typically less than 100 lines of code.

Documentation:

Online documentation only, in English. Currently in plain ASCII text; texinfo and HTML versions are in preparation.

Product support:

Normally included in license; by EMail, phone, and fax.

Extra features and add-ons:

Each input language is priced separately, with a discount for multiple languages.

Available since:

1988 as free software, 1991 commercially.

Countries with distribution:

World wide.

Price range:

Negotiated for each customer.

Vendor:

Artifex Software Inc.

```
454 Las Gallinas Ave., Suite 108
San Rafael, CA 94903
U.S.A.
```

Phone:

+1 415 492 9861

Fax:

+1 415 492 9862

EMail:

info@arsoft.com `<mailto:info@arsoft.com>`

URL:

http://www.cs.wisc.edu/~ghost/index.html `<http://www.cs.wisc.edu/~ghost/index.html>`

20.4 journyx WebTime

Description:

A web based time and attendance tracking software product. You can record and report on employee time worldwide using the power of the Internet, or across your entire enterprise on your Intranet.

Distribution media:

3.5" diskettes and Internet (FTP).

Licensing policy:

Free for first 60 days of use, US$1000 plus US$25 per user thereafter.

OS provisions:

Runs on any version of Linux.

Documentation:

All documentation is in HTML and included online with the product.

Product support:

A maintenance contract is 15% of the purchase price per annum.

Extra features and add-ons:

Works with any browser including text based browsers such as lynx. Easy export of data to Microsoft Excel or Quickbooks. Free webserver and SQL database engine included in the package.

Available since:

August 1, 1997.

Countries with distribution:

World wide.

Price range:

U$1000-$10,000.

Vendor:

journyx

```
6716 Beauford Drive
Austin, TX 78750
U.S.A.
```

Phone:

+1 512 345 8282

Fax:

+1 512 342 9379

EMail:

info@journyx.com `<mailto:info@journyx.com>`

URL:

http://journyx.com `<http://journyx.com>`

Contact:

Curt Finch

20.5   LanSafe

Description:

LanSafe III is a UPS Power Management application. It provides automatic orderly shutdown functionality in case of an extended power failure that should outlast the UPS battery run time. LanSafe III enables broadcast messages and EMail to be sent according to user defined power condition changes.

LanSafe III is bundled with the following Exide Electronics UPSs: OneUPS Plus, NetUPS, PowerWare Prestige, PowerWare Profile, PowerWare Plus 5xx. It also ships with FPS Power Systems UPSs: PowerRite Plus, PowerRite Max, PowerWorks A30, PowerWorks A40, Series 9000 and Series 10000.

It is also possible to purchase a separate software license to use with a previous UPS model or an other manufactures UPS.

Distribution media:

CD-ROM.

OS provisions:

Linux kernel 2.0. Both X/Motif based and character based user interfaces provided.

Documentation:

Online help. Online manual.

Product support:

Available.

Extra features and add-ons:

Support for other manufacturer's UPS.

Available since:

May, 1997.

Countries with distribution:

World wide.

Price range:

US$149.

Vendor (USA):

Exide Electronics

        8609 Six Forks Road
        Raleigh, NC 27615
        U.S.A.

Vendor (Europe/Middle East/Africa):

Exide Electronics S.A.

        MPL House, Prescott Road
        Poyle, Colnbrook
        Berkshire, SL3 0AE
        UK

Phone:

+1 800 554 3448, +1 919 872 3020, +44 1753 686200

Fax:

+1 800 75 EXIDE, +44 1753 686827

EMail:

info@exide.com <mailto:info@exide.com>, *info@deltecpower.com* <mailto:info@deltecpower.com>, *sales_support@exide.co.uk* <mailto:sales_support@exide.co.uk>

URL:

http://www.exide.com <http://www.exide.com>, *http://www.deltecpower.com* <http://www. deltecpower.com>, *http://www.fpsUPS.com* <http://www.fpsUPS.com>

20.6 LjetMgr

Description:

Printers from Hewlett-Packard (both laser and ink variants) have an extensive set of configurable options. These options are normally set on the front panel of the printer.

The most notable options are:

- Ccono-mode to save toner
- Powersave mode
- Page format selection
- Font/typeface and language selection

With LjetManager you can directly modify these settings on your screen. It is especially usefull for printers that lack front panel configurability (like the LaserJet 5L) or if you have more than one printer at your disposal.

LjetManager sports a graphical user interface, is fully localizable and comes with documentation and help pages in HTML format.

Distribution media:

3.5" diskettes, Internet (EMail and WWW).

Licensing policy:

You can download a demo version version of LjetMgr from the following location and the corresponding mirror sites: ftp://sunsite.unc.edu/pub/Linux/system/Printing Just have a look for ljetmgr-2.6.README and the accompanying files.

OS provisions:

Needs a printer that supports PJL. Available for Linux on Intel.

Documentation:

Complete context sensitive Help and documentation in HTML format. A PostScript version is available on request.

Product support:

Prices include installation support and one year of free upgrades. Additional support available on request.

Available since:

May, 1996.

Countries with distribution:

World wide.

Price range:

Please contact softWorks for current prices. Discounts for educational institutions and students available.

Vendor:

softWorks, Richard Schwaninger

```
Theodor-Körnerstr. 173
A-8010 Graz
Austria
```

Phone:

+43 316 686590

Fax:

+43 316 686590

EMail:

risc@ping.at <mailto:risc@ping.at>

URL:

http://members.ping.at/risc <http://members.ping.at/risc>

Contact:

Richard Schwaninger

20.7   Synchronize/CyberScheduler

Description:

Calendaring and scheduling software for LANS, WANs and Intranets.

Distribution media:

Internet (FTP).

Licensing policy:

Per user.

OS provisions:

Linux.

Documentation:

Take a look at our *web site* `<http://www.crosswind.com>`.

Available since:

1989.

Countries with distribution:

World wide.

Price range:

US$100 per user.

Vendor:

CrossWind Technologies Inc.

```
1505 Ocean Street, Suite 1
Santa Cruz, CA 95060
U.S.A.
```

Phone:

+1 408 469 1780

Fax:

+1 408 469 1750

EMail:

info@crosswind.com `<mailto:info@crosswind.com>`

URL:

http://www.crosswind.com `<http://www.crosswind.com>`

Contact:

Anne Becker

21   Free Software for Commercial Hardware

This section covers free Linux software (e.g. drivers) for specialized hardware.

21.1   Stallion Technologies Multiport Serial Boards

Description:

Stallion provides Linux support for its EasyIO and EasyConnection range of multiport cards. EasyIO is available with either 4 asynchronous serial ports with RJ45 connectors, or 8 asynchronous serial ports with RJ45 or DB25 connectors. EasyIO supports data rates of up to 145 Kbits/sec or 460 Kbits/sec per port (depending on the model) and full modem signaling. Drivers are available for most Intel-based operating systems, including Linux. EasyIO is available for the ISA bus.

EasyConnection is an expandable multiport solution that provides from 8 to 64 asynchronous serial ports in 8 or 16 port increments. Both RJ45 and DB25 connectors are available. Features include full surge suppression, full modem signaling, and data rates of up to 145 Kbits/sec or 460 Kbits/sec per port (depending on the panel version). Drivers are available for most Intel-based operating systems, including Linux. EasyConnection is available for the ISA, EISA and PCI bus.

Distribution media:

Internet (FTP).

Licensing policy:

The Linux driver is available at no charge and is copyrighted under the GNU General Public License. Source code is provided.

OS provisions:

The most current driver supports all 2.0.x kernel versions. The drivers are updated regularly to keep pace with kernel changes.

Documentation:

Hardware reference documentation provided with the boards. The Linux driver package contains a README file with driver installation and usage information.

Product support:

Stallion Technologies now fully supports the Stallion board Linux drivers. Software updates are available from the Internet. Stallion also provides technical support for the hardware. Contact *Stallion support* <mailto:www-support@stallion.com> for assistance.

Available since:

October, 1994.

Countries with distribution:

World wide distribution. Available in most countries.

Price range:

Prices for the serial boards vary from country to country. Contact your nearest Stallion Technologies office for local availability and pricing. The driver package contains a file with contact information for all Stallion Technologies offices.

Vendor:

Stallion Technologies Pty Ltd.

```
2880 Research Park Drive, Suite 160
Soquel, CA 95073
U.S.A.
```

Phone:

+1 800 347 7979

Fax:

+1 408 477 0444

EMail:
    info@stallion.com `<mailto:info@stallion.com>`

URL:
    http://www.stallion.com `<http://www.stallion.com>`

FTP:
    ftp://ftp.stallion.com `<ftp://ftp.stallion.com>`

The teTeX HOWTO: The Linux-teTeX Local Guide

Robert Kiesling   v2.9.1, 21 August 1997

This document covers the basic installation and usage of the teTeX TeX and LaTeX implementation under the major U.S. Linux distributions, and auxiliary packages like Ghostscript. Contents of the teTeX HOWTO: The Linux-teTeX Local Guide are Copyright (c) 1997 by Robert A. Kiesling. Permission is granted to copy this document, in whole or in part, provided that credit is given to the author and the Linux Documentation Project. Registered trademarks are the property of their respective holders. Please send all complaints, suggestions, errata, and any miscellany to *kiesling@terracom.net* <mailto:kiesling@terracom.net>, so I can keep this document as complete and up to date as possible.

Contents

1 Introduction.

FAQ No. 1. My computer just ate NINE high density diskettes' worth of data. WHAT HAPPENED?

Answer: Installing teTeX on Chanel3, my Compaq laptop, was like dropping a 20-foot concrete bridge section exactly into place from a height of 50 feet. teTeX is a *big package.* Even so, it is a moderately complete implementation of TeX 3.1415 and LaTeX 2e for Linux systems. TeX is a big subject anyway, so you can expect to spend the rest of your computing career keeping up-to-date on the latest in the world of TeX. That is to say, installing and using teTeX is not for the faint of heart. Nor is it for day trippers. This package requires serious quality time.

Thomas Esser, the author of teTeX, has gone to great lengths to make the package fast, complete, and easy to use. Because TeX is implemented for practically every serious computer system in the world—and quite a few "non-serious" ones—implementors must provide the installation facilities for all of them. This accounts in part for teTeX's size. It also accounts for the fact that the pieces necessary to make a workable teTeX installation are spread all over your friendly neighborhood CTAN archive.

CTAN is the Comprehensive TeX Archive Network, a series of anonymous FTP sites which archive TeX programs, macros, fonts, and documentation. You'll probably become familiar with at least one CTAN site. In this document, a pathname like `~CTAN/contrib/pstricks` means "look in the directory `contrib/pstricks` of your nearest CTAN site." See section 8 (Appendix A) for a current list of CTAN sites and their mirror sites.

Fortunately, some considerate Linux Distribution implementors have assembled the necessary pieces for us. teTeX comes with all the major Linux distributions.

However, if you don't have the Slackware, RedHat, or Debian GNU/Linux distribution, you can install teTeX from its official CTAN distribution. In some cases this may be more desirable. See **Section 3** for details.

If you already have teTeX installed on your system and want to jump directly into figuring out how to use it, skip this section and the next, and go directly to section 5 (Using teTeX).

2 What is TeX? What is LaTeX? What is teTeX?

teTeX is an implementation of TeX for UNIX systems. It is the work of Thomas Esser, *te@informatik.uni-hannover.de* <mailto:te@informatik.uni-hannover.de>. In the Linux versions of teTeX, the executable programs themselves run under Linux and the fonts are provided in form usable by the Linux-teTeX system. (The sections covering teTeX installation concentrate on the i386 versions of Linux. Installing teTeX for MkLinux or Linux for the Alpha should require only substituting the appropriate binary-program archive in the installation process.) The rest of the code, TeX and LaTeX itself, is portable across various machines.

In addition to the executable programs, the distribution includes all of the TeX and LaTeX package, metafont and its sources, bibtex(1), makeindex(1), and *all* of the documentation... more than 4 megabytes' worth. The documentation covers everything you will forseeably need to know to get started. So, you should install all of the documents. Not only will you eventually read them, the documents themselves provide many examples of "live" TeX and LaTeX code.

In comparison with other implementations of TeX, the installation of teTeX is almost trivial, even without the Linux distribution packages, if you don't count the effort necessary acquire the distributions via anonymous FTP or insert and remove several dozen distribution diskettes by hand. If your teTeX distribution arrived on a CD-ROM, even less effort is required to install it.

TeX is a typesetting system developed by Professor Donald Knuth of Stanford University. It is a lower-level typesetting language that powers all of the higher-level packages like LaTeX. Essentially, LaTeX is a set of TeX macros which provide convenient, predefined document formats for end users. If you like the formats provided by LaTeX, you may never need to learn bare-bones TeX programming. The difference between the two languages is like the difference between assembly language and C. You can have the speed and flexibility of TeX, or the convenience of LaTeX. Which brings us to the next answer,

Answer: You have it backwards! I want to know what exactly I need to get before I can have TeX on my system!

It's important to remember that TeX only handles the typesetting part of the document preparation. Generating output with TeX is like compiling source code into object code, which still needs to be linked. You prepare an input file with a text editor – what most people think of as "word processing" – and typeset the input file document with TeX to produce a device-independent output file, called a .dvi file.

You also need output drivers for your printer and video display. These output drivers translate TeX's .dvi output to display your typeset document on the screen or on paper. This software is collectively known as "dviware." For example, TeX itself only makes requests for fonts. It is up to the .dvi output translator to provide the actual font to the display device if necessary, regardless of whether it is the screen or a printer. This extra step may seem overly complicated, but the abstraction allows documents to display the same on different devices with no change to the original document.

In fact, much of TeX's, and therefore LaTeX's, complexity, arises from its implementation of various font systems, and the way these fonts are specified. A major improvement of LaTeX 2e over its predecessor was the way users specify fonts, the former New Font Selection Scheme. (See the sections 5.2.2 (Characters and type styles) and 7 (Using PostScript Fonts).)

teTeX comes distributed with about a dozen standard fonts preloaded, which is enough to get you started. Also provided are the font metrics descriptions, in .tfm (TeX font metric) files. To generate the other fonts you will need, it is simply a matter of installing the metafont sources. teTeX's .dvi utilities will invoke metafont automatically and generate the Computer Modern fonts you need, on-the-fly.

By the way, the letters of the word "TeX" are Greek, tau-epsilon-chi. This is *not* a fraternity. Instead, it is the root of the Greek word, *techne,* which means art and/or science. "TeX" is not pronounced like the first syllable in "Texas." The *chi* has no English equivalent, but TeX is generally pronounced so that it rhymes with "yecch," to use Professor Knuth's example from *The TeXBook* (see below). When writing, "TeX," on character devices, always use the standard capitalization, or the \TeX{} macro in typesetting. This is how TeX is distinguished from other typesetting systems.

Speaking of typing, any of the editors which work under Linux— nvi(1), jed(1), joe(1), jove(1), vi(1), vim(1), stevie(1), emacs(1), microemacs—will work to prepare a TeX input file, as long as the editor reads and writes plain-vanilla ASCII text. My preference is emacs(1), the GNU version. There are several reasons for this:

- Emacs' TeX and LaTeX modes obviate the need for a stand-alone TeX shell.
- Emacs can automatically insert TeX-style, "curly quotes," as you type, rather than the "ASCII-vanilla" kind.

- Emacs has integrated support for `texinfo` and `makeinfo,` a hypertext documentation system.
- Emacs is widely supported. Version 19.34, for example, is included in the major U.S. Linux distributions.
- Emacs does everything except butter the toast in the morning.
- Emacs is free.

There's a lot of software to assemble. In the meantime, you can start in "learning" TeX and LaTeX. Remember that teTeX and the font packages have been designed as two separate entities: The teTeX executable programs and shell scripts, as distributed with Linux, have been built specifically for the system, but the CM, DC, American Mathematical Society, or other font distributions work on many different platforms. While you are working on assembling the files, you can take a few breaks to locate some of the documentation you will need.

2.1   Resources for further information.

There are user manuals available both commercially and via the Internet. Judging by the number of mentions they receive in the Usenet `comp.text.tex` newsgroup, the most useful—and definitive—commercially available texts for beginners are:

LaTeX: A Document Preparation System, by Leslie Lamport, 272 pp. If you're using LaTeX instead of plain TeX (highly recommended), this is the definitive reference.

If you must use plain TeX, *The TeXBook* by Donald Knuth, 483 pp., is the definitive reference. It is also necessary if you plan to do any serious class, package, or macro writing for LaTeX.

The LaTeX Companion, by Michel Goosens, Frank Mittelbach, and Alexander Samarin, 530 pp., is more advanced than the Lamport, above. If you are approaching TeX or LaTeX for the first time, you may feel lost reading this. (I was.) However, when you need to add extension packages, like PSNFSS (See the section titled, 7 (Using PostScript fonts).), or `bibtex(1)`, a bibliography indexing program, this book is one of the most highly regarded on the market.

At your nearest CTAN site you can retrieve these documents for free:

The Not So Short Introduction to LaTeX2e, by Tobias Oetiker, Hubert Partl, Irene Hyna, and Elisabeth Schlegl, 69 pp. This wonderful document is located at `~CTAN/packages/TeX/info/lshort/*`.

You can get a PostScript or `.dvi` version of the document ready for printing, or the native LaTeX document. There is also a version available in German: `lkurz.*`. Make sure to read the `README` file before assembling!

A Gentle Introduction to TeX: A Manual for Self-Study, by Michael Doob, 91 pp. You can find this document at: `~CTAN:packages/TeX/info/gentle.tex`. Almost of necessity, this document covers less ground than its LaTeX counterpart, above. However, it will get you to the same place as the LaTeX manuals. If you must use plain TeX for your documents, this document clarifies many of the complexities of plain TeX and makes its use almost easy.

"IMPRINT: The Newsletter of Digital Typography," edited by Robert Kiesling. I realize that this is BLATANT and SHAMELESS self-promotion. But, you should know anyway, that IMPRINT is a free, ASCII-text newsletter which is available via e-mail. IMPRINT appears approximately monthly and covers a broad range of text processing and digital imaging topics, both beginning and advanced. Many of the items covered apply directly or indirectly to TeX'ing. The emphasis is on production of industry-standard typeset and printed material. To subscribe to IMPRINT, send a brief, human-readable message to me at *imprint@macline.com.* `<mailto:imprint@macline.com>`

The LaTeX Catalogue is a `bibtex(1)` database of available LaTeX packages, compiled and maintained by Graham Williams. It's included with teTeX, and the most recent version is available on the World Wide Web. Do you need a package that prints borders, or makes margin notes? You'll find that the package you need is listed here. *The LaTeX Catalogue* is located in your local teTeX library in the directory `teTeX/texmf/doc/Catalog`, and on the Web at *http://cbr.dit.csiro.au/~gjw* <http://www.cbr.dit.csiro.au/~gjw/>. See section 5.3 (LaTeX extension packages and other resources) for further details about LaTeX packages.

Thomas Merz's Ghostscript Manual, which is the Ghostscript appendix of his book, *PostScript \& Acrobat/PDF: Applications, Troubleshooting, and Cross-Platform Publishing*. It is available from the Ghostscript Home Page (see the section 3.3 (Ghosctscript V. 5.03)), or from Merz's home page, *http://www.muc.de/~tm/* <http://www.muc.de/~tm/>.

There are, of course, other guides available to using TeX and LaTeX. They cover different aspects of these systems to varying degrees. The reference documents cited above, however, are the most comprehensive in scope that I have seen and are aimed at beginners (or near-beginners).

If the going gets especially tough, you can probably do a little extra shopping at Office Max, Office Depot, Staples, or your local stationer, and pick up several reams of three-hole punched, photocopy paper, two or three, three-inch binders, and some index tabs. When it comes time to print the documents, you'll need a place to keep them, and they seem to be more useful if they are kept on paper. This must be one of the stranger phenomena of technical documentation.

You will note, however, that the references mentioned above are hardware-independent. They won't tell you a thing about running teTeX specifically. Many of them, in fact, refer to some mythical "Local Guide." This, and several of the documents that come bundled with teTeX, comprise the less-than-mythical Local Guide to installing and operating teTeX with Linux.

3 Installation notes.

All of the major Linux distributions include packaged versions of teTeX, and each distribution has its own idiosyncrasies. The packaging methods of each distribution are, for the most part, incompatible. If you try to install teTeX from another distribution, you *may* succeed in installing the package, but you're certain to mess up the package-management database on your system. When installing teTeX, please consult the section below that corresponds to your Linux distribution.

Installing teTeX is surprisingly easy for a package of this magnitude. This document covers only the major free U.S. Linux distributions, because I haven't had time to obtain or install European Linux distributions like S.u.S.E.

However, the generic, teTeX distribution isn't any harder to install than the Linux packages. See section 3.1 (Generic CTAN distribution), below.

You should consider installing the generic teTeX distribution from the CTAN archives if:

- Your system isn't based on one of the standard Linux distributions.
- You don't have root privileges on your system.
- You want or need to have the very latest version of teTeX, or LaTeX.
- You don't have enough disk space available for a full installation.
- You want to install teTeX somewhere instead of the `/usr` file system.
- You would like to share your teTeX installation with other UNIX variants or platforms on a network. In this case, you should strongly consider installing from the *source* distribution. See section 3.1.2 (Installing the source distribution), below.
- You want the latest versions of teTeX's public domain Type 1 fonts, which are significantly better than the fonts included in earlier releases.

A complete installation of the binary distribution requires 40-50 Mb of disk space, and building the distribution from the source code takes about 75 Mb, so you should make sure that the disk space is available before you start. You don't need to have the `gcc(1)` compiler or the X Windows System installed (although X certainly helps because it is much easier to preview documents on-screen). All you need is an editor that is capable of producing plain ASCII, text (see section 2). What could be simpler?

Ghostscript V. 5.03 allows printing of PostScript documents on non-PostScript printers, and allows previewing of PostScript documents on VGA monitors and X Window System displays. If you already have a PostScript printer, you won't need Ghostscript simply to print PostScript documents. Ghostscript has many other capabilities, however, which are beyond the scope of this HOWTO.

APSFILTER can automate document post processing and printing, and make life with your printer a lot easier. See the section titled 3.4 (APSFILTER).

For information on how to install a printer daemon and generally configure printers for Linux, see the section titled 3.5 (The lpd(8) daemon), and consult the Printing-HOWTO.

3.1 Generic CTAN distribution, V. 0.4.

You can retrieve the files from one of the CTAN archives listed in section 8 (Appendix A). In the examples below, the files were retrieved from the CTAN archive at *ftp.tex.ac.uk*. `<ftp://ftp.tex.ac.uk>`

3.1.1 Installing the binary distribution.

Minimal installation.   First, FTP to *ftp.tex.ac.uk* `<ftp://ftp.tex.ac.uk/ctan/tex-archive/` `systems/unix/teTeX/contrib>` and `cd` to the directory

```
ctan/tex-archive/systems/unix/teTeX/distrib/
```

Retrieve the files

```
INSTALL.bin
install.sh
```

and place them in the top-level directory where you want to install teTeX, for example, `/var/teTeX` if you plan to install teTeX in the `/var` file system.

Print out the `INSTALL.bin` file. Keep this file handy, because it describes how to install a minimal teTeX installation. The minimal installation requires only 10-15 MB of disk space, but it is recommended that you install the complete teTeX package if at all possible. For a minimum installation, you'll need the files

```
ctan/tex-archive/systems/unix/teTeX/distrib/base/latex-base.tar.gz
ctan/tex-archive/systems/unix/teTeX/distrib/base/tetex-base.tar.gz
```

You'll also need one of two archives which contain the executable teTeX programs. Retrieve the archive file

```
ctan/tex-archive/systems/unix/teTeX/distrib/binaries/i386-linux.tar.gz
```

if your system uses the Linux ELF shared libraries, `ld.so(1)` of at least version 1.73, and clibs of at least version 5.09. If it doesn't, retrieve the archive

```
ctan/tex-archive/systems/unix/teTeX/distrib/binaries/i386-linuxaout.tar.gz
```

which is compiled for systems that use the older, a.out-format static libraries.

Then, following the instructions in the file INSTALL.bin, execute the command

```
sh ./install.sh
```

while in the top-level teTeX installation directory. (Make sure that the teTeX archives are located there, too.) After a few moments, the installation program will warn you that you are missing some of the teTeX packages. However, if you're planning only a minimal teTeX installation, you should ignore the warnings and proceed. To configure the basic teTeX system, see section 3.1.1 (Base system configuration), below.

To install the remaining packages, see the next section.

Complete installation. To perform a complete teTeX installation, retrieve the archive files listed in the previous section, as well as the following files:

```
ctan/tex-archive/systems/unix/teTeX/distrib/doc/ams-doc.tar.gz
ctan/tex-archive/systems/unix/teTeX/distrib/doc/bibtex-doc.tar.gz
ctan/tex-archive/systems/unix/teTeX/distrib/doc/eplain-doc.tar.gz
ctan/tex-archive/systems/unix/teTeX/distrib/doc/fonts-doc.tar.gz
ctan/tex-archive/systems/unix/teTeX/distrib/doc/general-doc.tar.gz
ctan/tex-archive/systems/unix/teTeX/distrib/doc/generic-doc.tar.gz
ctan/tex-archive/systems/unix/teTeX/distrib/doc/latex-doc.tar.gz
ctan/tex-archive/systems/unix/teTeX/distrib/doc/makeindex-doc.tar.gz
ctan/tex-archive/systems/unix/teTeX/distrib/doc/metapost-doc.tar.gz
ctan/tex-archive/systems/unix/teTeX/distrib/doc/programs-doc.tar.gz
ctan/tex-archive/systems/unix/teTeX/distrib/fonts/ams-fonts.tar.gz
ctan/tex-archive/systems/unix/teTeX/distrib/fonts/dc-fonts.tar.gz
ctan/tex-archive/systems/unix/teTeX/distrib/fonts/ec-fonts.tar.gz
ctan/tex-archive/systems/unix/teTeX/distrib/fonts/misc-fonts.tar.gz
ctan/tex-archive/systems/unix/teTeX/distrib/fonts/postscript-fonts.tar.gz
ctan/tex-archive/systems/unix/teTeX/distrib/fonts/sauter-fonts.tar.gz
ctan/tex-archive/systems/unix/teTeX/distrib/goodies/amstex.tar.gz
ctan/tex-archive/systems/unix/teTeX/distrib/goodies/bibtex.tar.gz
ctan/tex-archive/systems/unix/teTeX/distrib/goodies/eplain.tar.gz
ctan/tex-archive/systems/unix/teTeX/distrib/goodies/latex-extra.tar.gz
ctan/tex-archive/systems/unix/teTeX/distrib/goodies/metapost.tar.gz
ctan/tex-archive/systems/unix/teTeX/distrib/goodies/pictex.tar.gz
ctan/tex-archive/systems/unix/teTeX/distrib/goodies/pstricks.tar.gz
ctan/tex-archive/systems/unix/teTeX/distrib/goodies/texdraw.tar.gz
ctan/tex-archive/systems/unix/teTeX/distrib/goodies/xypic.tar.gz
```

All of these files should be placed in the top-level directory where you want teTeX to reside. As with the minimal installation, execute the command

```
sh ./install.sh
```

Base system configuration. The install.sh script, after determining which teTeX archive series are present, will present you with a menu of options. The only setting you need to make at this point is to set the top-level directory where you want teTeX installed, by selecting the "D" option. You must, of course, choose a directory in whose parent directory you have write permissions. For example, if you are installing teTeX in your home directory, you would specify the teTeX installation directory as

```
/home/john.q.public/teTeX
```

and, after returning to the main menu, select "I" to proceed with the installation. Note that the directory must not exist already: the `install.sh` script must be able to create it.

An option which you should consider enabling, is setting an alternative directory for generated fonts. Even if you plan to use only PostScript-format, Type 1 scalable fonts, occasionally you'll process a file that requires the Computer Modern fonts. Enabling this option requires that you enter the directory to use. You must have write permissions for the parent directory. Following the example above, you could specify

```
/home/john.q.public/texfonts
```

or, if you want the generated fonts to be accessible by all users on the system, specify a directory like

```
/var/texfonts
```

I would recommend that you *not,* however, use the default `/var/tmp/texfonts` directory for this option, because the generated fonts could be deleted after the next reboot, and the fonts will need to be generated again the next time they're needed.

After you've selected the option "I", and `install.sh` has installed the archives, set various permissions, and generated its links and format files, the program will exit with a message telling you to add the teTeX binary directory to your `$PATH` environment variable, and the directories where the man pages and info files reside to your `$MANPATH` and `$INFOPATH` environment variables. For example, add the statements

```
export PATH=$PATH:"/home/john.q.public/teTeX/bin"
export MANPATH=$MANPATH":/home/john.q.public/teTeX/man"
export INFOPATH$=INFOPATH":/home/john.q.public/teTeX/info"
```

to your `~/.bash_profile` if you use `bash(1)` as your shell, or to your `~/.profile` if you use another shell for logins.

Log out, and then log in again, so the environment variables are registered. Then, run the command

```
texconfig confall
```

to insure that the installation is correct.

Next, you can configure teTeX for you specific hardware. See section 4 (Post-installation configuration details), below.

3.1.2   Installing the source distribution.

To install teTeX V. 0.4 from the source code, `ftp` to a CTAN site like *ftp://ftp.tex.ac.uk* `<ftp://ftp.tex.ac.uk>` and retrieve the files

```
ctan/tex-archive/systems/unix/teTeX/distrib/INSTALL.src
ctan/tex-archive/systems/unix/teTeX/distrib/sources/README.texmf-src
ctan/tex-archive/systems/unix/teTeX/distrib/sources/teTeX-lib-0.4pl8.tar.gz
ctan/tex-archive/systems/unix/teTeX/distrib/sources/teTeX-src-0.4pl7.tar.gz
```

Read over the instructions in INSTALL.src, then su to root and unpack the files in a directory for which you have read-write-execute permissions.

Remember to use the p argument to tar(1), and also remember to unset the noclobber option of bash(1). You can do this with the counterintuitive command

```
set +o noclobber
```

Note that the argument +o to set *unsets* a variable, just exactly backwards from what you might expect.

The file teTeX-lib-0.4p18.tar.gz will create the directory ./teTeX. The file teTeX-src-0.4p17.tar.gz will create the directory teTeX-src-0.4 Print out the file INSTALL.src and keep it nearby for the following steps. cd to the ./teTeX-src-0.4 directory, and, per the instructions in the INSTALL.src file, edit ./Makefile. You need to set the TETEXDIR variable to the absolute path of the parent teTeX directory. This will be the subdirectory teTeX of the directory where you unpacked the source and library archives. For example, if you unpacked the archives in your home directory, you would set TETEXDIR to

```
/home/john.q.public/teTeX
```

The rest of the Makefile options are pretty generic. With gcc(1) version 2.7.2 and later, you should not need to make any further adjustments unless you have a non-standard compiler and library setup, or want the compiler to perform some further optimizations, or for some other reason. Check that the USE_DIALOG, USE_NCURSES, and HAVE_NCURSES variables are set correctly for your system, because the dialog program needs the ncurses library to be installed. A ncurses(3x) library is included in the source distribution, so the default values in the Makefile should work fine. If you can't get ncurses(3x) to compile or link, texconfig(1) can also be run from the command line.

If you've done everything correctly up to this point, you should be able to type make world in the top-level source directory, and relax until the teTeX executables are built. This can take a few hours.

After the build has completed, set the environment variables $PATH, $MANPATH, and $INFOPATH to include the teTeX directories. The statements which would be added to the file ~/.bash_profile, in the example, above, would be

```
export PATH=$PATH":/home/john.q.public/teTeX/bin/i386-linux"
export MANPATH=$MANPATH":/home/john.q.public/teTeX/man"
export INFOPATH=$INFOPATH":/home/john.q.public/teTeX/info"
```

The $PATH variable is different in the source distribution than in the binary distribution. Note that here the path to the binaries is teTeX/bin/i386-linux instead of simply teTeX/bin as in the binary distribution.

At this point you can run texconfig confall to ensure that the paths have been set correctly, and then proceed to configure teTeX as in the binary distribution. See the section 4 (Post-installation configuration details), below.

3.2 Linux packages.

3.2.1 Slackware 3.2.

First, ftp to your nearest Linux archive site. Mine is wuarchive.wustl.edu. Then find the directory with the Slackware distribution diskettes. On wuarchive.wustl.edu, this is

```
systems/linux/sunsite/distributions/Slackware/slakware/.
```

Linux sites which mirror sunsite.unc.edu will store these diskettes in the directory distributions/Slackware/slakware/. teTeX, the full package, is contained on the Slackware disk series t. So, grab all nine disks' worth of the t series, disks t1 - t9. Be sure to keep them in order, too. Either store the files in separate subdirectories labeled t1 - t9 on a hard drive partition, or on diskettes, and label the diskettes t1 through t9. We're going to install them by hand.

This isn't difficult. The Slackware installer creates the directories and unpacks the files. It also provides descriptions of each module in the distribution, which allows you to decide whether you want to install it or not. In the case of teTeX, however, you are simply going to install everything, because that's what you should do anyway.

Let's assume that you have all nine diskettes' worth of the Slackware teTeX distribution ready at hand, organized as described above. You'll have a lot of files which have the extension .tgz. This is shorthand for a tar(1) archive compressed with gzip(1). The names all fit the 8+3 filename limitations of MS-DOG. Aren't you glad you decided to scrap your DOG partitions and install Linux instead? You can use a MS-DOG hard disk partition or DOG-format diskettes to store the files. The archives also begin with the letters tb, td, or tm, and so on, which is the implementors' shorthand for TeX binary, TeX documentation, TeX macro, and so on. The difference to you is academic, because you'll be installing everything anyway.

Simply fire up the Slackware install utility. You needn't concern yourself with reconfiguring the system, so select the option to add new software. Select the appropriate source media (diskettes, HD partition, or CD-ROM), specify that you want to install the Slackware t series, and that you do *not* want to be prompted – simply install all the archives on the Slackware t series diskettes. You'll be prompted to insert each diskette in the floppy drive if you're installing from diskettes. If you're installing from a hard drive or CD-ROM, no more intervention is required by you.

Manual Slackware install. This section is for people who, for one reason or another, would like to install teTeX manually from a Linux package.

Let's assume that you've assembled the Slackware teTeX distribution on floppy diskettes labelled t1 thru t9. Mount the t1 diskette like this

```
mount /dev/fd0 /mnt
```

if your Linux configuration is a standard configuration. Actually, any mount point will do. You'll simply need to substitute the appropriate path spec in the next few steps.

The next thing you want to do is create the teTeX top-level directory. teTeX's internal paths are specified relative to its binary program files, but the Slackware distribution is archived relative to the root directory. So the top-level teTeX directory is:

```
/usr/lib/teTeX
```

For each of the .tgz archive files in the distribution, copy the archive file to the /usr/lib/teTeX directory and repeat the following commands:

You should be logged in as root and in the top-level directory, /, for these steps. I've used the tb-xfig.tgz archive for demonstration purposes. Of course, you'll want to substitute the name of whichever archive you're unpacking.

```
cp /mnt/tb-xfig.tgz /usr/lib/teTeX
tar -zxvf /usr/lib/teTeX/tb-xfig.tar  # v to see what's going on!
rm /usr/lib/teTeX/tb-xfig.tgz
```

Most Slackware packages that I've seen also include an install script, which the Slackware installer executes after unpacking the files. Look in the directory /install after you've unpacked the files. If there's a script there called doinst.sh, execute that, as root, by typing

```
sh < /install/doinst.sh
```

It may be alarming to watch all those filenames scrolling of the top of the screen as the archives are unpacked. Relax! Take a break, and freshen up your coffee (or grab another JOLT from the refrigerator, or otherwise replenish whatever you're drinking). There's only a few more steps you need to perform to install teTeX. They're covered in **Section 4.**

3.2.2 Debian GNU/Linux, V. 1.3.

Installing teTeX from Debian packages is truly trivial. `ftp` the most recent *stable* versions of the teTeX archive files from *ftp.debian.org* `<ftp://ftp.debian.org>`. The teTeX distribution is located in the directory

```
pub/debian/bo/binary-i386/tex
```

Retrieve the following Debian archive files via anonymous FTP (remembering to set *binary* mode for the transfers).

```
tetex-base_0.4pl6-5.deb
tetex-bin_0.4pl6-8.deb
tetex-dev_0.4pl6-8.deb
tetex-doc_0.4pl6-1.deb
tetex-extra_0.4pl6-4.deb
```

Once the files are safely transferred to your local hard disk, **su** to root, and install them using the `dpkg(1)` utility:

```
dpkg -i tetex-base_0.4pl6-5.deb
dpkg -i tetex-bin_0.4pl6-8.deb
dpkg -i tetex-dev_0.4pl6-8.deb
dpkg -i tetex-doc_0.4pl6-1.deb
dpkg -i tetex-extra_0.4pl6-4.deb
```

Installation will take some time, because the Debian archives contain the shell scripts necessary to check for old TeX installations, build the TeX and LaTeX `.fmt` files, build the path-searching database, and see to other configuration details. However, once they are finished, you should have an operational teTeX installation that needs only to be configured for the details of your local system; see section 4 (Post-installation configuration details).

3.2.3 RedHat V. 4.2.

Presumably, you could install only selected portions of the teTeX RedHat distribution, but consistent with the philosophy of the other sections, it is assumed that you will eventually need all of the facilities provided by teTeX, and so you should install the complete distribution.

To install teTeX from RedHat Linux RPM packages, under RedHat Linux v. 4.2, `ftp`to *sunsite.unc.edu* `<ftp://sunsite.unc.edu>` and **cd** to the directory

```
pub/Linux/distributions/redhat/current/i386/RedHat/RPMS/
```

Set *binary* mode for the transfers and retrieve the following files:

```
tetex-0.4pl8-5.i386.rpm
tetex-latex-0.4pl8-5.i386.rpm
tetex-afm-0.4pl8-5.i38 6.rpm
tetex-dvilj-0.4pl8-5.i386.rpm
tetex-dvips-0.4pl8-5.i386.rpm
tetex-xdvi-0.4pl8-5.i386.rpm
tetex-texmf-src-0.4pl8-5.i386.rpm
```

This last file may not be strictly necessary. It contains the LaTeX sources, if you want to install LaTeX yourself. If you're thinking of upgrading LaTeX independently of the binaries in the future, this archive could be useful to have around:

Simply install the files above in the order given, using the `rpm -i` command, and proceed to the section, 4 (Post-installation configuration details).

3.3   Ghostscript V. 5.03.

Ghostscript development is rapid, and the changes which are incorporated into every new version are significant. Therefore, it's worth the effort to install the version of Ghostscript that is available on its home page, *http://www.cs.wisc.edu/~ghost* `<http://www.cs.wisc.edu/~ghost>`.

At the time of this writing, the current version is 5.03. The Ghostscript archive for Linux is composed of the following files:

```
ghostscript-5.03gnu.tar.gz
ghostscript-5.03jpeg.tar.gz
ghostscript-5.03libpng.tar.gz
ghostscript-5.03zlib.tar.gz
ghostscript-fonts-std-5.03.tar.gz
ghostscript-fonts-other-5.03.tar.gz
```

What is Ghostscript, and why do you need it? Technically, Ghostscript is a Raster Image Processor. It translates PostScript code into many common, bit-mapped formats, like those understood by your printer or screen, whether or not they are equipped with PostScript. In practical terms, Ghostscript allows you to use Type 1 fonts, and mix text and graphics on any printer or video display that Ghostscript knows about.

The quality of the fonts which come with the program have improved steadily in the last several versions as well. Or maybe it's that more recent versions of Ghostscript have improved font rendering. In either case, this is of real benefit for Linux users, who may not be able to spend hundreds of dollars on commercial fonts. Because Ghostscript is able to read the font requests made by `dvips(1)`, Ghostscript's font library provides the fonts, not teTeX. But the font metrics files for Ghostscript's font library, which have the extension `.afm`, are already included in the teTeX distribution.

For information about using Ghostscript, see the file `use.txt` in the Ghostscript distribution, and the Linux Documentation Project's Printing-HOWTO. There's also a Ghostscript manual available from the Internet. See section 2.1 (Resources for further information)

Or, install APSFILTER and let that run Ghostscript automatically. (See section 3.4 (APSFILTER)).

A final, significant note: I would recommend that you compile Ghostscript for your own system, if possible. Combining different versions of Ghostscript and svgalib can quickly become confusing. The version of Ghostscript which is included in the Slackware `AP` set is version 2.6.2 and does not have X support compiled in. You might also have trouble finding the correct svgalib versions for it. There is supposedly a version of Ghostscript with X11 support in the Slackware `XAP` distribution series, and presumably in the other Linux distributions, though I haven't tried them. Compiling Ghostscript for your own system is far easier, it seems to me.

It's also important to remember that there are two Ghostscript releases in distribution: the commercial, Aladdin Ghostscript, and GNU Ghostscript, which lags behind Aladdin Ghostscript by several years. This is due to Ghostscript's unique licensing arrangement. See the Printing-HOWTO for more information about Ghostscript licensing.

svgalib support for GNU Ghostscript 3.33 is included in a small archive which contains a .diff file. Ghostscript 3.33 for X is also configured for JPEG support, so you should include the JPEG library sources as well. The relevant archives can be found at any GNU distribution site, like *ftp://prep.ai.mit.edu/pub/gnu* <ftp://prep.ai.mit.edu/pub/gnu>.

3.4   APSFILTER.

There are software packages which will simplify your life, and APSFILTER is one of them. Written by Andreas Klemm, APSFILTER works with any BSD-compatible printer daemon (which means that you have the `lpd(8)` program and an `/etc/printcap` file; see below), and provides transparent printer support for ASCII, DVI, and PostScript files, as well as files compressed by `gzip(1)`, `compress(1)`, and other data compression software.

Once you have successfully installed APSFILTER, you can print a PostScript file to whatever printer you have, by typing

```
lpr file.ps
```

Or, to print an ASCII file without PostScript translation, you can type

```
lpr -Praw file.asc
```

Amazing.

APSFILTER is surprisingly easy to install, considering that it works with many disparate elements of your system. Installing the generic APSFILTER distribution, however, does require that you have a current `gcc(1)` compiler on hand, because APSFILTER builds some of its filters during installation. Some distributions of Linux, however, provide a pre-built version, so check your specific distribution first.

In any event, you will need a correctly installed Ghostscript and `lpd(8)` installation for APSFILTER to work. The most recent APSFILTER is located in the Linux Archives at *ftp://sunsite.unc.edu/pub/Linux/system/printing/*   <ftp://sunsite.unc.edu/pub/Linux/system/printing/>.

3.5   The `lpd(8)` daemon.

There are wide variations in printers and configurations. Setting up a working printer daemon is no mean feat. If you're using teTeX on an individual system, you could simply dump the output to the printer device driver file, but this is less than desirable. You lose the filtering capabilities of the printer daemon. If you're printing on a network, having a working printer daemon is a must.

The basic UNIX program for printer management on BSD-style systems is `lpd(8)`. When you print a file with `lpr(1)` you are really sending the file to a print queue. `lpd(8)` prints files in the order they're queued. Other printer utilities include `lpq(1)`, which displays the contents of the print queue, and `lprm(1)`, which removes (dequeues) files from the print queue.

The printer daemon can perform other tasks, like transparently filtering output from various programs (using filter programs like APSFILTER, above), accept print jobs from other machines on a network, send print jobs to various printers if you have more than one connected, and hold print output until you've refilled the paper feed tray.

The Printing-HOWTO explains the process of setting up a working printer daemon in detail. Many Linux distributions already have configured `lpd(8)` suites. Check there first, because it will save you considerable work. They're usually archived, strangely enough, using the name `lpr`, so search for that program. There is also a printer daemon suite available from the Linux archives, at *ftp://sunsite.unc.edu/pub/Linux/system/printing* `<ftp://sunsite.unc.edu/pub/Linux/system/printing>`.

4   Post-installation configuration details.

The first thing you'll want to do is look at Thomas Esser's `README` file. It contains a lot of hints on how to configure teTeX for your output device (i.e., printer). The `README` file is located in the directory

`/usr/lib/teTeX/texmf/doc/tetex`

Read the file over with the command (the path in the following examples is that of the Slackware distribution):

`less /usr/lib/teTeX/texmf/doc/tetex/README`

or, print it out with the command

`cat /usr/lib/teTeX/texmf/doc/tetex/README >/dev/lp0`

assuming that your printer is connected to `/dev/lp0`. Substitute the device driver file that your printer is connected to, as appropriate.

Or, better still, print it using the `lpr(1)` command:

`lpr /usr/lib/teTeX/texmf/doc/tetex/README`

You should have installed the printer daemon that is included with your distribution of Linux. If not, do that now, per the instructions that come with the package. If you don't have one of the packages, or want to install a printer daemon yourself, see section 3.5 (The lpd(8) daemon)

Print out the `teTeX-FAQ`. Keep the FAQ handy because it contains useful hints for configuring teTeX's output drivers for your printer. We'll get to that in a moment. In more recent releases of teTeX, the `teTeX-FAQ` is viewable via the `texconfig` utility.

Next, you want to define a directory to store your own TeX format files. teTeX searches the directories listed by the `$TEXINPUTS` environment variable for local TeX input files. On Chanel3, I added the line

`export TEXINPUTS=".:~/texinputs:"`

to the system-wide `/etc/profile` file. Individual users can set their own local `$TEXINPUTS` directory, by adding the line in their `~/.profile` or `~/.bash_profile` if `bash(1)` is the default shell. The `$TEXINPUTS` environment variable tells teTeX to look for users' individual TeX style files in the `~/texinputs` directories under each user's home directory. It is *critical* that a colon appear before and after this directory. teTeX is going to append its own directory searches to your own. You want to have teTeX search the local format files first, so it uses the local versions of any of the standard files you have edited.

Add the `/usr/lib/teTeX/bin` directory to the system-wide path if you're installing teTeX as root. Again, if you're installing a personal copy of teTeX, add the directory where the teTeX binaries are located to *the front* your `$PATH` with the following line in your `~/.profile` or `~/.bash_profile`:

```
export PATH="~/tetex/bin:"$PATH
```

Now, log in as `root` and run `texconfig` per the instructions in the `teTeX-FAQ` and choose the printer that is attached to your system. Make sure that you configure teTeX for both the correct printer and printer resolution.

Finally, run the `texhash` program. This ensures that teTeX's internal database is up to date. The database is actually a `ls-lR` file. You *must* run `texhash` every time you change the system configuration, or teTeX will not be able to locate your changes.

4.1 What if my printer isn't included?

The teTeX distribution comes with only a limited selection of DVI output drivers: `dvips(1)`, drivers for Hewlett Packard LaserJets, and nothing else. You have two options if you have a printer which isn't LaserJet-compatible: You can use `dvips(1)` and Ghostscript, which I would recommend anyway, for reasons already mentioned, or you can investigate other dviware sources.

A limited number of DVI drivers have been ported to Linux and are available as pre-built binaries. They are located in the Linux archives at *ftp://sunsite.unc.edu/pub/Linux/apps/tex/dvi/* `<ftp://sunsite.unc.edu/pub/Linux/apps/tex/dvi/>`.

The master dviware libraries are maintained at the University of Utah archives. If you can't find a DVI driver there that supports your printer, chances are that it doesn't exist. You can also write your *own* DVI driver using the templates available there. The library's URL is *ftp://ftp.math.utah.edu/pub/tex/dvi/* `<ftp://ftp.math.utah.edu/pub/tex/dvi/>`.

5   Using teTeX.

Theoretically, at least, everything is installed correctly and is ready to run. teTeX is a very large software package. As with any complex software package, you'll want to start by learning teTeX slowly, instead of being overwhelmed by its complexity.

At the same time, we want the software to do something useful. So instead of watching TeX typeset

```
''Hello, World!''
```

as Professor Knuth suggests in the *The TeXBook,* we'll produce a couple of teTeX's own documents in order to test it.

The next section, 5.1 (Printing the documentation), is really a tutorial for operating teTeX. It covers printing the documentation included with teTeX (which is in LaTeX and `.dvi` format, of course). The following section, 5.2 (TeX and LaTeX commands), is more of a "cookbook" than a tutorial. It discusses how to format LaTeX documents, and covers a few of the commands and environments of the more commonly used document classes.

The section 5.3 (LaTeX extension packages and other resources) tells how to use the many pre-existing LaTeX packages to customize documents to your specifications.

5.1   Printing the documentation.

You should be logged in as `root` the first few times you run teTeX. If you aren't, metafont may not be able to create the necessary directories for its fonts. The `texconfig` program includes an option to make the font directories world-writable, but if you're working on a multi-user system, security considerations may make this option impractical or undesirable.

In either instance, if you don't have the appropriate permissions to write to the directories where the fonts are stored, `metafont` will complain loudly because it can't make the directories. You won't see any output because you have a bunch of zero-length font characters. This is no problem. Simply log out, re-login as `root,` and repeat the offending operation.

The nice thing about teTeX is that, if you blow it, no real harm is done. It's not like a compiler, where, say, you will trash the root partition if a pointer goes astray. What, you haven't read the teTeX manual yet? Of course you haven't. It's still in the distribution, in source code form, waiting to be output.

So, without further delay, you will want to read the teTeX manual. It's located in the directory

`/usr/lib/teTeX/texmf/doc/tetex.`

The LaTeX source for the manual is called `TETEXDOC.tex`. (The `.tex` extension is used for both TeX and LaTeX files. Some editors, like `emacs(1)`, can tell the difference.) There is also a file `TETEXDOC.dvi` included with the distribution, which you might want to keep in a safe place—say, another directory —in case you want to test your `.dvi` drivers later. With that out of the way, type

`latex TETEXDOC.tex`

LaTeX will print several warnings. The first,

`LaTeX Warning: Label(s) may have changed. Rerun to get the`
`cross-references right.`

is standard. It's common to build a document's Table of Contents by LaTeXing the document twice. So, repeat the command. The other warnings can be safely ignored. They simply are informing you that some of the FTP paths mentioned in the documentation are too wide for their alloted spaces. (If you're really inquisitive, look at one of the TeX references for a discussion of `\hbox` and `\vbox`.)

teTeX will have generated several files from `TETEXDOC.tex`. The one that we're interested in is `TETEXDOC.dvi`. This is the device-independent output which you can send either to the screen or the printer. If you're running teTeX under the X Windows System, you can preview the document with `xdvi(1)`.

For the present, let's assume that you have a HP LaserJet II. You would give the command

`dvilj2 TETEXDOC.dvi`

which will write a PCL output file from `TETEXDOC.dvi`, including soft fonts which will be downloaded to the LaserJet. This is *not* a feature of TeX or LaTeX, but a feature provided by `dvilj2(1)`. Other `.dvi` drivers provide features which are relevant to the devices they support. `dvilj2(1)` will fill the font requests which were made in the original LaTeX document with the the closest equivalents available on the system. In the case of a plain-text document like `TETEXDOC.tex,` there isn't much difficulty. All of the fonts requested by `TETEXDOC.tex` will be generated by metafont, which is automatically invoked by `dvilj2(1)` and generates the fonts if they aren't already present. (If you're running `dvilj2(1)` for the first time, the program needs to generate all of the fonts, which could take up to several days if you're using a *really* slow machine.) There are several options which control font generation via `dvilj2(1)`; they're outlined in the manual page. At this point, you shouldn't need to operate metafont directly. If you do, then something has gone awry with your installation. All of the `.dvi` drivers will invoke metafont directly via the kpathsea path-searching library—also beyond the scope of this document—and you don't need to do any more work with metafont for the present—all of the metafont sources for the Computer Modern font library are provided.

You can print `TETEXDOC.lj` with the command

```
lpr TETEXDOC.lj
```

You may need to install a printer filter that understands PCL. Look at the Printing-HOWTO for details.

The nine-page *teTeX Guide* provides some useful information for further configuring your system, some of which I have mentioned, much which this document doesn't cover.

Some of the information in the next section I haven't been able to test, because I have a non-PostScript HP Deskjet 400 color ink jet printer connected to Chanel3's parallel port. However, not owning a PostScript printer is no barrier to printing text and graphics from your text documents. See the section 3.3 (Ghostscript) to install Ghostscript, if it isn't already installed on your system.

5.2 TeX and LaTeX commands.

5.2.1 Document structure.

Preparing documents for TeX typesetting is easy. Make sure there's a blank line between the paragraphs of a plain text file, and run file through the TeX program with the command

```
TeX your_text_file
```

The result will be a file of the same base name and the extension `.dvi`. The text is set in 10-point, Computer Modern Roman, single-spaced, with justified left and right margins. If you receive error messages from special characters like dollar signs, escape them with a backslash character, \, and run TeX on the file again. You should be able to process the resulting file with the `.dvi` file translator of your choice (see above) to get printed output.

The only other peculiarity of TeX input files is to make sure that you use opening and closing quotes, which are denoted in the input file with the grave accent and single quote characters. Emacs' TeX mode will do this for you automatically.

```
"These are ascii-type quotes."
``These are `TeX-style' quotes.''
```

You can consult a guide like *A Gentle Introduction to TeX,* described above, for hints on how to make modifications to the default TeX page format.

Documents formatted for LaTeX have a few more rules, but with complex documents, LaTeX can greatly simplify the formatting process.

Essentially, LaTeX is a document markup language which tries to separate the output style from the document's logical content. For example, formatting a section heading with TeX would require specifying 36 points of white space above the heading, then the heading itself set in bold, 24-point type, then copying the heading text and page number to the Table of Contents, then leaving 24 points of white space after the heading. By contrast, LaTeX has the `\section{}` command, which does all of the work for you. If you need to change the format of the section headings throughout your document, you can change the definition of `\section{}` instead of the text in the document. You can see where this would save hours of reformatting for documents of more than a dozen pages in length.

All LaTeX documents have three sections: a *preamble,* the *body* text, and a *postamble.* These terms are standard jargon and are widely used by TeXperts.

The preamble, at a minimum, specifies the type of document to be produced—the *document class*—and a statement which signals the beginning of the document's body text. For example:

```
\documentclass{article}
\makeindex
\begin{document}
```

The document's postamble is usually very simple. Except in specialized cases, it contains only the statement:

```
\end{document}
```

Note the \begin{document} and \end{document} pairing. In LaTeX, this is called an *environment.* All text must appear within an environment, and many commands are effective only in the environments in which they're called. The document environment is the only instance where LaTeX enforces this convention, however. That is, it's the only environment that is required in a document. (An exception is letter class, which also requires you to declare \begin{letter} and \end{letter}. See the section 5.2.4 (Letters).) However, many formatting features are specified as environments. They're described in the following sections.

The document classes can be called with arguments. For example, instead of the default, 10-point type used as the base point size, as in the previous example, we could have specified

```
\documentclass[a4paper,twoside]{article}
\makeindex
```

to produce the document using 12 points as the base point size. The document class, *article,* makes the necessary adjustments.

There are a few document classes which are commonly used. They're described below. The *report* class is similar to *article* class, but produces a title page and starts each section on a new page. The *letter* class includes special definitions for addresses, salutations, and closings, a few of which are described below.

You can include canned LaTeX code, commonly known as a *package,* with the \usepackage{} command.

```
\usepackage{fancyhdr}
```

The command above would include the LaTeX style file fancyhdr.sty from one of the TEXINPUTS directories, which you and teTeX specified during installation and setup processes.

```
\documentclass{article}
\makeindex
\usepackage{fancyhdr}
\begin{document}
```

Note that the \usepackage{} declarations are given before the \begin{document} statement; that is, in the document preamble.

fancyhdr.sty extends the \pagestyle{} command so that you can create custom headers and footers. Most LaTeX document classes provide headers and footers of the following standard page styles:

```
\pagestyle{plain}         % default pages style -- page number centered at
                          % the bottom of the page.
\pagestyle{empty}         % no headers or footers
\pagestyle{headings}      % print section number and page number at the
                          % top of the page.
\pagestyle{myheadings}    % print custom information in the page heading.
```

Everything on a line to the right of the percent sign is a comment.

The \pagestyle{} command doesn't take effect until the following page. To change the headers and footers on the current page, use the command

```
\thispagestyle{the_pagestyle}
```

5.2.2 Characters and type styles.

Character styles are partially a function of the fonts specified in the document. However, bold and italic character emphasis should be available for every font present on the system. Underlining, too, can be used, though its formatting presents special problems. See section 5.3 (LaTeX extension packages and other resources), below.

You can specify text to be emphasized in several ways. The most portable is the \em command. All text within its scope is italicized by default. For example:

```
This word will be {\em emphasized.}
```

If you have italicized text that runs into text which is not italicized, you can specify an italic correction factor to be used. The command for this is \/; that is, a backslash and a forward slash.

```
This example {\em will\/} print correctly.
```

```
This example will {\em not} print correctly.
```

Slightly less portable, but still acceptable in situations where they're used singly, are the commands \it, \bf, and \tt, which specify that the characters within their scope be printed using italic, bold, and monospaced (teletype) typefaces, respectively.

```
{\tt This text will be printed monospaced,}
{\it this text will be italic,} and
{\bf this text will be bold\dots} all in one paragraph.
```

The command \dots prints a series of three periods for ellipses, which will not break across a line.

The most recent version of LaTeX, which is what you have, includes commands which account for instances where one emphasis command would supersede another.

```
This is {\it not {\bf bold italic!}}
```

What happens is that teTeX formats the text with the italic typeface until it encounters the \bf command, at which point it switches to boldface type.

To get around this, the NFSS scheme of selecting font shapes requires three parameters for each typeface: shape, series, and family. Not all font sets will include all of these styles. LaTeX will print a warning, however, if it needs to substitute another font.

You can specify the following font shapes:

```
\textup{text}           % upright shape (the default)
\textit{text}           % italic
\textsl{text}           % slanted
\textsc{text}           % small caps
```

These are the two series that most fonts have:

```
\textmd{text}           % medium series (the default)
\textbf{text}           % boldface series.
```

There are generally three families of type available.

```
\textrm{text}           % roman (the default)
\textsf{text}           % sans serif
\texttt{text}           % typewriter (monospaced, Courier-like)
```

Setting font styles using these parameters, you can combine effects.

```
\texttt{\textit{This example likely will result in a font
substitution, because many fonts don't include a typewriter italic
typeface.}}
```

The font family defaults to Computer Modern, which is a bit-mapped font. Other font families are usually PostScript-format Type 1 fonts. See section 7 (Using PostScript fonts) for details on how to specify them.

There are also many forms of accents and special characters which are available for typesetting. This is only a few of them. (Try typesetting these on your own printer.)

```
\'{o}   \`{e}   \^{o}   \"{u}   \={o}   \c{c}   `? `!
\copyright       \pounds        \dag
```

Finally, there are characters which are used as meta- or escape characters in TeX and LaTeX. One of them, the dollar sign, is mentioned above. The complete set of metacharacters, which need to be escaped with a backslash to be used literally, is:

```
# $ % & _ { }
```

There are also different alphabets available, like Greek and Cyrillic. LaTeX provides many facilities for setting non-English text, which are covered by some of the other references mentioned here

5.2.3   Margins and line spacing.

Changing margins in a TeX or LaTeX document is not a straightforward task. A lot depends on the relative indent of the text you're trying to adjust the margin for. The placement of the margin-changing command is also significant.

For document-wide changes to LaTeX documents, the \evensidemargin and \oddsidemargin commands are available. They affect the left-hand margins of the even-numbered and odd-numbered pages, respectively. For example,

```
\evensidemargin=1in
\oddsidemargin=1in
```

adds on inch to the left-hand margin of the even and odd pages *in addition* to the standard one-inch, left-hand margin. These commands affect the entire document and will shift the entire body of the text right and left across a page, regardless of any local indent, so they're safe to use with LaTeX environments like `verse` and `list`.

Below is a set of margin-changing macros which I wrote. They have a different effect than the commands mentioned above. Because they use plain TeX commands, they're not guaranteed to honor the margins of any LaTeX environments which may be in effect, but you can place them anywhere in a document and change the margins from that point on.

```
%%  margins.sty -- v. 0.1   by Robert Kiesling
%%  Copies of this code may be freely distributed in verbatim form.
%%
%%  Some elementary plain TeX margin-changing commands. Lengths are
%%  in inches:
%%  \leftmargin{1}    %% sets the document's left margin in 1 inch.
%%  \leftindent{1}    %% sets the following paragraphs' indent in
%%                       1 inch.
%%  \rightindent{1}   %% sets the following paragraphs' right margins
%%                       %% in 1 inch.
%%  \llength{3}       %% sets the following lines' lengths to 3 inches.
%%
\message{Margins macros...}
\def\lmargin#1{\hoffset = #1 in}
\def\lindent#1{\leftskip = #1 in}
\def\rindent#1{\rightskip = #1 in}
\def\llength#1{\hsize = #1 in}
%%
%% (End of margins macros.}
```

Place this code in a file called `margins.sty` in your local `$TEXINPUTS` directory. The commands are explained in the commented section of the file. To include them in a document, use the command

```
\usepackage{margins}
```

in the document preamble.

While we're on the subject, if you don't want the right margin to be justified, which is the default, you can tell LaTeX to use ragged right margins by giving the command:

```
\raggedright
```

Setting line spacing also has its complexities.

The *baselineskip* measurement is the distance between lines of text. It is given as an absolute measurement. For example,

```
\baselineskip=24pt
```

or even better:

```
\setlength{\baselineskip}{24pt}
```

The difference between the two forms is that *setlength* will respect any scoping rules that may be in effect when you use the command.

The problem with using baselineskip is that it also affects the distance between section headings, footnotes, and the like. You need to take care that baselineskip is correct for whatever text elements you're formatting. There are, however, LaTeX macro packages, like `setspace.sty,` which will help you in these circumstances. See section 5.3 (LaTeX extension packages and other resources).

5.2.4   Document classes.

LaTeX provides document classes which provide standardized formats for documents. They provide environments to format lists, quotations, footnotes, and other text elements. Commonly used document classes are covered in the following sections.

Articles and reports.   As mentioned above, the `article` class and the `report` class are similar. The main differences are that the report class creates a title page by default and begins each section on a new page. Mostly, though, the two document classes are similar.

To create titles, abstracts, and bylines in these document classes, you can type, for example,

```
\title{The Breeding Habits of Cacti}
\author{John Q. Public}
\abstract{Description of how common desert cacti search
for appropriate watering holes to perform their breeding
rituals.}
```

in the document preamble. Then, the command

```
\maketitle
```

given at the start of the text, will generate either a title page in the report class, or the title and abstract at the top of the first page, in the article class.

Sections can be defined with commands that include the following:

```
\section
\subsection
\subsubsection
```

These commands will produce the standard, numbered sections used in technical documents. For unnumbered sections, use

```
\section*
\subsection*
\subsubsection*
```

and so on.

LaTeX provides many environments for formatting displayed material. You can include quoted text with the `quotation` environment.

```
\begin{quotation}
Start of paragraph to be quoted...

... end of paragraph.
\end{quotation}
```

For shorter quotes, you can use the **quote** environment.

To format verse, use the **verse** environment.

```
\begin{verse}
Because I could not stop for death\\
He kindly stopped for me
\end{verse}
```

Notice that you must use the double backslashes to break lines in the correct places. Otherwise, LaTeX fills the lines in a verse environment, just like any other environment.

Lists come in several flavors. To format a bulleted list, the **list** environment is used:

```
\begin{list}
\item
This is the first item of the list.
\item
This is the second item of the list...
\item
... and so on.
\end{list}
```

A numbered list uses the **enumerate** environment:

```
\begin{enumerate}
\item
Item No. 1.
\item
Item No. 2.
\item
\dots
\end{enumerate}
```

A descriptive list uses the **description** environment.

```
\begin{description}
\item{Oven} Dirty, needs new burner.
\item{Refrigerator}  Dirty.  Sorry.
\item{Sink and drainboard}  Stained, drippy, cold water faucet.
\end{description}
```

Letters.   The **letter** class uses special definitions to format business letters.

The **letter** environment takes one argument, the address of the letter's addressee. The **address** command, which must appear in the document preamble, defines the return address. The **signature** command defines the sender's name as it appears after the closing.

The LaTeX source of a simple business letter might look like this.

```
\documentclass[a4paper,twoside]{letter}
\makeindex
\signature{John Q. Public}
\address{123 Main St.\\Los Angeles, CA.  96005\\Tel: 123/456-7890}
\begin{document}
\begin{letter}{ACME Brick Co.\\100 Ash St.\\San Diego, CA 96403}
\opening{Dear Sir/Madam:}

With regard to one of your bricks that I found on my living room
carpet surrounded by shards of my broken front window...

(Remainder of the body of the letter.)

\closing{Sincerely,}

\end{letter}
\end{document}
```

Note that the addresses include double backslashes, which specify where the line breaks should occur.

5.3   LaTeX extension packages and other resources.

We mentioned above that using underlining as a form of text emphasis presents special problems. Actually, TeX has no problem underlining text, because it is a convention of mathematical typesetting. In LaTeX, you can underline words with the command:

```
\underline{text to be underlined}
```

The problem is that underlining will not break across lines, and, in some circumstances, underlining can be uneven. However, there is a LaTeX macro packagem, ready-made, that makes underlining the default mode of text emphasis. It's called `ulem.sty`, and is one of the many contributed LaTeX packages that are freely available via the Internet.

To use `ulem.sty`, include the command

```
\usepackage{ulem}
```

in the document preamble.

The LaTeX Catalogue provides one-line descriptions of every LaTeX package available, their names and CTAN paths. For the URL of the most current edition of the Catalogue, see the section 2.1 (Resources for further information).

The packages which are available for LaTeX include:

ifthen
> Include conditional statements in your documents.

initials
> Defines a font for initial dropped capitals.

sanskrit
> Font and preprocessor for producing documents in Sanskrit.

recipe

A LaTeX2e class to typeset recipes.

refman

Variant report and article styles.

To make the path given in the Catalogue into a fully-qualified URL, concatenate the path to the hostname URL and top-level path of the CTAN archive you wish to contact. For example, the top-level CTAN directory of the site *ftp.tex.ac.uk* `<ftp://ftp.tex.ac.uk>` is `ctan/tex-archive`. The complete URL of the directory of the **refman** package would be:

```
ftp://ftp.tex.ac.uk/ctan/tex-archive/     +
macros/latex/contrib/supported/refman     =

ftp://ftp.tex.ac.uk/ctan/tex-archive/macros/latex/contrib/supported/refman/
```

Some packages have more than one file, so only the path to the package's directory is given.

When you have the URL in hand, you can retrieve the package from one of the CTAN archive sites listed in section 8 (Appendix A). You can download a complete list of the archive's contents as the file `FILES.byname`, in the archive's top-level directory. You can also search the archive on line for a keyword with the `ftp(1)` command

```
quote site index <keyword>
```

6   Mixing text and graphics with dvips(1).

In general, this section applies to any TeX or LaTeX document which mixes text and graphics. teTeX, like most other TeX distributions, is configured to request Computer Modern fonts by default. When printing documents with Type 1 scalable fonts or graphics, font and graphics imaging is the job of `dvips(1)`. `dvips(1)` can use either Computer Modern bit mapped fonts or Type 1 scalable fonts, or any combination of the two. First, let's concentrate on printing and previewing some graphics.

In general, you will want to follow this procedure any time a LaTeX source document has the statement

```
\includepackage{graphics}
```

in the document preamble. This statement tells LaTeX to include the text of the `graphics.sty` package in the source document. There are other commands to perform graphics operations, and the statements in plain-TeX documents may not clue you in whether you need to use `dvips(1)`. The difference will be apparent in the output, though, when the document is printed with missing figures and other graphics.

So, for now, we'll concentrate on printing documents which use the LaTeX `graphics.sty` package. You might want to take a look at the original TeX input. It isn't included in the teTeX distribution, but it is available at

```
~CTAN/macros/latex/packages/graphics/grfguide.tex.
```

What the teTeX distribution does include is the `.dvi` output file, and it is already TeXed for you. There is a reason for this, and it has to do with the necessity of including Type 1 fonts in the output in order for the document to print properly. If you want to LaTeX `grfguide.tex,` see the next section. For now, however, we'll work on getting usable output using `dvips(1)`.

The file `grfguide.dvi` is located in the directory

`texmf/doc/latex/graphics`

The first step in outputting `grfguide.dvi` is to translate it to PostScript. The program `dvips(1)` is used for this. It does just exactly what its name implies. There are many options available for invoking `dvips(1)`, but the simplest (nearly) form is

`dvips -f -r <grfguide.dvi >grfguide.ps`

The `-f` command switch tells `dvips(1)` to operate as a filter, reading from standard input and writing to standard output. `dvips(1)` output can be configured so its output defaults to `lpr(1)`. (Mine does, which allows me to print directly from `dvips(1)`.) Post processors like Ghostscript and printing filters like APSFILTER (see section 3.4 () name="APSFILTER"), can be configured for your own needs. If you need to feed the output manually to a post-processor, the `-f` option is generally the first you should include in the `dvips(1)` command line. This form also seems to be easier to use in shell scripts.

If you can print PostScript directly to your printer via `lpr(1)`, you can simply type

`dvips -r grfguide.dvi`

The `-r` option tells dvips to output the pages in reverse order so they stack correctly when they exit a printer. Use it or not, as appropriate for your output device.

Depending on whether you still have the fonts that `dvilj2(1)` generated from the last document, `dvips(1)` and metafont may or may not need to create new fonts needed by `grfguide.dvi`. Eventually, though, `dvips(1)` will output a list of the pages translated to PostScript, and you will have your PostScript output ready to be rendered on whatever output device you have available.

If you're lucky (and rich), then you have a PostScript-capable printer already and will be able to print `grfguide.ps` directly. You can either spool the output to the printer using `lpr(1)`. If for some reason your printer software doesn't work right with PostScript files, you can, in a pinch, simply dump the file to printer, with

`cat grfguide.ps >/dev/lp0`

or whichever port your printer is attached to, though this is not recommended for everyday use.

If you want or need to invoke Ghostscript manually, this is the standard procedure for its operation. The first thing you want to do is invoke Ghostscript to view its command line arguments, like this:

`gs -help | less`

You'll see a list of supported output devices and sundry other commands. Pick the output device which most nearly matches your printer. On Chanel3, because I generally produce black-and-white text, I use the `cdjmono` driver, which drives a color Deskjet in monochrome (black and white) mode.

The command line I would use is:

`gs -dNOPAUSE -sDEVICE=cdjmono -sOutputFile=/tmp/gs.out grfguide.ps -c quit`

This will produce my HP-compatible output in the `/tmp` directory. It's a good idea to use a directory like `/tmp`, because `gs(1)` can be particular about access permissions, and you can't (and shouldn't) always count on being logged in as `root` to perform these steps. Now you can print the file:

`lpr /tmp/gs.out`

Obviously, this can all go into a shell script. On my system, I have two simple scripts written, `pv` and `pr`, which simply outputs the PostScript file either to the display or the printer. Screen previewing is possible without X, but it's far from ideal. So, it's definitely worth the effort to install XFree86, or TinyX (which is what I did) to view the output on the screen.

The order of commands in a `gs(1)` command line is significant, because some of the options tell Ghostscript to look for pieces of PostScript code from its library.

The important thing to remember is that `grfguide.dvi` makes requests for both Computer Modern bit mapped and Type 1 scaled fonts. If you can mix scalable and bit mapped fonts in a document, you're well on the way to becoming a TeXpert.

7 Using PostScript fonts.

It used to be that public domain, Type 1 fonts were much poorer quality than Computer Modern bit mapped fonts. This situation has improved in the last several years, though, but matching the fonts is up to you. Having several different font systems on one machine can seem redundant and an unnecessary waste of disk space. And the Computer Modern fonts can seem, well, a little too *formal* to be suitable for everyday use. It reminds me sometimes of bringing out the good China to feed the dog. At least you don't need to spend a bundle on professional quality fonts any longer.

One of the major improvements of LaTeX2e over its predecessor was the inclusion of the New Font Selection Scheme. (It's now called PSNFSS.) Formerly, TeX authors would specify fonts with commands like

```
\font=bodyroman = cmr10 scaled \magstep 1
```

which provides precision but requires the skills of a type designer and mathematician to make good use of. Also, it's not very portable. If another system didn't have the font `cmr10` (this is TeX nomenclature for Computer Modern Roman, 10 point, with the default medium stroke weight), somebody would have to re-code the fonts specifications for the entire document. PSNFSS, however, allows you specify fonts by family (Computer Modern, URW Nimbus, Helvetica, Utopia, and so forth), weight (light, medium, bold), orientation (upright or oblique), face (Roman, Italic), and base point size. (See the section 5.2.2 (Characters and type styles) for a description of the commands to specify typefaces.) Many fonts are packaged as families. For example, a Roman-type font may come packaged with a sans serif font, like Helvetica, and a monospaced font, like Courier. You, as the author of a LaTeX document, can specify an entire font family with one command.

There are, as I said, several high-quality font sets available in the public domain. One of them is Adobe Utopia. Another is Bitstream Charter. Both are commercial quality fonts which have been donated to the public domain.

These happen to be two of my favorites. If you look around one of the CTAN sites, you will find these and other fonts archived there. There are enough fonts around that you'll be able to design documents the way you want them to look, and not just English text, either. TeX was originally designed for mathematical typesetting, so there is a full range of mathematical fonts available, as well as Cyrillic, Greek, Kana, and other alphabets too numerous to mention.

The important thing to look for is files which have either the `.pfa` or `.pfb` extension. They indicate that these are the scalable fonts themselves, not simply the metrics files. Type 1 fonts use `.pfm` metric files, as opposed to the `.tfm` metric files which bit mapped fonts use. The two font sets I mentioned above are included in teTeX distributions, as well as separately.

What I said above, concerning the ease of font selection under PSNFSS, is true in this instance. If we want to use the Charter fonts in our document instead of Computer Modern bit mapped, all that is necessary is include the LaTeX statement

```
\renewcommand{\familydefault}{bch}
```

in the document preamble, where "bch" is the common designation for Bitstream Charter. The Charter fonts reside in the directory

```
/usr/lib/teTeX/texmf/fonts/type1/bitstrea/charter
```

There you'll see the `.pfb` files of the Charter fonts: `bchb8a.pfb` for Charter Bold, `bchr8a.pfb` for Charter Roman, `bchbi8a.pfb` for Charter Bold Italic. The "8a" in the font names indicates the character encoding. At this point you shouldn't need to worry much about them, because the encodings mostly differ for 8-bit characters, which have numeric values above 128 decimal. They mostly define accents and non-English characters. The Type 1 font encodings generally work well for Western alphabets because they conform to the ISO 8859 standards for international character sets, so this is an added benefit of using them.

To typeset a document which has Charter fonts selected, you would give the command

```
pslatex document.tex
```

`pslatex` is a variant of teTeX's standard `latex(1)` command which defines the directories where the Type 1 fonts are, as well as some additional LaTeX code to load. You'll see the notice screen for `pslatex` followed by the status output of the TeX job itself. In a moment, you'll have a `.dvi` file which includes the Charter font requests. You can then print the file with `dvips(1)`, and `gs(1)` if necessary.

Installing a Type 1 font set is not difficult, as long as you follow a few basic steps. You should unpack the fonts in a subdirectory of the `/usr/lib/teTeX/texmf/fonts/type1` directory, where your other Type 1 fonts are located, and then run `texhash` to let the directory search routines know that the fonts have been added. Then you need to add the font descriptions to the file `psfonts.map` so `dvips(1)` knows they're on the system. The format of the `psfonts.map` file is covered in a couple different places in the references mentioned above. Again, remember to run the `texhash` program to update the teTeX directory database.

It is definitely an advantage to use the X Windows System with teTeX– XFree86 under Linux – because it allows for superior document previewing. It's not required, but in general, anything that allows for easier screen previewing is going to benefit your work, in terms of the quality of the output. However, there is a tradeoff with speed of editing, which is much quicker on character-mode displays. Having an editor which is slower than molasses in Minnesota can definitely hinder your work.

Anyway, whether or not you are able to view documents easily on-screen, please recycle your paper, and use both sides of each sheet. If possible, purchase recycled photocopy paper to print on. You don't want your workplace to look like a branch office of a paper company.

Remember: Save a tree... kill an editor.

Robert Kiesling

kiesling@terracom.net <mailto:kiesling@terracom.net>

8   Appendix: CTAN Site Listing

This is the text of the file `CTAN.sites`, which is available in the top-level directory of each CTAN archive or mirror site.

```
In order to reduce network load, it is recommended that you use the
Comprehensive TeX Archive Network (CTAN) host which is located in the
closest network proximity to your site.  Alternatively, you may wish to
```

obtain a copy of the CTAN via CD-ROM (see help/CTAN.cdrom for details).

Known mirrors of the CTAN reside on (alphabetically):
```
  cis.utovrm.it (Italia)                  /TeX
  ctan.unsw.edu.au (NSW, Australia)       /tex-archive
  dongpo.math.ncu.edu.tw (Taiwan)         /tex-archive
  ftp.belnet.be (Belgium)                 /packages/TeX
  ftp.ccu.edu.tw (Taiwan)                 /pub/tex
  ftp.cdrom.com (West coast, USA)         /pub/tex/ctan
  ftp.comp.hkbu.edu.hk (Hong Kong)        /pub/TeX/CTAN
  ftp.cs.rmit.edu.au  (Australia)         /tex-archive
  ftp.cs.ruu.nl (The Netherlands)         /pub/tex-archive
  ftp.cstug.cz (The Czech Republic)       /pub/tex/CTAN
  ftp.duke.edu (North Carolina, USA)      /tex-archive
  ftp.funet.fi (Finland)                  /pub/TeX/CTAN
  ftp.gwdg.de (Deutschland)               /pub/dante
  ftp.jussieu.fr (France)                 /pub4/TeX/CTAN
  ftp.kreonet.re.kr (Korea)               /pub/CTAN
  ftp.loria.fr (France)                   /pub/unix/tex/ctan
  ftp.mpi-sb.mpg.de (Deutschland)         /pub/tex/mirror/ftp.dante.de
  ftp.nada.kth.se (Sweden)                /pub/tex/ctan-mirror
  ftp.oleane.net (France)                 /pub/mirrors/CTAN/
  ftp.rediris.es (Espa\~na)               /mirror/tex-archive
  ftp.rge.com (New York, USA)             /pub/tex
  ftp.riken.go.jp (Japan)                 /pub/tex-archive
  ftp.tu-chemnitz.de (Deutschland)        /pub/tex
  ftp.u-aizu.ac.jp (Japan)                /pub/tex/CTAN
  ftp.uni-augsburg.de (Deutschland)       /tex-archive
  ftp.uni-bielefeld.de (Deutschland)      /pub/tex
  ftp.unina.it (Italia)                   /pub/TeX
  ftp.uni-stuttgart.de (Deutschland)      /tex-archive (/pub/tex)
  ftp.univie.ac.at (\"Osterreich)         /packages/tex
  ftp.ut.ee (Estonia)                     /tex-archive
  ftpserver.nus.sg (Singapore)            /pub/zi/TeX
  src.doc.ic.ac.uk (England)              /packages/tex/uk-tex
  sunsite.auc.dk (Denmark)                /pub/tex/ctan
  sunsite.cnlab-switch.ch (Switzerland)   /mirror/tex
  sunsite.icm.edu.pl (Poland)             /pub/CTAN
  sunsite.unc.edu (North Carolina, USA)   /pub/packages/TeX
  wuarchive.wustl.edu (Missouri, USA)     /packages/TeX
```

Known partial mirrors of the CTAN reside on (alphabetically):
```
  ftp.adfa.oz.au (Australia)              /pub/tex/ctan
  ftp.fcu.edu.tw (Taiwan)                 /pub2/tex
  ftp.germany.eu.net (Deutschland)        /pub/packages/TeX
  ftp.gust.org.pl (Poland)                /pub/TeX
  ftp.jaist.ac.jp (Japan)                 /pub/TeX/tex-archive
  ftp.uu.net (Virginia, USA)              /pub/text-processing/TeX
  nic.switch.ch (Switzerland)             /mirror/tex
  sunsite.dsi.unimi.it (Italia)           /pub/TeX
  sunsite.snu.ac.kr (Korea)               /shortcut/CTAN
```

Please send updates to this list to <ctan@urz.uni-heidelberg.de>.

```
The participating hosts in the Comprehensive TeX Archive Network are:
  ftp.dante.de  (Deutschland)
      -- anonymous ftp                   /tex-archive (/pub/tex /pub/archive)
      -- gopher on node gopher.dante.de
      -- e-mail via ftpmail@dante.de
      -- World Wide Web access on www.dante.de
      -- Administrator: <ftpmaint@dante.de>

  ftp.tex.ac.uk (England)
      -- anonymous ftp                   /tex-archive (/pub/tex /pub/archive)
      -- gopher on node gopher.tex.ac.uk
      -- NFS mountable from nfs.tex.ac.uk:/public/ctan/tex-archive
      -- World Wide Web access on www.tex.ac.uk
      -- Administrator: <ctan-uk@tex.ac.uk>
```

Linux Benchmarking HOWTO

by André D. Balsa, *andrewbalsa@usa.net* `<mailto:andrewbalsa@usa.net>`   v0.12, 15 August 1997

The Linux Benchmarking HOWTO discusses some issues associated with the benchmarking of Linux systems and presents a basic benchmarking toolkit, as well as an associated form, which enable one to produce significant benchmarking information in a couple of hours. Perhaps it will also help diminish the amount of useless articles in comp.os.linux.hardware...

Contents

1 Introduction

"What we cannot speak about we must pass over in silence."

     Ludwig Wittgenstein (1889-1951), Austrian philosopher

Benchmarking means **measuring** the speed with which a computer system will execute a computing task, in a way that will allow comparison between different hard/software combinations. It **does not** involve user-friendliness, aesthetic or ergonomic considerations or any other subjective judgment.

Benchmarking is a tedious, repetitive task, and takes attention to details. Very often the results are not what one would expect, and subject to interpretation (which actually may be the most important part of a benchmarking procedure).

Finally, benchmarking deals with facts and figures, not opinion or approximation.

1.1 Why is benchmarking so important ?

Apart from the reasons pointed out in the BogoMips Mini-HOWTO (section 7, paragraph 2), one occasionally is confronted with a limited budget and/or minimum performance requirements while putting together a Linux box. In other words, when confronted with the following questions:

- How do I maximize performance within a given budget ?

- How do I minimize costs for a required minimum performance level ?

- How do I obtain the best performance/cost ratio (within a given budget or given performance requirements)?

one will have to examine, compare and/or produce benchmarks. Minimizing costs with no performance requirements usually involves putting together a machine with leftover parts (that old 386SX-16 box lying around in the garage will do fine) and does not require benchmarks, and maximizing performance with no cost ceiling is not a realistic situation (unless one is willing to put a Cray box in his/her living room - the leather-covered power supplies around it look nice, don't they ?).

Benchmarking per se is senseless, a waste of time and money; it is only meaningful as part of a decision process, i.e. if one has to make a choice between two or more alternatives.

Usually another parameter in the decision process is **cost**, but it could be availability, service, reliability, strategic considerations or any other rational, measurable characteristic of a computer system. When comparing the performance of different Linux kernel versions, for example, **stability** is almost always more important than speed.

1.2 Invalid benchmarking considerations

Very often read in newsgroups and mailing lists, unfortunately:

1. Reputation of manufacturer (unmeasurable and meaningless).

2. Market share of manufacturer (meaningless and irrelevant).

3. Irrational parameters (for example, superstition or prejudice: would you buy a processor labeled 131313ZAP and painted pink ?)

4. Perceived value (meaningless, unmeasurable and irrational).

5. Amount of marketing hype: this one is the worst, I guess. I personally am fed up with the "XXX inside" or "kkkkkws compatible" logos (now the "aaaaaPowered" has joined the band - what next ?). IMHO, the billions of dollars spent on such campaigns would be better used by research teams on the design of new, faster, (cheaper :-) bug-free processors. No amount of marketing hype will remove a floating-point bug in the FPU of the brand-new processor you just plugged in your motherboard, but an exchange against a redesigned processor will.

6. "You get what you pay for" opinions are just that: opinions. Give me the facts, please.

2 Benchmarking procedures and interpretation of results

A few semi-obvious recommendations:

1. First and foremost, **identify your benchmarking goals**. What is it you are exactly trying to benchmark ? In what way will the benchmarking process help later in your decision making ? How much time and resources are you willing to put into your benchmarking effort ?

2. **Use standard tools.** Use a current, stable kernel version, standard, current gcc and libc and a standard benchmark. In short, use the LBT (see below).

3. Give a **complete description** of your setup (see the LBT report form below).

4. Try to **isolate a single variable**. Comparative benchmarking is more informative than "absolute" benchmarking. **I cannot stress this enough.**

5. **Verify your results**. Run your benchmarks a few times and verify the variations in your results, if any. Unexplained variations will invalidate your results.

6. If you think your benchmarking effort produced meaningful information, **share it** with the Linux community in a **precise** and **concise** way.

7. Please **forget about BogoMips**. I promise myself I shall someday implement a very fast ASIC with the BogoMips loop wired in. Then we shall see what we shall see !

2.1   Understanding benchmarking choices

2.1.1   Synthetic vs. applications benchmarks

Before spending any amount of time on benchmarking chores, a basic choice must be made between "synthetic" benchmarks and "applications" benchmarks.

Synthetic benchmarks are specifically designed to measure the performance of individual components of a computer system, usually by exercising the chosen component to its maximum capacity. An example of a well-known synthetic benchmark is the **Whetstone** suite, originally programmed in 1972 by Harold Curnow in FORTRAN (or was that ALGOL ?) and still in widespread use nowadays. The Whestone suite will measure the floating-point performance of a CPU.

The main critic that can be made to synthetic benchmarks is that they do not represent a computer system's performance in real-life situations. Take for example the Whetstone suite: the main loop is very short and will easily fit in the primary cache of a CPU, keeping the FPU pipeline constantly filled and so exercising the FPU to its maximum speed. We cannot really criticize the Whetstone suite if we remember it was programmed 25 years ago (its design dates even earlier than that !), but we must make sure we interpret its results with care, when it comes to benchmarking modern microprocessors.

Another very important point to note about synthetic benchmarks is that, ideally, they should tell us something about a **specific** aspect of the system being tested, independently of all other aspects: a synthetic benchmark for Ethernet card I/O throughput should result in the same or similar figures whether it is run on a 386SX-16 with 4 MBytes of RAM or a Pentium 200 MMX with 64 MBytes of RAM. Otherwise, the test will be measuring the overall performance of the CPU/Motherboard/Bus/Ethernet card/Memory subsystem/DMA combination: not very useful since the variation in CPU will cause a greater impact than the change in Ethernet network card (this of course assumes we are using the same kernel/driver combination, which could cause an even greater variation)!

Finally, a very common mistake is to average various synthetic benchmarks and claim that such an average is a good representation of real-life performance for any given system.

Here is a comment on FPU benchmarks quoted with permission from the Cyrix Corp. Web site:

> "A Floating Point Unit (FPU) accelerates software designed to use floating point mathematics : typically CAD programs, spreadsheets, 3D games and design applications. However, today's most popular PC applications make use of both floating point and integer instructions. As a result, Cyrix chose to emphasize "parallelism" in the design of the 6x86 processor to speed up software that intermixes these two instruction types.

> The x86 floating point exception model allows integer instructions to issue and complete while a floating point instruction is executing. In contrast, a second floating point instruction cannot begin execution while a previous floating point instruction is executing. To remove the performance limitation created by the floating point exception model, the 6x86 can speculatively issue up to four floating point instructions to the on-chip FPU while continuing to issue and execute integer instructions. As an example, in a code sequence of two floating point instructions (FLTs) followed by six integer instructions (INTs) followed by two FLTs, the 6x86 processor can issue all ten instructions to the appropriate execution units prior to completion of the first FLT. If none of the instructions fault (the typical case), execution continues with both the integer and floating point units completing instructions in parallel. If one of the FLTs faults (the atypical case), the speculative execution capability of the 6x86 allows the processor state to be restored in such a way that it is compatible with the x86 floating point exception model.

> Examination of benchmark tests reveals that synthetic floating point benchmarks use a pure floating point-only code stream not found in real-world applications. This type of benchmark does not take advantage of the speculative execution capability of the 6x86 processor. Cyrix

believes that non-synthetic benchmarks based on real-world applications better reflect the actual performance users will achieve. Real-world applications contain intermixed integer and floating point instructions and therefore benefit from the 6x86 speculative execution capability."

So, the recent trend in benchmarking is to choose common applications and use them to test the performance of complete computer systems. For example, **SPEC**, the non-profit corporation that designed the well-known SPECINT and SPECFP synthetic benchmark suites, has launched a project for a new applications benchmark suite. But then again, it is very unlikely that such commercial benchmarks will ever include any Linux code.

Summarizing, synthetic benchmarks are valid as long as you understand their purposes and limitations. Applications benchmarks will better reflect a computer system's performance, but none are available for Linux.

2.1.2 High-level vs. low-level benchmarks

Low-level benchmarks will directly measure the performance of the hardware: CPU clock, DRAM and cache SRAM cycle times, hard disk average access time, latency, track-to-track stepping time, etc... This can be useful in case you bought a system and are wondering what components it was built with, but a better way to check these figures would be to open the case, list whatever part numbers you can find and somehow obtain the data sheet for each part (usually on the Web).

Another use for low-level benchmarks is to check that a kernel driver was correctly configured for a specific piece of hardware: if you have the data sheet for the component, you can compare the results of the low-level benchmarks to the theoretical, printed specs.

High-level benchmarks are more concerned with the performance of the hardware/driver/OS combination for a specific aspect of a microcomputer system, for example file I/O performance, or even for a specific hardware/driver/OS/application performance, e.g. an Apache benchmark on different microcomputer systems.

Of course, all low-level benchmarks are synthetic. High-level benchmarks may be synthetic or applications benchmarks.

2.2 Standard benchmarks available for Linux

IMHO a simple test that anyone can do while upgrading any component in his/her Linux box is to launch a kernel compile before and after the hard/software upgrade and compare compilation times. If all other conditions are kept equal then the test is valid as a measure of compilation performance and one can be confident to say that:

> "Changing A to B led to an improvement of x % in the compile time of the Linux kernel under such and such conditions".

No more, no less !

Since kernel compilation is a very usual task under Linux, and since it exercises most functions that get exercised by normal benchmarks (except floating-point performance), it constitutes a rather good **individual** test. In most cases, however, results from such a test cannot be reproduced by other Linux users because of variations in hard/software configurations and so this kind of test cannot be used as a "yardstick" to compare dissimilar systems (unless we all agree on a standard kernel to compile - see below).

Unfortunately, there are no Linux-specific benchmarking tools, except perhaps the Byte Linux Benchmarks which are a slightly modified version of the Byte Unix Benchmarks dating back from May 1991 (Linux mods by Jon Tombs, original authors Ben Smith, Rick Grehan and Tom Yager).

There is a central *Web site* `<http://www.silkroad.com/bass/linux/bm.html>`for the Byte Linux Benchmarks.

An improved, updated version of the Byte Unix Benchmarks was put together by David C. Niemi. It is called UnixBench 4.01 to avoid confusion with earlier versions. Here is what David wrote about his mods:

> *"The original and slightly modified BYTE Unix benchmarks are broken in quite a number of ways which make them an unusually unreliable indicator of system performance. I intentionally made my "index" values look a lot different to avoid confusion with the old benchmarks."*

David has setup a majordomo mailing list for discussion of benchmarking on Linux and competing OSs. Join with "subscribe bench" sent in the body of a message to *majordomo@wauug.erols.com* `<mailto:majordomo@ wauug.erols.com>`. The Washington Area Unix User Group is also in the process of setting up a *Web site* `<http://wauug.erols.com/bench>`for Linux benchmarks.

Also recently, Uwe F. Mayer, *mayer@math.vanderbilt.edu* `<mailto:mayer@math.vanderbilt.edu>`ported the BYTE Bytemark suite to Linux. This is a modern suite carefully put together by Rick Grehan at BYTE Magazine to test the CPU, FPU and memory system performance of modern microcomputer systems (these are strictly processor-performance oriented benchmarks, no I/O or system performance is taken into account).

Uwe has also put together a *Web site* `<http://math.vanderbilt.edu:80/~mayer/linux/bmark.html>`with a database of test results for his version of the Linux BYTEmark benchmarks.

While searching for synthetic benchmarks for Linux, you will notice that sunsite.unc.edu carries few benchmarking tools. To test the relative speed of X servers and graphics cards, the xbench-0.2 suite by Claus Gittinger is available from sunsite.unc.edu, ftp.x.org and other sites. Xfree86.org refuses (wisely) to carry or recommend any benchmarks.

The *XFree86-benchmarks Survey* `<http://www.goof.com/xbench/>`is a Web site with a database of x-bench results.

For pure disk I/O throughput, the hdparm program (included with most distributions, otherwise available from sunsite.unc.edu) will measure transfer rates if called with the -t and -T switches.

There are many other tools freely available on the Internet to test various performance aspects of your Linux box.

2.3   Links and references

The comp.benchmarks.faq by Dave Sill is the standard reference for benchmarking. It is not Linux specific, but recommended reading for anybody serious about benchmarking. It is available from a number of FTP and web sites and lists **56 different benchmarks**, with links to FTP or Web sites that carry them. Some of the benchmarks listed are commercial (SPEC for example), though.

I will not go through each one of the benchmarks mentionned in the comp.benchmarks.faq, but there is at least one low-level suite which I would like to comment on: the *lmbench suite* `<http://reality.sgi.com/ lm/lmbench/lmbench.html>`, by Larry McVoy. Quoting David C. Niemi:

> *"Linus and David Miller use this a lot because it does some useful low-level measurements and can also measure network throughput and latency if you have 2 boxes to test with. But it does not attempt to come up with anything like an overall "figure of merit"..."*

A rather complete *FTP site* `<ftp://ftp.nosc.mil/pub/aburto>`for **freely** available benchmarks was put together by Alfred Aburto. The Whetstone suite used in the LBT can be found at this site.

There is a **multipart FAQ by Eugene Miya** that gets posted regularly to comp.benchmarks; it is an excellent reference.

3 The Linux Benchmarking Toolkit (LBT)

I will propose a basic benchmarking toolkit for Linux. This is a preliminary version of a comprehensive Linux Benchmarking Toolkit, to be expanded and improved. Take it for what it's worth, i.e. as a proposal. If you don't think it is a valid test suite, feel free to email me your critics and I will be glad to make the changes and improve it if I can. Before getting into an argument, however, read this HOWTO and the mentionned references: informed criticism is welcomed, empty criticism is not.

3.1 Rationale

This is just common sense:

1. It should not take a whole day to run. When it comes to comparative benchmarking (various runs), nobody wants to spend days trying to figure out the fastest setup for a given system. Ideally, the entire benchmark set should take about 15 minutes to complete on an average machine.

2. All source code for the software used must be freely available on the Net, for obvious reasons.

3. Benchmarks should provide simple figures reflecting the measured performance.

4. There should be a mix of synthetic benchmarks and application benchmarks (with separate results, of course).

5. Each **synthetic** benchmarks should exercise a particular subsystem to its maximum capacity.

6. Results of **synthetic** benchmarks should **not** be averaged into a single figure of merit (that defeats the whole idea behind synthetic benchmarks, with considerable loss of information).

7. Applications benchmarks should consist of commonly executed tasks on Linux systems.

3.2 Benchmark selection

I have selected five different benchmark suites, trying as much as possible to avoid overlap in the tests:

1. Kernel 2.0.0 (default configuration) compilation using gcc.

2. Whetstone version 10/03/97 (latest version by Roy Longbottom).

3. xbench-0.2 (with fast execution parameters).

4. UnixBench benchmarks version 4.01 (partial results).

5. BYTE Magazine's BYTEmark benchmarks beta release 2 (partial results).

For tests 4 and 5, "(partial results)" means that not all results produced by these benchmarks are considered.

3.3 Test duration

1. Kernel 2.0.0 compilation: 5 - 30 minutes, depending on the **real** performance of your system.

2. Whetstone: 100 seconds.

3. Xbench-0.2: < 1 hour.

4. UnixBench benchmarks version 4.01: approx. 15 minutes.

5. BYTE Magazine's BYTEmark benchmarks: approx. 10 minutes.

3.4   Comments

3.4.1   Kernel 2.0.0 compilation:

- **What:** it is the only application benchmark in the LBT.
- The code is widely available (i.e. I finally found some use for my old Linux CD-ROMs).
- Most linuxers recompile the kernel quite often, so it is a significant measure of overall performance.
- The kernel is large and gcc uses a large chunk of memory: attenuates L2 cache size bias with small tests.
- It does frequent I/O to disk.
- Test procedure: get a pristine 2.0.0 source, compile with default options (make config, press Enter repeatedly). The reported time should be the time spent on compilation i.e. after you type make zImage, **not** including make dep, make clean. Note that the default target architecture for the kernel is the i386, so if compiled on another architecture, gcc too should be set to cross-compile, with i386 as the target architecture.
- **Results:** compilation time in minutes and seconds (please don't report fractions of seconds).

3.4.2   Whetstone:

- **What:** measures pure floating point performance with a short, tight loop. The source (in C) is quite readable and it is very easy to see which floating-point operations are involved.
- Shortest test in the LBT :-).
- It's an "Old Classic" test: comparable figures are available, its flaws and shortcomings are well known.
- Test procedure: the newest C source should be obtained from Aburto's site. Compile and run in double precision mode. Specify gcc and -O2 as precompiler and precompiler options, and define POSIX 1 to specify machine type.
- **Results:** a floating-point performance figure in MWIPS.

3.4.3   Xbench-0.2:

- **What:** measures X server performance.
- The xStones measure provided by xbench is a weighted average of several tests indexed to an old Sun station with a single-bit-depth display. Hmmm... it is questionable as a test of modern X servers, but it's still the best tool I have found.
- Test procedure: compile with -O2. We specify a few options for a shorter run:./xbench -timegoal 3 > results/name_of_your_linux_box.out. To get the xStones rating, we must run an awk script; the simplest way is to type make summary.ms. Check the summary.ms file: the xStone rating for your system is in the last column of the line with your machine name specified during the test.
- **Results:** an X performance figure in xStones.
- Note: this test, as it stands, is outdated. It should be re-coded.

3.4.4   UnixBench version 4.01:

- **What:** measures overall Unix performance. This test will exercice the file I/O and kernel multitasking performance.
- I have discarded all arithmetic test results, keeping only the system-related test results.

- Test procedure: make with -O2. Execute with ./Run -1 (run each test once). You will find the results in the ./results/report file. Calculate the geometric mean of the EXECL THROUGHPUT, FILECOPY 1, 2, 3, PIPE THROUGHPUT, PIPE-BASED CONTEXT SWITCHING, PROCESS CREATION, SHELL SCRIPTS and SYSTEM CALL OVERHEAD indexes.
- **Results:** a system index.

3.4.5 BYTE Magazine's BYTEmark benchmarks:

- **What:** provides a good measure of CPU performance. Here is an excerpt from the documentation: *"These benchmarks are meant to expose the theoretical upper limit of the CPU, FPU, and memory architecture of a system. They cannot measure video, disk, or network throughput (those are the domains of a different set of benchmarks). You should, therefore, use the results of these tests as part, not all, of any evaluation of a system."*
- I have discarded the FPU test results since the Whetstone test is just as representative of FPU performance.
- I have split the integer tests in two groups: those more representative of memory-cache-CPU performance and the CPU integer tests.
- Test procedure: make with -O2. Run the test with ./nbench > myresults.dat or similar. Then, from myresults.dat, calculate geometric mean of STRING SORT, ASSIGNMENT and BITFIELD test indexes; this is the **memory index**; calculate the geometric mean of NUMERIC SORT, IDEA, HUFFMAN and FP EMULATION test indexes; this is the **integer index**.
- **Results:** a memory index and an integer index calculated as explained above.

3.5 Possible improvements

The ideal benchmark suite would run in a few minutes, with synthetic benchmarks testing every subsystem separately and applications benchmarks providing results for different applications. It would also automatically generate a complete report and eventually email the report to a central database on the Web.

We are not really interested in portability here, but it should at least run on all recent (> 2.0.0) versions and flavours (i386, Alpha, Sparc...) of Linux.

If anybody has any idea about benchmarking network performance in a simple, easy and reliable way, with a short (less than 30 minutes to setup and run) test, please contact me.

3.6 LBT Report Form

Besides the tests, the benchmarking procedure would not be complete without a form describing the setup, so here it is (following the guidelines from comp.benchmarks.faq):

```
LINUX BENCHMARKING TOOLKIT REPORT FORM


CPU
==
Vendor:
Model:
Core clock:
Motherboard vendor:
```

```
Mbd. model:
Mbd. chipset:
Bus type:
Bus clock:
Cache total:
Cache type/speed:
SMP (number of processors):
```

```
RAM
====
Total:
Type:
Speed:
```

```
Disk
====
Vendor:
Model:
Size:
Interface:
Driver/Settings:
```

```
Video board
===========
Vendor:
Model:
Bus:
Video RAM type:
Video RAM total:
X server vendor:
X server version:
X server chipset choice:
Resolution/vert. refresh rate:
Color depth:
```

```
Kernel
======
Version:
Swap size:
```

```
gcc
===
Version:
Options:
libc version:
```

```
Test notes
==========
```

```
RESULTS
========
Linux kernel 2.0.0 Compilation Time: (minutes and seconds)
Whetstones: results are in MWIPS.
Xbench: results are in xstones.
Unixbench Benchmarks 4.01 system INDEX:
BYTEmark integer INDEX:
BYTEmark memory INDEX:
```

```
Comments*
=========
* This field is included for possible interpretations of the results, and as
such, it is optional. It could be the most significant part of your report,
though, specially if you are doing comparative benchmarking.
```

3.7   Network performance tests

Testing network performance is a challenging task since it involves at least two machines, a server and a client machine, hence twice the time to setup and many more variables to control, etc... On an ethernet network, I guess your best bet would be the ttcp package. (to be expanded)

3.8   SMP tests

SMP tests are another challenge, and any benchmark specifically designed for SMP testing will have a hard time proving itself valid in real-life settings, since algorithms that can take advantage of SMP are hard to come by. It seems later versions of the Linux kernel (> 2.1.30 or around that) will do "fine-grained" multiprocessing, but I have no more information than that for the moment.

According to David Niemi, " ... shell8 [part of the Unixbench 4.01 benchmaks]does a good job at comparing similar hardware/OS in SMP and UP modes."

4   Example run and results

The LBT was run on my home machine, a Pentium-class Linux box that I put together myself and that I used to write this HOWTO. Here is the LBT Report Form for this system:

```
LINUX BENCHMARKING TOOLKIT REPORT FORM
```

```
CPU
```

```
==
```

Vendor: Cyrix/IBM

Model: 6x86L P166+

Core clock: 133 MHz

Motherboard vendor: Elite Computer Systems (ECS)

Mbd. model: P5VX-Be

Mbd. chipset: Intel VX

Bus type: PCI

Bus clock: 33 MHz

Cache total: 256 KB

Cache type/speed: Pipeline burst 6 ns

SMP (number of processors): 1

RAM

====

Total: 32 MB

Type: EDO SIMMs

Speed: 60 ns

Disk

====

Vendor: IBM

Model: IBM-DAQA-33240

Size: 3.2 GB

Interface: EIDE

Driver/Settings: Bus Master DMA mode 2

Video board

==========

Vendor: Generic S3

Model: Trio64-V2

Bus: PCI

Video RAM type: EDO DRAM

Video RAM total: 2 MB

X server vendor: XFree86

X server version: 3.3

X server chipset choice: S3 accelerated

Resolution/vert. refresh rate: 1152x864 @ 70 Hz

Color depth: 16 bits

Kernel

=====

Version: 2.0.29

Swap size: 64 MB

gcc

===

Version: 2.7.2.1

Options: -O2

libc version: 5.4.23

Test notes

==========

Very light load. The above tests were run with some of the special
Cyrix/IBM 6x86 features enabled with the setx86 program: fast ADS,
fast IORT, Enable DTE, fast LOOP, fast Lin. VidMem.

RESULTS

========

Linux kernel 2.0.0 Compilation Time: 7m12s

Whetstones: 38.169 MWIPS.

Xbench: 97243 xStones.

BYTE Unix Benchmarks 4.01 system INDEX: 58.43

BYTEmark integer INDEX: 1.50

BYTEmark memory INDEX: 2.50

Comments

=========

This is a very stable system with homogeneous performance, ideal
for home use and/or Linux development. I will report results
with a 6x86MX processor as soon as I can get my hands on one!

5   Pitfalls and caveats of benchmarking

After putting together this HOWTO I began to understand why the words "pitfalls" and "caveats" are so
often associated with benchmarking...

5.1   Comparing apples and oranges

Or should I say Apples and PCs ? This is so obvious and such an old dispute that I won't go into any
details. I doubt the time it takes to load Word on a Mac compared to an average Pentium is a real measure
of anything. Likewise booting Linux and Windows NT, etc... Try as much as possible to compare identical
machines with a single modification.

5.2   Incomplete information

A single example will illustrate this very common mistake. One often reads in comp.os.linux.hardware the
following or similar statement: "I just plugged in processor XYZ running at nnn MHz and now compiling
the linux kernel only takes i minutes" (adjust XYZ, nnn and i as required). This is irritating, because no
other information is given, i.e. we don't even know the amount of RAM, size of swap, other tasks running
simultaneously, kernel version, modules selected, hard disk type, gcc version, etc... I recommend you use
the LBT Report Form, which at least provides a standard information framework.

5.3   Proprietary hardware/software

A well-known processor manufacturer once published results of benchmarks produced by a special, customized version of gcc. Ethical considerations apart, those results were meaningless, since 100% of the Linux community would go on using the standard version of gcc. The same goes for proprietary hardware. Benchmarking is much more useful when it deals with off-the-shelf hardware and free (in the GNU/GPL sense) software.

5.4   Relevance

We are talking Linux, right ? So we should forget about benchmarks produced on other operating systems (this is a special case of the "Comparing apples and oranges" pitfall above). Also, if one is going to benchmark Web server performance, **do not** quote FPU performance and other irrelevant information. In such cases, less is more. Also, you do **not** need to mention the age of your cat, your mood while benchmarking, etc..

6   FAQ

Q1.

Is there any single figure of merit for Linux systems ?

A:

No, thankfully nobody has yet come up with a Lhinuxstone (tm) measurement. And if there was one, it would not make much sense: Linux systems are used for many different tasks, from heavily loaded Web servers to graphics workstations for individual use. No single figure of merit can describe the performance of a Linux system under such different situations.

Q2.

Then, how about a dozen figures summarizing the performance of diverse Linux systems ?

A:

That would be the ideal situation. I would like to see that come true. Anybody volunteers for a **Linux Benchmarking Project** ? With a Web site and an on-line, complete, well-designed reports database ?

Q3.

... BogoMips ... ?

A:

BogoMips has nothing to do with the performance of your system. Check the BogoMips Mini-HOWTO.

Q4.

What is the "best" benchmark for Linux ?

A:

It all depends on which performance aspect of a Linux system one wants to measure. There are different benchmarks to measure the network (Ethernet sustained transfer rates), file server (NFS), disk I/O, FPU, integer, graphics, 3D, processor-memory bandwidth, CAD performance, transaction time, SQL performance, Web server performance, real-time performance, CD-ROM performance, Quake performance (!), etc ... AFAIK no bechmark suite exists for Linux that supports all these tests.

Q5.

What is the fastest processor under Linux ?

A:

Fastest at what task ? If one is heavily number-crunching oriented, a very high clock rate Alpha (600 MHz and going) should be faster than anything else, since Alphas have been designed for that kind of performance. If, on the other hand, one wants to put together a very fast news server, it is probable that the choice of a fast hard disk subsystem and lots of RAM will result in higher performance improvements than a change of processor, for the same amount of $.

Q6.

Let me rephrase the last question, then: is there a processor that is fastest for general purpose applications ?

A:

This is a tricky question but it takes a very simple answer: **NO**. One can always design a faster system even for general purpose applications, independent of the processor. Usually, all other things being equal, higher clock rates will result in higher performance systems (and more headaches too). Taking out an old 100 MHz Pentium from an (usually not) upgradable motherboard, and plugging in the 200 MHz version, one should feel the extra "hummph". Of course, with only 16 MBytes of RAM, the same investment would have been more wisely spent on extra SIMMs...

Q7.

So clock rates influence the performance of a system ?

A:

For most tasks except for NOP empty loops (BTW these get removed by modern optimizing compilers), an increase in clock rate will not give you a linear increase in performance. Very small processor intensive programs that will fit entirely in the primary cache inside the processor (the L1 cache, usually 8 or 16 K) will have a performance increase equivalent to the clock rate increase, but most "true" programs are much larger than that, have loops that do not fit in the L1 cache, share the L2 (external) cache with other processes, depend on external components and will give much smaller performance increases. This is because the L1 cache runs at the same clock rate as the processor, whereas most L2 caches and all other subsystems (DRAM, for example) will run asynchronously at lower clock rates.

Q8.

OK, then, one last question on that matter: which is the processor with the best price/performance ratio for general purpose Linux use ?

A:

Defining "general purpose Linux use" in not an easy thing ! For any particular application, there is always a processor with THE BEST price/performance ratio at any given time, but it changes rather frequently as manufacturers release new processors, so answering Processor XYZ running at n MHz would be a snapshot answer. However, the price of the processor is insignificant when compared to the price of the whole system one will be putting together. So, really, the question should be how can one maximize the price/performance ratio for a given system ? And the answer to that question depends heavily on the minimum performance requirements and/or maximum cost established for the configuration being considered. Sometimes, off-the-shelf hardware will not meet minimum performance requirements and expensive RISC systems will be the only alternative. For home use, I recommend a balanced, homogeneous system for overall performance (now go figure what I mean by balanced and homogeneous :-); the choice of a processor is an important decision , but no more than choosing hard disk type and capacity, amount of RAM, video card, etc...

Q9.

What is a "significant" increase in performance ?

A:

I would say that anything under 1% is not significant (could be described as "marginal"). We, humans, will hardly perceive the difference between two systems with a 5 % difference in response time. Of course some hard-core benchmarkers are not humans and will tell you that, when comparing systems with 65.9 and 66.5 performance indexes, the later is "definitely faster".

Q10.

How do I obtain "significant" increases in performance at the lowest cost ?

A:

Since most source code is available for Linux, careful examination and algorithmic redesign of key subroutines could yield order-of-magnitude increases in performance in some cases. If one is dealing with a commercial project and does not wish to delve deeply in C source code a **Linux consultant should be called in**. See the Consultants-HOWTO.

7 Copyright, acknowledgments and miscellaneous

7.1 How this document was produced

The first step was reading section 4 "Writing and submitting a HOWTO" of the HOWTO Index by Greg Hankins.

I knew absolutely nothing about SGML or LaTeX, but was tempted to use an automated documentation generation package after reading the various comments about SGML-Tools. However, inserting tags manually in a document reminds me of the days I hand-assembled a 512 byte monitor program for a now defunct 8-bit microprocessor, so I got hold of the LyX sources, compiled it, and used its LinuxDoc mode. Highly recommended combination: **LyX and SGML-Tools**.

7.2 Copyright

7.3 New versions of this document

New versions of the Linux Benchmarking-HOWTO will be placed on sunsite.unc.edu and mirror sites. There are other formats, such as a Postscript and dvi version in the other-formats directory. The Linux Benchmarking-HOWTO is also available for WWW clients such as Grail, a Web browser written in Python. It will also be posted regularly to comp.os.linux.answers.

7.4 Feedback

Suggestions, corrections, additions wanted. Contributors wanted and acknowledged. Flames not wanted.

I can always be reached at andrewbalsa@usa.net.

7.5 Acknowledgments

David Niemi, the author of the Unixbench suite, has proved to be an endless source of information and (valid) criticism.

I also want to thank Greg Hankins, the Linux HOWTO coordinator and one of the main contributors to the SGML-tools package, Linus Torvalds and the entire Linux community. This HOWTO is my way of giving back.

7.6 Disclaimer

Your mileage may, and will, vary. Be aware that benchmarking is a touchy subject and a great time-and-energy consuming activity.

7.7 Trademarks

Pentium and Windows NT are trademarks of Intel and Microsoft Corporations respectively.

BYTE and BYTEmark are trademarks of McGraw-Hill, Inc.

Cyrix and 6x86 are trademarks of Cyrix Corporation.

Linux is not a trademark, hopefully never will be.

BogoMips mini-Howto

Wim van Dorst, *baron@clifton.hobby.nl* `<mailto:baron@clifton.hobby.nl>`

1997-12-13

This text gives some information about BogoMips, compiled from various sources such as news and e-mail. This text is retrievable from the various Linux archives in *.../HOWTO/mini/BogoMips* `<http://www.hobby.nl/user/clifton/bogomips.html>`. An article was published in the Linux Journal, issue January 1996. New entries for unlisted CPUs will be highly appreciated. They can be send per e-mail to the author.

Contents

1 Lowest and highest single CPU Linux BogoMips ratings

The following are the lowest and the highest BogoMips ratings, to date, on single CPU Linux systems.

1.1 The Lowest

- Tim Van der Linden, `timvdl@innet.be`
- Intel 8088, 4.77 MHz, ELKS
- 0.02 BogoMips

1.2 The Highest

- Jay Estabrook `jay.estabrook@digital.com`
- Alpha 21264, 400 MHz, Pass-1
- 794.82 BogoMips

2 What are BogoMips

>From Lars Wirzenius,' `wirzeniu@kruuna.Helsinki.FI` mail of 9 September 1993, explaining Bogomips, with additional detailed information by Wim van Dorst:

'MIPS is short for Millions of Instructions Per Second. It is a measure for the computation speed of a program. Like most such measures, it is more often abused than used properly (it is very difficult to justly compare MIPS for different kinds of computers). BogoMips are Linus's invention. The kernel (or was it a device driver?) needs a timing loop (the time is too short and/or needs to be too exact for a non-busy-loop method of waiting), which must be calibrated to the processor speed of the machine. Hence, the kernel measures at boot time how fast a certain kind of busy loop runs on a computer. "Bogo" comes from "bogus", i.e, something which is a fake. Hence, the BogoMips value gives some indication of the processor speed, but it is way too unscientific to be called anything but BogoMips.

The reasons (there are two) it is printed during bootup is that a) it is slightly useful for debugging and for checking that the computers caches and turbo button work, and b) Linus loves to chuckle when he sees confused people on the news.'

BogoMips are being determined in `/usr/src/linux/init/main.c` (simple C algorithm), and the pertaining kernel variable `loops_per_sec` is used in various drivers of the net, scsi, and char sections. The actual delay functions are in assembler, and therefore each port has their own in `/include/asm/delay.h`. This `loops_per_sec` variable is used in various drivers for char, net, and scsi devices, see:

```
find /usr/src/linux -name '*.[hcS]' -print -exec fgrep loops_per_sec {} \;
```

3   How to estimate what the proper BogoMips rating should be

>From a initiative by Ian Jackson, `ijackson@nyx.cs.du.edu`, and Przemek Klosowski, much updated and expanded by Wim van Dorst for current data, as listed below:

As a very approximate guide, the BogoMips can be calculated by:

```
System              BogoMips                              Comparison
Intel 8088          clock * (0.004 plusminus 0.001)       0.02
Intel/AMD 386SX     clock * (0.14  plusminus 0.01)        0.8
Intel/AMD 386DX     clock * (0.18  plusminus 0.01)        1 (definition)
Motorola 68030      clock * (0.25  plusminus 0.005)       1.4
Cyrix/IBM 486       clock * (0.34  plusminus 0.065)       1.8
Intel Pentium       clock * (0.40  plusminus 0.035)       2.2
Intel 486/AMD 5x86  clock * (0.50  plusminus 0.01)        2.8
Mips R4000/R4400    clock * (0.50  plusminus 0.015)       2.3
Nexgen Nx586        clock * (0.75  plusminus 0.010)       4.2
PowerPC 601         clock * (0.84  plusminus 0.015)       4.7
Alpha (all CPUs)    clock * (0.99  plusminus 0.005)       5.5
Intel Pentium Pro   clock * (0.99  plusminus 0.005)       5.5
Cyrix 5x86/6x86     clock * (1.00  plusminus 0.005)       5.6
Intel Pentium II    clock * (1.00)                        5.6
Mips R4600          clock * (1.00)                        5.6
Alpha 21264         clock * (1.99)                        11.1
AMD K5/K6           clock * (2.00  plusminus 0.010)       11.1
Pentium MMX         clock * (2.00)                        11.1
Motorola 68060      clock * (2.01)                        11.2


Motorola 68040      (insufficient data yet)
Sparc               (insufficient data yet)
```

Note that the BogoMips calculation loop does not take advantage of the parallelism of various processors, such as the Intel Pentium and the Alpha 21164.

Note that the BogoMips calculation loop for the non-Intel CPUs is similar but not the same.

4   How to determine what the current BogoMips rating is

There are three methods to determing the current BogoMips, viz.

1. looking in `/proc/cpuinfo`, e.g., with 'cat /proc/cpuinfo'.
2. looking in the syslog output to see what was printed there during booting (if necessary retrieving the information explicitly with dmesg or syslogk) or
3. using the standalone bogomips program.

And non determinative alternative may be, also applicable for non-Linux systems, such as Crays an so on, the standalone BogoMips program. From the readme file by Jeff Tranter, jeff_tranter@mitel.com:

> 'Tired of rebooting your system so you can see how many BogoMIPS it's running at today? [...] "Bogomips" is a standalone program that displays your system performance using one of the world's most recognized benchmarks. It uses the same code that is used in the Linux kernel while booting, but runs as a user program. [...] Version 1.3 of BogoMIPS is now portable and should run on any system that supports an ANSI C compiler and library.'

Note that due to system load values calculated with the standalone program may be lower than registered in the list below. Intrinsically the standalone cannot give precisely similar information to the boot sequence BogoMips, since system load will compete with this program run by an ordinary user.

Be aware that the file sunsite.unc.edu:/pub/Linux/system/status/bogo-1.2.tar.gz/ contains the latest version 1.3 (sic), which is yet rather outdated.

5   Variations in BogoMips rating

>From Linus Torvalds, torvalds@cc.helsinki.fi, explaining about the variation one may see in the BogoMips rating, in c.o.l.development, at 28 April 1994

> 'The BogoMips calculation loop is "quantizised", so you're most likely to get the exact same number all the time. You usually will get different numbers only if the speed is just on the "edge", when small variations (different time for interrupt ticks etc) will make it jump from one value to the other.'

6   BogoMips ... failed

Suggested by various questions on the net and private mail, e.g., by Lily, lbliao@alumni.caltech.edu, and by Pierre Frenkiel, frenkiel@cdfap2.in2p3.fr. In March 1995 they asked:

> 'When I boot Linux I get the message:
>
> ```
> Calibrating delay loop.. ok - 23.96 BogoMips
> failed
> ```
>
> Where/why has the calibration delay loop failed?'

It didn't fail. If it had failed the text would have been

```
Calibrating delay loop.. failed
```

What likely did fail was a driver for some gadget which you may not have in your machine. Just after calculating the BogoMips rating all device drivers are initiated. First the SCSI devices, then Net devices, etc. Any failure is duly reported. Noteworthy is the AHA152x driver. Other effects of failing drivers (and not of failing BogoMips calculations) are systems crashes, long waits, and complete system locks.

Since Linux 1.2 many error messages have improved, so upgrade to at least that version to find out which particular driver it is that is failing.

7   What about clone CPUs (Cyrix, NexGen, AMD, etc)

Cyrix 486-like CPUs need cache enabling software, sometimes referred to as BogoBoost software. Cyrix 5x86 and 6x86 CPUs may have their BogoMips improved drastically by branch-prediction (BIOS option). Note that the performance improvement may be marginal. There are several packages available for adjusting Cyrix CPUs, such as the bogoboost patch, cx5x86mod, and set6x86, all from the normal archives, in obvious places. It is reported the Cyrix 6x86 CPUs may give better performance when the kernel is compiled with 486-optimization, instead Pentium-optimization.

NexGen 386-enhanced CPUs, marked as Nx586, are listed as 386-like, since the fact that they are performing like Pentium machines is not relevant to BogoMips.

AMD 5x86, also denoted as AMD 486DX5, are quadrupled 486/33 machines. They are fully in line with other 486 CPUs. The AMD K5 and the K6 are Pentium-like CPUs, with their own BogoMips multipliers.

8   Why to pay attention to BogoMips

Let me add that there are only two reasons for paying attention to the BogoMips rating that is presented on booting Linux:

1. To see whether it is in the proper range for the particular processor, its clock frequency, and the potentially present cache. Many CPUs are prone to faulty setups of

   - memory cache setting (write-back is wrong for BogoMips, often reported lower than 5; write-through is ok)
   - turbo-buttons (should be ON)
   - BIOS-software emulated fake cache (change it for real cache)
   - similar cache and clock related things.

2. To see whether your system is faster than mine. Of course this is completely wrong, unreliable, ill-founded, and utterly useless, but all benchmarks suffer from this same problem. So why not use it? This inherent stupidity has never before stopped people from using benchmarks, has it? :-)

Note that more serious uses for real benchmarking are addressed in the Linux Benchmarking Howto by André D. Balsa.

9   Compilation of ratings

The following table gives some reported BogoMips ratings for various systems (over 800 entries by about 700 different persons, from about 50 different countries. Note that the ratings here are from the Linux actual booting sequence, except of course for the section on Non-Linux Systems.

9.1   Oddly or faultly configured 386 systems

```
System                  BogoMips   Reporter
386DX/16 387 nocache     0.57      H. Peter Anvin <hpa@nwu.edu>
386DX/25                 0.82      P Wright <philip.wright@purplet.demon.co.uk>
386DX/25 nocache         1.03      Mark A. Horton <mahmha@crl.com>
386SX/16                 1.5       Stefan Kromer <sk@galaxy.sunflower.sub.org>
```

386SX/16	1.6	Bill Davidsen <davidsen@tmr.com>
386SX/20	1.87	Paul C. Dulany <pcdulany@wam.umd.edu>
386SX/20	2.45	Roger Harkess <roger@visi.com>
386DX/25(?) 128c	6.03	Chuck Meo <meo@solbourne.com>
386DX/20	13	Ed Runnion <erunnio@hubcap.clemson.edu>

9.2 Normal 386 systems: SX, DX, Nexgen

System	BogoMips	Reporter
386SX/8 undercl	1.04	Andrew Costa <c_chaos@wahnapitae.on.ca>
386SX/16	1.99	James Vahn <jvahn@short.circuit.com>
386SX/16 Packard Bell	2.05	<root@Belvedere\%hip-hop.suvl.ca.us>
386SX/16	2.09	David E. Fox <dfox@belvedere.sbay.org>
386SX/16	2.15	W Stevens <wgsteven@math.uwaterloo.co>
386SX/16	2.2	Lech Marcinkowski <puolalm@tekla.fi>
386SX/16	2.23	Andrew Bulhak <acb@yoyo.cc.monash.edu.au>
386SX/16	2.23	Steven M. Gallo <smgallo@cs.buffalo.edu>
386SX/16	2.34	Kevin Burtch <kburtch@pts.mot.com>
386SX/16 turbo	2.38	Andrew Haylett <ajh@gec-mrc.co.uk>
386SX/16 0c	2.43	Adam Clarke <adamc@loose.apana.org.au>
386SX/16	2.49	Waymon <waymon@pacifier.com>
386SX/20	2.7	Alex Strasheim <astrashe@nyx.cs.du.edu>
386SX/20	2.70	J.L. Brothers <brothers@halcyon.com>
386SXL/25 AMD	2.9	Vaughan R. Pratt <pratt@sunburn.stanford.edu>
386SX/25 AMD 0c	3.06	K.J. MacDonald <kenny@festival.ed.ac.uk>
386SX/25 AMD	3.38	Hamish Coleman <hamish@zot.apana.org.au>
386SX/25 0c	3.52	Rogier Wolff <r.e.wolff@et.tudelft.nl>
386SL/25 Intel	3.57	S Harris <harris@teaching.physics.ox.ac.uk>
386SX/25 AMD	3.62	S Harris <harris@teaching.physics.ox.ac.uk>
386SXL/25 AMD 0c	3.71	David E.A. Wilson <david@cs.uow.edu.au>
386SX/33 Intel	4.06	Kenneth J. Hoover <ken@psuedvax.psu.edu>
386SX/33	4.71	Alexander Komlik <apkom@l.ukrcom.kherson.ua>
386SX/40 Intel 0c	6.03	Michael Kenyon <u3g12@keele.ac.uk>
386DX/16	2.49	Mike <mike@emgee.demon.co.uk>
386DX/20 Intel	3.0	Malcolm Reeves <reeves@rocky1.usask.cs>
386DX/20 Intel	3.08	Si. Harris <harris@teaching.physics.ox.ac.uk>
386DX/20 Nec Powermate	3.22	David J Dawkins <davidd@isl.co.uk>
386DX/20 Micronics	3.25	M Haardt <u31b3hs@informatik.rwth-aachen.de>
386DX/20	3.67	Joost Helberg <jhelberg@nlsun8.oracle.nl>
386DX/25	3.91	Ian McCloghrie <imcclogh@cs.ucsd.edu>
386DX/25	3.95	Grant Edwards <grante@aquarius.rosemount.com>
386DX/25 0cache	3.96	J.O. Williams <jow@techbase.com>
386DX/25 32cache	4.53	J.M.A. Lahtinen <jmalahti@klaava.Helsinki.FI>
386DX/33	5.86	Tim Lacy <timla@microsoft.com>
386DX/33 64cache	5.99	Lars Wirzenius <wirzeniu@kruuna.Helsinki.FI>
386DX/33 Intel	5.99	Harri Pasanen <hpasanen@cs.hut.fi>
386DX/33 no387	6.03	Joel B.Levin <levin@bbn.com>
386DX/33 387	6.03	Peter Bechtold <peter@fns.greenie.muc.de>
386DX/40	6.21	J.L. Brothers <brothers@halcyon.com>
386DX/33	6.46	Dennis Robinson <djrobins@uxa.cso.uiuc.edu>
386DX/33	6.5	Dean Nelson <deannelson@aol.com>

```
386DX/33 387 256cache   6.65    Wim van Dorst <baron@clifton.hobby.nl>
386DX/33                6.65    Rick Lim <ricklim@opus.freenet.vancouver.bc.ca>
386DX/33                6.7     Craig Hagan <hagan@cih.com>
386DX/40                6.99    Ken Wilcox <wilcox@math.psu.edu>
386DX/40 AMD            7.76    Joe Phillips <rchandra@letter.com>
386DX/40 AMD            7.10    Kerry Person <kperson@plains.NoDak.edu>
386DX/40                7.10    D. Bikram Singh <a336dhal@cdf.toronto.edu>
386DX/40 128cache       7.23    Julian Francis Day <jfd0@aber.ac.uk>
386DX/40 bogoboosted    7.23    Pat St Jean <stjean@math.enmu.edu>
386DX/40 AMD 128cache   7.23    R.Bergs <rabe@akela.informatik.rwth-aachen.de>
386DX/40 slow DRAM      7.26    John Lockwood <lockwood@pan.vlsi.uiuc.edu>
386DX/40 128c           7.29    Karsten Friese <ftdkafr@ftd.ericsson.se>
386DX/40                7.29    E.C. Garrison <ericg@nickel.ucs.indiana.edu>
386DX/40                7.29    Darin Cowan <cowan@rubicon.org>
386DX/40                7.29    Bonne van Dijk <bonne@cs.utwente.nl>
386DX/40 AMD            7.76    Todd Lindner <tlindner@panix.com>
386DX/40                7.76    Bear Giles <bear@indra.com>
386DX/40 AMD 387 64c    7.91    <wires@gnu.ai.mit.edu>
386DX/40                7.98    Frank Pilhofer <fp@informatik.uni-frankfurt.de>
386DX/40 64c            7.98    Dean Junk <dpjunk@mm.com>
386DX/40 AMD 32c        7.98    Tommy Olsen <tommyo@ifi.uio.no>
386DX/40 AMD            7.98    James Reith <reith@racores.com>
386DX/40                7.98    Aaron T. Baldie <atb@u.washington.edu>
386DX/40 128c           7.98    John Pate <jpate@easynet.co.uk>
386DX/40                7.98    Christian Nelson <cnelson@csugrad.cs.vt.edu>
386DX/40                7.98    Alan Peckham <peckham@drei.enet.dec.com>
386DX/40                8.06    Michael Guslick <michaelg@alpha2.csd.uwm.edu>
386DX/40                8.06    Richard Brown <brown@midget.towson.edu>
386DX/40                8.06    Bill G. Bohling <bs146@tali.uchsc.edu>

Nx586/90 NexGen         67.44   <root@wgw.mnsinc.com>
Nx586/90 NexGen         67.44   Robert Gehring <rag@cs.tu-berlin.de>
Nx586/90 NexGen         67.48   David G. Eckard <dgeckard@eos.ncsu.edu>
Nx586/100 NexGen        74.34   Cameron L. Spitzer <cls@truffala.sj.ca.us>
Nx586/100 NexGen 256c   74.56   Marius Groenendijk <marius@cray-systems.lu>
Nx586/110 NexGen 256c   81.51   Michael J. Micek <mmicek@muddcs.cs.hmc.edu>
Nx586/110 NexGen        81.51   Ron Marsh <rmarsh@plains.nodak.edu>
```

9.3   Oddly or faultly configured 486 systems

```
System              BogoMips  Reporter
486DX/33 0c         1.45      Mark Gray <vatavian@gvu1.gatech.edu>
486SL/25 0c         1.95      Paraskevas Evripidou <skevos@seas.smu.edu>
486DLC/40 0c        2.45      S.Schendel <sschend@magnus.acs.ohio-state.edu>
486DX/33 128c       2.94      P.J. Nefkens <p.nefkens@student.utwente.nl>
486DX4/120 AMD      3.04      Andrew Steinbach <stei0113@maroon.tc.umn.edu>
486DX5/133 AMD      3.05      Eric Hagen <ehagen@hawaii.edu>
486DX4/100 Cyrix    3.06      Stuart Harvey <sharvey@primenet.com>
486DX5/133 AMD      3.06      Charles Galpin <chg@severn.wash.inmet.com>
486DX4/100          3.06      Bear Giles <bear@indra.com>
486DX2/80           3.08      Gerald E. Butler <gbutler@phoenix.kent.edu>
486DX4/120 AMD      3.08      Charles Hines <chuck_hines@vnet.ibm.com>
```

```
486DX4/66 256c         3.10   Riccardo Capella <mc8508@mclink.it>
486DX4/100 wb-cache    3.10   Paul Close <pdc@sgi.com>
486DX4/120             3.13   Brian Perkins <bperkins@netspace.com>
486DX4/120 AMD         3.15   <eruston@net2.intserv.com>
486DX4/100             3.17   Thomas Sudbrak <sudbrak@borneo.gmd.de>
486SLC2/50 Cyrix       3.30   Colin J. Wynne <cwynne@sage.wlu.edu>
486DX/33               3.61   Marten van de Laan <marten@cs.rug.nl>
486DX/33 noturbo       3.61   Dimitris Evmorfopoulos <devmorfo@mtu.edu>
486DX4/120             3.74   Brian Wheeler <bdwheele@indiana.edu>
486DX4/120 AMD         3.74   Frank Pilhofer <fp@informatik.uni-frankfurt.de>
486DX4/100 Cyrix 256c  4      Joel Kelso <joel@cs.murdoch.edu.au>
486DX/33 256c noturbo  4.25   Wouter Liefting <wlieftin@cs.vu.nl>
486DX/33               4.66   Mark Gray <vatavian@gvu1.gatech.edu>
486Rx2 Cyrix 25/50     4.85   <cosc19v2@menudo.uh.edu>
486SX/33 noturbo       5.21   Scott D. Heavner <sdh@fishmonger.nouucp>
486DX2/66 overdrive    5.37   Jeremy Orr <jeremy@careercenter.sfsu.edu>
486DX/33               5.66   Ryan Tucker <rtucker@ttgcitn.com>
486DX2/66              5.88   P.J. Nefkens <p.nefkens@student.utwente.nl>
486DX4/100             5.94   Howard Goldstein <hg@n2wx.ampr.org>
486DX4/100 AMD         5.94   Mr Pink <vince@dallas.demon.co.uk>
486DX4/100 notebook    6.55   Thomas <tom@dirac.physik.uni-konstanz.de>
486DX4/100 notebook    6.55   Hugh McCurdy <hmccurdy@ix.netcom.com>
486SLC Cyrix           7      Pieter Verhaeghe <pive@uia.ac.be>
486SX/33               7.84   Paul Hedderly <prh6@unix.york.ac.uk>
486DLC/40              7.98   Wil Cromer <nwc2@Ra.MsState.Edu>
486DX/33 256c          8.27   Rohan Tronson <rohan@kihi.com.au>
486DX4/100             11.11  NN <usenet@uxmail.ust.hk>
486DX4/100             11.3   Earl Gooch <egooch@mc.com>
486/66 Cyrix           13.02  Mike Baptiste <baptiste@bnr.ca>
486SLC2/25             14.6   Vaughan R. Pratt <pratt@Sunburn.Stanford.EDU>
486DX2/66 laptop       14.46  Robert Knop <rknop@netcom.com>
486SLC2/66             18.94  <root@avalon.net>
486DX/33 turbo         19.98  C Vetter <cbvetter@informatik.th-darmstadt.de>
486DX4/75              21.5   Theo Scott <rkwtgs@pukrs3.puk.ac.za>
486DX4/75              24.13  Sherman Hsieh <shieh@csua.berkeley.edu>
486DX2/58              26.3   Vassili Leonov <leonov@iedv7.acd.com>
486DX4/100 overclock   28.67  Theo Scott <rkwtgs@pukrs3.puk.ac.za>
486DX2/80              36     Mark Lee <mlee@heartlab.rri.uwo.ca>
486DX2/80              50.08  Mark Lee <mlee@heartlab.rri.uwo.ca>
486DX4/100             60     Sebastien Dedieu <dedieu@emi.u-bordeaux.fr>
486DX2/100 overclock   60.45  Tony D Shan <tdsst9+@pitt.edu>
486DX5/133 AMD         75.40  Jeff Hyche <jwhyche@scott.net>
486DX5/133 AMD         80.08  NN <guesta@slip-29-7.ots.utexas.edu>
486DX5/133 AMD         87     John Wiggins <jwiggins@comp.uark.edu>
```

9.4   Normal 486 systems

System	BogoMips	Reporter
486SX/20 DECpc	9.98	Thomas Pfau <pfau@cnj.digex.com>
486SX/25	12.24	M. Buchenrieder <mibu@scrum.greenie.muc.de>
486SX/25	12.3	Darren McKay <e9bh@unb.ca>
486SX/25	12.42	Mark R. Lindsey <mlindsey@nyx.cs.du.edu>

```
486DX/25            12.5    Phillip Hardy <phillip@mserve.kiwi.gen.nz>
486SX/25            12.52   Emmanual Emore <emor7672@elan.rowan.edu>
486DX/33 256c       16.33   Eric Kemminan <ekemmina@pms709.ms.ford.com>
486DX/33            16.35   Christopher L. Morrow <cm43@andrew.cmu.edu>
486DX/33            16.43   Rob Janssen <pe1chl@amsat.org>
486DX/33 64cache    16.44   H. Peter Anvin <hpa@nwu.edu>
486DX/33 256c DIY   16.44   Wouter Liefting <wlieftin@cs.vu.nl>
486DX/33 Intel 128c 16.44   Rafal Kustra <g1krakow@cdf.toronto.edu>
486DX/33            16.5    Alex Freed <freed@europa.orion.adobe.com>
486DX/33            16.6    Vaughan R. Pratt <pratt@Sunburn.Stanford.EDU>
486DX/33 noturbo    16.61   C Vetter <cbvetter@informatik.th-darmstadt.de>
486DX/33            16.61   Jeffrey L. Newbern <jnewbern@athena.mit.edu>
486DX/33            16.61   Giuseppe De Marco <gdemarco@freenet.hut.fi>
486DX/33            16.61   M Heuler <heuler@informatik.uni-wuerzburg.de>
486DX/33            16.61   Frank Lofaro <ftlofaro@unlv.edu>
486DX/33            16.77   Donald Lewis <dlewis@jackson.freenet.org>
486DX/33            16.77   Stephan Boettcher <staphan@alzt.tau.ac.il>
486DX/33 256c       16.77   David Manchester <mustang@tartarus.uwa.edu.au>
486DX/40            19.8    Jose Calhariz <cal@minerva.inesc.pt>
486DX/40            19.91   M Heuler <heuler@informatik.uni-wuerzburg.de>
486DX/40            19.96   David A. Ranch <dranch@ecst.csuchico.edu>
486DX/40 AMD        19.97   M Haardt <u31b3hs@informatik.RWTH-Aachen.DE>
486DX/40 Intel      19.97   Paul van Spronsen <vspr@teppic.sun.ac.za>
486DX/40            19.97   Ulf Tietz <ulf@rio70.bln.sni.de>
486DX/40            19.97   <Eberhard_Moenkeberg@p27.rollo.central.de>
486DX/40            19.97   Zoltan Lajber <lajbi@lajli.gau.hu>
486DX/40            19.97   Wim van Dorst <baron@wiesje.hobby.nl>
486DX/40 AMD        20      Chuck Munro <chuckm@canada.hp.com>
486DX/40 AMD        20.09   Pieter Eendebak <peendebak@bbsw.idn.nl>
486DX/50            24.48   Arnd Gehrmann <arnd@rea>
486DX/50 AMD        24.85   Klaas Hemstra <hst@mh.nl>
486DX/50 DTK        24.85   Randolph Christophers <randyc@lna.oz.au>
486DX/50            24.85   Kevin Lentin <kevinl@bruce.cs.monash.edu.au>
486DX2/50           24.85   Jason Matthew <jmatthew@kn.pacbell.com>
486DX2/50           24.85   Gregory P. Smith <smithgr@cs.colorado.edu>
486DX/50 VLB        24.97   Tom Miller <tvtom@en.com>
486DX/50            24.99   Jeff <css@erols.com>
486DX/50 Intel 256c 24.99   Mike <mike@emgee.demon.co.uk>
486DX/50            25      Robert Herzog <rherzog@rc1.vub.ac.be>
486DX2/50           25      M. Abrahamsson <swmike@uplift.df.lth.se>
486DX2/50           25.0    Christian Holtje <choltje@ux1.cso.uiuc.edu>
486DX2/50 DECpc     25.04   Thomas Pfau <pfau@cnj.digex.com>
486DX2/50 Eisa      25.04   John Willing <willing@cimage.com>
486DX2/50 256c      25.04   Zhou Yanmo <zhou@gauss.math.usf.edu>
486DX/50            25.04   Michael Kress <kress@hal.saar.de>
486DX2/50           25.04   Mats Wikholm <mwikholm@news.abo.fi>
486DX2/50           25.04   Jean C Delepine <delepine@linux.u-picardia.fr>
486DX/50            25.04   Jean C Delepine <delepine@linux.u-picardia.fr>
486DX/50            25.04   Kevin Burtch <kburtch@pts.mot.com>
486DX/50 notebook   25.04   Pierre Frenkiel <frenkiel@cdfap1.in2p3.fr>
486DX/50            25.10   M Heuler <heuler@informatik.uni-wuerzburg.edu>
486DX2/50           25.4    Brian Kennedy <bkenned@hubcap.clemson.edu>
486DX2/66           32      Lee Sau Dan <h9210876@khuxa.hku.hk>
486DX2/66           32.9    Frederick <niles@axp745.gsfc.nasa.gov>
```

```
486DX2/80  AMD            39.94   Pete Krawczyk <pkrawczy@uiuc.edu>
486DX2/80  AMD            40      Rene Baart <baart@simplex.nl>
486DX2/80  AMD            40      Wolfgang Kalthoff <wo@rio70.bln.sni.de>
486DX2/80                 40.0    Rick Brown <ccastrb@prism.gatech.edu>
486DX2/80  AMD            40.14   Jon Lewis <jlewis@inorganic5.chem.ufl.edu>
486DX2/80  AMD            40.14   Richard S. Stone <rstone@edgp.com>
486DX2/80                 40.15   Oleg <oleg@hpcms.co.il>
486DX2/80  AMD            40.18   Adri Verhoef <a3@a3.xs4all.nl>
486DX2/80                 40.18   Mats Andtbacka <mandtback@abo.fi>
486DX2/100 AMD overcl     49.14   Jon Lewis <jlewis@inorganic5.chem.ufl.edu>
5x86/100 AMD undercl      49.66   NN <root@tailor.aleim.net>
486DX4/100 256c           49.71   Lutz Pressler <lutz.pressler@med-stat.GWDG.de>
486DX4/100                49.71   Brett Gersekowski <bgrerseko@powerup.com.au>
486DX4/100 Intel 256c     49.77   Angelo Haritsis <ah@doc.ic.ac.uk>
5x86/100 AMB undercl      49.77   Bernd Hentig <bernd.hentig@guug.de>
486DX4/100                49.78   Aurel Balmosan <aurel@xylo.owl.de>
486DX4/100                49.87   Chris Saia <minkie@concentric.net>
486DX4/100                50      Donald Lewis <dlewis@jackson.freenet.org>
486DX4/100                50.02   Peter Skov Knudsen <gogol@ask.diku.dk>
486DX4/100                50.02   Shadow Weaver <djamison@students.wisc.edu>
486DX4/100 AMD            50.3    Dave <shodan@shodan.clark.net>
486DX4/100 AMD            50.04   Tony Smolar <asmolar@fast.net>
486DX4/100                50.05   fredk <fredk@shadow.net>
486DX4/100                50.06   Ronald Prague <ronp@fisnet.net>
486DX4/100                50.08   Matt Gisher <matt@matt.fidalgo.net>
486DX4/100                50.08   Steven A. Duchene <sduchene@cis.ysu.edu>
486DX4/100                50.08   Miles O'Neal <meo@schoneal.com>
486DX4/100                50.08   Will <zxmvg07@hp12.zdv.uni-tuebingen.de>
486DX4/100                50.08   Piet de Bondt <bondt@dutiws.twi.tudelft.nl>
486DX4/100 laptop         50.08   Karl Kleinpaste <karl_kleinpaste@cs.cmu.edu>
486DX4/100 256c           50.08   Thomas Kanschik <y0000997@ws.rz.tu-bs.de>
486DX4/100                50.08   Linas Vepstas <linas@fc.net>
486DX4/100                50.08   Ed Daiga <daiga@engin.umich.edu>
486DX4/100 notebook       50.08   Gerry Quejada <fd863@cleveland.freenet.edu>
486DX4/100 AMD            50.08   B Schuller <schuller@ind136a.wi.leidenuniv.nl>
486DX4/100                50.08   J.L. Brothers <brothers@halcyon.com>
486DX4/100                50.08   David E.A. Wilson <david@cs.uow.edu.au>
486DX4/100                50.08   Mark Lumsden <root@titan2.physics.mcmaster.ca>
486DX4/100                50.08   Ashar <ashar@netcom12.netcom.com>
486DX4/100                50.08   Jacob Waltz <waltz@pcjiw.lampf.lanl.gov>
486DX4/100                50.08   Tom Sinclair <sinner@cafe.net>
486DX4/100 AMD            50.08   G. Skinner <gskinner@gwsunix1.crystalball.com>
486DX4/100 AMD            50.08   Nick Savoiu <nick@ritz.mordor.com>
486DX4/100                50.08   Thomas J Fisher <twb5odt@nmia.com>
486DX4/100                50.08   Pascal Pensa <pensa@aurora.unice.fr>
486DX4/100                50.08   Julian Bradbury <julian@xabcs.demon.co.uk>
486DX4/100                50.51   Frederic Potter <frederic@swing.ibp.fr>
486DX4/100                50.66   Bill Stegers <bill_ste@zeelandnet.nl>
486DX4/120 256c           59.1    Kevin <kalichwa@oakland.edu>
486DX4/120 AMD            59.80   Mark Tranchant <mat92@ecs.soton.ac.uk>
486DX4/120 AMD            59.80   Fred Broce <fbroce@atlanta.com>
486DX4/120 AMD            59.90   Marko Ovaska <ovaska@cc.helsinki.fi>
486DX4/120 AMD            59.80   Bob Purdon <bobp@mpx.com.au>
486DX4/120 AMD            59.80   Pat Young <dice@netbsd.warped.com>
```

```
486DX4/120              59.91   Will <zxmvg07@hp12.zdv.uni-tuebingen.de>
486DX4/120 AMD 256c     60.01   Angelo Haritsis <ah@doc.ic.ac.uk>
486DX4/120 overcl       60.45   Pascal Pensa <pensa@aurora.unice.fr>
486DX4/120              60.45   Neal Howard <neal@metronet.com>
486DX4/120 AMD          60.45   Oscar Belmar Madrid <obelmar@anakena.usach.cl>
486DX4/120              60.45   Jason Buchanan <jsb@digistar.com>
486DX4/120              60.45   Foersterling <dirk@informatik.uni-frankfurt.de>
486DX4/120              60.45   Bernd Hentig <bernd@finow.snafu.de>
5x86/133 AMD            66.15   NN <root@tailor.aleim.net>
5x86/133 AMD            66.15   Brad Wilson <bwilson@deltanet.com>
5x86/133 AMD            66.44   P Yli-Krekola <perttu@ntcmar01ba.ntc.nokia.com>
5x86/133 AMD            66.44   V. Tailor <vtailor@ibm.net>
5x86/133 AMD            66.55   Andrew B. Cramer <cramer@ripco.com>
5x86/133 AMD            66.56   Bob Nielsen <nielsen@primenet.com>
5x86/133 AMD            66.65   Geoff Raye <gtraye@igsrsparc2.er.usgs.gov>
5x86/133 AMD            66.7    Klaas Hemstra <hst@mh.nl>
5x86/133 AMD            66.80   N.N. <vp24njcb@ubvms.cc.buffalo.edu>
5x86/133 AMD      256c  67.10   Vasily Lewis
5x86/133 AMD            67.10   James Reith <reith@racores.com>
5x86/133 AMD      256c  67.10   Yves Rougy <yrougy%siam@cal.fr>
5x86/133 AMD      256c  67.10   Peter A. Koren <pkoren@lvdc20.dseg.ti.com>
5x86/133 AMD      256c  67.10   Wim Joppe <joppe@xs4all.nl>
5x86/133 AMD      256c  67.10   Gunnar Stefansson <gunnars@rhi.hi.is>
5x86/133 AMD      256c  67.10   Vernard Martin <vernard.martin@cc.gatech.edu>
5x86/150 AMD overcl     74.75   Sergio Riveros <riveros@musca.unm.edu>
5x86/150 AMD overcl     74.75   Arthur K. Chan <artchan@cs.ucr.edu>
5x86/160 AMD overcl     79.87   M.Suencksen <msuencks@techfak.uni-bielefeld.de>
5x86/160 AMD overcl     79.87   J. Chris Hammond <cosmo@pcisys.net>
5x86/160 AMD overcl     79.87   Bird Chen <luca@linux.taiwan.hp.com>
5x86/160 AMD overcl     79.89   Geir Skaugen <geir.skaugen@energy.sintef.no>
5x86/160 AMD overcl     79.89   Martin Vernon <martin@gw6hva.demon.co.uk>
5x86/160 AMD overcl     79.92   T. Zerucha <zerucha@shell.portal.com>
5x86/160 AMD overcl     80.36   Paul Colucci <pcolucci@acsu.buffalo.edu>
5x86/160 AMD overcl     80.36   Steinar Haug <sthaug@nethelp.no>
5x86/160 AMD overcl     80.36   James Daniel <triadmin@bga.com>
5x86/160 AMD            80.36   David H.S. Oh <david@std.net>
```

9.5   Normal 486 variations: Cyrix/IBM, UMC

```
System                  BogoMips  Reporter
486DLC/33                  9.42   Dennis Robinson <djrobins@uxa.cso.uiuc.edu>
486DLC/33 387DX/40         9.47   Denis Solaro <drzob@vectrex.login.qc.ca>
486DLC/33 Cyrix wb         9.5    M. Asplund <matt@xenon.cchem.berkely.edu>
486DLC/33 Cyrix 386       11.2    Alex Freed <freed@europa.orion.adobe.com>
486DLC/40 256c            11.33   Schendel <sschend@magnus.acs.ohio-state.edu>
486Dx/40 Cyrix            11.73   Malcolm Bremer <malcolm@strw.LeidenUniv.nl>
486DRx2/40 Cyrix          13.10   Christopher Lau <clau@acs.ucalgary.ca>
486DX/33 Cyrix            13.21   M Haardt <u31b3hs@informatik.RWTH-Aachen.DE>
486DLC/40 bogoboost       13.21   Harry Pasanen <ps@tekla.fi>
486DLC/40 487 Cyrix       13.21   Ian A. Verschuren <iav@po.CWRU.Edu>
486DCL Cyrix              13.3    Tracer Bullet P.I. <ges@earth.baylor.edu>
486DLC/40                 13.31   Adam Frampton <frampton@access2.digex.net>
```

```
486DLC/40                13.31   Rick Chow <crc@cacs.usl.edu>
486SLC-S/33              13.51   Brad Pepers <pepersb@cuug.ab.ca>
486DLC/40 no Cxpatch     15.47   Sergei O. Naoumov <serge@envy.astro.unc.edu>
486DLC/40 TI 128c        15.97   Philip K. Roban <phil@seal.micro.umn.edu>
486DLC/40 Cyrix          15.97   L.J. LaBash <labash@lcjones.aclib.siue.edu>
486DRx2/40               15.99   Christopher Lau <lauc@fusion.cuc.ab.ca>
486DX2/66 IBM no-FF      19      NN <coolefa@pmifeg.com>
486SLC2/66 IBM 64c       18.95   Sujat Jamil <sujat@shasta.ee.umn.edu>
486SLC2/66 IBM 128c      18.95   Sujat Jamil <sujat@shasta.ee.umn.edu>
486SLC2/66               19.02   Harry Mangalam <mangalam@uci.edu>
486SLC/50                19.28   Sion Arrowsmith <sion@bast.demon.co.uk>
486BL3/75 IBM 256c       21.40   Anders Stenback <stenback@kuai.se>
486BL3/75 IBM 256c       21.50   Ming S. Chan <ming.chan@canrem.com>
486DX2/66 Cyrix 128c     26.63   Derek Kwan <dkwan@zeus.UWaterloo.ca>
486DX2/66 Cyrix          26.63   Adrian Parker <adrian@willen.demon.co.uk>
486DX2-S/66 256c         26.63   Jean-Marc Wislez <JeanMarc.Wislez@rug.ac.be>
486DX2/66 Cyrix          26.63   Curran W. Fey <fey@biotech.washington.edu>
486BL3/100 IBM 256c      28.36   Anders Stenback <stenback@kuai.se>

486SX-S/33 UMC 0c        20.20   Hynek Med <xmedh02@manes.vse.cz>
486SX-S/40 UMC 0c        26.52   Hynek Med <xmedh02@manes.vse.cz>
486SX-U5/40 UMC 0c       26.63   Dusan Mihajlovic <zdule@herkules.co.yu>
```

9.6   Oddly or faultly configured Pentium systems, or variations

```
System                 BogoMips   Reporter
Pentium/66                 2.18   Bob Myers <root@shyguy.lonestar.org>
Pentium/90 notebook        9.5    Mark Maybee <markm@cs.colorado.edu>
6x86/120 Cyrix            52.32   Joel Boring <dwild@eskimo.com>
Pentium/83 Overdrive      82.85   Brian Smith <smithb@laraby.tiac.net>
Pentium/83 Overdrive      83.32   Scott Francis <mord@netcom.com>
Pentium/83 Overdrive      82.94   G. Spiegelberg <greg@owens.ridgecrest.ca.us>
Pentium/83 Overdrive      83.35   Jacek Polewczak <jacek.polewczak@csun.edu>
6x86/120 P120+overcl     104.86   Howard Poe <falcor@kingsnet.com>
Pentium MMX/263 overcl   392.40   John Appleby <jma24@cam.ac.uk>
Pentium MMX/231          419.43   Juan Domenech <domenech@mail.seric.es>
Pentium MMX/263 overcl   435.87   Juan Domenech <domenech@mail.seric.es>
SMP4 Pentium Pro/200     700.13   R. Carrico <robert_carrico@themoneystore.com>
```

9.7   Normal Pentium systems

```
System                 BogoMips   Reporter
Pentium/60             23         Chien-An Chen <giant@nwu.edu>
Pentium/60             23.96      Joost Helberg <jhelberg@nlsun8.oracle.nl>
Pentium/60             23.96      Ulf Tietz <ulf@rio70.bln.sni.de>
Pentium/60 Gateway     23.96      Manoj Kasichainula <mvkasich@eos.ncsu.edu>
Pentium/60             23.96      Pierre Frenkiel <frenkiel@cdfap1.in2p3.fr>
Pentium/60             23.96      Tim Oosterbroek <tim@astro.uva.nl>
Pentium/60 NCR 3455    24         Mathias Koerber <mathias@solomon.technet.sg>
Pentium/60             24         Joe Sloan <jjs@engr.ucr.edu>
Pentium/60             24.0       Mark H. Wood <mwood@indyvax.iupui.edu>
```

```
Pentium/100 overcl      39.94   Donar G.E. Alofs <donar@cs.vu.nl>
Pentium/100             39.94   Larry Snyder <larry@trauma.iag.net>
Pentium/100             39.94   Ian Hill <ian@hecate.phy.queensu.ca>
Pentium/100             39.94   John Crawford <link@spu.edu>
Pentium/100             39.94   Jered <jered@mit.edu>
Pentium/100 overcl      39.94   Ian <irs2@tweedledum.amp.york.ac.uk>
Pentium/100             39.94   Brian McGhee <brianm@iceonline.com>
Pentium/100             39.94   M Skjelland <morten.skjelland@pvv.unit.no>
Pentium/100             39.96   Dan Kha <dkha@yorku.ca>
Pentium/100             39.98   Phillipe Charon <charron@ecoledoc.ibp.fr>
Pentium/100             40.03   <bon@elektron.ikp.physik.th-darmstadt.de>
Pentium/100             40.08   Ronny Spiegel <rspiegel@htwm.de>
Pentium/100             40.18   David Baldwin <davidb@exis.net>
Pentium/100             40.18   <habibie@catevr.fiu.edu>
Pentium/120 Cyrix       47.8    Simon Ho <simon@epsilon.win-uk.net>
Pentium/120             47.82   Jorge Juan-Chico <jjchico@imse.cnm.es>
Pentium/120 Cyrix       47.92   Joel N. Squire <squire@colorado.edu>
Pentium/120             47.93   Umberto d'Ortona <umberto@grenet.fr>
Pentium/120 Cyrix       47.93   Jim T. Polk <jtpolk@cris.com>
Pentium/120             47.93   Jon Trowbridge <trow@mcs.com>
Pentium/120             47.98   Craig Bates <cbates@psu.edu>
Pentium/120 Cyrix       48      Steve <horne@mhd2.pfc.mit.edu>
Pentium/120             48.00   Michael Wazenski <mwazenski@dsrnet.com>
Pentium/120 Intel       48.02   Scott M. Grim <sgrim@netwalk.com>
Pentium/120 Cyrix       48.27   Glenn T. Jayaputera <gjt@budgie.apana.org.au>
Pentium/120             48.27   Roman Mitnitski <mitnits@shany.net>
Pentium/120             48.27   Peter Walsh <pwalsh@rain.org>
Pentium/120 Cyrix       48.2    Viznyuk <sviznyuk@magnus.acs.ohio-state.edu>
Pentium/120             49.27   Simon Hargrave <simon@revell.demon.co.uk>
Pentium/133             53.04   Wayne Roberts <wroberts@aug.com>
Pentium/133             53.04   Gregory Travis <greg@indiana.edu>
Pentium/133 overcl      53.04   A. Kunigelis <algikun@santaka.sc-uni.ktu.lt>
Pentium/133 Intel       53.04   Jimmie Farmer <calvin@malchick.com>
Pentium/133             53.25   Chuck Mattern <cmattern@mindspring.com>
Pentium/133             53.26   Glenn Holt <gholt@lsil.com>
Pentium/133             53.26   Heikki Levanto <heikki@lsd.ping.dk>
Pentium/133             53.26   Chaim Tarshish <chaim@ipl.med.nyu.edu>
Pentium/133             53.26   Mitchell B. Hamm <hamm@one.net>
Pentium/133             53.26   Donald Lewis <dlewis@jackson.freenet.org>
Pentium/133             53.26   Jon Trowbridge <trow@kremlin.emccta.com>
Pentium/133             53.26   Charny Peete Mitchell <cpmiche@eos.ncsu.edu>
Pentium/133 256c        53.26   David Wuertele <dave@gctech.com>
Pentium/133 256c        53.68   Guiseppe Miceli <ferdy@ccii.unipi.it>
Pentium/133             53.68   Michael Kress <kress@hal.saar.de>
Pentium/150 Intel       59.80   Joel D. Young <jdyoung@afit.af.mil>
Pentium/150             60.01   Joost de Greef <joost@stack.nl>
Pentium/150 overcl      60.21   Duarte Cordeiro <l38404@alfa.ist.utl.pt>
Pentium/166             66.16   Pedro Soria-Rodriguez <sorrodp@wpi.edu>
Pentium/166             66.35   K. Visweswaran <kvisweswa@lehman.com>
Pentium/166             66.36   T. Endo <enchan@trc.rwcp.or.jp>
Pentium/166             66.44   Donald Lewis <dlewis@jackson.freenet.org>
Pentium/166             66.76   F. Baitinger <baiti@herrenberg.netsurf.de>
Pentium/166             67.10   Jon Trowbridge <trow@mcs.com>
Pentium/166             67.10   Dylan <dylan@ert.com>
```

```
Pentium/166 512c        67.10   Dirk Freese <freese@infra.de>
Pentium/200             79.66   Piete Brooks <Piete.Brooks@cl.cam.ac.uk>
Pentium/200             79.69   Timm Gleason <timm@bess.net>
Pentium/200             79.89   Dave S. Baker <dave@acedia.demon.co.uk>
Pentium/200             78.87   Nick D'Apice <ndapice@erols.com>
Pentium/200             81.92   Steve Baur <steve@xemacs.org>
```

9.8 Normal Pentium variations: MMX, Pro, II, Cyrix, AMD

```
System                  BogoMips   Reporter

Pentium MMX/133         265.77   Ron Peters <rpeters@f15fast.al.intel.com>
Pentium MMX/150         307.53   Sami Sihvonen <buggy@fix.no>
Pentium MMX/166 notebk  331.75   n.n. <visionary@aura.title14.com>
Pentium MMX/166         331.78   Rob Janssen <pe1chl@amsat.org>
Pentium MMX/166         331.78   Dave Page <dave@vale-housing.co.uk>
Pentium MMX/166         331.78   Matthew C. Sell <amtmcs@amsta.leeds.ac.uk>
Pentium MMX/166         333.41   Sjoelie <patrick@sjoel.xs4all.nl>
Pentium MMX/180         358.81   David Efflandt <efflandt@xnet.com>
Pentium MMX/200         398.13   Andy Saunders <andi@numenor.oucs.ox.ac.uk>
Pentium MMX/200         398.13   A. James Lewis <james@vrtx.net>
Pentium MMX/200         398.95   Reinhold J. Gerharz <rgerharx@erols.com>
Pentium MMX/200         398.95   Eric Beymer <beymer@soundex.com>
Pentium MMX/200         398.95   Duane Steel <dsteele@direct.ca>
Pentium MMX/200         400      Rob Jokinen <rjokinen@rt66.com>
Pentium MMX/200         400.59   Paul Black <paul@darwin.demon.co.uk>
Pentium MMX/200         400.59   Bart <bart@aceonline.com.au>
Pentium MMX/210 overcl  416.97   John Saunders <john@nlc.net.au>
Pentium MMX/225 overcl  448.92   Ingo Reimann <reimann@uni-muenster.de>
Pentium MMX/250 overcl  498.07   Maarten van Rossum <m@vr.xs4all.nl>

Pentium Pro/133         132.88   John D. Sundberg <jdsundberg@mmm.com>
Pentium Pro/150         149.50   Rogier Wolff <wolff@bitwizard.nl>
Pentium Pro/180         179.61   Chuck Fee <fee@ch4549.org>
Pentium Pro/200         197.42   Michael Griffith <grif@cs.ucr.edu>
Pentium Pro/200         197.42   Curtis Varner <carner@cs.ucr.edu>
Pentium Pro/200         198.84   Erik Max Francis <max@alcyone.com>
Pentium Pro/200         198.84   Marc Winkler <marcus@healthchex.com>
Pentium Pro/200         199.04   V. Bostrom <Vareck_Bostrom@ccm.jf.intel.com>
Pentium Pro/200         199.06   Justin Clancy <justin@hippos.demon.co.uk>
Pentium Pro/200         199.06   Glenn Lamb <mumford@netcom15.netcom.com>
Pentium Pro/200         199.06   Laszlo Herczeg <las@light-house.com>
Pentium Pro/200         199.07   Stefan <boresch@schuber.u-strasbg.fr>
Pentium Pro/200         199.07   Greg Fausak <lgfausak@august.com>
Pentium Pro/200         199.07   Chris Jones <chris@planetsymphone.com>
Pentium Pro/200         199.07   Matthew S. Crocker <matthew@crocker.com>
Pentium Pro/200         199.95   Reinhold J. Gerharz <rgerharx@erols.com>
Pentium Pro/200         200.32   Gil Megidish <gmegidis@ort.org.il>
Pentium Pro/200         200.32   Jose Navarro <jnavarro@aoc.nrao.edu>
Pentium Pro/200         200.32   <Eric_Zucker@om.hp.com>
Pentium Pro/200         200.32   Wayne Scott <wscott@ichips.intel.com>
Pentium Pro/200         200.32   Adrian L. Hosey <ahosey@cs.indiana.edu>
```

```
Pentium Pro/233 overcl    234.43   S. Curtarolo <auro@spiro.fisica.unipd.it>

Pentium II/266            265.42   Jon Trowbridge <trow@kremlin.emccta.com>
Pentium II/266            265.44   Nick Ullman <nick@avenza.com>
Pentium II/266            267.06   James McKinnon <jmack@phys.ualberta.ca>
Pentium II/300 overcl     299.01   Martin Lathoud <nytral@endirect.qc.ca>

5x86/100 Cyrix            100.16   NN <root@anxa04.cc.ic.ac.uk>
5x86/100                  100.19   Valient Gough <vgough@teton.mines.edu>
5x86/100 Cyrix            100.47   C.Chan <chan@alfrothul.uchicago.edu>
5x86/120 Cyrix P150+      119.60   Wynstan Tong <wynstan@eecg.toronto.ca>
5x86/120 Cyrix P150+      119.60   Joel N. Squire <squire@colorado.edu>
5x86/120 Cyrix P150+      119.83   Leland Olds <olds@eskimo.com>
5x86/120 Cyrix P150+      119.83   NN <root@anxa04.cc.ic.ac.uk>
5x86/120 Cyrix P150+      120.68   C.Chan <chan@alfrothul.uchicago.edu>
5x86/120 Cyrix P150+      122.01   Andre Coetzee <acoetzee@ctcc.gov.za>

6x86/100 Cyrix             99.42   Stig M. Valstad <svalstad@sn.no>
6x86/110 Cyrix P133+      109.77   Matthew Flint <matthew@philtrum.demon.co.uk>
6x86/110 Cyrix P133+      109.77   John Merriam <suprnaut@esslink.com>
6x86/110 Cyrix P133+      109.77   Keith Smith <keith@ksmith.com>
6x86/120 Cyrix P150+      119      Jean-Claude Gouiran <jcg13@ibm.net>
6x86/120 Cyrix P150+      119.60   Taso Lyristis <taso@remus.rutgers.edu>
6x86/120 Cyrix P150+      119.60   Hrvoje Stipetic <stipe@zemris.fer.hr>
6x86/120 Cyrix           119.60   Yakko J. Warner <yakko@wtower.com>
6x86/120 Cyrix P150+      119.60   B. James Philippe <bryan@terran.org>
6x86/120 Cyrix P150+      119.83   Roger Merchberger <zmerch@northernway.net>
6x86/120 Cyrix           119.83   Daniel Wold <danw@panix.com>
6x86/120 Cyrix           120      John C. Beasley <beaslej1@nevada.edu>
6x86/120 Cyrix P150+      120.01   Jay Thorne <jay@result.com>
6x86/120 Cyrix P150+      120.01   Jeawan Kim <jaewan@harc.edu>
6x86/120 Cyrix P150+      120.91   Cymen <cymen@ziplink.net>
6x86/133 Cyrix P166+      132.71   Holger Kemper <hok@balu.ping.de>
6x86/133 Cyrix P166+      132.71   Hrvoje Stipetic <stipe@zemris.fer.hr>
6x86/133 Cyrix P166+      132.82   Alex Liffers <aliffers@tartarus.uwa.edu.au>
6x86/133 Cyrix P166+      132.82   Brian C. Theobald <theobald@nortel.ca>
6x86/133 Cyrix P166+      132.88   Alvaro Lopes <alvieboy@utad.pt>
6x86/133 Cyrix P166+      132.88   Craig Andersen <andersen@fastlane.net>
6x86/133 Cyrix P166+      133.73   C. Drews <drews_c@informatik.fh-hamburg.de>
6x86/133 Cyrix P166+      133.12   Daniel Gritter <dgritt47@calvin.edu>
6x86/150 Cyrix P200+      149.50   Evan L. Schemm <elschemm@mtu.edu>
6x86/150 Cyrix P200+      149.50   Steven Rainwater <srainwater@ncc.com>
6x86/150 Cyrix P200+      149.91   Sid Boyce <szb50@amdahl.com>
6x86MX/166 Cyrix A-Step   166.71   David Anderson <rovaughn@infoave.net>

K5/75 AMD                 149.91   Simon Karpen <slk@linux-shell.net>
K5/90 AMD                 179.40   <root@krabi.mbp.ee>
K5/90 AMD                 179.40   Ken Edwards <edwards@thor.xon.cuug.ab.ca>
K5/90 AMD                 180.22   Hector DC Gonzalez <turbo@linux.lsl.com.mx>
K5/90 AMD                 181.00   Drew Golden <golden@platinum.nb.net>
K5/100 AMD PR133          198.66   Trond Solem <trond.solem@homemail.com>
K5/100 AMD PR133          199.07   Henri Jamgotchian <hjamgot@planete.net>
K5/100 AMD PR133          199.48   Dark Mind <root@dmh.ml.org>
K5/100 AMD PR133          199.88   J. Grassel <grassel@heart.cas.und.nodak.edu>
```

```
K5/100 AMD PR133          199.88  Berend Reitsma <berend@united-info.com>
K5/100 AMD PR133          200.29  Tilman Sommer <sommer@vsun02.ag01.kodak.com>
K5/100 AMD PR133          200.32  Carlo Politi <cpoliti@mare.gol.grosseto.it>
K5/100 AMD PR133          199.07  Franco De Angelis <fda@ied.unipr.it>
K5/100 AMD PR133          199.07  HaJo Simons <hajo@frodo.com>
K5/116 AMD PR166          233.47  Hans-Joachim Baader <hans@grumber.ika.de>
K5/120 AMD PR133 overcl   239.21  Chris Harshman <harshman@paradigm.uor.edu>

K6/166                    332.60  David Parsons <orc@pell.chi.il.us>
K6/166                    331     Bill Petersen <brp@cuberramp.net>
K6/200                    398.85  n.n. <uh886@freenet.victoria.bc.ca>
K6/200                    398.89  Ian Hanschen <hanschen@uwyo.edu>
K6/200                    399.77  Murtaza Amiji <murti@wpi.edu>
K6/200                    399.78  Dan Hetzel <dan@icor.fr>
K6/200                    400.58  Paco Culebras Amigo <paco@hades.udg.es>
K6/200                    400.59  Sverre H. Huseby <s.h.huseby@usit.uio.no>
K6/200                    400.59  Steve Conley <sconley@muck.leonine.com>
K6/200                    400.59  Mark Lehrer <edge@dux.raex.com>
K6/200                    400.59  Chris Esser <ksqueak@erols.com>
K6/200                    400.59  Federico Pellegrin <fede@triangolo.it>
K6/200                    400.59  Howard Poe <falcor@kingsnet.com>
K6/208 overcl             416.15  Jani Halme <jaadha@utu.fi>
K6/208 overcl             416.15  Donnie Savage <dsavage@cris.com>
K6/208                    417.97  J.F. Ursetto <ursetto@uiuc.edu>
K6/225                    440     n.n. <uh886@freenet.victoria.bc.ca>
K6/225 overcl             448.92  Paco Culebras Amigo <paco@hades.udg.es>
K6/225 overcl             450.56  M. Cramer <mccramer@stuttgart.netscape.de>
K6/233                    466.5   R. Garcia <rgarciaitt@aol.com>
K6/233 overcl             466.84  Francesco <root@fly.cnuce.cnr.it>
K6/233 overcl             466.94  Paco Culebras Amigo <paco@hades.udg.es>
K6/233                    466.94  Howard Poe <hpoe@nyx.net>
K6/233                    466.94  Andreas Haumer <andreas@xss.co.at>
K6/233                    466.94  Damien Castelltort <eznerald@mail.mnet.fr>
K6/233                    466.94  G. Cantallops Ramis <gcantallopsr@jet.se>
```

9.9   Normal Alpha systems

```
System                BogoMips  Reporter
21064/150 Jensen       148.37   Linus Torvalds <torvalds@cc.helsinki.fi>
21064/150 Jensen       149.49   J.L. Brothers <brothers@halcyon.com>
21064/150 Jensen       148.89   Martin Osterman <ost@comnets.rwth-aachen.de>

21064A/275 Cabriolet   271.58   <michal@ellpspace.math.ualberta.ca>
21064A/275 Cabriolet   272      Linus Torvalds <torvalds@cc.helsinki.fi>
21064A/275             272      Stephen Gaudet <sjg@tiac.net>
21064A/275 Cabriolet   272.63   Jay Estabrook <jestabro@amt.tay1.dec.com>
21064A/275 Cabriolet   273.37   David Mosberger-Tang <davidm@cs.arizona.edu>
21064A/275             274.11   Kevin Jacobs <jacobs@eek.cwru.edu>
21064A/300 Cabriolet   298      Jay Estabrook <jestabro@amt.tay1.dec.com>
21064A/300             298      Stephen Gaudet <sjg@tiac.net>

21066/166              162.53   Phil Bostley <pbostley@qualcomm.com>
```

```
21066/166                    163.05   Matthew Jacob <mjacob@feral.com>
21066/166                    164.59   David Mosberger-Tang <davidm@cs.arizona.edu>
21066/166 Multia             164.63   Rudolf Gabler <rug@usm.uni-muenchen.de>
21066/166                    165      Gareth Bult <gareth@ftech.net>
21066/166                    165.04   Craig Ruff <cruff@ncar.ucar.edu>
21066/200                    196.9    Danny ter Haar <danny@cistron.nl>
21066/200 UDB overcl         198      Kari Davidsson <d154402@cs.tut.fi>

21066A/233 UDB               229.63   Toon van der Pas <toon@vdpas.hobby.nl>
21066A/233 AS400             230.16   Ophir Ronen <ophir@connectsoft.com>
21066A/233 NoName            230.67   T. Bogendoerfer <tsbogend@bigbug.franken.de>
21066A/233 UDB               230.68   Ted Schipper <ted@tedux.hobby.nl>
21066A/233 NoName            230.76   Mikael Nykvist <viper@ludd.luth.se>
21066A/233 UDB               231.21   Eric Smith <eric@goonsquad.spies.com>
21066A/233 NoName            231.21   Jay Estabrook <jestabro@amt.tay1.dec.com>
21066A/266 NoName ov.cl      261.62   Andreas Johansson <ajo@ludd.luth.se>
21066A/266 UDB overcl        261.62   Michael Brennen <mbrennen@fni.net>
21066A/266 NoName ov.cl      262.14   Wim van Dorst <baron@clifton.hobby.nl>
21066A/266 Multia            264      Joshua Grubman <joshg@dn.net>
21066A/284 NoName ov.cl      281.0    <imakino@gloria.cord.edu>
21066A/297 NoName ov.cl      293.6    <imakino@gloria.cord.edu>
21066A/300 UDB ov.cl         294.65   Topi Kanerva <tkanerva@nks.oulu.fi>

21164/266 EB164              265.29   Jay Estabrook <jestabro@amt.tay1.dec.com>
21164/300 EB164              297.79   Hilarius <maurice@ellpspace.math.ualberta.ca>
21164/300 XLT Alcor          297.79   Dave Wreski <dave@nic.com>
21164/300 AS1000             297.79   Salvador Pinto Abreu <spa@sc.uevora.pt>
21164/333 Alcor              331.35   Linus Torvalds <torvalds@cs.helsinki.fi>
21164/333 Alcor              331.35   David Mosberger-Tang <davidm@azstarnet.com>
21164/366 PC164 Durango      363.85   Geerten Kuiper <geerten@bart.nl>
21164/433 PC164              429.89   Paul D. Robertson <proberts@clark.net>
21164/433 PC164              429.91   Bernd Meyer <bmeyer@cs.monash.edu.au>
21164/433 Maita              429.91   Bill Broadley <bill@math.ucdavis.edu>
21164/433 PC164              430.96   <rainer.landes@physik.uni-karlsruhe.de>
21164/433 EB164              430.96   <Metod.Kozelj@rzs-hm.si>
21164/433 PC164              430.96   H. Sumargo <habibie@robotic.eng.fiu.edu>
21164/433 PC164              431.94   Timm Gleason <timm@bess.com>
21164/466 PC164              464.51   Daryll Strauss <daryll@d2.com>
21164/500                    497      Alex Butcher <alex@asimov.annex.co.uk>
21164/500 PC164              497.02   C.J. Grayce <cgrayce@wasatch.ps.uci.edu>
21164/500                    497.05   Heiner Kruener <hk@martian.ping.de>
21164/500 AS500              497.03   Jim Nance <jlnance@avanticorp.com>
21164/500 P7                 497.03   Jan guldentops <jacko@ba.be>
21164/500 EB164 Durango      497.43   Kevin Jacobs <jacobs@eek.cwru.edu>

21164A/500 PWS               497.02   Robert Harley <robert.harley@inria.fr>
21164A/500 PC164             497.02   Stephen Oberski <sfo@deterministic.com>
21164A/533 PC164LX           529.53   Harvey J. Stein <hjstein@bfr.co.il>
21164A/533 PC164LX           530.57   Ronny Ranerup <ronny@axis.com>
21164A/600 PC164LX           595.59   L.F. Donaldson <donaldlf@cs.rose-hulman.edu>

21264/400 Pass-1             794.82   Jay Estabrook <jay.estabrook@digital.com>
```

9.10 Normal Motorola systems

System	BogoMips	Reporter
68030/16 Atari Falcon	3.90	Jay T. Millar <jmillar@eaglequest.com>
68030/16 Atari Falcon	3.95	J.L. Brothers <brothers@halcyon.com>
68030/16 Atari Falcon	3.98	<Roman.Hodek@informatik.uni-erlangen.de>
68030/20 0c	4.92	Chris Nadigh <chrnadig@iiic.ethz.ch>
68030 Amiga 3000	6.08	Andy Wick <awick@vt.edu>
68030/30 Amiga 4000	6.09	Karsten Merker <km@golf.dinet.com>
68030/25 Amiga 3000	6.12	Glen Hewlett <hewlett@planeteer.com>
68030/25 Amiga 3000	6.21	Hamish Macdonald <hamish@bnr.ca>
68030/25 Amiga 3000	6.21	J.L. Brothers <brothers@halcyon.com>
68030/32 Atari Falcon	7.91	Franz Korntner <fkorntne@bazis.nl>
68030 Atari TT	7.96	<schwab@issan.informatik.uni-dortmund.de>
68030/32 Atari MegaST	7.98	E.J. van den Bussche <busscheh@ksepl.nl>
68030/33 Atari TT	7.98	<Roman.Hodek@informatik.uni-erlangen.de>
68030 Atari TT	7.98	Wayne Booth <trek@ihgp114r.ih.att.com>
68030/60	8.06	Korey Budgen <kbudgen@st.nepean.uws.edu.au>
68030/33 Amiga 2000	8.14	W. Haidinger <e9225662@stud1.tuwien.ac.at>
68030/48 32c	11.89	Martin Rogge <Martin_Rogge@ki.maus.de>
68030/50 Atari	12	<Roman.Hodek@informatik.uni-erlangen.de>
68030/50 Amiga 1200	12.36	Chris Sumner <chris@ganymede.sonnet.co.uk>
68030/50 Amiga 1200	12.4	Richard Jerome <etlrdje@tigger.ericsson.se>
68030/50 32c	12.42	Michael Plonus <michi@pluto.ping.de>
68030/50 Amiga 1200	12.33	Detrix <detrix@popd.ix.netcom.com>
68040/24 Amiga 4000-40	16.6	Hamish Macdonald <hamish@bnr.ca>
68040/24 Amiga 4000-20	16.60	J.L. Brothers <brothers@halcyon.com>
68040/25 Amiga 4000-040	16.61	<Geert.Uytterhoeven@cs.ku-leuven.ac.be>
68040/25 Amiga 4000	16.61	Lawrence <lawrenc@nextwork.rose-hulmand.edu>
68040/60 Amiga 4000-40	18.99	Darren Enns <dmenns@surf.pangea.ca>
68040/32 Medusa T40	21.25	<Hartmut.Koptein@et-inf.fho-emden.de>
68040 Amiga 2000	21.86	Ron Flory <rjflory@feist.com>
68060/50 Amiga 1200	99.53	baba <baba@pa.yokogawa.jp>
68060/50 Amiga 4000	99.74	Stefan Tauche <otauche@uni-paderborn.de>
68060/50 Amiga 4000	100.16	Jan Johansson <jj@mordor.it.kth.se>

9.11 Other Systems: Sparc, PowerPC, Mips, Intel 8088/286 ELKS

System	BogoMips	Reporter
Sparc Sun4c	17.94	J.L. Brothers <brothers@halcyon.com>
Sparc SLC/20 S1	19.86	Simon Karpen <slk@linux-shell.net>
Sparc IPX 4c	39.83	Paul D. Robertson <proberts@clark.net>
Sparc SS10 super50 4m	39.93	Juan Cespedes <cespedes@etsit.upm.es>
Sparc microS/50 SS-LX	49.76	Will Shaw <romulan@netwatch.clemson.edu>
Sparc SS20	49.86	Gary A. Donahue <lordgad@webspan.net>
Sparc hyperS Classic 4m	49.86	Juan Cespedes <cespedes@etsit.upm.es>
Sparc Voyager portable	59.80	Edward Austin <eastin@shl.com>
Sparc SS5 Netra	68	Craig Falconer <cf@papanui.school.nz>
Sparc SS50	74.95	Kaz <kaz@latte.cafe.net>
Sparc SS10 hyperS	99.73	Thomas B. Fox <tfox@oliverdesign.com>

```
Sparc SS5/66              109.77   Lance S. Nehring <lnehrin@uswest.com>
Sparc hSparc/150 Sun4m    150.32   Tethys <tethys@ml.com>
Sparc Ultra1 sun4u        284.05   Iban Cardona <icc@seric.es>

PowerPC 601/60 Mac6100     45.24   J.L. Brothers <brothers@halcyon.com>
PowerPC 601/66 Mac         51.62   Fred Klein <klein@des3.u-strasbg.fr>
PowerPC 601/60 Mac6100     59.38   Kent Radek <goo@itd.sterling.com>
PowerPC 601/75 Mac7200     73.93   Dimitris Tsifakis <jimmy@typhoeus.dg.uoa.gr>
PowerPC 601/100 Mac7500    98.91   Russ Hoffman <reh@fore.com>
PowerPC 601/110 Mac8100   108      Charles Eicher <ceicher@inav.net>

PowerPC 603/100            66.56   A. Costa <c_chaos@chaosnet.wahnapitae.on.ca>

PowerPC 604/100 PPS6050    99.74   Evaldas Darcianovas <evaldas@isi.kvm.lt>
PowerPC 604/100           199      Hamish Marson <hamish@aixrules.nz.ibm.com>
PowerPC 604/100 PPS7248   199.48   Evaldas Darcianovas <evaldas@isi.kvm.lt>
PowerPC 604/133 MOT PS    266.24   Christoper Harrel <cnh@eng.mindspring.net>
PowerPC 604/150 Mac9500   297.73   Jean-Philippe Lord <jpl@binex.com>
PowerPC 604/200 Mac8600   320      Julien Sebot <sebot@lri.fr>

Mips R4000/100             48.30   J.L. Brothers <brothers@halcyon.com>
Mips R4000/100 Magnum      50.03   Andreas Busse <andy@soft-n-hard.de>
Mips R4400/134 Acer Pica   67.10   Andreas Busse <andy@soft-n-hard.de>
Mips R4400/134 Acer Pica   67.10   Ralf Baechle <ralf@waldorf-gmbh.de>
Mips R4600/133 Tyne       133.12   Ralf Baechle <ralf@waldorf-gmbh.de>
Mips R4600/133 RM200      133.08   Ralf Baechle <ralf@julia.de>
Mips R5000/150 Indy       154.83   Ralf Baechle <ralf@julie.de>

Intel 8088/4.77            0.02    Tim Van der Linden <timvdl@innet.be>
Intel 8088/10              0.05    Tim Van der Linden <timvdl@innet.be>
Intel 8086                 0.5     Kin Lau <gabe@zot.io.org>
Intel 286 Tandy            0.75    Joey Hess <joey@kite.ml.org>
Intel 286/8 VAXMate        1.03    Andrew Costa <c_chaos@wahnapitae.on.ca>
Intel 286/10 Commodore     1.30    Hans-Joachim Baader <hans@grumber.inka.de>
Intel 286 PS2              2.32    Morillas C.H. Antonio <morilla@fie.us.es>
Intel 286 PS2              2.34    Joey Hess <joey@kite.ml.org>
```

9.12 Normal Multi CPU systems

```
System                BogoMips   Reporter
SMP2 Pentium/75         59.50    Michael Engel <engel@unix-ag.uni-siegen.de>
SMP2 Pentium/90         71.68    Edwin Whitelaw <elw@ivc.com>
SMP2 Pentium/90         71.98    Daniel Luhde-Thompson <dl10010@cam.ac.uk>
SMP2 Pentium/90         72.08    Alan Cox <alan@cymru.net>
SMP2 Pentium/100        79.46    Lam Dang <dangit@ix.netcom.com>
SMP2 Pentium/100        80.08    Christian Tan <pigeon@xs4all.nl>
SMP2 Pentium/100        80.08    McNalley <jmcnalle@attila.stevens-tech.edu>
SMP2 Pentium/166       133.53    <Reinhard.Simkovics@jk.uni-linz.ac.at>

SMP2 Pentium MMX/200   794.62    Kristian Koehntopp <kris@koehntopp.de>
SMP2 Pentium MMX/200   796.26    Eric Clark <eclark@opencominc.com>
SMP2 Pentium MMX/233   927.33    Jeff White <jwhite@ghq.com>
```

```
SMP2 Pentium Pro/150    299.00   Steven Gallo <smgallo@numenor.csgeeks.org>
SMP2 Pentium Pro/150    299.01   Eric van Dijken <E.vanDijken@PTT-Telecom.nl>
SMP2 Pentium Pro/166    331.78   Eric van Dijken <E.vanDijken@PTT-Telecom.nl>
SMP2 Pentium Pro/180    358.81   Eric van Dijken <E.vanDijken@PTT-Telecom.nl>
SMP2 Pentium Pro/180    358.81   Frankie East <fae2401@rit.edu>
SMP2 Pentium Pro/180    358.81   James K. Wiggs <wiggs@wolfenet.com>
SMP2 Pentium Pro/200    396.25   Will Shaw <shaww@dialup.dstm.com>
SMP2 Pentium Pro/200    398.13   David Konerding <dek@cgl.ucsf.edu>
SMP2 Pentium Pro/200    398.13   B. Heinen <benedikt.heinen@infrasys.ascom.ch>
SMP2 Pentium Pro/200    398.14   C.-A. Possamai <camille@sugiton.cnrs-mrs.fr>
SMP2 Pentium Pro/200    398.14   Leland <llucius@millcom.com>
SMP2 Pentium Pro/200    398.14   John Lellis <lellis@dmccorp.com>
SMP2 Pentium Pro/200    398.14   Jim Gifford <jim@mail.rath.peachnet.edu>
SMP2 Pentium Pro/200    398.6    Bill Davidsen <davidsen@tmr.com>
SMP2 Pentium Pro/200    398.95   Fons Rademakers <f.rademakers@cern.ch>
SMP2 Pentium Pro/200    398.98   Greg Fausak <glfausak@august.com>
SMP2 Pentium Pro/200    400.18   Attila Karpati <karpati@cs.elte.hu>
SMP4 Pentium Pro/133    532.07   Erik Walthinsen <omega@sequent.com>
SMP4 Pentium Pro/200    794.62   Kenneth Hedlund <c415khd@nll.se>
SMP4 Pentium Pro/200    796.28   John Pelan <j.pelan@am.qub.ac.uk>

SMP2 Pentium II/233     466.94   Eli Kane <eli@crl.nmsu.edu>
SMP2 Pentium II/266     530.84   Shon Martin <cshoon@oberlin.edu>
SMP2 Pentium II/266     534.12   n.n. <service@cprompt.sk.ca>
SMP2 Pentium II/266     534.12   Emmanuel Tychon <manu@acm.org>
```

9.13   Non-Linux systems (reference only)

System	OS	BogoMips	Reporter
68000/8 Macintosh Classic	MacOS	0.53	<jimmy@typhoeus.dg.uoa.gr>
68020/20 Sun 3	SUNOS	2.0	<korpela@ssl.berkeley.edu>
68020/16 Macintosh LC	MacOS	3.09	<jimmy@typhoeus.dg.uoa.gr>
68020/25 Sun 3-180	SUNOS	4.0	<korpela@ssl.berkeley.edu>
Sparc Sun 3-60	SUNOS	4.00	<tranter@software.mitel.com>
Sparc Sun 3-80	SUNOS	4.00	<tranter@software.mitel.com>
68030/25 Macintosh IIci	NetBSD	5.62	<kirk-corey@uiowa.edu>
68040/25 Macintosh LC475	MacOS	12.27	<jimmy@typhoeus.dg.uoa.gr>
68040/33 HP9000-280	HP-UX	14	<niles@axp745.gsfc.nasa.gov>
68040/25 Apollo 5500	DomainOS	14.00	<kirk-corey@uiowa.edu>
Sparc Sun 4-280	SUNOS	16.0	<korpela@ssl.berkeley.edu>
Sparc Sun IPC/40	Solaris	16.00	<gong@cs.msu.su>
68040/25 HP9000-425	DomainOS	16.00	<kirk-corey@uiowa.edu>
68040 NextStep	(?)	16.26	<petergun@coffeehaus.com>
Sparc Sun SS1	SUNOS	18.00	<tranter@software.mitel.com>
Sparc Sun SS1	SUNOS	18.00	<jimmy@typhoeus.dg.uoa.gr>
Sparc Sun SS1+	SUNOS	19	<swmike@uplift.df.lth.se>
Sparc Sun SS1+	SUNOS	24.00	<tranter@software.mitel.com>
Sparc Sun IPC	SUNOS	24.00	<tranter@software.mitel.com>
Sparc Sun Sparcstation2	SUNOS	26.00	<gong@cs.msu.su>
SparcClassic/50	Solaris	32.00	<gong@cs.msu.su>

Sparc Sun ELC	SUNOS	32.00	<tranter@software.mitel.com>
HP-PA 9000-720	HP-UX	32.00	<metod.kozelj@rzs-hm.si>
Sparc Sun SS10	SUNOS	34.00	<tranter@software.mitel.com>
Sparc Sun SS10	SUNOS	34.00	<makler@man.torun.pl>
Pentium/100	Win-NT	36.21	<marcus@healthchex.com>
Sparc Sun Sparcstation2	SUNOS	38.0	<korpela@ssl.berkeley.edu>
Mips R4000/100 Indy	(?)	48.00	<p.verwer@organon.akzonobel.nl>
Mips R4000/100 SGI IndySC	Irix	48.00	<lziegler@csbsju.edu>
HP-PA 9000-720	HP-UX	48.00	<metod.kozelj@rzs-hm.si>
Sparc SS10	SUNOS	48.00	<makler@man.torun.pl>
Sparc Sun Sparcstation10d	SUNOS	54.0	<korpela@ssl.berkeley.edu>
Sparc SS1000 2CPU	SUNOS	58.00	<gong@cs.msu.su>
Sparc SS20	SUNOS	60.00	<makler@man.torun.pl>
Alpha 21064/133 Decstation	OSF1	64	<niles@axp745.gsfc.nasa.gov>
Alpha 21064/133 Dec3000	OSF1	66.00	<daniels@helplaxp1.harvard.edu>
Sparc Sun SS5	SUNOS	68.00	<tranter@software.mitel.com>
Sparc Sun SS20	SUNOS	72.00	<tranter@software.mitel.com>
Sparc Sun SS20/712	Solaris	74	<spohr@qmos>
Mips R4400/150 Challenge	(?)	74.00	<p.verwer@organon.akzonobel.nl>
Mips R4400/150 Indigo2Extr	(?)	74.00	<p.verwer@organon.akzonobel.nl>
HP-PA 9000-715	HP-UX	74.00	<metod.kozelj@rzs-hm.si>
Sparc SS5 sun4m	SUNOS	84.00	<chrisv@allegria.com>
Sparc SS1000E	SUNOS	84.00	<makler@man.torun.pl>
Alpha	OSF1	92.00	<petergun@coffeehaus.com>
Mips R4400/200 Indigo2Extr	(?)	98.00	<p.verwer@organon.akzonobel.nl>
HP-PA 9000-735/99	HP-UX	98.00	<lankhors@cs.rug.nl>
Sparc SS5	SUNOS	104.00	<makler@man.torun.pl>
Sparc Sun SS4/110	Solaris	108	<spohr@qmos>
Sparc Sun SS4	Solaris	108.00	<jimmy@typhoeus.dg.uoa.gr>
Sparc Sun SS5	SUNOS	110	<swmike@uplift.df.lth.se>
Alpha 21064A/233	OSF1	114	<niles@axp745.gsfc.nasa.gov>
HP-PA 700/125	HP-UX	122	<niles@axp745.gsfc.nasa.gov>
HP-PA 9000-735/125	HP-UX	122.00	<lankhors@cs.rug.nl>
Mips R4600/133 SGI Indy	Irix	132	<lziegler@csbsju.edu>
Alpha	OSF1	180.0	<mauger@ensinfo.univ-nantes.fr>
Alpha 21164/333 AS500	OSF1	222.00	<daniels@helplaxp1.harvard.edu>
Sparc Ultra-1 sun4u	Solaris	254.00	<alternat@rwth-aachen.de>
PPC604/133 IBM RS6000	AIX	254.00	<kirk-corey@uiowa.edu>
Alpha 21164/433 DPW433au	OSF1	286.00	<daniels@helplaxp1.harvard.edu>
HP9000-C160/160	HP-UX	316.00	<nicolai@prz.tu-berlin.de>
Sparc Sun US1/170	Solaris	330	<spohr@qmos>
Sparc Sun US1/167	Solaris	330	<jimmy@typhoeus.dg.uoa.gr>
Sparc Ultra-1 sun4u	SUNOS	334.00	<chrisv@allegria.com>
Alpha 3000-600S	VMS	348.61	<metod.kozelj@rzs-hm.si>
Alpha server 1000-4/200	VMS	397.68	<metod.kozelj@rzs-hm.si>
Sparc US2/296 2cpu	SUNOS	596.00	<manu@acm.org>
Cray J90 Y-MP/100 16cpu	Unicos	912.00	<lankhors@cs.rug.nl>
Sequent Symmetry 6xP5/166	Dynix	984.00	<omega@sequent.com>
Sequent Symmetry 16xP5/66	Dynix	1056.00	<omega@sequent.com>
HP9000-C160/160	HP-UX	1278.00	<nicolai@prz.tu-berlin.de>
Sequent NUMA-Q 12x P6/180	Dynix	1416.00	<omega@sequent.com>
Sequent NUMA-Q 32x P6/180	Dynix	3776.00	<omega@sequent.com>

10   Signature

Roderick `<mailto:roderick@clifton.hobby.nl>` and *Isolde* `<mailto:isolde@clifton.hobby.nl>` are two very friendly children: Although Roderick's vocabulary is only three words (Op, Open, Papa), he insists on joining in with his sister in Sinterklaas-songs and Christmas carols.

Met vriendelijke groeten, Wim van Dorst.

```
-----------------------------------------------------------------
Blue Baron = Wim van Dorst, Voice (+31) 33 4676365, (+31) 35 5242319
(-:      baron@clifton.hobby.nl      WvD@Chem.AkzoNobel.nl       :-)
-----------------------------------------------------------------
```

From DOS/Windows to Linux HOWTO

By Guido Gonzato, *guido@ibogfs.cineca.it* <mailto:guido@ibogfs.cineca.it>   v1.2.2, 31 October 1997

This HOWTO is dedicated to all the (soon to be former?) DOS and Windows users who have just taken the plunge and decided to switch to Linux, the free UNIX clone. Given the similarities between DOS and UNIX, the purpose of this document is to help the reader translate his or her knowledge of DOS and Windows into the Linux environment, so as to be productive ASAP.

Contents

1 Introduction

1.1 Is Linux Right for You?

You want to switch from DOS/Windows to Linux? Good idea, but beware: it might not be useful for you. IMHO, there is no such thing as "the best computer" or "the best operating system": it depends on what one has to do. That's why I don't believe that Linux is the best solution for everyone, even if it's technically superior to many commercial OS's. You're going to benefit immensely from Linux if what you need is sw for programming, the Internet, TeX... technical sw in general, but if you mostly need commercial sw, or if you don't feel like learning and typing commands, look elsewhere.

Linux is not (for now) as easy to use and configure as Windows or the Mac, so be prepared to hack quite a bit. In spite of these warnings, let me tell you that I'm 100% confident that if you belong to the right user type you'll find in Linux your computer Nirvana. It's up to you. And remember that Linux + DOS/Windows can coexist on the same machine, anyway.

Prerequisites for this howto: I'll assume that

- you know the basic DOS commands and concepts;

- Linux, possibly with X Window System, is properly installed on your PC;

- your shell—the equivalent of COMMAND.COM—is bash;

- you understand that this guide is only an incomplete primer. For more information, please refer to Matt Welsh's "Linux Installation and Getting Started" and/or Larry Greenfield's "Linux User Guide" (*sunsite.unc.edu:/pub/Linux/docs/LDP* <ftp://sunsite.unc.edu:/pub/Linux/docs/LDP>).

This howto replaces the old "From DOS to Linux — Quick!" mini-howto. Also note that, unless specified, all information in this work is aimed at bad ol' DOS. There's a section about Windows, but bear in mind that Windows and Linux are totally different, unlike DOS which is sort of a UNIX poor relation.

1.2 It Is. Tell Me More

You installed Linux and the programs you needed on the PC. You gave yourself an account (if not, type `adduser` *now!*) and Linux is running. You've just entered your name and password, and now you are looking at the screen thinking: "Well, now what?"

Now, don't despair. You're almost ready to do the same things you used to do with DOS, and many more. If you were running DOS instead of Linux, you would be doing some of the following tasks:

- running programs and creating, copying, viewing, deleting, printing, renaming files;
- CD'ing, MD'ing, RD'ing, and DIR'ring your directories;
- formatting floppies and copying files from/to them;
- mending your `AUTOEXEC.BAT` and `CONFIG.SYS`;
- writing your own .BAT files and/or `QBasic` and/or C/Pascal programs;
- the remaining 1%.

You'll be glad to know that these tasks can be accomplished under Linux in a fashion similar to DOS. Under DOS, the average user uses very few of the 100+ commands available: the same, up to a point, holds for Linux.

A few things to point out before going on:

- first, how to get out. To quit Linux: if you see a text mode screen, press CTRL-ALT-DEL, wait for the system to fix its innards and tell you everything is OK, then switch off the PC. If you are working under X Window System, press CTRL-ALT-BACKSPACE first, then CTRL-ALT-DEL. *Never* switch off or reset the PC directly: this could damage the file system;
- unlike DOS, Linux has built-in security mechanisms, due to its multiuser nature. Files and directories have permissions associated to them, and therefore some cannot be accessed by the normal user; (see Section 2.3 (Permissions)). Only the user whose login name is "root" has the power. (This guy's the system administrator. If you work on your own PC, you'll be root as well.) DOS, on the contrary, will let you wipe out the entire contents of your hard disk;
- you are strongly encouraged to experiment, play, try by yourself: it surely won't hurt. If you need help, you can do the following:
  - to get some help about the "internal commands" of the shell, type `help`;
  - to get help on a command, type `man command` that invokes the manual ("man") page pertinent to `command`. Alternatively, type `info command` that invokes, if available, the info page pertinent to `command`. Info is a hypertext-based documentation system, perhaps not intuitive to use at first. Finally, you may try `apropos command` or `whatis command` pressing then 'q' to exit;
- most of the power and flexibility of UNIX comes from the simple concepts of redirection and piping, more powerful than under DOS. Simple commands can be strung together to accomplish complex tasks. Do use these features!
- conventions: <...> means something that must be specified, while [...] something optional. Example:

  ```
  $ tar -tf <file.tar> [> redir_file]
  ```

  `file.tar` must be indicated, but redirection to `redir_file` is optional.
- from now on "RMP" means "please read the man pages for further information".

1.3   For the Impatient

Want to strike out? Have a look at this:

```
         DOS                  Linux                  Notes
         ---------------------------------------------------------------------

         BACKUP               tar -Mcvf device dir/  completely different
         CD dirname\          cd dirname/            almost the same syntax
         COPY file1 file2     cp file1 file2         ditto
         DEL file             rm file                beware - no undelete
         DELTREE dirname      rm -R dirname/         ditto
         DIR                  ls                     not exactly the same syntax
         DIR file /S          find . -name file      completely different
         EDIT file            vi file                I think you won't like it
                              emacs file             this is better
                              jstar file             feels like dos' edit
         FORMAT               fdformat,
                              mount, umount          quite different syntax
         HELP command         man command           same philosophy
         MD dirname           mkdir dirname/         almost the same syntax
         MOVE file1 file2     mv file1 file2         ditto
         NUL                  /dev/null              ditto
         PRINT file           lpr file               ditto
         PRN                  /dev/lp0,
                              /dev/lp1               ditto
         RD dirname           rmdir dirname/         almost the same syntax
         REN file1 file2      mv file1 file2         not for multiple files
         RESTORE              tar -Mxpvf device      different syntax
         TYPE file            less file              much better
         WIN                  startx                 poles apart!
```

If you need more than a table of commands, please refer to the following sections.

2   Files and Programs

2.1   Files: Preliminary Notions

Linux has a file system—meaning by that "the structure of directories and files therein"—very similar to that of DOS. Files have filenames that obey special rules, are stored in directories, some are executable, and among these most have command switches. Moreover, you can use wildcard characters, redirection, and piping. There are only a few minor differences:

- under DOS, file names are in the so-called 8.3 form; e.g. NOTENOUG.TXT. Under Linux we can do better. If you installed Linux using a file system like ext2 or umsdos, you can use longer filenames (up to

255 characters), and with more than one dot in them: for example, `This_is.a.VERY_long.filename`. Please note that I used both upper and lower case characters: in fact...

- upper and lower case characters in file names or commands are different. Therefore, `FILENAME.tar.gz` and `filename.tar.gz` are two different files. `ls` is a command, `LS` is a mistake;

- Windows 95 users will want to use long file names under Linux, of course. If a file name contains spaces (not recommended but possible), you must enclose the file in double quotes whenever your refer to it. For example:

```
$ # the following command makes a directory called "My old files"
$ mkdir "My old files"
$ ls
My old files    bin    tmp
```

Some characters shouldn't but can be used: some are `!*$&`. I won't tell you how, though.

- there are no compulsory extensions like .COM and ..EXE for programs, or .BAT for batch files. Executable files are marked by an asterisk '`*`' at the end of their name when you issue the `ls -F` command. For example:

```
$ ls -F
I_am_a_dir/    cindy.jpg    cjpg*    letter_to_Joe    my_1st_script* old~
```

The files `cjpg*` and `my_1st_script*` are executable—"programs". Under DOS, backup files end in .BAK, while under Linux they end with a tilde '`~`'. Further, a file whose name starts with a dot is considered as hidden. Example: the file `.I.am.a.hidden.file` won't show up after the `ls` command;

- DOS program switches are obtained with /switch, Linux switches with `-switch` or `--switch`. Example: `dir /s` becomes `ls -R`. Note that many DOS programs, like `PKZIP` or `ARJ`, use UNIX-style switches.

You can now jump to Section 2.4 (Translating Commands from DOS to Linux), but if I were you I'd read on.

2.2 Symbolic Links

UNIX has a type of file that doesn't exist under DOS: the symbolic link. This can be thought of as a pointer to a file or to a directory, and can be used instead of the file or directory it points to; it's similar to Windows 95 shortcuts. Examples of symbolic links are `/usr/X11`, which points to `/usr/X11R6`; `/dev/modem`, which points to either `/dev/cua0` or `/dev/cua1`.

To make a symbolic link:

```
$ ln -s <file_or_dir> <linkname>
```

Example:

```
$ ln -s /usr/doc/g77/DOC g77manual.txt
```

Now you can refer to `g77manual.txt` instead of `/usr/doc/g77/DOC`. Links appear like this in directory listings:

```
$ ls -F
g77manual.txt@
$ ls -l
(various things...)          g77manual.txt -> /usr/doc/g77/DOC
```

2.3   Permissions and Ownership

DOS files and directories have the following attributes: A (archive), H (hidden), R (read-only), and S (system). Only H and R make sense under Linux: hidden files start with a dot, and for the R attribute, read on.

Under UNIX a file has "permissions" and an owner, who in turn belongs to a "group". Look at this example:

```
$ ls -l /bin/ls
-rwxr-xr-x  1  root  bin  27281 Aug 15 1995 /bin/ls*
```

The first field contains the permissions of the file **/bin/ls**, which belongs to root, group bin. Leaving the remaining information aside (Matt's book is there for that purpose), remember that **-rwxr-xr-x** means, from left to right:

- is the file type (- = ordinary file, d = directory, l = link, etc); **rwx** are the permissions for the file owner (read, write, execute); **r-x** are the permissions for the group of the file owner (read, execute); (I won't cover the concept of group, you can survive without it as long as you're a beginner ;-) **r-x** are the permissions for all other users (read, execute).

This is why you can't delete the file **/bin/ls** unless you are root: you don't have the write permission to do so. To change a file's permissions, the command is:

```
$ chmod <whoXperm> <file>
```

where who is u (user, that is owner), **g** (group), **o** (other), X is either + or -, perm is **r** (read), **w** (write), or **x** (execute). Examples:

```
$ chmod u+x file
```

this sets the execute permission for the file owner. Shortcut: **chmod +x file**.

```
$ chmod go-wx file
```

this removes write and execute permission for everyone but the owner.

```
$ chmod ugo+rwx file
```

this gives everyone read, write, and execute permission.

```
# chmod +s file
```

this makes a so-called "setuid" or "suid" file—a file that everyone can execute with its owner's privileges. Typically, you'll come across root suid files.

A shorter way to refer to permissions is with numbers: **rwxr-xr-x** can be expressed as 755 (every letter corresponds to a bit: **---** is 0, **--x** is 1, **-w-** is 2, **-wx** is 3...). It looks difficult, but with a bit of practice you'll understand the concept.

root, being the so-called superuser, can change everyone's file permissions. There's more to it—RMP.

2.4 Translating Commands from DOS to Linux

On the left, the DOS commands; on the right, their Linux counterpart.

```
COPY:        cp
DEL:         rm
MOVE:        mv
REN:         mv
TYPE:        more, less, cat
```

Redirection and plumbing operators: < > >> |

Wildcards: * ?

nul: /dev/null

prn, lpt1: /dev/lp0 or /dev/lp1; lpr

- EXAMPLES -

```
DOS                                Linux
--------------------------------------------------------------------

C:\GUIDO>COPY JOE.TXT JOE.DOC      $ cp joe.txt joe.doc
C:\GUIDO>COPY *.* TOTAL           $ cat * > total
C:\GUIDO>COPY FRACTALS.DOC PRN    $ lpr fractals.doc
C:\GUIDO>DEL TEMP                 $ rm temp
C:\GUIDO>DEL *.BAK                $ rm *~
C:\GUIDO>MOVE PAPER.TXT TMP\      $ mv paper.txt tmp/
C:\GUIDO>REN PAPER.TXT PAPER.ASC  $ mv paper.txt paper.asc
C:\GUIDO>PRINT LETTER.TXT         $ lpr letter.txt
C:\GUIDO>TYPE LETTER.TXT          $ more letter.txt
C:\GUIDO>TYPE LETTER.TXT          $ less letter.txt
C:\GUIDO>TYPE LETTER.TXT > NUL    $ cat letter.txt > /dev/null
         n/a                      $ more *.txt *.asc
         n/a                      $ cat section*.txt | less
```

Notes:

- * is smarter under Linux: * matches all files except the hidden ones; .* matches all hidden files; *.* matches only those that have a '.' in the middle, followed by other characters; p*r matches both 'peter' and 'piper'; *c* matches both 'picked' and 'peck';

- when using more, press SPACE to read through the file, 'q' or CTRL-C to exit. less is more intuitive and lets you use the arrow keys;

- there is no UNDELETE, so *think twice* before deleting anything;

- in addition to DOS < > >>, Linux has 2> to redirect error messages (stderr); moreover, 2>&1 redirects stderr to stdout, while 1>&2 redirects stdout to stderr;

- Linux has another wildcard: the []. Use: [abc]* matches files starting with a, b, c; *[I-N,1,2,3] matches files ending with I, J, K, L, M, N, 1, 2, 3;

- there is no DOS-like RENAME; that is, mv *.xxx *.yyy won't work. You could try this simple script; see Section 7.1 (Shell Scripts) for details.

```
#!/bin/sh
# ren: rename multiple files according to several rules

if [ $# -lt 3 ] ; then
  echo "usage: ren \"pattern\" \"replacement\" files..."
  exit 1
fi

OLD=$1 ; NEW=$2 ; shift ; shift

for file in $*
do
  new=`echo ${file} | sed s/${OLD}/${NEW}/g`
  mv ${file} $new
done
```

Beware: it doesn't behave like DOS REN, as it uses "regular expressions" that you still don't know. Shortly, if you simply want to change file extensions, use it as in: ren "htm$" "html" *htm. Don't forget the $ sign.

- use cp -i and mv -i to be warned when a file is going to be overwritten.

2.5   Running Programs: Multitasking and Sessions

To run a program, type its name as you would do under DOS. If the directory (Section 3 (Directories)) where the program is stored is included in the PATH (Section 6.1 (System Initialisation)), the program will start. Exception: unlike DOS, under Linux a program located in the current directory won't run unless the directory is included in the PATH. Escamotage: being prog your program, type ./prog.

This is what the typical command line looks like:

```
$ command -s1 -s2 ... -sn par1 par2 ... parn < input > output
```

where -s1, ..., -sn are the program switches, par1, ..., parn are the program parameters. You can issue several commands on the command line:

```
$ command1 ; command2 ; ... ; commandn
```

That's all about running programs, but it's easy to go a step beyond. One of the main reasons for using Linux is that it is a multitasking os—it can run several programs (from now on, processes) at the same time. You can launch processes in background and continue working straight away. Moreover, Linux lets you have several sessions: it's like having many computers to work on at once!

- To switch to session 1..6:

    ```
    $ ALT-F1 ... ALT-F6
    ```

- To start a new session without leaving the current one:

    ```
    $ su - <loginname>
    ```

Example:

```
$ su - root
```

This is useful, for one, when you need to mount a disk (Section 4 (Floppies)): normally, only root can do that.

- To end a session:

```
$ exit
```

If there are stopped jobs (see later), you'll be warned.

- To launch a process in foreground:

```
$ progname [-switches] [parameters] [< input] [> output]
```

- To launch a process in background, add an ampersand '&' at the end of the command line:

```
$ progname [-switches] [parameters] [< input] [> output] &
[1] 123
```

the shell identifies the process with a job number (e.g. [1]; see below), and with a PID (123 in our example).

- To see how many processes there are:

```
$ ps -a
```

This will output a list of currently running processes.

- To kill a process:

```
$ kill <PID>
```

You may need to kill a process when you don't know how to quit it the right way... ;-). Sometimes, a process will only be killed by either of the following:

```
$ kill -15 <PID>
$ kill -9 <PID>
```

In addition to this, the shell allows you to stop or temporarily suspend a process, send a process to background, and bring a process from background to foreground. In this context, processes are called "jobs".

- To see how many jobs there are:

```
$ jobs
```

here jobs are identified by their job number, not by their PID.

- To stop a process running in foreground (it won't always work):

```
$ CTRL-C
```

- To suspend a process running in foreground (ditto):

```
$ CTRL-Z
```

- To send a suspended process into background (it becomes a job):

```
$ bg <job>
```

- To bring a job to foreground:

```
$ fg <job>
```

- To kill a job:

```
$ kill <%job>
```

where <job> may be 1, 2, 3, ... Using these commands you can format a disk, zip a bunch of files, compile a program, and unzip an archive all at the same time, and still have the prompt at your disposal. Try this with DOS! And try with Windows, just to see the difference in performance.

2.6   Running Programs on Remote Computers

To run a program on a remote machine whose IP address is `remote.bigone.edu`, you do:

```
$ telnet remote.bigone.edu
```

After logging in, start your favourite program. Needless to say, you must have an account on the remote machine.

If you have X11, you can even run an X application on a remote computer, displaying it on your X screen. Let `remote.bigone.edu` be the remote X computer and `local.linux.box` be your Linux machine. To run from `local.linux.box` an X program that resides on `remote.bigone.edu`, do the following:

- fire up X11, start an **xterm** or equivalent terminal emulator, then type:

```
$ xhost +remote.bigone.edu
$ telnet remote.bigone.edu
```

- after logging in, type:

```
remote:$ DISPLAY=local.linux.box:0.0
remote:$ progname &
```

(instead of `DISPLAY...`, you may have to write `setenv DISPLAY local.linux.box:0.0`. It depends on the remote shell.)

Et voila! Now `progname` will start on `remote.bigone.edu` and will be displayed on your machine. Don't try this over a ppp line though, for it's too slow to be usable.

3   Using Directories

3.1   Directories: Preliminary Notions

We have seen the differences between files under DOS and Linux. As for directories, under DOS the root directory is \, under Linux / is. Similarly, nested directories are separated by \ under DOS, by / under Linux. Example of file paths:

```
DOS:      C:\PAPERS\GEOLOGY\MID_EOC.TEX
Linux:    /home/guido/papers/geology/mid_eocene.tex
```

As usual, .. is the parent directory, . is the current directory. Remember that the system won't let you cd, rd, or md everywhere you want. Each user starts from his or her own directory called 'home', given by the system administrator; for instance, on my PC my home dir is /home/guido.

3.2 Directories Permissions

Directories, too, have permissions. What we have seen in Section 2.3 (Permissions) holds for directories as well (user, group, and other). For a directory, rx means you can cd to that directory, and w means that you can delete a file in the directory (according to the file's permissions, of course), or the directory itself.

For example, to prevent other users from snooping in /home/guido/text:

```
$ chmod o-rwx /home/guido/text
```

3.3 Translating Commands from DOS to Linux

```
DIR:       ls, find, du
CD:        cd, pwd
MD:        mkdir
RD:        rmdir
DELTREE:   rm -R
MOVE:      mv
```

- EXAMPLES -

```
DOS                              Linux
----------------------------------------------------------------------

C:\GUIDO>DIR                     $ ls
C:\GUIDO>DIR FILE.TXT            $ ls file.txt
C:\GUIDO>DIR *.H *.C             $ ls *.h *.c
C:\GUIDO>DIR/P                   $ ls | more
C:\GUIDO>DIR/A                   $ ls -l
C:\GUIDO>DIR *.TMP /S            $ find / -name "*.tmp"
C:\GUIDO>CD                      $ pwd
       n/a - see note            $ cd
       ditto                     $ cd ~
       ditto                     $ cd ~/temp
C:\GUIDO>CD \OTHER               $ cd /other
C:\GUIDO>CD ..\TEMP\TRASH        $ cd ../temp/trash
C:\GUIDO>MD NEWPROGS             $ mkdir newprogs
C:\GUIDO>MOVE PROG ..            $ mv prog ..
C:\GUIDO>MD \PROGS\TURBO         $ mkdir /progs/turbo
```

```
C:\GUIDO>DELTREE TEMP\TRASH          $ rm -R temp/trash
C:\GUIDO>RD NEWPROGS                 $ rmdir newprogs
C:\GUIDO>RD \PROGS\TURBO             $ rmdir /progs/turbo
```

Notes:

1. when using **rmdir**, the directory to remove must be empty. To delete a directory and all of its contents, use **rm -R** (at your own risk).

2. the character '~' is a shortcut for the name of your home directory. The commands **cd** or **cd ~** will take you to your home directory from wherever you are; the command **cd ~/tmp** will take you to /home/your_home/tmp.

3. **cd -** "undoes" the last **cd**.

4 Floppies, Hard Disks, and the Like

4.1 Managing Devices

You have never thought about it, but the DOS command **FORMAT A:** does a lot more work than it seems. In fact, when you issue the command **FORMAT** it will: 1) physically format the disk; 2) create the A:\ directory (= create a filesystem); 3) make the disk available to the user (= mount the disk).

These three steps are addressed separately under Linux. You can use floppies in MS-DOS format, though other formats are available and are better—the MS-DOS format won't let you use long filenames. Here is how to prepare a disk (you'll need to start a session as root):

- To format a standard 1.44 meg floppy disk (A:):

  ```
  # fdformat /dev/fd0H1440
  ```

- To create a filesystem:

  ```
  # mkfs -t ext2 -c /dev/fd0H1440
  ```

  To create an MS-DOS filesystem, use **msdos** instead of **ext2**. Before using the disk, you must mount it.

- To mount the disk:

  ```
  # mount -t ext2 /dev/fd0 /mnt
  ```

  or

  ```
  # mount -t msdos /dev/fd0 /mnt
  ```

  Now you can address the files in the floppy. When you've finished, before extracting the disk you *must* unmount it.

- To unmount the disk:

  ```
  # umount /mnt
  ```

Now you can extract the disk. Obviously, you have to fdformat and mkfs only unformatted disks, not previously used ones. If you want to use drive B:, refer to fd1H1440 and fd1 instead of fd0H1440 and fd0 in the examples above.

All you used to do with A: or B: is now done using /mnt instead. Examples:

```
DOS                                        Linux
------------------------------------------------------------------

C:\GUIDO>DIR A:                            $ ls /mnt
C:\GUIDO>COPY A:*.*                        $ cp /mnt/* /docs/temp
C:\GUIDO>COPY *.ZIP A:                      $ cp *.zip /mnt/zip
C:\GUIDO>A:                                 $ cd /mnt
A:>_                                        /mnt/$ _
```

If you don't like this mounting/unmounting thing, use the mtools suite: it's a set of commands that are perfectly equivalent to their DOS counterpart, but start with an 'm': i.e., mformat, mdir, mdel, and so on. They can even preserve long file names, but not file permissions. Use these commands as you'd use the DOS commands and rest in peace.

Needless to say, what holds for floppies also holds for other devices; for instance, you may want to mount another hard disk or a CD-ROM drive. Here's how to mount the CD-ROM:

```
# mount -t iso9660 /dev/cdrom /mnt
```

This was the "official" way to mount your disks, but there's a trick in store. Since it's a bit of a nuisance having to be root to mount a floppy or a CD-ROM, every user can be allowed to mount them this way:

- as root, do the following:

```
~# mkdir /mnt/a: ; mkdir /mnt/a ; mkdir /mnt/cdrom
~# chmod 777 /mnt/a* /mnt/cd*
~# # make sure that the CD-ROM device is right
~# chmod 666 /dev/hdb ; chmod 666 /dev/fd*
```

- add in /etc/fstab the following lines:

```
/dev/cdrom      /mnt/cdrom   iso9660  ro,user,noauto    0    0
/dev/fd0        /mnt/a:      msdos    user,noauto       0    0
/dev/fd0        /mnt/a       ext2     user,noauto       0    0
```

Now, to mount a DOS floppy, an ext2 floppy, and a CD-ROM:

```
$ mount /mnt/a:
$ mount /mnt/a
$ mount /mnt/cdrom
```

/mnt/a, /mnt/a:, and /mnt/cdrom can now be accessed by every user. Remember that allowing everyone to mount disks this way is a gaping security hole, if you care.

4.2 Backing Up

Now that you know how to handle floppies etc., a couple of lines to see how to do your backup. There are several packages to help you, but the very least you can do for a multi-volume backup is (as root):

```
# tar -M -cvf /dev/fd0H1440 dir_to_backup/
```

Make sure to have a formatted floppy in the drive, and several more ready. To restore your stuff, insert the first floppy in the drive and do:

```
# tar -M -xpvf /dev/fd0H1440
```

5 What About Windows?

The "equivalent" of Windows is the graphic system X11. Unlike Windows or the Mac, X11 wasn't designed for ease of use or to look good, but just to provide graphic facilities to UNIX workstations. These are the main differences:

- while Windows looks and feels the same all over the world, X11 doesn't: it's much more configurable. X11's overall look is given by a key component called "window manager"; there are many you can choose from. The most common are fvwm, basic but nice and memory efficient, fvwm2-95 and The Next Level that give X11 a Windows 95–like taste, plus several others. Some look really beautiful;

- your window manager can be configured so as a window acts as in, er, Windows: you click on it and it comes to foreground. Another possibility is that it comes to foreground when the mouse is located on it. This feature ("focus") and many others can be altered by editing one or more configuration files. Read the docs of your window manager;

- X applications are written using special libraries ("widget sets"); as several are available, applications look different. The most basic ones are those that use the Athena widgets (2–D look; xdvi, xman, xcalc); others use Motif (netscape), others still use Tcl/Tk, XForms, Qt and what have you. Some— not all—of these libraries provide roughly the same look and feel as Windows;

- so much for the look of X11, but what about the feel? Unfortunately, all applications behave differently. For instance, if you select a line of text using the mouse and press BACKSPACE, you'd expect the line to disappear, right? This doesn't work with Athena–based apps, but it does with Motif, Qt, and Tcl/Tk ones;

- scrollbars, resizing, and iconisation: these, too, depend on the window manager and the widget set. Too many different things to mention here, just a couple of points. When using Athena–based apps the scrollbars are better moved with the central button. If you don't have a three–button mouse, try pressing the two buttons together;

- applications don't have an icon by default, but they can have many. It depends on the window manager. The desktop is called "root window", and you can change its appearance with apps like xsetroot or xloadimage;

- the clipboard can only contain text, and behaves strange. Once you've selected text, it's already copied to the clipboard: move elsewhere and press the central button. There's an application, xclipboard, that provides for multiple clipboard buffers;

- drag and drop is an option, and is only available if you use X applications that support it.

To save memory, it's better to use applications that use the same libraries, but this is difficult to do in practice. There's a project called the K Desktop Environment that aims at making X11 look and behave as coherently as Windows; it's currently in early beta stage but, believe me, it's awesome. It's going to put Windows' interface to shame. Point your browser to *http://www.kde.org* <http://www.kde.org>.

6   Tailoring the System

6.1   System Initialisation Files

Two important files under DOS are `AUTOEXEC.BAT` and `CONFIG.SYS`, which are used at boot time to initialise the system, set some environment variables like PATH and FILES, and possibly launch a program or batch file. Under Linux there are several initialisation files, some of which you had better not tamper with until you know exactly what you are doing. I'll tell you what the most important are, anyway:

FILES	NOTES
/etc/inittab	don't touch for now!
/etc/rc.d/*	ditto

If all you need is setting the `$PATH` and other environment variables, or you want to change the login messages or automatically launch a program after the login, have a look at the following files:

FILES	NOTES
/etc/issue	sets pre-login message
/etc/motd	sets post-login message
/etc/profile	sets $PATH and other variables, etc.
/etc/bashrc	sets aliases and functions, etc.
/home/your_home/.bashrc	sets your aliases + functions
/home/your_home/.bash_profile or	
/home/your_home/.profile	sets environment + starts your progs

If the latter file exists (note that it is a hidden file), it will be read after the login and the commands in it will be executed.

Example—look at this `.bash_profile`:

```
# I am a comment
echo Environment:
printenv | less    # equivalent of command SET under DOS
alias d='ls -l'    # easy to understand what an alias is
alias up='cd ..'
echo "I remind you that the path is "$PATH
echo "Today is `date`"  # use the output of command 'date'
echo "Have a good day, "$LOGNAME
# The following is a "shell function"
ctgz() # List the contents of a .tar.gz archive.
{
  for file in $*
  do
    gzip -dc ${file} | tar tf -
  done
}
# end of .profile
```

$PATH and $LOGNAME, you guessed right, are environment variables. There are many others to play with; for instance, RMP for apps like less or bash.

6.2   Program Initialisation Files

Under Linux, virtually everything can be tailored to your needs. Most programs have one or more initialisation files you can fiddle with, often as a .prognamerc in your home dir. The first ones you'll want to modify are:

- .inputrc: used by bash to define keybindings;
- .xinitrc: used by startx to initialise X Window System;
- .fvwmrc: used by the window manager fvwm. A sample is in: /usr/lib/X11/fvwm/system.fvwmrc;
- .Xdefault: used by rxvt, a terminal emulator for X, and other programs.

For all of these and the others you'll come across sooner or later, RMP.

7   A Bit of Programming

7.1   Shell Scripts: .BAT Files on Steroids

If you used .BAT files to create shortcuts of long command lines (I did a lot), this goal can be attained by inserting appropriate alias lines (see example above) in profile or .profile. But if your .BATs were more complicated, then you'll love the scripting language made available by the shell: it's as powerful as QBasic, if not more. It has variables, structures like while, for, case, if... then... else, and lots of other features: it can be a good alternative to a "real" programming language.

To write a script—the equivalent of a .BAT file under DOS—all you have to do is write a standard ASCII file containing the instructions, save it, then make it executable with the command chmod +x <scriptfile>. To execute it, type its name.

A word of warning. The system editor is called vi, and in my experience most new users find it very difficult to use. I'm not going to explain how to use it, because I don't like it and don't use it, so there. See Matt Welsh's "Linux installation...", pag. 109. (You had better get hold of another editor like joe, jed or emacs for X.) Suffice it here to say that:

- to insert some text, type 'i' then your text;
- to quit vi whithout saving, type ESC then :q!
- to save and quit, type ESC then :wq

Writing scripts under bash is such a vast subject it would require a book by itself, and I will not delve into the topic any further. I'll just give you an example of shell script, from which you can extract some basic rules:

```
#!/bin/sh
# sample.sh
# I am a comment
# don't change the first line, it must be there
```

```
echo "This system is: 'uname -a'" # use the output of the command
echo "My name is $0" # built-in variables
echo "You gave me the following $# parameters: "$*
echo "The first parameter is: "$1
echo -n "What's your name? " ; read your_name
echo notice the difference: "hi $your_name" # quoting with "
echo notice the difference: 'hi $your_name' # quoting with '
DIRS=0 ; FILES=0
for file in 'ls .' ; do
  if [ -d ${file} ] ; then # if file is a directory
    DIRS='expr $DIRS + 1'  # DIRS = DIRS + 1
  elif [ -f ${file} ] ; then
    FILES='expr $FILES + 1'
  fi
  case ${file} in
    *.gif|*jpg) echo "${file}: graphic file" ;;
    *.txt|*.tex) echo "${file}: text file" ;;
    *.c|*.f|*.for) echo "${file}: source file" ;;
    *) echo "${file}: generic file" ;;
  esac
done
echo "there are ${DIRS} directories and ${FILES} files"
ls | grep "ZxY--!!!WKW"
if [ $? != 0 ] ; then # exit code of last command
  echo "ZxY--!!!WKW not found"
fi
echo "enough... type 'man bash' if you want more info."
```

7.2   C for Yourself

Under UNIX, the system language is C, love it or hate it. Scores of other languages (FORTRAN, Pascal, Lisp, Basic, Perl, awk...) are also available.

Taken for granted that you know C, here are a couple of guidelines for those of you who have been spoilt by Turbo C++ or one of its DOS kin. Linux's C compiler is called **gcc** and lacks all the bells and whistles that usually accompany its DOS counterparts: no IDE, on-line help, integrated debugger, etc. It's just a rough command-line compiler, very powerful and efficient. To compile your standard **hello.c** you'll do:

```
$ gcc hello.c
```

which will create an executable file called **a.out**. To give the executable a different name, do

```
$ gcc -o hola hello.c
```

To link a library against a program, add the switch -l<libname>. For example, to link in the math library:

```
$ gcc -o mathprog mathprog.c -lm
```

(The -l<libname> switch forces **gcc** to link the library /usr/lib/lib<libname>.a; so -lm links /usr/lib/libm.a).

So far, so good. But when your prog is made of several source files, you'll need to use the utility **make**. Let's suppose you have written an expression parser: its source file is called **parser.c** and #includes two header files, `parser.h` and `xy.h`. Then you want to use the routines in `parser.c` in a program, say, `calc.c`, which in turn #includes `parser.h`. What a mess! What do you have to do to compile `calc.c`?

You'll have to write a so-called `makefile`, which teaches the compiler the dependencies between sources and objects files. In our example:

```
# This is makefile, used to compile calc.c
# Press the <TAB> key at appropriate positions!

calc: calc.o parser.o
<TAB>gcc -o calc calc.o parser.o -lm
# calc depends on two object files: calc.o and parser.o

calc.o: calc.c parser.h
<TAB>gcc -c calc.c
# calc.o depends on two source files

parser.o:  parser.c parser.h xy.h
<TAB>gcc -c parser.c
# parser.o depends on three source files

# end of makefile.
```

Save this file as `makefile` and type `make` to compile your program; alternatively, save it as `calc.mak` and type `make -f calc.mak`, and of course RMP. You can invoke some help about the C functions, that are covered by man pages, section 3; for example,

```
$ man 3 printf
```

There are lots of libraries available out there; among the first you'll want to use are `ncurses`, to handle textmode effects, and `svgalib`, to do graphics. If you feel brave enough to tackle X programming, get XForms (*ftp://bloch.phys.uwm.edu/pub/xforms* <ftp://bloch.phys.uwm.edu/pub/xforms>) and/or one of the many libraries that make writing X programs a breeze. Have a look at *http://www.xnet.com/~blatura/linapp6.html* <http://www.xnet.com/~blatura/linapp6.html> .

Many editors can act as an IDE; `emacs` and `jed`, for instance, also feature syntax highlighting, automatic indent and so on. Alternatively, get the package `rhide` from *sunsite.unc.edu:/pub/Linux/devel/debuggers/* <ftp://sunsite.unc.edu:/pub/Linux/devel/debuggers/>. It's a Borland IDE clone, and chances are that you'll like it.

8   The Remaining 1%

8.1   Using tar & gzip

Under UNIX there are some widely used applications to archive and compress files. `tar` is used to make archives—it's like PKZIP but it doesn't compress, it only archives. To make a new archive:

```
$ tar -cvf <archive_name.tar> <file> [file...]
```

To extract files from an archive:

```
$ tar -xpvf <archive_name.tar> [file...]
```

To list the contents of an archive:

```
$ tar -tf <archive_name.tar> | less
```

You can compress files using **compress**, which is obsolete and shouldn't be used any more, or **gzip**:

```
$ compress <file>
$ gzip <file>
```

that creates a compressed file with extension .Z (**compress**) or .gz (**gzip**). These programs can compress only one file at a time. To decompress, use:

```
$ compress -d <file.Z>
$ gzip -d <file.gz>
```

RMP.

The **unarj**, **zip** and **unzip** (PK??ZIP compatible) utilities are also available. Files with extension .tar.gz or .tgz (archived with **tar**, then compressed with **gzip**) are as common in the UNIX world as .ZIP files are under DOS. Here's how to list the contents of a .tar.gz archive:

```
$ gzip -dc <file.tar.gz> | tar tf - | less
```

or, equivalently,

```
$ tar -ztf <file.tar.gz> | less
```

8.2   Installing Applications

First of all: installing packages is root's work. Some Linux applications are distributed as .tar.gz or .tgz archives, specifically prepared so that they can be decompressed from / typing the following command:

```
# gzip -dc <file.tar.gz> | tar xvf -
```

or, equivalently,

```
$ tar -zxf <file.tar.gz>
```

The files will be decompressed in the right directory, which will be created on the fly. Users of the Slackware distribution have a user-friendly **pkgtool** program; another is **rpm**, which is available on all distributions thanks to Red Hat.

Most programs shouldn't be installed from /; typically, the archive will contain a directory called **pkgname/** and a lot of files and/or subdirectories under **pkgname/**. A good rule is to install those packages from /usr/local. Besides, some programs are distributed as C or C++ source files, which you'll have to compile to create the binaries. In most cases, all you have to do is issue **make**. Obviously, you'll need the **gcc** or **g++** compiler.

8.3   Tips You Can't Do Without

Command completion: pressing <TAB> when issuing a command will complete the command line for you. Example: you have to type `gcc this_is_a_long_name.c`; typing `gcc thi<TAB>` will suffice. (If you have other files that start with the same characters, supply enough characters to resolve any ambiguity.)

Backscrolling: pressing SHIFT + PAG UP (the grey key) allows you to backscroll a few pages, depending on how much video memory you have.

Resetting the screen: if you happen to `more` or `cat` a binary file, your screen may end up full of garbage. To fix things, blind type `reset` or this sequence of characters: `echo CTRL-V ESC c RETURN`.

Pasting text: in console, see below; in X, click and drag to select the text in an `xterm` window, then click the middle button (or the two buttons together if you have a two-button mouse) to paste. There is also `xclipboard` (alas, only for text); don't get confused by its very slow response.

Using the mouse: install `gpm`, a mouse driver for the console. Click and drag to select text, then right click to paste the selected text. It works across different VCs.

Messages from the kernel: have a look at `/var/adm/messages` or `/var/log/messages` as root to see what the kernel has to tell you, including bootup messages. The command `dmesg` is also handy.

8.4   Useful Programs and Commands

This list reflects my personal preferences and needs, of course. First of all, where to find them. Since you all know how to surf the Net and how to use `archie` and `ftp`, I'll just give you three of the most important addresses for Linux: *ftp://sunsite.unc.edu* <ftp://sunsite.unc.edu>, *ftp://tsx-11.mit.edu* <ftp://tsx-11.mit.edu>, and *ftp://nic.funet.fi* <ftp://nic.funet.fi>. Please use your nearest mirror.

- `at` allows you to run programs at a specified time;
- `awk` is a simple yet powerful language to manipulate data files (and not only). For example, being `data.dat` your multi field data file,

    `$ awk '$2 ~ "abc" {print $1, "\t", $4}' data.dat`

  prints out fields 1 and 4 of every line in `data.dat` whose second field contains "abc".
- `cron` is useful to perform tasks periodically, at specified date and time;
- `delete-undelete` do what their name means;
- `df` gives you info about all mounted disk(s);
- `dosemu` allows you to run several (not all) DOS programs—including Windows 3.x, with a bit of hacking;
- `file <filename>` tells you what `filename` is (ASCII text, executable, archive, etc.);
- `find` (see also Section 3.3 (dir)) is one of the most powerful and useful commands. It's used to find files that match several characteristics and perform actions on them. General use of `find` is:

    `$ find <directory> <expression>`

  where <expression> includes search criteria and actions. Examples:

    `$ find . -type l -exec ls -l {} \;`

  finds all the files that are symbolic links and shows what they point to.

    `$ find / -name "*.old" -ok rm {} \;`

finds all the files matching the pattern and deletes them, asking for your permission first.

> $ find . -perm +111

finds all the files whose permissions match 111 (executable).

> $ find . -user root

finds all the files that belong to root. Lots of possibilities here—RMP.

- gnuplot is a brilliant program for scientific plotting;
- grep finds text patterns in files. For example,

> $ grep -l "geology" *.tex

lists the files *.tex that contain the word "geology". The variant zgrep works on gzipped files. RMP;

- tcx compresses executable binaries keeping them executable;
- joe is an excellent editor. Invoking it by typing jstar you'll get the same key bindings as WordStar and its offspring, including DOS and Borland's Turbo languages editors;
- less is probably the best text browser, and if properly configured lets you browse gzipped, tarred, and zipped files as well;
- lpr <file> prints a file in background. To check the status of the printing queue, use lpq; to remove a file from the printing queue, use lprm;
- mc is a great file manager;
- pine is a nice e-mailing program;
- script <script_file> copies to script_file what appears on screen until you issue the command exit. Useful for debugging;
- sudo allows users to perform some of root's tasks (e.g. formatting and mounting disks; RMP);
- uname -a gives you info about your system;
- zcat and zless are useful for viewing gzipped text files without ungzipping them. Possible use:

> $ zless textfile.gz
> $ zcat textfile.gz | lpr

- The following commands often come in handy: bc, cal, chsh, cmp, cut, fmt, head, hexdump, nl, passwd, printf, sort, split, strings, tac, tail, tee, touch, uniq, w, wall, wc, whereis, write, xargs, znew. RMP.

8.5 Common Extensions and Related Programs

You may come across scores of file extensions. Excluding the more exotic ones (i.e. fonts, etc.), here's a list of who's what:

- 1 ... 8: man pages. Get man.
- arj: archive made with arj. unarj to unpack.
- dvi: output file produced by TeX (see below). xdvi to visualise it; dvips to turn it into a PostScript .ps file.
- gif: graphic file. Get seejpeg or xpaint.
- gz: archive made with gzip.

- `info`: info file (sort of alternative to man pages). Get `info`.
- `jpg`, `jpeg`: graphic file. Get `seejpeg`.
- `lsm`: Linux Software Map file. It's a plain ASCII file containing the description of a package.
- `ps`: PostScript file. To visualise or print it get `gs` and, optionally, `ghostview`.
- `rpm`: Red Hat package. You can install it on any system using the package manager `rpm`.
- `tgz`, `tar.gz`: archive made with `tar` and compressed with `gzip`.
- `tex`: text file to submit to TeX, a powerful typesetting program. Get the package `tex`, available in many distributions; but beware of NTeX, which has corrupted fonts and is included in some Slackware versions.
- `texi`: texinfo file, can produce both TeX and info files (cp. `info`). Get `texinfo`.
- `xbm`, `xpm`, `xwd`: graphic file. Get `xpaint`.
- `Z`: archive made with `compress`.
- `zip`: archive made with `zip`. Get `zip` and `unzip`.

9   The End, for Now

Congratulations! You have now grasped a little bit of UNIX and are ready to start working. Remember that your knowledge of the system is still limited, and that you are expected to do more practice with Linux to use it comfortably. But if all you had to do was get a bunch of applications and start working with them, I bet that what I included here is enough.

I'm sure you'll enjoy using Linux and will keep learning more about it—everybody does. I bet, too, that you'll never go back to DOS! I hope I made myself understood and did a good service to my 3 or 4 readers.

9.1   Copyright

Unless otherwise stated, Linux HOWTO documents are copyrighted by their respective authors. Linux HOWTO documents may be reproduced and distributed in whole or in part, in any medium physical or electronic, as long as this copyright notice is retained on all copies. Commercial redistribution is allowed and encouraged; however, the author would like to be notified of any such distributions.

All translations, derivative works, or aggregate works incorporating any Linux HOWTO documents must be covered under this copyright notice. That is, you may not produce a derivative work from a HOWTO and impose additional restrictions on its distribution. Exceptions to these rules may be granted under certain conditions; please contact the Linux HOWTO coordinator at the address given below.

In short, we wish to promote dissemination of this information through as many channels as possible. However, we do wish to retain copyright on the HOWTO documents, and would like to be notified of any plans to redistribute the HOWTOs.

If you have questions, please contact Greg Hankins, the Linux HOWTO coordinator, at gregh@sunsite.unc.edu via email.

9.2   Disclaimer

"From DOS to Linux HOWTO" was written by Guido Gonzato, *guido@ibogfs.cineca.it* <mailto:guido@ibogfs.cineca.it>. Many thanks to Matt Welsh, the author of "Linux Installation and Getting Started", to Ian Jackson, the author of "Linux frequently asked questions with answers", to Giuseppe Zanetti, the author of "Linux", to all the folks who emailed me suggestions, and especially to Linus Torvalds and GNU who gave us Linux.

This document is provided "as is". I put great effort into writing it as accurately as I could, but you use the information contained in it at your own risk. In no event shall I be liable for any damages resulting from the use of this work.

Feedback is welcome. For any requests, suggestions, flames, etc., feel free to contact me.

Enjoy Linux and life,

Guido =8-)

The dosemu HOWTO

by Mike Deisher.   Updated by Uwe Bonnes,   *bon@elektron.ikp.physik.th-darmstadt.de*
`<mailto:bon@elektron.ikp.physik.th-darmstadt.de>`   v0.64.4, 15 March 1997 for dosemu-0.64.4 (in progress)

This is the 'Frequently Asked Questions' (FAQ) / HOWTO document for dosemu. The most up-to-date version of the dosemu-HOWTO may be found in **ftp.mathematik.th-darmstadt.de:/pub/linux/bonnes/** `<ftp://ftp.mathematik.th-darmstadt.de:/pub/linux/bonnes/>`.

Contents

1   The preliminaries

1.1   What is dosemu, anyway?

To quote the manual, "dosemu" is a user-level program which uses certain special features of the Linux kernel and the 80386 processor to run MS-DOS in what we in the biz call a 'DOS box.' The DOS box, a combination of hardware and software trickery, has these capabilities:

o the ability to virtualize all input/output and processor control instructions

o the ability to support the word size and addressing modes of the iAPX86 processor family's "real mode," while still running within the full protected mode environment

o the ability to trap all DOS and BIOS system calls and emulate such calls as are necessary for proper operation and good performance

o the ability to simulate a hardware environment over which DOS programs are accustomed to having control.

o the ability to provide MS-DOS services through native Linux services; for example, dosemu can provide a virtual hard disk drive which is actually a Linux directory hierarchy."

1.2 Names and numbers

(xx/yy/zz) means day zz in month yy in year xx(97/2/9).

winemu mean WinOS/2 running in dosemu(97/2/10).

1.3 What version of Dosemu should I use?

Dosemu uses the same numbering scheme as the kernel. Uneven second numbers are for possible unstable developper releases, even second numbers are for releases considered stable. At the time of writing, **0.64.4** is the latest stable release, while **0.65.0.6** ist the latest developper's release. So if you want to use dosemu, get the latest **stable** release (97/02/28).

(xx/yy/zz) means day zz in month yy in year xx(97/2/9).

winemu mean WinOS/2 running in dosemu(97/2/10).

1.4 What's the newest version of dosemu and where can I get it?

The newest version of dosemu as of (97/2/9) is **dosemu0.64.4** and can be ftp'ed from:

tsx-11.mit.edu:/pub/linux/ALPHA/dosemu/ <ftp://tsx-11.mit.edu:/pub/linux/ALPHA/dosemu/>

ftp.suse.com:/pub/dosemu/ <ftp://ftp.suse.com:/pub/dosemu/>

However, pre-release versions are also available for developers and ALPHA testers. They can be retrieved from:

http://www.ednet.ns.ca/auto/rddc <http://www.ednet.ns.ca/auto/rddc>

Remember that this is ALPHA code, however: there may be serious bugs and very little documentation for new features. At present, the development version is known to have bugs. Please use it only if you like to do active development. Don't report bugs in the development version, fix them instead.

1.5   Where can I ask questions?

If you have problems regarding installing and running dosemu after reading the documentation, first try to help yourself: Your question has probably been asked and perhaps answered before. Try some search engine on the internet to retrieve that information. E.g. you can ask

    http://www.dejanews.com <http://www.dejanews.com>

to find all newsnet articles containing the keywords of your question. Helping yourself will probably be faster than asking a well known question. It too frees up the time of developpers from answering trivial question and so helps the further development of dosemu(97/2/9) .

1.6   Where can I report bugs and ask questions?

If you want to ask questions and report bugs regarding dosemu, you should consider subscribing to the linux-msdos-digest mailing list. To subscribe, send mail to *Majordomo@vger.rutgers.edu* <mailto:Majordomo@vger.rutgers.edu> with the following command in the body of your email message:

    subscribe linux-msdos-digest your_username@your.email.address

If you ever want to remove yourself from the mailing list, you can send mail to *Majordomo@vger.rutgers.edu* <mailto:Majordomo@vger.rutgers.edu> with the following command in the body of your email message:

    unsubscribe linux-msdos-digest your_username@your.email.address

(95/8/11).   When you are subscribed to linux-msdos, you can send your report as mail to linux-msdos@vger.rutgers.edu. There is a gate that send mails to linux-msdos@vger.rutgers.edu as postings to the newsgroup named **linux.dev.msdos**. If your News provider doesn't carry that group, ask her(him) to add that group(97/2/10).

1.7   Where can I follow the development?

If you want to follow the development of dosemu, there is a mailing list for developpers. To subscribe, send mail to *Majordomo@ednet.ns.ca* <mailto:Majordomo@ednet.ns.ca> with the following command in the body of your email message:

    subscribe msdos-devel your_username@your.email.address

If you ever want to remove yourself from the mailing list, you can send mail to *Majordomo@ednet.ns.ca* <mailto:Majordomo@ednet.ns.ca> with the following command in the body of your email message:

    unsubscribe dosemu-devel your_username@your.email.address

Please, don't use this list for the things linux-dosemu-digest is thought for. Contributions to msdos-devel should concern the further development of dosemu. Normal installation problems shouldn't be reported here, and are normally ignored by those reading that list(97/2/9).

1.8   What documentation is available for dosemu?

The dosemu manual (**dosemu.texinfo**) written by Robert Sanders has not been updated in some time but is still a good source of information. It is distributed with dosemu.

The "dosemu Novice's Altering Guide" or DANG is a road map to the inner workings of dosemu. It is designed for the adventurous, those who wish to modify the source code themselves. The DANG is maintained by Alistair MacDonald (*alistair@slitesys.demon.co.uk* <mailto:alistair@slitesys.demon. co.uk>) and is found in the doc-directory of the dosemu source tree.

The EMU failure list (EMUfailure.txt) is a list of all programs known **not** to work under dosemu.

And then, of course, there is the dosemu FAQ/HOWTO. But you already know about that, don't you. It is also posted once in a while to the mailing list and found in the doc-directory. The most recent version can be found in *ftp.mathematik.th-darmstadt.de:/pub/linux/bonnes/* <ftp://ftp.mathematik. th-darmstadt.de:/pub/linux/bonnes/>(97/2/9).

1.9   I have a program that fails, not listed in EMUfailure

First check, if the failure of your program is not caused by some of the fundamental incapabilities of dosemu, listed in EMUfailure. If you think you have something new, please report to *linux-msdos@vger.rutgers.edu* <mailto:linux-msdos@vger.rutgers.edu>. Perhaps it can be made going with the help others. Give detailed information about your setup, tell the version of kernel, dosemu etc and name the observed errors. You can use xdos to cut and paste the error message into your report. But keep your report in a readable form. We know the content of ../etc/config.dist. So only send the active lines from your dosemu.conf. And scan through your debug output and at first only send those parts you think are relevant. Few people are willing to decode some long attachment to a mail, to do debugging for others. But keeps your logs at hand, if others ask detailed(97/2/10).

1.10   How do I submit changes or additions to the HOWTO?

The preferred method is to edit the file **dosemu-HOWTO-xx.x.sgml** to incorporate the changes, create a diff file by typing something like

```
diff -uw original-file new-file
```

and send it to *bon@elektron.ikp.physik.th-darmstadt.de* <mailto:bon@elektron.ikp.physik. th-darmstadt.de>. If you do not know SGML, that's ok. Changes or new information in any form will be accepted. Creating the diff file just makes it easier on the HOWTO maintainer. :-)(97/2/9)

1.11   Message from Greg...

Unless otherwise stated, Linux HOWTO documents are copyrighted by their respective authors. Linux HOWTO documents may be reproduced and distributed in whole or in part, in any medium physical or electronic, as long as this copyright notice is retained on all copies. Commercial redistribution is allowed and encouraged; however, the author would like to be notified of any such distributions.

All translations, derivative works, or aggregate works incorporating any Linux HOWTO documents must be covered under this copyright notice. That is, you may not produce a derivative work from a HOWTO and impose additional restrictions on its distribution. Exceptions to these rules may be granted under certain conditions; please contact the Linux HOWTO coordinator at the address given below.

In short, we wish to promote dissemination of this information through as many channels as possible. However, we do wish to retain copyright on the HOWTO documents, and would like to be notified of any plans to redistribute the HOWTOs.

If you have questions, please contact Greg Hankins, the Linux HOWTO coordinator, at gregh@cc.gatech.edu(95/8/11).

2 Compiling and installing dosemu

2.1 Where are the installation instructions?

The installation instructions are in the file, "QuickStart", included in the distribution.

2.2 Top ten problems while compiling and installing dosemu.

1. Forgetting to read the **QuickStart** Guide.

2. Try to compile some old version of dosemu.

3. Try to compile with a kernel older than 2.0.28 or 2.1.15.

4.   Having   the   wrong   linux   kernel   source   sitting   in   **/usr/src/linux**   or   missing **/usr/src/linux/include/version.h**

5. Use dosemu with a kernel that does not have **IPC** compiled in.

6. Compile with gcc older than 2.7.2 or libc older than x.x.x.

7. Forget to edit your **/etc/dosemu.conf** file.

8. Run DOSEMU with partition access while they are already mounted.

9. Don't install dosemu with sufficient privileges (i.e., root). (97/04/08)

2.3 How can I use dosemu on an older version of the Linux Kernel.

If you still use 1.2.13 and can't upgarde for some reasons, use **dosemu-0.60.4**. If you use some version of dosemu below 2.0.28 and 2.1.15, Hans Lermen (*lermen@elserv.ffm.fgan.de* <mailto:lermen@elserv. ffm.fgan.de>) reported (97/1/25 and 97/2/11)

```
> Is the dosemu-0.64.3.tgz version of dosemulator for the 2.xx.yy versions > of
the linux kernel ??

Yes, but ...

  if ( ((xx == 0) && (yy >= 28)) || ((xx >= 1) && (yy >= 15)) )
    take_dosemu_0_64_4();
  else {
    if (xx == 1)  exit(1);
    take_dosemu_0_64_2_x();
  }
```

;-)

2.4 How do I make aout binaries?

Starting with version 0.64.4 there is no a.out support any more. If you absolutely need it, you must use version 0.64.3.1. The configure script then should take care for this, if you setup is a standard setup(97/2/11).

2.5 How do I compile dosemu on a machine with low memory?

Marty Leisner (**leisner@sdsp.mc.xerox.com**) reported (95/4/8) that

If you have problems with running out of swap space you may want to add `CFLAGS+=-fno-inline` after `CFLAGS` is defined in **dpmi/Makefile**. Be careful before you do this and check for the existence of swap space. I found Linux crashes a times when it has no swap space.

2.6 Compilation fails with some strange error regarding "slang"

You probably have installed your own version of the Slang library. Hans Lermen <**lermen@elserv.ffm.fgan.de**> writes(97/2/11):

```
configure --enable-force-slang
```

2.7 What configurabe options are available

Try

```
configure --help
```

to get the list of configurable options listed (97/2/12)

2.8 How can I speed up compilation?

Marty Leisner (**leisner@sdsp.mc.xerox.com**) reported (95/4/8) that

The default optimization is -O2. You may want edit the makefile to use -O (compiled somewhat faster/smaller).

2.9 More compilation tips from Marty...

Marty Leisner (**leisner@sdsp.mc.xerox.com**) reported (95/4/8) that

You need to have build the kernel on your system to get the current version. If not, you may want to hand modify KERNEL_VERSION in the top level Makefile. The number is of the form, "nmmmppp", where "n" is the version, "mmm" is the minor version, and "ppp" is the patchlevel. For example, kernel 1.1.88 corresponds to "1001088" and kernel 1.2.1 to "1002001".

Addition from (**lermen@elserv.ffm.fgan.de**):

For versions greater 0.64.3 this no longer is true. You need to have a valid <linux/version.h>, which has to be part off your standard /usr/include. If you don't have it, you either did a 'make clean' on your kernel source or your distributor failed to support you with this.

2.10   Do I need to compile dosemu as root?

(95/4/8)

No. You must install it as root, though.

Marty Leisner (**leisner@sdsp.mc.xerox.com**) adds

In order to access I/O ports (including the console) dosemu needs to run as root. Running dosemu on an xterm or in X windows and requiring now direct hardware access allows you to run dosemu as a user. The security/setuid implications will be worked on in development releases(95/8/11).

Have a look at ..;/**doc/SECURITY.readme** too(97/2/9).

2.11   How to I patch dosemu.

If you do patch dosemu from one version to another, do "make pristine;./configure; make". If you don't make pristine, at least the version of the new executable will be wrong, if the whole thing compiles at all(97/2/9).

2.12   What versions of DOS are known to run with dosemu.

Caldera's OpenDos (formerly known as DrDOS) is reported to work with dosemu (**Nicolas St-Pierre** <**draggy@kosmic.org**>. As OpenDos can be used free of charge for non-commercial use, it is preferred. However as of now, redistribution is not allowed. You must get OpenDos youself from Caldera's site *http://www.caldera.com/dos* <http://www.caldera.com/dos> Hopefully this will change soon, so dosemu can distribute a bootable hdimage. **MsDos-6.22** is known to work with dosemu. **MsDos-7** aka **Win95** works with dosemu to, supposed you have the boot logo switched off and you don't start the graphic shell at bootup. If you make the hdimage bootable with the so called "Rescue Disk" you are offered to make during the Windows installation, you get the right settings. If you use your normal Win95 installation to transfer the system files, have a look at the msdos.sys written on the hdimage and change the settings under the section [Options] to have entries like [Options] Logo=0 BootGUI=0

(97/3/7)

2.13   Versions known not to run

DOS 4.01 had problems by itself, do it won't work with dosemu either (Mattias Hembruch <mghembru@ece.uwaterloo.ca> 97/04/03)

3   Hard disk setup

3.1   How do I use my hard disk with dosemu?

First, mount your dos hard disk partition as a Linux subdirectory. For example, you could create a directory in Linux such as /dos (mkdir -m 755 /dos) and add a line like

```
   /dev/hda1          /dos      msdos    umask=022
```

to your /etc/fstab. (In this example, the hard disk is mounted read-only. You may want to mount it read/write by replacing "022" with "000" and using the -m 777 option with mkdir). Now **mount /dos**. Now you can add a line like

```
   lredir d: linux\fs/dos
```

to the AUTOEXEC.BAT file in your hdimage (see the comments on LREDIR below). On a multi-user system you may want to use

```
   lredir d: linux\fs\${home}
```

where "home" is the name of an environmental variable that contains the location of the dos directory (/dos in this example)(95/8/11).

Tim Bird (Tim_R_Bird@Novell.COM) states that LREDIR users should be careful when they use LREDIR in the autoexec, because COMMAND.COM will continue parsing the autoexec.bat from the redirected drive as the same file offset where it left off in the autoexec.bat on the physical drive. For this reason, it is safest to have the autoexec.bat on the redirected drive and the physical drive (diskimage) be the same(95/8/11).

Robert D. Warren (**rw11258@xx.acs.appstate.edu**) reported (94/4/28) that

I boot off a small hdimage file (less than 1 MB - and twice as large as needs be at that), and the next to last line in my config.sys file on the hdimage boot image is:

```
        install=c:\lredir.exe c: LINUX\FS\home/dos
```

This will execute lredir just before the command interpreter runs. And I have successfully run it with both command.com and 4DOS. This eliminates the offset problem using lredir in autoexec.bat.

Uwe Bonnes (**bon@elektron.ikp.physik.th-darmstadt.de**) adds (95/8/11) that

It is usefull to do:

```
install=C:\subst.exe g: c:
```

before that, so you have still access to your hdimage as drive g: Another useful tip in that circumstance is to configure dosemu to use "**autoexec.emu**" to keep dos and dosemu apart.

3.2   How can I access the hdimage from Linux?

Use the recent mtools, version 3.0 at the time of writing. With a line in **/etc/mtools.conf** like

```
   drive g:  file="/var/lib/dosemu/hdimage" Offset=8832
```

you can use the mtools on the hdimage, like "mdir g:". "mcopy g:/config.emu /tmp" copies the config.emu file from the hdimage to /tmp/config.emu. You can edit it there and copy it back. Use a drive letter you find sensible. "G:" is only an example(07/2/9).

3.3   Can I use my stacked/double-spaced/super-stored disk?

At this time, compressed drives cannot be accessed via the redirector (lredir or emufs) on a standard kernel. There is a patch for the kernel to mount compressed files under the name "dmsdosfs". Find it on sunsite.unc.edu and its mirrors

> *http://sunsite.unc.edu:/pub/Linux/system/Filesystems/dosfs/* `<http://sunsite.unc.`
> `edu:/pub/Linux/system/Filesystems/dosfs/>`

A good idea is also to look in *http://sunsite.unc.edu:/pub/Linux/Incoming* `<http://sunsite.unc.edu:/pub/`
`Linux/Incoming>` for a newer version. However, many people have had success by simply uncommenting the

```
disk { wholedisk "/dev/hda" }          # 1st partition on 1st disk
```

line in their dosemu config file. Others have had success using

```
disk { partition "/dev/hda1" }
```

Do that on the risk to loose data on a dosemu crash(97/2/9)!

If your dos partition is already mounted with write access and you try to run dosemu with partition or whole disk access, dosemu will print a warning message and abort. This prevents DOS and Linux from making independent writes to your disk and trashing the data on your dos partition(95/8/11).

If LILO is installed, the above will not work. However...

Thomas Mockridge (**thomas@aztec.co.za**) reported (94/8/5) that

To boot dosemu with LILO and Stacker 4.0 I did a little work around...

1. **dd** the MBR to a file. (or norton utility, etc., first 512 bytes)

2. Boot dos (from full boot not emu), do a fdisk /mbr, make your dos partition active with (dos) fdisk.

3. Copy the new MBR to a file.

4. Replace the original MBR

5. Copy the second MBR to /var/lib/dosemu/partition.hda? (Whichever is your dos partition)

6. Set dosemu.conf

```
disk {partition "/dev/hda? ?"}
```

7. Start dosemu and and voila! No LILO.

Holger Schemel (**q99492@pbhrzx.uni-paderborn.de**) reported (94/2/10) that

Works even fine under dosemu with MS-DOS 6.0. If you have problems, then you have to edit the file 'DBLSPACE.INI' manually and change the disk letter to the letter your drive gets under dosemu.

Darren J Moffat (**moffatd@dcs.gla.ac.uk**) also reported (94/3/27)

"...use 6.2 if you can get it!! Just make sure you have a LILO boot disk on hand since dos 6{.2} will change the MBR of the boot HZ."

4   Parallel ports, serial ports and mice

4.1   Port access worked with older version, but doesn't work now!

Read ../**doc/README.port-io** and the port-section in ../**etc/config.dist**

4.2   Port access was faster with older versions!

To have a chance to log port access, by default every port access produces an exception out of vm86-mode.
This takes some time. If you don't want to log port access, use the keyword **"fast"** in the appropriate port
statement.

4.3   Where are the (microsoft compatible) mouse drivers?

Tom Kimball (**tk@pssparc2.oc.com**) reported (93/11/24) that

Several people said to use a different mouse driver and suggested some. I found a couple that seem to work
fine.

```
oak.oakland.edu:/pub/msdos/mouse/mouse701.zip    (mscmouse)
oak.oakland.edu:/pub/msdos/mouse/gmous102.zip    (gmouse)
```

Normally you can use dosemu's internaldriver, so you don't need any additional mousedriver in dosemu
outside winemu(97/2/10).

4.4   Why doesn't the mouse driver work?

Mark Rejhon (**mdrejhon@magi.com**) reported (95/4/7) that

If you start the mouse driver and it just hangs (it might actually take 30-60s), but if you are waiting longer
than a minute for the mouse driver to start, try specifying the COM port that the mouse is on, at the mouse
driver command line.

4.5   Why does dosemu clobber COM4?

Rob Janssen (**rob@pe1chl.ampr.org**) reported (94/3/24) that

According to **jmorriso@bogomips.ee.ubc.ca**, "dosemu still clobbers COM4 (0x2e8, IRQ 5). 0x2e8 isn't
in ports{} in config. I have to run setserial /dev/cua3 irq 5 on it after dosemu exits."

This is caused by your VGA BIOS. I have found that by enabling the IO port trace and seeing where it was
clobbered.

Disable the "`allowvideoportaccess on`" line in config and it will work fine. When you then have problems
with the video, try to enable more selective ranges of IO addresses (e.g., 40-43).

4.6   How do I use dosemu over the serial ports?

4.7   How can I switch between dosemu and a shell over the serial line?

John Taylor (**taylor@pollux.cs.uga.edu**) reported (94/5/25) that

I am running Linux 1.1.13 and want to point out a great feature that should be protected and not taken out (IMHO). With the 52 version, I can run the program, "screen." From screen, i can invoke dos -D-a. What is really great (IMHO) is the screen commands (the CTRL-A cmds) still work. This means I can do a CTRL-A C and add another unix shell, and switch between the two (DOS / UNIX). This allows me to use dosemu over the serial line really well, because switching is made easy.

4.8   How can I get the parallel ports to work?

The dosemu.conf has lines at the end to redirect printers to either lpr or a file. If you want direct access to the bare metal, comment out these emulation lines, and add the line

```
    ports { device /dev/lp0 fast range 0x3bc 0x3bf } # lpt0
```

for the "monitor card" printer port (corresponds to /dev/lp0), or

```
    ports { device /dev/lp1 fast range 0x378 0x37f } # lpt1
```

```
    ports { device /dev/lp1 fast range 0x278 0x27f } # lpt2
```

for LPT1 (/dev/lp1) and LPT2 (/dev/lp2) respectively(97/2/9).

5   Multiple users and Non-interactive sessions

5.1   Can I use dosemu on a multi-user system?

Corey Sweeney (**corey@amiganet.xnet.com**) reported (93/12/8) that

If you are running dosemu on a system in which more then one person may want to run dosemu, then you may want to change the directory of your hard drive image. Currently in the **/etc/dosemu.conf** file there exists the line saying that the hard drive image is "hdimage". If you change this to **/var/lib/dosemu/hdimage** then people do not have to worry about what directory they are in when they run dosemu, and hdimage does not have to be moved each time you upgrade to the next patch level.

If you do do this for multi-user dosemu, then you will want to make the hdimage in **/var/lib/dosemu** read-only for everyone but the dosemu administrator.

Note that you can use the new emufs.sys thing to mount a "public" directory and/or a "private" directory (a sub-directory in each person's home directory).

[Note: Users may also create a personal configuration file named **/.dosrc** (same format as **/etc/dosemu.conf**) to run their own copy of dos.]

5.2 How can I run dos commands non-interactively?

I have been meaning to write an article on this for quite some time but have not gotten around to it. Here are some hints from others:

Dan Newcombe (**newcombe@aa.csc.peachnet.edu**) reported (94/1/27) that

Here is an idea (untested) to be able to run a DOS command from the command line (or menu choice, etc...) without modifying the actual emulator. [Your dos partition is assumed to be mounted under Linux, already.]

Suppose you wanted to run wp60.exe with the parameter "**wp60 d:\doc\paper.txt**". You would do something like "**dosrun wp60 d:\doc\paper.txt**". "**dosrun**" would be a linux shell program that would a) edit/modify/recreate the dos **autoexec.bat** from your dos partition and b) simply run dosemu (e.g., "**dos -C >/dev/null**". Step a) would somehow keep all the stuff you'd normally want in **autoexec.bat** (e.g., mouse.com) and the last line would be "**wp60 d:\doc\paper.txt**".

On the dosemu side, beforehand, you would have to modify the **config.sys** file (located in hdimage) so that it 1) uses emufs to access the dos partition as **D:**, 2) sets "**COMPSEC=D:** (I think. I don't have a DOS manual around.), and 3) sets "**shell=c:\command.com /p**".

The idea is that for each time that you load the DOS emulator, you will recreate an autoexec.bat that is specific to that session. What makes it specific is that the last line will execute the program you want. The modifications on the hdimage are to tell the emulator/DOS that you want to use (and effectively) boot off of D:, which will be the actual DOS partition.

If you do not use hdimage and access the DOS filesystem directly upon boot-up of dosemu, then this will work, and you don't have to go through the hdimage part of this all.

Daniel T. Schwager (**danny@dragon.s.bawue.de**) reported (94/7/2) that

You can use different dosemu.conf files (and different hd-boot-images with different autoexec.bat's) and call dosemu like

```
$ dos -F my_quicken_q_exe_dosemu.conf
```

Dietmar Braun (**braun@math20.mathematik.uni-bielefeld.de**) reported (94/7/4) that

This is no problem at all when you use the redirector of dosemu. It is possible to redirect a drive letter to a linux path given by an environment variable.

So I have a shell script named "**DOS**" which does something like

```
mkdir /tmp/dos.$$
DOSTMP=/tmp/dos.$$; export DOSTMP
```

and then a little trick to get "**echo $* > $DOSTMP/startup.bat**" really working (actually a small C Program which turns '/' in '\' and terminates lines correctly for messy dos with cr/lf pairs and adds ^**Z** at the end of the file), creates startup files, links and so on in this directory, and then starts dosemu. Within "**autoexec.bat**" drive c: is redirected from hdimage to this tmp-directory, which has links for **$HOME** and **$PWD**.

So if I want to see my filenames shortened to 8.3 I can type "**DOS dir**" and I get my current directory listing. So I have full DOS multi user (I don't have any DOS partition and redirecting to Linux preserves user permissions) and multi tasking. (dosemu sessions are completely independent). I did this once to be able to use a dos driver for my printer. My printcap df is actually a DOS program. So you can even make DOS executables act as lpr filters.

6 dosemu and Netware

6.1 How do I get Netware access from dosemu?

As always, access through the Linux filesystem is preferred. Mount your Netware drives with Caldera's Netware utilities or Volker Lendecke's free ncpfs utility (*ftp://ftp.gwdg.de:/pub/linux/misc/ncpfs* <ftp: //ftp.gwdg.de:/pub/linux/misc/ncpfs>). If you need real IPX access, e.g. to run Novell's "syscon", read ../doc/**NOVELL-HOWTO**.txt.

7 dosemu and X-windows(97/2/9).

7.1 Can I run dosemu in console mode while running X?

Ronald Schalk (**R.Schalk@uci.kun.nl**) reported (94/1/17) that

Yes, no problem. Just remember to use ctrl-alt-<Fn> to go to a Virtual Console (VC), and you can run any Linux application (dosemu is a linux-application). I've got almost always WP5.1 in a dos session.

[Note: Use ctrl-alt-F7 to switch back to X from dosemu, if X runs on VC7.]

7.2 Is it possible to run dosemu in a window in X-windows?

If you have X installed and you have successfully compiled dosemu and run it successfully outside X-windows, you should be able to run "xdos" or "dos -X" right away to bring up a dosemu window. If this does not work, make sure:

```
1. Dosemu has X support compiled in. This is default, however
   if you you have configured dosemu with
   "./configured --without-x", you don't have X support. So make
   "make pristine; ./configure; make; make install" should build
   you a dosemu-executable with X support, if you have the
   X-libraries installed in /usr/X11R6.
2. Set up your X key-mappings.  In an xterm, type

   xmodmap -e "keycode 22 = 0xff08"
   xmodmap -e "keycode 107 = 0xffff"

   These lines fixes the backspace and delete keys respectively.
3. Configured the X-related configuration options in your
   /etc/dosemu.conf file.
```

Alternatively, you can run dosemu inside a color xterm, which is not recommended because many color xterms have buggy support for the complex text display capabilities of dosemu. This does not require X_SUPPORT to be compiled into dosemu. However, if you really want to do this, do the following steps:

```
1. Install ansi_xterm.  The recommended package is available as:
   tsx-11.mit.edu:/pub/linux/ALPHA/dosemu/Development/ansi-xterm-R6.tar.gz

2. Set up your X key-mappings.  In an xterm, type
```

```
xmodmap -e "keycode 22 = 0xff08"
xmodmap -e "keycode 107 = 0xffff"
```

These lines fixes the backspace and delete keys, respectively.

3. Configured the terminal-related (not X-related) settings in /etc/dosemu.conf

(972/9).

Marty Leisner (**leisner@sdsp.mc.xerox.com**) reported (95/3/31) that

I have xrdb log the following resources

```
dosxterm*Font:  vga dosxterm*geometry:  80x25 dosxterm*saveLines:  25
```

or I alias "dosxterm" to "term -fn vga -title dosxterm -geometry 80x25 -sl 25"

If you use the xrdb method, all you have to do is run "xterm -name dosxterm"

7.3 Xdos dosen't work on a remote X-display!

At present, dosemu is set up to use the MIT shared memory extensions. This extension only works on a local display. If you want to run xdos on a remote display, configure dosemu with "./configure –enable-nomitshm" after a "make pristine" or on the clean source tree(97/2/9).

7.4 Xdos dosen't find the VGA font

Check that the vga fonts you installed are listed in the font.dir of the directory you installed the fonts in:

```
hertz:~> grep misc /usr/X11R6/lib/X11/XF86Config
    FontPath    "/usr/X11R6/lib/X11/fonts/misc/"
hertz:~> grep vga /usr/X11R6/lib/X11/fonts/misc/fonts.dir
vga.pcf vga
vga11x19.pcf vga11x19
hertz:~> ls /usr/X11R6/lib/X11/fonts/misc/vga*
/usr/X11R6/lib/X11/fonts/misc/vga.pcf
/usr/X11R6/lib/X11/fonts/misc/vga11x19.bdf
/usr/X11R6/lib/X11/fonts/misc/vga11x19.pcf
```

If you installed some X-fonts, like you did when you installed dosemu with X-Support for the first time, "mkfontdir" and then "xset fp rehash" needs to be run. The dosemu install should take care for "mkfontdir" and tells you about "xset fp rehash". Tell us if it dosen't work for you. (97/2/13)

7.5 The vga font is very smal on my high resolution Display

Look for the vga11x19 font. (97/2/13)

7.6   Dosemu compilation fails with some strange error regarding X!

As stated above, dosemu uses the MIT shared memory extensions by default. Under XFree86 they are only available with Version 3.1.2 and above. If you have an older version, consider to upgrade, or configure dosemu to not use this extension (see last section)(97/2/9).

7.7   Does ansi emulation work properly?

Marty Leisner (**leisner@sdsp.mc.xerox.com**) reported (95/3/31) that

Yes. I use **nnansi.com** under X windows. I find 25, 43 and 50 line mode work properly, however 50 line mode is difficult to use on a 1024x768 screen (unless smaller fonts are used are you use a bigger screen. 43 line mode will resize the **xterm** window to use 43 lines.

8   dosemu and MS-Windows 3.1

8.1   Is it possible to run MS-Windows 3.1 under dosemu?

The **../doc/README.Windows** file says:

```
******************************************************************
*    WARNING!!! WARNING!!! WARNING!!! WARNING!!! WARNING!!!    *
*                                                              *
*  Danger Will Robinson!!!  This is not yet fully supported    *
*  and there are many known bugs!  Large programs will almost  *
*  certainly NOT WORK!!!  BE PREPARED FOR SYSTEM CRASHES IF    *
*  YOU TRY THIS!!!                                             *
*                                                              *
*    WARNING!!! WARNING!!! WARNING!!! WARNING!!! WARNING!!!    *
******************************************************************
```

Okay, it is possible to boot WINOS2 (the modified version of Windows 3.1 that OS/2 uses) under DOSEMU. Many kudos to Lutz & Dong!

However, YOU NEED BOTH LICENSES, for WINDOWS-3.1 as well OS/2 !!!

There are many known problems. Windows is prone to crash, could take data with it, large programs will not load, etc. etc. etc. In other words, it is NOT ready for daily use. Many video cards are known to have problems (you may see a nice white screen, however, look below for win31-in-xdos). Your program groups are all likely to disappear. ... Basically, it's a pain.

On the other hand, if you're dying to see the little Windows screen running under Linux and you have read this CAREFULLY and PROMISE NOT TO BOMBARD THE DOSEMU DEVELOPERS WITH "MS Word 6.0 doesn't run!!!" MESSAGES...

1. Get DOSEMU & the Linux source distributions.
2. Unpack DOSEMU.
3. Configure DOSEMU typing './configure' and do _not_ disable vm86plus.
4. Compile DOSEMU typing 'make'.
5. Get the OS2WIN31.ZIP distribution from ... ????
    ... oh well, and now you have the first problem.

It _was_ on ibm.com sometime ago, but has vanished from that site, and
as long as it was there, we could mirror it. ... you see the problem?
However, use 'archie' to find it, it will be around somewhere on the net
... for some time ;-)
5. Unpack the OS2WIN31 files into your WINDOWS\SYSTEM directory.
   (Infact you only need WINDOWS/SYSTEM/os2k386.exe and the mouse driver)
7. Startup dosemu (make certain that DPMI is set to a value such as 4096)
8. Copy the file winemu.bat to your c: drive.
9. Cross your fingers.

Good luck!

REMEMBER: THIS IS NOT AT ALL RECOMMENDED!!! THIS IS NOT RECOMMENDED!!!
           WE DO NOT RECOMMEND YOU TRY THIS!!!

8.2   Windows 3.x in xdos:

As of version 0.64.3 DOSEMU is able to run Windows in xdos. Of course, this is not recommended at all,
but if you really want to try, it is safer then starting windows-31 on the console, because _when_ it crashes,
it doesn't block your keyboard or freeze your screen.

Hints:

1. Get Dosemu & Linux source.
2. Unpack dosemu.
3. Run "./configure" to configure Dosemu (it will enable vm86plus as a
   default).
4. Type "make" to compile.
5. Get a Trident SVGA drivers for Windows. The files are tvgaw31a.zip
   and/or tvgaw31b.zip. They are available at garbo.uwasa.fi in
   /windows/drivers (any mirrors?).
6. Unpack the Trident drivers.
7. In Windows setup, install the Trident "800x600 256 color for 512K
   boards" driver.
8. Do the things described above to get and install OS2WIN31.
10. Start xdos.
11. In Dosemu, go to windows directory and start winemu.
12. Cross your fingers.

8.3   Can I install windows from within dosemu?

No you cant't. Dos will tell you something like

        The XMS driver you have on your system is not compatible with Windows...

You need to install windows from Dos. You can copy the windows tree to somewhere on your Linux
Filesystem and use lredir to mount it on the same place as it is in dos. Example:

```
You have windows in d:\windows You have d:\ mounted as /dosc in Linux You copy
the windows tree to Linux, e.g.  "cp -a /dosd/windows /usr/share Inside dosemu
you redirect the copied tree like lredir d:  linux\fs\dosd
```

Now dosemu can't mess around in you windows directory, but changes in the windows directory aren't seen by dosemu too. If you want to do the same with windows on drive c:> look in this FAQ how to redirect c:.

But you can use "setup" from inside the windows directory to install drivers and change some settings. (97/2/1497)

8.4   Notes for the mouse under win31-in-xdos:

1. Use the mouse driver "mouse.drv" from WinOS2

2. In order to let the mouse properly work you need the following in your win.ini file:

```
[windows]
MouseThreshold1=0
MouseThreshold2=0
MouseSpeed=0
```

3. The mouse cursor gets not painted by X, but by windows itself, so it depends on the refresh rate how often it gets updated, though the mouse coordinates movement itself will not get delayed. (In fact you have 2 cursors, but the X-cursor is given an 'invisible' cursor shape while within the DOS-Box.)

4. Because the coordinates passed to windows are interpreted relatively, we need to calibrate the cursor. This is done automatically whenever you enter the DOS-Box window: The cursor gets forced to 0,0 and then back to its right coordinates. Hence, if you want to re-calibrate the cursor, just move the cursor outside and then inside the DOS-Box again. (97/2/10)

8.5   Why did my Icon dissapear from the Programmanager?

MS-Windows and WinOS2 handle the program manager group different. While MS-Win store the setup in progman.ini, WinOS2 what's the conted of progman.ini in system.ini. Her a tip from (**friest@acm.org** (**Todd T. Fries**)):

```
cat progman.ini >> system.ini
```

Be sure to use >> :-)

9   Video and sound

9.1   Can I run 32-bit video games under dosemu?

Mark Rejhon (**mdrejhon@magi.com**) reported (95/4/8) that

With the recent DPMI improvements that has gone into 0.60, you can now run some 32-bit video games in dosemu. If the game is compatible in an OS/2 DOS box, there are chances that it will work in dosemu. (Example 32-bit games include Descent, Dark Forces, Mortal Kombat 2, Rise of The Triad, which have all successfully been tested in recent dosemu releases).

Before you attempt to run a video game, you must have the keyboard configured in raw keyboard mode and enabled VGA graphics modes, in the **/etc/dosemu.conf** file. If you have successfully run graphics programs in dosemu, and are prepared to take the risk of a possible system crash (this is because you are letting dosemu run with root access to the video card, and leaves the possibility of putting the video card in a bad state that is difficult to recover from) then you can go ahead and try running the video game.

Note, however, you will have to turn off the sound in the game. (Someone will have to program in sound board emulation before we can avoid this). Note that game timers can be a little bit slow, due to Linux multitasking and lack of high-frequency timer support. So the games may run from anywhere from 5 to 100 percent speed. Typically, the speed is approximately 50 percent in recent dosemu releases and is expected to improve eventually.

Who knows, it might even work. If you can't get it to work, check EMUfailure if the program is listed there, or falls in a category of programs that at present don't or probably never work with dosemu. If you think, it should be listed in EMUfailure, report to **linux-msdos@vger.rutgers.edu**

Addition from (**lermen@elserv.ffm.fgan.de**(97/2/11)):

There is a security hole when having enabled DPMI and having dosemu suid root (especially when using dos4gw-based games), the client is able to access the whole user space, hence also can modify the dosemu code itself. Use of the 'secure on' option in /etc/dosemu.conf disables this, but then you can't run those games.

9.2   Exiting from dosemu gives me a screen full of garbage.

(95/4/8)

The problem is that the font information for the VGA text screen is not being saved. Get a copy of the svgalib package. The current source is in

```
sunsite.unc.edu:/pub/Linux/libs/graphics/svgalib125.tar.gz
```

It may also be available as a pre-compiled package in your favorite Linux distribution (e.g., Slackware, etc.). Use `savetextmode` to save the current text mode and font to a file in **/tmp** before running dosemu. Then run `textmode` upon exiting dosemu to restore it.

Addition from (**lermen@elserv.ffm.fgan.de**(97/2/11)):

Have a look also at src/arch/linux/debugger/README.recover and README.dosdebug, dosdebug can aid you recovering.

9.3   How do I get dosemu to work with my Trident/Actix/other video card?

[The screen flickers violently, displays the video BIOS startup message, and hangs.]

Andrew Tridgell (**tridge@nimbus.anu.edu.au**) reported (94/1/29) that

I found with early versions it would work if I used:

```
ports { 0x42 }
```

but that sometimes my machine would crash when it was cycling the video BIOS in dosemu. This is because you're allowing the VGA BIOS to re-program your clock, which severely stuffs with Linux.

This prompted me to write the read-only and masking patches for dosemu, which I believe are still in the latest version. I now use:

```
ports { readonly 0x42 }
```

and it boots dosemu more slowly, but more reliably.

Tim Shnaider (**tims@kcbbs.gen.nz**) also reported (94/1/18) that

One way of fixing this is to use the GETROM program to dump your video BIOS to a file and edit the config file in the **/etc/dosemu** directory There will be a few video lines. Here is my video line

```
video { vga console graphics chipset trident memsize 1024 vbios_file
/etc/dosemu/vbios }
```

where vbios is the file generated by typing

```
getrom > vbios
```

Douglas Gleichman (**p86884@tcville.edsg.hac.com**) reported (94/9/1) that (with the ATI Graphics Ultra)

For dosemu 0.52 you need to add this line to your dosemu.conf file:

```
ports   { 0x1ce 0x1cf 0x238 0x23b 0x23c 0x23f 0x9ae8 0x9ae9 0x9aee 0x9aef }
```

The board self test will list a failure but graphics programs will run fine.

9.4   Why doesn't my soundcard software work with dosemu?

Hannu Savolainen (**hsavolai@cs.Helsinki.FI**) reported (94/3/21) that

The dosemu and any DOS program with it run under control of a protected mode operating system. This means that the memory is not mapped as the program expects. If it somehow manages to start DMA based recording with SB, the recorded sound doesn't find it's way to the application. It just destroys some data in the memory.

James B. MacLean (**macleajb@ednet.ns.ca**) reported (94/6/19) that

Sorry to disappoint, but at this time dosemu does not support directly the necessary interception of interrupts or DMA generally required for sound card access via dosemu :-(.

It's bound to happen at some future date though :-),

And **Corey Sweeney (orey@d94.nnb.interaccess.com)** reports (97/2/15)

```
Sound code is being currectly being worked on
```

10   Games

10.1   Duke3d dosen't work

Hans Lermen <**lermen@elserv.ffm.fgan.de**> said (97/2/16): duke3d must be 'configured' via a setup, within this setup you have to choose 'keyboard + mouse', else it won't work.

11   Other Hardware

11.1   How do I get my xxxxx device working under dosemu?

Corey Sweeney (**corey@bbs.xnet.com**) reported (94/5/30) that

Here is a log of my adventures trying to get devices working under dosemu. So far I've gotten my voice mail system working and my scanner half working. Here's how:

1. Look in your manual and find if your card uses any ports. If your manual gives you some, put them in your config file at the "ports" line. Remember that sometimes you need to have several ports in a row, and the first one might be the only one documented.

2. Try it out. If it doesn't work, or you don't have a manual (or your manual is as crappy as my AT&T manual:) then run dosemu with "**dos -D+T 2> /tmp/io.debug**". Run your device software, then exit dosemu. Look through **/tmp/io.debug** and find any port numbers it might give you. Try adding those to the port lines and try running dosemu again. Ports below 0x400 with the keyword fast don't get logged(97/2/9)!

3. If you still fail then you may need interrupts.

Find out what interrupt the card uses and verify, that the kernel isn't using the IRQ in question (cat /proc/interrupts). Hans Lermen wrote (97/2/17):

```
1. Make sure Linux doesn't use this network card

2. Set 'sillyint { use_sigio 5 }' in /etc/dosemu.conf
```

(some addittions (97/2/11)) and that's about it...

Question: What if my card uses DMA? Answer: Your screwed.

12   Problems and fixes

12.1   Security issues

A full featured Dosemu needs to be suid root, e.g to access ports. Dosemu runs as suid "root" only where it is needed, and releases this right thereafter. But with DPMI, the Dos client programm can access the whole user space, hence also can modify the dosemu code itself. Use of the 'secure on' option in /etc/dosemu.conf disables this, but then you can't run any more some applications like 32-bit video games (**lermen@elserv.ffm.fgan.de**(97/2/11)). E.g. running a well known compiler with full access might have smaller security implications then some game, obtained by some obscure source.

12.2   Dosemu dies when booting. I have Win95 installed.

Dosemu relies that the Dos-Version on the hdimage and the Drive you map to contain command.com are the same. If not, dosemu will crash sooner or later. With the dual boot option Win95 offers when pressing the F4,F5 and F8 Keys with the "Starting Win95" text, versions on the Win95 drive may swap. Take special care for command.com. Let your shell variable in config.emu point to the correct static version of command.com, e.g.: shell=c:\win95\command.com c:\ /P /E:1024 (97/02/28)

Learn about **dosdebug** and use it to control a dosemu session(97/2/9)

12.3   Dosemu hangs! How can I kill it?

Learn about **dosdebug** and use it to control a dosemu session(97/2/9)

12.4   Dosemu crashed and now I can't type anything.

Daniel Barlow(**jo95004@sable.ox.ac.uk**) reported (95/4/8) that

If you have no terminal or network access that you can use to log in, you may have to press the reset button. If you can still get a usable shell somehow, run "kbd_mode -a" to switch the keyboard out of raw mode, and/or "stty sane" on the console so that you can see what you're typing.

A useful thing to do is to use a script to run dosemu, and run "kbd_mode -a" automatically right after dosemu. When dosemu crashes, the script usually will resume running, and execute the "kbd_mode -a" command.

12.5   I've enabled EMS memory in dosemu.conf but it does not help.

Rob Janssen (**rob@pe1chl.ampr.org**) reported (94/7/11)

Don't forget to load the provided ems.sys from the config.sys file.

12.6   How do I get rid of all those annoying "disk change" messages?

(94/8/11)

Grab and install klogd. Try

```
sunsite.unc.edu:/pub/Linux/system/Daemons/sysklogd1.2.tgz
```

12.7   Why won't dosemu run a second time after exiting in console mode?

Aldy Hernandez (**aldy@sauron.cc.andrews.edu**) reported (94/7/8) that

You should disable your video and/or BIOS caching.

12.8   Why will dosemu run in a term but not in the console?

JyiJiin Luo (**jjluo@casbah.acns.nwu.edu**) reported (94/4/19) that

I experienced exactly the same problem before. I figured out all the video shadow in my AMI BIOS must be disabled. Now dosemu runs fine on my system.

12.9   How can I speed up dosemu?

In some cases it is useful to play with the value of the `HogThreshold` variable in your `dosemu.conf` file.

Daniel Barlow(**jo95004@sable.ox.ac.uk**) reported (95/4/8) that

HogThreshold should now be set to approximately half of the BogoMips value that the system reports on boot.

12.10   My CDROM drive has problems reading some files under dosemu.

Vinod G Kulkarni (**vinod@cse.iitb.ernet.in**) reported (94/4/7) that

When a CDROM is mounted from linux and used from within dosemu (mapped drive), there could be some problems. The CD-ROM driver (iso9660) in the kernel tries to find out the type of the file (i.e. binary or text). If it can't find, it tries to guess the type of the file using a heuristic. This heuristic fails under some circumstances when a (almost) text file is to be treated as binary. (I do not know if it is a bug or feature.)

The result of this is that if you copy such a file from CD-ROM (from linux itself, and not necessarily dosemu), the resulting file will be usually bigger than original file. (Blanks get added before ^J,^M.) So a program running in dosemu gives an error or hangs, which may be mistaken as problem of dosemu.

Rob Janssen (**pe1chl@rabo.nl**) reported (94/8/10) that

The way to solve this is to turn off conversion altogether. Pass the option "**-o conv=binary**" to the mount command mounting the CD-ROM, or use the following in **/etc/fstab**:

```
/dev/cdrom      /cdrom          iso9660 conv=binary,ro
```

No patches to the kernel are necessary.

12.11   How do I see debugging output?

Daniel Barlow(**jo95004@sable.ox.ac.uk**) reported (95/4/8) that

As of dosemu 0.60, debugging output is redirected to a file specified on the command line. Use "**dos -D+a -o /tmp/debug**" to log all debug output to **/tmp/debug**. There should no longer be any need to redirect `stderr`.

12.12   Why are my keystrokes echoed ttwwiiccee??

Nick Holloway (**alfie@dcs.warwick.ac.uk**) reported (94/2/22) that

After running dos after playing with some stty settings, I was getting doubled key presses. I can now reveal what the reason is!

It only happens when dos is run on the console with 'istrip' set. This is (I think) because the raw scancodes are mutilated by the 'istrip', so that key release events look like key press events.

So, the input processing needs to be turned off when using the scan codes on a console (it wouldn't be a good idea to do it for tty lines).

12.13   Dosemu scrambles my screen?

For those graphics cards not fully supported in dosemu, with allowed console graphics a dosemu crash may leave your console in a scrambles and nearly unusable way. To prepare for that situation, Spudgun <spudgun@earthlight.co.nz> posted following solution. First save your registers when running on the console ~> cat /usr/bin/savetextmode ~> restoretextmode -w /etc/textregs ~> restorefont -w /etc/fontdata Then, when a crash happened, run following script: restoretextmode -r /etc/textregs restorefont -r /etc/fontdata restorepalette

If it doesn't fix it nothing will I also found having an X server running sometimes put my Vid card's registers into a strange state where this script made things worse I think since changing X servers and/or running savetextmode on a vt while X was running helped. (97/04/08)

12.14   MS FoxPro 2.6 won't run

FoxPro 2.6 doesn't run on network drives. Alexey Naidyonov <growler@growler.tsu.tula.ru> states on that problem: And I guess your FoxPro files are on lredir'ed disk, yeah? The matter is that FoxPro doesn't run on such disk, but when I said disk { partition ... } in /etc/dosemu/conf, it runs.

13   Contributing to the dosemu project

13.1   Who is responsible for dosemu?

(97/2/9)

Dosemu is built upon the work of Matthias Lautner and Robert Sanders. James B. MacLean (**jmaclean@ednet.ns.ca**) is responsible for organizing the latest releases of dosemu.

```
                History of dosemu

    Version     Date                Person
    -------------------------------------------------
    0.1         September 3, 1992   Matthias Lautner
    0.2         September 13, 1992  Matthias Lautner
    0.3         ???                 Matthias Lautner
    0.4         November 26, 1992   Matthias Lautner
    0.47        January 27, 1993    Robert Sanders
    0.47.7      February 5, 1993    Robert Sanders
    0.48        February 16, 1993   Robert Sanders
    0.48pl1     February 18, 1993   Robert Sanders
    0.49        May 20, 1993        Robert Sanders
    0.49pl2     November 18, 1993   James MacLean
    0.49pl3     November 30, 1993   James MacLean
    0.49pl3.3   December 3, 1993    James MacLean
```

0.50	March 4, 1994	James MacLean
0.50pl1	March 18, 1994	James MacLean
0.52	June 16, 1994	James MacLean
0.60	April 9, 1995	James MacLean
0.64.4	February 9,1997	Hans Lermen

13.2   I want to help. Who should I contact?

The dosemu project is a team effort. If you wish to contribute, see the DPR (dosemu Project Registry). A current copy may be found in ../**doc/DANG** (97/2/9).

The Linux "Linux-DOS-Win95-OS2" mini-HOWTO

Mike Harlan, `r3mdh@raex.com` v1.3.1, 11 November 1997

This document presents a procedure to make 4 operating systems co-exist on a single hard disk.

Contents

Disclaimer:

Any damages inflicted on any machine by you as a result of your reading of this HOWTO is still YOUR FAULT. When you read about deleting partitions and formatting disks, be smart. Realize that doing any of the above will result in loss of data. So, BACKUP SOON, BACKUP OFTEN. This is your second-to-the-last warning.

Stuff to make the lawyers happy:

Unless otherwise stated, Linux HOWTO documents are copyrighted by their respective authors. Linux HOWTO documents may be reproduced and distributed in whole or in part, in any medium physical or electronic, as long as this copyright notice is retained on all copies. Commercial redistribution is allowed and encouraged; however, the author would like to be notified of any such distributions.

All translations, derivative works, or aggregate works incorporating Linux HOWTO documents must be covered under this copyright notice. That is, you may not produce a derivative work from a HOWTO and impose additional restrictions on its distribution. Exceptions to these rules may be granted under certain conditions; please contact the Linux HOWTO coordinator at the address given below.

In short, we wish to promote dissemination of this information through as many channels as possible. However, we do wish to retain copyright on the HOWTO documents, and would like to be notified of any plans to redistribute the HOWTOs.

If you have any questions, please contact Greg Hankins, the Linux HOWTO coordinator, at *gregh@sunsite.unc.edu* `<mailto:gregh@sunsite.unc.edu>` via email, or at +1 404 853 9989.

Updates from v1.3:

- Updated my e-mail address. My address has changed from *r3mdh@imperium.net* `<mailto: r3mdh@imperium.net>` to *r3mdh@raex.com* `<mailto:r3mdh@raex.com>`.

Updates from v1.0:

- Updated my e-mail address. My address has changed from *r3mdh@dax.cc.uakron.edu* `<mailto: r3mdh@dax.cc.uakron.edu>` to *r3mdh@imperium.net* `<mailto:r3mdh@imperium.net>`.

Now...........on with the show!

1 Introduction

After many days of struggle and frustration, I finally figured out how to accomplish what I wanted. I have a 1.2GB HD and 16MB RAM PC. I wanted to have 4 operating systems on my system: MSDOS v6.22,

Windows 95, OS/2, and Linux. Until now, I have found no Linux HOWTO to perform the task of getting each and every one of these operating systems on one machine and still have the ability to boot each (it is possible to write the OSs to different partitions, but getting them to boot and not hang at the "Starting MSDOS" message, for example, is something that I had to figure out. Well, after much trial and error, I have come up with the following recipe to perform this feat:

Before I begin going through the procedure step-by-step, let me first clue you in on what I eventually wish to accomplish:

```
<NAME>                          <SIZE>   <LABEL>   <PARTITION NUMBER>
--------------------------------------------------------------------
MSDOS v6.22                     11MB     P1        Primary Partition 1
--------------------------------------------------------------------
Windows '95                     350MB    P2        Primary Partition 2
--------------------------------------------------------------------
OS/2 Boot Manager               2MB      P3        Primary Partition 3
--------------------------------------------------------------------
DOS/Win Data                    511MB    E1        Primary Partition 4
OS/2 Warp 3.0                   127MB    E2        Extended into 4 logical
Linux Slakware 3.2 Swap         XMB      E3        drives (sub-partitions)
Linux Slakware 3.2 Native       219-XMB  E4        labeled E1-E4
--------------------------------------------------------------------
```

What does all of this mean? Well, let me talk you through it. First, we need to use up all 4 partitions on our 1 harddrive. Partitions 1 through 3 are PRIMARY partitions. We will store MSDOS, Win95 and the OS/2 Boot Manager (which inefficiently requires its OWN partition) on these partitions, respectively. We then have 1 partition left. But, we want to have a drive just for DOS/Win95 data (this gives us a large place to dump all of those ZIP files we so often download from the Internet as well as a place to store Win95 programs and data that we don't have enough room for on the Win95 partition), OS/2, and Linux (both a Linux native as well as Linux swap partition).

Now, I've been getting a lot of grief through e-mail lately about why I have a separate partition for Win95 and one for DOS and one for Win95/DOS data. Here's my answer: having separate Win95 and DOS partitions isn't for everyone. Perhaps you don't even use DOS anymore. Perhaps Windows '95 is your answer for any software written for a Microsoft platform. Well, there are some people out there who still use DOS and can't live without it. Whether it's because DOS can run 16-bit applications faster and more efficient, or because the certain DOS program that you may use won't run under a Windows environment (the Gravis Ultrasound soundcard setup program comes to mind), you simply MUST be able to boot into DOS from time to time. This HOWTO was written with those people in mind. If you still have difficulty swallowing the fact that the word "MSDOS" is included in this HOWTO, then feel free to sit down and write a Linux-Win95-OS/2-only HOWTO. :)

Now, back to the diagram above. Like I said, we have 1 partition to cram 4 things onto: DOS/Win data, OS/2, and Linux native & swap. This can be done by creating what are called logical drives (or logical partitions, depending on which book you read) within the 1 primary partition. When we create these logical drives within a primary partition, we refer to this primary partition as an EXTENDED PARTITION (because it is extended beyond the scope of a single, primary partition and instead contains up to 3 subpartitions (logical drives)). Confused? If so, you might want to read the OS/2 manual about this topic. It will explain it better than I have here.

Now, you might be scratching your head saying "he wants to cram 4 things onto that extended partition, but he just got done saying we can only have 3 subpartitions to put them on!" This is true, at least in MS-DOS's and OS/2's reasoning. But, here one of the many powerful advantages to Linux comes to save the day. Linux can create more than 3 subpartitions on an extended drive. Just how many, I don't know.

But, I know it can create at LEAST 4 (what we need). So, when we go through the steps of the installation procedure below, keep in mind that when we create partitions using an MSDOS or OS/2 program, we will only create 3 logical drives. Then, when we go to Linux, we will split one of them into two. Essentially, you can think of it as "tricking" MSDOS and OS/2 into seeing only 3 logical drives, but in reality (and to Linux), there will be 4.

2   The Procedure

NOTE:

Numbers in parentheses were the number of megabytes that I used on my 1.2GB harddrive.

Now, let's move on to the step-by-step procedure:

1. Run `view.exe` on the Linux Slakware CD and create the Linux Boot and Linux Root floppies. For some reason, the Linux bootstrap program calls the Root disk the Ramdisk floppy. I'll refer to this disk from now on as the Ramdisk (Root) floppy.

2. Backup any information that you wish to keep to tape (or whatever media you have available to you).

3. Boot your original MSDOS installation floppy, disk 1.

4. When "`Starting MSDOS`" appears, press F5 to bypass `config.sys` and `autoexec.bat`.

5. Run `a:\fdisk.exe`.

6. Delete all partitions (you have been warned: DELETING / MODIFYING OF ANY PARTITION WILL RESULT IN THE LOSS OF ALL DATA ON THE DISK!).

7. Add an MSDOS primary partition. (11MB)

8. `Format` this partition.

9. Run `a:\setup.exe` to install MSDOS on this partition.

10. Boot OS/2.

11. Select Advanced installation.

12. Run `FDISK`. (this will eventually popup for you if you run through the OS/2 installation)

13. Add 1 primary partition after the MSDOS one. This will become our Windows 95 partition. (349MB)

14. Add the Boot Manager to the next primary partition. (2MB)

15. Add an extended partition.

16. Add a logical drive to the extended partition. This will become the data portion of our MSDOS system. (511MB)

17. Add another logical drive to the extended partition. This will become our OS/2 HPFS ("High Performance File System") partition. (127MB)

18. Add 1 last logical drive to the extended partition using the remaining space on the drive. This will later become 2 partitions under Linux — our swap partition and our native Linux partition. But, since OS/2 (and DOS as well) can only write up to 6 partitions per drive (3 primary and 3 logical drives housed within 1 extended partition), we have to create only one at this time. And we DO have to create this partition. Don't leave this as free space and expect Linux to be able to create the two partitions. Due to the way that OS/2's FDISK works, where you add your last logical drive to the extended partition marks the END of the extended partition. You can**not** add partitions beyond this point. So, in other words, creating this one last logical drive serves as a space-filler for Linux. Later we will delete this partition and add 2 new ones in the space that it once took up.

19. Add partitions 1, 2, and 5 to the Boot Manager.

20. Make partition 5 installable.

    Your FDISK screen should now look like this (or something like this):

```
                              FDISK


     Disk 1

     ------------------------------------------------------------------------

     Partition Information
     Name            Status              Access          FS Type         MBytes

     ------------------------------------------------------------------------


     MSDOS           Bootable        C: Primary          FAT                11
     WIN 95          Bootable         : Primary          FAT               350
                     Startable        : Primary          BOOT MANAGER        2
                     None            D: Logical          Unformatted       511
     OS/2            Installable     E: Logical          FAT               127
                     None            F: Logical          Unformatted       219
```

---

21. Continue on with the OS/2 installation process.

22. Reboot and select partition 2 (Windows 95) from the Boot Manager.

23. When the missing operating system error pops up, boot your MSDOS installation disk. We selected this partition in order to "hide" the MSDOS partition. OS/2's Boot Manager is a bit strange. For every bootable partition you have (in our case, MSDOS and OS/2), you can have only one of them visible at a time. What this means is that if you boot into one partition, MSDOS for example, the other partition (Win95) is invisible. The MSDOS partition and Win95 essentially SHARE a drive letter. That's why under "Access" above, MSDOS has drive letter C and Win95 has no drive letter. Under the current circumstances, MSDOS is visible with drive letter C and Win95 is invisible with no drive letter. If we were to boot Win95, the opposite would be true: MSDOS would be invisible with no drive letter and Win95 would be visible with drive letter C. **An invisible drive cannot be accessed AT ALL.** If you wish to copy files between two drives in which only one can be visible at one time, you must use a common (non-bootable) drive to swap files. In our case, the DOS/Win95 Data drive (drive D 511MB above) will serve as this common drive. You might be asking "Won't we eventually be booting Linux also?". The answer is yes, we will. But let's not get into that just yet.

24. Install MSDOS to Partition 2 (we'll need this in order to install Windows 95).

25. Boot Partition 2.

26. Install Windows 95 to this partition (if you are running the upgrade version of Win95, you may need to have your Win3.1 installation disk 1 ready to insert).

27. Boot Partition 1.

28. Format Partition 4.

29. Restore DOS data from tape (if any) to partitions 1 and 4.

30. Boot the Linux Boot Floppy.

31. Follow up with the Linux Ramdisk (Root) floppy.

32. When you log in as root and get to the # prompt, type "fdisk" and press enter.

33. Delete the last partition (the one we created in step 18).

34. Add 1 16MB partition and tag it as filesystem type Linux Swap. (17MB)

35. Add 1 last partition with the remaining cylinders on the disk and tag this as filesystem type Linux native. (198MB)

36. Write the changes to the boot sector and reboot.

37. When you get to the **#** prompt again, run **setup**.

38. Install Linux to the last partition.

39. When you install LILO, be sure to install it to the root of the last partition (NOT to the MBR, as you will destroy all of your previous work in this HOWTO if you do so). Add only the last partition to LILO and set the timer to zero. By doing this, when you select Linux from the OS/2 Boot Manager, LILO will activate and will then boot Linux from the logical drive on the extended partition. Since Linux is the only partition that we wish to activate from LILO, we don't need a timer on it (unless you have more than one Kernel that you wish to load. In this case, you may want to set the timer to something more than 0 seconds).

40. Activate the Linux swap partition (refer to the Linux Installation and Getting Started Manual by Matt Welsh for this).

41. Boot OS/2.

42. Run FDISK.

43. Add Linux to the Boot Manager using the Linux NATIVE partition (type **83 not** 82!).

Your FDISK screen should now look like this (or something like this):

```
                              FDISK


        Disk 1
        ------------------------------------------------------------------

        Partition Information
        Name        Status        Access         FS Type        MBytes
        ------------------------------------------------------------------


        MSDOS       Bootable      C: Primary     FAT               11
        WIN 95      Bootable      :  Primary     FAT              350
                    Startable     :  Primary     BOOT MANAGER       2
                    None          D: Logical     FAT              511
        OS/2        Bootable      E: Logical     HPFS             127
                    None          :  Logical     Type 82           17
        Linux       Bootable      :  Logical     Type 83          198
```

...And you're done!

Send any comments/suggestions/problems (as a last resort, please!) to me at *r3mdh@raex.com* <mailto: r3mdh@raex.com>.

Mike Harlan, 11 NOV 1997

NT OS Loader + Linux mini-HOWTO

Bernd Reichert, <reichert@dial.eunet.ch>   v1.11, 2 September 1997

1   Abstract

This document describes the use of the Windows NT boot loader to start Linux. This procedures have been tested with Windows NT 4.0 WS and Linux 2.0.

2   How does the NT OS Loader work

The NT OS loader likes to have the boot sector from the other operating systems available as a file. It reads this file and starts the operating system selected, i.e. either Windows NT in different Modes or any other OS.

3   Tips on how to install Windows NT and Linux on the same System

3.1   Windows NT installation

Try to install Windows NT first. If you want to use NTFS for your Windows NT-partition, keep in mind, that the todays production version of Linux cannot access NTFS partitions. An alpha driver that can read NTFS-Partitions is available at `http://www.informatik.hu-berlin.de/~loewis/ntfs`. You may create a separate FAT-Partition for data exchange or you have to use DOS-formatted floppies.

3.2   Partitioning

Another Mini-howto recommends not to use NTs "Disk Administartor" to create the Linux swap- and root-partitions. It is sufficient to see the free space there. I also recommend to use linux's fdisk later.

3.3   Linux installation

Now boot linux from diskettes, create the swap and root-partition. Fdisk assumes the ntfs-partition to be a HPFS-partition. This is normal. Boot again from diskettes and install Linux as you like.

Just in case the installation procedure suggests that you could mount the HPFS partition which it has found: Ignore it.

3.4 Lilo

When you come to the Lilo-Section, specify your Linux-root-partition as your boot device because the Master Boot Record (MBR) of your harddisk is owned by Windows NT. This means that the root-entry and the boot-entry in your /etc/lilo.conf have the same value. If you have a IDE-harddisk and your Linux-partition is is the second partition, your boot-entry in /etc/lilo.conf looks like:

```
boot=/dev/hda2
```

If you have two disks and your Linux resides on the first partition of your second disk, your boot-entry in /etc/lilo.conf looks like:

```
boot=/dev/hdb1
```

Run lilo with a kernel that matches your system. Check the kernel by booting from diskette first if you are not sure.

If you cannot boot Windows NT now, you have a problem. I hope you have created a repair-disk recently.

4 Bootpart

There is a NT-programm called bootpart written by G. Vollant that can do the jobs from the next two points for you. Bootpart is available at http://ourworld.compuserve.com/homepages/gvollant/bootpart.htm.

If you want to know how things are working together, use the procedures described in point 5 and 6.

5 The Linux part of the work

You have to boot from diskettes until the NT-part is fixed.

Now you have to peel the bootsector from your Linux-root-Partition. With /dev/hda2 as your linux-partition, the dd-command is:

```
# dd if=/dev/hda2 of=/bootsect.lnx bs=512 count=1
```

There is something wrong if your bootsect.lnx has more than 512 bytes.

Now copy the file bootsect.lnx to a DOS-formated floppy if this is your way to transfer files to the NTFS-Windows-partition.

You can copy it with

```
# mcopy /bootsect.lnx a:
```

or with

```
# mount -t msdos /dev/fd0 /mnt
# copy /bootsect.lnx /mnt
# umount /mnt
```

6   The Windows NT part of the work

Copy the file from the diskette to C:\\bootsect.lnx. I don't tell you how to do that.

What lilo.conf is for linux is c:\\boot.ini for Windows NT. Remove the, system- and the read-only-attribute before you can modify it with:

```
C:\attrib -s -r c:\boot.ini
```

Now change the file boot.ini with an editor, notepad for example, as follows:

```
[boot loader]
timeout=30
default=multi(0)disk(0)rdisk(0)partition(1)\WINNT
[operating systems]
multi(0)disk(0)rdisk(0)partition(1)\WINNT="Windows NT Workstation ...
multi(0)disk(0)rdisk(0)partition(1)\WINNT="Windows NT Workstation ...
C:\BOOTSECT.LNX="Linux"
```

Only the last line has been added in this example. Restore the attributes after you have saved boot.ini with:

```
C:\attrib +s +r c:\boot.ini
```

After a shutdown of your Windows NT and a restart your should see the following:

```
OS Loader V4.00

Please select the operating system to start:

Windows NT Workstation Version 4.0
Windows NT Workstation Version 4.0 [VGA mode]
Linux
```

```
Select Linux and see

LILO loading zImage ....
```

7   Play it again Sam

A new copy of bootsect.lnx must be transfererd to C:\BOOTSECT.LNX evry time the bootsector of your linux-partition has been modified. This happens for example when you install a new kernel with lilo. As you can see such a system in not ideal for testing experimental kernels.

8 Troubleshooting

If things do not work as expected, check bootability with a floppy disk. With **/dev/hdb1** as your Linux-partition, your **/etc/lilo.conf** has the following entries:

```
root=/dev/hdb1
boot=/dev/fd0
```

Run lilo with a diskette inserted. Now try to boot from the diskette. If your Linux on **/dev/hdb1** can't be started, the NT OS loader will also fail to start it. If you see a lot of 01 01 01 01, your root-disk is not accessible. Check whether all your disks are known by the bios.

If the floppy boots your Linux partition, you can peel of your boot-sector for the NT OS loader with:

```
# dd if=/dev/fd0 of=/bootsect.lnx bs=512 count=1
```

You can keep this diskette as your rescue-diskette just in case your Windows NT installation breaks.

9 References

- The Linux+WindowsNT mini-HOWTO
- The FAQ for FreeBSD 2.X

10 Acknowledgements

- Thanks to Xiaoming Yi <z3c20@ttacs.ttu.edu> for the tip that the procedures work also with other disks than the first one.
- Thanks to Frank Dennler <Frank.Dennler@zkb.ch> for the diskette-trick.

11 Feedback

Any comments are welcome.

The Linux+FreeBSD mini-HOWTO

Niels Kristian Bech Jensen, nkbj@image.dk   v1.5.1, 7 February 1998

This document describes how to use Linux and FreeBSD on the same system. It introduces FreeBSD and discuss how the two operating systems can interact, e.g. by sharing swap space. You should probably have some experience with Linux and hard drive partitioning (`fdisk`) before you read this document. Do not hesitate to mail me if you have comments, questions or suggestions about this document. I would also like to hear from people who have experience using Linux together with NetBSD or OpenBSD.

Contents

1   What is FreeBSD?

FreeBSD is a free Unix-like operating system much like Linux. The main difference is that, while the Linux kernel has been written from scratch, FreeBSD is based on the freely redistributable parts of 4.4BSD (Berkeley Software Distribution) known as 4.4BSD-lite. This fact might lead some people to suggest that FreeBSD is closer to being "real" UNIX(TM) than Linux. FreeBSD runs only on the Intel PC platform (i386 and higher); a port to the DEC Alpha platform is being discussed at the moment. Hardware requirements for FreeBSD are much like those for Linux.

The development of FreeBSD is more "closed" than the Linux development. A core team of developers makes the key decisions concerning the project. Big changes are discussed in advance on the mailing lists. The FreeBSD project has two development trees (just like Linux): "-current" and "-stable". The "-current" development tree is where the development of new features is going on, while changes to the "-stable" tree mainly are bug fixes.

FreeBSD can be used and (re-)distributed freely just as Linux. Most parts of the system are released under the BSD copyright; the rest is under the GNU GPL or the GNU LGPL.

You can find more information about FreeBSD (and download the whole system) at *FreeBSD Inc.* <http://www.freebsd.org/>. The newest "-stable" releases and snapshots of the "-current" development code are sold on CDROMs by *Walnut Creek CDROM* <http://www.cdrom.com/> (their web- and ftp-servers are running FreeBSD.)

2   The FreeBSD way of labelling hard drives

Linux and FreeBSD label hard drives and partitions after two differents schemes. This section explains the main differences between the two schemes.

2.1   FreeBSD "slices" and "partitions"

FreeBSD needs only one entry in the primary partition table on your hard drive. This primary partition is called a *"slice"* in FreeBSD terminology. It then uses the program `disklabel` to make several logical partitions in this primary partition. These logical partitions are called *"partitions"* in FreeBSD terminology. This concept is similar to the way Linux (and DOS) handles logical partitions in an extended partition. Note that the Linux `fdisk` program doesn't display the partitions in a FreeBSD slice from the main menu, but it can display BSD disklabel information if you give the command 'b'. The output is something like this (`/dev/hda4` is the FreeBSD slice):

```
# fdisk /dev/hda

Command (m for help): p

Disk /dev/hda: 64 heads, 63 sectors, 621 cylinders
Units = cylinders of 4032 * 512 bytes

     Device Boot    Begin    Start     End    Blocks    Id  System
   /dev/hda1    *       1        1      27    54400+    83  Linux native
   /dev/hda2           28       28      55    56448     83  Linux native
   /dev/hda3           56       56     403    701568    83  Linux native
   /dev/hda4          404      404     621    439488    a5  BSD/386
```

```
Command (m for help): b
Reading disklabel of /dev/hda4 at sector 1624897.


BSD disklabel command (m for help): p


8 partitions:
#       size    offset   fstype   [fsize bsize    cpg]
  a:    64512   1624896   4.2BSD       0     0       0  # (Cyl.  404 - 419)
  b:   104832   1689408    swap                         # (Cyl.  420 - 445)
  c:   878976   1624896   unused       0     0          # (Cyl.  404 - 621)
  e:    64512   1794240   4.2BSD       0     0       0  # (Cyl.  446 - 461)
  f:   645120   1858752   4.2BSD       0     0       0  # (Cyl.  462 - 621)


BSD disklabel command (m for help): q
#
```

The letters 'a'...'f' in the first column are the same labels as shown below in the example for a FreeBSD slice. The letter 'b' designates the swap partition while 'c' designates the whole slice. See the FreeBSD documentation for more information on the "standard" way of assigning these letters to different partition types.

2.2 Drive and partition labelling in Linux and FreeBSD

The hard drives are labelled in the following way in Linux and FreeBSD:

	Linux	FreeBSD
First IDE drive	/dev/hda	/dev/wd0
Second IDE drive	/dev/hdb	/dev/wd1
First SCSI drive	/dev/sda	/dev/sd0
Second SCSI drive	/dev/sdb	/dev/sd1

The partitions (FreeBSD slices) on a drive are labelled in the following way (/dev/hda is used as an example):

	Linux	FreeBSD
First primary partition	/dev/hda1	/dev/wd0s1
Second primary partition	/dev/hda2	/dev/wd0s2
Third primary partition	/dev/hda3	/dev/wd0s3
Fourth primary partition	/dev/hda4	/dev/wd0s4

The partitions in a FreeBSD slice is labelled in the following way (/dev/hda4 is the FreeBSD slice in the example):

Linux label	FreeBSD label	Default FreeBSD mount point
/dev/hda5	/dev/wd0s4a	/
/dev/hda6	/dev/wd0s4b	swap
/dev/hda7	/dev/wd0s4e	/var
/dev/hda8	/dev/wd0s4f	/usr

If you run `dmesg` in Linux you will see this as (The linux kernel must be build with **UFS filesystem support** for this to work. See section 3.1 (Installing and preparing Linux)):

```
Partition check:
hda: hda1 hda2 hda3 hda4 < hda5 hda6 hda7 hda8 >
```

If you have installed FreeBSD in the `/dev/sdb3` slice, and `/dev/sdb2` is a Linux extended partition containing two logical partitions (`/dev/sdb5` and `/dev/sdb6`), the previous example would look like this:

Linux label	FreeBSD label	Default FreeBSD mount point
/dev/sdb7	/dev/sd1s3a	/
/dev/sdb8	/dev/sd1s3b	swap
/dev/sdb9	/dev/sd1s3e	/var
/dev/sdb10	/dev/sd1s3f	/usr

This will be shown as

```
Partition check:
sdb: sdb1 sdb2 < sdb5 sdb6 > sdb3 < sdb7 sdb8 sdb9 sdb10 >
```

in the output from `dmesg`.

If you have a Linux extended partition *after* your FreeBSD slice your in for trouble. Since most Linux kernels installation floppies are build without UFS support, they will not recognise the FreeBSD partitions inside the slice. What should have have been seen as (`/dev/hda3` is the FreeBSD slice and `/dev/hda4` is the Linux extended partition)

```
Partition check:
hda: hda1 hda2 hda3 < hda5 hda6 hda7 hda8 > hda4 < hda9 hda10 >
```

is seen as:

```
Partition check:
hda: hda1 hda2 hda3 hda4 < hda5 hda6 >
```

This can give you the wrong device assignment and cause the loss of data. My advice is to *always put your FreeBSD slice after any Linux extended partitions, and do not change any logical partitions in your Linux extended partitions after installing FreeBSD!*

3 Sharing swap space between Linux and FreeBSD

This section describes how I got Linux and FreeBSD to share a swap partition. There may be other ways to get the same result. This is based on Red Hat Linux release 4.1 and 4.2 (Linux kernel 2.0.29 and 2.0.30) and FreeBSD 2.2.2. You can install FreeBSD before Linux if you want to, just pay attention to the order of the partitions in the FreeBSD slice.

3.1 Installing and preparing Linux

The first step is to install Linux as normal. You have to leave space for the FreeBSD slice at you hard drive. You don't have to make a Linux swap partition, but if you want one, put it in the space you want to allocate for FreeBSD. That way you can delete the Linux swap partition later and use the space for FreeBSD.

When you have installed Linux you have to build a new kernel. Read **The Linux Kernel HOWTO** if this is new to you. You *have* to include both **UFS filesystem support (read only)** and **BSD disklabel (FreeBSD partition tables) support**.

```
UFS filesystem support (read only) (CONFIG_UFS_FS) [N/y/m/?] y
BSD disklabel (FreeBSD partition tables) support (CONFIG_BSD_DISKLABEL) [N/y/?]
(NEW) y
```

Install the new kernel and reboot. Remove any line including the word *swap* from your `/etc/fstab` file if you have made a Linux swap partition. *Make sure you have a working Linux boot floppy with the new kernel.* Now you are ready to install FreeBSD.

3.2 Installing FreeBSD

Install FreeBSD as described in the FreeBSD documentation. Remove the Linux swap partition is you have made one (you can use the FreeBSD `fdisk` program.) Pay attention to the order of the partitions in the FreeBSD slice. If you use the default labelling the second partition will be the swap partition. Complete the installation of FreeBSD and reboot into Linux *using the new Linux boot floppy*.

3.3 Setting up the FreeBSD swap partition in Linux

Run `dmesg` when you have booted into Linux. In the output you should see something like this:

```
Partition check:
 hda: hda1 hda2 hda3 hda4 < hda5 hda6 hda7 hda8 >
```

This means that `/dev/hda4` is your FreeBSD slice, while `/dev/hda5`, `/dev/hda6`, `/dev/hda7` and `/dev/hda8` are the FreeBSD partitions. If your swap partition is the second partition in the slice, it will be `/dev/hda6`.

You have to put the following line into your `/etc/fstab` file to enable the swap partition:

```
/dev/hda6        none        swap        sw        0        0
```

While FreeBSD can use any type of partition as swap space, Linux needs a special signature in the swap partition. This signature is made by `mkswap`. FreeBSD ruins this signature when it uses the shared swap partition, so you will have to run `mkswap` each time you boot into Linux. To do this automagically you have to find the script that runs `swapon` at boot time. In Red Hat Linux it is `/etc/rc.d/rc.sysinit`. Put the following line into that file just *before* `swapon -a`:

```
awk -- '/swap/ && ($1 !~ /#/) { system("mkswap "$1"") }' /etc/fstab
```

This will run `mkswap` on any swap partitions in `/etc/fstab` every time you boot except if they are commented out (having "#" as the first character in the line.)

Run `free` to check out the size of the swap space when you have rebooted into Linux. You should also reboot into FreeBSD to make sure everything works as expected. If it does not, you have probably used the wrong partition as swap partition. The only solution to that problem is to reinstall FreeBSD and try again. Experience is a great teacher. :-)

4 Booting FreeBSD using LILO

You can easily boot FreeBSD with LILO. Do not install the FreeBSD boot loader (`Booteasy`) if you want to use LILO. Append the following lines to your `/etc/lilo.conf` file and run `lilo` (the FreeBSD slice being `/dev/hda4`):

```
other=/dev/hda4
        table=/dev/hda
        label=FreeBSD
```

If you have installed FreeBSD on the second SCSI drive, use something like this (the FreeBSD slice being `/dev/sdb2`):

```
other=/dev/sdb2
        table=/dev/sdb
        loader=/boot/chain.b
        label=FreeBSD
```

5 Mounting file systems

5.1 Mounting UFS file systems under Linux

Unfortunately the UFS driver in the Linux 2.0.xx kernels (and 2.1.xx kernels; but that is being worked on) does not include support for FreeBSD. When you try to mount a FreeBSD file system, you just get some error messages (the file system actually gets mounted, but you cannot read anything from it.)

There is another version of the UFS driver for Linux 2.0.xx kernels (xx <= 30) on *SunSite* <ftp://sunsite.unc.edu/pub/Linux/ALPHA/ufs/>. It is called **U2FS** and the current version is `u2fs-0.4.3.tar.gz`. A version of U2FS (`ufs-0.4.4.tar.gz`) for Linux 2.0.31 and higher (2.0.xx; not 2.1.xx) can be found at *this site* <http://www.mathi.uni-heidelberg.de/~flight/projects/u2fs/> along with further information about U2FS (and UFS.)

Now you have to build a new kernel with support for the U2FS file system and BSD disklabels. See section 3.1 (Installing and preparing Linux) for more information on this. You can leave out **UFS filesystem support** from the kernel when you use U2FS.

When you have installed the new kernel, you can mount your UFS file systems (all the partitions in the FreeBSD slice except the swap partition) with a command like this:

```
mount -t u2fs /dev/hda8 /mnt
```

The UFS driver is read-only. That is; you can read from the UFS file systems but you cannot write to them.

5.2 Mounting ext2fs file systems under FreeBSD

To mount ext2fs file systems under FreeBSD, you first have to build a new kernel with ext2fs support. Read the FreeBSD documentation to learn how to do that. Put the line

```
options         "EXT2FS"
```

in your kernel configuration file for the new kernel.

When you have booted with the new kernel, you can mount an ext2fs file system by giving a command like:

```
mount -t ext2fs /dev/wd0s3 /mnt
```

Note that you cannot mount ext2fs file systems in extended partitions from FreeBSD.

Due to a bug in FreeBSD you will have to unmount all ext2fs file systems *before* you shut down FreeBSD. If you shut down FreeBSD with an ext2fs file system mounted, FreeBSD cannot sync the UFS file systems. This results in `fsck` being run the next time FreeBSD is booted. This bug is reported to have been fixed in the "-current" development tree.

6 Running foreign binaries

6.1 Running FreeBSD binaries under Linux

The `iBCS` package has support for running FreeBSD binaries under Linux; but it's old and unmaintained. I can't get it to work. Please let me know if you have had better luck with this.

6.2 Running Linux binaries under FreeBSD

FreeBSD has the ability to run Linux binaries, both in a.out and ELF formats. To do this you have to take the following three steps:

1. You have to enable Linux compatibility. To do this (in FreeBSD 2.2.2 — details may vary in other versions) you have to edit your `/etc/rc.conf` file and change

   ```
   linux_enable="NO"
   ```

   to

   ```
   linux_enable="YES"
   ```

2. You have to install the Linux shared libraries. They are included in FreeBSD 2.2.2 as the package `linux_lib-2.4.tgz` (a newer version might be out now.) Run the command

   ```
   pkg_add <path_to_package>/linux_lib-2.4.tgz
   ```

   to install the package. <path_to_package> is the directory where the package is stored.

3. Install the Linux program(s) you want to run. The program(s) can be installed on either UFS or ext2fs file systems. See section 5.2 (Mounting ext2fs file systems under FreeBSD) for more information about using ext2fs file systems under FreeBSD.

I have successfully run the Linux versions of Applixware 4.3 and Netscape 3.01 (both ELF format) under FreeBSD 2.2.2 using this method (yes, I know there is a native FreeBSD version of Netscape 4.) Read the FreeBSD documentation for more information on this topic.

7 References and other documents of interest

The latest version of this mini-HOWTO can be downloaded from *my homepage* `<http://www.image.dk/nkbj/>` in several formats (including SGML and PostScript.) The document has been translated into Japanese by Mr. Teruyoshi Fujiwara as part of *the JF project* `<ftp://jf.linux.or.jp/pub/JF/other-formats/>`.

Gregor Hoffleit maintains a *homepage* `<http://www.mathi.uni-heidelberg.de/~flight/projects/u2fs/>` with information about the developement of U2FS and UFS.

The FreeBSD Handbook and The FreeBSD FAQ are distributed with FreeBSD. They can also be found at *FreeBSD Inc.* `<http://www.freebsd.org/>`. This site has a lot of other information about FreeBSD too.

The Linux Kernel HOWTO is released as part of *The Linux Documentation Project* `<http://sunsite.unc.edu/LDP/>`.

8 Acknowledgments and Copyright

Thanks to the members of the **BSD user group in Denmark* `<http://hotel.prosa.dk/bsd-dk/>` for answering the questions of a FreeBSD newbie and to Mr. Takeshi Okazaki for bringing the existence of U2FS to my attention.

8.1 Disclaimer

Although the information given in this document is believed to be correct, the authors will accept no liability for the content of this document. Use the tips and examples given herein at your own risk.

8.2 Copyright

Copyright (c) 1997, 1998 by Niels Kristian Bech Jensen. This document may be distributed only subject to the terms and conditions set forth in *the LDP license* `<http://sunsite.unc.edu/LDP/LICENSE.html>`.

Linux Access HOWTO

Michael De La Rue, <*access-howto@ed.ac.uk*> `<mailto:access-howto@ed.ac.uk>`   v2.11, 28 March 1997

The Linux Access HOWTO covers the use of adaptive technology with Linux, In particular, using adaptive technology to make Linux accessible to those who could not use it otherwise. It also covers areas where Linux can be used within more general adaptive technology solutions.

Contents

1   Introduction

The aim of this document is to serve as an introduction to the technologies which are available to make Linux usable by people who, through some disability would otherwise have problems with it. In other words the target groups of the technologies are, the blind, the partially sighted, deaf and the physically disabled. As any other technologies or pieces of information are discovered they will be added.

The information here not just for these people (although that is probably the main aim) but also to allow developers of Linux to become aware of the difficulties involved here. Possibly the biggest problem is that, right now, very few of the developers of Linux are aware of the issues and various simple ways to make life simpler for implementors of these systems. This has, however, changed noticeably since the introduction of this document, and at least to a small extent because of this document, but also to a large extent due to the work of some dedicated developers, many of whom are mentioned in the document's Acknowledgements.

Please send any comments or extra information or offers of assistance to *<access-howto@ed.ac.uk>* `<mailto:access-howto@ed.ac.uk>` This address might become a mailing list in future, or be automatically handed over to a future maintainer of the HOWTO, so please don't use it for personal email.

I don't have time to follow developments in all areas. I probably won't even read a mail until I have time to update this document. It's still gratefully received. If a mail is sent to the blind-list or the access-list, I *will* eventually read it and put any useful information into the document. Otherwise, please send a copy of anything interesting to the above email address.

Normal mail can be sent to

```
Linux Access HOWTO
23 Kingsborough Gardens
Glasgow G12 9NH
Scotland
U.K.
```

And will gradually make its way round the world to me. Email will be faster by weeks.

I can be personally contacted using *<miked@ed.ac.uk>* `<mailto:miked@ed.ac.uk>`. Since I use mail filtering on all mail I receive, please use the other address except for personal email. This is most likely to lead to an appropriate response.

1.1 Distribution Policy

```
The ACCESS-HOWTO is copyrighted (c) 1996 Michael De La Rue

The ACCESS-HOWTO may be distributed, at your choice, under either the terms of
the GNU Public License version 2 or later or the standard Linux Documentation
project terms.  These licenses should be available from where you got this
document.  Please note that since the LDP terms don't allow modification (other
than translation), modified versions can be assumed to be distributed under the
GPL.
```

2 Comparing Linux with other Operating Systems

2.1 General Comparison

The best place to find out about this is in such documents as the 'Linux Info Sheet', 'Linux Meta FAQ' and 'Linux FAQ' (see 7.1 (Linux Documentation)). Major reasons for a visually impaired person to use Linux would include it's inbuilt networking which gives full access to the Internet. More generally, users are attracted by the full development environment included. Also, unlike most other modern GUI environments, the graphical front end to Linux (X Windows) is clearly separated from the underlying environment and there is a complete set of modern programs such as World Wide Web browsers and fax software which work directly in the non graphical environment. This opens up the way to provide alternative access paths to the systems functionality; Emacspeak is a good example.

For other users, the comparison is probably less favourable and less clear. People with very specific and complex needs will find that the full development system included allows properly customised solutions. However, much of the software which exists on other systems is only just beginning to become available. More development is being done however in almost all directions.

2.2   Availability of Adaptive Technology

There is almost nothing commercial available *specifically* for Linux. There is a noticeable amount of free software which would be helpful in adaptation, for example, a free speech synthesiser and some free voice control software. There are also a number of free packages which provide good support for certain Braille terminals, for example.

2.3   Inherent Usability

Linux has the vast advantage over Windows that most of it's software is command line oriented. This is now changing and almost everything is now available with a graphical front end. However, because it is in origin a programmers operating system, line oriented programs are still being written covering almost all new areas of interest. For the physically disabled, this means that it is easy to build custom programs to suit their needs. For the visually impaired, this should make use with a speech synthesiser or Braille terminal easy and useful for the foreseeable future.

Linux's multiple virtual consoles system make it practical to use as a multi-tasking operating system by a visually impaired person working directly through Braille.

The windowing system used by Linux (X11) comes with many programming tools, and should be adaptable. However, in practice, the adaptive programs available up till now have been more primitive than those on the Macintosh or Windows. They are, however, completely free (as opposed to hundreds of pounds) and the quality is definitely improving.

In principle it should be possible to put together a complete, usable Linux system for a visually impaired person for about $500 (cheap & nasty PC + sound card). This compares with many thousands of dollars for other operating systems (screen reader software/ speech synthesiser hardware). I have yet to see this. I doubt it would work in practice because the software speech synthesisers available for Linux aren't yet sufficiently good. For a physically disabled person, the limitation will still be the expense of input hardware.

3   Visually Impaired

I'll use two general categories here. People who are partially sighted and need help seeing / deciphering / following the text and those who are unable to use any visual interface whatsoever.

3.1   Seeing the Screen with Low Vision

There are many different problems here. Often magnification can be helpful, but that's not the full story. Sometimes people can't track motion, sometimes people can't find the cursor unless it moves. This calls for a range of techniques, the majority of which are only just being added to X.

3.1.1   SVGATextMode

This program is useful for improving the visibility of the normal text screen that Linux provides. The normal screen that Linux provides shows 80 characters across by 25 vertically. This can be changed (and the quality of those characters improved) using SVGATextMode. The program allows full access to the possible modes of an SVGA graphics card. For example, the text can be made larger so that only 50 by 15 characters appear on the screen. There isn't any easy way to zoom in on sections of a screen, but you can resize when needed.

3.1.2   X Window System

For people who can see the screen there are a large number of ways of improving X. They don't add up to a coherent set of features yet, but if set up correctly could solve many problems.

Different Screen Resolutions   The X server can be set up with many different resolutions. A single key press can then change between them allowing difficult to read text to be seen.

In the file /etc/XF86Config, you have an entry in the Screen section with a line beginning with modes. If, for example, you set this to

```
Modes        "1280x1024" "1024x768" "800x600" "640x480" "320x240"
```

with each mode set up correctly (which requires a reasonably good monitor for the highest resolution mode), you will be able to have four times screen magnification, switching between the different levels using

Ctrl+Alt+Keypad-Plus and **Ctrl+Alt+Keypad-Minus**

Moving the mouse around the screen will scroll you to different parts of the screen. For more details on how to set this up you should see the documentation which comes with the **XFree86** X server.

Screen Magnification   There are several known screen magnification programs, xmag which will magnify a portion of the screen as much as needed but is very primitive. Another one is xzoom. Previously I said that there had to be something better than xmag, well this is it. See section 8.6 (xzoom).

Another program which is available is puff. This is specifically oriented towards visually impaired users. It provides such features as a box around the pointer which makes it easier to locate. Other interesting features of puff are that, if correctly set up, it is able to select and magnify portions of the screen as they are updated. However, there seem to be interacations between xpuff and the window manager which could make it difficult to use. When used with my fvwm setup, it didn't respond at all to key presses. However using twm improved the situation.

The final program which I have seen working is dynamag. This again has some specific advantages such as the ability to select a specific area of the screen and monitor it, refreshing the magnified display at regular intervals between a few tenths of a second at twenty seconds. dynamag is part of the UnWindows distribution. See 8.8 (UnWindows) for more details.

Change Screen Font   The screen fonts all properly written X software should be changeable. You can simply make it big enough for you to read. This is generally accomplished by putting a line the file .Xdefaults which should be in your home directory. By putting the correct lines in this you can change the fonts of your programs, for example

```
Emacs.font: -sony-fixed-medium-r-normal--16-150-75-75-c-80-iso8859-*
```

To see what fonts are available, use the program xfontsel under X.

There should be some way of changing things at a more fundamental level so that everything comes out with a magnified font. This could be done by renaming fonts, and by telling telling font generating programs to use a different level of scaling. If someone gets this to work properly, please send me the details of how you did it.

Cross Hair Cursors etc.. For people that have problems following cursors there are many things which can help;

- cross-hair cursors (horizontal and vertical lines from the edge of the screen)
- flashing cursors (flashes when you press a key)

No software I know of specifically provides a cross hair cursor. `puff`, mentioned in the previous section does however provide a flashing box around the cursor which can make it considerably easier to locate.

For now the best that can be done is to change the cursor bitmap. Make a bitmap file as you want it, and another one which is the same size, but completely black. Convert them to the XBM format and run

```
xsetroot -cursor cursorfile.xbm black-file.xbm
```

actually, if you understand masks, then the black-file doesn't have to be completely black, but start with it like that. The `.Xdefaults` file controls cursors used by actual applications. For much more information, please see the X Big Cursor mini-HOWTO, by Joerg Schneider <*schneid@ira.uka.de*> <mailto:schneid@ ira.uka.de>.

3.1.3 Audio

Provided that the user can hear, audio input can be very useful for making a more friendly and communicative computing environment. For a person with low vision, audio clues can be used to help locate the pointer (see 8.8 (UnWindows)). For a console mode user using Emacspeak (see 8.1 (Emacspeak)), the audio icons available will provide very many useful facilities.

Setting up Linux audio is covered in the Linux Sound HOWTO (see 7.1 (Linux Documentation)). Once sound is set up, sounds can be played with the `play` command which is included with most versions of Linux. This is the way to use my version of UnWindows.

3.1.4 Producing Large Print

Using large print with Linux is quite easy. There are several techniques.

LaTeX / TeX LaTeX is an extremely powerful document preparation system. It may be used to produce large print documents of almost any nature. Though somewhat complicated to learn, many documents are produced using LaTeX or the underlying typesetting program, TeX.

this will produce some reasonably large text

```
\font\magnifiedtenrm=cmr10 at 20pt  % setup a big font
\magnifiedtenrm
this is some large text
\bye
```

For more details, see the LaTeX book which is available in any computer book shop. There are also a large number of introductions available on the internet.

3.1.5   Outputting Large Text

Almost all Linux printing uses postscript, and Linux can drive almost any printer using it. I output large text teaching materials using a standard Epson dot matrix printer.

For users of X, there are various tools available which can produce large Text. These include `LyX`, and many commercial word processors.

3.2   Aids for Those Who Can't Use Visual Output

For someone who is completely unable to use a normal screen there are two alternatives Braille and Speech. Obviously for people who also have hearing loss, speech isn't always useful, so Braille will always be important.

If you can choose, which should you choose? This is a matter of 'vigorous' debate. Speech is rapid to use, reasonably cheap and especially good for textual applications (e.g. reading a long document like this one). Problems include needing a quiet environment, possibly needing headphones to work without disturbing others and avoid being listened in on by them (not available for all speech synthesisers).

Braille is better for applications where precise layout is important (e.g. spreadsheets). Also can be somewhat more convenient if you want to check the beginning of a sentence when you get to the end. Braille is, however, much more expensive and slower for reading text. Obviously, the more you use Braille, the faster you get. Grade II Braille is difficult to learn, but is almost certainly worth it since it is much faster. This means that if you don't use Braille for a fair while you can never discover its full potential and decide for yourself. Anyway, enough said on this somewhat controversial topic.

based on original by James Bowden <*jrbowden@bcs.org.uk*> `<mailto:jrbowden@bcs.org.uk>`

3.2.1   Braille Terminals

Braille terminals are normally a line or two of Braille. Since these are at most 80 characters wide and normally 40 wide, they are somewhat limited. I know of two kinds

- Hardware driven Braille terminals.
- Software driven Braille terminals.

The first kind works only when the computer is in text mode and reads the screen memory directly. See section 9.1 (hardware driven Braille terminals).

The second kind of Braille terminal is similar, in many ways, to a normal terminal screen of the kind Linux supports automatically. Unfortunately, they need special software to make them usable.

There are two packages which help with these. The first, `BRLTTY`, works with several Braille display types and the authors are keen to support more as information becomes available. Currently `BRLTTY` supports Tieman B.V.'s CombiBraille series, Alva B.V.'s ABT3 series and Telesensory Systems Inc.'s PowerBraille and Navigator series displays. The use of Blazie Engineering's Braille Lite as a Braille display is discouraged, but support may be renewed on demand. See section 9.2 (Software Braille Terminals).

The other package I am aware of is Braille Enhanced Screen. This is designed to work on other UNIX systems as well as Linux. This should allow user access to a Braille terminal with many useful features such as the ability to run different programs in different 'virtual terminals' at the same time.

3.2.2   Speech Synthesis

Speech Synthesisers take (normally) ASCII text and convert it into actual spoken output. It is possible to have these implemented as either hardware or software. Unfortunately, the free Linux speech synthesisers are, reportedly, not good enough to use as a sole means of output.

Hardware speech synthesisers are the alternative. The main one that I know of that works is DECtalk from Digital, driven by `emacspeak`. However, at this time (March 1997) a driver for the Doubletalk synthesiser has been announced. Using `emacspeak` full access to all of the facilities of Linux is fairly easy. This includes the normal use of the shell, a world wide web browser and many other similar features, such as email. Although, it only acts as a plain text reader (similar to IBM's one for the PC) when controling programs it doesn't understand, with those that it does, it can provide much more sophisticated control. See section 8.1 (Emacspeak) for more information about `emacspeak`.

3.2.3   Handling Console Output

When it starts up, Linux at present puts all of its messages straight to the normal (visual) screen. This could be changed if anyone with a basic level of kernel programming ability wants to do it. This means that it is impossible for most Braille devices to get information about what Linux is doing before the operating system is completely working.

It is only at that stage that you can start the program that you need for access. If the `BRLTTY` program is used and run very early in the boot process, then from this stage on the messages on the screen can be read. Most hardware and software will still have to wait until the system is completely ready. This makes administering a Linux system difficult, but not impossible for a visually impaired person. Once the system is ready however, you can scroll back by pressing (on the default keyboard layout) Shift-PageUP.

There is one Braille system that can use the console directly, called the Braillex. This is designed to read directly from the screen memory. Unfortunately the normal scrolling of the terminal gets in the way of this. If you are using a Kernel newer than 1.3.75, just type `linux no-scroll` at the LILO prompt or configure LILO to do this automatically. If you have an earlier version of Linux, see section 9.1 (Screen Memory Braille Terminals)

The other known useful thing to do is to use sounds to say when each stage of the boot process has been reached. (T.V. Raman suggestion)

3.2.4   Optical Character Recognition

There is a free Optical Character Recognition (OCR) program for Linux called `xocr`. In principle, if it is good enough, this program would allow visually impaired people to read normal books to some extent (accuracy of OCR is never high enough..). However, according to the documentation, this program needs training to recognise the particular font that it is going to use and I have no idea how good it is since I don't have the hardware to test it.

3.3   Beginning to Learn Linux

Beginning to learn Linux can seem difficult and daunting for someone who is either coming from no computing background or from a pure DOS background. Doing the following things may help:

- Learn to use Linux (or UNIX) on someone else's system before setting up your own.

- Initially control Linux from your own known speaking/Braille terminal. If you plan to use speech, you may want to learn `emacs` now. You can learn it as you go along though. See below

- If you come from an MS-DOS background, read the DOS2Linux Mini HOWTO for help with converting (see 7.1.4 (The Linux HOWTO Documents)).

The Emacspeak HOWTO written by Jim Van Zandt (<*jrv@vanzandt.mv.com*> <mailto:jrv@vanzandt.mv.com>) covers this in much more detail (see 7.1.4 (The Linux HOWTO Documents)).

If you are planning to use Emacspeak, you should know that Emacspeak does not attempt to teach Emacs, so in this sense, prior knowledge of Emacs would always be useful. This said, you certainly do not need to know much about Emacs to start using Emacspeak. In fact, once Emacspeak is installed and running, it provides a fluent interface to the rich set of online documentation including the info pages, and makes learning what you need a lot easier.

"In summary: starting to use Emacspeak takes little learning. Getting the full mileage out of Emacs and Emacspeak, especially if you intend using it as a replacement for X Windows as I do does involve eventually becoming familiar with a lot of the Emacs extensions; but this is an incremental process and does not need to be done in a day." - *T.V.Raman*

One other option which may be interesting are the RNIB training tapes which include one covering UNIX. These can be got from

```
RNIB
Customer Services
PO Box 173
Peterborough
Cambridgeshire PE2 6WS
Tel: 01345 023153 (probably only works in UK)
```

3.4   Braille Embossing

Linux should be the perfect platform to drive a Braille embosser from. There are many formatting tools which are aimed specifically at the fixed width device. A Braille embosser can just be connected to the serial port using the standard Linux printing mechanisms. For more info see the Linux Printing HOWTO.

There is a free software package which acts as a multi-lingual grade two translator available for Linux from the American "National Federation for the Blind". This is called NFBtrans. See section 8.7 (NFB translator) for more details.

4   Hearing Problems

For the most part there is little problem using a computer for people with hearing problems. Almost all of the output is visual. There are some situations where sound output is used though. For these, the problem can sometimes be worked round by using visual output instead.

4.1   Visual Bells

By tradition, computers go 'beep' when some program sends them a special code. This is generally used to get attention to the program and for little else. Most of the time, it's possible to replace this by making the entire screen (or terminal emulator) flash. How to do this is very variable though.

xterm (under X)

for xterm, you can either change the setting by pressing the middle mouse button while holding down the control key, or by putting a line with just 'XTerm*visualBell: true' (not the quotes of course) in the file .Xdefaults in your home directory.

the console (otherwise)

The console is slightly more complex. Please see Alessandro Rubini's Visual Bell mini HOWTO for details on this. Available along with all the other Linux documentation (see section 7.1 (other Linux documents)). Mostly the configuration has to be done on a per application basis, or by changing the Linux Kernel its self.

5   Physical Problems

Many of these problems have to be handled individually. The needs of the individual, the ways that they can generate input and other factors vary so much that all that this HOWTO can provide is a general set of pointers to useful software and expertise.

5.1   Unable to Use a Mouse/Pointer

Limited mobility can make it difficult to use a mouse. For some people a tracker ball can be a very good solution, but for others the only possible input device is a keyboard (or even something which simulates a keyboard). For normal use of Linux this shouldn't be a problem (but see the section 5.3 (Making the keyboard behave)), but for users of X, this may cause major problems under some circumstances.

Fortunately, the fvwm window manager has been designed for use without a pointer and most things can be done using this. I actually do this myself when I lose my mouse (don't ask) or want to just keep typing. fvwm is included with all distributions of Linux that I know of. Actually using other programs will depend on their ability to accept key presses. Many X programs do this for all functions. Many don't. I sticky mouse keys, which are supposedly present in the current release of X should make this easier.

5.1.1   Unable to Use a Keyboard

People who are unable to use a keyboard normally can sometimes use one through a headstick or a mouth-stick. This calls for special setup of the keyboard. Please see also the section 5.3 (Making the keyboard behave).

Other Input Hardware (X Windows System only)   For others, the keyboard cannot be used at all and only pointing devices are available. In this case, no solution is available under the standard Linux Console and X will have to be used. If the X-Input extension can be taught to use the device and the correct software for converting pointer input to characters can be found (I haven't seen it yet) then any pointing should be usable without a keyboard.

There are a number of devices worth considering for such input such as touch screens and eye pointers. Many of these will need a 'device driver' written for them. This is not terribly difficult if the documentation is available, but requires someone with good C programming skills. Please see the *Linux Kernel Hackers guide* and other kernel reference materials for more information. Once this is set up, it should be possible to use these devices like a normal mouse.

5.1.2 Controlling Physical Hardware From Linux

The main group of interest here are the Linux Lab Project. Generally, much GPIB (a standard interface to scientific equipment, also known as the IEEE bus) hardware can be controlled. This potentially gives much potential for very ambitious accessibility projects. As far as I know none have yet been attempted.

5.2 Speech Recognition

Speech recognition is a very powerful tool for enabling computer use. There are two recognition systems that I know of for Linux, the first is **ears** which is described as "recognition is not optimal. But it is fine for playing and will be improved", the second is **AbbotDemo** "A speaker independent continuous speech recognition system" which may well be more interesting, though isn't available for commercial use without prior arrangement. See the Linux software map for details (see section 7.1 (other Linux documents)).

5.3 Making the Keyboard Behave

5.3.1 X Window System.

The latest X server which comes with Linux can include many features which assist in input. This includes such features as StickKeys, MouseKeys, RepeatKeys, BounceKeys, SlowKeys, and TimeOut. These allow customisation of the keyboard to the needs of the user. These are provided as part of the XKB> extension in versions of X after version 6.1. To find out your version and see whether you have the extension installed, you can try.

```
xdpyinfo -queryExtensions
```

5.3.2 Getting Rid of Auto Repeat

To turn off key repeat on the Linux console run this command (I think it has to be run once per console; a good place to run it would be in your login files, `.profile` or `.login` in your home directory).

```
setterm -repeat off
```

To get rid of auto repeat on any X server, you can use the command

```
xset -r
```

which you could put into the file which get runs when you start using X (often `.xsession` or `.xinit` under some setups)

Both of these commands are worth looking at for more ways of changing behaviour of the console.

5.3.3 Macros / Much input, few key presses

Often in situations such as this, the biggest problem is speed of input. Here the most important thing to aim for is the most number of commands with the fewest key presses. For users of the shell (`bash` / `tcsh`) you should look at the manual page, in particular command and filename completion (press the tab key and bash tries to guess what should come next). For information on macros which provide sequences of commands for just one key press, have a look at the Keystroke HOWTO.

5.3.4 Sticky Keys

Sticky keys are a feature that allow someone who can only reliably press one button at a time to use a keyboard with all of the various modifier keys such as shift and control. These keys, instead of having to be held on at the same time as the other key instead become like the caps lock key and stay on while the other key is pressed. They may then either switch off or stay on for the next key depending on what is needed. For information about how to set this up please see the Linux Keyboard HOWTO, especially section 'I can use only one finger to type with' (section 15 in the version I have) for more information on this. - Information from Toby Reed.

6   General Programming Issues

Many of the issues worth taking into account are the same when writing software which is designed to be helpful for access as when trying to follow good design.

6.1   Try to Make it Easy to Provide Multiple Interfaces

If your software is only usable through a graphical interface then it can be very hard to make it usable for someone who can't see. If it's only usable through a line oriented interface, then someone who can't type will have difficulties.

Provide keyboard shortcuts as well as the use of the normal X pointer (generally the mouse). You can almost certainly rely on the user being able to generate key presses to your application.

6.2   Make software configurable.

If it's easy to change fonts then people will be able to change to one they can read. If the colour scheme can be changed then people who are colour blind will be more likely to be able to use it. If fonts can be changed easily then the visually impaired will find your software more useful.

6.3   Test the Software on Users.

If you have a number of people use your software, each with different access problems then they will be more likely to point up specific problems. Obviously, this won't be practical for everybody, but you can always ask for feedback.

6.4   Make Output Distinct

Where possible, make it clear what different parts of your program are what. Format error messages in a specific way to identify them. Under X, make sure each pane of your window has a name so that any screen reader software can identify it.

6.5   Licenses

Some software for Linux (though none of the key programs) has license like 'not for commercial use'. This could be quite bad for a person who starts using the software for their personal work and then possibly begins to be able to do work they otherwise couldn't with it. This could be something which frees them from financial and other dependence on others people. Even if the author of the software is willing to make exceptions, it makes the user vulnerable both to changes of commercial conditions (some company buys up the rights) and to refusal from people they could work for (many companies are overly paranoid about licenses). It is much better to avoid this kind of licensing where possible. Protection from commercial abuse of software can be obtained through more specific licenses like the GNU Public License or Artistic License where needed.

7   Other Information

7.1   Linux Documentation

The Linux documentation is critical to the use of Linux and most of the documents mentioned here should be included in recent versions of Linux, from any source I know of.

If you want to get the documentation on the Internet, here are some example sites. These should be mirrored at most of the major FTP sites in the world.

- ftp.funet.fi (128.214.6.100) : */pub/OS/Linux/doc/* <ftp://ftp.funet.fi/pub/OS/Linux/doc/>
- tsx-11.mit.edu (18.172.1.2) : */pub/linux/docs/* <ftp://tsx-11.mit.edu/pub/linux/docs/>
- sunsite.unc.edu (152.2.22.81) : */pub/Linux/docs/* <ftp://sunsite.unc.edu/pub/Linux/docs/>

7.1.1   The Linux Info Sheet

A simple and effective explanation of what Linux is. This is one of the things that you should hand over when you want to explain why you want Linux and what it is good for.

The Linux Info Sheet is available on the World Wide Web from <http://sunsite.unc.edu/mdw/HOWTO/INFO-SHEET.html> and other mirrors.

7.1.2   The Linux Meta FAQ

A list of other information resources, much more complete than this one. The meta FAQ is available on the World Wide Web from <http://sunsite.unc.edu/mdw/HOWTO/META-FAQ.html> and other mirrors

7.1.3   The Linux Software Map

The list of software available for Linux on the Internet. Many of the packages listed here were found through this. The LSM is available in a searchable form from <http://www.boutell.com/lsm/>. It is also available in a single text file in all of the FTP sites mentioned in section 7.1 (Linux Documentation).

7.1.4   The Linux HOWTO documents

The HOWTO documents are the main documentation of Linux. This Access HOWTO is an example of one.

The home site for the Linux Documentation Project which produces this information is <http://sunsite.unc.edu/mdw/linux.html>. There are also many companies producing these in book form. Contact a local Linux supplier for more details.

The Linux HOWTO documents will be in the directory HOWTO in all of the FTP sites mentioned in section 7.1 (Linux Documentation).

7.1.5   The Linux FAQ

A list of 'Frequently Asked Questions' with answers which should solve many common questions. The FAQ list is available from `<http://www.cl.cam.ac.uk/users/iwj10/linux-faq/>` as well as all of the FTP sites mentioned in section 7.1 (Linux Documentation).

7.2   Mailing Lists

There are two lists that I know of covering these issues specifically for Linux. There are also others which it is worth researching which cover computer use more generally. Incidentally, if a mail is sent to these lists I *will* read it eventually and include any important information in the Access-HOWTO, so you don't need to send me a separate copy unless it's urgent in some way.

7.2.1   The Linux Access List

This is a general list covering Linux access issues. It is designed 'to service the needs of users and developers of the Linux OS and software who are either disabled or want to help make Linux more accessible'. To subscribe send email to *<majordomo@ssv1.union.utah.edu>* `<mailto:majordomo@ssv1.union.utah.edu>` and in the BODY (not the subject) of the email message put:

```
subscribe linux-access <your-email-address>
```

7.2.2   The Linux Blind List

This is a mailing list covering Linux use for blind users. There is also a list of important and useful software being gathered in the list's archive. To subscribe send mail to *<blinux-list-request@redhat.com>* `<mailto:blinux-list-request@redhat.com>` with the subject: help. This list is now moderated.

7.3   WWW References

The World Wide Web is, by it's nature, very rapidly changing. If you are reading this document in an old version then some of these are likely to be out of date. The original version that I maintain on the WWW shouldn't go more than a month or two out of date, so refer to that please.

Linux Documentation is available from `<http://sunsite.unc.edu/mdw/linux.html>`

Linux Access On the Web `<http://www.tardis.ed.ac.uk/mikedlr/access/>` with all of the versions of the HOWTO in `<http://www.tardis.ed.ac.uk/mikedlr/access/HOWTO/>`. Preferably, however, download from one of the main Linux FTP sites. If I get a vast amount of traffic I'll have to close down these pages and move them elsewhere.

The BLINUX Documentation and Development Project `<http://leb.net/blinux/>`. "The purpose of The BLINUX Documentation and Development Project is to serve as a catalyst which will both spur and speed the development of software and documentation which will enable the blind user to run his or her own Linux workstation."

Emacspeak WWW page `<http://cs.cornell.edu/home/raman/emacspeak/emacspeak.html>`

BRLTTY unofficial WWW page `<http://www.sf.co.kr/t.linux/new/brltty.html>`

Yahoo (one of the most major Internet catalogues) `<http://www.yahoo.com/Society_and_Culture/Disabilities/Adaptive_Technology/>`

The Linux Lab Project `<http://www.fu-berlin.de/clausi/>`.

The BLYNX pages: Lynx Support Files Tailored For Blind and Visually Handicapped Users `<http://leb.net/blinux/blynx/>`.

7.4   Suppliers

This is a UK supplier for the Braillex.

```
Alphavision Limited
```

7.5   Manufacturers

7.5.1   Alphavision

I think that they are a manufacturer? RNIB only lists them as a supplier, but others say they make the Braillex.

```
Alphavision Ltd
Seymour House
Copyground Lane
High Wycombe
Bucks HP12 3HE
England
U.K.
```

Phone
        +44 1494-530 555

Linux Supported Alphavision AT Products

- Braillex

7.5.2   Blazie Engineering

The Braille Lite was supported in the original version of BRLTTY. That support has now been discontinued. If you have one and want to use it with Linux then that may be possible by using this version of the software.

```
Blazie Engineering
105 East Jarrettsville Rd.
Forest Hill, MD 21050
U.S.A.
```

Phone
        +1 (410) 893-9333

FAX

> +1 (410) 836-5040

BBS

> +1 (410) 893-8944

E-Mail

> <*info@blazie.com*> `<mailto:info@blazie.com>`

WWW

> `<http://www.blazie.com/>`

Blazie AT Products

- Braille Lite (support discontinued)

7.5.3 Digital Equipment Corporation

```
Digital Equipment Corporation
P.O. Box CS2008
Nashua
NH 03061-2008
U.S.A
```

Order

> +1 800-722-9332

Tech info

> +1 800-722-9332

FAX

> +1 603-884-5597

WWW

> `<http://www.digital.com/>`

Linux Supported DEC AT Products

- DECTalk Express

7.5.4 Kommunikations-Technik Stolper GmbH

```
KTS Stolper GmbH
Herzenhaldenweg 10
73095 Albershausen
Germany
```

Phone

> +49 7161 37023

Fax

> +49 7161 32632

Linux Supported KTG AT Products

- Brailloterm

8   Software Packages

References in this section are taken directly from the Linux Software map which can be found in all standard places for Linux documentation and which lists almost all of the software available for Linux.

8.1   Emacspeak

Emacspeak is the software side of a speech interface to Linux. Any other character based program, such as a WWW browser, or `telnet` or another editor can potentially be used within `emacspeak`. The main difference between it and normal screen reader software for such operating systems as DOS is that it also has a load more extra features. It is based in the emacs text editor.

A text editor is generally just a program which allows you to change the contents of a file, for example, adding new information to a letter. Emacs is in fact far beyond a normal text editor, and so this package is much more useful than you might imagine. You can run any other program from within emacs, getting any output it generates to appear in the emacs terminal emulator.

The reason that emacs is a better environment for Emacspeak is that it can can understand the layout of the screen and can intelligently interpret the meaning of, for example, a calendar, which would just be a messy array of numbers otherwise. The originator of the package manages to look after his own Linux machine entirely, doing all of the administration from within emacs. He also uses it to control a wide variety of other machines and software directly from that machine.

Emacspeak is included within the Debian Linux distribution and is included as contributed software within the Slakware distribution. This means that it is available on many of the CDROM distributions of Linux. By the time this is published, the version included should be 5 or better, but at present I only have version 4 available for examination.

```
Begin3
Title:          emacspeak - a speech output interface to Emacs
Version:        4.0
Entered-date:   30MAY96
Description:    Emacspeak is the first full-fledged speech output
                system that will allow someone who cannot see to work
                directly on a UNIX system. (Until now, the only option
                available to visually impaired users has been to use a
                talking PC as a terminal.) Emacspeak is built on top
                of Emacs. Once you start emacs with emacspeak loaded,
                you get spoken feedback for everything you do. Your
                mileage will vary depending on how well you can use
                Emacs.  There is nothing that you cannot do inside
                Emacs:-)
Keywords:       handicap access visually impaired blind speech emacs
Author:         raman@adobe.com (T. V. Raman)
Maintained-by:  jrv@vanzandt.mv.com (Jim Van Zandt)
```

```
Primary-site:    sunsite.unc.edu apps/sound/speech
                 124kB   emacspeak-4.0.tgz
Alternate-site:
Original-site:   http://www.cs.cornell.edu /pub/raman/emacspeak
                 123kB   emacspeak.tar.gz/Info/People/raman/emacspeak/emacspeak.tar.gz
Platforms:       DECtalk Express or DEC Multivoice speech synthesizer,
                 GNU FSF Emacs 19 (version 19.23 or later) and TCLX
                 7.3B (Extended TCL).
Copying-policy: GPL
End
```

8.2   BRLTTY

This is a program for running a serial port Braille terminal. It has been widely tested and used, and supports a number of different kinds of hardware (see the Linux Software Map entry below).

The maintainer is, Nikhil Nair <*nn201@cus.cam.ac.uk*> <mailto:nn201@cus.cam.ac.uk>. The other people working on it are Nicolas Pitre <*nico@cam.org*> <mailto:nico@cam.org> and Stephane Doyon <*doyons@jsp.umontreal.ca*> <mailto:doyons@jsp.umontreal.ca>. Send any comments to all of them.

The authors seem keen to get support in for more different devices, so if you have one you should consider contacting them. They will almost certainly need programming information for the device, so if you can contact your manufacturer and get that they are much more likely to be able to help you.

A brief feature list (from their README file) to get you interested

- Full implementation of the standard screen review facilities.
- A wide range of additional optional features, including blinking cursor and capital letters, screen freezing for leisurely review, attribute display to locate highlighted text, hypertext links, etc.
- 'Intelligent' cursor routing. This allows easy movement of the cursor in text editors etc. without moving the hands from the Braille display.
- A cut & paste function. This is particularly useful for copying long filenames, complicated commands etc.
- An on-line help facility.
- Support for multiple Braille codes.
- Modular design allows relatively easy addition of drivers for other Braille displays, or even (hopefully) porting to other Unix-like platforms.

```
Begin3
Title:           BRLTTY - Access software for Unix for a blind person
                         using a soft Braille terminal
Version:         1.0.2, 17SEP96
Entered-date:    17SEP96
Description:     BRLTTY is a daemon which provides access to a Unix console
                 for a blind person using a soft Braille display (see the
                 README file for a full explanation).

                 BRLTTY only works with text-mode applications.
```

We hope that this system will be expanded to support
other soft Braille displays, and possibly even other
Unix-like platforms.

Keywords:	Braille console access visually impaired blind
Author:	nn201@cus.cam.ac.uk (Nikhil Nair)
	nico@cam.org (Nicolas Pitre)
	doyons@jsp.umontreal.ca (Stephane Doyon)
	jrbowden@bcs.org.uk (James Bowden)
Maintained-by:	nn201@cus.cam.ac.uk (Nikhil Nair)
Primary-site:	sunsite.unc.edu /pub/Linux/system/Access
	110kb brltty-1.0.2.tar.gz (includes the README file)
	6kb brltty-1.0.2.README
	1kb brltty-1.0.2.lsm
Platforms:	Linux (kernel 1.1.92 or later) running on a PC or DEC Alpha.
	Not X/graphics.
	Supported Braille displays (serial communication only):
	- Tieman B.V.: CombiBraille 25/45/85;
	- Alva B.V.: ABT3xx series;
	- Telesensory Systems Inc.: PowerBraille 40 (not 65/80),
	Navigator 20/40/80 (latest firmware version only?).
Copying-policy:	GPL
End	

8.3 Screen

Screen is a standard piece of software to allow many different programs to run at the same time on one terminal. It has been enhanced to support some Braille terminals (those from Telesensory) directly.

8.4 Rsynth

This is a speech synthesiser listed in the Linux Software Map. It doesn't apparently work well enough for use by a visually impaired person. Use hardware instead, or improve it.. a free speech synthesiser would be really really useful.

8.5 xocr

xocr is a package which implements optical character recognition for Linux. As with Rsynth, I don't think that this will be acceptable as a package for use as a sole means of input by a visually impaired person. I suspect that the algorithm used means that it will need to be watched over by someone who can check that it is reading correctly. I would love to be proved wrong.

8.6 xzoom

xzoom is a screen magnifier, in the same vein as xmag, but sufficiently better to be very useful to a visually impaired person. The main disadvantages of xzoom are that it can't magnify under itself, that some of the key controls aren't compatible with fvwm, the normal Linux window manager and that it's default configuration doesn't run over a network (this can be fixed at some expense to speed). Apart from that though, it's excellent. It does continuous magnification which allows you to, for example, scroll a document up and down, whilst keeping the section you are reading magnified. Alternatively, you can move a little box around the screen, magnifying the contents and letting you search for the area you want to see. xzoom is also available as an rpm from the normal RedHat sites, making it very easy to install for people using the rpm system (such as Redhat users).

```
Begin3
Title:          xzoom
Version:        0.1
Entered-date:   Mar 30 1996
Description:    xzoom can magnify (by integer value) rotate
                (by a multiple if 90 degrees) and mirror about
                the X or Y axes areas on X11 screen
                and display them in it's window.
Keywords:       X11 zoom magnify xmag
Author:         Itai Nahshon <nahshon@best.com>
Maintained-by:  Itai Nahshon <nahshon@best.com>
Primary-site:   sunsite.unc.edu
                probably in /pub/Linux/X11/xutils/xzoom-0.1.tgz
Platforms:      Linux+11. Support only for 8-bit depth.
                Tested only in Linux 1.3.* with the XSVGA 3.1.2
driver.
                        Needs the XSHM extension.
Copying-policy: Free
End
```

8.7 NFBtrans

nfbtrans is a multi-grade Braille translation program distributed by the National Federation for the Blind in the U.S.A. It is released for free in the hope that someone will improve it. Languages covered are USA English, UK English, Spanish, Russian, Esperanto, German, Biblical Hebrew and Biblical Greek, though others could be added just by writing a translation table. Also covered are some computer and math forms. I have managed to get it to compile under Linux, though, not having a Braille embosser available at the present moment I have not been able to test it.

NFBtrans is available from <ftp://nfb.org/ftp/nfb/braille/nfbtrans/>. After downloading it, you will have to compile it.

8.7.1 Compiling NFBtrans on Linux

I have returned this patch to the maintainer of NFBtrans and he says that he has included it, so if you get a version later than 740, you probably won't have to do anything special. Just follow the instructions included in the package.

```
unzip -L NFBTR740.ZIP    #or whatever filename you have
mv makefile Makefile
```

Next save the following to a file (e.g. `patch-file`)

```
*** nfbpatch.c.orig     Tue Mar 12 11:37:28 1996
--- nfbpatch.c  Tue Mar 12 11:37:06 1996
***************
*** 185,190 ****
--- 185,193 ----
    return (finfo.st_size);
  }                 /* filelength */


+ #ifndef linux
+ /* pretty safe to assume all linux has usleep I think ?? this should be
+ done properly anyway */
  #ifdef SYSVR4
  void usleep(usec)
    int usec;
***************
*** 195,200 ****
--- 198,204 ----
UKP  }                  /* usleep */

  #endif
+ #endif

  void beep(count)
    int count;
```

and run

```
patch < patch-file
```

then type

```
make
```

and the program should compile.

8.8   UnWindows

UnWindows is a package of access utilities for X which provides many useful facilities for the visually impaired (not blind). It includes a screen magnifier and other customised utilities to help locate the pointer. UnWindows can be downloaded from <ftp://ftp.cs.rpi.edu/pub/unwindows>.

As it comes by default, the package will not work on Linux because it relies on special features of Suns. However, some of the utilities do work and I have managed to port most of the rest so this package may be interesting to some people. My port will either be incorporated back into the original or will be available in the BLINUX archives (see 7.3 (WWW references)). The remaining utility which doesn't yet work is the configuration utility.

In my version the programs, instead of generating sounds themselves, just call another program. The other program could for example be

```
play /usr/lib/games/xboing/sounds/ouch.au
```

Which would make the xboing ouch noise, for example it could do this as the pointer hit the left edge of the screen.

8.8.1   dynamag

dynamag is a screen magnification program. please see the section on Screen magnification (3.1.2 (magnification)). This program worked in the default distribution.

8.8.2   coloreyes

coloreyes makes it easy to find the pointer (mouse) location. It consists of a pair of eyes which always look in the direction of the pointer (like xeyes) and change color depending on how far away the mouse is (unlike xeyes). This doesn't work in the default distribution, but the test version, at the same location, seems to work.

8.8.3   border

border is a program which detects when the pointer (mouse) has moved to the edge of the screen and makes a sound according to which edge of the screen has been approached. The version which is available uses a SUN specific sound system. I have now changed this so that instead of that, it just runs a command, which could be any Linux sound program.

8.8.4   un-twm

The window manager is a special program which controls the location of all of the other windows (programs) displayed on the X screen. un-twm is a special version which will make a sound as the pointer enters different windows. The sound will depend on what window has been entered. The distributed version doesn't work on linux because, like border it relies on SUN audio facilities. Again I already have a special version which will be avaliable by the time you read this.

9   Hardware

9.1   Braille terminals driven from Screen Memory

These are Braille terminals that can read the screen memory directly in a normal text mode. It is possible to use it to work with Linux for almost all of the things that a seeing user can do on the console, including installation. However, it has a problem with the scrolling of the normal Linux kernel, so a kernel patch needs to be applied. See 9.1.3 (Patching the Kernel for Braillex and Brailloterm).

9.1.1 Braillex

The Braillex is a terminal which is designed to read directly from the Screen memory, thus getting round any problems with MS-DOS programs which don't behave strangely. If you could see it on screen, then this terminal should be able to display it in Braille. In Linux, unfortunately, screen handling is done differently from MS-DOS, so this has to be changed somewhat.

To get this terminal to work, you have to apply the patch given below in section 9.1.3 (Patching the Kernel). Once this is done, the Braillex becomes one of the most convenient ways to use Linux as it allows all of the information normally available to a seeing person to be read. Other terminals don't start working until the operating system has completely booted.

The Braillex is available with two arrangements of Braille cells (80x1 or 40x2) and there is a model, called the IB 2-D which also has a vertical bar to show information about all of the lines of the screen (using 4 programmable dots per screen line)

```
Price: 8,995  (pounds sterling) or 11495 UKP for 2-D
Manufacturer: Alphavision Limited (UK)
Suppliers: ????
```

9.1.2 Brailloterm

"What is Brailloterm?

It's a refreshable display Braille, made by KTS Kommunikations-Technik Stolper GmbH. It has 80 Braille cells in an unique line. Each cell has 8 dots that are combined (up/down) to represent a character. By default, Brailloterm shows me the line in which the screen cursor is. I can use some functions in Brailloterm to see any line in the screen." - *Jose Vilmar Estacio de Souza <jvilmar@embratel.net.br>* <mailto:jvilmar@embratel.net.br>

Jose then goes on to say that the terminal can also use the serial port under DOS but that it needs a special program. I don't know if any of the ones for Linux would work.

As with Braillex, this needs a special patch to the kernel work properly. See section 9.1.3 (Patching the Kernel).

```
Price: about 23.000,- DM /  $ 15.000,
Manufacturer: Kommunikations-Technik Stolper GmbH
Suppliers: ????
```

9.1.3 Patching the Kernel for Braillex and Brailloterm

This probably also applies to any other terminals which read directly from screen memory to work under MS-DOS. Mail me to confirm any terminals that you find work. This does not apply and will actually lose some features for terminals driven using the BRLTTY software.

I am told this patch applies to all Kernels version 1.2.X. It should also work on all Kernel versions from 1.1.X to 1.3.72, with just a warning from patch (I've tested that the patch applies to 1.3.68 at least). **From 1.3.75 the patch is no longer needed** because the Kernel can be configured not to scroll using 'linux no-scroll' at the LILO prompt. See the Boot Prompt HOWTO for more details.

```
*** drivers/char/console.c     Fri Mar 17 07:31:40 1995
--- drivers/char/console.c     Tue Mar  5 04:34:47 1996
```

```
**************
*** 601,605 ****
  static void scrup(int currcons, unsigned int t, unsigned int b)
  {
!         int hardscroll = 1;

        if (b > video_num_lines || t >= b)
--- 601,605 ----
  static void scrup(int currcons, unsigned int t, unsigned int b)
  {
!         int hardscroll = 0;

        if (b > video_num_lines || t >= b)
```

To apply it:

1. Save the above text to a file (say patch-file)
2. change to the drivers/char directory of your kernel sources
3. run

```
                patch < patch-file
```

4. Compile your kernel as normal

Apply those patches and you should be able to use the Braille terminal as normal to read the Linux Console.

Put in words, the patch just means 'change the 1 to a 0 in the first line of the function **scrup** which should be near line 603 in the file drivers/char/console.c'. The main thing about **patch** is that program understands this, and that it knows how to guess what to do when the Linux developers change things in that file.

If you want to use a more modern kernel with completely disabled scrolling, (instead of the boot prompt solution I already mentioned), please use the following patch. **This does not apply to kernels earlier than 1.3.75.**

```
*** console.c   Fri Mar 15 04:01:45 1996
--- console.c   Thu Apr  4 13:29:48 1996
**************
*** 516,520 ****
  unsigned char has_wrapped;              /* all of videomem is data of fg_console */
  static unsigned char hardscroll_enabled;
! static unsigned char hardscroll_disabled_by_init = 0;

  void no_scroll(char *str, int *ints)
--- 516,520 ----
  unsigned char has_wrapped;              /* all of videomem is data of fg_console */
  static unsigned char hardscroll_enabled;
! static unsigned char hardscroll_disabled_by_init = 1;

  void no_scroll(char *str, int *ints)
```

9.2   Software Driven Braille Terminals

The principle of operation of these terminal is very close to that of a CRT terminal such as the vt100. They connect to the serial port and the computer has to run a program which sends them output. At present there are two known programs for Linux. BRLTTY, see section 8.2 (BRLTTY)) and Braille enhanced screen.

9.2.1   Tieman B.V.

CombiBraille   This Braille terminal is supported by the BRLTTY software. It comes in three versions with 25, 45 or 85 Braille cells. The extra five cells over a standard display are used for status information.

```
Price: around 4600 UKP for the 45 cell model ...
Manufacturer: Tieman B.V.
Suppliers: Concept Systems, Nottingham, England (voice +44 115 925 5988)
```

9.2.2   Alva B.V.

The ABT3xx series is supported in BRLTTY. Only the ABT340 has been confirmed to work at this time. Please pass back information to the BRLTTY authors on other models.

```
Price: 20 cell - 2200 UKP; 40 cell 4500 UKP; 80 cell 8000 UKP
Manufacturer: Alva
Suppliers: Professional Vision Services LTD, Hertshire, England
          (+44 1462 677331)
```

9.2.3   Telesensory Systems Inc. displays

Because they have provided programming information to the developers, the Telesensory displays are supported both by BRLTTY and screen.

Powerbraille   There are three models the 40, the 65 and the 80. Only the 40 is known to be supported by BRLTTY.

```
Price: 20 cell - 2200 UKP; 40 cell 4500 UKP; 80 cell 8000 UKP
Manufacturer: Alva
Suppliers: Professional Vision Services LTD, Hertshire, England
          (+44 1462 677331)
```

Navigator   Again there are three models the 20, the 60 and the 80. Recent versions are all known to work with BRLTTY but whether earlier ones (with earlier firmware) also work has not been confirmed.

```
Price: 80 cell 7800 UKP
Manufacturer: Alva
Suppliers: Professional Vision Services LTD, Hertshire, England
          (+44 1462 677331)
```

9.2.4   Braille Lite

This is more a portable computer than a terminal. It could, however, be used with BRLTTY version 0.22 (but not newer versions) as if it was a normal Braille terminal. Unfortunately, many of the features available with the CombiBraille cannot be used with the Braille Lite. This means that it should be avoided for Linux use where possible.

```
Price: $3,395.00
Manufacturer: Blazie Engineering
```

9.3   Speech Synthesisers

Speech synthesisers normally connect to the serial port of a PC. Useful features include

- Braille labels on parts
- Many voices to allow different parts of document to be spoken differently
- Use with headphones (not available on all models)

The critical problem is that the quality of the speech. This is much more important to someone who is using the speech synthesiser as their main source of information than to someone who is just getting neat sounds out of a game. For this reason T.V. Raman seems to only recommend the DECTalk. Acceptable alternatives would be good.

9.3.1   DECTalk Express

This is a hardware speech synthesiser. It is recommended for use with Emacspeak and in fact the DECTalk range are the only speech synthesisers which work with that package at present. This synthesiser has every useful feature that I know about. The only disadvantage that I know of at present is price.

```
Price: $1195.00
Manufacturer: Digital Equipment Corporation

Suppliers: Many.  I'd like details of those with Specific Linux
        support / delivering international or otherwise of note only
        please.  Otherwise refer to local organisations.
        Digital themselves or the Emacspeak WWW pages.
```

9.3.2   Accent SA

This is a synthesiser made by Aicom Corporation. An effort has begun to write a driver for it however help is needed. Please see <http://www.cyberspc.mb.ca/~astrope/speak.html> if you think you can help.

9.3.3   SPO256-AL2 Speak and Spell chip.

Some interest has been expressed in using this chip in self built talking circuits. I'd be interested to know if anyone has found this useful. A software package speak-0.2pl1.tar.gz was produced by David Sugar <*dyfet@tycho.com*> <mailto:dyfet@tycho.com>. My suspicion, though, is that the quality of the output wouldn't be good enough for regular use.

10 Acknowledgements

Much of this document was created from various information sources on the Internet, many found from Yahoo and DEC's Alta Vista Search engine. Included in this was the documentation of most of the software packages mentioned in the text. Some information was also gleaned from the Royal National Institute for the Blind's helpsheets.

T.V. Raman, the author of Emacspeak has reliably contributed comments, information and text as well as putting me in touch with other people who he knew on the Internet.

Kenneth Albanowski <*kjahds@kjahds.com*> `<mailto:kjahds@kjahds.com>` provided the patch needed for the Brailloterm and information about it.

Roland Dyroff of *S.u.S.E. GmbH* `<http://www.suse.de/>` (Linux distributors and makers of S.u.S.E. Linux (English/German)) looked up KTS Stolper GmbH at my request and got some hardware details and information on the Brailloterm.

The most major and careful checks over of this document were done by James Bowden, <*jrbowden@bcs.org.uk*> `<mailto:jrbowden@bcs.org.uk>` and Nikhil Nair <*nn201@cus.cam.ac.uk*> `<mailto:nn201@cus.cam.ac.uk>`, the BRLTTY authors who suggested a large number of corrections as well as extra information for some topics.

The contributors to the blinux and linux-access mailing lists have contributed to this document by providng information for me to read.

Mark E. Novak of the Trace R&D centre `<http://trace.wisc.edu/>` pointed me in the direction of several packages of software and information which I had not seen before. He also made some comments on the structure of the document which I have partially taken into account and should probably do more about.

Other contributors include Nicolas Pitrie and Stephane Doyon.

A number of other people have contributed comments and information. Specific contributions are acknowledged within the document.

This version was specifically produced for *RedHat* `<http://www.redhat.com/>`'s Dr. Linux book. This is because they provided warning of it's impending release to myself and other LDP authors. Their doing this is strongly appreciated since wrong or old information sits around much longer in a book than on the Internet.

No doubt you made a contribution and I haven't mentioned it. Don't worry, it was an accident. I'm sorry. Just tell me and I will add you to the next version.

The Linux Emacspeak HOWTO

Jim Van Zandt, jrv@vanzandt.mv.com   v1.4, 21 Dececember 1997

This document describes how a blind user can use Linux with a speech synthesizer to replace the video display. It describes how to get Linux running on your own PC, and how to set it up for speech output. It suggests how to learn about Unix.

Contents

1   Introduction

Emacspeak is an Emacs subsystem that allows the user to get feedback using synthesized speech.

Screen reading programs allow a visually impaired user to get feedback using synthesized speech. Such programs have been commercially available for well over a decade. Most of them run on PC's under DOS, and there are now a few screen-readers for the Windows platform. However, screen-readers for the UNIX environment have been conspicuous in their absence.

This means that most visually impaired computer users face the additional handicap of being DOS-impaired – a far more serious problem:-)

Emacspeak is an emacs subsystem that provides basic speech access. Emacspeak will always have the shortcoming that it will only work under Emacs. This said, there is very little that cannot be done inside Emacs, so it's not a real shortcoming:-) Within Emacs, you can open a "shell window" where you can run commands and examine their output, even output which has scrolled out of the window. Emacs provides special modes for running certain commands. For example, it can parse error messages printed by a compiler and open a separate edit window with the cursor at the point of the error. It can also run a debugger and keep a separate edit window open at the point in the source code corresponding to the program counter.

Emacspeak does have a significant advantage: since it runs inside Emacs, a structure-sensitive, fully customizable editor, Emacspeak often has more context-specific information about what it is speaking than its commercial counterparts. In this sense, Emacspeak is not a "screenreader", it is a subsystem that produces speech output. A traditional screen-reader speaks the content of the screen, leaving it to the user to interpret the visually laid-out information. Emacspeak, on the other hand, treats speech as a first-class output mode; it speaks the information in a manner that is easy to comprehend when listening.

This initial version provides a basic speech subsystem for Emacs; using Emacs' power and flexibility, it has proven straightforward to add modules that customize how things are spoken, e.g. depending on the major/minor mode of a given buffer. Note that the basic speech functionality provided by Emacspeak is sufficient to use most Emacs packages effectively; adding package-specific customizations makes the interaction much smoother. This is because package-specific extensions can take advantage of the current context.

Emacspeak will only work with emacs. However, emacs can be used to run any program that has a command-line interface (ls, cd, rm, adduser, etc.). You can even run those like less or lynx which use escape sequences to control the appearance of the screen. The key to this is eterm mode, which you get with the emacs command M-x term.

Emacs is a large program, but it does not all have to be in RAM, because Linux has virtual memory. You can designate a swap partition, so that programs (or parts of programs) can be swapped out when they are not being used. You can comfortably run emacs with 8 MB of ram plus 8 MB of swap space.

This document is limited to the following:

- Linux (not Free BSD)
- The Slackware distribution (not Red Hat, Debian, etc.)
- Speech output only (not Braille - see the Access HOWTO)
- DECtalk (Dectalk Express and MultiVoice), DoubleTalk, and LiteTalk synthesizers (–not the Accent, SmarTalk, a sound card, etc.)
- Use of Emacs, with T. V. Raman's Emacspeak package, to drive the synthesizer.

The use of adaptive technology with Linux, and in particular, using adaptive technology to make Linux accessible to those who could not use it otherwise, is covered in the Linux Access HOWTO.

If you would like to help extend this document to cover one or more of the other alternatives, or point me to a discussion somewhere else, please contact me.

Emacspeak was written by T. V. Raman `raman@adobe.com`. Emacspeak has a Web page at `<http://www.cs.cornell.edu/Info/People/raman/emacspeak/emacspeak.html>`.

Emacspeak supports several speech synthesizers. The software required depends on which you have.

If you have a DECtalk Express or Multivoice, you need the basic Emacspeak package, tcl (an interpreter), and tclx (extensions for tcl). You can get the source package for Emacspeak from the Emacspeak web page, or a binary package in one of the popular distributions of Linux (Slackware, Red Hat, or Debian). I build each of these packages. Since I normally run Debian, the Debian package will be available a little sooner than the others. At this writing, the most recent release of Emacspeak is version 7.0. Here are some URLs:

```
<http://leb.net/pub/blinux/emacspeak/cornell.mirror>   <ftp://leb.net/pub/blinux/
emacspeak/blinux/emacspeak-6.0-2.i386.rpm>
```

Note: there are European mirrors of the blinux site which you should use if they closer:

```
<ftp://ftp.uni-muenster.de/share/public6/>   <ftp://ftp.gwdg.de/pub/linux/misc/
blinux/>
```

For the external DoubleTalk or LiteTalk synthesizers, you need the Emacspeak package and a separate driver which comes in the emacspeak-dt package:

```
<ftp://leb.net/pub/blinux/emacspeak/blinux/emacspeak-dt-0.27.tar.gz>   <ftp:
//leb.net/pub/blinux/emacspeak/blinux/emacspeak-dt-0.27-1.i386.rpm>   <http:
//www.mv.com/ipusers/vanzandt/emacspeak-dt_0.27-1_i386.deb>
```

For the internal DoubleTalk, you need three pieces of software: the basic Emacspeak package, the emacspeak-dt package, and a device driver. Here are some URLs for the device driver:

```
<ftp://leb.net/pub/blinux/emacspeak/blinux/dtlk-1.12.tar.gz>   <http://www.mv.com/
ipusers/vanzandt/dtlk-1.12.tar.gz>   <http://www.mv.com/ipusers/vanzandt/dtlk_1.
12-1_i386.deb>
```

There is an alpha test version of a driver for the Braille 'n Speak, Braille Lite, and Type 'n Speak devices used in "speech box" mode:

```
<ftp://leb.net/pub/blinux/emacspeak/blinux/emacspeak-bs-0.3.tar.gz>
```

Computer hardware, Unix user commands, Unix system administration, Emacs, and Emacspeak are each substantial subjects. Attempting to learn all of them at once is likely to lead to frustration. Instead, I suggest that the new user go through a sequence of stages, learning about only one system at a time.

2   Stage 1. DOS with speech

Most blind computer users have speech synthesizers with a screen reader program like JAWS [6.1 (JAWS)]. (References in this format refer to entries in the "Footnotes and References" section below.) Using this setup, install and become familiar with some terminal emulator like Telix [6.2 (TELIX)] or Commo [6.3 (COMMO)], which are available from the SimTel archive [6.4 (SimTel)] among others.

2.1   Getting Linux on CDROM

If you have or can borrow a CDROM drive, I recommend you get one of the many good distributions of Linux on that medium. The instructions below are for the Slackware distribution. I am most familiar with disks from InfoMagic [6.5 (InfoMagic)]. Another source is Walnut Creek [6.6 (Walnut Creek)] (where the whole idea of inexpensive CDROMS full of programs from Internet archives got its start). Distributions other than Slackware are available from Red Hat [6.7 (Red Hat)], Craftwork [6.8 (Craftwork)], and Yggdrasil [6.9 (Yggdrasil)]. As a rule, these CDROMS use the "ISO 9660" format, which can be read under DOS. (They also use the "Rock Ridge extensions" which add extra files in each directory. Linux uses the extra information to give you long filenames, both upper and lower case characters in filenames, and file permissions.)

2.2   Getting Linux by FTP

Another way to get Linux and its documentation is by FTP over the Internet. The home site for the Slackware distribution is Walnut Creek [6.6 (Walnut Creek)]. It is also carried by sunsite and many of it mirror sites. Here is a partial list:

- USA (home site) `<ftp://ftp.cdrom.com/pub/linux/slackware>`

- UK/Europe `<ftp://src.doc.ic.ac.uk/public/Mirrors/ftp.cdrom.com/pub/linux/slackware-3.1>`

- Japan `<ftp://ftp.cs.titech.ac.jp/pub/os/linux/slackware>`

- Taiwan `<ftp://NCTUCCCA.edu.tw/OS/Linux/Slackware>`

- Hong Kong `<ftp://ftp.cs.cuhk.hk/pub/slackware>`

- USA `<ftp://sunsite.unc.edu/pub/Linux/distributions/slackware>`

- USA `<ftp://uiarchive.cso.uiuc.edu/pub/systems/linux/sunsite/distributions/slackware>`

More sites are listed in the INFO-SHEET:

```
<http://sunsite.unc.edu/pub/Linux/welcome.html>  <ftp://sunsite.unc.edu/pub/
Linux/docs/HOWTO/INFO-SHEET>  <ftp://uiarchive.cso.uiuc.edu/pub/systems/linux/
sunsite/docs/HOWTO/INFO-SHEET>
```

2.3 Linux Documentation

Read the Linux documentation. I will quote here the file names and locations on the first disk of InfoMagic's December 1996 "Developer's Resource" set of six CDROMS, as seen under DOS. Other CDROM sets should have similar information, though perhaps differently arranged. The Slackware distribution is on disk 2 of the set. Matt Welsh's step by step guide to installing Slackware is in \doc\install-\install-.002. (This is a 245 page book!)

More general information is in the Linux "Frequently Asked Questions" list in \docs\linux.faq\linux-fa.asc. Longer descriptions are in "HOWTO" documents (of which this is one). They are found in \docs. Note particularly \docs\hardware, which lists which kinds of hardware are supported by Linux, \docs\meta-faq, which points to sources of information (that is, a more extensive version of this paragraph), and \help\index, which is a list of the HOWTO documents with short descriptions. The Linux installation HOWTO, \docs\installation, is another (much shorter, somewhat older) version of Matt Welsh's installation instructions.

One note on reading the documentation. You may run into files with ASCII highlighting, where character-backspace-character stands for "bold", and underscore-backspace-character stands for "italics". One way to handle this is to use the less program, which displays these sequences in alternate colors. A DOS screenreader can, for example, search for such highlighted text. A DOS version of less can be obtained by FTP from the SimTel archive [6.4 (SimTel)]. Within the SimTel collection, look for directory msdos/textutil. For example, try <ftp://ftp.coast.net/pub/SimTel/msdos/textutil>.

I will suggest four alternatives for learning Emacs commands (see section [3.2 (Learning Emacs)]). The first option is to install Emacs under DOS and learn it while using the DOS screen reader. Where to get Emacs for DOS is a "frequently asked question" [6.10 (Emacs for DOS)].

The source code for Emacs (about 10 MB) can be gotten from <ftp://prep.ai.mit.edu/pub/gnu/> (look for emacs-19.34b.tar.gz or similar), or from one of many mirrors of the GNU collection [6.11 (Gnu Mirrors)].

3 Stage 2. Terminal to remote UNIX system

Arrange for what is called a "shell account" on some Unix system. Most Internet Service Providers (ISPs) can provide this service. Use the terminal emulator program and a modem to dial in. Learn the basic Unix commands. If the system has Emacs installed, or you can persuade the system administrator to install it, this is your second chance to learn it. It is probably best to learn it at this point, because administering a Unix system (the next stage) will call for you to edit files. Therefore, I include here my suggestions for learning both Unix and Emacs.

3.1 Learning Unix

When you arrange for a shell account, or set up a new account on your own machine, you will have to decide on a username and a password. Your username will also be used in your email address, so try to find something short and memorable. Your password is important, and should be hard to guess. That usually means at least six characters, including at least one non-alphanumeric character.

When a Unix system is ready for you to log in, it normally displays a prompt ending with "login:". At this point you should type in your username. It will then prompt you for your password, and will turn off command echoing while you type it in.

The command to finish a terminal session is logout.

To learn about a command, use the man command to type its manual page ("man page" for short). For example, to learn more about the cp command by typing man cp. Of course, this helps only if you know or can guess the command name. However, each man page has a line near the beginning with the command name and a short description of what the command does. You can search a database of these lines using the command apropos. Thus, typing apropos working will list lines that include the word "working". Here's what that command prints here:

```
cd (n)                      - Change working directory
pwd (n)                     - Return the current working directory
Cwd (3pm)                   - get pathname of current working directory
chdir (2)                   - change working directory
fchdir (2)                  - change working directory
get_current_dir_name (3) - Get current working directory
getcwd (3)                  - Get current working directory
getwd (3)                   - Get current working directory
pwd (1)                     - print name of current/working directory
rcsclean (1)                - clean up working files
```

The numbers in parentheses are sections of the manual. User commands are in section 1. Functions called from within programs are in sections 2 and 3. Commands used mostly by the system administrator are in section 8. You can find out more about the on-line manual with the command man man.

Under Unix, commands normally accept options starting with a minus sign rather than the forward slash used under DOS. In a path, directory names are separated by forward slashes rather than backward slashes. Both operating systems have a "standard input", by default the keyboard, and a "standard output", by default the display screen. You can redirect the standard input using "<", and redirect the output using ">". You can use the output from one command as the input of another by separating the two commands with "|". This is called the "pipe" symbol.

The program that interprets your command is a "shell". Under DOS, COMMAND.COM is the shell. Most Unix shells are decendents of either the Bourne shell sh or the C shell csh. The shell most commonly used with Linux is the "Bourne again shell", or bash. It has several features which can reduce the need for typing. You can use the cursor up key key to bring previous commands to the command line. The cursor will be at the end of the command. You can use cursor left and right to move the cursor within the command, and edit it with Emacs style commands (control-D or DEL to delete the character to the right, et cetera). Also, you can insert the last word in the previous command with ESC-. (escape period). You can learn about these and other commands from the bash man page, in the section entitled "READLINE".

If a program gets "stuck", here is a sequence of keystrokes to try:

- Control-Q. You may have sent a control-S, which halts all output, without realizing it. The control-Q will restart it.

- Control-D, which signals "end of file" under Unix (similar to control-Z under DOS), in case the program expects input which you are not prepared to supply.

- Control-C is an interrupt, which may halt the program.

- Control-Z puts the program in the background. At this point you may simply log out, although you will be warned about the background process and will have to repeat the logout command. You can instead kill the process, as follows: Run ps with no arguments. It will list a header line, then one line for each of your processes. The first item on each line is the process id number, or PID. The command used to start the process (or at least the beginning of it) appears at the end of the line. If the PID were 117, you would kill the process with the command kill -9 117.

- If running Linux from the console, alt-2, or some other alt-number combination, will switch to a different virtual console. You can log in there just as if you had sat down to a different terminal.

- If your machine is connected to a network, you can log in from another machine.

- Control-alt-del should reboot the computer nondestructively.

- As a last resort, you can hit "reset" or cycle the power. This will leave the filesystems in an invalid state, since some buffers will not have been written to disk. The kernel will discover this while booting, and will take time to check and repair the filesystems. Actual data loss is unlikely unless you had something else going on at the time.

Guido Gonzato Guido@ibogfs.cineca.it has written an excellent guide to Linux for (former) DOS users, the DOS2Linux mini-HOWTO. You can probably find it where you found this document, or else at `<ftp://sunsite.unc.edu/pub/Linux/docs/HOWTO/mini/>`.

You can find general Unix information, including manual pages for several systems at `<http://www.cis.ohio-state.edu/hypertext/man_pages.html>`

There is a tutorial entitled "Beginning Unix and the C Shell" at `<http://www.eng.hawaii.edu:80/Courses/C.unix/page-03.html>`.

You can get general help from `<http://www.nova.edu/Inter-Links/UNIXhelp/TOP_.html>` or `<http://www.eecs.nwu.edu/unix.html>`

You can find a list of books on UNIX at `<http://www.eskimo.com/~cher/eskimospace/booklist.html>`.

3.2 Learning Emacs

When you start Emacs, you will normally list on the command line one or more files which you will be editing. To edit a file named "foobar" with Emacs, you would enter the command `emacs foobar`. If you enter the command `emacs` with no arguments, GNU Emacs will print out an introduction which includes the first five commands you need to learn, approximately as follows:

```
Type C-h for help;   ('C-' means use CTRL key.)
Type C-x u to undo changes.
Type C-h t for a tutorial on using Emacs.
Type C-h i to enter Info, which you can use to read GNU documentation.
To kill the Emacs job, type C-x C-c.
```

Note the way Emacs documentation refers to key combinations. C-h means hold the control key down while typing "h". You will also run into key combinations like M-v, which is pronounced "meta v". The tutorial suggests holding down the key labeled "edit" or "meta" then typing "v". I have never run across a keyboard with those keys, so I always use the escape key instead: typing "Esc" then "v" (two separate keystrokes). After using Emacs for a long time, I discovered that under Linux, the left "Alt" key works like a "meta" key. You may want to use this. On the other hand, some of these key combinations may conflict with your screen reader or communications program under DOS. Using the escape key is more reliable.

Three of the above commands start with C-h, which may be treated as a backspace by your communications program. In that case, you may access the help command using the long form M-x help. Conversely, you may find that pressing the backspace key starts the help command. This issue is treated in the Emacs FAQ, which is available within Emacs using C-h F or M-x help F. Look for the question "Why does the 'Backspace' key invoke help?". In the mean time, you can end the help session with the command C-g. (This is the keyboard-quit command, which cancels any prefix keys you have typed.)

You may also find that C-s and C-q are unavailable because they are used for flow control (XON and XOFF). You should look at the question "How do I handle C-s and C-q being used for flow control?" in the FAQ. For the particular command C-x C-s (save buffer), you may substitute the command C-x s (save-some-buffers). The former command saves the current buffer, while the latter asks the user about each of the modified buffers.

Note in particular the command "C-h t" to start the Emacs tutorial. That is one the first things you will want to try. I will only make a couple of comments on the tutorial. To move the cursor, it gives the four commands C-f, C-b, C-p, and C-n (for forward, back, previous line, and next line). These commands always work. However, with a properly installed Emacs, the regular arrow keys should also work. Try them out and use them if you are more comfortable with them. Similarly, you may be able to use home, end, page down, and page up keys in place of the standard commands C-a, C-e, C-v, and M-v. Finally, all Emacspeak commands begin with C-e. Once you start using Emacspeak, you will have to type it twice to get the end of line function. (The "End" key should be unaffected by Emacspeak.)

4   Stage 3. Terminal to local Linux system

This arrangement again requires a DOS machine with a speech synthesizer and a terminal emulator program. However, instead of dialing up a remote computer, it is used as a terminal to a local computer running Linux. To get to this point, you need to install Linux on a machine. You may be able to prevail on a knowledgable friend to help you with this. However, it is also possible to install it yourself with speech feedback for almost the whole procedure.

4.1   Installing Linux

First, some background. Even the simplest Unix system requires a program called the kernel and a root file system. The kernel has all the device drivers and resource management functions. One normally thinks of a "file system" as residing on a hard disk or floppy disk, but during an installation it is usually in ram. Linux is normally installed by writing a kernel image to a floppy disk, called the "boot floppy", configuring it to reserve a section of RAM for a ramdisk, then filling that ramdisk with data from a second floppy disk, called the "root floppy". As soon as both floppies have been read in, the user can log in as "root" and complete the installation. The sighted user logs in on the "system console", that is, the computer's own keyboard and video display. However, remember that Unix has been a multiprocessing operating system from the very beginning. Even this very primitive Unix system, running out of a small ramdisk, also supports logins from a terminal connected to a serial port. This is what a blind user can use.

To connect the two computers, you can use a "null modem", a serial cable that connects ground to ground, and transmit on each end to receive on the other. The cable that comes with the DOS application LapLink will work fine. It is particularly handy, in fact, because it has both a 9 pin and a 25 pin connector on each end. If you want to check a cable or have one made, here are the required connections:

For two 9 pin connectors, connect pin 2 (receive data) to pin 3, pin 3 (transmit data) to pin 2, and pin 5 (signal ground) to pin 5.

For two 25 pin connectors, connect pin 2 (receive data) to pin 3, pin 3 (transmit data) to pin 2, and pin 7 (signal ground) to pin 7.

For a 9 pin connector (first) to a 25 pin connector (second), connect pin 2 (receive data) to pin 2 (transmit data), pin 3 (transmit data) to pin 3 (receive data), and pin 5 (signal ground) to pin 7 (signal ground).

You may have noted that I have included no connections for the "handshaking" signals. During login, the serial port is handled by the program `agetty`. Recent versions of this program accept a -L switch which tells it not to expect modem control signals. The version in Slackware 3.0 does, but the one on the 3.0 (and earlier) installation root disks does not. However, Pat Volkerding has assured me that the root disks in the next release of Slackware will have the updated version of `agetty`. It is also possible to use the earlier root disks [6.12 (Emacspeak with Earlier Slackware Releases)].

Consult the documentation on your CDROM, or downloaded from an FTP site, and choose a boot disk with the proper kernel features for your hardware (IDE or SCSI, CDROM driver, etc.). I have the InfoMagic

September 1996 "Developer's Resource" set of six CDROMS. Slackware 3.1 is on disk 1 of that set, mostly in the two directories slackwar and slakware. (Note the difference in spelling. You will access them in alphabetical order: first slackwar, then slakware.)

Documentation on the boot floppies is in \bootdsks.144\which.one. A copy of the DOS program for writing boot images to a floppy, rawrite.exe, is in the same directory. Assuming the cdrom is the M drive under DOS, one might use these commands to write to a floppy disk in the A drive:

```
C>m:
M>cd \bootdsks.144
M>rawrite scsinet.s a:
```

Similarly, to write the "text" root disk:

```
C>m:
M>cd \rootdsks
M>rawrite text.gz a:
```

If you install from floppies, you should also copy the Emacspeak package onto a floppy with a command like this:

```
C>copy m:\contrib\emacspea.tgz a:
```

For the actual installation, proceed as follows: Use the null modem to connect the computer running DOS and equipped with speech output (which I will call the "DOS machine") to the computer into which you want to install Linux (the "Linux machine").

Boot the DOS machine, and start your terminal emulation program. Set it up for 9600 baud, no parity, eight data bits, 1 stop bit.

On the Linux machine, insert the "boot" disk and boot (power up, cntl-alt-del, or hit the reset switch). It should read the disk for five seconds or so, beep, and stop with the following text:

(Note: in the following, the large blocks of text quoted from the installation disks are preceded by "– begin quote" and followed by "– end quote". To skip to the end of a quote, you may search for two dashes starting in the first column. I have word wrapped some sections to limit the line lengths.)

```
-- begin quote

    Welcome to the Slackware96 Linux (v. 3.1.0) bootkernel disk!

    If you have any extra parameters to pass to the kernel, enter them at
    the prompt below after one of the valid configuration names (ramdisk,
    mount, drive2)

    Here are some examples (and more can be found in the BOOTING file):

     ramdisk hd=cyl,hds,secs    (Where "cyl", "hds", and "secs" are the
                                 number of cylinders, sectors, and heads
                                 on the drive.  Most machines won't need
                                 this.)
```

In a pinch, you can boot your system with a command like:
  mount root=/dev/hda1

On machines with low memory, you can use mount root=/dev/fd1 or mount
root=/dev/fd0 to install without a ramdisk. See LOWMEM.TXT for
details.

If you would rather load the root/install disk from your second
floppy drive: drive2 (or even this: ramdisk root=/dev/fd1)

DON'T SWITCH ANY DISKS YET! This prompt is just for entering extra
parameters. If you don't need to enter any parameters, hit ENTER to
continue.

boot:

-- end quote

I have almost always been able to just hit "enter" at this point.

After your entry, the Linux machine should read the floppy for another twenty seconds or so, then boot
the kernel. The first thing it prints is "Loading ramdisk...", which is somewhat misleading. In this case,
"ramdisk" is actually the name of the kernel configuration.

Each device driver in the kernel displays a line or two. The particular disk I'm using (the "bare.i" bootdisk)
displays more than one screen's worth. It is possible to type shift-page up to scroll the text back. On my
machine, the boot messages are as follows:

-- begin quote

    Loading ramdisk.....
    Uncompressing Linux...done.
    Now booting the kernel
    Console: colour VGA+ 80x25, 1 virtual console (max 63)
    Calibrating delay loop.. ok - 35.94 BogoMIPS
    Memory: 23028k/24768k available (688k kernel code, 384k reserved,
      668k data)
    Swansea University Computer Society NET3.035 for Linux 2.0
    NET3: Unix domain sockets 0.12 for Linux NET3.035.
    Swansea University Computer Society TCP/IP for NET3.034
    IP Protocols: ICMP, UDP, TCP
    VFS: Diskquotas version dquot_5.6.0 initialized
    Checking 386/387 coupling... Ok, fpu using exception 16 error reporting.
    Checking 'hlt' instruction... Ok.
    Linux version 2.0.0 (root@darkstar) (gcc version 2.7.2) #1 Mon Jun 10
    21:11:56 CDT 1996
    Serial driver version 4.13 with no serial options enabled
    tty00 at 0x03f8 (irq = 4) is a 16550A

```
PS/2 auxiliary pointing device detected -- driver installed.
Ramdisk driver initialized : 16 ramdisks of 49152K size
hda: IBM-DBOA-2720, 689MB w/64KB Cache, LBA, CHS=700/32/63
ide0: at 0x1f0-0x1f7,0x3f6 on irq 14
Floppy drive(s): fd0 is 1.44M
Started kswapd v 1.4.2.2
FDC 0 is a 8272A
Partition check:
   hda: hda1 hda2 hda3
VFS: Insert root floppy disk to be loaded into ramdisk and press ENTER
```

-- end quote

Some messages will of course be different on a machine with different hardware. Now, insert the "text"
rootdisk and press ENTER. After it is read, the following is displayed on the console:

-- begin quote

```
RAMDISK: Compressed image found at block 0
JAVA Binary support v1.01 for Linux 1.3.98 (C)1996 Brian A. Lantz
VFS: Mounted root (minix filesystem).
INIT: version 2.60 booting
none on /proc type proc (rw)
INIT: Entering runlevel: 4


Welcome to the Slackware Linux installation disk ,version 3.1.0-text!
### READ THE INSTRUCTIONS BELOW CAREFULLY! ###

You will need one or more partitions of type "Linux native"
prepared. It is also recommended that you create a swap partition
(type "Linux swap") prior to installation. Most users can use the
Linux "fdisk" utility to create and tag the types of all these
partitions. OS/2 Boot Manager users, however, should create their
Linux partitions with OS/2 "fdisk", add the bootable (root) partition
to the Boot Manager menu, and then use the Linux "fdisk" to tag the
partitions as type "Linux native".

If you have 4 megabytes or less of RAM, you MUST ACTIVATE a swap
partition before running setup. After making the partition with fdisk,
use:

mkswap /dev/<partition> <number of blocks> ; swapon /dev/<partition>

Once you have prepared the disk partitions for Linux, type "setup" to
begin the installation process.
```

```
You may now login as "root".

slackware login:
```

-- end quote

The program that prints the login prompt is called `agetty`. The Slackware 3.1 root disks are set up to allow logins only from the computer's own keyboard. You will have to reconfigure it to also allow logins from a serial port. This requires typing four lines on the Linux machine keyboard, with no voice feedback. If you realize you have made a mistake before hitting the carriage return, you can erase it with the backspace key. You can also discard what you have typed on a line with control-C. Here is what you type:

```
root
cat >>/etc/inittab
s1:45:respawn:/sbin/agetty 9600 ttyS0
control-D
init q
```

I will repeat that with explanations of what is going on.

First, type "root" and a single carriage return to log in (no password is needed). Next, you need to append one line to `/etc/inittab`. Type the following two lines:

```
cat >>/etc/inittab
s1:45:respawn:/sbin/agetty 9600 ttyS0
```

Finish each line with the "enter" key. Then type a control-D, which signals end of file to a Unix program. (Note: In the second line, the next to last character is an upper case "S". Everything else is in lower case.) This adds a line to the configuration file of the program `init`, to instruct it to use `agetty` to watch for logins on the first serial port on the Linux machine, called "COM1" under DOS, or "/dev/ttyS0" under Linux. To use the second port instead, change the last item on the above line to "ttyS1".

Then type

```
init q
```

which causes `init` to reread `/etc/inittab`. At this point the DOS machine should display the login prompt (the third of the blocks of text quoted above). On the DOS machine, type `root`, and finish the installation. (The next thing you should do is create and enable a swap partition.)

If you don't get the Slackware installation disk prompt, try the following:

- Type a single carriage return on the DOS machine.
- Recheck the terminal setup (9600 baud, no parity, eight data bits, 1 stop bit).
- Disconnect the null modem from the DOS machine. In its place, connect a modem which supports the Hayes "AT" commands. Type `AT` and a carriage return. You should get a reply of "OK" from the modem.

Once you get the above prompt on the DOS machine, you may type `root` and a carriage return to log in, and complete the installation like any other user. Of course, you must remember to include these packages: emacs, tcl, and tclX.

The installation script will offer to prepare a boot floppy. You should do this, since it is the most foolproof way to boot Linux. You will probably also want to install `lilo` (which is an abbreviation for "Linux loader") and/or `loadlin` (which is an abbreviation for "load Linux"). The installation script can install lilo. Loadlin is a DOS program that will let you boot from DOS to Linux. Install it on a DOS partition, and copy a compressed kernel file (usually named `zImage`) to the same partition. While running DOS, you may boot Linux with a command like `loadlin zimage root=/dev/hda3 ro/`. (I have assumed here that the kernel image is in the same directory as the loadlin program. You may find it more convenient to store kernel images in subdirectories named for the kernel version.)

After the Slackware setup script finishes the main installation, it will tell you to restart by pressing cntl-alt-del. Before doing that, you should install emacspeak. It can be found with the other "contributed" software. In the InfoMagic set, it is in slackwar/contrib. Assuming you are installing Linux directly from a cdrom, the setup script will mount the cdrom under /CDROM, and you may install emacspeak with the following command:

```
# installpkg /CDROM/slackwar/contrib/emacspeak.tgz
```

If you install from floppies, insert the floppy you made earlier and type this:

```
# mount -tmsdos /dev/fd0 /floppy
# cp /floppy/emacspea.tgz /tmp/emacspeak.tgz
# installpkg /tmp/emacspeak.tgz
```

You should not install the package directly off the floppy disk, because the DOS filesystem will not allow the full filename, so the installpkg program will think the package name is "emacspea" and will store its records under that name.

If you have a DoubleTalk or LiteTalk speech synthesizer, you should also install the emacspeak-dt package.

Reboot the Linux machine with the new boot floppy, with the DOS machine still connected. You should get a login prompt on the DOS machine. Celebrate! After getting this system working, you need to learn emacs (third option) and Unix system administration.

4.2   Learning Unix System Administration

Mostly you will learn system administration as the need arises. First adding a user (yourself), then installing programs, and so forth. The exception to this is making backups, which you should learn **before** you need them.

Among the many programs you will need to learn are these:

adduser

Register a new user, including creating a home directory and adding an entry in /etc/passwd.

tar

Create and unpack `.tar` files, which are collections of files (something like `.zip` files). To list the contents of an archive, use `tar -tf foobar.tar`. For a more verbose listing, use `tar -tvf foobar.tar`. To unpack an archive, use `tar -xf foobar.tar`.

chmod

Change permissions of a file or directory.

chown

Change ownership of a file or directory.

find

> Search directories recursively. For example, the command find . -name '*alpha*' -print means: search starting in the current directory (.) for a file whose name contains the string "alpha" (-name '*alpha*'), and print its path and name (-print). (With GNU find, the -print is optional.)

du

> Display the amount of space occupied by files or subdirectories. For a file with "holes", this may be much less than the length of the file.

df

> Display filesystem capacities, free space, and where they are mounted.

mount

> Display filesystems, where they are mounted, and the mount flags.

ifconfig

> Configure and check internet protocol (IP) network interfaces, including Ethernet cards, SLIP links, and PLIP links.

route

> Configure and check IP network routing, after the interface is configured.

ping

> Check IP network connectivity, after the interfaces and routes are configured.

ftp

> Transfer files across the Internet.

Here are some programs you may want to install:

agrep

> Approximate grep searches for approximate, not exact, string matches (also called "fuzzy string searches").

archie

> Search Internet archives for files.

flip

> Convert text files between Unix and DOS formats.

glimpse

> Fuzzy string searches in large collection of files (uses agrep).

lynx

> Text mode web browser.

Here are some Web pages related to Unix system administration:

General information <http://www.ensta.fr/internet/unix/sys_admin/> or <http://www.sai.msu.su/sysadm.html>

There is a Unix system administration tutorial at <http://www.iem.ac.ru/sysadm.html>

UnixWorld Online Magazine Home Page <http://www.wcmh.com/uworld/>

Internet Essentials for UNIX System Administrators Tutorial <http://www.greatcircle.com/tutorials/ieusa.html>

Pointers to Unix goodies available on the Internet <http://www.ensta.fr/internet/unix/>

Pointers to Unix system administration "goodies" available on the Internet <http://www.ensta.fr/internet/unix/sys_admin/>

5   Stage 4. Emacspeak under Linux

The Slackware setup script for Emacspeak should create the needed environment variables and install a script `emacspeak` that starts emacs with emacspeak. This is your fourth option for learning Emacs. This is the first time you will be able to actually use Emacspeak. A short tutorial appears below. Within Emacs, you may type C-h C-e to get a list of the commands. To search for a command, use C-h a. To get an explanation for a key sequence, use C-h k. There is also an info file which is part of the Emacspeak distribution. Within emacs, you may type C-h i to open the directory to the info pages. Search for the emacspeak menu item by typing C-s emacspeak, then two carriage returns (one to terminate the search, and a second one to go to the info page. If you have the standalone info program installed, you can consult the info file with the command `info Emacspeak`.

5.1   Emacspeak Introduction - Speech Enabled Normal Commands

All of the normal Emacs movement commands will speak the relevant information after moving. Here are some of the cursor movement functions that have been speech enabled. Note that this list only enumerates a few of these speech enabled commands; the purpose of emacspeak is to speech-enable all of emacs and provide you spoken feedback as you work. Thus, this list is here only as a representative example of the kind of speech-enabling extensions Emacspeak provides.

'C-n' or 'M-x next-line' or 'down'

Moves the cursor to the next line and speaks it.

'C-p' or 'M-x previous-line' or 'up'

Moves the cursor to the previous line and speaks it.

'M-f' or 'M-x forward-word' or

Moves the cursor to the next word and speaks it. Places point on the first character of the next work, rather than on the space preceding it (This is my personal preference).

'M-b' or 'M-x backward-word'

Moves the cursor to the previous word and speaks it.

'M-C-b' or 'M-x backward-sexp'

Moves the cursor to the previous sexp and speaks it. If the sexp spans more than a line, only the first line is spoken.

'M-<' or 'M-x beginning-of-buffer'

Speaks line moved to.

'M->' or 'M-x end-of-buffer'

Speaks line moved to.

'M-m' or 'M-x back-to-indentation'

Speaks entire current line. A useful way of hearing the current line.

5.2   Emacspeak Introduction - New Commands

Emacspeak provides a number of commands for reading portions of the current buffer, getting status information, and modifying Emacspeak's state.

All of the commands are documented in the subsequent sections. They can be classified into types:

Emacspeak commands for listening to chunks of information. The names of these commands all start with the common prefix 'emacspeak-'. All Emacspeak commands are bound to the keymap EMACSPEAK-KEYMAP and are accessed with the key 'Control e'. Thus, the Emacspeak command "emacspeak-speak-line" is bound to 'l' in keymap EMACSPEAK-KEYMAP and can be accessed with the keystroke 'Control-e l'.

Here are some of the commands for reading text:

'C-e c' or 'M-x emacspeak-speak-char'

Speak current character, using the phonetic alphabet.

'C-e w' or 'M-x emacspeak-speak-word'

Speak current word.

'C-e l' or 'M-x emacspeak-speak-line'

Speak current line. With prefix 'C-u', speaks the rest of the line from point. With negative prefix 'C-u -', speaks from start of line to point. Voicifies if voice-lock-mode is on. Indicates indentation with a tone if audio indentation is in use. Indicates position of point with an aural highlight if option emacspeak-show-point is turned on –see command 'M-x emacspeak-show-point'.

'C-e .' or 'M-x emacspeak-speak-sentence'

Speak the current sentence.

'C-e C-c' or 'M-x emacspeak-speak-current-window'

Speak everything in the current window.

'C-e =' or 'M-x emacspeak-speak-current-column'

State the column where point is.

The second category of commands provided by Emacspeak manipulate the state of the speech device. The names of these commands start with the common prefix 'dtk-'. You can access these commands via the prefix 'Control-e d'. Thus, the command "dtk-set-rate" is bound to 'r' in keymap EMACSPEAK-DTK-SUBMAP and can be executed by pressing 'Control e d r'.

'C-e s' or 'M-x dtk-stop'

Stop speech now. In addition, any command that causes speech output will discard anything in the speech buffer.

'C-e d I' or 'M-x dtk-toggle-stop-immediately-while-typing'

Toggle state of variable dtk-stop-immediately-while-typing. As the name implies, if true then speech flushes immediately as you type.

'C-e d i' or 'M-x emacspeak-toggle-audio-indentation'

Toggle state of Emacspeak audio indentation. Specifying the method of indentation as 'tone' results in the DECtalk producing a tone whose length is a function of the line's indentation. Specifying 'speak' results in the number of initial spaces being spoken.

'C-e d k' or 'M-x emacspeak-toggle-character-echo'

Toggle state of Emacspeak character echo (that is, whether typed characters are echoed).

'C-e d w' or 'M-x emacspeak-toggle-word-echo'

Toggle state of Emacspeak word echo (initially on).

'C-e d l' or 'M-x emacspeak-toggle-line-echo'

Toggle state of Emacspeak line echo (that is, whether typed text is echoed after typing enter).

'C-e d p' or 'M-x dtk-set-punctuations'

Set punctuation state. Possible values are 'some', 'all', or 'none'.

'C-e d q' or 'M-x dtk-toggle-quiet'

Toggle state of the speech device between being quiet and talkative. Useful if you want to continue using an emacs session that has emacspeak loaded but wish to make the speech shut up.

'C-e d R' or 'M-x dtk-reset-state'

Restore sanity to the Dectalk. Typically used after the Dectalk has been power cycled.

'C-e d SPC' or 'M-x dtk-toggle-splitting-on-white-space'

Toggle state of emacspeak that decides if we split text purely by clause boundaries, or also include whitespace.

'C-e d r' or 'M-x dtk-set-rate'

Set speaking rate for the dectalk.

'C-e d s' or 'M-x dtk-toggle-split-caps'

Toggle split caps mode. In split caps mode, a transition from lower case to upper case is treated like the beginning of a new word. This is useful when reading Hungarian notation in program source code.

'C-e d v' or 'M-x voice-lock-mode'

Toggle Voice Lock mode (initially off). When Voice Lock mode is enabled, text is voiceified as you type it, as follows:

- Comments are spoken in `voice-lock-comment-personality`; (That is a variable whose value should be a personality name.)

- Strings are spoken in `voice-lock-string-personality`.

- Documentation strings are spoken in `voice-lock-doc-string-personality`.

- Function and variable names in their defining forms are spoken in `voice-lock-function-name-personality`.

- Certain other expressions are spoken in other personalities according to the value of the variable `voice-lock-keywords`.

'C-e d V' or 'M-x emacspeak-dtk-speak-version'

Use this to find out which version of the Dectalk firmware you have.

5.3   Emacspeak Introduction - Using the Help System

When you press C-h to get the help index, the screen will appear, but Emacspeak will not speak the window. The only thing spoken is "Type one of the options listed or Space to scroll:".

Here is the menu that Emacspeak is not speaking:

– begin quote

You have typed C-h, the help character. Type a Help option: (Use SPC or DEL to scroll through this text. Type q to exit the Help command.)

a command-apropos. Give a substring, and see a list of commands (functions interactively callable) that contain that substring. See also the apropos command. b describe-bindings. Display table of all key bindings. c describe-key-briefly. Type a command key sequence; it prints the function name that sequence runs. f describe-function. Type a function name and get documentation of it. C-f Info-goto-emacs-command-node. Type a function name; it takes you to the Info node for that command. F view-emacs-FAQ. Shows emacs frequently asked questions file. i info. The info documentation reader. k describe-key. Type a command key sequence; it displays the full documentation. C-k Info-goto-emacs-key-command-node. Type a command key sequence; it takes you to the Info node for the command bound to that key. l view-lossage. Shows last 100 characters you typed. m describe-mode. Print documentation of current major mode, which describes the commands peculiar to it. n view-emacs-news. Shows emacs news file. p finder-by-keyword. Find packages matching a given topic keyword. s describe-syntax. Display contents of syntax table, plus explanations t help-with-tutorial. Select the Emacs learn-by-doing tutorial. v describe-variable. Type name of a variable; it displays the variable's documentation and value. w where-is. Type command name; it prints which keystrokes invoke that command. C-c print Emacs copying permission (General Public License). C-d print

Emacs ordering information. C-n print news of recent Emacs changes. C-p print information about the GNU project. C-w print information on absence of warranty for GNU Emacs.

– end quote

Suppose you type "a", for command-apropos.

The next spoken prompt is "Apropos command (regexp):"

Now you type some word you think is part of an emacs command, like "visit".

The help system will display the first section of the help, but will leave the cursor in the other window. The spoken text is "Type C-x 1 to remove help window. M-C-v to scroll the help." At this point, I think it's more helpful to move point to the other window with C-x o, then you can use regular navigation commands to speak the help text. You can delete the help window with C-x 0, which will also put point back where it was.

The complete menu displayed by help-for-help is also visible if you do a describe function on help-for-help. In a future version of Emacspeak, Raman plans to add a message to that effect when the user presses C-h ?

6   Footnotes and References

6.1   JAWS

Job Access With Speech (JAWS) is a screen reader which runs under Microsoft MSDOS. It is a product of Henter-Joyce, Inc., 2100 62nd Avenue Nort, St. Petersburg, FL 33702, telephone: 800-336-5658. A demo of JAWS for DOS is available at `<ftp://ftp.hj.com/pub/jh/dosdemos/JAWS231D.EXE>`.

6.2   TELIX

TELIX is a shareware terminal emulator for MSDOS. It can be obtained by FTP from the SimTel archive [6.4 (SimTel)]. Within the SimTel collection, look for directory msdos/telix. For example, try `<ftp://ftp.coast.net/pub/SimTel/msdos/telix>`. The latest version of the program itself is in the four files tlx322-1.zip, tlx322-2.zip, tlx322-3.zip, and tlx322-4.zip.

6.3   COMMO

COMMO is another shareware terminal emulator for DOS. In the SimTel archive [6.4 (SimTel)], it is in directory msdos/commprog, file `commo66.zip`. For example, try `<ftp://ftp.coast.net/pub/SimTel/msdos/commprog/commo66.zip>`.

6.4   SimTel

The SimTel archive is maintained by Keith Petersen `w8sdz@Simtel.Net`. CD-ROM copies of Simtel.Net collections are available from Walnut Creek CDROM [6.6 (Walnut Creek)]. The primary ftp sites are `<ftp://ftp.simtel.net/pub/simtelnet>`, and `<oak.oakland.edu://pub/simtelnet>`. There are many mirror sites, as listed in the following table:

- US, ALL (primary) `<ftp://ftp.simtel.net/pub/simtelnet>`
- US, California `<ftp://ftp.cdrom.com/pub/simtelnet>`

- US, California `<ftp://ftp.digital.com/pub/micro/pc/simtelnet>`
- US, California `<ftp://ftp.lib.sonoma.edu/pub/simtelnet>`
- US, Illinois `<ftp://uiarchive.cso.uiuc.edu/pub/systems/pc/simtelnet>`
- US, Massachusetts `<ftp://ftp.bu.edu/pub/mirrors/simtelnet>`
- US, Michigan `<ftp://oak.oakland.edu/pub/simtelnet>`
- US, New York `<ftp://ftp.rge.com/pub/systems/simtelnet>`
- US, Oklahoma `<ftp://ftp.ou.edu/pub/simtelnet>`
- US, Oregon `<ftp://ftp.orst.edu/pub/simtelnet>`
- US, Pennsylvania `<ftp://ftp.epix.net/pub/simtelnet>`
- US, Utah `<ftp://ftp.cyber-naut.com/pub/simtelnet>`
- US, Virginia `<ftp://mirrors.aol.com/pub/simtelnet>`
- Argentina `<ftp://ftp.satlink.com/pub/mirrors/simtelnet>`
- Australia `<ftp://ftp.iniaccess.net.au/pub/simtelnet>`
- Australia `<ftp://sunsite.anu.edu.au/pub/pc/simtelnet>`
- Austria, Vienna `<ftp://ftp.univie.ac.at/mirror/simtelnet>`
- Belgium `<ftp://ftp.linkline.be/mirror/simtelnet>`
- Belgium `<ftp://ftp.tornado.be/pub/simtelnet>`
- Bulgaria `<ftp://ftp.eunet.bg/pub/simtelnet>`
- Brazil `<ftp://ftp.iis.com.br/pub/simtelnet>`
- Brazil `<ftp://ftp.unicamp.br/pub/simtelnet>`
- Canada, Ottawa `<ftp://ftp.crc.doc.ca/systems/ibmpc/simtelnet>`
- Canada, Vancouver `<ftp://ftp.direct.ca/pub/simtelnet>`
- Chile `<ftp://sunsite.dcc.uchile.cl/pub/Mirror/simtelnet>`
- China `<ftp://ftp.pku.edu.cn/pub/simtelnet>`
- Czech Republic `<ftp://ftp.eunet.cz/pub/simtelnet>`
- Czech Republic `<ftp://ftp.zcu.cz/pub/simtelnet>`
- Czech Republic `<ftp://pub.vse.cz/pub/simtelnet>`
- Finland `<ftp://ftp.funet.fi/mirrors/ftp.simtel.net/pub/simtelnet>`
- France `<ftp://ftp.grolier.fr/pub/simtelnet>`
- France `<ftp://ftp.ibp.fr/pub/simtelnet>`
- Germany `<ftp://ftp.mpi-sb.mpg.de/pub/simtelnet>`
- Germany `<ftp://ftp.rz.ruhr-uni-bochum.de/pub/simtelnet>`
- Germany `<ftp://ftp.tu-chemnitz.de/pub/simtelnet>`
- Germany `<ftp://ftp.uni-heidelberg.de/pub/simtelnet>`
- Germany `<ftp://ftp.uni-magdeburg.de/pub/mirrors/simtelnet>`
- Germany `<ftp://ftp.uni-paderborn.de/pub/simtelnet>`
- Germany `<ftp://ftp.uni-trier.de/pub/pc/mirrors/Simtel.net>`
- Germany `<ftp://ftp.rz.uni-wuerzburg.de/pub/pc/simtelnet>`
- Greece `<ftp://ftp.ntua.gr/pub/pc/simtelnet>`
- Hong Kong `<ftp://ftp.cs.cuhk.hk/pub/simtelnet>`

- Hong Kong <ftp://ftp.hkstar.com/pub/simtelnet>
- Hong Kong <ftp://sunsite.ust.hk/pub/simtelnet>
- Ireland <ftp://ftp.iol.ie/pub/simtelnet>
- Israel <ftp://ftp.huji.ac.il/pub/simtelnet>
- Italy <ftp://cis.utovrm.it/simtelnet>
- Italy <ftp://ftp.flashnet.it/pub/simtelnet>
- Italy <ftp://ftp.unina.it/pub/simtelnet>
- Italy <ftp://mcftp.mclink.it/pub/simtelnet>
- Japan <ftp://ftp.iij.ad.jp/pub/simtelnet>
- Japan <ftp://ftp.riken.go.jp/pub/simtelnet>
- Japan <ftp://ftp.saitama-u.ac.jp/pub/simtelnet>
- Japan <ftp://ftp.u-aizu.ac.jp/pub/PC/simtelnet>
- Japan <ftp://ftp.web.ad.jp/pub/simtelnet>
- Japan <ftp://ring.aist.go.jp/pub/simtelnet>
- Japan <ftp://ring.asahi-net.or.jp/pub/simtelnet>
- Latvia <ftp://ftp.lanet.lv/pub/mirror/simtelnet>
- Malaysia <ftp://ftp.jaring.my/pub/simtelnet>
- Malaysia <ftp://ftp.mimos.my/pub/simtelnet>
- Mexico <ftp://ftp.gdl.iteso.mx/pub/simtelnet>
- Netherlands <ftp://ftp.euro.net/d5/simtelnet>
- Netherlands <ftp://ftp.nic.surfnet.nl/mirror-archive/software/simtelnet>
- New Zealand <ftp://ftp.vuw.ac.nz/pub/simtelnet>
- Norway <ftp://ftp.bitcon.no/pub/simtelnet>
- Poland <ftp://ftp.cyf-kr.edu.pl/pub/mirror/Simtel.Net>
- Poland <ftp://ftp.icm.edu.pl/pub/simtelnet>
- Poland <ftp://ftp.man.poznan.pl/pub/simtelnet>
- Portugal <ftp://ftp.ip.pt/pub/simtelnet>
- Portugal <ftp://ftp.ua.pt/pub/simtelnet>
- Romania <ftp://ftp.sorostm.ro/pub/simtelnet>
- Singapore <ftp://ftp.nus.sg/pub/simtelnet>
- Slovakia <ftp://ftp.uakom.sk/pub/simtelnet>
- Slovenia <ftp://ftp.arnes.si/software/simtelnet>
- South Africa <ftp://ftp.is.co.za/pub/simtelnet>
- South Africa <ftp://ftp.sun.ac.za/pub/simtelnet>
- South Korea <ftp://ftp.nuri.net/pub/simtelnet>
- South Korea <ftp://ftp.sogang.ac.kr/pub/simtelnet>
- South Korea <ftp://sunsite.snu.ac.kr/pub/simtelnet>
- Spain <ftp://ftp.rediris.es/mirror/simtelnet>
- Sweden <ftp://ftp.sunet.se/pub/simtelnet>
- Switzerland <ftp://sunsite.cnlab-switch.ch/mirror/simtelnet>

- Taiwan `<ftp://ftp.ncu.edu.tw/Packages/simtelnet>`
- Taiwan `<ftp://nctuccca.edu.tw/mirror/simtelnet>`
- Thailand `<ftp://ftp.nectec.or.th/pub/mirrors/simtelnet>`
- UK, Edinburgh `<ftp://emwac.ed.ac.uk/mirrors/simtelnet>`
- UK, London `<ftp://ftp.demon.co.uk/pub/simtelnet>`
- UK, Lancaster `<ftp://micros.hensa.ac.uk/pub/simtelnet>`
- UK, London `<ftp://sunsite.doc.ic.ac.uk/packages/simtelnet>`

6.5   InfoMagic

InfoMagic is at 11950 N. Highway 89, Flagstaff AZ 86004, telephone 800-800-6613 or 520-526-9565, fax 520-526-9573, email: info@infomagic.com, web: `<http://www.infomagic.com>`.

6.6   Walnut Creek

Walnut Creek CDROM has many useful CDROMs. They are at 4041 Pike Lane, Ste D-Simtel, Concord, CA 94520, USA. Telephone (800) 786-9907 or (510) 674-0783, or FAX (510) 674-0821. email: orders@cdrom.com. Web: `<http://www.cdrom.com/>`

6.7   Red Hat

Red Hat Software: telephone 800-454-5502 or 203-454-5500, fax: 203-454-2582, email: sales@redhat.com. Web: `<http://www.redhat.com>`.

6.8   Craftwork

CraftWork Solutions, 4320 Stevens Creek Blvd, Suite 170, San Jose CA 95129, telephone 800-985-1878, email: info@craftwork.com, web: `<http://www.craftwork.com>`.

6.9   Yggdrasil

Yggdrasil Computing, 4880 Stevens Creek Blvd., Suite 205, San Jose CA 95129-1024, telephone 800-261-6630 or 408-261-6630, fax: 408-261-6631, email: info@yggdrasil.com, web: `<http://www.yggdrasil.com>`.

6.10   Emacs for DOS

From the Emacs FAQ of November 11, 1996:

```
--begin quote
```

93: Where can I get Emacs for my PC running MS-DOS?

A pre-built binary distribution of Emacs 19.34 should be available by the beginning of November 1996 from the Simtel archives, the main site of which is at

`<ftp://ftp.simtel.net/pub/simtelnet/gnu/djgpp/v2gnu/>`

If you prefer to compile Emacs for yourself, you will need a 386 (or better) processor, and are running MS-DOS 3.0 or later. According to Eli Zaretskii `eliz@is.elta.co.il` and Darrel Hankerson `hankedr@dms.auburn.edu`, you will need the following:

Compiler: djgpp version 1.12 maint 1 or later. Djgpp 2.0 or later is recommended, since 1.x is being phased out. Djgpp 2 supports long filenames under Windows 95.

You can get the latest release of djgpp by retrieving all of the files in

`<ftp://ftp.simtel.net/pub/simtelnet/gnu/djgpp>`

Gunzip and tar:

The easiest way is to use "djtar" which comes with djgpp v2.x, because it can open gzip'ed tarfiles (i.e., those ending with ".tar.gz") in one step. Djtar comes in "djdev201.zip", from the URL mentioned above.

Utilities: make, mv, sed, rm.

All of these utilities are available at

`<ftp://ftp.simtel.net/pub/simtelnet/gnu/djgpp/v2gnu>`

16-bit utilities can be found in GNUish:

`<ftp://ftp.simtel.net/pub/simtelnet/gnu/gnuish>`

The file INSTALL in the top-level directory of the Emacs source contains some additional information regarding Emacs under MS-DOS. In addition, the file etc/MSDOS contains some information on the differences between the Unix and MS-DOS versions of Emacs.

For the most comprehensive information on running GNU Emacs on a PC, see the file prepared by Michael Ernst `mernst@theory.lcs.mit.edu` at

`<ftp://theory.lcs.mit.edu/pub/emacs/pc-emacs.gz>`

For a list of other MS-DOS implementations of Emacs (and Emacs look-alikes), consult the list of "Emacs implementations and literature," available at

`<ftp://rtfm.mit.edu/pub/usenet/comp.emacs/>`

Note that while many of these programs look similar to Emacs, they often lack certain features, such as the Emacs Lisp extension language.

`--end quote`

6.11   GNU Mirror Sites

The GNU collection at `<ftp://prep.ai.mit.edu/pub/gnu>` is mirrored at many sites. Mirrors in USA include these:

- `<ftp://labrea.stanford.edu/pub/gnu>`
- `<ftp://wuarchive.wustl.edu/systems/gnu>`
- `<ftp://ftp.kpc.com/pub/mirror/gnu>`
- `<ftp://f.ms.uky.edu/pub3/gnu>`
- `<ftp://jaguar.utah.edu/gnustuff>`
- `<ftp://ftp.hawaii.edu/mirrors/gnu>`
- `<ftp://uiarchive.cso.uiuc.edu/gnu>`

- `<ftp://uiarchive.cso.uiuc.edu/pub/gnu>`
- `<ftp://ftp.cs.columbia.edu/archives/gnu/prep>`
- `<ftp://gatekeeper.dec.com/pub/GNU>`
- `<ftp://ftp.uu.net/systems/gnu>`

6.12 Emacspeak with Earlier Slackware Releases

If you want to install Slackware 3.0 or earlier, you will need to prepare a full null modem cable, including modem control signals.

For two DB25 (25 pin) connectors, the required connections are:

- 1 (Frame Ground) - 1 (Frame Ground)
- 2 (Receive Data) - 3 (Transmit Data)
- 3 (Transmit Data) - 2 (Receive Data)
- 4 (Request To Send) - 5 (Clear To Send)
- 5 (Clear To Send) - 4 (Request To Send)
- 6 (Data Set Ready) - 20 (Data Terminal Ready)
- 7 (Signal Ground) - 7 (Signal Ground)
- 8 (Carrier Detect) - 20 (Data Terminal Ready)
- 20 (Data Terminal Ready) - 6 (Data Set Ready)
- 20 (Data Terminal Ready) - 8 (Carrier Detect)

For two DB9 connectors, the connections are:

- 1 (Carrier Detect) - 4 (Data Terminal Ready)
- 2 (Receive Data) - 3 (Transmit Data)
- 3 (Transmit Data) - 2 (Receive Data)
- 4 (Data Terminal Ready) - 6 (Data Set Ready)
- 4 (Data Terminal Ready) - 1 (Carrier Detect)
- 5 (Signal Ground) - 5 (Signal Ground)
- 6 (Data Set Ready) - 4 (Data Terminal Ready)
- 7 (Request To Send) - 8 (Clear To Send)
- 8 (Clear To Send) - 7 (Request To Send)
- 9 (Ring Indicator) not connected

For a DB9 (listed first) to a DB25 (second), the connections are:

- 1 (Carrier Detect) - 20 (Data Terminal Ready)
- 2 (Receive Data) - 2 (Transmit Data)
- 3 (Transmit Data) - 3 (Receive Data)
- 4 (Data Terminal Ready) - 6 (Data Set Ready)
- 4 (Data Terminal Ready) - 8 (Carrier Detect)
- 5 (Signal Ground) - 7 (Signal Ground)
- 6 (Data Set Ready) - 20(Data Terminal Ready)
- 7 (Request To Send) - 5 (Clear To Send)
- 8 (Clear To Send) - 4 (Request To Send)
- 9 (Ring Indicator) not connected

7   Frequently Asked Questions (FAQ)

7.1   Why does it say "space" after each character?

Your DECtalk Express has old firmware. Use the Emacspeak command 'C-e d V' to find out your version. You should be running a version no older than 4.2bw from March 1995. If you have an earlier version, you can find an updated version at `<http://www.ultranet.com/~rongemma/tips_upd.htm>`, a WWW site maintained by Ron Jemma of the Dectalk Group at DEC. Alternatively, you can send email to Anne Nelson at DECnelson@dectlk.enet.dec.com. The most recent version at this writing is 4.3 release AA X01 May 20 1996.

7.2   On occasion when reading the dectalk will produce high pitch tones that last for several words or more, if this happens in a buffer it will often repeat within the same buffer.

The problem is due to remaining bugs in the Dectalk firmware. When emacspeak produces tones, especially when split caps is on, the dtk sometime goes into squealing mode.

If you notice this happening in particular text documents, just turn off split caps mode locally with 'C-e d s'.

7.3   What is the significance of the message "No library autorevert in search path" which is spoken (or at least queued for speech) when emacspeak 7.0 starts?

It's completely insignificant. autorevert is a new minor mode provided by emacs 20 and emacspeak looks for it and if found speech-enables it.

8   Legalese

Copyright (c) 1997 by James R. Van Zandt jrv@vanzandt.mv.com. This document may be distributed under the terms set forth in the LDP license at `<http://sunsite.unc.edu/LDP/COPYRIGHT.html>`.

If you have questions, please contact Greg Hankins, the Linux HOWTO coordinator, at gregh@sunsite.unc.edu via email.

Linux Advocacy mini-HOWTO

Paul L. Rogers, *Paul.L.Rogers@li.org* `<mailto:Paul.L.Rogers@li.org>`   v0.4, 6 February 1997

This document provides suggestions for how the Linux community can effectively advocate the use of Linux.

Contents

1 About this document

This is the Linux Advocacy mini-HOWTO and is intended to provide guidelines and ideas to assist with *your* Linux advocacy efforts.

This mini-HOWTO was inspired by Jon "maddog" Hall when he responded to a request for feedback on guidelines for advocating Linux during *NetDay96* `<http://www.netday96.com>` activities. He responded positively to the guidelines and observed that they were the basis of a list of "canons of conduct" that would benefit the Linux community.

This document is available in HTML form at *http://www.datasync.com/˜rogerspl/Advocacy-HOWTO.html* `<http://www.datasync.com/~rogerspl/Advocacy-HOWTO.html>`.

Nat Makarevitch *<nat@nataa.fr.eu.org>* `<mailto:nat@nataa.fr.eu.org>` is in the process of translating this document into French.

Chie Nakatani *<jeanne@mbox.kyoto-inet.or.jp>* `<mailto:jeanne@mbox.kyoto-inet.or.jp>` has translated this document into *Japanese* `<http://jf.gee.kyoto-u.ac.jp/JF/JF-ftp/euc/Advocacy.euc>`.

The author and maintainer of the Linux Advocacy mini-HOWTO is Paul L. Rogers *<Paul.L.Rogers@li.org>* `<mailto:Paul.L.Rogers@li.org>`.

Comments and proposed additions are welcome.

If you need to know more about the *Linux Documentation Project* `<http://sunsite.unc.edu/mdw/linux.html>` or about Linux HOWTO's, feel free to contact the supervisor *Greg Hankins* `<http://www.cc.gatech.edu/staff/h/Greg.Hankins>` *<gregh@sunsite.unc.edu>* `<mailto:gregh@sunsite.unc.edu>`.

Greg Hankins will post this document to several national and international newsgroups on a monthly basis.

2   Copyright Information

This mini-HOWTO is Copyright © 1996 by Paul L. Rogers. All rights reserved.

A verbatim copy may be reproduced or distributed in any medium physical or electronic without permission of the author. Translations are similarly permitted without express permission if it includes a notice on who translated it.

Short quotes may be used without prior consent by the author. Derivative work and partial distributions of the Advocacy mini-HOWTO must be accompanied with either a verbatim copy of this file or a pointer to the verbatim copy.

Commercial redistribution is allowed and encouraged; however, the author would like to be notified of any such distributions.

In short, we wish to promote dissemination of this information through as many channels as possible. However, we do wish to retain copyright on the HOWTO documents, and would like to be notified of any plans to redistribute the HOWTOs.

We further want that *all* information provided in the HOWTOs is disseminated. If you have questions, please contact Greg Hankins, the Linux HOWTO coordinator, at *gregh@sunsite.unc.edu* `<mailto:gregh@sunsite.unc.edu>`.

3   Introduction

The Linux community has known for some time that for many applications, Linux is a stable, reliable, robust (although not perfect) product. Unfortunately, there are still many people, including key decision-makers, that are not aware of the existence of Linux and its capabilities.

If Linux and the many other components that make up a Linux distribution are to reach their full potential, it is critical that we reach out to prospective "customers" and advocate (being careful not to promise too much) the use of Linux for appropriate applications. The reason that many company's products have done well in the marketplace is not so much due to the product's technical superiority but the company's marketing abilities.

If you enjoy using Linux and would like to contribute something to the Linux community, please consider acting on one or more of the ideas in this mini-HOWTO and help others learn more about Linux.

4   Related Information

Lars Wirzenius, the *comp.os.linux.announce* `<news:comp.os.linux.announce>` moderator, also has some *thoughts* `<http://www.iki.fi/liw/texts/advocating-linux.html>` about Linux advocacy.

Linux International's `<http://www.li.org>` goal is to promote the development and use of Linux.

The *Linux Documentation Project* `<http://sunsite.unc.edu/mdw/linux.html>` is an invaluable resource for Linux advocates.

The *Linux Business Applications* `<http://www.m-tech.ab.ca/linux-biz>` site provides a forum for organizations that depend on Linux for day-to-day business operations to share their experiences.

The *Linux Advocacy Project's* `<http://www.10mb.com/linux/>` goal is to encourage commercial application developers to provide native Linux versions of their software.

The *Linux CD and Support Giveaway* `<http://emile.math.ucsb.edu:8000/giveaway.html>` program is helping make Linux more widely available by encouraging the reuse of Linux CD-ROMs.

Specialized Systems Consultants, Inc. (SSC) `<http://www.ssc.com/>` publishes the Linux Journal `<http://www.ssc.com/lj/>` as well as the Linux Gazette `<http://www.ssc.com/lg/>`, an online newsletter.

5 Advocating Linux

- Share your personal experiences (good and bad) with Linux. Everyone knows that software has bugs and limitations and if we only have glowing comments about Linux, we aren't being honest. I *love* to tell people about having to reboot four times (three scheduled) in three years.

- If someone has a problem that Linux may be able to solve, offer to provide pointers to appropriate information (Web pages, magazine articles, books, consultants, ...). If you haven't actually used the proposed solution, say so.

- Offer to help someone start using Linux.

- Try to respond to one "newbie" posting each week. Seek out the tough questions, you may be the only one to respond and you may learn something in the process. However, if you aren't confident that you can respond with the correct answer, find someone that can.

- Seek out small software development firms and offer to make a presentation about Linux.

- If the opportunity arises, make a presentation to your employer's Information Technology group.

- Participate in community events such as *NetDay96* `<http://www.netday96.com>`. While your first priority must be to contribute to the success of the event, use the opportunity to let others know what Linux can do for them.

- Always consider the viewpoints of the person to which you are "selling" Linux. Support, reliability, interoperability and cost are all factors that a decision-maker must consider. Of the above, cost is often the least important portion of the equation.

- Point out that the production of freely available software takes place in an environment of open collaboration between system architects, programmers, writers, alpha/beta testers and end users which often results in well documented, robust products such as Emacs, Perl and the Linux kernel.

- Report successful efforts of promoting Linux to *Linux International* `<http://www.li.org>` (*li@li.org* `<mailto:li@li.org>`) and similar organizations.

- Find a new home for Linux CD-ROMs and books that you no longer need. Give them to someone interested in Linux, a public library or a school computer club. A book and its CD-ROM would be most appropriate for a library. However, please be sure that making the CD-ROM publicly available does not violate a licensing agreement or copyright. Also, inform the library staff that the material on the CD-ROM is freely distributable. Follow up to make sure it is available on the shelves.

- When purchasing books about software distributed with Linux, give preference to books written by the author of the software. The royalties that authors receive from book sales may be the only monetary compensation received for their efforts.

6   Canons of Conduct

- As a representative of the Linux community, participate in mailing list and newsgroup discussions in a professional manner. Refrain from name-calling and use of vulgar language. Consider yourself a member of a virtual corporation with Mr. Torvalds as your Chief Executive Officer. Your words will either enhance or degrade the image the reader has of the Linux community.

- Avoid hyperbole and unsubstantiated claims at all costs. It's unprofessional and will result in unproductive discussions.

- A thoughtful, well-reasoned response to a posting will not only provide insight for your readers, but will also increase their respect for your knowledge and abilities.

- Don't bite if offered flame-bait. Too many threads degenerate into a "My O/S is better than your O/S" argument. Let's accurately describe the capabilities of Linux and leave it at that.

- Always remember that if you insult or are disrespectful to someone, their negative experience may be shared with many others. If you do offend someone, please try to make amends.

- Focus on what Linux has to offer. There is no need to bash the competition. We have a good, solid product that stands on its own.

- Respect the use of other operating systems. While Linux is a wonderful platform, it does not meet everyone's needs.

- Refer to another product by its proper name. There's nothing to be gained by attempting to ridicule a company or its products by using "creative spelling". If we expect respect for Linux, we must respect other products.

- Give credit where credit is due. Linux is just the kernel. Without the efforts of people involved with the GNU project, MIT, Berkeley and others too numerous to mention, the Linux kernel would not be very useful to most people.

- Don't insist that Linux is the only answer for a particular application. Just as the Linux community cherishes the freedom that Linux provides them, Linux only solutions would deprive others of their freedom.

- There will be cases where Linux is not the answer. Be the first to recognize this and offer another solution.

7   User Groups

- Participate in a local user group. If one does not exist in your area, start one. The *Groups of Linux Users* <http://www.ssc.com/glue/> information page allows you to search for a local user group and also contains suggestions on how to start a user group.

- Make speakers available to organizations interested in Linux.

- Issue press releases about your activities to your local media.

- Volunteer to configure a Linux system to meet the needs of local community organizations. Of course, the installation process must include training the user community to use the system and adequate documentation for ongoing maintenance.

- Discus the Linux Advocacy mini-HOWTO at a meeting. Brainstorm and submit new ideas.

8   Vendor Relations

- When contemplating a hardware purchase, ask the vendor about Linux support and other user's experiences with the product in a Linux environment.

- Consider supporting vendors that sell Linux based products and services.

- Support vendors that donate a portion of their income to organizations such as the *Free Software Foundation* <http://www.gnu.ai.mit.edu/>, the *Linux Development Grant Fund* <http://www.li.org/About/Fund/Welcome.html>, the *XFree86 Project* <http://www.xfree86.org/donations.html> or *Software in the Public Interest* <mailto:bruce@pixar.com>. If possible, make a personal donation to these or other organizations that support freely available software.

- If you need an application that is not supported on Linux, contact the vendor and request a native Linux version.

9   Media Relations

- Linux International is collecting *press clippings* <http://www.li.org/Products/Articles/Welcome.html> that mention Linux, GNU or freely redistributable software. When you see such an article, please send the following information to *clippings@li.org* <mailto:clippings@li.org>:

    - Name of publication
    - Publisher's contact address
    - Name of author
    - Author's contact address
    - Title of article
    - Page number where the article starts
    - The URL if available online
    - A summary of the article, including your opinion

- If you believe that Linux was not given fair treatment in an article, review or news story, send the details, including the above information, to *li@li.org* <mailto:li@li.org> so that an appropriate response can be sent to the publisher. If you contact the publisher directly, be professional and sure of your facts.

10   Acknowledgements

Grateful acknowledgement is made to all contributors, including:

```
Jon "maddog" Hall     <maddog@zk3.digital.com>
Greg Hankins          <gregh@cc.gatech.edu>
Eric Ladner           <eladner@goldinc.com>
Chie Nakatani         <jeanne@mbox.kyoto-inet.or.jp>
Nat Makarevitch       <nat@nataa.fr.eu.org>
Martin Michlmayr      <tbm@cyrius.com>
Idan Shoham           <idan@m-tech.ab.ca>
Adam Spiers           <adam.spiers@new.ox.ac.uk>
C. J. Suire           <suire@datasync.com>
Lars Wirzenius        <liw@iki.fi>
```

Linux User Group HOWTO

Kendall Grant Clark <mailto:kclark@cmpu.net>   v1.6, 1 January 1998

The Linux User Group HOWTO is a guide to founding, maintaining, and growing a Linux User Group.

Contents

1 Introduction

1.1 Purpose

The Linux User Group HOWTO is meant to serve as a guide to founding, maintaining, and growing a Linux User Group.

Linux is a freely-distributable implementation of Unix for personal computers, servers and workstations. It was developed on the i386 and now supports i486, Pentium, Pentium Pro, and Pentium II processors, as well as x86-clones from AMD, Cyrix, and others. It also supports many SPARC, DEC Alpha, PowerPC/PowerMac, Motorola 68x0 Mac/Amiga machines.

1.2 Other sources of information

If you want to learn more about Linux, the *Linux Documentation Project* <http://sunsite.unc.edu/LDP/> is a good place to start.

For general information about computer user groups, please see the *Association of PC Users Groups* <http://www.apcug.org/>.

2   What is a Linux User Group?

2.1   What is Linux?

In order to appreciate and understand fully the significant role of LUGs in the Linux Movement, it is important to understand what makes Linux unique among computer operating systems.

Linux as an operating system is very efficient and very powerful. But, Linux as an *idea* about how software ought to be developed is even more powerful. Linux is a **free** operating system: it is licensed under the GNU Public License. The source code is freely available to anyone who wants it and always will be. It is developed by a unstructured group of programmers from around the world, under the technical direction of Linus Torvalds and other key developers. Linux is a world-wide movement without any central structure, bureaucracy, or entity to control, coordinate, or otherwise direct its affairs. While this situation is a powerful part of the appeal and technical quality of Linux as an computer operating system, it can make for inefficient allocation of human resources, ineffective and even detrimental advocacy, public relations, user education and training.

2.2   How is Linux unique?

This loose structure is not likely to change with regard to Linux as a software project. And it's a good thing, too. Linux works precisely because people are free to come and go as they please: **free programmers are happy programmers are effective programmers**.

But this loose structure can make the average Linux user's life a little complicated–especially if that user isn't a programmer by profession or by vocation. Who does she call for support, training, or education? How does she know the kinds of uses for which Linux is well-suited?

In large part local LUGs provide the answers to these kinds of question. This is why LUGs are a crucial part of the Linux Movement. Because there is no "regional office" of the Linux Corporation in your town or village or metropolis, the local LUG takes on many of the same roles that a regional office does for a large multi-national corporation..

Linux is unique because it does not have, nor is it burdened by, a central structure or bureaucracy to allocate its resources, train its users, or provide support for its products. These jobs get done in a variety of ways: the Internet, consultants, VARs, support companies, colleges and universities. But, increasingly, in many places around the globe, they get done by a local LUG.

2.3   What is a user group?

Computer user groups, at least in the United States, are not a new phenomenon; in fact, they played an important role in the history of the personal computer. The personal computer arose in large part to satisfy the demand of electronics, Ham Radio, and other hobbyist user groups, as well as trade shows and swap meets, for affordable, personal access to computing resources. Of course eventually giants like IBM discovered that the PC was a good and profitable thing, but the impetus for the PC came from the people, by the people, and for the people.

In the United States, user groups have changed, and many for the worse, with the times. The financial woes of the largest user group ever, the *Boston Computer Society* <http://www.bcs.org/> have been well-reported; but all over the U.S. most of the big PC user groups have seen a decline in real membership. American user groups in their heyday concentrated on the production of newsletters, the maintenance of shareware and diskette libraries, meetings, social events, and, sometimes, even Bulletin Board Systems. With the advent of the Internet, however, many of the services that user groups once provided were transferred to things like CompuServe, AOL, and the Web.

The rise of Linux, however, coincided with and was intensified by general public's "discovery" of the Internet. As the Internet grew more popular, so did Linux: the Internet brought new users, developers, and vendors to the Linux Movement.

So just when traditional PC user groups were declining because of the Internet's popularity, this popularity propelled Linux forward, creating new demand for new user groups dedicated exclusively to Linux. To give just one indication of the ways in which a LUG is different than a traditional user group, I call the reader's attention to a curious fact: traditional user groups have had to maintain a fairly tight control over the kinds of software that its users copy and trade at its meetings. While illegal copying of commercial software certainly occurred at these meetings, it was officially discouraged and for good reason.

At a LUG meeting, however, this entire mindset simply does not apply. Far from being the kind of thing that a LUG ought to discourage, the free copying of Linux itself ought to be one of the primary activities of a LUG. In fact there is anecdotal evidence that traditional user groups sometimes have a difficult time adapting to the fact that Linux can be freely copied as many times as one needs or wants.

2.4 Summary

In order for the Linux Movement to continue to flourish, the proliferation and success of local LUGs, along with other factors, is an absolute requirement. Because of the unique status of Linux, the local LUG must provide some of the same functions that a "regional office" provides for large computer corporations like IBM, Microsoft, or Sun. LUGs can and must train, support, and educate Linux users, coordinate Linux consultants, advocate Linux as a computing solution, and even serve as a liason to local media outlets like newspapers and television.

3 What LUGs are there?

Since this document is meant as a guide not only to maintaining and growing LUGs but also to founding them, it would be well before we go much further to determine what LUGs there are.

3.1 Lists of LUGs

There are several lists of LUGs available on the Web. If you want to found a local LUG, one of the first things to do is to determine where the nearest LUG is. *Your best bet may be to join a LUG that is already established in your area rather than founding a new one.*

As of the mid-1997, there are LUGs in all 50 states, the District of Columbia, and 26 other countries, including India, Russia, and most of Western and Eastern Europe.

Note: the biggest untapped computing market on the planet, China, does not yet appear to have a LUG, and India, the second most populous country on the planet, has only a few.

- *Finding Groups of Linux Users Everywhere* <http://www.ssc.com/glue/groups/>
- *LUG List Project* <http://www.nllgg.nl/lugww/>

It appears that the GLUE list is more comprehensive for American LUGs, while the LUG List Project offers more comprehensive international coverage.

3.2   Solidarity versus convenience

While the lists of LUGs on the Web are well-maintained, it is likely that they do not list every LUG. In addition to consulting these lists, I suggest, if you are considering founding a LUG, that you post a short message asking about the existence of a local LUG to *comp.os.linux.announce* `<news:comp.os.linux.announce>`, *comp.os.linux.misc* `<news:comp.os.linux.misc>`, or an appropriate regional Usenet hierarchy. If there isn't a LUG already in your area, then posting mesages to these groups will alert potential members of your plans.

If you plan to found a local LUG, you should carefully balance convenience against solidarity. In other words, if there is a LUG in your metropolitan area, but on the other side of the city, it may be better to start a new group for the sake of convenience. But it may be better to join the pre-existing group for the sake of unity and solidarity. *Greater numbers almost always means greater power, influence, and efficiency*. While it might be nice to have two groups of 100 members each, there are certain advantages to one group of 200 members. Of course if you live in a small town or village, any group is better than no group at all.

The point is that starting a LUG is an arduous undertaking, and one that ought to be entered into with all the relevant facts, and with some appreciation of the effect on other groups.

4   What does a LUG do?

The goals of local LUGs are as varied as the locales in which they operate. There is no master plan for LUGs, nor is this document meant to supply one. Remember: Linux is free from bureaucracy and centralized control and so are local LUGs.

It is possible, however, to identify a core set of goals for a local LUG:

- advocacy
- education
- support
- socializing

Each local LUG will combine these and other goals in a unique way in order to satisfy the unique needs of its membership.

4.1   Linux advocacy

The urge to advocate the use of Linux is as natural to computer users as is eating or sleeping. When you find something that works and works well, the natural urge is to tell as many people about it as you can. The role of LUGs in Linux advocacy cannot be overestimated, especially since the wide-scale commercial acceptance of Linux which it so richly deserves has not yet been achieved. While it is certainly beneficial to the Linux Movement each and every time a computer journalist writes a positive review of Linux, it is also beneficial every time satisfied Linux users tell their friends, colleagues, employees or employers about Linux.

There is effective advocacy and there is ineffective carping: as Linux users, we must be constantly vigilant to advocate Linux in such a way as to reflect positively on both the product, its creators and developers, and our fellow users. The Linux Advocacy mini-HOWTO, available at the Linux Documentation Project, gives some helpful suggestions in this regard. Suffice it to say that advocacy is an important aspect of the mission of a local LUG.

There may come a time when Linux advocacy is pretty much beside the point because Linux has more or less won the day, when the phrase "No one ever got fired for using Linux" becomes a reality. Until that time, however, the local LUG plays an indispensable role in promoting the use of Linux. It does so because its advocacy is free, well-intentioned, and backed up by organizational commitment. If a person comes to know about Linux through the efforts of a local LUG, then that person, as a new Linux user, is already ahead of the game: *she is already aware of the existence of an organization that will help her install, configure, and even maintain Linux on whatever computers she is willing to dedicate to it.*

New Linux users who are already in contact with a local LUG are ahead of those whose interest in Linux has been piqued by a computer journalist, but who have no one to whom to turn to aid them in their quest to install, run, and learn Linux.

It is, therefore, important for local LUGs to advocate Linux because their advocacy is effective, well-supported, and free.

4.2   Linux education

Not only is it the business of a local LUG to advocate the use of Linux, it may also turn its efforts to training its member, as well as the computing public in its area, about Linux and associated components. In my own estimation, the goal of user education is the single most important goal a LUG may undertake. Of course, as I have already pointed out, LUGs are perfectly free to organize themselves and their activities around any of these, or other, goals. I believe, however, that LUGs can have the greatest impact on the Linux Movement by educating and training Linux users.

Local LUGs may choose to undertake the goal of education simply because there is no other local entity from which a Linux user may receive technically-oriented education. While it is certainly the case that universities, colleges, and junior colleges are increasingly turning to Linux as a way to educate their students, both efficiently and cheaply, about Unix-like operating systems, some Linux users are either unable or unwilling to register for courses in order to learn Linux. For these users the local LUG is a valuable resource for enhancement or creation of advanced computer skills: Unix-like system administration, system programming, support and creation of Internet and Intranet technologies, etc.

In an ironic twist, many local LUGs are even sharing the burden of worker training with large corporations. Every worker at Acme Corp that expands her computer skills by participating in a local LUG is one less worker Acme Corp has to train or pay to train. Even though using and administering a Linux PC at home isn't the same as administering a corporate data warehouse, call center, or similar high-availability facility, it is light years more complex, more rewarding, and more educational than using and administering a Windows 95 PC at home. As Linux itself advances toward things like journalling filesystems, high-availability, real-time capacity, and other high-end Unix features, the already blurry line between Linux and the "real" Unixes will get even more indistinct.

Not only is such education a form of worker training, but it will also serve, as information technology becomes an increasingly vital part of the global economy, as a kind of community service. In most metropolitan areas in the United States, for example, it is possible for a local LUG to take Linux into local schools, small businesses, community and social organizations, and other non-corporate environments. This accomplishes the task of Linux advocacy and also helps train the general public about Linux as a Unix-like operating system. As more and more of these kinds of organizations seek to establish an Internet presence or provide dial-in access to their workers, students, and constituents, the opportunities arise for local LUGs to participate in the life of their community by educating it about a free and freely-available operating system. This kind of community service allows the average Linux user to emulate the kind of generosity that has characterized Linux, and the free software community, from the very beginning. Most Linux users can't program like Linus Torvalds, but we can all all give our time and abilities to other Linux users, the Linux community, and the broader community in which work and live.

Linux is a natural fit for these kinds of organization because deploying it doesn't commit them to expensive license, upgrade, or maintenance fees. Because Linux is also technically elegant and economical, it runs very well on the the kinds of disposable hardware that corporations typically cast off and that non-profit organizations are only too happy to use. As more and more people discover every day, that old 486 collecting dust in the closet can do **real work** if someone will install Linux on it.

In addition, Linux education has a cumulative effect on the other goals of a local LUG, in particular the goal of Linux support discussed below. Better Linux education means better Linux support. The more people that a LUG can count on to reach its support goals, the easier support becomes and, therefore, the more of it can be done. The more new and inexperienced users a local LUG can support and eventually educate about Linux, the larger and more effective the LUG can become. In other words, if a LUG focuses solely on Linux support to the neglect of Linux education, the natural barriers to organizational growth will be more restrictive. If only two or three percent of the members of a LUG take upon themselves the task of supporting the others, the growth of the LUG will be stifled. One thing you can count on: *if new and inexperienced users don't get the help with Linux they need from a local LUG, they won't participate in that LUG for very long*. If a larger percentage of members support the others, the LUG will be able to grow much larger. Linux education is the key to this dynamic: education turns new Linux users into experienced ones.

Free education about free Linux also highlights the degree to which Linux is part and parcel of the free software Community. So it seems appropriate that local LUGs focus not solely on Linux education but also education about all of the various software systems and technologies that run under Linux. These include, for instance, the GNU suite of programs and utilities, the Apache Web server, the XFree86 implementation of X Windows, TeX, LaTeX, etc. Fortunately the list of free software that runs under Linux is a long and diverse one.

Finally, Linux is a self-documenting operating environment; in other words, if we don't write the documentation, nobody is going to do it for us. Toward that end, make sure that LUG members are well aware of the *Linux Documentation Project* `<http://sunsite.unc.edu/LDP/>`, which can be found at mirrors worldwide. Consider providing an LDP mirror for the local Linux community and for LUG members. Also make sure to publicize—through `comp.os.linux.announce`, the LDP, and other pertinent sources of Linux information— any relevant documentation that is developed by the LUG: technical presentations, tutorials, local FAQs, etc. There is a lot of Linux documentation produced in LUGs that doesn't benefit the worldwide Linux community because no one outside the LUG knows about it. Don't let the LUGs efforts in this regard go to waste: it is highly probable that if someone at one LUG had a question or problem with something, then people at other LUGs around the world will have the same questions and problems.

4.3 Linux support

Of course for the desperate **newbie** the primary role of a local LUG is Linux support. But it is a mistake to suppose that Linux support only means *technical* support for new Linux users. It can and should mean much more.

Local LUGs have the opportunity to support:

- users
- consultants
- businesses, non-profit organizations, and schools
- the Linux Movement

4.3.1 Users

The most frequent complaint from new Linux users, once they have gotten Linux installed, is the steep learning curve which is not at all unique to Linux but is, rather, a characteristic of all modern Unixes. With the steepness of the learning curve, however, comes the power and flexibility of a complex operating system. A local LUG is often the only resource that a new Linux user has available to help flatten out the learning curve.

But even if a new Linux user doesn't know it yet, she needs more than just technical support: Linux and the free software worlds are both rapidly moving targets. The local LUGs form an invaluable conduit of information about Linux and other free software products. Not only does Linux lack a central bureaucracy, but it also for the most part lacks the kind of journalistic infrastructure from which users of other computer systems benefit. The Linux Movement does have resources like *Linux Journal* <http://www.ssc.com/lj/> and *Linux Gazette* <http://www.ssc.com/lg/>, but many new Linux users are unaware of these resources. In addition, as *monthly* publications they are often already out of date about bugfixes, security problems, patches, new kernels, etc. This is where the local LUG as a source and conduit of timely information is so vital to new and experienced Linux users alike.

For example, until a new Linux user knows that the newest kernels are available from *ftp.kernel.org* <ftp://ftp.kernel.org> or that the **Linux Documentation Project** usually has newer versions of Linux HOWTOs than a CD-based Linux distribution, it is up to the local LUG, as the primary support entity, to be a conduit of timely and useful information.

In fact it may be just a bit misleading to focus on the support role that local LUGs provide to new users: intermediate and advanced users also benefit from the proliferation of timely and useful tips, facts, and secrets about Linux. Because of the complexity of Linux, even advanced users often learn new tricks or techniques simply by becoming involved in a local LUG. Sometimes they learn about software packages they didn't know existed, sometimes they just remember that arcane `vi` command sequence they've not used since college.

4.3.2 Consultants

It is, I think, rather obvious to claim that local LUGs ought to be in the business of supporting new Linux users. After all, if they're not supposed to be doing that, what are they to do? It may not be as obvious that local LUGs can play an important role in supporting local Linux consultants. Whether they do Linux consulting full-time or only part-time, consultants can be an important part of a local LUG. How can the LUG support them?

The answer to that question is just the answer to another question: what is it that Linux consultants want and need? *They need someone for whom to consult.* A local LUG provides the best way for those who *offer* Linux consulting to find those who *need* Linux consulting. The local LUG can informally broker connections between consulting suppliers and consulting consumers simply by getting all, or as many as possible, of the people interested in Linux in a local area together and talking with one another. How LUGs do that will occupy us below. What is important here is to point out that LUGs can and should play this role as well. The Linux Consultants HOWTO is an important document in this regard, but it is surely the case that only a fraction of the full-time and part-time Linux consultants worldwide are registered in the Consultants HOWTO.

The relationship is mutually beneficial. Consultants aid LUGs by providing experienced leadership, both technically and organizationally, while LUGs aid consultants by putting them in contact with the kinds of people who need their services. New and inexperienced users gain benefit from both LUGs and consultants since their routine or simple requests for support are handled by LUGs *gratis*, and their complex needs and problems—the kind that obviously require the services of a paid consultant—can be handled by the consultants whom the local LUG helps them contact.

The line between support requests that need a consultant and those that do not is sometimes indistinct; but in most cases the difference is clear. While a local LUG doesn't want to gain the reputation for pawning new users off unnecessarily on consultants–as this is simply rude and very anti-Linux behavior–there is no reason for LUGs not to help broker contacts between the users who need consulting services and the professionals who offer them.

Please see Martin Michlmayr's *Linux Consultants HOWTO* <http://sunsite.unc.edu/LDP/HOWTO/Consultants-HOWTO.html> for an international list of Linux consultants.

4.3.3 Businesses, non-profit organizations, and schools

LUGs also have the opportunity to support local businesses and organizations. This support has two aspects. First, LUGs can support businesses and organizations that want to use Linux as a part of their computing and IT efforts. Second, LUGs can support local businesses and organizations that develop for Linux, cater to Linux users, support or install Linux, etc.

The kinds of support that LUGs can provide to local businesses that want to use Linux as a part of their computing operations isn't really all that different from the kinds of support LUGs give to individuals who want to run Linux at home. For example, compiling the Linux kernel doesn't really vary from home to business. Supporting businesses using Linux, however, may mean that a LUG needs to concentrate on commercial software that runs on Linux, rather than concentrating solely on free software. If Linux is going to continue to maintain its momentum as a viable computing alternative, then it's going to take software vendors who are willing to write for and port to Linux as a commercially-viable platform. If local LUGs can play a role in helping business users evaluate commercial Linux solutions, then more software vendors will be encouraged to consider Linux in their development and planning.

This leads us directly to the second kind of support that a local LUG can give to local businesses. Local LUGs can serve as a clearing house for the kind of information that is available in very few other places. For example:

- Which local ISP is Linux-friendly?
- Are there any local hardware vendors that build Linux PCs?
- Does anyone sell Linux CDs locally?

Maintaining and making this kind of information public not only helps the members of a local LUG, but it also helps Linux-friendly local businesses as well, and it encourages them to continue to be Linux-friendly. It may even, in some cases, help contribute to a competitive atmosphere in which other businesses are encouraged to become Linux-friendly too.

4.3.4 Free software development

Finally, LUGs may also support the Linux Movement by soliciting and organizing charitable giving. *Chris Browne* <mailto:cbbrowne@hex.het> has thought about this issue as much as anyone I know, and he contributes the following.

Chris Browne on free software philanthropy A further involvement can be to encourage sponsorship of various Linux-related organizations in a financial way. With the *multiple millions* <http://counter.li.org> of Linux users, it would be entirely plausible for grateful users to individually contribute a little. Given millions of users, and the not unreasonable sum of a hundred dollars of "gratefulness" per Linux user ($100 being roughly the sum *not* spent this year upgrading a Microsoft OS), that could add up to *hundreds of millions* of dollars towards development of improved tools and applications for Linux.

A users group can encourage members to contribute to various "development projects." If it has some form of "charitable tax exemption" status, that can encourage members to contribute directly to the group, getting tax deductions as appropriate, with contributions flowing on to other organizations.

It is appropriate, in any case, to encourage LUG members to direct contributions to organizations with projects and goals that they individually wish to support.

This section lists possible candidates. None are explicitly being recommended here, but the list can represent useful "food for thought." Many are registered as charities in the United States, thus making U.S. contributions tax deductible.

Here are organizations with activities particularly directed towards development of software that works with Linux:

- *Linux International Project Sponsorship Fund* `<http://www.li.org/About/Fund/Welcome.html>`
- *Debian/Software In the Public Interest* `<http://www.debian.org/donations.html>`
- *Free Software Foundation* `<http://www.fsf.org/help/donate.html>`
- *The XFree86 Project* `<http://www.xfree86.org/donations.html>`

Contributions to these organizations has the direct effect of supporting the creation of freely redistributable software usable with Linux. Dollar for dollar, such contributions almost certainly have greater effect on the Linux community as a whole than any other specific kind of spending.

There are also organizations that are less directly associated with Linux that may nonetheless be worthy of assistance, such as:

- *League for Programming Freedom* `<http://www.lpf.org>`

  This is not a Linux-specific organization; they are involved in general advocacy activities that touch on people involved with software development. Involvement in this organization represents something closer to involvement in a "political lobby" group.

  There is somewhat of a "USA bias;" there are nonetheless international implications, and the international community as often follows the American lead in computing-related matters as vice-versa.

- The LaTeX3 Project Fund

  The *TeX Users Group (TUG)* `<http://www.tug.org>` is working on the "next generation" version of the LaTeX publishing system, known as LaTeX3. Linux is one of the platforms on which TeX and LaTeX are best supported.

  Donations for the project can be sent to:

  ```
  TeX Users Group
  P.O. Box 1239
  Three Rivers, CA 93271-1239
  USA
  ```

  or, for those in Europe,

  ```
  UK TUG
  1 Eymore Close
  Selly Oaks
  Burmingham B29 4LB
  UK
  ```

- *Project Gutenberg* `<http://www.promo.net/pg/lists/list.html>`

  Their purpose is to make freely available in electronic form the texts of out-of-copyright books. This isn't directly a "Linux thing," but it seems fairly worthy, and they actively encourage platform independence, which that their "products" are quite usable with Linux.

4.3.5 Linux Movement

I have referred throughout this HOWTO to something I call the **Linux Movement**. There really is no better way to describe the international Linux phenomenon than to call it a movement: it isn't a bureaucracy, but it is organized; it isn't a corporation, but it is important to businesses all over the world. The best way for a local LUG to support the international Linux movement is to work to insure that the local Linux community is robust, vibrant, and growing. Linux is *developed* internationally, which is easy enough to see by reading `/usr/src/linux/MAINTAINERS`. But Linux is also *used* internationally. And this ever-expanding user base is the key to Linux's continued success. And that is where the local LUG plays an incalculably important role.

The strength of the Linux Movement internationally is the simple fact that Linux offers unprecedented computing power and sophistication for its cost and for its freedom. The keys are value and independence from proprietary control. Every time a new person, group, business, or organization has the opportunity to be exposed to Linux's inherent value the Linux Movement grows in strength and numbers. Local LUGs can make that happen.

4.4 Linux socializing

The last goal of a local LUG that I will mention here is socializing. In some ways this is the most difficult goal to discuss because it is not clear how many or to what degree LUGs engage in it. While it would be strange to have a local LUG that didn't engage in the other goals, there very well may be local LUGs somewhere in the world for which socialization isn't an important consideration.

It seems, however, that whenever two or three Linux users get together fun, highjinks, and, often, beer are sure to follow. Linus Tovalds has always had one enduring goal for Linux: to have more fun. For hackers, kernel developers, and Linux users, there's nothing quite like downloading a new kernel, recompiling an old one, twittering with a window manager, or hacking some code. It is the sheer fun of Linux that keeps many LUGs together, and it is this kind of fun that leads many LUGs naturally to socializing.

By "socializing" here I mean primarily sharing experiences, forming friendships, and mutually-shared admiration and respect. There is another meaning, however, one that social scientists call *socialization*. In any movement, institution, or human community, there is the need for some process or pattern of events in and by which, to put it in Linux terms, newbies are turned into hackers. In other words, socialization turns you from "one of them" to "one of us".

For armed forces in the U.S. and in most countries, this process is called boot camp or basic training. This is the process whereby civilians are transformed into soldiers. The Linux movement has analogous requirements. It is important that new Linux users come to learn what it means to be a Linux user, what is expected of them as a member of an international community, the special vocabulary of the Linux movement, its unique requirements and opportunities. This may be as simple as how Linux users in a partcicular locale pronounce "Linux". It may be as profound as the ways in which Linux users should advocate, and the ways in which they should, more importantly, *refrain* from advocating Linux.

Linux socialization, unlike 'real world' socialization, can occur on mailing lists and Usenet, although the efficacy of the latter is constantly challenged precisely by poorly socialized users. In my view, socialization and socializing are both done best in the company of real, flesh-and-blood fellow human beings, and not by incorporeal voices on a mailing list or Usenet group.

5 Local LUG activities

In the previous section I focused exclusively on what LUGs do and what they ought to be doing. In this section the focus shifts to practical strategies for accomplishing these goals.

There are, despite the endless permutations of form, two basic things that local LUGs do: first, they meet together in physical space; second, they communicate with each other in cyberspace. Everything or nearly everything that LUGs do can be seen in terms of meetings and online resources.

5.1 Meetings

As I said above, physical meetings are synonymous with LUGs and with most computer user groups. LUGs have these kinds of meetings:

- social
- technical presentations
- informal discussion groups
- user group business
- Linux installation
- configuration and bug-squashing

What do LUGs do at these meetings?

- Install Linux for newbies and strangers
- Teach members about Linux
- Compare Linux to other operating systems
- Teach members about the software that runs on Linux
- Discuss the ways in which Linux can be advocated
- Discuss the importance of the Free Software Movement
- Discuss the business of the user group
- Eat, drink, and be merry

5.2 Online resources

The commercial rise of the Internet coincided roughly with the rise of Linux, and the latter in large part owes something to the former. The Internet has always been an important asset for Linux development. It is no different for LUGs. Most LUGs have web pages if not whole Web sites. In fact, I am not sure how else to find a local LUG but to check the Web.

It makes sense, then, for a local LUG to make use of whatever Internet technologies they can appropriate: Web sites, mailing lists, gopher, FTP, e-mail, WAIS, finger, news, etc. As the world of commerce is discovering, the Internet can be an effective way to advertise, inform, educate, and even sell. The other reason that LUGs make extensive use of Internet technologies is that it is the very essence of Linux to *provide* a stable and rich platform for the deployment of these technologies. So not only do LUGs benefit from, say, the establishment of a Web site because it advertizes their existence and helps organize their members, but in deploying these technologies, the members of the LUG are provided an opportunity to learn about this technology and see Linux at work.

Some LUGs that use the Internet effectively:

- *Atlanta Linux Enthusiasts* <http://www.ale.org/>
- *North Texas Linux Users Group* <http://www.ntlug.org/>

- *Boston Linux and Unix* `<http://www.blu.org/>`
- *Colorado Linux Users and Enthusiasts* `<http://spot.elfwerks.com/~clue/>`
- *BLUG - BHZ Linux Users Group (Brazil)* `<http://www.bhz.ampr.org/~linux/>`
- *Ottawa Carleton Linux Users Group* `<http://www.oclug.on.ca/>`
- *Provence Linux Users Group* `<http://www.pipo.com/plug/>`
- *Duesseldorf Linux Users Group* `<http://www.hsp.de/~dlug/>`
- *Israeli Linux Users Group* `<http://www.linux.org.il/>`
- *Tokyo Linux Users Group* `<http://www.twics.co.jp/~tlug/>`
- *Linux in Mexico* `<http://www.linux.org.mx/>`
- *Netherlands Linux Users Group (NLLGG)* `<http://www.nllgg.nl/>`
- *St. Petersburg Linux User Group* `<http://ethereal.ru/~mbravo/spblug/index.html>`
- *Linux User Group of Singapore* `<http://www.lugs.org.sg/>`
- *Victoria Linux User Group* `<http://www.linux.victoria.bc.ca/>`
- *Essex Linux User Group* `<http://www.epos.demon.co.uk/>`
- *Turkish Linux User Group* `<http://www.linux.org.tr/>`
- *Linux User Group of Rochester* `<http://www.lugor.org/>`
- *Korean Linux Users Group* `<http://www.linux-kr.org>`

Please let me know if your LUG uses the Internet in an important or interesting way; I'd like this list to include your group.

6   Practical suggestions

Finally, I want to make some very practical, even mundane, suggestions for anyone wanting to found, maintain, or grow a LUG.

6.1   LUG support organizations

There are several organizations that offer assistance to local LUGs.

GLUE

> Groups of Linux Users Everywhere is a user group coordination and support program started by SSC, the same people who publish *Linux Journal*. The *GLUE program* `<http://www.ssc.com/glue/>` is an inexpensive way for a local LUG to provide some benefits to its membership.

Linux Systems Labs

> *LSL* `<http://www.lsl.com/>` offers their Tri-Linux Disk set (Three Linux distributions on four CDs: Red Hat, Slackware, and Debian) to LUGs for resale at a considerable discount.

Linux Mall User Group Program

> Sponsored by WorkGroup Solutions, the *Linux Mall User Group Program* `<http://www.LinuxMall.com/usergrp.program.html>` offers a range of benefits for participating User Groups. LUGs are also free to participate in *Linux Mall's Referral Program* `<http://www.LinuxMall.com/mallrfr.html>` as well.

Cleveland Linux User's Group

Owns the Internet domain, `lug.net`. They will provide your LUG an Internet domain name at `lug.net`: your-LUG-name-or-citylug.net. More information may be found at *LUG.NET* `<http://www.lug.net/>` or by e-mailing *Jeff Garvas* `<mailto:jeff@cia.net>`.

Red Hat Software's User Group Program

Assists LUGs to develop and grow. More information may be found at *Red Hat Web site* `<http://www.redhat.com/redhat/rhug.html>`

6.2 Founding a LUG

- Determine the nearest pre-existing LUG
- Announce your intentions on `comp.os.linux.announce` and on an appropriate regional hierarchy
- Announce your intention wherever computer users are in your area: bookstores, swap meets, cyber-cafes, colleges and universities, corporations, Internet service providers, etc.
- Find Linux-friendly businesses or institutions in your area that may be willing to help you form the LUG
- Form a mailing list or some means of communication between the people who express an interest in forming a LUG
- Ask key people specifically for help in spreading the word about your intention to form a LUG
- Solicit space on a Web server to put a few HTML pages together about the group
- Begin looking for a meeting place
- Schedule an initial meeting
- Discuss at the initial meeting the goals for the LUG

6.3 Maintaining and growing a LUG

- Make the barriers to LUG membership as low as possible
- Make the LUG's Web site a priority: keep all information current, make it easy to find details about meetings (who, what, and where), and make contact information and feedback mechanisms prominent
- Install Linux for anyone who wants it
- Post flyers, messages, or handbills wherever computer users are in your area
- Secure dedicated leadership
- Follow Linus's *benevolent dictator* model of leadership
- Take the big decisions to the members for a vote
- Start a mailing list devoted to technical support and ask the "gurus" to participate on it
- Schedule a mixture of advanced and basic, formal and informal, presentations
- Support the software development efforts of your members
- Find way to raise money without dues: for instance, selling Linux merchandise to your members and to others
- Consider securing formal legal standing for the group, such as incorporation or tax-exempt status
- Find out if your meeting place is restricting growth of the LUG
- Meet in conjunction with swap meets, computer shows, or other community events where computer users—i.e., potential Linux converts—are likely to gather

- Elect formal leadership for the LUG as soon as is practical: some helpful officers might include President, Treasurer, Secretary, Meeting Host (general announcements, speaker introductions, opening and closing remarks, etc.), Publicity Coordinator (handles Usenet and e-mail postings, local publicity), and Program Coordinator (organizes and schedules speakers at LUG meetings)

- Provide ways for members and others to give feedback about the direction, goals, and strategies of the LUG

- Support Linux and Free Software development efforts by donating Web space, a mailing list, or FTP site

- Establish an FTP site for relevant software

- Archive everything the LUG does for the Web site

- Solicit "door prizes" from Linux vendors, VARs, etc. to give away at meetings

- Give credit where credit is due

- Join SSC's GLUE (Groups of Linux Users Everywhere) but be aware they charge a membership fee

- Submit your LUG's information to all of the Lists of LUGs

- Publicize your meetings on appropriate Usenet groups and in local computer publications and newspapers

- Compose promotional materials, like Postscript files, for instance, that members can use to help publicize the LUG at workplaces, bookstores, computer stores, etc.

- Make sure you know what LUG members want the LUG to do

- Release press releases to local media outlets about any unusual LUG events like an Installation Fest, Net Day, etc.

- Use LUG resources and members to help local non-profit organizations and schools with their Information Technology needs

- Advocate the use of Linux zealously but responsibly

- Play to the strengths of LUG members

- Maintain good relations with Linux vendors, VARs, developers, etc.

- Identify and contact Linux consultants in your area

- Network with the leaders of other LUGs in your area, state, region, or country to share experiences, tricks, and resources

- Keep LUG members advised on the state of Linux software—new kernels, bugs, fixes, patches, security advisories—and the state of the Linux world at large—new ports, trademark and licensing issues, where Linus is living and working, etc.

- Notify the Linux Documentation Project—and other pertinent sources of Linux information—about the documentation that the LUG produces: technical presentations, tutorials, local HOWTOs, etc.

7 Legal and political issues

7.1 Legal issues

7.2 United States

There is a strong case to be made for formal organization of local LUGs. I will not make that case here. If, however, you are interested in formally organizing your local LUG, then this section will introduce you to some of the relevant issues.

Note: this section should not be construed as competent legal counsel. These issues require the expertise of competent legal counsel; you should, before acting on any of the statements made in this section, consult an attorney.

There are at least two different legal statuses that a local LUG in the United States may attain:

1. incorporation as a non-profit entity
2. tax-exemption

Although the relevant statutes differ from state to state, most states allow user groups to incorporate as non-profit entitites. The benefits of incorporation for a local LUG may include limitations of liability of LUG members and volunteers, as well as limitation or even exemption from state corporate franchise taxes.

While you should consult competent legal counsel before incorporating your LUG as a non-profit entity, you can probably reduce your legal fees if you are acquainted with the relevant issues before consulting with an attorney. I recommend the *Non-Lawyers Non-Profit Corporation Kit* (ISBN 0-937434-35-3).

As for the second status, tax-exemption, this is not a legal status so much as a judgment by the Internal Revenue Service. It is important for you to know that incorporation as a non-profit entity **does not** insure that the IRS will rule that your LUG is to be tax-exempt. It is possible to have a non-profit corporation that is **not** also tax-exempt.

The IRS has a relatively simple document that explains the criteria and process for tax-exemption. It is **Publication 557:** *Tax-Exempt Status for Your Organization*. It is available as an Adobe Acrobat file from the IRS's Web site. I strongly recommend that you read this document **before** filing for incorporation as a non-profit entity. While becoming a non-profit corporation cannot insure that your LUG will be declared tax-exempt by the IRS, there are ways to incorporate that will **prevent** the IRS from declaring your LUG to be tax-exempt. *Tax-Exempt Status for Your Organization* clearly sets out the necessary conditions for your LUG to be declared tax-exempt.

Finally, there are resources available on the Internet for non-profit and tax-exempt organizations. Some of the material is probably relevant to your local LUG.

7.3 Canada

Thanks to *Chris Browne* <mailto:cbbrowne@hex.net> for the following comments about the Canadian situation.

The Canadian tax environment strongly parallels the US environment, in that the "charitable organization" status confers similar tax advantages for donors over mere "not for profit" status, while requiring that similar sorts of added paperwork be filed by the "charity" with the tax authorities in order to attain and maintain certified charity status.

7.4 Political issues

Chris Browne <mailto:cbbrowne@hex.net> has the following to say about the kinds of inter-LUG political dynamics that often crop up.

7.4.1 People have different feelings about free software.

Linux users are a diverse bunch. As soon as you try to put a lot of them together, there are *some* problem issues that can come up.There are those that are nearly political radicals that believe that all software, always, should be "free." Because Caldera charges quite a lot of money for their distribution, and doesn't give all profits over to *(pick favorite advocacy organization)*, they must be "evil." Ditto for Red Hat or S.u.S.E. Keep in mind that all three of these companies have made and continue to make significant contributions to free software.

Others may figure that they can find some way to highly exploit the "freeness" of the Linux platform for their fun and profit. Be aware that many users of the BSD UNIX variants consider that *their* licenses that *do* permit companies to build "privatized" custom versions of their OSes are preferable to the "enforced permanent freeness" of the GPL as applied to Linux. Do not presume that all people promoting this sort of view are necessarily greedy leeches.

If these people are put together in one place, disagreements can occur.

Leaders should be clear on the following facts:

- There are a lot of opinions about the GPL and how it is supposed to work. It is easy to misunderstand both the GPL and alternative licensing schemes.

- Linux benefits from contributions from many places, and can support some freeloaders, particularly if this encourages more people to get involved, thus pulling in further contributors.

- Many significant contributions have been made to Linux by commercial enterprises. Examining the sources to the Linux kernel, and notable subsystems such as XFree86 and GCC show a surprising number of commercial contributors.

- Commercial does not always imply "better," but it also does not always imply "horrible."

The main principle can be extended well beyond this; computer "holy wars" have long been waged over the virtues of one system over another, whether that be (in modern day) between Linux, other UNIX variants, and Microsoft OSes, or between the "IBM PC" and the various Motorola 68000-based systems, or between the many 8 bit systems of the 1970s. Or of KDE versus GNOME.

A wise LUG leader will seek to smooth over such differences, rather than inciting them. LUG leaders *must* have thick skins.

There *will* be disagreements at some point as diverse views collide with one another, and leaders must be able to cope with this, resolving disagreements rather than contributing to the problem.

7.4.2   Nonprofit organizations and money don't mix terribly well.

It is important to be quite careful in dealing with finances in a nonprofit organization of any sort. In businesses, where profitable flows of monies are the goal, people are not typically too worried about "nagging details" such as possible misspending of immaterial sums of money.

The same cannot be said about nonprofit organizations. Some people are involved for reasons of principle, and can easily give minor problems inordinate attention. And the potential for wide participation at business meetings correspondingly expands the potential for inordinate attention to be drawn to things.

As a result, it is probably preferable for there to *not* be a membership fee for a LUG, as that provides a specific thing for which people can reasonably demand accountability. Fees that are not collected cannot, by virtue of the fact that they don't exist, be misused.

If there *is* a lot of money and/or other such resources floating around, it is important for the user group to be accountable to its members for it.

In a vital, growing group, there should be more than one person involved. In troubled nonprofit organizations, financial information is often tightly held by someone who will not willingly relinquish control of funds. Ideally, there should be *some* rotation of duties in a LUG including that of control of the finances.

Regular useful financial reports should be made available to those that wish them. A LUG that maintains an official "charitable status" for tax purposes will have to file at least annual financial reports with the local tax authorities, which would represent a minimum financial disclosure for the purposes of the members.

With the growth of Linux-based financial software, it should be readily possible to create reports on a regular basis. With the growth of the Internet, it should even be possible to publish these on the World Wide Web.

8   About this document

8.1   Terms of use

Copyright (c) 1997 by Kendall Grant Clark. This document may be distributed under the terms set forth in the LDP license at *http://sunsite.unc.edu/LDP/COPYRIGHT.html* `<http://sunsite.unc.edu/LDP/COPYRIGHT.html>`.

8.2   New versions

New versions of the Linux User Group HOWTO will be periodically uploaded to various Linux WWW and FTP sites, principally *my homepage* `<http://www.cmpu.net/public/kclark/linux/>` and the *Linux Documentation Project* `<http://sunsite.unc.edu/LDP/>`

8.3   Please contribute to this HOWTO

I welcome questions about and feedback on this document. Please send them to me at *kclark@cmpu.net* `<mailto:kclark@cmpu.net>`. *I am especially interested in hearing from leaders of LUGs from around the world*. I would like to include real-life examples of the things described here. I would also like to include a section on LUGs outside the United States, since this HOWTO as it stands now is rather US-centric. Please let me know if your group does things that should be mentioned in this HOWTO.

8.4   Document history

- 1.0 released on 13 July 1997
- 1.1: expanded online resources section
- 1.3: added LUG Support Organizations and expanded the Legal and Organizational Issues section
- 1.3.1: general editing for clarity and conciseness
- 1.4: general editing, added new LUG resources
- 1.4.1: general editing for clarity
- 1.5: added some resources, some discussion of LUG documentation, also general editing
- 1.5.1: changed Web location for this document and author's email address.
- 1.5.2: new copyright and license
- 1.5.3: miscellaneous edits and minor re-organizations
- 1.6: added Chris Browne's material: Linux philanthropic donations and LUG political considerations

8.5   Acknowledgements

I want to thank all the great people I met and worked with during 1996–1997 when I served as President of the North Texas Linux Users Group. They helped inspire me to use Linux full-time. The best thing about Linux really is the people you meet.

I especially want to thank *Chris Browne* `<mailto:cbbrowne@hex.net>` for describing the situation with non-profit and charitable groups in Canada, his thoughts on financial donations as a way to participate in Linux and the free software movement, and his ideas about the kinds of political issues that may arise within LUGs.

In addition, the following people have made helpful comments and suggestions:

- Hugo van der Kooij
- Greg Hankins
- Charles Lindahl
- Rick Moen
- Jeff Garvas

The Linux Reading List HOWTO

by Eric S. Raymond   1.2, 29 November 1997

This document lists the book I think are most valuable to a person trying to learn Unix (especially Linux) top to bottom.

Contents

1   Introduction

1.1   Purpose of this document

This document lists what I consider to be the essential book-length references for learning Unix (especially Linux) and how to program under it.

1.2   New versions of this document

New versions of the Linux Reading List HOWTO will be periodically posted to *comp.os.linux.answers* <news:comp.os.linux.answers>. They will also be uploaded to various Linux WWW and FTP sites, including the LDP home page.

You can also view the latest version of this on the World Wide Web via the URL <http://sunsite.unc.edu/LDP/HOWTO/Reading-List-HOWTO.html>.

1.3   Feedback and Corrections

If you have questions or comments about this document (or just want to suggest a book that you think should be on it), please feel free to mail Eric S. Raymond, at *esr@thyrsus.com* <mailto:esr@thyrsus.com>. I welcome any suggestions or criticisms.

1.4   Related Resources

For on-line HOWTOs, magazines, and other non-book material, see the *Linux Documentation Project home page* <http://sunsite.unc.edu/LDP/HOWTO>.

Some years ago I wrote a less Linux-focused Unix bibliography that may still be of some interest and retains a certain amusement value. You can find the Loginataka at <http://www.ccil.org/~esr/faqs/loginataka.html>.

1.5   Conventions Used In This Document

Comments not in quotes below are either mine, or I have seen no reason to change them from those of Jim Haynes (previous maintainer of this document). Comments sent in by others are in quotes, and have the name of the commentator before them (JH is Jim Haynes).

"See" URLs attached to publishing information point directly into the publisher's web catalog and typically take you to a page containing a cover shot, blurbs, and ordering information. Books that don't have these lack them because the publisher is using frames and the catalog pages can't be bookmarked.

Topic listings go roughly from the outside in (culture to user-land programming to kernel programming to hardware). Within sections I have tried to list the most useful books first insofar as I am familiar with them. It's just an embarrassing coincidence that this lists one of my books first, honest! (Suggestions for a better organization cheerfully accepted.)

2 Books on Culture, History, and Pragmatics

The New Hacker's Dictionary (Third Edition)

Raymond, Eric S.; MIT Press; 1996; ISBN 0-262-68092-0; 547pp.

See `<http://www-mitpress.mit.edu/book-home.tcl?isbn=0262680920>`.

Um, er. A guide to Internet culture. Lots of people like it. HTML at the *Jargon File Resource Page* `<http://www.ccil.org>`.

A Quarter Century of Unix

Salus, Peter H.; Addison-Wesley; 1994; ISBN 0-201-54777-5; 256pp.

See `<http://www.awl.com/cp/authors/salus/unix/unix.html>`

Linux is part of the Unix tradition. This book is an oral history of Unix – how it originated, how it evolved, how it spread – by the people who were there.

The Mythical Man Month (Anniversary Edition)

Brooks, Frederick P.; Addison-Wesley 1995 (ISBN 0-201-83595-9).

See `<http://heg-school.awl.com/cseng/authors/brooks/mmm-ae/mmm-ae.html>`.

The one book on software engineering that everyone should read.

Alan Cox: "This I'd recommend not for its technical value but for its application of common sense and reality to computing projects." JH: "Ah, yes. What if Linus had been given 200 programmers and had been told to produce Linux in 3 months!"

Bell System Technical Journal, July-August 1978, Vol. 57, No. 6, part 2

AT&T; 416 pp.

Many early papers on Unix, including Ritchie & Thompson, "The UNIX Time Sharing System"; Thompson, "UNIX Implementation"; Ritchie, "A Retrospective"; Bourne, "The UNIX Shell"...

3 Books on General Unix/Linux

3.1 Linux Installation and Administration

Linux Installation and Getting Started

Welsh, Matt; LDP; 1997. Available on the LDP home page, or directly at `<http://sunsite.unc.edu/LDP/gs>`.

How to bring up Linux. Explains a lot of Linux basics. Covers basic system administration.

Linux System Administtrator's Guide

Wirzenius, Lars; LDP; 1997. Available on the LDP home page, or directly at `<http://sunsite.unc.edu/LDP/sag>`.

An excellent first book on how to maintain and administer a Linux system.

Essential System Administration (Second Edition)

Frisch, Aeleen; O'Reilly; 1995; ISBN 0-937175-80-3; 788 pp; $32.95.

See `<http://www.ora.com/catalog/esa2/noframes.html>`.

More in-depth coverage of normal system-administration tasks. Not Linux-specific but contains Linux material.

3.2   Using Unix & Linux

Linux in a Nutshell

> Hekman, Jessica P. et al.; O'Reilly; 1997; ISBN 1-56592-167-4; 438 pp. $9.95.
> See <http://www.ora.com/catalog/linuxnut/noframes.html>.
>
> According to O'Reilly, "The Desktop Reference for Linux". For Linux users this obsoletes their "Unix In a Nutshell" which was SVr4/Solaris-oriented.

Running Linux (Second Edition)

> Welsh, Matt, & Kaufman, Lar; O'Reilly; ISBN 1-56592-151-8; 1996; 650pp; $24.95.
> See <http://www.ora.com/catalog/runux2/noframes.html>.
>
> Everything you need in order to understand, install, and use the Linux operating system. Excellent beginner's book.

3.3   System Security

Practical Unix Security

> Garfinkel, Simpson, and Spafford, Gene; O'Reilly Associates; ISBN 0-56592-148-8; 1991.
> See <http://www.ora.com/catalog/puis/noframes.html>.
>
> Ronald P. Miller: "Some overlap with Essential System Admin., but all in all a solid book on security, especially for those aspiring to allow multiple-user, dial-up/net access to their Linux boxes."

Firewalls & Internet Security

> Cheswick, William R. & Bellovin, Steven M.; Addison-Wesley; 1994; ISBN 0-201-63357-4; 320pp.
> See <http://www.awl.com/cp/Ches.html>.

4   Books on Shell, Script, and Web Programming

Programming Perl (Second Edition)

> Wall, Larry & Christiansen, Tom & Schwartz, Randal; O'Reilly; 1997; ISBN 0-56592-149-6; 644pp.
> See <http://www.ora.com/catalog/pperl2/noframes.html>.
>
> Shell (as a programming language for more than trivial scripting) is dead. Perl rules in its place. This is the second edition of the definitive Perl book – vastly better organized than the first, and it covers Perl 5.

Programming Python

> Lutz, Mark; O'Reilly; 1997; ISBN 0-56592-197-6; 880pp.
> See <http://www.ora.com/catalog/python/noframes.html>.
>
> The next step beyond Perl. Python is beautifully designed, has better integration with C, and scales up better to large projects.

HTML: The Definitive Guide (2nd Edition)

> Musciano, Chuck & Kennedy. Bill; O'Reilly; 1997; ISBN 0-56592-235-2; 552pp.
> See <http://www.ora.com/catalog/html2/noframes.html>.
>
> The best HTML tutorial/reference I have ever seen, and the only HTML book you need unless you want to do CGI.

The Unix Programming Environment

> Kernighan, Brian, and Pike, Rob; Prentice-Hall; 1984; ISBN 0-13-937681-X; 1984.
>
> A true classic – possibly the best single-book exposition of the Unix philosophy.

5 Books on Text Formatting

5.1 Tex and LaTeX

The LaTeX Companion

Goossens, Michael & Mittlebach, Frank, & Samarin, Alexander; Addison-Wesley; 1994; ISBN 0-201-54199-8; 530pp.

See <http://www.awl.com/cp/tlc.html>.

'If you are one of those users who would like to know how LaTeX can be extended to create the nicest documents possible without becoming a (La)TeX guru, then this book is for you' — from the Preface. Bruce Thompson adds: "A very nice book providing a lot of information about the new extensions to LaTeX, provides a large number of examples showing precisely how your document's layout can be manipulated"

LaTeX: A Document Preparation System (Second Edition)

Lamport, Leslie; Addison-Wesley; 1994; ISBN 0-201-52983-1; 256pp.

See <http://heg-school.awl.com/cseng/authors/lamport/latex/latex.html>.

Bruce Thompson: "The ultimate reference on LaTeX 2.09 by its author. A new edition covering LaTeX2e (the version included in the current TeX/LaTeX distribution) is in preparation. LaTeX 2.09 is fully supported by LaTeX2e. A must for anyone wanting to use LaTeX. Provides a gentle introduction to document preparation and the various tools that LaTeX provides for producing professional quality documents. Lots of examples."

The TeXbook, Volume A of Computers and Typesetting; Knuth, Donald A.

Addison-Wesley; 1986, ISBN 0-201-13448; 496pp. See <http://www.awl.com/cp/TeXbook.html>

Bruce Thompson: "The definitive user's guide and complete reference manual for TeX. Probably not needed for casual LaTeX use, but a fascinating book nonetheless." I'll strengthen that by adding that this book is not for the faint of heart.

The METAFONT book, Volume C of Computers and Typesetting

Knuth, Donald A.; Addison-Wesley; 1986; 0-201-13444-6, 1986; 384pp.

See <http://www.awl.com/cp/METAFONTbook.html>

Bruce Thompson: "The definitive user's guide and reference manual for METAFONT, the companion program to TeX for designing fonts. An excellent work if you're planning to design your own fonts for use in TeX and LaTeX. METAFONT is included with the normal TeX/LaTeX distribution." This book is *definitely* not for the faint of heart.

6 Books on C and C++ Programming

6.1 C and C++

The C Programming Language (Second Edition)

Kernighan, Brian W.; Ritchie, Dennis M; Prentice-Hall; 1988; ISBN 0-13-110362-8, 272pp.

The improved second edition, covering ANSI C, of the original classic C book coauthored by C's designer, "K&R". Still the best!

Who's Afraid of C++?

Heller, Steve; Academic Press; 1996; ISBN 0-12-339097; 508pp.

The best introductory book on C++ I have seen.

6.2   C System Call Interface

POSIX Programmer's Guide: Writing Portable Unix Programs

> Lewine, Donald; O'Reilly; 1992; ISBN 0-937175-73-0; 607pp.
> See <http://www.ora.com/catalog/posix/noframes.html>.
> An excellent programmer's reference on the POSIX.1 standard. I like this one better than JH's choice.

The Posix.1 Standard: A Programmer's Guide

> Zlotnick, Fred; Benjamin/ Cummings; 1991; ISBN 0-8053-9605-5; 379pp.; $35.95 (USA).
>
> JH: "When I complained about the lack of Section 2 man pages in Linux, somebody told me just to get a POSIX book, because that's what Linux does. I like this book because I'm not a professional programmer and the author gives copious explanations and examples."

7   Books on Networking

Unix Network Programming

> Stevens, W. Richard; Prentice Hall; 1990; ISBN 0-13-949876-1; 772 pp.; $54 (USA).
>
> Everything you might want to know about the subject, and some things you probably didn't want to know (really, XNS!?). Generally regarded as definitive on the basics, though it's pre-Web.

Linux Network Administrator's Guide

> Kirch, Olaf; O'Reilly; 1995; ISBN 1-56592-087-2; 335pp.
> See <http://www.ora.com/catalog/linag/noframes.html>.
> A practical guide to Linux's TCP/IP and related services. Accessible on the Web at the *Linux Documentation Project* <http://sunsite.unc.edu/LDP> page, or directly at <http://sunsite.unc.edu/LDP/LDP/nag/nag.html>.

TCP/IP Network Adminstration

> Hunt, Craig; O'Reilly Associates, ISBN 0-937175-82-X; 1992; 472pp.
> See <http://www.ora.com/catalog/tcp2/noframes.html>.
> Less Linux-specific than the Kirch book. Features deeper coverage of the TCP/IP core, including routing and BGP.

DNS and BIND (Second Edition)

> Albitz, Paul, and Liu, Cricket; O'Reilly; 1996; ISBN 1-56592-236-0; 1992; 438pp; $32.95.
> See <http://www.ora.com/catalog/dns2/noframes.html>.
> In-depth coverage of DNS, useful for people running complicated multiple-subnet installations. Covers BIND library programming.

Sendmail (Second Edition)

> Costales, Bryan & Allman, Eric; O'Reilly; ISBN 1-56592-222-0; 1997; 1050 pp; $32.95
> See <http://www.ora.com/catalog/sendmail2/noframes.html>.
> An exhaustive (and exhausting) guide to Linux's and Unix's default mail-transfer agent.

8   Books on Unix Kernel Implementation

8.1   Ancestors of Linux

The Design of the Unix Operating System

Bach, Maurice J.; Prentice-Hall; ISBN 0-13-201799-7; 470pp.; $60 (USA).

The book that got Linus started.

Operating Systems, Design and Implementation;

Tanenbaum, Andrew S.; Prentice-Hall; 1987.

Alan Cox (one of the core kernel people) likes this book. Tanenbaum designed Minix, which is the system Linus bootstrapped Linux up from.

8.2 Linux

Linux Kernel Hackers' Guide

Johnson, Michael K.

Accessible on the Web at the *Linux Documentation Project* `<http://sunsite.unc.edu/LDP>` page, or directly at `<http://www.redhat.com:8080/HyperNews/get/khg.html>`.

LINUX Kernel Internals

Beck, Michael & Bohme, Harold & Mirko, Dziadzka & Kunitz, Ulrich & Magnus, Robert & Verworner, Dick; Addison Wesley; 1996; ISBN: 0-201-87741-4; 480pp.
See `<http://heg-school.awl.com/cseng/authors/beck.m/linux/linux.html>`.

A guide to Linux kernel programming; covers 1.2, slightly out of date now.

8.3 Relatives of Linux

The Design and Implementation of the 4.4BSD Unix Operating System

McKusick, Marshall Kirk, Bostic, Keith, Karels, Michael J., and Quarterman, John S.; Addison-Wesley; 1996; ISBN 0-201-54979-4; 608pp.
See `<http://heg-school.awl.com/cseng/authors/mckusick/4.4bsd/4.4bsd.html>`.

The successor to a classic book on the implementation of the 4.3 BSD kernel, which influenced Linux's design (especially near sockets and networking). This book covers the 4.4BSD base of BSD/OS, FreeBSD, and NetBSD.

Porting Unix to the 386; Jolitz, William F., and Jolitz, Lynne G.

Dr. Dobb's Journal; Jan 1991-July 1992.

9 Books on Intel processor architecture and programming

80386 Programmer's Reference Manual

Intel Corp.; ISBN 1-55512-022-9; 1986;

Part I. Applications Programming, data types, memory model, instruction set. Part II. Systems Programming, architecture, memory management, protection, multitasking, I/O, exceptions and interrupts, initialization, coprocessing and multiprocessing. Part III. Compatibility (with earlier x86 machines). Part IV. Instruction Set.

80386 System Software Writer's Guide

Intel Corp.; ISBN 1-55512-023-7; 1987.

This explains the 386 features for operating system writers. It includes a chapter on Unix implementation. A lot of the 80386 architecture seems to have been designed with Multics in mind; the features are not used by DOS or by Unix.

Programming the 80386

Crawford, John H & Gelsinger, Patrick P.; Sybex; ISBN 0-89588-381-3; 774pp.; $26.95 (USA).

This is the book the Jolitzes used when they ported BSD to the 386 architecture.

Pentium Processor User's Manual: Volume 3, Architecture and Programming Manual
> Intel Corp.; 1993; ISBN 1-55512-195-0;
> Pretty much the Pentium version of the 80386 Programmer's manual listed above.

10   Books on PC-Class Hardware

Note: these books are four or five years old and possibly out of date. I don't really grok hardware...

80386 Hardware Reference Manual
> Intel Corp.; 1986; ISBN 1-55512-024-5;
> Pin connections, timing, waveforms, block diagrams, voltages, all that kind of stuff.

The Indispensable PC Hardware Book
> Messmer, Hans-Peter; Addison-Wesley; 1993; ISBN 0-201-62424-9; 1000 pp.
> JH: "Covers the more recent stuff like EIDE and PCI."

11   Administrivia

11.1   Terms of Use

This document is copyright 1997 by Eric S. Raymond. You may use, disseminate, and reproduce it freely, provided you:

- Do not omit or alter this copyright notice.
- Do not omit or alter or omit the version number and date.
- Do not omit or alter the document's pointer to the current WWW version.
- Clearly mark any condensed, altered or versions as such.

These restrictions are intended to protect potential readers from stale or mangled versions. If you think you have a good case for an exception, ask me.

11.2   History

This was originally a mini-HOWTO maintained by Jim Haynes. I have changed the emphasis somewhat, trying to make it more a standalone document and less reliant on the various USENET bibliographic postings. The unattrbuted mini-reviews are mine rather than his.

Index